The Proper Name Version of the King James Bible

First Edition

The KJBPNV is based on the King James Version of the Bible,
in which the Word of God has been preserved.
It restores the proper name of God,
rather than using a traditional title in place of His name.
His name is written as Yahweh and as its short form, Yah.
The name of the Messiah is written as Yahshua,
thus retaining the meaning of His name as
Yah is Salvation.

The text is made more readable
by updating thousands of words into modern English.
Significant changes, which might affect the meaning of the Scriptures,
are not made in sentence structure or biblical content.

Publishers

Addison, Michigan
U. S. A.

©2010 LRI Publishers, U. S. A.
All rights reserved.

All Scriptures are based on the *Authorized King James Version of the Bible*, 1769 Edition.

The Proper Name Version of the King James Bible text may be quoted and/or reprinted up to and inclusive of one thousand (1,000) verses without express written permission of the copyright holder, provided that the verses quoted do not constitute a complete book of the Bible, nor account for as much as 50 percent of the total work in which they are quoted.

Notice of copyright must appear on the title or copyright page of the work as follows:

"Scriptures taken from *The Proper Name Version of the King James Bible*, Copyright 2010. Used by permission."

International Standard Book Number: 978-0-944835-08-1

Library of Congress Control Number: 2010932540

Printed in the United States of America

Table of Contents

Preface..v

Old Testament

Section 1: The Law
Genesis	Ge	1
Exodus	Ex	39
Leviticus	Le	70
Numbers	Nu	93
Deuteronomy	De	126

Section 2: History
Joshua	Jos	155
Judges	Jud	173
Ruth	Ru	192
1 Samuel	1Sa	194
2 Samuel	2Sa	218
1 Kings	1Ki	238
2 Kings	2Ki	262
1 Chronicles	1Ch	284
2 Chronicles	2Ch	306
Ezra	Ezr	332
Nehemiah	Ne	340
Esther	Es	351

Section 3: Poetic
Job	Job	357
Psalms	Ps	377
Proverbs	Pr	428
Ecclesiastes	Ec	445
Song of Solomon	So	451

Section 4: Prophecy
Isaiah	Isa	455
Jeremiah	Jer	492
Lamentations	La	533
Ezekiel	Eze	537
Daniel	Da	575
Hosea	Ho	586
Joel	Joe	592
Amos	Am	594
Obadiah	Ob	598
Jonah	Jon	599
Micah	Mic	600
Nahum	Na	604
Habakkuk	Hab	605
Zephaniah	Zep	607
Haggai	Hag	608
Zechariah	Zec	609
Malachi	Mal	616

New Testament

Section 5: The Gospels and Acts
Matthew	Mt	619
Mark	Mk	643
Luke	Lu	659
John	Joh	685
Acts	Ac	705

Section 6: The Epistles
Romans	Ro	731
1 Corinthians	1Co	741
2 Corinthians	2Co	750
Galatians	Ga	757
Ephesians	Eph	760
Philippians	Php	764
Colossians	Col	766
1 Thessalonians	1Th	768
2 Thessalonians	2Th	770
1 Timothy	1Ti	772
2 Timothy	2Ti	774
Titus	Ti	776
Philemon	Phm	777
Hebrews	Heb	778
James	Jas	785
1 Peter	1Pe	788
2 Peter	2Pe	791
1 John	1Jo	792
2 John	2Jo	795
3 John	3Jo	795
Jude	Jude	796

Section 7: Prophecy
Revelation	Re	797

Section 8: Concordance..................................809

Preface

The *Authorized King James Version of the Bible* of 1611 has preserved the Word of God in the English language. While God's Word does not change, languages do. Words that were once commonly known and understood fall out of usage and lose their meaning to new generations of modern English readers. To help preserve its meaning to readers, numerous updates in the language of the *Authorized King James Version of the Bible* have been made since the first edition was published. The most widely used edition of the *Authorized King James Version of the Bible* is that which was completed in 1769. Unfortunately, as changes in the English language continue, there is a widespread resistance to using the 1769 Edition of the *Authorized King James Version of the Bible* by those who claim that too many words in that version have become archaic to readers of modern English.

Following an increased emphasis on human reason, there was an advancement of the art of "textual criticism" in the early 1800s. As the demand for a "more readable" Bible intensified, biblical manuscripts that had been either discarded or ignored were resurrected. The result of applying textual criticism techniques combined with a zealous emphasis on the reliability of the limited number of rediscovered "old" manuscripts was the development of a new "Critical Text" of the Greek New Testament. That text was used to replace the "Received Text" on which the *Authorized King James Version of the Bible* was based.

The newly developed "Critical Text" was used to introduce a new English version of the Bible to the world in the late 1800s. Even though the "Revised Version" claimed to be a revision of the *Authorized King James Version of the Bible*, it was actually based on different underlying manuscripts from the Bible that it claimed to revise. After that "Revised Version" was introduced, it opened the gate for a flood of new versions, which were processed through the authority of human reason and presented as the "Holy Bible." Many of these versions either lack important passages or contain passages that are in total conflict with each other. As a result, they have brought confusion to their readers. This has led to increased questions concerning the reliability, and hence the authority, of the Scriptures.

Many of the versions that have actually updated the language of the *Authorized King James Version of the Bible* have sought to maintain their identity with the 1611 Bible by retaining the term "King James" in their names. This distinction is important because it helps readers distinguish between versions based on the Greek "Received Text" (on which the New Testament of the *Authorized King James Version of the Bible* is based) and those that are based on the Greek "Critical Text" (on which the New Testament of many other modern versions is based). Discerning readers know that there are significant differences between these two types of Greek texts. Therefore, the use of the term "King James" in the name of a version of the Bible is a method of clarifying which family of manuscripts the Bible version is based upon.

In addition to the confusion over the Word of God, there is also confusion over the Name of God. Since the translation of the Hebrew Old Testament in the Greek Septuagint during the third and second centuries B. C., a title has been traditionally used in place of His name. Consequently, many have taught that we no longer need to know His name. However, the Word of God itself tells us to call upon Him through His name and to praise Him by His name.

The term, "Proper Name," as used in *The Proper Name Version of the King James Bible*, denotes the use of a proper noun, rather than a common noun, for the name of God. A proper noun, which is also called a proper name, is a noun that designates a particular person, place, or thing and is usually not preceded by an article, such as "the." A common noun, however, does not identify a specific individual and is often preceded by an article. It refers to any or all of a group or class. Therefore, *The Proper Name Version of the King James Bible* is used to describe this version of the Bible as one that restores the proper name of God and is based on the translation known as the *King James Version of the Bible*.

Preface

The publication of *The Proper Name Version of the King James Bible* was prompted by the need expressed by many for a version of the Bible that:

(1) is edited with the understanding that it is the inspired Word of God and, therefore, it cannot be changed by the will or desires of man;

(2) is based on manuscripts translated before textual criticism theories were widely used to place the Scriptures and their revision under the authority of human reason;

(3) remains faithful to the word meanings of Hebrew and/or Greek manuscripts, which were translated into the *Authorized King James Version of the Bible*;

(4) retains the italics in the words provided for enhanced readability by the translators of the *Authorized King James Version of the Bible*, to distinguish them from the words of God;

(5) aids Scripture memory and retention by striving to retain the familiar sentence structures of the *Authorized King James Version of the Bible*;

(6) updates thousands of archaic English words into modern English, making it easier for many readers of modern English to read and understand;

(7) clarifies the meaning of the Greek word εκκλησια (ekklesia) as the congregation of those who are summoned or called out unto God;

(8) restores the Hebrew-based proper name of God (יהוה, and its short form יה, written in English as Yahweh and Yah), that was removed and replaced by the generic title κυριος (written in English as the LORD) during the translation in Egypt of the Greek Septuagint;

(9) shows the Hebrew-based proper name of God, Yahweh, in italics in the New Testament where there is clear evidence that the text references a passage containing His name in the Old Testament Hebrew manuscripts;

(10) restores the Hebrew-based proper name of the Messiah (יהושע, written in English as Yahshua, meaning Yah is salvation), given by the angel Gabriel, which has been continually revised, with its meaning obscured, as it was translated through Greek, Latin, and English languages.

The Proper Name Version of the King James Bible is presented in the belief that it will enable a greater depth of study and understanding of Yahweh and His Word.

Because I will publish the name of Yahweh: ascribe you greatness unto our God.
-Deuteronomy 32:3

Section 1
The Law

Genesis

Genesis 1

1 ¶ In the beginning God created the heaven and the earth.
2 And the earth was without form, and void; and darkness *was* upon the face of the deep. And the Spirit of God moved upon the face of the waters.
3 ¶ And God said, Let there be light: and there was light.
4 And God saw the light, that *it was* good: and God divided the light from the darkness.
5 And God called the light Day, and the darkness he called Night. And the evening and the morning were the first day.
6 ¶ And God said, Let there be a firmament in the midst of the waters, and let it divide the waters from the waters.
7 And God made the firmament, and divided the waters which *were* under the firmament from the waters which *were* above the firmament: and it was so.
8 And God called the firmament Heaven. And the evening and the morning were the second day.
9 ¶ And God said, Let the waters under the heaven be gathered together to one place, and let the dry *land* appear: and it was so.
10 And God called the dry *land* Earth; and the gathering together of the waters called he Seas: and God saw that *it was* good.
11 And God said, Let the earth bring forth grass, the herb yielding seed, *and* the fruit tree yielding fruit after his kind, whose seed *is* in itself, on the earth: and it was so.
12 And the earth brought forth grass, *and* herb yielding seed after his kind, and the tree yielding fruit, whose seed *was* in itself, after his kind: and God saw that *it was* good.
13 And the evening and the morning were the third day
14 ¶ And God said, Let there be lights in the firmament of the heaven to divide the day from the night; and let them be for signs, and for seasons, and for days, and years:
15 And let them be for lights in the firmament of the heaven to give light upon the earth: and it was so.
16 And God made two great lights; the greater light to rule the day, and the lesser light to rule the night: *he made* the stars also.
17 And God set them in the firmament of the heaven to give light upon the earth,
18 And to rule over the day and over the night, and to divide the light from the darkness: and God saw that *it was* good.
19 And the evening and the morning were the fourth day.
20 ¶ And God said, Let the waters bring forth abundantly the moving creatures that have life, and fowls *that* may fly above the earth in the open firmament of heaven.
21 And God created great whales, and every living creature that moves, which the waters brought forth abundantly, after their kind, and every winged fowl after his kind: and God saw that *it was* good.
22 And God blessed them, saying, Be fruitful, and multiply, and fill the waters in the seas, and let fowl multiply in the earth.
23 And the evening and the morning were the fifth day.
24 ¶ And God said, Let the earth bring forth the living creature after his kind, cattle, and creeping thing, and beast of the earth after his kind: and it was so.
25 And God made the beast of the earth after his kind, and cattle after their kind, and every thing that creeps upon the earth after his kind: and God saw that *it was* good.
26 ¶ And God said, Let us make man in our image, after our likeness: and let them have dominion over the fish of the sea, and over the fowl of the air, and over the cattle, and over all the earth, and over every creeping thing that creeps upon the earth.
27 So God created man in his *own* image, in the image of God created he him; male and female created he them.
28 And God blessed them, and God said unto them, Be fruitful, and multiply, and replenish the earth, and subdue it: and have dominion over the fish of the sea, and over the fowl of the air, and over every living thing that moves upon the earth.
29 ¶ And God said, Behold, I have given you every herb bearing seed, which *is* upon the face of all the earth, and every tree, in which *is* the fruit of a tree yielding seed; to you it shall be for food.
30 And to every beast of the earth, and to every fowl of the air, and to every thing that creeps upon the earth, wherein *there is* life, *I have given* every green herb for food: and it was so.
31 ¶ And God saw every thing that he had made, and, behold, *it was* very good. And the evening and the morning were the sixth day.

Genesis 2

2:1 ¶ Thus the heavens and the earth were finished, and all the host of them.
2 And on the seventh day God ended his work which he had made; and he rested on the seventh day from all his work which he had made.
3 And God blessed the seventh day, and sanctified it: because that in it he had rested from all his work which God created and made.

Genesis 2

4 ¶ These *are* the generations of the heavens and of the earth when they were created, in the day that Yahweh God made the earth and the heavens,
5 And every plant of the field before it was in the earth, and every herb of the field before it grew: for Yahweh God had not caused it to rain upon the earth, and *there was* not a man to till the ground.
6 But there went up a mist from the earth, and watered the whole face of the ground.
7 And Yahweh God formed man *of* the dust of the ground, and breathed into his nostrils the breath of life; and man became a living soul.
8 ¶ And Yahweh God planted a garden eastward in Eden; and there he put the man whom he had formed.
9 And out of the ground made Yahweh God to grow every tree that is pleasant to the sight, and good for food; the tree of life also in the midst of the garden, and the tree of knowledge of good and evil.
10 And a river went out of Eden to water the garden; and from there it was parted, and became into four heads.
11 The name of the first *is* Pison: that *is* it which encompasses the whole land of Havilah, where *there is* gold;
12 And the gold of that land *is* good: there *is* bdellium and the onyx stone.
13 And the name of the second river *is* Gihon: the same *is* it that encompasses the whole land of Ethiopia.
14 And the name of the third river *is* Hiddekel: that *is* it which goes toward the east of Assyria. And the fourth river *is* Euphrates.
15 And Yahweh God took the man, and put him into the garden of Eden to dress it and to keep it.
16 ¶ And Yahweh God commanded the man, saying, Of every tree of the garden you may freely eat:
17 But of the tree of the knowledge of good and evil, you shall not eat of it: for in the day that you eat thereof you shall surely die.
18 ¶ And Yahweh God said, *It is* not good that the man should be alone; I will make him a help match for him.
19 And out of the ground Yahweh God formed every beast of the field, and every fowl of the air; and brought *them* to Adam to see what he would call them: and whatever Adam called every living creature, that *was* the name thereof.
20 And Adam gave names to all cattle, and to the fowl of the air, and to every beast of the field; but for Adam there was not found a help match for him.
21 ¶ And Yahweh God caused a deep sleep to fall upon Adam, and he slept: and he took one of his ribs, and closed up the flesh instead thereof;
22 And the rib, which Yahweh God had taken from man, made he a woman, and brought her to the man.
23 And Adam said, This *is* now bone of my bones, and flesh of my flesh: she shall be called Woman, because she was taken out of Man.
24 Therefore shall a man leave his father and his mother, and shall join to his wife: and they shall be one flesh.
25 And they were both naked, the man and his wife, and were not ashamed.

Genesis 3

3:1 ¶ Now the serpent was more subtle than any beast of the field which Yahweh God had made. And he said to the woman, Indeed, has God said, You shall not eat of every tree of the garden?
2 And the woman said unto the serpent, We may eat of the fruit of the trees of the garden:
3 But of the fruit of the tree which *is* in the midst of the garden, God has said, You shall not eat of it, neither shall you touch it, lest you die.
4 And the serpent said unto the woman, You shall not surely die:
5 For God does know that in the day you eat thereof, then your eyes shall be opened, and you shall be as gods, knowing good and evil.
6 ¶ And when the woman saw that the tree *was* good for food, and that it *was* pleasant to the eyes, and a tree to be desired to make *one* wise, she took of the fruit thereof, and did eat, and gave also to her husband with her; and he did eat.
7 And the eyes of them both were opened, and they knew that they *were* naked; and they sewed fig leaves together, and made themselves aprons.
8 And they heard the voice of Yahweh God walking in the garden in the cool of the day: and Adam and his wife hid themselves from the presence of Yahweh God among the trees of the garden.
9 ¶ And Yahweh God called to Adam, and said to him, Where *are* you?
10 And he said, I heard your voice in the garden, and I was afraid, because I *was* naked; and I hid myself.
11 ¶ And he said, Who told you that you *were* naked? Have you eaten of the tree, whereof I commanded you that you should not eat?
12 And the man said, The woman whom you gave *to be* with me, she gave me of the tree, and I did eat.
13 And Yahweh God said unto the woman, What *is* this *that* you have done? And the woman said, The serpent beguiled me, and I did eat.
14 ¶ And Yahweh God said to the serpent, Because you have done this, you *are* cursed above all cattle, and above every beast of the field; upon your belly shall you go, and dust shall you eat all the days of your life:
15 And I will put enmity between you and the woman, and between your seed and her seed; it shall bruise your head, and you shall bruise his heel.
16 ¶ Unto the woman he said, I will greatly multiply your sorrow and your conception; in sorrow you shall bring forth children; and your desire *shall be* to your husband, and he shall rule over you.
17 ¶ And to Adam he said, Because you have listened to the voice of your wife, and have eaten of the tree, of which I commanded you, saying, You shall not eat of it: cursed *is* the ground for your sake; in sorrow shall you eat *of* it all the days of your life;
18 Thorns also and thistles shall it bring forth to you; and you shall eat the herb of the field;

19 In the sweat of your face shall you eat bread, till you return to the ground; for out of it were you taken: for dust you *are*, and to dust shall you return.
20 ¶ And Adam called his wife's name Eve; because she was the mother of all living.
21 ¶ Unto Adam also and to his wife did Yahweh God make coats of skins, and clothed them.
22 ¶ And Yahweh God said, Behold, the man has become as one of us, to know good and evil: and now, lest he puts forth his hand, and takes also of the tree of life, and eats, and lives forever:
23 Therefore Yahweh God sent him forth from the garden of Eden, to till the ground from where he was taken.
24 So he drove out the man; and he placed at the east of the garden of Eden Cherubims, and a flaming sword which turned every way, to keep the way of the tree of life.

Genesis 4

4:1 ¶ And Adam knew Eve his wife; and she conceived, and bore Cain, and said, I have gotten a man from Yahweh.
2 And she again bore his brother Abel. And Abel was a keeper of sheep, but Cain was a tiller of the ground.
3 ¶ And in *the* process of time it came to pass, that Cain brought of the fruit of the ground an offering unto Yahweh.
4 And Abel, he also brought of the firstborn of his flock and of the fat thereof. And Yahweh had respect unto Abel and to his offering:
5 But unto Cain and to his offering he had not respect. And Cain was very angry, and his countenance fell.
6 ¶ And Yahweh said unto Cain, Why are you angry? and why is your countenance fallen?
7 If you do well, shall you not be accepted? and if you do not well, sin lies at the door. And unto you *shall be* his desire, and you shall rule over him.
8 ¶ And Cain talked with Abel his brother: and it came to pass, when they were in the field, that Cain rose up against Abel his brother, and slew him.
9 ¶ And Yahweh said unto Cain, Where *is* Abel your brother? And he said, I know not: *Am* I my brother's keeper?
10 And he said, What have you done? the voice of your brother's blood cries to me from the ground.
11 And now *are* you cursed from the earth, which has opened her mouth to receive your brother's blood from your hand;
12 When you till the ground, it shall not henceforth yield to you her strength; a fugitive and a vagabond shall you be in the earth.
13 ¶ And Cain said unto Yahweh, My punishment *is* greater than I can bear.
14 Behold, you have driven me out this day from the face of the earth; and from your face shall I be hidden; and I shall be a fugitive and a vagabond in the earth; and it shall come to pass, *that* every one that finds me shall slay me.
15 And Yahweh said to him, Therefore whoever slays Cain, vengeance shall be taken upon him sevenfold. And Yahweh set a mark upon Cain, lest any finding him should kill him.
16 ¶ And Cain went out from the presence of Yahweh, and dwelt in the land of Nod, on the east of Eden.
17 And Cain knew his wife; and she conceived, and bore Enoch: and he built a city, and called the name of the city, after the name of his son, Enoch.
18 And to Enoch was born Irad: and Irad begot Mehujael: and Mehujael begot Methusael: and Methusael begot Lamech.
19 ¶ And Lamech took unto him two wives: the name of the one *was* Adah, and the name of the other Zillah.
20 And Adah bore Jabal: he was the father of such as dwell in tents, and *of such as have* cattle.
21 And his brother's name *was* Jubal: he was the father of all such as handle the harp and organ.
22 And Zillah, she also bore Tubalcain, an instructor of every craftsman in brass and iron: and the sister of Tubalcain *was* Naamah.
23 ¶ And Lamech said to his wives, Adah and Zillah, Hear my voice; you wives of Lamech, listen to my speech: for I have slain a man for my wounding, and a young man for my hurt.
24 If Cain shall be avenged sevenfold, truly Lamech seventy and sevenfold.
25 ¶ And Adam knew his wife again; and she bore a son, and called his name Seth: For God, *said she*, has appointed me another seed instead of Abel, whom Cain slew.
26 And to Seth, to him also there was born a son; and he called his name Enos: then began men to call upon the name of Yahweh.

Genesis 5

5:1 ¶ This *is* the book of the generations of Adam. In the day that God created man, in the likeness of God made he him;
2 Male and female created he them; and blessed them, and called their name Adam, in the day when they were created.
3 And Adam lived a hundred and thirty years, and begot *a son* in his own likeness, after his image; and called his name Seth:
4 And the days of Adam after he had begotten Seth were eight hundred years: and he begot sons and daughters:
5 And all the days that Adam lived were nine hundred and thirty years: and he died.
6 ¶ And Seth lived a hundred and five years, and begot Enos:
7 And Seth lived after he begot Enos eight hundred and seven years, and begot sons and daughters:
8 And all the days of Seth were nine hundred and twelve years: and he died.
9 And Enos lived ninety years, and begot Cainan:

Genesis 5

10 And Enos lived after he begot Cainan eight hundred and fifteen years, and begot sons and daughters:
11 And all the days of Enos were nine hundred and five years: and he died.
12 And Cainan lived seventy years, and begot Mahalaleel:
13 And Cainan lived after he begot Mahalaleel eight hundred and forty years, and begot sons and daughters:
14 And all the days of Cainan were nine hundred and ten years: and he died.
15 And Mahalaleel lived sixty and five years, and begot Jared:
16 And Mahalaleel lived after he begot Jared eight hundred and thirty years, and begot sons and daughters:
17 And all the days of Mahalaleel were eight hundred ninety and five years: and he died.
18 And Jared lived a hundred sixty and two years, and he begot Enoch:
19 And Jared lived after he begot Enoch eight hundred years, and begot sons and daughters:
20 And all the days of Jared were nine hundred sixty and two years: and he died.
21 ¶ And Enoch lived sixty and five years, and begot Methuselah:
22 And Enoch walked with God after he begot Methuselah three hundred years, and begot sons and daughters:
23 And all the days of Enoch were three hundred sixty and five years:
24 And Enoch walked with God: and he *was* not; for God took him.
25 ¶ And Methuselah lived a hundred eighty and seven years, and begot Lamech:
26 And Methuselah lived after he begot Lamech seven hundred eighty and two years, and begot sons and daughters:
27 And all the days of Methuselah were nine hundred sixty and nine years: and he died.
28 ¶ And Lamech lived a hundred eighty and two years, and begot a son:
29 And he called his name Noah, saying, This *same* shall comfort us concerning our work and toil of our hands, because of the ground which Yahweh has cursed.
30 And Lamech lived after he begot Noah five hundred ninety and five years, and begot sons and daughters:
31 And all the days of Lamech were seven hundred seventy and seven years: and he died.
32 And Noah was five hundred years old: and Noah begot Shem, Ham, and Japheth.

Genesis 6

6:1 ¶ And it came to pass, when men began to multiply on the face of the earth, and daughters were born to them,
2 That the sons of God saw the daughters of men that they *were* fair; and they took them wives of all which they chose.
3 ¶ And Yahweh said, My spirit shall not always strive with man, for that he also *is* flesh: yet his days shall be a hundred and twenty years.
4 ¶ There were giants in the earth in those days; and also after that, when the sons of God came in unto the daughters of men, and they bore *children* to them, the same *became* mighty men which *were* of old, men of renown.
5 And Yahweh saw that the wickedness of man *was* great in the earth, and *that* every imagination of the thoughts of his heart *was* only evil continually.
6 ¶ And it repented Yahweh that he had made man on the earth, and it grieved him at his heart.
7 And Yahweh said, I will destroy man whom I have created from the face of the earth; both man, and beast, and the creeping thing, and the fowls of the air; for it repents me that I have made them.
8 ¶ But Noah found grace in the eyes of Yahweh.
9 These *are* the generations of Noah: Noah was a just man *and* perfect in his generations, *and* Noah walked with God.
10 And Noah begot three sons, Shem, Ham, and Japheth.
11 ¶ The earth also was corrupt before God, and the earth was filled with violence.
12 And God looked upon the earth, and, behold, it was corrupt; for all flesh had corrupted his way upon the earth.
13 ¶ And God said to Noah, The end of all flesh has come before me; for the earth is filled with violence through them; and, behold, I will destroy them with the earth.
14 Make you an ark of gopher wood; rooms shall you make in the ark, and shall pitch it within and without with pitch.
15 And this *is the fashion* which you shall make it *of*: The length of the ark *shall be* three hundred cubits, the breadth of it fifty cubits, and the height of it thirty cubits.
16 A window shall you make for the ark, and in a cubit shall you finish it above; and the door of the ark shall you set in the side thereof; *with* lower, second, and third *stories* shall you make it.
17 And, behold, I, even I, do bring a flood of waters upon the earth, to destroy all flesh, wherein *is* the breath of life, from under heaven; *and* every thing that *is* in the earth shall die.
18 But with you shall I establish my covenant; and you shall come into the ark, you, and your sons, and your wife, and your sons' wives with you.
19 And of every living thing of all flesh, two of every *sort* shall you bring into the ark, to keep *them* alive with you; they shall be male and female.
20 Of fowls after their kind, and of cattle after their kind, of every creeping thing of the earth after his kind, two of every *sort* shall come to you, to keep *them* alive.
21 And take you unto you of all food that is eaten, and you shall gather *it* to you; and it shall be for food for you, and for them.

22 ¶ Thus did Noah; according to all that God commanded him, so did he.

Genesis 7

7:1 ¶ And Yahweh said unto Noah, Come you and all your house into the ark; for you have I seen righteous before me in this generation.

2 Of every clean beast you shall take to you by sevens, the male and his female: and of beasts that *are* not clean by two, the male and his female.

3 Of fowls also of the air by sevens, the male and the female; to keep seed alive upon the face of all the earth.

4 For yet seven days, and I will cause it to rain upon the earth forty days and forty nights; and every living substance that I have made will I destroy from off the face of the earth.

5 ¶ And Noah did according to all that Yahweh commanded him.

6 And Noah *was* six hundred years old when the flood of waters was upon the earth.

7 And Noah went in, and his sons, and his wife, and his sons' wives with him, into the ark, because of the waters of the flood.

8 Of clean beasts, and of beasts that *are* not clean, and of fowls, and of every thing that creeps upon the earth,

9 There went in two by two unto Noah into the ark, the male and the female, as God had commanded Noah.

10 And it came to pass after seven days, that the waters of the flood were upon the earth.

11 ¶ In the six hundredth year of Noah's life, in the second month, the seventeenth day of the month, the same day were all the fountains of the great deep broken up, and the windows of heaven were opened.

12 And the rain was upon the earth forty days and forty nights.

13 ¶ In the very same day entered Noah, and Shem, and Ham, and Japheth, the sons of Noah, and Noah's wife, and the three wives of his sons with them, into the ark;

14 They, and every beast after his kind, and all the cattle after their kind, and every creeping thing that creeps upon the earth after his kind, and every fowl after his kind, every bird of every sort.

15 And they went in unto Noah into the ark, two and two of all flesh, wherein *is* the breath of life

16 And they that went in, went in male and female of all flesh, as God had commanded him: and Yahweh shut him in.

17 ¶ And the flood was forty days upon the earth; and the waters increased, and bore up the ark, and it was lifted up above the earth.

18 And the waters prevailed, and were increased greatly upon the earth; and the ark went upon the face of the waters.

19 And the waters prevailed exceedingly upon the earth; and all the high hills, that *were* under the whole heaven, were covered.

20 Fifteen cubits upward did the waters prevail; and the mountains were covered.

21 ¶ And all flesh died that moved upon the earth, both of fowl, and of cattle, and of beast, and of every creeping thing that creeps upon the earth, and every man:

22 All in whose nostrils *was* the breath of life, of all that *was* in the dry *land*, died.

23 And every living substance was destroyed which was upon the face of the ground, both man, and cattle, and the creeping things, and the fowl of the heaven; and they were destroyed from the earth: and Noah only remained *alive*, and they that *were* with him in the ark.

24 And the waters prevailed upon the earth a hundred and fifty days.

Genesis 8

8:1 ¶ And God remembered Noah, and every living thing, and all the cattle that *was* with him in the ark: and God made a wind to pass over the earth, and the waters subsided;

2 The fountains also of the deep and the windows of heaven were stopped, and the rain from heaven was restrained;

3 And the waters returned from off the earth continually: and after the end of the hundred and fifty days the waters were abated.

4 ¶ And the ark rested in the seventh month, on the seventeenth day of the month, upon the mountains of Ararat.

5 And the waters decreased continually until the tenth month: in the tenth *month*, on the first *day* of the month, were the tops of the mountains seen.

6 ¶ And it came to pass at the end of forty days, that Noah opened the window of the ark which he had made:

7 And he sent forth a raven, which went forth to and fro, until the waters were dried up from off the earth.

8 Also he sent forth a dove from him, to see if the waters were abated from off the face of the ground;

9 But the dove found no rest for the sole of her foot, and she returned unto him into the ark, for the waters *were* on the face of the whole earth: then he put forth his hand, and took her, and pulled her in to him into the ark.

10 And he stayed yet another seven days; and again he sent forth the dove out of the ark;

11 And the dove came in to him in the evening; and, behold, in her mouth *was* an olive leaf plucked off: so Noah knew that the waters were abated from off the earth.

12 And he stayed yet another seven days; and sent forth the dove; which returned not again to him any more.

13 ¶ And it came to pass in the six hundredth and first year, in the first *month*, the first *day* of the month, the waters were dried up from off the earth: and Noah removed the covering of the ark, and looked, and, behold, the face of the ground was dry.

Genesis 8

14 And in the second month, on the seven and twentieth day of the month, was the earth dried.
15 ¶ And God spoke unto Noah, saying,
16 Go forth from the ark, you, and your wife, and your sons, and your sons' wives with you.
17 Bring forth with you every living thing that *is* with you, of all flesh, *both* of fowl, and of cattle, and of every creeping thing that creeps upon the earth; that they may breed abundantly in the earth, and be fruitful, and multiply upon the earth.
18 And Noah went forth, and his sons, and his wife, and his sons' wives with him:
19 Every beast, every creeping thing, and every fowl, *and* whatever creeps upon the earth, after their kinds, went forth out of the ark.
20 ¶ And Noah built an altar unto Yahweh; and took of every clean beast, and of every clean fowl, and offered burnt offerings upon the altar.
21 And Yahweh smelled a sweet savor; and Yahweh said in his heart, I will not again curse the ground any more for man's sake; for the imagination of man's heart *is* evil from his youth; neither will I again smite any more every thing living, as I have done.
22 While the earth remains, seedtime and harvest, and cold and heat, and summer and winter, and day and night shall not cease.

Genesis 9

9:1 ¶ And God blessed Noah and his sons, and said to them, Be fruitful, and multiply, and replenish the earth.
2 And the fear of you and the dread of you shall be upon every beast of the earth, and upon every fowl of the air, upon all that moves *upon* the earth, and upon all the fishes of the sea; into your hand are they delivered.
3 Every moving thing that lives shall be food for you; even as the green herb have I given you all things.
4 But flesh with the life thereof, *which is* the blood thereof, shall you not eat.
5 And surely your blood of your lives will I require; at the hand of every beast will I require it, and at the hand of man; at the hand of every man's brother will I require the life of man.
6 Whoever sheds man's blood, by man shall his blood be shed: for in the image of God made he man.
7 And you, be you fruitful, and multiply; bring forth abundantly in the earth, and multiply therein.
8 ¶ And God spoke to Noah, and to his sons with him, saying,
9 And I, behold, I establish my covenant with you, and with your seed after you;
10 And with every living creature that *is* with you, of the fowl, of the cattle, and of every beast of the earth with you; from all that go out of the ark, to every beast of the earth.
11 And I will establish my covenant with you; neither shall all flesh be cut off any more by the waters of a flood; neither shall there any more be a flood to destroy the earth.
12 ¶ And God said, This *is* the token of the covenant which I make between me and you and every living creature that *is* with you, for perpetual generations:
13 I do set my bow in the cloud, and it shall be for a token of a covenant between me and the earth.
14 And it shall come to pass, when I bring a cloud over the earth, that the bow shall be seen in the cloud:
15 And I will remember my covenant, which *is* between me and you and every living creature of all flesh; and the waters shall no more become a flood to destroy all flesh.
16 And the bow shall be in the cloud; and I will look upon it, that I may remember the everlasting covenant between God and every living creature of all flesh that *is* upon the earth.
17 And God said to Noah, This *is* the token of the covenant, which I have established between me and all flesh that *is* upon the earth.
18 ¶ And the sons of Noah, that went forth of the ark, were Shem, and Ham, and Japheth: and Ham *is* the father of Canaan.
19 These *are* the three sons of Noah: and of them was the whole earth overspread.
20 And Noah began *to be* a husbandman, and he planted a vineyard:
21 And he drank of the wine, and was drunken; and he was uncovered within his tent.
22 And Ham, the father of Canaan, saw the nakedness of his father, and told his two brothers outside.
23 And Shem and Japheth took a garment, and laid *it* upon both their shoulders, and went backward, and covered the nakedness of their father; and their faces *were* backward, and they saw not their father's nakedness.
24 ¶ And Noah awoke from his wine, and knew what his younger son had done unto him.
25 And he said, Cursed *be* Canaan; a servant of servants shall he be unto his brethren.
26 And he said, Blessed *be* Yahweh God of Shem; and Canaan shall be his servant.
27 God shall enlarge Japheth, and he shall dwell in the tents of Shem; and Canaan shall be his servant.
28 ¶ And Noah lived after the flood three hundred and fifty years.
29 And all the days of Noah were nine hundred and fifty years: and he died.

Genesis 10

10:1 ¶ Now these *are* the generations of the sons of Noah, Shem, Ham, and Japheth: and unto them were sons born after the flood.
2 The sons of Japheth; Gomer, and Magog, and Madai, and Javan, and Tubal, and Meshech, and Tiras.
3 And the sons of Gomer; Ashkenaz, and Riphath, and Togarmah.
4 And the sons of Javan; Elishah, and Tarshish, Kittim, and Dodanim.

5 By these were the isles of the Gentiles divided in their lands; every one after his tongue, after their families, in their nations.
6 ¶ And the sons of Ham; Cush, and Mizraim, and Phut, and Canaan.
7 And the sons of Cush; Seba, and Havilah, and Sabtah, and Raamah, and Sabtecha: and the sons of Raamah; Sheba, and Dedan.
8 And Cush begot Nimrod: he began to be a mighty one in the earth.
9 He was a mighty hunter before Yahweh: therefore it is said, Even as Nimrod the mighty hunter before Yahweh.
10 And the beginning of his kingdom was Babel, and Erech, and Accad, and Calneh, in the land of Shinar.
11 Out of that land went forth Asshur, and built Nineveh, and the city Rehoboth, and Calah,
12 And Resen between Nineveh and Calah: the same *is* a great city.
13 And Mizraim begot Ludim, and Anamim, and Lehabim, and Naphtuhim,
14 And Pathrusim, and Casluhim, (out of whom came Philistim,) and Caphtorim.
15 ¶ And Canaan begot Sidon his firstborn, and Heth,
16 And the Jebusite, and the Amorite, and the Girgasite,
17 And the Hivite, and the Arkite, and the Sinite,
18 And the Arvadite, and the Zemarite, and the Hamathite: and afterward were the families of the Canaanites spread abroad.
19 And the border of the Canaanites was from Sidon, as you come to Gerar, to Gaza; as you go, to Sodom, and Gomorrah, and Admah, and Zeboim, even to Lasha.
20 These *are* the sons of Ham, after their families, after their tongues, in their countries, *and* in their nations.
21 ¶ Unto Shem also, the father of all the children of Eber, the brother of Japheth the elder, even to him were *children* born.
22 The children of Shem; Elam, and Asshur, and Arphaxad, and Lud, and Aram.
23 And the children of Aram; Uz, and Hul, and Gether, and Mash.
24 And Arphaxad begot Salah; and Salah begot Eber.
25 And to Eber were born two sons: the name of one *was* Peleg; for in his days was the earth divided; and his brother's name *was* Joktan.
26 And Joktan begot Almodad, and Sheleph, and Hazarmaveth, and Jerah,
27 And Hadoram, and Uzal, and Diklah,
28 And Obal, and Abimael, and Sheba,
29 And Ophir, and Havilah, and Jobab: all these *were* the sons of Joktan.
30 And their dwelling was from Mesha, as you go unto Sephar a mount of the east.
31 These *are* the sons of Shem, after their families, after their tongues, in their lands, after their nations.
32 These *are* the families of the sons of Noah, after their generations, in their nations: and by these were the nations divided in the earth after the flood.

Genesis 11

11:1 ¶ And the whole earth was of one language, and of one speech.
2 And it came to pass, as they journeyed from the east, that they found a plain in the land of Shinar; and they dwelt there.
3 And they said one to another, Go to, let us make brick, and burn them thoroughly. And they had brick for stone, and slime had they for mortar.
4 And they said, Go to, let us build us a city and a tower, whose top *may reach* unto heaven; and let us make us a name, lest we be scattered abroad upon the face of the whole earth.
5 ¶ And Yahweh came down to see the city and the tower, which the children of men built.
6 And Yahweh said, Behold, the people *are* one, and they have all one language; and this they begin to do: and now nothing will be restrained from them, which they have imagined to do.
7 Go to, let us go down, and there confound their language, that they may not understand one another's speech.
8 So Yahweh scattered them abroad from there upon the face of all the earth: and they ceased to build the city.
9 Therefore is the name of it called Babel; because Yahweh did there confound the language of all the earth: and from there did Yahweh scatter them abroad upon the face of all the earth.
10 ¶ These *are* the generations of Shem: Shem *was* a hundred years old, and begot Arphaxad two years after the flood:
11 And Shem lived after he begot Arphaxad five hundred years, and begot sons and daughters.
12 And Arphaxad lived five and thirty years, and begot Salah:
13 And Arphaxad lived after he begot Salah four hundred and three years, and begot sons and daughters.
14 And Salah lived thirty years, and begot Eber:
15 And Salah lived after he begot Eber four hundred and three years, and begot sons and daughters.
16 And Eber lived four and thirty years, and begot Peleg:
17 And Eber lived after he begot Peleg four hundred and thirty years, and begot sons and daughters.
18 And Peleg lived thirty years, and begot Reu:
19 And Peleg lived after he begot Reu two hundred and nine years, and begot sons and daughters.
20 And Reu lived two and thirty years, and begot Serug:
21 And Reu lived after he begot Serug two hundred and seven years, and begot sons and daughters.
22 And Serug lived thirty years, and begot Nahor:
23 And Serug lived after he begot Nahor two hundred years, and begot sons and daughters.
24 And Nahor lived nine and twenty years, and begot Terah:
25 And Nahor lived after he begot Terah a hundred and nineteen years, and begot sons and daughters.

Genesis 11

26 And Terah lived seventy years, and begot Abram, Nahor, and Haran.
27 ¶ Now these *are* the generations of Terah: Terah begot Abram, Nahor, and Haran; and Haran begot Lot.
28 And Haran died before his father Terah in the land of his nativity, in Ur of the Chaldees.
29 And Abram and Nahor took them wives: the name of Abram's wife *was* Sarai; and the name of Nahor's wife, Milcah, the daughter of Haran, the father of Milcah, and the father of Iscah.
30 But Sarai was barren; she *had* no child.
31 And Terah took Abram his son, and Lot the son of Haran his son's son, and Sarai his daughter-in-law, his son Abram's wife; and they went forth with them from Ur of the Chaldees, to go into the land of Canaan; and they came to Haran, and dwelt there.
32 And the days of Terah were two hundred and five years: and Terah died in Haran.

Genesis 12

12:1 ¶ Now Yahweh had said to Abram, Get you out of your country, and from your kindred, and from your father's house, to a land that I will show you:
2 And I will make of you a great nation, and I will bless you, and make your name great; and you shall be a blessing:
3 And I will bless them that bless you, and curse him that curses you: and in you shall all families of the earth be blessed.
4 ¶ So Abram departed, as Yahweh had spoken to him; and Lot went with him: and Abram *was* seventy and five years old when he departed out of Haran.
5 And Abram took Sarai his wife, and Lot his brother's son, and all their substance that they had gathered, and the souls that they had gotten in Haran; and they went forth to go into the land of Canaan; and into the land of Canaan they came.
6 ¶ And Abram passed through the land to the place of Sichem, to the plain of Moreh. And the Canaanite *was* then in the land.
7 And Yahweh appeared to Abram, and said, Unto your seed will I give this land: and there built he an altar unto Yahweh, who appeared to him.
8 And he removed from there to a mountain upon the east of Bethel, and pitched his tent, *having* Bethel on the west, and Hai on the east: and there he built an altar unto Yahweh, and called upon the name of Yahweh.
9 And Abram journeyed, going on still toward the south.
10 ¶ And there was a famine in the land: and Abram went down into Egypt to sojourn there; for the famine *was* grievous in the land.
11 And it came to pass, when he had come near to enter into Egypt, that he said to Sarai his wife, Behold now, I know that you *are* a fair woman to look upon:
12 Therefore it shall come to pass, when the Egyptians shall see you, that they shall say, This *is* his wife: and they will kill me, but they will save you alive.
13 Say, I pray you, you *are* my sister: that it may be well with me for your sake; and my soul shall live because of you.
14 ¶ And it came to pass, that, when Abram had come into Egypt, the Egyptians saw the woman that she *was* very fair.
15 The princes also of Pharaoh saw her, and commended her before Pharaoh: and the woman was taken into Pharaoh's house.
16 And he treated Abram well for her sake: and he had sheep, and oxen, and he donkeys, and menservants, and maidservants, and she donkeys, and camels.
17 And Yahweh plagued Pharaoh and his house with great plagues because of Sarai Abram's wife.
18 And Pharaoh called Abram, and said, What *is* this *that* you have done to me? why did you not tell me that she *was* your wife?
19 Why said you, She *is* my sister? so I might have taken her to me to wife: now therefore behold your wife, take *her*, and go your way.
20 And Pharaoh commanded *his* men concerning him: and they sent him away, and his wife, and all that he had.

Genesis 13

13:1 ¶ And Abram went up out of Egypt, he, and his wife, and all that he had, and Lot with him, into the south.
2 And Abram *was* very rich in cattle, in silver, and in gold.
3 And he went on his journeys from the south even to Bethel, to the place where his tent had been at the beginning, between Bethel and Hai;
4 Unto the place of the altar, which he had made there at the first: and there Abram called on the name of Yahweh.
5 ¶ And Lot also, which went with Abram, had flocks, and herds, and tents.
6 And the land was not able to bear them, that they might dwell together: for their substance was great, so that they could not dwell together.
7 And there was a strife between the herdsmen of Abram's cattle and the herdsmen of Lot's cattle: and the Canaanite and the Perizzite dwelt then in the land.
8 And Abram said to Lot, Let there be no strife, I pray you, between me and you, and between my herdsmen and your herdsmen; for we *are* brethren.
9 *Is* not the whole land before you? separate yourself, I pray you, from me: if *you will take* the left hand, then I will go to the right; or if *you depart* to the right hand, then I will go to the left.
10 ¶ And Lot lifted up his eyes, and saw all the plain of Jordan, that it *was* well watered every where, before Yahweh destroyed Sodom and Gomorrah, *even* as the garden of Yahweh, like the land of Egypt, as you come unto Zoar.
11 Then Lot chose him all the plain of Jordan; and Lot journeyed east: and they separated themselves the one from the other.

12 Abram dwelt in the land of Canaan, and Lot dwelt in the cities of the plain, and pitched *his* tent toward Sodom.
13 But the men of Sodom *were* wicked and sinners before Yahweh exceedingly.
14 ¶ And Yahweh said to Abram, after that Lot was separated from him, Lift up now your eyes, and look from the place where you are northward, and southward, and eastward, and westward:
15 For all the land which you see, to you will I give it, and to your seed forever.
16 And I will make your seed as the dust of the earth: so that if a man can number the dust of the earth, *then* shall your seed also be numbered.
17 Arise, walk through the land in the length of it and in the breadth of it; for I will give it to you.
18 Then Abram removed *his* tent, and came and dwelt in the plain of Mamre, which *is* in Hebron, and built there an altar unto Yahweh.

Genesis 14

14:1 ¶ And it came to pass in the days of Amraphel king of Shinar, Arioch king of Ellasar, Chedorlaomer king of Elam, and Tidal king of nations;
2 *That these* made war with Bera king of Sodom, and with Birsha king of Gomorrah, Shinab king of Admah, and Shemeber king of Zeboiim, and the king of Bela, which is Zoar.
3 All these were joined together in the valley of Siddim, which is the salt sea.
4 Twelve years they served Chedorlaomer, and in the thirteenth year they rebelled.
5 And in the fourteenth year came Chedorlaomer, and the kings that *were* with him, and smote the Rephaims in Ashteroth Karnaim, and the Zuzims in Ham, and the Emims in Shaveh Kiriathaim,
6 And the Horites in their mount Seir, unto Elparan, which *is* by the wilderness.
7 And they returned, and came to Enmishpat, which *is* Kadesh, and smote all the country of the Amalekites, and also the Amorites, that dwelt in Hazezontamar.
8 And there went out the king of Sodom, and the king of Gomorrah, and the king of Admah, and the king of Zeboiim, and the king of Bela (the same *is* Zoar;) and they joined battle with them in the valley of Siddim;
9 With Chedorlaomer the king of Elam, and with Tidal king of nations, and Amraphel king of Shinar, and Arioch king of Ellasar; four kings against five.
10 And the valley of Siddim *was full of* slime pits; and the kings of Sodom and Gomorrah fled, and fell there; and they that remained fled to the mountain.
11 And they took all the goods of Sodom and Gomorrah, and all their victuals, and went their way.
12 And they took Lot, Abram's brother's son, who dwelt in Sodom, and his goods, and departed.
13 ¶ And there came one that had escaped, and told Abram the Hebrew; for he dwelt in the plain of Mamre the Amorite, brother of Eshcol, and brother of Aner: and these *were* confederate with Abram.

14 And when Abram heard that his brother was taken captive, he armed his trained *servants*, born in his own house, three hundred and eighteen, and pursued *them* unto Dan.
15 And he divided himself against them, he and his servants, by night, and smote them, and pursued them to Hobah, which *is* on the left hand of Damascus.
16 And he brought back all the goods, and also brought again his brother Lot, and his goods, and the women also, and the people.
17 ¶ And the king of Sodom went out to meet him after his return from the slaughter of Chedorlaomer, and of the kings that *were* with him, at the valley of Shaveh, which *is* the king's valley.
18 And Melchizedek king of Salem brought forth bread and wine: and he *was* the priest of the most high God.
19 And he blessed him, and said, Blessed *be* Abram of the most high God, possessor of heaven and earth:
20 And blessed be the most high God, which has delivered your enemies into your hand. And he gave him tithes of all.
21 ¶ And the king of Sodom said to Abram, Give me the persons, and take the goods to yourself.
22 And Abram said to the king of Sodom, I have lifted up my hand unto Yahweh, the most high God, the possessor of heaven and earth,
23 That I will not *take* from a thread even to a shoe latch, and that I will not take anything that *is* yours, lest you should say, I have made Abram rich:
24 Save only that which the young men have eaten, and the portion of the men which went with me, Aner, Eshcol, and Mamre; let them take their portion.

Genesis 15

15:1 ¶ After these things the word of Yahweh came to Abram in a vision, saying, Fear not, Abram: I *am* your shield, *and* your exceedingly great reward.
2 ¶ And Abram said, Lord Yahweh, what will you give me, seeing I go childless, and the steward of my house *is* this Eliezer of Damascus?
3 And Abram said, Behold, to me you have given no seed: and, look, one born in my house is my heir.
4 And, behold, the word of Yahweh *came* to him, saying, This shall not be your heir; but he that shall come forth out of your own bowels shall be your heir.
5 And he brought him forth abroad, and said, Look now toward heaven, and tell the stars, if you are able to number them: and he said to him, So shall your seed be.
6 And he believed in Yahweh; and he counted it to him for righteousness.
7 ¶ And he said to him, I *am* Yahweh that brought you out of Ur of the Chaldees, to give you this land to inherit it.
8 And he said, Lord Yahweh, whereby shall I know that I shall inherit it?
9 And he said to him, Take me a heifer of three years old, and a she goat of three years old, and a ram of three years old, and a turtledove, and a young pigeon.

Genesis 15

10 And he took to him all these, and divided them in the middle, and laid each piece one against another: but the birds divided he not.
11 And when the fowls came down upon the carcasses, Abram drove them away.
12 ¶ And when the sun was going down, a deep sleep fell upon Abram; and, behold, a horror of great darkness fell upon him.
13 And he said to Abram, Know for certain that your seed shall be a stranger in a land *that is* not theirs, and shall serve them; and they shall afflict them four hundred years;
14 And also that nation, whom they shall serve, will I judge: and afterward shall they come out with great substance.
15 And you shall go to your fathers in peace; you shall be buried in a good old age.
16 But in the fourth generation they shall come here again: for the iniquity of the Amorites *is* not yet full.
17 ¶ And it came to pass, that, when the sun went down, and it was dark, behold a smoking furnace, and a burning lamp that passed between those pieces.
18 In the same day Yahweh made a covenant with Abram, saying, Unto your seed have I given this land, from the river of Egypt to the great river, the river Euphrates:
19 The Kenites, and the Kenizzites, and the Kadmonites,
20 And the Hittites, and the Perizzites, and the Rephaims,
21 And the Amorites, and the Canaanites, and the Girgashites, and the Jebusites.

Genesis 16

16:1 ¶ Now Sarai Abram's wife bore him no children: and she had a handmaid, an Egyptian, whose name *was* Hagar.
2 And Sarai said to Abram, Behold now, Yahweh has restrained me from bearing: I pray you, go in to my maid; it may be that I may obtain children by her. And Abram listened to the voice of Sarai.
3 And Sarai Abram's wife took Hagar her maid the Egyptian, after Abram had dwelt ten years in the land of Canaan, and gave her to her husband Abram to be his wife.
4 ¶ And he went in to Hagar, and she conceived: and when she saw that she had conceived, her mistress was despised in her eyes.
5 And Sarai said to Abram, My wrong *be* upon you: I have given my maid into your bosom; and when she saw that she had conceived, I was despised in her eyes: Yahweh judge between me and you.
6 But Abram said to Sarai, Behold, your maid *is* in your hand; do to her as it pleases you. And when Sarai dealt hardly with her, she fled from her face.
7 ¶ And the angel of Yahweh found her by a fountain of water in the wilderness, by the fountain in the way to Shur.
8 And he said, Hagar, Sarai's maid, from where came you? and where will you go? And she said, I flee from the face of my mistress Sarai.

9 And the angel of Yahweh said to her, Return to your mistress, and submit yourself under her hands.
10 ¶ And the angel of Yahweh said to her, I will multiply your seed exceedingly, that it shall not be numbered for multitude.
11 And the angel of Yahweh said to her, Behold, you *are* with child, and shall bear a son, and shall call his name Ishmael; because Yahweh has heard your affliction.
12 And he will be a wild man; his hand *will be* against every man, and every man's hand against him; and he shall dwell in the presence of all his brethren.
13 And she called the name of Yahweh that spoke to her, You God sees me: for she said, Have I also here looked after him that sees me?
14 Therefore the well was called Beerlahairoi; behold, *it is* between Kadesh and Bered.
15 ¶ And Hagar bore Abram a son: and Abram called his son's name, which Hagar bore, Ishmael.
16 And Abram *was* fourscore and six years old, when Hagar bore Ishmael to Abram.

Genesis 17

17:1 ¶ And when Abram was ninety years old and nine, Yahweh appeared to Abram, and said to him, I *am* the Almighty God; walk before me, and be you perfect.
2 And I will make my covenant between me and you, and will multiply you exceedingly.
3 And Abram fell on his face: and God talked with him, saying,
4 ¶ As for me, behold, my covenant *is* with you, and you shall be a father of many nations.
5 Neither shall your name any more be called Abram, but your name shall be Abraham; for a father of many nations have I made you.
6 And I will make you exceedingly fruitful, and I will make nations of you, and kings shall come out of you.
7 ¶ And I will establish my covenant between me and you and your seed after you in their generations for an everlasting covenant, to be a God to you, and to your seed after you.
8 And I will give to you, and to your seed after you, the land wherein you are a stranger, all the land of Canaan, for an everlasting possession; and I will be their God.
9 And God said to Abraham, You shall keep my covenant therefore, you, and your seed after you in their generations.
10 This *is* my covenant, which you shall keep, between me and you and your seed after you; Every man child among you shall be circumcised.
11 And you shall circumcise the flesh of your foreskin; and it shall be a token of the covenant between me and you.
12 And he that is eight days old shall be circumcised among you, every man child in your generations, he that is born in the house, or bought with money of any stranger, which *is* not of your seed.
13 He that is born in your house, and he that is bought with your money, must need *to* be circumcised: and my covenant shall be in your flesh for an everlasting covenant.

14 And the uncircumcised man child whose flesh of his foreskin is not circumcised, that soul shall be cut off from his people; he has broken my covenant.

15 ¶ And God said to Abraham, As for Sarai your wife, you shall not call her name Sarai, but Sarah *shall* her name *be*.

16 And I will bless her, and give you a son also of her: yes, I will bless her, and she shall be *a mother* of nations; kings of people shall be of her.

17 Then Abraham fell upon his face, and laughed, and said in his heart, Shall *a child* be born to him that is a hundred years old? and shall Sarah, that is ninety years old, bear?

18 And Abraham said to God, O that Ishmael might live before you!

19 And God said, Sarah your wife shall bear you a son indeed; and you shall call his name Isaac: and I will establish my covenant with him for an everlasting covenant, *and* with his seed after him.

20 And as for Ishmael, I have heard you: Behold, I have blessed him, and will make him fruitful, and will multiply him exceedingly; twelve princes shall he beget, and I will make him a great nation.

21 But my covenant will I establish with Isaac, which Sarah shall bear to you at this set time in the next year.

22 And he ceased talking with him, and God went up from Abraham.

23 ¶ And Abraham took Ishmael his son, and all that were born in his house, and all that were bought with his money, every male among the men of Abraham's house; and circumcised the flesh of their foreskin in the very same day, as God had said to him.

24 And Abraham *was* ninety years old and nine, when he was circumcised in the flesh of his foreskin.

25 And Ishmael his son *was* thirteen years old, when he was circumcised in the flesh of his foreskin.

26 In the very same day was Abraham circumcised, and Ishmael his son.

27 And all the men of his house, born in the house, and bought with money of the stranger, were circumcised with him.

Genesis 18

18:1 ¶ And Yahweh appeared to him in the plains of Mamre: and he sat in the tent door in the heat of the day;

2 And he lifted up his eyes and looked, and, behold, three men stood by him: and when he saw *them*, he ran to meet them from the tent door, and bowed himself toward the ground,

3 And said, My Lord, if now I have found favor in your sight, pass not away, I pray you, from your servant:

4 Let a little water, I pray you, be fetched, and wash your feet, and rest yourselves under the tree:

5 And I will fetch a morsel of bread, and comfort you your hearts; after that you shall pass on: for therefore have you come to your servant. And they said, So do, as you have said.

6 And Abraham hastened into the tent to Sarah, and said, Make ready quickly three measures of fine meal, knead *it*, and make cakes upon the hearth.

7 And Abraham ran to the herd, and fetched a calf tender and good, and gave *it* to a young man; and he hurried to dress it.

8 And he took butter, and milk, and the calf which he had dressed, and set *it* before them; and he stood by them under the tree, and they did eat.

9 ¶ And they said to him, Where *is* Sarah your wife? And he said, Behold, in the tent.

10 And he said, I will certainly return to you according to the time of life; and, behold, Sarah your wife shall have a son. And Sarah heard *it* in the tent door, which *was* behind him.

11 Now Abraham and Sarah *were* old *and* well stricken in age; *and* it ceased to be with Sarah after the manner of women.

12 Therefore Sarah laughed within herself, saying, After I have become old shall I have pleasure, my lord being old also?

13 And Yahweh said to Abraham, Why did Sarah laugh, saying, Shall I truly bear a child, for I am old?

14 Is anything too hard for Yahweh? At the time appointed I will return to you, according to the time of life, and Sarah shall have a son.

15 Then Sarah denied, saying, I laughed not; for she was afraid. And he said, No; but you did laugh.

16 ¶ And the men rose up from there, and looked toward Sodom: and Abraham went with them to bring them on the way.

17 And Yahweh said, Shall I hide from Abraham that thing which I do;

18 Seeing that Abraham shall surely become a great and mighty nation, and all the nations of the earth shall be blessed in him?

19 For I know him, that he will command his children and his household after him, and they shall keep the way of Yahweh, to do justice and judgment; that Yahweh may bring upon Abraham that which he has spoken of him.

20 And Yahweh said, Because the cry of Sodom and Gomorrah is great, and because their sin is very grievous;

21 I will go down now, and see whether they have done altogether according to the cry of it, which is come to me; and if not, I will know.

22 And the men turned their faces from there, and went toward Sodom: but Abraham stood yet before Yahweh.

23 ¶ And Abraham drew near, and said, Will you also destroy the righteous with the wicked?

24 Perhaps there are fifty righteous within the city: will you also destroy and not spare the place for the fifty righteous that *are* therein?

25 That be far from you to do after this manner, to slay the righteous with the wicked: and that the righteous should be as the wicked, that be far from you: Shall not the Judge of all the earth do right?

26 And Yahweh said, If I find in Sodom fifty righteous within the city, then I will spare all the place for their sakes.

Genesis 18

27 And Abraham answered and said, Behold now, I have taken upon me to speak to the Lord, which *am but* dust and ashes:
28 Perhaps there shall lack five of the fifty righteous: will you destroy all the city for *lack of* five? And he said, If I find there forty and five, I will not destroy *it*.
29 And he spoke to him yet again, and said, Perhaps there shall be forty found there. And he said, I will not do *it* for forty's sake.
30 And he said *to him*, Oh let not the Lord be angry, and I will speak: Perhaps there shall thirty be found there. And he said, I will not do *it*, if I find thirty there.
31 And he said, Behold now, I have taken upon me to speak to the Lord: Perhaps there shall be twenty found there. And he said, I will not destroy *it* for twenty's sake.
32 And he said, Oh let not the Lord be angry, and I will speak yet but this once: Perhaps ten shall be found there. And he said, I will not destroy *it* for ten's sake.
33 And Yahweh went his way, as soon as he had left communing with Abraham: and Abraham returned to his place.

Genesis 19

19:1 ¶ And there came two angels to Sodom at evening; and Lot sat in the gate of Sodom: and Lot seeing *them* rose up to meet them; and he bowed himself with his face toward the ground;
2 And he said, Behold now, my lords, turn in, I pray you, into your servant's house, and lodge all night, and wash your feet, and you shall rise up early, and go on your ways. And they said, No; but we will remain in the street all night.
3 And he pressed upon them greatly; and they turned in to him, and entered into his house; and he made them a feast, and did bake unleavened bread, and they did eat.
4 ¶ But before they lay down, the men of the city, *even* the men of Sodom, compassed the house round, both old and young, all the people from every quarter:
5 And they called to Lot, and said to him, Where *are* the men which came in to you this night? bring them out to us, that we may know them.
6 And Lot went out at the door to them, and shut the door after him,
7 And said, I pray you, brethren, do not so wickedly.
8 Behold now, I have two daughters which have not known *a* man; let me, I pray you, bring them out to you, and do you to them as *is* good in your eyes: only to these men do nothing; for therefore came they under the shadow of my roof.
9 And they said, Stand back. And they said *again*, This one *fellow* came in to dwell, and he will need *to* be a judge: now will we deal worse with you, than with them. And they pressed greatly upon the man, *even* Lot, and came near to break the door.
10 But the men put forth their hand, and pulled Lot into the house to them, and shut to the door.
11 And they smote the men that *were* at the door of the house with blindness, both small and great: so that they wearied themselves to find the door.
12 ¶ And the men said to Lot, Have you here any besides? son-in-law, and your sons, and your daughters, and whatever you have in the city, bring *them* out of this place:
13 For we will destroy this place, because the cry of them is grown great before the face of Yahweh; and Yahweh has sent us to destroy it.
14 And Lot went out, and spoke to his sons-in-law, which married his daughters, and said, Up, get you out of this place; for Yahweh will destroy this city. But he seemed as one that mocked to his sons-in-law.
15 ¶ And when the morning arose, then the angels hastened Lot, saying, Arise, take your wife, and your two daughters, which are here; lest you be consumed in the iniquity of the city.
16 And while he lingered, the men laid hold upon his hand, and upon the hand of his wife, and upon the hand of his two daughters; Yahweh being merciful unto him: and they brought him forth, and set him outside the city.
17 And it came to pass, when they had brought them forth abroad, that he said, Escape for your life; look not behind you, neither stay you in all the plain; escape to the mountain, lest you be consumed.
18 And Lot said to them, Oh, not so, my Lord:
19 Behold now, your servant has found grace in your sight, and you have magnified your mercy, which you have shown to me in saving my life; and I cannot escape to the mountain, lest some evil take me, and I die:
20 Behold now, this city *is* near to flee to, and it *is* a little one: Oh, let me escape there, (*is* it not a little one?) and my soul shall live.
21 And he said to him, See, I have accepted you concerning this thing also, that I will not overthrow this city, for which you have spoken.
22 Haste you, escape there; for I cannot do anything till you have come there. Therefore the name of the city was called Zoar.
23 The sun had risen upon the earth when Lot entered into Zoar.
24 ¶ Then Yahweh rained upon Sodom and upon Gomorrah brimstone and fire from Yahweh out of heaven;
25 And he overthrew those cities, and all the plain, and all the inhabitants of the cities, and that which grew upon the ground.
26 ¶ But his wife looked back from behind him, and she became a pillar of salt.
27 ¶ And Abraham got up early in the morning to the place where he stood before Yahweh:
28 And he looked toward Sodom and Gomorrah, and toward all the land of the plain, and saw, and, behold, the smoke of the country went up as the smoke of a furnace.
29 And it came to pass, when God destroyed the cities of the plain, that God remembered Abraham, and sent Lot out of the midst of the overthrow, when he overthrew the cities in which Lot dwelt.

30 ¶ And Lot went up out of Zoar, and dwelt in the mountain, and his two daughters with him; for he feared to dwell in Zoar: and he dwelt in a cave, he and his two daughters.
31 And the firstborn said to the younger, Our father *is* old, and *there is* not a man in the earth to come in to us after the manner of all the earth:
32 Come, let us make our father drink wine, and we will lie with him, that we may preserve seed of our father.
33 And they made their father drink wine that night: and the firstborn went in, and lay with her father; and he perceived not when she lay down, nor when she arose.
34 And it came to pass on the next day, that the firstborn said to the younger, Behold, I lay last night with my father: let us make him drink wine this night also; and go you in, *and* lie with him, that we may preserve seed of our father.
35 And they made their father drink wine that night also: and the younger arose, and lay with him; and he perceived not when she lay down, nor when she arose.
36 Thus were both the daughters of Lot with child by their father.
37 And the firstborn bore a son, and called his name Moab: the same *is* the father of the Moabites unto this day.
38 And the younger, she also bore a son, and called his name Benammi: the same *is* the father of the children of Ammon unto this day.

Genesis 20

20:1 ¶ And Abraham journeyed from there toward the south country, and dwelt between Kadesh and Shur, and sojourned in Gerar.
2 And Abraham said of Sarah his wife, She *is* my sister: and Abimelech king of Gerar sent, and took Sarah.
3 ¶ But God came to Abimelech in a dream by night, and said to him, Behold, you *are but* a dead man, for the woman which you have taken; for she *is* a man's wife.
4 But Abimelech had not come near her: and he said, Lord, will you slay also a righteous nation?
5 Said he not to me, She *is* my sister? and she, even she herself said, He *is* my brother: in the integrity of my heart and innocence of my hands have I done this.
6 And God said to him in a dream, Yes, I know that you did this in the integrity of your heart; for I also withheld you from sinning against me: therefore permitted I you not to touch her.
7 Now therefore restore the man *his* wife; for he *is* a prophet, and he shall pray for you, and you shall live: and if you restore *her* not, know you that you shall surely die, you, and all that *are* yours.
8 ¶ Therefore Abimelech rose early in the morning, and called all his servants, and told all these things in their ears: and the men were very afraid.
9 Then Abimelech called Abraham, and said to him, What have you done to us? and what have I offended you, that you have brought on me and on my kingdom a great sin? you have done deeds unto me that ought not to be done.
10 And Abimelech said to Abraham, What saw you, that you have done this thing?
11 And Abraham said, Because I thought, Surely the fear of God *is* not in this place; and they will slay me for my wife's sake.
12 And yet indeed *she is* my sister; she *is* the daughter of my father, but not the daughter of my mother; and she became my wife.
13 And it came to pass, when God caused me to wander from my father's house, that I said to her, This *is* your kindness which you shall show to me; at every place where we shall come, say of me, He *is* my brother.
14 ¶ And Abimelech took sheep, and oxen, and menservants, and women servants, and gave *them* to Abraham, and restored him Sarah his wife.
15 And Abimelech said, Behold, my land *is* before you: dwell where it pleases you.
16 And to Sarah he said, Behold, I have given your brother a thousand *pieces* of silver: behold, he *is* to you a covering of the eyes, unto all that *are* with you, and with all *other*: thus she was reproved.
17 So Abraham prayed to God: and God healed Abimelech, and his wife, and his maidservants; and they bore *children*.
18 For Yahweh had fast closed up all the wombs of the house of Abimelech, because of Sarah Abraham's wife.

Genesis 21

21:1 ¶ And Yahweh visited Sarah as he had said, and Yahweh did to Sarah as he had spoken.
2 For Sarah conceived, and bore Abraham a son in his old age, at the set time of which God had spoken to him.
3 And Abraham called the name of his son that was born unto him, whom Sarah bore to him, Isaac.
4 And Abraham circumcised his son Isaac being eight days old, as God had commanded him.
5 And Abraham was a hundred years old, when his son Isaac was born unto him.
6 And Sarah said, God has made me to laugh, *so that* all that hear will laugh with me.
7 And she said, Who would have said to Abraham, that Sarah should have given children suck? for I have born *him* a son in his old age.
8 And the child grew, and was weaned: and Abraham made a great feast the *same* day that Isaac was weaned.
9 ¶ And Sarah saw the son of Hagar the Egyptian, which she had born unto Abraham, mocking.
10 Therefore she said to Abraham, Cast out this bondwoman and her son: for the son of this bondwoman shall not be heir with my son, *even* with Isaac.
11 And the thing was very grievous in Abraham's sight because of his son.
12 And God said to Abraham, Let it not be grievous in your sight because of the lad, and because of your bondwoman; in all that Sarah has said to you, listen to her voice; for in Isaac shall your seed be called.

Genesis 21

13 And also of the son of the bondwoman will I make a nation, because he *is* your seed.

14 ¶ And Abraham rose up early in the morning, and took bread, and a bottle of water, and gave *it* to Hagar, putting *it* on her shoulder, and the child, and sent her away: and she departed, and wandered in the wilderness of Beersheba.

15 And the water was spent in the bottle, and she cast the child under one of the shrubs.

16 And she went, and sat her down over before *him* a good way off, as it were a bowshot: for she said, Let me not see the death of the child. And she sat over before *him*, and lifted up her voice, and wept.

17 And God heard the voice of the lad; and the angel of God called to Hagar out of heaven, and said to her, What ails you, Hagar? fear not; for God has heard the voice of the lad where he *is*.

18 Arise, lift up the lad, and hold him in your hand; for I will make him a great nation.

19 And God opened her eyes, and she saw a well of water; and she went, and filled the bottle with water, and gave the lad drink.

20 And God was with the lad; and he grew, and dwelt in the wilderness, and became an archer.

21 And he dwelt in the wilderness of Paran: and his mother took him a wife out of the land of Egypt.

22 ¶ And it came to pass at that time, that Abimelech and Phichol the chief captain of his host spoke to Abraham, saying, God *is* with you in all that you do:

23 Now therefore swear to me here by God that you will not deal falsely with me, nor with my son, nor with my son's son: *but* according to the kindness that I have done to you, you shall do to me, and to the land wherein you have dwelt.

24 And Abraham said, I will swear.

25 And Abraham reproved Abimelech because of a well of water, which Abimelech's servants had violently taken away.

26 And Abimelech said, I know not who has done this thing: neither did you tell me, neither yet heard I *of it*, but today.

27 And Abraham took sheep and oxen, and gave them to Abimelech; and both of them made a covenant.

28 And Abraham set seven ewe lambs of the flock by themselves.

29 And Abimelech said to Abraham, What *mean* these seven ewe lambs which you have set by themselves?

30 And he said, For *these* seven ewe lambs shall you take of my hand, that they may be a witness to me, that I have dug this well.

31 Therefore he called that place Beersheba; because there they swore both of them.

32 Thus they made a covenant at Beersheba: then Abimelech rose up, and Phichol the chief captain of his host, and they returned into the land of the Philistines.

33 ¶ And *Abraham* planted a grove in Beersheba, and called there on the name of Yahweh, the everlasting God.

34 And Abraham sojourned in the Philistines' land many days.

Genesis 22

22:1 ¶ And it came to pass after these things, that God did tempt Abraham, and said to him, Abraham: and he said, Behold, *here* I *am*.

2 And he said, Take now your son, your only *son* Isaac, whom you love, and get you into the land of Moriah; and offer him there for a burnt offering upon one of the mountains which I will tell you of.

3 ¶ And Abraham rose up early in the morning, and saddled his donkey, and took two of his young men with him, and Isaac his son, and split the wood for the burnt offering, and rose up, and went to the place of which God had told him.

4 Then on the third day Abraham lifted up his eyes, and saw the place afar off.

5 And Abraham said to his young men, Abide you here with the donkey; and I and the lad will go yonder and worship, and come again to you.

6 And Abraham took the wood of the burnt offering, and laid *it* upon Isaac his son; and he took the fire in his hand, and a knife; and they went both of them together.

7 And Isaac spoke to Abraham his father, and said, My father: and he said, Here *am* I, my son. And he said, Behold the fire and the wood: but where *is* the lamb for a burnt offering?

8 And Abraham said, My son, God will provide himself a lamb for a burnt offering: so they went both of them together.

9 And they came to the place which God had told him of; and Abraham built an altar there, and laid the wood in order, and bound Isaac his son, and laid him on the altar upon the wood.

10 And Abraham stretched forth his hand, and took the knife to slay his son.

11 ¶ And the angel of Yahweh called to him out of heaven, and said, Abraham, Abraham: and he said, Here *am* I.

12 And he said, Lay not your hand upon the lad, neither do you anything to him: for now I know that you fear God, seeing you have not withheld your son, your only *son* from me.

13 And Abraham lifted up his eyes, and looked, and behold behind *him* a ram caught in a thicket by his horns: and Abraham went and took the ram, and offered him up for a burnt offering in the stead of his son.

14 And Abraham called the name of that place Yahwehyireh: as it is said *to* this day, In the mount of Yahweh it shall be seen.

15 ¶ And the angel of Yahweh called to Abraham out of heaven the second time,

16 And said, By myself have I sworn, says Yahweh, for because you have done this thing, and have not withheld your son, your only *son*:

17 That in blessing I will bless you, and in multiplying I will multiply your seed as the stars of the heaven, and as the sand which *is* upon the sea shore; and your seed shall possess the gate of his enemies;

18 And in your seed shall all the nations of the earth be blessed; because you have obeyed my voice.
19 So Abraham returned to his young men, and they rose up and went together to Beersheba; and Abraham dwelt at Beersheba.
20 ¶ And it came to pass after these things, that it was told to Abraham, saying, Behold, Milcah, she has also born children unto your brother Nahor;
21 Huz his firstborn, and Buz his brother, and Kemuel the father of Aram,
22 And Chesed, and Hazo, and Pildash, and Jidlaph, and Bethuel.
23 And Bethuel begot Rebekah: these eight Milcah did bear to Nahor, Abraham's brother.
24 And his concubine, whose name *was* Reumah, she bore also Tebah, and Gaham, and Thahash, and Maachah.

Genesis 23

23:1 ¶ And Sarah was a hundred and seven and twenty years old: *these were* the years of the life of Sarah.
2 And Sarah died in Kirjatharba; the same *is* Hebron in the land of Canaan: and Abraham came to mourn for Sarah, and to weep for her.
3 ¶ And Abraham stood up from before his dead, and spoke to the sons of Heth, saying,
4 I *am* a stranger and a foreigner with you: give me a possession of a burying place with you, that I may bury my dead out of my sight.
5 And the children of Heth answered Abraham, saying to him,
6 Hear us, my lord: you *are* a mighty prince among us: in the choice of our sepulchers bury your dead; none of us shall withhold from you his sepulcher, but that you may bury your dead.
7 And Abraham stood up, and bowed himself to the people of the land, *even* to the children of Heth.
8 And he communed with them, saying, If it is your mind that I should bury my dead out of my sight; hear me, and intercede for me to Ephron the son of Zohar,
9 That he may give me the cave of Machpelah, which he has, which *is* in the end of his field; for as much money as it is worth he shall give it *to* me for a possession of a burying place among you.
10 And Ephron dwelt among the children of Heth: and Ephron the Hittite answered Abraham in the audience of the children of Heth, *even* of all that went in at the gate of his city, saying,
11 No, my lord, hear me: the field give I *to* you, and the cave that *is* therein, I give it *to* you; in the presence of the sons of my people give I it *to* you: bury your dead.
12 And Abraham bowed down himself before the people of the land.
13 And he spoke to Ephron in the audience of the people of the land, saying, But if you *will give it*, I pray you, hear me: I will give you money for the field; take *it* from me, and I will bury my dead there.

14 And Ephron answered Abraham, saying to him,
15 My lord, listen to me: the land *is worth* four hundred shekels of silver; what *is* that between me and you? bury therefore your dead.
16 ¶ And Abraham listened to Ephron; and Abraham weighed to Ephron the silver, which he had named in the audience of the sons of Heth, four hundred shekels of silver, current *money* with the merchant.
17 And the field of Ephron, which *was* in Machpelah, which *was* before Mamre, the field, and the cave which *was* therein, and all the trees that *were* in the field, that *were* in all the borders round about, were made sure
18 Unto Abraham for a possession in the presence of the children of Heth, before all that went in at the gate of his city.
19 And after this, Abraham buried Sarah his wife in the cave of the field of Machpelah before Mamre: the same *is* Hebron in the land of Canaan.
20 And the field, and the cave that *is* therein, were made sure unto Abraham for a possession of a burying place by the sons of Heth.

Genesis 24

24:1 ¶ And Abraham was old, *and* well stricken in age: and Yahweh had blessed Abraham in all things.
2 And Abraham said to his oldest servant of his house, that ruled over all that he had, Put, I pray you, your hand under my thigh:
3 And I will make you swear by Yahweh, the God of heaven, and the God of the earth, that you shall not take a wife unto my son of the daughters of the Canaanites, among whom I dwell:
4 But you shall go to my country, and to my kindred, and take a wife unto my son Isaac.
5 And the servant said to him, Perhaps the woman will not be willing to follow me unto this land: must I need *to* bring your son again to the land from where you came?
6 And Abraham said to him, Beware you that you bring not my son there again.
7 Yahweh God of heaven, which took me from my father's house, and from the land of my kindred, and which spoke unto me, and that swore unto me, saying, Unto your seed will I give this land; he shall send his angel before you, and you shall take a wife unto my son from there.
8 And if the woman will not be willing to follow you, then you shall be clear from this my oath: only bring not my son there again.
9 And the servant put his hand under the thigh of Abraham his master, and swore to him concerning that matter.
10 ¶ And the servant took ten camels of the camels of his master, and departed; for all the goods of his master *were* in his hand: and he arose, and went to Mesopotamia, to the city of Nahor.
11 And he made his camels to kneel down outside the city by a well of water at the time of the evening, *even* the time that women go out to draw *water*.

Genesis 24

12 And he said, O Yahweh God of my master Abraham, I pray you, send me good speed this day, and show kindness to my master Abraham.

13 Behold, I stand *here* by the well of water; and the daughters of the men of the city come out to draw water:

14 And let it come to pass, that the damsel to whom I shall say, Let down your pitcher, I pray you, that I may drink; and she shall say, Drink, and I will give your camels drink also: *let the same be* she *that* you have appointed for your servant Isaac; and thereby shall I know that you have shown kindness to my master.

15 And it came to pass, before he had finished speaking, that, behold, Rebekah came out, who was born to Bethuel, son of Milcah, the wife of Nahor, Abraham's brother, with her pitcher upon her shoulder.

16 And the damsel *was* very fair to look upon, a virgin, neither had any man known her: and she went down to the well, and filled her pitcher, and came up.

17 And the servant ran to meet her, and said, Let me, I pray you, drink a little water from your pitcher.

18 And she said, Drink, my lord: and she hurried, and let down her pitcher upon her hand, and gave him drink.

19 And when she had finished giving him drink, she said, I will draw *water* for your camels also, until they have finished drinking.

20 And she hurried, and emptied her pitcher into the trough, and ran again to the well to draw *water*, and drew for all his camels.

21 And the man wondering at her held his peace, to know whether Yahweh had made his journey prosperous or not.

22 And it came to pass, as the camels had finished drinking, that the man took a golden earring of half a shekel weight, and two bracelets for her hands of ten *shekels* weight of gold;

23 And said, Whose daughter *are* you? tell me, I pray you: is there room *in* your father's house for us to lodge in?

24 And she said to him, I *am* the daughter of Bethuel the son of Milcah, which she bore unto Nahor.

25 She said moreover to him, We have both straw and feed enough, and room to lodge in.

26 And the man bowed down his head, and worshipped Yahweh.

27 And he said, Blessed *be* Yahweh God of my master Abraham, who has not left destitute my master of his mercy and his truth: I *being* in the way, Yahweh led me to the house of my master's brothers.

28 And the damsel ran, and told *them of* her mother's house these things.

29 ¶ And Rebekah had a brother, and his name *was* Laban: and Laban ran out unto the man, unto the well.

30 And it came to pass, when he saw the earring and bracelets upon his sister's hands, and when he heard the words of Rebekah his sister, saying, Thus spoke the man unto me; that he came to the man; and, behold, he stood by the camels at the well.

31 And he said, Come in, you blessed of Yahweh; why stand you outside? for I have prepared the house, and room for the camels.

32 And the man came into the house: and he ungirded his camels, and gave straw and feed for the camels, and water to wash his feet, and the men's feet that *were* with him.

33 And there was set *food* before him to eat: but he said, I will not eat, until I have told my errand. And he said, Speak on.

34 And he said, I *am* Abraham's servant.

35 And Yahweh has blessed my master greatly; and he has become great: and he has given him flocks, and herds, and silver, and gold, and menservants, and maidservants, and camels, and donkeys.

36 And Sarah my master's wife bore a son to my master when she was old: and to him has he given all that he has.

37 And my master made me swear, saying, You shall not take a wife unto my son of the daughters of the Canaanites, in whose land I dwell:

38 But you shall go to my father's house, and to my kindred, and take a wife unto my son.

39 And I said to my master, Perhaps the woman will not follow me.

40 And he said to me, Yahweh, before whom I walk, will send his angel with you, and prosper your way; and you shall take a wife for my son of my kindred, and of my father's house:

41 Then shall you be clear from *this* my oath, when you come to my kindred; and if they give not you *one*, you shall be clear from my oath.

42 And I came this day to the well, and said, O Yahweh God of my master Abraham, if now you do prosper my way which I go:

43 Behold, I stand by the well of water; and it shall come to pass, that when the virgin comes forth to draw *water*, and I say to her, Give me, I pray you, a little water of your pitcher to drink;

44 And she says to me, Both drink you, and I will also draw for your camels: *let* the same *be* the woman whom Yahweh has appointed out for my master's son.

45 And before I had finished speaking in my heart, behold, Rebekah came forth with her pitcher on her shoulder; and she went down to the well, and drew *water*: and I said to her, Let me drink, I pray you.

46 And she made haste, and let down her pitcher from her *shoulder*, and said, Drink, and I will give your camels drink also: so I drank, and she made the camels drink also.

47 And I asked her, and said, Whose daughter *are* you? And she said, The daughter of Bethuel, Nahor's son, whom Milcah bore unto him: and I put the earring upon her face, and the bracelets upon her hands.

48 And I bowed down my head, and worshipped Yahweh, and blessed Yahweh God of my master Abraham, which had led me in the right way to take my master's brother's daughter unto his son.

49 And now if you will deal kindly and truly with my master, tell me: and if not, tell me; that I may turn to the right hand, or to the left.

50 Then Laban and Bethuel answered and said, The thing proceeds from Yahweh: we cannot speak to you bad or good.

51 Behold, Rebekah *is* before you, take *her*, and go, and let her be your master's son's wife, as Yahweh has spoken.
52 And it came to pass, that, when Abraham's servant heard their words, he worshipped Yahweh, *bowing himself* to the earth.
53 And the servant brought forth jewels of silver, and jewels of gold, and clothing, and gave *them* to Rebekah: he gave also to her brother and to her mother precious things.
54 ¶ And they did eat and drink, he and the men that *were* with him, and stayed all night; and they rose up in the morning, and he said, Send me away to my master.
55 And her brother and her mother said, Let the damsel stay with us *a few* days, at the least ten; after that she shall go.
56 And he said to them, Hinder me not, seeing Yahweh has prospered my way; send me away that I may go to my master.
57 And they said, We will call the damsel, and inquire at her mouth.
58 And they called Rebekah, and said to her, Will you go with this man? And she said, I will go.
59 And they sent away Rebekah their sister, and her nurse, and Abraham's servant, and his men.
60 And they blessed Rebekah, and said to her, You *are* our sister, be you *the mother* of thousands of millions, and let your seed possess the gate of those which hate them.
61 And Rebekah arose, and her damsels, and they rode upon the camels, and followed the man: and the servant took Rebekah, and went his way.
62 ¶ And Isaac came from the way of the well Lahairoi; for he dwelt in the south country.
63 And Isaac went out to meditate in the field at the evening: and he lifted up his eyes, and saw, and, behold, the camels *were* coming.
64 And Rebekah lifted up her eyes, and when she saw Isaac, she lighted off the camel.
65 For she *had* said to the servant, What man *is* this that walks in the field to meet us? And the servant *had* said, It *is* my master: therefore she took a veil, and covered herself.
66 And the servant told Isaac all things that he had done.
67 And Isaac brought her into his mother Sarah's tent, and took Rebekah, and she became his wife; and he loved her: and Isaac was comforted after his mother's *death*.

Genesis 25

25:1 ¶ Then again Abraham took a wife, and her name *was* Keturah.
2 And she bore him Zimran, and Jokshan, and Medan, and Midian, and Ishbak, and Shuah.
3 And Jokshan begot Sheba, and Dedan. And the sons of Dedan were Asshurim, and Letushim, and Leummim.
4 And the sons of Midian; Ephah, and Epher, and Hanoch, and Abida, and Eldaah. All these *were* the children of Keturah.
5 And Abraham gave all that he had to Isaac.
6 But to the sons of the concubines, which Abraham had, Abraham gave gifts, and sent them away from Isaac his son, while he yet lived, eastward, to the east country.
7 And these *are* the days of the years of Abraham's life which he lived, a hundred threescore and fifteen years.
8 Then Abraham gave up the ghost, and died in a good old age, an old man, and full *of years*; and was gathered to his people.
9 And his sons Isaac and Ishmael buried him in the cave of Machpelah, in the field of Ephron the son of Zohar the Hittite, which *is* before Mamre;
10 The field which Abraham purchased of the sons of Heth: there was Abraham buried, and Sarah his wife.
11 ¶ And it came to pass after the death of Abraham, that God blessed his son Isaac; and Isaac dwelt by the well Lahairoi.
12 Now these *are* the generations of Ishmael, Abraham's son, whom Hagar the Egyptian, Sarah's handmaid, bore unto Abraham:
13 And these *are* the names of the sons of Ishmael, by their names, according to their generations: the firstborn of Ishmael, Nebajoth; and Kedar, and Adbeel, and Mibsam,
14 And Mishma, and Dumah, and Massa,
15 Hadar, and Tema, Jetur, Naphish, and Kedemah:
16 These *are* the sons of Ishmael, and these *are* their names, by their towns, and by their castles; twelve princes according to their nations.
17 And these *are* the years of the life of Ishmael, a hundred and thirty and seven years: and he gave up the ghost and died; and was gathered to his people.
18 And they dwelt from Havilah unto Shur, that *is* before Egypt, as you go toward Assyria: *and* he died in the presence of all his brethren.
19 ¶ And these *are* the generations of Isaac, Abraham's son: Abraham begot Isaac:
20 And Isaac was forty years old when he took Rebekah to wife, the daughter of Bethuel the Syrian of Padanaram, the sister to Laban the Syrian.
21 And Isaac prayed to Yahweh for his wife, because she *was* barren: and Yahweh was entreated of him, and Rebekah his wife conceived.
22 And the children struggled together within her; and she said, If *it is* so, why *am* I thus? And she went to inquire of Yahweh.
23 And Yahweh said to her, Two nations *are* in your womb, and two manner of people shall be separated from your womb; and *the one* people shall be stronger than *the other* people; and the elder shall serve the younger.
24 And when her days to be delivered were fulfilled, behold, *there were* twins in her womb.
25 And the first came out red, all over like a hairy garment; and they called his name Esau.
26 And after that came his brother out, and his hand took hold on Esau's heel; and his name was called Jacob: and Isaac *was* threescore years old when she bore them.

Genesis 25

27 And the boys grew: and Esau was a cunning hunter, a man of the field; and Jacob *was* a plain man, dwelling in tents.
28 And Isaac loved Esau, because he did eat of *his* venison: but Rebekah loved Jacob.
29 ¶ And Jacob boiled pottage: and Esau came from the field, and he *was* faint:
30 And Esau said to Jacob, Feed me, I pray you, with that same red *pottage*; for I *am* faint: therefore was his name called Edom.
31 And Jacob said, Sell me this day your birthright.
32 And Esau said, Behold, I *am* at the point to die: and what profit shall this birthright do to me?
33 And Jacob said, Swear to me this day; and he swore to him: and he sold his birthright to Jacob.
34 Then Jacob gave Esau bread and pottage of lentils; and he did eat and drink, and rose up, and went his way: thus Esau despised *his* birthright.

Genesis 26

26:1 ¶ And there was a famine in the land, besides the first famine that was in the days of Abraham. And Isaac went to Abimelech king of the Philistines unto Gerar.
2 And Yahweh appeared unto him, and said, Go not down into Egypt; dwell in the land which I shall tell you of:
3 Dwell in this land, and I will be with you, and will bless you; for unto you, and unto your seed, I will give all these countries, and I will perform the oath which I swore to Abraham your father;
4 And I will make your seed to multiply as the stars of heaven, and will give to your seed all these countries; and in your seed shall all the nations of the earth be blessed;
5 Because that Abraham obeyed my voice, and kept my charge, my commandments, my statutes, and my laws.
6 ¶ And Isaac dwelt in Gerar:
7 And the men of the place asked *him* of his wife; and he said, She *is* my sister: for he feared to say, *She is* my wife; lest, *said he*, the men of the place should kill me for Rebekah; because she *was* fair to look upon.
8 And it came to pass, when he had been there a long time, that Abimelech king of the Philistines looked out through a window, and saw, and, beheld, Isaac *was* sporting with Rebekah his wife.
9 And Abimelech called Isaac, and said, Behold, certainly she *is* your wife: and how said you, She *is* my sister? And Isaac said to him, Because I said, Lest I die for her.
10 And Abimelech said, What *is* this you have done unto us? one of the people might lightly have lain with your wife, and you should have brought guiltiness upon us.
11 And Abimelech charged all *his* people, saying, He that touches this man or his wife shall surely be put to death.
12 ¶ Then Isaac sowed in that land, and received in the same year a hundred times: and Yahweh blessed him.
13 And the man became great, and went forward, and grew until he became very great:
14 For he had possessions of flocks, and possessions of herds, and great store of servants: and the Philistines envied him.
15 For all the wells which his father's servants had dug in the days of Abraham his father, the Philistines had stopped them, and filled them with earth.
16 And Abimelech said to Isaac, Go from us; for you are much mightier than we.
17 And Isaac departed therefrom, and pitched his tent in the valley of Gerar, and dwelt there.
18 And Isaac dug again the wells of water, which they had dug in the days of Abraham his father; for the Philistines had stopped them after the death of Abraham: and he called their names after the names by which his father had called them.
19 And Isaac's servants dug in the valley, and found there a well of springing water.
20 And the herdsmen of Gerar did strive with Isaac's herdsmen, saying, The water *is* ours: and he called the name of the well Esek; because they strove with him.
21 And they dug another well, and strove for that also: and he called the name of it Sitnah.
22 And he removed from there, and dug another well; and for that they strove not: and he called the name of it Rehoboth; and he said, For now Yahweh has made room for us, and we shall be fruitful in the land.
23 And he went up from there to Beersheba.
24 And Yahweh appeared to him the same night, and said, I *am* the God of Abraham your father: fear not, for I *am* with you, and will bless you, and multiply your seed for my servant Abraham's sake.
25 And he built an altar there, and called upon the name of Yahweh, and pitched his tent there: and there Isaac's servants dug a well.
26 ¶ Then Abimelech went to him from Gerar, and Ahuzzath one of his friends, and Phichol the chief captain of his army.
27 And Isaac said unto them, Why come you to me, seeing you hate me, and have sent me away from you?
28 And they said, We saw certainly that Yahweh was with you: and we said, Let there be now an oath between us, *even* between us and you, and let us make a covenant with you;
29 That you will do us no harm, as we have not touched you, and as we have done to you nothing but good, and have sent you away in peace: you *are* now the blessed of Yahweh.
30 And he made them a feast, and they did eat and drink.
31 And they rose up early in the morning, and swore one to another: and Isaac sent them away, and they departed from him in peace.
32 And it came to pass the same day, that Isaac's servants came, and told him concerning the well which they had dug, and said unto him, We have found water.
33 And he called it Shebah: therefore the name of the city *is* Beersheba unto this day.
34 ¶ And Esau was forty years old when he took to wife Judith the daughter of Beeri the Hittite, and Bashemath the daughter of Elon the Hittite:
35 Which were a grief of mind to Isaac and to Rebekah.

Genesis 27

27:1 ¶ And it came to pass, that when Isaac was old, and his eyes were dim, so that he could not see, he called Esau his oldest son, and said unto him, My son: and he said unto him, Behold, *here am* I.
2 And he said, Behold now, I am old, I know not the day of my death:
3 Now therefore take, I pray you, your weapons, your quiver and your bow, and go out to the field, and take me *some* venison;
4 And make me savory meat, such as I love, and bring *it* to me, that I may eat; that my soul may bless you before I die.
5 And Rebekah heard when Isaac spoke to Esau his son. And Esau went to the field to hunt *for* venison, *and to* bring *it*.
6 ¶ And Rebekah spoke to Jacob her son, saying, Behold, I heard your father speak to Esau your brother, saying,
7 Bring me venison, and make me savory meat, that I may eat, and bless you before Yahweh before my death.
8 Now therefore, my son, obey my voice according to that which I command you.
9 Go now to the flock, and fetch me from there two good kids of the goats; and I will make them savory meat for your father, such as he loves:
10 And you shall bring *it* to your father, that he may eat, and that he may bless you before his death.
11 And Jacob said to Rebekah his mother, Behold, Esau my brother *is* a hairy man, and I *am* a smooth man:
12 My father perhaps will feel me, and I shall seem to him as a deceiver; and I shall bring a curse upon me, and not a blessing.
13 And his mother said to him, Upon me *be* your curse, my son: only obey my voice, and go fetch me *them*.
14 And he went, and fetched, and brought *them* to his mother: and his mother made savory meat, such as his father loved.
15 And Rebekah took goodly clothing of her oldest son Esau, which *were* with her in the house, and put them upon Jacob her younger son:
16 And she put the skins of the kids of the goats upon his hands, and upon the smooth of his neck:
17 And she gave the savory meat and the bread, which she had prepared, into the hand of her son Jacob.
18 ¶ And he came unto his father, and said, My father: and he said, Here *am* I; who *are* you, my son?
19 And Jacob said to his father, I *am* Esau your firstborn; I have done according as you told me: arise, I pray you, sit and eat of my venison, that your soul may bless me.
20 And Isaac said to his son, How *is it* that you have found *it* so quickly, my son? And he said, Because Yahweh your God brought *it* to me.
21 And Isaac said to Jacob, Come near, I pray you, that I may feel you, my son, whether you *be* my very son Esau or not.
22 And Jacob went near to Isaac his father; and he felt him, and said, The voice *is* Jacob's voice, but the hands *are* the hands of Esau.
23 And he discerned him not, because his hands were hairy, as his brother Esau's hands: so he blessed him.
24 And he said, *Are* you my very son Esau? And he said, I *am*.
25 And he said, Bring *it* near to me, and I will eat of my son's venison, that my soul may bless you. And he brought *it* near to him, and he did eat: and he brought him wine, and he drank.
26 And his father Isaac said to him, Come near now, and kiss me, my son.
27 And he came near, and kissed him: and he smelled the smell of his clothing, and blessed him, and said, See, the smell of my son *is* as the smell of a field which Yahweh has blessed:
28 Therefore *may* God give you of the dew of heaven, and the fatness of the earth, and plenty of corn and *new* wine:
29 Let people serve you, and nations bow down to you: be lord over your brethren, and let your mother's sons bow down to you: cursed *be* every one that curses you, and blessed *be* he that blesses you.
30 ¶ And it came to pass, as soon as Isaac had made an end of blessing Jacob, and Jacob was yet scarcely gone out from the presence of Isaac his father, that Esau his brother came in from his hunting.
31 And he also had made savory meat, and brought it unto his father, and said to his father, Let my father arise, and eat of his son's venison, that your soul may bless me.
32 And Isaac his father said to him, Who *are* you? And he said, I *am* your son, your firstborn Esau.
33 And Isaac trembled very exceedingly, and said, Who? where *is* he that has taken venison, and brought *it to* me, and I have eaten of all before you came, and have blessed him? yes, *and* he shall be blessed.
34 And when Esau heard the words of his father, he cried with a great and exceedingly bitter cry, and said to his father, Bless me, *even* me also, O my father.
35 And he said, Your brother came with deceit, and has taken away your blessing.
36 And he said, Is not he rightly named Jacob? for he has supplanted me these two times: he took away my birthright; and, behold, now he has taken away my blessing. And he said, Have you not reserved a blessing for me?
37 And Isaac answered and said to Esau, Behold, I have made him your lord, and all his brethren have I given to him for servants; and with corn and *new* wine have I sustained him: and what shall I do now unto you, my son?
38 And Esau said to his father, Have you but one blessing, my father? bless me, *even* me also, O my father. And Esau lifted up his voice, and wept.
39 And Isaac his father answered and said to him, Behold, your dwelling shall be the fatness of the earth, and of the dew of heaven from above;
40 And by your sword shall you live, and shall serve your brother; and it shall come to pass when you shall have the dominion, that you shall break his yoke from off your neck.

Genesis 27

41 ¶ And Esau hated Jacob because of the blessing with which his father blessed him: and Esau said in his heart, The days of mourning for my father are at hand; then will I slay my brother Jacob.

42 And these words of Esau her elder son were told to Rebekah: and she sent and called Jacob her younger son, and said to him, Behold, your brother Esau, as touching you, does comfort himself, *purposing* to kill you.

43 Now therefore, my son, obey my voice; and arise, flee you to Laban my brother to Haran;

44 And stay with him a few days, until your brother's fury turns away;

45 Until your brother's anger turns away from you, and he forgets *that* which you have done to him: then I will send, and fetch you from there: why should I be deprived also of you both in one day?

46 And Rebekah said to Isaac, I am weary of my life because of the daughters of Heth: if Jacob takes a wife of the daughters of Heth, such as these *which are* of the daughters of the land, what good shall my life do me?

Genesis 28

28:1 ¶ And Isaac called Jacob, and blessed him, and charged him, and said to him, You shall not take a wife of the daughters of Canaan.

2 Arise, go to Padanaram, to the house of Bethuel your mother's father; and take you a wife from there of the daughters of Laban your mother's brother.

3 And God Almighty bless you, and make you fruitful, and multiply you, that you may be a multitude of people;

4 And give you the blessing of Abraham, to you, and to your seed with you; that you may inherit the land wherein you are a stranger, which God gave to Abraham.

5 And Isaac sent away Jacob: and he went to Padanaram to Laban, son of Bethuel the Syrian, the brother of Rebekah, Jacob's and Esau's mother.

6 ¶ When Esau saw that Isaac had blessed Jacob, and sent him away to Padanaram, to take him a wife from there; and that as he blessed him he gave him a charge, saying you shall not take a wife of the daughters of Canaan;

7 And that Jacob obeyed his father and his mother, and had gone to Padanaram;

8 And Esau seeing that the daughters of Canaan pleased not Isaac his father;

9 Then went Esau to Ishmael, and took unto the wives which he had Mahalath the daughter of Ishmael Abraham's son, the sister of Nebajoth, to be his wife.

10 ¶ And Jacob went out from Beersheba, and went toward Haran.

11 And he lighted upon a certain place, and stayed there all night, because the sun was set; and he took of the stones of that place, and put *them for* his pillows, and lay down in that place to sleep.

12 And he dreamed, and behold a ladder set up on the earth, and the top of it reached to heaven: and behold the angels of God ascending and descending on it.

13 And, behold, Yahweh stood above it, and said, I *am* Yahweh God of Abraham your father, and the God of Isaac: the land whereon you lie, to you will I give it, and to your seed;

14 And your seed shall be as the dust of the earth, and you shall spread abroad to the west, and to the east, and to the north, and to the south: and in you and in your seed shall all the families of the earth be blessed.

15 And, behold, I *am* with you, and will keep you in all *places* where you go, and will bring you again into this land; for I will not leave you, until I have done *that* which I have spoken to you of.

16 ¶ And Jacob woke out of his sleep, and he said, Surely Yahweh is in this place; and I knew *it* not.

17 And he was afraid, and said, How dreadful *is* this place! this *is* none other but the house of God, and this *is* the gate of heaven.

18 And Jacob rose up early in the morning, and took the stone that he had put *for* his pillows, and set it up *for* a pillar, and poured oil upon the top of it.

19 And he called the name of that place Bethel: but the name of that city *was called* Luz at first.

20 And Jacob vowed a vow, saying, If God will be with me, and will keep me in this way that I go, and will give me bread to eat, and clothing to put on,

21 So that I come again to my father's house in peace; then shall Yahweh be my God:

22 And this stone, which I have set *for* a pillar, shall be God's house: and of all that you shall give me I will surely give the tenth unto you.

Genesis 29

29:1 ¶ Then Jacob went on his journey, and came into the land of the people of the east.

2 And he looked, and saw a well in the field, and, behold, there *were* three flocks of sheep lying by it; for out of that well they watered the flocks: and a great stone *was* upon the well's mouth.

3 And there were all the flocks gathered: and they rolled the stone from the well's mouth, and watered the sheep, and put the stone again upon the well's mouth in his place.

4 And Jacob said to them, My brethren, *from* where *are* you? And they said, Of Haran *are* we.

5 And he said to them, Know you Laban the son of Nahor? And they said, We know *him*.

6 And he said to them, *Is* he well? And they said, *He is* well: and, behold, Rachel his daughter comes with the sheep.

7 And he said, Behold, *it is* yet high day, neither *is it* time that the cattle should be gathered together: water you the sheep, and go *and* feed *them*.

8 And they said, We cannot, until all the flocks are gathered together, and *till* they roll the stone from the well's mouth; then we water the sheep.

9 ¶ And while he yet spoke with them, Rachel came with her father's sheep: for she kept them.

10 And it came to pass, when Jacob saw Rachel the daughter of Laban his mother's brother, and the sheep

of Laban his mother's brother, that Jacob went near, and rolled the stone from the well's mouth, and watered the flock of Laban his mother's brother.
11 And Jacob kissed Rachel, and lifted up his voice, and wept.
12 And Jacob told Rachel that he *was* her father's brother, and that he *was* Rebekah's son: and she ran and told her father.
13 And it came to pass, when Laban heard the tidings of Jacob his sister's son, that he ran to meet him, and embraced him, and kissed him, and brought him to his house. And he told Laban all these things.
14 And Laban said to him, Surely you *are* my bone and my flesh. And he stayed with him the space of a month.
15 ¶ And Laban said to Jacob, Because you *are* my brother, should you therefore serve me for nothing? tell me, what *shall* your wages *be*?
16 And Laban had two daughters: the name of the elder *was* Leah, and the name of the younger *was* Rachel.
17 Leah *was* tender eyed; but Rachel was beautiful and well favored.
18 And Jacob loved Rachel; and said, I will serve you seven years for Rachel your younger daughter.
19 And Laban said, *It is* better that I give her to you, than that I should give her to another man: stay with me.
20 And Jacob served seven years for Rachel; and they seemed unto him *but* a few days, for the love he had for her.
21 And Jacob said to Laban, Give *me* my wife, for my days are fulfilled, that I may go in unto her.
22 And Laban gathered together all the men of the place, and made a feast.
23 And it came to pass in the evening, that he took Leah his daughter, and brought her to him; and he went in unto her.
24 And Laban gave to his daughter Leah Zilpah his maid *for* a handmaid.
25 And it came to pass, that in the morning, behold, it *was* Leah: and he said to Laban, What *is* this you have done to me? did not I serve with you for Rachel? why then have you deceived me?
26 And Laban said, It must not be so done in our country, to give the younger before the firstborn.
27 Fulfill her week, and we will give you this also for the service which you shall serve with me yet seven other years.
28 And Jacob did so, and fulfilled her week: and he gave him Rachel his daughter to wife also.
29 And Laban gave to Rachel his daughter Bilhah his handmaid to be her maid.
30 And he went in also to Rachel, and he loved also Rachel more than Leah, and served with him yet seven other years.
31 ¶ And when Yahweh saw that Leah *was* hated, he opened her womb: but Rachel *was* barren.
32 And Leah conceived, and bore a son, and she called his name Reuben: for she said, Surely Yahweh has looked upon my affliction; now therefore my husband will love me.
33 And she conceived again, and bore a son; and said, Because Yahweh has heard that I *was* hated, he has therefore given me this *son* also: and she called his name Simeon.
34 And she conceived again, and bore a son; and said, Now this time will my husband be joined unto me, because I have born him three sons: therefore was his name called Levi.
35 And she conceived again, and bore a son: and she said, Now will I praise Yahweh: therefore she called his name Judah and stopped bearing.

Genesis 30

30:1 ¶ And when Rachel saw that she bore Jacob no children, Rachel envied her sister; and said to Jacob, Give me children, or else I die.
2 And Jacob's anger was kindled against Rachel: and he said, *Am* I in God's stead, who has withheld from you the fruit of the womb?
3 And she said, Behold my maid Bilhah, go in unto her; and she shall bear upon my knees, that I may also have children by her.
4 And she gave him Bilhah her handmaid to wife: and Jacob went in unto her.
5 And Bilhah conceived, and bore Jacob a son.
6 And Rachel said, God has judged me, and has also heard my voice, and has given me a son: therefore called she his name Dan.
7 And Bilhah Rachel's maid conceived again, and bore Jacob a second son.
8 And Rachel said, With great wrestlings have I wrestled with my sister, and I have prevailed: and she called his name Naphtali.
9 When Leah saw that she had stopped bearing, she took Zilpah her maid, and gave her Jacob to wife.
10 And Zilpah Leah's maid bore Jacob a son.
11 And Leah said, Good fortune comes: and she called his name Gad.
12 And Zilpah Leah's maid bore Jacob a second son.
13 And Leah said, Happy am I, for the daughters will call me blessed: and she called his name Asher.
14 ¶ And Reuben went in the days of wheat harvest, and found mandrakes in the field, and brought them to his mother Leah. Then Rachel said to Leah, Give me, I pray you, of your son's mandrakes.
15 And she said to her, *Is it* a small matter that you have taken my husband? and would you take away my son's mandrakes also? And Rachel said, Therefore he shall lie with you tonight for your son's mandrakes.
16 And Jacob came out of the field in the evening, and Leah went out to meet him, and said, You must come in unto me; for surely I have hired you with my son's mandrakes. And he lay with her that night.
17 And God listened to Leah, and she conceived, and bore Jacob the fifth son.
18 And Leah said, God has given me my hire, because I have given my maiden to my husband: and she called his name Issachar.
19 And Leah conceived again, and bore Jacob the sixth son.

Genesis 30

20 And Leah said, God has endued me *with* a good dowry; now will my husband dwell with me, because I have born him six sons: and she called his name Zebulun.

21 And afterward she bore a daughter, and called her name Dinah.

22 And God remembered Rachel, and God listened to her, and opened her womb.

23 And she conceived, and bore a son; and said, God has taken away my reproach:

24 And she called his name Joseph; and said, Yahweh shall add to me another son.

25 ¶ And it came to pass, when Rachel had birthed Joseph, that Jacob said to Laban, Send me away, that I may go to my own place, and to my country.

26 Give *me* my wives and my children, for whom I have served you, and let me go: for you know my service which I have served you.

27 And Laban said to him, I pray you, if I have found favor in your eyes, *stay: for* I have learned by experience that Yahweh has blessed me for your sake.

28 And he said, Name me your wages, and I will give *it*.

29 And he said to him, You know how I have served you, and how your cattle was with me.

30 For *it was* little which you had before I *came*, and it is *now* increased to a multitude; and Yahweh has blessed you since my coming: and now when shall I provide for my own house also?

31 And he said, What shall I give you? And Jacob said, You shall not give me anything: if you will do this thing for me, I will again feed *and* keep your flock:

32 I will pass through all your flock today, removing from there all the speckled and spotted cattle, and all the brown cattle among the sheep, and the spotted and speckled among the goats: and *of such* shall be my hire.

33 So shall my righteousness answer for me in time to come, when it shall come for my hire before your face: every one that *is* not speckled and spotted among the goats, and brown among the sheep, that shall be counted stolen with me.

34 And Laban said, Behold, I would it might be according to your word.

35 And he removed that day the he goats that were striped and spotted, and all the she goats that were speckled and spotted, *and* every one that had *some* white in it, and all the brown among the sheep, and gave *them* into the hand of his sons.

36 And he set three days' journey between himself and Jacob: and Jacob fed the rest of Laban's flocks.

37 ¶ And Jacob took him rods of green poplar, and of the hazel and chestnut tree; and peeled white strips in them, and made the white appear which *was* in the rods.

38 And he set the rods which he had peeled before the flocks in the gutters in the watering troughs when the flocks came to drink, that they should conceive when they came to drink.

39 And the flocks conceived before the rods, and brought forth cattle striped, speckled, and spotted.

40 And Jacob did separate the lambs, and set the faces of the flocks toward the striped, and all the brown in the flock of Laban; and he put his own flocks by themselves, and put them not to Laban's cattle.

41 And it came to pass, whenever the stronger cattle did conceive, that Jacob laid the rods before the eyes of the cattle in the gutters, that they might conceive among the rods.

42 But when the cattle were feeble, he put *them* not in: so the feebler were Laban's, and the stronger Jacob's.

43 And the man increased exceedingly, and had much cattle, and maidservants, and menservants, and camels, and donkeys.

Genesis 31

31:1 ¶ And he heard the words of Laban's sons, saying, Jacob has taken away all that *was* our father's; and of *that* which *was* our father's has he gotten all this glory.

2 And Jacob beheld the countenance of Laban, and, behold, it *was* not toward him as before.

3 And Yahweh said unto Jacob, Return to the land of your fathers, and to your kindred; and I will be with you.

4 And Jacob sent and called Rachel and Leah to the field unto his flock,

5 And said to them, I see your father's countenance, that it *is* not toward me as before; but the God of my father has been with me.

6 And you know that with all my power I have served your father.

7 And your father has deceived me, and changed my wages ten times; but God permitted him not to hurt me.

8 If he said thus, The speckled shall be your wages; then all the cattle bore speckled: and if he said thus, The striped shall be your hire; then bore all the cattle striped.

9 Thus God has taken away the cattle of your father, and given *them* to me.

10 And it came to pass at the time that the cattle conceived, that I lifted up my eyes, and saw in a dream, and, behold, the rams which leaped upon the cattle *were* striped, speckled, and grisled.

11 And the angel of God spoke to me in a dream, *saying*, Jacob: And I said, Here *am* I.

12 And he said, Lift up now your eyes, and see, all the rams which leap upon the cattle *are* striped, speckled, and grisled: for I have seen all that Laban does unto you.

13 I *am* the God of Bethel, where you anointed the pillar, *and* where you vowed a vow unto me: now arise, get you out from this land, and return to the land of your kindred.

14 And Rachel and Leah answered and said to him, *Is there* yet any portion or inheritance for us in our father's house?

15 Are we not counted of him strangers? for he has sold us, and has quite devoured also our money.

16 For all the riches which God has taken from our father, that *is* ours, and our children's: now then, whatever God has said unto you, do.

17 ¶ Then Jacob rose up, and set his sons and his wives upon camels;

18 And he carried away all his cattle, and all his goods which he had gotten, the cattle of his getting, which he had gotten in Padanaram, for to go to Isaac his father in the land of Canaan.
19 And Laban went to shear his sheep: and Rachel had stolen the images that *were* her father's.
20 And Jacob stole away unaware to Laban the Syrian, in that he told him not that he fled.
21 So he fled with all that he had; and he rose up, and passed over the river, and set his face *toward* the mount Gilead.
22 And it was told *to* Laban on the third day that Jacob had fled.
23 And he took his brethren with him, and pursued after him seven days' journey; and they overtook him in the mount Gilead.
24 And God came to Laban the Syrian in a dream by night, and said unto him, Take heed that you speak not to Jacob either good or bad.
25 ¶ Then Laban overtook Jacob. Now Jacob had pitched his tent in the mount: and Laban with his brethren pitched in the mount of Gilead.
26 And Laban said to Jacob, What have you done, that you have stolen away unaware to me, and carried away my daughters, as captives *taken* with the sword?
27 Why did you flee away secretly, and steal away from me; and did not tell me, that I might have sent you away with gladness, and with songs, with tambourine, and with harp?
28 And have not permitted me to kiss my sons and my daughters? you have now done foolishly in *so* doing.
29 It is in the power of my hand to do you hurt: but the God of your father spoke to me last night, saying, Take you heed that you speak not to Jacob either good or bad.
30 And now, *though* you would need to go, because you greatly longed after your father's house, *but* why have you stolen my gods?
31 And Jacob answered and said to Laban, Because I was afraid: for I said, Perhaps you would take by force your daughters from me.
32 With whomever you find your gods, let him not live: before our brethren discern you what *is* yours with me, and take *it* with you. For Jacob knew not that Rachel had stolen them.
33 And Laban went into Jacob's tent, and into Leah's tent, and into the two maidservants' tents; but he found *them* not. Then went he out of Leah's tent, and entered into Rachel's tent.
34 Now Rachel had taken the images, and put them in the camel's furniture, and sat upon them. And Laban searched all the tent, but found *them* not.
35 And she said to her father, Let it not displease my lord that I cannot rise up before you; for the custom of women *is* upon me. And he searched, but found not the images.
36 ¶ And Jacob was angry, and strived with Laban: and Jacob answered and said to Laban, What *is* my trespass? what *is* my sin, that you have so hotly pursued after me?
37 Whereas you have searched all my stuff, what have you found of all your household stuff? set *it* here before my brethren and your brethren, that they may judge between us both. 38 This twenty years *have* I *been* with you; your ewes and your she goats have not cast their young, and the rams of your flock have I not eaten.
39 That which was torn *of beasts* I brought not unto you; I bore the loss of it; of my hand did you require it, *whether* stolen by day, or stolen by night.
40 *Thus* I was; in the day the drought consumed me, and the frost by night; and my sleep departed from my eyes.
41 Thus have I been twenty years in your house; I served you fourteen years for your two daughters, and six years for your cattle: and you have changed my wages ten times.
42 Except the God of my father, the God of Abraham, and the fear of Isaac, had been with me, surely you had sent me away now empty. God has seen my affliction and the labor of my hands, and rebuked *you* last night.
43 ¶ And Laban answered and said to Jacob, *These* daughters *are* my daughters, and *these* children *are* my children, and *these* cattle *are* my cattle, and all that you see *is* mine: and what can I do this day to these my daughters, or to their children which they have born?
44 Now therefore come you, let us make a covenant, I and you; and let it be for a witness between me and you.
45 And Jacob took a stone, and set it up *for* a pillar.
46 And Jacob said to his brethren, Gather stones; and they took stones, and made a heap: and they did eat there upon the heap.
47 And Laban called it Jegarsahadutha: but Jacob called it Galeed.
48 And Laban said, This heap *is* a witness between me and you this day. Therefore was the name of it called Galeed;
49 And Mizpah; for he said, Yahweh watch between me and you, when we are absent one from another.
50 If you shall afflict my daughters, or if you shall take *other* wives besides my daughters, no man *is* with us; see, God *is* witness between me and you.
51 And Laban said to Jacob, Behold this heap, and behold *this* pillar, which I have cast between me and you;
52 This heap *is* witness, and *this* pillar *is* witness, that I will not pass over this heap to you, and that you shall not pass over this heap and this pillar unto me, for harm.
53 The God of Abraham, and the God of Nahor, the God of their father, judge between us. And Jacob swore by the fear of his father Isaac.
54 Then Jacob offered sacrifice upon the mount, and called his brethren to eat bread: and they did eat bread, and stayed all night in the mount.
55 And early in the morning Laban rose up, and kissed his sons and his daughters, and blessed them: and Laban departed, and returned to his place.

Genesis 32

32:1 ¶ And Jacob went on his way, and the angels of God met him.

2 And when Jacob saw them, he said, This *is* God's host: and he called the name of that place Mahanaim.

3 ¶ And Jacob sent messengers before him to Esau his brother unto the land of Seir, the country of Edom.

4 And he commanded them, saying, Thus shall you speak unto my lord Esau; Your servant Jacob says thus, I have sojourned with Laban, and stayed there until now:

5 And I have oxen, and donkeys, flocks, and menservants, and women servants: and I have sent to tell my lord, that I may find grace in your sight.

6 And the messengers returned to Jacob, saying, We came to your brother Esau, and also he comes to meet you, and four hundred men with him.

7 Then Jacob was greatly afraid and distressed: and he divided the people that *were* with him, and the flocks, and herds, and the camels, into two bands;

8 And said, If Esau comes to the one company, and smites it, then the other company which is left shall escape.

9 ¶ And Jacob said, O God of my father Abraham, and God of my father Isaac, Yahweh which said unto me, Return to your country, and to your kindred, and I will deal well with you:

10 I am not worthy of the least of all the mercies, and of all the truth, which you have shown unto your servant; for with my staff I passed over this Jordan; and now I have become two bands.

11 Deliver me, I pray you, from the hand of my brother, from the hand of Esau: for I fear him, lest he will come and smite me, *and* the mother with the children.

12 And you said, I will surely do you good, and make your seed as the sand of the sea, which cannot be numbered for multitude.

13 ¶ And he lodged there that same night; and took of that which came to his hand a present for Esau his brother;

14 Two hundred she goats, and twenty he goats, two hundred ewes, and twenty rams,

15 Thirty milk camels with their colts, forty cows, and ten bulls, twenty she donkeys, and ten foals.

16 And he delivered *them* into the hand of his servants, every herd by themselves; and said to his servants, Pass over before me, and put a space between herd and herd.

17 And he commanded the foremost, saying, When Esau my brother meets you, and asks you, saying, Whose *are* you? and where go you? and whose *are* these before you?

18 Then you shall say, *They are* your servant Jacob's; it *is* a present sent unto my lord Esau: and, behold, also he *is* behind us.

19 And so commanded he the second, and the third, and all that followed the herds, saying, On this manner shall you speak to Esau, when you find him.

20 And say you moreover, Behold, your servant Jacob *is* behind us. For he said, I will appease him with the present that goes before me, and afterward I will see his face; perhaps he will accept of me.

21 So went the present over before him: and himself lodged that night in the company.

22 And he rose up that night, and took his two wives, and his two women servants, and his eleven sons, and passed over the ford Jabbok.

23 And he took them, and sent them over the brook, and sent over what he had.

24 ¶ And Jacob was left alone; and there wrestled a man with him until the breaking of the day.

25 And when he saw that he prevailed not against him, he touched the hollow of his thigh; and the hollow of Jacob's thigh was out of joint, as he wrestled with him.

26 And he said, Let me go, for the day breaks. And he said, I will not let you go, unless you bless me.

27 And he said to him, What *is* your name? And he said, Jacob.

28 And he said, Your name shall be called no more Jacob, but Israel: for as a prince have you power with God and with men, and have prevailed.

29 And Jacob asked *him*, and said, Tell *me*, I pray you, your name. And he said, Why *is* it *that* you do ask after my name? And he blessed him there.

30 And Jacob called the name of the place Peniel: for I have seen God face to face, and my life is preserved.

31 And as he passed over Penuel the sun rose upon him, and he limped upon his thigh.

32 Therefore the children of Israel eat not *of* the sinew which shrank, which *is* upon the hollow of the thigh, unto this day: because he touched the hollow of Jacob's thigh in the sinew that shrank.

Genesis 33

33:1 ¶ And Jacob lifted up his eyes, and looked, and, behold, Esau came, and with him four hundred men. And he divided the children unto Leah, and unto Rachel, and unto the two handmaids.

2 And he put the handmaids and their children foremost, and Leah and her children after, and Rachel and Joseph last.

3 And he passed over before them, and bowed himself to the ground seven times, until he came near to his brother.

4 And Esau ran to meet him, and embraced him, and fell on his neck, and kissed him: and they wept.

5 ¶ And he lifted up his eyes, and saw the women and the children; and said, Who *are* those with you? And he said, The children which God has graciously given your servant.

6 Then the handmaidens came near, they and their children, and they bowed themselves.

7 And Leah also with her children came near, and bowed themselves: and afterward came Joseph near and Rachel, and they bowed themselves.

8 And he said, What *mean* you by all this company which I met? And he said, *These are* to find grace in the sight of my lord.

9 And Esau said, I have enough, my brother; keep what you have to yourself.

10 And Jacob said, No, I pray you, if now I have found grace in your sight, then receive my present at my hand: for therefore I have seen your face, as though I had seen the face of God, and you were pleased with me.

11 Take, I pray you, my blessing that is brought to you: because God has dealt graciously with me, and because I have enough. And he urged him, and he took *it*.

12 And he said, Let us take our journey, and let us go, and I will go before you.

13 And he said to him, My lord knows that the children *are* tender, and the flocks and herds with young *are* with me: and if men should overdrive them one day, all the flock will die.

14 Let my lord, I pray you, pass over before his servant: and I will lead on softly, according as the cattle that goes before me and the children be able to endure, until I come unto my lord unto Seir.

15 And Esau said, Let me now leave with you *some* of the folk that *are* with me. And he said, What needs it? let me find grace in the sight of my lord.

16 ¶ So Esau returned that day on his way to Seir.

17 And Jacob journeyed to Succoth, and built him a house, and made booths for his cattle: therefore the name of the place is called Succoth.

18 And Jacob came to Shalem, a city of Shechem, which *is* in the land of Canaan, when he came from Padanaram; and pitched his tent before the city.

19 And he bought a parcel of a field, where he had spread his tent, at the hand of the children of Hamor, Shechem's father, for a hundred pieces of money.

20 And he erected there an altar, and called it El-elohe-Israel.

Genesis 34

34:1 ¶ And Dinah the daughter of Leah, which she bore unto Jacob, went out to see the daughters of the land.

2 And when Shechem the son of Hamor the Hivite, prince of the country, saw her, he took her, and lay with her, and defiled her.

3 And his soul clung unto Dinah the daughter of Jacob, and he loved the damsel, and spoke kindly to the damsel.

4 And Shechem spoke to his father Hamor, saying, Get me this damsel to wife.

5 And Jacob heard that he had defiled Dinah his daughter: now his sons were with his cattle in the field: and Jacob held his peace until they had come.

6 ¶ And Hamor the father of Shechem went out to Jacob to commune with him.

7 And the sons of Jacob came out of the field when they heard *it*: and the men were grieved, and they were very angry, because he had worked folly in Israel in lying with Jacob's daughter; which thing ought not to be done.

8 And Hamor communed with them, saying, The soul of my son Shechem longs for your daughter: I pray you give her him to wife.

9 And make you marriages with us, *and* give your daughters to us, and take our daughters unto you.

10 And you shall dwell with us: and the land shall be before you; dwell and trade you therein, and get you possessions therein.

11 And Shechem said to her father and to her brothers, Let me find grace in your eyes, and what you shall say to me I will give.

12 Ask me never so much dowry and gift, and I will give according as you shall say to me: but give me the damsel to wife.

13 And the sons of Jacob answered Shechem and Hamor his father deceitfully, and said, because he had defiled Dinah their sister:

14 And they said to them, We cannot do this thing, to give our sister to one that is uncircumcised; for that *is* a reproach unto us:

15 But in this will we consent to you: If you will be as we *be*, that every male of you be circumcised;

16 Then will we give our daughters to you, and we will take your daughters to us, and we will dwell with you, and we will become one people.

17 But if you will not listen to us, to be circumcised; then will we take our daughter, and we will be gone.

18 ¶ And their words pleased Hamor, and Shechem Hamor's son.

19 And the young man deferred not to do the thing, because he had delight in Jacob's daughter: and he *was* more honorable than all the house of his father.

20 And Hamor and Shechem his son came to the gate of their city, and spoke with the men of their city, saying,

21 These men *are* peaceable with us; therefore let them dwell in the land, and trade therein; for the land, behold, *it is* large enough for them; let us take their daughters to us for wives, and let us give them our daughters.

22 Only herein will the men consent to us for to dwell with us, to be one people, if every male among us is circumcised, as they *are* circumcised.

23 *Shall* not their cattle and their substance and every beast of theirs *be* ours? only let us consent to them, and they will dwell with us.

24 And to Hamor and to Shechem his son heard all that went out of the gate of his city; and every male was circumcised, all that went out of the gate of his city.

25 ¶ And it came to pass on the third day, when they were sore, that two of the sons of Jacob, Simeon and Levi, Dinah's brothers, took each man his sword, and came upon the city boldly, and slew all the males.

26 And they slew Hamor and Shechem his son with the edge of the sword, and took Dinah out of Shechem's house, and went out.

27 The sons of Jacob came upon the slain, and spoiled the city, because they had defiled their sister.

28 They took their sheep, and their oxen, and their donkeys, and that which *was* in the city, and that which *was* in the field,

29 And all their wealth, and all their little ones, and their wives took they captive, and spoiled even all that *was* in the house.

Genesis 34

30 And Jacob said to Simeon and Levi, You have troubled me to make me to stink among the inhabitants of the land, among the Canaanites and the Perizzites: and I *being* few in number, they shall gather themselves together against me, and slay me; and I shall be destroyed, I and my house.

31 And they said, Should he deal with our sister as with a harlot?

Genesis 35

35:1 ¶ And God said unto Jacob, Arise, go up to Bethel, and dwell there: and make there an altar unto God, that appeared to you when you fled from the face of Esau your brother.

2 Then Jacob said to his household, and to all that *were* with him, Put away the strange gods that *are* among you, and be clean, and change your garments:

3 And let us arise, and go up to Bethel; and I will make there an altar to God, who answered me in the day of my distress, and was with me in the way which I went.

4 And they gave to Jacob all the strange gods which *were* in their hand, and *all their* earrings which *were* in their ears; and Jacob hid them under the oak which *was* by Shechem.

5 And they journeyed: and the terror of God was upon the cities that *were* round about them, and they did not pursue after the sons of Jacob.

6 ¶ So Jacob came to Luz, which *is* in the land of Canaan, that *is*, Bethel, he and all the people that *were* with him.

7 And he built there an altar, and called the place Elbethel: because there God appeared unto him, when he fled from the face of his brother.

8 But Deborah Rebekah's nurse died, and she was buried beneath Bethel under an oak: and the name of it was called Allonbachuth.

9 And God appeared unto Jacob again, when he came out of Padanaram, and blessed him.

10 And God said unto him, Your name *is* Jacob: your name shall not be called any more Jacob, but Israel shall be your name: and he called his name Israel.

11 And God said unto him, I *am* God Almighty: be fruitful and multiply; a nation and a company of nations shall be of you, and kings shall come out of your loins;

12 And the land which I gave Abraham and Isaac, to you I will give it, and to your seed after you will I give the land.

13 And God went up from him in the place where he talked with him.

14 And Jacob set up a pillar in the place where he talked with him, *even* a pillar of stone: and he poured a drink offering thereon, and he poured oil thereon.

15 And Jacob called the name of the place where God spoke with him, Bethel.

16 ¶ And they journeyed from Bethel; and there was but a little way to come to Ephrath: and Rachel travailed, and she had hard labor.

17 And it came to pass, when she was in hard labor, that the midwife said to her, Fear not; you shall have this son also.

18 And it came to pass, as her soul was departing, (for she died) that she called his name Benoni: but his father called him Benjamin.

19 And Rachel died, and was buried in the way to Ephrath, which *is* Bethlehem.

20 And Jacob set a pillar upon her grave: that *is* the pillar of Rachel's grave unto this day.

21 ¶ And Israel journeyed, and spread his tent beyond the tower of Edar.

22 And it came to pass, when Israel dwelt in that land, that Reuben went and lay with Bilhah his father's concubine: and Israel heard *it*. Now the sons of Jacob were twelve:

23 The sons of Leah; Reuben, Jacob's firstborn, and Simeon, and Levi, and Judah, and Issachar, and Zebulun:

24 The sons of Rachel; Joseph, and Benjamin:

25 And the sons of Bilhah, Rachel's handmaid; Dan, and Naphtali:

26 And the sons of Zilpah, Leah's handmaid; Gad, and Asher: these *are* the sons of Jacob, which were born to him in Padanaram.

27 And Jacob came to Isaac his father to Mamre, to the city of Arbah, which *is* Hebron, where Abraham and Isaac dwelt.

28 And the days of Isaac were a hundred and fourscore years.

29 And Isaac gave up the ghost, and died, and was gathered unto his people, *being* old and full of days: and his sons Esau and Jacob buried him.

Genesis 36

36:1 ¶ Now these *are* the generations of Esau, who *is* Edom.

2 Esau took his wives from the daughters of Canaan; Adah the daughter of Elon the Hittite, and Aholibamah the daughter of Anah the daughter of Zibeon the Hivite;

3 And Bashemath Ishmael's daughter, sister of Nebajoth.

4 And Adah bore to Esau Eliphaz; and Bashemath bore Reuel;

5 And Aholibamah bore Jeush, and Jaalam, and Korah: these *are* the sons of Esau, which were born to him in the land of Canaan.

6 And Esau took his wives, and his sons, and his daughters, and all the persons of his house, and his cattle, and all his beasts, and all his substance, which he had gotten in the land of Canaan; and went into the country from the face of his brother Jacob.

7 For their riches were more than that they might dwell together; and the land wherein they were strangers could not bear them because of their cattle.

8 Thus dwelt Esau in mount Seir: Esau *is* Edom.

9 ¶ And these *are* the generations of Esau the father of the Edomites in mount Seir:

10 These *are* the names of Esau's sons; Eliphaz the son of Adah the wife of Esau, Reuel the son of Bashemath the wife of Esau.

11 And the sons of Eliphaz were Teman, Omar, Zepho, and Gatam, and Kenaz.
12 And Timna was concubine to Eliphaz Esau's son; and she bore to Eliphaz Amalek: these *were* the sons of Adah Esau's wife.
13 And these *are* the sons of Reuel; Nahath, and Zerah, Shammah, and Mizzah: these were the sons of Bashemath Esau's wife.
14 And these were the sons of Aholibamah, the daughter of Anah the daughter of Zibeon, Esau's wife: and she bore to Esau Jeush, and Jaalam, and Korah.
15 These *were* dukes of the sons of Esau: the sons of Eliphaz the firstborn *son* of Esau; duke Teman, duke Omar, duke Zepho, duke Kenaz,
16 Duke Korah, duke Gatam, *and* duke Amalek: these *are* the dukes *that came* of Eliphaz in the land of Edom; these *were* the sons of Adah.
17 And these *are* the sons of Reuel Esau's son; duke Nahath, duke Zerah, duke Shammah, duke Mizzah: these *are* the dukes *that came* of Reuel in the land of Edom; these *are* the sons of Bashemath Esau's wife.
18 And these *are* the sons of Aholibamah Esau's wife; duke Jeush, duke Jaalam, duke Korah: these *were* the dukes *that came* of Aholibamah the daughter of Anah, Esau's wife.
19 These *are* the sons of Esau, who *is* Edom, and these *are* their dukes.
20 ¶ These *are* the sons of Seir the Horite, who inhabited the land; Lotan, and Shobal, and Zibeon, and Anah,
21 And Dishon, and Ezer, and Dishan: these *are* the dukes of the Horites, the children of Seir in the land of Edom.
22 And the children of Lotan were Hori and Hemam; and Lotan's sister *was* Timna.
23 And the children of Shobal *were* these; Alvan, and Manahath, and Ebal, Shepho, and Onam.
24 And these *are* the children of Zibeon; both Ajah, and Anah: this *was that* Anah that found the mules in the wilderness, as he fed the donkeys of Zibeon his father.
25 And the children of Anah *were* these; Dishon, and Aholibamah the daughter of Anah.
26 And these *are* the children of Dishon; Hemdan, and Eshban, and Ithran, and Cheran.
27 The children of Ezer *are* these; Bilhan, and Zaavan, and Akan.
28 The children of Dishan *are* these; Uz, and Aran.
29 These *are* the dukes *that came* of the Horites; duke Lotan, duke Shobal, duke Zibeon, duke Anah,
30 Duke Dishon, duke Ezer, duke Dishan: these *are* the dukes *that came* of Hori, among their dukes in the land of Seir.
31 ¶ And these *are* the kings that reigned in the land of Edom, before there reigned any king over the children of Israel.
32 And Bela the son of Beor reigned in Edom: and the name of his city *was* Dinhabah.
33 And Bela died, and Jobab the son of Zerah of Bozrah reigned in his stead.
34 And Jobab died, and Husham of the land of Temani reigned in his stead.
35 And Husham died, and Hadad the son of Bedad, who smote Midian in the field of Moab, reigned in his stead: and the name of his city *was* Avith.
36 And Hadad died, and Samlah of Masrekah reigned in his stead.
37 And Samlah died, and Saul of Rehoboth *by* the river reigned in his stead.
38 And Saul died, and Baalhanan the son of Achbor reigned in his stead.
39 And Baalhanan the son of Achbor died, and Hadar reigned in his stead: and the name of his city *was* Pau; and his wife's name *was* Mehetabel, the daughter of Matred, the daughter of Mezahab.
40 And these *are* the names of the dukes *that came* of Esau, according to their families, after their places, by their names: duke Timnah, duke Alvah, duke Jetheth,
41 Duke Aholibamah, duke Elah, duke Pinon,
42 Duke Kenaz, duke Teman, duke Mibzar,
43 Duke Magdiel, duke Iram: these *be* the dukes of Edom, according to their habitations in the land of their possession: he *is* Esau the father of the Edomites.

Genesis 37

37:1 ¶ And Jacob dwelt in the land wherein his father was a stranger, in the land of Canaan.
2 These *are* the generations of Jacob. Joseph, *being* seventeen years old, was feeding the flock with his brothers; and the lad *was* with the sons of Bilhah, and with the sons of Zilpah, his father's wives: and Joseph brought to his father their evil report.
3 Now Israel loved Joseph more than all his children, because he *was* the son of his old age: and he made him a coat of *many* colors.
4 And when his brothers saw that their father loved him more than all his brothers, they hated him, and could not speak peaceably unto him.
5 ¶ And Joseph dreamed a dream, and he told *it* to his brothers: and they hated him yet the more.
6 And he said to them, Hear, I pray you, this dream which I have dreamed:
7 For, behold, we *were* binding sheaves in the field, and, behold, my sheaf arose, and also stood upright; and, behold, your sheaves stood round about, and made obeisance unto my sheaf.
8 And his brothers said to him, Shall you indeed reign over us? or shall you indeed have dominion over us? And they hated him yet the more for his dreams, and for his words.
9 And he dreamed yet another dream, and told it *to* his brothers, and said, Behold, I have dreamed a dream more; and, behold, the sun and the moon and the eleven stars made obeisance to me.
10 And he told *it* to his father, and to his brothers: and his father rebuked him, and said to him, What *is* this dream that you have dreamed? Shall I and your mother and your brothers indeed come to bow down ourselves to you to the earth?
11 And his brothers envied him; but his father observed the saying.

Genesis 37

12 ¶ And his brothers went to feed their father's flock in Shechem.
13 And Israel said to Joseph, Do not your brothers feed *the flock* in Shechem? come, and I will send you to them. And he said to him, Here *am* I.
14 And he said to him, Go, I pray you, see whether it is well with your brothers, and well with the flocks; and bring me word again. So he sent him out of the valley of Hebron, and he came to Shechem.
15 And a certain man found him, and, behold, *he was* wandering in the field: and the man asked him, saying, What seek you?
16 And he said, I seek my brothers: tell me, I pray you, where they feed *their flocks*.
17 And the man said, They are departed away; for I heard them say, Let us go to Dothan. And Joseph went after his brothers, and found them in Dothan.
18 And when they saw him afar off, even before he came near to them, they conspired against him to slay him.
19 And they said one to another, Behold, this dreamer comes.
20 Come now therefore, and let us slay him, and cast him into some pit, and we will say, Some evil beast has devoured him: and we shall see what will become of his dreams.
21 And Reuben heard *it*, and he delivered him out of their hands; and said, Let us not kill him.
22 And Reuben said to them, Shed no blood, *but* cast him into this pit that *is* in the wilderness, and lay no hand upon him; that he might rescue him out of their hands, to deliver him to his father again.
23 ¶ And it came to pass, when Joseph had come to his brothers, that they stripped Joseph out of his coat, *his* coat of *many* colors that *was* on him;
24 And they took him, and cast him into a pit: and the pit *was* empty, *there was* no water in it.
25 And they sat down to eat bread: and they lifted up their eyes and looked, and, behold, a company of Ishmeelites came from Gilead with their camels bearing spices and balm and myrrh, going to carry *it* down to Egypt.
26 And Judah said to his brothers, What profit *is it* if we slay our brother, and conceal his blood?
27 Come, and let us sell him to the Ishmeelites, and let not our hand be upon him; for he *is* our brother *and* our flesh. And his brothers were content.
28 Then there passed by Midianite merchantmen; and they drew and lifted up Joseph out of the pit, and sold Joseph to the Ishmeelites for twenty *pieces* of silver: and they brought Joseph into Egypt.
29 And Reuben returned to the pit; and, behold, Joseph *was* not in the pit; and he tore his clothes.
30 And he returned to his brothers, and said, The child *is* not; and I, where shall I go?
31 ¶ And they took Joseph's coat, and killed a kid of the goats, and dipped the coat in the blood;
32 And they sent the coat of *many* colors, and they brought *it* to their father; and said, This have we found: know now whether it *is* your son's coat or not.
33 And he knew it, and said, *It is* my son's coat; an evil beast has devoured him; Joseph is without doubt torn in pieces.
34 And Jacob tore his clothes, and put sackcloth upon his loins, and mourned for his son many days.
35 And all his sons and all his daughters rose up to comfort him; but he refused to be comforted; and he said, For I will go down into the grave unto my son mourning. Thus his father wept for him.
36 And the Midianites sold him into Egypt to Potiphar, an officer of Pharaoh's, *and* captain of the guard.

Genesis 38

38:1 ¶ And it came to pass at that time, that Judah went down from his brothers, and turned in to a certain Adullamite, whose name *was* Hirah.
2 And Judah saw there a daughter of a certain Canaanite, whose name *was* Shuah; and he took her, and went in unto her.
3 And she conceived, and bore a son; and he called his name Er.
4 And she conceived again, and bore a son; and she called his name Onan.
5 And she yet again conceived, and bore a son; and called his name Shelah: and he was at Chezib, when she bore him.
6 And Judah took a wife for Er his firstborn, whose name *was* Tamar.
7 And Er, Judah's firstborn, was wicked in the sight of Yahweh; and Yahweh slew him.
8 And Judah said to Onan, Go in unto your brother's wife, and marry her, and raise up seed to your brother.
9 And Onan knew that the seed should not be his; and it came to pass, when he went in unto his brother's wife, that he spilled *it* on the ground, lest that he should give seed to his brother.
10 And the thing which he did displeased Yahweh: therefore he slew him also.
11 Then said Judah to Tamar his daughter-in-law, Remain a widow at your father's house, till Shelah my son is grown: for he said, Lest perhaps he dies also, as his brothers *did*. And Tamar went and dwelt in her father's house.
12 ¶ And in *the* process of time the daughter of Shuah Judah's wife died; and Judah was comforted, and went up unto his sheep shearers to Timnath, he and his friend Hirah the Adullamite.
13 And it was told *to* Tamar, saying, Behold your father-in-law goes up to Timnath to shear his sheep.
14 And she put her widow's garments off from her, and covered her with a veil, and wrapped herself, and sat in an open place, which *is* by the way to Timnath; for she saw that Shelah was grown, and she was not given unto him to wife.
15 When Judah saw her, he thought her *to be* a harlot; because she had covered her face.

16 And he turned to her by the way, and said, Go to, I pray you, let me come in unto you; (for he knew not that she *was* his daughter-in-law.) And she said, What will you give me, that you may come in unto me?

17 And he said, I will send *you* a kid from the flock. And she said, Will you give *me* a pledge, till you send *it*?

18 And he said, What pledge shall I give you? And she said, Your signet, and your bracelets, and your staff that *is* in your hand. And he gave *them to* her, and came in unto her, and she conceived by him.

19 And she arose, and went away, and laid by her veil from her, and put on the garments of her widowhood.

20 And Judah sent the kid by the hand of his friend the Adullamite, to receive *his* pledge from the woman's hand: but he found her not.

21 Then he asked the men of that place, saying, Where *is* the harlot, that *was* openly by the way side? And they said, There was no harlot in this *place*.

22 And he returned to Judah, and said, I cannot find her; and also the men of the place said, *that* there was no harlot in this *place*.

23 And Judah said, Let her take *it* to her, lest we be shamed: behold, I sent this kid, and you have not found her.

24 ¶ And it came to pass about three months after, that it was told *to* Judah, saying, Tamar your daughter-in-law has played the harlot; and also, behold, she *is* with child by whoredom. And Judah said, Bring her forth, and let her be burnt.

25 When she *was* brought forth, she sent to her father-in-law, saying, By the man, whose these *are, am* I with child: and she said, Discern, I pray you, whose *are* these, the signet, and bracelets, and staff.

26 And Judah acknowledged *them*, and said, She has been more righteous than I; because that I gave her not to Shelah my son. And he knew her again no more.

27 And it came to pass in the time of her labor, that, behold, twins *were* in her womb.

28 And it came to pass, when she labored, that *the one* put out *his* hand: and the midwife took and bound upon his hand a scarlet thread, saying, This came out first.

29 And it came to pass, as he drew back his hand, that, behold, his brother came out: and she said, How have you broken forth? *this* breach *be* upon you: therefore his name was called Pharez.

30 And afterward came out his brother, that had the scarlet thread upon his hand: and his name was called Zarah.

Genesis 39

39:1 ¶ And Joseph was brought down to Egypt; and Potiphar, an officer of Pharaoh, captain of the guard, an Egyptian, bought him of the hands of the Ishmeelites, which had brought him down there.

2 And Yahweh was with Joseph, and he was a prosperous man; and he was in the house of his master the Egyptian.

3 And his master saw that Yahweh *was* with him, and that Yahweh made all that he did to prosper in his hand.

4 And Joseph found grace in his sight, and he served him: and he made him overseer over his house, and all *that* he had he put into his hand.

5 And it came to pass from the time *that* he had made him overseer in his house, and over all that he had, that Yahweh blessed the Egyptian's house for Joseph's sake; and the blessing of Yahweh was upon all that he had in the house, and in the field.

6 And he left all that he had in Joseph's hand; and he knew not anything he had, save the bread which he did eat. And Joseph was *a* goodly *person*, and well favored.

7 ¶ And it came to pass after these things, that his master's wife cast her eyes upon Joseph; and she said, Lie with me.

8 But he refused, and said to his master's wife, Behold, my master knows not what *is* with me in the house, and he has committed all that he has to my hand;

9 *There is* none greater in this house than I; neither has he kept back anything from me but you, because you *are* his wife: how then can I do this great wickedness, and sin against God?

10 And it came to pass, as she spoke to Joseph day by day, that he listened not to her, to lie by her, *or* to be with her.

11 And it came to pass about this time, that *Joseph* went into the house to do his business; and *there was* none of the men of the house there within.

12 And she caught him by his garment, saying, Lie with me: and he left his garment in her hand, and fled, and got him out.

13 ¶ And it came to pass, when she saw that he had left his garment in her hand, and had fled forth,

14 That she called to the men of her house, and spoke to them, saying, See, he has brought in a Hebrew to us to mock us; he came in unto me to lie with me, and I cried with a loud voice:

15 And it came to pass, when he heard that I lifted up my voice and cried, that he left his garment with me, and fled, and got him out.

16 And she laid up his garment by her, until his lord came home

17 And she spoke to him according to these words, saying, The Hebrew servant, which you have brought to us, came in unto me to mock me:

18 And it came to pass, as I lifted up my voice and cried, that he left his garment with me, and fled out.

19 ¶ And it came to pass, when his master heard the words of his wife, which she spoke to him, saying, After this manner did your servant to me; that his wrath was kindled.

20 And Joseph's master took him, and put him into the prison, a place where the king's prisoners *were* bound: and he was there in the prison.

21 But Yahweh was with Joseph, and showed him mercy, and gave him favor in the sight of the keeper of the prison.

22 And the keeper of the prison committed to Joseph's hand all the prisoners that *were* in the prison; and whatever they did there, he was the doer *of it*.

Genesis 39

23 The keeper of the prison looked not to anything *that was* under his hand; because Yahweh was with him, and *that* which he did, Yahweh made *it* to prosper.

Genesis 40

40:1 ¶ And it came to pass after these things, *that* the butler of the king of Egypt and *his* baker had offended their lord the king of Egypt.
2 And Pharaoh was angry against two *of* his officers, against the chief of the butlers, and against the chief of the bakers.
3 And he put them in ward in the house of the captain of the guard, into the prison, the place where Joseph *was* bound.
4 And the captain of the guard charged Joseph with them, and he served them: and they continued a season in ward.
5 ¶ And they dreamed a dream both of them, each man his dream in one night, each man according to the interpretation of his dream, the butler and the baker of the king of Egypt, which *were* bound in the prison.
6 And Joseph came in unto them in the morning, and looked upon them, and, behold, they *were* sad.
7 And he asked Pharaoh's officers that *were* with him in the ward of his lord's house, saying, Why look you *so* sadly today?
8 And they said to him, We have dreamed a dream, and *there is* no interpreter of it. And Joseph said to them, *Do* not interpretations *belong* to God? tell me *them*, I pray you.
9 And the chief butler told his dream to Joseph, and said to him, In my dream, behold, a vine *was* before me;
10 And in the vine *were* three branches: and it *was* as though it budded, *and* her blossoms shot forth; and the clusters thereof brought forth ripe grapes:
11 And Pharaoh's cup *was* in my hand: and I took the grapes, and pressed them into Pharaoh's cup, and I gave the cup into Pharaoh's hand.
12 And Joseph said to him, This *is* the interpretation of it: The three branches *are* three days:
13 Yet within three days shall Pharaoh lift up your head, and restore you to your place: and you shall deliver Pharaoh's cup into his hand, after the former manner when you were his butler.
14 But think on me when it shall be well with you, and show kindness, I pray you, unto me, and make mention of me to Pharaoh, and bring me out of this house:
15 For indeed I was stolen away out of the land of the Hebrews: and here also have I done nothing that they should put me into the dungeon.
16 When the chief baker saw that the interpretation was good, he said to Joseph, I also *was* in my dream, and, behold, *I had* three white baskets on my head:
17 And in the uppermost basket *there was* of all manner of baked goods for Pharaoh; and the birds did eat them out of the basket on my head.
18 And Joseph answered and said, This *is* the interpretation thereof: The three baskets *are* three days:
19 Yet within three days shall Pharaoh lift up your head from off you, and shall hang you on a tree; and the birds shall eat your flesh from off you.
20 ¶ And it came to pass the third day, *which was* Pharaoh's birthday, that he made a feast unto all his servants: and he lifted up the head of the chief butler and of the chief baker among his servants.
21 And he restored the chief butler to his butlership again; and he gave the cup into Pharaoh's hand:
22 But he hanged the chief baker: as Joseph had interpreted to them.
23 Yet did not the chief butler remember Joseph, but forgot him.

Genesis 41

41:1 ¶ And it came to pass at the end of two full years, that Pharaoh dreamed: and, behold, he stood by the river.
2 And, behold, there came up out of the river seven well favored cows and fat; and they fed in a meadow.
3 And, behold, seven other cows came up after them out of the river, ill favored and thin; and stood by the *other* cows upon the brink of the river.
4 And the ill favored and thin cows did eat up the seven well favored and fat cows. So Pharaoh awoke.
5 And he slept and dreamed the second time: and, behold, seven ears of corn came up on one stalk, plump and good.
6 And, behold, seven thin ears and blasted with the east wind sprung up after them.
7 And the seven thin ears devoured the seven plump and full ears. And Pharaoh awoke, and, behold, *it was* a dream.
8 And it came to pass in the morning that his spirit was troubled; and he sent and called for all the magicians of Egypt, and all the wise men thereof: and Pharaoh told them his dream; but *there was* none that could interpret them to Pharaoh.
9 ¶ Then spoke the chief butler to Pharaoh, saying, I do remember my faults this day:
10 Pharaoh was angry with his servants, and put me in ward in the captain of the guard's house, *both* me and the chief baker:
11 And we dreamed a dream in one night, I and he; we dreamed each man according to the interpretation of his dream.
12 And *there was* there with us a young man, a Hebrew, servant to the captain of the guard; and we told him, and he interpreted to us our dreams; to each man according to his dream he did interpret.
13 And it came to pass, as he interpreted to us, so it was; me he restored to my office, and him he hanged.
14 Then Pharaoh sent and called Joseph, and they brought him hastily out of the dungeon: and he shaved *himself*, and changed his clothing, and came in to Pharaoh.
15 And Pharaoh said to Joseph, I have dreamed a dream, and *there is* none that can interpret it: and I have heard say of you, *that* you can understand a dream to interpret

it.

16 And Joseph answered Pharaoh, saying, *It is* not in me: God shall give Pharaoh an answer of peace.

17 ¶ And Pharaoh said to Joseph, In my dream, behold, I stood upon the bank of the river:

18 And, behold, there came up out of the river seven cows, fat and well favored; and they fed in a meadow:

19 And, behold, seven other cows came up after them, poor and very ill favored and thin, such as I never saw in all the land of Egypt for badness:

20 And the lean and the ill favored cows did eat up the first seven fat cows:

21 And when they had eaten them up, it could not be known that they had eaten them; but they *were* still ill favored, as at the beginning. So I awoke.

22 And I saw in my dream, and, behold, seven ears came up in one stalk, full and good:

23 And, behold, seven ears, withered, thin, *and* blasted with the east wind, sprung up after them:

24 And the thin ears devoured the seven good ears: and I told *this* to the magicians; but *there was* none that could declare *it* to me.

25 And Joseph said to Pharaoh, The dream of Pharaoh *is* one: God has shown Pharaoh what he *is* about to do.

26 The seven good cows *are* seven years; and the seven good ears *are* seven years: the dream *is* one.

27 And the seven thin and ill favored cows that came up after them *are* seven years; and the seven empty ears blasted with the east wind shall be seven years of famine.

28 This *is* the thing which I have spoken to Pharaoh: What God *is* about to do he shows to Pharaoh.

29 Behold, there come seven years of great plenty throughout all the land of Egypt:

30 And there shall arise after them seven years of famine; and all the plenty shall be forgotten in the land of Egypt; and the famine shall consume the land;

31 And the plenty shall not be known in the land by reason of that famine following; for it *shall be* very grievous.

32 And for that the dream was doubled to Pharaoh twice; *it is* because the thing *is* established by God, and God will shortly bring it to pass.

33 ¶ Now therefore let Pharaoh look out a man discreet and wise, and set him over the land of Egypt.

34 Let Pharaoh do *this*, and let him appoint officers over the land, and take up the fifth part of the land of Egypt in the seven plenteous years.

35 And let them gather all the food of those good years that come, and lay up corn under the hand of Pharaoh, and let them keep food in the cities.

36 And that food shall be for store to the land against the seven years of famine, which shall be in the land of Egypt; that the land perish not through the famine.

37 And the thing was good in the eyes of Pharaoh, and in the eyes of all his servants.

38 And Pharaoh said to his servants, Can we find *such a one* as this *is*, a man in whom the Spirit of God *is*?

39 And Pharaoh said to Joseph, Forasmuch as God has shown you all this, *there is* none so discreet and wise as you *are*:

40 You shall be over my house, and according to your word shall all my people be ruled: only in the throne will I be greater than you.

41 And Pharaoh said to Joseph, See, I have set you over all the land of Egypt.

42 And Pharaoh took off his ring from his hand, and put it upon Joseph's hand, and arrayed him in garments of fine linen, and put a gold chain about his neck;

43 And he made him to ride in the second chariot which he had; and they cried before him, Bow the knee: and he made him *ruler* over all the land of Egypt.

44 And Pharaoh said to Joseph, I *am* Pharaoh, and without you shall no man lift up his hand or foot in all the land of Egypt.

45 And Pharaoh called Joseph's name Zaphnathpaaneah; and he gave him to wife Asenath the daughter of Potipherah priest of On. And Joseph went out over *all* the land of Egypt.

46 ¶ And Joseph *was* thirty years old when he stood before Pharaoh king of Egypt. And Joseph went out from the presence of Pharaoh, and went throughout all the land of Egypt.

47 And in the seven plenteous years the earth brought forth by handfuls.

48 And he gathered up all the food of the seven years, which were in the land of Egypt, and laid up the food in the cities: the food of the field, which *was* round about every city, laid he up in the same.

49 And Joseph gathered corn as the sand of the sea, very much, until he ceased numbering; for *it was* without number.

50 And to Joseph were born two sons before the years of famine came, which Asenath the daughter of Potipherah priest of On bore unto him.

51 And Joseph called the name of the firstborn Manasseh: For God, *said he*, has made me forget all my toil, and all my father's house.

52 And the name of the second called he Ephraim: For God has caused me to be fruitful in the land of my affliction.

53 And the seven years of plenty, that was in the land of Egypt, were ended.

54 And the seven years of famine began to come, according as Joseph had said: and the famine was in all lands; but in all the land of Egypt there was bread.

55 And when all the land of Egypt was famished, the people cried to Pharaoh for bread: and Pharaoh said to all the Egyptians, Go to Joseph; what he says to you, do.

56 And the famine was over all the face of the earth: And Joseph opened all the storehouses, and sold to the Egyptians; and the famine became severe in the land of Egypt.

57 And all countries came into Egypt to Joseph to buy *corn*; because that the famine was *so* severe in all lands.

Genesis 42

42:1 ¶ Now when Jacob saw that there was corn in Egypt, Jacob said to his sons, Why do you look one upon another?
2 And he said, Behold, I have heard that there is corn in Egypt: get you down there, and buy for us from there; that we may live, and not die.
3 And Joseph's ten brothers went down to buy corn in Egypt.
4 But Benjamin, Joseph's brother, Jacob sent not with his brothers; for he said, Lest perhaps mischief befalls him.
5 And the sons of Israel came to buy *corn* among those that came: for the famine was in the land of Canaan.
6 And Joseph *was* the governor over the land, *and* he *it was* that sold to all the people of the land: and Joseph's brothers came, and bowed down themselves before him *with* their faces to the earth.
7 ¶ And Joseph saw his brothers, and he knew them, but made himself strange unto them, and spoke roughly unto them; and he said to them, Wherefrom come you? And they said, From the land of Canaan to buy food.
8 And Joseph knew his brothers, but they knew not him.
9 And Joseph remembered the dreams which he dreamed of them, and said to them, You *are* spies; to see the nakedness of the land you have come.
10 And they said unto him, No, my lord, but to buy food have your servants come.
11 We *are* all one man's sons; we *are* true *men*, your servants are no spies.
12 And he said to them, No, but to see the nakedness of the land you have come.
13 And they said, Your servants *are* twelve brothers, the sons of one man in the land of Canaan; and, behold, the youngest *is* this day with our father, and one *is* not.
14 And Joseph said to them, That *is it* that I spoke unto you, saying, You *are* spies:
15 Hereby you shall be proved: By the life of Pharaoh you shall not go forth away, unless your youngest brother comes here.
16 Send one of you, and let him fetch your brother, and you shall be kept in prison, that your words may be proved, whether *there is any* truth in you: or else by the life of Pharaoh surely you *are* spies.
17 And he put them all together into prison three days.
18 And Joseph said unto them the third day, This do, and live; *for* I fear God:
19 If you *are* true *men*, let one of your brothers be bound in the house of your prison: go you, carry corn for the famine of your houses:
20 But bring your youngest brother unto me; so shall your words be verified, and you shall not die. And they did so.
21 ¶ And they said one to another, We *are* truly guilty concerning our brother, in that we saw the anguish of his soul, when he pleaded *with* us, and we would not hear; therefore has this distress come upon us.
22 And Reuben answered them, saying, Spoke I not unto you, saying, Do not sin against the child; and you would not hear? therefore, behold, also his blood is required.
23 And they knew not that Joseph understood *them*; for he spoke to them by an interpreter.
24 And he turned himself about from them, and wept; and returned to them again, and spoke with them, and took from them Simeon, and bound him before their eyes.
25 Then Joseph commanded to fill their sacks with corn, and to restore every man's money into his sack, and to give them provision for the journey: and thus did he unto them.
26 And they loaded their donkeys with the corn, and departed therefrom.
27 And as one of them opened his sack to give his donkey feed in the inn, he saw his money; for, behold, it *was* in his sack's mouth.
28 And he said unto his brothers, My money is restored; and, behold, *it is* even in my sack: and their hearts failed *them*, and they were afraid, saying one to another, What *is* this *that* God has done unto us?
29 ¶ And they came unto Jacob their father to the land of Canaan, and told him all that befell unto them; saying,
30 The man, *who is* the lord of the land, spoke roughly to us, and took us for spies of the country.
31 And we said unto him, We *are* true *men*; we are no spies:
32 We *are* twelve brothers, sons of our father; one *is* not, and the youngest *is* this day with our father in the land of Canaan.
33 And the man, the lord of the country, said unto us, Hereby shall I know that you *are* true *men*; leave one of your brothers *here* with me, and take *food for* the famine of your households, and be gone:
34 And bring your youngest brother unto me: then shall I know that you *are* no spies, but *that* you *are* true *men*: so will I deliver you your brother, and you shall trade in the land.
35 And it came to pass as they emptied their sacks, that, behold, every man's bundle of money *was* in his sack: and when *both* they and their father saw the bundles of money, they were afraid.
36 And Jacob their father said unto them, Me have you bereaved *of my children*: Joseph *is* not, and Simeon *is* not, and you will take Benjamin *away*: all these things are against me.
37 And Reuben spoke unto his father, saying, Slay my two sons, if I bring him not to you: deliver him into my hand, and I will bring him to you again.
38 And he said, My son shall not go down with you; for his brother is dead, and he is left alone: if mischief befalls him by the way in which you go, then shall you bring down my gray hairs with sorrow to the grave.

Genesis 43

43:1 ¶ And the famine *was* severe in the land.
2 And it came to pass, when they had eaten up the corn which they had brought out of Egypt, their father said to them, Go again, buy us a little food.

3 And Judah spoke unto him, saying, The man did solemnly protest unto us, saying, You shall not see my face, unless your brother *is* with you.

4 If you will send our brother with us, we will go down and buy you food:

5 But if you will not send *him*, we will not go down: for the man said to us, You shall not see my face, unless your brother *is* with you.

6 And Israel said, Why dealt you *so* ill with me, *as* to tell the man whether you had yet a brother?

7 And they said, The man asked us earnestly of our state, and of our kindred, saying, *Is* your father yet alive? have you *another* brother? and we told him according to the tenor of these words: could we certainly know that he would say, Bring your brother down?

8 And Judah said unto Israel his father, Send the lad with me, and we will arise and go; that we may live, and not die, both we, and you, *and* also our little ones.

9 I will be surety for him; of my hand shall you require him: if I bring him not to you, and set him before you, then let me bear the blame forever:

10 For except we had lingered, surely *by* now we *would* have returned this second time.

11 ¶ And their father Israel said unto them, If *it must be* so now, do this; take of the best fruits in the land in your vessels, and carry down the man a present, a little balm, and a little honey, spices, and myrrh, nuts, and almonds:

12 And take double money in your hand; and the money that was brought again in the mouth of your sacks, carry *it* again in your hand; perhaps it *was* an oversight:

13 Take also your brother, and arise, go again to the man:

14 And God Almighty give you mercy before the man, that he may send away your other brother, and Benjamin. If I am bereaved *of my children*, I am bereaved.

15 ¶ And the men took that present, and they took double money in their hand, and Benjamin; and rose up, and went down to Egypt, and stood before Joseph.

16 And when Joseph saw Benjamin with them, he said to the ruler of his house, Bring *these* men home, and slay, and make ready; for *these* men shall dine with me at noon.

17 And the man did as Joseph said; and the man brought the men into Joseph's house.

18 And the men were afraid, because they were brought into Joseph's house; and they said, Because of the money that was returned in our sacks at the first time are we brought in; that he may seek occasion against us, and fall upon us, and take us for bondmen, and our donkeys.

19 And they came near to the steward of Joseph's house, and they spoke with him at the door of the house,

20 And said, O sir, we came indeed down the first time to buy food:

21 And it came to pass, when we came to the inn, that we opened our sacks, and, behold, *every* man's money *was* in the mouth of his sack, our money in full weight: and we have brought it again in our hand.

22 And other money have we brought down in our hands to buy food: we cannot tell who put our money in our sacks.

23 And he said, Peace *be* to you, fear not: your God, and the God of your father, has given you treasure in your sacks: I had your money. And he brought Simeon out to them.

24 And the man brought the men into Joseph's house, and gave *them* water, and they washed their feet; and he gave their donkeys feed.

25 And they made ready the present until Joseph came at noon: for they heard that they should eat bread there.

26 ¶ And when Joseph came home, they brought him the present which *was* in their hand into the house, and bowed themselves to him to the earth.

27 And he asked them of *their* welfare, and said, *Is* your father well, the old man of whom you spoke? *Is* he yet alive?

28 And they answered, Your servant our father *is* in good health, he *is* yet alive. And they bowed down their heads, and made obeisance.

29 And he lifted up his eyes, and saw his brother Benjamin, his mother's son, and said, *Is* this your younger brother, of whom you spoke to me? And he said, God be gracious to you, my son.

30 And Joseph made haste; for his compassion did yearn upon his brother: and he sought *where* to weep; and he entered into *his* chamber, and wept there.

31 And he washed his face, and went out, and refrained himself, and said, Set on bread.

32 And they set on for him by himself, and for them by themselves, and for the Egyptians, which did eat with him, by themselves: because the Egyptians might not eat bread with the Hebrews; for that *is* an abomination to the Egyptians.

33 And they sat before him, the firstborn according to his birthright, and the youngest according to his youth: and the men marveled one at another.

34 And he took *and sent* portions to them from before him: but Benjamin's portion was five times as much as any of theirs. And they drank, and were merry with him.

Genesis 44

44:1 ¶ And he commanded the steward of his house, saying, Fill the men's sacks *with* food, as much as they can carry, and put every man's money in his sack's mouth.

2 And put my cup, the silver cup, in the sack's mouth of the youngest, and his corn money. And he did according to the word that Joseph had spoken.

3 As soon as the morning was light, the men were sent away, they and their donkeys.

4 *And* when they had gone out of the city, *and* not *yet* far off, Joseph said to his steward, Up, follow after the men; and when you do overtake them, say to them, Why have you rewarded evil for good?

Genesis 44

5 *Is* not this *it* in which my lord drinks, and whereby indeed he divines? you have done evil in so doing.
6 And he overtook them, and he spoke to them these same words.
7 And they said to him, Why said my lord these words? God forbid that your servants should do according to this thing:
8 Behold, the money, which we found in our sacks' mouths, we brought again unto you out of the land of Canaan: how then should we steal out of your lord's house silver or gold?
9 With whomever of your servants it is found, both let him die, and we also will be my lord's bondmen.
10 And he said, Now also *let* it *be* according to your words: he with whom it is found shall be my servant; and you shall be blameless.
11 Then they speedily took down every man his sack to the ground, and opened every man his sack.
12 And he searched, *and* began at the oldest, and left at the youngest: and the cup was found in Benjamin's sack.
13 Then they tore their clothes, and loaded every man his donkey, and returned to the city.
14 And Judah and his brothers came to Joseph's house; for he *was* yet there: and they fell before him on the ground.
15 And Joseph said to them, What deed *is* this that you have done? know you not that such a man as I can certainly divine?
16 And Judah said, What shall we say to my lord? what shall we speak? or how shall we clear ourselves? God has found out the iniquity of your servants: behold, we *are* my lord's servants, both we, and *he* also with whom the cup is found.
17 And he said, God forbid that I should do so: *but* the man in whose hand the cup is found, he shall be my servant; and as for you, get you up in peace unto your father.
18 ¶ Then Judah came near to him, and said, Oh my lord, let your servant, I pray you, speak a word in my lord's ears, and let not your anger burn against your servant: for you *are* even as Pharaoh.
19 My lord asked his servants, saying, Have you a father, or a brother?
20 And we said to my lord, We have a father, an old man, and a child of his old age, a little one; and his brother is dead, and he alone is left of his mother, and his father loves him.
21 And you said to your servants, Bring him down to me, that I may set my eyes upon him.
22 And we said to my lord, The lad cannot leave his father: for *if* he should leave his father, *his father* would die.
23 And you said to your servants, Unless your youngest brother comes down with you, you shall see my face no more.
24 And it came to pass when we came up to your servant my father, we told him the words of my lord.
25 And our father said, Go again, *and* buy us a little food.
26 And we said, We cannot go down: if our youngest brother is with us, then will we go down: for we may not see the man's face, unless our youngest brother *is* with us.
27 And your servant my father said to us, You know that my wife bore me two *sons*:
28 And the one went out from me, and I said, Surely he is torn in pieces; and I saw him not since:
29 And if you take this also from me, and mischief befalls him, you shall bring down my gray hairs with sorrow to the grave.
30 Now therefore when I come to your servant my father, and the lad *is* not with us; seeing that his life is bound up in the lad's life;
31 It shall come to pass, when he sees that the lad *is* not *with us*, that he will die: and your servants shall bring down the gray hairs of your servant our father with sorrow to the grave.
32 For your servant became surety for the lad to my father, saying, If I bring him not to you, then I shall bear the blame to my father forever.
33 Now therefore, I pray you, let your servant stay instead of the lad a bondman to my lord; and let the lad go up with his brothers.
34 For how shall I go up to my father, and the lad *is* not with me? lest perhaps I see the evil that shall come on my father.

Genesis 45

45:1 ¶ Then Joseph could not refrain himself before all them that stood by him; and he cried, Cause every man to go out from me. And there stood no man with him, while Joseph made himself known to his brothers.
2 And he wept aloud: and the Egyptians and the house of Pharaoh heard.
3 And Joseph said to his brothers, I *am* Joseph; does my father yet live? And his brothers could not answer him; for they were troubled at his presence.
4 And Joseph said to his brothers, Come near to me, I pray you. And they came near. And he said, I *am* Joseph your brother, whom you sold into Egypt.
5 Now therefore be not grieved, nor angry with yourselves, that you sold me here: for God did send me before you to preserve life.
6 For these two years *has* the famine *been* in the land: and yet *there are* five years, in which *there shall* neither *be* plowing nor harvest.
7 And God sent me before you to preserve you a posterity in the earth, and to save your lives by a great deliverance.
8 So now *it was* not you *that* sent me here, but God: and he has made me a father to Pharaoh, and lord of all his house, and a ruler throughout all the land of Egypt.
9 Haste you, and go up to my father, and say to him, Thus says your son Joseph, God has made me lord of all Egypt: come down unto me, wait not:
10 And you shall dwell in the land of Goshen, and you shall be near to me, you, and your children, and your children's children, and your flocks, and your herds, and all that you have:

11 And there will I nourish you; for yet *there are* five years of famine; lest you, and your household, and all that you have, come to poverty.
12 And, behold, your eyes see, and the eyes of my brother Benjamin, that *it is* my mouth that speaks to you.
13 And you shall tell my father of all my glory in Egypt, and of all that you have seen; and you shall haste and bring down my father here.
14 And he fell upon his brother Benjamin's neck, and wept; and Benjamin wept upon his neck.
15 Moreover he kissed all his brothers, and wept upon them: and after that his brothers talked with him.
16 ¶ And the fame thereof was heard in Pharaoh's house, saying, Joseph's brothers have come: and it pleased Pharaoh well, and his servants.
17 And Pharaoh said to Joseph, Say to your brothers, This do you; load your beasts, and go, get you to the land of Canaan;
18 And take your father and your households, and come unto me: and I will give you the good of the land of Egypt, and you shall eat the fat of the land.
19 Now you are commanded, this do you; take you wagons out of the land of Egypt for your little ones, and for your wives, and bring your father, and come.
20 Also regard not your stuff; for the good of all the land of Egypt *is* yours.
21 And the children of Israel did so: and Joseph gave them wagons, according to the commandment of Pharaoh, and gave them provision for the way.
22 To all of them he gave each man changes of clothing; but to Benjamin he gave three hundred *pieces* of silver, and five changes of clothing.
23 And to his father he sent after this *manner*; ten donkeys loaded with the good things of Egypt, and ten she donkeys loaded with corn and bread and food for his father by the way.
24 So he sent his brothers away, and they departed: and he said to them, See that you fall not out by the way.
25 ¶ And they went up out of Egypt, and came into the land of Canaan to Jacob their father,
26 And told him, saying, Joseph *is* yet alive, and he *is* governor over all the land of Egypt. And Jacob's heart fainted, for he believed them not.
27 And they told him all the words of Joseph, which he had said to them: and when he saw the wagons which Joseph had sent to carry him, the spirit of Jacob their father revived:
28 And Israel said, *It is* enough; Joseph my son *is* yet alive: I will go and see him before I die.

Genesis 46

46:1 ¶ And Israel took his journey with all that he had, and came to Beersheba, and offered sacrifices to the God of his father Isaac.
2 And God spoke to Israel in the visions of the night, and said, Jacob, Jacob. And he said, Here *am* I.
3 And he said, I *am* God, the God of your father: fear not to go down into Egypt; for I will there make of you a great nation:
4 I will go down with you into Egypt; and I will also surely bring you up *again*: and Joseph shall put his hand upon your eyes.
5 ¶ And Jacob rose up from Beersheba: and the sons of Israel carried Jacob their father, and their little ones, and their wives, in the wagons which Pharaoh had sent to carry him.
6 And they took their cattle, and their goods, which they had gotten in the land of Canaan, and came into Egypt, Jacob, and all his seed with him:
7 His sons, and his sons' sons with him, his daughters, and his sons' daughters, and all his seed brought he with him into Egypt.
8 And these *are* the names of the children of Israel, which came into Egypt, Jacob and his sons: Reuben, Jacob's firstborn.
9 And the sons of Reuben; Hanoch, and Phallu, and Hezron, and Carmi.
10 And the sons of Simeon; Jemuel, and Jamin, and Ohad, and Jachin, and Zohar, and Shawl the son of a Canaanitish woman.
11 And the sons of Levi; Gershon, Kohath, and Merari.
12 And the sons of Judah; Er, and Onan, and Shelah, and Pharez, and Zerah: but Er and Onan died in the land of Canaan. And the sons of Pharez were Hezron and Hamul.
13 And the sons of Issachar; Tola, and Phuvah, and Job, and Shimron.
14 And the sons of Zebulun; Sered, and Elon, and Jahleel.
15 These *are* the sons of Leah, which she bore to Jacob in Padanaram, with his daughter Dinah: all the souls of his sons and his daughters *were* thirty and three.
16 And the sons of Gad; Ziphion, and Haggi, Shuni, and Ezbon, Eri, and Arodi, and Areli.
17 And the sons of Asher; Jimnah, and Ishuah, and Isui, and Beriah, and Serah their sister: and the sons of Beriah; Heber, and Malchiel.
18 These *are* the sons of Zilpah, whom Laban gave to Leah his daughter, and these she bore to Jacob, *even* sixteen souls.
19 The sons of Rachel Jacob's wife; Joseph, and Benjamin.
20 And to Joseph in the land of Egypt were born Manasseh and Ephraim, which Asenath the daughter of Potipherah priest of On bore to him.
21 And the sons of Benjamin *were* Belah, and Becher, and Ashbel, Gera, and Naaman, Ehi, and Rosh, Muppim, and Huppim, and Ard.
22 These *are* the sons of Rachel, which were born to Jacob: all the souls *were* fourteen.
23 And the sons of Dan; Hushim.
24 And the sons of Naphtali; Jahzeel, and Guni, and Jezer, and Shillem.
25 These *are* the sons of Bilhah, which Laban gave to Rachel his daughter, and she bore these to Jacob: all the souls *were* seven.
26 All the souls that came with Jacob into Egypt, which came out of his loins, besides Jacob's sons' wives, all the souls *were* threescore and six;

Genesis 46

27 And the sons of Joseph, which were born him in Egypt, *were* two souls: all the souls of the house of Jacob, which came into Egypt, *were* threescore and ten.

28 ¶ And he sent Judah before him to Joseph, to direct his face to Goshen; and they came into the land of Goshen.

29 And Joseph made ready his chariot, and went up to meet Israel his father, to Goshen, and presented himself to him; and he fell upon his neck, and wept upon his neck a good while.

30 And Israel said to Joseph, Now let me die, since I have seen your face, because you *are* yet alive.

31 And Joseph said to his brothers, and to his father's house, I will go up, and show Pharaoh, and say to him, My brothers, and my father's house, which *were* in the land of Canaan, have come unto me;

32 And the men *are* shepherds, for their trade has been to feed cattle; and they have brought their flocks, and their herds, and all that they have.

33 And it shall come to pass, when Pharaoh shall call you, and shall say, What *is* your occupation?

34 That you shall say, Your servants' trade has been about cattle from our youth even until now, both we, *and* also our fathers: that you may dwell in the land of Goshen; for every shepherd *is* an abomination to the Egyptians.

Genesis 47

47:1 ¶ Then Joseph came and told Pharaoh, and said, My father and my brothers, and their flocks, and their herds, and all that they have, have come out of the land of Canaan; and, behold, they *are* in the land of Goshen.

2 And he took some of his brothers, *even* five men, and presented them to Pharaoh.

3 And Pharaoh said to his brothers, What *is* your occupation? And they said to Pharaoh, Your servants *are* shepherds, both we, *and* also our fathers.

4 They said moreover to Pharaoh, For to dwell in the land have we come; for your servants have no pasture for their flocks; for the famine *is* severe in the land of Canaan: now therefore, we pray you, let your servants dwell in the land of Goshen.

5 And Pharaoh spoke to Joseph, saying, Your father and your brothers have come to you:

6 The land of Egypt *is* before you; in the best of the land make your father and brothers to dwell; in the land of Goshen let them dwell: and if you know *any* men of ability among them, then make them rulers over my cattle.

7 And Joseph brought in Jacob his father, and set him before Pharaoh: and Jacob blessed Pharaoh.

8 And Pharaoh said to Jacob, How old *are* you?

9 And Jacob said to Pharaoh, The days of the years of my pilgrimage *are* a hundred and thirty years: few and evil have the days of the years of my life been, and have not attained to the days of the years of the life of my fathers in the days of their pilgrimage.

10 And Jacob blessed Pharaoh, and went out from before Pharaoh.

11 And Joseph placed his father and his brothers, and gave them a possession in the land of Egypt, in the best of the land, in the land of Rameses, as Pharaoh had commanded.

12 And Joseph nourished his father, and his brothers, and all his father's household, with bread, according to *their* families.

13 ¶ And *there was* no bread in all the land; for the famine *was* very severe, so that the land of Egypt and *all* the land of Canaan fainted by reason of the famine.

14 And Joseph gathered up all the money that was found in the land of Egypt, and in the land of Canaan, for the corn which they bought: and Joseph brought the money into Pharaoh's house.

15 And when money failed in the land of Egypt, and in the land of Canaan, all the Egyptians came to Joseph, and said, Give us bread: for why should we die in your presence? for the money fails.

16 And Joseph said, Give your cattle; and I will give you for your cattle, if money fails.

17 And they brought their cattle to Joseph: and Joseph gave them bread *in exchange* for horses, and for the flocks, and for the cattle of the herds, and for the donkeys: and he fed them with bread for all their cattle for that year.

18 When that year had ended, they came to him the second year, and said to him, We will not hide *it* from my lord, how that our money is spent; my lord also has our herds of cattle; there is not anything left in the sight of my lord, but our bodies, and our lands:

19 Why shall we die before your eyes, both we and our land? buy us and our land for bread, and we and our land will be servants to Pharaoh: and give *us* seed, that we may live, and not die, that the land be not desolate.

20 And Joseph bought all the land of Egypt for Pharaoh; for the Egyptians sold every man his field, because the famine prevailed over them: so the land became Pharaoh's.

21 And as for the people, he removed them to cities from *one* end of the borders of Egypt even to the *other* end thereof.

22 Only the land of the priests bought he not; for the priests had a portion *assigned them* by Pharaoh, and did eat their portion which Pharaoh gave them: therefore they sold not their lands.

23 Then Joseph said to the people, Behold, I have bought you this day and your land for Pharaoh: behold, *here is* seed for you, and you shall sow the land.

24 And it shall come to pass in the increase, that you shall give the fifth *part* to Pharaoh, and four parts shall be your own, for seed of the field, and for your food, and for them of your households, and for food for your little ones.

25 And they said, You have saved our lives: let us find grace in the sight of my lord, and we will be Pharaoh's servants.

26 And Joseph made it a law over the land of Egypt unto this day, *that* Pharaoh should have the fifth *part*; except the land of the priests only, *which* became not Pharaoh's.

27 ¶ And Israel dwelt in the land of Egypt, in the country of Goshen; and they had possessions therein, and grew, and multiplied exceedingly.

28 And Jacob lived in the land of Egypt seventeen years: so the whole age of Jacob was a hundred forty and seven years.

29 And the time drew near that Israel must die: and he called his son Joseph, and said to him, If now I have found grace in your sight, put, I pray you, your hand under my thigh, and deal kindly and truly with me; bury me not, I pray you, in Egypt:

30 But I will lie with my fathers, and you shall carry me out of Egypt, and bury me in their burying place. And he said, I will do as you have said.

31 And he said, Swear to me. And he swore to him. And Israel bowed himself upon the bed's head.

Genesis 48

48:1 ¶ And it came to pass after these things, that one told Joseph, Behold, your father *is* sick: and he took with him his two sons, Manasseh and Ephraim.

2 And *one* told Jacob, and said, Behold, your son Joseph comes to you: and Israel strengthened himself, and sat upon the bed.

3 And Jacob said to Joseph, God Almighty appeared to me at Luz in the land of Canaan, and blessed me,

4 And said to me, Behold, I will make you fruitful, and multiply you, and I will make of you a multitude of people; and will give this land to your seed after you *for* an everlasting possession.

5 And now your two sons, Ephraim and Manasseh, which were born to you in the land of Egypt before I came to you into Egypt, *are* mine; as Reuben and Simeon, they shall be mine.

6 And your offspring, which you beget after them, shall be yours, *and* shall be called after the name of their brothers in their inheritance.

7 And as for me, when I came from Padan, Rachel died by me in the land of Canaan in the way, when yet *there was* but a little way to come to Ephrath: and I buried her there in the way of Ephrath; the same *is* Bethlehem.

8 ¶ And Israel saw Joseph's sons, and said, Who *are* these?

9 And Joseph said to his father, They *are* my sons, whom God has given me in this *place*. And he said, Bring them, I pray you, to me, and I will bless them.

10 Now the eyes of Israel were dim for age, *so that* he could not see. And he brought them near to him; and he kissed them, and embraced them.

11 And Israel said to Joseph, I had not thought to see your face: and, behold, God has shown me also your seed.

12 And Joseph brought them out from between his knees, and he bowed himself with his face to the earth.

13 And Joseph took them both, Ephraim in his right hand toward Israel's left hand, and Manasseh in his left hand toward Israel's right hand, and brought *them* near to him.

14 And Israel stretched out his right hand, and laid *it* upon Ephraim's head, who *was* the younger, and his left hand upon Manasseh's head, guiding his hands wittingly; for Manasseh *was* the firstborn.

15 And he blessed Joseph, and said, God, before whom my fathers Abraham and Isaac did walk, the God which fed me all my life long unto this day,

16 The Angel which redeemed me from all evil, bless the lads; and let my name be named on them, and the name of my fathers Abraham and Isaac; and let them grow into a multitude in the midst of the earth.

17 And when Joseph saw that his father laid his right hand upon the head of Ephraim, it displeased him: and he held up his father's hand, to remove it from Ephraim's head to Manasseh's head.

18 And Joseph said to his father, Not so, my father: for this *is* the firstborn; put your right hand upon his head.

19 And his father refused, and said, I know *it*, my son, I know *it*: he also shall become a people, and he also shall be great: but truly his younger brother shall be greater than he, and his seed shall become a multitude of nations.

20 And he blessed them that day, saying, In you shall Israel bless, saying, God make you as Ephraim and as Manasseh: and he set Ephraim before Manasseh.

21 And Israel said to Joseph, Behold, I die: but God shall be with you, and bring you again to the land of your fathers.

22 Moreover I have given to you one portion above your brothers, which I took out of the hand of the Amorite with my sword and with my bow.

Genesis 49

49:1 ¶ And Jacob called to his sons, and said, Gather yourselves together, that I may tell you *that* which shall befall you in the last days.

2 Gather yourselves together, and hear, you sons of Jacob; and listen to Israel your father.

3 Reuben, you *are* my firstborn, my might, and the beginning of my strength, the excellency of dignity, and the excellency of power:

4 Unstable as water, you shall not excel; because you went up to your father's bed; then defiled you *it*: he went up to my couch.

5 ¶ Simeon and Levi *are* brothers; instruments of cruelty *are in* their habitations.

6 O my soul, come not you into their secret; to their assembly, my honor, be not you united: for in their anger they slew a man, and in their self-will they dug down a wall.

7 Cursed *be* their anger, for *it was* fierce; and their wrath, for it was cruel: I will divide them in Jacob, and scatter them in Israel.

8 ¶ Judah, you *are he* whom your brothers shall praise: your hand *shall be* in the neck of your enemies; your father's children shall bow down before you.

9 Judah *is* a lion's cub: from the prey, my son, you are gone up: he stooped down, he couched as a lion, and as an old lion; who shall rouse him up?

10 The scepter shall not depart from Judah, nor a lawgiver from between his feet, until Shiloh comes; and to him *shall* the gathering of the people *be*.

11 Binding his foal to the vine, and his donkey's colt to the choice vine; he washed his garments in wine, and his clothes in the blood of grapes:

12 His eyes *shall be* red with wine, and his teeth white with milk.

13 ¶ Zebulun shall dwell at the haven of the sea; and he *shall be* for a haven of ships; and his border *shall be* unto Zidon.

14 Issachar *is* a strong donkey couching down between two burdens:

15 And he saw that rest *was* good, and the land that *it was* pleasant; and bowed his shoulder to bear, and became a servant unto tribute.

16 Dan shall judge his people, as one of the tribes of Israel.

17 Dan shall be a serpent by the way, an adder in the path, that bites the horse's heels, so that his rider shall fall backward.

18 I have waited for your salvation, O Yahweh.

19 Gad, a troop shall overcome him: but he shall overcome at the last.

20 Out of Asher his bread *shall be* fat, and he shall yield royal dainties.

21 Naphtali *is* a hind let loose: he gives goodly words.

22 ¶ Joseph *is* a fruitful bough, *even* a fruitful bough by a well; *whose* branches run over the wall:

23 The archers have greatly grieved him, and shot *at him*, and hated him:

24 But his bow stayed in strength, and the arms of his hands were made strong by the hands of the mighty *God* of Jacob; (from there *is* the shepherd, the stone of Israel:)

25 *Even* by the God of your father, who shall help you; and by the Almighty, who shall bless you with blessings of heaven above, blessings of the deep that lies under, blessings of the breasts, and of the womb:

26 The blessings of your father have prevailed above the blessings of my progenitors to the utmost bound of the everlasting hills: they shall be on the head of Joseph, and on the crown of the head of him that was separate from his brothers.

27 Benjamin shall tear *as* a wolf: in the morning he shall devour the prey, and at night he shall divide the spoil.

28 ¶ All these *are* the twelve tribes of Israel: and this *is it* that their father spoke to them, and blessed them; every one according to his blessing he blessed them.

29 And he charged them, and said to them, I am to be gathered to my people: bury me with my fathers in the cave that *is* in the field of Ephron the Hittite,

30 In the cave that *is* in the field of Machpelah, which *is* before Mamre, in the land of Canaan, which Abraham bought with the field of Ephron the Hittite for a possession of a burying place.

31 There they buried Abraham and Sarah his wife; there they buried Isaac and Rebekah his wife; and there I buried Leah.

32 The purchase of the field and of the cave that *is* therein *was* from the children of Heth.

33 And when Jacob had made an end of commanding his sons, he gathered up his feet into the bed, and yielded up the ghost, and was gathered to his people.

Genesis 50

50:1 ¶ And Joseph fell upon his father's face, and wept upon him, and kissed him.

2 And Joseph commanded his servants the physicians to embalm his father: and the physicians embalmed Israel.

3 And forty days were fulfilled for him; for so are fulfilled the days of those which are embalmed: and the Egyptians mourned for him threescore and ten days.

4 And when the days of his mourning were past, Joseph spoke to the house of Pharaoh, saying, If now I have found grace in your eyes, speak, I pray you, in the ears of Pharaoh, saying,

5 My father made me swear, saying, Behold, I die: in my grave which I have dug for me in the land of Canaan, there shall you bury me. Now therefore let me go up, I pray you, and bury my father, and I will come again.

6 And Pharaoh said, Go up, and bury your father, according as he made you swear.

7 ¶ And Joseph went up to bury his father: and with him went up all the servants of Pharaoh, the elders of his house, and all the elders of the land of Egypt,

8 And all the house of Joseph, and his brothers, and his father's house: only their little ones, and their flocks, and their herds, they left in the land of Goshen.

9 And there went up with him both chariots and horsemen: and it was a very great company.

10 And they came to the threshingfloor of Atad, which *is* beyond *the* Jordan, and there they mourned with a great and very grievous lamentation: and he made a mourning for his father seven days.

11 And when the inhabitants of the land, the Canaanites, saw the mourning in the floor of Atad, they said, This *is* a grievous mourning to the Egyptians: therefore the name of it was called Abelmizraim, which *is* beyond *the* Jordan.

12 And his sons did to him according as he commanded them:

13 For his sons carried him into the land of Canaan, and buried him in the cave of the field of Machpelah, which Abraham bought with the field for a possession of a burying place of Ephron the Hittite, before Mamre.

14 And Joseph returned into Egypt, he, and his brothers, and all that went up with him to bury his father, after he had buried his father.

15 ¶ And when Joseph's brothers saw that their father was dead, they said, Joseph will perhaps hate us, and will certainly return *to* us all the evil which we did unto him.

16 And they sent a messenger to Joseph, saying, Your father did command before he died, saying,

17 So shall you say to Joseph, Forgive, I pray you now, the trespass of your brothers, and their sin; for they did unto you evil: and now, we pray you, forgive the trespass of the servants of the God of your father. And Joseph wept when they spoke to him.

18 And his brothers also went and fell down before his face; and they said, Behold, we *are* your servants.

19 And Joseph said to them, Fear not: for *am* I in the place of God?

20 But as for you, you thought evil against me; *but* God meant it unto good, to bring to pass, as *it is* this day, to save many people alive.

21 Now therefore fear you not: I will nourish you, and your little ones. And he comforted them, and spoke kindly to them.

22 ¶ And Joseph dwelt in Egypt, he, and his father's house: and Joseph lived a hundred and ten years.

23 And Joseph saw Ephraim's children of the third *generation*: the children also of Machir the son of Manasseh were brought up on Joseph's knees.

24 And Joseph said to his brothers, I die: and God will surely visit you, and bring you out of this land to the land which he swore to Abraham, to Isaac, and to Jacob.

25 And Joseph took an oath of the children of Israel, saying, God will surely visit you, and you shall carry up my bones from here.

26 So Joseph died, *being* a hundred and ten years old: and they embalmed him, and he was put in a coffin in Egypt.

Exodus

Exodus 1

1:1 ¶ Now these *are* the names of the children of Israel, which came into Egypt; every man and his household came with Jacob.

2 Reuben, Simeon, Levi, and Judah,

3 Issachar, Zebulun, and Benjamin,

4 Dan, and Naphtali, Gad, and Asher.

5 And all the souls that came out of the loins of Jacob were seventy souls: for Joseph was in Egypt *already*.

6 And Joseph died, and all his brothers, and all that generation.

7 And the children of Israel were fruitful, and increased abundantly, and multiplied, and grew exceedingly mighty; and the land was filled with them.

8 ¶ Now there arose up a new king over Egypt, which knew not Joseph.

9 And he said to his people, Behold, the people of the children of Israel *are* more and mightier than we:

10 Come on, let us deal wisely with them; lest they multiply, and it comes to pass, that, when there falls out any war, they join also with our enemies, and fight against us, and *so* get them up out of the land.

11 Therefore they did set over them taskmasters to afflict them with their burdens. And they built for Pharaoh treasure cities, Pithom and Raamses.

12 But the more they afflicted them, the more they multiplied and grew. And they were grieved because of the children of Israel.

13 And the Egyptians made the children of Israel to serve with rigor:

14 And they made their lives bitter with hard bondage, in mortar, and in brick, and in all manner of service in the field: all their service, wherein they made them serve, *was* with rigor.

15 ¶ And the king of Egypt spoke to the Hebrew midwives, of which the name of the one *was* Shiphrah, and the name of the other Puah:

16 And he said, When you do the office of a midwife to the Hebrew women, and see *them* upon the stools; if it *is* a son, then you shall kill him: but if it *is* a daughter, then she shall live.

17 But the midwives feared God, and did not as the king of Egypt commanded them, but saved the men children alive.

18 And the king of Egypt called for the midwives, and said to them, Why have you done this thing, and have saved the men children alive?

19 And the midwives said to Pharaoh, Because the Hebrew women *are* not as the Egyptian women; for they *are* lively, and are delivered before the midwives come in to them.

20 Therefore God dealt well with the midwives: and the people multiplied, and grew very mighty.

21 And it came to pass, because the midwives feared God, that he made them houses.

22 And Pharaoh charged all his people, saying, Every son that is born you shall cast into the river, and every daughter you shall save alive.

Exodus 2

2:1 ¶ And there went a man of the house of Levi, and took *to wife* a daughter of Levi.

2 And the woman conceived, and bore a son: and when she saw him that he *was a* goodly *child*, she hid him three months.

3 And when she could no longer hide him, she took for him an ark of bulrushes, and daubed it with slime and with pitch, and put the child therein; and she laid *it* in the flags by the river's brink.

4 And his sister stood afar off, to know what would be done to him.

5 ¶ And the daughter of Pharaoh came down to wash *herself* at the river; and her maidens walked along by the river's side; and when she saw the ark among the flags, she sent her maid to fetch it.

6 And when she had opened *it*, she saw the child: and, behold, the babe wept. And she had compassion on him, and said, This *is one* of the Hebrews' children.

7 Then said his sister to Pharaoh's daughter, Shall I go and call to you a nurse of the Hebrew women, that she may nurse the child for you?

8 And Pharaoh's daughter said to her, Go. And the maid went and called the child's mother.

Exodus 2

9 And Pharaoh's daughter said to her, Take this child away, and nurse it for me, and I will give *you* your wages. And the woman took the child, and nursed it.

10 And the child grew, and she brought him to Pharaoh's daughter, and he became her son. And she called his name Moses: and she said, Because I drew him out of the water.

11 ¶ And it came to pass in those days, when Moses was grown, that he went out to his brethren, and looked on their burdens: and he saw an Egyptian smiting a Hebrew, one of his brethren.

12 And he looked this way and that way, and when he saw that *there was* no man, he slew the Egyptian, and hid him in the sand.

13 And when he went out the second day, behold, two men of the Hebrews strove together: and he said to him that did the wrong, Why smite you your fellow?

14 And he said, Who made you a prince and a judge over us? intend you to kill me, as you killed the Egyptian? And Moses feared, and said, Surely this thing is known.

15 Now when Pharaoh heard this thing, he sought to slay Moses. But Moses fled from the face of Pharaoh, and dwelt in the land of Midian: and he sat down by a well.

16 ¶ Now the priest of Midian had seven daughters: and they came and drew *water*, and filled the troughs to water their father's flock.

17 And the shepherds came and drove them away: but Moses stood up and helped them, and watered their flock.

18 And when they came to Reuel their father, he said, How *is it that* you have come so soon today?

19 And they said, An Egyptian delivered us out of the hand of the shepherds, and also drew *water* enough for us, and watered the flock.

20 And he said to his daughters, And where *is* he? why *is it that* you have left the man? call him, that he may eat bread.

21 And Moses was content to dwell with the man: and he gave Moses Zipporah his daughter.

22 And she bore *him* a son, and he called his name Gershom: for he said, I have been a stranger in a strange land.

23 ¶ And it came to pass in *the* process of time, that the king of Egypt died: and the children of Israel groaned by reason of the bondage, and they cried, and their cry came up to God by reason of the bondage.

24 And God heard their groaning, and God remembered his covenant with Abraham, with Isaac, and with Jacob.

25 And God looked upon the children of Israel, and God had respect unto *them*.

Exodus 3

3:1 ¶ Now Moses kept the flock of Jethro his father-in-law, the priest of Midian: and he led the flock to the backside of the desert, and came to the mountain of God, *even* to Horeb.

2 And the angel of Yahweh appeared to him in a flame of fire out of the midst of a bush: and he looked, and, behold, the bush burned with fire, and the bush *was* not consumed.

3 And Moses said, I will now turn aside, and see this great sight, why the bush is not burnt.

4 And when Yahweh saw that he turned aside to see, God called to him out of the midst of the bush, and said, Moses, Moses. And he said, Here *am* I.

5 And he said, Draw not near here: put off your shoes from off your feet, for the place whereon you stand *is* holy ground.

6 Moreover he said, I *am* the God of your father, the God of Abraham, the God of Isaac, and the God of Jacob. And Moses hid his face; for he was afraid to look upon God.

7 ¶ And Yahweh said, I have surely seen the affliction of my people which *are* in Egypt, and have heard their cry by reason of their taskmasters; for I know their sorrows;

8 And I have come down to deliver them out of the hand of the Egyptians, and to bring them up out of that land to a good land and a large, to a land flowing with milk and honey; to the place of the Canaanites, and the Hittites, and the Amorites, and the Perizzites, and the Hivites, and the Jebusites.

9 Now therefore, behold, the cry of the children of Israel has come to me: and I have also seen the oppression with which the Egyptians oppress them.

10 Come now therefore, and I will send you to Pharaoh, that you may bring forth my people the children of Israel out of Egypt.

11 ¶ And Moses said to God, Who *am* I, that I should go to Pharaoh, and that I should bring forth the children of Israel out of Egypt?

12 And he said, Certainly I will be with you; and this *shall be* a token to you, that I have sent you: When you have brought forth the people out of Egypt, you shall serve God upon this mountain.

13 And Moses said to God, Behold, *when* I come to the children of Israel, and shall say to them, The God of your fathers has sent me to you; and they shall say to me, What *is* his name? what shall I say to them?

14 And God said to Moses, I AM THAT I AM: and he said, Thus shall you say to the children of Israel, I AM has sent me to you.

15 And God said moreover to Moses, Thus shall you say to the children of Israel, Yahweh God of your fathers, the God of Abraham, the God of Isaac, and the God of Jacob, has sent me to you: this *is* my name forever, and this *is* my memorial unto all generations.

16 ¶ Go, and gather the elders of Israel together, and say to them, Yahweh God of your fathers, the God of Abraham, of Isaac, and of Jacob, appeared to me, saying, I have surely visited you, and *seen* that which is done to you in Egypt:

17 And I have said, I will bring you up out of the affliction of Egypt to the land of the Canaanites, and the Hittites, and the Amorites, and the Perizzites, and the Hivites, and the Jebusites, to a land flowing with milk and honey.

18 And they shall listen to your voice: and you shall come, you and the elders of Israel, to the king of Egypt, and you shall say to him, Yahweh God of the Hebrews has met with us: and now let us go, we beseech you, three days' journey into the wilderness, that we may sacrifice to Yahweh our God.

19 And I am sure that the king of Egypt will not let you go, no, not by a mighty hand.
20 And I will stretch out my hand, and smite Egypt with all my wonders which I will do in the midst thereof: and after that he will let you go.
21 And I will give this people favor in the sight of the Egyptians: and it shall come to pass, that, when you go, you shall not go empty:
22 But every woman shall borrow of her neighbor, and of her that dwells in her house, jewels of silver, and jewels of gold, and clothing: and you shall put *them* upon your sons, and upon your daughters; and you shall spoil the Egyptians.

Exodus 4

4:1 ¶ And Moses answered and said, But, behold, they will not believe me, nor listen to my voice: for they will say, Yahweh has not appeared to you.
2 And Yahweh said to him, What *is* that in your hand? And he said, A rod.
3 And he said, Cast it on the ground. And he cast it on the ground, and it became a serpent; and Moses fled from before it.
4 And Yahweh said to Moses, Put forth your hand, and take it by the tail. And he put forth his hand, and caught it, and it became a rod in his hand:
5 That they may believe that Yahweh God of their fathers, the God of Abraham, the God of Isaac, and the God of Jacob, has appeared to you.
6 And Yahweh said furthermore to him, Put now your hand into your bosom. And he put his hand into his bosom: and when he took it out, behold, his hand *was* leprous as snow.
7 And he said, Put your hand into your bosom again. And he put his hand into his bosom again; and plucked it out of his bosom, and, behold, it was turned again as his *other* flesh.
8 And it shall come to pass, if they will not believe you, neither listen to the voice of the first sign, that they will believe the voice of the latter sign.
9 And it shall come to pass, if they will not believe also these two signs, neither listen to your voice, that you shall take of the water of the river, and pour *it* upon the dry *land*: and the water which you take out of the river shall become blood upon the dry *land*.
10 ¶ And Moses said unto Yahweh, O my Lord, I *am* not eloquent, neither before, nor since you have spoken to your servant: but I *am* slow of speech, and of a slow tongue.
11 And Yahweh said to him, Who has made man's mouth? or who makes the dumb, or deaf, or the seeing, or the blind? have not I Yahweh?
12 Now therefore go, and I will be with your mouth, and teach you what you shall say.
13 And he said, O my Lord, send, I pray you, by the hand *of him whom* you will send.
14 And the anger of Yahweh was kindled against Moses, and he said, *Is* not Aaron the Levite your brother? I know that he can speak well. And also, behold, he comes forth to meet you: and when he sees you, he will be glad in his heart.
15 And you shall speak to him, and put words in his mouth: and I will be with your mouth, and with his mouth, and will teach you what you shall do.
16 And he shall be your spokesman to the people: and he shall be, *even* he shall be to you instead of a mouth, and you shall be to him instead of God.
17 And you shall take this rod in your hand, with which you shall do signs.
18 ¶ And Moses went and returned to Jethro his father-in-law, and said to him, Let me go, I pray you, and return to my brethren which *are* in Egypt, and see whether they are yet alive. And Jethro said to Moses, Go in peace.
19 And Yahweh said to Moses in Midian, Go, return into Egypt: for all the men are dead which sought your life.
20 And Moses took his wife and his sons, and set them upon a donkey, and he returned to the land of Egypt: and Moses took the rod of God in his hand.
21 And Yahweh said to Moses, When you go to return into Egypt, see that you do all those wonders before Pharaoh, which I have put in your hand: but I will harden his heart, that he shall not let the people go.
22 And you shall say to Pharaoh, Thus says Yahweh, Israel *is* my son, *even* my firstborn:
23 And I say to you, Let my son go, that he may serve me: and if you refuse to let him go, behold, I will slay your son, *even* your firstborn.
24 ¶ And it came to pass by the way in the inn, that Yahweh met him, and sought to kill him.
25 Then Zipporah took a sharp stone, and cut off the foreskin of her son, and cast *it* at his feet, and said, Surely a bloody husband *are* you to me.
26 So he let him go: then she said, A bloody husband *you are*, because of the circumcision.
27 And Yahweh said to Aaron, Go into the wilderness to meet Moses. And he went, and met him in the mount of God, and kissed him.
28 And Moses told Aaron all the words of Yahweh who had sent him, and all the signs which he had commanded him.
29 And Moses and Aaron went and gathered together all the elders of the children of Israel:
30 And Aaron spoke all the words which Yahweh had spoken to Moses, and did the signs in the sight of the people.
31 And the people believed: and when they heard that Yahweh had visited the children of Israel, and that he had looked upon their affliction, then they bowed their heads and worshipped.

Exodus 5

5:1 ¶ And afterward Moses and Aaron went in, and told Pharaoh, Thus says Yahweh God of Israel, Let my people go, that they may hold a feast to me in the wilderness.
2 And Pharaoh said, Who *is* Yahweh, that I should obey his voice to let Israel go? I know not Yahweh, neither will I let Israel go.
3 ¶ And they said, The God of the Hebrews has met with us: let us go, we pray you, three days' journey into the desert, and sacrifice unto Yahweh our God; lest he falls upon us with pestilence, or with the sword.

Exodus 5

4 And the king of Egypt said to them, Why do you, Moses and Aaron, loose the people from their work? get you to your burdens.

5 And Pharaoh said, Behold, the people of the land now *are* many, and you make them rest from their burdens.

6 And Pharaoh commanded the same day the taskmasters of the people, and their officers, saying,

7 You shall no more give the people straw to make brick, as before: let them go and gather straw for themselves.

8 And the tally of the bricks, which they did make before, you shall lay upon them; you shall not diminish anything thereof: for they *are* idle; therefore they cry, saying, Let us go *and* sacrifice to our God.

9 Let there more work be laid upon the men, that they may labor therein; and let them not regard vain words.

10 ¶ And the taskmasters of the people went out, and their officers, and they spoke to the people, saying, Thus says Pharaoh, I will not give you straw.

11 Go you, get you straw where you can find it: yet nothing of your work shall be diminished.

12 So the people were scattered abroad throughout all the land of Egypt to gather stubble instead of straw.

13 And the taskmasters hurried *them*, saying, Fulfill your works, *your* daily tasks, as when there was straw.

14 And the officers of the children of Israel, which Pharaoh's taskmasters had set over them, were beaten, *and* demanded, Why have you not fulfilled your task in making brick both yesterday and today, as before?

15 ¶ Then the officers of the children of Israel came and cried to Pharaoh, saying, Why deal you thus with your servants?

16 There is no straw given to your servants, and they say to us, Make brick: and, behold, your servants *are* beaten; but the fault *is* in your own people.

17 But he said, You *are* idle, *you are* idle: therefore you say, Let us go *and* do sacrifice to Yahweh.

18 Go therefore now, *and* work; for there shall no straw be given *to* you, yet shall you deliver the tally of bricks.

19 And the officers of the children of Israel did see *that* they *were* in evil *case*, after it was said, You shall not diminish *any* from your bricks of your daily task.

20 And they met Moses and Aaron, who stood in the way, as they came forth from Pharaoh:

21 And they said to them, Yahweh look upon you, and judge; because you have made our scent to be abhorred in the eyes of Pharaoh, and in the eyes of his servants, to put a sword in their hand to slay us.

22 And Moses returned unto Yahweh, and said, Lord, why have you *so* evilly treated this people? why *is* it *that* you have sent me?

23 For since I came to Pharaoh to speak in your name, he has done evil to this people; neither have you delivered your people at all.

Exodus 6

6:1 ¶ Then Yahweh said to Moses, Now shall you see what I will do to Pharaoh: for with a strong hand shall he let them go, and with a strong hand shall he drive them out of his land.

2 And God spoke to Moses, and said to him, I *am* Yahweh:

3 And I appeared to Abraham, to Isaac, and to Jacob, by *the name of* God Almighty, but by my name Yahweh was I not known to them.

4 And I have also established my covenant with them, to give them the land of Canaan, the land of their pilgrimage, wherein they were strangers.

5 And I have also heard the groaning of the children of Israel, whom the Egyptians keep in bondage; and I have remembered my covenant.

6 Therefore say to the children of Israel, I *am* Yahweh, and I will bring you out from under the burdens of the Egyptians, and I will rid you out of their bondage, and I will redeem you with a stretched out arm, and with great judgments:

7 And I will take you to me for a people, and I will be to you a God: and you shall know that I *am* Yahweh your God, which brings you out from under the burdens of the Egyptians.

8 And I will bring you in to the land, concerning which I did swear to give it to Abraham, to Isaac, and to Jacob; and I will give it *to* you for a heritage: I *am* Yahweh.

9 And Moses spoke so to the children of Israel: but they listened not to Moses for anguish of spirit, and for cruel bondage.

10 ¶ And Yahweh spoke to Moses, saying,

11 Go in, speak to Pharaoh king of Egypt, that he let the children of Israel go out of his land.

12 And Moses spoke before Yahweh, saying, Behold, the children of Israel have not listened to me; how then shall Pharaoh hear me, who *am* of uncircumcised lips?

13 And Yahweh spoke to Moses and to Aaron, and gave them a charge to the children of Israel, and to Pharaoh king of Egypt, to bring the children of Israel out of the land of Egypt.

14 ¶ These *are* the heads of their fathers' houses: The sons of Reuben the firstborn of Israel; Hanoch, and Pallu, Hezron, and Carmi: these *are* the families of Reuben.

15 And the sons of Simeon; Jemuel, and Jamin, and Ohad, and Jachin, and Zohar, and Shawl the son of a Canaanitish woman: these *are* the families of Simeon.

16 And these *are* the names of the sons of Levi according to their generations; Gershon, and Kohath, and Merari: and the years of the life of Levi *were* a hundred thirty and seven years.

17 The sons of Gershon; Libni, and Shimi, according to their families.

18 And the sons of Kohath; Amram, and Izhar, and Hebron, and Uzziel: and the years of the life of Kohath *were* a hundred thirty and three years.

19 And the sons of Merari; Mahali and Mushi: these *are* the families of Levi according to their generations.

20 And Amram took him Jochebed his father's sister to wife; and she bore him Aaron and Moses: and the years of the life of Amram *were* a hundred and thirty and seven years.

21 And the sons of Izhar; Korah, and Nepheg, and Zichri.

22 And the sons of Uzziel; Mishael, and Elzaphan, and Zithri.

23 And Aaron took him Elisheba, daughter of Amminadab, sister of Naashon, to wife; and she bore him Nadab, and Abihu, Eleazar, and Ithamar.

24 And the sons of Korah; Assir, and Elkanah, and Abiasaph: these *are* the families of the Korhites.
25 And Eleazar Aaron's son took him *one* of the daughters of Putiel to wife; and she bore him Phinehas: these *are* the heads of the fathers of the Levites according to their families.
26 These *are* that Aaron and Moses, to whom Yahweh said, Bring out the children of Israel from the land of Egypt according to their armies.
27 These *are* they which spoke to Pharaoh king of Egypt, to bring out the children of Israel from Egypt: these *are* that Moses and Aaron.
28 And it came to pass on the day *when* Yahweh spoke to Moses in the land of Egypt,
29 That Yahweh spoke to Moses, saying, I *am* Yahweh: speak you to Pharaoh king of Egypt all that I say to you.
30 And Moses said before Yahweh, Behold, I *am* of uncircumcised lips, and how shall Pharaoh listen to me?

Exodus 7

7:1 ¶ And Yahweh said to Moses, See, I have made you a god to Pharaoh: and Aaron your brother shall be your prophet.
2 You shall speak all that I command you: and Aaron your brother shall speak to Pharaoh, that he send the children of Israel out of his land.
3 And I will harden Pharaoh's heart, and multiply my signs and my wonders in the land of Egypt.
4 But Pharaoh shall not listen to you, that I may lay my hand upon Egypt, and bring forth my armies, *and* my people the children of Israel, out of the land of Egypt by great judgments.
5 And the Egyptians shall know that I *am* Yahweh, when I stretch forth my hand upon Egypt, and bring out the children of Israel from among them.
6 And Moses and Aaron did as Yahweh commanded them, so did they.
7 And Moses *was* fourscore years old, and Aaron fourscore and three years old, when they spoke to Pharaoh.
8 ¶ And Yahweh spoke to Moses and to Aaron, saying,
9 When Pharaoh shall speak to you, saying, Show a miracle for you: then you shall say to Aaron, Take your rod, and cast *it* before Pharaoh, *and* it shall become a serpent.
10 And Moses and Aaron went in to Pharaoh, and they did so as Yahweh had commanded: and Aaron cast down his rod before Pharaoh, and before his servants, and it became a serpent.
11 Then Pharaoh also called the wise men and the sorcerers: now the magicians of Egypt, they also did in like manner with their enchantments.
12 For they cast down every man his rod, and they became serpents: but Aaron's rod swallowed up their rods.
13 And he hardened Pharaoh's heart, that he listened not to them; as Yahweh had said.
14 ¶ And Yahweh said to Moses, Pharaoh's heart *is* hardened, he refuses to let the people go.
15 Get you to Pharaoh in the morning; behold, he goes out to the water; and you shall stand by the river's bank *to* meet his coming; and the rod which was turned to a serpent shall you take in your hand.
16 And you shall say to him, Yahweh God of the Hebrews has sent me to you, saying, Let my people go, that they may serve me in the wilderness: and, behold, till now you would not hear.
17 Thus says Yahweh, In this you shall know that I *am* Yahweh: behold, I will smite with the rod that *is* in my hand upon the waters which *are* in the river, and they shall be turned to blood.
18 And the fish that *are* in the river shall die, and the river shall stink; and the Egyptians shall loathe to drink of the water of the river.
19 And Yahweh spoke to Moses, Say to Aaron, Take your rod, and stretch out your hand upon the waters of Egypt, upon their streams, upon their rivers, and upon their ponds, and upon all their pools of water, that they may become blood; and *that* there may be blood throughout all the land of Egypt, both in *vessels of* wood, and in *vessels of* stone.
20 And Moses and Aaron did so, as Yahweh commanded; and he lifted up the rod, and smote the waters that *were* in the river, in the sight of Pharaoh, and in the sight of his servants; and all the waters that *were* in the river were turned to blood.
21 And the fish that *were* in the river died; and the river stunk, and the Egyptians could not drink of the water of the river; and there was blood throughout all the land of Egypt.
22 And the magicians of Egypt did so with their enchantments: and Pharaoh's heart was hardened, neither did he listen to them; as Yahweh had said.
23 And Pharaoh turned and went into his house, neither did he set his heart to this also.
24 And all the Egyptians dug round about the river for water to drink; for they could not drink of the water of the river.
25 And seven days were fulfilled, after that Yahweh had smitten the river.

Exodus 8

8:1 ¶ And Yahweh spoke to Moses, Go to Pharaoh, and say to him, Thus says Yahweh, Let my people go, that they may serve me.
2 And if you refuse to let *them* go, behold, I will smite all your borders with frogs:
3 And the river shall bring forth frogs abundantly, which shall go up and come into your house, and into your bedchamber, and upon your bed, and into the house of your servants, and upon your people, and into your ovens, and into your kneading troughs:
4 And the frogs shall come up both on you, and upon your people, and upon all your servants.
5 And Yahweh spoke to Moses, Say to Aaron, Stretch forth your hand with your rod over the streams, over the rivers, and over the ponds, and cause frogs to come up upon the land of Egypt.
6 And Aaron stretched out his hand over the waters of Egypt; and the frogs came up, and covered the land of Egypt.
7 And the magicians did so with their enchantments, and brought up frogs upon the land of Egypt.
8 Then Pharaoh called for Moses and Aaron, and said, Entreat Yahweh, that he may take away the frogs from me, and from my people; and I will let the people go, that they may do sacrifice unto Yahweh.

Exodus 8

9 And Moses said to Pharaoh, Glory over me: when shall I entreat for you, and for your servants, and for your people, to destroy the frogs from you and your houses, *that* they may remain in the river only?

10 And he said, Tomorrow. And he said, *Be it* according to your word: that you may know that *there is* none like unto Yahweh our God.

11 And the frogs shall depart from you, and from your houses, and from your servants, and from your people; they shall remain in the river only.

12 And Moses and Aaron went out from Pharaoh: and Moses cried unto Yahweh because of the frogs which he had brought against Pharaoh.

13 And Yahweh did according to the word of Moses; and the frogs died out of the houses, out of the villages, and out of the fields.

14 And they gathered them together upon heaps: and the land stunk.

15 But when Pharaoh saw that there was relief, he hardened his heart, and listened not to them; as Yahweh had said.

16 ¶ And Yahweh said to Moses, Say to Aaron, Stretch out your rod, and smite the dust of the land, that it may become lice throughout all the land of Egypt.

17 And they did so; for Aaron stretched out his hand with his rod, and smote the dust of the earth, and it became lice in man, and in beast; all the dust of the land became lice throughout all the land of Egypt.

18 And the magicians did so with their enchantments to bring forth lice, but they could not: so there were lice upon man, and upon beast.

19 Then the magicians said to Pharaoh, This *is* the finger of God: and Pharaoh's heart was hardened, and he listened not to them; as Yahweh had said.

20 ¶ And Yahweh said to Moses, Rise up early in the morning, and stand before Pharaoh; behold, he comes forth to the water; and say to him, Thus says Yahweh, Let my people go, that they may serve me.

21 Else, if you will not let my people go, behold, I will send swarms *of flies* upon you, and upon your servants, and upon your people, and into your houses: and the houses of the Egyptians shall be full of swarms *of flies*, and also the ground whereon they *are*.

22 And I will separate in that day the land of Goshen, in which my people dwell, that no swarms *of flies* shall be there; to the end you may know that I *am* Yahweh in the midst of the earth.

23 And I will put a division between my people and your people: tomorrow shall this sign be.

24 And Yahweh did so; and there came a grievous swarm *of flies* into the house of Pharaoh, and *into* his servants' houses, and into all the land of Egypt: the land was corrupted by reason of the swarm *of flies*.

25 And Pharaoh called for Moses and for Aaron, and said, Go you, sacrifice to your God in the land.

26 And Moses said, It is not right to do so; for we shall sacrifice the abomination of the Egyptians to Yahweh our God: behold, shall we sacrifice the abomination of the Egyptians before their eyes, and will they not stone us?

27 We will go three days' journey into the wilderness, and sacrifice to Yahweh our God, as he shall command us.

28 And Pharaoh said, I will let you go, that you may sacrifice to Yahweh your God in the wilderness; only you shall not go very far away: entreat for me.

29 And Moses said, Behold, I go out from you, and I will entreat Yahweh that the swarms *of flies* may depart from Pharaoh, from his servants, and from his people, tomorrow: but let not Pharaoh deal deceitfully any more in not letting the people go to sacrifice to Yahweh.

30 And Moses went out from Pharaoh, and entreated Yahweh.

31 And Yahweh did according to the word of Moses; and he removed the swarms *of flies* from Pharaoh, from his servants, and from his people; there remained not one.

32 And Pharaoh hardened his heart at this time also, neither would he let the people go.

Exodus 9

9:1 ¶ Then Yahweh said to Moses, Go in to Pharaoh, and tell him, Thus says Yahweh God of the Hebrews, Let my people go, that they may serve me.

2 For if you refuse to let *them* go, and will hold them still,

3 Behold, the hand of Yahweh is upon your cattle which *is* in the field, upon the horses, upon the donkeys, upon the camels, upon the oxen, and upon the sheep: *there shall be* a very grievous plague.

4 And Yahweh shall distinguish between the cattle of Israel and the cattle of Egypt: and there shall nothing die of all *that is* the children's of Israel.

5 And Yahweh appointed a set time, saying, Tomorrow Yahweh shall do this thing in the land.

6 And Yahweh did that thing on the next day, and all the cattle of Egypt died: but of the cattle of the children of Israel died not one.

7 And Pharaoh sent, and, behold, there was not one of the cattle of the Israelites dead. And the heart of Pharaoh was hardened, and he did not let the people go.

8 ¶ And Yahweh said to Moses and to Aaron, Take to you handfuls of ashes of the furnace, and let Moses sprinkle it toward the heaven in the sight of Pharaoh.

9 And it shall become small dust in all the land of Egypt, and shall be a boil breaking forth *with* blisters upon man, and upon beast, throughout all the land of Egypt.

10 And they took ashes of the furnace, and stood before Pharaoh; and Moses sprinkled it up toward heaven; and it became a boil breaking forth *with* blisters upon man, and upon beast.

11 And the magicians could not stand before Moses because of the boils; for the boils were upon the magicians, and upon all the Egyptians.

12 And Yahweh hardened the heart of Pharaoh, and he listened not to them; as Yahweh had spoken to Moses.

13 ¶ And Yahweh said to Moses, Rise up early in the morning, and stand before Pharaoh, and say to him, Thus says Yahweh God of the Hebrews, Let my people go, that they may serve me.

14 For I will at this time send all my plagues upon your heart, and upon your servants, and upon your people; that you may know that *there is* none like me in all the earth.

15 For now I will stretch out my hand, that I may smite you and your people with pestilence; and you shall be cut off from the earth.

16 And in very deed for this *cause* have I raised you up, for to show *in* you my power; and that my name may be declared throughout all the earth.

17 As yet exalt you yourself against my people, that you will not let them go?
18 Behold, tomorrow about this time I will cause it to rain a very grievous hail, such as has not been in Egypt since the foundation thereof even until now.
19 Send therefore now, *and* gather your cattle, and all that you have in the field; *for upon* every man and beast which shall be found in the field, and shall not be brought home, the hail shall come down upon them, and they shall die.
20 He that feared the word of Yahweh among the servants of Pharaoh made his servants and his cattle flee into the houses:
21 And he that regarded not the word of Yahweh left his servants and his cattle in the field.
22 ¶ And Yahweh said to Moses, Stretch forth your hand toward heaven, that there may be hail in all the land of Egypt, upon man, and upon beast, and upon every herb of the field, throughout the land of Egypt.
23 And Moses stretched forth his rod toward heaven: and Yahweh sent thunder and hail, and the fire ran along upon the ground; and Yahweh rained hail upon the land of Egypt.
24 So there was hail, and fire mingled with the hail, very grievous, such as there was none like it in all the land of Egypt since it became a nation.
25 And the hail smote throughout all the land of Egypt all that *was* in the field, both man and beast; and the hail smote every herb of the field, and broke every tree of the field.
26 Only in the land of Goshen, where the children of Israel *were*, was there no hail.
27 And Pharaoh sent, and called for Moses and Aaron, and said to them, I have sinned this time: Yahweh *is* righteous, and I and my people *are* wicked.
28 Entreat Yahweh (for *it is* enough) that there be no *more* mighty thunderings and hail; and I will let you go, and you shall stay no longer.
29 And Moses said to him, As soon as I have gone out of the city, I will spread abroad my hands unto Yahweh; *and* the thunder shall cease, neither shall there be any more hail; that you may know how that the earth *is* Yahweh's.
30 But as for you and your servants, I know that you will not yet fear Yahweh God.
31 And the flax and the barley was smitten: for the barley *was* in the ear, and the flax *was* budded.
32 But the wheat and the rye were not smitten: for they *had* not grown up.
33 And Moses went out of the city from Pharaoh, and spread abroad his hands unto Yahweh: and the thunders and hail ceased, and the rain was not poured upon the earth.
34 And when Pharaoh saw that the rain and the hail and the thunders had ceased, he sinned yet more, and hardened his heart, he and his servants.
35 And the heart of Pharaoh was hardened, neither would he let the children of Israel go; as Yahweh had spoken by Moses.

Exodus 10

10:1 ¶ And Yahweh said to Moses, Go in to Pharaoh: for I have hardened his heart, and the heart of his servants, that I might show these my signs before him:
2 And that you may tell in the ears of your son, and of your son's son, what things I have worked in Egypt, and my signs which I have done among them; that you may know how that I *am* Yahweh.
3 And Moses and Aaron came in unto Pharaoh, and said to him, Thus says Yahweh God of the Hebrews, How long will you refuse to humble yourself before me? let my people go, that they may serve me.
4 Else, if you refuse to let my people go, behold, tomorrow will I bring the locusts into your border:
5 And they shall cover the face of the earth, that one cannot be able to see the earth: and they shall eat the residue of that which is escaped, which remains to you from the hail, and shall eat every tree which grows for you out of the field:
6 And they shall fill your houses, and the houses of all your servants, and the houses of all the Egyptians; which neither your fathers, nor your fathers' fathers have seen, since the day that they were upon the earth unto this day. And he turned himself, and went out from Pharaoh.
7 And Pharaoh's servants said to him, How long shall this man be a snare to us? let the men go, that they may serve Yahweh their God: know you not yet that Egypt is destroyed?
8 And Moses and Aaron were brought again unto Pharaoh: and he said to them, Go, serve Yahweh your God: *but* who *are* they that shall go?
9 And Moses said, We will go with our young and with our old, with our sons and with our daughters, with our flocks and with our herds will we go; for we *must hold* a feast unto Yahweh.
10 And he said to them, Let Yahweh be so with you, as I will let you go, and your little ones: look *to it*; for evil *is* before you.
11 Not so: go now you *that are* men, and serve Yahweh; for that you did desire. And they were driven out from Pharaoh's presence.
12 ¶ And Yahweh said to Moses, Stretch out your hand over the land of Egypt for the locusts, that they may come upon the land of Egypt, and eat every herb of the land, *even* all that the hail has left.
13 And Moses stretched forth his rod over the land of Egypt, and Yahweh brought an east wind upon the land all that day, and all *that* night; *and* when it was morning, the east wind brought the locusts.
14 And the locusts went up over all the land of Egypt, and rested in all the coasts of Egypt: very grievous *were they*; before them there were no such locusts as they, neither after them shall be such.
15 For they covered the face of the whole earth, so that the land was darkened; and they did eat every herb of the land, and all the fruit of the trees which the hail had left: and there remained not any green thing in the trees, or in the herbs of the field, throughout all the land of Egypt.
16 Then Pharaoh called for Moses and Aaron in haste; and he said, I have sinned against Yahweh your God, and against you.
17 Now therefore forgive, I pray you, my sin only this once, and entreat Yahweh your God, that he may take away from me this death only.
18 And he went out from Pharaoh, and entreated Yahweh.

Exodus 10

19 And Yahweh turned a mighty strong west wind, which took away the locusts, and cast them into the Red Sea; there remained not one locust in all the coasts of Egypt.
20 But Yahweh hardened Pharaoh's heart, so that he would not let the children of Israel go.
21 ¶ And Yahweh said to Moses, Stretch out your hand toward heaven, that there may be darkness over the land of Egypt, even darkness *which* may be felt.
22 And Moses stretched forth his hand toward heaven; and there was a thick darkness in all the land of Egypt three days:
23 They saw not one another, neither rose any from his place for three days: but all the children of Israel had light in their dwellings.
24 And Pharaoh called to Moses, and said, Go you, serve Yahweh; only let your flocks and your herds be left: let your little ones also go with you.
25 And Moses said, You must give us also sacrifices and burnt offerings, that we may sacrifice unto Yahweh our God.
26 Our cattle also shall go with us; there shall not a hoof be left behind; for thereof must we take to serve Yahweh our God; and we know not with what we must serve Yahweh, until we come there.
27 But Yahweh hardened Pharaoh's heart, and he would not let them go.
28 And Pharaoh said to him, Get you from me, take heed to yourself, see my face no more; for in *that* day you see my face you shall die.
29 And Moses said, You have spoken well, I will see your face again no more.

Exodus 11

11:1 ¶ And Yahweh said to Moses, Yet will I bring one plague *more* upon Pharaoh, and upon Egypt; afterward he will let you go away: when he shall let *you* go, he shall surely thrust you out away altogether.
2 Speak now in the ears of the people, and let every man borrow of his neighbor, and every woman of her neighbor, jewels of silver, and jewels of gold.
3 And Yahweh gave the people favor in the sight of the Egyptians. Moreover the man Moses *was* very great in the land of Egypt, in the sight of Pharaoh's servants, and in the sight of the people.
4 ¶ And Moses said, Thus says Yahweh, About midnight will I go out into the midst of Egypt:
5 And all the firstborn in the land of Egypt shall die, from the firstborn of Pharaoh that sits upon his throne, even to the firstborn of the maidservant that *is* behind the mill; and all the firstborn of beasts.
6 And there shall be a great cry throughout all the land of Egypt, such as there was none like it, nor shall be like it any more.
7 But against any of the children of Israel shall not a dog move his tongue, against man or beast: that you may know how that Yahweh does put a difference between the Egyptians and Israel.
8 And all these your servants shall come down unto me, and bow down themselves unto me, saying, Get you out, and all the people that follow you: and after that I will go out. And he went out from Pharaoh in a great anger.
9 And Yahweh said to Moses, Pharaoh shall not listen to you; that my wonders may be multiplied in the land of Egypt.
10 And Moses and Aaron did all these wonders before Pharaoh: and Yahweh hardened Pharaoh's heart, so that he would not let the children of Israel go out of his land.

Exodus 12

12:1 ¶ And Yahweh spoke to Moses and Aaron in the land of Egypt, saying,
2 This month *shall be* to you the beginning of months: it *shall be* the first month of the year to you.
3 Speak you to all the congregation of Israel, saying, In the tenth *day* of this month they shall take to them every man a lamb, according to the house of *their* fathers, a lamb for a house:
4 And if the household is too little for the lamb, let him and his neighbor next to his house take *it* according to the number of the souls; every man according to his eating shall make your count for the lamb.
5 Your lamb shall be without blemish, a male of the first year: you shall take *it* out from the sheep, or from the goats:
6 And you shall keep it up until the fourteenth day of the same month: and the whole assembly of the congregation of Israel shall kill it in the evening.
7 And they shall take of the blood, and put *it* on the two side posts and on the upper door post of the houses, wherein they shall eat it.
8 And they shall eat the flesh in that night, roasted with fire, and unleavened bread; *and* with bitter *herbs* they shall eat it.
9 Eat not of it raw, nor boiled at all with water, but roasted *with* fire; his head with his legs, and with the entrails thereof.
10 And you shall let nothing of it remain until the morning; and that which remains of it until the morning you shall burn with fire.
11 And thus shall you eat it; *with* your loins girded, your shoes on your feet, and your staff in your hand; and you shall eat it in haste: it *is* Yahweh's passover.
12 For I will pass through the land of Egypt this night, and will smite all the firstborn in the land of Egypt, both man and beast; and against all the gods of Egypt I will execute judgment: I *am* Yahweh.
13 And the blood shall be to you for a token upon the houses where you *are*: and when I see the blood, I will pass over you, and the plague shall not be upon you to destroy *you*, when I smite the land of Egypt.
14 And this day shall be to you for a memorial; and you shall keep it a feast to Yahweh throughout your generations; you shall keep it a feast by an ordinance forever.
15 Seven days shall you eat unleavened bread; even the first day you shall put away leaven out of your houses: for whoever eats leavened bread from the first day until the seventh day, that soul shall be cut off from Israel.
16 And in the first day *there shall be* a holy convocation, and in the seventh day there shall be a holy convocation to you; no manner of work shall be done in them, save *that* which every man must eat, that only may be done by you.
17 And you shall observe *the feast of* unleavened bread; for in this very same day have I brought your armies out of the land of Egypt: therefore shall you observe this day in your generations by an ordinance forever.
18 In the first *month*, on the fourteenth day of the month at evening, you shall eat unleavened bread, until the one and twentieth day of the month at evening.

19 Seven days shall there be no leaven found in your houses: for whoever eats that which is leavened, even that soul shall be cut off from the congregation of Israel, whether he is a stranger, or born in the land.
20 You shall eat nothing leavened; in all your habitations shall you eat unleavened bread.
21 ¶ Then Moses called for all the elders of Israel, and said to them, Draw out and take you a lamb according to your families, and kill the passover.
22 And you shall take a bunch of hyssop, and dip *it* in the blood that *is* in the basin, and strike the upper door post and the two side posts with the blood that *is* in the basin; and none of you shall go out at the door of his house until the morning.
23 For Yahweh will pass through to smite the Egyptians; and when he sees the blood upon the lintel, and on the two side posts, Yahweh will pass over the door, and will not allow the destroyer to come in to your houses to smite *you*.
24 And you shall observe this thing for an ordinance to you and to your sons forever.
25 And it shall come to pass, when you have come to the land which Yahweh will give you, according as he has promised, that you shall keep this service.
26 And it shall come to pass, when your children shall say to you, What mean you by this service?
27 That you shall say, It *is* the sacrifice of Yahweh's passover, who passed over the houses of the children of Israel in Egypt, when he smote the Egyptians, and delivered our houses. And the people bowed the head and worshipped.
28 And the children of Israel went away, and did as Yahweh had commanded Moses and Aaron, so did they.
29 ¶ And it came to pass, that at midnight Yahweh smote all the firstborn in the land of Egypt, from the firstborn of Pharaoh that sat on his throne to the firstborn of the captive that *was* in the dungeon; and all the firstborn of cattle.
30 And Pharaoh rose up in the night, he, and all his servants, and all the Egyptians; and there was a great cry in Egypt; for *there was* not a house where *there was* not one dead.
31 And he called for Moses and Aaron by night, and said, Rise up, *and* get you forth from among my people, both you and the children of Israel; and go, serve Yahweh, as you have said.
32 Also take your flocks and your herds, as you have said, and be gone; and bless me also.
33 And the Egyptians were urgent upon the people, that they might send them out of the land in haste; for they said, We *are* all dead *men*.
34 And the people took their dough before it was leavened, their kneading troughs being bound up in their clothes upon their shoulders.
35 And the children of Israel did according to the word of Moses; and they borrowed of the Egyptians jewels of silver, and jewels of gold, and clothing:
36 And Yahweh gave the people favor in the sight of the Egyptians, so that they lent to them *such things as they required*. And they plundered the Egyptians.
37 ¶ And the children of Israel journeyed from Rameses to Succoth, about six hundred thousand on foot *that were* men, besides children.
38 And a mixed multitude went up also with them; and flocks, and herds, *even* very much cattle.
39 And they baked unleavened cakes of the dough which they brought forth out of Egypt, for it was not leavened; because they were thrust out of Egypt, and could not linger, neither had they prepared for themselves any provisions.
40 Now the sojourning of the children of Israel, who dwelt in Egypt, *was* four hundred and thirty years.
41 And it came to pass at the end of the four hundred and thirty years, even the very same day it came to pass, that all the hosts of Yahweh went out from the land of Egypt.
42 It *is* a night to be much observed unto Yahweh for bringing them out from the land of Egypt: this *is* that night of Yahweh to be observed by all the children of Israel in their generations.
43 ¶ And Yahweh said to Moses and Aaron, This *is* the ordinance of the passover: There shall no stranger eat thereof:
44 But every man's servant that is bought for money, when you have circumcised him, then shall he eat thereof.
45 A foreigner and a hired servant shall not eat thereof.
46 In one house shall it be eaten; you shall not carry forth any of the flesh abroad out of the house; neither shall you break a bone thereof.
47 All the congregation of Israel shall keep it.
48 And when a stranger shall sojourn with you, and will keep the passover to Yahweh, let all his males be circumcised, and then let him come near and keep it; and he shall be as one that is born in the land: for no uncircumcised person shall eat thereof.
49 One law shall be to him that is home born, and to the stranger that sojourns among you.
50 Thus did all the children of Israel; as Yahweh commanded Moses and Aaron, so did they.
51 And it came to pass the very same day, *that* Yahweh did bring the children of Israel out of the land of Egypt by their armies.

Exodus 13

13:1 ¶ And Yahweh spoke to Moses, saying,
2 Sanctify unto me all the firstborn, whatever opens the womb among the children of Israel, *both* of man and of beast: it *is* mine.
3 And Moses said to the people, Remember this day, in which you came out from Egypt, out of the house of bondage; for by strength of hand Yahweh brought you out from this *place*: there shall no leavened bread be eaten.
4 This day came you out in the month *of* Abib.
5 And it shall be when Yahweh shall bring you into the land of the Canaanites, and the Hittites, and the Amorites, and the Hivites, and the Jebusites, which he swore to your fathers to give you, a land flowing with milk and honey, that you shall keep this service in this month.
6 Seven days you shall eat unleavened bread, and in the seventh day *shall be* a feast to Yahweh.
7 Unleavened bread shall be eaten seven days; and there shall no leavened bread be seen with you, neither shall there be leaven seen with you in all your quarters.
8 And you shall show your son in that day, saying, *This is done* because of that *which* Yahweh did unto me when I came forth out of Egypt.

Exodus 13

9 And it shall be for a sign to you upon your hand, and for a memorial between your eyes, that Yahweh's law may be in your mouth: for with a strong hand has Yahweh brought you out of Egypt.
10 You shall therefore keep this ordinance in its season from year to year.
11 ¶ And it shall be when Yahweh shall bring you into the land of the Canaanites, as he swore to you and to your fathers, and shall give it you,
12 That you shall set apart unto Yahweh all that opens the womb, and every firstborn that comes from a beast which you have; the males *shall be* Yahweh's.
13 And every firstborn of a donkey you shall redeem with a lamb; and if you shall not redeem it, then you shall break his neck: and all the firstborn of man among your children shall you redeem.
14 And it shall be when your son asks you in time to come, saying, What *is* this? that you shall say to him, By strength of hand Yahweh brought us out from Egypt, from the house of bondage:
15 And it came to pass, when Pharaoh would hardly let us go, that Yahweh slew all the firstborn in the land of Egypt, both the firstborn of man, and the firstborn of beast: therefore I sacrifice to Yahweh all that opens the womb, being males; but all the firstborn of my children I redeem.
16 And it shall be for a token upon your hand, and for frontlets between your eyes: for by strength of hand Yahweh brought us forth out of Egypt.
17 ¶ And it came to pass, when Pharaoh had let the people go, that God led them not *through* the way of the land of the Philistines, although that *was* near; for God said, Lest perhaps the people repent when they see war, and they return to Egypt:
18 But God led the people about, *through* the way of the wilderness of the Red Sea: and the children of Israel went up armed out of the land of Egypt.
19 And Moses took the bones of Joseph with him: for he had straightly sworn the children of Israel, saying, God will surely visit you; and you shall carry up my bones away from here with you.
20 And they took their journey from Succoth, and encamped in Etham, at the edge of the wilderness.
21 And Yahweh went before them by day in a pillar of a cloud, to lead them the way; and by night in a pillar of fire, to give them light; to go by day and night:
22 He took not away the pillar of the cloud by day, nor the pillar of fire by night, *from* before the people.

Exodus 14

14:1 ¶ And Yahweh spoke to Moses, saying,
2 Speak to the children of Israel, that they turn and encamp before Pihahiroth, between Migdol and the sea, over against Baalzephon: before it shall you encamp by the sea.
3 For Pharaoh will say of the children of Israel, They *are* entangled in the land, the wilderness has shut them in.
4 And I will harden Pharaoh's heart, that he shall follow after them; and I will be honored upon Pharaoh, and upon all his host; that the Egyptians may know that I *am* Yahweh. And they did so.
5 And it was told *to* the king of Egypt that the people fled: and the heart of Pharaoh and of his servants was turned against the people, and they said, Why have we done this, that we have let Israel go from serving us?
6 And he made ready his chariot, and took his people with him:
7 And he took six hundred chosen chariots, and all the chariots of Egypt, and captains over every one of them.
8 And Yahweh hardened the heart of Pharaoh king of Egypt, and he pursued after the children of Israel: and the children of Israel went out with a high hand.
9 But the Egyptians pursued after them, all the horses *and* chariots of Pharaoh, and his horsemen, and his army, and overtook them encamping by the sea, beside Pihahiroth, before Baalzephon.
10 ¶ And when Pharaoh drew nigh, the children of Israel lifted up their eyes, and, behold, the Egyptians marched after them; and they were very afraid: and the children of Israel cried out unto Yahweh.
11 And they said to Moses, Because *there were* no graves in Egypt, have you taken us away to die in the wilderness? why have you dealt thus with us, to carry us forth out of Egypt?
12 *Is* not this the word that we did tell you in Egypt, saying, Let us alone, that we may serve the Egyptians? For *it had been* better for us to serve the Egyptians, than that we should die in the wilderness.
13 And Moses said to the people, Fear you not, stand still, and see the salvation of Yahweh, which he will show to you today: for the Egyptians whom you have seen today, you shall see them again no more forever.
14 Yahweh shall fight for you, and you shall hold your peace.
15 ¶ And Yahweh said to Moses, Why cry you to me? speak to the children of Israel, that they go forward:
16 But lift you up your rod, and stretch out your hand over the sea, and divide it: and the children of Israel shall go on dry *ground* through the midst of the sea.
17 And I, behold, I will harden the hearts of the Egyptians, and they shall follow them: and I will get me honor upon Pharaoh, and upon all his host, upon his chariots, and upon his horsemen.
18 And the Egyptians shall know that I *am* Yahweh, when I have gotten me honor upon Pharaoh, upon his chariots, and upon his horsemen.
19 And the angel of God, which went before the camp of Israel, removed and went behind them; and the pillar of the cloud went from before their face, and stood behind them:
20 And it came between the camp of the Egyptians and the camp of Israel; and it was a cloud and darkness *to them*, but it gave light by night *to these*: so that the one came not near the other all the night.
21 ¶ And Moses stretched out his hand over the sea; and Yahweh caused the sea to go *back* by a strong east wind all that night, and made the sea dry *land*, and the waters were divided.
22 And the children of Israel went into the midst of the sea upon the dry *ground*: and the waters *were* a wall to them on their right hand, and on their left.
23 And the Egyptians pursued, and went in after them to the midst of the sea, *even* all Pharaoh's horses, his chariots, and his horsemen.

24 And it came to pass, that in the morning watch Yahweh looked to the host of the Egyptians through the pillar of fire and of the cloud, and troubled the host of the Egyptians,
25 And took off their chariot wheels, that they drove them heavily: so that the Egyptians said, Let us flee from the face of Israel; for Yahweh fights for them against the Egyptians.
26 And Yahweh said to Moses, Stretch out your hand over the sea, that the waters may come again upon the Egyptians, upon their chariots, and upon their horsemen.
27 And Moses stretched forth his hand over the sea, and the sea returned to its strength when the morning appeared; and the Egyptians fled against it; and Yahweh overthrew the Egyptians in the midst of the sea.
28 And the waters returned, and covered the chariots, and the horsemen, *and* all the host of Pharaoh that came into the sea after them; there remained not so much as one of them.
29 But the children of Israel walked upon dry *land* in the midst of the sea; and the waters *were* a wall to them on their right hand, and on their left.
30 Thus Yahweh saved Israel that day out of the hand of the Egyptians; and Israel saw the Egyptians dead upon the sea shore.
31 And Israel saw that great work which Yahweh did upon the Egyptians: and the people feared Yahweh, and believed Yahweh, and his servant Moses.

Exodus 15

15:1 ¶ Then sang Moses and the children of Israel this song unto Yahweh, and spoke, saying, I will sing to Yahweh, for he has triumphed gloriously: the horse and his rider has he thrown into the sea.
2 Yah *is* my strength and song, and he has become my salvation: he *is* my God, and I will prepare him a habitation; my father's God, and I will exalt him.
3 Yahweh *is* a man of war: Yahweh *is* his name.
4 Pharaoh's chariots and his host has he cast into the sea: his chosen captains also are drowned in the Red Sea.
5 The depths have covered them: they sank into the bottom as a stone.
6 Your right hand, O Yahweh, has become glorious in power: your right hand, O Yahweh, has dashed in pieces the enemy.
7 And in the greatness of your excellency you have overthrown them that rose up against you: you sent forth your wrath, *which* consumed them as stubble.
8 And with the blast of your nostrils the waters were gathered together, the floods stood upright as a heap, *and* the depths were congealed in the heart of the sea.
9 The enemy said, I will pursue, I will overtake, I will divide the spoil; my lust shall be satisfied upon them; I will draw my sword, my hand shall destroy them.
10 You did blow with your wind, the sea covered them: they sank as lead in the mighty waters.
11 Who *is* like unto you, O Yahweh, among the gods? who *is* like you, glorious in holiness, fearful *in* praises, doing wonders?
12 You stretched out your right hand, the earth swallowed them.
13 You in your mercy have led forth the people *which* you have redeemed: you have guided *them* in your strength unto your holy habitation.
14 The people shall hear, *and* be afraid: sorrow shall take hold on the inhabitants of Palestina.
15 Then the dukes of Edom shall be amazed; the mighty men of Moab, trembling shall take hold upon them; all the inhabitants of Canaan shall melt away.
16 Fear and dread shall fall upon them; by the greatness of your arm they shall be *as* still as a stone; till your people pass over, O Yahweh, till the people pass over, *which* you have purchased.
17 You shall bring them in, and plant them in the mountain of your inheritance, *in* the place, O Yahweh, *which* you have made for you to dwell in, *in* the Sanctuary, O Lord, *which* your hands have established.
18 Yahweh shall reign forever and ever.
19 For the horse of Pharaoh went in with his chariots and with his horsemen into the sea, and Yahweh brought again the waters of the sea upon them; but the children of Israel went on dry *land* in the midst of the sea.
20 And Miriam the prophetess, the sister of Aaron, took a tambourine in her hand; and all the women went out after her with tambourines and with dances.
21 And Miriam answered them, Sing you to Yahweh, for he has triumphed gloriously; the horse and his rider has he thrown into the sea.
22 ¶ So Moses brought Israel from the Red Sea, and they went out into the wilderness of Shur; and they went three days in the wilderness, and found no water.
23 And when they came to Marah, they could not drink of the waters of Marah, for they *were* bitter: therefore the name of it was called Marah.
24 And the people murmured against Moses, saying, What shall we drink?
25 And he cried unto Yahweh; and Yahweh showed him a tree, *which* when he had cast into the waters, the waters were made sweet: there he made for them a statute and an ordinance, and there he proved them,
26 And said, If you will diligently listen to the voice of Yahweh your God, and will do that which is right in his sight, and will give ear to his commandments, and keep all his statutes, I will put none of these diseases upon you, which I have brought upon the Egyptians: for I *am* Yahweh that heals you.
27 And they came to Elim, where *were* twelve wells of water, and threescore and ten palm trees: and they encamped there by the waters.

Exodus 16

16:1 ¶ And they took their journey from Elim, and all the congregation of the children of Israel came to the wilderness of Sin, which *is* between Elim and Sinai, on the fifteenth day of the second month after their departing out of the land of Egypt.
2 And the whole congregation of the children of Israel murmured against Moses and Aaron in the wilderness:
3 And the children of Israel said to them, Would *to God* that we had died by the hand of Yahweh in the land of Egypt,

Exodus 16

when we sat by the flesh pots, *and* when we did eat bread to the full; for you have brought us forth into this wilderness, to kill this whole assembly with hunger.

4 Then said Yahweh to Moses, Behold, I will rain bread from heaven for you; and the people shall go out and gather a certain rate every day, that I may prove them, whether they will walk in my law, or not.

5 And it shall come to pass, that on the sixth day they shall prepare *that* which they bring in; and it shall be twice as much as they gather daily.

6 And Moses and Aaron said to all the children of Israel, At evening, then you shall know that Yahweh has brought you out from the land of Egypt:

7 And in the morning, then you shall see the glory of Yahweh; for that he hears your murmurings against Yahweh: and what *are* we, that you murmur against us?

8 And Moses said, *This shall be*, when Yahweh shall give you in the evening flesh to eat, and in the morning bread to the full; for that Yahweh hears your murmurings which you murmur against him: and what *are* we? your murmurings *are* not against us, but against Yahweh.

9 And Moses spoke to Aaron, Say to all the congregation of the children of Israel, Come near before Yahweh: for he has heard your murmurings.

10 And it came to pass, as Aaron spoke to the whole congregation of the children of Israel, that they looked toward the wilderness, and, behold, the glory of Yahweh appeared in the cloud.

11 And Yahweh spoke to Moses, saying,

12 I have heard the murmurings of the children of Israel: speak to them, saying, At evening you shall eat flesh, and in the morning you shall be filled with bread; and you shall know that I *am* Yahweh your God.

13 ¶ And it came to pass, that at evening the quails came up, and covered the camp: and in the morning the dew lay round about the host.

14 And when the dew that lay had gone up, behold, upon the face of the wilderness *there lay* a small round thing, *as* small as the gray frost on the ground.

15 And when the children of Israel saw *it*, they said one to another, It *is* manna: for they knew not what it *was*. And Moses said to them, This *is* the bread which Yahweh has given you to eat.

16 This *is* the thing which Yahweh has commanded, Gather of it every man according to his eating, an omer for every man, *according to* the number of your persons; take you every man for *them* which *are* in his tents.

17 And the children of Israel did so, and gathered, some more, some less.

18 And when they did measure *it* with an omer, he that gathered much had nothing over, and he that gathered little had no lack; they gathered every man according to his eating.

19 And Moses said, Let no man leave of it till the morning.

20 Notwithstanding they listened not to Moses; but some of them left of it until the morning, and it bred worms, and stunk: and Moses was angry with them.

21 And they gathered it every morning, every man according to his eating: and when the sun became hot, it melted.

22 ¶ And it came to pass, *that* on the sixth day they gathered twice as much bread, two omers for one *man*: and all the rulers of the congregation came and told Moses.

23 And he said to them, This *is that* which Yahweh has said, Tomorrow *is* the rest of the holy sabbath unto Yahweh: bake *that* which you will bake *today*, and boil what you will boil; and that which remains over lay up for you to be kept until the morning.

24 And they laid it up till the morning, as Moses commanded: and it did not stink, neither was there any worm therein.

25 And Moses said, Eat that today; for today *is* a sabbath unto Yahweh: today you shall not find it in the field.

26 Six days you shall gather it; but on the seventh day, *which is* the sabbath, in it there shall be none.

27 And it came to pass, *that* there went out *some* of the people on the seventh day for to gather, and they found none.

28 And Yahweh said to Moses, How long refuse you to keep my commandments and my laws?

29 See, for that Yahweh has given you the sabbath, therefore he gives you on the sixth day the bread of two days; remain you every man in his place, let no man go out of his place on the seventh day.

30 So the people rested on the seventh day.

31 And the house of Israel called the name thereof Manna: and it *was* like coriander seed, white; and the taste of it *was* like wafers *made* with honey.

32 ¶ And Moses said, This *is* the thing which Yahweh commands, Fill an omer of it to be kept for your generations; that they may see the bread with which I have fed you in the wilderness, when I brought you forth from the land of Egypt.

33 And Moses said to Aaron, Take a pot, and put an omer full of manna therein, and lay it up before Yahweh, to be kept for your generations.

34 As Yahweh commanded Moses, so Aaron laid it up before the Testimony, to be kept.

35 And the children of Israel did eat manna forty years, until they came to a land inhabited; they did eat manna, until they came to the borders of the land of Canaan.

36 Now an omer *is* the tenth *part* of an ephah.

Exodus 17

17:1 ¶ And all the congregation of the children of Israel journeyed from the wilderness of Sin, after their journeys, according to the commandment of Yahweh, and pitched in Rephidim: and *there was* no water for the people to drink.

2 Therefore the people did strive with Moses, and said, Give us water that we may drink. And Moses said to them, Why strive you with me? why do you tempt Yahweh?

3 And the people thirsted there for water; and the people murmured against Moses, and said, Why *is* this *that* you have brought us up out of Egypt, to kill us and our children and our cattle with thirst?

4 And Moses cried unto Yahweh, saying, What shall I do unto this people? they are almost ready to stone me.

5 And Yahweh said to Moses, Go on before the people, and take with you of the elders of Israel; and your rod, with which you smote the river, take in your hand, and go.

6 Behold, I will stand before you there upon the rock in Horeb; and you shall smite the rock, and there shall come water out of it, that the people may drink. And Moses did so in the sight of the elders of Israel.

7 And he called the name of the place Massah, and Meribah, because of the chiding of the children of Israel, and because they tempted Yahweh, saying, Is Yahweh among us, or not?

8 ¶ Then came Amalek, and fought with Israel in Rephidim.

9 And Moses said to Joshua, Choose us out men, and go out, fight with Amalek: tomorrow I will stand on the top of the hill with the rod of God in my hand.

10 So Joshua did as Moses had said to him, and fought with Amalek: and Moses, Aaron, and Hur went up to the top of the hill.

11 And it came to pass, when Moses held up his hand, that Israel prevailed: and when he let down his hand, Amalek prevailed.

12 But Moses' hands *were* heavy; and they took a stone, and put *it* under him, and he sat thereon; and Aaron and Hur held up his hands, the one on the one side, and the other on the other side; and his hands were steady until the going down of the sun.

13 And Joshua weakened Amalek and his people with the edge of the sword.

14 And Yahweh said to Moses, Write this *for* a memorial in a book, and rehearse *it* in the ears of Joshua: for I will utterly put out the remembrance of Amalek from under heaven.

15 And Moses built an altar, and called the name of it Yahweh-nissi:

16 For he said, Because Yah has sworn *that* Yahweh will have war with Amalek from generation to generation.

Exodus 18

18:1 ¶ When Jethro, the priest of Midian, Moses' father-in-law, heard of all that God had done for Moses, and for Israel his people, *and* that Yahweh had brought Israel out of Egypt;

2 Then Jethro, Moses' father-in-law, took Zipporah, Moses' wife, after he had sent her back,

3 And her two sons; of which the name of the one *was* Gershom; for he said, I have been an alien in a strange land:

4 And the name of the other *was* Eliezer; for the God of my father, *said he, was* my help, and delivered me from the sword of Pharaoh:

5 And Jethro, Moses' father-in-law, came with his sons and his wife to Moses into the wilderness, where he encamped at the mount of God:

6 And he said to Moses, I your father-in-law Jethro have come to you, and your wife, and her two sons with her.

7 ¶ And Moses went out to meet his father-in-law, and bowed down, and kissed him; and they asked each other of *their* welfare; and they came into the tent.

8 And Moses told his father-in-law all that Yahweh had done to Pharaoh and to the Egyptians for Israel's sake, *and* all the hardship that had come upon them by the way, and *how* Yahweh delivered them.

9 And Jethro rejoiced for all the goodness which Yahweh had done to Israel, whom he had delivered out of the hand of the Egyptians.

10 And Jethro said, Blessed *be* Yahweh, who has delivered you out of the hand of the Egyptians, and out of the hand of Pharaoh, who has delivered the people from under the hand of the Egyptians.

11 Now I know that Yahweh *is* greater than all gods: for in the thing wherein they dealt proudly *he was* above them.

12 And Jethro, Moses' father-in-law, took a burnt offering and sacrifices for God: and Aaron came, and all the elders of Israel, to eat bread with Moses' father-in-law before God.

13 ¶ And it came to pass on the next day, that Moses sat to judge the people: and the people stood by Moses from the morning to the evening.

14 And when Moses' father-in-law saw all that he did to the people, he said, What *is* this thing that you do to the people? why sit you yourself alone, and all the people stand by you from morning unto evening?

15 And Moses said to his father-in-law, Because the people come to me to inquire of God:

16 When they have a matter, they come to me; and I judge between one and another, and I do make *them* know the statutes of God, and his laws.

17 And Moses' father-in-law said to him, The thing that you do *is* not good.

18 You will surely wear away, both you, and this people that *is* with you: for this thing *is* too heavy for you; you are not able to perform it yourself alone.

19 Listen now to my voice, I will give you counsel, and God shall be with you: Be you for the people before God, that you may bring the causes to God:

20 And you shall teach them ordinances and laws, and shall show them the way wherein they must walk, and the work that they must do.

21 Moreover you shall provide out of all the people able men, such as fear God, men of truth, hating covetousness; and place *such* over them, *to be* rulers of thousands, *and* rulers of hundreds, rulers of fifties, and rulers of tens:

22 And let them judge the people at all seasons: and it shall be, *that* every great matter they shall bring to you, but every small matter they shall judge: so shall it be easier for yourself, and they shall bear *the burden* with you.

23 If you shall do this thing, and God commands you *so*, then you shall be able to endure, and all this people shall also go to their place in peace.

24 So Moses listened to the voice of his father-in-law, and did all that he had said.

25 And Moses chose able men out of all Israel, and made them heads over the people, rulers of thousands, rulers of hundreds, rulers of fifties, and rulers of tens.

26 And they judged the people at all seasons: the hard causes they brought to Moses, but every small matter they judged themselves.

27 And Moses let his father-in-law depart; and he went his way into his own land.

Exodus 19

19:1 ¶ In the third month, when the children of Israel had gone forth out of the land of Egypt, the same day came they *into* the wilderness of Sinai.
2 For they had departed from Rephidim, and had come *to* the desert of Sinai, and had pitched in the wilderness; and there Israel camped before the mount.
3 And Moses went up to God, and Yahweh called to him out of the mountain, saying, Thus shall you say to the house of Jacob, and tell the children of Israel;
4 You have seen what I did to the Egyptians, and *how* I bore you on eagles' wings, and brought you to myself.
5 Now therefore, if you will obey my voice indeed, and keep my covenant, then you shall be a peculiar treasure to me above all people: for all the earth *is* mine:
6 And you shall be to me a kingdom of priests, and a holy nation. These *are* the words which you shall speak to the children of Israel.
7 And Moses came and called for the elders of the people, and laid before their faces all these words which Yahweh commanded him.
8 And all the people answered together, and said, All that Yahweh has spoken we will do. And Moses returned the words of the people to Yahweh.
9 ¶ And Yahweh said to Moses, Behold, I come to you in a thick cloud, that the people may hear when I speak with you, and believe you forever. And Moses told the words of the people to Yahweh.
10 And Yahweh said to Moses, Go to the people, and sanctify them today and tomorrow, and let them wash their clothes,
11 And be ready against the third day: for the third day Yahweh will come down in the sight of all the people upon mount Sinai.
12 And you shall set bounds unto the people round about, saying, Take heed to yourselves, *that you* go *not* up into the mount, or touch the border of it: whoever touches the mount shall be surely put to death:
13 There shall not a hand touch it, but he shall surely be stoned, or shot through; whether *it is* beast or man, it shall not live: when the trumpet sounds long, they shall come up to the mount.
14 And Moses went down from the mount to the people, and sanctified the people; and they washed their clothes.
15 And he said to the people, Be ready against the third day: come not at *your* wives.
16 ¶ And it came to pass on the third day in the morning, that there were thunders and lightnings, and a thick cloud upon the mount, and the voice of the trumpet exceedingly loud; so that all the people that *were* in the camp trembled.
17 And Moses brought forth the people out of the camp to meet with God; and they stood at the lower part of the mount.
18 And mount Sinai was altogether in a smoke, because Yahweh descended upon it in fire: and the smoke thereof ascended as the smoke of a furnace, and the whole mount quaked greatly.
19 And when the voice of the trumpet sounded long, and grew louder and louder, Moses spoke, and God answered him by a voice.
20 And Yahweh came down upon mount Sinai, on the top of the mount: and Yahweh called Moses *up* to the top of the mount; and Moses went up.
21 And Yahweh said to Moses, Go down, charge the people, lest they break through unto Yahweh to gaze, and many of them perish.
22 And let the priests also, which come near to Yahweh, sanctify themselves, lest Yahweh breaks forth upon them.
23 And Moses said unto Yahweh, The people cannot come up to mount Sinai: for you charged us, saying, Set bounds about the mount, and sanctify it.
24 And Yahweh said to him, Away, get you down, and you shall come up, you, and Aaron with you: but let not the priests and the people break through to come up unto Yahweh, lest he breaks forth upon them.
25 So Moses went down to the people, and spoke to them.

Exodus 20

20:1 ¶ And God spoke all these words, saying,
2 I *am* Yahweh your God, which has brought you out of the land of Egypt, out of the house of bondage.
3 You shall have no other gods before me.
4 You shall not make to you any graven image, or any likeness *of anything* that *is* in heaven above, or that *is* in the earth beneath, or that *is* in the water under the earth:
5 You shall not bow down yourself to them, nor serve them: for I Yahweh your God *am* a jealous God, visiting the iniquity of the fathers upon the children to the third and fourth *generation* of them that hate me;
6 And showing mercy to thousands of them that love me, and keep my commandments.
7 You shall not take the name of Yahweh your God in vain; for Yahweh will not hold him guiltless that takes his name in vain.
8 Remember the sabbath day, to keep it holy.
9 Six days shall you labor, and do all your work:
10 But the seventh day *is* the sabbath of Yahweh your God: *in it* you shall not do any work, you, nor your son, nor your daughter, your manservant, nor your maidservant, nor your cattle, nor your stranger that *is* within your gates:
11 For *in* six days Yahweh made heaven and earth, the sea, and all that in them *is*, and rested the seventh day: therefore Yahweh blessed the sabbath day, and hallowed it.
12 ¶ Honor your father and your mother: that your days may be long upon the land which Yahweh your God gives you.

13 You shall not kill.
14 You shall not commit adultery.
15 You shall not steal.
16 You shall not bear false witness against your neighbor.
17 You shall not covet your neighbor's house, you shall not covet your neighbor's wife, nor his manservant, nor his maidservant, nor his ox, nor his donkey, nor anything that *is* your neighbor's.
18 ¶ And all the people saw the thunderings, and the lightnings, and the noise of the trumpet, and the mountain smoking: and when the people saw *it*, they trembled, and stood afar off.
19 And they said to Moses, Speak you with us, and we will hear: but let not God speak with us, lest we die.
20 And Moses said to the people, Fear not: for God has come to prove you, and that his fear may be before your faces, that you sin not.
21 And the people stood afar off, and Moses drew near unto the thick darkness where God *was*.
22 ¶ And Yahweh said to Moses, Thus you shall say to the children of Israel, You have seen that I have talked with you from heaven.
23 You shall not make with me gods of silver, neither shall you make unto you gods of gold.
24 An altar of earth you shall make unto me, and shall sacrifice thereon your burnt offerings, and your peace offerings, your sheep, and your oxen: in all places where I record my name I will come to you, and I will bless you.
25 And if you will make me an altar of stone, you shall not build it of hewn stone: for if you lift up your tool upon it, you have polluted it.
26 Neither shall you go up by steps to my altar, that your nakedness be not uncovered thereon.

Exodus 21

21:1 ¶ Now these *are* the judgments which you shall set before them.
2 If you buy a Hebrew servant, six years he shall serve: and in the seventh he shall go out free for nothing.
3 If he came in by himself, he shall go out by himself: if he were married, then his wife shall go out with him.
4 If his master has given him a wife, and she has born him sons or daughters; the wife and her children shall be her master's, and he shall go out by himself.
5 And if the servant shall plainly say, I love my master, my wife, and my children; I will not go out free:
6 Then his master shall bring him to the judges; he shall also bring him to the door, or to the door post; and his master shall bore his ear through with an awl; and he shall serve him forever.
7 And if a man sells his daughter to be a maidservant, she shall not go out as the menservants do.
8 If she pleases not her master, who has betrothed her to himself, then shall he let her be redeemed: to sell her to a strange nation he shall have no power, seeing he has dealt deceitfully with her.
9 And if he has betrothed her to his son, he shall deal with her after the manner of daughters.
10 If he takes him another *wife*; her food, her clothing, and her duty of marriage, shall he not diminish.
11 And if he does not these three to her, then shall she go out free without money.
12 ¶ He that smites a man, so that he dies, shall be surely put to death.
13 And if a man lies not in wait, but God delivers *him* into his hand; then I will appoint you a place where he shall flee.
14 But if a man comes presumptuously upon his neighbor, to slay him with guile; you shall take him from my altar, that he may die.
15 And he that smites his father, or his mother, shall be surely put to death.
16 And he that steals a man, and sells him, or if he is found in his hand, he shall surely be put to death.
17 And he that curses his father, or his mother, shall surely be put to death.
18 And if men strive together, and one smites another with a stone, or with *his* fist, and he dies not, but lies in *his* bed:
19 If he rises again, and walks abroad upon his staff, then shall he that smote *him* be acquitted: only he shall pay *for* the loss of his time, and shall cause *him* to be thoroughly healed.
20 And if a man smites his servant, or his maid, with a rod, and he dies under his hand; he shall be surely punished.
21 Notwithstanding, if he continues a day or two, he shall not be punished: for he *is* his money.
22 ¶ If men strive, and hurt a woman with child, so that her child departs *from her*, and yet no harm follows: he shall be surely punished, accordingly as the woman's husband will impose upon him; and he shall pay as the judges *determine*.
23 And if *any* harm follows, then you shall give life for life,
24 Eye for eye, tooth for tooth, hand for hand, foot for foot,
25 Burning for burning, wound for wound, stripe for stripe.
26 And if a man smites the eye of his servant, or the eye of his maid, that it perishes; he shall let him go free for his eye's sake.
27 And if he smites out his manservant's tooth, or his maidservant's tooth; he shall let him go free for his tooth's sake.
28 If an ox gores a man or a woman, that they die: then the ox shall be surely stoned, and his flesh shall not be eaten; but the owner of the ox *shall be* acquitted.
29 But if the ox were inclined to push with his horn in times past, and it has been testified to his owner, and he has not kept him in, but that he has killed a man or a woman; the ox shall be stoned, and his owner also shall be put to death.
30 If there is laid upon him a sum of money, then he shall give for the ransom of his life whatever is laid upon him.
31 Whether he has gored a son, or has gored a daughter, according to this judgment shall it be done to him.
32 If the ox shall push a manservant or a maidservant; he shall give to their master thirty shekels of silver, and the ox shall be stoned.
33 And if a man shall open a pit, or if a man shall dig a pit, and not cover it, and an ox or a donkey falls therein;
34 The owner of the pit shall make *it* good, *and* give money to the owner of them; and the dead *beast* shall be his.

Exodus 21

35 And if one man's ox hurts another's, that he dies; then they shall sell the live ox, and divide the money of it; and the dead *ox* also they shall divide.

36 Or if it is known that the ox was prone to goring in times past, and his owner has not kept him in; he shall surely pay ox for ox; and the dead shall be his own.

Exodus 22

22:1 ¶ If a man shall steal an ox, or a sheep, and kill it, or sell it; he shall restore five oxen for an ox, and four sheep for a sheep.

2 If a thief is found breaking in, and is smitten *so* that he dies, *there shall* no blood *be shed* for him.

3 If the sun has risen upon him, *there shall be* blood *shed* for him; *for* he should make full restitution; if he has nothing, then he shall be sold for his theft.

4 If the theft is certainly found in his hand alive, whether it is ox, or donkey, or sheep; he shall restore double.

5 If a man shall cause a field or vineyard to be eaten, and shall put in his beast, and shall feed in another man's field; of the best of his own field, and of the best of his own vineyard, shall he make restitution.

6 If fire breaks out, and catches in thorns, so that the stacks of corn, or the standing corn, or the field, are consumed *therewith*; he that kindled the fire shall surely make restitution.

7 ¶ If a man shall deliver to his neighbor money or stuff to keep, and it is stolen out of the man's house; if the thief is found, let him pay double.

8 If the thief is not found, then the master of the house shall be brought to the judges, *to see* whether he has put his hand to his neighbor's goods.

9 For all manner of trespass, *whether it is* for ox, for donkey, for sheep, for clothing, *or* for any manner of lost thing, which *another* challenges to be his, the cause of both parties shall come before the judges; *and* whom the judges shall condemn, he shall pay double to his neighbor.

10 If a man delivers to his neighbor a donkey, or an ox, or a sheep, or any beast, to keep; and it dies, or is hurt, or driven away, no man seeing *it*:

11 *Then* shall an oath of Yahweh be between them both, that he has not put his hand to his neighbor's goods; and the owner of it shall accept *thereof*, and he shall not make *it* good.

12 And if it is stolen from him, he shall make restitution to the owner thereof.

13 If it is torn in pieces, *then* let him bring it *for* witness, *and* he shall not make good that which was torn.

14 And if a man borrows *anything* from his neighbor, and it is broken, or dies, the owner thereof *being* not with it, he shall surely make *it* good.

15 *But* if the owner thereof *is* with it, he shall not make *it* good: if it is a hired *thing*, it came for his hire.

16 ¶ And if a man entices a maid that is not betrothed, and lies with her, he shall surely endow her to be his wife.

17 If her father utterly refuses to give her to him, he shall pay money according to the dowry of virgins.

18 You shall not allow a witch to live.

19 Whoever lies with a beast shall surely be put to death.

20 He that sacrifices to *any* god, save unto Yahweh only, he shall be utterly destroyed.

21 You shall neither mistreat a stranger, nor oppress him: for you were strangers in the land of Egypt.

22 You shall not afflict any widow, or fatherless child.

23 If you afflict them in any way, and they cry at all to me, I will surely hear their cry;

24 And my wrath shall grow hot, and I will kill you with the sword; and your wives shall be widows, and your children fatherless.

25 ¶ If you lend money to *any of* my people *that are* poor by you, you shall not be to him as a creditor, neither shall you lay upon him interest.

26 If you at all take your neighbor's garment to pledge, you shall deliver it to him by when the sun goes down:

27 For that *is* his covering only, it *is* his clothing for his skin: wherein shall he sleep? and it shall come to pass, when he cries to me, that I will hear; for I *am* gracious.

28 You shall not revile the gods, nor curse the ruler of your people.

29 You shall not delay *to offer* the first of your ripe fruits, and of your juices: the firstborn of your sons shall you give to me.

30 Likewise shall you do with your oxen, *and* with your sheep: seven days it shall be with his mother; on the eighth day you shall give it me.

31 And you shall be holy men to me: neither shall you eat *any* flesh *that is* torn of beasts in the field; you shall cast it to the dogs.

Exodus 23

23:1 ¶ You shall not raise a false report: put not your hand with the wicked to be an unrighteous witness.

2 You shall not follow a multitude to *do* evil; neither shall you speak in a cause to bow after many to pervert *judgment*:

3 Neither shall you adorn a poor man in his cause.

4 If you meet your enemy's ox or his donkey going astray, you shall surely bring it back to him again.

5 If you see the donkey of him that hates you lying under his burden, and would forbear to help him, you shall surely help with him.

6 You shall not pervert the judgment of your poor in his cause.

7 Keep you far from a false matter; and the innocent and righteous slay you not: for I will not justify the wicked.

8 And you shall take no gift: for the gift blinds the wise, and perverts the words of the righteous.

9 Also you shall not oppress a stranger: for you know the heart of a stranger, seeing you were strangers in the land of Egypt.

10 ¶ And six years you shall sow your land, and shall gather in the fruits thereof:

11 But the seventh *year* you shall let it rest and lie still; that the poor of your people may eat: and what they leave

the beasts of the field shall eat. In like manner you shall deal with your vineyard, *and* with your olive grove.

12 Six days you shall do your work, and on the seventh day you shall rest: that your ox and your donkey may rest, and the son of your handmaid, and the stranger, may be refreshed.

13 And in all *things* that I have said to you be circumspect: and make no mention of the name of other gods, neither let it be heard out of your mouth.

14 Three times you shall keep a feast to me in the year.

15 You shall keep the feast of unleavened bread: (you shall eat unleavened bread seven days, as I commanded you, in the time appointed of the month *of* Abib; for in it you came out from Egypt: and none shall appear before me empty:)

16 And the feast of harvest, the firstfruits of your labors, which you have sown in the field: and the feast of ingathering, *which is* in the end of the year, when you have gathered in your labors out of the field.

17 Three times in the year all your males shall appear before the Lord Yahweh.

18 You shall not offer the blood of my sacrifice with leavened bread; neither shall the fat of my sacrifice remain until the morning.

19 The first of the firstfruits of your land you shall bring into the house of Yahweh your God. You shall not boil a kid in his mother's milk.

20 ¶ Behold, I send an Angel before you, to keep you in the way, and to bring you into the place which I have prepared.

21 Beware of him, and obey his voice, provoke him not; for he will not pardon your transgressions: for my name *is* in him.

22 But if you shall indeed obey his voice, and do all that I speak; then I will be an enemy to your enemies, and an adversary to your adversaries.

23 For my Angel shall go before you, and bring you in to the Amorites, and the Hittites, and the Perizzites, and the Canaanites, the Hivites, and the Jebusites: and I will cut them off.

24 You shall not bow down to their gods, nor serve them, nor do after their works: but you shall utterly overthrow them, and quite break down their images.

25 And you shall serve Yahweh your God, and he shall bless your bread, and your water; and I will take sickness away from the midst of you.

26 There shall nothing miscarry their young, nor be barren, in your land: the number of your days I will fulfill.

27 I will send my fear before you, and will destroy all the people to whom you shall come, and I will make all your enemies turn their backs unto you.

28 And I will send hornets before you, which shall drive out the Hivite, the Canaanite, and the Hittite, from before you.

29 I will not drive them out from before you in one year; lest the land becomes desolate, and the beasts of the field multiply against you.

30 By little and little I will drive them out from before you, until you be increased, and inherit the land.

31 And I will set your bounds from the Red Sea even to the sea of the Philistines, and from the desert unto the river: for I will deliver the inhabitants of the land into your hand; and you shall drive them out before you.

32 You shall make no covenant with them, nor with their gods.

33 They shall not dwell in your land, lest they make you sin against me: for if you serve their gods, it will surely be a snare to you.

Exodus 24

24:1 ¶ And he said to Moses, Come up unto Yahweh, you, and Aaron, Nadab, and Abihu, and seventy of the elders of Israel; and worship you afar off.

2 And Moses alone shall come near Yahweh: but they shall not come near; neither shall the people go up with him.

3 And Moses came and told the people all the words of Yahweh, and all the judgments: and all the people answered with one voice, and said, All the words which Yahweh has said will we do.

4 And Moses wrote all the words of Yahweh, and rose up early in the morning, and built an altar under the hill, and twelve pillars, according to the twelve tribes of Israel.

5 And he sent young men of the children of Israel, which offered burnt offerings, and sacrificed peace offerings of oxen unto Yahweh.

6 And Moses took half of the blood, and put *it* in basins; and half of the blood he sprinkled on the altar.

7 And he took the book of the covenant, and read in the audience of the people: and they said, All that Yahweh has said will we do, and be obedient.

8 And Moses took the blood, and sprinkled *it* on the people, and said, Behold the blood of the covenant, which Yahweh has made with you concerning all these words.

9 ¶ Then went up Moses, and Aaron, Nadab, and Abihu, and seventy of the elders of Israel:

10 And they saw the God of Israel: and *there was* under his feet as it were a paved work of a sapphire stone, and as it were the body of heaven in *his* clearness.

11 And upon the nobles of the children of Israel he laid not his hand: also they saw God, and did eat and drink.

12 ¶ And Yahweh said to Moses, Come up to me into the mount, and be there: and I will give you tables of stone, and a law, and commandments which I have written; that you may teach them.

13 And Moses rose up, and his minister Joshua: and Moses went up into the mount of God.

14 And he said to the elders, Stay you here for us, until we come again to you: and, behold, Aaron and Hur *are* with you: if any man has any matters to do, let him come to them.

15 And Moses went up into the mount, and a cloud covered the mount.

16 And the glory of Yahweh stayed upon mount Sinai, and the cloud covered it six days: and the seventh day he called to Moses out of the midst of the cloud.

Exodus 24

17 And the sight of the glory of Yahweh *was* like devouring fire on the top of the mount in the eyes of the children of Israel.
18 And Moses went into the midst of the cloud, and got him up into the mount: and Moses was in the mount forty days and forty nights.

Exodus 25

25:1 ¶ And Yahweh spoke to Moses, saying,
2 Speak to the children of Israel, that they bring me an offering: of every man that gives it willingly with his heart you shall take my offering.
3 And this *is* the offering which you shall take of them; gold, and silver, and brass,
4 And blue, and purple, and scarlet, and fine linen, and goats' *hair*,
5 And rams' skins dyed red, and badgers' skins, and shittim wood,
6 Oil for the light, spices for anointing oil, and for sweet incense,
7 Onyx stones, and stones to be set in the ephod, and in the breastplate.
8 And let them make me a sanctuary; that I may dwell among them.
9 According to all that I show you, *after* the pattern of the tabernacle, and the pattern of all the instruments thereof, even so shall you make *it*.
10 ¶ And they shall make an ark *of* shittim wood: two cubits and a half *shall be* the length thereof, and a cubit and a half the breadth thereof, and a cubit and a half the height thereof.
11 And you shall overlay it with pure gold, within and without shall you overlay it, and shall make upon it a crown of gold round about.
12 And you shall cast four rings of gold for it, and put *them* in the four corners thereof; and two rings *shall be* in the one side of it, and two rings in the other side of it.
13 And you shall make staves *of* shittim wood, and overlay them with gold.
14 And you shall put the staves into the rings by the sides of the ark, that the ark may be borne with them.
15 The staves shall be in the rings of the ark: they shall not be taken from it.
16 And you shall put into the ark the testimony which I shall give you.
17 And you shall make a mercy seat *of* pure gold: two cubits and a half *shall be* the length thereof, and a cubit and a half the breadth thereof.
18 And you shall make two cherubims *of* gold, *of* beaten work shall you make them, in the two ends of the mercy seat.
19 And make one cherub on the one end, and the other cherub on the other end: *even* of the mercy seat shall you make the cherubims on the two ends thereof.
20 And the cherubims shall stretch forth *their* wings on high, covering the mercy seat with their wings, and their faces *shall look* one to another; toward the mercy seat shall the faces of the cherubims be.
21 And you shall put the mercy seat above upon the ark; and in the ark you shall put the testimony that I shall give you.
22 And there I will meet with you, and I will speak with you from above the mercy seat, from between the two cherubims which *are* upon the ark of the testimony, of all *things* which I will give you in commandment to the children of Israel.
23 ¶ You shall also make a table *of* shittim wood: two cubits *shall be* the length thereof, and a cubit the breadth thereof, and a cubit and a half the height thereof.
24 And you shall overlay it with pure gold, and make thereto a crown of gold round about.
25 And you shall make unto it a border of a hand breadth round about, and you shall make a golden crown to the border thereof round about.
26 And you shall make for it four rings of gold, and put the rings in the four corners that *are* on the four feet thereof.
27 Over against the border shall the rings be for places of the staves to bear the table.
28 And you shall make the staves *of* shittim wood, and overlay them with gold, that the table may be borne with them.
29 And you shall make the dishes thereof, and spoons thereof, and covers thereof, and bowls thereof, to pour therewith: *of* pure gold shall you make them.
30 And you shall set upon the table showbread before me always.
31 ¶ And you shall make a candlestick *of* pure gold: *of* beaten work shall the candlestick be made: his shaft, and his branches, his bowls, his knops, and his flowers, shall be of the same.
32 And six branches shall come out of the sides of it; three branches of the candlestick out of the one side, and three branches of the candlestick out of the other side:
33 Three bowls made like unto almonds, *with* a knop and a flower in one branch; and three bowls made like almonds in the other branch, *with* a knop and a flower: so in the six branches that come out of the candlestick.
34 And in the candlestick *shall be* four bowls made like unto almonds, *with* their knops and their flowers.
35 And *there shall be* a knop under two branches of the same, and a knop under two branches of the same, and a knop under two branches of the same, according to the six branches that proceed out of the candlestick.
36 Their knops and their branches shall be of the same: all it *shall be* one beaten work *of* pure gold.
37 And you shall make the seven lamps thereof: and they shall light the lamps thereof, that they may give light over against it.
38 And the tongs thereof, and the fire-holders thereof, *shall be of* pure gold.
39 *Of* a talent of pure gold shall he make it, with all these vessels.
40 And look that you make *them* after their pattern, which was shown you in the mount.

Exodus 26

26:1 ¶ Moreover you shall make the tabernacle *with* ten curtains *of* fine twined linen, and blue, and purple, and scarlet: *with* cherubims of cunning work shall you make them.

2 The length of one curtain *shall be* eight and twenty cubits, and the breadth of one curtain four cubits: and every one of the curtains shall have one measure.

3 The five curtains shall be coupled together one to another; and *the other* five curtains *shall be* coupled one to another.

4 And you shall make loops of blue upon the edge of the one curtain from the selvedge in the coupling; and likewise shall you make in the utmost edge of *another* curtain, in the coupling of the second.

5 Fifty loops shall you make in the one curtain, and fifty loops shall you make in the edge of the curtain that *is* in the coupling of the second; that the loops may take hold one of another.

6 And you shall make fifty clasps of gold, and couple the curtains together with the clasps: and it shall be one tabernacle.

7 ¶ And you shall make curtains *of* goats' *hair* to be a covering upon the tabernacle: eleven curtains shall you make.

8 The length of one curtain *shall be* thirty cubits, and the breadth of one curtain four cubits: and the eleven curtains *shall be all* of one measure.

9 And you shall couple five curtains by themselves, and six curtains by themselves, and shall double the sixth curtain in the forefront of the tabernacle.

10 And you shall make fifty loops on the edge of the one curtain *that is* outmost in the coupling, and fifty loops in the edge of the curtain which couples the second.

11 And you shall make fifty clasps of brass, and put the clasps into the loops, and couple the tent together, that it may be one.

12 And the remnant that remains of the curtains of the tent, the half curtain that remains, shall hang over the backside of the tabernacle.

13 And a cubit on the one side, and a cubit on the other side of that which remains in the length of the curtains of the tent, it shall hang over the sides of the tabernacle on this side and on that side, to cover it.

14 And you shall make a covering for the tent *of* rams' skins dyed red, and a covering above *of* badgers' skins.

15 ¶ And you shall make boards for the tabernacle *of* shittim wood standing up.

16 Ten cubits *shall be* the length of a board, and a cubit and a half *shall be* the breadth of one board.

17 Two tenons *shall there be* in one board, set in order one against another: thus shall you make for all the boards of the tabernacle.

18 And you shall make the boards for the tabernacle, twenty boards on the south side southward.

19 And you shall make forty sockets of silver under the twenty boards; two sockets under one board for his two tenons, and two sockets under another board for his two tenons.

20 And for the second side of the tabernacle on the north side *there shall be* twenty boards:

21 And their forty sockets *of* silver; two sockets under one board, and two sockets under another board.

22 And for the sides of the tabernacle westward you shall make six boards.

23 And two boards shall you make for the corners of the tabernacle in the two sides.

24 And they shall be coupled together beneath, and they shall be coupled together above the head of it unto one ring: thus shall it be for them both; they shall be for the two corners.

25 And they shall be eight boards, and their sockets *of* silver, sixteen sockets; two sockets under one board, and two sockets under another board.

26 And you shall make bars *of* shittim wood; five for the boards of the one side of the tabernacle,

27 And five bars for the boards of the other side of the tabernacle, and five bars for the boards of the side of the tabernacle, for the two sides westward.

28 And the middle bar in the midst of the boards shall reach from end to end.

29 And you shall overlay the boards with gold, and make their rings *of* gold *for* places for the bars: and you shall overlay the bars with gold.

30 And you shall rear up the tabernacle according to the fashion thereof which was shown you in the mount.

31 ¶ And you shall make a veil *of* blue, and purple, and scarlet, and fine twined linen of cunning work: with cherubims shall it be made:

32 And you shall hang it upon four pillars of shittim *wood* overlaid with gold: their hooks *shall be of* gold, upon the four sockets of silver.

33 And you shall hang up the veil under the clasps, that you may bring in there within the veil the ark of the testimony: and the veil shall divide unto you between the holy *place* and the most holy.

34 And you shall put the mercy seat upon the ark of the testimony in the most holy *place*.

35 And you shall set the table outside the veil, and the candlestick over against the table on the side of the tabernacle toward the south: and you shall put the table on the north side.

36 And you shall make a hanging for the door of the tent, *of* blue, and purple, and scarlet, and fine twined linen, worked with needlework.

37 And you shall make for the hanging five pillars *of* shittim *wood*, and overlay them with gold, *and* their hooks *shall be of* gold: and you shall cast five sockets of brass for them.

Exodus 27

27:1 ¶ And you shall make an altar *of* shittim wood, five cubits long, and five cubits broad; the altar shall be foursquare: and the height thereof *shall be* three cubits.

2 And you shall make the horns of it upon the four corners thereof: his horns shall be of the same: and you shall overlay it with brass.

3 And you shall make his pans to receive his ashes, and his shovels, and his basins, and his meat hooks, and his firepans: all the vessels thereof you shall make *of* brass.

4 And you shall make for it a grate of network *of* brass; and upon the net shall you make four brazen rings in the four corners thereof.

5 And you shall put it under the edge of the altar beneath, that the net may be even to the middle of the altar.

6 And you shall make staves for the altar, staves *of* shittim wood, and overlay them with brass.

7 And the staves shall be put into the rings, and the staves shall be upon the two sides of the altar, to bear it.

8 Hollow with boards shall you make it: as it was shown you in the mount, so shall they make *it*.

9 ¶ And you shall make the court of the tabernacle: for the south side southward *there shall be* hangings for the court *of* fine twined linen of a hundred cubits long for one side:

10 And the twenty pillars thereof and their twenty sockets *shall be of* brass; the hooks of the pillars and their fillets *shall be of* silver.

11 And likewise for the north side in length *there shall be* hangings of a hundred *cubits* long, and his twenty pillars and their twenty sockets *of* brass; the hooks of the pillars and their fillets *of* silver.

12 And *for* the breadth of the court on the west side *shall be* hangings of fifty cubits: their pillars ten, and their sockets ten.

13 And the breadth of the court on the east side eastward *shall be* fifty cubits.

14 The hangings of one side *of the gate shall be* fifteen cubits: their pillars three, and their sockets three.

15 And on the other side *shall be* hangings fifteen *cubits*: their pillars three, and their sockets three.

16 And for the gate of the court *shall be* a hanging of twenty cubits, *of* blue, and purple, and scarlet, and fine twined linen, worked with needlework: *and* their pillars *shall be* four, and their sockets four.

17 All the pillars round about the court *shall be* filleted with silver; their hooks *shall be of* silver, and their sockets *of* brass.

18 The length of the court *shall be* a hundred cubits, and the breadth fifty every where, and the height five cubits *of* fine twined linen, and their sockets *of* brass.

19 All the vessels of the tabernacle in all the service thereof, and all the pins thereof, and all the pins of the court, *shall be of* brass.

20 ¶ And you shall command the children of Israel, that they bring you pure olive oil beaten for the light, to cause the lamp to burn always.

21 In the tabernacle of the congregation outside the veil, which *is* before the testimony, Aaron and his sons shall order it from evening to morning before Yahweh: *it shall be* a statute forever unto their generations on the behalf of the children of Israel.

Exodus 28

28:1 ¶ And take you unto you Aaron your brother, and his sons with him, from among the children of Israel, that he may minister to me in the priest's office, *even* Aaron, Nadab and Abihu, Eleazar and Ithamar, Aaron's sons.

2 And you shall make holy garments for Aaron your brother for glory and for beauty.

3 And you shall speak to all *that are* wise hearted, whom I have filled with the spirit of wisdom, that they may make Aaron's garments to consecrate him, that he may minister to me in the priest's office.

4 And these *are* the garments which they shall make; a breastplate, and an ephod, and a robe, and a broidered coat, a turban, and a girdle: and they shall make holy garments for Aaron your brother, and his sons, that he may minister to me in the priest's office.

5 And they shall take gold, and blue, and purple, and scarlet, and fine linen.

6 ¶ And they shall make the ephod *of* gold, *of* blue, and *of* purple, *of* scarlet, and fine twined linen, with cunning work.

7 It shall have the two shoulder pieces thereof joined at the two edges thereof; and *so* it shall be joined together.

8 And the curious girdle of the ephod, which *is* upon it, shall be of the same, according to the work thereof; *even of* gold, *of* blue, and purple, and scarlet, and fine twined linen.

9 And you shall take two onyx stones, and engrave on them the names of the children of Israel:

10 Six of their names on one stone, and *the other* six names of the rest on the other stone, according to their birth.

11 With the work of an engraver in stone, *like* the engravings of a signet, shall you engrave the two stones with the names of the children of Israel: you shall make them to be set in settings of gold.

12 And you shall put the two stones upon the shoulders of the ephod *for* stones of memorial to the children of Israel: and Aaron shall bear their names before Yahweh upon his two shoulders for a memorial.

13 And you shall make settings *of* gold;

14 And two chains *of* pure gold at the ends; *of* wreathen work shall you make them, and fasten the wreathen chains to the settings.

15 ¶ And you shall make the breastplate of judgment with cunning work; after the work of the ephod you shall make it; *of* gold, *of* blue, and *of* purple, and *of* scarlet, and *of* fine twined linen, shall you make it.

16 Foursquare it shall be *being* doubled; a span *shall be* the length thereof, and a span *shall be* the breadth thereof.

17 And you shall set in it settings of stones, *even* four rows of stones: *the first* row *shall be* a sardius, a topaz, and a carbuncle: *this shall be* the first row.
18 And the second row *shall be* an emerald, a sapphire, and a diamond.
19 And the third row a ligure, an agate, and an amethyst.
20 And the fourth row a beryl, and an onyx, and a jasper: they shall be set in gold in their settings.
21 And the stones shall be with the names of the children of Israel, twelve, according to their names, *like* the engravings of a signet; every one with his name shall they be according to the twelve tribes.
22 And you shall make upon the breastplate chains at the ends *of* wreathen work *of* pure gold.
23 And you shall make upon the breastplate two rings of gold, and shall put the two rings on the two ends of the breastplate.
24 And you shall put the two wreathen *chains* of gold in the two rings *which are* on the ends of the breastplate.
25 And *the other* two ends of the two wreathen *chains* you shall fasten in the two settings, and put *them* on the shoulder pieces of the ephod before it.
26 And you shall make two rings of gold, and you shall put them upon the two ends of the breastplate in the border thereof, which *is* in the side of the ephod inward.
27 And two *other* rings of gold you shall make, and shall put them on the two sides of the ephod underneath, toward the forepart thereof, over against the *other* coupling thereof, above the curious girdle of the ephod.
28 And they shall bind the breastplate by the rings thereof to the rings of the ephod with a lace of blue, that *it* may be above the curious girdle of the ephod, and that the breastplate be not loosed from the ephod.
29 And Aaron shall bear the names of the children of Israel in the breastplate of judgment upon his heart, when he goes in to the holy *place*, for a memorial before Yahweh continually.
30 And you shall put in the breastplate of judgment the Urim and the Thummim; and they shall be upon Aaron's heart, when he goes in before Yahweh: and Aaron shall bear the judgment of the children of Israel upon his heart before Yahweh continually.
31 ¶ And you shall make the robe of the ephod all *of* blue.
32 And there shall be a hole in the top of it, in the midst thereof: it shall have a binding of woven work round about the hole of it, as it were the hole of a corselet, that it be not torn.
33 And *beneath* upon the hem of it you shall make pomegranates *of* blue, and *of* purple, and *of* scarlet, round about the hem thereof; and bells of gold between them round about:
34 A golden bell and a pomegranate, a golden bell and a pomegranate, upon the hem of the robe round about.
35 And it shall be upon Aaron to minister: and his sound shall be heard when he goes in to the holy *place* before Yahweh, and when he comes out, that he dies not.
36 And you shall make a plate *of* pure gold, and engrave upon it, *like* the engravings of a signet, HOLINESS TO YAHWEH.
37 And you shall put it on a blue lace, that it may be upon the turban; upon the forefront of the turban it shall be.
38 And it shall be upon Aaron's forehead, that Aaron may bear the iniquity of the holy things, which the children of Israel shall hallow in all their holy gifts; and it shall be always upon his forehead, that they may be accepted before Yahweh.
39 And you shall embroider the coat of fine linen, and you shall make the turban *of* fine linen, and you shall make the girdle *of* needlework.
40 ¶ And for Aaron's sons you shall make coats, and you shall make for them girdles, and bonnets shall you make for them, for glory and for beauty.
41 And you shall put them upon Aaron your brother, and his sons with him; and shall anoint them, and consecrate them, and sanctify them, that they may minister to me in the priest's office.
42 And you shall make them linen breeches to cover their nakedness; from the loins even to the thighs they shall reach:
43 And they shall be upon Aaron, and upon his sons, when they come in to the tabernacle of the congregation, or when they come near to the altar to minister in the holy *place*: that they bear not iniquity, and die: *it shall be* a statute forever unto him and his seed after him.

Exodus 29

29:1 ¶ And this *is* the thing that you shall do to them to hallow them, to minister unto me in the priest's office: Take one young bullock, and two rams without blemish,
2 And unleavened bread, and cakes unleavened mixed with oil, and wafers unleavened anointed with oil: *of* wheaten flour shall you make them.
3 And you shall put them into one basket, and bring them in the basket, with the bullock and the two rams.
4 And Aaron and his sons you shall bring to the door of the tabernacle of the congregation, and shall wash them with water.
5 And you shall take the garments, and put upon Aaron the coat, and the robe of the ephod, and the ephod, and the breastplate, and gird him with the curious girdle of the ephod:
6 And you shall put the turban upon his head, and put the holy crown upon the turban.
7 Then shall you take the anointing oil, and pour *it* upon his head, and anoint him.
8 And you shall bring his sons, and put coats upon them.
9 And you shall gird them with girdles, Aaron and his sons, and put the bonnets on them: and the priest's office shall be theirs for a perpetual statute: and you shall consecrate Aaron and his sons.
10 And you shall cause a bullock to be brought before the tabernacle of the congregation: and Aaron and his sons shall put their hands upon the head of the bullock.

Exodus 29

11 And you shall kill the bullock before Yahweh, *by* the door of the tabernacle of the congregation.

12 And you shall take of the blood of the bullock, and put *it* upon the horns of the altar with your finger, and pour all the blood beside the bottom of the altar.

13 And you shall take all the fat that covers the inwards, and the lobe *that is* above the liver, and the two kidneys, and the fat that *is* upon them, and burn *them* upon the altar.

14 But the flesh of the bullock, and his skin, and his dung, shall you burn with fire outside the camp: it *is* a sin offering.

15 You shall also take one ram; and Aaron and his sons shall put their hands upon the head of the ram.

16 And you shall slay the ram, and you shall take his blood, and sprinkle *it* round about upon the altar.

17 And you shall cut the ram in pieces, and wash the inwards of him, and his legs, and put *them* unto his pieces, and unto his head.

18 And you shall burn the whole ram upon the altar: it *is* a burnt offering to Yahweh: it *is* a sweet savor, an offering made by fire to Yahweh.

19 And you shall take the other ram; and Aaron and his sons shall put their hands upon the head of the ram.

20 Then shall you kill the ram, and take of his blood, and put *it* upon the tip of the right ear of Aaron, and upon the tip of the right ear of his sons, and upon the thumb of their right hand, and upon the great toe of their right foot, and sprinkle the blood upon the altar round about.

21 And you shall take of the blood that *is* upon the altar, and of the anointing oil, and sprinkle *it* upon Aaron, and upon his garments, and upon his sons, and upon the garments of his sons with him: and he shall be hallowed, and his garments, and his sons, and his sons' garments with him.

22 Also you shall take of the ram the fat and the rump, and the fat that covers the inwards, and the lobe *above* the liver, and the two kidneys, and the fat that *is* upon them, and the right shoulder; for it *is* a ram of consecration:

23 And one loaf of bread, and one cake of oiled bread, and one wafer out of the basket of the unleavened bread that *is* before Yahweh:

24 And you shall put all in the hands of Aaron, and in the hands of his sons; and shall wave them *for* a wave offering before Yahweh.

25 And you shall receive them from their hands, and burn *them* upon the altar for a burnt offering, for a sweet savor before Yahweh: it *is* an offering made by fire unto Yahweh.

26 And you shall take the breast of the ram of Aaron's consecration, and wave it *for* a wave offering before Yahweh: and it shall be your part.

27 And you shall sanctify the breast of the wave offering, and the shoulder of the heave offering, which is waved, and which is heaved up, of the ram of the consecration, *even* of *that* which *is* for Aaron, and of *that* which is for his sons:

28 And it shall be Aaron's and his sons' by a statute forever from the children of Israel: for it *is* a heave offering: and it shall be a heave offering from the children of Israel of the sacrifice of their peace offerings, *even* their heave offering unto Yahweh.

29 And the holy garments of Aaron shall be his sons' after him, to be anointed therein, and to be consecrated in them.

30 *And* that son that is priest in his stead shall put them on seven days, when he comes into the tabernacle of the congregation to minister in the holy *place*.

31 And you shall take the ram of the consecration, and boil his flesh in the holy place.

32 And Aaron and his sons shall eat the flesh of the ram, and the bread that *is* in the basket, *by* the door of the tabernacle of the congregation.

33 And they shall eat those things with which the atonement was made, to consecrate *and* to sanctify them: but a stranger shall not eat *thereof*, because they *are* holy.

34 And if any of the flesh of the consecrations, or of the bread, remains unto the morning, then you shall burn the remainder with fire: it shall not be eaten, because it *is* holy.

35 And thus shall you do to Aaron, and to his sons, according to all *things* which I have commanded you: seven days shall you consecrate them.

36 And you shall offer every day a bullock *for* a sin offering for atonement: and you shall cleanse the altar, when you have made an atonement for it, and you shall anoint it, to sanctify it.

37 Seven days you shall make an atonement for the altar, and sanctify it; and it shall be an altar most holy: whatever touches the altar shall be holy.

38 ¶ Now this *is that* which you shall offer upon the altar; two lambs of the first year day by day continually.

39 The one lamb you shall offer in the morning; and the other lamb you shall offer at evening:

40 And with the one lamb a tenth deal of flour mingled with the fourth part of a hin of beaten oil; and the fourth part of a hin of wine *for* a drink offering.

41 And the other lamb you shall offer at evening, and shall do thereto according to the meat offering of the morning, and according to the drink offering thereof, for a sweet savor, an offering made by fire unto Yahweh.

42 *This shall be* a continual burnt offering throughout your generations *at* the door of the tabernacle of the congregation before Yahweh: where I will meet you, to speak there unto you.

43 And there I will meet with the children of Israel, and *the tabernacle* shall be sanctified by my glory.

44 And I will sanctify the tabernacle of the congregation, and the altar: I will sanctify also both Aaron and his sons, to minister to me in the priest's office.

45 And I will dwell among the children of Israel, and will be their God.

46 And they shall know that I *am* Yahweh their God, that brought them forth out of the land of Egypt, that I may dwell among them: I *am* Yahweh their God.

Exodus 30

30:1 ¶ And you shall make an altar to burn incense upon: *of* shittim wood shall you make it.

2 A cubit *shall be* the length thereof, and a cubit the breadth thereof; foursquare shall it be: and two cubits *shall be* the height thereof: the horns thereof *shall be* of the same.

3 And you shall overlay it with pure gold, the top thereof, and the sides thereof round about, and the horns thereof; and you shall make unto it a crown of gold round about.

4 And two golden rings shall you make unto it under the crown of it, by the two corners thereof, on the two sides of it shall you make *it*; and they shall be for places for the staves to bear it therewith.

5 And you shall make the staves *of* shittim wood, and overlay them with gold.

6 And you shall put it before the veil that *is* by the ark of the testimony, before the mercy seat that *is* over the testimony, where I will meet with you.

7 And Aaron shall burn thereon sweet incense every morning: when he dresses the lamps, he shall burn incense upon it.

8 And when Aaron lights the lamps at evening, he shall burn incense upon it, a perpetual incense before Yahweh throughout your generations.

9 You shall offer no strange incense thereon, nor burnt sacrifice, nor meat offering; neither shall you pour *a* drink offering thereon.

10 And Aaron shall make an atonement upon the horns of it once in a year with the blood of the sin offering of atonement: once in the year shall he make atonement upon it throughout your generations: it *is* most holy unto Yahweh.

11 ¶ And Yahweh spoke to Moses, saying,

12 When you take the sum of the children of Israel after their number, then shall they give every man a ransom for his soul unto Yahweh, when you number them; that there be no plague among them, when *you* number them.

13 This they shall give, every one that passes among them that are numbered, half a shekel after the shekel of the sanctuary: (a shekel *is* twenty gerahs:) a half shekel *shall be* the offering of Yahweh.

14 Every one that passes among them that are numbered, from twenty years old and above, shall give an offering unto Yahweh.

15 The rich shall not give more, and the poor shall not give less than half a shekel, when *they* give an offering unto Yahweh, to make an atonement for your souls.

16 And you shall take the atonement money of the children of Israel, and shall appoint it for the service of the tabernacle of the congregation; that it may be a memorial to the children of Israel before Yahweh, to make an atonement for your souls.

17 ¶ And Yahweh spoke to Moses, saying,

18 You shall also make a laver *of* brass, and his foot *also of* brass, to wash *therewith*: and you shall put it between the tabernacle of the congregation and the altar, and you shall put water therein.

19 For Aaron and his sons shall wash their hands and their feet thereat:

20 When they go into the tabernacle of the congregation, they shall wash with water, that they die not; or when they come near to the altar to minister, to burn offering made by fire unto Yahweh:

21 So they shall wash their hands and their feet, that they die not: and it shall be a statute forever to them, *even* to him and to his seed throughout their generations.

22 ¶ Moreover Yahweh spoke to Moses, saying,

23 Take you also unto you principal spices, of pure myrrh five hundred *shekels*, and of sweet cinnamon half so much, *even* two hundred and fifty *shekels*, and of sweet calamus two hundred and fifty *shekels*,

24 And of cassia five hundred *shekels*, after the shekel of the sanctuary, and of olive oil a hin:

25 And you shall make it an oil of holy ointment, an ointment compound after the art of the apothecary: it shall be a holy anointing oil.

26 And you shall anoint the tabernacle of the congregation therewith, and the ark of the testimony,

27 And the table and all his vessels, and the candlestick and his vessels, and the altar of incense,

28 And the altar of burnt offering with all his vessels, and the basin and his foot.

29 And you shall sanctify them, that they may be most holy: whatever touches them shall be holy.

30 And you shall anoint Aaron and his sons, and consecrate them, that *they* may minister unto me in the priest's office.

31 And you shall speak to the children of Israel, saying, This shall be a holy anointing oil unto me throughout your generations.

32 Upon man's flesh shall it not be poured, neither shall you make *any other* like it, after the composition of it: it *is* holy, *and* it shall be holy unto you.

33 Whoever compounds *any* like it, or whoever puts *any* of it upon a stranger, shall even be cut off from his people.

34 And Yahweh said to Moses, Take unto you sweet spices, stacte, and onycha, and galbanum; *these* sweet spices with pure frankincense: of each shall there be a like *weight*:

35 And you shall make it a perfume, a confection after the art of the apothecary, tempered together, pure *and* holy:

36 And you shall beat *some* of it very small, and put of it before the testimony in the tabernacle of the congregation, where I will meet with you: it shall be unto you most holy.

37 And *as for* the perfume which you shall make, you shall not make to yourselves according to the composition thereof: it shall be unto you holy for Yahweh.

38 Whoever shall make like unto that, to smell thereto, shall even be cut off from his people.

Exodus 31

31:1 ¶ And Yahweh spoke to Moses, saying,
2 See, I have called by name Bezaleel the son of Uri, the son of Hur, of the tribe of Judah:
3 And I have filled him with the spirit of God, in wisdom, and in understanding, and in knowledge, and in all manner of workmanship,
4 To devise cunning works, to work in gold, and in silver, and in brass,
5 And in cutting of stones, to set *them*, and in carving of timber, to work in all manner of workmanship.
6 And I, behold, I have given with him Aholiab, the son of Ahisamach, of the tribe of Dan: and in the hearts of all that are wise hearted I have put wisdom, that they may make all that I have commanded you;
7 The tabernacle of the congregation, and the ark of the testimony, and the mercy seat that *is* thereupon, and all the furniture of the tabernacle,
8 And the table and his furniture, and the pure candlestick with all his furniture, and the altar of incense,
9 And the altar of burnt offering with all his furniture, and the laver and his foot,
10 And the cloths of service, and the holy garments for Aaron the priest, and the garments of his sons, to minister in the priest's office,
11 And the anointing oil, and sweet incense for the holy *place*: according to all that I have commanded you shall they do.
12 ¶ And Yahweh spoke to Moses, saying,
13 Speak you also to the children of Israel, saying, Truly my sabbaths you shall keep: for it *is* a sign between me and you throughout your generations; that *you* may know that I *am* Yahweh that does sanctify you.
14 You shall keep the sabbath therefore; for it *is* holy unto you: every one that defiles it shall surely be put to death: for whoever does *any* work therein, that soul shall be cut off from among his people.
15 Six days may work be done; but in the seventh *is* the sabbath of rest, holy to Yahweh: whoever does *any* work in the sabbath day, he shall surely be put to death.
16 Therefore the children of Israel shall keep the sabbath, to observe the sabbath throughout their generations, *for* a perpetual covenant.
17 It *is* a sign between me and the children of Israel forever: for *in* six days Yahweh made heaven and earth, and on the seventh day he rested, and was refreshed.
18 And he gave to Moses, when he had made an end of speaking with him upon mount Sinai, two tables of testimony, tables of stone, written with the finger of God.

Exodus 32

32:1 ¶ And when the people saw that Moses delayed to come down out of the mount, the people gathered themselves together unto Aaron, and said to him, Arise, make us gods, which shall go before us; for *as for* this Moses, the man that brought us up out of the land of Egypt, we know not what has become of him.
2 And Aaron said to them, Break off the golden earrings, which *are* in the ears of your wives, of your sons, and of your daughters, and bring *them* to me.
3 And all the people broke off the golden earrings which *were* in their ears, and brought *them* to Aaron.
4 And he received *them* from their hands, and fashioned it with an engraving tool, after he had made it a molten calf: and they said, These *are* your gods, O Israel, which brought you up out of the land of Egypt.
5 And when Aaron saw *it*, he built an altar before it; and Aaron made proclamation, and said, Tomorrow *is* a feast to Yahweh.
6 And they rose up early on the next day, and offered burnt offerings, and brought peace offerings; and the people sat down to eat and to drink, and rose up to play.
7 ¶ And Yahweh said to Moses, Go, get you down; for your people, which you brought out of the land of Egypt, have corrupted *themselves*:
8 They have turned aside quickly out of the way which I commanded them: they have made them a molten calf, and have worshipped it, and have sacrificed thereunto, and said, These *are* your gods, O Israel, which have brought you up out of the land of Egypt.
9 And Yahweh said to Moses, I have seen this people, and, behold, it *is* a stiffnecked people:
10 Now therefore let me alone, that my wrath may grow hot against them, and that I may consume them: and I will make of you a great nation.
11 And Moses sought Yahweh his God, and said, Yahweh, why does your wrath grow hot against your people, which you have brought forth out of the land of Egypt with great power, and with a mighty hand?
12 Why should the Egyptians speak, and say, For mischief did he bring them out, to slay them in the mountains, and to consume them from the face of the earth? Turn from your fierce wrath, and repent of this evil against your people.
13 Remember Abraham, Isaac, and Israel, your servants, to whom you swore by your own self, and said to them, I will multiply your seed as the stars of heaven, and all this land that I have spoken of will I give to your seed, and they shall inherit *it* forever.
14 And Yahweh repented of the evil which he thought to do to his people.
15 ¶ And Moses turned, and went down from the mount, and the two tables of the testimony *were* in his hand: the tables *were* written on both their sides; on the one side and on the other *were* they written.
16 And the tables *were* the work of God, and the writing *was* the writing of God, engraved upon the tables.
17 And when Joshua heard the noise of the people as they shouted, he said to Moses, *There is* a noise of war in the camp.
18 And he said, *It is* not the voice of *them that* shout for mastery, neither *is it* the voice of *them that* cry for being overcome: *but* the noise of *them that* sing do I hear.
19 And it came to pass, as soon as he came near to the camp, that he saw the calf, and the dancing: and Moses' anger grew hot, and he cast the tables out of his hands, and broke them beneath the mount.

20 And he took the calf which they had made, and burnt *it* in the fire, and ground *it* to powder, and scattered *it* upon the water, and made the children of Israel drink *of it*.

21 ¶ And Moses said to Aaron, What did this people unto you, that you have brought so great a sin upon them?

22 And Aaron said, Let not the anger of my lord grow hot: you know the people, that they *are set* on mischief.

23 For they said to me, Make us gods, which shall go before us: for *as for* this Moses, the man that brought us up out of the land of Egypt, we know not what has become of him.

24 And I said to them, Whoever has any gold, let them break *it* off. So they gave *it to* me: then I cast it into the fire, and there came out this calf.

25 And when Moses saw that the people were naked; (for Aaron had made them naked to *their* shame among their enemies:)

26 Then Moses stood in the gate of the camp, and said, Who *is* on Yahweh's side? *let him come* to me. And all the sons of Levi gathered themselves together unto him.

27 And he said to them, Thus says Yahweh God of Israel, Put every man his sword by his side, *and* go in and out from gate to gate throughout the camp, and slay every man his brother, and every man his companion, and every man his neighbor.

28 And the children of Levi did according to the word of Moses: and there fell of the people that day about three thousand men.

29 For Moses had said, Consecrate yourselves today to Yahweh, even every man upon his son, and upon his brother; that he may bestow upon you a blessing this day.

30 ¶ And it came to pass on the next day, that Moses said to the people, You have sinned a great sin: and now I will go up unto Yahweh; perhaps I shall make an atonement for your sin.

31 And Moses returned unto Yahweh, and said, Oh, these people have sinned a great sin, and have made them gods of gold.

32 Yet now, if you will forgive their sin—; and if not, blot me, I pray you, out of your book which you have written.

33 And Yahweh said to Moses, Whoever has sinned against me, him will I blot out of my book.

34 Therefore now go, lead the people to *the place* of which I have spoken to you: behold, my Angel shall go before you: nevertheless in the day when I visit I will visit their sin upon them.

35 And Yahweh plagued the people, because they made the calf, which Aaron made.

Exodus 33

33:1 ¶ And Yahweh said to Moses, Depart, *and* go up away, you and the people which you have brought up out of the land of Egypt, to the land which I swore to Abraham, to Isaac, and to Jacob, saying, Unto your seed will I give it:

2 And I will send an angel before you; and I will drive out the Canaanite, the Amorite, and the Hittite, and the Perizzite, the Hivite, and the Jebusite:

3 Unto a land flowing with milk and honey: for I will not go up in the midst of you; for you *are* a stiffnecked people: lest I consume you in the way.

4 And when the people heard these evil tidings, they mourned: and no man did put on him his ornaments.

5 For Yahweh had said to Moses, Say to the children of Israel, You *are* a stiffnecked people: I will come up into the midst of you in a moment, and consume you: therefore now put off your ornaments from you, that I may know what to do to you.

6 And the children of Israel stripped themselves of their ornaments by the mount Horeb.

7 ¶ And Moses took the tabernacle, and pitched it outside the camp, afar off from the camp, and called it the Tabernacle of the congregation. And it came to pass, *that* every one which sought Yahweh went out to the tabernacle of the congregation, which *was* outside the camp.

8 And it came to pass, when Moses went out to the tabernacle, *that* all the people rose up, and stood every man *at* his tent door, and looked after Moses, until he had gone into the tabernacle.

9 And it came to pass, as Moses entered into the tabernacle, the cloudy pillar descended, and stood *at* the door of the tabernacle, and *Yahweh* talked with Moses.

10 And all the people saw the cloudy pillar stand *at* the tabernacle door: and all the people rose up and worshipped, every man *in* his tent door.

11 And Yahweh spoke to Moses face to face, as a man speaks to his friend. And he turned again into the camp: but his servant Joshua, the son of Nun, a young man, departed not out of the tabernacle.

12 ¶ And Moses said unto Yahweh, See, you say to me, Bring up this people and you have not let me know whom you will send with me. Yet you have said, I know you by name, and you have also found grace in my sight.

13 Now therefore, I pray you, if I have found grace in your sight, show me now your way, that I may know you, that I may find grace in your sight: and consider that this nation *is* your people.

14 And he said, My presence shall go *with you*, and I will give you rest.

15 And he said to him, If your presence goes not *with me*, carry us not up away.

16 For wherein shall it be known here that I and your people have found grace in your sight? *is it* not in that you go with us? so shall we be separated, I and your people, from all the people that *are* upon the face of the earth.

17 And Yahweh said to Moses, I will do this thing also that you have spoken: for you have found grace in my sight, and I know you by name.

18 And he said, I beseech you, show me your glory.

Exodus 33

19 And he said, I will make all my goodness pass before you, and I will proclaim the name of Yahweh before you; and will be gracious to whom I will be gracious, and will show mercy on whom I will show mercy.
20 And he said, You can not see my face: for there shall no man see me, and live.
21 And Yahweh said, Behold, *there is* a place by me, and you shall stand upon a rock:
22 And it shall come to pass, while my glory passes by, that I will put you in a cleft of the rock, and will cover you with my hand while I pass by:
23 And I will take away my hand, and you shall see my back parts: but my face shall not be seen.

Exodus 34

34:1 ¶ And Yahweh said to Moses, Hew you two tables of stone like unto the first: and I will write upon *these* tables the words that were in the first tables, which you broke.
2 And be ready in the morning, and come up in the morning to mount Sinai, and present yourself there to me in the top of the mount.
3 And no man shall come up with you, neither let any man be seen throughout all the mount; neither let the flocks nor herds feed before that mount.
4 And he hewed two tables of stone like unto the first; and Moses rose up early in the morning, and went up to mount Sinai, as Yahweh had commanded him, and took in his hand the two tables of stone.
5 ¶ And Yahweh descended in the cloud, and stood with him there, and proclaimed the name of Yahweh.
6 And Yahweh passed by before him, and proclaimed, Yahweh, Yahweh God, merciful and gracious, longsuffering, and abundant in goodness and truth,
7 Keeping mercy for thousands, forgiving iniquity and transgression and sin, and that will by no means clear *the guilty*; visiting the iniquity of the fathers upon the children, and upon the children's children, to the third and to the fourth *generation*.
8 And Moses made haste, and bowed his head toward the earth, and worshipped.
9 And he said, If now I have found grace in your sight, O Lord, let my Lord, I pray you, go among us; for it *is* a stiffnecked people; and pardon our iniquity and our sin, and take us for your inheritance.
10 ¶ And he said, Behold, I make a covenant: before all your people I will do marvels, such as have not been done in all the earth, nor in any nation: and all the people among which you *are* shall see the work of Yahweh: for it *is* an awesome thing that I will do with you.
11 Observe you that which I command you this day: behold, I drive out before you the Amorite, and the Canaanite, and the Hittite, and the Perizzite, and the Hivite, and the Jebusite.
12 Take heed to yourself, lest you make a covenant with the inhabitants of the land where you go, lest it be for a snare in the midst of you:
13 But you shall destroy their altars, break their images, and cut down their groves:
14 For you shall worship no other god: for Yahweh, whose name *is* Jealous, *is* a jealous God:
15 Lest you make a covenant with the inhabitants of the land, and they go a whoring after their gods, and do sacrifice to their gods, and *one* calls you, and you eat of his sacrifice;
16 And you take of their daughters unto your sons, and their daughters go a whoring after their gods, and make your sons go a whoring after their gods.
17 You shall make you no molten gods.
18 ¶ The feast of unleavened bread shall you keep. Seven days you shall eat unleavened bread, as I commanded you, in the time of the month *of* Abib: for in the month *of* Abib you came out from Egypt.
19 All that opens the womb *is* mine; and every firstborn among your cattle, *whether* ox or sheep, *that is* male.
20 But the firstborn of a donkey you shall redeem with a lamb: and if you redeem *him* not, then shall you break his neck. All the firstborn of your sons you shall redeem. And none shall appear before me empty.
21 Six days you shall work, but on the seventh day you shall rest: in earing time and in harvest you shall rest.
22 And you shall observe the feast of weeks, of the firstfruits of wheat harvest, and the feast of ingathering at the year's end.
23 Three times in the year shall all your men children appear before the Lord Yahweh, the God of Israel.
24 For I will cast out the nations before you, and enlarge your borders: neither shall any man desire your land, when you shall go up to appear before Yahweh your God three times in the year.
25 You shall not offer the blood of my sacrifice with leaven; neither shall the sacrifice of the feast of the passover be left unto the morning.
26 The first of the firstfruits of your land you shall bring to the house of Yahweh your God. You shall not boil a kid in his mother's milk.
27 And Yahweh said to Moses, Write you these words: for after the tenor of these words I have made a covenant with you and with Israel.
28 ¶ And he was there with Yahweh forty days and forty nights; he did neither eat bread, nor drink water. And he wrote upon the tables the words of the covenant, the ten commandments.
29 And it came to pass, when Moses came down from mount Sinai with the two tables of testimony in Moses' hand, when he came down from the mount, that Moses knew not that the skin of his face shone while he talked with him.
30 And when Aaron and all the children of Israel saw Moses, behold, the skin of his face shone; and they were afraid to come near him.
31 And Moses called to them; and Aaron and all the rulers of the congregation returned to him: and Moses talked with them.
32 And afterward all the children of Israel came nigh: and he gave them in commandment all that Yahweh had spoken with him in mount Sinai.
33 And *until* Moses had finished speaking with them, he put a veil on his face.

34 But when Moses went in before Yahweh to speak with him, he took the veil off, until he came out. And he came out, and spoke to the children of Israel *that* which he was commanded.

35 And the children of Israel saw the face of Moses, that the skin of Moses' face shone: and Moses put the veil upon his face again, until he went in to speak with him.

Exodus 35

35:1 ¶ And Moses gathered all the congregation of the children of Israel together, and said to them, These *are* the words which Yahweh has commanded, that *you* should do them.

2 Six days shall work be done, but on the seventh day there shall be to you a holy day, a sabbath of rest to Yahweh: whoever does work therein shall be put to death.

3 You shall kindle no fire throughout your habitations on the sabbath day.

4 And Moses spoke to all the congregation of the children of Israel, saying, This *is* the thing which Yahweh commanded, saying,

5 Take you from among you an offering unto Yahweh: whoever *is* of a willing heart, let him bring it, an offering of Yahweh; gold, and silver, and brass,

6 And blue, and purple, and scarlet, and fine linen, and goats' *hair*,

7 And rams' skins dyed red, and badgers' skins, and shittim wood,

8 And oil for the light, and spices for anointing oil, and for the sweet incense,

9 And onyx stones, and stones to be set for the ephod, and for the breastplate.

10 And every wise hearted among you shall come, and make all that Yahweh has commanded;

11 The tabernacle, his tent, and his covering, his clasps, and his boards, his bars, his pillars, and his sockets,

12 The ark, and the staves thereof, *with* the mercy seat, and the veil of the covering,

13 The table, and his staves, and all his vessels, and the showbread,

14 The candlestick also for the light, and his furniture, and his lamps, with the oil for the light,

15 And the incense altar, and his staves, and the anointing oil, and the sweet incense, and the hanging for the door at the entering in of the tabernacle,

16 The altar of burnt offering, with his brazen grate, his staves, and all his vessels, the laver and his foot,

17 The hangings of the court, his pillars, and their sockets, and the hanging for the door of the court,

18 The pins of the tabernacle, and the pins of the court, and their cords,

19 The cloths of service, to do service in the holy *place*, the holy garments for Aaron the priest, and the garments of his sons, to minister in the priest's office.

20 ¶ And all the congregation of the children of Israel departed from the presence of Moses.

21 And they came, every one whose heart stirred him up, and every one whom his spirit made willing, *and* they brought Yahweh's offering to the work of the tabernacle of the congregation, and for all his service, and for the holy garments.

22 And they came, both men and women, as many as were willing hearted, *and* brought bracelets, and earrings, and rings, and tablets, all jewels of gold: and every man that offered *offered* an offering of gold unto Yahweh.

23 And every man, with whom was found blue, and purple, and scarlet, and fine linen, and goats' *hair*, and red skins of rams, and badgers' skins, brought *them*.

24 Every one that did offer an offering of silver and brass brought Yahweh's offering: and every man, with whom was found shittim wood for any work of the service, brought *it*.

25 And all the women that were wise hearted did spin with their hands, and brought that which they had spun, *both* of blue, and of purple, *and* of scarlet, and of fine linen.

26 And all the women whose heart stirred them up in wisdom spun goats' *hair*.

27 And the rulers brought onyx stones, and stones to be set, for the ephod, and for the breastplate;

28 And spice, and oil for the light, and for the anointing oil, and for the sweet incense.

29 The children of Israel brought a willing offering unto Yahweh, every man and woman, whose heart made them willing to bring for all manner of work, which Yahweh had commanded to be made by the hand of Moses.

30 ¶ And Moses said to the children of Israel, See, Yahweh has called by name Bezaleel the son of Uri, the son of Hur, of the tribe of Judah;

31 And he has filled him with the spirit of God, in wisdom, in understanding, and in knowledge, and in all manner of workmanship;

32 And to devise curious works, to work in gold, and in silver, and in brass,

33 And in the cutting of stones, to set *them*, and in carving of wood, to make any manner of cunning work.

34 And he has put in his heart that he may teach, *both* he, and Aholiab, the son of Ahisamach, of the tribe of Dan.

35 Them has he filled with wisdom of heart, to work all manner of work, of the engraver, and of the cunning workman, and of the embroiderer, in blue, and in purple, in scarlet, and in fine linen, and of the weaver, *even* of them that do any work, and of those that devise cunning work.

Exodus 36

36:1 ¶ Then worked Bezaleel and Aholiab, and every wise hearted man, in whom Yahweh put wisdom and understanding to know how to work all manner of work for the service of the sanctuary, according to all that Yahweh had commanded.

Exodus 36

2 And Moses called Bezaleel and Aholiab, and every wise hearted man, in whose heart Yahweh had put wisdom, *even* every one whose heart stirred him up to come unto the work to do it:

3 And they received from Moses all the offering, which the children of Israel had brought for the work of the service of the sanctuary, to make it *therewith*. And they brought yet to him free offerings every morning.

4 And all the wise men, that worked all the work of the sanctuary, came every man from his work which they made;

5 And they spoke to Moses, saying, The people bring much more than enough for the service of the work, which Yahweh commanded to make.

6 And Moses gave commandment, and they caused it to be proclaimed throughout the camp, saying, Let neither man nor woman make any more work for the offering of the sanctuary. So the people were restrained from bringing.

7 For the goods they had was sufficient for all the work to make it, and too much.

8 ¶ And every wise hearted man among them that worked the work of the tabernacle made ten curtains *of* fine twined linen, and blue, and purple, and scarlet: *with* cherubims of cunning work made he them.

9 The length of one curtain *was* twenty and eight cubits, and the breadth of one curtain four cubits: the curtains *were* all of one size.

10 And he coupled the five curtains one to another: and *the other* five curtains he coupled one to another.

11 And he made loops of blue on the edge of one curtain from the selvedge in the coupling: likewise he made in the outermost side of *another* curtain, in the coupling of the second.

12 Fifty loops made he in one curtain, and fifty loops made he in the edge of the curtain which *was* in the coupling of the second: the loops held one *curtain* to another.

13 And he made fifty clasps of gold, and coupled the curtains one to another with the clasps: so it became one tabernacle.

14 ¶ And he made curtains *of* goats' *hair* for the tent over the tabernacle: eleven curtains he made them.

15 The length of one curtain *was* thirty cubits, and four cubits *was* the breadth of one curtain: the eleven curtains *were* of one size.

16 And he coupled five curtains by themselves, and six curtains by themselves.

17 And he made fifty loops upon the outermost edge of the curtain in the coupling, and fifty loops made he upon the edge of the curtain which couples the second.

18 And he made fifty clasps *of* brass to couple the tent together, that it might be one.

19 And he made a covering for the tent *of* rams' skins dyed red, and a covering *of* badgers' skins above *that*.

20 And he made boards for the tabernacle *of* shittim wood, standing up.

21 The length of a board *was* ten cubits, and the breadth of a board one cubit and a half.

22 One board had two tenons, equally distant one from another: thus did he make for all the boards of the tabernacle.

23 And he made boards for the tabernacle; twenty boards for the south side southward:

24 And forty sockets of silver he made under the twenty boards; two sockets under one board for his two tenons, and two sockets under another board for his two tenons.

25 And for the other side of the tabernacle, *which is* toward the north corner, he made twenty boards,

26 And their forty sockets of silver; two sockets under one board, and two sockets under another board.

27 And for the sides of the tabernacle westward he made six boards.

28 And two boards made he for the corners of the tabernacle in the two sides.

29 And they were coupled beneath, and coupled together at the head thereof, to one ring: thus he did to both of them in both the corners.

30 And there were eight boards; and their sockets *were* sixteen sockets of silver, under every board two sockets.

31 And he made bars of shittim wood; five for the boards of the one side of the tabernacle,

32 And five bars for the boards of the other side of the tabernacle, and five bars for the boards of the tabernacle for the sides westward.

33 And he made the middle bar to shoot through the boards from the one end to the other.

34 And he overlaid the boards with gold, and made their rings *of* gold *to be* places for the bars, and overlaid the bars with gold.

35 ¶ And he made a veil *of* blue, and purple, and scarlet, and fine twined linen: *with* cherubims made he it of cunning work.

36 And he made thereunto four pillars *of* shittim *wood*, and overlaid them with gold: their hooks *were of* gold; and he cast for them four sockets of silver.

37 And he made a hanging for the tabernacle door *of* blue, and purple, and scarlet, and fine twined linen, of needlework;

38 And the five pillars of it with their hooks: and he overlaid their capitals and their fillets with gold: but their five sockets *were of* brass.

Exodus 37

37:1 ¶ And Bezaleel made the ark *of* shittim wood: two cubits and a half *was* the length of it, and a cubit and a half the breadth of it, and a cubit and a half the height of it:

2 And he overlaid it with pure gold within and without, and made a crown of gold to it round about.

3 And he cast for it four rings of gold, *to be set* by the four corners of it; even two rings upon the one side of it, and two rings upon the other side of it.

4 And he made staves *of* shittim wood, and overlaid them with gold.

5 And he put the staves into the rings by the sides of the ark, to bear the ark.

6 And he made the mercy seat *of* pure gold: two cubits and a half *was* the length thereof, and one cubit and a half the breadth thereof.

7 And he made two cherubims *of* gold, beaten out of one piece made he them, on the two ends of the mercy seat;

8 One cherub on the end on this side, and another cherub on the *other* end on that side: out of the mercy seat made he the cherubims on the two ends thereof.

9 And the cherubims spread out *their* wings on high, *and* covered with their wings over the mercy seat, with their faces one to another; *even* to the mercy seat were the faces of the cherubims.

10 ¶ And he made the table *of* shittim wood: two cubits *was* the length thereof, and a cubit the breadth thereof, and a cubit and a half the height thereof:

11 And he overlaid it with pure gold, and made thereunto a crown of gold round about.

12 Also he made thereunto a border of a handbreadth round about; and made a crown of gold for the border thereof round about.

13 And he cast for it four rings of gold, and put the rings upon the four corners that *were* in the four feet thereof.

14 Over against the border were the rings, the places for the staves to bear the table.

15 And he made the staves *of* shittim wood, and overlaid them with gold, to bear the table.

16 And he made the vessels which *were* upon the table, his dishes, and his spoons, and his bowls, and his covers to cover therewith, *of* pure gold.

17 And he made the candlestick *of* pure gold: *of* beaten work made he the candlestick; his shaft, and his branch, his bowls, his knops, and his flowers, were of the same:

18 And six branches going out of the sides thereof; three branches of the candlestick out of the one side thereof, and three branches of the candlestick out of the other side thereof:

19 Three bowls made after the fashion of almonds in one branch, a knop and a flower; and three bowls made like almonds in another branch, a knop and a flower: so throughout the six branches going out of the candlestick.

20 And in the candlestick *were* four bowls made like almonds, his knops, and his flowers:

21 And a knop under two branches of the same, and a knop under two branches of the same, and a knop under two branches of the same, according to the six branches going out of it.

22 Their knops and their branches were of the same: all of it *was* one beaten work *of* pure gold.

23 And he made his seven lamps, and his snuffers, and his firepans, *of* pure gold.

24 *Of* a talent of pure gold made he it, and all the vessels thereof.

25 ¶ And he made the incense altar *of* shittim wood: the length of it *was* a cubit, and the breadth of it a cubit; *it was* foursquare; and two cubits *was* the height of it; the horns thereof were of the same.

26 And he overlaid it with pure gold, *both* the top of it, and the sides thereof round about, and the horns of it: also he made to it a crown of gold round about.

27 And he made two rings of gold for it under the crown thereof, by the two corners of it, upon the two sides thereof, to be places for the staves to bear it therewith.

28 And he made the staves *of* shittim wood, and overlaid them with gold.

29 And he made the holy anointing oil, and the pure incense of sweet spices, according to the work of the apothecary.

Exodus 38

38:1 ¶ And he made the altar of burnt offering *of* shittim wood: five cubits *was* the length thereof, and five cubits the breadth thereof; *it was* foursquare; and three cubits the height thereof.

2 And he made the horns thereof on the four corners of it; the horns thereof were of the same: and he overlaid it with brass.

3 And he made all the vessels of the altar, the pots, and the shovels, and the basins, *and* the meat hooks, and the firepans: all the vessels thereof made he *of* brass.

4 And he made for the altar a brazen grate of network under the edge thereof beneath to the middle of it.

5 And he cast four rings for the four ends of the grate of brass, *to be* places for the staves.

6 And he made the staves *of* shittim wood, and overlaid them with brass.

7 And he put the staves into the rings on the sides of the altar, to bear it therewith; he made the altar hollow with boards.

8 And he made the laver *of* brass, and the foot of it *of* brass, of the looking glasses of *the women* assembling, which assembled *at* the door of the tabernacle of the congregation.

9 ¶ And he made the court: on the south side southward the hangings of the court *were of* fine twined linen, a hundred cubits:

10 Their pillars *were* twenty, and their brazen sockets twenty; the hooks of the pillars and their fillets *were of* silver.

11 And for the north side *the hangings were* a hundred cubits, their pillars *were* twenty, and their sockets of brass twenty; the hooks of the pillars and their fillets *of* silver.

12 And for the west side *were* hangings of fifty cubits, their pillars ten, and their sockets ten; the hooks of the pillars and their fillets *of* silver.

13 And for the east side eastward fifty cubits.

14 The hangings of the one side *of the gate were* fifteen cubits; their pillars three, and their sockets three.

15 And for the other side of the court gate, on this hand and that hand, *were* hangings of fifteen cubits; their pillars three, and their sockets three.

16 All the hangings of the court round about *were* of fine twined linen.

17 And the sockets for the pillars *were of* brass; the hooks of the pillars and their fillets *of* silver; and the overlaying of their capitals *of* silver; and all the pillars of the court *were* filleted with silver.

Exodus 38

18 And the hanging for the gate of the court *was* needlework, *of* blue, and purple, and scarlet, and fine twined linen: and twenty cubits *was* the length, and the height in the breadth *was* five cubits, answerable to the hangings of the court.
19 And their pillars *were* four, and their sockets *of* brass four; their hooks *of* silver, and the overlaying of their capitals and their fillets *of* silver.
20 And all the pins of the tabernacle, and of the court round about, *were of* brass.
21 ¶ This is the sum of the tabernacle, *even* of the tabernacle of testimony, as it was counted, according to the commandment of Moses, *for* the service of the Levites, by the hand of Ithamar, son of Aaron the priest.
22 And Bezaleel the son of Uri, the son of Hur, of the tribe of Judah, made all that Yahweh commanded Moses.
23 And with him *was* Aholiab, son of Ahisamach, of the tribe of Dan, an engraver, and a cunning workman, and an embroiderer in blue, and in purple, in scarlet, and fine linen.
24 All the gold that was occupied for the work in all the work of the holy *place*, even the gold of the offering, was twenty and nine talents, and seven hundred and thirty shekels, after the shekel of the sanctuary.
25 And the silver of them that were numbered of the congregation *was* a hundred talents, and a thousand seven hundred and threescore and fifteen shekels, after the shekel of the sanctuary:
26 A bekah for every man, *that is*, half a shekel, after the shekel of the sanctuary, for every one that went to be numbered, from twenty years old and upward, for six hundred thousand and three thousand and five hundred and fifty *men*.
27 And of the hundred talents of silver were cast the sockets of the sanctuary, and the sockets of the veil; a hundred sockets of the hundred talents, a talent for a socket.
28 And of the thousand seven hundred seventy and five shekels he made hooks for the pillars, and overlaid their capitals, and filleted them.
29 And the brass of the offering *was* seventy talents, and two thousand and four hundred shekels.
30 And therewith he made the sockets to the door of the tabernacle of the congregation, and the brazen altar, and the brazen grate for it, and all the vessels of the altar,
31 And the sockets of the court round about, and the sockets of the court gate, and all the pins of the tabernacle, and all the pins of the court round about.

Exodus 39

39:1 ¶ And of the blue, and purple, and scarlet, they made cloths of service, to do service in the holy *place*, and made the holy garments for Aaron; as Yahweh commanded Moses.
2 And he made the ephod *of* gold, blue, and purple, and scarlet, and fine twined linen.
3 And they did beat the gold into thin plates, and cut *it into* wires, to work *it* in the blue, and in the purple, and in the scarlet, and in the fine linen, *with* cunning work.
4 They made shoulder pieces for it, to couple *it* together: by the two edges was it coupled together.
5 And the curious girdle of his ephod, that *was* upon it, *was* of the same, according to the work thereof; *of* gold, blue, and purple, and scarlet, and fine twined linen; as Yahweh commanded Moses.
6 And they worked onyx stones enclosed in settings of gold, graven, as signets are graven, with the names of the children of Israel.
7 And he put them on the shoulders of the ephod, *that they should be* stones for a memorial to the children of Israel; as Yahweh commanded Moses.
8 And he made the breastplate *of* cunning work, like the work of the ephod; *of* gold, blue, and purple, and scarlet, and fine twined linen.
9 It was foursquare; they made the breastplate double: a span *was* the length thereof, and a span the breadth thereof, *being* doubled.
10 And they set in it four rows of stones: *the first* row *was* a sardius, a topaz, and a carbuncle: this *was* the first row.
11 And the second row, an emerald, a sapphire, and a diamond.
12 And the third row, a ligure, an agate, and an amethyst.
13 And the fourth row, a beryl, an onyx, and a jasper: *they were* enclosed in settings of gold in their enclosures.
14 And the stones *were* according to the names of the children of Israel, twelve, according to their names, *like* the engravings of a signet, every one with his name, according to the twelve tribes.
15 And they made upon the breastplate chains at the ends, *of* wreathen work *of* pure gold.
16 And they made two settings *of* gold, and two gold rings; and put the two rings in the two ends of the breastplate.
17 And they put the two wreathen chains of gold in the two rings on the ends of the breastplate.
18 And the two ends of the two wreathen chains they fastened in the two settings, and put them on the shoulder pieces of the ephod, before it.
19 And they made two rings of gold, and put *them* on the two ends of the breastplate, upon the border of it, which *was* on the side of the ephod inward.
20 And they made two *other* golden rings, and put them on the two sides of the ephod underneath, toward the forepart of it, over against the *other* coupling thereof, above the curious girdle of the ephod.
21 And they did bind the breastplate by his rings unto the rings of the ephod with a lace of blue, that it might be above the curious girdle of the ephod, and that the breastplate might not be loosed from the ephod; as Yahweh commanded Moses.
22 And he made the robe of the ephod *of* woven work, all *of* blue.

23 And *there was* a hole in the midst of the robe, as the hole of an corselet, *with* a band round about the hole, that it should not tear.
24 And they made upon the hems of the robe pomegranates *of* blue, and purple, and scarlet, *and* twined *linen.*
25 And they made bells *of* pure gold, and put the bells between the pomegranates upon the hem of the robe, round about between the pomegranates;
26 A bell and a pomegranate, a bell and a pomegranate, round about the hem of the robe to minister *in*; as Yahweh commanded Moses.
27 And they made coats *of* fine linen *of* woven work for Aaron, and for his sons,
28 And a turban *of* fine linen, and goodly bonnets *of* fine linen, and linen breeches *of* fine twined linen,
29 And a sash *of* fine twined linen, and blue, and purple, and scarlet, *of* needlework; as Yahweh commanded Moses.
30 And they made the plate of the holy crown *of* pure gold, and wrote upon it a writing, *like to* the engravings of a signet, HOLINESS TO YAHWEH.
31 And they tied to it a lace of blue, to fasten *it* on high upon the turban; as Yahweh commanded Moses.
32 ¶ Thus was all the work of the tabernacle of the tent of the congregation finished: and the children of Israel did according to all that Yahweh commanded Moses, so did they.
33 And they brought the tabernacle to Moses, the tent, and all his furniture, his clasps, his boards, his bars, and his pillars, and his sockets,
34 And the covering of rams' skins dyed red, and the covering of badgers' skins, and the veil of the covering,
35 The ark of the testimony, and the staves thereof, and the mercy seat,
36 The table, *and* all the vessels thereof, and the showbread,
37 The pure candlestick, *with* the lamps thereof, *even with* the lamps to be set in order, and all the vessels thereof, and the oil for light,
38 And the golden altar, and the anointing oil, and the sweet incense, and the hanging for the tabernacle door,
39 The brazen altar, and his grate of brass, his staves, and all his vessels, the laver and his foot,
40 The hangings of the court, his pillars, and his sockets, and the hanging for the court gate, his cords, and his pins, and all the vessels of the service of the tabernacle, for the tent of the congregation,
41 The cloths of service to do service in the holy *place*, and the holy garments for Aaron the priest, and his sons' garments, to minister in the priest's office.
42 According to all that Yahweh commanded Moses, so the children of Israel made all the work.
43 And Moses did look upon all the work, and, behold, they had done it as Yahweh had commanded, even so had they done it: and Moses blessed them.

Exodus 40

40:1 ¶ And Yahweh spoke to Moses, saying,
2 On the first day of the first month shall you set up the tabernacle of the tent of the congregation.
3 And you shall put therein the ark of the testimony, and cover the ark with the veil.
4 And you shall bring in the table, and set in order the things that are to be set in order upon it; and you shall bring in the candlestick, and light the lamps thereof.
5 And you shall set the altar of gold for the incense before the ark of the testimony, and put the hanging of the door to the tabernacle.
6 And you shall set the altar of the burnt offering before the door of the tabernacle of the tent of the congregation.
7 And you shall set the laver between the tent of the congregation and the altar, and shall put water therein.
8 And you shall set up the court round about, and hang up the hanging at the court gate.
9 And you shall take the anointing oil, and anoint the tabernacle, and all that *is* therein, and shall hallow it, and all the vessels thereof: and it shall be holy.
10 And you shall anoint the altar of the burnt offering, and all his vessels, and sanctify the altar: and it shall be an altar most holy.
11 And you shall anoint the laver and his foot, and sanctify it.
12 And you shall bring Aaron and his sons to the door of the tabernacle of the congregation, and wash them with water.
13 And you shall put upon Aaron the holy garments, and anoint him, and sanctify him; that he may minister to me in the priest's office.
14 And you shall bring his sons, and clothe them with coats:
15 And you shall anoint them, as you did anoint their father, that they may minister to me in the priest's office: for their anointing shall surely be an everlasting priesthood throughout their generations.
16 ¶ Thus did Moses: according to all that Yahweh commanded him, so did he.
17 And it came to pass in the first month in the second year, on the first *day* of the month, *that* the tabernacle was reared up.
18 And Moses reared up the tabernacle, and fastened his sockets, and set up the boards thereof, and put in the bars thereof, and reared up his pillars.
19 And he spread abroad the tent over the tabernacle, and put the covering of the tent above upon it; as Yahweh commanded Moses.
20 And he took and put the testimony into the ark, and set the staves on the ark, and put the mercy seat above upon the ark:
21 And he brought the ark into the tabernacle, and set up the veil of the covering, and covered the ark of the testimony; as Yahweh commanded Moses.

Exodus 40

22 And he put the table in the tent of the congregation, upon the side of the tabernacle northward, outside the veil.
23 And he set the bread in order upon it before Yahweh; as Yahweh had commanded Moses.
24 And he put the candlestick in the tent of the congregation, over against the table, on the side of the tabernacle southward.
25 And he lit the lamps before Yahweh; as Yahweh commanded Moses.
26 And he put the golden altar in the tent of the congregation before the veil:
27 And he burnt sweet incense thereon; as Yahweh commanded Moses.
28 And he set up the hanging *at* the door of the tabernacle.
29 And he put the altar of burnt offering *by* the door of the tabernacle of the tent of the congregation, and offered upon it the burnt offering and the meat offering; as Yahweh commanded Moses.
30 And he set the laver between the tent of the congregation and the altar, and put water there, to wash *therewith*.
31 And Moses and Aaron and his sons washed their hands and their feet thereat:
32 When they went into the tent of the congregation, and when they came near to the altar, they washed; as Yahweh commanded Moses.
33 And he reared up the court round about the tabernacle and the altar, and set up the hanging of the court gate. So Moses finished the work.
34 ¶ Then a cloud covered the tent of the congregation, and the glory of Yahweh filled the tabernacle.
35 And Moses was not able to enter into the tent of the congregation, because the cloud stayed thereon, and the glory of Yahweh filled the tabernacle.
36 And when the cloud was taken up from over the tabernacle, the children of Israel went onward in all their journeys:
37 But if the cloud was not taken up, then they journeyed not till the day that it was taken up.
38 For the cloud of Yahweh *was* upon the tabernacle by day, and fire was on it by night, in the sight of all the house of Israel, throughout all their journeys.

Leviticus

Leviticus 1

1:1 ¶ And Yahweh called to Moses, and spoke to him out of the tabernacle of the congregation, saying,
2 Speak to the children of Israel, and say to them, If any man of you brings an offering unto Yahweh, you shall bring your offering of the cattle, *even* of the herd, and of the flock.
3 ¶ If his offering *is* a burnt sacrifice of the herd, let him offer a male without blemish: he shall offer it of his own voluntary will at the door of the tabernacle of the congregation before Yahweh.
4 And he shall put his hand upon the head of the burnt offering; and it shall be accepted for him to make atonement for him.
5 And he shall kill the bullock before Yahweh: and the priests, Aaron's sons, shall bring the blood, and sprinkle the blood round about upon the altar that *is by* the door of the tabernacle of the congregation.
6 And he shall skin the burnt offering, and cut it into his pieces.
7 And the sons of Aaron the priest shall put fire upon the altar, and lay the wood in order upon the fire:
8 And the priests, Aaron's sons, shall lay the parts, the head, and the fat, in order upon the wood that *is* on the fire which *is* upon the altar:
9 But his inwards and his legs shall he wash in water: and the priest shall burn all on the altar, *to be* a burnt sacrifice, an offering made by fire, of a sweet savor unto Yahweh.
10 ¶ And if his offering *is* of the flocks, *namely*, of the sheep, or of the goats, for a burnt sacrifice; he shall bring it a male without blemish.
11 And he shall kill it on the side of the altar northward before Yahweh: and the priests, Aaron's sons, shall sprinkle his blood round about upon the altar.
12 And he shall cut it into his pieces, with his head and his fat: and the priest shall lay them in order on the wood that *is* on the fire which *is* upon the altar:
13 But he shall wash the inwards and the legs with water: and the priest shall bring *it* all, and burn *it* upon the altar: it *is* a burnt sacrifice, an offering made by fire, of a sweet savor unto Yahweh.
14 And if the burnt sacrifice for his offering to Yahweh *is* of fowls, then he shall bring his offering of turtledoves, or of young pigeons.
15 And the priest shall bring it to the altar, and wring off his head, and burn *it* on the altar; and the blood thereof shall be wrung out at the side of the altar:
16 And he shall pluck away his crop with his feathers, and cast it beside the altar on the east part, by the place of the ashes:
17 And he shall cleave it with the wings thereof, *but* shall not divide *it* apart: and the priest shall burn it upon the altar, upon the wood that *is* upon the fire: it *is* a burnt sacrifice, an offering made by fire, of a sweet savor unto Yahweh.

Leviticus 2

2:1 ¶ And when any will offer a meat offering unto Yahweh, his offering shall be *of* fine flour; and he shall pour oil upon it, and put frankincense thereon:
2 And he shall bring it to Aaron's sons the priests: and he shall take there out his handful of the flour thereof, and of the oil thereof, with all the frankincense thereof; and the priest shall burn the memorial of it upon the altar, *to be* an offering made by fire, of a sweet savor unto Yahweh:
3 And the remnant of the meat offering *shall be* Aaron's and his sons': *it is* a thing most holy of the offerings of Yahweh made by fire.

4 And if you bring an oblation of a meat offering baked in the oven, *it shall be* unleavened cakes of fine flour mingled with oil, or unleavened wafers anointed with oil.

5 And if your oblation *is* a meat offering *baked* in a pan, it shall be *of* fine flour unleavened, mingled with oil.

6 You shall part it in pieces, and pour oil thereon: it *is* a meat offering.

7 And if your oblation *is* a meat offering *baked* in the frying pan, it shall be made *of* fine flour with oil.

8 And you shall bring the meat offering that is made of these things unto Yahweh: and when it is presented to the priest, he shall bring it to the altar.

9 And the priest shall take from the meat offering a memorial thereof, and shall burn *it* upon the altar: *it is* an offering made by fire, of a sweet savor unto Yahweh.

10 And that which is left of the meat offering *shall be* Aaron's and his sons': *it is* a thing most holy of the offerings of Yahweh made by fire.

11 ¶ No meat offering, which you shall bring unto Yahweh, shall be made with leaven: for you shall burn no leaven, nor any honey, in any offering of Yahweh made by fire.

12 As for the oblation of the firstfruits, you shall offer them unto Yahweh: but they shall not be burnt on the altar for a sweet savor.

13 And every oblation of your meat offering shall you season with salt; neither shall you allow the salt of the covenant of your God to be lacking from your meat offering: with all your offerings you shall offer salt.

14 And if you offer a meat offering of your firstfruits unto Yahweh, you shall offer for the meat offering of your firstfruits green ears of corn dried by the fire, *even* corn beaten out of full ears.

15 And you shall put oil upon it, and lay frankincense thereon: it *is* a meat offering.

16 And the priest shall burn the memorial of it, *part* of the beaten corn thereof, and *part* of the oil thereof, with all the frankincense thereof: *it is* an offering made by fire unto Yahweh.

Leviticus 3

3:1 ¶ And if his oblation *is* a sacrifice of peace offering, if he offers *it* of the herd; whether *it is* a male or female, he shall offer it without blemish before Yahweh.

2 And he shall lay his hand upon the head of his offering, and kill it *at* the door of the tabernacle of the congregation: and Aaron's sons the priests shall sprinkle the blood upon the altar round about.

3 And he shall offer of the sacrifice of the peace offering an offering made by fire unto Yahweh; the fat that covers the inwards, and all the fat that *is* upon the inwards,

4 And the two kidneys, and the fat that *is* on them, which *is* by the flanks, and the lobe above the liver, with the kidneys, it shall he take away.

5 And Aaron's sons shall burn it on the altar upon the burnt sacrifice, which *is* upon the wood that *is* on the fire: *it is* an offering made by fire, of a sweet savor unto Yahweh.

6 ¶ And if his offering for a sacrifice of peace offering unto Yahweh *is* of the flock; male or female, he shall offer it without blemish.

7 If he offers a lamb for his offering, then shall he offer it before Yahweh.

8 And he shall lay his hand upon the head of his offering, and kill it before the tabernacle of the congregation: and Aaron's sons shall sprinkle the blood thereof round about upon the altar.

9 And he shall offer of the sacrifice of the peace offering an offering made by fire unto Yahweh; the fat thereof, *and* the whole rump, it shall he take off hard by the backbone; and the fat that covers the inwards, and all the fat that *is* upon the inwards,

10 And the two kidneys, and the fat that *is* upon them, which *is* by the flanks, and the lobe above the liver, with the kidneys, it shall he take away.

11 And the priest shall burn it upon the altar: *it is* the food of the offering made by fire unto Yahweh.

12 And if his offering *is* a goat, then he shall offer it before Yahweh.

13 And he shall lay his hand upon the head of it, and kill it before the tabernacle of the congregation: and the sons of Aaron shall sprinkle the blood thereof upon the altar round about.

14 And he shall offer thereof his offering, *even* an offering made by fire unto Yahweh; the fat that covers the inwards, and all the fat that *is* upon the inwards,

15 And the two kidneys, and the fat that *is* upon them, which *is* by the flanks, and the lobe above the liver, with the kidneys, it shall he take away.

16 And the priest shall burn them upon the altar: *it is* the food of the offering made by fire for a sweet savor: all the fat *is* Yahweh's.

17 *It shall be* a perpetual statute for your generations throughout all your dwellings, that you eat neither fat nor blood.

Leviticus 4

4:1 ¶ And Yahweh spoke to Moses, saying,

2 Speak to the children of Israel, saying, If a soul shall sin through ignorance against any of the commandments of Yahweh *concerning things* which ought not to be done, and shall do against any of them:

3 If the priest that is anointed does sin according to the sin of the people; then let him bring for his sin, which he has sinned, a young bullock without blemish unto Yahweh for a sin offering.

4 And he shall bring the bullock to the door of the tabernacle of the congregation before Yahweh; and shall lay his hand upon the bullock's head, and kill the bullock before Yahweh.

5 And the priest that is anointed shall take of the bullock's blood, and bring it to the tabernacle of the congregation:

Leviticus 4

6 And the priest shall dip his finger in the blood, and sprinkle of the blood seven times before Yahweh, before the veil of the sanctuary.

7 And the priest shall put *some* of the blood upon the horns of the altar of sweet incense before Yahweh, which *is* in the tabernacle of the congregation; and shall pour all the blood of the bullock at the bottom of the altar of the burnt offering, which *is at* the door of the tabernacle of the congregation.

8 And he shall take off from it all the fat of the bullock for the sin offering; the fat that covers the inwards, and all the fat that *is* upon the inwards,

9 And the two kidneys, and the fat that *is* upon them, which *is* by the flanks, and the lobe above the liver, with the kidneys, it shall he take away,

10 As it was taken off from the bullock of the sacrifice of peace offerings: and the priest shall burn them upon the altar of the burnt offering.

11 And the skin of the bullock, and all his flesh, with his head, and with his legs, and his inwards, and his dung,

12 Even the whole bullock shall he carry forth outside the camp to a clean place, where the ashes are poured out, and burn him on the wood with fire: where the ashes are poured out shall he be burnt.

13 ¶ And if the whole congregation of Israel sins through ignorance, and the thing be hidden from the eyes of the assembly, and they have done *somewhat against* any of the commandments of Yahweh *concerning things* which should not be done, and are guilty;

14 When the sin, which they have sinned against it, is known, then the congregation shall offer a young bullock for the sin, and bring him before the tabernacle of the congregation.

15 And the elders of the congregation shall lay their hands upon the head of the bullock before Yahweh: and the bullock shall be killed before Yahweh.

16 And the priest that is anointed shall bring of the bullock's blood to the tabernacle of the congregation:

17 And the priest shall dip his finger *in some* of the blood, and sprinkle *it* seven times before Yahweh, *even* before the veil.

18 And he shall put *some* of the blood upon the horns of the altar which *is* before Yahweh, that *is* in the tabernacle of the congregation, and shall pour out all the blood at the bottom of the altar of the burnt offering, which *is at* the door of the tabernacle of the congregation.

19 And he shall take all his fat from him, and burn *it* upon the altar.

20 And he shall do with the bullock as he did with the bullock for a sin offering, so shall he do with this: and the priest shall make an atonement for them, and it shall be forgiven them.

21 And he shall carry forth the bullock outside the camp, and burn him as he burned the first bullock: it *is* a sin offering for the congregation.

22 ¶ When a ruler has sinned, and done *something* through ignorance *against* any of the commandments of Yahweh his God *concerning things* which should not be done, and is guilty;

23 Or if his sin, wherein he has sinned, comes to his knowledge; he shall bring his offering, a kid of the goats, a male without blemish:

24 And he shall lay his hand upon the head of the goat, and kill it in the place where they kill the burnt offering before Yahweh: it *is* a sin offering.

25 And the priest shall take of the blood of the sin offering with his finger, and put *it* upon the horns of the altar of burnt offering, and shall pour out his blood at the bottom of the altar of burnt offering.

26 And he shall burn all his fat upon the altar, as the fat of the sacrifice of peace offerings: and the priest shall make an atonement for him as concerning his sin, and it shall be forgiven him.

27 ¶ And if any one of the common people sins through ignorance, while he does *somewhat against* any of the commandments of Yahweh *concerning things* which ought not to be done, and is guilty;

28 Or if his sin, which he has sinned, comes to his knowledge: then he shall bring his offering, a kid of the goats, a female without blemish, for his sin which he has sinned.

29 And he shall lay his hand upon the head of the sin offering, and slay the sin offering in the place of the burnt offering.

30 And the priest shall take of the blood thereof with his finger, and put *it* upon the horns of the altar of burnt offering, and shall pour out all the blood thereof at the bottom of the altar.

31 And he shall take away all the fat thereof, as the fat is taken away from off the sacrifice of peace offerings; and the priest shall burn *it* upon the altar for a sweet savor unto Yahweh; and the priest shall make an atonement for him, and it shall be forgiven him.

32 And if he brings a lamb for a sin offering, he shall bring it a female without blemish.

33 And he shall lay his hand upon the head of the sin offering, and slay it for a sin offering in the place where they kill the burnt offering.

34 And the priest shall take of the blood of the sin offering with his finger, and put *it* upon the horns of the altar of burnt offering, and shall pour out all the blood thereof at the bottom of the altar:

35 And he shall take away all the fat thereof, as the fat of the lamb is taken away from the sacrifice of the peace offerings; and the priest shall burn them upon the altar, according to the offerings made by fire unto Yahweh: and the priest shall make an atonement for his sin that he has committed, and it shall be forgiven him.

Leviticus 5

5:1 ¶ And if a soul sins, and hears the voice of swearing, and *is* a witness, whether he has seen or known *of it*; if he does not tell *it*, then he shall bear his iniquity.

2 Or if a soul touches any unclean thing, whether *it is* a carcass of an unclean beast, or a carcass of unclean cattle, or the carcass of unclean creeping things, and *if* it is hidden from him; he also shall be unclean, and guilty.

3 Or if he touches the uncleanness of man, whatever uncleanness *it is* that a man shall be defiled therewith, and it is hidden from him; when he knows *of it*, then he shall be guilty.

4 Or if a soul swears, pronouncing with *his* lips to do evil, or to do good, whatever *it is* that a man shall pronounce with an oath, and it is hidden from him; when he knows *of it*, then he shall be guilty in one of these.

5 And it shall be, when he shall be guilty in one of these *things*, that he shall confess that he has sinned in that *thing*:

6 And he shall bring his trespass offering unto Yahweh for his sin which he has sinned, a female from the flock, a lamb or a kid of the goats, for a sin offering; and the priest shall make an atonement for him concerning his sin.

7 ¶ And if he is not able to bring a lamb, then he shall bring for his trespass, which he has committed, two turtledoves, or two young pigeons, unto Yahweh; one for a sin offering, and the other for a burnt offering.

8 And he shall bring them to the priest, who shall offer *that* which *is* for the sin offering first, and wring off his head from his neck, but shall not divide *it* apart:

9 And he shall sprinkle of the blood of the sin offering upon the side of the altar; and the rest of the blood shall be wrung out at the bottom of the altar: it *is* a sin offering.

10 And he shall offer the second *for* a burnt offering, according to the manner: and the priest shall make an atonement for him for his sin which he has sinned, and it shall be forgiven him.

11 But if he is not able to bring two turtledoves, or two young pigeons, then he that sinned shall bring for his offering the tenth part of an ephah of fine flour for a sin offering; he shall put no oil upon it, neither shall he put *any* frankincense thereon: for it *is* a sin offering.

12 Then shall he bring it to the priest, and the priest shall take his handful of it, *even* a memorial thereof, and burn *it* on the altar, according to the offerings made by fire unto Yahweh: it *is* a sin offering.

13 And the priest shall make an atonement for him as touching his sin that he has sinned in one of these, and it shall be forgiven him: and *the remnant* shall be the priest's, as a meat offering.

14 ¶ And Yahweh spoke to Moses, saying,

15 If a soul commits a trespass, and sins through ignorance, in the holy things of Yahweh; then he shall bring for his trespass unto Yahweh a ram without blemish out of the flocks, with your estimation by shekels of silver, after the shekel of the sanctuary, for a trespass offering:

16 And he shall make amends for the harm that he has done in the holy thing, and shall add the fifth part thereto, and give it to the priest: and the priest shall make an atonement for him with the ram of the trespass offering, and it shall be forgiven him.

17 And if a soul sins, and commits any of these things which are forbidden to be done by the commandments of Yahweh; though he knew *it* not, yet is he guilty, and shall bear his iniquity.

18 And he shall bring a ram without blemish out of the flock, with your estimation, for a trespass offering, to the priest: and the priest shall make an atonement for him concerning his ignorance wherein he erred and knew *it* not, and it shall be forgiven him.

19 It *is* a trespass offering: he has certainly trespassed against Yahweh.

Leviticus 6

6:1 ¶ And Yahweh spoke to Moses, saying,

2 If a soul sins, and commits a trespass against Yahweh, and lies to his neighbor in that which was delivered him to keep, or in fellowship, or in a thing taken away by violence, or has deceived his neighbor;

3 Or has found that which was lost, and lies concerning it, and swears falsely; in any of all these that a man does, sinning therein:

4 Then it shall be, because he has sinned, and is guilty, that he shall restore that which he took violently away, or the thing which he has deceitfully gotten, or that which was delivered him to keep, or the lost thing which he found,

5 Or all that about which he has sworn falsely; he shall even restore it in the principal, and shall add the fifth part more thereto, *and* give it to him to whom it belongs, in the day of his trespass offering.

6 And he shall bring his trespass offering unto Yahweh, a ram without blemish out of the flock, with your estimation, for a trespass offering, unto the priest:

7 And the priest shall make an atonement for him before Yahweh: and it shall be forgiven him for anything of all that he has done in trespassing therein.

8 ¶ And Yahweh spoke to Moses, saying,

9 Command Aaron and his sons, saying, This *is* the law of the burnt offering: It *is* the burnt offering, because of the burning upon the altar all night to the morning, and the fire of the altar shall be burning in it.

10 And the priest shall put on his linen garment, and his linen breeches shall he put upon his flesh, and take up the ashes which the fire has consumed with the burnt offering on the altar, and he shall put them beside the altar.

11 And he shall strip off his garments, and put on other garments, and carry forth the ashes outside the camp to a clean place.

12 And the fire upon the altar shall be burning in it; it shall not be put out: and the priest shall burn wood on it every morning, and lay the burnt offering in order upon it; and he shall burn thereon the fat of the peace offerings.

13 The fire shall ever be burning upon the altar; it shall never go out.

14 ¶ And this *is* the law of the meat offering: the sons of Aaron shall offer it before Yahweh, before the altar.

15 And he shall take of it his handful, of the flour of the meat offering, and of the oil thereof, and all the frankincense which *is* upon the meat offering, and shall burn *it* upon the altar *for* a sweet savor, *even* the memorial of it, unto Yahweh.

Leviticus 6

16 And the remainder thereof shall Aaron and his sons eat: with unleavened bread shall it be eaten in the holy place; in the court of the tabernacle of the congregation they shall eat it.
17 It shall not be baked with leaven. I have given it *to them for* their portion of my offerings made by fire; it *is* most holy, as *is* the sin offering, and as the trespass offering.
18 All the males among the children of Aaron shall eat of it. *It shall be* a statute forever in your generations concerning the offerings of Yahweh made by fire: every one that touches them shall be holy.
19 And Yahweh spoke to Moses, saying,
20 This *is* the offering of Aaron and of his sons, which they shall offer unto Yahweh in the day when he is anointed; the tenth part of an ephah of fine flour for a meat offering perpetual, half of it in the morning, and half thereof at night.
21 In a pan it shall be made with oil; *and when it is* baked, you shall bring it in: *and* the baked pieces of the meat offering shall you offer *for* a sweet savor unto Yahweh.
22 And the priest of his sons that is anointed in his stead shall offer it: *it is* a statute forever unto Yahweh; it shall be wholly burnt.
23 For every meat offering for the priest shall be wholly burnt: it shall not be eaten.
24 ¶ And Yahweh spoke to Moses, saying,
25 Speak to Aaron and to his sons, saying, This *is* the law of the sin offering: In the place where the burnt offering is killed shall the sin offering be killed before Yahweh: it *is* most holy.
26 The priest that offers it for sin shall eat it: in the holy place shall it be eaten, in the court of the tabernacle of the congregation.
27 Whatever shall touch the flesh thereof shall be holy: and when there is sprinkled of the blood thereof upon any garment, you shall wash that on which it was sprinkled in the holy place.
28 But the earthen vessel wherein it is boiled shall be broken: and if it is boiled in a brazen pot, it shall be both scoured, and rinsed in water.
29 All the males among the priests shall eat thereof: it *is* most holy.
30 And no sin offering, whereof *any* of the blood is brought into the tabernacle of the congregation to reconcile *therewith* in the holy *place*, shall be eaten: it shall be burnt in the fire.

Leviticus 7

7:1 ¶ Likewise this *is* the law of the trespass offering: it *is* most holy.
2 In the place where they kill the burnt offering shall they kill the trespass offering: and the blood thereof shall he sprinkle round about upon the altar.
3 And he shall offer of it all the fat thereof; the rump, and the fat that covers the inwards,
4 And the two kidneys, and the fat that *is* on them, which *is* by the flanks, and the lobe *that is* above the liver, with the kidneys, it shall he take away:

5 And the priest shall burn them upon the altar *for* an offering made by fire unto Yahweh: it *is* a trespass offering.
6 Every male among the priests shall eat thereof: it shall be eaten in the holy place: it *is* most holy.
7 As the sin offering *is*, so *is* the trespass offering: *there is* one law for them: the priest that makes atonement therewith shall have *it*.
8 And the priest that offers any man's burnt offering, *even* the priest shall have to himself the skin of the burnt offering which he has offered.
9 And all the meat offering that is baked in the oven, and all that is dressed in the frying pan, and in the pan, shall be the priest's that offers it.
10 And every meat offering, mingled with oil, and dry, shall all the sons of Aaron have, one *as much* as another.
11 ¶ And this *is* the law of the sacrifice of peace offerings, which he shall offer unto Yahweh.
12 If he offers it for a thanksgiving, then he shall offer with the sacrifice of thanksgiving unleavened cakes mingled with oil, and unleavened wafers anointed with oil, and cakes mingled with oil, of fine flour, fried.
13 Besides the cakes, he shall offer *for* his offering leavened bread with the sacrifice of thanksgiving of his peace offerings.
14 And of it he shall offer one out of the whole oblation *for* a heave offering unto Yahweh, *and* it shall be the priest's that sprinkles the blood of the peace offerings.
15 And the flesh of the sacrifice of his peace offerings for thanksgiving shall be eaten the same day that it is offered; he shall not leave any of it until the morning.
16 But if the sacrifice of his offering *is* a vow, or a voluntary offering, it shall be eaten the same day that he offers his sacrifice: and on the next day also the remainder of it shall be eaten:
17 But the remainder of the flesh of the sacrifice on the third day shall be burnt with fire.
18 And if *any* of the flesh of the sacrifice of his peace offerings is eaten at all on the third day, it shall not be accepted, neither shall it be imputed unto him that offers it: it shall be an abomination, and the soul that eats of it shall bear his iniquity.
19 And the flesh that touches any unclean *thing* shall not be eaten; it shall be burnt with fire: and as for the flesh, all that are clean shall eat thereof.
20 But the soul that eats *of* the flesh of the sacrifice of peace offerings, that *pertain* unto Yahweh, having his uncleanness upon him, even that soul shall be cut off from his people.
21 Moreover the soul that shall touch any unclean *thing, as* the uncleanness of man, or *any* unclean beast, or any abominable unclean *thing*, and eats of the flesh of the sacrifice of peace offerings, which *pertain* unto Yahweh, even that soul shall be cut off from his people.
22 And Yahweh spoke to Moses, saying,
23 Speak to the children of Israel, saying, You shall eat no manner of fat, of ox, or of sheep, or of goat.

24 And the fat of the beast that dies of itself, and the fat of that which is torn with beasts, may be used in any other use: but you shall in no wise eat of it.
25 For whoever eats the fat of the beast, of which men offer an offering made by fire unto Yahweh, even the soul that eats *it* shall be cut off from his people.
26 Moreover you shall eat no manner of blood, *whether it is* of fowl or of beast, in any of your dwellings.
27 Whatever soul *it is* that eats any manner of blood, even that soul shall be cut off from his people.
28 And Yahweh spoke to Moses, saying,
29 Speak to the children of Israel, saying, He that offers the sacrifice of his peace offerings unto Yahweh shall bring his oblation unto Yahweh of the sacrifice of his peace offerings.
30 His own hands shall bring the offerings of Yahweh made by fire, the fat with the breast, it shall he bring, that the breast may be waved *for* a wave offering before Yahweh.
31 And the priest shall burn the fat upon the altar: but the breast shall be Aaron's and his sons'.
32 And the right shoulder shall you give to the priest *for* a heave offering of the sacrifices of your peace offerings.
33 He among the sons of Aaron, that offers the blood of the peace offerings, and the fat, shall have the right shoulder for *his* part.
34 For the wave breast and the heave shoulder have I taken of the children of Israel from off the sacrifices of their peace offerings, and have given them to Aaron the priest and to his sons by a statute forever from among the children of Israel.
35 ¶ This *is the portion* of the anointing of Aaron, and of the anointing of his sons, out of the offerings of Yahweh made by fire, in the day *when* he presented them to minister unto Yahweh in the priest's office;
36 Which Yahweh commanded to be given them of the children of Israel, in the day that he anointed them, *by* a statute forever throughout their generations.
37 This *is* the law of the burnt offering, of the meat offering, and of the sin offering, and of the trespass offering, and of the consecrations, and of the sacrifice of the peace offerings;
38 Which Yahweh commanded Moses in mount Sinai, in the day that he commanded the children of Israel to offer their oblations unto Yahweh, in the wilderness of Sinai.

Leviticus 8

8:1 ¶ And Yahweh spoke to Moses, saying,
2 Take Aaron and his sons with him, and the garments, and the anointing oil, and a bullock for the sin offering, and two rams, and a basket of unleavened bread;
3 And gather you all the congregation together to the door of the tabernacle of the congregation.
4 And Moses did as Yahweh commanded him; and the assembly was gathered together to the door of the tabernacle of the congregation.
5 And Moses said to the congregation, This *is* the thing which Yahweh commanded to be done.
6 And Moses brought Aaron and his sons, and washed them with water.
7 And he put upon him the coat, and girded him with the sash, and clothed him with the robe, and put the ephod upon him, and he girded him with the curious girdle of the ephod, and bound *it* unto him therewith.
8 And he put the breastplate upon him: also he put in the breastplate the Urim and the Thummim.
9 And he put the turban upon his head; also upon the turban, *even* upon his forefront, did he put the golden plate, the holy crown; as Yahweh commanded Moses.
10 And Moses took the anointing oil, and anointed the tabernacle and all that *was* therein, and sanctified them.
11 And he sprinkled thereof upon the altar seven times, and anointed the altar and all his vessels, both the laver and his foot, to sanctify them.
12 And he poured of the anointing oil upon Aaron's head, and anointed him, to sanctify him.
13 And Moses brought Aaron's sons, and put coats upon them, and girded them with sashes, and put bonnets upon them; as Yahweh commanded Moses.
14 ¶ And he brought the bullock for the sin offering: and Aaron and his sons laid their hands upon the head of the bullock for the sin offering.
15 And he slew *it*; and Moses took the blood, and put *it* upon the horns of the altar round about with his finger, and purified the altar, and poured the blood at the bottom of the altar, and sanctified it, to make reconciliation upon it.
16 And he took all the fat that *was* upon the inwards, and the lobe *above* the liver, and the two kidneys, and their fat, and Moses burned *them* upon the altar.
17 But the bullock, and his hide, his flesh, and his dung, he burnt with fire outside the camp; as Yahweh commanded Moses.
18 And he brought the ram for the burnt offering: and Aaron and his sons laid their hands upon the head of the ram.
19 And he killed *it*; and Moses sprinkled the blood upon the altar round about.
20 And he cut the ram into pieces; and Moses burnt the head, and the pieces, and the fat.
21 And he washed the inwards and the legs in water; and Moses burnt the whole ram upon the altar: it *was* a burnt sacrifice for a sweet savor, *and* an offering made by fire unto Yahweh; as Yahweh commanded Moses.
22 And he brought the other ram, the ram of consecration: and Aaron and his sons laid their hands upon the head of the ram.
23 And he slew *it*; and Moses took of the blood of it, and put *it* upon the tip of Aaron's right ear, and upon the thumb of his right hand, and upon the great toe of his right foot.
24 And he brought Aaron's sons, and Moses put of the blood upon the tip of their right ear, and upon the thumbs of their right hands, and upon the great toes of their right feet: and Moses sprinkled the blood upon the altar round about.
25 And he took the fat, and the rump, and all the fat that *was* upon the inwards, and the lobe *above* the liver, and the two kidneys, and their fat, and the right shoulder:

Leviticus 8

26 And out of the basket of unleavened bread, that *was* before Yahweh, he took one unleavened cake, and a cake of oiled bread, and one wafer, and put *them* on the fat, and upon the right shoulder:
27 And he put all upon Aaron's hands, and upon his sons' hands, and waved them *for* a wave offering before Yahweh.
28 And Moses took them from off their hands, and burnt *them* on the altar upon the burnt offering: they *were* consecrations for a sweet savor: it *is* an offering made by fire unto Yahweh.
29 And Moses took the breast, and waved it *for* a wave offering before Yahweh: *for* of the ram of consecration it was Moses' part; as Yahweh commanded Moses.
30 And Moses took of the anointing oil, and of the blood which *was* upon the altar, and sprinkled *it* upon Aaron, *and* upon his garments, and upon his sons, and upon his sons' garments with him; and sanctified Aaron, *and* his garments, and his sons, and his sons' garments with him.
31 ¶ And Moses said to Aaron and to his sons, Boil the flesh *at* the door of the tabernacle of the congregation: and there eat it with the bread that *is* in the basket of consecrations, as I commanded, saying, Aaron and his sons shall eat it.
32 And that which remains of the flesh and of the bread shall you burn with fire.
33 And you shall not go out of the door of the tabernacle of the congregation *for* seven days, until the days of your consecration are at an end: for seven days shall he consecrate you.
34 As he has done this day, *so* Yahweh has commanded to do, to make an atonement for you.
35 Therefore shall you remain *at* the door of the tabernacle of the congregation day and night seven days, and keep the charge of Yahweh, that you die not: for so I am commanded.
36 So Aaron and his sons did all things which Yahweh commanded by the hand of Moses.

Leviticus 9

9:1 ¶ And it came to pass on the eighth day, *that* Moses called Aaron and his sons, and the elders of Israel;
2 And he said to Aaron, Take you a young calf for a sin offering, and a ram for a burnt offering, without blemish, and offer *them* before Yahweh.
3 And to the children of Israel you shall speak, saying, Take you a kid of the goats for a sin offering; and a calf and a lamb, *both* of the first year, without blemish, for a burnt offering;
4 Also a bullock and a ram for peace offerings, to sacrifice before Yahweh; and a meat offering mingled with oil: for today Yahweh will appear to you.
5 And they brought *that* which Moses commanded before the tabernacle of the congregation: and all the congregation drew near and stood before Yahweh.
6 And Moses said, This *is* the thing which Yahweh commanded that you should do: and the glory of Yahweh shall appear to you.
7 And Moses said to Aaron, Go to the altar, and offer your sin offering, and your burnt offering, and make an atonement for yourself, and for the people: and offer the offering of the people, and make an atonement for them; as Yahweh commanded.
8 ¶ Aaron therefore went to the altar, and slew the calf of the sin offering, which *was* for himself.
9 And the sons of Aaron brought the blood to him: and he dipped his finger in the blood, and put *it* upon the horns of the altar, and poured out the blood at the bottom of the altar:
10 But the fat, and the kidneys, and the lobe above the liver of the sin offering, he burnt upon the altar; as Yahweh commanded Moses.
11 And the flesh and the hide he burnt with fire outside the camp.
12 And he slew the burnt offering; and Aaron's sons presented to him the blood, which he sprinkled round about upon the altar.
13 And they presented the burnt offering to him, with the pieces thereof, and the head: and he burnt *them* upon the altar.
14 And he did wash the inwards and the legs, and burnt *them* upon the burnt offering on the altar.
15 And he brought the people's offering, and took the goat, which *was* the sin offering for the people, and slew it, and offered it for sin, as the first.
16 And he brought the burnt offering, and offered it according to the manner.
17 And he brought the meat offering, and took a handful thereof, and burnt *it* upon the altar, beside the burnt sacrifice of the morning.
18 He slew also the bullock and the ram *for* a sacrifice of peace offerings, which *was* for the people: and Aaron's sons presented to him the blood, which he sprinkled upon the altar round about,
19 And the fat of the bullock and of the ram, the rump, and that which covers *the inwards*, and the kidneys, and the lobe *above* the liver:
20 And they put the fat upon the breasts, and he burnt the fat upon the altar:
21 And the breasts and the right shoulder Aaron waved *for* a wave offering before Yahweh; as Moses commanded.
22 And Aaron lifted up his hand toward the people, and blessed them, and came down from offering of the sin offering, and the burnt offering, and peace offerings.
23 ¶ And Moses and Aaron went into the tabernacle of the congregation, and came out, and blessed the people: and the glory of Yahweh appeared to all the people.
24 And there came a fire out from before Yahweh, and consumed upon the altar the burnt offering and the fat: *which* when all the people saw, they shouted, and fell on their faces.

Leviticus 10

10:1 ¶ And Nadab and Abihu, the sons of Aaron, took either of them his censer, and put fire therein, and put incense thereon, and offered strange fire before Yahweh, which he commanded them not.

2 And there went out fire from Yahweh, and devoured them, and they died before Yahweh.

3 ¶ Then Moses said to Aaron, This *is it* that Yahweh spoke, saying, I will be sanctified in them that come near me, and before all the people I will be glorified. And Aaron held his peace.

4 And Moses called Mishael and Elzaphan, the sons of Uzziel the uncle of Aaron, and said to them, Come near, carry your brethren from before the sanctuary out of the camp.

5 So they went near, and carried them in their coats out of the camp; as Moses had said.

6 And Moses said to Aaron, and to Eleazar and to Ithamar, his sons, Uncover not your heads, neither tear your clothes; lest you die, and lest wrath comes upon all the people: but let your brethren, the whole house of Israel, bewail the burning which Yahweh has kindled.

7 And you shall not go out from the door of the tabernacle of the congregation, lest you die: for the anointing oil of Yahweh *is* upon you. And they did according to the word of Moses.

8 ¶ And Yahweh spoke to Aaron, saying,

9 Do not drink wine nor strong drink, you, nor your sons with you, when you go into the tabernacle of the congregation, lest you die: *it shall be* a statute forever throughout your generations:

10 And that you may put difference between holy and unholy, and between unclean and clean;

11 And that you may teach the children of Israel all the statutes which Yahweh has spoken to them by the hand of Moses.

12 ¶ And Moses spoke to Aaron, and to Eleazar and to Ithamar, his sons that were left, Take the meat offering that remains of the offerings of Yahweh made by fire, and eat it without leaven beside the altar: for it *is* most holy:

13 And you shall eat it in the holy place, because it *is* your due, and your sons' due, of the sacrifices of Yahweh made by fire: for so I am commanded.

14 And the wave breast and heave shoulder shall you eat in a clean place; you, and your sons, and your daughters with you: for *they are* your due, and your sons' due, *which* are given out of the sacrifices of peace offerings of the children of Israel.

15 The heave shoulder and the wave breast shall they bring with the offerings made by fire of the fat, to wave *it for* a wave offering before Yahweh; and it shall be yours, and your sons' with you, by a statute forever; as Yahweh has commanded.

16 And Moses diligently sought the goat of the sin offering, and, behold, it was burnt: and he was angry with Eleazar and Ithamar, the sons of Aaron *which were* left alive, saying,

17 Why have you not eaten the sin offering in the holy place, seeing it *is* most holy, and *God* has given it *to* you to bear the iniquity of the congregation, to make atonement for them before Yahweh?

18 Behold, the blood of it was not brought in within the holy *place*: you should indeed have eaten it in the holy *place*, as I commanded.

19 And Aaron said to Moses, Behold, this day have they offered their sin offering and their burnt offering before Yahweh; and such things have befallen me: and *if* I had eaten the sin offering today, should it have been accepted in the sight of Yahweh?

20 And when Moses heard *that*, he was content.

Leviticus 11

11:1 ¶ And Yahweh spoke to Moses and to Aaron, saying to them,

2 Speak to the children of Israel, saying, These *are* the beasts which you shall eat among all the beasts that *are* on the earth.

3 Whatever parts the hoof, and is cloven footed, *and* chews the cud, among the beasts, that shall you eat.

4 Nevertheless these shall you not eat of them that chew the cud, or of them that divide the hoof: *as* the camel, because he chews the cud, but divides not the hoof; he *is* unclean to you.

5 And the coney, because he chews the cud, but divides not the hoof; he *is* unclean to you.

6 And the hare, because he chews the cud, but divides not the hoof; he *is* unclean to you.

7 And the swine, though he divides the hoof, and is cloven footed, yet he chews not the cud; he *is* unclean to you.

8 Of their flesh shall you not eat, and their carcass shall you not touch; they *are* unclean to you.

9 ¶ These shall you eat of all that *are* in the waters: whatever has fins and scales in the waters, in the seas, and in the rivers, them shall you eat.

10 And all that have not fins and scales in the seas, and in the rivers, of all that move in the waters, and of any living thing which *is* in the waters, they *shall be* an abomination to you:

11 They shall be even an abomination to you; you shall not eat of their flesh, but you shall have their carcasses in abomination.

12 Whatever has no fins nor scales in the waters, that *shall be* an abomination to you.

13 And these *are they which* you shall have in abomination among the fowls; they shall not be eaten, they *are* an abomination: the eagle, and the ossifrage, and the ospray,

14 And the vulture, and the kite after his kind;

15 Every raven after his kind;

16 And the owl, and the night hawk, and the cuckow, and the hawk after his kind,

17 And the little owl, and the cormorant, and the great owl,

18 And the swan, and the pelican, and the gier eagle,

19 And the stork, the heron after her kind, and the lapwing, and the bat.

20 ¶ All fowls that creep, going upon *all* four, *shall be* an abomination to you.

21 Yet these may you eat of every flying creeping thing that goes upon *all* four, which have legs above their feet, to leap therewith upon the earth;

22 *Even* these of them you may eat; the locust after his kind, and the bald locust after his kind, and the beetle after his kind, and the grasshopper after his kind.

Leviticus 11

23 But all *other* flying creeping things, which have four feet, *shall be* an abomination to you.

24 And for these you shall be unclean: whoever touches the carcass of them shall be unclean until the evening.

25 And whoever bears *any* of the carcass of them shall wash his clothes, and be unclean until the evening.

26 *The carcasses* of every beast which divides the hoof, and *is* not cloven footed, nor chews the cud, *are* unclean to you: every one that touches them shall be unclean.

27 And whatever goes upon his paws, among all manner of beasts that go on *all* four, those *are* unclean to you: whoever touches their carcass shall be unclean until the evening.

28 And he that bears the carcass of them shall wash his clothes, and be unclean until the evening: they *are* unclean to you.

29 These also *shall be* unclean to you among the creeping things that creep upon the earth; the weasel, and the mouse, and the tortoise after his kind,

30 And the ferret, and the chameleon, and the lizard, and the snail, and the mole.

31 These *are* unclean to you among all that creep: whoever does touch them, when they are dead, shall be unclean until the evening.

32 And upon whatever *any* of them, when they are dead, does fall, it shall be unclean; whether *it is* any vessel of wood, or clothing, or skin, or sack, whatever vessel *it is*, wherein *any* work is done, it must be put into water, and it shall be unclean until the evening; so it shall be cleansed.

33 And every earthen vessel, where into *any* of them falls, whatever *is* in it shall be unclean; and you shall break it.

34 Of all meat which may be eaten, *that* on which *such* water comes shall be unclean: and all drink that may be drunk in every *such* vessel shall be unclean.

35 And every *thing* whereupon *any part* of their carcass falls shall be unclean; *whether it is an* oven, or ranges for pots, they shall be broken down: *for* they *are* unclean, and shall be unclean to you.

36 Nevertheless a fountain or pit, *wherein there is* plenty of water, shall be clean: but that which touches their carcass shall be unclean.

37 And if *any part* of their carcass falls upon any sowing seed which is to be sown, it *shall be* clean.

38 But if *any* water is put upon the seed, and *any part* of their carcass falls thereon, it *shall be* unclean to you.

39 And if any beast, of which you may eat, dies; he that touches the carcass thereof shall be unclean until the evening.

40 And he that eats of the carcass of it shall wash his clothes, and be unclean until the evening: he also that bears the carcass of it shall wash his clothes, and be unclean until the evening.

41 And every creeping thing that creeps upon the earth *shall be* an abomination; it shall not be eaten.

42 Whatever goes upon the belly, and whatever goes upon *all* fours, or whatever has more feet among all creeping things that creep upon the earth, them you shall not eat; for they *are* an abomination.

43 ¶ You shall not make yourselves abominable with any creeping thing that creeps, neither shall you make yourselves unclean with them, that you should be defiled thereby.

44 For I *am* Yahweh your God: you shall therefore sanctify yourselves, and you shall be holy; for I *am* holy: neither shall you defile yourselves with any manner of creeping thing that creeps upon the earth.

45 For I *am* Yahweh that brought you up out of the land of Egypt, to be your God: you shall therefore be holy, for I *am* holy.

46 This *is* the law of the beasts, and of the fowl, and of every living creature that moves in the waters, and of every creature that creeps upon the earth:

47 To make a difference between the unclean and the clean, and between the beast that may be eaten and the beast that may not be eaten.

Leviticus 12

12:1 ¶ And Yahweh spoke to Moses, saying,

2 Speak to the children of Israel, saying, If a woman has conceived seed, and bears a man child: then she shall be unclean seven days; according to the days of the separation for her infirmity shall she be unclean.

3 And in the eighth day the flesh of his foreskin shall be circumcised.

4 And she shall then continue in the blood of her purifying three and thirty days; she shall touch no hallowed thing, nor come into the sanctuary, until the days of her purifying are fulfilled.

5 But if she bears a maid child, then she shall be unclean two weeks, as in her separation: and she shall continue in the blood of her purifying threescore and six days.

6 ¶ And when the days of her purifying are fulfilled, for a son, or for a daughter, she shall bring a lamb of the first year for a burnt offering, and a young pigeon, or a turtledove, for a sin offering, to the door of the tabernacle of the congregation, unto the priest:

7 Who shall offer it before Yahweh, and make an atonement for her; and she shall be cleansed from the issue of her blood. This *is* the law for her that has borne a male or a female.

8 And if she is not able to bring a lamb, then she shall bring two turtledoves, or two young pigeons; the one for the burnt offering, and the other for a sin offering: and the priest shall make an atonement for her, and she shall be clean.

Leviticus 13

13:1 ¶ And Yahweh spoke to Moses and Aaron, saying,

2 When a man shall have in the skin of his flesh a rising, a scab, or bright spot, and it is in the skin of his flesh *like* the plague of leprosy; then he shall be brought to Aaron the priest, or to one of his sons the priests:

3 And the priest shall look on the plague in the skin of the flesh: and *when* the hair in the plague has turned

white, and the plague in sight *is* deeper than the skin of his flesh, it *is* a plague of leprosy: and the priest shall look on him, and pronounce him unclean.

4 If the bright spot *is* white in the skin of his flesh, and in sight *is* not deeper than the skin, and the hair thereof has not turned white; then the priest shall shut up *him that has* the plague seven days:

5 And the priest shall look on him the seventh day: and, behold, *if* the plague in his sight is at a stay, *and* the plague spreads not in the skin; then the priest shall shut him up seven days more:

6 And the priest shall look on him again the seventh day: and, behold, *if* the plague *is* somewhat dark, *and* the plague spreads not in the skin, the priest shall pronounce him clean: it *is but* a scab: and he shall wash his clothes, and be clean.

7 But if the scab spreads much abroad in the skin, after that he has been seen by the priest for his cleansing, he shall be seen by the priest again:

8 And *if* the priest sees that, behold, the scab spreads in the skin, then the priest shall pronounce him unclean: it *is* a leprosy.

9 When the plague of leprosy is in a man, then he shall be brought to the priest;

10 And the priest shall see *him*: and, behold, *if* the rising *is* white in the skin, and it has turned the hair white, and *there is* tender raw flesh in the rising;

11 It *is* an old leprosy in the skin of his flesh, and the priest shall pronounce him unclean, and shall not shut him up: for he *is* unclean.

12 And if a leprosy breaks out abroad in the skin, and the leprosy covers all the skin of *him that has* the plague from his head even to his foot, wherever the priest looks;

13 Then the priest shall consider: and, behold, *if* the leprosy has covered all his flesh, he shall pronounce *him* clean *that has* the plague: it is all turned white: he *is* clean.

14 But when raw flesh appears in him, he shall be unclean.

15 And the priest shall see the raw flesh, and pronounce him to be unclean: *for* the raw flesh *is* unclean: it *is* a leprosy.

16 Or if the raw flesh turns again, and is changed to white, he shall come to the priest;

17 And the priest shall see him: and, behold, *if* the plague is turned into white; then the priest shall pronounce *him* clean *that has* the plague: he *is* clean.

18 ¶ The flesh also, in which, *even* in the skin thereof, was a boil, and is healed,

19 And in the place of the boil there is a white rising, or a bright spot, white, and somewhat reddish, and it is shown to the priest;

20 And if, when the priest sees it, behold, it *is* in sight lower than the skin, and the hair thereof is turned white; the priest shall pronounce him unclean: it *is* a plague of leprosy broken out of the boil.

21 But if the priest looks on it, and, behold, *there are* no white hairs therein, and *if* it *is* not lower than the skin, but *is* somewhat dark; then the priest shall shut him up seven days

22 And if it spreads much abroad in the skin, then the priest shall pronounce him unclean: it *is* a plague.

23 But if the bright spot stays in his place, *and* spreads not, it *is* a burning boil; and the priest shall pronounce him clean.

24 Or if there is *any* flesh, in the skin whereof *there is* a hot burning, and the quick *flesh* that burns has a white bright spot, somewhat reddish, or white;

25 Then the priest shall look upon it: and, behold, *if* the hair in the bright spot has turned white, and it *is in* sight deeper than the skin; it *is* a leprosy broken out of the burning: therefore the priest shall pronounce him unclean: it *is* the plague of leprosy.

26 But if the priest looks on it, and, behold, *there is* no white hair in the bright spot, and it *is* no lower than the *other* skin, but *is* somewhat dark; then the priest shall shut him up seven days:

27 And the priest shall look upon him the seventh day: *and* if it is spread much abroad in the skin, then the priest shall pronounce him unclean: it *is* the plague of leprosy.

28 And if the bright spot stays in his place, *and* spreads not in the skin, but it *is* somewhat dark; it *is* a rising of the burning, and the priest shall pronounce him clean: for it *is* an inflammation of the burning.

29 If a man or woman has a plague upon the head or the beard;

30 Then the priest shall see the plague: and, behold, if it *is* in sight deeper than the skin; *and there is* in it a yellow thin hair; then the priest shall pronounce him unclean: it *is* a dry scale, *even* a leprosy upon the head or beard.

31 And if the priest looks upon the plague of the scale, and, behold, it *is* not in sight deeper than the skin, and *that there is* no black hair in it; then the priest shall shut up *him that has* the plague of the scale seven days:

32 And in the seventh day the priest shall look on the plague: and, behold, *if* the scale spreads not, and there is in it no yellow hair, and the scale *is* not in sight deeper than the skin;

33 He shall be shaven, but the scale shall he not shave; and the priest shall shut up *him that has* the scale seven days more:

34 And in the seventh day the priest shall look on the scale: and, behold, *if* the scale is not spread in the skin, nor *is* in sight deeper than the skin; then the priest shall pronounce him clean: and he shall wash his clothes, and be clean.

35 But if the scale spreads much in the skin after his cleansing;

36 Then the priest shall look on him: and, behold, if the scale has spread in the skin, the priest shall not seek for yellow hair; he *is* unclean.

37 But if the scale is in his sight at a stay, and *that* there is black hair grown up therein; the scale is healed, he *is* clean: and the priest shall pronounce him clean.

38 ¶ If a man also or a woman has in the skin of their flesh bright spots, *even* white bright spots;

Leviticus 13

39 Then the priest shall look: and, behold, *if* the bright spots in the skin of their flesh *are* darkish white; it *is* a freckled spot *that* grows in the skin; he *is* clean.

40 And the man whose hair has fallen off his head, he *is* bald; *yet is* he clean.

41 And he that has his hair fallen off from the part of his head toward his face, he *is* forehead bald: *yet is* he clean.

42 And if there is in the bald head, or bald forehead, a white reddish sore; it *is* a leprosy sprung up in his bald head, or his bald forehead.

43 Then the priest shall look upon it: and, behold, *if* the rising of the sore *is* white reddish in his bald head, or in his bald forehead, as the leprosy appears in the skin of the flesh;

44 He is a leprous man, he *is* unclean: the priest shall pronounce him utterly unclean; his plague *is* in his head.

45 And the leper in whom the plague *is*, his clothes shall be torn, and his head bear, and he shall put a covering upon his upper lip, and shall cry, Unclean, unclean.

46 All the days wherein the plague *shall be* in him he shall be defiled; he *is* unclean: he shall dwell alone; outside the camp *shall* his habitation *be*.

47 ¶ The garment also that the plague of leprosy is in, *whether it is* a woolen garment, or a linen garment;

48 Whether *it is* in the warp, or woof; of linen, or of woolen; whether in a skin, or in anything made of skin;

49 And if the plague is greenish or reddish in the garment, or in the skin, either in the warp, or in the woof, or in anything of skin; it *is* a plague of leprosy, and shall be shown to the priest:

50 And the priest shall look upon the plague, and shut up *it that has* the plague seven days:

51 And he shall look on the plague on the seventh day: if the plague is spread in the garment, either in the warp, or in the woof, or in a skin, *or* in any work that is made of skin; the plague *is* a fretting leprosy; it *is* unclean.

52 He shall therefore burn that garment, whether warp or woof, in woolen or in linen, or anything of skin, wherein the plague is: for it *is* a fretting leprosy; it shall be burnt in the fire.

53 And if the priest shall look, and, behold, the plague has not spread in the garment, either in the warp, or in the woof, or in anything of skin;

54 Then the priest shall command that they wash *the thing* wherein the plague *is*, and he shall shut it up seven days more:

55 And the priest shall look on the plague, after that it is washed: and, behold, *if* the plague has not changed his color, and the plague is not spread; it *is* unclean; you shall burn it in the fire; it *is* boring inward, *whether* it *is* bare within or without.

56 And if the priest looks, and, behold, the plague *is* somewhat dark after the washing of it; then he shall rend it out of the garment, or out of the skin, or out of the warp, or out of the woof:

57 And if it appears still in the garment, either in the warp, or in the woof, or in anything of skin; it *is* a spreading *plague*: you shall burn that wherein the plague *is* with fire.

58 And the garment, either warp, or woof, or whatever thing of skin *it is*, which you shall wash, if the plague has departed from them, then it shall be washed the second time, and shall be clean.

59 This *is* the law of the plague of leprosy in a garment of woolen or linen, either in the warp, or woof, or anything of skins, to pronounce it clean, or to pronounce it unclean.

Leviticus 14

14:1 ¶ And Yahweh spoke to Moses, saying,

2 This shall be the law of the leper in the day of his cleansing: He shall be brought to the priest:

3 And the priest shall go forth out of the camp; and the priest shall look, and, behold, *if* the plague of leprosy is healed in the leper;

4 Then shall the priest command to take for him that is to be cleansed two birds alive *and* clean, and cedar wood, and scarlet, and hyssop:

5 And the priest shall command that one of the birds be killed in an earthen vessel over running water:

6 As for the living bird, he shall take it, and the cedar wood, and the scarlet, and the hyssop, and shall dip them and the living bird in the blood of the bird *that was* killed over the running water:

7 And he shall sprinkle upon him that is to be cleansed from the leprosy seven times, and shall pronounce him clean, and shall let the living bird loose into the open field.

8 And he that is to be cleansed shall wash his clothes, and shave off all his hair, and wash himself in water, that he may be clean: and after that he shall come into the camp, and shall remain outside out of his tent seven days.

9 But it shall be on the seventh day, that he shall shave all his hair off his head and his beard and his eyebrows, even all his hair he shall shave off: and he shall wash his clothes, also he shall wash his flesh in water, and he shall be clean.

10 ¶ And on the eighth day he shall take two he lambs without blemish, and one ewe lamb of the first year without blemish, and three tenths deals of fine flour *for* a meat offering, mingled with oil, and one log of oil.

11 And the priest that makes *him* clean shall present the man that is to be made clean, and those things, before Yahweh, *at* the door of the tabernacle of the congregation:

12 And the priest shall take one he lamb, and offer him for a trespass offering, and the log of oil, and wave them *for* a wave offering before Yahweh:

13 And he shall slay the lamb in the place where he shall kill the sin offering and the burnt offering, in the holy place: for as the sin offering *is* the priest's, *so is* the trespass offering: it *is* most holy:

14 And the priest shall take *some* of the blood of the trespass offering, and the priest shall put *it* upon the tip of the right ear of him that is to be cleansed, and upon the thumb of his right hand, and upon the great toe of his right foot:

15 And the priest shall take *some* of the log of oil, and pour *it* into the palm of his own left hand:

16 And the priest shall dip his right finger in the oil that *is* in his left hand, and shall sprinkle of the oil with his finger seven times before Yahweh:

17 And of the rest of the oil that *is* in his hand shall the priest put upon the tip of the right ear of him that is to be cleansed, and upon the thumb of his right hand, and upon the great toe of his right foot, upon the blood of the trespass offering:

18 And the remnant of the oil that *is* in the priest's hand he shall pour upon the head of him that is to be cleansed: and the priest shall make an atonement for him before Yahweh.

19 And the priest shall offer the sin offering, and make an atonement for him that is to be cleansed from his uncleanness; and afterward he shall kill the burnt offering:

20 And the priest shall offer the burnt offering and the meat offering upon the altar: and the priest shall make an atonement for him, and he shall be clean.

21 ¶ And if he *is* poor, and cannot get so much; then he shall take one lamb *for* a trespass offering to be waved, to make an atonement for him, and one tenth deal of fine flour mingled with oil for a meat offering, and a log of oil;

22 And two turtledoves, or two young pigeons, such as he is able to get; and the one shall be a sin offering, and the other a burnt offering.

23 And he shall bring them on the eighth day for his cleansing to the priest, to the door of the tabernacle of the congregation, before Yahweh.

24 And the priest shall take the lamb of the trespass offering, and the log of oil, and the priest shall wave them *for* a wave offering before Yahweh:

25 And he shall kill the lamb of the trespass offering, and the priest shall take *some* of the blood of the trespass offering, and put *it* upon the tip of the right ear of him that is to be cleansed, and upon the thumb of his right hand, and upon the great toe of his right foot:

26 And the priest shall pour of the oil into the palm of his own left hand:

27 And the priest shall sprinkle with his right finger *some* of the oil that *is* in his left hand seven times before Yahweh:

28 And the priest shall put of the oil that *is* in his hand upon the tip of the right ear of him that is to be cleansed, and upon the thumb of his right hand, and upon the great toe of his right foot, upon the place of the blood of the trespass offering:

29 And the rest of the oil that *is* in the priest's hand he shall put upon the head of him that is to be cleansed, to make an atonement for him before Yahweh.

30 And he shall offer one of the turtledoves, or of the young pigeons, such as he can get;

31 *Even* such as he is able to get, the one *for* a sin offering, and the other *for* a burnt offering, with the meat offering: and the priest shall make an atonement for him that is to be cleansed before Yahweh.

32 This *is* the law *of him* in whom *is* the plague of leprosy, whose hand is not able to get *that which pertains* to his cleansing.

33 ¶ And Yahweh spoke to Moses and to Aaron, saying,

34 When you come into the land of Canaan, which I give to you for a possession, and I put the plague of leprosy in a house of the land of your possession;

35 And he that owns the house shall come and tell the priest, saying, It seems to me *there is* as it were a plague in the house:

36 Then the priest shall command that they empty the house, before the priest goes *into it* to see the plague, that all that *is* in the house is not made unclean: and afterward the priest shall go in to see the house:

37 And he shall look on the plague, and, behold, *if* the plague *is* in the walls of the house with hollow streaks, greenish or reddish, which in sight *are* lower than the wall;

38 Then the priest shall go out of the house to the door of the house, and shut up the house seven days:

39 And the priest shall come again the seventh day, and shall look: and, behold, *if* the plague has spread in the walls of the house;

40 Then the priest shall command that they take away the stones in which the plague *is*, and they shall cast them into an unclean place outside the city:

41 And he shall cause the house to be scraped within round about, and they shall pour out the dust that they scrape off outside the city into an unclean place:

42 And they shall take other stones, and put *them* in the place of those stones; and he shall take other mortar, and shall plaster the house.

43 And if the plague comes again, and break out in the house, after that he has taken away the stones, and after he has scraped the house, and after it is plastered;

44 Then the priest shall come and look, and, behold, *if* the plague has spread in the house, it *is* a fretting leprosy in the house: it *is* unclean.

45 And he shall break down the house, the stones of it, and the timber thereof, and all the mortar of the house; and he shall carry *them* forth out of the city into an unclean place.

46 Moreover he that goes into the house all the while that it is shut up shall be unclean until the evening.

47 And he that lies in the house shall wash his clothes; and he that eats in the house shall wash his clothes.

48 And if the priest shall come in, and look upon *it*, and, behold, the plague has not spread in the house, after the house was plastered: then the priest shall pronounce the house clean, because the plague is healed.

49 And he shall take to cleanse the house two birds, and cedar wood, and scarlet, and hyssop:

50 And he shall kill one of the birds in an earthen vessel over running water:

51 And he shall take the cedar wood, and the hyssop, and the scarlet, and the living bird, and dip them in the blood of the slain bird, and in the running water, and sprinkle the house seven times:

52 And he shall cleanse the house with the blood of the bird, and with the running water, and with the living bird, and with the cedar wood, and with the hyssop, and with the scarlet:

Leviticus 14

53 But he shall let go the living bird out of the city into the open fields, and make an atonement for the house: and it shall be clean.
54 ¶ This *is* the law for all manner of plague of leprosy, and scale,
55 And for the leprosy of a garment, and of a house,
56 And for a rising, and for a scab, and for a bright spot:
57 To teach when *it is* unclean, and when *it is* clean: this *is* the law of leprosy.

Leviticus 15

15:1 ¶ And Yahweh spoke to Moses and to Aaron, saying,
2 Speak to the children of Israel, and say to them, When any man has a running issue out of his flesh, *because of* his issue he *is* unclean.
3 And this shall be his uncleanness in his issue: whether his flesh runs with his issue, or his flesh is stopped from his issue, it *is* his uncleanness.
4 Every bed, whereon he lies that has the issue, is unclean: and every thing, whereon he sits, shall be unclean.
5 And whoever touches his bed shall wash his clothes, and bathe *himself* in water, and be unclean until the evening.
6 And he that sits on *any* thing whereon he sat that has the issue shall wash his clothes, and bathe *himself* in water, and be unclean until the evening.
7 And he that touches the flesh of him that has the issue shall wash his clothes, and bathe *himself* in water, and be unclean until the evening.
8 And if he that has the issue spits upon him that is clean; then he shall wash his clothes, and bathe *himself* in water, and be unclean until the evening.
9 And whatever saddle he rides upon that has the issue shall be unclean.
10 And whoever touches anything that was under him shall be unclean until the evening: and he that bears *any of* those things shall wash his clothes, and bathe *himself* in water, and be unclean until the evening.
11 And whomever he touches that has the issue, and has not rinsed his hands in water, he shall wash his clothes, and bathe *himself* in water, and be unclean until the evening.
12 And the vessel of earth, that he touches which has the issue, shall be broken: and every vessel of wood shall be rinsed in water.
13 And when he that has an issue is cleansed of his issue; then he shall number to himself seven days for his cleansing, and wash his clothes, and bathe his flesh in running water, and shall be clean.
14 And on the eighth day he shall take to him two turtledoves, or two young pigeons, and come before Yahweh to the door of the tabernacle of the congregation, and give them to the priest:
15 And the priest shall offer them, the one *for* a sin offering, and the other *for* a burnt offering; and the priest shall make an atonement for him before Yahweh for his issue.
16 And if any man's seed of copulation goes out from him, then he shall wash all his flesh in water, and be unclean until the evening.
17 And every garment, and every skin, whereon is the seed of copulation, shall be washed with water, and be unclean until the evening.
18 The woman also with whom man shall lie *with* seed of copulation, they shall *both* bathe *themselves* in water, and be unclean until the evening.
19 ¶ And if a woman has an issue, *and* her issue in her flesh is blood, she shall be put apart seven days: and whoever touches her shall be unclean until the evening.
20 And every thing that she lies upon in her separation shall be unclean: every thing also that she sits upon shall be unclean.
21 And whoever touches her bed shall wash his clothes, and bathe *himself* in water, and be unclean until the evening.
22 And whoever touches anything that she sat upon shall wash his clothes, and bathe *himself* in water, and be unclean until the evening.
23 And if it *is* on *her* bed, or on anything whereon she sits, when he touches it, he shall be unclean until the evening.
24 And if any man lies with her at all, and her impurity is upon him, he shall be unclean seven days; and all the beds whereon he lies shall be unclean.
25 And if a woman has an issue of her blood many days out of the time of her separation, or if it runs beyond the time of her separation; all the days of the issue of her uncleanness shall be as the days of her separation: she *shall be* unclean.
26 Every bed whereon she lies all the days of her issue shall be to her as the bed of her separation: and whatever she sits upon shall be unclean, as the uncleanness of her separation.
27 And whoever touches those things shall be unclean, and shall wash his clothes, and bathe *himself* in water, and be unclean until the evening.
28 But if she is cleansed of her issue, then she shall number to herself seven days, and after that she shall be clean.
29 And on the eighth day she shall take to her two turtledoves, or two young pigeons, and bring them to the priest, to the door of the tabernacle of the congregation.
30 And the priest shall offer the one *for* a sin offering, and the other *for* a burnt offering; and the priest shall make an atonement for her before Yahweh for the issue of her uncleanness.
31 Thus shall you separate the children of Israel from their uncleanness; that they die not in their uncleanness, when they defile my tabernacle that *is* among them.
32 This *is* the law of him that has an issue, and *of him* whose seed goes from him, and is defiled therewith;
33 And of her that is sick of her impurity, and of him that has an issue, of the man, and of the woman, and of him that lies with her that is unclean.

Leviticus 16

16:1 ¶ And Yahweh spoke to Moses after the death of the two sons of Aaron, when they offered before Yahweh, and died;

2 And Yahweh said to Moses, Speak to Aaron your brother, that he comes not at all times into the holy *place* within the veil before the mercy seat, which *is* upon the ark; that he dies not: for I will appear in the cloud upon the mercy seat.

3 Thus shall Aaron come into the holy *place*: with a young bullock for a sin offering, and a ram for a burnt offering.

4 He shall put on the holy linen coat, and he shall have the linen breeches upon his flesh, and shall be girded with a linen girdle, and with the linen turban shall he be attired: these *are* holy garments; therefore shall he wash his flesh in water, and *so* put them on.

5 ¶ And he shall take of the congregation of the children of Israel two kids of the goats for a sin offering, and one ram for a burnt offering.

6 And Aaron shall offer his bullock of the sin offering, which *is* for himself, and make an atonement for himself, and for his house.

7 And he shall take the two goats, and present them before Yahweh *at* the door of the tabernacle of the congregation.

8 And Aaron shall cast lots upon the two goats; one lot for Yahweh, and the other lot for the scapegoat.

9 And Aaron shall bring the goat upon which Yahweh's lot fell, and offer him *for* a sin offering.

10 But the goat, on which the lot fell to be the scapegoat, shall be presented alive before Yahweh, to make an atonement with him, *and* to let him go for a scapegoat into the wilderness.

11 And Aaron shall bring the bullock of the sin offering, which *is* for himself, and shall make an atonement for himself, and for his house, and shall kill the bullock of the sin offering which *is* for himself:

12 And he shall take a censer full of burning coals of fire from off the altar before Yahweh, and his hands full of sweet incense beaten small, and bring *it* within the veil:

13 And he shall put the incense upon the fire before Yahweh, that the cloud of the incense may cover the mercy seat that *is* upon the testimony, that he dies not:

14 And he shall take of the blood of the bullock, and sprinkle *it* with his finger upon the mercy seat eastward; and before the mercy seat shall he sprinkle of the blood with his finger seven times.

15 ¶ Then shall he kill the goat of the sin offering, that *is* for the people, and bring his blood within the veil, and do with that blood as he did with the blood of the bullock, and sprinkle it upon the mercy seat, and before the mercy seat:

16 And he shall make an atonement for the holy *place*, because of the uncleanness of the children of Israel, and because of their transgressions in all their sins: and so shall he do for the tabernacle of the congregation, that remains among them in the midst of their uncleanness.

17 And there shall be no man in the tabernacle of the congregation when he goes in to make an atonement in the holy *place*, until he comes out, and has made an atonement for himself, and for his household, and for all the congregation of Israel.

18 And he shall go out to the altar that *is* before Yahweh, and make an atonement for it; and shall take of the blood of the bullock, and of the blood of the goat, and put *it* upon the horns of the altar round about.

19 And he shall sprinkle of the blood upon it with his finger seven times, and cleanse it, and hallow it from the uncleanness of the children of Israel.

20 ¶ And when he has made an end of reconciling the holy *place*, and the tabernacle of the congregation, and the altar, he shall bring the live goat:

21 And Aaron shall lay both his hands upon the head of the live goat, and confess over him all the iniquities of the children of Israel, and all their transgressions in all their sins, putting them upon the head of the goat, and shall send *him* away by the hand of a fit man into the wilderness:

22 And the goat shall bear upon him all their iniquities unto a land not inhabited: and he shall let go the goat in the wilderness.

23 And Aaron shall come into the tabernacle of the congregation, and shall put off the linen garments, which he put on when he went into the holy *place*, and shall leave them there:

24 And he shall wash his flesh with water in the holy place, and put on his garments, and come forth, and offer his burnt offering, and the burnt offering of the people, and make an atonement for himself, and for the people.

25 And the fat of the sin offering shall he burn upon the altar.

26 And he that let go the goat for the scapegoat shall wash his clothes, and bathe his flesh in water, and afterwards come into the camp.

27 And the bullock *for* the sin offering, and the goat *for* the sin offering, whose blood was brought in to make atonement in the holy *place*, shall *one* carry forth outside the camp; and they shall burn in the fire their skins, and their flesh, and their dung.

28 And he that burns them shall wash his clothes, and bathe his flesh in water, and afterwards he shall come into the camp.

29 ¶ And *this* shall be a statute forever unto you: *that* in the seventh month, on the tenth *day* of the month, you shall afflict your souls, and do no work at all, *whether it is* one of your own country, or a stranger that sojourns among you:

30 For on that day shall *the priest* make an atonement for you, to cleanse you, *that* you may be clean from all your sins before Yahweh.

31 It *shall be* a sabbath of rest to you, and you shall afflict your souls, by a statute forever.

32 And the priest, whom he shall anoint, and whom he shall consecrate to minister in the priest's office in his father's stead, shall make the atonement, and shall put on the linen clothes, *even* the holy garments:

Leviticus 16

33 And he shall make an atonement for the holy sanctuary, and he shall make an atonement for the tabernacle of the congregation, and for the altar, and he shall make an atonement for the priests, and for all the people of the congregation.

34 And this shall be an everlasting statute unto you, to make an atonement for the children of Israel for all their sins once a year. And he did as Yahweh commanded Moses.

Leviticus 17

17:1 ¶ And Yahweh spoke to Moses, saying,

2 Speak to Aaron, and to his sons, and to all the children of Israel, and say to them; This *is* the thing which Yahweh has commanded, saying,

3 Whatever man *there is* of the house of Israel, that kills an ox, or lamb, or goat, in the camp, or that kills *it* out of the camp,

4 And brings it not to the door of the tabernacle of the congregation, to offer an offering unto Yahweh before the tabernacle of Yahweh; blood shall be imputed unto that man; he has shed blood; and that man shall be cut off from among his people:

5 To the end that the children of Israel may bring their sacrifices, which they offer in the open field, even that they may bring them unto Yahweh, to the door of the tabernacle of the congregation, to the priest, and offer them *for* peace offerings unto Yahweh.

6 And the priest shall sprinkle the blood upon the altar of Yahweh *at* the door of the tabernacle of the congregation, and burn the fat for a sweet savor unto Yahweh.

7 And they shall no more offer their sacrifices to devils, after whom they have gone a whoring. This shall be a statute forever to them throughout their generations.

8 And you shall say to them, Whatever man *there is* of the house of Israel, or of the strangers which sojourn among you, that offers a burnt offering or sacrifice,

9 And brings it not to the door of the tabernacle of the congregation, to offer it unto Yahweh; even that man shall be cut off from among his people.

10 ¶ And whatever man *there is* of the house of Israel, or of the strangers that sojourn among you, that eats any manner of blood; I will even set my face against that soul that eats blood, and will cut him off from among his people.

11 For the life of the flesh *is* in the blood: and I have given it to you upon the altar to make an atonement for your souls: for it *is* the blood *that* makes an atonement for the soul.

12 Therefore I said to the children of Israel, No soul of you shall eat blood, neither shall any stranger that sojourns among you eat blood.

13 And whatever man *there is* of the children of Israel, or of the strangers that sojourn among you, which hunts and catches any beast or fowl that may be eaten; he shall even pour out the blood thereof, and cover it with dust.

14 For *it is* the life of all flesh; the blood of it *is* for the life thereof: therefore I said to the children of Israel, You shall eat the blood of no manner of flesh: for the life of all flesh *is* the blood thereof: whoever eats it shall be cut off.

15 And every soul that eats that which died *of itself*, or that which was torn *by beasts, whether it is* one of your own country, or a stranger, he shall both wash his clothes, and bathe *himself* in water, and be unclean until the evening: then shall he be clean.

16 But if he washes *them* not, nor bathes his flesh; then he shall bear his iniquity.

Leviticus 18

18:1 ¶ And Yahweh spoke to Moses, saying,

2 Speak to the children of Israel, and say to them, I am Yahweh your God.

3 After the doings of the land of Egypt, wherein you dwelt, shall you not do: and after the doings of the land of Canaan, where I bring you, shall you not do: neither shall you walk in their ordinances.

4 You shall do my judgments, and keep my ordinances, to walk therein: I *am* Yahweh your God.

5 You shall therefore keep my statutes, and my judgments: which if a man does, he shall live in them: I *am* Yahweh.

6 ¶ None of you shall approach to any that is near of kin to him, to uncover *their* nakedness: I *am* Yahweh.

7 The nakedness of your father, or the nakedness of your mother, shall you not uncover: she *is* your mother; you shall not uncover her nakedness.

8 The nakedness of your father's wife shall you not uncover: it *is* your father's nakedness.

9 The nakedness of your sister, the daughter of your father, or daughter of your mother, *whether she is* born at home, or born abroad, *even* their nakedness you shall not uncover.

10 The nakedness of your son's daughter, or of your daughter's daughter, *even* their nakedness you shall not uncover: for theirs *is* your own nakedness.

11 The nakedness of your father's wife's daughter, begotten of your father, she *is* your sister, you shall not uncover her nakedness.

12 You shall not uncover the nakedness of your father's sister: she *is* your father's near kinswoman.

13 You shall not uncover the nakedness of your mother's sister: for she *is* your mother's near kinswoman.

14 You shall not uncover the nakedness of your father's brother, you shall not approach to his wife: she *is* your aunt.

15 You shall not uncover the nakedness of your daughter-in-law: she *is* your son's wife; you shall not uncover her nakedness.

16 You shall not uncover the nakedness of your brother's wife: it *is* your brother's nakedness.

17 You shall not uncover the nakedness of a woman and her daughter, neither shall you take her son's daughter, or her daughter's daughter, to uncover her nakedness; *for* they *are* her near kinswomen: it *is* wickedness.

18 Neither shall you take a wife to her sister, to distress *her*, to uncover her nakedness, beside the other in her life *time*.
19 ¶ Also you shall not approach to a woman to uncover her nakedness, as long as she is put apart for her uncleanness.
20 Moreover you shall not lie carnally with your neighbor's wife, to defile yourself with her.
21 And you shall not let any of your seed pass through *the fire* to Molech, neither shall you profane the name of your God: I *am* Yahweh.
22 You shall not lie with mankind, as with womankind: it *is* abomination.
23 Neither shall you lie with any beast to defile yourself therewith: neither shall any woman stand before a beast to lie down thereto: it *is* confusion.
24 Defile not you yourselves in any of these things: for in all these the nations are defiled which I cast out before you:
25 And the land is defiled: therefore I do visit the iniquity thereof upon it, and the land itself vomits out her inhabitants.
26 You shall therefore keep my statutes and my judgments, and shall not commit *any* of these abominations; *neither* any of your own nation, nor any stranger that sojourns among you:
27 (For all these abominations have the men of the land done, which *were* before you, and the land is defiled;)
28 That the land spew not you out also, when you defile it, as it spewed out the nations that *were* before you.
29 For whoever shall commit any of these abominations, even the souls that commits *them* shall be cut off from among their people.
30 Therefore shall you keep my ordinance, that *you* commit not *any one* of these abominable customs, which were committed before you, and that you defile not yourselves therein: I *am* Yahweh your God.

Leviticus 19

19:1 ¶ And Yahweh spoke to Moses, saying,
2 Speak to all the congregation of the children of Israel, and say to them, You shall be holy: for I Yahweh your God *am* holy.
3 You shall fear every man his mother, and his father, and keep my sabbaths: I *am* Yahweh your God.
4 Turn you not unto idols, nor make to yourselves molten gods: I *am* Yahweh your God.
5 And if you offer a sacrifice of peace offerings unto Yahweh, you shall offer it at your own will.
6 It shall be eaten the same day you offer it, and on the next day: and if any remains until the third day, it shall be burnt in the fire.
7 And if it is eaten at all on the third day, it *is* abominable; it shall not be accepted.
8 Therefore *every one* that eats it shall bear his iniquity, because he has profaned the hallowed thing of Yahweh: and that soul shall be cut off from among his people.

9 And when you reap the harvest of your land, you shall not wholly reap the corners of your field, neither shall you gather the gleanings of your harvest.
10 And you shall not glean your vineyard, neither shall you gather *every* grape of your vineyard; you shall leave them for the poor and stranger: I *am* Yahweh your God.
11 ¶ You shall not steal, neither deal falsely, neither lie one to another.
12 And you shall not swear by my name falsely, neither shall you profane the name of your God: I *am* Yahweh.
13 You shall not defraud your neighbor, neither rob *him*: the wages of him that is hired shall not lodge with you all night until the morning.
14 You shall not curse the deaf, nor put a stumbling block before the blind, but shall fear your God: I *am* Yahweh.
15 You shall do no unrighteousness in judgment: you shall not respect the person of the poor, nor honor the person of the mighty: *but* in righteousness shall you judge your neighbor.
16 You shall not go up and down *as* a talebearer among your people: neither shall you stand against the blood of your neighbor: I *am* Yahweh.
17 You shall not hate your brother in your heart: you shall in any way rebuke your neighbor, and not bear sin upon him.
18 You shall not avenge, nor bear any grudge against the children of your people, but you shall love your neighbor as yourself: I *am* Yahweh.
19 ¶ You shall keep my statutes. You shall not let your cattle breed with a diverse kind: you shall not sow your field with mingled seed: neither shall a garment mingled of linen and woolen come upon you.
20 And whoever lies carnally with a woman, that *is* a bondmaid, betrothed to a husband, and not at all redeemed, nor freedom given her; she shall be scourged; they shall not be put to death, because she was not free.
21 And he shall bring his trespass offering unto Yahweh, to the door of the tabernacle of the congregation, *even* a ram for a trespass offering.
22 And the priest shall make an atonement for him with the ram of the trespass offering before Yahweh for his sin which he has done: and the sin which he has done shall be forgiven him.
23 And when you shall come into the land, and shall have planted all manner of trees for food, then you shall count the fruit thereof as uncircumcised: three years shall it be as uncircumcised unto you: it shall not be eaten of.
24 But in the fourth year all the fruit thereof shall be holy to praise Yahweh *therewith*.
25 And in the fifth year shall you eat of the fruit thereof, that it may yield to you the increase thereof: I *am* Yahweh your God.
26 You shall not eat *anything* with the blood: neither shall you use enchantments, nor observe times.
27 You shall not round the corners of your heads, neither shall you mar the corners of your beard.
28 You shall not make any cuttings in your flesh for the dead, nor print any marks upon you: I *am* Yahweh.

Leviticus 19

29 Do not prostitute your daughter, to cause her to be a whore; lest the land falls to whoredom, and the land becomes full of wickedness.

30 ¶ You shall keep my sabbaths, and reverence my sanctuary: I *am* Yahweh.

31 Regard not them that have familiar spirits, neither seek after wizards, to be defiled by them: I *am* Yahweh your God.

32 You shall rise up before the gray head, and honor the face of the old man, and fear your God: I *am* Yahweh.

33 And if a stranger sojourns with you in your land, you shall not oppress him.

34 *But* the stranger that dwells with you shall be to you as one born among you, and you shall love him as yourself; for you were strangers in the land of Egypt: I *am* Yahweh your God.

35 You shall do no unrighteousness in judgment, in length, in weight, or in measure.

36 Just balances, just weights, a just ephah, and a just hin, shall you have: I *am* Yahweh your God, which brought you out of the land of Egypt.

37 Therefore shall you observe all my statutes, and all my judgments, and do them: I *am* Yahweh.

Leviticus 20

20:1 ¶ And Yahweh spoke to Moses, saying,

2 Again, you shall say to the children of Israel, Whoever *he is* of the children of Israel, or of the strangers that sojourn in Israel, that gives *any* of his seed to Molech; he shall surely be put to death: the people of the land shall stone him with stones.

3 And I will set my face against that man, and will cut him off from among his people; because he has given of his seed to Molech, to defile my sanctuary, and to profane my holy name.

4 And if the people of the land do any way hide their eyes from the man, when he gives of his seed to Molech, and kill him not:

5 Then I will set my face against that man, and against his family, and will cut him off, and all that go a whoring after him, to commit whoredom with Molech, from among their people.

6 And the soul that turns after such as have familiar spirits, and after wizards, to go a whoring after them, I will even set my face against that soul, and will cut him off from among his people.

7 Sanctify yourselves therefore, and be you holy: for I *am* Yahweh your God.

8 And you shall keep my statutes, and do them: I *am* Yahweh which sanctifies you.

9 For every one that curses his father or his mother shall be surely put to death: he has cursed his father or his mother; his blood *shall be* upon him.

10 ¶ And the man that commits adultery with *another* man's wife, *even he* that commits adultery with his neighbor's wife, the adulterer and the adulteress shall surely be put to death.

11 And the man that lies with his father's wife has uncovered his father's nakedness: both of them shall surely be put to death; their blood *shall be* upon them.

12 And if a man lies with his daughter-in-law, both of them shall surely be put to death: they have worked confusion; their blood *shall be* upon them.

13 If a man also lies with mankind, as he lies with a woman, both of them have committed an abomination: they shall surely be put to death; their blood *shall be* upon them.

14 And if a man takes a wife and her mother, it *is* wickedness: they shall be burnt with fire, both he and they; that there be no wickedness among you.

15 And if a man lies with a beast, he shall surely be put to death: and you shall slay the beast.

16 And if a woman approaches unto any beast, and lies down thereto, you shall kill the woman, and the beast: they shall surely be put to death; their blood *shall be* upon them.

17 And if a man shall take his sister, his father's daughter, or his mother's daughter, and see her nakedness, and she sees his nakedness; it *is* a wicked thing; and they shall be cut off in the sight of their people: he has uncovered his sister's nakedness; he shall bear his iniquity.

18 And if a man shall lie with a woman having her sickness, and shall uncover her nakedness; he has discovered her fountain, and she has uncovered the fountain of her blood: and both of them shall be cut off from among their people.

19 And you shall not uncover the nakedness of your mother's sister, nor of your father's sister: for he uncovers his near kin: they shall bear their iniquity.

20 And if a man shall lie with his uncle's wife, he has uncovered his uncle's nakedness: they shall bear their sin; they shall die childless.

21 And if a man shall take his brother's wife, it *is* an unclean thing: he has uncovered his brother's nakedness; they shall be childless.

22 ¶ You shall therefore keep all my statutes, and all my judgments, and do them: that the land, where I bring you to dwell therein, spew you not out.

23 And you shall not walk in the manners of the nation, which I cast out before you: for they committed all these things, and therefore I abhorred them.

24 But I have said unto you, You shall inherit their land, and I will give it to you to possess it, a land that flows with milk and honey: I *am* Yahweh your God, which have separated you from *other* people.

25 You shall therefore put difference between clean beasts and unclean, and between unclean fowls and clean: and you shall not make your souls abominable by beast, or by fowl, or by any manner of living thing that creeps on the ground, which I have separated from you as unclean.

26 And you shall be holy to me: for I Yahweh *am* holy, and have severed you from *other* people, that you should be mine.

27 A man also or woman that has a familiar spirit, or that is a wizard, shall surely be put to death: they shall stone them with stones: their blood *shall be* upon them.

Leviticus 21

21:1 ¶ And Yahweh said to Moses, Speak to the priests the sons of Aaron, and say to them, There shall none be defiled for the dead among his people:
2 But for his kin, that is near to him, *that is*, for his mother, and for his father, and for his son, and for his daughter, and for his brother,
3 And for his sister a virgin, that is near to him, which has had no husband; for her may he be defiled.
4 *But* he shall not defile himself, *being* a chief man among his people, to profane himself.
5 They shall not make baldness upon their head, neither shall they shave off the corner of their beard, nor make any cuttings in their flesh.
6 They shall be holy to their God, and not profane the name of their God: for the offerings of Yahweh made by fire, *and* the bread of their God, they do offer: therefore they shall be holy.
7 They shall not take a wife *that is* a whore, or profane; neither shall they take a woman put away from her husband: for he *is* holy to his God.
8 You shall sanctify him therefore; for he offers the bread of your God: he shall be holy to you: for I Yahweh, which sanctifies you, *am* holy.
9 And the daughter of any priest, if she profanes herself by playing the whore, she profanes her father: she shall be burnt with fire.
10 ¶ And *he that is* the high priest among his brethren, upon whose head the anointing oil was poured, and that is consecrated to put on the garments, shall not uncover his head, nor tear his clothes;
11 Neither shall he go in to any dead body, nor defile himself for his father, or for his mother;
12 Neither shall he go out of the sanctuary, nor profane the sanctuary of his God; for the crown of the anointing oil of his God *is* upon him: I *am* Yahweh.
13 And he shall take a wife in her virginity.
14 A widow, or a divorced woman, or profane, *or* a harlot, these shall he not take: but he shall take a virgin of his own people to wife.
15 Neither shall he profane his seed among his people: for I Yahweh do sanctify him.
16 ¶ And Yahweh spoke to Moses, saying,
17 Speak to Aaron, saying, Whoever *he is* of your seed in their generations that has *any* blemish, let him not approach to offer the bread of his God.
18 For whatever man *he is* that has a blemish, he shall not approach: a blind man, or a lame, or he that has a flat nose, or anything superfluous,
19 Or a man that is broken footed, or broken handed,
20 Or hunch back, or a dwarf, or that has a blemish in his eye, or has scurvy, or scabbed, or has his testicles broken;
21 No man that has a blemish of the seed of Aaron the priest shall come near to offer the offerings of Yahweh made by fire: he has a blemish; he shall not come near to offer the bread of his God.
22 He shall eat the bread of his God, *both* of the most holy, and of the holy.
23 Only he shall not go in to the veil, nor come near to the altar, because he has a blemish; that he profane not my sanctuaries: for I Yahweh do sanctify them.
24 And Moses told *it* to Aaron, and to his sons, and to all the children of Israel.

Leviticus 22

22:1 ¶ And Yahweh spoke to Moses, saying,
2 Speak to Aaron and to his sons, that they separate themselves from the holy things of the children of Israel, and that they profane not my holy name *in those things* which they hallow unto me: I *am* Yahweh.
3 Say to them, Whoever *he is* of all your seed among your generations, that goes unto the holy things, which the children of Israel hallow unto Yahweh, having his uncleanness upon him, that soul shall be cut off from my presence: I *am* Yahweh.
4 Whatever man of the seed of Aaron *is* a leper, or has a running issue; he shall not eat of the holy things, until he is clean. And whoever touches anything *that is* unclean *by* the dead, or a man whose seed goes from him;
5 Or whoever touches any creeping thing, whereby he may be made unclean, or a man of whom he may take uncleanness, whatever uncleanness he has;
6 The soul which has touched any such shall be unclean until evening, and shall not eat of the holy things, unless he washes his flesh with water.
7 And when the sun is down, he shall be clean, and shall afterwards eat of the holy things; because it *is* his food.
8 That which dies of itself, or is torn *by beasts*, he shall not eat to defile himself therewith: I *am* Yahweh.
9 They shall therefore keep my ordinance, lest they bear sin for it, and die therefore, if they profane it: I Yahweh do sanctify them.
10 ¶ There shall no stranger eat *of* the holy thing: a sojourner of the priest, or a hired servant, shall not eat *of* the holy thing.
11 But if the priest buys *any* soul with his money, he shall eat of it, and he that is born in his house: they shall eat of his food.
12 If the priest's daughter also is *married* to a stranger, she may not eat of an offering of the holy things.
13 But if the priest's daughter is a widow, or divorced, and has no child, and is returned to her father's house, as in her youth, she shall eat of her father's food: but there shall no stranger eat thereof.
14 And if a man eats *of* the holy thing unwittingly, then he shall put the fifth *part* thereof unto it, and shall give *it* to the priest with the holy thing.
15 And they shall not profane the holy things of the children of Israel, which they offer unto Yahweh;
16 Or allow them to bear the iniquity of trespass, when they eat their holy things: for I Yahweh do sanctify them.
17 ¶ And Yahweh spoke to Moses, saying,

Leviticus 22

18 Speak to Aaron, and to his sons, and to all the children of Israel, and say to them, Whoever *he is* of the house of Israel, or of the strangers in Israel, that will offer his oblation for all his vows, and for all his freewill offerings, which they will offer unto Yahweh for a burnt offering;
19 *You shall offer* at your own will a male without blemish, of the cattle, of the sheep, or of the goats.
20 *But* whatever has a blemish, *that* shall you not offer: for it shall not be acceptable for you.
21 And whoever offers a sacrifice of peace offerings unto Yahweh to accomplish *his* vow, or a freewill offering in cattle or sheep, it shall be perfect to be accepted; there shall be no blemish therein.
22 Blind, or broken, or maimed, or having an ulcer, or scurvy, or scabbed, you shall not offer these to Yahweh, nor make an offering by fire of them upon the altar to Yahweh.
23 Either a bullock or a lamb that has anything superfluous or lacking in his parts, that may you offer *for* a freewill offering; but for a vow it shall not be accepted.
24 You shall not offer unto Yahweh that which is bruised, or crushed, or broken, or cut; neither shall you make *any offering thereof* in your land.
25 Neither from a stranger's hand shall you offer the bread of your God of any of these; because their corruption *is* in them, *and* blemishes *are* in them: they shall not be accepted for you.
26 And Yahweh spoke to Moses, saying,
27 When a bullock, or a sheep, or a goat, is brought forth, then it shall be seven days under the mother; and from the eighth day and thereafter it shall be accepted for an offering made by fire to Yahweh.
28 And *whether it is* cow or ewe, you shall not kill it and her young both in one day.
29 And when you will offer a sacrifice of thanksgiving to Yahweh, offer *it* at your own will.
30 On the same day it shall be eaten up; you shall leave none of it until the next day: I *am* Yahweh.
31 Therefore shall you keep my commandments, and do them: I *am* Yahweh.
32 Neither shall you profane my holy name; but I will be hallowed among the children of Israel: I *am* Yahweh which hallows you,
33 That brought you out of the land of Egypt, to be your God: I *am* Yahweh.

Leviticus 23

23:1 ¶ And Yahweh spoke to Moses, saying,
2 Speak to the children of Israel, and say to them, *Concerning* the feasts of Yahweh, which you shall proclaim *to be* holy convocations, *even* these *are* my feasts.
3 Six days shall work be done: but the seventh day *is* the sabbath of rest, a holy convocation; you shall do no work *therein*: it *is* the sabbath of Yahweh in all your dwellings.
4 ¶ These *are* the feasts of Yahweh, *even* holy convocations, which you shall proclaim in their seasons.
5 In the fourteenth *day* of the first month at evening *is* Yahweh's passover.
6 And on the fifteenth day of the same month *is* the feast of unleavened bread unto Yahweh: seven days you must eat unleavened bread.
7 In the first day you shall have a holy convocation: you shall do no laborious work therein.
8 But you shall offer an offering made by fire unto Yahweh seven days: in the seventh day *is* a holy convocation: you shall do no laborious work *therein*.
9 And Yahweh spoke to Moses, saying,
10 Speak to the children of Israel, and say to them, When you have come into the land which I give to you, and shall reap the harvest thereof, then you shall bring a sheaf of the firstfruits of your harvest to the priest:
11 And he shall wave the sheaf before Yahweh, to be accepted for you: on the next day after the sabbath the priest shall wave it.
12 And you shall offer that day when you wave the sheaf a he lamb without blemish of the first year for a burnt offering unto Yahweh.
13 And the meat offering thereof *shall be* two tenths deals of fine flour mingled with oil, an offering made by fire unto Yahweh *for* a sweet savor: and the drink offering thereof *shall be* of wine, the fourth *part* of a hin.
14 And you shall eat neither bread, nor parched corn, nor green ears, until the very same day that you have brought an offering to your God: *it shall be* a statute forever throughout your generations in all your dwellings.
15 ¶ And you shall count unto you from the next day after the sabbath, from the day that you brought the sheaf of the wave offering; seven sabbaths shall be complete:
16 Even to the next day after the seventh sabbath shall you number fifty days; and you shall offer a new meat offering unto Yahweh.
17 You shall bring out of your habitations two wave loaves of two tenths deals: they shall be of fine flour; they shall be baked with leaven; *they are* the firstfruits unto Yahweh.
18 And you shall offer with the bread seven lambs without blemish of the first year, and one young bullock, and two rams: they shall be *for* a burnt offering unto Yahweh, with their meat offering, and their drink offerings, *even* an offering made by fire, of sweet savor unto Yahweh.
19 Then you shall sacrifice one kid of the goats for a sin offering, and two lambs of the first year for a sacrifice of peace offerings.
20 And the priest shall wave them with the bread of the firstfruits *for* a wave offering before Yahweh, with the two lambs: they shall be holy unto Yahweh for the priest.
21 And you shall proclaim on the very same day, *that* it may be a holy convocation unto you: you shall do no laborious work *therein: it shall be* a statute forever in all your dwellings throughout your generations.
22 And when you reap the harvest of your land, you shall not make clean riddance of the corners of your field when you reap, neither shall you gather any gleaning of your harvest: you shall leave them to the poor, and to the stranger: I *am* Yahweh your God.

23 ¶ And Yahweh spoke to Moses, saying,
24 Speak to the children of Israel, saying, In the seventh month, in the first *day* of the month, shall you have a sabbath, a memorial of blowing of trumpets, a holy convocation.
25 You shall do no laborious work *therein*: but you shall offer an offering made by fire unto Yahweh.
26 And Yahweh spoke to Moses, saying,
27 Also on the tenth *day* of this seventh month *there shall be* a day of atonement: it shall be a holy convocation unto you; and you shall afflict your souls, and offer an offering made by fire unto Yahweh.
28 And you shall do no work in that same day: for it *is* a day of atonement, to make an atonement for you before Yahweh your God.
29 For whatever soul *it is* that shall not be afflicted in that same day, he shall be cut off from among his people.
30 And whatever soul *it is* that does any work in that same day, the same soul will I destroy from among his people.
31 You shall do no manner of work: *it shall be* a statute forever throughout your generations in all your dwellings.
32 It *shall be* to you a sabbath of rest, and you shall afflict your souls: in the ninth *day* of the month at evening, from evening to evening, shall you celebrate your sabbath.
33 ¶ And Yahweh spoke to Moses, saying,
34 Speak to the children of Israel, saying, The fifteenth day of this seventh month *shall be* the feast of tabernacles *for* seven days unto Yahweh.
35 On the first day *shall be* a holy convocation: you shall do no laborious work *therein*.
36 Seven days you shall offer an offering made by fire unto Yahweh: on the eighth day shall be a holy convocation unto you; and you shall offer an offering made by fire unto Yahweh: it *is* a solemn assembly; *and* you shall do no laborious work *therein*.
37 These *are* the feasts of Yahweh, which you shall proclaim *to be* holy convocations, to offer an offering made by fire unto Yahweh, a burnt offering, and a meat offering, a sacrifice, and drink offerings, every thing upon his day:
38 Besides the sabbaths of Yahweh, and besides your gifts, and besides all your vows, and besides all your freewill offerings, which you give unto Yahweh.
39 Also in the fifteenth day of the seventh month, when you have gathered in the fruit of the land, you shall keep a feast unto Yahweh seven days: on the first day *shall be* a sabbath, and on the eighth day *shall be* a sabbath.
40 And you shall take you on the first day the boughs of goodly trees, branches of palm trees, and the boughs of thick trees, and willows of the brook; and you shall rejoice before Yahweh your God seven days.
41 And you shall keep it a feast unto Yahweh seven days in the year. *It shall be* a statute forever in your generations: you shall celebrate it in the seventh month.
42 You shall dwell in booths seven days; all that are Israelites born shall dwell in booths:
43 That your generations may know that I made the children of Israel to dwell in booths, when I brought them out of the land of Egypt: I *am* Yahweh your God.
44 And Moses declared to the children of Israel the feasts of Yahweh.

Leviticus 24

24:1 ¶ And Yahweh spoke to Moses, saying,
2 Command the children of Israel, that they bring to you pure olive oil beaten for the light, to cause the lamps to burn continually.
3 Outside the veil of the testimony, in the tabernacle of the congregation, shall Aaron order it from the evening to the morning before Yahweh continually: *it shall be* a statute forever in your generations.
4 He shall order the lamps upon the pure candlestick before Yahweh continually.
5 And you shall take fine flour, and bake twelve cakes thereof: two tenths deals shall be in one cake.
6 And you shall set them in two rows, six on a row, upon the pure table before Yahweh.
7 And you shall put pure frankincense upon *each* row, that it may be on the bread for a memorial, *even* an offering made by fire unto Yahweh.
8 Every sabbath he shall set it in order before Yahweh continually, *being taken* from the children of Israel by an everlasting covenant.
9 And it shall be Aaron's and his sons'; and they shall eat it in the holy place: for it *is* most holy unto him of the offerings of Yahweh made by fire by a perpetual statute.
10 ¶ And the son of an Israelite woman, whose father *was* an Egyptian, went out among the children of Israel: and this son of the Israelite *woman* and a man of Israel strove together in the camp;
11 And the Israelite woman's son blasphemed the name *of Yahweh*, and cursed. And they brought him to Moses: (and his mother's name *was* Shelomith, the daughter of Dibri, of the tribe of Dan:)
12 And they put him in custody, that the mind of Yahweh might be shown them.
13 And Yahweh spoke to Moses, saying,
14 Bring forth him that has cursed outside the camp; and let all that heard *him* lay their hands upon his head, and let all the congregation stone him.
15 And you shall speak to the children of Israel, saying, Whoever curses his God shall bear his sin.
16 And he that blasphemes the name of Yahweh, he shall surely be put to death, *and* all the congregation shall certainly stone him: as well the stranger, as he that is born in the land, when he blasphemes the name *of Yahweh*, shall be put to death.
17 And he that kills any man shall surely be put to death.
18 And he that kills a beast shall make it good; beast for beast.
19 And if a man causes a blemish in his neighbor; as he has done, so shall it be done to him;
20 Breach for breach, eye for eye, tooth for tooth: as he has caused a blemish in a man, so shall it be done to him *again*

Leviticus 24

21 And he that kills a beast, he shall restore it: and he that kills a man, he shall be put to death.
22 You shall have one manner of law, as well for the stranger, as for one of your own country: for I *am* Yahweh your God.
23 And Moses spoke to the children of Israel, that they should bring forth him that had cursed out of the camp, and stone him with stones. And the children of Israel did as Yahweh commanded Moses.

Leviticus 25

25:1 ¶ And Yahweh spoke to Moses in mount Sinai, saying,
2 Speak to the children of Israel, and say to them, When you come into the land which I give you, then shall the land keep a sabbath unto Yahweh.
3 Six years you shall sow your field, and six years you shall prune your vineyard, and gather in the fruit thereof;
4 But in the seventh year shall be a sabbath of rest unto the land, a sabbath for Yahweh: you shall neither sow your field, nor prune your vineyard.
5 That which grows of its own accord of your harvest you shall not reap, neither gather the grapes of your vine undressed: *for* it is a year of rest unto the land.
6 And the sabbath of the land shall be food for you; for you, and for your servant, and for your maid, and for your hired servant, and for your stranger that sojourns with you,
7 And for your cattle, and for the beasts that *are* in your land, shall all the increase thereof be meat.
8 ¶ And you shall number seven sabbaths of years unto you, seven times seven years; and the space of the seven sabbaths of years shall be unto you forty and nine years.
9 Then shall you cause the trumpet of the jubilee to sound on the tenth *day* of the seventh month, in the day of atonement shall you make the trumpet sound throughout all your land.
10 And you shall hallow the fiftieth year, and proclaim liberty throughout *all* the land to all the inhabitants thereof: it shall be a jubilee unto you; and you shall return every man to his possession, and you shall return every man to his family.
11 A jubilee shall that fiftieth year be unto you: you shall not sow, neither reap that which grows of itself in it, nor gather *the grapes* in it of your vine undressed.
12 For it *is* the jubilee; it shall be holy unto you: you shall eat the increase thereof out of the field.
13 In the year of this jubilee you shall return every man to his possession.
14 And if you sell anything to your neighbor, or buy *anything* of your neighbor's hand, you shall not oppress one another:
15 According to the number of years after the jubilee you shall buy of your neighbor, *and* according to the number of years of the fruits he shall sell to you:
16 According to the multitude of years you shall increase the price thereof, and according to the fewness of years you shall diminish the price of it: for *according* to the number *of the years* of the fruits does he sell to you.

17 You shall not therefore oppress one another; but you shall fear your God: for I *am* Yahweh your God.
18 Therefore you shall do my statutes, and keep my judgments, and do them; and you shall dwell in the land in safety.
19 And the land shall yield her fruit, and you shall eat your fill, and dwell therein in safety.
20 And if you shall say, What shall we eat the seventh year? behold, we shall not sow, nor gather in our increase:
21 Then I will command my blessing upon you in the sixth year, and it shall bring forth fruit for three years.
22 And you shall sow the eighth year, and eat *yet* of old fruit until the ninth year; until her fruits come in you shall eat *of* the old *store*.
23 ¶ The land shall not be sold forever: for the land *is* mine; for you *are* strangers and sojourners with me.
24 And in all the land of your possession you shall grant a redemption for the land.
25 If your brother has become poor, and has sold away *some* of his possessions, and if any of his kin comes to redeem it, then shall he redeem that which his brother sold.
26 And if the man has nothing to redeem it, and himself is able to redeem it;
27 Then let him count the years of the sale thereof, and restore the remainder to the man to whom he sold it; that he may return to his possession.
28 But if he is not able to restore *it* to him, then that which is sold shall remain in the hand of him that has bought it until the year of jubilee: and in the jubilee it shall go out, and he shall return to his possession.
29 And if a man sells a dwelling house in a walled city, then he may redeem it within a whole year after it is sold; *within* a full year may he redeem it.
30 And if it is not redeemed within the space of a full year, then the house that *is* in the walled city shall be established forever to him that bought it throughout his generations: it shall not go out in the jubilee.
31 But the houses of the villages which have no wall round about them shall be counted as the fields of the country: they may be redeemed, and they shall go out in the jubilee.
32 Notwithstanding the cities of the Levites, *and* the houses of the cities of their possession, may the Levites redeem at any time.
33 And if a man purchases of the Levites, then the house that was sold, and the city of his possession, shall go out in *the year of* jubilee: for the houses of the cities of the Levites *are* their possession among the children of Israel.
34 But the field of the suburbs of their cities may not be sold; for it *is* their perpetual possession.
35 And if your brother has become poor, and fallen in decay with you; then you shall relieve him: *yes, though he is* a stranger, or a sojourner; that he may live with you.
36 Take you no usury of him, or increase: but fear your God; that your brother may live with you.
37 You shall not give him your money upon usury, nor lend him your food for increase.
38 I *am* Yahweh your God, which brought you forth out of the land of Egypt, to give you the land of Canaan, *and* to be your God.

39 ¶ And if your brother *that dwells* by you has become poor, and is sold to you; you shall not compel him to serve as a bondservant:

40 *But* as a hired servant, *and* as a sojourner, he shall be with you, *and* shall serve you unto the year of jubilee:

41 And *then* shall he depart from you, *both* he and his children with him, and shall return unto his own family, and unto the possession of his fathers shall he return.

42 For they *are* my servants, which I brought forth out of the land of Egypt: they shall not be sold as bondmen.

43 You shall not rule over him with rigor; but shall fear your God.

44 Both your bondmen, and your bondmaids, which you shall have, *shall be* of the heathen that are round about you; of them shall you buy bondmen and bondmaids.

45 Moreover of the children of the strangers that do sojourn among you, of them shall you buy, and of their families that *are* with you, which they begot in your land: and they shall be your possession.

46 And you shall take them as an inheritance for your children after you, to inherit *them for* a possession; they shall be your bondmen forever: but over your brethren the children of Israel, you shall not rule one over another with rigor.

47 And if a sojourner or stranger becomes rich by you, and your brother *that dwells* by him becomes poor, and sells himself to the stranger *or* sojourner by you, or to the stock of the stranger's family:

48 After that he is sold he may be redeemed again; one of his brothers may redeem him:

49 Either his uncle, or his uncle's son, may redeem him, or *any* that is near of kin to him of his family may redeem him; or if he is able, he may redeem himself.

50 And he shall reckon with him that bought him from the year that he was sold to him unto the year of jubilee: and the price of his sale shall be according to the number of years, according to the time of a hired servant shall it be with him.

51 If *there are* yet many years *behind*, according to them he shall give again the price of his redemption out of the money that he was bought for.

52 And if there remain but few years unto the year of jubilee, then he shall count with him, *and* according to his years shall he give him again the price of his redemption.

53 *And* as a yearly hired servant shall he be with him: *and the other* shall not rule with rigor over him in your sight.

54 And if he is not redeemed in these *years*, then he shall go out in the year of jubilee, *both* he, and his children with him.

55 For unto me the children of Israel *are* servants; they *are* my servants whom I brought forth out of the land of Egypt: I *am* Yahweh your God.

Leviticus 26

26:1 ¶ You shall make you no idols nor graven image, neither rear you up a standing image, neither shall you set up *any* image of stone in your land, to bow down to it: for I *am* Yahweh your God.

2 You shall keep my sabbaths, and reverence my sanctuary: I *am* Yahweh.

3 If you walk in my statutes, and keep my commandments, and do them;

4 Then I will give you rain in due season, and the land shall yield her increase, and the trees of the field shall yield their fruit.

5 And your threshing shall reach to the vintage, and the vintage shall reach unto the sowing time: and you shall eat your bread to the full, and dwell in your land safely.

6 And I will give peace in the land, and you shall lie down, and none shall make *you* afraid: and I will rid evil beasts out of the land, neither shall the sword go through your land.

7 And you shall chase your enemies, and they shall fall before you by the sword.

8 And five of you shall chase a hundred, and a hundred of you shall put ten thousand to flight: and your enemies shall fall before you by the sword.

9 For I will have respect unto you, and make you fruitful, and multiply you, and establish my covenant with you.

10 And you shall eat old store, and bring forth the old because of the new.

11 And I will set my tabernacle among you: and my soul shall not abhor you.

12 And I will walk among you, and will be your God, and you shall be my people.

13 I *am* Yahweh your God, which brought you forth out of the land of Egypt, that you should not be their bondmen; and I have broken the bands of your yoke, and made you go upright.

14 ¶ But if you will not listen to me, and will not do all these commandments;

15 And if you shall despise my statutes, or if your soul abhor my judgments, so that you will not do all my commandments, *but* that you break my covenant:

16 I also will do this to you; I will even appoint over you terror, consumption, and the burning fever, that shall consume the eyes, and cause sorrow of heart: and you shall sow your seed in vain, for your enemies shall eat it.

17 And I will set my face against you, and you shall be slain before your enemies: they that hate you shall reign over you; and you shall flee when none pursues you.

18 And if you will not yet for all this listen to me, then I will punish you seven times more for your sins.

19 And I will break the pride of your power; and I will make your heaven as iron, and your earth as brass:

20 And your strength shall be spent in vain: for your land shall not yield her increase, neither shall the trees of the land yield their fruits.

21 And if you walk contrary to me, and will not listen to me; I will bring seven times more plagues upon you according to your sins.

22 I will also send wild beasts among you, which shall rob you of your children, and destroy your cattle, and make you few in number; and your *high* ways shall be desolate.

23 And if you will not be reformed by me by these things, but will walk contrary to me;

Leviticus 26

24 Then will I also walk contrary to you, and will punish you yet seven times for your sins.
25 And I will bring a sword upon you, that shall avenge the quarrel of *my* covenant: and when you are gathered together within your cities, I will send the pestilence among you; and you shall be delivered into the hand of the enemy.
26 *And* when I have broken the staff of your bread, ten women shall bake your bread in one oven, and they shall deliver *you* your bread again by weight: and you shall eat, and not be satisfied.
27 And if you will not for all this listen to me, but walk contrary to me;
28 Then I will walk contrary to you also in fury; and I, even I, will chastise you seven times for your sins.
29 And you shall eat the flesh of your sons, and the flesh of your daughters shall you eat.
30 And I will destroy your high places, and cut down your images, and cast your carcasses upon the carcasses of your idols, and my soul shall abhor you.
31 And I will make your cities waste, and bring your sanctuaries unto desolation, and I will not smell the savor of your sweet odors.
32 And I will bring the land into desolation: and your enemies which dwell therein shall be astonished at it.
33 And I will scatter you among the heathen, and will draw out a sword after you: and your land shall be desolate, and your cities waste.
34 Then shall the land enjoy her sabbaths, as long as it lies desolate, and you *are* in your enemies' land; *even* then shall the land rest, and enjoy her sabbaths.
35 As long as it lies desolate it shall rest; because it did not rest in your sabbaths, when you dwelt upon it.
36 And upon them that are left *alive* of you I will send a faintness into their hearts in the lands of their enemies; and the sound of a shaken leaf shall chase them; and they shall flee, as fleeing from a sword; and they shall fall when none pursues.
37 And they shall fall one upon another, as it were before a sword, when none pursues: and you shall have no power to stand before your enemies.
38 And you shall perish among the heathen, and the land of your enemies shall eat you up.
39 And they that are left of you shall pine away in their iniquity in your enemies' lands; and also in the iniquities of their fathers shall they pine away with them.
40 ¶ If they shall confess their iniquity, and the iniquity of their fathers, with their trespass which they trespassed against me, and that also they have walked contrary to me;
41 And *that* I also have walked contrary to them, and have brought them into the land of their enemies; if then their uncircumcised hearts are humbled, and they then accept of the punishment of their iniquity:
42 Then will I remember my covenant with Jacob, and also my covenant with Isaac, and also my covenant with Abraham will I remember; and I will remember the land.
43 The land also shall be left of them, and shall enjoy her sabbaths, while she lies desolate without them: and they shall accept of the punishment of their iniquity: because, even because they despised my judgments, and because their soul abhorred my statutes.
44 And yet for all that, when they are in the land of their enemies, I will not cast them away, neither will I abhor them, to destroy them utterly, and to break my covenant with them: for I *am* Yahweh their God.
45 But I will for their sakes remember the covenant of their ancestors, whom I brought forth out of the land of Egypt in the sight of the heathen, that I might be their God: I *am* Yahweh.
46 These *are* the statutes and judgments and laws, which Yahweh made between him and the children of Israel in mount Sinai by the hand of Moses.

Leviticus 27

27:1 ¶ And Yahweh spoke to Moses, saying,
2 Speak to the children of Israel, and say to them, When a man shall make a singular vow, the persons *shall be* for Yahweh by your estimation.
3 And your estimation shall be of the male from twenty years old even to sixty years old, even your estimation shall be fifty shekels of silver, after the shekel of the sanctuary.
4 And if it *is* a female, then your estimation shall be thirty shekels.
5 And if *it is* from five years old even to twenty years old, then your estimation shall be of the male twenty shekels, and for the female ten shekels.
6 And if *it is* from a month old even to five years old, then your estimation shall be of the male five shekels of silver, and for the female your estimation *shall be* three shekels of silver.
7 And if *it is* from sixty years old and above; if *it is* a male, then your estimation shall be fifteen shekels, and for the female ten shekels.
8 But if he is poorer than your estimation, then he shall present himself before the priest, and the priest shall value him; according to his ability that vowed shall the priest value him.
9 And if *it is* a beast, whereof men bring an offering unto Yahweh, all that *any man* gives of such unto Yahweh shall be holy.
10 He shall not alter it, nor change it, a good for a bad, or a bad for a good: and if he shall at all change beast for beast, then it and the exchange thereof shall be holy.
11 And if *it is* any unclean beast, of which they do not offer a sacrifice unto Yahweh, then he shall present the beast before the priest:
12 And the priest shall value it, whether it is good or bad: as you value it, *who are* the priest, so shall it be.
13 But if he will at all redeem it, then he shall add a fifth *part* thereof unto your estimation.
14 ¶ And when a man shall sanctify his house *to be* holy unto Yahweh, then the priest shall estimate it, whether it is good or bad: as the priest shall estimate it, so shall it stand.

15 And if he that sanctified it will redeem his house, then he shall add the fifth *part* of the money of your estimation unto it, and it shall be his.

16 And if a man shall sanctify unto Yahweh *some part* of a field of his possession, then your estimation shall be according to the seed thereof: a homer of barley seed *shall be valued* at fifty shekels of silver.

17 If he sanctifies his field from the year of jubilee, according to your estimation it shall stand.

18 But if he sanctifies his field after the jubilee, then the priest shall reckon to him the money according to the years that remain, even unto the year of the jubilee, and it shall be diminished from your estimation.

19 And if he that sanctified the field will in any way redeem it, then he shall add the fifth *part* of the money of your estimation unto it, and it shall be assured to him.

20 And if he will not redeem the field, or if he has sold the field to another man, it shall not be redeemed any more.

21 But the field, when it goes out in the jubilee, shall be holy unto Yahweh, as a field devoted; the possession thereof shall be the priest's.

22 And if *a man* sanctifies unto Yahweh a field which he has bought, which *is* not of the fields of his possession;

23 Then the priest shall reckon unto him the worth of your estimation, *even* unto the year of the jubilee: and he shall give your estimation in that day, *as* a holy thing unto Yahweh.

24 In the year of the jubilee the field shall return unto him of whom it was bought, *even* unto him to whom the possession of the land *did belong*.

25 And all your estimations shall be according to the shekel of the sanctuary: twenty gerahs shall be the shekel.

26 ¶ Only the firstborn of the beasts, which should be Yahweh's firstborn, no man shall sanctify it; whether *it is* ox, or sheep: it *is* Yahweh's.

27 And if *it is* of an unclean beast, then he shall redeem *it* according unto your estimation, and shall add a fifth *part* of it thereto: or if it is not redeemed, then it shall be sold according to your estimation.

28 Notwithstanding no devoted thing, that a man shall devote unto Yahweh of all that he has, *both* of man and beast, and of the field of his possession, shall be sold or redeemed: every devoted thing *is* most holy unto Yahweh.

29 None devoted, which shall be devoted of men, shall be redeemed; *but* shall surely be put to death.

30 And all the tithe of the land, *whether* of the seed of the land, *or* of the fruit of the tree, *is* Yahweh's: *it is* holy unto Yahweh.

31 And if a man will at all redeem *any* of his tithes, he shall add thereto the fifth *part* thereof.

32 And concerning the tithe of the herd, or of the flock, *even* of whatever passes under the rod, the tenth shall be holy unto Yahweh.

33 He shall not search whether it is good or bad, neither shall he change it: and if he changes it at all, then both it and the change thereof shall be holy; it shall not be redeemed.

34 These *are* the commandments, which Yahweh commanded Moses for the children of Israel in mount Sinai.

Numbers

Numbers 1

1:1 ¶ And Yahweh spoke to Moses in the wilderness of Sinai, in the tabernacle of the congregation, on the first *day* of the second month, in the second year after they had come out of the land of Egypt, saying,

2 Take you the sum of all the congregation of the children of Israel, after their families, by the house of their fathers, with the number of *their* names, every male by their heads;

3 From twenty years old and upward, all that are able to go forth to war in Israel: you and Aaron shall number them by their armies.

4 And with you there shall be a man of every tribe; every one head of the house of his fathers.

5 And these *are* the names of the men that shall stand with you: of *the tribe of* Reuben; Elizur the son of Shedeur.

6 Of Simeon; Shelumiel the son of Zurishaddai.

7 Of Judah; Nahshon the son of Amminadab.

8 Of Issachar; Nethaneel the son of Zuar.

9 Of Zebulun; Eliab the son of Helon.

10 Of the children of Joseph: of Ephraim; Elishama the son of Ammihud: of Manasseh; Gamaliel the son of Pedahzur.

11 Of Benjamin; Abidan the son of Gideoni.

12 Of Dan; Ahiezer the son of Ammishaddai.

13 Of Asher; Pagiel the son of Ocran.

14 Of Gad; Eliasaph the son of Deuel.

15 Of Naphtali; Ahira the son of Enan.

16 These *were* the renowned of the congregation, princes of the tribes of their fathers, heads of thousands in Israel.

17 ¶ And Moses and Aaron took these men which are expressed by *their* names:

18 And they assembled all the congregation together on the first *day* of the second month, and they declared their pedigrees after their families, by the house of their fathers, according to the number of the names, from twenty years old and upward, by their heads.

19 As Yahweh commanded Moses, so he numbered them in the wilderness of Sinai.

20 And the children of Reuben, Israel's oldest son, by their generations, after their families, by the house of their fathers, according to the number of the names, by their heads, every male from twenty years old and upward, all that were able to go forth to war;

21 Those that were numbered of them, *even* of the tribe of Reuben, *were* forty and six thousand and five hundred.

22 Of the children of Simeon, by their generations, after their families, by the house of their fathers, those that were numbered of them, according to the number of the names, by their heads, every male from twenty years old and upward, all that were able to go forth to war;

Numbers 1

23 Those that were numbered of them, *even* of the tribe of Simeon, *were* fifty and nine thousand and three hundred.
24 Of the children of Gad, by their generations, after their families, by the house of their fathers, according to the number of the names, from twenty years old and upward, all that were able to go forth to war;
25 Those that were numbered of them, *even* of the tribe of Gad, *were* forty and five thousand six hundred and fifty.
26 Of the children of Judah, by their generations, after their families, by the house of their fathers, according to the number of the names, from twenty years old and upward, all that were able to go forth to war;
27 Those that were numbered of them, *even* of the tribe of Judah, *were* threescore and fourteen thousand and six hundred.
28 Of the children of Issachar, by their generations, after their families, by the house of their fathers, according to the number of the names, from twenty years old and upward, all that were able to go forth to war;
29 Those that were numbered of them, *even* of the tribe of Issachar, *were* fifty and four thousand and four hundred.
30 Of the children of Zebulun, by their generations, after their families, by the house of their fathers, according to the number of the names, from twenty years old and upward, all that were able to go forth to war;
31 Those that were numbered of them, *even* of the tribe of Zebulun, *were* fifty and seven thousand and four hundred.
32 Of the children of Joseph, *namely*, of the children of Ephraim, by their generations, after their families, by the house of their fathers, according to the number of the names, from twenty years old and upward, all that were able to go forth to war;
33 Those that were numbered of them, *even* of the tribe of Ephraim, *were* forty thousand and five hundred.
34 Of the children of Manasseh, by their generations, after their families, by the house of their fathers, according to the number of the names, from twenty years old and upward, all that were able to go forth to war;
35 Those that were numbered of them, *even* of the tribe of Manasseh, *were* thirty and two thousand and two hundred.
36 Of the children of Benjamin, by their generations, after their families, by the house of their fathers, according to the number of the names, from twenty years old and upward, all that were able to go forth to war;
37 Those that were numbered of them, *even* of the tribe of Benjamin, *were* thirty and five thousand and four hundred.
38 Of the children of Dan, by their generations, after their families, by the house of their fathers, according to the number of the names, from twenty years old and upward, all that were able to go forth to war;
39 Those that were numbered of them, *even* of the tribe of Dan, *were* threescore and two thousand and seven hundred.
40 Of the children of Asher, by their generations, after their families, by the house of their fathers, according to the number of the names, from twenty years old and upward, all that were able to go forth to war;
41 Those that were numbered of them, *even* of the tribe of Asher, *were* forty and one thousand and five hundred.
42 Of the children of Naphtali, throughout their generations, after their families, by the house of their fathers, according to the number of the names, from twenty years old and upward, all that were able to go forth to war;
43 Those that were numbered of them, *even* of the tribe of Naphtali, *were* fifty and three thousand and four hundred.
44 ¶ These *are* those that were numbered, which Moses and Aaron numbered, and the princes of Israel, *being* twelve men: each one was for the house of his fathers.
45 So were all those that were numbered of the children of Israel, by the house of their fathers, from twenty years old and upward, all that were able to go forth to war in Israel;
46 Even all they that were numbered were six hundred thousand and three thousand and five hundred and fifty.
47 ¶ But the Levites after the tribe of their fathers were not numbered among them.
48 For Yahweh had spoken to Moses, saying,
49 Only you shall not number the tribe of Levi, neither take the sum of them among the children of Israel:
50 But you shall appoint the Levites over the tabernacle of testimony, and over all the vessels thereof, and over all things that *belong* to it: they shall bear the tabernacle, and all the vessels thereof; and they shall minister unto it, and shall encamp round about the tabernacle.
51 And when the tabernacle sets forward, the Levites shall take it down: and when the tabernacle is to be pitched, the Levites shall set it up: and the stranger that comes near shall be put to death.
52 And the children of Israel shall pitch their tents, every man by his own camp, and every man by his own standard, throughout their hosts.
53 But the Levites shall pitch round about the tabernacle of testimony, that there be no wrath upon the congregation of the children of Israel: and the Levites shall keep the charge of the tabernacle of testimony.
54 And the children of Israel did according to all that Yahweh commanded Moses, so did they.

Numbers 2

2:1 ¶ And Yahweh spoke to Moses and to Aaron, saying,
2 Every man of the children of Israel shall pitch by his own standard, with the sign of their father's house: far off about the tabernacle of the congregation shall they pitch.
3 ¶ And on the east side toward the rising of the sun shall they of the standard of the camp of Judah pitch throughout their armies: and Nahshon the son of Amminadab *shall be* captain of the children of Judah.
4 And his host, and those that were numbered of them, *were* threescore and fourteen thousand and six hundred.

5 And those that do pitch next to him *shall be* the tribe of Issachar: and Nethaneel the son of Zuar *shall be* captain of the children of Issachar.
6 And his host, and those that were numbered thereof, *were* fifty and four thousand and four hundred.
7 *Then* the tribe of Zebulun: and Eliab the son of Helon *shall be* captain of the children of Zebulun.
8 And his host, and those that were numbered thereof, *were* fifty and seven thousand and four hundred.
9 All that were numbered in the camp of Judah *were* a hundred thousand and fourscore thousand and six thousand and four hundred, throughout their armies. These shall first set forth.
10 On the south side *shall be* the standard of the camp of Reuben according to their armies: and the captain of the children of Reuben *shall be* Elizur the son of Shedeur.
11 And his host, and those that were numbered thereof, *were* forty and six thousand and five hundred.
12 And those which pitch by him *shall be* the tribe of Simeon: and the captain of the children of Simeon *shall be* Shelumiel the son of Zurishaddai.
13 And his host, and those that were numbered of them, *were* fifty and nine thousand and three hundred.
14 Then the tribe of Gad: and the captain of the sons of Gad *shall be* Eliasaph the son of Reuel.
15 And his host, and those that were numbered of them, *were* forty and five thousand and six hundred and fifty.
16 All that were numbered in the camp of Reuben *were* a hundred thousand and fifty and one thousand and four hundred and fifty, throughout their armies. And they shall set forth in the second rank.
17 Then the tabernacle of the congregation shall set forward with the camp of the Levites in the midst of the camp: as they encamp, so shall they set forward, every man in his place by their standards.
18 On the west side *shall be* the standard of the camp of Ephraim according to their armies: and the captain of the sons of Ephraim *shall be* Elishama the son of Ammihud.
19 And his host, and those that were numbered of them, *were* forty thousand and five hundred.
20 And by him *shall be* the tribe of Manasseh: and the captain of the children of Manasseh *shall be* Gamaliel the son of Pedahzur.
21 And his host, and those that were numbered of them, *were* thirty and two thousand and two hundred.
22 Then the tribe of Benjamin: and the captain of the sons of Benjamin *shall be* Abidan the son of Gideoni.
23 And his host, and those that were numbered of them, *were* thirty and five thousand and four hundred.
24 All that were numbered of the camp of Ephraim *were* a hundred thousand and eight thousand and a hundred, throughout their armies. And they shall go forward in the third rank.
25 The standard of the camp of Dan *shall be* on the north side by their armies: and the captain of the children of Dan *shall be* Ahiezer the son of Ammishaddai.
26 And his host, and those that were numbered of them, *were* threescore and two thousand and seven hundred.
27 And those that encamp by him *shall be* the tribe of Asher: and the captain of the children of Asher *shall be* Pagiel the son of Ocran.
28 And his host, and those that were numbered of them, *were* forty and one thousand and five hundred.
29 Then the tribe of Naphtali: and the captain of the children of Naphtali *shall be* Ahira the son of Enan.
30 And his host, and those that were numbered of them, *were* fifty and three thousand and four hundred.
31 All they that were numbered in the camp of Dan *were* a hundred thousand and fifty and seven thousand and six hundred. They shall go last with their standards.
32 These *are* those which were numbered of the children of Israel by the house of their fathers: all those that were numbered of the camps throughout their hosts *were* six hundred thousand and three thousand and five hundred and fifty.
33 But the Levites were not numbered among the children of Israel; as Yahweh commanded Moses.
34 And the children of Israel did according to all that Yahweh commanded Moses: so they pitched by their standards, and so they set forward, every one after their families, according to the house of their fathers.

Numbers 3

3:1 ¶ These also *are* the generations of Aaron and Moses in the day *that* Yahweh spoke with Moses in mount Sinai.
2 And these *are* the names of the sons of Aaron; Nadab the firstborn, and Abihu, Eleazar, and Ithamar.
3 These *are* the names of the sons of Aaron, the priests which were anointed, whom he consecrated to minister in the priest's office.
4 And Nadab and Abihu died before Yahweh, when they offered strange fire before Yahweh, in the wilderness of Sinai, and they had no children: and Eleazar and Ithamar ministered in the priest's office in the sight of Aaron their father.
5 And Yahweh spoke to Moses, saying,
6 Bring the tribe of Levi near, and present them before Aaron the priest, that they may minister to him.
7 And they shall keep his charge, and the charge of the whole congregation before the tabernacle of the congregation, to do the service of the tabernacle.
8 And they shall keep all the instruments of the tabernacle of the congregation, and the charge of the children of Israel, to do the service of the tabernacle.
9 And you shall give the Levites to Aaron and to his sons: they *are* wholly given unto him out of the children of Israel.
10 And you shall appoint Aaron and his sons, and they shall wait on their priest's office: and the stranger that comes near shall be put to death.
11 And Yahweh spoke to Moses, saying,
12 And I, behold, I have taken the Levites from among the children of Israel instead of all the firstborn that opens the womb among the children of Israel: therefore the Levites shall be mine;

Numbers 3

13 Because all the firstborn *are* mine; *for* on the day that I smote all the firstborn in the land of Egypt I hallowed unto me all the firstborn in Israel, both man and beast: mine shall they be: I *am* Yahweh.

14 ¶ And Yahweh spoke to Moses in the wilderness of Sinai, saying,

15 Number the children of Levi after the house of their fathers, by their families: every male from a month old and upward shall you number them.

16 And Moses numbered them according to the word of Yahweh, as he was commanded.

17 And these were the sons of Levi by their names; Gershon, and Kohath, and Merari.

18 And these *are* the names of the sons of Gershon by their families; Libni, and Shimei.

19 And the sons of Kohath by their families; Amram, and Izehar, Hebron, and Uzziel.

20 And the sons of Merari by their families; Mahli, and Mushi. These *are* the families of the Levites according to the house of their fathers.

21 Of Gershon *was* the family of the Libnites, and the family of the Shimites: these *are* the families of the Gershonites.

22 Those that were numbered of them, according to the number of all the males, from a month old and upward, *even* those that were numbered of them *were* seven thousand and five hundred.

23 The families of the Gershonites shall pitch behind the tabernacle westward.

24 And the chief of the house of the father of the Gershonites *shall be* Eliasaph the son of Lael.

25 And the charge of the sons of Gershon in the tabernacle of the congregation *shall be* the tabernacle, and the tent, the covering thereof, and the hanging for the door of the tabernacle of the congregation,

26 And the hangings of the court, and the curtain for the door of the court, which *is* by the tabernacle, and by the altar round about, and the cords of it for all the service thereof.

27 And of Kohath *was* the family of the Amramites, and the family of the Izeharites, and the family of the Hebronites, and the family of the Uzzielites: these *are* the families of the Kohathites.

28 In the number of all the males, from a month old and upward, *were* eight thousand and six hundred, keeping the charge of the sanctuary.

29 The families of the sons of Kohath shall pitch on the side of the tabernacle southward.

30 And the chief of the house of the father of the families of the Kohathites *shall be* Elizaphan the son of Uzziel.

31 And their charge *shall be* the ark, and the table, and the candlestick, and the altars, and the vessels of the sanctuary with which they minister, and the hanging, and all the service thereof.

32 And Eleazar the son of Aaron the priest *shall be* chief over the chief of the Levites, *and have* the oversight of them that keep the charge of the sanctuary.

33 Of Merari *was* the family of the Mahlites, and the family of the Mushites: these *are* the families of Merari.

34 And those that were numbered of them, according to the number of all the males, from a month old and upward, *were* six thousand and two hundred.

35 And the chief of the house of the father of the families of Merari *was* Zuriel the son of Abihail: *these* shall pitch on the side of the tabernacle northward.

36 And *under* the custody and charge of the sons of Merari *shall be* the boards of the tabernacle, and the bars thereof, and the pillars thereof, and the sockets thereof, and all the vessels thereof, and all that serves thereto,

37 And the pillars of the court round about, and their sockets, and their pins, and their cords.

38 But those that encamp before the tabernacle toward the east, *even* before the tabernacle of the congregation eastward, *shall be* Moses, and Aaron and his sons, keeping the charge of the sanctuary for the charge of the children of Israel; and the stranger that comes near shall be put to death.

39 All that were numbered of the Levites, which Moses and Aaron numbered at the commandment of Yahweh, throughout their families, all the males from a month old and upward, *were* twenty and two thousand.

40 ¶ And Yahweh said to Moses, Number all the firstborn of the males of the children of Israel from a month old and upward, and take the number of their names.

41 And you shall take the Levites for me (I *am* Yahweh) instead of all the firstborn among the children of Israel; and the cattle of the Levites instead of all the firstborn among the cattle of the children of Israel.

42 And Moses numbered, as Yahweh commanded him, all the firstborn among the children of Israel.

43 And all the firstborn males by the number of names, from a month old and upward, of those that were numbered of them, were twenty and two thousand two hundred and threescore and thirteen.

44 And Yahweh spoke to Moses, saying,

45 Take the Levites instead of all the firstborn among the children of Israel, and the cattle of the Levites instead of their cattle; and the Levites shall be mine: I *am* Yahweh.

46 And for those that are to be redeemed of the two hundred and threescore and thirteen of the firstborn of the children of Israel, which are more than the Levites;

47 You shall even take five shekels apiece by the poll, after the shekel of the sanctuary shall you take *them*: (the shekel *is* twenty gerahs:)

48 And you shall give the money, with which the excess number of them is to be redeemed, to Aaron and to his sons.

49 And Moses took the redemption money of them that were over and above them that were redeemed by the Levites:

50 Of the firstborn of the children of Israel took he the money; a thousand three hundred and threescore and five *shekels*, after the shekel of the sanctuary:

51 And Moses gave the money of them that were redeemed to Aaron and to his sons, according to the word of Yahweh, as Yahweh commanded Moses.

Numbers 4

4:1 ¶ And Yahweh spoke to Moses and to Aaron, saying,
2 Take the sum of the sons of Kohath from among the sons of Levi, after their families, by the house of their fathers,
3 From thirty years old and upward even until fifty years old, all that enter into the host, to do the work in the tabernacle of the congregation.
4 This *shall be* the service of the sons of Kohath in the tabernacle of the congregation, *about* the most holy things:
5 And when the camp sets forward, Aaron shall come, and his sons, and they shall take down the covering veil, and cover the ark of testimony with it:
6 And shall put thereon the covering of badgers' skins, and shall spread over *it* a cloth wholly of blue, and shall put in the staves thereof.
7 And upon the table of showbread they shall spread a cloth of blue, and put thereon the dishes, and the spoons, and the bowls, and covers to cover therewith: and the continual bread shall be thereon:
8 And they shall spread upon them a cloth of scarlet, and cover the same with a covering of badgers' skins, and shall put in the staves thereof.
9 And they shall take a cloth of blue, and cover the candlestick of the light, and his lamps, and his tongs, and his firepans, and all the oil vessels thereof, with which they minister unto it:
10 And they shall put it and all the vessels thereof within a covering of badgers' skins, and shall put *it* upon a bar.
11 And upon the golden altar they shall spread a cloth of blue, and cover it with a covering of badgers' skins, and shall put to the staves thereof:
12 And they shall take all the instruments of ministry, with which they minister in the sanctuary, and put *them* in a cloth of blue, and cover them with a covering of badgers' skins, and shall put *them* on a bar:
13 And they shall take away the ashes from the altar, and spread a purple cloth thereon:
14 And they shall put upon it all the vessels thereof, with which they minister about it, *even* the censers, the meat hooks, and the shovels, and the basins, all the vessels of the altar; and they shall spread upon it a covering of badgers' skins, and put to the staves of it.
15 And when Aaron and his sons have made an end of covering the sanctuary, and all the vessels of the sanctuary, as the camp is to set forward; after that, the sons of Kohath shall come to bear *it*: but they shall not touch *any* holy thing, lest they die. These *things are* the burden of the sons of Kohath in the tabernacle of the congregation.
16 And to the office of Eleazar the son of Aaron the priest *pertains* the oil for the light, and the sweet incense, and the daily meat offering, and the anointing oil, *and* the oversight of all the tabernacle, and of all that therein *is*, in the sanctuary, and in the vessels thereof.
17 And Yahweh spoke to Moses and to Aaron, saying,
18 Cut you not off the tribe of the families of the Kohathites from among the Levites:
19 But thus do unto them, that they may live, and not die, when they approach unto the most holy things: Aaron and his sons shall go in, and appoint them every one to his service and to his burden:
20 But they shall not go in to see when the holy things are covered, lest they die.
21 ¶ And Yahweh spoke to Moses, saying,
22 Take also the sum of the sons of Gershon, throughout the houses of their fathers, by their families;
23 From thirty years old and upward until fifty years old shall you number them; all that enter in to perform the service, to do the work in the tabernacle of the congregation.
24 This *is* the service of the families of the Gershonites, to serve, and for burdens:
25 And they shall bear the curtains of the tabernacle, and the tabernacle of the congregation, his covering, and the covering of the badgers' skins that *is* above upon it, and the hanging for the door of the tabernacle of the congregation,
26 And the hangings of the court, and the hanging for the door of the gate of the court, which *is* by the tabernacle and by the altar round about, and their cords, and all the instruments of their service, and all that is made for them: so shall they serve.
27 At the appointment of Aaron and his sons shall be all the service of the sons of the Gershonites, in all their burdens, and in all their service: and you shall appoint to them in charge all their burdens.
28 This *is* the service of the families of the sons of Gershon in the tabernacle of the congregation: and their charge *shall be* under the hand of Ithamar the son of Aaron the priest.
29 As for the sons of Merari, you shall number them after their families, by the house of their fathers;
30 From thirty years old and upward even to fifty years old shall you number them, every one that enters into the service, to do the work of the tabernacle of the congregation.
31 And this *is* the charge of their burden, according to all their service in the tabernacle of the congregation; the boards of the tabernacle, and the bars thereof, and the pillars thereof, and sockets thereof,
32 And the pillars of the court round about, and their sockets, and their pins, and their cords, with all their instruments, and with all their service: and by name you shall reckon the instruments of the charge of their burden.
33 This *is* the service of the families of the sons of Merari, according to all their service, in the tabernacle of the congregation, under the hand of Ithamar the son of Aaron the priest.
34 ¶ And Moses and Aaron and the chief of the congregation numbered the sons of the Kohathites after their families, and after the house of their fathers,
35 From thirty years old and upward even to fifty years old, every one that enters into the service, for the work in the tabernacle of the congregation:

Numbers 4

36 And those that were numbered of them by their families were two thousand seven hundred and fifty.
37 These *were* they that were numbered of the families of the Kohathites, all that might do service in the tabernacle of the congregation, which Moses and Aaron did number according to the commandment of Yahweh by the hand of Moses.
38 And those that were numbered of the sons of Gershon, throughout their families, and by the house of their fathers,
39 From thirty years old and upward even to fifty years old, every one that enters into the service, for the work in the tabernacle of the congregation,
40 Even those that were numbered of them, throughout their families, by the house of their fathers, were two thousand and six hundred and thirty.
41 These *are* they that were numbered of the families of the sons of Gershon, of all that might do service in the tabernacle of the congregation, whom Moses and Aaron did number according to the commandment of Yahweh.
42 And those that were numbered of the families of the sons of Merari, throughout their families, by the house of their fathers,
43 From thirty years old and upward even to fifty years old, every one that enters into the service, for the work in the tabernacle of the congregation,
44 Even those that were numbered of them after their families, were three thousand and two hundred.
45 These *are* those that were numbered of the families of the sons of Merari, whom Moses and Aaron numbered according to the word of Yahweh by the hand of Moses.
46 All those that were numbered of the Levites, whom Moses and Aaron and the chief of Israel numbered, after their families, and after the house of their fathers,
47 From thirty years old and upward even to fifty years old, every one that came to do the service of the ministry, and the service of the burden in the tabernacle of the congregation,
48 Even those that were numbered of them, were eight thousand and five hundred and fourscore.
49 According to the commandment of Yahweh they were numbered by the hand of Moses, every one according to his service, and according to his burden: thus were they numbered of him, as Yahweh commanded Moses.

Numbers 5

5:1 ¶ And Yahweh spoke to Moses, saying,
2 Command the children of Israel, that they put out of the camp every leper, and every one that has an issue, and whoever is defiled by the dead:
3 Both male and female shall you put out, outside the camp shall you put them; that they defile not their camps, in the midst whereof I dwell.
4 And the children of Israel did so, and put them out outside the camp: as Yahweh spoke to Moses, so did the children of Israel.
5 And Yahweh spoke to Moses, saying,
6 Speak to the children of Israel, When a man or woman shall commit any sin that men commit, to do a trespass against Yahweh, and that person is guilty;
7 Then they shall confess their sin which they have done: and he shall recompense his trespass with the principal thereof, and add to it the fifth *part* thereof, and give *it* to *him* against whom he has trespassed.
8 But if the man has no kinsman to recompense the trespass unto, let the trespass be recompensed unto Yahweh, *even* to the priest; beside the ram of the atonement, whereby an atonement shall be made for him.
9 And every offering of all the holy things of the children of Israel, which they bring to the priest, shall be his.
10 And every man's hallowed things shall be his: whatever any man gives the priest, it shall be his.
11 ¶ And Yahweh spoke to Moses, saying,
12 Speak to the children of Israel, and say to them, If any man's wife goes aside, and commits a trespass against him,
13 And a man lies with her carnally, and it is hidden from the eyes of her husband, and is kept secret, and she is defiled, and *there is* no witness against her, nor she is caught *in the matter*;
14 And the spirit of jealousy comes upon him, and he is jealous of his wife, and she is defiled: or if the spirit of jealousy comes upon him, and he is jealous of his wife, and she is not defiled:
15 Then shall the man bring his wife to the priest, and he shall bring her offering for her, the tenth *part* of an ephah of barley meal; he shall pour no oil upon it, nor put frankincense thereon; for it *is* an offering of jealousy, an offering of memorial, bringing iniquity to remembrance.
16 And the priest shall bring her near, and set her before Yahweh:
17 And the priest shall take holy water in an earthen vessel; and of the dust that is in the floor of the tabernacle the priest shall take, and put *it* into the water:
18 And the priest shall set the woman before Yahweh, and uncover the woman's head, and put the offering of memorial in her hands, which *is* the jealousy offering: and the priest shall have in his hand the bitter water that causes the curse:
19 And the priest shall charge her by an oath, and say to the woman, If no man has lain with you, and if you have not gone aside to uncleanness *with another* instead of your husband, be you free from this bitter water that causes the curse:
20 But if you have gone aside *to another* instead of your husband, and if you are defiled, and some man has lain with you besides your husband:
21 Then the priest shall charge the woman with an oath of cursing, and the priest shall say to the woman, Yahweh makes you a curse and an oath among your people, when Yahweh does make your thigh to rot, and your belly to swell;
22 And this water that causes the curse shall go into your bowels, to make *your* belly to swell, and *your* thigh to rot: And the woman shall say, Amen, amen.
23 And the priest shall write these curses in a book, and he shall blot *them* out with the bitter water:

24 And he shall cause the woman to drink the bitter water that causes the curse: and the water that causes the curse shall enter into her, *and become* bitter.
25 Then the priest shall take the jealousy offering out of the woman's hand, and shall wave the offering before Yahweh, and offer it upon the altar:
26 And the priest shall take a handful of the offering, *even* the memorial thereof, and burn *it* upon the altar, and afterward shall cause the woman to drink the water.
27 And when he has made her to drink the water, then it shall come to pass, *that,* if she is defiled, and has done trespass against her husband, that the water that causes the curse shall enter into her, *and become* bitter, and her belly shall swell, and her thigh shall rot: and the woman shall be a curse among her people.
28 And if the woman is not defiled, but is clean; then she shall be free, and shall conceive seed.
29 This *is* the law of jealousies, when a wife goes aside *to another* instead of her husband, and is defiled;
30 Or when the spirit of jealousy comes upon him, and he is jealous over his wife, and shall set the woman before Yahweh, and the priest shall execute upon her all this law.
31 Then shall the man be guiltless from iniquity, and this woman shall bear her iniquity.

Numbers 6

6:1 ¶ And Yahweh spoke to Moses, saying,
2 Speak to the children of Israel, and say to them, When either man or woman shall separate *themselves* to vow a vow of a Nazarite, to separate *themselves* unto Yahweh:
3 He shall separate *himself* from wine and strong drink, and shall drink no vinegar of wine, or vinegar of strong drink, neither shall he drink any liquor of grapes, nor eat moist grapes, or dried.
4 All the days of his separation shall he eat nothing that is made of the vine tree, from the kernels even to the husk.
5 All the days of the vow of his separation there shall no razor come upon his head: until the days are fulfilled, in which he separates *himself* unto Yahweh, he shall be holy, *and* shall let the locks of the hair of his head grow.
6 All the days that he separates *himself* unto Yahweh he shall come at no dead body.
7 He shall not make himself unclean for his father, or for his mother, for his brother, or for his sister, when they die: because the consecration of his God *is* upon his head.
8 All the days of his separation he *is* holy unto Yahweh.
9 And if any man dies very suddenly by him, and he has defiled the head of his consecration; then he shall shave his head in the day of his cleansing, on the seventh day shall he shave it.
10 And on the eighth day he shall bring two turtledoves, or two young pigeons, to the priest, to the door of the tabernacle of the congregation:
11 And the priest shall offer the one for a sin offering, and the other for a burnt offering, and make an atonement for him, for that he sinned by the dead, and shall hallow his head that same day.

12 And he shall consecrate unto Yahweh the days of his separation, and shall bring a lamb of the first year for a trespass offering: but the days that were before shall be lost, because his separation was defiled.
13 And this *is* the law of the Nazarite, when the days of his separation are fulfilled: he shall be brought to the door of the tabernacle of the congregation:
14 And he shall offer his offering unto Yahweh, one he lamb of the first year without blemish for a burnt offering, and one ewe lamb of the first year without blemish for a sin offering, and one ram without blemish for peace offerings,
15 And a basket of unleavened bread, cakes of fine flour mingled with oil, and wafers of unleavened bread anointed with oil, and their meat offering, and their drink offerings.
16 And the priest shall bring *them* before Yahweh, and shall offer his sin offering, and his burnt offering:
17 And he shall offer the ram *for* a sacrifice of peace offerings unto Yahweh, with the basket of unleavened bread: the priest shall offer also his meat offering, and his drink offering.
18 And the Nazarite shall shave the head of his separation *at* the door of the tabernacle of the congregation, and shall take the hair of the head of his separation, and put *it* in the fire which *is* under the sacrifice of the peace offerings.
19 And the priest shall take the boiled shoulder of the ram, and one unleavened cake out of the basket, and one unleavened wafer, and shall put *them* upon the hands of the Nazarite, after *the hair of* his separation is shaven:
20 And the priest shall wave them *for* a wave offering before Yahweh: this *is* holy for the priest, with the wave breast and heave shoulder: and after that the Nazarite may drink wine.
21 This *is* the law of the Nazarite who has vowed, *and of* his offering unto Yahweh for his separation, besides *that* that his hand shall get: according to the vow which he vowed, so he must do after the law of his separation.
22 ¶ And Yahweh spoke to Moses, saying,
23 Speak to Aaron and to his sons, saying, In this manner you shall bless the children of Israel, saying to them,
24 Yahweh bless you, and keep you:
25 Yahweh make his face shine upon you, and be gracious unto you:
26 Yahweh lift up his countenance upon you, and give you peace.
27 And they shall put my name upon the children of Israel; and I will bless them.

Numbers 7

7:1 ¶ And it came to pass on the day that Moses had fully set up the tabernacle, and had anointed it, and sanctified it, and all the instruments thereof, both the altar and all the vessels thereof, and had anointed them, and sanctified them;
2 That the princes of Israel, heads of the house of their fathers, who *were* the princes of the tribes, and were over them that *were* numbered, offered:

Numbers 7

3 And they brought their offering before Yahweh, six covered wagons, and twelve oxen; a wagon for two of the princes, and for each one an ox: and they brought them before the tabernacle.

4 And Yahweh spoke to Moses, saying,

5 Take *it* of them, that they may be to do the service of the tabernacle of the congregation; and you shall give them to the Levites, to every man according to his service.

6 And Moses took the wagons and the oxen, and gave them to the Levites.

7 Two wagons and four oxen he gave to the sons of Gershon, according to their service:

8 And four wagons and eight oxen he gave to the sons of Merari, according to their service, under the hand of Ithamar the son of Aaron the priest.

9 But to the sons of Kohath he gave none: because the service of the sanctuary belonging to them *was that* they should bear upon their shoulders.

10 ¶ And the princes offered for dedicating of the altar in the day that it was anointed, even the princes offered their offering before the altar.

11 And Yahweh said to Moses, They shall offer their offering, each prince on his day, for the dedicating of the altar.

12 And he that offered his offering the first day was Nahshon the son of Amminadab, of the tribe of Judah:

13 And his offering *was* one silver platter, the weight thereof *was* a hundred and thirty *shekels*, one silver bowl of seventy shekels, after the shekel of the sanctuary; both of them *were* full of fine flour mingled with oil for a meat offering:

14 One spoon of ten *shekels* of gold, full of incense:

15 One young bullock, one ram, one lamb of the first year, for a burnt offering:

16 One kid of the goats for a sin offering:

17 And for a sacrifice of peace offerings, two oxen, five rams, five he goats, five lambs of the first year: this *was* the offering of Nahshon the son of Amminadab.

18 On the second day Nethaneel the son of Zuar, prince of Issachar, did offer:

19 He offered *for* his offering one silver platter, the weight thereof *was* a hundred and thirty *shekels*, one silver bowl of seventy shekels, after the shekel of the sanctuary; both of them full of fine flour mingled with oil for a meat offering:

20 One spoon of gold of ten *shekels*, full of incense:

21 One young bullock, one ram, one lamb of the first year, for a burnt offering:

22 One kid of the goats for a sin offering:

23 And for a sacrifice of peace offerings, two oxen, five rams, five he goats, five lambs of the first year: this *was* the offering of Nethaneel the son of Zuar.

24 On the third day Eliab the son of Helon, prince of the children of Zebulun, *did offer*:

25 His offering *was* one silver platter, the weight thereof *was* a hundred and thirty *shekels*, one silver bowl of seventy shekels, after the shekel of the sanctuary; both of them full of fine flour mingled with oil for a meat offering:

26 One golden spoon of ten *shekels*, full of incense:

27 One young bullock, one ram, one lamb of the first year, for a burnt offering:

28 One kid of the goats for a sin offering:

29 And for a sacrifice of peace offerings, two oxen, five rams, five he goats, five lambs of the first year: this *was* the offering of Eliab the son of Helon.

30 On the fourth day Elizur the son of Shedeur, prince of the children of Reuben, *did offer*:

31 His offering *was* one silver platter of the weight of a hundred and thirty *shekels*, one silver bowl of seventy shekels, after the shekel of the sanctuary; both of them full of fine flour mingled with oil for a meat offering:

32 One golden spoon of ten *shekels*, full of incense:

33 One young bullock, one ram, one lamb of the first year, for a burnt offering:

34 One kid of the goats for a sin offering:

35 And for a sacrifice of peace offerings, two oxen, five rams, five he goats, five lambs of the first year: this *was* the offering of Elizur the son of Shedeur.

36 On the fifth day Shelumiel the son of Zurishaddai, prince of the children of Simeon, *did offer*:

37 His offering *was* one silver platter, the weight thereof *was* a hundred and thirty *shekels*, one silver bowl of seventy shekels, after the shekel of the sanctuary; both of them full of fine flour mingled with oil for a meat offering:

38 One golden spoon of ten *shekels*, full of incense:

39 One young bullock, one ram, one lamb of the first year, for a burnt offering:

40 One kid of the goats for a sin offering:

41 And for a sacrifice of peace offerings, two oxen, five rams, five he goats, five lambs of the first year: this *was* the offering of Shelumiel the son of Zurishaddai.

42 On the sixth day Eliasaph the son of Deuel, prince of the children of Gad, *offered*:

43 His offering *was* one silver platter of the weight of a hundred and thirty *shekels*, a silver bowl of seventy shekels, after the shekel of the sanctuary; both of them full of fine flour mingled with oil for a meat offering:

44 One golden spoon of ten *shekels*, full of incense:

45 One young bullock, one ram, one lamb of the first year, for a burnt offering:

46 One kid of the goats for a sin offering:

47 And for a sacrifice of peace offerings, two oxen, five rams, five he goats, five lambs of the first year: this *was* the offering of Eliasaph the son of Deuel.

48 On the seventh day Elishama the son of Ammihud, prince of the children of Ephraim, *offered*:

49 His offering *was* one silver platter, the weight thereof *was* a hundred and thirty *shekels*, one silver bowl of seventy shekels, after the shekel of the sanctuary; both of them full of fine flour mingled with oil for a meat offering:

50 One golden spoon of ten *shekels*, full of incense:

51 One young bullock, one ram, one lamb of the first year, for a burnt offering:

52 One kid of the goats for a sin offering:

53 And for a sacrifice of peace offerings, two oxen, five rams, five he goats, five lambs of the first year: this was the offering of Elishama the son of Ammihud.
54 On the eighth day offered Gamaliel the son of Pedahzur, prince of the children of Manasseh:
55 His offering was one silver platter of the weight of a hundred and thirty *shekels*, one silver bowl of seventy shekels, after the shekel of the sanctuary; both of them full of fine flour mingled with oil for a meat offering:
56 One golden spoon of ten *shekels*, full of incense:
57 One young bullock, one ram, one lamb of the first year, for a burnt offering:
58 One kid of the goats for a sin offering:
59 And for a sacrifice of peace offerings, two oxen, five rams, five he goats, five lambs of the first year: this was the offering of Gamaliel the son of Pedahzur.
60 On the ninth day Abidan the son of Gideoni, prince of the children of Benjamin, *offered*:
61 His offering was one silver platter, the weight thereof was a hundred and thirty *shekels*, one silver bowl of seventy shekels, after the shekel of the sanctuary; both of them full of fine flour mingled with oil for a meat offering:
62 One golden spoon of ten *shekels*, full of incense:
63 One young bullock, one ram, one lamb of the first year, for a burnt offering:
64 One kid of the goats for a sin offering:
65 And for a sacrifice of peace offerings, two oxen, five rams, five he goats, five lambs of the first year: this was the offering of Abidan the son of Gideoni.
66 On the tenth day Ahiezer the son of Ammishaddai, prince of the children of Dan, *offered*:
67 His offering was one silver platter, the weight thereof was a hundred and thirty *shekels*, one silver bowl of seventy shekels, after the shekel of the sanctuary; both of them full of fine flour mingled with oil for a meat offering:
68 One golden spoon of ten *shekels*, full of incense:
69 One young bullock, one ram, one lamb of the first year, for a burnt offering:
70 One kid of the goats for a sin offering:
71 And for a sacrifice of peace offerings, two oxen, five rams, five he goats, five lambs of the first year: this was the offering of Ahiezer the son of Ammishaddai.
72 On the eleventh day Pagiel the son of Ocran, prince of the children of Asher, *offered*:
73 His offering was one silver platter, the weight thereof was a hundred and thirty *shekels*, one silver bowl of seventy shekels, after the shekel of the sanctuary; both of them full of fine flour mingled with oil for a meat offering:
74 One golden spoon of ten *shekels*, full of incense:
75 One young bullock, one ram, one lamb of the first year, for a burnt offering:
76 One kid of the goats for a sin offering:
77 And for a sacrifice of peace offerings, two oxen, five rams, five he goats, five lambs of the first year: this was the offering of Pagiel the son of Ocran.
78 On the twelfth day Ahira the son of Enan, prince of the children of Naphtali, *offered*:
79 His offering was one silver platter, the weight thereof was a hundred and thirty *shekels*, one silver bowl of seventy shekels, after the shekel of the sanctuary; both of them full of fine flour mingled with oil for a meat offering:
80 One golden spoon of ten *shekels*, full of incense:
81 One young bullock, one ram, one lamb of the first year, for a burnt offering:
82 One kid of the goats for a sin offering:
83 And for a sacrifice of peace offerings, two oxen, five rams, five he goats, five lambs of the first year: this was the offering of Ahira the son of Enan.
84 This was the dedication of the altar, in the day when it was anointed, by the princes of Israel: twelve platters of silver, twelve silver bowls, twelve spoons of gold:
85 Each platter of silver *weighing* a hundred and thirty *shekels*, each bowl seventy: all the silver vessels *weighed* two thousand and four hundred *shekels*, after the shekel of the sanctuary:
86 The golden spoons were twelve, full of incense, *weighing* ten *shekels* apiece, after the shekel of the sanctuary: all the gold of the spoons was a hundred and twenty *shekels*.
87 All the oxen for the burnt offering were twelve bullocks, the rams twelve, the lambs of the first year twelve, with their meat offering: and the kids of the goats for sin offering twelve.
88 And all the oxen for the sacrifice of the peace offerings were twenty and four bullocks, the rams sixty, the he goats sixty, the lambs of the first year sixty. This was the dedication of the altar, after that it was anointed.
89 And when Moses had gone into the tabernacle of the congregation to speak with him, then he heard the voice of one speaking to him from off the mercy seat that was upon the ark of testimony, from between the two cherubims: and he spoke to him.

Numbers 8

8:1 ¶ And Yahweh spoke to Moses, saying,
2 Speak to Aaron, and say to him, When you light the lamps, the seven lamps shall give light over against the candlestick.
3 And Aaron did so; he lit the lamps thereof over against the candlestick, as Yahweh commanded Moses.
4 And this work of the candlestick *was of* beaten gold, unto the shaft thereof, unto the flowers thereof, was beaten work: according to the pattern which Yahweh had shown Moses, so he made the candlestick.
5 ¶ And Yahweh spoke to Moses, saying,
6 Take the Levites from among the children of Israel, and cleanse them.
7 And thus shall you do to them, to cleanse them: Sprinkle water of purifying upon them, and let them shave all their flesh, and let them wash their clothes, and *so* make themselves clean.
8 Then let them take a young bullock with his meat offering, *even* fine flour mingled with oil, and another young bullock shall you take for a sin offering.

Numbers 8

9 And you shall bring the Levites before the tabernacle of the congregation: and you shall gather the whole assembly of the children of Israel together:
10 And you shall bring the Levites before Yahweh: and the children of Israel shall put their hands upon the Levites:
11 And Aaron shall offer the Levites before Yahweh *for* an offering of the children of Israel, that they may execute the service of Yahweh.
12 And the Levites shall lay their hands upon the heads of the bullocks: and you shall offer the one *for* a sin offering, and the other *for* a burnt offering, unto Yahweh, to make an atonement for the Levites.
13 And you shall set the Levites before Aaron, and before his sons, and offer them *for* an offering unto Yahweh.
14 Thus shall you separate the Levites from among the children of Israel: and the Levites shall be mine.
15 And after that shall the Levites go in to do the service of the tabernacle of the congregation: and you shall cleanse them, and offer them *for* an offering.
16 For they *are* wholly given unto me from among the children of Israel; instead of such as open every womb, *even instead of* the firstborn of all the children of Israel, have I taken them unto me.
17 For all the firstborn of the children of Israel *are* mine, *both* man and beast: on the day that I smote every firstborn in the land of Egypt I sanctified them for myself.
18 And I have taken the Levites for all the firstborn of the children of Israel.
19 And I have given the Levites *as* a gift to Aaron and to his sons from among the children of Israel, to do the service of the children of Israel in the tabernacle of the congregation, and to make an atonement for the children of Israel: that there be no plague among the children of Israel, when the children of Israel come near unto the sanctuary.
20 And Moses, and Aaron, and all the congregation of the children of Israel, did to the Levites according to all that Yahweh commanded Moses concerning the Levites, so did the children of Israel unto them.
21 And the Levites were purified, and they washed their clothes; and Aaron offered them *as* an offering before Yahweh; and Aaron made an atonement for them to cleanse them.
22 And after that went the Levites in to do their service in the tabernacle of the congregation before Aaron, and before his sons: as Yahweh had commanded Moses concerning the Levites, so did they unto them.
23 And Yahweh spoke to Moses, saying,
24 This *is it* that *belongs* to the Levites: from twenty and five years old and upward they shall go in to wait upon the service of the tabernacle of the congregation:
25 And from the age of fifty years they shall cease waiting upon the service *thereof*, and shall serve no more:
26 But shall minister with their brethren in the tabernacle of the congregation, to keep the charge, and shall do no service. Thus shall you do to the Levites touching their charge.

Numbers 9

9:1 ¶ And Yahweh spoke to Moses in the wilderness of Sinai, in the first month of the second year after they had come out of the land of Egypt, saying,
2 Let the children of Israel also keep the passover at his appointed season.
3 In the fourteenth day of this month, at evening, you shall keep it in his appointed season: according to all the rites of it, and according to all the ceremonies thereof, shall you keep it.
4 And Moses spoke to the children of Israel, that they should keep the passover.
5 And they kept the passover on the fourteenth day of the first month at evening in the wilderness of Sinai: according to all that Yahweh commanded Moses, so did the children of Israel.
6 And there were certain men, who were defiled by the dead body of a man, that they could not keep the passover on that day: and they came before Moses and before Aaron on that day:
7 And those men said to him, We *are* defiled by the dead body of a man: why are we kept back, that we may not offer an offering of Yahweh in his appointed season among the children of Israel?
8 And Moses said to them, Stand still, and I will hear what Yahweh will command concerning you.
9 And Yahweh spoke to Moses, saying,
10 Speak to the children of Israel, saying, If any man of you or of your posterity shall be unclean by reason of a dead body, or *is* in a journey afar off, yet he shall keep the passover unto Yahweh.
11 The fourteenth day of the second month at evening they shall keep it, *and* eat it with unleavened bread and bitter *herbs*.
12 They shall leave none of it unto the morning, nor break any bone of it: according to all the ordinances of the passover they shall keep it.
13 But the man that *is* clean, and is not in a journey, and forbears to keep the passover, even the same soul shall be cut off from among his people: because he brought not the offering of Yahweh in his appointed season, that man shall bear his sin.
14 And if a stranger shall sojourn among you, and will keep the passover unto Yahweh; according to the ordinance of the passover, and according to the manner thereof, so shall he do: you shall have one ordinance, both for the stranger, and for him that was born in the land.
15 ¶ And on the day that the tabernacle was reared up the cloud covered the tabernacle, *namely*, the tent of the testimony: and at evening there was upon the tabernacle as it were the appearance of fire, until the morning.
16 So it was always: the cloud covered it *by day*, and the appearance of fire by night.
17 And when the cloud was taken up from the tabernacle, then after that the children of Israel journeyed: and in the place where the cloud stayed, there the children of Israel pitched their tents.

18 At the commandment of Yahweh the children of Israel journeyed, and at the commandment of Yahweh they pitched: as long as the cloud stayed upon the tabernacle they rested in their tents.
19 And when the cloud tarried long upon the tabernacle many days, then the children of Israel kept the charge of Yahweh, and journeyed not.
20 And *so* it was, when the cloud was a few days upon the tabernacle; according to the commandment of Yahweh they stayed in their tents, and according to the commandment of Yahweh they journeyed.
21 And *so* it was, when the cloud stayed from evening unto the morning, and *that* the cloud was taken up in the morning, then they journeyed: whether *it was* by day or by night that the cloud was taken up, they journeyed.
22 Or *whether it was* two days, or a month, or a year, that the cloud tarried upon the tabernacle, remaining thereon, the children of Israel stayed in their tents, and journeyed not: but when it was taken up, they journeyed.
23 At the commandment of Yahweh they rested in the tents, and at the commandment of Yahweh they journeyed: they kept the charge of Yahweh, at the commandment of Yahweh by the hand of Moses.

Numbers 10

10:1 ¶ And Yahweh spoke to Moses, saying.
2 Make you two trumpets of silver; of a whole piece shall you make them: that you may use them for the calling of the assembly, and for the journeying of the camps.
3 And when they shall blow with them, all the assembly shall assemble themselves to you at the door of the tabernacle of the congregation.
4 And if they blow *but* with one *trumpet*, then the princes, *which are* heads of the thousands of Israel, shall gather themselves unto you.
5 When you blow an alarm, then the camps that lie on the east parts shall go forward.
6 When you blow an alarm the second time, then the camps that lie on the south side shall take their journey: they shall blow an alarm for their journeys.
7 But when the congregation is to be gathered together, you shall blow, but you shall not sound an alarm.
8 And the sons of Aaron, the priests, shall blow with the trumpets; and they shall be to you for an ordinance forever throughout your generations.
9 And if you go to war in your land against the enemy that oppresses you, then you shall blow an alarm with the trumpets; and you shall be remembered before Yahweh your God, and you shall be saved from your enemies.
10 Also in the day of your gladness, and in your solemn days, and in the beginnings of your months, you shall blow with the trumpets over your burnt offerings, and over the sacrifices of your peace offerings; that they may be to you for a memorial before your God: I *am* Yahweh your God.
11 ¶ And it came to pass on the twentieth *day* of the second month, in the second year, that the cloud was taken up from off the tabernacle of the testimony.
12 And the children of Israel took their journeys out of the wilderness of Sinai; and the cloud rested in the wilderness of Paran.
13 And they first took their journey according to the commandment of Yahweh by the hand of Moses.
14 In the first *place* went the standard of the camp of the children of Judah according to their armies: and over his host *was* Nahshon the son of Amminadab.
15 And over the host of the tribe of the children of Issachar *was* Nethaneel the son of Zuar.
16 And over the host of the tribe of the children of Zebulun *was* Eliab the son of Helon.
17 And the tabernacle was taken down; and the sons of Gershon and the sons of Merari set forward, bearing the tabernacle.
18 And the standard of the camp of Reuben set forward according to their armies: and over his host *was* Elizur the son of Shedeur.
19 And over the host of the tribe of the children of Simeon *was* Shelumiel the son of Zurishaddai.
20 And over the host of the tribe of the children of Gad *was* Eliasaph the son of Deuel.
21 And the Kohathites set forward, bearing the sanctuary: and *the others* did set up the tabernacle for their coming.
22 And the standard of the camp of the children of Ephraim set forward according to their armies: and over his host *was* Elishama the son of Ammihud.
23 And over the host of the tribe of the children of Manasseh *was* Gamaliel the son of Pedahzur.
24 And over the host of the tribe of the children of Benjamin *was* Abidan the son of Gideoni.
25 And the standard of the camp of the children of Dan set forward, *which was* the rear guard of all the camps throughout their hosts: and over his host *was* Ahiezer the son of Ammishaddai.
26 And over the host of the tribe of the children of Asher *was* Pagiel the son of Ocran.
27 And over the host of the tribe of the children of Naphtali *was* Ahira the son of Enan.
28 Thus *were* the journeys of the children of Israel according to their armies, when they set forward.
29 ¶ And Moses said to Hobab, the son of Raguel the Midianite, Moses' father-in-law, We are journeying to the place of which Yahweh said, I will give it *to* you: come you with us, and we will do you good: for Yahweh has spoken good concerning Israel.
30 And he said to him, I will not go; but I will depart to my own land, and to my kindred.
31 And he said, Leave us not, I pray you; forasmuch as you know how we are to encamp in the wilderness, and you may be to us instead of eyes.
32 And it shall be, if you go with us, yes, it shall be, that what goodness Yahweh shall do to us, the same will we do to you.
33 And they departed from the mount of Yahweh three days' journey: and the ark of the covenant of Yahweh went before them in the three days' journey, to search out a resting place for them.

Numbers 10

34 And the cloud of Yahweh *was* upon them by day, when they went out of the camp.
35 And it came to pass, when the ark set forward, that Moses said, Rise up, Yahweh, and let your enemies be scattered; and let them that hate you flee before you.
36 And when it rested, he said, Return, O Yahweh, to the many thousands of Israel.

Numbers 11

11:1 ¶ And *when* the people complained, it displeased Yahweh: and Yahweh heard *it*; and his anger was kindled; and the fire of Yahweh burnt among them, and consumed *them that were* in the outermost parts of the camp.
2 And the people cried to Moses; and when Moses prayed unto Yahweh, the fire was quenched.
3 And he called the name of the place Taberah: because the fire of Yahweh burnt among them.
4 ¶ And the mixed multitude that *was* among them fell a lusting: and the children of Israel also wept again, and said, Who shall give us flesh to eat?
5 We remember the fish, which we did eat in Egypt freely; the cucumbers, and the melons, and the leeks, and the onions, and the garlic:
6 But now our soul *is* dried away: *there is* nothing at all, besides this manna, *before* our eyes.
7 And the manna *was* as coriander seed, and the color thereof as the color of bdellium.
8 *And* the people went about, and gathered *it*, and ground *it* in mills, or beat *it* in a mortar, and baked *it* in pans, and made cakes of it: and the taste of it was as the taste of fresh oil.
9 And when the dew fell upon the camp in the night, the manna fell upon it.
10 Then Moses heard the people weep throughout their families, every man in the door of his tent: and the anger of Yahweh was kindled greatly; Moses also was displeased.
11 And Moses said unto Yahweh, Why have you afflicted your servant? and why have I not found favor in your sight, that you lay the burden of all this people upon me?
12 Have I conceived all these people? have I begotten them, that you should say to me, Carry them in your bosom, as a nursing father bears the sucking child, to the land which you swore unto their fathers?
13 Wherefrom should I get flesh to give to all this people? for they weep unto me, saying, Give us flesh, that we may eat.
14 I am not able to bear all this people alone, because *it is* too heavy for me.
15 And if you deal thus with me, kill me, I pray you, out of hand, if I have found favor in your sight; and let me not see my wretchedness.
16 ¶ And Yahweh said to Moses, Gather unto me seventy men of the elders of Israel, whom you know to be the elders of the people, and officers over them; and bring them to the tabernacle of the congregation, that they may stand there with you.
17 And I will come down and talk with you there: and I will take of the spirit which *is* upon you, and will put *it* upon them; and they shall bear the burden of the people with you, that you bear *it* not yourself alone.
18 And say you to the people, Sanctify yourselves against tomorrow, and you shall eat flesh: for you have wept in the ears of Yahweh, saying, Who shall give us flesh to eat? for *it was* well with us in Egypt: therefore Yahweh will give you flesh, and you shall eat.
19 You shall not eat one day, nor two days, nor five days, neither ten days, nor twenty days;
20 *But* even a whole month, until it comes out at your nostrils, and it is loathsome unto you: because that you have despised Yahweh which *is* among you, and have wept before him, saying, Why came we forth out of Egypt?
21 And Moses said, The people, among whom I *am, are* six hundred thousand footmen; and you have said, I will give them flesh, that they may eat a whole month.
22 Shall the flocks and the herds be slain for them, to suffice them? or shall all the fish of the sea be gathered together for them, to suffice them?
23 And Yahweh said to Moses, Is Yahweh's hand grown short? you shall see now whether my word shall come to pass unto you or not.
24 ¶ And Moses went out, and told the people the words of Yahweh, and gathered the seventy men of the elders of the people, and set them round about the tabernacle.
25 And Yahweh came down in a cloud, and spoke to him, and took of the spirit that *was* upon him, and gave *it* to the seventy elders: and it came to pass, *that*, when the spirit rested upon them, they prophesied, and did not cease.
26 But there remained two *of the* men in the camp, the name of the one *was* Eldad, and the name of the other Medad: and the spirit rested upon them; and they *were* of them that were written, but went not out to the tabernacle: and they prophesied in the camp.
27 And there ran a young man, and told Moses, and said, Eldad and Medad do prophesy in the camp.
28 And Joshua the son of Nun, the servant of Moses, *one* of his young men, answered and said, My lord Moses, forbid them.
29 And Moses said to him, Envy you for my sake? would God that all Yahweh's people were prophets, *and* that Yahweh would put his spirit upon them!
30 And Moses gathered himself into the camp, he and the elders of Israel.
31 ¶ And there went forth a wind from Yahweh, and brought quails from the sea, and let *them* fall by the camp, as it were a day's journey on this side, and as it were a day's journey on the other side, round about the camp, and as it were two cubits *high* upon the face of the earth.
32 And the people stood up all that day, and all *that* night, and all the next day, and they gathered the quails: he that gathered least gathered ten homers: and they spread *them* all abroad for themselves round about the camp.
33 And while the flesh *was* yet between their teeth, before it was chewed, the wrath of Yahweh was kindled against the people, and Yahweh smote the people with a very great plague.

34 And he called the name of that place Kibrothhattaavah: because there they buried the people that lusted.
35 *And* the people journeyed from Kibrothhattaavah to Hazeroth; and stayed at Hazeroth.

Numbers 12

12:1 ¶ And Miriam and Aaron spoke against Moses because of the Ethiopian woman whom he had married: for he had married an Ethiopian woman.
2 And they said, Has Yahweh indeed spoken only by Moses? has he not spoken also by us? And Yahweh heard *it*.
3 (Now the man Moses *was* very meek, above all the men which *were* upon the face of the earth.)
4 ¶ And Yahweh spoke suddenly to Moses, and to Aaron, and to Miriam, Come out you three to the tabernacle of the congregation. And they three came out.
5 And Yahweh came down in the pillar of the cloud, and stood *in* the door of the tabernacle, and called Aaron and Miriam: and they both came forth.
6 And he said, Hear now my words: If there is a prophet among you, *I* Yahweh will make myself known to him in a vision, *and* will speak to him in a dream.
7 My servant Moses *is* not so, who *is* faithful in all my house.
8 With him will I speak mouth to mouth, even apparently, and not in dark speeches; and the likeness of Yahweh shall he behold: why then were you not afraid to speak against my servant Moses?
9 And the anger of Yahweh was kindled against them; and he departed.
10 ¶ And the cloud departed from off the tabernacle; and, behold, Miriam *became* leprous, *white* as snow: and Aaron looked upon Miriam, and, behold, *she was* leprous.
11 And Aaron said to Moses, Alas, my lord, I beseech you, lay not the sin upon us, wherein we have done foolishly, and wherein we have sinned.
12 Let her not be as one dead, of whom the flesh is half consumed when he comes out of his mother's womb.
13 And Moses cried unto Yahweh, saying, Heal her now, O God, I beseech you.
14 And Yahweh said to Moses, If her father had but spit in her face, should she not be ashamed seven days? let her be shut out from the camp seven days, and after that let her be received in *again*.
15 And Miriam was shut out from the camp seven days: and the people journeyed not till Miriam was brought in *again*.
16 And afterward the people departed from Hazeroth, and pitched in the wilderness of Paran.

Numbers 13

13:1 ¶ And Yahweh spoke to Moses, saying,
2 Send you men, that they may search the land of Canaan, which I give to the children of Israel: of every tribe of their fathers shall you send a man, every one a ruler among them.
3 And Moses by the commandment of Yahweh sent them from the wilderness of Paran: all those men *were* heads of the children of Israel.
4 And these *were* their names: of the tribe of Reuben, Shammua the son of Zaccur.
5 Of the tribe of Simeon, Shaphat the son of Hori.
6 Of the tribe of Judah, Caleb the son of Jephunneh.
7 Of the tribe of Issachar, Igal the son of Joseph.
8 Of the tribe of Ephraim, Oshea the son of Nun.
9 Of the tribe of Benjamin, Palti the son of Raphu.
10 Of the tribe of Zebulun, Gaddiel the son of Sodi.
11 Of the tribe of Joseph, *namely*, of the tribe of Manasseh, Gaddi the son of Susi.
12 Of the tribe of Dan, Ammiel the son of Gemalli.
13 Of the tribe of Asher, Sethur the son of Michael.
14 Of the tribe of Naphtali, Nahbi the son of Vophsi.
15 Of the tribe of Gad, Geuel the son of Machi.
16 These *are* the names of the men which Moses sent to spy out the land. And Moses called Oshea the son of Nun Jehoshua.
17 And Moses sent them to spy out the land of Canaan, and said to them, Get you up this *way* southward, and go up into the mountain:
18 And see the land, what it *is*; and the people that dwell therein, whether they *are* strong or weak, few or many;
19 And what the land *is* that they dwell in, whether it *is* good or bad; and what cities *they have* that they dwell in, whether in tents, or in strong holds;
20 And what the land *is*, whether it *is* fat or lean, whether there is wood therein, or not. And be you of good courage, and bring of the fruit of the land. Now the time *was* the time of the first ripe grapes.
21 ¶ So they went up, and searched the land from the wilderness of Zin to Rehob, as men come to Hamath.
22 And they ascended by the south, and came to Hebron; where Ahiman, Sheshai, and Talmai, the children of Anak, *were* (Now Hebron was built seven years before Zoan in Egypt.)
23 And they came to the brook of Eshcol, and cut down from there a branch with one cluster of grapes, and they bore it between two upon a staff; and *they brought* of the pomegranates, and of the figs.
24 The place was called the brook Eshcol, because of the cluster of grapes which the children of Israel cut down from there.
25 And they returned from searching of the land after forty days.
26 ¶ And they went and came to Moses, and to Aaron, and to all the congregation of the children of Israel, to the wilderness of Paran, to Kadesh; and brought back word to them, and to all the congregation, and showed them the fruit of the land.
27 And they told him, and said, We came to the land where you sent us, and surely it flows with milk and honey; and *this is* the fruit of it.
28 Nevertheless the people *are* strong that dwell in the land, and the cities *are* walled, *and* very great: and moreover we saw the children of Anak there.

Numbers 13

29 The Amalekites dwell in the land of the south: and the Hittites, and the Jebusites, and the Amorites, dwell in the mountains: and the Canaanites dwell by the sea, and by the coast of *the* Jordan.
30 And Caleb stilled the people before Moses, and said, Let us go up at once, and possess it; for we are well able to overcome it.
31 But the men that went up with him said, We are not able to go up against the people; for they *are* stronger than we.
32 And they brought up an evil report of the land which they had searched to the children of Israel, saying, The land, through which we have gone to search it, *is* a land that eats up the inhabitants thereof; and all the people that we saw in it *are* men of a great stature.
33 And there we saw the giants, the sons of Anak, *which come* of the giants: and we were in our own sight as grasshoppers, and so we were in their sight.

Numbers 14

14:1 ¶ And all the congregation lifted up their voice, and cried; and the people wept that night.
2 And all the children of Israel murmured against Moses and against Aaron: and the whole congregation said to them, Would God that we had died in the land of Egypt! or would God we had died in this wilderness!
3 And why has Yahweh brought us to this land, to fall by the sword, that our wives and our children should be a prey? were it not better for us to return into Egypt?
4 And they said one to another, Let us make a captain, and let us return into Egypt.
5 ¶ Then Moses and Aaron fell on their faces before all the assembly of the congregation of the children of Israel.
6 And Joshua the son of Nun, and Caleb the son of Jephunneh, *which were* of them that searched the land, tore their clothes:
7 And they spoke to all the company of the children of Israel, saying, The land, which we passed through to search it, *is* an exceedingly good land.
8 If Yahweh delights in us, then he will bring us into this land, and give it us; a land which flows with milk and honey.
9 Only rebel not you against Yahweh, neither fear you the people of the land; for they *are* bread for us: their defense has departed from them, and Yahweh *is* with us: fear them not.
10 But all the congregation said stone them with stones. And the glory of Yahweh appeared in the tabernacle of the congregation before all the children of Israel.
11 ¶ And Yahweh said to Moses, How long will this people provoke me? and how long will it be before they believe me, for all the signs which I have shown among them?
12 I will smite them with the pestilence, and disinherit them, and will make of you a greater nation and mightier than they.
13 And Moses said unto Yahweh, Then the Egyptians shall hear *it*, (for you brought up this people in your might from among them;)
14 And they will tell *it* to the inhabitants of this land: *for* they have heard that you Yahweh *are* among this people, that you Yahweh are seen face to face, and *that* your cloud stands over them, and *that* you go before them, by day time in a pillar of a cloud, and in a pillar of fire by night.
15 Now *if* you shall kill *all* this people as one man, then the nations which have heard the fame of you will speak, saying,
16 Because Yahweh was not able to bring this people into the land which he swore to them, therefore he has slain them in the wilderness.
17 And now, I beseech you, let the power of my Lord be great, according as you have spoken, saying,
18 Yahweh *is* longsuffering, and of great mercy, forgiving iniquity and transgression, and by no means clearing *the guilty*, visiting the iniquity of the fathers upon the children to the third and fourth *generation*.
19 Pardon, I beseech you, the iniquity of this people according to the greatness of your mercy, and as you have forgiven this people, from Egypt even until now.
20 ¶ And Yahweh said, I have pardoned according to your word:
21 But *as* truly *as* I live, all the earth shall be filled with the glory of Yahweh.
22 Because all those men which have seen my glory, and my miracles, which I did in Egypt and in the wilderness, and have tempted me now these ten times, and have not listened to my voice;
23 Surely they shall not see the land which I swore to their fathers, neither shall any of them that provoked me see it:
24 But my servant Caleb, because he had another spirit with him, and has followed me fully, him will I bring into the land where into he went; and his seed shall possess it.
25 (Now the Amalekites and the Canaanites dwelt in the valley.) Tomorrow turn you, and get you into the wilderness by the way of the Red Sea.
26 And Yahweh spoke to Moses and to Aaron, saying,
27 How long *shall I bear with* this evil congregation, which murmur against me? I have heard the murmurings of the children of Israel, which they murmur against me.
28 Say to them, *As truly as* I live, says Yahweh, as you have spoken in my ears, so will I do to you:
29 Your carcasses shall fall in this wilderness; and all that were numbered of you, according to your whole number, from twenty years old and upward, which have murmured against me,
30 Doubtless you shall not come into the land, *concerning* which I swore to make you dwell therein, save Caleb the son of Jephunneh, and Joshua the son of Nun.
31 But your little ones, which you said should be a prey, them will I bring in, and they shall know the land which you have despised.
32 But *as for* you, your carcasses, they shall fall in this wilderness.
33 And your children shall wander in the wilderness forty years, and bear your whoredoms, until your carcasses are wasted in the wilderness.

34 After the number of the days in which you searched the land, *even* forty days, each day for a year, shall you bear your iniquities, *even* forty years, and you shall know my breach of promise.

35 I Yahweh have said, I will surely do it to all this evil congregation, that are gathered together against me: in this wilderness they shall be consumed, and there they shall die.

36 ¶ And the men, which Moses sent to search the land, who returned, and made all the congregation to murmur against him, by bringing up a slander upon the land,

37 Even those men that did bring up the evil report upon the land, died by the plague before Yahweh.

38 But Joshua the son of Nun, and Caleb the son of Jephunneh, *which were* of the men that went to search the land, lived *still*.

39 And Moses told these sayings to all the children of Israel: and the people mourned greatly.

40 And they rose up early in the morning, and got them up into the top of the mountain, saying, Behold, we *are here*, and will go up to the place which Yahweh has promised: for we have sinned.

41 And Moses said, Why now do you transgress the commandment of Yahweh? but it shall not prosper.

42 Go not up, for Yahweh *is* not among you; that you be not smitten before your enemies.

43 For the Amalekites and the Canaanites *are* there before you, and you shall fall by the sword: because you are turned away from Yahweh, therefore Yahweh will not be with you.

44 But they presumed to go up to the hill top: nevertheless the ark of the covenant of Yahweh, and Moses, departed not out of the camp.

45 Then the Amalekites came down, and the Canaanites which dwelt in that hill, and smote them, and discomfited them, *even* to Hormah.

Numbers 15

15:1 ¶ And Yahweh spoke to Moses, saying,

2 Speak to the children of Israel, and say to them, When you have come into the land of your habitations, which I give unto you,

3 And will make an offering by fire unto Yahweh, a burnt offering, or a sacrifice in performing a vow, or in a freewill offering, or in your solemn feasts, to make a sweet savor unto Yahweh, of the herd, or of the flock:

4 Then shall he that offers his offering unto Yahweh bring a meat offering of a tenth deal of flour mingled with the fourth *part* of a hin of oil.

5 And the fourth *part* of a hin of wine for a drink offering shall you prepare with the burnt offering or sacrifice, for one lamb.

6 Or for a ram, you shall prepare *for* a meat offering two tenths deals of flour mingled with the third *part* of a hin of oil.

7 And for a drink offering you shall offer the third *part* of a hin of wine, *for* a sweet savor unto Yahweh.

8 And when you prepare a bullock *for* a burnt offering, or *for* a sacrifice in performing a vow, or peace offerings unto Yahweh:

9 Then shall he bring with a bullock a meat offering of three tenths deals of flour mingled with half a hin of oil.

10 And you shall bring for a drink offering half a hin of wine, *for* an offering made by fire, of a sweet savor unto Yahweh.

11 Thus shall it be done for one bullock, or for one ram, or for a lamb, or a kid.

12 According to the number that you shall prepare, so shall you do to every one according to their number.

13 All that are born of the country shall do these things after this manner, in offering an offering made by fire, of a sweet savor unto Yahweh.

14 And if a stranger sojourns with you, or whoever *is* among you in your generations, and will offer an offering made by fire, of a sweet savor unto Yahweh; as you do, so he shall do.

15 One ordinance *shall be both* for you of the congregation, and also for the stranger that sojourns *with you*, an ordinance forever in your generations: as you *are*, so shall the stranger be before Yahweh.

16 One law and one manner shall be for you, and for the stranger that sojourns with you.

17 And Yahweh spoke to Moses, saying,

18 Speak to the children of Israel, and say to them, When you come into the land where I bring you,

19 Then it shall be, that, when you eat of the bread of the land, you shall offer up a heave offering unto Yahweh.

20 You shall offer up a cake of the first of your dough *for* a heave offering: as *you do* the heave offering of the threshingfloor, so shall you heave it.

21 Of the first of your dough you shall give unto Yahweh a heave offering in your generations.

22 ¶ And if you have erred, and *do* not observed all these commandments, which Yahweh has spoken to Moses,

23 *Even* all that Yahweh has commanded you by the hand of Moses, from the day that Yahweh commanded *Moses*, and henceforward among your generations;

24 Then it shall be, if *it* is committed by ignorance without the knowledge of the congregation, that all the congregation shall offer one young bullock for a burnt offering, for a sweet savor unto Yahweh, with his meat offering, and his drink offering, according to the manner, and one kid of the goats for a sin offering.

25 And the priest shall make an atonement for all the congregation of the children of Israel, and it shall be forgiven them; for it *is* ignorance: and they shall bring their offering, a sacrifice made by fire unto Yahweh, and their sin offering before Yahweh, for their ignorance:

26 And it shall be forgiven all the congregation of the children of Israel, and the stranger that sojourns among them; seeing all the people *were* in ignorance.

27 And if any soul sins through ignorance, then he shall bring a she goat of the first year for a sin offering.

28 And the priest shall make an atonement for the soul that sins ignorantly, when he sins by ignorance before Yahweh, to make an atonement for him; and it shall be forgiven him.

Numbers 15

29 You shall have one law for him that sins through ignorance, *both for* him that is born among the children of Israel, and for the stranger that sojourns among them.

30 ¶ But the soul that does *anything* presumptuously, *whether he is* born in the land, or a stranger, the same reproaches Yahweh; and that soul shall be cut off from among his people.

31 Because he has despised the word of Yahweh, and has broken his commandment, that soul shall utterly be cut off; his iniquity *shall be* upon him.

32 And while the children of Israel were in the wilderness, they found a man that gathered sticks upon the sabbath day.

33 And they that found him gathering sticks brought him to Moses and Aaron, and to all the congregation.

34 And they put him in custody, because it was not declared what should be done to him.

35 And Yahweh said to Moses, The man shall be surely put to death: all the congregation shall stone him with stones outside the camp.

36 And all the congregation brought him outside the camp, and stoned him with stones, and he died; as Yahweh commanded Moses.

37 ¶ And Yahweh spoke to Moses, saying,

38 Speak to the children of Israel, and bid them that they make them fringes in the borders of their garments throughout their generations, and that they put upon the fringe of the borders a ribbon of blue:

39 And it shall be unto you for a fringe, that you may look upon it, and remember all the commandments of Yahweh, and do them; and that you seek not after your own heart and your own eyes, after which you use to go a whoring:

40 That you may remember, and do all my commandments, and be holy unto your God.

41 I *am* Yahweh your God, which brought you out of the land of Egypt, to be your God: I *am* Yahweh your God.

Numbers 16

16:1 ¶ Now Korah, the son of Izhar, the son of Kohath, the son of Levi, and Dathan and Abiram, the sons of Eliab, and On, the son of Peleth, sons of Reuben, took *men*:

2 And they rose up before Moses, with certain of the children of Israel, two hundred and fifty princes of the assembly, famous in the congregation, men of renown:

3 And they gathered themselves together against Moses and against Aaron, and said to them, *You take* too much upon you, seeing all the congregation *is* holy, every one of them, and Yahweh *is* among them: why then lift you up yourselves above the congregation of Yahweh?

4 And when Moses heard *it*, he fell upon his face:

5 And he spoke to Korah and to all his company, saying, Even tomorrow Yahweh will show who *are* his, and *who is* holy; and will cause *him* to come near to him: even *him* whom he has chosen will he cause to come near to him.

6 This do; Take you censers, Korah, and all his company;

7 And put fire therein, and put incense in them before Yahweh tomorrow: and it shall be *that* the man whom Yahweh does choose, he *shall be* holy: *you take* too much upon you, you sons of Levi.

8 And Moses said to Korah, Hear, I pray you, you sons of Levi:

9 *Seem it but* a small thing to you, that the God of Israel has separated you from the congregation of Israel, to bring you near to himself to do the service of the tabernacle of Yahweh, and to stand before the congregation to minister to them?

10 And he has brought you near *to him*, and all your brothers the sons of Levi with you: and seek you the priesthood also?

11 For which cause *both* you and all your company *are* gathered together against Yahweh: and what *is* Aaron, that you murmur against him?

12 ¶ And Moses sent to call Dathan and Abiram, the sons of Eliab: which said, We will not come up:

13 *Is it* a small thing that you have brought us up out of a land that flows with milk and honey, to kill us in the wilderness, except you make yourself altogether a prince over us?

14 Moreover you have not brought us into a land that flows with milk and honey, or given us inheritance of fields and vineyards: will you put out the eyes of these men? we will not come up.

15 And Moses was very angry, and said unto Yahweh, Respect not you their offering: I have not taken one donkey from them, neither have I hurt one of them.

16 And Moses said to Korah, Be you and all your company before Yahweh, you, and they, and Aaron, tomorrow:

17 And take every man his censer, and put incense in them, and bring you before Yahweh every man his censer, two hundred and fifty censers; you also, and Aaron, each *of you* his censer.

18 And they took every man his censer, and put fire in them, and laid incense thereon, and stood in the door of the tabernacle of the congregation with Moses and Aaron.

19 And Korah gathered all the congregation against them to the door of the tabernacle of the congregation: and the glory of Yahweh appeared to all the congregation.

20 And Yahweh spoke to Moses and to Aaron, saying,

21 Separate yourselves from among this congregation, that I may consume them in a moment.

22 And they fell upon their faces, and said, O God, the God of the spirits of all flesh, shall one man sin, and will you be angry with all the congregation?

23 ¶ And Yahweh spoke to Moses, saying,

24 Speak to the congregation, saying, Get you up from about the tabernacle of Korah, Dathan, and Abiram.

25 And Moses rose up and went to Dathan and Abiram; and the elders of Israel followed him.

26 And he spoke to the congregation, saying, Depart, I pray you, from the tents of these wicked men, and touch nothing of theirs, lest you be consumed in all their sins.

27 So they got up from the tabernacle of Korah, Dathan,

and Abiram, on every side: and Dathan and Abiram came out, and stood in the door of their tents, and their wives, and their sons, and their little children.
28 And Moses said, Hereby you shall know that Yahweh has sent me to do all these works; for *I have not done them* of my own mind.
29 If these men die the common death of all men, or if they are visited after the visitation of all men; *then* Yahweh has not sent me.
30 But if Yahweh makes a new thing, and the earth opens her mouth, and swallows them up, with all that *appertains* to them, and they go down alive into the pit; then you shall understand that these men have provoked Yahweh.
31 And it came to pass, as he had made an end of speaking all these words, that the ground divided apart that *was* under them:
32 And the earth opened her mouth, and swallowed them up, and their houses, and all the men that *appertained to* Korah, and all *their* goods.
33 They, and all that *appertained* to them, went down alive into the pit, and the earth closed upon them: and they perished from among the congregation.
34 And all Israel that *were* round about them fled at the cry of them: for they said, Lest the earth swallow us up *also*.
35 ¶ And there came out a fire from Yahweh, and consumed the two hundred and fifty men that offered incense.
36 And Yahweh spoke to Moses, saying,
37 Speak to Eleazar the son of Aaron the priest, that he take up the censers out of the burning, and scatter you the fire yonder; for they are hallowed.
38 The censers of these sinners against their own souls, let them make them broad plates *for* a covering of the altar: for they offered them before Yahweh, therefore they are hallowed: and they shall be a sign to the children of Israel.
39 And Eleazar the priest took the brazen censers, with which they that were burnt had offered; and they were made broad *plates for* a covering of the altar:
40 *To be* a memorial to the children of Israel, that no stranger, which *is* not of the seed of Aaron, come near to offer incense before Yahweh; that he be not as Korah, and as his company: as Yahweh said to him by the hand of Moses.
41 ¶ But on the next day all the congregation of the children of Israel murmured against Moses and against Aaron, saying, You have killed the people of Yahweh.
42 And it came to pass, when the congregation had gathered against Moses and against Aaron, that they looked toward the tabernacle of the congregation: and, behold, the cloud covered it, and the glory of Yahweh appeared.
43 And Moses and Aaron came before the tabernacle of the congregation.
44 And Yahweh spoke to Moses, saying,
45 Get you up from among this congregation, that I may consume them as in a moment. And they fell upon their faces.
46 And Moses said to Aaron, Take a censer, and put fire therein from off the altar, and put on incense, and go quickly to the congregation, and make an atonement for them: for there is wrath gone out from Yahweh; the plague is begun.
47 And Aaron took as Moses commanded, and ran into the midst of the congregation; and, behold, the plague had begun among the people: and he put on incense, and made an atonement for the people.
48 And he stood between the dead and the living; and the plague was stayed.
49 Now they that died in the plague were fourteen thousand and seven hundred, besides them that died about the matter of Korah.
50 And Aaron returned to Moses to the door of the tabernacle of the congregation: and the plague was stayed.

Numbers 17

17:1 ¶ And Yahweh spoke to Moses, saying,
2 Speak to the children of Israel, and take of every one of them a rod according to the house of *their* fathers, of all their princes according to the house of their fathers twelve rods: write you every man's name upon his rod.
3 And you shall write Aaron's name upon the rod of Levi: for one rod *shall be* for the head of the house of their fathers.
4 And you shall lay them up in the tabernacle of the congregation before the testimony, where I will meet with you.
5 And it shall come to pass, *that* the man's rod, whom I shall choose, shall blossom: and I will make to cease from me the murmurings of the children of Israel, whereby they murmur against you.
6 And Moses spoke to the children of Israel, and every one of their princes gave him a rod apiece, for each prince one, according to their fathers' houses, *even* twelve rods: and the rod of Aaron *was* among their rods.
7 And Moses laid up the rods before Yahweh in the tabernacle of witness.
8 ¶ And it came to pass, that on the next day Moses went into the tabernacle of witness; and, behold, the rod of Aaron for the house of Levi was budded, and brought forth buds, and bloomed blossoms, and yielded almonds.
9 And Moses brought out all the rods from before Yahweh to all the children of Israel: and they looked, and took every man his rod.
10 And Yahweh said to Moses, Bring Aaron's rod again before the testimony, to be kept for a token against the rebels; and you shall quite take away their murmurings from me, that they die not.
11 And Moses did *so*: as Yahweh commanded him, so did he.

Numbers 17

12 And the children of Israel spoke to Moses, saying, Behold, we die, we perish, we all perish.
13 Whoever comes anywhere near to the tabernacle of Yahweh shall die: shall we be consumed with dying?

Numbers 18

18:1 ¶ And Yahweh said to Aaron, You and your sons and your father's house with you shall bear the iniquity of the sanctuary: and you and your sons with you shall bear the iniquity of your priesthood.
2 And your brethren also of the tribe of Levi, the tribe of your father, bring you with you, that they may be joined to you, and minister to you: but you and your sons with you *shall minister* before the tabernacle of witness.
3 And they shall keep your charge, and the charge of all the tabernacle: only they shall not come near the vessels of the sanctuary and the altar, that neither they, nor you also, die.
4 And they shall be joined to you, and keep the charge of the tabernacle of the congregation, for all the service of the tabernacle: and a stranger shall not come near to you.
5 And you shall keep the charge of the sanctuary, and the charge of the altar: that there be no wrath any more upon the children of Israel.
6 And I, behold, I have taken your brethren the Levites from among the children of Israel: to you *they are* given *as* a gift for Yahweh, to do the service of the tabernacle of the congregation.
7 Therefore you and your sons with you shall keep your priest's office for every thing of the altar, and within the veil; and you shall serve: I have given your priest's office *to you* as a service of gift: and the stranger that comes near shall be put to death.
8 ¶ And Yahweh spoke to Aaron, Behold, I also have given you the charge of my heave offerings of all the hallowed things of the children of Israel; to you have I given them by reason of the anointing, and to your sons, by an ordinance forever.
9 This shall be yours of the most holy things, *reserved* from the fire: every oblation of theirs, every meat offering of theirs, and every sin offering of theirs, and every trespass offering of theirs, which they shall render to me, *shall be* most holy for you and for your sons.
10 In the most holy *place* shall you eat it; every male shall eat it: it shall be holy to you.
11 And this *is* yours; the heave offering of their gift, with all the wave offerings of the children of Israel: I have given them to you, and to your sons and to your daughters with you, by a statute forever: every one that is clean in your house shall eat of it.
12 All the best of the oil, and all the best of the *new* wine, and of the wheat, the firstfruits of them which they shall offer unto Yahweh, them have I given you.
13 *And* whatever is first ripe in the land, which they shall bring unto Yahweh, shall be yours; every one that is clean in your house shall eat *of* it.
14 Every thing devoted in Israel shall be yours.
15 Every thing that opens the womb in all flesh, which they bring unto Yahweh, *whether it is* of men or beasts, shall be yours: nevertheless the firstborn of man shall you surely redeem, and the firstborn of unclean beasts shall you redeem.
16 And those that are to be redeemed from a month old shall you redeem, according to your estimation, for the money of five shekels, after the shekel of the sanctuary, which *is* twenty gerahs.
17 But the firstborn of a cow, or the firstborn of a sheep, or the firstborn of a goat, you shall not redeem; they *are* holy: you shall sprinkle their blood upon the altar, and shall burn their fat *for* an offering made by fire, for a sweet savor unto Yahweh.
18 And the flesh of them shall be yours, as the wave breast and as the right shoulder are yours.
19 All the heave offerings of the holy things, which the children of Israel offer unto Yahweh, have I given you, and your sons and your daughters with you, by a statute forever: it *is* a covenant of salt forever before Yahweh to you and to your seed with you.
20 ¶ And Yahweh spoke to Aaron, You shall have no inheritance in their land, neither shall you have any part among them: I *am* your part and your inheritance among the children of Israel.
21 And, behold, I have given the children of Levi all the tenth in Israel for an inheritance, for their service which they serve, *even* the service of the tabernacle of the congregation.
22 Neither must the children of Israel henceforth come near the tabernacle of the congregation, lest they bear sin, and die.
23 But the Levites shall do the service of the tabernacle of the congregation, and they shall bear their iniquity: *it shall be* a statute forever throughout your generations, that among the children of Israel they have no inheritance.
24 But the tithes of the children of Israel, which they offer *as* a heave offering unto Yahweh, I have given to the Levites to inherit: therefore I have said to them, Among the children of Israel they shall have no inheritance.
25 And Yahweh spoke to Moses, saying,
26 Thus speak to the Levites, and say to them, When you take of the children of Israel the tithes which I have given you from them for your inheritance, then you shall offer up a heave offering of it for Yahweh, *even* a tenth *part* of the tithe.
27 And *this* your heave offering shall be reckoned unto you, as though *it were* the corn of the threshingfloor, and as the fullness of the winepress.
28 Thus you also shall offer a heave offering unto Yahweh of all your tithes, which you receive of the children of Israel; and you shall give thereof Yahweh's heave offering to Aaron the priest.
29 Out of all your gifts you shall offer every heave offering of Yahweh, of all the best thereof, *even* the hallowed part thereof out of it.
30 Therefore you shall say to them, When you have

heaved the best thereof from it, then it shall be counted to the Levites as the increase of the threshingfloor, and as the increase of the winepress.

31 And you shall eat it in every place, you and your households: for it *is* your reward for your service in the tabernacle of the congregation.

32 And you shall bear no sin by reason of it, when you have heaved from it the best of it: neither shall you pollute the holy things of the children of Israel, lest you die.

Numbers 19

19:1 ¶ And Yahweh spoke to Moses and to Aaron, saying,
2 This *is* the ordinance of the law which Yahweh has commanded, saying, Speak to the children of Israel, that they bring you a red heifer without spot, wherein *is* no blemish, *and* upon which never came yoke:
3 And you shall give her to Eleazar the priest, that he may bring her forth outside the camp, and one shall slay her before his face:
4 And Eleazar the priest shall take of her blood with his finger, and sprinkle of her blood directly before the tabernacle of the congregation seven times:
5 And *one* shall burn the heifer in his sight; her skin, and her flesh, and her blood, with her dung, shall he burn:
6 And the priest shall take cedar wood, and hyssop, and scarlet, and cast *it* into the midst of the burning of the heifer.
7 Then the priest shall wash his clothes, and he shall bathe his flesh in water, and afterward he shall come into the camp, and the priest shall be unclean until the evening.
8 And he that burns her shall wash his clothes in water, and bathe his flesh in water, and shall be unclean until the evening.
9 And a man *that is* clean shall gather up the ashes of the heifer, and lay *them* up outside the camp in a clean place, and it shall be kept for the congregation of the children of Israel for a water of separation: it *is* a purification for sin.
10 And he that gathers the ashes of the heifer shall wash his clothes, and be unclean until the evening: and it shall be to the children of Israel, and to the stranger that sojourns among them, for a statute forever.
11 ¶ He that touches the dead body of any man shall be unclean seven days.
12 He shall purify himself with it on the third day, and on the seventh day he shall be clean: but if he purifies not himself the third day, then the seventh day he shall not be clean.
13 Whoever touches the dead body of any man that is dead, and purifies not himself, defiles the tabernacle of Yahweh; and that soul shall be cut off from Israel: because the water of separation was not sprinkled upon him, he shall be unclean; his uncleanness *is* yet upon him.
14 This *is* the law, when a man dies in a tent: all that come into the tent, and all that *is* in the tent, shall be unclean seven days.
15 And every open vessel, which has no covering bound upon it, *is* unclean.

16 And whoever touches one that is slain with a sword in the open fields, or a dead body, or a bone of a man, or a grave, shall be unclean seven days.
17 And for an unclean *person* they shall take of the ashes of the burnt heifer of purification for sin, and running water shall be put thereto in a vessel:
18 And a clean person shall take hyssop, and dip *it* in the water, and sprinkle *it* upon the tent, and upon all the vessels, and upon the persons that were there, and upon him that touched a bone, or one slain, or one dead, or a grave:
19 And the clean *person* shall sprinkle upon the unclean on the third day, and on the seventh day: and on the seventh day he shall purify himself, and wash his clothes, and bathe himself in water, and shall be clean at evening.
20 But the man that shall be unclean, and shall not purify himself, that soul shall be cut off from among the congregation, because he has defiled the sanctuary of Yahweh: the water of separation has not been sprinkled upon him; he *is* unclean.
21 And it shall be a perpetual statute to them, that he that sprinkles the water of separation shall wash his clothes; and he that touches the water of separation shall be unclean until evening.
22 And whatever the unclean *person* touches shall be unclean; and the soul that touches *it* shall be unclean until evening.

Numbers 20

20:1 ¶ Then came the children of Israel, *even* the whole congregation, into the desert of Zin in the first month: and the people stayed in Kadesh; and Miriam died there, and was buried there.
2 And there was no water for the congregation: and they gathered themselves together against Moses and against Aaron.
3 And the people strove with Moses, and spoke, saying, Would God that we had died when our brethren died before Yahweh!
4 And why have you brought up the congregation of Yahweh into this wilderness, that we and our cattle should die here?
5 And why have you made us to come up out of Egypt, to bring us in to this evil place? it *is* no place of seed, or of figs, or of vines, or of pomegranates; neither *is* there any water to drink.
6 And Moses and Aaron went from the presence of the assembly to the door of the tabernacle of the congregation, and they fell upon their faces: and the glory of Yahweh appeared to them.
7 And Yahweh spoke to Moses, saying,
8 Take the rod, and gather you the assembly together, you, and Aaron your brother, and speak you to the rock before their eyes; and it shall give forth his water, and you shall bring forth to them water out of the rock: so you shall give the congregation and their beasts drink.
9 And Moses took the rod from before Yahweh, as he commanded him.

Numbers 20

10 And Moses and Aaron gathered the congregation together before the rock, and he said to them, Hear now, you rebels; must we fetch you water out of this rock?

11 And Moses lifted up his hand, and with his rod he smote the rock twice: and the water came out abundantly, and the congregation drank, and their beasts *also*.

12 And Yahweh spoke to Moses and Aaron, Because you believed me not, to sanctify me in the eyes of the children of Israel, therefore you shall not bring this congregation into the land which I have given them.

13 This *is* the water of Meribah; because the children of Israel strove with Yahweh, and he was sanctified in them.

14 ¶ And Moses sent messengers from Kadesh to the king of Edom, Thus says your brother Israel, You know all the trouble that has befallen us:

15 How our fathers went down into Egypt, and we have dwelt in Egypt a long time; and the Egyptians afflicted us, and our fathers:

16 And when we cried unto Yahweh, he heard our voice, and sent an angel, and has brought us forth out of Egypt: and, behold, we *are* in Kadesh, a city in the outermost of your border:

17 Let us pass, I pray you, through your country: we will not pass through the fields, or through the vineyards, neither will we drink *of* the water of the wells: we will go by the king's *high* way, we will not turn to the right hand nor to the left, until we have passed your borders.

18 And Edom said to him, You shall not pass by me, lest I come out against you with the sword.

19 And the children of Israel said unto him, We will go by the high way: and if I and my cattle drink of your water, then I will pay for it: I will only, without *doing* anything *else*, go through on my feet.

20 And he said, You shall not go through. And Edom came out against them with much people, and with a strong hand.

21 Thus Edom refused to give Israel passage through his border: therefore Israel turned away from him.

22 ¶ And the children of Israel, *even* the whole congregation, journeyed from Kadesh, and came to mount Hor.

23 And Yahweh spoke to Moses and Aaron in mount Hor, by the coast of the land of Edom, saying,

24 Aaron shall be gathered to his people: for he shall not enter into the land which I have given to the children of Israel, because you rebelled against my word at the water of Meribah.

25 Take Aaron and Eleazar his son, and bring them up to mount Hor:

26 And strip Aaron of his garments, and put them upon Eleazar his son: and Aaron shall be gathered *to his people*, and shall die there.

27 And Moses did as Yahweh commanded: and they went up into mount Hor in the sight of all the congregation.

28 And Moses stripped Aaron of his garments, and put them upon Eleazar his son; and Aaron died there in the top of the mount: and Moses and Eleazar came down from the mount.

29 And when all the congregation saw that Aaron was dead, they mourned for Aaron thirty days, *even* all the house of Israel.

Numbers 21

21:1 ¶ And *when* king Arad the Canaanite, which dwelt in the south, heard tell that Israel came by the way of the spies; then he fought against Israel, and took *some* of them prisoners.

2 And Israel vowed a vow unto Yahweh, and said, If you will indeed deliver this people into my hand, then I will utterly destroy their cities.

3 And Yahweh listened to the voice of Israel, and delivered up the Canaanites; and they utterly destroyed them and their cities: and he called the name of the place Hormah.

4 ¶ And they journeyed from mount Hor by the way of the Red Sea, to encompass the land of Edom: and the soul of the people was much discouraged because of the way.

5 And the people spoke against God, and against Moses, Why have you brought us up out of Egypt to die in the wilderness? for *there is* no bread, neither *is there any* water; and our soul loathes this light bread.

6 And Yahweh sent fiery serpents among the people, and they bit the people; and much people of Israel died.

7 Therefore the people came to Moses, and said, We have sinned, for we have spoken against Yahweh, and against you; pray unto Yahweh, that he take away the serpents from us. And Moses prayed for the people.

8 And Yahweh said to Moses, Make you a fiery serpent, and set it upon a pole: and it shall come to pass, that every one that is bitten, when he looks upon it, shall live.

9 And Moses made a serpent of brass, and put it upon a pole, and it came to pass, that if a serpent had bitten any man, when he saw the serpent of brass, he lived.

10 ¶ And the children of Israel set forward, and pitched in Oboth.

11 And they journeyed from Oboth, and pitched at Ijeabarim, in the wilderness which *is* before Moab, toward the sunrising.

12 From there they removed, and pitched in the valley of Zared.

13 From there they removed, and pitched on the other side of Arnon, which *is* in the wilderness that comes out of the coasts of the Amorites: for Arnon *is* the border of Moab, between Moab and the Amorites.

14 Therefore it is said in the book of the wars of Yahweh, What he did in the Red Sea, and in the brooks of Arnon,

15 And at the stream of the brooks that goes down to the dwelling of Ar, and lies upon the border of Moab.

16 And from there *they went* to Beer: that *is* the well whereof Yahweh spoke to Moses, Gather the people together, and I will give them water.

17 Then Israel sang this song, Spring up, O well; sing you to it:

18 The princes dug the well, the nobles of the people dug it, by *the direction of* the lawgiver, with their staves. And from the wilderness *they went* to Mattanah:
19 And from Mattanah to Nahaliel: and from Nahaliel to Bamoth:
20 And from Bamoth *in* the valley, that *is* in the country of Moab, to the top of Pisgah, which looks toward Jeshimon.
21 ¶ And Israel sent messengers to Sihon king of the Amorites, saying,
22 Let me pass through your land: we will not turn into the fields, or into the vineyards; we will not drink *of* the waters of the well: *but* we will go along by the king's *high* way, until we are past your borders.
23 And Sihon would not allow Israel to pass through his border: but Sihon gathered all his people together, and went out against Israel into the wilderness: and he came to Jahaz, and fought against Israel.
24 And Israel smote him with the edge of the sword, and possessed his land from Arnon to Jabbok, even to the children of Ammon: for the border of the children of Ammon *was* strong.
25 And Israel took all these cities: and Israel dwelt in all the cities of the Amorites, in Heshbon, and in all the villages thereof.
26 For Heshbon *was* the city of Sihon the king of the Amorites, who had fought against the former king of Moab, and taken all his land out of his hand, even to Arnon.
27 Therefore they that speak in proverbs say, Come into Heshbon, let the city of Sihon be built and prepared:
28 For there is a fire gone out of Heshbon, a flame from the city of Sihon: it has consumed Ar of Moab, *and* the lords of the high places of Arnon.
29 Woe to you, Moab! you are undone, O people of Chemosh: he has given his sons that escaped, and his daughters, into captivity to Sihon king of the Amorites.
30 We have shot at them; Heshbon is perished even to Dibon, and we have laid them waste even to Nophah, which *reaches* to Medeba.
31 Thus Israel dwelt in the land of the Amorites.
32 And Moses sent to spy out Jaazer, and they took the villages thereof, and drove out the Amorites that *were* there.
33 And they turned and went up by the way of Bashan: and Og the king of Bashan went out against them, he, and all his people, to the battle at Edrei.
34 And Yahweh said to Moses, Fear him not: for I have delivered him into your hand, and all his people, and his land; and you shall do to him as you did to Sihon king of the Amorites, which dwelt at Heshbon.
35 So they smote him, and his sons, and all his people, until there was none left alive: and they possessed his land.

Numbers 22

22:1 ¶ And the children of Israel set forward, and pitched in the plains of Moab on this side *of the* Jordan *by* Jericho.
2 And Balak the son of Zippor saw all that Israel had done to the Amorites.
3 And Moab was very afraid of the people, because they *were* many: and Moab was distressed because of the children of Israel.
4 And Moab said to the elders of Midian, Now shall this company lick up all *that are* round about us, as the ox licks up the grass of the field. And Balak the son of Zippor *was* king of the Moabites at that time.
5 He sent messengers therefore to Balaam the son of Beor to Pethor, which *is* by the river of the land of the children of his people, to call him, saying, Behold, there is a people come out from Egypt: behold, they cover the face of the earth, and they inhabit over against me:
6 Come now therefore, I pray you, curse me this people; for they *are* too mighty for me: perhaps I shall prevail, *that* we may smite them, and *that* I may drive them out of the land: for I know that he whom you bless *is* blessed, and he whom you curse is cursed.
7 And the elders of Moab and the elders of Midian departed with the rewards of divination in their hand; and they came to Balaam, and spoke to him the words of Balak.
8 And he said to them, Lodge here this night, and I will bring you word again, as Yahweh shall speak to me: and the princes of Moab stayed with Balaam.
9 And God came to Balaam, and said, What men *are* these with you?
10 And Balaam said to God, Balak the son of Zippor, king of Moab, has sent unto me, *saying*,
11 Behold, *there is* a people come out of Egypt, which covers the face of the earth: come now, curse me them; perhaps I shall be able to overcome them, and drive them out.
12 And God said to Balaam, You shall not go with them; you shall not curse the people: for they *are* blessed.
13 And Balaam rose up in the morning, and said to the princes of Balak, Get you into your land: for Yahweh refuses to give me leave to go with you.
14 And the princes of Moab rose up, and they went to Balak, and said, Balaam refuses to come with us.
15 ¶ And Balak sent yet again princes, more, and more honorable than they.
16 And they came to Balaam, and said to him, Thus says Balak the son of Zippor, Let nothing, I pray you, hinder you from coming to me:
17 For I will promote you unto very great honor, and I will do whatever you say to me: come therefore, I pray you, curse me this people.
18 And Balaam answered and said to the servants of Balak, If Balak would give me his house full of silver and gold, I cannot go beyond the word of Yahweh my God, to do less or more.
19 Now therefore, I pray you, tarry you also here this night, that I may know what Yahweh will say to me more.
20 And God came to Balaam at night, and said to him, If the men come to call you, rise up, *and* go with them; but yet the word which I shall say to you, that shall you do.

Numbers 22

21 And Balaam rose up in the morning, and saddled his donkey, and went with the princes of Moab.
22 ¶ And God's anger was kindled because he went: and the angel of Yahweh stood in the way for an adversary against him. Now he was riding upon his donkey, and his two servants *were* with him.
23 And the donkey saw the angel of Yahweh standing in the way, and his sword drawn in his hand: and the donkey turned aside out of the way, and went into the field: and Balaam struck the donkey, to turn her into the way.
24 But the angel of Yahweh stood in a path of the vineyards, a wall *being* on this side, and a wall on that side.
25 And when the donkey saw the angel of Yahweh, she thrust herself unto the wall, and crushed Balaam's foot against the wall: and he struck her again.
26 And the angel of Yahweh went further, and stood in a narrow place, where *was* no way to turn either to the right hand or to the left.
27 And when the donkey saw the angel of Yahweh, she fell down under Balaam: and Balaam's anger was kindled, and he struck the donkey with a staff.
28 And Yahweh opened the mouth of the donkey, and she said to Balaam, What have I done to you, that you have struck me these three times?
29 And Balaam said to the donkey, Because you have mocked me: I would there were a sword in my hand, for now would I kill you.
30 And the donkey said to Balaam, *Am* not I your donkey, upon which you have ridden ever since *I was* yours unto this day? was I ever inclined to do so to you? And he said, No.
31 Then Yahweh opened the eyes of Balaam, and he saw the angel of Yahweh standing in the way, and his sword drawn in his hand: and he bowed down his head, and fell flat on his face.
32 And the angel of Yahweh said to him, Why have you struck your donkey these three times? behold, I went out to withstand you, because *your* way is perverse before me:
33 And the donkey saw me, and turned from me these three times: unless she had turned from me, surely now also I had slain you, and saved her alive.
34 And Balaam said to the angel of Yahweh, I have sinned; for I knew not that you stood in the way against me: now therefore, if it displeases you, I will get me back again.
35 And the angel of Yahweh said to Balaam, Go with the men: but only the word that I shall speak to you, that you shall speak. So Balaam went with the princes of Balak.
36 ¶ And when Balak heard that Balaam had come, he went out to meet him to a city of Moab, which *is* in the border of Arnon, which *is* in the utmost coast.
37 And Balak said to Balaam, Did I not earnestly send to you to call you? why came you not to me? am I not able indeed to promote you to honor?
38 And Balaam said to Balak, Behold, I have come to you: have I now any power at all to say anything? the word that God puts in my mouth, that I shall speak.
39 And Balaam went with Balak, and they came to Kirjathhuzoth.
40 And Balak offered oxen and sheep, and sent to Balaam, and to the princes that *were* with him.
41 And it came to pass on the next day, that Balak took Balaam, and brought him up into the high places of Baal, that there he might see the utmost *part* of the people.

Numbers 23

23:1 ¶ And Balaam said to Balak, Build me here seven altars, and prepare me here seven oxen and seven rams.
2 And Balak did as Balaam had spoken; and Balak and Balaam offered on *every* altar a bullock and a ram.
3 And Balaam said to Balak, Stand by your burnt offering, and I will go: perhaps Yahweh will come to meet me: and whatever he shows me I will tell you. And he went to a high place.
4 And God met Balaam: and he said to him, I have prepared seven altars, and I have offered upon *every* altar a bullock and a ram.
5 And Yahweh put a word in Balaam's mouth, and said, Return to Balak, and thus you shall speak.
6 And he returned to him, and, behold, he stood by his burnt sacrifice, he, and all the princes of Moab.
7 And he took up his parable, and said, Balak the king of Moab has brought me from Aram, out of the mountains of the east, *saying*, Come, curse me Jacob, and come, defy Israel.
8 How shall I curse, whom God has not cursed? or how shall I defy, *whom* Yahweh has not defied?
9 For from the top of the rocks I see him, and from the hills I behold him: lo, the people shall dwell alone, and shall not be reckoned among the nations.
10 Who can count the dust of Jacob, and the number of the fourth *part* of Israel? Let me die the death of the righteous, and let my last end be like his!
11 And Balak said to Balaam, What have you done unto me? I took you to curse my enemies, and, behold, you have blessed *them* altogether.
12 And he answered and said, Must I not take heed to speak that which Yahweh has put in my mouth?
13 ¶ And Balak said to him, Come, I pray you, with me to another place, from where you may see them: you shall see but the utmost part of them, and shall not see them all: and curse me them from there.
14 And he brought him into the field of Zophim, to the top of Pisgah, and built seven altars, and offered a bullock and a ram on *every* altar.
15 And he said to Balak, Stand here by your burnt offering, while I meet *Yahweh* yonder.
16 And Yahweh met Balaam, and put a word in his mouth, and said, Go again to Balak, and say thus.
17 And when he came to him, behold, he stood by his burnt offering, and the princes of Moab with him. And Balak said to him, What has Yahweh spoken?
18 And he took up his parable, and said, Rise up, Balak, and hear; listen to me, you son of Zippor:

19 God *is* not a man, that he should lie; neither the son of man, that he should repent: has he said, and shall he not do *it*? or has he spoken, and shall he not make it good?
20 Behold, I have received *commandment* to bless: and he has blessed; and I cannot reverse it.
21 He has not beheld iniquity in Jacob, neither has he seen perverseness in Israel: Yahweh his God *is* with him, and the shout of a king *is* among them.
22 God brought them out of Egypt; he has as it were the strength of an unicorn.
23 Surely *there is* no enchantment against Jacob, neither *is there* any divination against Israel: according to this time it shall be said of Jacob and of Israel, What has God worked!
24 Behold, the people shall rise up as a great lion, and lift up himself as a young lion: he shall not lie down until he eats *of* the prey, and drinks the blood of the slain.
25 And Balak said to Balaam, Neither curse them at all, nor bless them at all.
26 But Balaam answered and said to Balak, Told not I you, saying, All that Yahweh speaks, that I must do?
27 And Balak said to Balaam, Come, I pray you, I will bring you to another place; perhaps it will please God that you may curse me them from there.
28 And Balak brought Balaam to the top of Peor, that looks toward Jeshimon.
29 And Balaam said to Balak, Build me here seven altars, and prepare me here seven bullocks and seven rams.
30 And Balak did as Balaam had said, and offered a bullock and a ram on *every* altar.

Numbers 24

24:1 ¶ And when Balaam saw that it pleased Yahweh to bless Israel, he went not, as at other times, to seek for enchantments, but he set his face toward the wilderness.
2 And Balaam lifted up his eyes, and he saw Israel dwelling *in his tents* according to their tribes; and the spirit of God came upon him.
3 And he took up his parable, and said, Balaam the son of Beor has said, and the man whose eyes are open has said:
4 He has said, which heard the words of God, which saw the vision of the Almighty, falling *into a trance*, but having his eyes open:
5 How goodly are your tents, O Jacob, *and* your tabernacles, O Israel!
6 As the valleys are they spread forth, as gardens by the river's side, as the trees of lign aloes which Yahweh has planted, *and* as cedar trees beside the waters.
7 He shall pour the water out of his buckets, and his seed *shall be* in many waters, and his king shall be higher than Agag, and his kingdom shall be exalted.
8 God brought him forth out of Egypt; he has as it were the strength of a unicorn: he shall eat up the nations his enemies, and shall break their bones, and pierce *them* through with his arrows.

9 He bowed, he lies down as a lion, and as a great lion: who shall stir him up? Blessed *is* he that blesses you, and cursed *is* he that curses you.
10 ¶ And Balak's anger was kindled against Balaam, and he smote his hands together: and Balak said to Balaam, I called you to curse my enemies, and, behold, you have altogether blessed *them* these three times.
11 Therefore now flee you to your place: I thought to promote you unto great honor; but, lo, Yahweh has kept you back from honor.
12 And Balaam said to Balak, Spoke I not also to your messengers which you sent to me, saying,
13 If Balak would give me his house full of silver and gold, I cannot go beyond the commandment of Yahweh, to do *either* good or bad of my own mind; *but* what Yahweh says, that will I speak?
14 And now, behold, I go to my people: come *therefore, and* I will advise you what this people shall do to your people in the latter days.
15 ¶ And he took up his parable, and said, Balaam the son of Beor has said, and the man whose eyes are open has said:
16 He has said, which heard the words of God, and knew the knowledge of the most High, *which* saw the vision of the Almighty, falling *into a trance*, but having his eyes open:
17 I shall see him, but not now: I shall behold him, but not nigh: there shall come a Star out of Jacob, and a Scepter shall rise out of Israel, and shall smite the corners of Moab, and destroy all the children of Sheth.
18 And Edom shall be a possession, Seir also shall be a possession for his enemies; and Israel shall do valiantly.
19 Out of Jacob shall come he that shall have dominion, and shall destroy him that remains of the city.
20 And when he looked on Amalek, he took up his parable, and said, Amalek *was* the first of the nations; but his latter end *shall be* that he perishes forever.
21 And he looked on the Kenites, and took up his parable, and said, Strong is your dwelling place, and you put your nest in a rock.
22 Nevertheless the Kenite shall be wasted, until Asshur shall carry you away captive.
23 And he took up his parable, and said, Alas, who shall live when God does this!
24 And ships *shall come* from the coast of Chittim, and shall afflict Asshur, and shall afflict Eber, and he also shall perish forever.
25 And Balaam rose up, and went and returned to his place: and Balak also went his way.

Numbers 25

25:1 ¶ And Israel stayed in Shittim, and the people began to commit whoredom with the daughters of Moab.
2 And they called the people to the sacrifices of their gods: and the people did eat, and bowed down to their gods.
3 And Israel joined himself to Baalpeor: and the anger of Yahweh was kindled against Israel.

Numbers 25

4 And Yahweh said to Moses, Take all the heads of the people, and hang them up before Yahweh against the sun, that the fierce anger of Yahweh may be turned away from Israel.
5 And Moses said to the judges of Israel, Slay you every one his men that were joined to Baalpeor.
6 ¶ And, behold, one of the children of Israel came and brought to his brethren a Midianitish woman in the sight of Moses, and in the sight of all the congregation of the children of Israel, who *were* weeping *before* the door of the tabernacle of the congregation.
7 And when Phinehas, the son of Eleazar, the son of Aaron the priest, saw *it*, he rose up from among the congregation, and took a javelin in his hand;
8 And he went after the man of Israel into the tent, and thrust both of them through, the man of Israel, and the woman through her belly. So the plague was stayed from the children of Israel.
9 And those that died in the plague were twenty and four thousand.
10 And Yahweh spoke to Moses, saying,
11 Phinehas, the son of Eleazar, the son of Aaron the priest, has turned my wrath away from the children of Israel, while he was zealous for my sake among them, that I consumed not the children of Israel in my jealousy.
12 Therefore say, Behold, I give to him my covenant of peace:
13 And he shall have it, and his seed after him, *even* the covenant of an everlasting priesthood; because he was zealous for his God, and made an atonement for the children of Israel.
14 Now the name of the Israelite that was slain, *even* that was slain with the Midianitish woman, *was* Zimri, the son of Salu, a prince of a chief house among the Simeonites.
15 And the name of the Midianitish woman that was slain *was* Cozbi, the daughter of Zur; he *was* head over a people, *and* of a chief house in Midian.
16 ¶ And Yahweh spoke to Moses, saying,
17 Afflict the Midianites, and smite them:
18 For they afflict you with their deceit, with which they have beguiled you in the matter of Peor, and in the matter of Cozbi, the daughter of a prince of Midian, their sister, which was slain in the day of the plague for Peor's sake.

Numbers 26

26:1 ¶ And it came to pass after the plague, that Yahweh spoke to Moses and to Eleazar the son of Aaron the priest, saying,
2 Take the sum of all the congregation of the children of Israel, from twenty years old and upward, throughout their fathers' house, all that are able to go to war in Israel.
3 And Moses and Eleazar the priest spoke with them in the plains of Moab by *the* Jordan *near* Jericho, saying,
4 *Take the sum of the people*, from twenty years old and upward; as Yahweh commanded Moses and the children of Israel, which went forth out of the land of Egypt.
5 ¶ Reuben, the oldest son of Israel: the children of Reuben; Hanoch, *of whom comes* the family of the Hanochites: of Pallu, the family of the Palluites:
6 Of Hezron, the family of the Hezronites: of Carmi, the family of the Carmites.
7 These *are* the families of the Reubenites: and they that were numbered of them were forty and three thousand and seven hundred and thirty.
8 And the sons of Pallu; Eliab.
9 And the sons of Eliab; Nemuel, and Dathan, and Abiram. This *is that* Dathan and Abiram, *which were* famous in the congregation, who strove against Moses and against Aaron in the company of Korah, when they strove against Yahweh:
10 And the earth opened her mouth, and swallowed them up together with Korah, when that company died, the time the fire devoured two hundred and fifty men: and they became a sign.
11 Notwithstanding the children of Korah died not.
12 The sons of Simeon after their families: of Nemuel, the family of the Nemuelites: of Jamin, the family of the Jaminites: of Jachin, the family of the Jachinites:
13 Of Zerah, the family of the Zarhites: of Shawl, the family of the Shawlites.
14 These *are* the families of the Simeonites, twenty and two thousand and two hundred.
15 The children of Gad after their families: of Zephon, the family of the Zephonites: of Haggi, the family of the Haggites: of Shuni, the family of the Shunites:
16 Of Ozni, the family of the Oznites: of Eri, the family of the Erites:
17 Of Arod, the family of the Arodites: of Areli, the family of the Arelites.
18 These *are* the families of the children of Gad according to those that were numbered of them, forty thousand and five hundred.
19 The sons of Judah *were* Er and Onan: and Er and Onan died in the land of Canaan.
20 And the sons of Judah after their families were; of Shelah, the family of the Shelanites: of Pharez, the family of the Pharzites: of Zerah, the family of the Zarhites.
21 And the sons of Pharez were; of Hezron, the family of the Hezronites: of Hamul, the family of the Hamulites.
22 These *are* the families of Judah according to those that were numbered of them, threescore and sixteen thousand and five hundred.
23 *Of* the sons of Issachar after their families: *of* Tola, the family of the Tolaites: of Pua, the family of the Punites:
24 Of Jashub, the family of the Jashubites: of Shimron, the family of the Shimronites.
25 These *are* the families of Issachar according to those that were numbered of them, threescore and four thousand and three hundred.
26 *Of* the sons of Zebulun after their families: of Sered, the family of the Sardites: of Elon, the family of the Elonites: of Jahleel, the family of the Jahleelites.
27 These *are* the families of the Zebulunites according to those that were numbered of them, threescore thousand and five hundred.

28 The sons of Joseph after their families *were* Manasseh and Ephraim.
29 Of the sons of Manasseh: of Machir, the family of the Machirites: and Machir begot Gilead: of Gilead came the family of the Gileadites.
30 These *are* the sons of Gilead: *of* Jeezer, the family of the Jeezerites: of Helek, the family of the Helekites:
31 And *of* Asriel, the family of the Asrielites: and *of* Shechem, the family of the Shechemites:
32 And *of* Shemida, the family of the Shemidaites: and *of* Hepher, the family of the Hepherites.
33 And Zelophehad the son of Hepher had no sons, but daughters: and the names of the daughters of Zelophehad *were* Mahlah, and Noah, Hoglah, Milcah, and Tirzah.
34 These *are* the families of Manasseh, and those that were numbered of them, fifty and two thousand and seven hundred.
35 These *are* the sons of Ephraim after their families: of Shuthelah, the family of the Shuthalhites: of Becher, the family of the Bachrites: of Tahan, the family of the Tahanites.
36 And these *are* the sons of Shuthelah: of Eran, the family of the Eranites.
37 These *are* the families of the sons of Ephraim according to those that were numbered of them, thirty and two thousand and five hundred. These *are* the sons of Joseph after their families.
38 The sons of Benjamin after their families: of Bela, the family of the Belaites: of Ashbel, the family of the Ashbelites: of Ahiram, the family of the Ahiramites:
39 Of Shupham, the family of the Shuphamites: of Hupham, the family of the Huphamites.
40 And the sons of Bela were Ard and Naaman: *of Ard*, the family of the Ardites: *and* of Naaman, the family of the Naamites.
41 These *are* the sons of Benjamin after their families: and they that were numbered of them *were* forty and five thousand and six hundred.
42 These *are* the sons of Dan after their families: of Shuham, the family of the Shuhamites. These *are* the families of Dan after their families.
43 All the families of the Shuhamites, according to those that were numbered of them, *were* threescore and four thousand and four hundred.
44 *Of* the children of Asher after their families: of Jimna, the family of the Jimnites: of Jesui, the family of the Jesuites: of Beriah, the family of the Beriites.
45 Of the sons of Beriah: of Heber, the family of the Heberites: of Malchiel, the family of the Malchielites.
46 And the name of the daughter of Asher *was* Sarah.
47 These *are* the families of the sons of Asher according to those that were numbered of them; *who were* fifty and three thousand and four hundred.
48 *Of* the sons of Naphtali after their families: of Jahzeel, the family of the Jahzeelites: of Guni, the family of the Gunites:
49 Of Jezer, the family of the Jezerites: of Shillem, the family of the Shillemites.

50 These *are* the families of Naphtali according to their families: and they that were numbered of them *were* forty and five thousand and four hundred.
51 These *were* the numbered of the children of Israel, six hundred thousand and a thousand seven hundred and thirty.
52 ¶ And Yahweh spoke to Moses, saying,
53 Unto these the land shall be divided for an inheritance according to the number of names.
54 To many you shall give the more inheritance, and to few you shall give the less inheritance: to every one shall his inheritance be given according to those that were numbered of him.
55 Notwithstanding the land shall be divided by lot: according to the names of the tribes of their fathers they shall inherit.
56 According to the lot shall the possession thereof be divided between many and few.
57 ¶ And these *are* they that were numbered of the Levites after their families: of Gershon, the family of the Gershonites: of Kohath, the family of the Kohathites: of Merari, the family of the Merarites.
58 These *are* the families of the Levites: the family of the Libnites, the family of the Hebronites, the family of the Mahlites, the family of the Mushites, the family of the Korathites. And Kohath begot Amram.
59 And the name of Amram's wife *was* Jochebed, the daughter of Levi, whom *her mother* bore to Levi in Egypt: and she bore to Amram Aaron and Moses, and Miriam their sister.
60 And to Aaron was born Nadab, and Abihu, Eleazar, and Ithamar.
61 And Nadab and Abihu died, when they offered strange fire before Yahweh.
62 And those that were numbered of them were twenty and three thousand, all males from a month old and upward: for they were not numbered among the children of Israel, because there was no inheritance given them among the children of Israel.
63 ¶ These *are* they that were numbered by Moses and Eleazar the priest, who numbered the children of Israel in the plains of Moab by *the* Jordan *near* Jericho.
64 But among these there was not a man of them whom Moses and Aaron the priest numbered, when they numbered the children of Israel in the wilderness of Sinai.
65 For Yahweh had said of them, They shall surely die in the wilderness. And there was not left a man of them, save Caleb the son of Jephunneh, and Joshua the son of Nun.

Numbers 27

27:1 ¶ Then came the daughters of Zelophehad, the son of Hepher, the son of Gilead, the son of Machir, the son of Manasseh, of the families of Manasseh the son of Joseph: and these *are* the names of his daughters; Mahlah, Noah, and Hoglah, and Milcah, and Tirzah.
2 And they stood before Moses, and before Eleazar the priest, and before the princes and all the congregation, *by* the door of the tabernacle of the congregation, saying,

Numbers 27

3 Our father died in the wilderness, and he was not in the company of them that gathered themselves together against Yahweh in the company of Korah; but died in his own sin, and had no sons.

4 Why should the name of our father be done away from among his family, because he has no son? Give to us *therefore* a possession among the brothers of our father.

5 And Moses brought their cause before Yahweh.

6 And Yahweh spoke to Moses, saying,

7 The daughters of Zelophehad speak right: you shall surely give them a possession of an inheritance among their father's brothers; and you shall cause the inheritance of their father to pass unto them.

8 And you shall speak to the children of Israel, saying, If a man dies, and has no son, then you shall cause his inheritance to pass to his daughter.

9 And if he has no daughter, then you shall give his inheritance unto his brothers.

10 And if he has no brothers, then you shall give his inheritance unto his father's brothers.

11 And if his father has no brothers, then you shall give his inheritance unto his kinsman that is next to him of his family, and he shall possess it: and it shall be to the children of Israel a statute of judgment, as Yahweh commanded Moses.

12 ¶ And Yahweh said to Moses, Get you up into this mount Abarim, and see the land which I have given to the children of Israel.

13 And when you have seen it, you also will be gathered to your people, as Aaron your brother was gathered.

14 For you rebelled against my commandment in the desert of Zin, in the strife of the congregation, to sanctify me at the water before their eyes: that *is* the water of Meribah in Kadesh in the wilderness of Zin.

15 ¶ And Moses spoke unto Yahweh, saying,

16 Let Yahweh, the God of the spirits of all flesh, set a man over the congregation,

17 Which may go out before them, and which may go in before them, and which may lead them out, and which may bring them in; that the congregation of Yahweh be not as sheep which have no shepherd.

18 And Yahweh said to Moses, Take you Joshua the son of Nun, a man in whom *is* the spirit, and lay your hand upon him;

19 And set him before Eleazar the priest, and before all the congregation; and give him a charge in their sight.

20 And you shall put *some* of your honor upon him, that all the congregation of the children of Israel may be obedient.

21 And he shall stand before Eleazar the priest, who shall ask *counsel* for him after the judgment of Urim before Yahweh: at his word shall they go out, and at his word they shall come in, *both* he, and all the children of Israel with him, even all the congregation.

22 And Moses did as Yahweh commanded him: and he took Joshua, and set him before Eleazar the priest, and before all the congregation:

23 And he laid his hands upon him, and gave him a charge, as Yahweh commanded by the hand of Moses.

Numbers 28

28:1 ¶ And Yahweh spoke to Moses, saying,

2 Command the children of Israel, and say to them, My offering, *and* my bread for my sacrifices made by fire, *for* a sweet savor unto me, shall you observe unto offer unto me in their due season.

3 And you shall say to them, This *is* the offering made by fire which you shall offer unto Yahweh; two lambs of the first year without spot day by day, *for* a continual burnt offering.

4 The one lamb shall you offer in the morning, and the other lamb shall you offer at evening;

5 And a tenth *part* of an ephah of flour for a meat offering, mingled with the fourth *part* of a hin of beaten oil.

6 *It is* a continual burnt offering, which was ordained in mount Sinai for a sweet savor, a sacrifice made by fire unto Yahweh.

7 And the drink offering thereof *shall be* the fourth *part* of a hin for the one lamb: in the holy *place* shall you cause the strong wine to be poured unto Yahweh *for* a drink offering.

8 And the other lamb shall you offer at evening: as the meat offering of the morning, and as the drink offering thereof, you shall offer *it*, a sacrifice made by fire, of a sweet savor unto Yahweh.

9 ¶ And on the sabbath day two lambs of the first year without spot, and two tenths deals of flour *for* a meat offering, mingled with oil, and the drink offering thereof:

10 *This is* the burnt offering of every sabbath, besides the continual burnt offering, and his drink offering.

11 And in the beginnings of your months you shall offer a burnt offering unto Yahweh; two young bullocks, and one ram, seven lambs of the first year without spot;

12 And three tenths deals of flour *for* a meat offering, mingled with oil, for one bullock; and two tenths deals of flour *for* a meat offering, mingled with oil, for one ram;

13 And a single tenth deal of flour mingled with oil *for* a meat offering unto one lamb; *for* a burnt offering of a sweet savor, a sacrifice made by fire unto Yahweh.

14 And their drink offerings shall be half a hin of wine unto a bullock, and the third *part* of a hin unto a ram, and a fourth *part* of a hin unto a lamb: this *is* the burnt offering of every month throughout the months of the year.

15 And one kid of the goats for a sin offering unto Yahweh shall be offered, besides the continual burnt offering, and his drink offering.

16 ¶ And in the fourteenth day of the first month *is* the passover of Yahweh.

17 And in the fifteenth day of this month *is* the feast: seven days shall unleavened bread be eaten.

18 In the first day *shall be* a holy convocation; you shall do no manner of laborious work *therein*:

19 But you shall offer a sacrifice made by fire *for* a burnt offering unto Yahweh; two young bullocks, and one ram, and seven lambs of the first year: they shall be unto you without blemish:

20 And their meat offering *shall be of* flour mingled with oil: three tenths deals shall you offer for a bullock, and two tenths deals for a ram;

21 A single tenth deal shall you offer for every lamb, throughout the seven lambs:

22 And one goat *for* a sin offering, to make an atonement for you.

23 You shall offer these besides the burnt offering in the morning, which *is* for a continual burnt offering.

24 After this manner you shall offer daily, throughout the seven days, the meat of the sacrifice made by fire, of a sweet savor unto Yahweh: it shall be offered besides the continual burnt offering, and his drink offering.

25 And on the seventh day you shall have a holy convocation; you shall do no laborious work.

26 Also in the day of the firstfruits, when you bring a new meat offering unto Yahweh, after your weeks *are out*, you shall have a holy convocation; you shall do no laborious work:

27 But you shall offer the burnt offering for a sweet savor unto Yahweh; two young bullocks, one ram, seven lambs of the first year;

28 And their meat offering of flour mingled with oil, three tenths deals unto one bullock, two tenths deals unto one ram,

29 A single tenth deal unto one lamb, throughout the seven lambs;

30 *And* one kid of the goats, to make an atonement for you.

31 You shall offer *them* besides the continual burnt offering, and his meat offering, (they shall be unto you without blemish) and their drink offerings.

Numbers 29

29:1 ¶ And in the seventh month, on the first *day* of the month, you shall have a holy convocation; you shall do no laborious work: it is a day of blowing the trumpets unto you.

2 And you shall offer a burnt offering for a sweet savor unto Yahweh; one young bullock, one ram, *and* seven lambs of the first year without blemish:

3 And their meat offering *shall be of* flour mingled with oil, three tenths deals for a bullock, *and* two tenths deals for a ram,

4 And one tenth deal for one lamb, throughout the seven lambs:

5 And one kid of the goats *for* a sin offering, to make an atonement for you:

6 Besides the burnt offering of the month, and his meat offering, and the daily burnt offering, and his meat offering, and their drink offerings, according to their manner, for a sweet savor, a sacrifice made by fire unto Yahweh.

7 And you shall have on the tenth *day* of this seventh month a holy convocation; and you shall afflict your souls: you shall not do any work *therein*:

8 But you shall offer a burnt offering unto Yahweh *for* a sweet savor; one young bullock, one ram, *and* seven lambs of the first year; they shall be unto you without blemish:

9 And their meat offering *shall be of* flour mingled with oil, three tenths deals to a bullock, *and* two tenths deals to one ram,

10 A single tenth deal for one lamb, throughout the seven lambs:

11 One kid of the goats *for* a sin offering; besides the sin offering of atonement, and the continual burnt offering, and the meat offering of it, and their drink offerings.

12 ¶ And on the fifteenth day of the seventh month you shall have a holy convocation; you shall do no laborious work, and you shall keep a feast unto Yahweh seven days:

13 And you shall offer a burnt offering, a sacrifice made by fire, of a sweet savor unto Yahweh; thirteen young bullocks, two rams, *and* fourteen lambs of the first year; they shall be without blemish:

14 And their meat offering *shall be of* flour mingled with oil, three tenths deals unto every bullock of the thirteen bullocks, two tenths deals to each ram of the two rams,

15 And a single tenth deal to each lamb of the fourteen lambs:

16 And one kid of the goats *for* a sin offering; besides the continual burnt offering, his meat offering, and his drink offering.

17 And on the second day *you shall offer* twelve young bullocks, two rams, fourteen lambs of the first year without spot:

18 And their meat offering and their drink offerings for the bullocks, for the rams, and for the lambs, *shall be* according to their number, after the manner:

19 And one kid of the goats *for* a sin offering; besides the continual burnt offering, and the meat offering thereof, and their drink offerings.

20 And on the third day eleven bullocks, two rams, fourteen lambs of the first year without blemish;

21 And their meat offering and their drink offerings for the bullocks, for the rams, and for the lambs, *shall be* according to their number, after the manner:

22 And one goat *for* a sin offering; besides the continual burnt offering, and his meat offering, and his drink offering.

23 And on the fourth day ten bullocks, two rams, *and* fourteen lambs of the first year without blemish:

24 Their meat offering and their drink offerings for the bullocks, for the rams, and for the lambs, *shall be* according to their number, after the manner:

25 And one kid of the goats *for* a sin offering; besides the continual burnt offering, his meat offering, and his drink offering.

26 And on the fifth day nine bullocks, two rams, *and* fourteen lambs of the first year without spot:

27 And their meat offering and their drink offerings for the bullocks, for the rams, and for the lambs, *shall be* according to their number, after the manner:

28 And one goat *for* a sin offering; besides the continual burnt offering, and his meat offering, and his drink offering.

29 And on the sixth day eight bullocks, two rams, *and* fourteen lambs of the first year without blemish:

Numbers 29

30 And their meat offering and their drink offerings for the bullocks, for the rams, and for the lambs, *shall be* according to their number, after the manner:
31 And one goat *for* a sin offering; besides the continual burnt offering, his meat offering, and his drink offering.
32 And on the seventh day seven bullocks, two rams, *and* fourteen lambs of the first year without blemish:
33 And their meat offering and their drink offerings for the bullocks, for the rams, and for the lambs, *shall be* according to their number, after the manner:
34 And one goat *for* a sin offering; besides the continual burnt offering, his meat offering, and his drink offering.
35 On the eighth day you shall have a solemn assembly: you shall do no laborious work *therein*:
36 But you shall offer a burnt offering, a sacrifice made by fire, of a sweet savor unto Yahweh: one bullock, one ram, seven lambs of the first year without blemish:
37 Their meat offering and their drink offerings for the bullock, for the ram, and for the lambs, *shall be* according to their number, after the manner:
38 And one goat *for* a sin offering; besides the continual burnt offering, and his meat offering, and his drink offering.
39 These *things* you shall do unto Yahweh in your set feasts, besides your vows, and your freewill offerings, for your burnt offerings, and for your meat offerings, and for your drink offerings, and for your peace offerings.
40 And Moses told the children of Israel according to all that Yahweh commanded Moses.

Numbers 30

30:1 ¶ And Moses spoke to the heads of the tribes concerning the children of Israel, saying, This *is* the thing which Yahweh has commanded.
2 If a man vows a vow unto Yahweh, or swears an oath to bind his soul with a bond; he shall not break his word, he shall do according to all that proceeds out of his mouth.
3 ¶ If a woman also vows a vow unto Yahweh, and binds herself by a bond, *being* in her father's house in her youth;
4 And her father hears her vow, and her bond with which she has bound her soul, and her father shall hold his peace at her: then all her vows shall stand, and every bond with which she has bound her soul shall stand.
5 But if her father disallows her in the day that he hears; not any of her vows, or of her bonds with which she has bound her soul, shall stand: and Yahweh shall forgive her, because her father disallowed her.
6 And if she had at all a husband, when she vowed, or uttered anything out of her lips, with which she bound her soul;
7 And her husband heard *it,* and held his peace at her in the day that he heard *it*: then her vows shall stand, and her bonds with which she bound her soul shall stand.
8 But if her husband disallowed her on the day that he heard *it*; then he shall make her vow which she vowed, and that which she uttered with her lips, with which she bound her soul, of no effect: and Yahweh shall forgive her.
9 But every vow of a widow, and of her that is divorced, with which they have bound their souls, shall stand against her.
10 And if she vowed in her husband's house, or bound her soul by a bond with an oath;
11 And her husband heard *it*, and held his peace at her, *and* disallowed her not: then all her vows shall stand, and every bond with which she bound her soul shall stand.
12 But if her husband has utterly made them void on the day he heard *them; then* whatever proceeded out of her lips concerning her vows, or concerning the bond of her soul, shall not stand: her husband has made them void; and Yahweh shall forgive her.
13 Every vow, and every binding oath to afflict the soul, her husband may establish it, or her husband may make it void.
14 But if her husband altogether holds his peace at her from day to day; then he establishes all her vows, or all her bonds, which *are* upon her: he confirms them, because he held his peace at her in the day that he heard *them.*
15 But if he shall in any way make them void after that he has heard *them*; then he shall bear her iniquity.
16 These *are* the statutes, which Yahweh commanded Moses, between a man and his wife, between the father and his daughter, *being yet* in her youth in her father's house.

Numbers 31

31:1 ¶ And Yahweh spoke to Moses, saying,
2 Avenge the children of Israel of the Midianites: afterward shall you be gathered to your people.
3 And Moses spoke to the people, saying, Arm some of yourselves unto the war, and let them go against the Midianites, and avenge Yahweh of Midian.
4 Of every tribe a thousand, throughout all the tribes of Israel, shall you send to the war.
5 So there were delivered out of the thousands of Israel, a thousand of *every* tribe, twelve thousand armed for war.
6 And Moses sent them to the war, a thousand of *every* tribe, them and Phinehas the son of Eleazar the priest, to the war, with the holy instruments, and the trumpets to blow in his hand.
7 ¶ And they warred against the Midianites, as Yahweh commanded Moses; and they slew all the males.
8 And they slew the kings of Midian, besides the rest of them that were slain; *namely*, Evi, and Rekem, and Zur, and Hur, and Reba, five kings of Midian: Balaam also the son of Beor they slew with the sword.
9 And the children of Israel took *all* the women of Midian captives, and their little ones, and took the spoil of all their cattle, and all their flocks, and all their goods.
10 And they burnt all their cities wherein they dwelt, and all their goodly castles, with fire.
11 And they took all the spoil, and all the prey, *both* of men and of beasts.

12 And they brought the captives, and the prey, and the spoil, to Moses, and Eleazar the priest, and to the congregation of the children of Israel, to the camp at the plains of Moab, which are by the Jordan near Jericho.

13 ¶ And Moses, and Eleazar the priest, and all the princes of the congregation, went forth to meet them outside the camp.

14 And Moses was angry with the officers of the host, with the captains over thousands, and captains over hundreds, which came from the battle.

15 And Moses said to them, Have you saved all the women alive?

16 Behold, these caused the children of Israel, through the counsel of Balaam, to commit trespass against Yahweh in the matter of Peor, and there was a plague among the congregation of Yahweh.

17 Now therefore kill every male among the little ones, and kill every woman that has known man by lying with him.

18 But all the female children, that have not known a man by lying with him, keep alive for yourselves.

19 And do you abide outside the camp seven days: whoever has killed any person, and whoever has touched any slain, purify both yourselves and your captives on the third day, and on the seventh day.

20 And purify all your clothing, and all that is made of skins, and all work of goats' hair, and all things made of wood.

21 And Eleazar the priest said to the men of war which went to the battle, This is the ordinance of the law which Yahweh commanded Moses;

22 Only the gold, and the silver, the brass, the iron, the tin, and the lead,

23 Every thing that may pass the fire, you shall make it go through the fire, and it shall be clean: nevertheless it shall be purified with the water of separation: and all that passes not the fire you shall make go through the water.

24 And you shall wash your clothes on the seventh day, and you shall be clean, and afterward you shall come into the camp.

25 ¶ And Yahweh spoke to Moses, saying,

26 Take the sum of the prey that was taken, both of man and of beast, you, and Eleazar the priest, and the chief fathers of the congregation:

27 And divide the prey into two parts; between them that took the war upon them, who went out to battle, and between all the congregation:

28 And levy a tribute unto Yahweh of the men of war which went out to battle: one soul of five hundred, both of the persons, and of the cattle, and of the donkeys, and of the sheep:

29 Take it of their half, and give it to Eleazar the priest, for a heave offering of Yahweh.

30 And of the children of Israel's half, you shall take one portion of fifty, of the persons, of the cattle, of the donkeys, and of the flocks, of all manner of beasts, and give them to the Levites, which keep the charge of the tabernacle of Yahweh.

31 And Moses and Eleazar the priest did as Yahweh commanded Moses.

32 And the booty, being the rest of the prey which the men of war had caught, was six hundred thousand and seventy thousand and five thousand sheep,

33 And threescore and twelve thousand cattle,

34 And threescore and one thousand donkeys,

35 And thirty and two thousand persons in all, of women that had not known man by lying with him.

36 And the half, which was the portion of them that went out to war, was in number three hundred thousand and seven and thirty thousand and five hundred sheep:

37 And Yahweh's tribute of the sheep was six hundred and threescore and fifteen.

38 And the cattle were thirty and six thousand; of which Yahweh's tribute was threescore and twelve.

39 And the donkeys were thirty thousand and five hundred; of which Yahweh's tribute was threescore and one.

40 And the persons were sixteen thousand; of which Yahweh's tribute was thirty and two persons.

41 And Moses gave the tribute, which was Yahweh's heave offering, to Eleazar the priest, as Yahweh commanded Moses.

42 And of the children of Israel's half, which Moses divided from the men that warred,

43 (Now the half that pertained to the congregation was three hundred thousand and thirty thousand and seven thousand and five hundred sheep,

44 And thirty and six thousand cattle,

45 And thirty thousand donkeys and five hundred,

46 And sixteen thousand persons;)

47 Even of the children of Israel's half, Moses took one portion of fifty, both of man and of beast, and gave them to the Levites, which kept the charge of the tabernacle of Yahweh; as Yahweh commanded Moses.

48 ¶ And the officers which were over thousands of the host, the captains of thousands, and captains of hundreds, came near to Moses:

49 And they said to Moses, Your servants have taken the sum of the men of war which are under our charge, and there lacks not one man of us.

50 We have therefore brought an oblation for Yahweh, what every man has gotten, of jewels of gold, chains, and bracelets, rings, earrings, and tablets, to make an atonement for our souls before Yahweh.

51 And Moses and Eleazar the priest took the gold of them, even all worked jewels.

52 And all the gold of the offering that they offered up to Yahweh, of the captains of thousands, and of the captains of hundreds, was sixteen thousand seven hundred and fifty shekels

53 (For the men of war had taken spoil, every man for himself.)

54 And Moses and Eleazar the priest took the gold of the captains of thousands and of hundreds, and brought it into the tabernacle of the congregation, for a memorial for the children of Israel before Yahweh.

Numbers 32

32:1 ¶ Now the children of Reuben and the children of Gad had a very great multitude of cattle: and when they saw the land of Jazer, and the land of Gilead, that, behold, the place *was* a place for cattle;

2 The children of Gad and the children of Reuben came and spoke to Moses, and to Eleazar the priest, and to the princes of the congregation, saying,

3 Ataroth, and Dibon, and Jazer, and Nimrah, and Heshbon, and Elealeh, and Shebam, and Nebo, and Beon,

4 *Even* the country which Yahweh smote before the congregation of Israel, *is* a land for cattle, and your servants have cattle:

5 Therefore, said they, if we have found grace in your sight, let this land be given to your servants for a possession, *and* bring us not over *the* Jordan.

6 And Moses said to the children of Gad and to the children of Reuben, Shall your brethren go to war, and shall you sit here?

7 And why discourage you the heart of the children of Israel from going over into the land which Yahweh has given them?

8 Thus did your fathers, when I sent them from Kadeshbarnea to see the land.

9 For when they went up to the valley of Eshcol, and saw the land, they discouraged the heart of the children of Israel, that they should not go into the land which Yahweh had given them.

10 And Yahweh's anger was kindled the same time, and he swore, saying,

11 Surely none of the men that came up out of Egypt, from twenty years old and upward, shall see the land which I swore to Abraham, to Isaac, and to Jacob; because they have not wholly followed me:

12 Save Caleb the son of Jephunneh the Kenezite, and Joshua the son of Nun: for they have wholly followed Yahweh.

13 And Yahweh's anger was kindled against Israel, and he made them wander in the wilderness forty years, until all the generation, that had done evil in the sight of Yahweh, was consumed.

14 And, behold, you have risen up in your fathers' stead, an increase of sinful men, to augment yet the fierce anger of Yahweh toward Israel.

15 For if you turn away from after him, he will yet again leave them in the wilderness; and you shall destroy all this people.

16 ¶ And they came near to him, and said, We will build sheepfolds here for our cattle, and cities for our little ones:

17 But we ourselves will go ready armed before the children of Israel, until we have brought them to their place: and our little ones shall dwell in the fenced cities because of the inhabitants of the land.

18 We will not return to our houses, until the children of Israel have inherited every man his inheritance.

19 For we will not inherit with them on *the* yonder side *of the* Jordan, or forward; because our inheritance is fallen to us on this side *the* Jordan eastward.

20 And Moses said to them, If you will do this thing, if you will go armed before Yahweh to war,

21 And will go all of you armed over *the* Jordan before Yahweh, until he has driven out his enemies from before him,

22 And the land is subdued before Yahweh: then afterward you shall return, and be guiltless before Yahweh, and before Israel; and this land shall be your possession before Yahweh.

23 But if you will not do so, behold, you have sinned against Yahweh: and be sure your sin will find you out.

24 Build you cities for your little ones, and folds for your sheep; and do that which has proceeded out of your mouth.

25 And the children of Gad and the children of Reuben spoke to Moses, saying, Your servants will do as my lord commands.

26 Our little ones, our wives, our flocks, and all our cattle, shall be there in the cities of Gilead:

27 But your servants will pass over, every man armed for war, before Yahweh to battle, as my lord said.

28 ¶ So concerning them Moses commanded Eleazar the priest, and Joshua the son of Nun, and the chief fathers of the tribes of the children of Israel:

29 And Moses said to them, If the children of Gad and the children of Reuben will pass with you over *the* Jordan, every man armed to battle, before Yahweh, and the land shall be subdued before you; then you shall give them the land of Gilead for a possession:

30 But if they will not pass over with you armed, they shall have possessions among you in the land of Canaan.

31 And the children of Gad and the children of Reuben answered, saying, As Yahweh has said to your servants, so will we do.

32 We will pass over armed before Yahweh into the land of Canaan, that the possession of our inheritance on this side *of the* Jordan *may be* ours.

33 And Moses gave to them, *even* to the children of Gad, and to the children of Reuben, and to half the tribe of Manasseh the son of Joseph, the kingdom of Sihon king of the Amorites, and the kingdom of Og king of Bashan, the land, with the cities thereof in the coasts, *even* the cities of the country round about.

34 And the children of Gad built Dibon, and Ataroth, and Aroer,

35 And Atroth, Shophan, and Jaazer, and Jogbehah,

36 And Bethnimrah, and Bethharan, fenced cities: and folds for sheep.

37 And the children of Reuben built Heshbon, and Elealeh, and Kirjathaim,

38 And Nebo, and Baalmeon, (their names being changed,) and Shibmah: and gave other names to the cities which they built.

39 And the children of Machir the son of Manasseh went to Gilead, and took it, and dispossessed the Amorite which *was* in it.

40 And Moses gave Gilead to Machir the son of Manasseh; and he dwelt therein.
41 And Jair the son of Manasseh went and took the small towns thereof, and called them Havothjair.
42 And Nobah went and took Kenath, and the villages thereof, and called it Nobah, after his own name.

Numbers 33

33:1 ¶ These *are* the journeys of the children of Israel, which went forth out of the land of Egypt with their armies under the hand of Moses and Aaron.
2 And Moses wrote their goings out according to their journeys by the commandment of Yahweh: and these *are* their journeys according to their goings out.
3 And they departed from Rameses in the first month, on the fifteenth day of the first month; on the next day after the passover the children of Israel went out with a high hand in the sight of all the Egyptians.
4 For the Egyptians buried all *their* firstborn, which Yahweh had smitten among them: upon their gods also Yahweh executed judgments.
5 And the children of Israel removed from Rameses, and pitched in Succoth.
6 And they departed from Succoth, and pitched in Etham, which *is* in the edge of the wilderness.
7 And they removed from Etham, and turned again to Pihahiroth, which *is* before Baalzephon: and they pitched before Migdol.
8 And they departed from before Pihahiroth, and passed through the midst of the sea into the wilderness, and went three days' journey in the wilderness of Etham, and pitched in Marah.
9 And they removed from Marah, and came to Elim: and in Elim *were* twelve fountains of water, and threescore and ten palm trees; and they pitched there.
10 And they removed from Elim, and encamped by the Red Sea.
11 And they removed from the Red Sea, and encamped in the wilderness of Sin.
12 And they took their journey out of the wilderness of Sin, and encamped in Dophkah.
13 And they departed from Dophkah, and encamped in Alush.
14 And they removed from Alush, and encamped at Rephidim, where was no water for the people to drink.
15 And they departed from Rephidim, and pitched in the wilderness of Sinai.
16 And they removed from the desert of Sinai, and pitched at Kibrothhattaavah.
17 And they departed from Kibrothhattaavah, and encamped at Hazeroth.
18 And they departed from Hazeroth, and pitched in Rithmah.
19 And they departed from Rithmah, and pitched at Rimmonparez.
20 And they departed from Rimmonparez, and pitched in Libnah.
21 And they removed from Libnah, and pitched at Rissah.
22 And they journeyed from Rissah, and pitched in Kehelathah.
23 And they went from Kehelathah, and pitched in mount Shapher.
24 And they removed from mount Shapher, and encamped in Haradah.
25 And they removed from Haradah, and pitched in Makheloth.
26 And they removed from Makheloth, and encamped at Tahath.
27 And they departed from Tahath, and pitched at Tarah.
28 And they removed from Tarah, and pitched in Mithcah.
29 And they went from Mithcah, and pitched in Hashmonah.
30 And they departed from Hashmonah, and encamped at Moseroth.
31 And they departed from Moseroth, and pitched in Benejaakan.
32 And they removed from Benejaakan, and encamped at Horhagidgad.
33 And they went from Horhagidgad, and pitched in Jotbathah.
34 And they removed from Jotbathah, and encamped at Ebronah.
35 And they departed from Ebronah, and encamped at Eziongaber.
36 And they removed from Eziongaber, and pitched in the wilderness of Zin, which *is* Kadesh.
37 And they removed from Kadesh, and pitched in mount Hor, in the edge of the land of Edom.
38 And Aaron the priest went up into mount Hor at the commandment of Yahweh, and died there, in the fortieth year after the children of Israel had come out of the land of Egypt, in the first *day* of the fifth month.
39 And Aaron *was* a hundred and twenty and three years old when he died in mount Hor.
40 And king Arad the Canaanite, which dwelt in the south in the land of Canaan, heard of the coming of the children of Israel.
41 And they departed from mount Hor, and pitched in Zalmonah
42 And they departed from Zalmonah, and pitched in Punon.
43 And they departed from Punon, and pitched in Oboth.
44 And they departed from Oboth, and pitched in Ijeabarim, in the border of Moab.
45 And they departed from Iim, and pitched in Dibongad.
46 And they removed from Dibongad, and encamped in Almondiblathaim.
47 And they removed from Almondiblathaim, and pitched in the mountains of Abarim, before Nebo.
48 And they departed from the mountains of Abarim, and pitched in the plains of Moab by *the* Jordan *near* Jericho.

Numbers 33

49 And they pitched by *the* Jordan, from Bethjesimoth *even* to Abelacacia in the plains of Moab.
50 ¶ And Yahweh spoke to Moses in the plains of Moab by *the* Jordan *near* Jericho, saying,
51 Speak to the children of Israel, and say to them, When you have passed over *the* Jordan into the land of Canaan;
52 Then you shall drive out all the inhabitants of the land from before you, and destroy all their pictures, and destroy all their molten images, and quite pluck down all their high places:
53 And you shall dispossess *the inhabitants* of the land, and dwell therein: for I have given you the land to possess it.
54 And you shall divide the land by lot for an inheritance among your families: *and* to the more you shall give the more inheritance, and to the fewer you shall give the less inheritance: every man's *inheritance* shall be in the place where his lot falls; according to the tribes of your fathers you shall inherit.
55 But if you will not drive out the inhabitants of the land from before you; then it shall come to pass, that those which you let remain of them *shall be* pricks in your eyes, and thorns in your sides, and shall trouble you in the land wherein you dwell.
56 Moreover it shall come to pass, *that* I shall do to you, as I thought to do to them.

Numbers 34

34:1 ¶ And Yahweh spoke to Moses, saying,
2 Command the children of Israel, and say to them, When you come into the land of Canaan; (this *is* the land that shall fall to you for an inheritance, *even* the land of Canaan with the coasts thereof:)
3 Then your south quarter shall be from the wilderness of Zin along by the coast of Edom, and your south border shall be the outmost coast of the salt sea eastward:
4 And your border shall turn from the south to the ascent of Akrabbim, and pass on to Zin: and the going forth thereof shall be from the south to Kadeshbarnea, and shall go on to Hazaraddar, and pass on to Azmon:
5 And the border shall turn about from Azmon to the river of Egypt, and the goings out of it shall be at the sea.
6 And *as for* the western border, you shall even have the great sea for a border: this shall be your west border.
7 And this shall be your north border: from the great sea you shall point out for you mount Hor:
8 From mount Hor you shall point out *your border* to the entrance of Hamath; and the goings forth of the border shall be to Zedad:
9 And the border shall go on to Ziphron, and the goings out of it shall be at Hazarenan: this shall be your north border.
10 And you shall point out your east border from Hazarenan to Shepham:
11 And the coast shall go down from Shepham to Riblah, on the east side of Ain; and the border shall descend, and shall reach to the side of the sea of Chinnereth eastward:
12 And the border shall go down to *the* Jordan, and the goings out of it shall be at the salt sea: this shall be your land with the coasts thereof round about.
13 And Moses commanded the children of Israel, saying, This *is* the land which you shall inherit by lot, which Yahweh commanded to give to the nine tribes, and to the half tribe:
14 For the tribe of the children of Reuben according to the house of their fathers, and the tribe of the children of Gad according to the house of their fathers, have received *their inheritance*; and half the tribe of Manasseh have received their inheritance:
15 The two tribes and the half tribe have received their inheritance on this side *of the* Jordan *near* Jericho eastward, toward the sunrising.
16 ¶ And Yahweh spoke to Moses, saying,
17 These *are* the names of the men which shall divide the land to you: Eleazar the priest, and Joshua the son of Nun.
18 And you shall take one prince of every tribe, to divide the land by inheritance.
19 And the names of the men *are* these: Of the tribe of Judah, Caleb the son of Jephunneh.
20 And of the tribe of the children of Simeon, Shemuel the son of Ammihud.
21 Of the tribe of Benjamin, Elidad the son of Chislon.
22 And the prince of the tribe of the children of Dan, Bukki the son of Jogli.
23 The prince of the children of Joseph, for the tribe of the children of Manasseh, Hanniel the son of Ephod.
24 And the prince of the tribe of the children of Ephraim, Kemuel the son of Shiphtan.
25 And the prince of the tribe of the children of Zebulun, Elizaphan the son of Parnach.
26 And the prince of the tribe of the children of Issachar, Paltiel the son of Azzan.
27 And the prince of the tribe of the children of Asher, Ahihud the son of Shelomi.
28 And the prince of the tribe of the children of Naphtali, Pedahel the son of Ammihud.
29 These *are they* whom Yahweh commanded to divide the inheritance unto the children of Israel in the land of Canaan.

Numbers 35

35:1 ¶ And Yahweh spoke to Moses in the plains of Moab by *the* Jordan *near* Jericho, saying,
2 Command the children of Israel, that they give to the Levites of the inheritance of their possession cities to dwell in; and you shall give *also* to the Levites suburbs for the cities round about them.
3 And the cities shall they have to dwell in; and the suburbs of them shall be for their cattle, and for their goods, and for all their beasts.
4 And the suburbs of the cities, which you shall give to the Levites, *shall reach* from the wall of the city and outward a thousand cubits round about.

5 And you shall measure from outside the city on the east side two thousand cubits, and on the south side two thousand cubits, and on the west side two thousand cubits, and on the north side two thousand cubits; and the city *shall be* in the midst: this shall be to them the suburbs of the cities.

6 And among the cities which you shall give to the Levites *there shall be* six cities for refuge, which you shall appoint for the manslayer, that he may flee there: and to them you shall add forty and two cities.

7 *So* all the cities which you shall give to the Levites *shall be* forty and eight cities: them *shall you give* with their suburbs.

8 And the cities which you shall give *shall be* of the possession of the children of Israel: from *them that have* many you shall give many; but from *them that have* few you shall give few: every one shall give of his cities to the Levites according to his inheritance which he inherits

9 ¶ And Yahweh spoke to Moses, saying,

10 Speak to the children of Israel, and say to them, When you have come over *the* Jordan into the land of Canaan;

11 Then you shall appoint you cities to be cities of refuge for you; that the slayer may flee there, which kills any person unwittingly.

12 And they shall be to you cities for refuge from the avenger; that the manslayer dies not, until he stands before the congregation in judgment.

13 And of these cities which you shall give six cities shall you have for refuge.

14 You shall give three cities on this side *of the* Jordan, and three cities shall you give in the land of Canaan, *which* shall be cities of refuge.

15 These six cities shall be a refuge, *both* for the children of Israel, and for the stranger, and for the sojourner among them: that every one that kills any person unwittingly may flee there.

16 And if he smites him with an instrument of iron, so that he dies, he *is* a murderer: the murderer shall surely be put to death.

17 And if he smites him with throwing a stone, with which he may die, and he dies, he *is* a murderer: the murderer shall surely be put to death.

18 Or *if* he smites him with a hand weapon of wood, with which he may die, and he dies, he *is* a murderer: the murderer shall surely be put to death.

19 The revenger of blood himself shall slay the murderer: when he meets him, he shall slay him.

20 But if he thrusts him *out* of hatred, or hurls at him by lying in wait, that he dies;

21 Or in enmity smites him with his hand, that he dies: he that smote *him* shall surely be put to death; *for* he *is* a murderer: the revenger of blood shall slay the murderer, when he meets him.

22 But if he thrusts him suddenly without enmity, or has cast upon him anything without lying in wait,

23 Or with any stone, with which a man may die, seeing *him* not, and cast *it* upon him, that he dies, and *was* not his enemy, neither sought his harm:

24 Then the congregation shall judge between the slayer and the revenger of blood according to these judgments:

25 And the congregation shall deliver the slayer out of the hand of the revenger of blood, and the congregation shall restore him to the city of his refuge, where he has fled: and he shall dwell in it unto the death of the high priest, which was anointed with the holy oil.

26 But if the slayer shall at any time come outside the border of the city of his refuge, where he has fled;

27 And the revenger of blood finds him outside the borders of the city of his refuge, and the revenger of blood kills the slayer; he shall not be guilty of blood:

28 Because he should have remained in the city of his refuge until the death of the high priest: but after the death of the high priest the slayer shall return into the land of his possession.

29 So these *things* shall be for a statute of judgment unto you throughout your generations in all your dwellings.

30 Whoever kills any person, the murderer shall be put to death by the mouth of witnesses: but one witness shall not testify against any person *to cause him* to die.

31 Moreover you shall take no satisfaction for the life of a murderer, which *is* guilty of death: but he shall be surely put to death.

32 And you shall take no satisfaction for him that has fled to the city of his refuge, that he should come again to dwell in the land, until the death of the priest.

33 So you shall not pollute the land wherein you *are*: for blood it defiles the land: and the land cannot be cleansed of the blood that is shed therein, but by the blood of him that shed it.

34 Defile not therefore the land which you shall inhabit, wherein I dwell: for I Yahweh dwell among the children of Israel.

Numbers 36

36:1 ¶ And the chief fathers of the families of the children of Gilead, the son of Machir, the son of Manasseh, of the families of the sons of Joseph, came near, and spoke before Moses, and before the princes, the chief fathers of the children of Israel:

2 And they said, Yahweh commanded my lord to give the land for an inheritance by lot to the children of Israel: and my lord was commanded by Yahweh to give the inheritance of Zelophehad our brother to his daughters.

3 And if they are married to any of the sons of the *other* tribes of the children of Israel, then shall their inheritance be taken from the inheritance of our fathers, and shall be put to the inheritance of the tribe whereunto they are received: so shall it be taken from the lot of our inheritance.

4 And when the jubilee of the children of Israel shall be, then shall their inheritance be put to the inheritance of the tribe whereunto they are received: so shall their inheritance be taken away from the inheritance of the tribe of our fathers.

5 ¶ And Moses commanded the children of Israel according to the word of Yahweh, saying, The tribe of the sons of Joseph has said well.

Numbers 36

6 This *is* the thing which Yahweh does command concerning the daughters of Zelophehad, saying, Let them marry to whom they think best; only to the family of the tribe of their father shall they marry.

7 So shall not the inheritance of the children of Israel remove from tribe to tribe: for every one of the children of Israel shall keep himself to the inheritance of the tribe of his fathers.

8 And every daughter, that possesses an inheritance in any tribe of the children of Israel, shall be wife to one of the family of the tribe of her father, that the children of Israel may enjoy every man the inheritance of his fathers.

9 Neither shall the inheritance remove from *one* tribe to another tribe; but every one of the tribes of the children of Israel shall keep himself to his own inheritance.

10 Even as Yahweh commanded Moses, so did the daughters of Zelophehad:

11 For Mahlah, Tirzah, and Hoglah, and Milcah, and Noah, the daughters of Zelophehad, were married to their father's brothers' sons:

12 *And* they were married into the families of the sons of Manasseh the son of Joseph, and their inheritance remained in the tribe of the family of their father.

13 These *are* the commandments and the judgments, which Yahweh commanded by the hand of Moses to the children of Israel in the plains of Moab by *the* Jordan *near* Jericho.

Deuteronomy

Deuteronomy 1

1:1 ¶ These *are* the words which Moses spoke to all Israel on this side *of the* Jordan in the wilderness, in the plain over against the Red *Sea*, between Paran, and Tophel, and Laban, and Hazeroth, and Dizahab.

2 (*There are* eleven days' *journey* from Horeb by the way of mount Seir to Kadeshbarnea.)

3 And it came to pass in the fortieth year, in the eleventh month, on the first *day* of the month, *that* Moses spoke to the children of Israel, according to all that Yahweh had given him in commandment unto them;

4 After he had slain Sihon the king of the Amorites, which dwelt in Heshbon, and Og the king of Bashan, which dwelt at Astaroth in Edrei:

5 On this side *of the* Jordan, in the land of Moab, began Moses to declare this law, saying,

6 Yahweh our God spoke to us in Horeb, saying, You have dwelt long enough in this mount:

7 Turn you, and take your journey, and go to the mount of the Amorites, and to all *the places* near thereunto, in the plain, in the hills, and in the vale, and in the south, and by the sea side, to the land of the Canaanites, and to Lebanon, to the great river, the river Euphrates.

8 Behold, I have set the land before you: go in and possess the land which Yahweh swore to your fathers, Abraham, Isaac, and Jacob, to give to them and to their seed after them.

9 ¶ And I spoke to you at that time, saying, I am not able to bear you myself alone:

10 Yahweh your God has multiplied you, and, behold, you *are* this day as the stars of heaven for multitude.

11 (Yahweh God of your fathers make you a thousand times so many more as you *are*, and bless you, as he has promised you!)

12 How can I myself alone bear your trouble, and your burden, and your strife?

13 Take you wise men, and understanding, and known among your tribes, and I will make them rulers over you.

14 And you answered me, and said, The thing which you have spoken *is* good *for us* to do.

15 So I took the chief of your tribes, wise men, and known, and made them heads over you, captains over thousands, and captains over hundreds, and captains over fifties, and captains over tens, and officers among your tribes.

16 And I charged your judges at that time, saying, Hear *the causes* between your brethren, and judge righteously between *every* man and his brother, and the stranger *that is* with him.

17 You shall not respect persons in judgment; *but* you shall hear the small as well as the great; you shall not be afraid of the face of man; for the judgment *is* God's: and the cause that is too hard for you, bring *it* to me, and I will hear it.

18 And I commanded you at that time all the things which you should do.

19 ¶ And when we departed from Horeb, we went through all that great and terrible wilderness, which you saw by the way of the mountain of the Amorites, as Yahweh our God commanded us; and we came to Kadeshbarnea.

20 And I said to you, You have come to the mountain of the Amorites, which Yahweh our God does give to us.

21 Behold, Yahweh your God has set the land before you: go up *and* possess *it*, as Yahweh God of your fathers has said to you; fear not, neither be discouraged.

22 And you came near to me every one of you, and said, We will send men before us, and they shall search us out the land, and bring us word again by what way we must go up, and into what cities we shall come.

23 And the saying pleased me well: and I took twelve men of you, one of a tribe:

24 And they turned and went up into the mountain, and came to the valley of Eshcol, and searched it out.

25 And they took of the fruit of the land in their hands, and brought *it* down to us, and brought us word again, and said, *It is* a good land which Yahweh our God does give us.

26 Notwithstanding you would not go up, but rebelled against the commandment of Yahweh your God:

27 And you murmured in your tents, and said, Because Yahweh hated us, he has brought us forth out of the land of Egypt, to deliver us into the hand of the Amorites, to destroy us.

28 Where shall we go up? our brethren have discouraged our heart, saying, The people *are* greater and taller than we; the cities *are* great and walled up to heaven; and moreover we have seen the sons of the Anakims there.

29 Then I said to you, Dread not, neither be afraid of them.
30 Yahweh your God which goes before you, he shall fight for you, according to all that he did for you in Egypt before your eyes;
31 And in the wilderness, where you have seen how that Yahweh your God bore you, as a man does bear his son, in all the way that you went, until you came into this place.
32 Yet in this thing you did not believe Yahweh your God,
33 Who went in the way before you, to search you out a place to pitch your tents *in*, in fire by night, to show you by what way you should go, and in a cloud by day.
34 And Yahweh heard the voice of your words, and was angry, and swore, saying,
35 Surely there shall not one of these men of this evil generation see that good land, which I swore to give to your fathers,
36 Save Caleb the son of Jephunneh; he shall see it, and to him will I give the land that he has trodden upon, and to his children, because he has wholly followed Yahweh.
37 Also Yahweh was angry with me for your sakes, saying, You also shall not go in there.
38 *But* Joshua the son of Nun, which stands before you, he shall go in there: encourage him: for he shall cause Israel to inherit it.
39 Moreover your little ones, which you said should be a prey, and your children, which in that day had no knowledge between good and evil, they shall go in there, and to them will I give it, and they shall possess it.
40 But *as for* you, turn you, and take your journey into the wilderness by the way of the Red Sea.
41 Then you answered and said to me, We have sinned against Yahweh, we will go up and fight, according to all that Yahweh our God commanded us. And when you had girded on every man his weapons of war, you were ready to go up into the hill.
42 And Yahweh said to me, Say to them, Go not up, neither fight; for I *am* not among you; lest you be smitten before your enemies.
43 So I spoke to you; and you would not hear, but rebelled against the commandment of Yahweh, and went presumptuously up into the hill.
44 And the Amorites, which dwelt in that mountain, came out against you, and chased you, as bees do, and destroyed you in Seir, *even* to Hormah.
45 And you returned and wept before Yahweh; but Yahweh would not listen to your voice, nor give ear to you.
46 So you stayed in Kadesh many days, according to the days that you stayed *there*.

Deuteronomy 2

2:1 ¶ Then we turned, and took our journey into the wilderness by the way of the Red Sea, as Yahweh spoke to me: and we compassed mount Seir many days.

2 And Yahweh spoke to me, saying,
3 You have compassed this mountain long enough: turn you northward.
4 And command you the people, saying, You *are* to pass through the coast of your brethren the children of Esau, which dwell in Seir; and they shall be afraid of you: take you good heed to yourselves therefore:
5 Meddle not with them; for I will not give you of their land, no, not so much as a foot breadth; because I have given mount Seir to Esau *for* a possession.
6 You shall buy food from them for money, that you may eat; and you shall also buy water from them for money, that you may drink.
7 For Yahweh your God has blessed you in all the works of your hand: he knows your walking through this great wilderness: these forty years Yahweh your God *has been* with you; you have lacked nothing.
8 ¶ And when we passed by from our brethren the children of Esau, which dwelt in Seir, through the way of the plain from Elath, and from Eziongaber, we turned and passed by the way of the wilderness of Moab.
9 And Yahweh said to me, Distress not the Moabites, neither contend with them in battle: for I will not give you of their land *for* a possession; because I have given Ar to the children of Lot *for* a possession.
10 The Emims dwelt therein in times past, a people great, and many, and tall, as the Anakims;
11 Which also were accounted giants, as the Anakims; but the Moabites call them Emims.
12 The Horims also dwelt in Seir before; but the children of Esau succeeded them, when they had destroyed them from before them, and dwelt in their stead; as Israel did to the land of his possession, which Yahweh gave to them.
13 Now rise up, *said I*, and get you over the brook Zered. And we went over the brook Zered.
14 And the space in which we came from Kadeshbarnea, until we had come over the brook Zered, *was* thirty and eight years; until all the generation of the men of war was wasted out from among the host, as Yahweh swore to them.
15 For indeed the hand of Yahweh was against them, to destroy them from among the host, until they were consumed.
16 So it came to pass, when all the men of war were consumed and dead from among the people,
17 That Yahweh spoke to me, saying,
18 You are to pass over through Ar, the coast of Moab, this day:
19 And *when* you come near over against the children of Ammon, distress them not, nor meddle with them: for I will not give you of the land of the children of Ammon *any* possession; because I have given it to the children of Lot *for* a possession.
20 (That also was accounted a land of giants: giants dwelt therein in old time; and the Ammonites call them Zamzummims;
21 A people great, and many, and tall, as the Anakims; but Yahweh destroyed them before them; and they succeeded them, and dwelt in their stead:

22 As he did to the children of Esau, which dwelt in Seir, when he destroyed the Horims from before them; and they succeeded them, and dwelt in their stead even unto this day:

23 And the Avims which dwelt in Hazerim, *even* to Azzah, the Caphtorims, which came forth out of Caphtor, destroyed them, and dwelt in their stead.)

24 ¶ Rise you up, take your journey, and pass over the river Arnon: behold, I have given into your hand Sihon the Amorite, king of Heshbon, and his land: begin to possess *it*, and contend with him in battle.

25 This day will I begin to put the dread of you and the fear of you upon the nations *that are* under the whole heaven, who shall hear report of you, and shall tremble, and be in anguish because of you.

26 And I sent messengers out of the wilderness of Kedemoth to Sihon king of Heshbon with words of peace, saying,

27 Let me pass through your land: I will go along by the high way, I will neither turn to the right hand nor to the left.

28 You shall sell me food for money, that I may eat; and give me water for money, that I may drink: only I will pass through on my feet;

29 (As the children of Esau which dwell in Seir, and the Moabites which dwell in Ar, did to me;) until I shall pass over *the* Jordan into the land which Yahweh our God gives us.

30 But Sihon king of Heshbon would not let us pass by him: for Yahweh your God hardened his spirit, and made his heart obstinate, that he might deliver him into your hand, as *appears* this day.

31 And Yahweh said to me, Behold, I have begun to give Sihon and his land before you: begin to possess, that you may inherit his land.

32 Then Sihon came out against us, he and all his people, to fight at Jahaz.

33 And Yahweh our God delivered him before us; and we smote him, and his sons, and all his people.

34 And we took all his cities at that time, and utterly destroyed the men, and the women, and the little ones, of every city, we left none to remain:

35 Only the cattle we took for a prey to ourselves, and the spoil of the cities which we took.

36 From Aroer, which *is* by the brink of the river of Arnon, and *from* the city that *is* by the river, even unto Gilead, there was not one city too strong for us: Yahweh our God delivered all unto us:

37 Only to the land of the children of Ammon you came not, *nor* to any place of the river Jabbok, nor to the cities in the mountains, nor to whatever Yahweh our God forbade us.

Deuteronomy 3

3:1 ¶ Then we turned, and went up the way to Bashan: and Og the king of Bashan came out against us, he and all his people, to battle at Edrei.

2 And Yahweh said to me, Fear him not: for I will deliver him, and all his people, and his land, into your hand; and you shall do to him as you did to Sihon king of the Amorites, which dwelt at Heshbon.

3 So Yahweh our God delivered into our hands Og also, the king of Bashan, and all his people: and we smote him until none was left to him remaining.

4 And we took all his cities at that time, there was not a city which we took not from them, threescore cities, all the region of Argob, the kingdom of Og in Bashan.

5 All these cities *were* fenced with high walls, gates, and bars; besides unwalled towns a great many.

6 And we utterly destroyed them, as we did to Sihon king of Heshbon, utterly destroying the men, women, and children, of every city.

7 But all the cattle, and the spoil of the cities, we took for a prey to ourselves.

8 And we took at that time out of the hand of the two kings of the Amorites the land that *was* on this side *of the* Jordan, from the river of Arnon to mount Hermon;

9 (*Which* Hermon the Sidonians call Sirion; and the Amorites call it Shenir;)

10 All the cities of the plain, and all Gilead, and all Bashan, to Salchah and Edrei, cities of the kingdom of Og in Bashan.

11 For only Og king of Bashan remained of the remnant of giants; behold, his bedstead *was* a bedstead of iron; *is* it not in Rabbath of the children of Ammon? nine cubits *was* the length thereof, and four cubits the breadth of it, after the cubit of a man.

12 ¶ And this land, *which* we possessed at that time, from Aroer, which *is* by the river Arnon, and half mount Gilead, and the cities thereof, gave I to the Reubenites and to the Gadites.

13 And the rest of Gilead, and all Bashan, *being* the kingdom of Og, gave I to the half tribe of Manasseh; all the region of Argob, with all Bashan, which was called the land of giants.

14 Jair the son of Manasseh took all the country of Argob to the coasts of Geshuri and Maachathi; and called them after his own name, Bashanhavothjair, unto this day.

15 And I gave Gilead to Machir.

16 And to the Reubenites and to the Gadites I gave from Gilead even to the river Arnon half the valley, and the border even to the river Jabbok, *which is* the border of the children of Ammon;

17 The plain also, and *the* Jordan, and the coast *thereof*, from Chinnereth even to the sea of the plain, *even* the salt sea, under Ashdothpisgah eastward.

18 And I commanded you at that time, saying, Yahweh your God has given you this land to possess it: you shall pass over armed before your brethren the children of Israel, all *that are* able for the war.

19 But your wives, and your little ones, and your cattle, (*for* I know that you have much cattle,) shall stay in your cities which I have given you;

20 Until Yahweh has given rest to your brethren, as well as to you, and *until* they also possess the land which Yahweh your God has given them beyond *the* Jordan: and *then* shall you return every man unto his possession, which I have given you.

21 ¶ And I commanded Joshua at that time, saying, Your eyes have seen all that Yahweh your God has done to these two kings: so shall Yahweh do to all the kingdoms where you pass.

22 You shall not fear them: for Yahweh your God he shall fight for you.

23 And I sought Yahweh at that time, saying,

24 O Lord Yahweh, you have begun to show your servant your greatness, and your mighty hand: for what God *is there* in heaven or in earth, that can do according to your works, and according to your might?

25 I pray you, let me go over, and see the good land that *is* beyond *the* Jordan, that goodly mountain, and Lebanon.

26 But Yahweh was angry with me for your sakes, and would not hear me: and Yahweh said to me, Let it suffice you; speak no more to me of this matter.

27 Get you up into the top of Pisgah, and lift up your eyes westward, and northward, and southward, and eastward, and behold *it* with your eyes: for you shall not go over this Jordan.

28 But charge Joshua, and encourage him, and strengthen him: for he shall go over before this people, and he shall cause them to inherit the land which you shall see.

29 So we stayed in the valley over against Bethpeor.

Deuteronomy 4

4:1 ¶ Now therefore listen, O Israel, to the statutes and to the judgments, which I teach you, for to do *them*, that you may live, and go in and possess the land which Yahweh God of your fathers gives you.

2 You shall not add to the word which I command you, neither shall you diminish *anything* from it, that you may keep the commandments of Yahweh your God which I command you.

3 Your eyes have seen what Yahweh did because of Baalpeor: for all the men that followed Baalpeor, Yahweh your God has destroyed them from among you.

4 But you that did cling unto Yahweh your God *are* alive every one of you this day.

5 Behold, I have taught you statutes and judgments, even as Yahweh my God commanded me, that you should do so in the land where you go to possess it.

6 Keep therefore and do *them*; for this *is* your wisdom and your understanding in the sight of the nations, which shall hear all these statutes, and say, Surely this great nation *is* a wise and understanding people.

7 For what nation *is there so* great, who *has* God *so* near to them, as Yahweh our God *is* in all *things that* we call upon him *for*?

8 And what nation *is there so* great, that has statutes and judgments *so* righteous as all this law, which I set before you this day?

9 Only take heed to yourself, and keep your soul diligently, lest you forget the things which your eyes have seen, and lest they depart from your heart all the days of your life: but teach them *to* your sons, and your sons' sons;

10 *Specially* the day that you stood before Yahweh your God in Horeb, when Yahweh said to me, Gather me the people together, and I will make them hear my words, that they may learn to fear me all the days that they shall live upon the earth, and *that* they may teach their children.

11 And you came near and stood under the mountain; and the mountain burned with fire unto the midst of heaven, with darkness, clouds, and thick darkness.

12 And Yahweh spoke unto you out of the midst of the fire: you heard the voice of the words, but saw no likeness; only *you heard* a voice.

13 And he declared unto you his covenant, which he commanded you to perform, *even* ten commandments; and he wrote them upon two tables of stone.

14 And Yahweh commanded me at that time to teach you statutes and judgments, that you might do them in the land where you go over to possess it.

15 Take you therefore good heed unto yourselves; for you saw no manner of likeness on the day *that* Yahweh spoke unto you in Horeb out of the midst of the fire:

16 Lest you corrupt *yourselves*, and make you a graven image, the similitude of any figure, the likeness of male or female,

17 The likeness of any beast that *is* on the earth, the likeness of any winged fowl that flies in the air,

18 The likeness of anything that creeps on the ground, the likeness of any fish that *is* in the waters beneath the earth:

19 And lest you lift up your eyes unto heaven, and when you see the sun, and the moon, and the stars *even* all the host of heaven, should be driven to worship them, and serve them, which Yahweh your God has divided to all nations under the whole heaven.

20 But Yahweh has taken you, and brought you forth out of the iron furnace, *even* out of Egypt, to be unto him a people of inheritance, as *you are* this day.

21 Furthermore Yahweh was angry with me for your sakes, and swore that I should not go over *the* Jordan, and that I should not go in to that good land, which Yahweh your God gives you *for* an inheritance:

22 But I must die in this land, I must not go over *the* Jordan: but you shall go over, and possess that good land.

23 Take heed unto yourselves, lest you forget the covenant of Yahweh your God, which he made with you, and make you a graven image, *or* the likeness of any *thing*, which Yahweh your God has forbidden you.

24 For Yahweh your God *is* a consuming fire, *even* a jealous God.

25 When you shall beget children, and children's children, and you shall have remained long in the land, and shall corrupt *yourselves*, and make a graven image, *or* the likeness of any *thing*, and shall do evil in the sight of Yahweh your God, to provoke him to anger:

26 I call heaven and earth to witness against you this day, that you shall soon utterly perish from off the land whereunto

Deuteronomy 4

you go over *the* Jordan to possess it; you shall not prolong *your* days upon it, but shall utterly be destroyed.
27 And Yahweh shall scatter you among the nations, and you shall be left few in number among the heathen, where Yahweh shall lead you.
28 And there you shall serve gods, the work of men's hands, wood and stone, which neither see, nor hear, nor eat, nor smell.
29 But if from there you shall seek Yahweh your God, you shall find *him*, if you seek him with all your heart and with all your soul.
30 When you are in tribulation, and all these things have come upon you, *even* in the latter days, if you turn to Yahweh your God, and shall be obedient to his voice;
31 (For Yahweh your God *is* a merciful God;) he will not forsake you, neither destroy you, nor forget the covenant of your fathers which he swore to them.
32 For ask now of the days that are past, which were before you, since the day that God created man upon the earth, and *ask* from the one side of heaven to the other, whether there has been *any such thing* as this great thing *is*, or has been heard like it?
33 Did *ever* people hear the voice of God speaking out of the midst of the fire, as you have heard, and live?
34 Or has God tried to go *and* take him a nation from the midst of *another* nation, by temptations, by signs, and by wonders, and by war, and by a mighty hand, and by a stretched out arm, and by great terrors, according to all that Yahweh your God did for you in Egypt before your eyes?
35 Unto you it was shown, that you might know that Yahweh he *is* God; *there is* none else beside him.
36 Out of heaven he made you to hear his voice, that he might instruct you: and upon earth he showed you his great fire; and you heard his words out of the midst of the fire.
37 And because he loved your fathers, therefore he chose their seed after them, and brought you out in his sight with his mighty power out of Egypt;
38 To drive out nations from before you greater and mightier than you *are*, to bring you in, to give you their land *for* an inheritance, as *it is* this day.
39 Know therefore this day, and consider *it* in your heart, that Yahweh he *is* God in heaven above, and upon the earth beneath: *there is* none else.
40 You shall keep therefore his statutes, and his commandments, which I command you this day, that it may go well with you, and with your children after you, and that you may prolong *your* days upon the earth, which Yahweh your God gives you, forever.
41 ¶ Then Moses separated three cities on this side *of the* Jordan toward the sunrising;
42 That the slayer might flee there, which should kill his neighbor unwittingly, and hated him not in times past; and that fleeing to one of these cities he might live:
43 *Namely*, Bezer in the wilderness, in the plain country, of the Reubenites; and Ramoth in Gilead, of the Gadites; and Golan in Bashan, of the Manassites.
44 And this *is* the law which Moses set before the children of Israel:
45 These *are* the testimonies, and the statutes, and the judgments, which Moses spoke to the children of Israel, after they came forth out of Egypt,
46 On this side *of the* Jordan, in the valley over against Bethpeor, in the land of Sihon king of the Amorites, who dwelt at Heshbon, whom Moses and the children of Israel smote, after they had come forth out of Egypt:
47 And they possessed his land, and the land of Og king of Bashan, two kings of the Amorites, which *were* on this side *of the* Jordan toward the sunrising;
48 From Aroer, which *is* by the bank of the river Arnon, even to mount Sion, which *is* Hermon,
49 And all the plain on this side *of the* Jordan eastward, even to the sea of the plain, under the springs of Pisgah.

Deuteronomy 5

5:1 ¶ And Moses called all Israel, and said to them, Hear, O Israel, the statutes and judgments which I speak in your ears this day, that you may learn them, and keep, and do them.
2 Yahweh our God made a covenant with us in Horeb.
3 Yahweh made not this covenant with our fathers, but with us, *even* us, who *are* all of us here alive this day.
4 Yahweh talked with you face to face in the mount out of the midst of the fire,
5 (I stood between Yahweh and you at that time, to show you the word of Yahweh: for you were afraid by reason of the fire, and went not up into the mount;) saying,
6 ¶ I *am* Yahweh your God, which brought you out of the land of Egypt, from the house of bondage.
7 You shall have no other gods before me.
8 You shall not make you *any* graven image, *or* any likeness *of any thing* that *is* in heaven above, or that *is* in the earth beneath, or that *is* in the waters beneath the earth:
9 You shall not bow down yourself unto them, nor serve them: for I Yahweh your God *am* a jealous God, visiting the iniquity of the fathers upon the children to the third and fourth *generation* of them that hate me,
10 And showing mercy unto thousands of them that love me and keep my commandments.
11 You shall not take the name of Yahweh your God in vain: for Yahweh will not hold *him* guiltless that takes his name in vain.
12 Keep the sabbath day to sanctify it, as Yahweh your God has commanded you.
13 Six days you shall labor, and do all your work:
14 But the seventh day *is* the sabbath of Yahweh your God: *in it* you shall not do any work, you, nor your son, nor your daughter, nor your manservant, nor your maidservant, nor your ox, nor your donkey, nor any of your cattle, nor your stranger that *is* within your gates; that your manservant and your maidservant may rest as well as you.
15 And remember that you were a servant in the land of Egypt, and *that* Yahweh your God brought you out *of* there through a mighty hand and by a stretched out arm: therefore Yahweh your God commanded you to keep the sabbath day.

16 Honor your father and your mother, as Yahweh your God has commanded you; that your days may be prolonged, and that it may go well with you, in the land which Yahweh your God gives you.
17 You shall not kill.
18 Neither shall you commit adultery.
19 Neither shall you steal.
20 Neither shall you bear false witness against your neighbor.
21 Neither shall you desire your neighbor's wife, neither shall you covet your neighbor's house, his field, or his manservant, or his maidservant, his ox, or his donkey, or any *thing* that *is* your neighbor's.
22 These words Yahweh spoke to all your assembly in the mount out of the midst of the fire, of the cloud, and of the thick darkness, with a great voice: and he added no more. And he wrote them in two tables of stone, and delivered them to me.
23 ¶ And it came to pass, when you heard the voice out of the midst of the darkness, (for the mountain did burn with fire,) that you came near to me, *even* all the heads of your tribes, and your elders;
24 And you said, Behold, Yahweh our God has shown us his glory and his greatness, and we have heard his voice out of the midst of the fire: we have seen this day that God does talk with man, and he lives.
25 Now therefore why should we die? for this great fire will consume us: if we hear the voice of Yahweh our God any more, then we shall die.
26 For who *is there of* all flesh, that has heard the voice of the living God speaking out of the midst of the fire, as we *have*, and lived?
27 Go you near, and hear all that Yahweh our God shall say: and speak you to us all that Yahweh our God shall speak to you; and we will hear *it*, and do *it*.
28 And Yahweh heard the voice of your words, when you spoke to me; and Yahweh said to me, I have heard the voice of the words of this people, which they have spoken to you: they have well said all that they have spoken.
29 O that there were such a heart in them, that they would fear me, and keep all my commandments always, that it might be well with them, and with their children forever!
30 Go say to them, Get you into your tents again.
31 But as for you, stand you here by me, and I will speak to you all the commandments, and the statutes, and the judgments, which you shall teach them, that they may do *them* in the land which I give them to possess it.
32 You shall observe to do therefore as Yahweh your God has commanded you: you shall not turn aside to the right hand or to the left.
33 You shall walk in all the ways which Yahweh your God has commanded you, that you may live, and *that it may be* well with you, and *that* you may prolong *your* days in the land which you shall possess.

Deuteronomy 6

6:1 ¶ Now these *are* the commandments, the statutes, and the judgments, which Yahweh your God commanded to teach you, that you might do *them* in the land where you go to possess it:
2 That you might fear Yahweh your God, to keep all his statutes and his commandments, which I command you, you, and your son, and your son's son, all the days of your life; and that your days may be prolonged.
3 Hear therefore, O Israel, and observe to do *it*; that it may be well with you, and that you may increase mightily, as Yahweh God of your fathers has promised you, in the land that flows with milk and honey.
4 ¶ Hear, O Israel: Yahweh our God *is* one Yahweh:
5 And you shall love Yahweh your God with all your heart, and with all your soul, and with all your might.
6 And these words, which I command you this day, shall be in your heart:
7 And you shall teach them diligently to your children, and shall talk of them when you sit in your house, and when you walk by the way, and when you lie down, and when you rise up.
8 And you shall bind them for a sign upon your hand, and they shall be as frontlets between your eyes.
9 And you shall write them upon the posts of your house, and on your gates.
10 And it shall be, when Yahweh your God shall have brought you into the land which he swore to your fathers, to Abraham, to Isaac, and to Jacob, to give you great and goodly cities, which you built not,
11 And houses full of all good *things*, which you filled not, and wells dug, which you dug not, vineyards and olive trees, which you planted not; when you shall have eaten and be full;
12 *Then* beware lest you forget Yahweh, which brought you forth out of the land of Egypt, from the house of bondage.
13 You shall fear Yahweh your God, and serve him, and shall swear by his name.
14 You shall not go after other gods, of the gods of the people which *are* round about you;
15 (For Yahweh your God *is* a jealous God among you) lest the anger of Yahweh your God be kindled against you, and destroy you from off the face of the earth.
16 You shall not tempt Yahweh your God, as you tempted *him* in Massah.
17 ¶ You shall diligently keep the commandments of Yahweh your God, and his testimonies, and his statutes, which he has commanded you.
18 And you shall do *that which is* right and good in the sight of Yahweh: that it may be well with you, and that you may go in and possess the good land which Yahweh swore unto your fathers,
19 To cast out all your enemies from before you, as Yahweh has spoken.

Deuteronomy 6

20 *And* when your son asks you in time to come, saying, What *mean* the testimonies, and the statutes, and the judgments, which Yahweh our God has commanded you?
21 Then you shall say to your son, We were Pharaoh's bondmen in Egypt; and Yahweh brought us out of Egypt with a mighty hand:
22 And Yahweh showed signs and wonders, great and grievous, upon Egypt, upon Pharaoh, and upon all his household, before our eyes:
23 And he brought us out from there, that he might bring us in, to give us the land which he swore unto our fathers.
24 And Yahweh commanded us to do all these statutes, to fear Yahweh our God, for our good always, that he might preserve us alive, as *it is* at this day.
25 And it shall be our righteousness, if we observe to do all these commandments before Yahweh our God, as he has commanded us.

Deuteronomy 7

7:1 ¶ When Yahweh your God shall bring you into the land where you go to possess it, and has cast out many nations before you, the Hittites, and the Girgashites, and the Amorites, and the Canaanites, and the Perizzites, and the Hivites, and the Jebusites, seven nations greater and mightier than you;
2 And when Yahweh your God shall deliver them before you; you shall smite them, *and* utterly destroy them; you shall make no covenant with them, nor show mercy to them:
3 Neither shall you make marriages with them; your daughter you shall not give to his son, nor his daughter shall you take to your son.
4 For they will turn away your son from following me, that they may serve other gods: so will the anger of Yahweh be kindled against you, and destroy you suddenly.
5 But thus shall you deal with them; you shall destroy their altars, and break down their images, and cut down their groves, and burn their graven images with fire.
6 For you *are* a holy people unto Yahweh your God: Yahweh your God has chosen you to be a special people unto himself, above all people that *are* upon the face of the earth.
7 Yahweh did not set his love upon you, nor choose you, because you were more in number than any people; for you *were* the fewest of all people:
8 But because Yahweh loved you, and because he would keep the oath which he had sworn to your fathers, has Yahweh brought you out with a mighty hand, and redeemed you out of the house of bondmen, from the hand of Pharaoh king of Egypt.
9 Know therefore that Yahweh your God, he *is* God, the faithful God, which keeps covenant and mercy with them that love him and keep his commandments to a thousand generations;
10 And repays them that hate him to their face, to destroy them: he will not be slack to him that hates him, he will repay him to his face.
11 You shall therefore keep the commandments, and the statutes, and the judgments, which I command you this day, to do them.
12 ¶ Therefore it shall come to pass, if you listen to these judgments, and keep, and do them, that Yahweh your God shall keep unto you the covenant and the mercy which he swore to your fathers:
13 And he will love you, and bless you, and multiply you: he will also bless the fruit of your womb, and the fruit of your land, your corn, and your *new* wine, and your oil, the increase of your cattle, and the flocks of your sheep, in the land which he swore to your fathers to give you.
14 You shall be blessed above all people: there shall not be male or female barren among you, or among your cattle.
15 And Yahweh will take away from you all sickness, and will put none of the evil diseases of Egypt, which you know, upon you; but will lay them upon all *them* that hate you.
16 And you shall consume all the people which Yahweh your God shall deliver you; your eye shall have no pity upon them: neither shall you serve their gods; for that *will be* a snare to you.
17 If you shall say in your heart, These nations *are* more than I; how can I dispossess them?
18 You shall not be afraid of them: *but* will well remember what Yahweh your God did to Pharaoh, and to all Egypt;
19 The great temptations which your eyes saw, and the signs, and the wonders, and the mighty hand, and the stretched out arm, whereby Yahweh your God brought you out: so shall Yahweh your God do to all the people of whom you are afraid.
20 Moreover Yahweh your God will send the hornet among them, until they that are left, and hide themselves from you, are destroyed.
21 You shall not be frightened by them: for Yahweh your God *is* among you, a mighty God and fearful.
22 And Yahweh your God will put out those nations before you by little and little: you may not consume them at once, lest the beasts of the field increase upon you.
23 But Yahweh your God shall deliver them to you, and shall destroy them with a mighty destruction, until they are destroyed.
24 And he shall deliver their kings into your hand, and you shall destroy their name from under heaven: there shall no man be able to stand before you, until you have destroyed them.
25 The graven images of their gods shall you burn with fire: you shall not desire the silver or gold *that is* on them, nor take *it* to you, lest you be snared therein: for it *is* an abomination to Yahweh your God.
26 Neither shall you bring an abomination into your house, lest you be a cursed thing like it: *but* you shall utterly detest it, and you shall utterly abhor it; for it *is* a cursed thing.

Deuteronomy 8

8:1 ¶ All the commandments which I command you this day shall you observe to do, that you may live, and multiply, and go in and possess the land which Yahweh swore unto your fathers.

2 And you shall remember all the way which Yahweh your God led you these forty years in the wilderness, to humble you, *and* to prove you, to know what *was* in your heart, whether you would keep his commandments, or not.

3 And he humbled you, and allowed you to hunger, and fed you with manna, which you knew not, neither did your fathers know; that he might make you know that man does not live by bread only, but by every *word* that proceeds out of the mouth of Yahweh does man live.

4 Your clothing became not old upon you, neither did your foot swell, these forty years.

5 You shall also consider in your heart, that, as a man chastens his son, *so* Yahweh your God chastens you.

6 Therefore you shall keep the commandments of Yahweh your God, to walk in his ways, and to fear him.

7 For Yahweh your God brings you into a good land, a land of brooks of water, of fountains and depths that spring out of valleys and hills;

8 A land of wheat, and barley, and vines, and fig trees, and pomegranates; a land of olive oil, and honey;

9 A land wherein you shall eat bread without scarceness, you shall not lack any *thing* in it; a land whose stones *are* iron, and out of whose hills you may dig brass.

10 ¶ When you have eaten and are full, then you shall bless Yahweh your God for the good land which he has given you.

11 Beware that you forget not Yahweh your God, in not keeping his commandments, and his judgments, and his statutes, which I command you this day:

12 Lest *when* you have eaten and are full, and have built fine houses, and dwelt *therein*;

13 And *when* your herds and your flocks multiply, and your silver and your gold is multiplied, and all that you have is multiplied;

14 Then your heart is lifted up, and you forget Yahweh your God, which brought you forth out of the land of Egypt, from the house of bondage;

15 Who led you through that great and terrible wilderness, *wherein were* fiery serpents, and scorpions, and drought, where *there was* no water; who brought you forth water out of the rock of flint;

16 Who fed you in the wilderness with manna, which your fathers knew not, that he might humble you, and that he might prove you, to do you good at your latter end;

17 And you say in your heart, My power and the might of *my* hand has gotten me this wealth.

18 But you shall remember Yahweh your God: for *it is* he that gives you power to get wealth, that he may establish his covenant which he swore to your fathers, as *it is* this day.

19 And it shall be, if you do at all forget Yahweh your God, and walk after other gods, and serve them, and worship them, I testify against you this day that you shall surely perish.

20 As the nations which Yahweh destroys before your face, so shall you perish; because you would not be obedient to the voice of Yahweh your God.

Deuteronomy 9

9:1 ¶ Hear, O Israel: You *are* to pass over *the* Jordan this day, to go in to possess nations greater and mightier than yourself, cities great and fenced up to heaven.

2 A people great and tall, the children of the Anakims, whom you know, and *of whom* you have heard *say*, Who can stand before the children of Anak!

3 Understand therefore this day, that Yahweh your God *is* he which goes over before you; *as* a consuming fire he shall destroy them, and he shall bring them down before your face: so shall you drive them out, and destroy them quickly, as Yahweh has said to you.

4 Speak not you in your heart, after that Yahweh your God has cast them out from before you, saying, For my righteousness Yahweh has brought me in to possess this land: but for the wickedness of these nations Yahweh does drive them out from before you.

5 Not for your righteousness, or for the uprightness of your heart, do you go to possess their land: but for the wickedness of these nations Yahweh your God does drive them out from before you, and that he may perform the word which Yahweh swore to your fathers, Abraham, Isaac, and Jacob.

6 Understand therefore, that Yahweh your God gives you not this good land to possess it for your righteousness; for you *are* a stiffnecked people.

7 ¶ Remember, *and* forget not, how you provoked Yahweh your God to wrath in the wilderness: from the day that you did depart out of the land of Egypt, until you came to this place, you have been rebellious against Yahweh.

8 Also in Horeb you provoked Yahweh to wrath, so that Yahweh was angry with you to have destroyed you.

9 When I had gone up into the mount to receive the tables of stone, *even* the tables of the covenant which Yahweh made with you, then I stayed in the mount forty days and forty nights, I neither did eat bread nor drink water:

10 And Yahweh delivered to me two tables of stone written with the finger of God; and on them *was written* according to all the words, which Yahweh spoke with you in the mount out of the midst of the fire in the day of the assembly.

11 And it came to pass at the end of forty days and forty nights, *that* Yahweh gave me the two tables of stone, *even* the tables of the covenant.

12 And Yahweh said to me, Arise, get you down quickly from here; for your people which you have brought forth out of Egypt have corrupted *themselves*; they have quickly turned aside out of the way which I commanded them; they have made them a molten image.

13 Furthermore Yahweh spoke to me, saying, I have seen this people, and, behold, it *is* a stiffnecked people:

14 Let me alone, that I may destroy them, and blot out their name from under heaven: and I will make of you a nation mightier and greater than they.

Deuteronomy 9

15 So I turned and came down from the mount, and the mount burned with fire: and the two tables of the covenant *were* in my two hands.

16 And I looked, and, behold, you had sinned against Yahweh your God, *and* had made you a molten calf: you had turned aside quickly out of the way which Yahweh had commanded you.

17 And I took the two tables, and cast them out of my two hands, and broke them before your eyes.

18 And I fell down before Yahweh, as at the first, forty days and forty nights: I did neither eat bread, nor drink water, because of all your sins which you sinned, in doing wickedly in the sight of Yahweh, to provoke him to anger.

19 For I was afraid of the anger and hot displeasure, with which Yahweh was angry against you to destroy you. But Yahweh listened to me at that time also.

20 And Yahweh was very angry with Aaron to have destroyed him: and I prayed for Aaron also the same time.

21 And I took your sin, the calf which you had made, and burnt it with fire, and crushed it, *and* ground *it* very small, *even* until it was as small as dust: and I cast the dust thereof into the brook that descended out of the mount.

22 And at Taberah, and at Massah, and at Kibrothhattaavah, you provoked Yahweh to wrath.

23 Likewise when Yahweh sent you from Kadeshbarnea, saying, Go up and possess the land which I have given you; then you rebelled against the commandment of Yahweh your God, and you believed him not, nor listened to his voice.

24 You have been rebellious against Yahweh from the day that I knew you.

25 Thus I fell down before Yahweh forty days and forty nights, as I fell down *at the first*; because Yahweh had said he would destroy you.

26 I prayed therefore unto Yahweh, and said, O Lord Yahweh, destroy not your people and your inheritance, which you have redeemed through your greatness, which you have brought forth out of Egypt with a mighty hand.

27 Remember your servants, Abraham, Isaac, and Jacob; look not to the stubbornness of this people, nor to their wickedness, nor to their sin:

28 Lest the land wherefrom you brought us out say, Because Yahweh was not able to bring them into the land which he promised them, and because he hated them, he has brought them out to slay them in the wilderness.

29 Yet they *are* your people and your inheritance, which you brought out by your mighty power and by your stretched out arm.

Deuteronomy 10

10:1 ¶ At that time Yahweh said to me, Hew you two tables of stone like unto the first, and come up to me into the mount, and make you an ark of wood.

2 And I will write on the tables the words that were in the first tables which you broke, and you shall put them in the ark.

3 And I made an ark *of* shittim wood, and hewed two tables of stone like unto the first, and went up into the mount, having the two tables in my hand.

4 And he wrote on the tables, according to the first writing, the ten commandments, which Yahweh spoke to you in the mount out of the midst of the fire in the day of the assembly: and Yahweh gave them to me.

5 And I turned myself and came down from the mount, and put the tables in the ark which I had made; and there they are, as Yahweh commanded me.

6 And the children of Israel took their journey from Beeroth of the children of Jaakan to Mosera: there Aaron died, and there he was buried; and Eleazar his son ministered in the priest's office in his stead.

7 From there they journeyed to Gudgodah; and from Gudgodah to Jotbath, a land of rivers of waters.

8 At that time Yahweh separated the tribe of Levi, to bear the ark of the covenant of Yahweh, to stand before Yahweh to minister to him, and to bless in his name, unto this day.

9 Therefore Levi has no part nor inheritance with his brethren; Yahweh *is* his inheritance, according as Yahweh your God promised him.

10 And I stayed in the mount, according to the first time, forty days and forty nights; and Yahweh listened to me at that time also, *and* Yahweh would not destroy you.

11 And Yahweh said to me, Arise, take *your* journey before the people, that they may go in and possess the land, which I swore to their fathers to give to them.

12 ¶ And now, Israel, what does Yahweh your God require of you, but to fear Yahweh your God, to walk in all his ways, and to love him, and to serve Yahweh your God with all your heart and with all your soul,

13 To keep the commandments of Yahweh, and his statutes, which I command you this day for your good?

14 Behold, the heaven and the heaven of heavens *is* Yahweh's your God, the earth *also*, with all that therein *is*.

15 Only Yahweh had a delight in your fathers to love them, and he chose their seed after them, *even* you above all people, as *it is* this day.

16 Circumcise therefore the foreskin of your heart, and be no more stiffnecked.

17 For Yahweh your God *is* God of gods, and Lord of lords, a great God, a mighty, and a fearful, which regards not persons, nor takes reward:

18 He does execute the judgment of the fatherless and widow, and loves the stranger, in giving him food and clothing.

19 Love you therefore the stranger: for you were strangers in the land of Egypt.

20 You shall fear Yahweh your God; him shall you serve, and to him shall you cling, and swear by his name.

21 He *is* your praise, and he *is* your God, that has done for you these great and fearful things, which your eyes have seen.

22 Your fathers went down into Egypt with threescore and ten persons; and now Yahweh your God has made you as the stars of heaven for multitude.

Deuteronomy 11

11:1 ¶ Therefore you shall love Yahweh your God, and keep his charge, and his statutes, and his judgments, and his commandments, always.

2 And know you this day: for *I speak* not with your children which have not known, and which have not seen the chastisement of Yahweh your God, his greatness, his mighty hand, and his stretched out arm,

3 And his miracles, and his acts, which he did in the midst of Egypt to Pharaoh the king of Egypt, and to all his land;

4 And what he did to the army of Egypt, to their horses, and to their chariots; how he made the water of the Red Sea to overflow them as they pursued after you, and *how* Yahweh has destroyed them unto this day;

5 And what he did to you in the wilderness, until you came into this place;

6 And what he did to Dathan and Abiram, the sons of Eliab, the son of Reuben: how the earth opened her mouth, and swallowed them up, and their households, and their tents, and all the substance that *was* in their possession, in the midst of all Israel:

7 But your eyes have seen all the great acts of Yahweh which he did.

8 ¶ Therefore shall you keep all the commandments which I command you this day, that you may be strong, and go in and possess the land, where you go to possess it;

9 And that you may prolong *your* days in the land, which Yahweh swore to your fathers to give to them and to their seed, a land that flows with milk and honey.

10 For the land, where you go in to possess it, *is* not as the land of Egypt, from where you came out, where you sowed your seed, and watered *it* with your foot, as a garden of herbs:

11 But the land, where you go to possess it, *is* a land of hills and valleys, *and* drinks water of the rain of heaven:

12 A land which Yahweh your God cares for: the eyes of Yahweh your God *are* always upon it, from the beginning of the year even to the end of the year.

13 And it shall come to pass, if you shall listen diligently to my commandments which I command you this day, to love Yahweh your God, and to serve him with all your heart and with all your soul,

14 That I will give *you* the rain of your land in his due season, the first rain and the latter rain, that you may gather in your corn, and your *new* wine, and your oil.

15 And I will send grass in your fields for your cattle, that you may eat and be full.

16 Take heed to yourselves, that your heart is not deceived, and you turn aside, and serve other gods, and worship them;

17 And *then* Yahweh's wrath be kindled against you, and he shut up the heaven, that there be no rain, and that the land yield not her fruit; and *lest* you perish quickly from off the good land which Yahweh gives you.

18 ¶ Therefore shall you lay up these my words in your heart and in your soul, and bind them for a sign upon your hand, that they may be as frontlets between your eyes.

19 And you shall teach them your children, speaking of them when you sit in your house, and when you walk by the way, when you lie down, and when you rise up.

20 And you shall write them upon the door posts of your house, and upon your gates:

21 That your days may be multiplied, and the days of your children, in the land which Yahweh swore to your fathers to give them, as the days of heaven upon the earth.

22 For if you shall diligently keep all these commandments which I command you, to do them, to love Yahweh your God, to walk in all his ways, and to cling to him;

23 Then will Yahweh drive out all these nations from before you, and you shall possess greater nations and mightier than yourselves.

24 Every place whereon the soles of your feet shall tread shall be yours: from the wilderness and Lebanon, from the river, the river Euphrates, even to the utmost sea shall your coast be.

25 There shall no man be able to stand before you: *for* Yahweh your God shall lay the fear of you and the dread of you upon all the land that you shall tread upon, as he has said to you.

26 ¶ Behold, I set before you this day a blessing and a curse;

27 A blessing, if you obey the commandments of Yahweh your God, which I command you this day:

28 And a curse, if you will not obey the commandments of Yahweh your God, but turn aside out of the way which I command you this day, to go after other gods, which you have not known.

29 And it shall come to pass, when Yahweh your God has brought you in to the land where you go to possess it, that you shall put the blessing upon mount Gerizim, and the curse upon mount Ebal.

30 *Are* they not on the other side *of the* Jordan, by the way where the sun goes down, in the land of the Canaanites, which dwell in the desert over against Gilgal, beside the plains of Moreh?

31 For you shall pass over *the* Jordan to go in to possess the land which Yahweh your God gives you, and you shall possess it, and dwell therein.

32 And you shall observe to do all the statutes and judgments which I set before you this day.

Deuteronomy 12

12:1 ¶ These *are* the statutes and judgments, which you shall observe to do in the land, which Yahweh God of your fathers gives you to possess it, all the days that you live upon the earth.

2 You shall utterly destroy all the places, wherein the nations which you shall possess served their gods, upon the high mountains, and upon the hills, and under every green tree:

3 And you shall overthrow their altars, and break their pillars, and burn their groves with fire; and you shall hew down the graven images of their gods, and destroy the names of them out of that place.

Deuteronomy 12

4 You shall not do so unto Yahweh your God.
5 ¶ But to the place which Yahweh your God shall choose out of all your tribes to put his name there, *even* unto his habitation shall you seek, and there you shall come:
6 And there you shall bring your burnt offerings, and your sacrifices, and your tithes, and heave offerings of your hand, and your vows, and your freewill offerings, and the firstborn of your herds and of your flocks:
7 And there you shall eat before Yahweh your God, and you shall rejoice in all that you put your hand to, you and your households, wherein Yahweh your God has blessed you.
8 You shall not do after all *the things* that we do here this day, every man whatever *is* right in his own eyes.
9 For you are not as yet come to the rest and to the inheritance, which Yahweh your God gives you.
10 But *when* you go over *the* Jordan, and dwell in the land which Yahweh your God gives you to inherit, and *when* he gives you rest from all your enemies round about, so that you dwell in safety;
11 Then there shall be a place which Yahweh your God shall choose to cause his name to dwell there; there shall you bring all that I command you; your burnt offerings, and your sacrifices, your tithes, and the heave offering of your hand, and all your choice vows which you vow unto Yahweh:
12 And you shall rejoice before Yahweh your God, you, and your sons, and your daughters, and your menservants, and your maidservants, and the Levite that *is* within your gates; forasmuch as he has no part nor inheritance with you.
13 Take heed to yourself that you offer not your burnt offerings in every place that you see:
14 But in the place which Yahweh shall choose in one of your tribes, there you shall offer your burnt offerings, and there you shall do all that I command you.
15 Notwithstanding you may kill and eat flesh in all your gates, whatever your soul lusts after, according to the blessing of Yahweh your God which he has given you: the unclean and the clean may eat thereof, as of the roebuck, and as of the hart.
16 Only you shall not eat the blood; you shall pour it upon the earth as water.
17 You may not eat within your gates the tithe of your corn, or of your *new* wine, or of your oil, or the firstborn of your herds or of your flock, nor any of your vows which you vow, nor your freewill offerings, or heave offering of your hand:
18 But you must eat them before Yahweh your God in the place which Yahweh your God shall choose, you, and your son, and your daughter, and your manservant, and your maidservant, and the Levite that *is* within your gates: and you shall rejoice before Yahweh your God in all that you put your hands to.
19 Take heed to yourself that you forsake not the Levite as long as you live upon the earth.
20 When Yahweh your God shall enlarge your border, as he has promised you, and you shall say, I will eat flesh, because your soul longs to eat flesh; you may eat flesh, whatever your soul lusts after.
21 If the place which Yahweh your God has chosen to put his name there is too far from you, then you shall kill of your herd and of your flock, which Yahweh has given you, as I have commanded you, and you shall eat in your gates whatever your soul lusts after.
22 Even as the roebuck and the hart are eaten, so you shall eat them: the unclean and the clean shall eat *of* them alike.
23 Only be sure that you eat not the blood: for the blood *is* the life; and you may not eat the life with the flesh.
24 You shall not eat it; you shall pour it upon the earth as water.
25 You shall not eat it; that it may go well with you, and with your children after you, when you shall do *that which is* right in the sight of Yahweh.
26 Only your holy things which you have, and your vows, you shall take, and go to the place which Yahweh shall choose:
27 And you shall offer your burnt offerings, the flesh and the blood, upon the altar of Yahweh your God: and the blood of your sacrifices shall be poured out upon the altar of Yahweh your God, and you shall eat the flesh.
28 Observe and hear all these words which I command you, that it may go well with you, and with your children after you forever, when you do *that which is* good and right in the sight of Yahweh your God.
29 When Yahweh your God shall cut off the nations from before you, where you go to possess them, and you succeed them, and dwell in their land;
30 Take heed to yourself that you are not snared by following them, after that they are destroyed from before you; and that you inquire not after their gods, saying, How did these nations serve their gods? even so will I do likewise.
31 You shall not do so unto Yahweh your God: for every abomination to Yahweh, which he hates, have they done to their gods; for even their sons and their daughters they have burnt in the fire to their gods.
32 Whatever thing I command you, observe to do it: you shall not add thereto, nor diminish from it.

Deuteronomy 13

13:1 ¶ If there arises among you a prophet, or a dreamer of dreams, and gives you a sign or a wonder,
2 And the sign or the wonder comes to pass, whereof he spoke to you, saying, Let us go after other gods, which you have not known, and let us serve them;
3 You shall not listen to the words of that prophet, or that dreamer of dreams: for Yahweh your God proves you, to know whether you love Yahweh your God with all your heart and with all your soul.
4 You shall walk after Yahweh your God, and fear him, and keep his commandments, and obey his voice, and you shall serve him, and cling to him.
5 And that prophet, or that dreamer of dreams, shall be put to death; because he has spoken to turn *you* away from Yahweh your God, which brought you out of the land of Egypt, and redeemed you out of the house of bondage, to thrust you out of the way which Yahweh your God commanded you to walk in. So shall you put the evil away from the midst of you.

6 ¶ If your brother, the son of your mother, or your son, or your daughter, or the wife of your bosom, or your friend, which *is* as your own soul, entices you secretly, saying, Let us go and serve other gods, which you have not known, you, nor your fathers;

7 *Namely*, of the gods of the people which *are* round about you, near to you, or far off from you, from the *one* end of the earth even to the *other* end of the earth;

8 You shall not consent to him, nor listen to him; neither shall your eye pity him, neither will you spare, neither will you conceal him:

9 But you shall surely kill him; your hand shall be first upon him to put him to death, and afterward the hand of all the people.

10 And you shall stone him with stones, that he dies; because he has sought to thrust you away from Yahweh your God, which brought you out of the land of Egypt, from the house of bondage.

11 And all Israel shall hear, and fear, and shall do no more any such wickedness as this is among you.

12 ¶ If you shall hear *said* in one of your cities, which Yahweh your God has given you to dwell therein, saying,

13 *Certain* men, the children of Belial, have gone out from among you, and have withdrawn the inhabitants of their city, saying, Let us go and serve other gods, which you have not known;

14 Then shall you inquire, and make search, and ask diligently; and, behold, *if it is* truth, *and* the thing certain, *that* such abomination was performed among you;

15 You shall surely smite the inhabitants of that city with the edge of the sword, destroying it utterly, and all that *is* therein, and the cattle thereof, with the edge of the sword.

16 And you shall gather all the spoil of it into the midst of the street thereof, and shall burn with fire the city, and all the spoil thereof completely, for Yahweh your God: and it shall be a heap forever; it shall not be built again.

17 And there shall cling nothing of the cursed thing to your hand: that Yahweh may turn from the fierceness of his anger, and show you mercy, and have compassion upon you, and multiply you, as he has sworn to your fathers;

18 When you shall listen to the voice of Yahweh your God, to keep all his commandments which I command you this day, to do *that which is* right in the eyes of Yahweh your God.

Deuteronomy 14

14:1 ¶ You *are* the children of Yahweh your God: you shall not cut yourselves, nor make any baldness between your eyes for the dead.

2 For you *are* a holy people unto Yahweh your God, and Yahweh has chosen you to be a peculiar people unto himself, above all the nations that *are* upon the earth.

3 You shall not eat any abominable thing.

4 These *are* the beasts which you shall eat: the ox, the sheep, and the goat,

5 The hart, and the roebuck, and the fallow deer, and the wild goat, and the pygarg, and the wild ox, and the chamois.

6 And every beast that parts the hoof, and cleaves the cleft into two claws, *and* chews the cud among the beasts, that you shall eat.

7 Nevertheless these you shall not eat of them that chew the cud, or of them that divide the cloven hoof; *as* the camel, and the hare, and the coney: for they chew the cud, but divide not the hoof; *therefore* they *are* unclean to you.

8 And the swine, because it divides the hoof, yet chews not the cud, it *is* unclean to you: you shall not eat of their flesh, nor touch their dead carcass.

9 These you shall eat of all that *are* in the waters: all that have fins and scales shall you eat:

10 And whatever has not fins and scales you may not eat; it *is* unclean to you.

11 *Of* all clean birds you shall eat.

12 But these *are they* of which you shall not eat: the eagle, and the ossifrage, and the ospray,

13 And the glede, and the kite, and the vulture after his kind,

14 And every raven after his kind,

15 And the owl, and the night hawk, and the cuckow, and the hawk after his kind,

16 The little owl, and the great owl, and the swan,

17 And the pelican, and the gier eagle, and the cormorant,

18 And the stork, and the heron after her kind, and the lapwing, and the bat.

19 And every creeping thing that flies *is* unclean to you: they shall not be eaten.

20 *But of* all clean fowls you may eat.

21 You shall not eat *of* anything that dies of itself: you shall give it to the stranger that *is* in your gates, that he may eat it; or you may sell it to an alien: for you *are* a holy people unto Yahweh your God. You shall not boil a kid in his mother's milk.

22 ¶ You shall truly tithe all the increase of your seed, that the field brings forth year by year.

23 And you shall eat before Yahweh your God, in the place which he shall choose to place his name there, the tithe of your corn, of your *new* wine, and of your oil, and the firstborn of your herds and of your flocks; that you may learn to fear Yahweh your God always.

24 And if the way is too long for you, so that you are not able to carry it; *or* if the place is too far from you, which Yahweh your God shall choose to set his name there, when Yahweh your God has blessed you:

25 Then shall you turn *it* into money, and bind up the money in your hand, and shall go to the place which Yahweh your God shall choose:

26 And you shall bestow that money for whatever your soul lusts after, for oxen, or for sheep, or for wine, or for strong drink, or for whatever your soul desires: and you shall eat there before Yahweh your God, and you shall rejoice, you, and your household,

Deuteronomy 14

27 And the Levite that *is* within your gates; you shall not forsake him; for he has no part nor inheritance with you.
28 At the end of three years you shall bring forth all the tithe of your increase the same year, and shall lay *it* up within your gates:
29 And the Levite, (because he has no part nor inheritance with you,) and the stranger, and the fatherless, and the widow, which *are* within your gates, shall come, and shall eat and be satisfied; that Yahweh your God may bless you in all the work of your hand which you do.

Deuteronomy 15

15:1 ¶ At the end of *every* seven years you shall make a release.
2 And this *is* the manner of the release: Every creditor that lent *anything* to his neighbor shall release *it*; he shall not require *it* of his neighbor, or of his brother; because it is called Yahweh's release.
3 Of a foreigner you may require *it again*: but *that* which is yours with your brother your hand shall release;
4 Save when there shall be no poor among you; for Yahweh shall greatly bless you in the land which Yahweh your God gives you *for* an inheritance to possess it:
5 Only if you carefully listen to the voice of Yahweh your God, to observe to do all these commandments which I command you this day.
6 For Yahweh your God blesses you, as he promised you: and you shall lend to many nations, but you shall not borrow; and you shall reign over many nations, but they shall not reign over you.
7 If there is among you a poor man of one of your brethren within any of your gates in your land which Yahweh your God gives you, you shall not harden your heart, nor shut your hand from your poor brother:
8 But you shall open your hand wide to him, and shall surely lend him sufficient for his need, *in that* which he wants.
9 Beware that there is not a thought in your wicked heart, saying, The seventh year, the year of release, is at hand; and your eye is evil against your poor brother, and you give him nothing; and he cries unto Yahweh against you, and it is sin unto you.
10 You shall surely give *to* him, and your heart shall not be grieved when you give to him: because that for this thing Yahweh your God shall bless you in all your works, and in all that you put your hand unto.
11 For the poor shall never cease out of the land: therefore I command you, saying, You shall open your hand wide to your brother, to your poor, and to your needy, in your land.
12 ¶ *And* if your brother, a Hebrew man, or a Hebrew woman, is sold to you, and serves you six years; then in the seventh year you shall let him go free from you.
13 And when you send him out free from you, you shall not let him go away empty:
14 You shall furnish him liberally out of your flock, and out of your floor, and out of your winepress: *of that* with which Yahweh your God has blessed you you shall give to him.
15 And you shall remember that you were a bondman in the land of Egypt, and Yahweh your God redeemed you: therefore I command you this thing today.
16 And it shall be, if he says unto you, I will not go away from you; because he loves you and your house, because he is well with you;
17 Then you shall take an awl, and thrust *it* through his ear to the door, and he shall be your servant forever. And also to your maidservant you shall do likewise.
18 It shall not seem hard to you, when you send him away free from you; for he has been worth a double hired servant *to you*, in serving you six years: and Yahweh your God shall bless you in all that you do.
19 ¶ All the firstborn males that come of your herd and of your flock you shall sanctify unto Yahweh your God: you shall do no work with the firstborn of your bullock, nor shear the firstborn of your sheep.
20 You shall eat *it* before Yahweh your God year by year in the place which Yahweh shall choose, you and your household.
21 And if there is *any* blemish therein, *as if it is* lame, or blind, *or has* any ill blemish, you shall not sacrifice it unto Yahweh your God.
22 You shall eat it within your gates: the unclean and the clean *person shall eat it* alike, as the roebuck, and as the hart.
23 Only you shall not eat the blood thereof; you shall pour it upon the ground as water.

Deuteronomy 16

16:1 ¶ Observe the month of Abib, and keep the passover unto Yahweh your God: for in the month of Abib Yahweh your God brought you forth out of Egypt by night.
2 You shall therefore sacrifice the passover unto Yahweh your God, of the flock and the herd, in the place which Yahweh shall choose to place his name there.
3 You shall eat no leavened bread with it; seven days shall you eat unleavened bread therewith, *even* the bread of affliction; for you came forth out of the land of Egypt in haste: that you may remember the day when you came forth out of the land of Egypt all the days of your life.
4 And there shall be no leavened bread seen with you in all your coast seven days; neither shall there *any thing* of the flesh, which you sacrificed the first day at evening, remain all night until the morning.
5 You may not sacrifice the passover within any of your gates, which Yahweh your God gives you:
6 But at the place which Yahweh your God shall choose to place his name in, there you shall sacrifice the passover at evening, at the going down of the sun, at the season that you came forth out of Egypt.
7 And you shall roast and eat *it* in the place which Yahweh your God shall choose: and you shall turn in the morning, and go to your tents.

8 Six days you shall eat unleavened bread: and on the seventh day *shall be* a solemn assembly unto Yahweh your God: you shall do no work *therein*.

9 Seven weeks shall you number to you: begin to number the seven weeks from *such time as* you begin *to put* the sickle to the corn.

10 And you shall keep the feast of weeks unto Yahweh your God with a tribute of a freewill offering of your hand, which you shall give *unto Yahweh your God*, according as Yahweh your God has blessed you:

11 And you shall rejoice before Yahweh your God, you, and your son, and your daughter, and your manservant, and your maidservant, and the Levite that *is* within your gates, and the stranger, and the fatherless, and the widow, that *are* among you, in the place which Yahweh your God has chosen to place his name there.

12 And you shall remember that you were a bondman in Egypt: and you shall observe and do these statutes.

13 You shall observe the feast of tabernacles seven days, after that you have gathered in your corn and your wine:

14 And you shall rejoice in your feast, you, and your son, and your daughter, and your manservant, and your maidservant, and the Levite, the stranger, and the fatherless, and the widow, that *are* within your gates.

15 Seven days shall you keep a solemn feast unto Yahweh your God in the place which Yahweh shall choose: because Yahweh your God shall bless you in all your increase, and in all the works of your hands, therefore you shall surely rejoice.

16 Three times in a year shall all your males appear before Yahweh your God in the place which he shall choose; in the feast of unleavened bread, and in the feast of weeks, and in the feast of tabernacles: and they shall not appear before Yahweh empty:

17 Every man *shall give* as he is able, according to the blessing of Yahweh your God which he has given you.

18 ¶ Judges and officers shall you make you in all your gates, which Yahweh your God gives you, throughout your tribes: and they shall judge the people with just judgment.

19 You shall not pervert judgment; you shall not respect persons, neither take a gift: for a gift does blind the eyes of the wise, and pervert the words of the righteous.

20 That which is altogether just shall you follow, that you may live, and inherit the land which Yahweh your God gives you.

21 You shall not plant you a grove of any trees near to the altar of Yahweh your God, which you shall make you.

22 Neither shall you set you up *any* image; which Yahweh your God hates.

Deuteronomy 17

17:1 ¶ You shall not sacrifice unto Yahweh your God any bullock, or sheep, wherein is blemish, *or* any defect: for that *is* an abomination unto Yahweh your God.

2 If there is found among you, within any of your gates which Yahweh your God gives you, man or woman, that has performed wickedness in the sight of Yahweh your God, in transgressing his covenant,

3 And has gone and served other gods, and worshipped them, either the sun, or moon, or any of the host of heaven, which I have not commanded;

4 And it is told *to* you, and you have heard *of it*, and inquired diligently, and, behold, *it is* true, *and* the thing certain, *that* such abomination is performed in Israel:

5 Then shall you bring forth that man or that woman, which has committed that wicked thing, to your gates, *even* that man or that woman, and shall stone them with stones, till they die.

6 At the mouth of two witnesses, or three witnesses, shall he that is worthy of death be put to death; *but* at the mouth of one witness he shall not be put to death.

7 The hands of the witnesses shall be first upon him to put him to death, and afterward the hands of all the people. So you shall put the evil away from among you.

8 ¶ If there arises a matter too hard for you in judgment, between blood and blood, between plea and plea, and between stroke and stroke, *being* matters of controversy within your gates: then shall you arise, and get you up into the place which Yahweh your God shall choose;

9 And you shall come to the priests the Levites, and to the judge that shall be in those days, and inquire; and they shall show you the sentence of judgment:

10 And you shall do according to the sentence, which they of that place which Yahweh shall choose shall show you; and you shall observe to do according to all that they inform you:

11 According to the sentence of the law which they shall teach you, and according to the judgment which they shall tell you, you shall do: you shall not decline from the sentence which they shall show you, *to* the right hand, nor to the left.

12 And the man that will do presumptuously, and will not listen to the priest that stands to minister there before Yahweh your God, or to the judge, even that man shall die: and you shall put away the evil from Israel

13 And all the people shall hear, and fear, and do no more presumptuously.

14 ¶ When you have come unto the land which Yahweh your God gives you, and shall possess it, and shall dwell therein, and shall say, I will set a king over me, like as all the nations that *are* about me;

15 You shall in any wise set *him* king over you, whom Yahweh your God shall choose: *one* from among your brethren shall you set king over you: you may not set a stranger over you, which *is* not your brother

16 But he shall not multiply horses to himself, nor cause the people to return to Egypt, to the end that he should multiply horses: forasmuch as Yahweh has said to you, You shall henceforth return no more that way

17 Neither shall he multiply wives to himself, that his heart turn not away: neither shall he greatly multiply to himself silver and gold.

Deuteronomy 17

18 And it shall be, when he sits upon the throne of his kingdom, that he shall write him a copy of this law in a book out of *that which is* before the priests the Levites:
19 And it shall be with him, and he shall read therein all the days of his life: that he may learn to fear Yahweh his God, to keep all the words of this law and these statutes, to do them:
20 That his heart is not lifted up above his brethren, and that he turns not aside from the commandment, *to* the right hand, or *to* the left: to the end that he may prolong *his* days in his kingdom, he, and his children, in the midst of Israel.

Deuteronomy 18

18:1 ¶ The priests the Levites, *and* all the tribe of Levi, shall have no part nor inheritance with Israel: they shall eat the offerings of Yahweh made by fire, and his inheritance.
2 Therefore shall they have no inheritance among their brethren: Yahweh *is* their inheritance, as he has said to them.
3 And this shall be the priest's due from the people, from them that offer a sacrifice, whether *it is* ox or sheep; and they shall give to the priest the shoulder, and the two cheeks, and the stomach.
4 The first fruit *also* of your corn, of your *new* wine, and of your oil, and the first of the fleece of your sheep, shall you give him.
5 For Yahweh your God has chosen him out of all your tribes, to stand to minister in the name of Yahweh, him and his sons forever.
6 And if a Levite comes from any of your gates out of all Israel, where he sojourned, and comes with all the desire of his mind to the place which Yahweh shall choose;
7 Then he shall minister in the name of Yahweh his God, as all his brethren the Levites *do*, which stand there before Yahweh.
8 They shall have like portions to eat, besides that which comes of the sale of his patrimony.
9 ¶ When you have come into the land which Yahweh your God gives you, you shall not learn to do after the abominations of those nations.
10 There shall not be found among you *any one* that makes his son or his daughter to pass through the fire, *or* that uses divination, *or* an observer of times, or an enchanter, or a witch,
11 Or a charmer, or a consulter with familiar spirits, or a wizard, or a necromancer.
12 For all that do these things *are* an abomination unto Yahweh: and because of these abominations Yahweh your God does drive them out from before you.
13 You shall be perfect with Yahweh your God.
14 For these nations, which you shall possess, listened to observers of times, and to diviners: but as for you, Yahweh your God has not allowed you so *to do*.
15 ¶ Yahweh your God will raise up to you a Prophet from the midst of you, of your brethren, like unto me; unto him you shall listen;
16 According to all that you desired of Yahweh your God in Horeb in the day of the assembly, saying, Let me not hear again the voice of Yahweh my God, neither let me see this great fire any more, that I die not.
17 And Yahweh said to me, They have well *spoken that* which they have spoken.
18 I will raise them up a Prophet from among their brethren, like unto you, and will put my words in his mouth; and he shall speak to them all that I shall command him.
19 And it shall come to pass, *that* whoever will not listen to my words which he shall speak in my name, I will require *it* of him.
20 But the prophet, which shall presume to speak a word in my name, which I have not commanded him to speak, or that shall speak in the name of other gods, even that prophet shall die.
21 And if you say in your heart, How shall we know the word which Yahweh has not spoken?
22 When a prophet speaks in the name of Yahweh, if the thing follows not, nor comes to pass, that *is* the thing which Yahweh has not spoken, *but* the prophet has spoken it presumptuously: you shall not be afraid of him.

Deuteronomy 19

19:1 ¶ When Yahweh your God has cut off the nations, whose land Yahweh your God gives you, and you succeed them, and dwell in their cities, and in their houses;
2 You shall separate three cities for you in the midst of your land, which Yahweh your God gives you to possess it.
3 You shall prepare you a way, and divide the coasts of your land, which Yahweh your God gives you to inherit, into three parts, that every slayer may flee there.
4 And this *is* the case of the slayer, which shall flee there, that he may live: Whoever kills his neighbor ignorantly, whom he hated not in time past;
5 As when a man goes into the woods with his neighbor to hew wood, and his hand swings a stroke with the ax to cut down the tree, and the head slips from the handle, and lights upon his neighbor, that he dies; he shall flee to one of those cities, and live:
6 Lest the avenger of the blood pursues the slayer, while his heart is hot, and overtakes him, because the way is long, and slays him; whereas he *was* not worthy of death, inasmuch as he hated him not in time past.
7 Therefore I command you, saying, You shall separate three cities for you.
8 And if Yahweh your God enlarges your coast, as he has sworn to your fathers, and gives you all the land which he promised to give to your fathers;
9 If you shall keep all these commandments to do them, which I command you this day, to love Yahweh your God, and to walk ever in his ways; then shall you add three cities more for you, besides these three:
10 That innocent blood is not shed in your land, which Yahweh your God gives you *for* an inheritance, and *so* blood is upon you.

11 But if any man hates his neighbor, and lies in wait for him, and rises up against him, and smites him mortally that he dies, and flees into one of these cities:
12 Then the elders of his city shall send and fetch him there, and deliver him into the hand of the avenger of blood, that he may die.
13 Your eye shall not pity him, but you shall put away *the guilt of* innocent blood from Israel, that it may go well with you.
14 ¶ You shall not remove your neighbor's landmark, which they of old time have set in your inheritance, which you shall inherit in the land that Yahweh your God gives you to possess it.
15 One witness shall not rise up against a man for any iniquity, or for any sin, in any sin that he sins: at the mouth of two witnesses, or at the mouth of three witnesses, shall the matter be established.
16 If a false witness rises up against any man to testify against him *that which is* wrong;
17 Then both the men, between whom the controversy *is*, shall stand before Yahweh, before the priests and the judges, which shall be in those days;
18 And the judges shall make diligent inquisition: and, behold, *if* the witness *is* a false witness, *and* has testified falsely against his brother;
19 Then shall you do to him, as he had thought to have done to his brother: so shall you put the evil away from among you.
20 And those which remain shall hear, and fear, and shall henceforth commit no more any such evil among you.
21 And your eye shall not pity; *but* life *shall go* for life, eye for eye, tooth for tooth, hand for hand, foot for foot.

Deuteronomy 20

20:1 ¶ When you go out to battle against your enemies, and see horses, and chariots, *and* a people more than you, be not afraid of them: for Yahweh your God *is* with you, which brought you up out of the land of Egypt.
2 And it shall be, when you have come near to the battle, that the priest shall approach and speak to the people,
3 And shall say to them, Hear, O Israel, you approach this day to battle against your enemies: let not your hearts faint, fear not, and do not tremble, neither be you terrified because of them;
4 For Yahweh your God *is* he that goes with you, to fight for you against your enemies, to save you.
5 And the officers shall speak to the people, saying, What man *is there* that has built a new house, and has not dedicated it? let him go and return to his house, lest he dies in the battle, and another man dedicates it.
6 And what man *is he* that has planted a vineyard, and has not *yet* eaten of it? let him *also* go and return to his house, lest he dies in the battle, and another man eats of it.
7 And what man *is there* that has betrothed a wife, and has not taken her? let him go and return to his house, lest he dies in the battle, and another man takes her.

8 And the officers shall speak further to the people, and they shall say, What man *is there that is* fearful and fainthearted? let him go and return to his house, lest his brethren's heart faint as well as his heart.
9 And it shall be, when the officers have made an end of speaking to the people, that they shall make captains of the armies to lead the people.
10 ¶ When you come near to a city to fight against it, then proclaim peace to it.
11 And it shall be, if it makes you answer of peace, and opens to you, then it shall be, *that* all the people *that are* found therein shall be tributaries unto you, and they shall serve you.
12 And if it will make no peace with you, but will make war against you, then you shall besiege it:
13 And when Yahweh your God has delivered it into your hands, you shall smite every male thereof with the edge of the sword:
14 But the women, and the little ones, and the cattle, and all that are in the city, *even* all the spoil thereof, shall you take to yourself; and you shall eat the spoil of your enemies, which Yahweh your God has given you.
15 Thus shall you do to all the cities which *are* very far off from you, which *are* not of the cities of these nations.
16 But of the cities of these people, which Yahweh your God does give you *for* an inheritance, you shall save alive nothing that breathes:
17 But you shall utterly destroy them; *namely*, the Hittites, and the Amorites, the Canaanites, and the Perizzites, the Hivites, and the Jebusites; as Yahweh your God has commanded you:
18 That they teach you not to do after all their abominations, which they have done unto their gods; so should you sin against Yahweh your God.
19 When you shall besiege a city a long time, in making war against it to take it, you shall not destroy the trees thereof by forcing an ax against them: for you may eat of them, and you shall not cut them down (for the tree of the field *is* man's *life*) to employ *them* in the siege:
20 Only the trees which you know that they *are* not trees for food, you shall destroy and cut them down; and you shall build bulwarks against the city that makes war with you, until it is subdued.

Deuteronomy 21

21:1 ¶ If *one* is found slain in the land which Yahweh your God gives you to possess it, lying in the field, *and* it is not known who has slain him:
2 Then your elders and your judges shall come forth, and they shall measure unto the cities which *are* round about him that is slain:
3 And it shall be, *that* the city *which is* next to the slain man, even the elders of that city shall take a heifer, which has not been worked with, *and* which has not drawn in the yoke;
4 And the elders of that city shall bring down the heifer to a rough valley, which is neither tilled nor sown, and shall strike off the heifer's neck there in the valley:

Deuteronomy 21

5 And the priests the sons of Levi shall come near; for them Yahweh your God has chosen to minister to him, and to bless in the name of Yahweh; and by their word shall every controversy and every stroke be *tried*:

6 And all the elders of that city, *that are* next to the slain *man*, shall wash their hands over the heifer that is beheaded in the valley:

7 And they shall answer and say, Our hands have not shed this blood, neither have our eyes seen *it*.

8 Be merciful, O Yahweh, to your people Israel, whom you have redeemed, and lay not innocent blood to your people of Israel's charge. And the blood shall be forgiven them.

9 So shall you put away the *guilt of* innocent blood from among you, when you shall do *that which is* right in the sight of Yahweh.

10 ¶ When you go forth to war against your enemies, and Yahweh your God has delivered them into your hands, and you have taken them captive,

11 And see among the captives a beautiful woman, and have a desire unto her, that you would have her to your wife;

12 Then you shall bring her home to your house; and she shall shave her head, and pare her nails;

13 And she shall put the clothing of her captivity from off her, and shall remain in your house, and bewail her father and her mother a full month: and after that you shall go in to her, and be her husband, and she shall be your wife.

14 And it shall be, if you have no delight in her, then you shall let her go where she will; but you shall not sell her at all for money, you shall not make merchandise of her, because you have humbled her.

15 ¶ If a man has two wives, one beloved, and another hated, and they have born him children, *both* the beloved and the hated; and *if* the firstborn son is hers that was hated:

16 Then it shall be, when he makes his sons to inherit *that* which he has, *that* he may not make the son of the beloved firstborn before the son of the hated, *which is indeed* the firstborn:

17 But he shall acknowledge the son of the hated *for* the firstborn, by giving him a double portion of all that he has: for he *is* the beginning of his strength; the right of the firstborn *is* his.

18 ¶ If a man has a stubborn and rebellious son, which will not obey the voice of his father, or the voice of his mother, and *that*, when they have chastened him, will not listen to them:

19 Then shall his father and his mother lay hold on him, and bring him out to the elders of his city, and to the gate of his place;

20 And they shall say to the elders of his city, This our son *is* stubborn and rebellious, he will not obey our voice; *he is* a glutton, and a drunkard.

21 And all the men of his city shall stone him with stones, that he dies: so shall you put evil away from among you; and all Israel shall hear, and fear.

22 And if a man has committed a sin worthy of death, and he is to be put to death, and you hang him on a tree:

23 His body shall not remain all night upon the tree, but you shall in any wise bury him that day; (for he that is hanged *is* accursed of God;) that your land is not defiled, which Yahweh your God gives you *for* an inheritance.

Deuteronomy 22

22:1 ¶ You shall not see your brother's ox or his sheep go astray, and hide yourself from them: you shall in any case bring them again to your brother.

2 And if your brother *is* not near to you, or if you know him not, then you shall bring it to your own house, and it shall be with you until your brother seeks after it, and you shall restore it to him again.

3 In like manner shall you do with his donkey; and so shall you do with his garment; and with all lost things of your brother's, which he has lost, and you have found, shall you do likewise: you may not hide yourself.

4 You shall not see your brother's donkey or his ox fall down by the way, and hide yourself from them: you shall surely help him to lift *them* up again.

5 ¶ The woman shall not wear that which pertains to a man, neither shall a man put on a woman's garment: for all that do so *are* abominations unto Yahweh your God.

6 If a bird's nest chances to be before you in the way in any tree, or on the ground, *whether they are* young ones, or eggs, and the mother sitting upon the young, or upon the eggs, you shall not take the mother with the young:

7 *But* you shall in any wise let the mother go, and take the young to you; that it may be well with you, and *that* you may prolong *your* days.

8 When you build a new house, then you shall make a battlement for your roof, that you bring not blood upon your house, if any man falls from there.

9 You shall not sow your vineyard with diverse seeds: lest the fruit of your seed which you have sown, and the fruit of your vineyard, is defiled.

10 You shall not plow with an ox and a donkey together.

11 You shall not wear a garment of diverse sorts, *as of* woolen and linen together.

12 You shall make you fringes upon the four quarters of your coat, with which you cover *yourself*.

13 ¶ If any man takes a wife, and goes in to her, and hates her,

14 And gives occasions of speech against her, and brings up an evil name upon her, and says, I took this woman, and when I came to her, I found her not a maid:

15 Then shall the father of the damsel, and her mother, take and bring forth *the evidence of* the damsel's virginity to the elders of the city in the gate:

16 And the damsel's father shall say to the elders, I gave my daughter to this man to wife, and he hates her;

17 And, lo, he has given occasions of speech *against her*, saying, I found not your daughter a maid; and yet these *are the tokens of* my daughter's virginity. And they shall spread the cloth before the elders of the city.

18 And the elders of that city shall take that man and chastise him;
19 And they shall fine him a hundred *shekels* of silver, and give *them* to the father of the damsel, because he has brought up an evil name upon a virgin of Israel: and she shall be his wife; he may not put her away all his days.
20 But if this thing is true, *and the tokens of* virginity are not found for the damsel:
21 Then they shall bring out the damsel to the door of her father's house, and the men of her city shall stone her with stones that she dies: because she has worked folly in Israel, to play the whore in her father's house: so shall you put evil away from among you.
22 If a man is found lying with a woman married to a husband, then they shall both of them die, *both* the man that lay with the woman, and the woman: so shall you put away evil from Israel.
23 If a damsel *that is* a virgin is betrothed to a husband, and a man finds her in the city, and lies with her;
24 Then you shall bring them both out to the gate of that city, and you shall stone them with stones that they die; the damsel, because she cried not, *being* in the city; and the man, because he has humbled his neighbor's wife: so you shall put away evil from among you.
25 But if a man finds a betrothed damsel in the field, and the man forces her, and lies with her: then the man only that lay with her shall die:
26 But to the damsel you shall do nothing; *there is* in the damsel no sin *worthy* of death: for as when a man rises against his neighbor, and slays him, even so *is* this matter:
27 For he found her in the field, *and* the betrothed damsel cried, and *there was* none to save her.
28 If a man finds a damsel *that is* a virgin, which is not betrothed, and lay hold on her, and lies with her, and they are found;
29 Then the man that lay with her shall give to the damsel's father fifty *shekels* of silver, and she shall be his wife; because he has humbled her, he may not put her away all his days.
30 A man shall not take his father's wife, nor uncover his father's skirt.

Deuteronomy 23

23:1 ¶ He that is wounded in the stones, or has his male organ cut off, shall not enter into the congregation of Yahweh.
2 A bastard shall not enter into the congregation of Yahweh; even to his tenth generation shall he not enter into the congregation of Yahweh.
3 An Ammonite or Moabite shall not enter into the congregation of Yahweh; even to their tenth generation shall they not enter into the congregation of Yahweh forever:
4 Because they met you not with bread and with water in the way, when you came forth out of Egypt; and because they hired against you Balaam the son of Beor of Pethor of Mesopotamia, to curse you.
5 Nevertheless Yahweh your God would not listen to Balaam; but Yahweh your God turned the curse into a blessing unto you, because Yahweh your God loved you.
6 You shall not seek their peace nor their prosperity all your days forever.
7 You shall not abhor an Edomite; for he *is* your brother: you shall not abhor an Egyptian; because you were a stranger in his land.
8 The children that are begotten of them shall enter into the congregation of Yahweh in their third generation.
9 ¶ When the host goes forth against your enemies, then keep you from every wicked thing.
10 If there is among you any man, that is not clean by reason of uncleanness that chances him by night, then shall he go abroad out of the camp, he shall not come within the camp:
11 But it shall be, when evening comes on, he shall wash *himself* with water: and when the sun is down, he shall come into the camp *again*.
12 You shall have a place also outside the camp, where you shall go forth abroad:
13 And you shall have a paddle upon your weapon; and it shall be, when you shall ease yourself abroad, you shall dig therewith, and shall turn back and cover that which comes from you:
14 For Yahweh your God walks in the midst of your camp, to deliver you, and to give up your enemies before you; therefore shall your camp be holy: that he sees no unclean thing in you, and turn away from you.
15 ¶ You shall not deliver to his master the servant which is escaped from his master to you:
16 He shall dwell with you, *even* among you, in that place which he shall choose in one of your gates, where it suites him best: you shall not oppress him.
17 There shall be no whore of the daughters of Israel, nor a sodomite of the sons of Israel.
18 You shall not bring the hire of a whore, or the price of a dog, into the house of Yahweh your God for any vow: for even both these *are* abominations unto Yahweh your God.
19 You shall not lend upon usury to your brother; usury of money, usury of victuals, usury of anything that is lent upon usury:
20 Unto a stranger you may lend upon usury; but to your brother you shall not lend upon usury: that Yahweh your God may bless you in all that you set your hand to in the land where you go to possess it.
21 When you shall vow a vow unto Yahweh your God, you shall not slack to pay it: for Yahweh your God will surely require it of you; and it would be sin in you.
22 But if you shall forbear to vow, it shall be no sin in you.
23 That which is gone out of your lips you shall keep and perform; *even* a freewill offering, according as you have vowed unto Yahweh your God, which you have promised with your mouth.
24 When you come into your neighbor's vineyard, then you may eat grapes your fill at your own pleasure; but you shall not put *any* in your vessel.

Deuteronomy 23

25 When you come into the standing corn of your neighbor, then you may pluck the ears with your hand; but you shall not move a sickle to your neighbor's standing corn.

Deuteronomy 24

24:1 ¶ When a man has taken a wife, and married her, and it comes to pass that she finds no favor in his eyes, because he has found some uncleanness in her: then let him write her a bill of divorce, and give *it* in her hand, and send her out of his house.
2 And when she has departed out of his house, she may go and be another man's *wife*.
3 And *if* the latter husband hates her, and writes her a bill of divorce, and gives *it* in her hand, and sends her out of his house; or if the latter husband dies, which took her *to be* his wife;
4 Her former husband, which sent her away, may not take her again to be his wife, after that she is defiled; for that *is* abomination before Yahweh: and you shall not cause the land to sin, which Yahweh your God gives you *for* an inheritance.
5 ¶ When a man has taken a new wife, he shall not go out to war, neither shall he be charged with any business: *but* he shall be free at home one year, and shall cheer up his wife which he has taken.
6 No man shall take the lower or the upper millstone to pledge: for he takes *a man's* life to pledge.
7 If a man is found stealing any of his brethren of the children of Israel, and makes merchandise of him, or sells him; then that thief shall die; and you shall put evil away from among you.
8 Take heed in the plague of leprosy, that you observe diligently, and do according to all that the priests the Levites shall teach you: as I commanded them, *so* you shall observe to do.
9 Remember what Yahweh your God did unto Miriam by the way, after that you were come forth out of Egypt.
10 When you do lend your brother anything, you shall not go into his house to fetch his pledge.
11 You shall stand outside, and the man to whom you did lend shall bring out the pledge outside to you.
12 And if the man *is* poor, you shall not sleep with his pledge:
13 In any case you shall deliver him the pledge again when the sun goes down, that he may sleep in his own garment, and bless you: and it shall be righteousness to you before Yahweh your God.
14 ¶ You shall not oppress a hired servant *that is* poor and needy, *whether he is* of your brethren, or of your strangers that *are* in your land within your gates:
15 At his day you shall give *him* his hire, neither shall the sun go down upon it; for he *is* poor, and sets his heart upon it: lest he cries against you unto Yahweh, and it is sin unto you.
16 The fathers shall not be put to death for the children, neither shall the children be put to death for the fathers: every man shall be put to death for his own sin.
17 You shall not pervert the judgment of the stranger, *nor* of the fatherless; nor take a widow's garment to pledge:
18 But you shall remember that you were a bondman in Egypt, and Yahweh your God redeemed you there: therefore I command you to do this thing.
19 When you cut down your harvest in your field, and have forgotten a sheaf in the field, you shall not go again to fetch it: it shall be for the stranger, for the fatherless, and for the widow: that Yahweh your God may bless you in all the work of your hands.
20 When you beat your olive tree, you shall not go over the boughs again: it shall be for the stranger, for the fatherless, and for the widow.
21 When you gather the grapes of your vineyard, you shall not glean *it* afterward: it shall be for the stranger, for the fatherless, and for the widow.
22 And you shall remember that you were a bondman in the land of Egypt: therefore I command you to do this thing.

Deuteronomy 25

25:1 ¶ If there is a controversy between men, and they come to judgment, that *the judges* may judge them; then they shall justify the righteous, and condemn the wicked.
2 And it shall be, if the wicked man *is* worthy to be beaten, that the judge shall cause him to lie down, and to be beaten before his face, according to his fault, by a certain number.
3 Forty stripes he may give him, *and* not exceed: lest, *if* he should exceed, and beat him above these with many stripes, then your brother should seem vile unto you.
4 You shall not muzzle the ox when he treads out *the corn*.
5 ¶ If brothers dwell together, and one of them dies, and has no child, the wife of the dead shall not marry outside to a stranger: her husband's brother shall go in unto her, and take her to him to wife, and perform the duty of a husband's brother unto her.
6 And it shall be, *that* the firstborn which she bears shall succeed in the name of his brother *which is* dead, that his name is not put out of Israel.
7 And if the man likes not to take his brother's wife, then let his brother's wife go up to the gate to the elders, and say, My husband's brother refuses to raise up to his brother a name in Israel, he will not perform the duty of my husband's brother.
8 Then the elders of his city shall call him, and speak to him: and *if* he stands *to it*, and says, I like not to take her;
9 Then shall his brother's wife come to him in the presence of the elders, and loose his shoe from off his foot, and spit in his face, and shall answer and say, So shall it be done to that man that will not build up his brother's house.

10 And his name shall be called in Israel, The house of him that has his shoe loosed.
11 When men strive together one with another, and the wife of the one draws near for to deliver her husband out of the hand of him that smites him, and puts forth her hand, and takes him by the genitals:
12 Then you shall cut off her hand, your eye shall not pity *her*.
13 ¶ You shall not have in your bag diverse weights, a great and a small.
14 You shall not have in your house diverse measures, a great and a small.
15 *But* you shall have a perfect and just weight, a perfect and just measure shall you have: that your days may be lengthened in the land which Yahweh your God gives you.
16 For all that do such things, *and* all that do unrighteously, *are* an abomination unto Yahweh your God.
17 Remember what Amalek did to you by the way, when you had come forth out of Egypt;
18 How he met you by the way, and smote the hindmost of you, *even* all *that were* feeble behind you, when you *were* faint and weary; and he feared not God.
19 Therefore it shall be, when Yahweh your God has given you rest from all your enemies round about, in the land which Yahweh your God gives you *for* an inheritance to possess it, *that* you shall blot out the remembrance of Amalek from under heaven; you shall not forget *it*.

Deuteronomy 26

26:1 ¶ And it shall be, when you *have* come in to the land which Yahweh your God gives you *for* an inheritance, and possess it, and dwell therein;
2 That you shall take of the first of all the fruit of the earth, which you shall bring of your land that Yahweh your God gives you, and shall put *it* in a basket, and shall go to the place which Yahweh your God shall choose to place his name there.
3 And you shall go to the priest that shall be in those days, and say unto him, I profess this day unto Yahweh your God, that I have come to the country which Yahweh swore unto our fathers for to give us.
4 And the priest shall take the basket out of your hand, and set it down before the altar of Yahweh your God.
5 And you shall speak and say before Yahweh your God, A Syrian ready to perish *was* my father, and he went down into Egypt, and sojourned there with a few, and became there a nation, great, mighty, and populous:
6 And the Egyptians evilly treated us, and afflicted us, and laid upon us hard bondage:
7 And when we cried unto Yahweh God of our fathers, Yahweh heard our voice, and looked on our affliction, and our labor, and our oppression:
8 And Yahweh brought us forth out of Egypt with a mighty hand, and with an outstretched arm, and with great terribleness, and with signs, and with wonders:
9 And he has brought us into this place, and has given us this land, *even* a land that flows with milk and honey.
10 And now, behold, I have brought the firstfruits of the land, which you, O Yahweh, have given me. And you shall set it before Yahweh your God, and worship before Yahweh your God:
11 And you shall rejoice in every good *thing* which Yahweh your God has given to you, and to your house, you, and the Levite, and the stranger that *is* among you.
12 ¶ When you have made an end of tithing all the tithes of your increase the third year, *which is* the year of tithing, and have given *it* to the Levite, the stranger, the fatherless, and the widow, that they may eat within your gates, and be filled;
13 Then you shall say before Yahweh your God, I have brought away the hallowed things out of *my* house, and also have given them to the Levite, and to the stranger, to the fatherless, and to the widow, according to all your commandments which you have commanded me: I have not transgressed your commandments, neither have I forgotten *them*:
14 I have not eaten thereof in my mourning, neither have I taken away *anything* thereof for *any* unclean *use*, nor given *anything* thereof for the dead: *but* I have listened to the voice of Yahweh my God, *and* have done according to all that you have commanded me.
15 Look down from your holy habitation, from heaven, and bless your people Israel, and the land which you have given us, as you swore unto our fathers, a land that flows with milk and honey.
16 ¶ This day Yahweh your God has commanded you to do these statutes and judgments: you shall therefore keep and do them with all your heart, and with all your soul.
17 You have avouched Yahweh this day to be your God, and to walk in his ways, and to keep his statutes, and his commandments, and his judgments, and to listen to his voice:
18 And Yahweh has avouched you this day to be his peculiar people, as he has promised you, and that *you* should keep all his commandments;
19 And to make you high above all nations which he has made, in praise, and in name, and in honor; and that you may be a holy people unto Yahweh your God, as he has spoken.

Deuteronomy 27

27:1 ¶ And Moses with the elders of Israel commanded the people, saying, Keep all the commandments which I command you this day.
2 And it shall be on the day when you shall pass over *the* Jordan to the land which Yahweh your God gives you, that you shall set you up great stones, and plaster them with plaster:
3 And you shall write upon them all the words of this law, when you have passed over, that you may go in to the land which Yahweh your God gives you, a land that flows with milk and honey; as Yahweh God of your fathers has promised you.

Deuteronomy 27

4 Therefore it shall be when you have gone over *the* Jordan, *that* you shall set up these stones, which I command you this day, in mount Ebal, and you shall plaster them with plaster.
5 And there shall you build an altar unto Yahweh your God, an altar of stones: you shall not lift up *any* iron *tool* upon them.
6 You shall build the altar of Yahweh your God of whole stones: and you shall offer burnt offerings thereon unto Yahweh your God:
7 And you shall offer peace offerings, and shall eat there, and rejoice before Yahweh your God.
8 And you shall write upon the stones all the words of this law very plainly.
9 And Moses and the priests the Levites spoke unto all Israel, saying, Take heed, and listen, O Israel; this day you have become the people of Yahweh your God.
10 You shall therefore obey the voice of Yahweh your God, and do his commandments and his statutes, which I command you this day.
11 ¶ And Moses charged the people the same day, saying,
12 These shall stand upon mount Gerizim to bless the people, when you have come over *the* Jordan; Simeon, and Levi, and Judah, and Issachar, and Joseph, and Benjamin:
13 And these shall stand upon mount Ebal to curse; Reuben, Gad, and Asher, and Zebulun, Dan, and Naphtali.
14 And the Levites shall speak, and say to all the men of Israel with a loud voice,
15 Cursed *is* the man that makes *any* graven or molten image, an abomination unto Yahweh, the work of the hands of the craftsman, and puts *it* in *a* secret *place*. And all the people shall answer and say, Amen.
16 Cursed *is* he that brings disgrace to his father or his mother. And all the people shall say, Amen.
17 Cursed *is* he that removes his neighbor's landmark. And all the people shall say, Amen.
18 Cursed *is* he that makes the blind to wander out of the way. And all the people shall say, Amen.
19 Cursed *is* he that perverts the judgment of the stranger, fatherless, and widow. And all the people shall say, Amen.
20 Cursed *is* he that lies with his father's wife; because he uncovers his father's skirt. And all the people shall say, Amen.
21 Cursed *is* he that lies with any manner of beast. And all the people shall say, Amen.
22 Cursed *is* he that lies with his sister, the daughter of his father, or the daughter of his mother. And all the people shall say, Amen.
23 Cursed *is* he that lies with his mother-in-law. And all the people shall say, Amen.
24 Cursed *is* he that smites his neighbor secretly. And all the people shall say, Amen.
25 Cursed *is* he that takes reward to slay an innocent person. And all the people shall say, Amen.
26 Cursed *is* he that confirms not *all* the words of this law to do them. And all the people shall say, Amen.

Deuteronomy 28

28:1 ¶ And it shall come to pass, if you shall listen diligently to the voice of Yahweh your God, to observe *and* to do all his commandments which I command you this day, that Yahweh your God will set you on high above all nations of the earth:
2 And all these blessings shall come on you, and overtake you, if you shall listen to the voice of Yahweh your God.
3 Blessed *shall* you *be* in the city, and blessed *shall* you *be* in the field.
4 Blessed *shall be* the fruit of your body, and the fruit of your ground, and the fruit of your cattle, the increase of your cows, and the flocks of your sheep.
5 Blessed *shall be* your basket and your store.
6 Blessed *shall* you *be* when you come in, and blessed *shall* you *be* when you go out.
7 Yahweh shall cause your enemies that rise up against you to be smitten before your face: they shall come out against you one way, and flee before you seven ways.
8 Yahweh shall command the blessing upon you in your storehouses, and in all that you set your hand unto; and he shall bless you in the land which Yahweh your God gives you.
9 Yahweh shall establish you a holy people unto himself, as he has sworn to you, if you shall keep the commandments of Yahweh your God, and walk in his ways.
10 And all people of the earth shall see that you are called by the name of Yahweh; and they shall be afraid of you.
11 And Yahweh shall make you plenteous in goods, in the fruit of your body, and in the fruit of your cattle, and in the fruit of your ground, in the land which Yahweh swore unto your fathers to give you.
12 Yahweh shall open to you his good treasure, the heaven to give the rain to your land in his season, and to bless all the work of your hand: and you shall lend to many nations, and you shall not borrow.
13 And Yahweh shall make you the head, and not the tail; and you shall be above only, and you shall not be beneath; if that you listen unto the commandments of Yahweh your God, which I command you this day, to observe and to do *them*:
14 And you shall not go aside from any of the words which I command you this day, *to* the right hand, or *to* the left, to go after other gods to serve them.
15 ¶ But it shall come to pass, if you will not listen unto the voice of Yahweh your God, to observe to do all his commandments and his statutes which I command you this day; that all these curses shall come upon you, and overtake you:
16 Cursed *shall* you *be* in the city, and cursed *shall* you *be* in the field.
17 Cursed *shall be* your basket and your store.

18 Cursed *shall be* the fruit of your body, and the fruit of your land, the increase of your cows, and the flocks of your sheep.
19 Cursed *shall* you *be* when you come in, and cursed *shall* you *be* when you go out.
20 Yahweh shall send upon you cursing, trouble, and rebuke, in all that you set your hand to for to do, until you are destroyed, and until you perish quickly; because of the wickedness of your doings, whereby you have forsaken me.
21 Yahweh shall make the pestilence cling unto you, until he has consumed you from off the land, where you go to possess it.
22 Yahweh shall smite you with a consumption, and with a fever, and with an inflammation, and with an extreme burning, and with the sword, and with blasting, and with mildew; and they shall pursue you until you perish.
23 And your heaven that *is* over your head shall be brass, and the earth that is under you *shall be* iron.
24 Yahweh shall make the rain of your land powder and dust: from heaven shall it come down upon you, until you are destroyed.
25 Yahweh shall cause you to be smitten before your enemies: you shall go out one way against them, and flee seven ways before them: and shall be removed into all the kingdoms of the earth.
26 And your carcass shall be meat unto all fowls of the air, and unto the beasts of the earth, and no man shall frighten *them* away.
27 Yahweh will smite you with the boils of Egypt, and with the tumors, and with the scab, and with the itch, whereof you can not be healed.
28 Yahweh shall smite you with madness, and blindness, and astonishment of heart:
29 And you shall grope at noonday, as the blind gropes in darkness, and you shall not prosper in your ways: and you shall be only oppressed and spoiled evermore, and no man shall save *you*.
30 You shall betroth a wife, and another man shall lie with her: you shall build a house, and you shall not dwell therein: you shall plant a vineyard, and shall not gather the grapes thereof.
31 Your ox *shall be* slain before your eyes, and you shall not eat thereof: your donkey *shall be* violently taken away from before your face, and shall not be restored to you: your sheep *shall be* given to your enemies, and you shall have none to rescue *them*.
32 Your sons and your daughters *shall be* given to another people, and your eyes shall look, and fail *with longing* for them all the day long: and *there shall be no* might in your hand.
33 The fruit of your land, and all your labors, shall a nation which you know not eat up; and you shall be only oppressed and crushed always:
34 So that you shall be mad for the sight of your eyes which you shall see.
35 Yahweh shall smite you in the knees, and in the legs, with grievous boils that cannot be healed, from the sole of your foot to the top of your head.

36 Yahweh shall bring you, and your king which you shall set over you, unto a nation which neither you nor your fathers have known; and there shall you serve other gods, wood and stone.
37 And you shall become an astonishment, a proverb, and a byword, among all nations where Yahweh shall lead you.
38 You shall carry much seed out into the field, and shall gather *but* little in; for the locust shall consume it.
39 You shall plant vineyards, and dress *them*, but will neither drink *of* the wine, nor gather *the grapes*; for the worms shall eat them.
40 You shall have olive trees throughout all your coasts, but you shall not anoint *yourself* with the oil; for your olive shall cast *his fruit*.
41 You shall beget sons and daughters, but you shall not enjoy them; for they shall go into captivity.
42 All your trees and fruit of your land shall the locust consume.
43 The stranger that *is* among you shall get up above you very high; and you shall come down very low.
44 He shall lend to you, and you shall not lend to him: he shall be the head, and you shall be the tail.
45 ¶ Moreover all these curses shall come upon you, and shall pursue you, and overtake you, till you are destroyed; because you listened not to the voice of Yahweh your God, to keep his commandments and his statutes which he commanded you:
46 And they shall be upon you for a sign and for a wonder, and upon your seed forever.
47 Because you served not Yahweh your God with joyfulness, and with gladness of heart, for the abundance of all *things*;
48 Therefore shall you serve your enemies which Yahweh shall send against you, in hunger, and in thirst, and in nakedness, and in want of all *things*: and he shall put a yoke of iron upon your neck, until he has destroyed you.
49 Yahweh shall bring a nation against you from far, from the end of the earth, *as swift* as the eagle flies; a nation whose tongue you shall not understand;
50 A nation of fierce countenance, which shall not regard the person of the old, nor show favor to the young:
51 And he shall eat the fruit of your cattle, and the fruit of your land, until you are destroyed: which *also* shall not leave you *either* corn, *new* wine, or oil, *or* the increase of your cows, or flocks of your sheep, until he has destroyed you.
52 And he shall besiege you in all your gates, until your high and fenced walls come down, wherein you trusted, throughout all your land: and he shall besiege you in all your gates throughout all your land, which Yahweh your God has given you.
53 And you shall eat the fruit of your own body, the flesh of your sons and of your daughters, which Yahweh your God has given you, in the siege, and in the anguish, with which your enemies shall distress you:
54 *So that* the man *that is* tender among you, and very delicate, his eye shall be evil toward his brother, and toward the wife of his bosom, and toward the remnant of his children which he shall leave:

Deuteronomy 28

55 So that he will not give to any of them of the flesh of his children whom he shall eat: because he has nothing left him in the siege, and in the anguish, with which your enemies shall distress you in all your gates.

56 The tender and delicate woman among you, which would not adventure to set the sole of her foot upon the ground for delicateness and tenderness, her eye shall be evil toward the husband of her bosom, and toward her son, and toward her daughter,

57 And toward her young one that comes out from between her feet, and toward her children which she shall bear: for she shall eat them for want of all *things* secretly in the siege and anguish, with which your enemy shall distress you in your gates.

58 If you shall not observe to do all the words of this law that are written in this book, that you may fear this glorious and fearful name, Yahweh your God;

59 Then Yahweh will make your plagues extraordinary, and the plagues of your seed, *even* great plagues, and of long continuance, and grievous sicknesses, and of long continuance.

60 Moreover he will bring upon you all the diseases of Egypt, which you were afraid of; and they shall cling unto you.

61 Also every sickness, and every plague, which *is* not written in the book of this law, them will Yahweh bring upon you, until you are destroyed.

62 And you shall be left few in number, whereas you were as the stars of heaven for multitude; because you would not obey the voice of Yahweh your God.

63 And it shall come to pass, *that* as Yahweh rejoiced over you to do you good, and to multiply you; so Yahweh will rejoice over you to destroy you, and to bring you to nothing; and you shall be plucked from off the land where you go to possess it.

64 And Yahweh shall scatter you among all people, from the one end of the earth even to the other; and there you shall serve other gods, which neither you nor your fathers have known, *even* wood and stone.

65 And among these nations shall you find no ease, neither shall the sole of your foot have rest: but Yahweh shall give you there a trembling heart, and failing of eyes, and sorrow of mind:

66 And your life shall hang in doubt before you; and you shall fear day and night, and shall have no assurance of your life:

67 In the morning you shall say, Would God it were evening! and at evening you shall say, Would God it were morning! for the fear of your heart with which you shall fear, and for the sight of your eyes which you shall see.

68 And Yahweh shall bring you into Egypt again with ships, by the way whereof I spoke to you, You shall see it no more again: and there you shall be sold to your enemies for bondmen and bondwomen, and no man shall buy *you*.

Deuteronomy 29

29:1 ¶ These *are* the words of the covenant, which Yahweh commanded Moses to make with the children of Israel in the land of Moab, besides the covenant which he made with them in Horeb.

2 And Moses called to all Israel, and said to them, You have seen all that Yahweh did before your eyes in the land of Egypt to Pharaoh, and to all his servants, and to all his land;

3 The great temptations which your eyes have seen, the signs, and those great miracles:

4 Yet Yahweh has not given you a heart to perceive, and eyes to see, and ears to hear, unto this day.

5 And I have led you forty years in the wilderness: your clothes have not grown old upon you, and your shoe has not grown old upon your foot.

6 You have not eaten bread, neither have you drunk wine or strong drink: that you might know that I *am* Yahweh your God.

7 And when you came to this place, Sihon the king of Heshbon, and Og the king of Bashan, came out against us to battle, and we smote them:

8 And we took their land, and gave it for an inheritance unto the Reubenites, and to the Gadites, and to the half tribe of Manasseh.

9 Keep therefore the words of this covenant, and do them, that you may prosper in all that you do.

10 ¶ You stand this day all of you before Yahweh your God; your captains of your tribes, your elders, and your officers, *with* all the men of Israel,

11 Your little ones, your wives, and your stranger that *is* in your camp, from the hewer of your wood to the drawer of your water:

12 That you should enter into covenant with Yahweh your God, and into his oath, which Yahweh your God makes with you this day:

13 That he may establish you today for a people to himself, and *that* he may be to you a God, as he has said to you, and as he has sworn to your fathers, to Abraham, to Isaac, and to Jacob.

14 Neither with you only do I make this covenant and this oath;

15 But with *him* that stands here with us this day before Yahweh our God, and also with *him* that *is* not here with us this day:

16 (For you know how we have dwelt in the land of Egypt; and how we came through the nations which you passed by;

17 And you have seen their abominations, and their idols, wood and stone, silver and gold, which *were* among them:)

18 Lest there should be among you man, or woman, or family, or tribe, whose heart turns away this day from Yahweh our God, to go *and* serve the gods of these nations; lest there should be among you a root that bears gall and wormwood;

19 And it comes to pass, when he hears the words of this curse, that he blesses himself in his heart, saying, I shall have peace, though I walk in the imagination of my heart, to add drunkenness to thirst:
20 Yahweh will not spare him, but then the anger of Yahweh and his jealousy shall smoke against that man, and all the curses that are written in this book shall lie upon him, and Yahweh shall blot out his name from under heaven.
21 And Yahweh shall separate him unto evil out of all the tribes of Israel, according to all the curses of the covenant that are written in this book of the law:
22 So that the generation to come of your children that shall rise up after you, and the stranger that shall come from a far land, shall say, when they see the plagues of that land, and the sicknesses which Yahweh has laid upon it;
23 *And that* the whole land thereof *is* brimstone, and salt, *and* burning, *that* it is not sown, nor *does it* bear, nor any grass grows therein, like the overthrow of Sodom, and Gomorrah, Admah, and Zeboim, which Yahweh overthrew in his anger, and in his wrath:
24 Even all nations shall say, Why has Yahweh done thus to this land? what *means* the heat of this great anger?
25 Then men shall say, Because they have forsaken the covenant of Yahweh God of their fathers, which he made with them when he brought them forth out of the land of Egypt:
26 For they went and served other gods, and worshipped them, gods whom they knew not, and *whom* he had not given to them:
27 And the anger of Yahweh was kindled against this land, to bring upon it all the curses that are written in this book:
28 And Yahweh rooted them out of their land in anger, and in wrath, and in great indignation, and cast them into another land, as *it is* this day.
29 The secret *things belong* unto Yahweh our God: but those *things which are* revealed *belong* to us and to our children forever, that *we* may do all the words of this law.

Deuteronomy 30

30:1 ¶ And it shall come to pass, when all these things have come upon you, the blessing and the curse, which I have set before you, and you shall call *them* to mind among all the nations, where Yahweh your God has driven you,
2 And shall return unto Yahweh your God, and shall obey his voice according to all that I command you this day, you and your children, with all your heart, and with all your soul;
3 That then Yahweh your God will turn your captivity, and have compassion upon you, and will return and gather you from all the nations, where Yahweh your God has scattered you.
4 If *any* of yours are driven out to the outmost *parts* of heaven, from there will Yahweh your God gather you, and from there will he fetch you:
5 And Yahweh your God will bring you into the land which your fathers possessed, and you shall possess it; and he will do you good, and multiply you above your fathers.
6 And Yahweh your God will circumcise your heart, and the heart of your seed, to love Yahweh your God with all your heart, and with all your soul, that you may live.
7 And Yahweh your God will put all these curses upon your enemies, and on them that hate you, which persecuted you.
8 And you shall return and obey the voice of Yahweh, and do all his commandments which I command you this day.
9 And Yahweh your God will make you plenteous in every work of your hand, in the fruit of your body, and in the fruit of your cattle, and in the fruit of your land, for good: for Yahweh will again rejoice over you for good, as he rejoiced over your fathers:
10 If you shall listen to the voice of Yahweh your God, to keep his commandments and his statutes which are written in this book of the law, *and* if you turn unto Yahweh your God with all your heart, and with all your soul.
11 ¶ For this commandment which I command you this day, it *is* not hidden from you, neither *is* it far off.
12 It *is* not in heaven, that you should say, Who shall go up for us to heaven, and bring it to us, that we may hear it, and do it?
13 Neither *is* it beyond the sea, that you should say, Who shall go over the sea for us, and bring it to us, that we may hear it, and do it?
14 But the word *is* very near to you, in your mouth, and in your heart, that you may do it.
15 ¶ See, I have set before you this day life and good, and death and evil;
16 In that I command you this day to love Yahweh your God, to walk in his ways, and to keep his commandments and his statutes and his judgments, that you may live and multiply: and Yahweh your God shall bless you in the land whither you go to possess it.
17 But if your heart turns away, so that you will not hear, but will be drawn away, and worship other gods, and serve them;
18 I announce unto you this day, that you shall surely perish, *and that* you shall not prolong *your* days upon the land, where you pass over *the* Jordan to go to possess it.
19 I call heaven and earth to record this day against you, *that* I have set before you life and death, blessing and cursing: therefore choose life, that both you and your seed may live:
20 That you may love Yahweh your God, *and* that you may obey his voice, and that you may cling unto him: for he *is* your life, and the length of your days: that you may dwell in the land which Yahweh swore to your fathers, to Abraham, to Isaac, and to Jacob, to give them.

Deuteronomy 31

31:1 ¶ And Moses went and spoke these words to all Israel.

2 And he said to them, I *am* a hundred and twenty years old this day; I can no more go out and come in: also Yahweh has said to me, You shall not go over this Jordan.

3 Yahweh your God, he will go over before you, *and* he will destroy these nations from before you, and you shall possess them: *and* Joshua, he shall go over before you, as Yahweh has said.

4 And Yahweh shall do to them as he did to Sihon and to Og, kings of the Amorites, and to the land of them, whom he destroyed.

5 And Yahweh shall give them up before your face, that you may do to them according to all the commandments which I have commanded you.

6 Be strong and of a good courage, fear not, nor be afraid of them: for Yahweh your God, he *it is* that does go with you; he will not fail you, nor forsake you.

7 And Moses called to Joshua, and said to him in the sight of all Israel, Be strong and of a good courage: for you must go with this people to the land which Yahweh has sworn unto their fathers to give them; and you shall cause them to inherit it.

8 And Yahweh, he *it is* that does go before you; he will be with you, he will not fail you, neither forsake you: fear not, neither be dismayed.

9 ¶ And Moses wrote this law, and delivered it to the priests the sons of Levi, which bore the ark of the covenant of Yahweh, and to all the elders of Israel.

10 And Moses commanded them, saying, At the end of *every* seven years, in the solemnity of the year of release, in the feast of tabernacles,

11 When all Israel has come to appear before Yahweh your God in the place which he shall choose, you shall read this law before all Israel in their hearing.

12 Gather the people together, men, and women, and children, and your stranger that *is* within your gates, that they may hear, and that they may learn, and fear Yahweh your God, and observe to do all the words of this law:

13 And *that* their children, which have not known *anything*, may hear, and learn to fear Yahweh your God, as long as you live in the land where you go over *the* Jordan to possess it.

14 ¶ And Yahweh said to Moses, Behold, your days approach that you must die: call Joshua, and present yourselves in the tabernacle of the congregation, that I may give him a charge. And Moses and Joshua went, and presented themselves in the tabernacle of the congregation.

15 And Yahweh appeared in the tabernacle in a pillar of a cloud: and the pillar of the cloud stood over the door of the tabernacle.

16 And Yahweh said to Moses, Behold, you shall sleep with your fathers; and this people will rise up, and go a whoring after the gods of the strangers of the land, where they go *to be* among them, and will forsake me, and break my covenant which I have made with them.

17 Then my anger shall be kindled against them in that day, and I will forsake them, and I will hide my face from them, and they shall be devoured, and many evils and troubles shall befall them; so that they will say in that day, Have not these evils come upon us, because our God *is* not among us?

18 And I will surely hide my face in that day for all the evils which they shall have performed, in that they have turned to other gods.

19 Now therefore write you this song for you, and teach it the children of Israel: put it in their mouths, that this song may be a witness for me against the children of Israel.

20 For when I shall have brought them into the land which I swore to their fathers, that flows with milk and honey; and they shall have eaten and filled themselves, and become fat; then will they turn to other gods, and serve them, and provoke me, and break my covenant.

21 And it shall come to pass, when many evils and troubles have found them, that this song shall testify against them as a witness; for it shall not be forgotten out of the mouths of their seed: for I know their imagination which they go about, even now, before I have brought them into the land which I swore.

22 ¶ Moses therefore wrote this song the same day, and taught it *to* the children of Israel.

23 And he gave Joshua the son of Nun a charge, and said, Be strong and of a good courage: for you shall bring the children of Israel into the land which I swore unto them: and I will be with you.

24 And it came to pass, when Moses had made an end of writing the words of this law in a book, until they were finished,

25 That Moses commanded the Levites, which bore the ark of the covenant of Yahweh, saying,

26 Take this book of the law, and put it in the side of the ark of the covenant of Yahweh your God, that it may be there for a witness against you.

27 For I know your rebellion, and your stiff neck: behold, while I am yet alive with you this day, you have been rebellious against Yahweh; and how much more after my death?

28 Gather to me all the elders of your tribes, and your officers, that I may speak these words in their ears, and call heaven and earth to record against them.

29 For I know that after my death you will utterly corrupt *yourselves*, and turn aside from the way which I have commanded you; and evil will befall you in the latter days; because you will do evil in the sight of Yahweh, to provoke him to anger through the work of your hands.

30 And Moses spoke in the ears of all the congregation of Israel the words of this song, until they were ended.

Deuteronomy 32

32:1 ¶ Give ear, O you heavens, and I will speak; and hear, O earth, the words of my mouth.

2 My doctrine shall drop as the rain, my speech shall distill as the dew, as the small rain upon the tender herb, and as the showers upon the grass:

3 Because I will publish the name of Yahweh: ascribe you greatness unto our God.

4 *He is* the Rock, his work *is* perfect: for all his ways *are* judgment: a God of truth and without iniquity, just and right *is* he.

5 They have corrupted themselves, their spot *is* not *the spot* of his children: *they are* a perverse and crooked generation.

6 Do you thus repay Yahweh, O foolish people and unwise? *is* not he your father *that* has bought you? has he not made you, and established you?

7 ¶ Remember the days of old, consider the years of many generations: ask your father, and he will show you; your elders, and they will tell you.

8 When the most High divided to the nations their inheritance, when he separated the sons of Adam, he set the bounds of the people according to the number of the children of Israel.

9 For Yahweh's portion *is* his people; Jacob *is* the lot of his inheritance.

10 He found him in a desert land, and in the waste howling wilderness; he led him about, he instructed him, he kept him as the apple of his eye.

11 As an eagle stirs up her nest, flutters over her young, spreads abroad her wings, takes them, bears them on her wings:

12 *So* Yahweh alone did lead him, and *there was* no strange god with him.

13 He made him ride on the high places of the earth, that he might eat the increase of the fields; and he made him to suck honey out of the rock, and oil out of the flinty rock:

14 Butter of cows, and milk of sheep, with fat of lambs, and rams of the breed of Bashan, and goats, with the fat of kidneys of wheat; and you did drink the pure blood of the grape.

15 ¶ But Jeshurun grew fat, and kicked: you have grown fat, you have grown thick, you are covered *with fatness*; then he forsook God *which* made him, and lightly esteemed the Rock of his salvation.

16 They provoked him to jealousy with strange *gods*, with abominations provoked they him to anger.

17 They sacrificed unto devils, not to God; to gods whom they knew not, to new *gods that* came newly up, whom your fathers feared not.

18 Of the Rock *that* begot you, you are unmindful, and have forgotten God that formed you.

19 ¶ And when Yahweh saw *it*, he abhorred *them*, because of the provoking of his sons, and of his daughters.

20 And he said, I will hide my face from them, I will see what their end *shall be*: for they *are* a very perverse generation, children in whom *is* no faith.

21 They have moved me to jealousy with *that which is* not God; they have provoked me to anger with their vanities: and I will move them to jealousy with *those which are* not a people; I will provoke them to anger with a foolish nation.

22 For a fire is kindled in my anger, and shall burn to the lowest hell, and shall consume the earth with her increase, and set on fire the foundations of the mountains.

23 I will heap afflictions upon them; I will spend my arrows upon them.

24 *They shall be* burnt with hunger, and devoured with burning heat, and with bitter destruction: I will also send the teeth of beasts upon them, with the poison of serpents of the dust.

25 The sword outside, and terror within, shall destroy both the young man and the virgin, the suckling *also* with the man of gray hairs.

26 ¶ I said, I would scatter them into corners, I would make the remembrance of them to cease from among men:

27 Were it not that I feared the wrath of the enemy, lest their adversaries should behave themselves strangely, *and* lest they should say, Our hand *is* high, and Yahweh has not done all this.

28 For they *are* a nation void of counsel, neither *is there any* understanding in them.

29 O that they were wise, *that* they understood this, *that* they would consider their latter end!

30 How should one chase a thousand, and two put ten thousand to flight, except their Rock had sold them, and Yahweh had shut them up?

31 For their rock *is* not as our Rock, even our enemies themselves *being* judges.

32 For their vine *is* of the vine of Sodom, and of the fields of Gomorrah: their grapes *are* grapes of gall, their clusters *are* bitter:

33 Their wine *is* the poison of dragons, and the cruel venom of asps.

34 *Is* not this laid up in store with me, *and* sealed up among my treasures?

35 To me *belongs* vengeance, and recompense; their foot shall slide in *due* time: for the day of their calamity *is* at hand, and the things that shall come upon them make haste.

36 For Yahweh shall judge his people, and repent himself for his servants, when he sees that *their* power is gone, and *there is* none shut up, or left.

37 And he shall say, Where *are* their gods, *their* rock in whom they trusted,

38 Which did eat the fat of their sacrifices, *and* drank the wine of their drink offerings? let them rise up and help you, *and* be your protection.

39 ¶ See now that I, *even* I, *am* he, and *there is* no god with me: I kill, and I make alive; I wound, and I heal: neither *is there any* that can deliver out of my hand.

40 For I lift up my hand to heaven, and say, I live forever.

41 If I sharpen my glittering sword, and my hand takes hold on judgment; I will render vengeance to my enemies, and will reward them that hate me.

Deuteronomy 32

42 I will make my arrows drunk with blood, and my sword shall devour flesh; *and that* with the blood of the slain and of the captives, from the beginning of revenges upon the enemy.

43 Rejoice, O you nations, *with* his people: for he will avenge the blood of his servants, and will render vengeance to his adversaries, and will be merciful to his land, *and* to his people.

44 ¶ And Moses came and spoke all the words of this song in the ears of the people, he, and Hoshea the son of Nun.

45 And Moses made an end of speaking all these words to all Israel:

46 And he said to them, Set your hearts to all the words which I testify among you this day, which you shall command your children to observe to do, all the words of this law.

47 For it *is* not a vain thing for you; because it *is* your life: and through this thing you shall prolong *your* days in the land, where you go over *the* Jordan to possess it.

48 And Yahweh spoke to Moses that very same day, saying,

49 Get you up into this mountain Abarim, *to* mount Nebo, which *is* in the land of Moab, that *is* over against Jericho; and behold the land of Canaan, which I give to the children of Israel for a possession:

50 And die in the mount where you go up, and be gathered to your people; as Aaron your brother died in mount Hor, and was gathered to his people:

51 Because you trespassed against me among the children of Israel at the waters of Meribah-Kadesh, in the wilderness of Zin; because you sanctified me not in the midst of the children of Israel.

52 Yet you shall see the land before *you*; but you shall not go there unto the land which I give the children of Israel.

Deuteronomy 33

33:1 ¶ And this *is* the blessing, with which Moses the man of God blessed the children of Israel before his death.

2 And he said, Yahweh came from Sinai, and rose up from Seir unto them; he shined forth from mount Paran, and he came with ten thousands of saints: from his right hand *went* a fiery law for them.

3 Yes, he loves the people; all his saints *are* in your hand: and they sit down at your feet; *every one* shall receive of your words.

4 Moses commanded us a law, *even* the inheritance of the congregation of Jacob.

5 And he was king in Jeshurun, when the heads of the people *and* the tribes of Israel were gathered together.

6 ¶ Let Reuben live, and not die; and let *not* his men be few.

7 And this *is the blessing* of Judah: and he said, Hear, Yahweh, the voice of Judah, and bring him to his people: let his hands be sufficient for him; and be you a help *to him* from his enemies.

8 ¶ And of Levi he said, *Let* your Thummim and your Urim *be* with your holy one, whom you did prove at Massah, *and with* whom you did strive at the waters of Meribah;

9 Who said to his father and to his mother, I have not seen him; neither did he acknowledge his brethren, nor knew his own children: for they have observed your word, and kept your covenant.

10 They shall teach Jacob your judgments, and Israel your law: they shall put incense before you, and whole burnt sacrifice upon your altar.

11 Bless, Yahweh, his substance, and accept the work of his hands: smite through the loins of them that rise against him, and of them that hate him, that they rise not again.

12 ¶ *And* of Benjamin he said, The beloved of Yahweh shall dwell in safety by him; *and Yahweh* shall cover him all the day long, and he shall dwell between his shoulders.

13 And of Joseph he said, Blessed of Yahweh *be* his land, for the precious things of heaven, for the dew, and for the deep that couches beneath,

14 And for the precious fruits *brought forth* by the sun, and for the precious things put forth by the moon,

15 And for the chief things of the ancient mountains, and for the precious things of the lasting hills,

16 And for the precious things of the earth and fullness thereof, and *for* the good will of him that dwelt in the bush: let *the blessing* come upon the head of Joseph, and upon the top of the head of him *that was* separated from his brethren.

17 His glory *is like* the firstborn of his bullock, and his horns *are like* the horns of unicorns: with them he shall push the people together to the ends of the earth: and they *are* the ten thousands of Ephraim, and they *are* the thousands of Manasseh.

18 ¶ And of Zebulun he said, Rejoice, Zebulun, in your going out; and, Issachar, in your tents.

19 They shall call the people to the mountain; there they shall offer sacrifices of righteousness: for they shall suck *of* the abundance of the seas, and *of* treasures hidden in the sand.

20 And of Gad he said, Blessed *is* he that enlarges Gad: he dwells as a lion, and tears the arm with the crown of the head.

21 And he provided the first part for himself, because there, *in* a portion of the lawgiver, *was he* seated; and he came with the heads of the people, he executed the justice of Yahweh, and his judgments with Israel.

22 ¶ And of Dan he said, Dan *is* a lion's cub: he shall leap from Bashan.

23 And of Naphtali he said, O Naphtali, satisfied with favor, and full with the blessing of Yahweh: possess you the west and the south.

24 And of Asher he said, *Let* Asher *be* blessed with children; let him be acceptable to his brethren, and let him dip his foot in oil.

25 Your shoes *shall be* iron and brass; and as your days, *so shall* your strength *be*.

26 ¶ *There is* none like unto the God of Jeshurun, who rides upon the heaven in your help, and in his excellency on the sky.
27 The eternal God *is your* refuge, and underneath *are* the everlasting arms: and he shall thrust out the enemy from before you; and shall say, Destroy *them*.
28 Israel then shall dwell in safety alone: the fountain of Jacob *shall be* upon a land of corn and *new* wine; also his heavens shall drop down dew.
29 Happy *are* you, O Israel: who *is* like unto you, O people saved by Yahweh, the shield of your help, and who *is* the sword of your excellency! and your enemies shall be found liars unto you; and you shall tread upon their high places.

Deuteronomy 34

34:1 ¶ And Moses went up from the plains of Moab to the mountain of Nebo, to the top of Pisgah, that *is* over against Jericho. And Yahweh showed him all the land of Gilead, unto Dan,
2 And all Naphtali, and the land of Ephraim, and Manasseh, and all the land of Judah, unto the utmost sea,
3 And the south, and the plain of the valley of Jericho, the city of palm trees, unto Zoar.
4 And Yahweh said to him, This *is* the land which I swore to Abraham, to Isaac, and to Jacob, saying, I will give it to your seed: I have caused you to see *it* with your eyes, but you shall not go over there.
5 ¶ So Moses the servant of Yahweh died there in the land of Moab, according to the word of Yahweh.
6 And he buried him in a valley in the land of Moab, over against Bethpeor: but no man knows of his sepulcher unto this day.
7 And Moses *was* a hundred and twenty years old when he died: his eye was not dim, nor his natural force abated.
8 And the children of Israel wept for Moses in the plains of Moab thirty days: so the days of weeping *and* mourning for Moses were ended.
9 ¶ And Joshua the son of Nun was full of the spirit of wisdom; for Moses had laid his hands upon him: and the children of Israel listened to him, and did as Yahweh commanded Moses.
10 And there arose not a prophet since in Israel like unto Moses, whom Yahweh knew face to face,
11 In all the signs and the wonders, which Yahweh sent him to do in the land of Egypt to Pharaoh, and to all his servants, and to all his land,
12 And in all that mighty hand, and in all the great terror which Moses showed in the sight of all Israel.

Section 2

History

Joshua

Joshua 1

1:1 ¶ Now after the death of Moses the servant of Yahweh it came to pass, that Yahweh spoke to Joshua the son of Nun, Moses' minister, saying,
2 Moses my servant is dead; now therefore arise, go over this Jordan, you, and all this people, to the land which I do give to them, *even* to the children of Israel.
3 Every place that the sole of your foot shall tread upon, that have I given to you, as I said to Moses.
4 From the wilderness and this Lebanon even to the great river, the river Euphrates, all the land of the Hittites, and to the great sea toward the going down of the sun, shall be your coast.
5 There shall not any man be able to stand before you all the days of your life: as I was with Moses, *so* I will be with you: I will not fail you, nor forsake you.
6 Be strong and of a good courage: for to this people shall you divide for an inheritance the land, which I swore to their fathers to give them.
7 Only be you strong and very courageous, that you may observe to do according to all the law, which Moses my servant commanded you: turn not from it *to* the right hand or *to* the left, that you may prosper wherever you go.
8 This book of the law shall not depart out of your mouth; but you shall meditate therein day and night, that you may observe to do according to all that is written therein: for then you shall make your way prosperous, and then you shall have good success.
9 Have not I commanded you? Be strong and of a good courage; be not afraid, neither be you dismayed: for Yahweh your God *is* with you wherever you go.
10 ¶ Then Joshua commanded the officers of the people, saying,
11 Pass through the host, and command the people, saying, Prepare you food; for within three days you shall pass over this Jordan, to go in to possess the land, which Yahweh your God gives you to possess it.
12 And to the Reubenites, and to the Gadites, and to half the tribe of Manasseh, spoke Joshua, saying,
13 Remember the word which Moses the servant of Yahweh commanded you, saying, Yahweh your God has given you rest, and has given you this land.
14 Your wives, your little ones, and your cattle, shall remain in the land which Moses gave you on this side *of the* Jordan; but you shall pass before your brethren armed, all the mighty men of valor, and help them;

15 Until Yahweh has given your brethren rest, as *he has given* you, and they also have possessed the land which Yahweh your God gives them: then you shall return to the land of your possession, and enjoy it, which Moses Yahweh's servant gave you on this side *of the* Jordan toward the sunrising.
16 ¶ And they answered Joshua, saying, All that you command us we will do, and wherever you send us, we will go.
17 According as we listened to Moses in all things, so will we listen to you: only Yahweh your God be with you, as he was with Moses.
18 Whoever *he is* that does rebel against your commandment, and will not listen to your words in all that you command him, he shall be put to death: only be strong and of a good courage.

Joshua 2

2:1 ¶ And Joshua the son of Nun sent out of Shittim two men to spy secretly, saying, Go view the land, even Jericho. And they went, and came into a harlot's house, named Rahab, and lodged there.
2 And it was told *to* the king of Jericho, saying, Behold, there came men in here tonight of the children of Israel to search out the country.
3 And the king of Jericho sent to Rahab, saying, Bring forth the men that have come to you, which have entered into your house: for they have come to search out all the country.
4 And the woman took the two men, and hid them, and said thus, There came men to me, but I knew not *from* where they *were*:
5 And it came to pass *about the time* of shutting of the gate, when it was dark, that the men went out: where the men went I know not: pursue after them quickly; for you shall overtake them.
6 But she had brought them up to the roof of the house, and hid them with the stalks of flax, which she had laid in order upon the roof.
7 And the men pursued after them the way to *the* Jordan to the fords: and as soon as they which pursued after them had gone out, they shut the gate.
8 ¶ And before they were laid down, she came up to them upon the roof;
9 And she said to the men, I know that Yahweh has given you the land, and that your terror has fallen upon us, and that all the inhabitants of the land faint because of you.
10 For we have heard how Yahweh dried up the water of the Red Sea for you, when you came out of Egypt; and what you did to the two kings of the Amorites, that *were*

on the other side *of the* Jordan, Sihon and Og, whom you utterly destroyed.

11 And as soon as we had heard *these things*, our hearts did melt, neither did there remain any more courage in any man, because of you: for Yahweh your God, he *is* God in heaven above, and in earth beneath.

12 Now therefore, I pray you, swear to me by Yahweh, since I have shown you kindness, that you will also show kindness to my father's house, and give me a true token:

13 And *that* you will save alive my father, and my mother, and my brothers, and my sisters, and all that they have, and deliver our lives from death.

14 And the men answered her, Our life for yours, if you utter not this our business. And it shall be, when Yahweh has given us the land, that we will deal kindly and truly with you.

15 Then she let them down by a cord through the window: for her house *was* upon the town wall, and she dwelt upon the wall.

16 And she said to them, Get you to the mountain, lest the pursuers meet you; and hide yourselves there three days, until the pursuers have returned: and afterward may you go your way.

17 And the men said to her, We *will be* blameless of this your oath which you have made us swear.

18 Behold, *when* we come into the land, you shall bind this line of scarlet thread in the window which you did let us down by: and you shall bring your father, and your mother, and your brothers, and all your father's household, home to you.

19 And it shall be, *that* whoever shall go out of the doors of your house into the street, his blood *shall be* upon his head, and we *will be* guiltless: and whoever shall be with you in the house, his blood *shall be* on our head, if *any* hand be upon him.

20 And if you utter this our business, then we will be free from your oath which you have made us to swear.

21 And she said, According to your words, so *be* it. And she sent them away, and they departed: and she bound the scarlet line in the window.

22 ¶ And they went, and came to the mountain, and stayed there three days, until the pursuers had returned: and the pursuers sought *them* throughout all the way, but found *them* not.

23 So the two men returned, and descended from the mountain, and passed over, and came to Joshua the son of Nun, and told him all *things* that befell them:

24 And they said to Joshua, Truly Yahweh has delivered into our hands all the land; for even all the inhabitants of the country do faint because of us.

Joshua 3

3:1 ¶ And Joshua rose early in the morning; and they removed from Shittim, and came to *the* Jordan, he and all the children of Israel, and lodged there before they passed over.

2 And it came to pass after three days, that the officers went through the host;

3 And they commanded the people, saying, When you see the ark of the covenant of Yahweh your God, and the priests the Levites bearing it, then you shall remove from your place, and go after it.

4 Yet there shall be a space between you and it, about two thousand cubits by measure: come not near to it, that you may know the way by which you must go: for you have not passed *this* way before.

5 And Joshua said to the people, Sanctify yourselves: for tomorrow Yahweh will do wonders among you.

6 And Joshua spoke to the priests, saying, Take up the ark of the covenant, and pass over before the people. And they took up the ark of the covenant, and went before the people.

7 ¶ And Yahweh said to Joshua, This day will I begin to magnify you in the sight of all Israel, that they may know that, as I was with Moses, *so* I will be with you.

8 And you shall command the priests that bear the ark of the covenant, saying, When you have come to the brink of the water of *the* Jordan, you shall stand still in *the* Jordan.

9 And Joshua said to the children of Israel, Come here, and hear the words of Yahweh your God.

10 And Joshua said, Hereby you shall know that the living God *is* among you, and *that* he will without fail drive out from before you the Canaanites, and the Hittites, and the Hivites, and the Perizzites, and the Girgashites, and the Amorites, and the Jebusites.

11 Behold, the ark of the covenant of the Lord of all the earth passes over before you into *the* Jordan.

12 Now therefore take you twelve men out of the tribes of Israel, out of every tribe a man.

13 And it shall come to pass, as soon as the soles of the feet of the priests that bear the ark of Yahweh, the Lord of all the earth, shall rest in the waters of *the* Jordan, *that* the waters of *the* Jordan shall be cut off *from* the waters that come down from above; and they shall stand upon a heap.

14 ¶ And it came to pass, when the people removed from their tents, to pass over *the* Jordan, and the priests bearing the ark of the covenant before the people;

15 And as they that bore the ark had come to *the* Jordan, and the feet of the priests that bore the ark were dipped in the brim of the water, (for *the* Jordan overflows all his banks all the time of harvest,)

16 That the waters which came down from above stood *and* rose up upon a heap very far from the city Adam, that *is* beside Zaretan: and those that came down toward the sea of the plain, *even* the salt sea, failed, *and* were cut off: and the people passed over right against Jericho.

17 And the priests that bore the ark of the covenant of Yahweh stood firm on dry ground in the midst of *the* Jordan, and all the Israelites passed over on dry ground, until all the people had passed completely over *the* Jordan.

Joshua 4

4:1 ¶ And it came to pass, when all the people had completely passed over *the* Jordan, that Yahweh spoke to Joshua, saying.

2 Take you twelve men out of the people, out of every tribe a man,

3 And command you them, saying, Take you away out of the midst of *the* Jordan, out of the place where the priests' feet stood firm, twelve stones, and you shall carry them over with you, and leave them in the lodging place, where you shall lodge this night.

4 Then Joshua called the twelve men, whom he had prepared of the children of Israel, out of every tribe a man:

5 And Joshua said to them, Pass over before the ark of Yahweh your God into the midst of *the* Jordan, and take you up every man of you a stone upon his shoulder, according to the number of the tribes of the children of Israel:

6 That this may be a sign among you, *that* when your children ask *their fathers* in time to come, saying, What *mean* you by these stones?

7 Then you shall answer them, That the waters of *the* Jordan were cut off before the ark of the covenant of Yahweh; when it passed over *the* Jordan, the waters of *the* Jordan were cut off: and these stones shall be for a memorial to the children of Israel forever.

8 And the children of Israel did so as Joshua commanded, and took up twelve stones out of the midst of *the* Jordan, as Yahweh spoke to Joshua, according to the number of the tribes of the children of Israel, and carried them over with them to the place where they lodged, and laid them down there.

9 And Joshua set up twelve stones in the midst of *the* Jordan, in the place where the feet of the priests which bore the ark of the covenant stood: and they are there unto this day.

10 ¶ For the priests which bore the ark stood in the midst of *the* Jordan, until every thing was finished that Yahweh commanded Joshua to speak to the people, according to all that Moses commanded Joshua: and the people hurried and passed over.

11 And it came to pass, when all the people had completely passed over, that the ark of Yahweh passed over, and the priests, in the presence of the people.

12 And the children of Reuben, and the children of Gad, and half the tribe of Manasseh, passed over armed before the children of Israel, as Moses spoke to them:

13 About forty thousand prepared for war passed over before Yahweh unto battle, to the plains of Jericho.

14 On that day Yahweh magnified Joshua in the sight of all Israel; and they feared him, as they feared Moses, all the days of his life.

15 And Yahweh spoke to Joshua, saying,

16 Command the priests that bore the ark of the testimony, that they come up out of *the* Jordan.

17 Joshua therefore commanded the priests, saying, Come you up out of *the* Jordan.

18 And it came to pass, when the priests that bore the ark of the covenant of Yahweh had come up out of the midst of *the* Jordan, *and* the soles of the priests' feet were lifted up to the dry land, that the waters of *the* Jordan returned to their place, and flowed over all his banks, as *they did* before.

19 And the people came up out of *the* Jordan on the tenth *day* of the first month, and encamped in Gilgal, in the east border of Jericho.

20 ¶ And those twelve stones, which they took out of *the* Jordan, did Joshua pitch in Gilgal.

21 And he spoke to the children of Israel, saying, When your children shall ask their fathers in time to come, saying, What *mean* these stones?

22 Then you shall let your children know, saying, Israel came over this Jordan on dry land.

23 For Yahweh your God dried up the waters of *the* Jordan from before you, until you had passed over, as Yahweh your God did to the Red Sea, which he dried up from before us, until we had gone over:

24 That all the people of the earth might know the hand of Yahweh, that it *is* mighty: that you might fear Yahweh your God forever.

Joshua 5

5:1 ¶ And it came to pass, when all the kings of the Amorites, which *were* on the side of *the* Jordan westward, and all the kings of the Canaanites, which *were* by the sea, heard that Yahweh had dried up the waters of *the* Jordan from before the children of Israel, until we had passed over, that their heart melted, neither was there spirit in them any more, because of the children of Israel.

2 At that time Yahweh said to Joshua, Make you sharp knives, and circumcise again the children of Israel the second time.

3 And Joshua made him sharp knives, and circumcised the children of Israel at the hill of the foreskins.

4 And this *is* the cause why Joshua did circumcise: All the people that came out of Egypt, *that were* males, *even* all the men of war, died in the wilderness by the way, after they came out of Egypt.

5 Now all the people that came out were circumcised: but all the people *that were* born in the wilderness by the way as they came forth out of Egypt, *them* they had not circumcised.

6 For the children of Israel walked forty years in the wilderness, till all the people *that were* men of war, which came out of Egypt, were consumed, because they obeyed not the voice of Yahweh: to whom Yahweh swore that he would not show them the land, which Yahweh swore to their fathers that he would give us, a land that flows with milk and honey.

7 And their children, *whom* he raised up in their stead, them Joshua circumcised: for they were uncircumcised, because they had not circumcised them by the way.

8 And it came to pass, when they were done circumcising all the people, that they stayed in their places in the camp, till they were whole.

Joshua 5

9 And Yahweh said to Joshua, This day have I rolled away the reproach of Egypt from off you. Therefore the name of the place is called Gilgal unto this day.

10 ¶ And the children of Israel encamped in Gilgal, and kept the passover on the fourteenth day of the month at evening in the plains of Jericho.

11 And they did eat of the old corn of the land on the next day after the passover, unleavened cakes, and parched *corn* in the very same day.

12 And the manna ceased on the next day after they had eaten of the old corn of the land; neither had the children of Israel manna any more; but they did eat of the fruit of the land of Canaan that year.

13 ¶ And it came to pass, when Joshua was by Jericho, that he lifted up his eyes and looked, and, behold, there stood a man over against him with his sword drawn in his hand: and Joshua went to him, and said to him, *Are* you for us, or for our adversaries?

14 And he said, No; but *as* captain of the host of Yahweh have I now come. And Joshua fell on his face to the earth, and did worship, and said to him, What said my lord to his servant?

15 And the captain of Yahweh's host said to Joshua, Loose your shoe from off your foot; for the place whereon you stand *is* holy. And Joshua did so.

Joshua 6

6:1 ¶ Now Jericho was closely shut up because of the children of Israel: none went out, and none came in.

2 And Yahweh said to Joshua, See, I have given into your hand Jericho, and the king thereof, *and* the mighty men of valor.

3 And you shall compass the city, all *you* men of war, *and* go round about the city once. Thus shall you do six days.

4 And seven priests shall bear before the ark seven trumpets of rams' horns: and the seventh day you shall compass the city seven times, and the priests shall blow with the trumpets.

5 And it shall come to pass, that when they make a long *blast* with the ram's horn, *and* when you hear the sound of the trumpet, all the people shall shout with a great shout; and the wall of the city shall fall down flat, and the people shall ascend up every man straight before him.

6 ¶ And Joshua the son of Nun called the priests, and said to them, Take up the ark of the covenant, and let seven priests bear seven trumpets of rams' horns before the ark of Yahweh.

7 And he said to the people, Pass on, and compass the city, and let him that is armed pass on before the ark of Yahweh.

8 And it came to pass, when Joshua had spoken to the people, that the seven priests bearing the seven trumpets of rams' horns passed on before Yahweh, and blew with the trumpets: and the ark of the covenant of Yahweh followed them.

9 And the armed men went before the priests that blew with the trumpets, and the rear guard came after the ark, *the priests* going on, and blowing with the trumpets.

10 And Joshua had commanded the people, saying, You shall not shout, nor make any noise with your voice, neither shall *any* word proceed out of your mouth, until the day I bid you shout; then shall you shout.

11 So the ark of Yahweh compassed the city, going about *it* once: and they came into the camp, and lodged in the camp.

12 And Joshua rose early in the morning, and the priests took up the ark of Yahweh.

13 And seven priests bearing seven trumpets of rams' horns before the ark of Yahweh went on continually, and blew with the trumpets: and the armed men went before them; but the rear guard came after the ark of Yahweh, *the priests* going on, and blowing with the trumpets.

14 And the second day they compassed the city once, and returned into the camp: so they did six days.

15 And it came to pass on the seventh day, that they rose early about the dawning of the day, and compassed the city after the same manner seven times: only on that day they compassed the city seven times.

16 And it came to pass at the seventh time, when the priests blew with the trumpets, Joshua said to the people, Shout; for Yahweh has given you the city.

17 ¶ And the city shall be accursed, *even* it, and all that *are* therein, to Yahweh: only Rahab the harlot shall live, she and all that *are* with her in the house, because she hid the messengers that we sent.

18 And you, in any wise keep *yourselves* from the accursed thing, lest you make *yourselves* accursed, when you take of the accursed thing, and make the camp of Israel a curse, and trouble it.

19 But all the silver, and gold, and vessels of brass and iron, *are* consecrated unto Yahweh: they shall come into the treasury of Yahweh.

20 So the people shouted when *the priests* blew with the trumpets: and it came to pass, when the people heard the sound of the trumpet, and the people shouted with a great shout, that the wall fell down flat, so that the people went up into the city, every man straight before him, and they took the city.

21 And they utterly destroyed all that *was* in the city, both man and woman, young and old, and ox, and sheep, and donkey, with the edge of the sword.

22 But Joshua had said to the two men that had spied out the country, Go into the harlot's house, and bring out thereof the woman, and all that she has, as you swore to her.

23 And the young men that were spies went in, and brought out Rahab, and her father, and her mother, and her brothers, and all that she had; and they brought out all her kindred, and left them outside the camp of Israel.

24 And they burnt the city with fire, and all that *was* therein: only the silver, and the gold, and the vessels of brass and of iron, they put into the treasury of the house of Yahweh.

25 And Joshua saved Rahab the harlot alive, and her father's household, and all that she had; and she dwells in Israel *even* unto this day; because she hid the messengers, which Joshua sent to spy out Jericho.

26 And Joshua adjured *them* at that time, saying, Cursed *be* the man before Yahweh, that rises up and builds this city Jericho: he shall lay the foundation thereof in his firstborn, and in his youngest *son* shall he set up the gates of it.
27 So Yahweh was with Joshua; and his fame was *spread* throughout all the country.

Joshua 7

7:1 ¶ But the children of Israel committed a trespass in the accursed thing: for Achan, the son of Carmi, the son of Zabdi, the son of Zerah, of the tribe of Judah, took of the accursed thing: and the anger of Yahweh was kindled against the children of Israel.
2 And Joshua sent men from Jericho to Ai, which *is* beside Bethaven, on the east side of Bethel, and spoke to them, saying, Go up and view the country. And the men went up and viewed Ai.
3 And they returned to Joshua, and said to him, Let not all the people go up; but let about two or three thousand men go up and smite Ai; *and* make not all the people to labor there; for they *are but* few.
4 So there went up there of the people about three thousand men: and they fled before the men of Ai.
5 And the men of Ai smote of them about thirty and six men: for they chased them *from* before the gate *even* to Shebarim, and smote them in the going down: therefore the hearts of the people melted, and became as water.
6 ¶ And Joshua tore his clothes, and fell to the earth upon his face before the ark of Yahweh until the evening, he and the elders of Israel, and put dust upon their heads.
7 And Joshua said, Alas, O Lord Yahweh, why have you at all brought this people over *the* Jordan, to deliver us into the hand of the Amorites, to destroy us? would to God we had been content, and dwelt on the other side *of the* Jordan!
8 O Lord, what shall I say, when Israel turns their backs before their enemies!
9 For the Canaanites and all the inhabitants of the land shall hear *of it*, and shall surround us, and cut off our name from the earth: and what will you do to your great name?
10 ¶ And Yahweh said to Joshua, Get you up; why lie you thus upon your face?
11 Israel has sinned, and they have also transgressed my covenant which I commanded them: for they have even taken of the accursed thing, and have also stolen, and deceived also, and they have put *it* even among their own stuff.
12 Therefore the children of Israel could not stand before their enemies, *but* turned *their* backs before their enemies, because they were accursed: neither will I be with you any more, unless you destroy the accursed from among you.
13 Up, sanctify the people, and say, Sanctify yourselves against tomorrow: for thus says Yahweh God of Israel, *There is* an accursed thing in the midst of you, O Israel: you cannot stand before your enemies, until you take away the accursed thing from among you.
14 In the morning therefore you shall be brought according to your tribes: and it shall be, *that* the tribe which Yahweh takes shall come according to the families *thereof*; and the family which Yahweh shall take shall come by households; and the household which Yahweh shall take shall come man by man.
15 And it shall be, *that* he that is taken with the accursed thing shall be burnt with fire, he and all that he has: because he has transgressed the covenant of Yahweh, and because he has worked folly in Israel.
16 ¶ So Joshua rose up early in the morning, and brought Israel by their tribes; and the tribe of Judah was taken:
17 And he brought the family of Judah; and he took the family of the Zarhites: and he brought the family of the Zarhites man by man; and Zabdi was taken:
18 And he brought his household man by man; and Achan, the son of Carmi, the son of Zabdi, the son of Zerah, of the tribe of Judah, was taken.
19 And Joshua said to Achan, My son, give, I pray you, glory to Yahweh God of Israel, and make confession to him; and tell me now what you have done; hide *it* not from me.
20 And Achan answered Joshua, and said, Indeed I have sinned against Yahweh God of Israel, and thus and thus have I done:
21 When I saw among the spoils a goodly Babylonish garment, and two hundred shekels of silver, and a wedge of gold of fifty shekels weight, then I coveted them, and took them; and, behold, they *are* hidden in the earth in the midst of my tent, and the silver under it.
22 So Joshua sent messengers, and they ran to the tent; and, behold, *it was* hidden in his tent, and the silver under it.
23 And they took them out of the midst of the tent, and brought them to Joshua, and to all the children of Israel, and laid them out before Yahweh.
24 And Joshua, and all Israel with him, took Achan the son of Zerah, and the silver, and the garment, and the wedge of gold, and his sons, and his daughters, and his oxen, and his donkeys, and his sheep, and his tent, and all that he had: and they brought them to the valley of Achor.
25 And Joshua said, Why have you troubled us? Yahweh shall trouble you this day. And all Israel stoned him with stones, and burned them with fire, after they had stoned them with stones.
26 And they raised over him a great heap of stones unto this day. So Yahweh turned from the fierceness of his anger. Therefore the name of that place was called, The valley of Achor, unto this day.

Joshua 8

8:1 ¶ And Yahweh said to Joshua, Fear not, neither be you dismayed: take all the people of war with you, and arise, go up to Ai: see, I have given into your hand the king of Ai, and his people, and his city, and his land:

Joshua 8

2 And you shall do to Ai and her king as you did to Jericho and her king: only the spoil thereof, and the cattle thereof, shall you take for a prey to yourselves: lay you an ambush for the city behind it.

3 ¶ So Joshua arose, and all the people of war, to go up against Ai: and Joshua chose out thirty thousand mighty men of valor, and sent them away by night.

4 And he commanded them, saying, Behold, you shall lie in wait against the city, *even* behind the city: go not very far from the city, but be you all ready:

5 And I, and all the people that *are* with me, will approach to the city: and it shall come to pass, when they come out against us, as at the first, that we will flee before them,

6 (For they will come out after us) till we have drawn them from the city; for they will say, They flee before us, as at the first: therefore we will flee before them.

7 Then you shall rise up from the ambush, and seize upon the city: for Yahweh your God will deliver it into your hand.

8 And it shall be, when you have taken the city, *that* you shall set the city on fire: according to the commandment of Yahweh shall you do. See, I have commanded you.

9 Joshua therefore sent them forth: and they went to lie in ambush, and stayed between Bethel and Ai, on the west side of Ai: but Joshua lodged that night among the people.

10 And Joshua rose up early in the morning, and numbered the people, and went up, he and the elders of Israel, before the people to Ai.

11 And all the people, *even the people* of war that *were* with him, went up, and drew nigh, and came before the city, and pitched on the north side of Ai: now *there was* a valley between them and Ai.

12 And he took about five thousand men, and set them to lie in ambush between Bethel and Ai, on the west side of the city.

13 And when they had set the people, *even* all the host that *was* on the north of the city, and their liers in wait on the west of the city, Joshua went that night into the midst of the valley.

14 And it came to pass, when the king of Ai saw *it*, that they hurried and rose up early, and the men of the city went out against Israel to battle, he and all his people, at a time appointed, before the plain; but he knew not that *there were* liers in ambush against him behind the city.

15 And Joshua and all Israel made as if they were beaten before them, and fled by the way of the wilderness.

16 And all the people that *were* in Ai were called together to pursue after them: and they pursued after Joshua, and were drawn away from the city.

17 And there was not a man left in Ai or Bethel, that went not out after Israel: and they left the city open, and pursued after Israel.

18 And Yahweh said to Joshua, Stretch out the spear that *is* in your hand toward Ai; for I will give it into your hand. And Joshua stretched out the spear that *he had* in his hand toward the city.

19 And the ambush arose quickly out of their place, and they ran as soon as he had stretched out his hand: and they entered into the city, and took it, and hurried and set the city on fire.

20 And when the men of Ai looked behind them, they saw, and, behold, the smoke of the city ascended up to heaven, and they had no power to flee this way or that way: and the people that fled to the wilderness turned back upon the pursuers.

21 And when Joshua and all Israel saw that the ambush had taken the city, and that the smoke of the city ascended, then they turned again, and slew the men of Ai.

22 And the others came out of the city against them; so they were in the midst of Israel, some on this side, and some on that side: and they smote them, so that they let none of them remain or escape.

23 ¶ And the king of Ai they took alive, and brought him to Joshua.

24 And it came to pass, when Israel had made an end of slaying all the inhabitants of Ai in the field, in the wilderness wherein they chased them, and when they had all fallen on the edge of the sword, until they were consumed, that all the Israelites returned to Ai, and smote it with the edge of the sword.

25 And *so* it was, *that* all that fell that day, both of men and women, *were* twelve thousand, *even* all the men of Ai.

26 For Joshua drew not his hand back, with which he stretched out the spear, until he had utterly destroyed all the inhabitants of Ai.

27 Only the cattle and the spoil of that city Israel took for a prey to themselves, according to the word of Yahweh which he commanded Joshua.

28 And Joshua burnt Ai, and made it a heap forever, *even* a desolation unto this day.

29 And the king of Ai he hanged on a tree until evening: and as soon as the sun was down, Joshua commanded that they should take his carcass down from the tree, and cast it at the entering of the gate of the city, and raise thereon a great heap of stones, *that remains* unto this day.

30 ¶ Then Joshua built an altar unto Yahweh God of Israel in mount Ebal,

31 As Moses the servant of Yahweh commanded the children of Israel, as it is written in the book of the law of Moses, an altar of whole stones, over which no man has lifted up *any* iron: and they offered thereon burnt offerings unto Yahweh, and sacrificed peace offerings.

32 And he wrote there upon the stones a copy of the law of Moses, which he wrote in the presence of the children of Israel.

33 And all Israel, and their elders, and officers, and their judges, stood on this side *of* the ark and on that side before the priests the Levites, which bore the ark of the covenant of Yahweh, as well the stranger, as he that was born among them; half of them over against mount Gerizim, and half of them over against mount Ebal; as Moses the servant of Yahweh had commanded before, that they should bless the people of Israel.

34 And afterward he read all the words of the law, the blessings and cursings, according to all that is written in the book of the law.

35 There was not a word of all that Moses commanded, which Joshua read not before all the congregation of Israel, with the women, and the little ones, and the strangers that were living among them.

Joshua 9

9:1 ¶ And it came to pass, when all the kings which were on this side of the Jordan, in the hills, and in the valleys, and in all the coasts of the great sea over against Lebanon, the Hittite, and the Amorite, the Canaanite, the Perizzite, the Hivite, and the Jebusite, heard thereof;

2 That they gathered themselves together, to fight with Joshua and with Israel, with one accord.

3 ¶ And when the inhabitants of Gibeon heard what Joshua had done to Jericho and to Ai,

4 They did work craftily, and went and made as if they had been ambassadors, and took old sacks upon their donkeys, and wine bottles, old, and broken, and bound up;

5 And old shoes and patched upon their feet, and old garments upon them; and all the bread of their provision was dry and moldy.

6 And they went to Joshua to the camp at Gilgal, and said to him, and to the men of Israel, We have come from a far country: now therefore make you a league with us.

7 And the men of Israel said to the Hivites, Perhaps you dwell among us; and how shall we make a league with you?

8 And they said to Joshua, We are your servants. And Joshua said to them, Who are you? and from where come you?

9 And they said to him, From a very far country your servants have come because of the name of Yahweh your God: for we have heard the fame of him, and all that he did in Egypt,

10 And all that he did to the two kings of the Amorites, that were beyond the Jordan, to Sihon king of Heshbon, and to Og king of Bashan, which was at Ashtaroth.

11 Therefore our elders and all the inhabitants of our country spoke to us, saying, Take victuals with you for the journey, and go to meet them, and say to them, We are your servants: therefore now make you a league with us.

12 This our bread we took hot for our provision out of our houses on the day we came forth to go to you; but now, behold, it is dry, and it is moldy:

13 And these bottles of wine, which we filled, were new; and, behold, they are broken: and these our garments and our shoes have become old by reason of the very long journey.

14 And the men took of their victuals, and asked not counsel at the mouth of Yahweh.

15 ¶ And Joshua made peace with them, and made a league with them, to let them live: and the princes of the congregation swore to them.

16 And it came to pass at the end of three days after they had made a league with them, that they heard that they were their neighbors, and that they dwelt among them.

17 And the children of Israel journeyed, and came to their cities on the third day. Now their cities were Gibeon, and Chephirah, and Beeroth, and Kirjathjearim.

18 And the children of Israel smote them not, because the princes of the congregation had sworn to them by Yahweh God of Israel. And all the congregation murmured against the princes.

19 But all the princes said to all the congregation, We have sworn to them by Yahweh God of Israel: now therefore we may not touch them.

20 This we will do to them; we will even let them live, lest wrath be upon us, because of the oath which we swore to them.

21 And the princes said to them, Let them live; but let them be hewers of wood and drawers of water unto all the congregation; as the princes had promised them.

22 ¶ And Joshua called for them, and he spoke to them, saying, Why have you deceived us, saying, We are very far from you; when you dwell among us?

23 Now therefore you are cursed, and there shall none of you be freed from being bondmen, and hewers of wood and drawers of water for the house of my God.

24 And they answered Joshua, and said, Because it was certainly told your servants, how that Yahweh your God commanded his servant Moses to give you all the land, and to destroy all the inhabitants of the land from before you, therefore we were very afraid for our lives because of you, and have done this thing.

25 And now, behold, we are in your hand: as it seems good and right to you to do to us, do.

26 And so did he to them, and delivered them out of the hand of the children of Israel, that they slew them not.

27 And Joshua made them that day hewers of wood and drawers of water for the congregation, and for the altar of Yahweh, even unto this day, in the place which he should choose.

Joshua 10

10:1 ¶ Now it came to pass, when Adonizedek king of Jerusalem had heard how Joshua had taken Ai, and had utterly destroyed it; as he had done to Jericho and her king, so he had done to Ai and her king; and how the inhabitants of Gibeon had made peace with Israel, and were among them;

2 That they feared greatly, because Gibeon was a great city, as one of the royal cities, and because it was greater than Ai, and all the men thereof were mighty.

3 Therefore Adonizedek king of Jerusalem sent unto Hoham king of Hebron, and to Piram king of Jarmuth, and to Japhia king of Lachish, and to Debir king of Eglon, saying,

4 Come up to me, and help me, that we may smite Gibeon: for it has made peace with Joshua and with the children of Israel.

Joshua 10

5 Therefore the five kings of the Amorites, the king of Jerusalem, the king of Hebron, the king of Jarmuth, the king of Lachish, the king of Eglon, gathered themselves together, and went up, they and all their hosts, and encamped before Gibeon, and made war against it.

6 And the men of Gibeon sent to Joshua to the camp to Gilgal, saying, Slack not your hand from your servants; come up to us quickly, and save us, and help us: for all the kings of the Amorites that dwell in the mountains have gathered together against us.

7 ¶ So Joshua ascended from Gilgal, he, and all the people of war with him, and all the mighty men of valor.

8 And Yahweh said to Joshua, Fear them not: for I have delivered them into your hand; there shall not a man of them stand before you.

9 Joshua therefore came to them suddenly, *and* went up from Gilgal all night.

10 And Yahweh discomfited them before Israel, and slew them with a great slaughter at Gibeon, and chased them along the way that goes up to Bethhoron, and smote them to Azekah, and to Makkedah.

11 And it came to pass, as they fled from before Israel, *and* were in the going down to Bethhoron, that Yahweh cast down great stones from heaven upon them to Azekah, and they died: *there were* more which died with hailstones than *they* whom the children of Israel slew with the sword.

12 Then spoke Joshua to Yahweh in the day when Yahweh delivered up the Amorites before the children of Israel, and he said in the sight of Israel, Sun, stand you still upon Gibeon; and you, Moon, in the valley of Ajalon.

13 And the sun stood still, and the moon stayed, until the people had avenged themselves upon their enemies. *Is* not this written in the book of Jasher? So the sun stood still in the midst of heaven, and hurried not to go down about a whole day.

14 And there was no day like that before it or after it, that Yahweh listened to the voice of a man: for Yahweh fought for Israel.

15 ¶ And Joshua returned, and all Israel with him, unto the camp to Gilgal.

16 But these five kings fled, and hid themselves in a cave at Makkedah.

17 And it was told *to* Joshua, saying, The five kings are found hidden in a cave at Makkedah.

18 And Joshua said, Roll great stones upon the mouth of the cave, and set men by it for to keep them:

19 And stay you not, *but* pursue after your enemies, and smite the hindmost of them; permit them not to enter into their cities: for Yahweh your God has delivered them into your hand.

20 And it came to pass, when Joshua and the children of Israel had made an end of slaying them with a very great slaughter, till they were consumed, that the rest *which* remained of them entered into fenced cities.

21 And all the people returned to the camp to Joshua at Makkedah in peace: none moved his tongue against any of the children of Israel.

22 Then said Joshua, Open the mouth of the cave, and bring out those five kings to me out of the cave.

23 And they did so, and brought forth those five kings to him out of the cave, the king of Jerusalem, the king of Hebron, the king of Jarmuth, the king of Lachish, *and* the king of Eglon.

24 And it came to pass, when they brought out those kings to Joshua, that Joshua called for all the men of Israel, and said to the captains of the men of war which went with him, Come near, put your feet upon the necks of these kings. And they came near, and put their feet upon the necks of them.

25 And Joshua said to them, Fear not, nor be dismayed, be strong and of good courage: for thus shall Yahweh do to all your enemies against whom you fight.

26 And afterward Joshua smote them, and slew them, and hanged them on five trees: and they were hanging upon the trees until the evening.

27 And it came to pass at the time of the going down of the sun, *that* Joshua commanded, and they took them down off the trees, and cast them into the cave wherein they had been hidden, and laid great stones in the cave's mouth, *which remain* until this very day.

28 ¶ And that day Joshua took Makkedah, and smote it with the edge of the sword, and the king thereof he utterly destroyed, them, and all the souls that *were* therein; he let none remain: and he did to the king of Makkedah as he did to the king of Jericho.

29 Then Joshua passed from Makkedah, and all Israel with him, to Libnah, and fought against Libnah:

30 And Yahweh delivered it also, and the king thereof, into the hand of Israel; and he smote it with the edge of the sword, and all the souls that *were* therein; he let none remain in it; but did unto the king thereof as he did to the king of Jericho.

31 And Joshua passed from Libnah, and all Israel with him, to Lachish, and encamped against it, and fought against it:

32 And Yahweh delivered Lachish into the hand of Israel, which took it on the second day, and smote it with the edge of the sword, and all the souls that *were* therein, according to all that he had done to Libnah.

33 Then Horam king of Gezer came up to help Lachish; and Joshua smote him and his people, until he had left him none remaining.

34 And from Lachish Joshua passed to Eglon, and all Israel with him; and they encamped against it, and fought against it:

35 And they took it on that day, and smote it with the edge of the sword, and all the souls that *were* therein he utterly destroyed that day, according to all that he had done to Lachish.

36 And Joshua went up from Eglon, and all Israel with him, to Hebron; and they fought against it:

37 And they took it, and smote it with the edge of the sword, and the king thereof, and all the cities thereof, and all the souls that *were* therein; he let none remaining, according to all that he had done to Eglon; but destroyed it utterly, and all the souls that *were* therein.

38 And Joshua returned, and all Israel with him, to Debir; and fought against it:
39 And he took it, and the king thereof, and all the cities thereof; and they smote them with the edge of the sword, and utterly destroyed all the souls that *were* therein; he left none remaining: as he had done to Hebron, so he did to Debir, and to the king thereof; as he had done also to Libnah, and to her king.
40 So Joshua smote all the country of the hills, and of the south, and of the vale, and of the springs, and all their kings: he left none remaining, but utterly destroyed all that breathed, as Yahweh God of Israel commanded.
41 And Joshua smote them from Kadeshbarnea even to Gaza, and all the country of Goshen, even to Gibeon.
42 And all these kings and their land did Joshua take at one time, because Yahweh God of Israel fought for Israel.
43 And Joshua returned, and all Israel with him, to the camp to Gilgal.

Joshua 11

11:1 ¶ And it came to pass, when Jabin king of Hazor had heard *those things*, that he sent to Jobab king of Madon, and to the king of Shimron, and to the king of Achshaph,
2 And to the kings that *were* on the north of the mountains, and of the plains south of Chinneroth, and in the valley, and in the borders of Dor on the west,
3 *And to* the Canaanite on the east and on the west, and *to* the Amorite, and the Hittite, and the Perizzite, and the Jebusite in the mountains, and *to* the Hivite under Hermon in the land of Mizpeh.
4 And they went out, they and all their hosts with them, much people, even as the sand that *is* upon the sea shore in multitude, with horses and chariots very many.
5 And when all these kings were had together, they came and pitched together at the waters of Merom, to fight against Israel.
6 And Yahweh said to Joshua, Be not afraid because of them: for tomorrow about this time will I deliver them up all slain before Israel: you shall cripple their horses, and burn their chariots with fire.
7 So Joshua came, and all the people of war with him, against them by the waters of Merom suddenly; and they fell upon them.
8 And Yahweh delivered them into the hand of Israel, who smote them, and chased them to great Zidon, and to Misrephothmaim, and to the valley of Mizpeh eastward; and they smote them, until they left them none remaining.
9 And Joshua did to them as Yahweh told him: he crippled their horses, and burnt their chariots with fire.
10 ¶ And Joshua at that time turned back, and took Hazor, and smote the king thereof with the sword: for Hazor before was the head of all those kingdoms.
11 And they smote all the souls that *were* therein with the edge of the sword, utterly destroying *them*: there was not any left to breathe: and he burnt Hazor with fire.
12 And all the cities of those kings, and all the kings of them, did Joshua take, and smote them with the edge of the sword, *and* he utterly destroyed them, as Moses the servant of Yahweh commanded.
13 But *as for* the cities that stood still in their strength, Israel burned none of them, save Hazor only; *that* did Joshua burn.
14 And all the spoil of these cities, and the cattle, the children of Israel took for a prey to themselves; but every man they smote with the edge of the sword, until they had destroyed them, neither left they any to breathe.
15 ¶ As Yahweh commanded Moses his servant, so did Moses command Joshua, and so did Joshua; he left nothing undone of all that Yahweh commanded Moses.
16 So Joshua took all that land, the hills, and all the south country, and all the land of Goshen, and the valley, and the plain, and the mountain of Israel, and the valley of the same;
17 *Even* from the mount Halak, that goes up to Seir, even to Baalgad in the valley of Lebanon under mount Hermon: and all their kings he took, and smote them, and slew them.
18 Joshua made war a long time with all those kings.
19 There was not a city that made peace with the children of Israel, save the Hivites the inhabitants of Gibeon: all *others* they took in battle.
20 For it was of Yahweh to harden their hearts, that they should come against Israel in battle, that he might destroy them utterly, *and* that they might have no favor, but that he might destroy them, as Yahweh commanded Moses.
21 And at that time came Joshua, and cut off the Anakims from the mountains, from Hebron, from Debir, from Anab, and from all the mountains of Judah, and from all the mountains of Israel: Joshua destroyed them utterly with their cities.
22 There was none of the Anakims left in the land of the children of Israel: only in Gaza, in Gath, and in Ashdod, there remained.
23 So Joshua took the whole land, according to all that Yahweh said to Moses; and Joshua gave it for an inheritance unto Israel according to their divisions by their tribes. And the land rested from war.

Joshua 12

12:1 ¶ Now these *are* the kings of the land, which the children of Israel smote, and possessed their land on the other side *of the* Jordan toward the rising of the sun, from the river Arnon to mount Hermon, and all the plain on the east:
2 Sihon king of the Amorites, who dwelt in Heshbon, *and* ruled from Aroer, which *is* upon the bank of the river Arnon, and from the middle of the river, and from half Gilead, even to the river Jabbok, *which is* the border of the children of Ammon;
3 And from the plain to the sea of Chinneroth on the east, and to the sea of the plain, *even* the salt sea on the east, the way to Bethjeshimoth; and from the south, under Ashdothpisgah:

Joshua 12

4 And the coast of Og king of Bashan, *which was* of the remnant of the giants, that dwelt at Ashtaroth and at Edrei,
5 And reigned in mount Hermon, and in Salcah, and in all Bashan, to the border of the Geshurites and the Maachathites, and half Gilead, the border of Sihon king of Heshbon.
6 Them did Moses the servant of Yahweh and the children of Israel smite: and Moses the servant of Yahweh gave it *for* a possession to the Reubenites, and the Gadites, and the half tribe of Manasseh.
7 ¶ And these *are* the kings of the country which Joshua and the children of Israel smote on this side *of the* Jordan on the west, from Baalgad in the valley of Lebanon even to the mount Halak, that goes up to Seir; which Joshua gave to the tribes of Israel *for* a possession according to their divisions;
8 In the mountains, and in the valleys, and in the plains, and in the springs, and in the wilderness, and in the south country; the Hittites, the Amorites, and the Canaanites, the Perizzites, the Hivites, and the Jebusites:
9 The king of Jericho, one; the king of Ai, which *is* beside Bethel, one;
10 The king of Jerusalem, one; the king of Hebron, one;
11 The king of Jarmuth, one; the king of Lachish, one;
12 The king of Eglon, one; the king of Gezer, one;
13 The king of Debir, one; the king of Geder, one;
14 The king of Hormah, one; the king of Arad, one;
15 The king of Libnah, one; the king of Adullam, one;
16 The king of Makkedah, one; the king of Bethel, one;
17 The king of Tappuah, one; the king of Hepher, one;
18 The king of Aphek, one; the king of Lasharon, one;
19 The king of Madon, one; the king of Hazor, one;
20 The king of Shimronmeron, one; the king of Achshaph, one;
21 The king of Taanach, one; the king of Megiddo, one;
22 The king of Kedesh, one; the king of Jokneam of Carmel, one;
23 The king of Dor in the coast of Dor, one; the king of the nations of Gilgal, one;
24 The king of Tirzah, one: all the kings thirty and one.

Joshua 13

13:1 ¶ Now Joshua was old *and* stricken in years; and Yahweh said to him, You are old *and* stricken in years, and there remains yet very much land to be possessed.
2 This *is* the land that yet remains: all the borders of the Philistines, and all Geshuri,
3 From Sihor, which *is* before Egypt, even to the borders of Ekron northward, *which* is counted to the Canaanite: five lords of the Philistines; the Gazathites, and the Ashdothites, the Eshkalonites, the Gittites, and the Ekronites; also the Avites:
4 From the south, all the land of the Canaanites, and Mearah that *is* beside the Sidonians, to Aphek, to the borders of the Amorites:
5 And the land of the Giblites, and all Lebanon, toward the sunrising, from Baalgad under mount Hermon unto the entering into Hamath.
6 All the inhabitants of the hill country from Lebanon to Misrephothmaim, *and* all the Sidonians, them will I drive out from before the children of Israel: only divide you it by lot to the Israelites for an inheritance, as I have commanded you.
7 ¶ Now therefore divide this land for an inheritance unto the nine tribes, and the half tribe of Manasseh,
8 With whom the Reubenites and the Gadites have received their inheritance, which Moses gave them, beyond *the* Jordan eastward, *even* as Moses the servant of Yahweh gave them;
9 From Aroer, that *is* upon the bank of the river Arnon, and the city that *is* in the midst of the river, and all the plain of Medeba unto Dibon;
10 And all the cities of Sihon king of the Amorites, which reigned in Heshbon, unto the border of the children of Ammon;
11 And Gilead, and the border of the Geshurites and Maachathites, and all mount Hermon, and all Bashan unto Salcah;
12 All the kingdom of Og in Bashan, which reigned in Ashtaroth and in Edrei, who remained of the remnant of the giants: for these did Moses smite, and cast them out.
13 Nevertheless the children of Israel expelled not the Geshurites, nor the Maachathites: but the Geshurites and the Maachathites dwell among the Israelites until this day.
14 Only to the tribe of Levi he gave no inheritance; the sacrifices of Yahweh God of Israel made by fire *are* their inheritance, as he said to them.
15 And Moses gave to the tribe of the children of Reuben *inheritance* according to their families.
16 And their coast was from Aroer, that *is* on the bank of the river Arnon, and the city that *is* in the midst of the river, and all the plain by Medeba;
17 Heshbon, and all her cities that *are* in the plain; Dibon, and Bamothbaal, and Bethbaalmeon,
18 And Jahazah, and Kedemoth, and Mephaath,
19 And Kirjathaim, and Sibmah, and Zarethshahar in the mount of the valley,
20 And Bethpeor, and Ashdothpisgah, and Bethjeshimoth,
21 And all the cities of the plain, and all the kingdom of Sihon king of the Amorites, which reigned in Heshbon, whom Moses smote with the princes of Midian, Evi, and Rekem, and Zur, and Hur, and Reba, *which were* dukes of Sihon, dwelling in the country.
22 Balaam also the son of Beor, the soothsayer, did the children of Israel slay with the sword among them that were slain by them.
23 And the border of the children of Reuben was *the* Jordan, and the border *thereof*. This *was* the inheritance of the children of Reuben after their families, the cities and the villages thereof.
24 And Moses gave *inheritance* unto the tribe of Gad, *even* to the children of Gad according to their families.
25 And their coast was Jazer, and all the cities of Gilead, and half the land of the children of Ammon, to Aroer that *is* before Rabbah;

26 And from Heshbon unto Ramathmizpeh, and Betonim; and from Mahanaim unto the border of Debir;

27 And in the valley, Betharam, and Bethnimrah, and Succoth, and Zaphon, the rest of the kingdom of Sihon king of Heshbon, *the* Jordan and *his* border, *even* unto the edge of the sea of Chinnereth on the other side *of the* Jordan eastward.

28 This *is* the inheritance of the children of Gad after their families, the cities, and their villages.

29 And Moses gave *inheritance* unto the half tribe of Manasseh: and *this* was *the possession* of the half tribe of the children of Manasseh by their families.

30 And their coast was from Mahanaim, all Bashan, all the kingdom of Og king of Bashan, and all the towns of Jair, which *are* in Bashan, threescore cities:

31 And half Gilead, and Ashtaroth, and Edrei, cities of the kingdom of Og in Bashan, *were pertaining* to the children of Machir the son of Manasseh, *even* to the one half of the children of Machir by their families.

32 These *are the countries* which Moses did distribute for inheritance in the plains of Moab, on the other side *of the* Jordan, by Jericho, eastward.

33 But to the tribe of Levi Moses gave not *any* inheritance: Yahweh God of Israel *was* their inheritance, as he said to them.

Joshua 14

14:1 ¶ And these *are the countries* which the children of Israel inherited in the land of Canaan, which Eleazar the priest, and Joshua the son of Nun, and the heads of the fathers of the tribes of the children of Israel, distributed for inheritance to them.

2 By lot *was* their inheritance, as Yahweh commanded by the hand of Moses, for the nine tribes, and *for* the half tribe.

3 For Moses had given the inheritance of two tribes and a half tribe on the other side *of the* Jordan: but to the Levites he gave no inheritance among them.

4 For the children of Joseph were two tribes, Manasseh and Ephraim: therefore they gave no part to the Levites in the land, save cities to dwell *in*, with their suburbs for their cattle and for their substance.

5 As Yahweh commanded Moses, so the children of Israel did, and they divided the land.

6 ¶ Then the children of Judah came to Joshua in Gilgal: and Caleb the son of Jephunneh the Kenezite said to him, You know the thing that Yahweh said to Moses the man of God concerning me and you in Kadeshbarnea.

7 Forty years old *was* I when Moses the servant of Yahweh sent me from Kadeshbarnea to spy out the land; and I brought him word again as *it was* in my heart.

8 Nevertheless my brethren that went up with me made the heart of the people melt: but I wholly followed Yahweh my God.

9 And Moses swore on that day, saying, Surely the land whereon your feet have trodden shall be your inheritance, and your children's forever, because you have wholly followed Yahweh my God.

10 And now, behold, Yahweh has kept me alive, as he said, these forty and five years, even since Yahweh spoke this word to Moses, while *the children of* Israel wandered in the wilderness: and now, lo, I *am* this day fourscore and five years old.

11 As yet I *am as* strong this day as *I was* in the day that Moses sent me: as my strength *was* then, even so *is* my strength now, for war, both to go out, and to come in.

12 Now therefore give me this mountain, whereof Yahweh spoke in that day; for you heard in that day how the Anakims *were* there, and *that* the cities *were* great *and* fenced: if so be Yahweh *will be* with me, then I shall be able to drive them out, as Yahweh said.

13 And Joshua blessed him, and gave to Caleb the son of Jephunneh Hebron for an inheritance.

14 Hebron therefore became the inheritance of Caleb the son of Jephunneh the Kenezite unto this day, because that he wholly followed Yahweh God of Israel.

15 And the name of Hebron before *was* Kirjatharba; *which Arba was* a great man among the Anakims. And the land had rest from war.

Joshua 15

15:1 ¶ *This* then was the lot of the tribe of the children of Judah by their families; *even* to the border of Edom the wilderness of Zin southward *was* the utmost part of the south coast.

2 And their south border was from the shore of the salt sea, from the bay that looks southward:

3 And it went out to the south side to Maalehacrabbim, and passed along to Zin, and ascended up on the south side to Kadeshbarnea, and passed along to Hezron, and went up to Adar, and circled around to Karkaa:

4 *From there* it passed toward Azmon, and went out to the river of Egypt; and the goings out of that coast were at the sea: this shall be your south coast.

5 And the east border *was* the salt sea, *even* to the end of *the* Jordan. And *their* border in the north quarter *was* from the bay of the sea at the utmost part of *the* Jordan:

6 And the border went up to Bethhogla, and passed along by the north of Betharabah; and the border went up to the stone of Bohan the son of Reuben:

7 And the border went up toward Debir from the valley of Achor, and so northward, looking toward Gilgal, that *is* before the going up to Adummim, which *is* on the south side of the river: and the border passed toward the waters of Enshemesh, and the goings out thereof were at Enrogel:

8 And the border went up by the valley of the son of Hinnom to the south side of the Jebusite; the same *is* Jerusalem: and the border went up to the top of the mountain that *lies* before the valley of Hinnom westward, which *is* at the end of the valley of the giants northward:

Joshua 15

9 And the border was drawn from the top of the hill to the fountain of the water of Nephtoah, and went out to the cities of mount Ephron; and the border was drawn to Baalah, which *is* Kirjathjearim:

10 And the border turned from Baalah westward to mount Seir, and passed along to the side of mount Jearim, which *is* Chesalon, on the north side, and went down to Bethshemesh, and passed on to Timnah:

11 And the border went out to the side of Ekron northward: and the border was drawn to Shicron, and passed along to mount Baalah, and went out to Jabneel; and the goings out of the border were at the sea.

12 And the west border *was* to the great sea, and the coast *thereof*. This *is* the coast of the children of Judah round about according to their families.

13 ¶ And to Caleb the son of Jephunneh he gave a part among the children of Judah, according to the commandment of Yahweh to Joshua, *even* the city of Arba the father of Anak, which *city is* Hebron.

14 And Caleb drove therefrom the three sons of Anak, Sheshai, and Ahiman, and Talmai, the children of Anak.

15 And he went up there to the inhabitants of Debir: and the name of Debir before *was* Kirjathsepher.

16 And Caleb said, He that smites Kirjathsepher, and takes it, to him will I give Achsah my daughter to wife.

17 And Othniel the son of Kenaz, the brother of Caleb, took it: and he gave him Achsah his daughter to wife.

18 And it came to pass, as she came *to him*, that she moved him to ask of her father a field: and she lighted off *her* donkey; and Caleb said to her, What would you?

19 Who answered, Give me a blessing; for you have given me a south land; give me also springs of water. And he gave her the upper springs, and the lower springs.

20 ¶ This *is* the inheritance of the tribe of the children of Judah according to their families.

21 And the utmost cities of the tribe of the children of Judah toward the coast of Edom southward were Kabzeel, and Eder, and Jagur,

22 And Kinah, and Dimonah, and Adadah,

23 And Kedesh, and Hazor, and Ithnan,

24 Ziph, and Telem, and Bealoth,

25 And Hazor, Hadattah, and Kerioth, *and* Hezron, which *is* Hazor,

26 Amam, and Shema, and Moladah,

27 And Hazargaddah, and Heshmon, and Bethpalet,

28 And Hazarshual, and Beersheba, and Bizjothjah,

29 Baalah, and Iim, and Azem,

30 And Eltolad, and Chesil, and Hormah,

31 And Ziklag, and Madmannah, and Sansannah,

32 And Lebaoth, and Shilhim, and Ain, and Rimmon: all the cities *are* twenty and nine, with their villages:

33 *And* in the valley, Eshtaol, and Zoreah, and Ashnah,

34 And Zanoah, and Engannim, Tappuah, and Enam,

35 Jarmuth, and Adullam, Socoh, and Azekah,

36 And Sharaim, and Adithaim, and Gederah, and Gederothaim; fourteen cities with their villages:

37 Zenan, and Hadashah, and Migdalgad,

38 And Dilean, and Mizpeh, and Joktheel,

39 Lachish, and Bozkath, and Eglon,

40 And Cabbon, and Lahmam, and Kithlish,

41 And Gederoth, Bethdagon, and Naamah, and Makkedah; sixteen cities with their villages:

42 Libnah, and Ether, and Ashan,

43 And Jiphtah, and Ashnah, and Nezib,

44 And Keilah, and Achzib, and Mareshah; nine cities with their villages:

45 Ekron, with her towns and her villages:

46 From Ekron even to the sea, all that *lay* near Ashdod, with their villages:

47 Ashdod with her towns and her villages, Gaza with her towns and her villages, to the river of Egypt, and the great sea, and the border *thereof*:

48 And in the mountains, Shamir, and Jattir, and Socoh,

49 And Dannah, and Kirjathsannah, which *is* Debir,

50 And Anab, and Eshtemoh, and Anim,

51 And Goshen, and Holon, and Giloh; eleven cities with their villages:

52 Arab, and Dumah, and Eshean,

53 And Janum, and Bethtappuah, and Aphekah,

54 And Humtah, and Kirjatharba, which *is* Hebron, and Zior; nine cities with their villages:

55 Maon, Carmel, and Ziph, and Juttah,

56 And Jezreel, and Jokdeam, and Zanoah,

57 Cain, Gibeah, and Timnah; ten cities with their villages:

58 Halhul, Bethzur, and Gedor,

59 And Maarath, and Bethanoth, and Eltekon; six cities with their villages:

60 Kirjathbaal, which *is* Kirjathjearim, and Rabbah; two cities with their villages:

61 In the wilderness, Betharabah, Middin, and Secacah,

62 And Nibshan, and the city of Salt, and Engedi; six cities with their villages.

63 As for the Jebusites the inhabitants of Jerusalem, the children of Judah could not drive them out: but the Jebusites dwell with the children of Judah at Jerusalem unto this day.

Joshua 16

16:1 ¶ And the lot of the children of Joseph fell from *the* Jordan by Jericho, to the water of Jericho on the east, to the wilderness that goes up from Jericho throughout mount Bethel,

2 And goes out from Bethel to Luz, and passes along to the borders of Archi to Ataroth,

3 And goes down westward to the coast of Japhleti, to the coast of Bethhoron the lower, and to Gezer: and the goings out thereof are at the sea.

4 So the children of Joseph, Manasseh and Ephraim, took their inheritance.

5 ¶ And the border of the children of Ephraim according to their families was *thus*: even the border of their inheritance on the east side was Atarothaddar, to Bethhoron the upper;

6 And the border went out toward the sea to Michmethah on the north side; and the border went about eastward to Taanathshiloh, and passed by it on the east to Janohah;
7 And it went down from Janohah to Ataroth, and to Naarath, and came to Jericho, and went out at *the* Jordan.
8 The border went out from Tappuah westward to the river Kanah; and the goings out thereof were at the sea. This *is* the inheritance of the tribe of the children of Ephraim by their families.
9 And the separate cities for the children of Ephraim *were* among the inheritance of the children of Manasseh, all the cities with their villages.
10 And they drove not out the Canaanites that dwelt in Gezer: but the Canaanites dwell among the Ephraimites unto this day, and serve under tribute.

Joshua 17

17:1 ¶ There was also a lot for the tribe of Manasseh; for he *was* the firstborn of Joseph; *that is*, for Machir the firstborn of Manasseh, the father of Gilead: because he was a man of war, therefore he had Gilead and Bashan.
2 There was also *a lot* for the rest of the children of Manasseh by their families; for the children of Abiezer, and for the children of Helek, and for the children of Asriel, and for the children of Shechem, and for the children of Hepher, and for the children of Shemida: these *were* the male children of Manasseh the son of Joseph by their families.
3 But Zelophehad, the son of Hepher, the son of Gilead, the son of Machir, the son of Manasseh, had no sons, but daughters: and these *are* the names of his daughters, Mahlah, and Noah, Hoglah, Milcah, and Tirzah.
4 And they came near before Eleazar the priest, and before Joshua the son of Nun, and before the princes, saying, Yahweh commanded Moses to give us an inheritance among our brethren. Therefore according to the commandment of Yahweh he gave them an inheritance among the brothers of their father.
5 And there fell ten portions to Manasseh, beside the land of Gilead and Bashan, which *were* on the other side *of the* Jordan;
6 Because the daughters of Manasseh had an inheritance among his sons: and the rest of Manasseh's sons had the land of Gilead.
7 ¶ And the coast of Manasseh was from Asher to Michmethah, that *lies* before Shechem; and the border went along on the right hand to the inhabitants of Entappuah.
8 *Now* Manasseh had the land of Tappuah: but Tappuah on the border of Manasseh *belonged* to the children of Ephraim;
9 And the coast descended to the river Kanah, southward of the river: these cities of Ephraim *are* among the cities of Manasseh: the coast of Manasseh also *was* on the north side of the river, and the outgoings of it were at the sea:
10 Southward *it was* Ephraim's, and northward *it was* Manasseh's, and the sea is his border; and they met together in Asher on the north, and in Issachar on the east.

11 And Manasseh had in Issachar and in Asher Bethshean and her towns, and Ibleam and her towns, and the inhabitants of Dor and her towns, and the inhabitants of Endor and her towns, and the inhabitants of Taanach and her towns, and the inhabitants of Megiddo and her towns, *even* three countries.
12 Yet the children of Manasseh could not drive out *the inhabitants of* those cities; but the Canaanites would dwell in that land.
13 Yet it came to pass, when the children of Israel had grown strong, that they put the Canaanites to forced labor; but did not utterly drive them out.
14 ¶ And the children of Joseph spoke to Joshua, saying, Why have you given me *but* one lot and one portion to inherit, seeing I *am* a great people, forasmuch as Yahweh has blessed me till now?
15 And Joshua answered them, If you *are* a great people, *then* get you up to the wood *country*, and cut down for yourself there in the land of the Perizzites and of the giants, if mount Ephraim is too narrow for you.
16 And the children of Joseph said, The hill is not enough for us: and all the Canaanites that dwell in the land of the valley have chariots of iron, *both they* who *are* of Bethshean and her towns, and *they* who *are* of the valley of Jezreel.
17 And Joshua spoke to the house of Joseph, *even* to Ephraim and to Manasseh, saying, You *are* a great people, and have great power: you shall not have one lot *only*:
18 But the mountain shall be yours; for it *is* a woods, and you shall cut it down: and the outgoings of it shall be yours: for you shall drive out the Canaanites, though they have iron chariots, *and* though they *are* strong.

Joshua 18

18:1 ¶ And the whole congregation of the children of Israel assembled together at Shiloh, and set up the tabernacle of the congregation there. And the land was subdued before them.
2 ¶ And there remained among the children of Israel seven tribes, which had not yet received their inheritance.
3 And Joshua said to the children of Israel, How long *will* you slack to go to possess the land, which Yahweh God of your fathers has given you?
4 Give out from among you three men for *each* tribe: and I will send them, and they shall rise, and go through the land, and describe it according to the inheritance of them; and they shall come *again* to me.
5 And they shall divide it into seven parts: Judah shall remain in their coast on the south, and the house of Joseph shall remain in their coasts on the north.
6 You shall therefore describe the land *into* seven parts, and bring *the description* here to me, that I may cast lots for you here before Yahweh our God.
7 But the Levites have no part among you; for the priesthood of Yahweh *is* their inheritance: and Gad, and Reuben, and half the tribe of Manasseh, have received

Joshua 18

their inheritance beyond *the* Jordan on the east, which Moses the servant of Yahweh gave them.

8 And the men arose, and went away: and Joshua charged them that went to describe the land, saying, Go and walk through the land, and describe it, and come again to me, that I may here cast lots for you before Yahweh in Shiloh.

9 And the men went and passed through the land, and described it by cities into seven parts in a book, and came *again* to Joshua to the host at Shiloh.

10 And Joshua cast lots for them in Shiloh before Yahweh: and there Joshua divided the land unto the children of Israel according to their divisions.

11 ¶ And the lot of the tribe of the children of Benjamin came up according to their families: and the coast of their lot came forth between the children of Judah and the children of Joseph.

12 And their border on the north side was from *the* Jordan; and the border went up to the side of Jericho on the north side, and went up through the mountains westward; and the goings out thereof were at the wilderness of Bethaven.

13 And the border went over from there toward Luz, to the side of Luz, which *is* Bethel, southward; and the border descended to Atarothadar, near the hill that *lies* on the south side of the lower Bethhoron.

14 And the border was drawn *therefrom*, and turned the corner of the sea southward, from the hill that *lies* before Bethhoron southward; and the goings out thereof were at Kirjathbaal, which *is* Kirjathjearim, a city of the children of Judah: this *was* the west quarter.

15 And the south quarter *was* from the end of Kirjathjearim, and the border went out on the west, and went out to the well of *the* waters of Nephtoah:

16 And the border came down to the end of the mountain that *lies* before the valley of the son of Hinnom, *and* which *is* in the valley of the giants on the north, and descended to the valley of Hinnom, to the side of Jebusi on the south, and descended to Enrogel,

17 And was drawn from the north, and went forth to Enshemesh, and went forth toward Geliloth, which *is* over against the going up of Adummim, and descended to the stone of Bohan the son of Reuben,

18 And passed along toward the side over against Arabah northward, and went down to Arabah:

19 And the border passed along to the side of Bethhoglah northward: and the outgoings of the border were at the north bay of the salt sea at the south end of *the* Jordan: this *was* the south coast.

20 And *the* Jordan was the border of it on the east side. This *was* the inheritance of the children of Benjamin, by the coasts thereof round about, according to their families.

21 Now the cities of the tribe of the children of Benjamin according to their families were Jericho, and Bethhoglah, and the valley of Keziz,

22 And Betharabah, and Zemaraim, and Bethel,

23 And Avim, and Parah, and Ophrah,

24 And Chepharhaammonai, and Ophni, and Gaba; twelve cities with their villages:

25 Gibeon, and Ramah, and Beeroth,

26 And Mizpeh, and Chephirah, and Mozah,

27 And Rekem, and Irpeel, and Taralah,

28 And Zelah, Eleph, and Jebusi, which *is* Jerusalem, Gibeath, *and* Kirjath; fourteen cities with their villages. This *is* the inheritance of the children of Benjamin according to their families.

Joshua 19

19:1 ¶ And the second lot came forth to Simeon, *even* for the tribe of the children of Simeon according to their families: and their inheritance was within the inheritance of the children of Judah.

2 And they had in their inheritance Beersheba, or Sheba, and Moladah,

3 And Hazarshual, and Balah, and Azem,

4 And Eltolad, and Bethul, and Hormah,

5 And Ziklag, and Bethmarcaboth, and Hazarsusah,

6 And Bethlebaoth, and Sharuhen; thirteen cities and their villages:

7 Ain, Remmon, and Ether, and Ashan; four cities and their villages:

8 And all the villages that *were* round about these cities to Baalathbeer, Ramath of the south. This *is* the inheritance of the tribe of the children of Simeon according to their families.

9 Out of the portion of the children of Judah *was* the inheritance of the children of Simeon: for the part of the children of Judah was too much for them: therefore the children of Simeon had their inheritance within the inheritance of them.

10 ¶ And the third lot came up for the children of Zebulun according to their families: and the border of their inheritance was to Sarid:

11 And their border went up toward the sea, and Maralah, and reached to Dabbasheth, and reached to the river that *is* before Jokneam;

12 And turned from Sarid eastward toward the sunrising to the border of Chislothtabor, and then goes out to Daberath, and goes up to Japhia,

13 And from there passed on along on the east to Gittahhepher, to Ittahkazin, and goes out to Remmonmethoar to Neah;

14 And the border surrounded it on the north side to Hannathon: and the outgoings thereof are in the valley of Jiphthahel:

15 And Kattath, and Nahallal, and Shimron, and Idalah, and Bethlehem: twelve cities with their villages.

16 This *is* the inheritance of the children of Zebulun according to their families, these cities with their villages.

17 ¶ *And* the fourth lot came out to Issachar, for the children of Issachar according to their families.

18 And their border was toward Jezreel, and Chesulloth, and Shunem,

19 And Hapharaim, and Shion, and Anaharath,

20 And Rabbith, and Kishion, and Abez,
21 And Remeth, and Engannim, and Enhaddah, and Bethpazzez;
22 And the coast reaches to Tabor, and Shahazimah, and Bethshemesh; and the outgoings of their border were at *the* Jordan: sixteen cities with their villages.
23 This *is* the inheritance of the tribe of the children of Issachar according to their families, the cities and their villages.
24 ¶ And the fifth lot came out for the tribe of the children of Asher according to their families.
25 And their border was Helkath, and Hali, and Beten, and Achshaph,
26 And Alammelech, and Amad, and Misheal; and reaches to Carmel westward, and to Shihorlibnath;
27 And turns toward the sunrising to Bethdagon, and reaches to Zebulun, and to the valley of Jiphthahel toward the north side of Bethemek, and Neiel, and goes out to Cabul on the left hand,
28 And Hebron, and Rehob, and Hammon, and Kanah, *even* to great Zidon;
29 And *then* the coast turns to Ramah, and to the strong city Tyre; and the coast turns to Hosah; and the outgoings thereof are at the sea from the coast to Achzib:
30 Ummah also, and Aphek, and Rehob: twenty and two cities with their villages.
31 This *is* the inheritance of the tribe of the children of Asher according to their families, these cities with their villages.
32 ¶ The sixth lot came out to the children of Naphtali, *even* for the children of Naphtali according to their families.
33 And their coast was from Heleph, from Allon to Zaanannim, and Adami, Nekeb, and Jabneel, to Lakum; and the outgoings thereof were at *the* Jordan:
34 And *then* the coast turns westward to Aznothtabor, and goes out from there to Hukkok, and reaches to Zebulun on the south side, and reaches to Asher on the west side, and to Judah upon *the* Jordan toward the sunrising.
35 And the fenced cities *are* Ziddim, Zer, and Hammath, Rakkath, and Chinnereth,
36 And Adamah, and Ramah, and Hazor,
37 And Kedesh, and Edrei, and Enhazor,
38 And Iron, and Migdalel, Horem, and Bethanath, and Bethshemesh; nineteen cities with their villages.
39 This *is* the inheritance of the tribe of the children of Naphtali according to their families, the cities and their villages.
40 ¶ *And* the seventh lot came out for the tribe of the children of Dan according to their families.
41 And the coast of their inheritance was Zorah, and Eshtaol, and Irshemesh,
42 And Shaalabbin, and Ajalon, and Jethlah,
43 And Elon, and Thimnathah, and Ekron,
44 And Eltekeh, and Gibbethon, and Baalath,
45 And Jehud, and Beneberak, and Gathrimmon,
46 And Mejarkon, and Rakkon, with the border before Japho.
47 And the coast of the children of Dan went forth *too small* for them: therefore the children of Dan went up to fight against Leshem, and took it, and smote it with the edge of the sword, and possessed it, and dwelt therein, and called Leshem, Dan, after the name of Dan their father.
48 This *is* the inheritance of the tribe of the children of Dan according to their families, these cities with their villages.
49 ¶ When they had made an end of dividing the land for inheritance by their coasts, the children of Israel gave an inheritance to Joshua the son of Nun among them:
50 According to the word of Yahweh they gave him the city which he asked, *even* Timnathserah in mount Ephraim: and he built the city, and dwelt therein.
51 These *are* the inheritances, which Eleazar the priest, and Joshua the son of Nun, and the heads of the fathers of the tribes of the children of Israel, divided for an inheritance by lot in Shiloh before Yahweh, at the door of the tabernacle of the congregation. So they made an end of dividing the country.

Joshua 20

20:1 ¶ Yahweh also spoke to Joshua, saying,
2 Speak to the children of Israel, saying, Appoint out for you cities of refuge, whereof I spoke to you by the hand of Moses:
3 That the slayer that kills *any* person unaware *and* unwittingly may flee there: and they shall be your refuge from the avenger of blood.
4 And when he that does flee to one of those cities shall stand at the entering of the gate of the city, and shall declare his cause in the ears of the elders of that city, they shall take him into the city to them, and give him a place, that he may dwell among them.
5 And if the avenger of blood pursues after him, then they shall not deliver the slayer up into his hand; because he smote his neighbor unwittingly, and hated him not before.
6 And he shall dwell in that city, until he stands before the congregation for judgment, *and* until the death of the high priest that shall be in those days: then shall the slayer return, and come to his own city, and to his own house, to the city from where he fled.
7 ¶ And they appointed Kedesh in Galilee in mount Naphtali, and Shechem in mount Ephraim, and Kirjatharba, which *is* Hebron, in the mountain of Judah.
8 And on the other side *of the* Jordan by Jericho eastward, they assigned Bezer in the wilderness upon the plain out of the tribe of Reuben, and Ramoth in Gilead out of the tribe of Gad, and Golan in Bashan out of the tribe of Manasseh.
9 These were the cities appointed for all the children of Israel, and for the stranger that sojourns among them, that whoever kills *any* person unwittingly might flee there, and not die by the hand of the avenger of blood, until he stood before the congregation.

Joshua 21

21:1 ¶ Then came near the heads of the fathers of the Levites to Eleazar the priest, and to Joshua the son of Nun, and to the heads of the fathers of the tribes of the children of Israel;

2 And they spoke to them at Shiloh in the land of Canaan, saying, Yahweh commanded by the hand of Moses to give us cities to dwell in, with the suburbs thereof for our cattle.

3 And the children of Israel gave to the Levites out of their inheritance, at the commandment of Yahweh, these cities and their suburbs.

4 And the lot came out for the families of the Kohathites: and the children of Aaron the priest, *which were* of the Levites, had by lot out of the tribe of Judah, and out of the tribe of Simeon, and out of the tribe of Benjamin, thirteen cities.

5 And the rest of the children of Kohath *had* by lot out of the families of the tribe of Ephraim, and out of the tribe of Dan, and out of the half tribe of Manasseh, ten cities.

6 And the children of Gershon *had* by lot out of the families of the tribe of Issachar, and out of the tribe of Asher, and out of the tribe of Naphtali, and out of the half tribe of Manasseh in Bashan, thirteen cities.

7 The children of Merari by their families *had* out of the tribe of Reuben, and out of the tribe of Gad, and out of the tribe of Zebulun, twelve cities.

8 And the children of Israel gave by lot to the Levites these cities with their suburbs, as Yahweh commanded by the hand of Moses.

9 ¶ And they gave out of the tribe of the children of Judah, and out of the tribe of the children of Simeon, these cities which are *here* mentioned by name,

10 Which the children of Aaron, *being* of the families of the Kohathites, *who were* of the children of Levi, had: for theirs was the first lot.

11 And they gave them the city of Arba the father of Anak, which *city is* Hebron, in the hill *country* of Judah, with the suburbs thereof round about it.

12 But the fields of the city, and the villages thereof, gave they to Caleb the son of Jephunneh for his possession.

13 Thus they gave to the children of Aaron the priest Hebron with her suburbs, *to be* a city of refuge for the slayer; and Libnah with her suburbs,

14 And Jattir with her suburbs, and Eshtemoa with her suburbs,

15 And Holon with her suburbs, and Debir with her suburbs,

16 And Ain with her suburbs, and Juttah with her suburbs, *and* Bethshemesh with her suburbs; nine cities out of those two tribes.

17 And out of the tribe of Benjamin, Gibeon with her suburbs, Geba with her suburbs,

18 Anathoth with her suburbs, and Almon with her suburbs; four cities.

19 All the cities of the children of Aaron, the priests, *were* thirteen cities with their suburbs.

20 And the families of the children of Kohath, the Levites which remained of the children of Kohath, even they had the cities of their lot out of the tribe of Ephraim.

21 For they gave them Shechem with her suburbs in mount Ephraim, *to be* a city of refuge for the slayer; and Gezer with her suburbs,

22 And Kibzaim with her suburbs, and Bethhoron with her suburbs; four cities.

23 And out of the tribe of Dan, Eltekeh with her suburbs, Gibbethon with her suburbs,

24 Aijalon with her suburbs, Gathrimmon with her suburbs; four cities.

25 And out of the half tribe of Manasseh, Tanach with her suburbs, and Gathrimmon with her suburbs; two cities.

26 All the cities *were* ten with their suburbs for the families of the children of Kohath that remained.

27 And to the children of Gershon, of the families of the Levites, out of the *other* half tribe of Manasseh *they gave* Golan in Bashan with her suburbs, *to be* a city of refuge for the slayer; and Beeshterah with her suburbs; two cities.

28 And out of the tribe of Issachar, Kishon with her suburbs, Dabareh with her suburbs,

29 Jarmuth with her suburbs, Engannim with her suburbs; four cities.

30 And out of the tribe of Asher, Mishal with her suburbs, Abdon with her suburbs,

31 Helkath with her suburbs, and Rehob with her suburbs; four cities.

32 And out of the tribe of Naphtali, Kedesh in Galilee with her suburbs, *to be* a city of refuge for the slayer; and Hammothdor with her suburbs, and Kartan with her suburbs; three cities.

33 All the cities of the Gershonites according to their families *were* thirteen cities with their suburbs.

34 And to the families of the children of Merari, the rest of the Levites, out of the tribe of Zebulun, Jokneam with her suburbs, and Kartah with her suburbs,

35 Dimnah with her suburbs, Nahalal with her suburbs; four cities.

36 And out of the tribe of Reuben, Bezer with her suburbs, and Jahazah with her suburbs,

37 Kedemoth with her suburbs, and Mephaath with her suburbs; four cities.

38 And out of the tribe of Gad, Ramoth in Gilead with her suburbs, *to be* a city of refuge for the slayer; and Mahanaim with her suburbs,

39 Heshbon with her suburbs, Jazer with her suburbs; four cities in all.

40 So all the cities for the children of Merari by their families, which were remaining of the families of the Levites, were *by* their lot twelve cities.

41 All the cities of the Levites within the possession of the children of Israel *were* forty and eight cities with their suburbs.

42 These cities were every one with their suburbs round about them: thus *were* all these cities.

43 ¶ And Yahweh gave to Israel all the land which he swore to give to their fathers; and they possessed it, and dwelt therein.

44 And Yahweh gave them rest round about, according to all that he swore to their fathers: and there stood not a man of all their enemies before them; Yahweh delivered all their enemies into their hand.
45 There failed no word of any good thing which Yahweh had spoken to the house of Israel; all came to pass.

Joshua 22

22:1 ¶ Then Joshua called the Reubenites, and the Gadites, and the half tribe of Manasseh,
2 And said to them, You have kept all that Moses the servant of Yahweh commanded you, and have obeyed my voice in all that I commanded you:
3 You have not left your brethren these many days unto this day, but have kept the charge of the commandment of Yahweh your God.
4 And now Yahweh your God has given rest unto your brethren, as he promised them: therefore now return you, and get you to your tents, *and* to the land of your possession, which Moses the servant of Yahweh gave you on the other side *of the* Jordan.
5 But take diligent heed to do the commandment and the law, which Moses the servant of Yahweh charged you, to love Yahweh your God, and to walk in all his ways, and to keep his commandments, and to cling to him, and to serve him with all your heart and with all your soul.
6 So Joshua blessed them, and sent them away: and they went to their tents.
7 Now to the *one* half of the tribe of Manasseh Moses had given *possession* in Bashan: but to the *other* half thereof gave Joshua among their brethren on this side *of the* Jordan westward. And when Joshua sent them away also to their tents, then he blessed them,
8 And he spoke to them, saying, Return with much riches to your tents, and with very much cattle, with silver, and with gold, and with brass, and with iron, and with very many garments: divide the spoil of your enemies with your brethren.
9 And the children of Reuben and the children of Gad and the half tribe of Manasseh returned, and departed from the children of Israel out of Shiloh, which *is* in the land of Canaan, to go to the country of Gilead, to the land of their possession, whereof they were possessed, according to the word of Yahweh by the hand of Moses.
10 ¶ And when they came to the borders of *the* Jordan, that *are* in the land of Canaan, the children of Reuben and the children of Gad and the half tribe of Manasseh built there an altar by *the* Jordan, a great altar to see to.
11 And the children of Israel heard say, Behold, the children of Reuben and the children of Gad and the half tribe of Manasseh have built an altar over against the land of Canaan, in the borders of *the* Jordan, at the passage of the children of Israel.
12 And when the children of Israel heard *of it*, the whole congregation of the children of Israel gathered themselves together at Shiloh, to go up to war against them.
13 And the children of Israel sent to the children of Reuben, and to the children of Gad, and to the half tribe of Manasseh, into the land of Gilead, Phinehas the son of Eleazar the priest,
14 And with him ten princes, of each chief house a prince throughout all the tribes of Israel; and each one *was* a head of the house of their fathers among the thousands of Israel.
15 And they came to the children of Reuben, and to the children of Gad, and to the half tribe of Manasseh, to the land of Gilead, and they spoke with them, saying,
16 Thus says the whole congregation of Yahweh, What trespass *is* this that you have committed against the God of Israel, to turn away this day from following Yahweh, in that you have built you an altar, that you might rebel this day against Yahweh?
17 *Is* the iniquity of Peor too little for us, from which we are not cleansed until this day, although there was a plague in the congregation of Yahweh,
18 But that you must turn away this day from following Yahweh? and it will be, *seeing* you rebel today against Yahweh, that tomorrow he will be angry with the whole congregation of Israel.
19 Notwithstanding, if the land of your possession *is* unclean, *then* pass you over to the land of the possession of Yahweh, wherein Yahweh's tabernacle dwells, and take possession among us: but rebel not against Yahweh, nor rebel against us, in building you an altar besides the altar of Yahweh our God.
20 Did not Achan the son of Zerah commit a trespass in the accursed thing, and wrath fell on all the congregation of Israel? and that man perished not alone in his iniquity.
21 ¶ Then the children of Reuben and the children of Gad and the half tribe of Manasseh answered, and said to the heads of the thousands of Israel,
22 Yahweh God of gods, Yahweh God of gods, he knows, and Israel he shall know; if *it is* in rebellion, or if in transgression against Yahweh, (save us not this day,)
23 That we have built us an altar to turn from following Yahweh, or if to offer thereon burnt offering or meat offering, or if to offer peace offerings thereon, let Yahweh himself require *it*;
24 And if we have not *rather* done it for fear of *this* thing, saying, In time to come your children might speak to our children, saying, What have you to do with Yahweh God of Israel?
25 For Yahweh has made *the* Jordan a border between us and you, you children of Reuben and children of Gad; you have no part in Yahweh: so shall your children make our children cease from fearing Yahweh.
26 Therefore we said, Let us now prepare to build us an altar, not for burnt offering, nor for sacrifice:
27 But *that* it *may be* a witness between us, and you, and our generations after us, that we might do the service of Yahweh before him with our burnt offerings, and with our sacrifices, and with our peace offerings; that your children may not say to our children in time to come, You have no part in Yahweh.

Joshua 22

28 Therefore said we, that it shall be, when they should *so* say to us or to our generations in time to come, that we may say *again*, Behold the pattern of the altar of Yahweh, which our fathers made, not for burnt offerings, nor for sacrifices; but it *is* a witness between us and you.

29 God forbid that we should rebel against Yahweh, and turn this day from following Yahweh, to build an altar for burnt offerings, for meat offerings, or for sacrifices, besides the altar of Yahweh our God that *is* before his tabernacle.

30 ¶ And when Phinehas the priest, and the princes of the congregation and heads of the thousands of Israel which *were* with him, heard the words that the children of Reuben and the children of Gad and the children of Manasseh spoke, it pleased them.

31 And Phinehas the son of Eleazar the priest said to the children of Reuben, and to the children of Gad, and to the children of Manasseh, This day we perceive that Yahweh *is* among us, because you have not committed this trespass against Yahweh: now you have delivered the children of Israel out of the hand of Yahweh.

32 And Phinehas the son of Eleazar the priest, and the princes, returned from the children of Reuben, and from the children of Gad, out of the land of Gilead, to the land of Canaan, to the children of Israel, and brought them word again.

33 And the thing pleased the children of Israel; and the children of Israel blessed God, and did not intend to go up against them in battle, to destroy the land wherein the children of Reuben and Gad dwelt.

34 And the children of Reuben and the children of Gad called the altar *Ed*: for it *shall be* a witness between us that Yahweh *is* God.

Joshua 23

23:1 ¶ And it came to pass a long time after that Yahweh had given rest to Israel from all their enemies round about, that Joshua grew old *and* stricken in age.

2 And Joshua called for all Israel, *and* for their elders, and for their heads, and for their judges, and for their officers, and said to them, I am old *and* stricken in age:

3 And you have seen all that Yahweh your God has done to all these nations because of you; for Yahweh your God *is* he that has fought for you.

4 Behold, I have divided to you by lot these nations that remain, to be an inheritance for your tribes, from *the* Jordan, with all the nations that I have cut off, even to the great sea westward.

5 And Yahweh your God, he shall expel them from before you, and drive them from out of your sight; and you shall possess their land, as Yahweh your God has promised to you.

6 Be you therefore very courageous to keep and to do all that is written in the book of the law of Moses, that you turn not aside therefrom *to* the right hand or *to* the left;

7 That you come not among these nations, these that remain among you; neither make mention of the name of their gods, nor cause to swear *by them*, neither serve them, nor bow yourselves unto them:

8 But cling unto Yahweh your God, as you have done unto this day.

9 For Yahweh has driven out from before you great nations and strong: but *as for* you, no man has been able to stand before you unto this day.

10 One man of you shall chase a thousand: for Yahweh your God, he *it is* that fights for you, as he has promised you.

11 ¶ Take good heed therefore unto yourselves, that you love Yahweh your God.

12 Else if you do in any way go back, and cling to the remnant of these nations, *even* these that remain among you, and shall make marriages with them, and go in unto them, and they to you:

13 Know for a certainty that Yahweh your God will no more drive out *any of* these nations from before you; but they shall be snares and traps to you, and scourges in your sides, and thorns in your eyes, until you perish from off this good land which Yahweh your God has given you.

14 And, behold, this day I *am* going the way of all the earth: and you know in all your hearts and in all your souls, that not one thing has failed of all the good things which Yahweh your God spoke concerning you; all have come to pass unto you, *and* not one thing has failed thereof.

15 Therefore it shall come to pass, *that* as all good things have come upon you, which Yahweh your God promised you; so shall Yahweh bring upon you all evil things, until he has destroyed you from off this good land which Yahweh your God has given you.

16 When you have transgressed the covenant of Yahweh your God, which he commanded you, and have gone and served other gods, and bowed yourselves to them; then shall the anger of Yahweh be kindled against you, and you shall perish quickly from off the good land which he has given to you.

Joshua 24

24:1 ¶ And Joshua gathered all the tribes of Israel to Shechem, and called for the elders of Israel, and for their heads, and for their judges, and for their officers; and they presented themselves before God.

2 And Joshua said to all the people, Thus says Yahweh God of Israel, Your fathers dwelt on the other side of the river in old times, *even* Terah, the father of Abraham, and the father of Nachor: and they served other gods.

3 And I took your father Abraham from the other side of the river, and led him throughout all the land of Canaan, and multiplied his seed, and gave him Isaac.

4 And I gave to Isaac Jacob and Esau: and I gave to Esau mount Seir, to possess it; but Jacob and his children went down into Egypt.

5 I sent Moses also and Aaron, and I plagued Egypt, according to that which I did among them: and afterward I brought you out.

6 And I brought your fathers out of Egypt: and you came to the sea; and the Egyptians pursued after your fathers with chariots and horsemen unto the Red Sea.

7 And when they cried unto Yahweh, he put darkness between you and the Egyptians, and brought the sea upon them, and covered them; and your eyes have seen what I have done in Egypt: and you dwelt in the wilderness a long season.

8 And I brought you into the land of the Amorites, which dwelt on the other side *of the* Jordan; and they fought with you: and I gave them into your hand, that you might possess their land; and I destroyed them from before you.

9 Then Balak the son of Zippor, king of Moab, arose and warred against Israel, and sent and called Balaam the son of Beor to curse you:

10 But I would not listen to Balaam; therefore he blessed you still: so I delivered you out of his hand.

11 And you went over *the* Jordan, and came to Jericho: and the men of Jericho fought against you, the Amorites, and the Perizzites, and the Canaanites, and the Hittites, and the Girgashites, the Hivites, and the Jebusites; and I delivered them into your hand.

12 And I sent the hornet before you, which drove them out from before you, *even* the two kings of the Amorites; *but* not with your sword, nor with your bow.

13 And I have given you a land for which you did not labor, and cities which you built not, and you dwell in them; of the vineyards and olive groves which you planted not do you eat.

14 Now therefore fear Yahweh, and serve him in sincerity and in truth: and put away the gods which your fathers served on the other side of the river, and in Egypt; and serve you Yahweh.

15 ¶ And if it seems evil to you to serve Yahweh, choose you this day whom you will serve; whether the gods which your fathers served that *were* on the other side of the river, or the gods of the Amorites, in whose land you dwell: but as for me and my house, we will serve Yahweh.

16 And the people answered and said, God forbid that we should forsake Yahweh, to serve other gods;

17 For Yahweh our God, he *it is* that brought us up and our fathers out of the land of Egypt, from the house of bondage, and which did those great signs in our sight, and preserved us in all the way wherein we went, and among all the people through whom we passed:

18 And Yahweh drove out from before us all the people, even the Amorites which dwelt in the land: *therefore* will we also serve Yahweh; for he *is* our God.

19 And Joshua said to the people, You cannot serve Yahweh: for he *is* a holy God; he *is* a jealous God: he will not forgive your transgressions nor your sins.

20 If you forsake Yahweh, and serve strange gods, then he will turn and do you hurt, and consume you, after that he has done you good.

21 And the people said to Joshua, No; but we will serve Yahweh.

22 And Joshua said to the people, You *are* witnesses against yourselves that you have chosen you Yahweh, to serve him. And they said, *We are* witnesses.

23 Now therefore put away, *said he*, the strange gods which *are* among you, and incline your heart unto Yahweh God of Israel.

24 And the people said to Joshua, Yahweh our God will we serve, and his voice will we obey.

25 So Joshua made a covenant with the people that day, and set them a statute and an ordinance in Shechem.

26 And Joshua wrote these words in the book of the law of God, and took a great stone, and set it up there under an oak, that *was* by the sanctuary of Yahweh.

27 And Joshua said to all the people, Behold, this stone shall be a witness to us; for it has heard all the words of Yahweh which he spoke to us: it shall be therefore a witness to you, lest you deny your God.

28 So Joshua let the people depart, every man to his inheritance.

29 ¶ And it came to pass after these things, that Joshua the son of Nun, the servant of Yahweh, died, *being* a hundred and ten years old.

30 And they buried him in the border of his inheritance in Timnathserah, which *is* in mount Ephraim, on the north side of the hill of Gaash.

31 And Israel served Yahweh all the days of Joshua, and all the days of the elders that outlived Joshua, and which had known all the works of Yahweh, that he had done for Israel.

32 And the bones of Joseph, which the children of Israel brought up out of Egypt, buried they in Shechem, in a parcel of ground which Jacob bought of the sons of Hamor the father of Shechem for a hundred pieces of silver: and it became the inheritance of the children of Joseph.

33 And Eleazar the son of Aaron died; and they buried him in a hill *that pertained to* Phinehas his son, which was given him in mount Ephraim.

Judges

Judges 1

1:1 ¶ Now after the death of Joshua it came to pass, that the children of Israel asked Yahweh, saying, Who shall go up for us against the Canaanites first, to fight against them?

2 And Yahweh said, Judah shall go up: behold, I have delivered the land into his hand.

3 And Judah said to Simeon his brother, Come up with me into my lot, that we may fight against the Canaanites; and I likewise will go with you into your lot. So Simeon went with him.

4 And Judah went up; and Yahweh delivered the Canaanites and the Perizzites into their hand: and they slew of them in Bezek ten thousand men.

5 And they found Adonibezek in Bezek: and they fought against him, and they slew the Canaanites and the Perizzites.

Judges 1

6 But Adonibezek fled; and they pursued after him, and caught him, and cut off his thumbs and his great toes.

7 And Adonibezek said, Threescore and ten kings, having their thumbs and their great toes cut off, gathered *their meat* under my table: as I have done, so God has repaid me. And they brought him to Jerusalem, and there he died.

8 Now the children of Judah had fought against Jerusalem, and had taken it, and smitten it with the edge of the sword, and set the city on fire.

9 ¶ And afterward the children of Judah went down to fight against the Canaanites, that dwelt in the mountain, and in the south, and in the valley.

10 And Judah went against the Canaanites that dwelt in Hebron: (now the name of Hebron before *was* Kirjatharba:) and they slew Sheshai, and Ahiman, and Talmai.

11 And from there he went against the inhabitants of Debir: and the name of Debir before *was* Kirjathsepher:

12 And Caleb said, He that smites Kirjathsepher, and takes it, to him will I give Achsah my daughter to wife.

13 And Othniel the son of Kenaz, Caleb's younger brother, took it: and he gave him Achsah his daughter to wife.

14 And it came to pass, when she came *to him*, that she moved him to ask of her father a field: and she lighted from off *her* donkey; and Caleb said to her, What will you?

15 And she said to him, Give me a blessing: for you have given me a south land; give me also springs of water. And Caleb gave her the upper springs and the lower springs.

16 And the children of the Kenite, Moses' father-in-law, went up out of the city of palm trees with the children of Judah into the wilderness of Judah, which *lies* in the south of Arad; and they went and dwelt among the people.

17 And Judah went with Simeon his brother, and they slew the Canaanites that inhabited Zephath, and utterly destroyed it. And the name of the city was called Hormah.

18 Also Judah took Gaza with the coast thereof, and Askelon with the coast thereof, and Ekron with the coast thereof.

19 And Yahweh was with Judah; and he drove out *the inhabitants of* the mountain; but could not drive out the inhabitants of the valley, because they had chariots of iron.

20 And they gave Hebron to Caleb, as Moses said: and he expelled therefrom the three sons of Anak.

21 ¶ And the children of Benjamin did not drive out the Jebusites that inhabited Jerusalem; but the Jebusites dwell with the children of Benjamin in Jerusalem unto this day.

22 And the house of Joseph, they also went up against Bethel: and Yahweh *was* with them.

23 And the house of Joseph sent to spy out Bethel. (Now the name of the city before *was* Luz.)

24 And the spies saw a man come forth out of the city, and they said to him, Show us, we pray you, the entrance into the city, and we will show you mercy.

25 And when he showed them the entrance into the city, they smote the city with the edge of the sword; but they let go the man and all his family.

26 And the man went into the land of the Hittites, and built a city, and called the name thereof Luz: which *is* the name thereof unto this day.

27 Neither did Manasseh drive out *the inhabitants of* Bethshean and her towns, nor Taanach and her towns, nor the inhabitants of Dor and her towns, nor the inhabitants of Ibleam and her towns, nor the inhabitants of Megiddo and her towns: but the Canaanites would dwell in that land.

28 And it came to pass, when Israel was strong, that they put the Canaanites to tribute, and did not utterly drive them out.

29 Neither did Ephraim drive out the Canaanites that dwelt in Gezer; but the Canaanites dwelt in Gezer among them.

30 Neither did Zebulun drive out the inhabitants of Kitron, nor the inhabitants of Nahalol; but the Canaanites dwelt among them, and became tributaries.

31 Neither did Asher drive out the inhabitants of Accho, nor the inhabitants of Zidon, nor of Ahlab, nor of Achzib, nor of Helbah, nor of Aphik, nor of Rehob:

32 But the Asherites dwelt among the Canaanites, the inhabitants of the land: for they did not drive them out.

33 Neither did Naphtali drive out the inhabitants of Bethshemesh, nor the inhabitants of Bethanath; but he dwelt among the Canaanites, the inhabitants of the land: nevertheless the inhabitants of Bethshemesh and of Bethanath became tributaries unto them.

34 And the Amorites forced the children of Dan into the mountain: for they would not permit them to come down to the valley:

35 But the Amorites would dwell in mount Heres in Aijalon, and in Shaalbim: yet the hand of the house of Joseph prevailed, so that they became tributaries.

36 And the coast of the Amorites *was* from the going up to Akrabbim, from the rock, and upward.

Judges 2

2:1 ¶ And an angel of Yahweh came up from Gilgal to Bochim, and said, I made you to go up out of Egypt, and have brought you to the land which I swore to your fathers; and I said, I will never break my covenant with you.

2 And you shall make no league with the inhabitants of this land; you shall throw down their altars: but you have not obeyed my voice: why have you done this?

3 Therefore I also said, I will not drive them out from before you; but they shall be *as thorns* in your sides, and their gods shall be a snare to you.

4 And it came to pass, when the angel of Yahweh spoke these words to all the children of Israel, that the people lifted up their voice, and wept.

5 And they called the name of that place Bochim: and they sacrificed there unto Yahweh.

6 ¶ And when Joshua had let the people go, the children of Israel went every man to his inheritance to possess the land.

7 And the people served Yahweh all the days of Joshua, and all the days of the elders that outlived Joshua, who had seen all the great works of Yahweh, that he did for Israel.

8 And Joshua the son of Nun, the servant of Yahweh, died, *being* a hundred and ten years old.

9 And they buried him in the border of his inheritance in Timnathheres, in the mount of Ephraim, on the north side of the hill Gaash.

10 And also all that generation were gathered to their fathers: and there arose another generation after them, which knew not Yahweh, nor yet the works which he had done for Israel.

11 And the children of Israel did evil in the sight of Yahweh, and served Baalim:

12 And they forsook Yahweh God of their fathers, which brought them out of the land of Egypt, and followed other gods, of the gods of the people that *were* round about them, and bowed themselves to them, and provoked Yahweh to anger.

13 And they forsook Yahweh, and served Baal and Ashtaroth.

14 And the anger of Yahweh was hot against Israel, and he delivered them into the hands of spoilers that spoiled them, and he sold them into the hands of their enemies round about, so that they could not any longer stand before their enemies.

15 Wherever they went out, the hand of Yahweh was against them for evil, as Yahweh had said, and as Yahweh had sworn to them: and they were greatly distressed.

16 Nevertheless Yahweh raised up judges, which delivered them out of the hand of those that spoiled them.

17 And yet they would not listen to their judges, but they went a whoring after other gods, and bowed themselves to them: they turned quickly out of the way which their fathers walked in, obeying the commandments of Yahweh; *but* they did not so.

18 And when Yahweh raised them up judges, then Yahweh was with the judge, and delivered them out of the hand of their enemies all the days of the judge: for it repented Yahweh because of their groanings by reason of them that oppressed them and vexed them.

19 And it came to pass, when the judge was dead, *that* they returned, and corrupted *themselves* more than their fathers, in following other gods to serve them, and to bow down to them; they ceased not from their own doings, nor from their stubborn way.

20 And the anger of Yahweh was hot against Israel; and he said, Because that this people has transgressed my covenant which I commanded their fathers, and have not listened to my voice;

21 I also will not henceforth drive out any from before them of the nations which Joshua left when he died:

22 That through them I may prove Israel, whether they will keep the way of Yahweh to walk therein, as their fathers did keep *it*, or not.

23 Therefore Yahweh left those nations, without driving them out hastily; neither delivered he them into the hand of Joshua.

Judges 3

3:1 ¶ Now these *are* the nations which Yahweh left, to prove Israel by them, *even* as many *of Israel* as had not known all the wars of Canaan;

2 Only that the generations of the children of Israel might know, to teach them war, at the least such as before knew nothing thereof;

3 *Namely*, five lords of the Philistines, and all the Canaanites, and the Sidonians, and the Hivites that dwelt in mount Lebanon, from mount Baalhermon to the entering in of Hamath.

4 And they were to prove Israel by them, to know whether they would listen to the commandments of Yahweh, which he commanded their fathers by the hand of Moses.

5 And the children of Israel dwelt among the Canaanites, Hittites, and Amorites, and Perizzites, and Hivites, and Jebusites:

6 And they took their daughters to be their wives, and gave their daughters to their sons, and served their gods.

7 And the children of Israel did evil in the sight of Yahweh, and forgot Yahweh their God, and served Baalim and the groves.

8 ¶ Therefore the anger of Yahweh was hot against Israel, and he sold them into the hand of Chushanrishathaim king of Mesopotamia: and the children of Israel served Chushanrishathaim eight years.

9 And when the children of Israel cried unto Yahweh, Yahweh raised up a deliverer to the children of Israel, who delivered them, *even* Othniel the son of Kenaz, Caleb's younger brother.

10 And the Spirit of Yahweh came upon him, and he judged Israel, and went out to war: and Yahweh delivered Chushanrishathaim king of Mesopotamia into his hand; and his hand prevailed against Chushanrishathaim.

11 And the land had rest *for* forty years. And Othniel the son of Kenaz died.

12 ¶ And the children of Israel did evil again in the sight of Yahweh: and Yahweh strengthened Eglon the king of Moab against Israel, because they had done evil in the sight of Yahweh.

13 And he gathered to him the children of Ammon and Amalek, and went and smote Israel, and possessed the city of palm trees.

14 So the children of Israel served Eglon the king of Moab eighteen years.

15 But when the children of Israel cried unto Yahweh, Yahweh raised them up a deliverer, Ehud the son of Gera, a Benjamite, a man left handed: and by him the children of Israel sent a present to Eglon the king of Moab.

16 But Ehud made him a dagger which had two edges, of a cubit length; and he did gird it under his clothing upon his right thigh.

17 And he brought the present to Eglon king of Moab: and Eglon *was* a very fat man.

18 And when he had finished offering the present, he sent away the people that bore the present.

Judges 3

19 But he himself turned again from the quarries that *were* by Gilgal, and said, I have a secret errand unto you, O king: who said, Keep silent. And all that stood by him went out from him.
20 And Ehud came to him; and he was sitting in a summer parlor, which he had for himself alone. And Ehud said, I have a message from God unto you. And he arose out of *his* seat.
21 And Ehud put forth his left hand, and took the dagger from his right thigh, and thrust it into his belly:
22 And the handle also went in after the blade; and the fat closed upon the blade, so that he could not draw the dagger out of his belly; and the dirt came out.
23 Then Ehud went forth through the porch, and shut the doors of the parlor upon him, and locked them.
24 When he had gone out, his servants came; and when they saw that, behold, the doors of the parlor *were* locked, they said, Surely he covers his feet in his summer chamber.
25 And they tarried till they were ashamed: and, behold, he opened not the doors of the parlor; therefore they took a key, and opened *them*: and, behold, their lord *was* fallen down dead on the earth.
26 And Ehud escaped while they tarried, and passed beyond the quarries, and escaped to Seirath.
27 And it came to pass, when he had come, that he blew a trumpet in the mountain of Ephraim, and the children of Israel went down with him from the mount, and he before them.
28 And he said to them, Follow after me: for Yahweh has delivered your enemies the Moabites into your hand. And they went down after him, and took the fords of *the* Jordan toward Moab, and permitted not a man to pass over.
29 And they slew of Moab at that time about ten thousand men, all stout, and all men of valor; and there escaped not a man.
30 So Moab was subdued that day under the hand of Israel. And the land had rest fourscore years.
31 ¶ And after him was Shamgar the son of Anath, which slew of the Philistines six hundred men with an ox goad: and he also delivered Israel.

Judges 4

4:1 ¶ And the children of Israel again did evil in the sight of Yahweh, when Ehud was dead.
2 And Yahweh sold them into the hand of Jabin king of Canaan, that reigned in Hazor; the captain of whose host *was* Sisera, which dwelt in Harosheth of the Gentiles.
3 And the children of Israel cried unto Yahweh: for he had nine hundred chariots of iron; and twenty years he mightily oppressed the children of Israel.
4 ¶ And Deborah, a prophetess, the wife of Lapidoth, she judged Israel at that time.
5 And she dwelt under the palm tree of Deborah between Ramah and Bethel in mount Ephraim: and the children of Israel came up to her for judgment.
6 And she sent and called Barak the son of Abinoam out of Kedeshnaphtali, and said to him, Has not Yahweh God of Israel commanded, *saying*, Go and draw toward mount Tabor, and take with you ten thousand men of the children of Naphtali and of the children of Zebulun?
7 And I will draw unto you to the river Kishon Sisera, the captain of Jabin's army, with his chariots and his multitude; and I will deliver him into your hand.
8 And Barak said to her, If you will go with me, then I will go: but if you will not go with me, *then* I will not go.
9 And she said, I will surely go with you: notwithstanding the journey that you take shall not be for your honor; for Yahweh shall sell Sisera into the hand of a woman. And Deborah arose, and went with Barak to Kedesh.
10 ¶ And Barak called Zebulun and Naphtali to Kedesh; and he went up with ten thousand men at his feet: and Deborah went up with him.
11 Now Heber the Kenite, *which was* of the children of Hobab the father-in-law of Moses, had severed himself from the Kenites, and pitched his tent unto the plain of Zaanaim, which *is* by Kedesh.
12 And they showed Sisera that Barak the son of Abinoam had gone up to mount Tabor.
13 And Sisera gathered together all his chariots, *even* nine hundred chariots of iron, and all the people that *were* with him, from Harosheth of the Gentiles to the river of Kishon.
14 And Deborah said to Barak, Up; for this *is* the day in which Yahweh has delivered Sisera into your hand: has not Yahweh gone out before you? So Barak went down from mount Tabor, and ten thousand men after him.
15 And Yahweh discomfited Sisera, and all *his* chariots, and all *his* host, with the edge of the sword before Barak; so that Sisera lighted down off *his* chariot, and fled away on his feet.
16 But Barak pursued after the chariots, and after the host, to Harosheth of the Gentiles: and all the host of Sisera fell upon the edge of the sword; *and* there was not a man left.
17 ¶ However Sisera fled away on his feet to the tent of Jael the wife of Heber the Kenite: for *there was* peace between Jabin the king of Hazor and the house of Heber the Kenite.
18 And Jael went out to meet Sisera, and said to him, Turn in, my lord, turn in to me; fear not. And when he had turned in unto her into the tent, she covered him with a mantle.
19 And he said to her, Give me, I pray you, a little water to drink; for I am thirsty. And she opened a bottle of milk, and gave him drink, and covered him.
20 Again he said to her, Stand in the door of the tent, and it shall be, when any man does come and inquire of you, and say, Is there any man here? that you shall say, No.
21 Then Jael Heber's wife took a nail of the tent, and took a hammer in her hand, and went softly to him, and smote the nail into his temples, and fastened it into the ground: for he was fast asleep and weary. So he died.
22 And, behold, as Barak pursued Sisera, Jael came out to meet him, and said to him, Come, and I will show you the

man whom you seek. And when he came into her *tent*, behold, Sisera lay dead, and the nail *was* in his temples.

23 So God subdued on that day Jabin the king of Canaan before the children of Israel.

24 And the hand of the children of Israel prospered, and prevailed against Jabin the king of Canaan, until they had destroyed Jabin king of Canaan.

Judges 5

5:1 ¶ Then sang Deborah and Barak the son of Abinoam on that day, saying,

2 Praise you Yahweh for the avenging of Israel, when the people willingly offered themselves.

3 Hear, O you kings; give ear, O you princes; I, *even* I, will sing unto Yahweh; I will sing *praise* to Yahweh God of Israel.

4 Yahweh, when you went out of Seir, when you marched out of the field of Edom, the earth trembled, and the heavens dropped, the clouds also dropped water.

5 The mountains melted from before Yahweh, *even* that Sinai from before Yahweh God of Israel.

6 ¶ In the days of Shamgar the son of Anath, in the days of Jael, the highways were unoccupied, and the travelers walked through byways.

7 *The inhabitants of* the villages ceased, they ceased in Israel, until that I Deborah arose, that I arose a mother in Israel.

8 They chose new gods; then *was* war in the gates: was there a shield or spear seen among forty thousand in Israel?

9 My heart *is* toward the governors of Israel, that offered themselves willingly among the people. Bless you Yahweh.

10 Speak, you that ride on white donkeys, you that sit in judgment, and walk by the way.

11 *They that are delivered* from the noise of archers in the places of drawing water, there shall they rehearse the righteous acts of Yahweh, *even* the righteous acts *toward the inhabitants* of his villages in Israel: then shall the people of Yahweh go down to the gates.

12 ¶ Awake, awake, Deborah: awake, awake, utter a song: arise, Barak, and lead your captivity captive, you son of Abinoam.

13 Then he made him that remains have dominion over the nobles among the people: Yahweh made me have dominion over the mighty.

14 Out of Ephraim *was there* a root of them against Amalek; after you, Benjamin, among your people; out of Machir came down governors, and out of Zebulun they that handle the pen of the writer.

15 And the princes of Issachar *were* with Deborah; even Issachar, and also Barak: he was sent on foot into the valley. For the divisions of Reuben *there were* great thoughts of heart.

16 Why stayed you among the sheepfolds, to hear the bleatings of the flocks? For the divisions of Reuben *there were* great searchings of heart.

17 Gilead stayed beyond *the* Jordan: and why did Dan remain in ships? Asher continued on the sea shore, and stayed in his landings.

18 Zebulun and Naphtali *were* a people *that* jeopardized their lives unto the death in the high places of the field.

19 The kings came *and* fought, then fought the kings of Canaan in Taanach by the waters of Megiddo; they took no gain of money.

20 They fought from heaven; the stars in their courses fought against Sisera.

21 The river of Kishon swept them away, that ancient river, the river Kishon. O my soul, you have trodden down strength.

22 Then were the horse hoofs broken by the means of the prancings, the prancings of their mighty ones.

23 Curse you Meroz, said the angel of Yahweh, curse you bitterly the inhabitants thereof; because they came not to the help of Yahweh, to the help of Yahweh against the mighty.

24 ¶ Blessed above women shall Jael the wife of Heber the Kenite be, blessed shall she be above women in the tent.

25 He asked water, *and* she gave *him* milk; she brought forth butter in a lordly dish.

26 She put her hand to the nail, and her right hand to the workmen's hammer; and with the hammer she smote Sisera, she smote off his head, when she had pierced and stricken through his temples.

27 At her feet he bowed, he fell, he lay down: at her feet he bowed, he fell: where he bowed, there he fell down dead.

28 The mother of Sisera looked out at a window, and cried through the lattice, Why is his chariot *so* long in coming? why tarry the wheels of his chariots?

29 Her wise ladies answered her, yes, she returned answer to herself,

30 Have they not found? have they *not* divided the prey; to every man a damsel *or* two; to Sisera a prey of diverse colors, a prey of diverse colors of needlework, of diverse colors of needlework on both sides, *fit* for the necks of *them that take* the spoil?

31 So let all your enemies perish, O Yahweh: but *let* them that love him *be* as the sun when he goes forth in his might. And the land had rest *for* forty years.

Judges 6

6:1 ¶ And the children of Israel did evil in the sight of Yahweh: and Yahweh delivered them into the hand of Midian *for* seven years.

2 And the hand of Midian prevailed against Israel: *and* because of the Midianites the children of Israel made them the dens which *are* in the mountains, and caves, and strong holds.

3 And *so* it was, when Israel had sown, that the Midianites came up, and the Amalekites, and the children of the east, even they came up against them;

4 And they encamped against them, and destroyed the increase of the earth, till you come unto Gaza, and left no sustenance for Israel, neither sheep, nor ox, nor donkey.

Judges 6

5 For they came up with their cattle and their tents, and they came as grasshoppers for multitude; *for* both they and their camels were without number: and they entered into the land to destroy it.

6 And Israel was greatly impoverished because of the Midianites; and the children of Israel cried unto Yahweh.

7 ¶ And it came to pass, when the children of Israel cried unto Yahweh because of the Midianites,

8 That Yahweh sent a prophet to the children of Israel, which said to them, Thus says Yahweh God of Israel, I brought you up from Egypt, and brought you forth out of the house of bondage;

9 And I delivered you out of the hand of the Egyptians, and out of the hand of all that oppressed you, and drove them out from before you, and gave you their land;

10 And I said to you, I *am* Yahweh your God; fear not the gods of the Amorites, in whose land you dwell: but you have not obeyed my voice.

11 ¶ And there came an angel of Yahweh, and sat under an oak which *was* in Ophrah, that *pertained* to Joash the Abiezrite: and his son Gideon threshed wheat by the winepress, to hide *it* from the Midianites.

12 And the angel of Yahweh appeared to him, and said to him, Yahweh *is* with you, you mighty man of valor.

13 And Gideon said to him, Oh my Lord, if Yahweh is with us, why then is all this befallen us? and where *are* all his miracles which our fathers told us of, saying, Did not Yahweh bring us up from Egypt? but now Yahweh has forsaken us, and delivered us into the hands of the Midianites.

14 And Yahweh looked upon him, and said, Go in this your might, and you shall save Israel from the hand of the Midianites: have not I sent you?

15 And he said to him, Oh my Lord, with what shall I save Israel? behold, my family *is* poor in Manasseh, and I *am* the least in my father's house.

16 And Yahweh said to him, Surely I will be with you, and you shall smite the Midianites as one man.

17 And he said to him, If now I have found grace in your sight, then show me a sign that you talk with me.

18 Depart not away, I pray you, until I come to you, and bring forth my present, and set *it* before you. And he said, I will tarry until you come again.

19 And Gideon went in, and made ready a kid, and unleavened cakes of an ephah of flour: the flesh he put in a basket, and he put the broth in a pot, and brought *it* out to him under the oak, and presented *it*.

20 And the angel of God said to him, Take the flesh and the unleavened cakes, and lay *them* upon this rock, and pour out the broth. And he did so.

21 Then the angel of Yahweh put forth the end of the staff that *was* in his hand, and touched the flesh and the unleavened cakes; and there rose up fire out of the rock, and consumed the flesh and the unleavened cakes. Then the angel of Yahweh departed out of his sight.

22 And when Gideon perceived that he *was* an angel of Yahweh, Gideon said, Alas, O Lord Yahweh! for because I have seen an angel of Yahweh face to face.

23 And Yahweh said to him, Peace *be* to you; fear not: you shall not die.

24 Then Gideon built an altar there unto Yahweh, and called it Yahweh-shalom: unto this day it *is* yet in Ophrah of the Abiezrites.

25 ¶ And it came to pass the same night, that Yahweh said to him, Take your father's young bullock, even the second bullock of seven years old, and throw down the altar of Baal that your father has, and cut down the grove that *is* by it:

26 And build an altar unto Yahweh your God upon the top of this rock, in the ordered place, and take the second bullock, and offer a burnt sacrifice with the wood of the grove which you shall cut down.

27 Then Gideon took ten men of his servants, and did as Yahweh had said to him: and *so* it was, because he feared his father's household, and the men of the city, that he could not do *it* by day, that he did *it* by night.

28 And when the men of the city arose early in the morning, behold, the altar of Baal was cast down, and the grove was cut down that *was* by it, and the second bullock was offered upon the altar *that was* built.

29 And they said one to another, Who has done this thing? And when they inquired and asked, they said, Gideon the son of Joash has done this thing.

30 Then the men of the city said to Joash, Bring out your son, that he may die: because he has cast down the altar of Baal, and because he has cut down the grove that *was* by it.

31 And Joash said to all that stood against him, Will you plead for Baal? will you save him? he that will plead for him, let him be put to death while *it is yet* morning: if he *is* a god, let him plead for himself, because *one* has cast down his altar.

32 Therefore on that day he called him Jerubbaal, saying, Let Baal plead against him, because he has thrown down his altar.

33 ¶ Then all the Midianites and the Amalekites and the children of the east were gathered together, and went over, and pitched in the valley of Jezreel.

34 But the Spirit of Yahweh came upon Gideon, and he blew a trumpet; and Abiezer was gathered after him.

35 And he sent messengers throughout all Manasseh; who also was gathered after him: and he sent messengers to Asher, and to Zebulun, and to Naphtali; and they came up to meet them.

36 And Gideon said to God, If you will save Israel by my hand, as you have said,

37 Behold, I will put a fleece of wool on the floor; *and* if the dew is on the fleece only, and *it is* dry upon all the earth *beside*, then shall I know that you will save Israel by my hand, as you have said.

38 And it was so: for he rose up early on the next day, and thrust the fleece together, and wrung the dew out of the fleece, a bowl full of water.

39 And Gideon said to God, Let not your anger be hot against me, and I will speak but this once: let me prove, I pray you, but this once with the fleece; let it now be dry only upon the fleece, and upon all the ground let there be dew.

40 And God did so that night: for it was dry upon the fleece only, and there was dew on all the ground.

Judges 7

7:1 ¶ Then Jerubbaal, who *is* Gideon, and all the people that *were* with him, rose up early, and pitched beside the well of Harod: so that the host of the Midianites were on the north side of them, by the hill of Moreh, in the valley.
2 And Yahweh said to Gideon, The people that *are* with you *are* too many for me to give the Midianites into their hands, lest Israel vaunt themselves against me, saying, My own hand has saved me.
3 Now therefore go to, proclaim in the ears of the people, saying, Whoever *is* fearful and afraid, let him return and depart early from mount Gilead. And there returned of the people twenty and two thousand; and there remained ten thousand.
4 And Yahweh said to Gideon, The people *are* yet too many; bring them down to the water, and I will try them for you there: and it shall be, *that* of whom I say to you, This shall go with you, the same shall go with you; and of whomever I say to you, This shall not go with you, the same shall not go.
5 So he brought down the people to the water: and Yahweh said to Gideon, Every one that laps of the water with his tongue, as a dog laps, him shall you set by himself; likewise every one that bows down upon his knees to drink.
6 And the number of them that lapped, *putting* their hand to their mouth, were three hundred men: but all the rest of the people bowed down upon their knees to drink water.
7 And Yahweh said to Gideon, By the three hundred men that lapped will I save you, and deliver the Midianites into your hand: and let all the *other* people go every man to his place.
8 So the people took provisions in their hand, and their trumpets: and he sent all *the rest of* Israel every man to his tent, and retained those three hundred men: and the host of Midian was beneath him in the valley.
9 ¶ And it came to pass the same night, that Yahweh said to him, Arise, get you down to the host; for I have delivered it into your hand.
10 But if you fear to go down, go you with Phurah your servant down to the host:
11 And you shall hear what they say; and afterward shall your hands be strengthened to go down to the host. Then went he down with Phurah his servant to the outside of the armed men that *were* in the host.
12 And the Midianites and the Amalekites and all the children of the east lay along in the valley like grasshoppers for multitude; and their camels *were* without number, as the sand by the sea side for multitude.
13 And when Gideon had come, behold, *there was* a man that told a dream to his fellow, and said, Behold, I dreamed a dream, and, lo, a cake of barley bread tumbled into the host of Midian, and came to a tent, and smote it that it fell, and overturned it, that the tent lay along.

14 And his fellow answered and said, This *is* nothing else save the sword of Gideon the son of Joash, a man of Israel: *for* into his hand has God delivered Midian, and all the host.
15 And it was *so*, when Gideon heard the telling of the dream, and the interpretation thereof, that he worshipped, and returned into the host of Israel, and said, Arise; for Yahweh has delivered into your hand the host of Midian.
16 ¶ And he divided the three hundred men *into* three companies, and he put a trumpet in every man's hand, with empty pitchers, and lamps within the pitchers.
17 And he said to them, Look on me, and do likewise: and, behold, when I come to the outside of the camp, it shall be *that*, as I do, so shall you do.
18 When I blow with a trumpet, I and all that *are* with me, then blow you the trumpets also on every side of all the camp, and say, *The sword* of Yahweh, and of Gideon.
19 So Gideon, and the hundred men that *were* with him, came to the outside of the camp in the beginning of the middle watch; and they had but newly set the watch: and they blew the trumpets, and broke the pitchers that *were* in their hands.
20 And the three companies blew the trumpets, and broke the pitchers, and held the lamps in their left hands, and the trumpets in their right hands to blow *therewith*: and they cried, The sword of Yahweh, and of Gideon.
21 And they stood every man in his place round about the camp: and all the host ran, and cried, and fled.
22 And the three hundred blew the trumpets, and Yahweh set every man's sword against his fellow, even throughout all the host and the host fled to Bethshittah in Zererath, *and* to the border of Abelmeholah, to Tabbath.
23 ¶ And the men of Israel gathered themselves together out of Naphtali, and out of Asher, and out of all Manasseh, and pursued after the Midianites.
24 And Gideon sent messengers throughout all mount Ephraim, saying, Come down against the Midianites, and take before them the waters to Bethbarah and *the* Jordan. Then all the men of Ephraim gathered themselves together, and took the waters to Bethbarah and *the* Jordan.
25 And they took two princes of the Midianites, Oreb and Zeeb; and they slew Oreb upon the rock Oreb, and Zeeb they slew at the winepress of Zeeb, and pursued Midian, and brought the heads of Oreb and Zeeb to Gideon on the other side *of the* Jordan.

Judges 8

8:1 ¶ And the men of Ephraim said to him, Why have you served us thus, that you called us not, when you went to fight with the Midianites? And they did chide with him sharply.
2 And he said to them, What have I done now in comparison of you? *Is* not the gleaning of the grapes of Ephraim better than the vintage of Abiezer?

Judges 8

3 God has delivered into your hands the princes of Midian, Oreb and Zeeb: and what was I able to do in comparison of you? Then their anger was abated toward him, when he had said that.

4 ¶ And Gideon came to the Jordan, and passed over, he, and the three hundred men that were with him, faint, yet pursuing them.

5 And he said to the men of Succoth, Give, I pray you, loaves of bread to the people that follow me; for they are faint, and I am pursuing after Zebah and Zalmunna, kings of Midian.

6 And the princes of Succoth said, Are the hands of Zebah and Zalmunna now in your hand, that we should give bread to your army?

7 And Gideon said, Therefore when Yahweh has delivered Zebah and Zalmunna into my hand, then I will tear your flesh with the thorns of the wilderness and with briers.

8 And he went up there to Penuel, and spoke to them likewise: and the men of Penuel answered him as the men of Succoth had answered him.

9 And he spoke also to the men of Penuel, saying, When I come again in peace, I will break down this tower.

10 Now Zebah and Zalmunna were in Karkor, and their hosts with them, about fifteen thousand men, all that were left of all the hosts of the children of the east: for there fell a hundred and twenty thousand men that drew the sword.

11 And Gideon went up by the way of them that dwelt in tents on the east of Nobah and Jogbehah, and smote the host: for the host was secure.

12 And when Zebah and Zalmunna fled, he pursued after them, and took the two kings of Midian, Zebah and Zalmunna, and discomfited all the host.

13 And Gideon the son of Joash returned from battle before the sun was up,

14 And caught a young man of the men of Succoth, and inquired of him: and he described to him the princes of Succoth, and the elders thereof, even threescore and seventeen men.

15 And he came to the men of Succoth, and said, Behold Zebah and Zalmunna, with whom you did upbraid me, saying, Are the hands of Zebah and Zalmunna now in your hand, that we should give bread to your men that are weary?

16 And he took the elders of the city, and thorns of the wilderness and briers, and with them he taught the men of Succoth.

17 And he beat down the tower of Penuel, and slew the men of the city.

18 ¶ Then said he to Zebah and Zalmunna, What manner of men were they whom you slew at Tabor? And they answered, As you are, so were they; each one resembled the children of a king.

19 And he said, They were my brothers, even the sons of my mother: as Yahweh lives, if you had saved them alive, I would not slay you.

20 And he said to Jether his firstborn, Up, and slay them. But the youth drew not his sword: for he feared, because he was yet a youth.

21 Then Zebah and Zalmunna said, Rise you, and fall upon us: for as the man is, so is his strength. And Gideon arose, and slew Zebah and Zalmunna, and took away the ornaments that were on their camels' necks.

22 ¶ Then the men of Israel said to Gideon, Rule you over us, both you, and your son, and your son's son also: for you have delivered us from the hand of Midian.

23 And Gideon said to them, I will not rule over you, neither shall my son rule over you: Yahweh shall rule over you.

24 And Gideon said to them, I would desire a request of you, that you would give me every man the earrings of his prey. (For they had golden earrings, because they were Ishmaelites.)

25 And they answered, We will willingly give them. And they spread a garment, and did cast therein every man the earrings of his prey.

26 And the weight of the golden earrings that he requested was a thousand and seven hundred shekels of gold; besides ornaments, and collars, and purple robes that were on the kings of Midian, and besides the chains that were about their camels' necks.

27 And Gideon made an ephod thereof, and put it in his city, even in Ophrah: and all Israel went there a whoring after it: which thing became a snare to Gideon, and to his house.

28 Thus was Midian subdued before the children of Israel, so that they lifted up their heads no more. And the country was in quietness for forty years in the days of Gideon.

29 ¶ And Jerubbaal the son of Joash went and dwelt in his own house.

30 And Gideon had threescore and ten sons of his body begotten: for he had many wives.

31 And his concubine that was in Shechem, she also bore him a son, whose name he called Abimelech.

32 And Gideon the son of Joash died in a good old age, and was buried in the sepulcher of Joash his father, in Ophrah of the Abiezrites.

33 And it came to pass, as soon as Gideon was dead, that the children of Israel turned again, and went a whoring after Baalim, and made Baalberith their god.

34 And the children of Israel remembered not Yahweh their God, who had delivered them out of the hands of all their enemies on every side:

35 Neither showed they kindness to the house of Jerubbaal, namely, Gideon, according to all the goodness which he had shown to Israel.

Judges 9

9:1 ¶ And Abimelech the son of Jerubbaal went to Shechem to his mother's brothers, and communed with them, and with all the family of the house of his mother's father, saying,

2 Speak, I pray you, in the ears of all the men of Shechem, Whether is better for you, either that all the sons of Jerubbaal, which are threescore and ten persons, reign over you, or that one reigns over you? remember also that I am your bone and your flesh.

3 And his mother's brothers spoke of him in the ears of all the men of Shechem all these words: and their hearts inclined to follow Abimelech; for they said, He *is* our brother.

4 And they gave him threescore and ten *pieces* of silver out of the house of Baalberith, with which Abimelech hired vain and reckless persons, which followed him.

5 And he went to his father's house at Ophrah, and slew his brothers the sons of Jerubbaal, *being* threescore and ten persons, upon one stone: notwithstanding yet Jotham the youngest son of Jerubbaal was left; for he hid himself.

6 And all the men of Shechem gathered together, and all the house of Millo, and went, and made Abimelech king, by the plain of the pillar that *was* in Shechem.

7 ¶ And when they told *it* to Jotham, he went and stood in the top of mount Gerizim, and lifted up his voice, and cried, and said to them, Listen to me, you men of Shechem, that God may listen to you.

8 The trees went forth *once* to anoint a king over them; and they said to the olive tree, Reign you over us.

9 But the olive tree said to them, Should I leave my fatness, with which by me they honor God and man, and go to be promoted over the trees?

10 And the trees said to the fig tree, Come you, *and* reign over us.

11 But the fig tree said to them, Should I forsake my sweetness, and my good fruit, and go to be promoted over the trees?

12 Then said the trees to the vine, Come you, *and* reign over us.

13 And the vine said to them, Should I leave my *new* wine, which cheers God and man, and go to be promoted over the trees?

14 Then said all the trees to the bramble, Come you, *and* reign over us.

15 And the bramble said to the trees, If in truth you anoint me king over you, *then* come *and* put your trust in my shadow: and if not, let fire come out of the bramble, and devour the cedars of Lebanon.

16 Now therefore, if you have done truly and sincerely, in that you have made Abimelech king, and if you have dealt well with Jerubbaal and his house, and have done to him according to the deserving of his hands;

17 (For my father fought for you, and adventured his life far, and delivered you out of the hand of Midian:

18 And you have risen up against my father's house this day, and have slain his sons, threescore and ten persons, upon one stone, and have made Abimelech, the son of his maidservant, king over the men of Shechem, because he *is* your brother;)

19 If you then have dealt truly and sincerely with Jerubbaal and with his house this day, *then* rejoice you in Abimelech, and let him also rejoice in you:

20 But if not, let fire come out from Abimelech, and devour the men of Shechem, and the house of Millo; and let fire come out from the men of Shechem, and from the house of Millo, and devour Abimelech.

21 And Jotham ran away, and fled, and went to Beer, and dwelt there, for fear of Abimelech his brother.

22 ¶ When Abimelech had reigned three years over Israel,

23 Then God sent an evil spirit between Abimelech and the men of Shechem; and the men of Shechem dealt treacherously with Abimelech:

24 That the cruelty *done* to the threescore and ten sons of Jerubbaal might come, and their blood be laid upon Abimelech their brother, which slew them; and upon the men of Shechem, which aided him in the killing of his brothers.

25 And the men of Shechem set liers in wait for him in the top of the mountains, and they robbed all that came along that way by them: and it was told *to* Abimelech.

26 And Gaal the son of Ebed came with his brethren, and went over to Shechem: and the men of Shechem put their confidence in him.

27 And they went out into the fields, and gathered their vineyards, and trod *the grapes*, and made merry, and went into the house of their god, and did eat and drink, and cursed Abimelech.

28 And Gaal the son of Ebed said, Who *is* Abimelech, and who *is* Shechem, that we should serve him? *is* not *he* the son of Jerubbaal? and Zebul his officer? serve the men of Hamor the father of Shechem: for why should we serve him?

29 And would to God this people were under my hand! then would I remove Abimelech. And he said to Abimelech, Increase your army, and come out.

30 And when Zebul the ruler of the city heard the words of Gaal the son of Ebed, his anger was kindled.

31 And he sent messengers to Abimelech privately, saying, Behold, Gaal the son of Ebed and his brethren have come to Shechem; and, behold, they fortify the city against you.

32 Now therefore up by night, you and the people that *are* with you, and lie in wait in the field:

33 And it shall be, *that* in the morning, as soon as the sun is up, you shall rise early, and set upon the city: and, behold, *when* he and the people that *are* with him come out against you, then may you do to them as you shall find occasion.

34 And Abimelech rose up, and all the people that *were* with him, by night, and they laid wait against Shechem in four companies.

35 And Gaal the son of Ebed went out, and stood in the entering of the gate of the city: and Abimelech rose up, and the people that *were* with him, from lying in wait.

36 And when Gaal saw the people, he said to Zebul, Behold, there come people down from the top of the mountains. And Zebul said to him, You see the shadow of the mountains as *if they were* men.

37 And Gaal spoke again and said, See there come people down by the middle of the land, and another company comes along by the plain of Meonenim.

38 Then said Zebul to him, Where *is* now your mouth, with which you said, Who *is* Abimelech, that we should serve him? *is* not this the people that you have despised? go out, I pray now, and fight with them.

Judges 9

39 And Gaal went out before the men of Shechem, and fought with Abimelech.
40 And Abimelech chased him, and he fled before him, and many were overthrown *and* wounded, *even* to the entering of the gate.
41 And Abimelech dwelt at Arumah: and Zebul thrust out Gaal and his brethren, that they should not dwell in Shechem.
42 And it came to pass on the next day, that the people went out into the field; and they told Abimelech.
43 And he took the people, and divided them into three companies, and laid wait in the field, and looked, and, behold, the people *were* coming forth out of the city; and he rose up against them, and smote them.
44 And Abimelech, and the company that *was* with him, rushed forward, and stood in the entering of the gate of the city: and the two *other* companies ran upon all *the* people that *were* in the fields, and slew them.
45 And Abimelech fought against the city all that day; and he took the city, and slew the people that *were* therein, and beat down the city, and sowed it with salt.
46 And when all the men of the tower of Shechem heard *that*, they entered into a hold of the house of the god Berith.
47 And it was told *to* Abimelech, that all the men of the tower of Shechem were gathered together.
48 And Abimelech got him up to mount Zalmon, he and all the people that *were* with him; and Abimelech took an ax in his hand, and cut down a bough from the trees, and took it, and laid *it* on his shoulder, and said to the people that *were* with him, What you have seen me do, make haste, *and* do as I *have* done.
49 And all the people likewise cut down every man his bough, and followed Abimelech, and put *them* to the hold, and set the hold on fire upon them; so that all the men of the tower of Shechem died also, about a thousand men and women.
50 ¶ Then went Abimelech to Thebez, and encamped against Thebez, and took it.
51 But there was a strong tower within the city, and there fled all the men and women, and all they of the city, and shut *it* to them, and got them up to the top of the tower.
52 And Abimelech came to the tower, and fought against it, and went hard to the door of the tower to burn it with fire.
53 And a certain woman cast a piece of a millstone upon Abimelech's head, and crushed his skull.
54 Then he called hastily to the young man his armor bearer, and said to him, Draw your sword, and slay me, that men say not of me, A woman slew him. And his young man thrust him through, and he died.
55 And when the men of Israel saw that Abimelech was dead, they departed every man to his place.
56 Thus God rendered the wickedness of Abimelech, which he did to his father, in slaying his seventy brothers:
57 And all the evil of the men of Shechem did God render upon their heads: and upon them came the curse of Jotham the son of Jerubbaal.

Judges 10

10:1 ¶ And after Abimelech there arose to defend Israel Tola the son of Puah, the son of Dodo, a man of Issachar; and he dwelt in Shamir in mount Ephraim.
2 And he judged Israel *for* twenty and three years, and died, and was buried in Shamir.
3 And after him arose Jair, a Gileadite, and judged Israel *for* twenty and two years.
4 And he had thirty sons that rode on thirty donkey colts, and they had thirty cities, which are called Havothjair unto this day, which *are* in the land of Gilead.
5 And Jair died, and was buried in Camon.
6 ¶ And the children of Israel did evil again in the sight of Yahweh, and served Baalim, and Ashtaroth, and the gods of Syria, and the gods of Zidon, and the gods of Moab, and the gods of the children of Ammon, and the gods of the Philistines, and forsook Yahweh, and served not him.
7 And the anger of Yahweh was hot against Israel, and he sold them into the hands of the Philistines, and into the hands of the children of Ammon.
8 And that year they vexed and oppressed the children of Israel: eighteen years, all the children of Israel that *were* on the other side *of the* Jordan in the land of the Amorites, which *is* in Gilead.
9 Moreover the children of Ammon passed over *the* Jordan to fight also against Judah, and against Benjamin, and against the house of Ephraim; so that Israel was greatly distressed.
10 ¶ And the children of Israel cried unto Yahweh, saying, We have sinned against you, both because we have forsaken our God, and also served Baalim.
11 And Yahweh said to the children of Israel, *Did* not *I deliver you* from the Egyptians, and from the Amorites, from the children of Ammon, and from the Philistines?
12 The Zidonians also, and the Amalekites, and the Maonites, did oppress you; and you cried to me, and I delivered you out of their hand.
13 Yet you have forsaken me, and served other gods: therefore I will deliver you no more.
14 Go and cry to the gods which you have chosen; let them deliver you in the time of your tribulation.
15 And the children of Israel said unto Yahweh, We have sinned: do you to us whatever seems good to you; deliver us only, we pray you, this day.
16 And they put away the strange gods from among them, and served Yahweh: and his soul was grieved for the misery of Israel.
17 Then the children of Ammon were gathered together, and encamped in Gilead. And the children of Israel assembled themselves together, and encamped in Mizpeh.
18 And the people *and* princes of Gilead said one to another, What man *is he* that will begin to fight against the children of Ammon? he shall be head over all the inhabitants of Gilead.

Judges 11

11:1 ¶ Now Jephthah the Gileadite was a mighty man of valor, and he *was* the son of a harlot: and Gilead begot Jephthah.

2 And Gilead's wife bore him sons; and his wife's sons grew up, and they thrust out Jephthah, and said to him, You shall not inherit in our father's house; for you *are* the son of a strange woman.

3 Then Jephthah fled from his brothers, and dwelt in the land of Tob: and there were gathered vain men to Jephthah, and went out with him.

4 ¶ And it came to pass in *the* process of time, that the children of Ammon made war against Israel.

5 And it was so, that when the children of Ammon made war against Israel, the elders of Gilead went to fetch Jephthah out of the land of Tob:

6 And they said to Jephthah, Come, and be our captain, that we may fight with the children of Ammon.

7 And Jephthah said to the elders of Gilead, Did not you hate me, and expel me out of my father's house? and why have you come to me now when you are in distress?

8 And the elders of Gilead said to Jephthah, Therefore we turn again to you now, that you may go with us, and fight against the children of Ammon, and be our head over all the inhabitants of Gilead.

9 And Jephthah said to the elders of Gilead, If you bring me home again to fight against the children of Ammon, and Yahweh delivers them before me, shall I be your head?

10 And the elders of Gilead said to Jephthah, Yahweh be witness between us, if we do not so according to your words.

11 Then Jephthah went with the elders of Gilead, and the people made him head and captain over them: and Jephthah uttered all his words before Yahweh in Mizpeh.

12 ¶ And Jephthah sent messengers to the king of the children of Ammon, saying, What have you to do with me, that you have come against me to fight in my land?

13 And the king of the children of Ammon answered to the messengers of Jephthah, Because Israel took away my land, when they came up out of Egypt, from Arnon even to Jabbok, and unto *the* Jordan: now therefore restore those *lands* again peaceably.

14 And Jephthah sent messengers again to the king of the children of Ammon:

15 And said to him, Thus says Jephthah, Israel took not away the land of Moab, nor the land of the children of Ammon:

16 But when Israel came up from Egypt, and walked through the wilderness unto the Red Sea, and came to Kadesh;

17 Then Israel sent messengers to the king of Edom, saying, Let me, I pray you, pass through your land: but the king of Edom would not listen *thereto*. And in like manner they sent to the king of Moab: but he would not *consent*: and Israel stayed in Kadesh.

18 Then they went along through the wilderness, and compassed the land of Edom, and the land of Moab, and came by the east side of the land of Moab, and pitched on the other side of Arnon, but came not within the border of Moab: for Arnon *was* the border of Moab.

19 And Israel sent messengers to Sihon king of the Amorites, the king of Heshbon; and Israel said to him, Let us pass, we pray you, through your land into my place.

20 But Sihon trusted not Israel to pass through his coast: but Sihon gathered all his people together, and pitched in Jahaz, and fought against Israel.

21 And Yahweh God of Israel delivered Sihon and all his people into the hand of Israel, and they smote them: so Israel possessed all the land of the Amorites, the inhabitants of that country.

22 And they possessed all the coasts of the Amorites, from Arnon even to Jabbok, and from the wilderness even to *the* Jordan.

23 So now Yahweh God of Israel has dispossessed the Amorites from before his people Israel, and should you possess it?

24 Will not you possess that which Chemosh your god gives you to possess? So whomever Yahweh our God shall drive out from before us, them will we possess.

25 And now *are* you anything better than Balak the son of Zippor, king of Moab? did he ever strive against Israel, or did he ever fight against them,

26 While Israel dwelt in Heshbon and her towns, and in Aroer and her towns, and in all the cities that *are* along by the coasts of Arnon, *for* three hundred years? why therefore did you not recover *them* within that time?

27 Therefore I have not sinned against you, but you do me wrong to war against me: Yahweh the Judge is judge this day between the children of Israel and the children of Ammon.

28 However the king of the children of Ammon listened not to the words of Jephthah which he sent him.

29 ¶ Then the Spirit of Yahweh came upon Jephthah, and he passed over Gilead, and Manasseh, and passed over Mizpeh of Gilead, and from Mizpeh of Gilead he passed over *to* the children of Ammon.

30 And Jephthah vowed a vow unto Yahweh, and said, If you shall without fail deliver the children of Ammon into my hands,

31 Then it shall be, that whatever comes forth of the doors of my house to meet me, when I return in peace from the children of Ammon, shall surely be Yahweh's, and I will offer it up for a burnt offering.

32 So Jephthah passed over to the children of Ammon to fight against them; and Yahweh delivered them into his hands.

33 And he smote them from Aroer, even till you come to Minnith, *even* twenty cities, and to the plain of the vineyards, with a very great slaughter. Thus the children of Ammon were subdued before the children of Israel.

34 And Jephthah came to Mizpeh to his house, and, behold, his daughter came out to meet him with tambourines and with dances: and she *was his* only child; besides her he had neither son nor daughter.

Judges 11

35 And it came to pass, when he saw her, that he tore his clothes, and said, Alas, my daughter! you have brought me very low, and you are one of them that troubles me: for I have opened my mouth unto Yahweh, and I cannot go back.
36 And she said to him, My father, *if* you have opened your mouth unto Yahweh, do to me according to that which has proceeded out of your mouth; forasmuch as Yahweh has taken vengeance for you of your enemies, *even* of the children of Ammon.
37 And she said to her father, Let this thing be done for me: let me alone two months, that I may go up and down upon the mountains, and bewail my virginity, I and my companions.
38 And he said, Go. And he sent her away *for* two months: and she went with her companions, and bewailed her virginity upon the mountains.
39 And it came to pass at the end of two months, that she returned to her father, who did with her *according* to his vow which he had vowed: and she knew no man. And it was a custom in Israel,
40 *That* the daughters of Israel went yearly to lament the daughter of Jephthah the Gileadite four days in a year.

Judges 12

12:1 ¶ And the men of Ephraim gathered themselves together, and went northward, and said to Jephthah, Why passed you over to fight against the children of Ammon, and did not call us to go with you? we will burn your house upon you with fire.
2 And Jephthah said to them, I and my people were at great strife with the children of Ammon; and when I called you, you delivered me not out of their hands.
3 And when I saw that you delivered *me* not, I put my life in my hands, and passed over against the children of Ammon, and Yahweh delivered them into my hand: why then have you come up to me this day, to fight against me?
4 Then Jephthah gathered together all the men of Gilead, and fought with Ephraim: and the men of Gilead smote Ephraim, because they said, You Gileadites *are* fugitives of Ephraim among the Ephraimites, *and* among the Manassites.
5 And the Gileadites took the passages of *the* Jordan before the Ephraimites: and it was *so*, that when those Ephraimites which were escaped said, Let me go over; that the men of Gilead said to him, *Are* you an Ephraimite? If he said, No;
6 Then said they to him, Say now Shibboleth: and he said Sibboleth: for he could not establish to pronounce *it* right. Then they took him, and slew him at the passages of *the* Jordan: and there fell at that time of the Ephraimites forty and two thousand.
7 And Jephthah judged Israel *for* six years. Then died Jephthah the Gileadite, and was buried in *one of* the cities of Gilead.
8 ¶ And after him Ibzan of Bethlehem judged Israel.
9 And he had thirty sons, and thirty daughters, *whom* he sent abroad, and took in thirty daughters from abroad for his sons. And he judged Israel *for* seven years.
10 Then died Ibzan, and was buried at Bethlehem.
11 And after him Elon, a Zebulonite, judged Israel; and he judged Israel *for* ten years.
12 And Elon the Zebulonite died, and was buried in Aijalon in the country of Zebulun.
13 And after him Abdon the son of Hillel, a Pirathonite, judged Israel.
14 And he had forty sons and thirty nephews, that rode on threescore and ten donkey colts: and he judged Israel *for* eight years.
15 And Abdon the son of Hillel the Pirathonite died, and was buried in Pirathon in the land of Ephraim, in the mount of the Amalekites.

Judges 13

13:1 ¶ And the children of Israel did evil again in the sight of Yahweh; and Yahweh delivered them into the hand of the Philistines *for* forty years.
2 And there was a certain man of Zorah, of the family of the Danites, whose name *was* Manoah; and his wife *was* barren, and bore not.
3 And the angel of Yahweh appeared to the woman, and said to her, Behold now, you *are* barren, and bear not: but you shall conceive, and bear a son.
4 Now therefore beware, I pray you, and drink not wine nor strong drink, and eat not any unclean *thing*:
5 For, lo, you shall conceive, and bear a son; and no razor shall come on his head: for the child shall be a Nazarite unto God from the womb: and he shall begin to deliver Israel out of the hand of the Philistines.
6 Then the woman came and told her husband, saying, A man of God came to me, and his countenance *was* like the countenance of an angel of God, very awesome: but I asked him not *from* where he *was*, neither told he me his name:
7 But he said to me, Behold, you shall conceive, and bear a son; and now drink no wine nor strong drink, neither eat any unclean *thing*: for the child shall be a Nazarite to God from the womb to the day of his death.
8 ¶ Then Manoah entreated Yahweh, and said, O my Lord, let the man of God which you did send come again to us, and teach us what we shall do to the child that shall be born.
9 And God listened to the voice of Manoah; and the angel of God came again to the woman as she sat in the field: but Manoah her husband *was* not with her.
10 And the woman made haste, and ran, and showed her husband, and said to him, Behold, the man has appeared to me, that came to me the *other* day.
11 And Manoah arose, and went after his wife, and came to the man, and said to him, *Are* you the man that spoke to the woman? And he said, I *am*.
12 And Manoah said, Now let your words come to pass. How shall we order the child, and *how* shall we do unto him?
13 And the angel of Yahweh said to Manoah, Of all that I said to the woman let her beware.

14 She may not eat of any *thing* that comes of the vine, neither let her drink wine or strong drink, nor eat any unclean *thing*: all that I commanded her let her observe.
15 ¶ And Manoah said to the angel of Yahweh, I pray you, let us detain you, until we shall have made ready a kid for you.
16 And the angel of Yahweh said to Manoah, Though you detain me, I will not eat of your bread: and if you shall offer a burnt offering, you must offer it unto Yahweh. For Manoah knew not that he *was* an angel of Yahweh.
17 And Manoah said to the angel of Yahweh, What *is* your name, that when your sayings come to pass we may do you honor?
18 And the angel of Yahweh said to him, Why ask you thus after my name, seeing it *is* secret?
19 So Manoah took a kid with a meat offering, and offered *it* upon a rock unto Yahweh: and *the angel* did wondrously; and Manoah and his wife looked on.
20 For it came to pass, when the flame went up toward heaven from off the altar, that the angel of Yahweh ascended in the flame of the altar. And Manoah and his wife looked on *it*, and fell on their faces to the ground.
21 But the angel of Yahweh did no more appear to Manoah and to his wife. Then Manoah knew that he *was* an angel of Yahweh.
22 And Manoah said to his wife, We shall surely die, because we have seen God.
23 But his wife said to him, If Yahweh were pleased to kill us, he would not have received a burnt offering and a meat offering at our hands, neither would he have shown us all these *things*, nor would as at this time have told us *such things* as these.
24 ¶ And the woman bore a son, and called his name Samson: and the child grew, and Yahweh blessed him.
25 And the Spirit of Yahweh began to move him at times in the camp of Dan between Zorah and Eshtaol.

Judges 14

14:1 ¶ And Samson went down to Timnath, and saw a woman in Timnath of the daughters of the Philistines.
2 And he came up, and told his father and his mother, and said, I have seen a woman in Timnath of the daughters of the Philistines: now therefore get her for me to wife.
3 Then his father and his mother said to him, *Is there* not a woman among the daughters of your brethren, or among all my people, that you go to take a wife of the uncircumcised Philistines? And Samson said to his father, Get her for me; for she pleases me well.
4 But his father and his mother knew not that it *was* of Yahweh, that he sought an occasion against the Philistines: for at that time the Philistines had dominion over Israel.
5 Then went Samson down, and his father and his mother, to Timnath, and came to the vineyards of Timnath: and, behold, a young lion roared against him.
6 And the Spirit of Yahweh came mightily upon him, and he split him as he would have split a kid, and *he* had nothing in his hand: but he told not his father or his mother what he had done.
7 And he went down, and talked with the woman; and she pleased Samson well.
8 And after a time he returned to take her, and he turned aside to see the carcass of the lion: and, behold, *there was* a swarm of bees and honey in the carcass of the lion.
9 And he took thereof in his hands, and went on eating, and came to his father and mother, and he gave them, and they did eat: but he told not them that he had taken the honey out of the carcass of the lion.
10 ¶ So his father went down to the woman: and Samson made there a feast; such as used the young men to do.
11 And it came to pass, when they saw him, that they brought thirty companions to be with him.
12 And Samson said to them, I will now put forth a riddle to you: if you can certainly declare it *to* me within the seven days of the feast, and find *it* out, then I will give you thirty sheets and thirty changes of garments:
13 But if you cannot declare *it to* me, then shall you give me thirty sheets and thirty changes of garments. And they said to him, Put forth your riddle, that we may hear it.
14 And he said to them, Out of the eater came forth meat, and out of the strong came forth sweetness. And they could not in three days expound the riddle.
15 And it came to pass on the seventh day, that they said to Samson's wife, Entice your husband, that he may declare to us the riddle, lest we burn you and your father's house with fire: have you called us to take that we have? *is it* not *so*?
16 And Samson's wife wept before him, and said, You do but hate me, and love me not: you have put forth a riddle to the children of my people, and have not told *it to* me. And he said to her, Behold, I have not told *it* my father nor my mother, and shall I tell *it* you?
17 And she wept before him the seven days, while their feast lasted: and it came to pass on the seventh day, that he told her, because she put pressure upon him: and she told the riddle to the children of her people.
18 And the men of the city said to him on the seventh day before the sun went down, What *is* sweeter than honey? and what *is* stronger than a lion? And he said to them, If you had not plowed with my heifer, you had not found out my riddle.
19 And the Spirit of Yahweh came upon him, and he went down to Ashkelon, and slew thirty men of them, and took their spoil, and gave changes of garments to them which expounded the riddle. And his anger was kindled, and he went up to his father's house.
20 But Samson's wife was *given* to his companion, whom he had used as his friend.

Judges 15

15:1 ¶ But it came to pass within a while after, in the time of wheat harvest, that Samson visited his wife with a kid; and he said, I will go in to my wife into the chamber. But her father would not permit him to go in.

Judges 15

2 And her father said, I truly thought that you had utterly hated her; therefore I gave her to your companion: *is* not her younger sister fairer than she? take her, I pray you, instead of her.

3 And Samson said concerning them, Now shall I be more blameless than the Philistines, though I do them a displeasure.

4 And Samson went and caught three hundred foxes, and took firebrands, and turned tail to tail, and put a firebrand in the midst between two tails.

5 And when he had set the brands on fire, he let *them* go into the standing corn of the Philistines, and burnt up both the shocks, and also the standing corn, with the vineyards *and* olives.

6 Then the Philistines said, Who has done this? And they answered, Samson, the son-in-law of the Timnite, because he had taken his wife, and given her to his companion. And the Philistines came up, and burnt her and her father with fire.

7 And Samson said to them, Though you have done this, yet will I be avenged of you, and after that I will cease.

8 And he smote them hip and thigh with a great slaughter: and he went down and dwelt in the top of the rock Etam.

9 ¶ Then the Philistines went up, and pitched in Judah, and spread themselves in Lehi.

10 And the men of Judah said, Why have you come up against us? And they answered, To bind Samson have we come up, to do to him as he has done to us.

11 Then three thousand men of Judah went to the top of the rock Etam, and said to Samson, Know you not that the Philistines *are* rulers over us? what *is* this *that* you have done to us? And he said to them, As they did to me, so have I done to them.

12 And they said to him, We have come down to bind you, that we may deliver you into the hands of the Philistines. And Samson said to them, Swear to me, that you will not fall upon me yourselves.

13 And they spoke to him, saying, No; but we will bind you fast, and deliver you into their hand: but surely we will not kill you. And they bound him with two new cords, and brought him up from the rock.

14 *And* when he came to Lehi, the Philistines shouted against him: and the Spirit of Yahweh came mightily upon him, and the cords that *were* upon his arms became as flax that was burnt with fire, and his bands loosed from off his hands.

15 And he found a new jawbone of a donkey, and put forth his hand, and took it, and slew a thousand men therewith.

16 And Samson said, With the jawbone of a donkey, heaps upon heaps, with the jaw of a donkey have I slain a thousand men.

17 And it came to pass, when he had made an end of speaking, that he cast away the jawbone out of his hand, and called that place Ramathlehi.

18 ¶ And he was very thirsty, and called on Yahweh, and said, You have given this great deliverance into the hands of your servant: and now shall I die for thirst, and fall into the hand of the uncircumcised?

19 But God broke open a hollow place that *was* in the jaw, and there came water there out; and when he had drunk, his spirit came again, and he revived: therefore he called the name thereof Enhakkore, which *is* in Lehi unto this day.

20 And he judged Israel in the days of the Philistines *for* twenty years.

Judges 16

16:1 ¶ Then went Samson to Gaza, and saw there a harlot, and went in unto her.

2 *And it was told to* the Gazites, saying, Samson has come here. And they encircled *him* in, and laid wait for him all night in the gate of the city, and were quiet all the night, saying, In the morning, when it is day, we shall kill him.

3 And Samson lay till midnight, and arose at midnight, and took the doors of the gate of the city, and the two posts, and went away with them, bar and all, and put *them* upon his shoulders, and carried them up to the top of a hill that *is* before Hebron.

4 ¶ And it came to pass afterward, that he loved a woman in the valley of Sorek, whose name *was* Delilah.

5 And the lords of the Philistines came up to her, and said to her, Entice him, and see wherein his great strength *lies*, and by what *means* we may prevail against him, that we may bind him to afflict him: and we will give you every one of us eleven hundred *pieces* of silver.

6 And Delilah said to Samson, Tell me, I pray you, wherein your great strength *lies*, and with what you might be bound to afflict you.

7 And Samson said to her, If they bind me with seven green cords that were never dried, then shall I be weak, and be as another man.

8 Then the lords of the Philistines brought up to her seven green cords which had not been dried, and she bound him with them.

9 Now *there were* men lying in wait, staying with her in the chamber. And she said to him, The Philistines *are* upon you, Samson. And he broke the cords, as a thread of flax is broken when it touches the fire. So his strength was not known.

10 And Delilah said to Samson, Behold, you have mocked me, and told me lies: now tell me, I pray you, with what you might be bound.

11 And he said to her, If they bind me fast with new ropes that never were occupied, then shall I be weak, and be as another man.

12 Delilah therefore took new ropes, and bound him therewith, and said to him, The Philistines *are* upon you, Samson. And *there were* liers in wait staying in the chamber. And he broke them from off his arms like a thread.

13 And Delilah said to Samson, Till now you have mocked me, and told me lies: tell me with what you might be bound. And he said to her, If you weave the seven locks of my head with the web.

14 And she fastened *it* with the pin, and said to him, The Philistines *are* upon you, Samson. And he awoke out of

his sleep, and went away with the pin of the beam, and with the web.

15 And she said to him, How can you say, I love you, when your heart *is* not with me? you have mocked me these three times, and have not told me wherein your great strength *lies*.

16 And it came to pass, when she pressed him daily with her words, and urged him, *so* that his soul was grieved unto death;

17 That he told her all his heart, and said to her, There has not come a razor upon my head; for I *have been* a Nazarite unto God from my mother's womb: if I am shaven, then my strength will go from me, and I shall become weak, and be like any *other* man.

18 ¶ And when Delilah saw that he had told her all his heart, she sent and called for the lords of the Philistines, saying, Come up this once, for he has shown me all his heart. Then the lords of the Philistines came up to her, and brought money in their hand.

19 And she made him sleep upon her knees; and she called for a man, and she caused him to shave off the seven locks of his head; and she began to afflict him, and his strength went from him.

20 And she said, The Philistines *are* upon you, Samson. And he awoke out of his sleep, and said, I will go out as at other times before, and shake myself. And he knew not that Yahweh had departed from him.

21 But the Philistines took him, and put out his eyes, and brought him down to Gaza, and bound him with fetters of brass; and he did grind in the prison house.

22 ¶ However the hair of his head began to grow again after he was shaven.

23 Then the lords of the Philistines gathered them together for to offer a great sacrifice to Dagon their god, and to rejoice: for they said, Our god has delivered Samson our enemy into our hands.

24 And when the people saw him, they praised their god: for they said, Our god has delivered into our hands our enemy, and the destroyer of our country, which slew many of us.

25 And it came to pass, when their hearts were merry, that they said, Call for Samson, that he may make us sport. And they called for Samson out of the prison house; and he made them laugh: and they set him between the pillars.

26 And Samson said to the lad that held him by the hand, Allow me that I may feel the pillars whereupon the house stands, that I may lean upon them.

27 Now the house was full of men and women; and all the lords of the Philistines *were* there; and *there were* upon the roof about three thousand men and women, that watched while Samson made sport.

28 And Samson called unto Yahweh, and said, O Lord Yahweh, remember me, I pray you, and strengthen me, I pray you, only this once, O God, that I may be at once avenged of the Philistines for my two eyes.

29 And Samson took hold of the two middle pillars upon which the house stood, and on which it was borne up, of the one with his right hand, and of the other with his left.

30 And Samson said, Let me die with the Philistines. And he bowed himself with *all his* might; and the house fell upon the lords, and upon all the people that *were* therein. So the dead which he slew at his death were more than *they* which he slew in his life.

31 Then his brethren and all the house of his father came down, and took him, and brought *him* up, and buried him between Zorah and Eshtaol in the burying place of Manoah his father. And he judged Israel *for* twenty years.

Judges 17

17:1 ¶ And there was a man of mount Ephraim, whose name *was* Micah.

2 And he said to his mother, The eleven hundred *shekels* of silver that were taken from you, about which you cursed, and spoke of also in my ears, behold, the silver *is* with me; I took it. And his mother said, Blessed *be you* of Yahweh, my son.

3 And when he had restored the eleven hundred *shekels* of silver to his mother, his mother said, I had wholly dedicated the silver unto Yahweh from my hand for my son, to make a graven image and a molten image: now therefore I will restore it to you.

4 Yet he restored the money to his mother; and his mother took two hundred *shekels* of silver, and gave them to the founder, who made thereof a graven image and a molten image: and they were in the house of Micah.

5 And the man Micah had a house of gods, and made an ephod, and teraphim, and consecrated one of his sons, who became his priest.

6 In those days *there was* no king in Israel, *but* every man did *that which was* right in his own eyes.

7 ¶ And there was a young man out of Bethlehemjudah of the family of Judah, who *was* a Levite, and he sojourned there.

8 And the man departed out of the city from Bethlehemjudah to sojourn where he could find *a place*: and he came to mount Ephraim to the house of Micah, as he journeyed.

9 And Micah said to him, Wherefrom come you? And he said to him, I *am* a Levite of Bethlehemjudah, and I go to sojourn where I may find *a place*.

10 And Micah said to him, Dwell with me, and be to me a father and a priest, and I will give you ten *shekels* of silver by the year, and a suit of apparel, and your victuals. So the Levite went in.

11 And the Levite was content to dwell with the man; and the young man was to him as one of his sons.

12 And Micah consecrated the Levite; and the young man became his priest, and was in the house of Micah.

13 Then said Micah, Now know I that Yahweh will do me good, seeing I have a Levite for *my* priest.

Judges 18

18:1 ¶ In those days *there was* no king in Israel: and in those days the tribe of the Danites sought them an inheritance to dwell in; for to that day *all their* inheritance had not fallen to them among the tribes of Israel.

2 And the children of Dan sent of their family five men from their coasts, men of valor, from Zorah, and from Eshtaol, to spy out the land, and to search it; and they said to them, Go, search the land: who when they came to mount Ephraim, to the house of Micah, they lodged there.

3 When they *were* by the house of Micah, they knew the voice of the young man the Levite: and they turned in there, and said to him, Who brought you here? and what do you in this *place*? and what have you here?

4 And he said to them, Thus and thus deals Micah with me, and has hired me, and I am his priest.

5 And they said to him, Ask counsel, we pray you, of God, that we may know whether our way which we go shall be prosperous.

6 And the priest said to them, Go in peace: before Yahweh *is* your way wherein you go.

7 ¶ Then the five men departed, and came to Laish, and saw the people that *were* therein, how they dwelt carelessly, after the manner of the Zidonians, quiet and secure; and *there was* no magistrate in the land, that might put *them* to shame in *any* thing; and they *were* far from the Zidonians, and had no business with *any* man.

8 And they came to their brethren to Zorah and Eshtaol: and their brethren said to them, What *say* you?

9 And they said, Arise, that we may go up against them: for we have seen the land, and, behold, it *is* very good: and *are* you still? be not slothful to go, *and* to enter to possess the land.

10 When you go, you shall come to a people secure, and to a large land: for God has given it into your hands; a place where *there is* no want of anything that *is* in the earth.

11 And there went from there of the family of the Danites, out of Zorah and out of Eshtaol, six hundred men appointed with weapons of war.

12 And they went up, and pitched in Kirjathjearim, in Judah: therefore they called that place Mahanehdan unto this day: behold, *it is* behind Kirjathjearim.

13 And they passed *from* there to mount Ephraim, and came to the house of Micah.

14 ¶ Then answered the five men that went to spy out the country of Laish, and said to their brethren, Do you know that there is in these houses an ephod, and teraphim, and a graven image, and a molten image? now therefore consider what you have to do.

15 And they turned toward there, and came to the house of the young man the Levite, *even* to the house of Micah, and saluted him.

16 And the six hundred men appointed with their weapons of war, which *were* of the children of Dan, stood by the entering of the gate.

17 And the five men that went to spy out the land went up, *and* came in there, *and* took the graven image, and the ephod, and the teraphim, and the molten image: and the priest stood in the entering of the gate with the six hundred men *that were* appointed with weapons of war.

18 And these went into Micah's house, and fetched the carved image, the ephod, and the teraphim, and the molten image. Then said the priest to them, What do you?

19 And they said to him, Hold your peace, lay your hand upon your mouth, and go with us, and be to us a father and a priest: *is it* better for you to be a priest to the house of one man, or that you be a priest to a tribe and a family in Israel?

20 And the priest's heart was glad, and he took the ephod, and the teraphim, and the graven image, and went in the midst of the people.

21 So they turned and departed, and put the little ones and the cattle and the carriage before them.

22 *And* when they were a good way from the house of Micah, the men that *were* in the houses near to Micah's house were gathered together, and overtook the children of Dan.

23 And they cried to the children of Dan. And they turned their faces, and said to Micah, What ails you, that you come with such a company?

24 And he said, You have taken away my gods which I made, and the priest, and you have gone away: and what have I more? and what *is* this *that* you say to me, What ails you?

25 And the children of Dan said to him, Let not your voice be heard among us, lest angry fellows run upon you, and you lose your life, with the lives of your household.

26 And the children of Dan went their way: and when Micah saw that they *were* too strong for him, he turned and went back to his house.

27 ¶ And they took *the things* which Micah had made, and the priest which he had, and came to Laish, to a people *that were* at peace and secure: and they smote them with the edge of the sword, and burnt the city with fire.

28 And *there was* no deliverer, because it *was* far from Zidon, and they had no business with *any* man; and it was in the valley that *lies* by Bethrehob. And they built a city, and dwelt therein.

29 And they called the name of the city Dan, after the name of Dan their father, who was born unto Israel: however the name of the city *was* Laish at the first.

30 And the children of Dan set up the graven image: and Jonathan, the son of Gershom, the son of Manasseh, he and his sons were priests to the tribe of Dan until the day of the captivity of the land.

31 And they set them up Micah's graven image, which he made, all the time that the house of God was in Shiloh.

Judges 19

19:1 ¶ And it came to pass in those days, when *there was* no king in Israel, that there was a certain Levite sojourning on the side of mount Ephraim, who took to him a concubine out of Bethlehemjudah.

2 And his concubine played the whore against him, and went away from him to her father's house to Bethlehemjudah, and was there four whole months.

3 And her husband arose, and went after her, to speak friendly to her, *and* to bring her again, having his servant with him, and a couple of donkeys: and she brought him into her father's house: and when the father of the damsel saw him, he rejoiced to meet him.

4 And his father-in-law, the damsel's father, retained him; and he stayed with him three days: so they did eat and drink, and lodged there.

5 And it came to pass on the fourth day, when they arose early in the morning, that he rose up to depart: and the damsel's father said to his son-in-law, Comfort your heart with a morsel of bread, and afterward go your way.

6 And they sat down, and did eat and drink both of them together: for the damsel's father had said to the man, Be content, I pray you, and tarry all night, and let your heart be merry.

7 And when the man rose up to depart, his father-in-law urged him: therefore he lodged there again.

8 And he arose early in the morning on the fifth day to depart: and the damsel's father said, Comfort your heart, I pray you. And they tarried until afternoon, and they did eat both of them.

9 And when the man rose up to depart, he, and his concubine, and his servant, his father-in-law, the damsel's father, said to him, Behold, now the day draws toward evening, I pray you tarry all night: behold, the day grows to an end, lodge here, that your heart may be merry; and tomorrow get you early on your way, that you may go home.

10 But the man would not tarry that night, but he rose up and departed, and came over against Jebus, which *is* Jerusalem; and *there were* with him two donkeys saddled, his concubine also *was* with him.

11 *And* when they *were* by Jebus, the day was far spent; and the servant said to his master, Come, I pray you, and let us turn in into this city of the Jebusites, and lodge in it.

12 And his master said to him, We will not turn aside here into the city of a stranger, that *is* not of the children of Israel; we will pass over to Gibeah.

13 And he said to his servant, Come, and let us draw near to one of these places to lodge all night, in Gibeah, or in Ramah.

14 And they passed on and went their way; and the sun went down upon them *when they were* by Gibeah, which *belongs* to Benjamin.

15 And they turned aside there, to go in *and* to lodge in Gibeah: and when he went in, he sat him down in a street of the city: for *there was* no man that took them into his house to lodge.

16 ¶ And, behold, there came an old man from his work out of the field at evening, which *was* also of mount Ephraim; and he sojourned in Gibeah: but the men of the place *were* Benjamites.

17 And when he had lifted up his eyes, he saw a wayfaring man in the street of the city: and the old man said, Where go you? and *from* where come you?

18 And he said to him, We *are* passing from Bethlehemjudah toward the side of mount Ephraim; from there *am* I: and I went to Bethlehemjudah, but I *am* now going to the house of Yahweh; and there *is* no man that receives me into *his* house.

19 Yet there is both straw and feed for our donkeys; and there is bread and wine also for me, and for your handmaid, and for the young man *which is* with your servants: *there is* no want of anything.

20 And the old man said, Peace *be* with you; however *let* all your wants *lie* upon me; only lodge not in the street.

21 So he brought him into his house, and gave feed to the donkeys: and they washed their feet, and did eat and drink.

22 ¶ *Now* as they were making their hearts merry, behold, the men of the city, certain sons of Belial, surrounded the house round about, *and* beat at the door, and spoke to the master of the house, the old man, saying, Bring forth the man that came into your house, that we may know him.

23 And the man, the master of the house, went out to them, and said to them, No, my brethren, *no*, I pray you, do not *so* wickedly; seeing that this man has come into my house, do not this disgrace.

24 Behold, *here is* my daughter a maiden, and his concubine; them I will bring out now, and humble you them, and do with them what seems good to you: but to this man do not so vile a thing.

25 But the men would not listen to him: so the man took his concubine, and brought her forth to them; and they knew her, and abused her all the night until the morning: and when the day began to spring, they let her go.

26 Then came the woman in the dawning of the day, and fell down at the door of the man's house where her lord *was*, till it was light.

27 And her lord rose up in the morning, and opened the doors of the house, and went out to go his way: and, behold, the woman his concubine was fallen down *at* the door of the house, and her hands *were* upon the threshold.

28 And he said to her, Up, and let us be going. But *there was* no answer. Then the man took her *up* upon a donkey, and the man rose up, and got him to his place.

29 And when he had come into his house, he took a knife, and laid hold on his concubine, and divided her, *together* with her bones, into twelve pieces, and sent her into all the coasts of Israel.

30 And it was so, that all that saw it said, There was no such deed done nor seen from the day that the children of Israel came up out of the land of Egypt unto this day: consider of it, take advice, and speak *your minds*.

Judges 20

20:1 ¶ Then all the children of Israel went out, and the congregation was gathered together as one man, from Dan even to Beersheba, with the land of Gilead, unto Yahweh in Mizpeh.

2 And the chief of all the people, *even* of all the tribes of Israel, presented themselves in the assembly of the people of God, four hundred thousand footmen that drew *the* sword.

Judges 20

3 (Now the children of Benjamin heard that the children of Israel had gone up to Mizpeh.) Then said the children of Israel, Tell *us*, how became this wickedness?
4 And the Levite, the husband of the woman that was slain, answered and said, I came into Gibeah that *belongs* to Benjamin, I and my concubine, to lodge.
5 And the men of Gibeah rose against me, and surrounded the house round about upon me by night, *and* thought to have slain me: and my concubine have they forced, *so* that she was dead.
6 And I took my concubine, and cut her in pieces, and sent her throughout all the country of the inheritance of Israel: for they have committed lewdness and disgrace in Israel.
7 Behold, you *are* all children of Israel; give here your advice and counsel.
8 And all the people arose as one man, saying, We will not any *of us* go to his tent, neither will we any *of us* turn into his house.
9 But now this *shall be* the thing which we will do to Gibeah; *we will go up* by lot against it;
10 And we will take ten men of a hundred throughout all the tribes of Israel, and a hundred of a thousand, and a thousand out of ten thousand, to fetch provisions for the people, that they may do, when they come to Gibeah of Benjamin, according to all the disgrace that they have committed in Israel.
11 So all the men of Israel were gathered against the city, knit together as one man.
12 ¶ And the tribes of Israel sent men through all the tribe of Benjamin, saying, What wickedness *is* this that is done among you?
13 Now therefore deliver *us* the men, the children of Belial, which *are* in Gibeah, that we may put them to death, and put away evil from Israel. But the children of Benjamin would not listen to the voice of their brethren the children of Israel:
14 But the children of Benjamin gathered themselves together out of the cities to Gibeah, to go out to battle against the children of Israel.
15 And the children of Benjamin were numbered at that time out of the cities twenty and six thousand men that drew *the* sword, besides the inhabitants of Gibeah, which were numbered seven hundred chosen men.
16 Among all this people *there were* seven hundred chosen men left handed; every one could sling stones at a hair's *breadth*, and not miss.
17 And the men of Israel, besides Benjamin, were numbered four hundred thousand men that drew *the* sword: all these *were* men of war.
18 ¶ And the children of Israel arose, and went up to the house of God, and asked counsel of God, and said, Which of us shall go up first to the battle against the children of Benjamin? And Yahweh said, Judah *shall go up* first.
19 And the children of Israel rose up in the morning, and encamped against Gibeah.
20 And the men of Israel went out to battle against Benjamin; and the men of Israel put themselves in array to fight against them at Gibeah.
21 And the children of Benjamin came forth out of Gibeah, and destroyed down to the ground of the Israelites that day twenty and two thousand men.
22 And the people the men of Israel encouraged themselves, and set their battle again in array in the place where they put themselves in array the first day.
23 (And the children of Israel went up and wept before Yahweh until evening, and asked counsel of Yahweh, saying, Shall I go up again to battle against the children of Benjamin my brother? And Yahweh said, Go up against him.)
24 And the children of Israel came near against the children of Benjamin the second day.
25 And Benjamin went forth against them out of Gibeah the second day, and destroyed down to the ground of the children of Israel again eighteen thousand men; all these drew the sword.
26 ¶ Then all the children of Israel, and all the people, went up, and came to the house of God, and wept, and sat there before Yahweh, and fasted that day until evening, and offered burnt offerings and peace offerings before Yahweh.
27 And the children of Israel inquired of Yahweh, (for the ark of the covenant of God *was* there in those days,
28 And Phinehas, the son of Eleazar, the son of Aaron, stood before it in those days,) saying, Shall I yet again go out to battle against the children of Benjamin my brother, or shall I cease? And Yahweh said, Go up; for tomorrow I will deliver them into your hand.
29 And Israel set liers in wait round about Gibeah.
30 And the children of Israel went up against the children of Benjamin on the third day, and put themselves in array against Gibeah, as at other times.
31 And the children of Benjamin went out against the people, *and* were drawn away from the city; and they began to smite of the people, *and* kill, as at other times, in the highways, of which one goes up to the house of God, and the other to Gibeah in the field, about thirty men of Israel.
32 And the children of Benjamin said, They *are* smitten down before us, as at the first. But the children of Israel said, Let us flee, and draw them from the city to the highways.
33 And all the men of Israel rose up out of their place, and put themselves in array at Baaltamar: and the liers in wait of Israel came forth out of their places, *even* out of the meadows of Gibeah.
34 And there came against Gibeah ten thousand chosen men out of all Israel, and the battle was great: but they knew not that evil *was* near them.
35 And Yahweh smote Benjamin before Israel: and the children of Israel destroyed of the Benjamites that day twenty and five thousand and a hundred men: all these drew the sword.
36 So the children of Benjamin saw that they were smitten: for the men of Israel gave place to the Benjamites, because they trusted to the liers in wait which they had set beside Gibeah.

37 And the liers in wait hurried, and rushed upon Gibeah; and the liers in wait drew *themselves* along, and smote all the city with the edge of the sword.
38 Now there was an appointed sign between the men of Israel and the liers in wait, that they should make a great flame with smoke rise up out of the city.
39 And when the men of Israel retired in the battle, Benjamin began to smite *and* kill of the men of Israel about thirty persons: for they said, Surely they are smitten down before us, as *in* the first battle.
40 But when the flame began to arise up out of the city with a pillar of smoke, the Benjamites looked behind them, and, behold, the flame of the city ascended up to heaven.
41 And when the men of Israel turned again, the men of Benjamin were amazed: for they saw that evil had come upon them.
42 Therefore they turned *their backs* before the men of Israel unto the way of the wilderness; but the battle overtook them; and them which *came* out of the cities they destroyed in the midst of them.
43 *Thus* they enclosed the Benjamites round about, *and* chased them, *and* trod them down with ease over against Gibeah toward the sunrising.
44 And there fell of Benjamin eighteen thousand men; all these *were* men of valor.
45 And they turned and fled toward the wilderness to the rock of Rimmon: and they gleaned of them in the highways five thousand men; and pursued hard after them to Gidom, and slew two thousand men of them.
46 So that all which fell that day of Benjamin were twenty and five thousand men that drew the sword; all these *were* men of valor.
47 But six hundred men turned and fled to the wilderness to the rock Rimmon, and stayed in the rock Rimmon four months.
48 And the men of Israel turned again upon the children of Benjamin, and smote them with the edge of the sword, as well the men of *every* city, as the beast, and all that came to hand: also they set on fire all the cities that they came to.

Judges 21

21:1 ¶ Now the men of Israel had sworn in Mizpeh, saying, There shall not any of us give his daughter to Benjamin to wife.
2 And the people came to the house of God, and stayed there till evening before God, and lifted up their voices, and wept greatly;
3 And said, O Yahweh God of Israel, why has this come to pass in Israel, that there should be today one tribe lacking in Israel?
4 And it came to pass on the next day, that the people rose early, and built there an altar, and offered burnt offerings and peace offerings.
5 And the children of Israel said, Who *is there* among all the tribes of Israel that came not up with the congregation unto Yahweh? For they had made a great oath concerning him that came not up to Yahweh to Mizpeh, saying, He shall surely be put to death.
6 And the children of Israel grieved themselves for Benjamin their brother, and said, There is one tribe cut off from Israel this day.
7 How shall we do for wives for them that remain, seeing we have sworn by Yahweh that we will not give them of our daughters as wives?
8 And they said, What one *is there* of the tribes of Israel that came not up to Mizpeh to Yahweh? And, behold, there came none to the camp from Jabeshgilead to the assembly.
9 For the people were numbered, and, behold, *there were* none of the inhabitants of Jabeshgilead there.
10 And the congregation sent there twelve thousand men of the most valiant, and commanded them, saying, Go and smite the inhabitants of Jabeshgilead with the edge of the sword, with the women and the children.
11 And this *is* the thing that you shall do, You shall utterly destroy every male, and every woman that has lain with *a* man.
12 And they found among the inhabitants of Jabeshgilead four hundred young virgins, that had known no man by lying with any male: and they brought them to the camp to Shiloh, which *is* in the land of Canaan.
13 And the whole congregation sent *some* to speak to the children of Benjamin that *were* in the rock Rimmon, and to call peaceably to them.
14 And Benjamin came again at that time; and they gave them wives which they had saved alive of the women of Jabeshgilead: and yet so they sufficed them not.
15 And the people repented them for Benjamin, because that Yahweh had made a breach in the tribes of Israel.
16 ¶ Then the elders of the congregation said, How shall we do for wives for them that remain, seeing the women are destroyed out of Benjamin?
17 And they said, *There must be* an inheritance for them that have escaped of Benjamin, that a tribe be not destroyed out of Israel.
18 However we may not give them wives of our daughters: for the children of Israel have sworn, saying, Cursed be he that gives a wife to Benjamin.
19 Then they said, Behold, *there is* a feast of Yahweh in Shiloh yearly *in a place* which *is* on the north side of Bethel, on the east side of the highway that goes up from Bethel to Shechem, and on the south of Lebonah.
20 Therefore they commanded the children of Benjamin, saying, Go and lie in wait in the vineyards;
21 And see, and, behold, if the daughters of Shiloh come out to dance in dances, then come you out of the vineyards, and catch you every man his wife of the daughters of Shiloh, and go to the land of Benjamin.
22 And it shall be, when their fathers or their brothers come to us to complain, that we will say to them, Be favorable to them for our sakes: because we reserved not to each man his wife in the war: for you did not give to them at this time, *that* you should be guilty.
23 And the children of Benjamin did so, and took *them* wives, according to their number, of them that danced,

Judges 21

whom they caught: and they went and returned to their inheritance, and repaired the cities, and dwelt in them.

24 And the children of Israel departed therefrom at that time, every man to his tribe and to his family, and they went out from there every man to his inheritance.

25 In those days *there was* no king in Israel: every man did *that which was* right in his own eyes.

Ruth

Ruth 1

1:1 ¶ Now it came to pass in the days when the judges ruled, that there was a famine in the land. And a certain man of Bethlehemjudah went to dwell in the country of Moab, he, and his wife, and his two sons.

2 And the name of the man *was* Elimelech, and the name of his wife Naomi, and the name of his two sons Mahlon and Chilion, Ephrathites of Bethlehemjudah. And they came into the country of Moab, and continued there.

3 And Elimelech Naomi's husband died; and she was left, and her two sons.

4 And they took them wives of the women of Moab; the name of the one *was* Orpah, and the name of the other Ruth: and they dwelt there about ten years.

5 And Mahlon and Chilion died also both of them; and the woman was left of her two sons and her husband.

6 ¶ Then she arose with her daughters-in-law, that she might return from the country of Moab: for she had heard in the country of Moab how that Yahweh had visited his people in giving them bread.

7 Therefore she went forth out of the place where she was, and her two daughters-in-law with her; and they went on the way to return to the land of Judah.

8 And Naomi said to her two daughters-in-law, Go, return each to her mother's house: Yahweh deal kindly with you, as you have dealt with the dead, and with me.

9 Yahweh grant you that you may find rest, each *of you* in the house of her husband. Then she kissed them; and they lifted up their voice, and wept.

10 And they said to her, Surely we will return with you to your people.

11 And Naomi said, Turn again, my daughters: why will you go with me? *are* there yet *any more* sons in my womb, that they may be your husbands?

12 Turn again, my daughters, go *your way*; for I am too old to have a husband. If I should say, I have hope, *if* I should have a husband also tonight, and should also bear sons;

13 Would you wait for them till they were grown? would you stay for them from having husbands? no, my daughters; for it grieves me much for your sakes that the hand of Yahweh has gone out against me.

14 And they lifted up their voice, and wept again: and Orpah kissed her mother-in-law; but Ruth clung to her.

15 And she said, Behold, your sister-in-law has gone back to her people, and to her gods: return you after your sister-in-law.

16 And Ruth said, Entreat me not to leave you, *or* to return from following after you: for where you go, I will go; and where you lodge, I will lodge: your people *shall be* my people, and your God my God:

17 Where you die, will I die, and there will I be buried: Yahweh do so to me, and more also, *if anything* but death part you and me.

18 When she saw that she was steadfastly minded to go with her, then she left speaking to her.

19 ¶ So they two went until they came to Bethlehem. And it came to pass, when they had come to Bethlehem, that all the city was moved about them, and they said, *Is* this Naomi?

20 And she said to them, Call me not Naomi, call me Mara: for the Almighty has dealt very bitterly with me.

21 I went out full, and Yahweh has brought me home again empty: why *then* call you me Naomi, seeing Yahweh has testified against me, and the Almighty has afflicted me?

22 So Naomi returned, and Ruth the Moabitess, her daughter-in-law, with her, which returned out of the country of Moab: and they came to Bethlehem in the beginning of barley harvest.

Ruth 2

2:1 ¶ And Naomi had a kinsman of her husband's, a mighty man of wealth, of the family of Elimelech; and his name *was* Boaz.

2 And Ruth the Moabitess said to Naomi, Let me now go to the field, and glean ears of corn after *him* in whose sight I shall find grace. And she said to her, Go, my daughter.

3 And she went, and came, and gleaned in the field after the reapers: and she happened to come upon a part of the field *belonging* to Boaz, who *was* of the kindred of Elimelech.

4 ¶ And, behold, Boaz came from Bethlehem, and said to the reapers, Yahweh *be* with you. And they answered him, Yahweh bless you.

5 Then said Boaz to his servant that was set over the reapers, Whose damsel *is* this?

6 And the servant that was set over the reapers answered and said, It *is* the Moabitish damsel that came back with Naomi out of the country of Moab:

7 And she said, I pray you, let me glean and gather after the reapers among the sheaves: so she came, and has continued even from the morning until now, that she tarried a little in the house.

8 Then said Boaz to Ruth, Hear you not, my daughter? Go not to glean in another field, neither go from here, but stay here close by my maidens:

9 *Let* your eyes *be* on the field that they do reap, and go you after them: have I not charged the young men that they shall not touch you? and when you are thirsty, go to the vessels, and drink of *that* which the young men have drawn.

10 Then she fell on her face, and bowed herself to the ground, and said to him, Why have I found grace in your eyes, that you should take knowledge of me, seeing I *am* a stranger?

11 And Boaz answered and said to her, It has fully been shown *to* me, all that you have done to your mother-in-law since the death of your husband: and *how* you have left your father and your mother, and the land of your birth, and have come to a people which you knew not before.

12 Yahweh repay your work, and a full reward be given *to* you from Yahweh God of Israel, under whose wings you have come to trust.

13 Then she said, Let me find favor in your sight, my lord; for that you have comforted me, and for that you have spoken friendly to your handmaid, though I am not like unto one of your handmaidens.

14 And Boaz said to her, At mealtime come you here, and eat of the bread, and dip your morsel in the vinegar. And she sat beside the reapers: and he reached her parched *corn*, and she did eat, and was satisfied, and left.

15 And when she had risen up to glean, Boaz commanded his young men, saying, Let her glean even among the sheaves, and reproach her not:

16 And let fall also *some* of the handfuls on purpose for her, and leave *them*, that she may glean *them*, and rebuke her not.

17 ¶ So she gleaned in the field until evening, and beat out that *which* she had gleaned: and it was about an ephah of barley.

18 And she took *it* up, and went into the city: and her mother-in-law saw what she had gleaned: and she brought forth, and gave to her that *which* she had reserved after she was satisfied.

19 And her mother-in-law said to her, Where have you gleaned today? and where worked you? blessed be he that did take knowledge of you. And she showed her mother-in-law with whom she had worked, and said, The man's name with whom I worked today *is* Boaz.

20 And Naomi said to her daughter-in-law, Blessed *be* he of Yahweh, who has not left off his kindness to the living and to the dead. And Naomi said to her, The man *is* near of kin to us, one of our next kinsmen.

21 And Ruth the Moabitess said, He said to me also, You shall keep close by my young men, until they have ended all my harvest.

22 And Naomi said to Ruth her daughter-in-law, *It is* good, my daughter, that you go out with his maidens, that they meet you not in any other field.

23 So she kept close by the maidens of Boaz to glean to the end of barley harvest and of wheat harvest; and dwelt with her mother-in-law.

Ruth 3

3:1 ¶ Then Naomi her mother-in-law said to her, My daughter, shall I not seek rest for you, that it may be well with you?

2 And now *is* not Boaz of our kindred, with whose maidens you were? Behold, he winnows barley tonight in the threshingfloor.

3 Wash yourself therefore, and anoint you, and put your clothing upon you, and get you down to the floor: *but* make not yourself known to the man, until he shall have finished eating and drinking.

4 And it shall be, when he lies down, that you shall mark the place where he shall lie, and you shall go in, and uncover his feet, and lay you down; and he will tell you what you shall do.

5 And she said to her, All that you say to me I will do.

6 ¶ And she went down to the floor, and did according to all that her mother-in-law told her.

7 And when Boaz had eaten and drunk, and his heart was merry, he went to lie down at the end of the heap of corn: and she came softly, and uncovered his feet, and laid herself down.

8 And it came to pass at midnight, that the man was afraid, and turned himself: and, behold, a woman lay at his feet.

9 And he said, Who *are* you? And she answered, I *am* Ruth your handmaid: spread therefore your skirt over your handmaid; for you *are* a near kinsman.

10 And he said, Blessed *be* you of Yahweh, my daughter: *for* you have shown more kindness in the latter end than at the beginning, inasmuch as you followed not young men, whether poor or rich.

11 And now, my daughter, fear not; I will do to you all that you require: for all the city of my people does know that you *are* a virtuous woman.

12 And now it is true that I *am your* near kinsman: however there is a kinsman nearer than I.

13 Tarry this night, and it shall be in the morning, *that* if he will perform to you the part of a kinsman, well; let him do the kinsman's part: but if he will not do the part of a kinsman to you, then will I do the part of a kinsman to you, *as* Yahweh lives: lie down until the morning.

14 ¶ And she lay at his feet until the morning: and she rose up before one could recognize another. And he said, Let it not be known that a woman came into the floor.

15 Also he said, Bring the veil that *you have* upon you, and hold it. And when she held it, he measured six *measures* of barley, and laid *it* on her: and she went into the city.

16 And when she came to her mother-in-law, she said, Who *are* you, my daughter? And she told her all that the man had done to her.

17 And she said, These six *measures* of barley gave he *to* me; for he said to me, Go not empty unto your mother-in-law.

18 Then said she, Sit still, my daughter, until you know how the matter will fall: for the man will not be in rest, until he has finished the matter this day.

Ruth 4

4:1 ¶ Then went Boaz up to the gate, and sat him down there: and, behold, the kinsman of whom Boaz spoke came by; to whom he said, Ho, such a one! turn aside, sit down here. And he turned aside, and sat down.

2 And he took ten men of the elders of the city, and said, Sit you down here. And they sat down.

3 And he said to the kinsman, Naomi, that has come again out of the country of Moab, sells a parcel of land, which *was* our brother Elimelech's:

4 And I thought to reveal *to* you, saying, Buy *it* before the inhabitants, and before the elders of my people. If you will redeem *it*, redeem *it*: but if you will not redeem *it, then* tell me, that I may know: for *there is* none to redeem *it* besides you; and I *am* after you. And he said, I will redeem *it*.

5 Then said Boaz, The day you buy the field of the hand of Naomi, you must buy *it* also from Ruth the Moabitess, the wife of the dead, to raise up the name of the dead upon his inheritance.

6 And the kinsman said, I cannot redeem *it* for myself, lest I mar my own inheritance: redeem you my right to yourself; for I cannot redeem *it*.

7 Now this *was the manner* in former time in Israel concerning redeeming and concerning changing, for to confirm all things; a man plucked off his shoe, and gave *it* to his neighbor: and this *was* a testimony in Israel.

8 Therefore the kinsman said to Boaz, Buy *it* for yourself. So he drew off his shoe.

9 ¶ And Boaz said to the elders, and *to* all the people, You *are* witnesses this day, that I have bought all that *was* Elimelech's, and all that *was* Chilion's and Mahlon's, from the hand of Naomi.

10 Moreover Ruth the Moabitess, the wife of Mahlon, have I purchased to be my wife, to raise up the name of the dead upon his inheritance, that the name of the dead be not cut off from among his brethren, and from the gate of his place: you *are* witnesses this day.

11 And all the people that *were* in the gate, and the elders, said, We *are* witnesses. Yahweh make the woman that has come into your house like Rachel and like Leah, which two did build the house of Israel: and do you worthily in Ephratah, and be famous in Bethlehem:

12 And let your house be like the house of Pharez, whom Tamar bore unto Judah, of the seed which Yahweh shall give you from this young woman.

13 ¶ So Boaz took Ruth, and she was his wife: and when he went in unto her, Yahweh gave her conception, and she bore a son.

14 And the women said to Naomi, Blessed *be* Yahweh, which has not left you this day without a kinsman, that his name may be famous in Israel.

15 And he shall be to you a restorer of *your* life, and a nourisher of your old age: for your daughter-in-law, which loves you, which is better to you than seven sons, has borne him.

16 And Naomi took the child, and laid it in her bosom, and became *a* nurse to it.

17 And the women her neighbors gave it a name, saying, There is a son born to Naomi; and they called his name Obed: he *is* the father of Jesse, the father of David.

18 Now these *are* the generations of Pharez: Pharez begot Hezron,

19 And Hezron begot Ram, and Ram begot Amminadab,

20 And Amminadab begot Nahshon, and Nahshon begot Salmon,

21 And Salmon begot Boaz, and Boaz begot Obed,

22 And Obed begot Jesse, and Jesse begot David.

1 Samuel

1 Samuel 1

1:1 ¶ Now there was a certain man of Ramathaimzophim, of mount Ephraim, and his name *was* Elkanah, the son of Jeroham, the son of Elihu, the son of Tohu, the son of Zuph, an Ephrathite:

2 And he had two wives; the name of the one *was* Hannah, and the name of the other Peninnah: and Peninnah had children, but Hannah had no children.

3 And this man went up out of his city yearly to worship and to sacrifice unto Yahweh of hosts in Shiloh. And the two sons of Eli, Hophni and Phinehas, the priests of Yahweh, *were* there.

4 And when the time came that Elkanah offered, he gave to Peninnah his wife, and to all her sons and her daughters, portions:

5 But to Hannah he gave a worthy portion; for he loved Hannah: but Yahweh had shut up her womb.

6 And her adversary also provoked her grief, for to make her fret, because Yahweh had shut up her womb.

7 And *as* he did so year by year, when she went up to the house of Yahweh, so she provoked her; therefore she wept, and did not eat.

8 Then said Elkanah her husband to her, Hannah, why weep you? and why eat you not? and why is your heart grieved? *am* not I better to you than ten sons?

9 ¶ So Hannah rose up after they had eaten in Shiloh, and after they had drunk. Now Eli the priest sat upon a seat by a post of the temple of Yahweh.

10 And she *was* in bitterness of soul, and prayed unto Yahweh, and wept tearfully.

11 And she vowed a vow, and said, O Yahweh of hosts, if you will indeed look upon the affliction of your handmaid, and remember me, and not forget your handmaid, but will give to your handmaid a man child, then I will give him unto Yahweh all the days of his life, and there shall no razor come upon his head.

12 And it came to pass, as she continued praying before Yahweh, that Eli observed her mouth.

13 Now Hannah, she spoke in her heart; only her lips moved, but her voice was not heard: therefore Eli thought she was drunk.

14 And Eli said to her, How long will you be drunk? put away your wine from you.

15 And Hannah answered and said, No, my lord, I *am* a woman of a sorrowful spirit: I have drunk neither wine nor strong drink, but have poured out my soul before Yahweh.

16 Count not your handmaid for a daughter of Belial: for out of the abundance of my complaint and grief have I spoken till now.

17 Then Eli answered and said, Go in peace: and the God of Israel grant *you* your petition that you have asked of him.

18 And she said, Let your handmaid find grace in your sight. So the woman went her way, and did eat, and her countenance was no more *sad*.

19 ¶ And they rose up in the morning early, and worshipped before Yahweh, and returned, and came to their house to Ramah: and Elkanah knew Hannah his wife; and Yahweh remembered her.

20 Therefore it came to pass, when the time had come about after Hannah had conceived, that she bore a son, and called his name Samuel, *saying*, Because I have asked him of Yahweh.

21 And the man Elkanah, and all his house, went up to offer unto Yahweh the yearly sacrifice, and his vow.

22 But Hannah went not up; for she said to her husband, *I will not go up* until the child is weaned, and *then* I will bring him, that he may appear before Yahweh, and there remain forever.

23 And Elkanah her husband said to her, Do what seems you good; tarry until you have weaned him; only Yahweh establish his word. So the woman stayed, and gave her son suck until she weaned him.

24 And when she had weaned him, she took him up with her, with three bullocks, and one ephah of flour, and a bottle of wine, and brought him to the house of Yahweh in Shiloh: and the child *was* young.

25 And they slew a bullock, and brought the child to Eli.

26 And she said, Oh my lord, *as* your soul lives, my lord, I *am* the woman that stood by you here, praying unto Yahweh.

27 For this child I prayed; and Yahweh has given me my petition which I asked of him:

28 Therefore also I have lent him to Yahweh; as long as he lives he shall be lent to Yahweh. And he worshipped Yahweh there.

1 Samuel 2

2:1 ¶ And Hannah prayed, and said, My heart rejoices in Yahweh, my horn is exalted in Yahweh: my mouth is enlarged over my enemies; because I rejoice in your salvation.

2 *There is* none holy as Yahweh: for *there is* none besides you: neither *is there* any rock like our God.

3 Talk no more so exceedingly proud; let *not* arrogance come out of your mouth: for Yahweh *is* a God of knowledge, and by him actions are weighed.

4 The bows of the mighty men *are* broken, and they that stumbled are girded with strength.

5 *They that were* full have hired out themselves for bread; and *they that were* hungry ceased: so that the barren has born seven; and she that has many children has grown feeble.

6 Yahweh kills, and makes alive: he brings down to the grave, and brings up.

7 Yahweh makes poor, and makes rich: he brings low, and lifts up.

8 He raises up the poor out of the dust, *and* lifts up the beggar from the dunghill, to set *them* among princes, and to make them inherit the throne of glory: for the pillars of the earth *are* Yahweh's, and he has set the world upon them.

9 He will keep the feet of his saints, and the wicked shall be silent in darkness; for by strength shall no man prevail.

10 The adversaries of Yahweh shall be broken to pieces; out of heaven shall he thunder upon them: Yahweh shall judge the ends of the earth; and he shall give strength to his king, and exalt the horn of his anointed.

11 ¶ And Elkanah went to Ramah to his house. And the child did minister unto Yahweh before Eli the priest.

12 Now the sons of Eli *were* sons of Belial; they knew not Yahweh.

13 And the priests' custom with the people *was, that*, when any man offered sacrifice, the priest's servant came, while the flesh was in seething, with a meat hook of three teeth in his hand;

14 And he struck *it* into the pan, or kettle, or caldron, or pot; all that the meat hook brought up the priest took for himself. So they did in Shiloh to all the Israelites that came there.

15 Also before they burnt the fat, the priest's servant came, and said to the man that sacrificed, Give flesh to roast for the priest; for he will not have boiled flesh of you, but raw.

16 And *if* any man said to him, Let them not fail to burn the fat presently, and *then* take *as* much as your soul desires; then he would answer him, *No*; but you shall give *it to me* now: and if not, I will take *it* by force.

17 Therefore the sin of the young men was very great before Yahweh: for men abhorred the offering of Yahweh.

18 But Samuel ministered before Yahweh, *being* a child, girded with a linen ephod.

19 Moreover his mother made him a little coat, and brought *it* to him from year to year, when she came up with her husband to offer the yearly sacrifice.

20 And Eli blessed Elkanah and his wife, and said, Yahweh give you seed of this woman for the loan which is lent to Yahweh. And they went to their own home.

21 And Yahweh visited Hannah, so that she conceived, and bore three sons and two daughters. And the child Samuel grew before Yahweh.

22 Now Eli was very old, and heard all that his sons did to all Israel; and how they lay with the women that assembled *at* the door of the tabernacle of the congregation.

23 And he said to them, Why do you such things? for I hear of your evil dealings by all this people.

1 Samuel 2

24 No, my sons; for *it is* no good report that I hear: you make Yahweh's people to transgress.
25 If one man sins against another, the judge shall judge him: but if a man sins against Yahweh, who shall intercede for him? Notwithstanding they listened not to the voice of their father, because Yahweh would slay them.
26 And the child Samuel grew on, and was in favor both with Yahweh, and also with men.
27 ¶ And there came a man of God to Eli, and said to him, Thus says Yahweh, Did I plainly appear to the house of your father, when they were in Egypt in Pharaoh's house?
28 And did I choose him out of all the tribes of Israel *to be* my priest, to offer upon my altar, to burn incense, to wear an ephod before me? and did I give to the house of your father all the offerings made by fire of the children of Israel?
29 Why kick you at my sacrifice and at my offering, which I have commanded *in my* habitation; and honor your sons above me, to make yourselves fat with the most chief of all the offerings of Israel my people?
30 Therefore Yahweh God of Israel says, I said indeed *that* your house, and the house of your father, should walk before me forever: but now Yahweh says, Be it far from me; for them that honor me I will honor, and they that despise me shall be lightly esteemed.
31 Behold, the days come, that I will cut off your arm, and the arm of your father's house, that there shall not be an old man in your house.
32 And you shall see an enemy *in my* dwelling place, in all *the wealth* which *God* shall give Israel: and there shall not be an old man in your house forever.
33 And the man of yours, *whom* I shall not cut off from my altar, *shall be* to consume your eyes, and to grieve your heart: and all the increase of your house shall die in the flower of their age.
34 And this *shall be* a sign to you, that shall come upon your two sons, on Hophni and Phinehas; in one day they shall die both of them.
35 And I will raise me up a faithful priest, *that* shall do according to *that* which *is* in my heart and in my mind: and I will build him a sure house; and he shall walk before my anointed forever.
36 And it shall come to pass, *that* every one that is left in your house shall come *and* bow to him for a piece of silver and a morsel of bread, and shall say, Put me, I pray you, into one of the priests' offices, that I may eat a piece of bread.

1 Samuel 3

3:1 ¶ And the child Samuel ministered unto Yahweh before Eli. And the word of Yahweh was precious in those days; *there was* no open vision.
2 And it came to pass at that time, when Eli *had* lain down in his place, and his eyes began to grow dim, *that* he could not see;
3 And before the lamp of God went out in the temple of Yahweh, where the ark of God *was*, and Samuel had lain down *to sleep*;
4 That Yahweh called Samuel: and he answered, Here *am* I.
5 And he ran to Eli, and said, Here *am* I; for you called me. And he said, I called not; lie down again. And he went and lay down.
6 And Yahweh called yet again, Samuel. And Samuel arose and went to Eli, and said, Here *am* I; for you did call me. And he answered, I called not, my son; lie down again.
7 Now Samuel did not yet know Yahweh, neither was the word of Yahweh yet revealed to him.
8 And Yahweh called Samuel again the third time. And he arose and went to Eli, and said, Here *am* I; for you did call me. And Eli perceived that Yahweh had called the child.
9 Therefore Eli said to Samuel, Go, lie down: and it shall be, if he calls you, that you shall say, Speak, Yahweh; for your servant hears. So Samuel went and lay down in his place.
10 And Yahweh came, and stood, and called as at other times, Samuel, Samuel. Then Samuel answered, Speak; for your servant hears.
11 ¶ And Yahweh said to Samuel, Behold, I will do a thing in Israel, at which both the ears of everyone that hears it shall tingle.
12 In that day I will perform against Eli all *things* which I have spoken concerning his house: when I begin, I will also make an end.
13 For I have told him that I will judge his house forever for the iniquity which he knows; because his sons made themselves vile, and he restrained them not.
14 And therefore I have sworn to the house of Eli, that the iniquity of Eli's house shall not be purged with sacrifice nor offering forever.
15 And Samuel lay until the morning, and opened the doors of the house of Yahweh. And Samuel feared to show Eli the vision.
16 Then Eli called Samuel, and said, Samuel, my son. And he answered, Here *am* I.
17 And he said, What *is* the thing that *Yahweh* has said to you? I pray you hide *it* not from me: God do so to you, and more also, if you hide *any* thing from me of all the things that he said to you.
18 And Samuel told him everything, and hid nothing from him. And he said, It *is* Yahweh: let him do what seems him good.
19 ¶ And Samuel grew, and Yahweh was with him, and did let none of his words fall to the ground.
20 And all Israel from Dan even to Beersheba knew that Samuel *was* established *to be* a prophet of Yahweh.
21 And Yahweh appeared again in Shiloh: for Yahweh revealed himself to Samuel in Shiloh by the word of Yahweh.

1 Samuel 4

4:1 ¶ And the word of Samuel came to all Israel. Now Israel went out against the Philistines to battle, and pitched beside Ebenezer: and the Philistines pitched in Aphek.

2 And the Philistines put themselves in array against Israel: and when they joined battle, Israel was smitten before the Philistines: and they slew of the army in the field about four thousand men.

3 And when the people had come into the camp, the elders of Israel said, Why has Yahweh smitten us today before the Philistines? Let us fetch the ark of the covenant of Yahweh out of Shiloh unto us, that, when it comes among us, it may save us out of the hand of our enemies.

4 So the people sent to Shiloh, that they might bring from there the ark of the covenant of Yahweh of hosts, which dwells *between* the cherubims: and the two sons of Eli, Hophni and Phinehas, *were* there with the ark of the covenant of God.

5 And when the ark of the covenant of Yahweh came into the camp, all Israel shouted with a great shout, so that the earth rang again.

6 And when the Philistines heard the noise of the shout, they said, What *means* the noise of this great shout in the camp of the Hebrews? And they understood that the ark of Yahweh had come into the camp.

7 And the Philistines were afraid, for they said, God has come into the camp. And they said, Woe unto us! for there has not been such a thing before.

8 Woe unto us! who shall deliver us out of the hand of these mighty Gods? these *are* the Gods that smote the Egyptians with all the plagues in the wilderness.

9 Be strong, and be yourselves like men, O you Philistines, that you be not servants to the Hebrews, as they have been to you: be yourselves like men, and fight.

10 ¶ And the Philistines fought, and Israel was smitten, and they fled every man into his tent: and there was a very great slaughter; for there fell of Israel thirty thousand footmen.

11 And the ark of God was taken; and the two sons of Eli, Hophni and Phinehas, were slain.

12 ¶ And there ran a man of Benjamin out of the army, and came to Shiloh the same day with his clothes torn, and with earth upon his head.

13 And when he came, lo, Eli sat upon a seat by the wayside watching: for his heart trembled for the ark of God. And when the man came into the city, and told *it*, all the city cried out.

14 And when Eli heard the noise of the crying, he said, What *means* the noise of this tumult? And the man came in hastily, and told Eli.

15 Now Eli was ninety and eight years old; and his eyes were dim, that he could not see.

16 And the man said to Eli, I *am* he that came out of the army, and I fled today out of the army. And he said, What is there done, my son?

17 And the messenger answered and said, Israel has fled before the Philistines, and there has been also a great slaughter among the people, and your two sons also, Hophni and Phinehas, are dead, and the ark of God was taken.

18 And it came to pass, when he made mention of the ark of God, that he fell from off the seat backward by the side of the gate, and his neck broke, and he died: for he was an old man, and heavy. And he had judged Israel *for* forty years.

19 ¶ And his daughter-in-law, Phinehas' wife, was with child, *near* to be delivered: and when she heard the tidings that the ark of God was taken, and that her father-in-law and her husband were dead, she bowed herself and labored; for her pains came upon her.

20 And about the time of her death the women that stood by her said to her, Fear not; for you have born a son. But she answered not, neither did she regard *it*.

21 And she named the child Ichabod, saying, The glory is departed from Israel: because the ark of God was taken, and because of her father-in-law and her husband.

22 And she said, The glory has departed from Israel: for the ark of God was taken.

1 Samuel 5

5:1 ¶ And the Philistines took the ark of God, and brought it from Ebenezer to Ashdod.

2 When the Philistines took the ark of God, they brought it into the house of Dagon, and set it by Dagon.

3 And when they of Ashdod arose early on the next day, behold, Dagon *had* fallen upon his face to the earth before the ark of Yahweh. And they took Dagon, and set him in his place again.

4 And when they arose early on the next day's morning, behold, Dagon *had* fallen upon his face to the ground before the ark of Yahweh; and the head of Dagon and both the palms of his hands *were* cut off upon the threshold; only *the stump of* Dagon was left to him.

5 Therefore neither the priests of Dagon, nor any that come into Dagon's house, tread on the threshold of Dagon in Ashdod unto this day.

6 ¶ But the hand of Yahweh was heavy upon them of Ashdod, and he destroyed them, and smote them with tumors, *even* Ashdod and the coasts thereof.

7 And when the men of Ashdod saw that *it was* so, they said, The ark of the God of Israel shall not remain with us: for his hand is severe upon us, and upon Dagon our god.

8 They sent therefore and gathered all the lords of the Philistines unto them, and said, What shall we do with the ark of the God of Israel? And they answered, Let the ark of the God of Israel be carried about to Gath. And they carried the ark of the God of Israel about *there*.

9 And it was *so*, that, after they had carried it about, the hand of Yahweh was against the city with a very great destruction: and he smote the men of the city, both small and great, and they had tumors in their secret parts.

10 Therefore they sent the ark of God to Ekron. And it came to pass, as the ark of God came to Ekron, that the Ekronites cried out, saying, They have brought about the ark of the God of Israel to us, to slay us and our people.

11 So they sent and gathered together all the lords of the Philistines and said, Send away the ark of the God of Israel, and let it go again to his own place, that it slay us

1 Samuel 5

not, and our people: for there was a deadly destruction throughout all the city; the hand of God was very heavy there.

12 And the men that died not were smitten with the tumors: and the cry of the city went up to heaven.

1 Samuel 6

6:1 ¶ And the ark of Yahweh was in the country of the Philistines *for* seven months.

2 And the Philistines called for the priests and the diviners, saying, What shall we do to the ark of Yahweh? tell us with what we shall send it to his place.

3 And they said, If you send away the ark of the God of Israel, send it not empty; but in any way return him a trespass offering: then you shall be healed, and it shall be known to you why his hand is not removed from you.

4 Then said they, What *shall be* the trespass offering which we shall return to him? They answered, Five golden tumors, and five golden mice, *according to* the number of the lords of the Philistines: for one plague *was* on you all, and on your lords.

5 Therefore you shall make images of your tumors, and images of your mice that mar the land; and you shall give glory to the God of Israel: perhaps he will lighten his hand from off you, and from off your gods, and from off your land.

6 Why then do you harden your hearts, as the Egyptians and Pharaoh hardened their hearts? when he had worked wonderfully among them, did they not let the people go, and they departed?

7 Now therefore make a new cart, and take two milk cows, on which there has come no yoke, and tie the cows to the cart, and bring their calves home from them:

8 And take the ark of Yahweh, and lay it upon the cart; and put the jewels of gold, which you return *to* him *for* a trespass offering, in a coffer by the side thereof; and send it away, that it may go.

9 And see, if it goes up by the way of his own coast to Bethshemesh, *then* he has done us this great evil: but if not, then we shall know that *it is* not his hand *that* smote us: it *was* a chance *that* happened to us.

10 ¶ And the men did so; and took two milk cows, and tied them to the cart, and shut up their calves at home:

11 And they laid the ark of Yahweh upon the cart, and the coffer with the mice of gold and the images of their tumors.

12 And the cows took the straight way to the way of Bethshemesh, *and* went along the highway, lowing as they went, and turned not aside *to* the right hand or *to* the left; and the lords of the Philistines went after them to the border of Bethshemesh.

13 And *they of* Bethshemesh *were* reaping their wheat harvest in the valley: and they lifted up their eyes, and saw the ark, and rejoiced to see *it*.

14 And the cart came into the field of Joshua, a Bethshemite, and stood there, where *there was* a great stone: and they split the wood of the cart, and offered the cows *as* a burnt offering unto Yahweh.

15 And the Levites took down the ark of Yahweh, and the coffer that *was* with it, wherein the jewels of gold *were*, and put *them* on the great stone: and the men of Bethshemesh offered burnt offerings and sacrificed sacrifices the same day unto Yahweh.

16 And when the five lords of the Philistines had seen *it*, they returned to Ekron the same day.

17 And these *are* the golden tumors which the Philistines returned *for* a trespass offering unto Yahweh; for Ashdod one, for Gaza one, for Askelon one, for Gath one, for Ekron one;

18 And the golden mice, *according to* the number of all the cities of the Philistines *belonging* to the five lords, *both* of fenced cities, and of country villages, even to the great *stone of* Abel, whereon they set down the ark of Yahweh: *which stone remains* unto this day in the field of Joshua, the Bethshemite.

19 ¶ And he smote the men of Bethshemesh, because they had looked into the ark of Yahweh, even he smote of the people fifty thousand and threescore and ten men: and the people lamented, because Yahweh had smitten *many* of the people with a great slaughter.

20 And the men of Bethshemesh said, Who is able to stand before this holy Yahweh God? and to whom shall he go up from us?

21 And they sent messengers to the inhabitants of Kirjathjearim, saying, The Philistines have brought again the ark of Yahweh; come you down, *and* fetch it up to you.

1 Samuel 7

7:1 ¶ And the men of Kirjathjearim came, and fetched up the ark of Yahweh, and brought it into the house of Abinadab in the hill, and sanctified Eleazar his son to keep the ark of Yahweh.

2 And it came to pass, while the ark stayed in Kirjathjearim, that the time was long; for it was twenty years: and all the house of Israel lamented after Yahweh.

3 ¶ And Samuel spoke to all the house of Israel, saying, If you do return unto Yahweh with all your hearts, *then* put away the strange gods and Ashtaroth from among you, and prepare your hearts unto Yahweh, and serve him only: and he will deliver you out of the hand of the Philistines.

4 Then the children of Israel did put away Baalim and Ashtaroth, and served Yahweh only.

5 And Samuel said, Gather all Israel to Mizpeh, and I will pray for you unto Yahweh.

6 And they gathered together to Mizpeh, and drew water, and poured *it* out before Yahweh, and fasted on that day, and said there, We have sinned against Yahweh. And Samuel judged the children of Israel in Mizpeh.

7 ¶ And when the Philistines heard that the children of Israel had gathered together to Mizpeh, the lords of the Philistines went up against Israel. And when the children of Israel heard *it*, they were afraid of the Philistines.

8 And the children of Israel said to Samuel, Cease not to cry unto Yahweh our God for us, that he will save us out of the hand of the Philistines.

9 And Samuel took a suckling lamb, and offered *it for* a burnt offering wholly unto Yahweh: and Samuel cried unto Yahweh for Israel; and Yahweh heard him.

10 And as Samuel was offering up the burnt offering, the Philistines drew near to battle against Israel: but Yahweh thundered with a great thunder on that day upon the Philistines, and troubled them; and they were smitten before Israel.

11 And the men of Israel went out of Mizpeh, and pursued the Philistines, and smote them, until *they came* under Bethcar.

12 Then Samuel took a stone, and set *it* between Mizpeh and Shen, and called the name of it Ebenezer, saying, Till now has Yahweh helped us.

13 ¶ So the Philistines were subdued, and they came no more into the coast of Israel: and the hand of Yahweh was against the Philistines all the days of Samuel.

14 And the cities which the Philistines had taken from Israel were restored to Israel, from Ekron even to Gath; and the coasts thereof did Israel deliver out of the hands of the Philistines. And there was peace between Israel and the Amorites.

15 And Samuel judged Israel all the days of his life.

16 And he went from year to year in circuit to Bethel, and Gilgal, and Mizpeh, and judged Israel in all those places.

17 And his return *was* to Ramah; for there *was* his house; and there he judged Israel; and there he built an altar unto Yahweh.

1 Samuel 8

8:1 ¶ And it came to pass, when Samuel was old, that he made his sons judges over Israel.

2 Now the name of his firstborn was Joel; and the name of his second, Abiah: *they were* judges in Beersheba.

3 And his sons walked not in his ways, but turned aside after profit, and took bribes, and perverted judgment.

4 ¶ Then all the elders of Israel gathered themselves together, and came to Samuel to Ramah,

5 And said to him, Behold, you are old, and your sons walk not in your ways: now make us a king to judge us like all the nations.

6 But the thing displeased Samuel, when they said, Give us a king to judge us. And Samuel prayed unto Yahweh.

7 And Yahweh said to Samuel, Listen to the voice of the people in all that they say to you: for they have not rejected you, but they have rejected me, that I should not reign over them.

8 According to all the works which they have done since the day that I brought them up out of Egypt even unto this day, with which they have forsaken me, and served other gods, so do they also to you.

9 Now therefore listen to their voice: however yet protest solemnly to them, and show them the manner of the king that shall reign over them.

10 And Samuel told all the words of Yahweh to the people that asked of him a king.

11 And he said, This will be the manner of the king that shall reign over you: He will take your sons, and appoint *them* for himself, for his chariots, and *to be* his horsemen; and *some* shall run before his chariots.

12 And he will appoint him captains over thousands, and captains over fifties; and *will set them* to plow his ground, and to reap his harvest, and to make his instruments of war, and instruments of his chariots.

13 And he will take your daughters *to be* confectioners, and *to be* cooks, and *to be* bakers.

14 And he will take your fields, and your vineyards, and your olive groves, *even* the best *of them*, and give *them* to his servants.

15 And he will take the tenth of your seed, and of your vineyards, and give to his officers, and to his servants.

16 And he will take your menservants, and your maidservants, and your best young men, and your donkeys, and put *them* to his work.

17 He will take the tenth of your sheep: and you shall be his servants.

18 And you shall cry out in that day because of your king which you shall have chosen you; and Yahweh will not hear you in that day.

19 Nevertheless the people refused to obey the voice of Samuel; and they said, No; but we will have a king over us;

20 That we also may be like all the nations; and that our king may judge us, and go out before us, and fight our battles.

21 And Samuel heard all the words of the people, and he rehearsed them in the ears of Yahweh.

22 And Yahweh said to Samuel, Listen to their voice, and make them a king. And Samuel said to the men of Israel, Go you every man to his city.

1 Samuel 9

9:1 ¶ Now there was a man of Benjamin, whose name *was* Kish, the son of Abiel, the son of Zeror, the son of Bechorath, the son of Aphiah, a Benjamite, a mighty man of power.

2 And he had a son, whose name *was* Saul, a choice young man, and goodly: and *there was* not among the children of Israel a better person than he: from his shoulders and upward *he was* higher than any of the people.

3 ¶ And the donkeys of Kish Saul's father were lost. And Kish said to Saul his son, Take now one of the servants with you, and arise, go seek the donkeys.

4 And he passed through mount Ephraim, and passed through the land of Shalisha, but they found *them* not: then they passed through the land of Shalim, and *there they were* not: and he passed through the land of the Benjamites, but they found *them* not.

5 *And* when they had come to the land of Zuph, Saul said to his servant that *was* with him, Come, and let us return; lest my father leaves *off caring* for the donkeys, and takes thought for us.

1 Samuel 9

6 And he said to him, Behold now, *there is* in this city a man of God, and *he is* an honorable man; all that he says comes surely to pass: now let us go there; perhaps he can show us our way that we should go.

7 Then said Saul to his servant, But, behold, *if* we go, what shall we bring the man? for the bread is spent in our vessels, and *there is* not a present to bring to the man of God: what have we?

8 And the servant answered Saul again, and said, Behold, I have here at hand the fourth part of a shekel of silver: *that* will I give to the man of God, to tell us our way.

9 (Before in Israel, when a man went to inquire of God, thus he spoke, Come, and let us go to the seer: for *he that is* now *called* a Prophet was before called a Seer.)

10 Then said Saul to his servant, Well said; come, let us go. So they went to the city where the man of God *was*.

11 ¶ *And* as they went up the hill to the city, they found young maidens going out to draw water, and said to them, Is the seer here?

12 And they answered them, and said, He is; behold, *he is* before you: make haste now, for he came today to the city; for *there is* a sacrifice of the people today in the high place:

13 As soon as you have come into the city, you shall surely find him, before he goes up to the high place to eat: for the people will not eat until he comes, because he does bless the sacrifice; *and* afterward they eat that are invited. Now therefore get you up; for about this time you shall find him.

14 And they went up into the city: *and* when they had come into the city, behold, Samuel came out against them, for to go up to the high place.

15 Now Yahweh had told Samuel in his ear a day before Saul came, saying,

16 Tomorrow about this time I will send you a man out of the land of Benjamin, and you shall anoint him *to be* captain over my people Israel, that he may save my people out of the hand of the Philistines: for I have looked upon my people, because their cry has come unto me.

17 And when Samuel saw Saul, Yahweh said to him, Behold the man whom I spoke to you of! this same shall reign over my people.

18 ¶ Then Saul drew near to Samuel in the gate, and said, Tell me, I pray you, where the seer's house *is*.

19 And Samuel answered Saul, and said, I *am* the seer: go up before me to the high place; for you shall eat with me today, and tomorrow I will let you go, and will tell you all that *is* in your heart.

20 And as for your donkeys that were lost three days ago, set not your mind on them; for they are found. And on whom *is* all the desire of Israel? *Is it* not on you, and on all your father's house?

21 And Saul answered and said, *Am* not I a Benjamite, of the smallest of the tribes of Israel? and my family least of all the families of the tribe of Benjamin? why then speak you so to me?

22 And Samuel took Saul and his servant, and brought them into the parlor, and made them sit in the most chief place among them that were invited, which *were* about thirty persons.

23 And Samuel said to the cook, Bring the portion which I gave you, of which I said to you, Set it by you.

24 And the cook took up the shoulder, and *that* which *was* upon it, and set *it* before Saul. And *Samuel* said, Behold that which is left! set *it* before you, *and* eat: for unto this time has it been kept for you since I said, I have invited the people. So Saul did eat with Samuel that day.

25 And when they had come down from the high place into the city, *Samuel* communed with Saul upon the top of the house.

26 And they arose early: and it came to pass about the spring of the day, that Samuel called Saul to the top of the house, saying, Up, that I may send you away. And Saul arose, and they went out both of them, he and Samuel, abroad.

27 *And* as they were going down to the end of the city, Samuel said to Saul, Bid the servant *to* pass on before us, (and he passed on,) but stand you still a while, that I may show you the word of God.

1 Samuel 10

10:1 ¶ Then Samuel took a vial of oil, and poured *it* upon his head, and kissed him, and said, *Is it* not because Yahweh has anointed you *to be* captain over his inheritance?

2 When you have departed from me today, then you shall find two men by Rachel's sepulcher in the border of Benjamin at Zelzah; and they will say to you, The donkeys which you went to seek are found: and, lo, your father has left the care of the donkeys, and sorrows for you, saying, What shall I do for my son?

3 Then shall you go on forward from there, and you shall come to the plain of Tabor, and there shall meet you three men going up to God to Bethel, one carrying three kids, and another carrying three loaves of bread, and another carrying a bottle of wine:

4 And they will salute you, and give you two *loaves* of bread; which you shall receive of their hands.

5 After that you shall come to the hill of God, where *is* the garrison of the Philistines: and it shall come to pass, when you have come there to the city, that you shall meet a company of prophets coming down from the high place with a psaltery, and a tambourine, and a pipe, and a harp, before them; and they shall prophesy:

6 And the Spirit of Yahweh will come upon you, and you shall prophesy with them, and shall be turned into another man.

7 And let it be, when these signs have come to you, *that* you do as *the* occasion serves you; for God *is* with you.

8 And you shall go down before me to Gilgal; and, behold, I will come down to you, to offer burnt offerings, *and* to sacrifice sacrifices of peace offerings: seven days shall you tarry, till I come to you, and show you what you shall do.

9 ¶ And it was *so*, that when he had turned his back to go from Samuel, God gave him another heart: and all those signs came to pass that day.

10 And when they came there to the hill, behold, a company of prophets met him; and the Spirit of God came upon him, and he prophesied among them.

11 And it came to pass, when all that knew him before saw that, behold, he prophesied among the prophets, then the people said one to another, What *is* this *that* has come unto the son of Kish? *Is* Saul also among the prophets?

12 And one of the same place answered and said, But who *is* their father? Therefore it became a proverb, *Is* Saul also among the prophets?

13 And when he had made an end of prophesying, he came to the high place.

14 And Saul's uncle said to him and to his servant, Where went you? And he said, To seek the donkeys: and when we saw that *they were* no where, we came to Samuel

15 And Saul's uncle said, Tell me, I pray you, what Samuel said to you.

16 And Saul said to his uncle, He told us plainly that the donkeys were found. But of the matter of the kingdom, whereof Samuel spoke, he told him not.

17 ¶ And Samuel called the people together unto Yahweh to Mizpeh;

18 And said to the children of Israel, Thus says Yahweh God of Israel, I brought up Israel out of Egypt, and delivered you out of the hand of the Egyptians, and out of the hand of all kingdoms, *and* of them that oppressed you:

19 And you have this day rejected your God, who himself saved you out of all your adversities and your tribulations; and you have said to him, *No*, but set a king over us. Now therefore present yourselves before Yahweh by your tribes, and by your thousands.

20 And when Samuel had caused all the tribes of Israel to come near, the tribe of Benjamin was taken.

21 When he had caused the tribe of Benjamin to come near by their families, the family of Matri was taken, and Saul the son of Kish was taken: and when they sought him, he could not be found.

22 Therefore they inquired of Yahweh further, if the man should yet come there. And Yahweh answered, Behold, he has hidden himself among the stuff.

23 And they ran and fetched him there: and when he stood among the people, he was higher than any of the people from his shoulders and upward.

24 And Samuel said to all the people, See you him whom Yahweh has chosen, that *there is* none like him among all the people? And all the people shouted, and said, God save the king.

25 Then Samuel told the people the manner of the kingdom, and wrote *it* in a book, and laid *it* up before Yahweh. And Samuel sent all the people away, every man to his house.

26 And Saul also went home to Gibeah; and there went with him a band of men, whose hearts God had touched.

27 But the children of Belial said, How shall this man save us? And they despised him, and brought him no presents. But he held his peace.

1 Samuel 11

11:1 ¶ Then Nahash the Ammonite came up, and encamped against Jabeshgilead: and all the men of Jabesh said to Nahash, Make a covenant with us, and we will serve you.

2 And Nahash the Ammonite answered them, On this *condition* will I make *a covenant* with you, that I may thrust out all your right eyes, and lay it *for* a reproach upon all Israel.

3 And the elders of Jabesh said to him, Give us seven days' respite, that we may send messengers to all the coasts of Israel: and then, if *there is* no man to save us, we will come out to you.

4 Then came the messengers to Gibeah of Saul, and told the tidings in the ears of the people: and all the people lifted up their voices, and wept.

5 ¶ And, behold, Saul came after the herd out of the field; and Saul said, What ails the people that they weep? And they told him the tidings of the men of Jabesh.

6 And the Spirit of God came upon Saul when he heard those tidings, and his anger was kindled greatly.

7 And he took a yoke of oxen, and hewed them in pieces, and sent *them* throughout all the coasts of Israel by the hands of messengers, saying, Whoever comes not forth after Saul and after Samuel, so shall it be done to his oxen. And the fear of Yahweh fell on the people, and they came out with one consent.

8 And when he numbered them in Bezek, the children of Israel were three hundred thousand, and the men of Judah thirty thousand.

9 And they said to the messengers that came, Thus shall you say to the men of Jabeshgilead, Tomorrow, by *that time* the sun is hot, you shall have help. And the messengers came and showed *it* to the men of Jabesh; and they were glad.

10 Therefore the men of Jabesh said, Tomorrow we will come out to you, and you shall do with us all that seems good to you.

11 And it was *so* on the next day, that Saul put the people in three companies; and they came into the midst of the host in the morning watch, and slew the Ammonites until the heat of the day: and it came to pass, that they which remained were scattered, so that two of them were not left together.

12 ¶ And the people said to Samuel, Who *is* he that said, Shall Saul reign over us? bring the men, that we may put them to death.

13 And Saul said, There shall not a man be put to death this day: for today Yahweh has worked salvation in Israel.

14 Then said Samuel to the people, Come, and let us go to Gilgal, and renew the kingdom there.

15 And all the people went to Gilgal; and there they made Saul king before Yahweh in Gilgal; and there they sacrificed sacrifices of peace offerings before Yahweh; and there Saul and all the men of Israel rejoiced greatly.

1 Samuel 12

12:1 ¶ And Samuel said to all Israel, Behold, I have listened to your voice in all that you said to me, and have made a king over you.

2 And now, behold, the king walks before you: and I am old and grayheaded; and, behold, my sons *are* with you: and I have walked before you from my childhood unto this day.

3 Behold, here I *am*: witness against me before Yahweh, and before his anointed: whose ox have I taken? or whose donkey have I taken? or whom have I defrauded? whom have I oppressed? or of whose hand have I received *any* bribe to blind my eyes therewith? and I will restore it you.

4 And they said, You have not defrauded us, nor oppressed us, neither have you taken anything of any man's hand.

5 And he said to them, Yahweh *is* witness against you, and his anointed *is* witness this day, that you have not found anything in my hand. And they answered, *He is* witness.

6 ¶ And Samuel said to the people, *It is* Yahweh that advanced Moses and Aaron, and that brought your fathers up out of the land of Egypt.

7 Now therefore stand still, that I may reason with you before Yahweh of all the righteous acts of Yahweh, which he did to you and to your fathers.

8 When Jacob had come into Egypt, and your fathers cried unto Yahweh, then Yahweh sent Moses and Aaron, which brought forth your fathers out of Egypt, and made them dwell in this place.

9 And when they forgot Yahweh their God, he sold them into the hand of Sisera, captain of the host of Hazor, and into the hand of the Philistines, and into the hand of the king of Moab, and they fought against them.

10 And they cried unto Yahweh, and said, We have sinned, because we have forsaken Yahweh, and have served Baalim and Ashtaroth: but now deliver us out of the hand of our enemies, and we will serve you.

11 And Yahweh sent Jerubbaal, and Bedan, and Jephthah, and Samuel, and delivered you out of the hand of your enemies on every side, and you dwelt safely.

12 And when you saw that Nahash the king of the children of Ammon came against you, you said to me, No; but a king shall reign over us: when Yahweh your God *was* your king.

13 Now therefore behold the king whom you have chosen, *and* whom you have desired! and, behold, Yahweh has set a king over you.

14 If you will fear Yahweh, and serve him, and obey his voice, and not rebel against the commandment of Yahweh, then shall both you and also the king that reigns over you continue following Yahweh your God:

15 But if you will not obey the voice of Yahweh, but rebel against the commandment of Yahweh, then shall the hand of Yahweh be against you, as *it was* against your fathers.

16 ¶ Now therefore stand and see this great thing, which Yahweh will do before your eyes.

17 *Is it* not wheat harvest today? I will call unto Yahweh, and he shall send thunder and rain; that you may perceive and see that your wickedness *is* great, which you have done in the sight of Yahweh, in asking you *for* a king.

18 So Samuel called unto Yahweh; and Yahweh sent thunder and rain that day: and all the people greatly feared Yahweh and Samuel.

19 And all the people said to Samuel, Pray for your servants unto Yahweh your God, that we die not: for we have added to all our sins *this* evil, to ask us *for* a king.

20 And Samuel said to the people, Fear not: you have done all this wickedness: yet turn not aside from following Yahweh, but serve Yahweh with all your heart;

21 And turn you not aside: for *then should you go* after vain *things*, which cannot profit nor deliver; for they *are* vain.

22 For Yahweh will not forsake his people for his great name's sake: because it has pleased Yahweh to make you his people.

23 Moreover as for me, God forbid that I should sin against Yahweh in ceasing to pray for you: but I will teach you the good and the right way:

24 Only fear Yahweh, and serve him in truth with all your heart: for consider how great *things* he has done for you.

25 But if you shall still do wickedly, you shall be consumed, both you and your king.

1 Samuel 13

13:1 ¶ Saul reigned one year; and when he had reigned two years over Israel,

2 Saul chose him three thousand *men* of Israel; *whereof* two thousand were with Saul in Michmash and in mount Bethel, and a thousand were with Jonathan in Gibeah of Benjamin: and the rest of the people he sent every man to his tent.

3 And Jonathan smote the garrison of the Philistines that *was* in Geba, and the Philistines heard *of it*. And Saul blew the trumpet throughout all the land, saying, Let the Hebrews hear.

4 And all Israel heard say *that* Saul had smitten a garrison of the Philistines, and *that* Israel also had become an abomination to the Philistines. And the people were called together after Saul to Gilgal.

5 And the Philistines gathered themselves together to fight with Israel, thirty thousand chariots, and six thousand horsemen, and people as the sand which *is* on the sea shore in multitude: and they came up, and pitched in Michmash, eastward from Bethaven.

6 When the men of Israel saw that they were in a bind, (for the people were distressed,) then the people did hide themselves in caves, and in thickets, and in rocks, and in high places, and in pits.

7 And *some of* the Hebrews went over *the* Jordan to the land of Gad and Gilead. As for Saul, he *was* yet in Gilgal, and all the people followed him trembling.

8 ¶ And he tarried seven days, according to the set time that Samuel *had appointed*: but Samuel came not to Gilgal; and the people were scattered from him.
9 And Saul said, Bring here a burnt offering to me, and peace offerings. And he offered the burnt offering.
10 And it came to pass, that as soon as he had made an end of offering the burnt offering, behold, Samuel came; and Saul went out to meet him, that he might salute him.
11 And Samuel said, What have you done? And Saul said, Because I saw that the people were scattered from me, and *that* you came not within the days appointed, and *that* the Philistines gathered themselves together at Michmash;
12 Therefore said I, The Philistines will come down now upon me to Gilgal, and I have not made supplication unto Yahweh: I forced myself therefore, and offered a burnt offering.
13 And Samuel said to Saul, You have done foolishly: you have not kept the commandment of Yahweh your God, which he commanded you: for now would Yahweh have established your kingdom upon Israel forever.
14 But now your kingdom shall not continue: Yahweh has sought him a man after his own heart, and Yahweh has commanded him *to be* captain over his people, because you have not kept *that* which Yahweh commanded you.
15 ¶ And Samuel arose, and got him up from Gilgal to Gibeah of Benjamin. And Saul numbered the people *that were* present with him, about six hundred men.
16 And Saul, and Jonathan his son, and the people *that were* present with them, stayed in Gibeah of Benjamin: but the Philistines encamped in Michmash.
17 And the spoilers came out of the camp of the Philistines in three companies: one company turned to the way *that leads to* Ophrah, to the land of Shual:
18 And another company turned the way *to* Bethhoron: and another company turned *to* the way of the border that looked to the valley of Zeboim toward the wilderness
19 Now there was no smith found throughout all the land of Israel: for the Philistines said, Lest the Hebrews make *them* swords or spears:
20 But all the Israelites went down to the Philistines, to sharpen every man his share, and his coulter, and his ax, and his mattock.
21 Yet they had a file for the mattocks, and for the coulters, and for the forks, and for the axes, and to sharpen the goads.
22 So it came to pass in the day of battle, that there was neither sword nor spear found in the hand of any of the people that *were* with Saul and Jonathan: but with Saul and with Jonathan his son was there found.
23 And the garrison of the Philistines went out to the passage of Michmash.

1 Samuel 14

14:1 ¶ Now it came to pass upon a day, that Jonathan the son of Saul said to the young man that bore his armor, Come, and let us go over to the Philistines' garrison, that *is* on the other side. But he told not his father.
2 And Saul tarried in the utmost part of Gibeah under a pomegranate tree which *is* in Migron: and the people that *were* with him *were* about six hundred men;
3 And Ahiah, the son of Ahitub, Ichabod's brother, the son of Phinehas, the son of Eli, Yahweh's priest in Shiloh, wearing an ephod. And the people knew not that Jonathan was gone.
4 And between the passages, by which Jonathan sought to go over to the Philistines' garrison, *there was* a sharp rock on the one side, and a sharp rock on the other side: and the name of the one *was* Bozez, and the name of the other Seneh.
5 The forefront of the one *was* situated northward over against Michmash, and the other southward over against Gibeah.
6 And Jonathan said to the young man that bore his armor, Come, and let us go over to the garrison of these uncircumcised: it may be that Yahweh will work for us: for *there is* no restraint to Yahweh to save by many or by few.
7 And his armor bearer said to him, Do all that *is* in your heart: turn you; behold, I *am* with you according to your heart.
8 Then said Jonathan, Behold, we will pass over to *these* men, and we will show ourselves to them.
9 If they say thus to us, Tarry until we come to you; then we will stand still in our place, and will not go up to them.
10 But if they say thus, Come up to us; then we will go up: for Yahweh has delivered them into our hand: and this *shall be* a sign to us.
11 And both of them showed themselves to the garrison of the Philistines: and the Philistines said, Behold, the Hebrews come forth out of the holes where they have hidden themselves.
12 And the men of the garrison answered Jonathan and his armor bearer, and said, Come up to us, and we will show you a thing. And Jonathan said to his armor bearer, Come up after me: for Yahweh has delivered them into the hand of Israel.
13 And Jonathan climbed up upon his hands and upon his feet, and his armor bearer after him: and they fell before Jonathan; and his armor bearer slew behind him.
14 And that first slaughter, which Jonathan and his armor bearer made, was about twenty men, within as it were a half acre of land, *which* a yoke *of oxen might plow*.
15 And there was trembling in the host, in the field, and among all the people: the garrison, and the spoilers, they also trembled, and the earth quaked: so it was a very great trembling.
16 ¶ And the watchmen of Saul in Gibeah of Benjamin looked; and, behold, the multitude melted away, and they went on beating down *one another*.
17 Then said Saul to the people that *were* with him, Number now, and see who is gone from us. And when they had numbered, behold, Jonathan and his armor bearer *were* not *there*.

1 Samuel 14

18 And Saul said to Ahiah, Bring here the ark of God. For the ark of God was at that time with the children of Israel.

19 And it came to pass, while Saul talked to the priest, that the noise that *was* in the host of the Philistines went on and increased: and Saul said to the priest, Withdraw your hand.

20 And Saul and all the people that *were* with him assembled themselves, and they came to the battle: and, behold, every man's sword was against his fellow, *and there was* a very great confusion.

21 Moreover the Hebrews *that* were with the Philistines before that time, which went up with them into the camp *from the country* round about, even they also *turned* to be with the Israelites that *were* with Saul and Jonathan.

22 Likewise all the men of Israel which had hidden themselves in mount Ephraim, *when* they heard that the Philistines fled, even they also followed hard after them in the battle.

23 So Yahweh saved Israel that day: and the battle passed over to Bethaven.

24 ¶ And the men of Israel were distressed that day: for Saul had adjured the people, saying, Cursed *is* the man that eats *any* food until evening, that I may be avenged on my enemies. So none of the people tasted *any* food.

25 And all *they of* the land came to a woods; and there was honey upon the ground.

26 And when the people had come into the woods, behold, the honey dropped; but no man put his hand to his mouth: for the people feared the oath.

27 But Jonathan heard not when his father charged the people with the oath: therefore he put forth the end of the rod that *was* in his hand, and dipped it in a honeycomb, and put his hand to his mouth; and his eyes were enlightened.

28 Then answered one of the people, and said, Your father straightly charged the people with an oath, saying, Cursed *is* the man that eats *any* food this day. And the people were faint.

29 Then said Jonathan, My father has troubled the land: see, I pray you, how my eyes have been enlightened, because I tasted a little of this honey.

30 How much more, if only the people had eaten freely today of the spoil of their enemies which they found? for had there not been now a much greater slaughter among the Philistines?

31 And they smote the Philistines that day from Michmash to Aijalon: and the people were very faint.

32 And the people flew upon the spoil, and took sheep, and oxen, and calves, and slew *them* on the ground: and the people did eat *them* with the blood.

33 Then they told Saul, saying, Behold, the people sin against Yahweh, in that they eat with the blood. And he said, You have transgressed: roll a great stone unto me this day.

34 And Saul said, Disperse yourselves among the people, and say to them, Bring me here every man his ox, and every man his sheep, and slay *them* here, and eat; and sin not against Yahweh in eating with the blood. And all the people brought every man his ox with him that night, and slew *them* there.

35 And Saul built an altar unto Yahweh: the same was the first altar that he built unto Yahweh.

36 ¶ And Saul said, Let us go down after the Philistines by night, and spoil them until the morning light, and let us not leave a man of them. And they said, Do whatever seems good to you. Then said the priest, Let us draw near here unto God.

37 And Saul asked counsel of God, Shall I go down after the Philistines? will you deliver them into the hand of Israel? But he answered him not that day.

38 And Saul said, Draw you near here, all the chief of the people: and know and see wherein this sin has been this day.

39 For, *as* Yahweh lives, which saves Israel, though it be in Jonathan my son, he shall surely die. But *there was* not a man among all the people *that* answered him.

40 Then said he to all Israel, Be you on one side, and I and Jonathan my son will be on the other side. And the people said to Saul, Do what seems good to you.

41 Therefore Saul said unto Yahweh God of Israel, Give a perfect *lot*. And Saul and Jonathan were taken: but the people escaped.

42 And Saul said, Cast *lots* between me and Jonathan my son. And Jonathan was taken.

43 Then Saul said to Jonathan, Tell me what you have done. And Jonathan told him, and said, I did but taste a little honey with the end of the rod that *was* in my hand, *and*, lo, I must die.

44 And Saul answered, God do so and more also: for you shall surely die, Jonathan.

45 And the people said to Saul, Shall Jonathan die, who has worked this great salvation in Israel? God forbid: *as* Yahweh lives, there shall not one hair of his head fall to the ground; for he has worked with God this day. So the people rescued Jonathan, *so* that he died not.

46 Then Saul went up from following the Philistines: and the Philistines went to their own place.

47 ¶ So Saul took the kingdom over Israel, and fought against all his enemies on every side, against Moab, and against the children of Ammon, and against Edom, and against the kings of Zobah, and against the Philistines: and wherever he turned himself, he condemned *them*.

48 And he gathered a host, and smote the Amalekites, and delivered Israel out of the hands of them that spoiled them.

49 Now the sons of Saul were Jonathan, and Ishui, and Melchishua: and the names of his two daughters *were these*; the name of the firstborn Merab, and the name of the younger Michal:

50 And the name of Saul's wife *was* Ahinoam, the daughter of Ahimaaz: and the name of the captain of his host *was* Abner, the son of Ner, Saul's uncle.

51 And Kish *was* the father of Saul; and Ner the father of Abner *was* the son of Abiel.

52 And there was mighty war against the Philistines all the days of Saul: and when Saul saw any strong man, or any valiant man, he took him unto him.

1 Samuel 15

15:1 ¶ Samuel also said to Saul, Yahweh sent me to anoint you *to be* king over his people, over Israel: now therefore listen you to the voice of the words of Yahweh.

2 Thus says Yahweh of hosts, I remember *that* which Amalek did to Israel, how he laid *wait* for him in the way, when he came up from Egypt.

3 Now go and smite Amalek, and utterly destroy all that they have, and spare them not; but slay both man and woman, infant and suckling, ox and sheep, camel and donkey.

4 And Saul gathered the people together, and numbered them in Telaim, two hundred thousand footmen, and ten thousand men of Judah.

5 And Saul came to a city of Amalek, and laid wait in the valley.

6 And Saul said to the Kenites, Go, depart, get you down from among the Amalekites, lest I destroy you with them: for you showed kindness to all the children of Israel, when they came up out of Egypt. So the Kenites departed from among the Amalekites.

7 And Saul smote the Amalekites from Havilah *until* you come to Shur, that *is* over against Egypt.

8 And he took Agag the king of the Amalekites alive, and utterly destroyed all the people with the edge of the sword.

9 But Saul and the people spared Agag, and the best of the sheep, and of the oxen, and of the fatted calves, and the lambs, and all *that was* good, and would not utterly destroy them: but every thing *that was* vile and refuse, that they destroyed utterly.

10 ¶ Then came the word of Yahweh to Samuel, saying,

11 It repents me that I have set up Saul *to be* king: for he has turned back from following me, and has not performed my commandments. And it grieved Samuel; and he cried unto Yahweh all night.

12 And when Samuel rose early to meet Saul in the morning, it was told *to* Samuel, saying, Saul came to Carmel, and, behold, he set him up a place, and has gone about, and passed on, and gone down to Gilgal.

13 And Samuel came to Saul: and Saul said to him, Blessed *are* you of Yahweh: I have performed the commandment of Yahweh.

14 And Samuel said, What *means* then this bleating of the sheep in my ears, and the lowing of the oxen which I hear?

15 And Saul said, They have brought them from the Amalekites: for the people spared the best of the sheep and of the oxen, to sacrifice unto Yahweh your God; and the rest we have utterly destroyed.

16 Then Samuel said to Saul, Stay, and I will tell you what Yahweh has said to me this night. And he said to him, Say on.

17 And Samuel said, When you *were* little in your own sight, *were* you not *made* the head of the tribes of Israel, and Yahweh anointed you king over Israel?

18 And Yahweh sent you on a journey, and said, Go and utterly destroy the sinners the Amalekites, and fight against them until they are consumed.

19 Why then did you not obey the voice of Yahweh, but did rush upon the spoil, and do evil in the sight of Yahweh?

20 And Saul said to Samuel, Yes, I have obeyed the voice of Yahweh, and have gone the way which Yahweh sent me, and have brought Agag the king of Amalek, and have utterly destroyed the Amalekites.

21 But the people took of the spoil, sheep and oxen, the chief of the things which should have been utterly destroyed, to sacrifice unto Yahweh your God in Gilgal.

22 And Samuel said, Has Yahweh *as great* delight in burnt offerings and sacrifices, as in obeying the voice of Yahweh? Behold, to obey *is* better than sacrifice, *and* to listen than the fat of rams.

23 For rebellion *is as* the sin of witchcraft, and stubbornness *is as* iniquity and idolatry. Because you have rejected the word of Yahweh, he has also rejected you from *being* king.

24 ¶ And Saul said to Samuel, I have sinned: for I have transgressed the commandment of Yahweh, and your words: because I feared the people, and obeyed their voice.

25 Now therefore, I pray you, pardon my sin, and turn again with me, that I may worship Yahweh.

26 And Samuel said to Saul, I will not return with you: for you have rejected the word of Yahweh, and Yahweh has rejected you from being king over Israel.

27 And as Samuel turned about to go away, he laid hold upon the skirt of his mantle, and it tore.

28 And Samuel said to him, Yahweh has torn the kingdom of Israel from you this day, and has given it to a neighbor of yours, *that is* better than you.

29 And also the Strength of Israel will not lie nor repent: for he *is* not a man, that he should repent.

30 Then he said, I have sinned: *yet* honor me now, I pray you, before the elders of my people, and before Israel, and turn again with me, that I may worship Yahweh your God.

31 So Samuel turned again after Saul; and Saul worshipped Yahweh.

32 ¶ Then said Samuel, Bring you here to me Agag the king of the Amalekites. And Agag came to him delicately. And Agag said, Surely the bitterness of death is past.

33 And Samuel said, As your sword has made women childless, so shall your mother be childless among women. And Samuel hewed Agag in pieces before Yahweh in Gilgal.

34 Then Samuel went to Ramah; and Saul went up to his house to Gibeah of Saul.

35 And Samuel came no more to see Saul until the day of his death: nevertheless Samuel mourned for Saul: and Yahweh repented that he had made Saul king over Israel.

1 Samuel 16

16:1 ¶ And Yahweh said to Samuel, How long will you mourn for Saul, seeing I have rejected him from reigning over Israel? fill your horn with oil, and go, I will send you to Jesse the Bethlehemite: for I have provided me a king among his sons.
2 And Samuel said, How can I go? if Saul hears *it*, he will kill me. And Yahweh said, Take a heifer with you, and say, I have come to sacrifice to Yahweh.
3 And call Jesse to the sacrifice, and I will show you what you shall do: and you shall anoint to me *him* whom I name to you.
4 And Samuel did that which Yahweh spoke, and came to Bethlehem. And the elders of the town trembled at his coming, and said, Come you peaceably?
5 And he said, Peaceably: I have come to sacrifice unto Yahweh: sanctify yourselves, and come with me to the sacrifice. And he sanctified Jesse and his sons, and called them to the sacrifice.
6 ¶ And it came to pass, when they had come, that he looked on Eliab, and said, Surely Yahweh's anointed *is* before him.
7 But Yahweh said to Samuel, Look not on his countenance, or on the height of his stature; because I have refused him: for *Yahweh sees* not as man sees; for man looks on the outward appearance, but Yahweh looks on the heart.
8 Then Jesse called Abinadab, and made him pass before Samuel. And he said, Neither has Yahweh chosen this.
9 Then Jesse made Shammah to pass by. And he said, Neither has Yahweh chosen this.
10 Again, Jesse made seven of his sons to pass before Samuel. And Samuel said to Jesse, Yahweh has not chosen these.
11 And Samuel said to Jesse, Are here all *your* children? And he said, There remains yet the youngest, and, behold, he keeps the sheep. And Samuel said to Jesse, Send and fetch him: for we will not sit down till he comes here.
12 And he sent, and brought him in. Now he *was* ruddy, *and* with a beautiful countenance, and pleasant to look to. And Yahweh said, Arise, anoint him: for this *is* he.
13 Then Samuel took the horn of oil, and anointed him in the midst of his brothers: and the Spirit of Yahweh came upon David from that day forward. So Samuel rose up, and went to Ramah.
14 ¶ But the Spirit of Yahweh departed from Saul, and an evil spirit from Yahweh troubled him.
15 And Saul's servants said to him, Behold now, an evil spirit from God troubles you.
16 Let our lord now command your servants, *which are* before you, to seek out a man, *who is* a knowledgeable player on a harp: and it shall come to pass, when the evil spirit from God is upon you, that he shall play with his hand, and you shall be well.
17 And Saul said to his servants, Provide me now a man that can play well, and bring *him* to me.
18 Then answered one of the servants, and said, Behold, I have seen a son of Jesse the Bethlehemite, *that is* knowledgeable in playing, and a mighty valiant man, and a man of war, and prudent in matters, and a handsome person, and Yahweh *is* with him.
19 Therefore Saul sent messengers to Jesse, and said, Send me David your son, which *is* with the sheep.
20 And Jesse took a donkey *loaded* with bread, and a bottle of wine, and a kid, and sent *them* by David his son to Saul.
21 And David came to Saul, and stood before him: and he loved him greatly; and he became his armor bearer.
22 And Saul sent to Jesse, saying, Let David, I pray you, stand before me; for he has found favor in my sight.
23 And it came to pass, when the *evil* spirit from God was upon Saul, that David took a harp, and played with his hand: so Saul was refreshed, and was well, and the evil spirit departed from him.

1 Samuel 17

17:1 ¶ Now the Philistines gathered together their armies to battle, and were gathered together at Shochoh, which *belongs* to Judah, and pitched between Shochoh and Azekah, in Ephesdammim.
2 And Saul and the men of Israel were gathered together, and pitched by the valley of Elah, and set the battle in array against the Philistines.
3 And the Philistines stood on a mountain on the one side, and Israel stood on a mountain on the other side: and *there was* a valley between them.
4 And there went out a champion out of the camp of the Philistines, named Goliath, of Gath, whose height *was* six cubits and a span.
5 And *he had* a helmet of brass upon his head, and he *was* armed with a coat of mail; and the weight of the coat *was* five thousand shekels of brass.
6 And *he had* leg armor of brass upon his legs, and a target of brass between his shoulders.
7 And the staff of his spear *was* like a weaver's beam; and his spear's head *weighed* six hundred shekels of iron: and one bearing a shield went before him.
8 And he stood and cried to the armies of Israel, and said to them, Why have you come out to set *your* battle in array? *am* not I a Philistine, and you servants to Saul? choose you a man for you, and let him come down to me.
9 If he is able to fight with me, and to kill me, then will we be your servants: but if I prevail against him, and kill him, then shall you be our servants, and serve us.
10 And the Philistine said, I defy the armies of Israel this day; give me a man, that we may fight together.
11 When Saul and all Israel heard those words of the Philistine, they were dismayed, and greatly afraid.
12 ¶ Now David *was* the son of that Ephrathite of Bethlehemjudah, whose name *was* Jesse; and he had eight sons: and the man went among men *for* an old man in the days of Saul.

13 And the three oldest sons of Jesse went *and* followed Saul to the battle: and the names of his three sons that went to the battle *were* Eliab the firstborn, and next to him Abinadab, and the third Shammah.

14 And David *was* the youngest: and the three oldest followed Saul.

15 But David went and returned from Saul to feed his father's sheep at Bethlehem.

16 And the Philistine drew near morning and evening, and presented himself *for* forty days.

17 And Jesse said to David his son, Take now for your brothers an ephah of this parched *corn*, and these ten loaves, and run to the camp to your brothers;

18 And carry these ten cheeses to the captain of *their* thousand, and look how your brothers fare, and take their pledge.

19 Now Saul, and they, and all the men of Israel, *were* in the valley of Elah, fighting with the Philistines.

20 And David rose up early in the morning, and left the sheep with a keeper, and took, and went, as Jesse had commanded him; and he came to the trench, as the host was going forth to the fight, and shouted for the battle.

21 For Israel and the Philistines had put the battle in array, army against army.

22 And David left his carriage in the hand of the keeper of the carriage, and ran into the army, and came and saluted his brothers.

23 And as he talked with them, behold, there came up the champion, the Philistine of Gath, Goliath by name, out of the armies of the Philistines, and spoke according to the same words: and David heard *them*.

24 And all the men of Israel, when they saw the man, fled from him, and were very afraid.

25 And the men of Israel said, Have you seen this man that has come up? surely to defy Israel has he come up: and it shall be, *that* the man who kills him, the king will enrich him with great riches, and will give him his daughter, and make his father's house free in Israel.

26 And David spoke to the men that stood by him, saying, What shall be done to the man that kills this Philistine, and takes away the reproach from Israel? for who *is* this uncircumcised Philistine, that he should defy the armies of the living God?

27 And the people answered him after this manner, saying, So shall it be done to the man that kills him.

28 And Eliab his oldest brother heard when he spoke to the men; and Eliab's anger was kindled against David, and he said, Why came you down here? and with whom have you left those few sheep in the wilderness? I know your pride, and the naughtiness of your heart; for you have come down that you might see the battle.

29 And David said, What have I now done? *Is there not* a cause?

30 And he turned from him toward another, and spoke after the same manner: and the people answered him again after the former manner.

31 ¶ And when the words were heard which David spoke, they rehearsed *them* before Saul: and he sent for him.

32 And David said to Saul, Let no man's heart fail because of him; your servant will go and fight with this Philistine.

33 And Saul said to David, You are not able to go against this Philistine to fight with him: for you *are but* a youth, and he a man of war from his youth.

34 And David said to Saul, Your servant kept his father's sheep, and there came a lion, and a bear, and took a lamb out of the flock:

35 And I went out after him, and smote him, and delivered *it* out of his mouth: and when he arose against me, I caught *him* by his beard, and smote him, and slew him.

36 Your servant slew both the lion and the bear: and this uncircumcised Philistine shall be as one of them, seeing he has defied the armies of the living God.

37 David said moreover, Yahweh that delivered me out of the paw of the lion, and out of the paw of the bear, he will deliver me out of the hand of this Philistine. And Saul said to David, Go, and Yahweh be with you.

38 And Saul armed David with his armor, and he put a helmet of brass upon his head; also he armed him with a coat of mail.

39 And David girded his sword upon his armor, and he assayed to go; for he had not proved *it*. And David said to Saul, I cannot go with these; for I have not proved *them*. And David put them off him.

40 ¶ And he took his staff in his hand, and chose him five smooth stones out of the brook, and put them in a shepherd's bag which he had, even in a pouch; and his sling *was* in his hand: and he drew near to the Philistine.

41 And the Philistine came on and drew near unto David; and the man that bore the shield *went* before him.

42 And when the Philistine looked about, and saw David, he disdained him: for he was *but* a youth, and ruddy, and of a fair countenance.

43 And the Philistine said to David, *Am* I a dog, that you come to me with sticks? And the Philistine cursed David by his gods.

44 And the Philistine said to David, Come to me, and I will give your flesh to the fowls of the air, and to the beasts of the field.

45 Then said David to the Philistine, You come to me with a sword, and with a spear, and with a shield: but I come to you in the name of Yahweh of hosts, the God of the armies of Israel, whom you have defied.

46 This day will Yahweh deliver you into my hand; and I will smite you, and take your head from you; and I will give the carcasses of the host of the Philistines this day to the fowls of the air, and to the wild beasts of the earth; that all the earth may know that there is a God in Israel.

47 And all this assembly shall know that Yahweh saves not with sword and spear: for the battle *is* Yahweh's, and he will give you into our hands.

48 ¶ And it came to pass, when the Philistine arose, and came and drew near to meet David, that David hurried, and ran toward the army to meet the Philistine.

49 And David put his hand in his bag, and took therefrom a stone, and slung *it*, and smote the Philistine in his forehead, that the stone sank into his forehead; and he fell upon his face to the earth.

1 Samuel 17

50 So David prevailed over the Philistine with a sling and with a stone, and smote the Philistine, and slew him; but *there was* no sword in the hand of David.

51 Therefore David ran, and stood upon the Philistine, and took his sword, and drew it out of the sheath thereof, and slew him, and cut off his head therewith. And when the Philistines saw their champion was dead, they fled.

52 And the men of Israel and of Judah arose, and shouted, and pursued the Philistines, until you come to the valley, and to the gates of Ekron. And the wounded of the Philistines fell down by the way to Shaaraim, even to Gath, and to Ekron.

53 And the children of Israel returned from chasing after the Philistines, and they spoiled their tents.

54 And David took the head of the Philistine, and brought it to Jerusalem; but he put his armor in his tent.

55 And when Saul saw David go forth against the Philistine, he said to Abner, the captain of the host, Abner, whose son *is* this youth? And Abner said, *As* your soul lives, O king, I cannot tell.

56 And the king said, Inquire you whose son the young man *is*.

57 And as David returned from the slaughter of the Philistine, Abner took him, and brought him before Saul with the head of the Philistine in his hand.

58 And Saul said to him, Whose son *are* you, *you* young man? And David answered, I *am* the son of your servant Jesse the Bethlehemite.

1 Samuel 18

18:1 ¶ And it came to pass, when he had made an end of speaking to Saul, that the soul of Jonathan was knit with the soul of David, and Jonathan loved him as his own soul.

2 And Saul took him that day, and would let him go no more home to his father's house.

3 Then Jonathan and David made a covenant, because he loved him as his own soul.

4 And Jonathan stripped himself of the robe that *was* upon him, and gave it to David, and his garments, even to his sword, and to his bow, and to his girdle.

5 And David went out wherever Saul sent him, *and* behaved himself wisely: and Saul set him over the men of war, and he was accepted in the sight of all the people, and also in the sight of Saul's servants.

6 ¶ And it came to pass as they came, when David had returned from the slaughter of the Philistine, that the women came out of all cities of Israel, singing and dancing, to meet king Saul, with tambourines, with joy, and with instruments of music.

7 And the women answered *one another* as they played, and said, Saul has slain his thousands, and David his ten thousands.

8 And Saul was very angry, and the saying displeased him; and he said, They have ascribed to David ten thousands, and to me they have ascribed *but* thousands: and *what* can he have more but the kingdom?

9 And Saul eyed David from that day and forward.

10 And it came to pass on the next day, that the evil spirit from God came upon Saul, and he prophesied in the midst of the house: and David played with his hand, as at other times: and *thereof was* a javelin in Saul's hand.

11 And Saul cast the javelin; for he said, I will smite David even to the wall *with it*. And David avoided out of his presence twice.

12 ¶ And Saul was afraid of David, because Yahweh was with him, and was departed from Saul.

13 Therefore Saul removed him from him, and made him his captain over a thousand; and he went out and came in before the people.

14 And David behaved himself wisely in all his ways; and Yahweh *was* with him.

15 Therefore when Saul saw that he behaved himself very wisely, he was afraid of him.

16 But all Israel and Judah loved David, because he went out and came in before them.

17 And Saul said to David, Behold my elder daughter Merab, her will I give you to wife: only be you valiant for me, and fight Yahweh's battles. For Saul said, Let not my hand be upon him, but let the hand of the Philistines be upon him.

18 And David said to Saul, Who *am* I? and what *is* my life, *or* my father's family in Israel, that I should be son-in-law to the king?

19 But it came to pass at the time when Merab Saul's daughter should have been given to David, that she was given to Adriel the Meholathite to wife.

20 And Michal, Saul's daughter, loved David: and they told Saul, and the thing pleased him.

21 And Saul said, I will give him her, that she may be a snare to him, and that the hand of the Philistines may be against him. Therefore Saul said to David, You shall this day be my son-in-law in *the one of* the two.

22 And Saul commanded his servants, *saying*, Commune with David secretly, and say, Behold, the king has delight in you, and all his servants love you: now therefore be the king's son-in-law.

23 And Saul's servants spoke those words in the ears of David. And David said, Seems it to you *a* light *thing* to be a king's son-in-law, seeing that I *am* a poor man, and lightly esteemed?

24 And the servants of Saul told him, saying, On this manner spoke David.

25 And Saul said, Thus shall you say to David, The king desires not any dowry, but a hundred foreskins of the Philistines, to be avenged of the king's enemies. But Saul thought to make David fall by the hand of the Philistines.

26 And when his servants told David these words, it pleased David well to be the king's son-in-law: and the days were not expired.

27 Therefore David arose and went, he and his men, and slew of the Philistines two hundred men; and David

brought their foreskins, and they gave them in full number to the king, that he might be the king's son-in-law. And Saul gave him Michal his daughter to wife.

28 And Saul saw and knew that Yahweh *was* with David, and *that* Michal, Saul's daughter, loved him.

29 And Saul was yet the more afraid of David; and Saul became David's enemy continually.

30 Then the princes of the Philistines went forth: and it came to pass, after they went forth, *that* David behaved himself more wisely than all the servants of Saul; so that his name was greatly esteemed.

1 Samuel 19

19:1 ¶ And Saul spoke to Jonathan his son, and to all his servants, that they should kill David.

2 But Jonathan Saul's son delighted much in David: and Jonathan told David, saying, Saul my father seeks to kill you: now therefore, I pray you, take heed to yourself until the morning, and stay in a secret *place*, and hide yourself:

3 And I will go out and stand beside my father in the field where you *are*, and I will commune with my father of you; and what I see, that I will tell you.

4 And Jonathan spoke good of David to Saul his father, and said to him, Let not the king sin against his servant, against David; because he has not sinned against you, and because his works *have been* to toward you very good:

5 For he did put his life in his hand, and slew the Philistine, and Yahweh worked a great salvation for all Israel: you saw *it*, and did rejoice: why then will you sin against innocent blood, to slay David without a cause?

6 And Saul listened to the voice of Jonathan: and Saul swore, *As* Yahweh lives, he shall not be slain.

7 And Jonathan called David, and Jonathan showed him all those things. And Jonathan brought David to Saul, and he was in his presence, as in times past.

8 ¶ And there was war again: and David went out, and fought with the Philistines, and slew them with a great slaughter; and they fled from him.

9 And the evil spirit from Yahweh was upon Saul, as he sat in his house with his javelin in his hand: and David played with *his* hand.

10 And Saul sought to smite David even to the wall with the javelin; but he slipped away out of Saul's presence, and he smote the javelin into the wall: and David fled, and escaped that night.

11 ¶ Saul also sent messengers to David's house, to watch him, and to slay him in the morning: and Michal, David's wife, told him, saying, If you save not your life tonight, tomorrow you shall be slain.

12 So Michal let David down through a window: and he went, and fled, and escaped.

13 And Michal took an image, and laid *it* in the bed, and put a pillow of goats' *hair* for his pillow, and covered *it* with a cloth.

14 And when Saul sent messengers to take David, she said, He *is* sick.

15 And Saul sent the messengers *again* to see David, saying, Bring him up to me in the bed, that I may slay him.

16 And when the messengers had come in, behold, *there was* an image in the bed, with a pillow of goats' *hair* for his pillow.

17 And Saul said to Michal, Why have you deceived me so, and sent away my enemy, that he has escaped? And Michal answered Saul, He said to me, Let me go; why should I kill you?

18 ¶ So David fled, and escaped, and came to Samuel to Ramah, and told him all that Saul had done to him. And he and Samuel went and dwelt in Naioth.

19 And it was told *to* Saul, saying, Behold, David *is* at Naioth in Ramah.

20 And Saul sent messengers to take David: and when they saw the company of the prophets prophesying, and Samuel standing *as* appointed over them, the Spirit of God was upon the messengers of Saul, and they also prophesied.

21 And when it was told *to* Saul, he sent other messengers, and they prophesied likewise. And Saul sent messengers again the third time, and they prophesied also.

22 Then went he also to Ramah, and came to a great well that *is* in Sechu: and he asked and said, Where *are* Samuel and David? And *one* said, Behold, *they are* at Naioth in Ramah.

23 And he went there to Naioth in Ramah: and the Spirit of God was upon him also, and he went on, and prophesied, until he came to Naioth in Ramah.

24 And he stripped off his clothes also, and prophesied before Samuel in like manner, and lay down naked all that day and all that night. Therefore they say, *Is* Saul also among the prophets?

1 Samuel 20

20:1 ¶ And David fled from Naioth in Ramah, and came and said before Jonathan, What have I done? what *is* my iniquity? and what *is* my sin before your father, that he seeks my life?

2 And he said to him, God forbid; you shall not die: behold, my father will do nothing either great or small, but that he will show it *to* me: and why should my father hide this thing from me? it *is* not *so*.

3 And David swore moreover, and said, Your father certainly knows that I have found grace in your eyes; and he said, Let not Jonathan know this, lest he be grieved: but truly *as* Yahweh lives, and *as* your soul lives, *there is* but a step between me and death.

4 Then said Jonathan to David, Whatever your soul desires, I will even do *it* for you.

5 And David said to Jonathan, Behold, tomorrow *is* the new moon, and I should not fail to sit with the king to eat: but let me go, that I may hide myself in the field to the third *day* at evening.

1 Samuel 20

6 If your father at all misses me, then say, David earnestly asked *leave* of me that he might run to Bethlehem his city: for *there is* a yearly sacrifice there for all the family.

7 If he says thus, *It is* well; your servant shall have peace: but if he is very angry, *then* be sure that evil is determined by him.

8 Therefore you shall deal kindly with your servant; for you have brought your servant into a covenant of Yahweh with you: notwithstanding, if there is in me iniquity, slay me yourself; for why should you bring me to your father?

9 ¶ And Jonathan said, Far be it from you: for if I knew certainly that evil was determined by my father to come upon you, then would not I tell it you?

10 Then said David to Jonathan, Who shall tell me? or what *if* your father answers you roughly?

11 And Jonathan said to David, Come, and let us go out into the field. And they went out both of them into the field.

12 And Jonathan said to David, O Yahweh God of Israel, when I have sounded my father out tomorrow anytime, *or* the third *day*, and, behold, *if there is* good toward David, and I then send not to you, and show it *to* you;

13 Yahweh do so and much more to Jonathan: but if it pleases my father *to do* you evil, then I will show it *to* you, and send you away, that you may go in peace: and Yahweh be with you, as he has been with my father.

14 And you shall not only while yet I live show me the kindness of Yahweh, that I die not:

15 But *also* you shall not cut off your kindness from my house forever: no, not when Yahweh has cut off the enemies of David every one from the face of the earth.

16 So Jonathan made *a covenant* with the house of David, *saying*, Let Yahweh even require *it* at the hand of David's enemies.

17 And Jonathan caused David to swear again, because he loved him: for he loved him as he loved his own soul.

18 Then Jonathan said to David, Tomorrow *is* the new moon: and you shall be missed, because your seat will be empty.

19 And *when* you have stayed three days, *then* you shall go down quickly, and come to the place where you did hide yourself when the business was *in hand*, and shall remain by the stone Ezel.

20 And I will shoot three arrows on the side *thereof*, as though I shot at a mark.

21 And, behold, I will send a lad, *saying*, Go, find out the arrows. If I expressly say to the lad, Behold, the arrows *are* on this side of you, take them; then come you: for *there is* peace to you, and no hurt; *as* Yahweh lives.

22 But if I say thus to the young man, Behold, the arrows *are* beyond you; go your way: for Yahweh has sent you away.

23 And *as touching* the matter which you and I have spoken of, behold, Yahweh *be* between you and me forever.

24 ¶ So David hid himself in the field: and when the new moon had come, the king sat him down to eat meat.

25 And the king sat upon his seat, as at other times, *even* upon a seat by the wall: and Jonathan arose, and Abner sat by Saul's side, and David's place was empty.

26 Nevertheless Saul spoke not anything that day: for he thought, Something has befallen him, he *is* not clean; surely he *is* not clean.

27 And it came to pass on the next day, *which was* the second *day* of the month, that David's place was empty: and Saul said to Jonathan his son, Why came not the son of Jesse to eat, neither yesterday, nor today?

28 And Jonathan answered Saul, David earnestly asked *leave* of me *to go* to Bethlehem:

29 And he said, Let me go, I pray you; for our family has a sacrifice in the city; and my brother, he has commanded me *to be there*: and now, if I have found favor in your eyes, let me get away, I pray you, and see my brothers. Therefore he came not to the king's table.

30 Then Saul's anger was kindled against Jonathan, and he said to him, You son of the perverse rebellious *woman*, do not I know that you have chosen the son of Jesse to your own shame, and to the shame of your mother's nakedness?

31 For as long as the son of Jesse lives upon the ground, you shall not be established, nor your kingdom. Therefore now send and fetch him unto me, for he shall surely die.

32 And Jonathan answered Saul his father, and said to him, Why shall he be slain? what has he done?

33 And Saul cast a javelin at him to smite him: whereby Jonathan knew that it was determined of his father to slay David.

34 So Jonathan arose from the table in fierce anger, and did eat no meat the second day of the month: for he was grieved for David, because his father had done him shame.

35 ¶ And it came to pass in the morning, that Jonathan went out into the field at the time appointed with David, and a little lad with him.

36 And he said to his lad, Run, find out now the arrows which I shoot. *And* as the lad ran, he shot an arrow beyond him.

37 And when the lad had come to the place of the arrow which Jonathan had shot, Jonathan cried after the lad, and said, *Is* not the arrow beyond you?

38 And Jonathan cried after the lad, Make speed, haste, stay not. And Jonathan's lad gathered up the arrows, and came to his master.

39 But the lad knew not anything: only Jonathan and David knew the matter.

40 And Jonathan gave his artillery to his lad, and said to him, Go, carry *them* to the city.

41 *And* as soon as the lad was gone, David arose out of *a place* toward the south, and fell on his face to the ground, and bowed himself three times: and they kissed one another, and wept one with another, until David exceeded.

42 And Jonathan said to David, Go in peace, forasmuch as we have sworn both of us in the name of Yahweh,

saying, Yahweh be between me and you, and between my seed and your seed forever. And he arose and departed: and Jonathan went into the city.

1 Samuel 21

21:1 ¶ Then came David to Nob to Ahimelech the priest: and Ahimelech was afraid at the meeting of David, and said to him, Why *are* you alone, and no man with you?
2 And David said to Ahimelech the priest, The king has commanded me a business, and has said to me, Let no man know anything of the business about which I send you, and what I have commanded you: and I have appointed *my* servants to such and such a place.
3 Now therefore what is under your hand? give *me* five *loaves of* bread in my hand, or what there is present.
4 And the priest answered David, and said, There *is* no common bread under my hand, but there is hallowed bread; if the young men have kept themselves at least from women.
5 And David answered the priest, and said to him, Of a truth women *have been* kept from us about these three days, since I came out, and the vessels of the young men are holy, and *the bread is* in a manner common, yes, though it were sanctified this day in the vessel.
6 So the priest gave him hallowed *bread*: for there was no bread there but the showbread, that was taken from before Yahweh, to put hot bread in the day when it was taken away.
7 Now a certain man of the servants of Saul *was* there that day, detained before Yahweh; and his name *was* Doeg, an Edomite, the chiefest of the herdsmen that *belonged* to Saul.
8 And David said to Ahimelech, And is there not here under your hand spear or sword? for I have neither brought my sword nor my weapons with me, because the king's business required haste.
9 And the priest said, The sword of Goliath the Philistine, whom you slew in the valley of Elah, behold, it *is* here wrapped in a cloth behind the ephod: if you shall take that, take *it*: for *there is* no other except that here. And David said, *There is* none like that; give it *to* me.
10 ¶ And David arose, and fled that day for fear of Saul, and went to Achish the king of Gath.
11 And the servants of Achish said to him, *Is* not this David the king of the land? did they not sing one to another of him in dances, saying, Saul has slain his thousands, and David his ten thousands?
12 And David laid up these words in his heart, and was very afraid of Achish the king of Gath.
13 And he changed his behavior before them, and feigned himself mad in their hands, and scrabbled on the doors of the gate, and let his spittle fall down upon his beard.
14 Then said Achish to his servants, Lo, you see the man is mad: why *then* have you brought him to me?
15 Have I need of mad men, that you have brought this *fellow* to play the mad man in my presence? shall this *fellow* come into my house?

1 Samuel 22

22:1 ¶ David therefore departed therefrom, and escaped to the cave Adullam: and when his brothers and all his father's house heard *it*, they went down there to him.
2 And every one *that was* in distress, and every one that *was* in debt, and every one *that was* discontented, gathered themselves to him; and he became a captain over them: and there were with him about four hundred men.
3 And David went there to Mizpeh of Moab: and he said to the king of Moab, Let my father and my mother, I pray you, come forth, *and be* with you, till I know what God will do for me.
4 And he brought them before the king of Moab: and they dwelt with him all the while that David was in the hold.
5 And the prophet Gad said to David, Abide not in the hold; depart, and get you into the land of Judah. Then David departed, and came into the forest of Hareth.
6 ¶ When Saul heard that David was discovered, and the men that *were* with him, (now Saul stayed in Gibeah under a tree in Ramah, having his spear in his hand, and all his servants *were* standing about him;)
7 Then Saul said to his servants that stood about him, Hear now, you Benjamites; will the son of Jesse give every one of you fields and vineyards, *and* make you all captains of thousands, and captains of hundreds;
8 That all of you have conspired against me, and *there is* none that shows me that my son has made a league with the son of Jesse, and *there is* none of you that is sorry for me, or shows to me that my son has stirred up my servant against me, to lie in wait, as at this day?
9 Then answered Doeg the Edomite, which was set over the servants of Saul, and said, I saw the son of Jesse coming to Nob, to Ahimelech the son of Ahitub.
10 And he inquired of Yahweh for him, and gave him victuals, and gave him the sword of Goliath the Philistine.
11 Then the king sent to call Ahimelech the priest, the son of Ahitub, and all his father's house, the priests that *were* in Nob: and they came all of them to the king.
12 And Saul said, Hear now, you son of Ahitub. And he answered, Here I *am*, my lord.
13 And Saul said to him, Why have you conspired against me, you and the son of Jesse, in that you have given him bread, and a sword, and have inquired of God for him, that he should rise against me, to lie in wait, as at this day?
14 Then Ahimelech answered the king, and said, And who *is so* faithful among all your servants as David, which is the king's son-in-law, and goes at your bidding, and is honorable in your house?
15 Did I then begin to inquire of God for him? be it far from me: let not the king impute *any* thing to his servant, *nor* to all the house of my father: for your servant knew nothing of all this, less or more.

1 Samuel 22

16 And the king said, You shall surely die, Ahimelech, you, and all your father's house.

17 And the king said to the footmen that stood about him, Turn, and slay the priests of Yahweh; because their hand also *is* with David, and because they knew when he fled, and did not show it to me. But the servants of the king would not put forth their hand to fall upon the priests of Yahweh.

18 And the king said to Doeg, Turn you, and fall upon the priests. And Doeg the Edomite turned, and he fell upon the priests, and slew on that day fourscore and five persons that did wear a linen ephod.

19 And Nob, the city of the priests, smote he with the edge of the sword, both men and women, children and sucklings, and oxen, and donkeys, and sheep, with the edge of the sword.

20 ¶ And one of the sons of Ahimelech the son of Ahitub, named Abiathar, escaped, and fled after David.

21 And Abiathar told David that Saul had slain Yahweh's priests.

22 And David said to Abiathar, I knew *it* that day, when Doeg the Edomite *was* there, that he would surely tell Saul: I have occasioned *the death* of all the persons of your father's house.

23 Stay you with me, fear not: for he that seeks my life seeks your life: but with me you *shall be* in safeguard.

1 Samuel 23

23:1 ¶ Then they told David, saying, Behold, the Philistines fight against Keilah, and they rob the threshing floors.

2 Therefore David inquired of Yahweh, saying, Shall I go and smite these Philistines? And Yahweh said to David, Go, and smite the Philistines, and save Keilah.

3 And David's men said to him, Behold, we are afraid here in Judah: how much more then if we come to Keilah against the armies of the Philistines?

4 Then David inquired of Yahweh yet again. And Yahweh answered him and said, Arise, go down to Keilah; for I will deliver the Philistines into your hand.

5 So David and his men went to Keilah, and fought with the Philistines, and brought away their cattle, and smote them with a great slaughter. So David saved the inhabitants of Keilah.

6 And it came to pass, when Abiathar the son of Ahimelech fled to David to Keilah, *that* he came down *with* an ephod in his hand.

7 ¶ And it was told *to* Saul that David had come to Keilah. And Saul said, God has delivered him into my hand; for he is shut in, by entering into a town that has gates and bars.

8 And Saul called all the people together to war, to go down to Keilah, to besiege David and his men.

9 And David knew that Saul secretly practiced mischief against him; and he said to Abiathar the priest, Bring here the ephod.

10 Then said David, O Yahweh God of Israel, your servant has certainly heard that Saul seeks to come to Keilah, to destroy the city for my sake.

11 Will the men of Keilah deliver me up into his hand? will Saul come down, as your servant has heard? O Yahweh God of Israel, I beseech you, tell your servant. And Yahweh said, He will come down.

12 Then said David, Will the men of Keilah deliver me and my men into the hand of Saul? And Yahweh said, They will deliver *you* up.

13 Then David and his men, *which were* about six hundred, arose and departed out of Keilah, and went wherever they could go. And it was told *to* Saul that David had escaped from Keilah; and he ceased to go forth.

14 ¶ And David stayed in the wilderness in strong holds, and remained in a mountain in the wilderness of Ziph. And Saul sought him every day, but God delivered him not into his hand.

15 And David saw that Saul had come out to seek his life: and David *was* in the wilderness of Ziph in a woods.

16 And Jonathan Saul's son arose, and went to David into the woods, and strengthened his hand in God.

17 And he said to him, Fear not: for the hand of Saul my father shall not find you; and you shall be king over Israel, and I shall be next to you; and that also Saul my father knows.

18 And they two made a covenant before Yahweh: and David stayed in the woods, and Jonathan went to his house.

19 ¶ Then came up the Ziphytes to Saul to Gibeah, saying, Does not David hide himself with us in strong holds in the woods, in the hill of Hachilah, which *is* on the south of Jeshimon?

20 Now therefore, O king, come down according to all the desire of your soul to come down; and our part *shall be* to deliver him into the king's hand.

21 And Saul said, Blessed *be* you of Yahweh; for you have compassion on me.

22 Go, I pray you, prepare yet, and know and see his place where his haunt is, *and* who has seen him there: for it is told me *that* he deals very subtly.

23 See therefore, and take knowledge of all the lurking places where he hides himself, and come you again to me with the certainty, and I will go with you: and it shall come to pass, if he is in the land, that I will search him out throughout all the thousands of Judah.

24 And they arose, and went to Ziph before Saul: but David and his men *were* in the wilderness of Maon, in the plain on the south of Jeshimon.

25 Saul also and his men went to seek *him*. And they told David: therefore he came down into a rock, and stayed in the wilderness of Maon. And when Saul heard *that*, he pursued after David in the wilderness of Maon.

26 And Saul went on this side of the mountain, and David and his men on that side of the mountain: and David made haste to get away for fear of Saul; for Saul

and his men compassed David and his men round about to take them.

27 But there came a messenger to Saul, saying, Hasten you, and come; for the Philistines have invaded the land.

28 Therefore Saul returned from pursuing after David, and went against the Philistines: therefore they called that place Selahammahlekoth.

29 And David went up from there, and dwelt in strong holds at Engedi.

1 Samuel 24

24:1 ¶ And it came to pass, when Saul had returned from following the Philistines, that it was told *to* him, saying, Behold, David *is* in the wilderness of Engedi.

2 Then Saul took three thousand chosen men out of all Israel, and went to seek David and his men upon the rocks of the wild goats.

3 And he came to the sheepfolds by the way, where *was* a cave; and Saul went in to cover his feet: and David and his men remained in the sides of the cave.

4 And the men of David said to him, Behold the day of which Yahweh said to you, Behold, I will deliver your enemy into your hand, that you may do to him as it shall seem good to you. Then David arose, and cut off the skirt of Saul's robe privately.

5 And it came to pass afterward, that David's heart smote him, because he had cut off Saul's skirt.

6 And he said to his men, Yahweh forbid that I should do this thing to my master, Yahweh's anointed, to stretch forth my hand against him, seeing he *is* the anointed of Yahweh.

7 So David stayed his servants with these words, and allowed them not to rise against Saul. But Saul rose up out of the cave, and went on *his* way.

8 David also arose afterward, and went out of the cave, and cried after Saul, saying, My lord the king. And when Saul looked behind him, David stooped with his face to the earth, and bowed himself.

9 ¶ And David said to Saul, Why hear you men's words, saying, Behold, David seeks your harm?

10 Behold, this day your eyes have seen how that Yahweh had delivered you today into my hand in the cave: and *some* urged *me* to kill you: but *my eye* spared you; and I said, I will not put forth my hand against my lord; for he *is* Yahweh's anointed.

11 Moreover, my father, see, yes, see the skirt of your robe in my hand: for in that I cut off the skirt of your robe, and killed you not, know you and see that *there is* neither evil nor transgression in mine hand, and I have not sinned against you; yet you hunt my soul to take it.

12 Yahweh judge between me and you, and Yahweh avenge me of you: but my hand shall not be upon you.

13 As said the proverb of the ancients, Wickedness proceeds from the wicked: but my hand shall not be upon you.

14 After whom has the king of Israel come out? after whom do you pursue? after a dead dog, after a flea.

15 Yahweh therefore be judge, and judge between me and you, and see, and plead my cause, and deliver me out of your hand.

16 ¶ And it came to pass, when David had made an end of speaking these words to Saul, that Saul said, *Is* this your voice, my son David? And Saul lifted up his voice, and wept.

17 And he said to David, You *are* more righteous than I: for you have rewarded me good, whereas I have rewarded you evil.

18 And you have shown this day how that you have dealt well with me: forasmuch as when Yahweh had delivered me into your hand, you killed me not.

19 For if a man finds his enemy, will he let him go well away? therefore *may* Yahweh reward you good for that you have done to me this day.

20 And now, behold, I know well that you shall surely be king, and that the kingdom of Israel shall be established in your hand.

21 Swear now therefore to me by Yahweh, that you will not cut off my seed after me, and that you will not destroy my name out of my father's house.

22 And David swore to Saul. And Saul went home; but David and his men got them up to the hold.

1 Samuel 25

25:1 ¶ And Samuel died; and all the Israelites were gathered together, and lamented him, and buried him in his house at Ramah. And David arose, and went down to the wilderness of Paran.

2 ¶ And *there was* a man in Maon, whose possessions *were* in Carmel; and the man *was* very great, and he had three thousand sheep, and a thousand goats: and he was shearing his sheep in Carmel.

3 Now the name of the man *was* Nabal; and the name of his wife Abigail: and *she was* a woman of good understanding, and of a beautiful countenance: but the man *was* churlish and evil in his doings; and he *was* of the house of Caleb.

4 And David heard in the wilderness that Nabal did shear his sheep.

5 And David sent out ten young men, and David said to the young men, Get you up to Carmel, and go to Nabal, and greet him in my name:

6 And thus shall you say to him that lives *in prosperity*, Peace *be* both to you, and peace *be* to your house, and peace *be* to all that you have.

7 And now I have heard that you have shearers: now your shepherds which were with us, we hurt them not, neither was there anything missing to them, all the while they were in Carmel.

8 Ask your young men, and they will tell you. Therefore let the young men find favor in your eyes: for we come in a good day: give, I pray you, whatever comes to your hand to your servants, and to your son David.

9 And when David's young men came, they spoke to Nabal according to all those words in the name of David, and ceased.

1 Samuel 25

10 And Nabal answered David's servants, and said, Who *is* David? and who *is* the son of Jesse? there are many servants now a days that break away every man from his master.

11 Shall I then take my bread, and my water, and my flesh that I have killed for my shearers, and give *it* to men, whom I know not *from* where they *are*?

12 ¶ So David's young men turned their way, and went again, and came and told him all those sayings.

13 And David said to his men, Gird you on every man his sword. And they girded on every man his sword; and David also girded on his sword: and there went up after David about four hundred men; and two hundred stayed by the stuff.

14 But one of the young men told Abigail, Nabal's wife, saying, Behold, David sent messengers out of the wilderness to salute our master; and he railed on them.

15 But the men *were* very good to us, and we were not hurt, neither missed we anything, as long as we were walking with them, when we were in the fields:

16 They were a wall to us both by night and day, all the while we were with them keeping the sheep.

17 Now therefore know and consider what you will do; for evil is determined against our master, and against all his household: for he *is such* a son of Belial, that *a man* cannot speak to him.

18 ¶ Then Abigail made haste, and took two hundred loaves, and two bottles of wine, and five sheep ready dressed, and five measures of parched *corn*, and a hundred clusters of raisins, and two hundred cakes of figs, and laid *them* on donkeys.

19 And she said to her servants, Go on before me; behold, I come after you. But she told not her husband Nabal.

20 And it was *so, as* she rode on the donkey, that she came down by the covert of the hill, and, behold, David and his men came down against her; and she met them.

21 Now David had said, Surely in vain have I kept all that this *fellow* has in the wilderness, so that nothing was missed of all that *pertained* to him: and he has requited me evil for good.

22 So and more also do God to the enemies of David, if I leave of all that *pertain* to him by the morning light any that urinates against the wall.

23 And when Abigail saw David, she hurried, and lighted off the donkey, and fell before David on her face, and bowed herself to the ground,

24 And fell at his feet, and said, Upon me, my lord, upon me *let this* iniquity *be*: and let your handmaid, I pray you, speak in your audience, and hear the words of your handmaid.

25 Let not my lord, I pray you, regard this man of Belial, *even* Nabal: for as his name *is*, so *is* he; Nabal *is* his name, and folly *is* with him: but I your handmaid saw not the young men of my lord, whom you did send.

26 Now therefore, my lord, *as* Yahweh lives, and *as* your soul lives, seeing Yahweh has withheld you from coming to *shed* blood, and from avenging yourself with your own hand, now let your enemies, and they that seek evil to my lord, be as Nabal.

27 And now this blessing which your handmaid has brought to my lord, let it even be given to the young men that follow my lord.

28 I pray you, forgive the trespass of your handmaid: for Yahweh will certainly make my lord a sure house; because my lord fights the battles of Yahweh, and evil has not been found in you *all* your days.

29 Yet a man is risen to pursue you, and to seek your soul: but the soul of my lord shall be bound in the bundle of life with Yahweh your God; and the souls of your enemies, them shall he sling out, *as out* of the middle of a sling.

30 And it shall come to pass, when Yahweh shall have done to my lord according to all the good that he has spoken concerning you, and shall have appointed you ruler over Israel;

31 That this shall be no grief to you, nor offense of heart to my lord, either that you have shed blood without cause, or that my lord has avenged himself: but when Yahweh shall have dealt well with my lord, then remember your handmaid.

32 ¶ And David said to Abigail, Blessed *be* Yahweh God of Israel, which sent you this day to meet me:

33 And blessed *be* your advice, and blessed *be* you, which have kept me this day from coming to *shed* blood, and from avenging myself with my own hand.

34 For in very deed, *as* Yahweh God of Israel lives, which has kept me back from hurting you, unless you had hurried and come to meet me, surely there had not been left to Nabal by the morning light any that urinates against the wall.

35 So David received of her hand *that* which she had brought him, and said to her, Go up in peace to your house; see, I have listened to your voice, and have accepted your person.

36 ¶ And Abigail came to Nabal; and, behold, he held a feast in his house, like the feast of a king; and Nabal's heart *was* merry within him, for he *was* very drunken: therefore she told him nothing, less or more, until the morning light.

37 But it came to pass in the morning, when the wine was gone out of Nabal, and his wife had told him these things, that his heart died within him, and he became *as* a stone.

38 And it came to pass about ten days *after*, that Yahweh smote Nabal, that he died.

39 And when David heard that Nabal was dead, he said, Blessed *be* Yahweh, that has pleaded the cause of my reproach from the hand of Nabal, and has kept his servant from evil: for Yahweh has returned the wickedness of Nabal upon his own head. And David sent and communed with Abigail, to take her to him to wife.

40 And when the servants of David had come to Abigail to Carmel, they spoke to her, saying, David sent us to you, to take you to him to wife.

41 And she arose, and bowed herself on *her* face to the earth, and said, Behold, *let* your handmaid *be* a servant to wash the feet of the servants of my lord.

42 And Abigail hurried, and arose, and rode upon a donkey, with five damsels of hers that went after her; and she went after the messengers of David, and became his wife.

43 David also took Ahinoam of Jezreel; and they were also both of them his wives.

44 But Saul had given Michal his daughter, David's wife, to Phalti the son of Laish, which *was* of Gallim.

1 Samuel 26

26:1 ¶ And the Ziphytes came to Saul to Gibeah, saying, Does not David hide himself in the hill of Hachilah, *which is* before Jeshimon?

2 Then Saul arose, and went down to the wilderness of Ziph, having three thousand chosen men of Israel with him, to seek David in the wilderness of Ziph.

3 And Saul pitched in the hill of Hachilah, which *is* before Jeshimon, by the way. But David stayed in the wilderness, and he saw that Saul came after him into the wilderness.

4 David therefore sent out spies, and understood that Saul had come in very deed.

5 And David arose, and came to the place where Saul had pitched: and David beheld the place where Saul lay, and Abner the son of Ner, the captain of his host: and Saul lay in the trench, and the people pitched round about him.

6 ¶ Then answered David and said to Ahimelech the Hittite, and to Abishai the son of Zeruiah, brother to Joab, saying, Who will go down with me to Saul to the camp? And Abishai said, I will go down with you.

7 So David and Abishai came to the people by night: and, behold, Saul lay sleeping within the trench, and his spear stuck in the ground at his pillow: but Abner and the people lay round about him.

8 Then said Abishai to David, God has delivered your enemy into your hand this day: now therefore let me smite him, I pray you, with the spear even to the earth at once, and I will not *smite* him the second time.

9 And David said to Abishai, Destroy him not: for who can stretch forth his hand against Yahweh's anointed, and be guiltless?

10 David said furthermore, *As* Yahweh lives, Yahweh shall smite him; or his day shall come to die; or he shall descend into battle, and perish.

11 Yahweh forbid that I should stretch forth my hand against Yahweh's anointed: but, I pray you, take you now the spear that *is* at his pillow, and the cruse of water, and let us go.

12 So David took the spear and the cruse of water from Saul's pillow; and they got them away, and no man saw *it*, nor knew *it*, neither awoke: for they *were* all asleep; because a deep sleep from Yahweh had fallen upon them.

13 ¶ Then David went over to the other side, and stood on the top of a hill afar off; a great space *being* between them:

14 And David cried to the people, and to Abner the son of Ner, saying, Answer you not, Abner? Then Abner answered and said, Who *are* you *that* cry to the king?

15 And David said to Abner, *Are* not you a *valiant* man? and who *is* like to you in Israel? why then have you not kept your lord the king? for there came one of the people in to destroy the king your lord.

16 This thing *is* not good that you have done. *As* Yahweh lives, you *are* worthy to die, because you have not kept your master, Yahweh's anointed. And now see where the king's spear *is*, and the cruse of water that *was* at his pillow.

17 And Saul knew David's voice, and said, *Is* this your voice, my son David? And David said, *It is* my voice, my lord, O king.

18 And he said, Why does my lord thus pursue after his servant? for what have I done? or what evil *is* in my hand?

19 Now therefore, I pray you, let my lord the king hear the words of his servant. If Yahweh has stirred you up against me, let him accept an offering: but if *they are* the children of men, cursed *are* they before Yahweh; for they have driven me out this day from joining in the inheritance of Yahweh, saying, Go, serve other gods.

20 Now therefore, let not my blood fall to the earth before the face of Yahweh: for the king of Israel has come out to seek a flea, as when one does hunt a partridge in the mountains.

21 ¶ Then said Saul, I have sinned: return, my son David: for I will no more do you harm, because my soul was precious in your eyes this day: behold, I have played the fool, and have erred exceedingly.

22 And David answered and said, Behold the king's spear! and let one of the young men come over and fetch it.

23 Yahweh render to every man his righteousness and his faithfulness: for Yahweh delivered you into *my* hand today, but I would not stretch forth my hand against Yahweh's anointed.

24 And, behold, as your life was much set by this day in my eyes, so let my life be much set by in the eyes of Yahweh, and let him deliver me out of all tribulation.

25 Then Saul said to David, Blessed *be* you, my son David: you shall both do great *things*, and also will still prevail. So David went on his way, and Saul returned to his place.

1 Samuel 27

27:1 ¶ And David said in his heart, I shall now perish one day by the hand of Saul: *there is* nothing better for me than that I should speedily escape into the land of the Philistines; and Saul shall despair of me, to seek me any more in any coast of Israel: so shall I escape out of his hand.

2 And David arose, and he passed over with the six hundred men that *were* with him to Achish, the son of Maoch, king of Gath.

1 Samuel 27

3 And David dwelt with Achish at Gath, he and his men, every man with his household, *even* David with his two wives, Ahinoam the Jezreelitess, and Abigail the Carmelitess, Nabal's wife.

4 And it was told *to* Saul that David was fled to Gath: and he sought no more again for him.

5 And David said to Achish, If I have now found grace in your eyes, let them give me a place in some town in the country, that I may dwell there: for why should your servant dwell in the royal city with you?

6 Then Achish gave him Ziklag that day: therefore Ziklag pertains to the kings of Judah unto this day.

7 And the time that David dwelt in the country of the Philistines was a full year and four months.

8 ¶ And David and his men went up, and invaded the Geshurites, and the Gezrites, and the Amalekites: for those *nations were* of old the inhabitants of the land, as you go to Shur, even to the land of Egypt.

9 And David smote the land, and left neither man nor woman alive, and took away the sheep, and the oxen, and the donkeys, and the camels, and the apparel, and returned, and came to Achish.

10 And Achish said, Where have you made a road today? And David said, Against the south of Judah, and against the south of the Jerahmeelites, and against the south of the Kenites.

11 And David saved neither man nor woman alive, to bring *tidings* to Gath, saying, Lest they should tell on us, saying, So did David, and so *will be* his manner all the while he dwells in the country of the Philistines.

12 And Achish believed David, saying, He has made his people Israel utterly to abhor him; therefore he shall be my servant forever.

1 Samuel 28

28:1 ¶ And it came to pass in those days, that the Philistines gathered their armies together for warfare, to fight with Israel. And Achish said to David, Know you assuredly, that you shall go out with me to battle, you and your men.

2 And David said to Achish, Surely you shall know what your servant can do. And Achish said to David, Therefore will I make you keeper of my head forever.

3 Now Samuel was dead, and all Israel had lamented him, and buried him in Ramah, even in his own city. And Saul had put away those that had familiar spirits, and the wizards, out of the land.

4 And the Philistines gathered themselves together, and came and pitched in Shunem: and Saul gathered all Israel together, and they pitched in Gilboa.

5 And when Saul saw the host of the Philistines, he was afraid, and his heart greatly trembled.

6 And when Saul inquired of Yahweh, Yahweh answered him not, neither by dreams, nor by Urim, nor by prophets.

7 ¶ Then said Saul to his servants, Seek me a woman that has a familiar spirit, that I may go to her, and inquire of her. And his servants said to him, Behold, *there is* a woman that has a familiar spirit at Endor.

8 And Saul disguised himself, and put on other clothes, and he went, and two men with him, and they came to the woman by night: and he said, I pray you, divine to me by the familiar spirit, and bring me *him* up, whom I shall name to you.

9 And the woman said to him, Behold, you know what Saul has done, how he has cut off those that have familiar spirits, and the wizards, out of the land: why then lay you a snare for my life, to cause me to die?

10 And Saul swore to her by Yahweh, saying, *As* Yahweh lives, there shall no punishment happen to you for this thing.

11 Then said the woman, Whom shall I bring up to you? And he said, Bring me up Samuel.

12 And when the woman saw Samuel, she cried with a loud voice: and the woman spoke to Saul, saying, Why have you deceived me? for you *are* Saul.

13 And the king said to her, Be not afraid: for what saw you? And the woman said to Saul, I saw gods ascending out of the earth.

14 And he said to her, What form *is* he of? And she said, An old man comes up; and he *is* covered with a mantle. And Saul perceived that it *was* Samuel, and he stooped with *his* face to the ground, and bowed himself.

15 ¶ And Samuel said to Saul, Why have you disquieted me, to bring me up? And Saul answered, I am greatly distressed; for the Philistines make war against me, and God is departed from me, and answers me no more, neither by prophets, nor by dreams: therefore I have called you, that you may make known to me what I shall do.

16 Then said Samuel, Why then do you ask of me, seeing Yahweh has departed from you, and has become your enemy?

17 And Yahweh has done to him, as he spoke by me: for Yahweh has torn the kingdom out of your hand, and given it to your neighbor, *even* to David:

18 Because you obeyed not the voice of Yahweh, nor executed his fierce wrath upon Amalek, therefore has Yahweh done this thing to you this day.

19 Moreover Yahweh will also deliver Israel with you into the hand of the Philistines: and tomorrow *shall* you and your sons *be* with me: Yahweh also shall deliver the host of Israel into the hand of the Philistines.

20 ¶ Then Saul fell suddenly all along on the earth, and was very afraid, because of the words of Samuel: and there was no strength in him; for he had eaten no bread all the day, nor all the night.

21 And the woman came to Saul, and saw that he was greatly troubled, and said unto him, Behold, your handmaid has obeyed your voice, and I have put my life in my hand, and have listened to your words which you spoke to me.

22 Now therefore, I pray you, listen you also to the voice of your handmaid, and let me set a morsel of bread before you; and eat, that you may have strength, when you go on your way.

1 Samuel 28 (continued)

23 But he refused, and said, I will not eat. But his servants, together with the woman, compelled him; and he listened to their voice. So he arose from the earth, and sat on the bed.
24 And the woman had a fat calf in the house; and she hurried, and killed it, and took flour, and kneaded *it*, and did bake unleavened bread thereof:
25 And she brought *it* before Saul, and before his servants; and they did eat. Then they rose up, and went away that night.

1 Samuel 29

29:1 ¶ Now the Philistines gathered together all their armies to Aphek: and the Israelites pitched by a fountain which *is* in Jezreel.
2 And the lords of the Philistines passed on by hundreds, and by thousands: but David and his men passed on in the rear guard with Achish.
3 Then said the princes of the Philistines, What *do* these Hebrews *here*? And Achish said to the princes of the Philistines, *Is* not this David, the servant of Saul the king of Israel, which has been with me these days, or these years, and I have found no fault in him since he fell *unto me* unto this day?
4 And the princes of the Philistines were angry with him; and the princes of the Philistines said to him, Make this fellow return, that he may go again to his place which you have appointed him, and let him not go down with us to battle, lest in the battle he *becomes* an adversary to us: for with what should he reconcile himself to his master? *should it* not *be* with the heads of these men?
5 *Is* not this David, of whom they sang one to another in dances, saying, Saul slew his thousands, and David his ten thousands?
6 ¶ Then Achish called David, and said to him, Surely, *as* Yahweh lives, you have been upright, and your going out and your coming in with me in the host *is* good in my sight: for I have not found evil in you since the day of your coming to me unto this day: nevertheless the lords favor you not.
7 Therefore now return, and go in peace, that you displease not the lords of the Philistines.
8 And David said to Achish, But what have I done? and what have you found in your servant so long as I have been with you unto this day, that I may not go fight against the enemies of my lord the king?
9 And Achish answered and said to David, I know that you *are* good in my sight, as an angel of God: notwithstanding the princes of the Philistines have said, He shall not go up with us to the battle.
10 Therefore now rise up early in the morning with your master's servants that have come with you: and as soon as you are up early in the morning, and have light, depart.
11 So David and his men rose up early to depart in the morning, to return into the land of the Philistines. And the Philistines went up to Jezreel.

1 Samuel 30

30:1 ¶ And it came to pass, when David and his men had come to Ziklag on the third day, that the Amalekites had invaded the south, and Ziklag, and smitten Ziklag, and burned it with fire;
2 And had taken the women captives, that *were* therein: they slew not any, either great or small, but carried *them* away, and went on their way.
3 So David and his men came to the city, and, behold, *it was* burned with fire; and their wives, and their sons, and their daughters, were taken captives.
4 Then David and the people that *were* with him lifted up their voice and wept, until they had no more power to weep.
5 And David's two wives were taken captives, Ahinoam the Jezreelitess, and Abigail the wife of Nabal the Carmelite.
6 And David was greatly distressed; for the people spoke of stoning him, because the souls of all the people were grieved, every man for his sons and for his daughters: but David encouraged himself in Yahweh his God.
7 ¶ And David said to Abiathar the priest, Ahimelech's son, I pray you, bring me here the ephod. And Abiathar brought there the ephod to David.
8 And David inquired at Yahweh, saying, Shall I pursue after this troop? shall I overtake them? And he answered him, Pursue: for you shall surely overtake *them*, and without fail recover *all*.
9 So David went, he and the six hundred men that *were* with him, and came to the brook Besor, where those that were left behind stayed.
10 But David pursued, he and four hundred men: for two hundred stayed behind, which were so faint that they could not go over the brook Besor.
11 And they found an Egyptian in the field, and brought him to David, and gave him bread, and he did eat; and they made him drink water;
12 And they gave him a piece of a cake of figs, and two clusters of raisins: and when he had eaten, his spirit came again to him: for he had eaten no bread, nor drunk *any* water, three days and three nights.
13 And David said to him, To whom *belong* you? and *from* where *are* you? And he said, I *am* a young man of Egypt, servant to an Amalekite; and my master left me, because three days ago I fell sick.
14 We made an invasion *upon* the south of the Cherethites, and upon *the coast* which *belongs* to Judah, and on the south of Caleb; and we burned Ziklag with fire.
15 And David said to him, Can you bring me down to this company? And he said, Swear to me by God, that you will neither kill me, nor deliver me into the hands of my master, and I will bring you down to this company.
16 And when he had brought him down, behold, *they were* spread abroad upon all the earth, eating and drinking, and dancing, because of all the great spoil that they had taken out of the land of the Philistines, and out of the land of Judah.

1 Samuel 30

17 And David smote them from the twilight even unto the evening of the next day: and there escaped not a man of them, save four hundred young men, which rode upon camels, and fled.
18 And David recovered all that the Amalekites had carried away: and David rescued his two wives.
19 And there was nothing lacking to them, neither small nor great, neither sons nor daughters, neither spoil, nor any *thing* that they had taken to them: David recovered all.
20 And David took all the flocks and the herds, *which* they drove before those *other* cattle, and said, This *is* David's spoil.
21 ¶ And David came to the two hundred men, which were so faint that they could not follow David, whom they had made also to remain at the brook Besor: and they went forth to meet David, and to meet the people that *were* with him: and when David came near to the people, he saluted them.
22 Then answered all the wicked men and *men* of Belial, of those that went with David, and said, Because they went not with us, we will not give them *anything* of the spoil that we have recovered, except to every man his wife and his children, that they may lead *them* away, and depart.
23 Then said David, You shall not do so, my brethren, with that which Yahweh has given us, who has preserved us, and delivered the company that came against us into our hand.
24 For who will listen to you in this matter? but as his part *is* that goes down to the battle, so *shall* his part *be* that tarries by the stuff: they shall share alike.
25 And it was *so* from that day forward, that he made it a statute and an ordinance for Israel unto this day.
26 And when David came to Ziklag, he sent of the spoil to the elders of Judah, *even* to his friends, saying, Behold a present for you of the spoil of the enemies of Yahweh;
27 To *them* which *were* in Bethel, and to *them* which *were* in south Ramoth, and to *them* which *were* in Jattir,
28 And to *them* which *were* in Aroer, and to *them* which *were* in Siphmoth, and to *them* which *were* in Eshtemoa,
29 And to *them* which *were* in Rachal, and to *them* which *were* in the cities of the Jerahmeelites, and to *them* which *were* in the cities of the Kenites,
30 And to *them* which *were* in Hormah, and to *them* which *were* in Chorashan, and to *them* which *were* in Athach,
31 And to *them* which *were* in Hebron, and to all the places where David himself and his men were inclined to go.

1 Samuel 31

31:1 ¶ Now the Philistines fought against Israel: and the men of Israel fled from before the Philistines, and fell down slain in mount Gilboa.
2 And the Philistines followed hard upon Saul and upon his sons; and the Philistines slew Jonathan, and Abinadab, and Malchishua, Saul's sons.
3 And the battle went grievously against Saul, and the archers hit him; and he was severely wounded of the archers.
4 Then said Saul to his armor bearer, Draw your sword, and thrust me through therewith; lest these uncircumcised come and thrust me through, and abuse me. But his armor bearer would not; for he was very afraid. Therefore Saul took a sword, and fell upon it.
5 And when his armor bearer saw that Saul was dead, he fell likewise upon his sword, and died with him.
6 So Saul died, and his three sons, and his armor bearer, and all his men, that same day together.
7 And when the men of Israel that *were* on the other side of the valley, and *they* that *were* on the other side *of the* Jordan, saw that the men of Israel fled, and that Saul and his sons were dead, they forsook the cities, and fled; and the Philistines came and dwelt in them.
8 ¶ And it came to pass on the next day, when the Philistines came to strip the slain, that they found Saul and his three sons fallen in mount Gilboa.
9 And they cut off his head, and stripped off his armor, and sent into the land of the Philistines round about, to publish *it in* the house of their idols, and among the people.
10 And they put his armor in the house of Ashtaroth: and they fastened his body to the wall of Bethshan.
11 And when the inhabitants of Jabeshgilead heard of that which the Philistines had done to Saul;
12 All the valiant men arose, and went all night, and took the body of Saul and the bodies of his sons from the wall of Bethshan, and came to Jabesh, and burnt them there.
13 And they took their bones, and buried *them* under a tree at Jabesh, and fasted seven days.

2 Samuel

2 Samuel 1

1:1 ¶ Now it came to pass after the death of Saul, when David had returned from the slaughter of the Amalekites, and David had stayed two days in Ziklag;
2 It came even to pass on the third day, that, behold, a man came out of the camp from Saul with his clothes torn, and earth upon his head: and *so* it was, when he came to David, that he fell to the earth, and did obeisance.
3 And David said to him, From where come you? And he said to him, Out of the camp of Israel have I escaped.
4 And David said to him, How went the matter? I pray you, tell me. And he answered, That the people have fled from the battle, and many of the people also have fallen and *are* dead; and Saul and Jonathan his son are dead also.
5 And David said to the young man that told him, How know you that Saul and Jonathan his son are dead?
6 And the young man that told him said, As I happened by chance upon mount Gilboa, behold, Saul leaned upon

his spear; and, lo, the chariots and horsemen followed hard after him.

7 And when he looked behind him, he saw me, and called to me. And I answered, Here *am* I.

8 And he said to me, Who *are* you? And I answered him, I *am* an Amalekite.

9 He said to me again, Stand, I pray you, upon me, and slay me: for anguish has come upon me, because my life *is* yet whole in me.

10 So I stood upon him, and slew him, because I was sure that he could not live after that he was fallen: and I took the crown that *was* upon his head, and the bracelet that *was* on his arm, and have brought them here to my lord.

11 ¶ Then David took hold on his clothes, and tore them; and likewise all the men that *were* with him:

12 And they mourned, and wept, and fasted until evening, for Saul, and for Jonathan his son, and for the people of Yahweh, and for the house of Israel; because they had fallen by the sword.

13 And David said to the young man that told him, *From* where *are* you? And he answered, I *am* the son of a stranger, an Amalekite.

14 And David said to him, How were you not afraid to stretch forth your hand to destroy Yahweh's anointed?

15 And David called one of the young men, and said, Go near, *and* fall upon him. And he smote him that he died.

16 And David said to him, Your blood *be* upon your head; for your mouth has testified against you, saying, I have slain Yahweh's anointed.

17 ¶ And David lamented with this lamentation over Saul and over Jonathan his son:

18 (Also he told them to teach the children of Judah *the use of* the bow: behold, *it* is written in the book of Jasher.)

19 The beauty of Israel is slain upon your high places: how are the mighty fallen!

20 Tell *it* not in Gath, publish *it* not in the streets of Askelon; lest the daughters of the Philistines rejoice, lest the daughters of the uncircumcised triumph.

21 You mountains of Gilboa, *let there be* no dew, neither *let there be* rain, upon you, nor fields of offerings: for there the shield of the mighty is vilely cast away, the shield of Saul, *as though he had* not *been* anointed with oil.

22 From the blood of the slain, from the fat of the mighty, the bow of Jonathan turned not back, and the sword of Saul returned not empty.

23 Saul and Jonathan *were* lovely and pleasant in their lives, and in their death they were not divided: they were swifter than eagles, they were stronger than lions.

24 You daughters of Israel, weep over Saul, who clothed you in scarlet, with *other* delights, who put on ornaments of gold upon your apparel.

25 How have the mighty fallen in the midst of the battle! O Jonathan, *you were* slain in your high places.

26 I am distressed for you, my brother Jonathan: very pleasant have you been to me: your love to me was wonderful, passing the love of women.

27 How have the mighty fallen, and the weapons of war perished!

2 Samuel 2

2:1 ¶ And it came to pass after this, that David inquired of Yahweh, saying, Shall I go up into any of the cities of Judah? And Yahweh said to him, Go up. And David said, Where shall I go up? And he said, Unto Hebron.

2 So David went up there, and his two wives also, Ahinoam the Jezreelitess, and Abigail Nabal's wife the Carmelite.

3 And his men that *were* with him did David bring up, every man with his household: and they dwelt in the cities of Hebron.

4 And the men of Judah came, and there they anointed David king over the house of Judah. And they told David, saying, *That* the men of Jabeshgilead *were they* that buried Saul.

5 And David sent messengers to the men of Jabeshgilead, and said to them, Blessed *be* you of Yahweh, that you have shown this kindness to your lord, *even* to Saul, and have buried him.

6 And now Yahweh show kindness and truth to you: and I also will offer you this kindness, because you have done this thing.

7 Therefore now let your hands be strengthened, and be you valiant: for your master Saul is dead, and also the house of Judah has anointed me king over them.

8 ¶ But Abner the son of Ner, captain of Saul's host, took Ishbosheth the son of Saul, and brought him over to Mahanaim;

9 And made him king over Gilead, and over the Ashurites, and over Jezreel, and over Ephraim, and over Benjamin, and over all Israel.

10 Ishbosheth Saul's son *was* forty years old when he began to reign over Israel, and reigned two years. But the house of Judah followed David.

11 And the time that David was king in Hebron over the house of Judah was seven years and six months.

12 And Abner the son of Ner, and the servants of Ishbosheth the son of Saul, went out from Mahanaim to Gibeon.

13 And Joab the son of Zeruiah, and the servants of David, went out, and met together by the pool of Gibeon: and they sat down, the one on the one side of the pool, and the other on the other side of the pool.

14 And Abner said to Joab, Let the young men now arise, and play before us. And Joab said, Let them arise.

15 Then there arose and went over by number twelve of Benjamin, which *pertained* to Ishbosheth the son of Saul, and twelve of the servants of David.

16 And they caught every one his fellow by the head, and *thrust* his sword in his fellow's side; so they fell down together: therefore that place was called Helkathhazzurim, which *is* in Gibeon.

17 And there was a very fierce battle that day; and Abner was beaten, and the men of Israel, before the servants of David.

18 ¶ And there were three sons of Zeruiah there, Joab, and Abishai, and Asahel: and Asahel *was as* light of foot as a wild roe.

19 And Asahel pursued after Abner; and in going he turned not to the right hand nor to the left from following Abner.

20 Then Abner looked behind him, and said, *Are* you Asahel? And he answered, I *am*.

21 And Abner said to him, Turn you aside to your right hand or to your left, and lay you hold on one of the young men, and take you his armor. But Asahel would not turn aside from following of him.

22 And Abner said again to Asahel, Turn you aside from following me: why should I smite you to the ground? how then should I hold up my face to Joab your brother?

23 However he refused to turn aside: therefore Abner with the hind end of the spear smote him under the fifth *rib*, *so* that the spear came out behind him; and he fell down there, and died in the same place: and it came to pass, *that* as many as came to the place where Asahel fell down and died stood still.

24 Joab also and Abishai pursued after Abner: and the sun went down when they had come to the hill of Ammah, that *lies* before Giah by the way of the wilderness of Gibeon.

25 ¶ And the children of Benjamin gathered themselves together behind Abner, and became one troop, and stood on the top of a hill.

26 Then Abner called to Joab, and said, Shall the sword devour forever? know you not that it will be bitterness in the latter end? how long shall it be then, before you bid the people return from following their brother?

27 And Joab said, *As* God lives, unless you had spoken, surely then in the morning the people had gone up every one from following his brother.

28 So Joab blew a trumpet, and all the people stood still, and pursued after Israel no more, neither fought they any more.

29 And Abner and his men walked all that night through the plain, and passed over *the* Jordan, and went through all Bithron, and they came to Mahanaim.

30 And Joab returned from following Abner: and when he had gathered all the people together, there lacked of David's servants nineteen men and Asahel.

31 But the servants of David had smitten of Benjamin, and of Abner's men, *so that* three hundred and threescore men died.

32 And they took up Asahel, and buried him in the sepulcher of his father, which *was in* Bethlehem. And Joab and his men went all night, and they came to Hebron at *the* break of day.

2 Samuel 3

3:1 ¶ Now there was long war between the house of Saul and the house of David: but David grew stronger and stronger, and the house of Saul grew weaker and weaker.

2 And to David were sons born in Hebron: and his firstborn was Amnon, of Ahinoam the Jezreelitess;

3 And his second, Chileab, of Abigail the wife of Nabal the Carmelite; and the third, Absalom the son of Maacah the daughter of Talmai king of Geshur;

4 And the fourth, Adonijah the son of Haggith; and the fifth, Shephatiah the son of Abital;

5 And the sixth, Ithream, by Eglah David's wife. These were born to David in Hebron.

6 And it came to pass, while there was war between the house of Saul and the house of David, that Abner made himself strong for the house of Saul.

7 ¶ And Saul had a concubine, whose name *was* Rizpah, the daughter of Aiah: and *Ishbosheth* said to Abner, Why have you gone in unto my father's concubine?

8 Then was Abner very angry for the words of Ishbosheth, and said, *Am* I a dog's head, which against Judah do show kindness this day unto the house of Saul your father, to his brothers, and to his friends, and have not delivered you into the hand of David, that you charge me today with a fault concerning this woman?

9 So do God to Abner, and more also, except, as Yahweh has sworn to David, even so I do to him;

10 To translate the kingdom from the house of Saul, and to set up the throne of David over Israel and over Judah, from Dan even to Beersheba.

11 And he could not answer Abner a word again, because he feared him.

12 And Abner sent messengers to David on his behalf, saying, Whose *is* the land? saying *also*, Make your league with me, and, behold, my hand *shall be* with you, to bring about all Israel to you.

13 And he said, Well; I will make a league with you: but one thing I require of you, that is, You shall not see my face, except you first bring Michal, Saul's daughter, when you come to see my face.

14 And David sent messengers to Ishbosheth Saul's son, saying, Deliver *me* my wife Michal, which I espoused to me for a hundred foreskins of the Philistines.

15 And Ishbosheth sent, and took her from *her* husband, *even* from Phaltiel the son of Laish.

16 And her husband went with her along weeping behind her to Bahurim. Then said Abner to him, Go, return. And he returned.

17 And Abner had communication with the elders of Israel, saying, You sought for David in times past *to be* king over you:

18 Now then do *it*: for Yahweh has spoken of David, saying, By the hand of my servant David I will save my people Israel out of the hand of the Philistines, and out of the hand of all their enemies.

19 And Abner also spoke in the ears of Benjamin: and Abner went also to speak in the ears of David in Hebron all that seemed good to Israel, and that seemed good to the whole house of Benjamin.

20 So Abner came to David at Hebron, and twenty men with him. And David made Abner and the men that *were* with him a feast.

21 And Abner said to David, I will arise and go, and will gather all Israel to my lord the king, that they may make a league with you, and that you may reign over all that your heart desires. And David sent Abner away; and he went in peace.

22 ¶ And, behold, the servants of David and Joab came from *pursuing* a troop, and brought in a great spoil with them: but Abner *was* not with David in Hebron; for he had sent him away, and he had gone in peace.

23 When Joab and all the host that *were* with him had come, they told Joab, saying, Abner the son of Ner came to the king, and he has sent him away, and he has gone in peace.

24 Then Joab came to the king, and said, What have you done? behold, Abner came to you; why *is* it *that* you have sent him away, and he is quite gone?

25 You know Abner the son of Ner, that he came to deceive you, and to know your going out and your coming in, and to know all that you do.

26 And when Joab had come out from David, he sent messengers after Abner, which brought him again from the well of Sirah: but David knew *it* not.

27 And when Abner was returned to Hebron, Joab took him aside in the gate to speak with him quietly, and smote him there under the fifth *rib*, *so* that he died, for the blood of Asahel his brother.

28 And afterward when David heard *it*, he said, I and my kingdom *are* guiltless before Yahweh forever from the blood of Abner the son of Ner:

29 Let it rest on the head of Joab, and on all his father's house; and let there not fail from the house of Joab one that has an issue, or that is a leper, or that leans on a staff, or that falls on the sword, or that lacks bread.

30 So Joab and Abishai his brother slew Abner, because he had slain their brother Asahel at Gibeon in the battle.

31 And David said to Joab, and to all the people that *were* with him, Tear your clothes, and gird you with sackcloth, and mourn before Abner. And king David *himself* followed the coffin.

32 And they buried Abner in Hebron: and the king lifted up his voice, and wept at the grave of Abner; and all the people wept.

33 And the king lamented over Abner, and said, Died Abner as a fool dies?

34 Your hands *were* not bound, nor your feet put into fetters: as a man falls before wicked men, *so* fell you. And all the people wept again over him.

35 And when all the people came to cause David to eat food while it was yet day, David swore, saying, So do God to me, and more also, if I taste bread, or anything else, till the sun is down.

36 And all the people took notice *of it*, and it pleased them: as whatever the king did pleased all the people.

37 For all the people and all Israel understood that day that it was not of the king to slay Abner the son of Ner.

38 And the king said to his servants, Know you not that there is a prince and a great man fallen this day in Israel?

39 And I *am* this day weak, though anointed king; and these men the sons of Zeruiah *are* too hard for me: Yahweh shall reward the doer of evil according to his wickedness.

2 Samuel 4

4:1 ¶ And when Saul's son heard that Abner was dead in Hebron, his hands were feeble, and all the Israelites were troubled.

2 And Saul's son had two men *that were* captains of bands: the name of the one *was* Baanah, and the name of the other Rechab, the sons of Rimmon a Beerothite, of the children of Benjamin: (for Beeroth also was reckoned to Benjamin:

3 And the Beerothites fled to Gittaim, and were sojourners there until this day.)

4 And Jonathan, Saul's son, had a son *that was* lame of *his* feet. He was five years old when the tidings came of Saul and Jonathan out of Jezreel, and his nurse took him up, and fled: and it came to pass, as she made haste to flee, that he fell, and became lame. And his name *was* Mephibosheth.

5 And the sons of Rimmon the Beerothite, Rechab and Baanah, went, and came *at* about the heat of the day to the house of Ishbosheth, who lay on a bed at noon.

6 And they came there into the midst of the house, *as though* they would have fetched wheat; and they smote him under the fifth *rib*: and Rechab and Baanah his brother escaped.

7 For when they came into the house, he lay on his bed in his bedchamber, and they smote him, and slew him, and beheaded him, and took his head, and got them away through the plain all night.

8 And they brought the head of Ishbosheth to David to Hebron, and said to the king, Behold the head of Ishbosheth the son of Saul your enemy, which sought your life; and Yahweh has avenged my lord the king this day of Saul, and of his seed.

9 ¶ And David answered Rechab and Baanah his brother, the sons of Rimmon the Beerothite, and said to them, *As* Yahweh lives, who has redeemed my soul out of all adversity,

10 When one told me, saying, Behold, Saul is dead, thinking to have brought good tidings, I took hold of him, and slew him in Ziklag, who *thought* that I would have given him a reward for his tidings:

11 How much more, when wicked men have slain a righteous person in his own house upon his bed? shall I not therefore now require his blood of your hand, and take you away from the earth?

12 And David commanded his young men, and they slew them, and cut off their hands and their feet, and hanged *them* up over the pool in Hebron. But they took the head of Ishbosheth, and buried *it* in the sepulcher of Abner in Hebron.

2 Samuel 5

5:1 ¶ Then came all the tribes of Israel to David to Hebron, and spoke, saying, Behold, we *are* your bone and your flesh.

2 Samuel 5

2 Also in time past, when Saul was king over us, you were he that led out and brought in Israel: and Yahweh said to you, You shall feed my people Israel, and you shall be a captain over Israel.

3 So all the elders of Israel came to the king at Hebron; and king David made a league with them in Hebron before Yahweh: and they anointed David king over Israel.

4 David *was* thirty years old when he began to reign, *and* he reigned *for* forty years.

5 In Hebron he reigned over Judah seven years and six months: and in Jerusalem he reigned thirty and three years over all Israel and Judah.

6 ¶ And the king and his men went to Jerusalem to the Jebusites, the inhabitants of the land: which spoke to David, saying, Unless you take away the blind and the lame, you shall not come in here: thinking, David cannot come in here.

7 Nevertheless David took the strong hold of Zion: the same *is* the city of David.

8 And David said on that day, Whoever gets up to the gutter, and smites the Jebusites, and the lame and the blind, *that are* hated of David's soul, *he shall be chief and captain*. Therefore they said, The blind and the lame shall not come into the house.

9 So David dwelt in the fort, and called it the city of David. And David built round about from Millo and inward.

10 And David went on, and grew great, and Yahweh God of hosts *was* with him.

11 ¶ And Hiram king of Tyre sent messengers to David, and cedar trees, and carpenters, and masons: and they built David a house.

12 And David perceived that Yahweh had established him king over Israel, and that he had exalted his kingdom for his people Israel's sake.

13 And David took *him* more concubines and wives out of Jerusalem, after he had come from Hebron: and there were yet sons and daughters born to David.

14 And these *are* the names of those that were born to him in Jerusalem; Shammua, and Shobab, and Nathan, and Solomon,

15 Ibhar also, and Elishua, and Nepheg, and Japhia,

16 And Elishama, and Eliada, and Eliphalet.

17 ¶ But when the Philistines heard that they had anointed David king over Israel, all the Philistines came up to seek David; and David heard *of it*, and went down to the hold.

18 The Philistines also came and spread themselves in the valley of Rephaim.

19 And David inquired of Yahweh, saying, Shall I go up to the Philistines? will you deliver them into my hand? And Yahweh said to David, Go up: for I will doubtless deliver the Philistines into your hand.

20 And David came to Baalperazim, and David smote them there, and said, Yahweh has broken forth upon my enemies before me, as the breach of waters. Therefore he called the name of that place Baalperazim.

21 And there they left their images, and David and his men burned them.

22 And the Philistines came up yet again, and spread themselves in the valley of Rephaim.

23 And when David inquired of Yahweh, he said, You shall not go up; *but* circle around behind them, and come upon them over against the mulberry trees.

24 And let it be, when you hear the sound of a going in the tops of the mulberry trees, that then you shall move yourself: for then shall Yahweh go out before you, to smite the host of the Philistines.

25 And David did so, as Yahweh had commanded him; and smote the Philistines from Geba until you come to Gazer.

2 Samuel 6

6:1 ¶ Again, David gathered together all *the* chosen *men* of Israel, thirty thousand.

2 And David arose, and went with all the people that *were* with him from Baale of Judah, to bring up from there the ark of God, whose name is called by the name of Yahweh of hosts that dwells *between* the cherubims.

3 And they set the ark of God upon a new cart, and brought it out of the house of Abinadab that *was* in Gibeah: and Uzzah and Ahio, the sons of Abinadab, drove the new cart.

4 And they brought it out of the house of Abinadab which *was* at Gibeah, accompanying the ark of God: and Ahio went before the ark.

5 And David and all the house of Israel played before Yahweh on all manner of *instruments made of* fir wood, even on harps, and on psalteries, and on tambourines, and on cornets, and on cymbals.

6 ¶ And when they came to Nachon's threshingfloor, Uzzah put forth *his hand* to the ark of God, and took hold of it; for the oxen shook *it*.

7 And the anger of Yahweh was kindled against Uzzah; and God smote him there for *his* error; and there he died by the ark of God.

8 And David was displeased, because Yahweh had made a breach upon Uzzah: and he called the name of the place Perezuzzah unto this day.

9 And David was afraid of Yahweh that day, and said, How shall the ark of Yahweh come to me?

10 So David would not remove the ark of Yahweh unto him into the city of David: but David carried it aside into the house of Obededom the Gittite.

11 And the ark of Yahweh continued in the house of Obededom the Gittite *for* three months: and Yahweh blessed Obededom, and all his household.

12 ¶ And it was told *to* king David, saying, Yahweh has blessed the house of Obededom, and all that *pertains* to him, because of the ark of God. So David went and brought up the ark of God from the house of Obededom into the city of David with gladness.

13 And it was *so*, that when they that bore the ark of Yahweh had gone six paces, he sacrificed oxen and fatted calves.

14 And David danced before Yahweh with all *his* might; and David *was* girded with a linen ephod.

15 So David and all the house of Israel brought up the ark of Yahweh with shouting, and with the sound of the trumpet.

16 And as the ark of Yahweh came into the city of David, Michal, Saul's daughter, looked through a window, and saw king David leaping and dancing before Yahweh; and she despised him in her heart.

17 And they brought in the ark of Yahweh, and set it in his place, in the midst of the tabernacle that David had pitched for it: and David offered burnt offerings and peace offerings before Yahweh.

18 And as soon as David had made an end of offering burnt offerings and peace offerings, he blessed the people in the name of Yahweh of hosts.

19 And he dealt among all the people, *even* among the whole multitude of Israel, as well to the women as men, to every one a cake of bread, and a good piece *of flesh*, and a flagon *of wine*. So all the people departed every one to his house.

20 ¶ Then David returned to bless his household. And Michal the daughter of Saul came out to meet David, and said, How glorious was the king of Israel today, who uncovered himself today in the eyes of the handmaids of his servants, as one of the vain fellows shamelessly uncovers himself!

21 And David said to Michal, *It was* before Yahweh, which chose me before your father, and before all his house, to appoint me ruler over the people of Yahweh, over Israel: therefore will I play before Yahweh.

22 And I will yet be more vile than thus, and will be base in my own sight: and of the maidservants which you have spoken of, of them shall I be had in honor.

23 Therefore Michal the daughter of Saul had no child to the day of her death.

2 Samuel 7

7:1 ¶ And it came to pass, when the king sat in his house, and Yahweh had given him rest round about from all his enemies;

2 That the king said to Nathan the prophet, See now, I dwell in a house of cedar, but the ark of God dwells within curtains.

3 And Nathan said to the king, Go, do all that *is* in your heart; for Yahweh *is* with you.

4 ¶ And it came to pass that night, that the word of Yahweh came to Nathan, saying,

5 Go and tell my servant David, Thus says Yahweh, Shall you build me a house for me to dwell in?

6 Whereas I have not dwelt in *any* house since the time that I brought up the children of Israel out of Egypt, even unto this day, but have walked in a tent and in a tabernacle.

7 In all *the places* wherein I have walked with all the children of Israel spoke I a word with any of the tribes of Israel, whom I commanded to feed my people Israel, saying, Why build you not me a house of cedar?

8 Now therefore so shall you say to my servant David, Thus says Yahweh of hosts, I took you from the sheepfold, from following the sheep, to be ruler over my people, over Israel:

9 And I was with you wherever you went, and have cut off all your enemies out of your sight, and have made you a great name, like unto the name of the great *men* that *are* in the earth.

10 Moreover I will appoint a place for my people Israel, and will plant them, that they may dwell in a place of their own, and move no more; neither shall the children of wickedness afflict them any more, as before,

11 And as since the time that I commanded judges *to be* over my people Israel, and have caused you to rest from all your enemies. Also Yahweh tells you that he will make you a house.

12 And when your days are fulfilled, and you shall sleep with your fathers, I will set up your seed after you, which shall proceed out of your bowels, and I will establish his kingdom.

13 He shall build a house for my name, and I will establish the throne of his kingdom forever.

14 I will be his father, and he shall be my son. If he commits iniquity, I will chasten him with the rod of men, and with the stripes of the children of men:

15 But my mercy shall not depart away from him, as I took *it* from Saul, whom I put away before you.

16 And your house and your kingdom shall be established forever before you: your throne shall be established forever.

17 According to all these words, and according to all this vision, so did Nathan speak to David.

18 ¶ Then went king David in, and sat before Yahweh, and he said, Who *am* I, O Lord Yahweh? and what *is* my house, that you have brought me till now?

19 And this was yet a small thing in your sight, O Lord Yahweh; but you have spoken also of your servant's house for a great while to come. And *is* this the manner of man, O Lord Yahweh?

20 And what can David say more to you? for you, Lord Yahweh, know your servant.

21 For your word's sake, and according to your own heart, have you done all these great things, to make your servant know *them*.

22 Therefore you are great, O Yahweh God: for *there is* none like you, neither *is there any* God besides you, according to all that we have heard with our ears.

23 And what one nation in the earth *is* like your people, *even* like Israel, whom God went to redeem for a people to himself, and to make him a name, and to do for you great things and terrible, for your land, before your people, which you redeemed to you from Egypt, *from* the nations and their gods?

24 For you have confirmed to yourself your people Israel *to be* a people to you forever: and you, Yahweh, have become their God.

25 And now, O Yahweh God, the word that you have spoken concerning your servant, and concerning his house, establish *it* forever, and do as you have said.

26 And let your name be magnified forever, saying, Yahweh of hosts *is* the God over Israel: and let the house of your servant David be established before you.
27 For you, O Yahweh of hosts, God of Israel, have revealed to your servant, saying, I will build you a house: therefore has your servant found in his heart to pray this prayer to you.
28 And now, O Lord Yahweh, you *are* that God, and your words are true, and you have promised this goodness to your servant:
29 Therefore now let it please you to bless the house of your servant, that it may continue forever before you: for you, O Lord Yahweh, have spoken *it*: and with your blessing let the house of your servant be blessed forever.

2 Samuel 8

8:1 ¶ And after this it came to pass, that David smote the Philistines, and subdued them: and David took Methegammah out of the hand of the Philistines.
2 And he smote Moab, and measured them with a line, casting them down to the ground; even with two lines measured he to put to death, and with one full line to keep alive. And *so* the Moabites became David's servants, *and* brought gifts.
3 David smote also Hadadezer, the son of Rehob, king of Zobah, as he went to recover his border at the river Euphrates.
4 And David took from him a thousand *chariots*, and seven hundred horsemen, and twenty thousand footmen: and David crippled all the chariot *horses*, but reserved of them *for* a hundred chariots.
5 And when the Syrians of Damascus came to help Hadadezer king of Zobah, David slew of the Syrians two and twenty thousand men.
6 Then David put garrisons in Syria of Damascus: and the Syrians became servants to David, *and* brought gifts. And Yahweh preserved David wherever he went.
7 And David took the shields of gold that were on the servants of Hadadezer, and brought them to Jerusalem.
8 And from Betah, and from Berothai, cities of Hadadezer, king David took exceedingly much brass.
9 ¶ When Toi king of Hamath heard that David had smitten all the host of Hadadezer,
10 Then Toi sent Joram his son to king David, to salute him, and to bless him, because he had fought against Hadadezer, and smitten him: for Hadadezer had wars with Toi. And *Joram* brought with him vessels of silver, and vessels of gold, and vessels of brass:
11 Which also king David did dedicate unto Yahweh, with the silver and gold that he had dedicated of all nations which he subdued;
12 Of Syria, and of Moab, and of the children of Ammon, and of the Philistines, and of Amalek, and of the spoil of Hadadezer, son of Rehob, king of Zobah.
13 And David got *him* a name when he returned from smiting of the Syrians in the valley of salt, *being* eighteen thousand *men*.
14 And he put garrisons in Edom; throughout all Edom put he garrisons, and all they of Edom became David's servants. And Yahweh preserved David wherever he went.
15 ¶ And David reigned over all Israel; and David executed judgment and justice to all his people.
16 And Joab the son of Zeruiah *was* over the host; and Jehoshaphat the son of Ahilud *was* recorder;
17 And Zadok the son of Ahitub, and Ahimelech the son of Abiathar, *were* the priests; and Seraiah *was* the scribe;
18 And Benaiah the son of Jehoiada *was over* both the Cherethites and the Pelethites; and David's sons were chief rulers.

2 Samuel 9

9:1 ¶ And David said, Is there yet any that is left of the house of Saul, that I may show him kindness for Jonathan's sake?
2 And *there was* of the house of Saul a servant whose name *was* Ziba. And when they had called him to David, the king said to him, *Are* you Ziba? And he said, Your servant *is* he.
3 And the king said, *Is* there not yet any of the house of Saul, that I may show the kindness of God to him? And Ziba said to the king, Jonathan has yet a son, *which is* lame on *his* feet.
4 And the king said to him, Where *is* he? And Ziba said to the king, Behold, he *is* in the house of Machir, the son of Ammiel, in Lodebar.
5 Then king David sent, and fetched him out of the house of Machir, the son of Ammiel, from Lodebar.
6 Now when Mephibosheth, the son of Jonathan, the son of Saul, had come to David, he fell on his face, and did reverence. And David said, Mephibosheth. And he answered, Behold your servant!
7 And David said to him, Fear not: for I will surely show you kindness for Jonathan your father's sake, and will restore *to* you all the land of Saul your father; and you shall eat bread at my table continually.
8 And he bowed himself, and said, What *is* your servant, that you should look upon such a dead dog as I *am*?
9 ¶ Then the king called to Ziba, Saul's servant, and said to him, I have given to your master's son all that pertained to Saul and to all his house.
10 You therefore, and your sons, and your servants, shall till the land for him, and you shall bring in *the fruits*, that your master's son may have food to eat: but Mephibosheth your master's son shall eat bread always at my table. Now Ziba had fifteen sons and twenty servants.
11 Then said Ziba to the king, According to all that my lord the king has commanded his servant, so shall your servant do. As for Mephibosheth, *said the king*, he shall eat at my table, as one of the king's sons.
12 And Mephibosheth had a young son, whose name *was* Micha. And all that dwelt in the house of Ziba *were* servants to Mephibosheth.

13 So Mephibosheth dwelt in Jerusalem: for he did eat continually at the king's table; and was lame on both his feet.

2 Samuel 10

10:1 ¶ And it came to pass after this, that the king of the children of Ammon died, and Hanun his son reigned in his stead.

2 Then said David, I will show kindness to Hanun the son of Nahash, as his father showed kindness to me. And David sent to comfort him by the hand of his servants for his father. And David's servants came into the land of the children of Ammon.

3 And the princes of the children of Ammon said to Hanun their lord, Think you that David does honor your father, that he has sent comforters to you? has not David *rather* sent his servants to you, to search the city, and to spy it out, and to overthrow it?

4 Therefore Hanun took David's servants, and shaved off the one half of their beards, and cut off their garments in the middle, *even* to their buttocks, and sent them away.

5 When they told *it* to David, he sent to meet them, because the men were greatly ashamed: and the king said, Tarry at Jericho until your beards are grown, and *then* return.

6 ¶ And when the children of Ammon saw that they stank before David, the children of Ammon sent and hired the Syrians of Bethrehob, and the Syrians of Zoba, twenty thousand footmen, and of king Maacah a thousand men, and of Ishtob twelve thousand men.

7 And when David heard of *it*, he sent Joab, and all the host of the mighty men.

8 And the children of Ammon came out, and put the battle in array at the entering in of the gate: and the Syrians of Zoba, and of Rehob, and Ishtob, and Maacah, *were* by themselves in the field.

9 When Joab saw that the front of the battle was against him before and behind, he chose of all the choice *men* of Israel, and put *them* in array against the Syrians:

10 And the rest of the people he delivered into the hand of Abishai his brother, that he might put *them* in array against the children of Ammon.

11 And he said, If the Syrians are too strong for me, then you shall help me: but if the children of Ammon are too strong for you, then I will come and help you.

12 Be of good courage, and let us strengthen the men for our people, and for the cities of our God: and Yahweh do that which seems him good.

13 And Joab drew nigh, and the people that *were* with him, to the battle against the Syrians: and they fled before him.

14 And when the children of Ammon saw that the Syrians had fled, then fled they also before Abishai, and entered into the city. So Joab returned from the children of Ammon, and came to Jerusalem.

15 ¶ And when the Syrians saw that they were smitten before Israel, they gathered themselves together.

16 And Hadarezer sent, and brought out the Syrians that *were* beyond the river: and they came to Helam; and Shobach the captain of the host of Hadarezer *went* before them.

17 And when it was told David, he gathered all Israel together, and passed over *the* Jordan, and came to Helam. And the Syrians set themselves in array against David, and fought with him.

18 And the Syrians fled before Israel; and David slew *the men of* seven hundred chariots of the Syrians, and forty thousand horsemen, and smote Shobach the captain of their host, who died there.

19 And when all the kings *that were* servants to Hadarezer saw that they were smitten before Israel, they made peace with Israel, and served them. So the Syrians feared to help the children of Ammon any more.

2 Samuel 11

11:1 ¶ And it came to pass, after the year was expired, at the time when kings go forth *to battle*, that David sent Joab, and his servants with him, and all Israel; and they destroyed the children of Ammon, and besieged Rabbah. But David tarried still at Jerusalem.

2 And it came to pass in an evening, that David arose from off his bed, and walked upon the roof of the king's house: and from the roof he saw a woman washing herself; and the woman *was* very beautiful to look upon.

3 And David sent and inquired after the woman. And *one* said, *Is* not this Bathsheba, the daughter of Eliam, the wife of Uriah the Hittite?

4 And David sent messengers, and took her; and she came in unto him, and he lay with her; for she was purified from her uncleanness: and she returned to her house.

5 And the woman conceived, and sent and told David, and said, I *am* with child.

6 ¶ And David sent to Joab, *saying*, Send me Uriah the Hittite. And Joab sent Uriah to David.

7 And when Uriah had come to him, David demanded *of him* how Joab did, and how the people did, and how the war prospered.

8 And David said to Uriah, Go down to your house, and wash your feet. And Uriah departed out of the king's house, and there followed him a gift *of food* from the king.

9 But Uriah slept at the door of the king's house with all the servants of his lord, and went not down to his house.

10 And when they had told David, saying, Uriah went not down to his house, David said to Uriah, Came you not from *your* journey? why *then* did you not go down to your house?

11 And Uriah said to David, The ark, and Israel, and Judah, dwell in tents; and my lord Joab, and the servants of my lord, are encamped in the open fields; shall I then go into my house, to eat and to drink, and to lie with my wife? *as* you live, and *as* your soul lives, I will not do this thing.

2 Samuel 11

12 And David said to Uriah, Tarry here today also, and tomorrow I will let you depart. So Uriah stayed in Jerusalem that day, and the next day.

13 And when David had called him, he did eat and drink before him; and he made him drunk: and at evening he went out to lie on his bed with the servants of his lord, but went not down to his house.

14 ¶ And it came to pass in the morning, that David wrote a letter to Joab, and sent *it* by the hand of Uriah.

15 And he wrote in the letter, saying, Set you Uriah in the forefront of the hottest battle, and retire you from him, that he may be smitten, and die.

16 And it came to pass, when Joab observed the city, that he assigned Uriah to a place where he knew that valiant men *were*.

17 And the men of the city went out, and fought with Joab: and there fell *some* of the people of the servants of David; and Uriah the Hittite died also.

18 Then Joab sent and told David all the things concerning the war;

19 And charged the messenger, saying, When you have made an end of telling the matters of the war to the king,

20 And if so be that the king's wrath arises, and he says to you, Why approached you so near to the city when you did fight? knew you not that they would shoot from the wall?

21 Who smote Abimelech the son of Jerubbesheth? did not a woman cast a piece of a millstone upon him from the wall, that he died in Thebez? why went you near the wall? then say you, Your servant Uriah the Hittite is dead also.

22 So the messenger went, and came and showed David all that Joab had sent him for.

23 And the messenger said to David, Surely the men prevailed against us, and came out to us into the field, and we were upon them even to the entering of the gate.

24 And the shooters shot from off the wall upon your servants; and *some* of the king's servants are dead, and your servant Uriah the Hittite is dead also.

25 Then David said to the messenger, Thus shall you say to Joab, Let not this thing displease you, for the sword devours one as well as another: make your battle more strong against the city, and overthrow it: and encourage you him.

26 And when the wife of Uriah heard that Uriah her husband was dead, she mourned for her husband.

27 And when the mourning was past, David sent and fetched her to his house, and she became his wife, and bore him a son. But the thing that David had done displeased Yahweh.

2 Samuel 12

12:1 ¶ And Yahweh sent Nathan to David. And he came to him, and said to him, There were two men in one city; the one rich, and the other poor.

2 The rich *man* had exceedingly many flocks and herds:

3 But the poor *man* had nothing, save one little ewe lamb, which he had bought and nourished up: and it grew up together with him, and with his children; it did eat of his own food, and drank of his own cup, and lay in his bosom, and was to him as a daughter.

4 And there came a traveler to the rich man, and he spared to take of his own flock and of his own herd, to dress for the wayfaring man that had come to him; but took the poor man's lamb, and dressed it for the man that had come to him.

5 And David's anger was greatly kindled against the man; and he said to Nathan, *As* Yahweh lives, the man that has done this *thing* shall surely die:

6 And he shall restore the lamb fourfold, because he did this thing, and because he had no pity.

7 And Nathan said to David, You *are* the man. Thus says Yahweh God of Israel, I anointed you king over Israel, and I delivered you out of the hand of Saul;

8 And I gave you your master's house, and your master's wives into your bosom, and gave you the house of Israel and of Judah; and if *that had been* too little, I would moreover have given to you such and such things.

9 Why have you despised the commandment of Yahweh, to do evil in his sight? you have killed Uriah the Hittite with the sword, and have taken his wife *to be* your wife, and have slain him with the sword of the children of Ammon.

10 Now therefore the sword shall never depart from your house; because you have despised me, and have taken the wife of Uriah the Hittite to be your wife.

11 Thus says Yahweh, Behold, I will raise up evil against you out of your own house, and I will take your wives before your eyes, and give *them* to your neighbor, and he shall lie with your wives in the sight of this sun.

12 For you did *it* secretly: but I will do this thing before all Israel, and before the sun.

13 And David said to Nathan, I have sinned against Yahweh. And Nathan said to David, Yahweh also has put away your sin; you shall not die.

14 However, because by this deed you have given great occasion to the enemies of Yahweh to blaspheme, the child also *that is* born to you shall surely die.

15 ¶ And Nathan departed to his house. And Yahweh struck the child that Uriah's wife bore unto David, and it was very sick.

16 David therefore sought God for the child; and David fasted, and went in, and lay all night upon the earth.

17 And the elders of his house arose, *and went* to him, to raise him up from the earth: but he would not, neither did he eat bread with them.

18 And it came to pass on the seventh day, that the child died. And the servants of David feared to tell him that the child was dead: for they said, Behold, while the child was yet alive, we spoke to him, and he would not listen to our voice: how will he then harm himself, if we tell him that the child is dead?

19 But when David saw that his servants whispered, David perceived that the child was dead: therefore David

said to his servants, Is the child dead? And they said, He is dead.

20 Then David arose from the earth, and washed, and anointed *himself*, and changed his apparel, and came into the house of Yahweh, and worshipped: then he came to his own house; and when he required, they set bread before him, and he did eat.

21 Then said his servants to him, What thing *is* this that you have done? you did fast and weep for the child, *while it was* alive; but when the child was dead, you did rise and eat bread.

22 And he said, While the child was yet alive, I fasted and wept: for I said, Who can tell *whether* Yahweh will be gracious to me, that the child may live?

23 But now he is dead, why should I fast? can I bring him back again? I shall go to him, but he shall not return to me.

24 And David comforted Bathsheba his wife, and went in to her, and lay with her: and she bore a son, and he called his name Solomon: and Yahweh loved him.

25 And he sent by the hand of Nathan the prophet; and he called his name Jedidiah, because of Yahweh.

26 ¶ And Joab fought against Rabbah of the children of Ammon, and took the royal city.

27 And Joab sent messengers to David, and said, I have fought against Rabbah, and have taken the city of waters.

28 Now therefore gather the rest of the people together, and encamp against the city, and take it: lest I take the city, and it be called after my name.

29 And David gathered all the people together, and went to Rabbah, and fought against it, and took it.

30 And he took their king's crown from off his head, the weight thereof *was* a talent of gold with the precious stones: and it was *set* on David's head. And he brought forth the spoil of the city in great abundance.

31 And he brought forth the people that *were* therein, and put *them* under saws, and under cutting tools of iron, and under axes of iron, and made them pass through the brick kiln: and thus did he to all the cities of the children of Ammon. So David and all the people returned to Jerusalem.

2 Samuel 13

13:1 ¶ And it came to pass after this, that Absalom the son of David had a fair sister, whose name *was* Tamar; and Amnon the son of David loved her.

2 And Amnon was so distressed, that he fell sick for his sister Tamar; for she *was* a virgin; and Amnon thought it hard for him to do anything to her.

3 But Amnon had a friend, whose name *was* Jonadab, the son of Shimeah David's brother: and Jonadab *was* a very subtle man.

4 And he said to him, Why *are* you, *being* the king's son, lean from day to day? will you not tell me? And Amnon said to him, I love Tamar, my brother Absalom's sister.

5 And Jonadab said to him, Lay you down on your bed, and make yourself sick: and when your father comes to see you, say to him, I pray you, let my sister Tamar come, and give me food, and prepare the food in my sight, that I may see *it*, and eat *it* from her hand.

6 So Amnon lay down, and made himself sick: and when the king had come to see him, Amnon said to the king, I pray you, let Tamar my sister come, and make me a couple of cakes in my sight, that I may eat from her hand.

7 Then David sent home to Tamar, saying, Go now to your brother Amnon's house, and prepare him food.

8 So Tamar went to her brother Amnon's house; and he was laying down. And she took flour, and kneaded *it*, and made cakes in his sight, and did bake the cakes.

9 And she took a pan, and poured *them* out before him; but he refused to eat. And Amnon said, Have out all men from me. And they went out every man from him.

10 And Amnon said to Tamar, Bring the food into the chamber, that I may eat of your hand. And Tamar took the cakes which she had made, and brought *them* into the chamber to Amnon her brother.

11 And when she had brought *them* to him to eat, he took hold of her, and said to her, Come lie with me, my sister.

12 And she answered him, No, my brother, do not force me; for no such thing ought to be done in Israel: do not you this folly.

13 And I, where shall I cause my shame to go? and as for you, you shall be as one of the fools in Israel. Now therefore, I pray you, speak to the king; for he will not withhold me from you.

14 However he would not listen to her voice: but, being stronger than her, forced her, and lay with her.

15 Then Amnon hated her exceedingly; so that the hatred with which he hated her *was* greater than the love with which he had loved her. And Amnon said to her, Arise, be gone.

16 And she said to him, *There is* no cause: this evil in sending me away *is* greater than the other that you did to me. But he would not listen to her.

17 Then he called his servant that ministered to him, and said, Put now this *woman* out from me, and bolt the door after her.

18 And *she had* a garment of diverse colors upon her: for with such robes were the king's daughters *that were* virgins appareled. Then his servant brought her out, and bolted the door after her.

19 And Tamar put ashes on her head, and tore her garment of diverse colors that *was* on her, and laid her hand on her head, and went on crying.

20 And Absalom her brother said to her, Has Amnon your brother been with you? but hold now your peace, my sister: he *is* your brother; regard not this thing. So Tamar remained desolate in her brother Absalom's house.

21 ¶ But when king David heard of all these things, he was very angry.

2 Samuel 13

22 And Absalom spoke to his brother Amnon neither good nor bad: for Absalom hated Amnon, because he had forced his sister Tamar.

23 And it came to pass after two full years, that Absalom had sheep shearers in Baalhazor, which *is* beside Ephraim: and Absalom invited all the king's sons.

24 And Absalom came to the king, and said, Behold now, your servant has sheep shearers; let the king, I beseech you, and his servants go with your servant.

25 And the king said to Absalom, No, my son, let us not all now go, lest we be chargeable to you. And he pressed him: however he would not go, but blessed him.

26 Then said Absalom, If not, I pray you, let my brother Amnon go with us. And the king said to him, Why should he go with you?

27 But Absalom pressed him, that he let Amnon and all the king's sons go with him.

28 Now Absalom had commanded his servants, saying, Mark you now when Amnon's heart is merry with wine, and when I say to you, Smite Amnon; then kill him, fear not: have not I commanded you? be courageous, and be valiant.

29 And the servants of Absalom did to Amnon as Absalom had commanded. Then all the king's sons arose, and every man got him up upon his mule, and fled.

30 ¶ And it came to pass, while they were in the way, that tidings came to David, saying, Absalom has slain all the king's sons, and there is not one of them left.

31 Then the king arose, and tore his garments, and lay on the earth; and all his servants stood by with their clothes torn.

32 And Jonadab, the son of Shimeah David's brother, answered and said, Let not my lord suppose *that* they have slain all the young men the king's sons; for Amnon only is dead: for by the appointment of Absalom this has been determined from the day that he forced his sister Tamar.

33 Now therefore let not my lord the king take the thing to his heart, to think that all the king's sons are dead: for Amnon only is dead.

34 But Absalom fled. And the young man that kept the watch lifted up his eyes, and looked, and, behold, there came many people by the way of the hill side behind him.

35 And Jonadab said to the king, Behold, the king's sons come: as your servant said, so it is.

36 And it came to pass, as soon as he had made an end of speaking, that, behold, the king's sons came, and lifted up their voice and wept: and the king also and all his servants wept very greatly.

37 But Absalom fled, and went to Talmai, the son of Ammihud, king of Geshur. And *David* mourned for his son every day.

38 So Absalom fled, and went to Geshur, and was there three years.

39 And *the soul of* king David longed to go forth to Absalom: for he was comforted concerning Amnon, seeing he was dead.

2 Samuel 14

14:1 ¶ Now Joab the son of Zeruiah perceived that the king's heart *was* toward Absalom.

2 And Joab sent to Tekoah, and fetched there a wise woman, and said to her, I pray you, pretend yourself to be a mourner, and put on now mourning apparel, and anoint not yourself with oil, but be as a woman that had a long time mourned for the dead:

3 And come to the king, and speak on this manner to him. So Joab put the words in her mouth.

4 And when the woman of Tekoah spoke to the king, she fell on her face to the ground, and did obeisance, and said, Help, O king.

5 And the king said to her, What ails you? And she answered, I *am* indeed a widow woman, and my husband is dead.

6 And your handmaid had two sons, and they two strove together in the field, and *there was* none to part them, but the one smote the other, and slew him.

7 And, behold, the whole family is risen against your handmaid, and they said, Deliver him that smote his brother, that we may kill him, for the life of his brother whom he slew; and we will destroy the heir also: and so they shall quench my coal which is left, and shall not leave to my husband *neither* name nor remainder upon the earth.

8 And the king said to the woman, Go to your house, and I will give charge concerning you.

9 And the woman of Tekoah said to the king, My lord, O king, the iniquity *be* on me, and on my father's house: and the king and his throne *be* guiltless.

10 And the king said, Whoever says *anything* to you, bring him to me, and he shall not touch you any more.

11 Then said she, I pray you, let the king remember Yahweh your God, that you would not allow the revengers of blood to destroy any more, lest they destroy my son. And he said, *As* Yahweh lives, there shall not one hair of your son fall to the earth.

12 Then the woman said, Let your handmaid, I pray you, speak *one* word unto my lord the king. And he said, Say on.

13 And the woman said, Why then have you thought such a thing against the people of God? for the king does speak this thing as one which is faulty, in that the king does not fetch home again his banished.

14 For we must surely die, and *are* as water spilt on the ground, which cannot be gathered up again; neither does God respect *any* person: yet does he devise means, that his banished be not expelled from him.

15 Now therefore that I have come to speak of this thing to my lord the king, *it is* because the people have made me afraid: and your handmaid said, I will now speak to the king; it may be that the king will perform the request of his handmaid.

16 For the king will hear, to deliver his handmaid out of the hand of the man *that would* destroy me and my son together out of the inheritance of God.

17 Then your handmaid said, The word of my lord the king shall now be comfortable: for as an angel of God, so *is* my lord the king to discern good and bad: therefore Yahweh your God will be with you.

18 Then the king answered and said to the woman, Hide not from me, I pray you, the thing that I shall ask you. And the woman said, Let my lord the king now speak.

19 And the king said, *Is not* the hand of Joab with you in all this? And the woman answered and said, *As* your soul lives, my lord the king, none can turn to the right hand or to the left from anything that my lord the king has spoken: for your servant Joab, he commanded me, and he put all these words in the mouth of your handmaid:

20 To fetch about this form of speech has your servant Joab done this thing: and my lord *is* wise, according to the wisdom of an angel of God, to know all *things* that *are* in the earth.

21 ¶ And the king said to Joab, Behold now, I have done this thing: go therefore, bring the young man Absalom again.

22 And Joab fell to the ground on his face, and bowed himself, and thanked the king: and Joab said, Today your servant knows that I have found grace in your sight, my lord, O king, in that the king has fulfilled the request of his servant.

23 So Joab arose and went to Geshur, and brought Absalom to Jerusalem.

24 And the king said, Let him return to his own house, and let him not see my face. So Absalom returned to his own house, and saw not the king's face.

25 But in all Israel there was none to be so much praised as Absalom for his beauty: from the sole of his foot even to the crown of his head there was no blemish in him.

26 And when he shaved his head, (for it was at every year's end that he shaved *it*: because *the hair* was heavy on him, therefore he shaved it:) he weighed the hair of his head at two hundred shekels after the king's weight.

27 And to Absalom there were born three sons, and one daughter, whose name *was* Tamar: she was a woman of a fair countenance.

28 ¶ So Absalom dwelt two full years in Jerusalem, and saw not the king's face.

29 Therefore Absalom sent for Joab, to have sent him to the king; but he would not come to him: and when he sent again the second time, he would not come.

30 Therefore he said to his servants, See, Joab's field is near mine, and he has barley there; go and set it on fire. And Absalom's servants set the field on fire.

31 Then Joab arose, and came to Absalom to *his* house, and said to him, Why have your servants set my field on fire?

32 And Absalom answered Joab, Behold, I sent to you, saying, Come here, that I may send you to the king, to say, Why have I come from Geshur? *it would have been* good for me *to have been* there still: now therefore let me see the king's face; and if there is *any* iniquity in me, let him kill me.

33 So Joab came to the king, and told him: and when he had called for Absalom, he came to the king, and bowed himself on his face to the ground before the king: and the king kissed Absalom.

2 Samuel 15

15:1 ¶ And it came to pass after this, that Absalom prepared him chariots and horses, and fifty men to run before him.

2 And Absalom rose up early, and stood beside the way of the gate: and it was *so*, that when any man that had a controversy came to the king for judgment, then Absalom called to him, and said, Of what city *are* you? And he said, Your servant *is* of one of the tribes of Israel.

3 And Absalom said to him, See, your matters *are* good and right; but *there is* no man *deputized* of the king to hear you.

4 Absalom said moreover, Oh that I were made judge in the land, that every man which has any suit or cause might come to me, and I would do him justice!

5 And it was *so*, that when any man came near *to him* to do him obeisance, he put forth his hand, and took him, and kissed him.

6 And on this manner did Absalom to all Israel that came to the king for judgment: so Absalom stole the hearts of the men of Israel.

7 ¶ And it came to pass after forty years, that Absalom said to the king, I pray you, let me go and pay my vow, which I have vowed unto Yahweh, in Hebron.

8 For your servant vowed a vow while I stayed at Geshur in Syria, saying, If Yahweh shall bring me again indeed to Jerusalem, then I will serve Yahweh.

9 And the king said to him, Go in peace. So he arose, and went to Hebron.

10 But Absalom sent spies throughout all the tribes of Israel, saying, As soon as you hear the sound of the trumpet, then you shall say, Absalom reigns in Hebron.

11 And with Absalom went two hundred men out of Jerusalem, *that were* called; and they went in their simplicity, and they knew not anything.

12 And Absalom sent for Ahithophel the Gilonite, David's counselor, from his city, *even* from Giloh, while he offered sacrifices. And the conspiracy was strong; for the people increased continually with Absalom.

13 ¶ And there came a messenger to David, saying, The hearts of the men of Israel are after Absalom.

14 And David said to all his servants that *were* with him at Jerusalem, Arise, and let us flee; for we shall not *else* escape from Absalom: make speed to depart, lest he overtakes us suddenly, and brings evil upon us, and smites the city with the edge of the sword.

15 And the king's servants said to the king, Behold, your servants *are ready to do* whatever my lord the king shall appoint.

16 And the king went forth, and all his household after him. And the king left ten women, *which were* concubines, to keep the house.

17 And the king went forth, and all the people after him, and waited in a place that was far off.

2 Samuel 15

18 And all his servants passed on before him; and all the Cherethites, and all the Pelethites, and all the Gittites, six hundred men which came after him from Gath, passed on before the king.

19 Then said the king to Ittai the Gittite, Why go you also with us? return to your place, and remain with the king: for you *are* a stranger, and also an exile.

20 Whereas you came *but* yesterday, should I this day make you go up and down with us? seeing I go where I may, return you, and take back your brothers: mercy and truth *be* with you.

21 And Ittai answered the king, and said, *As* Yahweh lives, and *as* my lord the king lives, surely in what place my lord the king shall be, whether in death or life, even there also will your servant be.

22 And David said to Ittai, Go and pass over. And Ittai the Gittite passed over, and all his men, and all the little ones that *were* with him.

23 And all the country wept with a loud voice, and all the people passed over: the king also himself passed over the brook Kidron, and all the people passed over, toward the way of the wilderness.

24 ¶ And lo Zadok also, and all the Levites *were* with him, bearing the ark of the covenant of God: and they set down the ark of God; and Abiathar went up, until all the people had finished passing out of the city.

25 And the king said to Zadok, Carry back the ark of God into the city: if I shall find favor in the eyes of Yahweh, he will bring me again, and show me *both* it, and his habitation:

26 But if he thus says, I have no delight in you; behold, *here am* I, let him do to me as seems good to him.

27 The king said also to Zadok the priest, *Are not* you a seer? return into the city in peace, and your two sons with you, Ahimaaz your son, and Jonathan the son of Abiathar.

28 See, I will wait in the plain of the wilderness, until there comes word from you to inform me.

29 Zadok therefore and Abiathar carried the ark of God again to Jerusalem: and they remained there.

30 And David went up by the ascent of *the mount of* Olives, and wept as he went up, and had his head covered, and he went barefoot: and all the people that *were* with him covered every man his head, and they went up, weeping as they went up.

31 ¶ And *one* told David, saying, Ahithophel *is* among the conspirators with Absalom. And David said, O Yahweh, I pray you, turn the counsel of Ahithophel into foolishness.

32 And it came to pass, that *when* David had come to the top *of the mount*, where he worshipped God, behold, Hushai the Archite came to meet him with his coat torn, and earth upon his head:

33 Unto whom David said, If you pass on with me, then you shall be a burden to me:

34 But if you return to the city, and say to Absalom, I will be your servant, O king; *as* I *have been* your father's servant till now, so *will* I now also *be* your servant: then may you for me defeat the counsel of Ahithophel.

35 And *have you* not there with you Zadok and Abiathar the priests? therefore it shall be, *that* what thing soever you shall hear out of the king's house, you shall tell *it* to Zadok and Abiathar the priests.

36 Behold, *they have* there with them their two sons, Ahimaaz Zadok's *son*, and Jonathan Abiathar's *son*; and by them you shall send to me every thing that you can hear.

37 So Hushai David's friend came into the city, and Absalom came into Jerusalem.

2 Samuel 16

16:1 ¶ And when David was a little past the top *of the hill*, behold, Ziba the servant of Mephibosheth met him, with a couple of donkeys saddled, and upon them two hundred *loaves* of bread, and a hundred bunches of raisins, and a hundred of summer fruits, and a bottle of wine.

2 And the king said to Ziba, What mean you by these? And Ziba said, The donkeys *are* for the king's household to ride on; and the bread and summer fruit for the young men to eat; and the wine, that such are faint in the wilderness may drink.

3 And the king said, And where *is* your master's son? And Ziba said to the king, Behold, he stays at Jerusalem: for he said, Today shall the house of Israel restore *to* me the kingdom of my father.

4 Then said the king to Ziba, Behold, yours *are* all that *pertained* to Mephibosheth. And Ziba said, I humbly beseech you *that* I may find grace in your sight, my lord, O king.

5 ¶ And when king David came to Bahurim, behold, there came out a man of the family of the house of Saul, whose name *was* Shimei, the son of Gera: he came forth, and cursed still as he came.

6 And he cast stones at David, and at all the servants of king David: and all the people and all the mighty men *were* upon his right hand and upon his left.

7 And thus said Shimei when he cursed, Come out, come out, you bloody man, and you man of Belial:

8 Yahweh has returned upon you all the blood of the house of Saul, in whose stead you have reigned; and Yahweh has delivered the kingdom into the hand of Absalom your son: and, behold, you *are taken* in your mischief, because you *are* a bloody man.

9 Then said Abishai the son of Zeruiah to the king, Why should this dead dog curse my lord the king? let me go over, I pray you, and take off his head.

10 And the king said, What have I to do with you, you sons of Zeruiah? so let him curse, because Yahweh has said to him, Curse David. Who shall then say, Why have you done so?

11 And David said to Abishai, and to all his servants, Behold, my son, which came forth of my bowels, seeks my life: how much more now *may this* Benjamite *do it*? let him alone, and let him curse; for Yahweh has invited him.

12 It may be that Yahweh will look on my affliction, and that Yahweh will return me good for his cursing this day.

13 And as David and his men went by the way, Shimei went along on the hill's side over against him, and cursed as he went, and threw stones at him, and cast dust.

14 And the king, and all the people that *were* with him, became weary, and refreshed themselves there.

15 ¶ And Absalom, and all the people the men of Israel, came to Jerusalem, and Ahithophel with him.

16 And it came to pass, when Hushai the Archite, David's friend, had come to Absalom, that Hushai said to Absalom, God save the king, God save the king.

17 And Absalom said to Hushai, *Is* this your kindness to your friend? why went you not with your friend?

18 And Hushai said to Absalom, No; but whom Yahweh, and this people, and all the men of Israel, choose, his will I be, and with him will I remain.

19 And again, whom should I serve? *should I* not *serve* in the presence of his son? as I have served in your father's presence, so will I be in your presence.

20 Then said Absalom to Ahithophel, Give counsel among you what we shall do.

21 And Ahithophel said to Absalom, Go in to your father's concubines, which he has left to keep the house; and all Israel shall hear that you are abhorred of your father: then shall the hands of all that *are* with you be strong.

22 So they spread Absalom a tent on the top of the house; and Absalom went in unto his father's concubines in the sight of all Israel.

23 And the counsel of Ahithophel, which he counseled in those days, *was* as if a man had inquired at the oracle of God: so *was* all the counsel of Ahithophel both with David and with Absalom.

2 Samuel 17

17:1 ¶ Moreover Ahithophel said to Absalom, Let me now choose out twelve thousand men, and I will arise and pursue after David this night:

2 And I will come upon him while he *is* weary and weak handed, and will make him afraid: and all the people that *are* with him shall flee; and I will smite the king only:

3 And I will bring back all the people to you: the man whom you seek *is* as if all returned: *so* all the people shall be in peace.

4 And the saying pleased Absalom well, and all the elders of Israel.

5 Then said Absalom, Call now Hushai the Archite also, and let us hear likewise what he says.

6 And when Hushai had come to Absalom, Absalom spoke to him, saying, Ahithophel has spoken after this manner: shall we do *after* his saying? if not; speak you.

7 And Hushai said to Absalom, The counsel that Ahithophel has given *is* not good at this time.

8 For, said Hushai, you know your father and his men, that they *are* mighty men, and they *are* chafed in their minds, as a bear robbed of her cubs in the field: and your father *is* a man of war, and will not lodge with the people.

9 Behold, he is hidden now in some pit, or in some *other* place: and it will come to pass, when some of them are overthrown at the first, that whoever hears it will say, There is a slaughter among the people that follow Absalom.

10 And he also *that is* valiant, whose heart *is* as the heart of a lion, shall utterly melt: for all Israel knows that your father *is* a mighty man, and *they* which *are* with him *are* valiant men.

11 Therefore I counsel that all Israel be generally gathered to you, from Dan even to Beersheba, as the sand that *is* by the sea for multitude; and that you go to battle in your own person.

12 So shall we come upon him in some place where he shall be found, and we will light upon him as the dew falls on the ground: and of him and of all the men that *are* with him there shall not be left so much as one.

13 Moreover, if he has gotten into a city, then shall all Israel bring ropes to that city, and we will draw it into the river, until there is not one small stone found there.

14 And Absalom and all the men of Israel said, The counsel of Hushai the Archite *is* better than the counsel of Ahithophel. For Yahweh had appointed to defeat the good counsel of Ahithophel, to the intent that Yahweh might bring evil upon Absalom.

15 ¶ Then said Hushai to Zadok and to Abiathar the priests, Thus and thus did Ahithophel counsel Absalom and the elders of Israel; and thus and thus have I counseled.

16 Now therefore send quickly, and tell David, saying, Lodge not this night in the plains of the wilderness, but speedily pass over; lest the king be swallowed up, and all the people that *are* with him.

17 Now Jonathan and Ahimaaz stayed by Enrogel; for they could not be seen to come into the city: and a wench went and told them; and they went and told king David.

18 Nevertheless a lad saw them, and told Absalom: but they went both of them away quickly, and came to a man's house in Bahurim, which had a well in his court; where they went down.

19 And the woman took and spread a covering over the well's mouth, and spread ground corn thereon; and the thing was not known.

20 And when Absalom's servants came to the woman at the house, they said, Where *is* Ahimaaz and Jonathan? And the woman said to them, They have gone over the brook of water. And when they had sought and could not find *them*, they returned to Jerusalem.

21 And it came to pass, after they had departed, that they came up out of the well, and went and told king David, and said to David, Arise, and pass quickly over the water: for thus has Ahithophel counseled against you.

22 ¶ Then David arose, and all the people that *were* with him, and they passed over *the* Jordan: by the morning light there lacked not one of them that was not gone over *the* Jordan.

23 And when Ahithophel saw that his counsel was not followed, he saddled *his* donkey, and arose, and got him home to his house, to his city, and put his household in order, and hanged himself, and died, and was buried in the sepulcher of his father.

2 Samuel 17

24 Then David came to Mahanaim. And Absalom passed over *the* Jordan, he and all the men of Israel with him.
25 And Absalom made Amasa captain of the host instead of Joab: which Amasa *was* a man's son, whose name *was* Ithra, an Israelite, that went in to Abigail the daughter of Nahash, sister to Zeruiah Joab's mother.
26 So Israel and Absalom pitched in the land of Gilead.
27 And it came to pass, when David had come to Mahanaim, that Shobi the son of Nahash of Rabbah of the children of Ammon, and Machir the son of Ammiel of Lodebar, and Barzillai the Gileadite of Rogelim,
28 Brought beds, and basins, and earthen vessels, and wheat, and barley, and flour, and parched *corn*, and beans, and lentils, and parched *vegetables*,
29 And honey, and butter, and sheep, and cheese of cows, for David, and for the people that *were* with him, to eat: for they said, The people *are* hungry, and weary, and thirsty, in the wilderness.

2 Samuel 18

18:1 ¶ And David numbered the people that *were* with him, and set captains of thousands and captains of hundreds over them.
2 And David sent forth a third part of the people under the hand of Joab, and a third part under the hand of Abishai the son of Zeruiah, Joab's brother, and a third part under the hand of Ittai the Gittite. And the king said to the people, I will surely go forth with you myself also.
3 But the people answered, You shall not go forth: for if we flee away, they will not care for us; neither if half of us die, will they care for us: but now *you are* worth ten thousand of us: therefore now *it is* better that you help us out of the city.
4 And the king said to them, What seems you best I will do. And the king stood by the gate side, and all the people came out by hundreds and by thousands.
5 And the king commanded Joab and Abishai and Ittai, saying, *Deal* gently for my sake with the young man, *even* with Absalom. And all the people heard when the king gave all the captains charge concerning Absalom.
6 So the people went out into the field against Israel: and the battle was in the woods of Ephraim;
7 Where the people of Israel were slain before the servants of David, and there was there a great slaughter that day of twenty thousand *men*.
8 For the battle was there scattered over the face of all the country: and the woods devoured more people that day than the sword devoured.
9 ¶ And Absalom met the servants of David. And Absalom rode upon a mule, and the mule went under the thick boughs of a great oak, and his head caught hold of the oak, and he was taken up between the heaven and the earth; and the mule that *was* under him went away.
10 And a certain man saw *it*, and told Joab, and said, Behold, I saw Absalom hanged in an oak.
11 And Joab said to the man that told him, And, behold, you saw *him*, and why did you not smite him there to the ground? and I would have given you ten *shekels* of silver, and a belt.
12 And the man said to Joab, Though I should receive a thousand *shekels* of silver in my hand, *yet* would I not put forth my hand against the king's son: for in our hearing the king charged you and Abishai and Ittai, saying, Beware that none *touch* the young man Absalom.
13 Otherwise I should have worked falsehood against my own life: for there is no matter hidden from the king, and you yourself would have set yourself against *me*.
14 Then said Joab, I may not wait thus with you. And he took three darts in his hand, and thrust them through the heart of Absalom, while he *was* yet alive in the midst of the oak.
15 And ten young men that bore Joab's armor turned about and smote Absalom, and slew him.
16 And Joab blew the trumpet, and the people returned from pursuing after Israel: for Joab held back the people.
17 And they took Absalom, and cast him into a great pit in the woods, and laid a very great heap of stones upon him: and all Israel fled every one to his tent.
18 Now Absalom in his lifetime had taken and reared up for himself a pillar, which *is* in the king's valley: for he said, I have no son to keep my name in remembrance: and he called the pillar after his own name: and it is called unto this day, Absalom's place.
19 ¶ Then said Ahimaaz the son of Zadok, Let me now run, and bear the king tidings, how that Yahweh has avenged him of his enemies.
20 And Joab said to him, You shall not bear tidings this day, but you shall bear tidings another day: but this day you shall bear no tidings, because the king's son is dead.
21 Then said Joab to Cushi, Go tell the king what you have seen. And Cushi bowed himself to Joab, and ran.
22 Then said Ahimaaz the son of Zadok yet again to Joab, But, whatever, let me, I pray you, also run after Cushi. And Joab said, Why will you run, my son, seeing that you have no tidings ready?
23 But *whatever*, *said he*, let me run. And he said to him, Run. Then Ahimaaz ran by the way of the plain, and overran Cushi.
24 And David sat between the two gates: and the watchman went up to the roof over the gate to the wall, and lifted up his eyes, and looked, and beheld a man running alone.
25 And the watchman cried, and told the king. And the king said, If he is alone, *there is* tidings in his mouth. And he came walking, and drew near.
26 And the watchman saw another man running: and the watchman called to the porter, and said, Behold *another* man running alone. And the king said, He also brings tidings.
27 And the watchman said, I think the running of the foremost is like the running of Ahimaaz the son of Zadok. And the king said, He *is* a good man, and comes with good tidings.

28 And Ahimaaz called, and said to the king, All is well. And he fell down to the earth upon his face before the king, and said, Blessed *be* Yahweh your God, which has delivered up the men that lifted up their hand against my lord the king.

29 And the king said, Is the young man Absalom safe? And Ahimaaz answered, When Joab sent the king's servant, and *me* your servant, I saw a great tumult, but I knew not what *it was*.

30 And the king said *to him*, Turn aside, *and* stand here. And he turned aside, and stood still.

31 And, behold, Cushi came; and Cushi said, Tidings, my lord the king: for Yahweh has avenged you this day of all them that rose up against you.

32 And the king said to Cushi, Is the young man Absalom safe? And Cushi answered, The enemies of my lord the king, and all that rise against you to do *you* hurt, be as *that* young man *is*.

33 And the king was much moved, and went up to the chamber over the gate, and wept: and as he went, thus he said, O my son Absalom, my son, my son Absalom! would God I had died for you, O Absalom, my son, my son!

2 Samuel 19

19:1 ¶ And it was told *to* Joab, Behold, the king weeps and mourns for Absalom.

2 And the victory that day was *turned* into mourning to all the people: for the people heard say that day how the king was grieved for his son.

3 And the people got them by stealth that day into the city, as people being ashamed steal away when they flee in battle.

4 But the king covered his face, and the king cried with a loud voice, O my son Absalom, O Absalom, my son, my son!

5 And Joab came into the house to the king, and said, You have shamed this day the faces of all your servants, which this day have saved your life, and the lives of your sons and of your daughters, and the lives of your wives, and the lives of your concubines;

6 In that you love your enemies, and hate your friends. For you have declared this day, that you regard neither princes nor servants: for this day I perceive, that if Absalom had lived, and all we had died this day, then it had pleased you well.

7 Now therefore arise, go forth, and speak comfortably to your servants: for I swear by Yahweh, if you go not forth, there will not tarry one with you this night: and that will be worse to you than all the evil that befell you from your youth until now.

8 Then the king arose, and sat in the gate. And they told to all the people, saying, Behold, the king does sit in the gate. And all the people came before the king: for Israel had fled every man to his tent.

9 ¶ And all the people were at strife throughout all the tribes of Israel, saying, The king saved us out of the hand of our enemies, and he delivered us out of the hand of the Philistines; and now he has fled out of the land for Absalom.

10 And Absalom, whom we anointed over us, is dead in battle. Now therefore why speak you not a word of bringing the king back?

11 And king David sent to Zadok and to Abiathar the priests, saying, Speak to the elders of Judah, saying, Why are you the last to bring the king back to his house? seeing the speech of all Israel has come to the king, *even* to his house.

12 You *are* my brethren, you *are* my bones and my flesh: why then are you the last to bring back the king?

13 And say you to Amasa, *Are* you not of my bone, and of my flesh? God do so to me, and more also, if you are not captain of the host before me continually in the room of Joab.

14 And he bowed the heart of all the men of Judah, even as *the heart of* one man; so that they sent *this word* to the king, Return you, and all your servants.

15 So the king returned, and came to *the* Jordan. And Judah came to Gilgal, to go to meet the king, to conduct the king over *the* Jordan.

16 ¶ And Shimei the son of Gera, a Benjamite, which *was* of Bahurim, hurried and came down with the men of Judah to meet king David.

17 And *there were* a thousand men of Benjamin with him, and Ziba the servant of the house of Saul, and his fifteen sons and his twenty servants with him; and they went over *the* Jordan before the king.

18 And there went over a ferry boat to carry over the king's household, and to do what he thought good. And Shimei the son of Gera fell down before the king, as he had come over *the* Jordan;

19 And said to the king, Let not my lord impute iniquity to me, neither do you remember that which your servant did perversely the day that my lord the king went out of Jerusalem, that the king should take it to his heart.

20 For your servant does know that I have sinned: therefore, behold, I have come, the first this day of all the house of Joseph, to go down to meet my lord the king.

21 But Abishai the son of Zeruiah answered and said, Shall not Shimei be put to death for this, because he cursed Yahweh's anointed?

22 And David said, What have I to do with you, you sons of Zeruiah, that you should this day be adversaries to me? shall there any man be put to death this day in Israel? for do not I know that I *am* this day king over Israel?

23 Therefore the king said to Shimei, You shall not die. And the king swore to him.

24 ¶ And Mephibosheth the son of Saul came down to meet the king, and had neither dressed his feet, nor trimmed his beard, nor washed his clothes, from the day the king departed until the day he came *again* in peace.

25 And it came to pass, when he had come to Jerusalem to meet the king, that the king said to him, Why went not you with me, Mephibosheth?

26 And he answered, My lord, O king, my servant deceived me: for your servant said, I will saddle me

2 Samuel 19

a donkey, that I may ride thereon, and go to the king; because your servant *is* lame.

27 And he has slandered your servant to my lord the king; but my lord the king *is* as an angel of God: do therefore *what is* good in your eyes.

28 For all *of* my father's house were but dead men before my lord the king: yet did you set your servant among them that did eat at your own table. What right therefore have I yet to cry any more to the king?

29 And the king said to him, Why speak you any more of your matters? I have said, You and Ziba divide the land.

30 And Mephibosheth said to the king, Yes, let him take all, forasmuch as my lord the king has come again in peace to his own house.

31 ¶ And Barzillai the Gileadite came down from Rogelim, and went over *the* Jordan with the king, to conduct him over *the* Jordan.

32 Now Barzillai was a very aged man, *even* fourscore years old: and he had provided the king of sustenance while he lay at Mahanaim; for he *was* a very great man.

33 And the king said to Barzillai, Come you over with me, and I will feed you with me in Jerusalem.

34 And Barzillai said to the king, How long have I to live, that I should go up with the king to Jerusalem?

35 I *am* this day fourscore years old: *and* can I discern between good and evil? can your servant taste what I eat or what I drink? can I hear any more the voice of singing men and singing women? why then should your servant be yet a burden to my lord the king?

36 Your servant will go a little way over *the* Jordan with the king: and why should the king recompense it *to* me with such a reward?

37 Let your servant, I pray you, turn back again, that I may die in my own city, *and be buried* by the grave of my father and of my mother. But behold your servant Chimham; let him go over with my lord the king; and do to him what shall seem good to you.

38 And the king answered, Chimham shall go over with me, and I will do to him that which shall seem good to you: and whatever you shall require of me, *that* will I do for you.

39 And all the people went over *the* Jordan. And when the king had come over, the king kissed Barzillai, and blessed him; and he returned to his own place.

40 ¶ Then the king went on to Gilgal, and Chimham went on with him: and all the people of Judah conducted the king, and also half the people of Israel.

41 And, behold, all the men of Israel came to the king, and said to the king, Why have our brethren the men of Judah stolen you away, and have brought the king, and his household, and all David's men with him, over *the* Jordan?

42 And all the men of Judah answered the men of Israel, Because the king *is* near of kin to us: why then are you angry for this matter? have we eaten at all of the king's *cost*? or has he given us any gift?

43 And the men of Israel answered the men of Judah, and said, We have ten parts in the king, and we have also more *right* in David than you: why then did you despise us, that our advice should not be first had in bringing back our king? And the words of the men of Judah were fiercer than the words of the men of Israel.

2 Samuel 20

20:1 ¶ And there happened to be there a man of Belial, whose name *was* Sheba, the son of Bichri, a Benjamite: and he blew a trumpet, and said, We have no part in David, neither have we inheritance in the son of Jesse: every man to his tents, O Israel.

2 So every man of Israel went up from after David, *and* followed Sheba the son of Bichri: but the men of Judah clung to their king, from *the* Jordan even to Jerusalem.

3 And David came to his house at Jerusalem; and the king took the ten women *his* concubines, whom he had left to keep the house, and put them in confinement, and fed them, but went not in unto them. So they were shut up to the day of their death, living in widowhood.

4 ¶ Then said the king to Amasa, Assemble me the men of Judah within three days, and be you here present.

5 So Amasa went to assemble *the men of* Judah: but he delayed longer than the set time which he had appointed him.

6 And David said to Abishai, Now shall Sheba the son of Bichri do us more harm than *did* Absalom: take you your lord's servants, and pursue after him, lest he finds him fenced cities, and escapes us.

7 And there went out after him Joab's men, and the Cherethites, and the Pelethites, and all the mighty men: and they went out of Jerusalem, to pursue after Sheba the son of Bichri.

8 When they *were* at the great stone which *is* in Gibeon, Amasa went before them. And Joab's garment that he had put on was girded to him, and upon it a girdle *with* a sword fastened upon his loins in the sheath thereof; and as he went forth it fell out.

9 And Joab said to Amasa, *Are* you in health, my brother? And Joab took Amasa by the beard with the right hand to kiss him.

10 But Amasa took no heed to the sword that *was* in Joab's hand: so he smote him therewith in the fifth *rib*, and shed out his bowels to the ground, and struck him not again; and he died. So Joab and Abishai his brother pursued after Sheba the son of Bichri.

11 And one of Joab's men stood by him, and said, He that favors Joab, and he that *is* for David, *let him go* after Joab.

12 And Amasa wallowed in blood in the midst of the highway. And when the man saw that all the people stood still, he removed Amasa out of the highway into the field, and cast a cloth upon him, when he saw that every one that came by him stood still.

13 When he was removed out of the highway, all the people went on after Joab, to pursue after Sheba the son of Bichri.

14 ¶ And he went through all the tribes of Israel to Abel, and to Bethmaachah, and all the Berites: and they were gathered together, and went also after him.

15 And they came and besieged him in Abel of Bethmaachah, and they cast up a bank against the city, and it stood in the trench: and all the people that *were* with Joab battered the wall, to throw it down.

16 Then cried a wise woman out of the city, Hear, hear; say, I pray you, to Joab, Come near here, that I may speak with you.

17 And when he had come near to her, the woman said, *Are* you Joab? And he answered, I *am he*. Then she said to him, Hear the words of your handmaid. And he answered, I do hear.

18 Then she spoke, saying, They were inclined to speak in old time, saying, They shall surely ask *counsel* at Abel: and so they ended *the matter*.

19 I *am one of them that are* peaceable *and* faithful in Israel: you seek to destroy a city and a mother in Israel: why will you swallow up the inheritance of Yahweh?

20 And Joab answered and said, Far be it, far be it from me, that I should swallow up or destroy.

21 The matter *is* not so: but a man of mount Ephraim, Sheba the son of Bichri by name, has lifted up his hand against the king, *even* against David: deliver him only, and I will depart from the city. And the woman said to Joab, Behold, his head shall be thrown to you over the wall.

22 Then the woman went to all the people in her wisdom. And they cut off the head of Sheba the son of Bichri, and cast *it* out to Joab. And he blew a trumpet, and they retired from the city, every man to his tent. And Joab returned to Jerusalem to the king.

23 ¶ Now Joab *was* over all the host of Israel: and Benaiah the son of Jehoiada *was* over the Cherethites and over the Pelethites:

24 And Adoram *was* over the tribute: and Jehoshaphat the son of Ahilud *was* recorder:

25 And Sheva *was* scribe: and Zadok and Abiathar *were* the priests:

26 And Ira also the Jairite was a chief ruler about David.

2 Samuel 21

21:1 ¶ Then there was a famine in the days of David for three years, year after year; and David inquired of Yahweh. And Yahweh answered, *It is* for Saul, and for *his* bloody house, because he slew the Gibeonites.

2 And the king called the Gibeonites, and said to them; (now the Gibeonites *were* not of the children of Israel, but of the remnant of the Amorites; and the children of Israel had sworn to them: and Saul sought to slay them in his zeal to the children of Israel and Judah.)

3 Therefore David said to the Gibeonites, What shall I do for you? and with what shall I make the atonement, that you may bless the inheritance of Yahweh?

4 And the Gibeonites said to him, We will have no silver nor gold of Saul, nor of his house; neither for us shall you kill any man in Israel. And he said, What you shall say, *that* will I do for you.

5 And they answered the king, The man that consumed us, and that devised against us *that* we should be destroyed from remaining in any of the coasts of Israel,

6 Let seven men of his sons be delivered to us, and we will hang them up unto Yahweh in Gibeah of Saul, *whom* Yahweh did choose. And the king said, I will give *them*.

7 But the king spared Mephibosheth, the son of Jonathan the son of Saul, because of Yahweh's oath that *was* between them, between David and Jonathan the son of Saul.

8 But the king took the two sons of Rizpah the daughter of Aiah, whom she bore to Saul, Armoni and Mephibosheth; and the five sons of Michal the daughter of Saul, whom she brought up for Adriel the son of Barzillai the Meholathite:

9 And he delivered them into the hands of the Gibeonites, and they hanged them in the hill before Yahweh: and they fell *all* seven together, and were put to death in the days of harvest, in the first *days*, in the beginning of barley harvest.

10 ¶ And Rizpah the daughter of Aiah took sackcloth, and spread it for her upon the rock, from the beginning of harvest until water dropped upon them out of heaven, and allowed neither the birds of the air to rest on them by day, nor the beasts of the field by night.

11 And it was told *to* David what Rizpah the daughter of Aiah, the concubine of Saul, had done.

12 And David went and took the bones of Saul and the bones of Jonathan his son from the men of Jabeshgilead, which had stolen them from the street of Bethshan, where the Philistines had hanged them, when the Philistines had slain Saul in Gilboa:

13 And he brought up from there the bones of Saul and the bones of Jonathan his son; and they gathered the bones of them that were hanged.

14 And the bones of Saul and Jonathan his son buried they in the country of Benjamin in Zelah, in the sepulcher of Kish his father: and they performed all that the king commanded. And after that God was entreated for the land

15 ¶ Moreover the Philistines had yet war again with Israel; and David went down, and his servants with him, and fought against the Philistines: and David grew faint.

16 And Ishbibenob, which *was* of the sons of the giant, the weight of whose spear *weighed* three hundred *shekels* of brass in weight, he being girded with a new *sword*, thought to have slain David.

17 But Abishai the son of Zeruiah helped him, and smote the Philistine, and killed him. Then the men of David swore to him, saying, You shall go no more out with us to battle, that you quench not the light of Israel.

18 And it came to pass after this, that there was again a battle with the Philistines at Gob: then Sibbechai the Hushathite slew Saph, which *was* of the sons of the giant.

19 And there was again a battle in Gob with the Philistines, where Elhanan the son of Jaareoregim, a Bethlehemite, slew *the brother of* Goliath the Gittite, the staff of whose spear *was* like a weaver's beam.

2 Samuel 21

20 And there was yet a battle in Gath, where was a man of *great* stature, that had on every hand six fingers, and on every foot six toes, four and twenty in number; and he also was born to the giant.

21 And when he defied Israel, Jonathan the son of Shimea the brother of David slew him.

22 These four were born to the giant in Gath, and fell by the hand of David, and by the hand of his servants.

2 Samuel 22

22:1 ¶ And David spoke unto Yahweh the words of this song in the day *that* Yahweh had delivered him out of the hand of all his enemies, and out of the hand of Saul:

2 ¶ And he said, Yahweh *is* my rock, and my fortress, and my deliverer;

3 The God of my rock; in him will I trust: *he is* my shield, and the horn of my salvation, my high tower, and my refuge, my savior; you save me from violence.

4 I will call on Yahweh, *who is* worthy to be praised: so shall I be saved from my enemies.

5 When the waves of death encompassed me, the floods of ungodly men made me afraid;

6 The sorrows of hell compassed me about; the snares of death prevented me;

7 In my distress I called upon Yahweh, and cried to my God: and he did hear my voice out of his temple, and my cry *did enter* into his ears.

8 Then the earth shook and trembled; the foundations of heaven moved and shook, because he was angry.

9 There went up a smoke out of his nostrils, and fire out of his mouth devoured: coals were kindled by it.

10 He bowed the heavens also, and came down; and darkness *was* under his feet.

11 And he rode upon a cherub, and did fly: and he was seen upon the wings of the wind.

12 And he made darkness pavilions round about him, dark waters, *and* thick clouds of the skies.

13 Through the brightness before him were coals of fire kindled.

14 Yahweh thundered from heaven, and the most High uttered his voice.

15 And he sent out arrows, and scattered them; lightning, and discomfited them.

16 And the channels of the sea appeared, the foundations of the world were discovered, at the rebuking of Yahweh, at the blast of the breath of his nostrils.

17 He sent from above, he took me; he drew me out of many waters;

18 He delivered me from my strong enemy, *and* from them that hated me: for they were too strong for me.

19 They prevented me in the day of my calamity: but Yahweh was my support.

20 He brought me forth also into a large place: he delivered me, because he delighted in me.

21 Yahweh rewarded me according to my righteousness: according to the cleanness of my hands has he recompensed me.

22 For I have kept the ways of Yahweh, and have not wickedly departed from my God.

23 For all his judgments *were* before me: and *as for* his statutes, I did not depart from them.

24 I was also upright before him, and have kept myself from my iniquity.

25 Therefore Yahweh has recompensed me according to my righteousness; according to my cleanness in his eye sight.

26 With the merciful you will show yourself merciful, *and* with the upright man you will show yourself upright.

27 With the pure you will show yourself pure; and with the perverse you will show yourself unsavory.

28 And the afflicted people you will save: but your eyes *are* upon the haughty, *that* you may bring *them* down.

29 For you *are* my lamp, O Yahweh: and Yahweh will lighten my darkness.

30 For by you I have run through a troop: by my God have I leaped over a wall.

31 *As for* God, his way *is* perfect; the word of Yahweh *is* tried: he *is* a buckler to all them that trust in him.

32 For who *is* God, save Yahweh? and who *is* a rock, save our God?

33 God *is* my strength *and* power: and he makes my way perfect.

34 He makes my feet like deer's *feet*: and sets me upon my high places.

35 He teaches my hands to war; so that a bow of steel is broken by my arms.

36 You have also given me the shield of your salvation: and your gentleness has made me great.

37 You have enlarged my steps under me; so that my feet did not slip.

38 I have pursued my enemies, and destroyed them; and turned not again until I had consumed them.

39 And I have consumed them, and wounded them, that they could not arise: yes, they are fallen under my feet.

40 For you have girded me with strength to battle: them that rose up against me have you subdued under me.

41 You have also given me the necks of my enemies, that I might destroy them that hate me.

42 They looked, but *there was* none to save; *even* unto Yahweh, but he answered them not.

43 Then did I beat them as small as the dust of the earth, I did stamp them as the mire of the street, *and* did spread them abroad.

44 You also have delivered me from the strivings of my people, you have kept me *to be* head of the heathen: a people *which* I knew not shall serve me.

45 Strangers shall submit themselves to me: as soon as they hear, they shall be obedient to me.

46 Strangers shall fade away, and they shall be afraid out of their close places.

47 Yahweh lives; and blessed *be* my rock; and exalted be the God of the rock of my salvation.

48 It *is* God that avenges me, and that brings down the people under me,

49 And that brings me forth from my enemies: you also have lifted me up on high above them that rose up against me: you have delivered me from the violent man.
50 Therefore I will give thanks to you, O Yahweh, among the heathen, and I will sing praises to your name.
51 *He is* the tower of salvation for his king: and shows mercy to his anointed, to David, and to his seed forevermore.

2 Samuel 23

23:1 ¶ Now these *are* the last words of David. David the son of Jesse said, and the man *who was* raised up on high, the anointed of the God of Jacob, and the sweet psalmist of Israel, said,
2 The Spirit of Yahweh spoke by me, and his word *was* in my tongue.
3 The God of Israel said, the Rock of Israel spoke to me, He that rules over men *must be* just, ruling in the fear of God.
4 And *he shall be* as the light of the morning, *when* the sun rises, *even* a morning without clouds; *as* the tender grass *springing* out of the earth by clear shining after rain.
5 Although my house *is* not so with God; yet he has made with me an everlasting covenant, ordered in all *things*, and sure: for *this is* all my salvation, and all *my* desire, although he makes *it* not to grow.
6 But *the sons* of Belial *shall be* all of them as thorns thrust away, because they cannot be taken with hands:
7 But the man *that* shall touch them must be fenced with iron and the staff of a spear; and they shall be utterly burned with fire in the *same* place.
8 ¶ These *are* the names of the mighty men whom David had: The Tachmonite that sat in the seat, chief among the captains; the same *was* Adino the Eznite: *he lifted up his spear* against eight hundred, whom he slew at one time.
9 And after him *was* Eleazar the son of Dodo the Ahohite, *one* of the three mighty men with David, when they defied the Philistines *that* were there gathered together to battle, and the men of Israel had gone away:
10 He arose, and smote the Philistines until his hand was weary, and his hand clung to the sword: and Yahweh worked a great victory that day; and the people returned after him only to spoil.
11 And after him *was* Shammah the son of Agee the Hararite. And the Philistines had gathered together into a troop, where was a piece of ground full of lentils: and the people fled from the Philistines.
12 But he stood in the midst of the ground, and defended it, and slew the Philistines: and Yahweh worked a great victory.
13 And three of the thirty chiefs went down, and came to David in the harvest time to the cave of Adullam: and the troop of the Philistines pitched in the valley of Rephaim.
14 And David *was* then in a hold, and the garrison of the Philistines *was* then *in* Bethlehem.
15 And David longed, and said, Oh that one would give me drink of the water of the well of Bethlehem, which *is* by the gate!
16 And the three mighty men broke through the host of the Philistines, and drew water out of the well of Bethlehem, that *was* by the gate, and took *it*, and brought *it* to David: nevertheless he would not drink thereof, but poured it out unto Yahweh.
17 And he said, Be it far from me, O Yahweh, that I should do this: *is not this* the blood of the men that went in jeopardy of their lives? therefore he would not drink it. These things did these three mighty men.
18 And Abishai, the brother of Joab, the son of Zeruiah, was chief among three. And he lifted up his spear against three hundred, *and* slew *them*, and had the name among three.
19 Was he not most honorable of three? therefore he was their captain: however he attained not to the *first* three.
20 And Benaiah the son of Jehoiada, the son of a valiant man, of Kabzeel, who had done many acts, he slew two lionlike men of Moab: he went down also and slew a lion in the midst of a pit in time of snow:
21 And he slew an Egyptian, a goodly man: and the Egyptian had a spear in his hand; but he went down to him with a staff, and plucked the spear out of the Egyptian's hand, and slew him with his own spear.
22 These *things* did Benaiah the son of Jehoiada, and had the name among three mighty men.
23 He was more honorable than the thirty, but he attained not to the *first* three. And David set him over his guard.
24 Asahel the brother of Joab *was* one of the thirty; Elhanan the son of Dodo of Bethlehem,
25 Shammah the Harodite, Elika the Harodite,
26 Helez the Paltite, Ira the son of Ikkesh the Tekoite,
27 Abiezer the Anethothite, Mebunnai the Hushathite,
28 Zalmon the Ahohite, Maharai the Netophathite,
29 Heleb the son of Baanah, a Netophathite, Ittai the son of Ribai out of Gibeah of the children of Benjamin,
30 Benaiah the Pirathonite, Hiddai of the brooks of Gaash,
31 Abialbon the Arbathite, Azmaveth the Barhumite,
32 Eliahba the Shaalbonite, of the sons of Jashen, Jonathan,
33 Shammah the Hararite, Ahiam the son of Sharar the Hararite,
34 Eliphelet the son of Ahasbai, the son of the Maachathite, Eliam the son of Ahithophel the Gilonite,
35 Hezrai the Carmelite, Paarai the Arbite,
36 Igal the son of Nathan of Zobah, Bani the Gadite,
37 Zelek the Ammonite, Naharai the Beerothite, armor bearer to Joab the son of Zeruiah,
38 Ira an Ithrite, Gareb an Ithrite,
39 Uriah the Hittite: thirty and seven in all.

2 Samuel 24

24:1 ¶ And again the anger of Yahweh was kindled against Israel, and he moved David against them to say, Go, number Israel and Judah.
2 For the king said to Joab the captain of the host, which *was* with him, Go now through all the tribes of Israel, from Dan even to Beersheba, and number you the people, that I may know the number of the people.
3 And Joab said to the king, Now Yahweh your God add to the people, how many soever they are, a hundred

times, and that the eyes of my lord the king may see *it*: but why does my lord the king delight in this thing?
4 Notwithstanding the king's word prevailed against Joab, and against the captains of the host. And Joab and the captains of the host went out from the presence of the king, to number the people of Israel.
5 And they passed over *the* Jordan, and pitched in Aroer, on the right side of the city that *lies* in the midst of the river of Gad, and toward Jazer:
6 Then they came to Gilead, and to the land of Tahtimhodshi; and they came to Danjaan, and about to Zidon,
7 And came to the strong hold of Tyre, and to all the cities of the Hivites, and of the Canaanites: and they went out to the south of Judah, *even* to Beersheba.
8 So when they had gone through all the land, they came to Jerusalem at the end of nine months and twenty days.
9 And Joab gave up the sum of the number of the people to the king: and there were in Israel eight hundred thousand valiant men that drew the sword; and the men of Judah *were* five hundred thousand men.
10 ¶ And David's heart smote him after that he had numbered the people. And David said unto Yahweh, I have sinned greatly in that I have done: and now, I beseech you, O Yahweh, take away the iniquity of your servant; for I have done very foolishly.
11 For when David was up in the morning, the word of Yahweh came to the prophet Gad, David's seer, saying,
12 Go and say to David, Thus says Yahweh, I offer you three *things*; choose you one of them, that I may *do it* to you.
13 So Gad came to David, and told him, and said to him, Shall seven years of famine come to you in your land? or will you flee three months before your enemies, while they pursue you? or that there be three days' pestilence in your land? now advise, and see what answer I shall return to him that sent me.
14 And David said to Gad, I am in a great bind: let us fall now into the hand of Yahweh; for his mercies *are* great: and let me not fall into the hand of man.
15 So Yahweh sent a pestilence upon Israel from the morning even to the time appointed: and there died of the people from Dan even to Beersheba seventy thousand men.
16 And when the angel stretched out his hand upon Jerusalem to destroy it, Yahweh repented him of the evil, and said to the angel that destroyed the people, It is enough: stay now your hand. And the angel of Yahweh was by the threshing place of Araunah the Jebusite.
17 And David spoke unto Yahweh when he saw the angel that smote the people, and said, Lo, I have sinned, and I have done wickedly: but these sheep, what have they done? let your hand, I pray you, be against me, and against my father's house.
18 ¶ And Gad came that day to David, and said to him, Go up, rear an altar unto Yahweh in the threshingfloor of Araunah the Jebusite.
19 And David, according to the saying of Gad, went up as Yahweh commanded.

20 And Araunah looked, and saw the king and his servants coming on toward him: and Araunah went out, and bowed himself before the king upon his face upon the ground.
21 And Araunah said, Why has my lord the king come to his servant? And David said, To buy the threshingfloor of you, to build an altar unto Yahweh, that the plague may be stayed from the people.
22 And Araunah said to David, Let my lord the king take and offer up what *seems* good to him: behold, *here are* oxen for burnt sacrifice, and threshing instruments and *other* instruments of the oxen for wood.
23 All these *things* did Araunah, *as* a king, give to the king. And Araunah said to the king, Yahweh your God accept you.
24 And the king said to Araunah, No; but I will surely buy *it* of you at a price: neither will I offer burnt offerings unto Yahweh my God of that which does cost me nothing. So David bought the threshingfloor and the oxen for fifty shekels of silver.
25 And David built there an altar unto Yahweh, and offered burnt offerings and peace offerings. So Yahweh was entreated for the land, and the plague was stayed from Israel.

1 Kings

1 Kings 1

1:1 ¶ Now king David was old *and* stricken in years; and they covered him with clothes, but he got no heat.
2 Therefore his servants said to him, Let there be sought for my lord the king a young virgin: and let her stand before the king, and let her cherish him, and let her lie in your bosom, that my lord the king may get heat.
3 So they sought for a fair damsel throughout all the coasts of Israel, and found Abishag a Shunammite, and brought her to the king.
4 And the damsel *was* very fair, and cherished the king, and ministered to him: but the king knew her not.
5 ¶ Then Adonijah the son of Haggith exalted himself, saying, I will be king: and he prepared him chariots and horsemen, and fifty men to run before him.
6 And his father had not displeased him at any time in saying, Why have you done so? and he also *was a* very goodly *man*; and *his mother* bore him after Absalom.
7 And he conferred with Joab the son of Zeruiah, and with Abiathar the priest: and they following Adonijah helped *him*.
8 But Zadok the priest, and Benaiah the son of Jehoiada, and Nathan the prophet, and Shimei, and Rei, and the mighty men which *belonged* to David, were not with Adonijah.
9 And Adonijah slew sheep and oxen and fat cattle by the stone of Zoheleth, which *is* by Enrogel, and called all

his brothers the king's sons, and all the men of Judah the king's servants:

10 But Nathan the prophet, and Benaiah, and the mighty men, and Solomon his brother, he called not.

11 ¶ Therefore Nathan spoke to Bathsheba the mother of Solomon, saying, Have you not heard that Adonijah the son of Haggith does reign, and David our lord knows *it* not?

12 Now therefore come, let me, I pray you, give you counsel, that you may save your own life, and the life of your son Solomon.

13 Go and get you in unto king David, and say to him, Did not you, my lord, O king, swear to your handmaid, saying, Assuredly Solomon your son shall reign after me, and he shall sit upon my throne? why then does Adonijah reign?

14 Behold, while you yet talk there with the king, I also will come in after you, and confirm your words.

15 And Bathsheba went in to the king into the chamber: and the king was very old; and Abishag the Shunammite ministered to the king.

16 And Bathsheba bowed, and did obeisance unto the king. And the king said, What would you?

17 And she said to him, My lord, you swore by Yahweh your God to your handmaid, *saying*, Assuredly Solomon your son shall reign after me, and he shall sit upon my throne.

18 And now, behold, Adonijah reigns; and now, my lord the king, you know *it* not:

19 And he has slain oxen and fat cattle and sheep in abundance, and has called all the sons of the king, and Abiathar the priest, and Joab the captain of the host: but Solomon your servant has he not called.

20 And you, my lord, O king, the eyes of all Israel *are* upon you, that you should tell them who shall sit on the throne of my lord the king after him.

21 Otherwise it shall come to pass, when my lord the king shall sleep with his fathers, that I and my son Solomon shall be counted offenders.

22 And, lo, while she yet talked with the king, Nathan the prophet also came in.

23 And they told the king, saying, Behold Nathan the prophet. And when he had come in before the king, he bowed himself before the king with his face to the ground.

24 And Nathan said, My lord, O king, have you said, Adonijah shall reign after me, and he shall sit upon my throne?

25 For he has gone down this day, and has slain oxen and fat cattle and sheep in abundance, and has called all the king's sons, and the captains of the host, and Abiathar the priest; and, behold, they eat and drink before him, and say, God save king Adonijah.

26 But me, *even* me your servant, and Zadok the priest, and Benaiah the son of Jehoiada, and your servant Solomon, has he not called.

27 Is this thing done by my lord the king, and you have not shown *it* to your servant, who should sit on the throne of my lord the king after him?

28 Then king David answered and said, Call me Bathsheba. And she came into the king's presence, and stood before the king.

29 And the king swore, and said, *As* Yahweh lives, that has redeemed my soul out of all distress,

30 Even as I swore to you by Yahweh God of Israel, saying, Assuredly Solomon your son shall reign after me, and he shall sit upon my throne in my stead; even so will I certainly do this day.

31 Then Bathsheba bowed with *her* face to the earth, and did reverence to the king, and said, Let my lord king David live forever.

32 ¶ And king David said, Call me Zadok the priest, and Nathan the prophet, and Benaiah the son of Jehoiada. And they came before the king.

33 The king also said to them, Take with you the servants of your lord, and cause Solomon my son to ride upon my own mule, and bring him down to Gihon:

34 And let Zadok the priest and Nathan the prophet anoint him there king over Israel: and blow you with the trumpet, and say, God save king Solomon.

35 Then you shall come up after him, that he may come and sit upon my throne; for he shall be king in my stead: and I have appointed him to be ruler over Israel and over Judah.

36 And Benaiah the son of Jehoiada answered the king, and said, Amen: Yahweh God of my lord the king say so *too*.

37 As Yahweh has been with my lord the king, even so be he with Solomon, and make his throne greater than the throne of my lord king David.

38 So Zadok the priest, and Nathan the prophet, and Benaiah the son of Jehoiada, and the Cherethites, and the Pelethites, went down, and caused Solomon to ride upon king David's mule, and brought him to Gihon.

39 And Zadok the priest took a horn of oil out of the tabernacle, and anointed Solomon. And they blew the trumpet; and all the people said, God save king Solomon.

40 And all the people came up after him, and the people piped with pipes, and rejoiced with great joy, so that the earth split with the sound of them.

41 ¶ And Adonijah and all the guests that *were* with him heard *it* as they had made an end of eating. And when Joab heard the sound of the trumpet, he said, Why *is this* noise of the city being in an uproar?

42 And while he yet spoke, behold, Jonathan the son of Abiathar the priest came: and Adonijah said to him, Come in; for you *are* a valiant man, and bring good tidings.

43 And Jonathan answered and said to Adonijah, Truly our lord king David has made Solomon king.

44 And the king has sent with him Zadok the priest, and Nathan the prophet, and Benaiah the son of Jehoiada, and the Cherethites, and the Pelethites, and they have caused him to ride upon the king's mule:

45 And Zadok the priest and Nathan the prophet have anointed him king in Gihon: and they have come up from there rejoicing, so that the city rang again. This *is* the noise that you have heard.

1 Kings 1

46 And also Solomon sits on the throne of the kingdom.
47 And moreover the king's servants came to bless our lord king David, saying, God make the name of Solomon better than your name, and make his throne greater than your throne. And the king bowed himself upon the bed.
48 And also thus said the king, Blessed *be* Yahweh God of Israel, which has given *one* to sit on my throne this day, my eyes even seeing *it*.
49 And all the guests that *were* with Adonijah were afraid, and rose up, and went every man his way.
50 And Adonijah feared because of Solomon, and arose, and went, and caught hold on the horns of the altar.
51 And it was told *to* Solomon, saying, Behold, Adonijah fears king Solomon: for, lo, he has caught hold on the horns of the altar, saying, Let king Solomon swear to me today that he will not slay his servant with the sword.
52 And Solomon said, If he will show himself a worthy man, there shall not a hair of him fall to the earth: but if wickedness shall be found in him, he shall die.
53 So king Solomon sent, and they brought him down from the altar. And he came and bowed himself to king Solomon: and Solomon said to him, Go to your house.

1 Kings 2

2:1 ¶ Now the days of David drew near that he should die; and he charged Solomon his son, saying,
2 I go the way of all the earth: be you strong therefore, and show yourself a man;
3 And keep the charge of Yahweh your God, to walk in his ways, to keep his statutes, and his commandments, and his judgments, and his testimonies, as it is written in the law of Moses, that you may prosper in all that you do, and wherever you turn yourself:
4 That Yahweh may continue his word which he spoke concerning me, saying, If your children take heed to their way, to walk before me in truth with all their heart and with all their soul, there shall not fail you (said he) a man on the throne of Israel.
5 Moreover you know also what Joab the son of Zeruiah did to me, *and* what he did to the two captains of the hosts of Israel, to Abner the son of Ner, and to Amasa the son of Jether, whom he slew, and shed the blood of war in peace, and put the blood of war upon his girdle that *was* about his loins, and in his shoes that *were* on his feet.
6 Do therefore according to your wisdom, and let not his gray head go down to the grave in peace.
7 But show kindness to the sons of Barzillai the Gileadite, and let them be of those that eat at your table: for so they came to me when I fled because of Absalom your brother.
8 And, behold, *you have* with you Shimei the son of Gera, a Benjamite of Bahurim, which cursed me with a grievous curse in the day when I went to Mahanaim: but he came down to meet me at *the* Jordan, and I swore to him by Yahweh, saying, I will not put you to death with the sword.
9 Now therefore hold him not guiltless: for you *are* a wise man, and know what you ought to do to him; but his gray head bring you down to the grave with blood.
10 So David slept with his fathers, and was buried in the city of David.
11 And the days that David reigned over Israel *were* forty years: seven years reigned he in Hebron, and thirty and three years reigned he in Jerusalem.
12 ¶ Then sat Solomon upon the throne of David his father; and his kingdom was established greatly.
13 And Adonijah the son of Haggith came to Bathsheba the mother of Solomon. And she said, Come you peaceably? And he said, Peaceably.
14 He said moreover, I have something to say to you. And she said, Say on.
15 And he said, You know that the kingdom was mine, and *that* all Israel set their faces on me, that I should reign: however the kingdom has turned about, and has become my brother's: for it was his from Yahweh.
16 And now I ask one petition of you, deny me not. And she said to him, Say on.
17 And he said, Speak, I pray you, to Solomon the king, (for he will not say you no,) that he give me Abishag the Shunammite to wife.
18 And Bathsheba said, Well; I will speak for you to the king.
19 Bathsheba therefore went to king Solomon, to speak to him for Adonijah. And the king rose up to meet her, and bowed himself to her, and sat down on his throne, and caused a seat to be set for the king's mother; and she sat on his right hand.
20 Then she said, I desire one small petition of you; *I pray you*, say me not no. And the king said to her, Ask on, my mother: for I will not say you no.
21 And she said, Let Abishag the Shunammite be given to Adonijah your brother to wife.
22 And king Solomon answered and said to his mother, And why do you ask Abishag the Shunammite for Adonijah? ask for him the kingdom also; for he *is* my elder brother; even for him, and for Abiathar the priest, and for Joab the son of Zeruiah.
23 Then king Solomon swore by Yahweh, saying, God do so to me, and more also, if Adonijah has not spoken this word against his own life.
24 Now therefore, *as* Yahweh lives, which has established me, and set me on the throne of David my father, and who has made me a house, as he promised, Adonijah shall be put to death this day.
25 And king Solomon sent by the hand of Benaiah the son of Jehoiada; and he fell upon him that he died.
26 ¶ And to Abiathar the priest said the king, Get you to Anathoth, to your own fields; for you *are* worthy of death: but I will not at this time put you to death, because you bore the ark of the Lord Yahweh before David my father, and because you have been afflicted in all wherein my father was afflicted.
27 So Solomon thrust out Abiathar from being priest unto Yahweh; that he might fulfill the word of Yahweh, which he spoke concerning the house of Eli in Shiloh.
28 Then tidings came to Joab: for Joab had turned after Adonijah, though he turned not after Absalom. And Joab

fled to the tabernacle of Yahweh, and caught hold on the horns of the altar.

29 And it was told *to* king Solomon that Joab was fled to the tabernacle of Yahweh; and, behold, *he is* by the altar. Then Solomon sent Benaiah the son of Jehoiada, saying, Go, fall upon him.

30 And Benaiah came to the tabernacle of Yahweh, and said to him, Thus says the king, Come forth. And he said, No; but I will die here. And Benaiah brought the king word again, saying, Thus said Joab, and thus he answered me.

31 And the king said to him, Do as he has said, and fall upon him, and bury him; that you may take away the innocent blood, which Joab shed, from me, and from the house of my father.

32 And Yahweh shall return his blood upon his own head, who fell upon two men more righteous and better than he, and slew them with the sword, my father David not knowing *thereof, to know*, Abner the son of Ner, captain of the host of Israel, and Amasa the son of Jether, captain of the host of Judah.

33 Their blood shall therefore return upon the head of Joab, and upon the head of his seed forever: but upon David, and upon his seed, and upon his house, and upon his throne, shall there be peace forever from Yahweh.

34 So Benaiah the son of Jehoiada went up, and fell upon him, and slew him: and he was buried in his own house in the wilderness.

35 ¶ And the king put Benaiah the son of Jehoiada in his room over the host: and Zadok the priest did the king put in the room of Abiathar.

36 And the king sent and called for Shimei, and said to him, Build you a house in Jerusalem, and dwell there, and go not forth there any where.

37 For it shall be, *that* on the day you go out, and pass over the brook Kidron, you shall know for certain that you shall surely die: your blood shall be upon your own head.

38 And Shimei said to the king, The saying *is* good: as my lord the king has said, so will your servant do. And Shimei dwelt in Jerusalem many days.

39 And it came to pass at the end of three years, that two of the servants of Shimei ran away unto Achish son of Maachah king of Gath. And they told Shimei, saying, Behold, your servants *are* in Gath.

40 And Shimei arose, and saddled his donkey, and went to Gath to Achish to seek his servants: and Shimei went, and brought his servants from Gath.

41 And it was told *to* Solomon that Shimei had gone from Jerusalem to Gath, and had come again.

42 And the king sent and called for Shimei, and said to him, Did I not make you to swear by Yahweh, and protested to you, saying, Know for a certain, on the day you go out, and walk abroad any where, that you shall surely die? and you said to me, The word *that* I have heard *is* good.

43 Why then have you not kept the oath of Yahweh, and the commandment that I have charged you with?

44 The king said moreover to Shimei, You know all the wickedness which your heart is privy to, that you did to David my father: therefore Yahweh shall return your wickedness upon your own head;

45 And king Solomon *shall be* blessed, and the throne of David shall be established before Yahweh forever.

46 So the king commanded Benaiah the son of Jehoiada; which went out, and fell upon him, that he died. And the kingdom was established in the hand of Solomon.

1 Kings 3

3:1 ¶ And Solomon made affinity with Pharaoh king of Egypt, and took Pharaoh's daughter, and brought her into the city of David, until he had made an end of building his own house, and the house of Yahweh, and the wall of Jerusalem round about.

2 Only the people sacrificed in high places, because there was no house built unto the name of Yahweh, until those days.

3 And Solomon loved Yahweh, walking in the statutes of David his father: only he sacrificed and burnt incense in high places.

4 And the king went to Gibeon to sacrifice there; for that *was* the great high place: a thousand burnt offerings did Solomon offer upon that altar.

5 ¶ In Gibeon Yahweh appeared to Solomon in a dream by night: and God said, Ask what I shall give you.

6 And Solomon said, You have shown to your servant David my father great mercy, according as he walked before you in truth, and in righteousness, and in uprightness of heart with you; and you have kept for him this great kindness, that you have given him a son to sit on his throne, as *it is* this day.

7 And now, O Yahweh my God, you have made your servant king instead of David my father: and I *am but* a little child: I know not *how* to go out or come in.

8 And your servant *is* in the midst of your people which you have chosen, a great people, that cannot be numbered nor counted for multitude.

9 Give therefore your servant an understanding heart to judge your people, that I may discern between good and bad: for who is able to judge this your so great a people?

10 And the speech pleased the Lord, that Solomon had asked this thing.

11 And God said to him, Because you have asked this thing, and have not asked for yourself long life; neither have asked riches for yourself, nor have asked the life of your enemies; but have asked for yourself understanding to discern judgment;

12 Behold, I have done according to your words: lo, I have given you a wise and an understanding heart; so that there was none like you before you, neither after you shall any arise like unto you.

13 And I have also given you that which you have not asked, both riches, and honor: so that there shall not be any among the kings like unto you all your days.

1 Kings 3

14 And if you will walk in my ways, to keep my statutes and my commandments, as your father David did walk, then I will lengthen your days.

15 And Solomon awoke; and, behold, *it was* a dream. And he came to Jerusalem, and stood before the ark of the covenant of Yahweh, and offered up burnt offerings, and offered peace offerings, and made a feast to all his servants.

16 ¶ Then came there two women, *that were* harlots, to the king, and stood before him.

17 And the one woman said, O my lord, I and this woman dwell in one house; and I was delivered of a child with her in the house.

18 And it came to pass the third day after that I was delivered, that this woman was delivered also: and we *were* together; *there was* no stranger with us in the house, save we two in the house.

19 And this woman's child died in the night; because she overlaid it.

20 And she arose at midnight, and took my son from beside me, while your handmaid slept, and laid it in her bosom, and laid her dead child in my bosom.

21 And when I rose in the morning to give my child suck, behold, it was dead: but when I had considered it in the morning, behold, it was not my son, which I did bear.

22 And the other woman said, No; but the living *is* my son, and the dead *is* your son. And this *woman* said, No; but the dead *is* your son, and the living *is* my son. Thus they spoke before the king.

23 Then said the king, The one says, This *is* my son that lives, and your son *is* the dead: and the other says, No; but your son *is* the dead, and my son *is* the living.

24 And the king said, Bring me a sword. And they brought a sword before the king.

25 And the king said, Divide the living child in two, and give half to the one, and half to the other.

26 Then spoke the woman whose the living child *was* unto the king, for her mercy yearned upon her son, and she said, O my lord, give her the living child, and in no way slay it. But the other said, Let it be neither my nor yours, *but* divide *it*.

27 Then the king answered and said, Give her the living child, and in no way slay it: she *is* the mother thereof.

28 And all Israel heard of the judgment which the king had judged; and they feared the king: for they saw that the wisdom of God *was* in him, to do judgment.

1 Kings 4

4:1 ¶ So king Solomon was king over all Israel.

2 And these *were* the princes which he had; Azariah the son of Zadok the priest,

3 Elihoreph and Ahiah, the sons of Shisha, scribes; Jehoshaphat the son of Ahilud, the recorder.

4 And Benaiah the son of Jehoiada *was* over the host: and Zadok and Abiathar *were* the priests:

5 And Azariah the son of Nathan *was* over the officers: and Zabud the son of Nathan *was* principal officer, *and* the king's friend:

6 And Ahishar *was* over the household: and Adoniram the son of Abda *was* over the tribute.

7 And Solomon had twelve officers over all Israel, which provided victuals for the king and his household: each man his month in a year made provision.

8 And these *are* their names: The son of Hur, in mount Ephraim:

9 The son of Dekar, in Makaz, and in Shaalbim, and Bethshemesh, and Elonbethhanan:

10 The son of Hesed, in Aruboth; to him *pertained* Sochoh, and all the land of Hepher:

11 The son of Abinadab, in all the region of Dor; which had Taphath the daughter of Solomon to wife:

12 Baana the son of Ahilud; *to him pertained* Taanach and Megiddo, and all Bethshean, which *is* by Zartanah beneath Jezreel, from Bethshean to Abelmeholah, *even* to *the place that is* beyond Jokneam:

13 The son of Geber, in Ramothgilead; to him *pertained* the towns of Jair the son of Manasseh, which *are* in Gilead; to him *also pertained* the region of Argob, which *is* in Bashan, threescore great cities with walls and brazen bars:

14 Ahinadab the son of Iddo *had* Mahanaim:

15 Ahimaaz *was* in Naphtali; he also took Basmath the daughter of Solomon to wife:

16 Baanah the son of Hushai *was* in Asher and in Aloth:

17 Jehoshaphat the son of Paruah, in Issachar:

18 Shimei the son of Elah, in Benjamin:

19 Geber the son of Uri *was* in the country of Gilead, *in* the country of Sihon king of the Amorites, and of Og king of Bashan; and *he was* the only officer which *was* in the land.

20 ¶ Judah and Israel *were* many, as the sand which *is* by the sea in multitude, eating and drinking, and making merry.

21 And Solomon reigned over all kingdoms from the river to the land of the Philistines, and to the border of Egypt: they brought presents, and served Solomon all the days of his life.

22 And Solomon's provision for one day was thirty measures of fine flour, and threescore measures of meal,

23 Ten fat oxen, and twenty oxen out of the pastures, and a hundred sheep, besides harts, and roebucks, and fallow deer, and fatted fowl.

24 For he had dominion over all *the region* on this side *of* the river, from Tiphsah even to Azzah, over all the kings on this side *of* the river: and he had peace on all sides round about him.

25 And Judah and Israel dwelt safely, every man under his vine and under his fig tree, from Dan even to Beersheba, all the days of Solomon.

26 And Solomon had forty thousand stalls of horses for his chariots, and twelve thousand horsemen.

27 And those officers provided victual for king Solomon, and for all that came to king Solomon's table, every man in his month: they lacked nothing.

28 Barley also and straw for the horses and dromedaries brought they to the place where *the officers* were, every man according to his charge.

29 ¶ And God gave Solomon wisdom and understanding exceedingly much, and largeness of heart, even as the sand that *is* on the sea shore.
30 And Solomon's wisdom excelled the wisdom of all the children of the east country, and all the wisdom of Egypt.
31 For he was wiser than all men; than Ethan the Ezrahite, and Heman, and Chalcol, and Darda, the sons of Mahol: and his fame was in all nations round about.
32 And he spoke three thousand proverbs: and his songs were a thousand and five.
33 And he spoke of trees, from the cedar tree that *is* in Lebanon even to the hyssop that springs out of the wall: he spoke also of beasts, and of fowl, and of creeping things, and of fishes.
34 And there came of all people to hear the wisdom of Solomon, from all kings of the earth, which had heard of his wisdom.

1 Kings 5

5:1 ¶ And Hiram king of Tyre sent his servants to Solomon; for he had heard that they had anointed him king in the room of his father: for Hiram was ever a lover of David.
2 And Solomon sent to Hiram, saying,
3 You know how that David my father could not build a house unto the name of Yahweh his God for the wars which were about him on every side, until Yahweh put them under the soles of his feet.
4 But now Yahweh my God has given me rest on every side, *so that there is* neither adversary nor evil occurring.
5 And, behold, I purpose to build a house unto the name of Yahweh my God, as Yahweh spoke to David my father, saying, Your son, whom I will set on your throne in your room, he shall build a house unto my name.
6 Now therefore command you that they hew me cedar trees out of Lebanon; and my servants shall be with your servants: and to you will I give hire for your servants according to all that you shall appoint: for you know that *there is* not among us any that can skill to hew timber like unto the Sidonians.
7 And it came to pass, when Hiram heard the words of Solomon, that he rejoiced greatly, and said, Blessed *be* Yahweh this day, which has given to David a wise son over this great people.
8 And Hiram sent to Solomon, saying, I have considered the things which you sent to me for: *and* I will do all your desire concerning timber of cedar, and concerning timber of fir.
9 My servants shall bring *them* down from Lebanon to the sea: and I will convey them by sea in floats to the place that you shall appoint me, and will cause them to be discharged there, and you shall receive *them*: and you shall accomplish my desire, in giving food for my household.
10 ¶ So Hiram gave Solomon cedar trees and fir trees *according to* all his desire.
11 And Solomon gave Hiram twenty thousand measures of wheat *for* food to his household, and twenty measures of pure oil: thus gave Solomon to Hiram year by year.
12 And Yahweh gave Solomon wisdom, as he promised him: and there was peace between Hiram and Solomon; and they two made a league together.
13 And king Solomon raised a levy out of all Israel; and the levy was thirty thousand men.
14 And he sent them to Lebanon, ten thousand a month by courses: a month they were in Lebanon, *and* two months at home: and Adoniram *was* over the levy.
15 And Solomon had threescore and ten thousand that bore burdens, and fourscore thousand hewers in the mountains;
16 Besides the chief of Solomon's officers which *were* over the work, three thousand and three hundred, which ruled over the people that performed in the work.
17 And the king commanded, and they brought great stones, costly stones, *and* hewn stones, to lay the foundation of the house.
18 And Solomon's builders and Hiram's builders did hew *them*, and the stonesquarers: so they prepared timber and stones to build the house.

1 Kings 6

6:1 ¶ And it came to pass in the four hundred and eightieth year after the children of Israel had come out of the land of Egypt, in the fourth year of Solomon's reign over Israel, in the month *of* Ziv, which *is* the second month, that he began to build the house of Yahweh.
2 And the house which king Solomon built for Yahweh, the length thereof *was* threescore cubits, and the breadth thereof twenty *cubits*, and the height thereof thirty cubits.
3 And the porch before the temple of the house, twenty cubits *was* the length thereof, according to the breadth of the house; *and* ten cubits *was* the breadth thereof before the house.
4 And for the house he made windows of narrow lights.
5 And against the wall of the house he built chambers round about, *against* the walls of the house round about, *both* of the temple and of the oracle: and he made chambers round about:
6 The lowest chamber *was* five cubits broad, and the middle *was* six cubits broad, and the third *was* seven cubits broad: for outside *in the wall* of the house he made narrowed ledges round about, that *the beams* should not be fastened in the walls of the house.
7 And the house, when it was being built, was built of stone made ready before it was brought there: so that there was neither hammer nor ax *nor* any tool of iron heard in the house, while it was being built.
8 The door for the middle chamber *was* in the right side of the house: and they went up with winding stairs into the middle *chamber*, and out of the middle into the third.
9 So he built the house, and finished it; and covered the house with beams and boards of cedar.
10 And *then* he built chambers against all the house, five cubits high: and they rested on the house *with* timber of cedar.

1 Kings 6

11 ¶ And the word of Yahweh came to Solomon, saying,
12 *Concerning* this house which you are building, if you will walk in my statutes, and execute my judgments, and keep all my commandments to walk in them; then will I perform my word with you, which I spoke to David your father:
13 And I will dwell among the children of Israel, and will not forsake my people Israel.
14 So Solomon built the house, and finished it.
15 ¶ And he built the walls of the house within with boards of cedar, both the floor of the house, and the walls of the ceiling: *and* he covered *them* on the inside with wood, and covered the floor of the house with planks of fir.
16 And he built twenty cubits on the sides of the house, both the floor and the walls with boards of cedar: he even built *them* for it within, *even* for the oracle, *even* for the most holy *place*.
17 And the house, that *is*, the temple before it, was forty cubits *long*.
18 And the cedar of the house within *was* carved with knops and open flowers: all *was* cedar; there was no stone seen.
19 And the oracle he prepared in the house within, to set there the ark of the covenant of Yahweh.
20 And the oracle in the forepart *was* twenty cubits in length, and twenty cubits in breadth, and twenty cubits in the height thereof: and he overlaid it with pure gold; and *so* covered the altar *which was of* cedar.
21 So Solomon overlaid the house within with pure gold: and he made a partition by the chains of gold before the oracle; and he overlaid it with gold.
22 And the whole house he overlaid with gold, until he had finished all the house: also the whole altar that *was* by the oracle he overlaid with gold.
23 And within the oracle he made two cherubims *of* olive tree, *each* ten cubits high.
24 And five cubits *was* the one wing of the cherub, and five cubits the other wing of the cherub: from the utmost part of the one wing to the utmost part of the other *was* ten cubits.
25 And the other cherub *was* ten cubits: both the cherubims *were* of one measure and one size.
26 The height of the one cherub *was* ten cubits, and so *was it* of the other cherub.
27 And he set the cherubims within the inner house: and they stretched forth the wings of the cherubims, so that the wing of the one touched the *one* wall, and the wing of the other cherub touched the other wall; and their wings touched one another in the middle of the house.
28 And he overlaid the cherubims with gold.
29 And he carved all the walls of the house round about with carved figures of cherubims and palm trees and open flowers, within and without.
30 And the floor of the house he overlaid with gold, within and without.
31 And for the entering of the oracle he made doors *of* olive tree: the lintel *and* side posts *were* a fifth part *of the wall*.
32 The two doors also *were of* olive tree; and he carved on them carvings of cherubims and palm trees and open flowers, and overlaid *them* with gold, and spread gold on the cherubims, and on the palm trees.
33 So also made he for the door of the temple posts *of* olive tree, a fourth part *of the wall*.
34 And the two doors *were of* fir tree: the two leaves of the one door *were* folding, and the two leaves of the other door *were* folding.
35 And he carved *thereon* cherubims and palm trees and open flowers: and covered *them* with gold fitted upon the carved work.
36 And he built the inner court with three rows of hewn stone, and a row of cedar beams.
37 In the fourth year was the foundation of the house of Yahweh laid, in the month *of* Ziv:
38 And in the eleventh year, in the month *of* Bul, which *is* the eighth month, was the house finished throughout all the parts thereof, and according to all the fashion of it. So was he seven years in building it.

1 Kings 7

7:1 ¶ But Solomon was building his own house thirteen years, and he finished all his house.
2 He built also the house of the forest of Lebanon; the length thereof *was* a hundred cubits, and the breadth thereof fifty cubits, and the height thereof thirty cubits, upon four rows of cedar pillars, with cedar beams upon the pillars.
3 And *it was* covered with cedar above upon the beams, that *lay* on forty five pillars, fifteen *in* a row.
4 And *there were* windows *in* three rows, and light *was* against light *in* three ranks.
5 And all the doors and posts *were* square, with the windows: and light *was* against light *in* three ranks.
6 And he made a porch of pillars; the length thereof *was* fifty cubits, and the breadth thereof thirty cubits: and the porch *was* before them: and the *other* pillars and the thick beam *were* before them.
7 Then he made a porch for the throne where he might judge, *even* the porch of judgment: and *it was* covered with cedar from one side of the floor to the other.
8 And his house where he dwelt *had* another court within the porch, *which* was of the like work. Solomon made also a house for Pharaoh's daughter, whom he had taken *to wife*, like unto this porch.
9 All these *were of* costly stones, according to the measures of hewn stones, sawed with saws, within and without, even from the foundation to the coping, and *so* on the outside toward the great court.
10 And the foundation *was of* costly stones, even great stones, stones of ten cubits, and stones of eight cubits.
11 And above *were* costly stones, after the measures of hewed stones, and cedars.
12 And the great court round about *was* with three rows of hewn stones, and a row of cedar beams, both for the inner court of the house of Yahweh, and for the porch of the house.

1 Kings 7

13 ¶ And king Solomon sent and fetched Hiram out of Tyre.

14 He *was* a widow's son of the tribe of Naphtali, and his father *was* a man of Tyre, a worker in brass: and he was filled with wisdom, and understanding, and cunning to work all works in brass. And he came to king Solomon, and worked all his work.

15 For he cast two pillars of brass, of eighteen cubits high apiece: and a line of twelve cubits did compass either of them about.

16 And he made two capitals *of* molten brass, to set upon the tops of the pillars: the height of the one capital *was* five cubits, and the height of the other capital *was* five cubits:

17 *And* nets of checker work, and wreaths of chain work, for the capitals which *were* upon the top of the pillars; seven for the one capital, and seven for the other capital.

18 And he made the pillars, and two rows round about upon the one network, to cover the capitals that *were* upon the top, with pomegranates: and so did he for the other capital.

19 And the capitals that *were* upon the top of the pillars *were* of lily work in the porch, four cubits.

20 And the capitals upon the two pillars *had pomegranates* also above, over against the belly which *was* by the network: and the pomegranates *were* two hundred in rows round about upon the other capital.

21 And he set up the pillars in the porch of the temple: and he set up the right pillar, and called the name thereof Jachin: and he set up the left pillar, and called the name thereof Boaz.

22 And upon the top of the pillars *was* lily work: so was the work of the pillars finished.

23 And he made a molten sea, ten cubits from the one brim to the other: *it was* round all about, and his height *was* five cubits: and a line of thirty cubits did compass it round about.

24 And under the brim of it round about *there were* knops compassing it, ten in a cubit, compassing the sea round about: the knops *were* cast in two rows, when it was cast.

25 It stood upon twelve oxen, three looking toward the north, and three looking toward the west, and three looking toward the south, and three looking toward the east: and the sea *was set* above upon them, and all their hinder parts *were* inward.

26 And it *was* a hand breadth thick, and the brim thereof was worked like the brim of a cup, with flowers of lilies: it contained two thousand baths.

27 And he made ten bases of brass; four cubits *was* the length of one base, and four cubits the breadth thereof, and three cubits the height of it.

28 And the work of the bases *was* on this *manner*: they had borders, and the borders *were* between the ledges:

29 And on the borders that *were* between the ledges *were* lions, oxen, and cherubims: and upon the ledges *there was* a base above: and beneath the lions and oxen *were* certain additions made of thin work.

30 And every base had four brazen wheels, and plates of brass: and the four corners thereof had supports: under the laver *were* supports molten, at the side of every addition.

31 And the mouth of it within the capital and above *was* a cubit: but the mouth thereof *was* round *after* the work of the base, a cubit and a half: and also upon the mouth of it *were* engravings with their borders, foursquare, not round.

32 And under the borders *were* four wheels; and the axles of the wheels *were joined* to the base: and the height of a wheel *was* a cubit and half a cubit.

33 And the work of the wheels *was* like the work of a chariot wheel: their axles, and their rims, and their spokes, and their hubs, *were* all molten.

34 And *there were* four supports to the four corners of one base: *and* the supports *were* of the very base itself.

35 And in the top of the base *was there* a round compass of half a cubit high: and on the top of the base the ledges thereof and the borders thereof *were* of the same.

36 For on the plates of the ledges thereof, and on the borders thereof, he engraved cherubims, lions, and palm trees, according to the proportion of every one, and additions round about.

37 After this *manner* he made the ten bases: all of them had one casting, one measure, *and* one size.

38 Then made he ten lavers of brass: one laver contained forty baths: *and* every laver was four cubits: *and* upon every one of the ten bases one laver.

39 And he put five bases on the right side of the house, and five on the left side of the house: and he set the sea on the right side of the house eastward over against the south.

40 And Hiram made the lavers, and the shovels, and the basins. So Hiram made an end of doing all the work that he made king Solomon for the house of Yahweh:

41 The two pillars, and the *two* bowls of the capitals that *were* on the top of the two pillars; and the two networks, to cover the two bowls of the capitals which *were* upon the top of the pillars;

42 And four hundred pomegranates for the two networks, *even* two rows of pomegranates for one network, to cover the two bowls of the capitals that *were* upon the pillars;

43 And the ten bases, and ten lavers on the bases;

44 And one sea, and twelve oxen under the sea;

45 And the pots, and the shovels, and the basins: and all these vessels, which Hiram made to king Solomon for the house of Yahweh, *were of* bright brass.

46 In the plain of Jordan did the king cast them, in the clay ground between Succoth and Zarthan.

47 And Solomon left all the vessels *unweighed*, because they were exceedingly many: neither was the weight of the brass found out.

48 ¶ And Solomon made all the vessels that *pertained* to the house of Yahweh: the altar of gold, and the table of gold, whereupon the showbread *was*,

49 And the candlesticks of pure gold, five on the right *side*, and five on the left, before the oracle, with the flowers, and the lamps, and the tongs *of* gold,

1 Kings 7

50 And the bowls, and the snuffers, and the basins, and the spoons, and the censers *of* pure gold; and the hinges *of* gold, *both* for the doors of the inner house, the most holy *place, and* for the doors of the house, *to know,* of the temple.

51 So was ended all the work that king Solomon made for the house of Yahweh. And Solomon brought in the things which David his father had dedicated; *even* the silver, and the gold, and the vessels, did he put among the treasuries of the house of Yahweh.

1 Kings 8

8:1 ¶ Then Solomon assembled the elders of Israel, and all the heads of the tribes, the chief of the fathers of the children of Israel, unto king Solomon in Jerusalem, that they might bring up the ark of the covenant of Yahweh out of the city of David, which *is* Zion.

2 And all the men of Israel assembled themselves unto king Solomon at the feast in the month *of* Ethanim, which *is* the seventh month.

3 And all the elders of Israel came, and the priests took up the ark.

4 And they brought up the ark of Yahweh, and the tabernacle of the congregation, and all the holy vessels that *were* in the tabernacle, even those did the priests and the Levites bring up.

5 And king Solomon, and all the congregation of Israel, that were assembled to him, *were* with him before the ark, sacrificing sheep and oxen, that could not be told nor numbered for multitude.

6 And the priests brought in the ark of the covenant of Yahweh to his place, into the oracle of the house, to the most holy *place, even* under the wings of the cherubims.

7 For the cherubims spread forth *their* two wings over the place of the ark, and the cherubims covered the ark and the staves thereof above.

8 And they drew out the staves, that the ends of the staves were seen out in the holy *place* before the oracle, and they were not seen outside: and there they are unto this day.

9 *There was* nothing in the ark save the two tables of stone, which Moses put there at Horeb, when Yahweh made *a covenant* with the children of Israel, when they came out of the land of Egypt.

10 And it came to pass, when the priests had come out of the holy *place,* that the cloud filled the house of Yahweh,

11 So that the priests could not stand to minister because of the cloud: for the glory of Yahweh had filled the house of Yahweh.

12 ¶ Then spoke Solomon, Yahweh said that he would dwell in the thick darkness.

13 I have surely built you a house to dwell in, a settled place for you to inhabit forever.

14 And the king turned his face about, and blessed all the congregation of Israel: (and all the congregation of Israel stood;)

15 And he said, Blessed *be* Yahweh God of Israel, which spoke with his mouth to David my father, and has with his hand fulfilled *it,* saying,

16 Since the day that I brought forth my people Israel out of Egypt, I chose no city out of all the tribes of Israel to build a house, that my name might be therein; but I chose David to be over my people Israel.

17 And it was in the heart of David my father to build a house for the name of Yahweh God of Israel.

18 And Yahweh said to David my father, Whereas it was in your heart to build a house unto my name, you did well that it was in your heart.

19 Nevertheless you shall not build the house; but your son that shall come forth out of your loins, he shall build the house unto my name.

20 And Yahweh has performed his word that he spoke, and I have risen up in the room of David my father, and sit on the throne of Israel, as Yahweh promised, and have built a house for the name of Yahweh God of Israel.

21 And I have set there a place for the ark, wherein *is* the covenant of Yahweh, which he made with our fathers, when he brought them out of the land of Egypt.

22 ¶ And Solomon stood before the altar of Yahweh in the presence of all the congregation of Israel, and spread forth his hands toward heaven:

23 And he said, Yahweh God of Israel, *there is* no God like you, in heaven above, or on earth beneath, who keeps covenant and mercy with your servants that walk before you with all their heart:

24 Who has kept with your servant David my father that you promised him: you spoke also with your mouth, and have fulfilled *it* with your hand, as *it is* this day.

25 Therefore now, Yahweh God of Israel, keep with your servant David my father that you promised him, saying, There shall not fail you a man in my sight to sit on the throne of Israel; so that your children take heed to their way, that they walk before me as you have walked before me.

26 And now, O God of Israel, let your word, I pray you, be verified, which you spoke to your servant David my father.

27 But will God indeed dwell on the earth? behold, the heaven and heaven of heavens cannot contain you; how much less this house that I have built?

28 Yet have you respect to the prayer of your servant, and to his supplication, O Yahweh my God, to listen to the cry and to the prayer, which your servant prays before you today:

29 That your eyes may be open toward this house night and day, *even* toward the place of which you have said, My name shall be there: that you may listen to the prayer which your servant shall make toward this place.

30 And listen you to the supplication of your servant, and of your people Israel, when they shall pray toward this place: and hear you in heaven your dwelling place: and when you hear, forgive.

31 If any man trespasses against his neighbor, and an oath is laid upon him to cause him to swear, and the oath comes before your altar in this house:

32 Then hear you in heaven, and do, and judge your servants, condemning the wicked, to bring his way upon his head; and justifying the righteous, to give him according to his righteousness.

33 When your people Israel are smitten down before the enemy, because they have sinned against you, and shall turn again to you, and confess your name, and pray, and make supplication unto you in this house:

34 Then hear you in heaven, and forgive the sin of your people Israel, and bring them again to the land which you gave to their fathers.

35 When heaven is shut up, and there is no rain, because they have sinned against you; if they pray toward this place, and confess your name, and turn from their sin, when you afflict them:

36 Then hear you in heaven, and forgive the sin of your servants, and of your people Israel, that you teach them the good way wherein they should walk, and give rain upon your land, which you have given to your people for an inheritance.

37 If there is in the land famine, if there is pestilence, blasting, mildew, locust, *or* if there are caterpillars. if their enemy besieges them in the land of their cities; whatever plague, whatever sickness *there is*;

38 What prayer and supplication soever is *made* by any man, *or* by all your people Israel, which shall know every man the plague of his own heart, and spread forth his hands toward this house:

39 Then hear you in heaven your dwelling place, and forgive, and do, and give to every man according to his ways, whose heart you know; (for you, *even* you only, know the hearts of all the children of men;)

40 That they may fear you all the days that they live in the land which you gave to our fathers.

41 Moreover concerning a stranger, that *is* not of your people Israel, but comes out of a far country for your name's sake;

42 (For they shall hear of your great name, and of your strong hand, and of your stretched out arm;) when he shall come and pray toward this house;

43 Hear you in heaven your dwelling place, and do according to all that the stranger calls to you for: that all people of the earth may know your name, to fear you, as *do* your people Israel; and that they may know that this house, which I have built, is called by your name.

44 If your people go out to battle against their enemy, wherever you shall send them, and shall pray unto Yahweh toward the city which you have chosen, and *toward* the house that I have built for your name:

45 Then hear you in heaven their prayer and their supplication, and maintain their cause.

46 If they sin against you, (for *there is* no man that sins not,) and you are angry with them, and deliver them to the enemy, so that they carry them away captives to the land of the enemy, far or near;

47 *Yet* if they shall return *to* themselves in the land where they were carried captives, and repent, and make supplication unto you in the land of them that carried them captives, saying, We have sinned, and have done perversely, we have committed wickedness;

48 And *so* return unto you with all their heart, and with all their soul, in the land of their enemies, which led them away captive, and pray unto you toward their land, which you gave to their fathers, the city which you have chosen, and the house which I have built for your name:

49 Then hear you their prayer and their supplication in heaven your dwelling place, and maintain their cause,

50 And forgive your people that have sinned against you, and all their transgressions wherein they have transgressed against you, and give them compassion before them who carried them captive, that they may have compassion on them:

51 For they *are* your people, and your inheritance, which you brought forth out of Egypt, from the midst of the furnace of iron:

52 That your eyes may be open to the supplication of your servant, and to the supplication of your people Israel, to listen to them in all that they call for unto you.

53 For you did separate them from among all the people of the earth, *to be* your inheritance, as you spoke by the hand of Moses your servant, when you brought our fathers out of Egypt, O Lord Yahweh.

54 ¶ And it was *so*, that when Solomon had made an end of praying all this prayer and supplication unto Yahweh, he arose from before the altar of Yahweh, from kneeling on his knees with his hands spread up to heaven.

55 And he stood, and blessed all the congregation of Israel with a loud voice, saying,

56 Blessed *be* Yahweh, that has given rest to his people Israel, according to all that he promised: there has not failed one word of all his good promise, which he promised by the hand of Moses his servant.

57 Yahweh our God be with us, as he was with our fathers: let him not leave us, nor forsake us:

58 That he may incline our hearts unto him, to walk in all his ways, and to keep his commandments, and his statutes, and his judgments, which he commanded our fathers.

59 And let these my words, with which I have made supplication before Yahweh, be near unto Yahweh our God day and night, that he maintain the cause of his servant, and the cause of his people Israel at all times, as the matter shall require:

60 That all the people of the earth may know that Yahweh *is* God, *and that there is* none else.

61 Let your heart therefore be perfect with Yahweh our God, to walk in his statutes, and to keep his commandments, as at this day.

62 ¶ And the king, and all Israel with him, offered sacrifice before Yahweh.

63 And Solomon offered a sacrifice of peace offerings, which he offered unto Yahweh, two and twenty thousand oxen, and a hundred and twenty thousand sheep. So the king and all the children of Israel dedicated the house of Yahweh.

64 The same day did the king hallow the middle of the court that *was* before the house of Yahweh: for there he offered burnt offerings, and meat offerings, and the fat of

the peace offerings: because the brazen altar that *was* before Yahweh *was* too little to receive the burnt offerings, and meat offerings, and the fat of the peace offerings.

65 And at that time Solomon held a feast, and all Israel with him, a great congregation, from the entering in of Hamath to the river of Egypt, before Yahweh our God, seven days and seven days, *even* fourteen days.

66 On the eighth day he sent the people away: and they blessed the king, and went to their tents joyful and glad of heart for all the goodness that Yahweh had done for David his servant, and for Israel his people.

1 Kings 9

9:1 ¶ And it came to pass, when Solomon had finished the building of the house of Yahweh, and the king's house, and all Solomon's desire which he was pleased to do,

2 That Yahweh appeared to Solomon the second time, as he had appeared to him at Gibeon.

3 And Yahweh said to him, I have heard your prayer and your supplication, that you have made before me: I have hallowed this house, which you have built, to put my name there forever; and my eyes and my heart shall be there perpetually.

4 And if you will walk before me, as David your father walked, in integrity of heart, and in uprightness, to do according to all that I have commanded you, *and* will keep my statutes and my judgments:

5 Then I will establish the throne of your kingdom upon Israel forever, as I promised to David your father, saying, There shall not fail you a man upon the throne of Israel.

6 *But* if you shall at all turn from following me, you or your children, and will not keep my commandments *and* my statutes which I have set before you, but go and serve other gods, and worship them:

7 Then will I cut off Israel out of the land which I have given them; and this house, which I have hallowed for my name, will I cast out of my sight; and Israel shall be a proverb and a byword among all people:

8 And at this house, *which* is high, every one that passes by it shall be astonished, and shall hiss; and they shall say, Why has Yahweh done thus to this land, and to this house?

9 And they shall answer, Because they forsook Yahweh their God, who brought forth their fathers out of the land of Egypt, and have taken hold upon other gods, and have worshipped them, and served them: therefore has Yahweh brought upon them all this evil.

10 ¶ And it came to pass at the end of twenty years, when Solomon had built the two houses, the house of Yahweh, and the king's house,

11 (*Now* Hiram the king of Tyre had furnished Solomon with cedar trees and fir trees, and with gold, according to all his desire,) that then king Solomon gave Hiram twenty cities in the land of Galilee.

12 And Hiram came out from Tyre to see the cities which Solomon had given him; and they pleased him not.

13 And he said, What cities *are* these which you have given me, my brother? And he called them the land of Cabul unto this day.

14 And Hiram sent to the king six score talents of gold.

15 ¶ And this *is* the reason of the levy which king Solomon raised; for to build the house of Yahweh, and his own house, and Millo, and the wall of Jerusalem, and Hazor, and Megiddo, and Gezer.

16 *For* Pharaoh king of Egypt had gone up, and taken Gezer, and burnt it with fire, and slain the Canaanites that dwelt in the city, and given it *for* a present to his daughter, Solomon's wife.

17 And Solomon built Gezer, and Bethhoron the lower,

18 And Baalath, and Tadmor in the wilderness, in the land,

19 And all the cities of store that Solomon had, and cities for his chariots, and cities for his horsemen, and that which Solomon desired to build in Jerusalem, and in Lebanon, and in all the land of his dominion.

20 *And* all the people *that were* left of the Amorites, Hittites, Perizzites, Hivites, and Jebusites, which *were* not of the children of Israel,

21 Their children that were left after them in the land, whom the children of Israel also were not able utterly to destroy, upon those did Solomon levy a tribute of slavery unto this day.

22 But of the children of Israel did Solomon make no bondmen: but they *were* men of war, and his servants, and his princes, and his captains, and rulers of his chariots, and his horsemen.

23 These *were* the chief of the officers that *were* over Solomon's work, five hundred and fifty, which bear rule over the people that worked in the work.

24 But Pharaoh's daughter came up out of the city of David to her house which *Solomon* had built for her: then did he build Millo.

25 And three times in a year did Solomon offer burnt offerings and peace offerings upon the altar which he built unto Yahweh, and he burnt incense upon the altar that *was* before Yahweh. So he finished the house.

26 And king Solomon made a navy of ships in Eziongeber, which *is* beside Eloth, on the shore of the Red Sea, in the land of Edom.

27 And Hiram sent in the navy his servants, shipmen that had knowledge of the sea, with the servants of Solomon.

28 And they came to Ophir, and fetched from there gold, four hundred and twenty talents, and brought *it* to king Solomon.

1 Kings 10

10:1 ¶ And when the queen of Sheba heard of the fame of Solomon concerning the name of Yahweh, she came to prove him with hard questions.

2 And she came to Jerusalem with a very great train, with camels that bear spices, and very much gold, and precious stones: and when she had come to Solomon, she communed with him of all that was in her heart.

3 And Solomon told her all her questions: there was not *any* thing hidden from the king, which he told her not.

4 And when the queen of Sheba had seen all Solomon's wisdom, and the house that he had built,

5 And the food of his table, and the sitting of his servants, and the attendance of his ministers, and their apparel, and his cup bearers, and his ascent by which he went up to the house of Yahweh; there was no more spirit in her.

6 And she said to the king, It was a true report that I heard in my own land of your acts and of your wisdom.

7 However I believed not the words, until I came, and my eyes had seen *it*: and, behold, the half was not told me: your wisdom and prosperity exceeds the fame which I heard.

8 Happy *are* your men, happy *are* these your servants, which stand continually before you, *and* that hear your wisdom.

9 Blessed be Yahweh your God, which delighted in you, to set you on the throne of Israel: because Yahweh loved Israel forever, therefore made he you king, to do judgment and justice.

10 And she gave the king a hundred and twenty talents of gold, and of spices *a* very great store, and precious stones: there came no more such abundance of spices as these which the queen of Sheba gave to king Solomon.

11 And the navy also of Hiram, that brought gold from Ophir, brought in from Ophir great plenty of almug trees, and precious stones.

12 And the king made of the almug trees pillars for the house of Yahweh, and for the king's house, harps also and psalteries for singers: there came no such almug trees, nor were seen unto this day.

13 And king Solomon gave to the queen of Sheba all her desire, whatever she asked, besides *that* which Solomon gave her of his royal bounty. So she turned and went to her own country, she and her servants.

14 ¶ Now the weight of gold that came to Solomon in one year was six hundred threescore and six talents of gold,

15 Besides *that he had* of the merchantmen, and of the traffic of the spice merchants, and of all the kings of Arabia, and of the governors of the country.

16 And king Solomon made two hundred targets *of* beaten gold: six hundred *shekels* of gold went to one target.

17 And *he made* three hundred shields *of* beaten gold; three pounds of gold went to one shield: and the king put them in the house of the forest of Lebanon.

18 Moreover the king made a great throne of ivory, and overlaid it with the best gold.

19 The throne had six steps, and the top of the throne *was* round behind: and *there were* stays on either side on the place of the seat, and two lions stood beside the stays.

20 And twelve lions stood there on the one side and on the other upon the six steps: there was not the like made in any kingdom.

21 And all king Solomon's drinking vessels *were of* gold, and all the vessels of the house of the forest of Lebanon *were of* pure gold; none *were of* silver: it was nothing accounted of in the days of Solomon.

22 For the king had at sea a navy of Tharshish with the navy of Hiram: once in three years came the navy of Tharshish, bringing gold, and silver, ivory, and apes, and peacocks.

23 So king Solomon exceeded all the kings of the earth for riches and for wisdom.

24 And all the earth sought to Solomon, to hear his wisdom, which God had put in his heart.

25 And they brought every man his present, vessels of silver, and vessels of gold, and garments, and armor, and spices, horses, and mules, a rate year by year.

26 And Solomon gathered together chariots and horsemen: and he had a thousand and four hundred chariots, and twelve thousand horsemen, whom he bestowed in the cities for chariots, and with the king at Jerusalem.

27 And the king made silver *to be* in Jerusalem as stones, and cedars made he *to be* as the sycamore trees that *are* in the vale, for abundance.

28 And Solomon had horses brought out of Egypt, and linen yarn the king's merchants received the linen yarn at a price.

29 And a chariot came up and went out of Egypt for six hundred *shekels* of silver, and a horse for a hundred and fifty: and so for all the kings of the Hittites, and for the kings of Syria, did they bring *them* out by their means.

1 Kings 11

11:1 ¶ But king Solomon loved many strange women, together with the daughter of Pharaoh, women of the Moabites, Ammonites, Edomites, Zidonians, *and* Hittites;

2 Of the nations *concerning* which Yahweh said to the children of Israel, You shall not go in to them, neither shall they come in unto you: *for* surely they will turn away your heart after their gods: Solomon clung to these in love.

3 And he had seven hundred wives, princesses, and three hundred concubines: and his wives turned away his heart.

4 For it came to pass, when Solomon was old, *that* his wives turned away his heart after other gods: and his heart was not perfect with Yahweh his God, as *was* the heart of David his father.

5 For Solomon went after Ashtoreth the goddess of the Zidonians, and after Milcom the abomination of the Ammonites.

6 And Solomon did evil in the sight of Yahweh, and went not fully after Yahweh, as *did* David his father.

7 Then did Solomon build a high place for Chemosh, the abomination of Moab, in the hill that *is* before Jerusalem, and for Molech, the abomination of the children of Ammon.

1 Kings 11

8 And likewise did he for all his strange wives, which burnt incense and sacrificed to their gods.

9 ¶ And Yahweh was angry with Solomon, because his heart was turned from Yahweh God of Israel, which had appeared to him twice,

10 And had commanded him concerning this thing, that he should not go after other gods: but he kept not that which Yahweh commanded.

11 Therefore Yahweh said to Solomon, Forasmuch as this is done of you, and you have not kept my covenant and my statutes, which I have commanded you, I will surely tear the kingdom from you, and will give it to your servant.

12 Notwithstanding in your days I will not do it for David your father's sake: *but* I will rend it out of the hand of your son.

13 However I will not rend away all the kingdom; *but* will give one tribe to your son for David my servant's sake, and for Jerusalem's sake which I have chosen.

14 ¶ And Yahweh stirred up an adversary unto Solomon, Hadad the Edomite: he *was* of the king's seed in Edom.

15 For it came to pass, when David was in Edom, and Joab the captain of the host had gone up to bury the slain, after he had smitten every male in Edom;

16 (For six months did Joab remain there with all Israel, until he had cut off every male in Edom:)

17 That Hadad fled, he and certain Edomites of his father's servants with him, to go into Egypt; Hadad *being* yet a little child.

18 And they arose out of Midian, and came to Paran: and they took men with them out of Paran, and they came to Egypt, to Pharaoh king of Egypt; which gave him a house, and appointed him victuals, and gave him land.

19 And Hadad found great favor in the sight of Pharaoh, so that he gave him to wife the sister of his own wife, the sister of Tahpenes the queen.

20 And the sister of Tahpenes bore him Genubath his son, whom Tahpenes weaned in Pharaoh's house: and Genubath was in Pharaoh's household among the sons of Pharaoh.

21 And when Hadad heard in Egypt that David slept with his fathers, and that Joab the captain of the host was dead, Hadad said to Pharaoh, Let me depart, that I may go to my own country.

22 Then Pharaoh said to him, But what have you lacked with me, that, behold, you seek to go to your own country? And he answered, Nothing: however let me go anyway.

23 And God stirred him up *another* adversary, Rezon the son of Eliadah, which fled from his lord Hadadezer king of Zobah:

24 And he gathered men to him, and became captain over a band, when David slew them *of Zobah*: and they went to Damascus, and dwelt therein, and reigned in Damascus.

25 And he was an adversary to Israel all the days of Solomon, besides the mischief that Hadad *did*: and he abhorred Israel, and reigned over Syria.

26 ¶ And Jeroboam the son of Nebat, an Ephrathite of Zereda, Solomon's servant, whose mother's name *was* Zeruah, a widow woman, even he lifted up *his* hand against the king.

27 And this *was* the cause that he lifted up *his* hand against the king: Solomon built Millo, *and* repaired the breaches of the city of David his father.

28 And the man Jeroboam *was* a mighty man of valor: and Solomon seeing the young man that he was industrious, he made him ruler over all the charge of the house of Joseph.

29 And it came to pass at that time when Jeroboam went out of Jerusalem, that the prophet Ahijah the Shilonite found him in the way; and he had clothed himself with a new garment; and they two *were* alone in the field:

30 And Ahijah caught the new garment that *was* on him, and tore it *in* twelve pieces:

31 And he said to Jeroboam, Take you ten pieces: for thus says Yahweh, the God of Israel, Behold, I will tear the kingdom out of the hand of Solomon, and will give ten tribes to you:

32 (But he shall have one tribe for my servant David's sake, and for Jerusalem's sake, the city which I have chosen out of all the tribes of Israel:)

33 Because that they have forsaken me, and have worshipped Ashtoreth the goddess of the Zidonians, Chemosh the god of the Moabites, and Milcom the god of the children of Ammon, and have not walked in my ways, to do *that which is* right in my eyes, and *to keep* my statutes and my judgments, as *did* David his father.

34 However I will not take the whole kingdom out of his hand: but I will make him prince all the days of his life for David my servant's sake, whom I chose, because he kept my commandments and my statutes:

35 But I will take the kingdom out of his son's hand, and will give it to you, *even* ten tribes.

36 And to his son will I give one tribe, that David my servant may have a light always before me in Jerusalem, the city which I have chosen me to put my name there.

37 And I will take you, and you shall reign according to all that your soul desires, and shall be king over Israel.

38 And it shall be, if you will listen to all that I command you, and will walk in my ways, and do *what is* right in my sight, to keep my statutes and my commandments, as David my servant did; that I will be with you, and build you a sure house, as I built for David, and will give Israel to you.

39 And I will for this afflict the seed of David, but not forever.

40 Solomon sought therefore to kill Jeroboam. And Jeroboam arose, and fled into Egypt, to Shishak king of Egypt, and was in Egypt until the death of Solomon.

41 ¶ And the rest of the acts of Solomon, and all that he did, and his wisdom, *are* they not written in the book of the acts of Solomon?

42 And the time that Solomon reigned in Jerusalem over all Israel *was* forty years.

43 And Solomon slept with his fathers, and was buried in the city of David his father: and Rehoboam his son reigned in his stead.

1 Kings 12

12:1 ¶ And Rehoboam went to Shechem: for all Israel had come to Shechem to make him king.
2 And it came to pass, when Jeroboam the son of Nebat, who was yet in Egypt, heard *of it*, (for he had fled from the presence of king Solomon, and Jeroboam dwelt in Egypt;)
3 That they sent and called him. And Jeroboam and all the congregation of Israel came, and spoke to Rehoboam, saying,
4 Your father made our yoke grievous: now therefore make you the grievous service of your father, and his heavy yoke which he put upon us, lighter, and we will serve you.
5 And he said to them, Depart yet *for* three days, then come again to me. And the people departed.
6 And king Rehoboam consulted with the old men, that stood before Solomon his father while he yet lived, and said, How do you advise that I may answer this people?
7 And they spoke to him, saying, If you will be a servant to this people this day, and will serve them, and answer them, and speak good words to them, then they will be your servants forever.
8 But he forsook the counsel of the old men, which they had given him, and consulted with the young men that had grown up with him, *and* which stood before him:
9 And he said to them, What counsel give you that we may answer this people, who have spoken to me, saying, Make the yoke which your father did put upon us lighter?
10 And the young men that had grown up with him spoke to him, saying, Thus shall you speak to this people that spoke to you, saying, Your father made our yoke heavy, but make you *it* lighter to us; thus shall you say to them, My little *finger* shall be thicker than my father's loins.
11 And now whereas my father did load you with a heavy yoke, I will add to your yoke: my father has chastised you with whips, but I will chastise you with scorpions.
12 So Jeroboam and all the people came to Rehoboam the third day, as the king had appointed, saying, Come to me again the third day.
13 And the king answered the people roughly, and forsook the old men's counsel that they gave him;
14 And spoke to them after the counsel of the young men, saying, My father made your yoke heavy, and I will add to your yoke: my father *also* chastised you with whips, but I will chastise you with scorpions.
15 Therefore the king listened not to the people; for the cause was from Yahweh, that he might perform his saying, which Yahweh spoke by Ahijah the Shilonite to Jeroboam the son of Nebat.
16 ¶ So when all Israel saw that the king listened not to them, the people answered the king, saying, What portion have we in David? neither *have we* inheritance in the son of Jesse: to your tents, O Israel: now see to your own house, David. So Israel departed to their tents.
17 But *as for* the children of Israel which dwelt in the cities of Judah, Rehoboam reigned over them.
18 Then king Rehoboam sent Adoram, who *was* over the tribute; and all Israel stoned him with stones, that he died. Therefore king Rehoboam made speed to get him up to his chariot, to flee to Jerusalem.
19 So Israel rebelled against the house of David unto this day.
20 And it came to pass, when all Israel heard that Jeroboam had come again, that they sent and called him to the congregation, and made him king over all Israel: there was none that followed the house of David, but the tribe of Judah only.
21 And when Rehoboam had come to Jerusalem, he assembled all the house of Judah, with the tribe of Benjamin, a hundred and fourscore thousand chosen men, which were warriors, to fight against the house of Israel, to bring the kingdom again to Rehoboam the son of Solomon.
22 But the word of God came to Shemaiah the man of God, saying,
23 Speak to Rehoboam, the son of Solomon, king of Judah, and to all the house of Judah and Benjamin, and to the remnant of the people, saying,
24 Thus says Yahweh, You shall not go up, nor fight against your brethren the children of Israel: return every man to his house; for this thing is from me. They listened therefore to the word of Yahweh, and returned to depart, according to the word of Yahweh.
25 ¶ Then Jeroboam built Shechem in mount Ephraim, and dwelt therein; and went out from there, and built Penuel.
26 And Jeroboam said in his heart, Now shall the kingdom return to the house of David:
27 If this people go up to do sacrifice in the house of Yahweh at Jerusalem, then shall the heart of this people turn again to their lord, *even* to Rehoboam king of Judah, and they shall kill me, and go again to Rehoboam king of Judah.
28 Whereupon the king took counsel, and made two calves *of* gold, and said to them, It is too much for you to go up to Jerusalem: behold your gods, O Israel, which brought you up out of the land of Egypt.
29 And he set the one in Bethel, and the other put he in Dan.
30 And this thing became a sin: for the people went *to worship* before the one, *even* unto Dan.
31 And he made a house of high places, and made priests of the lowest of the people, which were not of the sons of Levi.
32 And Jeroboam ordained a feast in the eighth month, on the fifteenth day of the month, like unto the feast that *is* in Judah, and he offered upon the altar. So did he in Bethel, sacrificing to the calves that he had made: and he placed in Bethel the priests of the high places which he had made.

1 Kings 12

33 So he offered upon the altar which he had made in Bethel the fifteenth day of the eighth month, *even* in the month which he had devised of his own heart; and ordained a feast to the children of Israel: and he offered upon the altar, and burnt incense.

1 Kings 13

13:1 ¶ And, behold, there came a man of God out of Judah by the word of Yahweh to Bethel: and Jeroboam stood by the altar to burn incense.
2 And he cried against the altar in the word of Yahweh, and said, O altar, altar, thus says Yahweh; Behold, a child shall be born to the house of David, Josiah by name; and upon you shall he offer the priests of the high places that burn incense upon you, and men's bones shall be burnt upon you.
3 And he gave a sign the same day, saying, This *is* the sign which Yahweh has spoken; Behold, the altar shall be torn, and the ashes that *are* upon it shall be poured out.
4 And it came to pass, when king Jeroboam heard the saying of the man of God, which had cried against the altar in Bethel, that he put forth his hand from the altar, saying, Lay hold on him. And his hand, which he put forth against him, dried up, so that he could not pull it in again to him.
5 The altar also was torn, and the ashes poured out from the altar, according to the sign which the man of God had given by the word of Yahweh.
6 And the king answered and said to the man of God, Entreat now the face of Yahweh your God, and pray for me, that my hand may be restored *to* me again. And the man of God sought Yahweh, and the king's hand was restored *to* him again, and became as *it was* before.
7 And the king said to the man of God, Come home with me, and refresh yourself, and I will give you a reward.
8 And the man of God said to the king, If you will give me half your house, I will not go in with you, neither will I eat bread nor drink water in this place:
9 For so was it charged me by the word of Yahweh, saying, Eat no bread, nor drink water, nor turn again by the same way that you came.
10 So he went another way, and returned not by the way that he came to Bethel.
11 ¶ Now there dwelt an old prophet in Bethel; and his sons came and told him all the works that the man of God had done that day in Bethel: the words which he had spoken to the king, them they told also to their father.
12 And their father said to them, What way went he? For his sons had seen what way the man of God went, which came from Judah.
13 And he said to his sons, Saddle me the donkey. So they saddled him the donkey: and he rode thereon,
14 And went after the man of God, and found him sitting under an oak: and he said to him, *Are* you the man of God that came from Judah? And he said, I *am*.
15 Then he said to him, Come home with me, and eat bread.
16 And he said, I may not return with you, nor go in with you: neither will I eat bread nor drink water with you in this place:
17 For it was said to me by the word of Yahweh, You shall eat no bread nor drink water there, nor turn again to go by the way that you came.
18 He said to him, I *am* a prophet also as you *are*; and an angel spoke to me by the word of Yahweh, saying, Bring him back with you into your house, that he may eat bread and drink water. *But* he lied to him.
19 So he went back with him, and did eat bread in his house, and drank water.
20 And it came to pass, as they sat at the table, that the word of Yahweh came to the prophet that brought him back:
21 And he cried to the man of God that came from Judah, saying, Thus says Yahweh, Forasmuch as you have disobeyed the mouth of Yahweh, and have not kept the commandment which Yahweh your God commanded you,
22 But came back, and have eaten bread and drank water in the place, of the which *Yahweh* did say to you, Eat no bread, and drink no water; your carcass shall not come to the sepulcher of your fathers.
23 ¶ And it came to pass, after he had eaten bread, and after he had drunk, that he saddled for him the donkey, *that is*, for the prophet whom he had brought back.
24 And when he had gone, a lion met him by the way, and slew him: and his carcass was cast in the way, and the donkey stood by it, the lion also stood by the carcass.
25 And, behold, men passed by, and saw the carcass cast in the way, and the lion standing by the carcass: and they came and told *it* in the city where the old prophet dwelt.
26 And when the prophet that brought him back from the way heard *thereof*, he said, It *is* the man of God, who was disobedient to the word of Yahweh: therefore Yahweh has delivered him to the lion, which has torn him, and slain him, according to the word of Yahweh, which he spoke to him.
27 And he spoke to his sons, saying, Saddle me the donkey. And they saddled *him*.
28 And he went and found his carcass cast in the way, and the donkey and the lion standing by the carcass: the lion had not eaten the carcass, nor torn the donkey.
29 And the prophet took up the carcass of the man of God, and laid it upon the donkey, and brought it back: and the old prophet came to the city, to mourn and to bury him.
30 And he laid his carcass in his own grave; and they mourned over him, *saying*, Alas, my brother!
31 And it came to pass, after he had buried him, that he spoke to his sons, saying, When I am dead, then bury me in the sepulcher wherein the man of God *is* buried; lay my bones beside his bones:
32 For the saying which he cried by the word of Yahweh against the altar in Bethel, and against all the houses of the high places which *are* in the cities of Samaria, shall surely come to pass.

33 After this thing Jeroboam returned not from his evil way, but made again of the lowest of the people priests of the high places: whoever would, he consecrated him, and he became *one* of the priests of the high places.

34 And this thing became sin to the house of Jeroboam, even to cut *it* off, and to destroy *it* from off the face of the earth.

1 Kings 14

14:1 ¶ At that time Abijah the son of Jeroboam fell sick.

2 And Jeroboam said to his wife, Arise, I pray you, and disguise yourself, that you are not known to be the wife of Jeroboam; and get you to Shiloh: behold, there *is* Ahijah the prophet, which told me that *I should be* king over this people.

3 And take with you ten loaves, and hard biscuits, and a cruse of honey, and go to him: he shall tell you what shall become of the child.

4 And Jeroboam's wife did so, and arose, and went to Shiloh, and came to the house of Ahijah. But Ahijah could not see; for his eyes were set by reason of his age.

5 And Yahweh said to Ahijah, Behold, the wife of Jeroboam comes to ask a thing of you for her son; for he *is* sick: thus and thus shall you say to her: for it shall be, when she comes in, that she shall feign herself *to be* another *woman*.

6 And it was *so*, when Ahijah heard the sound of her feet, as she came in at the door, that he said, Come in, you wife of Jeroboam; why feign you yourself *to be* another? for I *am* sent to you *with* heavy *tidings*.

7 ¶ Go, tell Jeroboam, Thus says Yahweh God of Israel, Forasmuch as I exalted you from among the people, and made you prince over my people Israel,

8 And tore the kingdom away from the house of David, and gave it *to* you: and *yet* you have not been as my servant David, who kept my commandments, and who followed me with all his heart, to do *that* only *which was* right in my eyes;

9 But have done evil above all that were before you: for you have gone and made you other gods, and molten images, to provoke me to anger, and have cast me behind your back:

10 Therefore, behold, I will bring evil upon the house of Jeroboam, and will cut off from Jeroboam him that urinates against the wall, *and* him that is shut up and left in Israel, and will take away the remnant of the house of Jeroboam, as a man takes away dung, till it is all gone.

11 Him that dies of Jeroboam in the city shall the dogs eat; and him that dies in the field shall the fowls of the air eat: for Yahweh has spoken *it*.

12 Arise you therefore, get you to your own house: *and* when your feet enter into the city, the child shall die.

13 And all Israel shall mourn for him, and bury him: for he only of Jeroboam shall come to the grave, because in him there is found *some* good thing toward Yahweh God of Israel in the house of Jeroboam.

14 Moreover Yahweh shall raise him up a king over Israel, who shall cut off the house of Jeroboam that day: but what? even now.

15 For Yahweh shall smite Israel, as a reed is shaken in the water, and he shall root up Israel out of this good land, which he gave to their fathers, and shall scatter them beyond the river, because they have made their groves, provoking Yahweh to anger.

16 And he shall give Israel up because of the sins of Jeroboam, who did sin, and who made Israel to sin.

17 And Jeroboam's wife arose, and departed, and came to Tirzah: *and* when she came to the threshold of the door, the child died;

18 And they buried him; and all Israel mourned for him, according to the word of Yahweh, which he spoke by the hand of his servant Ahijah the prophet.

19 And the rest of the acts of Jeroboam, how he warred, and how he reigned, behold, they *are* written in the book of the chronicles of the kings of Israel.

20 And the days which Jeroboam reigned *were* two and twenty years: and he slept with his fathers, and Nadab his son reigned in his stead.

21 ¶ And Rehoboam the son of Solomon reigned in Judah. Rehoboam *was* forty and one years old when he began to reign, and he reigned seventeen years in Jerusalem, the city which Yahweh did choose out of all the tribes of Israel, to put his name there. And his mother's name *was* Naamah an Ammonitess.

22 And Judah did evil in the sight of Yahweh, and they provoked him to jealousy with their sins which they had committed, above all that their fathers had done.

23 For they also built them high places, and images, and groves, on every high hill, and under every green tree.

24 And there were also sodomites in the land: *and* they did according to all the abominations of the nations which Yahweh cast out before the children of Israel.

25 And it came to pass in the fifth year of king Rehoboam, *that* Shishak king of Egypt came up against Jerusalem:

26 And he took away the treasures of the house of Yahweh, and the treasures of the king's house; he even took away all: and he took away all the shields of gold which Solomon had made.

27 And king Rehoboam made in their stead brazen shields, and committed *them* to the hands of the chief of the guard, which kept the door of the king's house.

28 And it was *so*, when the king went into the house of Yahweh, that the guard bore them, and brought them back into the guard chamber.

29 Now the rest of the acts of Rehoboam, and all that he did, *are* they not written in the book of the chronicles of the kings of Judah?

30 And there was war between Rehoboam and Jeroboam all *their* days.

31 And Rehoboam slept with his fathers, and was buried with his fathers in the city of David. And his mother's name *was* Naamah an Ammonitess. And Abijam his son reigned in his stead.

1 Kings 15

15:1 ¶ Now in the eighteenth year of king Jeroboam the son of Nebat reigned Abijam over Judah.

2 Three years reigned he in Jerusalem. And his mother's name *was* Maachah, the daughter of Abishalom.

3 And he walked in all the sins of his father, which he had done before him: and his heart was not perfect with Yahweh his God, as the heart of David his father.

4 Nevertheless for David's sake did Yahweh his God give him a lamp in Jerusalem, to set up his son after him, and to establish Jerusalem:

5 Because David did *that which was* right in the eyes of Yahweh, and turned not aside from any *thing* that he commanded him all the days of his life, save only in the matter of Uriah the Hittite.

6 And there was war between Rehoboam and Jeroboam all the days of his life.

7 Now the rest of the acts of Abijam, and all that he did, *are* they not written in the book of the chronicles of the kings of Judah? And there was war between Abijam and Jeroboam.

8 And Abijam slept with his fathers; and they buried him in the city of David: and Asa his son reigned in his stead.

9 ¶ And in the twentieth year of Jeroboam king of Israel reigned Asa over Judah.

10 And forty and one years reigned he in Jerusalem. And his mother's name *was* Maachah, the daughter of Abishalom.

11 And Asa did *that which was* right in the eyes of Yahweh, as *did* David his father.

12 And he took away the sodomites out of the land, and removed all the idols that his fathers had made.

13 And also Maachah his mother, even her he removed from *being* queen, because she had made an idol in a grove; and Asa destroyed her idol, and burnt *it* by the brook Kidron.

14 But the high places were not removed: nevertheless Asa's heart was perfect with Yahweh all his days.

15 And he brought in the things which his father had dedicated, and the things which himself had dedicated, into the house of Yahweh, silver, and gold, and vessels.

16 And there was war between Asa and Baasha king of Israel all their days.

17 And Baasha king of Israel went up against Judah, and built Ramah, that he might not grant any to go out or come in to Asa king of Judah.

18 Then Asa took all the silver and the gold *that were* left in the treasuries of the house of Yahweh, and the treasuries of the king's house, and delivered them into the hand of his servants: and king Asa sent them to Benhadad, the son of Tabrimon, the son of Hezion, king of Syria, that dwelt at Damascus, saying,

19 *There is* a league between me and you, *and* between my father and your father: behold, I have sent to you a present of silver and gold; come and break your league with Baasha king of Israel, that he may depart from me.

20 So Benhadad listened to king Asa, and sent the captains of the hosts which he had against the cities of Israel, and smote Ijon, and Dan, and Abelbethmaachah, and all Cinneroth, with all the land of Naphtali.

21 And it came to pass, when Baasha heard *thereof*, that he left off building of Ramah, and dwelt in Tirzah.

22 Then king Asa made a proclamation throughout all Judah; none *was* exempted: and they took away the stones of Ramah, and the timber thereof, with which Baasha had built; and king Asa built with them Geba of Benjamin, and Mizpah.

23 The rest of all the acts of Asa, and all his might, and all that he did, and the cities which he built, *are* they not written in the book of the chronicles of the kings of Judah? Nevertheless in the time of his old age he was diseased in his feet.

24 And Asa slept with his fathers, and was buried with his fathers in the city of David his father: and Jehoshaphat his son reigned in his stead.

25 ¶ And Nadab the son of Jeroboam began to reign over Israel in the second year of Asa king of Judah, and reigned over Israel two years.

26 And he did evil in the sight of Yahweh, and walked in the way of his father, and in his sin with which he made Israel to sin.

27 And Baasha the son of Ahijah, of the house of Issachar, conspired against him; and Baasha smote him at Gibbethon, which *belonged* to the Philistines; for Nadab and all Israel laid siege to Gibbethon.

28 Even in the third year of Asa king of Judah did Baasha slay him, and reigned in his stead.

29 And it came to pass, when he reigned, *that* he smote all the house of Jeroboam; he left not to Jeroboam any that breathed, until he had destroyed him, according to the saying of Yahweh, which he spoke by his servant Ahijah the Shilonite:

30 Because of the sins of Jeroboam which he sinned, and which he made Israel sin, by his provocation with which he provoked Yahweh God of Israel to anger.

31 Now the rest of the acts of Nadab, and all that he did, *are* they not written in the book of the chronicles of the kings of Israel?

32 And there was war between Asa and Baasha king of Israel all their days.

33 In the third year of Asa king of Judah began Baasha the son of Ahijah to reign over all Israel in Tirzah, twenty and four years.

34 And he did evil in the sight of Yahweh, and walked in the way of Jeroboam, and in his sin with which he made Israel to sin.

1 Kings 16

16:1 ¶ Then the word of Yahweh came to Jehu the son of Hanani against Baasha, saying,

2 Forasmuch as I exalted you out of the dust, and made you prince over my people Israel; and you have walked in

the way of Jeroboam, and have made my people Israel to sin, to provoke me to anger with their sins;

3 Behold, I will take away the posterity of Baasha, and the posterity of his house; and will make your house like the house of Jeroboam the son of Nebat.

4 Him that dies of Baasha in the city shall the dogs eat; and him that dies of his in the fields shall the fowls of the air eat.

5 Now the rest of the acts of Baasha, and what he did, and his might, *are* they not written in the book of the chronicles of the kings of Israel?

6 So Baasha slept with his fathers, and was buried in Tirzah: and Elah his son reigned in his stead.

7 And also by the hand of the prophet Jehu the son of Hanani came the word of Yahweh against Baasha, and against his house, even for all the evil that he did in the sight of Yahweh, in provoking him to anger with the work of his hands, in being like the house of Jeroboam; and because he killed him.

8 In the twenty and sixth year of Asa king of Judah began Elah the son of Baasha to reign over Israel in Tirzah, two years.

9 And his servant Zimri, captain of half *his* chariots, conspired against him, as he was in Tirzah, drinking himself drunk in the house of Arza steward of *his* house in Tirzah.

10 And Zimri went in and smote him, and killed him in the twenty and seventh year of Asa king of Judah, and reigned in his stead.

11 And it came to pass, when he began to reign, as soon as he sat on his throne, *that* he slew all the house of Baasha: he left him not one that urinates against a wall, neither of his relatives, nor of his friends.

12 Thus did Zimri destroy all the house of Baasha, according to the word of Yahweh, which he spoke against Baasha by Jehu the prophet,

13 For all the sins of Baasha, and the sins of Elah his son, by which they sinned, and by which they made Israel to sin, in provoking Yahweh God of Israel to anger with their vanities.

14 Now the rest of the acts of Elah, and all that he did, *are* they not written in the book of the chronicles of the kings of Israel?

15 ¶ In the twenty and seventh year of Asa king of Judah did Zimri reign seven days in Tirzah. And the people *were* encamped against Gibbethon, which *belonged* to the Philistines.

16 And the people *that were* encamped heard say, Zimri has conspired, and has also slain the king: therefore all Israel made Omri, the captain of the host, king over Israel that day in the camp.

17 And Omri went up from Gibbethon, and all Israel with him, and they besieged Tirzah.

18 And it came to pass, when Zimri saw that the city was taken, that he went into the palace of the king's house, and burnt the king's house over him with fire, and died.

19 For his sins which he sinned in doing evil in the sight of Yahweh, in walking in the way of Jeroboam, and in his sin which he did, to make Israel to sin.

20 Now the rest of the acts of Zimri, and his treason that he worked, *are* they not written in the book of the chronicles of the kings of Israel?

21 Then were the people of Israel divided into two parts: half of the people followed Tibni the son of Ginath, to make him king; and half followed Omri.

22 But the people that followed Omri prevailed against the people that followed Tibni the son of Ginath: so Tibni died, and Omri reigned.

23 In the thirty and first year of Asa king of Judah began Omri to reign over Israel, twelve years: six years reigned he in Tirzah.

24 And he bought the hill Samaria of Shemer for two talents of silver, and built on the hill, and called the name of the city which he built, after the name of Shemer, owner of the hill, Samaria.

25 But Omri worked evil in the eyes of Yahweh, and did worse than all that *were* before him.

26 For he walked in all the way of Jeroboam the son of Nebat, and in his sin with which he made Israel to sin, to provoke Yahweh God of Israel to anger with their vanities.

27 Now the rest of the acts of Omri which he did, and his might that he showed, *are* they not written in the book of the chronicles of the kings of Israel?

28 So Omri slept with his fathers, and was buried in Samaria: and Ahab his son reigned in his stead.

29 ¶ And in the thirty and eighth year of Asa king of Judah began Ahab the son of Omri to reign over Israel: and Ahab the son of Omri reigned over Israel in Samaria twenty and two years.

30 And Ahab the son of Omri did evil in the sight of Yahweh above all that *were* before him.

31 And it came to pass, as if it had been a light thing for him to walk in the sins of Jeroboam the son of Nebat, that he took to wife Jezebel the daughter of Ethbaal king of the Zidonians, and went and served Baal, and worshipped him.

32 And he reared up an altar for Baal in the house of Baal, which he had built in Samaria.

33 And Ahab made a grove; and Ahab did more to provoke Yahweh God of Israel to anger than all the kings of Israel that were before him.

34 In his days did Hiel the Bethelite build Jericho: he laid the foundation thereof in Abiram his firstborn, and set up the gates thereof in his youngest son Segub, according to the word of Yahweh, which he spoke by Joshua the son of Nun.

1 Kings 17

17:1 ¶ And Elijah the Tishbite, *who was* of the inhabitants of Gilead, said to Ahab, As Yahweh God of Israel lives, before whom I stand, there shall not be dew nor rain these years, but according to my word.

2 And the word of Yahweh came to him, saying,

3 Get you away, and turn you eastward, and hide yourself by the brook Cherith, that *is* before *the* Jordan.

1 Kings 17

4 And it shall be, *that* you shall drink of the brook; and I have commanded the ravens to feed you there.

5 So he went and did according to the word of Yahweh: for he went and dwelt by the brook Cherith, that *is* before *the* Jordan.

6 And the ravens brought him bread and flesh in the morning, and bread and flesh in the evening; and he drank of the brook.

7 And it came to pass after a while, that the brook dried up, because there had been no rain in the land.

8 ¶ And the word of Yahweh came to him, saying,

9 Arise, get you to Zarephath, which *belongs* to Zidon, and dwell there: behold, I have commanded a widow woman there to sustain you.

10 So he arose and went to Zarephath. And when he came to the gate of the city, behold, the widow woman *was* there gathering of sticks: and he called to her, and said, Fetch me, I pray you, a little water in a vessel, that I may drink.

11 And as she was going to fetch *it*, he called to her, and said, Bring me, I pray you, a morsel of bread in your hand.

12 And she said, *As* Yahweh your God lives, I have not a cake, but a handful of meal in a barrel, and a little oil in a cruse: and, behold, I *am* gathering two sticks, that I may go in and prepare it for me and my son, that we may eat it, and die.

13 And Elijah said to her, Fear not; go *and* do as you have said: but make me thereof a little cake first, and bring *it* to me, and after make for you and for your son.

14 For thus says Yahweh God of Israel, The barrel of meal shall not waste, neither shall the cruse of oil fail, until the day *that* Yahweh sends rain upon the earth.

15 And she went and did according to the saying of Elijah: and she, and he, and her house, did eat *many* days.

16 *And* the barrel of meal wasted not, neither did the cruse of oil fail, according to the word of Yahweh, which he spoke by Elijah.

17 ¶ And it came to pass after these things, *that* the son of the woman, the mistress of the house, fell sick; and his sickness was so severe, that there was no breath left in him.

18 And she said to Elijah, What have I to do with you, O you man of God? have you come to me to call my sin to remembrance, and to slay my son?

19 And he said to her, Give me your son. And he took him out of her bosom, and carried him up into a loft, where he stayed, and laid him upon his own bed.

20 And he cried unto Yahweh, and said, O Yahweh my God, have you also brought evil upon the widow with whom I sojourn, by slaying her son?

21 And he stretched himself upon the child three times, and cried unto Yahweh, and said, O Yahweh my God, I pray you, let this child's soul come into him again.

22 And Yahweh heard the voice of Elijah; and the soul of the child came into him again, and he revived.

23 And Elijah took the child, and brought him down out of the chamber into the house, and delivered him to his mother: and Elijah said, See, your son lives.

24 And the woman said to Elijah, Now by this I know that you *are* a man of God, *and* that the word of Yahweh in your mouth *is* truth.

1 Kings 18

18:1 ¶ And it came to pass *after* many days, that the word of Yahweh came to Elijah in the third year, saying, Go, show yourself to Ahab; and I will send rain upon the earth.

2 And Elijah went to show himself to Ahab. And *there was* a severe famine in Samaria.

3 And Ahab called Obadiah, which *was* the governor of *his* house. (Now Obadiah feared Yahweh greatly:

4 For it was *so*, when Jezebel cut off the prophets of Yahweh, that Obadiah took a hundred prophets, and hid them by fifty in a cave, and fed them with bread and water.)

5 And Ahab said to Obadiah, Go into the land, to all fountains of water, and to all brooks: perhaps we may find grass to save the horses and mules alive, that we lose not all the beasts.

6 So they divided the land between them to pass throughout it: Ahab went one way by himself, and Obadiah went another way by himself.

7 And as Obadiah was in the way, behold, Elijah met him: and he knew him, and fell on his face, and said, *Are* you that my lord Elijah?

8 And he answered him, I *am*: go, tell your lord, Behold, Elijah *is here*.

9 And he said, What have I sinned, that you would deliver your servant into the hand of Ahab, to slay me?

10 *As* Yahweh your God lives, there is no nation or kingdom, where my lord has not sent to seek you: and when they said, *He is* not *there*; he took an oath of the kingdom and nation, that they found you not.

11 And now you say, Go, tell your lord, Behold, Elijah *is here*.

12 And it shall come to pass, *as soon as* I am gone from you, that the Spirit of Yahweh shall carry you where I know not; and *so* when I come and tell Ahab, and he cannot find you, he shall slay me: but I your servant feared Yahweh from my youth.

13 Was it not told my lord what I did when Jezebel slew the prophets of Yahweh, how I hid a hundred men of Yahweh's prophets by fifty in a cave, and fed them with bread and water?

14 And now you say, Go, tell your lord, Behold, Elijah *is here*: and he shall slay me.

15 And Elijah said, *As* Yahweh of hosts lives, before whom I stand, I will surely show myself to him today.

16 So Obadiah went to meet Ahab, and told him: and Ahab went to meet Elijah.

17 ¶ And it came to pass, when Ahab saw Elijah, that Ahab said to him, *Are* you he that troubles Israel?

18 And he answered, I have not troubled Israel; but you, and your father's house, in that you have forsaken the commandments of Yahweh, and you have followed Baalim.

19 Now therefore send, *and* gather to me all Israel to mount Carmel, and the prophets of Baal four hundred and fifty, and the prophets of the groves four hundred, which eat at Jezebel's table.

20 So Ahab sent to all the children of Israel, and gathered the prophets together to mount Carmel.

21 ¶ And Elijah came to all the people, and said, How long halt you between two opinions? if Yahweh *is* God, follow him: but if Baal, *then* follow him. And the people answered him not a word.

22 Then said Elijah to the people, I, *even* I only, remain a prophet of Yahweh; but Baal's prophets *are* four hundred and fifty men.

23 Let them therefore give us two bullocks; and let them choose one bullock for themselves, and cut it in pieces, and lay *it* on wood, and put no fire *under*: and I will dress the other bullock, and lay *it* on wood, and put no fire *under*:

24 And call you on the name of your gods, and I will call on the name of Yahweh: and the God that answers by fire, let him be God. And all the people answered and said, It is well spoken.

25 And Elijah said to the prophets of Baal, Choose you one bullock for yourselves, and dress *it* first; for you *are* many; and call on the name of your gods, but put no fire *under*.

26 And they took the bullock which was given them, and they dressed *it*, and called on the name of Baal from morning even until noon, saying, O Baal, hear us. But *there was* no voice, nor any that answered. And they leaped upon the altar which was made.

27 And it came to pass at noon, that Elijah mocked them, and said, Cry aloud: for he *is* a god; either he is talking, or he is pursuing, or he is on a journey, *or* perhaps he sleeps, and must be awakened.

28 And they cried aloud, and cut themselves after their manner with knives and lancets, till the blood gushed out upon them.

29 And it came to pass, when midday was past, and they prophesied until the *time* of the offering of the *evening* sacrifice, that *there was* neither voice, nor any to answer, nor any that regarded.

30 And Elijah said to all the people, Come near to me. And all the people came near to him. And he repaired the altar of Yahweh *that was* broken down.

31 And Elijah took twelve stones, according to the number of the tribes of the sons of Jacob, to whom the word of Yahweh came, saying, Israel shall be your name:

32 And with the stones he built an altar in the name of Yahweh: and he made a trench about the altar, as great as would contain two measures of seed.

33 And he put the wood in order, and cut the bullock in pieces, and laid *him* on the wood, and said, Fill four barrels with water, and pour *it* on the burnt sacrifice, and on the wood.

34 And he said, Do *it* the second time. And they did *it* the second time. And he said, Do *it* the third time. And they did *it* the third time.

35 And the water ran round about the altar; and he filled the trench also with water.

36 And it came to pass at *the time of* the offering of the *evening* sacrifice, that Elijah the prophet came near, and said, Yahweh God of Abraham, Isaac, and of Israel, let it be known this day that you *are* God in Israel, and *that* I *am* your servant, and *that* I have done all these things at your word.

37 Hear me, O Yahweh, hear me, that this people may know that you *are* Yahweh God, and *that* you have turned their heart back again.

38 Then the fire of Yahweh fell, and consumed the burnt sacrifice, and the wood, and the stones, and the dust, and licked up the water that *was* in the trench

39 And when all the people saw *it*, they fell on their faces: and they said, Yahweh, he *is* the God; Yahweh, he *is* the God.

40 And Elijah said to them, Take the prophets of Baal; let not one of them escape. And they took them: and Elijah brought them down to the brook Kishon, and slew them there.

41 ¶ And Elijah said to Ahab, Get you up, eat and drink; for *there is* a sound of abundance of rain.

42 So Ahab went up to eat and to drink. And Elijah went up to the top of Carmel; and he cast himself down upon the earth, and put his face between his knees,

43 And said to his servant, Go up now, look toward the sea. And he went up, and looked, and said, *There is* nothing. And he said, Go again seven times.

44 And it came to pass at the seventh time, that he said, Behold, there rises a little cloud out of the sea, like a man's hand. And he said, Go up, say to Ahab, Prepare *your chariot*, and get you down, that the rain stop you not.

45 And it came to pass in the mean while, that the heaven was black with clouds and wind, and there was a great rain. And Ahab rode, and went to Jezreel.

46 And the hand of Yahweh was on Elijah; and he girded up his loins, and ran before Ahab to the entrance of Jezreel.

1 Kings 19

19:1 ¶ And Ahab told Jezebel all that Elijah had done, and therewith how he had slain all the prophets with the sword.

2 Then Jezebel sent a messenger to Elijah, saying, So let the gods do *to me*, and more also, if I make not your life as the life of one of them by tomorrow about this time.

3 And when he saw *that*, he arose, and went for his life, and came to Beersheba, which *belongs* to Judah, and left his servant there.

4 But he himself went a day's journey into the wilderness, and came and sat down under a juniper tree: and he requested for himself that he might die; and said, It is enough; now, O Yahweh, take away my life; for I *am* not better than my fathers.

5 And as he lay and slept under a juniper tree, behold, then an angel touched him, and said to him, Arise *and* eat.

1 Kings 19

6 And he looked, and, behold, *there was* a cake baked on the coals, and a cruse of water at his head. And he did eat and drink, and laid him down again.

7 And the angel of Yahweh came again the second time, and touched him, and said, Arise *and* eat; because the journey *is* too great for you.

8 And he arose, and did eat and drink, and went in the strength of that food *for* forty days and forty nights unto Horeb the mount of God.

9 ¶ And he came there to a cave, and lodged there; and, behold, the word of Yahweh *came* to him, and he said to him, What do you here, Elijah?

10 And he said, I have been very jealous for Yahweh God of hosts: for the children of Israel have forsaken your covenant, thrown down your altars, and slain your prophets with the sword; and I, *even* I only, am left; and they seek my life, to take it away.

11 And he said, Go forth, and stand upon the mount before Yahweh. And, behold, Yahweh passed by, and a great and strong wind tore the mountains, and broke in pieces the rocks before Yahweh; *but* Yahweh *was* not in the wind: and after the wind an earthquake; *but* Yahweh *was* not in the earthquake:

12 And after the earthquake a fire; *but* Yahweh *was* not in the fire: and after the fire a still small voice.

13 And it was *so*, when Elijah heard *it*, that he wrapped his face in his mantle, and went out, and stood in the entering in of the cave. And, behold, *there came* a voice to him, and said, What do you here, Elijah?

14 And he said, I have been very jealous for Yahweh God of hosts: because the children of Israel have forsaken your covenant, thrown down your altars, and slain your prophets with the sword; and I, *even* I only, am left; and they seek my life, to take it away.

15 And Yahweh said to him, Go, return on your way to the wilderness of Damascus: and when you come, anoint Hazael *to be* king over Syria:

16 And Jehu the son of Nimshi shall you anoint *to be* king over Israel: and Elisha the son of Shaphat of Abelmeholah shall you anoint *to be* prophet in your room.

17 And it shall come to pass, *that* him that escapes the sword of Hazael shall Jehu slay: and him that escapes from the sword of Jehu shall Elisha slay.

18 Yet I have left *me* seven thousand in Israel, all the knees which have not bowed to Baal, and every mouth which has not kissed him.

19 ¶ So he departed therefrom, and found Elisha the son of Shaphat, who *was* plowing *with* twelve yoke *of* oxen before him, and he with the twelfth: and Elijah passed by him, and cast his mantle upon him.

20 And he left the oxen, and ran after Elijah, and said, Let me, I pray you, kiss my father and my mother, and *then* I will follow you. And he said to him, Go back again: for what have I done to you?

21 And he returned back from him, and took a yoke of oxen, and slew them, and boiled their flesh with the instruments of the oxen, and gave *it* to the people, and they did eat. Then he arose, and went after Elijah, and ministered to him.

1 Kings 20

20:1 ¶ And Benhadad the king of Syria gathered all his host together: and *there were* thirty and two kings with him, and horses, and chariots: and he went up and besieged Samaria, and warred against it.

2 And he sent messengers to Ahab king of Israel into the city, and said to him, Thus says Benhadad,

3 Your silver and your gold *are* mine; your wives also and your children, *even* the best, *are* mine.

4 And the king of Israel answered and said, My lord, O king, according to your saying, I *am* yours, and all that I have.

5 And the messengers came again, and said, Thus speaks Benhadad, saying, Although I have sent to you, saying, You shall deliver me your silver, and your gold, and your wives, and your children;

6 Yet I will send my servants to you tomorrow about this time, and they shall search your house, and the houses of your servants; and it shall be, *that* whatever is pleasant in your eyes, they shall put *it* in their hand, and take *it* away.

7 Then the king of Israel called all the elders of the land, and said, Mark, I pray you, and see how this *man* seeks mischief: for he sent to me for my wives, and for my children, and for my silver, and for my gold; and I denied him not.

8 And all the elders and all the people said to him, Listen not *to him*, nor consent.

9 Therefore he said to the messengers of Benhadad, Tell my lord the king, All that you did send for to your servant at the first I will do: but this thing I may not do. And the messengers departed, and brought him word again.

10 And Benhadad sent to him, and said, The gods do so unto me, and more also, if the dust of Samaria shall suffice for handfuls for all the people that follow me.

11 And the king of Israel answered and said, Tell *him*, Let not him that girds on *his harness* boast himself as he that puts it off.

12 ¶ And it came to pass, when *Benhadad* heard this message, as he *was* drinking, he and the kings in the pavilions, that he said to his servants, Set *yourselves in array*. And they set *themselves in array* against the city.

13 And, behold, there came a prophet to Ahab king of Israel, saying, Thus says Yahweh, Have you seen all this great multitude? behold, I will deliver it into your hand this day; and you shall know that I *am* Yahweh.

14 And Ahab said, By whom? And he said, Thus says Yahweh, *Even* by the young men of the princes of the provinces. Then he said, Who shall order the battle? And he answered, You.

15 Then he numbered the young men of the princes of the provinces, and they were two hundred and thirty two:

and after them he numbered all the people, *even* all the children of Israel, *being* seven thousand.

16 And they went out at noon. But Benhadad *was* drinking himself drunk in the pavilions, he and the kings, the thirty and two kings that helped him.

17 And the young men of the princes of the provinces went out first; and Benhadad sent out, and they told him, saying, There are men come out of Samaria.

18 And he said, Whether they have come out for peace, take them alive; or whether they have come out for war, take them alive.

19 So these young men of the princes of the provinces came out of the city, and the army which followed them.

20 And they slew every one his man: and the Syrians fled; and Israel pursued them: and Benhadad the king of Syria escaped on a horse with the horsemen.

21 And the king of Israel went out, and smote the horses and chariots, and slew the Syrians with a great slaughter.

22 ¶ And the prophet came to the king of Israel, and said to him, Go, strengthen yourself, and mark, and see what you do: for at the return of the year the king of Syria will come up against you.

23 And the servants of the king of Syria said to him, Their gods *are* gods of the hills; therefore they were stronger than we; but let us fight against them in the plain, and surely we shall be stronger than they.

24 And do this thing, Take the kings away, every man out of his place, and put captains in their places:

25 And number you an army, like the army that you have lost, horse for horse, and chariot for chariot: and we will fight against them in the plain, *and* surely we shall be stronger than they. And he listened to their voice, and did so.

26 And it came to pass at the return of the year, that Benhadad numbered the Syrians, and went up to Aphek, to fight against Israel.

27 And the children of Israel were numbered, and were all present, and went against them: and the children of Israel pitched before them like two little flocks of kids; but the Syrians filled the country.

28 And there came a man of God, and spoke to the king of Israel, and said, Thus says Yahweh, Because the Syrians have said, Yahweh *is* God of the hills, but he *is* not God of the valleys, therefore will I deliver all this great multitude into your hand, and you shall know that I *am* Yahweh.

29 And they pitched one over against the other seven days. And so it was, that in the seventh day the battle was joined: and the children of Israel slew of the Syrians a hundred thousand footmen in one day.

30 But the rest fled to Aphek, into the city; and *there* a wall fell upon twenty and seven thousand of the men *that were* left. And Benhadad fled, and came into the city, into an inner chamber.

31 ¶ And his servants said to him, Behold now, we have heard that the kings of the house of Israel *are* merciful kings: let us, I pray you, put sackcloth on our loins, and ropes upon our heads, and go out to the king of Israel: perhaps he will save your life.

32 So they girded sackcloth on their loins, and *put* ropes on their heads, and came to the king of Israel, and said, Your servant Benhadad said, I pray you, let me live. And he said, *is* he yet alive? he *is* my brother.

33 Now the men did diligently observe whether *anything would come* from him, and did hastily catch *it*: and they said, Your brother Benhadad. Then he said, Go you, bring him. Then Benhadad came forth to him; and he caused him to come up into the chariot.

34 And *Benhadad* said unto him, The cities, which my father took from your father, I will restore; and you shall make streets for you in Damascus, as my father made in Samaria. Then *said Ahab*, I will send you away with this covenant. So he made a covenant with him, and sent him away.

35 And a certain man of the sons of the prophets said to his neighbor in the word of Yahweh, Smite me, I pray you. And the man refused to smite him.

36 Then said he to him, Because you have not obeyed the voice of Yahweh, behold, as soon as you have departed from me, a lion shall slay you. And as soon as he had departed from him, a lion found him, and slew him.

37 Then he found another man, and said, Smite me, I pray you. And the man smote him, so that in smiting he wounded *him*.

38 So the prophet departed, and waited for the king by the way, and disguised himself with ashes upon his face.

39 And as the king passed by, he cried to the king: and he said, Your servant went out into the midst of the battle; and, behold, a man turned aside, and brought a man to me, and said, Keep this man: if by any means he is missing, then shall your life be for his life, or else you shall pay a talent of silver.

40 And as your servant was busy here and there, he was gone. And the king of Israel said to him, So *shall* your judgment *be*; yourself have decided *it*.

41 And he hurried, and took the ashes away from his face; and the king of Israel discerned him that he *was* of the prophets.

42 And he said to him, Thus says Yahweh, Because you have let go out of *your* hand a man whom I appointed to utter destruction, therefore your life shall go for his life, and your people for his people.

43 And the king of Israel went to his house heavy and displeased, and came to Samaria.

1 Kings 21

21:1 ¶ And it came to pass after these things *that* Naboth the Jezreelite had a vineyard, which *was* in Jezreel, next to the palace of Ahab king of Samaria.

2 And Ahab spoke to Naboth, saying, Give me your vineyard, that I may have it for a garden of herbs, because it *is* near to my house: and I will give you for it a better vineyard than it; *or*, if it seems good to you, I will give you the worth of it in money.

3 And Naboth said to Ahab, Yahweh forbid it *to* me, that I should give the inheritance of my fathers to you.

1 Kings 21

4 And Ahab came into his house heavy and displeased because of the word which Naboth the Jezreelite had spoken to him: for he had said, I will not give you the inheritance of my fathers. And he laid him down upon his bed, and turned away his face, and would eat no bread.

5 ¶ But Jezebel his wife came to him, and said to him, Why is your spirit so sad, that you eat no bread?

6 And he said to her, Because I spoke to Naboth the Jezreelite, and said to him, Give me your vineyard for money; or else, if it pleases you, I will give you *another* vineyard for it: and he answered, I will not give you my vineyard.

7 And Jezebel his wife said to him, Do you now govern the kingdom of Israel? arise, *and* eat bread, and let your heart be merry: I will give you the vineyard of Naboth the Jezreelite.

8 So she wrote letters in Ahab's name, and sealed *them* with his seal, and sent the letters to the elders and to the nobles that *were* in his city, dwelling with Naboth.

9 And she wrote in the letters, saying, Proclaim a fast, and set Naboth on high among the people:

10 And set two men, sons of Belial, before him, to bear witness against him, saying, You did blaspheme God and the king. And *then* carry him out, and stone him, that he may die.

11 And the men of his city, *even* the elders and the nobles who were the inhabitants in his city, did as Jezebel had sent to them, *and* as it *was* written in the letters which she had sent to them.

12 They proclaimed a fast, and set Naboth on high among the people.

13 And there came in two men, children of Belial, and sat before him: and the men of Belial witnessed against him, *even* against Naboth, in the presence of the people, saying, Naboth did blaspheme God and the king. Then they carried him forth out of the city, and stoned him with stones, that he died.

14 Then they sent to Jezebel, saying, Naboth is stoned, and is dead.

15 And it came to pass, when Jezebel heard that Naboth was stoned, and was dead, that Jezebel said to Ahab, Arise, take possession of the vineyard of Naboth the Jezreelite, which he refused to give you for money: for Naboth is not alive, but dead.

16 And it came to pass, when Ahab heard that Naboth was dead, that Ahab rose up to go down to the vineyard of Naboth the Jezreelite, to take possession of it.

17 ¶ And the word of Yahweh came to Elijah the Tishbite, saying,

18 Arise, go down to meet Ahab king of Israel, which *is* in Samaria: behold, *he is* in the vineyard of Naboth, where he has gone down to possess it.

19 And you shall speak to him, saying, Thus says Yahweh, Have you killed, and also taken possession? And you shall speak to him, saying, Thus says Yahweh, In the place where dogs licked the blood of Naboth shall dogs lick your blood, even yours.

20 And Ahab said to Elijah, Have you found me, O my enemy? And he answered, I have found *you*: because you have sold yourself to work evil in the sight of Yahweh.

21 Behold, I will bring evil upon you, and will take away your posterity, and will cut off from Ahab him that urinates against the wall, and him that is shut up and left in Israel,

22 And will make your house like the house of Jeroboam the son of Nebat, and like the house of Baasha the son of Ahijah, for the provocation with which you have provoked *me* to anger, and made Israel to sin.

23 And of Jezebel also spoke Yahweh, saying, The dogs shall eat Jezebel by the wall of Jezreel.

24 Him that dies of Ahab in the city the dogs shall eat; and him that dies in the field shall the fowls of the air eat.

25 But there was none like unto Ahab, which did sell himself to work wickedness in the sight of Yahweh, whom Jezebel his wife stirred up.

26 And he did very abominably in following idols, according to all *things* as did the Amorites, whom Yahweh cast out before the children of Israel.

27 And it came to pass, when Ahab heard those words, that he tore his clothes, and put sackcloth upon his flesh, and fasted, and lay in sackcloth, and went softly.

28 And the word of Yahweh came to Elijah the Tishbite, saying,

29 See you how Ahab humbles himself before me? because he humbles himself before me, I will not bring the evil in his days: *but* in his son's days will I bring the evil upon his house.

1 Kings 22

22:1 ¶ And they continued three years without war between Syria and Israel.

2 And it came to pass in the third year, that Jehoshaphat the king of Judah came down to the king of Israel.

3 And the king of Israel said to his servants, Know you that Ramoth in Gilead *is* ours, and we *are* still, *and* take it not out of the hand of the king of Syria?

4 And he said to Jehoshaphat, Will you go with me to battle to Ramothgilead? And Jehoshaphat said to the king of Israel, I *am* as you *are*, my people as your people, my horses as your horses.

5 And Jehoshaphat said to the king of Israel, Inquire, I pray you, at the word of Yahweh today.

6 Then the king of Israel gathered the prophets together, about four hundred men, and said to them, Shall I go against Ramothgilead to battle, or shall I forbear? And they said, Go up; for the Lord shall deliver *it* into the hand of the king.

7 And Jehoshaphat said, *Is there* not here a prophet of Yahweh besides, that we might inquire of him?

8 And the king of Israel said to Jehoshaphat, *There is* yet one man, Micaiah the son of Imlah, by whom we may inquire of Yahweh: but I hate him; for he does not prophesy good concerning me, but evil. And Jehoshaphat said, Let not the king say so.

9 Then the king of Israel called an officer, and said, Hurry *here* Micaiah the son of Imlah.

10 And the king of Israel and Jehoshaphat the king of Judah sat each on his throne, having put on their robes, in a void place in the entrance of the gate of Samaria; and all the prophets prophesied before them.

11 And Zedekiah the son of Chenaanah made him horns of iron: and he said, Thus says Yahweh, With these shall you push the Syrians, until you have consumed them.

12 And all the prophets prophesied so, saying, Go up to Ramothgilead, and prosper: for Yahweh shall deliver *it* into the king's hand.

13 And the messenger that had gone to call Micaiah spoke to him, saying, Behold now, the words of the prophets *declare* good to the king with one mouth: let your word, I pray you, be like the word of one of them, and speak *that which is* good.

14 And Micaiah said, *As* Yahweh lives, what Yahweh says to me, that will I speak.

15 ¶ So he came to the king. And the king said to him, Micaiah, shall we go against Ramothgilead to battle, or shall we forbear? And he answered him, Go, and prosper: for Yahweh shall deliver *it* into the hand of the king.

16 And the king said to him, How many times shall I adjure you that you tell me nothing but *that which is* true in the name of Yahweh?

17 And he said, I saw all Israel scattered upon the hills, as sheep that have not a shepherd: and Yahweh said, These have no master: let them return every man to his house in peace.

18 And the king of Israel said to Jehoshaphat, Did I not tell you that he would prophesy no good concerning me, but evil?

19 And he said, Hear you therefore the word of Yahweh: I saw Yahweh sitting on his throne, and all the host of heaven standing by him on his right hand and on his left.

20 And Yahweh said, Who shall persuade Ahab, that he may go up and fall at Ramothgilead? And one said on this manner, and another said on that manner.

21 And there came forth a spirit, and stood before Yahweh, and said, I will persuade him.

22 And Yahweh said to him, Wherewith? And he said, I will go forth, and I will be a lying spirit in the mouth of all his prophets. And he said, You shall persuade *him*, and prevail also: go forth, and do so.

23 Now therefore, behold, Yahweh has put a lying spirit in the mouth of all these your prophets, and Yahweh has spoken evil concerning you.

24 But Zedekiah the son of Chenaanah went near, and smote Micaiah on the cheek, and said, Which way went the Spirit of Yahweh from me to speak to you?

25 And Micaiah said, Behold, you shall see in that day, when you shall go into an inner chamber to hide yourself.

26 And the king of Israel said, Take Micaiah, and carry him back to Amon the governor of the city, and to Joash the king's son;

27 And say, Thus says the king, Put this *fellow* in the prison, and feed him with bread of affliction and with water of affliction, until I come in peace.

28 And Micaiah said, If you return at all in peace, Yahweh has not spoken by me. And he said, Listen, O people, every one of you.

29 ¶ So the king of Israel and Jehoshaphat the king of Judah went up to Ramothgilead.

30 And the king of Israel said to Jehoshaphat, I will disguise myself, and enter into the battle; but put you on your robes. And the king of Israel disguised himself, and went into the battle.

31 But the king of Syria commanded his thirty and two captains that had rule over his chariots, saying, Fight neither with small nor great, save only with the king of Israel.

32 And it came to pass, when the captains of the chariots saw Jehoshaphat, that they said, Surely it *is* the king of Israel. And they turned aside to fight against him: and Jehoshaphat cried out.

33 And it came to pass, when the captains of the chariots perceived that it *was* not the king of Israel, that they turned back from pursuing him.

34 And a *certain* man drew a bow at a venture, and smote the king of Israel between the joints of the harness: therefore he said to the driver of his chariot, Turn your hand, and carry me out of the host; for I am wounded.

35 And the battle increased that day: and the king was stood up in his chariot against the Syrians, and died at evening: and the blood ran out of the wound into the midst of the chariot.

36 And there went a proclamation throughout the host about the going down of the sun, saying, Every man to his city, and every man to his own country.

37 So the king died, and was brought to Samaria; and they buried the king in Samaria.

38 And *one* washed the chariot in the pool of Samaria; and the dogs licked up his blood; and they washed his armor; according to the word of Yahweh which he spoke.

39 Now the rest of the acts of Ahab, and all that he did, and the ivory house which he made, and all the cities that he built, *are* they not written in the book of the chronicles of the kings of Israel?

40 So Ahab slept with his fathers; and Ahaziah his son reigned in his stead.

41 ¶ And Jehoshaphat the son of Asa began to reign over Judah in the fourth year of Ahab king of Israel.

42 Jehoshaphat *was* thirty and five years old when he began to reign; and he reigned twenty and five years in Jerusalem. And his mother's name *was* Azubah the daughter of Shilhi.

43 And he walked in all the ways of Asa his father; he turned not aside from them, doing *that which was* right in the eyes of Yahweh: nevertheless the high places were not taken away; *for* the people offered and burnt incense yet in the high places.

44 And Jehoshaphat made peace with the king of Israel.

45 Now the rest of the acts of Jehoshaphat, and his might that he showed, and how he warred, *are* they not written in the book of the chronicles of the kings of Judah?

46 And the remnant of the sodomites, which remained in the days of his father Asa, he took out of the land.

47 *There was* then no king in Edom: a deputy *was* king.
48 Jehoshaphat made ships of Tharshish to go to Ophir for gold: but they went not; for the ships were broken at Eziongeber.
49 Then said Ahaziah the son of Ahab to Jehoshaphat, Let my servants go with your servants in the ships. But Jehoshaphat would not.
50 And Jehoshaphat slept with his fathers, and was buried with his fathers in the city of David his father: and Jehoram his son reigned in his stead.
51 Ahaziah the son of Ahab began to reign over Israel in Samaria the seventeenth year of Jehoshaphat king of Judah, and reigned two years over Israel.
52 And he did evil in the sight of Yahweh, and walked in the way of his father, and in the way of his mother, and in the way of Jeroboam the son of Nebat, who made Israel to sin:
53 For he served Baal, and worshipped him, and provoked to anger Yahweh God of Israel, according to all that his father had done.

2 Kings

2 Kings 1

1:1 ¶ Then Moab rebelled against Israel after the death of Ahab.
2 And Ahaziah fell down through a lattice in his upper chamber that *was* in Samaria, and was sick: and he sent messengers, and said to them, Go, inquire of Baalzebub the god of Ekron whether I shall recover of this disease.
3 But the angel of Yahweh said to Elijah the Tishbite, Arise, go up to meet the messengers of the king of Samaria, and say to them, *Is it* not because *there is* not a God in Israel, *that* you go to inquire of Baalzebub the god of Ekron?
4 Now therefore thus says Yahweh, You shall not come down from that bed on which you have gone up, but will surely die. And Elijah departed.
5 And when the messengers turned back to him, he said to them, Why have you now turned back?
6 And they said to him, There came a man up to meet us, and said to us, Go, turn back unto the king that sent you, and say to him, Thus says Yahweh, *Is it* not because *there is* not a God in Israel, *that* you send to inquire of Baalzebub the god of Ekron? therefore you shall not come down from that bed on which you have gone up, but will surely die.
7 And he said to them, What manner of man *was he* which came up to meet you, and told you these words?
8 And they answered him, *He was* a hairy man, and girded with a girdle of leather about his loins. And he said, It *is* Elijah the Tishbite.
9 ¶ Then the king sent to him a captain of fifty with his fifty. And he went up to him: and, behold, he sat on the top of a hill. And he spoke to him, You man of God, the king has said, Come down.
10 And Elijah answered and said to the captain of fifty, If I *am* a man of God, then let fire come down from heaven, and consume you and your fifty. And there came down fire from heaven, and consumed him and his fifty.
11 Again also he sent to him another captain of fifty with his fifty. And he answered and said to him, O man of God, thus has the king said, Come down quickly.
12 And Elijah answered and said to them, If I *am* a man of God, let fire come down from heaven, and consume you and your fifty. And the fire of God came down from heaven, and consumed him and his fifty.
13 And he sent again a captain of the third fifty with his fifty. And the third captain of fifty went up, and came and fell on his knees before Elijah, and besought him, and said to him, O man of God, I pray you, let my life, and the life of these fifty your servants, be precious in your sight.
14 Behold, there came fire down from heaven, and burnt up the two captains of the former fifties with their fifties: therefore let my life now be precious in your sight.
15 And the angel of Yahweh said to Elijah, Go down with him: be not afraid of him. And he arose, and went down with him to the king.
16 And he said to him, Thus says Yahweh, Forasmuch as you have sent messengers to inquire of Baalzebub the god of Ekron, *is it* not because *there is* no God in Israel to inquire of his word? therefore you shall not come down off that bed on which you have gone up, but will surely die.
17 So he died according to the word of Yahweh which Elijah had spoken. And Jehoram reigned in his stead in the second year of Jehoram the son of Jehoshaphat king of Judah; because he had no son.
18 Now the rest of the acts of Ahaziah which he did, *are* they not written in the book of the chronicles of the kings of Israel?

2 Kings 2

2:1 ¶ And it came to pass, when Yahweh would take up Elijah into heaven by a whirlwind, that Elijah went with Elisha from Gilgal.
2 And Elijah said to Elisha, Remain here, I pray you; for Yahweh has sent me to Bethel. And Elisha said *to him, As* Yahweh lives, and *as* your soul lives, I will not leave you. So they went down to Bethel.
3 And the sons of the prophets that *were* at Bethel came forth to Elisha, and said to him, Know you that Yahweh will take away your master from your head today? And he said, Yes, I know *it*; hold you your peace.
4 And Elijah said to him, Elisha, remain here, I pray you; for Yahweh has sent me to Jericho. And he said, *As* Yahweh lives, and *as* your soul lives, I will not leave you. So they came to Jericho.
5 And the sons of the prophets that *were* at Jericho came to Elisha, and said to him, Know you that Yahweh will

take away your master from your head today? And he answered, Yes, I know it; hold you your peace.

6 And Elijah said to him, Remain, I pray you, here; for Yahweh has sent me to the Jordan. And he said, As Yahweh lives, and as your soul lives, I will not leave you. And they two went on.

7 And fifty men of the sons of the prophets went, and stood to view afar off: and they two stood by the Jordan.

8 And Elijah took his mantle, and wrapped it together, and smote the waters, and they were divided here and there, so that they two went over on dry ground.

9 ¶ And it came to pass, when they had gone over, that Elijah said to Elisha, Ask what I shall do for you, before I am taken away from you. And Elisha said, I pray you, let a double portion of your spirit be upon me.

10 And he said, You have asked a hard thing: nevertheless, if you see me when I am taken from you, it shall be so unto you; but if not, it shall not be so.

11 And it came to pass, as they still went on, and talked, that, behold, there appeared a chariot of fire, and horses of fire, and parted them both apart; and Elijah went up by a whirlwind into heaven.

12 And Elisha saw it, and he cried, My father, my father, the chariot of Israel, and the horsemen thereof. And he saw him no more: and he took hold of his own clothes, and tore them in two pieces.

13 ¶ He took up also the mantle of Elijah that fell from him, and went back, and stood by the bank of the Jordan;

14 And he took the mantle of Elijah that fell from him, and smote the waters, and said, Where is Yahweh God of Elijah? and when he also had smitten the waters, they parted here and there: and Elisha went over.

15 And when the sons of the prophets which were to view at Jericho saw him, they said, The spirit of Elijah does rest on Elisha. And they came to meet him, and bowed themselves to the ground before him.

16 And they said to him, Behold now, there are with your servants fifty strong men; let them go, we pray you, and seek your master: lest perhaps the Spirit of Yahweh has taken him up, and cast him upon some mountain, or into some valley. And he said, You shall not send.

17 And when they urged him till he was ashamed, he said, Send. They sent therefore fifty men; and they sought three days, but found him not.

18 And when they came again to him, (for he remained at Jericho,) he said to them, Did I not say to you, Go not?

19 ¶ And the men of the city said to Elisha, Behold, I ask you, the situation of this city is pleasant, as my lord sees: but the water is bad, and the ground barren.

20 And he said, Bring me a new cruse, and put salt therein. And they brought it to him.

21 And he went forth to the spring of the waters, and cast the salt in there, and said, Thus says Yahweh, I have healed these waters; there shall not be from there any more death or barren land.

22 So the waters were healed unto this day, according to the saying of Elisha which he spoke.

23 And he went up from there to Bethel: and as he was going up by the way, there came forth little children out of the city, and mocked him, and said to him, Go up, you bald head; go up, you bald head.

24 And he turned back, and looked on them, and cursed them in the name of Yahweh. And there came forth two she bears out of the woods, and tore forty and two children of them.

25 And he went from there to mount Carmel, and from there he returned to Samaria.

2 Kings 3

3:1 ¶ Now Jehoram the son of Ahab began to reign over Israel in Samaria the eighteenth year of Jehoshaphat king of Judah, and reigned twelve years.

2 And he worked evil in the sight of Yahweh; but not like his father, and like his mother: for he put away the image of Baal that his father had made.

3 Nevertheless he clung to the sins of Jeroboam the son of Nebat, which made Israel to sin; he departed not therefrom.

4 And Mesha king of Moab was a sheepmaster, and rendered to the king of Israel a hundred thousand lambs, and a hundred thousand rams, with the wool.

5 But it came to pass, when Ahab was dead, that the king of Moab rebelled against the king of Israel.

6 ¶ And king Jehoram went out of Samaria the same time, and numbered all Israel.

7 And he went and sent to Jehoshaphat the king of Judah, saying, The king of Moab has rebelled against me: will you go with me against Moab to battle? And he said, I will go up: I am as you are, my people as your people, and my horses as your horses.

8 And he said, Which way shall we go up? And he answered, The way through the wilderness of Edom.

9 So the king of Israel went, and the king of Judah, and the king of Edom: and they walked around for seven days' journey: and there was no water for the host, and for the cattle that followed them.

10 And the king of Israel said, Alas! that Yahweh has called these three kings together, to deliver them into the hand of Moab!

11 But Jehoshaphat said, Is there not here a prophet of Yahweh, that we may inquire of Yahweh by him? And one of the king of Israel's servants answered and said, Here is Elisha the son of Shaphat, which poured water on the hands of Elijah.

12 And Jehoshaphat said, The word of Yahweh is with him. So the king of Israel and Jehoshaphat and the king of Edom went down to him.

13 And Elisha said to the king of Israel, What have I to do with you? get you to the prophets of your father, and to the prophets of your mother. And the king of Israel said to him, No: for Yahweh has called these three kings together, to deliver them into the hand of Moab.

14 And Elisha said, As Yahweh of hosts lives, before whom I stand, surely, were it not that I regard the presence of Jehoshaphat the king of Judah, I would not look toward you, nor see you.

2 Kings 3

15 But now bring me a minstrel. And it came to pass, when the minstrel played, that the hand of Yahweh came upon him.
16 And he said, Thus says Yahweh, Make this valley full of ditches.
17 For thus says Yahweh, You shall not see wind, neither shall you see rain; yet that valley shall be filled with water, that you may drink, both you, and your cattle, and your beasts.
18 And this is *but* a light thing in the sight of Yahweh: he will deliver the Moabites also into your hand.
19 And you shall smite every fenced city, and every choice city, and shall fell every good tree, and stop all wells of water, and mar every good piece of land with stones.
20 ¶ And it came to pass in the morning, when the meat offering was offered, that, behold, there came water by the way of Edom, and the country was filled with water.
21 And when all the Moabites heard that the kings had come up to fight against them, they gathered all that were able to put on armor, and upward, and stood in the border.
22 And they rose up early in the morning, and the sun shone upon the water, and the Moabites saw the water on the other side *as* red as blood:
23 And they said, This *is* blood: the kings are surely slain, and they have smitten one another: now therefore, Moab, to the spoil.
24 And when they came to the camp of Israel, the Israelites rose up and smote the Moabites, so that they fled before them: but they went forward smiting the Moabites, even in *their* country.
25 And they beat down the cities, and on every good piece of land cast every man his stone, and filled it; and they stopped all the wells of water, and felled all the good trees: only in Kirharaseth left they the stones thereof; however the slingers went about *it*, and smote it.
26 And when the king of Moab saw that the battle was too strong for him, he took with him seven hundred men that drew swords, to break through *even* to the king of Edom: but they could not.
27 Then he took his oldest son that should have reigned in his stead, and offered him *for* a burnt offering upon the wall. And there was great indignation against Israel: and they departed from him, and returned to *their own* land.

2 Kings 4

4:1 ¶ Now there cried a certain woman of the wives of the sons of the prophets unto Elisha, saying, Your servant my husband is dead; and you know that your servant did fear Yahweh: and the creditor is coming to take unto him my two sons to be bondmen.
2 And Elisha said to her, What shall I do for you? tell me, what have you in the house? And she said, Your handmaid has not anything in the house, save a pot of oil.
3 Then he said, Go, borrow you vessels abroad of all your neighbors, *even* empty vessels; borrow not a few.
4 And when you have come in, you will shut the door upon you and upon your sons, and shall pour out into all those vessels, and you shall set aside that which is full.
5 So she went from him, and shut the door upon her and upon her sons, who brought *the vessels* to her; and she poured out.
6 And it came to pass, when the vessels were full, that she said to her son, Bring me yet a vessel. And he said to her, *There is* not a vessel more. And the oil stayed.
7 Then she came and told the man of God. And he said, Go, sell the oil, and pay your debt, and live you and your children of the rest.
8 ¶ And it fell on a day, that Elisha passed to Shunem, where *was* a great woman; and she constrained him to eat bread. And *so* it was, *that* as often as he passed by, he turned in there to eat bread.
9 And she said to her husband, Behold now, I perceive that this *is* a holy man of God, which passes by us continually.
10 Let us make a little chamber, I pray you, on the wall; and let us set for him there a bed, and a table, and a stool, and a candlestick: and it shall be, when he comes to us, that he shall turn in there.
11 And it fell on a day, that he came there, and he turned into the chamber, and lay there.
12 And he said to Gehazi his servant, Call this Shunammite. And when he had called her, she stood before him.
13 And he said to him, Say now to her, Behold, you have been careful for us with all this care; what *is* to be done for you? would you be spoken for to the king, or to the captain of the host? And she answered, I dwell among my own people.
14 And he said, What then *is* to be done for her? And Gehazi answered, Truly she has no child, and her husband is old.
15 And he said, Call her. And when he had called her, she stood in the door.
16 And he said, About this season, according to the time of life, you shall embrace a son. And she said, No, my lord, *you* man of God, do not lie to your handmaid.
17 And the woman conceived, and bore a son at that season that Elisha had said to her, according to the time of life.
18 ¶ And when the child was grown, it fell on a day, that he went out to his father to the reapers.
19 And he said to his father, My head, my head. And he said to a lad, Carry him to his mother.
20 And when he had taken him, and brought him to his mother, he sat on her knees till noon, and *then* died.
21 And she went up, and laid him on the bed of the man of God, and shut *the door* upon him, and went out.
22 And she called to her husband, and said, Send me, I pray you, one of the young men, and one of the donkeys, that I may run to the man of God, and come again.
23 And he said, Why will you go to him today? *it is* neither new moon, nor sabbath. And she said, *It shall be* well.
24 Then she saddled a donkey, and said to her servant, Drive, and go forward; slack not *your* riding for me, unless I bid you.

25 So she went and came to the man of God to mount Carmel. And it came to pass, when the man of God saw her afar off, that he said to Gehazi his servant, Behold, *yonder is* that Shunammite:

26 Run now, I pray you, to meet her, and say to her, *Is it* well with you? *is it* well with your husband? *is it* well with the child? And she answered, *It is* well.

27 And when she came to the man of God to the hill, she caught him by the feet: but Gehazi came near to thrust her away. And the man of God said, Let her alone: for her soul *is* bitter within her: and Yahweh has hidden *it* from me, and has not told me.

28 Then she said, Did I desire a son of my lord? did I not say, Do not deceive me?

29 Then he said to Gehazi, Gird up your loins, and take my staff in your hand, and go your way: if you meet any man, salute him not; and if any salutes you, answer him not again: and lay my staff upon the face of the child.

30 And the mother of the child said, *As* Yahweh lives, and *as* your soul lives, I will not leave you. And he arose, and followed her.

31 And Gehazi passed on before them, and laid the staff upon the face of the child; but *there was* neither voice, nor hearing. Therefore he went again to meet him, and told him, saying, The child is not awake.

32 And when Elisha had come into the house, behold, the child was dead, *and* laid upon his bed.

33 He went in therefore, and shut the door upon them both, and prayed unto Yahweh.

34 And he went up, and lay upon the child, and put his mouth upon his mouth, and his eyes upon his eyes, and his hands upon his hands: and he stretched himself upon the child; and the flesh of the child became warm.

35 Then he returned, and walked in the house to and fro; and went up, and stretched himself upon him: and the child sneezed seven times, and the child opened his eyes.

36 And he called Gehazi, and said, Call this Shunammite. So he called her. And when she had come in to him, he said, Take up your son.

37 Then she went in, and fell at his feet, and bowed herself to the ground, and took up her son, and went out.

38 ¶ And Elisha came again to Gilgal: and *there was* a famine in the land; and the sons of the prophets *were* sitting before him: and he said to his servant, Set on the great pot, and boil pottage for the sons of the prophets.

39 And one went out into the field to gather herbs, and found a wild vine, and gathered thereof wild gourds his lap full, and came and shred *them* into the pot of pottage: for they knew *them* not.

40 So they poured out for the men to eat. And it came to pass, as they were eating of the pottage, that they cried out, and said, O *you* man of God, *there is* death in the pot. And they could not eat *thereof*.

41 But he said, Then bring meal. And he cast *it* into the pot; and he said, Pour out for the people, that they may eat. And there was no harm in the pot.

42 And there came a man from Baalshalisha, and brought the man of God bread of the firstfruits, twenty loaves of barley, and full ears of corn in the husk thereof. And he said, Give to the people, that they may eat.

43 And his servant said, What, should I set this before a hundred men? He said again, Give the people, that they may eat: for thus says Yahweh, They shall eat, and shall leave *thereof*.

44 So he set *it* before them, and they did eat, and left *thereof*, according to the word of Yahweh.

2 Kings 5

5:1 ¶ Now Naaman, captain of the host of the king of Syria, was a great man with his master, and honorable, because by him Yahweh had given deliverance to Syria: he was also a mighty man in valor, *but he was* a leper.

2 And the Syrians had gone out by companies, and had brought away captive out of the land of Israel a little maid; and she waited upon Naaman's wife.

3 And she said to her mistress, Would God my lord *were* with the prophet that *is* in Samaria! for he would recover him of his leprosy.

4 And *one* went in, and told his lord, saying, Thus and thus said the maid that *is* of the land of Israel.

5 And the king of Syria said, Go to, go, and I will send a letter to the king of Israel. And he departed, and took with him ten talents of silver, and six thousand *pieces* of gold, and ten changes of clothing.

6 And he brought the letter to the king of Israel, saying, Now when this letter has come to you, behold, I have *therewith* sent Naaman my servant to you, that you may recover him of his leprosy.

7 And it came to pass, when the king of Israel had read the letter, that he tore his clothes, and said, *Am* I God, to kill and to make alive, that this man does send to me to recover a man of his leprosy? therefore consider, I pray you, and see how he seeks a quarrel against me.

8 And it was *so*, when Elisha the man of God had heard that the king of Israel had torn his clothes, that he sent to the king, saying, Why have you torn your clothes? let him come now to me, and he shall know that there is a prophet in Israel.

9 ¶ So Naaman came with his horses and with his chariot, and stood at the door of the house of Elisha.

10 And Elisha sent a messenger to him, saying, Go and wash in *the* Jordan seven times, and your flesh shall come again to you, and you shall be clean.

11 But Naaman was angry, and went away, and said, Behold, I thought, He will surely come out to me, and stand, and call upon the name of Yahweh his God, and strike his hand over the place, and recover the leper.

12 *Are* not Abana and Pharpar, rivers of Damascus, better than all the waters of Israel? may I not wash in them, and be clean? So he turned and went away in a rage.

13 And his servants came near, and spoke to him, and said, My father, *if* the prophet had bid you *to do some great thing*, would you not have done *it*? how much rather then, when he said to you, Wash, and be clean?

2 Kings 5

14 Then went he down, and dipped himself seven times in *the* Jordan, according to the saying of the man of God: and his flesh came again like unto the flesh of a little child, and he was clean.

15 ¶ And he returned to the man of God, he and all his company, and came, and stood before him: and he said, Behold, now I know that *there is* no God in all the earth, but in Israel: now therefore, I pray you, take a blessing of your servant.

16 But he said, *As* Yahweh lives, before whom I stand, I will receive none. And he urged him to take *it*; but he refused.

17 And Naaman said, Shall there not then, I pray you, be given to your servant two mules' burden of earth? for your servant will henceforth offer neither burnt offering nor sacrifice unto other gods, but unto Yahweh.

18 In this thing Yahweh pardon your servant, *that* when my master goes into the house of Rimmon to worship there, and he leans upon my hand, and I bow myself in the house of Rimmon: when I bow down myself in the house of Rimmon, Yahweh pardon your servant in this thing.

19 And he said to him, Go in peace. So he departed from him a little way.

20 ¶ But Gehazi, the servant of Elisha the man of God, said, Behold, my master has spared Naaman this Syrian, in not receiving at his hands that which he brought: but, *as* Yahweh lives, I will run after him, and take something from him.

21 So Gehazi followed after Naaman. And when Naaman saw *him* running after him, he lighted down from the chariot to meet him, and said, *Is* all well?

22 And he said, All *is* well. My master has sent me, saying, Behold, even now there has come to me from mount Ephraim two young men of the sons of the prophets: give them, I pray you, a talent of silver, and two changes of garments.

23 And Naaman said, Be content, take two talents. And he urged him, and bound two talents of silver in two bags, with two changes of garments, and laid *them* upon two of his servants; and they bore *them* before him.

24 And when he came to the tower, he took *them* from their hand, and bestowed *them* in the house: and he let the men go, and they departed.

25 But he went in, and stood before his master. And Elisha said to him, Where *went you*, Gehazi? And he said, Your servant went no where.

26 And he said to him, Went not my heart *with you*, when the man turned again from his chariot to meet you? *Is it* a time to receive money, and to receive garments, and olive groves, and vineyards, and sheep, and oxen, and menservants, and maidservants?

27 The leprosy therefore of Naaman shall cling to you, and to your seed forever. And he went out from his presence a leper *as white* as snow.

2 Kings 6

6:1 ¶ And the sons of the prophets said to Elisha, Behold now, the place where we dwell with you is too tight for us.

2 Let us go, we pray you, to *the* Jordan, and take there every man a beam, and let us make us a place there, where we may dwell. And he answered, Go you.

3 And one said, Be content, I pray you, and go with your servants. And he answered, I will go.

4 So he went with them. And when they came to *the* Jordan, they cut down wood.

5 But as one was felling a beam, the ax head fell into the water: and he cried, and said, Alas, master! for it was borrowed.

6 And the man of God said, Where fell it? And he showed him the place. And he cut down a stick, and cast *it* in there; and the iron did swim.

7 Therefore said he, Take *it* up to you. And he put out his hand, and took it.

8 ¶ Then the king of Syria warred against Israel, and took counsel with his servants, saying, In such and such a place *shall be* my camp.

9 And the man of God sent to the king of Israel, saying, Beware that you pass not such a place; for there the Syrians are coming down.

10 And the king of Israel sent to the place which the man of God told him and warned him of, and saved himself there, not once nor twice.

11 Therefore the heart of the king of Syria was very troubled for this thing; and he called his servants, and said to them, Will you not show me which of us *is* for the king of Israel?

12 And one of his servants said, None, my lord, O king: but Elisha, the prophet that *is* in Israel, tells the king of Israel the words that you speak in your bedchamber.

13 ¶ And he said, Go and spy where he *is*, that I may send and fetch him. And it was told *to* him, saying, Behold, *he is* in Dothan.

14 Therefore sent he there horses, and chariots, and a great host: and they came by night, and compassed the city about.

15 And when the servant of the man of God had risen early, and gone forth, behold, a host compassed the city both with horses and chariots. And his servant said to him, Alas, my master! how shall we do?

16 And he answered, Fear not: for they that *are* with us *are* more than they that *are* with them.

17 And Elisha prayed, and said, Yahweh, I pray you, open his eyes, that he may see. And Yahweh opened the eyes of the young man; and he saw: and, behold, the mountain *was* full of horses and chariots of fire round about Elisha.

18 And when they came down to him, Elisha prayed unto Yahweh, and said, Smite this people, I pray you, with blindness. And he smote them with blindness according to the word of Elisha.

19 And Elisha said to them, This *is* not the way, neither *is* this the city: follow me, and I will bring you to the man whom you seek. But he led them to Samaria.

20 And it came to pass, when they had come into Samaria, that Elisha said, Yahweh, open the eyes of these *men*, that they may see. And Yahweh opened their

eyes, and they saw; and, behold, *they were* in the midst of Samaria.

21 And the king of Israel said to Elisha, when he saw them, My father, shall I smite *them*? shall I smite *them*?

22 And he answered, You shall not smite *them*: would you smite those whom you have taken captive with your sword and with your bow? set bread and water before them, that they may eat and drink, and go to their master.

23 And he prepared great provision for them: and when they had eaten and drunk, he sent them away, and they went to their master. So the bands of Syria came no more into the land of Israel.

24 ¶ And it came to pass after this, that Benhadad king of Syria gathered all his host, and went up, and besieged Samaria.

25 And there was a great famine in Samaria: and, behold, they besieged it, until a donkey's head was sold for fourscore *pieces* of silver, and the fourth part of a cab of dove's dung for five *pieces* of silver.

26 And as the king of Israel was passing by upon the wall, there cried a woman to him, saying, Help, my lord, O king.

27 And he said, If Yahweh does not help you, where shall I help you? out of the barn floor, or out of the winepress?

28 And the king said to her, What ails you? And she answered, This woman said to me, Give your son, that we may eat him today, and we will eat my son tomorrow.

29 So we boiled my son, and did eat him: and I said to her on the next day, Give your son, that we may eat him: and she has hidden her son.

30 And it came to pass, when the king heard the words of the woman, that he tore his clothes; and he passed by upon the wall, and the people looked, and, behold, *he had* sackcloth within upon his flesh.

31 Then he said, God do so and more also to me, if the head of Elisha the son of Shaphat shall stand on him this day.

32 But Elisha sat in his house, and the elders sat with him; and *the king* sent a man from before him: but before the messenger came to him, he said to the elders, See you how this son of a murderer has sent to take away my head? look, when the messenger comes, shut the door, and hold him fast at the door: *is* not the sound of his master's feet behind him?

33 And while he yet talked with them, behold, the messenger came down to him: and he said, Behold, this evil *is* of Yahweh; why should I wait for Yahweh any longer?

2 Kings 7

7:1 ¶ Then Elisha said, Hear you the word of Yahweh; Thus says Yahweh, Tomorrow about this time *shall* a measure of fine flour *be sold* for a shekel, and two measures of barley for a shekel, in the gate of Samaria.

2 Then a lord on whose hand the king leaned answered the man of God, and said, Behold, *if* Yahweh would make windows in heaven, might this thing be? And he said, Behold, you shall see *it* with your eyes, but shall not eat thereof.

3 ¶ And there were four leprous men at the entering in of the gate: and they said one to another, Why sit we here until we die?

4 If we say, We will enter into the city, then the famine *is* in the city, and we shall die there: and if we sit still here, we die also. Now therefore come, and let us fall to the host of the Syrians: if they save us alive, we shall live; and if they kill us, we shall but die.

5 And they rose up in the twilight, to go to the camp of the Syrians: and when they had come to the utmost part of the camp of Syria, behold, *there was* no man there.

6 For the Lord had made the host of the Syrians to hear a noise of chariots, and a noise of horses, *even* the noise of a great host: and they said one to another, Lo, the king of Israel has hired against us the kings of the Hittites, and the kings of the Egyptians, to come upon us.

7 Therefore they arose and fled in the twilight, and left their tents, and their horses, and their donkeys, even the camp as it *was*, and fled for their lives.

8 And when these lepers came to the utmost part of the camp, they went into one tent, and did eat and drink, and carried there silver, and gold, and clothing, and went and hid *it*; and came again, and entered into another tent, and carried there *also*, and went and hid *it*.

9 Then they said one to another, We do not well: this day *is* a day of good tidings, and we hold our peace: if we wait till the morning light, some mischief will come upon us: now therefore come, that we may go and tell the king's household.

10 So they came and called to the porter of the city: and they told them, saying, We came to the camp of the Syrians, and, behold, *there was* no man there, neither voice of man, but horses tied, and donkeys tied, and the tents as they *were*.

11 And he called the porters; and they told *it* to the king's house within.

12 ¶ And the king arose in the night, and said to his servants, I will now show you what the Syrians have done to us. They know that we *are* hungry; therefore have they gone out of the camp to hide themselves in the field, saying, When they come out of the city, we shall catch them alive, and get into the city.

13 And one of his servants answered and said, Let *some* take, I pray you, five of the horses that remain, which are left in the city, (behold, they *are* as all the multitude of Israel that are left in it: behold, *I say*, they *are* even as all the multitude of the Israelites that are consumed:) and let us send and see.

14 They took therefore two chariot horses; and the king sent after the host of the Syrians, saying, Go and see.

15 And they went after them unto *the* Jordan: and, lo, all the way *was* full of garments and vessels, which the Syrians had cast away in their haste. And the messengers returned, and told the king.

16 And the people went out, and spoiled the tents of the Syrians. So a measure of fine flour was *sold* for a shekel, and two measures of barley for a shekel, according to the word of Yahweh.

17 And the king appointed the lord on whose hand he leaned to have the charge of the gate: and the people trampled upon him in the gate, and he died, as the man of God had said, who spoke when the king came down to him.

18 And it came to pass as the man of God had spoken to the king, saying, Two measures of barley for a shekel, and a measure of fine flour for a shekel, shall be tomorrow about this time in the gate of Samaria:

19 And that lord answered the man of God, and said, Now, behold, *if* Yahweh should make windows in heaven, might such a thing be? And he said, Behold, you shall see it with your eyes, but will not eat thereof.

20 And so it fell out unto him: for the people trampled upon him in the gate, and he died.

2 Kings 8

8:1 ¶ Then spoke Elisha to the woman, whose son he had restored to life, saying, Arise, and go you and your household, and sojourn wherever you can sojourn: for Yahweh has called for a famine; and it shall also come upon the land *for* seven years.

2 And the woman arose, and did after the saying of the man of God: and she went with her household, and sojourned in the land of the Philistines *for* seven years.

3 And it came to pass at the seven years' end, that the woman returned out of the land of the Philistines: and she went forth to cry unto the king for her house and for her land.

4 And the king talked with Gehazi the servant of the man of God, saying, Tell me, I pray you, all the great things that Elisha has done.

5 And it came to pass, as he was telling the king how he had restored a dead body to life, that, behold, the woman, whose son he had restored to life, cried to the king for her house and for her land. And Gehazi said, My lord, O king, this *is* the woman, and this *is* her son, whom Elisha restored to life.

6 And when the king asked the woman, she told him. So the king appointed unto her a certain officer, saying, Restore all that *was* hers, and all the fruits of the field since the day that she left the land, even until now.

7 ¶ And Elisha came to Damascus; and Benhadad the king of Syria was sick; and it was told *to* him, saying, The man of God has come here.

8 And the king said to Hazael, Take a present in your hand, and go, meet the man of God, and inquire of Yahweh by him, saying, Shall I recover from this disease?

9 So Hazael went to meet him, and took a present with him, even of every good thing of Damascus, forty camels' burden, and came and stood before him, and said, Your son Benhadad king of Syria has sent me to you, saying, Shall I recover from this disease?

10 And Elisha said to him, Go, say to him, You may certainly recover: however Yahweh has shown me that he shall surely die.

11 And he settled his countenance steadfastly, until he was ashamed: and the man of God wept.

12 And Hazael said, Why weep my lord? And he answered, Because I know the evil that you will do to the children of Israel: their strong holds will you set on fire, and their young men will you slay with the sword, and will dash their children, and rip up their women with child.

13 And Hazael said, But what, *is* your servant a dog, that he should do this great thing? And Elisha answered, Yahweh has shown me that you *shall be* king over Syria.

14 So he departed from Elisha, and came to his master; who said to him, What said Elisha to you? And he answered, He told me *that* you should surely recover.

15 And it came to pass on the next day, that he took a thick cloth, and dipped *it* in water, and spread *it* on his face, so that he died: and Hazael reigned in his stead.

16 ¶ And in the fifth year of Joram the son of Ahab king of Israel, Jehoshaphat *being* then king of Judah, Jehoram the son of Jehoshaphat king of Judah began to reign.

17 Thirty and two years old was he when he began to reign; and he reigned eight years in Jerusalem.

18 And he walked in the way of the kings of Israel, as did the house of Ahab: for the daughter of Ahab was his wife: and he did evil in the sight of Yahweh.

19 Yet Yahweh would not destroy Judah for David his servant's sake, as he promised him to give him always a light, *and* to his children.

20 In his days Edom revolted from under the hand of Judah, and made a king over themselves.

21 So Joram went over to Zair, and all the chariots with him: and he rose by night, and smote the Edomites which compassed him about, and the captains of the chariots: and the people fled into their tents.

22 Yet Edom revolted from under the hand of Judah unto this day. Then Libnah revolted at the same time.

23 And the rest of the acts of Joram, and all that he did, *are* they not written in the book of the chronicles of the kings of Judah?

24 And Joram slept with his fathers, and was buried with his fathers in the city of David: and Ahaziah his son reigned in his stead.

25 ¶ In the twelfth year of Joram the son of Ahab king of Israel did Ahaziah the son of Jehoram king of Judah begin to reign.

26 Two and twenty years old *was* Ahaziah when he began to reign; and he reigned one year in Jerusalem. And his mother's name *was* Athaliah, the daughter of Omri king of Israel.

27 And he walked in the way of the house of Ahab, and did evil in the sight of Yahweh, as *did* the house of Ahab: for he *was* the son-in-law of the house of Ahab.

28 And he went with Joram the son of Ahab to the war against Hazael king of Syria in Ramothgilead; and the Syrians wounded Joram.

29 And king Joram went back to be healed in Jezreel of the wounds which the Syrians had given him at Ramah, when he fought against Hazael king of Syria. And Ahaziah the son of Jehoram king of Judah went down to see Joram the son of Ahab in Jezreel, because he was sick.

2 Kings 9

9:1 ¶ And Elisha the prophet called one of the children of the prophets, and said to him, Gird up your loins, and take this box of oil in your hand, and go to Ramothgilead:
2 And when you get there, look out there Jehu the son of Jehoshaphat the son of Nimshi, and go in, and make him arise up from among his brethren, and carry him to an inner chamber;
3 Then take the box of oil, and pour *it* on his head, and say, Thus says Yahweh, I have anointed you king over Israel. Then open the door, and flee, and wait not.
4 So the young man, *even* the young man the prophet, went to Ramothgilead.
5 And when he came, behold, the captains of the host *were* sitting; and he said, I have a matter for you, O captain. And Jehu said, Unto which of all *of* us? And he said, To you, O captain.
6 And he arose, and went into the house; and he poured the oil on his head, and said to him, Thus says Yahweh God of Israel, I have anointed you king over the people of Yahweh, *even* over Israel.
7 And you shall smite the house of Ahab your master, that I may avenge the blood of my servants the prophets, and the blood of all the servants of Yahweh, at the hand of Jezebel.
8 For the whole house of Ahab shall perish: and I will cut off from Ahab him that urinates against the wall, and him that is shut up and left in Israel:
9 And I will make the house of Ahab like the house of Jeroboam the son of Nebat, and like the house of Baasha the son of Ahijah:
10 And the dogs shall eat Jezebel in the portion of Jezreel, and *there shall be* none to bury *her*. And he opened the door, and fled.
11 ¶ Then Jehu came forth to the servants of his lord: and *one* said to him, *Is* all well? why came this mad *fellow* to you? And he said to them, You know the man, and his communication.
12 And they said, *It is* false; tell us now. And he said, Thus and thus spoke he to me, saying, Thus says Yahweh, I have anointed you king over Israel.
13 Then they hurried, and took every man his garment, and put *it* under him on the top of the stairs, and blew with trumpets, saying, Jehu is king.
14 So Jehu the son of Jehoshaphat the son of Nimshi conspired against Joram. (Now Joram had kept Ramothgilead, he and all Israel, because of Hazael king of Syria.
15 But king Joram was returned to be healed in Jezreel of the wounds which the Syrians had given him, when he fought with Hazael king of Syria.) And Jehu said, If it is your mind, *then* let none go forth *nor* escape out of the city to go to tell *it* in Jezreel.
16 ¶ So Jehu rode in a chariot, and went to Jezreel; for Joram lay there. And Ahaziah king of Judah had come down to see Joram.
17 And there stood a watchman on the tower in Jezreel, and he spied the company of Jehu as he came, and said, I see a company. And Joram said, Take a horseman, and send to meet them, and let him say, *Is it* peace?
18 So there went one on horseback to meet him, and said, Thus says the king, *Is it* peace? And Jehu said, What have you to do with peace? turn you behind me. And the watchman told, saying, The messenger came to them, but he comes not again.
19 Then he sent out a second on horseback, which came to them, and said, Thus says the king, *Is it* peace? And Jehu answered, What have you to do with peace? turn you behind me.
20 And the watchman told, saying, He came even to them, and comes not again: and the driving *is* like the driving of Jehu the son of Nimshi; for he drives furiously
21 And Joram said, Make ready. And his chariot was made ready. And Joram king of Israel and Ahaziah king of Judah went out, each in his chariot, and they went out against Jehu, and met him in the portion of Naboth the Jezreelite.
22 And it came to pass, when Joram saw Jehu, that he said, *Is it* peace, Jehu? And he answered, What peace, so long as the whoredoms of your mother Jezebel and her witchcrafts *are so* many?
23 And Joram turned his hands, and fled, and said to Ahaziah, *There is* treachery, O Ahaziah.
24 And Jehu drew a bow with his full strength, and smote Jehoram between his arms, and the arrow went out at his heart, and he sunk down in his chariot.
25 Then said *Jehu* to Bidkar his captain, Take up, *and* cast him in the portion of the field of Naboth the Jezreelite: for remember how that, when I and you rode together after Ahab his father, Yahweh laid this burden upon him;
26 Surely I have seen yesterday the blood of Naboth, and the blood of his sons, says Yahweh; and I will repay you in this plat, says Yahweh. Now therefore take *and* cast him into the plat *of ground*, according to the word of Yahweh.
27 But when Ahaziah the king of Judah saw *this*, he fled by the way of the garden house. And Jehu followed after him, and said, Smite him also in the chariot. *And they did so* at the going up to Gur, which *is* by Ibleam. And he fled to Megiddo, and died there.
28 And his servants carried him in a chariot to Jerusalem, and buried him in his sepulcher with his fathers in the city of David.
29 And in the eleventh year of Joram the son of Ahab began Ahaziah to reign over Judah.
30 ¶ And when Jehu had come to Jezreel, Jezebel heard *of it*; and she painted her face, and adorned her head, and looked out at a window.

2 Kings 9

31 And as Jehu entered in at the gate, she said, *Had* Zimri peace, who slew his master?

32 And he lifted up his face to the window, and said, Who *is* on my side? who? And there looked out to him two *or* three eunuchs.

33 And he said, Throw her down. So they threw her down: and *some* of her blood was sprinkled on the wall, and on the horses: and he trampled her under foot.

34 And when he had come in, he did eat and drink, and said, Go, see now this cursed *woman*, and bury her: for she *is* a king's daughter.

35 And they went to bury her: but they found no more of her than the skull, and the feet, and the palms of *her* hands.

36 Therefore they came again, and told him. And he said, This *is* the word of Yahweh, which he spoke by his servant Elijah the Tishbite, saying, In the portion of Jezreel shall dogs eat the flesh of Jezebel:

37 And the carcass of Jezebel shall be as dung upon the face of the field in the portion of Jezreel; *so* that they shall not say, This *is* Jezebel.

2 Kings 10

10:1 ¶ And Ahab had seventy sons in Samaria. And Jehu wrote letters, and sent to Samaria, to the rulers of Jezreel, to the elders, and to them that brought up Ahab's *children*, saying,

2 Now as soon as this letter comes to you, seeing your master's sons *are* with you, and *there are* with you chariots and horses, a fenced city also, and armor;

3 Look even out the best and *most* upright of your master's sons, and set *him* on his father's throne, and fight for your master's house.

4 But they were exceedingly afraid, and said, Behold, two kings stood not before him: how then shall we stand?

5 And he that *was* over the house, and he that *was* over the city, the elders also, and the bringers up *of the children*, sent to Jehu, saying, We *are* your servants, and will do all that you shall bid us; we will not make any king: do you *that which is* good in your eyes.

6 Then he wrote a letter the second time to them, saying, If you *are* mine, and *if* you will listen to my voice, take you the heads of the men your master's sons, and come to me to Jezreel by tomorrow this time. Now the king's sons, *being* seventy persons, *were* with the great men of the city, which brought them up.

7 And it came to pass, when the letter came to them, that they took the king's sons, and slew seventy persons, and put their heads in baskets, and sent him *them* to Jezreel.

8 And there came a messenger, and told him, saying, They have brought the heads of the king's sons. And he said, Lay you them in two heaps at the entering in of the gate until the morning.

9 And it came to pass in the morning, that he went out, and stood, and said to all the people, You *are* righteous: behold, I conspired against my master, and slew him: but who slew all these?

10 Know now that there shall fall to the earth nothing of the word of Yahweh, which Yahweh spoke concerning the house of Ahab: for Yahweh has done *that* which he spoke by his servant Elijah.

11 So Jehu slew all that remained of the house of Ahab in Jezreel, and all his great men, and his relatives, and his priests, until he left him none remaining.

12 And he arose and departed, and came to Samaria. *And* as he *was* at the shearing house in the way,

13 Jehu met with the brothers of Ahaziah king of Judah, and said, Who *are* you? And they answered, We *are* the brothers of Ahaziah; and we go down to salute the children of the king and the children of the queen.

14 And he said, Take them alive. And they took them alive, and slew them at the pit of the shearing house, *even* two and forty men; neither left he any of them.

15 ¶ And when he had departed therefrom, he lighted on Jehonadab the son of Rechab *coming* to meet him: and he saluted him, and said to him, Is your heart right, as my heart *is* with your heart? And Jehonadab answered, It is. If it is, give *me* your hand. And he gave *him* his hand; and he took him up to him into the chariot.

16 And he said, Come with me, and see my zeal for Yahweh. So they made him ride in his chariot.

17 And when he came to Samaria, he slew all that remained unto Ahab in Samaria, till he had destroyed him, according to the saying of Yahweh, which he spoke to Elijah.

18 And Jehu gathered all the people together, and said to them, Ahab served Baal a little; *but* Jehu shall serve him much.

19 Now therefore call to me all the prophets of Baal, all his servants, and all his priests; let none be wanting: for I have a great sacrifice *to do* to Baal; whoever shall be wanting, he shall not live. But Jehu did *it* in subtlety, to the intent that he might destroy the worshippers of Baal.

20 And Jehu said, Proclaim a solemn assembly for Baal. And they proclaimed *it*.

21 And Jehu sent through all Israel: and all the worshippers of Baal came, so that there was not a man left that came not. And they came into the house of Baal; and the house of Baal was full from one end to another.

22 And he said to him that *was* over the vestry, Bring forth vestments for all the worshippers of Baal. And he brought them forth vestments.

23 And Jehu went, and Jehonadab the son of Rechab, into the house of Baal, and said to the worshippers of Baal, Search, and look that there is here with you none of the servants of Yahweh, but the worshippers of Baal only.

24 And when they went in to offer sacrifices and burnt offerings, Jehu appointed fourscore men outside, and said, *If* any of the men whom I have brought into your hands escapes, *he that lets him go*, his life *shall be* for the life of him.

25 And it came to pass, as soon as he had made an end of offering the burnt offering, that Jehu said to the guard

and to the captains, Go in, *and* slay them; let none come forth. And they smote them with the edge of the sword; and the guard and the captains cast *them* out, and went to the city of the house of Baal.

26 And they brought forth the images out of the house of Baal, and burned them.

27 And they broke down the image of Baal, and broke down the house of Baal, and made it a draught house unto this day.

28 Thus Jehu destroyed Baal out of Israel.

29 ¶ However *from* the sins of Jeroboam the son of Nebat, who made Israel to sin, Jehu departed not from after them, *that is*, the golden calves that *were* in Bethel, and that *were* in Dan.

30 And Yahweh said to Jehu, Because you have done well in executing *that which is* right in my eyes, *and* have done to the house of Ahab according to all that *was* in my heart, your children of the fourth *generation* shall sit on the throne of Israel.

31 But Jehu took no heed to walk in the law of Yahweh God of Israel with all his heart: for he departed not from the sins of Jeroboam, which made Israel to sin.

32 In those days Yahweh began to cut Israel short: and Hazael smote them in all the coasts of Israel;

33 From *the* Jordan eastward, all the land of Gilead, the Gadites, and the Reubenites, and the Manassites, from Aroer, which *is* by the river Arnon, even Gilead and Bashan.

34 Now the rest of the acts of Jehu, and all that he did, and all his might, *are* they not written in the book of the chronicles of the kings of Israel?

35 And Jehu slept with his fathers: and they buried him in Samaria. And Jehoahaz his son reigned in his stead.

36 And the time that Jehu reigned over Israel in Samaria *was* twenty and eight years.

2 Kings 11

11:1 ¶ And when Athaliah the mother of Ahaziah saw that her son was dead, she arose and destroyed all the seed royal.

2 But Jehosheba, the daughter of king Joram, sister of Ahaziah, took Joash the son of Ahaziah, and stole him from among the king's sons *which were* slain; and they hid him, *even* him and his nurse, in the bedchamber from Athaliah, so that he was not slain.

3 And he was with her hidden in the house of Yahweh *for* six years. And Athaliah did reign over the land.

4 ¶ And the seventh year Jehoiada sent and fetched the rulers over hundreds, with the captains and the guard, and brought them to him into the house of Yahweh, and made a covenant with them, and took an oath of them in the house of Yahweh, and showed them the king's son.

5 And he commanded them, saying, This *is* the thing that you shall do; A third part of you that enter in on the sabbath shall even be keepers of the watch of the king's house;

6 And a third part *shall be* at the gate of Sur; and a third part at the gate behind the guard: so shall you keep the watch of the house, that it be not broken down.

7 And two parts of all you that go forth on the sabbath, even they shall keep the watch of the house of Yahweh about the king.

8 And you shall compass the king round about, every man with his weapons in his hand: and he that comes within the ranges, let him be slain: and be you with the king as he goes out and as he comes in.

9 And the captains over the hundreds did according to all *things* that Jehoiada the priest commanded: and they took every man his men that were to come in on the sabbath, with them that should go out on the sabbath, and came to Jehoiada the priest.

10 And to the captains over hundreds did the priest give king David's spears and shields, that *were* in the temple of Yahweh.

11 And the guard stood, every man with his weapons in his hand, round about the king, from the right corner of the temple to the left corner of the temple, *along* by the altar and the temple.

12 And he brought forth the king's son, and put the crown upon him, and *gave him* the testimony; and they made him king, and anointed him; and they clapped their hands, and said, God save the king.

13 ¶ And when Athaliah heard the noise of the guard *and* of the people, she came to the people into the temple of Yahweh.

14 And when she looked, behold, the king stood by a pillar, as the manner *was*, and the princes and the trumpeters by the king, and all the people of the land rejoiced, and blew with trumpets: and Athaliah tore her clothes, and cried, Treason, Treason.

15 But Jehoiada the priest commanded the captains of the hundreds, the officers of the host, and said to them, Bring her forth outside the ranges: and him that follows her kill with the sword. For the priest had said, Let her not be slain in the house of Yahweh.

16 And they laid hands on her; and she went by the way by the which the horses came into the king's house: and there was she slain.

17 ¶ And Jehoiada made a covenant between Yahweh and the king and the people, that they should be Yahweh's people; between the king also and the people.

18 And all the people of the land went into the house of Baal, and broke it down; his altars and his images broke they in pieces thoroughly, and slew Mattan the priest of Baal before the altars. And the priest appointed officers over the house of Yahweh.

19 And he took the rulers over hundreds, and the captains, and the guard, and all the people of the land; and they brought down the king from the house of Yahweh, and came by the way of the gate of the guard to the king's house. And he sat on the throne of the kings.

20 And all the people of the land rejoiced, and the city was in quiet: and they slew Athaliah with the sword *beside* the king's house.

21 Seven years old *was* Jehoash when he began to reign.

2 Kings 12

12:1 ¶ In the seventh year of Jehu Jehoash began to reign; and forty years reigned he in Jerusalem. And his mother's name *was* Zibiah of Beersheba.
2 And Jehoash did *that which was* right in the sight of Yahweh all his days wherein Jehoiada the priest instructed him.
3 But the high places were not taken away: the people still sacrificed and burnt incense in the high places.
4 ¶ And Jehoash said to the priests, All the money of the dedicated things that is brought into the house of Yahweh, *even* the money of every one that passes *the account*, the money that every man is set at, *and* all the money that comes into any man's heart to bring into the house of Yahweh,
5 Let the priests take *it* to them, every man of his acquaintance: and let them repair the breaches of the house, wherever any breach shall be found.
6 But it was *so, that* in the three and twentieth year of king Jehoash, the priests had not repaired the breaches of the house.
7 Then king Jehoash called for Jehoiada the priest, and the *other* priests, and said to them, Why repair you not the breaches of the house? now therefore receive no *more* money of your acquaintance, but deliver it for the breaches of the house.
8 And the priests consented to receive no *more* money of the people, neither to repair the breaches of the house.
9 But Jehoiada the priest took a chest, and bored a hole in the lid of it, and set it beside the altar, on the right side as one comes into the house of Yahweh: and the priests that kept the door put therein all the money *that was* brought into the house of Yahweh.
10 And it was *so*, when they saw that *there was* much money in the chest, that the king's scribe and the high priest came up, and they put *it* up in bags, and counted the money that was found in the house of Yahweh.
11 And they gave the money, being told, into the hands of them that did the work, that had the oversight of the house of Yahweh: and they laid it out to the carpenters and builders, that worked upon the house of Yahweh,
12 And to masons, and hewers of stone, and to buy timber and hewed stone to repair the breaches of the house of Yahweh, and for all that was laid out for the house to repair *it*.
13 However there were not made for the house of Yahweh bowls of silver, snuffers, basins, trumpets, any vessels of gold, or vessels of silver, of the money *that was* brought into the house of Yahweh:
14 But they gave that to the workmen, and repaired therewith the house of Yahweh.
15 Moreover they reckoned not with the men, into whose hand they delivered the money to be bestowed on workmen: for they dealt faithfully.
16 The trespass money and sin money was not brought into the house of Yahweh: it was the priests'.
17 ¶ Then Hazael king of Syria went up, and fought against Gath, and took it: and Hazael set his face to go up to Jerusalem.
18 And Jehoash king of Judah took all the hallowed things that Jehoshaphat, and Jehoram, and Ahaziah, his fathers, kings of Judah, had dedicated, and his own hallowed things, and all the gold *that was* found in the treasuries of the house of Yahweh, and in the king's house, and sent *it* to Hazael king of Syria: and he went away from Jerusalem.
19 And the rest of the acts of Joash, and all that he did, *are* they not written in the book of the chronicles of the kings of Judah?
20 And his servants arose, and made a conspiracy, and slew Joash in the house of Millo, which goes down to Silla.
21 For Jozachar the son of Shimeath, and Jehozabad the son of Shomer, his servants, smote him, and he died; and they buried him with his fathers in the city of David: and Amaziah his son reigned in his stead.

2 Kings 13

13:1 ¶ In the three and twentieth year of Joash the son of Ahaziah king of Judah, Jehoahaz the son of Jehu began to reign over Israel in Samaria, *and reigned* seventeen years.
2 And he did *that which was* evil in the sight of Yahweh, and followed the sins of Jeroboam the son of Nebat, which made Israel to sin; he departed not therefrom.
3 And the anger of Yahweh was kindled against Israel, and he delivered them into the hand of Hazael king of Syria, and into the hand of Benhadad the son of Hazael, all *their* days.
4 And Jehoahaz besought Yahweh, and Yahweh listened to him: for he saw the oppression of Israel, because the king of Syria oppressed them.
5 (And Yahweh gave Israel a savior, so that they went out from under the hand of the Syrians: and the children of Israel dwelt in their tents, as before.
6 Nevertheless they departed not from the sins of the house of Jeroboam, who made Israel sin, *but* walked therein: and there remained the grove also in Samaria.)
7 Neither did he leave of the people to Jehoahaz but fifty horsemen, and ten chariots, and ten thousand footmen; for the king of Syria had destroyed them, and had made them like the dust by threshing.
8 Now the rest of the acts of Jehoahaz, and all that he did, and his might, *are* they not written in the book of the chronicles of the kings of Israel?
9 And Jehoahaz slept with his fathers; and they buried him in Samaria: and Joash his son reigned in his stead.
10 ¶ In the thirty and seventh year of Joash king of Judah began Jehoash the son of Jehoahaz to reign over Israel in Samaria, *and reigned* sixteen years.
11 And he did *that which was* evil in the sight of Yahweh; he departed not from all the sins of Jeroboam the son of Nebat, who made Israel sin: *but* he walked therein.

12 And the rest of the acts of Joash, and all that he did, and his might with which he fought against Amaziah king of Judah, are they not written in the book of the chronicles of the kings of Israel?

13 And Joash slept with his fathers; and Jeroboam sat upon his throne: and Joash was buried in Samaria with the kings of Israel.

14 Now Elisha had fallen sick of his sickness whereof he died. And Joash the king of Israel came down to him, and wept over his face, and said, O my father, my father, the chariot of Israel, and the horsemen thereof.

15 And Elisha said to him, Take bow and arrows. And he took unto him bow and arrows.

16 And he said to the king of Israel, Put your hand upon the bow. And he put his hand *upon it*: and Elisha put his hands upon the king's hands.

17 And he said, Open the window eastward. And he opened *it*. Then Elisha said, Shoot. And he shot. And he said, The arrow of Yahweh's deliverance, and the arrow of deliverance from Syria: for you shall smite the Syrians in Aphek, till you have consumed *them*.

18 And he said, Take the arrows. And he took *them*. And he said to the king of Israel, Smite upon the ground. And he smote three times, and stood.

19 And the man of God was angry with him, and said, You should have smitten five or six times; then had you smitten Syria till you had consumed *it*: whereas now you shall smite Syria *but* three times.

20 ¶ And Elisha died, and they buried him. And the bands of the Moabites invaded the land at the coming in of the year.

21 And it came to pass, as they were burying a man, that, behold, they spied a band *of men*; and they cast the man into the sepulcher of Elisha: and when the man was let down, and touched the bones of Elisha, he revived, and stood up on his feet.

22 But Hazael king of Syria oppressed Israel all the days of Jehoahaz.

23 And Yahweh was gracious to them, and had compassion on them, and had respect unto them, because of his covenant with Abraham, Isaac, and Jacob, and would not destroy them, neither cast he them from his presence as yet.

24 So Hazael king of Syria died; and Benhadad his son reigned in his stead.

25 And Jehoash the son of Jehoahaz took again out of the hand of Benhadad the son of Hazael the cities, which he had taken out of the hand of Jehoahaz his father by war. Three times did Joash beat him, and recovered the cities of Israel.

2 Kings 14

14:1 ¶ In the second year of Joash son of Jehoahaz king of Israel reigned Amaziah the son of Joash king of Judah.

2 He was twenty and five years old when he began to reign, and reigned twenty and nine years in Jerusalem. And his mother's name *was* Jehoaddan of Jerusalem.

3 And he did *that which was* right in the sight of Yahweh, yet not like David his father: he did according to all things as Joash his father did.

4 However the high places were not taken away: as yet the people did sacrifice and burnt incense on the high places.

5 And it came to pass, as soon as the kingdom was confirmed in his hand, that he slew his servants which had slain the king his father.

6 But the children of the murderers he slew not: according to that which is written in the book of the law of Moses, wherein Yahweh commanded, saying, The fathers shall not be put to death for the children, nor the children be put to death for the fathers; but every man shall be put to death for his own sin.

7 He slew of Edom in the valley of salt ten thousand, and took Selah by war, and called the name of it Joktheel unto this day.

8 ¶ Then Amaziah sent messengers to Jehoash, the son of Jehoahaz son of Jehu, king of Israel, saying, Come, let us look one another in the face.

9 And Jehoash the king of Israel sent to Amaziah king of Judah, saying, The thistle that *was* in Lebanon sent to the cedar that *was* in Lebanon, saying, Give your daughter to my son to wife: and there passed by a wild beast that *was* in Lebanon, and trampled down the thistle.

10 You have indeed smitten Edom, and your heart has lifted you up: glory *of this*, and remain at home: for why should you meddle to *your* hurt, that you should fall, *even* you, and Judah with you?

11 But Amaziah would not hear. Therefore Jehoash king of Israel went up; and he and Amaziah king of Judah looked one another in the face at Bethshemesh, which *belongs* to Judah.

12 And Judah was put to the worse before Israel; and they fled every man to their tents.

13 And Jehoash king of Israel took Amaziah king of Judah, the son of Jehoash the son of Ahaziah, at Bethshemesh, and came to Jerusalem, and broke down the wall of Jerusalem from the gate of Ephraim to the corner gate, four hundred cubits.

14 And he took all the gold and silver, and all the vessels that were found in the house of Yahweh, and in the treasuries of the king's house, and hostages, and returned to Samaria.

15 ¶ Now the rest of the acts of Jehoash which he did, and his might, and how he fought with Amaziah king of Judah, are they not written in the book of the chronicles of the kings of Israel?

16 And Jehoash slept with his fathers, and was buried in Samaria with the kings of Israel; and Jeroboam his son reigned in his stead.

17 And Amaziah the son of Joash king of Judah lived after the death of Jehoash son of Jehoahaz king of Israel fifteen years.

18 And the rest of the acts of Amaziah, *are* they not written in the book of the chronicles of the kings of Judah?

19 Now they made a conspiracy against him in Jerusalem: and he fled to Lachish; but they sent after him to Lachish, and slew him there.
20 And they brought him on horses: and he was buried at Jerusalem with his fathers in the city of David.
21 And all the people of Judah took Azariah, which *was* sixteen years old, and made him king instead of his father Amaziah.
22 He built Elath, and restored it to Judah, after that the king slept with his fathers.
23 ¶ In the fifteenth year of Amaziah the son of Joash king of Judah Jeroboam the son of Joash king of Israel began to reign in Samaria, *and reigned for* forty and one years.
24 And he did *that which was* evil in the sight of Yahweh: he departed not from all the sins of Jeroboam the son of Nebat, who made Israel to sin.
25 He restored the coast of Israel from the entering of Hamath to the sea of the plain, according to the word of Yahweh God of Israel, which he spoke by the hand of his servant Jonah, the son of Amittai, the prophet, which *was* of Gathhepher.
26 For Yahweh saw the affliction of Israel, *that it was* very bitter: for *there was* not any shut up, nor any left, nor any helper for Israel.
27 And Yahweh said not that he would blot out the name of Israel from under heaven: but he saved them by the hand of Jeroboam the son of Joash.
28 Now the rest of the acts of Jeroboam, and all that he did, and his might, how he warred, and how he recovered Damascus, and Hamath, *which belonged* to Judah, for Israel, are they not written in the book of the chronicles of the kings of Israel?
29 And Jeroboam slept with his fathers, *even* with the kings of Israel; and Zachariah his son reigned in his stead.

2 Kings 15

15:1 ¶ In the twenty and seventh year of Jeroboam king of Israel began Azariah son of Amaziah king of Judah to reign.
2 Sixteen years old was he when he began to reign, and he reigned two and fifty years in Jerusalem. And his mother's name *was* Jecholiah of Jerusalem.
3 And he did *that which was* right in the sight of Yahweh, according to all that his father Amaziah had done;
4 Save that the high places were not removed: the people sacrificed and burnt incense still on the high places.
5 And Yahweh smote the king, so that he was a leper to the day of his death, and dwelt in a separate house. And Jotham the king's son *was* over the house, judging the people of the land.
6 And the rest of the acts of Azariah, and all that he did, *are* they not written in the book of the chronicles of the kings of Judah?
7 So Azariah slept with his fathers; and they buried him with his fathers in the city of David: and Jotham his son reigned in his stead.

8 ¶ In the thirty and eighth year of Azariah king of Judah did Zachariah the son of Jeroboam reign over Israel in Samaria six months.
9 And he did *that which was* evil in the sight of Yahweh, as his fathers had done: he departed not from the sins of Jeroboam the son of Nebat, who made Israel to sin.
10 And Shallum the son of Jabesh conspired against him, and smote him before the people, and slew him, and reigned in his stead.
11 And the rest of the acts of Zachariah, behold, they *are* written in the book of the chronicles of the kings of Israel.
12 This *was* the word of Yahweh which he spoke to Jehu, saying, Your sons shall sit on the throne of Israel unto the fourth *generation*. And so it came to pass.
13 Shallum the son of Jabesh began to reign in the nine and thirtieth year of Uzziah king of Judah; and he reigned a full month in Samaria.
14 For Menahem the son of Gadi went up from Tirzah, and came to Samaria, and smote Shallum the son of Jabesh in Samaria, and slew him, and reigned in his stead.
15 And the rest of the acts of Shallum, and his conspiracy which he made, behold, they *are* written in the book of the chronicles of the kings of Israel.
16 Then Menahem smote Tiphsah, and all that *were* therein, and the coasts thereof from Tirzah: because they opened not *to him*, therefore he smote *it; and* all the women therein that were with child he ripped up.
17 In the nine and thirtieth year of Azariah king of Judah began Menahem the son of Gadi to reign over Israel, *and reigned* ten years in Samaria.
18 And he did *that which was* evil in the sight of Yahweh: he departed not all his days from the sins of Jeroboam the son of Nebat, who made Israel to sin.
19 *And* Pul the king of Assyria came against the land: and Menahem gave Pul a thousand talents of silver, that his hand might be with him to confirm the kingdom in his hand.
20 And Menahem exacted the money of Israel, *even* of all the mighty men of wealth, of each man fifty shekels of silver, to give to the king of Assyria. So the king of Assyria turned back, and stayed not there in the land.
21 And the rest of the acts of Menahem, and all that he did, *are* they not written in the book of the chronicles of the kings of Israel?
22 And Menahem slept with his fathers; and Pekahiah his son reigned in his stead.
23 In the fiftieth year of Azariah king of Judah, Pekahiah the son of Menahem began to reign over Israel in Samaria, *and reigned* two years.
24 And he did *that which was* evil in the sight of Yahweh: he departed not from the sins of Jeroboam the son of Nebat, who made Israel to sin.
25 But Pekah the son of Remaliah, a captain of his, conspired against him, and smote him in Samaria, in the palace of the king's house, with Argob and Arieh, and with him fifty men of the Gileadites: and he killed him, and reigned in his place.
26 And the rest of the acts of Pekahiah, and all that he did, behold, they *are* written in the book of the chronicles of the kings of Israel.

27 In the two and fiftieth year of Azariah king of Judah, Pekah the son of Remaliah began to reign over Israel in Samaria, *and reigned for* twenty years.

28 And he did *that which was* evil in the sight of Yahweh: he departed not from the sins of Jeroboam the son of Nebat, who made Israel to sin.

29 In the days of Pekah king of Israel came Tiglathpileser king of Assyria, and took Ijon, and Abelbethmaachah, and Janoah, and Kedesh, and Hazor, and Gilead, and Galilee, all the land of Naphtali, and carried them captive to Assyria.

30 And Hoshea the son of Elah made a conspiracy against Pekah the son of Remaliah, and smote him, and slew him, and reigned in his stead, in the twentieth year of Jotham the son of Uzziah.

31 And the rest of the acts of Pekah, and all that he did, behold, they *are* written in the book of the chronicles of the kings of Israel.

32 ¶ In the second year of Pekah the son of Remaliah king of Israel began Jotham the son of Uzziah king of Judah to reign.

33 Five and twenty years old was he when he began to reign, and he reigned sixteen years in Jerusalem. And his mother's name *was* Jerusha, the daughter of Zadok.

34 And he did *that which was* right in the sight of Yahweh: he did according to all that his father Uzziah had done.

35 However the high places were not removed: the people sacrificed and burned incense still in the high places. He built the higher gate of the house of Yahweh.

36 Now the rest of the acts of Jotham, and all that he did, *are* they not written in the book of the chronicles of the kings of Judah?

37 In those days Yahweh began to send against Judah Rezin the king of Syria, and Pekah the son of Remaliah.

38 And Jotham slept with his fathers, and was buried with his fathers in the city of David his father: and Ahaz his son reigned in his stead.

2 Kings 16

16:1 ¶ In the seventeenth year of Pekah the son of Remaliah, Ahaz the son of Jotham king of Judah began to reign.

2 Twenty years old *was* Ahaz when he began to reign, and reigned sixteen years in Jerusalem, and did not *that which was* right in the sight of Yahweh his God, like David his father.

3 But he walked in the way of the kings of Israel, yes, and made his son to pass through the fire, according to the abominations of the heathen, whom Yahweh cast out from before the children of Israel.

4 And he sacrificed and burnt incense in the high places, and on the hills, and under every green tree.

5 ¶ Then Rezin king of Syria and Pekah son of Remaliah king of Israel came up to Jerusalem to war: and they besieged Ahaz, but could not overcome *him*.

6 At that time Rezin king of Syria recovered Elath to Syria, and drove the Jews from Elath: and the Syrians came to Elath, and dwelt there unto this day.

7 So Ahaz sent messengers to Tiglathpileser king of Assyria, saying, I *am* your servant and your son: come up, and save me out of the hand of the king of Syria, and out of the hand of the king of Israel, which rise up against me.

8 And Ahaz took the silver and gold that was found in the house of Yahweh, and in the treasuries of the king's house, and sent *it for* a present to the king of Assyria.

9 And the king of Assyria listened to him: for the king of Assyria went up against Damascus, and took it, and carried *the people of* it captive to Kir, and slew Rezin.

10 ¶ And king Ahaz went to Damascus to meet Tiglathpileser king of Assyria, and saw an altar that *was* at Damascus: and king Ahaz sent to Urijah the priest the fashion of the altar, and the pattern of it, according to all the workmanship thereof.

11 And Urijah the priest built an altar according to all that king Ahaz had sent from Damascus: so Urijah the priest made *it* before king Ahaz came from Damascus.

12 And when the king had come from Damascus, the king saw the altar: and the king approached to the altar, and offered thereon.

13 And he burnt his burnt offering and his meat offering, and poured his drink offering, and sprinkled the blood of his peace offerings, upon the altar.

14 And he brought also the brazen altar, which *was* before Yahweh, from the forefront of the house, from between the altar and the house of Yahweh, and put it on the north side of the altar.

15 And king Ahaz commanded Urijah the priest, saying, Upon the great altar burn the morning burnt offering, and the evening meat offering, and the king's burnt sacrifice, and his meat offering, with the burnt offering of all the people of the land, and their meat offering, and their drink offerings; and sprinkle upon it all the blood of the burnt offering, and all the blood of the sacrifice: and the brazen altar shall be for me to inquire *by*.

16 Thus did Urijah the priest, according to all that king Ahaz commanded.

17 ¶ And king Ahaz cut off the borders of the bases, and removed the lavers from off them; and took down the sea from off the brazen oxen that *were* under it, and put it upon a pavement of stones.

18 And the covert for the sabbath that they had built in the house, and the king's entry outside, turned he from the house of Yahweh for the king of Assyria.

19 Now the rest of the acts of Ahaz which he did, *are* they not written in the book of the chronicles of the kings of Judah?

20 And Ahaz slept with his fathers, and was buried with his fathers in the city of David: and Hezekiah his son reigned in his stead.

2 Kings 17

17:1 ¶ In the twelfth year of Ahaz king of Judah began Hoshea the son of Elah to reign in Samaria over Israel nine years.

2 Kings 17

2 And he did *that which was* evil in the sight of Yahweh, but not as the kings of Israel that were before him.
3 Against him came up Shalmaneser king of Assyria; and Hoshea became his servant, and gave him presents.
4 And the king of Assyria found conspiracy in Hoshea: for he had sent messengers to So, king of Egypt, and brought no present to the king of Assyria, as *he had done* year by year: therefore the king of Assyria shut him up, and bound him in prison.
5 Then the king of Assyria came up throughout all the land, and went up to Samaria, and besieged it *for* three years.
6 In the ninth year of Hoshea the king of Assyria took Samaria, and carried Israel away into Assyria, and placed them in Halah and in Habor *by* the river of Gozan, and in the cities of the Medes.
7 ¶ For *so* it was, that the children of Israel had sinned against Yahweh their God, which had brought them up out of the land of Egypt, from under the hand of Pharaoh king of Egypt, and had feared other gods,
8 And walked in the statutes of the heathen, whom Yahweh cast out from before the children of Israel, and of the kings of Israel, which they had made.
9 And the children of Israel did secretly *those* things that *were* not right against Yahweh their God, and they built them high places in all their cities, from the tower of the watchmen to the fenced city.
10 And they set them up images and groves in every high hill, and under every green tree:
11 And there they burnt incense in all the high places, as *did* the heathen whom Yahweh carried away before them; and worked wicked things to provoke Yahweh to anger:
12 For they served idols, whereof Yahweh had said to them, You shall not do this thing.
13 Yet Yahweh testified against Israel, and against Judah, by all the prophets, *and by* all the seers, saying, Turn you from your evil ways, and keep my commandments *and* my statutes, according to all the law which I commanded your fathers, and which I sent to you by my servants the prophets.
14 Notwithstanding they would not hear, but hardened their necks, like to the neck of their fathers, that did not believe in Yahweh their God.
15 And they rejected his statutes, and his covenant that he made with their fathers, and his testimonies which he testified against them; and they followed vanity, and became vain, and went after the heathen that *were* round about them, *concerning* whom Yahweh had charged them, that they should not do like them.
16 And they left all the commandments of Yahweh their God, and made them molten images, *even* two calves, and made a grove, and worshipped all the host of heaven, and served Baal.
17 And they caused their sons and their daughters to pass through the fire, and used divination and enchantments, and sold themselves to do evil in the sight of Yahweh, to provoke him to anger.
18 Therefore Yahweh was very angry with Israel, and removed them out of his sight: there was none left but the tribe of Judah only.
19 Also Judah kept not the commandments of Yahweh their God, but walked in the statutes of Israel which they made.
20 And Yahweh rejected all the seed of Israel, and afflicted them, and delivered them into the hand of spoilers, until he had cast them out of his sight.
21 For he tore Israel from the house of David; and they made Jeroboam the son of Nebat king: and Jeroboam drove Israel from following Yahweh, and made them sin a great sin.
22 For the children of Israel walked in all the sins of Jeroboam which he did; they departed not from them;
23 Until Yahweh removed Israel out of his sight, as he had said by all his servants the prophets. So was Israel carried away out of their own land to Assyria unto this day.
24 ¶ And the king of Assyria brought *men* from Babylon, and from Cuthah, and from Ava, and from Hamath, and from Sepharvaim, and placed *them* in the cities of Samaria instead of the children of Israel: and they possessed Samaria, and dwelt in the cities thereof.
25 And *so* it was at the beginning of their dwelling there, *that* they feared not Yahweh: therefore Yahweh sent lions among them, which slew *some* of them.
26 Therefore they spoke to the king of Assyria, saying, The nations which you have removed, and placed in the cities of Samaria, know not the manner of the God of the land: therefore he has sent lions among them, and, behold, they slay them, because they know not the manner of the God of the land.
27 Then the king of Assyria commanded, saying, Carry there one of the priests whom you brought from there; and let them go and dwell there, and let him teach them the manner of the God of the land.
28 Then one of the priests whom they had carried away from Samaria came and dwelt in Bethel, and taught them how they should fear Yahweh.
29 However, every nation made gods of their own, and put *them* in the houses of the high places which the Samaritans had made, every nation in their cities wherein they dwelt.
30 And the men of Babylon made Succothbenoth, and the men of Cuth made Nergal, and the men of Hamath made Ashima,
31 And the Avites made Nibhaz and Tartak, and the Sepharvites burnt their children in fire to Adrammelech and Anammelech, the gods of Sepharvaim.
32 So they feared Yahweh, and made unto themselves of the lowest of them priests of the high places, which sacrificed for them in the houses of the high places.
33 They feared Yahweh, and served their own gods, after the manner of the nations whom they carried away from there.
34 Unto this day they do after the former manners: they fear not Yahweh, neither do they after their statutes, or

after their ordinances, or after the law and commandment which Yahweh commanded the children of Jacob, whom he named Israel;
35 With whom Yahweh had made a covenant, and charged them, saying, You shall not fear other gods, nor bow yourselves to them, nor serve them, nor sacrifice to them:
36 But Yahweh, who brought you up out of the land of Egypt with great power and a stretched out arm, him shall you fear, and him shall you worship, and to him shall you do sacrifice.
37 And the statutes, and the ordinances, and the law, and the commandment, which he wrote for you, you shall observe to do forevermore; and you shall not fear other gods.
38 And the covenant that I have made with you you shall not forget; neither shall you fear other gods.
39 But Yahweh your God you shall fear; and he shall deliver you out of the hand of all your enemies.
40 However they did not listen, but they did after their former manner.
41 So these nations feared Yahweh, and served their graven images, both their children, and their children's children: as did their fathers, so do they unto this day.

2 Kings 18

18:1 ¶ Now it came to pass in the third year of Hoshea son of Elah king of Israel, *that* Hezekiah the son of Ahaz king of Judah began to reign.
2 Twenty and five years old was he when he began to reign; and he reigned twenty and nine years in Jerusalem. His mother's name also *was* Abi, the daughter of Zachariah.
3 And he did *that which was* right in the sight of Yahweh, according to all that David his father did.
4 He removed the high places, and broke the images, and cut down the groves, and broke in pieces the brazen serpent that Moses had made: for unto those days the children of Israel did burn incense to it: and he called it Nehushtan.
5 He trusted in Yahweh God of Israel; so that after him was none like him among all the kings of Judah, nor *any* that were before him.
6 For he clung to Yahweh, *and* departed not from following him, but kept his commandments, which Yahweh commanded Moses.
7 And Yahweh was with him; *and* he prospered wherever he went forth: and he rebelled against the king of Assyria, and served him not.
8 He smote the Philistines, *even* unto Gaza, and the borders thereof, from the tower of the watchmen to the fenced city.
9 ¶ And it came to pass in the fourth year of king Hezekiah, which *was* the seventh year of Hoshea son of Elah king of Israel, *that* Shalmaneser king of Assyria came up against Samaria, and besieged it.
10 And at the end of three years they took it: *even* in the sixth year of Hezekiah, that *is* the ninth year of Hoshea king of Israel, Samaria was taken.
11 And the king of Assyria did carry away Israel to Assyria, and put them in Halah and in Habor *by* the river of Gozan, and in the cities of the Medes:
12 Because they obeyed not the voice of Yahweh their God, but transgressed his covenant, *and* all that Moses the servant of Yahweh commanded, and would not hear *them*, nor do *them*.
13 Now in the fourteenth year of king Hezekiah did Sennacherib king of Assyria come up against all the fenced cities of Judah, and took them.
14 And Hezekiah king of Judah sent to the king of Assyria to Lachish, saying, I have offended; return from me: that which you put on me will I bear. And the king of Assyria appointed to Hezekiah king of Judah three hundred talents of silver and thirty talents of gold.
15 And Hezekiah gave *him* all the silver that was found in the house of Yahweh, and in the treasuries of the king's house.
16 At that time did Hezekiah cut off *the gold from* the doors of the temple of Yahweh, and *from* the pillars which Hezekiah king of Judah had overlaid, and gave it to the king of Assyria.
17 ¶ And the king of Assyria sent Tartan and Rabsaris and Rabshakeh from Lachish to king Hezekiah with a great host against Jerusalem. And they went up and came to Jerusalem. And when they had come up, they came and stood by the conduit of the upper pool, which *is* in the highway of the fuller's field.
18 And when they had called to the king, there came out to them Eliakim the son of Hilkiah, which *was* over the household, and Shebna the scribe, and Joah the son of Asaph the recorder.
19 And Rabshakeh said to them, Speak you now to Hezekiah, Thus says the great king, the king of Assyria, What confidence *is* this wherein you trust?
20 You say, (but *they are but* vain words,) *I have* counsel and strength for the war. Now on whom do you trust, that you rebel against me?
21 Now, behold, you trust upon the staff of this bruised reed, *even* upon Egypt, on which if a man leans, it will go into his hand, and pierce it: so *is* Pharaoh king of Egypt to all that trust on him.
22 But if you say to me, We trust in Yahweh our God: *is* not that he, whose high places and whose altars Hezekiah has taken away, and has said to Judah and Jerusalem, You shall worship before this altar in Jerusalem?
23 Now therefore, I pray you, give pledges to my lord the king of Assyria, and I will deliver you two thousand horses, if you are able on your part to set riders upon them.
24 How then will you turn away the face of one captain of the least of my master's servants, and put your trust on Egypt for chariots and for horsemen?
25 Have I now come up without Yahweh against this place to destroy it? Yahweh said to me, Go up against this land, and destroy it.
26 Then said Eliakim the son of Hilkiah, and Shebna, and Joah, to Rabshakeh, Speak, I pray you, to your servants in the Syrian language; for we understand *it*: and talk not with us in the Jews' language in the ears of the people that *are* on the wall.

2 Kings 18

27 But Rabshakeh said to them, Has my master sent me to your master, and to you, to speak these words? *has he* not *sent me* to the men which sit on the wall, that they may eat their own dung, and drink their own urine with you?

28 Then Rabshakeh stood and cried with a loud voice in the Jews' language, and spoke, saying, Hear the word of the great king, the king of Assyria:

29 Thus says the king, Let not Hezekiah deceive you: for he shall not be able to deliver you out of his hand:

30 Neither let Hezekiah make you trust in Yahweh, saying, Yahweh will surely deliver us, and this city shall not be delivered into the hand of the king of Assyria.

31 Listen not to Hezekiah: for thus says the king of Assyria, Make *an agreement* with me by a present, and come out to me, and *then* eat you every man of his own vine, and every one of his fig tree, and drink you every one the waters of his cistern:

32 Until I come and take you away to a land like your own land, a land of corn and *new* wine, a land of bread and vineyards, a land of olive oil and of honey, that you may live, and not die: and listen not to Hezekiah, when he persuades you, saying, Yahweh will deliver us.

33 Has any of the gods of the nations delivered at all his land out of the hand of the king of Assyria?

34 Where *are* the gods of Hamath, and of Arpad? where *are* the gods of Sepharvaim, Hena, and Ivah? have they delivered Samaria out of my hand?

35 Who *are* they among all the gods of the countries, that have delivered their country out of my hand, that Yahweh should deliver Jerusalem out of my hand?

36 But the people held their peace, and answered him not a word: for the king's commandment was, saying, Answer him not.

37 Then came Eliakim the son of Hilkiah, which *was* over the household, and Shebna the scribe, and Joah the son of Asaph the recorder, to Hezekiah with *their* clothes torn, and told him the words of Rabshakeh.

2 Kings 19

19:1 ¶ And it came to pass, when king Hezekiah heard *it*, that he tore his clothes, and covered himself with sackcloth, and went into the house of Yahweh.

2 And he sent Eliakim, which *was* over the household, and Shebna the scribe, and the elders of the priests, covered with sackcloth, to Isaiah the prophet the son of Amoz.

3 And they said to him, Thus says Hezekiah, This day *is* a day of trouble, and of rebuke, and blasphemy: for the children have come to the birth, and *there is* not strength to bring forth.

4 It may be Yahweh your God will hear all the words of Rabshakeh, whom the king of Assyria his master has sent to reproach the living God; and will reprove the words which Yahweh your God has heard: therefore lift up *your* prayer for the remnant that are left.

5 So the servants of king Hezekiah came to Isaiah.

6 And Isaiah said to them, Thus shall you say to your master, Thus says Yahweh, Be not afraid of the words which you have heard, with which the servants of the king of Assyria have blasphemed me.

7 Behold, I will send a spirit upon him, and he shall hear a rumor, and shall return to his own land; and I will cause him to fall by the sword in his own land.

8 ¶ So Rabshakeh returned, and found the king of Assyria warring against Libnah: for he had heard that he had departed from Lachish.

9 And when he heard say of Tirhakah king of Ethiopia, Behold, he has come out to fight against you: he sent messengers again to Hezekiah, saying,

10 Thus shall you speak to Hezekiah king of Judah, saying, Let not your God in whom you trust deceive you, saying, Jerusalem shall not be delivered into the hand of the king of Assyria.

11 Behold, you have heard what the kings of Assyria have done to all lands, by destroying them utterly: and shall you be delivered?

12 Have the gods of the nations delivered them which my fathers have destroyed; *as* Gozan, and Haran, and Rezeph, and the children of Eden which *were* in Thelasar?

13 Where *is* the king of Hamath, and the king of Arpad, and the king of the city of Sepharvaim, of Hena, and Ivah?

14 And Hezekiah received the letter from the hand of the messengers, and read it: and Hezekiah went up into the house of Yahweh, and spread it before Yahweh.

15 And Hezekiah prayed before Yahweh, and said, O Yahweh God of Israel, which dwell *between* the cherubims, you are the God, *even* you alone, of all the kingdoms of the earth; you have made heaven and earth.

16 Yahweh, bow down your ear, and hear: open, Yahweh, your eyes, and see: and hear the words of Sennacherib, which has sent him to reproach the living God.

17 Of a truth, Yahweh, the kings of Assyria have destroyed the nations and their lands,

18 And have cast their gods into the fire: for they *were* no gods, but the work of men's hands, wood and stone: therefore they have destroyed them.

19 Now therefore, O Yahweh our God, I beseech you, save you us out of his hand, that all the kingdoms of the earth may know that you *are* Yahweh God, *even* you only.

20 ¶ Then Isaiah the son of Amoz sent to Hezekiah, saying, Thus says Yahweh God of Israel, *That* which you have prayed to me against Sennacherib king of Assyria I have heard.

21 This *is* the word that Yahweh has spoken concerning him; The virgin the daughter of Zion has despised you, *and* laughed you to scorn; the daughter of Jerusalem has shaken her head at you.

22 Whom have you reproached and blasphemed? and against whom have you exalted *your* voice, and lifted up your eyes on high? *even* against the Holy *One* of Israel.

23 By your messengers you have reproached the Lord, and have said, With the multitude of my chariots I have come up

to the height of the mountains, to the sides of Lebanon, and will cut down the tall cedar trees thereof, *and* the choice fir trees thereof: and I will enter into the lodgings of his borders, *and into* the forest of his Carmel.

24 I have dug and drank strange waters, and with the sole of my feet have I dried up all the rivers of besieged places.

25 Have you not heard long ago *how* I have done it, *and* of ancient times that I have formed it? now have I brought it to pass, that you should be to lay waste fenced cities *into* ruinous heaps.

26 Therefore their inhabitants were of small power, they were dismayed and confounded; they were *as* the grass of the field, and *as* the green herb, *as* the grass on the housetops, and *as corn* blighted before it is grown up.

27 But I know your dwelling, and your going out, and your coming in, and your rage against me.

28 Because your rage against me and your tumult have come up into my ears, therefore I will put my hook in your nose, and my bridle in your lips, and I will turn you back by the way by which you came.

29 And this *shall be* a sign to you, You shall eat this year such things as grow of themselves, and in the second year that which springs of the same; and in the third year sow you, and reap, and plant vineyards, and eat the fruits thereof.

30 And the remnant that has escaped of the house of Judah shall yet again take root downward, and bear fruit upward.

31 For out of Jerusalem shall go forth a remnant, and they that escape out of mount Zion: the zeal of Yahweh *of hosts* shall do this.

32 Therefore thus says Yahweh concerning the king of Assyria, He shall not come into this city, nor shoot an arrow there, nor come before it with shield, nor cast a bank against it.

33 By the way that he came, by the same shall he return, and shall not come into this city, says Yahweh.

34 For I will defend this city, to save it, for my own sake, and for my servant David's sake.

35 ¶ And it came to pass that night, that the angel of Yahweh went out, and smote in the camp of the Assyrians a hundred fourscore and five thousand: and when they arose early in the morning, behold, they *were* all dead corpses.

36 So Sennacherib king of Assyria departed, and went and returned, and dwelt at Nineveh.

37 And it came to pass, as he was worshipping in the house of Nisroch his god, that Adrammelech and Sharezer his sons smote him with the sword: and they escaped into the land of Armenia. And Esarhaddon his son reigned in his stead.

2 Kings 20

20:1 ¶ In those days was Hezekiah sick unto death. And the prophet Isaiah the son of Amoz came to him, and said to him, Thus says Yahweh, Set your house in order; for you shall die, and not live.

2 Then he turned his face to the wall, and prayed unto Yahweh, saying,

3 I beseech you, O Yahweh, remember now how I have walked before you in truth and with a perfect heart, and have done *that which is* good in your sight. And Hezekiah wept greatly.

4 And it came to pass, before Isaiah had gone out into the middle court, that the word of Yahweh came to him, saying,

5 Turn again, and tell Hezekiah the captain of my people, Thus says Yahweh, the God of David your father, I have heard your prayer, I have seen your tears: behold, I will heal you: on the third day you shall go up to the house of Yahweh.

6 And I will add to your days fifteen years; and I will deliver you and this city out of the hand of the king of Assyria; and I will defend this city for my own sake, and for my servant David's sake.

7 And Isaiah said, Take a lump of figs. And they took and laid *it* on the boil, and he recovered.

8 And Hezekiah said to Isaiah, What *shall be* the sign that Yahweh will heal me, and that I shall go up into the house of Yahweh the third day?

9 And Isaiah said, This sign shall you have of Yahweh, that Yahweh will do the thing that he has spoken: shall the shadow go forward ten degrees, or go back ten degrees?

10 And Hezekiah answered, It is a light thing for the shadow to go down ten degrees: no, but let the shadow return backward ten degrees.

11 And Isaiah the prophet cried unto Yahweh: and he brought the shadow ten degrees backward, by which it had gone down in the dial of Ahaz.

12 ¶ At that time Berodachbaladan, the son of Baladan, king of Babylon, sent letters and a present to Hezekiah: for he had heard that Hezekiah had been sick.

13 And Hezekiah listened to them, and showed them all the house of his precious things, the silver, and the gold, and the spices, and the precious ointment, and *all* the house of his armor, and all that was found in his treasures: there was nothing in his house, nor in all his dominion, that Hezekiah showed them not.

14 Then came Isaiah the prophet to king Hezekiah, and said to him, What said these men? and from where came they to you? And Hezekiah said, They have come from a far country, *even* from Babylon.

15 And he said, What have they seen in your house? And Hezekiah answered, All *the things* that *are* in my house have they seen: there is nothing among my treasures that I have not shown them.

16 And Isaiah said to Hezekiah, Hear the word of Yahweh.

17 Behold, the days come, that all that *is* in your house, and that which your fathers have laid up in store unto this day, shall be carried into Babylon: nothing shall be left, says Yahweh.

18 And of your sons that shall issue from you, which you shall beget, shall they take away; and they shall be eunuchs in the palace of the king of Babylon.

19 Then said Hezekiah to Isaiah, Good *is* the word of Yahweh which you have spoken. And he said, *Is it* not *good*, if peace and truth be in my days?
20 And the rest of the acts of Hezekiah, and all his might, and how he made a pool, and a conduit, and brought water into the city, *are* they not written in the book of the chronicles of the kings of Judah?
21 And Hezekiah slept with his fathers: and Manasseh his son reigned in his stead.

2 Kings 21

21:1 ¶ Manasseh *was* twelve years old when he began to reign, and reigned fifty and five years in Jerusalem. And his mother's name *was* Hephzibah.
2 And he did *that which was* evil in the sight of Yahweh, after the abominations of the heathen, whom Yahweh cast out before the children of Israel.
3 For he built up again the high places which Hezekiah his father had destroyed; and he reared up altars for Baal, and made a grove, as did Ahab king of Israel; and worshipped all the host of heaven, and served them.
4 And he built altars in the house of Yahweh, of which Yahweh said, In Jerusalem will I put my name.
5 And he built altars for all the host of heaven in the two courts of the house of Yahweh.
6 And he made his son pass through the fire, and observed times, and used enchantments, and dealt with familiar spirits and wizards: he worked much wickedness in the sight of Yahweh, to provoke *him* to anger.
7 And he set a graven image of the grove that he had made in the house, of which Yahweh said to David, and to Solomon his son, In this house, and in Jerusalem, which I have chosen out of all tribes of Israel, will I put my name forever:
8 Neither will I make the feet of Israel move any more out of the land which I gave their fathers; only if they will observe to do according to all that I have commanded them, and according to all the law that my servant Moses commanded them.
9 But they listened not: and Manasseh seduced them to do more evil than did the nations whom Yahweh destroyed before the children of Israel.
10 ¶ And Yahweh spoke by his servants the prophets, saying,
11 Because Manasseh king of Judah has done these abominations, *and* has done wickedly above all that the Amorites did, which *were* before him, and has made Judah also to sin with his idols:
12 Therefore thus says Yahweh God of Israel, Behold, I *am* bringing *such* evil upon Jerusalem and Judah, that whoever hears of it, both his ears shall tingle.
13 And I will stretch over Jerusalem the line of Samaria, and the plummet of the house of Ahab: and I will wipe Jerusalem as *a man* wipes a dish, wiping *it*, and turning *it* upside down.
14 And I will forsake the remnant of my inheritance, and deliver them into the hand of their enemies; and they shall become a prey and a spoil to all their enemies;
15 Because they have done *that which was* evil in my sight, and have provoked me to anger, since the day their fathers came forth out of Egypt, even unto this day.
16 Moreover Manasseh shed innocent blood very much, till he had filled Jerusalem from one end to another; besides his sin with which he made Judah to sin, in doing *that which was* evil in the sight of Yahweh.
17 Now the rest of the acts of Manasseh, and all that he did, and his sin that he sinned, *are* they not written in the book of the chronicles of the kings of Judah?
18 And Manasseh slept with his fathers, and was buried in the garden of his own house, in the garden of Uzza: and Amon his son reigned in his stead.
19 ¶ Amon *was* twenty and two years old when he began to reign, and he reigned two years in Jerusalem. And his mother's name *was* Meshullemeth, the daughter of Haruz of Jotbah.
20 And he did *that which was* evil in the sight of Yahweh, as his father Manasseh did.
21 And he walked in all the way that his father walked in, and served the idols that his father served, and worshipped them:
22 And he forsook Yahweh God of his fathers, and walked not in the way of Yahweh.
23 And the servants of Amon conspired against him, and slew the king in his own house.
24 And the people of the land slew all them that had conspired against king Amon; and the people of the land made Josiah his son king in his stead.
25 Now the rest of the acts of Amon which he did, *are* they not written in the book of the chronicles of the kings of Judah?
26 And he was buried in his sepulcher in the garden of Uzza: and Josiah his son reigned in his stead.

2 Kings 22

22:1 ¶ Josiah *was* eight years old when he began to reign, and he reigned thirty and one years in Jerusalem. And his mother's name *was* Jedidah, the daughter of Adaiah of Boscath.
2 And he did *that which was* right in the sight of Yahweh, and walked in all the way of David his father, and turned not aside to the right hand or to the left.
3 And it came to pass in the eighteenth year of king Josiah, *that* the king sent Shaphan the son of Azaliah, the son of Meshullam, the scribe, to the house of Yahweh, saying,
4 Go up to Hilkiah the high priest, that he may sum the silver which is brought into the house of Yahweh, which the keepers of the door have gathered of the people:
5 And let them deliver it into the hand of the doers of the work, that have the oversight of the house of Yahweh: and let them give it to the doers of the work which *is* in the house of Yahweh, to repair the breaches of the house,
6 Unto carpenters, and builders, and masons, and to buy timber and hewn stone to repair the house.

7 However there was no reckoning made with them of the money that was delivered into their hand, because they dealt faithfully.

8 And Hilkiah the high priest said to Shaphan the scribe, I have found the book of the law in the house of Yahweh. And Hilkiah gave the book to Shaphan, and he read it.

9 And Shaphan the scribe came to the king, and brought the king word again, and said, Your servants have gathered the money that was found in the house, and have delivered it into the hand of them that do the work, that have the oversight of the house of Yahweh.

10 And Shaphan the scribe showed the king, saying, Hilkiah the priest has delivered me a book. And Shaphan read it before the king.

11 ¶ And it came to pass, when the king had heard the words of the book of the law, that he tore his clothes.

12 And the king commanded Hilkiah the priest, and Ahikam the son of Shaphan, and Achbor the son of Michaiah, and Shaphan the scribe, and Asahiah a servant of the king's, saying,

13 Go you, inquire of Yahweh for me, and for the people, and for all Judah, concerning the words of this book that is found: for great *is* the wrath of Yahweh that is kindled against us, because our fathers have not listened to the words of this book, to do according to all that which is written concerning us.

14 So Hilkiah the priest, and Ahikam, and Achbor, and Shaphan, and Asahiah, went to Huldah the prophetess, the wife of Shallum the son of Tikvah, the son of Harhas, keeper of the wardrobe; (now she dwelt in Jerusalem in the college;) and they communed with her.

15 And she said to them, Thus says Yahweh God of Israel, Tell the man that sent you to me,

16 Thus says Yahweh, Behold, I will bring evil upon this place, and upon the inhabitants thereof, *even* all the words of the book which the king of Judah has read:

17 Because they have forsaken me, and have burned incense to other gods, that they might provoke me to anger with all the works of their hands; therefore my wrath shall be kindled against this place, and shall not be quenched.

18 But to the king of Judah which sent you to inquire of Yahweh, thus shall you say to him, Thus says Yahweh God of Israel, *As touching* the words which you have heard;

19 Because your heart was tender, and you have humbled yourself before Yahweh, when you heard what I spoke against this place, and against the inhabitants thereof, that they should become a desolation and a curse, and have torn your clothes, and wept before me; I also have heard *you*, says Yahweh.

20 Behold therefore, I will gather you to your fathers, and you shall be gathered into your grave in peace; and your eyes shall not see all the evil which I will bring upon this place. And they brought the king word again.

2 Kings 23

23:1 ¶ And the king sent, and they gathered to him all the elders of Judah and of Jerusalem.

2 And the king went up into the house of Yahweh, and all the men of Judah and all the inhabitants of Jerusalem with him, and the priests, and the prophets, and all the people, both small and great: and he read in their ears all the words of the book of the covenant which was found in the house of Yahweh.

3 And the king stood by a pillar, and made a covenant before Yahweh, to walk after Yahweh, and to keep his commandments and his testimonies and his statutes with all *their* heart and all *their* soul, to perform the words of this covenant that were written in this book. And all the people stood to the covenant.

4 ¶ And the king commanded Hilkiah the high priest, and the priests of the second order, and the keepers of the door, to bring forth out of the temple of Yahweh all the vessels that were made for Baal, and for the grove, and for all the host of heaven: and he burned them outside Jerusalem in the fields of Kidron, and carried the ashes of them to Bethel.

5 And he put down the idolatrous priests, whom the kings of Judah had ordained to burn incense in the high places in the cities of Judah, and in the places round about Jerusalem; them also that burned incense to Baal, to the sun, and to the moon, and to the planets, and to all the host of heaven.

6 And he brought out the grove from the house of Yahweh, outside Jerusalem, to the brook Kidron, and burned it at the brook Kidron, and stamped *it* small to powder, and cast the powder thereof upon the graves of the children of the people.

7 And he broke down the houses of the sodomites, that *were* by the house of Yahweh, where the women wove hangings for the grove.

8 And he brought all the priests out of the cities of Judah, and defiled the high places where the priests had burned incense, from Geba to Beersheba, and broke down the high places of the gates that *were* in the entering in of the gate of Joshua the governor of the city, which *were* on a man's left hand at the gate of the city.

9 Nevertheless the priests of the high places came not up to the altar of Yahweh in Jerusalem, but they did eat of the unleavened bread among their brethren.

10 And he defiled Topheth, which *is* in the valley of the children of Hinnom, that no man might make his son or his daughter to pass through the fire to Molech.

11 And he took away the horses that the kings of Judah had given to the sun, at the entering in of the house of Yahweh, by the chamber of Nathanmelech the chamberlain, which *was* in the suburbs, and burned the chariots of the sun with fire.

12 And the altars that *were* on the top of the upper chamber of Ahaz, which the kings of Judah had made, and the altars which Manasseh had made in the two courts of the house of Yahweh, did the king beat down,

and broke *them* down from there, and cast the dust of them into the brook Kidron.

13 And the high places that *were* before Jerusalem, which *were* on the right hand of the mount of corruption, which Solomon the king of Israel had built for Ashtoreth the abomination of the Zidonians, and for Chemosh the abomination of the Moabites, and for Milcom the abomination of the children of Ammon, did the king defile.

14 And he broke in pieces the images, and cut down the groves, and filled their places with the bones of men.

15 Moreover the altar that *was* at Bethel, *and* the high place which Jeroboam the son of Nebat, who made Israel to sin, had made, both that altar and the high place he broke down, and burned the high place, *and* stamped *it* small to powder, and burned the grove.

16 And as Josiah turned himself, he spied the sepulchers that *were* there in the mount, and sent, and took the bones out of the sepulchers, and burned *them* upon the altar, and polluted it, according to the word of Yahweh which the man of God proclaimed, who proclaimed these words.

17 Then he said, What title *is* that that I see? And the men of the city told him, *It is* the sepulcher of the man of God, which came from Judah, and proclaimed these things that you have done against the altar of Bethel.

18 And he said, Let him alone; let no man move his bones. So they let his bones alone, with the bones of the prophet that came out of Samaria.

19 And all the houses also of the high places that *were* in the cities of Samaria, which the kings of Israel had made to provoke *Yahweh* to anger, Josiah took away, and did to them according to all the acts that he had done in Bethel.

20 And he slew all the priests of the high places that *were* there upon the altars, and burned men's bones upon them, and returned to Jerusalem.

21 And the king commanded all the people, saying, Keep the passover unto Yahweh your God, as *it is* written in the book of this covenant.

22 Surely there was not held such a passover from the days of the judges that judged Israel, nor in all the days of the kings of Israel, nor of the kings of Judah;

23 But in the eighteenth year of king Josiah, *wherein* this passover was held to Yahweh in Jerusalem.

24 Moreover the *workers with* familiar spirits, and the wizards, and the images, and the idols, and all the abominations that were spied in the land of Judah and in Jerusalem, did Josiah put away, that he might perform the words of the law which were written in the book that Hilkiah the priest found in the house of Yahweh.

25 ¶ And like unto him was there no king before him, that turned to Yahweh with all his heart, and with all his soul, and with all his might, according to all the law of Moses; neither after him arose there *any* like him.

26 Notwithstanding Yahweh turned not from the fierceness of his great wrath, with which his anger was kindled against Judah, because of all the provocations that Manasseh had provoked him therewith.

27 And Yahweh said, I will remove Judah also out of my sight, as I have removed Israel, and will cast off this city Jerusalem which I have chosen, and the house of which I said, My name shall be there.

28 Now the rest of the acts of Josiah, and all that he did, *are* they not written in the book of the chronicles of the kings of Judah?

29 In his days Pharaohnechoh king of Egypt went up against the king of Assyria to the river Euphrates: and king Josiah went against him; and he slew him at Megiddo, when he had seen him.

30 And his servants carried him in a chariot dead from Megiddo, and brought him to Jerusalem, and buried him in his own sepulcher. And the people of the land took Jehoahaz the son of Josiah, and anointed him, and made him king in his father's stead.

31 ¶ Jehoahaz *was* twenty and three years old when he began to reign; and he reigned three months in Jerusalem. And his mother's name *was* Hamutal, the daughter of Jeremiah of Libnah.

32 And he did *that which was* evil in the sight of Yahweh, according to all that his fathers had done.

33 And Pharaohnechoh put him in bands at Riblah in the land of Hamath, that he might not reign in Jerusalem; and put the land to a tribute of a hundred talents of silver, and a talent of gold.

34 And Pharaohnechoh made Eliakim the son of Josiah king in the place of Josiah his father, and changed his name to Jehoiakim, and took Jehoahaz away: and he came to Egypt, and died there.

35 And Jehoiakim gave the silver and the gold to Pharaoh; but he taxed the land to give the money according to the commandment of Pharaoh: he exacted the silver and the gold from the people of the land, from every one according to his taxation, to give *it* to Pharaohnechoh.

36 Jehoiakim *was* twenty and five years old when he began to reign; and he reigned eleven years in Jerusalem. And his mother's name *was* Zebudah, the daughter of Pedaiah of Rumah.

37 And he did *that which was* evil in the sight of Yahweh, according to all that his fathers had done.

2 Kings 24

24:1 ¶ In his days Nebuchadnezzar king of Babylon came up, and Jehoiakim became his servant *for* three years: then he turned and rebelled against him.

2 And Yahweh sent against him bands of the Chaldees, and bands of the Syrians, and bands of the Moabites, and bands of the children of Ammon, and sent them against Judah to destroy it, according to the word of Yahweh, which he spoke by his servants the prophets.

3 Surely at the commandment of Yahweh came *this* upon Judah, to remove *them* out of his sight, for the sins of Manasseh, according to all that he did;

4 And also for the innocent blood that he shed: for he filled Jerusalem with innocent blood; which Yahweh would not pardon.

5 Now the rest of the acts of Jehoiakim, and all that he did, *are* they not written in the book of the chronicles of the kings of Judah?

6 So Jehoiakim slept with his fathers: and Jehoiachin his son reigned in his stead.

7 And the king of Egypt came not again any more out of his land: for the king of Babylon had taken from the river of Egypt to the river Euphrates all that pertained to the king of Egypt.

8 ¶ Jehoiachin *was* eighteen years old when he began to reign, and he reigned in Jerusalem three months. And his mother's name *was* Nehushta, the daughter of Elnathan of Jerusalem.

9 And he did *that which was* evil in the sight of Yahweh, according to all that his father had done.

10 At that time the servants of Nebuchadnezzar king of Babylon came up against Jerusalem, and the city was besieged.

11 And Nebuchadnezzar king of Babylon came against the city, and his servants did besiege it.

12 And Jehoiachin the king of Judah went out to the king of Babylon, he, and his mother, and his servants, and his princes, and his officers: and the king of Babylon took him in the eighth year of his reign.

13 And he carried out *from* there all the treasures of the house of Yahweh, and the treasures of the king's house, and cut in pieces all the vessels of gold which Solomon king of Israel had made in the temple of Yahweh, as Yahweh had said.

14 And he carried away all Jerusalem, and all the princes, and all the mighty men of valor, *even* ten thousand captives, and all the craftsmen and smiths: none remained, save the poorest sort of the people of the land.

15 And he carried away Jehoiachin to Babylon, and the king's mother, and the king's wives, and his officers, and the mighty of the land, *those* carried he into captivity from Jerusalem to Babylon.

16 And all the men of might, *even* seven thousand, and craftsmen and smiths a thousand, all *that were* strong *and* apt for war, even them the king of Babylon brought captive to Babylon.

17 And the king of Babylon made Mattaniah his father's brother king in his stead, and changed his name to Zedekiah.

18 Zedekiah *was* twenty and one years old when he began to reign, and he reigned eleven years in Jerusalem. And his mother's name *was* Hamutal, the daughter of Jeremiah of Libnah.

19 And he did *that which was* evil in the sight of Yahweh, according to all that Jehoiakim had done.

20 For through the anger of Yahweh it came to pass in Jerusalem and Judah, until he had cast them out from his presence, that Zedekiah rebelled against the king of Babylon.

2 Kings 25

25:1 ¶ And it came to pass in the ninth year of his reign, in the tenth month, in the tenth *day* of the month, *that* Nebuchadnezzar king of Babylon came, he, and all his host, against Jerusalem, and pitched against it; and they built forts against it round about.

2 And the city was besieged unto the eleventh year of king Zedekiah.

3 And on the ninth *day* of the *fourth* month the famine prevailed in the city, and there was no bread for the people of the land.

4 And the city was broken up, and all the men of war *fled* by night by the way of the gate between two walls, which *is* by the king's garden: (now the Chaldees *were* against the city round about:) and *the king* went the way toward the plain.

5 And the army of the Chaldees pursued after the king, and overtook him in the plains of Jericho: and all his army was scattered from him.

6 So they took the king, and brought him up to the king of Babylon to Riblah; and they gave judgment upon him.

7 And they slew the sons of Zedekiah before his eyes, and put out the eyes of Zedekiah, and bound him with fetters of brass, and carried him to Babylon.

8 ¶ And in the fifth month, on the seventh *day* of the month, which *is* the nineteenth year of king Nebuchadnezzar king of Babylon, came Nebuzaradan, captain of the guard, a servant of the king of Babylon, to Jerusalem:

9 And he burnt the house of Yahweh, and the king's house, and all the houses of Jerusalem, and every great *man's* house burnt he with fire.

10 And all the army of the Chaldees, that *were with* the captain of the guard, broke down the walls of Jerusalem round about.

11 Now the rest of the people *that were* left in the city, and the fugitives that fell away to the king of Babylon, with the remnant of the multitude, did Nebuzaradan the captain of the guard carry away.

12 But the captain of the guard left of the poor of the land *to be* vine dressers and husbandmen.

13 And the pillars of brass that *were* in the house of Yahweh, and the bases, and the brazen sea that *was* in the house of Yahweh, did the Chaldees break in pieces, and carried the brass of them to Babylon.

14 And the pots, and the shovels, and the snuffers, and the spoons, and all the vessels of brass with which they ministered, took they away.

15 And the firepans, and the bowls, *and* such things as *were* of gold, *in* gold, and of silver, *in* silver, the captain of the guard took away.

16 The two pillars, one sea, and the bases which Solomon had made for the house of Yahweh; the brass of all these vessels was without weight.

17 The height of the one pillar *was* eighteen cubits, and the capital upon it *was* brass: and the height of the capital three cubits; and the wreathen work, and pomegranates upon the capital round about, all of brass: and like unto these had the second pillar with wreathen work.

18 And the captain of the guard took Seraiah the chief priest, and Zephaniah the second priest, and the three keepers of the door:
19 And out of the city he took an officer that was set over the men of war, and five men of them that were in the king's presence, which were found in the city, and the principal scribe of the host, which mustered the people of the land, and threescore men of the people of the land *that were* found in the city:
20 And Nebuzaradan captain of the guard took these, and brought them to the king of Babylon to Riblah:
21 And the king of Babylon smote them, and slew them at Riblah in the land of Hamath. So Judah was carried away out of their land.
22 ¶ And *as for* the people that remained in the land of Judah, whom Nebuchadnezzar king of Babylon had left, even over them he made Gedaliah the son of Ahikam, the son of Shaphan, ruler.
23 And when all the captains of the armies, they and their men, heard that the king of Babylon had made Gedaliah governor, there came to Gedaliah to Mizpah, even Ishmael the son of Nethaniah, and Johanan the son of Careah, and Seraiah the son of Tanhumeth the Netophathite, and Jaazaniah the son of a Maachathite, they and their men.
24 And Gedaliah swore to them, and to their men, and said to them, Fear not to be the servants of the Chaldees: dwell in the land, and serve the king of Babylon; and it shall be well with you.
25 But it came to pass in the seventh month, that Ishmael the son of Nethaniah, the son of Elishama, of the seed royal, came, and ten men with him, and smote Gedaliah, that he died, and the Jews and the Chaldees that were with him at Mizpah.
26 And all the people, both small and great, and the captains of the armies, arose, and came to Egypt: for they were afraid of the Chaldees.
27 And it came to pass in the seven and thirtieth year of the captivity of Jehoiachin king of Judah, in the twelfth month, on the seven and twentieth *day* of the month, *that* Evilmerodach king of Babylon in the year that he began to reign did lift up the head of Jehoiachin king of Judah out of prison;
28 And he spoke kindly to him, and set his throne above the throne of the kings that *were* with him in Babylon;
29 And changed his prison garments: and he did eat bread continually before him all the days of his life.
30 And his allowance *was* a continual allowance given *to* him by the king, a daily rate for every day, all the days of his life.

1 Chronicles

1 Chronicles 1

1:1 ¶ Adam, Sheth, Enosh,
2 Kenan, Mahalaleel, Jered,
3 Henoch, Methuselah, Lamech,
4 Noah, Shem, Ham, and Japheth.
5 The sons of Japheth; Gomer, and Magog, and Madai, and Javan, and Tubal, and Meshech, and Tiras.
6 And the sons of Gomer; Ashchenaz, and Riphath, and Togarmah.
7 And the sons of Javan; Elishah, and Tarshish, Kittim, and Dodanim.
8 The sons of Ham; Cush, and Mizraim, Put, and Canaan.
9 And the sons of Cush; Seba, and Havilah, and Sabta, and Raamah, and Sabtecha. And the sons of Raamah; Sheba, and Dedan.
10 And Cush begot Nimrod: he began to be mighty upon the earth.
11 And Mizraim begot Ludim, and Anamim, and Lehabim, and Naphtuhim,
12 And Pathrusim, and Casluhim, (of whom came the Philistines,) and Caphthorim.
13 And Canaan begot Zidon his firstborn, and Heth,
14 The Jebusite also, and the Amorite, and the Girgashite,
15 And the Hivite, and the Arkite, and the Sinite,
16 And the Arvadite, and the Zemarite, and the Hamathite.
17 The sons of Shem; Elam, and Asshur, and Arphaxad, and Lud, and Aram, and Uz, and Hul, and Gether, and Meshech.
18 And Arphaxad begot Shelah, and Shelah begot Eber.
19 And to Eber were born two sons: the name of the one *was* Peleg; because in his days the earth was divided: and his brother's name *was* Joktan.
20 And Joktan begot Almodad, and Sheleph, and Hazarmaveth, and Jerah,
21 Hadoram also, and Uzal, and Diklah,
22 And Ebal, and Abimael, and Sheba,
23 And Ophir, and Havilah, and Jobab. All these *were* the sons of Joktan.
24 Shem, Arphaxad, Shelah,
25 Eber, Peleg, Reu,
26 Serug, Nahor, Terah,
27 Abram; the same *is* Abraham.
28 ¶ The sons of Abraham; Isaac, and Ishmael.
29 These *are* their generations: The firstborn of Ishmael, Nebaioth; then Kedar, and Adbeel, and Mibsam,
30 Mishma, and Dumah, Massa, Hadad, and Tema,
31 Jetur, Naphish, and Kedemah. These are the sons of Ishmael.
32 Now the sons of Keturah, Abraham's concubine: she bore Zimran, and Jokshan, and Medan, and Midian, and Ishbak, and Shuah. And the sons of Jokshan; Sheba, and Dedan.
33 And the sons of Midian; Ephah, and Epher, and Henoch, and Abida, and Eldaah. All these *are* the sons of Keturah.

34 And Abraham begot Isaac. The sons of Isaac; Esau and Israel.
35 The sons of Esau; Eliphaz, Reuel, and Jeush, and Jaalam, and Korah.
36 The sons of Eliphaz; Teman, and Omar, Zephi, and Gatam, Kenaz, and Timna, and Amalek.
37 The sons of Reuel; Nahath, Zerah, Shammah, and Mizzah.
38 And the sons of Seir; Lotan, and Shobal, and Zibeon, and Anah, and Dishon, and Ezer, and Dishan.
39 And the sons of Lotan; Hori, and Homam: and Timna *was* Lotan's sister.
40 The sons of Shobal; Alian, and Manahath, and Ebal, Shephi, and Onam. And the sons of Zibeon; Aiah, and Anah.
41 The son of Anah; Dishon. And the sons of Dishon; Amram, and Eshban, and Ithran, and Cheran.
42 The sons of Ezer; Bilhan, and Zavan, *and* Jakan. The sons of Dishan; Uz, and Aran.
43 Now these *are* the kings that reigned in the land of Edom before *any* king reigned over the children of Israel; Bela the son of Beor: and the name of his city *was* Dinhabah.
44 And when Bela was dead, Jobab the son of Zerah of Bozrah reigned in his stead.
45 And when Jobab was dead, Husham of the land of the Temanites reigned in his stead.
46 And when Husham was dead, Hadad the son of Bedad, which smote Midian in the field of Moab, reigned in his stead: and the name of his city *was* Avith.
47 And when Hadad was dead, Samlah of Masrekah reigned in his stead.
48 And when Samlah was dead, Shaul of Rehoboth by the river reigned in his stead.
49 And when Shaul was dead, Baalhanan the son of Achbor reigned in his stead.
50 And when Baalhanan was dead, Hadad reigned in his stead: and the name of his city *was* Pai; and his wife's name *was* Mehetabel, the daughter of Matred, the daughter of Mezahab.
51 Hadad died also. And the dukes of Edom were; duke Timnah, duke Aliah, duke Jetheth,
52 Duke Aholibamah, duke Elah, duke Pinon,
53 Duke Kenaz, duke Teman, duke Mibzar,
54 Duke Magdiel, duke Iram. These *are* the dukes of Edom.

1 Chronicles 2

2:1 ¶ These *are* the sons of Israel; Reuben, Simeon, Levi, and Judah, Issachar, and Zebulun,
2 Dan, Joseph, and Benjamin, Naphtali, Gad, and Asher.
3 The sons of Judah; Er, and Onan, and Shelah: *which* three were born to him of the daughter of Shua the Canaanitess. And Er, the firstborn of Judah, was evil in the sight of Yahweh; and he slew him.
4 And Tamar his daughter-in-law bore him Pharez and Zerah. All the sons of Judah *were* five.
5 The sons of Pharez; Hezron, and Hamul.
6 And the sons of Zerah; Zimri, and Ethan, and Heman, and Calcol, and Dara: five of them in all.
7 And the son of Carmi; Achar, the troubler of Israel, who transgressed in the thing accursed.
8 And the son of Ethan; Azariah.
9 The sons also of Hezron, that were born to him; Jerahmeel, and Ram, and Chelubai.
10 And Ram begot Amminadab; and Amminadab begot Nahshon, prince of the children of Judah;
11 And Nahshon begot Salma, and Salma begot Boaz,
12 And Boaz begot Obed, and Obed begot Jesse,
13 And Jesse begot his firstborn Eliab, and Abinadab the second, and Shimma the third,
Nethaneel the fourth, Raddai the fifth,
15 Ozem the sixth, *and* David the seventh:
16 Whose sisters *were* Zeruiah, and Abigail. And the sons of Zeruiah; Abishai, and Joab, and Asahel, three.
17 And Abigail bore Amasa: and the father of Amasa *was* Jether the Ishmeelite.
18 ¶ And Caleb the son of Hezron begot *children* of Azubah *his* wife, and of Jerioth: her sons *are* these; Jesher, and Shobab, and Ardon.
19 And when Azubah was dead, Caleb took to him Ephrath, which bore him Hur.
20 And Hur begot Uri, and Uri begot Bezaleel.
21 And afterward Hezron went in to the daughter of Machir the father of Gilead, whom he married when he *was* threescore years old; and she bore him Segub.
22 And Segub begot Jair, who had three and twenty cities in the land of Gilead.
23 And he took Geshur, and Aram, with the towns of Jair, from them, with Kenath, and the towns thereof, *even* threescore cities. All these *belonged to* the sons of Machir the father of Gilead.
24 And after that Hezron was dead in Calebephratah, then Abiah Hezron's wife bore him Ashur the father of Tekoa.
25 And the sons of Jerahmeel the firstborn of Hezron were, Ram the firstborn, and Bunah, and Oren, and Ozem, *and* Ahijah.
26 Jerahmeel had also another wife, whose name *was* Atarah; she *was* the mother of Onam.
27 And the sons of Ram the firstborn of Jerahmeel were, Maaz, and Jamin, and Eker.
28 And the sons of Onam were, Shammai, and Jada. And the sons of Shammai; Nadab, and Abishur.
29 And the name of the wife of Abishur *was* Abihail, and she bore him Ahban, and Molid.
30 And the sons of Nadab; Seled, and Appaim: but Seled died without children.
31 And the son of Appaim; Ishi. And the son of Ishi; Sheshan. And the child of Sheshan; Ahlai.
32 And the sons of Jada the brother of Shammai; Jether, and Jonathan: and Jether died without children.

33 And the sons of Jonathan; Peleth, and Zaza. These were the sons of Jerahmeel.
34 Now Sheshan had no sons, but daughters. And Sheshan had a servant, an Egyptian, whose name *was* Jarha.
35 And Sheshan gave his daughter to Jarha his servant to wife; and she bore him Attai.
36 And Attai begot Nathan, and Nathan begot Zabad,
37 And Zabad begot Ephlal, and Ephlal begot Obed,
38 And Obed begot Jehu, and Jehu begot Azariah,
39 And Azariah begot Helez, and Helez begot Eleasah,
40 And Eleasah begot Sisamai, and Sisamai begot Shallum,
41 And Shallum begot Jekamiah, and Jekamiah begot Elishama.
42 Now the sons of Caleb the brother of Jerahmeel *were*, Mesha his firstborn, which was the father of Ziph; and the sons of Mareshah the father of Hebron.
43 And the sons of Hebron; Korah, and Tappuah, and Rekem, and Shema.
44 And Shema begot Raham, the father of Jorkoam: and Rekem begot Shammai.
45 And the son of Shammai *was* Maon: and Maon *was* the father of Bethzur.
46 And Ephah, Caleb's concubine, bore Haran, and Moza, and Gazez: and Haran begot Gazez.
47 And the sons of Jahdai; Regem, and Jotham, and Geshan, and Pelet, and Ephah, and Shaaph.
48 Maachah, Caleb's concubine, bore Sheber, and Tirhanah.
49 She bore also Shaaph the father of Madmannah, Sheva the father of Machbenah, and the father of Gibea: and the daughter of Caleb *was* Achsah.
50 These were the sons of Caleb the son of Hur, the firstborn of Ephratah; Shobal the father of Kirjathjearim,
51 Salma the father of Bethlehem, Hareph the father of Bethgader.
52 And Shobal the father of Kirjathjearim had sons; Haroeh, *and* half of the Manahethites.
53 And the families of Kirjathjearim; the Ithrites, and the Puhites, and the Shumathites, and the Mishraites; of them came the Zareathites, and the Eshtaulites.
54 The sons of Salma; Bethlehem, and the Netophathites, Ataroth, the house of Joab, and half of the Manahethites, the Zorites.
55 And the families of the scribes which dwelt at Jabez; the Tirathites, the Shimeathites, *and* Suchathites. These *are* the Kenites that came of Hemath, the father of the house of Rechab.

1 Chronicles 3

3:1 ¶ Now these were the sons of David, which were born to him in Hebron; the firstborn Amnon, of Ahinoam the Jezreelitess; the second Daniel, of Abigail the Carmelitess:
2 The third, Absalom the son of Maachah the daughter of Talmai king of Geshur: the fourth, Adonijah the son of Haggith:
3 The fifth, Shephatiah of Abital: the sixth, Ithream by Eglah his wife.
4 *These* six were born unto him in Hebron; and there he reigned seven years and six months: and in Jerusalem he reigned thirty and three years.
5 And these were born unto him in Jerusalem; Shimea, and Shobab, and Nathan, and Solomon, four, of Bathshua the daughter of Ammiel:
6 Ibhar also, and Elishama, and Eliphelet,
7 And Nogah, and Nepheg, and Japhia,
8 And Elishama, and Eliada, and Eliphelet, nine.
9 *These were* all the sons of David, besides the sons of the concubines, and Tamar their sister.
10 ¶ And Solomon's son *was* Rehoboam, Abia his son, Asa his son, Jehoshaphat his son,
11 Joram his son, Ahaziah his son, Joash his son,
12 Amaziah his son, Azariah his son, Jotham his son,
13 Ahaz his son, Hezekiah his son, Manasseh his son,
14 Amon his son, Josiah his son.
15 And the sons of Josiah *were*, the firstborn Johanan, the second Jehoiakim, the third Zedekiah, the fourth Shallum.
16 And the sons of Jehoiakim: Jeconiah his son, Zedekiah his son.
17 And the sons of Jeconiah; Assir, Salathiel his son,
18 Malchiram also, and Pedaiah, and Shenazar, Jecamiah, Hoshama, and Nedabiah.
19 And the sons of Pedaiah *were*, Zerubbabel, and Shimei: and the sons of Zerubbabel; Meshullam, and Hananiah, and Shelomith their sister:
20 And Hashubah, and Ohel, and Berechiah, and Hasadiah, Jushabhesed, five.
21 And the sons of Hananiah; Pelatiah, and Jesaiah: the sons of Rephaiah, the sons of Arnan, the sons of Obadiah, the sons of Shechaniah.
22 And the son of Shechaniah; Shemaiah: and the sons of Shemaiah; Hattush, and Igeal, and Bariah, and Neariah, and Shaphat, six.
23 And the sons of Neariah; Elioenai, and Hezekiah, and Azrikam, three.
24 And the sons of Elioenai *were*, Hodaiah, and Eliashib, and Pelaiah, and Akkub, and Johanan, and Dalaiah, and Anani, seven.

1 Chronicles 4

4:1 ¶ The sons of Judah; Pharez, Hezron, and Carmi, and Hur, and Shobal.
2 And Reaiah the son of Shobal begot Jahath; and Jahath begot Ahumai, and Lahad. These *are* the families of the Zorathites.
3 And these *were of* the father of Etam; Jezreel, and Ishma, and Idbash: and the name of their sister *was* Hazelelponi:
4 And Penuel the father of Gedor, and Ezer the father of Hushah. These *are* the sons of Hur, the firstborn of Ephratah, the father of Bethlehem.
5 And Ashur the father of Tekoa had two wives, Helah and Naarah.
6 And Naarah bore him Ahuzam, and Hepher, and Temeni, and Haahashtari. These *were* the sons of Naarah.

7 And the sons of Helah *were*, Zereth, and Jezoar, and Ethnan.

8 And Coz begot Anub, and Zobebah, and the families of Aharhel the son of Harum.

9 And Jabez was more honorable than his brothers: and his mother called his name Jabez, saying, Because I bore him with sorrow.

10 And Jabez called on the God of Israel, saying, Oh that you would bless me indeed, and enlarge my coast, and that your hand might be with me, and that you would keep *me* from evil, that it may not grieve me! And God granted him that which he requested.

11 ¶ And Chelub the brother of Shuah begot Mehir, which *was* the father of Eshton.

12 And Eshton begot Bethrapha, and Paseah, and Tehinnah the father of Irnahash. These *are* the men of Rechah.

13 And the sons of Kenaz; Othniel, and Seraiah: and the son of Othniel; Hathath.

14 And Meonothai begot Ophrah: and Seraiah begot Joab, the father of the valley of Charashim; for they were craftsmen.

15 And the sons of Caleb the son of Jephunneh; Iru, Elah, and Naam: and the son of Elah, even Kenaz.

16 And the sons of Jehaleleel; Ziph, and Ziphah, Tiria, and Asareel.

17 And the sons of Ezra *were*, Jether, and Mered, and Epher, and Jalon: and she bore Miriam, and Shammai, and Ishbah the father of Eshtemoa.

18 And his wife Jehudijah bore Jered the father of Gedor, and Heber the father of Socho, and Jekuthiel the father of Zanoah. And these *are* the sons of Bithiah the daughter of Pharaoh, which Mered took.

19 And the sons of *his* wife Hodiah the sister of Naham, the father of Keilah the Garmite, and Eshtemoa the Maachathite.

20 And the sons of Shimon *were*, Amnon, and Rinnah, Benhanan, and Tilon. And the sons of Ishi *were*, Zoheth, and Benzoheth.

21 The sons of Shelah the son of Judah *were*, Er the father of Lecah, and Laadah the father of Mareshah, and the families of the house of them that worked fine linen, of the house of Ashbea,

22 And Jokim, and the men of Chozeba, and Joash, and Saraph, who had the dominion in Moab, and Jashubilehem. And *these are* ancient things.

23 These *were* the potters, and those that dwelt among plants and hedges: there they dwelt with the king for his work.

24 ¶ The sons of Simeon *were*, Nemuel, and Jamin, Jarib, Zerah, *and* Shaul:

25 Shallum his son, Mibsam his son, Mishma his son.

26 And the sons of Mishma; Hamuel his son, Zacchur his son, Shimei his son.

27 And Shimei had sixteen sons and six daughters; but his brethren had not many children, neither did all their family multiply, like to the children of Judah.

28 And they dwelt at Beersheba, and Moladah, and Hazarshual,

29 And at Bilhah, and at Ezem, and at Tolad,

30 And at Bethuel, and at Hormah, and at Ziklag,

31 And at Bethmarcaboth, and Hazarsusim, and at Bethbirei, and at Shaaraim. These *were* their cities unto the reign of David.

32 And their villages *were*, Etam, and Ain, Rimmon, and Tochen, and Ashan, five cities:

33 And all their villages that *were* round about the same cities, unto Baal. These *were* their habitations, and their genealogy.

34 And Meshobab, and Jamlech, and Joshah the son of Amaziah,

35 And Joel, and Jehu the son of Josibiah, the son of Seraiah, the son of Asiel,

36 And Elioenai, and Jaakobah, and Jeshohaiah, and Asaiah, and Adiel, and Jesimiel, and Benaiah,

37 And Ziza the son of Shiphi, the son of Allon, the son of Jedaiah, the son of Shimri, the son of Shemaiah;

38 These mentioned by *their* names *were* princes in their families: and the house of their fathers increased greatly.

39 And they went to the entrance of Gedor, *even* to the east side of the valley, to seek pasture for their flocks.

40 And they found fat pasture and good, and the land *was* wide, and quiet, and peaceable; for *they* of Ham had dwelt there of old.

41 And these written by name came in the days of Hezekiah king of Judah, and smote their tents, and the habitations that were found there, and destroyed them utterly unto this day, and dwelt in their place: because *there was* pasture there for their flocks.

42 And *some* of them, *even* of the sons of Simeon, five hundred men, went to mount Seir, having for their captains Pelatiah, and Neariah, and Rephaiah, and Uzziel, the sons of Ishi.

43 And they smote the rest of the Amalekites that had escaped, and dwelt there unto this day.

1 Chronicles 5

5:1 ¶ Now the sons of Reuben the firstborn of Israel, (for he *was* the firstborn; but, forasmuch as he defiled his father's bed, his birthright was given to the sons of Joseph the son of Israel: and the genealogy is not to be reckoned after the birthright.

2 For Judah prevailed above his brethren, and of him *came* the chief ruler; but the birthright *was* Joseph's:)

3 The sons, *I say*, of Reuben the firstborn of Israel *were*, Hanoch, and Pallu, Hezron, and Carmi.

4 The sons of Joel; Shemaiah his son, Gog his son, Shimei his son,

5 Micah his son, Reaia his son, Baal his son,

6 Beerah his son, whom Tilgathpilneser king of Assyria carried away *captive*: he *was* prince of the Reubenites.

7 And his brethren by their families, when the genealogy of their generations was reckoned, *were* the chief, Jeiel, and Zechariah,

1 Chronicles 5

8 And Bela the son of Azaz, the son of Shema, the son of Joel, who dwelt in Aroer, even unto Nebo and Baalmeon:
9 And eastward he inhabited unto the entering in of the wilderness from the river Euphrates: because their cattle had multiplied in the land of Gilead.
10 And in the days of Saul they made war with the Hagarites, who fell by their hand: and they dwelt in their tents throughout all the east *land* of Gilead.
11 And the children of Gad dwelt over against them, in the land of Bashan to Salchah:
12 Joel the chief, and Shapham the next, and Jaanai, and Shaphat in Bashan.
13 And their brethren of the house of their fathers *were*, Michael, and Meshullam, and Sheba, and Jorai, and Jachan, and Zia, and Heber, seven.
14 These *are* the children of Abihail the son of Huri, the son of Jaroah, the son of Gilead, the son of Michael, the son of Jeshishai, the son of Jahdo, the son of Buz;
15 Ahi the son of Abdiel, the son of Guni, chief of the house of their fathers.
16 And they dwelt in Gilead in Bashan, and in her towns, and in all the suburbs of Sharon, upon their borders.
17 All these were reckoned by genealogies in the days of Jotham king of Judah, and in the days of Jeroboam king of Israel.
18 ¶ The sons of Reuben, and the Gadites, and half the tribe of Manasseh, of valiant men, men able to bear shield and sword, and to shoot with bow, and skillful in war, *were* four and forty thousand seven hundred and threescore, that went out to the war.
19 And they made war with the Hagarites, with Jetur, and Nephish, and Nodab.
20 And they were helped against them, and the Hagarites were delivered into their hand, and all that *were* with them: for they cried to God in the battle, and he was entreated of them; because they put their trust in him.
21 And they took away their cattle; of their camels fifty thousand, and of sheep two hundred and fifty thousand, and of donkeys two thousand, and of men a hundred thousand.
22 For there fell down many slain, because the war *was* of God. And they dwelt in their places until the captivity.
23 And the children of the half tribe of Manasseh dwelt in the land: they increased from Bashan to Baalhermon and Senir, and to mount Hermon.
24 And these *were* the heads of the house of their fathers, even Epher, and Ishi, and Eliel, and Azriel, and Jeremiah, and Hodaviah, and Jahdiel, mighty men of valor, famous men, *and* heads of the house of their fathers.
25 And they transgressed against the God of their fathers, and went a whoring after the gods of the people of the land, whom God destroyed before them.
26 And the God of Israel stirred up the spirit of Pul king of Assyria, and the spirit of Tilgathpilneser king of Assyria, and he carried them away, even the Reubenites, and the Gadites, and the half tribe of Manasseh, and brought them to Halah, and Habor, and Hara, and to the river Gozan, unto this day.

1 Chronicles 6

6:1 ¶ The sons of Levi; Gershon, Kohath, and Merari.
2 And the sons of Kohath; Amram, Izhar, and Hebron, and Uzziel.
3 And the children of Amram; Aaron, and Moses, and Miriam. The sons also of Aaron; Nadab, and Abihu, Eleazar, and Ithamar.
4 Eleazar begot Phinehas, Phinehas begot Abishua,
5 And Abishua begot Bukki, and Bukki begot Uzzi,
6 And Uzzi begot Zerahiah, and Zerahiah begot Meraioth,
7 Meraioth begot Amariah, and Amariah begot Ahitub,
8 And Ahitub begot Zadok, and Zadok begot Ahimaaz,
9 And Ahimaaz begot Azariah, and Azariah begot Johanan,
10 And Johanan begot Azariah, (he *it is* that executed the priest's office in the temple that Solomon built in Jerusalem:)
11 And Azariah begot Amariah, and Amariah begot Ahitub,
12 And Ahitub begot Zadok, and Zadok begot Shallum,
13 And Shallum begot Hilkiah, and Hilkiah begot Azariah,
14 And Azariah begot Seraiah, and Seraiah begot Jehozadak,
15 And Jehozadak went *into captivity*, when Yahweh carried away Judah and Jerusalem by the hand of Nebuchadnezzar.
16 The sons of Levi; Gershom, Kohath, and Merari.
17 And these *are* the names of the sons of Gershom; Libni, and Shimei.
18 And the sons of Kohath *were*, Amram, and Izhar, and Hebron, and Uzziel.
19 The sons of Merari; Mahli, and Mushi. And these *are* the families of the Levites according to their fathers.
20 Of Gershom; Libni his son, Jahath his son, Zimmah his son,
21 Joah his son, Iddo his son, Zerah his son, Jeaterai his son.
22 The sons of Kohath; Amminadab his son, Korah his son, Assir his son,
23 Elkanah his son, and Ebiasaph his son, and Assir his son,
24 Tahath his son, Uriel his son, Uzziah his son, and Shawl his son.
25 And the sons of Elkanah; Amasai, and Ahimoth.
26 *As for* Elkanah: the sons of Elkanah; Zophai his son, and Nahath his son,
27 Eliab his son, Jeroham his son, Elkanah his son.
28 And the sons of Samuel; the firstborn Vashni, and Abiah.
29 The sons of Merari; Mahli, Libni his son, Shimei his son, Uzza his son,
30 Shimea his son, Haggiah his son, Asaiah his son.
31 ¶ And these *are they* whom David set over the service of song in the house of Yahweh, after that the ark had rest.
32 And they ministered before the dwelling place of the tabernacle of the congregation with singing, until Solomon had built the house of Yahweh in Jerusalem: and *then* they waited on their office according to their order.

33 And these *are* they that waited with their children. Of the sons of the Kohathites: Heman a singer, the son of Joel, the son of Shemuel,

34 The son of Elkanah, the son of Jeroham, the son of Eliel, the son of Toah,

35 The son of Zuph, the son of Elkanah, the son of Mahath, the son of Amasai,

36 The son of Elkanah, the son of Joel, the son of Azariah, the son of Zephaniah,

37 The son of Tahath, the son of Assir, the son of Ebiasaph, the son of Korah,

38 The son of Izhar, the son of Kohath, the son of Levi, the son of Israel.

39 And his brother Asaph, who stood on his right hand, *even* Asaph the son of Berachiah, the son of Shimea,

40 The son of Michael, the son of Baaseiah, the son of Malchiah,

41 The son of Ethni, the son of Zerah, the son of Adaiah,

42 The son of Ethan, the son of Zimmah, the son of Shimei,

43 The son of Jahath, the son of Gershom, the son of Levi.

44 And their brethren the sons of Merari *stood* on the left hand: Ethan the son of Kishi, the son of Abdi, the son of Malluch,

45 The son of Hashabiah, the son of Amaziah, the son of Hilkiah,

46 The son of Amzi, the son of Bani, the son of Shamer,

47 The son of Mahli, the son of Mushi, the son of Merari, the son of Levi.

48 Their brethren also the Levites *were* appointed to all manner of service of the tabernacle of the house of God.

49 But Aaron and his sons offered upon the altar of the burnt offering, and on the altar of incense, *and were appointed* for all the work of the *place* most holy, and to make an atonement for Israel, according to all that Moses the servant of God had commanded.

50 And these *are* the sons of Aaron; Eleazar his son, Phinehas his son, Abishua his son,

51 Bukki his son, Uzzi his son, Zerahiah his son,

52 Meraioth his son, Amariah his son, Ahitub his son,

53 Zadok his son, Ahimaaz his son.

54 ¶ Now these *are* their dwelling places throughout their castles in their coasts, of the sons of Aaron, of the families of the Kohathites: for theirs was the lot.

55 And they gave them Hebron in the land of Judah, and the suburbs thereof round about it.

56 But the fields of the city, and the villages thereof, they gave to Caleb the son of Jephunneh.

57 And to the sons of Aaron they gave the cities of Judah, *namely*, Hebron, *the city* of refuge, and Libnah with her suburbs, and Jattir, and Eshtemoa, with their suburbs,

58 And Hilen with her suburbs, Debir with her suburbs,

59 And Ashan with her suburbs, and Bethshemesh with her suburbs:

60 And out of the tribe of Benjamin; Geba with her suburbs, and Alemeth with her suburbs, and Anathoth with her suburbs. All their cities throughout their families *were* thirteen cities.

61 And to the sons of Kohath, which *were* left of the family of that tribe, *were* cities given out of the half tribe, *namely, out of* the half *tribe* of Manasseh, by lot, ten cities.

62 And to the sons of Gershom throughout their families out of the tribe of Issachar, and out of the tribe of Asher, and out of the tribe of Naphtali, and out of the tribe of Manasseh in Bashan, thirteen cities.

63 Unto the sons of Merari *were given* by lot, throughout their families, out of the tribe of Reuben, and out of the tribe of Gad, and out of the tribe of Zebulun, twelve cities.

64 And the children of Israel gave to the Levites *these* cities with their suburbs.

65 And they gave by lot out of the tribe of the children of Judah, and out of the tribe of the children of Simeon, and out of the tribe of the children of Benjamin, these cities, which are called by *their* names.

66 And *the residue* of the families of the sons of Kohath had cities of their coasts out of the tribe of Ephraim.

67 And they gave unto them, *of* the cities of refuge, Shechem in mount Ephraim with her suburbs; *they gave* also Gezer with her suburbs,

68 And Jokmeam with her suburbs, and Bethhoron with her suburbs,

69 And Aijalon with her suburbs, and Gathrimmon with her suburbs:

70 And out of the half tribe of Manasseh; Aner with her suburbs, and Bileam with her suburbs, for the family of the remnant of the sons of Kohath.

71 Unto the sons of Gershom *were given* out of the family of the half tribe of Manasseh, Golan in Bashan with her suburbs, and Ashtaroth with her suburbs:

72 And out of the tribe of Issachar; Kedesh with her suburbs, Daberath with her suburbs,

73 And Ramoth with her suburbs, and Anem with her suburbs:

74 And out of the tribe of Asher; Mashal with her suburbs, and Abdon with her suburbs,

75 And Hukok with her suburbs, and Rehob with her suburbs:

76 And out of the tribe of Naphtali; Kedesh in Galilee with her suburbs, and Hammon with her suburbs, and Kirjathaim with her suburbs.

77 Unto the rest of the children of Merari *were given* out of the tribe of Zebulun, Rimmon with her suburbs, Tabor with her suburbs:

78 And on the other side *of the* Jordan by Jericho, on the east side *of the* Jordan, *were given them* out of the tribe of Reuben, Bezer in the wilderness with her suburbs, and Jahzah with her suburbs,

79 Kedemoth also with her suburbs, and Mephaath with her suburbs

80 And out of the tribe of Gad; Ramoth in Gilead with her suburbs, and Mahanaim with her suburbs,

81 And Heshbon with her suburbs, and Jazer with her suburbs.

1 Chronicles 7

7:1 ¶ Now the sons of Issachar *were*, Tola, and Puah, Jashub, and Shimron, four.

2 And the sons of Tola; Uzzi, and Rephaiah, and Jeriel, and Jahmai, and Jibsam, and Shemuel, heads of their father's house, *to know*, of Tola: *they were* valiant men of might in their generations; whose number *was* in the days of David two and twenty thousand and six hundred.

3 And the son of Uzzi; Izrahiah: and the sons of Izrahiah; Michael, and Obadiah, and Joel, Ishiah, five: all of them chief men.

4 And with them, by their generations, after the house of their fathers, *were* bands of soldiers for war, six and thirty thousand *men*: for they had many wives and sons.

5 And their brethren among all the families of Issachar *were* valiant men of might, reckoned in all by their genealogies fourscore and seven thousand.

6 *The sons* of Benjamin; Bela, and Becher, and Jediael, three.

7 And the sons of Bela; Ezbon, and Uzzi, and Uzziel, and Jerimoth, and Iri, five; heads of the house of *their* fathers, mighty men of valor; and were reckoned by their genealogies twenty and two thousand and thirty and four.

8 And the sons of Becher; Zemira, and Joash, and Eliezer, and Elioenai, and Omri, and Jerimoth, and Abiah, and Anathoth, and Alameth. All these *are* the sons of Becher.

9 And the number of them, after their genealogy by their generations, heads of the house of their fathers, mighty men of valor, *was* twenty thousand and two hundred.

10 The son also of Jediael; Bilhan: and the sons of Bilhan; Jeush, and Benjamin, and Ehud, and Chenaanah, and Zethan, and Tharshish, and Ahishahar.

11 All these the sons of Jediael, by the heads of their fathers, mighty men of valor, *were* seventeen thousand and two hundred *soldiers*, fit to go out for war *and* battle.

12 Shuppim also, and Huppim, the children of Ir, *and* Hushim, the sons of Aher.

13 The sons of Naphtali; Jahziel, and Guni, and Jezer, and Shallum, the sons of Bilhah.

14 The sons of Manasseh; Ashriel, whom she bore: (*but* his concubine the Aramitess bore Machir the father of Gilead:

15 And Machir took to wife *the sister* of Huppim and Shuppim, whose sister's name *was* Maachah;) and the name of the second *was* Zelophehad: and Zelophehad had daughters.

16 And Maachah the wife of Machir bore a son, and she called his name Peresh; and the name of his brother *was* Sheresh; and his sons *were* Ulam and Rakem.

17 And the son of Ulam; Bedan. These *were* the sons of Gilead, the son of Machir, the son of Manasseh.

18 And his sister Hammoleketh bore Ishod, and Abiezer, and Mahalah.

19 And the sons of Shemida were, Ahian, and Shechem, and Likhi, and Aniam.

20 ¶ And the son of Ephraim; Shuthelah, and Bered his son, and Tahath his son, and Eladah his son, and Tahath his son,

21 And Zabad his son, and Shuthelah his son, and Ezer, and Elead, whom the men of Gath *that were* born in *that* land slew, because they came down to take away their cattle.

22 And Ephraim their father mourned many days, and his brethren came to comfort him.

23 And when he went in to his wife, she conceived, and bore a son, and he called his name Beriah, because it went evil with his house.

24 (And his daughter *was* Sherah, who built Bethhoron the lower, and the upper, and Uzzensherah.)

25 And Rephah *was* his son, also Resheph, and Telah his son, and Tahan his son,

26 Laadan his son, Ammihud his son, Elishama his son,

27 Non his son, Jehoshua his son.

28 And their possessions and habitations *were*, Bethel and the towns thereof, and eastward Naaran, and westward Gezer, with the towns thereof; Shechem also and the towns thereof, to Gaza and the towns thereof:

29 And by the borders of the children of Manasseh, Bethshean and her towns, Taanach and her towns, Megiddo and her towns, Dor and her towns. In these dwelt the children of Joseph the son of Israel.

30 The sons of Asher; Imnah, and Isuah, and Ishuai, and Beriah, and Serah their sister.

31 And the sons of Beriah; Heber, and Malchiel, who *is* the father of Birzavith.

32 And Heber begot Japhlet, and Shomer, and Hotham, and Shua their sister.

33 And the sons of Japhlet; Pasach, and Bimhal, and Ashvath. These *are* the children of Japhlet.

34 And the sons of Shamer; Ahi, and Rohgah, Jehubbah, and Aram.

35 And the sons of his brother Helem; Zophah, and Imna, and Shelesh, and Amal.

36 The sons of Zophah; Suah, and Harnepher, and Shual, and Beri, and Imrah,

37 Bezer, and Hod, and Shamma, and Shilshah, and Ithran, and Beera.

38 And the sons of Jether; Jephunneh, and Pispah, and Ara.

39 And the sons of Ulla; Arah, and Haniel, and Rezia.

40 All these *were* the children of Asher, heads of *their* father's house, choice *and* mighty men of valor, chief of the princes. And the number throughout the genealogy of them that were able for the war *and* to battle *was* twenty and six thousand men.

1 Chronicles 8

8:1 ¶ Now Benjamin begot Bela his firstborn, Ashbel the second, and Aharah the third,

2 Nohah the fourth, and Rapha the fifth.

3 And the sons of Bela were, Addar, and Gera, and Abihud,

4 And Abishua, and Naaman, and Ahoah,

5 And Gera, and Shephuphan, and Huram.

6 And these *are* the sons of Ehud: these are the heads of the fathers of the inhabitants of Geba, and they removed them to Manahath:

7 And Naaman, and Ahiah, and Gera, he removed them, and begot Uzza, and Ahihud.

8 And Shaharaim begot *children* in the country of Moab, after he had sent them away; Hushim and Baara *were* his wives.

9 And he begot of Hodesh his wife, Jobab, and Zibia, and Mesha, and Malcham,

10 And Jeuz, and Shachia, and Mirma. These *were* his sons, heads of the fathers.

11 And of Hushim he begot Abitub, and Elpaal.

12 The sons of Elpaal; Eber, and Misham, and Shamed, who built Ono, and Lod, with the towns thereof:

13 Beriah also, and Shema, who *were* heads of the fathers of the inhabitants of Aijalon, who drove away the inhabitants of Gath:

14 And Ahio, Shashak, and Jeremoth,

15 And Zebadiah, and Arad, and Ader,

16 And Michael, and Ispah, and Joha, the sons of Beriah;

17 And Zebadiah, and Meshullam, and Hezeki, and Heber,

18 Ishmerai also, and Jezliah, and Jobab, the sons of Elpaal;

19 And Jakim, and Zichri, and Zabdi,

20 And Elienai, and Zilthai, and Eliel,

21 And Adaiah, and Beraiah, and Shimrath, the sons of Shimhi;

22 And Ishpan, and Heber, and Eliel,

23 And Abdon, and Zichri, and Hanan,

24 And Hananiah, and Elam, and Antothijah,

25 And Iphedeiah, and Penuel, the sons of Shashak;

26 And Shamsherai, and Shehariah, and Athaliah,

27 And Jaresiah, and Eliah, and Zichri, the sons of Jeroham.

28 These *were* heads of the fathers, by their generations, chief *men*. These dwelt in Jerusalem.

29 And at Gibeon dwelt the father of Gibeon; whose wife's name *was* Maachah:

30 And his firstborn son Abdon, and Zur, and Kish, and Baal, and Nadab,

31 And Gedor, and Ahio, and Zacher.

32 And Mikloth begot Shimeah. And these also dwelt with their brethren in Jerusalem, over against them.

33 ¶ And Ner begot Kish, and Kish begot Saul, and Saul begot Jonathan, and Malchishua, and Abinadab, and Eshbaal.

34 And the son of Jonathan *was* Meribbaal; and Meribbaal begot Micah.

35 And the sons of Micah *were*, Pithon, and Melech, and Tarea, and Ahaz.

36 And Ahaz begot Jehoadah; and Jehoadah begot Alemeth, and Azmaveth, and Zimri; and Zimri begot Moza,

37 And Moza begot Binea: Rapha *was* his son, Eleasah his son, Azel his son:

38 And Azel had six sons, whose names *are* these, Azrikam, Bocheru, and Ishmael, and Sheariah, and Obadiah, and Hanan. All these *were* the sons of Azel.

39 And the sons of Eshek his brother *were*, Ulam his firstborn, Jehush the second, and Eliphelet the third.

40 And the sons of Ulam were mighty men of valor, archers, and had many sons, and sons' sons, a hundred and fifty. All these *are* of the sons of Benjamin.

1 Chronicles 9

9:1 ¶ So all Israel were reckoned by genealogies; and, behold, they *were* written in the book of the kings of Israel and Judah, *who* were carried away to Babylon for their transgression.

2 Now the first inhabitants that *dwelt* in their possessions in their cities *were*, the Israelites, the priests, Levites, and the Nethinims.

3 And in Jerusalem dwelt of the children of Judah, and of the children of Benjamin, and of the children of Ephraim, and Manasseh;

4 Uthai the son of Ammihud, the son of Omri, the son of Imri, the son of Bani, of the children of Pharez the son of Judah.

5 And of the Shilonites; Asaiah the firstborn, and his sons.

6 And of the sons of Zerah; Jeuel, and their brethren, six hundred and ninety.

7 And of the sons of Benjamin; Sallu the son of Meshullam, the son of Hodaviah, the son of Hasenuah,

8 And Ibneiah the son of Jeroham, and Elah the son of Uzzi, the son of Michri, and Meshullam the son of Shephathiah, the son of Reuel, the son of Ibnijah;

9 And their brethren, according to their generations, nine hundred and fifty and six. All these men *were* chief of the fathers in the house of their fathers.

10 And of the priests; Jedaiah, and Jehoiarib, and Jachin,

11 And Azariah the son of Hilkiah, the son of Meshullam, the son of Zadok, the son of Meraioth, the son of Ahitub, the ruler of the house of God;

12 And Adaiah the son of Jeroham, the son of Pashur, the son of Malchijah, and Maasiai the son of Adiel, the son of Jahzerah, the son of Meshullam, the son of Meshillemith, the son of Immer;

13 And their brethren, heads of the house of their fathers, a thousand and seven hundred and threescore; very able men for the work of the service of the house of God.

14 ¶ And of the Levites; Shemaiah the son of Hasshub, the son of Azrikam, the son of Hashabiah, of the sons of Merari;

15 And Bakbakkar, Heresh, and Galal, and Mattaniah the son of Micah, the son of Zichri, the son of Asaph;

16 And Obadiah the son of Shemaiah, the son of Galal, the son of Jeduthun, and Berechiah the son of Asa, the son of Elkanah, that dwelt in the villages of the Netophathites.

17 And the porters *were*, Shallum, and Akkub, and Talmon, and Ahiman, and their brethren: Shallum *was* the chief;

18 Who until now *waited* in the king's gate eastward: they *were* porters in the companies of the children of Levi.

1 Chronicles 9

19 And Shallum the son of Kore, the son of Ebiasaph, the son of Korah, and his brethren, of the house of his father, the Korahites, *were* over the work of the service, keepers of the gates of the tabernacle: and their fathers, *being* over the host of Yahweh, *were* keepers of the entry.

20 And Phinehas the son of Eleazar was the ruler over them in time past, *and* Yahweh *was* with him.

21 *And* Zechariah the son of Meshelemiah *was* porter of the door of the tabernacle of the congregation.

22 All these *which were* chosen to be porters in the gates *were* two hundred and twelve. These were reckoned by their genealogy in their villages, whom David and Samuel the seer did ordain in their set office.

23 So they and their children *had* the oversight of the gates of the house of Yahweh, *namely*, the house of the tabernacle, by wards.

24 In four quarters were the porters, toward the east, west, north, and south.

25 And their brethren, *which were* in their villages, *were* to come after seven days from time to time with them.

26 For these Levites, the four chief porters, were in *their* set office, and were over the chambers and treasuries of the house of God.

27 And they lodged round about the house of God, because the charge *was* upon them, and the opening thereof every morning *pertained* to them.

28 And *certain* of them had the charge of the ministering vessels, that they should bring them in and out by number.

29 *Some* of them also *were* appointed to oversee the vessels, and all the instruments of the sanctuary, and the fine flour, and the wine, and the oil, and the frankincense, and the spices.

30 And *some* of the sons of the priests made the ointment of the spices.

31 And Mattithiah, *one* of the Levites, who *was* the firstborn of Shallum the Korahite, had the set office over the things that were made in the pans.

32 And *other* of their brethren, of the sons of the Kohathites, *were* over the showbread, to prepare *it* every sabbath.

33 And these *are* the singers, chief of the fathers of the Levites, *who remaining* in the chambers *were* free: for they were employed in *that* work day and night.

34 These chief fathers of the Levites *were* chief throughout their generations; these dwelt at Jerusalem.

35 ¶ And in Gibeon dwelt the father of Gibeon, Jehiel, whose wife's name *was* Maachah:

36 And his firstborn son Abdon, then Zur, and Kish, and Baal, and Ner, and Nadab,

37 And Gedor, and Ahio, and Zechariah, and Mikloth.

38 And Mikloth begot Shimeam. And they also dwelt with their brethren at Jerusalem, over against their brethren.

39 And Ner begot Kish; and Kish begot Saul; and Saul begot Jonathan, and Malchishua, and Abinadab, and Eshbaal.

40 And the son of Jonathan *was* Meribbaal: and Meribbaal begot Micah.

41 And the sons of Micah *were*, Pithon, and Melech, and Tahrea, *and Ahaz*.

42 And Ahaz begot Jarah; and Jarah begot Alemeth, and Azmaveth, and Zimri; and Zimri begot Moza;

43 And Moza begot Binea; and Rephaiah his son, Eleasah his son, Azel his son.

44 And Azel had six sons, whose names *are* these, Azrikam, Bocheru, and Ishmael, and Sheariah, and Obadiah, and Hanan: these *were* the sons of Azel.

1 Chronicles 10

10:1 ¶ Now the Philistines fought against Israel; and the men of Israel fled from before the Philistines, and fell down slain in mount Gilboa.

2 And the Philistines followed hard after Saul, and after his sons; and the Philistines slew Jonathan, and Abinadab, and Malchishua, the sons of Saul.

3 And the battle went heavily against Saul, and the archers hit him, and he was wounded by the archers.

4 Then said Saul to his armor bearer, Draw your sword, and thrust me through therewith; lest these uncircumcised come and abuse me. But his armor bearer would not; for he was very afraid. So Saul took a sword, and fell upon it.

5 And when his armor bearer saw that Saul was dead, he fell likewise on the sword, and died.

6 So Saul died, and his three sons, and all his house died together.

7 And when all the men of Israel that *were* in the valley saw that they fled, and that Saul and his sons were dead, then they forsook their cities, and fled: and the Philistines came and dwelt in them.

8 ¶ And it came to pass on the next day, when the Philistines came to strip the slain, that they found Saul and his sons fallen in mount Gilboa.

9 And when they had stripped him, they took his head, and his armor, and sent into the land of the Philistines round about, to carry tidings to their idols, and to the people.

10 And they put his armor in the house of their gods, and fastened his head in the temple of Dagon.

11 And when all Jabeshgilead heard all that the Philistines had done to Saul,

12 They arose, all the valiant men, and took away the body of Saul, and the bodies of his sons, and brought them to Jabesh, and buried their bones under the oak in Jabesh, and fasted seven days.

13 So Saul died for his transgression which he committed against Yahweh, *even* against the word of Yahweh, which he kept not, and also for asking *counsel* of *one that had* a familiar spirit, to inquire *of it*;

14 And inquired not of Yahweh: therefore he slew him, and turned the kingdom unto David the son of Jesse.

1 Chronicles 11

11:1 ¶ Then all Israel gathered themselves to David unto Hebron, saying, Behold, we *are* your bone and your flesh.

2 And moreover in time past, even when Saul was king, you *were* he that led out and brought in Israel: and Yahweh your God said to you, You shall feed my people Israel, and you shall be ruler over my people Israel.

3 Therefore came all the elders of Israel to the king to Hebron; and David made a covenant with them in Hebron before Yahweh; and they anointed David king over Israel, according to the word of Yahweh by Samuel.

4 And David and all Israel went to Jerusalem, which *is* Jebus; where the Jebusites *were*, the inhabitants of the land.

5 And the inhabitants of Jebus said to David, You shall not come here. Nevertheless David took the castle of Zion, which *is* the city of David.

6 And David said, Whoever smites the Jebusites first shall be chief and captain. So Joab the son of Zeruiah went first up, and was chief.

7 And David dwelt in the castle; therefore they called it the city of David.

8 And he built the city round about, even from Millo round about: and Joab repaired the rest of the city.

9 So David grew greater and greater: for Yahweh of hosts *was* with him.

10 ¶ These also *are* the chief of the mighty men whom David had, who strengthened themselves with him in his kingdom, *and* with all Israel, to make him king, according to the word of Yahweh concerning Israel.

11 And this *is* the number of the mighty men whom David had; Jashobeam, a Hachmonite, the chief of the captains: he lifted up his spear against three hundred slain *by him* at one time.

12 And after him *was* Eleazar the son of Dodo, the Ahohite, who *was one* of the three mighties.

13 He was with David at Pasdammim, and there the Philistines were gathered together to battle, where was a parcel of ground full of barley; and the people fled from before the Philistines.

14 And they set themselves in the midst of *that* parcel, and delivered it, and slew the Philistines; and Yahweh saved *them* by a great deliverance.

15 Now three of the thirty captains went down to the rock to David, into the cave of Adullam; and the host of the Philistines encamped in the valley of Rephaim.

16 And David *was* then in the hold, and the Philistines' garrison *was* then at Bethlehem.

17 And David longed, and said, Oh that one would give me *a* drink of the water of the well of Bethlehem, that *is* at the gate!

18 And the three broke through the host of the Philistines, and drew water out of the well of Bethlehem, that *was* by the gate, and took *it*, and brought *it* to David: but David would not drink *of* it, but poured it out to Yahweh,

19 And said, My God forbid it *to* me, that I should do this thing: shall I drink the blood of these men that have put their lives in jeopardy? for with *the jeopardy of* their lives they brought it. Therefore he would not drink it. These things did these three mightiest.

20 And Abishai the brother of Joab, he was chief of the three: for lifting up his spear against three hundred, he slew *them*, and had a name among the three.

21 Of the three, he was more honorable than the two; for he was their captain: however he attained not to the *first* three.

22 Benaiah the son of Jehoiada, the son of a valiant man of Kabzeel, who had done many acts; he slew two lionlike men of Moab: also he went down and slew a lion in a pit on a snowy day.

23 And he slew an Egyptian, a man of *great* stature, five cubits high; and in the Egyptian's hand *was* a spear like a weaver's beam; and he went down to him with a staff, and plucked the spear out of the Egyptian's hand, and slew him with his own spear.

24 These *things* did Benaiah the son of Jehoiada, and had the name among the three mighties.

25 Behold, he was honorable among the thirty, but attained not to the *first* three: and David set him over his guard.

26 Also the valiant men of the armies *were*, Asahel the brother of Joab, Elhanan the son of Dodo of Bethlehem,

27 Shammoth the Harorite, Helez the Pelonite,

28 Ira the son of Ikkesh the Tekoite, Abiezer the Antothite,

29 Sibbecai the Hushathite, Ilai the Ahohite,

30 Maharai the Netophathite, Heled the son of Baanah the Netophathite,

31 Ithai the son of Ribai of Gibeah, *that pertained* to the children of Benjamin, Benaiah the Pirathonite,

32 Hurai of the brooks of Gaash, Abiel the Arbathite,

33 Azmaveth the Baharumite, Eliahba the Shaalbonite,

34 The sons of Hashem the Gizonite, Jonathan the son of Shage the Hararite,

35 Ahiam the son of Sacar the Hararite, Eliphal the son of Ur,

36 Hepher the Mecherathite, Ahijah the Pelonite,

37 Hezro the Carmelite, Naarai the son of Ezbai,

38 Joel the brother of Nathan, Mibhar the son of Haggeri,

39 Zelek the Ammonite, Naharai the Berothite, the armor bearer of Joab the son of Zeruiah,

40 Ira the Ithrite, Gareb the Ithrite,

41 Uriah the Hittite, Zabad the son of Ahlai,

42 Adina the son of Shiza the Reubenite, a captain of the Reubenites, and thirty with him,

43 Hanan the son of Maachah, and Joshaphat the Mithnite,

44 Uzzia the Ashterathite, Shama and Jehiel the sons of Hothan the Aroerite,

45 Jediael the son of Shimri, and Joha his brother, the Tizite,

46 Eliel the Mahavite, and Jeribai, and Joshaviah, the sons of Elnaam, and Ithmah the Moabite,

47 Eliel, and Obed, and Jasiel the Mesobaite.

1 Chronicles 12

12:1 ¶ Now these *are* they that came to David to Ziklag, while he yet kept himself restrained because of Saul the son of Kish: and they *were* among the mighty men, helpers of the war.

2 *They were* armed with bows, and could use both the right hand and the left in *hurling* stones and *shooting* arrows out of a bow, *even* of Saul's brethren of Benjamin.

3 The chief *was* Ahiezer, then Joash, the sons of Shemaah the Gibeathite; and Jeziel, and Pelet, the sons of Azmaveth; and Berachah, and Jehu the Antothite,

4 And Ismaiah the Gibeonite, a mighty man among the thirty, and over the thirty; and Jeremiah, and Jahaziel, and Johanan, and Josabad the Gederathite,

5 Eluzai, and Jerimoth, and Bealiah, and Shemariah, and Shephatiah the Haruphite,

6 Elkanah, and Jesiah, and Azareel, and Joezer, and Jashobeam, the Korhites,

7 And Joelah, and Zebadiah, the sons of Jeroham of Gedor.

8 And of the Gadites there separated themselves unto David into the hold to the wilderness men of might, *and* men of war *fit* for the battle, that could handle shield and spear, whose faces *were like* the faces of lions, and *were* as swift as the roes upon the mountains;

9 Ezer the first, Obadiah the second, Eliab the third,

10 Mishmannah the fourth, Jeremiah the fifth,

11 Attai the sixth, Eliel the seventh,

12 Johanan the eighth, Elzabad the ninth,

13 Jeremiah the tenth, Machbanai the eleventh.

14 These *were* of the sons of Gad, captains of the host: one of the least *was* over a hundred, and the greatest over a thousand.

15 These *are* they that went over *the* Jordan in the first month, when it had overflowed all his banks; and they put to flight all *them* of the valleys, *both* toward the east, and toward the west.

16 And there came of the children of Benjamin and Judah to the stronghold unto David.

17 And David went out to meet them, and answered and said to them, If you have come peaceably to me to help me, my heart shall be knit to you: but if *you have come* to betray me to my enemies, seeing *there is* no wrong in my hands, the God of our fathers look *thereon*, and rebuke *it*.

18 Then the spirit came upon Amasai, *who was* chief of the captains, *and he said*, Yours *are we*, David, and on your side, you son of Jesse: peace, peace *be* to you, and peace *be* to your helpers; for your God helps you. Then David received them, and made them captains of the band.

19 And there fell *some* of Manasseh to David, when he came with the Philistines against Saul to battle: but they helped them not: for the lords of the Philistines upon advisement sent him away, saying, He will fall to his master Saul to *the jeopardy of* our heads.

20 As he went to Ziklag, there fell to him of Manasseh, Adnah, and Jozabad, and Jediael, and Michael, and Jozabad, and Elihu, and Zilthai, captains of the thousands that *were* of Manasseh.

21 And they helped David against the band *of the rovers*: for they *were* all mighty men of valor, and were captains in the host.

22 For at *that* time day by day *they* came to David to help him, until *it was* a great host, like the host of God.

23 ¶ And these *are* the numbers of the bands *that were* ready armed to the war, *and* came to David to Hebron, to turn the kingdom of Saul to him, according to the word of Yahweh.

24 The children of Judah that bore shields and spears *were* six thousand and eight hundred, ready armed to the war.

25 Of the children of Simeon, mighty men of valor for the war, seven thousand and one hundred.

26 Of the children of Levi four thousand and six hundred.

27 And Jehoiada *was* the leader of the Aaronites, and with him *were* three thousand and seven hundred;

28 And Zadok, a young man mighty of valor, and of his father's house twenty and two captains.

29 And of the children of Benjamin, the kindred of Saul, three thousand: for till now the greatest part of them had kept the guard of the house of Saul.

30 And of the children of Ephraim twenty thousand and eight hundred, mighty men of valor, famous throughout the house of their fathers.

31 And of the half tribe of Manasseh eighteen thousand, which were expressed by name, to come and make David king.

32 And of the children of Issachar, *which were men* that had understanding of the times, to know what Israel ought to do; the heads of them *were* two hundred; and all their brethren *were* at their command.

33 Of Zebulun, such as went forth to battle, expert in war, with all instruments of war, fifty thousand, which could keep rank: *they were* not of double heart.

34 And of Naphtali a thousand captains, and with them with shields and spears thirty and seven thousand.

35 And of the Danites expert in war twenty and eight thousand and six hundred.

36 And of Asher, such as went forth to battle, expert in war, forty thousand.

37 And on the other side of *the* Jordan, of the Reubenites, and the Gadites, and of the half tribe of Manasseh, with all manner of instruments of war for the battle, a hundred and twenty thousand.

38 All these men of war, that could keep rank, came with a perfect heart to Hebron, to make David king over all Israel: and all the rest also of Israel *were* of one heart to make David king.

39 And there they were with David three days, eating and drinking: for their brethren had prepared for them.

40 Moreover they that were near them, *even* to Issachar and Zebulun and Naphtali, brought bread on donkeys, and on camels, and on mules, and on oxen, *and* meat, meal, cakes of figs, and bunches of raisins, and wine, and oil, and oxen, and sheep abundantly: for *there was* joy in Israel.

1 Chronicles 13

13:1 ¶ And David consulted with the captains of thousands and hundreds, *and* with every leader.

2 And David said to all the congregation of Israel, If *it seems* good to you, and *that it is* of Yahweh our God, let us send abroad to our brethren every where, *that are* left in all the land of Israel, and with them *also* to the priests and Levites *which are* in their cities *and* suburbs, that they may gather themselves unto us:

3 And let us bring again the ark of our God to us: for we inquired not at it in the days of Saul.

4 And all the congregation said that they would do so: for the thing was right in the eyes of all the people.

5 So David gathered all Israel together, from Shihor of Egypt even unto the entering of Hemath, to bring the ark of God from Kirjathjearim.

6 And David went up, and all Israel, to Baalah, *that is*, to Kirjathjearim, which *belonged* to Judah, to bring up therefrom the ark of God Yahweh, that dwells *between* the cherubims, whose name is called *on it*.

7 And they carried the ark of God in a new cart out of the house of Abinadab: and Uzza and Ahio drove the cart.

8 And David and all Israel played before God with all *their* might, and with singing, and with harps, and with psalteries, and with tambourines, and with cymbals, and with trumpets.

9 ¶ And when they came to the threshingfloor of Chidon, Uzza put forth his hand to hold the ark; for the oxen stumbled.

10 And the anger of Yahweh was kindled against Uzza, and he smote him, because he put his hand to the ark: and there he died before God.

11 And David was displeased, because Yahweh had made a breach upon Uzza: therefore that place is called Perezuzza unto this day.

12 And David was afraid of God that day, saying, How shall I bring the ark of God *home* to me?

13 So David brought not the ark *home* to himself to the city of David, but carried it aside into the house of Obededom the Gittite.

14 And the ark of God remained with the family of Obededom in his house three months. And Yahweh blessed the house of Obededom, and all that he had.

1 Chronicles 14

14:1 ¶ Now Hiram king of Tyre sent messengers to David, and timber of cedars, with masons and carpenters, to build him a house.

2 And David perceived that Yahweh had confirmed him king over Israel, for his kingdom was lifted up on high, because of his people Israel.

3 And David took more wives at Jerusalem: and David begot more sons and daughters.

4 Now these *are* the names of *his* children which he had in Jerusalem; Shammua, and Shobab, Nathan, and Solomon,

5 And Ibhar, and Elishua, and Elpalet,

6 And Nogah, and Nepheg, and Japhia,

7 And Elishama, and Beeliada, and Eliphalet.

8 ¶ And when the Philistines heard that David was anointed king over all Israel, all the Philistines went up to seek David. And David heard *of it*, and went out against them.

9 And the Philistines came and spread themselves in the valley of Rephaim.

10 And David inquired of God, saying, Shall I go up against the Philistines? and will you deliver them into my hand? And Yahweh said to him, Go up; for I will deliver them into your hand.

11 So they came up to Baalperazim; and David smote them there. Then David said, God has broken in upon my enemies by my hand like the breaking forth of waters: therefore they called the name of that place Baalperazim.

12 And when they had left their gods there, David gave a commandment, and they were burned with fire.

13 And the Philistines yet again spread themselves abroad in the valley.

14 Therefore David inquired again of God: and God said to him, Go not up after them; turn away from them, and come upon them over against the mulberry trees.

15 And it shall be, when you shall hear a sound of marching in the tops of the mulberry trees, *that* then you shall go out to battle: for God is gone forth before you to smite the host of the Philistines.

16 David therefore did as God commanded him: and they smote the host of the Philistines from Gibeon even to Gazer.

17 And the fame of David went out into all lands; and Yahweh brought the fear of him upon all nations.

1 Chronicles 15

15:1 ¶ And *David* made him houses in the city of David, and prepared a place for the ark of God, and pitched for it a tent.

2 Then David said, None ought to carry the ark of God but the Levites: for them has Yahweh chosen to carry the ark of God, and to minister unto him forever.

3 And David gathered all Israel together to Jerusalem, to bring up the ark of Yahweh to his place, which he had prepared for it.

4 And David assembled the children of Aaron, and the Levites:

5 Of the sons of Kohath; Uriel the chief, and his brethren a hundred and twenty:

6 Of the sons of Merari; Asaiah the chief, and his brethren two hundred and twenty:

7 Of the sons of Gershom; Joel the chief, and his brethren a hundred and thirty:

8 Of the sons of Elizaphan; Shemaiah the chief, and his brethren two hundred:

9 Of the sons of Hebron; Eliel the chief, and his brethren fourscore:

1 Chronicles 15

10 Of the sons of Uzziel; Amminadab the chief, and his brethren a hundred and twelve.

11 And David called for Zadok and Abiathar the priests, and for the Levites, for Uriel, Asaiah, and Joel, Shemaiah, and Eliel, and Amminadab,

12 And said to them, You *are* the chief of the fathers of the Levites: sanctify yourselves, *both* you and your brethren, that you may bring up the ark of Yahweh God of Israel to *the place that* I have prepared for it.

13 For because you *did it* not at the first, Yahweh our God made a breach upon us, for that we sought him not after the due order.

14 So the priests and the Levites sanctified themselves to bring up the ark of Yahweh God of Israel.

15 And the children of the Levites bore the ark of God upon their shoulders with the staves thereon, as Moses commanded according to the word of Yahweh.

16 And David spoke to the chief of the Levites to appoint their brethren *to be* the singers with instruments of music, psalteries and harps and cymbals, sounding, by lifting up the voice with joy.

17 So the Levites appointed Heman the son of Joel; and of his brethren, Asaph the son of Berechiah; and of the sons of Merari their brethren, Ethan the son of Kushaiah;

18 And with them their brethren of the second *degree*, Zechariah, Ben, and Jaaziel, and Shemiramoth, and Jehiel, and Unni, Eliab, and Benaiah, and Maaseiah, and Mattithiah, and Elipheleh, and Mikneiah, and Obededom, and Jeiel, the porters.

19 So the singers, Heman, Asaph, and Ethan, *were appointed* to sound with cymbals of brass;

20 And Zechariah, and Aziel, and Shemiramoth, and Jehiel, and Unni, and Eliab, and Maaseiah, and Benaiah, with psalteries on Alamoth;

21 And Mattithiah, and Elipheleh, and Mikneiah, and Obededom, and Jeiel, and Azaziah, with harps on the Sheminith to excel.

22 And Chenaniah, chief of the Levites, *was* for song: he instructed about the song, because he *was* skillful.

23 And Berechiah and Elkanah *were* doorkeepers for the ark.

24 And Shebaniah, and Jehoshaphat, and Nethaneel, and Amasai, and Zechariah, and Benaiah, and Eliezer, the priests, did blow with the trumpets before the ark of God: and Obededom and Jehiah *were* doorkeepers for the ark.

25 ¶ So David, and the elders of Israel, and the captains over thousands, went to bring up the ark of the covenant of Yahweh out of the house of Obededom with joy.

26 And it came to pass, when God helped the Levites that bore the ark of the covenant of Yahweh, that they offered seven bullocks and seven rams.

27 And David *was* clothed with a robe of fine linen, and all the Levites that bore the ark, and the singers, and Chenaniah the master of the song with the singers: David also *had* upon him an ephod of linen.

28 Thus all Israel brought up the ark of the covenant of Yahweh with shouting, and with sound of the cornet, and with trumpets, and with cymbals, making a noise with psalteries and harps.

29 And it came to pass, *as* the ark of the covenant of Yahweh came to the city of David, that Michal the daughter of Saul looking out at a window saw king David dancing and playing: and she despised him in her heart.

1 Chronicles 16

16:1 ¶ So they brought the ark of God, and set it in the midst of the tent that David had pitched for it: and they offered burnt sacrifices and peace offerings before God.

2 And when David had made an end of offering the burnt offerings and the peace offerings, he blessed the people in the name of Yahweh.

3 And he dealt to every one of Israel, both man and woman, to every one a loaf of bread, and a good piece of flesh, and a flagon *of wine*.

4 And he appointed *certain* of the Levites to minister before the ark of Yahweh, and to record, and to thank and praise Yahweh God of Israel:

5 Asaph the chief, and next to him Zechariah, Jeiel, and Shemiramoth, and Jehiel, and Mattithiah, and Eliab, and Benaiah, and Obededom: and Jeiel with psalteries and with harps; but Asaph made a sound with cymbals;

6 Benaiah also and Jahaziel the priests with trumpets continually before the ark of the covenant of God.

7 ¶ Then on that day David delivered first *this psalm* to thank Yahweh into the hand of Asaph and his brethren.

8 Give thanks unto Yahweh, call upon his name, make known his deeds among the people.

9 Sing unto him, sing psalms to him, talk you of all his wondrous works.

10 Glory you in his holy name: let the heart of them rejoice that seek Yahweh.

11 Seek Yahweh and his strength, seek his face continually.

12 Remember his marvelous works that he has done, his wonders, and the judgments of his mouth;

13 O you seed of Israel his servant, you children of Jacob, his chosen ones.

14 He *is* Yahweh our God; his judgments *are* in all the earth.

15 Be you mindful always of his covenant; the word *which* he commanded to a thousand generations;

16 *Even of the covenant* which he made with Abraham, and of his oath to Isaac;

17 And has confirmed the same to Jacob for a law, *and* to Israel *for* an everlasting covenant,

18 Saying, Unto you will I give the land of Canaan, the lot of your inheritance;

19 When you were but few, even a few, and strangers in it.

20 And *when* they went from nation to nation, and from *one* kingdom to another people;

21 He allowed no man to do them wrong: yes, he reproved kings for their sakes,

22 *Saying*, Touch not my anointed, and do my prophets no harm.

23 Sing unto Yahweh, all the earth; show forth from day to day his salvation.
24 Declare his glory among the heathen; his marvelous works among all nations.
25 For great *is* Yahweh, and greatly to be praised: he also *is* to be feared above all gods.
26 For all the gods of the people *are* idols: but Yahweh made the heavens.
27 Glory and honor *are* in his presence; strength and gladness *are* in his place.
28 Give unto Yahweh, you kindred of the people, give unto Yahweh glory and strength.
29 Give unto Yahweh the glory *due* unto his name: bring an offering, and come before him: worship Yahweh in the beauty of holiness.
30 Fear before him, all the earth: the world also shall be stable, that it be not moved.
31 Let the heavens be glad, and let the earth rejoice: and let *men* say among the nations, Yahweh reigns.
32 Let the sea roar, and the fullness thereof: let the fields rejoice, and all that *is* therein.
33 Then shall the trees of the woods sing out at the presence of Yahweh, because he comes to judge the earth.
34 O give thanks unto Yahweh; for *he is* good; for his mercy *endures* forever.
35 And say you, Save us, O God of our salvation, and gather us together, and deliver us from the heathen, that we may give thanks to your holy name, *and* glory in your praise.
36 Blessed *be* Yahweh God of Israel forever and ever. And all the people said, Amen, and praised Yahweh.
37 ¶ So he left there before the ark of the covenant of Yahweh Asaph and his brethren, to minister before the ark continually, as every day's work required:
38 And Obededom with their brethren, threescore and eight; Obededom also the son of Jeduthun and Hosah *to be* porters:
39 And Zadok the priest, and his brethren the priests, before the tabernacle of Yahweh in the high place that *was* at Gibeon,
40 To offer burnt offerings unto Yahweh upon the altar of the burnt offering continually morning and evening, and *to do* according to all that is written in the law of Yahweh, which he commanded Israel;
41 And with them Heman and Jeduthun, and the rest that were chosen, who were expressed by name, to give thanks to Yahweh, because his mercy *endures* forever;
42 And with them Heman and Jeduthun with trumpets and cymbals for those that should make a sound, and with musical instruments of God. And the sons of Jeduthun *were* porters.
43 And all the people departed every man to his house: and David returned to bless his house.

1 Chronicles 17

17:1 ¶ Now it came to pass, as David sat in his house, that David said to Nathan the prophet, Lo, I dwell in a house of cedars, but the ark of the covenant of Yahweh *remains* under curtains.
2 Then Nathan said to David, Do all that *is* in your heart; for God *is* with you.
3 And it came to pass the same night, that the word of God came to Nathan, saying,
4 Go and tell David my servant, Thus says Yahweh, You shall not build me a house to dwell in:
5 For I have not dwelt in a house since the day that I brought up Israel unto this day; but have gone from tent to tent, and from *one* tabernacle *to another*.
6 Wherever I have walked with all Israel, spoke I a word to any of the judges of Israel, whom I commanded to feed my people, saying, Why have you not built me a house of cedars?
7 Now therefore thus shall you say to my servant David, Thus says Yahweh of hosts, I took you from the sheepfold, *even* from following the sheep, that you should be ruler over my people Israel:
8 And I have been with you wherever you have walked, and have cut off all your enemies from before you, and have made you a name like the name of the great men that *are* in the earth.
9 Also I will ordain a place for my people Israel, and will plant them, and they shall dwell in their place, and shall be moved no more; neither shall the children of wickedness waste them any more, as at the beginning,
10 And since the time that I commanded judges *to be* over my people Israel. Moreover I will subdue all your enemies. Furthermore I tell you that Yahweh will build you a house.
11 And it shall come to pass, when your days are expired that you must go *to be* with your fathers, that I will raise up your seed after you, which shall be of your sons; and I will establish his kingdom.
12 He shall build me a house, and I will establish his throne forever.
13 I will be his father, and he shall be my son: and I will not take my mercy away from him, as I took *it* from *him* that was before you:
14 But I will settle him in my house and in my kingdom forever: and his throne shall be established forevermore.
15 According to all these words, and according to all this vision, so did Nathan speak to David.
16 ¶ And David the king came and sat before Yahweh, and said, Who *am* I, O Yahweh God, and what *is* my house, that you have brought me till now?
17 And *yet* this was a small thing in your eyes, O God; for you have *also* spoken of your servant's house for a great while to come, and have regarded me according to the estate of a man of high degree, O Yahweh God.
18 What can David *speak* more to you for the honor of your servant? for you know your servant.
19 O Yahweh, for your servant's sake, and according to your own heart, have you done all this greatness, in making known all *these* great things.
20 O Yahweh, *there is* none like you, neither *is there any* God besides you, according to all that we have heard with our ears.

21 And what one nation in the earth *is* like your people Israel, whom God went to redeem *to be* his own people, to make you a name of greatness and awe, by driving out nations from before your people, whom you have redeemed out of Egypt?

22 For your people Israel did you make your own people forever; and you, Yahweh, became their God.

23 Therefore now, Yahweh, let the thing that you have spoken concerning your servant and concerning his house be established forever, and do as you have said.

24 Let it even be established, that your name may be magnified forever, saying, Yahweh of hosts *is* the God of Israel, *even* a God to Israel: and *let* the house of David your servant *be* established before you.

25 For you, O my God, have told your servant that you will build him a house: therefore your servant has found *in his heart* to pray before you.

26 And now, Yahweh, you are God, and have promised this goodness to your servant:

27 Now therefore let it please you to bless the house of your servant, that it may be before you forever: for you bless, O Yahweh, and *it shall be* blessed forever.

1 Chronicles 18

18:1 ¶ Now after this it came to pass, that David smote the Philistines, and subdued them, and took Gath and her towns out of the hand of the Philistines.

2 And he smote Moab; and the Moabites became David's servants, *and* brought gifts.

3 And David smote Hadarezer king of Zobah to Hamath, as he went to establish his dominion by the river Euphrates.

4 And David took from him a thousand chariots, and seven thousand horsemen, and twenty thousand footmen: David also crippled all the chariot *horses*, but reserved of them a hundred chariots.

5 And when the Syrians of Damascus came to help Hadarezer king of Zobah, David slew of the Syrians two and twenty thousand men.

6 Then David put *garrisons* in Syriadamascus; and the Syrians became David's servants, *and* brought gifts. Thus Yahweh preserved David wherever he went.

7 And David took the shields of gold that were on the servants of Hadarezer, and brought them to Jerusalem.

8 Likewise from Tibhath, and from Chun, cities of Hadarezer, brought David very much brass, with which Solomon made the brazen sea, and the pillars, and the vessels of brass.

9 ¶ Now when Tou king of Hamath heard how David had smitten all the host of Hadarezer king of Zobah;

10 He sent Hadoram his son to king David, to inquire of his welfare, and to congratulate him, because he had fought against Hadarezer, and smitten him; (for Hadarezer had war with Tou;) and *with him* all manner of vessels of gold and silver and brass.

11 Those also king David dedicated unto Yahweh, with the silver and the gold that he brought from all *these* nations; from Edom, and from Moab, and from the children of Ammon, and from the Philistines, and from Amalek.

12 Moreover Abishai the son of Zeruiah slew of the Edomites in the valley of salt eighteen thousand.

13 And he put garrisons in Edom; and all the Edomites became David's servants. Thus Yahweh preserved David wherever he went.

14 So David reigned over all Israel, and executed judgment and justice among all his people.

15 And Joab the son of Zeruiah *was* over the host; and Jehoshaphat the son of Ahilud, recorder.

16 And Zadok the son of Ahitub, and Abimelech the son of Abiathar, *were* the priests; and Shavsha was *the* scribe;

17 And Benaiah the son of Jehoiada *was* over the Cherethites and the Pelethites; and the sons of David *were* chief about the king.

1 Chronicles 19

19:1 ¶ Now it came to pass after this, that Nahash the king of the children of Ammon died, and his son reigned in his stead.

2 And David said, I will show kindness to Hanun the son of Nahash, because his father showed kindness to me. And David sent messengers to comfort him concerning his father. So the servants of David came into the land of the children of Ammon to Hanun, to comfort him.

3 But the princes of the children of Ammon said to Hanun, Think you that David does honor your father, that he has sent comforters to you? are not his servants come to you for to search, and to overthrow, and to spy out the land?

4 Therefore Hanun took David's servants, and shaved them, and cut off their garments in the middle next to their buttocks, and sent them away.

5 Then there went *certain*, and told David how the men were served. And he sent to meet them: for the men were greatly ashamed. And the king said, Remain at Jericho until your beards are grown, and *then* return.

6 ¶ And when the children of Ammon saw that they had made themselves odious to David, Hanun and the children of Ammon sent a thousand talents of silver to hire them chariots and horsemen out of Mesopotamia, and out of Syriamaachah, and out of Zobah.

7 So they hired thirty and two thousand chariots, and the king of Maachah and his people; who came and pitched before Medeba. And the children of Ammon gathered themselves together from their cities, and came to battle.

8 And when David heard *of it*, he sent Joab, and all the host of the mighty men.

9 And the children of Ammon came out, and put the battle in array before the gate of the city: and the kings that had come *were* by themselves in the field.

10 Now when Joab saw that the battle was set against him before and behind, he chose out of all the choice of Israel, and put *them* in array against the Syrians.

11 And the rest of the people he delivered to the hand of Abishai his brother, and they set *themselves* in array against the children of Ammon.
12 And he said, If the Syrians are too strong for me, then you shall help me: but if the children of Ammon are too strong for you, then I will help you.
13 Be of good courage, and let us behave ourselves valiantly for our people, and for the cities of our God: and let Yahweh do *that which is* good in his sight.
14 So Joab and the people that *were* with him drew near before the Syrians unto the battle; and they fled before him.
15 And when the children of Ammon saw that the Syrians had fled, they likewise fled before Abishai his brother, and entered into the city. Then Joab came to Jerusalem.
16 And when the Syrians saw that they were put to the worse before Israel, they sent messengers, and drew forth the Syrians that *were* beyond the river: and Shophach the captain of the host of Hadarezer *went* before them.
17 And it was told *to* David; and he gathered all Israel, and passed over *the* Jordan, and came upon them, and set *the battle* in array against them. So when David had put the battle in array against the Syrians, they fought with him.
18 But the Syrians fled before Israel; and David slew of the Syrians seven thousand *men which fought in* chariots, and forty thousand footmen, and killed Shophach the captain of the host.
19 And when the servants of Hadarezer saw that they were put to the worse before Israel, they made peace with David, and became his servants: neither would the Syrians help the children of Ammon any more.

1 Chronicles 20

20:1 ¶ And it came to pass, that after the year was expired, at the time that kings go out *to battle*, Joab led forth the power of the army, and wasted the country of the children of Ammon, and came and besieged Rabbah. But David remained in Jerusalem. And Joab smote Rabbah, and destroyed it.
2 And David took the crown of their king from off his head, and found it to weigh a talent of gold, and *there were* precious stones in it; and it was set upon David's head: and he brought also exceedingly much spoil out of the city.
3 And he brought out the people that *were* in it, and cut *them* with saws, and with harrows of iron, and with axes. Even so dealt David with all the cities of the children of Ammon. And David and all the people returned to Jerusalem.
4 ¶ And it came to pass after this, that there arose war at Gezer with the Philistines; at which time Sibbechai the Hushathite slew Sippai, *that was* of the children of the giant: and they were subdued.
5 And there was war again with the Philistines; and Elhanan the son of Jair slew Lahmi the brother of Goliath the Gittite, whose spear staff *was* like a weaver's beam.
6 And yet again there was war at Gath, where was a man of *great* stature, whose fingers and toes *were* four and twenty, six *on each hand*, and six *on each foot*: and he also was the son of the giant.
7 But when he defied Israel, Jonathan the son of Shimea, David's brother, slew him.
8 These were born to the giant in Gath; and they fell by the hand of David, and by the hand of his servants.

1 Chronicles 21

21:1 ¶ And Satan stood up against Israel, and provoked David to number Israel.
2 And David said to Joab and to the rulers of the people, Go, number Israel from Beersheba even to Dan; and bring the number of them to me, that I may know *it*.
3 And Joab answered, Yahweh make his people a hundred times so many more as they *are*: but, my lord the king, *are* they not all my lord's servants? why then does my lord require this thing? why will he be a cause of trespass to Israel?
4 Nevertheless the king's word prevailed against Joab. Therefore Joab departed, and went throughout all Israel, and came to Jerusalem.
5 And Joab gave the sum of the number of the people to David. And all *they of* Israel were a thousand thousand and a hundred thousand men that drew *the* sword: and Judah *was* four hundred threescore and ten thousand men that drew *the* sword.
6 But Levi and Benjamin counted he not among them: for the king's word was abominable to Joab.
7 ¶ And God was displeased with this thing; therefore he smote Israel.
8 And David said to God, I have sinned greatly, because I have done this thing: but now, I beseech you, take away the iniquity of your servant; for I have done very foolishly.
9 And Yahweh spoke to Gad, David's seer, saying,
10 Go and tell David, saying, Thus says Yahweh, I offer you three *things*: choose you one of them, that I may do *it* to you.
11 So Gad came to David, and said to him, Thus says Yahweh, Choose you
12 Either three years *of* famine; or three months to be destroyed before your foes, while that the sword of your enemies overtakes *you*; or else *for* three days the sword of Yahweh, even the pestilence, in the land, and the angel of Yahweh destroying throughout all the coasts of Israel. Now therefore advise yourself what word I shall bring back to him that sent me.
13 And David said to Gad, I am in great distress: let me fall now into the hand of Yahweh; for very great *are* his mercies: but let me not fall into the hand of man.
14 So Yahweh sent pestilence upon Israel: and there fell of Israel seventy thousand men.
15 And God sent an angel to Jerusalem to destroy it: and as he was destroying, Yahweh beheld, and he repented him of

1 Chronicles 21

the evil, and said to the angel that destroyed, It is enough, stay now your hand. And the angel of Yahweh stood by the threshingfloor of Ornan the Jebusite.

16 And David lifted up his eyes, and saw the angel of Yahweh stand between the earth and the heaven, having a drawn sword in his hand stretched out over Jerusalem. Then David and the elders *of Israel, who were* clothed in sackcloth, fell upon their faces.

17 And David said to God, *Is it* not I *that* commanded the people to be numbered? even I it is that have sinned and done evil indeed; but *as for* these sheep, what have they done? let your hand, I pray you, O Yahweh my God, be on me, and on my father's house; but not on your people, that they should be plagued.

18 ¶ Then the angel of Yahweh commanded Gad to say to David, that David should go up, and set up an altar unto Yahweh in the threshingfloor of Ornan the Jebusite.

19 And David went up at the saying of Gad, which he spoke in the name of Yahweh.

20 And Ornan turned back, and saw the angel; and his four sons with him hid themselves. Now Ornan was threshing wheat.

21 And as David came to Ornan, Ornan looked and saw David, and went out of the threshingfloor, and bowed himself to David with *his* face to the ground.

22 Then David said to Ornan, Grant me the place of *this* threshingfloor, that I may build an altar therein unto Yahweh: you shall grant it *to* me for the full price: that the plague may be stayed from the people.

23 And Ornan said to David, Take *it* to you, and let my lord the king do *that which is* good in his eyes: lo, I give *you* the oxen *also* for burnt offerings, and the threshing instruments for wood, and the wheat for the meat offering; I give it all.

24 And king David said to Ornan, No; but I will truly buy it for the full price: for I will not take *that* which *is* yours for Yahweh, nor offer burnt offerings without cost.

25 So David gave to Ornan for the place six hundred shekels of gold by weight.

26 And David built there an altar unto Yahweh, and offered burnt offerings and peace offerings, and called upon Yahweh; and he answered him from heaven by fire upon the altar of burnt offering.

27 And Yahweh commanded the angel; and he put up his sword again into the sheath thereof.

28 At that time when David saw that Yahweh had answered him in the threshingfloor of Ornan the Jebusite, then he sacrificed there.

29 For the tabernacle of Yahweh, which Moses made in the wilderness, and the altar of the burnt offering, *were* at that season in the high place at Gibeon.

30 But David could not go before it to inquire of God: for he was afraid because of the sword of the angel of Yahweh.

1 Chronicles 22

22:1 ¶ Then David said, This *is* the house of Yahweh God, and this *is* the altar of the burnt offering for Israel.

2 And David commanded to gather together the strangers that *were* in the land of Israel; and he set masons to hew worked stones to build the house of God.

3 And David prepared iron in abundance for the nails for the doors of the gates, and for the joints; and brass in abundance without weight;

4 Also cedar trees in abundance: for the Zidonians and they of Tyre brought much cedar wood to David.

5 And David said, Solomon my son *is* young and tender, and the house *that is* to be built for Yahweh *must be* exceedingly magnificent, of fame and of glory throughout all countries: I will *therefore* now make preparation for it. So David prepared abundantly before his death.

6 ¶ Then he called for Solomon his son, and charged him to build a house for Yahweh God of Israel.

7 And David said to Solomon, My son, as for me, it was in my mind to build a house unto the name of Yahweh my God:

8 But the word of Yahweh came to me, saying, You have shed blood abundantly, and have made great wars: you shall not build a house unto my name, because you have shed much blood upon the earth in my sight.

9 Behold, a son shall be born to you, who shall be a man of rest; and I will give him rest from all his enemies round about: for his name shall be Solomon, and I will give peace and quietness to Israel in his days.

10 He shall build a house for my name; and he shall be my son, and I *will be* his father; and I will establish the throne of his kingdom over Israel forever.

11 Now, my son, Yahweh be with you; and prosper you, and build the house of Yahweh your God, as he has said to you.

12 Only Yahweh give you wisdom and understanding, and give you charge concerning Israel, that you may keep the law of Yahweh your God.

13 Then shall you prosper, if you take heed to fulfill the statutes and judgments which Yahweh charged Moses with concerning Israel: be strong, and of good courage; dread not, nor be dismayed.

14 Now, behold, in my trouble I have prepared for the house of Yahweh a hundred thousand talents of gold, and a thousand thousand talents of silver; and of brass and iron without weight; for it is in abundance: timber also and stone have I prepared; and you may add thereto.

15 Moreover *there are* workmen with you in abundance, hewers and workers of stone and timber, and all manner of cunning men for every manner of work.

16 Of the gold, the silver, and the brass, and the iron, *there is* no number. Arise *therefore*, and be doing, and Yahweh be with you.

17 ¶ David also commanded all the princes of Israel to help Solomon his son, *saying,*

18 *Is* not Yahweh your God with you? and has he *not* given you rest on every side? for he has given the

inhabitants of the land into my hand; and the land is subdued before Yahweh, and before his people.

19 Now set your heart and your soul to seek Yahweh your God; arise therefore, and build you the sanctuary of Yahweh God, to bring the ark of the covenant of Yahweh, and the holy vessels of God, into the house that is to be built to the name of Yahweh.

1 Chronicles 23

23:1 ¶ So when David was old and full of days, he made Solomon his son king over Israel.
2 And he gathered together all the princes of Israel, with the priests and the Levites.
3 Now the Levites were numbered from the age of thirty years and upward: and their number by their heads, man by man, was thirty and eight thousand.
4 Of which, twenty and four thousand *were* to set forward the work of the house of Yahweh; and six thousand *were* officers and judges:
5 Moreover four thousand *were* porters; and four thousand praised Yahweh with the instruments which I made, *said David*, to praise *therewith*.
6 And David divided them into courses among the sons of Levi, *namely*, Gershon, Kohath, and Merari.
7 Of the Gershonites *were*, Laadan, and Shimei.
8 The sons of Laadan; the chief *was* Jehiel, and Zetham, and Joel, three.
9 The sons of Shimei; Shelomith, and Haziel, and Haran, three. These *were* the chief of the fathers of Laadan.
10 And the sons of Shimei *were*, Jahath, Zina, and Jeush, and Beriah. These four *were* the sons of Shimei.
11 And Jahath was the chief, and Zizah the second: but Jeush and Beriah had not many sons; therefore they were in one reckoning, according to *their* father's house.
12 The sons of Kohath; Amram, Izhar, Hebron, and Uzziel, four.
13 The sons of Amram; Aaron and Moses: and Aaron was separated, that he should sanctify the most holy things, he and his sons forever, to burn incense before Yahweh, to minister unto him, and to bless in his name forever.
14 Now *concerning* Moses the man of God, his sons were named of the tribe of Levi.
15 The sons of Moses *were*, Gershom, and Eliezer.
16 Of the sons of Gershom, Shebuel *was* the chief.
17 And the son of Eliezer *was*, Rehabiah the chief. And Eliezer had no other sons; but the sons of Rehabiah were very many.
18 Of the sons of Izhar; Shelomith the chief.
19 Of the sons of Hebron; Jeriah the first, Amariah the second, Jahaziel the third, and Jekameam the fourth.
20 Of the sons of Uzziel; Michah the first, and Jesiah the second.
21 The sons of Merari; Mahli, and Mushi. The sons of Mahli; Eleazar, and Kish.
22 And Eleazar died, and had no sons, but daughters: and their brethren the sons of Kish took them.
23 The sons of Mushi; Mahli, and Eder, and Jeremoth, three.
24 ¶ These *were* the sons of Levi after the house of their fathers; *even* the chief of the fathers, as they were counted by number of names by their heads, that did the work for the service of the house of Yahweh, from the age of twenty years and upward.
25 For David said, Yahweh God of Israel has given rest to his people, that they may dwell in Jerusalem forever:
26 And also to the Levites; they shall no *more* carry the tabernacle, nor any vessels of it for the service thereof.
27 For by the last words of David the Levites *were* numbered from twenty years old and above:
28 Because their office *was* to wait on the sons of Aaron for the service of the house of Yahweh, in the courts, and in the chambers, and in the purifying of all holy things, and the work of the service of the house of God;
29 Both for the showbread, and for the fine flour for meat offering, and for the unleavened cakes, and for *that which is baked in* the pan, and for that which is fried, and for all manner of measure and size;
30 And to stand every morning to thank and praise Yahweh, and likewise at evening;
31 And to offer all burnt sacrifices unto Yahweh in the sabbaths, in the new moons, and on the set feasts, by number, according to the order commanded to them, continually before Yahweh:
32 And that they should keep the charge of the tabernacle of the congregation, and the charge of the holy *place*, and the charge of the sons of Aaron their brethren, in the service of the house of Yahweh.

1 Chronicles 24

24:1 ¶ Now *these are* the divisions of the sons of Aaron. The sons of Aaron; Nadab, and Abihu, Eleazar, and Ithamar.
2 But Nadab and Abihu died before their father, and had no children: therefore Eleazar and Ithamar executed the priest's office.
3 And David distributed them, both Zadok of the sons of Eleazar, and Ahimelech of the sons of Ithamar, according to their offices in their service.
4 And there were more chief men found of the sons of Eleazar than of the sons of Ithamar; and *thus* were they divided. Among the sons of Eleazar *there were* sixteen chief men of the house of *their* fathers, and eight among the sons of Ithamar according to the house of their fathers.
5 Thus were they divided by lot, one sort with another; for the governors of the sanctuary, and governors *of the house* of God, were of the sons of Eleazar, and of the sons of Ithamar.
6 And Shemaiah the son of Nethaneel the scribe, *one* of the Levites, wrote them before the king, and the princes, and Zadok the priest, and Ahimelech the son of Abiathar, and *before* the chief of the fathers of the priests and Levites: one principal household being taken for Eleazar, and *one* taken for Ithamar.

1 Chronicles 24

7 Now the first lot came forth to Jehoiarib, the second to Jedaiah,
8 The third to Harim, the fourth to Seorim,
9 The fifth to Malchijah, the sixth to Mijamin,
10 The seventh to Hakkoz, the eighth to Abijah,
11 The ninth to Jeshua, the tenth to Shecaniah,
12 The eleventh to Eliashib, the twelfth to Jakim,
13 The thirteenth to Huppah, the fourteenth to Jeshebeab,
14 The fifteenth to Bilgah, the sixteenth to Immer,
15 The seventeenth to Hezir, the eighteenth to Aphses,
16 The nineteenth to Pethahiah, the twentieth to Jehezekel,
17 The one and twentieth to Jachin, the two and twentieth to Gamul,
18 The three and twentieth to Delaiah, the four and twentieth to Maaziah.
19 These *were* the orderings of them in their service to come into the house of Yahweh, according to their manner, under Aaron their father, as Yahweh God of Israel had commanded him.
20 ¶ And the rest of the sons of Levi *were these*: Of the sons of Amram; Shubael: of the sons of Shubael; Jehdeiah.
21 Concerning Rehabiah: of the sons of Rehabiah, the first *was* Isshiah.
22 Of the Izharites; Shelomoth: of the sons of Shelomoth; Jahath.
23 And the sons *of Hebron*; Jeriah *the first*, Amariah the second, Jahaziel the third, Jekameam the fourth.
24 *Of* the sons of Uzziel; Michah: of the sons of Michah; Shamir.
25 The brother of Michah *was* Isshiah: of the sons of Isshiah; Zechariah.
26 The sons of Merari *were* Mahli and Mushi: the sons of Jaaziah; Beno.
27 The sons of Merari by Jaaziah; Beno, and Shoham, and Zaccur, and Ibri.
28 Of Mahli *came* Eleazar, who had no sons.
29 Concerning Kish: the son of Kish *was* Jerahmeel.
30 The sons also of Mushi; Mahli, and Eder, and Jerimoth. These *were* the sons of the Levites after the house of their fathers.
31 These likewise cast lots over against their brethren the sons of Aaron in the presence of David the king, and Zadok, and Ahimelech, and the chief of the fathers of the priests and Levites, even the principal fathers over against their younger brethren.

1 Chronicles 25

25:1 ¶ Moreover David and the captains of the host separated to the service of the sons of Asaph, and of Heman, and of Jeduthun, who should prophesy with harps, with psalteries, and with cymbals: and the number of the workmen according to their service was:
2 Of the sons of Asaph; Zaccur, and Joseph, and Nethaniah, and Asarelah, the sons of Asaph under the hands of Asaph, which prophesied according to the order of the king.
3 Of Jeduthun: the sons of Jeduthun; Gedaliah, and Zeri, and Jeshaiah, Hashabiah, and Mattithiah, six, under the hands of their father Jeduthun, who prophesied with a harp, to give thanks and to praise Yahweh.
4 Of Heman: the sons of Heman; Bukkiah, Mattaniah, Uzziel, Shebuel, and Jerimoth, Hananiah, Hanani, Eliathah, Giddalti, and Romamtiezer, Joshbekashah, Mallothi, Hothir, *and* Mahazioth:
5 All these *were* the sons of Heman the king's seer in the words of God, to lift up the horn. And God gave to Heman fourteen sons and three daughters.
6 All these *were* under the hands of their father for song *in* the house of Yahweh, with cymbals, psalteries, and harps, for the service of the house of God, according to the king's order to Asaph, Jeduthun, and Heman.
7 So the number of them, with their brethren that were instructed in the songs of Yahweh, *even* all that were cunning, was two hundred fourscore and eight.
8 ¶ And they cast lots, ward against *ward*, as well the small as the great, the teacher as the scholar.
9 Now the first lot came forth for Asaph to Joseph: the second to Gedaliah, who with his brethren and sons *were* twelve:
10 The third to Zaccur, *he*, his sons, and his brethren, *were* twelve:
11 The fourth to Izri, *he*, his sons, and his brethren, *were* twelve:
12 The fifth to Nethaniah, *he*, his sons, and his brethren, *were* twelve:
13 The sixth to Bukkiah, *he*, his sons, and his brethren, *were* twelve:
14 The seventh to Jesharelah, *he*, his sons, and his brethren, *were* twelve:
15 The eighth to Jeshaiah, *he*, his sons, and his brethren, *were* twelve:
16 The ninth to Mattaniah, *he*, his sons, and his brethren, *were* twelve:
17 The tenth to Shimei, *he*, his sons, and his brethren, *were* twelve:
18 The eleventh to Azareel, *he*, his sons, and his brethren, *were* twelve:
19 The twelfth to Hashabiah, *he*, his sons, and his brethren, *were* twelve:
20 The thirteenth to Shubael, *he*, his sons, and his brethren, *were* twelve:
21 The fourteenth to Mattithiah, *he*, his sons, and his brethren, *were* twelve:
22 The fifteenth to Jeremoth, *he*, his sons, and his brethren, *were* twelve:
23 The sixteenth to Hananiah, *he*, his sons, and his brethren, *were* twelve:
24 The seventeenth to Joshbekashah, *he*, his sons, and his brethren, *were* twelve:
25 The eighteenth to Hanani, *he*, his sons, and his brethren, *were* twelve:
26 The nineteenth to Mallothi, *he*, his sons, and his brethren, *were* twelve:
27 The twentieth to Eliathah, *he*, his sons, and his brethren, *were* twelve:

28 The one and twentieth to Hothir, *he*, his sons, and his brethren, *were* twelve:
29 The two and twentieth to Giddalti, *he*, his sons, and his brethren, *were* twelve:
30 The three and twentieth to Mahazioth, *he*, his sons, and his brethren, *were* twelve:
31 The four and twentieth to Romamtiezer, *he*, his sons, and his brethren, *were* twelve.

1 Chronicles 26

26:1 ¶ Concerning the divisions of the porters: Of the Korhites *was* Meshelemiah the son of Kore, of the sons of Asaph.
2 And the sons of Meshelemiah *were*, Zechariah the firstborn, Jediael the second, Zebadiah the third, Jathniel the fourth,
3 Elam the fifth, Jehohanan the sixth, Elioenai the seventh.
4 Moreover the sons of Obededom *were*, Shemaiah the firstborn, Jehozabad the second, Joah the third, and Sacar the fourth, and Nethaneel the fifth,
5 Ammiel the sixth, Issachar the seventh, Peulthai the eighth: for God blessed him.
6 Also unto Shemaiah his son were sons born, that ruled throughout the house of their father: for they *were* mighty men of valor.
7 The sons of Shemaiah; Othni, and Rephael, and Obed, Elzabad, whose brethren *were* strong men, Elihu, and Semachiah.
8 All these of the sons of Obededom: they and their sons and their brothers, able men for strength for the service, *were* threescore and two of Obededom.
9 And Meshelemiah had sons and brothers, strong men, eighteen.
10 Also Hosah, of the children of Merari, had sons; Simri the chief, (for *though* he was not the firstborn, yet his father made him the chief;)
11 Hilkiah the second, Tebaliah the third, Zechariah the fourth: all the sons and brothers of Hosah *were* thirteen.
12 Among these *were* the divisions of the porters, *even* among the chief men, *having* wards one against another, to minister in the house of Yahweh.
13 And they cast lots, as well the small as the great, according to the house of their fathers, for every gate.
14 And the lot eastward fell to Shelemiah. Then for Zechariah his son, a wise counselor, they cast lots; and his lot came out northward.
15 To Obededom southward; and to his sons the house of Asuppim.
16 To Shuppim and Hosah *the lot came forth* westward, with the gate Shallecheth, by the causeway of the going up, ward beside ward.
17 Eastward *were* six Levites, northward four a day, southward four a day, and toward Asuppim two *and* two.
18 At Parbar westward, four at the causeway, *and* two at Parbar.
19 These *are* the divisions of the porters among the sons of Kore, and among the sons of Merari.
20 ¶ And of the Levites, Ahijah *was* over the treasuries of the house of God, and over the treasuries of the dedicated things.
21 *As concerning* the sons of Laadan; the sons of the Gershonite Laadan, chief fathers, *even* of Laadan the Gershonite, *was* Jehieli.
22 The sons of Jehieli; Zetham, and Joel his brother, *which were* over the treasuries of the house of Yahweh.
23 Of the Amramites, *and* the Izharites, the Hebronites, *and* the Uzzielites:
24 And Shebuel the son of Gershom, the son of Moses, *was* ruler of the treasuries.
25 And his brethren by Eliezer; Rehabiah his son, and Jeshaiah his son, and Joram his son, and Zichri his son, and Shelomith his son.
26 Which Shelomith and his brethren *were* over all the treasures of the dedicated things, which David the king, and the chief fathers, the captains over thousands and hundreds, and the captains of the host, had dedicated.
27 Out of the spoils won in battles did they dedicate to maintain the house of Yahweh.
28 And all that Samuel the seer, and Saul the son of Kish, and Abner the son of Ner, and Joab the son of Zeruiah, had dedicated; *and* whoever had dedicated anything, *it was* under the hand of Shelomith, and of his brethren.
29 ¶ Of the Izharites, Chenaniah and his sons *were* for the outward business over Israel, for officers and judges.
30 *And* of the Hebronites, Hashabiah and his brethren, men of valor, a thousand and seven hundred, *were* officers among them of Israel on this side *of the* Jordan westward in all the business of Yahweh, and in the service of the king.
31 Among the Hebronites *was* Jerijah the chief, *even* among the Hebronites, according to the generations of his fathers. In the fortieth year of the reign of David they were sought for, and there were found among them mighty men of valor at Jazer of Gilead.
32 And his brethren, men of valor, *were* two thousand and seven hundred chief fathers, whom king David made rulers over the Reubenites, the Gadites, and the half tribe of Manasseh, for every matter pertaining to God, and affairs of the king.

1 Chronicles 27

27:1 ¶ Now the children of Israel after their number, *to know*, the chief fathers and captains of thousands and hundreds, and their officers that served the king in any matter of the courses, which came in and went out month by month throughout all the months of the year, of every course *were* twenty and four thousand.
2 Over the first course for the first month *was* Jashobeam the son of Zabdiel: and in his division *were* twenty and four thousand.
3 Of the children of Perez *was* the chief of all the captains of the host for the first month.

4 And over the course of the second month *was* Dodai an Ahohite, and of his course *was* Mikloth also the ruler: in his course likewise *were* twenty and four thousand.

5 The third captain of the host for the third month *was* Benaiah the son of Jehoiada, a chief priest: and in his course *were* twenty and four thousand.

6 This *is that* Benaiah, *who was* mighty *among* the thirty, and above the thirty: and in his course *was* Ammizabad his son.

7 The fourth *captain* for the fourth month *was* Asahel the brother of Joab, and Zebadiah his son after him: and in his course *were* twenty and four thousand.

8 The fifth captain for the fifth month *was* Shamhuth the Izrahite: and in his course *were* twenty and four thousand.

9 The sixth *captain* for the sixth month *was* Ira the son of Ikkesh the Tekoite: and in his course *were* twenty and four thousand.

10 The seventh *captain* for the seventh month *was* Helez the Pelonite, of the children of Ephraim: and in his course *were* twenty and four thousand.

11 The eighth *captain* for the eighth month *was* Sibbecai the Hushathite, of the Zarhites: and in his course *were* twenty and four thousand.

12 The ninth *captain* for the ninth month *was* Abiezer the Anetothite, of the Benjamites: and in his course *were* twenty and four thousand.

13 The tenth *captain* for the tenth month *was* Maharai the Netophathite, of the Zarhites: and in his course *were* twenty and four thousand.

14 The eleventh *captain* for the eleventh month *was* Benaiah the Pirathonite, of the children of Ephraim: and in his course *were* twenty and four thousand.

15 The twelfth *captain* for the twelfth month *was* Heldai the Netophathite, of Othniel: and in his course *were* twenty and four thousand.

16 ¶ Furthermore over the tribes of Israel: the ruler of the Reubenites *was* Eliezer the son of Zichri: of the Simeonites, Shephatiah the son of Maachah:

17 Of the Levites, Hashabiah the son of Kemuel: of the Aaronites, Zadok:

18 Of Judah, Elihu, *one* of the brethren of David: of Issachar, Omri the son of Michael:

19 Of Zebulun, Ishmaiah the son of Obadiah: of Naphtali, Jerimoth the son of Azriel:

20 Of the children of Ephraim, Hoshea the son of Azaziah: of the half tribe of Manasseh, Joel the son of Pedaiah:

21 Of the half *tribe* of Manasseh in Gilead, Iddo the son of Zechariah: of Benjamin, Jaasiel the son of Abner:

22 Of Dan, Azareel the son of Jeroham. These *were* the princes of the tribes of Israel.

23 But David took not the number of them from twenty years old and under: because Yahweh had said he would increase Israel like to the stars of the heavens.

24 Joab the son of Zeruiah began to number, but he finished not, because there fell wrath for it against Israel; neither was the number put in the account of the chronicles of king David.

25 And over the king's treasures *was* Azmaveth the son of Adiel: and over the storehouses in the fields, in the cities, and in the villages, and in the castles, *was* Jehonathan the son of Uzziah:

26 And over them that did the work of the field for tillage of the ground *was* Ezri the son of Chelub:

27 And over the vineyards *was* Shimei the Ramathite: over the increase of the vineyards for the wine cellars *was* Zabdi the Shiphmite:

28 And over the olive trees and the sycamore trees that *were* in the low plains *was* Baalhanan the Gederite: and over the cellars of oil *was* Joash:

29 And over the herds that fed in Sharon *was* Shitrai the Sharonite: and over the herds *that were* in the valleys *was* Shaphat the son of Adlai:

30 Over the camels also *was* Obil the Ishmaelite: and over the donkeys *was* Jehdeiah the Meronothite:

31 And over the flocks *was* Jaziz the Hagerite. All these *were* the rulers of the substance which *was* king David's.

32 Also Jonathan, David's uncle, was a counselor, a wise man, and a scribe: and Jehiel the son of Hachmoni *was* with the king's sons:

33 And Ahithophel *was* the king's counselor: and Hushai the Archite *was* the king's companion:

34 And after Ahithophel *was* Jehoiada the son of Benaiah, and Abiathar: and the general of the king's army *was* Joab.

1 Chronicles 28

28:1 ¶ And David assembled all the princes of Israel, the princes of the tribes, and the captains of the companies that ministered to the king by course, and the captains over the thousands, and captains over the hundreds, and the stewards over all the substance and possession of the king, and of his sons, with the officers, and with the mighty men, and with all the valiant men, to Jerusalem.

2 Then David the king stood up upon his feet, and said, Hear me, my brethren, and my people: *As for me*, I had in my heart to build a house of rest for the ark of the covenant of Yahweh, and for the footstool of our God, and had made ready for the building:

3 But God said to me, You shall not build a house for my name, because you *have been* a man of war, and have shed blood.

4 However Yahweh God of Israel chose me before all the house of my father to be king over Israel forever: for he has chosen Judah *to be* the ruler; and of the house of Judah, the house of my father; and among the sons of my father he liked me to make *me* king over all Israel:

5 And of all my sons, (for Yahweh has given me many sons,) he has chosen Solomon my son to sit upon the throne of the kingdom of Yahweh over Israel.

6 And he said to me, Solomon your son, he shall build my house and my courts: for I have chosen him *to be* my son, and I will be his father.

7 Moreover I will establish his kingdom forever, if he is constant to do my commandments and my judgments, as at this day.

8 Now therefore in the sight of all Israel the congregation of Yahweh, and in the audience of our God, keep and seek for all the commandments of Yahweh your God: that you may possess this good land, and leave *it* for an inheritance for your children after you forever.
9 And you, Solomon my son, know you the God of your father, and serve him with a perfect heart and with a willing mind: for Yahweh searches all hearts, and understands all the imaginations of the thoughts: if you seek him, he will be found by you; but if you forsake him, he will cast you off forever.
10 Take heed now; for Yahweh has chosen you to build a house for the sanctuary: be strong, and do *it*.
11 ¶ Then David gave to Solomon his son the pattern of the porch, and of the houses thereof, and of the treasuries thereof, and of the upper chambers thereof, and of the inner parlors thereof, and of the place of the mercy seat,
12 And the pattern of all that he had by the spirit, of the courts of the house of Yahweh, and of all the chambers round about, of the treasuries of the house of God, and of the treasuries of the dedicated things:
13 Also for the courses of the priests and the Levites, and for all the work of the service of the house of Yahweh, and for all the vessels of service in the house of Yahweh.
14 *He gave* of gold by weight for *things* of gold, for all instruments of all manner of service; *silver also* for all instruments of silver by weight, for all instruments of every kind of service:
15 Even the weight for the candlesticks of gold, and for their lamps of gold, by weight for every candlestick, and for the lamps thereof: and for the candlesticks of silver by weight, *both* for the candlestick, and *also* for the lamps thereof, according to the use of every candlestick.
16 And by weight *he gave* gold for the tables of showbread, for every table; and *likewise* silver for the tables of silver:
17 Also pure gold for the meat hooks, and the bowls, and the cups: and for the golden basins *he gave gold* by weight for every basin; and *likewise silver* by weight for every basin of silver:
18 And for the altar of incense refined gold by weight; and gold for the pattern of the chariot of the cherubims, that spread out *their wings*, and covered the ark of the covenant of Yahweh.
19 All *this, said David*, Yahweh made me understand in writing by *his* hand upon me, *even* all the works of this pattern.
20 And David said to Solomon his son, Be strong and of good courage, and do *it*: fear not, nor be dismayed: for Yahweh God, *even* my God, *will be* with you; he will not fail you, nor forsake you, until you have finished all the work for the service of the house of Yahweh.
21 And, behold, the courses of the priests and the Levites, *even they shall be with you* for all the service of the house of God: and *there shall be* with you for all manner of workmanship every willing skillful man, for any manner of service: also the princes and all the people *will be* wholly at your command.

1 Chronicles 29

29:1 ¶ Furthermore David the king said to all the congregation, Solomon my son, whom alone God has chosen, *is yet* young and tender, and the work *is* great: for the palace *is* not for man, but for Yahweh God.
2 Now I have prepared with all my might for the house of my God the gold for *things to be made* of gold, and the silver for *things* of silver, and the brass for *things* of brass, the iron for *things* of iron, and wood for *things* of wood; onyx stones, and *stones* to be set, glistening stones, and of diverse colors, and all manner of precious stones, and marble stones in abundance.
3 Moreover, because I have set my affection to the house of my God, I have of my own proper good, of gold and silver, *which* I have given to the house of my God, over and above all that I have prepared for the holy house,
4 *Even* three thousand talents of gold, of the gold of Ophir, and seven thousand talents of refined silver, to overlay the walls of the houses *therewith*:
5 The gold for *things* of gold, and the silver for *things* of silver, and for all manner of work *to be made* by the hands of craftsmen. And who *then* is willing to consecrate his service this day unto Yahweh?
6 Then the chief of the fathers and princes of the tribes of Israel, and the captains of thousands and of hundreds, with the rulers of the king's work, offered willingly,
7 And gave for the service of the house of God of gold five thousand talents and ten thousand drams, and of silver ten thousand talents, and of brass eighteen thousand talents, and one hundred thousand talents of iron.
8 And they with whom *precious* stones were found gave *them* to the treasury of the house of Yahweh, by the hand of Jehiel the Gershonite.
9 Then the people rejoiced, for that they offered willingly, because with perfect heart they offered willingly to Yahweh: and David the king also rejoiced with great joy.
10 ¶ Therefore David blessed Yahweh before all the congregation: and David said, Blessed *are* you, Yahweh God of Israel our father, forever and ever.
11 Yours, O Yahweh, *is* the greatness, and the power, and the glory, and the victory, and the majesty: for all *that is* in the heaven and in the earth *is yours*; yours *is* the kingdom, O Yahweh, and you are exalted as head above all.
12 Both riches and honor *come* from you, and you reign over all; and in your hand *is* power and might; and in your hand *it is* to make great, and to give strength to all.
13 Now therefore, our God, we thank you, and praise your glorious name.
14 But who *am* I, and what *is* my people, that we should be able to offer so willingly after this sort? for all things *come* from you, and of your own have we given you.
15 For we *are* strangers before you, and sojourners, as *were* all our fathers: our days on the earth *are* as a shadow, and *there is* no hope.

1 Chronicles 29

16 O Yahweh our God, all this store that we have prepared to build you a house for your holy name *comes* from your hand, and *is* all your own.

17 I know also, my God, that you try the heart, and have pleasure in uprightness. As for me, in the uprightness of my heart I have willingly offered all these things: and now have I seen with joy your people, which are present here, to offer willingly to you.

18 O Yahweh God of Abraham, Isaac, and of Israel, our fathers, keep this forever in the imagination of the thoughts of the heart of your people, and prepare their heart unto you:

19 And give to Solomon my son a perfect heart, to keep your commandments, your testimonies, and your statutes, and to do all *these things*, and to build the palace, *for* the which I have made provision.

20 And David said to all the congregation, Now bless Yahweh your God. And all the congregation blessed Yahweh God of their fathers, and bowed down their heads, and worshipped Yahweh, and the king.

21 And they sacrificed sacrifices unto Yahweh, and offered burnt offerings unto Yahweh, on the next day after that day, *even* a thousand bullocks, a thousand rams, *and* a thousand lambs, with their drink offerings, and sacrifices in abundance for all Israel:

22 And did eat and drink before Yahweh on that day with great gladness. And they made Solomon the son of David king the second time, and anointed *him* unto Yahweh *to be* the chief governor, and Zadok *to be* priest.

23 ¶ Then Solomon sat on the throne of Yahweh as king instead of David his father, and prospered; and all Israel obeyed him.

24 And all the princes, and the mighty men, and all the sons likewise of king David, submitted themselves to Solomon the king.

25 And Yahweh magnified Solomon exceedingly in the sight of all Israel, and bestowed upon him *such* royal majesty as had not been on any king before him in Israel.

26 Thus David the son of Jesse reigned over all Israel.

27 And the time that he reigned over Israel *was* forty years; seven years reigned he in Hebron, and thirty and three *years* reigned he in Jerusalem.

28 And he died in a good old age, full of days, riches, and honor: and Solomon his son reigned in his stead.

29 Now the acts of David the king, first and last, behold, they *are* written in the book of Samuel the seer, and in the book of Nathan the prophet, and in the book of Gad the seer,

30 With all his reign and his might, and the times that went over him, and over Israel, and over all the kingdoms of the countries.

2 Chronicles

2 Chronicles 1

1:1 ¶ And Solomon the son of David was strengthened in his kingdom, and Yahweh his God *was* with him, and magnified him exceedingly.

2 Then Solomon spoke to all Israel, to the captains of thousands and of hundreds, and to the judges, and to every governor in all Israel, the chief of the fathers.

3 So Solomon, and all the congregation with him, went to the high place that *was* at Gibeon; for there was the tabernacle of the congregation of God, which Moses the servant of Yahweh had made in the wilderness.

4 But the ark of God had David brought up from Kirjathjearim to *the place which* David had prepared for it: for he had pitched a tent for it at Jerusalem.

5 Moreover the brazen altar, that Bezaleel the son of Uri, the son of Hur, had made, he put before the tabernacle of Yahweh: and Solomon and the congregation sought unto it.

6 And Solomon went up there to the brazen altar before Yahweh, which *was* at the tabernacle of the congregation, and offered a thousand burnt offerings upon it.

7 In that night did God appear to Solomon, and said to him, Ask what I shall give you.

8 And Solomon said to God, You have shown great mercy to David my father, and have made me to reign in his stead.

9 Now, O Yahweh God, let your promise to David my father be established: for you have made me king over a people like the dust of the earth in multitude.

10 Give me now wisdom and knowledge, that I may go out and come in before this people: for who can judge this your people, *that is so* great?

11 And God said to Solomon, Because this was in your heart, and you have not asked riches, wealth, or honor, nor the life of your enemies, neither yet have asked long life; but have asked wisdom and knowledge for yourself, that you may judge my people, over whom I have made you king:

12 Wisdom and knowledge *is* granted unto you; and I will give you riches, and wealth, and honor, such as none of the kings have had that *have been* before you, neither shall there any after you have the like.

13 ¶ Then Solomon came *from his journey* to the high place that *was* at Gibeon to Jerusalem, from before the tabernacle of the congregation, and reigned over Israel.

14 And Solomon gathered chariots and horsemen: and he had a thousand and four hundred chariots, and twelve thousand horsemen, which he placed in the chariot cities, and with the king at Jerusalem.

15 And the king made silver and gold at Jerusalem *as plenteous* as stones, and cedar trees made he as the sycamore trees that *are* in the vale for abundance.

16 And Solomon had horses brought out of Egypt, and linen yarn: the king's merchants received the linen yarn at a price.

17 And they fetched up, and brought forth out of Egypt a chariot for six hundred *shekels* of silver, and a horse for a hundred and fifty: and so brought they out *horses* for all the kings of the Hittites, and for the kings of Syria, by their means.

2 Chronicles 2

2:1 ¶ And Solomon determined to build a house for the name of Yahweh, and a house for his kingdom.
2 And Solomon numbered threescore and ten thousand men to bear burdens, and fourscore thousand to hew in the mountain, and three thousand and six hundred to oversee them.
3 And Solomon sent to Huram the king of Tyre, saying, As you did deal with David my father, and did send him cedars to build him a house to dwell therein, *even so deal with me*.
4 Behold, I build a house to the name of Yahweh my God, to dedicate *it* to him, *and* to burn before him sweet incense, and for the continual showbread, and for the burnt offerings morning and evening, on the sabbaths, and on the new moons, and on the solemn feasts of Yahweh our God. This *is an ordinance* forever to Israel.
5 And the house which I build *is* great: for great *is* our God above all gods.
6 But who is able to build him a house, seeing the heaven and heaven of heavens cannot contain him? who *am* I then, that I should build him a house, save only to burn sacrifice before him?
7 Send me now therefore a man skillful to work in gold, and in silver, and in brass, and in iron, and in purple, and crimson, and blue, and that has skill to engrave with the skillful men that *are* with me in Judah and in Jerusalem, whom David my father did provide.
8 Send me also cedar trees, fir trees, and algum trees, out of Lebanon: for I know that your servants are skilled to cut timber in Lebanon; and, behold, my servants *shall be* with your servants,
9 Even to prepare me timber in abundance: for the house which I am about to build *shall be* wonderfully great.
10 And, behold, I will give to your servants, the hewers that cut timber, twenty thousand measures of beaten wheat, and twenty thousand measures of barley, and twenty thousand baths of wine, and twenty thousand baths of oil.
11 ¶ Then Huram the king of Tyre answered in writing, which he sent to Solomon, Because Yahweh has loved his people, he has made you king over them.
12 Huram said moreover, Blessed *be* Yahweh God of Israel, that made heaven and earth, who has given to David the king a wise son, endued with prudence and understanding, that might build a house for Yahweh, and a house for his kingdom.
13 And now I have sent a cunning man, endued with understanding, of Huram my father's,
14 The son of a woman of the daughters of Dan, and his father *was* a man of Tyre, skillful to work in gold, and in silver, in brass, in iron, in stone, and in timber, in purple, in blue, and in fine linen, and in crimson; also to engrave any manner of engraving, and to find out every device which shall be put to him, with your skillful men, and with the skillful men of my lord David your father.
15 Now therefore the wheat, and the barley, the oil, and the wine, which my lord has spoken of, let him send to his servants:
16 And we will cut wood out of Lebanon, as much as you shall need: and we will bring it to you in floats by sea to Joppa; and you shall carry it up to Jerusalem.
17 And Solomon numbered all the strangers that *were* in the land of Israel, after the numbering with which David his father had numbered them; and they were found a hundred and fifty thousand and three thousand and six hundred.
18 And he set threescore and ten thousand of them *to be* bearers of burdens, and fourscore thousand *to be* hewers in the mountain, and three thousand and six hundred overseers to set the people to work.

2 Chronicles 3

3:1 ¶ Then Solomon began to build the house of Yahweh at Jerusalem in mount Moriah, where *Yahweh* appeared to David his father, in the place that David had prepared in the threshingfloor of Ornan the Jebusite.
2 And he began to build in the second *day* of the second month, in the fourth year of his reign.
3 Now these *are the things wherein* Solomon was instructed for the building of the house of God. The length by cubits after the first measure *was* threescore cubits, and the breadth twenty cubits.
4 And the porch that *was* in the front *of the house*, the length *of it was* according to the breadth of the house, twenty cubits, and the height *was* a hundred and twenty: and he overlaid it within with pure gold.
5 And the greater house he paneled with fir tree, which he overlaid with fine gold, and set thereon palm trees and chains.
6 And he garnished the house with precious stones for beauty: and the gold *was* gold of Parvaim.
7 He overlaid also the house, the beams, the posts, and the walls thereof, and the doors thereof, with gold; and engraved cherubims on the walls.
8 And he made the most holy house, the length whereof *was* according to the breadth of the house, twenty cubits, and the breadth thereof twenty cubits: and he overlaid it with fine gold, *amounting* to six hundred talents.
9 And the weight of the nails *was* fifty shekels of gold. And he overlaid the upper chambers with gold.
10 ¶ And in the most holy house he made two cherubims of image work, and overlaid them with gold.
11 And the wings of the cherubims *were* twenty cubits long: one wing *of the one cherub was* five cubits, reaching

2 Chronicles 3

to the wall of the house: and the other wing was likewise five cubits, reaching to the wing of the other cherub.

12 And *one* wing of the other cherub *was* five cubits, reaching to the wall of the house: and the other wing *was* five cubits *also*, joining to the wing of the other cherub.

13 The wings of these cherubims spread themselves forth twenty cubits: and they stood on their feet, and their faces *were* inward.

14 And he made the veil *of* blue, and purple, and crimson, and fine linen, and put cherubims thereon.

15 Also he made before the house two pillars of thirty and five cubits high, and the capital that *was* on the top of each of them *was* five cubits.

16 And he made chains, *as* in the oracle, and put *them* on the heads of the pillars; and made a hundred pomegranates, and put *them* on the chains.

17 And he reared up the pillars before the temple, one on the right hand, and the other on the left; and called the name of that on the right hand Jachin, and the name of that on the left Boaz.

2 Chronicles 4

4:1 ¶ Moreover he made an altar of brass, twenty cubits the length thereof, and twenty cubits the breadth thereof, and ten cubits the height thereof.

2 Also he made a molten sea of ten cubits from brim to brim, round completely, and five cubits the height thereof; and a line of thirty cubits did compass it round about.

3 And under it *was* the likeness of oxen, which did compass it round about: ten in a cubit, compassing the sea round about. Two rows of oxen *were* cast, when it was cast.

4 It stood upon twelve oxen, three looking toward the north, and three looking toward the west, and three looking toward the south, and three looking toward the east: and the sea *was set* above upon them, and all their back parts *were* inward.

5 And the thickness of it *was* a handbreadth, and the brim of it like the work of the brim of a cup, with flowers of lilies; *and* it received and held three thousand baths.

6 He made also ten lavers, and put five on the right hand, and five on the left, to wash in them: such things as they offered for the burnt offering they washed in them; but the sea *was* for the priests to wash in.

7 And he made ten candlesticks of gold according to their form, and set *them* in the temple, five on the right hand, and five on the left.

8 He made also ten tables, and placed *them* in the temple, five on the right side, and five on the left. And he made a hundred basins of gold.

9 Furthermore he made the court of the priests, and the great court, and doors for the court, and overlaid the doors of them with brass.

10 And he set the sea on the right side of the east end, over against the south.

11 ¶ And Huram made the pots, and the shovels, and the basins. And Huram finished the work that he was to make for king Solomon for the house of God;

12 *To know*, the two pillars, and the pommels, and the capitals *which were* on the top of the two pillars, and the two wreaths to cover the two pommels of the capitals which *were* on the top of the pillars;

13 And four hundred pomegranates on the two wreaths; two rows of pomegranates on each wreath, to cover the two pommels of the capitals which *were* upon the pillars.

14 He made also bases, and lavers made he upon the bases;

15 One sea, and twelve oxen under it.

16 The pots also, and the shovels, and the meat hooks, and all their instruments, did Huram his father make for king Solomon for the house of Yahweh of bright brass.

17 In the plain of Jordan did the king cast them, in the clay ground between Succoth and Zeredathah.

18 Thus Solomon made all these vessels in great abundance: for the weight of the brass could not be found out.

19 And Solomon made all the vessels that *were for* the house of God, the golden altar also, and the tables whereon the showbread *was set*;

20 Moreover the candlesticks with their lamps, that they should burn after the manner before the oracle, of pure gold;

21 And the flowers, and the lamps, and the tongs, *made he of* gold, *and* that perfect gold;

22 And the snuffers, and the basins, and the spoons, and the censers, *of* pure gold: and the entry of the house, the inner doors thereof for the most holy *place*, and the doors of the house of the temple, *were of* gold.

2 Chronicles 5

5:1 ¶ Thus all the work that Solomon made for the house of Yahweh was finished: and Solomon brought in *all* the things that David his father had dedicated; and the silver, and the gold, and all the instruments, put he among the treasures of the house of God.

2 Then Solomon assembled the elders of Israel, and all the heads of the tribes, the chief of the fathers of the children of Israel, to Jerusalem, to bring up the ark of the covenant of Yahweh out of the city of David, which *is* Zion.

3 Therefore all the men of Israel assembled themselves unto the king in the feast which *was* in the seventh month.

4 And all the elders of Israel came; and the Levites took up the ark.

5 And they brought up the ark, and the tabernacle of the congregation, and all the holy vessels that *were* in the tabernacle, these did the priests *and* the Levites bring up.

6 Also king Solomon, and all the congregation of Israel that were assembled unto him before the ark, sacrificed sheep and oxen, which could not be told nor numbered for multitude.

7 And the priests brought in the ark of the covenant of Yahweh to its place, to the oracle of the house, into the most holy *place, even* under the wings of the cherubims:

8 For the cherubims spread forth *their* wings over the place of the ark, and the cherubims covered the ark and the staves thereof above.

9 And they drew out the staves *of the ark*, that the ends of the staves were seen from the ark before the oracle; but they were not seen outside. And there it is unto this day.

10 *There was* nothing in the ark save the two tables which Moses put *therein* at Horeb, when Yahweh made *a covenant* with the children of Israel, when they came out of Egypt.

11 ¶ And it came to pass, when the priests had come out of the holy *place*: (for all the priests *that were* present were sanctified, *and* did not *then* wait by course:

12 Also the Levites *which were* the singers, all of them of Asaph, of Heman, of Jeduthun, with their sons and their brethren, *being* arrayed in white linen, having cymbals and psalteries and harps, stood at the east end of the altar, and with them a hundred and twenty priests sounding with trumpets:)

13 It came even to pass, as the trumpeters and singers *were* as one, to make one sound to be heard in praising and thanking Yahweh; and when they lifted up *their* voice with the trumpets and cymbals and instruments of music, and praised Yahweh, *saying*, For *he is* good; for his mercy *endures* forever: that *then* the house was filled with a cloud, *even* the house of Yahweh;

14 So that the priests could not stand to minister by reason of the cloud: for the glory of Yahweh had filled the house of God.

2 Chronicles 6

6:1 ¶ Then said Solomon, Yahweh has said that he would dwell in the thick darkness.

2 But I have built a house of habitation for you, and a place for your dwelling forever.

3 And the king turned his face, and blessed the whole congregation of Israel: and all the congregation of Israel stood.

4 And he said, Blessed *be* Yahweh God of Israel, who has with his hands fulfilled *that* which he spoke with his mouth to my father David, saying,

5 Since the day that I brought forth my people out of the land of Egypt I chose no city among all the tribes of Israel to build a house in, that my name might be there; neither chose I any man to be a ruler over my people Israel:

6 But I have chosen Jerusalem, that my name might be there; and have chosen David to be over my people Israel.

7 Now it was in the heart of David my father to build a house for the name of Yahweh God of Israel.

8 But Yahweh said to David my father, Forasmuch as it was in your heart to build a house for my name, you did well in that it was in your heart:

9 Notwithstanding you shall not build the house; but your son which shall come forth out of your loins, he shall build the house for my name.

10 Yahweh therefore has performed his word that he has spoken: for I have risen up in the place of David my father, and am set on the throne of Israel, as Yahweh promised, and have built the house for the name of Yahweh God of Israel.

11 And in it have I put the ark, wherein *is* the covenant of Yahweh, that he made with the children of Israel.

12 ¶ And he stood before the altar of Yahweh in the presence of all the congregation of Israel, and spread forth his hands:

13 For Solomon had made a brazen scaffold, of five cubits long, and five cubits broad, and three cubits high, and had set it in the midst of the court: and upon it he stood, and kneeled down upon his knees before all the congregation of Israel, and spread forth his hands toward heaven,

14 And said, O Yahweh God of Israel, *there is* no God like you in the heaven, nor in the earth; which keeps covenant, and *shows* mercy to your servants, that walk before you with all their hearts:

15 You which have kept with your servant David my father that which you have promised him; and spoke with your mouth, and have fulfilled *it* with your hand, as *it is* this day.

16 Now therefore, O Yahweh God of Israel, keep with your servant David my father that which you have promised him, saying, There shall not fail you a man in my sight to sit upon the throne of Israel; yet so that your children take heed to their way to walk in my law, as you have walked before me.

17 Now then, O Yahweh God of Israel, let your word be verified, which you have spoken to your servant David.

18 But will God in very deed dwell with men on the earth? behold, heaven and the heaven of heavens cannot contain you; how much less this house which I have built!

19 Have respect therefore to the prayer of your servant, and to his supplication, O Yahweh my God, to listen unto the cry and the prayer which your servant prays before you:

20 That your eyes may be open upon this house day and night, upon the place whereof you have said that you would put your name there; to listen unto the prayer which your servant prays toward this place.

21 Listen therefore unto the supplications of your servant, and of your people Israel, which they shall make toward this place: hear you from your dwelling place, *even* from heaven; and when you hear, forgive.

22 If a man sins against his neighbor, and an oath is laid upon him to make him swear, and the oath comes before your altar in this house;

23 Then hear you from heaven, and do, and judge your servants, by requiting the wicked, by recompensing his way upon his own head; and by justifying the righteous, by giving him according to his righteousness.

24 And if your people Israel are put to the worse before the enemy, because they have sinned against you; and shall return and confess your name, and pray and make supplication before you in this house;

2 Chronicles 6

25 Then hear you from the heavens, and forgive the sin of your people Israel, and bring them again to the land which you gave to them and to their fathers.

26 When the heaven is shut up, and there is no rain, because they have sinned against you; *yet* if they pray toward this place, and confess your name, and turn from their sin, when you do afflict them;

27 Then hear you from heaven, and forgive the sin of your servants, and of your people Israel, when you have taught them the good way, wherein they should walk; and send rain upon your land, which you have given to your people for an inheritance.

28 If there is famine in the land, if there is pestilence, if there is blasting, or mildew, locusts, or caterpillars; if their enemies besiege them in the cities of their land; whatever plague or whatever sickness *there is*:

29 *Then* what prayer *or* what supplication soever shall be made of any man, or of all your people Israel, when every one shall know his own plague and his own grief, and shall spread forth his hands in this house:

30 Then hear you from heaven your dwelling place, and forgive, and render to every man according to all his ways, whose heart you know; (for you only know the hearts of the children of men:)

31 That they may fear you, to walk in your ways, so long as they live in the land which you gave to our fathers.

32 Moreover concerning the stranger, which is not of your people Israel, but has come from a far country for your great name's sake, and your mighty hand, and your stretched out arm; if they come and pray in this house;

33 Then hear you from the heavens, *even* from your dwelling place, and do according to all that the stranger calls to you for; that all people of the earth may know your name, and fear you, as *do* your people Israel, and may know that this house which I have built is called by your name.

34 If your people go out to war against their enemies by the way that you shall send them, and they pray to you toward this city which you have chosen, and the house which I have built for your name;

35 Then hear you from the heavens their prayer and their supplication, and maintain their cause.

36 If they sin against you, (for *there is* no man which sins not,) and you are angry with them, and deliver them over before *their* enemies, and they carry them away captives unto a land far off or near;

37 Yet *if* they turn back themselves in the land where they are carried captive, and turn and pray unto you in the land of their captivity, saying, We have sinned, we have done amiss, and have dealt wickedly;

38 If they return to you with all their heart and with all their soul in the land of their captivity, where they have carried them captives, and pray toward their land, which you gave unto their fathers, and *toward* the city which you have chosen, and toward the house which I have built for your name:

39 Then hear you from the heavens, *even* from your dwelling place, their prayer and their supplications, and maintain their cause, and forgive your people which have sinned against you.

40 Now, my God, let, I beseech you, your eyes be open, and *let* your ears *be* attentive to the prayer *that is made* in this place.

41 Now therefore arise, O Yahweh God, into your resting place, you, and the ark of your strength: let your priests, O Yahweh God, be clothed with salvation, and let your saints rejoice in goodness.

42 O Yahweh God, turn not away the face of your anointed: remember the mercies of David your servant.

2 Chronicles 7

7:1 ¶ Now when Solomon had made an end of praying, the fire came down from heaven, and consumed the burnt offering and the sacrifices; and the glory of Yahweh filled the house.

2 And the priests could not enter into the house of Yahweh, because the glory of Yahweh had filled Yahweh's house.

3 And when all the children of Israel saw how the fire came down, and the glory of Yahweh upon the house, they bowed themselves with their faces to the ground upon the pavement, and worshipped, and praised Yahweh, *saying*, For *he is* good; for his mercy *endures* forever.

4 Then the king and all the people offered sacrifices before Yahweh.

5 And king Solomon offered a sacrifice of twenty and two thousand oxen, and a hundred and twenty thousand sheep: so the king and all the people dedicated the house of God.

6 And the priests waited on their offices: the Levites also with instruments of music of Yahweh, which David the king had made to praise Yahweh, because his mercy *endures* forever, when David praised by their ministry; and the priests sounded trumpets before them, and all Israel stood.

7 Moreover Solomon hallowed the middle of the court that *was* before the house of Yahweh: for there he offered burnt offerings, and the fat of the peace offerings, because the brazen altar which Solomon had made was not able to receive the burnt offerings, and the meat offerings, and the fat.

8 Also at the same time Solomon kept the feast seven days, and all Israel with him, a very great congregation, from the entering in of Hamath to the river of Egypt.

9 And in the eighth day they made a solemn assembly: for they kept the dedication of the altar seven days, and the feast seven days.

10 And on the three and twentieth day of the seventh month he sent the people away into their tents, glad and merry in heart for the goodness that Yahweh had shown unto David, and to Solomon, and to Israel his people.

11 Thus Solomon finished the house of Yahweh, and the king's house: and all that came into Solomon's heart to make in the house of Yahweh, and in his own house, he prosperously completed.

12 ¶ And Yahweh appeared to Solomon by night, and said to him, I have heard your prayer, and have chosen this place to myself for a house of sacrifice.

13 If I shut up heaven that there is no rain, or if I command the locusts to devour the land, or if I send pestilence among my people;

14 If my people, which are called by my name, shall humble themselves, and pray, and seek my face, and turn from their wicked ways; then will I hear from heaven, and will forgive their sin, and will heal their land.

15 Now my eyes shall be open, and my ears attentive unto the prayer *that is made* in this place.

16 For now have I chosen and sanctified this house, that my name may be there forever: and my eyes and my heart shall be there perpetually.

17 And as for you, if you will walk before me, as David your father walked, and do according to all that I have commanded you, and shall observe my statutes and my judgments;

18 Then will I establish the throne of your kingdom, according as I have covenanted with David your father, saying, There shall not fail you a man *to be* ruler in Israel.

19 But if you turn away, and forsake my statutes and my commandments, which I have set before you, and shall go and serve other gods, and worship them;

20 Then will I pluck them up by the roots out of my land which I have given them; and this house, which I have sanctified for my name, will I cast out of my sight, and will make it *to be* a proverb and a byword among all nations.

21 And this house, which is high, shall be an astonishment to every one that passes by it; so that he shall say, Why has Yahweh done thus to this land, and to this house?

22 And it shall be answered, Because they forsook Yahweh God of their fathers, which brought them forth out of the land of Egypt, and laid hold on other gods, and worshipped them, and served them: therefore has he brought all this evil upon them.

2 Chronicles 8

8:1 ¶ And it came to pass at the end of twenty years, wherein Solomon had built the house of Yahweh, and his own house,

2 That the cities which Huram had restored to Solomon, Solomon built them, and caused the children of Israel to dwell there.

3 And Solomon went to Hamathzobah, and prevailed against it.

4 And he built Tadmor in the wilderness, and all the storage cities, which he built in Hamath.

5 Also he built Bethhoron the upper, and Bethhoron the lower, fenced cities, with walls, gates, and bars;

6 And Baalath, and all the storage cities that Solomon had, and all the chariot cities, and the cities of the horsemen, and all that Solomon desired to build in Jerusalem, and in Lebanon, and throughout all the land of his dominion.

7 *As for* all the people *that were* left of the Hittites, and the Amorites, and the Perizzites, and the Hivites, and the Jebusites, which *were* not of Israel,

8 *But* of their children, who were left after them in the land, whom the children of Israel consumed not, them did Solomon make to pay tribute until this day.

9 But of the children of Israel did Solomon make no servants for his work; but they *were* men of war, and chief of his captains, and captains of his chariots and horsemen.

10 And these *were* the chief of king Solomon's officers, *even* two hundred and fifty, that bore rule over the people.

11 And Solomon brought up the daughter of Pharaoh out of the city of David to the house that he had built for her: for he said, My wife shall not dwell in the house of David king of Israel, because *the places are* holy, whereunto the ark of Yahweh has come.

12 ¶ Then Solomon offered burnt offerings unto Yahweh on the altar of Yahweh, which he had built before the porch,

13 Even after a certain rate every day, offering according to the commandment of Moses, on the sabbaths, and on the new moons, and on the solemn feasts, three times in the year, *even* in the feast of unleavened bread, and in the feast of weeks, and in the feast of tabernacles.

14 And he appointed, according to the order of David his father, the courses of the priests to their service, and the Levites to their charges, to praise and minister before the priests, as the duty of every day required: the porters also by their courses at every gate: for so had David the man of God commanded.

15 And they departed not from the commandment of the king unto the priests and Levites concerning any matter, or concerning the treasuries.

16 Now all the work of Solomon was prepared unto the day of the foundation of the house of Yahweh, and until it was finished. So the house of Yahweh was perfected.

17 Then went Solomon to Eziongeber, and to Eloth, at the sea side in the land of Edom.

18 And Huram sent him by the hands of his servants ships, and servants that had knowledge of the sea; and they went with the servants of Solomon to Ophir, and took there four hundred and fifty talents of gold, and brought *them* to king Solomon.

2 Chronicles 9

9:1 ¶ And when the queen of Sheba heard of the fame of Solomon, she came to prove Solomon with hard questions at Jerusalem, with a very great company, and camels that bore spices, and gold in abundance, and precious stones: and when she had come to Solomon, she communed with him of all that was in her heart.

2 And Solomon told her all her questions: and there was nothing hidden by Solomon which he told her not.

3 And when the queen of Sheba had seen the wisdom of Solomon, and the house that he had built,

4 And the food of his table, and the sitting of his servants, and the attendance of his ministers, and their apparel; his cup bearers also, and their apparel; and his ascent by which he went up into the house of Yahweh; there was no more spirit in her.

5 And she said to the king, *It was* a true report which I heard in my own land of your acts, and of your wisdom:

6 However I believed not their words, until I came, and my eyes have seen *it*: and, behold, the one half of the greatness of your wisdom was not told me: *for* you exceed the fame that I heard.

7 Happy *are* your men, and happy *are* these your servants, which stand continually before you, and hear your wisdom.

8 Blessed be Yahweh your God, which delighted in you to set you on his throne, *to be* king for Yahweh your God: because your God loved Israel, to establish them forever, therefore made he you king over them, to do judgment and justice.

9 And she gave the king a hundred and twenty talents of gold, and of spices *in* great abundance, and precious stones: neither was there any such spices as the queen of Sheba gave *to* king Solomon.

10 And the servants also of Huram, and the servants of Solomon, which brought gold from Ophir, brought algum trees and precious stones.

11 And the king made *of* the algum trees terraces to the house of Yahweh, and to the king's palace, and harps and psalteries for singers: and there were none such seen before in the land of Judah.

12 And king Solomon gave to the queen of Sheba all her desire, whatever she asked, besides *that* which she had brought to the king. So she turned, and went away to her own land, she and her servants.

13 ¶ Now the weight of gold that came to Solomon in one year was six hundred and threescore and six talents of gold;

14 Besides *that which* merchantmen and traders brought. And all the kings of Arabia and governors of the country brought gold and silver to Solomon.

15 And king Solomon made two hundred targets *of* beaten gold: six hundred *shekels* of beaten gold went to one target.

16 And three hundred shields *made he of* beaten gold: three hundred *shekels* of gold went to one shield. And the king put them in the house of the forest of Lebanon.

17 Moreover the king made a great throne of ivory, and overlaid it with pure gold.

18 And *there were* six steps to the throne, with a footstool of gold, *which were* fastened to the throne, and stays on each side of the sitting place, and two lions standing by the stays:

19 And twelve lions stood there on the one side and on the other upon the six steps. There was not the like made in any kingdom.

20 And all the drinking vessels of king Solomon *were of* gold, and all the vessels of the house of the forest of Lebanon *were of* pure gold: none *were of* silver; it was nothing *to be* accounted of in the days of Solomon.

21 For the king's ships went to Tarshish with the servants of Huram: every three years once came the ships of Tarshish bringing gold, and silver, ivory, and apes, and peacocks.

22 And king Solomon passed all the kings of the earth in riches and wisdom.

23 And all the kings of the earth sought the presence of Solomon, to hear his wisdom, that God had put in his heart.

24 And they brought every man his present, vessels of silver, and vessels of gold, and garments, armor, and spices, horses, and mules, a rate year by year.

25 And Solomon had four thousand stalls for horses and chariots, and twelve thousand horsemen; whom he bestowed in the chariot cities, and with the king at Jerusalem.

26 And he reigned over all the kings from the river even to the land of the Philistines, and to the border of Egypt.

27 And the king made silver in Jerusalem as stones, and cedar trees made he as the sycamore trees that *are* in the low plains in abundance.

28 And they brought to Solomon horses out of Egypt, and out of all lands.

29 Now the rest of the acts of Solomon, first and last, *are* they not written in the book of Nathan the prophet, and in the prophecy of Ahijah the Shilonite, and in the visions of Iddo the seer against Jeroboam the son of Nebat?

30 And Solomon reigned in Jerusalem over all Israel *for* forty years.

31 And Solomon slept with his fathers, and he was buried in the city of David his father: and Rehoboam his son reigned in his stead.

2 Chronicles 10

10:1 ¶ And Rehoboam went to Shechem: for to Shechem did all Israel come to make him king.

2 And it came to pass, when Jeroboam the son of Nebat, who *was* in Egypt, where he had fled from the presence of Solomon the king, heard *it*, that Jeroboam returned out of Egypt.

3 And they sent and called him. So Jeroboam and all Israel came and spoke to Rehoboam, saying,

4 Your father made our yoke grievous: now therefore ease you somewhat the grievous servitude of your father, and his heavy yoke that he put upon us, and we will serve you.

5 And he said to them, Come again to me after three days. And the people departed.

6 And king Rehoboam took counsel with the old men that had stood before Solomon his father while he yet lived, saying, What counsel give you *me* to return answer to this people?

7 And they spoke to him, saying, If you are kind to this people, and please them, and speak good words to them, they will be your servants forever.

8 But he forsook the counsel which the old men gave him, and took counsel with the young men that were brought up with him, that stood before him.

9 And he said to them, What advice give you that we may return answer to this people, which have spoken to me, saying, Ease somewhat the yoke that your father did put upon us?

10 And the young men that were brought up with him spoke to him, saying, Thus shall you answer the people that spoke to you, saying, Your father made our yoke heavy, but make you *it* somewhat lighter for us; thus shall you say to them, My little *finger* shall be thicker than my father's loins.

11 For whereas my father put a heavy yoke upon you, I will put more to your yoke: my father chastised you with whips, but I *will chastise you* with scorpions.

12 ¶ So Jeroboam and all the people came to Rehoboam on the third day, as the king ordered, saying, Come again to me on the third day.

13 And the king answered them roughly; and king Rehoboam forsook the counsel of the old men,

14 And answered them after the advice of the young men, saying, My father made your yoke heavy, but I will add thereto: my father chastised you with whips, but I *will chastise you* with scorpions.

15 So the king listened not to the people: for the cause was of God, that Yahweh might perform his word, which he spoke by the hand of Ahijah the Shilonite to Jeroboam the son of Nebat.

16 And when all Israel *saw* that the king would not listen to them, the people answered the king, saying, What portion have we in David? and *we have* no inheritance in the son of Jesse: every man to your tents, O Israel: *and* now, David, see to your own house. So all Israel went to their tents.

17 But *as for* the children of Israel that dwelt in the cities of Judah, Rehoboam reigned over them.

18 Then king Rehoboam sent Hadoram that *was* over the tribute; and the children of Israel stoned him with stones, that he died. But king Rehoboam made speed to get him up to *his* chariot, to flee to Jerusalem.

19 And Israel has rebelled against the house of David unto this day.

2 Chronicles 11

11:1 ¶ And when Rehoboam had come to Jerusalem, he gathered of the house of Judah and Benjamin a hundred and fourscore thousand chosen *men*, which were warriors, to fight against Israel, that he might bring the kingdom again to Rehoboam.

2 But the word of Yahweh came to Shemaiah the man of God, saying,

3 Speak to Rehoboam the son of Solomon, king of Judah, and to all Israel in Judah and Benjamin, saying,

4 Thus says Yahweh, You shall not go up, nor fight against your brethren: return every man to his house: for this thing is done by me. And they obeyed the words of Yahweh, and returned from going against Jeroboam.

5 And Rehoboam dwelt in Jerusalem, and built cities for defense in Judah.

6 He built even Bethlehem, and Etam, and Tekoa,

7 And Bethzur, and Shoco, and Adullam,

8 And Gath, and Mareshah, and Ziph,

9 And Adoraim, and Lachish, and Azekah,

10 And Zorah, and Aijalon, and Hebron, which *are* in Judah and in Benjamin fenced cities.

11 And he fortified the strong holds, and put captains in them, and stores of victuals, and of oil and wine.

12 And in every separate city *he put* shields and spears, and made them exceedingly strong, having Judah and Benjamin on his side.

13 ¶ And the priests and the Levites that *were* in all Israel resorted to him out of all their coasts.

14 For the Levites left their suburbs and their possessions, and came to Judah and Jerusalem: for Jeroboam and his sons had cast them off from executing the priest's office unto Yahweh:

15 And he ordained him priests for the high places, and for the devils, and for the calves which he had made.

16 And after them out of all the tribes of Israel such as set their hearts to seek Yahweh God of Israel came to Jerusalem, to sacrifice unto Yahweh God of their fathers.

17 So they strengthened the kingdom of Judah, and made Rehoboam the son of Solomon strong, three years: for three years they walked in the way of David and Solomon.

18 And Rehoboam took him Mahalath the daughter of Jerimoth the son of David to wife, *and* Abihail the daughter of Eliab the son of Jesse;

19 Which bore him children; Jeush, and Shamariah, and Zaham.

20 And after her he took Maachah the daughter of Absalom; which bore him Abijah, and Attai, and Ziza, and Shelomith.

21 And Rehoboam loved Maachah the daughter of Absalom above all his wives and his concubines: (for he took eighteen wives, and threescore concubines; and begot twenty and eight sons, and threescore daughters.)

22 And Rehoboam made Abijah the son of Maachah the chief, *to be* ruler among his brethren: for *he thought* to make him king.

23 And he dealt wisely, and dispersed of all his children throughout all the countries of Judah and Benjamin, to every fenced city: and he gave them food in abundance. And he desired many wives.

2 Chronicles 12

12:1 ¶ And it came to pass, when Rehoboam had established the kingdom, and had strengthened himself, he forsook the law of Yahweh, and all Israel with him.

2 And it came to pass, *that* in the fifth year of king Rehoboam, Shishak king of Egypt came up against Jerusalem, because they had transgressed against Yahweh,

3 With twelve hundred chariots, and threescore thousand horsemen: and the people *were* without number that came with him out of Egypt; the Lubims, the Sukkiims, and the Ethiopians.
4 And he took the fenced cities which *pertained* to Judah, and came to Jerusalem.
5 Then came Shemaiah the prophet to Rehoboam, and *to* the princes of Judah, that were gathered together to Jerusalem because of Shishak, and said to them, Thus says Yahweh, You have forsaken me, and therefore have I also left you in the hand of Shishak.
6 Whereupon the princes of Israel and the king humbled themselves; and they said, Yahweh *is* righteous.
7 And when Yahweh saw that they humbled themselves, the word of Yahweh came to Shemaiah, saying, They have humbled themselves; *therefore* I will not destroy them, but I will grant them some deliverance; and my wrath shall not be poured out upon Jerusalem by the hand of Shishak.
8 Nevertheless they shall be his servants; that they may know my service, and the service of the kingdoms of the countries.
9 So Shishak king of Egypt came up against Jerusalem, and took away the treasures of the house of Yahweh, and the treasures of the king's house; he took all: he carried away also the shields of gold which Solomon had made.
10 Instead of which king Rehoboam made shields of brass, and committed *them* to the hands of the chief of the guard, that kept the entrance of the king's house.
11 And when the king entered into the house of Yahweh, the guard came and fetched them, and brought them again into the guard chamber.
12 And when he humbled himself, the wrath of Yahweh turned from him, that he would not destroy *him* altogether: and also in Judah things went well.
13 ¶ So king Rehoboam strengthened himself in Jerusalem, and reigned: for Rehoboam *was* one and forty years old when he began to reign, and he reigned seventeen years in Jerusalem, the city which Yahweh had chosen out of all the tribes of Israel, to put his name there. And his mother's name *was* Naamah an Ammonitess.
14 And he did evil, because he prepared not his heart to seek Yahweh.
15 Now the acts of Rehoboam, first and last, *are* they not written in the book of Shemaiah the prophet, and of Iddo the seer concerning genealogies? And *there were* wars between Rehoboam and Jeroboam continually.
16 And Rehoboam slept with his fathers, and was buried in the city of David: and Abijah his son reigned in his stead.

2 Chronicles 13

13:1 ¶ Now in the eighteenth year of king Jeroboam began Abijah to reign over Judah.
2 He reigned three years in Jerusalem. His mother's name also *was* Michaiah the daughter of Uriel of Gibeah. And there was war between Abijah and Jeroboam.
3 And Abijah set the battle in array with an army of valiant men of war, *even* four hundred thousand chosen men: Jeroboam also set the battle in array against him with eight hundred thousand chosen men, *being* mighty men of valor.
4 And Abijah stood up upon mount Zemaraim, which *is* in mount Ephraim, and said, Hear me, you Jeroboam, and all Israel;
5 Ought you not to know that Yahweh God of Israel gave the kingdom over Israel to David forever, *even* to him and to his sons by a covenant of salt?
6 Yet Jeroboam the son of Nebat, the servant of Solomon the son of David, has risen up, and has rebelled against his lord.
7 And there were gathered to him vain men, the children of Belial, and have strengthened themselves against Rehoboam the son of Solomon, when Rehoboam was young and tenderhearted, and could not withstand them.
8 And now you think to withstand the kingdom of Yahweh in the hand of the sons of David; and you *are* a great multitude, and *there are* with you golden calves, which Jeroboam made you for gods.
9 Have you not cast out the priests of Yahweh, the sons of Aaron, and the Levites, and have made you priests after the manner of the nations of *other* lands? so that whoever comes to consecrate himself with a young bullock and seven rams, *the same* may be a priest of *them that are* no gods.
10 But as for us, Yahweh *is* our God, and we have not forsaken him; and the priests, which minister unto Yahweh, *are* the sons of Aaron, and the Levites *wait* upon *their* business:
11 And they burn unto Yahweh every morning and every evening burnt sacrifices and sweet incense: the showbread also *set they in order* upon the pure table; and the candlestick of gold with the lamps thereof, to burn every evening: for we keep the charge of Yahweh our God; but you have forsaken him.
12 And, behold, God himself *is* with us for *our* captain, and his priests with sounding trumpets to cry alarm against you. O children of Israel, fight you not against Yahweh God of your fathers; for you shall not prosper.
13 ¶ But Jeroboam caused an ambush to come about behind them: so they were before Judah, and the ambush *was* behind them.
14 And when Judah looked back, behold, the battle *was* before and behind: and they cried unto Yahweh, and the priests sounded with the trumpets.
15 Then the men of Judah gave a shout: and as the men of Judah shouted, it came to pass, that God smote Jeroboam and all Israel before Abijah and Judah.
16 And the children of Israel fled before Judah: and God delivered them into their hand.
17 And Abijah and his people slew them with a great slaughter: so there fell down slain of Israel five hundred thousand chosen men.
18 Thus the children of Israel were brought under at that time, and the children of Judah prevailed, because they relied upon Yahweh God of their fathers.

19 And Abijah pursued after Jeroboam, and took cities from him, Bethel with the towns thereof, and Jeshanah with the towns thereof, and Ephrain with the towns thereof.
20 Neither did Jeroboam recover strength again in the days of Abijah: and Yahweh struck him, and he died.
21 But Abijah became mighty, and married fourteen wives, and begot twenty and two sons, and sixteen daughters.
22 And the rest of the acts of Abijah, and his ways, and his sayings, *are* written in the story of the prophet Iddo.

2 Chronicles 14

14:1 ¶ So Abijah slept with his fathers, and they buried him in the city of David: and Asa his son reigned in his stead. In his days the land was quiet *for* ten years.
2 And Asa did *that which was* good and right in the eyes of Yahweh his God:
3 For he took away the altars of the strange *gods*, and the high places, and broke down the images, and cut down the groves:
4 And commanded Judah to seek Yahweh God of their fathers, and to do the law and the commandment.
5 Also he took away out of all the cities of Judah the high places and the images: and the kingdom was quiet before him.
6 And he built fenced cities in Judah: for the land had rest, and he had no war in those years; because Yahweh had given him rest.
7 Therefore he said unto Judah, Let us build these cities, and make about *them* walls, and towers, gates, and bars, *while* the land *is* yet before us; because we have sought Yahweh our God, we have sought *him*, and he has given us rest on every side. So they built and prospered.
8 And Asa had an army *of men* that bore targets and spears, out of Judah three hundred thousand; and out of Benjamin, that bore shields and drew bows, two hundred and fourscore thousand: all these *were* mighty men of valor.
9 ¶ And there came out against them Zerah the Ethiopian with a host of a thousand thousand, and three hundred chariots; and came to Mareshah.
10 Then Asa went out against him, and they set the battle in array in the valley of Zephathah at Mareshah.
11 And Asa cried unto Yahweh his God, and said, Yahweh, *it is* nothing with you to help, whether with many, or with them that have no power: help us, O Yahweh our God; for we rest on you, and in your name we go against this multitude. O Yahweh, you *are* our God; let not man prevail against you.
12 So Yahweh smote the Ethiopians before Asa, and before Judah; and the Ethiopians fled.
13 And Asa and the people that *were* with him pursued them to Gerar: and the Ethiopians were overthrown, that they could not recover themselves; for they were destroyed before Yahweh, and before his host; and they carried away very much spoil.

14 And they smote all the cities round about Gerar; for the fear of Yahweh came upon them: and they spoiled all the cities; for there was exceedingly much spoil in them.
15 They smote also the places of cattle, and carried away sheep and camels in abundance, and returned to Jerusalem.

2 Chronicles 15

15:1 ¶ And the Spirit of God came upon Azariah the son of Oded:
2 And he went out to meet Asa, and said to him, Hear you me, Asa, and all Judah and Benjamin; Yahweh *is* with you, while you are with him; and if you seek him, he will be found by you; but if you forsake him, he will forsake you.
3 Now for a long season Israel *has been* without the true God, and without a teaching priest, and without law.
4 But when they in their trouble did turn unto Yahweh God of Israel, and sought him, he was found of them.
5 And in those times *there was* no peace to him that went out, nor to him that came in, but great turmoil *was* upon all the inhabitants of the countries.
6 And nation was destroyed by nation, and city by city: for God did trouble them with all adversity.
7 Be you strong therefore, and let not your hands be weak: for your work shall be rewarded.
8 ¶ And when Asa heard these words, and the prophecy of Oded the prophet, he took courage, and put away the abominable idols out of all the land of Judah and Benjamin, and out of the cities which he had taken from mount Ephraim, and renewed the altar of Yahweh, that *was* before the porch of Yahweh.
9 And he gathered all Judah and Benjamin, and the strangers with them out of Ephraim and Manasseh, and out of Simeon: for they fell to him out of Israel in abundance, when they saw that Yahweh his God *was* with him.
10 So they gathered themselves together at Jerusalem in the third month, in the fifteenth year of the reign of Asa.
11 And they offered unto Yahweh the same time, of the spoil *which* they had brought, seven hundred oxen and seven thousand sheep.
12 And they entered into a covenant to seek Yahweh God of their fathers with all their heart and with all their soul;
13 That whoever would not seek Yahweh God of Israel should be put to death, whether small or great, whether man or woman.
14 And they swore unto Yahweh with a loud voice, and with shouting, and with trumpets, and with cornets.
15 And all Judah rejoiced at the oath: for they had sworn with all their heart, and sought him with their whole desire; and he was found by them: and Yahweh gave them rest round about.
16 And also *concerning* Maachah the mother of Asa the king, he removed her from *being* queen, because she had made an idol in a grove: and Asa cut down her idol, and stamped *it*, and burnt *it* at the brook Kidron.

2 Chronicles 15

17 But the high places were not taken away out of Israel: nevertheless the heart of Asa was perfect all his days.
18 And he brought into the house of God the things that his father had dedicated, and that he himself had dedicated, silver, and gold, and vessels.
19 And there was no *more* war unto the five and thirtieth year of the reign of Asa.

2 Chronicles 16

16:1 ¶ In the six and thirtieth year of the reign of Asa, Baasha king of Israel came up against Judah, and built Ramah, to the intent that he might let none go out or come in to Asa king of Judah.
2 Then Asa brought out silver and gold out of the treasuries of the house of Yahweh and of the king's house, and sent to Benhadad king of Syria, that dwelt at Damascus, saying,
3 *There is* a league between me and you, as *there was* between my father and your father: behold, I have sent you silver and gold; go, break your league with Baasha king of Israel, that he may depart from me.
4 And Benhadad listened to king Asa, and sent the captains of his armies against the cities of Israel; and they smote Ijon, and Dan, and Abelmaim, and all the store cities of Naphtali.
5 And it came to pass, when Baasha heard *it*, that he left off building of Ramah, and let his work cease.
6 Then Asa the king took all Judah; and they carried away the stones of Ramah, and the timber thereof, with which Baasha was building; and he built therewith Geba and Mizpah.
7 ¶ And at that time Hanani the seer came to Asa king of Judah, and said to him, Because you have relied on the king of Syria, and not relied on Yahweh your God, therefore has the host of the king of Syria escaped out of your hand.
8 Were not the Ethiopians and the Lubims a huge host, with very many chariots and horsemen? yet, because you did rely on Yahweh, he delivered them into your hand.
9 For the eyes of Yahweh run to and fro throughout the whole earth, to show himself strong in the behalf of *them* whose heart *is* perfect toward him. Herein you have done foolishly: therefore from now on you shall have wars.
10 Then Asa was angry with the seer, and put him in a prison house; for *he was* in a rage with him because of this *thing*. And Asa oppressed *some* of the people *at* the same time.
11 And, behold, the acts of Asa, first and last, lo, they *are* written in the book of the kings of Judah and Israel.
12 And Asa in the thirty and ninth year of his reign was diseased in his feet, until his disease *was* exceedingly *great*: yet in his disease he sought not to Yahweh, but to the physicians.
13 And Asa slept with his fathers, and died in the one and fortieth year of his reign.
14 And they buried him in his own sepulcher, which he had made for himself in the city of David, and laid him in the bed which was filled with sweet odors and diverse kinds *of spices* prepared by the apothecaries' art: and they made a very great burning for him.

2 Chronicles 17

17:1 ¶ And Jehoshaphat his son reigned in his stead, and strengthened himself against Israel.
2 And he placed forces in all the fenced cities of Judah, and set garrisons in the land of Judah, and in the cities of Ephraim, which Asa his father had taken.
3 And Yahweh was with Jehoshaphat, because he walked in the first ways of his father David, and sought not unto Baalim;
4 But sought to Yahweh God of his father, and walked in his commandments, and not after the doings of Israel.
5 Therefore Yahweh established the kingdom in his hand; and all Judah brought to Jehoshaphat presents; and he had riches and honor in abundance.
6 And his heart was lifted up in the ways of Yahweh: moreover he took away the high places and groves out of Judah.
7 Also in the third year of his reign he sent to his princes, *even* to Benhail, and to Obadiah, and to Zechariah, and to Nethaneel, and to Michaiah, to teach in the cities of Judah.
8 And with them *he sent* Levites, *even* Shemaiah, and Nethaniah, and Zebadiah, and Asahel, and Shemiramoth, and Jehonathan, and Adonijah, and Tobijah, and Tobadonijah, Levites; and with them Elishama and Jehoram, priests.
9 And they taught in Judah, and had the book of the law of Yahweh with them, and went about throughout all the cities of Judah, and taught the people.
10 ¶ And the fear of Yahweh fell upon all the kingdoms of the lands that *were* round about Judah, so that they made no war against Jehoshaphat.
11 Also *some* of the Philistines brought Jehoshaphat presents, and tribute silver; and the Arabians brought him flocks, seven thousand and seven hundred rams, and seven thousand and seven hundred he goats.
12 And Jehoshaphat became great exceedingly; and he built in Judah castles, and cities for storage.
13 And he had much business in the cities of Judah: and the men of war, mighty men of valor, *were* in Jerusalem.
14 And these *are* the numbers of them according to the house of their fathers: Of Judah, the captains of thousands; Adnah the chief, and with him mighty men of valor three hundred thousand.
15 And next to him *was* Jehohanan the captain, and with him two hundred and fourscore thousand.
16 And next him *was* Amasiah the son of Zichri, who willingly offered himself unto Yahweh; and with him two hundred thousand mighty men of valor.
17 And of Benjamin; Eliada a mighty man of valor, and with him armed men with bow and shield two hundred thousand.
18 And next him *was* Jehozabad, and with him a hundred

and fourscore thousand ready prepared for the war.

19 These waited on the king, besides *those* whom the king put in the fenced cities throughout all Judah.

2 Chronicles 18

18:1 ¶ Now Jehoshaphat had riches and honor in abundance, and joined *in* affinity with Ahab.

2 And after *certain* years he went down to Ahab to Samaria. And Ahab killed sheep and oxen for him in abundance, and for the people that *he had* with him, and persuaded him to go up *with him* to Ramothgilead.

3 And Ahab king of Israel said to Jehoshaphat king of Judah, Will you go with me to Ramothgilead? And he answered him, I *am* as you *are*, and my people as your people; and *we will be* with you in the war.

4 ¶ And Jehoshaphat said to the king of Israel, Inquire, I pray you, at the word of Yahweh today.

5 Therefore the king of Israel gathered together of prophets four hundred men, and said to them, Shall we go to Ramothgilead to battle, or shall I forbear? And they said, Go up; for God will deliver *it* into the king's hand.

6 But Jehoshaphat said, *Is there* not here a prophet of Yahweh besides, that we might inquire of him?

7 And the king of Israel said to Jehoshaphat, *There is* yet one man, by whom we may inquire of Yahweh: but I hate him; for he never prophesied good to me, but always evil: the same *is* Micaiah the son of Imla. And Jehoshaphat said, Let not the king say so.

8 And the king of Israel called for one *of his* officers, and said, Fetch quickly Micaiah the son of Imla.

9 And the king of Israel and Jehoshaphat king of Judah sat either of them on his throne, clothed in *their* robes, and they sat in a void place at the entering in of the gate of Samaria; and all the prophets prophesied before them.

10 And Zedekiah the son of Chenaanah had made him horns of iron, and said, Thus says Yahweh, With these you shall push Syria until they are consumed.

11 And all the prophets prophesied so, saying, Go up to Ramothgilead, and prosper: for Yahweh shall deliver *it* into the hand of the king.

12 And the messenger that went to call Micaiah spoke to him, saying, Behold, the words of the prophets *declare* good to the king with one assent; let your word therefore, I pray you, be like one of theirs, and speak you good.

13 And Micaiah said, *As* Yahweh lives, even what my God says, that will I speak.

14 And when he had come to the king, the king said to him, Micaiah, shall we go to Ramothgilead to battle, or shall I forbear? And he said, Go you up, and prosper, and they shall be delivered into your hand.

15 And the king said to him, How many times shall I charge you that you say nothing but the truth to me in the name of Yahweh?

16 Then he said, I did see all Israel scattered upon the mountains, as sheep that have no shepherd: and Yahweh said, These have no master; let them return *therefore* every man to his house in peace.

17 And the king of Israel said to Jehoshaphat, Did I not tell you *that* he would not prophesy good unto me, but evil?

18 Again he said, Therefore hear the word of Yahweh; I saw Yahweh sitting upon his throne, and all the host of heaven standing on his right hand and *on* his left.

19 And Yahweh said, Who shall entice Ahab king of Israel, that he may go up and fall at Ramothgilead? And one spoke saying after this manner, and another saying after that manner.

20 Then there came out a spirit, and stood before Yahweh, and said, I will entice him. And Yahweh said to him, With what?

21 And he said, I will go out, and be a lying spirit in the mouth of all his prophets. And *Yahweh* said, You shall entice *him*, and you shall also prevail: go out, and do *even* so.

22 Now therefore, behold, Yahweh has put a lying spirit in the mouth of these your prophets, and Yahweh has spoken evil against you.

23 Then Zedekiah the son of Chenaanah came near, and smote Micaiah upon the cheek, and said, Which way went the Spirit of Yahweh from me to speak to you?

24 And Micaiah said, Behold, you shall see on that day when you shall go into an inner chamber to hide yourself.

25 Then the king of Israel said, Take you Micaiah, and carry him back to Amon the governor of the city, and to Joash the king's son;

26 And say, Thus says the king, Put this *fellow* in the prison, and feed him with bread of affliction and with water of affliction, until I return in peace.

27 And Micaiah said, If you certainly return in peace, *then* has not Yahweh spoken by me. And he said, Listen, all you people.

28 ¶ So the king of Israel and Jehoshaphat the king of Judah went up to Ramothgilead.

29 And the king of Israel said to Jehoshaphat, I will disguise myself, and will go to the battle; but put you on your robes. So the king of Israel disguised himself; and they went to the battle.

30 Now the king of Syria had commanded the captains of the chariots that *were* with him, saying, Fight you not with small or great, save only with the king of Israel.

31 And it came to pass, when the captains of the chariots saw Jehoshaphat, that they said, It *is* the king of Israel. Therefore they compassed about him to fight: but Jehoshaphat cried out, and Yahweh helped him; and God moved them *to depart* from him.

32 For it came to pass, that, when the captains of the chariots perceived that it was not the king of Israel, they turned back again from pursuing him.

33 And a *certain* man drew a bow at a venture, and smote the king of Israel between the joints of the harness: therefore he said to his chariot man, Turn your hand, that you may carry me out of the host; for I am wounded.

34 And the battle increased that day: however the king of Israel stayed *himself* up in *his* chariot against the Syrians until the evening: and about the time of the sun going down he died.

2 Chronicles 19

19:1 ¶ And Jehoshaphat the king of Judah returned to his house in peace to Jerusalem.

2 And Jehu the son of Hanani the seer went out to meet him, and said to king Jehoshaphat, Should you help the ungodly, and love them that hate Yahweh? therefore *is* wrath upon you from before Yahweh.

3 Nevertheless there are good things found in you, in that you have taken away the groves out of the land, and have prepared your heart to seek God.

4 And Jehoshaphat dwelt at Jerusalem: and he went out again through the people from Beersheba to mount Ephraim, and brought them back to Yahweh God of their fathers.

5 ¶ And he set judges in the land throughout all the fenced cities of Judah, city by city,

6 And said to the judges, Take heed what you do: for you judge not for man, but for Yahweh, who *is* with you in the judgment.

7 Therefore now let the fear of Yahweh be upon you; take heed and do *it*: for *there is* no iniquity with Yahweh our God, nor respect of persons, nor taking of gifts.

8 Moreover in Jerusalem did Jehoshaphat set of the Levites, and *of* the priests, and of the chief of the fathers of Israel, for the judgment of Yahweh, and for controversies, when they returned to Jerusalem.

9 And he charged them, saying, Thus shall you do in the fear of Yahweh, faithfully, and with a perfect heart.

10 And what cause soever shall come to you of your brethren that dwell in their cities, between blood and blood, between law and commandment, statutes and judgments, you shall even warn them that they trespass not against Yahweh, and *so* wrath comes upon you, and upon your brethren: this do, and you shall not trespass.

11 And, behold, Amariah the chief priest *is* over you in all matters of Yahweh; and Zebadiah the son of Ishmael, the ruler of the house of Judah, for all the king's matters: also the Levites *shall be* officers before you. Deal courageously, and Yahweh shall be with the good.

2 Chronicles 20

20:1 ¶ It came to pass after this also, *that* the children of Moab, and the children of Ammon, and with them *others* besides the Ammonites, came against Jehoshaphat to battle.

2 Then there came some that told Jehoshaphat, saying, There comes a great multitude against you from beyond the sea on this side *of* Syria; and, behold, they *are* in Hazazontamar, which *is* Engedi.

3 And Jehoshaphat feared, and set himself to seek Yahweh, and proclaimed a fast throughout all Judah.

4 And Judah gathered themselves together, to ask *help* of Yahweh: even out of all the cities of Judah they came to seek Yahweh.

5 And Jehoshaphat stood in the congregation of Judah and Jerusalem, in the house of Yahweh, before the new court,

6 And said, O Yahweh God of our fathers, *are* not you God in heaven? and rule *not* you over all the kingdoms of the heathen? and in your hand *is there not* power and might, so that none is able to withstand you?

7 *Are* not you our God, *who* did drive out the inhabitants of this land before your people Israel, and gave it to the seed of Abraham your friend forever?

8 And they dwelt therein, and have built you a sanctuary therein for your name, saying,

9 If, *when* evil comes upon us, *as* the sword, judgment, or pestilence, or famine, we stand before this house, and in your presence, (for your name *is* in this house,) and cry to you in our affliction, then you will hear and help.

10 And now, behold, the children of Ammon and Moab and mount Seir, whom you would not let Israel invade, when they came out of the land of Egypt, but they turned from them, and destroyed them not;

11 Behold, *I say, how* they reward us, to come to cast us out of your possession, which you have given us to inherit.

12 O our God, will you not judge them? for we have no might against this great company that comes against us; neither know we what to do: but our eyes *are* upon you.

13 And all Judah stood before Yahweh, with their little ones, their wives, and their children.

14 ¶ Then upon Jahaziel the son of Zechariah, the son of Benaiah, the son of Jeiel, the son of Mattaniah, a Levite of the sons of Asaph, came the Spirit of Yahweh in the midst of the congregation;

15 And he said, Listen you, all Judah, and you inhabitants of Jerusalem, and you king Jehoshaphat, Thus says Yahweh to you, Be not afraid nor dismayed by reason of this great multitude; for the battle *is* not yours, but God's.

16 Tomorrow go you down against them: behold, they come up by the cliff of Ziz; and you shall find them at the end of the brook, before the wilderness of Jeruel.

17 You shall not *need* to fight in this *battle*: set yourselves, stand you *still*, and see the salvation of Yahweh with you, O Judah and Jerusalem: fear not, nor be dismayed; tomorrow go out against them: for Yahweh *will be* with you.

18 And Jehoshaphat bowed his head with *his* face to the ground: and all Judah and the inhabitants of Jerusalem fell before Yahweh, worshipping Yahweh.

19 And the Levites, of the children of the Kohathites, and of the children of the Korhites, stood up to praise Yahweh God of Israel with a loud voice on high.

20 ¶ And they rose early in the morning, and went forth into the wilderness of Tekoa: and as they went forth, Jehoshaphat stood and said, Hear me, O Judah, and you inhabitants of Jerusalem; Believe in Yahweh your God, so shall you be established; believe his prophets, so shall you prosper.

21 And when he had consulted with the people, he appointed singers unto Yahweh, and that should praise the beauty of holiness, as they went out before the army, and to say, Praise Yahweh; for his mercy *endures* forever.

22 And when they began to sing and to praise, Yahweh set ambushes against the children of Ammon, Moab, and mount Seir, which had come against Judah; and they were smitten.

23 For the children of Ammon and Moab stood up against the inhabitants of mount Seir, utterly to slay and destroy *them*: and when they had made an end of the inhabitants of Seir, every one helped to destroy another.

24 And when Judah came toward the watch tower in the wilderness, they looked unto the multitude, and, behold, they *were* dead bodies fallen to the earth, and none escaped.

25 And when Jehoshaphat and his people came to take away the spoil of them, they found among them in abundance both riches with the dead bodies, and precious jewels, which they stripped off for themselves, more than they could carry away: and they were three days in gathering of the spoil, it was so much.

26 And on the fourth day they assembled themselves in the valley of Berachah; for there they blessed Yahweh: therefore the name of the same place was called, The valley of Berachah, unto this day.

27 Then they returned, every man of Judah and Jerusalem, and Jehoshaphat in the forefront of them, to go again to Jerusalem with joy; for Yahweh had made them to rejoice over their enemies.

28 And they came to Jerusalem with psalteries and harps and trumpets to the house of Yahweh.

29 And the fear of God was on all the kingdoms of *those* countries, when they had heard that Yahweh fought against the enemies of Israel.

30 So the realm of Jehoshaphat was quiet: for his God gave him rest round about.

31 ¶ And Jehoshaphat reigned over Judah: he *was* thirty and five years old when he began to reign, and he reigned twenty and five years in Jerusalem. And his mother's name *was* Azubah the daughter of Shilhi.

32 And he walked in the way of Asa his father, and departed not from it, doing *that which was* right in the sight of Yahweh.

33 However the high places were not taken away: for as yet the people had not prepared their hearts unto the God of their fathers.

34 Now the rest of the acts of Jehoshaphat, first and last, behold, they *are* written in the book of Jehu the son of Hanani, who *is* mentioned in the book of the kings of Israel.

35 And after this did Jehoshaphat king of Judah join himself with Ahaziah king of Israel, who did very wickedly:

36 And he joined himself with him to make ships to go to Tarshish: and they made the ships in Eziongeber.

37 Then Eliezer the son of Dodavah of Mareshah prophesied against Jehoshaphat, saying, Because you have joined yourself with Ahaziah, Yahweh has broken your works. And the ships were broken, that they were not able to go to Tarshish.

2 Chronicles 21

21:1 ¶ Now Jehoshaphat slept with his fathers, and was buried with his fathers in the city of David. And Jehoram his son reigned in his stead.

2 And he had brothers the sons of Jehoshaphat, Azariah, and Jehiel, and Zechariah, and Azariah, and Michael, and Shephatiah: all these *were* the sons of Jehoshaphat king of Israel.

3 And their father gave them great gifts of silver, and of gold, and of precious things, with fenced cities in Judah: but the kingdom gave he to Jehoram; because he *was* the firstborn.

4 Now when Jehoram had risen up to the kingdom of his father, he strengthened himself, and slew all his brothers with the sword, and *several* also of the princes of Israel.

5 Jehoram *was* thirty and two years old when he began to reign, and he reigned eight years in Jerusalem.

6 And he walked in the way of the kings of Israel, like as did the house of Ahab: for he had the daughter of Ahab to wife: and he worked *that which was* evil in the eyes of Yahweh.

7 However Yahweh would not destroy the house of David, because of the covenant that he had made with David, and as he promised to give a light to him and to his sons forever.

8 In his days the Edomites revolted from under the dominion of Judah, and made themselves a king.

9 Then Jehoram went forth with his princes, and all his chariots with him: and he rose up by night, and smote the Edomites which encircled him, and the captains of the chariots.

10 So the Edomites revolted from under the hand of Judah unto this day. The same time *also* did Libnah revolt from under his hand; because he had forsaken Yahweh God of his fathers.

11 Moreover he made high places in the mountains of Judah, and caused the inhabitants of Jerusalem to commit fornication, and compelled Judah *thereto*.

12 ¶ And there came a writing to him from Elijah the prophet, saying, Thus says Yahweh God of David your father, Because you have not walked in the ways of Jehoshaphat your father, nor in the ways of Asa king of Judah,

13 But have walked in the way of the kings of Israel, and have made Judah and the inhabitants of Jerusalem to go a whoring, like to the whoredoms of the house of Ahab, and also have slain your brethren of your father's house, *which were* better than yourself:

14 Behold, with a great plague will Yahweh smite your people, and your children, and your wives, and all your goods:

15 And you *shall have* great sickness by disease of your bowels, until your bowels fall out by reason of the sickness day by day.

16 Moreover Yahweh stirred up against Jehoram the spirit of the Philistines, and of the Arabians, that *were* near the Ethiopians:
17 And they came up into Judah, and broke into it, and carried away all the substance that was found in the king's house, and his sons also, and his wives; so that there was not a son left him, except Jehoahaz, the youngest of his sons.
18 And after all this Yahweh smote him in his bowels with an incurable disease.
19 And it came to pass, that in *the* process of time, after the end of two years, his bowels fell out by reason of his sickness: so he died of grievous diseases. And his people made no burning for him, like the burning of his fathers.
20 Thirty and two years old was he when he began to reign, and he reigned in Jerusalem eight years, and departed without being desired. However they buried him in the city of David, but not in the sepulchers of the kings.

2 Chronicles 22

22:1 ¶ And the inhabitants of Jerusalem made Ahaziah his youngest son king in his stead: for the band of men that came with the Arabians to the camp had slain all the oldest. So Ahaziah the son of Jehoram king of Judah reigned.
2 Forty and two years old *was* Ahaziah when he began to reign, and he reigned one year in Jerusalem. His mother's name also *was* Athaliah the daughter of Omri.
3 He also walked in the ways of the house of Ahab: for his mother was his counselor to do wickedly.
4 Therefore he did evil in the sight of Yahweh like the house of Ahab: for they were his counselors after the death of his father to his destruction.
5 He walked also after their counsel, and went with Jehoram the son of Ahab king of Israel to war against Hazael king of Syria at Ramothgilead: and the Syrians smote Joram.
6 And he returned to be healed in Jezreel because of the wounds which were given him at Ramah, when he fought with Hazael king of Syria. And Azariah the son of Jehoram king of Judah went down to see Jehoram the son of Ahab at Jezreel, because he was sick.
7 And the destruction of Ahaziah was of God by coming to Joram: for when he had come, he went out with Jehoram against Jehu the son of Nimshi, whom Yahweh had anointed to cut off the house of Ahab.
8 And it came to pass, that, when Jehu was executing judgment upon the house of Ahab, and found the princes of Judah, and the sons of the brothers of Ahaziah, that ministered to Ahaziah, he slew them.
9 And he sought Ahaziah: and they caught him, (for he was hidden in Samaria,) and brought him to Jehu: and when they had slain him, they buried him: Because, said they, he *is* the son of Jehoshaphat, who sought Yahweh with all his heart. So the house of Ahaziah had no power to keep still the kingdom.
10 ¶ But when Athaliah the mother of Ahaziah saw that her son was dead, she arose and destroyed all the seed royal of the house of Judah.
11 But Jehoshabeath, the daughter of the king, took Joash the son of Ahaziah, and stole him from among the king's sons that were slain, and put him and his nurse in a bedchamber. So Jehoshabeath, the daughter of king Jehoram, the wife of Jehoiada the priest, (for she was the sister of Ahaziah,) hid him from Athaliah, so that she slew him not.
12 And he was with them hidden in the house of God *for* six years: and Athaliah reigned over the land.

2 Chronicles 23

23:1 ¶ And in the seventh year Jehoiada strengthened himself, and took the captains of hundreds, Azariah the son of Jeroham, and Ishmael the son of Jehohanan, and Azariah the son of Obed, and Maaseiah the son of Adaiah, and Elishaphat the son of Zichri, into covenant with him.
2 And they went about in Judah, and gathered the Levites out of all the cities of Judah, and the chief of the fathers of Israel, and they came to Jerusalem.
3 And all the congregation made a covenant with the king in the house of God. And he said to them, Behold, the king's son shall reign, as Yahweh has said of the sons of David.
4 This *is* the thing that you shall do; A third part of you entering on the sabbath, of the priests and of the Levites, *shall be* porters of the doors;
5 And a third part *shall be* at the king's house; and a third part at the gate of the foundation: and all the people *shall be* in the courts of the house of Yahweh.
6 But let none come into the house of Yahweh, save the priests, and they that minister of the Levites; they shall go in, for they *are* holy: but all the people shall keep the watch of Yahweh.
7 And the Levites shall compass the king round about, every man with his weapons in his hand; and whoever *else* comes into the house, he shall be put to death: but be you with the king when he comes in, and when he goes out.
8 So the Levites and all Judah did according to all things that Jehoiada the priest had commanded, and took every man his men that were to come in on the sabbath, with them that were to go *out* on the sabbath: for Jehoiada the priest dismissed not the courses.
9 Moreover Jehoiada the priest delivered to the captains of hundreds spears, and bucklers, and shields, that *had been* king David's, which *were* in the house of God.
10 And he set all the people, every man having his weapon in his hand, from the right side of the temple to the left side of the temple, along by the altar and the temple, by the king round about.
11 Then they brought out the king's son, and put upon him the crown, and *gave him* the testimony, and made him king. And Jehoiada and his sons anointed him, and said, *God* save the king.

12 ¶ Now when Athaliah heard the noise of the people running and praising the king, she came to the people into the house of Yahweh:
13 And she looked, and, behold, the king stood at his pillar at the entering in, and the princes and the trumpets by the king: and all the people of the land rejoiced, and sounded with trumpets, also the singers with instruments of music, and such as knew to sing praise. Then Athaliah tore her clothes, and said, Treason, Treason.
14 Then Jehoiada the priest brought out the captains of hundreds that were set over the host, and said unto them, Bring her forth from the house: and whoever follows her, let him be slain with the sword. For the priest said, Slay her not in the house of Yahweh.
15 So they laid hands on her; and when she had come to the entering of the horse gate by the king's house, they slew her there.
16 And Jehoiada made a covenant between him, and between all the people, and between the king, that they should be Yahweh's people.
17 Then all the people went to the house of Baal, and broke it down, and broke his altars and his images in pieces, and slew Mattan the priest of Baal before the altars.
18 Also Jehoiada appointed the offices of the house of Yahweh by the hand of the priests the Levites, whom David had distributed in the house of Yahweh, to offer the burnt offerings of Yahweh, as *it is* written in the law of Moses, with rejoicing and with singing, *as it was ordained* by David.
19 And he set the porters at the gates of the house of Yahweh, that none *which were* unclean in any thing should enter in.
20 And he took the captains of hundreds, and the nobles, and the governors of the people, and all the people of the land, and brought down the king from the house of Yahweh: and they came through the high gate into the king's house, and set the king upon the throne of the kingdom.
21 And all the people of the land rejoiced: and the city was quiet, after that they had slain Athaliah with the sword.

2 Chronicles 24

24:1 ¶ Joash *was* seven years old when he began to reign, and he reigned *for* forty years in Jerusalem. His mother's name also *was* Zibiah of Beersheba.
2 And Joash did *that which was* right in the sight of Yahweh all the days of Jehoiada the priest.
3 And Jehoiada took for him two wives; and he begot sons and daughters.
4 And it came to pass after this, *that* Joash was minded to repair the house of Yahweh.
5 And he gathered together the priests and the Levites, and said to them, Go out to the cities of Judah, and gather of all Israel money to repair the house of your God from year to year, and see that you hasten the matter. However the Levites hastened *it* not.
6 And the king called for Jehoiada the chief, and said to him, Why have you not required of the Levites to bring in out of Judah and out of Jerusalem the collection, *according to the commandment* of Moses the servant of Yahweh, and of the congregation of Israel, for the tabernacle of witness?
7 For the sons of Athaliah, that wicked woman, had broken up the house of God; and also all the dedicated things of the house of Yahweh did they bestow upon Baalim.
8 And at the king's commandment they made a chest, and set it outside at the gate of the house of Yahweh.
9 And they made a proclamation through Judah and Jerusalem, to bring in to Yahweh the collection *that* Moses the servant of God *laid* upon Israel in the wilderness.
10 And all the princes and all the people rejoiced, and brought in, and cast into the chest, until they had finished.
11 Now it came to pass, that at what time the chest was brought to the king's office by the hand of the Levites, and when they saw that *there was* much money, the king's scribe and the high priest's officer came and emptied the chest, and took it, and carried it to his place again. Thus they did day by day, and gathered money in abundance.
12 And the king and Jehoiada gave it to such as did the work of the service of the house of Yahweh, and hired masons and carpenters to repair the house of Yahweh, and also such as worked iron and brass to mend the house of Yahweh.
13 So the workmen worked, and the work was perfected by them, and they set the house of God in his state, and strengthened it.
14 And when they had finished *it*, they brought the rest of the money before the king and Jehoiada, whereof were made vessels for the house of Yahweh, *even* vessels to minister, and to offer *therewith*, and spoons, and vessels of gold and silver. And they offered burnt offerings in the house of Yahweh continually all the days of Jehoiada.
15 ¶ But Jehoiada grew old, and was full of days when he died; a hundred and thirty years old *was he* when he died.
16 And they buried him in the city of David among the kings, because he had done good in Israel, both toward God, and toward his house.
17 Now after the death of Jehoiada came the princes of Judah, and made obeisance to the king. Then the king listened to them.
18 And they left the house of Yahweh God of their fathers, and served groves and idols: and wrath came upon Judah and Jerusalem for this their trespass.
19 Yet he sent prophets to them, to bring them again unto Yahweh; and they testified against them: but they would not give ear.
20 And the Spirit of God came upon Zechariah the son of Jehoiada the priest, which stood above the people, and said to them, Thus says God, Why transgress you the commandments of Yahweh, that you cannot prosper? because you have forsaken Yahweh, he has also forsaken you.

21 And they conspired against him, and stoned him with stones at the commandment of the king in the court of the house of Yahweh.

22 Thus Joash the king remembered not the kindness which Jehoiada his father had done to him, but slew his son. And when he died, he said, Yahweh look upon *it*, and require *it*.

23 And it came to pass at the end of the year, *that* the host of Syria came up against him: and they came to Judah and Jerusalem, and destroyed all the princes of the people from among the people, and sent all the spoil of them to the king of Damascus.

24 For the army of the Syrians came with a small company of men, and Yahweh delivered a very great host into their hand, because they had forsaken Yahweh God of their fathers. So they executed judgment against Joash.

25 And when they had departed from him, (for they left him in great diseases,) his own servants conspired against him for the blood of the sons of Jehoiada the priest, and slew him on his bed, and he died: and they buried him in the city of David, but they buried him not in the sepulchers of the kings.

26 And these are they that conspired against him; Zabad the son of Shimeath an Ammonitess, and Jehozabad the son of Shimrith a Moabitess.

27 Now *concerning* his sons, and the greatness of the burdens *laid* upon him, and the repairing of the house of God, behold, they *are* written in the story of the book of the kings. And Amaziah his son reigned in his stead.

2 Chronicles 25

25:1 ¶ Amaziah *was* twenty and five years old *when* he began to reign, and he reigned twenty and nine years in Jerusalem. And his mother's name *was* Jehoaddan of Jerusalem.

2 And he did *that which was* right in the sight of Yahweh, but not with a perfect heart.

3 Now it came to pass, when the kingdom was established to him, that he slew his servants that had killed the king his father.

4 But he slew not their children, but *did* as *it is* written in the law in the book of Moses, where Yahweh commanded, saying, The fathers shall not die for the children, neither shall the children die for the fathers, but every man shall die for his own sin.

5 Moreover Amaziah gathered Judah together, and made them captains over thousands, and captains over hundreds, according to the houses of *their* fathers, throughout all Judah and Benjamin: and he numbered them from twenty years old and above, and found them three hundred thousand choice *men, able* to go forth to war, that could handle spear and shield.

6 He hired also a hundred thousand mighty men of valor out of Israel for a hundred talents of silver.

7 But there came a man of God to him, saying, O king, let not the army of Israel go with you; for Yahweh *is* not with Israel, *to know, with* all the children of Ephraim.

8 But if you will go, do *it*, be strong for the battle: God shall make you fall before the enemy: for God has power to help, and to cast down.

9 And Amaziah said to the man of God, But what shall we do for the hundred talents which I have given to the army of Israel? And the man of God answered, Yahweh is able to give you much more than this.

10 Then Amaziah separated them, *to know*, the army that had come to him out of Ephraim, to go home again: therefore their anger was greatly kindled against Judah, and they returned home in great anger.

11 And Amaziah strengthened himself, and led forth his people, and went to the valley of salt, and smote of the children of Seir ten thousand.

12 And *other* ten thousand *left* alive did the children of Judah carry away captive, and brought them to the top of the rock, and cast them down from the top of the rock, *so* that they all were broken in pieces.

13 But the soldiers of the army which Amaziah sent back, that they should not go with him to battle, fell upon the cities of Judah, from Samaria even to Bethhoron, and smote three thousand of them, and took much spoil.

14 ¶ Now it came to pass, after that Amaziah had come from the slaughter of the Edomites, that he brought the gods of the children of Seir, and set them up *to be* his gods, and bowed down himself before them, and burned incense to them.

15 Therefore the anger of Yahweh was kindled against Amaziah, and he sent to him a prophet, which said to him, Why have you sought after the gods of the people, which could not deliver their own people out of your hand?

16 And it came to pass, as he talked with him, that *the king* said to him, Are you made of the king's counsel? cease; why should you be smitten? Then the prophet ceased, and said, I know that God has determined to destroy you, because you have done this, and have not listened to my counsel.

17 ¶ Then Amaziah king of Judah took advice, and sent to Joash, the son of Jehoahaz, the son of Jehu, king of Israel, saying, Come, let us see one another in the face.

18 And Joash king of Israel sent to Amaziah king of Judah, saying, The thistle that *was* in Lebanon sent to the cedar that *was* in Lebanon, saying, Give your daughter to my son to wife: and there passed by a wild beast that *was* in Lebanon, and trod down the thistle.

19 You say, Lo, you have smitten the Edomites; and your heart lifts you up to boast: stay now at home; why should you meddle to *your* hurt, that you should fall, *even* you, and Judah with you?

20 But Amaziah would not hear; for it came from God, that he might deliver them into the hand *of their enemies*, because they sought after the gods of Edom.

21 So Joash the king of Israel went up; and they saw one another in the face, *both* he and Amaziah king of Judah, at Bethshemesh, which *belongs* to Judah.

22 And Judah was put to the worse before Israel, and they fled every man to his tent.

23 And Joash the king of Israel took Amaziah king of Judah, the son of Joash, the son of Jehoahaz, at Bethshemesh, and brought him to Jerusalem, and broke down the wall of Jerusalem from the gate of Ephraim to the corner gate, four hundred cubits.
24 And *he took* all the gold and the silver, and all the vessels that were found in the house of God with Obededom, and the treasures of the king's house, the hostages also, and returned to Samaria.
25 And Amaziah the son of Joash king of Judah lived after the death of Joash son of Jehoahaz king of Israel fifteen years.
26 Now the rest of the acts of Amaziah, first and last, behold, *are* they not written in the book of the kings of Judah and Israel?
27 Now after the time that Amaziah did turn away from following Yahweh they made a conspiracy against him in Jerusalem; and he fled to Lachish: but they sent to Lachish after him, and slew him there.
28 And they brought him upon horses, and buried him with his fathers in the city of Judah.

2 Chronicles 26

26:1 ¶ Then all the people of Judah took Uzziah, who *was* sixteen years old, and made him king in the room of his father Amaziah.
2 He built Eloth, and restored it to Judah, after that the king slept with his fathers.
3 Sixteen years old *was* Uzziah when he began to reign, and he reigned fifty and two years in Jerusalem. His mother's name also *was* Jecoliah of Jerusalem.
4 And he did *that which was* right in the sight of Yahweh, according to all that his father Amaziah did.
5 And he sought God in the days of Zechariah, who had understanding in the visions of God: and as long as he sought Yahweh, God made him to prosper.
6 And he went forth and warred against the Philistines, and broke down the wall of Gath, and the wall of Jabneh, and the wall of Ashdod, and built cities about Ashdod, and among the Philistines.
7 And God helped him against the Philistines, and against the Arabians that dwelt in Gurbaal, and the Mehunims.
8 And the Ammonites gave gifts to Uzziah: and his name spread abroad *even* to the entering in of Egypt; for he strengthened *himself* exceedingly.
9 Moreover Uzziah built towers in Jerusalem at the corner gate, and at the valley gate, and at the turning *of the wall*, and fortified them.
10 Also he built towers in the desert, and dug many wells: for he had much cattle, both in the low country, and in the plains: husbandmen *also*, and vine dressers in the mountains, and in Carmel: for he loved husbandry.
11 Moreover Uzziah had a host of fighting men, that went out to war by bands, according to the number of their account by the hand of Jeiel the scribe and Maaseiah the ruler, under the hand of Hananiah, *one* of the king's captains.
12 The whole number of the chief of the fathers of the mighty men of valor *were* two thousand and six hundred.
13 And under their hand *was* an army, three hundred thousand and seven thousand and five hundred, that made war with mighty power, to help the king against the enemy.
14 And Uzziah prepared for them throughout all the host shields, and spears, and helmets, and body armor, and bows, and slings *to cast* stones.
15 And he made in Jerusalem engines, invented by cunning men, to be on the towers and upon the bulwarks, to shoot arrows and great stones therewith. And his name spread far abroad; for he was marvelously helped, till he was strong.
16 ¶ But when he was strong, his heart was lifted up to *his* destruction: for he transgressed against Yahweh his God, and went into the temple of Yahweh to burn incense upon the altar of incense.
17 And Azariah the priest went in after him, and with him fourscore priests of Yahweh, *that were* valiant men:
18 And they withstood Uzziah the king, and said to him, *It appertains* not unto you, Uzziah, to burn incense unto Yahweh, but to the priests the sons of Aaron, that are consecrated to burn incense: go out of the sanctuary; for you have trespassed; neither *shall it be* for your honor from Yahweh God.
19 Then Uzziah was angry, and *had* a censer in his hand to burn incense: and while he was angry with the priests, the leprosy even rose up in his forehead before the priests in the house of Yahweh, from beside the incense altar.
20 And Azariah the chief priest, and all the priests, looked upon him, and, behold, he *was* leprous in his forehead, and they thrust him out from there; yes, himself hurried also to go out, because Yahweh had smitten him.
21 And Uzziah the king was a leper to the day of his death, and dwelt in a separate house, *being* a leper; for he was cut off from the house of Yahweh: and Jotham his son *was* over the king's house, judging the people of the land.
22 Now the rest of the acts of Uzziah, first and last, did Isaiah the prophet, the son of Amoz, write.
23 So Uzziah slept with his fathers, and they buried him with his fathers in the field of the burial which *belonged* to the kings; for they said, He *is* a leper: and Jotham his son reigned in his stead.

2 Chronicles 27

27:1 ¶ Jotham *was* twenty and five years old when he began to reign, and he reigned sixteen years in Jerusalem. His mother's name also *was* Jerushah, the daughter of Zadok.
2 And he did *that which was* right in the sight of Yahweh, according to all that his father Uzziah did: however he entered not into the temple of Yahweh. And the people did yet corruptly.

3 He built the high gate of the house of Yahweh, and on the wall of Ophel he built much.

4 Moreover he built cities in the mountains of Judah, and in the forests he built castles and towers.

5 He fought also with the king of the Ammonites, and prevailed against them. And the children of Ammon gave him the same year a hundred talents of silver, and ten thousand measures of wheat, and ten thousand of barley. So much did the children of Ammon pay to him, both the second year, and the third.

6 So Jotham became mighty, because he prepared his ways before Yahweh his God.

7 Now the rest of the acts of Jotham, and all his wars, and his ways, lo, they *are* written in the book of the kings of Israel and Judah.

8 He was five and twenty years old when he began to reign, and reigned sixteen years in Jerusalem.

9 And Jotham slept with his fathers, and they buried him in the city of David: and Ahaz his son reigned in his stead.

2 Chronicles 28

28:1 ¶ Ahaz *was* twenty years old when he began to reign, and he reigned sixteen years in Jerusalem: but he did not *that which was* right in the sight of Yahweh, like David his father:

2 For he walked in the ways of the kings of Israel, and made also molten images for Baalim.

3 Moreover he burnt incense in the valley of the son of Hinnom, and burnt his children in the fire, after the abominations of the heathen whom Yahweh had cast out before the children of Israel.

4 He sacrificed also and burnt incense in the high places, and on the hills, and under every green tree.

5 Therefore Yahweh his God delivered him into the hand of the king of Syria; and they smote him, and carried away a great multitude of them captives, and brought *them* to Damascus. And he was also delivered into the hand of the king of Israel, who smote him with a great slaughter.

6 ¶ For Pekah the son of Remaliah slew in Judah a hundred and twenty thousand in one day, *which were* all valiant men; because they had forsaken Yahweh God of their fathers.

7 And Zichri, a mighty man of Ephraim, slew Maaseiah the king's son, and Azrikam the governor of the house, and Elkanah *that was* next to the king.

8 And the children of Israel carried away captive of their brethren two hundred thousand, women, sons, and daughters, and took also away much spoil from them, and brought the spoil to Samaria.

9 But a prophet of Yahweh was there, whose name *was* Oded: and he went out before the host that came to Samaria, and said to them, Behold, because Yahweh God of your fathers was angry with Judah, he has delivered them into your hand, and you have slain them in a rage *that* reaches up to heaven.

10 And now you purpose to keep under the children of Judah and Jerusalem for bondmen and bondwomen unto you: *but are there* not with you, even with you, sins against Yahweh your God?

11 Now hear me therefore, and deliver the captives again, which you have taken captive of your brethren: for the fierce wrath of Yahweh *is* upon you.

12 Then certain of the heads of the children of Ephraim, Azariah the son of Johanan, Berechiah the son of Meshillemoth, and Jehizkiah the son of Shallum, and Amasa the son of Hadlai, stood up against them that came from the war,

13 And said to them, You shall not bring in the captives here: for whereas we have offended against Yahweh *already*, you intend to add *more* to our sins and to our trespass: for our trespass is great, and *there is* fierce wrath against Israel.

14 So the armed men left the captives and the spoil before the princes and all the congregation.

15 And the men which were expressed by name rose up, and took the captives, and with the spoil clothed all that were naked among them, and arrayed them, and shod them, and gave them to eat and to drink, and anointed them, and carried all the feeble of them upon donkeys, and brought them to Jericho, the city of palm trees, to their brethren: then they returned to Samaria.

16 ¶ At that time did king Ahaz send to the kings of Assyria to help him.

17 For again the Edomites had come and smitten Judah, and carried away captives.

18 The Philistines also had invaded the cities of the low country, and of the south of Judah, and had taken Bethshemesh, and Ajalon, and Gederoth, and Shocho with the villages thereof, and Timnah with the villages thereof, Gimzo also and the villages thereof: and they dwelt there.

19 For Yahweh brought Judah low because of Ahaz king of Israel; for he made Judah naked, and transgressed grievously against Yahweh.

20 And Tilgathpilneser king of Assyria came to him, and distressed him, but strengthened him not.

21 For Ahaz took away a portion *out* of the house of Yahweh, and *out* of the house of the king, and of the princes, and gave *it* to the king of Assyria: but he helped him not.

22 And in the time of his distress did he trespass yet more against Yahweh: this *is that* king Ahaz.

23 For he sacrificed to the gods of Damascus, which smote him: and he said, Because the gods of the kings of Syria help them, *therefore* will I sacrifice to them, that they may help me. But they were the ruin of him, and of all Israel.

24 And Ahaz gathered together the vessels of the house of God, and cut in pieces the vessels of the house of God, and shut up the doors of the house of Yahweh, and he made him altars in every corner of Jerusalem.

25 And in every separate city of Judah he made high places to burn incense to other gods, and provoked to anger Yahweh God of his fathers.

26 Now the rest of his acts and of all his ways, first and last, behold, they *are* written in the book of the kings of Judah and Israel.

27 And Ahaz slept with his fathers, and they buried him in the city, *even* in Jerusalem: but they brought him not into the sepulchers of the kings of Israel: and Hezekiah his son reigned in his stead.

2 Chronicles 29

29:1 ¶ Hezekiah began to reign *when he was* five and twenty years old, and he reigned nine and twenty years in Jerusalem. And his mother's name *was* Abijah, the daughter of Zechariah.

2 And he did *that which was* right in the sight of Yahweh, according to all that David his father had done.

3 He in the first year of his reign, in the first month, opened the doors of the house of Yahweh, and repaired them.

4 And he brought in the priests and the Levites, and gathered them together into the east street,

5 And said to them, Hear me, you Levites, sanctify now yourselves, and sanctify the house of Yahweh God of your fathers, and carry forth the filthiness out of the holy *place*.

6 For our fathers have trespassed, and done *that which was* evil in the eyes of Yahweh our God, and have forsaken him, and have turned away their faces from the habitation of Yahweh, and turned *their* backs.

7 Also they have shut up the doors of the porch, and put out the lamps, and have not burned incense nor offered burnt offerings in the holy *place* to the God of Israel.

8 Therefore the wrath of Yahweh was upon Judah and Jerusalem, and he has delivered them to trouble, to astonishment, and to hissing, as you see with your eyes.

9 For, lo, our fathers have fallen by the sword, and our sons and our daughters and our wives *are* in captivity for this.

10 Now *it is* in my heart to make a covenant with Yahweh God of Israel, that his fierce wrath may turn away from us.

11 My sons, be not now negligent: for Yahweh has chosen you to stand before him, to serve him, and that you should minister to him, and burn incense.

12 ¶ Then the Levites arose, Mahath the son of Amasai, and Joel the son of Azariah, of the sons of the Kohathites: and of the sons of Merari, Kish the son of Abdi, and Azariah the son of Jehalelel: and of the Gershonites; Joah the son of Zimmah, and Eden the son of Joah:

13 And of the sons of Elizaphan; Shimri, and Jeiel: and of the sons of Asaph; Zechariah, and Mattaniah:

14 And of the sons of Heman; Jehiel, and Shimei: and of the sons of Jeduthun; Shemaiah, and Uzziel.

15 And they gathered their brethren, and sanctified themselves, and came, according to the commandment of the king, by the words of Yahweh, to cleanse the house of Yahweh.

16 And the priests went into the inner part of the house of Yahweh, to cleanse *it*, and brought out all the uncleanness that they found in the temple of Yahweh into the court of the house of Yahweh. And the Levites took *it*, to carry *it* out abroad into the brook Kidron.

17 Now they began on the first *day* of the first month to sanctify, and on the eighth day of the month came they to the porch of Yahweh: so they sanctified the house of Yahweh in eight days; and in the sixteenth day of the first month they made an end.

18 Then they went in to Hezekiah the king, and said, We have cleansed all the house of Yahweh, and the altar of burnt offering, with all the vessels thereof, and the showbread table, with all the vessels thereof.

19 Moreover all the vessels, which king Ahaz in his reign did cast away in his transgression, have we prepared and sanctified, and, behold, they *are* before the altar of Yahweh.

20 ¶ Then Hezekiah the king rose early, and gathered the rulers of the city, and went up to the house of Yahweh.

21 And they brought seven bullocks, and seven rams, and seven lambs, and seven he goats, for a sin offering for the kingdom, and for the sanctuary, and for Judah. And he commanded the priests the sons of Aaron to offer *them* on the altar of Yahweh.

22 So they killed the bullocks, and the priests received the blood, and sprinkled *it* on the altar: likewise, when they had killed the rams, they sprinkled the blood upon the altar: they killed also the lambs, and they sprinkled the blood upon the altar.

23 And they brought forth the he goats *for* the sin offering before the king and the congregation; and they laid their hands upon them:

24 And the priests killed them, and they made reconciliation with their blood upon the altar, to make an atonement for all Israel: for the king commanded *that* the burnt offering and the sin offering *should be made* for all Israel.

25 And he set the Levites in the house of Yahweh with cymbals, with psalteries, and with harps, according to the commandment of David, and of Gad the king's seer, and Nathan the prophet: for *so was* the commandment of Yahweh by his prophets.

26 And the Levites stood with the instruments of David, and the priests with the trumpets.

27 And Hezekiah commanded to offer the burnt offering upon the altar. And when the burnt offering began, the song of Yahweh began *also* with the trumpets, and with the instruments *ordained* by David king of Israel.

28 And all the congregation worshipped, and the singers sang, and the trumpeters sounded: *and* all *this continued* until the burnt offering was finished.

29 And when they had made an end of offering, the king and all that were present with him bowed themselves, and worshipped.

30 Moreover Hezekiah the king and the princes commanded the Levites to sing praise unto Yahweh with the words of David, and of Asaph the seer. And they sang praises with gladness, and they bowed their heads and worshipped.

2 Chronicles 29

31 Then Hezekiah answered and said, Now you have consecrated yourselves unto Yahweh, come near and bring sacrifices and thank offerings into the house of Yahweh. And the congregation brought in sacrifices and thank offerings; and as many as were of a free heart burnt offerings.

32 And the number of the burnt offerings, which the congregation brought, was threescore and ten bullocks, a hundred rams, *and* two hundred lambs: all these *were* for a burnt offering to Yahweh.

33 And the consecrated things *were* six hundred oxen and three thousand sheep.

34 But the priests were too few, so that they could not strip all the burnt offerings: therefore their brethren the Levites did help them, till the work was ended, and until the *other* priests had sanctified themselves: for the Levites *were* more upright in heart to sanctify themselves than the priests.

35 And also the burnt offerings *were* in abundance, with the fat of the peace offerings, and the drink offerings for every burnt offering. So the service of the house of Yahweh was set in order.

36 And Hezekiah rejoiced, and all the people, that God had prepared the people: for the thing was *done* suddenly.

2 Chronicles 30

30:1 ¶ And Hezekiah sent to all Israel and Judah, and wrote letters also to Ephraim and Manasseh, that they should come to the house of Yahweh at Jerusalem, to keep the passover unto Yahweh God of Israel.

2 For the king had taken counsel, and his princes, and all the congregation in Jerusalem, to keep the passover in the second month.

3 For they could not keep it at that time, because the priests had not sanctified themselves sufficiently, neither had the people gathered themselves together to Jerusalem.

4 And the thing pleased the king and all the congregation.

5 So they established a decree to make proclamation throughout all Israel, from Beersheba even to Dan, that they should come to keep the passover unto Yahweh God of Israel at Jerusalem: for they had not done *it* of a long *time in such sort* as it was written.

6 So the posts went with the letters from the king and his princes throughout all Israel and Judah, and according to the commandment of the king, saying, You children of Israel, turn again unto Yahweh God of Abraham, Isaac, and Israel, and he will return to the remnant of you, that have escaped out of the hand of the kings of Assyria.

7 And be not you like your fathers, and like your brethren, which trespassed against Yahweh God of their fathers, *who* therefore gave them up to desolation, as you see.

8 Now be you not stiffnecked, as your fathers *were,* but yield yourselves unto Yahweh, and enter into his sanctuary, which he has sanctified forever: and serve Yahweh your God, that the fierceness of his wrath may turn away from you.

9 For if you turn again unto Yahweh, your brethren and your children *shall find* compassion before them that lead them captive, so that they shall come again into this land: for Yahweh your God *is* gracious and merciful, and will not turn away *his* face from you, if you return to him.

10 So the posts passed from city to city through the country of Ephraim and Manasseh even to Zebulun: but they laughed them to scorn, and mocked them.

11 Nevertheless some of Asher and Manasseh and of Zebulun humbled themselves, and came to Jerusalem.

12 Also in Judah the hand of God was to give them one heart to do the commandment of the king and of the princes, by the word of Yahweh.

13 ¶ And there assembled at Jerusalem many people to keep the feast of unleavened bread in the second month, a very great congregation.

14 And they arose and took away the altars that *were* in Jerusalem, and all the altars for incense took they away, and cast *them* into the brook Kidron.

15 Then they killed the passover on the fourteenth *day* of the second month: and the priests and the Levites were ashamed, and sanctified themselves, and brought in the burnt offerings into the house of Yahweh.

16 And they stood in their place after their manner, according to the law of Moses the man of God: the priests sprinkled the blood, *which they received* of the hand of the Levites.

17 For *there were* many in the congregation that were not sanctified: therefore the Levites had the charge of the killing of the passovers for every one *that was* not clean, to sanctify *them* unto Yahweh.

18 For a multitude of the people, *even* many of Ephraim, and Manasseh, Issachar, and Zebulun, had not cleansed themselves, yet did they eat the passover otherwise than it was written. But Hezekiah prayed for them, saying, Good Yahweh pardon every one

19 *That* prepares his heart to seek God, Yahweh God of his fathers, though *he is* not *cleansed* according to the purification of the sanctuary.

20 And Yahweh listened to Hezekiah, and healed the people.

21 ¶ And the children of Israel that were present at Jerusalem kept the feast of unleavened bread seven days with great gladness: and the Levites and the priests praised Yahweh day by day, *singing* with loud instruments unto Yahweh.

22 And Hezekiah spoke comfortably to all the Levites that taught the good knowledge of Yahweh: and they did eat throughout the feast seven days, offering peace offerings, and making confession to Yahweh God of their fathers.

23 And the whole assembly took counsel to keep another seven days: and they kept *another* seven days with gladness.

24 For Hezekiah king of Judah did give to the congregation a thousand bullocks and seven thousand sheep; and the princes gave to the congregation a thousand bullocks and ten thousand sheep: and a great number of priests sanctified themselves.

25 And all the congregation of Judah, with the priests and the Levites, and all the congregation that came out of Israel, and the strangers that came out of the land of Israel, and that dwelt in Judah, rejoiced.

26 So there was great joy in Jerusalem: for since the time of Solomon the son of David king of Israel *there was* not the like in Jerusalem.

27 Then the priests the Levites arose and blessed the people: and their voice was heard, and their prayer came *up* to his holy dwelling place, *even* to heaven.

2 Chronicles 31

31:1 ¶ Now when all this was finished, all Israel that were present went out to the cities of Judah, and broke the images in pieces, and cut down the groves, and threw down the high places and the altars out of all Judah and Benjamin, in Ephraim also and Manasseh, until they had utterly destroyed them all. Then all the children of Israel returned, every man to his possession, into their own cities.

2 And Hezekiah appointed the courses of the priests and the Levites after their courses, every man according to his service, the priests and Levites for burnt offerings and for peace offerings, to minister, and to give thanks, and to praise in the gates of the tents of Yahweh.

3 *He appointed* also the king's portion of his substance for the burnt offerings, *to know*, for the morning and evening burnt offerings, and the burnt offerings for the sabbaths, and for the new moons, and for the set feasts, as *it is* written in the law of Yahweh.

4 Moreover he commanded the people that dwelt in Jerusalem to give the portion for the priests and the Levites, that they might be encouraged in the law of Yahweh.

5 And as soon as the commandment came abroad, the children of Israel brought in abundance the firstfruits of corn, *new* wine, and oil, and honey, and of all the increase of the field; and the tithe of all *things* brought they in abundantly.

6 And *concerning* the children of Israel and Judah, that dwelt in the cities of Judah, they also brought in the tithe of oxen and sheep, and the tithe of holy things which were consecrated unto Yahweh their God, and laid *them* by heaps.

7 In the third month they began to lay the foundation of the heaps, and finished *them* in the seventh month.

8 And when Hezekiah and the princes came and saw the heaps, they blessed Yahweh, and his people Israel.

9 Then Hezekiah questioned with the priests and the Levites concerning the heaps.

10 And Azariah the chief priest of the house of Zadok answered him, and said, Since *the people* began to bring the offerings into the house of Yahweh, we have had enough to eat, and have left plenty: for Yahweh has blessed his people; and that which is left *is* this great store.

11 ¶ Then Hezekiah commanded to prepare chambers in the house of Yahweh; and they prepared *them*,

12 And brought in the offerings and the tithes and the dedicated *things* faithfully: over which Cononiah the Levite *was* ruler, and Shimei his brother *was* the second.

13 And Jehiel, and Azaziah, and Nahath, and Asahel, and Jerimoth, and Jozabad, and Eliel, and Ismachiah, and Mahath, and Benaiah, *were* overseers under the hand of Cononiah and Shimei his brother, at the commandment of Hezekiah the king, and Azariah the ruler of the house of God.

14 And Kore the son of Imnah the Levite, the porter toward the east, *was* over the freewill offerings of God, to distribute the oblations of Yahweh, and the most holy things.

15 And under him *were* Eden, and Miniamin, and Jeshua, and Shemaiah, Amariah, and Shecaniah, in the cities of the priests, in *their* set office, to give to their brethren by courses, as well to the great as to the small:

16 Besides their genealogy of males, from three years old and upward, *even* to every one that enters into the house of Yahweh, his daily portion for their service in their charges according to their courses;

17 Both to the genealogy of the priests by the house of their fathers, and the Levites from twenty years old and upward, in their charges by their courses;

18 And to the genealogy of all their little ones, their wives, and their sons, and their daughters, through all the congregation: for in their set office they sanctified themselves in holiness:

19 Also of the sons of Aaron the priests, *which were* in the fields of the suburbs of their cities, in every separate city, the men that were expressed by name, to give portions to all the males among the priests, and to all that were reckoned by genealogies among the Levites.

20 And thus did Hezekiah throughout all Judah, and worked *that which was* good and right and truth before Yahweh his God.

21 And in every work that he began in the service of the house of God, and in the law, and in the commandments, to seek his God, he did *it* with all his heart, and prospered.

2 Chronicles 32

32:1 ¶ After these things, and the establishment thereof, Sennacherib king of Assyria came, and entered into Judah, and encamped against the fenced cities, and thought to win them for himself.

2 And when Hezekiah saw that Sennacherib had come, and that he had purposed to fight against Jerusalem,

3 He took counsel with his princes and his mighty men to stop the waters of the fountains which *were* outside the city: and they did help him.

4 So there was gathered much people together, who stopped all the fountains, and the brook that ran through the midst of the land, saying, Why should the kings of Assyria come, and find much water?

5 Also he strengthened himself, and built up all the wall that was broken, and raised *it* up to the towers, and another wall outside, and repaired Millo *in* the city of David, and made darts and shields in abundance.

6 And he set captains of war over the people, and gathered them together to him in the street of the gate of the city, and spoke comfortably to them, saying,

7 Be strong and courageous, be not afraid nor dismayed for the king of Assyria, nor for all the multitude that *is* with him: for *there are* more with us than with him:

8 With him *is* an arm of flesh; but with us *is* Yahweh our God to help us, and to fight our battles. And the people rested themselves upon the words of Hezekiah king of Judah.

9 ¶ After this did Sennacherib king of Assyria send his servants to Jerusalem, (but he *himself laid siege* against Lachish, and all his power with him,) to Hezekiah king of Judah, and to all Judah that *were* at Jerusalem, saying,

10 Thus says Sennacherib king of Assyria, Whereon do you trust, that you remain in the siege in Jerusalem?

11 Does not Hezekiah persuade you to give over yourselves to die by famine and by thirst, saying, Yahweh our God shall deliver us out of the hand of the king of Assyria?

12 Has not the same Hezekiah taken away his high places and his altars, and commanded Judah and Jerusalem, saying, You shall worship before one altar, and burn incense upon it?

13 Know you not what I and my fathers have done to all the people of *other* lands? were the gods of the nations of those lands any way able to deliver their lands out of my hand?

14 Who *was there* among all the gods of those nations that my fathers utterly destroyed, that could deliver his people out of my hand, that your God should be able to deliver you out of my hand?

15 Now therefore let not Hezekiah deceive you, nor persuade you on this manner, neither yet believe him: for no god of any nation or kingdom was able to deliver his people out of my hand, and out of the hand of my fathers: how much less shall your God deliver you out of my hand?

16 And his servants spoke yet *more* against Yahweh God, and against his servant Hezekiah.

17 He wrote also letters to rail on Yahweh God of Israel, and to speak against him, saying, As the gods of the nations of *other* lands have not delivered their people out of my hand, so shall not the God of Hezekiah deliver his people out of my hand.

18 Then they cried with a loud voice in the Jews' speech to the people of Jerusalem that *were* on the wall, to frighten them, and to trouble them; that they might take the city.

19 And they spoke against the God of Jerusalem, as against the gods of the people of the earth, *which were* the work of the hands of man.

20 And for this *cause* Hezekiah the king, and the prophet Isaiah the son of Amoz, prayed and cried to heaven.

21 And Yahweh sent an angel, which cut off all the mighty men of valor, and the leaders and captains in the camp of the king of Assyria. So he returned with shame of face to his own land. And when he had come into the house of his god, they that came forth of his own bowels slew him there with the sword.

22 Thus Yahweh saved Hezekiah and the inhabitants of Jerusalem from the hand of Sennacherib the king of Assyria, and from the hand of all *others*, and guided them on every side.

23 And many brought gifts unto Yahweh to Jerusalem, and presents to Hezekiah king of Judah: so that he was magnified in the sight of all nations from thereafter.

24 ¶ In those days Hezekiah was sick to the death, and prayed unto Yahweh: and he spoke to him, and he gave him a sign.

25 But Hezekiah rendered not again according to the benefit *done* to him; for his heart was lifted up: therefore there was wrath upon him, and upon Judah and Jerusalem.

26 Notwithstanding Hezekiah humbled himself for the pride of his heart, *both* he and the inhabitants of Jerusalem, so that the wrath of Yahweh came not upon them in the days of Hezekiah.

27 And Hezekiah had exceedingly much riches and honor: and he made himself treasuries for silver, and for gold, and for precious stones, and for spices, and for shields, and for all manner of pleasant jewels;

28 Storehouses also for the increase of corn, and *new* wine, and oil; and stalls for all manner of beasts, and stalls for flocks.

29 Moreover he provided him cities, and possessions of flocks and herds in abundance: for God had given him substance very much.

30 This same Hezekiah also stopped the upper watercourse of Gihon, and brought it straight down to the west side of the city of David. And Hezekiah prospered in all his works.

31 However in *the business of* the ambassadors of the princes of Babylon, who sent to him to inquire of the wonder that was *done* in the land, God left him, to try him, that he might know all *that was* in his heart.

32 Now the rest of the acts of Hezekiah, and his goodness, behold, they *are* written in the vision of Isaiah the prophet, the son of Amoz, *and* in the book of the kings of Judah and Israel.

33 And Hezekiah slept with his fathers, and they buried him in the most chief of the sepulchers of the sons of David: and all Judah and the inhabitants of Jerusalem did him honor at his death. And Manasseh his son reigned in his stead.

2 Chronicles 33

33:1 ¶ Manasseh *was* twelve years old when he began to reign, and he reigned fifty and five years in Jerusalem:

2 But did *that which was* evil in the sight of Yahweh, like unto the abominations of the heathen, whom Yahweh had cast out before the children of Israel.

3 For he built again the high places which Hezekiah his father had broken down, and he reared up altars for Baalim, and made groves, and worshipped all the host of heaven, and served them.

4 Also he built altars in the house of Yahweh, whereof Yahweh had said, In Jerusalem shall my name be forever.

5 And he built altars for all the host of heaven in the two courts of the house of Yahweh.

6 And he caused his children to pass through the fire in the valley of the son of Hinnom: also he observed times, and used enchantments, and used witchcraft, and dealt with a familiar spirit, and with wizards: he worked much evil in the sight of Yahweh, to provoke him to anger.

7 And he set a carved image, the idol which he had made, in the house of God, of which God had said to David and to Solomon his son, In this house, and in Jerusalem, which I have chosen before all the tribes of Israel, will I put my name forever:

8 Neither will I any more remove the foot of Israel from out of the land which I have appointed for your fathers; so that they will take heed to do all that I have commanded them, according to the whole law and the statutes and the ordinances by the hand of Moses.

9 So Manasseh made Judah and the inhabitants of Jerusalem to err, *and* to do worse than the heathen, whom Yahweh had destroyed before the children of Israel.

10 And Yahweh spoke to Manasseh, and to his people: but they would not listen.

11 ¶ Therefore Yahweh brought upon them the captains of the host of the king of Assyria, which took Manasseh among the thorns, and bound him with fetters, and carried him to Babylon.

12 And when he was in affliction, he sought Yahweh his God, and humbled himself greatly before the God of his fathers,

13 And prayed to him: and he was entreated of him, and heard his supplication, and brought him again to Jerusalem into his kingdom. Then Manasseh knew that Yahweh he *was* God.

14 Now after this he built a wall outside the city of David, on the west side of Gihon, in the valley, even to the entering in at the fish gate, and compassed about Ophel, and raised it up a very great height, and put captains of war in all the fenced cities of Judah.

15 And he took away the strange gods, and the idol out of the house of Yahweh, and all the altars that he had built in the mount of the house of Yahweh, and in Jerusalem, and cast *them* out of the city.

16 And he repaired the altar of Yahweh, and sacrificed thereon peace offerings and thank offerings, and commanded Judah to serve Yahweh God of Israel.

17 Nevertheless the people did sacrifice still in the high places, *yet* unto Yahweh their God only.

18 Now the rest of the acts of Manasseh, and his prayer to his God, and the words of the seers that spoke to him in the name of Yahweh God of Israel, behold, they *are* written in the book of the kings of Israel.

19 His prayer also, and *how God* was entreated of him, and all his sin, and his trespass, and the places wherein he built high places, and set up groves and graven images, before he was humbled: behold, they *are* written among the sayings of the seers.

20 So Manasseh slept with his fathers, and they buried him in his own house: and Amon his son reigned in his stead.

21 ¶ Amon *was* two and twenty years old when he began to reign, and reigned two years in Jerusalem.

22 But he did *that which was* evil in the sight of Yahweh, as did Manasseh his father: for Amon sacrificed to all the carved images which Manasseh his father had made, and served them;

23 And humbled not himself before Yahweh, as Manasseh his father had humbled himself; but Amon trespassed more and more.

24 And his servants conspired against him, and slew him in his own house.

25 But the people of the land slew all them that had conspired against king Amon; and the people of the land made Josiah his son king in his stead.

2 Chronicles 34

34:1 ¶ Josiah *was* eight years old when he began to reign, and he reigned in Jerusalem one and thirty years.

2 And he did *that which was* right in the sight of Yahweh, and walked in the ways of David his father, and declined *neither* to the right hand, nor to the left.

3 For in the eighth year of his reign, while he was yet young, he began to seek after the God of David his father: and in the twelfth year he began to purge Judah and Jerusalem from the high places, and the groves, and the carved images, and the molten images.

4 And they broke down the altars of Baalim in his presence; and the images, that *were* on high above them, he cut down; and the groves, and the carved images, and the molten images, he broke in pieces, and made dust *of them*, and strewed *it* upon the graves of them that had sacrificed to them.

5 And he burnt the bones of the priests upon their altars, and cleansed Judah and Jerusalem.

6 And *so did he* in the cities of Manasseh, and Ephraim, and Simeon, even unto Naphtali, with their axes round about.

7 And when he had broken down the altars and the groves, and had beaten the graven images into powder, and cut down all the idols throughout all the land of Israel, he returned to Jerusalem.

8 ¶ Now in the eighteenth year of his reign, when he had purged the land, and the house, he sent Shaphan the son of Azaliah, and Maaseiah the governor of the city, and Joah the son of Joahaz the recorder, to repair the house of Yahweh his God.

9 And when they came to Hilkiah the high priest, they delivered the money that was brought into the house of God, which the Levites that kept the doors had gathered of the hand of Manasseh and Ephraim, and of all the

2 Chronicles 34

remnant of Israel, and of all Judah and Benjamin; and they returned to Jerusalem.

10 And they put *it* in the hand of the workmen that had the oversight of the house of Yahweh, and they gave it to the workmen that worked in the house of Yahweh, to repair and strengthen the house:

11 Even to the craftsmen and builders gave they *it*, to buy hewn stone, and timber for couplings, and to floor the houses which the kings of Judah had destroyed.

12 And the men did the work faithfully: and the overseers of them *were* Jahath and Obadiah, the Levites, of the sons of Merari; and Zechariah and Meshullam, of the sons of the Kohathites, to set *it* forward; and *others of* the Levites, all that could instruct with instruments of music.

13 Also *they were* over the bearers of burdens, and *were* overseers of all that worked the work in any manner of service: and of the Levites *there were* scribes, and officers, and porters.

14 ¶ And when they brought out the money that was brought into the house of Yahweh, Hilkiah the priest found a book of the law of Yahweh *given* by Moses.

15 And Hilkiah answered and said to Shaphan the scribe, I have found the book of the law in the house of Yahweh. And Hilkiah delivered the book to Shaphan.

16 And Shaphan carried the book to the king, and brought the king word back again, saying, All that was committed to your servants, they do *it*.

17 And they have gathered together the money that was found in the house of Yahweh, and have delivered it into the hand of the overseers, and to the hand of the workmen.

18 Then Shaphan the scribe told the king, saying, Hilkiah the priest has given me a book. And Shaphan read it before the king.

19 And it came to pass, when the king had heard the words of the law, that he tore his clothes.

20 And the king commanded Hilkiah, and Ahikam the son of Shaphan, and Abdon the son of Micah, and Shaphan the scribe, and Asaiah a servant of the king's, saying,

21 Go, inquire of Yahweh for me, and for them that are left in Israel and in Judah, concerning the words of the book that is found: for great *is* the wrath of Yahweh that is poured out upon us, because our fathers have not kept the word of Yahweh, to do after all that is written in this book.

22 And Hilkiah, and *they* that the king *had appointed*, went to Huldah the prophetess, the wife of Shallum the son of Tikvath, the son of Hasrah, keeper of the wardrobe; (now she dwelt in Jerusalem in the college:) and they spoke to her to that *effect*.

23 And she answered them, Thus says Yahweh God of Israel, Tell you the man that sent you to me,

24 Thus says Yahweh, Behold, I will bring evil upon this place, and upon the inhabitants thereof, *even* all the curses that are written in the book which they have read before the king of Judah:

25 Because they have forsaken me, and have burned incense to other gods, that they might provoke me to anger with all the works of their hands; therefore my wrath shall be poured out upon this place, and shall not be quenched.

26 And as for the king of Judah, who sent you to inquire of Yahweh, so shall you say to him, Thus says Yahweh God of Israel *concerning* the words which you have heard;

27 Because your heart was tender, and you did humble yourself before God, when you heard his words against this place, and against the inhabitants thereof, and humbled yourself before me, and did tear your clothes, and weep before me; I have even heard *you* also, says Yahweh.

28 Behold, I will gather you to your fathers, and you shall be gathered to your grave in peace, neither shall your eyes see all the evil that I will bring upon this place, and upon the inhabitants of the same. So they brought the king word again.

29 ¶ Then the king sent and gathered together all the elders of Judah and Jerusalem.

30 And the king went up into the house of Yahweh, and all the men of Judah, and the inhabitants of Jerusalem, and the priests, and the Levites, and all the people, great and small: and he read in their ears all the words of the book of the covenant that was found in the house of Yahweh.

31 And the king stood in his place, and made a covenant before Yahweh, to walk after Yahweh, and to keep his commandments, and his testimonies, and his statutes, with all his heart, and with all his soul, to perform the words of the covenant which are written in this book.

32 And he caused all that were present in Jerusalem and Benjamin to stand *to it*. And the inhabitants of Jerusalem did according to the covenant of God, the God of their fathers.

33 And Josiah took away all the abominations out of all the countries that *pertained* to the children of Israel, and made all that were present in Israel to serve, *even* to serve Yahweh their God. *And* all his days they departed not from following Yahweh, the God of their fathers.

2 Chronicles 35

35:1 ¶ Moreover Josiah kept a passover unto Yahweh in Jerusalem: and they killed the passover on the fourteenth *day* of the first month.

2 And he set the priests in their charges, and encouraged them to the service of the house of Yahweh,

3 And said to the Levites that taught all Israel, which were holy unto Yahweh, Put the holy ark in the house which Solomon the son of David king of Israel did build; *it shall* not *be* a burden upon *your* shoulders: serve now Yahweh your God, and his people Israel,

4 And prepare *yourselves* by the houses of your fathers, after your courses, according to the writing of David king of Israel, and according to the writing of Solomon his son.

5 And stand in the holy *place* according to the divisions of the families of the fathers of your brethren the people, and *after* the division of the families of the Levites.
6 So kill the passover, and sanctify yourselves, and prepare your brethren, that *they* may do according to the word of Yahweh by the hand of Moses.
7 And Josiah gave to the people, of the flock, lambs and kids, all for the passover offerings, for all that were present, to the number of thirty thousand, and three thousand bullocks: these *were* of the king's substance.
8 And his princes gave willingly to the people, to the priests, and to the Levites: Hilkiah and Zechariah and Jehiel, rulers of the house of God, gave to the priests for the passover offerings two thousand and six hundred *small cattle*, and three hundred oxen.
9 Conaniah also, and Shemaiah and Nethaneel, his brethren, and Hashabiah and Jeiel and Jozabad, chief of the Levites, gave to the Levites for passover offerings five thousand *small cattle*, and five hundred oxen.
10 So the service was prepared, and the priests stood in their place, and the Levites in their courses, according to the king's commandment.
11 And they killed the passover, and the priests sprinkled *the blood* from their hands, and the Levites skinned *them*.
12 And they removed the burnt offerings, that they might give according to the divisions of the families of the people, to offer unto Yahweh, as *it is* written in the book of Moses. And so *did they* with the oxen.
13 And they roasted the passover with fire according to the ordinance: but the *other* holy *offerings* boiled they in pots, and in caldrons, and in pans, and divided *them* speedily among all the people.
14 And afterward they made ready for themselves, and for the priests: because the priests the sons of Aaron *were busied* in offering of burnt offerings and the fat until night; therefore the Levites prepared for themselves, and for the priests the sons of Aaron.
15 And the singers the sons of Asaph *were* in their place, according to the commandment of David, and Asaph, and Heman, and Jeduthun the king's seer; and the porters *waited* at every gate; they might not depart from their service; for their brethren the Levites prepared for them.
16 So all the service of Yahweh was prepared the same day, to keep the passover, and to offer burnt offerings upon the altar of Yahweh, according to the commandment of king Josiah.
17 And the children of Israel that were present kept the passover at that time, and the feast of unleavened bread *for* seven days.
18 And there was no passover like to that kept in Israel from the days of Samuel the prophet; neither did all the kings of Israel keep such a passover as Josiah kept, and the priests, and the Levites, and all Judah and Israel that were present, and the inhabitants of Jerusalem.
19 In the eighteenth year of the reign of Josiah was this passover kept.

20 ¶ After all this, when Josiah had prepared the temple, Necho king of Egypt came up to fight against Carchemish by *the* Euphrates: and Josiah went out against him.
21 But he sent ambassadors to him, saying, What have I to do with you, you king of Judah? *I come* not against you this day, but against the house with which I have war: for God commanded me to make haste: forbear you from *meddling with* God, who *is* with me, that he destroys you not.
22 Nevertheless Josiah would not turn his face from him, but disguised himself, that he might fight with him, and listened not to the words of Necho from the mouth of God, and came to fight in the valley of Megiddo.
23 And the archers shot at king Josiah, and the king said to his servants, Have me away; for I am greatly wounded.
24 His servants therefore took him out of that chariot, and put him in the second chariot that he had; and they brought him to Jerusalem, and he died, and was buried in *one of* the sepulchers of his fathers. And all Judah and Jerusalem mourned for Josiah.
25 And Jeremiah lamented for Josiah: and all the singing men and the singing women speak of Josiah in their lamentations to this day, and made them an ordinance in Israel: and, behold, they *are* written in the lamentations.
26 Now the rest of the acts of Josiah, and his goodness, according to *that which was* written in the law of Yahweh,
27 And his deeds, first and last, behold, they *are* written in the book of the kings of Israel and Judah.

2 Chronicles 36

36:1 ¶ Then the people of the land took Jehoahaz the son of Josiah, and made him king in his father's stead in Jerusalem.
2 Jehoahaz *was* twenty and three years old when he began to reign, and he reigned three months in Jerusalem.
3 And the king of Egypt put him down at Jerusalem, and fined the land for a hundred talents of silver and a talent of gold.
4 And the king of Egypt made Eliakim his brother king over Judah and Jerusalem, and changed his name to Jehoiakim. And Necho took Jehoahaz his brother, and carried him to Egypt.
5 Jehoiakim *was* twenty and five years old when he began to reign, and he reigned eleven years in Jerusalem: and he did *that which was* evil in the sight of Yahweh his God.
6 Against him came up Nebuchadnezzar king of Babylon, and bound him in fetters, to carry him to Babylon.
7 Nebuchadnezzar also carried of the vessels of the house of Yahweh to Babylon, and put them in his temple at Babylon.
8 Now the rest of the acts of Jehoiakim, and his abominations which he did, and that which was found in him, behold, they *are* written in the book of the kings of Israel and Judah: and Jehoiachin his son reigned in his stead.

2 Chronicles 36

9 Jehoiachin *was* eight years old when he began to reign, and he reigned three months and ten days in Jerusalem: and he did *that which was* evil in the sight of Yahweh.

10 And when the year was expired, king Nebuchadnezzar sent, and brought him to Babylon, with the goodly vessels of the house of Yahweh, and made Zedekiah his brother king over Judah and Jerusalem.

11 ¶ Zedekiah *was* one and twenty years old when he began to reign, and reigned eleven years in Jerusalem.

12 And he did *that which was* evil in the sight of Yahweh his God, *and* humbled not himself before Jeremiah the prophet *speaking* from the mouth of Yahweh.

13 And he also rebelled against king Nebuchadnezzar, who had made him swear by God: but he stiffened his neck, and hardened his heart from turning unto Yahweh God of Israel.

14 Moreover all the chief of the priests, and the people, transgressed very much after all the abominations of the heathen; and polluted the house of Yahweh which he had hallowed in Jerusalem.

15 And Yahweh God of their fathers sent to them by his messengers, rising up early, and sending; because he had compassion on his people, and on his dwelling place:

16 But they mocked the messengers of God, and despised his words, and misused his prophets, until the wrath of Yahweh arose against his people, till *there was* no remedy.

17 Therefore he brought upon them the king of the Chaldees, who slew their young men with the sword in the house of their sanctuary, and had no compassion upon young man or maiden, old man, or him that stooped for age: he gave *them* all into his hand.

18 And all the vessels of the house of God, great and small, and the treasures of the house of Yahweh, and the treasures of the king, and of his princes; all *these* he brought to Babylon.

19 And they burnt the house of God, and broke down the wall of Jerusalem, and burnt all the palaces thereof with fire, and destroyed all the goodly vessels thereof.

20 And them that had escaped from the sword carried he away to Babylon; where they were servants to him and his sons until the reign of the kingdom of Persia:

21 To fulfill the word of Yahweh by the mouth of Jeremiah, until the land had enjoyed her sabbaths: *for* as long as she lay desolate she kept sabbath, to fulfill threescore and ten years.

22 ¶ Now in the first year of Cyrus king of Persia, that the word of Yahweh *spoken* by the mouth of Jeremiah might be accomplished, Yahweh stirred up the spirit of Cyrus king of Persia, that he made a proclamation throughout all his kingdom, and *put it* also in writing, saying,

23 Thus says Cyrus king of Persia, All the kingdoms of the earth has Yahweh God of heaven given me; and he has charged me to build him a house in Jerusalem, which *is* in Judah. Who *is there* among you of all his people? Yahweh his God *be* with him, and let him go up.

Ezra

Ezra 1

1:1 ¶ Now in the first year of Cyrus king of Persia, that the word of Yahweh by the mouth of Jeremiah might be fulfilled, Yahweh stirred up the spirit of Cyrus king of Persia, *so* that he made a proclamation throughout all his kingdom, and *put it* also in writing, saying,

2 Thus says Cyrus king of Persia, Yahweh God of heaven has given me all the kingdoms of the earth; and he has charged me to build him a house at Jerusalem, which *is* in Judah.

3 Who *is there* among you of all his people? his God be with him, and let him go up to Jerusalem, which *is* in Judah, and build the house of Yahweh God of Israel, (he *is* the God,) which *is* in Jerusalem.

4 And whoever remains in any place where he sojourns, let the men of his place help him with silver, and with gold, and with goods, and with beasts, besides the freewill offering for the house of God that *is* in Jerusalem.

5 ¶ Then rose up the chief of the fathers of Judah and Benjamin, and the priests, and the Levites, with all *them* whose spirit God had raised, to go up to build the house of Yahweh which *is* in Jerusalem.

6 And all they that *were* about them strengthened their hands with vessels of silver, with gold, with goods, and with beasts, and with precious things, besides all *that* was willingly offered.

7 Also Cyrus the king brought forth the vessels of the house of Yahweh, which Nebuchadnezzar had brought forth out of Jerusalem, and had put them in the house of his gods;

8 Even those did Cyrus king of Persia bring forth by the hand of Mithredath the treasurer, and numbered them unto Sheshbazzar, the prince of Judah.

9 And this *is* the number of them: thirty platters of gold, a thousand platters of silver, nine and twenty knives,

10 Thirty basins of gold, silver basins of a second *sort* four hundred and ten, *and* other vessels a thousand.

11 All the vessels of gold and of silver *were* five thousand and four hundred. All *these* did Sheshbazzar bring up with *them of* the captivity that were brought up from Babylon to Jerusalem.

Ezra 2

2:1 ¶ Now these *are* the children of the province that went up out of the captivity, of those which had been carried away, whom Nebuchadnezzar the king of Babylon had carried away to Babylon, and came again to Jerusalem and Judah, every one to his city;

2 Which came with Zerubbabel: Jeshua, Nehemiah, Seraiah, Reelaiah, Mordecai, Bilshan, Mispar, Bigvai, Rehum, Baanah. The number of the men of the people of Israel:

3 The children of Parosh, two thousand a hundred seventy and two.
4 The children of Shephatiah, three hundred seventy and two.
5 The children of Arah, seven hundred seventy and five.
6 The children of Pahathmoab, of the children of Jeshua *and* Joab, two thousand eight hundred and twelve.
7 The children of Elam, a thousand two hundred fifty and four.
8 The children of Zattu, nine hundred forty and five.
9 The children of Zaccai, seven hundred and threescore.
10 The children of Bani, six hundred forty and two.
11 The children of Bebai, six hundred twenty and three.
12 The children of Azgad, a thousand two hundred twenty and two.
13 The children of Adonikam, six hundred sixty and six.
14 The children of Bigvai, two thousand fifty and six.
15 The children of Adin, four hundred fifty and four.
16 The children of Ater of Hezekiah, ninety and eight.
17 The children of Bezai, three hundred twenty and three.
18 The children of Jorah, a hundred and twelve.
19 The children of Hashum, two hundred twenty and three.
20 The children of Gibbar, ninety and five.
21 The children of Bethlehem, a hundred twenty and three.
22 The men of Netophah, fifty and six.
23 The men of Anathoth, a hundred twenty and eight.
24 The children of Azmaveth, forty and two.
25 The children of Kirjatharim, Chephirah, and Beeroth, seven hundred and forty and three.
26 The children of Ramah and Gaba, six hundred twenty and one.
27 The men of Michmas, a hundred twenty and two.
28 The men of Bethel and Ai, two hundred twenty and three.
29 The children of Nebo, fifty and two.
30 The children of Magbish, a hundred fifty and six.
31 The children of the other Elam, a thousand two hundred fifty and four.
32 The children of Harim, three hundred and twenty.
33 The children of Lod, Hadid, and Ono, seven hundred twenty and five.
34 The children of Jericho, three hundred forty and five.
35 The children of Senaah, three thousand and six hundred and thirty.
36 ¶ The priests: the children of Jedaiah, of the house of Jeshua, nine hundred seventy and three.
37 The children of Immer, a thousand fifty and two.
38 The children of Pashur, a thousand two hundred forty and seven.
39 The children of Harim, a thousand and seventeen.
40 The Levites: the children of Jeshua and Kadmiel, of the children of Hodaviah, seventy and four.
41 The singers: the children of Asaph, a hundred twenty and eight.
42 The children of the porters: the children of Shallum, the children of Ater, the children of Talmon, the children of Akkub, the children of Hatita, the children of Shobai, *in* all a hundred thirty and nine.
43 The Nethinims: the children of Ziha, the children of Hasupha, the children of Tabbaoth,
44 The children of Keros, the children of Siaha, the children of Padon,
45 The children of Lebanah, the children of Hagabah, the children of Akkub,
46 The children of Hagab, the children of Shalmai, the children of Hanan,
47 The children of Giddel, the children of Gahar, the children of Reaiah,
48 The children of Rezin, the children of Nekoda, the children of Gazzam,
49 The children of Uzza, the children of Paseah, the children of Besai,
50 The children of Asnah, the children of Mehunim, the children of Nephusim,
51 The children of Bakbuk, the children of Hakupha, the children of Harhur,
52 The children of Bazluth, the children of Mehida, the children of Harsha,
53 The children of Barkos, the children of Sisera, the children of Thamah,
54 The children of Neziah, the children of Hatipha.
55 The children of Solomon's servants: the children of Sotai, the children of Sophereth, the children of Peruda,
56 The children of Jaalah, the children of Darkon, the children of Giddel,
57 The children of Shephatiah, the children of Hattil, the children of Pochereth of Zebaim, the children of Ami.
58 All the Nethinims, and the children of Solomon's servants, *were* three hundred ninety and two.
59 And these *were* they which went up from Telmelah, Telharsa, Cherub, Addan, *and* Immer: but they could not show their father's house, and their seed, whether they *were* of Israel:
60 The children of Delaiah, the children of Tobiah, the children of Nekoda, six hundred fifty and two.
61 And of the children of the priests: the children of Habaiah, the children of Koz, the children of Barzillai; which took a wife of the daughters of Barzillai the Gileadite, and was called after their name:
62 These sought their register *among* those that were reckoned by genealogy, but they were not found: therefore were they, as polluted, put from the priesthood.
63 And the Tirshatha said to them, that they should not eat of the most holy things, till there stood up a priest with Urim and with Thummim.
64 ¶ The whole congregation together *was* forty and two thousand three hundred *and* threescore,
65 Besides their servants and their maids, of whom *there were* seven thousand three hundred thirty and seven: and *there were* among them two hundred singing men and singing women.
66 Their horses *were* seven hundred thirty and six; their mules, two hundred forty and five;
67 Their camels, four hundred thirty and five; *their* donkeys, six thousand seven hundred and twenty.
68 And *some* of the chief of the fathers, when they came

Ezra 2

to the house of Yahweh which *is* at Jerusalem, offered freely for the house of God to set it up in his place:
69 They gave after their ability to the treasury of the work threescore and one thousand drams of gold, and five thousand pounds of silver, and one hundred priests' garments.
70 So the priests, and the Levites, and *some* of the people, and the singers, and the porters, and the Nethinims, dwelt in their cities, and all Israel in their cities.

Ezra 3

3:1 ¶ And when the seventh month had come, and the children of Israel *were* in the cities, the people gathered themselves together as one man to Jerusalem.
2 Then stood up Jeshua the son of Jozadak, and his brethren the priests, and Zerubbabel the son of Shealtiel, and his brethren, and built the altar of the God of Israel, to offer burnt offerings thereon, as *it is* written in the law of Moses the man of God.
3 And they set the altar upon his bases; for fear *was* upon them because of the people of those countries: and they offered burnt offerings thereon unto Yahweh, *even* burnt offerings morning and evening.
4 They kept also the feast of tabernacles, as *it is* written, and *offered* the daily burnt offerings by number, according to the custom, as the duty of every day required;
5 And afterward *offered* the continual burnt offering, both of the new moons, and of all the set feasts of Yahweh that were consecrated, and of every one that willingly offered a freewill offering unto Yahweh.
6 From the first day of the seventh month began they to offer burnt offerings unto Yahweh. But the foundation of the temple of Yahweh was not *yet* laid.
7 They gave money also to the masons, and to the carpenters; and food, and drink, and oil, to them of Zidon, and to them of Tyre, to bring cedar trees from Lebanon to the sea of Joppa, according to the grant that they had of Cyrus king of Persia.
8 ¶ Now in the second year of their coming to the house of God at Jerusalem, in the second month, began Zerubbabel the son of Shealtiel, and Jeshua the son of Jozadak, and the remnant of their brethren the priests and the Levites, and all they that had come out of the captivity to Jerusalem; and appointed the Levites, from twenty years old and upward, to set forward the work of the house of Yahweh.
9 Then stood Jeshua *with* his sons and his brethren, Kadmiel and his sons, the sons of Judah, together, to set forward the workmen in the house of God: the sons of Henadad, *with* their sons and their brethren the Levites.
10 And when the builders laid the foundation of the temple of Yahweh, they set the priests in their apparel with trumpets, and the Levites the sons of Asaph with cymbals, to praise Yahweh, after the ordinance of David king of Israel.
11 And they sang together by course in praising and giving thanks unto Yahweh; because *he is* good, for his mercy *endures* forever toward Israel. And all the people shouted with a great shout, when they praised Yahweh, because the foundation of the house of Yahweh was laid.
12 But many of the priests and Levites and chief of the fathers, *who were* ancient men, that had seen the first house, when the foundation of this house was laid before their eyes, wept with a loud voice; and many shouted aloud for joy:
13 So that the people could not discern the noise of the shout of joy from the noise of the weeping of the people: for the people shouted with a loud shout, and the noise was heard afar off.

Ezra 4

4:1 ¶ Now when the adversaries of Judah and Benjamin heard that the children of the captivity built the temple unto Yahweh God of Israel;
2 Then they came to Zerubbabel, and to the chiefs of the fathers, and said to them, Let us build with you: for we seek your God, as you *do*; and we do sacrifice to him since the days of Esarhaddon king of Assur, which brought us up here.
3 But Zerubbabel, and Jeshua, and the rest of the chief of the fathers of Israel, said to them, You have nothing to do with us to build a house to our God; but we ourselves together will build unto Yahweh God of Israel, as king Cyrus the king of Persia has commanded us.
4 Then the people of the land weakened the hands of the people of Judah, and troubled them in building,
5 And hired counselors against them, to frustrate their purpose, all the days of Cyrus king of Persia, even until the reign of Darius king of Persia.
6 ¶ And in the reign of Ahasuerus, in the beginning of his reign, wrote they *to him* an accusation against the inhabitants of Judah and Jerusalem.
7 And in the days of Artaxerxes wrote Bishlam, Mithredath, Tabeel, and the rest of their companions, to Artaxerxes king of Persia; and the writing of the letter *was* written in the Syrian tongue, and interpreted in the Syrian tongue.
8 Rehum the chancellor and Shimshai the scribe wrote a letter against Jerusalem to Artaxerxes the king in this sort:
9 Then *wrote* Rehum the chancellor, and Shimshai the scribe, and the rest of their companions; the Dinaites, the Apharsathchites, the Tarpelites, the Apharsites, the Archevites, the Babylonians, the Susanchites, the Dehavites, *and* the Elamites,
10 And the rest of the nations whom the great and noble Asnappar brought over, and set in the cities of Samaria, and the rest *that are* on this side *of* the river, and at such a time.
11 This *is* the copy of the letter that they sent to him, *even* to Artaxerxes the king; Your servants the men on this side the river, and at such a time.
12 Be it known to the king, that the Jews which came up from you to us have come to Jerusalem, building the rebellious and the bad city, and have set up the walls *thereof*, and joined the foundations.

13 Be it known now to the king, that, if this city is built, and the walls set up *again, then* will they not pay toll, tribute, and custom, and *so* you shall damage the revenue of the kings.

14 Now because we have maintenance from *the king's* palace, and it was not proper for us to see the king's dishonor, therefore have we sent and informed the king;

15 That search may be made in the book of the records of your fathers: so shall you find in the book of the records, and know that this city *is* a rebellious city, and hurtful to kings and provinces, and that they have moved sedition within the same of old time: for which cause was this city destroyed.

16 We inform the king that, if this city is built *again*, and the walls thereof set up, by this means you shall have no portion on this side *of* the river.

17 ¶ *Then* sent the king an answer to Rehum the chancellor, and *to* Shimshai the scribe, and *to* the rest of their companions that dwell in Samaria, and *to* the rest beyond the river. Peace, and at such a time.

18 The letter which you sent to us has been plainly read before me.

19 And I commanded, and search has been made, and it is found that this city of old time has made insurrection against kings, and *that* rebellion and sedition have been made therein.

20 There have been mighty kings also over Jerusalem, which have ruled over all *countries* beyond the river; and toll, tribute, and custom, was paid to them.

21 Give you now commandment to cause these men to cease, and that this city be not built, until *another* commandment shall be given from me.

22 Take heed now that you fail not to do this: why should damage grow to the hurt of the kings?

23 Now when the copy of king Artaxerxes' letter *was* read before Rehum, and Shimshai the scribe, and their companions, they went up in haste to Jerusalem to the Jews, and made them to cease by force and power.

24 Then ceased the work of the house of God which *is* at Jerusalem. So it ceased unto the second year of the reign of Darius king of Persia.

Ezra 5

5:1 ¶ Then the prophets, Haggai the prophet, and Zechariah the son of Iddo, prophesied to the Jews that *were* in Judah and Jerusalem in the name of the God of Israel, *even* unto them.

2 Then rose up Zerubbabel the son of Shealtiel, and Jeshua the son of Jozadak, and began to build the house of God which *is* at Jerusalem: and with them *were* the prophets of God helping them.

3 ¶ At the same time came to them Tatnai, governor on this side *of* the river, and Shetharboznai, and their companions, and said thus to them, Who has commanded you to build this house, and to make up this wall?

4 Then said we to them after this manner, What are the names of the men that make this building?

5 But the eye of their God was upon the elders of the Jews, that they could not cause them to cease, till the matter came to Darius: and then they returned answer by letter concerning this *matter*.

6 The copy of the letter that Tatnai, governor on this side *of* the river, and Shetharboznai, and his companions the Apharsachites, which *were* on this side *of* the river, sent to Darius the king:

7 They sent a letter to him, wherein was written thus; Unto Darius the king, all peace.

8 Be it known unto the king, that we went into the province of Judea, to the house of the great God, which is built with great stones, and timber is laid in the walls, and this work goes fast on, and prospers in their hands.

9 Then asked we those elders, *and* said to them thus, Who commanded you to build this house, and to make up these walls?

10 We asked their names also, to inform you, that we might write the names of the men that *were* the chief of them.

11 And thus they returned us answer, saying, We are the servants of the God of heaven and earth, and build the house that was built these many years ago, which a great king of Israel built and set up.

12 But after that our fathers had provoked the God of heaven to wrath, he gave them into the hand of Nebuchadnezzar the king of Babylon, the Chaldean, who destroyed this house, and carried the people away into Babylon.

13 But in the first year of Cyrus the king of Babylon *the same* king Cyrus made a decree to build this house of God.

14 And the vessels also of gold and silver of the house of God, which Nebuchadnezzar took out of the temple that *was* in Jerusalem, and brought them into the temple of Babylon, those did Cyrus the king take out of the temple of Babylon, and they were delivered to *one*, whose name *was* Sheshbazzar, whom he had made governor;

15 And said to him, Take these vessels, go, carry them into the temple that *is* in Jerusalem, and let the house of God be built in his place.

16 Then came the same Sheshbazzar, *and* laid the foundation of the house of God which *is* in Jerusalem: and since that time even until now has it been in building, and *yet* it is not finished.

17 Now therefore, if *it seems* good to the king, let there be search made in the king's treasure house, which *is* there at Babylon, whether it is *so*, that a decree was made of Cyrus the king to build this house of God at Jerusalem, and let the king send his pleasure to us concerning this matter.

Ezra 6

6:1 ¶ Then Darius the king made a decree, and search was made in the house of the rolls, where the treasures were laid up in Babylon.

2 And there was found at Achmetha, in the palace that *is* in the province of the Medes, a roll, and therein *was* a record thus written:

Ezra 6

3 In the first year of Cyrus the king *the same* Cyrus the king made a decree *concerning* the house of God at Jerusalem, Let the house be built, the place where they offered sacrifices, and let the foundations thereof be strongly laid; the height thereof threescore cubits, *and* the breadth thereof threescore cubits;

4 *With* three rows of great stones, and a row of new timber: and let the expenses be given out of the king's house:

5 And also let the golden and silver vessels of the house of God, which Nebuchadnezzar took forth out of the temple which *is* at Jerusalem, and brought to Babylon, be restored, and brought again to the temple which *is* at Jerusalem, *every one* to his place, and place *them* in the house of God.

6 Now *therefore*, Tatnai, governor beyond the river, Shetharboznai, and your companions the Apharsachites, which *are* beyond the river, be you far from there:

7 Let the work of this house of God alone; let the governor of the Jews and the elders of the Jews build this house of God in his place.

8 Moreover I make a decree what you shall do to the elders of these Jews for the building of this house of God: that of the king's goods, *even* of the tribute beyond the river, immediately expenses be given to these men, that they be not hindered.

9 And that which they have need of, both young bullocks, and rams, and lambs, for the burnt offerings of the God of heaven, wheat, salt, wine, and oil, according to the appointment of the priests which *are* at Jerusalem, let it be given *to* them day by day without fail:

10 That they may offer sacrifices of sweet savors to the God of heaven, and pray for the life of the king, and of his sons.

11 Also I have made a decree, that whoever shall alter this word, let timber be pulled down from his house, and being set up, let him be hanged thereon; and let his house be made a dunghill for this.

12 And the God that has caused his name to dwell there destroy all kings and people, that shall put to their hand to alter *and* to destroy this house of God which *is* at Jerusalem. I Darius have made a decree; let it be done with speed.

13 ¶ Then Tatnai, governor on this side *of* the river, Shetharboznai, and their companions, according to that which Darius the king had sent, so they did speedily.

14 And the elders of the Jews built, and they prospered through the prophesying of Haggai the prophet and Zechariah the son of Iddo. And they built, and finished *it*, according to the commandment of the God of Israel, and according to the commandment of Cyrus, and Darius, and Artaxerxes king of Persia.

15 And this house was finished on the third day of the month *of* Adar, which was in the sixth year of the reign of Darius the king.

16 And the children of Israel, the priests, and the Levites, and the rest of the children of the captivity, kept the dedication of this house of God with joy,

17 And offered at the dedication of this house of God a hundred bullocks, two hundred rams, four hundred lambs; and for a sin offering for all Israel, twelve he goats, according to the number of the tribes of Israel.

18 And they set the priests in their divisions, and the Levites in their courses, for the service of God, which *is* at Jerusalem; as it is written in the book of Moses.

19 And the children of the captivity kept the passover upon the fourteenth *day* of the first month.

20 For the priests and the Levites were purified together, all of them *were* pure, and killed the passover for all the children of the captivity, and for their brethren the priests, and for themselves.

21 And the children of Israel, which had come again out of captivity, and all such as had separated themselves unto them from the filthiness of the heathen of the land, to seek Yahweh God of Israel, did eat,

22 And kept the feast of unleavened bread seven days with joy: for Yahweh had made them joyful, and turned the heart of the king of Assyria to them, to strengthen their hands in the work of the house of God, the God of Israel.

Ezra 7

7:1 ¶ Now after these things, in the reign of Artaxerxes king of Persia, Ezra the son of Seraiah, the son of Azariah, the son of Hilkiah,

2 The son of Shallum, the son of Zadok, the son of Ahitub,

3 The son of Amariah, the son of Azariah, the son of Meraioth,

4 The son of Zerahiah, the son of Uzzi, the son of Bukki,

5 The son of Abishua, the son of Phinehas, the son of Eleazar, the son of Aaron the chief priest:

6 This Ezra went up from Babylon; and he *was* a ready scribe in the law of Moses, which Yahweh God of Israel had given: and the king granted him all his request, according to the hand of Yahweh his God upon him.

7 And there went up *some* of the children of Israel, and of the priests, and the Levites, and the singers, and the porters, and the Nethinims, to Jerusalem, in the seventh year of Artaxerxes the king.

8 And he came to Jerusalem in the fifth month, which *was* in the seventh year of the king.

9 For upon the first *day* of the first month began he to go up from Babylon, and on the first *day* of the fifth month came he to Jerusalem, according to the good hand of his God upon him.

10 For Ezra had prepared his heart to seek the law of Yahweh, and to do *it*, and to teach in Israel statutes and judgments.

11 ¶ Now this *is* the copy of the letter that the king Artaxerxes gave to Ezra the priest, the scribe, *even* a scribe of the words of the commandments of Yahweh, and of his statutes to Israel.

12 Artaxerxes, king of kings, to Ezra the priest, a scribe of the law of the God of heaven, perfect *peace*, and at such a time.
13 I make a decree, that all they of the people of Israel, and *of* his priests and Levites, in my realm, which are minded of their own freewill to go up to Jerusalem, go with you.
14 Forasmuch as you are sent by the king, and of his seven counselors, to inquire concerning Judah and Jerusalem, according to the law of your God which *is* in your hand;
15 And to carry the silver and gold, which the king and his counselors have freely offered to the God of Israel, whose habitation *is* in Jerusalem,
16 And all the silver and gold that you can find in all the province of Babylon, with the freewill offering of the people, and of the priests, offering willingly for the house of their God which *is* in Jerusalem:
17 That you may buy speedily with this money bullocks, rams, lambs, with their meat offerings and their drink offerings, and offer them upon the altar of the house of your God which *is* in Jerusalem.
18 And whatever shall seem good to you, and to your brethren, to do with the rest of the silver and the gold, that do after the will of your God.
19 The vessels also that are given *to* you for the service of the house of your God, *those* deliver you before the God of Jerusalem.
20 And whatever more shall be needful for the house of your God, which you shall have occasion to bestow, bestow *it* out of the king's treasure house.
21 And I, *even* I Artaxerxes the king, do make a decree to all the treasurers which *are* beyond the river, that whatever Ezra the priest, the scribe of the law of the God of heaven, shall require of you, it be done speedily,
22 Unto a hundred talents of silver, and to a hundred measures of wheat, and to a hundred baths of wine, and to a hundred baths of oil, and salt without prescribing *how much*.
23 Whatever is commanded by the God of heaven, let it be diligently done for the house of the God of heaven: for why should there be wrath against the realm of the king and his sons?
24 Also we inform you, that touching any of the priests and Levites, singers, porters, Nethinims, or ministers of this house of God, it shall not be lawful to impose toll, tribute, or custom, upon them.
25 And you, Ezra, after the wisdom of your God, that *is* in your hand, set magistrates and judges, which may judge all the people that *are* beyond the river, all such as know the laws of your God; and teach you them that know *them* not.
26 And whoever will not do the law of your God, and the law of the king, let judgment be executed speedily upon him, whether *it is* unto death, or to banishment, or to confiscation of goods, or to imprisonment.
27 ¶ Blessed *be* Yahweh God of our fathers, which has put *such a thing* as this in the king's heart, to beautify the house of Yahweh which *is* in Jerusalem:
28 And has extended mercy to me before the king, and his counselors, and before all the king's mighty princes. And I was strengthened as the hand of Yahweh my God *was* upon me, and I gathered together out of Israel chief men to go up with me.

Ezra 8

8:1 ¶ These *are* now the chief of their fathers, and *this is* the genealogy of them that went up with me from Babylon, in the reign of Artaxerxes the king.
2 Of the sons of Phinehas; Gershom: of the sons of Ithamar; Daniel: of the sons of David; Hattush.
3 Of the sons of Shechaniah, of the sons of Pharosh; Zechariah: and with him were reckoned by genealogy of the males a hundred and fifty.
4 Of the sons of Pahathmoab; Elihoenai the son of Zerahiah, and with him two hundred males.
5 Of the sons of Shechaniah; the son of Jahaziel, and with him three hundred males.
6 Of the sons also of Adin; Ebed the son of Jonathan, and with him fifty males.
7 And of the sons of Elam; Jeshaiah the son of Athaliah, and with him seventy males.
8 And of the sons of Shephatiah; Zebadiah the son of Michael, and with him fourscore males.
9 Of the sons of Joab; Obadiah the son of Jehiel, and with him two hundred and eighteen males.
10 And of the sons of Shelomith; the son of Josiphiah, and with him a hundred and threescore males.
11 And of the sons of Bebai; Zechariah the son of Bebai, and with him twenty and eight males.
12 And of the sons of Azgad; Johanan the son of Hakkatan, and with him a hundred and ten males.
13 And of the last sons of Adonikam, whose names *are* these, Eliphelet, Jeiel, and Shemaiah, and with them threescore males.
14 Of the sons also of Bigvai; Uthai, and Zabbud, and with them seventy males.
15 And I gathered them together to the river that runs to Ahava; and there stayed we in tents three days: and I viewed the people, and the priests, and found there none of the sons of Levi.
16 Then sent I for Eliezer, for Ariel, for Shemaiah, and for Elnathan, and for Jarib, and for Elnathan, and for Nathan, and for Zechariah, and for Meshullam, chief men; also for Joiarib, and for Elnathan, men of understanding.
17 And I sent them with commandment to Iddo the chief at the place Casiphia, and I told them what they should say to Iddo, *and* to his brethren the Nethinims, at the place Casiphia, that they should bring to us ministers for the house of our God.
18 And by the good hand of our God upon us they brought us a man of understanding, of the sons of Mahli, the son of Levi, the son of Israel; and Sherebiah, with his sons and his brethren, eighteen;
19 And Hashabiah, and with him Jeshaiah of the sons of Merari, his brethren and their sons, twenty;

Ezra 8

20 Also of the Nethinims, whom David and the princes had appointed for the service of the Levites, two hundred and twenty Nethinims: all of them were expressed by name.
21 ¶ Then I proclaimed a fast there, at the river of Ahava, that we might afflict ourselves before our God, to seek of him a right way for us, and for our little ones, and for all our substance.
22 For I was ashamed to require of the king a band of soldiers and horsemen to help us against the enemy in the way: because we had spoken to the king, saying, The hand of our God *is* upon all them for good that seek him; but his power and his wrath *is* against all them that forsake him.
23 So we fasted and sought our God for this: and he was entreated of us.
24 ¶ Then I separated twelve of the chief of the priests, Sherebiah, Hashabiah, and ten of their brethren with them,
25 And weighed to them the silver, and the gold, and the vessels, *even* the offering of the house of our God, which the king, and his counselors, and his lords, and all Israel there present, had offered:
26 I even weighed unto their hand six hundred and fifty talents of silver, and silver vessels a hundred talents, *and* of gold a hundred talents;
27 Also twenty basins of gold, of a thousand drams; and two vessels of fine copper, precious as gold.
28 And I said to them, You *are* holy unto Yahweh; the vessels *are* holy also; and the silver and the gold *are* a freewill offering unto Yahweh God of your fathers.
29 Watch you, and keep *them*, until you weigh *them* before the chief of the priests and the Levites, and chief of the fathers of Israel, at Jerusalem, in the chambers of the house of Yahweh.
30 So took the priests and the Levites the weight of the silver, and the gold, and the vessels, to bring *them* to Jerusalem to the house of our God.
31 ¶ Then we departed from the river of Ahava on the twelfth *day* of the first month, to go to Jerusalem: and the hand of our God was upon us, and he delivered us from the hand of the enemy, and of such as lay in wait by the way.
32 And we came to Jerusalem, and stayed there three days.
33 Now on the fourth day was the silver and the gold and the vessels weighed in the house of our God by the hand of Meremoth the son of Uriah the priest; and with him *was* Eleazar the son of Phinehas; and with them *was* Jozabad the son of Jeshua, and Noadiah the son of Binnui, Levites;
34 By number *and* by weight of every one: and all the weight was written at that time.
35 *Also* the children of those that had been carried away, which had come out of the captivity, offered burnt offerings to the God of Israel, twelve bullocks for all Israel, ninety and six rams, seventy and seven lambs, twelve he goats *for* a sin offering: all *this was* a burnt offering unto Yahweh.
36 And they delivered the king's commissions to the king's lieutenants, and to the governors on this side *of* the river: and they supported the people, and the house of God.

Ezra 9

9:1 ¶ Now when these things were done, the princes came to me, saying, The people of Israel, and the priests, and the Levites, have not separated themselves from the people of the lands, *doing* according to their abominations, *even* of the Canaanites, the Hittites, the Perizzites, the Jebusites, the Ammonites, the Moabites, the Egyptians, and the Amorites.
2 For they have taken of their daughters for themselves, and for their sons: so that the holy seed have mingled themselves with the people of *those* lands: yes, the hand of the princes and rulers has been chief in this trespass.
3 And when I heard this thing, I tore my garment and my mantle, and plucked off the hair of my head and of my beard, and sat down astonished.
4 Then were assembled to me every one that trembled at the words of the God of Israel, because of the transgression of those that had been carried away; and I sat astonished until the evening sacrifice.
5 ¶ And at the evening sacrifice I arose up from my heaviness; and having torn my garment and my mantle, I fell upon my knees, and spread out my hands unto Yahweh my God,
6 And said, O my God, I am ashamed and blush to lift up my face to you, my God: for our iniquities have increased over *our* head, and our trespass has grown up to the heavens.
7 Since the days of our fathers *have* we *been* in a great trespass unto this day; and for our iniquities have we, our kings, *and* our priests, been delivered into the hand of the kings of the lands, to the sword, to captivity, and to a spoil, and to confusion of face, as *it is* this day.
8 And now for a little space grace has been *shown* from Yahweh our God, to leave us a remnant to escape, and to give us a nail in his holy place, that our God may lighten our eyes, and give us a little reviving in our bondage.
9 For we *were* bondmen; yet our God did not forsake us in our bondage, but has extended mercy to us in the sight of the kings of Persia, to give us a reviving, to set up the house of our God, and to repair the desolations thereof, and to give us a wall in Judah and in Jerusalem.
10 And now, O our God, what shall we say after this? for we have forsaken your commandments,
11 Which you have commanded by your servants the prophets, saying, The land, to which you go to possess it, is an unclean land with the filthiness of the people of the lands, with their abominations, which have filled it from one end to another with their uncleanness.
12 Now therefore give not your daughters to their sons, neither take their daughters to your sons, nor seek their peace or their wealth forever: that you may be strong, and

eat the good of the land, and leave *it* for an inheritance to your children forever.

13 And after all that has come upon us for our evil deeds, and for our great trespass, seeing that you our God have punished us less than our iniquities *deserve*, and have given us *such* deliverance as this;

14 Should we again break your commandments, and join in affinity with the people of these abominations? would not you be angry with us till you have consumed *us*, so that *there should be* no remnant nor escaping?

15 O Yahweh God of Israel, you *are* righteous: for we remain yet escaped, as *it is* this day: behold, we *are* before you in our trespasses: for we cannot stand before you because of this.

Ezra 10

10:1 ¶ Now when Ezra had prayed, and when he had confessed, weeping and casting himself down before the house of God, there assembled to him out of Israel a very great congregation of men and women and children: for the people wept very bitterly.

2 And Shechaniah the son of Jehiel, *one* of the sons of Elam, answered and said to Ezra, We have trespassed against our God, and have taken strange wives of the people of the land: yet now there is hope in Israel concerning this thing.

3 Now therefore let us make a covenant with our God to put away all the wives, and such as are born of them, according to the counsel of my lord, and of those that tremble at the commandment of our God; and let it be done according to the law.

4 Arise; for *this* matter *belongs* to you: we also *will be* with you: be of good courage, and do *it*.

5 Then arose Ezra, and made the chief priests, the Levites, and all Israel, to swear that they should do according to this word. And they swore.

6 ¶ Then Ezra rose up from before the house of God, and went into the chamber of Johanan the son of Eliashib: and *when* he came there, he did eat no bread, nor drink water: for he mourned because of the transgression of them that had been carried away.

7 And they made proclamation throughout Judah and Jerusalem to all the children of the captivity, that they should gather themselves together to Jerusalem;

8 And that whoever would not come within three days, according to the counsel of the princes and the elders, all his substance should be forfeited, and himself separated from the congregation of those that had been carried away.

9 Then all the men of Judah and Benjamin gathered themselves together to Jerusalem within three days. It *was* the ninth month, on the twentieth *day* of the month; and all the people sat in the street of the house of God, trembling because of *this* matter, and for the great rain.

10 And Ezra the priest stood up, and said to them, You have transgressed, and have taken strange wives, to increase the trespass of Israel.

11 Now therefore make confession unto Yahweh God of your fathers, and do his pleasure: and separate yourselves from the people of the land, and from the strange wives.

12 Then all the congregation answered and said with a loud voice, As you have said, so must we do.

13 But the people *are* many, and *it is* a time of much rain, and we are not able to stand outside, neither *is this* a work of one day or two: for we are many that have transgressed in this thing.

14 Let now our rulers of all the congregation stand, and let all them which have taken strange wives in our cities come at appointed times, and with them the elders of every city, and the judges thereof, until the fierce wrath of our God for this matter is turned from us.

15 ¶ Only Jonathan the son of Asahel and Jahaziah the son of Tikvah were employed about this *matter*: and Meshullam and Shabbethai the Levite helped them.

16 And the children of the captivity did so. And Ezra the priest *with* certain chief of the fathers, after the house of their fathers, and all of them by *their* names, were separated, and sat down in the first day of the tenth month to examine the matter.

17 And they made an end with all the men that had taken strange wives by the first day of the first month.

18 And among the sons of the priests there were found that had taken strange wives: *namely*, of the sons of Jeshua the son of Jozadak, and his brothers; Maaseiah, and Eliezer, and Jarib, and Gedaliah.

19 And they gave their hands that they would put away their wives; and *being* guilty, *they offered* a ram of the flock for their trespass.

20 And of the sons of Immer; Hanani, and Zebadiah.

21 And of the sons of Harim; Maaseiah, and Elijah, and Shemaiah, and Jehiel, and Uzziah.

22 And of the sons of Pashur; Elioenai, Maaseiah, Ishmael, Nethaneel, Jozabad, and Elasah.

23 Also of the Levites; Jozabad, and Shimei, and Kelaiah, (the same *is* Kelita,) Pethahiah, Judah, and Eliezer.

24 Of the singers also; Eliashib: and of the porters; Shallum, and Telem, and Uri.

25 Moreover of Israel: of the sons of Parosh; Ramiah, and Jeziah, and Malchiah, and Miamin, and Eleazar, and Malchijah, and Benaiah.

26 And of the sons of Elam; Mattaniah, Zechariah, and Jehiel, and Abdi, and Jeremoth, and Eliah.

27 And of the sons of Zattu; Elioenai, Eliashib, Mattaniah, and Jeremoth, and Zabad, and Aziza.

28 Of the sons also of Bebai; Jehohanan, Hananiah, Zabbai, *and* Athlai.

29 And of the sons of Bani; Meshullam, Malluch, and Adaiah, Jashub, and Sheal, and Ramoth.

30 And of the sons of Pahathmoab; Adna, and Chelal, Benaiah, Maaseiah, Mattaniah, Bezaleel, and Binnui, and Manasseh.

31 And *of* the sons of Harim; Eliezer, Ishijah, Malchiah, Shemaiah, Shimeon,

32 Benjamin, Malluch, *and* Shemariah.

33 Of the sons of Hashum; Mattenai, Mattathah, Zabad, Eliphelet, Jeremai, Manasseh, *and* Shimei.

Ezra 10

34 Of the sons of Bani; Maadai, Amram, and Uel,
35 Benaiah, Bedeiah, Chelluh,
36 Vaniah, Meremoth, Eliashib,
37 Mattaniah, Mattenai, and Jaasau,
38 And Bani, and Binnui, Shimei,
39 And Shelemiah, and Nathan, and Adaiah,
40 Machnadebai, Shashai, Sharai,
41 Azareel, and Shelemiah, Shemariah,
42 Shallum, Amariah, *and* Joseph.
43 Of the sons of Nebo; Jeiel, Mattithiah, Zabad, Zebina, Jadau, and Joel, Benaiah.
44 All these had taken strange wives: and *some* of them had wives by whom they had children.

Nehemiah

Nehemiah 1

1:1 ¶ The words of Nehemiah the son of Hachaliah. And it came to pass in the month *of* Chisleu, in the twentieth year, as I was in Shushan the palace,
2 That Hanani, one of my brethren, came, he and *certain* men of Judah; and I asked them concerning the Jews that had escaped, which were left of the captivity, and concerning Jerusalem.
3 And they said to me, The remnant that are left of the captivity there in the province *are* in great affliction and reproach: the wall of Jerusalem also *is* broken down, and the gates thereof are burned with fire.
4 And it came to pass, when I heard these words, that I sat down and wept, and mourned *certain* days, and fasted, and prayed before the God of heaven,
5 ¶ And said, I beseech you, O Yahweh God of heaven, the great and awesome God, that keeps covenant and mercy for them that love him and observe his commandments:
6 Let your ear now be attentive, and your eyes open, that you may hear the prayer of your servant, which I pray before you now, day and night, for the children of Israel your servants, and confess the sins of the children of Israel, which we have sinned against you: both I and my father's house have sinned.
7 We have dealt very corruptly against you, and have not kept the commandments, nor the statutes, nor the judgments, which you commanded your servant Moses.
8 Remember, I beseech you, the word that you commanded your servant Moses, saying, *If* you transgress, I will scatter you abroad among the nations:
9 But *if* you turn unto me, and keep my commandments, and do them; though there were of you cast out to the utmost part of the heaven, *yet* will I gather them from there, and will bring them to the place that I have chosen to set my name there.
10 Now these *are* your servants and your people, whom you have redeemed by your great power, and by your strong hand.
11 O Lord, I beseech you, let now your ear be attentive to the prayer of your servant, and to the prayer of your servants, who desire to fear your name: and prosper, I pray you, your servant this day, and grant him mercy in the sight of this man. For I was the king's cup bearer.

Nehemiah 2

2:1 ¶ And it came to pass in the month *of* Nisan, in the twentieth year of Artaxerxes the king, *that* wine *was* before him: and I took up the wine, and gave *it* to the king. Now I had not been *beforetime* sad in his presence.
2 Therefore the king said to me, Why *is* your countenance sad, seeing you *are* not sick? this *is* nothing *else* but sorrow of heart. Then I was very greatly afraid,
3 And said to the king, Let the king live forever: why should not my countenance be sad, when the city, the place of my fathers' sepulchers, *lays* waste, and the gates thereof are consumed with fire?
4 Then the king said to me, For what do you make request? So I prayed to the God of heaven.
5 And I said to the king, If it pleases the king, and if your servant has found favor in your sight, that you would send me to Judah, to the city of my fathers' sepulchers, that I may build it.
6 And the king said to me, (the queen also sitting by him,) For how long shall your journey be? and when will you return? So it pleased the king to send me; and I set him a time.
7 Moreover I said to the king, If it pleases the king, let letters be given me to the governors beyond the river, that they may convey me over till I come into Judah;
8 And a letter to Asaph the keeper of the king's forest, that he may give me timber to make beams for the gates of the palace which *pertained* to the house, and for the wall of the city, and for the house that I shall enter into. And the king granted *them to* me, according to the good hand of my God upon me.
9 ¶ Then I came to the governors beyond the river, and gave them the king's letters. Now the king had sent captains of the army and horsemen with me.
10 When Sanballat the Horonite, and Tobiah the servant, the Ammonite, heard *of it*, it grieved them exceedingly that there had come a man to seek the welfare of the children of Israel.
11 So I came to Jerusalem, and was there three days.
12 And I arose in the night, I and some few men with me; neither told I *any* man what my God had put in my heart to do at Jerusalem: neither *was there any* beast with me, save the beast that I rode upon.
13 And I went out by night by the gate of the valley, even before the dragon well, and to the dung port, and viewed the walls of Jerusalem, which were broken down, and the gates thereof were consumed with fire.
14 Then I went on to the gate of the fountain, and to the king's pool: but *there was* no place for the beast *that was* under me to pass.

15 Then went I up in the night by the brook, and viewed the wall, and turned back, and entered by the gate of the valley, and *so* returned.

16 And the rulers knew not where I went, or what I did; neither had I as yet told *it* to the Jews, nor to the priests, nor to the nobles, nor to the rulers, nor to the rest that did the work.

17 Then said I to them, You see the distress that we *are* in, how Jerusalem *lies* waste, and the gates thereof are burned with fire: come, and let us build up the wall of Jerusalem, that we be no more a reproach.

18 Then I told them of the hand of my God which was good upon me; as also the king's words that he had spoken to me. And they said, Let us rise up and build. So they strengthened their hands for *this* good *work*.

19 But when Sanballat the Horonite, and Tobiah the servant, the Ammonite, and Geshem the Arabian, heard *it*, they laughed us to scorn, and despised us, and said, What *is* this thing that you do? will you rebel against the king?

20 Then answered I them, and said to them, The God of heaven, he will prosper us; therefore we his servants will arise and build: but you have no portion, nor right, nor memorial, in Jerusalem.

Nehemiah 3

3:1 ¶ Then Eliashib the high priest rose up with his brethren the priests, and they built the sheep gate; they sanctified it, and set up the doors of it; even to the tower of Meah they sanctified it, to the tower of Hananeel.

2 And next to him built the men of Jericho. And next to them built Zaccur the son of Imri.

3 But the fish gate did the sons of Hassenaah build, who *also* laid the beams thereof, and set up the doors thereof, the locks thereof, and the bars thereof.

4 And next to them repaired Meremoth the son of Urijah, the son of Koz. And next to them repaired Meshullam the son of Berechiah, the son of Meshezabeel. And next to them repaired Zadok the son of Baana.

5 And next to them the Tekoites repaired; but their nobles put not their necks to the work of their Lord.

6 Moreover the old gate repaired Jehoiada the son of Paseah, and Meshullam the son of Besodeiah; they laid the beams thereof, and set up the doors thereof, and the locks thereof, and the bars thereof.

7 And next to them repaired Melatiah the Gibeonite, and Jadon the Meronothite, the men of Gibeon, and of Mizpah, unto the throne of the governor on this side *of* the river.

8 Next to him repaired Uzziel the son of Harhaiah, of the goldsmiths. Next to him also repaired Hananiah the son of *one of* the apothecaries, and they fortified Jerusalem unto the broad wall.

9 And next to them repaired Rephaiah the son of Hur, the ruler of the half part of Jerusalem.

10 And next to them repaired Jedaiah the son of Harumaph, even over against his house. And next to him repaired Hattush the son of Hashabniah.

11 Malchijah the son of Harim, and Hashub the son of Pahathmoab, repaired the other piece, and the tower of the furnaces.

12 And next to him repaired Shallum the son of Halohesh, the ruler of the half part of Jerusalem, he and his daughters.

13 The valley gate repaired Hanun, and the inhabitants of Zanoah; they built it, and set up the doors thereof, the locks thereof, and the bars thereof, and a thousand cubits on the wall unto the dung gate.

14 But the dung gate repaired Malchiah the son of Rechab, the ruler of part of Bethhaccerem; he built it, and set up the doors thereof, the locks thereof, and the bars thereof.

15 But the gate of the fountain repaired Shallun the son of Colhozeh, the ruler of part of Mizpah; he built it, and covered it, and set up the doors thereof, the locks thereof, and the bars thereof, and the wall of the pool of Siloah by the king's garden, and unto the stairs that go down from the city of David.

16 After him repaired Nehemiah the son of Azbuk, the ruler of the half part of Bethzur, to *the place* over against the sepulchers of David, and to the pool that was made, and to the house of the mighty.

17 After him repaired the Levites, Rehum the son of Bani. Next to him repaired Hashabiah, the ruler of the half part of Keilah, in his part.

18 After him repaired their brethren, Bavai the son of Henadad, the ruler of the half part of Keilah.

19 And next to him repaired Ezer the son of Jeshua, the ruler of Mizpah, another piece over against the going up to the armory at the turning *of the wall*.

20 After him Baruch the son of Zabbai earnestly repaired the other piece, from the turning *of the wall* to the door of the house of Eliashib the high priest.

21 After him repaired Meremoth the son of Urijah the son of Koz another piece, from the door of the house of Eliashib even to the end of the house of Eliashib.

22 And after him repaired the priests, the men of the plain.

23 After him repaired Benjamin and Hashub over against their house. After him repaired Azariah the son of Maaseiah the son of Ananiah by his house.

24 After him repaired Binnui the son of Henadad another piece, from the house of Azariah unto the turning *of the wall*, even to the corner.

25 Palal the son of Uzai, over against the turning *of the wall*, and the tower which lies out from the king's high house, that *was* by the court of the prison. After him Pedaiah the son of Parosh.

26 Moreover the Nethinims dwelt in Ophel, unto *the place* over against the water gate toward the east, and the tower that lies out.

27 After them the Tekoites repaired another piece, over against the great tower that lies out, even unto the wall of Ophel.

28 From above the horse gate repaired the priests, every one over against his house.

Nehemiah 3

29 After them repaired Zadok the son of Immer over against his house. After him repaired also Shemaiah the son of Shechaniah, the keeper of the east gate.

30 After him repaired Hananiah the son of Shelemiah, and Hanun the sixth son of Zalaph, another piece. After him repaired Meshullam the son of Berechiah over against his chamber.

31 After him repaired Malchiah the goldsmith's son unto the place of the Nethinims, and of the merchants, over against the gate Miphkad, and to the going up of the corner.

32 And between the going up of the corner unto the sheep gate repaired the goldsmiths and the merchants.

Nehemiah 4

4:1 ¶ But it came to pass, that when Sanballat heard that we built the wall, he was angry, and took great indignation, and mocked the Jews.

2 And he spoke before his brethren and the army of Samaria, and said, What do these feeble Jews? will they fortify themselves? will they sacrifice? will they make an end in a day? will they revive the stones out of the heaps of the rubbish which are burned?

3 Now Tobiah the Ammonite *was* by him, and he said, Even that which they build, if a fox goes up *it*, he shall even break down their stone wall.

4 Hear, O our God; for we are despised: and turn their reproach upon their own head, and give them for a prey in the land of captivity:

5 And cover not their iniquity, and let not their sin be blotted out from before you: for they have provoked *you* to anger before the builders.

6 So built we the wall; and all the wall was joined together unto the half thereof: for the people had a mind to work.

7 ¶ But it came to pass, *that* when Sanballat, and Tobiah, and the Arabians, and the Ammonites, and the Ashdodites, heard that the walls of Jerusalem were made up, *and* that the breaches began to be stopped, then they were very angry,

8 And conspired all of them together to come *and* to fight against Jerusalem, and to hinder it.

9 Nevertheless we made our prayer to our God, and set a watch against them day and night, because of them.

10 And Judah said, The strength of the bearers of burdens is decayed, and *there is* much rubbish; so that we are not able to build the wall.

11 And our adversaries said, They shall not know, neither see, till we come in the midst among them, and slay them, and cause the work to cease.

12 And it came to pass, that when the Jews which dwelt by them came, they said unto us ten times, From all places where you shall return unto us *they will be upon you.*

13 Therefore set I in the lower places behind the wall, *and* on the higher places, I even set the people after their families with their swords, their spears, and their bows.

14 And I looked, and rose up, and said to the nobles, and to the rulers, and to the rest of the people, Be not you afraid of them: remember the Lord, *which is* great and terrible, and fight for your brethren, your sons, and your daughters, your wives, and your houses.

15 And it came to pass, when our enemies heard that it was known to us, and God had brought their counsel to nothing, that we returned all of us to the wall, every one to his work.

16 ¶ And it came to pass from that time forth, *that* the half of my servants worked in the work, and the other half of them held both the spears, the shields, and the bows, and the body armor; and the rulers *were* behind all the house of Judah.

17 They which built on the wall, and they that bore burdens, with those that loaded, *every one* with one of his hands worked in the work, and with the other *hand* held a weapon.

18 For the builders, every one had his sword girded by his side, and *so* built. And he that sounded the trumpet *was* by me.

19 And I said to the nobles, and to the rulers, and to the rest of the people, The work *is* great and large, and we are separated upon the wall, one far from another.

20 In what place *therefore* you hear the sound of the trumpet, resort you there to us: our God shall fight for us.

21 So we labored in the work: and half of them held the spears from the rising of the morning till the stars appeared.

22 Likewise at the same time said I to the people, Let every one with his servant lodge within Jerusalem, that in the night they may be a guard to us, and labor on the day.

23 So neither I, nor my brethren, nor my servants, nor the men of the guard which followed me, none of us put off our clothes, *saving that* every one put them off for washing.

Nehemiah 5

5:1 ¶ And there was a great cry of the people and of their wives against their brethren the Jews.

2 For there were that said, We, our sons, and our daughters, *are* many: therefore we take up corn *for them*, that we may eat, and live.

3 *Some* also there were that said, We have mortgaged our lands, vineyards, and houses, that we might buy corn, because of the famine.

4 There were also that said, We have borrowed money for the king's tribute, *and that upon* our lands and vineyards.

5 Yet now our flesh *is* as the flesh of our brethren, our children as their children: and, lo, we bring into bondage our sons and our daughters to be servants, and *some* of our daughters are brought unto bondage *already*: neither *is it* in our power *to redeem them*; for other men have our lands and vineyards.

6 ¶ And I was very angry when I heard their cry and these words.

7 Then I consulted with myself, and I rebuked the nobles, and the rulers, and said to them, You exact usury, every one from his brother. And I set a great assembly against them.

8 And I said to them, We after our ability have redeemed our brethren the Jews, which were sold to the heathen; and will you even sell your brethren? or shall they be sold to us? Then held they their peace, and found nothing *to answer*.

9 Also I said, It *is* not good what you do: ought you not to walk in the fear of our God because of the reproach of the heathen our enemies?

10 I likewise, *and* my brethren, and my servants, might lend them money and corn: I pray you, let us leave off this usury.

11 Restore, I pray you, to them, even this day, their lands, their vineyards, their olive groves, and their houses, also the hundredth *part* of the money, and of the corn, the *new* wine, and the oil, that you exacted from them.

12 Then said they, We will restore *them*, and will require nothing from them; so will we do as you say. Then I called the priests, and took an oath from them, that they should do according to this promise.

13 Also I shook my lap, and said, So God shake out every man from his house, and from his labor, that performs not this promise, even thus be he shaken out, and emptied. And all the congregation said, Amen, and praised Yahweh. And the people did according to this promise.

14 ¶ Moreover from the time that I was appointed to be their governor in the land of Judah, from the twentieth year even to the two and thirtieth year of Artaxerxes the king, *that is*, twelve years, I and my brethren have not eaten the bread of the governor.

15 But the former governors that *had been* before me were chargeable to the people, and had taken from them bread and wine, besides forty shekels of silver; yes, even their servants bore rule over the people: but so did not I, because of the fear of God.

16 Yes, also I continued in the work of this wall, neither bought we any land: and all my servants *were* gathered there unto the work.

17 Moreover *there were* at my table a hundred and fifty of the Jews and rulers, besides those that came to us from among the heathen that *are* about us.

18 Now *that* which was prepared *for me* daily *was* one ox *and* six choice sheep; also fowls were prepared for me, and once in ten days an increase of all sorts of wine: yet for all this required not I the bread of the governor, because the bondage was heavy upon this people.

19 Think upon me, my God, for good, *according* to all that I have done for this people.

Nehemiah 6

6:1 ¶ Now it came to pass, when Sanballat, and Tobiah, and Geshem the Arabian, and the rest of our enemies, heard that I had built the wall, and *that* there was no breach left therein; (though at that time I had not set up the doors upon the gates;)

2 That Sanballat and Geshem sent to me, saying, Come, let us meet together in *some one of* the villages in the plain of Ono. But they thought to do me mischief.

3 And I sent messengers to them, saying, I *am* doing a great work, so that I cannot come down: why should the work cease, while I leave it, and come down to you?

4 Yet they sent to me four times after this sort; and I answered them after the same manner.

5 Then sent Sanballat his servant to me in like manner the fifth time with an open letter in his hand;

6 Wherein *was* written, It is reported among the heathen, and Gashmu said *it, that* you and the Jews think to rebel: for which cause you build the wall, that you may be their king, according to these words.

7 And you have also appointed prophets to preach of you at Jerusalem, saying, *There is* a king in Judah: and now shall it be reported to the king according to these words. Come now therefore, and let us take counsel together.

8 Then I sent to him, saying, There are no such things done as you say, but you devise them out of your own heart.

9 For they all made us afraid, saying, Their hands shall be weakened from the work, that it be not done. Now therefore, *O God*, strengthen my hands.

10 ¶ Afterward I came to the house of Shemaiah the son of Delaiah the son of Mehetabeel, who *was* shut up; and he said, Let us meet together in the house of God, within the temple, and let us shut the doors of the temple: for they will come to slay you; yes, in the night will they come to slay you.

11 And I said, Should such a man as I flee? and who *is there*, that, *being* as I *am*, would go into the temple to save his life? I will not go in.

12 And, lo, I perceived that God had not sent him; but that he pronounced this prophecy against me: for Tobiah and Sanballat had hired him.

13 Therefore *was* he hired, that I should be afraid, and do so, and sin, and *that* they might have *matter* for an evil report, that they might reproach me.

14 My God, think you upon Tobiah and Sanballat according to these their works, and on the prophetess Noadiah, and the rest of the prophets, that would have put me in fear.

15 ¶ So the wall was finished in the twenty and fifth *day* of *the month of* Elul, in fifty and two days.

16 And it came to pass, that when all our enemies heard *thereof*, and all the heathen that *were* about us saw *these things*, they were much cast down in their own eyes: for they perceived that this work was worked by our God.

17 Moreover in those days the nobles of Judah sent many letters to Tobiah, and *the letters* of Tobiah came to them.

Nehemiah 6

18 For *there were* many in Judah sworn to him, because he *was* the son-in-law of Shechaniah the son of Arah; and his son Johanan had taken the daughter of Meshullam the son of Berechiah.

19 Also they reported his good deeds before me, and uttered my words to him. *And* Tobiah sent letters to put me in fear.

Nehemiah 7

7:1 ¶ Now it came to pass, when the wall was built, and I had set up the doors, and the porters and the singers and the Levites were appointed,

2 That I gave my brother Hanani, and Hananiah the ruler of the palace, charge over Jerusalem: for he *was* a faithful man, and feared God above many.

3 And I said to them, Let not the gates of Jerusalem be opened until the sun is hot; and while they stand by, let them shut the doors, and bar *them*: and appoint watches of the inhabitants of Jerusalem, every one in his watch, and every one *to be* over against his house.

4 Now the city *was* large and great: but the people *were* few therein, and the houses *were* not built.

5 ¶ And my God put into my heart to gather together the nobles, and the rulers, and the people, that they might be reckoned by genealogy. And I found a register of the genealogy of them which came up at the first, and found written therein,

6 These *are* the children of the province, that went up out of the captivity, of those that had been carried away, whom Nebuchadnezzar the king of Babylon had carried away, and came again to Jerusalem and to Judah, every one to his city;

7 Who came with Zerubbabel, Jeshua, Nehemiah, Azariah, Raamiah, Nahamani, Mordecai, Bilshan, Mispereth, Bigvai, Nehum, Baanah. The number, *I say*, of the men of the people of Israel *was this*;

8 The children of Parosh, two thousand a hundred seventy and two.

9 The children of Shephatiah, three hundred seventy and two.

10 The children of Arah, six hundred fifty and two.

11 The children of Pahathmoab, of the children of Jeshua and Joab, two thousand and eight hundred *and* eighteen.

12 The children of Elam, a thousand two hundred fifty and four.

13 The children of Zattu, eight hundred forty and five.

14 The children of Zaccai, seven hundred and threescore.

15 The children of Binnui, six hundred forty and eight.

16 The children of Bebai, six hundred twenty and eight.

17 The children of Azgad, two thousand three hundred twenty and two.

18 The children of Adonikam, six hundred threescore and seven.

19 The children of Bigvai, two thousand threescore and seven.

20 The children of Adin, six hundred fifty and five.

21 The children of Ater of Hezekiah, ninety and eight.

22 The children of Hashum, three hundred twenty and eight.

23 The children of Bezai, three hundred twenty and four.

24 The children of Hariph, a hundred and twelve.

25 The children of Gibeon, ninety and five.

26 The men of Bethlehem and Netophah, a hundred fourscore and eight.

27 The men of Anathoth, a hundred twenty and eight.

28 The men of Bethazmaveth, forty and two.

29 The men of Kirjathjearim, Chephirah, and Beeroth, seven hundred forty and three.

30 The men of Ramah and Geba, six hundred twenty and one.

31 The men of Michmas, a hundred and twenty and two.

32 The men of Bethel and Ai, a hundred twenty and three.

33 The men of the other Nebo, fifty and two.

34 The children of the other Elam, a thousand two hundred fifty and four.

35 The children of Harim, three hundred and twenty.

36 The children of Jericho, three hundred forty and five.

37 The children of Lod, Hadid, and Ono, seven hundred twenty and one.

38 The children of Senaah, three thousand nine hundred and thirty.

39 The priests: the children of Jedaiah, of the house of Jeshua, nine hundred seventy and three.

40 The children of Immer, a thousand fifty and two.

41 The children of Pashur, a thousand two hundred forty and seven.

42 The children of Harim, a thousand and seventeen.

43 The Levites: the children of Jeshua, of Kadmiel, *and* of the children of Hodevah, seventy and four.

44 The singers: the children of Asaph, a hundred forty and eight.

45 The porters: the children of Shallum, the children of Ater, the children of Talmon, the children of Akkub, the children of Hatita, the children of Shobai, a hundred thirty and eight.

46 The Nethinims: the children of Ziha, the children of Hashupha, the children of Tabbaoth,

47 The children of Keros, the children of Sia, the children of Padon,

48 The children of Lebana, the children of Hagaba, the children of Shalmai,

49 The children of Hanan, the children of Giddel, the children of Gahar,

50 The children of Reaiah, the children of Rezin, the children of Nekoda,

51 The children of Gazzam, the children of Uzza, the children of Phaseah,

52 The children of Besai, the children of Meunim, the children of Nephishesim,

53 The children of Bakbuk, the children of Hakupha, the children of Harhur,
54 The children of Bazlith, the children of Mehida, the children of Harsha,
55 The children of Barkos, the children of Sisera, the children of Tamah,
56 The children of Neziah, the children of Hatipha.
57 The children of Solomon's servants: the children of Sotai, the children of Sophereth, the children of Perida,
58 The children of Jaala, the children of Darkon, the children of Giddel,
59 The children of Shephatiah, the children of Hattil, the children of Pochereth of Zebaim, the children of Amon.
60 All the Nethinims, and the children of Solomon's servants, *were* three hundred ninety and two.
61 And these *were* they which went up *also* from Telmelah, Telharesha, Cherub, Addon, and Immer: but they could not show their father's house, nor their seed, whether they *were* of Israel.
62 The children of Delaiah, the children of Tobiah, the children of Nekoda, six hundred forty and two.
63 And of the priests: the children of Habaiah, the children of Koz, the children of Barzillai, which took *one* of the daughters of Barzillai the Gileadite to wife, and was called after their name.
64 These sought their register *among* those that were reckoned by genealogy, but it was not found: therefore were they, as polluted, put from the priesthood.
65 And the Tirshatha said to them, that they should not eat of the most holy things, till there stood *up* a priest with Urim and Thummim.
66 The whole congregation together *was* forty and two thousand three hundred and threescore,
67 Besides their manservants and their maidservants, of whom *there were* seven thousand three hundred thirty and seven: and they had two hundred forty and five singing men and singing women.
68 Their horses, seven hundred thirty and six: their mules, two hundred forty and five:
69 *Their* camels, four hundred thirty and five: six thousand seven hundred and twenty donkeys.
70 And some of the chief of the fathers gave to the work. The Tirshatha gave to the treasury a thousand drams of gold, fifty basins, five hundred and thirty priests' garments.
71 And *some* of the chief of the fathers gave to the treasury of the work twenty thousand drams of gold, and two thousand and two hundred pounds of silver.
72 And *that* which the rest of the people gave *was* twenty thousand drams of gold, and two thousand pounds of silver, and threescore and seven priests' garments.
73 So the priests, and the Levites, and the porters, and the singers, and *some* of the people, and the Nethinims, and all Israel, dwelt in their cities; and when the seventh month came, the children of Israel *were* in their cities.

Nehemiah 8

8:1 ¶ And all the people gathered themselves together as one man into the street that *was* before the water gate; and they spoke to Ezra the scribe to bring the book of the law of Moses, which Yahweh had commanded to Israel.
2 And Ezra the priest brought the law before the congregation both of men and women, and all that could hear with understanding, on the first day of the seventh month.
3 And he read therein before the street that *was* before the water gate from the morning until midday, before the men and the women, and those that could understand; and the ears of all the people *were attentive* unto the book of the law.
4 And Ezra the scribe stood upon a pulpit of wood, which they had made for the purpose; and beside him stood Mattithiah, and Shema, and Anaiah, and Urijah, and Hilkiah, and Maaseiah, on his right hand; and on his left hand, Pedaiah, and Mishael, and Malchiah, and Hashum, and Hashbadana, Zechariah, *and* Meshullam.
5 And Ezra opened the book in the sight of all the people; (for he was above all the people;) and when he opened it, all the people stood up:
6 And Ezra blessed Yahweh, the great God. And all the people answered, Amen, Amen, with lifting up their hands: and they bowed their heads, and worshipped Yahweh with *their* faces to the ground.
7 Also Jeshua, and Bani, and Sherebiah, Jamin, Akkub, Shabbethai, Hodijah, Maaseiah, Kelita, Azariah, Jozabad, Hanan, Pelaiah, and the Levites, caused the people to understand the law: and the people *stood* in their place.
8 So they read in the book in the law of God distinctly, and gave the sense, and caused *them* to understand the reading.
9 ¶ And Nehemiah, which *is* the Tirshatha, and Ezra the priest the scribe, and the Levites that taught the people, said to all the people, This day *is* holy unto Yahweh your God; mourn not, nor weep. For all the people wept, when they heard the words of the law.
10 Then he said unto them, Go your way, eat the fat, and drink the sweet, and send portions to them for whom nothing is prepared: for *this* day *is* holy unto our Lord: neither be you sorry; for the joy of Yahweh is your strength.
11 So the Levites stilled all the people, saying, Hold your peace, for the day *is* holy; neither be you grieved.
12 And all the people went their way to eat, and to drink, and to send portions, and to make great gladness, because they had understood the words that were declared to them.
13 ¶ And on the second day were gathered together the chief of the fathers of all the people, the priests, and the Levites, unto Ezra the scribe, even to understand the words of the law.
14 And they found written in the law which Yahweh had commanded by Moses, that the children of Israel should dwell in booths in the feast of the seventh month:

Nehemiah 8

15 And that they should publish and proclaim in all their cities, and in Jerusalem, saying, Go forth unto the mount, and fetch olive branches, and pine branches, and myrtle branches, and palm branches, and branches of thick trees, to make booths, as *it is* written.

16 So the people went forth, and brought *them*, and made themselves booths, every one upon the roof of his house, and in their courts, and in the courts of the house of God, and in the street of the water gate, and in the street of the gate of Ephraim.

17 And all the congregation of them that had come again out of the captivity made booths, and sat under the booths: for since the days of Jeshua the son of Nun to that day had not the children of Israel done so. And there was very great gladness.

18 Also day by day, from the first day to the last day, he read in the book of the law of God. And they kept the feast seven days; and on the eighth day *was* a solemn assembly, according to the manner.

Nehemiah 9

9:1 ¶ Now in the twenty and fourth day of this month the children of Israel were assembled with fasting, and with sackcloth, and earth upon them.

2 And the seed of Israel separated themselves from all strangers, and stood and confessed their sins, and the iniquities of their fathers.

3 And they stood up in their place, and read in the book of the law of Yahweh their God *one* fourth part of the day; and *another* fourth part they confessed, and worshipped Yahweh their God.

4 ¶ Then stood up upon the stairs, of the Levites, Jeshua, and Bani, Kadmiel, Shebaniah, Bunni, Sherebiah, Bani, *and* Chenani, and cried with a loud voice unto Yahweh their God.

5 Then the Levites, Jeshua, and Kadmiel, Bani, Hashabniah, Sherebiah, Hodijah, Shebaniah, *and* Pethahiah, said, Stand up *and* bless Yahweh your God forever and ever: and blessed be your glorious name, which is exalted above all blessing and praise.

6 You, *even* you, *are* Yahweh alone; you have made heaven, the heaven of heavens, with all their host, the earth, and all *things* that *are* therein, the seas, and all that *is* therein, and you preserve them all; and the host of heaven worships you.

7 You *are* Yahweh the God, who did choose Abram, and brought him forth out of Ur of the Chaldees, and gave him the name of Abraham;

8 And found his heart faithful before you, and made a covenant with him to give the land of the Canaanites, the Hittites, the Amorites, and the Perizzites, and the Jebusites, and the Girgashites, to give *it, I say*, to his seed, and have performed your words; for you *are* righteous:

9 And did see the affliction of our fathers in Egypt, and heard their cry by the Red Sea;

10 And showed signs and wonders upon Pharaoh, and upon all his servants, and on all the people of his land: for you knew that they dealt proudly against them. So did you get you a name, as *it is* this day.

11 And you did divide the sea before them, so that they went through the midst of the sea on the dry land; and their persecutors you threw into the deeps, as a stone into the mighty waters.

12 Moreover you led them in the day by a cloudy pillar; and in the night by a pillar of fire, to give them light in the way wherein they should go.

13 You came down also upon mount Sinai, and spoke with them from heaven, and gave them right judgments, and true laws, good statutes and commandments:

14 And made known to them your holy sabbath, and commanded them precepts, statutes, and laws, by the hand of Moses your servant:

15 And gave them bread from heaven for their hunger, and brought forth water for them out of the rock for their thirst, and promised them that they should go in to possess the land which you had sworn to give them.

16 But they and our fathers dealt proudly, and hardened their necks, and listened not to your commandments,

17 And refused to obey, neither were mindful of your wonders that you did among them; but hardened their necks, and in their rebellion appointed a captain to return to their bondage: but you *are* a God ready to pardon, gracious and merciful, slow to anger, and of great kindness, and forsook them not.

18 Yes, when they had made them a molten calf, and said, This *is* your God that brought you up out of Egypt, and had worked great provocations;

19 Yet you in your manifold mercies forsook them not in the wilderness: the pillar of the cloud departed not from them by day, to lead them in the way; neither the pillar of fire by night, to show them light, and the way wherein they should go.

20 You gave also your good spirit to instruct them, and withheld not your manna from their mouth, and gave them water for their thirst.

21 Yes, forty years did you sustain them in the wilderness, *so that* they lacked nothing; their clothes became not old, and their feet swelled not.

22 Moreover you gave them kingdoms and nations, and did divide them into corners: so they possessed the land of Sihon, and the land of the king of Heshbon, and the land of Og king of Bashan.

23 Their children also multiplied you as the stars of heaven, and brought them into the land, concerning which you had promised to their fathers, that they should go in to possess *it*.

24 So the children went in and possessed the land, and you subdued before them the inhabitants of the land, the Canaanites, and gave them into their hands, with their kings, and the people of the land, that they might do with them as they would.

25 And they took strong cities, and a fat land, and possessed houses full of all goods, wells dug, vineyards,

and olive groves, and fruit trees in abundance: so they did eat, and were filled, and became fat, and delighted themselves in your great goodness.

26 Nevertheless they were disobedient, and rebelled against you, and cast your law behind their backs, and slew your prophets which testified against them to turn them to you, and they worked great provocations.

27 Therefore you delivered them into the hand of their enemies, who afflicted them: and in the time of their trouble, when they cried unto you, you heard *them* from heaven; and according to your manifold mercies you gave them saviors, who saved them out of the hand of their enemies.

28 But after they had rest, they did evil again before you: therefore left you them in the hand of their enemies, so that they had the dominion over them: yet when they returned, and cried unto you, you heard *them* from heaven; and many times did you deliver them according to your mercies;

29 And testified against them, that you might bring them again to your law: yet they dealt proudly, and listened not to your commandments, but sinned against your judgments, (which if a man does, he shall live in them;) and withdrew the shoulder, and hardened their neck, and would not hear.

30 Yet many years did you forbear them, and testified against them by your spirit in your prophets: yet would they not give ear: therefore gave you them into the hand of the people of the lands.

31 Nevertheless for your great mercies' sake you did not utterly consume them, nor forsake them; for you *are* a gracious and merciful God.

32 Now therefore, our God, the great, the mighty, and the awesome God, who keeps covenant and mercy, let not all the trouble seem little before you, that has come upon us, on our kings, on our princes, and on our priests, and on our prophets, and on our fathers, and on all your people, since the time of the kings of Assyria unto this day.

33 However you *are* just in all that is brought upon us; for you have done right, but we have done wickedly:

34 Neither have our kings, our princes, our priests, nor our fathers, kept your law, nor listened to your commandments and your testimonies, with which you did testify against them.

35 For they have not served you in their kingdom, and in your great goodness that you gave them, and in the large and fat land which you gave before them, neither turned they from their wicked works.

36 Behold, we *are* servants this day, and *for* the land that you gave to our fathers to eat the fruit thereof and the good thereof, behold, we *are* servants in it:

37 And it yields much increase to the kings whom you have set over us because of our sins: also they have dominion over our bodies, and over our cattle, at their pleasure, and we *are* in great distress.

38 And because of all this we make a sure *covenant*, and write *it*; and our princes, Levites, *and* priests, seal *unto it*.

Nehemiah 10

10:1 ¶ Now those that sealed *were*, Nehemiah, the Tirshatha, the son of Hachaliah, and Zidkijah,

2 Seraiah, Azariah, Jeremiah,

3 Pashur, Amariah, Malchijah,

4 Hattush, Shebaniah, Malluch,

5 Harim, Meremoth, Obadiah,

6 Daniel, Ginnethon, Baruch,

7 Meshullam, Abijah, Mijamin,

8 Maaziah, Bilgai, Shemaiah: these *were* the priests.

9 And the Levites: both Jeshua the son of Azaniah, Binnui of the sons of Henadad, Kadmiel;

10 And their brethren, Shebaniah, Hodijah, Kelita, Pelaiah, Hanan,

11 Micha, Rehob, Hashabiah,

12 Zaccur, Sherebiah, Shebaniah,

13 Hodijah, Bani, Beninu.

14 The chief of the people; Parosh, Pahathmoab, Elam, Zatthu, Bani,

15 Bunni, Azgad, Bebai,

16 Adonijah, Bigvai, Adin,

17 Ater, Hizkijah, Azzur,

18 Hodijah, Hashum, Bezai,

19 Hariph, Anathoth, Nebai,

20 Magpiash, Meshullam, Hezir,

21 Meshezabeel, Zadok, Jaddua,

22 Pelatiah, Hanan, Anaiah,

23 Hoshea, Hananiah, Hashub,

24 Hallohesh, Pileha, Shobek,

25 Rehum, Hashabnah, Maaseiah,

26 And Ahijah, Hanan, Anan,

27 Malluch, Harim, Baanah.

28 And the rest of the people, the priests, the Levites, the porters, the singers, the Nethinims, and all they that had separated themselves from the people of the lands unto the law of God, their wives, their sons, and their daughters, every one having knowledge, and having understanding;

29 They clung to their brethren, their nobles, and entered into a curse, and into an oath, to walk in God's law, which was given by Moses the servant of God, and to observe and do all the commandments of Yahweh our Lord, and his judgments and his statutes;

30 And that we would not give our daughters to the people of the land, nor take their daughters for our sons:

31 And *if* the people of the land bring wares or any corn on the sabbath day to sell, *that* we would not buy it of them on the sabbath, or on the holy day: and *that* we would leave the seventh year, and the exaction of every debt.

32 ¶ Also we made ordinances for us, to charge ourselves yearly with the third part of a shekel for the service of the house of our God;

33 For the showbread, and for the continual meat offering, and for the continual burnt offering, of the sabbaths, of the new moons, for the set feasts, and for the holy *things*, and for the sin offerings to make an atonement for Israel, and *for* all the work of the house of our God.

Nehemiah 10

34 And we cast the lots among the priests, the Levites, and the people, for the wood offering, to bring *it* into the house of our God, after the houses of our fathers, at times appointed year by year, to burn upon the altar of Yahweh our God, as *it is* written in the law:

35 And to bring the firstfruits of our ground, and the firstfruits of all fruit of all trees, year by year, to the house of Yahweh:

36 Also the firstborn of our sons, and of our cattle, as *it is* written in the law, and the firstborn of our herds and of our flocks, to bring to the house of our God, to the priests that minister in the house of our God:

37 And *that* we should bring the firstfruits of our dough, and our offerings, and the fruit of all manner of trees, of *new* wine and of oil, to the priests, to the chambers of the house of our God; and the tithes of our ground to the Levites, that the same Levites might have the tithes in all the cities of our tillage.

38 And the priest the son of Aaron shall be with the Levites, when the Levites take tithes: and the Levites shall bring up the tithe of the tithes to the house of our God, to the chambers, into the treasure house.

39 For the children of Israel and the children of Levi shall bring the offering of the corn, of the new wine, and the oil, to the chambers, where *are* the vessels of the sanctuary, and the priests that minister, and the porters, and the singers: and we will not forsake the house of our God.

Nehemiah 11

11:1 ¶ And the rulers of the people dwelt at Jerusalem: the rest of the people also cast lots, to bring one of ten to dwell in Jerusalem the holy city, and nine parts *to dwell* in *other* cities.

2 And the people blessed all the men, that willingly offered themselves to dwell at Jerusalem.

3 Now these *are* the chief of the province that dwelt in Jerusalem: but in the cities of Judah dwelt every one in his possession in their cities, *that is*, Israel, the priests, and the Levites, and the Nethinims, and the children of Solomon's servants.

4 And at Jerusalem dwelt *certain* of the children of Judah, and of the children of Benjamin. Of the children of Judah; Athaiah the son of Uzziah, the son of Zechariah, the son of Amariah, the son of Shephatiah, the son of Mahalaleel, of the children of Perez;

5 And Maaseiah the son of Baruch, the son of Colhozeh, the son of Hazaiah, the son of Adaiah, the son of Joiarib, the son of Zechariah, the son of Shiloni.

6 All the sons of Perez that dwelt at Jerusalem *were* four hundred threescore and eight valiant men.

7 And these *are* the sons of Benjamin; Sallu the son of Meshullam, the son of Joed, the son of Pedaiah, the son of Kolaiah, the son of Maaseiah, the son of Ithiel, the son of Jesaiah.

8 And after him Gabbai, Sallai, nine hundred twenty and eight.

9 And Joel the son of Zichri *was* their overseer: and Judah the son of Senuah *was* second over the city.

10 Of the priests: Jedaiah the son of Joiarib, Jachin.

11 Seraiah the son of Hilkiah, the son of Meshullam, the son of Zadok, the son of Meraioth, the son of Ahitub, *was* the ruler of the house of God.

12 And their brethren that did the work of the house *were* eight hundred twenty and two: and Adaiah the son of Jeroham, the son of Pelaliah, the son of Amzi, the son of Zechariah, the son of Pashur, the son of Malchiah,

13 And his brethren, chief of the fathers, two hundred forty and two: and Amashai the son of Azareel, the son of Ahasai, the son of Meshillemoth, the son of Immer,

14 And their brethren, mighty men of valor, a hundred twenty and eight: and their overseer *was* Zabdiel, the son of *one of* the great men.

15 Also of the Levites: Shemaiah the son of Hashub, the son of Azrikam, the son of Hashabiah, the son of Bunni;

16 And Shabbethai and Jozabad, of the chief of the Levites, had the oversight of the outward business of the house of God.

17 And Mattaniah the son of Micha, the son of Zabdi, the son of Asaph, *was* the principal to begin the thanksgiving in prayer: and Bakbukiah the second among his brethren, and Abda the son of Shammua, the son of Galal, the son of Jeduthun.

18 All the Levites in the holy city *were* two hundred fourscore and four.

19 Moreover the porters, Akkub, Talmon, and their brethren that kept the gates, *were* a hundred seventy and two.

20 ¶ And the residue of Israel, of the priests, *and* the Levites, *were* in all the cities of Judah, every one in his inheritance.

21 But the Nethinims dwelt in Ophel: and Ziha and Gispa *were* over the Nethinims.

22 The overseer also of the Levites at Jerusalem *was* Uzzi the son of Bani, the son of Hashabiah, the son of Mattaniah, the son of Micha. Of the sons of Asaph, the singers *were* over the business of the house of God.

23 For *it was* the king's commandment concerning them, that a certain portion should be for the singers, due for every day.

24 And Pethahiah the son of Meshezabeel, of the children of Zerah the son of Judah, *was* at the king's hand in all matters concerning the people.

25 And for the villages, with their fields, *some* of the children of Judah dwelt at Kirjatharba, and *in* the villages thereof, and at Dibon, and *in* the villages thereof, and at Jekabzeel, and *in* the villages thereof,

26 And at Jeshua, and at Moladah, and at Bethphelet,

27 And at Hazarshual, and at Beersheba, and *in* the villages thereof,

28 And at Ziklag, and at Mekonah, and in the villages thereof,

29 And at Enrimmon, and at Zareah, and at Jarmuth,

30 Zanoah, Adullam, and *in* their villages, at Lachish, and the fields thereof, at Azekah, and *in* the villages thereof. And they dwelt from Beersheba to the valley of Hinnom.

31 The children also of Benjamin from Geba dwelt at Michmash, and Aija, and Bethel, and *in* their villages,
32 *And* at Anathoth, Nob, Ananiah,
33 Hazor, Ramah, Gittaim,
34 Hadid, Zeboim, Neballat,
35 Lod, and Ono, the valley of craftsmen.
36 And of the Levites *were* divisions *in* Judah, *and* in Benjamin.

Nehemiah 12

12:1 ¶ Now these *are* the priests and the Levites that went up with Zerubbabel the son of Shealtiel, and Jeshua: Seraiah, Jeremiah, Ezra,
2 Amariah, Malluch, Hattush,
3 Shechaniah, Rehum, Meremoth,
4 Iddo, Ginnetho, Abijah,
5 Miamin, Maadiah, Bilgah,
6 Shemaiah, and Joiarib, Jedaiah,
7 Sallu, Amok, Hilkiah, Jedaiah. These *were* the chief of the priests and of their brethren in the days of Jeshua.
8 Moreover the Levites: Jeshua, Binnui, Kadmiel, Sherebiah, Judah, *and* Mattaniah, *which were* over the thanksgiving, he and his brethren.
9 Also Bakbukiah and Unni, their brethren, *were* over against them in the watches.
10 And Jeshua begot Joiakim, Joiakim also begot Eliashib, and Eliashib begot Joiada,
11 And Joiada begot Jonathan, and Jonathan begot Jaddua.
12 And in the days of Joiakim were priests, the chief of the fathers: of Seraiah, Meraiah; of Jeremiah, Hananiah;
13 Of Ezra, Meshullam; of Amariah, Jehohanan;
14 Of Melicu, Jonathan; of Shebaniah, Joseph;
15 Of Harim, Adna; of Meraioth, Helkai;
16 Of Iddo, Zechariah; of Ginnethon, Meshullam;
17 Of Abijah, Zichri; of Miniamin, of Moadiah, Piltai;
18 Of Bilgah, Shammua; of Shemaiah, Jehonathan;
19 And of Joiarib, Mattenai; of Jedaiah, Uzzi;
20 Of Sallai, Kallai; of Amok, Eber;
21 Of Hilkiah, Hashabiah; of Jedaiah, Nethaneel.
22 The Levites in the days of Eliashib, Joiada, and Johanan, and Jaddua, *were* recorded *as* chief of the fathers: also the priests, to the reign of Darius the Persian.
23 The sons of Levi, the chief of the fathers, *were* written in the book of the chronicles, even until the days of Johanan the son of Eliashib.
24 And the chief of the Levites: Hashabiah, Sherebiah, and Jeshua the son of Kadmiel, with their brethren over beside them, to praise *and* to give thanks, according to the commandment of David the man of God, ward over beside ward.
25 Mattaniah, and Bakbukiah, Obadiah, Meshullam, Talmon, Akkub, *were* porters keeping the ward at the thresholds of the gates.
26 These *were* in the days of Joiakim the son of Jeshua, the son of Jozadak, and in the days of Nehemiah the governor, and of Ezra the priest, the scribe.

27 ¶ And at the dedication of the wall of Jerusalem they sought the Levites out of all their places, to bring them to Jerusalem, to keep the dedication with gladness, both with thanksgivings, and with singing, *with* cymbals, psalteries, and with harps.
28 And the sons of the singers gathered themselves together, both out of the plain country round about Jerusalem, and from the villages of Netophathi;
29 Also from the house of Gilgal, and out of the fields of Geba and Azmaveth: for the singers had built them villages round about Jerusalem.
30 And the priests and the Levites purified themselves, and purified the people, and the gates, and the wall.
31 Then I brought up the princes of Judah upon the wall, and appointed two great *companies of them that gave* thanks, *whereof one* went on the right hand upon the wall toward the dung gate:
32 And after them went Hoshaiah, and half of the princes of Judah,
33 And Azariah, Ezra, and Meshullam,
34 Judah, and Benjamin, and Shemaiah, and Jeremiah,
35 And *certain* of the priests' sons with trumpets; *namely*, Zechariah the son of Jonathan, the son of Shemaiah, the son of Mattaniah, the son of Michaiah, the son of Zaccur, the son of Asaph:
36 And his brethren, Shemaiah, and Azarael, Milalai, Gilalai, Maai, Nethaneel, and Judah, Hanani, with the musical instruments of David the man of God, and Ezra the scribe before them.
37 And at the fountain gate, which was over against them, they went up by the stairs of the city of David, at the going up of the wall, above the house of David, even to the water gate eastward.
38 And the other *company of them that gave* thanks went over against *them*, and I after them, and the half of the people upon the wall, from beyond the tower of the furnaces even to the broad wall;
39 And from above the gate of Ephraim, and above the old gate, and above the fish gate, and the tower of Hananeel, and the tower of Meah, even to the sheep gate: and they stood still in the prison gate.
40 So stood the two *companies of them that gave* thanks in the house of God, and I, and the half of the rulers with me:
41 And the priests; Eliakim, Maaseiah, Miniamin, Michaiah, Elioenai, Zechariah, *and* Hananiah, with trumpets;
42 And Maaseiah, and Shemaiah, and Eleazar, and Uzzi, and Jehohanan, and Malchijah, and Elam, and Ezer. And the singers sang loudly, with Jezrahiah *their* overseer.
43 Also that day they offered great sacrifices, and rejoiced: for God had made them rejoice with great joy: the wives also and the children rejoiced: so that the joy of Jerusalem was heard even afar off.
44 ¶ And at that time were some appointed over the chambers for the treasures, for the offerings, for the firstfruits, and for the tithes, to gather into them out of the fields of the cities the portions of the law for the priests and Levites: for Judah rejoiced for the priests and for the Levites that waited.

Nehemiah 12

45 And both the singers and the porters kept the ward of their God, and the ward of the purification, according to the commandment of David, *and* of Solomon his son.
46 For in the days of David and Asaph of old *there were* chief of the singers, and songs of praise and thanksgiving to God.
47 And all Israel in the days of Zerubbabel, and in the days of Nehemiah, gave the portions of the singers and the porters, every day his portion: and they sanctified *holy things* unto the Levites; and the Levites sanctified *them* unto the children of Aaron.

Nehemiah 13

13:1 ¶ On that day they read in the book of Moses in the audience of the people; and therein was found written, that the Ammonite and the Moabite should not come into the congregation of God forever;
2 Because they met not the children of Israel with bread and with water, but hired Balaam against them, that he should curse them: however our God turned the curse into a blessing.
3 Now it came to pass, when they had heard the law, that they separated from Israel all the mixed multitude.
4 And before this, Eliashib the priest, having the oversight of the chamber of the house of our God, *was* allied unto Tobiah:
5 And he had prepared for him a great chamber, where beforetime they laid the meat offerings, the frankincense, and the vessels, and the tithes of the corn, the new wine, and the oil, which was commanded *to be given* to the Levites, and the singers, and the porters; and the offerings of the priests.
6 But in all this *time* was not I at Jerusalem: for in the two and thirtieth year of Artaxerxes king of Babylon came I to the king, and after certain days obtained I leave from the king:
7 And I came to Jerusalem, and understood of the evil that Eliashib did for Tobiah, in preparing him a chamber in the courts of the house of God.
8 And it grieved me greatly: therefore I cast forth all the household stuff of Tobiah out of the chamber.
9 Then I commanded, and they cleansed the chambers: and there brought I again the vessels of the house of God, with the meat offering and the frankincense.
10 ¶ And I perceived that the portions of the Levites had not been given *them*: for the Levites and the singers, that did the work, had fled every one to his field.
11 Then contended I with the rulers, and said, Why is the house of God forsaken? And I gathered them together, and set them in their place.
12 Then brought all Judah the tithe of the corn and the new wine and the oil to the treasuries.
13 And I made treasurers over the treasuries, Shelemiah the priest, and Zadok the scribe, and of the Levites, Pedaiah: and next to them *was* Hanan the son of Zaccur, the son of Mattaniah: for they were counted faithful, and their office *was* to distribute to their brethren.
14 Remember me, O my God, concerning this, and wipe not out my good deeds that I have done for the house of my God, and for the offices thereof.
15 ¶ In those days saw I in Judah *some* treading winepresses on the sabbath, and bringing in sheaves, and loading donkeys; as also wine, grapes, and figs, and all *manner of* burdens, which they brought into Jerusalem on the sabbath day: and I testified *against them* in the day wherein they sold victuals.
16 There dwelt men of Tyre also therein, which brought fish, and all manner of ware, and sold on the sabbath to the children of Judah, and in Jerusalem.
17 Then I contended with the nobles of Judah, and said to them, What evil thing *is* this that you do, and profane the sabbath day?
18 Did not your fathers thus, and did not our God bring all this evil upon us, and upon this city? yet you bring more wrath upon Israel by profaning the sabbath.
19 And it came to pass, that when the gates of Jerusalem began to be dark before the sabbath, I commanded that the gates should be shut, and charged that they should not be opened till after the sabbath: and *some* of my servants set I at the gates, *that* there should no burden be brought in on the sabbath day.
20 So the merchants and sellers of all kinds of ware lodged outside Jerusalem once or twice.
21 Then I testified against them, and said to them, Why lodge you about the wall? if you do *so* again, I will lay hands on you. From that time forth came they no *more* on the sabbath.
22 And I commanded the Levites that they should cleanse themselves, and *that* they should come *and* keep the gates, to sanctify the sabbath day. Remember me, O my God, *concerning* this also, and spare me according to the greatness of your mercy.
23 ¶ In those days also saw I Jews *that* had married wives of Ashdod, of Ammon, *and* of Moab:
24 And their children spoke half in the speech of Ashdod, and could not speak in the Jews' language, but according to the language of each people.
25 And I contended with them, and cursed them, and smote certain of them, and plucked off their hair, and made them swear by God, *saying*, You shall not give your daughters to their sons, nor take their daughters to your sons, or for yourselves.
26 Did not Solomon king of Israel sin by these things? yet among many nations was there no king like him, who was beloved of his God, and God made him king over all Israel: nevertheless even him did outlandish women cause to sin.
27 Shall we then listen to you to do all this great evil, to transgress against our God in marrying strange wives?
28 And *one* of the sons of Joiada, the son of Eliashib the high priest, *was* son-in-law to Sanballat the Horonite: therefore I chased him from me.
29 Remember them, O my God, because they have defiled the priesthood, and the covenant of the priesthood, and of the Levites.

30 Thus cleansed I them from all strangers, and appointed the wards of the priests and the Levites, every one in his business;
31 And for the wood offering, at times appointed, and for the firstfruits. Remember me, O my God, for good.

Esther

Esther 1

1:1 ¶ Now it came to pass in the days of Ahasuerus, (this is Ahasuerus which reigned, from India even to Ethiopia, over a hundred and seven and twenty provinces:)
2 That in those days, when the king Ahasuerus sat on the throne of his kingdom, which was in Shushan the palace,
3 In the third year of his reign, he made a feast unto all his princes and his servants; the power of Persia and Media, the nobles and princes of the provinces, being before him:
4 When he showed the riches of his glorious kingdom and the honor of his excellent majesty many days, even a hundred and fourscore days.
5 And when these days were expired, the king made a feast to all the people that were present in Shushan the palace, both to great and small, seven days, in the court of the garden of the king's palace;
6 Where were white, green, and blue, hangings, fastened with cords of fine linen and purple to silver rings and pillars of marble: the beds were of gold and silver, upon a pavement of red, and blue, and white, and black, marble.
7 And they gave them drink in vessels of gold, (the vessels being diverse one from another,) and royal wine in abundance, according to the state of the king.
8 And the drinking was according to the law; none did compel: for so the king had appointed to all the officers of his house, that they should do according to every man's pleasure.
9 Also Vashti the queen made a feast for the women in the royal house which belonged to king Ahasuerus.
10 ¶ On the seventh day, when the heart of the king was merry with wine, he commanded Mehuman, Biztha, Harbona, Bigtha, and Abagtha, Zethar, and Carcas, the seven chamberlains that served in the presence of Ahasuerus the king,
11 To bring Vashti the queen before the king with the crown royal, to show the people and the princes her beauty: for she was fair to look on.
12 But the queen Vashti refused to come at the king's command by his chamberlains: therefore was the king very angry, and his anger burned in him.
13 Then the king said to the wise men, which knew the times, (for so was the king's manner toward all that knew law and judgment:
14 And the next to him was Carshena, Shethar, Admatha, Tarshish, Meres, Marsena, and Memucan, the seven princes of Persia and Media, which saw the king's face, and which sat the first in the kingdom;)
15 What shall we do to the queen Vashti according to law, because she has not performed the commandment of the king Ahasuerus by the chamberlains?
16 And Memucan answered before the king and the princes, Vashti the queen has not done wrong to the king only, but also to all the princes, and to all the people that are in all the provinces of the king Ahasuerus.
17 For this deed of the queen shall come abroad to all women, so that they shall despise their husbands in their eyes, when it shall be reported, The king Ahasuerus commanded Vashti the queen to be brought in before him, but she came not.
18 Likewise shall the ladies of Persia and Media say this day to all the king's princes, which have heard of the deed of the queen. Thus shall there arise too much contempt and wrath.
19 If it pleases the king, let there go a royal commandment from him, and let it be written among the laws of the Persians and the Medes, that it be not altered, That Vashti comes no more before king Ahasuerus; and let the king give her royal estate to another that is better than she.
20 And when the king's decree which he shall make shall be published throughout all his empire, (for it is great,) all the wives shall give to their husbands honor, both to great and small.
21 And the saying pleased the king and the princes; and the king did according to the word of Memucan:
22 For he sent letters into all the king's provinces, into every province according to the writing thereof, and to every people after their language, that every man should bear rule in his own house, and that it should be published according to the language of every people.

Esther 2

2:1 ¶ After these things, when the wrath of king Ahasuerus was appeased, he remembered Vashti, and what she had done, and what was decreed against her.
2 Then said the king's servants that ministered to him, Let there be fair young virgins sought for the king:
3 And let the king appoint officers in all the provinces of his kingdom, that they may gather together all the fair young virgins to Shushan the palace, to the house of the women, to the custody of Hege the king's chamberlain, keeper of the women; and let their things for purification be given them:
4 And let the maiden which pleases the king be queen instead of Vashti. And the thing pleased the king; and he did so.
5 Now in Shushan the palace there was a certain Jew, whose name was Mordecai, the son of Jair, the son of Shimei, the son of Kish, a Benjamite;
6 Who had been carried away from Jerusalem with the captivity which had been carried away with Jeconiah king of Judah, whom Nebuchadnezzar the king of Babylon had carried away.

Esther 2

7 And he brought up Hadassah, that *is*, Esther, his uncle's daughter: for she had neither father nor mother, and the maid *was* fair and beautiful; whom Mordecai, when her father and mother were dead, took for his own daughter.

8 So it came to pass, when the king's commandment and his decree was heard, and when many maidens were gathered together to Shushan the palace, to the custody of Hegai, that Esther was brought also to the king's house, to the custody of Hegai, keeper of the women.

9 And the maiden pleased him, and she obtained kindness from him; and he speedily gave her her things for purification, with such things as belonged to her, and seven maidens, *which were* provided to be given *to* her, out of the king's house: and he changed her and her maids to the best *place* of the house of the women.

10 Esther had not shown her people nor her kindred: for Mordecai had charged her that she should not show *it*.

11 And Mordecai walked every day before the court of the women's house, to know how Esther did, and what should become of her.

12 Now when every maid's turn had come to go in to king Ahasuerus, after that she had been twelve months, according to the manner of the women, (for so were the days of their purification accomplished, *that is*, six months with oil of myrrh, and six months with sweet odors, and with *other* things for the purifying of the women;)

13 Then thus came *every* maiden to the king; whatever she desired was given *to* her to go with her out of the house of the women to the king's house.

14 In the evening she went, and on the next day she returned into the second house of the women, to the custody of Shaashgaz, the king's chamberlain, which kept the concubines: she came in to the king no more, unless the king delighted in her, and that she was called by name.

15 Now when the turn of Esther, the daughter of Abihail the uncle of Mordecai, who had taken her for his daughter, had come to go in to the king, she required nothing but what Hegai the king's chamberlain, the keeper of the women, appointed. And Esther obtained favor in the sight of all them that looked upon her.

16 So Esther was taken to king Ahasuerus into his house royal in the tenth month, which *is* the month *of* Tebeth, in the seventh year of his reign.

17 And the king loved Esther above all the women, and she obtained grace and favor in his sight more than all the virgins; so that he set the royal crown upon her head, and made her queen instead of Vashti.

18 Then the king made a great feast to all his princes and his servants, *even* Esther's feast; and he made a release to the provinces, and gave gifts, according to the state of the king.

19 And when the virgins were gathered together the second time, then Mordecai sat in the king's gate.

20 Esther had not *yet* shown her kindred nor her people; as Mordecai had charged her: for Esther did the commandment of Mordecai, like as when she was brought up with him.

21 ¶ In those days, while Mordecai sat in the king's gate, two of the king's chamberlains, Bigthan and Teresh, of those which kept the door, were angry, and sought to lay hand on the king Ahasuerus.

22 And the thing was known to Mordecai, who told *it* to Esther the queen; and Esther informed the king *thereof* in Mordecai's name.

23 And when *an* inquisition was made of the matter, it was found out; therefore they were both hanged on a tree: and it was written in the book of the chronicles before the king.

Esther 3

3:1 ¶ After these things did king Ahasuerus promote Haman the son of Hammedatha the Agagite, and advanced him, and set his seat above all the princes that *were* with him.

2 And all the king's servants, that *were* in the king's gate, bowed, and reverenced Haman: for the king had so commanded concerning him. But Mordecai bowed not, nor did *him* reverence.

3 Then the king's servants, which *were* in the king's gate, said to Mordecai, Why transgress you the king's commandment?

4 Now it came to pass, when they spoke daily to him, and he listened not to them, that they told Haman, to see whether Mordecai's matters would stand: for he had told them that he *was* a Jew.

5 And when Haman saw that Mordecai bowed not, nor did him reverence, then was Haman full of wrath.

6 And he thought scorn to lay hands on Mordecai alone; for they had shown him the people of Mordecai: therefore Haman sought to destroy all the Jews that *were* throughout the whole kingdom of Ahasuerus, *even* the people of Mordecai.

7 ¶ In the first month, that *is*, the month *of* Nisan, in the twelfth year of king Ahasuerus, they cast Pur, that *is*, the lot, before Haman from day to day, and from month to month, *to* the twelfth *month*, that *is*, the month *of* Adar.

8 And Haman said to king Ahasuerus, There is a certain people scattered abroad and dispersed among the people in all the provinces of your kingdom; and their laws *are* diverse from all people; neither keep they the king's laws: therefore it *is* not for the king's profit to leave them.

9 If it pleases the king, let it be written that they may be destroyed: and I will pay ten thousand talents of silver to the hands of those that have the charge of the business, to bring *it* into the king's treasuries.

10 And the king took his ring from his hand, and gave it to Haman the son of Hammedatha the Agagite, the Jews' enemy.

11 And the king said to Haman, The silver *is* given to you, the people also, to do with them as it seems good to you.

12 Then were the king's scribes called on the thirteenth day of the first month, and there was written according to all that Haman had commanded to the king's lieutenants, and

to the governors that *were* over every province, and to the rulers of every people of every province according to the writing thereof, and *to* every people after their language; in the name of king Ahasuerus was it written, and sealed with the king's ring.

13 And the letters were sent by posts into all the king's provinces, to destroy, to kill, and to cause to perish, all Jews, both young and old, little children and women, in one day, *even* upon the thirteenth *day* of the twelfth month, which is the month *of* Adar, and *to take* the spoil of them for a prey.

14 The copy of the writing for a commandment to be given in every province was published to all people, that they should be ready for that day.

15 The posts went out, being hastened by the king's commandment, and the decree was given in Shushan the palace. And the king and Haman sat down to drink; but the city Shushan was perplexed.

Esther 4

4:1 ¶ When Mordecai perceived all that was done, Mordecai tore his clothes, and put on sackcloth with ashes, and went out into the midst of the city, and cried with a loud and a bitter cry;

2 And came even before the king's gate: for none *might* enter into the king's gate clothed with sackcloth.

3 And in every province, wherever the king's commandment and his decree came, *there was* great mourning among the Jews, and fasting, and weeping, and wailing; and many lay in sackcloth and ashes.

4 So Esther's maids and her chamberlains came and told *it* to her. Then was the queen exceedingly grieved; and she sent clothing to clothe Mordecai, and to take away his sackcloth from him: but he received *it* not.

5 ¶ Then called Esther for Hatach, *one* of the king's chamberlains, whom he had appointed to attend upon her, and gave him a commandment to Mordecai, to know what it *was*, and why it *was*.

6 So Hatach went forth to Mordecai to the street of the city, which *was* before the king's gate.

7 And Mordecai told him of all that had happened to him, and of the sum of the money that Haman had promised to pay to the king's treasuries for the Jews, to destroy them.

8 Also he gave him the copy of the writing of the decree that was given at Shushan to destroy them, to show *it* to Esther, and to declare *it* to her, and to charge her that she should go in to the king, to make supplication to him, and to make request before him for her people.

9 And Hatach came and told Esther the words of Mordecai.

10 Again Esther spoke to Hatach, and gave him a commandment for Mordecai;

11 All the king's servants, and the people of the king's provinces, do know, that whoever, whether man or woman, shall come to the king into the inner court, who is not called, *there is* one law of his to put *him* to death,

except such to whom the king shall hold out the golden scepter, that he may live: but I have not been called to come in to the king these thirty days.

12 And they told to Mordecai Esther's words.

13 Then Mordecai commanded to answer Esther, Think not with yourself that you shall escape in the king's house, more than all the Jews.

14 For if you altogether hold your peace at this time, *then* shall there enlargement and deliverance arise to the Jews from another place; but you and your father's house shall be destroyed: and who knows whether you have come to the kingdom for *such* a time as this?

15 Then Esther told *them* to return Mordecai *this answer*,

16 Go, gather together all the Jews that are present in Shushan, and fast you for me, and neither eat nor drink three days, night or day: I also and my maidens will fast likewise; and so will I go in to the king, which *is* not according to the law: and if I perish, I perish.

17 So Mordecai went his way, and did according to all that Esther had commanded him.

Esther 5

5:1 ¶ Now it came to pass on the third day, that Esther put on *her* royal *apparel*, and stood in the inner court of the king's house, over against the king's house: and the king sat upon his royal throne in the royal house, over against the gate of the house.

2 And it was so, when the king saw Esther the queen standing in the court, *that* she obtained favor in his sight: and the king held out to Esther the golden scepter that *was* in his hand. So Esther drew near, and touched the top of the scepter.

3 Then said the king to her, What will you, queen Esther? and what *is* your request? it shall be even given you to the half of the kingdom.

4 And Esther answered, If *it seems* good to the king, let the king and Haman come this day to the banquet that I have prepared for him.

5 Then the king said, Cause Haman to make haste, that he may do as Esther has said. So the king and Haman came to the banquet that Esther had prepared.

6 And the king said to Esther at the banquet of wine, What *is* your petition? and it shall be granted you: and what *is* your request? even to the half of the kingdom it shall be performed.

7 Then answered Esther, and said, My petition and my request *is*;

8 If I have found favor in the sight of the king, and if it pleases the king to grant my petition, and to perform my request, let the king and Haman come to the banquet that I shall prepare for them, and I will do tomorrow as the king has said.

9 ¶ Then went Haman forth that day joyful and with a glad heart: but when Haman saw Mordecai in the king's gate, that he stood not up, nor moved for him, he was full of indignation against Mordecai.

10 Nevertheless Haman refrained himself: and when he came home, he sent and called for his friends, and Zeresh his wife.

11 And Haman told them of the glory of his riches, and the multitude of his children, and all *the things* wherein the king had promoted him, and how he had advanced him above the princes and servants of the king.

12 Haman said moreover, Yes, Esther the queen did let no man come in with the king to the banquet that she had prepared but myself; and tomorrow am I invited to her also with the king.

13 Yet all this avails me nothing, so long as I see Mordecai the Jew sitting at the king's gate.

14 Then said Zeresh his wife and all his friends to him, Let a gallows be made of fifty cubits high, and tomorrow speak you to the king that Mordecai may be hanged thereon: then go you in merrily with the king to the banquet. And the thing pleased Haman; and he caused the gallows to be made.

Esther 6

6:1 ¶ On that night could not the king sleep, and he commanded to bring the book of records of the chronicles; and they were read before the king.

2 And it was found written, that Mordecai had told of Bigthana and Teresh, two of the king's chamberlains, the keepers of the door, who sought to lay hand on the king Ahasuerus.

3 And the king said, What honor and dignity has been done to Mordecai for this? Then said the king's servants that ministered to him, There was nothing done for him.

4 ¶ And the king said, Who *is* in the court? Now Haman had come into the outward court of the king's house, to speak to the king to hang Mordecai on the gallows that he had prepared for him.

5 And the king's servants said to him, Behold, Haman stands in the court. And the king said, Let him come in.

6 So Haman came in. And the king said to him, What shall be done to the man whom the king delights to honor? Now Haman thought in his heart, To whom would the king delight to do honor more than to myself?

7 And Haman answered the king, For the man whom the king delights to honor,

8 Let the royal apparel be brought which the king *uses* to wear, and the horse that the king rides upon, and the crown royal which is set upon his head:

9 And let this apparel and horse be delivered to the hand of one of the king's most noble princes, that they may array the man *therewith* whom the king delights to honor, and bring him on horseback through the street of the city, and proclaim before him, Thus shall it be done to the man whom the king delights to honor.

10 Then the king said to Haman, Make haste, *and* take the apparel and the horse, as you have said, and do even so to Mordecai the Jew, that sits at the king's gate: let nothing fail of all that you have spoken.

11 Then took Haman the apparel and the horse, and arrayed Mordecai, and brought him on horseback through the street of the city, and proclaimed before him, Thus shall it be done to the man whom the king delights to honor.

12 ¶ And Mordecai came again to the king's gate. But Haman hurried to his house mourning, and having his head covered.

13 And Haman told Zeresh his wife and all his friends every *thing* that had befallen him. Then said his wise men and Zeresh his wife to him, If Mordecai *is* of the seed of the Jews, before whom you have begun to fall, you shall not prevail against him, but will surely fall before him.

14 And while they *were* yet talking with him, came the king's chamberlains, and hurried to bring Haman to the banquet that Esther had prepared.

Esther 7

7:1 ¶ So the king and Haman came to *the* banquet with Esther the queen.

2 And the king said again to Esther on the second day at the banquet of wine, What *is* your petition, queen Esther? and it shall be granted you: and what *is* your request? and it shall be performed, *even* to the half of the kingdom.

3 Then Esther the queen answered and said, If I have found favor in your sight, O king, and if it pleases the king, let my life be given me at my petition, and my people at my request:

4 For we are sold, I and my people, to be destroyed, to be slain, and to perish. But if we had been sold for bondmen and bondwomen, I had held my tongue, although the enemy could not countervail the king's damage.

5 Then the king Ahasuerus answered and said to Esther the queen, Who is he, and where is he, that dared presume in his heart to do so?

6 And Esther said, The adversary and enemy *is* this wicked Haman. Then Haman was afraid before the king and the queen.

7 ¶ And the king arising from the banquet of wine in his wrath *went* into the palace garden: and Haman stood up to make request for his life to Esther the queen; for he saw that there was evil determined against him by the king.

8 Then the king returned out of the palace garden into the place of the banquet of wine; and Haman had fallen upon the bed whereon Esther *was*. Then said the king, Will he force the queen also before me in the house? As the word went out of the king's mouth, they covered Haman's face.

9 And Harbonah, one of the chamberlains, said before the king, Behold also, the gallows *of* fifty cubits high, which Haman had made for Mordecai, who had spoken good for the king, stands in the house of Haman. Then the king said, Hang him thereon.

10 So they hanged Haman on the gallows that he had prepared for Mordecai. Then was the king's wrath pacified.

Esther 8

8:1 ¶ On that day did the king Ahasuerus give the house of Haman, the Jews' enemy, to Esther the queen. And Mordecai came before the king; for Esther had told what he *was* to her.

2 And the king took off his ring, which he had taken from Haman, and gave it to Mordecai. And Esther set Mordecai over the house of Haman.

3 ¶ And Esther spoke yet again before the king, and fell down at his feet, and besought him with tears to put away the mischief of Haman the Agagite, and his device that he had devised against the Jews.

4 Then the king held out the golden scepter toward Esther. So Esther arose, and stood before the king,

5 And said, If it pleases the king, and if I have found favor in his sight, and the thing *seems* right before the king, and I *am* pleasing in his eyes, let it be written to reverse the letters devised by Haman the son of Hammedatha the Agagite, which he wrote to destroy the Jews which *are* in all the king's provinces:

6 For how can I endure to see the evil that shall come to my people? or how can I endure to see the destruction of my kindred?

7 Then the king Ahasuerus said to Esther the queen and to Mordecai the Jew, Behold, I have given Esther the house of Haman, and him they have hanged upon the gallows, because he laid his hand upon the Jews.

8 Write you also for the Jews, as you like it, in the king's name, and seal *it* with the king's ring: for the writing which is written in the king's name, and sealed with the king's ring, may no man reverse.

9 Then were the king's scribes called at that time in the third month, that *is*, the month *of* Sivan, on the three and twentieth *day* thereof; and it was written according to all that Mordecai commanded to the Jews, and to the lieutenants, and the deputies and rulers of the provinces which *are* from India to Ethiopia, a hundred twenty and seven provinces, to every province according to the writing thereof, and unto every people after their language, and to the Jews according to their writing, and according to their language.

10 And he wrote in the king Ahasuerus' name, and sealed *it* with the king's ring, and sent letters by posts on horseback, *and* riders on mules, camels, *and* young dromedaries:

11 Wherein the king granted the Jews which *were* in every city to gather themselves together, and to stand for their life, to destroy, to slay, and to cause to perish, all the power of the people and province that would assault them, *both* little ones and women, and *to take* the spoil of them for a prey.

12 Upon one day in all the provinces of king Ahasuerus, *namely*, upon the thirteenth *day* of the twelfth month, which *is* the month *of* Adar.

13 The copy of the writing for a commandment to be given in every province *was* published to all people, and that the Jews should be ready against that day to avenge themselves on their enemies.

14 *So* the posts that rode upon mules *and* camels went out, being hastened and pressed on by the king's commandment. And the decree was given at Shushan the palace.

15 ¶ And Mordecai went out from the presence of the king in royal apparel of blue and white, and with a great crown of gold, and with a garment of fine linen and purple: and the city of Shushan rejoiced and was glad.

16 The Jews had light, and gladness, and joy, and honor.

17 And in every province, and in every city, wherever the king's commandment and his decree came, the Jews had joy and gladness, a feast and a good day. And many of the people of the land became Jews; for the fear of the Jews fell upon them.

Esther 9

9:1 ¶ Now in the twelfth month, that *is*, the month *of* Adar, on the thirteenth day of the same, when the king's commandment and his decree drew near to be put in execution, in the day that the enemies of the Jews hoped to have power over them, (though it was turned to the contrary, that the Jews had rule over them that hated them;)

2 The Jews gathered themselves together in their cities throughout all the provinces of the king Ahasuerus, to lay hands on such as sought their hurt: and no man could withstand them; for the fear of them fell upon all people.

3 And all the rulers of the provinces, and the lieutenants, and the deputies, and officers of the king, helped the Jews; because the fear of Mordecai fell upon them.

4 For Mordecai *was* great in the king's house, and his fame went out throughout all the provinces: for this man Mordecai became greater and greater.

5 Thus the Jews smote all their enemies with the stroke of the sword, and slaughter, and destruction, and did what they would to those that hated them.

6 And in Shushan the palace the Jews slew and destroyed five hundred men.

7 And Parshandatha, and Dalphon, and Aspatha,

8 And Poratha, and Adalia, and Aridatha,

9 And Parmashta, and Arisai, and Aridai, and Vajezatha,

10 The ten sons of Haman the son of Hammedatha, the enemy of the Jews, slew they; but on the spoil laid they not their hand.

11 On that day the number of those that were slain in Shushan the palace was brought before the king.

12 And the king said to Esther the queen, The Jews have slain and destroyed five hundred men in Shushan the palace, and the ten sons of Haman; what have they done in the rest of the king's provinces? now what *is* your petition? and it shall be granted you: or what *is* your request further? and it shall be done.

Esther 9

13 Then said Esther, If it pleases the king, let it be granted to the Jews which *are* in Shushan to do tomorrow also according unto this day's decree, and let Haman's ten sons be hanged upon the gallows.

14 And the king commanded it so to be done: and the decree was given at Shushan; and they hanged Haman's ten sons.

15 For the Jews that *were* in Shushan gathered themselves together on the fourteenth day also of the month *of* Adar, and slew three hundred men at Shushan; but on the prey they laid not their hand.

16 But the other Jews that *were* in the king's provinces gathered themselves together, and stood for their lives, and had rest from their enemies, and slew of their foes seventy and five thousand, but they laid not their hands on the prey,

17 On the thirteenth day of the month *of* Adar; and on the fourteenth day of the same rested they, and made it a day of feasting and gladness.

18 But the Jews that *were* at Shushan assembled together on the thirteenth *day* thereof, and on the fourteenth thereof; and on the fifteenth *day* of the same they rested, and made it a day of feasting and gladness.

19 Therefore the Jews of the villages, that dwelt in the unwalled towns, made the fourteenth day of the month *of* Adar *a day of* gladness and feasting, and a good day, and of sending portions one to another.

20 ¶ And Mordecai wrote these things, and sent letters to all the Jews that *were* in all the provinces of the king Ahasuerus, *both* near and far,

21 To establish *this* among them, that they should keep the fourteenth day of the month *of* Adar, and the fifteenth day of the same, yearly,

22 As the days wherein the Jews rested from their enemies, and the month which was turned to them from sorrow to joy, and from mourning into a good day: that they should make them days of feasting and joy, and of sending portions one to another, and gifts to the poor.

23 And the Jews undertook to do as they had begun, and as Mordecai had written to them;

24 Because Haman the son of Hammedatha, the Agagite, the enemy of all the Jews, had devised against the Jews to destroy them, and had cast Pur, that *is*, the lot, to consume them, and to destroy them;

25 But when *Esther* came before the king, he commanded by letters that his wicked device, which he devised against the Jews, should return upon his own head, and that he and his sons should be hanged on the gallows.

26 Therefore they called these days Purim after the name of Pur. Therefore for all the words of this letter, and *of that* which they had seen concerning this matter, and which had come to them,

27 The Jews ordained, and took upon them, and upon their seed, and upon all such as joined themselves to them, so as it should not fail, that they would keep these two days according to their writing, and according to their *appointed* time every year;

28 And *that* these days *should be* remembered and kept throughout every generation, every family, every province, and every city; and *that* these days of Purim should not fail from among the Jews, nor the memorial of them perish from their seed.

29 Then Esther the queen, the daughter of Abihail, and Mordecai the Jew, wrote with all authority, to confirm this second letter of Purim.

30 And he sent the letters to all the Jews, to the hundred twenty and seven provinces of the kingdom of Ahasuerus, *with* words of peace and truth,

31 To confirm these days of Purim in their times *appointed*, according as Mordecai the Jew and Esther the queen had enjoined them, and as they had decreed for themselves and for their seed, the matters of the fastings and their cry.

32 And the decree of Esther confirmed these matters of Purim; and it was written in the book.

Esther 10

10:1 ¶ And the king Ahasuerus laid a tribute upon the land, and *upon* the isles of the sea.

2 And all the acts of his power and of his might, and the declaration of the greatness of Mordecai, whereunto the king advanced him, *are* they not written in the book of the chronicles of the kings of Media and Persia?

3 For Mordecai the Jew *was* next to king Ahasuerus, and great among the Jews, and accepted of the multitude of his brethren, seeking the wealth of his people, and speaking peace to all his seed.

Section 3
Poetic

Job

Job 1

1:1 ¶ There was a man in the land of Uz, whose name *was* Job; and that man was perfect and upright, and one that feared God, and shunned evil.
2 And there was born unto him seven sons and three daughters.
3 His substance also was seven thousand sheep, and three thousand camels, and five hundred yoke of oxen, and five hundred she donkeys, and a very great household; so that this man was the greatest of all the men of the east.
4 ¶ And his sons went and feasted *in their* houses, every one his day; and sent and called for their three sisters to eat and to drink with them.
5 And it was so, when the days of *their* feasting were gone about, that Job sent and sanctified them, and rose up early in the morning, and offered burnt offerings *according* to the number of them all: for Job said, It may be that my sons have sinned, and cursed God in their hearts. Thus did Job continually.
6 ¶ Now there was a day when the sons of God came to present themselves before Yahweh, and Satan came also among them.
7 And Yahweh said to Satan, *From* where come you? Then Satan answered Yahweh, and said, From going to and fro in the earth, and from walking up and down in it.
8 And Yahweh said to Satan, Have you considered my servant Job, that *there is* none like him in the earth, a perfect and an upright man, one that fears God, and shuns evil?
9 Then Satan answered Yahweh, and said, Does Job fear God for nothing?
10 Have not you made a hedge about him, and about his house, and about all that he has on every side? you have blessed the work of his hands, and his substance is increased in the land.
11 But put forth your hand now, and touch all that he has, and he will curse you to your face.
12 And Yahweh said to Satan, Behold, all that he has *is* in your power; only upon himself put not forth your hand. So Satan went forth from the presence of Yahweh.
13 ¶ And there was a day when his sons and his daughters *were* eating and drinking wine in their oldest brother's house:
14 And there came a messenger to Job, and said, The oxen were plowing, and the donkeys feeding beside them:
15 And the Sabeans fell *upon them*, and took them away; yes, they have slain the servants with the edge of the sword; and I only have escaped alone to tell you.
16 While he *was* yet speaking, there came also another, and said, The fire of God has fallen from heaven, and has burned up the sheep, and the servants, and consumed them; and I only have escaped alone to tell you.
17 While he *was* yet speaking, there came also another, and said, The Chaldeans made out three bands, and fell upon the camels, and have carried them away, yes, and slain the servants with the edge of the sword; and I only have escaped alone to tell you.
18 While he *was* yet speaking, there came also another, and said, Your sons and your daughters *were* eating and drinking wine in their oldest brother's house:
19 And, behold, there came a great wind from the wilderness, and smote the four corners of the house, and it fell upon the young men, and they are dead; and I only have escaped alone to tell you.
20 ¶ Then Job arose, and tore his mantle, and shaved his head, and fell down upon the ground, and worshipped,
21 And said, Naked came I out of my mother's womb, and naked shall I return there: Yahweh gave, and Yahweh has taken away; blessed be the name of Yahweh.
22 In all this Job sinned not, nor charged God foolishly.

Job 2

2:1 ¶ Again there was a day when the sons of God came to present themselves before Yahweh, and Satan came also among them to present himself before Yahweh.
2 And Yahweh said to Satan, From where come you? And Satan answered Yahweh, and said, From going to and fro in the earth, and from walking up and down in it.
3 And Yahweh said to Satan, Have you considered my servant Job, that *there is* none like him in the earth, a perfect and an upright man, one that fears God, and shuns evil? and still he holds fast his integrity, although you moved me against him, to destroy him without cause.
4 And Satan answered Yahweh, and said, Skin for skin, yes, all that a man has will he give for his life.
5 But put forth your hand now, and touch his bone and his flesh, and he will curse you to your face.
6 And Yahweh said to Satan, Behold, he *is* in your hand; but save his life.
7 ¶ So went Satan forth from the presence of Yahweh, and smote Job with grievous boils from the sole of his foot to his crown.
8 And he took him a potsherd to scrape himself therewith; and he sat down among the ashes.
9 Then said his wife to him, Do you still retain your integrity? curse God, and die.
10 But he said to her, You speak as one of the foolish women speaks. What? shall we receive good at the hand

Job 2

of God, and shall we not receive evil? In all this did not Job sin with his lips.

11 ¶ Now when Job's three friends heard of all this evil that had come upon him, they came every one from his own place; Eliphaz the Temanite, and Bildad the Shuhite, and Zophar the Naamathite: for they had made an appointment together to come to mourn with him and to comfort him.

12 And when they lifted up their eyes afar off, and knew him not, they lifted up their voice, and wept; and they tore every one his mantle, and sprinkled dust upon their heads toward heaven.

13 So they sat down with him upon the ground seven days and seven nights, and none spoke a word to him: for they saw that *his* grief was very great.

Job 3

3:1 ¶ After this opened Job his mouth, and cursed his day.

2 And Job spoke, and said,

3 Let the day perish wherein I was born, and the night *in which* it was said, There is a man child conceived.

4 Let that day be darkness; let not God regard it from above, neither let the light shine upon it.

5 Let darkness and the shadow of death stain it; let a cloud dwell upon it; let the blackness of the day terrify it.

6 As *for* that night, let darkness seize upon it; let it not be joined to the days of the year, let it not come into the number of the months.

7 Lo, let that night be solitary, let no joyful voice come therein.

8 Let them curse it that curse the day, who are ready to raise up their mourning.

9 Let the stars of the twilight thereof be dark; let it look for light, but *have* none; neither let it see the dawning of the day:

10 Because it shut not up the doors of my *mother's* womb, nor hid sorrow from my eyes.

11 ¶ Why died I not from the womb? *why* did I *not* give up the ghost when I came out of the belly?

12 Why did the knees receive me? or why the breasts that I should suck?

13 For now should I have lain still and been quiet, I should have slept: then had I been at rest,

14 With kings and counselors of the earth, which built desolate places for themselves;

15 Or with princes that had gold, who filled their houses with silver:

16 Or as a hidden untimely birth I had not been; as infants *which* never saw light.

17 There the wicked cease *from* troubling; and there the weary are at rest.

18 *There* the prisoners rest together; they hear not the voice of the oppressor.

19 The small and great are there; and the servant *is* free from his master.

20 ¶ Why is light given to him that is in misery, and life to the bitter *in* soul;

21 Which longs for death, but it *comes* not; and digs for it more than for hidden treasures;

22 Which rejoice exceedingly, *and* are glad, when they can find the grave?

23 *Why is light given* to a man whose way is hidden, and whom God has hedged in?

24 For my sighing comes before I eat, and my roarings are poured out like the waters.

25 For the thing which I greatly feared has come upon me, and that which I was afraid of has come to me.

26 I was not in safety, neither had I rest, neither was I quiet; yet trouble came.

Job 4

4:1 ¶ Then Eliphaz the Temanite answered and said,

2 *If* we try to speak with you, will you be grieved? but who can withhold himself from speaking?

3 Behold, you have instructed many, and you have strengthened the weak hands.

4 Your words have upheld him that was falling, and you have strengthened the feeble knees.

5 But now it has come upon you, and you faint; it touches you, and you are troubled.

6 *Is* not *this* your fear, your confidence, your hope, and the uprightness of your ways?

7 ¶ Remember, I pray you, who *ever* perished, being innocent? or where were the righteous cut off?

8 Even as I have seen, they that plow iniquity, and sow wickedness, reap the same.

9 By the blast of God they perish, and by the breath of his nostrils are they consumed.

10 The roaring of the lion, and the voice of the fierce lion, and the teeth of the young lions, are broken.

11 The old lion perishes for lack of prey, and the stout lion's young are scattered abroad.

12 ¶ Now a thing was secretly brought to me, and my ear received a little thereof.

13 In thoughts from the visions of the night, when deep sleep falls on men,

14 Fear came upon me, and trembling, which made all my bones to shake.

15 Then a spirit passed before my face; the hair of my flesh stood up:

16 It stood still, but I could not discern the form thereof: an image *was* before my eyes, *there was* silence, and I heard a voice, *saying,*

17 Shall mortal man be more just than God? shall a man be more pure than his maker?

18 Behold, he put no trust in his servants; and his angels he charged with folly:

19 How much less *in* them that dwell in houses of clay, whose foundation *is* in the dust, *which* are crushed before the moth?

20 They are destroyed from morning to evening: they perish forever without any regarding *it*.

21 Does not their excellency *which is* in them go away? they die, even without wisdom.

Job 5

5:1 ¶ Call now, if there are any that will answer you; and to which of the saints will you turn?

2 For wrath kills the foolish man, and envy slays the silly one.

3 I have seen the foolish taking root: but suddenly I cursed his habitation.

4 His children are far from safety, and they are crushed in the gate, neither *is there* any to deliver *them*.

5 Whose harvest the hungry eats up, and takes it even out of the thorns, and the robber swallows up their substance.

6 ¶ Although affliction comes not forth of the dust, neither does trouble spring out of the ground;

7 Yet man is born to trouble, as the sparks fly upward.

8 I would seek to God, and to God would I commit my cause:

9 Which does great things and unsearchable; marvelous things without number:

10 Who gives rain upon the earth, and sends waters upon the fields:

11 To set up on high those that are low; that those which mourn may be exalted to safety.

12 He disappoints the devices of the crafty, so that their hands cannot perform *their* enterprise.

13 He takes the wise in their own craftiness: and the counsel of the shrewd is carried hastily.

14 They meet with darkness in the daytime, and grope in the noonday as in the night.

15 But he saves the poor from the sword, from their mouth, and from the hand of the mighty.

16 So the poor has hope, and iniquity stops her mouth.

17 ¶ Behold, happy *is* the man whom God corrects: therefore despise not you the chastening of the Almighty:

18 For he makes pain, and binds up: he wounds, and his hands make whole.

19 He shall deliver you in six troubles: yes, in seven there shall no evil touch you.

20 In famine he shall redeem you from death: and in war from the power of the sword.

21 You shall be hidden from the scourge of the tongue: neither shall you be afraid of destruction when it comes.

22 At destruction and famine you shall laugh: neither shall you be afraid of the beasts of the earth.

23 For you shall be in league with the stones of the field: and the beasts of the field shall be at peace with you.

24 And you shall know that your tabernacle *shall be* in peace; and you shall visit your habitation, and shall not sin.

25 You shall know also that your seed *shall be* great, and your offspring as the grass of the earth.

26 You shall come to *your* grave in a full age, like as a shock of corn comes in in his season.

27 Lo this, we have searched it, so it *is*; hear it, and know you *it* for your good.

Job 6

6:1 ¶ But Job answered and said,

2 Oh that my grief were thoroughly weighed, and my calamity laid in the balances together!

3 For now it would be heavier than the sand of the sea: therefore my words are swallowed up.

4 For the arrows of the Almighty *are* within me, the poison thereof drinks up my spirit: the terrors of God do set themselves in array against me.

5 Does the wild donkey bray when he has grass? or lows the ox over his fodder?

6 Can that which is unsavory be eaten without salt? or is there *any* taste in the white of an egg?

7 The things *that* my soul refused to touch *are* as my sorrowful meat.

8 ¶ Oh that I might have my request; and that God would grant *me* the thing that I long for!

9 Even that it would please God to destroy me; that he would let loose his hand, and cut me off!

10 Then should I yet have comfort; yes, I would harden myself in sorrow: let him not spare; for I have not concealed the words of the Holy One.

11 What *is* my strength, that I should hope? and what *is* my end, that I should prolong my life?

12 *Is* my strength the strength of stones? or *is* my flesh of brass?

13 *Is* not my help in me? and is wisdom driven quite from me?

14 ¶ To him that is afflicted pity *should be shown* from his friend; but he forsakes the fear of the Almighty.

15 My brethren have dealt deceitfully as a brook, *and* as the stream of brooks they pass away;

16 Which are blackish by reason of the ice, *and* wherein the snow is hidden:

17 When they become warm, they vanish: when it is hot, they are consumed out of their place.

18 The paths of their way are turned aside; they go to nothing, and perish.

19 The troops of Tema looked, the companies of Sheba waited for them.

20 They were confounded because they had hoped; they came there, and were ashamed.

21 For now you are nothing; you see *my* casting down, and are afraid.

22 ¶ Did I say, Bring to me? or, Give a reward for me of your substance?

23 Or, Deliver me from the enemy's hand? or, Redeem me from the hand of the mighty?

24 Teach me, and I will hold my tongue: and cause me to understand wherein I have erred.

25 How forcible are right words! but what does your arguing prove?

26 Do you imagine to reprove words, and the speeches of one that is desperate, *which are* as wind?

27 Yes, you overwhelm the fatherless, and you dig *a pit* for your friend.

28 Now therefore be content, look upon me; for *it is* evident to you if I lie.
29 Return, I pray you, let it not be iniquity; yes, return again, my righteousness *is* in it.
30 Is there iniquity in my tongue? cannot my taste discern perverse things?

Job 7

7:1 ¶ *Is there* not an appointed time to man upon earth? *are not* his days also like the days of a hireling?
2 As a servant earnestly desires the shadow, and as a hireling looks for *the reward of* his work:
3 So am I made to possess months of vanity, and wearisome nights are appointed to me.
4 When I lie down, I say, When shall I arise, and the night be gone? and I am full of tossing to and fro to the dawning of the day.
5 My flesh is clothed with worms and clods of dust; my skin is broken, and become loathsome.
6 My days are swifter than a weaver's shuttle, and are spent without hope.
7 ¶ O remember that my life *is* wind: my eye shall no more see good.
8 The eye of him that has seen me shall see me no *more*: your eyes *are* upon me, and I *am* not.
9 *As* the cloud is consumed and vanishes away: so he that goes down to the grave shall come up no *more*.
10 He shall return no more to his house, neither shall his place know him any more.
11 Therefore I will not restrain my mouth; I will speak in the anguish of my spirit; I will complain in the bitterness of my soul.
12 *Am* I a sea, or a whale, that you set a watch over me?
13 When I say, My bed shall comfort me, my couch shall ease my complaint;
14 Then you scare me with dreams, and terrify me through visions:
15 So that my soul chooses strangling, *and* death rather than my life.
16 I loathe *it*; I would not live always: let me alone; for my days *are* vanity.
17 ¶ What *is* man, that you should magnify him? and that you should set your heart upon him?
18 And *that* you should visit him every morning, *and* try him every moment?
19 How long will you not depart from me, nor let me alone till I swallow down my spittle?
20 I have sinned; what shall I do to you, O you preserver of men? why have you set me as a mark against you, so that I am a burden to myself?
21 And why do you not pardon my transgression, and take away my iniquity? for now shall I sleep in the dust; and you shall seek me in the morning, but I *shall* not *be*.

Job 8

8:1 ¶ Then answered Bildad the Shuhite, and said,
2 How long will you speak these *things*? and *how long shall* the words of your mouth *be like* a strong wind?
3 Does God pervert judgment? or does the Almighty pervert justice?
4 If your children have sinned against him, and he has cast them away for their transgression;
5 If you would seek to God early, and make your supplication to the Almighty;
6 If you *were* pure and upright; surely now he would awaken for you, and make the habitation of your righteousness prosperous.
7 Though your beginning was small, yet your latter end should greatly increase.
8 ¶ For inquire, I pray you, of the former age, and prepare yourself to the search of their fathers:
9 (For we *are but of* yesterday, and know nothing, because our days upon earth *are* a shadow:)
10 Shall not they teach you, *and* tell you, and utter words out of their heart?
11 Can the rush grow up without mire? can the reeds grow without water?
12 While it *is* yet in its greenness, *and* not cut down, it withers before any *other* herb.
13 So *are* the paths of all that forget God; and the hypocrite's hope shall perish:
14 Whose hope shall be cut off, and whose trust *shall be* a spider's web.
15 He shall lean upon his house, but it shall not stand: he shall hold it fast, but it shall not endure.
16 He *is* green before the sun, and his branch shoots forth in his garden.
17 His roots are wrapped about the heap, *and* sees the place of stones.
18 If he destroys him from his place, then *it* shall deny him, *saying*, I have not seen you.
19 Behold, this *is* the joy of his way, and out of the earth shall others grow.
20 ¶ Behold, God will not cast away a perfect *man*, neither will he help the evil doers:
21 Till he fills your mouth with laughing, and your lips with rejoicing.
22 They that hate you shall be clothed with shame; and the dwelling place of the wicked shall come to nothing.

Job 9

9:1 ¶ Then Job answered and said,
2 I know *it is* so of a truth: but how should man be just with God?
3 If he will contend with him, he cannot answer him one of a thousand.
4 *He is* wise in heart, and mighty in strength: who has hardened *himself* against him, and has prospered?
5 Which removes the mountains, and they know not: which overturns them in his anger.

6 Which shakes the earth out of her place, and the pillars thereof tremble.
7 Which commands the sun, and it rises not; and seals up the stars.
8 Which alone spreads out the heavens, and treads upon the waves of the sea.
9 Which makes Arcturus, Orion, and Pleiades, and the chambers of the south.
10 Which does great things past finding out; yes, and wonders without number.
11 Lo, he goes by me, and I see *him* not: he passes on also, but I perceive him not.
12 Behold, he takes away, who can hinder him? who will say to him, What do you?
13 *If* God will not withdraw his anger, the proud helpers do stoop under him.
14 ¶ How much less shall I answer him, *and* choose out my words *to reason* with him?
15 Whom, though I were righteous, *yet* would I not answer, *but* I would make supplication to my judge.
16 If I had called, and he had answered me; *yet* would I not believe that he had listened to my voice.
17 For he breaks me with a tempest, and multiplies my wounds without cause.
18 He will not allow me to take my breath, but fills me with bitterness.
19 If *I speak* of strength, lo, *he is* strong: and if of judgment, who shall set me a time *to plead*?
20 If I justify myself, my own mouth shall condemn me: *if I say*, I *am* perfect, it shall also prove me perverse.
21 *Though* I *were* perfect, *yet* would I not know my soul: I would despise my life.
22 ¶ This *is* one *thing*, therefore I said *it*, He destroys the perfect and the wicked.
23 If the scourge slays suddenly, he will laugh at the trial of the innocent.
24 The earth is given into the hand of the wicked: he covers the faces of the judges thereof; if not, where, *and* who *is* he?
25 ¶ Now my days are swifter than a post: they flee away, they see no good.
26 They are passed away as the swift ships: as the eagle *that* hurries to the prey.
27 If I say, I will forget my complaint, I will leave off my heaviness, and comfort *myself*:
28 I am afraid of all my sorrows, I know that you will not hold me innocent.
29 *If* I am wicked, why then labor I in vain?
30 If I wash myself with snow water, and make my hands never so clean;
31 Yet shall you plunge me in the ditch, and my own clothes shall abhor me.
32 For *he is* not a man, as I *am, that* I should answer him, *and* we should come together in judgment.
33 Neither is there any judge between us, *that* might lay his hand upon us both.
34 Let him take his rod away from me, and let not his fear terrify me:
35 *Then* would I speak, and not fear him; but *it is* not so with me.

Job 10

10:1 ¶ My soul is weary of my life; I will leave my complaint upon myself; I will speak in the bitterness of my soul.
2 I will say to God, Do not condemn me; show me why you contend with me.
3 *Is it* good to you that you should oppress, that you should despise the work of your hands, and shine upon the counsel of the wicked?
4 Have you eyes of flesh? or see you as man sees?
5 *Are* your days as the days of man? *are* your years as man's days,
6 That you inquire after my iniquity, and search after my sin?
7 You know that I am not wicked; and *there is* none that can deliver out of your hand.
8 ¶ Your hands have made me and fashioned me together round about; yet you do destroy me.
9 Remember, I beseech you, that you have made me as the clay; and will you bring me into dust again?
10 Have you not poured me out as milk, and curdled me like cheese?
11 You have clothed me with skin and flesh, and have fenced me with bones and sinews.
12 You have granted me life and favor, and your visitation has preserved my spirit.
13 And these *things* have you hidden in your heart: I know that this *is* with you.
14 ¶ If I sin, then you mark me, and you will not acquit me from my iniquity.
15 If I am wicked, woe to me; and *if* I am righteous, *yet* will I not lift up my head. *I am* full of confusion; therefore see you my affliction;
16 For it increases. You hunt me as a fierce lion: and again you show yourself marvelous upon me.
17 You renew your witnesses against me, and increase your indignation upon me; changes and war *are* against me.
18 Why then have you brought me forth out of the womb? Oh that I had given up the ghost, and no eye had seen me!
19 I should have been as though I had not been; I should have been carried from the womb to the grave.
20 *Are* not my days few? cease *then, and* let me alone, that I may take comfort a little,
21 Before I go *from where* I shall not return, *even* to the land of darkness and the shadow of death;
22 A land of darkness, as darkness *itself; and* of the shadow of death, without any order, and *where* the light *is* as darkness.

Job 11

11:1 ¶ Then answered Zophar the Naamathite, and said,
2 Should not the multitude of words be answered? and should a man full of talk be justified?

Job 11

3 Should your lies make men hold their peace? and when you mock, shall no man make you ashamed?
4 For you have said, My doctrine *is* pure, and I am clean in your eyes.
5 But oh that God would speak, and open his lips against you;
6 And that he would show you the secrets of wisdom, that *they are* double to that which is! Know therefore that God exacts of you *less* than your iniquity *deserves*.
7 ¶ Can you by searching find out God? can you find out the Almighty unto perfection?
8 *It is* as high as heaven; what can you do? deeper than hell; what can you know?
9 The measure thereof *is* longer than the earth, and broader than the sea.
10 If he cuts off, and shuts up, or gathers together, then who can hinder him?
11 For he knows vain men: he sees wickedness also; will he not then consider *it*?
12 For vain man would be wise, though man be born *like* a wild donkey's colt.
13 ¶ If you prepare your heart, and stretch out your hands toward him;
14 If iniquity *is* in your hand, put it far away, and let not wickedness dwell in your tabernacles.
15 For then shall you lift up your face without spot; yes, you shall be steadfast, and shall not fear:
16 Because you shall forget *your* misery, *and* remember *it* as waters *that* pass away:
17 And *your* age shall be clearer than the noonday; you shall shine forth, you shall be as the morning.
18 And you shall be secure, because there is hope; yes, you shall dig *about you, and* you shall take your rest in safety.
19 Also you shall lie down, and none shall make *you* afraid; yes, many shall become weak unto you.
20 But the eyes of the wicked shall fail, and they shall not escape, and their hope *shall be as* the giving up of the ghost.

Job 12

12:1 ¶ And Job answered and said,
2 No doubt but you *are* the people, and wisdom shall die with you.
3 But I have understanding as well as you; I *am* not inferior to you: yes, who knows not such things as these?
4 I am *as* one mocked by his neighbor, who calls upon God, and he answers him: the just upright *man is* laughed to scorn.
5 He that is ready to slip with *his* feet *is as* a lamp despised in the thought of him that is at ease.
6 ¶ The tabernacles of robbers prosper, and they that provoke God are secure; into whose hand God brings *abundantly*.
7 But ask now the beasts, and they shall teach you; and the fowls of the air, and they shall tell you:
8 Or speak to the earth, and it shall teach you: and the fishes of the sea shall declare unto you.
9 Who knows not in all these that the hand of Yahweh has done this?
10 In whose hand *is* the soul of every living thing, and the breath of all mankind.
11 Does not the ear try words? and the mouth taste his meat?
12 ¶ With the ancient *is* wisdom; and in length of days understanding.
13 With him *is* wisdom and strength, he has counsel and understanding.
14 Behold, he breaks down, and it cannot be built again: he shuts up a man, and there can be no opening.
15 Behold, he withholds the waters, and they dry up: also he sends them out, and they overturn the earth.
16 With him *is* strength and wisdom: the deceived and the deceiver *are* his.
17 He leads counselors away spoiled, and makes the judges fools.
18 He looses the bonds of kings, and girds their loins with a girdle.
19 He leads princes away spoiled, and overthrows the mighty.
20 He removes away the speech of the trusty, and takes away the understanding of the aged.
21 He pours contempt upon princes, and weakens the strength of the mighty.
22 He uncovers deep things out of darkness, and brings out to light the shadow of death.
23 He increases the nations, and destroys them: he enlarges the nations, and leads them *again*.
24 He takes away the heart of the chief of the people of the earth, and causes them to wander in a wilderness *where there is* no way.
25 They grope in the dark without light, and he makes them to stagger like *a* drunken *man*.

Job 13

13:1 ¶ Lo, my eye has seen all *this*, my ear has heard and understood it.
2 What you know, *the same* do I know also: I *am* not inferior to you.
3 Surely I would speak to the Almighty, and I desire to reason with God.
4 But you *are* forgers of lies, you *are* all physicians of no value.
5 O that you would altogether hold your peace! and it should be your wisdom.
6 Hear now my reasoning, and listen to the pleadings of my lips.
7 Will you speak wickedly for God? and talk deceitfully for him?
8 Will you accept his person? will you contend for God?
9 Is it good that he should search you out? or as one man mocks another, do you *so* mock him?
10 He will surely reprove you, if you do secretly accept persons.

11 Shall not his excellency make you afraid? and his dread fall upon you?
12 Your remembrances *are* like unto ashes, your bodies to bodies of clay.
13 ¶ Hold your peace, let me alone, that I may speak, and let come on me what *will*.
14 Why do I take my flesh in my teeth, and put my life in my hand?
15 Though he slays me, yet will I trust in him: but I will maintain my own ways before him.
16 He also *shall be* my salvation: for a hypocrite shall not come before him.
17 Hear diligently my speech, and my declaration with your ears.
18 Behold now, I have ordered *my* cause; I know that I shall be justified.
19 Who *is* he *that* will plead with me? for now, if I hold my tongue, I shall give up the ghost.
20 Only do not two *things* unto me: then will I not hide myself from you.
21 Withdraw your hand far from me: and let not your dread make me afraid.
22 Then call you, and I will answer: or let me speak, and answer you me.
23 ¶ How many *are* my iniquities and sins? make me to know my transgression and my sin.
24 Why hide you your face, and hold me for your enemy?
25 Will you break a leaf driven to and fro? and will you pursue the dry stubble?
26 For you write bitter things against me, and make me to possess the iniquities of my youth.
27 You put my feet also in the stocks, and look narrowly to all my paths; you set a print upon the heels of my feet.
28 And he, as a rotten thing, consumes, as a garment that is moth eaten.

Job 14

14:1 ¶ Man *that is* born of a woman *is* of few days, and full of trouble.
2 He comes forth like a flower, and is cut down: he flees also as a shadow, and continues not.
3 And do you open your eyes upon such a one, and bring me into judgment with you?
4 Who can bring a clean *thing* out of an unclean? not one.
5 Seeing his days *are* determined, the number of his months *are* with you, you have appointed his bounds that he cannot pass;
6 Turn from him, that he may rest, till he shall accomplish, as a hireling, his day.
7 ¶ For there is hope for a tree, if it is cut down, that it will sprout again, and that the tender branch thereof will not cease.
8 Though the root thereof grows old in the earth, and the stock thereof dies in the ground;
9 *Yet* through the scent of water it will bud, and bring forth boughs like a plant.
10 But man dies, and wastes away: yes, man gives up the ghost, and where *is* he?
11 *As* the waters fail from the sea, and the flood decays and dries up:
12 So man lies down, and rises not: till the heavens *are* no more, they shall not awake, nor be raised out of their sleep.
13 O that you would hide me in the grave, that you would keep me secret, until your wrath is past, that you would appoint me a set time, and remember me!
14 If a man dies, shall he live *again*? all the days of my appointed time will I wait, till my change comes.
15 You shall call, and I will answer you: you will have a desire to the work of your hands.
16 ¶ For now you number my steps: do you not watch over my sin?
17 My transgression *is* sealed up in a bag, and you sew up my iniquity.
18 And surely the mountain falling comes to nothing, and the rock is removed out of his place.
19 The waters wear the stones: you wash away the things which grow *out* of the dust of the earth; and you destroy the hope of man.
20 You prevail forever against him, and he passes: you change his countenance, and send him away.
21 His sons come to honor, and he knows *it* not; and they are brought low, but he perceives *it* not of them.
22 But his flesh upon him shall have pain, and his soul within him shall mourn.

Job 15

15:1 ¶ Then answered Eliphaz the Temanite, and said,
2 Should a wise man utter vain knowledge, and fill his belly with the east wind?
3 Should he reason with unprofitable talk? or with speeches with which he can do no good?
4 Yes, you cast off fear, and restrain prayer before God.
5 For your mouth utters your iniquity, and you choose the tongue of the crafty.
6 Your own mouth condemns you, and not I: yes, your own lips testify against you.
7 *Are* you the first man *that* was born? or were you made before the hills?
8 Have you heard the secret of God? and do you restrain wisdom to yourself?
9 What know you, that we know not? *what* understand you, which *is* not in us?
10 With us *are* both the grayheaded and very aged men, much older than your father.
11 *Are* the consolations of God small with you? is there any secret thing with you?
12 Why does your heart carry you away? and what do your eyes wink at,
13 That you turn your spirit against God, and let *such* words go out of your mouth?

Job 15

14 What *is* man, that he should be clean? and *he which is* born of a woman, that he should be righteous?
15 Behold, he puts no trust in his saints; yes, the heavens are not clean in his sight.
16 How much more abominable and filthy *is* man, which drinks iniquity like water?
17 ¶ I will show you, hear me; and that *which* I have seen I will declare;
18 Which wise men have told from their fathers, and have not hidden *it*:
19 Unto whom alone the earth was given, and no stranger passed among them.
20 The wicked man grieves with pain all *his* days, and the number of years is hidden to the oppressor.
21 A dreadful sound *is* in his ears: in prosperity the destroyer shall come upon him.
22 He believes not that he shall return out of darkness, and he is waited for by the sword.
23 He wanders abroad for bread, *saying*, Where *is it*? he knows that the day of darkness is ready at his hand.
24 Trouble and anguish shall make him afraid; they shall prevail against him, as a king ready to the battle.
25 For he stretches out his hand against God, and strengthens himself against the Almighty.
26 He runs upon him, *even* on *his* neck, upon the thick backs of his shields:
27 Because he covers his face with his fatness, and makes bulges of fat on *his* flanks.
28 And he dwells in desolate cities, *and* in houses which no man inhabits, which are ready to become heaps.
29 He shall not be rich, neither shall his substance continue, neither shall he prolong the perfection thereof upon the earth.
30 He shall not depart out of darkness; the flame shall dry up his branches, and by the breath of his mouth shall he go away.
31 Let not him that is deceived trust in vanity: for vanity shall be his recompense.
32 It shall be accomplished before his time, and his branch shall not be green.
33 He shall shake off his unripe grape as the vine, and shall cast off his flower as the olive.
34 For the congregation of hypocrites *shall be* desolate, and fire shall consume the tabernacles of bribery.
35 They conceive mischief, and bring forth vanity, and their belly prepares deceit.

Job 16

16:1 ¶ Then Job answered and said,
2 I have heard many such things: miserable comforters *are* you all.
3 Shall vain words have an end? or what emboldens you that you answer?
4 I also could speak as you *do*: if your soul were in my soul's stead, I could heap up words against you, and shake my head at you.
5 *But* I would strengthen you with my mouth, and the moving of my lips should relieve *your grief*.
6 ¶ Though I speak, my grief is not restrained: and *though* I forbear, what am I eased?
7 But now he has made me weary: you have made desolate all my company.
8 And you have filled me with wrinkles, *which* is a witness *against me*: and my leanness rising up in me bears witness to my face.
9 He tears *me* in his wrath, who hates me: he gnashes upon me with his teeth; my enemy sharpens his eyes upon me.
10 They have gaped upon me with their mouth; they have smitten me upon the cheek reproachfully; they have gathered themselves together against me.
11 God has delivered me to the ungodly, and turned me over into the hands of the wicked.
12 I was at ease, but he has broken me to bits: he has also taken *me* by my neck, and shaken me to pieces, and set me up for his mark.
13 His archers compass me round about, he cleaves my reins open, and does not spare; he pours out my gall upon the ground.
14 He breaks me with breach upon breach, he runs upon me like a giant.
15 I have sewed sackcloth upon my skin, and defiled my horn in the dust.
16 My face is foul with weeping, and on my eyelids *is* the shadow of death;
17 ¶ Not for *any* injustice in my hands: also my prayer *is* pure.
18 O earth, cover not you my blood, and let my cry have no place.
19 Also now, behold, my witness *is* in heaven, and my record *is* on high.
20 My friends scorn me: *but* my eye pours out *tears* to God.
21 O that one might plead for a man with God, as a man *pleads* for his neighbor!
22 When a few years have come, then I shall go the way *from where* I shall not return.

Job 17

17:1 ¶ My breath is corrupt, my days are extinct, the graves *are ready* for me.
2 *Are there* not mockers with me? and does not my eye continue in their provocation?
3 Lay down now, put me in a surety with you; who *is he that* will strike hands with me?
4 For you have hidden their heart from understanding: therefore shall you not exalt *them*.
5 He that speaks flattery to *his* friends, even the eyes of his children shall fail.
6 He has made me also a byword of the people; and to my face I was as a spittoon.
7 My eye also is dim by reason of sorrow, and all my members *are* as a shadow.
8 Upright *men* shall be astonished at this, and the innocent shall stir up himself against the hypocrite.
9 The righteous also shall hold on his way, and he that has clean hands shall be stronger and stronger.

10 ¶ But as for you all, do you return, and come now: for I cannot find *one* wise *man* among you.
11 My days are past, my purposes are broken off, *even* the thoughts of my heart.
12 They change the night into day: the light *is* short because of darkness.
13 If I wait, the grave *is* my house: I have made my bed in the darkness.
14 I have said to corruption, You *are* my father: to the worm, *You are* my mother, and my sister.
15 And where *is* now my hope? as for my hope, who shall see it?
16 They shall go down to the bars of the pit, when *our* rest together *is* in the dust.

Job 18

18:1 ¶ Then answered Bildad the Shuhite, and said,
2 How long *will it be before* you make an end of words? understand, and afterward we will speak.
3 Why are we counted as beasts, *and* reputed *as* vile in your sight?
4 He tears himself in his anger: shall the earth be forsaken for you? and shall the rock be removed out of his place?
5 ¶ Yes, the light of the wicked shall be put out, and the spark of his fire shall not shine.
6 The light shall be dark in his tabernacle, and his candle shall be put out with him.
7 The steps of his strength shall be distressed, and his own counsel shall cast him down.
8 For he is cast into a net by his own feet, and he walks upon a snare.
9 The snare shall take *him* by the heel, *and* the robber shall prevail against him.
10 The snare *is* laid for him in the ground, and a trap for him in the way.
11 ¶ Terrors shall make him afraid on every side, and shall drive him to his feet.
12 His strength shall be extremely hungry, and destruction *shall be* ready at his side.
13 It shall devour the strength of his skin: *even* the firstborn of death shall devour his strength.
14 His confidence shall be rooted out of his tabernacle, and it shall bring him to the king of terrors.
15 It shall dwell in his tabernacle, because *it is* none of his: brimstone shall be scattered upon his habitation.
16 His roots shall be dried up beneath, and above shall his branch be cut off.
17 His remembrance shall perish from the earth, and he shall have no name in the street.
18 He shall be driven from light into darkness, and chased out of the world.
19 He shall neither have son nor nephew among his people, nor any remaining in his dwellings.
20 They that come after *him* shall be astonished at his day, as they that went before were frightened.
21 Surely such *are* the dwellings of the wicked, and this *is* the place *of him that* knows not God.

Job 19

19:1 ¶ Then Job answered and said,
2 How long will you afflict my soul, and break me in pieces with words?
3 These ten times have you reproached me: you are not ashamed *that* you make yourselves strange to me.
4 And be it indeed *that* I have erred, my error remains with myself.
5 If indeed you will magnify *yourselves* against me, and plead against me my reproach:
6 Know now that God has overthrown me, and has compassed me with his net.
7 Behold, I cry out of wrong, but I am not heard: I cry aloud, but *there is* no judgment.
8 ¶ He has fenced up my way that I cannot pass, and he has set darkness in my paths.
9 He has stripped me of my glory, and taken the crown *from* my head.
10 He has destroyed me on every side, and I am gone: and my hope has he removed like a tree.
11 He has also kindled his wrath against me, and he counts me to him as *one of* his enemies.
12 His troops come together, and raise up their way against me, and encamp round about my tabernacle.
13 He has put my brothers far from me, and my acquaintances are truly estranged from me.
14 My kinsfolk have failed, and my familiar friends have forgotten me.
15 They that dwell in my house, and my maids, count me as a stranger: I am an alien in their sight.
16 I called my servant, and he gave *me* no answer; I entreated him with my mouth.
17 My breath is strange to my wife, though I entreated for the children's *sake* of my own body.
18 Yes, young children despised me; I arose, and they spoke against me.
19 All my close friends abhorred me: and they whom I loved are turned against me.
20 My bone clings to my skin and to my flesh, and I have escaped with the skin of my teeth.
21 Have pity upon me, have pity upon me, O you my friends; for the hand of God has touched me.
22 Why do you persecute me as God *does*, and are not satisfied with my flesh?
23 ¶ Oh that my words were now written! oh that they were printed in a book!
24 That they were engraved with an iron pen and lead in the rock forever!
25 For I know *that* my redeemer lives, and *that* he shall stand at the latter *day* upon the earth:
26 And *though* after my skin *worms* destroy this *body*, yet in my flesh shall I see God:
27 Whom I shall see for myself, and my eyes shall behold, and not another; *though* my reins be consumed within me.
28 But you should say, Why persecute we him, seeing the root of the matter is found in me?

Job 19

29 Be you afraid of the sword: for wrath *brings* the punishments of the sword, that you may know *there is* a judgment.

Job 20

20:1 ¶ Then answered Zophar the Naamathite, and said,
2 Therefore do my thoughts cause me to answer, and for *this* I make haste.
3 I have heard the correction of my reproach, and the spirit of my understanding causes me to answer.
4 Know you *not* this of old, since man was placed upon earth,
5 That the triumphing of the wicked *is* short, and the joy of the hypocrite *is but* for a moment?
6 Though his excellency mount up to the heavens, and his head reaches to the clouds;
7 *Yet* he shall perish forever like his own dung: they which have seen him shall say, Where *is* he?
8 He shall fly away as a dream, and shall not be found: yes, he shall be chased away as a vision of the night.
9 The eye also *which* saw him shall *see him* no more; neither shall his place any more behold him.
10 ¶ His children shall seek to please the poor, and his hands shall restore their goods.
11 His bones are full *of the sin* of his youth, which shall lie down with him in the dust.
12 Though wickedness is sweet in his mouth, *though* he hides it under his tongue;
13 *Though* he spares it, and forsakes it not; but keeps it still within his mouth:
14 *Yet* his food in his bowels is turned, *it is* the gall of asps within him.
15 He has swallowed down riches, and he shall vomit them up again: God shall cast them out of his belly.
16 He shall suck the poison of asps: the viper's tongue shall slay him.
17 He shall not see the rivers, the floods, the brooks of honey and butter.
18 That which he labored for shall he restore, and shall not swallow *it* down: according to *his* substance *shall* the restitution *be*, and he shall not rejoice *therein*.
19 Because he has oppressed *and* has forsaken the poor; *because* he has violently taken away a house which he built not;
20 Surely he shall not feel quietness in his belly, he shall not save of that which he desired.
21 There shall none of his meat be left; therefore shall no man look for his goods.
22 In the fullness of his sufficiency he shall be in distress: every hand of the wicked shall come upon him.
23 ¶ *When* he is about to fill his belly, *God* shall cast the fury of his wrath upon him, and shall rain *it* upon him while he is eating.
24 He shall flee from the iron weapon, *and* the bow of steel shall strike him through.
25 It is drawn, and comes out of the body; yes, the glittering sword comes out of his gall: terrors *are* upon him.
26 All darkness *shall be* hidden in his secret places: a fire not blown shall consume him; it shall go ill with him that is left in his tabernacle.
27 The heaven shall reveal his iniquity; and the earth shall rise up against him.
28 The increase of his house shall depart, *and his goods* shall flow away in the day of his wrath.
29 This *is* the portion of a wicked man from God, and the heritage appointed to him by God.

Job 21

21:1 ¶ But Job answered and said,
2 Hear diligently my speech, and let this be your consolations.
3 Bear with me that I may speak; and after that I have spoken, mock on.
4 As for me, *is* my complaint to man? and if *it were so*, why should not my spirit be troubled?
5 Look *at* me, and be astonished, and lay *your* hand upon *your* mouth.
6 Even when I remember I am afraid, and trembling takes hold on my flesh.
7 ¶ Why do the wicked live, become old, yes, are mighty in power?
8 Their seed is established in their sight with them, and their offspring before their eyes.
9 Their houses *are* safe from fear, neither *is* the rod of God upon them.
10 Their bull breeds, and fails not; their cow calves, and miscarries not her calf.
11 They send forth their little ones like a flock, and their children dance.
12 They take the tambourine and harp, and rejoice at the sound of the organ.
13 They spend their days in wealth, and in a moment go down to the grave.
14 Therefore they say to God, Depart from us; for we desire not the knowledge of your ways.
15 What *is* the Almighty, that we should serve him? and what profit should we have, if we pray to him?
16 Lo, their good *is* not in their hand: the counsel of the wicked is far from me.
17 ¶ How often is the candle of the wicked put out! and *how often* comes their destruction upon them! *God* distributes sorrows in his anger.
18 They are as stubble before the wind, and as chaff that the storm carries away.
19 God lays up his iniquity for his children: he rewards him, and he shall know *it*.
20 His eyes shall see his destruction, and he shall drink of the wrath of the Almighty.
21 For what pleasure *has* he in his house after him, when the number of his months is cut off in the midst?
22 Shall *anyone* teach God knowledge? seeing he judges those that are high.
23 One dies in his full strength, being wholly at ease and quiet.

24 His breasts are full of milk, and his bones are moistened with marrow.
25 And another dies in the bitterness of his soul, and never eats with pleasure.
26 They shall lie down alike in the dust, and the worms shall cover them.
27 ¶ Behold, I know your thoughts, and the devices *which* you wrongfully imagine against me.
28 For you say, Where *is* the house of the prince? and where *are* the dwelling places of the wicked?
29 Have you not asked them that go by the way? and do you not know their signs,
30 That the wicked is reserved to the day of destruction? they shall be brought forth to the day of wrath.
31 Who shall declare his way to his face? and who shall repay him *for what* he has done?
32 Yet shall he be brought to the grave, and shall remain in the tomb.
33 The clods of the valley shall be sweet to him, and every man shall draw after him, as *there were* innumerable before him.
34 How then comfort you me in vain, seeing in your answers there remains falsehood?

Job 22

22:1 ¶ Then Eliphaz the Temanite answered and said,
2 Can a man be profitable to God, as he that is wise may be profitable to himself?
3 *Is it* any pleasure to the Almighty, that you are righteous? or *is it* gain *to him*, that you make your ways perfect?
4 Will he reprove you for fear of you? will he enter with you into judgment?
5 ¶ *Is* not your wickedness great? and your iniquities infinite?
6 For you have taken a pledge from your brother for nothing, and stripped the naked of their clothing.
7 You have not given water to the weary to drink, and you have withheld bread from the hungry.
8 But *as for* the mighty man, he had the earth; and the honorable man dwelt in it.
9 You have sent widows away empty, and the arms of the fatherless have been broken.
10 Therefore snares *are* round about you, and sudden fear troubles you;
11 Or darkness, *that* you cannot see; and *the* abundance of waters covers you.
12 *Is* not God in the height of heaven? and behold the height of the stars, how high they are!
13 And you say, How does God know? can he judge through the dark cloud?
14 Thick clouds *are* a covering to him, that he sees not; and he walks in the circle of heaven.
15 ¶ Have you marked the old way which wicked men have trodden?
16 Which were cut down out of time, whose foundation was overflowed with a flood:
17 Which said to God, Depart from us: and what can the Almighty do for them?
18 Yet he filled their houses with good *things*: but the counsel of the wicked is far from me.
19 The righteous see *it*, and are glad: and the innocent laugh them to scorn.
20 Whereas our substance is not cut down, but the remnant of them the fire consumes.
21 ¶ Acquaint now yourself with him, and be at peace: thereby good shall come to you.
22 Receive, I pray you, the law from his mouth, and lay up his words in your heart.
23 If you return to the Almighty, you shall be built up, you shall put away iniquity far from your tabernacles.
24 Then shall you lay up gold as dust, and the *gold* of Ophir as the stones of the brooks.
25 Yes, the Almighty shall be your defense, and you shall have plenty of silver.
26 For then shall you have your delight in the Almighty, and shall lift up your face to God.
27 You shall make your prayer to him, and he shall hear you, and you shall pay your vows.
28 You shall also decree a thing, and it shall be established unto you: and the light shall shine upon your ways.
29 When *men* are cast down, then you shall say, *There is* lifting up; and he shall save the humble person.
30 He shall deliver the island of the innocent: and it is delivered by the pureness of your hands.

Job 23

23:1 ¶ Then Job answered and said,
2 Even today *is* my complaint bitter: my stroke is heavier than my groaning.
3 Oh that I knew where I might find him! *that* I might come *even* to his seat!
4 I would order *my* cause before him, and fill my mouth with arguments.
5 I would know the words *which* he would answer me, and understand what he would say to me.
6 Will he plead against me with *his* great power? No; but he would put *strength* in me.
7 There the righteous might dispute with him; so should I be delivered forever from my judge.
8 ¶ Behold, I go forward, but he *is* not *there*; and backward, but I cannot perceive him:
9 On the left hand, where he does work, but I cannot behold *him*: he hides himself on the right hand, that I cannot see *him*:
10 But he knows the way that I take: when he has tried me, I shall come forth as gold.
11 My foot has held his steps, his way have I kept, and not declined.
12 Neither have I gone back from the commandment of his lips; I have esteemed the words of his mouth more than my necessary *food*.
13 ¶ But he *is* in one *mind*, and who can turn him? and *what* his soul desires, even *that* he does.

14 For he performs *the thing that is* appointed for me: and many such *things are* with him.
15 Therefore am I troubled at his presence: when I consider, I am afraid of him.
16 For God makes my heart soft, and the Almighty troubles me:
17 Because I was not cut off before the darkness, *neither* has he covered the darkness from my face.

Job 24

24:1 ¶ Why, seeing times are not hidden from the Almighty, do they that know him not see his days?
2 *Some* remove the landmarks; they violently take away flocks, and feed *thereof*.
3 They drive away the donkey of the fatherless, they take the widow's ox for a pledge.
4 They turn the needy out of the way: the poor of the earth hide themselves together.
5 Behold, *as* wild donkeys in the desert, go they forth to their work; rising early for a prey: the wilderness *yields* food for them *and for their* children.
6 They reap *every one* his corn in the field: and they glean the vineyard of the wicked.
7 They cause the naked to lodge without clothing, that *they have* no covering in the cold.
8 They are wet with the showers of the mountains, and embrace the rock for want of a shelter.
9 They pluck the fatherless from the breast, and take a pledge from the poor.
10 They cause *him* to go naked without clothing, and they take away the sheaf *from* the hungry;
11 *Which* make oil within their walls, *and* tread *their* winepresses, and suffer thirst.
12 Men groan from out of the city, and the soul of the wounded cries out: yet God lays not folly *to them*.
13 ¶ They are of those that rebel against the light; they know not the ways thereof, nor remain in the paths thereof.
14 The murderer rising with the light kills the poor and needy, and in the night is as a thief.
15 The eye also of the adulterer waits for the twilight, saying, No eye shall see me: and disguises *his* face.
16 In the dark they dug through houses, *which* they had marked for themselves in the daytime: they know not the light.
17 For the morning *is* to them even as the shadow of death: if *one* knows *them, they are in* the terrors of the shadow of death.
18 ¶ He *is* swift as the waters; their portion is cursed in the earth: he beholds not the way of the vineyards.
19 Drought and heat consume the snow waters: *so does* the grave *those which* have sinned.
20 The womb shall forget him; the worm shall feed sweetly on him; he shall be no more remembered; and wickedness shall be broken as a tree.
21 He evilly feeds *upon* the barren *that* bear not: and does not good to the widow.
22 He draws also the mighty with his power: he rises up, and no *man* is sure of life.
23 *Though* it is given him *to be* in safety, whereon he rests; yet his eyes *are* upon their ways.
24 They are exalted for a little while, but are gone and brought low; they are taken out of the way as all *other*, and cut off as the tops of the ears of corn.
25 And if *it is* not *so* now, who will make me a liar, and make my speech nothing worth?

Job 25

25:1 ¶ Then answered Bildad the Shuhite, and said,
2 Dominion and fear *are* with him, he makes peace in his high places.
3 Is there any number of his armies? and upon whom does not his light arise?
4 How then can man be justified with God? or how can he be clean *that is* born of a woman?
5 Behold even to the moon, and it shines not; yes, the stars are not pure in his sight.
6 How much less man, *that is* a worm? and the son of man, *which is* a worm?

Job 26

26:1 ¶ But Job answered and said,
2 How have you helped *him that is* without power? *how* save you the arm *that has* no strength?
3 How have you counseled *him that has* no wisdom? and *how* have you plentifully declared the thing as it is?
4 To whom have you uttered words? and whose spirit came from you?
5 ¶ Dead *things* are formed from under the waters, and the inhabitants thereof.
6 Hell *is* naked before him, and destruction has no covering.
7 He stretches out the north over the empty place, *and* hangs the earth upon nothing.
8 He binds up the waters in his thick clouds; and the cloud is not broken under them.
9 He holds back the face of his throne, *and* spreads his cloud upon it.
10 He has compassed the waters with bounds, until the day and night come to an end.
11 The pillars of heaven tremble and are astonished at his reproof.
12 He divides the sea with his power, and by his understanding he smites through the proud.
13 By his spirit he has garnished the heavens; his hand has formed the crooked serpent.
14 Lo, these *are* parts of his ways: but how little a portion is heard of him? but the thunder of his power who can understand?

Job 27

27:1 ¶ Moreover Job continued his parable, and said,
2 *As* God lives, *who* has taken away my judgment; and the Almighty, *who* has grieved my soul;

3 All the while my breath *is* in me, and the spirit of God *is* in my nostrils;
4 My lips shall not speak wickedness, nor my tongue utter deceit.
5 God forbid that I should justify you: till I die I will not remove my integrity from me.
6 My righteousness I hold fast, and will not let it go my heart shall not reproach *me* so long as I live.
7 ¶ Let my enemy be as the wicked, and he that rises up against me as the unrighteous.
8 For what *is* the hope of the hypocrite, though he has gained, when God takes away his soul?
9 Will God hear his cry when trouble comes upon him?
10 Will he delight himself in the Almighty? will he always call upon God?
11 ¶ I will teach you by the hand of God: *that* which *is* with the Almighty will I not conceal.
12 Behold, all you yourselves have seen *it*; why then are you thus altogether vain?
13 This *is* the portion of a wicked man with God, and the heritage of oppressors, *which* they shall receive from the Almighty.
14 If his children are multiplied, *it is* for the sword: and his offspring shall not be satisfied with bread.
15 Those that remain of him shall be buried in death: and his widows shall not weep.
16 Though he heaps up silver as the dust, and prepares clothing as the clay;
17 He may prepare *it*, but the just shall put *it* on, and the innocent shall divide the silver.
18 He builds his house as a moth, and as a booth *that* the keeper makes.
19 The rich man shall lie down, but he shall not be gathered: he opens his eyes, and he *is* not.
20 Terrors take hold on him as waters, a tempest steals him away in the night.
21 The east wind carries him away, and he departs: and as a storm hurls him out of his place.
22 For *God* shall cast upon him, and not spare: he would hurriedly flee out of his hand.
23 *Men* shall clap their hands at him, and shall hiss him out of his place.

Job 28

28:1 ¶ Surely there is a vein for the silver, and a place for gold *where* they refine *it*.
2 Iron is taken out of the earth, and brass *is* molten *out of* the stone.
3 He sets an end to darkness, and searches out all perfection: the stones of darkness, and the shadow of death.
4 The flood breaks out from the inhabitant; *even the waters* forgotten of the foot: they are dried up, they are gone away from men.
5 *As for* the earth, out of it comes bread: and under it is turned up as it were fire.
6 The stones of it *are* the place of sapphires: and it has dust of gold.
7 *There is* a path which no fowl knows, and which the vulture's eye has not seen:
8 The lion's young have not trodden it, nor the fierce lion passed by it.
9 He puts forth his hand upon the rock; he overturns the mountains by the roots.
10 He cuts out rivers among the rocks; and his eye sees every precious thing.
11 He binds the floods from overflowing; and *the thing that is* hidden brings he forth to light.
12 But where shall wisdom be found? and where *is* the place of understanding?
13 Man knows not the price thereof; neither is it found in the land of the living.
14 ¶ The depth said, It *is* not in me: and the sea said, *It is* not with me.
15 It cannot be gotten for gold, neither shall silver be weighed *for* the price thereof.
16 It cannot be valued with the gold of Ophir, with the precious onyx, or the sapphire.
17 The gold and the crystal cannot equal it: and the exchange of it *shall not be for* jewels of fine gold.
18 No mention shall be made of coral, or of pearls: for the price of wisdom *is* above rubies.
19 The topaz of Ethiopia shall not equal it, neither shall it be valued with pure gold.
20 ¶ *From* where then comes wisdom? and where *is* the place of understanding?
21 Seeing it is hidden from the eyes of all living, and *kept* concealed from the fowls of the air.
22 Destruction and death say, We have heard the fame thereof with our ears.
23 God understands the way thereof, and he knows the place thereof.
24 For he looks to the ends of the earth, *and* sees under the whole heaven;
25 To make the weight for the winds; and he weighs the waters by measure.
26 When he made a decree for the rain, and a way for the lightning of the thunder:
27 Then did he see it, and declare it; he prepared it, yes, and searched it out.
28 And to man he said, Behold, the fear of the Lord, that *is* wisdom; and to depart from evil *is* understanding.

Job 29

29:1 ¶ Moreover Job continued his parable, and said,
2 Oh that I were as *in* months past, as *in* the days *when* God preserved me;
3 When his candle shone upon my head, *and when* by his light I walked *through* darkness;
4 As I was in the days of my youth, when the secret of God *was* upon my tabernacle;
5 When the Almighty *was* yet with me, *when* my children *were* about me;
6 When I washed my steps with butter, and the rock poured me out rivers of oil;

Job 29

7 ¶ When I went out to the gate through the city, *when* I prepared my seat in the street!
8 The young men saw me, and hid themselves: and the aged arose, *and* stood up.
9 The princes refrained talking, and laid *their* hand on their mouth.
10 The nobles held their peace, and their tongue clung to the roof of their mouth.
11 When the ear heard *me*, then it blessed me; and when the eye saw *me*, it gave witness to me:
12 Because I delivered the poor that cried, and the fatherless, and *him that had* none to help him.
13 The blessing of him that was ready to perish came upon me: and I caused the widow's heart to sing for joy.
14 I put on righteousness, and it clothed me: my judgment *was* as a robe and a diadem.
15 I was eyes to the blind, and feet *was* I to the lame.
16 I *was* a father to the poor: and the cause *which* I knew not I searched out.
17 And I broke the jaws of the wicked, and plucked the spoil out of his teeth.
18 ¶ Then I said, I shall die in my nest, and I shall multiply *my* days as the sand.
19 My root *was* spread out by the waters, and the dew lay all night upon my branch.
20 My glory *was* fresh in me, and my bow was renewed in my hand.
21 Unto me *men* gave ear, and waited, and kept silence at my counsel.
22 After my words they spoke not again; and my speech dropped upon them.
23 And they waited for me as for the rain; and they opened their mouth wide *as* for the latter rain.
24 *If* I laughed on them, they believed *it* not; and the light of my countenance they cast not down.
25 I chose out their way, and sat *as* chief, and dwelt as a king in the army, as one *that* comforts the mourners.

Job 30

30:1 ¶ But now *they that are* younger than I have me in derision, whose fathers I would have disdained to have set with the dogs of my flock.
2 Yes, whereto *might* the strength of their hands *profit* me, in whom old age has perished?
3 For want and famine *they were* solitary; fleeing into the wilderness in former time desolate and waste.
4 Who cut up mallows by the bushes, and juniper roots *for* their food.
5 They were driven forth from among *men*, (they cried after them as *after* a thief;)
6 To dwell in the cliffs of the valleys, *in* caves of the earth, and *in* the rocks.
7 Among the bushes they brayed; under the nettles they were gathered together.
8 *They were* children of fools, yes, children of base men: they were viler than the earth.
9 And now am I their song, yes, I am their byword.
10 They abhor me, they flee far from me, and spare not to spit in my face.
11 Because he has loosed my cord, and afflicted me, they have also let loose the bridle before me.
12 Upon *my* right *hand* rise the youth; they push away my feet, and they raise up against me the ways of their destruction.
13 They mar my path, they set forward my calamity, they have no helper.
14 They came *upon me* as a wide breaking in *of waters*: in the desolation they rolled themselves *upon me*.
15 ¶ Terrors are turned on me: they pursue my soul as the wind: and my welfare passes away as a cloud.
16 And now my soul is poured out upon me; the days of affliction have taken hold upon me.
17 My bones are pierced in me in the night season: and my sinews take no rest.
18 By the great force *of my disease* is my garment changed: it binds me about as the collar of my coat.
19 He has cast me into the mire, and I have become like dust and ashes.
20 I cry to you, and you do not hear me: I stand up, and you regard me *not*.
21 You have become cruel to me: with your strong hand you oppose yourself against me.
22 You lift me up to the wind; you cause me to ride *upon it*, and dissolve my substance.
23 For I know *that* you will bring me *to* death, and *to* the house appointed for all living.
24 However he will not stretch out *his* hand to the grave, though they cry in his destruction.
25 Did not I weep for him that was in trouble? was *not* my soul grieved for the poor?
26 When I looked for good, then evil came *unto me*: and when I waited for light, there came darkness.
27 My bowels boiled, and rested not: the days of affliction confronted me.
28 I went mourning without the sun: I stood up, *and* I cried in the congregation.
29 I am a brother to dragons, and a companion to owls.
30 My skin is black upon me, and my bones are burned with heat.
31 My harp also is *turned* to mourning, and my organ into the voice of them that weep.

Job 31

31:1 ¶ I made a covenant with my eyes; why then should I think upon a maiden?
2 For what portion of God *is there* from above? and *what* inheritance of the Almighty from on high?
3 *Is* not destruction to the wicked? and a strange *punishment* to the workers of iniquity?
4 Does not he see my ways, and count all my steps?
5 If I have walked with vanity, or if my foot has hurried to deceit;
6 Let me be weighed in an even balance, that God may know my integrity.

7 If my step has turned out of the way, and my heart walked after my eyes, and if any blot has clung to my hands;
8 *Then* let me sow, and let another eat; yes, let my offspring be rooted out.
9 ¶ If my heart has been deceived by a woman, or *if* I have laid wait at my neighbor's door;
10 *Then* let my wife grind to another, and let others bow down upon her.
11 For this *is* a heinous crime; yes, it *is* an iniquity *to be punished by* the judges.
12 For it *is* a fire *that* consumes to destruction, and would root out all my increase.
13 If I did despise the cause of my manservant or of my maidservant, when they contended with me;
14 What then shall I do when God rises up? and when he visits, what shall I answer him?
15 Did not he that made me in the womb make him? and did not one fashion us in the womb?
16 ¶ If I have withheld the poor from *their* desire, or have caused the eyes of the widow to fail;
17 Or have eaten my morsel myself alone, and the fatherless has not eaten thereof;
18 (For from my youth he was brought up with me, as *with* a father, and I have guided her from my mother's womb;)
19 If I have seen any perish for want of clothing, or any poor without covering;
20 If his loins have not blessed me, and *if* he were *not* warmed with the fleece of my sheep;
21 If I have lifted up my hand against the fatherless, when I saw my help in the gate:
22 *Then* let my arm fall from my shoulder blade, and my arm be broken from the bone.
23 For destruction *from* God *was* a terror to me, and by reason of his highness I could not endure.
24 ¶ If I have made gold my hope, or have said to the fine gold, *You are* my confidence;
25 If I rejoiced because my wealth *was* great, and because my hand had gotten much;
26 If I beheld the sun when it shined, or the moon walking *in* brightness;
27 And my heart has been secretly enticed, or my mouth has kissed my hand:
28 This also *was* an iniquity *to be punished by* the judge: for I should have denied the God *that is* above.
29 If I rejoiced at the destruction of him that hated me, or lifted up myself when evil found him:
30 Neither have I given my mouth to sin by wishing a curse to his soul.
31 If the men of my tabernacle said not, Oh that we had of his flesh! we cannot be satisfied.
32 The stranger did not lodge in the street: *but* I opened my doors to the traveler.
33 ¶ If I covered my transgressions as Adam, by hiding my iniquity in my bosom:
34 Did I fear a great multitude, or did the contempt of families terrify me, that I kept silence, *and* went not out of the door?
35 Oh that one would hear me! behold, my desire *is, that* the Almighty would answer me, and *that* my adversary had written a book.
36 Surely I would take it upon my shoulder, *and* bind it *as* a crown to me.
37 I would declare to him the number of my steps; as a prince would I go near to him.
38 If my land cry against me, or that the furrows likewise thereof complain;
39 If I have eaten the fruits thereof without money, or have caused the owners thereof to lose their life:
40 Let thistles grow instead of wheat, and weeds instead of barley. The words of Job are ended.

Job 32

32:1 ¶ So these three men ceased to answer Job, because he *was* righteous in his own eyes.
2 Then was kindled the wrath of Elihu the son of Barachel the Buzite, of the kindred of Ram: against Job was his wrath kindled, because he justified himself rather than God.
3 Also against his three friends was his wrath kindled, because they had found no answer, and *yet* had condemned Job.
4 Now Elihu had waited till Job had spoken, because they *were* older than he.
5 When Elihu saw that *there was* no answer in the mouth of *these* three men, then his wrath was kindled.
6 ¶ And Elihu the son of Barachel the Buzite answered and said, *I am* young, and you *are* very old; therefore I was afraid, and dared not show you my opinion.
7 I said, Days should speak, and multitude of years should teach wisdom.
8 But *there is* a spirit in man: and the inspiration of the Almighty gives them understanding.
9 Great men are not *always* wise: neither do the aged understand judgment.
10 Therefore I said, Listen to me; I also will show my opinion.
11 Behold, I waited for your words; I gave ear to your reasons, while you searched out what to say.
12 Yes, I attended to you, and, behold, *there was* none of you that convinced Job, *or* that answered his words:
13 Lest you should say, We have found out wisdom: God thrusts him down, not man.
14 Now he has not directed *his* words against me: neither will I answer him with your speeches.
15 ¶ They were amazed, they answered no more: they left off speaking.
16 When I had waited, (for they spoke not, but stood still, *and* answered no more;)
17 *I said*, I will answer also my part, I also will show my opinion.
18 For I am full of words, the spirit within me constrains me.
19 Behold, my belly *is* as wine *which* has no vent; it is ready to burst like new bottles.
20 I will speak, that I may be refreshed: I will open my lips and answer.

21 Let me not, I pray you, accept any man's person, neither let me give flattering titles to man.
22 For I know not to give flattering titles; *in so doing* my maker would soon take me away.

Job 33

33:1 ¶ Wherefore, Job, I pray you, hear my speeches, and listen to all my words.
2 Behold, now I have opened my mouth, my tongue has spoken in my mouth.
3 My words *shall be from* the uprightness of my heart: and my lips shall utter knowledge clearly.
4 The Spirit of God has made me, and the breath of the Almighty has given me life.
5 If you can answer me, set *your words* in order before me, stand up.
6 Behold, I *am* according to your wish in God's stead: I also am formed out of the clay.
7 Behold, my terror shall not make you afraid, neither shall my hand be heavy upon you.
8 ¶ Surely you have spoken in my hearing, and I have heard the voice of *your* words, *saying*,
9 I am clean without transgression, I *am* innocent; neither *is there* iniquity in me.
10 Behold, he finds occasions against me, he counts me for his enemy,
11 He puts my feet in the stocks, he marks all my paths.
12 Behold, *in* this you are not just: I will answer you, that God is greater than man.
13 Why do you strive against him? for he gives not account of any of his matters.
14 ¶ For God speaks once, yes twice, *yet man* perceives it not.
15 In a dream, in a vision of the night, when deep sleep falls upon men, in slumberings upon the bed;
16 Then he opens the ears of men, and seals their instruction,
17 That he may withdraw man *from his* purpose, and hide pride from man.
18 He keeps back his soul from the pit, and his life from perishing by the sword.
19 ¶ He is chastened also with pain upon his bed, and the multitude of his bones with strong *pain*:
20 So that his life abhors bread, and his soul desirable food.
21 His flesh is consumed away, that it cannot be seen; and his bones *that* were not seen stick out.
22 Yes, his soul draws near to the grave, and his life to the destroyers.
23 If there is a messenger with him, an interpreter, one among a thousand, to show to man his uprightness:
24 Then he is gracious to him, and says, Deliver him from going down to the pit: I have found a ransom.
25 His flesh shall be fresher than a child's: he shall return to the days of his youth:
26 He shall pray to God, and he will be favorable to him: and he shall see his face with joy: for he will render to man his righteousness.
27 He looks upon men, and *if any* say, I have sinned, and perverted *that which was* right, and it profited me not;
28 He will deliver his soul from going into the pit, and his life shall see the light.
29 ¶ Lo, all these *things* works God oftentimes with man,
30 To bring back his soul from the pit, to be enlightened with the light of the living.
31 Hear well, O Job, listen to me: hold your peace, and I will speak.
32 If you have anything to say, answer me: speak, for I desire to justify you.
33 If not, listen to me: hold your peace, and I shall teach you wisdom.

Job 34

34:1 ¶ Furthermore Elihu answered and said,
2 Hear my words, O you wise *men*; and give ear to me, you that have knowledge.
3 For the ear tries words, as the mouth tastes meat.
4 Let us choose to us judgment: let us know among ourselves what *is* good.
5 For Job has said, I am righteous: and God has taken away my judgment.
6 Should I lie against my right? my wound *is* incurable without transgression.
7 What man *is* like Job, *who* drinks up scorning like water?
8 Which goes in company with the workers of iniquity, and walks with wicked men.
9 For he has said, It profits a man nothing that he should delight himself with God.
10 ¶ Therefore listen to me, you men of understanding: far be it from God, *that he should do* wickedness; and *from* the Almighty, *that he should commit* iniquity.
11 For the work of a man shall he render unto him, and cause every man to find according to *his* ways.
12 Yes, surely God will not do wickedly, neither will the Almighty pervert judgment.
13 Who has given him a charge over the earth? or who has disposed the whole world?
14 If he set his heart upon man, *if* he gather to himself his spirit and his breath;
15 All flesh shall perish together, and man shall turn again to dust.
16 ¶ If now *you have* understanding, hear this: listen to the voice of my words.
17 Shall even he that hates right govern? and will you condemn him that is most just?
18 *Is it fit* to say to a king, *You are* wicked? *and* to princes, *You are* ungodly?
19 *How much less to him* that accepts not the persons of princes, nor regards the rich more than the poor? for they all *are* the work of his hands.

20 In a moment shall they die, and the people shall be troubled at midnight, and pass away: and the mighty shall be taken away without hand.
21 For his eyes *are* upon the ways of man, and he sees all his goings.
22 *There is* no darkness, nor shadow of death, where the workers of iniquity may hide themselves.
23 For he will not lay upon man more *than right*; that he should enter into judgment with God.
24 He shall break in pieces mighty men without number, and set others in their place.
25 Therefore he knows their works, and he overturns *them* in the night, so that they are destroyed.
26 He strikes them as wicked men in the open sight of others;
27 Because they turned back from him, and would not consider any of his ways:
28 So that they cause the cry of the poor to come unto him, and he hears the cry of the afflicted.
29 When he gives quietness, who then can make trouble? and when he hides *his* face, who then can behold him? whether *it is done* against a nation, or against a man only:
30 That the hypocrite reign not, lest the people be ensnared.
31 ¶ Surely it is fitting to be said unto God, I have borne *chastisement*, I will not offend *any more*:
32 *That which* I see not teach you me: if I have done iniquity, I will do no more.
33 *Should it be* according to your mind? he will recompense it, whether you refuse, or whether you choose; and not I: therefore speak what you know.
34 Let men of understanding tell me, and let a wise man listen to me.
35 Job has spoken without knowledge, and his words *were* without wisdom.
36 My desire *is that* Job may be tried to the end because of *his* answers for wicked men.
37 For he adds rebellion to his sin, he claps *his hands* among us, and multiplies his words against God.

Job 35

35:1 ¶ Elihu spoke moreover, and said,
2 Think you this to be right, *that* you said, My righteousness *is* more than God's?
3 For you said, What advantage will it be to you? *and*, What profit shall I have, *if I am cleansed* from my sin?
4 I will answer you, and your companions with you.
5 Look to the heavens, and see; and behold the clouds *which* are higher than you.
6 If you sin, what do you against him? or *if* your transgressions are multiplied, what do you unto him?
7 If you are righteous, what give you him? or what receives he of your hand?
8 Your wickedness *may hurt* a man as you *are*; and your righteousness *may profit* the son of man.
9 ¶ By reason of the multitude of oppressions they make *the oppressed* to cry: they cry out by reason of the arm of the mighty.

10 But none says, Where *is* God my maker, who gives songs in the night;
11 Who teaches us more than the beasts of the earth, and makes us wiser than the fowls of heaven?
12 There they cry, but none gives answer, because of the pride of evil men.
13 Surely God will not hear vanity, neither will the Almighty regard it.
14 ¶ Although you say you shall not see him, *yet* judgment *is* before him; therefore trust you in him.
15 But now, because *it is* not *so*, he has visited in his anger; yet he knows *it* not in great extremity:
16 Therefore does Job open his mouth in vain; he multiplies words without knowledge.

Job 36

36:1 ¶ Elihu also proceeded, and said,
2 Surround me a little, and I will show you that *I have* yet to speak on God's behalf.
3 I will fetch my knowledge from afar, and will ascribe righteousness to my Maker.
4 For truly my words *shall* not *be* false: he that is perfect in knowledge *is* with you.
5 ¶ Behold, God *is* mighty, and despises not *any:* he is mighty in strength *and* wisdom.
6 He preserves not the life of the wicked: but gives right to the poor.
7 He withdraws not his eyes from the righteous: but with kings *are they* on the throne; yes, he does establish them forever, and they are exalted.
8 And if *they are* bound in fetters, *and* are held in cords of affliction;
9 Then he shows them their work, and their transgressions that they have exceeded.
10 He opens also their ear to discipline, and commands that they return from iniquity.
11 If they obey and serve *him*, they shall spend their days in prosperity, and their years in pleasures.
12 But if they obey not, they shall perish by the sword, and they shall die without knowledge.
13 But the hypocrites in heart heap up wrath: they cry not when he binds them.
14 They die in youth, and their life *is* among the unclean.
15 ¶ He delivers the poor in his affliction, and opens their ears in oppression.
16 Even so would he have removed you out of the strait *into* a broad place, where *there is* no narrow place; and that which should be set on your table *should be* full of fatness.
17 But you have fulfilled the judgment of the wicked: judgment and justice take hold *on you*.
18 Because *there is* wrath, *beware* lest he takes you away with *his* stroke: then a great ransom cannot deliver you.
19 Will he esteem your riches? *no*, not gold, nor all the forces of strength.

Job 36

20 Desire not the night, when people are cut off in their place.
21 Take heed, regard not iniquity: for this have you chosen rather than affliction.
22 Behold, God exalts by his power: who teaches like him?
23 Who has enjoined him his way? or who can say, You have worked iniquity?
24 ¶ Remember that you magnify his work, which men behold.
25 Every man may see it; man may behold *it* afar off.
26 Behold, God *is* great, and we know *him* not, neither can the number of his years be searched out.
27 For he makes small the drops of water: they pour down rain according to the vapor thereof:
28 Which the clouds do drop *and* distill upon man abundantly.
29 Also can *any* understand the spreading of the clouds, *or* the noise of his tabernacle?
30 Behold, he spreads his light upon it, and covers the bottom of the sea.
31 For by them judges he the people; he gives food in abundance.
32 With clouds he covers the light; and commands it *not to shine* by *the cloud* that comes between.
33 The noise thereof shows concerning it, the cattle also concerning the vapor.

Job 37

37:1 ¶ At this also my heart trembles, and is moved out of his place.
2 Hear attentively the noise of his voice, and the sound *that* goes out of his mouth.
3 He directs it under the whole heaven, and his lightning to the ends of the earth.
4 After it a voice roars: he thunders with the voice of his excellency; and he will not stay them when his voice is heard.
5 God thunders marvelously with his voice; great things does he, which we cannot comprehend.
6 ¶ For he says to the snow, Be you *on* the earth; likewise to the small rain, and to the great rain of his strength.
7 He seals up the hand of every man; that all men may know his work.
8 Then the beasts go into dens, and remain in their places.
9 Out of the south comes the whirlwind: and cold out of the north.
10 By the breath of God frost is given: and the breadth of the waters is straitened.
11 Also by watering he wearies the thick cloud: he scatters his bright cloud:
12 And it is turned round about by his counsels: that they may do whatever he commands them upon the face of the world in the earth.
13 He causes it to come, whether for correction, or for his land, or for mercy.

14 ¶ Listen to this, O Job: stand still, and consider the wondrous works of God.
15 Do you know when God disposed them, and caused the light of his cloud to shine?
16 Do you know the balancing of the clouds, the wondrous works of him which is perfect in knowledge?
17 How your garments *are* warm, when he quiets the earth by the south *wind*?
18 Have you with him spread out the sky, *which is* strong, *and* as a molten looking glass?
19 Teach us what we shall say to him; *for* we cannot order *our speech* by reason of darkness.
20 Shall it be told him that I speak? if a man speaks, surely he shall be swallowed up.
21 ¶ And now *men* see not the bright light which *is* in the clouds: but the wind passes, and cleans them.
22 Fair weather comes out of the north: with God *is* awesome majesty.
23 *Touching* the Almighty, we cannot find him out: *he is* excellent in power, and in judgment, and in plenty of justice: he will not afflict.
24 Men do therefore fear him: he respects not any *that are* wise of heart.

Job 38

38:1 ¶ Then Yahweh answered Job out of the whirlwind, and said,
2 Who *is* this that darkens counsel by words without knowledge?
3 Gird up now your loins like a man; for I will demand of you, and answer you me.
4 ¶ Where were you when I laid the foundations of the earth? declare, if you have understanding.
5 Who has laid the measures thereof, if you know? or who has stretched the line upon it?
6 Whereupon are the foundations thereof fastened? or who laid the corner stone thereof;
7 When the morning stars sang together, and all the sons of God shouted for joy?
8 Or *who* shut up the sea with doors, when it broke forth, *as if* it had issued out of the womb?
9 When I made the cloud the garment thereof, and thick darkness a swaddling band for it,
10 And broke up for it my decreed *place*, and set bars and doors,
11 And said, This far shall you come, but no further: and here shall your proud waves be stayed?
12 ¶ Have you commanded the morning since your days; *and* caused the dayspring to know his place;
13 That it might take hold of the ends of the earth, that the wicked might be shaken out of it?
14 It is turned as clay *to* the seal; and they stand as a garment.
15 And from the wicked their light is withheld, and the high arm shall be broken.
16 Have you entered into the springs of the sea? or have you walked in the search of the depth?

17 Have the gates of death been opened unto you? or have you seen the doors of the shadow of death?
18 Have you perceived the breadth of the earth? declare if you know it all.
19 Where *is* the way *where* light dwells? and *as for* darkness, where *is* the place thereof,
20 That you should take it to the bound thereof, and that you should know the paths *to* the house thereof?
21 Know you *it*, because you were then born? or *because* the number of your days *is* great?
22 Have you entered into the treasuries of the snow? or have you seen the treasuries of the hail,
23 Which I have reserved against the time of trouble, against the day of battle and war?
24 By what way is the light parted, *which* scatters the east wind upon the earth?
25 ¶ Who has divided a watercourse for the overflowing of waters, or a way for the lightning of thunder;
26 To cause it to rain on the earth, *where* no man *is; on* the wilderness, wherein *there is* no man;
27 To satisfy the desolate and waste *ground*; and to cause the bud of the tender herb to spring forth?
28 Has the rain a father? or who has begotten the drops of dew?
29 Out of whose womb came the ice? and the gray frost of heaven, who has begotten it?
30 The waters are hidden as *with* a stone, and the face of the deep is frozen.
31 Can you bind the sweet influences of Pleiades, or loose the bands of Orion?
32 Can you bring forth Mazzaroth in his season? or can you guide Arcturus with his sons?
33 Know you the ordinances of heaven? can you set the dominion thereof in the earth?
34 Can you lift up your voice to the clouds, that abundance of waters may cover you?
35 Can you send lightnings, that they may go, and say to you, Here we *are*?
36 Who has put wisdom in the inward parts? or who has given understanding to the heart?
37 Who can number the clouds in wisdom? or who can stay the bottles of heaven,
38 When the dust grows into hardness, and the clods stick fast together?
39 Will you hunt the prey for the lion? or fill the appetite of the young lions,
40 When they crouch in *their* dens, *and* sit in the covert to lie in wait?
41 Who provides for the raven his food? when his young ones cry to God, they wander for lack of food.

Job 39

39:1 ¶ Know you the time when the wild goats of the rock bring forth? *or* can you mark when the does do calve?
2 Can you number the months *that* they fulfill? or know you the time when they bring forth?
3 They bow themselves, they bring forth their young ones, they cast out their sorrows.
4 Their young ones are in good health, they grow up with corn; they go forth, and return not to them.
5 Who has sent out the wild donkey free? or who has loosed the bands of the wild donkey?
6 Whose house I have made the wilderness, and the barren land his dwellings.
7 He scorns the multitude of the city, neither regards he the crying of the driver.
8 The range of the mountains *is* his pasture, and he searches after every green thing.
9 Will the unicorn be willing to serve you, or lodge by your crib?
10 Can you bind the unicorn with his band in the furrow? or will he till the valleys after you?
11 Will you trust him, because his strength *is* great? or will you leave your labor to him?
12 Will you believe him, that he will bring home your seed, and gather *it into* your barn?
13 ¶ *Gave you* the goodly wings to the peacocks? or wings and feathers to the ostrich?
14 Which leaves her eggs in the earth, and warms them in dust,
15 And forgets that the foot may crush them, or that the wild beast may break them.
16 She is hardened against her young ones, as though *they were* not hers: her labor is in vain without fear;
17 Because God has deprived her of wisdom, neither has he imparted to her understanding.
18 When she lifts up herself on high, she scorns the horse and his rider.
19 ¶ Have you given the horse strength? have you clothed his neck with thunder?
20 Can you make him afraid as a grasshopper? the glory of his nostrils *is* terrible.
21 He paws in the valley, and rejoices in *his* strength: he goes on to meet the armed men.
22 He mocks at fear, and is not frightened; neither turns he back from the sword.
23 The quiver rattles against him, the glittering spear and the shield.
24 He swallows the ground with fierceness and rage: neither believes he that *it is* the sound of the trumpet.
25 He said among the trumpets, Ha, ha; and he smells the battle afar off, the thunder of the captains, and the shouting.
26 ¶ Does the hawk fly by your wisdom, *and* stretch her wings toward the south?
27 Does the eagle mount up at your command, and make her nest on high?
28 She dwells and remains on the rock, upon the crag of the rock, and the strong place.
29 From there she seeks the prey, *and* her eyes behold afar off.
30 Her young ones also suck up blood: and where the slain *are*, there *is* she.

Job 40

40:1 ¶ Moreover Yahweh answered Job, and said,
2 Shall he that contends with the Almighty instruct *him*? he that reproves God, let him answer it.
3 Then Job answered Yahweh, and said,
4 Behold, I am vile; what shall I answer you? I will lay my hand upon my mouth.
5 Once have I spoken; but I will not answer: yes, twice; but I will proceed no further.
6 ¶ Then answered Yahweh to Job out of the whirlwind, and said,
7 Gird up your loins now like a man: I will demand of you, and declare you unto me.
8 Will you also annul my judgment? will you condemn me, that you may be righteous?
9 Have you an arm like God? or can you thunder with a voice like him?
10 Deck yourself now *with* majesty and excellency; and array yourself with glory and beauty.
11 Cast abroad the rage of your wrath: and behold every one *that is* proud, and abase him.
12 Look on every one *that is* proud, *and* bring him low; and tread down the wicked in their place.
13 Hide them in the dust together; *and* bind their faces in secret.
14 Then will I also confess to you that your own right hand can save you.
15 ¶ Behold now behemoth, which I made with you; he eats grass as an ox.
16 Lo now, his strength *is* in his loins, and his force *is* in the muscle of his belly.
17 He moves his tail like a cedar: the sinews of his thighs are wrapped together.
18 His bones *are as* strong pieces of brass; his bones *are* like bars of iron.
19 He *is* the chief of the ways of God: he that made him can make his sword to approach *unto him*.
20 Surely the mountains bring him forth food, where all the beasts of the field play.
21 He lies under the shady trees, in the covert of the reed, and mire.
22 The shady trees cover him *with* their shadow; the willows of the brook compass him about.
23 Behold, he drinks up a river, *and* hastes not: he trusts that he can draw up *the* Jordan into his mouth.
24 He takes it with his eyes: *his* nose pierces through snares.

Job 41

41:1 ¶ Can you draw out leviathan with a hook? or his tongue with a cord *which* you let down?
2 Can you put a hook into his nose? or bore his jaw through with a thorn?
3 Will he make many supplications to you? will he speak soft *words* to you?
4 Will he make a covenant with you? will you take him for a servant forever?
5 Will you play with him as *with* a bird? or will you bind him for your maidens?
6 Shall the companions make a banquet of him? shall they part him among the merchants?
7 Can you fill his skin with barbed irons? or his head with fish spears?
8 Lay your hand upon him, remember the battle, do no more.
9 Behold, the hope of him is in vain: shall not *one* be cast down even at the sight of him?
10 None *is so* fierce that dare stir him up: who then is able to stand before me?
11 ¶ Who has preceded me, that I should repay *him*? whatever *is* under the whole heaven is mine.
12 I will not conceal his parts, nor his power, nor his comely proportion.
13 Who can uncover the face of his garment? *or* who can come *to him* with his double bridle?
14 Who can open the doors of his face? his teeth *are* terrible round about.
15 *His* scales *are his* pride, shut up together *as with* a close seal.
16 One is so near to another, that no air can come between them.
17 They are joined one to another, they stick together, that they cannot be parted.
18 By his sneezing a light does shine, and his eyes *are* like the eyelids of the morning.
19 Out of his mouth go burning lamps, *and* sparks of fire leap out.
20 Out of his nostrils goes smoke, as *out* of a seething pot or caldron.
21 His breath kindles coals, and a flame goes out of his mouth.
22 In his neck remains strength, and sorrow is turned into joy before him.
23 The flakes of his flesh are joined together: they are firm in themselves; they cannot be moved.
24 His heart is as firm as a stone; yes, as hard as a piece of the lower *millstone*.
25 When he raises up himself, the mighty are afraid: by reason of breakings they purify themselves.
26 The sword of him that lays at him cannot hold: the spear, the dart, nor the habergeon.
27 He esteems iron as straw, *and* brass as rotten wood.
28 The arrow cannot make him flee: sling stones are turned with him into stubble.
29 Darts are counted as stubble: he laughs at the shaking of a spear.
30 Sharp stones *are* under him: he spreads sharp pointed things upon the mire.
31 He makes the deep to boil like a pot: he makes the sea like a pot of ointment.
32 He makes a path to shine after him; *one* would think the deep *to be* gray.
33 Upon earth there is not his like, who is made without fear.

34 He beholds all high *things*: he *is* a king over all the children of pride.

Job 42

42:1 ¶ Then Job answered Yahweh, and said,
2 I know that you can do every *thing*, and *that* no thought can be withheld from you.
3 Who *is* he that hides counsel without knowledge? therefore have I uttered that I understood not; things too wonderful for me, which I knew not.
4 Hear, I beseech you, and I will speak: I will demand of you, and declare you unto me.
5 I have heard of you by the hearing of the ear: but now my eye sees you.
6 Therefore I abhor *myself*, and repent in dust and ashes
7 ¶ And it was *so*, that after Yahweh had spoken these words to Job, Yahweh said to Eliphaz the Temanite, My wrath is kindled against you, and against your two friends: for you have not spoken of me *the thing that is* right, as my servant Job *has*.
8 Therefore take to you now seven bullocks and seven rams, and go to my servant Job, and offer up for yourselves a burnt offering; and my servant Job shall pray for you: for him will I accept: lest I deal with you *after your* folly, in that you have not spoken of me *the thing which is* right, like my servant Job.
9 So Eliphaz the Temanite and Bildad the Shuhite and Zophar the Naamathite went, and did according as Yahweh commanded them: Yahweh also accepted Job.
10 ¶ And Yahweh returned the captivity of Job, when he prayed for his friends: also Yahweh gave Job twice as much as he had before.
11 Then came there to him all his brothers, and all his sisters, and all they that had been of his acquaintance before, and did eat bread with him in his house: and they lamented *with* him, and comforted him over all the evil that Yahweh had brought upon him: every man also gave him a piece of money, and every one an earring of gold.
12 So Yahweh blessed the latter end of Job more than his beginning: for he had fourteen thousand sheep, and six thousand camels, and a thousand yoke of oxen, and a thousand she donkeys.
13 He had also seven sons and three daughters.
14 And he called the name of the first, Jemima; and the name of the second, Kezia; and the name of the third, Kerenhappuch.
15 And in all the land were no women found *so* fair as the daughters of Job: and their father gave them an inheritance among their brothers.
16 After this lived Job a hundred and forty years, and saw his sons, and his sons' sons, *even* four generations.
17 So Job died, *being* old and full of days.

Psalms

Psalms 1

1:1 ¶ Blessed *is* the man that walks not in the counsel of the ungodly, nor stands in the way of sinners, nor sits in the seat of the scornful.
2 But his delight *is* in the law of Yahweh; and in his law does he meditate day and night.
3 And he shall be like a tree planted by the rivers of water, that brings forth his fruit in his season; his leaf also shall not wither; and whatever he does shall prosper.
4 ¶ The ungodly *are* not so: but *are* like the chaff which the wind drives away.
5 Therefore the ungodly shall not stand in the judgment, nor sinners in the congregation of the righteous.
6 For Yahweh knows the way of the righteous: but the way of the ungodly shall perish.

Psalms 2

2:1 ¶ Why do the heathen rage, and the people imagine a vain thing?
2 The kings of the earth set themselves, and the rulers take counsel together, against Yahweh, and against his anointed, *saying*,
3 Let us break their bands apart, and cast away their cords from us.
4 He that sits in the heavens shall laugh: the Lord shall have them in derision.
5 Then shall he speak to them in his wrath, and trouble them in his great displeasure.
6 Yet have I set my king upon my holy hill of Zion.
7 ¶ I will declare the decree: Yahweh has said to me, You *are* my Son; this day have I begotten you.
8 Ask of me, and I shall give *you* the heathen *for* your inheritance, and the utmost parts of the earth *for* your possession.
9 You shall break them with a rod of iron; you shall dash them in pieces like a potter's vessel.
10 ¶ Be wise now therefore, O you kings: be instructed, you judges of the earth.
11 Serve Yahweh with fear, and rejoice with trembling.
12 Kiss the Son, lest he be angry, and you perish *from* the way, when his wrath is kindled but a little. Blessed *are* all they that put their trust in him.

Psalms 3

3:1 ¶ <<A Psalm of David, when he fled from Absalom his son.>> Yahweh, how are they increased that trouble me! many *are* they that rise up against me.
2 Many *there are* which say of my soul, *There is* no help for him in God. Selah.
3 But you, O Yahweh, *are* a shield for me; my glory, and the lifter up of my head.

Psalms 3

4 ¶ I cried unto Yahweh with my voice, and he heard me out of his holy hill. Selah.
5 I laid me down and slept; I awoke; for Yahweh sustained me.
6 I will not be afraid of ten thousands of people, that have set *themselves* against me round about.
7 Arise, O Yahweh; save me, O my God: for you have smitten all my enemies *upon* the cheek bone; you have broken the teeth of the ungodly.
8 Salvation *belongs* unto Yahweh: your blessing *is* upon your people. Selah.

Psalms 4

4:1 ¶ <<To the chief Musician on Neginoth, A Psalm of David.>> Hear me when I call, O God of my righteousness: you have enlarged me *when I was* in distress; have mercy upon me, and hear my prayer.
2 O you sons of men, how long *will you turn* my glory into shame? *how long* will you love vanity, *and* seek after lies? Selah.
3 But know that Yahweh has set apart him that is godly for himself: Yahweh will hear when I call unto him.
4 Stand in awe, and sin not: commune with your own heart upon your bed, and be still. Selah.
5 Offer the sacrifices of righteousness, and put your trust in Yahweh.
6 ¶ *There are* many that say, Who will show us *any* good? Yahweh, lift you up the light of your countenance upon us.
7 You have put gladness in my heart, more than in the time *that* their corn and their *new* wine increased.
8 I will both lay me down in peace, and sleep: for you, Yahweh, only make me dwell in safety.

Psalms 5

5:1 ¶ <<To the chief Musician upon Nehiloth, A Psalm of David.>> Give ear to my words, O Yahweh, consider my meditation.
2 Listen to the voice of my cry, my King, and my God: for unto you will I pray.
3 My voice shall you hear in the morning, O Yahweh; in the morning will I direct *my prayer* unto you, and will look up.
4 For you *are* not a God that has pleasure in wickedness: neither shall evil dwell with you.
5 The foolish shall not stand in your sight: you hate all workers of iniquity.
6 You shall destroy them that speak lies: Yahweh will abhor the bloody and deceitful man.
7 ¶ But as for me, I will come *into* your house in the multitude of your mercy: *and* in your fear will I worship toward your holy temple.
8 Lead me, O Yahweh, in your righteousness because of my enemies; make your way straight before my face.
9 For *there is* no faithfulness in their mouth; their inward part *is* great wickedness; their throat *is* an open sepulcher; they flatter with their tongue.
10 Destroy you them, O God; let them fall by their own counsels; cast them out in the multitude of their transgressions; for they have rebelled against you.
11 But let all those that put their trust in you rejoice: let them ever shout for joy, because you defend them: let them also that love your name be joyful in you.
12 For you, Yahweh, will bless the righteous; with favor will you compass him as *with* a shield.

Psalms 6

6:1 ¶ <<To the chief Musician on Neginoth upon Sheminith, A Psalm of David.>> O Yahweh, rebuke me not in your anger, neither chasten me in your hot displeasure.
2 Have mercy upon me, O Yahweh; for I *am* weak: O Yahweh, heal me; for my bones are troubled.
3 My soul is also greatly troubled: but you, O Yahweh, how long?
4 Return, O Yahweh, deliver my soul: oh save me for your mercies' sake.
5 For in death *there is* no remembrance of you: in the grave who shall give you thanks?
6 I am weary with my groaning; all the night make I my bed to swim; I water my couch with my tears.
7 My eye is consumed because of grief; it grows old because of all my enemies.
8 ¶ Depart from me, all you workers of iniquity; for Yahweh has heard the voice of my weeping.
9 Yahweh has heard my supplication; Yahweh will receive my prayer.
10 Let all my enemies be ashamed and greatly troubled: let them return *and* be ashamed suddenly.

Psalms 7

7:1 ¶ <<Shiggaion of David, which he sang unto Yahweh, concerning the words of Cush the Benjamite.>> O Yahweh my God, in you do I put my trust: save me from all them that persecute me, and deliver me:
2 Lest they tear my soul like a lion, tearing *it* in pieces, while *there is* none to deliver.
3 O Yahweh my God, if I have done this; if there is iniquity in my hands;
4 If I have rewarded evil unto him that was at peace with me; (yes, I have delivered him that without cause is my enemy:)
5 Let the enemy persecute my soul, and take *it*; yes, let him tread down my life upon the earth, and lay my honor in the dust. Selah.
6 Arise, O Yahweh, in your anger, lift up yourself because of the rage of my enemies: and awake for me *to* the judgment *that* you have commanded.
7 So shall the congregation of the people compass you about: for their sakes therefore return you on high.
8 Yahweh shall judge the people: judge me, O Yahweh, according to my righteousness, and according to my integrity *that is* in me.

9 Oh let the wickedness of the wicked come to an end; but establish the just: for the righteous God tries the hearts and reins.
10 ¶ My defense *is* of God, which saves the upright in heart.
11 God judges the righteous, and God is angry *with the wicked* every day.
12 If he turns not, he will sharpen his sword; he has bent his bow, and made it ready.
13 He has also prepared for him the instruments of death; he ordains his arrows against the persecutors.
14 Behold, he labors with iniquity, and has conceived mischief, and brought forth falsehood.
15 He made a pit, and dug it, and is fallen into the ditch *which* he made.
16 His mischief shall return upon his own head, and his violent dealing shall come down upon his own scalp.
17 I will praise Yahweh according to his righteousness: and will sing praise to the name of Yahweh most high.

Psalms 8

8:1 ¶ <<To the chief Musician upon Gittith, A Psalm of David.>> O Yahweh our Lord, how excellent *is* your name in all the earth! who have set your glory above the heavens.
2 Out of the mouth of babes and sucklings have you ordained strength because of your enemies, that you might still the enemy and the avenger.
3 ¶ When I consider your heavens, the work of your fingers, the moon and the stars, which you have ordained;
4 What is man, that you are mindful of him? and the son of man, that you visit him?
5 For you have made him a little lower than the angels, and have crowned him with glory and honor.
6 You made him to have dominion over the works of your hands; you have put all *things* under his feet:
7 All sheep and oxen, yes, and the beasts of the field;
8 The fowl of the air, and the fish of the sea, *and* whatever passes through the paths of the seas.
9 O Yahweh our Lord, how excellent *is* your name in all the earth!

Psalms 9

9:1 ¶ <<To the chief Musician upon Muthlabben, A Psalm of David.>> I will praise *you*, O Yahweh, with my whole heart; I will show forth all your marvelous works.
2 I will be glad and rejoice in you: I will sing praise to your name, O you most High.
3 When my enemies are turned back, they shall fall and perish at your presence.
4 For you have maintained my right and my cause; you sat in the throne judging right.
5 You have rebuked the heathen, you have destroyed the wicked, you have put out their name forever and ever.
6 O you enemy, destructions have come to a perpetual end: and you have destroyed cities; their memorial has perished with them.
7 But Yahweh shall endure forever: he has prepared his throne for judgment.
8 And he shall judge the world in righteousness, he shall minister judgment to the people in uprightness.
9 Yahweh also will be a refuge for the oppressed, a refuge in times of trouble.
10 And they that know your name will put their trust in you: for you, Yahweh, have not forsaken them that seek you.
11 ¶ Sing praises to Yahweh, which dwells in Zion: declare among the people his doings.
12 When he makes inquisition for blood, he remembers them: he forgets not the cry of the humble.
13 Have mercy upon me, O Yahweh; consider my trouble *which I suffer* of them that hate me, you that lift me up from the gates of death:
14 That I may show forth all your praise in the gates of the daughter of Zion: I will rejoice in your salvation.
15 The heathen have sunk down in the pit *that* they made: in the net which they hid is their own foot taken.
16 Yahweh is known *by* the judgment *which* he executes: the wicked is snared in the work of his own hands. Higgaion. Selah.
17 The wicked shall be turned into hell, *and* all the nations that forget God.
18 For the needy shall not always be forgotten: the expectation of the poor shall *not* perish forever.
19 Arise, O Yahweh; let not man prevail: let the heathen be judged in your sight.
20 Put them in fear, O Yahweh: *that* the nations may know themselves *to be but* men. Selah.

Psalms 10

10:1 ¶ Why stand you afar off, O Yahweh? *why* hide you *yourself* in times of trouble?
2 The wicked in *his* pride does persecute the poor: let them be taken in the devices that they have imagined.
3 For the wicked boasts of his heart's desire, and blesses the covetous, *whom* Yahweh abhors.
4 The wicked, through the pride of his countenance, will not seek *after God*: God *is* not in all his thoughts.
5 His ways are always grievous; your judgments *are* far above out of his sight: *as for* all his enemies, he puffs at them.
6 He has said in his heart, I shall not be moved: for *I shall* never *be* in adversity.
7 His mouth is full of cursing and deceit and fraud: under his tongue *is* mischief and vanity.
8 He sits in the lurking places of the villages: in the secret places does he murder the innocent: his eyes are privately set against the poor.
9 He lies in wait secretly as a lion in his den: he lies in wait to catch the poor: he does catch the poor, when he draws him into his net.

10 He crouches, *and* humbles himself, that the poor may fall by his strong ones.
11 He has said in his heart, God has forgotten: he hides his face; he will never see *it*.
12 ¶ Arise, O Yahweh; O God, lift up your hand: forget not the humble.
13 Why does the wicked scorn God? he has said in his heart, You will not require *it*.
14 You have seen *it*; for you behold mischief and spite, to requite *it* with your hand: the poor commits himself to you; you are the helper of the fatherless.
15 Break you the arm of the wicked and the evil *man*: seek out his wickedness *till* you find none.
16 Yahweh *is* King forever and ever: the heathen are perished out of his land.
17 Yahweh, you have heard the desire of the humble: you will prepare their heart, you will cause your ear to hear:
18 To judge the fatherless and the oppressed, that the man of the earth may no more oppress.

Psalms 11

11:1 ¶ <<To the chief Musician, *A Psalm* of David.>> In Yahweh put I my trust: how say you to my soul, Flee *as* a bird to your mountain?
2 For, lo, the wicked bend *their* bow, they make ready their arrow upon the string, that they may privately shoot at the upright in heart.
3 If the foundations are destroyed, what can the righteous do?
4 ¶ Yahweh *is* in his holy temple, Yahweh's throne *is* in heaven: his eyes behold, his eyelids try, the children of men.
5 Yahweh tries the righteous: but the wicked and him that loves violence his soul hates.
6 Upon the wicked he shall rain snares, fire and brimstone, and a horrible tempest: *this shall be* the portion of their cup.
7 For the righteous Yahweh loves righteousness; his countenance does behold the upright.

Psalms 12

12:1 ¶ <<To the chief Musician upon Sheminith, A Psalm of David.>> Help, Yahweh; for the godly man ceases; for the faithful fail from among the children of men.
2 They speak vanity every one with his neighbor: *with* flattering lips *and* with a double heart do they speak.
3 Yahweh shall cut off all flattering lips, *and* the tongue that speaks proud things:
4 Who have said, With our tongue will we prevail; our lips *are* our own: who *is* lord over us?
5 For the oppression of the poor, for the sighing of the needy, now will I arise, says Yahweh; I will set *him* in safety *from him that* puffs at him.
6 The words of Yahweh *are* pure words: *as* silver tried in a furnace of earth, purified seven times.
7 You shall keep them, O Yahweh, you shall preserve them from this generation forever.
8 The wicked walk on every side, when the vilest men are exalted.

Psalms 13

13:1 ¶ <<To the chief Musician, A Psalm of David.>> How long will you forget me, O Yahweh? forever? how long will you hide your face from me?
2 How long shall I take counsel in my soul, *having* sorrow in my heart daily? how long shall my enemy be exalted over me?
3 Consider *and* hear me, O Yahweh my God: lighten my eyes, lest I sleep the *sleep of* death;
4 Lest my enemy says, I have prevailed against him; *and* those that trouble me rejoice when I am moved.
5 But I have trusted in your mercy; my heart shall rejoice in your salvation.
6 I will sing unto Yahweh, because he has dealt bountifully with me.

Psalms 14

14:1 ¶ <<To the chief Musician, *A Psalm* of David.>> The fool has said in his heart, *There is* no God. They are corrupt, they have done abominable works, *there is* none that does good.
2 Yahweh looked down from heaven upon the children of men, to see if there were any that did understand, *and* seek God.
3 They are all gone aside, they are *all* together become filthy: *there is* none that does good, no, not one.
4 ¶ Have all the workers of iniquity no knowledge? who eat up my people *as* they eat bread, and call not upon Yahweh.
5 There were they in great fear: for God *is* in the generation of the righteous.
6 You have shamed the counsel of the poor, because Yahweh *is* his refuge.
7 Oh that the salvation of Israel *were come* out of Zion! when Yahweh brings back the captivity of his people, Jacob shall rejoice, *and* Israel shall be glad.

Psalms 15

15:1 ¶ <<A Psalm of David.>> Yahweh, who shall abide in your tabernacle? who shall dwell in your holy hill?
2 He that walks uprightly, and works righteousness, and speaks the truth in his heart.
3 *He that* backbites not with his tongue, nor does evil to his neighbor, nor takes up a reproach against his neighbor.
4 In whose eyes a vile person is despised; but he honors them that fear Yahweh. *He that* swears to *his own* hurt, and changes not.
5 *He that* puts not out his money to usury, nor takes reward against the innocent. He that does these *things* shall never be moved.

Psalms 16

16:1 ¶ <<Michtam of David.>> Preserve me, O God: for in you do I put my trust.

2 *O my soul*, you have said unto Yahweh, You *are* my Lord: my goodness *extends* not to you;

3 *But* to the saints that *are* in the earth, and *to* the excellent, in whom *is* all my delight.

4 Their sorrows shall be multiplied *that* hurry *after* another *god*: their drink offerings of blood will I not offer, nor take up their names into my lips.

5 Yahweh *is* the portion of my inheritance and of my cup: you maintain my lot.

6 The lines are fallen unto me in pleasant *places*; yes, I have a goodly heritage.

7 I will bless Yahweh, who has given me counsel: my reins also instruct me in the night seasons.

8 ¶ I have set Yahweh always before me: because *he is* at my right hand, I shall not be moved.

9 Therefore my heart is glad, and my glory rejoices: my flesh also shall rest in hope.

10 For you will not leave my soul in hell; neither will you allow your Holy One to see corruption.

11 You will show me the path of life: in your presence *is* fullness of joy; at your right hand *there are* pleasures forevermore.

Psalms 17

17:1 ¶ <<A Prayer of David.>> Hear the right, O Yahweh, attend unto my cry, give ear unto my prayer, *that goes* not out of feigned lips.

2 Let my sentence come forth from your presence; let your eyes behold the things that are equal.

3 You have proved my heart; you have visited *me* in the night; you have tried me, *and* shall find nothing; I have purposed *that* my mouth shall not transgress.

4 Concerning the works of men, by the word of your lips I have kept *me from* the paths of the destroyer.

5 Hold up my goings in your paths, *that* my footsteps slip not.

6 I have called upon you, for you will hear me, O God: incline your ear unto me, *and hear* my speech.

7 Show your marvelous loving kindness, O you that save by your right hand them which put their trust *in you* from those that rise up *against them*.

8 ¶ Keep me as the apple of the eye, hide me under the shadow of your wings,

9 From the wicked that oppress me, *from* my deadly enemies, *who* compass me about.

10 They are enclosed in their own fat: with their mouth they speak proudly.

11 They have now encompassed us in our steps: they have set their eyes bowing down to the earth;

12 Like as a lion *that* is greedy of his prey, and as *it* were a young lion lurking in secret places.

13 Arise, O Yahweh, disappoint him, cast him down: deliver my soul from the wicked, *which is* your sword:

14 From men *which are* your hand, O Yahweh, from men of the world, *which have* their portion in *this* life, and whose belly you fill with your hidden *treasure*: they are full of children, and leave the rest of their *substance* to their babes.

15 As for me, I will behold your face in righteousness: I shall be satisfied, when I awake, in your likeness.

Psalms 18

18:1 ¶ <<To the chief Musician, *A Psalm* of David, the servant of Yahweh, who spoke unto Yahweh the words of this song in the day *that* Yahweh delivered him from the hand of all his enemies, and from the hand of Saul: And he said,>> I will love you, O Yahweh, my strength.

2 Yahweh *is* my rock, and my fortress, and my deliverer; my God, my strength, in whom I will trust; my shield, and the horn of my salvation, *and* my high tower.

3 I will call upon Yahweh, *who is worthy* to be praised: so shall I be saved from my enemies.

4 The sorrows of death encompassed me, and the floods of ungodly men made me afraid.

5 The sorrows of hell compassed me about: the snares of death prevented me.

6 In my distress I called upon Yahweh, and cried unto my God: he heard my voice out of his temple, and my cry came before him, *even* into his ears.

7 Then the earth shook and trembled; the foundations also of the hills moved and were shaken, because he was angry.

8 There went up a smoke out of his nostrils, and fire out of his mouth devoured: coals were kindled by it.

9 He bowed the heavens also, and came down: and darkness *was* under his feet.

10 And he rode upon a cherub, and did fly: yes, he did fly upon the wings of the wind.

11 He made darkness his secret place; his pavilion round about him *were* dark waters *and* thick clouds of the skies.

12 At the brightness *that was* before him his thick clouds passed, hail *stones* and coals of fire.

13 Yahweh also thundered in the heavens, and the Highest gave his voice; hail *stones* and coals of fire.

14 Yes, he sent out his arrows, and scattered them; and he shot out lightnings, and discomfited them.

15 Then the channels of waters were seen, and the foundations of the world were discovered at your rebuke, O Yahweh, at the blast of the breath of your nostrils.

16 He sent from above, he took me, he drew me out of many waters.

17 He delivered me from my strong enemy, and from them which hated me: for they were too strong for me.

18 They prevented me in the day of my calamity: but Yahweh was my stay.

19 He brought me forth also into a large place; he delivered me, because he delighted in me.

Psalms 18

20 ¶ Yahweh rewarded me according to my righteousness; according to the cleanness of my hands has he recompensed me.

21 For I have kept the ways of Yahweh, and have not wickedly departed from my God.

22 For all his judgments *were* before me, and I did not put away his statutes from me.

23 I was also upright before him, and I kept myself from my iniquity.

24 Therefore has Yahweh recompensed me according to my righteousness, according to the cleanness of my hands in his eyesight.

25 With the merciful you will show yourself merciful; with an upright man you will show yourself upright;

26 With the pure you will show yourself pure; and with the perverse you will show yourself shrewd.

27 For you will save the afflicted people; but will bring down high looks.

28 For you will light my candle: Yahweh my God will enlighten my darkness.

29 ¶ For by you I have run through a troop; and by my God have I leaped over a wall.

30 *As for* God, his way *is* perfect: the word of Yahweh is tried: he *is* a shield to all those that trust in him.

31 For who *is* God save Yahweh? or who *is* a rock save our God?

32 *It is* God that girds me with strength, and makes my way perfect.

33 He makes my feet like deer's *feet*, and sets me upon my high places.

34 He teaches my hands to war, so that a bow of steel is broken by my arms.

35 You have also given me the shield of your salvation: and your right hand has held me up, and your gentleness has made me great.

36 You have enlarged my steps under me, that my feet did not slip.

37 I have pursued my enemies, and overtaken them: neither did I turn again till they were consumed.

38 I have wounded them *so* that they were not able to rise: they have fallen under my feet.

39 For you have girded me with strength to the battle: you have subdued under me those that rose up against me.

40 You have also given me the necks of my enemies; that I might destroy them that hate me.

41 They cried, but *there was* none to save *them: even* unto Yahweh, but he answered them not.

42 Then did I beat them small as the dust before the wind: I did cast them out as the dirt in the streets.

43 You have delivered me from the strivings of the people; *and* you have made me the head of the heathen: a people *whom* I have not known shall serve me.

44 As soon as they hear of me, they shall obey me: the strangers shall submit themselves unto me.

45 The strangers shall fade away, and be afraid out of their close places.

46 Yahweh lives; and blessed *be* my rock; and let the God of my salvation be exalted.

47 *It is* God that avenges me, and subdues the people under me.

48 He delivers me from my enemies: yes, you lift me up above those that rise up against me: you have delivered me from the violent man.

49 Therefore will I give thanks to you, O Yahweh, among the heathen, and sing praises unto your name.

50 Great deliverance gives he to his king; and shows mercy to his anointed, to David, and to his seed forevermore.

Psalms 19

19:1 ¶ <<To the chief Musician, A Psalm of David.>> The heavens declare the glory of God; and the firmament shows his handiwork.

2 Day unto day utters speech, and night unto night shows knowledge.

3 *There is* no speech nor language, *where* their voice is not heard.

4 Their line has gone out through all the earth, and their words to the end of the world. In them has he set a tabernacle for the sun,

5 Which *is* as a bridegroom coming out of his chamber, *and* rejoices as a strong man to run a race.

6 His going forth *is* from the end of the heaven, and his circuit to the ends of it: and there is nothing hidden from the heat thereof.

7 ¶ The law of Yahweh *is* perfect, converting the soul: the testimony of Yahweh *is* sure, making wise the simple.

8 The statutes of Yahweh *are* right, rejoicing the heart: the commandment of Yahweh *is* pure, enlightening the eyes.

9 The fear of Yahweh *is* clean, enduring forever: the judgments of Yahweh *are* true *and* righteous altogether.

10 More to be desired *are they* than gold, yes, than much fine gold: sweeter also than honey and the honeycomb.

11 Moreover by them is your servant warned: *and* in keeping of them *there is* great reward.

12 Who can understand *his* errors? cleanse you me from secret *faults*.

13 Keep back your servant also from presumptuous *sins*; let them not have dominion over me: then shall I be upright, and I shall be innocent from the great transgression.

14 Let the words of my mouth, and the meditation of my heart, be acceptable in your sight, O Yahweh, my strength, and my redeemer.

Psalms 20

20:1 ¶ <<To the chief Musician, A Psalm of David.>> Yahweh hear you in the day of trouble; the name of the God of Jacob defend you;

2 Send you help from the sanctuary, and strengthen you out of Zion;

3 Remember all your offerings, and accept your burnt sacrifice; Selah.

4 Grant you according to your own heart, and fulfill all your counsel.
5 We will rejoice in your salvation, and in the name of our God we will set up *our* banners: Yahweh fulfill all your petitions.
6 ¶ Now know I that Yahweh saves his anointed; he will hear him from his holy heaven with the saving strength of his right hand.
7 Some *trust* in chariots, and some in horses: but we will remember the name of Yahweh our God.
8 They are brought down and fallen: but we are risen, and stand upright.
9 Save, Yahweh: let the king hear us when we call.

Psalms 21

21:1 ¶ <<To the chief Musician, A Psalm of David.>> The king shall joy in your strength, O Yahweh; and in your salvation how greatly shall he rejoice!
2 You have given him his heart's desire, and have not withheld the request of his lips. Selah.
3 For you go before him with the blessings of goodness: you set a crown of pure gold on his head.
4 He asked life from you, *and* you gave *it* him, *even* length of days forever and ever.
5 His glory *is* great in your salvation: honor and majesty have you laid upon him.
6 For you have made him most blessed forever: you have made him exceedingly glad with your countenance.
7 ¶ For the king trusts in Yahweh, and through the mercy of the most High he shall not be moved.
8 Your hand shall find out all your enemies: your right hand shall find out those that hate you.
9 You shall make them as a fiery oven in the time of your anger: Yahweh shall swallow them up in his wrath, and the fire shall devour them.
10 Their fruit shall you destroy from the earth, and their seed from among the children of men.
11 For they intended evil against you: they imagined a mischievous device, *which* they are not able *to perform*.
12 Therefore shall you make them turn their back, *when* you shall make ready *your arrows* upon your strings against the face of them.
13 Be you exalted, Yahweh, in your own strength: *so* will we sing and praise your power.

Psalms 22

22:1 ¶ <<To the chief Musician upon Aijeleth Shahar, A Psalm of David.>> My God, my God, why have you forsaken me? *why are you so* far from helping me, *and from* the words of my roaring?
2 O my God, I cry in the daytime, but you hear not; and in the night season, and am not silent.
3 But you *are* holy, O *you* that inhabit the praises of Israel.
4 Our fathers trusted in you: they trusted, and you did deliver them.
5 They cried unto you, and were delivered: they trusted in you, and were not confounded.
6 But I *am* a worm, and no man; a reproach of men, and despised by the people.
7 All they that see me laugh me to scorn: they shoot out the lip, they shake the head, *saying*,
8 He trusted on Yahweh *that* he would deliver him: let him deliver him, seeing he delighted in him.
9 But you *are* he that took me out of the womb: you did make me hope *when I was* upon my mother's breasts.
10 I was cast upon you from the womb: you *are* my God from my mother's belly.
11 ¶ Be not far from me; for trouble *is* near; for *there is* none to help.
12 Many bulls have compassed me: strong *bulls* of Bashan have beset me round.
13 They gaped upon me *with* their mouths, *as* a ravening and a roaring lion.
14 I am poured out like water, and all my bones are out of joint: my heart is like wax; it is melted in the midst of my bowels.
15 My strength is dried up like a potsherd; and my tongue clings to my jaws; and you have brought me into the dust of death.
16 For dogs have compassed me: the assembly of the wicked have enclosed me: they pierced my hands and my feet.
17 I may tell all my bones: they look *and* stare upon me.
18 They part my garments among them, and cast lots upon my coat.
19 But be not you far from me, O Yahweh: O my strength, haste you to help me.
20 Deliver my soul from the sword; my darling from the power of the dog.
21 Save me from the lion's mouth: for you have heard me from the horns of the unicorns.
22 ¶ I will declare your name to my brethren: in the midst of the congregation will I praise you.
23 You that fear Yahweh, praise him; all you the seed of Jacob, glorify him; and fear him, all you the seed of Israel.
24 For he has not despised nor abhorred the affliction of the afflicted; neither has he hidden his face from him; but when he cried to him, he heard.
25 My praise *shall be* of you in the great congregation: I will pay my vows before them that fear him.
26 The meek shall eat and be satisfied: they shall praise Yahweh that seek him: your heart shall live forever.
27 All the ends of the world shall remember and turn unto Yahweh: and all the families of the nations shall worship before you.
28 For the kingdom *is* Yahweh's: and he *is* the governor among the nations.
29 All *they that are* fat upon earth shall eat and worship: all they that go down to the dust shall bow before him: and none can keep alive his own soul.

Psalms 22

30 A seed shall serve him; it shall be accounted to the Lord for a generation.
31 They shall come, and shall declare his righteousness to a people that shall be born, that he has done *this*.

Psalms 23

23:1 ¶ <<A Psalm of David.>> Yahweh *is* my shepherd; I shall not want.
2 He makes me to lie down in green pastures: he leads me beside the still waters.
3 He restores my soul: he leads me in the paths of righteousness for his name's sake.
4 Yes, though I walk through the valley of the shadow of death, I will fear no evil: for you *are* with me; your rod and your staff they comfort me.
5 You prepare a table before me in the presence of my enemies: you anoint my head with oil; my cup runs over.
6 Surely goodness and mercy shall follow me all the days of my life: and I will dwell in the house of Yahweh forever.

Psalms 24

24:1 ¶ <<A Psalm of David.>> The earth *is* Yahweh's, and the fullness thereof; the world, and they that dwell therein.
2 For he has founded it upon the seas, and established it upon the floods.
3 ¶ Who shall ascend into the hill of Yahweh? or who shall stand in his holy place?
4 He that has clean hands, and a pure heart; who has not lifted up his soul to vanity, nor sworn deceitfully.
5 He shall receive the blessing from Yahweh, and righteousness from the God of his salvation.
6 This *is* the generation of them that seek him, that seek your face, O Jacob. Selah.
7 ¶ Lift up your heads, O you gates; and be you lifted up, you everlasting doors; and the King of glory shall come in.
8 Who *is* this King of glory? Yahweh strong and mighty, Yahweh mighty in battle.
9 Lift up your heads, O you gates; even lift *them* up, you everlasting doors; and the King of glory shall come in.
10 Who is this King of glory? Yahweh of hosts, he *is* the King of glory. Selah.

Psalms 25

25:1 ¶ <<*A Psalm* of David.>> Unto you, O Yahweh, do I lift up my soul.
2 O my God, I trust in you: let me not be ashamed, let not my enemies triumph over me.
3 Yes, let none that wait on you be ashamed: let them be ashamed which transgress without cause.
4 Show me your ways, O Yahweh; teach me your paths.
5 Lead me in your truth, and teach me: for you *are* the God of my salvation; on you do I wait all the day.
6 Remember, O Yahweh, your tender mercies and your loving kindness; for they *have been* ever of old.
7 Remember not the sins of my youth, nor my transgressions: according to your mercy remember you me for your goodness' sake, O Yahweh.
8 ¶ Good and upright *is* Yahweh: therefore will he teach sinners in the way.
9 The meek will he guide in judgment: and the meek will he teach his way.
10 All the paths of Yahweh *are* mercy and truth to such as keep his covenant and his testimonies.
11 For your name's sake, O Yahweh, pardon my iniquity; for it *is* great.
12 What man *is* he that fears Yahweh? him shall he teach in the way *that* he shall choose.
13 His soul shall dwell at ease; and his seed shall inherit the earth.
14 The secret of Yahweh *is* with them that fear him; and he will show them his covenant.
15 ¶ My eyes *are* ever toward Yahweh; for he shall pluck my feet out of the net.
16 Turn you unto me, and have mercy upon me; for I *am* desolate and afflicted.
17 The troubles of my heart are enlarged: *O* bring you me out of my distresses.
18 Look upon my affliction and my pain; and forgive all my sins.
19 Consider my enemies; for they are many; and they hate me with cruel hatred.
20 O keep my soul, and deliver me: let me not be ashamed; for I put my trust in you.
21 Let integrity and uprightness preserve me; for I wait on you.
22 Redeem Israel, O God, out of all his troubles.

Psalms 26

26:1 ¶ <<*A Psalm* of David.>> Judge me, O Yahweh; for I have walked in my integrity: I have trusted also in Yahweh; *therefore* I shall not slide.
2 Examine me, O Yahweh, and prove me; try my reins and my heart.
3 For your loving kindness *is* before my eyes: and I have walked in your truth.
4 I have not sat with vain persons, neither will I go in with hypocrites.
5 I have hated the congregation of evil doers; and will not sit with the wicked.
6 ¶ I will wash my hands in innocence: so will I compass your altar, O Yahweh:
7 That I may publish with the voice of thanksgiving, and tell of all your wondrous works.
8 Yahweh, I have loved the habitation of your house, and the place where your honor dwells.
9 Gather not my soul with sinners, nor my life with bloody men:
10 In whose hands *is* mischief, and their right hand is full of bribes.

11 But as for me, I will walk in my integrity: redeem me, and be merciful unto me.
12 My foot stands in an even place: in the congregations will I bless Yahweh.

Psalms 27

27:1 ¶ <<*A Psalm* of David.>> Yahweh *is* my light and my salvation; whom shall I fear? Yahweh *is* the strength of my life; of whom shall I be afraid?
2 When the wicked, *even* my enemies and my foes, came upon me to eat up my flesh, they stumbled and fell.
3 Though a host should encamp against me, my heart shall not fear: though war should rise against me, in this *will* I *be* confident.
4 One *thing* have I desired of Yahweh, that will I seek after; that I may dwell in the house of Yahweh all the days of my life, to behold the beauty of Yahweh, and to inquire in his temple.
5 For in the time of trouble he shall hide me in his pavilion: in the secret of his tabernacle shall he hide me; he shall set me up upon a rock.
6 And now shall my head be lifted up above my enemies round about me: therefore will I offer in his tabernacle sacrifices of joy; I will sing, yes, I will sing praises unto Yahweh.
7 ¶ Hear, O Yahweh, *when* I cry with my voice: have mercy also upon me, and answer me.
8 *When you said*, Seek you my face; my heart said to you, Your face, Yahweh, will I seek.
9 Hide not your face *far* from me; put not your servant away in anger: you have been my help; leave me not, neither forsake me, O God of my salvation.
10 When my father and my mother forsake me, then Yahweh will take me up.
11 Teach me your way, O Yahweh, and lead me in a plain path, because of my enemies.
12 Deliver me not over to the will of my enemies: for false witnesses have risen up against me, and such as breathe out cruelty.
13 *I had fainted*, unless I had believed to see the goodness of Yahweh in the land of the living.
14 Wait on Yahweh: be of good courage, and he shall strengthen your heart: wait, I say, on Yahweh.

Psalms 28

28:1 ¶ <<*A Psalm* of David.>> Unto you will I cry, O Yahweh my rock; be not silent to me: lest, *if* you are silent to me, I become like them that go down into the pit.
2 Hear the voice of my supplications, when I cry unto you, when I lift up my hands toward your holy oracle.
3 Draw me not away with the wicked, and with the workers of iniquity, which speak peace to their neighbors, but mischief *is* in their hearts.
4 Give them according to their deeds, and according to the wickedness of their endeavors: give them after the work of their hands; render to them their reward.
5 Because they regard not the works of Yahweh, nor the operation of his hands, he shall destroy them, and not build them up.
6 ¶ Blessed *be* Yahweh, because he has heard the voice of my supplications.
7 Yahweh *is* my strength and my shield; my heart trusted in him, and I am helped: therefore my heart greatly rejoices; and with my song will I praise him.
8 Yahweh *is* their strength, and he *is* the saving strength of his anointed.
9 Save your people, and bless your inheritance: feed them also, and lift them up forever.

Psalms 29

29:1 ¶ <<A Psalm of David.>> Give unto Yahweh, O you mighty, give unto Yahweh glory and strength.
2 Give unto Yahweh the glory due unto his name; worship Yahweh in the beauty of holiness.
3 The voice of Yahweh *is* upon the waters: the God of glory thunders: Yahweh *is* upon many waters.
4 The voice of Yahweh *is* powerful; the voice of Yahweh *is* full of majesty.
5 The voice of Yahweh breaks the cedars; yes, Yahweh breaks the cedars of Lebanon.
6 He makes them also to skip like a calf; Lebanon and Sirion like a young unicorn.
7 The voice of Yahweh divides the flames of fire.
8 The voice of Yahweh shakes the wilderness; Yahweh shakes the wilderness of Kadesh.
9 The voice of Yahweh makes the does to calve, and discovers the forests: and in his temple does every one speak of *his* glory.
10 Yahweh sits upon the flood; yes, Yahweh sits King forever.
11 Yahweh will give strength to his people; Yahweh will bless his people with peace.

Psalms 30

30:1 ¶ <<A Psalm *and* Song *at* the dedication of the house of David.>> I will extol you, O Yahweh; for you have lifted me up, and have not made my foes to rejoice over me.
2 O Yahweh my God, I cried unto you, and you have healed me.
3 O Yahweh, you have brought up my soul from the grave: you have kept me alive, that I should not go down to the pit.
4 Sing unto Yahweh, O you saints of his, and give thanks at the remembrance of his holiness.
5 For his anger *endures but* a moment; in his favor *is* life: weeping may endure for a night, but joy *comes* in the morning.

6 ¶ And in my prosperity I said, I shall never be moved.
7 Yahweh, by your favor you have made my mountain to stand strong: you did hide your face, *and* I was troubled.
8 I cried to you, O Yahweh; and unto Yahweh I made supplication.
9 What profit *is there* in my blood, when I go down to the pit? Shall the dust praise you? shall it declare your truth?
10 Hear, O Yahweh, and have mercy upon me: Yahweh, be you my helper.
11 You have turned for me my mourning into dancing: you have put off my sackcloth, and girded me with gladness;
12 To the end that *my* glory may sing praise unto you, and not be silent. O Yahweh my God, I will give thanks to you forever.

Psalms 31

31:1 ¶ <<To the chief Musician, A Psalm of David.>> In you, O Yahweh, do I put my trust; let me never be ashamed: deliver me in your righteousness.
2 Bow down your ear to me; deliver me speedily: be you my strong rock, for a house of defense to save me.
3 For you *are* my rock and my fortress; therefore for your name's sake lead me, and guide me.
4 Pull me out of the net that they have laid secretly for me: for you *are* my strength.
5 Into your hand I commit my spirit: you have redeemed me, O Yahweh God of truth.
6 I have hated them that regard lying vanities: but I trust in Yahweh.
7 I will be glad and rejoice in your mercy: for you have considered my trouble; you have known my soul in adversities;
8 And have not shut me up into the hand of the enemy: you have set my feet in a large room.
9 ¶ Have mercy upon me, O Yahweh, for I am in trouble: my eye is consumed with grief, *yes,* my soul and my belly.
10 For my life is spent with grief, and my years with sighing: my strength fails because of my iniquity, and my bones are consumed.
11 I was a reproach among all my enemies, but especially among my neighbors, and a fear to my acquaintances: they that did see me outside fled from me.
12 I am forgotten as a dead man out of mind: I am like a broken vessel.
13 For I have heard the slander of many: fear *was* on every side: while they took counsel together against me, they devised to take away my life.
14 But I trusted in you, O Yahweh: I said, You *are* my God.
15 My times *are* in your hand: deliver me from the hand of my enemies, and from them that persecute me.
16 Make your face to shine upon your servant: save me for your mercies' sake.
17 Let me not be ashamed, O Yahweh; for I have called upon you: let the wicked be ashamed, *and* let them be silent in the grave.
18 Let the lying lips be put to silence; which speak grievous things proudly and contemptuously against the righteous.
19 ¶ *Oh* how great *is* your goodness, which you have laid up for them that fear you; *which* you have worked for them that trust in you before the sons of men!
20 You shall hide them in the secret of your presence from the pride of man: you shall keep them secretly in a pavilion from the strife of tongues.
21 Blessed *be* Yahweh: for he has shown me his marvelous kindness in a strong city.
22 For I said in my haste, I am cut off from before your eyes: nevertheless you heard the voice of my supplications when I cried unto you.
23 O love Yahweh, all you his saints: *for* Yahweh preserves the faithful, and plentifully rewards the proud doer.
24 Be of good courage, and he shall strengthen your heart, all you that hope in Yahweh.

Psalms 32

32:1 ¶ <<*A Psalm* of David, Maschil.>> Blessed *is he whose* transgression *is* forgiven, *whose* sin *is* covered.
2 Blessed *is* the man to whom Yahweh imputes not iniquity, and in whose spirit *there is* no guile.
3 When I kept silence, my bones grew old through my roaring all the day long.
4 For day and night your hand was heavy upon me: my moisture was turned into the drought of summer. Selah.
5 I acknowledged my sin unto you, and my iniquity have I not hidden. I said, I will confess my transgressions unto Yahweh; and you forgave the iniquity of my sin. Selah.
6 For this shall every one that is godly pray unto you in a time when you may be found: surely in the floods of great waters they shall not come near unto him.
7 ¶ You *are* my hiding place; you shall preserve me from trouble; you shall compass me about with songs of deliverance. Selah.
8 I will instruct you and teach you in the way which you shall go: I will guide you with my eye.
9 Be you not as the horse, *or* as the mule, *which* have no understanding: whose mouth must be held in with bit and bridle, lest they come near unto you.
10 Many sorrows *shall be* to the wicked: but he that trusts in Yahweh, mercy shall compass him about.
11 Be glad in Yahweh, and rejoice, you righteous: and shout for joy, all *you that are* upright in heart.

Psalms 33

33:1 ¶ Rejoice in Yahweh, O you righteous: *for* praise is beautiful for the upright.
2 Praise Yahweh with harp: sing to him with the psaltery *and* an instrument of ten strings.
3 Sing unto him a new song; play skillfully with a loud noise.

4 For the word of Yahweh *is* right; and all his works *are done* in truth.
5 He loves righteousness and judgment: the earth is full of the goodness of Yahweh.
6 By the word of Yahweh were the heavens made; and all the host of them by the breath of his mouth.
7 He gathers the waters of the sea together as a heap: he lays up the depth in storehouses.
8 Let all the earth fear Yahweh: let all the inhabitants of the world stand in awe of him.
9 For he spoke, and it was *done*; he commanded, and it stood fast.
10 Yahweh brings the counsel of the heathen to nothing: he makes the devices of the people of no effect.
11 The counsel of Yahweh stands forever, the thoughts of his heart to all generations.
12 ¶ Blessed *is* the nation whose God *is* Yahweh; *and* the people *whom* he has chosen for his own inheritance.
13 Yahweh looks from heaven; he beholds all the sons of men.
14 From the place of his habitation he looks upon all the inhabitants of the earth.
15 He fashions their hearts alike; he considers all their works.
16 There is no king saved by the multitude of a host: a mighty man is not delivered by much strength.
17 A horse *is* a vain thing for safety: neither shall he deliver *any* by his great strength.
18 Behold, the eye of Yahweh *is* upon them that fear him, upon them that hope in his mercy;
19 To deliver their soul from death, and to keep them alive in famine.
20 Our soul waits for Yahweh: he *is* our help and our shield.
21 For our heart shall rejoice in him, because we have trusted in his holy name.
22 Let your mercy, O Yahweh, be upon us, according as we hope in you.

Psalms 34

34:1 ¶ <<*A Psalm* of David, when he changed his behavior before Abimelech; who drove him away, and he departed.>> I will bless Yahweh at all times: his praise *shall* continually *be* in my mouth.
2 My soul shall make her boast in Yahweh: the humble shall hear *thereof*, and be glad.
3 O magnify Yahweh with me, and let us exalt his name together.
4 I sought Yahweh, and he heard me, and delivered me from all my fears.
5 They looked unto him, and were lightened: and their faces were not ashamed.
6 This poor man cried, and Yahweh heard *him*, and saved him out of all his troubles.
7 The angel of Yahweh encamps round about them that fear him, and delivers them.
8 O taste and see that Yahweh *is* good: blessed *is* the man *that* trusts in him.
9 O fear Yahweh, you his saints: for *there is* no want to them that fear him.
10 The young lions do lack, and suffer hunger: but they that seek Yahweh shall not want any good *thing*.
11 ¶ Come, you children, listen to me: I will teach you the fear of Yahweh.
12 What man *is he that* desires life, *and* loves *many* days, that he may see good?
13 Keep your tongue from evil, and your lips from speaking guile.
14 Depart from evil, and do good; seek peace, and pursue it.
15 The eyes of Yahweh *are* upon the righteous, and his ears *are* open unto their cry.
16 The face of Yahweh *is* against them that do evil, to cut off the remembrance of them from the earth.
17 *The righteous* cry, and Yahweh hears, and delivers them out of all their troubles.
18 Yahweh *is* near to them that are of a broken heart; and saves such as are of a contrite spirit.
19 Many *are* the afflictions of the righteous: but Yahweh delivers him out of them all.
20 He keeps all his bones: not one of them is broken.
21 Evil shall slay the wicked: and they that hate the righteous shall be desolate.
22 Yahweh redeems the soul of his servants: and none of them that trust in him shall be desolate.

Psalms 35

35:1 ¶ <<*A Psalm* of David.>> Plead *my cause*, O Yahweh, with them that strive with me: fight against them that fight against me.
2 Take hold of shield and buckler, and stand up for my help.
3 Draw out also the spear, and stop *the way* against them that persecute me: say to my soul, I *am* your salvation.
4 Let them be confounded and put to shame that seek after my soul: let them be turned back and brought to confusion that devise my hurt.
5 Let them be as chaff before the wind: and let the angel of Yahweh chase *them*.
6 Let their way be dark and slippery: and let the angel of Yahweh persecute them.
7 For without cause have they hidden for me their net *in* a pit, *which* without cause they have dug for my soul.
8 Let destruction come upon him unknowingly; and let his net that he has hidden catch himself: into that very destruction let him fall.
9 And my soul shall be joyful in Yahweh: it shall rejoice in his salvation.
10 All my bones shall say, Yahweh, who *is* like unto you, which delivers the poor from him that is too strong for him, yes, the poor and the needy from him that spoils him?

11 ¶ False witnesses did rise up; they laid to my charge *things* that I knew not.
12 They rewarded me evil for good *to* the spoiling of my soul.
13 But as for me, when they were sick, my clothing *was* sackcloth: I humbled my soul with fasting; and my prayer returned into my own bosom.
14 I behaved myself as though *he had been* my friend *or* brother: I bowed down heavily, as one that mourns *for his* mother.
15 But in my adversity they rejoiced, and gathered themselves together: *yes,* the attackers gathered themselves together against me, and I knew *it* not; they did tear *me,* and ceased not:
16 With hypocritical mockers in feasts, they gnashed upon me with their teeth.
17 ¶ Lord, how long will you look on? rescue my soul from their destruction, my darling from the lions.
18 I will give you thanks in the great congregation: I will praise you among much people.
19 Let not them that are my enemies wrongfully rejoice over me: *neither* let them wink with the eye that hate me without a cause.
20 For they speak not peace: but they devise deceitful matters against *them that are* quiet in the land.
21 Yes, they opened their mouth wide against me, *and* said, Aha, aha, our eye has seen *it.*
22 *This* you have seen, O Yahweh: keep not silence: O Lord, be not far from me.
23 Stir up yourself, and awake to my judgment, *even* to my cause, my God and my Lord.
24 Judge me, O Yahweh my God, according to your righteousness; and let them not rejoice over me.
25 Let them not say in their hearts, Ah, so would we have it: let them not say, We have swallowed him up.
26 Let them be ashamed and brought to confusion together that rejoice at my hurt: let them be clothed with shame and dishonor that magnify *themselves* against me.
27 Let them shout for joy, and be glad, that favor my righteous cause: yes, let them say continually, Let Yahweh be magnified, which has pleasure in the prosperity of his servant.
28 And my tongue shall speak of your righteousness *and* of your praise all the day long.

Psalms 36

36:1 ¶ <<To the chief Musician, *A Psalm* of David the servant of Yahweh.>> The transgression of the wicked says within my heart, *that there is* no fear of God before his eyes.
2 For he flatters himself in his own eyes, until his iniquity be found to be hateful.
3 The words of his mouth *are* iniquity and deceit: he has left off to be wise, *and* to do good.
4 He devises mischief upon his bed; he sets himself in a way *that is* not good; he abhors not evil.
5 ¶ Your mercy, O Yahweh, *is* in the heavens; *and* your faithfulness *reaches* to the clouds.
6 Your righteousness *is* like the great mountains; your judgments *are* a great deep: O Yahweh, you preserve man and beast.
7 How excellent *is* your loving kindness, O God! therefore the children of men put their trust under the shadow of your wings.
8 They shall be abundantly satisfied with the fatness of your house; and you shall make them drink of the river of your pleasures.
9 For with you *is* the fountain of life: in your light shall we see light.
10 O continue your loving kindness to them that know you; and your righteousness to the upright in heart.
11 Let not the foot of pride come against me, and let not the hand of the wicked remove me.
12 There are the workers of iniquity fallen: they are cast down, and shall not be able to rise.

Psalms 37

37:1 ¶ <<*A Psalm* of David.>> Fret not yourself because of evildoers, neither be you envious against the workers of iniquity.
2 For they shall soon be cut down like the grass, and wither as the green herb.
3 Trust in Yahweh, and do good; *so* shall you dwell in the land, and truly you shall be fed.
4 Delight yourself also in Yahweh; and he shall give you the desires of your heart.
5 Commit your way unto Yahweh; trust also in him; and he shall bring *it* to pass.
6 And he shall bring forth your righteousness as the light, and your judgment as the noonday.
7 ¶ Rest in Yahweh, and wait patiently for him: fret not yourself because of him who prospers in his way, because of the man who brings wicked devices to pass.
8 Cease from anger, and forsake wrath: fret not yourself in any wise to do evil.
9 For evildoers shall be cut off: but those that wait upon Yahweh, they shall inherit the earth.
10 For yet a little while, and the wicked *shall* not *be*: yes, you shall diligently consider his place, and it *shall* not *be*.
11 But the meek shall inherit the earth; and shall delight themselves in the abundance of peace.
12 The wicked plots against the just, and gnashes upon him with his teeth.
13 The Lord shall laugh at him: for he sees that his day is coming.
14 The wicked have drawn out the sword, and have bent their bow, to cast down the poor and needy, *and* to slay such as be of upright conversation.
15 Their sword shall enter into their own heart, and their bows shall be broken.

16 A little that a righteous man has *is* better than the riches of many wicked.
17 For the arms of the wicked shall be broken: but Yahweh upholds the righteous.
18 Yahweh knows the days of the upright: and their inheritance shall be forever.
19 They shall not be ashamed in the evil time: and in the days of famine they shall be satisfied.
20 But the wicked shall perish, and the enemies of Yahweh *shall be* as the fat of lambs: they shall consume; into smoke shall they consume away.
21 ¶ The wicked borrows, and pays not again: but the righteous shows mercy, and gives.
22 For *such as are* blessed of him shall inherit the earth; and *they that are* cursed of him shall be cut off.
23 The steps of a *good* man are ordered by Yahweh: and he delights in his way.
24 Though he falls, he shall not be utterly cast down: for Yahweh upholds *him with* his hand.
25 I have been young, and *now* am old; yet have I not seen the righteous forsaken, nor his seed begging bread.
26 *He is* ever merciful, and lends; and his seed *is* blessed.
27 Depart from evil, and do good; and dwell forevermore.
28 For Yahweh loves judgment, and forsakes not his saints; they are preserved forever: but the seed of the wicked shall be cut off.
29 The righteous shall inherit the land, and dwell therein forever.
30 The mouth of the righteous speaks wisdom, and his tongue talks of judgment.
31 The law of his God *is* in his heart; none of his steps shall slide.
32 The wicked watches the righteous, and seeks to slay him.
33 Yahweh will not leave him in his hand, nor condemn him when he is judged.
34 ¶ Wait on Yahweh, and keep his way, and he shall exalt you to inherit the land: when the wicked are cut off, you shall see *it*.
35 I have seen the wicked in great power, and spreading himself like a green bay tree.
36 Yet he passed away, and, lo, he *was* not: yes, I sought him, but he could not be found.
37 Mark the perfect *man*, and behold the upright: for the end of *that* man *is* peace.
38 But the transgressors shall be destroyed together: the end of the wicked shall be cut off.
39 But the salvation of the righteous *is* of Yahweh: he *is* their strength in the time of trouble.
40 And Yahweh shall help them, and deliver them: he shall deliver them from the wicked, and save them, because they trust in him.

Psalms 38

38:1 ¶ <<A Psalm of David, to bring to remembrance.>> O Yahweh, rebuke me not in your wrath: neither chasten me in your hot displeasure.
2 For your arrows stick fast in me, and your hand presses me down.
3 *There is* no soundness in my flesh because of your anger; neither *is there any* rest in my bones because of my sin.
4 For my iniquities have gone over my head: as a heavy burden they are too heavy for me.
5 My wounds stink *and* are corrupt because of my foolishness.
6 I am troubled; I am bowed down greatly; I go mourning all the day long.
7 For my loins are filled with a loathsome *disease*: and *there is* no soundness in my flesh.
8 I am feeble and very broken: I have roared by reason of the disquietness of my heart.
9 Lord, all my desire *is* before you; and my groaning is not hidden from you.
10 My heart pants, my strength fails me: as for the light of my eyes, it also has gone from me.
11 My lovers and my friends stand aloof from my plague; and my kinsmen stand afar off.
12 ¶ They also that seek after my life lay snares *for me*: and they that seek my hurt speak mischievous things, and imagine deceits all the day long.
13 But I, as a deaf *man*, heard not; and *I was* as a dumb man *that* opens not his mouth.
14 Thus I was as a man that hears not, and in whose mouth *are* no reproofs.
15 For in you, O Yahweh, do I hope: you shall hear, O Lord my God.
16 For I said, *Hear me*, lest *otherwise* they should rejoice over me: when my foot slips, they magnify *themselves* against me.
17 For I am ready to halt, and my sorrow *is* continually before me.
18 For I will declare my iniquity; I will be sorry for my sin.
19 But my enemies *are* lively, *and* they are strong: and they that hate me wrongfully have multiplied.
20 They also that render evil for good are my adversaries; because I follow *the thing that* good *is*.
21 Forsake me not, O Yahweh: O my God, be not far from me.
22 Make haste to help me, O Lord my salvation.

Psalms 39

39:1 ¶ <<To the chief Musician, *even* to Jeduthun, A Psalm of David.>> I said, I will take heed to my ways, that I sin not with my tongue: I will keep my mouth with a bridle, while the wicked are before me.
2 I was dumb with silence, I held my peace, *even* from good; and my sorrow was stirred.

Psalms 39

3 My heart was hot within me, while I was musing the fire burned: *then* spoke I with my tongue,
4 Yahweh, make me to know my end, and the measure of my days, what it *is; that* I may know how frail I *am*.
5 Behold, you have made my days *as* a handbreadth; and my age *is* as nothing before you: truly every man at his best state *is* altogether vanity. Selah.
6 Surely every man walks in a vain show: surely they are disquieted in vain: he heaps up *riches*, and knows not who shall gather them.
7 ¶ And now, Lord, what wait I for? my hope *is* in you.
8 Deliver me from all my transgressions: make me not the reproach of the foolish.
9 I was dumb, I opened not my mouth; because you did *it*.
10 Remove your stroke away from me: I am consumed by the blow of your hand.
11 When you with rebukes do correct man for iniquity, you make his beauty to consume away like a moth: surely every man *is* vanity. Selah.
12 Hear my prayer, O Yahweh, and give ear to my cry; hold not your peace at my tears: for I *am* a stranger with you, *and* a sojourner, as all my fathers *were*.
13 O spare me, that I may recover strength, before I go away, and be no more.

Psalms 40

40:1 ¶ <<To the chief Musician, A Psalm of David.>> I waited patiently for Yahweh; and he inclined unto me, and heard my cry.
2 He brought me up also out of a horrible pit, out of the miry clay, and set my feet upon a rock, *and* established my goings.
3 And he has put a new song in my mouth, *even* praise to our God: many shall see *it*, and fear, and shall trust in Yahweh.
4 Blessed *is* that man that makes Yahweh his trust, and respects not the proud, nor such as turn aside to lies.
5 Many, O Yahweh my God, *are* your wonderful works *which* you have done, and your thoughts *which are* toward us: they cannot be reckoned up in order unto you: *if* I would declare and speak *of them*, they are more than can be numbered.
6 ¶ Sacrifice and offering you did not desire; my ears have you opened: burnt offering and sin offering have you not required.
7 Then said I, Lo, I come: in the volume of the book *it is* written of me,
8 I delight to do your will, O my God: yes, your law *is* within my heart.
9 I have preached righteousness in the great congregation: lo, I have not refrained my lips, O Yahweh, you know.
10 I have not hidden your righteousness within my heart; I have declared your faithfulness and your salvation: I have not concealed your loving kindness and your truth from the great congregation.
11 ¶ Withhold not you your tender mercies from me, O Yahweh: let your loving kindness and your truth continually preserve me.
12 For innumerable evils have encompassed me about: my iniquities have taken hold upon me, so that I am not able to look up; they are more than the hairs of my head: therefore my heart fails me.
13 Be pleased, O Yahweh, to deliver me: O Yahweh, make haste to help me.
14 Let them be ashamed and confounded together that seek after my soul to destroy it; let them be driven backward and put to shame that wish me evil.
15 Let them be desolate for a reward of their shame that say to me, Aha, aha.
16 Let all those that seek you rejoice and be glad in you: let such as love your salvation say continually, Yahweh be magnified.
17 But I *am* poor and needy; *yet* the Lord thinks upon me: you *are* my help and my deliverer; make no tarrying, O my God.

Psalms 41

41:1 ¶ <<To the chief Musician, A Psalm of David.>> Blessed *is* he that considers the poor: Yahweh will deliver him in time of trouble.
2 Yahweh will preserve him, and keep him alive; *and* he shall be blessed upon the earth: and you shall not deliver him unto the will of his enemies.
3 Yahweh will strengthen him upon the bed of languishing: you will make all his bed in his sickness.
4 I said, Yahweh, be merciful unto me: heal my soul; for I have sinned against you.
5 ¶ My enemies speak evil of me, When shall he die, and his name perish?
6 And if he comes to see *me*, he speaks vanity: his heart gathers iniquity to itself; *when* he goes abroad, he tells *it*.
7 All that hate me whisper together against me: against me do they devise my hurt.
8 An evil disease, *say they*, clings fast to him: and *now* that he lies he shall rise up no more.
9 Yes, my own familiar friend, in whom I trusted, which did eat of my bread, has lifted up *his* heel against me.
10 But you, O Yahweh, be merciful unto me, and raise me up, that I may repay them.
11 By this I know that you favor me, because my enemy does not triumph over me.
12 And as for me, you uphold me in my integrity, and set me before your face forever.
13 Blessed *be* Yahweh God of Israel from everlasting, and to everlasting. Amen, and Amen.

Psalms 42

42:1 ¶ <<To the chief Musician, Maschil, for the sons of Korah.>> As the hart pants after the water brooks, so pants my soul after you, O God.

2 My soul thirsts for God, for the living God: when shall I come and appear before God?

3 My tears have been my bread day and night, while they continually say to me, Where *is* your God?

4 When I remember these *things*, I pour out my soul in me: for I had gone with the multitude, I went with them to the house of God, with the voice of joy and praise, with a multitude that kept *the* holy day.

5 Why are you cast down, O my soul? and *why* are you disquieted in me? hope you in God: for I shall yet praise him *for* the help of his countenance.

6 ¶ O my God, my soul is cast down within me: therefore will I remember you from the land of *the* Jordan, and of the Hermonites, from the hill Mizar.

7 Deep calls to deep at the noise of your waterspouts: all your waves and your billows are gone over me.

8 *Yet* Yahweh will command his loving kindness in the daytime, and in the night his song *shall be* with me, *and* my prayer unto the God of my life.

9 I will say to God my rock, Why have you forgotten me? why go I mourning because of the oppression of the enemy?

10 *As* with a sword in my bones, my enemies reproach me; while they say daily to me, Where *is* your God?

11 Why are you cast down, O my soul? and why are you disquieted within me? hope you in God: for I shall yet praise him, *who is* the health of my countenance, and my God.

Psalms 43

43:1 ¶ Judge me, O God, and plead my cause against an ungodly nation: O deliver me from the deceitful and unjust man.

2 For you *are* the God of my strength: why do you cast me off? why go I mourning because of the oppression of the enemy?

3 O send out your light and your truth: let them lead me; let them bring me to your holy hill, and to your tabernacles.

4 Then will I go to the altar of God, to God my exceeding joy: yes, upon the harp will I praise you, O God my God.

5 Why are you cast down, O my soul? and why are you disquieted within me? hope in God: for I shall yet praise him, *who is* the health of my countenance, and my God.

Psalms 44

44:1 ¶ <<To the chief Musician for the sons of Korah, Maschil.>> We have heard with our ears, O God, our fathers have told us, *what* work you did in their days, in the times of old.

2 *How* you did drive out the heathen with your hand, and planted them; *how* you did afflict the people, and cast them out.

3 For they got not the land in possession by their own sword, neither did their own arm save them: but your right hand, and your arm, and the light of your countenance, because you had favor unto them.

4 You are my King, O God: command deliverances for Jacob.

5 Through you will we push down our enemies: through your name will we tread them under that rise up against us.

6 For I will not trust in my bow, neither shall my sword save me.

7 But you have saved us from our enemies, and have put them to shame that hated us.

8 In God we boast all the day long, and praise your name forever. Selah.

9 ¶ But you have cast off, and put us to shame; and go not forth with our armies.

10 You make us to turn back from the enemy: and they which hate us spoil for themselves.

11 You have given us like sheep *appointed* for meat; and have scattered us among the heathen.

12 You sell your people for nothing, and do not increase *your wealth* by their price.

13 You make us a reproach to our neighbors, a scorn and a derision to them that are round about us.

14 You make us a byword among the heathen, a shaking of the head among the people.

15 My confusion *is* continually before me, and the shame of my face has covered me,

16 For the voice of him that reproaches and blasphemes; by reason of the enemy and avenger.

17 ¶ All this is come upon us; yet have we not forgotten you, neither have we dealt falsely in your covenant.

18 Our heart is not turned back, neither have our steps declined from your way;

19 Though you have severely broken us in the place of dragons, and covered us with the shadow of death.

20 If we have forgotten the name of our God, or stretched out our hands to a strange god;

21 Shall not God search this out? for he knows the secrets of the heart.

22 Yes, for your sake are we killed all the day long; we are counted as sheep for the slaughter.

23 Awake, why sleep you, O Lord? arise, cast *us* not off forever.

24 Why hide you your face, *and* forget our affliction and our oppression?

25 For our soul is bowed down to the dust: our belly clings to the earth.

26 Arise for our help, and redeem us for your mercies' sake.

Psalms 45

45:1 ¶ <<To the chief Musician upon Shoshannim, for the sons of Korah, Maschil, A Song of loves.>> My heart is stirring a good matter: I speak of the things which I have made touching the king: my tongue *is* the pen of a ready writer.

Psalms 45

2 You are fairer than the children of men: grace is poured into your lips: therefore God has blessed you forever.
3 Gird your sword upon *your* thigh, O *most* mighty, with your glory and your majesty.
4 And in your majesty ride prosperously because of truth and meekness *and* righteousness; and your right hand shall teach you terrible things.
5 Your arrows *are* sharp in the heart of the king's enemies; *whereby* the people fall under you.
6 ¶ Your throne, O God, *is* forever and ever: the scepter of your kingdom *is* a right scepter.
7 You love righteousness, and hate wickedness: therefore God, your God, has anointed you with the oil of gladness above your fellows.
8 All your garments *smell* of myrrh, and aloes, *and* cassia, out of the ivory palaces, whereby they have made you glad.
9 Kings' daughters *were* among your honorable women: upon your right hand did stand the queen in gold of Ophir.
10 ¶ Listen, O daughter, and consider, and incline your ear; forget also your own people, and your father's house;
11 So shall the king greatly desire your beauty: for he *is* your Lord; and worship you him.
12 And the daughter of Tyre *shall be there* with a gift; *even* the rich among the people shall entreat your favor.
13 The king's daughter *is* all glorious within: her clothing *is* of worked gold.
14 She shall be brought to the king in clothing of needlework: the virgins her companions that follow her shall be brought to you.
15 With gladness and rejoicing shall they be brought: they shall enter into the king's palace.
16 Instead of your fathers shall be your children, whom you may make princes in all the earth.
17 I will make your name to be remembered in all generations: therefore shall the people praise you forever and ever.

Psalms 46

46:1 ¶ <<To the chief Musician for the sons of Korah, A Song upon Alamoth.>> God *is* our refuge and strength, a very present help in trouble.
2 Therefore will not we fear, though the earth be removed, and though the mountains be carried into the midst of the sea;
3 *Though* the waters thereof roar *and* be troubled, *though* the mountains shake with the swelling thereof. Selah.
4 *There is* a river, the streams whereof shall make glad the city of God, the holy *place* of the tabernacles of the most High.
5 God *is* in the midst of her; she shall not be moved: God shall help her, *and that* right early.
6 ¶ The heathen raged, the kingdoms were moved: he uttered his voice, the earth melted.
7 Yahweh of hosts *is* with us; the God of Jacob *is* our refuge. Selah.
8 Come, behold the works of Yahweh, what desolations he has made in the earth.
9 He makes wars to cease unto the end of the earth; he breaks the bow, and cuts the spear in pieces; he burns the chariot in the fire.
10 Be still, and know that I *am* God: I will be exalted among the heathen, I will be exalted in the earth.
11 Yahweh of hosts *is* with us; the God of Jacob *is* our refuge. Selah.

Psalms 47

47:1 ¶ <<To the chief Musician, A Psalm for the sons of Korah.>> O clap your hands, all you people; shout unto God with the voice of triumph.
2 For Yahweh most high *is* fearful; *he is* a great King over all the earth.
3 He shall subdue the people under us, and the nations under our feet.
4 He shall choose our inheritance for us, the excellency of Jacob whom he loved. Selah.
5 ¶ God has gone up with a shout, Yahweh with the sound of a trumpet.
6 Sing praises to God, sing praises: sing praises to our King, sing praises.
7 For God *is* the King of all the earth: sing you praises with understanding.
8 God reigns over the heathen: God sits upon the throne of his holiness.
9 The princes of the people are gathered together, *even* the people of the God of Abraham: for the shields of the earth *belong* to God: he is greatly exalted.

Psalms 48

48:1 ¶ <<A Song *and* Psalm for the sons of Korah.>> Great *is* Yahweh, and greatly to be praised in the city of our God, *in* the mountain of his holiness.
2 Beautiful for situation, the joy of the whole earth, *is* mount Zion, *on* the sides of the north, the city of the great King.
3 God is known in her palaces for a refuge.
4 For, lo, the kings were assembled, they passed by together.
5 They saw *it, and* so they marveled; they were troubled, *and* hurried away.
6 Fear took hold upon them there, *and* pain, as of a woman in labor.
7 You break the ships of Tarshish with an east wind.
8 ¶ As we have heard, so have we seen in the city of Yahweh of hosts, in the city of our God: God will establish it forever. Selah.
9 We have thought of your loving kindness, O God, in the midst of your temple.

10 According to your name, O God, so *is* your praise to the ends of the earth: your right hand is full of righteousness.
11 Let mount Zion rejoice, let the daughters of Judah be glad, because of your judgments.
12 Walk about Zion, and go round about her: tell the towers thereof.
13 Mark you well her bulwarks, consider her palaces; that you may tell *it* to the generation following.
14 For this God *is* our God forever and ever: he will be our guide *even* unto death.

Psalms 49

49:1 ¶ <<To the chief Musician, A Psalm for the sons of Korah.>> Hear this, all *you* people; give ear, all *you* inhabitants of the world:
2 Both low and high, rich and poor, together.
3 My mouth shall speak of wisdom; and the meditation of my heart *shall be* of understanding.
4 I will incline my ear to a parable: I will open my dark saying upon the harp.
5 Why should I fear in the days of evil, *when* the iniquity of my heels shall compass me about?
6 ¶ They that trust in their wealth, and boast themselves in the multitude of their riches;
7 None *of them* can by any means redeem his brother, nor give to God a ransom for him:
8 (For the redemption of their soul *is* precious, and it ceases forever:)
9 That he should still live forever, *and* not see corruption.
10 For he sees *that* wise men die, likewise the fool and the brutish person perish, and leave their wealth to others.
11 Their inward thought *is, that* their houses *shall continue* forever, *and* their dwelling places to all generations; they call *their* lands after their own names.
12 Nevertheless man *being* in honor remains not: he is like the beasts *that* perish.
13 This their way *is* their folly: yet their posterity approves their sayings. Selah.
14 Like sheep they are laid in the grave; death shall feed on them; and the upright shall have dominion over them in the morning; and their beauty shall consume in the grave from their dwelling.
15 ¶ But God will redeem my soul from the power of the grave: for he shall receive me. Selah.
16 Be not you afraid when one is made rich, when the glory of his house is increased;
17 For when he dies he shall carry nothing away: his glory shall not descend after him.
18 Though while he lived he blessed his soul: and *men* will praise you, when you do well to yourself.
19 He shall go to the generation of his fathers; they shall never see light.
20 Man *that is* in honor, and understands not, is like the beasts *that* perish.

Psalms 50

50:1 ¶ <<A Psalm of Asaph.>> The mighty God, *even* Yahweh, has spoken, and called the earth from the rising of the sun to the going down thereof.
2 Out of Zion, the perfection of beauty, God has shined.
3 Our God shall come, and shall not keep silent: a fire shall devour before him, and it shall be very tempestuous round about him.
4 He shall call to the heavens from above, and to the earth, that he may judge his people.
5 Gather my saints together unto me; those that have made a covenant with me by sacrifice.
6 And the heavens shall declare his righteousness: for God *is* judge himself. Selah.
7 ¶ Hear, O my people, and I will speak; O Israel, and I will testify against you: I *am* God, *even* your God.
8 I will not reprove you for your sacrifices or your burnt offerings, *to have been* continually before me.
9 I will take no bullock out of your house, *nor* he goats out of your folds.
10 For every beast of the forest *is* mine, *and* the cattle upon a thousand hills.
11 I know all the fowls of the mountains: and the wild beasts of the field *are* mine.
12 If I were hungry, I would not tell you: for the world *is* mine, and the fullness thereof.
13 Will I eat the flesh of bulls, or drink the blood of goats?
14 Offer unto God thanksgiving; and pay your vows to the most High:
15 And call upon me in the day of trouble: I will deliver you, and you shall glorify me.
16 ¶ But to the wicked God said, What have you to do to declare my statutes, or *that* you should take my covenant in your mouth?
17 Seeing you hate instruction, and cast my words behind you.
18 When you saw a thief, then you consented with him, and have been *a* partaker with adulterers.
19 You give your mouth to evil, and your tongue frames deceit.
20 You sit *and* speak against your brother; you slander your own mother's son.
21 These *things* have you done, and I kept silence; you thought that I was altogether *such a one* as yourself: *but* I will reprove you, and set *them* in order before your eyes.
22 Now consider this, you that forget God, lest I tear *you* in pieces, and *there is* none to deliver.
23 Whoever offers praise glorifies me: and to him that orders *his* conversation *aright* will I show the salvation of God.

Psalms 51

51:1 ¶ <<To the chief Musician, A Psalm of David, when Nathan the prophet came to him, after he had gone in to Bathsheba.>> Have mercy upon me, O God, according to your loving kindness: according to the multitude of your tender mercies blot out my transgressions.
2 Wash me thoroughly from my iniquity, and cleanse me from my sin.
3 For I acknowledge my transgressions: and my sin *is* ever before me.
4 Against you, you only, have I sinned, and done *this* evil in your sight: that you might be justified when you speak, *and* be clear when you judge.
5 Behold, I was shaped in iniquity; and in sin did my mother conceive me.
6 Behold, you desire truth in the inward parts: and in the hidden *part* you shall make me to know wisdom.
7 ¶ Purge me with hyssop, and I shall be clean: wash me, and I shall be whiter than snow.
8 Make me to hear joy and gladness; *that* the bones *which* you have broken may rejoice.
9 Hide your face from my sins, and blot out all my iniquities.
10 Create in me a clean heart, O God; and renew a right spirit within me.
11 Cast me not away from your presence; and take not your holy spirit from me.
12 Restore unto me the joy of your salvation; and uphold me *with your* free spirit.
13 *Then* will I teach transgressors your ways; and sinners shall be converted unto you.
14 ¶ Deliver me from bloodguiltiness, O God, you God of my salvation: *and* my tongue shall sing aloud of your righteousness.
15 O Lord, open you my lips; and my mouth shall show forth your praise.
16 For you desire not sacrifice; *or* else would I give *it*: you delight not in burnt offering.
17 The sacrifices of God *are* a broken spirit: a broken and a contrite heart, O God, you will not despise.
18 Do good in your good pleasure unto Zion: build you the walls of Jerusalem.
19 Then shall you be pleased with the sacrifices of righteousness, with burnt offering and whole burnt offering: then shall they offer bullocks upon your altar.

Psalms 52

52:1 ¶ <<To the chief Musician, Maschil, *A Psalm* of David, when Doeg the Edomite came and told Saul, and said unto him, David has come to the house of Ahimelech.>> Why boast you yourself in mischief, O mighty man? the goodness of God *endures* continually.
2 Your tongue devises mischief; like a sharp razor, working deceitfully.
3 You love evil more than good; *and* lying rather than to speak righteousness. Selah.
4 You love all devouring words, O *you* deceitful tongue.
5 God shall likewise destroy you forever, he shall take you away, and pluck you out of *your* dwelling place, and root you out of the land of the living. Selah.
6 ¶ The righteous also shall see, and fear, and shall laugh at him:
7 Lo, *this is* the man *that* made not God his strength; but trusted in the abundance of his riches, *and* strengthened himself in his wickedness.
8 But I *am* like a green olive tree in the house of God: I trust in the mercy of God forever and ever.
9 I will praise you forever, because you have done *it*: and I will wait on your name; for *it is* good before your saints.

Psalms 53

53:1 ¶ <<To the chief Musician upon Mahalath, Maschil, *A Psalm* of David.>> The fool has said in his heart, *There is* no God. Corrupt are they, and have done abominable iniquity: *there is* none that does good.
2 God looked down from heaven upon the children of men, to see if there were *any* that did understand, that did seek God.
3 Every one of them has gone back: they have altogether become filthy; *there is* none that does good, no, not one.
4 Have the workers of iniquity no knowledge? who eat up my people *as* they eat bread: they have not called upon God.
5 There were they in great fear, *where* no fear was: for God has scattered the bones of him that encamps *against* you: you have put *them* to shame, because God has despised them.
6 Oh that the salvation of Israel *were come* out of Zion! When God brings back the captivity of his people, Jacob shall rejoice, *and* Israel shall be glad.

Psalms 54

54:1 ¶ <<To the chief Musician on Neginoth, Maschil, *A Psalm* of David, when the Ziphims came and said to Saul, Does not David hide himself with us?>> Save me, O God, by your name, and judge me by your strength.
2 Hear my prayer, O God; give ear to the words of my mouth.
3 For strangers are risen up against me, and oppressors seek after my soul: they have not set God before them. Selah.
4 ¶ Behold, God *is* my helper: the Lord *is* with them that uphold my soul.
5 He shall reward evil unto my enemies: cut them off in your truth.
6 I will freely sacrifice unto you: I will praise your name, O Yahweh; for *it is* good.
7 For he has delivered me out of all trouble: and my eye has seen *his desire* upon my enemies.

Psalms 55

55:1 ¶ <<To the chief Musician on Neginoth, Maschil, *A Psalm* of David.>> Give ear to my prayer, O God; and hide not yourself from my supplication.
2 Attend to me, and hear me: I mourn in my complaint, and make a noise;
3 Because of the voice of the enemy, because of the oppression of the wicked: for they cast iniquity upon me, and in wrath they hate me.
4 My heart is very pained within me: and the terrors of death have fallen upon me.
5 Fearfulness and trembling have come upon me, and horror has overwhelmed me.
6 And I said, Oh that I had wings like a dove! *for then* would I fly away, and be at rest.
7 Lo, *then* would I wander far off, *and* remain in the wilderness. Selah.
8 I would hurry my escape from the windy storm *and* tempest.
9 ¶ Destroy, O Lord, *and* divide their tongues: for I have seen violence and strife in the city.
10 Day and night they go about it upon the walls thereof: mischief also and sorrow *are* in the midst of it.
11 Wickedness *is* in the midst thereof: deceit and guile depart not from her streets.
12 For *it was* not an enemy *that* reproached me; then I could have borne *it*: neither *was it* he that hated me *that* did magnify *himself* against me; then I would have hidden myself from him:
13 But *it was* you, a man my equal, my guide, and my acquaintance.
14 We took sweet counsel together, *and* walked to the house of God in company.
15 Let death seize upon them, *and* let them go down quick into hell: for wickedness *is* in their dwellings, *and* among them.
16 ¶ As for me, I will call upon God; and Yahweh shall save me.
17 Evening, and morning, and at noon, will I pray, and cry aloud: and he shall hear my voice.
18 He has delivered my soul in peace from the battle *that was* against me: for there were many with me.
19 God shall hear, and afflict them, even he that remains of old. Selah. Because they have no changes, therefore they fear not God.
20 He has put forth his hands against such as are at peace with him: he has broken his covenant.
21 *The words* of his mouth were smoother than butter, but war *was* in his heart: his words were softer than oil, yet *were* they drawn swords.
22 Cast your burden upon Yahweh, and he shall sustain you: he shall never permit the righteous to be moved.
23 But you, O God, will bring them down into the pit of destruction: bloody and deceitful men shall not live out half their days; but I will trust in you.

Psalms 56

56:1 ¶ <<To the chief Musician upon Jonathelemrechokim, Michtam of David, when the Philistines took him in Gath.>> Be merciful unto me, O God: for man would swallow me up; he fighting daily oppresses me.
2 My enemies would daily swallow *me* up: for *they are* many that fight against me, O you most High.
3 Whenever I am afraid, I will trust in you.
4 In God I will praise his word, in God I have put my trust; I will not fear what flesh can do to me.
5 Every day they pervert my words: all their thoughts *are* against me for evil.
6 They gather themselves together, they hide themselves, they mark my steps, when they wait for my soul.
7 Shall they escape by iniquity? in *your* anger cast down the people, O God.
8 ¶ You tell my wanderings: put you my tears into your bottle: *are they* not in your book?
9 When I cry *unto you*, then shall my enemies turn back: this I know; for God *is* for me.
10 In God will I praise *his* word: in Yahweh will I praise *his* word.
11 In God have I put my trust: I will not be afraid what man can do unto me.
12 Your vows *are* upon me, O God: I will render praises to you.
13 For you have delivered my soul from death: *will not you deliver* my feet from falling, that I may walk before God in the light of the living?

Psalms 57

57:1 ¶ <<To the chief Musician, Altaschith, Michtam of David, when he fled from Saul in the cave.>> Be merciful unto me, O God, be merciful unto me: for my soul trusts in you: yes, in the shadow of your wings will I make my refuge, until *these* calamities are over.
2 I will cry unto God most high; unto God that performs *all things* for me.
3 He shall send from heaven, and save me *from* the reproach of him that would swallow me up. Selah. God shall send forth his mercy and his truth.
4 My soul *is* among lions: *and* I lie *even among* them that are set on fire, *even* the sons of men, whose teeth *are* spears and arrows, and their tongue a sharp sword.
5 Be you exalted, O God, above the heavens; *let* your glory *be* above all the earth.
6 They have prepared a net for my steps; my soul is bowed down: they have dug a pit before me, into the midst whereof they are fallen *themselves*. Selah.
7 ¶ My heart is fixed, O God, my heart is fixed: I will sing and give praise.
8 Wake up, my glory; awake, psaltery and harp: I *myself* will awake early.
9 I will praise you, O Lord, among the people: I will sing to you among the nations.

Psalms 57

10 For your mercy *is* great unto the heavens, and your truth unto the clouds.
11 Be you exalted, O God, above the heavens: *let* your glory *be* above all the earth.

Psalms 58

58:1 ¶ <<To the chief Musician, Altaschith, Michtam of David.>> Do you indeed speak righteousness, O congregation? do you judge uprightly, O you sons of men?
2 Yes, in heart you work wickedness; you weigh the violence of your hands in the earth.
3 The wicked are estranged from the womb: they go astray as soon as they are born, speaking lies.
4 Their poison *is* like the poison of a serpent: *they are* like the deaf adder *that* stops her ear;
5 Which will not listen to the voice of charmers, charming never so wisely.
6 ¶ Break their teeth, O God, in their mouth: break out the great teeth of the young lions, O Yahweh.
7 Let them melt away as waters *which* run continually: *when* he bends *his bow to shoot* his arrows, let them be as cut in pieces.
8 As a snail *which* melts, let *every one of them* pass away: *like* the untimely birth of a woman, *that* they may not see the sun.
9 Before your pots can feel the thorns, he shall take them away as with a whirlwind, both living, and in *his* wrath.
10 The righteous shall rejoice when he sees the vengeance: he shall wash his feet in the blood of the wicked.
11 So that a man shall say, Truly *there is* a reward for the righteous: truly he is a God that judges in the earth.

Psalms 59

59:1 ¶ <<To the chief Musician, Altaschith, Michtam of David; when Saul sent, and they watched the house to kill him.>> Deliver me from my enemies, O my God: defend me from them that rise up against me.
2 Deliver me from the workers of iniquity, and save me from bloody men.
3 For, lo, they lie in wait for my soul: the mighty are gathered against me; not *for* my transgression, nor *for* my sin, O Yahweh.
4 They run and prepare themselves without *my* fault: awake to help me, and behold.
5 You therefore, O Yahweh God of hosts, the God of Israel, awake to visit all the heathen: be not merciful to any wicked transgressors. Selah.
6 They return at evening: they make a noise like a dog, and go round about the city.
7 Behold, they belch out with their mouth: swords *are* in their lips: for who, *say they*, does hear?
8 ¶ But you, O Yahweh, shall laugh at them; you shall have all the heathen in derision.
9 *Because of* his strength will I wait upon you: for God *is* my defense.
10 The God of my mercy shall prevent me: God shall let me see *my desire* upon my enemies.
11 Slay them not, lest my people forget: scatter them by your power; and bring them down, O Lord our shield.
12 *For* the sin of their mouth *and* the words of their lips let them even be taken in their pride: and for cursing and lying *which* they speak.
13 Consume *them* in wrath, consume *them*, that they *may* not *be*: and let them know that God rules in Jacob to the ends of the earth. Selah.
14 And at evening let them return; *and* let them make a noise like a dog, and go round about the city.
15 Let them wander up and down for food, and grumble if they are not satisfied.
16 But I will sing of your power; yes, I will sing aloud of your mercy in the morning: for you have been my defense and refuge in the day of my trouble.
17 Unto you, O my strength, will I sing: for God *is* my defense, *and* the God of my mercy.

Psalms 60

60:1 ¶ <<To the chief Musician upon Shushaneduth, Michtam of David, to teach; when he strove with Aramnaharaim and with Aramzobah, when Joab returned, and smote of Edom in the valley of salt twelve thousand.>> O God, you have cast us off, you have scattered us, you have been displeased; O turn yourself to us again.
2 You have made the earth to tremble; you have broken it: heal the breaches thereof; for it shakes.
3 You have shown your people hard things: you have made us to drink the wine of astonishment.
4 You have given a banner to them that fear you, that it may be displayed because of the truth. Selah.
5 That your beloved may be delivered; save *with* your right hand, and hear me.
6 ¶ God has spoken in his holiness; I will rejoice, I will divide Shechem, and measure out the valley of Succoth.
7 Gilead *is* mine, and Manasseh *is* mine; Ephraim also *is* the strength of my head; Judah *is* my lawgiver;
8 Moab *is* my wash pot; over Edom will I cast out my shoe: Philistia, triumph you because of me.
9 Who will bring me *into* the strong city? who will lead me into Edom?
10 *Will* not you, O God, *which* had cast us off? and *you*, O God, *which* did not go out with our armies?
11 Give us help from trouble: for vain *is* the help of man.
12 Through God we shall do valiantly: for he *it is that* shall tread down our enemies.

Psalms 61

61:1 ¶ <<To the chief Musician upon Neginah, *A Psalm* of David.>> Hear my cry, O God; attend to my prayer.
2 From the end of the earth will I cry unto you, when my heart is overwhelmed: lead me to the rock *that* is higher than I.

3 For you have been a shelter for me, *and* a strong tower from the enemy.
4 I will remain in your tabernacle forever: I will trust in the covert of your wings. Selah.
5 ¶ For you, O God, have heard my vows: you have given *me* the heritage of those that fear your name.
6 You will prolong the king's life: *and* his years as many generations.
7 He shall remain before God forever: O prepare mercy and truth, *which* may preserve him.
8 So will I sing praise unto your name forever, that I may daily perform my vows.

Psalms 62

62:1 ¶ <<To the chief Musician, to Jeduthun, A Psalm of David.>> Truly my soul waits upon God: from him *comes* my salvation.
2 He only *is* my rock and my salvation; *he is* my defense; I shall not be greatly moved.
3 How long will you imagine mischief against a man? you shall be slain all of you: as a bowing wall *shall you be, and as* a tottering fence.
4 They only consult to cast *him* down from his excellency: they delight in lies: they bless with their mouth, but they curse inwardly. Selah.
5 My soul, wait you only upon God; for my expectation *is* from him.
6 He only *is* my rock and my salvation: *he is* my defense; I shall not be moved.
7 In God *is* my salvation and my glory: the rock of my strength, *and* my refuge, *is* in God.
8 ¶ Trust in him at all times; *you* people, pour out your heart before him: God *is* a refuge for us. Selah.
9 Surely men of low degree *are* vanity, *and* men of high degree *are* a lie: to be laid in the balance, they *are* altogether *lighter* than vanity.
10 Trust not in oppression, and become not vain in robbery: if riches increase, set not your heart *upon them*.
11 God has spoken once; twice have I heard this; that power *belongs* to God.
12 Also to you, O Lord, *belongs* mercy: for you render to every man according to his work.

Psalms 63

63:1 ¶ <<A Psalm of David, when he was in the wilderness of Judah.>> O God, you *are* my God; earnestly will I seek you: my soul thirsts for you, my flesh longs for you in a dry and thirsty land, where no water is;
2 To see your power and your glory, so *as* I have seen you in the sanctuary.
3 ¶ Because your loving kindness *is* better than life, my lips shall praise you.
4 Thus will I bless you while I live: I will lift up my hands in your name.
5 My soul shall be satisfied as *with* marrow and fatness; and my mouth shall praise *you* with joyful lips:
6 When I remember you upon my bed, *and* meditate on you in the *night* watches.
7 ¶ Because you have been my help, therefore in the shadow of your wings will I rejoice.
8 My soul follows hard after you: your right hand upholds me.
9 But those *that* seek my soul, to destroy *it*, shall go into the lower parts of the earth.
10 They shall fall by the sword: they shall be a portion for foxes.
11 But the king shall rejoice in God; every one that swears by him shall glory: but the mouth of them that speak lies shall be stopped.

Psalms 64

64:1 ¶ <<To the chief Musician, A Psalm of David.>> Hear my voice, O God, in my prayer: preserve my life from fear of the enemy.
2 Hide me from the secret counsel of the wicked; from the insurrection of the workers of iniquity:
3 Who sharpen their tongue like a sword, *and* bend *their bows to shoot* their arrows, *even* bitter words:
4 That they may shoot in secret at the perfect: suddenly do they shoot at him, and fear not.
5 They encourage themselves *in* an evil matter: they commune of laying snares privately; they say, Who shall see them?
6 They search out iniquities; they accomplish a diligent search: both the inward *thought* of every one *of them*, and the heart, *is* deep.
7 ¶ But God shall shoot at them *with* an arrow; suddenly shall they be wounded.
8 So they shall make their own tongue to fall upon themselves: all that see them shall flee away.
9 And all men shall fear, and shall declare the work of God; for they shall wisely consider of his doing.
10 The righteous shall be glad in Yahweh, and shall trust in him; and all the upright in heart shall glory.

Psalms 65

65:1 ¶ <<To the chief Musician, A Psalm *and* Song of David.>> Praise waits for you, O God, in Zion: and unto you shall the vow be performed.
2 O you that hear prayer, unto you shall all flesh come.
3 Iniquities prevail against me: *as for* our transgressions, you shall purge them away.
4 Blessed *is the man whom* you choose, and cause to approach *unto you, that* he may dwell in your courts: we shall be satisfied with the goodness of your house, *even* of your holy temple.
5 *By* fearful things in righteousness will you answer us, O God of our salvation; *who are* the confidence of all the ends of the earth, and of them that are afar off *upon* the sea:
6 ¶ Which by his strength sets fast the mountains; *being* girded with power:

Psalms 65

7 Which stills the noise of the seas, the noise of their waves, and the tumult of the people.
8 They also that dwell in the utmost parts are afraid at your tokens: you make the outgoings of the morning and evening to rejoice.
9 You visit the earth, and water it: you greatly enrich it with the river of God, *which* is full of water: you prepare them corn, when you have so provided for it.
10 You water the ridges thereof abundantly: you settle the furrows thereof: you make it soft with showers: you bless the springing thereof.
11 You crown the year with your goodness; and your paths drop fatness.
12 They drop *upon* the pastures of the wilderness: and the little hills rejoice on every side.
13 The pastures are clothed with flocks; the valleys also are covered over with corn; they shout for joy, they also sing.

Psalms 66

66:1 ¶ <<To the chief Musician, A Song *or* Psalm.>> Make a joyful noise unto God, all you lands:
2 Sing forth the honor of his name: make his praise glorious.
3 Say unto God, How awesome *are you in* your works! through the greatness of your power shall your enemies submit themselves unto you.
4 All the earth shall worship you, and shall sing unto you; they shall sing *unto* your name. Selah.
5 Come and see the works of God: *he is* awesome *in his* doing toward the children of men.
6 He turned the sea into dry *land*: they went through the flood on foot: there did we rejoice in him.
7 He rules by his power forever; his eyes behold the nations: let not the rebellious exalt themselves. Selah.
8 ¶ O bless our God, you people, and make the voice of his praise to be heard:
9 Which holds our souls in life, and allows not our feet to be moved.
10 For you, O God, have proven us: you have tried us, as silver is tried.
11 You brought us into the net; you laid affliction upon our loins.
12 You have caused men to ride over our heads; we went through fire and through water: but you brought us out into a wealthy *place*.
13 ¶ I will go into your house with burnt offerings: I will pay you my vows,
14 Which my lips have uttered, and my mouth has spoken, when I was in trouble.
15 I will offer unto you burnt sacrifices of fatted calves, with the incense of rams; I will offer bullocks with goats. Selah.
16 Come *and* hear, all you that fear God, and I will declare what he has done for my soul.
17 I cried unto him with my mouth, and he was extolled with my tongue.
18 If I regard iniquity in my heart, the Lord will not hear *me*:
19 *But* truly God has heard *me*; he has attended to the voice of my prayer.
20 Blessed *be* God, which has not turned away my prayer, nor his mercy from me.

Psalms 67

67:1 ¶ <<To the chief Musician on Neginoth, A Psalm *or* Song.>> God be merciful to us, and bless us; *and* cause his face to shine upon us; Selah.
2 That your way may be known upon earth, your saving health among all nations.
3 Let the people praise you, O God; let all the people praise you.
4 O let the nations be glad and sing for joy: for you shall judge the people righteously, and govern the nations upon earth. Selah.
5 Let the people praise you, O God; let all the people praise you.
6 *Then* shall the earth yield her increase; *and* God, *even* our own God, shall bless us.
7 God shall bless us; and all the ends of the earth shall fear him.

Psalms 68

68:1 ¶ <<To the chief Musician, A Psalm *or* Song of David.>> Let God arise, let his enemies be scattered: let them also that hate him flee before him.
2 As smoke is driven away, *so* drive *them* away: as wax melts before the fire, *so* let the wicked perish at the presence of God.
3 But let the righteous be glad; let them rejoice before God: yes, let them exceedingly rejoice.
4 Sing unto God, sing praises to his name: extol him that rides upon the heavens by his name YAH, and rejoice before him.
5 A father of the fatherless, and a judge of the widows, *is* God in his holy habitation.
6 God sets the solitary in families: he brings out those which are bound with chains: but the rebellious dwell in a dry *land*.
7 ¶ O God, when you went forth before your people, when you did march through the wilderness; Selah:
8 The earth shook, the heavens also dropped at the presence of God: *even* Sinai itself *was moved* at the presence of God, the God of Israel.
9 You, O God, did send a plentiful rain, whereby you did confirm your inheritance, when it was weary.
10 Your congregation has dwelt therein: you, O God, have prepared of your goodness for the poor.
11 The Lord gave the word: great *was* the company of those that published *it*.
12 Kings of armies did flee away: and she that tarried at home divided the spoil.
13 Though you have lain among the pots, *yet shall you be as* the wings of a dove covered with silver, and her feathers with yellow gold.

14 When the Almighty scattered kings in it, it was *white* as snow in Salmon.
15 ¶ The hill of God *is as* the hill of Bashan; a high hill *as* the hill of Bashan.
16 Why leap you, you high hills? *this is* the hill which God desires to dwell in; yes, Yahweh will dwell *in it* forever.
17 The chariots of God *are* twenty thousand, *even* thousands of angels: the Lord *is* among them, *as in* Sinai, in the holy *place*.
18 You have ascended on high, you have led captivity captive: you have received gifts for men; yes, *for* the rebellious also, that Yah God might dwell *among them*.
19 Blessed *be* the Lord, *who* daily loads us *with benefits, even* the God of our salvation. Selah.
20 *He that is* our God *is* the God of salvation; and unto Yahweh the Lord *belongs* the issues from death.
21 But God shall wound the head of his enemies, *and* the hairy scalp of such a one as goes on still in his trespasses.
22 ¶ The Lord said, I will bring again from Bashan, I will bring *my people* again from the depths of the sea:
23 That your foot may be dipped in the blood of *your* enemies, *and* the tongue of your dogs in the same.
24 They have seen your goings, O God; *even* the goings of my God, my King, in the sanctuary.
25 The singers went before, the players on instruments *followed* after; among *them were* the damsels playing with tambourines.
26 Bless you God in the congregations, *even* the Lord, from the fountain of Israel.
27 There *is* little Benjamin *with* their ruler, the princes of Judah *and* their council, the princes of Zebulun, *and* the princes of Naphtali.
28 Your God has commanded your strength: strengthen, O God, that which you have worked for us.
29 Because of your temple at Jerusalem shall kings bring presents to you.
30 Rebuke the company of spear men, the multitude of the bulls, with the calves of the people, *till every one* submits himself with pieces of silver: scatter you the people *that* delight in war.
31 Princes shall come out of Egypt; Ethiopia shall soon stretch out her hands to God.
32 ¶ Sing to God, you kingdoms of the earth; O sing praises unto the Lord; Selah:
33 To him that rides upon the heavens of heavens, *which were* of old; lo, he does send out his voice, *and that* a mighty voice.
34 Ascribe you strength unto God: his excellency *is* over Israel, and his strength *is* in the clouds.
35 O God, *you are* awesome out of your holy places: the God of Israel *is* he that gives strength and power to *his* people. Blessed *be* God.

Psalms 69

69:1 ¶ <<To the chief Musician upon Shoshannim, *A Psalm* of David.>> Save me, O God; for the waters have come in unto *my* soul.
2 I sink in deep mire, where *there is* no standing: I have come into deep waters, where the floods overflow me.
3 I am weary of my crying: my throat is dried: my eyes fail while I wait for my God.
4 They that hate me without a cause are more than the hairs of my head: they that would destroy me, *being* my enemies wrongfully, are mighty: then I restored *that* which I took not away.
5 O God, you know my foolishness; and my sins are not hidden from you.
6 Let not them that wait on you, O Lord Yahweh of hosts, be ashamed for my sake: let not those that seek you be confounded for my sake, O God of Israel.
7 Because for your sake I have borne reproach; shame has covered my face.
8 I have become a stranger to my brothers, and an alien to my mother's children.
9 For the zeal of your house has eaten me up; and the reproaches of them that reproached you have fallen upon me.
10 When I wept, *and chastened* my soul with fasting, that was to my reproach.
11 I made sackcloth also my garment; and I became a proverb to them.
12 They that sit in the gate speak against me; and I *was* the song of the drunkards.
13 ¶ But as for me, my prayer *is* unto you, O Yahweh, *in* an acceptable time: O God, in the multitude of your mercy hear me, in the truth of your salvation.
14 Deliver me out of the mire, and let me not sink: let me be delivered from them that hate me, and out of the deep waters.
15 Let not the water flood overflow me, neither let the deep swallow me up, and let not the pit shut her mouth upon me.
16 Hear me, O Yahweh; for your loving kindness *is* good: turn unto me according to the multitude of your tender mercies.
17 And hide not your face from your servant; for I am in trouble: hear me speedily.
18 Draw near unto my soul, *and* redeem it: deliver me because of my enemies.
19 You have known my reproach, and my shame, and my dishonor: my adversaries *are* all before you.
20 Reproach has broken my heart; and I am full of heaviness: and I looked *for someone* to take pity, but *there was* none; and for comforters, but I found none.
21 They gave me also gall for my food; and in my thirst they gave me vinegar to drink.
22 ¶ Let their table become a snare before them: and *that which should have been* for *their* welfare, *let it become* a trap.
23 Let their eyes be darkened, that they see not; and make their loins continually to shake.

24 Pour out your indignation upon them, and let your wrathful anger take hold of them.
25 Let their habitation be desolate; *and* let none dwell in their tents.
26 For they persecute *him* whom you have smitten; and they talk to the grief of those whom you have wounded.
27 Add iniquity to their iniquity: and let them not come into your righteousness.
28 Let them be blotted out of the book of the living, and not be written with the righteous.
29 But I *am* poor and sorrowful: let your salvation, O God, set me up on high.
30 ¶ I will praise the name of God with a song, and will magnify him with thanksgiving.
31 *This* also shall please Yahweh better than an ox *or* bullock that has horns and hoofs.
32 The humble shall see *this, and* be glad: and your heart shall live that seek God.
33 For Yahweh hears the poor, and despises not his prisoners.
34 Let the heaven and earth praise him, the seas, and everything that moves therein.
35 For God will save Zion, and will build the cities of Judah: that they may dwell there, and have it in possession.
36 The seed also of his servants shall inherit it: and they that love his name shall dwell therein.

Psalms 70

70:1 ¶ <<To the chief Musician, *A Psalm* of David, to bring to remembrance.>> *Make haste*, O God, to deliver me; make haste to help me, O Yahweh.
2 Let them be ashamed and confounded that seek after my soul: let them be turned backward, and put to confusion, that desire my hurt.
3 Let them be turned back for a reward of their shame that say, Aha, aha.
4 Let all those that seek you rejoice and be glad in you: and let such as love your salvation say continually, Let God be magnified.
5 But I *am* poor and needy: make haste unto me, O God: you *are* my help and my deliverer; O Yahweh, make no delay.

Psalms 71

71:1 ¶ In you, O Yahweh, do I put my trust: let me never be put to shame.
2 Deliver me in your righteousness, and cause me to escape: incline your ear unto me, and save me.
3 Be you my strong habitation, whereunto I may continually resort: you have given commandment to save me; for you *are* my rock and my fortress.
4 Deliver me, O my God, out of the hand of the wicked, out of the hand of the unrighteous and cruel man.
5 For you *are* my hope, O Lord Yahweh: *you are* my trust from my youth.

6 By you have I been held up from the womb: you are he that took me out of my mother's womb: my praise *shall be* continually of you.
7 I am as a wonder unto many; but you *are* my strong refuge.
8 Let my mouth be filled *with* your praise *and with* your honor all the day.
9 Cast me not off in the time of old age; forsake me not when my strength fails.
10 For my enemies speak against me; and they that lay wait for my soul take counsel together,
11 Saying, God has forsaken him: persecute and take him; for *there is* none to deliver *him*.
12 O God, be not far from me: O my God, make haste for my help.
13 Let them be confounded *and* consumed that are adversaries to my soul; let them be covered *with* reproach and dishonor that seek my hurt.
14 ¶ But I will hope continually, and will yet praise you more and more.
15 My mouth shall show forth your righteousness *and* your salvation all the day; for I know not the numbers *thereof*.
16 I will go in the strength of the Lord Yahweh: I will make mention of your righteousness, *even* of yours only.
17 O God, you have taught me from my youth: and till now have I declared your wondrous works.
18 Now also when I am old and grayheaded, O God, forsake me not; until I have shown your strength unto *this* generation, *and* your power to every one *that* is to come.
19 Your righteousness also, O God, *is* very high, who has done great things: O God, who *is* like unto you!
20 *You*, which have shown me great and grievous troubles, shall quicken me again, and shall bring me up again from the depths of the earth.
21 You shall increase my greatness, and comfort me on every side.
22 I will also praise you with the psaltery, *even* your truth, O my God: unto you will I sing with the harp, O you Holy One of Israel.
23 My lips shall greatly rejoice when I sing unto you; and my soul, which you have redeemed.
24 My tongue also shall talk of your righteousness all the day long: for they are confounded, for they are brought to shame, that seek my hurt.

Psalms 72

72:1 ¶ <<*A Psalm* for Solomon.>> Give the king your judgments, O God, and your righteousness unto the king's son.
2 ¶ He shall judge your people with righteousness, and your poor with judgment.
3 The mountains shall bring peace to the people, and the little hills, by righteousness.
4 He shall judge the poor of the people, he shall save the children of the needy, and shall break in pieces the oppressor.

5 They shall fear you as long as the sun and moon endure, throughout all generations.
6 He shall come down like rain upon the mown grass: as showers *that* water the earth.
7 In his days shall the righteous flourish; and abundance of peace so long as the moon endures.
8 He shall have dominion also from sea to sea, and from the river unto the ends of the earth.
9 They that dwell in the wilderness shall bow before him; and his enemies shall lick the dust.
10 The kings of Tarshish and of the isles shall bring presents: the kings of Sheba and Seba shall offer gifts.
11 Yes, all kings shall fall down before him: all nations shall serve him.
12 For he shall deliver the needy when he cries; the poor also, and *him* that has no helper.
13 He shall spare the poor and needy, and shall save the souls of the needy.
14 He shall redeem their soul from deceit and violence: and precious shall their blood be in his sight.
15 And he shall live, and to him shall be given of the gold of Sheba: prayer also shall be made for him continually; *and* daily shall he be praised.
16 There shall be a handful of corn in the earth upon the top of the mountains; the fruit thereof shall shake like Lebanon: and *they* of the city shall flourish like grass of the earth.
17 His name shall endure forever: his name shall be continued as long as the sun: and *men* shall be blessed in him: all nations shall call him blessed.
18 ¶ Blessed *be* Yahweh God, the God of Israel, who only does wondrous things.
19 And blessed *be* his glorious name forever: and let the whole earth be filled *with* his glory; Amen, and Amen.
20 The prayers of David the son of Jesse are ended.

Psalms 73

73:1 ¶ <<A Psalm of Asaph.>> Truly God *is* good to Israel, *even* to such as are of a clean heart.
2 But as for me, my feet were almost gone; my steps had well near slipped.
3 For I was envious at the foolish, *when* I saw the prosperity of the wicked.
4 For *there are* no bands in their death: but their strength *is* firm.
5 They *are* not in trouble *as other* men; neither are they plagued like *other* men.
6 Therefore pride compasses them about as a chain; violence covers them *as* a garment.
7 Their eyes stand out with fatness: they have more than heart could wish.
8 They are corrupt, and speak wickedly *concerning* oppression: they speak loftily.
9 They set their mouth against the heavens, and their tongue walks through the earth.
10 Therefore his people return here: and waters of a full *cup* are wrung out to them.
11 And they say, How does God know? and is there knowledge in the most High?
12 Behold, these *are* the ungodly, who prosper in the world; they increase *in* riches.
13 Truly I have cleansed my heart *in* vain, and washed my hands in innocence.
14 For all the day long have I been plagued, and chastened every morning.
15 ¶ If I say, I will speak thus; behold, I should offend *against* the generation of your children.
16 When I thought to know this, it *was* too painful for me;
17 Until I went into the sanctuary of God; *then* understood I their end.
18 Surely you did set them in slippery places: you cast them down into destruction.
19 How are they *brought* into desolation, as in a moment! they are utterly consumed with terrors.
20 As a dream when *one* wakes; so, O Lord, when you wake, you shall despise their image.
21 ¶ Thus my heart was grieved, and I was pricked in my reins.
22 So foolish *was* I, and ignorant: I was *as* a beast before you.
23 Nevertheless I *am* continually with you: you have held *me* by my right hand.
24 You shall guide me with your counsel, and afterward receive me *to* glory.
25 Whom have I in heaven *but you*? and *there is* none upon earth *that* I desire besides you.
26 My flesh and my heart fail: *but* God *is* the strength of my heart, and my portion forever.
27 For, lo, they that are far from you shall perish: you have destroyed all them that go a whoring from you.
28 But *it is* good for me to draw near to God: I have put my trust in the Lord Yahweh, that I may declare all your works.

Psalms 74

74:1 ¶ <<Maschil of Asaph.>> O God, why have you cast *us* off forever? why does your anger smoke against the sheep of your pasture?
2 Remember your congregation, *which* you have purchased of old; the rod of your inheritance, *which* you have redeemed; this mount Zion, wherein you have dwelt.
3 Lift up your feet to the perpetual desolations; *even* all *that* the enemy has done wickedly in the sanctuary.
4 Your enemies roar in the midst of your congregations; they set up their banners *for* signs.
5 *A man* was famous according as he had lifted up axes upon the thick trees.
6 But now they break down the carved work thereof at once with axes and hammers.
7 They have cast fire into your sanctuary, they have defiled *by casting down* the dwelling place of your name to the ground.
8 They said in their hearts, Let us destroy them together: they have burned up all the synagogues of God in the land.

9 We see not our signs: *there is* no more any prophet: neither *is there* among us any that knows how long.
10 O God, how long shall the adversary reproach? shall the enemy blaspheme your name forever?
11 Why withdraw you your hand, even your right hand? pluck *it* out of your bosom.
12 ¶ For God *is* my King of old, working salvation in the midst of the earth.
13 You did divide the sea by your strength: you broke the heads of the dragons in the waters.
14 You broke the heads of leviathan in pieces, *and* gave him *to be* meat to the people inhabiting the wilderness.
15 You did cleave the fountain and the flood: you dried up mighty rivers.
16 The day *is* yours, the night also *is* yours: you have prepared the light and the sun.
17 You have set all the borders of the earth: you have made summer and winter.
18 ¶ Remember this, *that* the enemy has reproached, O Yahweh, and *that* the foolish people have blasphemed your name.
19 O deliver not the soul of your turtledove to the multitude *of the wicked*: forget not the congregation of your poor forever.
20 Have respect unto the covenant: for the dark places of the earth are full of the habitations of cruelty.
21 O let not the oppressed return ashamed: let the poor and needy praise your name.
22 Arise, O God, plead your own cause: remember how the foolish man reproaches you daily.
23 Forget not the voice of your enemies: the tumult of those that rise up against you increases continually.

Psalms 75

75:1 ¶ <<To the chief Musician, Altaschith, A Psalm *or* Song of Asaph.>> Unto you, O God, do we give thanks, *to you* do we give thanks: for *that* your name is near your wondrous works declare.
2 When I shall receive the congregation I will judge uprightly.
3 The earth and all the inhabitants thereof are dissolved: I bear up the pillars of it. Selah.
4 I said to the fools, Deal not foolishly: and to the wicked, Lift not up the horn:
5 Lift not up your horn on high: speak *not with* a stiff neck.
6 ¶ For promotion *comes* neither from the east, nor from the west, nor from the south.
7 But God *is* the judge: he puts down one, and sets up another.
8 For in the hand of Yahweh *there is* a cup, and the wine is red; it is full of mixture; and he pours out of the same: but the dregs thereof, all the wicked of the earth shall wring *them* out, *and* drink *them*.
9 But I will declare forever; I will sing praises to the God of Jacob.
10 All the horns of the wicked also will I cut off; *but* the horns of the righteous shall be exalted.

Psalms 76

76:1 ¶ <<To the chief Musician on Neginoth, A Psalm *or* Song of Asaph.>> In Judah *is* God known: his name *is* great in Israel.
2 In Salem also is his tabernacle, and his dwelling place in Zion.
3 There broke he the arrows of the bow, the shield, and the sword, and the battle. Selah.
4 You *are* more glorious *and* excellent than the mountains of prey.
5 The stouthearted are spoiled, they have slept their sleep: and none of the men of might have found their hands.
6 At your rebuke, O God of Jacob, both the chariot and horse were cast into a dead sleep.
7 ¶ You, *even* you, *are* to be feared: and who may stand in your sight when once you are angry?
8 You did cause judgment to be heard from heaven; the earth feared, and was still,
9 When God arose to judgment, to save all the meek of the earth. Selah.
10 Surely the wrath of man shall praise you: the remainder of wrath shall you restrain.
11 Vow, and pay unto Yahweh your God: let all that are round about him bring presents to him that ought to be feared.
12 He shall cut off the spirit of princes: *he is* fearful to the kings of the earth.

Psalms 77

77:1 ¶ <<To the chief Musician, to Jeduthun, A Psalm of Asaph.>> I cried unto God with my voice, *even* unto God with my voice; and he gave ear unto me.
2 In the day of my trouble I sought the Lord: my sore ran in the night, and ceased not: my soul refused to be comforted.
3 I remembered God, and was troubled: I complained, and my spirit was overwhelmed. Selah.
4 You hold my eyes waking: I am so troubled that I cannot speak.
5 I have considered the days of old, the years of ancient times.
6 I call to remembrance my song in the night: I commune with my own heart: and my spirit made diligent search.
7 Will the Lord cast off forever? and will he be favorable no more?
8 Is his mercy clean gone forever? does *his* promise fail forevermore?
9 Has God forgotten to be gracious? has he in anger shut up his tender mercies? Selah.
10 And I said, This *is* my infirmity: *but I will remember* the years of the right hand of the most High.
11 ¶ I will remember the works of Yahweh: surely I will remember your wonders of old.

12 I will meditate also of all your work, and talk of your doings.
13 Your way, O God, *is* in the sanctuary: who *is so* great a God as *our* God?
14 You *are* the God that does wonders: you have declared your strength among the people.
15 You have with *your* arm redeemed your people, the sons of Jacob and Joseph. Selah.
16 The waters saw you, O God, the waters saw you; they were afraid: the depths also were troubled.
17 The clouds poured out water: the skies sent out a sound: your arrows also went abroad.
18 The voice of your thunder *was* in the heaven: the lightnings lightened the world: the earth trembled and shook.
19 Your way *is* in the sea, and your path in the great waters, and your footsteps are not known.
20 You led your people like a flock by the hand of Moses and Aaron.

Psalms 78

78:1 ¶ <<Maschil of Asaph.>> Give ear, O my people, *to* my law: incline your ears to the words of my mouth.
2 I will open my mouth in a parable: I will utter dark sayings of old:
3 Which we have heard and known, and our fathers have told us.
4 We will not hide *them* from their children, showing to the generation to come the praises of Yahweh, and his strength, and his wonderful works that he has done.
5 For he established a testimony in Jacob, and appointed a law in Israel, which he commanded our fathers, that they should make them known to their children:
6 That the generation to come might know *them, even* the children *which* should be born; *who* should arise and declare *them* to their children:
7 That they might set their hope in God, and not forget the works of God, but keep his commandments:
8 And might not be as their fathers, a stubborn and rebellious generation; a generation *that* set not their heart aright, and whose spirit was not steadfast with God.
9 ¶ The children of Ephraim, *being* armed, *and* carrying bows, turned back in the day of battle.
10 They kept not the covenant of God, and refused to walk in his law;
11 And forgot his works, and his wonders that he had shown them.
12 Marvelous things did he in the sight of their fathers, in the land of Egypt, *in* the field of Zoan.
13 He divided the sea, and caused them to pass through; and he made the waters to stand as a heap.
14 In the daytime also he led them with a cloud, and all the night with a light of fire.
15 He broke open the rocks in the wilderness, and gave *them* drink as *out of* the great depths.
16 He brought streams also out of the rock, and caused waters to run down like rivers.
17 And they sinned yet more against him by provoking the most High in the wilderness.
18 And they tempted God in their heart by asking food for their lust.
19 Yes, they spoke against God; they said, Can God furnish a table in the wilderness?
20 Behold, he smote the rock, that the waters gushed out, and the streams overflowed; can he give bread also? can he provide flesh for his people?
21 Therefore Yahweh heard *this*, and was angry: so a fire was kindled against Jacob, and anger also came up against Israel;
22 Because they believed not in God, and trusted not in his salvation:
23 Though he had commanded the clouds from above, and opened the doors of heaven,
24 And had rained down manna upon them to eat, and had given them of the corn of heaven.
25 Man did eat angels' food: he sent them food to the full.
26 He caused an east wind to blow in the heaven: and by his power he brought in the south wind.
27 He rained flesh also upon them as dust, and feathered fowls like as the sand of the sea:
28 And he let *it* fall in the midst of their camp, round about their habitations.
29 So they did eat, and were well filled: for he gave them their own desire;
30 They were not estranged from their lust. But while their food *was* yet in their mouths,
31 The wrath of God came upon them, and slew the fattest of them, and smote down the chosen *men* of Israel.
32 For all this they sinned still, and believed not for his wondrous works.
33 Therefore their days did he consume in vanity, and their years in trouble.
34 When he slew them, then they sought him: and they returned and inquired early after God.
35 And they remembered that God *was* their rock, and the high God their redeemer.
36 Nevertheless they did flatter him with their mouth, and they lied to him with their tongues.
37 For their heart was not right with him, neither were they steadfast in his covenant.
38 But he, *being* full of compassion, forgave *their* iniquity, and destroyed *them* not: yes, many a time turned he his anger away, and did not stir up all his wrath.
39 For he remembered that they *were but* flesh; a wind that passes away, and comes not again.
40 ¶ How often did they provoke him in the wilderness, *and* grieve him in the desert!
41 Yes, they turned back and tempted God, and limited the Holy One of Israel.
42 They remembered not his hand, *nor* the day when he delivered them from the enemy.
43 How he had worked his signs in Egypt, and his wonders in the field of Zoan:

Psalms 78

44 And had turned their rivers into blood; and their floods, that they could not drink.
45 He sent diverse sorts of flies among them, which devoured them; and frogs, which destroyed them.
46 He gave also their increase to the caterpillar, and their labor to the locust.
47 He destroyed their vines with hail, and their sycamore trees with frost.
48 He gave up their cattle also to the hail, and their flocks to hot thunderbolts.
49 He cast upon them the fierceness of his anger, wrath, and indignation, and trouble, by sending evil angels *among them*.
50 He made a way to his anger; he spared not their soul from death, but gave their life over to the pestilence;
51 And smote all the firstborn in Egypt; the chief of *their* strength in the tabernacles of Ham:
52 But made his own people to go forth like sheep, and guided them in the wilderness like a flock.
53 And he led them on safely, so that they feared not: but the sea overwhelmed their enemies.
54 And he brought them to the border of his sanctuary, *even to* this mountain, *which* his right hand had purchased.
55 He cast out the heathen also before them, and divided them an inheritance by line, and made the tribes of Israel to dwell in their tents.
56 Yet they tempted and provoked the most high God, and kept not his testimonies:
57 But turned back, and dealt unfaithfully like their fathers: they were turned aside like a deceitful bow.
58 For they provoked him to anger with their high places, and moved him to jealousy with their graven images.
59 When God heard *this*, he was angry, and greatly abhorred Israel:
60 So that he forsook the tabernacle of Shiloh, the tent *which* he placed among men;
61 And delivered his strength into captivity, and his glory into the enemy's hand.
62 He gave his people over also to the sword; and was angry with his inheritance.
63 The fire consumed their young men; and their maidens were not given to marriage.
64 Their priests fell by the sword; and their widows made no lamentation.
65 Then the Lord awoke as one out of sleep, *and* like a mighty man that shouts by reason of wine.
66 And he smote his enemies in the hinder parts: he put them to a perpetual reproach.
67 Moreover he refused the tabernacle of Joseph, and chose not the tribe of Ephraim:
68 But chose the tribe of Judah, the mount Zion which he loved.
69 And he built his sanctuary like high *palaces*, like the earth which he has established forever.
70 He chose David also his servant, and took him from the sheepfolds:
71 From following the ewes great with young he brought him to feed Jacob his people, and Israel his inheritance.
72 So he fed them according to the integrity of his heart; and guided them by the skillfulness of his hands.

Psalms 79

79:1 ¶ <<A Psalm of Asaph.>> O God, the heathen have come into your inheritance; your holy temple have they defiled; they have laid Jerusalem in heaps.
2 The dead bodies of your servants have they given *to be* meat to the fowls of the heaven, the flesh of your saints to the beasts of the earth.
3 Their blood have they shed like water round about Jerusalem; and *there was* none to bury *them*.
4 We have become a reproach to our neighbors, a scorn and derision to them that are round about us.
5 How long, Yahweh? will you be angry forever? shall your jealousy burn like fire?
6 ¶ Pour out your wrath upon the heathen that have not known you, and upon the kingdoms that have not called upon your name.
7 For they have devoured Jacob, and laid waste his dwelling place.
8 O remember not against us former iniquities: let your tender mercies speedily prevent us: for we are brought very low.
9 Help us, O God of our salvation, for the glory of your name: and deliver us, and purge away our sins, for your name's sake.
10 Why should the heathen say, Where *is* their God? let him be known among the heathen in our sight *by* the revenging of the blood of your servants *which is* shed.
11 Let the sighing of the prisoner come before you; according to the greatness of your power preserve you those that are appointed to die;
12 And render to our neighbors sevenfold into their bosom their reproach, with which they have reproached you, O Lord.
13 So we your people and sheep of your pasture will give you thanks forever: we will show forth your praise to all generations.

Psalms 80

80:1 ¶ <<To the chief Musician upon Shoshannimeduth, A Psalm of Asaph.>> Give ear, O Shepherd of Israel, you that lead Joseph like a flock; you that dwell *between* the cherubims, shine forth.
2 Before Ephraim and Benjamin and Manasseh stir up your strength, and come *and* save us.
3 Turn us again, O God, and cause your face to shine; and we shall be saved.
4 O Yahweh God of hosts, how long will you be angry against the prayer of your people?
5 You feed them with the bread of tears; and give them tears to drink in great measure.
6 You make us a strife to our neighbors: and our enemies laugh among themselves.

7 Turn us again, O God of hosts, and cause your face to shine; and we shall be saved.

8 ¶ You have brought a vine out of Egypt: you have cast out the heathen, and planted it.

9 You prepared *room* before it, and did cause it to take deep root, and it filled the land.

10 The hills were covered with the shadow of it, and the boughs thereof *were like* the goodly cedars.

11 She sent out her boughs to the sea, and her branches to the river.

12 Why have you *then* broken down her hedges, so that all they which pass by the way do pluck her?

13 The boar out of the wood does waste it, and the wild beast of the field does devour it.

14 Return, we beseech you, O God of hosts: look down from heaven, and behold, and visit this vine;

15 And the vineyard which your right hand has planted, and the branch *that* you made strong for yourself.

16 *It is* burned with fire, *it is* cut down: they perish at the rebuke of your countenance.

17 Let your hand be upon the man of your right hand, upon the son of man *whom* you made strong for yourself.

18 So will not we go back from you: quicken us, and we will call upon your name.

19 Turn us again, O Yahweh God of hosts, cause your face to shine; and we shall be saved.

Psalms 81

81:1 ¶ <<To the chief Musician upon Gittith, *A Psalm* of Asaph.>> Sing aloud to God our strength: make a joyful noise unto the God of Jacob.

2 Take a psalm, and bring here the tambourine, the pleasant harp with the psaltery.

3 Blow up the trumpet in the new moon, in the time appointed, on our solemn feast day.

4 For this *was* a statute for Israel, *and* a law of the God of Jacob.

5 This he ordained in Joseph *for* a testimony, when he went out through the land of Egypt: *where* I heard a language *that* I understood not.

6 I removed his shoulder from the burden: his hands were delivered from the pots.

7 You called in trouble, and I delivered you; I answered you in the secret place of thunder: I proved you at the waters of Meribah. Selah.

8 ¶ Hear, O my people, and I will testify to you: O Israel, if you will listen to me;

9 There shall no strange god be in you; neither shall you worship any strange god.

10 I *am* Yahweh your God, which brought you out of the land of Egypt: open your mouth wide, and I will fill it.

11 But my people would not listen to my voice; and Israel would *have* none of me.

12 So I gave them up to their own hearts' lust: *and* they walked in their own counsels.

13 Oh that my people had listened to me, *and* Israel had walked in my ways!

14 I should soon have subdued their enemies, and turned my hand against their adversaries.

15 The haters of Yahweh should have submitted themselves unto him: but their time should have endured forever.

16 He should have fed them also with the finest of the wheat: and with honey out of the rock should I have satisfied you.

Psalms 82

82:1 ¶ <<A Psalm of Asaph.>> God stands in the congregation of the mighty; he judges among the gods.

2 How long will you judge unjustly, and accept the persons of the wicked? Selah.

3 Defend the poor and fatherless: do justice to the afflicted and needy.

4 Deliver the poor and needy: rid *them* out of the hand of the wicked.

5 They know not, neither will they understand; they walk on in darkness: all the foundations of the earth are out of course.

6 ¶ I have said, You *are* gods; and all of you *are* children of the most High.

7 But you shall die like men, and fall like one of the princes.

8 Arise, O God, judge the earth: for you shall inherit all nations.

Psalms 83

83:1 ¶ <<A Song *or* Psalm of Asaph.>> Keep not you silence, O God: hold not your peace, and be not still, O God.

2 For, lo, your enemies make a tumult: and they that hate you have lifted up the head.

3 They have taken crafty counsel against your people, and consulted against your hidden ones.

4 They have said, Come, and let us cut them off from *being* a nation; that the name of Israel may be no more in remembrance.

5 For they have consulted together with one consent: they are confederate against you:

6 The tabernacles of Edom, and the Ishmaelites; of Moab, and the Hagarenes;

7 Gebal, and Ammon, and Amalek; the Philistines with the inhabitants of Tyre;

8 Assur also has joined with them: they have helped the children of Lot. Selah.

9 ¶ Do unto them as *to* the Midianites; as *to* Sisera, as *to* Jabin, at the brook of Kison:

10 *Which* perished at Endor: they became *as* dung for the earth.

11 Make their nobles like Oreb, and like Zeeb: yes, all their princes as Zebah, and as Zalmunna:

12 Who said, Let us take unto ourselves the houses of God in possession.

Psalms 83

13 O my God, make them like a wheel; as the stubble before the wind.
14 As the fire burns a woods, and as the flame sets the mountains on fire;
15 So persecute them with your tempest, and make them afraid with your storm.
16 Fill their faces with shame; that they may seek your name, O Yahweh.
17 Let them be confounded and troubled forever; yes, let them be put to shame, and perish:
18 That *men* may know that you, whose name alone *is* YAHWEH, *are* the most high over all the earth.

Psalms 84

84:1 ¶ <<To the chief Musician upon Gittith, A Psalm for the sons of Korah.>> How beloved *are* your tabernacles, O Yahweh of hosts!
2 My soul longs, yes, even faints for the courts of Yahweh: my heart and my flesh cry out for the living God.
3 Yes, the sparrow has found a house, and the swallow a nest for herself, where she may lay her young, *even* your altars, O Yahweh of hosts, my King, and my God.
4 Blessed *are* they that dwell in your house: they will be still praising you. Selah.
5 Blessed *is* the man whose strength *is* in you; in whose heart *are* the ways *of them*.
6 *Who* passing through the valley of Baca make it a well; the rain also fills the pools.
7 They go from strength to strength, *every one of them* in Zion appears before God.
8 ¶ O Yahweh God of hosts, hear my prayer: give ear, O God of Jacob. Selah.
9 Behold, O God our shield, and look upon the face of your anointed.
10 For a day in your courts *is* better than a thousand. I would rather be a doorkeeper in the house of my God, than to dwell in the tents of wickedness.
11 For Yahweh God *is* a sun and shield: Yahweh will give grace and glory: no good *thing* will he withhold from them that walk uprightly.
12 O Yahweh of hosts, blessed *is* the man that trusts in you.

Psalms 85

85:1 ¶ <<To the chief Musician, A Psalm for the sons of Korah.>> Yahweh, you have been favorable to your land: you have brought back the captivity of Jacob.
2 You have forgiven the iniquity of your people, you have covered all their sin. Selah.
3 You have taken away all your wrath: you have turned *yourself* from the fierceness of your anger.
4 Turn us, O God of our salvation, and cause your anger toward us to cease.
5 Will you be angry with us forever? will you draw out your anger to all generations?
6 Will you not revive us again: that your people may rejoice in you?
7 Show us your mercy, O Yahweh, and grant us your salvation.
8 ¶ I will hear what God Yahweh will speak: for he will speak peace to his people, and to his saints: but let them not turn again to folly.
9 Surely his salvation *is* near them that fear him; that glory may dwell in our land.
10 Mercy and truth are met together; righteousness and peace have kissed *each other*.
11 Truth shall spring out of the earth; and righteousness shall look down from heaven.
12 Yes, Yahweh shall give *that which is* good; and our land shall yield her increase.
13 Righteousness shall go before him; and shall set *us* in the way of his steps.

Psalms 86

86:1 ¶ <<A Prayer of David.>> Bow down your ear, O Yahweh, hear me: for I *am* poor and needy.
2 Preserve my soul; for I *am* holy: O you my God, save your servant that trusts in you.
3 Be merciful unto me, O Lord: for I cry unto you daily.
4 Rejoice the soul of your servant: for unto you, O Lord, do I lift up my soul.
5 For you, Lord, *are* good, and ready to forgive; and plenteous in mercy to all them that call upon you.
6 Give ear, O Yahweh, unto my prayer; and attend to the voice of my supplications.
7 In the day of my trouble I will call upon you: for you will answer me.
8 ¶ Among the gods *there is* none like unto you, O Lord; neither *are there any works* like unto your works.
9 All nations whom you have made shall come and worship before you, O Lord; and shall glorify your name.
10 For you *are* great, and do wondrous things: you *are* God alone.
11 Teach me your way, O Yahweh; I will walk in your truth: unite my heart to fear your name.
12 I will praise you, O Lord my God, with all my heart: and I will glorify your name forevermore.
13 For great *is* your mercy toward me: and you have delivered my soul from the lowest hell.
14 O God, the proud have risen against me, and the assemblies of violent *men* have sought after my soul; and have not set you before them.
15 But you, O Lord, *are* a God full of compassion, and gracious, longsuffering, and plenteous in mercy and truth.
16 O turn unto me, and have mercy upon me; give your strength to your servant, and save the son of your handmaid.
17 Show me a token for good; that they which hate me may see *it*, and be ashamed: because you, Yahweh, have helped me, and comforted me.

Psalms 87

87:1 ¶ <<A Psalm *or* Song for the sons of Korah.>> His foundation *is* in the holy mountains.
2 Yahweh loves the gates of Zion more than all the dwellings of Jacob.
3 Glorious things are spoken of you, O city of God. Selah.
4 ¶ I will make mention of Rahab and Babylon to them that know me: behold Philistia, and Tyre, with Ethiopia; this *man* was born there.
5 And of Zion it shall be said, This and that man was born in her: and the highest himself shall establish her.
6 Yahweh shall count, when he writes up the people, *that* this *man* was born there. Selah.
7 As well the singers as the players on instruments *shall be there*: all my springs *are* in you.

Psalms 88

88:1 ¶ <<A Song *or* Psalm for the sons of Korah, to the chief Musician upon Mahalath Leannoth, Maschil of Heman the Ezrahite.>> O Yahweh God of my salvation, I have cried day *and* night before you:
2 Let my prayer come before you: incline your ear unto my cry;
3 For my soul is full of troubles: and my life draws near to the grave.
4 I am counted with them that go down into the pit: I am as a man *that has* no strength:
5 Free among the dead, like the slain that lie in the grave, whom you remember no more: and they are cut off from your hand.
6 You have laid me in the lowest pit, in darkness, in the depths.
7 Your wrath lies hard upon me, and you have afflicted *me* with all your waves. Selah.
8 You have put away my acquaintances far from me; you have made me an abomination to them: *I am* shut up, and I cannot come forth.
9 My eye mourns by reason of affliction: Yahweh, I have called daily upon you, I have stretched out my hands unto you.
10 ¶ Will you show wonders to the dead? shall the dead arise *and* praise you? Selah.
11 Shall your loving kindness be declared in the grave? *or* your faithfulness in destruction?
12 Shall your wonders be known in the dark? and your righteousness in the land of forgetfulness?
13 But unto you have I cried, O Yahweh; and in the morning shall my prayer prevent you.
14 Yahweh, why cast you off my soul? *why* hide you your face from me?
15 I *am* afflicted and ready to die from *my* youth up: *while* I suffer your terrors I am distracted.
16 Your fierce wrath goes over me; your terrors have cut me off.
17 They came round about me daily like water; they compassed me about together.
18 Lover and friend have you put far from me, *and* my acquaintances into darkness.

Psalms 89

89:1 ¶ <<Maschil of Ethan the Ezrahite.>> I will sing of the mercies of Yahweh forever: with my mouth will I make known your faithfulness to all generations.
2 For I have said, Mercy shall be built up forever: your faithfulness shall you establish in the very heavens.
3 I have made a covenant with my chosen, I have sworn to David my servant,
4 Your seed will I establish forever, and build up your throne to all generations. Selah.
5 ¶ And the heavens shall praise your wonders, O Yahweh: your faithfulness also in the congregation of the saints
6 For who in the heaven can be compared unto Yahweh? *who* among the sons of the mighty can be likened unto Yahweh?
7 God is greatly to be feared in the assembly of the saints, and to be had in reverence of all *them that are* about him.
8 O Yahweh God of hosts, who *is* a strong Yah like unto you? or to your faithfulness round about you?
9 You rule the raging of the sea: when the waves thereof arise, you still them.
10 You have broken Rahab in pieces, as one that is slain; you have scattered your enemies with your strong arm.
11 The heavens *are* yours, the earth also *is* yours: *as for* the world and the fullness thereof, you have founded them.
12 The north and the south you have created them: Tabor and Hermon shall rejoice in your name.
13 You have a mighty arm: strong is your hand, *and* high is your right hand.
14 Justice and judgment *are* the habitation of your throne: mercy and truth shall go before your face.
15 ¶ Blessed *are* the people that know the joyful sound: they shall walk, O Yahweh, in the light of your countenance.
16 In your name shall they rejoice all the day: and in your righteousness shall they be exalted.
17 For you *are* the glory of their strength and in your favor our horn shall be exalted.
18 For Yahweh *is* our defense; and the Holy One of Israel *is* our king.
19 ¶ Then you spoke in *a* vision to your holy one, and said, I have laid help upon *one that is* mighty; I have exalted *one* chosen out of the people.
20 I have found David my servant; with my holy oil have I anointed him:
21 With whom my hand shall be established: my arm also shall strengthen him.
22 The enemy shall not exact upon him; nor the son of wickedness afflict him.

Psalms 89

23 And I will beat down his foes before his face, and plague them that hate him.
24 But my faithfulness and my mercy *shall be* with him: and in my name shall his horn be exalted.
25 I will set his hand also in the sea, and his right hand in the rivers.
26 He shall cry unto me, You *are* my father, my God, and the rock of my salvation.
27 Also I will make him *my* firstborn, higher than the kings of the earth.
28 My mercy will I keep for him forevermore, and my covenant shall stand fast with him.
29 His seed also will I make *to endure* forever, and his throne as the days of heaven.
30 If his children forsake my law, and walk not in my judgments;
31 If they break my statutes, and keep not my commandments;
32 Then will I visit their transgression with the rod, and their iniquity with stripes.
33 Nevertheless my loving kindness will I not utterly take from him, nor allow my faithfulness to fail.
34 My covenant will I not break, nor alter the thing that has gone out of my lips.
35 Once have I sworn by my holiness that I will not lie to David.
36 His seed shall endure forever, and his throne as the sun before me.
37 It shall be established forever as the moon, and *as a* faithful witness in heaven. Selah.
38 ¶ But you have cast off and abhorred, you have been angry with your anointed.
39 You have made void the covenant of your servant: you have profaned his crown *by casting it* to the ground.
40 You have broken down all his hedges; you have brought his strong holds to ruin.
41 All that pass by the way spoil him: he is a reproach to his neighbors.
42 You have set up the right hand of his adversaries; you have made all his enemies to rejoice.
43 You have also turned the edge of his sword, and have not made him to stand in the battle.
44 You have made his glory to cease, and cast his throne down to the ground.
45 The days of his youth have you shortened: you have covered him with shame. Selah.
46 How long, Yahweh? will you hide yourself forever? shall your wrath burn like fire?
47 Remember how short my time is: why have you made all men in vain?
48 What man *is he that* lives, and shall not see death? shall he deliver his soul from the hand of the grave? Selah.
49 Lord, where *are* your former loving kindnesses, *which* you swore to David in your truth?
50 Remember, Lord, the reproach of your servants; *how* I do bear in my bosom *the reproach of* all the mighty people;
51 With which your enemies have reproached, O Yahweh; with which they have reproached the footsteps of your anointed.
52 Blessed *be* Yahweh forevermore. Amen, and Amen.

Psalms 90

90:1 ¶ <<A Prayer of Moses the man of God.>> Lord, you have been our dwelling place in all generations.
2 Before the mountains were brought forth, or ever you had formed the earth and the world, even from everlasting to everlasting, you *are* God.
3 You turn man to destruction; and say, Return, you children of men.
4 For a thousand years in your sight *are but* as yesterday when it is past, and *as* a watch in the night.
5 You carry them away as with a flood; they are *as* a sleep: in the morning *they are* like grass *which* grows up.
6 In the morning it flourishes, and grows up; in the evening it is cut down, and withers.
7 ¶ For we are consumed by your anger, and by your wrath are we troubled.
8 You have set our iniquities before you, our secret *sins* in the light of your countenance.
9 For all our days are passed away in your wrath: we spend our years as a tale *that is told*.
10 The days of our years *are* threescore years and ten; and if by reason of strength *they be* fourscore years, yet *is* their strength labor and sorrow; for it is soon cut off, and we fly away.
11 Who knows the power of your anger? even according to your fear, *so is* your wrath.
12 ¶ So teach *us* to number our days, that we may apply *our* hearts unto wisdom.
13 Return, O Yahweh, how long? and let it repent you concerning your servants.
14 O satisfy us early with your mercy; that we may rejoice and be glad all our days.
15 Make us glad according to the days *wherein* you have afflicted us, *and* the years *wherein* we have seen evil.
16 Let your work appear to your servants, and your glory to their children.
17 And let the beauty of Yahweh our God be upon us: and establish you the work of our hands upon us; yes, the work of our hands establish you it.

Psalms 91

91:1 ¶ He that dwells in the secret place of the most High shall remain under the shadow of the Almighty.
2 I will say of Yahweh, *He is* my refuge and my fortress: my God; in him will I trust.
3 Surely he shall deliver you from the snare of the fowler, *and* from the noisome pestilence.
4 He shall cover you with his feathers, and under his wings shall you trust: his truth *shall be your* shield and buckler.

5 You shall not be afraid for the terror by night; *nor* for the arrow *that* flies by day;
6 *Nor* for the pestilence *that* walks in darkness; *nor* for the destruction *that* wastes at noonday.
7 A thousand shall fall at your side, and ten thousand at your right hand; *but* it shall not come near you.
8 Only with your eyes shall you behold and see the reward of the wicked.
9 ¶ Because you have made Yahweh, *which is* my refuge, *even* the most High, your habitation;
10 There shall no evil befall you, neither shall any plague come near your dwelling.
11 For he shall give his angels charge over you, to keep you in all your ways.
12 They shall bear you up in *their* hands, lest you dash your foot against a stone.
13 You shall tread upon the lion and adder: the young lion and the dragon shall you trample under feet.
14 Because he has set his love upon me, therefore will I deliver him: I will set him on high, because he has known my name.
15 He shall call upon me, and I will answer him: I *will be* with him in trouble; I will deliver him, and honor him.
16 With long life will I satisfy him, and show him my salvation.

Psalms 92

92:1 ¶ <<A Psalm *or* Song for the sabbath day.>> *It is a* good *thing* to give thanks unto Yahweh, and to sing praises unto your name, O most High:
2 To show forth your loving kindness in the morning, and your faithfulness every night,
3 Upon an instrument of ten strings, and upon the psaltery; upon the harp with a solemn sound.
4 For you, Yahweh, have made me glad through your work: I will triumph in the works of your hands.
5 O Yahweh, how great are your works! *and* your thoughts are very deep.
6 A brutish man knows not; neither does a fool understand this.
7 ¶ When the wicked spring as the grass, and when all the workers of iniquity do flourish; *it is* that they shall be destroyed forever:
8 But you, Yahweh, *are most* high forevermore.
9 For, lo, your enemies, O Yahweh, for, lo, your enemies shall perish; all the workers of iniquity shall be scattered.
10 But my horn shall you exalt like *the horn of* a unicorn: I shall be anointed with fresh oil.
11 My eye also shall see *my desire* on my enemies, *and* my ears shall hear *my desire* of the wicked that rise up against me.
12 The righteous shall flourish like the palm tree: he shall grow like a cedar in Lebanon.
13 Those that are planted in the house of Yahweh shall flourish in the courts of our God.
14 They shall still bring forth fruit in old age; they shall be fat and flourishing;
15 To show that Yahweh *is* upright: *he is* my rock, and *there is* no unrighteousness in him.

Psalms 93

93:1 ¶ Yahweh reigns, he is clothed with majesty; Yahweh is clothed with strength, *with which* he has girded himself: the world also is established, that it cannot be moved.
2 Your throne *is* established of old: you *are* from everlasting.
3 The floods have lifted up, O Yahweh, the floods have lifted up their voice; the floods lift up their waves.
4 Yahweh on high *is* mightier than the noise of many waters, *yes, than* the mighty waves of the sea.
5 Your testimonies are very sure: holiness becomes your house, O Yahweh, forever.

Psalms 94

94:1 ¶ O Yahweh God, to whom vengeance belongs; O God, to whom vengeance belongs, show yourself.
2 Lift up yourself, you judge of the earth: render a reward to the proud.
3 Yahweh, how long shall the wicked, how long shall the wicked triumph?
4 *How long* shall they utter *and* speak hard things? *and* all the workers of iniquity boast themselves?
5 They break in pieces your people, O Yahweh, and afflict your heritage.
6 They slay the widow and the stranger, and murder the fatherless.
7 Yet they say, Yah shall not see, neither shall the God of Jacob regard *it*.
8 Understand, you brutish among the people: and *you* fools, when will you be wise?
9 He that planted the ear, shall he not hear? he that formed the eye, shall he not see?
10 He that chastises the heathen, shall not he correct? he that teaches man knowledge, *shall not he know*?
11 Yahweh knows the thoughts of man, that they *are* vanity.
12 ¶ Blessed *is* the man whom you chasten, O Yah, and teach him out of your law;
13 That you may give him rest from the days of adversity, until the pit is dug for the wicked.
14 For Yahweh will not cast off his people, neither will he forsake his inheritance.
15 But judgment shall return to righteousness: and all the upright in heart shall follow it.
16 Who will rise up for me against the evildoers? *or* who will stand up for me against the workers of iniquity?
17 Unless Yahweh *had been* my help, my soul had almost dwelt in silence.
18 When I said, My foot slips; your mercy, O Yahweh, held me up.

Psalms 94

19 In the multitude of my thoughts within me your comforts delight my soul.
20 Shall the throne of iniquity have fellowship with you, which frames mischief by a law?
21 They gather themselves together against the soul of the righteous, and condemn the innocent blood.
22 But Yahweh is my defense; and my God *is* the rock of my refuge.
23 And he shall bring upon them their own iniquity, and shall cut them off in their own wickedness; *yes,* Yahweh our God shall cut them off.

Psalms 95

95:1 ¶ O come, let us sing unto Yahweh: let us make a joyful noise to the rock of our salvation.
2 Let us come before his presence with thanksgiving, and make a joyful noise unto him with psalms.
3 For Yahweh *is* a great God, and a great King above all gods.
4 In his hand *are* the deep places of the earth: the strength of the hills *is* his also.
5 The sea *is* his, and he made it: and his hands formed the dry *land*.
6 O come, let us worship and bow down: let us kneel before Yahweh our maker.
7 ¶ For he *is* our God; and we *are* the people of his pasture, and the sheep of his hand. Today if you will hear his voice,
8 Harden not your heart, as in the provocation, *and* as *in* the day of temptation in the wilderness:
9 When your fathers tempted me, proved me, and saw my work.
10 Forty years long was I grieved with *this* generation, and said, It *is* a people that do err in their heart, and they have not known my ways:
11 To whom I swore in my wrath that they should not enter into my rest.

Psalms 96

96:1 ¶ O sing unto Yahweh a new song: sing unto Yahweh, all the earth.
2 Sing unto Yahweh, bless his name; show forth his salvation from day to day.
3 Declare his glory among the heathen, his wonders among all people.
4 For Yahweh *is* great, and greatly to be praised: he *is* to be feared above all gods.
5 For all the gods of the nations *are* idols: but Yahweh made the heavens.
6 Honor and majesty *are* before him: strength and beauty *are* in his sanctuary.
7 Give unto Yahweh, O you kindreds of the people, give unto Yahweh glory and strength.
8 Give unto Yahweh the glory *due unto* his name: bring an offering, and come into his courts.
9 O worship Yahweh in the beauty of holiness: fear before him, all the earth.
10 ¶ Say among the heathen *that* Yahweh reigns: the world also shall be established that it shall not be moved: he shall judge the people righteously.
11 Let the heavens rejoice, and let the earth be glad; let the sea roar, and the fullness thereof.
12 Let the field be joyful, and all that *is* therein: then shall all the trees of the wood rejoice
13 Before Yahweh: for he comes, for he comes to judge the earth: he shall judge the world with righteousness, and the people with his truth.

Psalms 97

97:1 ¶ Yahweh reigns; let the earth rejoice; let the multitude of isles be glad *thereof*.
2 Clouds and darkness *are* round about him: righteousness and judgment *are* the habitation of his throne.
3 A fire goes before him, and burns up his enemies round about.
4 His lightnings enlightened the world: the earth saw, and trembled.
5 The hills melted like wax at the presence of Yahweh, at the presence of the Lord of the whole earth.
6 The heavens declare his righteousness, and all the people see his glory.
7 Confounded be all they that serve graven images, that boast themselves of idols: worship him, all *you* gods.
8 ¶ Zion heard, and was glad; and the daughters of Judah rejoiced because of your judgments, O Yahweh.
9 For you, Yahweh, *are* high above all the earth: you are exalted far above all gods.
10 You that love Yahweh, hate evil: he preserves the souls of his saints; he delivers them out of the hand of the wicked.
11 Light is sown for the righteous, and gladness for the upright in heart.
12 Rejoice in Yahweh, you righteous; and give thanks at the remembrance of his holiness.

Psalms 98

98:1 ¶ <<A Psalm.>> O sing unto Yahweh a new song; for he has done marvelous things: his right hand, and his holy arm, have gotten him the victory.
2 Yahweh has made known his salvation: his righteousness has he openly shown in the sight of the heathen.
3 He has remembered his mercy and his truth toward the house of Israel: all the ends of the earth have seen the salvation of our God.
4 ¶ Make a joyful noise unto Yahweh, all the earth: make a loud noise, and rejoice, and sing praise.
5 Sing unto Yahweh with the harp; with the harp, and the voice of a psalm.
6 With trumpets and sound of cornet make a joyful noise before Yahweh, the King.

7 Let the sea roar, and the fullness thereof; the world, and they that dwell therein.
8 Let the floods clap *their* hands: let the hills be joyful together
9 Before Yahweh; for he comes to judge the earth: with righteousness shall he judge the world, and the people with equity.

Psalms 99

99:1 ¶ Yahweh reigns; let the people tremble: he sits *between* the cherubims; let the earth be moved.
2 Yahweh *is* great in Zion; and he *is* high above all the people.
3 Let them praise your great and awesome name; *for* it *is* holy.
4 The king's strength also loves judgment; you do establish equity, you execute judgment and righteousness in Jacob.
5 Exalt you Yahweh our God, and worship at his footstool; *for* he *is* holy.
6 ¶ Moses and Aaron among his priests, and Samuel among them that call upon his name; they called upon Yahweh, and he answered them.
7 He spoke to them in the cloudy pillar: they kept his testimonies, and the ordinance *that* he gave them.
8 You answered them, O Yahweh our God: you were a God that forgave them, though you took vengeance of their inventions.
9 Exalt Yahweh our God, and worship at his holy hill; for Yahweh our God *is* holy.

Psalms 100

100:1 ¶ <<A Psalm of praise.>> Make a joyful noise unto Yahweh, all you lands.
2 Serve Yahweh with gladness: come before his presence with singing.
3 Know you that Yahweh he *is* God: *it is* he *that* has made us, and not we ourselves; *we are* his people, and the sheep of his pasture.
4 Enter into his gates with thanksgiving, *and* into his courts with praise: be thankful unto him, *and* bless his name.
5 For Yahweh *is* good; his mercy *is* everlasting; and his truth *endures* to all generations.

Psalms 101

101:1 ¶ <<A Psalm of David.>> I will sing of mercy and judgment: unto you, O Yahweh, will I sing.
2 I will behave myself wisely in a perfect way. O when will you come to me? I will walk within my house with a perfect heart.
3 I will set no wicked thing before my eyes: I hate the work of them that turn aside; *it* shall not cling to me.
4 A froward heart shall depart from me: I will not know a wicked *person*.
5 Whoever privately slanders his neighbor, him will I cut off: him that has a high look and a proud heart will not I endure.
6 My eyes *shall be* upon the faithful of the land, that they may dwell with me: he that walks in a perfect way, he shall serve me.
7 He that works deceit shall not dwell within my house: he that tells lies shall not tarry in my sight.
8 I will early destroy all the wicked of the land; that I may cut off all wicked doers from the city of Yahweh.

Psalms 102

102:1 ¶ <<A Prayer of the afflicted, when he is overwhelmed, and pours out his complaint before Yahweh.>> Hear my prayer, O Yahweh, and let my cry come unto you.
2 Hide not your face from me in the day *when* I am in trouble; incline your ear to me: in the day *when* I call answer me speedily.
3 For my days are consumed like smoke, and my bones are burned as a hearth.
4 My heart is smitten, and withered like grass; so that I forget to eat my bread.
5 By reason of the voice of my groaning my bones cling to my skin.
6 I am like a pelican of the wilderness: I am like an owl of the desert.
7 I watch, and am as a sparrow alone upon the house top.
8 My enemies reproach me all the day; *and* they that are mad against me have sworn against me.
9 For I have eaten ashes like bread, and mingled my drink with weeping,
10 Because of your indignation and your wrath: for you have lifted me up, and cast me down.
11 My days *are* like a shadow that declines; and I am withered like grass.
12 ¶ But you, O Yahweh, will endure forever; and your remembrance unto all generations.
13 You shall arise, *and* have mercy upon Zion: for the time to favor her, yes, the set time, has come.
14 For your servants take pleasure in her stones, and favor the dust thereof.
15 So the heathen shall fear the name of Yahweh, and all the kings of the earth your glory.
16 When Yahweh shall build up Zion, he shall appear in his glory.
17 He will regard the prayer of the destitute, and not despise their prayer.
18 This shall be written for the generation to come: and the people which shall be created shall praise Yah.
19 For he has looked down from the height of his sanctuary; from heaven did Yahweh behold the earth;
20 To hear the groaning of the prisoner; to loose those that are appointed to death;
21 To declare the name of Yahweh in Zion, and his praise in Jerusalem;

Psalms 102

22 When the people are gathered together, and the kingdoms, to serve Yahweh.
23 ¶ He weakened my strength in the way; he shortened my days.
24 I said, O my God, take me not away in the midst of my days: your years *are* throughout all generations.
25 Of old have you laid the foundation of the earth: and the heavens *are* the work of your hands.
26 They shall perish, but you shall endure: yes, all of them shall grow old like a garment; as a coat shall you change them, and they shall be changed:
27 But you *are* the same, and your years shall have no end.
28 The children of your servants shall continue, and their seed shall be established before you.

Psalms 103

103:1 ¶ <<*A Psalm* of David.>> Bless Yahweh, O my soul: and all that is within me, *bless* his holy name.
2 Bless Yahweh, O my soul, and forget not all his benefits:
3 Who forgives all your iniquities; who heals all your diseases;
4 Who redeems your life from destruction; who crowns you with loving kindness and tender mercies;
5 Who satisfies your mouth with good *things; so that* your youth is renewed like the eagle's.
6 ¶ Yahweh executes righteousness and judgment for all that are oppressed.
7 He made known his ways to Moses, his acts to the children of Israel.
8 Yahweh *is* merciful and gracious, slow to anger, and plenteous in mercy.
9 He will not always plead: neither will he keep *his anger* forever.
10 He has not dealt with us after our sins; nor rewarded us according to our iniquities.
11 For as the heaven is high above the earth, *so* great is his mercy toward them that fear him.
12 As far as the east is from the west, *so* far has he removed our transgressions from us.
13 Like as a father pities *his* children, *so* Yahweh pities them that fear him.
14 For he knows our frame; he remembers that we *are* dust.
15 *As for* man, his days *are* as grass: as a flower of the field, so he flourishes.
16 For the wind passes over it, and it is gone; and the place thereof shall know it no more.
17 But the mercy of Yahweh *is* from everlasting to everlasting upon them that fear him, and his righteousness unto children's children;
18 To such as keep his covenant, and to those that remember his commandments to do them.
19 ¶ Yahweh has prepared his throne in the heavens; and his kingdom rules over all.
20 Bless Yahweh, you his angels, that excel in strength, that do his commandments, hearkening to the voice of his word.
21 Bless you Yahweh, all *you* his hosts; *you* ministers of his, that do his pleasure.
22 Bless Yahweh, all his works in all places of his dominion: bless Yahweh, O my soul.

Psalms 104

104:1 ¶ Bless Yahweh, O my soul. O Yahweh my God, you are very great; you are clothed with honor and majesty.
2 Who covers *yourself* with light as *with* a garment: who stretches out the heavens like a curtain:
3 Who lays the beams of his chambers in the waters: who makes the clouds his chariot: who walks upon the wings of the wind:
4 Who makes his angels spirits; his ministers a flaming fire:
5 *Who* laid the foundations of the earth, *that* it should not be removed forever.
6 You covered it with the deep as *with* a garment: the waters stood above the mountains.
7 At your rebuke they fled; at the voice of your thunder they hurried away.
8 They go up by the mountains; they go down by the valleys to the place which you have founded for them.
9 You have set a bound that they may not pass over; that they turn not again to cover the earth.
10 ¶ He sends the springs into the valleys, *which* run among the hills.
11 They give drink to every beast of the field: the wild donkeys quench their thirst.
12 By them shall the fowls of the heaven have their habitation, *which* sing among the branches.
13 He waters the hills from his chambers: the earth is satisfied with the fruit of your works.
14 He causes the grass to grow for the cattle, and herb for the service of man: that he may bring forth food out of the earth;
15 And wine *that* makes glad the heart of man, *and* oil to make *his* face to shine, and bread *which* strengthens man's heart.
16 The trees of Yahweh are full *of sap;* the cedars of Lebanon, which he has planted;
17 Where the birds make their nests: *as for* the stork, the fir trees *are* her house.
18 The high hills *are* a refuge for the wild goats; *and* the rocks for the conies.
19 ¶ He appointed the moon for seasons: the sun knows his going down.
20 You make darkness, and it is night: wherein all the beasts of the forest do creep *forth*.
21 The young lions roar after their prey, and seek their meat from God.
22 The sun rises, they gather themselves together, and lay them down in their dens.
23 Man goes forth to his work and to his labor until the evening.
24 O Yahweh, how manifold are your works! in wisdom have you made them all: the earth is full of your riches.

25 *So is* this great and wide sea, wherein *are* things creeping innumerable, both small and great beasts.
26 There go the ships: *there is* that leviathan, *whom* you have made to play therein.
27 These wait all upon you; that you may give *them* their meat in due season.
28 *That* you give them they gather: you open your hand, they are filled with good.
29 You hide your face, they are troubled: you take away their breath, they die, and return to their dust.
30 You send forth your spirit, they are created: and you renew the face of the earth.
31 ¶ The glory of Yahweh shall endure forever: Yahweh shall rejoice in his works.
32 He looks on the earth, and it trembles: he touches the hills, and they smoke.
33 I will sing unto Yahweh as long as I live: I will sing praise unto my God while I have my being.
34 My meditation of him shall be sweet: I will be glad in Yahweh.
35 Let the sinners be consumed out of the earth, and let the wicked be no more. Bless you Yahweh, O my soul. Praise you Yah.

Psalms 105

105:1 ¶ O give thanks unto Yahweh; call upon his name: make known his deeds among the people.
2 Sing unto him, sing psalms unto him: talk you of all his wondrous works.
3 Glory you in his holy name: let the heart of them rejoice that seek Yahweh.
4 Seek Yahweh, and his strength: seek his face evermore.
5 Remember his marvelous works that he has done; his wonders, and the judgments of his mouth;
6 O you seed of Abraham his servant, you children of Jacob his chosen.
7 He *is* Yahweh our God: his judgments *are* in all the earth.
8 ¶ He has remembered his covenant forever, the word *which* he commanded to a thousand generations.
9 Which *covenant* he made with Abraham, and his oath to Isaac;
10 And confirmed the same to Jacob for a law, *and* to Israel *for* an everlasting covenant:
11 Saying, Unto you will I give the land of Canaan, the lot of your inheritance:
12 When they were *but* a few men in number; yes, very few, and strangers in it.
13 When they went from one nation to another, from *one* kingdom to another people;
14 He allowed no man to do them wrong: yes, he reproved kings for their sakes;
15 *Saying*, Touch not my anointed, and do my prophets no harm.
16 Moreover he called for a famine upon the land: he broke the whole staff of bread.
17 He sent a man before them, *even* Joseph, *who* was sold for a servant:
18 Whose feet they hurt with fetters: he was laid in iron:
19 Until the time that his word came: the word of Yahweh tried him.
20 The king sent and loosed him; *even* the ruler of the people, and let him go free.
21 He made him lord of his house, and ruler of all his substance:
22 To bind his princes at his pleasure: and teach his senators wisdom.
23 Israel also came into Egypt; and Jacob sojourned in the land of Ham.
24 And he increased his people greatly; and made them stronger than their enemies.
25 ¶ He turned their heart to hate his people, to deal subtly with his servants.
26 He sent Moses his servant; *and* Aaron whom he had chosen.
27 They showed his signs among them, and wonders in the land of Ham.
28 He sent darkness, and made it dark; and they rebelled not against his word.
29 He turned their waters into blood, and slew their fish.
30 Their land brought forth frogs in abundance, in the chambers of their kings.
31 He spoke, and there came diverse sorts of flies, *and* lice in all their coasts.
32 He gave them hail for rain, *and* flaming fire in their land.
33 He smote their vines also and their fig trees; and broke the trees of their coasts.
34 He spoke, and the locusts came, and caterpillars, and that without number,
35 And did eat up all the herbs in their land, and devoured the fruit of their ground.
36 He smote also all the firstborn in their land, the chief of all their strength.
37 He brought them forth also with silver and gold: and *there was* not one feeble *person* among their tribes.
38 Egypt was glad when they departed: for the fear of them fell upon them.
39 He spread a cloud for a covering; and fire to give light in the night.
40 *The people* asked, and he brought quails, and satisfied them with the bread of heaven.
41 He opened the rock, and the waters gushed out; they ran in the dry places *like* a river.
42 For he remembered his holy promise, *and* Abraham his servant.
43 And he brought forth his people with joy, *and* his chosen with gladness:
44 And gave them the lands of the heathen: and they inherited the labor of the people;
45 That they might observe his statutes, and keep his laws. Praise you Yah.

Psalms 106

106:1 ¶ Praise you Yah. O give thanks unto Yahweh; for *he is* good: for his mercy *endures* forever.

2 Who can utter the mighty acts of Yahweh? *who* can show forth all his praise?

3 Blessed *are* they that keep judgment, *and* he that does righteousness at all times.

4 Remember me, O Yahweh, with the favor *that you bear unto* your people: O visit me with your salvation;

5 That I may see the good of your chosen, that I may rejoice in the gladness of your nation, that I may glory with your inheritance.

6 ¶ We have sinned with our fathers, we have committed iniquity, we have done wickedly.

7 Our fathers understood not your wonders in Egypt; they remembered not the multitude of your mercies; but provoked *him* at the sea, *even* at the Red Sea.

8 Nevertheless he saved them for his name's sake, that he might make his mighty power to be known.

9 He rebuked the Red Sea also, and it was dried up: so he led them through the depths, as through the wilderness.

10 And he saved them from the hand of him that hated *them*, and redeemed them from the hand of the enemy.

11 And the waters covered their enemies: there was not one of them left.

12 Then believed they his words; they sang his praise.

13 ¶ They soon forgot his works; they waited not for his counsel:

14 But lusted exceedingly in the wilderness, and tempted God in the desert.

15 And he gave them their request; but sent leanness into their soul.

16 They envied Moses also in the camp, *and* Aaron the saint of Yahweh.

17 The earth opened and swallowed up Dathan, and covered the company of Abiram.

18 And a fire was kindled in their company; the flame burned up the wicked.

19 They made a calf in Horeb, and worshipped the molten image.

20 Thus they changed their glory into the likeness of an ox that eats grass.

21 They forgot God their savior, which had done great things in Egypt;

22 Wondrous works in the land of Ham, *and* awesome things by the Red Sea.

23 Therefore he said that he would destroy them, had not Moses his chosen stood before him in the breach, to turn away his wrath, lest he should destroy *them*.

24 Yes, they despised the pleasant land, they believed not his word:

25 But murmured in their tents, *and* listened not to the voice of Yahweh.

26 Therefore he lifted up his hand against them, to overthrow them in the wilderness:

27 To overthrow their seed also among the nations, and to scatter them in the lands.

28 They joined themselves also to Baalpeor, and ate the sacrifices of the dead.

29 Thus they provoked *him* to anger with their inventions: and the plague broke in upon them.

30 Then stood up Phinehas, and executed judgment: and *so* the plague was stayed.

31 And that was counted to him for righteousness to all generations forevermore.

32 They angered *him* also at the waters of strife, so that it went ill with Moses for their sakes:

33 Because they provoked his spirit, so that he spoke unadvisedly with his lips.

34 ¶ They did not destroy the nations, concerning whom Yahweh commanded them:

35 But were mingled among the heathen, and learned their works.

36 And they served their idols: which were a snare to them.

37 Yes, they sacrificed their sons and their daughters unto devils,

38 And shed innocent blood, *even* the blood of their sons and of their daughters, whom they sacrificed unto the idols of Canaan: and the land was polluted with blood.

39 Thus were they defiled with their own works, and went a whoring with their own inventions.

40 Therefore was the wrath of Yahweh kindled against his people, insomuch that he abhorred his own inheritance.

41 And he gave them into the hand of the heathen; and they that hated them ruled over them.

42 Their enemies also oppressed them, and they were brought into subjection under their hand.

43 Many times did he deliver them; but they provoked *him* with their counsel, and were brought low for their iniquity.

44 Nevertheless he regarded their affliction, when he heard their cry:

45 And he remembered for them his covenant, and repented according to the multitude of his mercies.

46 He made them also to be pitied of all those that carried them captives.

47 Save us, O Yahweh our God, and gather us from among the heathen, to give thanks unto your holy name, *and* to triumph in your praise.

48 Blessed *be* Yahweh God of Israel from everlasting to everlasting: and let all the people say, Amen. Praise you Yah.

Psalms 107

107:1 ¶ O give thanks unto Yahweh, for *he is* good: for his mercy *endures* forever.

2 Let the redeemed of Yahweh say *so*, whom he has redeemed from the hand of the enemy;

3 And gathered them out of the lands, from the east, and from the west, from the north, and from the south.

4 They wandered in the wilderness in a solitary way; they found no city to dwell in.

5 Hungry and thirsty, their soul fainted in them.

6 Then they cried unto Yahweh in their trouble, *and* he delivered them out of their distresses.

7 And he led them forth by the right way, that they might go to a city of habitation.

8 Oh that *men* would praise Yahweh *for* his goodness, and *for* his wonderful works to the children of men!

9 For he satisfies the longing soul, and fills the hungry soul with goodness.

10 ¶ Such as sit in darkness and in the shadow of death, *being* bound in affliction and iron;

11 Because they rebelled against the words of God, and despised the counsel of the most High:

12 Therefore he brought down their heart with labor; they fell down, and *there was* none to help.

13 Then they cried unto Yahweh in their trouble, *and* he saved them out of their distresses.

14 He brought them out of darkness and the shadow of death, and broke their bands in pieces.

15 Oh that *men* would praise Yahweh *for* his goodness, and *for* his wonderful works to the children of men!

16 For he has broken the gates of brass, and cut the bars of iron in two.

17 ¶ Fools because of their transgression, and because of their iniquities, are afflicted.

18 Their soul abhors all manner of food; and they draw near to the gates of death.

19 Then they cry unto Yahweh in their trouble, *and* he saves them out of their distresses.

20 He sent his word, and healed them, and delivered *them* from their destructions.

21 Oh that *men* would praise Yahweh *for* his goodness, and *for* his wonderful works to the children of men!

22 And let them sacrifice the sacrifices of thanksgiving, and declare his works with rejoicing.

23 ¶ They that go down to the sea in ships, that do business in great waters;

24 These see the works of Yahweh, and his wonders in the deep.

25 For he commands, and raises the stormy wind, which lifts up the waves thereof.

26 They mount up to the heaven, they go down again to the depths: their soul is melted because of trouble.

27 They reel to and fro, and stagger like a drunken man, and are at their wits' end.

28 Then they cry unto Yahweh in their trouble, and he brings them out of their distresses.

29 He makes the storm calm, so that the waves thereof are still.

30 Then are they glad because they are quiet; so he brings them to their desired haven.

31 Oh that *men* would praise Yahweh *for* his goodness, and *for* his wonderful works to the children of men!

32 Let them exalt him also in the congregation of the people, and praise him in the assembly of the elders.

33 ¶ He turns rivers into a wilderness, and the water springs into dry ground;

34 A fruitful land into barrenness, for the wickedness of them that dwell therein.

35 He turns the wilderness into a standing water, and dry ground into water springs.

36 And there he makes the hungry to dwell, that they may prepare a city for habitation;

37 And sow the fields, and plant vineyards, which may yield fruits of increase.

38 He blesses them also, so that they are multiplied greatly; and allows not their cattle to decrease.

39 Again, they are diminished and brought low through oppression, affliction, and sorrow.

40 He pours contempt upon princes, and causes them to wander in the wilderness, *where there is* no way.

41 Yet sets he the poor on high from affliction, and makes *him* families like a flock.

42 The righteous shall see *it*, and rejoice: and all iniquity shall stop her mouth.

43 Whoever *is* wise, and will observe these *things*, even they shall understand the loving kindness of Yahweh.

Psalms 108

108:1 ¶ <<A Song *or* Psalm of David.>> O God, my heart is fixed; I will sing and give praise, even with my glory.

2 Awake, psaltery and harp: I *myself* will awake early.

3 I will praise you, O Yahweh, among the people: and I will sing praises to you among the nations.

4 For your mercy *is* great above the heavens: and your truth *reaches* to the clouds.

5 Be you exalted, O God, above the heavens: and your glory above all the earth;

6 ¶ That your beloved may be delivered: save *with* your right hand, and answer me.

7 God has spoken in his holiness; I will rejoice, I will divide Shechem, and measure out the valley of Succoth.

8 Gilead *is* mine; Manasseh *is* mine; Ephraim also *is* the strength of my head; Judah *is* my lawgiver;

9 Moab *is* my wash pot; over Edom will I cast out my shoe; over Philistia will I triumph.

10 Who will bring me into the strong city? who will lead me into Edom?

11 *Will* not *you*, O God, *who* has cast us off? and will not you, O God, go forth with our hosts?

12 Give us help from trouble: for vain *is* the help of man.

13 Through God we shall do valiantly: for he *it is that* shall tread down our enemies.

Psalms 109

109:1 ¶ <<To the chief Musician, A Psalm of David.>> Hold not your peace, O God of my praise;

2 For the mouth of the wicked and the mouth of the deceitful are opened against me: they have spoken against me with a lying tongue.

3 They compassed me about also with words of hatred; and fought against me without a cause.

Psalms 109

4 For my love they are my adversaries: but I *give myself to* prayer.
5 And they have rewarded me evil for good, and hatred for my love.
6 ¶ Set you a wicked man over him: and let Satan stand at his right hand.
7 When he shall be judged, let him be condemned: and let his prayer become sin.
8 Let his days be few; *and* let another take his office.
9 Let his children be fatherless, and his wife a widow.
10 Let his children be continually vagabonds, and beg: let them seek *their bread* also out of their desolate places.
11 Let the extortioner catch all that he has; and let the strangers spoil his labor.
12 Let there be none to extend mercy to him: neither let there be any to favor his fatherless children.
13 Let his posterity be cut off; *and* in the generation following let their name be blotted out.
14 Let the iniquity of his fathers be remembered with Yahweh; and let not the sin of his mother be blotted out.
15 Let them be before Yahweh continually, that he may cut off the memory of them from the earth.
16 Because that he remembered not to show mercy, but persecuted the poor and needy man, that he might even slay the broken in heart.
17 As he loved cursing, so let it come to him: as he delighted not in blessing, so let it be far from him.
18 As he clothed himself with cursing like as with his garment, so let it come into his bowels like water, and like oil into his bones.
19 Let it be to him as the garment *which* covers him, and for a girdle with which he is girded continually.
20 *Let* this *be* the reward of my adversaries from Yahweh, and of them that speak evil against my soul.
21 ¶ But do you for me, O Yahweh the Lord, for your name's sake: because your mercy *is* good, deliver you me.
22 For I *am* poor and needy, and my heart is wounded within me.
23 I am gone like the shadow when it declines: I am tossed up and down as the locust.
24 My knees are weak through fasting; and my flesh fails of fatness.
25 I became also a reproach to them: *when* they looked upon me they shook their heads.
26 Help me, O Yahweh my God: O save me according to your mercy:
27 That they may know that this *is* your hand; *that* you, Yahweh, have done it.
28 Let them curse, but bless you: when they arise, let them be ashamed; but let your servant rejoice.
29 Let my adversaries be clothed with shame, and let them cover themselves with their own confusion, as with a mantle.
30 I will greatly praise Yahweh with my mouth; yes, I will praise him among the multitude.
31 For he shall stand at the right hand of the poor, to save *him* from those that condemn his soul.

Psalms 110

110:1 ¶ <<A Psalm of David.>> Yahweh said unto my Lord, Sit you at my right hand, until I make your enemies your footstool.
2 Yahweh shall send the rod of your strength out of Zion: rule you in the midst of your enemies.
3 Your people *shall be* willing in the day of your power, in the beauties of holiness from the womb of the morning: you have the dew of your youth.
4 Yahweh has sworn, and will not repent, You *are* a priest forever after the order of Melchizedek.
5 ¶ The Lord at your right hand shall strike through kings in the day of his wrath.
6 He shall judge among the heathen, he shall fill *the places* with the dead bodies; he shall wound the heads over many countries.
7 He shall drink of the brook in the way: therefore shall he lift up the head.

Psalms 111

111:1 ¶ Praise you Yah. I will praise Yahweh with *my* whole heart, in the assembly of the upright, and *in* the congregation.
2 The works of Yahweh *are* great, sought out of all them that have pleasure therein.
3 His work *is* honorable and glorious: and his righteousness endures forever.
4 He has made his wonderful works to be remembered: Yahweh *is* gracious and full of compassion.
5 He has given meat to them that fear him: he will ever be mindful of his covenant.
6 ¶ He has shown his people the power of his works, that he may give them the heritage of the heathen.
7 The works of his hands *are* verity and judgment; all his commandments *are* sure.
8 They stand fast forever and ever, *and are* done in truth and uprightness.
9 He sent redemption to his people: he has commanded his covenant forever: holy and reverend *is* his name.
10 The fear of Yahweh *is* the beginning of wisdom: a good understanding have all they that do *his commandments*: his praise endures forever.

Psalms 112

112:1 ¶ Praise you Yah. Blessed *is* the man *that* fears Yahweh, *that* delights greatly in his commandments.
2 His seed shall be mighty upon earth: the generation of the upright shall be blessed.
3 Wealth and riches *shall be* in his house: and his righteousness endures forever.
4 Unto the upright there rises light in the darkness: *he is* gracious, and full of compassion, and righteous.
5 A good man shows favor, and lends: he will guide his affairs with discretion.

6 ¶ Surely he shall not be moved forever: the righteous shall be in everlasting remembrance.
7 He shall not be afraid of evil tidings: his heart is fixed, trusting in Yahweh.
8 His heart *is* established, he shall not be afraid, until he sees *his desire* upon his enemies.
9 He has dispersed, he has given to the poor, his righteousness endures forever; his horn shall be exalted with honor.
10 The wicked shall see *it*, and be grieved; he shall gnash with his teeth, and melt away: the desire of the wicked shall perish.

Psalms 113

113:1 ¶ Praise you Yah. Praise, O you servants of Yahweh, praise the name of Yahweh.
2 Blessed be the name of Yahweh from this time forth and forevermore.
3 From the rising of the sun to the going down of the same Yahweh's name *is* to be praised.
4 Yahweh *is* high above all nations, *and* his glory above the heavens.
5 Who *is* like unto Yahweh our God, who dwells on high,
6 Who humbles *himself* to behold *the things that are* in heaven, and in the earth!
7 He raises up the poor out of the dust, *and* lifts the needy out of the dunghill;
8 That he may set *him* with princes, *even* with the princes of his people.
9 He makes the barren woman to keep house, *and to be* a joyful mother of children. Praise you Yah.

Psalms 114

114:1 ¶ When Israel went out of Egypt, the house of Jacob from a people of strange language;
2 Judah was his sanctuary, *and* Israel his dominion.
3 The sea saw *it*, and fled: *the* Jordan was driven back.
4 The mountains skipped like rams, *and* the little hills like lambs.
5 What *ailed* you, O you sea, that you fled? you Jordan, *that* you were driven back?
6 You mountains, *that* you skipped like rams; *and* you little hills, like lambs?
7 Tremble, you earth, at the presence of the Lord, at the presence of the God of Jacob;
8 Which turned the rock *into* a standing water, the flint into a fountain of waters.

Psalms 115

115:1 ¶ Not unto us, O Yahweh, not unto us, but unto your name give glory, for your mercy, *and* for your truth's sake.
2 Why should the heathen say, Where *is* now their God?
3 But our God *is* in the heavens: he has done whatever he has pleased.
4 Their idols *are* silver and gold, the work of men's hands.
5 They have mouths, but they speak not: eyes have they, but they see not:
6 They have ears, but they hear not: noses have they, but they smell not:
7 They have hands, but they handle not: feet have they, but they walk not: neither speak they through their throat.
8 They that make them are like unto them; *so is* every one that trusts in them.
9 ¶ O Israel, trust you in Yahweh: he *is* their help and their shield.
10 O house of Aaron, trust in Yahweh: he *is* their help and their shield.
11 You that fear Yahweh, trust in Yahweh: he *is* their help and their shield.
12 Yahweh has been mindful of us: he will bless *us*; he will bless the house of Israel; he will bless the house of Aaron.
13 He will bless them that fear Yahweh, *both* small and great.
14 Yahweh shall increase you more and more, you and your children.
15 You *are* blessed of Yahweh which made heaven and earth.
16 The heaven, *even* the heavens, *are* Yahweh's: but the earth has he given to the children of men.
17 The dead praise not Yahweh, neither any that go down into silence.
18 But we will bless Yahweh from this time forth and forevermore. Praise Yahweh.

Psalms 116

116:1 ¶ I love Yahweh, because he has heard my voice *and* my supplications.
2 Because he has inclined his ear unto me, therefore will I call upon *him* as long as I live.
3 The sorrows of death encompassed me, and the pains of hell got hold upon me: I found trouble and sorrow.
4 Then called I upon the name of Yahweh; O Yahweh, I beseech you, deliver my soul.
5 Gracious *is* Yahweh, and righteous; yes, our God *is* merciful.
6 Yahweh preserves the simple: I was brought low, and he helped me.
7 Return to your rest, O my soul; for Yahweh has dealt bountifully with you.
8 For you have delivered my soul from death, my eyes from tears, *and* my feet from falling.
9 I will walk before Yahweh in the land of the living.
10 ¶ I believed, therefore have I spoken: I was greatly afflicted:
11 I said in my haste, All men *are* liars.

Psalms 116

12 What shall I render unto Yahweh *for* all his benefits toward me?
13 I will take the cup of salvation, and call upon the name of Yahweh.
14 I will pay my vows unto Yahweh now in the presence of all his people.
15 Precious in the sight of Yahweh *is* the death of his saints.
16 O Yahweh, truly I *am* your servant; I *am* your servant, *and* the son of your handmaid: you have loosed my bonds.
17 I will offer unto you the sacrifice of thanksgiving, and will call upon the name of Yahweh.
18 I will pay my vows unto Yahweh now in the presence of all his people,
19 In the courts of Yahweh's house, in the midst of you, O Jerusalem. Praise you Yah.

Psalms 117

117:1 ¶ O praise Yahweh, all you nations: praise him, all you people.
2 For his merciful kindness is great toward us: and the truth of Yahweh *endures* forever. Praise you Yah.

Psalms 118

118:1 ¶ O give thanks unto Yahweh; for *he is* good: because his mercy *endures* forever.
2 Let Israel now say, that his mercy *endures* forever.
3 Let the house of Aaron now say, that his mercy *endures* forever.
4 Let them now that fear Yahweh say, that his mercy *endures* forever.
5 I called upon Yah in distress: Yah answered me, *and set me* in a large place.
6 Yahweh *is* on my side; I will not fear: what can man do unto me?
7 Yahweh takes my part with them that help me: therefore shall I see *my desire* upon them that hate me.
8 *It is* better to trust in Yahweh than to put confidence in man.
9 *It is* better to trust in Yahweh than to put confidence in princes.
10 All nations compassed me about: but in the name of Yahweh will I destroy them.
11 They compassed me about; yes, they compassed me about: but in the name of Yahweh I will destroy them.
12 They compassed me about like bees; they are quenched as the fire of thorns: for in the name of Yahweh I will destroy them.
13 You have thrust down at me that I might fall: but Yahweh helped me.
14 Yah *is* my strength and song, and has become my salvation.
15 The voice of rejoicing and salvation *is* in the tabernacles of the righteous: the right hand of Yahweh does valiantly.
16 The right hand of Yahweh is exalted: the right hand of Yahweh does valiantly.
17 I shall not die, but live, and declare the works of Yah.
18 Yah has chastened me severely: but he has not given me over unto death.
19 ¶ Open to me the gates of righteousness: I will go into them, *and* I will praise Yah:
20 This *is the* gate of Yahweh, into which the righteous shall enter.
21 I will praise you: for you have heard me, and have become my salvation.
22 The stone *which* the builders refused has become the head *stone* of the corner.
23 This is Yahweh's doing; it *is* marvelous in our eyes.
24 This *is* the day *which* Yahweh has made; we will rejoice and be glad in it.
25 Save now, I beseech you, O Yahweh: O Yahweh, I beseech you, send now prosperity.
26 Blessed *is* he that comes in the name of Yahweh: we have blessed you out of the house of Yahweh.
27 God *is* Yahweh, which has shown us light: bind the sacrifice with cords, *even* unto the horns of the altar.
28 You *are* my God, and I will praise you: *you are* my God, I will exalt you.
29 O give thanks unto Yahweh; for *he is* good: for his mercy *endures* forever.

Psalms 119

119:1 ¶ ALEPH. Blessed *are* the undefiled in the way, who walk in the law of Yahweh.
2 Blessed *are* they that keep his testimonies, *and that* seek him with the whole heart.
3 They also do no iniquity: they walk in his ways.
4 ¶ You have commanded *us* to keep your precepts diligently.
5 O that my ways were directed to keep your statutes!
6 Then shall I not be ashamed, when I have respect unto all your commandments.
7 ¶ I will praise you with uprightness of heart, when I shall have learned your righteous judgments.
8 I will keep your statutes: O forsake me not utterly.
9 ¶ BETH. Wherewithal shall a young man cleanse his way? by taking heed *thereto* according to your word.
10 ¶ With my whole heart have I sought you: O let me not wander from your commandments.
11 ¶ Your word have I hidden in my heart, that I might not sin against you.
12 ¶ Blessed *are* you, O Yahweh: teach me your statutes.
13 ¶ With my lips have I declared all the judgments of your mouth.
14 I have rejoiced in the way of your testimonies, as *much as* in all riches.
15 I will meditate in your precepts, and have respect unto your ways.

16 I will delight myself in your statutes: I will not forget your word.
17 ¶ GIMEL. Deal bountifully with your servant, *that* I may live, and keep your word.
18 ¶ Open you my eyes, that I may behold wondrous things out of your law.
19 ¶ I *am* a stranger in the earth: hide not your commandments from me.
20 ¶ My soul breaks for the longing *that it has* unto your judgments at all times.
21 ¶ You have rebuked the proud *that are* cursed, which do err from your commandments.
22 ¶ Remove from me reproach and contempt; for I have kept your testimonies.
23 ¶ Princes also did sit *and* speak against me: *but* your servant did meditate in your statutes.
24 ¶ Your testimonies also *are* my delight *and* my counselors.
25 ¶ DALETH. My soul clings to the dust: quicken you me according to your word.
26 ¶ I have declared my ways, and you heard me: teach me your statutes.
27 Make me to understand the way of your precepts: so shall I talk of your wondrous works.
28 ¶ My soul melts for heaviness: strengthen you me according to your word.
29 Remove from me the way of lying: and grant me your law graciously.
30 ¶ I have chosen the way of truth: your judgments have I laid *before me*.
31 I have stuck unto your testimonies: O Yahweh, put me not to shame.
32 I will run the way of your commandments, when you shall enlarge my heart.
33 ¶ HE. Teach me, O Yahweh, the way of your statutes; and I shall keep it *to* the end.
34 Give me understanding, and I shall keep your law; yes, I shall observe it with *my* whole heart.
35 ¶ Make me to go in the path of your commandments; for therein do I delight.
36 Incline my heart unto your testimonies, and not to covetousness.
37 ¶ Turn away my eyes from beholding vanity; *and* quicken you me in your way.
38 ¶ Establish your word to your servant, who *is devoted* to your fear.
39 ¶ Turn away my reproach which I fear: for your judgments *are* good.
40 ¶ Behold, I have longed after your precepts: quicken me in your righteousness.
41 ¶ VAU. Let your mercies come also unto me, O Yahweh, *even* your salvation, according to your word.
42 So shall I have sayings to answer him that reproaches me: for I trust in your word.
43 ¶ And take not the word of truth utterly out of my mouth; for I have hoped in your judgments.
44 So shall I keep your law continually forever and ever.
45 ¶ And I will walk at liberty: for I seek your precepts.
46 I will speak of your testimonies also before kings, and will not be ashamed.
47 And I will delight myself in your commandments, which I have loved.
48 My hands also will I lift up unto your commandments, which I have loved; and I will meditate in your statutes.
49 ¶ ZAIN. Remember the word unto your servant, upon which you have caused me to hope.
50 ¶ This *is* my comfort in my affliction: for your word has quickened me.
51 ¶ The proud have had me greatly in derision: *yet* have I not declined from your law.
52 ¶ I remembered your judgments of old, O Yahweh; and have comforted myself.
53 ¶ Horror has taken hold upon me because of the wicked that forsake your law.
54 ¶ Your statutes have been my songs in the house of my pilgrimage.
55 ¶ I have remembered your name, O Yahweh, in the night, and have kept your law.
56 This I had, because I kept your precepts.
57 ¶ CHETH. *You are* my portion, O Yahweh: I have said that I would keep your words.
58 ¶ I entreated your favor with *my* whole heart: be merciful unto me according to your word.
59 ¶ I thought on my ways, and turned my feet unto your testimonies.
60 I made haste, and delayed not to keep your commandments.
61 ¶ The bands of the wicked have robbed me: *but* I have not forgotten your law.
62 ¶ At midnight I will rise to give thanks to you because of your righteous judgments.
63 ¶ I *am* a companion of all *them* that fear you, and of them that keep your precepts.
64 ¶ The earth, O Yahweh, is full of your mercy: teach me your statutes.
65 ¶ TETH. You have dealt well with your servant, O Yahweh, according to your word.
66 Teach me good judgment and knowledge: for I have believed your commandments.
67 ¶ Before I was afflicted I went astray: but now have I kept your word.
68 ¶ You *are* good, and do good; teach me your statutes.
69 ¶ The proud have forged a lie against me: *but* I will keep your precepts with *my* whole heart.
70 Their heart is as fat as grease; *but* I delight in your law.
71 ¶ *It is* good for me that I have been afflicted; that I might learn your statutes.
72 ¶ The law of your mouth *is* better to me than thousands of gold and silver.
73 ¶ JOD. Your hands have made me and fashioned me: give me understanding, that I may learn your commandments.
74 ¶ They that fear you will be glad when they see me; because I have hoped in your word.

75 ¶ I know, O Yahweh, that your judgments *are* right, and *that* you in faithfulness have afflicted me.
76 ¶ Let, I pray you, your merciful kindness be for my comfort, according to your word to your servant.
77 Let your tender mercies come unto me, that I may live: for your law *is* my delight.
78 ¶ Let the proud be ashamed; for they dealt perversely with me without a cause: *but* I will meditate in your precepts.
79 Let those that fear you turn unto me, and those that have known your testimonies.
80 ¶ Let my heart be sound in your statutes; that I be not ashamed.
81 ¶ CAPH. My soul faints for your salvation: *but* I hope in your word.
82 My eyes fail for your word, saying, When will you comfort me?
83 ¶ For I have become like a bottle in the smoke; *yet* do I not forget your statutes.
84 ¶ How many *are* the days of your servant? when will you execute judgment on them that persecute me?
85 ¶ The proud have dug pits for me, which *are* not after your law.
86 All your commandments *are* faithful: they persecute me wrongfully; help you me.
87 They had almost consumed me upon earth; but I forsook not your precepts.
88 ¶ Quicken me after your loving kindness; so shall I keep the testimony of your mouth.
89 ¶ LAMED. Forever, O Yahweh, your word is settled in heaven.
90 Your faithfulness *is* unto all generations: you have established the earth, and it remains.
91 They continue this day according to your ordinances: for all *are* your servants.
92 ¶ Unless your law *had been* my delights, I should then have perished in my affliction.
93 ¶ I will never forget your precepts: for with them you have quickened me.
94 ¶ I *am* yours, save me; for I have sought your precepts.
95 ¶ The wicked have waited for me to destroy me: *but* I will consider your testimonies.
96 ¶ I have seen an end of all perfection: *but* your commandment *is* exceedingly broad.
97 ¶ MEM. O how love I your law! it *is* my meditation all the day.
98 ¶ You through your commandments have made me wiser than my enemies: for they *are* ever with me.
99 I have more understanding than all my teachers: for your testimonies *are* my meditation.
100 I understand more than the ancients, because I keep your precepts.
101 ¶ I have refrained my feet from every evil way, that I might keep your word.
102 ¶ I have not departed from your judgments: for you have taught me.
103 ¶ How sweet are your words to my taste! *yes, sweeter* than honey to my mouth!
104 Through your precepts I get understanding: therefore I hate every false way.
105 ¶ NUN. Your word *is* a lamp unto my feet, and a light unto my path.
106 ¶ I have sworn, and I will perform *it*, that I will keep your righteous judgments.
107 ¶ I am afflicted very much: quicken me, O Yahweh, according to your word.
108 ¶ Accept, I beseech you, the freewill offerings of my mouth, O Yahweh, and teach me your judgments.
109 ¶ My soul *is* continually in my hand: yet do I not forget your law.
110 The wicked have laid a snare for me: yet I erred not from your precepts.
111 ¶ Your testimonies have I taken as a heritage forever: for they *are* the rejoicing of my heart.
112 I have inclined my heart to perform your statutes always, *even unto* the end.
113 ¶ SAMECH. I hate *vain* thoughts: but your law do I love.
114 ¶ You *are* my hiding place and my shield: I hope in your word.
115 ¶ Depart from me, you evildoers: for I will keep the commandments of my God.
116 ¶ Uphold me according to your word, that I may live: and let me not be ashamed of my hope.
117 Hold you me up, and I shall be safe: and I will have respect unto your statutes continually.
118 ¶ You have trodden down all them that err from your statutes: for their deceit *is* falsehood.
119 You put away all the wicked of the earth *like* dross: therefore I love your testimonies.
120 My flesh trembles for fear of you; and I am afraid of your judgments.
121 ¶ AIN. I have done judgment and justice: leave me not to my oppressors.
122 Be surety for your servant for good: let not the proud oppress me.
123 ¶ My eyes fail for your salvation, and for the word of your righteousness.
124 ¶ Deal with your servant according to your mercy, and teach me your statutes.
125 I *am* your servant; give me understanding, that I may know your testimonies.
126 ¶ *It is* time for *you*, Yahweh, to work: *for* they have made void your law.
127 ¶ Therefore I love your commandments above gold; yes, above fine gold.
128 Therefore I esteem all *your* precepts *concerning* all *things to be* right; *and* I hate every false way.
129 ¶ PE. Your testimonies *are* wonderful: therefore does my soul keep them.
130 ¶ The entrance of your words gives light; it gives understanding to the simple.
131 ¶ I opened my mouth, and panted: for I longed for your commandments.
132 ¶ Look you upon me, and be merciful unto me, as you used to do unto those that love your name.

133 ¶ Order my steps in your word: and let not any iniquity have dominion over me.
134 ¶ Deliver me from the oppression of man: so will I keep your precepts.
135 ¶ Make your face to shine upon your servant; and teach me your statutes.
136 ¶ Rivers of waters run down my eyes, because they keep not your law.
137 ¶ TZADDI. Righteous *are* you, O Yahweh, and upright *are* your judgments.
138 Your testimonies *that* you have commanded *are* righteous and very faithful.
139 ¶ My zeal has consumed me, because my enemies have forgotten your words.
140 ¶ Your word *is* very pure: therefore your servant loves it.
141 ¶ I *am* small and despised: yet do not I forget your precepts.
142 ¶ Your righteousness *is* an everlasting righteousness, and your law *is* the truth.
143 ¶ Trouble and anguish have taken hold on me: *yet* your commandments *are* my delights.
144 The righteousness of your testimonies *is* everlasting: give me understanding, and I shall live.
145 ¶ KOPH. I cried with *my* whole heart; hear me, O Yahweh: I will keep your statutes.
146 I cried unto you; save me, and I shall keep your testimonies.
147 ¶ I prevented the dawning of the morning, and cried: I hoped in your word.
148 My eyes prevent the *night* watches, that I might meditate in your word.
149 ¶ Hear my voice according to your loving kindness: O Yahweh, quicken me according to your judgment.
150 ¶ They draw near that follow after mischief: they are far from your law.
151 You *are* near, O Yahweh; and all your commandments *are* truth.
152 ¶ Concerning your testimonies, I have known of old that you have founded them forever.
153 ¶ RESH. Consider my affliction, and deliver me: for I do not forget your law.
154 Plead my cause, and deliver me: quicken me according to your word.
155 ¶ Salvation *is* far from the wicked: for they seek not your statutes.
156 ¶ Great *are* your tender mercies, O Yahweh: quicken me according to your judgments.
157 ¶ Many *are* my persecutors and my enemies; *yet* do I not decline from your testimonies.
158 ¶ I beheld the transgressors, and was grieved; because they kept not your word.
159 ¶ Consider how I love your precepts: quicken me, O Yahweh, according to your loving kindness.
160 ¶ Your word *is* true *from* the beginning: and every one of your righteous judgments *endures* forever.
161 ¶ SCHIN. Princes have persecuted me without a cause: but my heart stands in awe of your word.
162 ¶ I rejoice at your word, as one that finds great spoil.
163 ¶ I hate and abhor lying: *but* your law do I love.
164 ¶ Seven times a day do I praise you because of your righteous judgments.
165 ¶ Great peace have they which love your law: and nothing shall offend them.
166 ¶ Yahweh, I have hoped for your salvation, and done your commandments.
167 ¶ My soul has kept your testimonies; and I love them exceedingly.
168 I have kept your precepts and your testimonies: for all my ways *are* before you.
169 ¶ TAU. Let my cry come near before you, O Yahweh: give me understanding according to your word.
170 Let my supplication come before you: deliver me according to your word.
171 ¶ My lips shall utter praise, when you have taught me your statutes.
172 ¶ My tongue shall speak of your word: for all your commandments *are* righteousness.
173 ¶ Let your hand help me; for I have chosen your precepts.
174 I have longed for your salvation, O Yahweh; and your law *is* my delight.
175 ¶ Let my soul live, and it shall praise you; and let your judgments help me.
176 ¶ I have gone astray like a lost sheep; seek your servant; for I do not forget your commandments.

Psalms 120

120:1 ¶ <<A Song of degrees.>> In my distress I cried unto Yahweh, and he heard me.
2 Deliver my soul, O Yahweh, from lying lips, *and* from a deceitful tongue.
3 What shall be given unto you? or what shall be done unto you, you false tongue?
4 Sharp arrows of the mighty, with coals of juniper.
5 ¶ Woe is me, that I sojourn in Mesech, *that* I dwell in the tents of Kedar!
6 My soul has long dwelt with him that hates peace.
7 I *am for* peace: but when I speak, they *are* for war.

Psalms 121

121:1 ¶ <<A Song of degrees.>> I will lift up my eyes unto the hills, from where comes my help.
2 My help *comes* from Yahweh, which made heaven and earth.
3 He will not permit your foot to be moved: he that keeps you will not slumber.
4 Behold, he that keeps Israel shall neither slumber nor sleep.
5 Yahweh *is* your keeper: Yahweh *is* your shade upon your right hand.
6 The sun shall not smite you by day, nor the moon by night.

Psalms 121

7 Yahweh shall preserve you from all evil: he shall preserve your soul.
8 Yahweh shall preserve your going out and your coming in from this time forth, and even forevermore.

Psalms 122

122:1 ¶ <<A Song of degrees of David.>> I was glad when they said to me, Let us go into the house of Yahweh.
2 Our feet shall stand within your gates, O Jerusalem.
3 Jerusalem is built as a city that is compact together:
4 Where the tribes go up, the tribes of Yah, to the testimony of Israel, to give thanks unto the name of Yahweh.
5 For there are set thrones of judgment, the thrones of the house of David.
6 ¶ Pray for the peace of Jerusalem: they shall prosper that love you.
7 Peace be within your walls, *and* prosperity within your palaces.
8 For my brethren and companions' sakes, I will now say, Peace *be* within you.
9 Because of the house of Yahweh our God I will seek your good.

Psalms 123

123:1 ¶ <<A Song of degrees.>> Unto you lift I up my eyes, O you that dwell in the heavens.
2 Behold, as the eyes of servants *look* unto the hand of their masters, *and* as the eyes of a maiden unto the hand of her mistress; so our eyes *wait* upon Yahweh our God, until that he has mercy upon us.
3 Have mercy upon us, O Yahweh, have mercy upon us: for we are exceedingly filled with contempt.
4 Our soul is exceedingly filled with the scorning of those that are at ease, *and* with the contempt of the proud.

Psalms 124

124:1 ¶ <<A Song of degrees of David.>> If *it had not been* Yahweh who was on our side, now may Israel say;
2 If *it had not been* Yahweh who was on our side, when men rose up against us:
3 Then they *would* have swallowed us up alive, when their wrath was kindled against us:
4 Then the waters *would* have overwhelmed us, the stream *would* have gone over our soul:
5 Then the proud waters *would* have gone over our soul.
6 ¶ Blessed *be* Yahweh, who has not given us *as* a prey to their teeth.
7 Our soul has escaped as a bird out of the snare of the fowlers: the snare is broken, and we have escaped.
8 Our help *is* in the name of Yahweh, who made heaven and earth.

Psalms 125

125:1 ¶ <<A Song of degrees.>> They that trust in Yahweh *shall be* as mount Zion, *which* cannot be removed, *but* remain forever.
2 As the mountains *are* round about Jerusalem, so Yahweh *is* round about his people from now on even forever.
3 For the rod of the wicked shall not rest upon the lot of the righteous; lest the righteous put forth their hands to iniquity.
4 ¶ Do good, O Yahweh, to *those that are* good, and *to them that are* upright in their hearts.
5 As for such as turn aside to their crooked ways, Yahweh shall lead them forth with the workers of iniquity: *but* peace *shall be* upon Israel.

Psalms 126

126:1 ¶ <<A Song of degrees.>> When Yahweh turned again the captivity of Zion, we were like them that dream.
2 Then was our mouth filled with laughter, and our tongue with singing: then said they among the heathen, Yahweh has done great things for them.
3 Yahweh has done great things for us; *whereof* we are glad.
4 ¶ Turn again our captivity, O Yahweh, as the streams in the south.
5 They that sow in tears shall reap in joy.
6 He that goes forth and weeps, bearing precious seed, shall doubtless come again with rejoicing, bringing his sheaves *with him*.

Psalms 127

127:1 ¶ <<A Song of degrees for Solomon.>> Unless Yahweh builds the house, they labor in vain that build it: unless Yahweh keeps the city, the watchman wakes *but* in vain.
2 *It is* vain for you to rise up early, to sit up late, to eat the bread of sorrows: *for* so he gives his beloved sleep.
3 Lo, children *are* a heritage of Yahweh: *and* the fruit of the womb *is his* reward.
4 As arrows *are* in the hand of a mighty man; so *are* children of the youth.
5 Happy *is* the man that has his quiver full of them: they shall not be ashamed, but they shall speak with the enemies in the gate.

Psalms 128

128:1 ¶ <<A Song of degrees.>> Blessed *is* every one that fears Yahweh; that walks in his ways.
2 For you shall eat the labor of your hands: happy *shall* you *be*, and *it shall be* well with you.

3 Your wife *shall be* as a fruitful vine by the sides of your house: your children like olive plants round about your table.
4 Behold, that thus shall the man be blessed that fears Yahweh.
5 Yahweh shall bless you out of Zion: and you shall see the good of Jerusalem all the days of your life.
6 Yes, you shall see your children's children, *and* peace upon Israel.

Psalms 129

129:1 ¶ <<A Song of degrees.>> Many a time have they afflicted me from my youth, may Israel now say:
2 Many a time have they afflicted me from my youth: yet they have not prevailed against me.
3 The plowers plowed upon my back: they made long their furrows.
4 Yahweh *is* righteous: he has cut in pieces the cords of the wicked.
5 ¶ Let them all be confounded and turned back that hate Zion.
6 Let them be as the grass *upon* the housetops, which withers before it grows up:
7 With which the mower fills not his hand; nor he that binds sheaves his bosom.
8 Neither do they which go by say, The blessing of Yahweh *be* upon you: we bless you in the name of Yahweh.

Psalms 130

130:1 ¶ <<A Song of degrees.>> Out of the depths have I cried unto you, O Yahweh.
2 Lord, hear my voice: let your ears be attentive to the voice of my supplications.
3 If you, Yah, should mark iniquities, O Lord, who shall stand?
4 But *there is* forgiveness with you, that you may be feared.
5 ¶ I wait for Yahweh, my soul does wait, and in his word do I hope.
6 My soul *waits* for the Lord more than they that watch for the morning: *I say, more than* they that watch for the morning.
7 Let Israel hope in Yahweh: for with Yahweh *there is* mercy, and with him *is* plenteous redemption.
8 And he shall redeem Israel from all his iniquities.

Psalms 131

131:1 ¶ <<A Song of degrees of David.>> Yahweh, my heart is not haughty, nor my eyes lofty: neither do I exercise myself in great matters, or in things too high for me.
2 Surely I have behaved and quieted myself, as a child that is weaned of his mother: my soul *is* even as a weaned child.
3 Let Israel hope in Yahweh from now on and forever.

Psalms 132

132:1 ¶ A Song of degrees. Yahweh, remember David, *and* all his afflictions:
2 How he swore unto Yahweh, *and* vowed unto the mighty *God* of Jacob;
3 Surely I will not come into the tabernacle of my house, nor go up into my bed;
4 I will not give sleep to my eyes, *or* slumber to my eyelids,
5 Until I find out a place for Yahweh, a habitation for the mighty *God* of Jacob.
6 Lo, we heard of it at Ephratah: we found it in the fields of the wood.
7 We will go into his tabernacles: we will worship at his footstool.
8 Arise, O Yahweh, into your rest; you, and the ark of your strength.
9 Let your priests be clothed with righteousness; and let your saints shout for joy.
10 For your servant David's sake turn not away the face of your anointed.
11 ¶ Yahweh has sworn *in* truth unto David; he will not turn from it; Of the fruit of your body will I set upon your throne.
12 If your children will keep my covenant and my testimony that I shall teach them, their children shall also sit upon your throne forevermore.
13 For Yahweh has chosen Zion; he has desired *it* for his habitation.
14 This *is* my rest forever: here will I dwell; for I have desired it.
15 I will abundantly bless her provision: I will satisfy her poor with bread.
16 I will also clothe her priests with salvation: and her saints shall shout aloud for joy.
17 There will I make the horn of David to bud: I have ordained a lamp for my anointed.
18 His enemies will I clothe with shame: but upon himself shall his crown flourish.

Psalms 133

133:1 ¶ <<A Song of degrees of David.>> Behold, how good and how pleasant *it is* for brethren to dwell together in unity!
2 *It is* like the precious ointment upon the head, that ran down upon the beard, *even* Aaron's beard: that went down to the skirts of his garments;
3 As the dew of Hermon, *and as the dew* that descended upon the mountains of Zion: for there Yahweh commanded the blessing, *even* life forevermore.

Psalms 134

134:1 ¶ <<A Song of degrees.>> Behold, bless you Yahweh, all *you* servants of Yahweh, which by night stand in the house of Yahweh.

2 Lift up your hands *in* the sanctuary, and bless Yahweh.
3 Yahweh that made heaven and earth bless you out of Zion.

Psalms 135

135:1 ¶ Praise you Yah. Praise you the name of Yahweh; praise *him*, O you servants of Yahweh.
2 You that stand in the house of Yahweh, in the courts of the house of our God,
3 Praise Yah; for Yahweh *is* good: sing praises unto his name; for *it is* pleasant.
4 For Yah has chosen Jacob unto himself, *and* Israel for his peculiar treasure.
5 ¶ For I know that Yahweh *is* great, and *that* our Lord *is* above all gods.
6 Whatever Yahweh pleased, *that* did he in heaven, and in earth, in the seas, and all deep places.
7 He causes the vapors to ascend from the ends of the earth; he makes lightnings for the rain; he brings the wind out of his treasuries.
8 Who smote the firstborn of Egypt, both of man and beast.
9 *Who* sent tokens and wonders into the midst of you, O Egypt, upon Pharaoh, and upon all his servants.
10 Who smote great nations, and slew mighty kings;
11 Sihon king of the Amorites, and Og king of Bashan, and all the kingdoms of Canaan:
12 And gave their land *for* a heritage, a heritage to Israel his people.
13 Your name, O Yahweh, *endures* forever; *and* your memorial, O Yahweh, throughout all generations.
14 For Yahweh will judge his people, and he will repent himself concerning his servants.
15 ¶ The idols of the heathen *are* silver and gold, the work of men's hands.
16 They have mouths, but they speak not; eyes have they, but they see not;
17 They have ears, but they hear not; neither is there *any* breath in their mouths.
18 They that make them are like unto them: *so is* every one that trusts in them.
19 Bless Yahweh, O house of Israel: bless Yahweh, O house of Aaron:
20 Bless Yahweh, O house of Levi: you that fear Yahweh, bless Yahweh.
21 Blessed be Yahweh out of Zion, which dwells at Jerusalem. Praise you Yah.

Psalms 136

136:1 ¶ O give thanks unto Yahweh; for *he is* good: for his mercy *endures* forever.
2 O give thanks unto the God of gods: for his mercy *endures* forever.
3 O give thanks unto the Lord of lords: for his mercy *endures* forever.
4 To him who alone does great wonders: for his mercy *endures* forever.
5 To him that by wisdom made the heavens: for his mercy *endures* forever.
6 To him that stretched out the earth above the waters: for his mercy *endures* forever.
7 To him that made great lights: for his mercy *endures* forever:
8 The sun to rule by day: for his mercy *endures* forever:
9 The moon and stars to rule by night: for his mercy *endures* forever.
10 ¶ To him that smote Egypt in their firstborn: for his mercy *endures* forever:
11 And brought out Israel from among them: for his mercy *endures* forever:
12 With a strong hand, and with a stretched out arm: for his mercy *endures* forever.
13 To him which divided the Red Sea into parts: for his mercy *endures* forever:
14 And made Israel to pass through the midst of it: for his mercy *endures* forever:
15 But overthrew Pharaoh and his host in the Red Sea: for his mercy *endures* forever.
16 To him which led his people through the wilderness: for his mercy *endures* forever.
17 To him which smote great kings: for his mercy *endures* forever:
18 And slew famous kings: for his mercy *endures* forever:
19 Sihon king of the Amorites: for his mercy *endures* forever:
20 And Og the king of Bashan: for his mercy *endures* forever:
21 And gave their land for a heritage: for his mercy *endures* forever:
22 *Even* a heritage unto Israel his servant: for his mercy *endures* forever.
23 ¶ Who remembered us in our low estate: for his mercy *endures* forever:
24 And has redeemed us from our enemies: for his mercy *endures* forever.
25 Who gives food to all flesh: for his mercy *endures* forever.
26 O give thanks unto the God of heaven: for his mercy *endures* forever.

Psalms 137

137:1 ¶ By the rivers of Babylon, there we sat down, yes, we wept, when we remembered Zion.
2 We hung our harps upon the willows in the midst thereof.
3 For there they that carried us away captive required of us a song; and they that wasted us *required of us* gladness, *saying*, Sing us *one* of the songs of Zion.
4 How shall we sing Yahweh's song in a strange land?

5 If I forget you, O Jerusalem, let my right hand forget *her cunning*.
6 If I do not remember you, let my tongue cling to the roof of my mouth; if I prefer not Jerusalem above my chief joy.
7 ¶ Remember, O Yahweh, the children of Edom in the day of Jerusalem; who said, Raze *it*, raze *it, even* to the foundation thereof.
8 O daughter of Babylon, who are to be destroyed; happy *shall he be*, that rewards you as you have served us.
9 Happy *shall he be*, that takes and dashes your little ones against the stones.

Psalms 138

138:1 ¶ <<*A Psalm* of David.>> I will praise you with my whole heart: before the gods will I sing praise unto you.
2 I will worship toward your holy temple, and praise your name for your loving kindness and for your truth: for you have magnified your word above all your name.
3 In the day when I cried you answered me, *and* strengthened me *with* strength in my soul.
4 All the kings of the earth shall praise you, O Yahweh, when they hear the words of your mouth.
5 Yes, they shall sing in the ways of Yahweh: for great *is* the glory of Yahweh.
6 ¶ Though Yahweh *is* high, yet has he respect unto the lowly: but the proud he knows afar off.
7 Though I walk in the midst of trouble, you will revive me: you shall stretch forth your hand against the wrath of my enemies, and your right hand shall save me.
8 Yahweh will perfect *that which* concerns me: your mercy, O Yahweh, *endures* forever: forsake not the works of your own hands.

Psalms 139

139:1 ¶ <<To the chief Musician, A Psalm of David.>> O Yahweh, you have searched me, and known *me*.
2 You know my sitting down and my rising up, you understand my thought afar off.
3 You compass my path and my lying down, and are acquainted *with* all my ways.
4 For *there is* not a word in my tongue, *but*, lo, O Yahweh, you know it altogether.
5 You have beset me behind and before, and laid your hand upon me.
6 *Such* knowledge *is* too wonderful for me; it is high, I cannot *attain* unto it.
7 ¶ Where shall I go from your spirit? or where shall I flee from your presence?
8 If I ascend up into heaven, you *are* there: if I make my bed in hell, behold, you *are there*.
9 *If* I take the wings of the morning, *and* dwell in the utmost parts of the sea;
10 Even there shall your hand lead me, and your right hand shall hold me.
11 If I say, Surely the darkness shall cover me; even the night shall be light about me.
12 Yes, the darkness hides not from you; but the night shines as the day: the darkness and the light *are* both alike *to you*.
13 For you have possessed my reins: you have covered me in my mother's womb.
14 I will praise you; for I am fearfully *and* wonderfully made: marvelous *are* your works; and *that* my soul knows right well.
15 My substance was not hidden from you, when I was made in secret, *and* curiously worked in the lowest parts of the earth.
16 Your eyes did see my substance, yet being imperfect; and in your book all *my members* were written, *which* in continuance were fashioned, when *as yet there was* none of them.
17 ¶ How precious also are your thoughts unto me, O God! how great is the sum of them!
18 *If* I should count them, they are more in number than the sand: when I awake, I am still with you.
19 Surely you will slay the wicked, O God: depart from me therefore, you bloody men.
20 For they speak against you wickedly, *and* your enemies take *your name* in vain.
21 Do not I hate them, O Yahweh, that hate you? and am not I grieved with those that rise up against you?
22 I hate them with perfect hatred: I count them my enemies.
23 Search me, O God, and know my heart: try me, and know my thoughts:
24 And see if *there is any* wicked way in me, and lead me in the way everlasting.

Psalms 140

140:1 ¶ <<To the chief Musician, A Psalm of David.>> Deliver me, O Yahweh, from the evil man: preserve me from the violent man;
2 Which imagine mischief in *their* heart; continually are they gathered together *for* war.
3 They have sharpened their tongues like a serpent; adders' poison *is* under their lips. Selah.
4 Keep me, O Yahweh, from the hands of the wicked; preserve me from the violent man; who has purposed to overthrow my goings.
5 The proud have hidden a snare for me, and cords; they have spread a net by the wayside; they have set gins for me. Selah.
6 I said unto Yahweh, You *are* my God: hear the voice of my supplications, O Yahweh.
7 O Yahweh the Lord, the strength of my salvation, you have covered my head in the day of battle.
8 ¶ Grant not, O Yahweh, the desires of the wicked: further not his wicked device; *lest* they exalt themselves. Selah.
9 *As for* the head of those that compass me about, let the mischief of their own lips cover them.

Psalms 140

10 Let burning coals fall upon them: let them be cast into the fire; into deep pits, that they rise not up again.
11 Let not an evil speaker be established in the earth: evil shall hunt the violent man to overthrow *him*.
12 I know that Yahweh will maintain the cause of the afflicted, *and* the right of the poor.
13 Surely the righteous shall give thanks unto your name: the upright shall dwell in your presence.

Psalms 141

141:1 ¶ <<A Psalm of David.>> Yahweh, I cry unto you: make haste unto me; give ear unto my voice, when I cry to you.
2 Let my prayer be set forth before you *as* incense; *and* the lifting up of my hands *as* the evening sacrifice.
3 Set a watch, O Yahweh, before my mouth; keep the door of my lips.
4 Incline not my heart to *any* evil thing, to practice wicked works with men that work iniquity: and let me not eat of their delicacies.
5 ¶ Let the righteous smite me; *it shall be* a kindness: and let him reprove me; *it shall be* an excellent oil, *which* shall not break my head: for yet my prayer also *shall be* in their calamities.
6 When their judges are overthrown in stony places, they shall hear my words; for they are sweet.
7 Our bones are scattered at the grave's mouth, as when one cuts and splits *wood* upon the earth.
8 But my eyes *are* unto you, O Yahweh the Lord: in you is my trust; leave not my soul destitute.
9 Keep me from the snares *which* they have laid for me, and the gins of the workers of iniquity.
10 Let the wicked fall into their own nets, while that I altogether escape.

Psalms 142

142:1 ¶ <<Maschil of David; A Prayer when he was in the cave.>> I cried unto Yahweh with my voice; with my voice unto Yahweh did I make my supplication.
2 I poured out my complaint before him; I declared before him my trouble.
3 When my spirit was overwhelmed within me, then you knew my path. In the way wherein I walked have they secretly laid a snare for me.
4 ¶ I looked on *my* right hand, and beheld, but *there was* no man that would know me: refuge failed me; no man cared for my soul.
5 I cried unto you, O Yahweh: I said, You *are* my refuge *and* my portion in the land of the living.
6 Attend unto my cry; for I am brought very low: deliver me from my persecutors; for they are stronger than I.
7 Bring my soul out of prison, that I may praise your name: the righteous shall compass me about; for you shall deal bountifully with me.

Psalms 143

143:1 ¶ <<A Psalm of David.>> Hear my prayer, O Yahweh, give ear unto my supplications: in your faithfulness answer me, *and* in your righteousness.
2 And enter not into judgment with your servant: for in your sight shall no man living be justified.
3 For the enemy has persecuted my soul; he has smitten my life down to the ground; he has made me to dwell in darkness, as those that have been long dead.
4 Therefore is my spirit overwhelmed within me; my heart within me is desolate.
5 I remember the days of old; I meditate on all your works; I muse on the work of your hands.
6 I stretch forth my hands unto you: my soul *thirsts* after you, as a thirsty land. Selah.
7 ¶ Hear me speedily, O Yahweh: my spirit fails: hide not your face from me, lest I be like unto them that go down into the pit.
8 Cause me to hear your loving kindness in the morning; for in you do I trust: cause me to know the way wherein I should walk; for I lift up my soul unto you.
9 Deliver me, O Yahweh, from my enemies: I flee unto you to hide me.
10 Teach me to do your will; for you *are* my God: your spirit *is* good; lead me into the land of uprightness.
11 Quicken me, O Yahweh, for your name's sake: for your righteousness' sake bring my soul out of trouble.
12 And of your mercy cut off my enemies, and destroy all them that afflict my soul: for I *am* your servant.

Psalms 144

144:1 ¶ <<*A Psalm* of David.>> Blessed *be* Yahweh my strength, which teaches my hands to war, *and* my fingers to fight:
2 My goodness, and my fortress; my high tower, and my deliverer; my shield, and *he* in whom I trust; who subdues my people under me.
3 Yahweh, what *is* man, that you take knowledge of him! *or* the son of man, that you make account of him!
4 Man is like to vanity: his days *are* as a shadow that passes away.
5 Bow your heavens, O Yahweh, and come down: touch the mountains, and they shall smoke.
6 Cast forth lightning, and scatter them: shoot out your arrows, and destroy them.
7 Send your hand from above; rid me, and deliver me out of great waters, from the hand of strange children;
8 Whose mouth speaks vanity, and their right hand *is* a right hand of falsehood.
9 ¶ I will sing a new song unto you, O God: upon a psaltery *and* an instrument of ten strings will I sing praises unto you.
10 *It is he* that gives salvation unto kings: who delivers David his servant from the hurtful sword.

11 Rid me, and deliver me from the hand of strange children, whose mouth speaks vanity, and their right hand *is* a right hand of falsehood:
12 That our sons *may be* as plants grown up in their youth; *that* our daughters *may be* as corner stones, polished *after* the pattern of a palace:
13 *That* our granaries *may be* full, furnishing all manner of store: *that* our sheep may bring forth thousands and ten thousands in our streets:
14 *That* our oxen *may be* strong to labor; *that there be* no breaking in, nor going out; that *there be* no complaining in our streets.
15 Happy *is that* people, that is in such a case: *yes,* happy *is that* people, whose God *is* Yahweh.

Psalms 145

145:1 ¶ <<David's *Psalm* of praise.>> I will extol you, my God, O king; and I will bless your name forever and ever.
2 Every day will I bless you; and I will praise your name forever and ever.
3 Great *is* Yahweh, and greatly to be praised; and his greatness *is* unsearchable.
4 One generation shall praise your works to another, and shall declare your mighty acts.
5 I will speak of the glorious honor of your majesty, and of your wondrous works.
6 And *men* shall speak of the might of your awesome acts: and I will declare your greatness.
7 They shall abundantly utter the memory of your great goodness, and shall sing of your righteousness.
8 Yahweh *is* gracious, and full of compassion; slow to anger, and of great mercy.
9 Yahweh *is* good to all: and his tender mercies *are* over all his works.
10 ¶ All your works shall praise you, O Yahweh; and your saints shall bless you.
11 They shall speak of the glory of your kingdom, and talk of your power;
12 To make known to the sons of men his mighty acts, and the glorious majesty of his kingdom.
13 Your kingdom *is* an everlasting kingdom, and your dominion *endures* throughout all generations.
14 Yahweh upholds all that fall, and raises up all *those that are* bowed down.
15 The eyes of all wait upon you; and you give them their meat in due season.
16 You open your hand, and satisfy the desire of every living thing.
17 Yahweh *is* righteous in all his ways, and holy in all his works.
18 Yahweh *is* near to all them that call upon him, to all that call upon him in truth.
19 He will fulfill the desire of them that fear him: he also will hear their cry, and will save them.
20 Yahweh preserves all them that love him: but all the wicked will he destroy.
21 My mouth shall speak the praise of Yahweh: and let all flesh bless his holy name forever and ever.

Psalms 146

146:1 ¶ Praise you Yah. Praise Yahweh, O my soul.
2 While I live will I praise Yahweh: I will sing praises unto my God while I have any being.
3 Put not your trust in princes, *nor* in the son of man, in whom *there is* no help.
4 His breath goes forth, he returns to his earth; in that very day his thoughts perish.
5 ¶ Happy *is he* that *has* the God of Jacob for his help, whose hope *is* in Yahweh his God:
6 Which made heaven, and earth, the sea, and all that therein *is*: which keeps truth forever:
7 Which executes judgment for the oppressed: which gives food to the hungry. Yahweh looses the prisoners:
8 Yahweh opens *the eyes of* the blind: Yahweh raises them that are bowed down: Yahweh loves the righteous:
9 Yahweh preserves the strangers; he relieves the fatherless and widow: but the way of the wicked he turns upside down.
10 Yahweh shall reign forever, *even* your God, O Zion, unto all generations. Praise you Yah.

Psalms 147

147:1 ¶ Praise you Yah: for *it is* good to sing praises unto our God; for *it is* pleasant; *and* praise is beautiful.
2 Yahweh does build up Jerusalem: he gathers together the outcasts of Israel.
3 He heals the broken in heart, and binds up their wounds.
4 He tells the number of the stars; he calls them all by *their* names.
5 Great *is* our Lord, and of great power: his understanding *is* infinite.
6 Yahweh lifts up the meek: he casts the wicked down to the ground.
7 Sing unto Yahweh with thanksgiving; sing praise upon the harp unto our God:
8 Who covers the heaven with clouds, who prepares rain for the earth, who makes grass to grow upon the mountains.
9 He gives to the beast his food, *and* to the young ravens which cry.
10 He delights not in the strength of the horse: he takes not pleasure in the legs of a man.
11 Yahweh takes pleasure in them that fear him, in those that hope in his mercy.
12 ¶ Praise Yahweh, O Jerusalem; praise your God, O Zion.
13 For he has strengthened the bars of your gates; he has blessed your children within you.
14 He makes peace *in* your borders, *and* fills you with the finest of the wheat.

Psalms 147

15 He sends forth his commandment *upon* earth: his word runs very swiftly.
16 He gives snow like wool: he scatters the hoarfrost like ashes.
17 He casts forth his ice like morsels: who can stand before his cold?
18 He sends out his word, and melts them: he causes his wind to blow, *and* the waters flow.
19 He shows his word to Jacob, his statutes and his judgments to Israel.
20 He has not dealt so with any nation: and *as for his* judgments, they have not known them. Praise you Yah.

Psalms 148

148:1 ¶ Praise you Yah. Praise you Yahweh from the heavens: praise him in the heights.
2 Praise you him, all his angels: praise you him, all his hosts.
3 Praise you him, sun and moon: praise him, all you stars of light.
4 Praise him, you heavens of heavens, and you waters that *are* above the heavens.
5 Let them praise the name of Yahweh: for he commanded, and they were created.
6 He has also established them forever and ever: he has made a decree which shall not pass.
7 ¶ Praise Yahweh from the earth, you dragons, and all depths:
8 Fire, and hail; snow, and vapor; stormy wind fulfilling his word:
9 Mountains, and all hills; fruitful trees, and all cedars:
10 Beasts, and all cattle; creeping things, and flying fowl:
11 Kings of the earth, and all people; princes, and all judges of the earth:
12 Both young men, and maidens; old men, and children:
13 Let them praise the name of Yahweh: for his name alone is excellent; his glory *is* above the earth and heaven.
14 He also exalts the horn of his people, the praise of all his saints; *even* of the children of Israel, a people near unto him. Praise you Yah.

Psalms 149

149:1 ¶ Praise you Yah. Sing unto Yahweh a new song, *and* his praise in the congregation of saints.
2 Let Israel rejoice in him that made him: let the children of Zion be joyful in their King.
3 Let them praise his name in the dance: let them sing praises unto him with the tambourine and harp.
4 For Yahweh takes pleasure in his people: he will beautify the meek with salvation.
5 Let the saints be joyful in glory: let them sing aloud upon their beds.
6 ¶ *Let* the high *praises* of God *be* in their mouth, and a two-edged sword in their hand;
7 To execute vengeance upon the heathen, *and* punishments upon the people;
8 To bind their kings with chains, and their nobles with fetters of iron;
9 To execute upon them the judgment written: this honor have all his saints. Praise you Yah.

Psalms 150

150:1 ¶ Praise you Yah. Praise God in his sanctuary: praise him in the firmament of his power.
2 Praise him for his mighty acts: praise him according to his excellent greatness.
3 Praise him with the sound of the trumpet: praise him with the psaltery and harp.
4 Praise him with the tambourine and dance: praise him with stringed instruments and organs.
5 Praise him upon the loud cymbals: praise him upon the high sounding cymbals.
6 Let every thing that has breath praise Yah. Praise you Yah.

Proverbs

Proverbs 1

1:1 ¶ The proverbs of Solomon the son of David, king of Israel;
2 To know wisdom and instruction; to perceive the words of understanding;
3 To receive the instruction of wisdom, justice, and judgment, and equity;
4 To give subtlety to the simple, to the young man knowledge and discretion.
5 A wise *man* will hear, and will increase learning; and a man of understanding shall attain unto wise counsels:
6 To understand a proverb, and the interpretation; the words of the wise, and their dark sayings.
7 ¶ The fear of Yahweh *is* the beginning of knowledge: *but* fools despise wisdom and instruction.
8 My son, hear the instruction of your father, and forsake not the law of your mother:
9 For they *shall be* an ornament of grace unto your head, and chains about your neck.
10 ¶ My son, if sinners entice you, consent you not.
11 If they say, Come with us, let us lay wait for blood, let us lurk privately for the innocent without cause:
12 Let us swallow them up alive as the grave; and whole, as those that go down into the pit:
13 We shall find all precious substance, we shall fill our houses with spoil:
14 Cast in your lot among us; let us all have one purse:

15 My son, walk not you in the way with them; refrain your foot from their path:
16 For their feet run to evil, and make haste to shed blood.
17 Surely in vain the net is spread in the sight of any bird.
18 And they lay wait for their *own* blood; they lurk privately for their *own* lives.
19 So *are* the ways of every one that is greedy of gain; *which* takes away the life of the owners thereof.
20 ¶ Wisdom cries outside; she utters her voice in the streets:
21 She cries in the chief place of concourse, in the openings of the gates: in the city she utters her words, *saying*,
22 How long, you simple ones, will you love simplicity? and the scorners delight in their scorning, and fools hate knowledge?
23 Turn you at my reproof: behold, I will pour out my spirit unto you, I will make known my words unto you.
24 Because I have called, and you refused; I have stretched out my hand, and no man regarded;
25 But you have set at nothing all my counsel, and would *have* none of my reproof:
26 I also will laugh at your calamity; I will mock when your fear comes;
27 When your fear comes as desolation, and your destruction comes as a whirlwind; when distress and anguish comes upon you.
28 Then shall they call upon me, but I will not answer; they shall seek me earnestly, but they shall not find me:
29 For that they hated knowledge, and did not choose the fear of Yahweh:
30 They would none of my counsel: they despised all my reproof.
31 Therefore shall they eat of the fruit of their own way, and be filled with their own devices.
32 For the turning away of the simple shall slay them, and the prosperity of fools shall destroy them.
33 But whoever listens to me shall dwell safely, and shall be quiet from fear of evil.

Proverbs 2

2:1 ¶ My son, if you will receive my words, and hide my commandments with you;
2 So that you incline your ear unto wisdom, *and* apply your heart unto understanding;
3 Yes, if you cry after knowledge, *and* lift up your voice for understanding;
4 If you seek her as silver, and search for her as *for* hidden treasures;
5 Then shall you understand the fear of Yahweh, and find the knowledge of God.
6 For Yahweh gives wisdom: out of his mouth *comes* knowledge and understanding.
7 He lays up sound wisdom for the righteous: *he is* a buckler to them that walk uprightly.
8 He keeps the paths of judgment, and preserves the way of his saints.
9 Then shall you understand righteousness, and judgment, and equity; *yes,* every good path.
10 ¶ When wisdom enters into your heart, and knowledge is pleasant unto your soul;
11 Discretion shall preserve you, understanding shall keep you:
12 To deliver you from the way of the evil *man*, from the man that speaks froward things;
13 Who leave the paths of uprightness, to walk in the ways of darkness;
14 Who rejoice to do evil, *and* delight in the perversity of the wicked;
15 Whose ways *are* crooked, and *they are* froward in their paths:
16 To deliver you from the strange woman, *even* from the stranger *which* flatters with her words;
17 Which forsakes the guide of her youth, and forgets the covenant of her God.
18 For her house inclines unto death, and her paths unto the dead.
19 None that go to her return again, neither take they hold of the paths of life.
20 That you may walk in the way of good *men*, and keep the paths of the righteous.
21 For the upright shall dwell in the land, and the perfect shall remain in it.
22 But the wicked shall be cut off from the earth, and the transgressors shall be rooted out of it.

Proverbs 3

3:1 ¶ My son, forget not my law; but let your heart keep my commandments:
2 For length of days, and long life, and peace, shall they add to you.
3 Let not mercy and truth forsake you: bind them about your neck; write them upon the table of your heart:
4 So shall you find favor and good understanding in the sight of God and man.
5 Trust in Yahweh with all your heart; and lean not unto your own understanding.
6 In all your ways acknowledge him, and he shall direct your paths.
7 ¶ Be not wise in your own eyes: fear Yahweh, and depart from evil.
8 It shall be health to your navel, and marrow to your bones.
9 Honor Yahweh with your substance, and with the firstfruits of all your increase:
10 So shall your barns be filled with plenty, and your presses shall burst out with new wine.
11 My son, despise not the chastening of Yahweh; neither be weary of his correction:
12 For whom Yahweh loves he corrects; even as a father the son *in whom* he delights.

Proverbs 3

13 ¶ Happy *is* the man *that* finds wisdom, and the man *that* gets understanding.
14 For the merchandise of it *is* better than the merchandise of silver, and the gain thereof than fine gold.
15 She *is* more precious than rubies: and all the things you can desire are not to be compared unto her.
16 Length of days *is* in her right hand; *and* in her left hand riches and honor.
17 Her ways *are* ways of pleasantness, and all her paths *are* peace.
18 She *is* a tree of life to them that lay hold upon her: and happy *is* every one that retains her.
19 Yahweh by wisdom has founded the earth; by understanding has he established the heavens.
20 By his knowledge the depths are broken up, and the clouds drop down the dew.
21 ¶ My son, let not them depart from your eyes: keep sound wisdom and discretion:
22 So shall they be life unto your soul, and grace to your neck.
23 Then shall you walk in your way safely, and your foot shall not stumble.
24 When you lie down, you shall not be afraid: yes, you shall lie down, and your sleep shall be sweet.
25 Be not afraid of sudden fear, neither of the desolation of the wicked, when it comes.
26 For Yahweh shall be your confidence, and shall keep your foot from being taken.
27 ¶ Withhold not good from them to whom it is due, when it is in the power of your hand to do *it*.
28 Say not unto your neighbor, Go, and come again, and tomorrow I will give; when you have it by you.
29 Devise not evil against your neighbor, seeing he dwells securely by you.
30 Strive not with a man without cause, if he has done you no harm.
31 Envy you not the oppressor, and choose none of his ways.
32 For the froward *is* abomination to Yahweh: but his secret *is* with the righteous.
33 The curse of Yahweh *is* in the house of the wicked: but he blesses the habitation of the just.
34 Surely he scorns the scorners: but he gives grace to the lowly.
35 The wise shall inherit glory: but shame shall be the promotion of fools.

Proverbs 4

4:1 ¶ Hear, you children, the instruction of a father, and attend to know understanding.
2 For I give you good doctrine, forsake you not my law.
3 For I was my father's son, tender and only *beloved* in the sight of my mother.
4 He taught me also, and said unto me, Let your heart retain my words: keep my commandments, and live.
5 Get wisdom, get understanding: forget *it* not; neither decline from the words of my mouth.
6 Forsake her not, and she shall preserve you: love her, and she shall keep you.
7 Wisdom *is* the principal thing; *therefore* get wisdom: and with all your getting get understanding.
8 Exalt her, and she shall promote you: she shall bring you to honor, when you do embrace her.
9 She shall give to your head an ornament of grace: a crown of glory shall she deliver to you.
10 Hear, O my son, and receive my sayings; and the years of your life shall be many.
11 I have taught you in the way of wisdom; I have led you in right paths.
12 When you go, your steps shall not be cramped; and when you run, you shall not stumble.
13 Take fast hold of instruction; let *her* not go: keep her; for she *is* your life.
14 ¶ Enter not into the path of the wicked, and go not in the way of evil *men*.
15 Avoid it, pass not by it, turn from it, and pass away.
16 For they sleep not, unless they have done mischief; and their sleep is taken away, unless they cause *some* to fall.
17 For they eat the bread of wickedness, and drink the wine of violence.
18 But the path of the just *is* as the shining light, that shines more and more unto the perfect day.
19 The way of the wicked *is* as darkness: they know not at what they stumble.
20 ¶ My son, attend to my words; incline your ear unto my sayings.
21 Let them not depart from your eyes; keep them in the midst of your heart.
22 For they *are* life to those that find them, and health to all their flesh.
23 Keep your heart with all diligence; for out of it *are* the issues of life.
24 Put away from you a froward mouth, and perverse lips put far from you.
25 Let your eyes look right on, and let your eyelids look straight before you.
26 Ponder the path of your feet, and let all your ways be established.
27 Turn not to the right hand nor to the left: remove your foot from evil.

Proverbs 5

5:1 ¶ My son, attend unto my wisdom, *and* bow your ear unto my understanding:
2 That you may regard discretion, and *that* your lips may keep knowledge.
3 For the lips of a strange woman drop *as* a honeycomb, and her mouth *is* smoother than oil:
4 But her end is bitter as wormwood, sharp as a two-edged sword.

5 Her feet go down to death; her steps take hold on hell.
6 Lest you should ponder the path of life, her ways are moveable, *that* you can not know *them*.
7 Hear me now therefore, O you children, and depart not from the words of my mouth.
8 Remove your way far from her, and come not near the door of her house:
9 Lest you give your honor unto others, and your years unto the cruel:
10 Lest strangers be filled with your wealth; and your labors *be* in the house of a stranger;
11 And you mourn at the last, when your flesh and your body are consumed,
12 And say, How have I hated instruction, and my heart despised reproof;
13 And have not obeyed the voice of my teachers, nor inclined my ear to them that instructed me!
14 I was almost in all evil in the midst of the congregation and assembly.
15 ¶ Drink waters out of your own cistern, and running waters out of your own well.
16 Let your fountains be dispersed abroad, *and* rivers of waters in the streets.
17 Let them be only your own, and not strangers' with you.
18 Let your fountain be blessed: and rejoice with the wife of your youth.
19 *Let her be as* the loving deer and pleasant roe; let her breasts satisfy you at all times; and be you ravished always with her love.
20 And why will you, my son, be ravished with a strange woman, and embrace the bosom of a stranger?
21 For the ways of man *are* before the eyes of Yahweh, and he ponders all his goings.
22 His own iniquities shall take the wicked himself, and he shall be held with the cords of his sins.
23 He shall die without instruction; and in the greatness of his folly he shall go astray.

Proverbs 6

6:1 ¶ My son, if you are surety for your friend, *if* you have stricken your hand with a stranger,
2 You are snared with the words of your mouth, you are taken with the words of your mouth.
3 Do this now, my son, and deliver yourself, when you have come into the hand of your friend; go, humble yourself, and make sure your friend.
4 Give not sleep to your eyes, nor slumber to your eyelids.
5 Deliver yourself as a roe from the hand *of the hunter*, and as a bird from the hand of the fowler.
6 ¶ Go to the ant, you sluggard; consider her ways, and be wise:
7 Which having no guide, overseer, or ruler,
8 Provides her meat in the summer, *and* gathers her food in the harvest.
9 How long will you sleep, O sluggard? when will you arise out of your sleep?
10 *Yet* a little sleep, a little slumber, a little folding of the hands to sleep:
11 So shall your poverty come as one that travels, and your want as an armed man.
12 ¶ A naughty person, a wicked man, walks with a froward mouth.
13 He winks with his eyes, he speaks with his feet, he teaches with his fingers;
14 Perversity *is* in his heart, he devises mischief continually; he sows discord.
15 Therefore shall his calamity come suddenly; suddenly shall he be broken without remedy.
16 These six *things* does Yahweh hate: yes, seven *are* an abomination to him:
17 A proud look, a lying tongue, and hands that shed innocent blood,
18 A heart that devises wicked imaginations, feet that are swift in running to mischief,
19 A false witness *that* speaks lies, and he that sows discord among brethren.
20 ¶ My son, keep your father's commandment, and forsake not the law of your mother:
21 Bind them continually upon your heart, *and* tie them about your neck.
22 When you go, it shall lead you; when you sleep, it shall keep you; and *when* you wake, it shall talk with you.
23 For the commandment *is* a lamp; and the law *is* light; and reproofs of instruction *are* the way of life:
24 To keep you from the evil woman, from the flattery of the tongue of a strange woman.
25 Lust not after her beauty in your heart; neither let her take you with her eyelids.
26 For by means of a whorish woman *a man is* brought to a piece of bread: and the adulteress will hunt for the precious life.
27 Can a man take fire in his bosom, and his clothes not be burned?
28 Can one go upon hot coals, and his feet not be burned?
29 So he that goes in to his neighbor's wife; whoever touches her shall not be innocent.
30 *Men* do not despise a thief, if he steals to satisfy his soul when he is hungry;
31 But *if* he is found, he shall restore sevenfold; he shall give all the substance of his house.
32 *But* whoever commits adultery with a woman lacks understanding: he *that* does it destroys his own soul.
33 A wound and dishonor shall he get; and his reproach shall not be wiped away.
34 For jealousy *is* the rage of a man: therefore he will not spare in the day of vengeance.
35 He will not regard any ransom; neither will he rest content, though you give many gifts.

Proverbs 7

7:1 ¶ My son, keep my words, and lay up my commandments with you.

2 Keep my commandments, and live; and my law as the apple of your eye.

3 Bind them upon your fingers, write them upon the table of your heart.

4 Say unto wisdom, You *are* my sister; and call understanding *your* kinswoman:

5 That they may keep you from the strange woman, from the stranger *which* flatters with her words.

6 ¶ For at the window of my house I looked through my casement,

7 And saw among the simple ones, I discerned among the youths, a young man void of understanding,

8 Passing through the street near her corner; and he went the way to her house,

9 In the twilight, in the evening, in the black and dark night:

10 And, behold, there met him a woman *with* the attire of a harlot, and subtle of heart.

11 (She *is* loud and stubborn; her feet stay not in her house:

12 Now *is she* without, now in the streets, and lies in wait at every corner.)

13 So she caught him, and kissed him, *and* with an impudent face said to him,

14 *I have* peace offerings with me; this day have I paid my vows.

15 Therefore came I forth to meet you, diligently to seek your face, and I have found you.

16 I have decked my bed with coverings of tapestry, with carved *works*, with fine linen of Egypt.

17 I have perfumed my bed with myrrh, aloes, and cinnamon.

18 Come, let us take our fill of love until the morning: let us solace ourselves with loves.

19 For my husband *is* not at home, he has gone *on* a long journey:

20 He has taken a bag of money with him, *and* will come home at the day appointed.

21 With her much fair speech she caused him to yield, with the flattering of her lips she forced him.

22 He goes after her suddenly, as an ox goes to the slaughter, or as a fool to the correction of the stocks;

23 Till a dart strikes through his liver; as a bird hastens to the snare, and knows not that it *is* for his life.

24 ¶ Listen unto me now therefore, O you children, and attend to the words of my mouth.

25 Let not your heart decline to her ways, go not astray in her paths.

26 For she has cast down many wounded: yes, many strong *men* have been slain by her.

27 Her house *is* the way to hell, going down to the chambers of death.

Proverbs 8

8:1 ¶ Does not wisdom cry? and understanding put forth her voice?

2 She stands in the top of high places, by the way in the places of the paths.

3 She cries at the gates, at the entry of the city, at the coming in at the doors.

4 Unto you, O men, I call; and my voice *is* to the sons of man.

5 O you simple, understand wisdom: and, you fools, be you of an understanding heart.

6 Hear; for I will speak of excellent things; and the opening of my lips *shall be* right things.

7 For my mouth shall speak truth; and wickedness *is* an abomination to my lips.

8 All the words of my mouth *are* in righteousness; *there is* nothing froward or perverse in them.

9 They *are* all plain to him that understands, and right to them that find knowledge.

10 Receive my instruction, and not silver; and knowledge rather than choice gold.

11 For wisdom *is* better than rubies; and all the things that may be desired are not to be compared to it.

12 ¶ I wisdom dwell with prudence, and find out knowledge of witty inventions.

13 The fear of Yahweh *is* to hate evil: pride, and arrogance, and the evil way, and the froward mouth, do I hate.

14 Counsel *is* mine, and sound wisdom: I *am* understanding; I have strength.

15 By me kings reign, and princes decree justice.

16 By me princes rule, and nobles, *even* all the judges of the earth.

17 I love them that love me; and those that seek me earnestly shall find me.

18 Riches and honor *are* with me; *yes,* durable riches and righteousness.

19 My fruit *is* better than gold, yes, than fine gold; and my revenue than choice silver.

20 I lead in the way of righteousness, in the midst of the paths of judgment:

21 That I may cause those that love me to inherit substance; and I will fill their treasures.

22 ¶ Yahweh possessed me in the beginning of his way, before his works of old.

23 I was set up from everlasting, from the beginning, or ever the earth was.

24 When *there were* no depths, I was brought forth; when *there were* no fountains abounding with water.

25 Before the mountains were settled, before the hills was I brought forth:

26 While as yet he had not made the earth, nor the fields, nor the highest part of the dust of the world.

27 When he prepared the heavens, I *was* there: when he set a compass upon the face of the depth:

28 When he established the clouds above: when he strengthened the fountains of the deep:

29 When he gave to the sea his decree, that the waters should not pass his commandment: when he appointed the foundations of the earth:
30 Then I was by him, *as* one brought up *with him*: and I was daily *his* delight, rejoicing always before him;
31 Rejoicing in the habitable part of his earth; and my delights *were* with the sons of men.
32 ¶ Now therefore listen unto me, O you children: for blessed *are they that* keep my ways.
33 Hear instruction, and be wise, and refuse it not.
34 Blessed *is* the man that hears me, watching daily at my gates, waiting at the posts of my doors.
35 For whoever finds me finds life, and shall obtain favor of Yahweh.
36 But he that sins against me wrongs his own soul: all they that hate me love death.

Proverbs 9

9:1 ¶ Wisdom has built her house, she has hewn out her seven pillars:
2 She has killed her beasts; she has mingled her wine; she has also furnished her table.
3 She has sent forth her maidens: she cries upon the highest places of the city,
4 Whoever *is* simple, let him turn in here: *as for* him that wants understanding, she says to him,
5 Come, eat of my bread, and drink of the wine *which* I have mingled.
6 Forsake the foolish, and live; and go in the way of understanding.
7 He that reproves a scorner gets to himself shame: and he that rebukes a wicked *man gets* himself a blot.
8 Reprove not a scorner, lest he hates you: rebuke a wise man, and he will love you.
9 Give *instruction* to a wise *man*, and he will be yet wiser: teach a just *man*, and he will increase in learning.
10 The fear of Yahweh *is* the beginning of wisdom: and the knowledge of the holy *is* understanding.
11 For by me your days shall be multiplied, and the years of your life shall be increased.
12 If you are wise, you shall be wise for yourself: but *if* you scorn, you alone will bear *it*.
13 ¶ A foolish woman *is* clamorous: *she is* simple, and knows nothing.
14 For she sits at the door of her house, on a seat in the high places of the city,
15 To call passengers who go right on their ways:
16 Whoever *is* simple, let him turn in here: and *as for* him that wants understanding, she says to him,
17 Stolen waters are sweet, and bread *eaten* in secret is pleasant.
18 But he knows not that the dead *are* there; *and that* her guests *are* in the depths of hell.

Proverbs 10

10:1 ¶ The proverbs of Solomon. A wise son makes a glad father: but a foolish son *is* the heaviness of his mother.
2 ¶ Treasures of wickedness profit nothing: but righteousness delivers from death.
3 Yahweh will not permit the soul of the righteous to famish: but he casts away the substance of the wicked.
4 ¶ He becomes poor that deals *with* a slack hand: but the hand of the diligent makes rich.
5 ¶ He that gathers in summer *is* a wise son: *but* he that sleeps in harvest *is* a son that causes shame.
6 ¶ Blessings *are* upon the head of the just: but violence covers the mouth of the wicked.
7 ¶ The memory of the just *is* blessed: but the name of the wicked shall rot.
8 ¶ The wise in heart will receive commandments: but a prating fool shall fall.
9 ¶ He that walks uprightly walks surely: but he that perverts his ways shall be known.
10 ¶ He that winks with the eye causes sorrow: but a prating fool shall fall.
11 ¶ The mouth of a righteous *man is* a well of life: but violence covers the mouth of the wicked.
12 ¶ Hatred stirs up strife: but love covers all sins.
13 ¶ In the lips of him that has understanding wisdom is found: but a rod *is* for the back of him that is void of understanding.
14 ¶ Wise *men* lay up knowledge: but the mouth of the foolish *is* near destruction.
15 ¶ The rich man's wealth *is* his strong city: the destruction of the poor *is* their poverty.
16 ¶ The labor of the righteous *tends* to life: the fruit of the wicked to sin.
17 ¶ He *is in* the way of life that keeps instruction: but he that refuses reproof errs.
18 ¶ He that hides hatred *with* lying lips, and he that utters a slander, *is* a fool.
19 ¶ In the multitude of words there ceases not sin: but he that refrains his lips *is* wise.
20 ¶ The tongue of the just *is as* choice silver: the heart of the wicked *is of* little worth.
21 The lips of the righteous feed many: but fools die for want of wisdom.
22 ¶ The blessing of Yahweh, it makes rich, and he adds no sorrow with it.
23 ¶ *It is* as sport to a fool to do mischief: but a man of understanding has wisdom.
24 ¶ The fear of the wicked, it shall come upon him: but the desire of the righteous shall be granted.
25 As the whirlwind passes, so *is* the wicked no *more*: but the righteous *has* an everlasting foundation.
26 ¶ As vinegar to the teeth, and as smoke to the eyes, so *is* the sluggard to them that send him.
27 ¶ The fear of Yahweh prolongs days: but the years of the wicked shall be shortened.

Proverbs 10

28 The hope of the righteous *shall be* gladness: but the expectation of the wicked shall perish.
29 ¶ The way of Yahweh *is* strength to the upright: but destruction *shall be* to the workers of iniquity.
30 The righteous shall never be removed: but the wicked shall not inhabit the earth.
31 ¶ The mouth of the just brings forth wisdom: but the froward tongue shall be cut out.
32 The lips of the righteous know what is acceptable: but the mouth of the wicked *speaks* perversity.

Proverbs 11

11:1 ¶ A false balance *is an* abomination to Yahweh: but a just weight *is* his delight.
2 ¶ *When* pride comes, then comes shame: but with the lowly *is* wisdom.
3 ¶ The integrity of the upright shall guide them: but the perverseness of transgressors shall destroy them.
4 ¶ Riches profit not in the day of wrath: but righteousness delivers from death.
5 ¶ The righteousness of the perfect shall direct his way: but the wicked shall fall by his own wickedness.
6 The righteousness of the upright shall deliver them: but transgressors shall be taken in *their own* naughtiness.
7 ¶ When a wicked man dies, *his* expectation shall perish: and the hope of unjust *men* perishes.
8 ¶ The righteous is delivered out of trouble, and the wicked comes in his stead.
9 ¶ A hypocrite with *his* mouth destroys his neighbor: but through knowledge shall the just be delivered.
10 ¶ When it goes well with the righteous, the city rejoices: and when the wicked perish, *there is* shouting.
11 By the blessing of the upright the city is exalted: but it is overthrown by the mouth of the wicked.
12 ¶ He that is void of wisdom despises his neighbor: but a man of understanding holds his peace.
13 A talebearer reveals secrets: but he that is of a faithful spirit conceals the matter.
14 ¶ Where no counsel *is*, the people fall: but in the multitude of counselors *there is* safety.
15 ¶ He that is surety for a stranger shall suffer *for it*: and he that hates being surety is secure.
16 ¶ A gracious woman retains honor: and strong *men* retain riches.
17 ¶ The merciful man does good to his own soul: but *he that is* cruel troubles his own flesh.
18 ¶ The wicked works a deceitful work: but to him that sows righteousness *shall be* a sure reward.
19 ¶ As righteousness *tends* to life: so he that pursues evil *pursues it* to his own death.
20 ¶ They that are of a froward heart *are* abomination to Yahweh: but *such as are* upright in *their* way *are* his delight.
21 ¶ *Though* hand *joins* in hand, the wicked shall not be unpunished: but the seed of the righteous shall be delivered.
22 ¶ *As* a jewel of gold in a swine's snout, *so is* a fair woman which is without discretion.
23 ¶ The desire of the righteous *is* only good: *but* the expectation of the wicked *is* wrath.
24 ¶ There is *one* that scatters, and yet increases; and *there is one* that withholds more than is right, but *it tends* to poverty.
25 ¶ The liberal soul shall be made fat: and he that waters shall be watered also himself.
26 ¶ He that withholds corn, the people shall curse him: but blessing *shall be* upon the head of him that sells *it*.
27 ¶ He that diligently seeks good procures favor: but he that seeks mischief, it shall come to him.
28 ¶ He that trusts in his riches shall fall: but the righteous shall flourish as a branch.
29 ¶ He that troubles his own house shall inherit the wind: and the fool *shall be* servant to the wise of heart.
30 ¶ The fruit of the righteous *is* a tree of life; and he that wins souls *is* wise.
31 ¶ Behold, the righteous shall be recompensed in the earth: much more the wicked and the sinner.

Proverbs 12

12:1 ¶ Whoever loves instruction loves knowledge: but he that hates reproof *is* brutish.
2 ¶ A good *man* obtains favor of Yahweh: but a man of wicked devices will he condemn.
3 ¶ A man shall not be established by wickedness: but the root of the righteous shall not be moved.
4 ¶ A virtuous woman *is* a crown to her husband: but she that makes ashamed *is* as rottenness in his bones.
5 ¶ The thoughts of the righteous *are* right: *but* the counsels of the wicked *are* deceit.
6 ¶ The words of the wicked *are* to lie in wait for blood: but the mouth of the upright shall deliver them.
7 ¶ The wicked are overthrown, and *are* not: but the house of the righteous shall stand.
8 ¶ A man shall be commended according to his wisdom: but he that is of a perverse heart shall be despised.
9 ¶ *He that is* despised, and has a servant, *is* better than he that honors himself, and lacks bread.
10 ¶ A righteous *man* regards the life of his beast: but the tender mercies of the wicked *are* cruel.
11 ¶ He that tills his land shall be satisfied with bread: but he that follows vain *persons is* void of understanding.
12 ¶ The wicked desires the net of evil *men*: but the root of the righteous yields *fruit*.
13 ¶ The wicked is snared by the transgression of *his* lips: but the just shall come out of trouble.
14 ¶ A man shall be satisfied with good by the fruit of *his* mouth: and the recompense of a man's hands shall be rendered unto him.
15 ¶ The way of a fool *is* right in his own eyes: but he that hearkens unto counsel *is* wise.
16 ¶ A fool's wrath is presently known: but a prudent *man* covers shame.
17 ¶ *He that* speaks truth shows forth righteousness: but a false witness deceit.

18 ¶ There is that speaks like the piercings of a sword: but the tongue of the wise *is* health.
19 ¶ The lip of truth shall be established forever: but a lying tongue *is* but for a moment.
20 ¶ Deceit *is* in the heart of them that imagine evil: but to the counselors of peace *is* joy.
21 ¶ There shall no evil happen to the just: but the wicked shall be filled with mischief.
22 ¶ Lying lips *are* abomination to Yahweh: but they that deal truly *are* his delight.
23 ¶ A prudent man conceals knowledge: but the heart of fools proclaims foolishness.
24 ¶ The hand of the diligent shall bear rule: but the slothful shall be under tribute.
25 ¶ Heaviness in the heart of man makes it stoop: but a good word makes it glad.
26 ¶ The righteous *is* more excellent than his neighbor: but the way of the wicked seduces them.
27 ¶ The slothful *man* roasts not that which he took in hunting: but the substance of a diligent man *is* precious.
28 ¶ In the way of righteousness *is* life; and *in* the pathway *thereof there is* no death.

Proverbs 13

13:1 ¶ A wise son *hears* his father's instruction: but a scorner hears not rebuke.
2 ¶ A man shall eat good by the fruit of *his* mouth: but the soul of the transgressors *shall eat* violence.
3 ¶ He that keeps his mouth keeps his life: *but* he that opens wide his lips shall have destruction.
4 ¶ The soul of the sluggard desires, and *has* nothing: but the soul of the diligent shall be made fat.
5 ¶ A righteous *man* hates lying: but a wicked *man* is loathsome, and comes to shame.
6 ¶ Righteousness keeps *him that is* upright in the way: but wickedness overthrows the sinner.
7 ¶ There is that *which* makes himself rich, yet *has* nothing: *there* is that *which* makes himself poor, yet *has* great riches.
8 ¶ The ransom of a man's life *are* his riches: but the poor hears not rebuke.
9 ¶ The light of the righteous rejoices: but the lamp of the wicked shall be put out.
10 ¶ Only by pride comes contention: but with the well advised *is* wisdom.
11 ¶ Wealth *gotten* by vanity shall be diminished: but he that gathers by labor shall increase.
12 ¶ Hope deferred makes the heart sick: but *when* the desire comes, it is a tree of life.
13 ¶ Whoever despises the word shall be destroyed: but he that fears the commandment shall be rewarded.
14 ¶ The law of the wise *is* a fountain of life, to depart from the snares of death.
15 ¶ Good understanding gives favor: but the way of transgressors *is* hard.

16 ¶ Every prudent *man* deals with knowledge: but a fool lays open *his* folly.
17 ¶ A wicked messenger falls into mischief: but a faithful ambassador *is* health.
18 ¶ Poverty and shame *shall be to* him that refuses instruction: but he that regards reproof shall be honored.
19 ¶ The desire accomplished is sweet to the soul: but *it is* abomination to fools to depart from evil.
20 ¶ He that walks with wise *men* shall be wise: but a companion of fools shall be destroyed.
21 ¶ Evil pursues sinners: but to the righteous good shall be repaid
22 ¶ A good *man* leaves an inheritance to his children's children: and the wealth of the sinner *is* laid up for the just.
23 ¶ Much food *is in* the tillage of the poor: but there is *that which is* destroyed for want of judgment.
24 ¶ He that spares his rod hates his son: but he that loves him chastens him early.
25 ¶ The righteous eats to the satisfying of his soul: but the belly of the wicked shall want.

Proverbs 14

14:1 ¶ Every wise woman builds her house: but the foolish plucks it down with her hands.
2 ¶ He that walks in his uprightness fears Yahweh: but *he that is* perverse in his ways despises him.
3 ¶ In the mouth of the foolish *is* a rod of pride: but the lips of the wise shall preserve them.
4 ¶ Where no oxen *are*, the crib *is* clean: but much increase *is* by the strength of the ox.
5 ¶ A faithful witness will not lie: but a false witness will utter lies.
6 ¶ A scorner seeks wisdom, and *finds it* not: but knowledge *is* easy unto him that understands.
7 ¶ Go from the presence of a foolish man, when you perceive not *in him* the lips of knowledge.
8 ¶ The wisdom of the prudent *is* to understand his way: but the folly of fools *is* deceit.
9 ¶ Fools make a mock at sin: but among the righteous *there is* favor.
10 ¶ The heart knows his own bitterness; and a stranger does not mingle with his joy.
11 ¶ The house of the wicked shall be overthrown: but the tabernacle of the upright shall flourish.
12 ¶ There is a way which seems right to a man, but the end thereof *are* the ways of death.
13 ¶ Even in laughter the heart is sorrowful; and the end of that gladness *is* heaviness.
14 ¶ The backslider in heart shall be filled with his own ways: and a good man *shall be satisfied* from himself.
15 ¶ The simple believes every word: but the prudent *man* looks well to his going.
16 ¶ A wise *man* fears, and departs from evil: but the fool rages, and is confident.
17 ¶ *He that is* soon angry deals foolishly: and a man of wicked devices is hated.

Proverbs 14

18 ¶ The simple inherit folly: but the prudent are crowned with knowledge.

19 ¶ The evil bow before the good; and the wicked at the gates of the righteous.

20 ¶ The poor is hated even of his own neighbor: but the rich *has* many friends.

21 ¶ He that despises his neighbor sins: but he that has mercy on the poor, happy *is* he.

22 ¶ Do they not err that devise evil? but mercy and truth *shall be* to them that devise good.

23 ¶ In all labor there is profit: but the talk of the lips *tends* only to poverty.

24 ¶ The crown of the wise *is* their riches: *but* the foolishness of fools *is* folly.

25 ¶ A true witness delivers souls: but a deceitful *witness* speaks lies.

26 ¶ In the fear of Yahweh *is* strong confidence: and his children shall have a place of refuge.

27 The fear of Yahweh *is* a fountain of life, to depart from the snares of death.

28 ¶ In the multitude of people *is* the king's honor: but in the want of people *is* the destruction of the prince.

29 ¶ *He that is* slow to wrath *is* of great understanding: but *he that is* hasty of spirit exalts folly.

30 ¶ A sound heart *is* the life of the flesh: but envy the rottenness of the bones.

31 ¶ He that oppresses the poor reproaches his Maker: but he that honors him has mercy on the poor.

32 ¶ The wicked is driven away in his wickedness: but the righteous has hope in his death.

33 ¶ Wisdom rests in the heart of him that has understanding: but *that which is* in the midst of fools is made known.

34 ¶ Righteousness exalts a nation: but sin *is* a reproach to any people.

35 ¶ The king's favor *is* toward a wise servant: but his wrath is *against* him that causes shame.

Proverbs 15

15:1 ¶ A soft answer turns away wrath: but grievous words stir up anger.

2 ¶ The tongue of the wise uses knowledge well: but the mouth of fools pours out foolishness.

3 ¶ The eyes of Yahweh *are* in every place, beholding the evil and the good.

4 ¶ A wholesome tongue *is* a tree of life: but perverseness therein *is* a breach in the spirit.

5 ¶ A fool despises his father's instruction: but he that regards reproof is prudent.

6 ¶ In the house of the righteous *is* much treasure: but in the revenues of the wicked is trouble.

7 ¶ The lips of the wise disperse knowledge: but the heart of the foolish *does* not so.

8 ¶ The sacrifice of the wicked *is* an abomination to Yahweh: but the prayer of the upright *is* his delight.

9 ¶ The way of the wicked *is* an abomination unto Yahweh: but he loves him that follows after righteousness.

10 ¶ Correction *is* grievous to him that forsakes the way: *and* he that hates reproof shall die.

11 ¶ Hell and destruction *are* before Yahweh: how much more then the hearts of the children of men?

12 ¶ A scorner loves not one that reproves him: neither will he go to the wise.

13 ¶ A merry heart makes a cheerful countenance: but by sorrow of the heart the spirit is broken.

14 ¶ The heart of him that has understanding seeks knowledge: but the mouth of fools feeds on foolishness.

15 ¶ All the days of the afflicted *are* evil: but he that is of a merry heart *has* a continual feast.

16 ¶ Better *is* little with the fear of Yahweh than great treasure and trouble therewith.

17 Better *is* a dinner of herbs where love is, than a stalled ox and hatred therewith.

18 ¶ A wrathful man stirs up strife: but *he that is* slow to anger appeases strife.

19 ¶ The way of the slothful *man is* as a hedge of thorns: but the way of the righteous *is* made plain.

20 ¶ A wise son makes a glad father: but a foolish man despises his mother.

21 ¶ Folly *is* joy to *him that is* destitute of wisdom: but a man of understanding walks uprightly.

22 ¶ Without counsel purposes are disappointed: but in the multitude of counselors they are established.

23 ¶ A man has joy by the answer of his mouth: and a word *spoken* in due season, how good *is it*!

24 ¶ The way of life *is* above to the wise, that he may depart from hell beneath.

25 ¶ Yahweh will destroy the house of the proud: but he will establish the border of the widow.

26 ¶ The thoughts of the wicked *are* an abomination to Yahweh: but *the words* of the pure *are* pleasant words.

27 ¶ He that is greedy for gain troubles his own house; but he that hates gifts shall live.

28 ¶ The heart of the righteous studies to answer: but the mouth of the wicked pours out evil things.

29 ¶ Yahweh *is* far from the wicked: but he hears the prayer of the righteous.

30 ¶ The light of the eyes rejoices the heart: *and* a good report makes the bones fat.

31 ¶ The ear that hears the reproof of life dwells among the wise.

32 ¶ He that refuses instruction despises his own soul: but he that hears reproof gets understanding.

33 ¶ The fear of Yahweh *is* the instruction of wisdom; and before honor *is* humility.

Proverbs 16

16:1 ¶ The preparations of the heart in man, and the answer of the tongue, *is* from Yahweh.

2 ¶ All the ways of a man *are* clean in his own eyes; but Yahweh weighs the spirits.

3 ¶ Commit your works unto Yahweh, and your thoughts shall be established.

4 ¶ Yahweh has made all *things* for himself: yes, even the wicked for the day of evil.

5 ¶ Every one *that is* proud in heart *is* an abomination to Yahweh: *though* hand *joins* in hand, he shall not be unpunished.
6 ¶ By mercy and truth iniquity is purged: and by the fear of Yahweh *men* depart from evil.
7 ¶ When a man's ways please Yahweh, he makes even his enemies to be at peace with him.
8 ¶ Better *is* a little with righteousness than great revenues without right.
9 ¶ A man's heart devises his way: but Yahweh directs his steps.
10 ¶ A divine sentence *is* in the lips of the king: his mouth transgresses not in judgment.
11 ¶ A just weight and balance *are* Yahweh's: all the weights of the bag *are* his work.
12 ¶ *It is* an abomination to kings to commit wickedness: for the throne is established by righteousness.
13 ¶ Righteous lips *are* the delight of kings; and they love him that speaks right.
14 ¶ The wrath of a king *is as* messengers of death: but a wise man will pacify it.
15 In the light of the king's countenance *is* life; and his favor *is* as a cloud of the latter rain.
16 ¶ How much better *is it* to get wisdom than gold! and to get understanding rather to be chosen than silver!
17 ¶ The highway of the upright *is* to depart from evil: he that keeps his way preserves his soul.
18 ¶ Pride *goes* before destruction, and a haughty spirit before a fall.
19 ¶ Better *it is to be* of a humble spirit with the lowly, than to divide the spoil with the proud.
20 ¶ He that handles a matter wisely shall find good: and whoever trusts in Yahweh, happy *is* he.
21 ¶ The wise in heart shall be called prudent: and the sweetness of the lips increases learning.
22 ¶ Understanding *is* a wellspring of life unto him that has it: but the instruction of fools *is* folly.
23 ¶ The heart of the wise teaches his mouth, and adds learning to his lips.
24 ¶ Pleasant words *are as* a honeycomb, sweet to the soul, and health to the bones.
25 ¶ There is a way that seems right unto a man, but the end thereof *are* the ways of death.
26 ¶ He that labors labors for himself; for his mouth craves it of him.
27 ¶ An ungodly man digs up evil: and in his lips *there is* as a burning fire.
28 A froward man sows strife: and a whisperer separates chief friends.
29 ¶ A violent man entices his neighbor, and leads him into the way *that is* not good.
30 He shuts his eyes to devise froward things: moving his lips he brings evil to pass.
31 ¶ The gray head *is* a crown of glory, *if* it is found in the way of righteousness.
32 ¶ *He that is* slow to anger *is* better than the mighty; and he that rules his spirit than he that takes a city.
33 ¶ The lot is cast into the lap; but the whole disposing thereof *is* of Yahweh.

Proverbs 17

17:1 ¶ Better *is* a dry morsel, and quietness therewith, than a house full of sacrifices *with* strife.
2 ¶ A wise servant shall have rule over a son that causes shame, and shall have part of the inheritance among the brothers.
3 ¶ The fining pot *is* for silver, and the furnace for gold: but Yahweh tries the hearts.
4 ¶ A wicked doer gives heed to false lips; *and* a liar gives ear to a naughty tongue.
5 ¶ Whoever mocks the poor reproaches his Maker: *and* he that is glad at calamities shall not be unpunished.
6 ¶ Children's children *are* the crown of old men; and the glory of children *are* their fathers.
7 ¶ Excellent speech becomes not a fool: much less do lying lips a prince.
8 ¶ A gift *is as* a precious stone in the eyes of him that has it: wherever it turns, it prospers.
9 ¶ He that covers a transgression seeks love; but he that repeats a matter separates *close* friends.
10 ¶ A reproof enters more into a wise man than a hundred stripes into a fool.
11 ¶ An evil *man* seeks only rebellion: therefore a cruel messenger shall be sent against him.
12 ¶ Let a bear robbed of her cubs meet a man, rather than a fool in his folly.
13 ¶ Whoever rewards evil for good, evil shall not depart from his house.
14 ¶ The beginning of strife *is as* when one lets out water: therefore leave off contention, before it is meddled with.
15 ¶ He that justifies the wicked, and he that condemns the just, even they both *are* abomination to Yahweh.
16 ¶ Why *is there* a price in the hand of a fool to get wisdom, seeing *he has* no heart *to it*?
17 ¶ A friend loves at all times, and a brother is born for adversity.
18 ¶ A man void of understanding strikes hands, *and* becomes surety in the presence of his friend.
19 ¶ He loves transgression that loves strife: *and* he that exalts his gate seeks destruction.
20 ¶ He that has a froward heart finds no good: and he that has a perverse tongue falls into mischief.
21 ¶ He that begets a fool *does it* to his sorrow: and the father of a fool has no joy.
22 ¶ A merry heart does good *like* a medicine: but a broken spirit dries the bones.
23 ¶ A wicked *man* takes a gift out of the bosom to pervert the ways of judgment.
24 ¶ Wisdom *is* before him that has understanding; but the eyes of a fool *are* in the ends of the earth.
25 ¶ A foolish son *is* a grief to his father, and bitterness to her that bore him.
26 ¶ Also to punish the just *is* not good, *nor* to strike princes for equity.

27 ¶ He that has knowledge spares his words: *and* a man of understanding is of an excellent spirit.
28 Even a fool, when he holds his peace, is counted wise: *and* he that shuts his lips *is esteemed* a man of understanding.

Proverbs 18

18:1 ¶ Through desire a man, having separated himself, seeks *and* intermeddles with all wisdom.
2 ¶ A fool has no delight in understanding, but that his heart may uncover itself.
3 ¶ When the wicked comes, *then* comes also contempt, and with shame reproach.
4 ¶ The words of a man's mouth *are as* deep waters, *and* the wellspring of wisdom *as* a flowing brook.
5 ¶ *It is* not good to accept the person of the wicked, to overthrow the righteous in judgment.
6 ¶ A fool's lips enter into contention, and his mouth calls for blows.
7 A fool's mouth *is* his destruction, and his lips *are* the snare of his soul.
8 ¶ The words of a talebearer *are* as wounds, and they go down into the innermost parts of the belly.
9 ¶ He also that is slothful in his work is brother to him that is a great waster.
10 ¶ The name of Yahweh *is* a strong tower: the righteous runs into it, and is safe.
11 ¶ The rich man's wealth *is* his strong city, and as a high wall in his own conceit.
12 ¶ Before destruction the heart of man is haughty, and before honor *is* humility.
13 ¶ He that answers a matter before he hears *it*, it *is* folly and shame unto him.
14 ¶ The spirit of a man will sustain his infirmity; but a wounded spirit who can bear?
15 ¶ The heart of the prudent gets knowledge; and the ear of the wise seeks knowledge.
16 ¶ A man's gift makes room for him, and brings him before great men.
17 ¶ *He that is* first in his own cause *seems* just; but his neighbor comes and searches him.
18 ¶ The lot causes contentions to cease, and parts between the mighty.
19 ¶ A brother offended *is harder to be won* than a strong city: and *their* contentions *are* like the bars of a castle.
20 ¶ A man's belly shall be satisfied with the fruit of his mouth; *and* with the increase of his lips shall he be filled.
21 ¶ Death and life *are* in the power of the tongue: and they that love it shall eat the fruit thereof.
22 ¶ *Whoever* finds a wife finds a good *thing*, and obtains favor of Yahweh.
23 ¶ The poor uses entreaties; but the rich answers roughly.
24 ¶ A man *that has* friends must show himself friendly: and there is a friend *that* sticks closer than a brother.

Proverbs 19

19:1 ¶ Better *is* the poor that walks in his integrity, than *he that is* perverse in his lips, and is a fool.
2 ¶ Also, *that* the soul *be* without knowledge, *it is* not good; and he that hastens with *his* feet sins.
3 ¶ The foolishness of man perverts his way: and his heart frets against Yahweh.
4 ¶ Wealth makes many friends; but the poor is separated from his neighbor.
5 ¶ A false witness shall not be unpunished, and *he that* speaks lies shall not escape.
6 ¶ Many will entreat the favor of the prince: and every man *is* a friend to him that gives gifts.
7 All the brethren of the poor do hate him: how much more do his friends go far from him? he pursues *them with* words, *yet* they *are* wanting *to him*.
8 ¶ He that gets wisdom loves his own soul: he that keeps understanding shall find good.
9 ¶ A false witness shall not be unpunished, and *he that* speaks lies shall perish.
10 ¶ Delight is not seemly for a fool; much less for a servant to have rule over princes.
11 ¶ The discretion of a man defers his anger; and *it is* his glory to pass over a transgression.
12 ¶ The king's wrath *is* as the roaring of a lion; but his favor *is* as dew upon the grass.
13 ¶ A foolish son *is* the calamity of his father: and the contentions of a wife *are* a continual dripping.
14 ¶ House and riches *are* the inheritance of fathers: and a prudent wife *is* from Yahweh.
15 ¶ Slothfulness casts into a deep sleep; and an idle soul shall suffer hunger.
16 ¶ He that keeps the commandment keeps his own soul; *but* he that despises his ways shall die.
17 ¶ He that has pity upon the poor lends unto Yahweh; and that which he has given will he pay him again.
18 ¶ Chasten your son while there is hope, and let not your soul spare for his crying.
19 ¶ A man of great wrath shall suffer punishment: for if you deliver *him*, yet you must do it again.
20 ¶ Hear counsel, and receive instruction, that you may be wise in your latter end.
21 ¶ *There are* many devices in a man's heart; nevertheless the counsel of Yahweh, that shall stand.
22 ¶ The desire of a man *is* his kindness: and a poor man *is* better than a liar.
23 ¶ The fear of Yahweh *tends* to life: and *he that has it* shall dwell satisfied; he shall not be visited with evil.
24 ¶ A slothful *man* hides his hand in *his* bosom, and will not so much as bring it to his mouth again.
25 ¶ Smite a scorner, and the simple will beware: and reprove one that has understanding, *and* he will understand knowledge.
26 ¶ He that wastes *his* father, *and* chases away *his* mother, *is* a son that causes shame, and brings reproach.
27 ¶ Cease, my son, to hear the instruction *and be caused* to err from the words of knowledge.

28 ¶ An ungodly witness scorns judgment: and the mouth of the wicked devours iniquity.
29 ¶ Judgments are prepared for scorners, and stripes for the back of fools.

Proverbs 20

20:1 ¶ Wine *is* a mocker, strong drink *is* raging: and whoever is deceived thereby is not wise.
2 ¶ The fear of a king *is* as the roaring of a lion: *whoever* provokes him to anger sins *against* his own soul.
3 ¶ *It is* an honor for a man to cease from strife: but every fool will be meddling.
4 ¶ The sluggard will not plow by reason of the cold; *therefore* shall he beg in harvest, and *have* nothing.
5 ¶ Counsel in the heart of man *is like* deep water; but a man of understanding will draw it out.
6 ¶ Most men will proclaim every one his own goodness: but a faithful man who can find?
7 ¶ The just *man* walks in his integrity: his children *are* blessed after him.
8 ¶ A king that sits in the throne of judgment scatters away all evil with his eyes.
9 ¶ Who can say, I have made my heart clean, I am pure from my sin?
10 ¶ Diverse weights, *and* diverse measures, both of them *are* alike abomination to Yahweh.
11 ¶ Even a child is known by his doings, whether his work *is* pure, and whether *it is* right.
12 ¶ The hearing ear, and the seeing eye, Yahweh has made even both of them.
13 ¶ Love not sleep, lest you come to poverty; open your eyes, *and* you shall be satisfied with bread.
14 ¶ *It is* bad, *it is* bad, says the buyer: but when he has gone his way, then he boasts.
15 ¶ There is gold, and a multitude of rubies: but the lips of knowledge *are* a precious jewel.
16 ¶ Take his garment that is surety *for* a stranger: and take a pledge of him for a strange woman.
17 ¶ Bread of deceit *is* sweet to a man; but afterward his mouth shall be filled with gravel.
18 ¶ *Every* purpose is established by counsel: and with good advice make war.
19 ¶ He that goes about *as* a talebearer reveals secrets: therefore meddle not with him that flatters with his lips.
20 ¶ Whoever curses his father or his mother, his lamp shall be put out in obscure darkness.
21 ¶ An inheritance *may be* gotten hastily at the beginning; but the end thereof shall not be blessed.
22 ¶ Say not you, I will recompense evil; *but* wait on Yahweh, and he shall save you.
23 ¶ Diverse weights *are* an abomination unto Yahweh; and a false balance *is* not good.
24 ¶ Man's goings *are* of Yahweh; how can a man then understand his own way?
25 ¶ *It is* a snare to the man *who* devours *that which is* holy, and after vows to make inquiry.
26 ¶ A wise king scatters the wicked, and brings the wheel over them.
27 ¶ The spirit of man *is* the candle of Yahweh, searching all the inward parts of the belly.
28 ¶ Mercy and truth preserve the king: and his throne is upheld by mercy.
29 ¶ The glory of young men *is* their strength: and the beauty of old men *is* the gray head.
30 ¶ The blueness of a wound cleans away evil: so *do* stripes the inward parts of the belly.

Proverbs 21

21:1 ¶ The king's heart *is* in the hand of Yahweh, *as* the rivers of water: he turns it wherever he will.
2 ¶ Every way of a man *is* right in his own eyes: but Yahweh ponders the hearts.
3 ¶ To do justice and judgment *is* more acceptable to Yahweh than sacrifice.
4 ¶ A high look, and a proud heart, *and* the plowing of the wicked, *is* sin.
5 ¶ The thoughts of the diligent *tend* only to plenty; but of every one *that is* hasty only to want.
6 ¶ The getting of treasures by a lying tongue *is* a vanity tossed to and fro of them that seek death.
7 ¶ The robbery of the wicked shall destroy them; because they refuse to do judgment.
8 ¶ The way of man *is* froward and strange: but *as for* the pure, his work *is* right.
9 ¶ *It is* better to dwell in a corner of the housetop, than with a brawling woman in a wide house.
10 ¶ The soul of the wicked desires evil: his neighbor finds no favor in his eyes.
11 ¶ When the scorner is punished, the simple is made wise: and when the wise is instructed, he receives knowledge.
12 ¶ The righteous *man* wisely considers the house of the wicked: *but God* overthrows the wicked for *their* wickedness.
13 ¶ Whoever stops his ears at the cry of the poor, he also shall cry himself, but shall not be heard.
14 ¶ A gift in secret pacifies anger: and a reward in the bosom strong wrath.
15 ¶ *It is* joy to the just to do judgment: but destruction *shall be* to the workers of iniquity.
16 ¶ The man that wanders out of the way of understanding shall remain in the congregation of the dead.
17 ¶ He that loves pleasure *shall be* a poor man: he that loves wine and oil shall not be rich.
18 ¶ The wicked *shall be* a ransom for the righteous, and the transgressor for the upright.
19 ¶ *It is* better to dwell in the wilderness, than with a contentious and an angry woman.
20 ¶ *There is* treasure to be desired and oil in the dwelling of the wise; but a foolish man spends it up.
21 ¶ He that follows after righteousness and mercy finds life, righteousness, and honor.

Proverbs 21

22 ¶ A wise *man* scales the city of the mighty, and casts down the strength of the confidence thereof.
23 ¶ Whoever keeps his mouth and his tongue keeps his soul from troubles.
24 ¶ Proud *and* haughty scorner *is* his name, who deals in proud wrath.
25 ¶ The desire of the slothful kills him; for his hands refuse to labor.
26 He covets greedily all the day long: but the righteous gives and spares not.
27 ¶ The sacrifice of the wicked *is* abomination: how much more, *when* he brings it with a wicked mind?
28 ¶ A false witness shall perish: but the man that hears speaks constantly.
29 ¶ A wicked man hardens his face: but *as for* the upright, he directs his way.
30 ¶ *There is* no wisdom nor understanding nor counsel against Yahweh.
31 The horse *is* prepared against the day of battle: but safety *is* of Yahweh.

Proverbs 22

22:1 ¶ A *good* name *is* rather to be chosen than great riches, *and* loving favor rather than silver and gold.
2 ¶ The rich and poor meet together: Yahweh *is* the maker of them all.
3 ¶ A prudent *man* foresees the evil, and hides himself: but the simple pass on, and are punished.
4 ¶ By humility *and* the fear of Yahweh *are* riches, and honor, and life.
5 ¶ Thorns *and* snares *are* in the way of the froward: he that does keep his soul shall be far from them.
6 ¶ Train up a child in the way he should go: and when he is old, he will not depart from it.
7 ¶ The rich rules over the poor, and the borrower *is* servant to the lender.
8 ¶ He that sows iniquity shall reap vanity: and the rod of his anger shall fail.
9 ¶ He that has a bountiful eye shall be blessed; for he gives of his bread to the poor.
10 ¶ Cast out the scorner, and contention shall go out; yes, strife and reproach shall cease.
11 ¶ He that loves pureness of heart, *for* the grace of his lips the king *shall be* his friend.
12 ¶ The eyes of Yahweh preserve knowledge, and he overthrows the words of the transgressor.
13 ¶ The slothful *man* says, *There is* a lion outside, I shall be slain in the streets.
14 ¶ The mouth of strange women *is* a deep pit: he that is abhorred of Yahweh shall fall therein.
15 ¶ Foolishness *is* bound in the heart of a child; *but* the rod of correction shall drive it far from him.
16 ¶ He that oppresses the poor to increase his *riches, and* he that gives to the rich, *shall* surely *come* to want.
17 ¶ Bow down your ear, and hear the words of the wise, and apply your heart unto my knowledge.
18 For *it is* a pleasant thing if you keep them within you; they shall therewith be fitted in your lips.
19 That your trust may be in Yahweh, I have made known to you this day, even to you.
20 Have not I written to you excellent things in counsels and knowledge,
21 That I might make you know the certainty of the words of truth; that you might answer the words of truth to them that send unto you?
22 ¶ Rob not the poor, because he *is* poor: neither oppress the afflicted in the gate:
23 For Yahweh will plead their cause, and spoil the soul of those that spoiled them.
24 ¶ Make no friendship with an angry man; and with a furious man you shall not go:
25 Lest you learn his ways, and get a snare to your soul.
26 ¶ Be not you *one* of them that strikes hands, *or* of them that are sureties for debts.
27 If you have nothing to pay, why should he take away your bed from under you?
28 ¶ Remove not the ancient landmark, which your fathers have set.
29 ¶ See you a man diligent in his business? he shall stand before kings; he shall not stand before mean *men*.

Proverbs 23

23:1 ¶ When you sit to eat with a ruler, consider diligently what *is* before you:
2 And put a knife to your throat, if you *are* a man given to appetite.
3 Be not desirous of his dainties: for they *are* deceitful bread.
4 ¶ Labor not to be rich: cease from your own wisdom.
5 Will you set your eyes upon that which is not? for *riches* certainly make themselves wings; they fly away as an eagle toward heaven.
6 ¶ Eat you not the bread of *him that has* an evil eye, neither desire you his delectable food:
7 For as he thinks in his heart, so *is* he: Eat and drink, said he to you; but his heart *is* not with you.
8 The morsel *which* you have eaten shall you vomit up, and lose your sweet words.
9 ¶ Speak not in the ears of a fool: for he will despise the wisdom of your words.
10 ¶ Remove not the old landmark; and enter not into the fields of the fatherless:
11 For their redeemer *is* mighty; he shall plead their cause with you.
12 ¶ Apply your heart unto instruction, and your ears to the words of knowledge.
13 Withhold not correction from the child: for *if* you beat him with the rod, he shall not die.
14 You shall beat him with the rod, and shall deliver his soul from hell.
15 My son, if your heart is wise, my heart shall rejoice, even mine.

16 Yes, my reins shall rejoice, when your lips speak right things.
17 ¶ Let not your heart envy sinners: but *be you* in the fear of Yahweh all the day long.
18 For surely there is an end; and your expectation shall not be cut off.
19 ¶ Hear you, my son, and be wise, and guide your heart in the way.
20 Be not among winebibbers; among riotous eaters of flesh:
21 For the drunkard and the glutton shall come to poverty: and drowsiness shall clothe *a man* with rags.
22 Listen unto your father that begot you, and despise not your mother when she is old.
23 Buy the truth, and sell *it* not; *also* wisdom, and instruction, and understanding.
24 The father of the righteous shall greatly rejoice: and he that begets a wise *child* shall have joy of him.
25 Your father and your mother shall be glad, and she that bore you shall rejoice.
26 My son, give me your heart, and let your eyes observe my ways.
27 For a whore *is* a deep ditch; and a strange woman *is* a narrow pit.
28 She also lies in wait as *for* a prey, and increases the transgressors among men.
29 ¶ Who has woe? who has sorrow? who has contentions? who has babbling? who has wounds without cause? who has redness of eyes?
30 They that tarry long at the wine; they that go to seek mixed wine.
31 Look not you upon the wine when it is red, when it gives his color in the cup, *when* it moves itself sweetly.
32 At the last it bites like a serpent, and stings like an adder.
33 Your eyes shall behold strange women, and your heart shall utter perverse things.
34 Yes, you shall be as he that lies down in the midst of the sea, or as he that lies upon the top of a mast.
35 They have stricken me, *shall you say, and* I was not sick; they have beaten me, *and* I felt *it* not: when shall I awake? I will seek it yet again.

Proverbs 24

24:1 ¶ Be not you envious against evil men, neither desire to be with them.
2 For their heart studies destruction, and their lips talk of mischief.
3 ¶ Through wisdom is a house built; and by understanding it is established:
4 And by knowledge shall the chambers be filled with all precious and pleasant riches.
5 A wise man *is* strong; yes, a man of knowledge increases strength.
6 For by wise counsel you shall make your war: and in multitude of counselors *there is* safety.
7 ¶ Wisdom *is* too high for a fool: he opens not his mouth in the gate.
8 He that devises to do evil shall be called a mischievous person.
9 The thought of foolishness *is* sin: and the scorner *is* an abomination to men.
10 ¶ *If* you faint in the day of adversity, your strength *is* small.
11 ¶ If you forbear to deliver *them that are* drawn unto death, and *those that are* ready to be slain;
12 If you say, Behold, we knew it not; does not he that ponders the heart consider *it*? and he that keeps your soul, does *not* he know *it*? and shall *not* he render to *every* man according to his works?
13 ¶ My son, eat you honey, because *it is* good; and the honeycomb, *which is* sweet to your taste:
14 So *shall* the knowledge of wisdom *be* to your soul: when you have found *it*, then there shall be a reward, and your expectation shall not be cut off.
15 ¶ Lay not wait, O wicked *man*, against the dwelling of the righteous; spoil not his resting place:
16 For a just *man* falls seven times, and rises up again: but the wicked shall fall into mischief.
17 ¶ Rejoice not when your enemy falls, and let not your heart be glad when he stumbles:
18 Lest Yahweh sees *it*, and it displeases him, and he turns away his wrath from him.
19 ¶ Fret not yourself because of evil *men*, neither be you envious at the wicked;
20 For there shall be no reward to the evil *man*; the candle of the wicked shall be put out.
21 ¶ My son, fear you Yahweh and the king: *and* meddle not with them that are given to change:
22 For their calamity shall rise suddenly; and who knows the ruin of them both?
23 ¶ These *things* also *belong* to the wise. *It is* not good to have respect of persons in judgment.
24 He that says to the wicked, You *are* righteous; him shall the people curse, nations shall abhor him:
25 But to them that rebuke *him* shall be delight, and a good blessing shall come upon them.
26 *Every man* shall kiss *his* lips that gives a right answer.
27 ¶ Prepare your work outside, and make it fit for yourself in the field; and afterward build your house.
28 ¶ Be not a witness against your neighbor without cause; and deceive *not* with your lips.
29 Say not, I will do so to him as he has done to me: I will render to the man according to his work.
30 ¶ I went by the field of the slothful, and by the vineyard of the man void of understanding;
31 And, lo, it was all grown over with thorns, *and* nettles had covered the face thereof, and the stone wall thereof was broken down.
32 Then I saw, *and* considered *it* well: I looked upon *it, and* received instruction.
33 *Yet* a little sleep, a little slumber, a little folding of the hands to sleep:
34 So shall your poverty come *as* one that travels; and your want as an armed man.

Proverbs 25

25:1 ¶ These *are* also proverbs of Solomon, which the men of Hezekiah king of Judah copied out.

2 ¶ *It is* the glory of God to conceal a thing: but the honor of kings *is* to search out a matter.

3 The heaven for height, and the earth for depth, and the heart of kings *is* unsearchable.

4 ¶ Take away the dross from the silver, and there shall come forth a vessel for the refiner.

5 Take away the wicked *from* before the king, and his throne shall be established in righteousness.

6 ¶ Put not forth yourself in the presence of the king, and stand not in the place of great *men*:

7 For better *it is* that it be said to you, Come up here; than that you should be put lower in the presence of the prince whom your eyes have seen.

8 ¶ Go not forth hastily to strive, lest *you know not* what to do in the end thereof, when your neighbor has put you to shame.

9 Debate your cause with your neighbor *himself*; and discover not a secret to another:

10 Lest he that hears *it* puts you to shame, and your infamy turns not away.

11 ¶ A word fitly spoken *is like* apples of gold in pictures of silver.

12 *As* an earring of gold, and an ornament of fine gold, *so is* a wise reprover upon an obedient ear.

13 ¶ As the cold of snow in the time of harvest, *so is* a faithful messenger to them that send him: for he refreshes the soul of his masters.

14 ¶ Whoever boasts himself of a false gift *is like* clouds and wind without rain.

15 ¶ By long forbearing is a prince persuaded, and a soft tongue breaks the bone.

16 ¶ Have you found honey? eat as much as is sufficient for you, lest you be filled therewith, and vomit it.

17 ¶ Withdraw your foot from your neighbor's house; lest he becomes weary of you, and *so* hates you.

18 ¶ A man that bears false witness against his neighbor *is* a maul, and a sword, and a sharp arrow.

19 ¶ Confidence in an unfaithful man in time of trouble *is like* a broken tooth, and a foot out of joint.

20 ¶ *As* he that takes away a garment in cold weather, *and as* vinegar upon soda, so *is* he that sings songs to a heavy heart.

21 ¶ If your enemy is hungry, give him bread to eat; and if he is thirsty, give him water to drink:

22 For you shall heap coals of fire upon his head, and Yahweh shall reward you.

23 ¶ The north wind drives away rain: so *does* an angry countenance a backbiting tongue.

24 ¶ *It is* better to dwell in the corner of the housetop, than with a brawling woman and in a wide house.

25 ¶ *As* cold waters to a thirsty soul, so *is* good news from a far country.

26 ¶ A righteous man falling down before the wicked *is as* a troubled fountain, and a corrupt spring.

27 ¶ *It is* not good to eat much honey: so *for men* to search their own glory *is not* glory.

28 ¶ He that *has* no rule over his own spirit *is like* a city *that is* broken down, *and* without walls.

Proverbs 26

26:1 ¶ As snow in summer, and as rain in harvest, so honor is not seemly for a fool.

2 ¶ As the bird by wandering, as the swallow by flying, so the curse without cause shall not come.

3 ¶ A whip for the horse, a bridle for the donkey, and a rod for the fool's back.

4 ¶ Answer not a fool according to his folly, lest you also be like unto him.

5 Answer a fool according to his folly, lest he be wise in his own conceit.

6 ¶ He that sends a message by the hand of a fool cuts off the feet, *and* drinks damage.

7 The legs of the lame are not equal: so *is* a parable in the mouth of fools.

8 As he that binds a stone in a sling, so *is* he that gives honor to a fool.

9 *As* a thorn goes up into the hand of a drunkard, so *is* a parable in the mouth of fools.

10 ¶ The great *God* that formed all *things* both rewards the fool, and rewards transgressors.

11 ¶ As a dog returns to his vomit, *so* a fool returns to his folly.

12 ¶ See you a man wise in his own conceit? *there is* more hope of a fool than of him.

13 ¶ The slothful *man* said, There is a lion in the way; a lion *is* in the streets.

14 ¶ *As* the door turns upon his hinges, so *does* the slothful upon his bed.

15 ¶ The slothful hides his hand in *his* bosom; it grieves him to bring it again to his mouth.

16 ¶ The sluggard *is* wiser in his own conceit than seven men that can render a reason.

17 ¶ He that passes by, *and* meddles with strife *belonging* not to him, *is like* one that takes a dog by the ears.

18 ¶ As a mad *man* who casts firebrands, arrows, and death,

19 So *is* the man *that* deceives his neighbor, and said, Am not I in sport?

20 ¶ Where no wood is, *there* the fire goes out: so where *there is* no talebearer, the strife ceases.

21 *As* coals *are* to burning coals, and wood to fire; so *is* a contentious man to kindle strife.

22 The words of a talebearer *are* as wounds, and they go down into the innermost parts of the belly.

23 ¶ Burning lips and a wicked heart *are like* pottery covered with silver dross.

24 ¶ He that hates disguises with his lips, and lays up deceit within him;

25 When he speaks graciously, believe him not: for *there are* seven abominations in his heart.
26 *Whose* hatred is covered by deceit, his wickedness shall be shown before the *whole* congregation.
27 ¶ Whoever digs a pit shall fall therein: and he that rolls a stone, it will return upon him.
28 ¶ A lying tongue hates *those that are* afflicted by it; and a flattering mouth works ruin.

Proverbs 27

27:1 ¶ Boast not yourself of tomorrow; for you know not what a day may bring forth.
2 ¶ Let another man praise you, and not your own mouth; a stranger, and not your own lips.
3 ¶ A stone *is* heavy, and the sand weighty; but a fool's wrath *is* heavier than them both.
4 Wrath *is* cruel, and anger *is* outrageous; but who *is* able to stand before envy?
5 ¶ Open rebuke *is* better than secret love.
6 Faithful *are* the wounds of a friend; but the kisses of an enemy *are* deceitful.
7 ¶ The full soul loathes a honeycomb; but to the hungry soul every bitter thing is sweet.
8 ¶ As a bird that wanders from her nest, so *is* a man that wanders from his place.
9 ¶ Ointment and perfume rejoice the heart: so *does* the sweetness of a man's friend by hearty counsel.
10 Your own friend, and your father's friend, forsake not; neither go into your brother's house in the day of your calamity: *for* better *is* a neighbor *that is* near than a brother far off.
11 ¶ My son, be wise, and make my heart glad, that I may answer him that reproaches me.
12 ¶ A prudent *man* foresees the evil, *and* hides himself; *but* the simple pass on, *and* are punished.
13 ¶ Take his garment that is surety for a stranger, and take a pledge of him for a strange woman.
14 ¶ He that blesses his friend with a loud voice, rising early in the morning, it shall be counted a curse to him.
15 ¶ A continual dripping in a very rainy day and a contentious woman are alike.
16 Whoever hides her hides the wind, and the ointment of his right hand, *which* proclaims *itself.*
17 ¶ Iron sharpens iron; so a man sharpens the countenance of his friend.
18 ¶ Whoever keeps the fig tree shall eat the fruit thereof: so he that waits on his master shall be honored.
19 ¶ As in water face *answers* to face, so the heart of man to man.
20 ¶ Hell and destruction are never full; so the eyes of man are never satisfied.
21 ¶ *As* the refining pot for silver, and the furnace for gold; so *is* a man to his praise.
22 ¶ Though you should pound a fool in a mortar among wheat with a pestle, *yet* will not his foolishness depart from him.

23 ¶ Be you diligent to know the state of your flocks, *and* look well to your herds.
24 For riches *are* not forever: and does the crown *endure* to every generation?
25 The hay appears, and the tender grass shows itself, and herbs of the mountains are gathered.
26 The lambs *are* for your clothing, and the goats *are* the price of the field.
27 And *you shall have* goats' milk enough for your food, for the food of your household, and *for* the maintenance for your maidens.

Proverbs 28

28:1 ¶ The wicked flee when no man pursues: but the righteous are bold as a lion.
2 ¶ For the transgression of a land many *are* the princes thereof: but by a man of understanding *and* knowledge the state *thereof* shall be prolonged.
3 ¶ A poor man that oppresses the poor *is like* a sweeping rain which leaves no food.
4 ¶ They that forsake the law praise the wicked: but such as keep the law contend with them.
5 ¶ Evil men understand not judgment: but they that seek Yahweh understand all *things.*
6 ¶ Better *is* the poor that walks in his uprightness, than *he that is* perverse *in* his ways, though he *is* rich.
7 ¶ Whoever keeps the law *is* a wise son: but he that is a companion of riotous *men* shames his father.
8 ¶ He that by usury and unjust gain increases his substance, he shall gather it for him that will pity the poor.
9 ¶ He that turns away his ear from hearing the law, even his prayer *shall be* abomination.
10 ¶ Whoever causes the righteous to go astray in an evil way, he shall fall himself into his own pit: but the upright shall have good *things* in possession.
11 ¶ The rich man *is* wise in his own conceit; but the poor that has understanding searches him out.
12 ¶ When righteous *men* do rejoice, *there is* great glory: but when the wicked rise, a man is hidden.
13 ¶ He that covers his sins shall not prosper: but whoever confesses and forsakes *them* shall have mercy.
14 ¶ Happy *is* the man that fears always: but he that hardens his heart shall fall into mischief.
15 ¶ *As* a roaring lion, and a ranging bear; *so is* a wicked ruler over the poor people.
16 ¶ The prince that wants understanding *is* also a great oppressor: *but* he that hates covetousness shall prolong *his* days.
17 ¶ A man that does violence to the blood of *any* person shall flee to the pit; let no man uphold him.
18 ¶ Whoever walks uprightly shall be saved: but *he that is* perverse *in* his ways shall fall at once.
19 ¶ He that tills his land shall have plenty of bread: but he that follows after vain *persons* shall have poverty enough.

Proverbs 28

20 ¶ A faithful man shall abound with blessings: but he that makes haste to be rich shall not be innocent.
21 ¶ To have respect of persons *is* not good: for for a piece of bread *that* man will transgress.
22 ¶ He that hastens to be rich *has* an evil eye, and considers not that poverty shall come upon him.
23 ¶ He that rebukes a man afterward shall find more favor than he that flatters with the tongue.
24 ¶ Whoever robs his father or his mother, and said, *It is* no transgression; the same *is* the companion of a destroyer.
25 ¶ He that is of a proud heart stirs up strife: but he that puts his trust in Yahweh shall be made fat.
26 ¶ He that trusts in his own heart is a fool: but whoever walks wisely, he shall be delivered.
27 ¶ He that gives to the poor shall not lack: but he that hides his eyes shall have many a curse.
28 ¶ When the wicked rise, men hide themselves: but when they perish, the righteous increase.

Proverbs 29

29:1 ¶ He, that being often reproved hardens *his* neck, shall suddenly be destroyed, and that without remedy.
2 ¶ When the righteous are in authority, the people rejoice: but when the wicked bear rule, the people mourn.
3 ¶ Whoever loves wisdom rejoices his father: but he that keeps company with harlots spends *his* substance.
4 ¶ The king by judgment establishes the land: but he that receives gifts overthrows it.
5 ¶ A man that flatters his neighbor spreads a net for his feet.
6 ¶ In the transgression of an evil man *there is* a snare: but the righteous does sing and rejoice.
7 ¶ The righteous considers the cause of the poor: *but* the wicked regards not to know *it*.
8 ¶ Scornful men bring a city into a snare: but wise *men* turn away wrath.
9 ¶ *If* a wise man contends with a foolish man, whether he rages or laughs, *there is* no rest.
10 ¶ The bloodthirsty hates the upright: but the just seek his soul.
11 ¶ A fool utters all his mind: but a wise *man* keeps it in till afterward.
12 ¶ If a ruler listens to lies, all his servants *are* wicked.
13 ¶ The poor and the deceitful man meet together: Yahweh lightens both their eyes.
14 ¶ The king that faithfully judges the poor, his throne shall be established forever.
15 ¶ The rod and reproof give wisdom: but a child left *to himself* brings his mother to shame.
16 ¶ When the wicked are multiplied, transgression increases: but the righteous shall see their fall.
17 ¶ Correct your son, and he shall give you rest; yes, he shall give delight to your soul.
18 ¶ Where *there is* no vision, the people perish: but he that keeps the law, happy *is* he.
19 ¶ A servant will not be corrected by words: for though he understands he will not answer.
20 ¶ See you a man *that is* hasty in his words? *there is* more hope of a fool than of him.
21 ¶ He that delicately brings up his servant from a child shall have him become *his* son in the end.
22 ¶ An angry man stirs up strife, and a furious man abounds in transgression.
23 ¶ A man's pride shall bring him low: but honor shall uphold the humble in spirit.
24 ¶ Whoever is partner with a thief hates his own soul: he hears cursing, and reports *it* not.
25 ¶ The fear of man brings a snare: but whoever puts his trust in Yahweh shall be safe.
26 ¶ Many seek the ruler's favor; but *every* man's judgment *comes* from Yahweh.
27 ¶ An unjust man *is* an abomination to the just: and *he that is* upright in the way *is* abomination to the wicked.

Proverbs 30

30:1 ¶ The words of Agur the son of Jakeh, *even* the prophecy: the man spoke to Ithiel, even to Ithiel and Ucal,
2 Surely I *am* more brutish than *any* man, and have not the understanding of a man.
3 I neither learned wisdom, nor have the knowledge of the holy.
4 Who has ascended up into heaven, or descended? who has gathered the wind in his fists? who has bound the waters in a garment? who has established all the ends of the earth? what *is* his name, and what *is* his son's name, if you can tell?
5 Every word of God *is* pure: he *is* a shield to them that put their trust in him.
6 Add you not to his words, lest he reprove you, and you be found a liar.
7 ¶ Two *things* have I required of you; deny me *them* not before I die:
8 Remove far from me vanity and lies: give me neither poverty nor riches; feed me with food convenient for me:
9 Lest I be full, and deny *you*, and say, Who *is* Yahweh? or lest I be poor, and steal, and take the name of my God *in vain*.
10 ¶ Accuse not a servant unto his master, lest he curses you, and you are found guilty.
11 *There is* a generation *that* curses their father, and does not bless their mother.
12 *There is* a generation *that are* pure in their own eyes, and *yet* is not washed from their filthiness.
13 *There is* a generation, O how lofty are their eyes! and their eyelids are lifted up.
14 *There is* a generation, whose teeth *are as* swords, and their jaw teeth *as* knives, to devour the poor from off the earth, and the needy from *among* men.
15 ¶ The leech has two daughters, *crying*, Give, give. There are three *things that* are never satisfied, *yes*, four *things* say not, *It is* enough:

16 The grave; and the barren womb; the earth *that* is not filled with water; and the fire *that* says not, *It is* enough.
17 The eye *that* mocks at *his* father, and despises to obey *his* mother, the ravens of the valley shall pick it out, and the young eagles shall eat it.
18 ¶ There are three *things which* are too wonderful for me, yes, four which I know not:
19 The way of an eagle in the air; the way of a serpent upon a rock; the way of a ship in the midst of the sea; and the way of a man with a maid.
20 Such *is* the way of an adulterous woman; she eats, and wipes her mouth, and says, I have done no wickedness.
21 For three *things* the earth is disquieted, and for four *which* it cannot bear:
22 For a servant when he reigns; and a fool when he is filled with meat;
23 For a hateful *woman* when she is married; and a handmaid that is heir to her mistress.
24 ¶ There are four *things which are* little upon the earth, but they *are* exceedingly wise:
25 The ants *are* a people not strong, yet they prepare their meat in the summer;
26 The conies *are but* a feeble folk, yet make they their houses in the rocks;
27 The locusts have no king, yet go they forth all of them by bands;
28 The spider takes hold with her hands, and is in kings' palaces.
29 ¶ There are three *things* which go well, yes, four are comely in going:
30 A lion *which is* strongest among beasts, and turns not away for any;
31 A greyhound; a he goat also; and a king, against whom *there is* no rising up.
32 If you have done foolishly in lifting up yourself, or if you have thought evil, *lay* your hand upon your mouth.
33 Surely the churning of milk brings forth butter, and the wringing of the nose brings forth blood: so the forcing of wrath brings forth strife.

Proverbs 31

31:1 ¶ The words of king Lemuel, the prophecy that his mother taught him.
2 What, my son? and what, the son of my womb? and what, the son of my vows?
3 Give not your strength unto women, nor your ways to that which destroys kings.
4 *It is* not for kings, O Lemuel, *it is* not for kings to drink wine; nor for princes strong drink:
5 Lest they drink, and forget the law, and pervert the judgment of any of the afflicted.
6 Give strong drink unto him that is ready to perish, and wine to those that are of heavy hearts.
7 Let him drink, and forget his poverty, and remember his misery no more.
8 Open your mouth for the dumb in the cause of all such as are appointed to destruction.

9 Open your mouth, judge righteously, and plead the cause of the poor and needy.
10 ¶ Who can find a virtuous woman? for her price *is* far above rubies.
11 The heart of her husband does safely trust in her, so that he shall have no need of spoil.
12 She will do him good and not evil all the days of her life.
13 She seeks wool, and flax, and works willingly with her hands.
14 She is like the merchants' ships; she brings her food from afar.
15 She rises also while it is yet night, and gives food to her household, and a portion to her maidens.
16 She considers a field, and buys it: with the fruit of her hands she plants a vineyard.
17 She girds her loins with strength, and strengthens her arms.
18 She perceives that her merchandise *is* good: her candle goes not out by night.
19 She lays her hands to the spindle, and her hands hold the fiber stick.
20 She stretches out her hand to the poor; yes, she reaches forth her hands to the needy.
21 She is not afraid of the snow for her household: for all her household *are* clothed with scarlet.
22 She makes herself coverings of tapestry; her clothing *is* silk and purple.
23 Her husband is known in the gates, when he sits among the elders of the land.
24 She makes fine linen, and sells *it*; and delivers girdles unto the merchant.
25 Strength and honor *are* her clothing; and she shall rejoice in time to come.
26 She opens her mouth with wisdom; and in her tongue *is* the law of kindness.
27 She looks well to the ways of her household, and eats not the bread of idleness.
28 Her children arise up, and call her blessed; her husband *also*, and he praises her.
29 Many daughters have done virtuously, but you excel them all.
30 Favor *is* deceitful, and beauty *is* vain: *but* a woman *that* fears Yahweh, she shall be praised.
31 Give her of the fruit of her hands; and let her own works praise her in the gates.

Ecclesiastes

Ecclesiastes 1

1:1 ¶ The words of the Preacher, the son of David, king in Jerusalem.
2 Vanity of vanities, says the Preacher, vanity of vanities; all *is* vanity.

Ecclesiastes 1

3 What profit has a man of all his labor which he takes under the sun?

4 ¶ *One* generation passes away, and *another* generation comes: but the earth remains forever.

5 The sun also rises, and the sun goes down, and hastens to his place where he arose.

6 The wind goes toward the south, and turns about to the north; it whirls about continually, and the wind returns again according to his circuits.

7 All the rivers run into the sea; yet the sea *is* not full; unto the place from where the rivers come, there they return again.

8 All things *are* full of labor; man cannot utter *it*: the eye is not satisfied with seeing, nor the ear filled with hearing.

9 ¶ The thing that has been, it *is that* which shall be; and that which is done *is* that which shall be done: and *there is* no new *thing* under the sun.

10 Is there *any* thing whereof it may be said, See, this *is* new? it has been already of old time, which was before us.

11 *There is* no remembrance of former *things*; neither shall there be *any* remembrance of *things* that are to come with *those* that shall come after.

12 ¶ I the Preacher was king over Israel in Jerusalem.

13 And I gave my heart to seek and search out by wisdom concerning all *things* that are done under heaven: this grievous job has God given to the sons of man to be exercised therewith.

14 I have seen all the works that are done under the sun; and, behold, all *is* vanity and longing of spirit.

15 *That which is* crooked cannot be made straight: and that which is wanting cannot be numbered.

16 I communed with my own heart, saying, Lo, I have come to great estate, and have gotten more wisdom than all *they* that have been before me in Jerusalem: yes, my heart had great experience of wisdom and knowledge.

17 And I gave my heart to know wisdom, and to know madness and folly: I perceived that this also is longing of spirit.

18 For in much wisdom *is* much grief: and he that increases knowledge increases sorrow.

Ecclesiastes 2

2:1 ¶ I said in my heart, Go to now, I will prove you with gladness, therefore enjoy pleasure: and, behold, this also *is* vanity.

2 I said of laughter, *It is* mad: and of gladness, What does it?

3 I sought in my heart to give myself unto wine, yet acquainting my heart with wisdom; and to lay hold on folly, till I might see what *was* that good for the sons of men, which they should do under the heaven all the days of their lives.

4 I made me great works; I built me houses; I planted me vineyards:

5 I made me gardens and orchards, and I planted trees in them of all *kind of* fruits:

6 I made me pools of water, to water therewith the woods that brings forth trees:

7 I got *me* servants and maidens, and had servants born in my house; also I had great possessions of great and small cattle above all that were in Jerusalem before me:

8 I gathered me also silver and gold, and the peculiar treasures of kings and of the provinces: I got me men singers and women singers, and the delights of the sons of men, *as* musical instruments, and that of all sorts.

9 So I was great, and increased more than all that were before me in Jerusalem: also my wisdom remained with me.

10 And whatever my eyes desired I kept not from them, I withheld not my heart from any joy; for my heart rejoiced in all my labor: and this was my portion of all my labor.

11 Then I looked on all the works that my hands had worked, and on the labor that I had labored to do: and, behold, all *was* vanity and longing of spirit, and *there was* no profit under the sun.

12 ¶ And I turned myself to behold wisdom, and madness, and folly: for what *can* the man *do* that comes after the king? *even* that which has been already done.

13 Then I saw that wisdom excels folly, as far as light excels darkness.

14 The wise man's eyes *are* in his head; but the fool walks in darkness: and I myself perceived also that one event happens to them all.

15 Then said I in my heart, As it happens to the fool, so it happens even to me; and why was I then more wise? Then I said in my heart, that this also *is* vanity.

16 For *there is* no remembrance of the wise more than of the fool forever; seeing that which now *is* in the days to come shall all be forgotten. And how dies the wise *man*? as the fool.

17 ¶ Therefore I hated life; because the work that is worked under the sun *is* grievous to me: for all *is* vanity and longing of spirit.

18 Yes, I hated all my labor which I had taken under the sun: because I should leave it to the man that shall be after me.

19 And who knows whether he shall be a wise *man* or a fool? yet shall he have rule over all my labor wherein I have labored, and wherein I have shown myself wise under the sun. This *is* also vanity.

20 Therefore I went about to cause my heart to despair of all the labor which I took under the sun.

21 For there is a man whose labor *is* in wisdom, and in knowledge, and in equity; yet to a man that has not labored therein shall he leave it *for* his portion. This also *is* vanity and a great evil.

22 For what has man of all his labor, and of the longing of his heart, wherein he has labored under the sun?

23 For all his days *are* sorrows, and his travail grief; yes, his heart takes not rest in the night. This is also vanity.

24 *There is* nothing better for a man, *than* that he should eat and drink, and *that* he should make his soul enjoy

good in his labor. This also I saw, that it *was* from the hand of God.

25 For who can eat, or who else can hurry *hereunto*, more than I?

26 For *God* gives to a man that *is* good in his sight wisdom, and knowledge, and joy: but to the sinner he gives work, to gather and to heap up, that he may give to *him that is* good before God. This also *is* vanity and longing of spirit.

Ecclesiastes 3

3:1 ¶ To every *thing there is* a season, and a time to every purpose under the heaven:

2 A time to be born, and a time to die; a time to plant, and a time to pluck up *that which is* planted;

3 A time to kill, and a time to heal; a time to break down, and a time to build up;

4 A time to weep, and a time to laugh; a time to mourn, and a time to dance;

5 A time to cast away stones, and a time to gather stones together; a time to embrace, and a time to refrain from embracing;

6 A time to get, and a time to lose; a time to keep, and a time to cast away;

7 A time to tear, and a time to sew; a time to keep silence, and a time to speak;

8 A time to love, and a time to hate; a time of war, and a time of peace.

9 What profit has he that works in that wherein he labors?

10 I have seen the job, which God has given to the sons of men to be exercised in it.

11 ¶ He has made every *thing* beautiful in his time: also he has set the world in their heart, so that no man can find out the work that God makes from the beginning to the end.

12 I know that *there is* no good in them, but for *a man* to rejoice, and to do good in his life.

13 And also that every man should eat and drink, and enjoy the good of all his labor, it *is* the gift of God.

14 I know that, whatever God does, it shall be forever: nothing can be put to it, nor anything taken from it: and God does *it*, that *men* should fear before him.

15 That which has been is now; and that which is to be has already been; and God requires that which is past.

16 ¶ And moreover I saw under the sun the place of judgment, *that* wickedness *was* there; and the place of righteousness, *that* iniquity *was* there.

17 I said in my heart, God shall judge the righteous and the wicked: for *there is* a time there for every purpose and for every work.

18 I said in my heart concerning the estate of the sons of men, that God might manifest them, and that they might see that they themselves are beasts.

19 For that which befalls the sons of men befalls beasts; even one thing befalls them: as the one dies, so dies the other; yes, they have all one breath; so that a man has no preeminence above a beast: for all *is* vanity.

20 All go to one place; all are of the dust, and all turn to dust again.

21 Who knows the spirit of man that goes upward, and the spirit of the beast that goes downward to the earth?

22 Therefore I perceive that *there is* nothing better, than that a man should rejoice in his own works; for that *is* his portion: for who shall bring him to see what shall be after him?

Ecclesiastes 4

4:1 ¶ So I returned, and considered all the oppressions that are done under the sun: and behold the tears of *such as were* oppressed, and they had no comforter; and on the side of their oppressors *there was* power; but they had no comforter.

2 Therefore I praised the dead which are already dead more than the living which are yet alive.

3 Yes, better *is he* than both they, which has not yet been, who has not seen the evil work that is done under the sun.

4 ¶ Again, I considered all labor, and every right work, that for this a man is envied by his neighbor. This *is* also vanity and longing of spirit.

5 The fool folds his hands together, and eats his own flesh.

6 Better *is* a handful *with* quietness, than both the hands full *with* labor and longing of spirit.

7 ¶ Then I returned, and I saw vanity under the sun.

8 There is one *alone*, and *there is* not a second; yes, he has neither child nor brother: yet *is there* no end of all his labor; neither is his eye satisfied with riches; neither *says he*, For whom do I labor, and bereave my soul of good? This *is* also vanity, yes, it *is* a grievous job.

9 Two *are* better than one; because they have a good reward for their labor.

10 For if they fall, the one will lift up his fellow: but woe to him *that is* alone when he falls; for *he has* not another to help him up.

11 Again, if two lie together, then they have heat: but how can one be warm *alone*?

12 And if one prevails against him, two shall withstand him; and a threefold cord is not quickly broken.

13 ¶ Better *is* a poor and a wise child than an old and foolish king, who will no more be admonished.

14 For out of prison he comes to reign; whereas also *he that is* born in his kingdom becomes poor.

15 I considered all the living which walk under the sun, with the second child that shall stand up in his stead.

16 *There is* no end of all the people, *even* of all that have been before them: they also that come after shall not rejoice in him. Surely this also *is* vanity and longing of spirit.

Ecclesiastes 5

5:1 ¶ Keep your foot when you go to the house of God, and be more ready to hear, than to give the sacrifice of fools: for they consider not that they do evil.
2 Be not rash with your mouth, and let not your heart be hasty to utter *any* thing before God: for God *is* in heaven, and you upon earth: therefore let your words be few.
3 For a dream comes through the multitude of business; and a fool's voice *is known* by *his* multitude of words.
4 ¶ When you vow a vow unto God, defer not to pay it; for *he has* no pleasure in fools: pay that which you have vowed.
5 Better *is it* that you should not vow, than that you should vow and not pay.
6 Allow not your mouth to cause your flesh to sin; neither say you before the angel, that it *was* an error: why should God be angry at your voice, and destroy the work of your hands?
7 For in the multitude of dreams and many words *there are* also *diverse* vanities: but fear you God.
8 If you see the oppression of the poor, and *the* violent perverting of judgment and justice in a province, marvel not at the matter: for *he that is* higher than the highest regards; and *there are* higher than they.
9 ¶ Moreover the profit of the earth is for all: the king *himself* is served by the field.
10 He that loves silver shall not be satisfied with silver; nor he that loves abundance with increase: this *is* also vanity.
11 When goods increase, they are increased that eat them: and what good *is there* to the owners thereof, saving the beholding *of them* with their eyes?
12 The sleep of a laboring man *is* sweet, whether he eats little or much: but the abundance of the rich will not permit him to sleep.
13 There is a grievous evil *which* I have seen under the sun, *namely*, riches kept for the owners thereof to their hurt.
14 But those riches perish by evil work: and he begets a son, and *there is* nothing in his hand.
15 As he came forth from his mother's womb, naked shall he return to go as he came, and shall take nothing of his labor, which he may carry away in his hand.
16 And this also *is* a grievous evil, *that* in all points as he came, so shall he go: and what profit has he that has labored for the wind?
17 All his days also he eats in darkness, and *he has* much sorrow and wrath with his sickness.
18 ¶ Behold *that* which I have seen: *it is* good and comely *for one* to eat and to drink, and to enjoy the good of all his labor that he takes under the sun all the days of his life, which God gives him: for it *is* his portion.
19 Every man also to whom God has given riches and wealth, and has given him power to eat thereof, and to take his portion, and to rejoice in his labor; this *is* the gift of God.
20 For he shall not much remember the days of his life; because God answers *him* in the joy of his heart.

Ecclesiastes 6

6:1 ¶ There is an evil which I have seen under the sun, and it *is* common among men:
2 A man to whom God has given riches, wealth, and honor, so that he wants nothing for his soul of all that he desires, yet God gives him not power to eat thereof, but a stranger eats it: this *is* vanity, and it *is* an evil disease.
3 If a man begets a hundred *children*, and lives many years, so that the days of his years are many, and his soul is not filled with good, and also *that* he has no burial; I say, *that* an untimely birth *is* better than he.
4 For he comes in with vanity, and departs in darkness, and his name shall be covered with darkness.
5 Moreover he has not seen the sun, nor known *any thing*: this has more rest than the other.
6 Yes, though he lives a thousand years twice *told*, yet has he seen no good: do not all go to one place?
7 ¶ All the labor of man *is* for his mouth, and yet the appetite is not filled.
8 For what has the wise more than the fool? what has the poor, that knows to walk before the living?
9 Better *is* the sight of the eyes than the wandering of the desire: this *is* also vanity and longing of spirit.
10 That which has been is named already, and it is known that it *is* man: neither may he contend with him that is mightier than he.
11 ¶ Seeing there are many things that increase vanity, what *is* man the better?
12 For who knows what *is* good for man in *this* life, all the days of his vain life which he spends as a shadow? for who can tell a man what shall be after him under the sun?

Ecclesiastes 7

7:1 ¶ A good name *is* better than precious ointment; and the day of death than the day of one's birth.
2 *It is* better to go to the house of mourning, than to go to the house of feasting: for that *is* the end of all men; and the living will lay *it* to his heart.
3 Sorrow *is* better than laughter: for by the sadness of the countenance the heart is made better.
4 The heart of the wise *is* in the house of mourning; but the heart of fools *is* in the house of gladness.
5 *It is* better to hear the rebuke of the wise, than for a man to hear the song of fools.
6 For as the crackling of thorns under a pot, so *is* the laughter of the fool: this also *is* vanity.
7 ¶ Surely oppression makes a wise man mad; and a gift destroys the heart.
8 Better *is* the end of a thing than the beginning thereof: *and* the patient in spirit *is* better than the proud in spirit.
9 Be not hasty in your spirit to be angry: for anger rests in the bosom of fools.
10 Say not you, What is *the cause* that the former days were better than these? for you do not inquire wisely concerning this.

11 ¶ Wisdom *is* good with an inheritance: and *by it there is* profit to them that see the sun.

12 For wisdom *is* a defense, *and* money *is* a defense: but the excellency of knowledge *is, that* wisdom gives life to them that have it.

13 Consider the work of God: for who can make *that* straight, which he has made crooked?

14 In the day of prosperity be joyful, but in the day of adversity consider: God also has set the one over against the other, to the end that man should find nothing after him.

15 All *things* have I seen in the days of my vanity: there is a just *man* that perishes in his righteousness, and there is a wicked *man* that prolongs *his life* in his wickedness.

16 Be not righteous exceedingly; neither make yourself overly wise: why should you destroy yourself?

17 Be not over much wicked, neither be you foolish: why should you die before your time?

18 *It is* good that you should take hold of this; yes, also from this withdraw not your hand: for he that fears God shall come forth of them all.

19 Wisdom strengthens the wise more than ten mighty *men* which are in the city.

20 For *there is* not a just man upon earth, that does good, and sins not.

21 Also take no heed to all words that are spoken; lest you hear your servant curse you:

22 For oftentimes also your own heart knows that you yourself likewise have cursed others.

23 ¶ All this have I proved by wisdom: I said, I will be wise; but it *was* far from me.

24 That which is far off, and exceedingly deep, who can find it out?

25 I applied my heart to know, and to search, and to seek out wisdom, and the reason *of things*, and to know the wickedness of folly, even of foolishness *and* madness:

26 And I find more bitter than death the woman, whose heart *is* snares and nets, *and* her hands *as* bands: whoever pleases God shall escape from her; but the sinner shall be taken by her.

27 Behold, this have I found, said the preacher, *counting* one by one, to find out the account:

28 Which yet my soul seeks, but I find not: one man among a thousand have I found; but a woman among all those have I not found.

29 Look, this only have I found, that God has made man upright; but they have sought out many inventions.

Ecclesiastes 8

8:1 ¶ Who *is* as the wise *man*? and who knows the interpretation of a thing? a man's wisdom makes his face to shine, and the boldness of his face shall be changed.

2 I *counsel you* to keep the king's commandment, and *that* in regard of the oath of God.

3 Be not hasty to go out of his sight: stand not in an evil thing; for he does whatever pleases him.

4 Where the word of a king *is, there is* power: and who may say unto him, What do you?

5 Whoever keeps the commandment shall feel no evil thing: and a wise man's heart discerns both time and judgment.

6 ¶ Because to every purpose there is time and judgment, therefore the misery of man *is* great upon him.

7 For he knows not that which shall be: for who can tell him when it shall be?

8 *There is* no man that has power over the spirit to retain the spirit; neither *has he* power in the day of death: and *there is* no discharge *in that* war; neither shall wickedness deliver those that are given to it.

9 ¶ All this have I seen, and applied my heart to every work that is done under the sun: *there is* a time wherein one man rules over another to his own hurt.

10 And so I saw the wicked buried, who had come and gone from the place of the holy, and they were forgotten in the city where they had so done: this *is* also vanity.

11 Because *the* sentence against an evil work is not executed speedily, therefore the heart of the sons of men is fully set in them to do evil.

12 Though a sinner does evil a hundred times, and his *days* are prolonged, yet surely I know that it shall be well with them that fear God, which fear before him:

13 But it shall not be well with the wicked, neither shall he prolong *his* days, *which are* as a shadow; because he fears not before God.

14 ¶ There is a vanity which is done upon the earth; that there are just *men*, to whom it happens according to the work of the wicked; again, there are wicked *men*, to whom it happens according to the work of the righteous: I said that this also *is* vanity.

15 Then I commended gladness, because a man has no better thing under the sun, than to eat, and to drink, and to be merry: for that shall join with him in his labor the days of his life, which God gives him under the sun.

16 When I applied my heart to know wisdom, and to see the business that is done upon the earth: (for also *there is that* neither day nor night sees sleep with his eyes:)

17 Then I saw all the work of God, that a man cannot find out the work that is done under the sun: because though a man labors to seek *it* out, yet he shall not find *it*; yes further; though a wise *man* thinks to know *it*, yet shall he not be able to find *it*.

Ecclesiastes 9

9:1 ¶ For all this I considered in my heart even to declare all this, that the righteous, and the wise, and their works, *are* in the hand of God: no man knows either love or hatred *by* all *that is* before them.

2 All *things come* alike to all: *there is* one event to the righteous, and to the wicked; to the good and to the clean, and to the unclean; to him that sacrifices, and to him that sacrifices not: as *is* the good, so *is* the sinner; *and* he that swears, as *he* that fears an oath.

Ecclesiastes 9

3 This *is* an evil among all *things* that are done under the sun, that *there is* one event unto all: yes, also the heart of the sons of men is full of evil, and madness *is* in their heart while they live, and after that *they go* to the dead.

4 ¶ For to him that is joined to all the living there is hope: for a living dog is better than a dead lion.

5 For the living know that they shall die: but the dead know not anything, neither have they any more a reward; for the memory of them is forgotten.

6 Also their love, and their hatred, and their envy, have now perished; neither have they any more a portion forever in any *thing* that is done under the sun.

7 Go your way, eat your bread with joy, and drink your wine with a merry heart; for God now accepts your works.

8 Let your garments be always white; and let your head lack no ointment.

9 Live joyfully with the wife whom you love all the days of the life of your vanity, which he has given you under the sun, all the days of your vanity: for that *is* your portion in *this* life, and in your labor which you take under the sun.

10 Whatever your hand finds to do, do *it* with your might; for *there is* no work, nor device, nor knowledge, nor wisdom, in the grave, where you go.

11 ¶ I returned, and saw under the sun, that the race *is* not to the swift, nor the battle to the strong, neither yet bread to the wise, nor yet riches to men of understanding, nor yet favor to men of skill; but time and chance happens to them all.

12 For man also knows not his time: as the fishes that are taken in an evil net, and as the birds that are caught in the snare; so *are* the sons of men snared in an evil time, when it falls suddenly upon them.

13 ¶ This wisdom have I seen also under the sun, and it *seemed* great to me:

14 *There was* a little city, and few men within it; and there came a great king against it, and besieged it, and built great bulwarks against it:

15 Now there was found in it a poor wise man, and he by his wisdom delivered the city; yet no man remembered that same poor man.

16 Then said I, Wisdom *is* better than strength: nevertheless the poor man's wisdom *is* despised, and his words are not heard.

17 The words of wise *men are* heard in quiet more than the cry of him that rules among fools.

18 Wisdom *is* better than weapons of war: but one sinner destroys much good.

Ecclesiastes 10

10:1 ¶ Dead flies cause the ointment of the apothecary to send forth a stinking savor: *so does* a little folly him that is in reputation for wisdom *and* honor.

2 A wise man's heart *is* at his right hand; but a fool's heart at his left.

3 Yes also, when he that is a fool walks by the way, his wisdom fails *him*, and he says to every one *that* he *is* a fool.

4 ¶ If the spirit of the ruler rises up against you, leave not your place; for yielding pacifies great offenses.

5 There is an evil *which* I have seen under the sun, as an error *which* proceeds from the ruler:

6 Folly is set in great dignity, and the rich sit in low places.

7 I have seen servants upon horses, and princes walking as servants upon the earth.

8 He that digs a pit shall fall into it; and whoever breaks a hedge, a serpent shall bite him.

9 Whoever removes stones shall be hurt therewith; *and* he that splits wood shall be endangered thereby.

10 If the iron is blunt, and he does not sharpen the edge, then must he put to more strength: but wisdom *is* profitable to direct.

11 Surely the serpent will bite without enchantment; and a babbler is no better.

12 ¶ The words of a wise man's mouth *are* gracious; but the lips of a fool will swallow up himself.

13 The beginning of the words of his mouth *is* foolishness: and the end of his talk *is* mischievous madness.

14 A fool also is full of words: a man cannot tell what shall be; and what shall be after him, who can tell him?

15 The labor of the foolish wearies every one of them, because he knows not how to go to the city.

16 ¶ Woe to you, O land, when your king *is* a child, and your princes eat in the morning!

17 Blessed *are* you, O land, when your king *is* the son of nobles, and your princes eat in due season, for strength, and not for drunkenness!

18 By much slothfulness the building decays; and through idleness of the hands the house drops through.

19 A feast is made for laughter, and wine makes merry: but money answers all *things*.

20 Curse not the king, no not in your thought; and curse not the rich in your bedchamber: for a bird of the air shall carry the voice, and that which has wings shall tell the matter.

Ecclesiastes 11

11:1 ¶ Cast your bread upon the waters: for you shall find it after many days.

2 Give a portion to seven, and also to eight; for you know not what evil shall be upon the earth.

3 If the clouds are full of rain, they empty *themselves* upon the earth: and if the tree falls toward the south, or toward the north, in the place where the tree falls, there it shall be.

4 He that observes the wind shall not sow; and he that regards the clouds shall not reap.

5 As you know not what *is* the way of the spirit, *nor* how the bones *do grow* in the womb of her that is with child: even so you know not the works of God who makes all.

6 In the morning sow your seed, and in the evening withhold not your hand: for you know not which shall prosper, either this or that, or whether they both *shall be* alike good.

7 ¶ Truly the light *is* sweet, and a pleasant *thing it is* for the eyes to behold the sun:

8 But if a man lives many years, *and* rejoices in them all; yet let him remember the days of darkness; for they shall be many. All that comes *is* vanity.

9 Rejoice, O young man, in your youth; and let your heart cheer you in the days of your youth, and walk in the ways of your heart, and in the sight of your eyes: but know you, that for all these *things* God will bring you into judgment.

10 Therefore remove sorrow from your heart, and put away evil from your flesh: for childhood and youth *are* vanity.

Ecclesiastes 12

12:1 ¶ Remember now your Creator in the days of your youth, while the evil days come not, nor the years draw nigh, when you shall say, I have no pleasure in them;

2 While the sun, or the light, or the moon, or the stars, are not darkened, nor the clouds return after the rain:

3 In the day when the keepers of the house shall tremble, and the strong men shall bow themselves, and the grinders cease because they are few, and those that look out of the windows are darkened,

4 And the doors shall be shut in the streets, when the sound of the grinding is low, and he shall rise up at the voice of the bird, and all the daughters of music shall be brought low;

5 Also *when* they shall be afraid of *that which is* high, and fears *shall be* in the way, and the almond tree shall flourish, and the grasshopper shall be a burden, and desire shall fail: because man goes to his long home, and the mourners go about the streets:

6 Before the silver cord is loosed, or the golden bowl is broken, or the pitcher is broken at the fountain, or the wheel broken at the cistern.

7 Then shall the dust return to the earth as it was: and the spirit shall return unto God who gave it.

8 ¶ Vanity of vanities, says the preacher; all *is* vanity.

9 And moreover, because the preacher was wise, he still taught the people knowledge; yes, he gave good heed, and sought out, *and* set in order many proverbs.

10 The preacher sought to find out acceptable words: and *that which was* written *was* upright, *even* words of truth.

11 The words of the wise *are* as goads, and as nails fastened *by* the masters of assemblies, *which* are given from one shepherd.

12 And further, by these, my son, be admonished: of making many books *there is* no end; and much study *is* a weariness of the flesh.

13 ¶ Let us hear the conclusion of the whole matter: Fear God, and keep his commandments: for this *is* the whole *duty* of man.

14 For God shall bring every work into judgment, with every secret thing, whether *it is* good, or whether *it is* evil.

Song of Solomon

Song of Solomon 1

1:1 ¶ The song of songs, which *is* Solomon's.

2 ¶ Let him kiss me with the kisses of his mouth: for your love *is* better than wine.

3 Because of the savor of your good ointments your name *is as* ointment poured forth, therefore do the virgins love you.

4 Draw me, we will run after you: the king has brought me into his chambers: we will be glad and rejoice in you, we will remember your love more than wine: the upright love you.

5 I *am* black, but comely, O you daughters of Jerusalem, as the tents of Kedar, as the curtains of Solomon.

6 Look not upon me, because I *am* black, because the sun has looked upon me: my mother's children were angry with me; they made me the keeper of the vineyards; *but* my own vineyard have I not kept.

7 ¶ Tell me, O you whom my soul loves, where you feed, where you make *your flock* to rest at noon: for why should I be as one that turns aside by the flocks of your companions?

8 If you know not, O you fairest among women, go your way forth by the footsteps of the flock, and feed your kids beside the shepherds' tents.

9 I have compared you, O my love, to a company of horses in Pharaoh's chariots.

10 Your cheeks are comely with rows *of jewels*, your neck with chains *of gold*.

11 We will make you borders of gold with studs of silver.

12 ¶ While the king *sits* at his table, my spikenard sends forth the smell thereof.

13 A bundle of myrrh *is* my wellbeloved unto me; he shall lie all night between my breasts.

14 My beloved *is* to me *as* a cluster of henna in the vineyards of Engedi.

15 Behold, you *are* fair, my love; behold, you *are* fair; you *have* doves' eyes.

16 Behold, you *are* fair, my beloved, yes, pleasant: also our bed *is* green.

17 The beams of our house *are* cedar, *and* our rafters of fir.

Song of Solomon 2

2:1 ¶ I *am* the rose of Sharon, *and* the lily of the valleys.

2 As the lily among thorns, so *is* my love among the daughters.

3 ¶ As the apple tree among the trees of the woods, so *is* my beloved among the sons. I sat down under his shadow with great delight, and his fruit *was* sweet to my taste.

4 He brought me to the banqueting house, and his banner over me *was* love.

Song of Solomon 2

5 Stay me with raisin cakes, comfort me with apples: for I *am* sick with love.
6 His left hand *is* under my head, and his right hand does embrace me.
7 I charge you, O you daughters of Jerusalem, by the roes, and by the does of the field, that you stir not up, nor awake *my* love, till he pleases.
8 ¶ The voice of my beloved! behold, he comes leaping upon the mountains, skipping upon the hills.
9 My beloved is like a roe or a young hart: behold, he stands behind our wall, he looks forth at the windows, showing himself through the lattice.
10 My beloved spoke, and said unto me, Rise up, my love, my fair one, and come away.
11 For, lo, the winter is past, the rain is over *and* gone;
12 The flowers appear on the earth; the time of the singing *of birds* has come, and the voice of the turtledove is heard in our land;
13 The fig tree puts forth her green figs, and the vines *with* the tender grapes give a *good* smell. Arise, my love, my fair one, and come away.
14 ¶ O my dove, *that is* in the clefts of the rock, in the secret *places* of the stairs, let me see your countenance, let me hear your voice; for sweet *is* your voice, and your countenance *is* comely.
15 Take us the foxes, the little foxes, that spoil the vines: for our vines *have* tender grapes.
16 My beloved *is* mine, and I *am* his: he feeds among the lilies.
17 Until the day breaks, and the shadows flee away, turn, my beloved, and be you like a roe or a young hart upon the mountains of Bether.

Song of Solomon 3

3:1 ¶ By night on my bed I sought him whom my soul loves: I sought him, but I found him not.
2 I will rise now, and go about the city in the streets, and in the broad ways I will seek him whom my soul loves: I sought him, but I found him not.
3 The watchmen that go about the city found me: *to whom I said*, Saw you him whom my soul loves?
4 *It was* but a little that I passed from them, but I found him whom my soul loves: I held him, and would not let him go, until I had brought him into my mother's house, and into the chamber of her that conceived me.
5 I charge you, O you daughters of Jerusalem, by the roes, and by the does of the field, that you stir not up, nor awake *my* love, till he pleases.
6 ¶ Who *is* this that comes out of the wilderness like pillars of smoke, perfumed with myrrh and frankincense, with all powders of the merchant?
7 ¶ Behold his bed, which *is* Solomon's; threescore valiant men *are* about it, of the valiant of Israel.
8 They all hold swords, *being* expert in war: every man *has* his sword upon his thigh because of fear in the night.
9 King Solomon made himself a chariot of the wood of Lebanon.
10 He made the pillars thereof *of* silver, the bottom thereof *of* gold, the covering of it *of* purple, the midst thereof being paved *with* love, for the daughters of Jerusalem.
11 Go forth, O you daughters of Zion, and behold king Solomon with the crown with which his mother crowned him in the day of his espousals, and in the day of the gladness of his heart.

Song of Solomon 4

4:1 ¶ Behold, you *are* fair, my love; behold, you *are* fair; you *have* doves' eyes within your locks: your hair *is* as a flock of goats, that appear from mount Gilead.
2 Your teeth *are* like a flock *of sheep that are even* shorn, which came up from the washing; whereof every one bears twins, and none *is* barren among them.
3 Your lips *are* like a thread of scarlet, and your speech *is* comely: your temples *are* like a piece of a pomegranate within your locks.
4 Your neck *is* like the tower of David built for an armory, whereon there hangs a thousand bucklers, all shields of mighty men.
5 Your two breasts *are* like two young roes that are twins, which feed among the lilies.
6 Until the day breaks, and the shadows flee away, I will get me to the mountain of myrrh, and to the hill of frankincense.
7 You *are* all fair, my love; *there is* no spot in you.
8 ¶ Come with me from Lebanon, *my* spouse, with me from Lebanon: look from the top of Amana, from the top of Shenir and Hermon, from the lions' dens, from the mountains of the leopards.
9 You have ravished my heart, my sister, *my* spouse; you have ravished my heart with one of your eyes, with one chain of your neck.
10 How fair is your love, my sister, *my* spouse! how much better is your love than wine! and the smell of your ointments than all spices!
11 Your lips, O *my* spouse, drop *as* the honeycomb: honey and milk *are* under your tongue; and the smell of your garments *is* like the smell of Lebanon.
12 A garden enclosed *is* my sister, *my* spouse; a spring shut up, a fountain sealed.
13 Your plants *are* an orchard of pomegranates, with pleasant fruits; henna, with spikenard,
14 Spikenard and saffron; calamus and cinnamon, with all trees of frankincense; myrrh and aloes, with all the chief spices:
15 ¶ A fountain of gardens, a well of living waters, and streams from Lebanon.
16 Awake, O north wind; and come, you south; blow upon my garden, *that* the spices thereof may flow out. Let my beloved come into his garden, and eat his pleasant fruits.

Song of Solomon 5

5:1 ¶ I have come into my garden, my sister, *my* spouse: I have gathered my myrrh with my spice; I have eaten my honeycomb with my honey; I have drunk my wine with my milk: eat, O friends; drink, yes, drink abundantly, O beloved.

2 ¶ I sleep, but my heart wakes: *it is* the voice of my beloved that knocks, *saying*, Open to me, my sister, my love, my dove, my undefiled: for my head is filled with dew, *and* my locks with the drops of the night.

3 I have put off my coat; how shall I put it on? I have washed my feet; how shall I defile them?

4 My beloved put in his hand by the hole *of the door*, and my heart was moved for him.

5 I rose up to open to my beloved; and my hands dropped *with* myrrh, and my fingers *with* sweet smelling myrrh, upon the handles of the lock.

6 I opened to my beloved; but my beloved had withdrawn himself, *and* was gone: my soul failed when he spoke: I sought him, but I could not find him; I called him, but he gave me no answer.

7 The watchmen that went about the city found me, they smote me, they wounded me; the keepers of the walls took away my veil from me.

8 I charge you, O daughters of Jerusalem, if you find my beloved, that you tell him, that I *am* sick with love.

9 ¶ What *is* your beloved more than *another* beloved, O you fairest among women? what *is* your beloved more than *another* beloved, that you do so charge us?

10 My beloved *is* white and ruddy, the most chief among ten thousand.

11 His head *is as* the most fine gold, his locks *are* bushy, *and* black as a raven.

12 His eyes *are* as *the eyes* of doves by the rivers of waters, washed with milk, *and* fitly set.

13 His cheeks *are* as a bed of spices, *as* sweet flowers: his lips *like* lilies, dropping sweet smelling myrrh.

14 His hands *are as* gold rings set with the beryl: his belly *is as* bright ivory overlaid *with* sapphires.

15 His legs *are as* pillars of marble, set upon sockets of fine gold: his countenance *is* as Lebanon, excellent as the cedars.

16 His mouth *is* most sweet: yes, he *is* altogether lovely. This *is* my beloved, and this *is* my friend, O daughters of Jerusalem.

Song of Solomon 6

6:1 ¶ Where has your beloved gone, O you fairest among women? where has your beloved turned aside? that we may seek him with you.

2 My beloved has gone down into his garden, to the beds of spices, to feed in the gardens, and to gather lilies.

3 I *am* my beloved's, and my beloved *is* mine: he feeds among the lilies.

4 ¶ You *are* beautiful, O my love, as Tirzah, comely as Jerusalem, awesome as *an army* with banners.

5 Turn away your eyes from me, for they have overcome me: your hair *is* as a flock of goats that appear from Gilead.

6 Your teeth *are* as a flock of sheep which go up from the washing, whereof every one bears twins, and *there is* not one barren among them.

7 As a piece of a pomegranate *are* your temples within your locks.

8 There are threescore queens, and fourscore concubines, and virgins without number.

9 My dove, my undefiled is *but* one; she *is* the *only* one of her mother, she *is* the choice *one* of her that bore her. The daughters saw her, and blessed her; *yes*, the queens and the concubines, and they praised her.

10 Who *is* she *that* looks forth as the morning, fair as the moon, clear as the sun, *and* awesome as *an army* with banners?

11 ¶ I went down into the garden of nuts to see the fruits of the valley, *and* to see whether the vine flourished, *and* the pomegranates budded.

12 Before I was aware, my soul made me *like* the chariots of Amminadib.

13 Return, return, O Shulamite; return, return, that we may look upon you. What will you see in the Shulamite? As it were the company of two armies.

Song of Solomon 7

7:1 ¶ How beautiful are your feet with shoes, O prince's daughter! the joints of your thighs *are* like jewels, the work of the hands of a cunning workman.

2 Your navel *is like* a round goblet, *which* wants not liquor: your belly *is like* a heap of wheat set about with lilies.

3 Your two breasts *are* like two young roes *that are* twins.

4 Your neck *is* as a tower of ivory; your eyes *like* the fish pools in Heshbon, by the gate of Bathrabbim: your nose *is* as the tower of Lebanon which looks toward Damascus.

5 Your head upon you *is* like Carmel, and the hair of your head like purple; the king *is* held in the galleries.

6 How fair and how pleasant are you, O love, for delights!

7 This your stature is like to a palm tree, and your breasts to clusters *of grapes*.

8 I said, I will go up to the palm tree, I will take hold of the boughs thereof: now also your breasts shall be as clusters of the vine, and the smell of your nose like apples;

9 And the roof of your mouth like the best wine for my beloved, that goes *down* sweetly, causing the lips of those that are asleep to speak.

10 ¶ I *am* my beloved's, and his desire *is* toward me.

11 Come, my beloved, let us go forth into the field; let us lodge in the villages.

Song of Solomon 7

12 Let us get up early to the vineyards; let us see if the vine flourishes, *whether* the tender grape appears, *and* the pomegranates bud forth: there will I give you my love.

13 The mandrakes give a smell, and at our gates *are* all manner of pleasant *fruits*, new and old, *which* I have laid up for you, O my beloved.

Song of Solomon 8

8:1 ¶ O that you *were* as my brother, that sucked the breasts of my mother! *when* I should find you outside, I would kiss you; yes, I should not be despised.

2 I would lead you, *and* bring you into my mother's house, *who* would instruct me: I would cause you to drink of spiced wine of the juice of my pomegranate.

3 His left hand *should be* under my head, and his right hand should embrace me.

4 I charge you, O daughters of Jerusalem, that you stir not up, nor awake *my* love, until he pleases.

5 ¶ Who *is* this that comes up from the wilderness, leaning upon her beloved? I raised you up under the apple tree: there your mother brought you forth: there she brought you forth *that* bore you.

6 Set me as a seal upon your heart, as a seal upon your arm: for love *is* strong as death; jealousy *is* cruel as the grave: the coals thereof *are* coals of fire, *which have a* most vehement flame.

7 Many waters cannot quench love, neither can the floods drown it: if *a* man would give all the substance of his house for love, it would utterly be despised.

8 ¶ We have a little sister, and she has no breasts: what shall we do for our sister in the day when she shall be spoken for?

9 If she *is* a wall, we will build upon her a palace of silver: and if she *is* a door, we will enclose her with boards of cedar.

10 I *am* a wall, and my breasts like towers: then was I in his eyes as one that found favor.

11 Solomon had a vineyard at Baalhamon; he let out the vineyard to keepers; every one for the fruit thereof was to bring a thousand *pieces* of silver.

12 My vineyard, which *is* mine, *is* before me: you, O Solomon, *must have* a thousand, and those that keep the fruit thereof two hundred.

13 ¶ You that dwell in the gardens, the companions listen to your voice: cause me to hear *it*.

14 Make haste, my beloved, and be you like to a roe or to a young hart upon the mountains of spices.

Section 4
Prophecy

Isaiah

Isaiah 1

1:1 ¶ The vision of Isaiah the son of Amoz, which he saw concerning Judah and Jerusalem in the days of Uzziah, Jotham, Ahaz, *and* Hezekiah, kings of Judah.

2 ¶ Hear, O heavens, and give ear, O earth: for Yahweh has spoken, I have nourished and brought up children, and they have rebelled against me.

3 The ox knows his owner, and the donkey his master's crib: *but* Israel does not know, my people do not consider.

4 Ah sinful nation, a people laden with iniquity, a seed of evildoers, children that are corrupters: they have forsaken Yahweh, they have provoked the Holy One of Israel to anger, they are gone away backward.

5 Why should you be stricken any more? you will revolt more and more: the whole head is sick, and the whole heart faint.

6 From the sole of the foot even unto the head *there is* no soundness in it; *but* wounds, and bruises, and putrefying sores: they have not been closed, neither bound up, neither soothed with ointment.

7 Your country *is* desolate, your cities *are* burned with fire: your land, strangers devour it in your presence, and *it is* desolate, as overthrown by strangers.

8 And the daughter of Zion is left as a cottage in a vineyard, as a lodge in a garden of cucumbers, as a besieged city.

9 Unless Yahweh of hosts had left unto us a very small remnant, we should have been as Sodom, *and* we should have been like unto Gomorrah.

10 ¶ Hear the word of Yahweh, you rulers of Sodom; give ear to the law of our God, you people of Gomorrah.

11 To what purpose *is* the multitude of your sacrifices unto me? says Yahweh: I am full of the burnt offerings of rams, and the fat of fed beasts; and I delight not in the blood of bullocks, or of lambs, or of he goats.

12 When you come to appear before me, who has required this at your hand, to tread my courts?

13 Bring no more vain oblations; incense is an abomination unto me; the new moons and sabbaths, the calling of assemblies, I cannot endure it; *it is* iniquity, even the solemn meeting.

14 Your new moons and your appointed feasts my soul hates: they are a trouble unto me; I am weary to bear *them*.

15 And when you spread forth your hands, I will hide my eyes from you: yes, when you make many prayers, I will not hear: your hands are full of blood.

16 ¶ Wash you, make you clean; put away the evil of your doings from before my eyes; cease to do evil;

17 Learn to do well; seek judgment, relieve the oppressed, judge the fatherless, plead for the widow.

18 Come now, and let us reason together, says Yahweh: though your sins are as scarlet, they shall be as white as snow; though they are red like crimson, they shall be as wool.

19 If you are willing and obedient, you shall eat the good of the land:

20 But if you refuse and rebel, you shall be devoured with the sword: for the mouth of Yahweh has spoken *it*.

21 ¶ How has the faithful city become a harlot! it was full of judgment; righteousness lodged in it; but now murderers.

22 Your silver has become dross, your wine mixed with water:

23 Your princes *are* rebellious, and companions of thieves: every one loves bribes, and follows after rewards: they judge not the fatherless, neither does the cause of the widow come to them.

24 Therefore says the Lord, Yahweh of hosts. the mighty One of Israel, Ah, I will ease me of my adversaries, and avenge me of my enemies:

25 And I will turn my hand upon you, and purely purge away your dross, and take away all your tin:

26 And I will restore your judges as at the first, and your counselors as at the beginning: afterward you shall be called, The city of righteousness, the faithful city.

27 Zion shall be redeemed with judgment, and her converts with righteousness.

28 And the destruction of the transgressors and of the sinners *shall be* together, and they that forsake Yahweh shall be consumed.

29 For they shall be ashamed of the oaks which you have desired, and you shall be confounded for the gardens that you have chosen.

30 For you shall be as an oak whose leaf fades, and as a garden that has no water.

31 And the strong shall be as flax fibers, and the maker of it as a spark, and they shall both burn together, and none shall quench *them*.

Isaiah 2

2:1 ¶ The word that Isaiah the son of Amoz saw concerning Judah and Jerusalem.

2 And it shall come to pass in the last days, *that* the mountain of Yahweh's house shall be established in the top of the mountains, and shall be exalted above the hills; and all nations shall flow unto it.

3 And many people shall go and say, Come you, and let us go up to the mountain of Yahweh, to the house of the

Isaiah 2

God of Jacob; and he will teach us of his ways, and we will walk in his paths: for out of Zion shall go forth the law, and the word of Yahweh from Jerusalem.

4 And he shall judge among the nations, and shall rebuke many people: and they shall beat their swords into plowshares, and their spears into pruning hooks: nation shall not lift up sword against nation, neither shall they learn war any more.

5 O house of Jacob, come you, and let us walk in the light of Yahweh.

6 ¶ Therefore you have forsaken your people the house of Jacob, because they are replenished from the east, and *are* soothsayers like the Philistines, and they please themselves in the children of strangers.

7 Their land also is full of silver and gold, neither *is there any* end to their treasures; their land is also full of horses, neither *is there any* end to their chariots:

8 Their land also is full of idols; they worship the work of their own hands, that which their own fingers have made:

9 And the mean man bows down, and the great man humbles himself: therefore forgive them not.

10 ¶ Enter into the rock, and hide you in the dust, for fear of Yahweh, and for the glory of his majesty.

11 The lofty looks of man shall be humbled, and the haughtiness of men shall be bowed down, and Yahweh alone shall be exalted in that day.

12 For the day of Yahweh of hosts *shall be* upon every *one that is* proud and lofty, and upon every *one that is* lifted up; and he shall be brought low:

13 And upon all the cedars of Lebanon, *that are* high and lifted up, and upon all the oaks of Bashan,

14 And upon all the high mountains, and upon all the hills *that are* lifted up,

15 And upon every high tower, and upon every fenced wall,

16 And upon all the ships of Tarshish, and upon all pleasant pictures.

17 And the loftiness of man shall be bowed down, and the haughtiness of men shall be made low: and Yahweh alone shall be exalted in that day.

18 And the idols he shall utterly abolish.

19 And they shall go into the holes of the rocks, and into the caves of the earth, for fear of Yahweh, and for the glory of his majesty, when he arises to shake terribly the earth.

20 In that day a man shall cast his idols of silver, and his idols of gold, which they made *each one* for himself to worship, to the moles and to the bats;

21 To go into the clefts of the rocks, and into the tops of the ragged rocks, for fear of Yahweh, and for the glory of his majesty, when he arises to shake terribly the earth.

22 Cease you from man, whose breath *is* in his nostrils: for wherein is he to be accounted of?

Isaiah 3

3:1 ¶ For, behold, the Lord, Yahweh of hosts, does take away from Jerusalem and from Judah the stay and the staff, the whole stay of bread, and the whole stay of water,

2 The mighty man, and the man of war, the judge, and the prophet, and the prudent, and the ancient,

3 The captain of fifty, and the honorable man, and the counselor, and the skillful craftsman, and the eloquent orator.

4 And I will give children *to be* their princes, and babes shall rule over them.

5 And the people shall be oppressed, every one by another, and every one by his neighbor: the child shall behave himself proudly against the ancient, and the base against the honorable.

6 When a man shall take hold of his brother of the house of his father, *saying*, You have clothing, be you our ruler, and *let* this ruin *be* under your hand:

7 In that day shall he swear, saying, I will not be a healer; for in my house *is* neither bread nor clothing: make me not a ruler of the people.

8 For Jerusalem is ruined, and Judah is fallen: because their tongue and their doings *are* against Yahweh, to provoke the eyes of his glory.

9 ¶ The show of their countenance does witness against them; and they declare their sin as Sodom, they hide *it* not. Woe unto their soul! for they have rewarded evil unto themselves.

10 Say you to the righteous, that *it shall be* well *with him*: for they shall eat the fruit of their doings.

11 Woe unto the wicked! *it shall be* ill *with him*: for the reward of his hands shall be given him.

12 *As for* my people, children *are* their oppressors, and women rule over them. O my people, they which lead you cause *you* to err, and destroy the way of your paths.

13 Yahweh stands up to plead, and stands to judge the people.

14 Yahweh will enter into judgment with the ancients of his people, and the princes thereof: for you have eaten up the vineyard; the spoil of the poor *is* in your houses.

15 What mean you *that* you beat my people to pieces, and grind the faces of the poor? says the Lord Yahweh of hosts.

16 ¶ Moreover Yahweh says, Because the daughters of Zion are haughty, and walk with stretched forth necks and wanton eyes, walking and mincing *as* they go, and making a tinkling with their feet:

17 Therefore the Lord will smite with a scab the crown of the head of the daughters of Zion, and Yahweh will uncover their secret parts.

18 In that day the Lord will take away the beauty of *their* tinkling ornaments *about their feet*, and *their* headbands, and *their* round ornaments like the moon,

19 The chains, and the bracelets, and the veils,

20 The bonnets, and the ornaments of the legs, and the headbands, and the tablets, and the earrings,

21 The rings, and nose jewels,

22 The changeable suits of apparel, and the mantles, and the cloaks, and the purses,

23 The glasses, and the fine linen, and the hoods, and the veils.

24 And it shall come to pass, *that* instead of sweet smell there shall be stink; and instead of a girdle a rope; and

instead of well set hair baldness; and instead of a rich robe a girding of sackcloth; *and* burning instead of beauty.
25 Your men shall fall by the sword, and your mighty in the war.
26 And her gates shall lament and mourn; and she *being* desolate shall sit upon the ground.

Isaiah 4

4:1 ¶ And in that day seven women shall take hold of one man, saying, We will eat our own bread, and wear our own apparel: only let us be called by your name, to take away our reproach.
2 ¶ In that day shall the branch of Yahweh be beautiful and glorious, and the fruit of the earth *shall be* excellent and comely for them that have escaped of Israel.
3 And it shall come to pass, *that he that is* left in Zion, and *he that* remains in Jerusalem, shall be called holy, *even* every one that is written among the living in Jerusalem:
4 When the Lord shall have washed away the filth of the daughters of Zion, and shall have purged the blood of Jerusalem from the midst thereof by the spirit of judgment, and by the spirit of burning.
5 And Yahweh will create upon every dwelling place of mount Zion, and upon her assemblies, a cloud and smoke by day, and the shining of a flaming fire by night: for upon all the glory *shall be* a defense.
6 And there shall be a tabernacle for a shadow in the daytime from the heat, and for a place of refuge, and for a covert from storm and from rain.

Isaiah 5

5:1 ¶ Now will I sing to my wellbeloved a song of my beloved touching his vineyard. My wellbeloved has a vineyard in a very fruitful hill:
2 And he fenced it, and gathered out the stones thereof, and planted it with the choicest vine, and built a tower in the midst of it, and also made a winepress therein: and he looked that it should bring forth grapes, and it brought forth wild grapes.
3 And now, O inhabitants of Jerusalem, and men of Judah, judge, I pray you, between me and my vineyard.
4 What could have been done more to my vineyard, that I have not done in it? why, when I looked that it should bring forth grapes, brought it forth wild grapes?
5 And now go to; I will tell you what I will do to my vineyard: I will take away the hedge thereof, and it shall be eaten up; *and* break down the wall thereof, and it shall be trodden down:
6 And I will lay it waste: it shall not be pruned, nor dug; but there shall come up briers and thorns: I will also command the clouds that they rain no rain upon it.
7 For the vineyard of Yahweh of hosts *is* the house of Israel, and the men of Judah his pleasant plant: and he looked for judgment, but behold oppression; for righteousness, but behold a cry.

8 ¶ Woe unto them that join house to house, *that* lay field to field, till *there is* no place, that they may be placed alone in the midst of the earth!
9 In my ears *says* Yahweh of hosts, Of a truth many houses shall be desolate, *even* great and fair, without inhabitant.
10 Yes, ten acres of vineyard shall yield one bath, and the seed of a homer shall yield an ephah.
11 Woe unto them that rise up early in the morning, *that* they may follow strong drink; that continue until night, *till* wine inflames them!
12 And the harp, and the viol, the tambourine, and flute, and wine, are in their feasts: but they regard not the work of Yahweh, neither consider the operation of his hands.
13 Therefore my people have gone into captivity, because *they have* no knowledge: and their honorable men *are* famished, and their multitude dried up with thirst.
14 Therefore hell has enlarged herself, and opened her mouth without measure: and their glory, and their multitude, and their pomp, and he that rejoices, shall descend into it.
15 And the mean man shall be brought down, and the mighty man shall be humbled, and the eyes of the lofty shall be humbled:
16 But Yahweh of hosts shall be exalted in judgment, and God that is holy shall be sanctified in righteousness.
17 Then shall the lambs feed after their manner, and the waste places of the fat ones shall strangers eat.
18 ¶ Woe unto them that draw iniquity with cords of vanity, and sin as it were with a cart rope:
19 That say, Let him make speed, *and* hurry his work, that we may see *it*: and let the counsel of the Holy One of Israel draw near and come, that we may know *it*!
20 Woe unto them that call evil good, and good evil; that put darkness for light, and light for darkness; that put bitter for sweet, and sweet for bitter!
21 Woe unto *them that are* wise in their own eyes, and prudent in their own sight!
22 Woe unto *them that are* mighty to drink wine, and men of strength to mingle strong drink:
23 Which justify the wicked for bribe, and take away the righteousness of the righteous from him!
24 Therefore as the fire devours the stubble, and the flame consumes the chaff, *so* their root shall be as rottenness, and their blossom shall go up as dust: because they have cast away the law of Yahweh of hosts, and despised the word of the Holy One of Israel.
25 Therefore is the anger of Yahweh kindled against his people, and he has stretched forth his hand against them, and has smitten them: and the hills did tremble, and their carcasses *were* torn in the midst of the streets. For all this his anger is not turned away, but his hand *is* stretched out still.
26 And he will lift up an ensign to the nations from afar, and will hiss to them from the end of the earth: and, behold, they shall come with speed swiftly:
27 None shall be weary nor stumble among them; none shall slumber nor sleep; neither shall the girdle of their loins be loosed, nor the lace of their shoes be broken:

Isaiah 5

28 Whose arrows *are* sharp, and all their bows bent, their horses' hoofs shall be counted like flint, and their wheels like a whirlwind:
29 Their roaring *shall be* like a lion, they shall roar like young lions: yes, they shall roar, and lay hold of the prey, and shall carry *it* away safely, and none shall deliver *it*.
30 And in that day they shall roar against them like the roaring of the sea: and if *one* looks unto the land, behold darkness *and* sorrow, and the light is darkened in the heavens thereof.

Isaiah 6

6:1 ¶ In the year that king Uzziah died I saw also the Lord sitting upon a throne, high and lifted up, and his train filled the temple.
2 Above it stood the seraphims: each one had six wings; with two he covered his face, and with two he covered his feet, and with two he did fly.
3 And one cried to another, and said, Holy, holy, holy, *is* Yahweh of hosts: the whole earth *is* full of his glory.
4 And the posts of the door moved at the voice of him that cried, and the house was filled with smoke.
5 ¶ Then said I, Woe *is* me! for I am undone; because I *am* a man of unclean lips, and I dwell in the midst of a people of unclean lips: for my eyes have seen the King, Yahweh of hosts.
6 Then flew one of the seraphims unto me, having a live coal in his hand, *which* he had taken with the tongs from off the altar:
7 And he laid *it* upon my mouth, and said, Lo, this has touched your lips; and your iniquity is taken away, and your sin purged.
8 Also I heard the voice of the Lord, saying, Whom shall I send, and who will go for us? Then said I, Here *am* I; send me.
9 ¶ And he said, Go, and tell this people, Hear you indeed, but understand not; and see you indeed, but perceive not.
10 Make the heart of this people fat, and make their ears heavy, and shut their eyes; lest they see with their eyes, and hear with their ears, and understand with their heart, and convert, and be healed.
11 Then said I, Lord, how long? And he answered, Until the cities are wasted without inhabitant, and the houses without man, and the land is utterly desolate,
12 And Yahweh has removed men far away, and *there is* a great forsaking in the midst of the land.
13 But yet in it *shall be* a tenth, and *it* shall return, and shall be eaten: as a teil tree, and as an oak, whose substance *is* in them, when they cast *their leaves: so* the holy seed *shall be* the substance thereof.

Isaiah 7

7:1 ¶ And it came to pass in the days of Ahaz the son of Jotham, the son of Uzziah, king of Judah, *that* Rezin the king of Syria, and Pekah the son of Remaliah, king of Israel, went up toward Jerusalem to war against it, but could not prevail against it.
2 And it was told *to* the house of David, saying, Syria is confederate with Ephraim. And his heart was moved, and the heart of his people, as the trees of the woods are moved with the wind.
3 Then said Yahweh unto Isaiah, Go forth now to meet Ahaz, you, and Shearjashub your son, at the end of the conduit of the upper pool in the highway of the fuller's field;
4 And say unto him, Take heed, and be quiet; fear not, neither be fainthearted for the two tails of these smoking firebrands, for the fierce anger of Rezin with Syria, and of the son of Remaliah.
5 Because Syria, Ephraim, and the son of Remaliah, have taken evil counsel against you, saying,
6 Let us go up against Judah, and distress it, and let us make a breach therein for us, and set a king in the midst of it, *even* the son of Tabeal:
7 Thus says the Lord Yahweh, It shall not stand, neither shall it come to pass.
8 For the head of Syria *is* Damascus, and the head of Damascus *is* Rezin; and within threescore and five years shall Ephraim be broken, that it be not a people.
9 And the head of Ephraim *is* Samaria, and the head of Samaria *is* Remaliah's son. If you will not believe, surely you shall not be established.
10 ¶ Moreover Yahweh spoke again to Ahaz, saying,
11 Ask you *for* a sign from Yahweh your God; ask it either in the depth, or in the height above.
12 But Ahaz said, I will not ask, neither will I tempt Yahweh.
13 And he said, Hear you now, O house of David; *Is it* a small thing for you to weary men, but will you weary my God also?
14 Therefore the Lord himself shall give you a sign; Behold, a virgin shall conceive, and bear a son, and shall call his name Immanuel.
15 Butter and honey shall he eat, that he may know to refuse the evil, and choose the good.
16 For before the child shall know to refuse the evil, and choose the good, the land that you abhor shall be forsaken of both her kings.
17 ¶ Yahweh shall bring upon you, and upon your people, and upon your father's house, days that have not come, from the day that Ephraim departed from Judah; *even* the king of Assyria.
18 And it shall come to pass in that day, *that* Yahweh shall hiss for the fly that *is* in the utmost part of the rivers of Egypt, and for the bee that *is* in the land of Assyria.
19 And they shall come, and shall rest all of them in the desolate valleys, and in the holes of the rocks, and upon all thorns, and upon all bushes.
20 In the same day shall the Lord shave with a razor that is hired, *namely*, by them beyond the river, by the king of Assyria, the head, and the hair of the feet: and it shall also consume the beard.

21 And it shall come to pass in that day, *that* a man shall nourish a young cow, and two sheep;
22 And it shall come to pass, for the abundance of milk *that* they shall give he shall eat butter: for butter and honey shall every one eat that is left in the land.
23 And it shall come to pass in that day, *that* every place shall be, where there were a thousand vines *worth* a thousand silver coins, it shall *even* be for briers and thorns.
24 With arrows and with bows shall *men* come there; because all the land shall become briers and thorns.
25 And *on* all hills that shall be dug with the hoe, there shall not come therein the fear of briers and thorns: but it shall be for the sending forth of oxen, and for the treading of lesser cattle.

Isaiah 8

8:1 ¶ Moreover Yahweh said unto me, Take you a great roll, and write in it with a man's pen concerning Mahershalalhashbaz.
2 And I took unto me faithful witnesses to record, Uriah the priest, and Zechariah the son of Jeberechiah.
3 And I went unto the prophetess; and she conceived, and bore a son. Then said Yahweh to me, Call his name Mahershalalhashbaz.
4 For before the child shall have knowledge to cry, My father, and my mother, the riches of Damascus and the spoil of Samaria shall be taken away before the king of Assyria.
5 Yahweh spoke also unto me again, saying,
6 Forasmuch as this people refuses the waters of Shiloah that go softly, and rejoice in Rezin and Remaliah's son;
7 Now therefore, behold, the Lord brings up upon them the waters of the river, strong and many, *even* the king of Assyria, and all his glory: and he shall come up over all his channels, and go over all his banks:
8 And he shall pass through Judah; he shall overflow and go over, he shall reach *even* to the neck; and the stretching out of his wings shall fill the breadth of your land, O Immanuel.
9 ¶ Associate yourselves, O you people, and you shall be broken in pieces; and give ear, all you of far countries: gird yourselves, and you shall be broken in pieces; gird yourselves, and you shall be broken in pieces.
10 Take counsel together, and it shall come to nothing; speak the word, and it shall not stand: for God *is* with us.
11 For Yahweh spoke thus to me with a strong hand, and instructed me that I should not walk in the way of this people, saying,
12 Say you not, A confederacy, to all *them to* whom this people shall say, A confederacy; neither fear you their fear, nor be afraid.
13 Sanctify Yahweh of hosts himself; and *let* him *be* your fear, and *let* him *be* your dread.
14 And he shall be for a sanctuary; but for a stone of stumbling and for a rock of offense to both the houses of Israel, for a gin and for a snare to the inhabitants of Jerusalem.
15 And many among them shall stumble, and fall, and be broken, and be snared, and be taken.
16 ¶ Bind up the testimony, seal the law among my disciples.
17 And I will wait upon Yahweh, that hides his face from the house of Jacob, and I will look for him.
18 Behold, I and the children whom Yahweh has given me *are* for signs and for wonders in Israel from Yahweh of hosts, which dwells in mount Zion.
19 And when they shall say unto you, Seek unto them that have familiar spirits, and unto wizards that peep, and that mutter: should not a people seek unto their God? for the living to the dead?
20 To the law and to the testimony: if they speak not according to this word, *it is* because *there is* no light in them.
21 And they shall pass through it, greatly distressed and hungry: and it shall come to pass, that when they shall be hungry, they shall fret themselves, and curse their king and their God, and look upward.
22 And they shall look unto the earth; and behold trouble and darkness, dimness of anguish; and *they shall be* driven to darkness.

Isaiah 9

9:1 ¶ Nevertheless the dimness *shall* not *be* such as *was* in her distress, when at the first he lightly afflicted the land of Zebulun and the land of Naphtali, and afterward did more grievously afflict *her by* the way of the sea, beyond *the* Jordan, in Galilee of the nations.
2 The people that walked in darkness have seen a great light: they that dwell in the land of the shadow of death, upon them has the light shined.
3 You have multiplied the nation, *and* not increased the joy: they joy before you according to the joy in harvest, *and* as *men* rejoice when they divide the spoil.
4 For you have broken the yoke of his burden, and the staff of his shoulder, the rod of his oppressor, as in the day of Midian.
5 For every battle of the warrior *is* with confused noise, and garments rolled in blood; but *this* shall be with burning *and* fuel of fire.
6 For unto us a child is born, unto us a son is given: and the government shall be upon his shoulder: and his name shall be called Wonderful, Counselor, The mighty God, The everlasting Father, The Prince of Peace.
7 Of the increase of *his* government and peace *there shall be* no end, upon the throne of David, and upon his kingdom, to order it, and to establish it with judgment and with justice from now on even forever The zeal of Yahweh of hosts will perform this.
8 ¶ The Lord sent a word into Jacob, and it has lighted upon Israel.
9 And all the people shall know, *even* Ephraim and the inhabitant of Samaria, that say in the pride and stoutness of heart,

Isaiah 9

10 The bricks have fallen down, but we will build with hewn stones: the sycamores are cut down, but we will change *them into* cedars.

11 Therefore Yahweh shall set up the adversaries of Rezin against him, and join his enemies together;

12 The Syrians before, and the Philistines behind; and they shall devour Israel with *an* open mouth. For all this his anger is not turned away, but his hand *is* stretched out still.

13 For the people turn not unto him that smites them, neither do they seek Yahweh of hosts.

14 Therefore Yahweh will cut off from Israel head and tail, branch and rush, in one day.

15 The ancient and honorable, he *is* the head; and the prophet that teaches lies, he *is* the tail.

16 For the leaders of this people cause *them* to err; and *they that are* led by them *are* destroyed.

17 Therefore the Lord shall have no joy in their young men, neither shall have mercy on their fatherless and widows: for every one *is* a hypocrite and an evildoer, and every mouth speaks folly. For all this his anger is not turned away, but his hand *is* stretched out still.

18 For wickedness burns as the fire: it shall devour the briers and thorns, and shall kindle in the thickets of the forest, and they shall mount up *like* the lifting up of smoke.

19 Through the wrath of Yahweh of hosts is the land darkened, and the people shall be as the fuel of the fire: no man shall spare his brother.

20 And he shall snatch on the right hand, and be hungry; and he shall eat on the left hand, and they shall not be satisfied: they shall eat every man the flesh of his own arm:

21 Manasseh, Ephraim; and Ephraim, Manasseh: *and* they together *shall be* against Judah. For all this his anger is not turned away, but his hand *is* stretched out still.

Isaiah 10

10:1 ¶ Woe unto them that decree unrighteous decrees, and that write grievousness *which* they have prescribed;

2 To turn aside the needy from judgment, and to take away the right from the poor of my people, that widows may be their prey, and *that* they may rob the fatherless!

3 And what will you do in the day of visitation, and in the desolation *which* shall come from afar? to whom will you flee for help? and where will you leave your glory?

4 Without me they shall bow down under the prisoners, and they shall fall under the slain. For all this his anger is not turned away, but his hand *is* stretched out still.

5 ¶ O Assyrian, the rod of my anger, and the staff in their hand is my indignation.

6 I will send him against a hypocritical nation, and against the people of my wrath will I give him a charge, to take the spoil, and to take the prey, and to tread them down like the mire of the streets.

7 However he means not so, neither does his heart think so; but *it is* in his heart to destroy and cut off nations not a few.

8 For he said, *Are* not my princes altogether kings?

9 *Is* not Calno as Carchemish? *is* not Hamath as Arpad? *is* not Samaria as Damascus?

10 As my hand has found the kingdoms of the idols, and whose graven images did excel them of Jerusalem and of Samaria;

11 Shall I not, as I have done to Samaria and her idols, so do to Jerusalem and her idols?

12 Therefore it shall come to pass, *that* when the Lord has performed his whole work upon mount Zion and on Jerusalem, I will punish the fruit of the stout heart of the king of Assyria, and the glory of his high looks.

13 For he says, By the strength of my hand I have done *it*, and by my wisdom; for I am prudent: and I have removed the bounds of the people, and have robbed their treasures, and I have put down the inhabitants like a valiant *man*:

14 And my hand has found as a nest the riches of the people: and as one gathers eggs *that are* left, have I gathered all the earth; and there was none that moved the wing, or opened the mouth, or peeped.

15 Shall the ax boast itself against him that hews therewith? *or* shall the saw magnify itself against him that moves it? as if the rod should shake *itself* against them that lift it up, *or* as if the staff should lift up *itself, as if it were* not wood.

16 Therefore shall the Lord, the Lord of hosts, send among his fat ones leanness; and under his glory he shall kindle a burning like the burning of a fire.

17 And the light of Israel shall be for a fire, and his Holy One for a flame: and it shall burn and devour his thorns and his briers in one day;

18 And shall consume the glory of his forest, and of his fruitful field, both soul and body: and they shall be as when a standardbearer faints.

19 And the rest of the trees of his forest shall be few, that a child may record them.

20 ¶ And it shall come to pass in that day, *that* the remnant of Israel, and such as have escaped of the house of Jacob, shall no more again rely upon him that smote them; but shall rely upon Yahweh, the Holy One of Israel, in truth.

21 The remnant shall return, *even* the remnant of Jacob, unto the mighty God.

22 For though your people Israel be as the sand of the sea, *yet* a remnant of them shall return: the destruction decreed shall overflow with righteousness.

23 For the Lord Yahweh of hosts shall make a completion, even determined, in the midst of all the land.

24 ¶ Therefore thus says the Lord Yahweh of hosts, O my people that dwell in Zion, be not afraid of the Assyrian: he shall smite you with a rod, and shall lift up his staff against you, after the manner of Egypt.

25 For yet a very little while, and the indignation shall cease, and my anger in their destruction.

26 And Yahweh of hosts shall stir up a scourge for him according to the slaughter of Midian at the rock of Oreb: and *as* his rod *was* upon the sea, so shall he lift it up after the manner of Egypt.

27 And it shall come to pass in that day, *that* his burden shall be taken away from off your shoulder, and his yoke from off your neck, and the yoke shall be destroyed because of the anointing.

28 He has come to Aiath, he has passed to Migron: at Michmash he has laid up his carriages:

29 They have gone over the passage: they have taken up their lodging at Geba; Ramah is afraid; Gibeah of Saul has fled.

30 Lift up your voice, O daughter of Gallim: cause it to be heard unto Laish, O poor Anathoth.

31 Madmenah is removed; the inhabitants of Gebim gather themselves to flee.

32 As yet shall he remain at Nob that day: he shall shake his hand *against* the mount of the daughter of Zion, the hill of Jerusalem.

33 Behold, the Lord, Yahweh of hosts, shall lop the bough with terror: and the high ones of stature *shall be* hewn down, and the haughty shall be humbled.

34 And he shall cut down the thickets of the forest with iron, and Lebanon shall fall by a mighty one.

Isaiah 11

11:1 ¶ And there shall come forth a rod out of the stem of Jesse, and a Branch shall grow out of his roots:

2 And the spirit of Yahweh shall rest upon him, the spirit of wisdom and understanding, the spirit of counsel and might, the spirit of knowledge and of the fear of Yahweh;

3 And shall make him of quick understanding in the fear of Yahweh: and he shall not judge after the sight of his eyes, neither reprove after the hearing of his ears:

4 But with righteousness shall he judge the poor, and reprove with equity for the meek of the earth: and he shall smite the earth with the rod of his mouth, and with the breath of his lips shall he slay the wicked.

5 And righteousness shall be the girdle of his loins, and faithfulness the girdle of his reins.

6 The wolf also shall dwell with the lamb, and the leopard shall lie down with the kid; and the calf and the young lion and the fatted calf together; and a little child shall lead them.

7 And the cow and the bear shall feed; their young ones shall lie down together: and the lion shall eat straw like the ox.

8 And the sucking child shall play on the hole of the asp, and the weaned child shall put his hand on the poisonous serpent's den.

9 They shall not hurt nor destroy in all my holy mountain: for the earth shall be full of the knowledge of Yahweh, as the waters cover the sea.

10 ¶ And in that day there shall be a root of Jesse, which shall stand for an ensign of the people; to it shall the Gentiles seek: and his rest shall be glorious.

11 And it shall come to pass in that day, *that* the Lord shall set his hand again the second time to recover the remnant of his people, which shall be left, from Assyria, and from Egypt, and from Pathros, and from Cush, and from Elam, and from Shinar, and from Hamath, and from the islands of the sea.

12 And he shall set up an ensign for the nations, and shall assemble the outcasts of Israel, and gather together the dispersed of Judah from the four corners of the earth.

13 The envy also of Ephraim shall depart, and the adversaries of Judah shall be cut off: Ephraim shall not envy Judah, and Judah shall not distress Ephraim.

14 But they shall fly upon the shoulders of the Philistines toward the west; they shall spoil them of the east together: they shall lay their hand upon Edom and Moab; and the children of Ammon shall obey them.

15 And Yahweh shall utterly destroy the tongue of the Egyptian sea; and with his mighty wind shall he shake his hand over the river, and shall smite it in the seven streams, and make *men* go over with dry sandals.

16 And there shall be a highway for the remnant of his people, which shall be left, from Assyria; like as it was to Israel in the day that he came up out of the land of Egypt.

Isaiah 12

12:1 ¶ And in that day you shall say, O Yahweh, I will praise you though you were angry with me, your anger is turned away, and you comforted me.

2 Behold, God *is* my salvation; I will trust, and not be afraid: for Yah Yahweh *is* my strength and *my* song; he also has become my salvation.

3 Therefore with joy shall you draw water out of the wells of salvation.

4 ¶ And in that day shall you say, Praise Yahweh, call upon his name, declare his doings among the people, make mention that his name is exalted.

5 Sing unto Yahweh; for he has done excellent things: this *is* known in all the earth.

6 Cry out and shout, you inhabitant of Zion: for great *is* the Holy One of Israel in the midst of you.

Isaiah 13

13:1 ¶ The burden of Babylon, which Isaiah the son of Amoz did see.

2 Lift you up a banner upon the high mountain, exalt the voice unto them, shake the hand, that they may go into the gates of the nobles.

3 I have commanded my sanctified ones, I have also called my mighty ones for my anger, *even* them that rejoice in my highness.

4 The noise of a multitude in the mountains, like as of a great people; a tumultuous noise of the kingdoms of nations gathered together: Yahweh of hosts musters the host of the battle.

5 They come from a far country, from the end of heaven, *even* Yahweh, and the weapons of his indignation, to destroy the whole land.

Isaiah 13

6 ¶ Howl you; for the day of Yahweh *is* at hand; it shall come as a destruction from the Almighty.

7 Therefore shall all hands be faint, and every man's heart shall melt:

8 And they shall be afraid: pangs and sorrows shall take hold of them; they shall be in pain as a woman that labors: they shall be amazed one at another; their faces *shall be as* flames.

9 Behold, the day of Yahweh comes, cruel both with wrath and fierce anger, to lay the land desolate: and he shall destroy the sinners thereof out of it.

10 For the stars of heaven and the constellations thereof shall not give their light: the sun shall be darkened in his going forth, and the moon shall not cause her light to shine.

11 And I will punish the world for *their* evil, and the wicked for their iniquity; and I will cause the arrogance of the proud to cease, and will lay low the haughtiness of the terrible.

12 I will make a man more precious than fine gold; even a man than the golden wedge of Ophir.

13 Therefore I will shake the heavens, and the earth shall remove out of her place, in the wrath of Yahweh of hosts, and in the day of his fierce anger.

14 And it shall be as the chased roe, and as a sheep that no man takes up: they shall every man turn to his own people, and flee every one into his own land.

15 Every one that is found shall be thrust through; and every one that is joined *unto them* shall fall by the sword.

16 Their children also shall be dashed to pieces before their eyes; their houses shall be spoiled, and their wives ravished.

17 Behold, I will stir up the Medes against them, which shall not regard silver; and *as for* gold, they shall not delight in it.

18 *Their* bows also shall dash the young men to pieces; and they shall have no pity on the fruit of the womb; their eye shall not spare children.

19 ¶ And Babylon, the glory of kingdoms, the beauty of the Chaldees' excellency, shall be as when God overthrew Sodom and Gomorrah.

20 It shall never be inhabited, neither shall it be dwelt in from generation to generation: neither shall the Arabian pitch tent there; neither shall the shepherds make their fold there.

21 But wild beasts of the desert shall lie there; and their houses shall be full of doleful creatures; and owls shall dwell there, and satyrs shall dance there.

22 And the wild beasts of the islands shall cry in their desolate houses, and dragons in *their* pleasant palaces: and her time *is* near to come, and her days shall not be prolonged.

Isaiah 14

14:1 ¶ For Yahweh will have mercy on Jacob, and will yet choose Israel, and set them in their own land: and the strangers shall be joined with them, and they shall cling to the house of Jacob.

2 And the people shall take them, and bring them to their place: and the house of Israel shall possess them in the land of Yahweh for servants and handmaids: and they shall take them captives, whose captives they were; and they shall rule over their oppressors.

3 And it shall come to pass in the day that Yahweh shall give you rest from your sorrow, and from your fear, and from the hard bondage wherein you were made to serve,

4 ¶ That you shall take up this proverb against the king of Babylon, and say, How has the oppressor ceased! the golden city ceased!

5 Yahweh has broken the staff of the wicked, *and* the scepter of the rulers.

6 He who smote the people in wrath with a continual stroke, he that ruled the nations in anger, is persecuted, *and* none hinders.

7 The whole earth is at rest, *and* is quiet: they break forth into singing.

8 Yes, the fir trees rejoice at you, *and* the cedars of Lebanon, *saying,* Since you were laid down, no woodsman has come up against us.

9 Hell from beneath is moved for you to meet *you* at your coming: it stirs up the dead for you, *even* all the chief ones of the earth; it has raised up from their thrones all the kings of the nations.

10 All they shall speak and say unto you, Have you also become weak as we? have you become like unto us?

11 Your pomp is brought down to the grave, *and* the noise of your viols: the worm is spread under you, and the worms cover you.

12 How are you fallen from heaven, O Lucifer, son of the morning! *how* are you cut down to the ground, which did weaken the nations!

13 For you have said in your heart, I will ascend into heaven, I will exalt my throne above the stars of God: I will sit also upon the mount of the congregation, in the sides of the north:

14 I will ascend above the heights of the clouds; I will be like the most High.

15 Yet you shall be brought down to hell, to the sides of the pit.

16 They that see you shall narrowly look upon you, *and* consider you, *saying, Is* this the man that made the earth to tremble, that did shake kingdoms;

17 *That* made the world as a wilderness, and destroyed the cities thereof; *that* opened not the house of his prisoners?

18 All the kings of the nations, *even* all of them, lie in glory, every one in his own house.

19 But you are cast out of your grave like an abominable branch, *and as* the clothing of those that are slain, thrust through with a sword, that go down to the stones of the pit; as a carcass trodden under feet.

20 You shall not be joined with them in burial, because you have destroyed your land, *and* slain your people: the seed of evildoers shall never be renowned.

21 Prepare slaughter for his children for the iniquity of their fathers; that they do not rise, nor possess the land, nor fill the face of the world with cities.

22 For I will rise up against them, says Yahweh of hosts, and cut off from Babylon the name, and remnant, and son, and nephew, says Yahweh.

23 I will also make it a possession for the bittern, and pools of water: and I will sweep it with the broom of destruction, says Yahweh of hosts.

24 ¶ Yahweh of hosts has sworn, saying, Surely as I have thought, so shall it come to pass; and as I have purposed, *so shall* it stand:

25 That I will break the Assyrian in my land, and upon my mountains tread him under foot: then shall his yoke depart from off them, and his burden depart from off their shoulders.

26 This *is* the purpose that is purposed upon the whole earth: and this *is* the hand that is stretched out upon all the nations.

27 For Yahweh of hosts has purposed, and who shall annul *it*? and his hand *is* stretched out, and who shall turn it back?

28 In the year that king Ahaz died was this burden.

29 Rejoice not you, whole Palestina, because the rod of him that smote you is broken: for out of the serpent's root shall come forth a poisonous serpent, and his fruit *shall be* a fiery flying serpent.

30 And the firstborn of the poor shall feed, and the needy shall lie down in safety: and I will kill your root with famine, and he shall slay your remnant.

31 Howl, O gate; cry, O city; you, whole Palestina, *are* dissolved: for there shall come from the north a smoke, and none *shall be* alone in his appointed times.

32 What shall *one* then answer the messengers of the nation? That Yahweh has founded Zion, and the poor of his people shall trust in it.

Isaiah 15

15:1 ¶ The burden of Moab. Because in the night Ar of Moab is laid waste, *and* brought to silence; because in the night Kir of Moab is laid waste, *and* brought to silence;

2 He has gone up to Bajith, and to Dibon, the high places, to weep: Moab shall howl over Nebo, and over Medeba: on all their heads *shall be* baldness, *and* every beard cut off.

3 In their streets they shall gird themselves with sackcloth: on the tops of their houses, and in their streets, every one shall howl, weeping abundantly.

4 And Heshbon shall cry, and Elealeh: their voice shall be heard *even* to Jahaz: therefore the armed soldiers of Moab shall cry out; his life shall be grievous unto him.

5 My heart shall cry out for Moab; his fugitives *shall flee* unto Zoar, a heifer of three years old: for by the mounting up of Luhith with weeping shall they go up; for in the way of Horonaim they shall raise up a cry of destruction.

6 ¶ For the waters of Nimrim shall be desolate: for the hay has withered away, the grass fails, there is no green thing.

7 Therefore the abundance they have gotten, and that which they have laid up, shall they carry away to the brook of the willows.

8 For the cry has gone round about the borders of Moab; the howling thereof to Eglaim, and the howling thereof to Beerelim.

9 For the waters of Dimon shall be full of blood: for I will bring more upon Dimon, lions upon him that escapes of Moab, and upon the remnant of the land.

Isaiah 16

16:1 ¶ Send you the lamb to the ruler of the land from Sela to the wilderness, unto the mount of the daughter of Zion.

2 For it shall be, *that*, as a wandering bird cast out of the nest, *so* the daughters of Moab shall be at the fords of Arnon.

3 Take counsel, execute judgment; make your shadow as the night in the midst of the noonday; hide the outcasts; reveal not him that wanders.

4 Let my outcasts dwell with you, Moab; be you a covert to them from the face of the spoiler: for the extortioner is at an end, the spoiler ceases, the oppressors are consumed out of the land.

5 And in mercy shall the throne be established: and he shall sit upon it in truth in the tabernacle of David, judging, and seeking judgment, and hastening righteousness.

6 ¶ We have heard of the pride of Moab; *he is* very proud: *even* of his haughtiness, and his pride, and his wrath: *but* his lies *shall* not *be* so.

7 Therefore shall Moab howl for Moab, every one shall howl for the foundations of Kirhareseth shall you mourn; surely *they are* stricken.

8 For the fields of Heshbon languish, *and* the vine of Sibmah: the lords of the heathen have broken down the principal plants thereof, they have come *even* to Jazer, they wandered *through* the wilderness: her branches were stretched out, they have gone over the sea.

9 Therefore I will bewail with the weeping of Jazer the vine of Sibmah: I will water you with my tears, O Heshbon, and Elealeh: for the shouting for your summer fruits and for your harvest has fallen.

10 And gladness is taken away, and joy out of the plentiful field; and in the vineyards there shall be no singing, neither shall there be shouting: the treaders shall tread out no wine in *their* presses; I have made *their vintage* shouting to cease.

11 Therefore my bowels shall sound like a harp for Moab, and my inward parts for Kirharesh.

12 And it shall come to pass, when it is seen that Moab is weary on the high place, that he shall come to his sanctuary to pray; but he shall not prevail.

13 This *is* the word that Yahweh has spoken concerning Moab since that time.

14 But now Yahweh has spoken, saying, Within three years, as the years of a hireling, and the glory of Moab shall be dishonored, with all that great multitude; and the remnant *shall be* very small *and* feeble.

Isaiah 17

17:1 ¶ The burden of Damascus. Behold, Damascus is taken away from *being* a city, and it shall be a ruinous heap.
2 The cities of Aroer *are* forsaken: they shall be for flocks, which shall lie down, and none shall make *them* afraid.
3 The fortress also shall cease from Ephraim, and the kingdom from Damascus, and the remnant of Syria: they shall be as the glory of the children of Israel, says Yahweh of hosts.
4 And in that day it shall come to pass, *that* the glory of Jacob shall be made thin, and the fatness of his flesh shall become lean.
5 And it shall be as when the harvest man gathers the corn, and reaps the ears with his arm; and it shall be as he that gathers ears in the valley of Rephaim.
6 ¶ Yet gleaning grapes shall be left in it, as the shaking of an olive tree, two *or* three olives in the top of the uppermost bough, four *or* five in the outmost fruitful branches thereof, says Yahweh God of Israel.
7 At that day shall a man look to his Maker, and his eyes shall have respect to the Holy One of Israel.
8 And he shall not look to the altars, the work of his hands, neither shall *he* respect *that* which his fingers have made, either the groves, or the images.
9 ¶ In that day shall his strong cities be as a forsaken bough, and an uppermost branch, which they left because of the children of Israel: and there shall be desolation.
10 Because you have forgotten the God of your salvation, and have not been mindful of the rock of your strength, therefore shall you plant pleasant plants, and shall set it with strange slips:
11 In the day shall you make your plant to grow, and in the morning shall you make your seed to flourish: *but* the harvest *shall be* a heap in the day of grief and of desperate sorrow.
12 ¶ Woe to the multitude of many people, *which* make a noise like the noise of the seas; and to the rushing of nations, *that* make a rushing like the rushing of mighty waters!
13 The nations shall rush like the rushing of many waters: but *God* shall rebuke them, and they shall flee far off, and shall be chased as the chaff of the mountains before the wind, and like a rolling thing before the whirlwind.
14 And behold at evening trouble; *and* before the morning he *is* not. This *is* the portion of them that spoil us, and the lot of them that rob us.

Isaiah 18

18:1 ¶ Woe to the land shadowing with wings, which *is* beyond the rivers of Ethiopia:
2 That sends ambassadors by the sea, even in vessels of bulrushes upon the waters, *saying*, Go, you swift messengers, to a nation scattered and peeled, to a people terrible from their beginning till now; a nation meted out and trodden down, whose land the rivers have spoiled!
3 All you inhabitants of the world, and dwellers on the earth, see you, when he lifts up an ensign on the mountains; and when he blows a trumpet, hear you.
4 For so Yahweh said unto me, I will take my rest, and I will consider in my dwelling place like a clear heat upon herbs, *and* like a cloud of dew in the heat of harvest.
5 For before the harvest, when the bud is perfect, and the sour grape is ripening in the flower, he shall both cut off the sprigs with pruning hooks, and take away *and* cut down the branches.
6 They shall be left together to the fowls of the mountains, and to the beasts of the earth: and the fowls shall summer upon them, and all the beasts of the earth shall winter upon them.
7 In that time shall the present be brought unto Yahweh of hosts of a people scattered and peeled, and from a people terrible from their beginning hitherto; a nation meted out and trodden under foot, whose land the rivers have spoiled, to the place of the name of Yahweh of hosts, the mount Zion.

Isaiah 19

19:1 ¶ The burden of Egypt. Behold, Yahweh rides upon a swift cloud, and shall come into Egypt: and the idols of Egypt shall be moved at his presence, and the heart of Egypt shall melt in the midst of it.
2 And I will set the Egyptians against the Egyptians: and they shall fight every one against his brother, and every one against his neighbor; city against city, *and* kingdom against kingdom.
3 And the spirit of Egypt shall fail in the midst thereof; and I will destroy the counsel thereof: and they shall seek to the idols, and to the charmers, and to them that have familiar spirits, and to the wizards.
4 And the Egyptians will I give over into the hand of a cruel lord; and a fierce king shall rule over them, says the Lord, Yahweh of hosts.
5 And the waters shall fail from the sea, and the river shall be wasted and dried up.
6 And they shall turn the rivers far away; *and* the brooks of defense shall be emptied and dried up: the reeds and rushes shall wither.
7 The paper reeds by the brooks, by the mouth of the brooks, and every thing sown by the brooks, shall wither, be driven away, and be no *more*.
8 The fishers also shall mourn, and all they that cast angle into the brooks shall lament, and they that spread nets upon the waters shall languish.
9 Moreover they that work in fine flax, and they that weave networks, shall be confounded.
10 And they shall be broken in the purposes thereof, all that make wages *and* ponds for fish.
11 Surely the princes of Zoan *are* fools, the counsel of the wise counselors of Pharaoh has become brutish: how say you unto Pharaoh, I *am* the son of the wise, the son of ancient kings?

12 Where *are* they? where *are* your wise *men*? and let them tell you now, and let them know what Yahweh of hosts has purposed upon Egypt.

13 The princes of Zoan have become fools, the princes of Noph are deceived; they have also seduced Egypt, *even they that are* the stay of the tribes thereof.

14 Yahweh has mingled a perverse spirit in the midst thereof: and they have caused Egypt to err in every work thereof, as a drunken *man* staggers in his vomit.

15 Neither shall there be *any* work for Egypt, which the head or tail, branch or rush, may do.

16 In that day shall Egypt be like unto women: and it shall be afraid and fear because of the shaking of the hand of Yahweh of hosts, which he shakes over it.

17 And the land of Judah shall be a terror to Egypt, every one that makes mention thereof shall be afraid in himself, because of the counsel of Yahweh of hosts, which he has determined against it.

18 ¶ In that day shall five cities in the land of Egypt speak the language of Canaan, and swear to Yahweh of hosts; one shall be called, The city of destruction.

19 In that day shall there be an altar to Yahweh in the midst of the land of Egypt, and a pillar at the border thereof to Yahweh.

20 And it shall be for a sign and for a witness unto Yahweh of hosts in the land of Egypt: for they shall cry unto Yahweh because of the oppressors, and he shall send them a savior, and a great one, and he shall deliver them.

21 And Yahweh shall be known to Egypt, and the Egyptians shall know Yahweh in that day, and shall do sacrifice and oblation; yes, they shall vow a vow unto Yahweh, and perform *it*.

22 And Yahweh shall smite Egypt: he shall smite and heal *it*: and they shall return *even* to Yahweh, and he shall be entreated of them, and shall heal them.

23 In that day shall there be a highway out of Egypt to Assyria, and the Assyrian shall come into Egypt, and the Egyptian into Assyria, and the Egyptians shall serve with the Assyrians.

24 In that day shall Israel be the third with Egypt and with Assyria, *even* a blessing in the midst of the land:

25 Whom Yahweh of hosts shall bless, saying, Blessed *be* Egypt my people, and Assyria the work of my hands, and Israel my inheritance.

Isaiah 20

20:1 ¶ In the year that Tartan came to Ashdod, (when Sargon the king of Assyria sent him,) and fought against Ashdod, and took it;

2 At the same time spoke Yahweh by Isaiah the son of Amoz, saying, Go and loose the sackcloth from off your loins, and put off your shoe from your foot. And he did so, walking naked and barefoot.

3 And Yahweh said, Like as my servant Isaiah has walked naked and barefoot three years *for* a sign and wonder upon Egypt and upon Ethiopia;

4 So shall the king of Assyria lead away the Egyptians prisoners, and the Ethiopians captives, young and old, naked and barefoot, even with *their* buttocks uncovered, to the shame of Egypt.

5 And they shall be afraid and ashamed of Ethiopia their expectation, and of Egypt their glory.

6 And the inhabitant of this isle shall say in that day, Behold, such *is* our expectation, wherever we flee for help to be delivered from the king of Assyria: and how shall we escape?

Isaiah 21

21:1 ¶ The burden of the desert of the sea. As whirlwinds in the south pass through; *so* it comes from the desert, from a terrible land.

2 A grievous vision is declared unto me; the treacherous dealer deals treacherously, and the spoiler spoils. Go up, O Elam: besiege, O Media; all the sighing thereof have I made to cease.

3 Therefore are my loins filled with pain: pangs have taken hold upon me, as the pangs of a woman that labors: I was bowed down at the hearing *of it*; I was dismayed at the seeing *of it*.

4 My heart panted, fearfulness frightened me: the night of my pleasure has he turned into fear unto me.

5 Prepare the table, watch in the watchtower, eat, drink: arise, you princes, *and* anoint the shield.

6 For thus has the Lord said to me, Go, set a watchman, let him declare what he sees.

7 And he saw a chariot *with* a couple of horsemen, a chariot of donkeys, *and* a chariot of camels; and he listened diligently with much heed:

8 And he cried, A lion: My lord, I stand continually upon the watchtower in the daytime, and I have set in my ward whole nights:

9 And, behold, here comes a chariot of men, *with* a couple of horsemen. And he answered and said, Babylon is fallen, is fallen; and all the graven images of her gods he has broken unto the ground.

10 O my threshing, and the corn of my floor: that which I have heard of Yahweh of hosts, the God of Israel, have I declared unto you.

11 ¶ The burden of Dumah. He calls to me out of Seir, Watchman, what of the night? Watchman, what of the night?

12 The watchman said, The morning comes, and also the night: if you will inquire, inquire you: return, come.

13 ¶ The burden upon Arabia. In the forest in Arabia shall you lodge, O you traveling companies of Dedanim.

14 The inhabitants of the land of Tema brought water to him that was thirsty, they met with their bread him that fled.

15 For they fled from the swords, from the drawn sword, and from the bent bow, and from the grievousness of war.

16 For thus has the Lord said to me, Within a year, according to the years of a hireling, and all the glory of Kedar shall fail:

17 And the residue of the number of archers, the mighty men of the children of Kedar, shall be diminished: for Yahweh God of Israel has spoken *it*.

Isaiah 22

22:1 ¶ The burden of the valley of vision. What ails you now, that you are wholly gone up to the housetops?
2 You that are full of noise, a tumultuous city, a joyous city: your slain *men are* not slain with the sword, nor dead in battle.
3 All your rulers have fled together, they are bound by the archers: all that are found in you are bound together, *which* have fled from afar.
4 Therefore said I, Look away from me; I will weep bitterly, labor not to comfort me, because of the spoiling of the daughter of my people.
5 For *it is* a day of trouble, and of treading down, and of perplexity by the Lord Yahweh of hosts in the valley of vision, breaking down the walls, and of crying to the mountains.
6 And Elam bore the quiver with chariots of men *and* horsemen, and Kir uncovered the shield.
7 And it shall come to pass, *that* your choicest valleys shall be full of chariots, and the horsemen shall set themselves in array at the gate.
8 ¶ And he discovered the covering of Judah, and you did look in that day to the armor of the house of the forest.
9 You have seen also the breaches of the city of David, that they are many: and you gathered together the waters of the lower pool.
10 And you have numbered the houses of Jerusalem, and the houses have you broken down to fortify the wall.
11 You made also a ditch between the two walls for the water of the old pool: but you have not looked unto the maker thereof, neither had respect unto him that fashioned it long ago.
12 And in that day did the Lord Yahweh of hosts call to weeping, and to mourning, and to baldness, and to girding with sackcloth:
13 And behold joy and gladness, slaying oxen, and killing sheep, eating flesh, and drinking wine: let us eat and drink; for tomorrow we shall die.
14 And it was revealed in my ears by Yahweh of hosts, Surely this iniquity shall not be purged from you till you die, says the Lord Yahweh of hosts.
15 ¶ Thus says the Lord Yahweh of hosts, Go, get you unto this treasurer, *even* to Shebna, which *is* over the house, *and say*,
16 What have you here? and whom have you here, that you have hewed you out a sepulcher here, *as* he that hews him out a sepulcher on high, *and* that carved a habitation for himself in a rock?
17 Behold, Yahweh will carry you away with a mighty captivity, and will surely cover you.
18 He will surely violently turn and toss you *like* a ball into a large country: there shall you die, and there the chariots of your glory *shall be* the shame of your lord's house.
19 And I will drive you from your station, and from your state shall he pull you down.
20 And it shall come to pass in that day, that I will call my servant Eliakim the son of Hilkiah:
21 And I will clothe him with your robe, and strengthen him with your girdle, and I will commit your government into his hand: and he shall be a father to the inhabitants of Jerusalem, and to the house of Judah.
22 And the key of the house of David will I lay upon his shoulder; so he shall open, and none shall shut; and he shall shut, and none shall open.
23 And I will fasten him *as* a nail in a sure place; and he shall be for a glorious throne to his father's house.
24 And they shall hang upon him all the glory of his father's house, the offspring and the issue, all vessels of small quantity, from the vessels of cups, even to all the vessels of bottles.
25 In that day, says Yahweh of hosts, shall the nail that is fastened in the sure place be removed, and be cut down, and fall; and the burden that *was* upon it shall be cut off: for Yahweh has spoken *it*.

Isaiah 23

23:1 ¶ The burden of Tyre. Howl, you ships of Tarshish; for it is laid waste, so that there is no house, no entering in: from the land of Chittim it is revealed to them.
2 Be still, you inhabitants of the isle; you whom the merchants of Zidon, that pass over the sea, have replenished.
3 And by great waters the seed of Sihor, the harvest of the river, *is* her revenue; and she is a mart of nations.
4 Be you ashamed, O Zidon: for the sea has spoken, *even* the strength of the sea, saying, I labor not, nor bring forth children, neither do I nourish up young men, *nor* bring up virgins.
5 As at the report concerning Egypt, *so* shall they be greatly pained at the report of Tyre.
6 Pass you over to Tarshish; howl, you inhabitants of the isle.
7 *Is* this your joyous *city*, whose antiquity *is* of ancient days? her own feet shall carry her afar off to dwell.
8 Who has taken this counsel against Tyre, the crowning *city*, whose merchants *are* princes, whose traders *are* the honorable of the earth?
9 Yahweh of hosts has purposed it, to stain the pride of all glory, *and* to bring into contempt all the honorable of the earth.
10 Pass through your land as a river, O daughter of Tarshish: *there is* no more strength.
11 He stretched out his hand over the sea, he shook the kingdoms: Yahweh has given a commandment against the merchant *city*, to destroy the strong holds thereof.
12 And he said, You shall no more rejoice, O you oppressed virgin, daughter of Zidon: arise, pass over to Chittim; there also shall you have no rest.
13 Behold the land of the Chaldeans; this people was not, *till* the Assyrian founded it for them that dwell in the

wilderness: they set up the towers thereof, they raised up the palaces thereof; *and* he brought it to ruin.

14 Howl, you ships of Tarshish: for your strength is laid waste.

15 ¶ And it shall come to pass in that day, that Tyre shall be forgotten seventy years, according to the days of one king: after the end of seventy years shall Tyre sing as a harlot.

16 Take a harp, go about the city, you harlot that has been forgotten; make sweet melody, sing many songs, that you may be remembered.

17 And it shall come to pass after the end of seventy years, that Yahweh will visit Tyre, and she shall turn to her hire, and shall commit fornication with all the kingdoms of the world upon the face of the earth.

18 And her merchandise and her hire shall be holiness to Yahweh: it shall not be treasured nor laid up; for her merchandise shall be for them that dwell before Yahweh, to eat sufficiently, and for durable clothing.

Isaiah 24

24:1 ¶ Behold, Yahweh makes the earth empty, and makes it waste, and turns it upside down, and scatters abroad the inhabitants thereof.

2 And it shall be, as with the people, so with the priest; as with the servant, so with his master; as with the maid, so with her mistress; as with the buyer, so with the seller; as with the lender, so with the borrower; as with the taker of usury, so with the giver of usury to him.

3 The land shall be utterly emptied, and utterly spoiled: for Yahweh has spoken this word.

4 The earth mourns *and* fades away, the world languishes *and* fades away, the haughty people of the earth do languish.

5 The earth also is defiled under the inhabitants thereof; because they have transgressed the laws, changed the ordinance, broken the everlasting covenant.

6 Therefore has the curse devoured the earth, and they that dwell therein are desolate: therefore the inhabitants of the earth are burned, and few men left.

7 The new wine mourns, the vine languishes, all the merry hearted do sigh.

8 The joy of tambourines ceases, the noise of them that rejoice ends, the joy of the harp ceases.

9 They shall not drink wine with a song; strong drink shall be bitter to them that drink it.

10 The city of confusion is broken down: every house is shut up, that no man may come in.

11 *There is* a crying for wine in the streets; all joy is darkened, the rejoicing of the land is gone.

12 In the city is left desolation, and the gate is smitten with destruction.

13 ¶ When thus it shall be in the midst of the land among the people, *there shall be* as the shaking of an olive tree, *and* as the gleaning grapes when the vintage is done.

14 They shall lift up their voice, they shall sing for the majesty of Yahweh, they shall cry aloud from the sea.

15 Therefore glorify you Yahweh in the fires, *even* the name of Yahweh God of Israel in the isles of the sea.

16 ¶ From the utmost part of the earth have we heard songs, *even* glory to the righteous. But I said, My leanness, my leanness, woe unto me! the treacherous dealers have dealt treacherously; yes, the treacherous dealers have dealt very treacherously.

17 Fear, and the pit, and the snare, *are* upon you, O inhabitant of the earth.

18 And it shall come to pass, *that* he who flees from the noise of the fear shall fall into the pit; and he that comes up out of the midst of the pit shall be taken in the snare: for the windows from on high are open, and the foundations of the earth do shake.

19 The earth is utterly broken down, the earth is clean dissolved, the earth is moved exceedingly

20 The earth shall reel to and fro like a drunkard, and shall be removed like a cottage; and the transgression thereof shall be heavy upon it; and it shall fall, and not rise again.

21 And it shall come to pass in that day, *that* Yahweh shall punish the host of the high ones *that are* on high, and the kings of the earth upon the earth.

22 And they shall be gathered together, *as* prisoners are gathered in the pit, and shall be shut up in the prison, and after many days shall they be visited.

23 Then the moon shall be confounded, and the sun ashamed, when Yahweh of hosts shall reign in mount Zion, and in Jerusalem, and before his ancients gloriously.

Isaiah 25

25:1 ¶ O Yahweh, you *are* my God; I will exalt you, I will praise your name; for you have done wonderful *things;* *your* counsels of old *are* faithfulness *and* truth.

2 For you have made of a city a heap; *of* a defensed city a ruin: a palace of strangers to be no city; it shall never be built.

3 Therefore shall the strong people glorify you, the city of the terrible nations shall fear you.

4 For you have been a strength to the poor, a strength to the needy in his distress, a refuge from the storm, a shadow from the heat, when the blast of the terrible ones *is* as a storm *against* the wall.

5 You shall bring down the noise of strangers, as the heat in a dry place; *even* the heat with the shadow of a cloud: the branch of the terrible ones shall be brought low.

6 ¶ And in this mountain shall Yahweh of hosts make unto all people a feast of fat things, a feast of wines on the lees, of fat things full of marrow, of wines on the lees well refined.

7 And he will destroy in this mountain the face of the covering cast over all people, and the veil that is spread over all nations.

8 He will swallow up death in victory; and the Lord Yahweh will wipe away tears from off all faces; and the rebuke of his people shall he take away from off all the earth: for Yahweh has spoken *it*.

9 ¶ And it shall be said in that day, Lo, this *is* our God; we have waited for him, and he will save us: this *is* Yahweh; we have waited for him, we will be glad and rejoice in his salvation.
10 For in this mountain shall the hand of Yahweh rest, and Moab shall be trodden down under him, even as straw is trodden down for the dunghill.
11 And he shall spread forth his hands in the midst of them, as he that swims spreads forth *his hands* to swim: and he shall bring down their pride together with the spoils of their hands.
12 And the fortress of the high fort of your walls shall he bring down, lay low, *and* bring to the ground, *even* to the dust.

Isaiah 26

26:1 ¶ In that day shall this song be sung in the land of Judah; We have a strong city; salvation will *God* appoint *for* walls and bulwarks.
2 Open you the gates, that the righteous nation which keeps the truth may enter in.
3 You will keep *him* in perfect peace, *whose* mind *is* stayed *on you*: because he trusts in you.
4 Trust you in Yahweh forever: for in Yah Yahweh *is* everlasting strength:
5 ¶ For he brings down them that dwell on high; the lofty city, he lays it low; he lays it low, *even* to the ground; he brings it *even* to the dust.
6 The foot shall tread it down, *even* the feet of the poor, *and* the steps of the needy.
7 The way of the just *is* uprightness: you, most upright, do weigh the path of the just.
8 Yes, in the way of your judgments, O Yahweh, have we waited for you; the desire of *our* soul *is* to your name, and to the remembrance of you.
9 With my soul have I desired you in the night; yes, with my spirit within me will I seek you earnestly: for when your judgments *are* in the earth, the inhabitants of the world will learn righteousness.
10 Let favor be shown to the wicked, *yet* will he not learn righteousness: in the land of uprightness will he deal unjustly, and will not behold the majesty of Yahweh.
11 Yahweh, *when* your hand is lifted up, they will not see: *but* they shall see, and be ashamed for *their* envy of the people; yes, the fire of your enemies shall devour them.
12 ¶ Yahweh, you will ordain peace for us: for you also have worked all our works in us.
13 O Yahweh our God, *other* lords besides you have had dominion over us: *but* by you only will we make mention of your name.
14 *They are* dead, they shall not live; *they are* deceased, they shall not rise: therefore have you visited and destroyed them, and made all their memory to perish.
15 You have increased the nation, O Yahweh, you have increased the nation: you are glorified: you had removed *it* far *to* all the ends of the earth.
16 Yahweh, in trouble have they visited you, they poured out a prayer *when* your chastening *was* upon them.
17 Like as a woman with child, *that* draws near the time of her delivery, is in pain, *and* cries out in her pangs; so have we been in your sight, O Yahweh.
18 We have been with child, we have been in pain, we have as it were brought forth wind; we have not worked any deliverance in the earth; neither have the inhabitants of the world fallen.
19 Your dead *men* shall live, *together with* my dead body shall they arise. Awake and sing, you that dwell in dust: for your dew *is as* the dew of herbs, and the earth shall cast out the dead.
20 ¶ Come, my people, enter you into your chambers, and shut your doors about you: hide yourself as it were for a little moment, until the indignation is over.
21 For, behold, Yahweh comes out of his place to punish the inhabitants of the earth for their iniquity: the earth also shall disclose her blood, and shall no more cover her slain.

Isaiah 27

27:1 ¶ In that day Yahweh with his severe and great and strong sword shall punish leviathan the piercing serpent, even leviathan that crooked serpent; and he shall slay the dragon that *is* in the sea.
2 In that day sing you unto her, A vineyard of red wine.
3 I Yahweh do keep it; I will water it every moment: lest *any* hurt it, I will keep it night and day.
4 Fury *is* not in me: who would set the briers *and* thorns against me in battle? I would go through them, I would burn them together.
5 Or let him take hold of my strength, *that* he may make peace with me; *and* he shall make peace with me.
6 He shall cause them that come of Jacob to take root: Israel shall blossom and bud, and fill the face of the world with fruit.
7 ¶ Has he smitten him, as he smote those that smote him? *or* is he slain according to the slaughter of them that are slain by him?
8 In measure, when it shoots forth, you will debate with it: he stays his rough wind in the day of the east wind.
9 By this therefore shall the iniquity of Jacob be purged; and this *is* all the fruit to take away his sin; when he makes all the stones of the altar as chalk that are beaten in pieces, the groves and images shall not stand up.
10 Yet the defensed city *shall be* desolate, *and* the habitation forsaken, and left like a wilderness: there shall the calf feed, and there shall he lie down, and consume the branches thereof.
11 When the boughs thereof are withered, they shall be broken off: the women come, *and* set them on fire: for it *is* a people of no understanding: therefore he that made them will not have mercy on them, and he that formed them will show them no favor.
12 And it shall come to pass in that day, *that* Yahweh shall thresh from the channel of the river unto the stream

of Egypt, and you shall be gathered one by one, O you children of Israel.

13 And it shall come to pass in that day, *that* the great trumpet shall be blown, and they shall come which were ready to perish in the land of Assyria, and the outcasts in the land of Egypt, and shall worship Yahweh in the holy mount at Jerusalem.

Isaiah 28

28:1 ¶ Woe to the crown of pride, to the drunkards of Ephraim, whose glorious beauty *is* a fading flower, which *are* on the head of the fat valleys of them that are overcome with wine!

2 Behold, the Lord has a mighty and strong one, *which* as a tempest of hail *and* a destroying storm, as a flood of mighty waters overflowing, shall cast down to the earth with the hand.

3 The crown of pride, the drunkards of Ephraim, shall be trodden under feet:

4 And the glorious beauty, which *is* on the head of the fat valley, shall be a fading flower, *and* as the hasty fruit before the summer; which *when* he that looks upon it sees, while it is yet in his hand he eats it up.

5 In that day shall Yahweh of hosts be for a crown of glory, and for a diadem of beauty, unto the residue of his people.

6 And for a spirit of judgment to him that sits in judgment, and for strength to them that turn the battle to the gate

7 But they also have erred through wine, and through strong drink are out of the way; the priest and the prophet have erred through strong drink, they are swallowed up of wine, they are out of the way through strong drink; they err in vision, they stumble *in* judgment.

8 For all tables are full of vomit *and* filthiness, *so that there is* no place *clean*.

9 ¶ Whom shall he teach knowledge? and whom shall he make to understand doctrine? *them that are* weaned from the milk, *and* drawn from the breasts.

10 For precept *must be* upon precept, precept upon precept; line upon line, line upon line; here a little, *and* there a little:

11 For with stammering lips and another tongue will he speak to this people.

12 To whom he said, This *is* the rest *with which* you may cause the weary to rest; and this *is* the refreshing: yet they would not hear.

13 But the word of Yahweh was unto them precept upon precept, precept upon precept; line upon line, line upon line; here a little, *and* there a little; that they might go, and fall backward, and be broken, and snared, and taken.

14 ¶ Therefore hear the word of Yahweh, you scornful men, that rule this people which *is* in Jerusalem.

15 Because you have said, We have made a covenant with death, and with hell are we at agreement; when the overflowing scourge shall pass through, it shall not come to us: for we have made lies our refuge, and under falsehood have we hidden ourselves:

16 Therefore thus says the Lord Yahweh, Behold, I lay in Zion for a foundation a stone, a tried stone, a precious corner *stone*, a sure foundation: he that believes shall not make haste.

17 Judgment also will I lay to the line, and righteousness to the plummet: and the hail shall sweep away the refuge of lies, and the waters shall overflow the hiding place.

18 And your covenant with death shall be annulled, and your agreement with hell shall not stand; when the overflowing scourge shall pass through, then you shall be trodden down by it.

19 From the time that it goes forth it shall take you: for morning by morning shall it pass over, by day and by night: and it shall be a horror only *to* understand the report.

20 For the bed is shorter than that *a man* can stretch himself *on it*: and the covering narrower than that he can wrap himself *in it*.

21 For Yahweh shall rise up as *in* mount Perazim, he shall be angry as *in* the valley of Gibeon, that he may do his work, his strange work; and bring to pass his act, his strange act.

22 Now therefore be you not mockers, lest your bands be made strong: for I have heard from the Lord Yahweh of hosts a consumption, even determined upon the whole earth.

23 ¶ Give you ear, and hear my voice; listen, and hear my speech.

24 Does the plowman plow all day to sow? does he open and break the clods of his ground?

25 When he has made plain the face thereof, does he not cast abroad the black cummin, and scatter the cummin, and cast in the principal wheat and the appointed barley and the rye in their place?

26 For his God does instruct him to discretion, *and* does teach him.

27 For the black cummin are not threshed with a threshing instrument, neither is a cart wheel turned about upon the cummin; but the black cummin are beaten out with a staff, and the cummin with a rod.

28 Bread *corn* is bruised; because he will not ever be threshing it, nor break *it with* the wheel of his cart, nor bruise it *with* his horsemen.

29 This also comes forth from Yahweh of hosts, *which* is wonderful in counsel, *and* excellent in working.

Isaiah 29

29:1 ¶ Woe to Ariel, to Ariel, the city *where* David dwelt! add you year to year; let them kill sacrifices.

2 Yet I will distress Ariel, and there shall be heaviness and sorrow: and it shall be unto me as Ariel.

3 And I will camp against you round about, and will lay siege against you with a mount, and I will raise forts against you.

4 And you shall be brought down, *and* shall speak out of the ground, and your speech shall be low out of the dust, and your voice shall be, as of one that has a familiar spirit, out of the ground, and your speech shall whisper out of the dust.

Isaiah 29

5 Moreover the multitude of your strangers shall be like small dust, and the multitude of the terrible ones *shall be* as chaff that passes away: yes, it shall be at an instant suddenly.

6 You shall be visited by Yahweh of hosts with thunder, and with earthquake, and great noise, with storm and tempest, and the flame of devouring fire.

7 And the multitude of all the nations that fight against Ariel, even all that fight against her and her stronghold, and that distress her, shall be as a dream of a night vision.

8 It shall even be as when a hungry *man* dreams, and, behold, he eats; but he wakes, and his soul is empty: or as when a thirsty man dreams, and, behold, he drinks; but he wakes, and, behold, *he is* faint, and his soul has appetite: so shall the multitude of all the nations be, that fight against mount Zion.

9 ¶ Stay yourselves, and wonder; cry you out, and cry: they are drunken, but not with wine; they stagger, but not with strong drink.

10 For Yahweh has poured out upon you the spirit of deep sleep, and has closed your eyes: the prophets and your rulers, the seers has he covered.

11 And the vision of all has become unto you as the words of a book that is sealed, which *men* deliver to one that is learned, saying, Read this, I pray you: and he says, I cannot; for it *is* sealed:

12 And the book is delivered to him that is not learned, saying, Read this, I pray you: and he says, I am not learned.

13 Therefore the Lord said, Forasmuch as this people draw near *me* with their mouth, and with their lips do honor me, but have removed their heart far from me, and their fear toward me is taught by the precept of men:

14 Therefore, behold, I will proceed to do a marvelous work among this people, *even* a marvelous work and a wonder: for the wisdom of their wise *men* shall perish, and the understanding of their prudent *men* shall be hidden.

15 Woe unto them that seek deep to hide their counsel from Yahweh, and their works are in the dark, and they say, Who sees us? and who knows us?

16 Surely your turning of things upside down shall be esteemed as the potter's clay: for shall the work say of him that made it, He made me not? or shall the thing framed say of him that framed it, He had no understanding?

17 ¶ *Is* it not yet a very little while, and Lebanon shall be turned into a fruitful field, and the fruitful field shall be esteemed as a forest?

18 And in that day shall the deaf hear the words of the book, and the eyes of the blind shall see out of obscurity, and out of darkness.

19 The meek also shall increase *their* joy in Yahweh, and the poor among men shall rejoice in the Holy One of Israel.

20 For the terrible one is brought to nothing, and the scorner is consumed, and all that watch for iniquity are cut off:

21 That make a man an offender for a word, and lay a snare for him that reproves in the gate, and turn aside the just for a thing of nothing.

22 Therefore thus says Yahweh, who redeemed Abraham, concerning the house of Jacob, Jacob shall not now be ashamed, neither shall his face now grow pale.

23 But when he sees his children, the work of my hands, in the midst of him, they shall sanctify my name, and sanctify the Holy One of Jacob, and shall fear the God of Israel.

24 They also that erred in spirit shall come to understanding, and they that murmured shall learn doctrine.

Isaiah 30

30:1 ¶ Woe to the rebellious children, says Yahweh, that take counsel, but not of me; and that cover with a covering, but not of my spirit, that they may add sin to sin:

2 That walk to go down into Egypt, and have not asked at my mouth; to strengthen themselves in the strength of Pharaoh, and to trust in the shadow of Egypt!

3 Therefore shall the strength of Pharaoh be your shame, and the trust in the shadow of Egypt *your* confusion.

4 For his princes were at Zoan, and his ambassadors came to Hanes.

5 They were all ashamed of a people *that* could not profit them, nor be a help nor profit, but a shame, and also a reproach.

6 The burden of the beasts of the south: into the land of trouble and anguish, from where *comes* the young and old lion, the viper and fiery flying serpent, they will carry their riches upon the shoulders of young donkeys, and their treasures upon the humps of camels, to a people *that* shall not profit *them*.

7 For the Egyptians shall help in vain, and to no purpose: therefore have I cried concerning this, Their strength *is* to sit still.

8 ¶ Now go, write it before them in a table, and note it in a book, that it may be for the time to come forever and ever:

9 That this *is* a rebellious people, lying children, children *that* will not hear the law of Yahweh:

10 Which say to the seers, See not; and to the prophets, Prophesy not unto us right things, speak unto us smooth things, prophesy deceits:

11 Get you out of the way, turn aside out of the path, cause the Holy One of Israel to cease from before us.

12 Therefore thus says the Holy One of Israel, Because you despise this word, and trust in oppression and perverseness, and rely thereon:

13 Therefore this iniquity shall be to you as a breach ready to fall, swelling out in a high wall, whose breaking comes suddenly at an instant.

14 And he shall break it as the breaking of the potters' vessel that is broken in pieces; he shall not spare: so that

there shall not be found in the bursting of it an earthen vessel to take fire from the hearth, or to take water *therewith* out of the pit.

15 For thus says the Lord Yahweh, the Holy One of Israel; In returning and rest shall you be saved; in quietness and in confidence shall be your strength: and you would not.

16 But you said, No; for we will flee upon horses; therefore shall you flee: and, We will ride upon the swift; therefore shall they that pursue you be swift.

17 One thousand *shall flee* at the rebuke of one; at the rebuke of five shall you flee: till you are left as a beacon upon the top of a mountain, and as an ensign on a hill

18 ¶ And therefore will Yahweh wait, that he may be gracious unto you, and therefore will he be exalted, that he may have mercy upon you: for Yahweh *is* a God of judgment: blessed *are* all they that wait for him.

19 For the people shall dwell in Zion at Jerusalem: you shall weep no more: he will be very gracious unto you at the voice of your cry; when he shall hear it, he will answer you.

20 And *though* the Lord gives you the bread of adversity, and the water of affliction, yet shall not your teachers be removed into a corner any more, but your eyes shall see your teachers:

21 And your ears shall hear a word behind you, saying, This *is* the way, walk you in it, when you turn to the right hand, and when you turn to the left.

22 You shall defile also the covering of your graven images of silver, and the ornament of your molten images of gold: you shall cast them away as a menstruous cloth; you shall say to them, Get you away.

23 Then shall he give the rain of your seed, that you shall sow the ground therewith; and bread of the increase of the earth, and it shall be fat and plenteous: in that day shall your cattle feed in large pastures.

24 The oxen likewise and the young donkeys that till the ground shall eat clean feed, which has been winnowed with the shovel and with the fan.

25 And there shall be upon every high mountain, and upon every high hill, rivers *and* streams of waters in the day of the great slaughter, when the towers fall.

26 Moreover the light of the moon shall be as the light of the sun, and the light of the sun shall be sevenfold, as the light of seven days, in the day that Yahweh binds up the breach of his people, and heals the stroke of their wound.

27 ¶ Behold, the name of Yahweh comes from afar, burning *with* his anger, and the burden *thereof is* heavy: his lips are full of indignation, and his tongue as a devouring fire:

28 And his breath, as an overflowing stream, shall reach to the midst of the neck, to sift the nations with the sieve of vanity: and *there shall be* a bridle in the jaws of the people, causing *them* to err.

29 You shall have a song, as in the night *when* a holy feast is kept; and gladness of heart, as when one goes with a pipe to come into the mountain of Yahweh, to the mighty One of Israel.

30 And Yahweh shall cause his glorious voice to be heard, and shall show the descent of his arm, with the indignation of *his* anger, and *with* the flame of a devouring fire, *with* scattering, and tempest, and hailstones.

31 For through the voice of Yahweh shall the Assyrian be beaten down, *which* smote with a rod.

32 And *in* every place where the grounded staff shall pass, which Yahweh shall lay upon him, *it* shall be with tambourines and harps: and in battles of shaking will he fight with it.

33 For Tophet *is* ordained of old; yes, for the king it is prepared; he has made *it* deep *and* large: the pile thereof *is* fire and much wood; the breath of Yahweh, like a stream of brimstone, does kindle it.

Isaiah 31

31:1 ¶ Woe to them that go down to Egypt for help; and rely on horses, and trust in chariots, because *they are* many; and in horsemen, because they are very strong; but they look not to the Holy One of Israel, neither seek Yahweh!

2 Yet he also *is* wise, and will bring evil, and will not call back his words: but will arise against the house of the evildoers, and against the help of them that work iniquity.

3 Now the Egyptians *are* men, and not God; and their horses flesh, and not spirit. When Yahweh shall stretch out his hand, both he that helps shall fall, and he that is helped shall fall down, and they all shall fail together.

4 For thus has Yahweh spoken unto me, Like as the lion and the young lion roaring on his prey, when a multitude of shepherds is called forth against him, *he* will not be afraid of their voice, nor abase himself for the noise of them: so shall Yahweh of hosts come down to fight for mount Zion, and for the hill thereof.

5 As birds flying, so will Yahweh of hosts defend Jerusalem; defending also he will deliver *it; and* passing over he will preserve it.

6 ¶ Turn you unto *him from* whom the children of Israel have deeply revolted.

7 For in that day every man shall cast away his idols of silver, and his idols of gold, which your own hands have made unto you *for* a sin.

8 Then shall the Assyrian fall with the sword, not of a mighty man; and the sword, not of a mean man, shall devour him: but he shall flee from the sword, and his young men shall be forced laborers.

9 And he shall pass over to his strong hold for fear, and his princes shall be afraid of the ensign, says Yahweh, whose fire *is* in Zion, and his furnace in Jerusalem.

Isaiah 32

32:1 ¶ Behold, a king shall reign in righteousness, and princes shall rule in judgment.

2 And a man shall be as a hiding place from the wind, and a covert from the tempest; as rivers of water in a dry place, as the shadow of a great rock in a weary land.

Isaiah 32

3 And the eyes of them that see shall not be dim, and the ears of them that hear shall listen.

4 The heart also of the rash shall understand knowledge, and the tongue of the stammerers shall be ready to speak plainly.

5 The vile person shall be no more called liberal, nor the scoundrel said *to be* bountiful.

6 For the vile person will speak vilely, and his heart will work iniquity, to practice hypocrisy, and to utter error against Yahweh, to make empty the soul of the hungry, and he will cause the drink of the thirsty to fail.

7 The instruments also of the scoundrel *are* evil: he devises wicked devices to destroy the poor with lying words, even when the needy speaks right.

8 But the liberal devises liberal things; and by liberal things shall he stand.

9 ¶ Rise up, you women that are at ease; hear my voice, you careless daughters; give ear unto my speech.

10 Many days and years shall you be troubled, you careless women: for the vintage shall fail, the gathering shall not come.

11 Tremble, you women that are at ease; be troubled, you careless ones: strip you, and make you bear, and gird *sackcloth* upon *your* loins.

12 They shall lament for the breasts, for the pleasant fields, for the fruitful vine.

13 Upon the land of my people shall come up thorns *and* briers; yes, upon all the houses of joy *in* the joyous city:

14 Because the palaces shall be forsaken; the multitude of the city shall be left; the forts and towers shall be for dens forever, a joy of wild donkeys, a pasture of flocks;

15 Until the spirit is poured upon us from on high, and the wilderness is a fruitful field, and the fruitful field is counted for a forest.

16 Then judgment shall dwell in the wilderness, and righteousness remain in the fruitful field.

17 And the work of righteousness shall be peace; and the effect of righteousness quietness and assurance forever.

18 And my people shall dwell in a peaceable habitation, and in sure dwellings, and in quiet resting places;

19 When it shall hail, coming down on the forest; and the city shall be low in a low place.

20 Blessed *are* you that sow beside all waters, that send forth *there* the feet of the ox and the donkey.

Isaiah 33

33:1 ¶ Woe to you that spoil, and you *were* not spoiled; and deal treacherously, and they dealt not treacherously with you! when you shall cease to spoil, you shall be spoiled; *and* when you shall make an end to deal treacherously, they shall deal treacherously with you.

2 O Yahweh, be gracious unto us; we have waited for you: be you their arm every morning, our salvation also in the time of trouble.

3 At the noise of the tumult the people fled; at the lifting up of yourself the nations were scattered.

4 And your spoil shall be gathered *like* the gathering of the caterpillar: as the running to and fro of locusts shall he run upon them.

5 Yahweh is exalted; for he dwells on high: he has filled Zion with judgment and righteousness.

6 And wisdom and knowledge shall be the stability of your times, *and* strength of salvation: the fear of Yahweh *is* his treasure.

7 Behold, their valiant ones shall cry outside: the ambassadors of peace shall weep bitterly.

8 The highways lie waste, the wayfaring man ceases: he has broken the covenant, he has despised the cities, he regards no man.

9 The earth mourns *and* languishes: Lebanon is ashamed *and* hewn down: Sharon is like a wilderness; and Bashan and Carmel shake off *their fruits*.

10 Now will I arise, says Yahweh; now will I be exalted; now will I lift up myself.

11 You shall conceive chaff, you shall bring forth stubble: your breath, *as* fire, shall devour you.

12 And the people shall be *as* the burnings of lime: *as* thorns cut up shall they be burned in the fire.

13 ¶ Hear, you *that are* far off, what I have done; and, you *that are* near, acknowledge my might.

14 The sinners in Zion are afraid; fearfulness has surprised the hypocrites. Who among us shall dwell with the devouring fire? who among us shall dwell with everlasting burnings?

15 He that walks righteously, and speaks uprightly; he that despises the gain of oppressions, that shakes his hands from holding of bribes, that stops his ears from hearing of blood, and shuts his eyes from seeing evil;

16 He shall dwell on high: his place of defense *shall be* the strongholds of rocks: bread shall be given him; his waters *shall be* sure.

17 Your eyes shall see the king in his beauty: they shall behold the land that is very far off.

18 Your heart shall meditate terror. Where *is* the scribe? where *is* the receiver? where *is* he that counted the towers?

19 You shall not see a fierce people, a people of a deeper speech than you can perceive; of a stammering tongue, *that you can* not understand.

20 Look upon Zion, the city of our solemnities: your eyes shall see Jerusalem a quiet habitation, a tabernacle *that* shall not be taken down; not one of the stakes thereof shall ever be removed, neither shall any of the cords thereof be broken.

21 But there the glorious Yahweh *will be* unto us a place of broad rivers *and* streams; wherein shall go no galley with oars, neither shall gallant ships pass thereby.

22 For Yahweh *is* our judge, Yahweh *is* our lawgiver, Yahweh *is* our king; he will save us.

23 Your tackle ropes are loosed; they could not well strengthen their mast, they could not spread the sail: then is the prey of a great spoil divided; the lame take the prey.

24 And the inhabitant shall not say, I am sick: the people that dwell therein *shall be* forgiven *their* iniquity.

Isaiah 34

34:1 ¶ Come near, you nations, to hear; and listen, you people: let the earth hear, and all that is therein; the world, and all things that come forth from it.
2 For the indignation of Yahweh *is* upon all nations, and *his* fury upon all their armies: he has utterly destroyed them, he has delivered them to the slaughter.
3 Their slain also shall be cast out, and their stink shall come up out of their carcasses, and the mountains shall be melted with their blood.
4 And all the host of heaven shall be dissolved, and the heavens shall be rolled together as a scroll: and all their host shall fall down, as the leaf falls off from the vine, and as a falling *fig* from the fig tree.
5 For my sword shall be bathed in heaven: behold, it shall come down upon Idumea, and upon the people of my curse, to judgment.
6 The sword of Yahweh is filled with blood, it is made fat with fatness, *and* with the blood of lambs and goats, with the fat of the kidneys of rams: for Yahweh has a sacrifice in Bozrah, and a great slaughter in the land of Idumea.
7 And the unicorns shall come down with them, and the bullocks with the bulls; and their land shall be soaked with blood, and their dust made fat with fatness.
8 For *it is* the day of Yahweh's vengeance, *and* the year of recompenses for the controversy of Zion.
9 ¶ And the streams thereof shall be turned into pitch, and the dust thereof into brimstone, and the land thereof shall become burning pitch.
10 It shall not be quenched night nor day; the smoke thereof shall go up forever: from generation to generation it shall lie waste; none shall pass through it forever and ever.
11 But the cormorant and the bittern shall possess it; the owl also and the raven shall dwell in it: and he shall stretch out upon it the line of confusion, and the stones of emptiness.
12 They shall call the nobles thereof to the kingdom, but none *shall be* there, and all her princes shall be nothing.
13 And thorns shall come up in her palaces, nettles and brambles in the fortresses thereof: and it shall be a habitation of dragons, *and* a court for owls.
14 The wild beasts of the desert shall also meet with the wild beasts of the island, and the satyr shall cry to his fellow; Lilith also shall rest there, and find for herself a place of rest.
15 There shall the great owl make her nest, and lay, and hatch, and gather under her shadow: there shall the vultures also be gathered, every one with her mate.
16 Seek you out of the book of Yahweh, and read: no one of these shall fail, none shall want her mate: for my mouth it has commanded, and his spirit it has gathered them.
17 And he has cast the lot for them, and his hand has divided it to them by line: they shall possess it forever, from generation to generation shall they dwell therein.

Isaiah 35

35:1 ¶ The wilderness and the solitary place shall be glad for them; and the desert shall rejoice, and blossom as the rose.
2 It shall blossom abundantly, and rejoice even with joy and singing: the glory of Lebanon shall be given unto it, the excellency of Carmel and Sharon, they shall see the glory of Yahweh, *and* the excellency of our God.
3 Strengthen you the weak hands, and confirm the feeble knees.
4 Say to them *that are* of a fearful heart, Be strong, fear not: behold, your God will come *with* vengeance, *even* God *with* a recompense; he will come and save you.
5 ¶ Then the eyes of the blind shall be opened, and the ears of the deaf shall be unstopped.
6 Then shall the lame *man* leap as a hart, and the tongue of the dumb sing: for in the wilderness shall waters break out, and streams in the desert.
7 And the parched ground shall become a pool, and the thirsty land springs of water: in the habitation of dragons, where each lay, *shall be* grass with reeds and rushes.
8 And a highway shall be there, and a way, and it shall be called The way of holiness; the unclean shall not pass over it; but it *shall be* for those: the wayfaring men, though fools, shall not err *therein*.
9 No lion shall be there, nor *any* ravenous beast shall go up thereon, it shall not be found there; but the redeemed shall walk *there*:
10 And the ransomed of Yahweh shall return, and come to Zion with songs and everlasting joy upon their heads: they shall obtain joy and gladness, and sorrow and sighing shall flee away.

Isaiah 36

36:1 ¶ Now it came to pass in the fourteenth year of king Hezekiah, *that* Sennacherib king of Assyria came up against all the defensed cities of Judah, and took them.
2 And the king of Assyria sent Rabshakeh from Lachish to Jerusalem unto king Hezekiah with a great army. And he stood by the conduit of the upper pool in the highway of the fuller's field.
3 Then came forth to him Eliakim, Hilkiah's son, which was over the house, and Shebna the scribe, and Joah, Asaph's son, the recorder.
4 And Rabshakeh said unto them, Say you now to Hezekiah, Thus says the great king, the king of Assyria, What confidence *is* this wherein you trust?
5 I say, *say you*, (but *they are but* vain words) *I have* counsel and strength for war: now on whom do you trust, that you rebel against me?
6 Lo, you trust in the staff of this broken reed, on Egypt; whereon if a man leans, it will go into his hand, and pierce it: so *is* Pharaoh king of Egypt to all that trust in him.

Isaiah 36

7 But if you say to me, We trust in Yahweh our God: *is it* not he, whose high places and whose altars Hezekiah has taken away, and said to Judah and to Jerusalem, You shall worship before this altar?
8 Now therefore give pledges, I pray you, to my master the king of Assyria, and I will give you two thousand horses, if you are able on your part to set riders upon them.
9 How then will you turn away the face of one captain of the least of my master's servants, and put your trust on Egypt for chariots and for horsemen?
10 And have I now come up without Yahweh against this land to destroy it? Yahweh said unto me, Go up against this land, and destroy it.
11 ¶ Then said Eliakim and Shebna and Joah to Rabshakeh, Speak, I pray you, unto your servants in the Syrian language; for we understand *it*: and speak not to us in the Jews' language, in the ears of the people that *are* on the wall.
12 But Rabshakeh said, Has my master sent me to your master and to you to speak these words? *has he* not *sent me* to the men that sit upon the wall, that they may eat their own dung, and drink their own urine with you?
13 Then Rabshakeh stood, and cried with a loud voice in the Jews' language, and said, Hear you the words of the great king, the king of Assyria.
14 Thus says the king, Let not Hezekiah deceive you: for he shall not be able to deliver you.
15 Neither let Hezekiah make you trust in Yahweh, saying, Yahweh will surely deliver us: this city shall not be delivered into the hand of the king of Assyria.
16 Listen not to Hezekiah: for thus says the king of Assyria, Make *an agreement* with me *by* a present, and come out to me: and eat you every one of his vine, and every one of his fig tree, and drink you every one the waters of his own cistern;
17 Until I come and take you away to a land like your own land, a land of corn and *new* wine, a land of bread and vineyards.
18 *Beware* lest Hezekiah persuades you, saying, Yahweh will deliver us. Have any of the gods of the nations delivered his land out of the hand of the king of Assyria?
19 Where *are* the gods of Hamath and Arphad? where *are* the gods of Sepharvaim? and have they delivered Samaria out of my hand?
20 Who *are they* among all the gods of these lands, that have delivered their land out of my hand, that Yahweh should deliver Jerusalem out of my hand?
21 But they held their peace, and answered him not a word: for the king's commandment was, saying, Answer him not.
22 Then came Eliakim, the son of Hilkiah, that *was* over the household, and Shebna the scribe, and Joah, the son of Asaph, the recorder, to Hezekiah with *their* clothes torn, and told him the words of Rabshakeh.

Isaiah 37

37:1 ¶ And it came to pass, when king Hezekiah heard *it*, that he tore his clothes, and covered himself with sackcloth, and went into the house of Yahweh.
2 And he sent Eliakim, who *was* over the household, and Shebna the scribe, and the elders of the priests covered with sackcloth, unto Isaiah the prophet the son of Amoz.
3 And they said unto him, Thus says Hezekiah, This day *is* a day of trouble, and of rebuke, and of blasphemy: for the children have come to the birth, and *there is* not strength to bring forth.
4 It may be Yahweh your God will hear the words of Rabshakeh, whom the king of Assyria his master has sent to reproach the living God, and will reprove the words which Yahweh your God has heard: therefore lift up *your* prayer for the remnant that is left.
5 So the servants of king Hezekiah came to Isaiah.
6 And Isaiah said unto them, Thus shall you say unto your master, Thus says Yahweh, Be not afraid of the words that you have heard, with which the servants of the king of Assyria have blasphemed me.
7 Behold, I will send a spirit upon him, and he shall hear a rumor, and return to his own land; and I will cause him to fall by the sword in his own land.
8 ¶ So Rabshakeh returned, and found the king of Assyria warring against Libnah: for he had heard that he had departed from Lachish.
9 And he heard say concerning Tirhakah king of Ethiopia, He has come forth to make war with you. And when he heard *it*, he sent messengers to Hezekiah, saying,
10 Thus shall you speak to Hezekiah king of Judah, saying, Let not your God, in whom you trust, deceive you, saying, Jerusalem shall not be given into the hand of the king of Assyria.
11 Behold, you have heard what the kings of Assyria have done to all lands by destroying them utterly; and shall you be delivered?
12 Have the gods of the nations delivered them which my fathers have destroyed, *as* Gozan, and Haran, and Rezeph, and the children of Eden which *were* in Telassar?
13 Where *is* the king of Hamath, and the king of Arphad, and the king of the city of Sepharvaim, Hena, and Ivah?
14 And Hezekiah received the letter from the hand of the messengers, and read it: and Hezekiah went up unto the house of Yahweh, and spread it before Yahweh.
15 And Hezekiah prayed unto Yahweh, saying,
16 O Yahweh of hosts, God of Israel, that dwells *between* the cherubims, you *are* the God, *even* you alone, of all the kingdoms of the earth: you have made heaven and earth.
17 Incline your ear, O Yahweh, and hear; open your eyes, O Yahweh, and see: and hear all the words of Sennacherib, which has sent to reproach the living God.
18 Of a truth, Yahweh, the kings of Assyria have laid waste all the nations, and their countries,

19 And have cast their gods into the fire: for they *were* no gods, but the work of men's hands, wood and stone: therefore they have destroyed them.
20 Now therefore, O Yahweh our God, save us from his hand, that all the kingdoms of the earth may know that you *are* Yahweh, *even* you only.
21 ¶ Then Isaiah the son of Amoz sent unto Hezekiah, saying, Thus says Yahweh God of Israel, Whereas you have prayed to me against Sennacherib king of Assyria:
22 This *is* the word which Yahweh has spoken concerning him; The virgin, the daughter of Zion, has despised you, *and* laughed you to scorn; the daughter of Jerusalem has shaken her head at you.
23 Whom have you reproached and blasphemed? and against whom have you exalted *your* voice, and lifted up your eyes on high? *even* against the Holy One of Israel.
24 By your servants have you reproached the Lord, and have said, By the multitude of my chariots have I come up to the height of the mountains, to the sides of Lebanon; and I will cut down the tall cedars thereof, *and* the choice fir trees thereof: and I will enter into the height of his border, *and* the forest of his Carmel.
25 I have dug, and drunk water; and with the sole of my feet have I dried up all the rivers of the besieged places.
26 Have you not heard long ago, *how* I have done it; *and* of ancient times, that I have formed it? now have I brought it to pass, that you should be to lay waste defensed cities *into* ruinous heaps.
27 Therefore their inhabitants *were* of small power, they were dismayed and confounded: they were *as* the grass of the field, and *as* the green herb, *as* the grass on the housetops, and *as corn* blighted before it is grown up.
28 But I know your habitation, and your going out, and your coming in, and your rage against me.
29 Because your rage against me, and your tumult, has come up into my ears, therefore will I put my hook in your nose, and my bridle in your lips, and I will turn you back by the way by which you came.
30 And this *shall be* a sign unto you, You shall eat *this* year such as grows of itself; and the second year that which springs of the same: and in the third year sow you, and reap, and plant vineyards, and eat the fruit thereof.
31 And the remnant that has escaped of the house of Judah shall again take root downward, and bear fruit upward:
32 For out of Jerusalem shall go forth a remnant, and they that escape out of mount Zion: the zeal of Yahweh of hosts shall do this.
33 Therefore thus says Yahweh concerning the king of Assyria, He shall not come into this city, nor shoot an arrow there, nor come before it with shields, nor cast a bank against it.
34 By the way that he came, by the same shall he return, and shall not come into this city, says Yahweh.
35 For I will defend this city to save it for my own sake, and for my servant David's sake.
36 Then the angel of Yahweh went forth, and smote in the camp of the Assyrians a hundred and fourscore and five thousand: and when they arose early in the morning, behold, they *were* all dead corpses.
37 So Sennacherib king of Assyria departed, and went and returned, and dwelt at Nineveh.
38 And it came to pass, as he was worshipping in the house of Nisroch his god, that Adrammelech and Sharezer his sons smote him with the sword; and they escaped into the land of Armenia: and Esarhaddon his son reigned in his stead.

Isaiah 38

38:1 ¶ In those days was Hezekiah sick unto death. And Isaiah the prophet the son of Amoz came unto him, and said unto him, Thus says Yahweh, Set your house in order: for you shall die, and not live.
2 Then Hezekiah turned his face toward the wall, and prayed unto Yahweh,
3 And said, Remember now, O Yahweh, I beseech you, how I have walked before you in truth and with a perfect heart, and have done *that which is* good in your sight. And Hezekiah wept greatly.
4 Then came the word of Yahweh to Isaiah, saying,
5 Go, and say to Hezekiah, Thus says Yahweh, the God of David your father, I have heard your prayer, I have seen your tears: behold, I will add unto your days fifteen years.
6 And I will deliver you and this city out of the hand of the king of Assyria: and I will defend this city.
7 And this *shall be* a sign unto you from Yahweh, that Yahweh will do this thing that he has spoken;
8 Behold, I will bring again the shadow of the degrees, which has gone down in the sun dial of Ahaz, ten degrees backward. So the sun returned ten degrees, by which degrees it was gone down.
9 ¶ The writing of Hezekiah king of Judah, when he had been sick, and had recovered from his sickness:
10 I said in the cutting off of my days, I shall go to the gates of the grave: I am deprived of the residue of my years.
11 I said, I shall not see Yah, *even* Yah, in the land of the living: I shall behold man no more with the inhabitants of the world.
12 My age is departed, and is removed from me as a shepherd's tent: I have cut off like a weaver my life: he will cut me off with pining sickness: from day *even* to night will you make an end of me.
13 I reckoned till morning, *that*, as a lion, so will he break all my bones: from day *even* to night will you make an end of me.
14 Like a crane *or* a swallow, so did I chatter: I did mourn as a dove: my eyes fail *with looking* upward: O Yahweh, I am oppressed; undertake for me.
15 What shall I say? he has both spoken to me, and himself has done *it*: I shall go softly all my years in the bitterness of my soul.

Isaiah 38

16 O Lord, by these *things men* live, and in all these *things is* the life of my spirit: so will you recover me, and make me to live.

17 Behold, for peace I had great bitterness: but you have in love to my soul *delivered it* from the pit of corruption: for you have cast all my sins behind your back.

18 For the grave cannot praise you, death can *not* celebrate you: they that go down into the pit cannot hope for your truth.

19 The living, the living, he shall praise you, as I *do* this day: the father to the children shall make known your truth.

20 Yahweh *was ready* to save me: therefore we will sing my songs with the stringed instruments all the days of our life in the house of Yahweh.

21 For Isaiah had said, Let them take a lump of figs, and lay *it* for a plaster upon the boil, and he shall recover.

22 Hezekiah also had said, What *is* the sign that I shall go up to the house of Yahweh?

Isaiah 39

39:1 ¶ At that time Merodachbaladan, the son of Baladan, king of Babylon, sent letters and a present to Hezekiah: for he had heard that he had been sick, and had recovered.

2 And Hezekiah was glad of them, and showed them the house of his precious things, the silver, and the gold, and the spices, and the precious ointment, and all the house of his armor, and all that was found in his treasures: there was nothing in his house, nor in all his dominion, that Hezekiah showed them not.

3 Then came Isaiah the prophet unto king Hezekiah, and said to him, What said these men? and from where came they to you? And Hezekiah said, They have come from a far country to me, *even* from Babylon.

4 Then said he, What have they seen in your house? And Hezekiah answered, All that *is* in my house have they seen: there is nothing among my treasures that I have not shown them.

5 ¶ Then said Isaiah to Hezekiah, Hear the word of Yahweh of hosts:

6 Behold, the days come, that all that *is* in your house, and *that* which your fathers have laid up in store until this day, shall be carried to Babylon: nothing shall be left, says Yahweh.

7 And of your sons that shall issue from you, which you shall beget, shall they take away; and they shall be eunuchs in the palace of the king of Babylon.

8 Then said Hezekiah to Isaiah, Good *is* the word of Yahweh which you have spoken. He said moreover, For there shall be peace and truth in my days.

Isaiah 40

40:1 ¶ Comfort you, comfort you my people, says your God.

2 Speak you comfortably to Jerusalem, and cry unto her, that her warfare is accomplished, that her iniquity is pardoned: for she has received from Yahweh's hand double for all her sins.

3 ¶ The voice of him that cries in the wilderness, Prepare you the way of Yahweh, make straight in the desert a highway for our God.

4 Every valley shall be exalted, and every mountain and hill shall be made low: and the crooked shall be made straight, and the rough places plain:

5 And the glory of Yahweh shall be revealed, and all flesh shall see *it* together: for the mouth of Yahweh has spoken *it*.

6 The voice said, Cry. And he said, What shall I cry? All flesh *is* grass, and all the goodness thereof *is* as the flower of the field:

7 The grass withers, the flower fades: because the spirit of Yahweh blows upon it: surely the people *are* grass.

8 The grass withers, the flower fades: but the word of our God shall stand forever.

9 ¶ O Zion, that brings good tidings, get you up into the high mountain; O Jerusalem, that brings good tidings, lift up your voice with strength; lift *it* up, be not afraid; say unto the cities of Judah, Behold your God!

10 Behold, the Lord Yahweh will come with *a* strong *hand*, and his arm shall rule for him: behold, his reward *is* with him, and his work before him.

11 He shall feed his flock like a shepherd: he shall gather the lambs with his arm, and carry *them* in his bosom, *and* shall gently lead those that are with young.

12 ¶ Who has measured the waters in the hollow of his hand, and measured out heaven with the span, and comprehended the dust of the earth in a measure, and weighed the mountains in scales, and the hills in a balance?

13 Who has directed the Spirit of Yahweh, or *being* his counselor has taught him?

14 With whom took he counsel, and *who* instructed him, and taught him in the path of judgment, and taught him knowledge, and showed to him the way of understanding?

15 Behold, the nations *are* as a drop in a bucket, and are counted as the small dust of the balance: behold, he takes up the isles as a very little thing.

16 And Lebanon *is* not sufficient to burn, nor the beasts thereof sufficient for a burnt offering.

17 All nations before him *are* as nothing; and they are counted to him less than nothing, and vanity.

18 ¶ To whom then will you liken God? or what likeness will you compare unto him?

19 The workman melts a graven image, and the goldsmith spreads it over with gold, and casts silver chains.

20 He that *is* so impoverished that he has no oblation chooses a tree *that* will not rot; he seeks unto him a cunning workman to prepare a graven image, *that* shall not be moved.

21 Have you not known? have you not heard? has it not been told you from the beginning? have you not understood from the foundations of the earth?

22 *It is* he that sits upon the circle of the earth, and the inhabitants thereof *are* as grasshoppers; that stretches out the heavens as a curtain, and spreads them out as a tent to dwell in:
23 That brings the princes to nothing; he makes the judges of the earth as vanity.
24 Yes, they shall not be planted; yes, they shall not be sown: yes, their stock shall not take root in the earth: and he shall also blow upon them, and they shall wither, and the whirlwind shall take them away as stubble.
25 To whom then will you liken me, or shall I be equal? says the Holy One.
26 Lift up your eyes on high, and behold who has created these *things*, that brings out their host by number: he calls them all by names by the greatness of his might, for that *he is* strong in power; not one fails.
27 ¶ Why say you, O Jacob, and speak, O Israel, My way is hidden from Yahweh, and my judgment is passed over from my God?
28 Have you not known? have you not heard, *that* the everlasting God, Yahweh, the Creator of the ends of the earth, faints not, neither is weary? *there is* no searching of his understanding.
29 He gives power to the faint; and to *them that have* no might he increases strength.
30 Even the youths shall faint and be weary, and the young men shall utterly fall:
31 But they that wait upon Yahweh shall renew *their* strength; they shall mount up with wings as eagles; they shall run, and not be weary; *and* they shall walk, and not faint.

Isaiah 41

41:1 ¶ Keep silence before me, O islands; and let the people renew *their* strength: let them come near; then let them speak: let us come near together to judgment.
2 Who raised up the righteous *man* from the east, called him to his feet, gave the nations before him, and made *him* rule over kings? he gave *them* as the dust to his sword, *and* as driven stubble to his bow.
3 He pursued them, *and* passed safely; *even* by the way *that* he had not gone with his feet.
4 Who has worked and done *it*, calling the generations from the beginning? I Yahweh, the first, and with the last; I *am* he.
5 The isles saw *it*, and feared; the ends of the earth were afraid, drew near, and came.
6 They helped every one his neighbor; and *every one* said to his brother, Be of good courage.
7 So the carpenter encouraged the goldsmith, *and* he that smoothed *with* the hammer him that smote the anvil, saying, It *is* ready for the soldering: and he fastened it with nails, *that* it should not be moved.
8 But you, Israel, *are* my servant, Jacob whom I have chosen, the seed of Abraham my friend.
9 *You* whom I have taken from the ends of the earth, and called you from the chief men thereof, and said unto you, You *are* my servant; I have chosen you, and not cast you away.
10 ¶ Fear you not; for I *am* with you: be not dismayed; for I *am* your God: I will strengthen you; yes, I will help you; yes, I will uphold you with the right hand of my righteousness.
11 Behold, all they that were incensed against you shall be ashamed and confounded: they shall be as nothing; and they that strive with you shall perish.
12 You shall seek them, and shall not find them, *even* them that contended with you: they that war against you shall be as nothing, and as a thing of nothing.
13 For I Yahweh your God will hold your right hand, saying unto you, Fear not; I will help you.
14 Fear not, you worm Jacob, *and* you men of Israel; I will help you, says Yahweh, and your redeemer, the Holy One of Israel.
15 Behold, I will make you a new sharp threshing instrument having teeth: you shall thresh the mountains, and beat *them* small, and shall make the hills as chaff.
16 You shall fan them, and the wind shall carry them away, and the whirlwind shall scatter them: and you shall rejoice in Yahweh, *and* shall glory in the Holy One of Israel.
17 *When* the poor and needy seek water, and *there is* none, *and* their tongue fails for thirst, I Yahweh will hear them, I the God of Israel will not forsake them.
18 I will open rivers in high places, and fountains in the midst of the valleys: I will make the wilderness a pool of water, and the dry land springs of water.
19 I will plant in the wilderness the cedar, the shittah tree, and the myrtle, and the oil tree; I will set in the desert the fir tree, *and* the pine, and the box tree together:
20 That they may see, and know, and consider, and understand together, that the hand of Yahweh has done this, and the Holy One of Israel has created it.
21 ¶ Produce your cause, says Yahweh; bring forth your strong *reasons*, says the King of Jacob.
22 Let them bring *them* forth, and show us what shall happen: let them show the former things, what they *are*, that we may consider them, and know the latter end of them; or declare *to* us things for to come.
23 Show the things that are to come hereafter, that we may know that you *are* gods: yes, do good, or do evil, that we may be dismayed, and behold *it* together.
24 Behold, you *are* of nothing, and your work of nothing: an abomination *is* he that chooses you.
25 I have raised up *one* from the north, and he shall come: from the rising of the sun shall he call upon my name: and he shall come upon princes as *upon* mortar, and as the potter treads clay.
26 Who has declared from the beginning, that we may know? and before, that we may say, *He is* righteous? yes, *there is* none that shows, yes, *there is* none that declares, yes, *there is* none that hears your words.
27 The first *shall say* to Zion, Behold, behold them: and I will give to Jerusalem one that brings good tidings.
28 For I beheld, and *there was* no man; even among them, and *there was* no counselor, that, when I asked of them, could answer a word.

Isaiah 41

29 Behold, they *are* all vanity; their works *are* nothing: their molten images *are* wind and confusion.

Isaiah 42

42:1 ¶ Behold my servant, whom I uphold; my elect, *in whom* my soul delights; I have put my spirit upon him: he shall bring forth judgment to the Gentiles.
2 He shall not cry, nor lift up, nor cause his voice to be heard in the street.
3 A bruised reed shall he not break, and the smoking flax shall he not quench: he shall bring forth judgment unto truth.
4 He shall not fail nor be discouraged, till he has set judgment in the earth: and the isles shall wait for his law.
5 ¶ Thus says God Yahweh, he that created the heavens, and stretched them out; he that spread forth the earth, and that which comes out of it; he that gives breath unto the people upon it, and spirit to them that walk therein:
6 I Yahweh have called you in righteousness, and will hold your hand, and will keep you, and give you for a covenant of the people, for a light of the Gentiles;
7 To open the blind eyes, to bring out the prisoners from the prison, *and* them that sit in darkness out of the prison house.
8 I *am* Yahweh: that *is* my name: and my glory will I not give to another, neither my praise to graven images.
9 Behold, the former things have come to pass, and new things do I declare: before they spring forth I tell you of them.
10 Sing unto Yahweh a new song, *and* his praise from the end of the earth, you that go down to the sea, and all that is therein; the isles, and the inhabitants thereof.
11 Let the wilderness and the cities thereof lift up *their voice*, the villages *that* Kedar does inhabit: let the inhabitants of the rock sing, let them shout from the top of the mountains.
12 Let them give glory unto Yahweh, and declare his praise in the islands.
13 ¶ Yahweh shall go forth as a mighty man, he shall stir up jealousy like a man of war: he shall cry, yes, roar; he shall prevail against his enemies.
14 I have *for a* long time held my peace; I have been still, *and* refrained myself: *now* will I cry like a laboring woman; I will destroy and devour at once.
15 I will make waste mountains and hills, and dry up all their herbs; and I will make the rivers islands, and I will dry up the pools.
16 And I will bring the blind by a way *that* they knew not; I will lead them in paths *that* they have not known: I will make darkness light before them, and crooked things straight. These things will I do unto them, and not forsake them.
17 They shall be turned back, they shall be greatly ashamed, that trust in graven images, that say to the molten images, You *are* our gods.
18 ¶ Hear, you deaf; and look, you blind, that you may see.
19 Who *is* blind, but my servant? or deaf, as my messenger *that* I sent? who *is* blind as *he that is* perfect, and blind as Yahweh's servant?
20 Seeing many things, but you observe not; opening the ears, but he hears not.
21 Yahweh is well pleased for his righteousness' sake; he will magnify the law, and make *it* honorable.
22 But this *is* a people robbed and spoiled; *they are* all of them snared in holes, and they are hidden in prison houses: they are for a prey, and none delivers; for a spoil, and none says, Restore.
23 Who among you will give ear to this? *who* will listen and hear for the time to come?
24 Who gave Jacob for a spoil, and Israel to the robbers? did not Yahweh, he against whom we have sinned? for they would not walk in his ways, neither were they obedient unto his law.
25 Therefore he has poured upon him the fury of his anger, and the strength of battle: and it has set him on fire round about, yet he knew not; and it burned him, yet he laid *it* not to heart.

Isaiah 43

43:1 ¶ But now thus says Yahweh that created you, O Jacob, and he that formed you, O Israel, Fear not: for I have redeemed you, I have called *you* by your name; you *are* mine.
2 When you pass through the waters, I *will be* with you; and through the rivers, they shall not overflow you: when you walk through the fire, you shall not be burned; neither shall the flame kindle upon you.
3 For I *am* Yahweh your God, the Holy One of Israel, your Savior: I gave Egypt *for* your ransom, Ethiopia and Seba for you.
4 Since you were precious in my sight, you have been honorable, and I have loved you: therefore will I give men for you, and people for your life.
5 Fear not: for I *am* with you: I will bring your seed from the east, and gather you from the west;
6 I will say to the north, Give up; and to the south, Keep not back: bring my sons from far, and my daughters from the ends of the earth;
7 *Even* every one that is called by my name: for I have created him for my glory, I have formed him; yes, I have made him.
8 ¶ Bring forth the blind people that have eyes, and the deaf that have ears.
9 Let all the nations be gathered together, and let the people be assembled: who among them can declare this, and show us former things? let them bring forth their witnesses, that they may be justified: or let them hear, and say, It is truth.
10 You *are* my witnesses, says Yahweh, and my servant whom I have chosen: that you may know and believe me, and understand that I *am* he: before me there was no God formed, neither shall there be after me.
11 I, *even* I, *am* Yahweh; and besides me *there is* no savior.

12 I have declared, and have saved, and I have shown, when *there was* no strange *god* among you: therefore you *are* my witnesses, says Yahweh, that I *am* God.
13 Yes, before the day *was* I *am* he; and *there is* none that can deliver out of my hand: I will work, and who shall hinder it?
14 ¶ Thus says Yahweh, your redeemer, the Holy One of Israel; For your sake I have sent to Babylon, and have brought down all their nobles, and the Chaldeans, whose cry *is* in the ships.
15 I *am* Yahweh, your Holy One, the creator of Israel, your King.
16 Thus says Yahweh, which makes a way in the sea, and a path in the mighty waters;
17 Which brings forth the chariot and horse, the army and the power; they shall lie down together, they shall not rise: they are extinct, they are quenched as a wick.
18 Remember you not the former things, neither consider the things of old.
19 Behold, I will do a new thing; now it shall spring forth; shall you not know it? I will even make a way in the wilderness, *and* rivers in the desert.
20 The beast of the field shall honor me, the dragons and the owls: because I give waters in the wilderness, *and* rivers in the desert, to give drink to my people, my chosen.
21 This people have I formed for myself; they shall show forth my praise.
22 ¶ But you have not called upon me, O Jacob; but you have been weary of me, O Israel.
23 You have not brought me the small cattle of your burnt offerings; neither have you honored me with your sacrifices. I have not caused you to serve with an offering, nor wearied you with incense.
24 You have bought me no sweet cane with money, neither have you filled me with the fat of your sacrifices: but you have made me to serve with your sins, you have wearied me with your iniquities.
25 I, *even* I, *am* he that blots out your transgressions for my own sake, and will not remember your sins.
26 Put me in remembrance: let us plead together: declare you, that you may be justified.
27 Your first father has sinned, and your teachers have transgressed against me.
28 Therefore I have profaned the princes of the sanctuary, and have given Jacob to the curse, and Israel to reproaches.

Isaiah 44

44:1 ¶ Yet now hear, O Jacob my servant; and Israel, whom I have chosen:
2 Thus says Yahweh that made you, and formed you from the womb, *which* will help you; Fear not, O Jacob, my servant; and you, Jesurun, whom I have chosen.
3 For I will pour water upon him that is thirsty, and floods upon the dry ground: I will pour my spirit upon your seed, and my blessing upon your offspring:
4 And they shall spring up *as* among the grass, as willows by the water courses.
5 One shall say, I *am* Yahweh's; and another shall call *himself* by the name of Jacob; and another shall subscribe *with* his hand unto Yahweh, and surname *himself* by the name of Israel.
6 Thus says Yahweh the King of Israel, and his redeemer Yahweh of hosts; I *am* the first, and I *am* the last; and besides me *there is* no God.
7 And who, as I, shall call, and shall declare it, and set it in order for me, since I appointed the ancient people? and the things that are coming, and shall come, let them show unto them.
8 Fear you not, neither be afraid: have not I told you from that time, and have declared *it*? you *are* even my witnesses Is there a God besides me? yes, *there is* no God; I know not *any*.
9 ¶ They that make a graven image *are* all of them vanity; and their delectable things shall not profit; and they *are* their own witnesses; they see not, nor know; that they may be ashamed.
10 Who has formed a god, or molten a graven image *that* is profitable for nothing?
11 Behold, all his fellows shall be ashamed: and the workmen, they *are* of men: let them all be gathered together, let them stand up; *yet* they shall fear, *and* they shall be ashamed together.
12 The smith with the tongs both works in the coals, and fashions it with hammers, and works it with the strength of his arms: yes, he is hungry, and his strength fails: he drinks no water, and is faint.
13 The carpenter stretches out *his* rule; he marks it out with a line; he fits it with planes, and he marks it out with the compass, and makes it after the figure of a man, according to the beauty of a man; that it may remain in the house.
14 He hews him down cedars, and takes the cypress and the oak, which he strengthens for himself among the trees of the forest: he plants an ash, and the rain does nourish *it*.
15 Then shall it be for a man to burn: for he will take thereof, and warm himself; yes, he kindles *it*, and bakes bread; yes, he makes a god, and worships *it*; he makes it a graven image, and falls down thereto.
16 He burns part thereof in the fire; with part thereof he eats flesh; he roasts roast, and is satisfied: yes, he warms *himself*, and says, Aha, I am warm, I have seen the fire:
17 And the residue thereof he makes a god, *even* his graven image: he falls down unto it, and worships *it*, and prays unto it, and says, Deliver me; for you *are* my god.
18 They have not known nor understood: for he has shut their eyes, that they cannot see; *and* their hearts, that they cannot understand.
19 And none considers in his heart, neither *is there* knowledge nor understanding to say, I have burned part of it in the fire; yes, also I have baked bread upon the coals thereof; I have roasted flesh, and eaten *it*: and shall I make the residue thereof an abomination? shall I fall down to the stock of a tree?

Isaiah 44

20 He feeds on ashes: a deceived heart has turned him aside, that he cannot deliver his soul, nor say, *Is there* not a lie in my right hand?

21 ¶ Remember these, O Jacob and Israel; for you *are* my servant: I have formed you; you *are* my servant: O Israel, you shall not be forgotten by me.

22 I have blotted out, as a thick cloud, your transgressions, and, as a cloud, your sins: return unto me; for I have redeemed you.

23 Sing, O you heavens; for Yahweh has done *it*: shout, you lower parts of the earth: break forth into singing, you mountains, O forest, and every tree therein: for Yahweh has redeemed Jacob, and glorified himself in Israel.

24 Thus says Yahweh, your redeemer, and he that formed you from the womb, I *am* Yahweh that makes all *things*; that stretches forth the heavens alone; that spreads abroad the earth by myself;

25 That frustrates the tokens of the liars, and makes diviners mad; that turns wise *men* backward, and makes their knowledge foolish;

26 That confirms the word of his servant, and performs the counsel of his messengers; that says to Jerusalem, You shall be inhabited; and to the cities of Judah, You shall be built, and I will raise up the decayed places thereof:

27 That says to the deep, Be dry, and I will dry up your rivers:

28 That says of Cyrus, *He is* my shepherd, and shall perform all my pleasure: even saying to Jerusalem, You shall be built; and to the temple, Your foundation shall be laid.

Isaiah 45

45:1 ¶ Thus says Yahweh to his anointed, to Cyrus, whose right hand I have held, to subdue nations before him; and I will loose the loins of kings, to open before him the two leaved gates; and the gates shall not be shut;

2 I will go before you, and make the crooked places straight: I will break in pieces the gates of brass, and cut down the bars of iron:

3 And I will give you the treasures of darkness, and hidden riches of secret places, that you may know that I, Yahweh, which call *you* by your name, *am* the God of Israel.

4 For Jacob my servant's sake, and Israel my elect, I have even called you by your name: I have surnamed you, though you have not known me.

5 ¶ I *am* Yahweh, and *there is* none else, *there is* no God besides me: I girded you, though you have not known me:

6 That they may know from the rising of the sun, and from the west, that *there is* none besides me. I *am* Yahweh, and *there is* none else.

7 I form the light, and create darkness: I make peace, and create evil: I Yahweh do all these *things*.

8 Drop down, you heavens, from above, and let the skies pour down righteousness: let the earth open, and let them bring forth salvation, and let righteousness spring up together; I Yahweh have created it.

9 Woe unto him that strives with his Maker! *Let* the potsherd *strive* with the potsherds of the earth. Shall the clay say to him that fashions it, What make you? or your work, He has no hands?

10 Woe unto him that says to *his* father, What beget you? or to the woman, What have you brought forth?

11 ¶ Thus says Yahweh, the Holy One of Israel, and his Maker, Ask me of things to come concerning my sons, and concerning the work of my hands command you me.

12 I have made the earth, and created man upon it: I, *even* my hands, have stretched out the heavens, and all their host have I commanded.

13 I have raised him up in righteousness, and I will direct all his ways: he shall build my city, and he shall let go my captives, not for price nor reward, says Yahweh of hosts.

14 Thus says Yahweh, The labor of Egypt, and merchandise of Ethiopia and of the Sabeans, men of stature, shall come over unto you, and they shall be yours: they shall come after you; in chains they shall come over, and they shall fall down unto you, they shall make supplication unto you, *saying*, Surely God *is* in you; and *there is* none else, *there is* no God.

15 Truly you *are* a God that hides yourself, O God of Israel, the Savior.

16 They shall be ashamed, and also confounded, all of them: they shall go to confusion together *that are* makers of idols.

17 *But* Israel shall be saved in Yahweh with an everlasting salvation: you shall not be ashamed nor confounded world without end.

18 For thus says Yahweh that created the heavens; God himself that formed the earth and made it; he has established it, he created it not in vain, he formed it to be inhabited: I *am* Yahweh; and *there is* none else.

19 I have not spoken in secret, in a dark place of the earth: I said not to the seed of Jacob, Seek you me in vain: I Yahweh speak righteousness, I declare things that are right.

20 ¶ Assemble yourselves and come; draw near together, you *that are* escaped of the nations: they have no knowledge that set up the wood of their graven image, and pray to a god *that* cannot save.

21 Tell you, and bring *them* near; yes, let them take counsel together: who has declared this from ancient time? *who* has told it from that time? *have* not I Yahweh? and *there is* no God else besides me; a just God and a Savior; *there is* none besides me.

22 Look unto me, and be you saved, all the ends of the earth: for I *am* God, and *there is* none else.

23 I have sworn by myself, the word has gone out of my mouth *in* righteousness, and shall not return, That unto me every knee shall bow, every tongue shall swear.

24 Surely, shall *one* say, in Yahweh have I righteousness and strength: *even* to him shall *men* come; and all that are incensed against him shall be ashamed.

25 In Yahweh shall all the seed of Israel be justified, and shall glory.

Isaiah 46

46:1 ¶ Bel bows down, Nebo stoops, their idols were upon the beasts, and upon the cattle: your carriages *were* heavily loaded; *they are* a burden to the weary *beast*.

2 They stoop, they bow down together; they could not deliver the burden, but themselves have gone into captivity.

3 Listen to me, O house of Jacob, and all the remnant of the house of Israel, which are borne *by me* from the belly, which are carried from the womb:

4 And *even to your* old age *I am* he; and *even to* gray hairs will I carry *you*: I have made, and I will bear; even I will carry, and will deliver *you*.

5 ¶ To whom will you liken me, and make *me* equal, and compare me, that we may be like?

6 They lavish gold out of the bag, and weigh silver in the balance, *and* hire a goldsmith; and he makes it a god: they fall down, yes, they worship.

7 They bear him upon the shoulder, they carry him, and set him in his place, and he stands; from his place shall he not remove: yes, *one* shall cry unto him, yet can he not answer, nor save him out of his trouble.

8 Remember this, and show yourselves men: bring *it* again to mind, O you transgressors.

9 Remember the former things of old: for I *am* God, and *there is* none else; *I am* God, and *there is* none like me,

10 Declaring the end from the beginning, and from ancient times *the things* that are not *yet* done, saying, My counsel shall stand, and I will do all my pleasure:

11 Calling a ravenous bird from the east, the man that executes my counsel from a far country: yes, I have spoken *it*, I will also bring it to pass; I have purposed *it*, I will also do it.

12 Listen unto me, you stouthearted, that *are* far from righteousness:

13 I bring near my righteousness; it shall not be far off, and my salvation shall not tarry: and I will place salvation in Zion for Israel my glory.

Isaiah 47

47:1 ¶ Come down, and sit in the dust, O virgin daughter of Babylon, sit on the ground: *there is* no throne, O daughter of the Chaldeans: for you shall no more be called tender and delicate.

2 Take the millstones, and grind meal: uncover your locks, make bare the leg, uncover the thigh, pass over the rivers.

3 Your nakedness shall be uncovered, yes, your shame shall be seen: I will take vengeance, and I will not meet *you as* a man.

4 *As for* our redeemer, Yahweh of hosts *is* his name, the Holy One of Israel.

5 Sit you silent, and get you into darkness, O daughter of the Chaldeans: for you shall no more be called, The lady of kingdoms.

6 I was angry with my people, I have polluted my inheritance, and given them into your hand: you did show them no mercy; upon the ancient have you very heavily laid your yoke.

7 ¶ And you said, I shall be a lady forever: *so* that you did not lay these *things* to your heart, neither did remember the latter end of it.

8 Therefore hear now this, *you that are* given to pleasures, that dwell carelessly, that say in your heart, I *am*, and none else besides me; I shall not sit *as* a widow, neither shall I know the loss of children:

9 But these two *things* shall come to you in a moment in one day, the loss of children, and widowhood: they shall come upon you in their perfection for the multitude of your sorceries, *and* for the great abundance of your enchantments.

10 For you have trusted in your wickedness: you have said, None sees me. Your wisdom and your knowledge, it has perverted you; and you have said in your heart, I *am*, and none else besides me.

11 Therefore shall evil come upon you; you shall not know from where it rises: and mischief shall fall upon you; you shall not be able to put it off: and desolation shall come upon you suddenly, *which* you shall not know.

12 Stand now with your enchantments, and with the multitude of your sorceries, wherein you have labored from your youth; if so be you shall be able to profit, if so be you may prevail.

13 You are wearied in the multitude of your counsels. Let now the astrologers, the stargazers, the monthly prognosticators, stand up, and save you from *these things* that shall come upon you.

14 Behold, they shall be as stubble; the fire shall burn them; they shall not deliver themselves from the power of the flame: *there shall* not *be* a coal to warm at, *nor* fire to sit before it.

15 Thus shall they be to you with whom you have labored, *even* your merchants, from your youth: they shall wander every one to his quarter; none shall save you.

Isaiah 48

48:1 ¶ Hear you this, O house of Jacob, which are called by the name of Israel, and have come forth out of the waters of Judah, which swear by the name of Yahweh, and make mention of the God of Israel, *but* not in truth, nor in righteousness.

2 For they call themselves of the holy city, and lean themselves upon the God of Israel; Yahweh of hosts *is* his name.

3 I have declared the former things from the beginning; and they went forth out of my mouth, and I showed them; I did *them* suddenly, and they came to pass.

Isaiah 48

4 Because I knew that you *are* obstinate, and your neck *is* an iron sinew, and your brow brass;
5 I have even from the beginning declared *it* to you; before it came to pass I showed *it to* you: lest you should say, My idol has done them, and my graven image, and my molten image, has commanded them.
6 You have heard, see all this; and will not you declare *it*? I have shown you new things from this time, even hidden things, and you did not know them.
7 They are created now, and not from the beginning; even before the day when you heard them not; lest you should say, Behold, I knew them.
8 Yes, you heard not; yes, you knew not; yes, from that time *that* your ear was not opened: for I knew that you would deal very treacherously, and were called a transgressor from the womb.
9 ¶ For my name's sake will I defer my anger, and for my praise will I refrain for you, that I cut you not off.
10 Behold, I have refined you, but not with silver; I have chosen you in the furnace of affliction.
11 For my own sake, *even* for my own sake, will I do *it*: for how should *my* name be polluted? and I will not give my glory to another.
12 Listen unto me, O Jacob and Israel, my called; I *am* he; I *am* the first, I also *am* the last.
13 My hand also has laid the foundation of the earth, and my right hand has spanned the heavens: *when* I call unto them, they stand up together.
14 All you, assemble yourselves, and hear; which among them has declared these *things*? Yahweh has loved him: he will do his pleasure on Babylon, and his arm *shall be on* the Chaldeans.
15 I, *even* I, have spoken; yes, I have called him: I have brought him, and he shall make his way prosperous.
16 ¶ Come you near unto me, hear you this; I have not spoken in secret from the beginning; from the time that it was, there *am* I: and now the Lord Yahweh, and his Spirit, has sent me.
17 Thus says Yahweh, your Redeemer, the Holy One of Israel; I *am* Yahweh your God which teaches you to profit, which leads you by the way *that* you should go.
18 O that you had listened to my commandments! then had your peace been as a river, and your righteousness as the waves of the sea:
19 Your seed also had been as the sand, and the offspring of your bowels like the gravel thereof; his name should not have been cut off nor destroyed from before me.
20 Go you forth from Babylon, flee you from the Chaldeans, with a voice of singing declare you, tell this, utter it *even* to the end of the earth; say you, Yahweh has redeemed his servant Jacob.
21 And they thirsted not *when* he led them through the deserts: he caused the waters to flow out of the rock for them: he broke open the rock also, and the waters gushed out.
22 *There is* no peace, says Yahweh, unto the wicked.

Isaiah 49

49:1 ¶ Listen, O isles, unto me; and listen, you people, from afar; Yahweh has called me from the womb; from the bowels of my mother has he made mention of my name.
2 And he has made my mouth like a sharp sword; in the shadow of his hand has he hidden me, and made me a polished shaft; in his quiver has he hidden me;
3 And said unto me, You *are* my servant, O Israel, in whom I will be glorified.
4 Then I said, I have labored in vain, I have spent my strength for nothing, and in vain: *yet* surely my judgment *is* with Yahweh, and my work with my God.
5 And now, says Yahweh that formed me from the womb *to be* his servant, to bring Jacob again to him, Though Israel is not gathered, yet shall I be glorious in the eyes of Yahweh, and my God shall be my strength.
6 And he said, It is a light thing that you should be my servant to raise up the tribes of Jacob, and to restore the preserved of Israel: I will also give you for a light to the Gentiles, that you may be my salvation unto the end of the earth.
7 ¶ Thus says Yahweh, the Redeemer of Israel, *and* his Holy One, to him whom man despises, to him whom the nation abhors, to a servant of rulers, Kings shall see and arise, princes also shall worship, because of Yahweh that is faithful, *and* the Holy One of Israel, and he shall choose you.
8 Thus says Yahweh, In an acceptable time have I heard you, and in a day of salvation have I helped you: and I will preserve you, and give you for a covenant of the people, to establish the earth, to cause to inherit the desolate heritages;
9 That you may say to the prisoners, Go forth; to them that *are* in darkness, Show yourselves. They shall feed in the ways, and their pastures *shall be* in all high places.
10 They shall not hunger nor thirst; neither shall the heat nor sun smite them: for he that has mercy on them shall lead them, even by the springs of water shall he guide them.
11 And I will make all my mountains a way, and my highways shall be exalted.
12 Behold, these shall come from afar: and, lo, these from the north and from the west; and these from the land of Sinim.
13 ¶ Sing, O heavens; and be joyful, O earth; and break forth into singing, O mountains: for Yahweh has comforted his people, and will have mercy upon his afflicted.
14 But Zion said, Yahweh has forsaken me, and my Lord has forgotten me.
15 Can a woman forget her sucking child, that she should not have compassion on the son of her womb? yes, they may forget, yet will I not forget you.
16 Behold, I have engraved you upon the palms of *my* hands; your walls *are* continually before me.
17 Your children shall make haste; your destroyers and they that made you waste shall go forth of you.

18 ¶ Lift up your eyes round about, and behold: all these gather themselves together, *and* come to you. *As* I live, says Yahweh, you shall surely clothe you with them all, as with an ornament, and bind them *on you*, as a bride *does*.

19 For your waste and your desolate places, and the land of your destruction, shall even now be too narrow by reason of the inhabitants, and they that swallowed you up shall be far away.

20 The children which you shall have, after you have lost the other, shall say again in your ears, The place *is* too narrow for me: give place to me that I may dwell.

21 Then shall you say in your heart, Who has begotten me these, seeing I have lost my children, and am desolate, a captive, and removing to and fro? and who has brought up these? Behold, I was left alone; these, where *had* they *been*?

22 Thus says the Lord Yahweh, Behold, I will lift up my hand to the Gentiles, and set up my standard to the people: and they shall bring your sons in *their* arms, and your daughters shall be carried upon *their* shoulders.

23 And kings shall be your nursing fathers, and their queens your nursing mothers: they shall bow down to you with *their* face toward the earth, and lick up the dust of your feet; and you shall know that I *am* Yahweh: for they shall not be ashamed that wait for me.

24 ¶ Shall the prey be taken from the mighty, or the lawful captive delivered?

25 But thus says Yahweh, Even the captives of the mighty shall be taken away, and the prey of the terrible shall be delivered: for I will contend with him that contends with you, and I will save your children.

26 And I will feed them that oppress you with their own flesh; and they shall be drunken with their own blood, as with sweet wine: and all flesh shall know that I Yahweh *am* your Savior and your Redeemer, the mighty One of Jacob.

Isaiah 50

50:1 ¶ Thus says Yahweh, Where *is* the bill of your mother's divorce, whom I have put away? or which of my creditors *is it* to whom I have sold you? Behold, for your iniquities have you sold yourselves, and for your transgressions is your mother put away.

2 Why, when I came, *was there* no man? when I called, *was there* none to answer? Is my hand shortened at all, that it cannot redeem? or have I no power to deliver? behold, at my rebuke I dry up the sea, I make the rivers a wilderness: their fish stinks, because *there is* no water, and die for thirst.

3 I clothe the heavens with blackness, and I make sackcloth their covering.

4 ¶ The Lord Yahweh has given me the tongue of the learned, that I should know how to speak a word in season to *him that is* weary: he awakens morning by morning, he awakens my ear to hear as the learned.

5 The Lord Yahweh has opened my ear, and I was not rebellious, neither turned away back.

6 I gave my back to the smiters, and my cheeks to them that plucked off the hair: I hid not my face from shame and spitting.

7 For the Lord Yahweh will help me; therefore shall I not be confounded: therefore have I set my face like a flint, and I know that I shall not be ashamed.

8 *He is* near that justifies me; who will contend with me? let us stand together: who *is* my adversary? let him come near to me.

9 Behold, the Lord Yahweh will help me; who *is* he *that* shall condemn me? lo, they all shall grow old as a garment; the moth shall eat them up.

10 ¶ Who *is* among you that fears Yahweh, that obeys the voice of his servant, that walks *in* darkness, and has no light? let him trust in the name of Yahweh, and lean upon his God.

11 Behold, all you that kindle a fire, that compass *yourselves* about with sparks: walk in the light of your fire, and in the sparks *that* you have kindled. This shall you have of my hand: you shall lie down in sorrow.

Isaiah 51

51:1 ¶ Listen to me, you that follow after righteousness, you that seek Yahweh: look unto the rock *wherefrom* you were hewn, and to the hole of the pit *wherefrom* you were dug.

2 Look to Abraham your father, and to Sarah *that* bore you: for I called him alone, and blessed him, and increased him.

3 For Yahweh shall comfort Zion: he will comfort all her waste places; and he will make her wilderness like Eden, and her desert like the garden of Yahweh; joy and gladness shall be found therein, thanksgiving, and the voice of melody.

4 ¶ Listen unto me, my people; and give ear unto me, O my nation: for a law shall proceed from me, and I will make my judgment to rest for a light of the people.

5 My righteousness *is* near; my salvation has gone forth, and my arms shall judge the people; the isles shall wait upon me, and on my arm shall they trust.

6 Lift up your eyes to the heavens, and look upon the earth beneath: for the heavens shall vanish away like smoke, and the earth shall grow old like a garment, and they that dwell therein shall die in like manner: but my salvation shall be forever, and my righteousness shall not be abolished.

7 Listen unto me, you that know righteousness, the people in whose heart *is* my law; fear you not the reproach of men, neither be you afraid of their revilings.

8 For the moth shall eat them up like a garment, and the worm shall eat them like wool: but my righteousness shall be forever, and my salvation from generation to generation.

9 ¶ Awake, awake, put on strength, O arm of Yahweh; awake, as in the ancient days, in the generations of old. *Are* you not it that has cut Rahab, *and* wounded the dragon?

Isaiah 51

10 *Are* you not it which has dried the sea, the waters of the great deep; that has made the depths of the sea a way for the ransomed to pass over?

11 Therefore the redeemed of Yahweh shall return, and come with singing unto Zion; and everlasting joy *shall be* upon their head: they shall obtain gladness and joy; *and* sorrow and mourning shall flee away.

12 I, *even* I, *am* he that comforts you: who *are* you, that you should be afraid of a man *that* shall die, and of the son of man *which* shall be made *as* grass;

13 And forget Yahweh your maker, that has stretched forth the heavens, and laid the foundations of the earth; and have feared continually every day because of the fury of the oppressor, as if he were ready to destroy? and where *is* the fury of the oppressor?

14 The captive exile hastens that he may be loosed, and that he should not die in the pit, nor that his bread should fail.

15 But I *am* Yahweh your God, that divided the sea, whose waves roared: Yahweh of hosts *is* his name.

16 And I have put my words in your mouth, and I have covered you in the shadow of my hand, that I may plant the heavens, and lay the foundations of the earth, and say unto Zion, You *are* my people.

17 ¶ Awake, awake, stand up, O Jerusalem, which have drunk at the hand of Yahweh the cup of his fury; you have drunk the dregs of the cup of trembling, *and* wrung *them* out.

18 *There is* none to guide her among all the sons *whom* she has brought forth; neither *is there any* that takes her by the hand of all the sons *that* she has brought up.

19 These two *things* have come unto you; who shall be sorry for you? desolation, and destruction, and the famine, and the sword: by whom shall I comfort you?

20 Your sons have fainted, they lie at the head of all the streets, as a wild bull in a net: they are full of the fury of Yahweh, the rebuke of your God.

21 Therefore hear now this, you afflicted, and drunken, but not with wine:

22 Thus says your Lord Yahweh, and your God *that* pleads the cause of his people, Behold, I have taken out of your hand the cup of trembling, *even* the dregs of the cup of my fury; you shall no more drink it again:

23 But I will put it into the hand of them that afflict you; which have said to your soul, Bow down, that we may go over: and you have laid your body as the ground, and as the street, to them that went over.

Isaiah 52

52:1 ¶ Awake, awake; put on your strength, O Zion; put on your beautiful garments, O Jerusalem, the holy city: for henceforth there shall no more come into you the uncircumcised and the unclean.

2 Shake yourself from the dust; arise, *and* sit down, O Jerusalem: loose yourself from the bands of your neck, O captive daughter of Zion.

3 For thus says Yahweh, You have sold yourselves for nothing; and you shall be redeemed without money.

4 For thus says the Lord Yahweh, My people went down aforetime into Egypt to dwell there; and the Assyrian oppressed them without cause.

5 Now therefore, what have I here, says Yahweh, that my people are taken away for nothing? they that rule over them make them to howl, says Yahweh; and my name continually every day *is* blasphemed.

6 Therefore my people shall know my name: therefore *they shall know* in that day that I *am* he that does speak: behold, *it is* I.

7 ¶ How beautiful upon the mountains are the feet of him that brings good tidings, that publishes peace; that brings good tidings of good, that publishes salvation; that says unto Zion, Your God reigns!

8 Your watchmen shall lift up the voice; with the voice together shall they sing: for they shall see eye to eye, when Yahweh shall bring again Zion.

9 Break forth into joy, sing together, you waste places of Jerusalem: for Yahweh has comforted his people, he has redeemed Jerusalem.

10 Yahweh has made bare his holy arm in the eyes of all the nations; and all the ends of the earth shall see the salvation of our God.

11 Depart you, depart you, go you out from there, touch no unclean *thing*; go you out of the midst of her; be you clean, that bear the vessels of Yahweh.

12 For you shall not go out with haste, nor go by flight: for Yahweh will go before you; and the God of Israel *will be* your rear guard.

13 ¶ Behold, my servant shall deal prudently, he shall be exalted and extolled, and be very high.

14 As many were astonished at you; his visage was so marred more than any man, and his form more than the sons of men:

15 So shall he sprinkle many nations; the kings shall shut their mouths at him: for *that* which had not been told them shall they see; and *that* which they had not heard shall they consider.

Isaiah 53

53:1 ¶ Who has believed our report? and to whom is the arm of Yahweh revealed?

2 For he shall grow up before him as a tender plant, and as a root out of a dry ground: he has no form nor comeliness; and when we shall see him, *there is* no beauty that we should desire him.

3 He is despised and rejected by men; a man of sorrows, and acquainted with grief: and we hid as it were *our* faces from him; he was despised, and we esteemed him not.

4 ¶ Surely he has borne our griefs, and carried our sorrows: yet we did esteem him stricken, smitten by God, and afflicted.

5 But he *was* wounded for our transgressions, *he was* bruised for our iniquities: the chastisement of our peace *was* upon him; and by his stripes we are healed.

6 All we like sheep have gone astray; we have turned every one to his own way; and Yahweh has laid on him the iniquity of us all.
7 He was oppressed, and he was afflicted, yet he opened not his mouth: he was brought as a lamb to the slaughter, and as a sheep before her shearers is dumb, so he opened not his mouth.
8 He was taken from prison and from judgment: and who shall declare his generation? for he was cut off out of the land of the living: for the transgression of my people was he stricken.
9 And he made his grave with the wicked, and with the rich in his death; because he had done no violence, neither *was any* deceit in his mouth.
10 ¶ Yet it pleased Yahweh to bruise him; he has put *him* to grief: when you shall make his soul an offering for sin, he shall see *his* seed, he shall prolong *his* days, and the pleasure of Yahweh shall prosper in his hand.
11 He shall see of the labor of his soul, *and* shall be satisfied: by his knowledge shall my righteous servant justify many; for he shall bear their iniquities.
12 Therefore will I divide him *a portion* with the great, and he shall divide the spoil with the strong; because he has poured out his soul unto death: and he was numbered with the transgressors; and he bore the sin of many, and made intercession for the transgressors.

Isaiah 54

54:1 ¶ Sing, O barren, you *that* did not bear; break forth into singing, and cry aloud, you *that* did not labor with child: for more *are* the children of the desolate than the children of the married wife, says Yahweh.
2 Enlarge the place of your tent, and let them stretch forth the curtains of your habitations: spare not, lengthen your cords, and strengthen your stakes;
3 For you shall break forth on the right hand and on the left; and your seed shall inherit the Gentiles, and make the desolate cities to be inhabited.
4 Fear not; for you shall not be ashamed: neither be you confounded; for you shall not be put to shame: for you shall forget the shame of your youth, and shall not remember the reproach of your widowhood any more.
5 For your Maker *is* your husband; Yahweh of hosts *is* his name; and your Redeemer the Holy One of Israel; The God of the whole earth shall he be called.
6 ¶ For Yahweh has called you as a woman forsaken and grieved in spirit, and a wife of youth, when you were refused, says your God.
7 For a small moment have I forsaken you; but with great mercies will I gather you.
8 In a little wrath I hid my face from you for a moment; but with everlasting kindness will I have mercy on you, says Yahweh your Redeemer.
9 For this *is as* the waters of Noah unto me: for *as* I have sworn that the waters of Noah should no more go over the earth; so have I sworn that I would not be angry with you, nor rebuke you.

10 For the mountains shall depart, and the hills be removed; but my kindness shall not depart from you, neither shall the covenant of my peace be removed, says Yahweh that has mercy on you.
11 ¶ O you afflicted, tossed with tempest, *and* not comforted, behold, I will lay your stones with fair colors, and lay your foundations with sapphires.
12 And I will make your windows of agates, and your gates of carbuncles, and all your borders of pleasant stones.
13 And all your children *shall be* taught of Yahweh; and great *shall be* the peace of your children.
14 In righteousness shall you be established: you shall be far from oppression; for you shall not fear: and from terror; for it shall not come near you.
15 Behold, they shall surely gather together, *but* not by me: whoever shall gather together against you shall fall for your sake.
16 Behold, I have created the smith that blows the coals in the fire, and that brings forth an instrument for his work; and I have created the waster to destroy.
17 No weapon that is formed against you shall prosper; and every tongue *that* shall rise against you in judgment you shall condemn. This *is* the heritage of the servants of Yahweh, and their righteousness *is* of me, says Yahweh.

Isaiah 55

55:1 ¶ Ho, every one that thirsts, come you to the waters, and he that has no money; come you, buy, and eat; yes, come, buy wine and milk without money and without price.
2 Why do you spend money for *that which is* not bread? and your labor for *that which* satisfies not? listen diligently unto me, and eat you *that which is* good, and let your soul delight itself in fatness.
3 Incline your ear, and come unto me: hear, and your soul shall live; and I will make an everlasting covenant with you, *even* the sure mercies of David.
4 Behold, I have given him *for* a witness to the people, a leader and commander to the people.
5 Behold, you shall call a nation *that* you know not, and nations *that* knew not you shall run unto you because of Yahweh your God, and for the Holy One of Israel; for he has glorified you.
6 ¶ Seek you Yahweh while he may be found, call you upon him while he is near:
7 Let the wicked forsake his way, and the unrighteous man his thoughts: and let him return unto Yahweh, and he will have mercy upon him; and to our God, for he will abundantly pardon.
8 For my thoughts *are* not your thoughts, neither *are* your ways my ways, says Yahweh.
9 For *as* the heavens are higher than the earth, so are my ways higher than your ways, and my thoughts than your thoughts.
10 For as the rain comes down, and the snow from heaven, and returns not there, but waters the earth, and makes it bring forth and bud, that it may give seed to the sower, and bread to the eater:

Isaiah 55

11 So shall my word be that goes forth out of my mouth: it shall not return unto me void, but it shall accomplish that which I please, and it shall prosper *in the thing* whereto I sent it.

12 For you shall go out with joy, and be led forth with peace: the mountains and the hills shall break forth before you into singing, and all the trees of the field shall clap *their* hands.

13 Instead of the thorn shall come up the fir tree, and instead of the brier shall come up the myrtle tree: and it shall be to Yahweh for a name, for an everlasting sign *that* shall not be cut off.

Isaiah 56

56:1 ¶ Thus says Yahweh, Keep you judgment, and do justice: for my salvation *is* near to come, and my righteousness to be revealed.

2 Blessed *is* the man *that* does this, and the son of man *that* lays hold on it; that keeps the sabbath from polluting it, and keeps his hand from doing any evil.

3 ¶ Neither let the son of the stranger, that has joined himself to Yahweh, speak, saying, Yahweh has utterly separated me from his people: neither let the eunuch say, Behold, I *am* a dry tree.

4 For thus says Yahweh unto the eunuchs that keep my sabbaths, and choose *the things* that please me, and take hold of my covenant;

5 Even unto them will I give in my house and within my walls a place and a name better than of sons and of daughters: I will give them an everlasting name, that shall not be cut off.

6 Also the sons of the stranger, that join themselves to Yahweh, to serve him, and to love the name of Yahweh, to be his servants, every one that keeps the sabbath from polluting it, and takes hold of my covenant;

7 Even them will I bring to my holy mountain, and make them joyful in my house of prayer: their burnt offerings and their sacrifices *shall be* accepted upon my altar; for my house shall be called a house of prayer for all people.

8 The Lord Yahweh which gathers the outcasts of Israel says, Yet will I gather *others* to him, besides those that are gathered unto him.

9 ¶ All you beasts of the field, come to devour, *yes,* all you beasts in the forest.

10 His watchmen *are* blind: they are all ignorant, they *are* all dumb dogs, they cannot bark; sleeping, lying down, loving to slumber.

11 Yes, *they are* greedy dogs *which* can never have enough, and they *are* shepherds *that* cannot understand: they all look to their own way, every one for his gain, from his quarter.

12 Come you, *say they,* I will fetch wine, and we will fill ourselves with strong drink; and tomorrow shall be as this day, *and* much more abundant.

Isaiah 57

57:1 ¶ The righteous perishes, and no man lays *it* to heart: and merciful men *are* taken away, none considering that the righteous are taken away from the evil *to come.*

2 He shall enter into peace: they shall rest in their beds, *each one* walking *in* his uprightness.

3 ¶ But draw near here, you sons of the sorceress, the seed of the adulterer and the whore.

4 Against whom do you delight yourselves? against whom make you a wide mouth, *and* draw out the tongue? *are* you not children of transgression, a seed of falsehood,

5 Inflaming yourselves with idols under every green tree, slaying the children in the valleys under the clefts of the rocks?

6 Among the smooth *stones* of the stream *is* your portion; they, they *are* your lot: even to them have you poured a drink offering, you have offered a meat offering. Should I receive comfort in these?

7 Upon a lofty and high mountain have you set your bed: even there went you up to offer sacrifice.

8 Behind the doors also and the posts have you set up your remembrance: for you have uncovered *yourself to another* than me, and have gone up; you have enlarged your bed, and made you *a covenant* with them; you loved their bed where you saw *it.*

9 And you went to the king with ointment, and did increase your perfumes, and did send your messengers far off, and did debase *yourself even* unto hell.

10 You are wearied in the greatness of your way; *yet* say you not, There is no hope: you have found the life of your hand; therefore you were not grieved.

11 And of whom have you been afraid or feared, that you have lied, and have not remembered me, nor laid *it* to your heart? have not I held my peace even of old, and you fear me not?

12 I will declare your righteousness, and your works; for they shall not profit you.

13 ¶ When you cry, let your companies deliver you; but the wind shall carry them all away; vanity shall take *them*: but he that puts his trust in me shall possess the land, and shall inherit my holy mountain;

14 And shall say, Cast you up, cast you up, prepare the way, take up the stumbling block out of the way of my people.

15 For thus says the high and lofty One that inhabits eternity, whose name *is* Holy; I dwell in the high and holy *place*, with him also *that is* of a contrite and humble spirit, to revive the spirit of the humble, and to revive the heart of the contrite ones.

16 For I will not contend forever, neither will I be always angry: for the spirit should fail before me, and the souls *which* I have made.

17 ¶ For the iniquity of his covetousness was I angry, and smote him: I hid me, and was angry, and he went on backsliding in the way of his heart.

18 I have seen his ways, and will heal him: I will lead him also, and restore comforts to him and to his mourners.

19 I create the fruit of the lips; Peace, peace to *him that is* far off, and to *him that is* near, says Yahweh; and I will heal him.
20 But the wicked *are* like the troubled sea, when it cannot rest, whose waters cast up mire and dirt.
21 *There is* no peace, says my God, to the wicked.

Isaiah 58

58:1 ¶ Cry aloud, spare not, lift up your voice like a trumpet, and show my people their transgression, and the house of Jacob their sins.
2 Yet they seek me daily, and delight to know my ways, as a nation that did righteousness, and forsook not the ordinance of their God: they ask of me the ordinances of justice; they take delight in approaching to God.
3 ¶ Why have we fasted, *say they*, and you see not? why have we afflicted our soul, and you take no knowledge? Behold, in the day of your fast you find pleasure, and exact all your labors.
4 Behold, you fast for strife and debate, and to smite with the fist of wickedness: you shall not fast as *you do this* day, to make your voice to be heard on high.
5 Is it such a fast that I have chosen? a day for a man to afflict his soul? *is it* to bow down his head as a bulrush, and to spread sackcloth and ashes *under him*? will you call this a fast, and an acceptable day to Yahweh?
6 *Is* not this the fast that I have chosen? to loose the bands of wickedness, to undo the heavy burdens, and to let the oppressed go free, and that you break every yoke?
7 *Is it* not to deal your bread to the hungry, and that you bring the poor that are cast out to your house? when you see the naked, that you cover him; and that you hide not yourself from your own flesh?
8 ¶ Then shall your light break forth as the morning, and your health shall spring forth speedily: and your righteousness shall go before you; the glory of Yahweh shall be your rear guard.
9 Then shall you call, and Yahweh shall answer; you shall cry, and he shall say, Here I *am*. If you take away from the midst of you the yoke, the putting forth of the finger, and speaking vanity;
10 And *if* you draw out your soul to the hungry, and satisfy the afflicted soul; then shall your light rise in obscurity, and your darkness *be* as the noonday:
11 And Yahweh shall guide you continually, and satisfy your soul in drought, and make fat your bones: and you shall be like a watered garden, and like a spring of water, whose waters fail not.
12 And *they that shall be* of you shall build the old waste places: you shall raise up the foundations of many generations; and you shall be called, The repairer of the breach, The restorer of paths to dwell in.
13 ¶ If you turn away your foot from the sabbath, *from* doing your pleasure on my holy day; and call the sabbath a delight, the holy of Yahweh, honorable; and shall honor him, not doing your own ways, nor finding your own pleasure, nor speaking *your own* words:
14 Then shall you delight yourself in Yahweh; and I will cause you to ride upon the high places of the earth, and feed you with the heritage of Jacob your father: for the mouth of Yahweh has spoken *it*.

Isaiah 59

59:1 ¶ Behold, Yahweh's hand is not shortened, that it cannot save; neither his ear heavy, that it cannot hear:
2 But your iniquities have separated between you and your God, and your sins have hidden *his* face from you, that he will not hear.
3 For your hands are defiled with blood, and your fingers with iniquity; your lips have spoken lies, your tongue has muttered perverseness.
4 None calls for justice, nor *any* pleads for truth: they trust in vanity, and speak lies; they conceive mischief, and bring forth iniquity.
5 They hatch poisonous serpent's eggs, and weave the spider's web: he that eats of their eggs dies, and that which is crushed breaks out into a viper.
6 Their webs shall not become garments, neither shall they cover themselves with their works: their works *are* works of iniquity, and the act of violence *is* in their hands.
7 Their feet run to evil, and they make haste to shed innocent blood: their thoughts *are* thoughts of iniquity; wasting and destruction *are* in their paths.
8 The way of peace they know not; and *there is* no judgment in their goings: they have made them crooked paths: whoever goes therein shall not know peace.
9 ¶ Therefore is judgment far from us, neither does justice overtake us: we wait for light, but behold obscurity; for brightness, *but* we walk in darkness.
10 We grope for the wall like the blind, and we grope as if *we had* no eyes: we stumble at noonday as in the night; *we are* in desolate places as dead *men*.
11 We roar all like bears, and mourn moaning like doves: we look for judgment, but *there is* none; for salvation, *but* it is far off from us.
12 For our transgressions are multiplied before you, and our sins testify against us: for our transgressions *are* with us; and *as for* our iniquities, we know them;
13 In transgressing and lying against Yahweh, and departing away from our God, speaking oppression and revolt, conceiving and uttering from the heart words of falsehood.
14 And judgment is turned away backward, and justice stands afar off: for truth has fallen in the street, and equity cannot enter.
15 Yes, truth fails; and he *that* departs from evil makes himself a prey: and Yahweh saw *it*, and it displeased him that *there was* no judgment.
16 ¶ And he saw that *there was* no man, and wondered that *there was* no intercessor: therefore his arm brought salvation unto him; and his righteousness, it sustained him.
17 For he put on righteousness as a breastplate, and a helmet of salvation upon his head; and he put on the

Isaiah 59

garments of vengeance *for* clothing, and was clad with zeal as a cloak.
18 According to *their* deeds, accordingly he will repay, fury to his adversaries, recompense to his enemies; to the islands he will repay recompense.
19 So shall they fear the name of Yahweh from the west, and his glory from the rising of the sun. When the enemy shall come in like a flood, the Spirit of Yahweh shall lift up a standard against him.
20 And the Redeemer shall come to Zion, and to them that turn from transgression in Jacob, says Yahweh.
21 As for me, this *is* my covenant with them, says Yahweh; My spirit that *is* upon you, and my words which I have put in your mouth, shall not depart out of your mouth, nor out of the mouth of your seed, nor out of the mouth of your seed's seed, says Yahweh, from now on and forever.

Isaiah 60

60:1 ¶ Arise, shine; for your light is come, and the glory of Yahweh is risen upon you.
2 For, behold, the darkness shall cover the earth, and gross darkness the people: but Yahweh shall arise upon you, and his glory shall be seen upon you.
3 And the Gentiles shall come to your light, and kings to the brightness of your rising.
4 Lift up your eyes round about, and see: all they gather themselves together, they come to you: your sons shall come from far, and your daughters shall be nursed at *your* side.
5 Then you shall see, and flow together, and your heart shall fear, and be enlarged; because the abundance of the sea shall be converted unto you, the forces of the Gentiles shall come unto you.
6 The multitude of camels shall cover you, the dromedaries of Midian and Ephah; all they from Sheba shall come: they shall bring gold and incense; and they shall show forth the praises of Yahweh.
7 All the flocks of Kedar shall be gathered together unto you, the rams of Nebaioth shall minister unto you: they shall come up with acceptance on my altar, and I will glorify the house of my glory.
8 Who *are* these *that* fly as a cloud, and as the doves to their windows?
9 ¶ Surely the isles shall wait for me, and the ships of Tarshish first, to bring your sons from far, their silver and their gold with them, unto the name of Yahweh your God, and to the Holy One of Israel, because he has glorified you.
10 And the sons of strangers shall build up your walls, and their kings shall minister unto you: for in my wrath I smote you, but in my favor have I had mercy on you.
11 Therefore your gates shall be open continually; they shall not be shut day nor night; that *men* may bring unto you the forces of the Gentiles, and *that* their kings *may be* brought.
12 For the nation and kingdom that will not serve you shall perish; yes, *those* nations shall be utterly wasted.
13 The glory of Lebanon shall come unto you, the fir tree, the pine tree, and the box together, to beautify the place of my sanctuary; and I will make the place of my feet glorious.
14 The sons also of them that afflicted you shall come bending unto you; and all they that despised you shall bow themselves down at the soles of your feet; and they shall call you, The city of Yahweh, The Zion of the Holy One of Israel.
15 ¶ Whereas you have been forsaken and hated, so that no man went through *you*, I will make you an eternal excellency, a joy of many generations.
16 You shall also suck the milk of the Gentiles, and shall suck the breast of kings: and you shall know that I Yahweh *am* your Savior and your Redeemer, the mighty One of Jacob.
17 For brass I will bring gold, and for iron I will bring silver, and for wood brass, and for stones iron: I will also make your officers peace, and your exactors righteousness.
18 Violence shall no more be heard in your land, wasting nor destruction within your borders; but you shall call your walls Salvation, and your gates Praise.
19 The sun shall be no more your light by day; neither for brightness shall the moon give light to you: but Yahweh shall be to you an everlasting light, and your God your glory.
20 Your sun shall no more go down; neither shall your moon withdraw itself: for Yahweh shall be your everlasting light, and the days of your mourning shall be ended.
21 Your people also *shall be* all righteous: they shall inherit the land forever, the branch of my planting, the work of my hands, that I may be glorified.
22 A little one shall become a thousand, and a small one a strong nation: I Yahweh will hurry it in his time.

Isaiah 61

61:1 ¶ The Spirit of the Lord Yahweh *is* upon me; because Yahweh has anointed me to preach good tidings to the meek; he has sent me to bind up the brokenhearted, to proclaim liberty to the captives, and the opening of the prison to *them that are* bound;
2 To proclaim the acceptable year of Yahweh, and the day of vengeance of our God; to comfort all that mourn;
3 To appoint to them that mourn in Zion, to give to them beauty for ashes, the oil of joy for mourning, the garment of praise for the spirit of heaviness; that they might be called trees of righteousness, the planting of Yahweh, that he might be glorified.
4 ¶ And they shall build the old wastes, they shall raise up the former desolations, and they shall repair the waste cities, the desolations of many generations.
5 And strangers shall stand and feed your flocks, and the sons of the alien *shall be* your plowmen and your vine dressers.
6 But you shall be named the Priests of Yahweh: *men* shall call you the Ministers of our God: you shall eat the

riches of the Gentiles, and in their glory shall you boast yourselves.

7 For your shame *you shall have* double; and *for* confusion they shall rejoice in their portion: therefore in their land they shall possess the double: everlasting joy shall be unto them.

8 For I Yahweh love judgment, I hate robbery for burnt offering; and I will direct their work in truth, and I will make an everlasting covenant with them.

9 And their seed shall be known among the Gentiles, and their offspring among the people: all that see them shall acknowledge them, that they *are* the seed which Yahweh has blessed.

10 ¶ I will greatly rejoice in Yahweh, my soul shall be joyful in my God; for he has clothed me with the garments of salvation, he has covered me with the robe of righteousness, as a bridegroom decks *himself* with ornaments, and as a bride adorns *herself* with her jewels.

11 For as the earth brings forth her bud, and as the garden causes the things that are sown in it to spring forth; so the Lord Yahweh will cause righteousness and praise to spring forth before all the nations.

Isaiah 62

62:1 ¶ For Zion's sake will I not hold my peace, and for Jerusalem's sake I will not rest, until the righteousness thereof goes forth as brightness, and the salvation thereof as a lamp *that* burns.

2 And the Gentiles shall see your righteousness, and all kings your glory: and you shall be called by a new name, which the mouth of Yahweh shall name.

3 You shall also be a crown of glory in the hand of Yahweh, and a royal diadem in the hand of your God.

4 You shall no more be termed Forsaken; neither shall your land any more be termed Desolate: but you shall be called Hephzibah, and your land Beulah: for Yahweh delights in you, and your land shall be married.

5 For *as* a young man marries a virgin, *so* shall your sons marry you: and *as* the bridegroom rejoices over the bride, *so* shall your God rejoice over you.

6 ¶ I have set watchmen upon your walls, O Jerusalem, *which* shall never hold their peace day nor night: you that make mention of Yahweh, keep not silence,

7 And give him no rest, till he establishes, and till he makes Jerusalem a praise in the earth.

8 Yahweh has sworn by his right hand, and by the arm of his strength, Surely I will no more give your corn *to be* food for your enemies; and the sons of the stranger shall not drink your *new* wine, for the which you have labored:

9 But they that have gathered it shall eat it, and praise Yahweh; and they that have brought it together shall drink it in the courts of my holiness.

10 ¶ Go through, go through the gates; prepare you the way of the people; cast up, cast up the highway; gather out the stones; lift up a standard for the people.

11 Behold, Yahweh has proclaimed unto the end of the world, Say you to the daughter of Zion, Behold, your salvation comes; behold, his reward *is* with him, and his work before him.

12 And they shall call them, The holy people, The redeemed of Yahweh: and you shall be called, Sought Out, A city not forsaken.

Isaiah 63

63:1 ¶ Who *is* this that comes from Edom, with dyed garments from Bozrah? this *that is* glorious in his apparel, traveling in the greatness of his strength? I that speak in righteousness, mighty to save.

2 Why *are you* red in your apparel, and your garments like him that treads in the wine vat?

3 I have trodden the winepress alone; and of the people *there were* none with me: for I will tread them in my anger, and trample them in my fury; and their blood shall be sprinkled upon my garments, and I will stain all my apparel.

4 For the day of vengeance *is* in my heart, and the year of my redeemed has come.

5 And I looked, and *there was* none to help; and I wondered that *there was* none to uphold: therefore my own arm brought salvation unto me; and my fury, it upheld me.

6 And I will tread down the people in my anger, and make them drunk in my fury, and I will bring down their strength to the earth.

7 ¶ I will mention the loving kindness of Yahweh, *and* the praises of Yahweh, according to all that Yahweh has bestowed on us, and the great goodness toward the house of Israel, which he has bestowed on them according to his mercies, and according to the multitude of his loving kindness.

8 For he said, Surely they *are* my people, children *that* will not lie so he was their Savior.

9 In all their affliction he was afflicted, and the angel of his presence saved them: in his love and in his pity he redeemed them; and he bore them, and carried them all the days of old.

10 But they rebelled, and grieved his holy Spirit: therefore he was turned to be their enemy, *and* he fought against them.

11 Then he remembered the days of old, Moses, *and* his people, *saying*, Where *is* he that brought them up out of the sea with the shepherd of his flock? where *is* he that put his holy Spirit within him?

12 That led *them* by the right hand of Moses with his glorious arm, dividing the water before them, to make himself an everlasting name?

13 That led them through the deep, as a horse in the wilderness, *that* they should not stumble?

14 As a beast goes down into the valley, the Spirit of Yahweh caused him to rest: so did you lead your people, to make yourself a glorious name.

Isaiah 63

15 ¶ Look down from heaven, and behold from the habitation of your holiness and of your glory: where *is* your zeal and your strength, the abundance of your heart and of your mercies toward me? are they restrained?
16 Doubtless you *are* our father, though Abraham was ignorant of us, and Israel acknowledges us not: you, O Yahweh, *are* our father, our redeemer; your name *is* from everlasting.
17 O Yahweh, why have you made us to err from your ways, *and* hardened our heart from your fear? Return for your servants' sake, the tribes of your inheritance.
18 The people of your holiness have possessed *it* but a little while: our adversaries have trodden down your sanctuary.
19 We are *yours*: you never bore rule over them; they were not called by your name.

Isaiah 64

64:1 ¶ Oh that you would rend the heavens, that you would come down, that the mountains might flow down at your presence,
2 As *when* the melting fire burns, the fire causes the waters to boil, to make your name known to your adversaries, *that* the nations may tremble at your presence!
3 When you did fearful things *which* we looked not for, you came down, the mountains flowed down at your presence.
4 For since the beginning of the world *men* have not heard, nor perceived by the ear, neither has the eye seen, O God, besides you, *what* he has prepared for him that waits for him.
5 You meet him that rejoices and works righteousness, *those that* remember you in your ways: behold, you are angry; for we have sinned: in those is continuance, and we shall be saved.
6 ¶ But we are all as an unclean *thing*, and all our righteousnesses *are* as filthy rags; and we all do fade as a leaf; and our iniquities, like the wind, have taken us away.
7 And *there is* none that calls on your name, that stirs up himself to take hold of you: for you have hidden your face from us, and have consumed us, because of our iniquities.
8 But now, O Yahweh, you *are* our father; we *are* the clay, and you our potter; and we all *are* the work of your hand.
9 Be not angry very much O Yahweh, neither remember iniquity forever: behold, see, we beseech you, we *are* all your people.
10 Your holy cities are a wilderness, Zion is a wilderness, Jerusalem a desolation.
11 Our holy and our beautiful house, where our fathers praised you, is burned up with fire: and all our pleasant things are laid waste.
12 Will you refrain yourself for these *things*, O Yahweh? will you hold your peace, and afflict us very greatly?

Isaiah 65

65:1 ¶ I am sought of *them that* asked not *for me*; I am found of *them that* sought me not: I said, Behold me, behold me, to a nation *that* was not called by my name.
2 I have spread out my hands all the day to a rebellious people, which walk in a way *that is* not good, after their own thoughts;
3 A people that provokes me to anger continually to my face; that sacrifices in gardens, and burns incense upon altars of brick;
4 Which remain among the graves, and lodge in the monuments, which eat swine's flesh, and broth of abominable *things is in* their vessels;
5 Which say, Stand by yourself, come not near to me; for I am holier than you. These *are* a smoke in my nose, a fire that burns all the day.
6 Behold, *it is* written before me: I will not keep silent, but will recompense, even recompense into their bosom,
7 Your iniquities, and the iniquities of your fathers together, says Yahweh, which have burned incense upon the mountains, and blasphemed me upon the hills: therefore will I measure their former work into their bosom.
8 ¶ Thus says Yahweh, As the new wine is found in the cluster, and *one* says, Destroy it not; for a blessing *is* in it: so will I do for my servants' sakes, that I may not destroy them all.
9 And I will bring forth a seed out of Jacob, and out of Judah an inheritor of my mountains: and my elect shall inherit it, and my servants shall dwell there.
10 And Sharon shall be a fold of flocks, and the valley of Achor a place for the herds to lie down in, for my people that have sought me.
11 ¶ But you *are* they that forsake Yahweh, that forget my holy mountain, that prepare a table for fortune, and that furnish the drink offering unto *the* god of fate.
12 Therefore will I number you to the sword, and you shall all bow down to the slaughter: because when I called, you did not answer; when I spoke, you did not hear; but did evil before my eyes, and did choose *that* wherein I delighted not.
13 Therefore thus says the Lord Yahweh, Behold, my servants shall eat, but you shall be hungry: behold, my servants shall drink, but you shall be thirsty: behold, my servants shall rejoice, but you shall be ashamed:
14 Behold, my servants shall sing for joy of heart, but you shall cry for sorrow of heart, and shall howl for hurting of spirit.
15 And you shall leave your name for a curse unto my chosen: for the Lord Yahweh shall slay you, and call his servants by another name:
16 That he who blesses himself in the earth shall bless himself in the God of truth; and he that swears in the earth shall swear by the God of truth; because the former troubles are forgotten, and because they are hidden from my eyes.

17 ¶ For, behold, I create new heavens and a new earth: and the former shall not be remembered, nor come into mind.
18 But be you glad and rejoice forever *in that* which I create: for, behold, I create Jerusalem a rejoicing, and her people a joy.
19 And I will rejoice in Jerusalem, and joy in my people: and the voice of weeping shall be no more heard in her, nor the voice of crying.
20 There shall be no more there an infant of days, nor an old man that has not filled his days: for the child shall die a hundred years old; but the sinner *being* a hundred years old shall be accursed.
21 And they shall build houses, and inhabit *them*; and they shall plant vineyards, and eat the fruit of them.
22 They shall not build, and another inhabit; they shall not plant, and another eat: for as the days of a tree *are* the days of my people, and my elect shall long enjoy the work of their hands.
23 They shall not labor in vain, nor bring forth for trouble; for they *are* the seed of the blessed of Yahweh, and their offspring with them.
24 And it shall come to pass, that before they call, I will answer; and while they are yet speaking, I will hear.
25 The wolf and the lamb shall feed together, and the lion shall eat straw like the bullock: and dust *shall be* the serpent's food. They shall not hurt nor destroy in all my holy mountain, says Yahweh.

Isaiah 66

66:1 ¶ Thus says Yahweh, The heaven *is* my throne, and the earth *is* my footstool: where *is* the house that you build unto me? and where *is* the place of my rest?
2 For all those *things* has my hand made, and all those *things* have been, says Yahweh: but to this *man* will I look, *even* to *him that is* poor and of a contrite spirit, and trembles at my word.
3 He that kills an ox *is as if* he slew a man; he that sacrifices a lamb, *as if* he cut off a dog's neck; he that offers an oblation, *as if he offered* swine's blood; he that burns incense, *as if* he blessed an idol. Yes, they have chosen their own ways, and their soul delights in their abominations.
4 I also will choose their delusions, and will bring their fears upon them; because when I called, none did answer; when I spoke, they did not hear: but they did evil before my eyes, and chose *that* in which I delighted not.
5 ¶ Hear the word of Yahweh, you that tremble at his word; Your brethren that hated you, that cast you out for my name's sake, said, Let Yahweh be glorified: but he shall appear to your joy, and they shall be ashamed.
6 A voice of noise from the city, a voice from the temple, a voice of Yahweh that renders recompense to his enemies.
7 Before she labored, she brought forth; before her pain came, she was delivered of a man child.
8 Who has heard such a thing? who has seen such things? Shall the earth be made to bring forth in one day? *or* shall a nation be born at once? for as soon as Zion labored, she brought forth her children.
9 Shall I bring to the birth, and not cause to bring forth? says Yahweh: shall I cause to bring forth, and shut *the womb*? says your God.
10 Rejoice you with Jerusalem, and be glad with her, all you that love her: rejoice for joy with her, all you that mourn for her:
11 That you may suck, and be satisfied with the breasts of her consolations; that you may milk out, and be delighted with the abundance of her glory.
12 For thus says Yahweh, Behold, I will extend peace to her like a river, and the glory of the Gentiles like a flowing stream: then shall you suck, you shall be borne upon *her* sides, and be dandled upon *her* knees.
13 As one whom his mother comforts, so will I comfort you; and you shall be comforted in Jerusalem.
14 And when you see *this*, your heart shall rejoice, and your bones shall flourish like a herb: and the hand of Yahweh shall be known toward his servants, and *his* indignation toward his enemies.
15 ¶ For, behold, Yahweh will come with fire, and with his chariots like a whirlwind, to render his anger with fury, and his rebuke with flames of fire.
16 For by fire and by his sword will Yahweh plead with all flesh: and the slain of Yahweh shall be many.
17 They that sanctify themselves, and purify themselves in the gardens behind one *tree* in the midst, eating swine's flesh, and the abomination, and the mouse, shall be consumed together, says Yahweh.
18 For I know their works and their thoughts: it shall come, that I will gather all nations and tongues; and they shall come, and see my glory.
19 And I will set a sign among them, and I will send those that escape of them to the nations, *to* Tarshish, Pul, and Lud, that draw the bow, *to* Tubal, and Javan, *to* the isles afar off, that have not heard my fame, neither have seen my glory; and they shall declare my glory among the Gentiles.
20 And they shall bring all your brethren *for* an offering unto Yahweh out of all nations upon horses, and in chariots, and in litters, and upon mules, and upon swift beasts, to my holy mountain Jerusalem, says Yahweh, as the children of Israel bring an offering in a clean vessel into the house of Yahweh.
21 And I will also take of them for priests *and* for Levites, says Yahweh.
22 For as the new heavens and the new earth, which I will make, shall remain before me, says Yahweh, so shall your seed and your name remain.
23 And it shall come to pass, *that* from one new moon to another, and from one sabbath to another, shall all flesh come to worship before me, says Yahweh.
24 And they shall go forth, and look upon the carcasses of the men that have transgressed against me: for their worm shall not die, neither shall their fire be quenched; and they shall be an abhorring unto all flesh.

Jeremiah

Jeremiah 1

1:1 ¶ The words of Jeremiah the son of Hilkiah, of the priests that *were* in Anathoth in the land of Benjamin:
2 To whom the word of Yahweh came in the days of Josiah the son of Amon king of Judah, in the thirteenth year of his reign.
3 It came also in the days of Jehoiakim the son of Josiah king of Judah, to the end of the eleventh year of Zedekiah the son of Josiah king of Judah, to the carrying away of Jerusalem captive in the fifth month.
4 ¶ Then the word of Yahweh came to me, saying,
5 Before I formed you in the belly I knew you; and before you came forth out of the womb I sanctified you, *and* I ordained you a prophet unto the nations.
6 Then said I, Ah, Lord Yahweh! behold, I cannot speak: for I *am* a child.
7 But Yahweh said to me, Say not, I *am* a child: for you shall go to all that I shall send you, and whatever I command you you shall speak.
8 Be not afraid of their faces: for I *am* with you to deliver you, says Yahweh.
9 Then Yahweh put forth his hand, and touched my mouth. And Yahweh said to me, Behold, I have put my words in your mouth.
10 See, I have this day set you over the nations and over the kingdoms, to root out, and to pull down, and to destroy, and to throw down, to build, and to plant.
11 ¶ Moreover the word of Yahweh came to me, saying, Jeremiah, what see you? And I said, I see a rod of an almond tree.
12 Then said Yahweh to me, You have well seen: for I will hasten my word to perform it.
13 And the word of Yahweh came to me the second time, saying, What see you? And I said, I see a seething pot; and the face thereof *is* toward the north.
14 Then Yahweh said to me, Out of the north an evil shall break forth upon all the inhabitants of the land.
15 For, lo, I will call all the families of the kingdoms of the north, says Yahweh; and they shall come, and they shall set every one his throne at the entering of the gates of Jerusalem, and against all the walls thereof round about, and against all the cities of Judah.
16 And I will utter my judgments against them touching all their wickedness, who have forsaken me, and have burned incense to other gods, and worshipped the works of their own hands.
17 You therefore gird up your loins, and arise, and speak to them all that I command you: be not dismayed at their faces, lest I confound you before them.
18 For, behold, I have made you this day a defensed city, and an iron pillar, and brazen walls against the whole land, against the kings of Judah, against the princes thereof, against the priests thereof, and against the people of the land.
19 And they shall fight against you; but they shall not prevail against you; for I *am* with you, says Yahweh, to deliver you.

Jeremiah 2

2:1 ¶ Moreover the word of Yahweh came to me, saying,
2 Go and cry in the ears of Jerusalem, saying, Thus says Yahweh; I remember you, the kindness of your youth, the love of your espousals, when you went after me in the wilderness, in a land *that was* not sown.
3 Israel *was* holiness unto Yahweh, *and* the firstfruits of his increase: all that devour him shall offend; evil shall come upon them, says Yahweh.
4 Hear you the word of Yahweh, O house of Jacob, and all the families of the house of Israel:
5 Thus says Yahweh, What iniquity have your fathers found in me, that they have gone far from me, and have walked after vanity, and have become vain?
6 Neither said they, Where *is* Yahweh that brought us up out of the land of Egypt, that led us through the wilderness, through a land of deserts and of pits, through a land of drought, and of the shadow of death, through a land that no man passed through, and where no man dwelt?
7 And I brought you into a plentiful country, to eat the fruit thereof and the goodness thereof; but when you entered, you defiled my land, and made my heritage an abomination.
8 The priests said not, Where *is* Yahweh? and they that handle the law knew me not: the pastors also transgressed against me, and the prophets prophesied by Baal, and walked after *things that* do not profit.
9 ¶ Therefore I will yet plead with you, says Yahweh, and with your children's children will I plead.
10 For pass over the isles of Chittim, and see; and send unto Kedar, and consider diligently, and see if there is such a thing.
11 Has a nation changed *their* gods, which *are* yet no gods? but my people have changed their glory for *that which* does not profit.
12 Be astonished, O you heavens, at this, and be horribly afraid, be you very desolate, says Yahweh.
13 For my people have committed two evils; they have forsaken me the fountain of living waters, *and* hewed them out cisterns, broken cisterns, that can hold no water.
14 ¶ *Is* Israel a servant? *is* he a home born *slave*? why is he spoiled?
15 The young lions roared upon him, *and* yelled, and they made his land waste: his cities are burned without inhabitant.
16 Also the children of Noph and Tahapanes have broken the crown of your head.
17 Have you not procured this unto yourself, in that you have forsaken Yahweh your God, when he led you by the way?
18 And now what have you to do in the way of Egypt, to drink the waters of Sihor? or what have you to do in the way of Assyria, to drink the waters of the river?

19 Your own wickedness shall correct you, and your backslidings shall reprove you: know therefore and see that *it is* an evil *thing* and bitter, that you have forsaken Yahweh your God, and that my fear *is* not in you, says the Lord Yahweh of hosts.

20 ¶ For of old time I have broken your yoke, *and* burst your bands; and you said, I will not transgress; when upon every high hill and under every green tree you wander, playing the harlot.

21 Yet I had planted you a noble vine, wholly a right seed: how then have you turned into the degenerate plant of a strange vine unto me?

22 For though you wash you with soda, and take you much soap, *yet* your iniquity is marked before me, says the Lord Yahweh.

23 How can you say, I am not polluted, I have not gone after Baalim? see your way in the valley, know what you have done: *you are* a swift dromedary traversing her ways;

24 A wild donkey used to the wilderness, *that* snuffs up the wind at her pleasure; in her occasion who can turn her away? all they that seek her will not weary themselves; in her month they shall find her.

25 Withhold your foot from being unshod, and your throat from thirst: but you said, There is no hope: no; for I have loved strangers, and after them will I go.

26 As the thief is ashamed when he is found, so is the house of Israel ashamed; they, their kings, their princes, and their priests, and their prophets,

27 Saying to a tree, You *are* my father; and to a stone, You have brought me forth: for they have turned *their* back unto me, and not *their* face: but in the time of their trouble they will say, Arise, and save us.

28 But where *are* your gods that you have made you? let them arise, if they can save you in the time of your trouble: for *according to* the number of your cities *are* your gods, O Judah.

29 ¶ Why will you plead with me? you all have transgressed against me, says Yahweh.

30 In vain have I smitten your children; they received no correction: your own sword has devoured your prophets, like a destroying lion.

31 O generation, see you the word of Yahweh. Have I been a wilderness to Israel? a land of darkness? why say my people, We are lords; we will come no more unto you?

32 Can a maid forget her ornaments, *or* a bride her attire? yet my people have forgotten me days without number.

33 Why trim you your way to seek love? therefore have you also taught the wicked ones your ways.

34 Also in your skirts is found the blood of the souls of the poor innocents: I have not found it by secret search, but upon all these.

35 Yet you say, Because I am innocent, surely his anger shall turn from me. Behold, I will plead with you, because you say, I have not sinned.

36 Why gad you about so much to change your way? you also will be ashamed of Egypt, as you were ashamed of Assyria.

37 Yes, you shall go forth from him, and your hands upon your head: for Yahweh has rejected your confidences, and you shall not prosper in them.

Jeremiah 3

3:1 ¶ They say, If a man puts away his wife, and she goes from him, and becomes another man's, shall he return to her again? shall not that land be greatly polluted? but you have played the harlot with many lovers; yet return again to me, says Yahweh.

2 Lift up your eyes to the high places, and see where you have not been lain with. In the ways have you sat for them, as the Arabian in the wilderness; and you have polluted the land with your whoredoms and with your wickedness.

3 Therefore the showers have been withheld, and there has been no latter rain; and you had a whore's forehead, you refused to be ashamed.

4 Will you not from this time cry unto me, My father, you *are* the guide of my youth?

5 Will he reserve *his anger* forever? will he keep *it* to the end? Behold, you have spoken and done evil things as you could.

6 ¶ Yahweh said also to me in the days of Josiah the king, Have you seen *that* which backsliding Israel has done? she has gone up upon every high mountain and under every green tree, and there has played the harlot.

7 And I said after she had done all these *things*, Turn you unto me. But she returned not. And her treacherous sister Judah saw *it*.

8 And I saw, when for all the causes whereby backsliding Israel committed adultery I had put her away, and given her a bill of divorce; yet her treacherous sister Judah feared not, but went and played the harlot also.

9 And it came to pass through the lightness of her whoredom, that she defiled the land, and committed adultery with stones and with trees.

10 And yet for all this her treacherous sister Judah has not turned unto me with her whole heart, but deceitfully, says Yahweh.

11 And Yahweh said to me, The backsliding Israel has justified herself more than treacherous Judah.

12 ¶ Go and proclaim these words toward the north, and say, Return, you backsliding Israel, says Yahweh; *and* I will not cause my anger to fall upon you: for I *am* merciful, says Yahweh, *and* I will not keep *anger* forever.

13 Only acknowledge your iniquity, that you have transgressed against Yahweh your God, and have scattered your ways to the strangers under every green tree, and you have not obeyed my voice, says Yahweh.

14 Turn, O backsliding children, says Yahweh; for I am married to you: and I will take you one of a city, and two of a family, and I will bring you to Zion:

15 And I will give you pastors according to my heart, which shall feed you with knowledge and understanding.

Jeremiah 3

16 And it shall come to pass, when you are multiplied and increased in the land, in those days, says Yahweh, they shall say no more, The ark of the covenant of Yahweh: neither shall it come to mind: neither shall they remember it; neither shall they visit *it*; neither shall *that* be done any more.

17 At that time they shall call Jerusalem the throne of Yahweh; and all the nations shall be gathered unto it, to the name of Yahweh, to Jerusalem: neither shall they walk any more after the imagination of their evil heart.

18 In those days the house of Judah shall walk with the house of Israel, and they shall come together out of the land of the north to the land that I have given for an inheritance unto your fathers.

19 But I said, How shall I put you among the children, and give you a pleasant land, a glorious inheritance of the hosts of nations? and I said, You shall call me, My father; and shall not turn away from me.

20 ¶ Surely *as* a wife treacherously departs from her husband, so have you dealt treacherously with me, O house of Israel, says Yahweh.

21 A voice was heard upon the high places, weeping *and* supplications of the children of Israel: for they have perverted their way, *and* they have forgotten Yahweh their God.

22 Return, you backsliding children, *and* I will heal your backslidings. Behold, we come to you; for you *are* Yahweh our God.

23 Truly in vain *is salvation hoped for* from the hills, *and from* the multitude of mountains: truly in Yahweh our God *is* the salvation of Israel.

24 For shame has devoured the labor of our fathers from our youth; their flocks and their herds, their sons and their daughters.

25 We lie down in our shame, and our confusion covers us: for we have sinned against Yahweh our God, we and our fathers, from our youth even unto this day, and have not obeyed the voice of Yahweh our God.

Jeremiah 4

4:1 ¶ If you will return, O Israel, says Yahweh, return unto me: and if you will put away your abominations out of my sight, then shall you not remove.

2 And you shall swear, Yahweh lives, in truth, in judgment, and in righteousness; and the nations shall bless themselves in him, and in him shall they glory.

3 ¶ For thus says Yahweh to the men of Judah and Jerusalem, Break up your fallow ground, and sow not among thorns.

4 Circumcise yourselves to Yahweh, and take away the foreskins of your heart, you men of Judah and inhabitants of Jerusalem: lest my fury come forth like fire, and burn that none can quench *it*, because of the evil of your doings.

5 ¶ Declare you in Judah, and publish in Jerusalem; and say, Blow you the trumpet in the land: cry, gather together, and say, Assemble yourselves, and let us go into the defensed cities.

6 Set up the standard toward Zion: flee, stay not: for I will bring evil from the north, and a great destruction.

7 The lion has come up from his thicket, and the destroyer of the Gentiles is on his way; he has gone forth from his place to make your land desolate; *and* your cities shall be laid waste, without an inhabitant.

8 For this gird you with sackcloth, lament and howl: for the fierce anger of Yahweh is not turned back from us.

9 And it shall come to pass at that day, says Yahweh, *that* the heart of the king shall perish, and the heart of the princes; and the priests shall be astonished, and the prophets shall wonder.

10 Then said I, Ah, Lord Yahweh! surely you have greatly deceived this people and Jerusalem, saying, You shall have peace; whereas the sword reaches unto the soul.

11 At that time shall it be said to this people and to Jerusalem, A dry wind of the high places in the wilderness toward the daughter of my people, not to fan, nor to cleanse,

12 *Even* a full wind from those *places* shall come to me: now also will I give sentence against them.

13 Behold, he shall come up as clouds, and his chariots *shall be* as a whirlwind: his horses are swifter than eagles. Woe unto us! for we are spoiled.

14 O Jerusalem, wash your heart from wickedness, that you may be saved. How long shall your vain thoughts lodge within you?

15 For a voice declares from Dan, and publishes affliction from mount Ephraim.

16 Make you mention to the nations; behold, publish against Jerusalem, *that* watchers come from a far country, and give out their voice against the cities of Judah.

17 As keepers of a field, are they against her round about; because she has been rebellious against me, says Yahweh.

18 Your way and your doings have procured these *things* unto you; this *is* your wickedness, because it is bitter, because it reaches unto your heart.

19 ¶ My bowels, my bowels! I am pained at my very heart; my heart makes a noise in me; I cannot hold my peace, because you have heard, O my soul, the sound of the trumpet, the alarm of war.

20 Destruction upon destruction is cried; for the whole land is spoiled: suddenly are my tents spoiled, *and* my curtains in a moment.

21 How long shall I see the standard, *and* hear the sound of the trumpet?

22 For my people *are* foolish, they have not known me; they *are* foolish children, and they have no understanding: they *are* wise to do evil, but to do good they have no knowledge.

23 I beheld the earth, and, lo, *it was* without form, and void; and the heavens, and they *had* no light.

24 I beheld the mountains, and, lo, they trembled, and all the hills moved lightly.

25 I beheld, and, lo, *there was* no man, and all the birds of the heavens had fled.

26 I beheld, and, lo, the fruitful place *was* a wilderness, and all the cities thereof were broken down at the presence of Yahweh, *and* by his fierce anger.

27 For thus has Yahweh said, The whole land shall be desolate; yet will I not make a full end.

28 For this shall the earth mourn, and the heavens above be black: because I have spoken *it*, I have purposed *it*, and will not repent, neither will I turn back from it.

29 The whole city shall flee for the noise of the horsemen and bow men; they shall go into thickets, and climb up upon the rocks: every city *shall be* forsaken, and not a man dwell therein.

30 And *when* you *are* spoiled, what shall you do? Though you clothe yourself with crimson, though you deck you with ornaments of gold, though you cover your face with painting, in vain will you make yourself fair; *your* lovers will despise you, they will seek your life.

31 For I have heard a voice as of a woman in labor, *and* the anguish as of her that brings forth her first child, the voice of the daughter of Zion, *that* bewails herself, *that* spreads her hands, *saying*, Woe *is* me now! for my soul is wearied because of murderers.

Jeremiah 5

5:1 ¶ Run you to and fro through the streets of Jerusalem, and see now, and know, and seek in the broad places thereof, if you can find a man, if there is *any* that executes judgment, that seeks the truth; and I will pardon it.

2 And though they say, Yahweh lives; surely they swear falsely.

3 O Yahweh, *are* not your eyes upon the truth? you have stricken them, but they have not grieved; you have consumed them, *but* they have refused to receive correction: they have made their faces harder than a rock; they have refused to return.

4 Therefore I said, Surely these *are* poor; they are foolish: for they know not the way of Yahweh, *nor* the judgment of their God.

5 I will get me to the great men, and will speak to them; for they have known the way of Yahweh, *and* the judgment of their God: but these have altogether broken the yoke, *and* burst the bonds.

6 Therefore a lion out of the forest shall slay them, *and* a wolf of the evenings shall spoil them, a leopard shall watch over their cities: every one that goes out there shall be torn in pieces: because their transgressions are many, *and* their backslidings are increased.

7 How shall I pardon you for this? your children have forsaken me, and sworn by *them that are* no gods: when I had fed them to the full, they then committed adultery, and assembled themselves by troops in the harlots' houses.

8 They were *as* fed horses in the morning: every one neighed after his neighbor's wife.

9 Shall I not visit for these *things*? says Yahweh: and shall not my soul be avenged on such a nation as this?

10 ¶ Go you up upon her walls, and destroy; but make not a full end: take away her battlements; for they *are* not Yahweh's.

11 For the house of Israel and the house of Judah have dealt very treacherously against me, says Yahweh.

12 They have belied Yahweh, and said, *it is* not he; neither shall evil come upon us; neither shall we see sword nor famine:

13 And the prophets shall become wind, and the word *is* not in them: thus shall it be done to them.

14 Therefore thus says Yahweh God of hosts, Because you speak this word, behold, I will make my words in your mouth fire, and this people wood, and it shall devour them.

15 Lo, I will bring a nation upon you from far, O house of Israel, says Yahweh: it *is* a mighty nation, it *is* an ancient nation, a nation whose language you know not, neither understand what they say.

16 Their quiver *is* as an open sepulcher, they *are* all mighty men.

17 And they shall eat up your harvest, and your bread, *which* your sons and your daughters should eat: they shall eat up your flocks and your herds: they shall eat up your vines and your fig trees: they shall impoverish your fenced cities, wherein you trusted, with the sword.

18 Nevertheless in those days, says Yahweh, I will not make a full end with you.

19 And it shall come to pass, when you shall say, Why does Yahweh our God all these *things* unto us? then shall you answer them, Like as you have forsaken me, and served strange gods in your land, so shall you serve strangers in a land *that is* not yours.

20 ¶ Declare this in the house of Jacob, and publish it in Judah, saying,

21 Hear now this, O foolish people, and without understanding; which have eyes, and see not; which have ears, and hear not:

22 Fear you not me? says Yahweh: will you not tremble at my presence, which have placed the sand *for* the bound of the sea by a perpetual decree, that it cannot pass it: and though the waves thereof toss themselves, yet can they not prevail; though they roar, yet can they not pass over it?

23 But this people has a revolting and a rebellious heart; they have revolted and *are* gone.

24 Neither say they in their heart, Let us now fear Yahweh our God, that gives rain, both the former and the latter, in his season: he reserves unto us the appointed weeks of the harvest.

25 ¶ Your iniquities have turned away these *things*, and your sins have withheld good *things* from you.

26 For among my people are found wicked *men*: they lay wait, as he that sets snares; they set a trap, they catch men.

27 As a cage is full of birds, so *are* their houses full of deceit: therefore they have become great, and grown rich.

28 They have grown fat, they shine: yes, they overpass the deeds of the wicked: they judge not the cause, the cause of the fatherless, yet they prosper; and the right of the needy do they not judge.

Jeremiah 5

29 Shall I not visit for these *things*? says Yahweh: shall not my soul be avenged on such a nation as this?
30 A wonderful and horrible thing is committed in the land;
31 The prophets prophesy falsely, and the priests bear rule by their means; and my people love *to have it* so: and what will you do in the end thereof?

Jeremiah 6

6:1 ¶ O you children of Benjamin, gather yourselves to flee out of the midst of Jerusalem, and blow the trumpet in Tekoa, and set up a sign of fire in Bethhaccerem: for evil appears out of the north, and great destruction.
2 I have likened the daughter of Zion to a comely and delicate *woman*.
3 The shepherds with their flocks shall come to her; they shall pitch *their* tents against her round about; they shall feed every one in his place.
4 Prepare you war against her; arise, and let us go up at noon. Woe unto us! for the day goes away, for the shadows of the evening are stretched out.
5 Arise, and let us go by night, and let us destroy her palaces.
6 For thus has Yahweh of hosts said, Hew you down trees, and cast a mount against Jerusalem: this *is* the city to be visited; she *is* wholly oppression in the midst of her.
7 As a fountain casts out her waters, so she casts out her wickedness: violence and spoil is heard in her; before me continually *is* grief and wounds.
8 Be you instructed, O Jerusalem, lest my soul departs from you; lest I make you desolate, a land not inhabited.
9 ¶ Thus says Yahweh of hosts, They shall thoroughly glean the remnant of Israel as a vine: turn back your hand as a grape gatherer into the baskets.
10 To whom shall I speak, and give warning, that they may hear? behold, their ear *is* uncircumcised, and they cannot listen: behold, the word of Yahweh is to them a reproach; they have no delight in it.
11 Therefore I am full of the fury of Yahweh; I am weary with holding in: I will pour it out upon the children abroad, and upon the assembly of young men together: for even the husband with the wife shall be taken, the aged with *him that is* full of days.
12 And their houses shall be turned unto others, *with their* fields and wives together: for I will stretch out my hand upon the inhabitants of the land, says Yahweh.
13 For from the least of them even to the greatest of them every one *is* given to covetousness; and from the prophet even to the priest every one deals falsely.
14 They have healed also the hurt *of the daughter* of my people slightly, saying, Peace, peace; when *there is* no peace.
15 Were they ashamed when they had committed abomination? no, they were not at all ashamed, neither could they blush: therefore they shall fall among them that fall: at the time *that* I visit them they shall be cast down, says Yahweh.
16 Thus says Yahweh, Stand you in the ways, and see, and ask for the old paths, where *is* the good way, and walk therein, and you shall find rest for your souls. But they said, We will not walk *therein*.
17 Also I set watchmen over you, *saying*, Listen to the sound of the trumpet. But they said, We will not listen.
18 ¶ Therefore hear, you nations, and know, O congregation, what *is* among them.
19 Hear, O earth: behold, I will bring evil upon this people, *even* the fruit of their thoughts, because they have not listened to my words, nor to my law, but rejected it.
20 To what purpose comes there to me incense from Sheba, and the sweet cane from a far country? your burnt offerings *are* not acceptable, nor your sacrifices sweet unto me.
21 Therefore thus says Yahweh, Behold, I will lay stumbling blocks before this people, and the fathers and the sons together shall fall upon them; the neighbor and his friend shall perish.
22 Thus says Yahweh, Behold, a people came from the north country, and a great nation shall be raised from the sides of the earth.
23 They shall lay hold on bow and spear; they *are* cruel, and have no mercy; their voice roars like the sea; and they ride upon horses, set in array as men for war against you, O daughter of Zion.
24 We have heard the fame thereof: our hands grow feeble: anguish has taken hold of us, *and* pain, as of a woman in labor.
25 Go not forth into the field, nor walk by the way; for the sword of the enemy *and* fear *is* on every side.
26 O daughter of my people, gird *you* with sackcloth, and wallow yourself in ashes: make you mourning, *as for* an only son, most bitter lamentation: for the spoiler shall suddenly come upon us.
27 I have set you *for* a tower *and* a fortress among my people, that you may know and try their way.
28 They *are* all grievous rebels, walking with slanders: *they are* brass and iron; they *are* all corrupters.
29 The bellows are burned, the lead is consumed of the fire; the founder melts in vain: for the wicked are not plucked away.
30 Reprobate silver shall *men* call them, because Yahweh has rejected them.

Jeremiah 7

7:1 ¶ The word that came to Jeremiah from Yahweh, saying,
2 Stand in the gate of Yahweh's house, and proclaim there this word, and say, Hear the word of Yahweh, all *you of* Judah, that enter in at these gates to worship Yahweh.
3 Thus says Yahweh of hosts, the God of Israel, Amend your ways and your doings, and I will cause you to dwell in this place.

4 Trust you not in lying words, saying, The temple of Yahweh, The temple of Yahweh, The temple of Yahweh, *are* these.

5 For if you thoroughly amend your ways and your doings; if you thoroughly execute judgment between a man and his neighbor;

6 *If* you oppress not the stranger, the fatherless, and the widow, and shed not innocent blood in this place, neither walk after other gods to your hurt:

7 Then will I cause you to dwell in this place, in the land that I gave to your fathers, forever and ever.

8 Behold, you trust in lying words, that cannot profit.

9 Will you steal, murder, and commit adultery, and swear falsely, and burn incense unto Baal, and walk after other gods whom you know not;

10 And come and stand before me in this house, which is called by my name, and say, We are delivered to do all these abominations?

11 Has this house, which is called by my name, become a den of robbers in your eyes? Behold, even I have seen *it*, says Yahweh.

12 But go you now to my place which *was* in Shiloh, where I set my name at the first, and see what I did to it for the wickedness of my people Israel.

13 And now, because you have done all these works, says Yahweh, and I spoke to you, rising up early and speaking, but you heard not; and I called you, but you answered not;

14 Therefore will I do to *this* house, which is called by my name, wherein you trust, and to the place which I gave to you and to your fathers, as I have done to Shiloh.

15 And I will cast you out of my sight, as I have cast out all your brethren, *even* the whole seed of Ephraim.

16 ¶ Therefore pray not you for this people, neither lift up cry nor prayer for them, neither make intercession to me: for I will not hear you.

17 See you not what they do in the cities of Judah and in the streets of Jerusalem?

18 The children gather wood, and the fathers kindle the fire, and the women knead *their* dough, to make cakes to the queen of heaven, and to pour out drink offerings to other gods, that they may provoke me to anger.

19 Do they provoke me to anger? says Yahweh: *do they* not *provoke* themselves to the confusion of their own faces?

20 Therefore thus says the Lord Yahweh; Behold, my anger and my fury shall be poured out upon this place, upon man, and upon beast, and upon the trees of the field, and upon the fruit of the ground; and it shall burn, and shall not be quenched.

21 ¶ Thus says Yahweh of hosts, the God of Israel; Put your burnt offerings unto your sacrifices, and eat flesh.

22 For I spoke not to your fathers, nor commanded them in the day that I brought them out of the land of Egypt, concerning burnt offerings or sacrifices:

23 But this thing commanded I them, saying, Obey my voice, and I will be your God, and you shall be my people: and walk you in all the ways that I have commanded you, that it may be well unto you.

24 But they listened not, nor inclined their ear, but walked in the counsels *and* in the imagination of their evil heart, and went backward, and not forward.

25 Since the day that your fathers came forth out of the land of Egypt unto this day I have even sent to you all my servants the prophets, daily rising up early and sending *them*:

26 Yet they listened not to me, nor inclined their ear, but hardened their neck: they did worse than their fathers.

27 Therefore you shall speak all these words to them; but they will not listen to you: you shall also call to them; but they will not answer you.

28 But you shall say to them, This *is* a nation that obeys not the voice of Yahweh their God, nor receives correction: truth is perished, and is cut off from their mouth.

29 ¶ Cut off your hair, *O Jerusalem*, and cast *it* away, and take up a lamentation on high places; for Yahweh has rejected and forsaken the generation of his wrath.

30 For the children of Judah have done evil in my sight, says Yahweh: they have set their abominations in the house which is called by my name, to pollute it.

31 And they have built the high places of Tophet, which *is* in the valley of the son of Hinnom, to burn their sons and their daughters in the fire; which I commanded *them* not, neither came it into my heart.

32 Therefore, behold, the days come, says Yahweh, that it shall no more be called Tophet, nor the valley of the son of Hinnom, but the valley of slaughter: for they shall bury in Tophet, till there is no place.

33 And the carcasses of this people shall be meat for the fowls of the heaven, and for the beasts of the earth; and none shall frighten *them* away.

34 Then will I cause to cease from the cities of Judah, and from the streets of Jerusalem, the voice of joy, and the voice of gladness, the voice of the bridegroom, and the voice of the bride: for the land shall be desolate.

Jeremiah 8

8:1 ¶ At that time, says Yahweh, they shall bring out the bones of the kings of Judah, and the bones of his princes, and the bones of the priests, and the bones of the prophets, and the bones of the inhabitants of Jerusalem, out of their graves:

2 And they shall spread them before the sun, and the moon, and all the host of heaven, whom they have loved, and whom they have served, and after whom they have walked, and whom they have sought, and whom they have worshipped: they shall not be gathered, nor be buried; they shall be for dung upon the face of the earth.

3 And death shall be chosen rather than life by all the residue of them that remain of this evil family, which remain in all the places where I have driven them, says Yahweh of hosts.

4 ¶ Moreover you shall say to them, Thus says Yahweh; Shall they fall, and not arise? shall he turn away, and not return?

Jeremiah 8

5 Why *then* has this people of Jerusalem slid back by a perpetual backsliding? they hold fast deceit, they refuse to return.

6 I listened and heard, *but* they spoke not aright: no man repented him of his wickedness, saying, What have I done? every one turned to his course, as the horse rushes into the battle.

7 Yes, the stork in the heaven knows her appointed times; and the turtle and the crane and the swallow observe the time of their coming; but my people know not the judgment of Yahweh.

8 How do you say, We *are* wise, and the law of Yahweh *is* with us? Lo, certainly in vain made he *it*; the pen of the scribes *is* in vain.

9 The wise *men* are ashamed, they are dismayed and taken: lo, they have rejected the word of Yahweh; and what wisdom *is* in them?

10 Therefore will I give their wives to others, *and* their fields to them that shall inherit *them*: for every one from the least even to the greatest is given to covetousness, from the prophet even to the priest every one deals falsely.

11 For they have healed the hurt of the daughter of my people slightly, saying, Peace, peace; when *there is* no peace.

12 Were they ashamed when they had committed abomination? no, they were not at all ashamed, neither could they blush: therefore shall they fall among them that fall: in the time of their visitation they shall be cast down, says Yahweh.

13 ¶ I will surely consume them, says Yahweh: *there shall be* no grapes on the vine, nor figs on the fig tree, and the leaf shall fade; and *the things that* I have given them shall pass away from them.

14 Why do we sit still? assemble yourselves, and let us enter into the defensed cities, and let us be silent there: for Yahweh our God has put us to silence, and given us water of gall to drink, because we have sinned against Yahweh.

15 We looked for peace, but no good *came; and* for a time of health, and behold trouble!

16 The snorting of his horses was heard from Dan: the whole land trembled at the sound of the neighing of his strong ones; for they have come, and have devoured the land, and all that is in it; the city, and those that dwell therein.

17 For, behold, I will send serpents, poisonous serpents, among you, which *will* not *be* charmed, and they shall bite you, says Yahweh.

18 *When* I would comfort myself against sorrow, my heart *is* faint in me.

19 Behold the voice of the cry of the daughter of my people because of them that dwell in a far country: *Is* not Yahweh in Zion? *is* not her king in her? Why have they provoked me to anger with their graven images, *and* with strange vanities?

20 The harvest is past, the summer is ended, and we are not saved.

21 For the hurt of the daughter of my people am I hurt; I am darkened; astonishment has taken hold on me.

22 *Is there* no balm in Gilead; *is there* no physician there? why then is not the health of the daughter of my people recovered?

Jeremiah 9

9:1 ¶ Oh that my head were waters, and my eyes a fountain of tears, that I might weep day and night for the slain of the daughter of my people!

2 Oh that I had in the wilderness a lodging place of wayfaring men; that I might leave my people, and go from them! for they *are* all adulterers, an assembly of treacherous men.

3 And they bend their tongues *like* their bow *for* lies: but they are not valiant for the truth upon the earth; for they proceed from evil to evil, and they know not me, says Yahweh.

4 Take you heed every one of his neighbor, and trust you not in any brother: for every brother will utterly supplant, and every neighbor will walk with slanders.

5 And they will deceive every one his neighbor, and will not speak the truth: they have taught their tongue to speak lies, *and* weary themselves to commit iniquity.

6 Your habitation *is* in the midst of deceit; through deceit they refuse to know me, says Yahweh.

7 Therefore thus says Yahweh of hosts, Behold, I will melt them, and try them; for how shall I do for the daughter of my people?

8 Their tongue *is as* an arrow shot out; it speaks deceit: *one* speaks peaceably to his neighbor with his mouth, but in *his* heart he lays in wait.

9 Shall I not visit them for these *things*? says Yahweh: shall not my soul be avenged on such a nation as this?

10 For the mountains will I take up a weeping and wailing, and for the habitations of the wilderness a lamentation, because they are burned up, so that none can pass through *them*; neither can *men* hear the voice of the cattle; both the fowl of the heavens and the beast have fled; they are gone.

11 And I will make Jerusalem heaps, *and* a den of dragons; and I will make the cities of Judah desolate, without an inhabitant.

12 ¶ Who *is* the wise man, that may understand this? and *who is he* to whom the mouth of Yahweh has spoken, that he may declare it, for what *does* the land perish *and* be burned up like a wilderness, that none passes through?

13 And Yahweh says, Because they have forsaken my law which I set before them, and have not obeyed my voice, neither walked therein;

14 But have walked after the imagination of their own heart, and after Baalim, which their fathers taught them:

15 Therefore thus says Yahweh of hosts, the God of Israel; Behold, I will feed them, *even* this people, with wormwood, and give them water of gall to drink.

16 I will scatter them also among the heathen, whom neither they nor their fathers have known: and I will send a sword after them, till I have consumed them.

17 Thus says Yahweh of hosts, Consider you, and call for the mourning women, that they may come; and send for cunning *women*, that they may come:

18 And let them make haste, and take up a wailing for us, that our eyes may run down with tears, and our eyelids gush out with waters.

19 For a voice of wailing is heard out of Zion, How are we spoiled! we are greatly confounded, because we have forsaken the land, because our dwellings have cast *us* out.

20 Yet hear the word of Yahweh, O you women, and let your ear receive the word of his mouth, and teach your daughters wailing, and every one her neighbor lamentation.

21 For death has come up into our windows, *and* has entered into our palaces, to cut off the children from outside, *and* the young men from the streets.

22 Speak, Thus says Yahweh, Even the carcasses of men shall fall as dung upon the open field, and as the handful after the harvest man, and none shall gather *them*.

23 ¶ Thus says Yahweh, Let not the wise *man* glory in his wisdom, neither let the mighty *man* glory in his might, let not the rich *man* glory in his riches:

24 But let him that glories glory in this, that he understands and knows me, that I *am* Yahweh which exercises loving kindness, judgment, and righteousness, in the earth: for in these *things* I delight, says Yahweh.

25 Behold, the days come, says Yahweh, that I will punish all *them* *which* *are* circumcised with the uncircumcised;

26 Egypt, and Judah, and Edom, and the children of Ammon, and Moab, and all *that* *are* in the utmost corners, that dwell in the wilderness: for all *these* nations *are* uncircumcised, and all the house of Israel *are* uncircumcised in the heart.

Jeremiah 10

10:1 ¶ Hear you the word which Yahweh speaks unto you, O house of Israel:

2 Thus says Yahweh, Learn not the way of the heathen, and be not dismayed at the signs of heaven; for the heathen are dismayed at them.

3 For the customs of the people *are* vain: for *one* cuts a tree out of the forest, the work of the hands of the workman, with the ax.

4 They deck it with silver and with gold; they fasten it with nails and with hammers, that it moves not.

5 They *are* upright as the palm tree, but speak not: they must need *to* be carried, because they cannot go. Be not afraid of them; for they cannot do evil, neither also *is* *it* in them to do good.

6 Forasmuch as *there* *is* none like unto you, O Yahweh; you *are* great, and your name *is* great in might.

7 Who would not fear you, O King of nations? for to you does it appertain: forasmuch as among all the wise *men* of the nations, and in all their kingdoms, *there* *is* none like unto you.

8 But they are altogether brutish and foolish: the tree *is* a doctrine of vanities.

9 Silver spread into plates is brought from Tarshish, and gold from Uphaz, the work of the workman, and of the hands of the founder: blue and purple *is* their clothing: they *are* all the work of cunning *men*.

10 But Yahweh *is* the true God, he *is* the living God, and an everlasting king: at his wrath the earth shall tremble, and the nations shall not be able to contain his indignation.

11 Thus shall you say to them, The gods that have not made the heavens and the earth, *even* they shall perish from the earth, and from under these heavens.

12 He has made the earth by his power, he has established the world by his wisdom, and has stretched out the heavens by his discretion.

13 When he utters his voice, *there* *is* a multitude of waters in the heavens, and he causes the vapors to ascend from the ends of the earth; he makes lightning with rain, and brings forth the wind out of his treasuries.

14 Every man is brutish in *his* knowledge: every founder is confounded by the graven image: for his molten image *is* falsehood, and *there* *is* no breath in them.

15 They *are* vanity, *and* the work of errors: in the time of their visitation they shall perish.

16 The portion of Jacob *is* not like them: for he *is* the former of all *things*; and Israel *is* the rod of his inheritance: Yahweh of hosts *is* his name.

17 ¶ Gather up your wares out of the land, O inhabitant of the fortress.

18 For thus says Yahweh, Behold, I will sling out the inhabitants of the land at this time, and will distress them, that they may find *it* *so*.

19 Woe is me for my hurt! my wound is grievous: but I said, Truly this *is* a grief, and I must bear it.

20 My tabernacle is spoiled, and all my cords are broken: my children have gone forth from me, and they *are* not: *there* *is* none to stretch forth my tent any more, and to set up my curtains.

21 For the pastors have become brutish, and have not sought Yahweh: therefore they shall not prosper, and all their flocks shall be scattered.

22 Behold, the noise of the rumor has come, and a great commotion out of the north country, to make the cities of Judah desolate, *and* a den of dragons.

23 O Yahweh, I know that the way of man *is* not in himself: *it* *is* not in man that walks to direct his steps.

24 O Yahweh, correct me, but with judgment; not in your anger, lest you bring me to nothing.

25 Pour out your fury upon the heathen that know you not, and upon the families that call not on your name: for they have eaten up Jacob, and devoured him, and consumed him, and have made his habitation desolate.

Jeremiah 11

11:1 ¶ The word that came to Jeremiah from Yahweh, saying,

Jeremiah 11

2 Hear you the words of this covenant, and speak to the men of Judah, and to the inhabitants of Jerusalem;

3 And say you to them, Thus says Yahweh God of Israel; Cursed *be* the man that obeys not the words of this covenant,

4 Which I commanded your fathers in the day *that* I brought them forth out of the land of Egypt, from the iron furnace, saying, Obey my voice, and do them, according to all which I command you: so shall you be my people, and I will be your God:

5 That I may perform the oath which I have sworn to your fathers, to give them a land flowing with milk and honey, as *it is* this day. Then answered I, and said, So be it, O Yahweh.

6 Then Yahweh said to me, Proclaim all these words in the cities of Judah, and in the streets of Jerusalem, saying, Hear you the words of this covenant, and do them.

7 For I earnestly charged to your fathers in the day *that* I brought them up out of the land of Egypt, *even* unto this day, rising early and warning, saying, Obey my voice.

8 Yet they obeyed not, nor inclined their ear, but walked every one in the imagination of their evil heart: therefore I will bring upon them all the words of this covenant, which I commanded *them* to do; but they did *them* not.

9 And Yahweh said to me, A conspiracy is found among the men of Judah, and among the inhabitants of Jerusalem.

10 They have turned back to the iniquities of their forefathers, which refused to hear my words; and they went after other gods to serve them: the house of Israel and the house of Judah have broken my covenant which I made with their fathers.

11 ¶ Therefore thus says Yahweh, Behold, I will bring evil upon them, which they shall not be able to escape; and though they shall cry unto me, I will not listen to them.

12 Then shall the cities of Judah and inhabitants of Jerusalem go, and cry unto the gods to whom they offer incense: but they shall not save them at all in the time of their trouble.

13 For *according to* the number of your cities were your gods, O Judah; and *according to* the number of the streets of Jerusalem have you set up altars to *that* shameful thing, *even* altars to burn incense unto Baal.

14 Therefore pray not you for this people, neither lift up a cry or prayer for them: for I will not hear *them* in the time that they cry unto me for their trouble.

15 What has my beloved to do in my house, *seeing* she has worked lewdness with many, and the holy flesh has passed from you? when you do evil, then you rejoice.

16 Yahweh called your name, A green olive tree, fair, *and* of goodly fruit: with the noise of a great tumult he has kindled fire upon it, and the branches of it are broken.

17 For Yahweh of hosts, that planted you, has pronounced evil against you, for the evil of the house of Israel and of the house of Judah, which they have done against themselves to provoke me to anger in offering incense to Baal.

18 ¶ And Yahweh has given me knowledge *of it*, and I know *it*: for you showed me their doings.

19 But I *was* like a lamb *or* an ox *that* is brought to the slaughter; and I knew not that they had devised devices against me, *saying*, Let us destroy the tree with the fruit thereof, and let us cut him off from the land of the living, that his name may be no more remembered.

20 But, O Yahweh of hosts, that judges righteously, that tries the reins and the heart, let me see your vengeance on them: for unto you have I revealed my cause.

21 Therefore thus says Yahweh of the men of Anathoth, that seek your life, saying, Prophesy not in the name of Yahweh, that you die not by our hand:

22 Therefore thus says Yahweh of hosts, Behold, I will punish them: the young men shall die by the sword; their sons and their daughters shall die by famine:

23 And there shall be no remnant of them: for I will bring evil upon the men of Anathoth, *even* the year of their punishment.

Jeremiah 12

12:1 ¶ Righteous *are* you, O Yahweh, when I plead with you: yet let me talk with you of *your* judgments: Why does the way of the wicked prosper? *why* are all they happy that deal very treacherously?

2 You have planted them, yes, they have taken root: they grow, yes, they bring forth fruit: you *are* near in their mouth, and far from their reins.

3 But you, O Yahweh, know me: you have seen me, and tried my heart toward you: pull them out like sheep for the slaughter, and prepare them for the day of slaughter.

4 How long shall the land mourn, and the herbs of every field wither, for the wickedness of them that dwell therein? the beasts are consumed, and the birds; because they said, He shall not see our last end.

5 If you have run with the footmen, and they have wearied you, then how can you contend with horses? and *if* in the land of peace, *wherein* you trusted, *they wearied you*, then how will you do in the swelling of *the* Jordan?

6 For even your brothers, and the house of your father, even they have dealt treacherously with you; yes, they have called a multitude after you: believe them not, though they speak fair words to you.

7 ¶ I have forsaken my house, I have left my heritage; I have given the dearly beloved of my soul into the hand of her enemies.

8 My heritage is unto me as a lion in the forest; it cries out against me: therefore have I hated it.

9 My heritage *is* unto me *as* a speckled bird, the birds round about *are* against her; come you, assemble all the beasts of the field, come to devour.

10 Many pastors have destroyed my vineyard, they have trodden my portion under foot, they have made my pleasant portion a desolate wilderness.

11 They have made it desolate, *and being* desolate it mourns unto me; the whole land is made desolate, because no man takes *it* to heart.

12 The spoilers have come upon all high places through the wilderness: for the sword of Yahweh shall devour from the *one* end of the land even to the *other* end of the land: no flesh shall have peace.

13 They have sown wheat, but shall reap thorns: they have put themselves to pain, *but* shall not profit: and they shall be ashamed of your revenues because of the fierce anger of Yahweh.

14 ¶ Thus says Yahweh against all my evil neighbors, that touch the inheritance which I have caused my people Israel to inherit; Behold, I will pluck them out of their land, and pluck out the house of Judah from among them.

15 And it shall come to pass, after that I have plucked them out I will return, and have compassion on them, and will bring them again, every man to his heritage, and every man to his land.

16 And it shall come to pass, if they will diligently learn the ways of my people, to swear by my name, Yahweh lives; as they taught my people to swear by Baal; then shall they be built in the midst of my people.

17 But if they will not obey, I will utterly pluck up and destroy that nation, says Yahweh.

Jeremiah 13

13:1 ¶ Thus said Yahweh to me, Go and get you a linen girdle, and put it upon your loins, and put it not in water.

2 So I got a girdle according to the word of Yahweh, and put *it* on my loins.

3 And the word of Yahweh came to me the second time, saying,

4 Take the girdle that you have gotten, which *is* upon your loins, and arise, go to *the* Euphrates, and hide it there in a hole of the rock.

5 So I went, and hid it by *the* Euphrates, as Yahweh commanded me.

6 And it came to pass after many days, that Yahweh said to me, Arise, go to *the* Euphrates, and take the girdle from there, which I commanded you to hide there.

7 Then I went to *the* Euphrates, and dug, and took the girdle from the place where I had hidden it: and, behold, the girdle was marred, it was profitable for nothing.

8 Then the word of Yahweh came to me, saying,

9 Thus says Yahweh, After this manner will I mar the pride of Judah, and the great pride of Jerusalem.

10 This evil people, which refuse to hear my words, which walk in the imagination of their heart, and walk after other gods, to serve them, and to worship them, shall even be as this girdle, which is good for nothing.

11 For as the girdle clings to the loins of a man, so have I caused to cling to me the whole house of Israel and the whole house of Judah, says Yahweh; that they might be unto me for a people, and for a name, and for a praise, and for a glory: but they would not hear.

12 ¶ Therefore you shall speak unto them this word; Thus says Yahweh God of Israel, Every bottle shall be filled with wine: and they shall say to you, Do we not certainly know that every bottle shall be filled with wine?

13 Then shall you say to them, Thus says Yahweh, Behold, I will fill all the inhabitants of this land, even the kings that sit upon David's throne, and the priests, and the prophets, and all the inhabitants of Jerusalem, with drunkenness.

14 And I will dash them one against another, even the fathers and the sons together, says Yahweh: I will not pity, nor spare, nor have mercy, but destroy them.

15 Hear you, and give ear; be not proud: for Yahweh has spoken.

16 Give glory to Yahweh your God, before he causes darkness, and before your feet stumble upon the dark mountains and, while you look for light, he turns it into the shadow of death, *and* makes *it* total darkness.

17 But if you will not hear it, my soul shall weep in secret places for *your* pride; and my eye shall weep much, and run down with tears, because Yahweh's flock is carried away captive.

18 Say to the king and to the queen, Humble yourselves, sit down: for your principalities shall come down, *even* the crown of your glory.

19 The cities of the south shall be shut up, and none shall open *them*: Judah shall be carried away captive all of it, it shall be wholly carried away captive.

20 Lift up your eyes, and behold them that come from the north: where *is* the flock *that* was given you, your beautiful flock?

21 What will you say when he shall punish you? for you have taught them *to be* captains, *and* as chiefs over you: shall not sorrows take you, as a woman in labor?

22 ¶ And if you say in your heart, Why come these things upon me? For the greatness of your iniquity are your skirts uncovered, *and* your heels made bare.

23 Can the Ethiopian change his skin, or the leopard his spots? *then* may you also do good, that are accustomed to do evil.

24 Therefore will I scatter them as the stubble that passes away by the wind of the wilderness.

25 This *is* your lot, the portion of your measures from me, says Yahweh; because you have forgotten me, and trusted in falsehood.

26 Therefore will I uncover your skirts upon your face, that your shame may appear.

27 I have seen your adulteries, and your neighings, the lewdness of your whoredom, *and* your abominations on the hills in the fields. Woe unto you, O Jerusalem! will you not be made clean? when *shall it* yet *be*?

Jeremiah 14

14:1 ¶ The word of Yahweh that came to Jeremiah concerning the famine.

2 Judah mourns, and the gates thereof languish; they are darkened unto the ground; and the cry of Jerusalem has gone up.

Jeremiah 14

3 And their nobles have sent their little ones to the waters: they came to the pits, *and* found no water; they returned with their vessels empty; they were ashamed and confounded, and covered their heads.

4 Because the ground is chapped, for there was no rain in the earth, the plowmen were ashamed, they covered their heads.

5 Yes, the deer also calved in the field, and forsook *it*, because there was no grass.

6 And the wild donkeys did stand in the high places, they snuffed up the wind like dragons; their eyes did fail, because *there was* no grass.

7 O Yahweh, though our iniquities testify against us, do you *it* for your name's sake: for our backslidings are many; we have sinned against you.

8 O the hope of Israel, the savior thereof in time of trouble, why should you be as a stranger in the land, and as a wayfaring man *that* turns aside to tarry for a night?

9 Why should you be as a man astonished, as a mighty man *that* cannot save? yet you, O Yahweh, *are* in the midst of us, and we are called by your name; leave us not.

10 ¶ Thus says Yahweh unto this people, Thus have they loved to wander, they have not refrained their feet, therefore Yahweh does not accept them; he will now remember their iniquity, and visit their sins.

11 Then said Yahweh to me, Pray not for this people for *their* good.

12 When they fast, I will not hear their cry; and when they offer burnt offering and an oblation, I will not accept them: but I will consume them by the sword, and by the famine, and by the pestilence.

13 Then said I, Ah, Lord Yahweh! behold, the prophets say to them, You shall not see the sword, neither shall you have famine; but I will give you assured peace in this place.

14 Then Yahweh said to me, The prophets prophesy lies in my name: I sent them not, neither have I commanded them, neither spoke to them: they prophesy to you a false vision and divination, and a thing of nothing, and the deceit of their heart.

15 Therefore thus says Yahweh concerning the prophets that prophesy in my name, and I sent them not, yet they say, Sword and famine shall not be in this land; By sword and famine shall those prophets be consumed.

16 And the people to whom they prophesy shall be cast out in the streets of Jerusalem because of the famine and the sword; and they shall have none to bury them, them, their wives, nor their sons, nor their daughters: for I will pour their wickedness upon them.

17 ¶ Therefore you shall say this word to them; Let my eyes run down with tears night and day, and let them not cease: for the virgin daughter of my people is broken with a great breach, with a very grievous blow.

18 If I go forth into the field, then behold the slain with the sword! and if I enter into the city, then behold them that are sick with famine! yes, both the prophet and the priest go about into a land that they know not.

19 Have you utterly rejected Judah? has your soul loathed Zion? why have you smitten us, and *there is* no healing for us? we looked for peace, and *there is* no good; and for the time of healing, and behold trouble!

20 We acknowledge, O Yahweh, our wickedness, *and* the iniquity of our fathers: for we have sinned against you.

21 Do not abhor *us*, for your name's sake, do not disgrace the throne of your glory: remember, break not your covenant with us.

22 Are there *any* among the vanities of the Gentiles that can cause rain? or can the heavens give showers? *are* not you he, O Yahweh our God? therefore we will wait upon you: for you have made all these *things*.

Jeremiah 15

15:1 ¶ Then said Yahweh to me, Though Moses and Samuel stood before me, *yet* my mind *could* not *be* toward this people: cast *them* out of my sight, and let them go forth.

2 And it shall come to pass, if they say to you, Where shall we go forth? then you shall tell them, Thus says Yahweh; Such as *are* for death, to death; and such as *are* for the sword, to the sword; and such as *are* for the famine, to the famine; and such as *are* for the captivity, to the captivity.

3 And I will appoint over them four kinds, says Yahweh: the sword to slay, and the dogs to tear, and the fowls of the heaven, and the beasts of the earth, to devour and destroy.

4 And I will cause them to be removed into all kingdoms of the earth, because of Manasseh the son of Hezekiah king of Judah, for *that* which he did in Jerusalem.

5 For who shall have pity upon you, O Jerusalem? or who shall bemoan you? or who shall go aside to ask how you do?

6 You have forsaken me, says Yahweh, you have gone backward: therefore will I stretch out my hand against you, and destroy you; I am weary with repenting.

7 And I will fan them with a fan in the gates of the land; I will bereave *them* of children, I will destroy my people, *since* they return not from their ways.

8 Their widows are increased to me above the sand of the seas: I have brought upon them against the mother of the young men a spoiler at noonday: I have caused *him* to fall upon it suddenly, and terrors upon the city.

9 She that has borne seven languishes: she has given up the ghost; her sun has gone down while *it was* yet day: she has been ashamed and confounded: and the residue of them will I deliver to the sword before their enemies, says Yahweh.

10 ¶ Woe is me, my mother, that you have borne me a man of strife and a man of contention to the whole earth! I have neither lent on usury, nor men have lent to me on usury; *yet* every one of them does curse me.

11 Yahweh said, Truly it shall be well with your remnant; truly I will cause the enemy to entreat you *well* in the time of evil and in the time of affliction.

12 Shall iron break the northern iron and the steel?

13 Your substance and your treasures will I give to the spoil without price, and *that* for all your sins, even in all your borders.

14 And I will make *you* to pass with your enemies into a land *which* you know not: for a fire is kindled in my anger, *which* shall burn upon you.

15 ¶ O Yahweh, you know: remember me, and visit me, and revenge me of my persecutors; take me not away in your longsuffering: know that for your sake I have suffered rebuke.

16 Your words were found, and I did eat them; and your word was to me the joy and rejoicing of my heart: for I am called by your name, O Yahweh God of hosts.

17 I sat not in the assembly of the mockers, nor rejoiced; I sat alone because of your hand: for you have filled me with indignation.

18 Why is my pain perpetual, and my wound incurable, *which* refuses to be healed? will you be altogether to me as a liar, *and as* waters *that* fail?

19 Therefore thus says Yahweh, If you return, then will I bring you again, *and* you shall stand before me: and if you take forth the precious from the vile, you shall be as my mouth: let them return unto you; but return not you unto them.

20 And I will make you unto this people a fenced brazen wall: and they shall fight against you, but they shall not prevail against you: for I *am* with you to save you and to deliver you, says Yahweh.

21 And I will deliver you out of the hand of the wicked, and I will redeem you out of the hand of the terrible.

Jeremiah 16

16:1 ¶ The word of Yahweh came also to me, saying,

2 You shall not take you a wife, neither shall you have sons or daughters in this place.

3 For thus says Yahweh concerning the sons and concerning the daughters that are born in this place, and concerning their mothers that bore them, and concerning their fathers that begot them in this land;

4 They shall die of grievous deaths; they shall not be lamented; neither shall they be buried; *but* they shall be as dung upon the face of the earth: and they shall be consumed by the sword, and by famine; and their carcasses shall be meat for the fowls of heaven, and for the beasts of the earth.

5 For thus says Yahweh, Enter not into the house of mourning, neither go to lament nor bemoan them: for I have taken away my peace from this people, says Yahweh, *even* loving kindness and mercies.

6 Both the great and the small shall die in this land: they shall not be buried, neither shall *men* lament for them, nor cut themselves, nor make themselves bald for them:

7 Neither shall *men* tear *themselves* for them in mourning, to comfort them for the dead; neither shall *men* give them the cup of consolation to drink for their father or for their mother.

8 You shall not also go into the house of feasting, to sit with them to eat and to drink.

9 For thus says Yahweh of hosts, the God of Israel; Behold, I will cause to cease out of this place in your eyes, and in your days, the voice of joy, and the voice of gladness, the voice of the bridegroom, and the voice of the bride.

10 ¶ And it shall come to pass, when you shall show this people all these words, and they shall say to you, Why has Yahweh pronounced all this great evil against us? or what *is* our iniquity? or what *is* our sin that we have committed against Yahweh our God?

11 Then shall you say to them, Because your fathers have forsaken me, says Yahweh, and have walked after other gods, and have served them, and have worshipped them, and have forsaken me, and have not kept my law;

12 And you have done worse than your fathers; for, behold, you walk every one after the imagination of his evil heart, that they may not listen to me:

13 Therefore will I cast you out of this land into a land that you know not, *neither* you nor your fathers; and there shall you serve other gods day and night; where I will not show you favor.

14 ¶ Therefore, behold, the days come, says Yahweh, that it shall no more be said, Yahweh lives, that brought up the children of Israel out of the land of Egypt;

15 But, Yahweh lives, that brought up the children of Israel from the land of the north, and from all the lands where he had driven them: and I will bring them again into their land that I gave to their fathers.

16 Behold, I will send for many fishers, says Yahweh, and they shall fish them; and after will I send for many hunters, and they shall hunt them from every mountain, and from every hill, and out of the holes of the rocks.

17 For my eyes *are* upon all their ways: they are not hidden from my face, neither is their iniquity hidden from my eyes.

18 And first I will recompense their iniquity and their sin double; because they have defiled my land, they have filled my inheritance with the carcasses of their detestable and abominable things.

19 O Yahweh, my strength, and my fortress, and my refuge in the day of affliction, the Gentiles shall come to you from the ends of the earth, and shall say, Surely our fathers have inherited lies, vanity, and *things* wherein *there is* no profit.

20 Shall a man make gods unto himself, and they *are* no gods?

21 Therefore, behold, I will this once cause them to know, I will cause them to know my hand and my might; and they shall know that my name *is* Yahweh.

Jeremiah 17

17:1 ¶ The sin of Judah *is* written with a pen of iron, *and* with the point of a diamond: *it is* engraved upon the table of their heart, and upon the horns of your altars;

2 While their children remember their altars and their groves by the green trees upon the high hills.

Jeremiah 17

3 O my mountain in the field, I will give your substance *and* all your treasures to the spoil, *and* your high places for sin, throughout all your borders.

4 And you, even yourself, will discontinue from your heritage that I gave you; and I will cause you to serve your enemies in the land which you know not: for you have kindled a fire in my anger, *which* shall burn forever.

5 ¶ Thus says Yahweh; Cursed *be* the man that trusts in man, and makes flesh his arm, and whose heart departs from Yahweh.

6 For he shall be like the destitute in the desert, and shall not see when good comes; but shall inhabit the parched places in the wilderness, *in* a salt land and not inhabited.

7 Blessed *is* the man that trusts in Yahweh, and whose hope Yahweh is.

8 For he shall be as a tree planted by the waters, and *that* spreads out her roots by the river, and shall not see when heat comes, but her leaf shall be green; and shall not be afraid in the year of drought, neither shall cease from yielding fruit.

9 The heart *is* deceitful above all *things*, and desperately wicked: who can know it?

10 I Yahweh search the heart, *I* try the reins, even to give every man according to his ways, *and* according to the fruit of his doings.

11 *As* the partridge sits *on eggs*, and hatches *them* not; *so* he that gets riches, and not by right, shall leave them in the midst of his days, and at his end shall be a fool.

12 ¶ A glorious high throne from the beginning *is* the place of our sanctuary.

13 O Yahweh, the hope of Israel, all that forsake you shall be ashamed, *and* they that depart from me shall be written in the earth, because they have forsaken Yahweh, the fountain of living waters.

14 Heal me, O Yahweh, and I shall be healed; save me, and I shall be saved: for you *are* my praise.

15 Behold, they say to me, Where *is* the word of Yahweh? let it come now.

16 As for me, I have not hastened from *being* a pastor to follow you: neither have I desired the woeful day; you know: that which came out of my lips was *right* before you.

17 Be not a terror to me: you *are* my hope in the day of evil.

18 Let them be confounded that persecute me, but let not me be confounded: let them be dismayed, but let not me be dismayed: bring upon them the day of evil, and destroy them with double destruction.

19 ¶ Thus said Yahweh to me; Go and stand in the gate of the children of the people, whereby the kings of Judah come in, and by which they go out, and in all the gates of Jerusalem;

20 And say to them, Hear you the word of Yahweh, you kings of Judah, and all Judah, and all the inhabitants of Jerusalem, that enter in by these gates:

21 Thus says Yahweh; Take heed to yourselves, and bear no burden on the sabbath day, nor bring *it* in by the gates of Jerusalem;

22 Neither carry forth a burden out of your houses on the sabbath day, neither do you any work, but hallow you the sabbath day, as I commanded your fathers.

23 But they obeyed not, neither inclined their ear, but made their neck stiff, that they might not hear, nor receive instruction.

24 And it shall come to pass, if you diligently listen to me, says Yahweh, to bring in no burden through the gates of this city on the sabbath day, but hallow the sabbath day, to do no work therein;

25 Then shall there enter into the gates of this city kings and princes sitting upon the throne of David, riding in chariots and on horses, they, and their princes, the men of Judah, and the inhabitants of Jerusalem: and this city shall remain forever.

26 And they shall come from the cities of Judah, and from the places about Jerusalem, and from the land of Benjamin, and from the plain, and from the mountains, and from the south, bringing burnt offerings, and sacrifices, and meat offerings, and incense, and bringing sacrifices of praise, unto the house of Yahweh.

27 But if you will not listen to me to hallow the sabbath day, and not to bear a burden, even entering in at the gates of Jerusalem on the sabbath day; then will I kindle a fire in the gates thereof, and it shall devour the palaces of Jerusalem, and it shall not be quenched.

Jeremiah 18

18:1 ¶ The word which came to Jeremiah from Yahweh, saying,

2 Arise, and go down to the potter's house, and there I will cause you to hear my words.

3 Then I went down to the potter's house, and, behold, he worked a work on the wheels.

4 And the vessel that he made of clay was marred in the hand of the potter: so he made it again another vessel, as seemed good to the potter to make *it*.

5 Then the word of Yahweh came to me, saying,

6 O house of Israel, cannot I do with you as this potter? says Yahweh. Behold, as the clay *is* in the potter's hand, so *are* you in my hand, O house of Israel.

7 *At what* instant I shall speak concerning a nation, and concerning a kingdom, to pluck up, and to pull down, and to destroy *it*;

8 If that nation, against whom I have pronounced, turns from their evil, I will repent of the evil that I thought to do unto them.

9 And *at what* instant I shall speak concerning a nation, and concerning a kingdom, to build and to plant *it*;

10 If it does evil in my sight, that it obeys not my voice, then I will repent of the good, with which I said I would benefit them.

11 ¶ Now therefore go to, speak to the men of Judah, and to the inhabitants of Jerusalem, saying, Thus says Yahweh; Behold, I frame evil against you, and devise a device against you: return you now every one from his evil way, and make your ways and your doings good.

12 And they said, There is no hope: but we will walk after our own devices, and we will every one do the imagination of his evil heart.

13 Therefore thus says Yahweh; Ask you now among the heathen, who has heard such things: the virgin of Israel has done a very horrible thing.

14 Will *a man* leave the snow of Lebanon *which comes* from the rock of the field? *or* shall the cold flowing waters that come from another place be forsaken?

15 Because my people has forgotten me, they have burned incense to vanity, and they have caused them to stumble in their ways *from* the ancient paths, to walk in paths, *in* a way not cast up;

16 To make their land desolate, *and* a perpetual hissing; every one that passes thereby shall be astonished, and wag his head.

17 I will scatter them as with an east wind before the enemy; I will show them the back, and not the face, in the day of their calamity.

18 ¶ Then said they, Come, and let us devise devices against Jeremiah; for the law shall not perish from the priest, nor counsel from the wise, nor the word from the prophet. Come, and let us smite him with the tongue, and let us not give heed to any of his words.

19 Give heed to me, O Yahweh, and listen to the voice of them that contend with me.

20 Shall evil be recompensed for good? for they have dug a pit for my soul. Remember that I stood before you to speak good for them, *and* to turn away your wrath from them.

21 Therefore deliver up their children to the famine, and pour out their *blood* by the force of the sword; and let their wives be bereaved of their children, and *be* widows; and let their men be put to death; *let* their young men *be* slain by the sword in battle.

22 Let a cry be heard from their houses, when you shall bring a troop suddenly upon them: for they have dug a pit to take me, and hidden snares for my feet.

23 Yet, Yahweh, you know all their counsel against me to slay *me*: forgive not their iniquity, neither blot out their sin from your sight, but let them be overthrown before you; deal *thus* with them in the time of your anger.

Jeremiah 19

19:1 ¶ Thus says Yahweh, Go and get a potter's earthen bottle, and *take* of the ancients of the people, and of the ancients of the priests;

2 And go forth unto the valley of the son of Hinnom, which *is* by the entry of the east gate, and proclaim there the words that I shall tell you,

3 And say, Hear you the word of Yahweh, O kings of Judah, and inhabitants of Jerusalem; Thus says Yahweh of hosts, the God of Israel; Behold, I will bring evil upon this place, the which whoever hears, his ears shall tingle.

4 Because they have forsaken me, and have estranged this place, and have burned incense in it unto other gods, whom neither they nor their fathers have known, nor the kings of Judah, and have filled this place with the blood of innocents;

5 They have built also the high places of Baal, to burn their sons with fire *for* burnt offerings to Baal, which I commanded not, nor spoke *it*, neither came *it* into my mind:

6 Therefore, behold, the days come, says Yahweh, that this place shall no more be called Tophet, nor The valley of the son of Hinnom, but The valley of slaughter.

7 And I will make void the counsel of Judah and Jerusalem in this place; and I will cause them to fall by the sword before their enemies, and by the hands of them that seek their lives: and their carcasses will I give to be meat for the fowls of the heaven, and for the beasts of the earth.

8 And I will make this city desolate, and a hissing; every one that passes thereby shall be astonished and hiss because of all the plagues thereof.

9 And I will cause them to eat the flesh of their sons and the flesh of their daughters, and they shall eat every one the flesh of his friend in the siege and distress, with which their enemies, and they that seek their lives, shall oppress them.

10 ¶ Then shall you break the bottle in the sight of the men that go with you,

11 And shall say to them, Thus says Yahweh of hosts; Even so will I break this people and this city, as *one* breaks a potter's vessel, that cannot be made whole again: and they shall bury *them* in Tophet, till *there is* no place to bury.

12 Thus will I do to this place, says Yahweh, and to the inhabitants thereof, and *even* make this city as Tophet:

13 And the houses of Jerusalem, and the houses of the kings of Judah, shall be defiled as the place of Tophet, because of all the houses upon whose roofs they have burned incense to all the host of heaven, and have poured out drink offerings unto other gods.

14 Then came Jeremiah from Tophet, where Yahweh had sent him to prophesy; and he stood in the court of Yahweh's house; and said to all the people,

15 Thus says Yahweh of hosts, the God of Israel; Behold, I will bring upon this city and upon all her towns all the evil that I have pronounced against it, because they have hardened their necks, that they might not hear my words.

Jeremiah 20

20:1 ¶ Now Pashur the son of Immer the priest, who *was* also chief governor in the house of Yahweh, heard that Jeremiah prophesied these things.

2 Then Pashur smote Jeremiah the prophet, and put him in the stocks that *were* in the high gate of Benjamin, which *was* by the house of Yahweh.

3 And it came to pass on the next day, that Pashur brought forth Jeremiah out of the stocks. Then said Jeremiah to him, Yahweh has not called your name Pashur, but Magormissabib.

Jeremiah 20

4 For thus says Yahweh, Behold, I will make you a terror to yourself, and to all your friends: and they shall fall by the sword of their enemies, and your eyes shall behold *it*: and I will give all Judah into the hand of the king of Babylon, and he shall carry them captive into Babylon, and shall slay them with the sword.

5 Moreover I will deliver all the strength of this city, and all the labors thereof, and all the precious things thereof, and all the treasures of the kings of Judah will I give into the hand of their enemies, which shall spoil them, and take them, and carry them to Babylon.

6 And you, Pashur, and all that dwell in your house shall go into captivity: and you shall come to Babylon, and there you shall die, and shall be buried there, you, and all your friends, to whom you have prophesied lies.

7 ¶ O Yahweh, you have deceived me, and I was deceived: you are stronger than I, and have prevailed: I am in derision daily, every one mocks me.

8 For since I spoke, I cried out, I cried violence and spoil; because the word of Yahweh was made a reproach unto me, and a derision, daily.

9 Then I said, I will not make mention of him, nor speak any more in his name. But *his word* was in my heart as a burning fire shut up in my bones, and I was weary with forbearing, and I could not *stay*.

10 For I heard the defaming of many, fear on every side. Report, *say they*, and we will report it. All my familiars watched for my halting, *saying*, Perhaps he will be enticed, and we shall prevail against him, and we shall take our revenge on him.

11 But Yahweh *is* with me as a mighty terrible one: therefore my persecutors shall stumble, and they shall not prevail: they shall be greatly ashamed; for they shall not prosper: *their* everlasting confusion shall never be forgotten.

12 But, O Yahweh of hosts, that try the righteous, *and* see the reins and the heart, let me see your vengeance on them: for unto you have I opened my cause.

13 Sing unto Yahweh, praise you Yahweh: for he has delivered the soul of the poor from the hand of evildoers.

14 ¶ Cursed *be* the day wherein I was born: let not the day wherein my mother bore me be blessed.

15 Cursed *be* the man who brought tidings to my father, saying, A man child is born to you; making him very glad.

16 And let that man be as the cities which Yahweh overthrew, and repented not: and let him hear the cry in the morning, and the shouting at noontime;

17 Because he slew me not from the womb; or that my mother might have been my grave, and her womb *to be* always pregnant *with me*.

18 Why came I forth out of the womb to see labor and sorrow, that my days should be consumed with shame?

Jeremiah 21

21:1 ¶ The word which came to Jeremiah from Yahweh, when king Zedekiah sent to him Pashur the son of Melchiah, and Zephaniah the son of Maaseiah the priest, saying,

2 Inquire, I pray you, of Yahweh for us; for Nebuchadrezzar king of Babylon makes war against us; if so be that Yahweh will deal with us according to all his wondrous works, that he may go up from us.

3 Then said Jeremiah to them, Thus shall you say to Zedekiah:

4 Thus says Yahweh God of Israel; Behold, I will turn back the weapons of war that *are* in your hands, with which you fight against the king of Babylon, and *against* the Chaldeans, which besiege you outside the walls, and I will assemble them into the midst of this city.

5 And I myself will fight against you with an outstretched hand and with a strong arm, even in anger, and in fury, and in great wrath.

6 And I will smite the inhabitants of this city, both man and beast: they shall die of a great pestilence.

7 And afterward, says Yahweh, I will deliver Zedekiah king of Judah, and his servants, and the people, and such as are left in this city from the pestilence, from the sword, and from the famine, into the hand of Nebuchadrezzar king of Babylon, and into the hand of their enemies, and into the hand of those that seek their life: and he shall smite them with the edge of the sword; he shall not spare them, neither have pity, nor have mercy.

8 ¶ And to this people you shall say, Thus says Yahweh; Behold, I set before you the way of life, and the way of death.

9 He that stays in this city shall die by the sword, and by the famine, and by the pestilence: but he that goes out, and falls to the Chaldeans that besiege you, he shall live, and his life shall be to him for a prey.

10 For I have set my face against this city for evil, and not for good, says Yahweh: it shall be given into the hand of the king of Babylon, and he shall burn it with fire.

11 And touching the house of the king of Judah, *say*, Hear you the word of Yahweh;

12 O house of David, thus says Yahweh; Execute judgment in the morning, and deliver *him that is* spoiled out of the hand of the oppressor, lest my fury goes out like fire, and burns *so* that none can quench *it*, because of the evil of your doings.

13 Behold, I *am* against you, O inhabitant of the valley, *and* rock of the plain, says Yahweh; which say, Who shall come down against us? or who shall enter into our habitations?

14 But I will punish you according to the fruit of your doings, says Yahweh: and I will kindle a fire in the forest thereof, and it shall devour all things round about it.

Jeremiah 22

22:1 ¶ Thus says Yahweh; Go down to the house of the king of Judah, and speak there this word,

2 And say, Hear the word of Yahweh, O king of Judah, that sits upon the throne of David, you, and your servants, and your people that enter in by these gates:

3 Thus says Yahweh; Execute you judgment and righteousness, and deliver the spoiled out of the hand

of the oppressor: and do no wrong, do no violence to the stranger, the fatherless, nor the widow, neither shed innocent blood in this place.

4 For if you do this thing indeed, then shall there enter in by the gates of this house kings sitting upon the throne of David, riding in chariots and on horses, he, and his servants, and his people.

5 But if you will not hear these words, I swear by myself, says Yahweh, that this house shall become a desolation.

6 For thus says Yahweh to the king's house of Judah; You *are* Gilead unto me, *and* the head of Lebanon: *yet* surely I will make you a wilderness, *and* cities *which* are not inhabited.

7 And I will prepare destroyers against you, every one with his weapons: and they shall cut down your choice cedars, and cast *them* into the fire.

8 And many nations shall pass by this city, and they shall say every man to his neighbor, Why has Yahweh done thus unto this great city?

9 Then they shall answer, Because they have forsaken the covenant of Yahweh their God, and worshipped other gods, and served them.

10 ¶ Weep you not for the dead, neither bemoan him: *but* weep sorrowfully for him that goes away: for he shall return no more, nor see his native country.

11 For thus says Yahweh touching Shallum the son of Josiah king of Judah, which reigned instead of Josiah his father, which went forth out of this place; He shall not return there any more:

12 But he shall die in the place where they have led him captive, and shall see this land no more.

13 Woe unto him that builds his house by unrighteousness, and his chambers by wrong; *that* uses his neighbor's service without wages, and gives him not for his work;

14 That says, I will build me a wide house and large chambers, and cuts him out windows; and *it is* paneled with cedar, and painted with bright red.

15 Shall you reign, because you close *yourself* in cedar? did not your father eat and drink, and do judgment and justice, *and* then *it was* well with him?

16 He judged the cause of the poor and needy; then *it was* well *with him: was* not this to know me? says Yahweh.

17 But your eyes and your heart *are* not but for your covetousness, and for to shed innocent blood, and for oppression, and for violence, to do *it*.

18 Therefore thus says Yahweh concerning Jehoiakim the son of Josiah king of Judah; They shall not lament for him, *saying*, Ah my brother! or, Ah sister! they shall not lament for him, *saying*, Ah lord! or, Ah his glory!

19 He shall be buried with the burial of a donkey, drawn and cast forth beyond the gates of Jerusalem.

20 ¶ Go up to Lebanon, and cry; and lift up your voice in Bashan, and cry from the passages: for all your lovers are destroyed.

21 I spoke to you in your prosperity; *but* you said, I will not hear. This *has been* your manner from your youth, that you obeyed not my voice.

22 The wind shall eat up all your pastors, and your lovers shall go into captivity: surely then shall you be ashamed and confounded for all your wickedness.

23 O inhabitant of Lebanon, that make your nest in the cedars, how gracious shall you be when pangs come upon you, the pain as of a woman in labor!

24 *As* I live, says Yahweh, though Coniah the son of Jehoiakim king of Judah were the signet upon my right hand, yet would I pluck you therefrom;

25 And I will give you into the hand of them that seek your life, and into the hand *of them* whose face you fear, even into the hand of Nebuchadrezzar king of Babylon, and into the hand of the Chaldeans.

26 And I will cast you out, and your mother that bore you, into another country, where you were not born; and there shall you die.

27 But to the land whereunto they desire to return, there shall they not return.

28 *Is* this man Coniah a despised broken idol? *is he* a vessel wherein *is* no pleasure? therefore are they cast out, he and his seed, and are cast into a land which they know not?

29 O earth, earth, earth, hear the word of Yahweh.

30 Thus says Yahweh, Write you this man *as* childless, a man *that* shall not prosper in his days: for no man of his seed shall prosper, sitting upon the throne of David, and ruling any more in Judah.

Jeremiah 23

23:1 ¶ Woe be unto the pastors that destroy and scatter the sheep of my pasture! says Yahweh.

2 Therefore thus says Yahweh God of Israel against the pastors that feed my people; You have scattered my flock, and driven them away, and have not visited them: behold, I will visit upon you the evil of your doings, says Yahweh.

3 And I will gather the remnant of my flock out of all countries where I have driven them, and will bring them again to their folds; and they shall be fruitful and increase.

4 And I will set up shepherds over them which shall feed them: and they shall fear no more, nor be dismayed, neither shall they be lacking, says Yahweh.

5 Behold, the days come, says Yahweh, that I will raise unto David a righteous Branch, and a King shall reign and prosper, and shall execute judgment and justice in the earth.

6 In his days Judah shall be saved, and Israel shall dwell safely: and this *is* his name whereby he shall be called, YAHWEH OUR RIGHTEOUSNESS.

7 Therefore, behold, the days come, says Yahweh, that they shall no more say, Yahweh lives, which brought up the children of Israel out of the land of Egypt;

8 But, Yahweh lives, which brought up and which led the seed of the house of Israel out of the north country, and from all countries where I had driven them; and they shall dwell in their own land.

Jeremiah 23

9 ¶ My heart within me is broken because of the prophets; all my bones shake; I am like a drunken man, and like a man whom wine has overcome, because of Yahweh, and because of the words of his holiness.

10 For the land is full of adulterers; for because of swearing the land mourns; the pleasant places of the wilderness are dried up, and their course is evil, and their force *is* not right.

11 For both prophet and priest are profane; yes, in my house have I found their wickedness, says Yahweh.

12 Therefore their way shall be to them as slippery *ways* in the darkness: they shall be driven on, and fall therein: for I will bring evil upon them, *even* the year of their visitation, says Yahweh.

13 And I have seen folly in the prophets of Samaria; they prophesied in Baal, and caused my people Israel to err.

14 I have seen also in the prophets of Jerusalem a horrible thing: they commit adultery, and walk in lies: they strengthen also the hands of evildoers, that none does return from his wickedness: they are all of them to me as Sodom, and the inhabitants thereof as Gomorrah.

15 Therefore thus says Yahweh of hosts concerning the prophets; Behold, I will feed them with wormwood, and make them drink the water of gall: for from the prophets of Jerusalem has profaneness gone forth into all the land.

16 Thus says Yahweh of hosts, Listen not to the words of the prophets that prophesy to you: they make you vain: they speak a vision of their own heart, *and* not out of the mouth of Yahweh.

17 They say still unto them that despise me, Yahweh has said, You shall have peace; and they say unto every one that walks after the imagination of his own heart, No evil shall come upon you.

18 For who has stood in the counsel of Yahweh, and has perceived and heard his word? who has marked his word, and heard *it*?

19 Behold, a whirlwind of Yahweh has gone forth in fury, even a grievous whirlwind: it shall fall grievously upon the head of the wicked.

20 The anger of Yahweh shall not return, until he has executed, and till he has performed the thoughts of his heart: in the latter days you shall consider it perfectly.

21 I have not sent these prophets, yet they ran: I have not spoken to them, yet they prophesied.

22 But if they had stood in my counsel, and had caused my people to hear my words, then they should have turned them from their evil way, and from the evil of their doings.

23 *Am* I a God at hand, says Yahweh, and not a God afar off?

24 Can any hide himself in secret places that I shall not see him? says Yahweh. Do not I fill heaven and earth? says Yahweh.

25 I have heard what the prophets said, that prophesy lies in my name, saying, I have dreamed, I have dreamed.

26 How long shall *this* be in the heart of the prophets that prophesy lies? yes, *they are* prophets of the deceit of their own heart;

27 Which think to cause my people to forget my name by their dreams which they tell every man to his neighbor, as their fathers have forgotten my name for Baal.

28 The prophet that has a dream, let him tell a dream; and he that has my word, let him speak my word faithfully. What *is* the chaff to the wheat? says Yahweh.

29 *Is* not my word like as a fire? says Yahweh; and like a hammer *that* breaks the rock in pieces?

30 Therefore, behold, I *am* against the prophets, says Yahweh, that steal my words every one from his neighbor.

31 Behold, I *am* against the prophets, says Yahweh, that use their tongues, and say, He says.

32 Behold, I *am* against them that prophesy false dreams, says Yahweh, and do tell them, and cause my people to err by their lies, and by their lightness; yet I sent them not, nor commanded them: therefore they shall not profit this people at all, says Yahweh.

33 ¶ And when this people, or the prophet, or a priest, shall ask you, saying, What *is* the burden of Yahweh? you shall then say to them, What burden? I will even forsake you, says Yahweh.

34 And *as for* the prophet, and the priest, and the people, that shall say, The burden of Yahweh, I will even punish that man and his house.

35 Thus shall you say every one to his neighbor, and every one to his brother, What has Yahweh answered? and, What has Yahweh spoken?

36 And the burden of Yahweh shall you mention no more: for every man's word shall be his burden; for you have perverted the words of the living God, of Yahweh of hosts our God.

37 Thus shall you say to the prophet, What has Yahweh answered you? and, What has Yahweh spoken?

38 But since you say, The burden of Yahweh; therefore thus says Yahweh; Because you say this word, The burden of Yahweh, and I have sent to you, saying, You shall not say, The burden of Yahweh;

39 Therefore, behold, I, even I, will utterly forget you, and I will forsake you, and the city that I gave you and your fathers, *and cast you* out of my presence:

40 And I will bring an everlasting reproach upon you, and a perpetual shame, which shall not be forgotten.

Jeremiah 24

24:1 ¶ Yahweh showed me, and, behold, two baskets of figs *were* set before the temple of Yahweh, after that Nebuchadrezzar king of Babylon had carried away captive Jeconiah the son of Jehoiakim king of Judah, and the princes of Judah, with the carpenters and smiths, from Jerusalem, and had brought them to Babylon.

2 One basket *had* very good figs, *even* like the figs *that are* first ripe: and the other basket *had* very naughty figs, which could not be eaten, they were so bad.

3 Then said Yahweh to me, What see you, Jeremiah? And I said, Figs; the good figs, very good; and the evil, very evil, that cannot be eaten, they are so evil.

4 Again the word of Yahweh came to me, saying,
5 Thus says Yahweh, the God of Israel; Like these good figs, so will I acknowledge them that are carried away captive from Judah, whom I have sent out of this place into the land of the Chaldeans for *their* good.
6 For I will set my eyes upon them for good, and I will bring them again to this land: and I will build them, and not pull *them* down; and I will plant them, and not pluck *them* up.
7 And I will give them a heart to know me, that I *am* Yahweh: and they shall be my people, and I will be their God: for they shall return to me with their whole heart.
8 And as the evil figs, which cannot be eaten, they are so evil; surely thus says Yahweh, So will I give Zedekiah the king of Judah, and his princes, and the residue of Jerusalem, that remain in this land, and them that dwell in the land of Egypt:
9 And I will deliver them to be removed into all the kingdoms of the earth for *their* hurt, *to be* a reproach and a proverb, a taunt and a curse, in all places where I shall drive them.
10 And I will send the sword, the famine, and the pestilence, among them, till they are consumed from off the land that I gave to them and to their fathers.

Jeremiah 25

25:1 ¶ The word that came to Jeremiah concerning all the people of Judah in the fourth year of Jehoiakim the son of Josiah king of Judah, that *was* the first year of Nebuchadrezzar king of Babylon;
2 The which Jeremiah the prophet spoke to all the people of Judah, and to all the inhabitants of Jerusalem, saying,
3 From the thirteenth year of Josiah the son of Amon king of Judah, even unto this day, that *is* the three and twentieth year, the word of Yahweh has come to me, and I have spoken to you, rising early and speaking; but you have not listened.
4 And Yahweh has sent to you all his servants the prophets, rising early and sending *them*; but you have not listened, nor inclined your ear to hear.
5 They said, Turn you again now every one from his evil way, and from the evil of your doings, and dwell in the land that Yahweh has given to you and to your fathers forever and ever:
6 And go not after other gods to serve them, and to worship them, and provoke me not to anger with the works of your hands; and I will do you no hurt.
7 Yet you have not listened to me, says Yahweh; that you might provoke me to anger with the works of your hands to your own hurt.
8 ¶ Therefore thus says Yahweh of hosts; Because you have not heard my words,
9 Behold, I will send and take all the families of the north, says Yahweh, and Nebuchadrezzar the king of Babylon, my servant, and will bring them against this land, and against the inhabitants thereof, and against all these nations round about, and will utterly destroy them, and make them an astonishment, and a hissing, and perpetual desolations.
10 Moreover I will take from them the voice of joy, and the voice of gladness, the voice of the bridegroom, and the voice of the bride, the sound of the millstones, and the light of the candle.
11 And this whole land shall be a desolation, *and* an astonishment; and these nations shall serve the king of Babylon seventy years.
12 And it shall come to pass, when seventy years are accomplished, *that* I will punish the king of Babylon, and that nation, says Yahweh, for their iniquity, and the land of the Chaldeans, and will make it perpetual desolations.
13 And I will bring upon that land all my words which I have pronounced against it, *even* all that is written in this book, which Jeremiah has prophesied against all the nations.
14 For many nations and great kings shall serve themselves of them also: and I will recompense them according to their deeds, and according to the works of their own hands.
15 ¶ For thus says Yahweh God of Israel to me; Take the wine cup of this fury at my hand, and cause all the nations, to whom I send you, to drink it.
16 And they shall drink, and be moved, and be mad, because of the sword that I will send among them.
17 Then took I the cup at Yahweh's hand, and made all the nations to drink, to whom Yahweh had sent me:
18 *That is*, Jerusalem, and the cities of Judah, and the kings thereof, and the princes thereof, to make them a desolation, an astonishment, a hissing, and a curse; as *it is* this day;
19 Pharaoh king of Egypt, and his servants, and his princes, and all his people;
20 And all the mingled people, and all the kings of the land of Uz, and all the kings of the land of the Philistines, and Ashkelon, and Azzah, and Ekron, and the remnant of Ashdod,
21 Edom, and Moab, and the children of Ammon,
22 And all the kings of Tyrus, and all the kings of Zidon, and the kings of the isles which *are* beyond the sea,
23 Dedan, and Tema, and Buz, and all *that are* in the utmost corners,
24 And all the kings of Arabia, and all the kings of the mingled people that dwell in the desert,
25 And all the kings of Zimri, and all the kings of Elam, and all the kings of the Medes,
26 And all the kings of the north, far and near, one with another, and all the kingdoms of the world, which *are* upon the face of the earth: and the king of Sheshach shall drink after them.
27 Therefore you shall say to them, Thus says Yahweh of hosts, the God of Israel; Drink you, and be drunken, and spew, and fall, and rise no more, because of the sword which I will send among you.
28 And it shall be, if they refuse to take the cup at your hand to drink, then shall you say to them, Thus says Yahweh of hosts; You shall certainly drink.

Jeremiah 25

29 For, lo, I begin to bring evil on the city which is called by my name, and should you be utterly unpunished? You shall not be unpunished: for I will call for a sword upon all the inhabitants of the earth, says Yahweh of hosts.
30 ¶ Therefore prophesy you against them all these words, and say to them, Yahweh shall roar from on high, and utter his voice from his holy habitation; he shall mightily roar upon his habitation; he shall give a shout, as they that tread *the grapes*, against all the inhabitants of the earth.
31 A noise shall come *even* to the ends of the earth; for Yahweh has a controversy with the nations, he will plead with all flesh; he will give them *that are* wicked to the sword, says Yahweh.
32 Thus says Yahweh of hosts, Behold, evil shall go forth from nation to nation, and a great whirlwind shall be raised up from the coasts of the earth.
33 And the slain of Yahweh shall be at that day from *one* end of the earth even to the *other* end of the earth: they shall not be lamented, neither gathered, nor buried; they shall be dung upon the ground.
34 Howl, you shepherds, and cry; and wallow yourselves *in the ashes*, you principal of the flock: for the days of your slaughter and of your dispersions are accomplished; and you shall fall like a pleasant vessel.
35 And the shepherds shall have no way to flee, nor the principal of the flock to escape.
36 A voice of the cry of the shepherds, and a howling of the principal of the flock, *shall be heard*: for Yahweh has spoiled their pasture.
37 And the peaceable habitations are cut down because of the fierce anger of Yahweh.
38 He has forsaken his den, as the lion: for their land is desolate because of the fierceness of the oppressor, and because of his fierce anger.

Jeremiah 26

26:1 ¶ In the beginning of the reign of Jehoiakim the son of Josiah king of Judah came this word from Yahweh, saying,
2 Thus says Yahweh; Stand in the court of Yahweh's house, and speak to all the cities of Judah, which come to worship in Yahweh's house, all the words that I command you to speak to them; diminish not a word:
3 If so be they will listen, and turn every man from his evil way, that I may repent me of the evil, which I purpose to do to them because of the evil of their doings.
4 And you shall say to them, Thus says Yahweh; If you will not listen to me, to walk in my law, which I have set before you,
5 To listen to the words of my servants the prophets, whom I sent to you, both rising up early, and sending *them*, but you have not listened;
6 Then will I make this house like Shiloh, and will make this city a curse to all the nations of the earth.
7 ¶ So the priests and the prophets and all the people heard Jeremiah speaking these words in the house of Yahweh.
8 Now it came to pass, when Jeremiah had made an end of speaking all that Yahweh had commanded *him* to speak to all the people, that the priests and the prophets and all the people took him, saying, You shall surely die.
9 Why have you prophesied in the name of Yahweh, saying, This house shall be like Shiloh, and this city shall be desolate without an inhabitant? And all the people were gathered against Jeremiah in the house of Yahweh.
10 When the princes of Judah heard these things, then they came up from the king's house to the house of Yahweh, and sat down in the entry of the new gate of Yahweh's *house*.
11 Then spoke the priests and the prophets to the princes and to all the people, saying, This man *is* worthy to die; for he has prophesied against this city, as you have heard with your ears.
12 Then spoke Jeremiah unto all the princes and to all the people, saying, Yahweh sent me to prophesy against this house and against this city all the words that you have heard.
13 Therefore now amend your ways and your doings, and obey the voice of Yahweh your God; and Yahweh will repent him of the evil that he has pronounced against you.
14 As for me, behold, I *am* in your hand: do with me as seems good and right unto you.
15 But know you for certain, that if you put me to death, you shall surely bring innocent blood upon yourselves, and upon this city, and upon the inhabitants thereof: for of a truth Yahweh has sent me unto you to speak all these words in your ears.
16 ¶ Then said the princes and all the people to the priests and to the prophets; This man *is* not worthy to die: for he has spoken to us in the name of Yahweh our God.
17 Then rose up certain of the elders of the land, and spoke to all the assembly of the people, saying,
18 Micah the Morasthite prophesied in the days of Hezekiah king of Judah, and spoke to all the people of Judah, saying, Thus says Yahweh of hosts; Zion shall be plowed *like* a field, and Jerusalem shall become heaps, and the mountain of the house as the high places of a forest.
19 Did Hezekiah king of Judah and all Judah put him at all to death? did he not fear Yahweh, and sought Yahweh, and Yahweh repented him of the evil which he had pronounced against them? Thus might we procure great evil against our souls.
20 And there was also a man that prophesied in the name of Yahweh, Urijah the son of Shemaiah of Kirjathjearim, who prophesied against this city and against this land according to all the words of Jeremiah:
21 And when Jehoiakim the king, with all his mighty men, and all the princes, heard his words, the king sought to put him to death: but when Urijah heard it, he was afraid, and fled, and went into Egypt;
22 And Jehoiakim the king sent men into Egypt, *namely*, Elnathan the son of Achbor, and *certain* men with him into Egypt.

23 And they fetched forth Urijah out of Egypt, and brought him to Jehoiakim the king; who slew him with the sword, and cast his dead body into the graves of the common people.
24 Nevertheless the hand of Ahikam the son of Shaphan was with Jeremiah, that they should not give him into the hand of the people to put him to death.

Jeremiah 27

27:1 ¶ In the beginning of the reign of Jehoiakim the son of Josiah king of Judah came this word to Jeremiah from Yahweh, saying,
2 Thus says Yahweh to me; Make you bonds and yokes, and put them upon your neck,
3 And send them to the king of Edom, and to the king of Moab, and to the king of the Ammonites, and to the king of Tyrus, and to the king of Zidon, by the hand of the messengers which come to Jerusalem to Zedekiah king of Judah;
4 And command them to say to their masters, Thus says Yahweh of hosts, the God of Israel; Thus shall you say to your masters;
5 I have made the earth, the man and the beast that *are* upon the ground, by my great power and by my outstretched arm, and have given it to whom it seemed pleasing to me.
6 And now have I given all these lands into the hand of Nebuchadnezzar the king of Babylon, my servant; and the beasts of the field have I given him also to serve him.
7 And all nations shall serve him, and his son, and his son's son, until the very time of his land comes: and then many nations and great kings shall serve themselves of him.
8 And it shall come to pass, *that* the nation and kingdom which will not serve the same Nebuchadnezzar the king of Babylon, and that will not put their neck under the yoke of the king of Babylon, that nation will I punish, says Yahweh, with the sword, and with the famine, and with the pestilence, until I have consumed them by his hand.
9 Therefore listen not you to your prophets, nor to your diviners, nor to your dreamers, nor to your enchanters, nor to your sorcerers, which speak to you, saying, You shall not serve the king of Babylon:
10 For they prophesy a lie unto you, to remove you far from your land; and that I should drive you out, and you should perish.
11 But the nations that bring their neck under the yoke of the king of Babylon, and serve him, those will I let remain still in their own land, says Yahweh; and they shall till it, and dwell therein.
12 ¶ I spoke also to Zedekiah king of Judah according to all these words, saying, Bring your necks under the yoke of the king of Babylon, and serve him and his people, and live.
13 Why will you die, you and your people, by the sword, by the famine, and by the pestilence, as Yahweh has spoken against the nation that will not serve the king of Babylon?
14 Therefore listen not to the words of the prophets that speak to you, saying, You shall not serve the king of Babylon: for they prophesy a lie unto you.
15 For I have not sent them, says Yahweh, yet they prophesy a lie in my name; that I might drive you out, and that you might perish, you, and the prophets that prophesy unto you.
16 Also I spoke to the priests and to all this people, saying, Thus says Yahweh; Listen not to the words of your prophets that prophesy to you, saying, Behold, the vessels of Yahweh's house shall now shortly be brought again from Babylon: for they prophesy a lie unto you.
17 Listen not to them; serve the king of Babylon, and live: why should this city be laid waste?
18 But if they *are* prophets, and if the word of Yahweh is with them, let them now make intercession to Yahweh of hosts, that the vessels which are left in the house of Yahweh, and *in* the house of the king of Judah, and at Jerusalem, go not to Babylon.
19 For thus says Yahweh of hosts concerning the pillars, and concerning the sea, and concerning the bases, and concerning the residue of the vessels that remain in this city,
20 Which Nebuchadnezzar king of Babylon took not, when he carried away captive Jeconiah the son of Jehoiakim king of Judah from Jerusalem to Babylon, and all the nobles of Judah and Jerusalem;
21 Yes, thus says Yahweh of hosts, the God of Israel, concerning the vessels that remain *in* the house of Yahweh, and *in* the house of the king of Judah and of Jerusalem;
22 They shall be carried to Babylon, and there shall they be until the day that I visit them, says Yahweh; then will I bring them up, and restore them to this place.

Jeremiah 28

28:1 ¶ And it came to pass the same year, in the beginning of the reign of Zedekiah king of Judah, in the fourth year, *and* in the fifth month, *that* Hananiah the son of Azur the prophet, which *was* of Gibeon, spoke to me in the house of Yahweh, in the presence of the priests and of all the people, saying,
2 Thus speaks Yahweh of hosts, the God of Israel, saying, I have broken the yoke of the king of Babylon.
3 Within two full years will I bring again into this place all the vessels of Yahweh's house, that Nebuchadnezzar king of Babylon took away from this place, and carried them to Babylon:
4 And I will bring again to this place Jeconiah the son of Jehoiakim king of Judah, with all the captives of Judah, that went into Babylon, says Yahweh: for I will break the yoke of the king of Babylon.

Jeremiah 28

5 Then the prophet Jeremiah said to the prophet Hananiah in the presence of the priests, and in the presence of all the people that stood in the house of Yahweh,

6 Even the prophet Jeremiah said, Amen: Yahweh do so: Yahweh perform your words which you have prophesied, to bring again the vessels of Yahweh's house, and all that is carried away captive, from Babylon into this place.

7 Nevertheless hear you now this word that I speak in your ears, and in the ears of all the people;

8 The prophets that have been before me and before you of old prophesied both against many countries, and against great kingdoms, of war, and of evil, and of pestilence.

9 The prophet which prophesies of peace, when the word of the prophet shall come to pass, *then* shall the prophet be known, that Yahweh has truly sent him.

10 ¶ Then Hananiah the prophet took the yoke from off the prophet Jeremiah's neck, and broke it.

11 And Hananiah spoke in the presence of all the people, saying, Thus says Yahweh; Even so will I break the yoke of Nebuchadnezzar king of Babylon from the neck of all nations within the space of two full years. And the prophet Jeremiah went his way.

12 Then the word of Yahweh came to Jeremiah *the prophet*, after that Hananiah the prophet had broken the yoke from off the neck of the prophet Jeremiah, saying,

13 Go and tell Hananiah, saying, Thus says Yahweh; You have broken the yokes of wood; but you shall make for them yokes of iron.

14 For thus says Yahweh of hosts, the God of Israel; I have put a yoke of iron upon the neck of all these nations, that they may serve Nebuchadnezzar king of Babylon; and they shall serve him: and I have given him the beasts of the field also.

15 Then said the prophet Jeremiah to Hananiah the prophet, Hear now, Hananiah; Yahweh has not sent you; but you make this people to trust in a lie.

16 Therefore thus says Yahweh; Behold, I will cast you from off the face of the earth: this year you shall die, because you have taught rebellion against Yahweh.

17 So Hananiah the prophet died the same year in the seventh month.

Jeremiah 29

29:1 ¶ Now these *are* the words of the letter that Jeremiah the prophet sent from Jerusalem to the residue of the elders which were carried away captives, and to the priests, and to the prophets, and to all the people whom Nebuchadnezzar had carried away captive from Jerusalem to Babylon;

2 (After that Jeconiah the king, and the queen, and the eunuchs, the princes of Judah and Jerusalem, and the carpenters, and the smiths, were departed from Jerusalem;)

3 By the hand of Elasah the son of Shaphan, and Gemariah the son of Hilkiah, (whom Zedekiah king of Judah sent to Babylon to Nebuchadnezzar king of Babylon) saying,

4 Thus says Yahweh of hosts, the God of Israel, unto all that are carried away captives, whom I have caused to be carried away from Jerusalem to Babylon;

5 Build you houses, and dwell *in them*; and plant gardens, and eat the fruit of them;

6 Take you wives, and beget sons and daughters; and take wives for your sons, and give your daughters to husbands, that they may bear sons and daughters; that you may be increased there, and not diminished.

7 And seek the peace of the city where I have caused you to be carried away captives, and pray unto Yahweh for it: for in the peace thereof shall you have peace.

8 ¶ For thus says Yahweh of hosts, the God of Israel; Let not your prophets and your diviners, that *are* in the midst of you, deceive you, neither listen to your dreams which you cause to be dreamed.

9 For they prophesy falsely to you in my name: I have not sent them, says Yahweh.

10 For thus says Yahweh, That after seventy years are accomplished at Babylon I will visit you, and perform my good word toward you, in causing you to return to this place.

11 For I know the thoughts that I think toward you, says Yahweh, thoughts of peace, and not of evil, to give you an expected end.

12 Then shall you call upon me, and you shall go and pray unto me, and I will listen to you.

13 And you shall seek me, and find *me*, when you shall search for me with all your heart.

14 And I will be found by you, says Yahweh: and I will turn away your captivity, and I will gather you from all the nations, and from all the places where I have driven you, says Yahweh; and I will bring you again into the place *from* where I caused you to be carried away captive.

15 ¶ Because you have said, Yahweh has raised us up prophets in Babylon;

16 *Know* that thus says Yahweh of the king that sits upon the throne of David, and of all the people that dwell in this city, *and* of your brethren that have not gone forth with you into captivity;

17 Thus says Yahweh of hosts; Behold, I will send upon them the sword, the famine, and the pestilence, and will make them like vile figs, that cannot be eaten, they are so evil.

18 And I will persecute them with the sword, with the famine, and with the pestilence, and will deliver them to be removed to all the kingdoms of the earth, to be a curse, and an astonishment, and a hissing, and a reproach, among all the nations where I have driven them:

19 Because they have not listened to my words, says Yahweh, which I sent to them by my servants the prophets, rising up early and sending *them*; but you would not hear, says Yahweh.

20 Hear you therefore the word of Yahweh, all you of the captivity, whom I have sent from Jerusalem to Babylon:

21 Thus says Yahweh of hosts, the God of Israel, of Ahab the son of Kolaiah, and of Zedekiah the son of Maaseiah, which prophesy a lie unto you in my name; Behold, I will deliver them into the hand of Nebuchadrezzar king of Babylon; and he shall slay them before your eyes;
22 And of them shall be taken up a curse by all the captivity of Judah which *are* in Babylon, saying, Yahweh make you like Zedekiah and like Ahab, whom the king of Babylon roasted in the fire;
23 Because they have committed villainy in Israel, and have committed adultery with their neighbors' wives, and have spoken lying words in my name, which I have not commanded them; even I know, and *am* a witness, says Yahweh.
24 ¶ *Thus* shall you also speak to Shemaiah the Nehelamite, saying,
25 Thus speaks Yahweh of hosts, the God of Israel, saying, Because you have sent letters in your name to all the people that *are* at Jerusalem, and to Zephaniah the son of Maaseiah the priest, and to all the priests, saying,
26 Yahweh has made you priest in the stead of Jehoiada the priest, that you should be officers in the house of Yahweh, for every man *that is* mad, and makes himself a prophet, that you should put him in prison, and in the stocks.
27 Now therefore why have you not reproved Jeremiah of Anathoth, which makes himself a prophet to you?
28 For therefore he sent to us *in* Babylon, saying, This *captivity is* long: build you houses, and dwell *in them*; and plant gardens, and eat the fruit of them.
29 And Zephaniah the priest read this letter in the ears of Jeremiah the prophet.
30 Then came the word of Yahweh to Jeremiah, saying,
31 Send to all them of the captivity, saying, Thus says Yahweh concerning Shemaiah the Nehelamite; Because that Shemaiah has prophesied to you, and I sent him not, and he caused you to trust in a lie:
32 Therefore thus says Yahweh; Behold, I will punish Shemaiah the Nehelamite, and his seed: he shall not have a man to dwell among this people; neither shall he behold the good that I will do for my people, says Yahweh; because he has taught rebellion against Yahweh.

Jeremiah 30

30:1 ¶ The word that came to Jeremiah from Yahweh, saying,
2 Thus speaks Yahweh God of Israel, saying, Write you all the words that I have spoken to you in a book.
3 For, lo, the days come, says Yahweh, that I will bring again the captivity of my people Israel and Judah, says Yahweh: and I will cause them to return to the land that I gave to their fathers, and they shall possess it.
4 And these *are* the words that Yahweh spoke concerning Israel and concerning Judah.
5 For thus says Yahweh; We have heard a voice of trembling, of fear, and not of peace.
6 Ask you now, and see whether a man does labor with child? why do I see every man with his hands on his loins, as a woman in labor, and all faces are turned into paleness?
7 Alas! for that day *is* great, so that none *is* like it: it *is* even the time of Jacob's trouble; but he shall be saved out of it.
8 For it shall come to pass in that day, says Yahweh of hosts, *that* I will break his yoke from off your neck, and will burst your bonds, and strangers shall no more serve themselves of him:
9 But they shall serve Yahweh their God, and David their king, whom I will raise up unto them.
10 ¶ Therefore fear you not, O my servant Jacob, says Yahweh; neither be dismayed, O Israel: for, lo, I will save you from afar, and your seed from the land of their captivity; and Jacob shall return, and shall be in rest, and be quiet, and none shall make *him* afraid.
11 For I *am* with you, says Yahweh, to save you: though I make a full end of all nations wherein I have scattered you, yet will I not make a full end of you: but I will correct you in measure, and will not leave you altogether unpunished.
12 For thus says Yahweh, Your bruise *is* incurable, *and* your wound *is* grievous.
13 *There is* none to plead your cause, that you may be bound up: you have no healing medicines.
14 All your lovers have forgotten you; they seek you not; for I have wounded you with the wound of an enemy, with the chastisement of a cruel one, for the multitude of your iniquity; *because* your sins were increased.
15 Why cry you for your affliction? your sorrow *is* incurable for the multitude of your iniquity: *because* your sins were increased, I have done these things to you.
16 Therefore all they that devour you shall be devoured; and all your adversaries, every one of them, shall go into captivity; and they that spoil you shall be a spoil, and all that prey upon you will I give for a prey.
17 For I will restore health unto you, and I will heal you of your wounds, says Yahweh; because they called you an Outcast, *saying*, This *is* Zion, whom no man seeks after.
18 ¶ Thus says Yahweh; Behold, I will bring again the captivity of Jacob's tents, and have mercy on his dwelling places; and the city shall be built upon her own heap, and the palace shall remain after the manner thereof.
19 And out of them shall proceed thanksgiving and the voice of them that make merry: and I will multiply them, and they shall not be few; I will also glorify them, and they shall not be small.
20 Their children also shall be as before, and their congregation shall be established before me, and I will punish all that oppress them.
21 And their nobles shall be of themselves, and their governor shall proceed from the midst of them; and I will cause him to draw near, and he shall approach unto me: for who *is* this that engaged his heart to approach unto me? says Yahweh.

Jeremiah 30

22 And you shall be my people, and I will be your God.
23 Behold, the whirlwind of Yahweh goes forth with fury, a continuing whirlwind: it shall fall with pain upon the head of the wicked.
24 The fierce anger of Yahweh shall not return, until he has done *it*, and until he has performed the intents of his heart: in the latter days you shall consider it.

Jeremiah 31

31:1 ¶ At the same time, says Yahweh, will I be the God of all the families of Israel, and they shall be my people.
2 Thus says Yahweh, The people *which were* left of the sword found grace in the wilderness; *even* Israel, when I went to cause him to rest.
3 Yahweh has appeared of old unto me, *saying*, Yes, I have loved you with an everlasting love: therefore with loving kindness have I drawn you.
4 Again I will build you, and you shall be built, O virgin of Israel: you shall again be adorned with your tambourines, and shall go forth in the dances of them that make merry.
5 You shall yet plant vines upon the mountains of Samaria: the planters shall plant, and shall eat *them* as common things.
6 For there shall be a day, *that* the watchmen upon mount Ephraim shall cry, Arise you, and let us go up to Zion unto Yahweh our God.
7 For thus says Yahweh; Sing with gladness for Jacob, and shout among the chief of the nations: publish you, praise you, and say, O Yahweh, save your people, the remnant of Israel.
8 Behold, I will bring them from the north country, and gather them from the coasts of the earth, *and* with them the blind and the lame, the woman with child and her that labors with child together: a great company shall return there.
9 They shall come with weeping, and with supplications will I lead them: I will cause them to walk by the rivers of waters in a straight way, wherein they shall not stumble: for I am a father to Israel, and Ephraim *is* my firstborn.
10 ¶ Hear the word of Yahweh, O you nations, and declare *it* in the isles afar off, and say, He that scattered Israel will gather him, and keep him, as a shepherd *does* his flock.
11 For Yahweh has redeemed Jacob, and ransomed him from the hand of *him that was* stronger than he.
12 Therefore they shall come and sing in the height of Zion, and shall flow together to the goodness of Yahweh, for wheat, and for *new* wine, and for oil, and for the young of the flock and of the herd: and their soul shall be as a watered garden; and they shall not sorrow any more at all.
13 Then shall the virgin rejoice in the dance, both young men and old together: for I will turn their mourning into joy, and will comfort them, and make them rejoice from their sorrow.
14 And I will satiate the soul of the priests with fatness, and my people shall be satisfied with my goodness, says Yahweh.
15 Thus says Yahweh; A voice was heard in Ramah, lamentation, *and* bitter weeping; Rachel weeping for her children refused to be comforted for her children, because they *were* not.
16 Thus says Yahweh; Refrain your voice from weeping, and your eyes from tears: for your work shall be rewarded, says Yahweh; and they shall come again from the land of the enemy.
17 And there is hope in your end, says Yahweh, that your children shall come again to their own border.
18 ¶ I have surely heard Ephraim bemoaning himself *thus*; You have chastised me, and I was chastised, as a bullock unaccustomed *to the yoke*: turn you me, and I shall be turned; for you *are* Yahweh my God.
19 Surely after that I was turned, I repented; and after that I was instructed, I smote upon *my* thigh: I was ashamed, yes, even confounded, because I did bear the reproach of my youth.
20 *Is* Ephraim my dear son? *is he* a pleasant child? for since I spoke against him, I do earnestly remember him still: therefore my heart is troubled for him; I will surely have mercy upon him, says Yahweh.
21 Set you up markers, make you high heaps: set your heart toward the highway, *even* the way *which* you went: turn again, O virgin of Israel, turn again to these your cities.
22 How long will you go about, O you backsliding daughter? for Yahweh has created a new thing in the earth, A woman shall compass a man.
23 Thus says Yahweh of hosts, the God of Israel; As yet they shall use this speech in the land of Judah and in the cities thereof, when I shall bring again their captivity; Yahweh bless you, O habitation of justice, *and* mountain of holiness.
24 And there shall dwell in Judah itself, and in all the cities thereof together, husbandmen, and they *that* go forth with flocks.
25 For I have satiated the weary soul, and I have replenished every sorrowful soul.
26 Upon this I awoke, and saw; and my sleep was sweet unto me.
27 ¶ Behold, the days come, says Yahweh, that I will sow the house of Israel and the house of Judah with the seed of man, and with the seed of beast.
28 And it shall come to pass, *that* like as I have watched over them, to pluck up, and to break down, and to throw down, and to destroy, and to afflict; so will I watch over them, to build, and to plant, says Yahweh.
29 In those days they shall say no more, The fathers have eaten a sour grape, and the children's teeth are set on edge.
30 But every one shall die for his own iniquity: every man that eats the sour grape, his teeth shall be set on edge.

31 Behold, the days come, says Yahweh, that I will make a new covenant with the house of Israel, and with the house of Judah:

32 Not according to the covenant that I made with their fathers in the day *that* I took them by the hand to bring them out of the land of Egypt; which my covenant they broke, although I was a husband to them, says Yahweh:

33 But this *shall be* the covenant that I will make with the house of Israel; After those days, says Yahweh, I will put my law in their inward parts, and write it in their hearts; and will be their God, and they shall be my people.

34 And they shall teach no more every man his neighbor, and every man his brother, saying, Know Yahweh: for they shall all know me, from the least of them to the greatest of them, says Yahweh: for I will forgive their iniquity, and I will remember their sin no more.

35 ¶ Thus says Yahweh, which gives the sun for a light by day, *and* the ordinances of the moon and of the stars for a light by night, which divides the sea when the waves thereof roar; Yahweh of hosts *is* his name:

36 If those ordinances depart from before me, says Yahweh, *then* the seed of Israel also shall cease from being a nation before me forever.

37 Thus says Yahweh; If heaven above can be measured, and the foundations of the earth searched out beneath, I will also cast off all the seed of Israel for all that they have done, says Yahweh.

38 Behold, the days come, says Yahweh, that the city shall be built to Yahweh from the tower of Hananeel to the gate of the corner.

39 And the measuring line shall yet go forth over against it upon the hill Gareb, and shall compass about to Goath.

40 And the whole valley of the dead bodies, and of the ashes, and all the fields to the brook of Kidron, to the corner of the horse gate toward the east, *shall be* holy unto Yahweh; it shall not be plucked up, nor thrown down any more forever.

Jeremiah 32

32:1 ¶ The word that came to Jeremiah from Yahweh in the tenth year of Zedekiah king of Judah, which *was* the eighteenth year of Nebuchadrezzar.

2 For then the king of Babylon's army besieged Jerusalem: and Jeremiah the prophet was shut up in the court of the prison, which *was* in the king of Judah's house.

3 For Zedekiah king of Judah had shut him up, saying, Why do you prophesy, and say, Thus says Yahweh, Behold, I will give this city into the hand of the king of Babylon, and he shall take it;

4 And Zedekiah king of Judah shall not escape out of the hand of the Chaldeans, but shall surely be delivered into the hand of the king of Babylon, and shall speak with him mouth to mouth, and his eyes shall behold his eyes;

5 And he shall lead Zedekiah to Babylon, and there shall he be until I visit him, says Yahweh: though you fight with the Chaldeans, you shall not prosper.

6 And Jeremiah said, The word of Yahweh came to me, saying,

7 Behold, Hanameel the son of Shallum your uncle shall come to you, saying, Buy you my field that *is* in Anathoth: for the right of redemption *is* yours to buy *it*.

8 So Hanameel my uncle's son came to me in the court of the prison according to the word of Yahweh, and said to me, Buy my field, I pray you, that *is* in Anathoth, which *is* in the country of Benjamin: for the right of inheritance *is* yours, and the redemption *is* yours; buy *it* for yourself. Then I knew that this *was* the word of Yahweh.

9 And I bought the field of Hanameel my uncle's son, that *was* in Anathoth, and weighed him the money, *even* seventeen shekels of silver.

10 And I signed the evidence, and sealed *it*, and took witnesses, and weighed *him* the money in the balances.

11 So I took the evidence of the purchase, *both* that which was sealed *according* to the law and custom, and that which was open:

12 And I gave the evidence of the purchase to Baruch the son of Neriah, the son of Maaseiah, in the sight of Hanameel my uncle's *son*, and in the presence of the witnesses that signed the book of the purchase, before all the Jews that sat in the court of the prison.

13 And I charged Baruch before them, saying,

14 Thus says Yahweh of hosts, the God of Israel; Take these documents, this evidence of the purchase, both which is sealed, and this evidence which is open; and put them in an earthen vessel, that they may continue many days.

15 For thus says Yahweh of hosts, the God of Israel; Houses and fields and vineyards shall be possessed again in this land.

16 ¶ Now when I had delivered the evidence of the purchase to Baruch the son of Neriah, I prayed unto Yahweh, saying,

17 Ah Lord Yahweh! behold, you have made the heaven and the earth by your great power and stretched out arm, *and* there is nothing too hard for you:

18 You show loving kindness to thousands, and recompense the iniquity of the fathers into the bosom of their children after them: the Great, the Mighty God, Yahweh of hosts, *is* his name,

19 Great in counsel, and mighty in work: for your eyes *are* open upon all the ways of the sons of men: to give every one according to his ways, and according to the fruit of his doings:

20 Which have set signs and wonders in the land of Egypt, *even* unto this day, and in Israel, and among *other* men; and have made you a name, as at this day;

21 And have brought forth your people Israel out of the land of Egypt with signs, and with wonders, and with a strong hand, and with a stretched out arm, and with great terror;

22 And have given them this land, which you did swear to their fathers to give them, a land flowing with milk and honey;

Jeremiah 32

23 And they came in, and possessed it; but they obeyed not your voice, neither walked in your law; they have done nothing of all that you commanded them to do: therefore you have caused all this evil to come upon them:
24 Behold the mounts, they have come unto the city to take it; and the city is given into the hand of the Chaldeans, that fight against it, because of the sword, and of the famine, and of the pestilence: and what you have spoken has come to pass; and, behold, you see *it*.
25 And you have said to me, O Lord Yahweh, Buy you the field for money, and take witnesses; for the city is given into the hand of the Chaldeans.
26 ¶ Then came the word of Yahweh to Jeremiah, saying,
27 Behold, I *am* Yahweh, the God of all flesh: is there anything too hard for me?
28 Therefore thus says Yahweh; Behold, I will give this city into the hand of the Chaldeans, and into the hand of Nebuchadrezzar king of Babylon, and he shall take it:
29 And the Chaldeans, that fight against this city, shall come and set fire on this city, and burn it with the houses, upon whose roofs they have offered incense to Baal, and poured out drink offerings to other gods, to provoke me to anger.
30 For the children of Israel and the children of Judah have only done evil before me from their youth: for the children of Israel have only provoked me to anger with the work of their hands, says Yahweh.
31 For this city has been to me *as* a provocation of my anger and of my fury from the day that they built it even unto this day; that I should remove it from before my face,
32 Because of all the evil of the children of Israel and of the children of Judah, which they have done to provoke me to anger, they, their kings, their princes, their priests, and their prophets, and the men of Judah, and the inhabitants of Jerusalem.
33 And they have turned unto me the back, and not the face: though I taught them, rising up early and teaching *them*, yet they have not listened to receive instruction.
34 But they set their abominations in the house, which is called by my name, to defile it.
35 And they built the high places of Baal, which *are* in the valley of the son of Hinnom, to cause their sons and their daughters to pass through *the fire* unto Molech; which I commanded them not, neither came it into my mind, that they should do this abomination, to cause Judah to sin.
36 And now therefore thus says Yahweh, the God of Israel, concerning this city, whereof you say, It shall be delivered into the hand of the king of Babylon by the sword, and by the famine, and by the pestilence;
37 Behold, I will gather them out of all countries, where I have driven them in my anger, and in my fury, and in great wrath; and I will bring them again to this place, and I will cause them to dwell safely:
38 And they shall be my people, and I will be their God:
39 And I will give them one heart, and one way, that they may fear me forever, for the good of them, and of their children after them:
40 And I will make an everlasting covenant with them, that I will not turn away from them, to do them good; but I will put my fear in their hearts, that they shall not depart from me.
41 Yes, I will rejoice over them to do them good, and I will plant them in this land assuredly with my whole heart and with my whole soul.
42 For thus says Yahweh; Like as I have brought all this great evil upon this people, so will I bring upon them all the good that I have promised them.
43 And fields shall be bought in this land, whereof you say, *It is* desolate without man or beast; it is given into the hand of the Chaldeans.
44 Men shall buy fields for money, and sign records, and seal *them*, and take witnesses in the land of Benjamin, and in the places about Jerusalem, and in the cities of Judah, and in the cities of the mountains, and in the cities of the valley, and in the cities of the south: for I will cause their captivity to return, says Yahweh.

Jeremiah 33

33:1 ¶ Moreover the word of Yahweh came to Jeremiah the second time, while he was yet shut up in the court of the prison, saying,
2 Thus says Yahweh the maker thereof, Yahweh that formed it, to establish it; Yahweh *is* his name;
3 Call unto me, and I will answer you, and show you great and mighty things, which you know not.
4 For thus says Yahweh, the God of Israel, concerning the houses of this city, and concerning the houses of the kings of Judah, which are thrown down by the mounts, and by the sword;
5 They come to fight with the Chaldeans, but *it is* to fill them with the dead bodies of men, whom I have slain in my anger and in my fury, and for all whose wickedness I have hidden my face from this city.
6 Behold, I will bring it health and cure, and I will cure them, and will reveal to them the abundance of peace and truth.
7 And I will cause the captivity of Judah and the captivity of Israel to return, and will build them, as at the first.
8 And I will cleanse them from all their iniquity, whereby they have sinned against me; and I will pardon all their iniquities, whereby they have sinned, and whereby they have transgressed against me.
9 And it shall be to me a name of joy, a praise and an honor before all the nations of the earth, which shall hear all the good that I do unto them: and they shall fear and tremble for all the goodness and for all the prosperity that I procure unto it.
10 ¶ Thus says Yahweh; Again there shall be heard in this place, which you say *shall be* desolate without man and without beast, *even* in the cities of Judah, and in the streets of Jerusalem, that are desolate, without man, and without inhabitant, and without beast,

11 The voice of joy, and the voice of gladness, the voice of the bridegroom, and the voice of the bride, the voice of them that shall say, Praise Yahweh of hosts: for Yahweh *is* good; for his mercy *endures* forever: *and* of them that shall bring the sacrifice of praise into the house of Yahweh. For I will cause to return the captivity of the land, as at the first, says Yahweh.
12 Thus says Yahweh of hosts; Again in this place, which is desolate without man and without beast, and in all the cities thereof, shall be a habitation of shepherds causing *their* flocks to lie down.
13 In the cities of the mountains, in the cities of the vale, and in the cities of the south, and in the land of Benjamin, and in the places about Jerusalem, and in the cities of Judah, shall the flocks pass again under the hands of him that tells *them*, says Yahweh.
14 Behold, the days come, says Yahweh, that I will perform that good thing which I have promised to the house of Israel and to the house of Judah.
15 In those days, and at that time, will I cause the Branch of righteousness to grow up unto David; and he shall execute judgment and righteousness in the land.
16 In those days shall Judah be saved, and Jerusalem shall dwell safely: and this *is the name* with which she shall be called, Yahweh our righteousness.
17 ¶ For thus says Yahweh; David shall never want a man to sit upon the throne of the house of Israel;
18 Neither shall the priests the Levites want a man before me to offer burnt offerings, and to kindle meat offerings, and to do sacrifice continually.
19 And the word of Yahweh came to Jeremiah, saying,
20 Thus says Yahweh; If you can break my covenant of the day, and my covenant of the night, and that there should not be day and night in their season;
21 *Then* may also my covenant be broken with David my servant, that he should not have a son to reign upon his throne; and with the Levites the priests, my ministers.
22 As the host of heaven cannot be numbered, neither the sand of the sea measured: so will I multiply the seed of David my servant, and the Levites that minister unto me.
23 Moreover the word of Yahweh came to Jeremiah, saying,
24 Consider you not what these people have spoken, saying, The two families which Yahweh has chosen, he has even cast them off? thus they have despised my people, that they should be no more a nation before them.
25 Thus says Yahweh; If my covenant *be* not with day and night, *and if* I have not appointed the ordinances of heaven and earth;
26 Then will I cast away the seed of Jacob, and David my servant, *so that* I will not take *any* of his seed *to be* rulers over the seed of Abraham, Isaac, and Jacob: for I will cause their captivity to return, and have mercy on them.

Jeremiah 34

34:1 ¶ The word which came to Jeremiah from Yahweh, when Nebuchadnezzar king of Babylon, and all his army, and all the kingdoms of the earth of his dominion, and all the people, fought against Jerusalem, and against all the cities thereof, saying,
2 Thus says Yahweh, the God of Israel; Go and speak to Zedekiah king of Judah, and tell him, Thus says Yahweh; Behold, I will give this city into the hand of the king of Babylon, and he shall burn it with fire:
3 And you shall not escape out of his hand, but will surely be taken, and delivered into his hand; and your eyes shall behold the eyes of the king of Babylon, and he shall speak with you mouth to mouth, and you shall go to Babylon.
4 Yet hear the word of Yahweh, O Zedekiah king of Judah; Thus says Yahweh of you, You shall not die by the sword:
5 *But* you shall die in peace: and with the burnings of your fathers, the former kings which were before you, so shall they burn *incense* for you; and they will lament you, *saying*, Ah lord! for I have pronounced the word, says Yahweh.
6 Then Jeremiah the prophet spoke all these words to Zedekiah king of Judah in Jerusalem,
7 When the king of Babylon's army fought against Jerusalem, and against all the cities of Judah that were left, against Lachish, and against Azekah: for these defensed cities remained of the cities of Judah.
8 ¶ *This is* the word that came to Jeremiah from Yahweh, after that the king Zedekiah had made a covenant with all the people which *were* at Jerusalem, to proclaim liberty unto them;
9 That every man should let his manservant, and every man his maidservant, *being* a Hebrew or a Hebrewess, go free; that none should serve himself of them, *that is*, of a Jew his brother.
10 Now when all the princes, and all the people, which had entered into the covenant, heard that every one should let his manservant, and every one his maidservant, go free, that none should serve themselves of them any more, then they obeyed, and let *them* go.
11 But afterward they turned, and caused the servants and the handmaids, whom they had let go free, to return, and brought them into subjection for servants and for handmaids.
12 Therefore the word of Yahweh came to Jeremiah from Yahweh, saying,
13 Thus says Yahweh, the God of Israel; I made a covenant with your fathers in the day that I brought them forth out of the land of Egypt, out of the house of bondmen, saying,
14 At the end of seven years let you go every man his brother a Hebrew, which has been sold to you; and when he has served you six years, you shall let him go free from you: but your fathers listened not unto me, neither inclined their ear.
15 And you were now turned, and had done right in my sight, in proclaiming liberty every man to his neighbor;

Jeremiah 34

and you had made a covenant before me in the house which is called by my name:

16 But you turned and polluted my name, and caused every man his servant, and every man his handmaid, whom you had set at liberty at their pleasure, to return, and brought them into subjection, to be unto you for servants and for handmaids.

17 Therefore thus says Yahweh; You have not listened unto me, in proclaiming liberty, every one to his brother, and every man to his neighbor: behold, I proclaim a liberty for you, says Yahweh, to the sword, to the pestilence, and to the famine; and I will make you to be removed into all the kingdoms of the earth.

18 And I will give the men that have transgressed my covenant, which have not performed the words of the covenant which they had made before me, when they cut the calf in two, and passed between the parts thereof,

19 The princes of Judah, and the princes of Jerusalem, the eunuchs, and the priests, and all the people of the land, which passed between the parts of the calf;

20 I will even give them into the hand of their enemies, and into the hand of them that seek their life: and their dead bodies shall be for meat to the fowls of the heaven, and to the beasts of the earth.

21 And Zedekiah king of Judah and his princes will I give into the hand of their enemies, and into the hand of them that seek their life, and into the hand of the king of Babylon's army, which have gone up from you.

22 Behold, I will command, says Yahweh, and cause them to return to this city; and they shall fight against it, and take it, and burn it with fire: and I will make the cities of Judah a desolation without an inhabitant.

Jeremiah 35

35:1 ¶ The word which came to Jeremiah from Yahweh in the days of Jehoiakim the son of Josiah king of Judah, saying,

2 Go to the house of the Rechabites, and speak to them, and bring them into the house of Yahweh, into one of the chambers, and give them wine to drink.

3 Then I took Jaazaniah the son of Jeremiah, the son of Habaziniah, and his brothers, and all his sons, and the whole house of the Rechabites;

4 And I brought them into the house of Yahweh, into the chamber of the sons of Hanan, the son of Igdaliah, a man of God, which *was* by the chamber of the princes, which *was* above the chamber of Maaseiah the son of Shallum, the keeper of the door:

5 And I set before the sons of the house of the Rechabites pots full of wine, and cups, and I said to them, Drink you wine.

6 But they said, We will drink no wine: for Jonadab the son of Rechab our father commanded us, saying, You shall drink no wine, *neither you*, nor your sons forever:

7 Neither shall you build houses, nor sow seed, nor plant vineyards, nor have *any*: but all your days you shall dwell in tents; that you may live many days in the land where you *are* strangers.

8 Thus have we obeyed the voice of Jonadab the son of Rechab our father in all that he has charged us, to drink no wine all our days, we, our wives, our sons, nor our daughters;

9 Nor to build houses for us to dwell in: neither have we vineyards, nor fields, nor seed:

10 But we have dwelt in tents, and have obeyed, and done according to all that Jonadab our father commanded us.

11 But it came to pass, when Nebuchadrezzar king of Babylon came up into the land, that we said, Come, and let us go to Jerusalem for fear of the army of the Chaldeans, and for fear of the army of the Syrians: so we dwell at Jerusalem.

12 ¶ Then came the word of Yahweh to Jeremiah, saying,

13 Thus says Yahweh of hosts, the God of Israel; Go and tell the men of Judah and the inhabitants of Jerusalem, Will you not receive instruction to listen to my words? says Yahweh.

14 The words of Jonadab the son of Rechab, that he commanded his sons not to drink wine, are performed; for unto this day they drink none, but obey their father's commandment: notwithstanding I have spoken to you, rising early and speaking; but you listened not unto me.

15 I have sent also to you all my servants the prophets, rising up early and sending *them*, saying, Return you now every man from his evil way, and amend your doings, and go not after other gods to serve them, and you shall dwell in the land which I have given to you and to your fathers: but you have not inclined your ear, nor listened unto me.

16 Because the sons of Jonadab the son of Rechab have performed the commandment of their father, which he commanded them; but this people has not listened unto me:

17 Therefore thus says Yahweh God of hosts, the God of Israel; Behold, I will bring upon Judah and upon all the inhabitants of Jerusalem all the evil that I have pronounced against them: because I have spoken to them, but they have not heard; and I have called to them, but they have not answered.

18 And Jeremiah said to the house of the Rechabites, Thus says Yahweh of hosts, the God of Israel; Because you have obeyed the commandment of Jonadab your father, and kept all his precepts, and done according to all that he has commanded you:

19 Therefore thus says Yahweh of hosts, the God of Israel; Jonadab the son of Rechab shall not want a man to stand before me forever.

Jeremiah 36

36:1 ¶ And it came to pass in the fourth year of Jehoiakim the son of Josiah king of Judah, *that* this word came to Jeremiah from Yahweh, saying,

2 Take you a roll of a book, and write therein all the words that I have spoken to you against Israel, and against Judah, and against all the nations, from the day I spoke to you, from the days of Josiah, even unto this day.
3 It may be that the house of Judah will hear all the evil which I purpose to do unto them; that they may return every man from his evil way; that I may forgive their iniquity and their sin.
4 Then Jeremiah called Baruch the son of Neriah: and Baruch wrote from the mouth of Jeremiah all the words of Yahweh, which he had spoken to him, upon a roll of a book.
5 And Jeremiah commanded Baruch, saying, I *am* shut up; I cannot go into the house of Yahweh:
6 Therefore go you, and read in the roll, which you have written from my mouth, the words of Yahweh in the ears of the people in Yahweh's house upon the fasting day: and also you shall read them in the ears of all Judah that come out of their cities.
7 It may be they will present their supplication before Yahweh, and will return every one from his evil way: for great *is* the anger and the fury that Yahweh has pronounced against this people.
8 And Baruch the son of Neriah did according to all that Jeremiah the prophet commanded him, reading in the book the words of Yahweh in Yahweh's house.
9 ¶ And it came to pass in the fifth year of Jehoiakim the son of Josiah king of Judah, in the ninth month, *that* they proclaimed a fast before Yahweh to all the people in Jerusalem, and to all the people that came from the cities of Judah to Jerusalem.
10 Then read Baruch in the book the words of Jeremiah in the house of Yahweh, in the chamber of Gemariah the son of Shaphan the scribe, in the higher court, at the entry of the new gate of Yahweh's house, in the ears of all the people.
11 When Michaiah the son of Gemariah, the son of Shaphan, had heard out of the book all the words of Yahweh,
12 Then he went down into the king's house, into the scribe's chamber: and, lo, all the princes sat there, *even* Elishama the scribe, and Delaiah the son of Shemaiah, and Elnathan the son of Achbor, and Gemariah the son of Shaphan, and Zedekiah the son of Hananiah, and all the princes.
13 Then Michaiah declared to them all the words that he had heard, when Baruch read the book in the ears of the people.
14 Therefore all the princes sent Jehudi the son of Nethaniah, the son of Shelemiah, the son of Cushi, to Baruch, saying, Take in your hand the roll wherein you have read in the ears of the people, and come. So Baruch the son of Neriah took the roll in his hand, and came to them.
15 And they said to him, Sit down now, and read it in our ears. So Baruch read *it* in their ears.
16 Now it came to pass, when they had heard all the words, they were afraid both one and another, and said to Baruch, We will surely tell the king of all these words.
17 And they asked Baruch, saying, Tell us now, How did you write all these words at his mouth?
18 Then Baruch answered them, He pronounced all these words to me with his mouth, and I wrote *them* with ink in the book.
19 Then said the princes to Baruch, Go, hide you, you and Jeremiah; and let no man know where you are.
20 ¶ And they went in to the king into the court, but they laid up the roll in the chamber of Elishama the scribe, and told all the words in the ears of the king.
21 So the king sent Jehudi to fetch the roll: and he took it out of Elishama the scribe's chamber. And Jehudi read it in the ears of the king, and in the ears of all the princes which stood beside the king.
22 Now the king sat in the winter house in the ninth month: and *there was a fire* on the hearth burning before him.
23 And it came to pass, *that* when Jehudi had read three or four leaves, he cut it with the penknife, and cast *it* into the fire that *was* on the hearth, until all the roll was consumed in the fire that *was* on the hearth.
24 Yet they were not afraid, nor tore their garments, *neither* the king, nor any of his servants that heard all these words.
25 Nevertheless Elnathan and Delaiah and Gemariah had made intercession to the king that he would not burn the roll: but he would not hear them.
26 But the king commanded Jerahmeel the son of Hammelech, and Seraiah the son of Azriel, and Shelemiah the son of Abdeel, to take Baruch the scribe and Jeremiah the prophet: but Yahweh hid them.
27 Then the word of Yahweh came to Jeremiah, after that the king had burned the roll, and the words which Baruch wrote at the mouth of Jeremiah, saying,
28 Take you again another roll, and write in it all the former words that were in the first roll, which Jehoiakim the king of Judah has burned.
29 And you shall say to Jehoiakim king of Judah, Thus says Yahweh; You have burned this roll, saying, Why have you written therein, saying, The king of Babylon shall certainly come and destroy this land, and shall cause to cease from there man and beast?
30 Therefore thus says Yahweh of Jehoiakim king of Judah; He shall have none to sit upon the throne of David: and his dead body shall be cast out in the day to the heat, and in the night to the frost.
31 And I will punish him and his seed and his servants for their iniquity; and I will bring upon them, and upon the inhabitants of Jerusalem, and upon the men of Judah, all the evil that I have pronounced against them; but they listened not.
32 Then took Jeremiah another roll, and gave it to Baruch the scribe, the son of Neriah; who wrote therein from the mouth of Jeremiah all the words of the book which Jehoiakim king of Judah had burned in the fire: and there were added besides to them many like words.

Jeremiah 37

37:1 ¶ And king Zedekiah the son of Josiah reigned instead of Coniah the son of Jehoiakim, whom Nebuchadrezzar king of Babylon made king in the land of Judah.
2 But neither he, nor his servants, nor the people of the land, did listen to the words of Yahweh, which he spoke by the prophet Jeremiah.
3 And Zedekiah the king sent Jehucal the son of Shelemiah and Zephaniah the son of Maaseiah the priest to the prophet Jeremiah, saying, Pray now unto Yahweh our God for us.
4 Now Jeremiah came in and went out among the people: for they had not put him into prison.
5 Then Pharaoh's army had come forth out of Egypt: and when the Chaldeans that besieged Jerusalem heard tidings of them, they departed from Jerusalem.
6 Then came the word of Yahweh to the prophet Jeremiah, saying,
7 Thus says Yahweh, the God of Israel; Thus shall you say to the king of Judah, that sent you to me to inquire of me; Behold, Pharaoh's army, which has come forth to help you, shall return to Egypt into their own land.
8 And the Chaldeans shall come again, and fight against this city, and take it, and burn it with fire.
9 Thus says Yahweh; Deceive not yourselves, saying, The Chaldeans shall surely depart from us: for they shall not depart.
10 For though you had smitten the whole army of the Chaldeans that fight against you, and there remained *but* wounded men among them, *yet* should they rise up every man in his tent, and burn this city with fire.
11 ¶ And it came to pass, that when the army of the Chaldeans had broken up from Jerusalem for fear of Pharaoh's army,
12 Then Jeremiah went forth out of Jerusalem to go into the land of Benjamin, to separate himself there in the midst of the people.
13 And when he was in the gate of Benjamin, a captain of the ward *was* there, whose name *was* Irijah, the son of Shelemiah, the son of Hananiah; and he took Jeremiah the prophet, saying, You fall down to the Chaldeans.
14 Then said Jeremiah, *It is* false; I fall not down to the Chaldeans. But he listened not to him: so Irijah took Jeremiah, and brought him to the princes.
15 Therefore the princes were angry with Jeremiah, and smote him, and put him in prison in the house of Jonathan the scribe: for they had made that the prison.
16 When Jeremiah had entered into the dungeon, and into the cells, and Jeremiah had remained there many days;
17 Then Zedekiah the king sent, and took him out: and the king asked him secretly in his house, and said, Is there *any* word from Yahweh? And Jeremiah said, There is: for, said he, you shall be delivered into the hand of the king of Babylon.
18 Moreover Jeremiah said to king Zedekiah, What have I offended against you, or against your servants, or against this people, that you have put me in prison?
19 Where *are* now your prophets which prophesied unto you, saying, The king of Babylon shall not come against you, nor against this land?
20 Therefore hear now, I pray you, O my lord the king: let my supplication, I pray you, be accepted before you; that you cause me not to return to the house of Jonathan the scribe, lest I die there.
21 Then Zedekiah the king commanded that they should commit Jeremiah into the court of the prison, and that they should give him daily a piece of bread out of the bakers' street, until all the bread in the city was spent. Thus Jeremiah remained in the court of the prison.

Jeremiah 38

38:1 ¶ Then Shephatiah the son of Mattan, and Gedaliah the son of Pashur, and Jucal the son of Shelemiah, and Pashur the son of Malchiah, heard the words that Jeremiah had spoken to all the people, saying,
2 Thus says Yahweh, He that remains in this city shall die by the sword, by the famine, and by the pestilence: but he that goes forth to the Chaldeans shall live; for he shall have his life for a prey, and shall live.
3 Thus says Yahweh, This city shall surely be given into the hand of the king of Babylon's army, which shall take it.
4 Therefore the princes said to the king, We beseech you, let this man be put to death: for thus he weakens the hands of the men of war that remain in this city, and the hands of all the people, in speaking such words to them: for this man seeks not the welfare of this people, but the hurt.
5 Then Zedekiah the king said, Behold, he *is* in your hand: for the king *is* not *he that* can do *any* thing against you.
6 Then took they Jeremiah, and cast him into the dungeon of Malchiah the son of Hammelech, that *was* in the court of the prison: and they let down Jeremiah with cords. And in the dungeon *there was* no water, but mire: so Jeremiah sunk in the mire.
7 Now when Ebedmelech the Ethiopian, one of the eunuchs which was in the king's house, heard that they had put Jeremiah in the dungeon; the king then sitting in the gate of Benjamin;
8 Ebedmelech went forth out of the king's house, and spoke to the king, saying,
9 My lord the king, these men have done evil in all that they have done to Jeremiah the prophet, whom they have cast into the dungeon; and he is likely to die from hunger in the place where he is: for *there is* no more bread in the city.
10 Then the king commanded Ebedmelech the Ethiopian, saying, Take from here thirty men with you, and take up Jeremiah the prophet out of the dungeon, before he dies.
11 So Ebedmelech took the men with him, and went into the house of the king under the treasury, and took there

old torn rags and old rotten rags, and let them down by ropes into the dungeon to Jeremiah.

12 And Ebedmelech the Ethiopian said to Jeremiah, Put now *these* old torn clothes and rotten rags under your armholes under the cords. And Jeremiah did so.

13 So they drew up Jeremiah with cords, and took him up out of the dungeon: and Jeremiah remained in the court of the prison.

14 ¶ Then Zedekiah the king sent, and took Jeremiah the prophet to him into the third entry that *is* in the house of Yahweh: and the king said unto Jeremiah, I will ask you a thing; hide nothing from me.

15 Then Jeremiah said to Zedekiah, If I declare *it* to you, will you not surely put me to death? and if I give you counsel, will you not listen to me?

16 So Zedekiah the king swore secretly to Jeremiah, saying, *As* Yahweh lives, that made us this soul, I will not put you to death, neither will I give you into the hand of these men that seek your life.

17 Then said Jeremiah to Zedekiah, Thus says Yahweh, the God of hosts, the God of Israel; If you will assuredly go forth to the king of Babylon's princes, then your soul shall live, and this city shall not be burned with fire; and you shall live, and your house:

18 But if you will not go forth to the king of Babylon's princes, then shall this city be given into the hand of the Chaldeans, and they shall burn it with fire, and you shall not escape out of their hand.

19 And Zedekiah the king said to Jeremiah, I am afraid of the Jews that have fallen to the Chaldeans, lest they deliver me into their hand, and they mock me.

20 But Jeremiah said, They shall not deliver *you*. Obey, I beseech you, the voice of Yahweh, which I speak to you: so it shall be well unto you, and your soul shall live.

21 But if you refuse to go forth, this *is* the word that Yahweh has shown me:

22 And, behold, all the women that are left in the king of Judah's house *shall be* brought forth to the king of Babylon's princes, and those *women* shall say, Your friends have enticed you, and have prevailed against you: your feet are sunk in the mire, *and* they are turned away back.

23 So they shall bring out all your wives and your children to the Chaldeans: and you shall not escape out of their hand, but will be taken by the hand of the king of Babylon: and you shall cause this city to be burned with fire.

24 Then said Zedekiah to Jeremiah, Let no man know of these words, and you shall not die.

25 But if the princes hear that I have talked with you, and they come to you, and say to you, Declare to us now what you have said to the king, hide it not from us, and we will not put you to death; also what the king said to you:

26 Then you shall say to them, I presented my supplication before the king, that he would not cause me to return to Jonathan's house, to die there

27 Then came all the princes to Jeremiah, and asked him: and he told them according to all these words that the king had commanded. So they left off speaking with him; for the matter was not perceived.

28 So Jeremiah stayed in the court of the prison until the day that Jerusalem was taken: and he was *there* when Jerusalem was taken.

Jeremiah 39

39:1 ¶ In the ninth year of Zedekiah king of Judah, in the tenth month, came Nebuchadrezzar king of Babylon and all his army against Jerusalem, and they besieged it.

2 *And* in the eleventh year of Zedekiah, in the fourth month, the ninth *day* of the month, the city was broken up.

3 And all the princes of the king of Babylon came in, and sat in the middle gate, *even* Nergalsharezer, Samgarnebo, Sarsechim, Rabsaris, Nergalsharezer, Rabmag, with all the residue of the princes of the king of Babylon.

4 And it came to pass, *that* when Zedekiah the king of Judah saw them, and all the men of war, then they fled, and went forth out of the city by night, by the way of the king's garden, by the gate between the two walls: and he went out the way of the plain.

5 But the Chaldeans' army pursued after them, and overtook Zedekiah in the plains of Jericho: and when they had taken him, they brought him up to Nebuchadnezzar king of Babylon to Riblah in the land of Hamath, where he gave judgment upon him.

6 Then the king of Babylon slew the sons of Zedekiah in Riblah before his eyes: also the king of Babylon slew all the nobles of Judah.

7 Moreover he put out Zedekiah's eyes, and bound him with chains, to carry him to Babylon.

8 And the Chaldeans burned the king's house, and the houses of the people, with fire, and broke down the walls of Jerusalem.

9 Then Nebuzaradan the captain of the guard carried away captive into Babylon the remnant of the people that remained in the city, and those that fell away, that fell to him, with the rest of the people that remained.

10 But Nebuzaradan the captain of the guard left of the poor of the people, which had nothing, in the land of Judah, and gave them vineyards and fields at the same time.

11 ¶ Now Nebuchadrezzar king of Babylon gave charge concerning Jeremiah to Nebuzaradan the captain of the guard, saying,

12 Take him, and look well to him, and do him no harm; but do to him even as he shall say unto you.

13 So Nebuzaradan the captain of the guard sent, and Nebushasban, Rabsaris, and Nergalsharezer, Rabmag, and all the king of Babylon's princes;

14 Even they sent, and took Jeremiah out of the court of the prison, and committed him to Gedaliah the son of Ahikam the son of Shaphan, that he should carry him home: so he dwelt among the people.

15 Now the word of Yahweh came to Jeremiah, while he was shut up in the court of the prison, saying,

Jeremiah 39

16 Go and speak to Ebedmelech the Ethiopian, saying, Thus says Yahweh of hosts, the God of Israel; Behold, I will bring my words upon this city for evil, and not for good; and they shall be *accomplished* in that day before you.
17 But I will deliver you in that day, says Yahweh: and you shall not be given into the hand of the men of whom you *are* afraid.
18 For I will surely deliver you, and you shall not fall by the sword, but your life shall be for a prey to you: because you have put your trust in me, says Yahweh.

Jeremiah 40

40:1 ¶ The word that came to Jeremiah from Yahweh, after that Nebuzaradan the captain of the guard had let him go from Ramah, when he had taken him being bound in chains among all that were carried away captive from Jerusalem and Judah, which were carried away captive to Babylon.
2 And the captain of the guard took Jeremiah, and said to him, Yahweh your God has pronounced this evil upon this place.
3 Now Yahweh has brought *it*, and done according as he has said: because you have sinned against Yahweh, and have not obeyed his voice, therefore this thing has come upon you.
4 And now, behold, I loose you this day from the chains which *were* upon your hand. If it seems good to you to come with me into Babylon, come; and I will look well unto you: but if it seems ill to you to come with me into Babylon, forbear: behold, all the land *is* before you: wherever it seems good and convenient for you to go, there go.
5 Now while he was not yet gone back, *he said*, Go back also to Gedaliah the son of Ahikam the son of Shaphan, whom the king of Babylon has made governor over the cities of Judah, and dwell with him among the people: or go wherever it seems convenient to you to go. So the captain of the guard gave him food and a reward, and let him go.
6 Then went Jeremiah to Gedaliah the son of Ahikam to Mizpah; and dwelt with him among the people that were left in the land.
7 ¶ Now when all the captains of the forces which *were* in the fields, *even* they and their men, heard that the king of Babylon had made Gedaliah the son of Ahikam governor in the land, and had committed to him men, and women, and children, and of the poor of the land, of them that were not carried away captive to Babylon;
8 Then they came to Gedaliah to Mizpah, even Ishmael the son of Nethaniah, and Johanan and Jonathan the sons of Kareah, and Seraiah the son of Tanhumeth, and the sons of Ephai the Netophathite, and Jezaniah the son of a Maachathite, they and their men.
9 And Gedaliah the son of Ahikam the son of Shaphan swore to them and to their men, saying, Fear not to serve the Chaldeans: dwell in the land, and serve the king of Babylon, and it shall be well with you.
10 As for me, behold, I will dwell at Mizpah to serve the Chaldeans, which will come to us: but you, gather you wine, and summer fruits, and oil, and put *them* in your vessels, and dwell in your cities that you have taken.
11 Likewise when all the Jews that *were* in Moab, and among the Ammonites, and in Edom, and that *were* in all the countries, heard that the king of Babylon had left a remnant of Judah, and that he had set over them Gedaliah the son of Ahikam the son of Shaphan;
12 Even all the Jews returned out of all places where they were driven, and came to the land of Judah, to Gedaliah, to Mizpah, and gathered wine and summer fruits very much.
13 Moreover Johanan the son of Kareah, and all the captains of the forces that *were* in the fields, came to Gedaliah to Mizpah,
14 And said to him, Do you certainly know that Baalis the king of the Ammonites has sent Ishmael the son of Nethaniah to slay you? But Gedaliah the son of Ahikam believed them not.
15 Then Johanan the son of Kareah spoke to Gedaliah in Mizpah secretly, saying, Let me go, I pray you, and I will slay Ishmael the son of Nethaniah, and no man shall know *it*: why should he slay you, that all the Jews which are gathered to you should be scattered, and the remnant in Judah perish?
16 But Gedaliah the son of Ahikam said to Johanan the son of Kareah, You shall not do this thing: for you speak falsely of Ishmael.

Jeremiah 41

41:1 ¶ Now it came to pass in the seventh month, *that* Ishmael the son of Nethaniah the son of Elishama, of the seed royal, and the princes of the king, even ten men with him, came to Gedaliah the son of Ahikam to Mizpah; and there they did eat bread together in Mizpah.
2 Then arose Ishmael the son of Nethaniah, and the ten men that were with him, and smote Gedaliah the son of Ahikam the son of Shaphan with the sword, and slew him, whom the king of Babylon had made governor over the land.
3 Ishmael also slew all the Jews that were with him, *even* with Gedaliah, at Mizpah, and the Chaldeans that were found there, *and* the men of war.
4 And it came to pass the second day after he had slain Gedaliah, and no man knew *it*,
5 That there came certain from Shechem, from Shiloh, and from Samaria, *even* fourscore men, having their beards shaven, and their clothes torn, and having cut themselves, with offerings and incense in their hand, to bring *them* to the house of Yahweh.
6 And Ishmael the son of Nethaniah went forth from Mizpah to meet them, weeping all along as he went: and it came to pass, as he met them, he said to them, Come to Gedaliah the son of Ahikam.
7 And it was *so*, when they came into the midst of the city, that Ishmael the son of Nethaniah slew them, *and*

cast them into the midst of the pit, he, and the men that *were* with him.

8 But ten men were found among them that said unto Ishmael, Slay us not: for we have treasures in the field, of wheat, and of barley, and of oil, and of honey. So he forbore, and slew them not among their brethren.

9 Now the pit wherein Ishmael had cast all the dead bodies of the men, whom he had slain because of Gedaliah, *was* it which Asa the king had made for fear of Baasha king of Israel: *and* Ishmael the son of Nethaniah filled it with *them that were* slain.

10 Then Ishmael carried away captive all the residue of the people that *were* in Mizpah, *even* the king's daughters, and all the people that remained in Mizpah, whom Nebuzaradan the captain of the guard had committed to Gedaliah the son of Ahikam: and Ishmael the son of Nethaniah carried them away captive, and departed to go over to the Ammonites.

11 ¶ But when Johanan the son of Kareah, and all the captains of the forces that *were* with him, heard of all the evil that Ishmael the son of Nethaniah had done,

12 Then they took all the men, and went to fight with Ishmael the son of Nethaniah, and found him by the great waters that *are* in Gibeon.

13 Now it came to pass, *that* when all the people which *were* with Ishmael saw Johanan the son of Kareah, and all the captains of the forces that *were* with him, then they were glad.

14 So all the people that Ishmael had carried away captive from Mizpah cast about and returned, and went to Johanan the son of Kareah.

15 But Ishmael the son of Nethaniah escaped from Johanan with eight men, and went to the Ammonites.

16 Then took Johanan the son of Kareah, and all the captains of the forces that *were* with him, all the remnant of the people whom he had recovered from Ishmael the son of Nethaniah, from Mizpah, after *that* he had slain Gedaliah the son of Ahikam, *even* mighty men of war, and the women, and the children, and the eunuchs, whom he had brought again from Gibeon:

17 And they departed, and dwelt in the habitation of Chimham, which is by Bethlehem, to go to enter into Egypt,

18 Because of the Chaldeans: for they were afraid of them, because Ishmael the son of Nethaniah had slain Gedaliah the son of Ahikam, whom the king of Babylon made governor in the land.

Jeremiah 42

42:1 ¶ Then all the captains of the forces, and Johanan the son of Kareah, and Jezaniah the son of Hoshaiah, and all the people from the least even to the greatest, came near,

2 And said to Jeremiah the prophet, Let, we beseech you, our supplication be accepted before you, and pray for us unto Yahweh your God, *even* for all this remnant; (for we are left *but* a few of many, as your eyes do behold us:)

3 That Yahweh your God may show us the way wherein we may walk, and the thing that we may do.

4 Then Jeremiah the prophet said to them, I have heard *you*; behold, I will pray unto Yahweh your God according to your words; and it shall come to pass, *that* whatever thing Yahweh shall answer you, I will declare *it* unto you; I will keep nothing back from you.

5 Then they said to Jeremiah, Yahweh be a true and faithful witness between us, if we do not even according to all things for which Yahweh your God shall send you to us.

6 Whether *it is* good, or whether *it is* evil, we will obey the voice of Yahweh our God, to whom we send you; that it may be well with us, when we obey the voice of Yahweh our God.

7 ¶ And it came to pass after ten days, that the word of Yahweh came to Jeremiah.

8 Then called he Johanan the son of Kareah, and all the captains of the forces which *were* with him, and all the people from the least even to the greatest,

9 And said to them, Thus says Yahweh, the God of Israel, to whom you sent me to present your supplication before him;

10 If you will still dwell in this land, then will I build you, and not pull *you* down, and I will plant you, and not pluck *you* up: for I repent me of the evil that I have done unto you.

11 Be not afraid of the king of Babylon, of whom you are afraid; be not afraid of him, says Yahweh: for I *am* with you to save you, and to deliver you from his hand.

12 And I will show mercies unto you, that he may have mercy upon you, and cause you to return to your own land.

13 But if you say, We will not dwell in this land, neither obey the voice of Yahweh your God,

14 Saying, No; but we will go into the land of Egypt, where we shall see no war, nor hear the sound of the trumpet, nor have hunger for bread; and there will we dwell:

15 And now therefore hear the word of Yahweh, you remnant of Judah; Thus says Yahweh of hosts, the God of Israel; If you wholly set your faces to enter into Egypt, and go to dwell there;

16 Then it shall come to pass, *that* the sword, which you feared, shall overtake you there in the land of Egypt, and the famine, whereof you were afraid, shall follow close after you there in Egypt; and there you shall die.

17 So shall it be with all the men that set their faces to go into Egypt to dwell there; they shall die by the sword, by the famine, and by the pestilence: and none of them shall remain or escape from the evil that I will bring upon them.

18 For thus says Yahweh of hosts, the God of Israel; As my anger and my fury has been poured forth upon the inhabitants of Jerusalem; so shall my fury be poured forth upon you, when you shall enter into Egypt: and you shall be a swearing, and an astonishment, and a curse, and a reproach; and you shall see this place no more.

Jeremiah 42

19 Yahweh has said concerning you, O you remnant of Judah; Go you not into Egypt: know certainly that I have admonished you this day.
20 For you deceived in your hearts, when you sent me unto Yahweh your God, saying, Pray for us unto Yahweh our God; and according to all that Yahweh our God shall say, so declare to us, and we will do *it*.
21 And *now* I have this day declared *it* to you; but you have not obeyed the voice of Yahweh your God, nor any *thing* for the which he has sent me to you.
22 Now therefore know certainly that you shall die by the sword, by the famine, and by the pestilence, in the place where you desire to go *and* to dwell.

Jeremiah 43

43:1 ¶ And it came to pass, *that* when Jeremiah had made an end of speaking to all the people all the words of Yahweh their God, for which Yahweh their God had sent him to them, *even* all these words,
2 Then spoke Azariah the son of Hoshaiah, and Johanan the son of Kareah, and all the proud men, saying to Jeremiah, You speak falsely: Yahweh our God has not sent you to say, Go not into Egypt to dwell there:
3 But Baruch the son of Neriah sets you on against us, for to deliver us into the hand of the Chaldeans, that they might put us to death, and carry us away captives into Babylon.
4 So Johanan the son of Kareah, and all the captains of the forces, and all the people, obeyed not the voice of Yahweh, to dwell in the land of Judah.
5 But Johanan the son of Kareah, and all the captains of the forces, took all the remnant of Judah, that had returned from all nations, where they had been driven, to dwell in the land of Judah;
6 *Even* men, and women, and children, and the king's daughters, and every person that Nebuzaradan the captain of the guard had left with Gedaliah the son of Ahikam the son of Shaphan, and Jeremiah the prophet, and Baruch the son of Neriah.
7 So they came into the land of Egypt: for they obeyed not the voice of Yahweh: thus came they *even* to Tahpanhes.
8 ¶ Then came the word of Yahweh to Jeremiah in Tahpanhes, saying,
9 Take great stones in your hand, and hide them in the clay in the brick kiln, which *is* at the entry of Pharaoh's house in Tahpanhes, in the sight of the men of Judah;
10 And say to them, Thus says Yahweh of hosts, the God of Israel; Behold, I will send and take Nebuchadrezzar the king of Babylon, my servant, and will set his throne upon these stones that I have hidden; and he shall spread his royal pavilion over them.
11 And when he comes, he shall smite the land of Egypt, *and deliver* such *as are* for death to death; and such *as are* for captivity to captivity; and such *as are* for the sword to the sword.
12 And I will kindle a fire in the houses of the gods of Egypt; and he shall burn them, and carry them away captives: and he shall array himself with the land of Egypt, as a shepherd puts on his garment; and he shall go forth from there in peace.
13 He shall break also the images of Bethshemesh, that *is* in the land of Egypt; and the houses of the gods of the Egyptians shall he burn with fire.

Jeremiah 44

44:1 ¶ The word that came to Jeremiah concerning all the Jews which dwell in the land of Egypt, which dwell at Migdol, and at Tahpanhes, and at Noph, and in the country of Pathros, saying,
2 Thus says Yahweh of hosts, the God of Israel; You have seen all the evil that I have brought upon Jerusalem, and upon all the cities of Judah; and, behold, this day they *are* a desolation, and no man dwells therein,
3 Because of their wickedness which they have committed to provoke me to anger, in that they went to burn incense, *and* to serve other gods, whom they knew not, *neither* they, you, nor your fathers.
4 However I sent to you all my servants the prophets, rising early and sending *them*, saying, Oh, do not this abominable thing that I hate.
5 But they listened not, nor inclined their ear to turn from their wickedness, to burn no incense to other gods.
6 Therefore my fury and my anger was poured forth, and was kindled in the cities of Judah and in the streets of Jerusalem; and they are wasted *and* desolate, as at this day.
7 Therefore now thus says Yahweh, the God of hosts, the God of Israel; Why commit you *this* great evil against your souls, to cut off from you man and woman, child and suckling, out of Judah, to leave you none to remain;
8 In that you provoke me to wrath with the works of your hands, burning incense to other gods in the land of Egypt, where you have gone to dwell, that you might cut yourselves off, and that you might be a curse and a reproach among all the nations of the earth?
9 Have you forgotten the wickedness of your fathers, and the wickedness of the kings of Judah, and the wickedness of their wives, and your own wickedness, and the wickedness of your wives, which they have committed in the land of Judah, and in the streets of Jerusalem?
10 They are not humbled *even* unto this day, neither have they feared, nor walked in my law, nor in my statutes, that I set before you and before your fathers.
11 Therefore thus says Yahweh of hosts, the God of Israel; Behold, I will set my face against you for evil, and to cut off all Judah.
12 And I will take the remnant of Judah, that have set their faces to go into the land of Egypt to dwell there, and they shall all be consumed, *and* fall in the land of Egypt; they shall *even* be consumed by the sword *and*

by the famine: they shall die, from the least even to the greatest, by the sword and by the famine: and they shall be a swearing, *and* an astonishment, and a curse, and a reproach.

13 For I will punish them that dwell in the land of Egypt, as I have punished Jerusalem, by the sword, by the famine, and by the pestilence:

14 So that none of the remnant of Judah, which have gone into the land of Egypt to sojourn there, shall escape or remain, that they should return into the land of Judah, to the which they have a desire to return to dwell there: for none shall return but such as shall escape.

15 ¶ Then all the men which knew that their wives had burned incense to other gods, and all the women that stood by, a great multitude, even all the people that dwelt in the land of Egypt, in Pathros, answered Jeremiah, saying,

16 *As for* the word that you have spoken to us in the name of Yahweh, we will not listen to you.

17 But we will certainly do whatever thing goes forth out of our own mouth, to burn incense to the queen of heaven, and to pour out drink offerings unto her, as we have done, we, and our fathers, our kings, and our princes, in the cities of Judah, and in the streets of Jerusalem: for *then* had we plenty of victuals, and were well, and saw no evil.

18 But since we left off to burn incense to the queen of heaven, and to pour out drink offerings unto her, we have wanted all *things*, and have been consumed by the sword and by the famine.

19 And when we burned incense to the queen of heaven, and poured out drink offerings to her, did we make her cakes to worship her, and pour out drink offerings to her, without our men?

20 ¶ Then Jeremiah said to all the people, to the men, and to the women, and to all the people which had given him *that* answer, saying,

21 The incense that you burned in the cities of Judah, and in the streets of Jerusalem, you, and your fathers, your kings, and your princes, and the people of the land, did not Yahweh remember them, and came it *not* into his mind?

22 So that Yahweh could no longer bear, because of the evil of your doings, *and* because of the abominations which you have committed; therefore is your land a desolation, and an astonishment, and a curse, without an inhabitant, as at this day.

23 Because you have burned incense, and because you have sinned against Yahweh, and have not obeyed the voice of Yahweh, nor walked in his law, nor in his statutes, nor in his testimonies; therefore this evil has happened unto you, as at this day.

24 Moreover Jeremiah said to all the people, and to all the women, Hear the word of Yahweh, all Judah that *are* in the land of Egypt:

25 Thus says Yahweh of hosts, the God of Israel, saying; You and your wives have both spoken with your mouths, and fulfilled with your hand, saying, We will surely perform our vows that we have vowed, to burn incense to the queen of heaven, and to pour out drink offerings unto her: you will surely accomplish your vows, and surely perform your vows.

26 Therefore hear you the word of Yahweh, all Judah that dwell in the land of Egypt; Behold, I have sworn by my great name, says Yahweh, that my name shall no more be named in the mouth of any man of Judah in all the land of Egypt, saying, The Lord Yahweh lives.

27 Behold, I will watch over them for evil, and not for good: and all the men of Judah that *are* in the land of Egypt shall be consumed by the sword and by the famine, until there is an end of them.

28 Yet a small number that escape the sword shall return out of the land of Egypt into the land of Judah, and all the remnant of Judah, that have gone into the land of Egypt to dwell there, shall know whose words shall stand, mine, or theirs.

29 And this *shall be* a sign unto you, says Yahweh, that I will punish you in this place, that you may know that my words shall surely stand against you for evil:

30 Thus says Yahweh; Behold, I will give Pharaohhophra king of Egypt into the hand of his enemies, and into the hand of them that seek his life; as I gave Zedekiah king of Judah into the hand of Nebuchadrezzar king of Babylon, his enemy, and that sought his life.

Jeremiah 45

45:1 ¶ The word that Jeremiah the prophet spoke to Baruch the son of Neriah, when he had written these words in a book at the mouth of Jeremiah, in the fourth year of Jehoiakim the son of Josiah king of Judah, saying,

2 Thus says Yahweh, the God of Israel, to you, O Baruch;

3 You did say, Woe is me now! for Yahweh has added grief to my sorrow; I fainted in my sighing, and I find no rest.

4 Thus shall you say to him, Yahweh says thus; Behold, *that* which I have built will I break down, and that which I have planted I will pluck up, even this whole land.

5 And seek you great things for yourself? seek *them* not: for, behold, I will bring evil upon all flesh, says Yahweh: but your life will I give to you for a prey in all places where you go.

Jeremiah 46

46:1 ¶ The word of Yahweh which came to Jeremiah the prophet against the Gentiles;

2 Against Egypt, against the army of Pharaohnecho king of Egypt, which was by the river Euphrates in Carchemish, which Nebuchadrezzar king of Babylon smote in the fourth year of Jehoiakim the son of Josiah king of Judah.

3 Order you the buckler and shield, and draw near to battle.

4 Harness the horses; and get up, you horsemen, and stand forth with *your* helmets; furbish the spears, *and* put on the armor.

Jeremiah 46

5 Why have I seen them dismayed *and* turned away back? and their mighty ones are beaten down, and are fled *to* escape, and look not back: *for* fear *was* round about, says Yahweh.

6 Let not the swift flee away, nor the mighty man escape; they shall stumble, and fall toward the north by the river Euphrates.

7 Who *is* this *that* comes up as a flood, whose waters are moved as the rivers?

8 Egypt rises up like a flood, and *his* waters are moved like the rivers; and he says, I will go up, *and* will cover the earth; I will destroy the city and the inhabitants thereof.

9 Come up, you horses; and rage, you chariots; and let the mighty men come forth; the Ethiopians and the Libyans, that handle the shield; and the Lydians, that handle *and* bend the bow.

10 For this *is* the day of the Lord Yahweh of hosts, a day of vengeance, that he may avenge him of his adversaries: and the sword shall devour, and it shall be satiated and made drunk with their blood: for the Lord Yahweh of hosts has a sacrifice in the north country by the river Euphrates.

11 Go up into Gilead, and take balm, O virgin, the daughter of Egypt: in vain shall you use many medicines; *for* you shall not be cured.

12 ¶ The nations have heard of your shame, and your cry has filled the land: for the mighty man has stumbled against the mighty, *and* they have fallen both together.

13 The word that Yahweh spoke to Jeremiah the prophet, how Nebuchadrezzar king of Babylon should come *and* smite the land of Egypt.

14 Declare you in Egypt, and publish in Migdol, and publish in Noph and in Tahpanhes: say you, Stand fast, and prepare you; for the sword shall devour round about you.

15 Why are your valiant *men* swept away? they stood not, because Yahweh did drive them.

16 He made many to fall, yes, one fell upon another: and they said, Arise, and let us go again to our own people, and to the land of our nativity, from the oppressing sword.

17 They did cry there, Pharaoh king of Egypt *is but* a noise; he has passed the time appointed.

18 *As* I live, says the King, whose name *is* Yahweh of hosts, Surely as Tabor *is* among the mountains, and as Carmel by the sea, *so* shall he come.

19 O you daughter dwelling in Egypt, furnish yourself to go into captivity: for Noph shall be waste and desolate without an inhabitant.

20 Egypt *is like* a very fair heifer, *but* destruction comes; it comes out of the north.

21 Also her hired men *are* in the midst of her like fatted bullocks; for they also have turned back, *and* have fled away together: they did not stand, because the day of their calamity had come upon them, *and* the time of their visitation.

22 The voice thereof shall go like a serpent; for they shall march with an army, and come against her with axes, as hewers of wood.

23 They shall cut down her forest, says Yahweh, though it cannot be searched; because they are more than the grasshoppers, and *are* innumerable.

24 The daughter of Egypt shall be confounded; she shall be delivered into the hand of the people of the north.

25 Yahweh of hosts, the God of Israel, says; Behold, I will punish the multitude of No, and Pharaoh, and Egypt, with their gods, and their kings; even Pharaoh, and *all* them that trust in him:

26 And I will deliver them into the hand of those that seek their lives, and into the hand of Nebuchadrezzar king of Babylon, and into the hand of his servants: and afterward it shall be inhabited, as in the days of old, says Yahweh.

27 But fear not you, O my servant Jacob, and be not dismayed, O Israel: for, behold, I will save you from afar off, and your seed from the land of their captivity; and Jacob shall return, and be in rest and at ease, and none shall make *him* afraid.

28 Fear you not, O Jacob my servant, says Yahweh: for I *am* with you; for I will make a full end of all the nations where I have driven you: but I will not make a full end of you, but correct you in measure; yet will I not leave you wholly unpunished.

Jeremiah 47

47:1 ¶ The word of Yahweh that came to Jeremiah the prophet against the Philistines, before that Pharaoh smote Gaza.

2 Thus says Yahweh; Behold, waters rise up out of the north, and shall be an overflowing flood, and shall overflow the land, and all that is therein; the city, and them that dwell therein: then the men shall cry, and all the inhabitants of the land shall howl.

3 At the noise of the stamping of the hoofs of his strong *horses*, at the rushing of his chariots, *and at* the rumbling of his wheels, the fathers shall not look back to *their* children for feebleness of hands;

4 Because of the day that comes to spoil all the Philistines, *and* to cut off from Tyrus and Zidon every helper that remains: for Yahweh will spoil the Philistines, the remnant of the country of Caphtor.

5 Baldness has come upon Gaza; Ashkelon is cut off *with* the remnant of their valley: how long will you cut yourself?

6 O you sword of Yahweh, how long *will it be* before you are quiet? put up yourself into your scabbard, rest, and be still.

7 How can it be quiet, seeing Yahweh has given it a charge against Ashkelon, and against the sea shore? there has he appointed it.

Jeremiah 48

48:1 ¶ Against Moab thus says Yahweh of hosts, the God of Israel; Woe unto Nebo! for it is spoiled: Kiriathaim is confounded *and* taken: Misgab is confounded and dismayed.

2 *There shall be* no more praise of Moab: in Heshbon they have devised evil against it; come, and let us cut it off from *being* a nation. Also you shall be cut down, O Madmen; the sword shall pursue you.

3 A voice of crying *shall be* from Horonaim, spoiling and great destruction.

4 Moab is destroyed; her little ones have caused a cry to be heard.

5 For in the going up of Luhith continual weeping shall go up; for in the going down of Horonaim the enemies have heard a cry of destruction.

6 Flee, save your lives, and be like the heath in the wilderness.

7 For because you have trusted in your works and in your treasures, you shall also be taken: and Chemosh shall go forth into captivity *with* his priests and his princes together.

8 And the spoiler shall come upon every city, and no city shall escape: the valley also shall perish, and the plain shall be destroyed, as Yahweh has spoken.

9 Give wings to Moab, that it may flee and get away: for the cities thereof shall be desolate, without any to dwell therein.

10 Cursed *be* he that does the work of Yahweh deceitfully, and cursed *be* he that keeps back his sword from blood.

11 Moab has been at ease from his youth, and he has settled on his dregs, and has not been emptied from vessel to vessel, neither has he gone into captivity: therefore his taste remained in him, and his scent has not changed.

12 Therefore, behold, the days come, says Yahweh, that I will send to him wanderers, that shall cause him to wander, and shall empty his vessels, and break their bottles.

13 And Moab shall be ashamed of Chemosh, as the house of Israel was ashamed of Bethel their confidence.

14 ¶ How say you, We *are* mighty and strong men for the war?

15 Moab is spoiled, and gone up *out of* her cities, and his chosen young men have gone down to the slaughter, says the King, whose name *is* Yahweh of hosts.

16 The calamity of Moab *is* near to come, and his affliction hastens fast.

17 All you that are about him, bemoan him; and all you that know his name, say, How is the strong staff broken, *and* the beautiful rod!

18 You daughter that does inhabit Dibon, come down from *your* glory, and sit in thirst; for the spoiler of Moab shall come upon you, *and* he shall destroy your strong holds.

19 O inhabitant of Aroer, stand by the way, and watch; ask him that flees, and her that escapes, *and* say, What is done?

20 Moab is confounded; for it is broken down: howl and cry; tell you it in Arnon, that Moab is spoiled,

21 And judgment has come upon the plain country; upon Holon, and upon Jahazah, and upon Mephaath,

22 And upon Dibon, and upon Nebo, and upon Bethdiblathaim,

23 And upon Kiriathaim, and upon Bethgamul, and upon Bethmeon,

24 And upon Kerioth, and upon Bozrah, and upon all the cities of the land of Moab, far or near.

25 The horn of Moab is cut off, and his arm is broken, says Yahweh.

26 Make you him drunken: for he magnified *himself* against Yahweh: Moab also shall wallow in his vomit, and he also shall be in derision.

27 For was not Israel a derision to you? was he found among thieves? for since you spoke of him, you skipped for joy.

28 O you that dwell in Moab, leave the cities, and dwell in the rock, and be like the dove *that* makes her nest in the sides of the snares's mouth.

29 We have heard the pride of Moab, (he is exceedingly proud) his loftiness, and his arrogance, and his pride, and the haughtiness of his heart.

30 I know his wrath, says Yahweh; but *it shall* not *be* so; his lies shall not so effect *it*.

31 Therefore will I howl for Moab, and I will cry out for all Moab; *my heart* shall mourn for the men of Kirheres.

32 O vine of Sibmah, I will weep for you with the weeping of Jazer: your plants have gone over the sea, they reach *even* to the sea of Jazer: the spoiler is fallen upon your summer fruits and upon your vintage.

33 And joy and gladness is taken from the plentiful field, and from the land of Moab; and I have caused wine to fail from the winepresses: none shall tread with shouting; *their* shouting *shall be* no shouting.

34 From the cry of Heshbon *even* to Elealeh, *and even* to Jahaz, have they uttered their voice, from Zoar *even* to Horonaim, *as* a heifer of three years old: for the waters also of Nimrim shall be desolate.

35 Moreover I will cause to cease in Moab, says Yahweh, him that offers in the high places, and him that burns incense to his gods.

36 Therefore my heart shall sound for Moab like pipes, and my heart shall sound like pipes for the men of Kirheres: because the riches *that* he has gotten have perished.

37 For every head *shall be* bald, and every beard clipped: upon all the hands *shall be* cuttings, and upon the loins sackcloth.

38 *There shall be* lamentation generally upon all the housetops of Moab, and in the streets thereof: for I have broken Moab like a vessel wherein *is* no pleasure, says Yahweh.

39 They shall howl, *saying*, How is it broken down! how has Moab turned the back with shame! so shall Moab be a derision and a dismaying to all them about him.

40 For thus says Yahweh; Behold, he shall fly as an eagle, and shall spread his wings over Moab.

41 Kerioth is taken, and the strong holds are surprised, and the mighty men's hearts in Moab at that day shall be as the heart of a woman in her pangs.

42 And Moab shall be destroyed from *being* a people, because he has magnified *himself* against Yahweh.

43 Fear, and the pit, and the snare, *shall be* upon you, O inhabitant of Moab, says Yahweh.

Jeremiah 48

44 He that flees from the fear shall fall into the pit; and he that gets up out of the pit shall be taken in the snare: for I will bring upon it, *even* upon Moab, the year of their visitation, says Yahweh.

45 They that fled stood under the shadow of Heshbon because of the force: but a fire shall come forth out of Heshbon, and a flame from the midst of Sihon, and shall devour the corner of Moab, and the crown of the head of the tumultuous ones.

46 Woe be unto you, O Moab! the people of Chemosh perish: for your sons are taken captives, and your daughters captives.

47 Yet will I bring again the captivity of Moab in the latter days, says Yahweh. Thus far *is* the judgment of Moab.

Jeremiah 49

49:1 ¶ Concerning the Ammonites, thus says Yahweh; Has Israel no sons? has he no heir? why *then* does their king inherit Gad, and his people dwell in his cities?

2 Therefore, behold, the days come, says Yahweh, that I will cause an alarm of war to be heard in Rabbah of the Ammonites; and it shall be a desolate heap, and her daughters shall be burned with fire: then shall Israel be heir to them that were his heirs, says Yahweh.

3 Howl, O Heshbon, for Ai is spoiled: cry, you daughters of Rabbah, gird you with sackcloth; lament, and run to and fro by the hedges; for their king shall go into captivity, *and* his priests and his princes together.

4 Why glory you in the valleys, your flowing valley, O backsliding daughter? that trusted in her treasures, *saying*, Who shall come unto me?

5 Behold, I will bring a fear upon you, says the Lord Yahweh of hosts, from all those that are about you; and you shall be driven out every man right forth; and none shall gather up him that wanders.

6 And afterward I will bring again the captivity of the children of Ammon, says Yahweh.

7 ¶ Concerning Edom, thus says Yahweh of hosts; *Is* wisdom no more in Teman? is counsel perished from the prudent? is their wisdom vanished?

8 Flee you, turn back, dwell deep, O inhabitants of Dedan; for I will bring the calamity of Esau upon him, the time *that* I will visit him.

9 If grape gatherers come to you, would they not leave *some* gleaning grapes? if thieves by night, they will destroy till they have enough.

10 But I have made Esau bare, I have uncovered his secret places, and he shall not be able to hide himself: his seed is spoiled, and his brethren, and his neighbors, and he *is* not.

11 Leave your fatherless children, I will preserve *them* alive; and let your widows trust in me.

12 For thus says Yahweh; Behold, they whose judgment *was* not to drink of the cup have assuredly drunk; and *are* you he *that* shall altogether go unpunished? you shall not go unpunished, but you shall surely drink *of it*.

13 For I have sworn by myself, says Yahweh, that Bozrah shall become a desolation, a reproach, a waste, and a curse; and all the cities thereof shall be perpetual wastes.

14 I have heard a rumor from Yahweh, and an ambassador is sent to the heathen, *saying*, Gather you together, and come against her, and rise up to the battle.

15 For, lo, I will make you small among the heathen, *and* despised among men.

16 Your terribleness has deceived you, *and* the pride of your heart, O you that dwell in the clefts of the rock, that hold the height of the hill: though you should make your nest as high as the eagle, I will bring you down from there, says Yahweh.

17 Also Edom shall be a desolation: every one that goes by it shall be astonished, and shall hiss at all the plagues thereof.

18 As in the overthrow of Sodom and Gomorrah and the neighbor *cities* thereof, says Yahweh, no man shall remain there, neither shall a son of man dwell in it.

19 Behold, he shall come up like a lion from the swelling of *the* Jordan against the habitation of the strong: but I will suddenly make him run away from her: and who *is* a chosen *man, that* I may appoint over her? for who *is* like me? and who will appoint me the time? and who *is* that shepherd that will stand before me?

20 Therefore hear the counsel of Yahweh, that he has taken against Edom; and his purposes, that he has purposed against the inhabitants of Teman: Surely the least of the flock shall draw them out: surely he shall make their habitations desolate with them.

21 The earth is moved at the noise of their fall, at the cry the noise thereof was heard in the Red Sea.

22 Behold, he shall come up and fly as the eagle, and spread his wings over Bozrah: and at that day shall the heart of the mighty men of Edom be as the heart of a woman in her pangs.

23 ¶ Concerning Damascus. Hamath is confounded, and Arpad: for they have heard evil tidings: they are fainthearted; *there is* sorrow on the sea; it cannot be quiet.

24 Damascus has grown feeble, *and* turns herself to flee, and fear has seized on *her*: anguish and sorrows have taken her, as a woman in labor.

25 How is the city of praise not left, the city of my joy!

26 Therefore her young men shall fall in her streets, and all the men of war shall be cut off in that day, says Yahweh of hosts.

27 And I will kindle a fire in the wall of Damascus, and it shall consume the palaces of Benhadad.

28 ¶ Concerning Kedar, and concerning the kingdoms of Hazor, which Nebuchadrezzar king of Babylon shall smite, thus says Yahweh; Arise you, go up to Kedar, and spoil the men of the east.

29 Their tents and their flocks shall they take away: they shall take to themselves their curtains, and all their vessels, and their camels; and they shall cry unto them, Fear *is* on every side.

30 Flee, get you far off, dwell deep, O you inhabitants of Hazor, says Yahweh; for Nebuchadrezzar king

of Babylon has taken counsel against you, and has conceived a purpose against you.

31 Arise, get you up to the wealthy nation, that dwells without care, says Yahweh, which have neither gates nor bars, *which* dwells alone.

32 And their camels shall be a booty, and the multitude of their cattle a spoil: and I will scatter into all winds them *that are* in the utmost corners; and I will bring their calamity from all sides thereof, says Yahweh.

33 And Hazor shall be a dwelling for dragons, *and* a desolation forever: there shall no man inhabit there, nor *any* son of man dwell in it.

34 ¶ The word of Yahweh that came to Jeremiah the prophet against Elam in the beginning of the reign of Zedekiah king of Judah, saying,

35 Thus says Yahweh of hosts; Behold, I will break the bow of Elam, the chief of their might.

36 And upon Elam will I bring the four winds from the four quarters of heaven, and will scatter them toward all those winds; and there shall be no nation where the outcasts of Elam shall not come.

37 For I will cause Elam to be dismayed before their enemies, and before them that seek their life: and I will bring evil upon them, *even* my fierce anger, says Yahweh; and I will send the sword after them, till I have consumed them:

38 And I will set my throne in Elam, and will destroy from there the king and the princes, says Yahweh.

39 But it shall come to pass in the latter days, *that* I will bring again the captivity of Elam, says Yahweh.

Jeremiah 50

50:1 ¶ The word that Yahweh spoke against Babylon *and* against the land of the Chaldeans by Jeremiah the prophet.

2 Declare you among the nations, and publish, and set up a standard; publish, *and* conceal not: say, Babylon is taken, Bel is confounded, Merodach is broken in pieces; her idols are confounded, her images are broken in pieces.

3 For out of the north there comes up a nation against her, which shall make her land desolate, and none shall dwell therein: they shall remove, they shall depart, both man and beast.

4 In those days, and in that time, says Yahweh, the children of Israel shall come, they and the children of Judah together, going and weeping: they shall go, and seek Yahweh their God.

5 They shall ask the way to Zion with their faces toward it, *saying*, Come, and let us join ourselves to Yahweh in a perpetual covenant *that* shall not be forgotten.

6 My people have been lost sheep: their shepherds have caused them to go astray, they have turned them away *on* the mountains: they have gone from mountain to hill, they have forgotten their resting place.

7 All that found them have devoured them: and their adversaries said, We offend not, because they have sinned against Yahweh, the habitation of justice, even Yahweh, the hope of their fathers.

8 Remove out of the midst of Babylon, and go forth out of the land of the Chaldeans, and be as the he goats before the flocks.

9 ¶ For, lo, I will raise and cause to come up against Babylon an assembly of great nations from the north country: and they shall set themselves in array against her; from there she shall be taken: their arrows *shall be* as of a mighty expert man; none shall return in vain.

10 And Chaldea shall be a spoil: all that spoil her shall be satisfied, says Yahweh.

11 Because you were glad, because you rejoiced, O you destroyers of my heritage, because you have grown fat as the heifer at grass, and bellow as bulls;

12 Your mother shall be greatly confounded; she that bore you shall be ashamed: behold, the last of the nations *shall be* a wilderness, a dry land, and a desert.

13 Because of the wrath of Yahweh it shall not be inhabited, but it shall be wholly desolate: every one that goes by Babylon shall be astonished, and hiss at all her plagues.

14 Put yourselves in array against Babylon round about: all you that bend the bow, shoot at her, spare no arrows: for she has sinned against Yahweh.

15 Shout against her round about: she has given her hand: her foundations are fallen, her walls are thrown down: for it *is* the vengeance of Yahweh: take vengeance upon her; as she has done, do unto her.

16 Cut off the sower from Babylon, and him that handles the sickle in the time of harvest: for fear of the oppressing sword they shall turn every one to his people, and they shall flee every one to his own land.

17 Israel *is* a scattered sheep; the lions have driven *him* away: first the king of Assyria has devoured him; and last this Nebuchadrezzar king of Babylon has broken his bones.

18 Therefore thus says Yahweh of hosts, the God of Israel; Behold, I will punish the king of Babylon and his land, as I have punished the king of Assyria.

19 And I will bring Israel again to his habitation, and he shall feed on Carmel and Bashan, and his soul shall be satisfied upon mount Ephraim and Gilead.

20 In those days, and in that time, says Yahweh, the iniquity of Israel shall be sought for, and *there shall be* none; and the sins of Judah, and they shall not be found: for I will pardon them whom I reserve.

21 ¶ Go up against the land of Merathaim, *even* against it, and against the inhabitants of Pekod: waste and utterly destroy after them, says Yahweh, and do according to all that I have commanded you.

22 A sound of battle *is* in the land, and of great destruction.

23 How is the hammer of the whole earth cut apart and broken! how has Babylon become a desolation among the nations!

24 I have laid a snare for you, and you are also taken, O Babylon, and you were not aware: you are found, and also caught, because you have striven against Yahweh.

25 Yahweh has opened his armory, and has brought forth the weapons of his indignation: for this *is* the work of the Lord Yahweh of hosts in the land of the Chaldeans.

Jeremiah 50

26 Come against her from the utmost border, open her storehouses: cast her up as heaps, and destroy her utterly: let nothing of her be left.

27 Slay all her bullocks; let them go down to the slaughter: woe unto them! for their day has come, the time of their visitation.

28 The voice of them that flee and escape out of the land of Babylon, to declare in Zion the vengeance of Yahweh our God, the vengeance of his temple.

29 Call together the archers against Babylon: all you that bend the bow, camp against it round about; let none thereof escape: recompense her according to her work; according to all that she has done, do unto her: for she has been proud against Yahweh, against the Holy One of Israel.

30 Therefore shall her young men fall in the streets, and all her men of war shall be cut off in that day, says Yahweh.

31 Behold, I *am* against you, *O you* most proud, says the Lord Yahweh of hosts: for your day has come, the time *that* I will visit you.

32 And the most proud shall stumble and fall, and none shall raise him up: and I will kindle a fire in his cities, and it shall devour all round about him.

33 ¶ Thus says Yahweh of hosts; The children of Israel and the children of Judah *were* oppressed together: and all that took them captives held them fast; they refused to let them go.

34 Their Redeemer *is* strong; Yahweh of hosts *is* his name: he shall thoroughly plead their cause, that he may give rest to the land, and disquiet the inhabitants of Babylon.

35 A sword *is* upon the Chaldeans, says Yahweh, and upon the inhabitants of Babylon, and upon her princes, and upon her wise *men*.

36 A sword *is* upon the liars; and they shall be foolish: a sword *is* upon her mighty men; and they shall be dismayed.

37 A sword *is* upon their horses, and upon their chariots, and upon all the mingled people that *are* in the midst of her; and they shall become as women: a sword *is* upon her treasures; and they shall be robbed.

38 A drought *is* upon her waters; and they shall be dried up: for it *is* the land of graven images, and they are mad upon *their* idols.

39 Therefore the wild beasts of the desert with the wild beasts of the islands shall dwell *there*, and the owls shall dwell therein: and it shall be no more inhabited forever; neither shall it be dwelt in from generation to generation.

40 As God overthrew Sodom and Gomorrah and the neighbor *cities* thereof, says Yahweh; *so* shall no man inhabit there, neither shall any son of man dwell therein.

41 Behold, a people shall come from the north, and a great nation, and many kings shall be raised up from the coasts of the earth.

42 They shall hold the bow and the lance: they *are* cruel, and will not show mercy: their voice shall roar like the sea, and they shall ride upon horses, *every one* put in array, like a man to the battle, against you, O daughter of Babylon.

43 The king of Babylon has heard the report of them, and his hands became feeble: anguish took hold of him, *and* pangs as of a woman in labor.

44 Behold, he shall come up like a lion from the swelling of *the* Jordan to the habitation of the strong: but I will make them suddenly run away from her: and who *is* a chosen *man, that* I may appoint over her? for who *is* like me? and who will appoint me the time? and who *is* that shepherd that will stand before me?

45 Therefore hear you the counsel of Yahweh, that he has taken against Babylon; and his purposes, that he has purposed against the land of the Chaldeans: Surely the least of the flock shall draw them out: surely he shall make *their* habitation desolate with them.

46 At the noise of the taking of Babylon the earth is moved, and the cry is heard among the nations.

Jeremiah 51

51:1 ¶ Thus says Yahweh; Behold, I will raise up against Babylon, and against them that dwell in the midst of them that rise up against me, a destroying wind;

2 And will send to Babylon fanners, that shall fan her, and shall empty her land: for in the day of trouble they shall be against her round about.

3 Against *him that* bends let the archer bend his bow, and against *him that* lifts himself up in his armor: and spare you not her young men; destroy you utterly all her host.

4 Thus the slain shall fall in the land of the Chaldeans, and *they that are* thrust through in her streets.

5 For Israel *has* not *been* forsaken, nor Judah of his God, of Yahweh of hosts; though their land was filled with sin against the Holy One of Israel.

6 Flee out of the midst of Babylon, and deliver every man his soul: be not cut off in her iniquity; for this *is* the time of Yahweh's vengeance; he will render to her a recompense.

7 Babylon *has been* a golden cup in Yahweh's hand, that made all the earth drunken: the nations have drunk of her wine; therefore the nations are mad.

8 Babylon is suddenly fallen and destroyed: howl for her; take balm for her pain, if so be she may be healed.

9 We would have healed Babylon, but she is not healed: forsake her, and let us go every one into his own country: for her judgment reaches to heaven, and is lifted up *even* to the skies.

10 Yahweh has brought forth our righteousness: come, and let us declare in Zion the work of Yahweh our God.

11 Make bright the arrows; gather the shields: Yahweh has raised up the spirit of the kings of the Medes: for his device *is* against Babylon, to destroy it; because it *is* the vengeance of Yahweh, the vengeance of his temple.

12 Set up the standard upon the walls of Babylon, make the watch strong, set up the watchmen, prepare the

ambushes: for Yahweh has both devised and done that which he spoke against the inhabitants of Babylon.

13 O you that dwell upon many waters, abundant in treasures, your end has come, *and* the measure of your covetousness.

14 Yahweh of hosts has sworn by himself, *saying*, Surely I will fill you with men, as with caterpillars; and they shall lift up a shout against you.

15 He has made the earth by his power, he has established the world by his wisdom, and has stretched out the heaven by his understanding.

16 When he utters *his* voice, *there is* a multitude of waters in the heavens; and he causes the vapors to ascend from the ends of the earth: he makes lightnings with rain, and brings forth the wind out of his treasuries.

17 Every man is brutish by *his* knowledge; every founder is confounded by the graven image: for his molten image *is* falsehood, and *there is* no breath in them.

18 They *are* vanity, the work of errors: in the time of their visitation they shall perish.

19 The portion of Jacob *is* not like them; for he *is* the former of all things: and *Israel is* the rod of his inheritance: Yahweh of hosts *is* his name.

20 You *are* my battle ax *and* weapons of war: for with you will I break in pieces the nations, and with you will I destroy kingdoms;

21 And with you will I break in pieces the horse and his rider; and with you will I break in pieces the chariot and his rider;

22 With you also will I break in pieces man and woman; and with you will I break in pieces old and young; and with you will I break in pieces the young man and the maid;

23 I will also break in pieces with you the shepherd and his flock; and with you will I break in pieces the plowman and his yoke of oxen; and with you will I break in pieces captains and rulers.

24 And I will render to Babylon and to all the inhabitants of Chaldea all their evil that they have done in Zion in your sight, says Yahweh.

25 Behold, I *am* against you, O destroying mountain, says Yahweh, which destroys all the earth: and I will stretch out my hand upon you, and roll you down from the rocks, and will make you a burnt mountain.

26 And they shall not take from you a stone for a corner, nor a stone for foundations; but you shall be desolate forever, says Yahweh.

27 Set you up a standard in the land, blow the trumpet among the nations, prepare the nations against her, call together against her the kingdoms of Ararat, Minni, and Ashchenaz; appoint a captain against her; cause the horses to come up as the rough caterpillars.

28 Prepare against her the nations with the kings of the Medes, the captains thereof, and all the rulers thereof, and all the land of his dominion.

29 And the land shall tremble and sorrow: for every purpose of Yahweh shall be performed against Babylon, to make the land of Babylon a desolation without an inhabitant.

30 The mighty men of Babylon have forborne to fight, they have remained in *their* holds: their might has failed; they became as women: they have burned her dwelling places; her bars are broken.

31 One runner shall run to meet another, and one messenger to meet another, to show the king of Babylon that his city is taken at *one* end,

32 And that the passages are stopped, and the reeds they have burned with fire, and the men of war are frightened.

33 For thus says Yahweh of hosts, the God of Israel; The daughter of Babylon *is* like a threshingfloor, *it is* time to thresh her: yet a little while, and the time of her harvest shall come.

34 Nebuchadrezzar the king of Babylon has devoured me, he has crushed me, he has made me an empty vessel, he has swallowed me up like a dragon, he has filled his belly with my delicacies, he has cast me out.

35 The violence done to me and to my flesh *be* upon Babylon, shall the inhabitant of Zion say; and my blood upon the inhabitants of Chaldea, shall Jerusalem say.

36 Therefore thus says Yahweh; Behold, I will plead your cause, and take vengeance for you; and I will dry up her sea, and make her springs dry.

37 And Babylon shall become heaps, a dwelling place for dragons, an astonishment, and a hissing, without an inhabitant.

38 They shall roar together like lions: they shall yell as lions' whelps.

39 In their heat I will make their feasts, and I will make them drunken, that they may rejoice, and sleep a perpetual sleep, and not awaken, says Yahweh.

40 I will bring them down like lambs to the slaughter, like rams with he goats.

41 How is Sheshach taken! and how is the praise of the whole earth surprised! how has Babylon become an astonishment among the nations!

42 The sea has come up upon Babylon: she is covered with the multitude of the waves thereof.

43 Her cities are a desolation, a dry land, and a wilderness, a land wherein no man dwells, neither does *any* son of man pass thereby.

44 And I will punish Bel in Babylon, and I will bring forth out of his mouth that which he has swallowed up: and the nations shall not flow together any more unto him: yes, the wall of Babylon shall fall.

45 My people, go you out of the midst of her, and deliver you every man his soul from the fierce anger of Yahweh.

46 And lest your heart faints, and you fear for the rumor that shall be heard in the land; a rumor shall both come *one* year, and after that in *another* year *shall come* a rumor, and violence in the land, ruler against ruler.

47 Therefore, behold, the days come, that I will do judgment upon the graven images of Babylon: and her whole land shall be confounded, and all her slain shall fall in the midst of her.

48 Then the heaven and the earth, and all that *is* therein, shall sing for Babylon: for the spoilers shall come to her from the north, says Yahweh.

Jeremiah 51

49 As Babylon *has caused* the slain of Israel to fall, so at Babylon shall fall the slain of all the earth.
50 You that have escaped the sword, go away, stand not still: remember Yahweh afar off, and let Jerusalem come into your mind.
51 We are confounded, because we have heard reproach: shame has covered our faces: for strangers have come into the sanctuaries of Yahweh's house.
52 Therefore, behold, the days come, says Yahweh, that I will do judgment upon her graven images: and through all her land the wounded shall groan.
53 Though Babylon should mount up to heaven, and though she should fortify the height of her strength, *yet* from me shall spoilers come unto her, says Yahweh.
54 A sound of a cry *comes* from Babylon, and great destruction from the land of the Chaldeans:
55 Because Yahweh has spoiled Babylon, and destroyed out of her the great voice; when her waves do roar like great waters, a noise of their voice is uttered:
56 Because the spoiler has come upon her, *even* upon Babylon, and her mighty men are taken, every one of their bows is broken: for Yahweh God of recompenses shall surely repay.
57 And I will make drunk her princes, and her wise *men*, her captains, and her rulers, and her mighty men: and they shall sleep a perpetual sleep, and not awaken, says the King, whose name *is* Yahweh of hosts.
58 Thus says Yahweh of hosts; The broad walls of Babylon shall be utterly broken, and her high gates shall be burned with fire; and the people shall labor in vain, and the folk in the fire, and they shall be weary.
59 ¶ The word which Jeremiah the prophet commanded Seraiah the son of Neriah, the son of Maaseiah, when he went with Zedekiah the king of Judah into Babylon in the fourth year of his reign. And *this* Seraiah *was* a quiet prince.
60 So Jeremiah wrote in a book all the evil that should come upon Babylon, *even* all these words that are written against Babylon.
61 And Jeremiah said to Seraiah, When you come to Babylon, and shall see, and shall read all these words;
62 Then shall you say, O Yahweh, you have spoken against this place, to cut it off, that none shall remain in it, neither man nor beast, but that it shall be desolate forever.
63 And it shall be, when you have made an end of reading this book, *that* you shall bind a stone to it, and cast it into the midst of *the* Euphrates:
64 And you shall say, Thus shall Babylon sink, and shall not rise from the evil that I will bring upon her: and they shall be weary. Thus far *are* the words of Jeremiah.

Jeremiah 52

52:1 ¶ Zedekiah *was* one and twenty years old when he began to reign, and he reigned eleven years in Jerusalem. And his mother's name *was* Hamutal the daughter of Jeremiah of Libnah.
2 And he did *that which was* evil in the eyes of Yahweh, according to all that Jehoiakim had done.
3 For through the anger of Yahweh it came to pass in Jerusalem and Judah, till he had cast them out from his presence, that Zedekiah rebelled against the king of Babylon.
4 And it came to pass in the ninth year of his reign, in the tenth month, in the tenth *day* of the month, *that* Nebuchadrezzar king of Babylon came, he and all his army, against Jerusalem, and pitched against it, and built forts against it round about.
5 So the city was besieged to the eleventh year of king Zedekiah.
6 And in the fourth month, in the ninth *day* of the month, the famine was severe in the city, so that there was no bread for the people of the land.
7 Then the city was broken up, and all the men of war fled, and went forth out of the city by night by the way of the gate between the two walls, which *was* by the king's garden; (now the Chaldeans *were* by the city round about:) and they went by the way of the plain.
8 But the army of the Chaldeans pursued after the king, and overtook Zedekiah in the plains of Jericho; and all his army was scattered from him.
9 Then they took the king, and carried him up to the king of Babylon to Riblah in the land of Hamath; where he gave judgment upon him.
10 And the king of Babylon slew the sons of Zedekiah before his eyes: he slew also all the princes of Judah in Riblah.
11 Then he put out the eyes of Zedekiah; and the king of Babylon bound him in chains, and carried him to Babylon, and put him in prison till the day of his death.
12 ¶ Now in the fifth month, in the tenth *day* of the month, which *was* the nineteenth year of Nebuchadrezzar king of Babylon, came Nebuzaradan, captain of the guard, *which* served the king of Babylon, into Jerusalem,
13 And burned the house of Yahweh, and the king's house; and all the houses of Jerusalem, and all the houses of the great *men*, burned he with fire:
14 And all the army of the Chaldeans, that *were* with the captain of the guard, broke down all the walls of Jerusalem round about.
15 Then Nebuzaradan the captain of the guard carried away captive *certain* of the poor of the people, and the residue of the people that remained in the city, and those that fell away, that fell to the king of Babylon, and the rest of the multitude.
16 But Nebuzaradan the captain of the guard left *certain* of the poor of the land for vine dressers and for husbandmen.
17 Also the pillars of brass that *were* in the house of Yahweh, and the bases, and the brazen sea that *was* in the house of Yahweh, the Chaldeans broke, and carried all the brass of them to Babylon.
18 The caldrons also, and the shovels, and the snuffers, and the bowls, and the spoons, and all the vessels of brass with which they ministered, took they away.

19 And the basins, and the firepans, and the bowls, and the caldrons, and the candlesticks, and the spoons, and the cups; *that* which *was* of gold *in* gold, and *that* which *was* of silver *in* silver, took the captain of the guard away.

20 The two pillars, one sea, and twelve brazen bulls that *were* under the bases, which king Solomon had made in the house of Yahweh: the brass of all these vessels was without weight.

21 And *concerning* the pillars, the height of one pillar *was* eighteen cubits; and a fillet of twelve cubits did compass it; and the thickness thereof *was* four fingers: *it was* hollow.

22 And a capital of brass *was* upon it; and the height of one capital *was* five cubits, with network and pomegranates upon the capitals round about, all *of* brass. The second pillar also and the pomegranates *were* like unto these.

23 And there were ninety and six pomegranates on a side; *and* all the pomegranates upon the network *were* a hundred round about.

24 ¶ And the captain of the guard took Seraiah the chief priest, and Zephaniah the second priest, and the three keepers of the door:

25 He took also out of the city a eunuch, which had the charge of the men of war; and seven men of them that were near the king's person, which were found in the city; and the principal scribe of the host, who mustered the people of the land; and threescore men of the people of the land, that were found in the midst of the city.

26 So Nebuzaradan the captain of the guard took them, and brought them to the king of Babylon to Riblah.

27 And the king of Babylon smote them, and put them to death in Riblah in the land of Hamath. Thus Judah was carried away captive out of his own land.

28 These *are* the people whom Nebuchadrezzar carried away captive: in the seventh year three thousand Jews and three and twenty:

29 In the eighteenth year of Nebuchadrezzar he carried away captive from Jerusalem eight hundred thirty and two persons:

30 In the three and twentieth year of Nebuchadrezzar Nebuzaradan the captain of the guard carried away captive of the Jews seven hundred forty and five persons: all the persons *were* four thousand and six hundred.

31 ¶ And it came to pass in the seven and thirtieth year of the captivity of Jehoiachin king of Judah, in the twelfth month, in the five and twentieth *day* of the month, *that* Evilmerodach king of Babylon in the *first* year of his reign lifted up the head of Jehoiachin king of Judah, and brought him forth out of prison,

32 And spoke kindly to him, and set his throne above the throne of the kings that *were* with him in Babylon,

33 And changed his prison garments: and he did continually eat bread before him all the days of his life.

34 And *for* his diet, there was a continual diet given him by the king of Babylon, every day a portion until the day of his death, all the days of his life.

Lamentations

Lamentations 1

1:1 ¶ How does the city sit solitary, *that was* full of people! *how* has she become as a widow! she *that was* great among the nations, *and* princess among the provinces, *how* has she become tributary!

2 She weeps tearfully in the night, and her tears *are* on her cheeks among all her lovers she has none to comfort *her*: all her friends have dealt treacherously with her, they have become her enemies.

3 Judah has gone into captivity because of affliction, and because of great servitude: she dwells among the heathen, she finds no rest: all her persecutors overtook her during the distress.

4 The ways of Zion do mourn, because none come to the solemn feasts: all her gates are desolate: her priests sigh, her virgins are afflicted, and she *is* in bitterness.

5 Her adversaries are the chief, her enemies prosper; for Yahweh has afflicted her for the multitude of her transgressions: her children have gone into captivity before the enemy.

6 And from the daughter of Zion all her beauty has departed: her princes have become like harts *that* find no pasture, and they have gone without strength before the pursuer.

7 Jerusalem remembered in the days of her affliction and of her miseries all her pleasant things that she had in the days of old, when her people fell into the hand of the enemy, and none did help her: the adversaries saw her, *and* did mock at her sabbaths.

8 Jerusalem has grievously sinned; therefore she is removed: all that honored her despise her, because they have seen her nakedness: yes, she sighs, and turns backward.

9 Her filthiness *is* in her skirts; she remembers not her last end; therefore she came down wonderfully: she had no comforter. O Yahweh, behold my affliction: for the enemy has magnified *himself*.

10 The adversary has spread out his hand upon all her pleasant things: for she has seen *that* the heathen entered into her sanctuary, whom you did command *that* they should not enter into your congregation.

11 All her people sigh, they seek bread; they have given their pleasant things for food to relieve the soul: see, O Yahweh, and consider; for I have become vile.

12 ¶ *Is it* nothing to you, all you that pass by? behold, and see if there is any sorrow like unto my sorrow, which is done unto me, with which Yahweh has afflicted *me* in the day of his fierce anger.

13 From above has he sent fire into my bones, and it prevails against them: he has spread a net for my feet, he has turned me back: he has made me desolate *and* faint all the day.

14 The yoke of my transgressions is bound by his hand: they are wreathed, *and* come up upon my neck: he has made my strength to fall, the Lord has delivered me into *their* hands, *from whom* I am not able to rise up.

Lamentations 1

15 The Lord has trodden under foot all my mighty *men* in the midst of me: he has called an assembly against me to crush my young men: the Lord has trodden the virgin, the daughter of Judah, *as* in a winepress.

16 For these *things* I weep; my eye, my eye runs down with water, because the comforter that should relieve my soul is far from me: my children are desolate, because the enemy prevailed.

17 Zion spreads forth her hands, *and there is* none to comfort her: Yahweh has commanded concerning Jacob, *that* his adversaries *should be* round about him: Jerusalem is as a menstruous woman among them.

18 Yahweh is righteous; for I have rebelled against his commandment: hear, I pray you, all people, and behold my sorrow: my virgins and my young men have gone into captivity.

19 I called for my lovers, *but* they deceived me: my priests and my elders gave up the ghost in the city, while they sought their food to relieve their souls.

20 Behold, O Yahweh; for I *am* in distress: my bowels are troubled; my heart is turned within me; for I have grievously rebelled: abroad the sword bereaves, at home *there is* as death.

21 They have heard that I sigh: *there is* none to comfort me: all my enemies have heard of my trouble; they are glad that you have done *it*: you will bring the day *that* you have called, and they shall be like unto me.

22 Let all their wickedness come before you; and do to them, as you have done unto me for all my transgressions: for my sighs *are* many, and my heart *is* faint.

Lamentations 2

2:1 ¶ How has the Lord covered the daughter of Zion with a cloud in his anger, *and* cast down from heaven to the earth the beauty of Israel, and remembered not his footstool in the day of his anger!

2 The Lord has swallowed up all the habitations of Jacob, and has not pitied: he has thrown down in his wrath the strong holds of the daughter of Judah; he has brought *them* down to the ground: he has polluted the kingdom and the princes thereof.

3 He has cut off in *his* fierce anger all the horn of Israel: he has drawn back his right hand from before the enemy, and he burned against Jacob like a flaming fire, *which* devours round about.

4 He has bent his bow like an enemy: he stood with his right hand as an adversary, and slew all *that were* pleasant to the eye in the tabernacle of the daughter of Zion: he poured out his fury like fire.

5 The Lord was as an enemy: he has swallowed up Israel, he has swallowed up all her palaces: he has destroyed his strong holds, and has increased in the daughter of Judah mourning and lamentation.

6 And he has violently taken away his tabernacle, as *if it were of* a garden: he has destroyed his places of the assembly: Yahweh has caused the solemn feasts and sabbaths to be forgotten in Zion, and has despised in the indignation of his anger the king and the priest.

7 The Lord has cast off his altar, he has abhorred his sanctuary, he has given up into the hand of the enemy the walls of her palaces; they have made a noise in the house of Yahweh, as in the day of a solemn feast.

8 Yahweh has purposed to destroy the wall of the daughter of Zion: he has stretched out a line, he has not withdrawn his hand from destroying: therefore he made the rampart and the wall to lament; they languished together.

9 Her gates are sunk into the ground; he has destroyed and broken her bars: her king and her princes *are* among the Gentiles: the law *is* no *more*; her prophets also find no vision from Yahweh.

10 ¶ The elders of the daughter of Zion sit upon the ground, *and* keep silence: they have cast up dust upon their heads; they have girded themselves with sackcloth: the virgins of Jerusalem hang down their heads to the ground.

11 My eyes do fail with tears, my bowels are troubled, my liver is poured upon the earth, for the destruction of the daughter of my people; because the children and the sucklings swoon in the streets of the city.

12 They say to their mothers, Where *is* corn and wine? when they swooned as the wounded in the streets of the city, when their soul was poured out into their mothers' bosom.

13 What thing shall I take to witness for you? what thing shall I liken to you, O daughter of Jerusalem? what shall I equal to you, that I may comfort you, O virgin daughter of Zion? for your breach *is* great like the sea: who can heal you?

14 Your prophets have seen vain and foolish things for you: and they have not discovered your iniquity, to turn away your captivity; but have seen for you false burdens and causes of banishment.

15 All that pass by clap *their* hands at you; they hiss and wag their head at the daughter of Jerusalem, *saying, Is* this the city that *men* call The perfection of beauty, The joy of the whole earth?

16 All your enemies have opened their mouths against you: they hiss and gnash the teeth: they say, We have swallowed *her* up: certainly this *is* the day that we looked for; we have found, we have seen *it*.

17 Yahweh has done *that* which he had devised; he has fulfilled his word that he had commanded in the days of old: he has thrown down, and has not pitied: and he has caused *your* enemy to rejoice over you, he has set up the horn of your adversaries.

18 Their heart cried unto the Lord, O wall of the daughter of Zion, let tears run down like a river day and night: give yourself no rest; let not the apple of your eye cease.

19 Arise, cry out in the night: in the beginning of the watches pour out your heart like water before the face of the Lord: lift up your hands toward him for the life of your young children, that faint for hunger in the top of every street.

20 Behold, O Yahweh, and consider to whom you have done this. Shall the women eat their offspring, *and* children of *their* tender care? shall the priest and the prophet be slain in the sanctuary of the Lord?

21 The young and the old lie on the ground in the streets: my virgins and my young men have fallen by the sword; you have slain *them* in the day of your anger; you have killed, *and* not pitied.
22 You have called as in a solemn day my terrors round about, so that in the day of Yahweh's anger none escaped nor remained: those that I have swaddled and brought up has my enemy consumed.

Lamentations 3

3:1 ¶ I *am* the man *that* has seen affliction by the rod of his wrath.
2 He has led me, and brought *me into* darkness, but not *into* light.
3 Surely against me is he turned; he turns his hand *against me* all the day.
4 My flesh and my skin has he made old; he has broken my bones.
5 He has built against me, and compassed *me* with gall and travail.
6 He has set me in dark places, as *they that are* dead of old.
7 He has hedged me about, that I cannot get out: he has made my chain heavy.
8 Also when I cry and shout, he shuts out my prayer.
9 He has enclosed my ways with hewn stone, he has made my paths crooked.
10 He *was* to me *as* a bear lying in wait, *and as* a lion in secret places.
11 He has turned aside my ways, and pulled me in pieces: he has made me desolate.
12 He has bent his bow, and set me as a mark for the arrow.
13 He has caused the arrows of his quiver to enter into my reins.
14 I was a derision to all my people; *and* their song all the day.
15 He has filled me with bitterness, he has made me drunken with wormwood.
16 He has also broken my teeth with gravel stones, he has covered me with ashes.
17 And you have removed my soul far off from peace: I forgot prosperity.
18 And I said, My strength and my hope have perished from Yahweh:
19 Remembering my affliction and my misery, the wormwood and the gall.
20 My soul has *them* still in remembrance, and is humbled in me.
21 ¶ This I recall to my mind, therefore have I hope.
22 *It is of* Yahweh's mercies that we are not consumed, because his compassions fail not.
23 *They are* new every morning: great *is* your faithfulness.
24 Yahweh *is* my portion, said my soul; therefore will I hope in him.
25 Yahweh *is* good to them that wait for him, to the soul *that* seeks him.
26 *It is* good that *a man* should both hope and quietly wait for the salvation of Yahweh.
27 *It is* good for a man that he bears the yoke in his youth.
28 He sits alone and keeps silent, because he has borne *it* upon him.
29 He puts his mouth in the dust; if so be there may be hope.
30 He gives *his* cheek to him that smites him: he is filled full with reproach.
31 For the Lord will not cast off forever:
32 But though he causes grief, yet will he have compassion according to the multitude of his mercies.
33 For he does not afflict willingly nor grieve the children of men.
34 To crush under his feet all the prisoners of the earth,
35 To turn aside the right of a man before the face of the most High,
36 To subvert a man in his cause, the Lord approves not.
37 ¶ Who *is* he *that* says, and it comes to pass, *when* the Lord commands *it* not?
38 Out of the mouth of the most High proceeds not evil and good?
39 Why does a living man complain, a man for the punishment of his sins?
40 Let us search and try our ways, and turn again to Yahweh.
41 Let us lift up our heart with *our* hands unto God in the heavens.
42 ¶ We have transgressed and have rebelled: you have not pardoned.
43 You have covered with anger, and persecuted us: you have slain, you have not pitied.
44 You have covered yourself with a cloud, that *our* prayer should not pass through.
45 You have made us *as* the offscouring and refuse in the midst of the people.
46 All our enemies have opened their mouths against us.
47 Fear and a snare has come upon us, desolation and destruction
48 My eye runs down with rivers of water for the destruction of the daughter of my people.
49 My eye trickles down, and ceases not, without any intermission,
50 Till Yahweh looks down, and beholds from heaven.
51 My eye affects my heart because of all the daughters of my city.
52 My enemies hunted me eagerly, like a bird, without cause.
53 They have cut off my life in the dungeon, and cast a stone upon me.
54 Waters flowed over my head; *then* I said, I am cut off.
55 ¶ I called upon your name, O Yahweh, out of the low dungeon.
56 You have heard my voice: hide not your ear at my breathing, at my cry.
57 You drew near in the day *that* I called upon you: you said, Fear not.

58 O Lord, you have pleaded the causes of my soul; you have redeemed my life.
59 O Yahweh, you have seen my wrong: judge you my cause.
60 You have seen all their vengeance *and* all their imaginations against me.
61 You have heard their reproach, O Yahweh, *and* all their imaginations against me;
62 The lips of those that rose up against me, and their device against me all the day.
63 Behold their sitting down, and their rising up; I *am* their music.
64 Render to them a recompense, O Yahweh, according to the work of their hands.
65 Give them sorrow of heart, your curse to them.
66 Persecute and destroy them in anger from under the heavens of Yahweh.

Lamentations 4

4:1 ¶ How has the gold become dim! *how* has the most fine gold changed! the stones of the sanctuary are poured out in the top of every street.
2 The precious sons of Zion, comparable to fine gold, how are they esteemed as earthen pitchers, the work of the hands of the potter!
3 Even the sea monsters draw out the breast, they give suck to their young ones: the daughter of my people *has become* cruel, like the ostriches in the wilderness.
4 The tongue of the sucking child clings to the roof of his mouth for thirst: the young children ask *for* bread, *and* no man breaks *it* unto them.
5 They that did feed delicately are desolate in the streets: they that were brought up in scarlet embrace dunghills.
6 For the punishment of the iniquity of the daughter of my people is greater than the punishment of the sin of Sodom, that was overthrown as in a moment, and no hands stayed on her.
7 Her Nazarites were purer than snow, they were whiter than milk, they were more ruddy in body than rubies, their polishing *was* of sapphire:
8 Their visage is blacker than a coal; they are not known in the streets: their skin clings to their bones; it is withered, it has become like a stick.
9 *They that are* slain with the sword are better than *they that are* slain with hunger: for these pine away, stricken through for *want of* the fruits of the field.
10 The hands of the pitiful women have boiled their own children: they were their meat in the destruction of the daughter of my people.
11 Yahweh has accomplished his fury; he has poured out his fierce anger, and has kindled a fire in Zion, and it has devoured the foundations thereof.
12 The kings of the earth, and all the inhabitants of the world, would not have believed that the adversary and the enemy should have entered into the gates of Jerusalem.
13 ¶ For the sins of her prophets, *and* the iniquities of her priests, that have shed the blood of the just in the midst of her,
14 They have wandered *as* blind *men* in the streets, they have polluted themselves with blood, so that men could not touch their garments.
15 They cried to them, Depart you; *it is* unclean; depart, depart, touch not: when they fled away and wandered, they said among the heathen, They shall no more sojourn *there*.
16 The anger of Yahweh has divided them; he will no more regard them: they respected not the persons of the priests, they favored not the elders.
17 As for us, our eyes as yet failed for our vain help: in our watching we have watched for a nation *that* could not save *us*.
18 They hunt our steps, that we cannot go in our streets: our end is near, our days are fulfilled; for our end has come.
19 Our persecutors are swifter than the eagles of the heaven: they pursued us upon the mountains, they laid wait for us in the wilderness.
20 The breath of our nostrils, the anointed of Yahweh, was taken in their pits, of whom we said, Under his shadow we shall live among the heathen.
21 ¶ Rejoice and be glad, O daughter of Edom, that dwell in the land of Uz; the cup also shall pass through to you: you shall be drunken, and shall make yourself naked.
22 The punishment of your iniquity is accomplished, O daughter of Zion; he will no more carry you away into captivity: he will visit your iniquity, O daughter of Edom; he will discover your sins.

Lamentations 5

5:1 ¶ Remember, O Yahweh, what has come upon us: consider, and behold our reproach.
2 Our inheritance is turned to strangers, our houses to aliens.
3 We are orphans and fatherless, our mothers *are* as widows.
4 We have drunk our water for money; our wood is sold to us.
5 Our necks *are* under persecution: we labor, *and* have no rest.
6 We have given the hand *to* the Egyptians, *and to* the Assyrians, to be satisfied with bread.
7 Our fathers have sinned, *and are* not; and we have borne their iniquities.
8 Servants have ruled over us: *there is* none that does deliver *us* out of their hand.
9 We got our bread with *the peril of* our lives because of the sword of the wilderness.
10 Our skin was black like an oven because of the terrible famine.
11 They ravished the women in Zion, *and* the maids in the cities of Judah.

12 Princes are hung up by their hands: the faces of elders were not honored.
13 They took the young men to grind, and the children fell under the wood.
14 The elders have ceased from the gate, the young men from their music.
15 The joy of our heart has ceased; our dance has turned into mourning.
16 The crown has fallen *from* our head: woe unto us, that we have sinned!
17 ¶ For this our heart is faint; for these *things* our eyes are dim.
18 Because of the mountain of Zion, which is desolate, the foxes walk upon it.
19 You, O Yahweh, remain forever; your throne from generation to generation.
20 Why do you forget us forever, *and* forsake us *for* so long *a* time?
21 Turn you us unto you, O Yahweh, and we shall be turned; renew our days as of old.
22 But you have utterly rejected us; you are very angry against us.

Ezekiel

Ezekiel 1

1:1 ¶ Now it came to pass in the thirtieth year, in the fourth *month*, in the fifth *day* of the month, as I *was* among the captives by the river of Chebar, *that* the heavens were opened, and I saw visions of God.
2 In the fifth *day* of the month, which *was* the fifth year of king Jehoiachin's captivity,
3 The word of Yahweh came expressly unto Ezekiel the priest, the son of Buzi, in the land of the Chaldeans by the river Chebar; and the hand of Yahweh was there upon him.
4 ¶ And I looked, and, behold, a whirlwind came out of the north, a great cloud, and a fire enfolding itself, and a brightness *was* about it, and out of the midst thereof as the color of amber, out of the midst of the fire.
5 Also out of the midst thereof *came* the likeness of four living creatures. And this *was* their appearance; they had the likeness of a man.
6 And every one had four faces, and every one had four wings.
7 And their feet *were* straight feet; and the soles of their feet *were* like the sole of a calf's foot: and they sparkled like the color of burnished brass.
8 And *they had* the hands of a man under their wings on their four sides; and they four had their faces and their wings.
9 Their wings *were* joined one to another; they turned not when they went; they went every one straight forward.
10 As for the likeness of their faces, they four had the face of a man, and the face of a lion, on the right side: and they four had the face of an ox on the left side; they four also had the face of an eagle.
11 Thus *were* their faces: and their wings *were* stretched upward; two *wings* of every one *were* joined one to another, and two covered their bodies.
12 And they went every one straight forward: wherever the spirit was to go, they went; *and* they turned not when they went.
13 As for the likeness of the living creatures, their appearance *was* like burning coals of fire, *and* like the appearance of lamps: it went up and down among the living creatures; and the fire was bright, and out of the fire went forth lightning.
14 And the living creatures ran and returned as the appearance of a flash of lightning.
15 ¶ Now as I beheld the living creatures, behold one wheel upon the earth by the living creatures, with his four faces.
16 The appearance of the wheels and their work *was* like unto the color of a beryl: and they four had one likeness: and their appearance and their work *was* as it were a wheel in the middle of a wheel.
17 When they went, they went upon their four sides: *and* they turned not when they went.
18 As for their rims, they were so high that they were dreadful; and their rims *were* full of eyes round about them four.
19 And when the living creatures went, the wheels went by them: and when the living creatures were lifted up from the earth, the wheels were lifted up.
20 Wherever the spirit was to go, they went, there *was* their spirit to go; and the wheels were lifted up over against them: for the spirit of the living creature *was* in the wheels.
21 When those went, *these* went; and when those stood, *these* stood; and when those were lifted up from the earth, the wheels were lifted up over against them: for the spirit of the living creature *was* in the wheels.
22 And the likeness of the firmament upon the heads of the living creature *was* as the color of the awesome crystal, stretched forth over their heads above.
23 And under the firmament *were* their wings straight, the one toward the other: every one had two, which covered on this side, and every one had two, which covered on that side, their bodies.
24 And when they went, I heard the noise of their wings, like the noise of great waters, as the voice of the Almighty, the voice of speech, as the noise of a host: when they stood, they let down their wings.
25 And there was a voice from the firmament that *was* over their heads, when they stood, *and* had let down their wings.
26 ¶ And above the firmament that *was* over their heads *was* the likeness of a throne, as the appearance of a sapphire stone: and upon the likeness of the throne *was* the likeness as the appearance of a man above upon it.
27 And I saw as the color of amber, as the appearance of fire round about within it, from the appearance of his loins even upward, and from the appearance of his loins even downward, I saw as it were the appearance of fire, and it had brightness round about.

Ezekiel 1

28 As the appearance of the bow that is in the cloud in the day of rain, so *was* the appearance of the brightness round about. This *was* the appearance of the likeness of the glory of Yahweh. And when I saw *it*, I fell upon my face, and I heard a voice of one that spoke.

Ezekiel 2

2:1 ¶ And he said to me, Son of man, stand upon your feet, and I will speak unto you.
2 And the spirit entered into me when he spoke to me, and set me upon my feet, that I heard him that spoke unto me.
3 And he said to me, Son of man, I send you to the children of Israel, to a rebellious nation that has rebelled against me: they and their fathers have transgressed against me, *even* unto this very day.
4 For *they are* impudent children and stiff hearted. I do send you unto them; and you shall say unto them, Thus says the Lord Yahweh.
5 And they, whether they will hear, or whether they will forbear, (for they *are* a rebellious house,) yet *they* shall know that there has been a prophet among them.
6 ¶ And you, son of man, be not afraid of them, neither be afraid of their words, though briers and thorns *be* with you, and you do dwell among scorpions: be not afraid of their words, nor be dismayed at their looks, though they *are* a rebellious house.
7 And you shall speak my words to them, whether they will hear, or whether they will forbear: for they *are* most rebellious.
8 But you, son of man, hear what I say unto you; Be not you rebellious like that rebellious house: open your mouth, and eat what I give you.
9 And when I looked, behold, a hand *was* sent to me; and, lo, a roll of a book *was* therein;
10 And he spread it before me; and it *was* written within and without: and *there was* written therein lamentations, and mourning, and woe.

Ezekiel 3

3:1 ¶ Moreover he said unto me, Son of man, eat what you find; eat this roll, and go speak to the house of Israel.
2 So I opened my mouth, and he caused me to eat that roll.
3 And he said unto me, Son of man, cause your belly to eat, and fill your bowels with this roll that I give you. Then did I eat *it*; and it was in my mouth as honey for sweetness.
4 And he said unto me, Son of man, go, get you unto the house of Israel, and speak with my words to them.
5 For you *are* not sent to a people of a strange speech and of a hard language, *but* to the house of Israel;
6 Not to many people of a strange speech and of a hard language, whose words you can not understand. Surely, had I sent you to them, they would have listened unto you.
7 But the house of Israel will not listen unto you; for they will not listen unto me: for all the house of Israel *are* impudent and hardhearted.
8 Behold, I have made your face strong against their faces, and your forehead strong against their foreheads.
9 As an adamant harder than flint have I made your forehead: fear them not, neither be dismayed at their looks, though they *are* a rebellious house.
10 Moreover he said unto me, Son of man, all my words that I shall speak unto you receive in your heart, and hear with your ears.
11 And go, get you to them of the captivity, to the children of your people, and speak to them, and tell them, Thus says the Lord Yahweh; whether they will hear, or whether they will forbear.
12 Then the spirit took me up, and I heard behind me a voice of a great rushing, *saying*, Blessed *be* the glory of Yahweh from his place.
13 *I heard* also the noise of the wings of the living creatures that touched one another, and the noise of the wheels over against them, and a noise of a great rushing.
14 So the spirit lifted me up, and took me away, and I went in bitterness, in the fury of my spirit; but the hand of Yahweh was strong upon me.
15 Then I came to them of the captivity at Telabib, that dwelt by the river of Chebar, and I sat where they sat, and remained there astonished among them seven days.
16 ¶ And it came to pass at the end of seven days, that the word of Yahweh came unto me, saying,
17 Son of man, I have made you a watchman unto the house of Israel: therefore hear the word at my mouth, and give them warning from me.
18 When I say to the wicked, You shall surely die; and you give him not warning, nor speak to warn the wicked from his wicked way, to save his life; the same wicked *man* shall die in his iniquity; but his blood will I require at your hand.
19 Yet if you warn the wicked, and he turns not from his wickedness, nor from his wicked way, he shall die in his iniquity; but you have delivered your soul.
20 Again, When a righteous *man* does turn from his righteousness, and commits iniquity, and I lay a stumbling block before him, he shall die: because you have not given him warning, he shall die in his sin, and his righteousness which he has done shall not be remembered; but his blood will I require at your hand.
21 Nevertheless if you warn the righteous *man*, that the righteous sins not, and he does not sin, he shall surely live, because he is warned; also you have delivered your soul.
22 ¶ And the hand of Yahweh was there upon me; and he said unto me, Arise, go forth into the plain, and I will there talk with you.
23 Then I arose, and went forth into the plain: and, behold, the glory of Yahweh stood there, as the glory which I saw by the river of Chebar: and I fell on my face.

24 Then the spirit entered into me, and set me upon my feet, and spoke with me, and said unto me, Go, shut yourself within your house.
25 But you, O son of man, behold, they shall put bands upon you, and shall bind you with them, and you shall not go out among them:
26 And I will make your tongue cling to the roof of your mouth, *so* that you shall be dumb, and shall not be to them a reprover: for they *are* a rebellious house.
27 But when I speak with you, I will open your mouth, and you shall say to them, Thus says the Lord Yahweh; He that hears, let him hear; and he that forbears, let him forbear: for they *are* a rebellious house.

Ezekiel 4

4:1 ¶ You also, son of man, take you a tile, and lay it before you, and portray upon it the city, *even* Jerusalem:
2 And lay siege against it, and build a fort against it, and cast a mount against it; set the camp also against it, and set *battering* rams against it round about.
3 Moreover take you unto you an iron pan, and set it *for* a wall of iron between you and the city: and set your face against it, and it shall be besieged, and you shall lay siege against it. This *shall be* a sign to the house of Israel.
4 Lie you also upon your left side, and lay the iniquity of the house of Israel upon it: *according* to the number of the days that you shall lie upon it you shall bear their iniquity.
5 For I have laid upon you the years of their iniquity, according to the number of the days, three hundred and ninety days: so shall you bear the iniquity of the house of Israel.
6 And when you have accomplished them, lie again on your right side, and you shall bear the iniquity of the house of Judah *for* forty days: I have appointed you each day for a year.
7 Therefore you shall set your face toward the siege of Jerusalem, and your arm *shall be* uncovered, and you shall prophesy against it.
8 And, behold, I will lay bands upon you, and you shall not turn you from one side to another, till you have ended the days of your siege.
9 ¶ Take you also unto you wheat, and barley, and beans, and lentils, and millet, and fitches, and put them in one vessel, and make you bread thereof, *according* to the number of the days that you shall lie upon your side, three hundred and ninety days shall you eat thereof.
10 And your food which you shall eat *shall be* by weight, twenty shekels a day: from time to time shall you eat it.
11 You shall drink also water by measure, the sixth part of a hin: from time to time shall you drink.
12 And you shall eat it *as* barley cakes, and you shall bake it with dung that comes out of man, in their sight.
13 And Yahweh said, Even thus shall the children of Israel eat their defiled bread among the Gentiles, where I will drive them.
14 Then said I, Ah Lord Yahweh! behold, my soul has not been polluted: for from my youth up even till now have I not eaten of that which dies of itself, or is torn in pieces; neither came there abominable flesh into my mouth.
15 Then he said to me, Lo, I have given you cow's dung for man's dung, and you shall prepare your bread therewith.
16 Moreover he said unto me, Son of man, behold, I will break the staff of bread in Jerusalem: and they shall eat bread by weight, and with care; and they shall drink water by measure, and with astonishment:
17 That they may want bread and water, and be astonished one with another, and consume away for their iniquity.

Ezekiel 5

5:1 ¶ And you, son of man, take you a sharp knife, take you a barber's razor, and cause *it* to pass upon your head and upon your beard: then take you balances to weigh, and divide the *hair*.
2 You shall burn with fire a third part in the midst of the city, when the days of the siege are fulfilled: and you shall take a third part, *and* smite about it with a knife: and a third part you shall scatter in the wind; and I will draw out a sword after them.
3 You shall also take thereof a few in number, and bind them in your skirts.
4 Then take of them again, and cast them into the midst of the fire, and burn them in the fire; *for* thereof shall a fire come forth into all the house of Israel.
5 ¶ Thus says the Lord Yahweh; This *is* Jerusalem: I have set it in the midst of the nations and countries *that are* round about her.
6 And she has changed my judgments into wickedness more than the nations, and my statutes more than the countries that *are* round about her: for they have refused my judgments and my statutes, they have not walked in them.
7 Therefore thus says the Lord Yahweh; Because you multiplied more than the nations that *are* round about you, *and* have not walked in my statutes, neither have kept my judgments, neither have done according to the judgments of the nations that *are* round about you;
8 Therefore thus says the Lord Yahweh; Behold, I, even I, *am* against you, and will execute judgments in the midst of you in the sight of the nations.
9 And I will do in you that which I have not done, and whereunto I will not do any more the like, because of all your abominations.
10 Therefore the fathers shall eat the sons in the midst of you, and the sons shall eat their fathers; and I will execute judgments in you, and the whole remnant of you will I scatter into all the winds.
11 Therefore, *as* I live, says the Lord Yahweh; Surely, because you have defiled my sanctuary with all your detestable things, and with all your abominations, therefore will I also diminish *you*; neither shall my eye spare, neither will I have any pity.

Ezekiel 5

12 A third part of you shall die with the pestilence, and with famine shall they be consumed in the midst of you: and a third part shall fall by the sword round about you; and I will scatter a third part into all the winds, and I will draw out a sword after them.

13 Thus shall my anger be accomplished, and I will cause my fury to rest upon them, and I will be comforted: and they shall know that I Yahweh have spoken *it* in my zeal, when I have accomplished my fury in them.

14 Moreover I will make you waste, and a reproach among the nations that *are* round about you, in the sight of all that pass by.

15 So it shall be a reproach and a taunt, an instruction and an astonishment unto the nations that *are* round about you, when I shall execute judgments in you in anger and in fury and in furious rebukes. I Yahweh have spoken *it*.

16 When I shall send upon them the evil arrows of famine, which shall be for *their* destruction, *and* which I will send to destroy you: and I will increase the famine upon you, and will break your staff of bread:

17 So will I send upon you famine and evil beasts, and they shall bereave you; and pestilence and blood shall pass through you; and I will bring the sword upon you. I Yahweh have spoken *it*.

Ezekiel 6

6:1 ¶ And the word of Yahweh came unto me, saying,

2 Son of man, set your face toward the mountains of Israel, and prophesy against them,

3 And say, You mountains of Israel, hear the word of the Lord Yahweh; Thus says the Lord Yahweh to the mountains, and to the hills, to the rivers, and to the valleys; Behold, I, *even* I, will bring a sword upon you, and I will destroy your high places.

4 And your altars shall be desolate, and your images shall be broken: and I will cast down your slain *men* before your idols.

5 And I will lay the dead carcasses of the children of Israel before their idols; and I will scatter your bones round about your altars.

6 In all your dwelling places the cities shall be laid waste, and the high places shall be desolate; that your altars may be laid waste and made desolate, and your idols may be broken and cease, and your images may be cut down, and your works may be abolished.

7 And the slain shall fall in the midst of you, and you shall know that I *am* Yahweh.

8 ¶ Yet will I leave a remnant, that you may have *some* that shall escape the sword among the nations, when you shall be scattered through the countries.

9 And they that escape of you shall remember me among the nations where they shall be carried captives, because I am broken with their whorish heart, which has departed from me, and with their eyes, which go a whoring after their idols: and they shall loathe themselves for the evils which they have committed in all their abominations.

10 And they shall know that I *am* Yahweh, *and that* I have not said in vain that I would do this evil unto them.

11 ¶ Thus says the Lord Yahweh; Smite with your hand, and stamp with your foot, and say, Alas for all the evil abominations of the house of Israel! for they shall fall by the sword, by the famine, and by the pestilence.

12 He that is far off shall die of the pestilence; and he that is near shall fall by the sword; and he that remains and is besieged shall die by the famine: thus will I accomplish my fury upon them.

13 Then shall you know that I *am* Yahweh, when their slain *men* shall be among their idols round about their altars, upon every high hill, in all the tops of the mountains, and under every green tree, and under every thick oak, the place where they did offer sweet savor to all their idols.

14 So will I stretch out my hand upon them, and make the land desolate, yes, more desolate than the wilderness toward Diblath, in all their habitations: and they shall know that I *am* Yahweh.

Ezekiel 7

7:1 ¶ Moreover the word of Yahweh came unto me, saying,

2 Also, you son of man, thus says the Lord Yahweh to the land of Israel; An end, the end is come upon the four corners of the land.

3 Now *is* the end *come* upon you, and I will send my anger upon you, and will judge you according to your ways, and will recompense upon you all your abominations.

4 And my eye shall not spare you, neither will I have pity: but I will recompense your ways upon you, and your abominations shall be in the midst of you: and you shall know that I *am* Yahweh.

5 Thus says the Lord Yahweh; An evil, an only evil, behold, is come.

6 An end is come, the end is come: it watches for you; behold, it is come.

7 The morning is come unto you, O you that dwell in the land: the time is come, the day of trouble *is* near, and not the sounding again of the mountains.

8 Now will I shortly pour out my fury upon you, and accomplish my anger upon you: and I will judge you according to your ways, and will recompense you for all your abominations.

9 And my eye shall not spare, neither will I have pity: I will recompense you according to your ways and your abominations *that* are in the midst of you; and you shall know that I *am* Yahweh that smites.

10 Behold the day, behold, it is come: the morning is gone forth; the rod has blossomed, pride has budded.

11 Violence is risen up into a rod of wickedness: none of them *shall remain*, nor of their multitude, nor of any of theirs: neither *shall there be* wailing for them.

12 The time is come, the day draws near: let not the buyer rejoice, nor the seller mourn: for wrath *is* upon all the multitude thereof.

13 For the seller shall not return to that which is sold, although they were yet alive: for the vision *is* touching the whole multitude thereof, *which* shall not return; neither shall any strengthen himself in the iniquity of his life.

14 They have blown the trumpet, even to make all ready; but none goes to the battle: for my wrath *is* upon all the multitude thereof.

15 The sword *is* outside, and the pestilence and the famine within: he that *is* in the field shall die with the sword; and he that *is* in the city, famine and pestilence shall devour him.

16 ¶ But they that escape of them shall escape, and shall be on the mountains like doves of the valleys, all of them mourning, every one for his iniquity.

17 All hands shall be feeble, and all knees shall be weak *as* water.

18 They shall also gird *themselves* with sackcloth, and horror shall cover them; and shame *shall be* upon all faces, and baldness upon all their heads.

19 They shall cast their silver in the streets, and their gold shall be unclean: their silver and their gold shall not be able to deliver them in the day of the wrath of Yahweh: they shall not satisfy their souls, neither fill their bowels: because it is the stumbling block of their iniquity.

20 As for the beauty of his ornament, he set it in majesty: but they made the images of their abominations *and* of their detestable things therein: therefore have I set it far from them.

21 And I will give it into the hands of the strangers for a prey, and to the wicked of the earth for a spoil; and they shall pollute it.

22 My face will I turn also from them, and they shall pollute my secret *place*: for the robbers shall enter into it, and defile it.

23 ¶ Make a chain: for the land is full of bloody crimes, and the city is full of violence.

24 Therefore I will bring the worst of the heathen, and they shall possess their houses: I will also make the pomp of the strong to cease; and their holy places shall be defiled.

25 Destruction comes; and they shall seek peace, and *there shall be* none.

26 Mischief shall come upon mischief, and rumor shall be upon rumor; then shall they seek a vision of the prophet; but the law shall perish from the priest, and counsel from the ancients.

27 The king shall mourn, and the prince shall be clothed with desolation, and the hands of the people of the land shall be troubled: I will do unto them after their way, and according to their manner will I judge them; and they shall know that I *am* Yahweh.

Ezekiel 8

8:1 ¶ And it came to pass in the sixth year, in the sixth *month*, in the fifth *day* of the month, *as* I sat in my house, and the elders of Judah sat before me, that the hand of the Lord Yahweh fell there upon me.

2 Then I beheld, and lo a likeness as the appearance of fire: from the appearance of his loins even downward, fire; and from his loins even upward, as the appearance of brightness, as the color of amber.

3 And he put forth the form of a hand, and took me by a lock of my head; and the spirit lifted me up between the earth and the heaven, and brought me in the visions of God to Jerusalem, to the door of the inner gate that looks toward the north; where *was* the seat of the image of jealousy. which provokes to jealousy.

4 And, behold, the glory of the God of Israel *was* there, according to the vision that I saw in the plain.

5 Then said he unto me, Son of man, lift up your eyes now the way toward the north. So I lifted up my eyes the way toward the north, and behold northward at the gate of the altar this image of jealousy in the entry

6 He said furthermore unto me, Son of man, see you what they do? *even* the great abominations that the house of Israel commits here, that I should go far off from my sanctuary? but turn you yet again, *and* you shall see greater abominations.

7 ¶ And he brought me to the door of the court, and when I looked, behold a hole in the wall.

8 Then said he unto me, Son of man, dig now in the wall: and when I had dug in the wall, behold a door.

9 And he said unto me, Go in, and behold the wicked abominations that they do here.

10 So I went in and saw; and behold every form of creeping things, and abominable beasts, and all the idols of the house of Israel, portrayed upon the wall round about.

11 And there stood before them seventy men of the ancients of the house of Israel, and in the midst of them stood Jaazaniah the son of Shaphan, with every man his censer in his hand; and a thick cloud of incense went up.

12 Then said he unto me, Son of man, have you seen what the ancients of the house of Israel do in the dark, every man in the chambers of his imagery? for they say, Yahweh sees us not; Yahweh has forsaken the earth.

13 ¶ He said also unto me, Turn you yet again, *and* you shall see greater abominations that they do.

14 Then he brought me to the door of the gate of Yahweh's house which *was* toward the north; and, behold, there sat women weeping for Tammuz.

15 Then said he unto me, Have you seen *this*, O son of man? turn you yet again, *and* you shall see greater abominations than these.

16 And he brought me into the inner court of Yahweh's house, and, behold, at the door of the temple of Yahweh, between the porch and the altar, *were* about five and twenty men, with their backs toward the temple of Yahweh, and their faces toward the east; and they worshipped the sun toward the east.

17 Then he said unto me, Have you seen *this*, O son of man? Is it a light thing to the house of Judah that they commit the abominations which they commit here? for they have filled the land with violence, and have returned to provoke me to anger: and, lo, they put the branch to their nose.

Ezekiel 8

18 Therefore will I also deal in fury: my eye shall not spare, neither will I have pity: and though they cry in my ears with a loud voice, *yet* will I not hear them.

Ezekiel 9

9:1 ¶ He cried also in my ears with a loud voice, saying, Cause them that have charge over the city to draw near, even every man *with* his destroying weapon in his hand.
2 And, behold, six men came from the way of the higher gate, which lies toward the north, and every man *with* a slaughter weapon in his hand; and one man among them *was* clothed with linen, with a writer's inkhorn by his side: and they went in, and stood beside the brazen altar.
3 And the glory of the God of Israel was gone up from the cherub, whereupon he was, to the threshold of the house. And he called to the man clothed with linen, which *had* the writer's inkhorn by his side;
4 And Yahweh said unto him, Go through the midst of the city, through the midst of Jerusalem, and set a mark upon the foreheads of the men that sigh and that cry for all the abominations that are done in the midst thereof.
5 ¶ And to the others he said in my hearing, Go you after him through the city, and smite: let not your eye spare, neither have you pity:
6 Slay utterly old *and* young, both maids, and little children, and women: but come not near any man upon whom *is* the mark; and begin at my sanctuary. Then they began at the ancient men which *were* before the house.
7 And he said unto them, Defile the house, and fill the courts with the slain: go you forth. And they went forth, and slew in the city.
8 And it came to pass, while they were slaying them, and I was left, that I fell upon my face, and cried, and said, Ah Lord Yahweh! will you destroy all the residue of Israel in your pouring out of your fury upon Jerusalem?
9 Then said he unto me, The iniquity of the house of Israel and Judah *is* exceedingly great, and the land is full of blood, and the city full of perverseness: for they say, Yahweh has forsaken the earth, and Yahweh sees not.
10 And as for me also, my eye shall not spare, neither will I have pity, *but* I will recompense their way upon their head.
11 And, behold, the man clothed with linen, which *had* the inkhorn by his side, reported the matter, saying, I have done as you have commanded me.

Ezekiel 10

10:1 ¶ Then I looked, and, behold, in the firmament that was above the head of the cherubims there appeared over them as it were a sapphire stone, as the appearance of the likeness of a throne.
2 And he spoke unto the man clothed with linen, and said, Go in between the wheels, *even* under the cherub, and fill your hand with coals of fire from between the cherubims, and scatter *them* over the city. And he went in in my sight.
3 Now the cherubims stood on the right side of the house, when the man went in; and the cloud filled the inner court.
4 Then the glory of Yahweh went up from the cherub, *and stood* over the threshold of the house; and the house was filled with the cloud, and the court was full of the brightness of Yahweh's glory.
5 And the sound of the cherubims' wings was heard *even* to the outer court, as the voice of the Almighty God when he speaks.
6 And it came to pass, *that* when he had commanded the man clothed with linen, saying, Take fire from between the wheels, from between the cherubims; then he went in, and stood beside the wheels.
7 And *one* cherub stretched forth his hand from between the cherubims to the fire that *was* between the cherubims, and took *thereof*, and put *it* into the hands of *him that was* clothed with linen: who took *it*, and went out.
8 ¶ And there appeared in the cherubims the form of a man's hand under their wings.
9 And when I looked, behold the four wheels by the cherubims, one wheel by one cherub, and another wheel by another cherub: and the appearance of the wheels *was* as the color of a beryl stone.
10 And *as for* their appearances, they four had one likeness, as if a wheel had been in the midst of a wheel.
11 When they went, they went upon their four sides; they turned not as they went, but to the place where the head looked they followed it; they turned not as they went.
12 And their whole body, and their backs, and their hands, and their wings, and the wheels, *were* full of eyes round about, *even* the wheels that they four had.
13 As for the wheels, it was cried unto them in my hearing, O wheel.
14 And every one had four faces: the first face *was* the face of a cherub, and the second face *was* the face of a man, and the third the face of a lion, and the fourth the face of an eagle.
15 And the cherubims were lifted up. This *is* the living creature that I saw by the river of Chebar.
16 And when the cherubims went, the wheels went by them: and when the cherubims lifted up their wings to mount up from the earth, the same wheels also turned not from beside them.
17 When they stood, *these* stood; and when they were lifted up, *these* lifted up themselves *also*: for the spirit of the living creature *was* in them.
18 Then the glory of Yahweh departed from off the threshold of the house, and stood over the cherubims.
19 And the cherubims lifted up their wings, and mounted up from the earth in my sight: when they went out, the wheels also *were* beside them, and *every one* stood at the door of the east gate of Yahweh's house; and the glory of the God of Israel *was* over them above.
20 This *is* the living creature that I saw under the God of Israel by the river of Chebar; and I knew that they *were* the cherubims.

21 Every one had four faces apiece, and every one four wings; and the likeness of the hands of a man *was* under their wings.
22 And the likeness of their faces *was* the same *as the* faces which I saw by the river of Chebar, their appearances and themselves: they went every one straight forward.

Ezekiel 11

11:1 ¶ Moreover the spirit lifted me up, and brought me unto the east gate of Yahweh's house, which looks eastward: and behold at the door of the gate five and twenty men; among whom I saw Jaazaniah the son of Azur, and Pelatiah the son of Benaiah, princes of the people.
2 Then said he unto me, Son of man, these *are* the men that devise mischief, and give wicked counsel in this city:
3 Which say, *It is* not near; let us build houses: this *city is* the caldron, and we *are* the flesh.
4 Therefore prophesy against them, prophesy, O son of man.
5 And the Spirit of Yahweh fell upon me, and said unto me, Speak; Thus says Yahweh; Thus have you said, O house of Israel: for I know the things that come into your mind, *every one of* them.
6 You have multiplied your slain in this city, and you have filled the streets thereof with the slain.
7 Therefore thus says the Lord Yahweh; Your slain whom you have laid in the midst of it, they *are* the flesh, and this *city is* the caldron: but I will bring you forth out of the midst of it.
8 You have feared the sword; and I will bring a sword upon you, says the Lord Yahweh.
9 And I will bring you out of the midst thereof, and deliver you into the hands of strangers, and will execute judgments among you.
10 You shall fall by the sword; I will judge you in the border of Israel; and you shall know that I *am* Yahweh.
11 This *city* shall not be your caldron, neither shall you be the flesh in the midst thereof; *but* I will judge you in the border of Israel:
12 And you shall know that I *am* Yahweh: for you have not walked in my statutes, neither executed my judgments, but have done after the manners of the heathen that *are* round about you.
13 And it came to pass, when I prophesied, that Pelatiah the son of Benaiah died. Then fell I down upon my face, and cried with a loud voice, and said, Ah Lord Yahweh! will you make a full end of the remnant of Israel?
14 ¶ Again the word of Yahweh came unto me, saying,
15 Son of man, your brethren, *even* your brothers, the men of your kindred, and all the house of Israel wholly, *are* they to whom the inhabitants of Jerusalem have said, Get you far from Yahweh: unto us is this land given in possession.
16 Therefore say, Thus says the Lord Yahweh: Although I have cast them far off among the heathen, and although I have scattered them among the countries, yet will I be to them as a little sanctuary in the countries where they shall come.
17 Therefore say, Thus says the Lord Yahweh; I will even gather you from the people, and assemble you out of the countries where you have been scattered, and I will give you the land of Israel.
18 And they shall come there, and they shall take away all the detestable things thereof and all the abominations thereof from there.
19 And I will give them one heart, and I will put a new spirit within you; and I will take the stony heart out of their flesh, and will give them a heart of flesh:
20 That they may walk in my statutes, and keep my ordinances, and do them: and they shall be my people, and I will be their God.
21 But *as for them* whose heart walks after the heart of their detestable things and their abominations, I will recompense their way upon their own heads, says the Lord Yahweh.
22 ¶ Then did the cherubims lift up their wings, and the wheels beside them; and the glory of the God of Israel *was* over them above.
23 And the glory of Yahweh went up from the midst of the city, and stood upon the mountain which *is* on the east side of the city.
24 Afterward the spirit took me up, and brought me in a vision by the Spirit of God into Chaldea, to them of the captivity. So the vision that I had seen went up from me.
25 Then I spoke unto them of the captivity all the things that Yahweh had shown me.

Ezekiel 12

12:1 ¶ The word of Yahweh also came unto me, saying,
2 Son of man, you dwell in the midst of a rebellious house, which have eyes to see, and see not; they have ears to hear, and hear not: for they *are* a rebellious house.
3 Therefore, you son of man, prepare you things for removing, and remove by day in their sight; and you shall remove from your place to another place in their sight: it may be they will consider, though they *are* a rebellious house.
4 Then shall you bring forth your things by day in their sight, as things for removing: and you shall go forth at evening in their sight, as they that go forth into captivity.
5 Dig you through the wall in their sight, and carry out thereby.
6 In their sight shall you bear *them* upon *your* shoulders, *and* carry *them* forth in the twilight: you shall cover your face, that you see not the ground: for I have set you *for* a sign to the house of Israel.
7 And I did so as I was commanded: I brought forth my things by day, as things for captivity, and in the evening I dug through the wall with my hand; I brought *them*

forth in the twilight, *and* I bore *them* upon *my* shoulder in their sight.

8 And in the morning came the word of Yahweh unto me, saying,

9 Son of man, has not the house of Israel, the rebellious house, said unto you, What do you?

10 Say you unto them, Thus says the Lord Yahweh; This burden *concerns* the prince in Jerusalem, and all the house of Israel that *are* among them.

11 Say, I *am* your sign: like as I have done, so shall it be done unto them: they shall remove *and* go into captivity.

12 And the prince that *is* among them shall bear upon *his* shoulder in the twilight, and shall go forth: they shall dig through the wall to carry out thereby: he shall cover his face, that he sees not the ground with *his* eyes.

13 My net also will I spread upon him, and he shall be taken in my snare: and I will bring him to Babylon *to* the land of the Chaldeans; yet shall he not see it, though he shall die there.

14 And I will scatter toward every wind all that *are* about him to help him, and all his bands; and I will draw out the sword after them.

15 And they shall know that I *am* Yahweh, when I shall scatter them among the nations, and disperse them in the countries.

16 But I will leave a few men of them from the sword, from the famine, and from the pestilence; that they may declare all their abominations among the heathen where they go; and they shall know that I *am* Yahweh.

17 ¶ Moreover the word of Yahweh came to me, saying,

18 Son of man, eat your bread with quaking, and drink your water with trembling and with anxiousness;

19 And say unto the people of the land, Thus says the Lord Yahweh of the inhabitants of Jerusalem, *and* of the land of Israel; They shall eat their bread with anxiousness, and drink their water with astonishment, that her land may be desolate from all that is therein, because of the violence of all them that dwell therein.

20 And the cities that are inhabited shall be laid waste, and the land shall be desolate; and you shall know that I *am* Yahweh.

21 ¶ And the word of Yahweh came unto me, saying,

22 Son of man, what *is* that proverb *that* you have in the land of Israel, saying, The days are prolonged, and every vision fails?

23 Tell them therefore, Thus says the Lord Yahweh; I will make this proverb to cease, and they shall no more use it as a proverb in Israel; but say unto them, The days are at hand, and the effect of every vision.

24 For there shall be no more any vain vision nor flattering divination within the house of Israel.

25 For I *am* Yahweh: I will speak, and the word that I shall speak shall come to pass; it shall be no more prolonged: for in your days, O rebellious house, will I say the word, and will perform it, says the Lord Yahweh.

26 Again the word of Yahweh came unto me, saying,

27 Son of man, behold, *they of* the house of Israel say, The vision that he sees *is* for many days *to come*, and he prophesies of the times *that are* far off.

28 Therefore say unto them, Thus says the Lord Yahweh; There shall none of my words be prolonged any more, but the word which I have spoken shall be done, says the Lord Yahweh.

Ezekiel 13

13:1 ¶ And the word of Yahweh came unto me, saying,

2 Son of man, prophesy against the prophets of Israel that prophesy, and say you unto them that prophesy out of their own hearts, Hear you the word of Yahweh;

3 Thus says the Lord Yahweh; Woe unto the foolish prophets, that follow their own spirit, and have seen nothing!

4 O Israel, your prophets are like the foxes in the deserts.

5 You have not gone up into the gaps, neither made up the hedge for the house of Israel to stand in the battle in the day of Yahweh.

6 They have seen vanity and lying divination, saying, Yahweh says: and Yahweh has not sent them: and they have made *others* to hope that they would confirm the word.

7 Have you not seen a vain vision, and have you not spoken a lying divination, whereas you say, Yahweh says *it*; although I have not spoken?

8 Therefore thus says the Lord Yahweh; Because you have spoken vanity, and seen lies, therefore, behold, I *am* against you, says the Lord Yahweh.

9 And my hand shall be upon the prophets that see vanity, and that divine lies: they shall not be in the assembly of my people, neither shall they be written in the writing of the house of Israel, neither shall they enter into the land of Israel; and you shall know that I *am* the Lord Yahweh.

10 ¶ Because, even because they have seduced my people, saying, Peace; and *there was* no peace; and one built up a wall, and, lo, others daubed it with untempered *mortar*:

11 Say to them which daub *it* with untempered *mortar*, that it shall fall: there shall be an overflowing shower; and you, O great hailstones, shall fall; and a stormy wind shall split *it*.

12 Lo, when the wall is fallen, shall it not be said unto you, Where *is* the daubing with which you have daubed *it*?

13 Therefore thus says the Lord Yahweh; I will even split *it* with a stormy wind in my fury; and there shall be an overflowing shower in my anger, and great hailstones in *my* fury to consume *it*.

14 So will I break down the wall that you have daubed with untempered *mortar*, and bring it down to the ground, so that the foundation thereof shall be uncovered, and it shall fall, and you shall be consumed in the midst thereof: and you shall know that I *am* Yahweh.

15 Thus will I accomplish my wrath upon the wall, and upon them that have daubed it with untempered *mortar*, and will say unto you, The wall *is* no *more*, neither they that daubed it;

16 *That is*, the prophets of Israel which prophesy concerning Jerusalem, and which see visions of peace for her, and *there is* no peace, says the Lord Yahweh.

17 ¶ Likewise, you son of man, set your face against the daughters of your people, which prophesy out of their own heart; and prophesy you against them,

18 And say, Thus says the Lord Yahweh; Woe to the *women* that sew pillows to all armholes, and make kerchiefs upon the heads of *those of* every stature to hunt souls! Will you hunt the souls of my people, and will you save the souls alive *that come* to you?

19 And will you pollute me among my people for handfuls of barley and for pieces of bread, to slay the souls that should not die, and to save the souls alive that should not live, by your lying to my people that hear *your* lies?

20 Therefore thus says the Lord Yahweh; Behold, I *am* against your pillows, with which you there hunt the souls to make *them* fly, and I will tear them from your arms, and will let the souls go, *even* the souls that you hunt to make *them* fly.

21 Your kerchiefs also will I tear, and deliver my people out of your hand, and they shall be no more in your hand to be hunted; and you shall know that I *am* Yahweh.

22 Because with lies you have made the heart of the righteous sad, whom I have not made sad; and strengthened the hands of the wicked, that he should not return from his wicked way, by promising him life:

23 Therefore you shall see no more vanity, nor divine divinations: for I will deliver my people out of your hand: and you shall know that I *am* Yahweh.

Ezekiel 14

14:1 ¶ Then came certain of the elders of Israel unto me, and sat before me.

2 And the word of Yahweh came unto me, saying,

3 Son of man, these men have set up their idols in their heart, and put the stumbling block of their iniquity before their face: should I be inquired of at all by them?

4 Therefore speak unto them, and say unto them, Thus says the Lord Yahweh; Every man of the house of Israel that sets up his idols in his heart, and puts the stumbling block of his iniquity before his face, and comes to the prophet; I Yahweh will answer him that comes according to the multitude of his idols;

5 That I may take the house of Israel in their own heart, because they are all estranged from me through their idols

6 Therefore say unto the house of Israel, Thus says the Lord Yahweh; Repent, and turn *yourselves* from your idols; and turn away your faces from all your abominations.

7 For every one of the house of Israel, or of the stranger that dwells in Israel, which separates himself from me, and sets up his idols in his heart, and puts the stumbling block of his iniquity before his face, and comes to a prophet to inquire of him concerning me; I Yahweh will answer him by myself:

8 And I will set my face against that man, and will make him a sign and a proverb, and I will cut him off from the midst of my people; and you shall know that I *am* Yahweh.

9 And if the prophet is deceived when he has spoken a thing, I Yahweh have deceived that prophet, and I will stretch out my hand upon him, and will destroy him from the midst of my people Israel.

10 And they shall bear the punishment of their iniquity: the punishment of the prophet shall be even as the punishment of him that seeks *unto him*;

11 That the house of Israel may go no more astray from me, neither be polluted any more with all their transgressions; but that they may be my people, and I may be their God, says the Lord Yahweh.

12 ¶ The word of Yahweh came again unto me, saying,

13 Son of man, when the land sins against me by trespassing grievously, then will I stretch out my hand upon it, and will break the staff of the bread thereof, and will send famine upon it, and will cut off man and beast from it:

14 Though these three men, Noah, Daniel, and Job, were in it, they should deliver *but* their own souls by their righteousness, says the Lord Yahweh.

15 If I cause noisome beasts to pass through the land, and they spoil it, so that it is desolate, that no man may pass through because of the beasts:

16 *Though* these three men *were* in it, *as* I live, says the Lord Yahweh, they shall deliver neither sons nor daughters; they only shall be delivered, but the land shall be desolate.

17 Or *if* I bring a sword upon that land, and say, Sword, go through the land; so that I cut off man and beast from it:

18 Though these three men *were* in it, *as* I live, says the Lord Yahweh, they shall deliver neither sons nor daughters, but they only shall be delivered themselves.

19 Or *if* I send a pestilence into that land, and pour out my fury upon it in blood, to cut off from it man and beast:

20 Though Noah, Daniel, and Job, *were* in it, *as* I live, says the Lord Yahweh, they shall deliver neither son nor daughter; they shall *but* deliver their own souls by their righteousness.

21 For thus says the Lord Yahweh; How much more when I send my four grievous judgments upon Jerusalem, the sword, and the famine, and the noisome beast, and the pestilence, to cut off from it man and beast?

22 Yet, behold, therein shall be left a remnant that shall be brought forth, *both* sons and daughters: behold, they shall come forth unto you, and you shall see their way and their doings: and you shall be comforted concerning the evil that I have brought upon Jerusalem, *even* concerning all that I have brought upon it.

23 And they shall comfort you, when you see their ways and their doings: and you shall know that I have not done without cause all that I have done in it, says the Lord Yahweh.

Ezekiel 15

15:1 ¶ And the word of Yahweh came unto me, saying,

2 Son of man, What is the vine tree more than any tree, *or than* a branch which is among the trees of the forest?

3 Shall wood be taken thereof to do any work? or will *men* take a pin of it to hang any vessel thereon?

4 Behold, it is cast into the fire for fuel; the fire devours both the ends of it, and the midst of it is burned. Is it good for *any* use?

5 Behold, when it was whole, it was made for no use: how much less shall it be made yet for *any* use, when the fire has devoured it, and it is burned?

6 Therefore thus says the Lord Yahweh; As the vine tree among the trees of the forest, which I have given to the fire for fuel, so will I give the inhabitants of Jerusalem.

7 And I will set my face against them; they shall go out from *one* fire, and *another* fire shall devour them; and you shall know that I *am* Yahweh, when I set my face against them.

8 And I will make the land desolate, because they have committed a trespass, says the Lord Yahweh.

Ezekiel 16

16:1 ¶ Again the word of Yahweh came unto me, saying,

2 Son of man, cause Jerusalem to know her abominations,

3 And say, Thus says the Lord Yahweh to Jerusalem; Your birth and your nativity *is* of the land of Canaan; your father *was* an Amorite, and your mother a Hittite.

4 And *as for* your nativity, in the day you were born your navel was not cut, neither were you washed in water to supple *you*; you were not salted at all, nor swaddled at all.

5 None eye pitied you, to do any of these to you, to have compassion upon you; but you were cast out in the open field, to the loathing of your person, in the day that you were born.

6 ¶ And when I passed by you, and saw you polluted in your own blood, I said unto you *when you were* in your blood, Live; yes, I said unto you *when you were* in your blood, Live.

7 I have caused you to multiply as the bud of the field, and you have increased and become great, and you have come to excellent ornaments: *your* breasts are fashioned, and your hair is grown, whereas you *were* naked and bare.

8 Now when I passed by you, and looked upon you, behold, your time *was* the time of love; and I spread my skirt over you, and covered your nakedness: yes, I swore unto you, and entered into a covenant with you, says the Lord Yahweh, and you became mine.

9 Then washed I you with water; yes, I thoroughly washed away your blood from you, and I anointed you with oil.

10 I clothed you also with embroidered work, and shod you with badger skin, and I girded you about with fine linen, and I covered you with silk.

11 I decked you also with ornaments, and I put bracelets upon your hands, and a chain on your neck.

12 And I put a jewel on your forehead, and earrings in your ears, and a beautiful crown upon your head.

13 Thus were you decked with gold and silver; and your clothing *was of* fine linen, and silk, and embroidered work; you did eat fine flour, and honey, and oil: and you were exceedingly beautiful, and you did prosper into a kingdom.

14 And your renown went forth among the heathen for your beauty: for it *was* perfect through my comeliness, which I had put upon you, says the Lord Yahweh.

15 ¶ But you did trust in your own beauty, and played the harlot because of your renown, and poured out your fornications on every one that passed by; his it was.

16 And of your garments you did take, and decked your high places with diverse colors, and played the harlot thereupon: *the like things* shall not come, neither shall it be *so*.

17 You have also taken your fair jewels of my gold and of my silver, which I had given you, and made to yourself images of men, and did commit whoredom with them,

18 And took your embroidered garments, and covered them: and you have set my oil and my incense before them.

19 My food also which I gave you, fine flour, and oil, and honey, *with which* I fed you, you have even set it before them for a sweet savor: and *thus* it was, says the Lord Yahweh.

20 Moreover you have taken your sons and your daughters, whom you have borne unto me, and these have you sacrificed to them to be devoured. *Is this* of your whoredoms a small matter,

21 That you have slain my children, and delivered them to cause them to pass through *the fire* for them?

22 And in all your abominations and your whoredoms you have not remembered the days of your youth, when you were naked and bare, *and* were polluted in your blood.

23 And it came to pass after all your wickedness, (woe, woe unto you! says the Lord Yahweh;)

24 *That* you have also built to you an eminent place, and have made you a high place in every street.

25 You have built your high place at every head of the way, and have made your beauty to be abhorred, and have opened your feet to every one that passed by, and multiplied your whoredoms.

26 You have also committed fornication with the Egyptians your neighbors, great of flesh; and have increased your whoredoms, to provoke me to anger.

27 Behold, therefore I have stretched out my hand over you, and have diminished your ordinary *food*, and delivered you to the will of them that hate you, the daughters of the Philistines, which are ashamed of your lewd way.

28 You have played the whore also with the Assyrians, because you were insatiable; yes, you have played the harlot with them, and yet could not be satisfied.

29 You have moreover multiplied your fornication in the land of Canaan to Chaldea; and yet you were not satisfied herewith.

30 How weak is your heart, says the Lord Yahweh, seeing you do all these *things*, the work of an imperious whorish woman;

31 In that you build your eminent place in the head of every way, and make your high place in every street; and have not been as a harlot, in that you scorn hire;

32 *But as* a wife that commits adultery, *which* takes strangers instead of her husband!

33 They give gifts to all whores: but you give your gifts to all your lovers, and hire them, that they may come to you on every side for your whoredom.

34 And the contrary is in you from *other* women in your whoredoms, whereas none follows you to commit whoredoms: and in that you give a reward, and no reward is given unto you, therefore you are contrary.

35 ¶ Therefore, O harlot, hear the word of Yahweh:

36 Thus says the Lord Yahweh; Because your filthiness was poured out, and your nakedness uncovered through your whoredoms with your lovers, and with all the idols of your abominations, and by the blood of your children, which you did give unto them;

37 Behold, therefore I will gather all your lovers, with whom you have taken pleasure, and all *them* that you have loved, with all *them* that you have hated; I will even gather them round about against you, and will uncover your nakedness unto them, that they may see all your nakedness.

38 And I will judge you, as women that break wedlock and shed blood are judged; and I will give you blood in fury and jealousy.

39 And I will also give you into their hand, and they shall throw down your eminent place, and shall break down your high places: they shall strip you also of your clothes, and shall take your fair jewels, and leave you naked and bare.

40 They shall also bring up a company against you, and they shall stone you with stones, and thrust you through with their swords.

41 And they shall burn your houses with fire, and execute judgments upon you in the sight of many women: and I will cause you to cease from playing the harlot, and you also will give no hire any more.

42 So will I make my fury toward you to rest, and my jealousy shall depart from you, and I will be quiet, and will be no more angry.

43 Because you have not remembered the days of your youth, but have fretted me in all these *things*; behold, therefore I also will recompense your way upon *your* head, says the Lord Yahweh: and you shall not commit this lewdness above all your abominations.

44 ¶ Behold, every one that uses proverbs shall use *this* proverb against you, saying, As *is* the mother, *so is* her daughter.

45 You *are* your mother's daughter, that loathes her husband and her children; and you *are* the sister of your sisters, which loathed their husbands and their children: your mother *was* a Hittite, and your father an Amorite.

46 And your elder sister *is* Samaria, she and her daughters that dwell at your left hand: and your younger sister, that dwells at your right hand, *is* Sodom and her daughters.

47 Yet have you not walked after their ways, nor done after their abominations: but, as *if that were* a very little *thing*, you were corrupted more than they in all your ways.

48 *As* I live, says the Lord Yahweh, Sodom your sister has not done, she nor her daughters, as you have done, you and your daughters.

49 Behold, this was the iniquity of your sister Sodom, pride, fullness of bread, and abundance of idleness was in her and in her daughters, neither did she strengthen the hand of the poor and needy.

50 And they were haughty, and committed abomination before me therefore I took them away as I saw *good*.

51 Neither has Samaria committed half of your sins; but you have multiplied your abominations more than they, and have justified your sisters in all your abominations which you have done

52 You also, which have judged your sisters, bear your own shame for your sins that you have committed *were* more abominable than theirs: they are more righteous than you: yes, be you confounded also, and bear your shame, in that you have justified your sisters.

53 When I shall bring again their captivity, the captivity of Sodom and her daughters, and the captivity of Samaria and her daughters, then *will I bring again* the captivity of your captives in the midst of them:

54 That you may bear your own shame, and may be confounded in all that you have done, in that you are a comfort unto them.

55 When your sisters, Sodom and her daughters, shall return to their former estate, and Samaria and her daughters shall return to their former estate, then you and your daughters shall return to your former estate.

56 For your sister Sodom was not mentioned by your mouth in the day of your pride,

57 Before your wickedness was discovered, as at the time of *your* reproach of the daughters of Syria, and all *that are* round about her, the daughters of the Philistines, which despise you round about.

58 You have borne your lewdness and your abominations, says Yahweh.

59 For thus says the Lord Yahweh; I will even deal with you as you have done, which have despised the oath in breaking the covenant.

60 ¶ Nevertheless I will remember my covenant with you in the days of your youth, and I will establish unto you an everlasting covenant.

61 Then you shall remember your ways, and be ashamed, when you shall receive your sisters, your elder and your younger: and I will give them unto you for daughters, but not by your covenant.

62 And I will establish my covenant with you; and you shall know that I *am* Yahweh:
63 That you may remember, and be ashamed, and never open your mouth any more because of your shame, when I am pacified toward you for all that you have done, says the Lord Yahweh.

Ezekiel 17

17:1 ¶ And the word of Yahweh came unto me, saying,
2 Son of man, put forth a riddle, and speak a parable unto the house of Israel;
3 And say, Thus says the Lord Yahweh; A great eagle with great wings, long winged, full of feathers, which had diverse colors, came unto Lebanon, and took the highest branch of the cedar:
4 He cropped off the top of his young twigs, and carried it into a land of traffic; he set it in a city of merchants.
5 He took also of the seed of the land, and planted it in a fruitful field; he placed *it* by great waters, *and* set it *as* a willow tree.
6 And it grew, and became a spreading vine of low stature, whose branches turned toward him, and the roots thereof were under him: so it became a vine, and brought forth branches, and shot forth sprigs.
7 There was also another great eagle with great wings and many feathers: and, behold, this vine did bend her roots toward him, and shot forth her branches toward him, that he might water it by the furrows of her plantation.
8 It was planted in a good soil by great waters, that it might bring forth branches, and that it might bear fruit, that it might be a goodly vine.
9 Say you, Thus says the Lord Yahweh; Shall it prosper? shall he not pull up the roots thereof, and cut off the fruit thereof, that it withers? it shall wither in all the leaves of her spring, even without great power or many people to pluck it up by the roots thereof.
10 Yes, behold, *being* planted, shall it prosper? shall it not utterly wither, when the east wind touches it? it shall wither in the furrows where it grew.
11 Moreover the word of Yahweh came unto me, saying,
12 Say now to the rebellious house, Know you not what these *things mean*? tell *them*, Behold, the king of Babylon has come to Jerusalem, and has taken the king thereof, and the princes thereof, and led them with him to Babylon;
13 And has taken of the king's seed, and made a covenant with him, and has taken an oath of him: he has also taken the mighty of the land:
14 That the kingdom might be base, that it might not lift itself up, *but* that by keeping of his covenant it might stand.
15 But he rebelled against him in sending his ambassadors into Egypt, that they might give him horses and much people. Shall he prosper? shall he escape that does such *things*? or shall he break the covenant, and be delivered?
16 *As* I live, says the Lord Yahweh, surely in the place *where* the king *dwells* that made him king, whose oath he despised, and whose covenant he broke, *even* with him in the midst of Babylon he shall die.
17 Neither shall Pharaoh with *his* mighty army and great company make for him in the war, by casting up mounts, and building forts, to cut off many persons:
18 Seeing he despised the oath by breaking the covenant, when, lo, he had given his hand, and has done all these *things*, he shall not escape.
19 Therefore thus says the Lord Yahweh; *As* I live, surely my oath that he has despised, and my covenant that he has broken, even it will I recompense upon his own head.
20 And I will spread my net upon him, and he shall be taken in my snare, and I will bring him to Babylon, and will plead with him there for his trespass that he has trespassed against me.
21 And all his fugitives with all his bands shall fall by the sword, and they that remain shall be scattered toward all winds: and you shall know that I Yahweh have spoken *it*.
22 ¶ Thus says the Lord Yahweh; I will also take of the highest branch of the high cedar, and will set *it*; I will crop off from the top of his young twigs a tender one, and will plant *it* upon a high and eminent mountain:
23 In the mountain of the height of Israel will I plant it: and it shall bring forth boughs, and bear fruit, and be a goodly cedar: and under it shall dwell all fowl of every wing; in the shadow of the branches thereof shall they dwell.
24 And all the trees of the field shall know that I Yahweh have brought down the high tree, have exalted the low tree, have dried up the green tree, and have made the dry tree to flourish: I Yahweh have spoken and have done *it*.

Ezekiel 18

18:1 ¶ The word of Yahweh came unto me again, saying,
2 What mean you, that you use this proverb concerning the land of Israel, saying, The fathers have eaten sour grapes, and the children's teeth are set on edge?
3 *As* I live, says the Lord Yahweh, you shall not have *occasion* any more to use this proverb in Israel.
4 Behold, all souls are mine; as the soul of the father, so also the soul of the son is mine: the soul that sins, it shall die.
5 But if a man is just, and does that which is lawful and right,
6 *And* has not eaten upon the mountains, neither has lifted up his eyes to the idols of the house of Israel, neither has defiled his neighbor's wife, neither has come near to a menstruous woman,
7 And has not oppressed any, *but* has restored to the debtor his pledge, has spoiled none by violence, has given his bread to the hungry, and has covered the naked with a garment;

8 He *that* has not given forth upon usury, neither has taken any increase, *that* has withdrawn his hand from iniquity, has executed true judgment between man and man,

9 Has walked in my statutes, and has kept my judgments, to deal truly; he *is* just, he shall surely live, says the Lord Yahweh.

10 ¶ If he begets a son *that is* a robber, a shedder of blood, and *that* does the like to *any* one of these *things*,

11 And that does not any of those *duties*, but even has eaten upon the mountains, and defiled his neighbor's wife,

12 Has oppressed the poor and needy, has spoiled by violence, has not restored the pledge, and has lifted up his eyes to the idols, has committed abomination,

13 Has given forth upon usury, and has taken increase: shall he then live? he shall not live: he has done all these abominations; he shall surely die; his blood shall be upon him.

14 Now, lo, *if* he begets a son, that sees all his father's sins which he has done, and considers, and does not such like,

15 *That* has not eaten upon the mountains, neither has lifted up his eyes to the idols of the house of Israel, has not defiled his neighbor's wife,

16 Neither has oppressed any, has not withheld the pledge, neither has spoiled by violence, *but* has given his bread to the hungry, and has covered the naked with a garment,

17 *That* has taken off his hand from the poor, *that* has not received usury nor increase, has executed my judgments, has walked in my statutes; he shall not die for the iniquity of his father, he shall surely live.

18 *As for* his father, because he cruelly oppressed, spoiled his brother by violence, and did *that* which *is* not good among his people, lo, even he shall die in his iniquity.

19 Yet say you, Why? does not the son bear the iniquity of the father? When the son has done that which is lawful and right, *and* has kept all my statutes, and has done them, he shall surely live.

20 The soul that sins, it shall die. The son shall not bear the iniquity of the father, neither shall the father bear the iniquity of the son: the righteousness of the righteous shall be upon him, and the wickedness of the wicked shall be upon him.

21 ¶ But if the wicked will turn from all his sins that he has committed, and keep all my statutes, and do that which is lawful and right, he shall surely live, he shall not die.

22 All his transgressions that he has committed, they shall not be mentioned unto him: in his righteousness that he has done he shall live.

23 Have I any pleasure at all that the wicked should die? says the Lord Yahweh: *and* not that he should return from his ways, and live?

24 But when the righteous turns away from his righteousness, and commits iniquity, *and* does according to all the abominations that the wicked *man* does, shall he live? All his righteousness that he has done shall not be mentioned: in his trespass that he has trespassed, and in his sin that he has sinned, in them shall he die.

25 Yet you say, The way of the Lord is not equal. Hear now, O house of Israel; Is not my way equal? are not your ways unequal?

26 When a righteous *man* turns away from his righteousness, and commits iniquity, and dies in them; for his iniquity that he has done shall he die.

27 Again, when the wicked *man* turns away from his wickedness that he has committed, and does that which is lawful and right, he shall save his soul alive.

28 Because he considers, and turns away from all his transgressions that he has committed, he shall surely live, he shall not die.

29 Yet says the house of Israel, The way of the Lord is not equal. O house of Israel, are not my ways equal? are not your ways unequal?

30 ¶ Therefore I will judge you, O house of Israel, every one according to his ways, says the Lord Yahweh. Repent, and turn *yourselves* from all your transgressions; so iniquity shall not be your ruin.

31 Cast away from you all your transgressions, whereby you have transgressed; and make you a new heart and a new spirit: for why will you die, O house of Israel?

32 For I have no pleasure in the death of him that dies, says the Lord Yahweh: therefore turn *yourselves*, and live you.

Ezekiel 19

19:1 ¶ Moreover take you up a lamentation for the princes of Israel,

2 And say, What *is* your mother? A lioness: she lay down among lions, she nourished her cubs among young lions.

3 And she brought up one of her cubs: it became a young lion, and it learned to catch the prey; it devoured men.

4 The nations also heard of him; he was taken in their pit, and they brought him with chains unto the land of Egypt.

5 Now when she saw that she had waited, *and* her hope was lost, then she took another of her cubs, *and* made him a young lion.

6 And he went up and down among the lions, he became a young lion, and learned to catch the prey, *and* devoured men.

7 And he knew their desolate palaces, and he laid waste their cities; and the land was desolate, and the fullness thereof, by the noise of his roaring.

8 Then the nations set against him on every side from the provinces, and spread their net over him: he was taken in their pit.

9 And they put him in ward in chains, and brought him to the king of Babylon: they brought him into holds, that his voice should no more be heard upon the mountains of Israel.

10 ¶ Your mother *is* like a vine in your blood, planted by the waters: she was fruitful and full of branches by reason of many waters.

Ezekiel 19

11 And she had strong rods for the scepters of them that bear rule, and her stature was exalted among the thick branches, and she appeared in her height with the multitude of her branches.
12 But she was plucked up in fury, she was cast down to the ground, and the east wind dried up her fruit: her strong rods were broken and withered; the fire consumed them.
13 And now she *is* planted in the wilderness, in a dry and thirsty ground.
14 And fire is gone out of a rod of her branches, *which* has devoured her fruit, so that she has no strong rod *to be* a scepter to rule. This *is* a lamentation, and shall be for a lamentation.

Ezekiel 20

20:1 ¶ And it came to pass in the seventh year, in the fifth *month*, the tenth *day* of the month, *that* certain of the elders of Israel came to inquire of Yahweh, and sat before me.
2 Then came the word of Yahweh unto me, saying,
3 Son of man, speak unto the elders of Israel, and say unto them, Thus says the Lord Yahweh; Have you come to inquire of me? *As* I live, says the Lord Yahweh, I will not be inquired of by you.
4 Will you judge them, son of man, will you judge *them*? cause them to know the abominations of their fathers:
5 ¶ And say unto them, Thus says the Lord Yahweh; In the day when I chose Israel, and lifted up my hand unto the seed of the house of Jacob, and made myself known unto them in the land of Egypt, when I lifted up my hand unto them, saying, I *am* Yahweh your God;
6 In the day *that* I lifted up my hand unto them, to bring them forth *out* of the land of Egypt into a land that I had searched out for them, flowing with milk and honey, which *is* the glory of all lands:
7 Then said I unto them, Cast you away every man the abominations of his eyes, and defile not yourselves with the idols of Egypt: I *am* Yahweh your God.
8 But they rebelled against me, and would not listen unto me: they did not every man cast away the abominations of their eyes, neither did they forsake the idols of Egypt: then I said, I will pour out my fury upon them, to accomplish my anger against them in the midst of the land of Egypt.
9 But I worked for my name's sake, that it should not be polluted before the heathen, among whom they *were*, in whose sight I made myself known unto them, in bringing them forth out of the land of Egypt.
10 ¶ Therefore I caused them to go forth out of the land of Egypt, and brought them into the wilderness.
11 And I gave them my statutes, and showed them my judgments, which *if* a man does, he shall even live in them.
12 Moreover also I gave them my sabbaths, to be a sign between me and them, that they might know that I *am* Yahweh that sanctifies them.
13 But the house of Israel rebelled against me in the wilderness: they walked not in my statutes, and they despised my judgments, which *if* a man does, he shall even live in them; and my sabbaths they greatly polluted: then I said, I would pour out my fury upon them in the wilderness, to consume them.
14 But I worked for my name's sake, that it should not be polluted before the heathen, in whose sight I brought them out.
15 Yet also I lifted up my hand unto them in the wilderness, that I would not bring them into the land which I had given *them*, flowing with milk and honey, which *is* the glory of all lands;
16 Because they despised my judgments, and walked not in my statutes, but polluted my sabbaths: for their heart went after their idols.
17 Nevertheless my eye spared them from destroying them, neither did I make an end of them in the wilderness.
18 But I said unto their children in the wilderness, Walk you not in the statutes of your fathers, neither observe their judgments, nor defile yourselves with their idols:
19 I *am* Yahweh your God; walk in my statutes, and keep my judgments, and do them;
20 And hallow my sabbaths; and they shall be a sign between me and you, that you may know that I *am* Yahweh your God.
21 Notwithstanding the children rebelled against me: they walked not in my statutes, neither kept my judgments to do them, which *if* a man does, he shall even live in them; they polluted my sabbaths: then I said, I would pour out my fury upon them, to accomplish my anger against them in the wilderness.
22 Nevertheless I withdrew my hand, and worked for my name's sake, that it should not be polluted in the sight of the heathen, in whose sight I brought them forth.
23 I lifted up my hand unto them also in the wilderness, that I would scatter them among the heathen, and disperse them through the countries;
24 Because they had not executed my judgments, but had despised my statutes, and had polluted my sabbaths, and their eyes were after their fathers' idols.
25 Therefore I gave them also statutes *that were* not good, and judgments whereby they should not live;
26 And I polluted them in their own gifts, in that they caused to pass through *the fire* all that opens the womb, that I might make them desolate, to the end that they might know that I *am* Yahweh.
27 ¶ Therefore, son of man, speak unto the house of Israel, and say unto them, Thus says the Lord Yahweh; Yet in this your fathers have blasphemed me, in that they have committed a trespass against me.
28 *For* when I had brought them into the land, *for* the which I lifted up my hand to give it to them, then they saw every high hill, and all the thick trees, and they offered there their sacrifices, and there they presented the provocation of their offering: there also they made their sweet savor, and poured out there their drink offerings.

29 Then I said unto them, What *is* the high place whereunto you go? And the name thereof is called Bamah unto this day.

30 Therefore say unto the house of Israel, Thus says the Lord Yahweh; Are you polluted after the manner of your fathers? and commit you whoredom after their abominations?

31 For when you offer your gifts, when you make your sons to pass through the fire, you pollute yourselves with all your idols, even unto this day: and shall I be inquired of by you, O house of Israel? *As* I live, says the Lord Yahweh, I will not be inquired of by you.

32 And that which comes into your mind shall not be at all, that you say, We will be as the heathen, as the families of the countries, to serve wood and stone.

33 ¶ *As* I live, says the Lord Yahweh, surely with a mighty hand, and with a stretched out arm, and with fury poured out, will I rule over you:

34 And I will bring you out from the people, and will gather you out of the countries wherein you are scattered, with a mighty hand, and with a stretched out arm, and with fury poured out.

35 And I will bring you into the wilderness of the people, and there will I plead with you face to face.

36 Like as I pleaded with your fathers in the wilderness of the land of Egypt, so will I plead with you, says the Lord Yahweh.

37 And I will cause you to pass under the rod, and I will bring you into the bond of the covenant:

38 And I will purge out from among you the rebels, and them that transgress against me: I will bring them forth out of the country where they dwell, and they shall not enter into the land of Israel: and you shall know that I *am* Yahweh.

39 As for you, O house of Israel, thus says the Lord Yahweh; Go you, serve you every one his idols, and hereafter *also*, if you will not listen unto me: but pollute you my holy name no more with your gifts, and with your idols.

40 For in my holy mountain, in the mountain of the height of Israel, says the Lord Yahweh, there shall all the house of Israel, all of them in the land, serve me: there will I accept them, and there will I require your offerings, and the firstfruits of your oblations, with all your holy things.

41 I will accept you with your sweet savor, when I bring you out from the people, and gather you out of the countries wherein you have been scattered; and I will be sanctified in you before the heathen.

42 And you shall know that I *am* Yahweh, when I shall bring you into the land of Israel, into the country *for* the which I lifted up my hand to give it to your fathers.

43 And there shall you remember your ways, and all your doings, wherein you have been defiled; and you shall loathe yourselves in your own sight for all your evils that you have committed.

44 And you shall know that I *am* Yahweh, when I have worked with you for my name's sake, not according to your wicked ways, nor according to your corrupt doings, O you house of Israel, says the Lord Yahweh.

45 ¶ Moreover the word of Yahweh came unto me, saying,

46 Son of man, set your face toward the south, and drop *your word* toward the south, and prophesy against the forest of the south field;

47 And say to the forest of the south, Hear the word of Yahweh; Thus says the Lord Yahweh; Behold, I will kindle a fire in you, and it shall devour every green tree in you, and every dry tree: the flaming flame shall not be quenched, and all faces from the south to the north shall be burned therein.

48 And all flesh shall see that I Yahweh have kindled it: it shall not be quenched.

49 Then said I, Ah Lord Yahweh! they say of me, Does he not speak parables?

Ezekiel 21

21:1 ¶ And the word of Yahweh came unto me, saying,

2 Son of man, set your face toward Jerusalem, and drop *your word* toward the holy places, and prophesy against the land of Israel,

3 And say to the land of Israel, Thus says Yahweh; Behold, I *am* against you, and will draw forth my sword out of his sheath, and will cut off from you the righteous and the wicked.

4 Seeing then that I will cut off from you the righteous and the wicked, therefore shall my sword go forth out of his sheath against all flesh from the south to the north:

5 That all flesh may know that I Yahweh have drawn forth my sword out of his sheath: it shall not return any more.

6 Sigh therefore, you son of man, with the breaking of *your* loins; and with bitterness sigh before their eyes.

7 And it shall be, when they say unto you, Why sigh you? that you shall answer, For the news; because it comes: and every heart shall melt, and all hands shall be feeble, and every spirit shall faint, and all knees shall be weak *as* water: behold, it comes, and shall be brought to pass, says the Lord Yahweh.

8 ¶ Again the word of Yahweh came unto me, saying,

9 Son of man, prophesy, and say, Thus says Yahweh; Say, A sword, a sword is sharpened, and also polished:

10 It is sharpened to make a ruthless slaughter; it is polished that it may glitter: should we then be rejoicing? it despises the rod of my son, *as* every tree.

11 And he has given it to be polished, that it may be handled: this sword is sharpened, and it is furbished, to give it into the hand of the slayer.

12 Cry and howl, son of man: for it shall be upon my people, it *shall be* upon all the princes of Israel: terrors by reason of the sword shall be upon my people: smite therefore upon *your* thigh.

13 Because *it is* a trial, and what if *the sword* despises even the scepter? it shall be no *more*, says the Lord Yahweh.

Ezekiel 21

14 You therefore, son of man, prophesy, and smite *your* hands together, and let the sword be doubled the third time, the sword of the slain: it *is* the sword of the great *men that are* slain, which enters into their private chambers.

15 I have set the point of the sword against all their gates, that *their* heart may faint, and *their* ruins be multiplied: ah! *it is* made bright, *it is* wrapped up for the slaughter.

16 Go you one way or *the* other, *either* on the right hand, *or* on the left, wherever your face *is* set.

17 I will also smite my hands together, and I will cause my fury to rest: I Yahweh have said *it*.

18 ¶ The word of Yahweh came unto me again, saying,

19 Also, you son of man, appoint you two ways, that the sword of the king of Babylon may come: both two shall come forth out of one land: and choose you a place, choose *it* at the head of the way to the city.

20 Appoint a way, that the sword may come to Rabbath of the Ammonites, and to Judah in Jerusalem the defensed.

21 For the king of Babylon stood at the parting of the way, at the head of the two ways, to use divination: he made *his* arrows bright, he consulted with images, he looked in the liver.

22 At his right hand was the divination for Jerusalem, to appoint captains, to open the mouth in the slaughter, to lift up the voice with shouting, to appoint *battering* rams against the gates, to cast a mount, *and* to build a fort.

23 And it shall be to them as a false divination in their sight, to them that have sworn oaths: but he will call to remembrance the iniquity, that they may be taken.

24 Therefore thus says the Lord Yahweh; Because you have made your iniquity to be remembered, in that your transgressions are uncovered, so that in all your doings your sins do appear; because, *I say*, that you have come to remembrance, you shall be taken with the hand.

25 And you, profane wicked prince of Israel, whose day has come, when iniquity *shall have* an end,

26 Thus says the Lord Yahweh; Remove the diadem, and take off the crown: this *shall* not *be* the same: exalt *him that is* low, and abase *him that is* high.

27 I will overturn, overturn, overturn, it: and it shall be no *more*, until he comes whose right it is; and I will give it *to him*.

28 ¶ And you, son of man, prophesy and say, Thus says the Lord Yahweh concerning the Ammonites, and concerning their reproach; even say you, The sword, the sword *is* drawn: for the slaughter *it is* polished, to consume because of the glittering:

29 While they see vanity unto you, while they divine a lie unto you, to bring you upon the necks of *them that are* slain, of the wicked, whose day has come, when their iniquity *shall have* an end.

30 Shall I cause *it* to return into his sheath? I will judge you in the place where you were created, in the land of your nativity.

31 And I will pour out my indignation upon you, I will blow against you in the fire of my wrath, and deliver you into the hand of brutish men, skillful to destroy.

32 You shall be for fuel to the fire; your blood shall be in the midst of the land; you shall be no *more* remembered: for I Yahweh have spoken *it*.

Ezekiel 22

22:1 ¶ Moreover the word of Yahweh came unto me, saying,

2 Now, you son of man, will you judge, will you judge the bloody city? yes, you shall show her all her abominations.

3 Then say you, Thus says the Lord Yahweh, The city sheds blood in the midst of it, that her time may come, and makes idols against herself to defile herself.

4 You have become guilty in your blood that you have shed; and have defiled yourself in your idols which you have made; and you have caused your days to draw near, and have come *even* to your years: therefore have I made you a reproach to the heathen, and a mocking to all countries.

5 *Those that are* near, and *those that are* far from you, shall mock you, *which are* infamous *and* much troubled.

6 Behold, the princes of Israel, every one was in you to their power to shed blood.

7 In you have they been vile to father and mother: in the midst of you have they dealt by oppression with the stranger: in you have they oppressed the fatherless and the widow.

8 You have despised my holy things, and have profaned my sabbaths.

9 In you are men that carry tales to shed blood: and in you they eat upon the mountains: in the midst of you they commit lewdness.

10 In you have they uncovered their fathers' nakedness: in you have they humbled her that was set apart for pollution.

11 And one has committed abomination with his neighbor's wife; and another has lewdly defiled his daughter-in-law; and another in you has humbled his sister, his father's daughter.

12 In you have they taken gifts to shed blood; you have taken usury and increase, and you have greedily gained of your neighbors by extortion, and have forgotten me, says the Lord Yahweh.

13 Behold, therefore I have smitten my hand at your dishonest gain which you have made, and at your blood which has been in the midst of you.

14 Can your heart endure, or can your hands be strong, in the days that I shall deal with you? I Yahweh have spoken *it*, and will do *it*.

15 And I will scatter you among the heathen, and disperse you in the countries, and will consume your filthiness out of you.

16 And you shall take your inheritance in yourself in the sight of the heathen, and you shall know that I *am* Yahweh.

17 ¶ And the word of Yahweh came unto me, saying,

18 Son of man, the house of Israel has to me become dross: all they *are* brass, and tin, and iron, and lead, in the midst of the furnace; they are *even* the dross of silver.
19 Therefore thus says the Lord Yahweh; Because you have all become dross, behold, therefore I will gather you into the midst of Jerusalem.
20 *As* they gather silver, and brass, and iron, and lead, and tin, into the midst of the furnace, to blow the fire upon it, to melt *it*; so will I gather *you* in my anger and in my fury, and I will leave *you there*, and melt you
21 Yes, I will gather you, and blow upon you in the fire of my wrath, and you shall be melted in the midst thereof.
22 As silver is melted in the midst of the furnace, so shall you be melted in the midst thereof; and you shall know that I Yahweh have poured out my fury upon you.
23 ¶ And the word of Yahweh came unto me, saying
24 Son of man, say unto her, You *are* the land that is not cleansed, nor rained upon in the day of indignation.
25 *There is* a conspiracy of her prophets in the midst thereof, like a roaring lion ravening the prey; they have devoured souls; they have taken the treasure and precious things; they have made her many widows in the midst thereof.
26 Her priests have violated my law, and have profaned my holy things: they have put no difference between the holy and profane, neither have they shown *difference* between the unclean and the clean, and have hidden their eyes from my sabbaths, and I am profaned among them.
27 Her princes in the midst thereof *are* like wolves ravening the prey, to shed blood, *and* to destroy souls, to get dishonest gain.
28 And her prophets have daubed them with untempered *mortar*, seeing vanity, and divining lies unto them, saying, Thus says the Lord Yahweh, when Yahweh has not spoken.
29 The people of the land have used oppression, and exercised robbery, and have oppressed the poor and needy: yes, they have oppressed the stranger wrongfully.
30 And I sought for a man among them, that should make up the hedge, and stand in the gap before me for the land, that I should not destroy it: but I found none.
31 Therefore have I poured out my indignation upon them; I have consumed them with the fire of my wrath: their own way have I recompensed upon their heads, says the Lord Yahweh.

Ezekiel 23

23:1 ¶ The word of Yahweh came again unto me, saying,
2 Son of man, there were two women, the daughters of one mother:
3 And they committed whoredoms in Egypt; they committed whoredoms in their youth: there were their breasts pressed, and there they bruised the teats of their virginity.
4 And the names of them *were* Aholah the elder, and Aholibah her sister: and they were mine, and they bore sons and daughters. Thus *were* their names; Samaria *is* Aholah, and Jerusalem Aholibah.
5 And Aholah played the harlot when she was mine; and she doted on her lovers, on the Assyrians *her* neighbors,
6 *Which were* clothed with blue, captains and rulers, all of them desirable young men, horsemen riding upon horses.
7 Thus she committed her whoredoms with them, with all them *that were* the chosen men of Assyria, and with all on whom she doted: with all their idols she defiled herself.
8 Neither left she her whoredoms *brought* from Egypt: for in her youth they lay with her, and they bruised the breasts of her virginity, and poured their whoredom upon her.
9 Therefore I have delivered her into the hand of her lovers, into the hand of the Assyrians, upon whom she doted.
10 These uncovered her nakedness: they took her sons and her daughters, and slew her with the sword: and she became famous among women; for they had executed judgment upon her.
11 ¶ And when her sister Aholibah saw *this*, she was more corrupt in her inordinate love than she, and in her whoredoms more than her sister in *her* whoredoms.
12 She doted upon the Assyrians *her* neighbors, captains and rulers clothed most gorgeously, horsemen riding upon horses, all of them desirable young men.
13 Then I saw that she was defiled, *that* they *took* both one way,
14 And *that* she increased her whoredoms: for when she saw men portrayed upon the wall, the images of the Chaldeans portrayed with bright red,
15 Girded with girdles upon their loins, overhanging with dyed attire upon their heads, all of them princes to look to, after the manner of the Babylonians of Chaldea, the land of their nativity:
16 And as soon as she saw them with her eyes, she doted upon them, and sent messengers to them into Chaldea.
17 And the Babylonians came to her into the bed of love, and they defiled her with their whoredom, and she was polluted with them, and her mind was alienated from them.
18 So she uncovered her whoredoms, and uncovered her nakedness: then my mind was alienated from her, like as my mind was alienated from her sister.
19 Yet she multiplied her whoredoms, in calling to remembrance the days of her youth, wherein she had played the harlot in the land of Egypt.
20 For she doted upon their concubines, whose flesh *is as* the flesh of donkeys, and whose issue *is like* the issue of horses.
21 Thus you called to remembrance the lewdness of your youth, in bruising your teats by the Egyptians for the breasts of your youth.
22 ¶ Therefore, O Aholibah, thus says the Lord Yahweh; Behold, I will raise up your lovers against you, from whom your mind is alienated, and I will bring them against you on every side;

Ezekiel 23

23 The Babylonians, and all the Chaldeans, Pekod, and Shoa, and Koa, *and* all the Assyrians with them: all of them desirable young men, captains and rulers, great lords and renowned, all of them riding upon horses.

24 And they shall come against you with chariots, wagons, and wheels, and with an assembly of people, *which* shall set against you buckler and shield and helmet round about: and I will set judgment before them, and they shall judge you according to their judgments.

25 And I will set my jealousy against you, and they shall deal furiously with you: they shall take away your nose and your ears; and your remnant shall fall by the sword: they shall take your sons and your daughters; and your residue shall be devoured by the fire.

26 They shall also strip you out of your clothes, and take away your fair jewels.

27 Thus will I make your lewdness to cease from you, and your whoredom *brought* from the land of Egypt: so that you shall not lift up your eyes unto them, nor remember Egypt any more.

28 For thus says the Lord Yahweh; Behold, I will deliver you into the hand *of them* whom you hate, into the hand *of them* from whom your mind is alienated:

29 And they shall deal with you hatefully, and shall take away all your labor, and shall leave you naked and bare: and the nakedness of your whoredoms shall be uncovered, both your lewdness and your whoredoms.

30 I will do these *things* unto you, because you have gone a whoring after the heathen, *and* because you are polluted with their idols.

31 You have walked in the way of your sister; therefore will I give her cup into your hand.

32 Thus says the Lord Yahweh; You shall drink of your sister's cup deep and large: you shall be laughed to scorn and had in derision; it contains much.

33 You shall be filled with drunkenness and sorrow, with the cup of astonishment and desolation, with the cup of your sister Samaria.

34 You shall even drink it and suck *it* out, and you shall break the earthen vessels thereof, and pluck off your own breasts: for I have spoken *it*, says the Lord Yahweh.

35 Therefore thus says the Lord Yahweh; Because you have forgotten me, and cast me behind your back, therefore bear you also your lewdness and your whoredoms.

36 ¶ Yahweh said moreover unto me; Son of man, will you judge Aholah and Aholibah? yes, declare to them their abominations;

37 That they have committed adultery, and blood *is* in their hands, and with their idols have they committed adultery, and have also caused their sons, whom they bore unto me, to pass for them through *the fire*, to devour *them*.

38 Moreover this they have done unto me: they have defiled my sanctuary in the same day, and have profaned my sabbaths.

39 For when they had slain their children to their idols, then they came the same day into my sanctuary to profane it; and, lo, thus have they done in the midst of my house.

40 And furthermore, that you have sent for men to come from far, to whom a messenger *was* sent; and, lo, they came: for whom you did wash yourself, painted your eyes, and decked yourself with ornaments,

41 And sat upon a stately bed, and a table prepared before it, whereupon you have set my incense and my oil.

42 And a voice of a multitude being at ease *was* with her: and with the men of the common sort *were* brought Sabeans from the wilderness, which put bracelets upon their hands, and beautiful crowns upon their heads.

43 Then said I to *her that was* old in adulteries, Will they now commit whoredoms with her, and she *with them*?

44 Yet they went in unto her, as they go in to a woman that plays the harlot: so went they in unto Aholah and unto Aholibah, the lewd women.

45 And the righteous men, they shall judge them after the manner of adulteresses, and after the manner of women that shed blood; because they *are* adulteresses, and blood *is* in their hands.

46 For thus says the Lord Yahweh; I will bring up a company upon them, and will give them to be removed and spoiled.

47 And the company shall stone them with stones, and dispatch them with their swords; they shall slay their sons and their daughters, and burn up their houses with fire.

48 Thus will I cause lewdness to cease out of the land, that all women may be taught not to do after your lewdness.

49 And they shall recompense your lewdness upon you, and you shall bear the sins of your idols: and you shall know that I *am* the Lord Yahweh.

Ezekiel 24

24:1 ¶ Again in the ninth year, in the tenth month, in the tenth *day* of the month, the word of Yahweh came unto me, saying,

2 Son of man, write you the name of the day, *even* of this same day: the king of Babylon set himself against Jerusalem this same day.

3 And utter a parable unto the rebellious house, and say unto them, Thus says the Lord Yahweh; Set on a pot, set *it* on, and also pour water into it:

4 Gather the pieces thereof into it, *even* every good piece, the thigh, and the shoulder; fill *it* with the choice bones.

5 Take the choice of the flock, and burn also the bones under it, *and* make it boil well, and let them boil the bones of it therein.

6 Therefore thus says the Lord Yahweh; Woe to the bloody city, to the pot whose scum *is* therein, and whose scum is not gone out of it! bring it out piece by piece; let no lot fall upon it.

7 For her blood is in the midst of her; she set it upon the top of a rock; she poured it not upon the ground, to cover it with dust;

8 That it might cause fury to come up to take vengeance; I have set her blood upon the top of a rock, that it should not be covered.

9 Therefore thus says the Lord Yahweh; Woe to the bloody city! I will even make the pile for fire great.
10 Heap on wood, kindle the fire, consume the flesh, and spice it well, and let the bones be burned.
11 Then set it empty upon the coals thereof, that the brass of it may be hot, and may burn, and *that* the filthiness of it may be molten in it, *that* the scum of it may be consumed.
12 She has wearied *herself* with lies, and her great scum went not forth out of her: her scum *shall be* in the fire.
13 In your filthiness *is* lewdness: because I have purged you, and you were not purged, you shall not be purged from your filthiness any more, till I have caused my fury to rest upon you.
14 I Yahweh have spoken *it*: it shall come to pass, and I will do *it*; I will not go back, neither will I spare, neither will I repent; according to your ways, and according to your doings, shall they judge you, says the Lord Yahweh.
15 ¶ Also the word of Yahweh came unto me, saying,
16 Son of man, behold, I take away from you the desire of your eyes with a stroke: yet neither shall you mourn nor weep, neither shall your tears run down.
17 Forbear to cry, make no mourning for the dead, bind the turban of your head upon you, and put upon your shoes on your feet, and cover not *your* lips, and eat not the bread of men.
18 So I spoke to the people in the morning: and at evening my wife died; and I did in the morning as I was commanded.
19 And the people said to me, Will you not tell us what these *things are* to us, that you do *so*?
20 Then I answered them, The word of Yahweh came unto me, saying,
21 Speak to the house of Israel, Thus says the Lord Yahweh; Behold, I will profane my sanctuary, the excellency of your strength, the desire of your eyes, and that which your soul pities; and your sons and your daughters whom you have left shall fall by the sword.
22 And you shall do as I have done: you shall not cover *your* lips, nor eat the bread of men.
23 And your turbans *shall be* upon your heads, and your shoes upon your feet: you shall not mourn nor weep; but you shall pine away for your iniquities, and mourn one toward another.
24 Thus Ezekiel is unto you a sign: according to all that he has done shall you do: and when this comes, you shall know that I *am* the Lord Yahweh.
25 Also, you son of man, *shall it* not *be* in the day when I take from them their strength, the joy of their glory, the desire of their eyes, and that whereupon they set their minds, their sons and their daughters,
26 *That* he that escapes in that day shall come unto you, to cause *you* to hear *it* with *your* ears?
27 In that day shall your mouth be opened to him which has escaped, and you shall speak, and be no more dumb: and you shall be a sign unto them; and they shall know that I *am* Yahweh.

Ezekiel 25

25:1 ¶ The word of Yahweh came again unto me, saying,
2 Son of man, set your face against the Ammonites, and prophesy against them;
3 And say unto the Ammonites, Hear the word of the Lord Yahweh; Thus says the Lord Yahweh; Because you said, Aha, against my sanctuary, when it was profaned; and against the land of Israel, when it was desolate; and against the house of Judah, when they went into captivity;
4 Behold, therefore I will deliver you to the men of the east for a possession, and they shall set their palaces in you, and make their dwellings in you: they shall eat your fruit, and they shall drink your milk.
5 And I will make Rabbah a stable for camels, and the Ammonites a couching place for flocks: and you shall know that I *am* Yahweh.
6 For thus says the Lord Yahweh; Because you have clapped *your* hands, and stamped with the feet, and rejoiced in heart with all your despite against the land of Israel;
7 Behold, therefore I will stretch out my hand upon you, and will deliver you for a spoil to the heathen; and I will cut you off from the people, and I will cause you to perish out of the countries: I will destroy you; and you shall know that I *am* Yahweh.
8 ¶ Thus says the Lord Yahweh; Because that Moab and Seir do say, Behold, the house of Judah *is* like unto all the heathen;
9 Therefore, behold, I will open the side of Moab from the cities, from his cities *which are* on his frontiers, the glory of the country, Bethjeshimoth, Baalmeon, and Kiriathaim,
10 Unto the men of the east with the Ammonites, and will give them in possession, that the Ammonites may not be remembered among the nations.
11 And I will execute judgments upon Moab; and they shall know that I *am* Yahweh.
12 Thus says the Lord Yahweh; Because that Edom has dealt against the house of Judah by taking vengeance, and has greatly offended, and revenged himself upon them;
13 Therefore thus says the Lord Yahweh; I will also stretch out my hand upon Edom, and will cut off man and beast from it; and I will make it desolate from Teman; and they of Dedan shall fall by the sword.
14 And I will lay my vengeance upon Edom by the hand of my people Israel: and they shall do in Edom according to my anger and according to my fury; and they shall know my vengeance, says the Lord Yahweh.
15 Thus says the Lord Yahweh; Because the Philistines have dealt by revenge, and have taken vengeance with a spiteful heart, to destroy *it* for the old hatred;
16 Therefore thus says the Lord Yahweh; Behold, I will stretch out my hand upon the Philistines, and I will cut off the Cherethims, and destroy the remnant of the sea coast.

17 And I will execute great vengeance upon them with furious rebukes; and they shall know that I *am* Yahweh, when I shall lay my vengeance upon them.

Ezekiel 26

26:1 ¶ And it came to pass in the eleventh year, in the first *day* of the month, *that* the word of Yahweh came unto me, saying,

2 Son of man, because that Tyrus has said against Jerusalem, Aha, she is broken *that was* the gates of the people: she is turned unto me: I shall be replenished, *now* she is laid waste:

3 Therefore thus says the Lord Yahweh; Behold, I *am* against you, O Tyrus, and will cause many nations to come up against you, as the sea causes his waves to come up.

4 And they shall destroy the walls of Tyrus, and break down her towers: I will also scrape her dust from her, and make her like the top of a rock.

5 It shall be *a place for* the spreading of nets in the midst of the sea: for I have spoken *it*, says the Lord Yahweh: and it shall become a spoil to the nations.

6 And her daughters which *are* in the field shall be slain by the sword; and they shall know that I *am* Yahweh.

7 For thus says the Lord Yahweh; Behold, I will bring upon Tyrus Nebuchadrezzar king of Babylon, a king of kings, from the north, with horses, and with chariots, and with horsemen, and companies, and many people.

8 He shall slay with the sword your daughters in the field: and he shall make a fort against you, and cast a mount against you, and lift up the buckler against you.

9 And he shall set engines of war against your walls, and with his axes he shall break down your towers.

10 By reason of the abundance of his horses their dust shall cover you: your walls shall shake at the noise of the horsemen, and of the wheels, and of the chariots, when he shall enter into your gates, as men enter into a city wherein is made a breach.

11 With the hoofs of his horses shall he tread down all your streets: he shall slay your people by the sword, and your strong garrisons shall go down to the ground.

12 And they shall make a spoil of your riches, and make a prey of your merchandise: and they shall break down your walls, and destroy your pleasant houses: and they shall lay your stones and your timber and your dust in the midst of the water.

13 And I will cause the noise of your songs to cease; and the sound of your harps shall be no more heard.

14 And I will make you like the top of a rock: you shall be *a place* to spread nets upon; you shall be built no more: for I Yahweh have spoken *it*, says the Lord Yahweh.

15 ¶ Thus says the Lord Yahweh to Tyrus; Shall not the isles shake at the sound of your fall, when the wounded cry, when the slaughter is made in the midst of you?

16 Then all the princes of the sea shall come down from their thrones, and lay away their robes, and put off their embroidered garments: they shall clothe themselves with trembling; they shall sit upon the ground, and shall tremble at *every* moment, and be astonished at you.

17 And they shall take up a lamentation for you, and say to you, How are you destroyed, *that were* inhabited of seafaring men, the renowned city, which were strong in the sea, she and her inhabitants, which cause their terror *to be* on all that haunt it!

18 Now shall the isles tremble in the day of your fall; yes, the isles that *are* in the sea shall be troubled at your departure.

19 For thus says the Lord Yahweh; When I shall make you a desolate city, like the cities that are not inhabited; when I shall bring up the deep upon you, and great waters shall cover you;

20 When I shall bring you down with them that descend into the pit, with the people of old time, and shall set you in the low parts of the earth, in places desolate of old, with them that go down to the pit, that you be not inhabited; and I shall set glory in the land of the living;

21 I will make you a terror, and you *shall be* no *more*: though you *will* be sought for, yet shall you never be found again, says the Lord Yahweh.

Ezekiel 27

27:1 ¶ The word of Yahweh came again unto me, saying,

2 Now, you son of man, take up a lamentation for Tyrus;

3 And say unto Tyrus, O you that are situated at the entry of the sea, *which are* a merchant of the people for many isles, Thus says the Lord Yahweh; O Tyrus, you have said, I *am* of perfect beauty.

4 Your borders *are* in the midst of the seas, your builders have perfected your beauty.

5 They have made all your *ship* boards of fir trees of Senir: they have taken cedars from Lebanon to make masts for you.

6 *Of* the oaks of Bashan have they made your oars; the company of the Ashurites have made your benches *of* ivory, *brought* out of the isles of Chittim.

7 Fine linen with embroidered work from Egypt was that which you spread forth to be your sail; blue and purple from the isles of Elishah was that which covered you.

8 The inhabitants of Zidon and Arvad were your mariners: your wise *men*, O Tyrus, *that* were in you, were your pilots.

9 The ancients of Gebal and the wise *men* thereof were in you, your caulkers: all the ships of the sea with their mariners were in you to occupy your merchandise.

10 They of Persia and of Lud and of Phut were in your army, your men of war: they hung the shield and helmet in you; they set forth your comeliness.

11 The men of Arvad with your army *were* upon your walls round about, and the Gammadims were in your towers: they hung their shields upon your walls round about; they have made your beauty perfect.

12 Tarshish *was* your merchant by reason of the multitude of all *kind of* riches; with silver, iron, tin, and lead, they traded in your fairs.
13 Javan, Tubal, and Meshech, they *were* your merchants: they traded the persons of men and vessels of brass in your market.
14 They of the house of Togarmah traded in your fairs with horses and horsemen and mules.
15 The men of Dedan *were* your merchants; many isles *were* the merchandise of your hand: they brought you *for* a present horns of ivory and ebony.
16 Syria *was* your merchant by reason of the multitude of the wares of your making: they occupied in your fairs with emeralds, purple, and embroidered work, and fine linen, and coral, and agate.
17 Judah, and the land of Israel, they *were* your merchants: they traded in your market wheat of Minnith, and Pannag, and honey, and oil, and balm.
18 Damascus *was* your merchant in the multitude of the wares of your making, for the multitude of all riches; in the wine of Helbon, and white wool.
19 Dan also and Javan going to and fro occupied in your fairs: bright iron, cassia, and calamus, were in your market.
20 Dedan *was* your merchant in precious clothes for chariots.
21 Arabia, and all the princes of Kedar, they occupied with you in lambs, and rams, and goats: in these *were they* your merchants.
22 The merchants of Sheba and Raamah, they *were* your merchants: they occupied in your fairs with chief of all spices, and with all precious stones, and gold.
23 Haran, and Canneh, and Eden, the merchants of Sheba, Asshur, *and* Chilmad, *were* your merchants.
24 These *were* your merchants in all sorts *of things*, in blue clothes, and embroidered work, and in chests of rich apparel, bound with cords, and made of cedar, among your merchandise.
25 The ships of Tarshish did sing of you in your market: and you were replenished, and made very glorious in the midst of the seas.
26 ¶ Your rowers have brought you into great waters: the east wind has broken you in the midst of the seas
27 Your riches, and your fairs, your merchandise, your mariners, and your pilots, your caulkers, and the occupiers of your merchandise, and all your men of war, that *are* in you, and in all your company which *is* in the midst of you, shall fall into the midst of the seas in the day of your ruin.
28 The suburbs shall shake at the sound of the cry of your pilots.
29 And all that handle the oar, the mariners, *and* all the pilots of the sea, shall come down from their ships, they shall stand upon the land;
30 And shall cause their voice to be heard against you, and shall cry bitterly, and shall cast up dust upon their heads, they shall wallow themselves in the ashes:
31 And they shall make themselves utterly bald for you, and gird them with sackcloth, and they shall weep for you with bitterness of heart *and* bitter wailing.

32 And in their wailing they shall take up a lamentation for you, and lament over you, *saying*, What *city is* like Tyrus, like the destroyed in the midst of the sea?
33 When your wares went forth out of the seas, you filled many people; you did enrich the kings of the earth with the multitude of your riches and of your merchandise.
34 In the time *when* you shall be broken by the seas in the depths of the waters your merchandise and all your company in the midst of you shall fall.
35 All the inhabitants of the isles shall be astonished at you, and their kings shall be horribly afraid, they shall be troubled in *their* countenance.
36 The merchants among the people shall hiss at you; you shall be a terror, and never *shall be* any more.

Ezekiel 28

28:1 ¶ The word of Yahweh came again unto me, saying,
2 Son of man, say to the prince of Tyrus, Thus says the Lord Yahweh; Because your heart *is* lifted up, and you have said, I *am* a God, I sit *in* the seat of God, in the midst of the seas; yet you *are* a man, and not God, though you set your heart as the heart of God:
3 Behold, you *are* wiser than Daniel; there is no secret that they can hide from you:
4 With your wisdom and with your understanding you have gotten yourself riches, and have gotten gold and silver into your treasuries:
5 By your great wisdom *and* by your traffic have you increased your riches, and your heart is lifted up because of your riches:
6 Therefore thus says the Lord Yahweh; Because you have set your heart as the heart of God;
7 Behold, therefore I will bring strangers upon you, the terrible of the nations: and they shall draw their swords against the beauty of your wisdom, and they shall defile your brightness.
8 They shall bring you down to the pit, and you shall die the deaths of *them that are* slain in the midst of the seas.
9 Will you yet say before him that slays you, I *am* God? but you *shall be* a man, and no God, in the hand of him that slays you.
10 You shall die the deaths of the uncircumcised by the hand of strangers: for I have spoken *it*, says the Lord Yahweh.
11 ¶ Moreover the word of Yahweh came to me, saying,
12 Son of man, take up a lamentation upon the king of Tyrus, and say to him, Thus says the Lord Yahweh; You seal up the sum, full of wisdom, and perfect in beauty.
13 You have been in Eden the garden of God; every precious stone *was* your covering, the sardius, topaz, and the diamond, the beryl, the onyx, and the jasper, the sapphire, the emerald, and the carbuncle, and gold: the workmanship of your tambourines and of your pipes was prepared in you in the day that you were created.
14 You *were* the anointed cherub that covers; and I have set you *so*: you were upon the holy mountain of God; you have walked up and down in the midst of the stones of fire.

15 You *were* perfect in your ways from the day that you were created, till iniquity was found in you.
16 By the multitude of your merchandise they have filled the midst of you with violence, and you have sinned: therefore I will cast you as profane out of the mountain of God: and I will destroy you, O covering cherub, from the midst of the stones of fire.
17 Your heart was lifted up because of your beauty, you have corrupted your wisdom by reason of your brightness: I will cast you to the ground, I will lay you before kings, that they may behold you.
18 You have defiled your sanctuaries by the multitude of your iniquities, by the iniquity of your traffic; therefore will I bring forth a fire from the midst of you, it shall devour you, and I will bring you to ashes upon the earth in the sight of all them that behold you.
19 All they that know you among the people shall be astonished at you: you shall be a terror, and never *shall* you *be* any more.
20 ¶ Again the word of Yahweh came unto me, saying,
21 Son of man, set your face against Zidon, and prophesy against it,
22 And say, Thus says the Lord Yahweh; Behold, I *am* against you, O Zidon; and I will be glorified in the midst of you: and they shall know that I *am* Yahweh, when I shall have executed judgments in her, and shall be sanctified in her.
23 For I will send into her pestilence, and blood into her streets; and the wounded shall be judged in the midst of her by the sword upon her on every side; and they shall know that I *am* Yahweh.
24 And there shall be no more a pricking brier unto the house of Israel, nor *any* grieving thorn of all *that are* round about them, that despised them; and they shall know that I *am* the Lord Yahweh.
25 Thus says the Lord Yahweh; When I shall have gathered the house of Israel from the people among whom they are scattered, and shall be sanctified in them in the sight of the heathen, then shall they dwell in their land that I have given to my servant Jacob.
26 And they shall dwell safely therein, and shall build houses, and plant vineyards; yes, they shall dwell with confidence, when I have executed judgments upon all those that despise them round about them; and they shall know that I *am* Yahweh their God.

Ezekiel 29

29:1 ¶ In the tenth year, in the tenth *month*, in the twelfth *day* of the month, the word of Yahweh came unto me, saying,
2 Son of man, set your face against Pharaoh king of Egypt, and prophesy against him, and against all Egypt:
3 Speak, and say, Thus says the Lord Yahweh; Behold, I *am* against you, Pharaoh king of Egypt, the great dragon that lies in the midst of his rivers, which has said, My river *is* my own, and I have made *it* for myself.
4 But I will put hooks in your jaws, and I will cause the fish of your rivers to stick unto your scales, and I will bring you up out of the midst of your rivers, and all the fish of your rivers shall stick unto your scales.
5 And I will leave you *thrown* into the wilderness, you and all the fish of your rivers: you shall fall upon the open fields; you shall not be brought together, nor gathered: I have given you for meat to the beasts of the field and to the fowls of the heaven.
6 And all the inhabitants of Egypt shall know that I *am* Yahweh, because they have been a staff of reed to the house of Israel.
7 When they took hold of you by your hand, you did break, and tear all their shoulders: and when they leaned upon you, you broke, and made all their loins to be at a stand.
8 ¶ Therefore thus says the Lord Yahweh; Behold, I will bring a sword upon you, and cut off man and beast out of you.
9 And the land of Egypt shall be desolate and waste; and they shall know that I *am* Yahweh: because he has said, The river *is* mine, and I have made *it*.
10 Behold, therefore I *am* against you, and against your rivers, and I will make the land of Egypt utterly waste *and* desolate, from the tower of Syene even to the border of Ethiopia.
11 No foot of man shall pass through it, nor foot of beast shall pass through it, neither shall it be inhabited *for* forty years.
12 And I will make the land of Egypt desolate in the midst of the countries *that are* desolate, and her cities among the cities *that are* laid waste shall be desolate *for* forty years: and I will scatter the Egyptians among the nations, and will disperse them through the countries.
13 Yet thus says the Lord Yahweh; At the end of forty years will I gather the Egyptians from the people where they were scattered:
14 And I will bring again the captivity of Egypt, and will cause them to return *into* the land of Pathros, into the land of their habitation; and they shall be there a base kingdom.
15 It shall be the basest of the kingdoms; neither shall it exalt itself any more above the nations: for I will diminish them, that they shall no more rule over the nations.
16 And it shall be no more the confidence of the house of Israel, which brings *their* iniquity to remembrance, when they shall look after them: but they shall know that I *am* the Lord Yahweh.
17 ¶ And it came to pass in the seven and twentieth year, in the first *month*, in the first *day* of the month, the word of Yahweh came unto me, saying,
18 Son of man, Nebuchadrezzar king of Babylon caused his army to serve a great service against Tyrus: every head *was* made bald, and every shoulder *was* peeled: yet had he no wages, nor his army, for Tyrus, for the service that he had served against it:
19 Therefore thus says the Lord Yahweh; Behold, I will give the land of Egypt to Nebuchadrezzar king of Babylon; and he shall take her multitude, and take her spoil, and take her prey; and it shall be the wages for his army.

20 I have given him the land of Egypt *for* his labor with which he served against it, because they worked for me, says the Lord Yahweh.

21 In that day will I cause the horn of the house of Israel to bud forth, and I will give you the opening of the mouth in the midst of them; and they shall know that I *am* Yahweh.

Ezekiel 30

30:1 ¶ The word of Yahweh came again unto me, saying,

2 Son of man, prophesy and say, Thus says the Lord Yahweh; Howl you, Alas the day!

3 For the day *is* near, even the day of Yahweh *is* near, a cloudy day; it shall be the time of the heathen.

4 And the sword shall come upon Egypt, and great pain shall be in Ethiopia, when the slain shall fall in Egypt, and they shall take away her multitude, and her foundations shall be broken down.

5 Ethiopia, and Libya, and Lydia, and all the mingled people, and Chub, and the men of the land that are in league, shall fall with them by the sword.

6 Thus says Yahweh; They also that uphold Egypt shall fall; and the pride of her power shall come down: from the tower of Syene shall they fall in it by the sword, says the Lord Yahweh.

7 And they shall be desolate in the midst of the countries *that are* desolate, and her cities shall be in the midst of the cities *that are* wasted.

8 And they shall know that I *am* Yahweh, when I have set a fire in Egypt, and *when* all her helpers shall be destroyed.

9 In that day shall messengers go forth from me in ships to make the careless Ethiopians afraid, and great pain shall come upon them, as in the day of Egypt: for, lo, it comes.

10 Thus says the Lord Yahweh; I will also make the multitude of Egypt to cease by the hand of Nebuchadrezzar king of Babylon.

11 He and his people with him, the terrible of the nations, shall be brought to destroy the land: and they shall draw their swords against Egypt, and fill the land with the slain.

12 And I will make the rivers dry, and sell the land into the hand of the wicked: and I will make the land waste, and all that is therein, by the hand of strangers: I Yahweh have spoken *it*.

13 Thus says the Lord Yahweh; I will also destroy the idols, and I will cause *their* images to cease out of Noph; and there shall be no more a prince of the land of Egypt: and I will put a fear in the land of Egypt.

14 And I will make Pathros desolate, and will set fire in Zoan, and will execute judgments in No.

15 And I will pour my fury upon Sin, the strength of Egypt; and I will cut off the multitude of No.

16 And I will set fire in Egypt: Sin shall have great pain, and No shall be torn apart, and Noph *shall have* distresses daily.

17 The young men of Aven and of Pibeseth shall fall by the sword: and these *cities* shall go into captivity.

18 At Tehaphnehes also the day shall be darkened, when I shall break there the yokes of Egypt: and the pomp of her strength shall cease in her: as for her, a cloud shall cover her, and her daughters shall go into captivity.

19 Thus will I execute judgments in Egypt: and they shall know that I *am* Yahweh.

20 ¶ And it came to pass in the eleventh year, in the first *month*, in the seventh *day* of the month, *that* the word of Yahweh came unto me, saying,

21 Son of man, I have broken the arm of Pharaoh king of Egypt; and, lo, it shall not be bound up to be healed, to put a roller to bind it, to make it strong to hold the sword.

22 Therefore thus says the Lord Yahweh; Behold, I *am* against Pharaoh king of Egypt, and will break his arms, the strong, and that which was broken; and I will cause the sword to fall out of his hand.

23 And I will scatter the Egyptians among the nations, and will disperse them through the countries.

24 And I will strengthen the arms of the king of Babylon, and put my sword in his hand: but I will break Pharaoh's arms, and he shall groan before him with the groanings of a deadly wounded *man*.

25 But I will strengthen the arms of the king of Babylon, and the arms of Pharaoh shall fall down; and they shall know that I *am* Yahweh, when I shall put my sword into the hand of the king of Babylon, and he shall stretch it out upon the land of Egypt.

26 And I will scatter the Egyptians among the nations, and disperse them among the countries; and they shall know that I *am* Yahweh.

Ezekiel 31

31:1 ¶ And it came to pass in the eleventh year, in the third *month*, in the first *day* of the month, *that* the word of Yahweh came unto me, saying,

2 Son of man, speak to Pharaoh king of Egypt, and to his multitude; Whom are you like in your greatness?

3 Behold, the Assyrian *was* a cedar in Lebanon with fair branches, and with a shadowing shroud, and of a high stature; and his top was among the thick boughs.

4 The waters made him great, the deep set him up on high with her rivers running round about his plants, and sent out her little rivers unto all the trees of the field.

5 Therefore his height was exalted above all the trees of the field, and his boughs were multiplied, and his branches became long because of the multitude of waters, when he shot forth.

6 All the fowls of heaven made their nests in his boughs, and under his branches did all the beasts of the field bring forth their young, and under his shadow dwelt all great nations.

7 Thus was he fair in his greatness, in the length of his branches: for his root was by great waters.

8 The cedars in the garden of God could not hide him: the fir trees were not like his boughs, and the chestnut

Ezekiel 31

trees were not like his branches; nor any tree in the garden of God was like unto him in his beauty.

9 I have made him fair by the multitude of his branches: so that all the trees of Eden, that *were* in the garden of God, envied him.

10 ¶ Therefore thus says the Lord Yahweh; Because you have lifted up yourself in height, and he has shot up his top among the thick boughs, and his heart is lifted up in his height;

11 I have therefore delivered him into the hand of the mighty one of the heathen; he shall surely deal with him: I have driven him out for his wickedness.

12 And strangers, the terrible of the nations, have cut him off, and have left him: upon the mountains and in all the valleys his branches are fallen, and his boughs are broken by all the rivers of the land; and all the people of the earth are gone down from his shadow, and have left him.

13 Upon his ruin shall all the fowls of the heaven remain, and all the beasts of the field shall be upon his branches:

14 To the end that none of all the trees by the waters exalt themselves for their height, neither shoot up their top among the thick boughs, neither their trees stand up in their height, all that drink water: for they are all delivered unto death, to the lower parts of the earth, in the midst of the children of men, with them that go down to the pit.

15 Thus says the Lord Yahweh; In the day when he went down to the grave I caused a mourning: I covered the deep for him, and I restrained the floods thereof, and the great waters were stayed: and I caused Lebanon to mourn for him, and all the trees of the field fainted for him.

16 I made the nations to shake at the sound of his fall, when I cast him down to hell with them that descend into the pit: and all the trees of Eden, the choice and best of Lebanon, all that drink water, shall be comforted in the lower parts of the earth.

17 They also went down into hell with him unto *them that were* slain with the sword; and *they that were* his arm, *that* dwelt under his shadow in the midst of the heathen.

18 To whom are you thus like in glory and in greatness among the trees of Eden? yet shall you be brought down with the trees of Eden to the lower parts of the earth: you shall lie in the midst of the uncircumcised with *them that are* slain by the sword. This *is* Pharaoh and all his multitude, says the Lord Yahweh.

Ezekiel 32

32:1 ¶ And it came to pass in the twelfth year, in the twelfth month, in the first *day* of the month, *that* the word of Yahweh came unto me, saying,

2 Son of man, take up a lamentation for Pharaoh king of Egypt, and say to him, You are like a young lion of the nations, and you *are* as a whale in the seas: and you came forth with your rivers, and troubled the waters with your feet, and fouled their rivers.

3 Thus says the Lord Yahweh; I will therefore spread out my net over you with a company of many people; and they shall bring you up in my net.

4 Then will I leave you upon the land, I will cast you forth upon the open field, and will cause all the fowls of the heaven to remain upon you, and I will fill the beasts of the whole earth with you.

5 And I will lay your flesh upon the mountains, and fill the valleys with your height.

6 I will also water with your blood the land wherein you swim, *even* to the mountains; and the rivers shall be full of you.

7 And when I shall put you out, I will cover the heaven, and make the stars thereof dark; I will cover the sun with a cloud, and the moon shall not give her light.

8 All the bright lights of heaven will I make dark over you, and set darkness upon your land, says the Lord Yahweh.

9 I will also anger the hearts of many people, when I shall bring your destruction among the nations, into the countries which you have not known.

10 Yes, I will make many people amazed at you, and their kings shall be horribly afraid for you, when I shall brandish my sword before them; and they shall tremble at *every* moment, every man for his own life, in the day of your fall.

11 For thus says the Lord Yahweh; The sword of the king of Babylon shall come upon you.

12 By the swords of the mighty will I cause your multitude to fall, the terrible of the nations, all of them: and they shall spoil the pomp of Egypt, and all the multitude thereof shall be destroyed.

13 I will destroy also all the beasts thereof from beside the great waters; neither shall the foot of man trouble them any more, nor the hoofs of beasts trouble them.

14 Then will I make their waters deep, and cause their rivers to run like oil, says the Lord Yahweh.

15 When I shall make the land of Egypt desolate, and the country shall be destitute of that whereof it was full, when I shall smite all them that dwell therein, then shall they know that I *am* Yahweh.

16 This *is* the lamentation with which they shall lament her: the daughters of the nations shall lament her: they shall lament for her, *even* for Egypt, and for all her multitude, says the Lord Yahweh.

17 ¶ It came to pass also in the twelfth year, in the fifteenth *day* of the month, *that* the word of Yahweh came to me, saying,

18 Son of man, wail for the multitude of Egypt, and cast them down, *even* her, and the daughters of the famous nations, to the lower parts of the earth, with them that go down into the pit.

19 Whom do you pass in beauty? go down, and be you laid with the uncircumcised.

20 They shall fall in the midst of *them that are* slain by the sword: she is delivered to the sword: draw her and all her multitudes.

21 The strong among the mighty shall speak to him out of the midst of hell with them that help him: they have gone down, they lie uncircumcised, slain by the sword.

22 Asshur *is* there and all her company: his graves *are* about him: all of them slain, fallen by the sword:
23 Whose graves are set in the sides of the pit, and her company is round about her grave: all of them slain, fallen by the sword, which caused terror in the land of the living.
24 There *is* Elam and all her multitude round about her grave, all of them slain, fallen by the sword, which are gone down uncircumcised into the lower parts of the earth, which caused their terror in the land of the living; yet have they borne their shame with them that go down to the pit.
25 They have set her a bed in the midst of the slain with all her multitude: her graves *are* round about him: all of them uncircumcised, slain by the sword: though their terror was caused in the land of the living, yet have they borne their shame with them that go down to the pit: he is put in the midst of *them that are* slain.
26 There *is* Meshech, Tubal, and all her multitude: her graves *are* round about him: all of them uncircumcised, slain by the sword, though they caused their terror in the land of the living.
27 And they shall not lie with the mighty *that have* fallen of the uncircumcised, which have gone down to hell with their weapons of war: and they have laid their swords under their heads, but their iniquities shall be upon their bones, though *they were* the terror of the mighty in the land of the living.
28 Yes, you shall be broken in the midst of the uncircumcised, and shall lie with *them that are* slain with the sword.
29 There *is* Edom, her kings, and all her princes, which with their might are laid by *them that were* slain by the sword: they shall lie with the uncircumcised, and with them that go down to the pit.
30 There *are* the princes of the north, all of them, and all the Zidonians, which have gone down with the slain; with their terror they are ashamed of their might; and they lie uncircumcised with *them that are* slain by the sword, and bear their shame with them that go down to the pit.
31 Pharaoh shall see them, and shall be comforted over all his multitude, *even* Pharaoh and all his army slain by the sword, says the Lord Yahweh.
32 For I have caused my terror in the land of the living: and he shall be laid in the midst of the uncircumcised with *them that are* slain with the sword, *even* Pharaoh and all his multitude, says the Lord Yahweh.

Ezekiel 33

33:1 ¶ Again the word of Yahweh came unto me, saying,
2 Son of man, speak to the children of your people, and say unto them, When I bring the sword upon a land, if the people of the land take a man of their coasts, and set him for their watchman:
3 If when he sees the sword come upon the land, he blows the trumpet, and warns the people;
4 Then whoever hears the sound of the trumpet, and takes not warning; if the sword comes, and takes him away, his blood shall be upon his own head.
5 He heard the sound of the trumpet, and took not warning; his blood shall be upon him. But he that takes warning shall deliver his soul.
6 But if the watchman sees the sword come, and blows not the trumpet, and the people are not warned; if the sword comes, and takes *any* person from among them, he is taken away in his iniquity; but his blood will I require at the watchman's hand.
7 So you, O son of man, I have set you a watchman unto the house of Israel; therefore you shall hear the word at my mouth, and warn them from me.
8 When I say unto the wicked, O wicked man, you shall surely die; if you do not speak to warn the wicked from his way, that wicked *man* shall die in his iniquity; but his blood will I require at your hand.
9 Nevertheless, if you warn the wicked of his way to turn from it; if he does not turn from his way, he shall die in his iniquity; but you have delivered your soul.
10 ¶ Therefore, O you son of man, speak unto the house of Israel; Thus you speak, saying, If our transgressions and our sins *are* upon us, and we pine away in them, how should we then live?
11 Say unto them, *As* I live, says the Lord Yahweh, I have no pleasure in the death of the wicked; but that the wicked turns from his way and live: turn you, turn you from your evil ways; for why will you die, O house of Israel?
12 Therefore, you son of man, say unto the children of your people, The righteousness of the righteous shall not deliver him in the day of his transgression: as for the wickedness of the wicked, he shall not fall thereby in the day that he turns from his wickedness; neither shall the righteous be able to live for his *righteousness* in the day that he sins.
13 When I shall say unto the righteous, *that* he shall surely live; if he trusts to his own righteousness, and commits iniquity, all his righteousness shall not be remembered; but for his iniquity that he has committed, he shall die for it.
14 Again, when I say unto the wicked, You shall surely die; if he turns from his sin, and does that which is lawful and right;
15 *If* the wicked restores the pledge, gives again that he had robbed, walks in the statutes of life, without committing iniquity; he shall surely live, he shall not die.
16 None of his sins that he has committed shall be mentioned unto him: he has done that which is lawful and right; he shall surely live.
17 Yet the children of your people say, The way of the Lord is not equal: but as for them, their way is not equal.
18 When the righteous turns from his righteousness, and commits iniquity, he shall even die thereby.

Ezekiel 33

19 But if the wicked turns from his wickedness, and does that which is lawful and right, he shall live thereby.
20 Yet you say, The way of the Lord is not equal. O you house of Israel, I will judge you every one after his ways.
21 ¶ And it came to pass in the twelfth year of our captivity, in the tenth *month*, in the fifth *day* of the month, *that* one that had escaped out of Jerusalem came unto me, saying, The city is smitten.
22 Now the hand of Yahweh was upon me in the evening, before he that was escaped came; and had opened my mouth, until he came to me in the morning; and my mouth was opened, and I was no more dumb.
23 Then the word of Yahweh came unto me, saying,
24 Son of man, they that inhabit those wastes of the land of Israel speak, saying, Abraham was one, and he inherited the land: but we *are* many; the land is given *to* us for inheritance.
25 Therefore say unto them, Thus says the Lord Yahweh; You eat with the blood, and lift up your eyes toward your idols, and shed blood: and shall you possess the land?
26 You stand upon your sword, you work abomination, and you defile every one his neighbor's wife: and shall you possess the land?
27 Say you thus to them, Thus says the Lord Yahweh; *As* I live, surely they that *are* in the wastes shall fall by the sword, and him that *is* in the open field will I give to the beasts to be devoured, and they that *are* in the forts and in the caves shall die of the pestilence.
28 For I will lay the land most desolate, and the pomp of her strength shall cease; and the mountains of Israel shall be desolate, that none shall pass through.
29 Then shall they know that I *am* Yahweh, when I have laid the land most desolate because of all their abominations which they have committed.
30 ¶ Also, you son of man, the children of your people still are talking against you by the walls and in the doors of the houses, and speak one to another, every one to his brother, saying, Come, I pray you, and hear what is the word that comes forth from Yahweh.
31 And they come unto you as the people come, and they sit before you *as* my people, and they hear your words, but they will not do them: for with their mouth they show much love, *but* their heart goes after their covetousness.
32 And, lo, you *are* unto them as a very lovely song of one that has a pleasant voice, and can play well on an instrument: for they hear your words, but they do them not.
33 And when this comes to pass, (lo, it will come,) then shall they know that a prophet has been among them.

Ezekiel 34

34:1 ¶ And the word of Yahweh came unto me, saying,
2 Son of man, prophesy against the shepherds of Israel, prophesy, and say unto them, Thus says the Lord Yahweh unto the shepherds; Woe *be* to the shepherds of Israel that do feed themselves! should not the shepherds feed the flocks?
3 You eat the fat, and you clothe yourselves with the wool, you kill them that are fed: *but* you feed not the flock.
4 The diseased have you not strengthened, neither have you healed that which was sick, neither have you bound up *that which was* broken, neither have you brought again that which was driven away, neither have you sought that which was lost; but with force and with cruelty have you ruled them.
5 And they were scattered, because *there was* no shepherd: and they became meat to all the beasts of the field, when they were scattered.
6 My sheep wandered through all the mountains, and upon every high hill: yes, my flock was scattered upon all the face of the earth, and none did search or seek *after them*.
7 ¶ Therefore, you shepherds, hear the word of Yahweh;
8 *As* I live, says the Lord Yahweh, surely because my flock became a prey, and my flock became meat to every beast of the field, because *there was* no shepherd, neither did my shepherds search for my flock, but the shepherds fed themselves, and fed not my flock;
9 Therefore, O you shepherds, hear the word of Yahweh;
10 Thus says the Lord Yahweh; Behold, I *am* against the shepherds; and I will require my flock at their hand, and cause them to cease from feeding the flock; neither shall the shepherds feed themselves any more; for I will deliver my flock from their mouth, that they may not be meat for them.
11 For thus says the Lord Yahweh; Behold, I, *even* I, will both search my sheep, and seek them out.
12 As a shepherd seeks out his flock in the day that he is among his sheep *that are* scattered; so will I seek out my sheep, and will deliver them out of all places where they have been scattered in the cloudy and dark day.
13 And I will bring them out from the people, and gather them from the countries, and will bring them to their own land, and feed them upon the mountains of Israel by the rivers, and in all the inhabited places of the country.
14 I will feed them in a good pasture, and upon the high mountains of Israel shall their fold be: there shall they lie in a good fold, and *in* a fat pasture shall they feed upon the mountains of Israel.
15 I will feed my flock, and I will cause them to lie down, says the Lord Yahweh.
16 I will seek that which was lost, and bring again that which was driven away, and will bind up *that which was* broken, and will strengthen that which was sick: but I will destroy the fat and the strong; I will feed them with judgment.
17 ¶ And *as for* you, O my flock, thus says the Lord Yahweh; Behold, I judge between cattle and cattle, between the rams and the he goats.
18 *Seems it* a small thing to you to have eaten up the good pasture, but you must tread down with your feet the

residue of your pastures? and to have drunk of the deep waters, but you must foul the residue with your feet?

19 And *as for* my flock, they eat that which you have trodden with your feet; and they drink that which you have fouled with your feet.

20 Therefore thus says the Lord Yahweh to them; Behold, I, *even* I, will judge between the fat cattle and between the lean cattle.

21 Because you have thrust with side and with shoulder, and pushed all the diseased with your horns, till you have scattered them abroad;

22 Therefore will I save my flock, and they shall no more be a prey; and I will judge between cattle and cattle.

23 And I will set up one shepherd over them, and he shall feed them, *even* my servant David; he shall feed them, and he shall be their shepherd.

24 And I Yahweh will be their God, and my servant David a prince among them; I Yahweh have spoken *it*.

25 And I will make with them a covenant of peace, and will cause the evil beasts to cease out of the land: and they shall dwell safely in the wilderness, and sleep in the woods.

26 And I will make them and the places round about my hill a blessing; and I will cause the shower to come down in his season; there shall be showers of blessing.

27 And the tree of the field shall yield her fruit, and the earth shall yield her increase, and they shall be safe in their land, and shall know that I *am* Yahweh, when I have broken the bands of their yoke, and delivered them out of the hand of those that served themselves of them.

28 And they shall no more be a prey to the heathen, neither shall the beast of the land devour them; but they shall dwell safely, and none shall make *them* afraid.

29 And I will raise up for them a plant of renown, and they shall be no more consumed with hunger in the land, neither bear the shame of the heathen any more.

30 Thus shall they know that I Yahweh their God *am* with them, and *that* they, *even* the house of Israel, *are* my people, says the Lord Yahweh.

31 And you my flock, the flock of my pasture, *are* men, *and* I *am* your God, says the Lord Yahweh.

Ezekiel 35

35:1 ¶ Moreover the word of Yahweh came to me, saying,

2 Son of man, set your face against mount Seir, and prophesy against it,

3 And say to it, Thus says the Lord Yahweh; Behold, O mount Seir, I *am* against you, and I will stretch out my hand against you, and I will make you most desolate.

4 I will lay your cities waste, and you shall be desolate, and you shall know that I *am* Yahweh.

5 Because you have had a perpetual hatred, and have shed *the blood of* the children of Israel by the force of the sword in the time of their calamity, in the time *that their* iniquity *had* an end:

6 Therefore, *as* I live, says the Lord Yahweh, I will prepare you unto blood, and blood shall pursue you: since you have not hated blood, even blood shall pursue you.

7 Thus will I make mount Seir most desolate, and cut off from it him that passes out and him that returns.

8 And I will fill his mountains with his slain *men*: in your hills, and in your valleys, and in all your rivers, shall they fall that are slain with the sword.

9 I will make you perpetual desolations, and your cities shall not return: and you shall know that I *am* Yahweh.

10 ¶ Because you have said, These two nations and these two countries shall be mine, and we will possess it; whereas Yahweh was there:

11 Therefore, *as* I live, says the Lord Yahweh, I will even do according to your anger, and according to your envy which you have used out of your hatred against them; and I will make myself known among them, when I have judged you.

12 And you shall know that I *am* Yahweh, *and that* I have heard all your blasphemies which you have spoken against the mountains of Israel, saying, They are laid desolate, they are given *to* us to consume.

13 Thus with your mouth you have boasted against me, and have multiplied your words against me: I have heard *them*.

14 Thus says the Lord Yahweh; When the whole earth rejoices, I will make you desolate.

15 As you did rejoice at the inheritance of the house of Israel, because it was desolate, so will I do to you: you shall be desolate, O mount Seir, and all Idumea, *even* all of it: and they shall know that I *am* Yahweh.

Ezekiel 36

36:1 ¶ Also, you son of man, prophesy to the mountains of Israel, and say, You mountains of Israel, hear the word of Yahweh:

2 Thus says the Lord Yahweh; Because the enemy has said against you, Aha, even the ancient high places are ours in possession:

3 Therefore prophesy and say, Thus says the Lord Yahweh; Because they have made *you* desolate, and swallowed you up on every side, that you might be a possession to the residue of the heathen, and you are taken up in the lips of talkers, and *are* an infamy of the people:

4 Therefore, you mountains of Israel, hear the word of the Lord Yahweh; Thus says the Lord Yahweh to the mountains, and to the hills, to the rivers, and to the valleys, to the desolate wastes, and to the cities that are forsaken, which became a prey and derision to the residue of the heathen that *are* round about.

5 Therefore thus says the Lord Yahweh; Surely in the fire of my jealousy have I spoken against the residue of the

Ezekiel 36

heathen, and against all Idumea, which have appointed my land into their possession with the joy of all *their* heart, with despiteful minds, to cast it out for a prey.

6 Prophesy therefore concerning the land of Israel, and say to the mountains, and to the hills, to the rivers, and to the valleys, Thus says the Lord Yahweh; Behold, I have spoken in my jealousy and in my fury, because you have borne the shame of the heathen:

7 Therefore thus says the Lord Yahweh; I have lifted up my hand, Surely the heathen that *are* about you, they shall bear their shame.

8 But you, O mountains of Israel, you shall shoot forth your branches, and yield your fruit to my people of Israel; for they are at hand to come.

9 For, behold, I *am* for you, and I will turn to you, and you shall be tilled and sown:

10 And I will multiply men upon you, all the house of Israel, *even* all of it: and the cities shall be inhabited, and the wastes shall be built:

11 And I will multiply upon you man and beast; and they shall increase and bring fruit: and I will settle you after your old estates, and will do better *to you* than at your beginnings: and you shall know that I *am* Yahweh.

12 Yes, I will cause men to walk upon you, *even* my people Israel; and they shall possess you, and you shall be their inheritance, and you shall no more henceforth bereave them *of men*.

13 Thus says the Lord Yahweh; Because they say to you, You *land* devour up men, and have bereaved your nations;

14 Therefore you shall devour men no more, neither bereave your nations any more, says the Lord Yahweh.

15 Neither will I cause *men* to hear in you the shame of the heathen any more, neither will you bear the reproach of the people any more, neither will you cause your nations to fall any more, says the Lord Yahweh.

16 ¶ Moreover the word of Yahweh came to me, saying,

17 Son of man, when the house of Israel dwelt in their own land, they defiled it by their own way and by their doings: their way was before me as the uncleanness of a removed woman.

18 Therefore I poured my fury upon them for the blood that they had shed upon the land, and for their idols *with which* they had polluted it:

19 And I scattered them among the heathen, and they were dispersed through the countries: according to their way and according to their doings I judged them.

20 And when they entered to the heathen, where they went, they profaned my holy name, when they said to them, These *are* the people of Yahweh, and are gone forth out of his land.

21 But I had pity for my holy name, which the house of Israel had profaned among the heathen, wherever they went.

22 Therefore say to the house of Israel, Thus says the Lord Yahweh; I do not *this* for your sakes, O house of Israel, but for my holy name's sake, which you have profaned among the heathen, wherever you went.

23 And I will sanctify my great name, which was profaned among the heathen, which you have profaned in the midst of them; and the heathen shall know that I *am* Yahweh, says the Lord Yahweh, when I shall be sanctified in you before their eyes.

24 For I will take you from among the heathen, and gather you out of all countries, and will bring you into your own land.

25 ¶ Then will I sprinkle clean water upon you, and you shall be clean: from all your filthiness, and from all your idols, will I cleanse you.

26 A new heart also will I give you, and a new spirit will I put within you: and I will take away the stony heart out of your flesh, and I will give you a heart of flesh.

27 And I will put my spirit within you, and cause you to walk in my statutes, and you shall keep my judgments, and do *them*.

28 And you shall dwell in the land that I gave to your fathers; and you shall be my people, and I will be your God.

29 I will also save you from all your uncleanness: and I will call for the corn, and will increase it, and lay no famine on you.

30 And I will multiply the fruit of the tree, and the increase of the field, that you shall receive no more reproach of famine among the heathen.

31 Then shall you remember your own evil ways, and your doings that *were* not good, and shall loathe yourselves in your own sight for your iniquities and for your abominations.

32 Not for your sakes do I *this*, says the Lord Yahweh, be it known to you: be ashamed and confounded for your own ways, O house of Israel.

33 Thus says the Lord Yahweh; In the day that I shall have cleansed you from all your iniquities I will also cause *you* to dwell in the cities, and the wastes shall be built.

34 And the desolate land shall be tilled, whereas it lay desolate in the sight of all that passed by.

35 And they shall say, This land that was desolate has become like the garden of Eden; and the waste and desolate and ruined cities *have become* fenced, *and* are inhabited.

36 Then the heathen that are left round about you shall know that I Yahweh build the ruined *places, and* plant that which was desolate: I Yahweh have spoken *it*, and I will do *it*.

37 Thus says the Lord Yahweh; I will yet *for* this be inquired of by the house of Israel, to do *it* for them; I will increase them with men like a flock.

38 As the holy flock, as the flock of Jerusalem in her solemn feasts; so shall the waste cities be filled with flocks of men: and they shall know that I *am* Yahweh.

Ezekiel 37

37:1 ¶ The hand of Yahweh was upon me, and carried me out in the spirit of Yahweh, and set me down in the midst of the valley which *was* full of bones,

2 And caused me to pass by them round about: and, behold, *there were* very many in the open valley; and, lo, *they were* very dry.

3 And he said unto me, Son of man, can these bones live? And I answered, O Lord Yahweh, you know.

4 Again he said unto me, Prophesy upon these bones, and say unto them, O you dry bones, hear the word of Yahweh.

5 Thus says the Lord Yahweh unto these bones; Behold, I will cause breath to enter into you, and you shall live:

6 And I will lay sinews upon you, and will bring up flesh upon you, and cover you with skin, and put breath in you, and you shall live; and you shall know that I *am* Yahweh.

7 So I prophesied as I was commanded: and as I prophesied, there was a noise, and behold a shaking, and the bones came together, bone to his bone.

8 And when I beheld, lo, the sinews and the flesh came up upon them, and the skin covered them above: but *there was* no breath in them.

9 Then said he unto me, Prophesy unto the wind, prophesy, son of man, and say to the wind, Thus says the Lord Yahweh; Come from the four winds, O breath, and breathe upon these slain, that they may live.

10 So I prophesied as he commanded me, and the breath came into them, and they lived, and stood up upon their feet, an exceedingly great army.

11 Then he said unto me, Son of man, these bones are the whole house of Israel: behold, they say, Our bones are dried, and our hope is lost: we are cut off for our parts.

12 Therefore prophesy and say to them, Thus says the Lord Yahweh; Behold, O my people, I will open your graves, and cause you to come up out of your graves, and bring you into the land of Israel.

13 And you shall know that I *am* Yahweh, when I have opened your graves, O my people, and brought you up out of your graves,

14 And shall put my spirit in you, and you shall live, and I shall place you in your own land: then shall you know that I Yahweh have spoken *it*, and performed *it*, says Yahweh.

15 ¶ The word of Yahweh came again unto me, saying,

16 Moreover, you son of man, take you one stick, and write upon it, For Judah, and for the children of Israel his companions: then take another stick, and write upon it, For Joseph, the stick of Ephraim, and *for* all the house of Israel his companions:

17 And join them one to another into one stick; and they shall become one in your hand.

18 And when the children of your people shall speak unto you, saying, Will you not show us what you *mean* by these?

19 Say unto them, Thus says the Lord Yahweh; Behold, I will take the stick of Joseph, which *is* in the hand of Ephraim, and the tribes of Israel his fellows, and will put them with him, *even* with the stick of Judah, and make them one stick, and they shall be one in my hand.

20 And the sticks whereon you write shall be in your hand before their eyes.

21 And say unto them, Thus says the Lord Yahweh; Behold, I will take the children of Israel from among the heathen, wherever they have gone, and will gather them on every side, and bring them into their own land:

22 And I will make them one nation in the land upon the mountains of Israel; and one king shall be king to them all: and they shall be no more two nations, neither shall they be divided into two kingdoms any more at all:

23 Neither shall they defile themselves any more with their idols, nor with their detestable things, nor with any of their transgressions: but I will save them out of all their dwelling places, wherein they have sinned, and will cleanse them: so shall they be my people, and I will be their God.

24 And David my servant *shall be* king over them; and they all shall have one shepherd: they shall also walk in my judgments, and observe my statutes, and do them.

25 And they shall dwell in the land that I have given unto Jacob my servant, wherein your fathers have dwelt; and they shall dwell therein, *even* they, and their children, and their children's children forever: and my servant David *shall be* their prince forever.

26 Moreover I will make a covenant of peace with them; it shall be an everlasting covenant with them: and I will place them, and multiply them, and will set my sanctuary in the midst of them forevermore.

27 My tabernacle also shall be with them: yes, I will be their God, and they shall be my people.

28 And the heathen shall know that I Yahweh do sanctify Israel, when my sanctuary shall be in the midst of them forevermore.

Ezekiel 38

38:1 ¶ And the word of Yahweh came unto me, saying,

2 Son of man, set your face against Gog, the land of Magog, the chief prince of Meshech and Tubal, and prophesy against him,

3 And say, Thus says the Lord Yahweh; Behold, I *am* against you, O Gog, the chief prince of Meshech and Tubal:

4 And I will turn you back, and put hooks into your jaws, and I will bring you forth, and all your army, horses and horsemen, all of them clothed with all sorts *of armor*, *even* a great company *with* bucklers and shields, all of them handling swords:

5 Persia, Ethiopia, and Libya with them: all of them with shield and helmet:

6 Gomer, and all his bands; the house of Togarmah of the north quarters, and all his bands: *and* many people with you.

7 Be you prepared, and prepare for yourself, you, and all your company that are assembled unto you, and be you a guard unto them.

8 After many days you shall be visited: in the latter years you shall come into the land *that is* brought back from the sword, *and is* gathered out of many people, against

the mountains of Israel, which have been always waste: but it is brought forth out of the nations, and they shall dwell safely all of them.

9 You shall ascend and come like a storm, you shall be like a cloud to cover the land, you, and all your bands, and many people with you.

10 Thus says the Lord Yahweh; It shall also come to pass, *that* at the same time shall things come into your mind, and you shall think an evil thought:

11 And you shall say, I will go up to the land of unwalled villages; I will go to them that are at rest, that dwell safely, all of them dwelling without walls, and having neither bars nor gates,

12 To take a spoil, and to take a prey; to turn your hand upon the desolate places *that are now* inhabited, and upon the people *that are* gathered out of the nations, which have gotten cattle and goods, that dwell in the midst of the land.

13 Sheba, and Dedan, and the merchants of Tarshish, with all the young lions thereof, shall say unto you, Have you come to take a spoil? have you gathered your company to take a prey? to carry away silver and gold, to take away cattle and goods, to take a great spoil?

14 ¶ Therefore, son of man, prophesy and say unto Gog, Thus says the Lord Yahweh; In that day when my people of Israel dwells safely, shall you not know *it*?

15 And you shall come from your place out of the north parts, you, and many people with you, all of them riding upon horses, a great company, and a mighty army:

16 And you shall come up against my people of Israel, as a cloud to cover the land; it shall be in the latter days, and I will bring you against my land, that the heathen may know me, when I shall be sanctified in you, O Gog, before their eyes.

17 Thus says the Lord Yahweh; *Are* you he of whom I have spoken in old time by my servants the prophets of Israel, which prophesied in those days *many* years that I would bring you against them?

18 And it shall come to pass at the same time when Gog shall come against the land of Israel, says the Lord Yahweh, *that* my fury shall come up in my face.

19 For in my jealousy *and* in the fire of my wrath have I spoken, Surely in that day there shall be a great shaking in the land of Israel;

20 So that the fishes of the sea, and the fowls of the heaven, and the beasts of the field, and all creeping things that creep upon the earth, and all the men that *are* upon the face of the earth, shall shake at my presence, and the mountains shall be thrown down, and the steep places shall fall, and every wall shall fall to the ground.

21 And I will call for a sword against him throughout all my mountains, says the Lord Yahweh: every man's sword shall be against his brother.

22 And I will plead against him with pestilence and with blood; and I will rain upon him, and upon his bands, and upon the many people that *are* with him, an overflowing rain, and great hailstones, fire, and brimstone.

23 Thus will I magnify myself, and sanctify myself; and I will be known in the eyes of many nations, and they shall know that I *am* Yahweh.

Ezekiel 39

39:1 ¶ Therefore, you son of man, prophesy against Gog, and say, Thus says the Lord Yahweh; Behold, I *am* against you, O Gog, the chief prince of Meshech and Tubal:

2 And I will turn you back, and leave but the sixth part of you, and will cause you to come up from the north parts, and will bring you upon the mountains of Israel:

3 And I will smite your bow out of your left hand, and will cause your arrows to fall out of your right hand.

4 You shall fall upon the mountains of Israel, you, and all your bands, and the people that *are* with you: I will give you to the ravenous birds of every sort, and *to* the beasts of the field to be devoured.

5 You shall fall upon the open field: for I have spoken *it*, says the Lord Yahweh.

6 And I will send a fire on Magog, and among them that dwell carelessly in the isles: and they shall know that I *am* Yahweh.

7 So will I make my holy name known in the midst of my people Israel; and I will not *let them* pollute my holy name any more: and the heathen shall know that I *am* Yahweh, the Holy One in Israel.

8 ¶ Behold, it has come, and it is done, says the Lord Yahweh; this *is* the day whereof I have spoken.

9 And they that dwell in the cities of Israel shall go forth, and shall set on fire and burn the weapons, both the shields and the bucklers, the bows and the arrows, and the javelins, and the spears, and they shall burn them with fire *for* seven years:

10 So that they shall take no wood out of the field, neither cut down *any* out of the forests; for they shall burn the weapons with fire: and they shall spoil those that spoiled them, and rob those that robbed them, says the Lord Yahweh.

11 And it shall come to pass in that day, *that* I will give unto Gog a place there of graves in Israel, the valley of the passengers on the east of the sea: and it shall stop the *noses* of the passengers: and there shall they bury Gog and all his multitude: and they shall call *it* The valley of Hamongog.

12 And seven months shall the house of Israel be burying of them, that they may cleanse the land.

13 Yes, all the people of the land shall bury *them*; and it shall be to them a renown the day that I shall be glorified, says the Lord Yahweh.

14 And they shall separate out men of continual employment, passing through the land to bury with the passengers those that remain upon the face of the earth, to cleanse it: after the end of seven months shall they search.

15 And the passengers *that* pass through the land, when *any* sees a man's bone, then shall he set up a sign by it, till the buriers have buried it in the valley of Hamongog.

16 And also the name of the city *shall be* Hamonah. Thus shall they cleanse the land.

17 And, you son of man, thus says the Lord Yahweh; Speak unto every feathered fowl, and to every beast of the field, Assemble yourselves, and come; gather yourselves on every side to my sacrifice that I do sacrifice for you, *even* a great sacrifice upon the mountains of Israel, that you may eat flesh, and drink blood.

18 You shall eat the flesh of the mighty, and drink the blood of the princes of the earth, of rams, of lambs, and of goats, of bullocks, all of them fatted calves of Bashan.

19 And you shall eat fat till you are full, and drink blood till you are drunken, of my sacrifice which I have sacrificed for you.

20 Thus you shall be filled at my table with horses and chariots, with mighty men, and with all men of war, says the Lord Yahweh.

21 And I will set my glory among the heathen, and all the heathen shall see my judgment that I have executed, and my hand that I have laid upon them.

22 So the house of Israel shall know that I *am* Yahweh their God from that day and forward.

23 ¶ And the heathen shall know that the house of Israel went into captivity for their iniquity: because they trespassed against me, therefore hid I my face from them, and gave them into the hand of their enemies: so fell they all by the sword.

24 According to their uncleanness and according to their transgressions have I done to them, and hidden my face from them.

25 Therefore thus says the Lord Yahweh; Now will I bring again the captivity of Jacob, and have mercy upon the whole house of Israel, and will be jealous for my holy name;

26 After that they have borne their shame, and all their trespasses whereby they have trespassed against me, when they dwelt safely in their land, and none made *them* afraid.

27 When I have brought them again from the people, and gathered them out of their enemies' lands, and am sanctified in them in the sight of many nations;

28 Then shall they know that I *am* Yahweh their God, which caused them to be led into captivity among the heathen: but I have gathered them unto their own land, and have left none of them any more there.

29 Neither will I hide my face any more from them: for I have poured out my spirit upon the house of Israel, says the Lord Yahweh.

Ezekiel 40

40:1 ¶ In the five and twentieth year of our captivity, in the beginning of the year, in the tenth *day* of the month, in the fourteenth year after that the city was smitten, in the very same day the hand of Yahweh was upon me, and brought me there.

2 In the visions of God brought he me into the land of Israel, and set me upon a very high mountain, by which *was* as the frame of a city on the south.

3 And he brought me there, and, behold, *there was* a man, whose appearance *was* like the appearance of brass, with a line of flax in his hand, and a measuring reed; and he stood in the gate.

4 And the man said to me, Son of man, behold with your eyes, and hear with your ears, and set your heart upon all that I shall show you; for to the intent that I might show *them* to you *are* you brought here: declare all that you see to the house of Israel.

5 ¶ And behold a wall on the outside of the house round about, and in the man's hand a measuring reed of six cubits *long* by the cubit and a hand breadth: so he measured the breadth of the building, one reed; and the height, one reed.

6 Then came he to the gate which looks toward the east, and went up the stairs thereof, and measured the threshold of the gate, *which was* one reed broad; and the other threshold *of the gate, which was* one reed broad.

7 And *every* little chamber *was* one reed long, and one reed broad; and between the little chambers *were* five cubits; and the threshold of the gate by the porch of the gate within *was* one reed.

8 He measured also the porch of the gate within, one reed.

9 Then measured he the porch of the gate, eight cubits; and the posts thereof, two cubits; and the porch of the gate *was* inward.

10 And the little chambers of the gate eastward *were* three on this side, and three on that side; they three *were* of one measure: and the posts had one measure on this side and on that side.

11 And he measured the breadth of the entry of the gate, ten cubits; *and* the length of the gate, thirteen cubits.

12 The space also before the little chambers *was* one cubit *on this side*, and the space *was* one cubit on that side: and the little chambers *were* six cubits on this side, and six cubits on that side.

13 He measured then the gate from the roof of *one* little chamber to the roof of another: the breadth *was* five and twenty cubits, door against door.

14 He made also posts of threescore cubits, even to the post of the court round about the gate.

15 And from the face of the gate of the entrance to the face of the porch of the inner gate *were* fifty cubits.

16 And *there were* narrow windows to the little chambers, and to their posts within the gate round about, and likewise to the arches: and windows *were* round about inward: and upon *each* post *were* palm trees.

17 Then brought he me into the outward court, and, lo, *there were* chambers, and a pavement made for the court round about: thirty chambers *were* upon the pavement.

18 And the pavement by the side of the gates over against the length of the gates *was* the lower pavement.

19 Then he measured the breadth from the forefront of the lower gate to the forefront of the inner court outside, a hundred cubits eastward and northward.

Ezekiel 40

20 And the gate of the outward court that looked toward the north, he measured the length thereof, and the breadth thereof.

21 And the little chambers thereof *were* three on this side and three on that side; and the posts thereof and the arches thereof were after the measure of the first gate: the length thereof *was* fifty cubits, and the breadth five and twenty cubits.

22 And their windows, and their arches, and their palm trees, *were* after the measure of the gate that looks toward the east; and they went up to it by seven steps; and the arches thereof *were* before them.

23 And the gate of the inner court *was* over against the gate toward the north, and toward the east; and he measured from gate to gate a hundred cubits.

24 After that he brought me toward the south, and behold a gate toward the south: and he measured the posts thereof and the arches thereof according to these measures.

25 And *there were* windows in it and in the arches thereof round about, like those windows: the length *was* fifty cubits, and the breadth five and twenty cubits.

26 And *there were* seven steps to go up to it, and the arches thereof *were* before them: and it had palm trees, one on this side, and another on that side, upon the posts thereof.

27 ¶ And *there was* a gate in the inner court toward the south: and he measured from gate to gate toward the south a hundred cubits.

28 And he brought me to the inner court by the south gate: and he measured the south gate according to these measures;

29 And the little chambers thereof, and the posts thereof, and the arches thereof, according to these measures: and *there were* windows in it and in the arches thereof round about: *it was* fifty cubits long, and five and twenty cubits broad.

30 And the arches round about *were* five and twenty cubits long, and five cubits broad.

31 And the arches thereof *were* toward the outer court; and palm trees *were* upon the posts thereof: and the going up to it *had* eight steps.

32 And he brought me into the inner court toward the east: and he measured the gate according to these measures.

33 And the little chambers thereof, and the posts thereof, and the arches thereof, *were* according to these measures: and *there were* windows therein and in the arches thereof round about: *it was* fifty cubits long, and five and twenty cubits broad.

34 And the arches thereof *were* toward the outward court; and palm trees *were* upon the posts thereof, on this side, and on that side: and the going up to it *had* eight steps.

35 And he brought me to the north gate, and measured *it* according to these measures;

36 The little chambers thereof, the posts thereof, and the arches thereof, and the windows to it round about: the length *was* fifty cubits, and the breadth five and twenty cubits.

37 And the posts thereof *were* toward the outer court; and palm trees *were* upon the posts thereof, on this side, and on that side: and the going up to it *had* eight steps.

38 And the chambers and the entries thereof *were* by the posts of the gates, where they washed the burnt offering.

39 ¶ And in the porch of the gate *were* two tables on this side, and two tables on that side, to slay thereon the burnt offering and the sin offering and the trespass offering.

40 And at the side without, as one goes up to the entry of the north gate, *were* two tables; and on the other side, which *was* at the porch of the gate, *were* two tables.

41 Four tables *were* on this side, and four tables on that side, by the side of the gate; eight tables, whereupon they slew *their sacrifices*.

42 And the four tables *were* of hewn stone for the burnt offering, of a cubit and a half long, and a cubit and a half broad, and one cubit high: whereupon also they laid the instruments with which they slew the burnt offering and the sacrifice.

43 And within *were* hooks, a hand broad, fastened round about: and upon the tables *was* the flesh of the offering.

44 And outside the inner gate *were* the chambers of the singers in the inner court, which *was* at the side of the north gate; and their prospect *was* toward the south: one at the side of the east gate *having* the prospect toward the north.

45 And he said to me, This chamber, whose prospect *is* toward the south, *is* for the priests, the keepers of the charge of the house.

46 And the chamber whose prospect *is* toward the north *is* for the priests, the keepers of the charge of the altar: these *are* the sons of Zadok among the sons of Levi, which come near to Yahweh to minister to him.

47 So he measured the court, a hundred cubits long, and a hundred cubits broad, foursquare; and the altar *that was* before the house.

48 And he brought me to the porch of the house, and measured *each* post of the porch, five cubits on this side, and five cubits on that side: and the breadth of the gate *was* three cubits on this side, and three cubits on that side.

49 The length of the porch *was* twenty cubits, and the breadth eleven cubits; and *he brought me* by the steps whereby they went up to it: and *there were* pillars by the posts, one on this side, and another on that side.

Ezekiel 41

41:1 ¶ Afterward he brought me to the temple, and measured the posts, six cubits broad on the one side, and six cubits broad on the other side, *which was* the breadth of the tabernacle.

2 And the breadth of the door *was* ten cubits; and the sides of the door *were* five cubits on the one side, and five cubits

on the other side: and he measured the length thereof, forty cubits: and the breadth, twenty cubits.

3 Then went he inward, and measured the post of the door, two cubits; and the door, six cubits; and the breadth of the door, seven cubits.

4 So he measured the length thereof, twenty cubits; and the breadth, twenty cubits, before the temple: and he said to me, This *is* the most holy *place*.

5 After he measured the wall of the house, six cubits; and the breadth of *every* side chamber, four cubits, round about the house on every side.

6 And the side chambers *were* three, one over another, and thirty in order; and they entered into the wall which *was* of the house for the side chambers round about, that they might be held, but they were not held in the wall of the house.

7 And *there was* an enlarging, and a winding about still upward to the side chambers: for the winding about of the house went still upward round about the house: therefore the breadth of the house *was still* upward, and so increased *from* the lowest *chamber* to the highest by the midst.

8 I saw also the height of the house round about: the foundations of the side chambers *were* a full reed of six great cubits.

9 The thickness of the wall, which *was* for the side chamber without, *was* five cubits: and *that* which *was* left *was* the place of the side chambers that *were* within.

10 And between the chambers *was* the wideness of twenty cubits round about the house on every side.

11 And the doors of the side chambers *were* toward *the place that was* left, one door toward the north, and another door toward the south: and the breadth of the place that was left *was* five cubits round about.

12 ¶ Now the building that *was* before the separate place at the end toward the west *was* seventy cubits broad; and the wall of the building *was* five cubits thick round about, and the length thereof ninety cubits.

13 So he measured the house, a hundred cubits long; and the separate place, and the building, with the walls thereof, a hundred cubits long;

14 Also the breadth of the face of the house, and of the separate place toward the east, a hundred cubits.

15 And he measured the length of the building over against the separate place which *was* behind it, and the galleries thereof on the one side and on the other side a hundred cubits, with the inner temple, and the porches of the court;

16 The door posts, and the narrow windows, and the galleries round about on their three stories, over against the door, paneled with wood round about, and from the ground up to the windows, and the windows *were* covered;

17 To that above the door, even to the inner house, and outside, and by all the wall round about within and without, by measure.

18 And *it was* made with cherubims and palm trees, so that a palm tree *was* between a cherub and a cherub; and *every* cherub had two faces;

19 So that the face of a man *was* toward the palm tree on the one side, and the face of a young lion toward the palm tree on the other side: *it was* made through all the house round about.

20 From the ground to above the door *were* cherubims and palm trees made, and *on* the wall of the temple.

21 The posts of the temple *were* squared, *and* the face of the sanctuary; the appearance *of the one* as the appearance *of the other*.

22 The altar of wood *was* three cubits high, and the length thereof two cubits; and the corners thereof, and the length thereof, and the walls thereof, *were* of wood: and he said to me, This *is* the table that *is* before Yahweh.

23 And the temple and the sanctuary had two doors.

24 And the doors had two leaves *apiece*, two turning leaves; two *leaves* for the one door, and two leaves for the other *door*.

25 And *there were* made on them, on the doors of the temple, cherubims and palm trees, like as *were* made upon the walls; and *there were* thick planks upon the face of the porch outside.

26 And *there were* narrow windows and palm trees on the one side and on the other side, on the sides of the porch, and *upon* the side chambers of the house, and thick planks.

Ezekiel 42

42:1 ¶ Then he brought me forth into the outer court, the way toward the north: and he brought me into the chamber that *was* over against the separate place, and which *was* before the building toward the north.

2 Before the length of a hundred cubits *was* the north door, and the breadth *was* fifty cubits.

3 Over against the twenty *cubits* which *were* for the inner court, and over against the pavement which *was* for the outer court, *was* gallery against gallery in three *stories*.

4 And before the chambers *was* a walk of ten cubits breadth inward, a way of one cubit; and their doors toward the north.

5 Now the upper chambers *were* shorter: for the galleries were higher than these, than the lower, and than the middlemost of the building.

6 For they *were* in three *stories*, but had not pillars as the pillars of the courts: therefore *the building* was straitened more than the lowest and the middlemost from the ground.

7 And the wall that *was* outside over against the chambers, toward the outer court on the forepart of the chambers, the length thereof *was* fifty cubits.

8 For the length of the chambers that *were* in the outer court *was* fifty cubits: and, lo, before the temple *was* a hundred cubits.

9 And from under these chambers *was* the entry on the east side, as one goes into them from the outer court.

10 The chambers *were* in the thickness of the wall of the court toward the east, over against the separate place, and over against the building.

Ezekiel 42

11 And the way before them *was* like the appearance of the chambers which *were* toward the north, as long as they, *and* as broad as they: and all their goings out *were* both according to their fashions, and according to their doors.

12 And according to the doors of the chambers that *were* toward the south *was* a door in the head of the way, *even* the way directly before the wall toward the east, as one enters into them.

13 Then said he to me, The north chambers *and* the south chambers, which *are* before the separate place, they *are* holy chambers, where the priests that approach unto Yahweh shall eat the most holy things: there shall they lay the most holy things, and the meat offering, and the sin offering, and the trespass offering; for the place *is* holy.

14 When the priests enter therein, then shall they not go out of the holy *place* into the outer court, but there they shall lay their garments wherein they minister; for they *are* holy; and shall put on other garments, and shall approach to *those things* which *are* for the people.

15 ¶ Now when he had made an end of measuring the inner house, he brought me forth toward the gate whose prospect *is* toward the east, and measured it round about.

16 He measured the east side with the measuring reed, five hundred reeds, with the measuring reed round about.

17 He measured the north side, five hundred reeds, with the measuring reed round about.

18 He measured the south side, five hundred reeds, with the measuring reed.

19 He turned about to the west side, *and* measured five hundred reeds with the measuring reed.

20 He measured it by the four sides: it had a wall round about, five hundred *reeds* long, and five hundred broad, to make a separation between the sanctuary and the profane place.

Ezekiel 43

43:1 ¶ Afterward he brought me to the gate, *even* the gate that looks toward the east:

2 And, behold, the glory of the God of Israel came from the way of the east: and his voice *was* like a noise of many waters: and the earth shined with his glory.

3 And *it was* according to the appearance of the vision which I saw, *even* according to the vision that I saw when I came to destroy the city: and the visions *were* like the vision that I saw by the river Chebar; and I fell upon my face.

4 And the glory of Yahweh came into the house by the way of the gate whose prospect *is* toward the east.

5 So the spirit took me up, and brought me into the inner court; and, behold, the glory of Yahweh filled the house.

6 And I heard *him* speaking to me out of the house; and the man stood by me.

7 ¶ And he said to me, Son of man, the place of my throne, and the place of the soles of my feet, where I will dwell in the midst of the children of Israel forever, and my holy name, shall the house of Israel no more defile, *neither* they, nor their kings, by their whoredom, nor by the carcasses of their kings in their high places.

8 In their setting of their threshold by my thresholds, and their post by my posts, and the wall between me and them, they have even defiled my holy name by their abominations that they have committed: therefore I have consumed them in my anger.

9 Now let them put away their whoredom, and the carcasses of their kings, far from me, and I will dwell in the midst of them forever.

10 You son of man, show the house to the house of Israel, that they may be ashamed of their iniquities: and let them measure the pattern.

11 And if they are ashamed of all that they have done, show them the form of the house, and the fashion thereof, and the goings out thereof, and the comings in thereof, and all the forms thereof, and all the ordinances thereof, and all the forms thereof, and all the laws thereof: and write *it* in their sight, that they may keep the whole form thereof, and all the ordinances thereof, and do them.

12 This *is* the law of the house; Upon the top of the mountain the whole limit thereof round about *shall be* most holy. Behold, this *is* the law of the house.

13 ¶ And these *are* the measures of the altar after the cubits: The cubit *is* a cubit and a hand breadth; even the bottom *shall be* a cubit, and the breadth a cubit, and the border thereof by the edge thereof round about *shall be* a span: and this *shall be* the higher place of the altar.

14 And from the bottom *upon* the ground *even* to the lower ledge *shall be* two cubits, and the breadth one cubit; and from the lesser ledge *even* to the greater ledge *shall be* four cubits, and the breadth *one* cubit.

15 So the altar *shall be* four cubits; and from the altar and upward *shall be* four horns.

16 And the altar *shall be* twelve *cubits* long, twelve broad, square in the four squares thereof.

17 And the ledge *shall be* fourteen *cubits* long and fourteen broad in the four squares thereof; and the border about it *shall be* half a cubit; and the bottom thereof *shall be* a cubit about; and his stairs shall look toward the east.

18 And he said to me, Son of man, thus says the Lord Yahweh; These *are* the ordinances of the altar in the day when they shall make it, to offer burnt offerings thereon, and to sprinkle blood thereon.

19 And you shall give to the priests the Levites that are of the seed of Zadok, which approach to me, to minister to me, says the Lord Yahweh, a young bullock for a sin offering.

20 And you shall take of the blood thereof, and put *it* on the four horns of it, and on the four corners of the ledge, and upon the border round about: thus shall you cleanse and purge it.

21 You shall take the bullock also of the sin offering, and he shall burn it in the appointed place of the house, outside the sanctuary.

22 And on the second day you shall offer a kid of the goats without blemish for a sin offering; and they shall cleanse the altar, as they did cleanse *it* with the bullock.
23 When you have made an end of cleansing *it*, you shall offer a young bullock without blemish, and a ram out of the flock without blemish.
24 And you shall offer them before Yahweh, and the priests shall cast salt upon them, and they shall offer them up *for* a burnt offering unto Yahweh.
25 Seven days shall you prepare every day a goat *for* a sin offering: they shall also prepare a young bullock, and a ram out of the flock, without blemish.
26 Seven days shall they purge the altar and purify it; and they shall consecrate themselves.
27 And when these days are expired, it shall be, *that* on the eighth day, and *so* forward, the priests shall make your burnt offerings upon the altar, and your peace offerings; and I will accept you, says the Lord Yahweh.

Ezekiel 44

44:1 ¶ Then he brought me back the way of the gate of the outward sanctuary which looks toward the east; and it *was* shut.
2 Then said Yahweh to me; This gate shall be shut, it shall not be opened, and no man shall enter in by it; because Yahweh, the God of Israel, has entered in by it, therefore it shall be shut.
3 *It is* for the prince; the prince, he shall sit in it to eat bread before Yahweh; he shall enter by the way of the porch of *that* gate, and shall go out by the way of the same.
4 ¶ Then brought he me the way of the north gate before the house: and I looked, and, behold, the glory of Yahweh filled the house of Yahweh: and I fell upon my face.
5 And Yahweh said to me, Son of man, mark well, and behold with your eyes, and hear with your ears all that I say to you concerning all the ordinances of the house of Yahweh, and all the laws thereof; and mark well the entering in of the house, with every going forth of the sanctuary.
6 And you shall say to the rebellious, *even* to the house of Israel, Thus says the Lord Yahweh; O you house of Israel, let it suffice you of all your abominations,
7 In that you have brought *into my sanctuary* strangers, uncircumcised in heart, and uncircumcised in flesh, to be in my sanctuary, to pollute it, *even* my house, when you offer my bread, the fat and the blood, and they have broken my covenant because of all your abominations.
8 And you have not kept the charge of my holy things: but you have set keepers of my charge in my sanctuary for yourselves.
9 Thus says the Lord Yahweh; No stranger, uncircumcised in heart, nor uncircumcised in flesh, shall enter into my sanctuary, of any stranger that *is* among the children of Israel.
10 ¶ And the Levites that have gone away far from me, when Israel went astray, which went astray away from me after their idols; they shall even bear their iniquity.
11 Yet they shall be ministers in my sanctuary, *having* charge at the gates of the house, and ministering to the house: they shall slay the burnt offering and the sacrifice for the people, and they shall stand before them to minister to them.
12 Because they ministered to them before their idols, and caused the house of Israel to fall into iniquity; therefore have I lifted up my hand against them, says the Lord Yahweh, and they shall bear their iniquity.
13 And they shall not come near to me, to do the office of a priest to me, nor to come near to any of my holy things, in the most holy *place*: but they shall bear their shame, and their abominations which they have committed.
14 But I will make them keepers of the charge of the house, for all the service thereof, and for all that shall be done therein.
15 But the priests the Levites, the sons of Zadok, that kept the charge of my sanctuary when the children of Israel went astray from me, they shall come near to me to minister to me, and they shall stand before me to offer to me the fat and the blood, says the Lord Yahweh:
16 They shall enter into my sanctuary, and they shall come near to my table, to minister to me, and they shall keep my charge.
17 ¶ And it shall come to pass, *that* when they enter in at the gates of the inner court, they shall be clothed with linen garments; and no wool shall come upon them, while they minister in the gates of the inner court, and within.
18 They shall have linen bonnets upon their heads, and shall have linen breeches upon their loins: they shall not gird *themselves* with anything that causes sweat.
19 And when they go forth into the outer court, *even* into the outer court to the people, they shall put off their garments wherein they ministered, and lay them in the holy chambers, and they shall put on other garments; and they shall not sanctify the people with their garments.
20 Neither shall they shave their heads, nor allow their locks to grow long; they shall only poll their heads.
21 Neither shall any priest drink wine, when they enter into the inner court.
22 Neither shall they take for their wives a widow, nor her that is put away: but they shall take maidens of the seed of the house of Israel, or a widow that had a priest before.
23 And they shall teach my people *the difference* between the holy and profane, and cause them to discern between the unclean and the clean.
24 And in controversy they shall stand in judgment; *and* they shall judge it according to my judgments: and they shall keep my laws and my statutes in all my assemblies; and they shall hallow my sabbaths.
25 And they shall come at no dead person to defile themselves: but for father, or for mother, or for son, or for daughter, for brother, or for sister that has had no husband, they may defile themselves.

Ezekiel 44

26 And after he is cleansed, they shall number unto him seven days.

27 And in the day that he goes into the sanctuary, to the inner court, to minister in the sanctuary, he shall offer his sin offering, says the Lord Yahweh.

28 And it shall be to them for an inheritance: I *am* their inheritance: and you shall give them no possession in Israel: I *am* their possession.

29 They shall eat the meat offering, and the sin offering, and the trespass offering; and every dedicated thing in Israel shall be theirs.

30 And the first of all the firstfruits of all *things*, and every oblation of all, of every *sort* of your oblations, shall be the priest's: you shall also give to the priest the first of your dough, that he may cause the blessing to rest in your house.

31 The priests shall not eat of anything that is dead of itself, or torn, whether it is fowl or beast.

Ezekiel 45

45:1 ¶ Moreover, when you shall divide by lot the land for inheritance, you shall offer an oblation unto Yahweh, a holy portion of the land: the length *shall be* the length of five and twenty thousand *reeds*, and the breadth *shall be* ten thousand. This *shall be* holy in all the borders thereof round about.

2 Of this there shall be for the sanctuary five hundred *in length*, with five hundred *in breadth*, square round about; and fifty cubits round about for the suburbs thereof.

3 And of this measure shall you measure the length of five and twenty thousand, and the breadth of ten thousand: and in it shall be the sanctuary *and* the most holy *place*.

4 The holy *portion* of the land shall be for the priests the ministers of the sanctuary, which shall come near to minister unto Yahweh: and it shall be a place for their houses, and a holy place for the sanctuary.

5 And the five and twenty thousand of length, and the ten thousand of breadth, shall also the Levites, the ministers of the house, have for themselves, for a possession for twenty chambers.

6 And you shall appoint the possession of the city five thousand broad, and five and twenty thousand long, over against the oblation of the holy *portion*: it shall be for the whole house of Israel.

7 And a *portion shall be* for the prince on the one side and on the other side of the oblation of the holy *portion*, and of the possession of the city, before the oblation of the holy *portion*, and before the possession of the city, from the west side westward, and from the east side eastward: and the length *shall be* over against one of the portions, from the west border to the east border.

8 In the land shall be his possession in Israel: and my princes shall no more oppress my people; and *the rest of* the land shall they give to the house of Israel according to their tribes.

9 ¶ Thus says the Lord Yahweh; Let it suffice you, O princes of Israel: remove violence and spoil, and execute judgment and justice, take away your exactions from my people, says the Lord Yahweh.

10 You shall have just balances, and a just ephah, and a just bath.

11 The ephah and the bath shall be of one measure, that the bath may contain the tenth part of a homer, and the ephah the tenth part of a homer: the measure thereof shall be after the homer.

12 And the shekel *shall be* twenty gerahs: twenty shekels, five and twenty shekels, fifteen shekels, shall be your maneh.

13 ¶ This *is* the oblation that you shall offer; the sixth part of an ephah of a homer of wheat, and you shall give the sixth part of an ephah of a homer of barley:

14 Concerning the ordinance of oil, the bath of oil, *you shall offer* the tenth part of a bath out of the kor, *which is* a homer of ten baths; for ten baths *are* a homer:

15 And one lamb out of the flock, out of two hundred, out of the fat pastures of Israel; for a meat offering, and for a burnt offering, and for peace offerings, to make reconciliation for them, says the Lord Yahweh.

16 All the people of the land shall give this oblation for the prince in Israel.

17 And it shall be the prince's part *to give* burnt offerings, and meat offerings, and drink offerings, in the feasts, and in the new moons, and in the sabbaths, in all solemnities of the house of Israel: he shall prepare the sin offering, and the meat offering, and the burnt offering, and the peace offerings, to make reconciliation for the house of Israel.

18 Thus says the Lord Yahweh; In the first *month*, in the first *day* of the month, you shall take a young bullock without blemish, and cleanse the sanctuary:

19 And the priest shall take of the blood of the sin offering, and put *it* upon the posts of the house, and upon the four corners of the ledge of the altar, and upon the posts of the gate of the inner court.

20 And so you shall do the seventh *day* of the month for every one that errs, and for *him that is* simple: so shall you reconcile the house.

21 In the first *month*, in the fourteenth day of the month, you shall have the passover, a feast of seven days; unleavened bread shall be eaten.

22 And upon that day shall the prince prepare for himself and for all the people of the land a bullock *for* a sin offering.

23 And seven days of the feast he shall prepare a burnt offering to Yahweh, seven bullocks and seven rams without blemish daily the seven days; and a kid of the goats daily *for* a sin offering.

24 And he shall prepare a meat offering of an ephah for a bullock, and an ephah for a ram, and a hin of oil for an ephah.

25 In the seventh *month*, in the fifteenth day of the month, shall he do the like in the feast of the seven days, according to the sin offering, according to the burnt offering, and according to the meat offering, and according to the oil.

Ezekiel 46

46:1 ¶ Thus says the Lord Yahweh; The gate of the inner court that looks toward the east shall be shut the six working days; but on the sabbath it shall be opened, and in the day of the new moon it shall be opened.

2 And the prince shall enter by the way of the porch of *that* gate without, and shall stand by the post of the gate, and the priests shall prepare his burnt offering and his peace offerings, and he shall worship at the threshold of the gate: then he shall go forth; but the gate shall not be shut until the evening.

3 Likewise the people of the land shall worship at the door of this gate before Yahweh in the sabbaths and in the new moons.

4 And the burnt offering that the prince shall offer unto Yahweh in the sabbath day *shall be* six lambs without blemish, and a ram without blemish.

5 And the meat offering *shall be* an ephah for a ram, and the meat offering for the lambs as he shall be able to give, and a hin of oil to an ephah.

6 And in the day of the new moon *it shall be* a young bullock without blemish, and six lambs, and a ram: they shall be without blemish.

7 And he shall prepare a meat offering, an ephah for a bullock, and an ephah for a ram, and for the lambs according as his hand shall attain to, and a hin of oil to an ephah.

8 And when the prince shall enter, he shall go in by the way of the porch of *that* gate, and he shall go forth by the way thereof.

9 But when the people of the land shall come before Yahweh in the solemn feasts, he that enters in by the way of the north gate to worship shall go out by the way of the south gate; and he that enters by the way of the south gate shall go forth by the way of the north gate: he shall not return by the way of the gate whereby he came in, but shall go forth over against it.

10 And the prince in the midst of them, when they go in, shall go in; and when they go forth, shall go forth.

11 And in the feasts and in the solemnities the meat offering shall be an ephah to a bullock, and an ephah to a ram, and to the lambs as he is able to give, and a hin of oil to an ephah.

12 Now when the prince shall prepare a voluntary burnt offering or peace offerings voluntarily unto Yahweh, *one* shall then open him the gate that looks toward the east, and he shall prepare his burnt offering and his peace offerings, as he did on the sabbath day: then he shall go forth; and after his going forth *one* shall shut the gate.

13 You shall daily prepare a burnt offering unto Yahweh *of* a lamb of the first year without blemish: you shall prepare it every morning.

14 And you shall prepare a meat offering for it every morning, the sixth part of an ephah, and the third part of a hin of oil, to temper with the fine flour; a meat offering continually by a perpetual ordinance unto Yahweh.

15 Thus shall they prepare the lamb, and the meat offering, and the oil, every morning *for* a continual burnt offering.

16 ¶ Thus says the Lord Yahweh; If the prince gives a gift to any of his sons, the inheritance thereof shall be his sons'; it *shall be* their possession by inheritance.

17 But if he gives a gift of his inheritance to one of his servants, then it shall be his unto the year of liberty; after it shall return to the prince: but his inheritance shall be his sons' for them.

18 Moreover the prince shall not take of the people's inheritance by oppression, to thrust them out of their possession; *but* he shall give his sons inheritance out of his own possession: that my people be not scattered every man from his possession.

19 ¶ After he brought me through the entry, which *was* at the side of the gate, into the holy chambers of the priests, which looked toward the north: and, behold, there *was* a place on the two sides westward.

20 Then said he to me, This *is* the place where the priests shall boil the trespass offering and the sin offering, where they shall bake the meat offering; that they bear *them* not out into the outer court, to sanctify the people.

21 Then he brought me forth into the outer court, and caused me to pass by the four corners of the court; and, behold, in every corner of the court *there was* a court.

22 In the four corners of the court *there were* courts joined of forty *cubits* long and thirty broad: these four corners *were* of one measure.

23 And *there was* a row *of building* round about in them, round about them four, and *it was* made with boiling places under the rows round about.

24 Then said he to me, These *are* the places of them that boil, where the ministers of the house shall boil the sacrifice of the people.

Ezekiel 47

47:1 ¶ Afterward he brought me again to the door of the house; and, behold, waters issued out from under the threshold of the house eastward: for the forefront of the house *stood toward* the east, and the waters came down from under from the right side of the house, at the south *side* of the altar.

2 Then brought he me out of the way of the gate northward, and led me about the way outside to the outer gate by the way that looks eastward; and, behold, there ran out waters on the right side.

3 And when the man that had the line in his hand went forth eastward, he measured a thousand cubits, and he brought me through the waters; the waters *were* to the ankles.

4 Again he measured a thousand, and brought me through the waters; the waters *were* to the knees. Again he measured a thousand, and brought me through; the waters *were* to the loins.

5 Afterward he measured a thousand; *and it was* a river that I could not pass over: for the waters had risen, waters to swim in, a river that could not be passed over.

Ezekiel 47

6 And he said to me, Son of man, have you seen *this*? Then he brought me, and caused me to return to the bank of the river.

7 Now when I had returned, behold, at the bank of the river *were* very many trees on the one side and on the other.

8 Then said he to me, These waters issue out toward the east country, and go down into the desert, and go into the sea: *which being* brought forth into the sea, the waters shall be healed.

9 And it shall come to pass, *that* every thing that lives, which moves, wherever the rivers shall come, shall live: and there shall be a very great multitude of fish, because these waters shall come there: for they shall be healed; and every thing shall live wherever the river comes.

10 And it shall come to pass, *that* the fishers shall stand upon it from Engedi even to Eneglaim; they shall be a *place* to spread forth nets; their fish shall be according to their kinds, as the fish of the great sea, exceedingly many.

11 But the miry places thereof and the marshes thereof shall not be healed; they shall be given to salt.

12 And by the river upon the bank thereof, on this side and on that side, shall grow all trees for food, whose leaf shall not fade, neither shall the fruit thereof be consumed: it shall bring forth new fruit according to his months, because their waters they issued out of the sanctuary: and the fruit thereof shall be for food, and the leaf thereof for medicine.

13 ¶ Thus says the Lord Yahweh; This *shall be* the border, whereby you shall inherit the land according to the twelve tribes of Israel: Joseph *shall have two* portions.

14 And you shall inherit it, one as well as another: *concerning* the which I lifted up my hand to give it to your fathers: and this land shall fall to you for inheritance.

15 And this *shall be* the border of the land toward the north side, from the great sea, the way of Hethlon, as men go to Zedad;

16 Hamath, Berothah, Sibraim, which *is* between the border of Damascus and the border of Hamath; Hazarhatticon, which *is* by the coast of Hauran.

17 And the border from the sea shall be Hazarenan, the border of Damascus, and the north northward, and the border of Hamath. And *this is* the north side.

18 And the east side you shall measure from Hauran, and from Damascus, and from Gilead, and from the land of Israel *by the* Jordan, from the border to the east sea. And *this is* the east side.

19 And the south side southward, from Tamar *even* to the waters of strife *in* Kadesh, the river to the great sea. And *this is* the south side southward.

20 The west side also *shall be* the great sea from the border, till a man comes over against Hamath. This *is* the west side.

21 So shall you divide this land to you according to the tribes of Israel.

22 And it shall come to pass, *that* you shall divide it by lot for an inheritance unto you, and to the strangers that sojourn among you, which shall beget children among you: and they shall be to you as born in the country among the children of Israel; they shall have inheritance with you among the tribes of Israel.

23 And it shall come to pass, *that* in whatever tribe the stranger sojourns, there shall you give *him* his inheritance, says the Lord Yahweh.

Ezekiel 48

48:1 ¶ Now these *are* the names of the tribes. From the north end to the coast of the way of Hethlon, as one goes to Hamath, Hazarenan, the border of Damascus northward, to the coast of Hamath; for these are his sides east *and* west; a *portion for* Dan.

2 And by the border of Dan, from the east side to the west side, a *portion for* Asher.

3 And by the border of Asher, from the east side even to the west side, a *portion for* Naphtali.

4 And by the border of Naphtali, from the east side to the west side, a *portion for* Manasseh.

5 And by the border of Manasseh, from the east side to the west side, a *portion for* Ephraim.

6 And by the border of Ephraim, from the east side even to the west side, a *portion for* Reuben.

7 And by the border of Reuben, from the east side to the west side, a *portion for* Judah.

8 And by the border of Judah, from the east side to the west side, shall be the offering which you shall offer of five and twenty thousand *reeds in* breadth, and *in* length as one of the *other* parts, from the east side to the west side: and the sanctuary shall be in the midst of it.

9 The oblation that you shall offer unto Yahweh *shall be* of five and twenty thousand in length, and of ten thousand in breadth.

10 And for them, *even* for the priests, shall be *this* holy oblation; toward the north five and twenty thousand *in length*, and toward the west ten thousand in breadth, and toward the east ten thousand in breadth, and toward the south five and twenty thousand in length: and the sanctuary of Yahweh shall be in the midst thereof.

11 *It shall be* for the priests that are sanctified of the sons of Zadok; which have kept my charge, which went not astray when the children of Israel went astray, as the Levites went astray.

12 And *this* oblation of the land that is offered shall be to them a thing most holy by the border of the Levites.

13 And over against the border of the priests the Levites *shall have* five and twenty thousand in length, and ten thousand in breadth: all the length *shall be* five and twenty thousand, and the breadth ten thousand.

14 And they shall not sell of it, neither exchange, nor alienate the firstfruits of the land: for *it is* holy unto Yahweh.

15 And the five thousand, that are left in the breadth over against the five and twenty thousand, shall be a profane *place* for the city, for dwelling, and for suburbs: and the city shall be in the midst thereof.

16 And these *shall be* the measures thereof; the north side four thousand and five hundred, and the south side four thousand and five hundred, and on the east side four thousand and five hundred, and the west side four thousand and five hundred.

17 And the suburbs of the city shall be toward the north two hundred and fifty, and toward the south two hundred and fifty, and toward the east two hundred and fifty, and toward the west two hundred and fifty.

18 And the residue in length over against the oblation of the holy *portion shall be* ten thousand eastward, and ten thousand westward: and it shall be over against the oblation of the holy *portion*; and the increase thereof shall be for food to them that serve the city.

19 And they that serve the city shall serve it out of all the tribes of Israel.

20 All the oblation *shall be* five and twenty thousand by five and twenty thousand: you shall offer the holy oblation foursquare, with the possession of the city.

21 And the residue *shall be* for the prince, on the one side and on the other of the holy oblation, and of the possession of the city, over against the five and twenty thousand of the oblation toward the east border, and westward over against the five and twenty thousand toward the west border, over against the portions for the prince: and it shall be the holy oblation; and the sanctuary of the house *shall be* in the midst thereof.

22 Moreover from the possession of the Levites, and from the possession of the city, *being* in the midst *of that* which is the prince's, between the border of Judah and the border of Benjamin, shall be for the prince.

23 As for the rest of the tribes, from the east side to the west side, Benjamin *shall have* a *portion*.

24 And by the border of Benjamin, from the east side to the west side, Simeon *shall have* a *portion*.

25 And by the border of Simeon, from the east side to the west side, Issachar a *portion*.

26 And by the border of Issachar, from the east side to the west side, Zebulun a *portion*.

27 And by the border of Zebulun, from the east side to the west side, Gad a *portion*.

28 And by the border of Gad, at the south side southward, the border shall be even from Tamar *to* the waters of strife *in* Kadesh, *and* to the river toward the great sea.

29 This *is* the land which you shall divide by lot to the tribes of Israel for inheritance, and these *are* their portions, says the Lord Yahweh.

30 And these *are* the goings out of the city on the north side, four thousand and five hundred measures.

31 ¶ And the gates of the city *shall be* after the names of the tribes of Israel: three gates northward; one gate of Reuben, one gate of Judah, one gate of Levi.

32 And at the east side four thousand and five hundred: and three gates; and one gate of Joseph, one gate of Benjamin, one gate of Dan.

33 And at the south side four thousand and five hundred measures: and three gates; one gate of Simeon, one gate of Issachar, one gate of Zebulun.

34 At the west side four thousand and five hundred, *with* their three gates; one gate of Gad, one gate of Asher, one gate of Naphtali.

35 *It was* round about eighteen thousand *measures*: and the name of the city from *that* day *shall be*, Yahweh *is* there.

Daniel

Daniel 1

1:1 ¶ In the third year of the reign of Jehoiakim king of Judah came Nebuchadnezzar king of Babylon to Jerusalem, and besieged it.

2 And the Lord gave Jehoiakim king of Judah into his hand, with part of the vessels of the house of God: which he carried into the land of Shinar to the house of his god; and he brought the vessels into the treasure house of his god.

3 And the king spoke to Ashpenaz the master of his eunuchs, that he should bring *certain* of the children of Israel, and of the king's seed, and of the princes;

4 Children in whom *was* no blemish, but well favored, and skillful in all wisdom, and cunning in knowledge, and understanding science, and such as *had* ability in them to stand in the king's palace, and whom they might teach the learning and the tongue of the Chaldeans.

5 And the king appointed them a daily provision of the king's meat, and of the wine which he drank: so nourishing them *for* three years, that at the end thereof they might stand before the king.

6 Now among these were of the children of Judah, Daniel, Hananiah, Mishael, and Azariah:

7 Unto whom the prince of the eunuchs gave names: for he gave to Daniel *the name* of Belteshazzar; and to Hananiah, of Shadrach; and to Mishael, of Meshach; and to Azariah, of Abednego.

8 ¶ But Daniel purposed in his heart that he would not defile himself with the portion of the king's meat, nor with the wine which he drank: therefore he requested of the prince of the eunuchs that he might not defile himself.

9 Now God had brought Daniel into favor and tender love with the prince of the eunuchs.

10 And the prince of the eunuchs said to Daniel, I fear my lord the king, who has appointed your meat and your drink: for why should he see your faces worse looking than the children which *are* of your sort? then shall you make *me* endanger my head to the king.

11 Then said Daniel to Melzar, whom the prince of the eunuchs had set over Daniel, Hananiah, Mishael, and Azariah,

12 Prove your servants, I beseech you, ten days; and let them give us vegetables to eat, and water to drink.

13 Then let our countenances be looked upon before you, and the countenance of the children that eat of the portion of the king's meat: and as you see, deal with your servants.

Daniel 1

14 So he consented to them in this matter, and proved them ten days.

15 And at the end of ten days their countenances appeared fairer and fatter in flesh than all the children which did eat the portion of the king's meat.

16 Thus Melzar took away the portion of their meat, and the wine that they should drink; and gave them vegetables.

17 ¶ As for these four children, God gave them knowledge and skill in all learning and wisdom: and Daniel had understanding in all visions and dreams.

18 Now at the end of the days that the king had said he should bring them in, then the prince of the eunuchs brought them in before Nebuchadnezzar.

19 And the king communed with them; and among them all was found none like Daniel, Hananiah, Mishael, and Azariah: therefore stood they before the king.

20 And in all matters of wisdom *and* understanding, that the king inquired of them, he found them ten times better than all the magicians *and* astrologers that *were* in all his realm.

21 And Daniel continued *even* unto the first year of king Cyrus.

Daniel 2

2:1 ¶ And in the second year of the reign of Nebuchadnezzar, Nebuchadnezzar dreamed dreams, with which his spirit was troubled, and his sleep broke from him.

2 Then the king commanded to call the magicians, and the astrologers, and the sorcerers, and the Chaldeans, for to show the king his dreams. So they came and stood before the king.

3 And the king said to them, I have dreamed a dream, and my spirit was troubled to know the dream.

4 Then spoke the Chaldeans to the king in Aramaic, O king, live forever: tell your servants the dream, and we will show the interpretation.

5 The king answered and said to the Chaldeans, The thing has gone from me: if you will not make known to me the dream, with the interpretation thereof, you shall be cut in pieces, and your houses shall be made a dunghill.

6 But if you show the dream, and the interpretation thereof, you shall receive of me gifts and rewards and great honor: therefore show me the dream, and the interpretation thereof.

7 They answered again and said, Let the king tell his servants the dream, and we will show the interpretation of it.

8 The king answered and said, I know of certainty that you would gain the time, because you see the thing has gone from me.

9 But if you will not make known to me the dream, *there is but* one decree for you: for you have prepared lying and corrupt words to speak before me, till the time is changed: therefore tell me the dream, and I shall know that you can show me the interpretation thereof.

10 The Chaldeans answered before the king, and said, There is not a man upon the earth that can show the king's matter: therefore *there is* no king, lord, nor ruler, *that* asked such things of any magician, or astrologer, or Chaldean.

11 And *it is* a rare thing that the king requires, and there is none other that can show it before the king, except the gods, whose dwelling is not with flesh.

12 For this cause the king was angry and very furious, and commanded to destroy all the wise *men* of Babylon.

13 And the decree went forth that the wise *men* should be slain; and they sought Daniel and his fellows to be slain.

14 ¶ Then Daniel answered with counsel and wisdom to Arioch the captain of the king's guard, which had gone forth to slay the wise *men* of Babylon:

15 He answered and said to Arioch the king's captain, Why *is* the decree *so* hasty from the king? Then Arioch made the thing known to Daniel.

16 Then Daniel went in, and desired of the king that he would give him time, and that he would show the king the interpretation.

17 Then Daniel went to his house, and made the thing known to Hananiah, Mishael, and Azariah, his companions:

18 That they would desire mercies of the God of heaven concerning this secret; that Daniel and his fellows should not perish with the rest of the wise *men* of Babylon.

19 Then was the secret revealed to Daniel in a night vision. Then Daniel blessed the God of heaven.

20 Daniel answered and said, Blessed be the name of God forever and ever: for wisdom and might are his:

21 And he changes the times and the seasons: he removes kings, and sets up kings: he gives wisdom to the wise, and knowledge to them that know understanding:

22 He reveals the deep and secret things: he knows what *is* in the darkness, and the light dwells with him.

23 I thank you, and praise you, O you God of my fathers, who has given me wisdom and might, and have made known to me now what we desired of you: for you have *now* made known to us the king's matter.

24 ¶ Therefore Daniel went in to Arioch, whom the king had ordained to destroy the wise *men* of Babylon: he went and said thus to him; Destroy not the wise *men* of Babylon: bring me in before the king, and I will show to the king the interpretation.

25 Then Arioch brought in Daniel before the king in haste, and said this to him, I have found a man of the captives of Judah, that will make known to the king the interpretation.

26 The king answered and said to Daniel, whose name *was* Belteshazzar, Are you able to make known to me the dream which I have seen, and the interpretation thereof?

27 Daniel answered in the presence of the king, and said, The secret which the king has demanded cannot the wise *men*, the astrologers, the magicians, the soothsayers, show to the king;

28 But there is a God in heaven that reveals secrets, and makes known to the king Nebuchadnezzar what shall be in the latter days. Your dream, and the visions of your head upon your bed, are these;

29 As for you, O king, your thoughts came *into your mind* upon your bed, what should come to pass hereafter: and he that reveals secrets makes known to you what shall come to pass.

30 But as for me, this secret is not revealed to me for *any* wisdom that I have more than any living, but for *their* sakes that shall make known the interpretation to the king, and that you might know the thoughts of your heart.

31 ¶ You, O king, saw, and behold a great image. This great image, whose brightness *was* excellent, stood before you; and the form thereof *was* terrible.

32 This image's head *was* of fine gold, his breast and his arms of silver, his belly and his thighs of brass,

33 His legs of iron, his feet part of iron and part of clay.

34 You saw till a stone was cut out without hands, which smote the image upon his feet *that were* of iron and clay, and broke them to pieces.

35 Then was the iron, the clay, the brass, the silver, and the gold, broken to pieces together, and became like the chaff of the summer threshing floors; and the wind carried them away, that no place was found for them: and the stone that smote the image became a great mountain, and filled the whole earth.

36 This *is* the dream; and we will tell the interpretation thereof before the king.

37 You, O king, *are* a king of kings: for the God of heaven has given you a kingdom, power, and strength, and glory.

38 And wherever the children of men dwell, the beasts of the field and the fowls of the heaven has he given into your hand, and has made you ruler over them all. You *are* this head of gold.

39 And after you shall arise another kingdom inferior to you, and another third kingdom of brass, which shall bear rule over all the earth.

40 And the fourth kingdom shall be strong as iron: forasmuch as iron breaks in pieces and subdues all *things*: and as iron that breaks all these, shall it break in pieces and bruise.

41 And whereas you saw the feet and toes, part of potters' clay, and part of iron, the kingdom shall be divided; but there shall be in it of the strength of the iron, forasmuch as you saw the iron mixed with miry clay.

42 And *as* the toes of the feet *were* part of iron, and part of clay, *so* the kingdom shall be partly strong, and partly broken.

43 And whereas you saw iron mixed with miry clay, they shall mingle themselves with the seed of men: but they shall not cling one to another, even as iron is not mixed with clay.

44 And in the days of these kings shall the God of heaven set up a kingdom, which shall never be destroyed: and the kingdom shall not be left to other people, *but* it shall break in pieces and consume all these kingdoms, and it shall stand forever.

45 Forasmuch as you saw that the stone was cut out of the mountain without hands, and that it broke in pieces the iron, the brass, the clay, the silver, and the gold; the great God has made known to the king what shall come to pass hereafter: and the dream *is* certain, and the interpretation thereof sure.

46 ¶ Then the king Nebuchadnezzar fell upon his face, and worshipped Daniel, and commanded that they should offer an oblation and sweet odors unto him.

47 The king answered to Daniel, and said, Of a truth *it is*, that your God *is* a God of gods, and a Lord of kings, and a revealer of secrets, seeing you could reveal this secret.

48 Then the king made Daniel a great man, and gave him many great gifts, and made him ruler over the whole province of Babylon, and chief of the governors over all the wise *men* of Babylon.

49 Then Daniel requested of the king, and he set Shadrach, Meshach, and Abednego, over the affairs of the province of Babylon: but Daniel *sat* in the gate of the king.

Daniel 3

3:1 ¶ Nebuchadnezzar the king made an image of gold, whose height *was* threescore cubits, *and* the breadth thereof six cubits: he set it up in the plain of Dura, in the province of Babylon.

2 Then Nebuchadnezzar the king sent to gather together the princes, the governors, and the captains, the judges, the treasurers, the counselors, the sheriffs, and all the rulers of the provinces, to come to the dedication of the image which Nebuchadnezzar the king had set up.

3 Then the princes, the governors, and captains, the judges, the treasurers, the counselors, the sheriffs, and all the rulers of the provinces, were gathered together to the dedication of the image that Nebuchadnezzar the king had set up; and they stood before the image that Nebuchadnezzar had set up.

4 Then a herald cried aloud, To you it is commanded, O people, nations, and languages,

5 *That* at what time you hear the sound of the cornet, flute, harp, sackbut, psaltery, dulcimer, and all kinds of music, you fall down and worship the golden image that Nebuchadnezzar the king has set up:

6 And whoever falls not down and worships shall the same hour be cast into the midst of a burning fiery furnace.

7 Therefore at that time, when all the people heard the sound of the cornet, flute, harp, sackbut, psaltery, and all kinds of music, all the people, the nations, and the languages, fell down *and* worshipped the golden image that Nebuchadnezzar the king had set up.

8 ¶ Therefore at that time certain Chaldeans came near, and accused the Jews.

9 They spoke and said to the king Nebuchadnezzar, O king, live forever.

10 You, O king, have made a decree, that every man that shall hear the sound of the cornet, flute, harp, sackbut, psaltery, and dulcimer, and all kinds of music, shall fall down and worship the golden image:

11 And whoever falls not down and worships, *that* he should be cast into the midst of a burning fiery furnace.

Daniel 3

12 There are certain Jews whom you have set over the affairs of the province of Babylon, Shadrach, Meshach, and Abednego; these men, O king, have not regarded you: they serve not your gods, nor worship the golden image which you have set up.

13 Then Nebuchadnezzar in *his* rage and fury commanded to bring Shadrach, Meshach, and Abednego. Then they brought these men before the king.

14 Nebuchadnezzar spoke and said to them, *Is it* true, O Shadrach, Meshach, and Abednego, do not you serve my gods, nor worship the golden image which I have set up?

15 Now if you are ready that at what time you hear the sound of the cornet, flute, harp, sackbut, psaltery, and dulcimer, and all kinds of music, you fall down and worship the image which I have made; *well*: but if you worship not, you shall be cast the same hour into the midst of a burning fiery furnace; and who *is* that God that shall deliver you out of my hands?

16 Shadrach, Meshach, and Abednego, answered and said to the king, O Nebuchadnezzar, we *are* not careful to answer you in this matter.

17 If it is *so*, our God whom we serve is able to deliver us from the burning fiery furnace, and he will deliver *us* out of your hand, O king.

18 But if not, be it known to you, O king, that we will not serve your gods, nor worship the golden image which you have set up.

19 ¶ Then was Nebuchadnezzar full of fury, and the form of his visage was changed against Shadrach, Meshach, and Abednego: *therefore* he spoke, and commanded that they should heat the furnace one seven times more than it was inclined to be heated.

20 And he commanded the most mighty men that *were* in his army to bind Shadrach, Meshach, and Abednego, *and* to cast *them* into the burning fiery furnace.

21 Then these men were bound in their coats, their hosen, and their hats, and their *other* garments, and were cast into the midst of the burning fiery furnace.

22 Therefore because the king's commandment was urgent, and the furnace exceedingly hot, the flame of the fire slew those men that took up Shadrach, Meshach, and Abednego.

23 And these three men, Shadrach, Meshach, and Abednego, fell down bound into the midst of the burning fiery furnace.

24 Then Nebuchadnezzar the king was astonished, and rose up in haste, *and* spoke, and said to his counselors, Did not we cast three men bound into the midst of the fire? They answered and said to the king, True, O king.

25 He answered and said, Lo, I see four men loose, walking in the midst of the fire, and they have no hurt; and the form of the fourth is like the Son of God.

26 Then Nebuchadnezzar came near to the mouth of the burning fiery furnace, *and* spoke, and said, Shadrach, Meshach, and Abednego, you servants of the most high God, come forth, and come *here*. Then Shadrach, Meshach, and Abednego, came forth from the midst of the fire.

27 And the princes, governors, and captains, and the king's counselors, being gathered together, saw these men, upon whose bodies the fire had no power, nor was a hair of their head singed, neither were their coats changed, nor the smell of fire had passed on them.

28 ¶ *Then* Nebuchadnezzar spoke, and said, Blessed *be* the God of Shadrach, Meshach, and Abednego, who has sent his angel, and delivered his servants that trusted in him, and have changed the king's word, and yielded their bodies, that they might not serve nor worship any god, except their own God.

29 Therefore I make a decree, That every people, nation, and language, which speak anything amiss against the God of Shadrach, Meshach, and Abednego, shall be cut in pieces, and their houses shall be made a dunghill: because there is no other God that can deliver after this sort.

30 Then the king promoted Shadrach, Meshach, and Abednego, in the province of Babylon.

Daniel 4

4:1 ¶ Nebuchadnezzar the king, unto all people, nations, and languages, that dwell in all the earth; Peace be multiplied unto you.

2 I thought it good to show the signs and wonders that the high God has worked toward me.

3 How great *are* his signs! and how mighty *are* his wonders! his kingdom *is* an everlasting kingdom, and his dominion *is* from generation to generation.

4 ¶ I Nebuchadnezzar was at rest in my house, and flourishing in my palace:

5 I saw a dream which made me afraid, and the thoughts upon my bed and the visions of my head troubled me.

6 Therefore made I a decree to bring in all the wise *men* of Babylon before me, that they might make known to me the interpretation of the dream.

7 Then came in the magicians, the astrologers, the Chaldeans, and the soothsayers: and I told the dream before them; but they did not make known to me the interpretation thereof.

8 But at the last Daniel came in before me, whose name *was* Belteshazzar, according to the name of my god, and in whom *is* the spirit of the holy gods: and before him I told the dream, *saying*,

9 O Belteshazzar, master of the magicians, because I know that the spirit of the holy gods *is* in you, and no secret troubles you, tell me the visions of my dream that I have seen, and the interpretation thereof.

10 Thus *were* the visions of my head in my bed; I saw, and behold a tree in the midst of the earth, and the height thereof *was* great.

11 The tree grew, and was strong, and the height thereof reached to heaven, and the sight thereof to the end of all the earth:

12 The leaves thereof *were* fair, and the fruit thereof much, and in it *was* food for all: the beasts of the field

had shadow under it, and the fowls of the heaven dwelt in the boughs thereof, and all flesh was fed of it.

13 I saw in the visions of my head upon my bed, and, behold, a watcher and a holy one came down from heaven;

14 He cried aloud, and said thus, Hew down the tree, and cut off his branches, shake off his leaves, and scatter his fruit: let the beasts get away from under it, and the fowls from his branches:

15 Nevertheless leave the stump of his roots in the earth, even with a band of iron and brass, in the tender grass of the field; and let it be wet with the dew of heaven, and *let* his portion *be* with the beasts in the grass of the earth:

16 Let his heart be changed from man's, and let a beast's heart be given to him; and let seven times pass over him.

17 This matter *is* by the decree of the watchers, and the demand by the word of the holy ones: to the intent that the living may know that the most High rules in the kingdom of men, and gives it to whomever he will, and sets up over it the basest of men.

18 This dream I king Nebuchadnezzar have seen. Now you, O Belteshazzar, declare the interpretation thereof, forasmuch as all the wise *men* of my kingdom are not able to make known to me the interpretation: but you *are* able; for the spirit of the holy gods *is* in you.

19 ¶ Then Daniel, whose name *was* Belteshazzar, was astonished for one hour, and his thoughts troubled him. The king spoke, and said, Belteshazzar, let not the dream, or the interpretation thereof, trouble you. Belteshazzar answered and said, My lord, the dream *is* to them that hate you, and the interpretation thereof to your enemies.

20 The tree that you saw, which grew, and was strong, whose height reached to the heaven, and the sight thereof to all the earth;

21 Whose leaves *were* fair, and the fruit thereof much, and in it *was* food for all; under which the beasts of the field dwelt, and upon whose branches the fowls of the heaven had their habitation:

22 It *is* you, O king, that have grown and become strong: for your greatness has grown, and reaches to heaven, and your dominion to the end of the earth.

23 And whereas the king saw a watcher and a holy one coming down from heaven, and saying, Hew the tree down, and destroy it; yet leave the stump of the roots thereof in the earth, even with a band of iron and brass, in the tender grass of the field; and let it be wet with the dew of heaven, and *let* his portion *be* with the beasts of the field, till seven times pass over him;

24 This *is* the interpretation, O king, and this *is* the decree of the most High, which has come upon my lord the king:

25 That they shall drive you from men, and your dwelling shall be with the beasts of the field, and they shall make you to eat grass as oxen, and they shall wet you with the dew of heaven, and seven times shall pass over you, till you know that the most High rules in the kingdom of men, and gives it to whomever he will.

26 And whereas they commanded to leave the stump of the tree roots; your kingdom shall be sure unto you, after that you shall have known that the heavens do rule.

27 Therefore, O king, let my counsel be acceptable to you, and break off your sins by righteousness, and your iniquities by showing mercy to the poor; if it may be a lengthening of your tranquillity.

28 ¶ All this came upon the king Nebuchadnezzar.

29 At the end of twelve months he walked in the palace of the kingdom of Babylon.

30 The king spoke, and said, Is not this great Babylon, that I have built for the house of the kingdom by the might of my power, and for the honor of my majesty?

31 While the word *was* in the king's mouth, there fell a voice from heaven, *saying*, O king Nebuchadnezzar, to you it is spoken; The kingdom is departed from you.

32 And they shall drive you from men, and your dwelling *shall be* with the beasts of the field: they shall make you to eat grass as oxen, and seven times shall pass over you, until you know that the most High rules in the kingdom of men, and gives it to whomever he will.

33 The same hour was the thing fulfilled upon Nebuchadnezzar: and he was driven from men, and did eat grass as oxen, and his body was wet with the dew of heaven, till his hair had grown like eagles' *feathers*, and his nails like birds' *claws*.

34 ¶ And at the end of the days I Nebuchadnezzar lifted up my eyes to heaven, and my understanding returned to me, and I blessed the most High, and I praised and honored him that lives forever, whose dominion *is* an everlasting dominion, and his kingdom *is* from generation to generation:

35 And all the inhabitants of the earth *are* reputed as nothing: and he does according to his will in the army of heaven, and *among* the inhabitants of the earth: and none can hinder his hand, or say to him, What do you?

36 At the same time my reason returned to me; and for the glory of my kingdom, my honor and brightness returned to me; and my counselors and my lords sought unto me; and I was established in my kingdom, and excellent majesty was added to me.

37 Now I Nebuchadnezzar praise and extol and honor the King of heaven, all whose works *are* truth, and his ways judgment: and those that walk in pride he is able to abase.

Daniel 5

5:1 ¶ Belshazzar the king made a great feast to a thousand of his lords, and drank wine before the thousand.

2 Belshazzar, while he tasted the wine, commanded to bring the golden and silver vessels which his father Nebuchadnezzar had taken out of the temple which *was* in Jerusalem; that the king, and his princes, his wives, and his concubines, might drink therein.

3 Then they brought the golden vessels that were taken out of the temple of the house of God which *was* at

Daniel 5

Jerusalem; and the king, and his princes, his wives, and his concubines, drank from them.

4 They drank wine, and praised the gods of gold, and of silver, of brass, of iron, of wood, and of stone.

5 In the same hour came forth fingers of a man's hand, and wrote over before the candlestick upon the plaster of the wall of the king's palace: and the king saw the part of the hand that wrote.

6 Then the king's countenance was changed, and his thoughts troubled him, so that the joints of his loins were loosed, and his knees smote one against another.

7 The king cried aloud to bring in the astrologers, the Chaldeans, and the soothsayers. *And* the king spoke, and said to the wise *men* of Babylon, Whoever shall read this writing, and show me the interpretation thereof, shall be clothed with scarlet, and *have* a chain of gold about his neck, and shall be the third ruler in the kingdom.

8 Then came in all the king's wise *men*: but they could not read the writing, nor make known to the king the interpretation thereof.

9 Then was king Belshazzar greatly troubled, and his countenance was changed in him, and his lords were astonished.

10 ¶ *Now* the queen, by reason of the words of the king and his lords, came into the banquet house: *and* the queen spoke and said, O king, live forever: let not your thoughts trouble you, nor let your countenance be changed:

11 There is a man in your kingdom, in whom *is* the spirit of the holy gods; and in the days of your father light and understanding and wisdom, like the wisdom of the gods, was found in him; whom the king Nebuchadnezzar your father, the king, *I say*, your father, made master of the magicians, astrologers, Chaldeans, *and* soothsayers;

12 Forasmuch as an excellent spirit, and knowledge, and understanding, interpreting of dreams, and showing of hard sentences, and dissolving of doubts, were found in the same Daniel, whom the king named Belteshazzar: now let Daniel be called, and he will show the interpretation.

13 Then was Daniel brought in before the king. *And* the king spoke and said to Daniel, *Are* you that Daniel, which *are* of the children of the captivity of Judah, whom the king my father brought out of Jewry?

14 I have even heard of you, that the spirit of the gods *is* in you, and *that* light and understanding and excellent wisdom is found in you.

15 And now the wise *men*, the astrologers, have been brought in before me, that they should read this writing, and make known to me the interpretation thereof: but they could not show the interpretation of the thing:

16 And I have heard of you, that you can make interpretations, and dissolve doubts: now if you can read the writing, and make known to me the interpretation thereof, you shall be clothed with scarlet, and *have* a chain of gold about your neck, and shall be the third ruler in the kingdom.

17 Then Daniel answered and said before the king, Let your gifts be to yourself, and give your rewards to another; yet I will read the writing to the king, and make known to him the interpretation.

18 O you king, the most high God gave Nebuchadnezzar your father a kingdom, and majesty, and glory, and honor:

19 And for the majesty that he gave him, all people, nations, and languages, trembled and feared before him: whom he would he slew; and whom he would he kept alive; and whom he would he set up; and whom he would he put down.

20 But when his heart was lifted up, and his mind hardened in pride, he was deposed from his kingly throne, and they took his glory from him:

21 And he was driven from the sons of men; and his heart was made like the beasts, and his dwelling *was* with the wild donkeys: they fed him with grass like oxen, and his body was wet with the dew of heaven; till he knew that the most high God ruled in the kingdom of men, and *that* he appoints over it whomever he will.

22 And you his son, O Belshazzar, have not humbled your heart, though you knew all this;

23 But have lifted up yourself against the Lord of heaven; and they have brought the vessels of his house before you, and you, and your lords, your wives, and your concubines, have drunk wine in them; and you have praised the gods of silver, and gold, of brass, iron, wood, and stone, which see not, nor hear, nor know: and the God in whose hand your breath *is*, and whose *are* all your ways, have you not glorified:

24 Then was the part of the hand sent from him; and this writing was written.

25 And this *is* the writing that was written, MENE, MENE, TEKEL, UPHARSIN.

26 This *is* the interpretation of the thing: MENE; God has numbered your kingdom, and finished it.

27 TEKEL; You are weighed in the balances, and are found wanting.

28 PERES; Your kingdom is divided, and given to the Medes and Persians.

29 Then commanded Belshazzar, and they clothed Daniel with scarlet, and *put* a chain of gold about his neck, and made a proclamation concerning him, that he should be the third ruler in the kingdom.

30 ¶ In that night was Belshazzar the king of the Chaldeans slain.

31 And Darius the Median took the kingdom, *being* about threescore and two years old.

Daniel 6

6:1 ¶ It pleased Darius to set over the kingdom a hundred and twenty princes, which should be over the whole kingdom;

2 And over these three presidents; of whom Daniel *was* first: that the princes might give accounts to them, and the king should have no damage.

3 Then this Daniel was preferred above the presidents and princes, because an excellent spirit *was* in him; and the king thought to set him over the whole realm.

4 Then the presidents and princes sought to find occasion against Daniel concerning the kingdom; but they could find no occasion nor fault; forasmuch as he *was* faithful, neither was there any error or fault found in him.

5 Then said these men, We shall not find any occasion against this Daniel, unless we find *it* against him concerning the law of his God.

6 ¶ Then these presidents and princes assembled together to the king, and said thus to him, King Darius, live forever.

7 All the presidents of the kingdom, the governors, and the princes, the counselors, and the captains, have consulted together to establish a royal statute, and to make a firm decree, that whoever shall ask a petition of any God or man for thirty days, except of you, O king, he shall be cast into the den of lions.

8 Now, O king, establish the decree, and sign the writing, that it be not changed, according to the law of the Medes and Persians, which alters not.

9 Therefore king Darius signed the writing and the decree.

10 Now when Daniel knew that the writing was signed, he went into his house; and his windows being open in his chamber toward Jerusalem, he knelt upon his knees three times a day, and prayed, and gave thanks before his God, as he did before.

11 ¶ Then these men assembled, and found Daniel praying and making supplication before his God.

12 Then they came near, and spoke before the king concerning the king's decree; Have you not signed a decree, that every man that shall ask *a petition* of any God or man within thirty days, except of you, O king, shall be cast into the den of lions? The king answered and said, The thing *is* true, according to the law of the Medes and Persians, which alters not.

13 Then answered they and said before the king, That Daniel, which *is* of the children of the captivity of Judah, regards not you, O king, nor the decree that you have signed, but makes his petition three times a day.

14 Then the king, when he heard *these* words, was greatly displeased with himself, and set *his* heart on Daniel to deliver him: and he labored till the going down of the sun to deliver him.

15 Then these men assembled to the king, and said to the king, Know, O king, that the law of the Medes and Persians *is*, That no decree nor statute which the king establishes may be changed.

16 Then the king commanded, and they brought Daniel, and cast *him* into the den of lions. *Now* the king spoke and said to Daniel, Your God whom you serve continually, he will deliver you.

17 And a stone was brought, and laid upon the mouth of the den; and the king sealed it with his own signet, and with the signet of his lords; that the purpose might not be changed concerning Daniel.

18 ¶ Then the king went to his palace, and passed the night fasting: neither were instruments of music brought before him: and his sleep went from him.

19 Then the king arose very early in the morning, and went in haste to the den of lions.

20 And when he came to the den, he cried with a lamentable voice to Daniel: *and* the king spoke and said to Daniel, O Daniel, servant of the living God, is your God, whom you serve continually, able to deliver you from the lions?

21 Then said Daniel to the king, O king, live forever.

22 My God has sent his angel, and has shut the lions' mouths, that they have not hurt me: forasmuch as before him innocence was found in me; and also before you, O king, have I done no hurt.

23 Then was the king exceedingly glad for him, and commanded that they should take Daniel up out of the den. So Daniel was taken up out of the den, and no manner of hurt was found upon him, because he believed in his God.

24 And the king commanded, and they brought those men which had accused Daniel, and they cast *them* into the den of lions, them, their children, and their wives; and the lions had the mastery of them, and broke all their bones in pieces or ever they came to the bottom of the den.

25 ¶ Then king Darius wrote to all people, nations, and languages, that dwelt in all the earth; Peace be multiplied unto you.

26 I make a decree, That in every dominion of my kingdom men tremble and fear before the God of Daniel: for he *is* the living God, and steadfast forever, and his kingdom *that* which shall not be destroyed, and his dominion *shall be even* to the end.

27 He delivers and rescues, and he works signs and wonders in heaven and in earth, who has delivered Daniel from the power of the lions.

28 So this Daniel prospered in the reign of Darius, and in the reign of Cyrus the Persian.

Daniel 7

7:1 ¶ In the first year of Belshazzar king of Babylon Daniel had a dream and visions of his head upon his bed: then he wrote the dream, *and* told the sum of the matters.

2 Daniel spoke and said, I saw in my vision by night, and, behold, the four winds of the heaven strove upon the great sea.

3 And four great beasts came up from the sea, diverse one from another.

4 The first *was* like a lion, and had eagle's wings: I beheld till the wings thereof were plucked, and it was lifted up from the earth, and made stand upon the feet as a man, and a man's heart was given to it.

5 And behold another beast, a second, like to a bear, and it raised up itself on one side, and *it had* three ribs in the mouth of it between the teeth of it: and they said thus to it, Arise, devour much flesh.

6 After this I beheld, and lo another, like a leopard, which had upon the back of it four wings of a fowl; the beast had also four heads; and dominion was given to it.

Daniel 7

7 After this I saw in the night visions, and behold a fourth beast, dreadful and terrible, and strong exceedingly; and it had great iron teeth: it devoured and broke in pieces, and stamped the residue with the feet of it: and it *was* diverse from all the beasts that *were* before it; and it had ten horns.

8 I considered the horns, and, behold, there came up among them another little horn, before whom there were three of the first horns plucked up by the roots: and, behold, in this horn *were* eyes like the eyes of man, and a mouth speaking great things.

9 ¶ I beheld till the thrones were cast down, and the Ancient of days did sit, whose garment *was* white as snow, and the hair of his head like the pure wool: his throne *was like* the fiery flame, *and* his wheels *as* burning fire.

10 A fiery stream issued and came forth from before him: thousand thousands ministered to him, and ten thousand times ten thousand stood before him: the judgment was set, and the books were opened.

11 I beheld then because of the voice of the great words which the horn spoke: I beheld *even* till the beast was slain, and his body destroyed, and given to the burning flame.

12 As concerning the rest of the beasts, they had their dominion taken away: yet their lives were prolonged for a season and time.

13 I saw in the night visions, and, behold, *one* like the Son of man came with the clouds of heaven, and came to the Ancient of days, and they brought him near before him.

14 And there was given him dominion, and glory, and a kingdom, that all people, nations, and languages, should serve him: his dominion *is* an everlasting dominion, which shall not pass away, and his kingdom *that* which shall not be destroyed.

15 ¶ I Daniel was grieved in my spirit in the midst of *my* body, and the visions of my head troubled me.

16 I came near to one of them that stood by, and asked him the truth of all this. So he told me, and made me know the interpretation of the things.

17 These great beasts, which are four, *are* four kings, *which* shall arise out of the earth.

18 But the saints of the most High shall take the kingdom, and possess the kingdom forever, even forever and ever.

19 Then I would know the truth of the fourth beast, which was diverse from all the others, exceedingly dreadful, whose teeth *were of* iron, and his nails *of* brass; *which* devoured, broke in pieces, and stamped the residue with his feet;

20 And of the ten horns that *were* in his head, and *of* the other which came up, and before whom three fell; even *of* that horn that had eyes, and a mouth that spoke very great things, whose look *was* more stout than his fellows.

21 I beheld, and the same horn made war with the saints, and prevailed against them;

22 Until the Ancient of days came, and judgment was given to the saints of the most High; and the time came that the saints possessed the kingdom.

23 Thus he said, The fourth beast shall be the fourth kingdom upon earth, which shall be diverse from all kingdoms, and shall devour the whole earth, and shall tread it down, and break it in pieces.

24 And the ten horns out of this kingdom *are* ten kings *that* shall arise: and another shall rise after them; and he shall be diverse from the first, and he shall subdue three kings.

25 And he shall speak *great* words against the most High, and shall wear out the saints of the most High, and think to change times and laws: and they shall be given into his hand until a time and times and the dividing of time.

26 But the judgment shall sit, and they shall take away his dominion, to consume and to destroy *it* to the end.

27 And the kingdom and dominion, and the greatness of the kingdom under the whole heaven, shall be given to the people of the saints of the most High, whose kingdom *is* an everlasting kingdom, and all dominions shall serve and obey him.

28 To here *is* the end of the matter. As for me Daniel, my cogitations much troubled me, and my countenance changed in me: but I kept the matter in my heart.

Daniel 8

8:1 ¶ In the third year of the reign of king Belshazzar a vision appeared to me, *even to* me Daniel, after that which appeared to me at the first.

2 And I saw in a vision; and it came to pass, when I saw, that I *was* at Shushan *in* the palace, which *is* in the province of Elam; and I saw in a vision, and I was by the river of Ulai.

3 Then I lifted up my eyes, and saw, and, behold, there stood before the river a ram which had *two* horns: and the *two* horns *were* high; but one *was* higher than the other, and the higher came up last.

4 I saw the ram pushing westward, and northward, and southward; so that no beasts might stand before him, neither *was there any* that could deliver out of his hand; but he did according to his will, and became great.

5 And as I was considering, behold, a he goat came from the west on the face of the whole earth, and touched not the ground: and the goat *had* a notable horn between his eyes.

6 And he came to the ram that had *two* horns, which I had seen standing before the river, and ran to him in the fury of his power.

7 And I saw him come close to the ram, and he was moved with bitterness against him, and smote the ram, and broke his two horns: and there was no power in the ram to stand before him, but he cast him down to the ground, and stamped upon him: and there was none that could deliver the ram out of his hand.

8 Therefore the he goat became very great: and when he was strong, the great horn was broken; and for it came up four notable ones toward the four winds of heaven.

9 And out of one of them came forth a little horn, which became exceedingly great, toward the south, and toward the east, and toward the pleasant *land*.
10 And it became great, *even* to the host of heaven; and it cast down *some* of the host and of the stars to the ground, and stamped upon them.
11 Yes, he magnified *himself* even to the prince of the host, and by him the daily *sacrifice* was taken away, and the place of his sanctuary was cast down.
12 And a host was given *him* against the daily *sacrifice* by reason of transgression, and it cast down the truth to the ground; and it practiced, and prospered.
13 Then I heard one saint speaking, and another saint said to that certain *saint* which spoke, How long *shall be* the vision *concerning* the daily *sacrifice*, and the transgression of desolation, to give both the sanctuary and the host to be trodden under foot?
14 And he said to me, Unto two thousand and three hundred days; then shall the sanctuary be cleansed.
15 ¶ And it came to pass, when I, *even* I Daniel, had seen the vision, and sought for the meaning, then, behold, there stood before me as the appearance of a man.
16 And I heard a man's voice between *the banks of* Ulai, which called, and said, Gabriel, make this *man* to understand the vision.
17 So he came near where I stood: and when he came, I was afraid, and fell upon my face: but he said to me, Understand, O son of man: for at the time of the end *shall be* the vision.
18 Now as he was speaking with me, I was in a deep sleep on my face toward the ground: but he touched me, and set me upright.
19 And he said, Behold, I will make you know what shall be in the last end of the indignation: for at the time appointed the end *shall be*.
20 The ram which you saw having *two* horns *are* the kings of Media and Persia.
21 And the rough goat *is* the king of Greece: and the great horn that *is* between his eyes *is* the first king.
22 Now that being broken, whereas four stood up for it, four kingdoms shall stand up out of the nation, but not in his power.
23 And in the latter time of their kingdom, when the transgressors have come to the full, a king of fierce countenance, and understanding dark sentences, shall stand up.
24 And his power shall be mighty, but not by his own power: and he shall destroy wonderfully, and shall prosper, and practice, and shall destroy the mighty and the holy people.
25 And through his policy also he shall cause craft to prosper in his hand; and he shall magnify *himself* in his heart, and by peace shall destroy many: he shall also stand up against the Prince of princes; but he shall be broken without hand.
26 And the vision of the evening and the morning which was told *is* true: therefore shut you up the vision; for it *shall be* for many days.
27 And I Daniel fainted, and was sick *certain* days; afterward I rose up, and did the king's business; and I was astonished at the vision, but none understood *it*.

Daniel 9

9:1 ¶ In the first year of Darius the son of Ahasuerus, of the seed of the Medes, which was made king over the realm of the Chaldeans;
2 In the first year of his reign I Daniel understood by books the number of the years, whereof the word of Yahweh came to Jeremiah the prophet, that he would accomplish seventy years in the desolations of Jerusalem.
3 And I set my face unto the Lord God, to seek by prayer and supplications, with fasting, and sackcloth, and ashes:
4 ¶ And I prayed unto Yahweh my God, and made my confession, and said, O Lord, the great and dreadful God, keeping the covenant and mercy to them that love him, and to them that keep his commandments;
5 We have sinned, and have committed iniquity, and have done wickedly, and have rebelled, even by departing from your precepts and from your judgments:
6 Neither have we listened to your servants the prophets, which spoke in your name to our kings, our princes, and our fathers, and to all the people of the land.
7 O Lord, righteousness *belongs* to you, but to us confusion of faces, as at this day; to the men of Judah, and to the inhabitants of Jerusalem, and to all Israel, *that are* near, and *that are* far off, through all the countries where you have driven them, because of their trespass that they have trespassed against you.
8 O Lord, to us *belongs* confusion of face, to our kings, to our princes, and to our fathers, because we have sinned against you.
9 To the Lord our God *belong* mercies and forgiveness, though we have rebelled against him;
10 Neither have we obeyed the voice of Yahweh our God, to walk in his laws, which he set before us by his servants the prophets.
11 Yes, all Israel has transgressed your law, even by departing, that they might not obey your voice; therefore the curse is poured upon us, and the oath that *is* written in the law of Moses the servant of God, because we have sinned against him.
12 And he has confirmed his words, which he spoke against us, and against our judges that judged us, by bringing upon us a great evil: for under the whole heaven has not been done as has been done upon Jerusalem.
13 As *it is* written in the law of Moses, all this evil has come upon us: yet made we not our prayer before Yahweh our God, that we might turn from our iniquities, and understand your truth.
14 Therefore has Yahweh watched upon the evil, and brought it upon us: for Yahweh our God *is* righteous in all his works which he does: for we obeyed not his voice.

Daniel 9

15 And now, O Lord our God, that have brought your people forth out of the land of Egypt with a mighty hand, and have gotten you renown, as at this day; we have sinned, we have done wickedly.

16 O Lord, according to all your righteousness, I beseech you, let your anger and your fury be turned away from your city Jerusalem, your holy mountain: because for our sins, and for the iniquities of our fathers, Jerusalem and your people *have become* a reproach to all *that are* about us.

17 Now therefore, O our God, hear the prayer of your servant, and his supplications, and cause your face to shine upon your sanctuary that is desolate, for the Lord's sake.

18 O my God, incline your ear, and hear; open your eyes, and behold our desolations, and the city which is called by your name: for we do not present our supplications before you for our righteousness, but for your great mercies.

19 O Lord, hear; O Lord, forgive; O Lord, listen and do; defer not, for your own sake, O my God: for your city and your people are called by your name.

20 ¶ And while I *was* speaking, and praying, and confessing my sin and the sin of my people Israel, and presenting my supplication before Yahweh my God for the holy mountain of my God;

21 Yes, while I *was* speaking in prayer, even the man Gabriel, whom I had seen in the vision at the beginning, being caused to fly swiftly, touched me about the time of the evening oblation.

22 And he informed *me*, and talked with me, and said, O Daniel, I have now come forth to give you skill and understanding.

23 At the beginning of your supplications the commandment came forth, and I have come to show *you*; for you *are* greatly beloved: therefore understand the matter, and consider the vision.

24 Seventy weeks are determined upon your people and upon your holy city, to finish the transgression, and to make an end of sins, and to make reconciliation for iniquity, and to bring in everlasting righteousness, and to seal up the vision and prophecy, and to anoint the most Holy.

25 Know therefore and understand, *that* from the going forth of the commandment to restore and to build Jerusalem to the Messiah the Prince *shall be* seven weeks, and threescore and two weeks: the street shall be built again, and the wall, even in troublesome times.

26 And after threescore and two weeks shall Messiah be cut off, but not for himself: and the people of the prince that shall come shall destroy the city and the sanctuary; and the end thereof *shall be* with a flood, and to the end of the war desolations are determined.

27 And he shall confirm the covenant with many for one week: and in the midst of the week he shall cause the sacrifice and the oblation to cease, and for the overspreading of abominations he shall make *it* desolate, even until the consummation, and that determined shall be poured upon the desolate.

Daniel 10

10:1 ¶ In the third year of Cyrus king of Persia a thing was revealed to Daniel, whose name was called Belteshazzar; and the thing *was* true, but the time appointed *was* long: and he understood the thing, and had understanding of the vision.

2 In those days I Daniel was mourning three full weeks.

3 I ate no pleasant bread, neither came flesh nor wine in my mouth, neither did I anoint myself at all, till three whole weeks were fulfilled.

4 And in the four and twentieth day of the first month, as I was by the side of the great river, which *is* Hiddekel;

5 Then I lifted up my eyes, and looked, and behold a certain man clothed in linen, whose loins *were* girded with fine gold of Uphaz:

6 His body also *was* like the beryl, and his face as the appearance of lightning, and his eyes as lamps of fire, and his arms and his feet like in color to polished brass, and the voice of his words like the voice of a multitude.

7 And I Daniel alone saw the vision: for the men that were with me saw not the vision; but a great quaking fell upon them, so that they fled to hide themselves.

8 Therefore I was left alone, and saw this great vision, and there remained no strength in me: for my comeliness was turned in me into corruption, and I retained no strength.

9 Yet heard I the voice of his words: and when I heard the voice of his words, then was I in a deep sleep on my face, and my face toward the ground.

10 ¶ And, behold, a hand touched me, which set me upon my knees and *upon* the palms of my hands.

11 And he said to me, O Daniel, a man greatly beloved, understand the words that I speak to you, and stand upright: for to you am I now sent. And when he had spoken this word to me, I stood trembling.

12 Then said he to me, Fear not, Daniel: for from the first day that you did set your heart to understand, and to chasten yourself before your God, your words were heard, and I have come for your words.

13 But the prince of the kingdom of Persia withstood me one and twenty days: but, lo, Michael, one of the chief princes, came to help me; and I remained there with the kings of Persia.

14 Now I have come to make you understand what shall befall your people in the latter days: for yet the vision *is* for *many* days.

15 And when he had spoken such words to me, I set my face toward the ground, and I became dumb.

16 And, behold, *one* like the likeness of the sons of men touched my lips: then I opened my mouth, and spoke, and said to him that stood before me, O my lord, by the vision my sorrows are turned upon me, and I have retained no strength.

17 For how can the servant of this my lord talk with this my lord? for as for me, now there remains no strength in me, neither is there breath left in me.

18 Then there came again and touched me *one* like the appearance of a man, and he strengthened me,

19 And said, O man greatly beloved, fear not: peace *be* unto you, be strong, yes, be strong. And when he had spoken to me, I was strengthened, and said, Let my lord speak; for you have strengthened me.

20 Then said he, Know you why I come to you? and now will I return to fight with the prince of Persia: and when I have gone forth, lo, the prince of Greece shall come.

21 But I will show you that which is noted in the scripture of truth: and *there is* none that holds with me in these things, but Michael your prince.

Daniel 11

11:1 ¶ Also I in the first year of Darius the Mede, *even* I, stood to confirm and to strengthen him.

2 And now will I show you the truth. Behold, there shall stand up yet three kings in Persia; and the fourth shall be far richer than *they* all: and by his strength through his riches he shall stir up all against the realm of Greece.

3 And a mighty king shall stand up, that shall rule with great dominion, and do according to his will.

4 And when he shall stand up, his kingdom shall be broken, and shall be divided toward the four winds of heaven; and not to his posterity, nor according to his dominion which he ruled: for his kingdom shall be plucked up, even for others besides those.

5 ¶ And the king of the south shall be strong, and *one* of his princes; and he shall be strong above him, and have dominion; his dominion *shall be* a great dominion.

6 And in the end of years they shall join themselves together; for the king's daughter of the south shall come to the king of the north to make an agreement: but she shall not retain the power of the arm; neither shall he stand, nor his arm: but she shall be given up, and they that brought her, and he that begot her, and he that strengthened her in *these* times.

7 But out of a branch of her roots shall *one* stand up in his estate, which shall come with an army, and shall enter into the fortress of the king of the north, and shall deal against them, and shall prevail:

8 And shall also carry captives into Egypt their gods, with their princes, *and* with their precious vessels of silver and of gold; and he shall continue *more* years than the king of the north.

9 So the king of the south shall come into *his* kingdom, and shall return into his own land.

10 But his sons shall be stirred up, and shall assemble a multitude of great forces: and *one* shall certainly come, and overflow, and pass through: then shall he return, and be stirred up, *even* to his fortress.

11 And the king of the south shall be moved with bitterness, and shall come forth and fight with him, *even* with the king of the north: and he shall set forth a great multitude; but the multitude shall be given into his hand.

12 *And* when he has taken away the multitude, his heart shall be lifted up; and he shall cast down *many* ten thousands: but he shall not be strengthened *by it*.

13 For the king of the north shall return, and shall set forth a multitude greater than the former, and shall certainly come after certain years with a great army and with much riches.

14 And in those times there shall many stand up against the king of the south: also the robbers of your people shall exalt themselves to establish the vision; but they shall fall.

15 So the king of the north shall come, and cast up a mount, and take the most fenced cities: and the arms of the south shall not withstand, neither his chosen people, neither *shall there be any* strength to withstand.

16 But he that comes against him shall do according to his own will, and none shall stand before him: and he shall stand in the glorious land, which by his hand shall be consumed.

17 He shall also set his face to enter with the strength of his whole kingdom, and upright ones with him; thus shall he do: and he shall give him the daughter of women, corrupting her: but she shall not stand *on his side*, neither be for him.

18 After this shall he turn his face to the isles, and shall take many: but a prince for his own behalf shall cause the reproach offered by him to cease; without his own reproach he shall cause *it* to turn upon him.

19 Then he shall turn his face toward the fort of his own land: but he shall stumble and fall, and not be found.

20 Then shall stand up in his estate a raiser of taxes *in* the glory of the kingdom: but within *a* few days he shall be destroyed, neither in anger, nor in battle.

21 ¶ And in his estate shall stand up a vile person, to whom they shall not give the honor of the kingdom: but he shall come in peaceably, and obtain the kingdom by flatteries.

22 And with the arms of a flood shall they be overflowed from before him, and shall be broken; yes, also the prince of the covenant.

23 And after the league *made* with him he shall work deceitfully: for he shall come up, and shall become strong with a small people.

24 He shall enter peaceably even upon the fattest places of the province; and he shall do *that* which his fathers have not done, nor his fathers' fathers; he shall scatter among them the prey, and spoil, and riches: *yes,* and he shall forecast his devices against the strong holds, even for a time.

25 And he shall stir up his power and his courage against the king of the south with a great army; and the king of the south shall be stirred up to battle with a very great and mighty army; but he shall not stand: for they shall forecast devices against him.

26 Yes, they that feed of the portion of his meat shall destroy him, and his army shall overflow: and many shall fall down slain.

27 And both these kings' hearts *shall be* to do mischief, and they shall speak lies at one table; but it shall not prosper: for yet the end *shall be* at the time appointed.

28 Then shall he return into his land with great riches; and his heart *shall be* against the holy covenant; and he shall do *exploits*, and return to his own land.
29 At the time appointed he shall return, and come toward the south; but it shall not be as the former, or as the latter.
30 For the ships of Chittim shall come against him: therefore he shall be grieved, and return, and have indignation against the holy covenant: so shall he do; he shall even return, and have intelligence with them that forsake the holy covenant.
31 And arms shall stand on his part, and they shall pollute the sanctuary of strength, and shall take away the daily *sacrifice*, and they shall place the abomination that makes desolate.
32 And such as do wickedly against the covenant shall he corrupt by flatteries: but the people that do know their God shall be strong, and do *exploits*.
33 And they that understand among the people shall instruct many: yet they shall fall by the sword, and by flame, by captivity, and by spoil, *many* days.
34 Now when they shall fall, they shall be helped with a little help: but many shall cling to them with flatteries.
35 And *some* of them of understanding shall fall, to try them, and to purge, and to make *them* white, *even* to the time of the end: because *it is* yet for a time appointed.
36 And the king shall do according to his will; and he shall exalt himself, and magnify himself above every god, and shall speak marvelous things against the God of gods, and shall prosper till the indignation is accomplished: for that that is determined shall be done.
37 Neither shall he regard the God of his fathers, nor the desire of women, nor regard any god: for he shall magnify himself above all.
38 But in his estate shall he honor the god of forces: and a god whom his fathers knew not shall he honor with gold, and silver, and with precious stones, and pleasant things.
39 Thus shall he do in the most strong holds with a strange god, whom he shall acknowledge *and* increase with glory: and he shall cause them to rule over many, and shall divide the land for gain.
40 And at the time of the end shall the king of the south push at him: and the king of the north shall come against him like a whirlwind, with chariots, and with horsemen, and with many ships; and he shall enter into the countries, and shall overflow and pass over.
41 He shall enter also into the glorious land, and many *countries* shall be overthrown: but these shall escape out of his hand, *even* Edom, and Moab, and the chief of the children of Ammon.
42 He shall stretch forth his hand also upon the countries: and the land of Egypt shall not escape.
43 But he shall have power over the treasures of gold and of silver, and over all the precious things of Egypt: and the Libyans and the Ethiopians *shall be* at his steps.
44 But tidings out of the east and out of the north shall trouble him: therefore he shall go forth with great fury to destroy, and utterly to make away many.
45 And he shall plant the tabernacles of his palace between the seas in the glorious holy mountain; yet he shall come to his end, and none shall help him.

Daniel 12

12:1 ¶ And at that time shall Michael stand up, the great prince which stands for the children of your people: and there shall be a time of trouble, such as never was since there was a nation *even* to that same time: and at that time your people shall be delivered, every one that shall be found written in the book.
2 And many of them that sleep in the dust of the earth shall awake, some to everlasting life, and some to shame *and* everlasting contempt.
3 And they that are wise shall shine as the brightness of the firmament; and they that turn many to righteousness as the stars forever and ever.
4 But you, O Daniel, shut up the words, and seal the book, *even* to the time of the end: many shall run to and fro, and knowledge shall be increased.
5 ¶ Then I Daniel looked, and, behold, there stood other two, the one on this side of the bank of the river, and the other on that side of the bank of the river.
6 And *one* said to the man clothed in linen, which *was* upon the waters of the river, How long *shall it be to* the end of these wonders?
7 And I heard the man clothed in linen, which *was* upon the waters of the river, when he held up his right hand and his left hand to heaven, and swore by him that lives forever that *it shall be* for a time, times, and a half; and when he shall have accomplished to scatter the power of the holy people, all these *things* shall be finished.
8 And I heard, but I understood not: then said I, O my Lord, what *shall be* the end of these *things*?
9 And he said, Go your way, Daniel: for the words *are* closed up and sealed till the time of the end.
10 Many shall be purified, and made white, and tried; but the wicked shall do wickedly: and none of the wicked shall understand; but the wise shall understand.
11 And from the time *that* the daily *sacrifice* shall be taken away, and the abomination that makes desolate set up, *there shall be* a thousand two hundred and ninety days.
12 Blessed *is* he that waits, and comes to the thousand three hundred and five and thirty days.
13 But go you your way till the end *is*: for you shall rest, and stand in your lot at the end of the days.

Hosea

Hosea 1

1:1 ¶ The word of Yahweh that came to Hosea, the son of Beeri, in the days of Uzziah, Jotham, Ahaz, *and* Hezekiah, kings of Judah, and in the days of Jeroboam the son of Joash, king of Israel.

2 ¶ The beginning of the word of Yahweh by Hosea. And Yahweh said to Hosea, Go, take to you a wife of whoredoms and children of whoredoms: for the land has committed great whoredom, *departing* from Yahweh.

3 So he went and took Gomer the daughter of Diblaim; which conceived, and bore him a son.

4 And Yahweh said to him, Call his name Jezreel; for yet a little *while*, and I will avenge the blood of Jezreel upon the house of Jehu, and will cause to cease the kingdom of the house of Israel.

5 And it shall come to pass at that day, that I will break the bow of Israel in the valley of Jezreel.

6 And she conceived again, and bore a daughter. And *God* said to him, Call her name Loruhamah: for I will no more have mercy upon the house of Israel; but I will utterly take them away.

7 But I will have mercy upon the house of Judah, and will save them by Yahweh their God, and will not save them by bow, nor by sword, nor by battle, by horses, nor by horsemen.

8 ¶ Now when she had weaned Loruhamah, she conceived, and bore a son.

9 Then said *God*, Call his name Loammi: for you *are* not my people, and I will not be your *God*.

10 Yet the number of the children of Israel shall be as the sand of the sea, which cannot be measured nor numbered; and it shall come to pass, *that* in the place where it was said to them, You *are* not my people, *there* it shall be said to them, *You are* the sons of the living God.

11 Then shall the children of Judah and the children of Israel be gathered together, and appoint themselves one head, and they shall come up out of the land: for great *shall be* the day of Jezreel.

Hosea 2

2:1 ¶ Say you to your brothers, Ammi; and to your sisters, Ruhamah.

2 Plead with your mother, plead: for she *is* not my wife, neither *am* I her husband: let her therefore put away her whoredoms out of her sight, and her adulteries from between her breasts;

3 Lest I strip her naked, and set her as in the day that she was born, and make her as a wilderness, and set her like a dry land, and slay her with thirst.

4 And I will not have mercy upon her children; for they *are* the children of whoredoms.

5 For their mother has played the harlot: she that conceived them has done shamefully: for she said, I will go after my lovers, that give *me* my bread and my water, my wool and my flax, my oil and my drink.

6 ¶ Therefore, behold, I will hedge up your way with thorns, and make a wall, that she shall not find her paths.

7 And she shall follow after her lovers, but she shall not overtake them; and she shall seek them, but shall not find *them*: then shall she say, I will go and return to my first husband; for then *was it* better with me than now.

8 For she did not know that I gave her corn, and *new* wine, and oil, and multiplied her silver and gold, *which* they prepared for Baal.

9 Therefore will I return, and take away my corn in the time thereof, and my *new* wine in the season thereof, and will recover my wool and my flax *given* to cover her nakedness.

10 And now will I discover her lewdness in the sight of her lovers, and none shall deliver her out of my hand.

11 I will also cause all her joy to cease, her feast days, her new moons, and her sabbaths, and all her solemn feasts.

12 And I will destroy her vines and her fig trees, whereof she has said, These *are* my rewards that my lovers have given me: and I will make them a forest, and the beasts of the field shall eat them.

13 And I will visit upon her the days of Baalim, wherein she burned incense to them, and she decked herself with her earrings and her jewels, and she went after her lovers, and forgot me, says Yahweh.

14 ¶ Therefore, behold, I will allure her, and bring her into the wilderness, and speak comfortably to her.

15 And I will give her her vineyards from there, and the valley of Achor for a door of hope: and she shall sing there, as in the days of her youth, and as in the day when she came up out of the land of Egypt.

16 And it shall be at that day, says Yahweh, *that* you shall call me Ishi; and shall call me no more Baali.

17 For I will take away the names of Baalim out of her mouth, and they shall no more be remembered by their name.

18 And in that day will I make a covenant for them with the beasts of the field, and with the fowls of heaven, and *with* the creeping things of the ground: and I will break the bow and the sword and the battle out of the earth, and will make them to lie down safely.

19 And I will betroth you to me forever; yes, I will betroth you to me in righteousness, and in judgment, and in loving kindness, and in mercies.

20 I will even betroth you to me in faithfulness: and you shall know Yahweh.

21 And it shall come to pass in that day, I will hear, says Yahweh, I will hear the heavens, and they shall hear the earth;

22 And the earth shall hear the corn, and the *new* wine, and the oil; and they shall hear Jezreel.

23 And I will sow her unto me in the earth; and I will have mercy upon her that had not obtained mercy; and I will say to *them which were* not my people, You *are* my people; and they shall say, *You are* my God.

Hosea 3

3:1 ¶ Then said Yahweh to me, Go yet, love a woman beloved of *her* friend, yet an adulteress, according to the love of Yahweh toward the children of Israel, who look to other gods, and love flagons of wine.

Hosea 3

2 So I bought her for me for fifteen *pieces* of silver, and *for* a homer of barley, and a half homer of barley:
3 And I said to her, You shall dwell with me many days; you shall not play the harlot, and you shall not be for *another* man: so *will* I also *be* for you.
4 For the children of Israel shall dwell many days without a king, and without a prince, and without a sacrifice, and without an image, and without an ephod, and *without* teraphim:
5 Afterward shall the children of Israel return, and seek Yahweh their God, and David their king; and shall fear Yahweh and his goodness in the latter days.

Hosea 4

4:1 ¶ Hear the word of Yahweh, you children of Israel: for Yahweh has a controversy with the inhabitants of the land, because *there is* no truth, nor mercy, nor knowledge of God in the land.
2 By swearing, and lying, and killing, and stealing, and committing adultery, they break out, and blood touches blood.
3 Therefore shall the land mourn, and every one that dwells therein shall languish, with the beasts of the field, and with the fowls of heaven; yes, the fishes of the sea also shall be taken away.
4 Yet let no man strive, nor reprove another: for your people *are* as they that strive with the priest.
5 Therefore shall you fall in the day, and the prophet also shall fall with you in the night, and I will destroy your mother.
6 ¶ My people are destroyed for lack of knowledge: because you have rejected knowledge, I will also reject you, that you shall be no priest to me: seeing you have forgotten the law of your God, I will also forget your children.
7 As they were increased, so they sinned against me: *therefore* will I change their glory into shame.
8 They eat up the sin of my people, and they set their heart on their iniquity.
9 And there shall be, like people, like priest: and I will punish them for their ways, and reward them *for* their doings.
10 For they shall eat, and not have enough: they shall commit whoredom, and shall not increase: because they have left off to take heed to Yahweh.
11 Whoredom and wine and new wine take away the heart.
12 ¶ My people ask counsel *from* their trees, and their staff declares unto them: for the spirit of whoredoms has caused *them* to err, and they have gone a whoring from under their God.
13 They sacrifice upon the tops of the mountains, and burn incense upon the hills, under oaks and poplars and elms, because the shadow thereof *is* good: therefore your daughters shall commit whoredom, and your spouses shall commit adultery.
14 I will not punish your daughters when they commit whoredom, nor your spouses when they commit adultery: for themselves are separated with whores, and they sacrifice with harlots: therefore the people *that* do not understand shall fall.
15 Though you, Israel, play the harlot, *yet* let not Judah offend; and come not you to Gilgal, neither go you up to Bethaven, nor swear, Yahweh lives.
16 For Israel slides back as a backsliding heifer: now Yahweh will feed them as a lamb in a large place.
17 Ephraim *is* joined to idols: let him alone.
18 Their drink is sour: they have committed whoredom continually: her rulers *with* shame do love, Give you.
19 The wind has bound her up in her wings, and they shall be ashamed because of their sacrifices.

Hosea 5

5:1 ¶ Hear you this, O priests; and listen, you house of Israel; and give you ear, O house of the king; for judgment *is* toward you, because you have been a snare on Mizpah, and a net spread upon Tabor.
2 And the rebels are profound to make slaughter, though I *have been* a rebuker of them all.
3 I know Ephraim, and Israel is not hidden from me: for now, O Ephraim, you commit whoredom, *and* Israel is defiled.
4 They will not frame their doings to turn to their God: for the spirit of whoredoms *is* in the midst of them, and they have not known Yahweh.
5 And the pride of Israel does testify to his face: therefore shall Israel and Ephraim fall in their iniquity; Judah also shall fall with them.
6 They shall go with their flocks and with their herds to seek Yahweh; but they shall not find *him*; he has withdrawn himself from them.
7 They have dealt treacherously against Yahweh: for they have begotten strange children: now shall a month devour them with their portions.
8 ¶ Blow you the cornet in Gibeah, *and* the trumpet in Ramah: cry aloud *at* Bethaven, after you, O Benjamin.
9 Ephraim shall be desolate in the day of rebuke: among the tribes of Israel have I made known that which shall surely be.
10 The princes of Judah were like them that remove the bound: *therefore* I will pour out my wrath upon them like water.
11 Ephraim *is* oppressed *and* broken in judgment, because he willingly walked after the commandment.
12 Therefore *will* I *be* to Ephraim as a moth, and to the house of Judah as rottenness.
13 When Ephraim saw his sickness, and Judah *saw* his wound, then went Ephraim to the Assyrian, and sent to king Jareb: yet could he not heal you, nor cure you of your wound.
14 For I *will be* to Ephraim as a lion, and as a young lion to the house of Judah: I, *even* I, will tear and go away; I will take away, and none shall rescue *him*.

15 I will go *and* return to my place, till they acknowledge their offense, and seek my face: in their affliction they will seek me earnestly.

Hosea 6

6:1 ¶ Come, and let us return unto Yahweh: for he has torn, and he will heal us; he has smitten, and he will bind us up.

2 After two days will he revive us: in the third day he will raise us up, and we shall live in his sight.

3 Then shall we know, *if* we follow on to know Yahweh: his going forth is prepared as the morning; and he shall come to us as the rain, as the latter *and* former rain to the earth.

4 ¶ O Ephraim, what shall I do unto you? O Judah, what shall I do unto you? for your goodness *is* as a morning cloud, and as the early dew it goes away.

5 Therefore have I hewed *them* by the prophets; I have slain them by the words of my mouth: and your judgments *are as* the light *that* goes forth.

6 For I desired mercy, and not sacrifice; and the knowledge of God more than burnt offerings.

7 But they like men have transgressed the covenant: there have they dealt treacherously against me.

8 Gilead *is* a city of them that work iniquity, *and is* polluted with blood.

9 And as troops of robbers wait for a man, *so* the company of priests murder in the way by consent: for they commit lewdness.

10 I have seen a horrible thing in the house of Israel: there *is* the whoredom of Ephraim, Israel is defiled.

11 Also, O Judah, he has set a harvest for you, when I returned the captivity of my people.

Hosea 7

7:1 ¶ When I would have healed Israel, then the iniquity of Ephraim was discovered, and the wickedness of Samaria: for they commit falsehood; and the thief comes in, *and* the troop of robbers spoils outside.

2 And they consider not in their hearts *that* I remember all their wickedness: now their own doings have beset them about; they are before my face.

3 They make the king glad with their wickedness, and the princes with their lies.

4 They *are* all adulterers, as an oven heated by the baker, *who* ceases from raising after he has kneaded the dough, until it is leavened.

5 In the day of our king the princes have made *him* sick with bottles of wine; he stretched out his hand with scorners.

6 For they have made ready their heart like an oven, while they lie in wait: their baker sleeps all the night; in the morning it burns as a flaming fire.

7 They are all hot as an oven, and have devoured their judges; all their kings have fallen: *there is* none among them that calls unto me.

8 ¶ Ephraim, he has mixed himself among the people; Ephraim is a cake not turned.

9 Strangers have devoured his strength, and he knows *it* not: yes, gray hairs are here and there upon him, yet he knows not.

10 And the pride of Israel testifies to his face: and they do not return to Yahweh their God, nor seek him for all this.

11 Ephraim also is like a silly dove without heart: they call to Egypt, they go to Assyria.

12 When they shall go, I will spread my net upon them; I will bring them down as the fowls of the heaven; I will chastise them, as their congregation has heard.

13 Woe unto them! for they have fled from me: destruction unto them! because they have transgressed against me: though I have redeemed them, yet they have spoken lies against me.

14 And they have not cried unto me with their heart, when they howled upon their beds: they assemble themselves for corn and *new* wine, *and* they rebel against me.

15 Though I have bound *and* strengthened their arms, yet do they imagine mischief against me.

16 They return, *but* not to the most High: they are like a deceitful bow: their princes shall fall by the sword for the rage of their tongue: this *shall be* their derision in the land of Egypt.

Hosea 8

8:1 ¶ *Set* the trumpet to your mouth. *He shall come* as an eagle against the house of Yahweh, because they have transgressed my covenant, and trespassed against my law.

2 Israel shall cry unto me, My God, we know you.

3 Israel has cast off *the thing that is* good: the enemy shall pursue him.

4 They have set up kings, but not by me: they have made princes, and I knew *it* not: of their silver and their gold have they made them idols, that they may be cut off.

5 Your calf, O Samaria, has cast *you* off; my anger is kindled against them: how long *will it be* before they attain to innocence?

6 For from Israel *was* it also: the workman made it; therefore it *is* not God: but the calf of Samaria shall be broken in pieces.

7 For they have sown the wind, and they shall reap the whirlwind: it has no stalk: the bud shall yield no meal: if so be it yields, the strangers shall swallow it up.

8 ¶ Israel is swallowed up: now shall they be among the Gentiles as a vessel wherein *is* no pleasure.

9 For they have gone up to Assyria, a wild donkey alone by himself: Ephraim has hired lovers.

10 Yes, though they have hired among the nations, now will I gather them, and they shall sorrow a little for the burden of the king of princes.

11 Because Ephraim has made many altars to sin, altars shall be unto him to sin.

12 I have written to him the great things of my law, *but* they were counted as a strange thing.

Hosea 8

13 They sacrifice flesh *for* the sacrifices of my offerings, and eat *it; but* Yahweh accepts them not; now will he remember their iniquity, and visit their sins: they shall return to Egypt.
14 For Israel has forgotten his Maker, and builds temples; and Judah has multiplied fenced cities: but I will send a fire upon his cities, and it shall devour the palaces thereof.

Hosea 9

9:1 ¶ Rejoice not, O Israel, for joy, as *other* people: for you have gone a whoring from your God, you have loved a reward upon every corn floor.
2 The floor and the winepress shall not feed them, and the new wine shall fail in her.
3 They shall not dwell in Yahweh's land; but Ephraim shall return to Egypt, and they shall eat unclean *things* in Assyria.
4 They shall not offer wine *offerings* to Yahweh, neither shall they be pleasing unto him: their sacrifices *shall be* to them as the bread of mourners; all that eat thereof shall be polluted: for their bread for their soul shall not come into the house of Yahweh.
5 What will you do in the solemn day, and in the day of the feast of Yahweh?
6 For, lo, they are gone because of destruction: Egypt shall gather them up, Memphis shall bury them: the pleasant *places* for their silver, nettles shall possess them: thorns *shall be* in their tabernacles.
7 ¶ The days of visitation are come, the days of recompense are come; Israel shall know *it*: the prophet *is* a fool, the spiritual man *is* mad, for the multitude of your iniquity, and the great hatred.
8 The watchman of Ephraim *was* with my God: *but* the prophet *is* a snare of a fowler in all his ways, *and* enmity in the house of his God.
9 They have deeply corrupted *themselves*, as in the days of Gibeah: *therefore* he will remember their iniquity, he will visit their sins.
10 I found Israel like grapes in the wilderness; I saw your fathers as the first ripe in the fig tree at her first time: *but* they went to Baalpeor, and separated themselves to *that* shame; and *their* abominations were according as they loved.
11 ¶ *As for* Ephraim, their glory shall fly away like a bird, from the birth, and from the womb, and from the conception.
12 Though they bring up their children, yet will I bereave them, *that there shall* not *be* a man *left*: yes, woe also to them when I depart from them!
13 Ephraim, as I saw Tyrus, *is* planted in a pleasant place: but Ephraim shall bring forth his children to the murderer.
14 Give them, O Yahweh: what will you give? give them a miscarrying womb and dry breasts.
15 All their wickedness *is* in Gilgal: for there I hated them: for the wickedness of their doings I will drive them out of my house, I will love them no more: all their princes *are* rebels.
16 Ephraim is smitten, their root is dried up, they shall bear no fruit: yes, though they bring forth, yet will I slay *even* the beloved *fruit* of their womb.
17 My God will cast them away, because they did not listen to him: and they shall be wanderers among the nations.

Hosea 10

10:1 ¶ Israel *is* an empty vine, he brings forth fruit unto himself: according to the multitude of his fruit he has increased the altars; according to the goodness of his land they have made goodly images.
2 Their heart is divided; now shall they be found faulty: he shall break down their altars, he shall spoil their images.
3 For now they shall say, We have no king, because we feared not Yahweh; what then should a king do to us?
4 They have spoken words, swearing falsely in making a covenant: thus judgment springs up as hemlock in the furrows of the field.
5 The inhabitants of Samaria shall fear because of the calf of Bethaven: for the people thereof shall mourn over it, and the priests thereof *that* rejoiced on it, for the glory thereof, because it has departed from it.
6 It shall be also carried to Assyria *for* a present to king Jareb: Ephraim shall receive shame, and Israel shall be ashamed of his own counsel.
7 *As for* Samaria, her king is cut off as the foam upon the water.
8 The high places also of Aven, the sin of Israel, shall be destroyed: the thorn and the thistle shall come up on their altars; and they shall say to the mountains, Cover us; and to the hills, Fall on us.
9 ¶ O Israel, you have sinned from the days of Gibeah: there they stood: the battle in Gibeah against the children of iniquity did not overtake them.
10 *It is* in my desire that I should chastise them; and the people shall be gathered against them, when they shall bind themselves in their two furrows.
11 And Ephraim *is as* a heifer *that is* taught, *and* loves to tread out *the corn*; but I passed over upon her fair neck: I will make Ephraim to ride; Judah shall plow, *and* Jacob shall break his clods.
12 Sow to yourselves in righteousness, reap in mercy; break up your fallow ground: for *it is* time to seek Yahweh, till he comes and rains righteousness upon you.
13 You have plowed wickedness, you have reaped iniquity; you have eaten the fruit of lies: because you did trust in your way, in the multitude of your mighty men.
14 Therefore shall a tumult arise among your people, and all your fortresses shall be spoiled, as Shalman spoiled Betharbel in the day of battle: the mother was dashed in pieces upon *her* children.
15 So shall Bethel do to you because of your great wickedness: in a morning shall the king of Israel utterly be cut off.

Hosea 11

11:1 ¶ When Israel *was* a child, then I loved him, and called my son out of Egypt.

2 *As* they called them, so they went from them: they sacrificed to Baalim, and burned incense to graven images.

3 I taught Ephraim also to go, taking them by their arms; but they knew not that I healed them.

4 I drew them with cords of a man, with bands of love: and I was to them as they that take off the yoke from their jaws, and I laid meat unto them.

5 He shall not return into the land of Egypt, but the Assyrian shall be his king, because they refused to return.

6 And the sword shall abide on his cities, and shall consume his branches, and devour *them*, because of their own counsels.

7 And my people are bent to backsliding from me: though they called them to the most High, none at all would exalt *him*.

8 ¶ How shall I give you up, Ephraim? *how* shall I deliver you, Israel? how shall I make you as Admah? *how* shall I set you as Zeboim? my heart is turned within me, my repentings are kindled together.

9 I will not execute the fierceness of my anger, I will not return to destroy Ephraim: for I *am* God, and not man; the Holy One in the midst of you: and I will not enter into the city.

10 They shall walk after Yahweh: he shall roar like a lion: when he shall roar, then the children shall tremble from the west.

11 They shall tremble as a bird out of Egypt, and as a dove out of the land of Assyria: and I will place them in their houses, says Yahweh.

12 Ephraim compasses me about with lies, and the house of Israel with deceit: but Judah yet rules with God, and is faithful with the saints.

Hosea 12

12:1 ¶ Ephraim feeds on wind, and follows after the east wind: he daily increases lies and desolation; and they do make a covenant with the Assyrians, and oil is carried into Egypt.

2 Yahweh has also a controversy with Judah, and will punish Jacob according to his ways; according to his doings will he recompense him.

3 He took his brother by the heel in the womb, and by his strength he had power with God:

4 Yes, he had power over the angel, and prevailed: he wept, and made supplication to him: he found him *in* Bethel, and there he spoke with us;

5 Even Yahweh God of hosts; Yahweh *is* his memorial.

6 Therefore turn you to your God: keep mercy and judgment, and wait on your God continually.

7 ¶ *He is* a merchant, the balances of deceit *are* in his hand: he loves to oppress.

8 And Ephraim said, Yet I have become rich, I have found me out wealth: *in* all my labors they shall find no iniquity in me that *is* sin.

9 And I *that am* Yahweh your God from the land of Egypt will yet make you to dwell in tabernacles, as in the days of the solemn feast.

10 I have also spoken by the prophets, and I have multiplied visions, and used similitudes, by the ministry of the prophets.

11 *Is there* iniquity *in* Gilead? surely they are vanity: they sacrifice bullocks in Gilgal; yes, their altars *are* as heaps in the furrows of the fields.

12 And Jacob fled into the country of Syria, and Israel served for a wife, and for a wife he kept *sheep*.

13 And by a prophet Yahweh brought Israel out of Egypt, and by a prophet was he preserved.

14 Ephraim provoked *him* to anger most bitterly: therefore shall he leave his blood upon him, and his reproach shall his Lord return to him.

Hosea 13

13:1 ¶ When Ephraim spoke trembling, he exalted himself in Israel; but when he offended in Baal, he died.

2 And now they sin more and more, and have made them molten images of their silver, *and* idols according to their own understanding, all of it the work of the craftsmen: they say of them, Let the men that sacrifice kiss the calves.

3 Therefore they shall be as the morning cloud, and as the early dew that passes away, as the chaff *that* is driven with the whirlwind out of the floor, and as the smoke out of the chimney.

4 Yet I *am* Yahweh your God from the land of Egypt, and you shall know no god but me: for *there is* no savior besides me.

5 ¶ I did know you in the wilderness, in the land of great drought.

6 According to their pasture, so were they filled; they were filled, and their heart was exalted; therefore have they forgotten me.

7 Therefore I will be unto them as a lion: as a leopard by the way will I observe *them*:

8 I will meet them as a bear *that is* bereaved *of her cubs*, and will tear the lobe of their heart, and there will I devour them like a lion: the wild beast shall tear them.

9 ¶ O Israel, you have destroyed yourself; but in me *is* your help.

10 I will be your king: where *is any other* that may save you in all your cities? and your judges of whom you said, Give me a king and princes?

11 I gave you a king in my anger, and took *him* away in my wrath.

12 The iniquity of Ephraim *is* bound up; his sin *is* hidden.

Hosea 13

13 The sorrows of a laboring woman shall come upon him: he *is* an unwise son; for he should not stay long in *the place of* the breaking forth of children.

14 I will ransom them from the power of the grave; I will redeem them from death: O death, I will be your plagues; O grave, I will be your destruction: repentance shall be hidden from my eyes.

15 Though he is fruitful among *the brethren*, an east wind shall come, the wind of Yahweh shall come up from the wilderness, and his spring shall become dry, and his fountain shall be dried up: he shall spoil the treasure of all pleasant vessels.

16 Samaria shall become desolate; for she has rebelled against her God: they shall fall by the sword: their infants shall be dashed in pieces, and their women with child shall be ripped up.

Hosea 14

14:1 ¶ O Israel, return unto Yahweh your God; for you have fallen by your iniquity.

2 Take with you words, and turn to Yahweh: say to him, Take away all iniquity, and receive *us* graciously: so will we render the calves of our lips.

3 Asshur shall not save us; we will not ride upon horses: neither will we say any more to the work of our hands, *You are* our gods: for in you the fatherless finds mercy.

4 ¶ I will heal their backsliding, I will love them freely: for my anger is turned away from him.

5 I will be as the dew unto Israel: he shall grow as the lily, and cast forth his roots as Lebanon.

6 His branches shall spread, and his beauty shall be as the olive tree, and his smell as Lebanon.

7 They that dwell under his shadow shall return; they shall revive *as* the corn, and grow as the vine: the scent thereof *shall be* as the wine of Lebanon.

8 ¶ Ephraim *shall say*, What have I to do any more with idols? I have heard *him*, and observed him: I *am* like a green fir tree. From me is your fruit found.

9 Who *is* wise, and he shall understand these *things*? prudent, and he shall know them? for the ways of Yahweh *are* right, and the just shall walk in them: but the transgressors shall fall therein.

Joel

Joel 1

1:1 ¶ The word of Yahweh that came to Joel the son of Pethuel.

2 Hear this, you old men, and give ear, all you inhabitants of the land. Has this been in your days, or even in the days of your fathers?

3 Tell you your children of it, and *let* your children *tell* their children, and their children another generation.

4 That which the palmerworm has left has the locust eaten; and that which the locust has left has the cankerworm eaten; and that which the cankerworm has left has the caterpillar eaten.

5 Awake, you drunkards, and weep; and howl, all you drinkers of wine, because of the new wine; for it is cut off from your mouth.

6 For a nation has come up upon my land, strong, and without number, whose teeth *are* the teeth of a lion, and he has the cheek teeth of a great lion.

7 He has laid my vine waste, and barked my fig tree: he has made it clean bare, and cast *it* away; the branches thereof are made white.

8 ¶ Lament like a virgin girded with sackcloth for the husband of her youth.

9 The meat offering and the drink offering is cut off from the house of Yahweh; the priests, Yahweh's ministers, mourn.

10 The field is wasted, the land mourns; for the corn is wasted: the new wine is dried up, the oil languishes.

11 Be you ashamed, O you husbandmen; howl, O you vine dressers, for the wheat and for the barley; because the harvest of the field has perished.

12 The vine is dried up, and the fig tree languishes; the pomegranate tree, the palm tree also, and the apple tree, *even* all the trees of the field, are withered: because joy is withered away from the sons of men.

13 Gird yourselves, and lament, you priests: howl, you ministers of the altar: come, lie all night in sackcloth, you ministers of my God: for the meat offering and the drink offering is withheld from the house of your God.

14 ¶ Sanctify you a fast, call a solemn assembly, gather the elders *and* all the inhabitants of the land *into* the house of Yahweh your God, and cry unto Yahweh,

15 Alas for the day! for the day of Yahweh *is* at hand, and as a destruction from the Almighty shall it come.

16 Is not the food cut off before our eyes, *yes,* joy and gladness from the house of our God?

17 The seed is rotten under their clods, the garners are laid desolate, the barns are broken down; for the corn is withered.

18 How do the beasts groan! the herds of cattle are perplexed, because they have no pasture; yes, the flocks of sheep are made desolate.

19 O Yahweh, to you will I cry: for the fire has devoured the pastures of the wilderness, and the flame has burned all the trees of the field.

20 The beasts of the field cry also to you: for the rivers of waters are dried up, and the fire has devoured the pastures of the wilderness.

Joel 2

2:1 ¶ Blow you the trumpet in Zion, and sound an alarm in my holy mountain: let all the inhabitants of the land tremble: for the day of Yahweh comes, for *it is* near at hand;

2 A day of darkness and of gloominess, a day of clouds and of thick darkness, as the morning spread upon the mountains: a great people and a strong; there has not been ever the like, neither shall be any more after it, *even* to the years of many generations.
3 A fire devours before them; and behind them a flame burns: the land *is* as the garden of Eden before them, and behind them a desolate wilderness; yes, and nothing shall escape them.
4 The appearance of them *is* as the appearance of horses; and as horsemen, so shall they run.
5 Like the noise of chariots on the tops of mountains shall they leap, like the noise of a flame of fire that devours the stubble, as a strong people set in battle array.
6 Before their face the people shall be much pained: all faces shall gather blackness.
7 They shall run like mighty men; they shall climb the wall like men of war; and they shall march every one on his ways, and they shall not break their ranks:
8 Neither shall one thrust another; they shall walk every one in his path: and *when* they fall upon the sword, they shall not be wounded.
9 They shall run to and fro in the city; they shall run upon the wall, they shall climb up upon the houses; they shall enter in at the windows like a thief.
10 The earth shall quake before them; the heavens shall tremble: the sun and the moon shall be dark, and the stars shall withdraw their shining:
11 And Yahweh shall utter his voice before his army: for his camp *is* very great: for *he is* strong that executes his word: for the day of Yahweh *is* great and very terrible; and who can endure it?
12 ¶ Therefore also now, says Yahweh, turn you *even* to me with all your heart, and with fasting, and with weeping, and with mourning:
13 And tear your heart, and not your garments, and turn unto Yahweh your God: for he *is* gracious and merciful, slow to anger, and of great kindness, and repents him of the evil.
14 Who knows *if* he will return and repent, and leave a blessing behind him; *even* a meat offering and a drink offering unto Yahweh your God?
15 Blow the trumpet in Zion, sanctify a fast, call a solemn assembly:
16 Gather the people, sanctify the congregation, assemble the elders, gather the children, and those that suck the breasts: let the bridegroom go forth from his chamber, and the bride out of her closet.
17 Let the priests, the ministers of Yahweh, weep between the porch and the altar, and let them say, Spare your people, O Yahweh, and give not your heritage to reproach, that the heathen should rule over them: why should they say among the people, Where *is* their God?
18 ¶ Then will Yahweh be jealous for his land, and pity his people.
19 Yes, Yahweh will answer and say to his people, Behold, I will send you corn, and *new* wine, and oil, and you shall be satisfied therewith: and I will no more make you a reproach among the heathen:
20 But I will remove far off from you the northern *army*, and will drive him into a land barren and desolate, with his face toward the east sea, and his hinder part toward the utmost sea, and his stink shall come up, and his ill savor shall come up, because he has done great things.
21 Fear not, O land; be glad and rejoice: for Yahweh will do great things.
22 Be not afraid, you beasts of the field: for the pastures of the wilderness do spring, for the tree bears her fruit, the fig tree and the vine do yield their strength.
23 Be glad then, you children of Zion, and rejoice in Yahweh your God: for he has given you the former rain moderately, and he will cause to come down for you the rain, the former rain, and the latter rain in the first *month*.
24 And the floors shall be full of wheat, and the vats shall overflow with *new* wine and oil.
25 And I will restore to you the years that the locust has eaten, the cankerworm, and the caterpillar, and the palmerworm, my great army which I sent among you.
26 And you shall eat in plenty, and be satisfied, and praise the name of Yahweh your God, that has dealt wondrously with you: and my people shall never be ashamed.
27 And you shall know that I *am* in the midst of Israel, and *that* I *am* Yahweh your God, and none else: and my people shall never be ashamed.
28 ¶ And it shall come to pass afterward, *that* I will pour out my spirit upon all flesh; and your sons and your daughters shall prophesy, your old men shall dream dreams, your young men shall see visions
29 And also upon the servants and upon the handmaids in those days will I pour out my spirit.
30 And I will show wonders in the heavens and in the earth, blood, and fire, and pillars of smoke.
31 The sun shall be turned into darkness, and the moon into blood, before the great and the terrible day of Yahweh comes.
32 And it shall come to pass, *that* whoever shall call on the name of Yahweh shall be delivered: for in mount Zion and in Jerusalem shall be deliverance, as Yahweh has said, and in the remnant whom Yahweh shall call.

Joel 3

3:1 ¶ For, behold, in those days, and in that time, when I shall bring again the captivity of Judah and Jerusalem,
2 I will also gather all nations, and will bring them down into the valley of Jehoshaphat, and will plead with them there for my people and *for* my heritage Israel, whom they have scattered among the nations, and parted my land.
3 And they have cast lots for my people; and have given a boy for a harlot, and sold a girl for wine, that they might drink.
4 Yes, and what have you to do with me, O Tyre, and Zidon, and all the coasts of Palestine? will you render me a recompense? and if you recompense me, swiftly *and* speedily will I return your recompense upon your own head;

5 Because you have taken my silver and my gold, and have carried into your temples my goodly pleasant things:
6 The children also of Judah and the children of Jerusalem have you sold to the Grecians, that you might remove them far from their border.
7 Behold, I will raise them out of the place where you have sold them, and will return your recompense upon your own head:
8 And I will sell your sons and your daughters into the hand of the children of Judah, and they shall sell them to the Sabeans, to a people far off: for Yahweh has spoken *it*.
9 ¶ Proclaim you this among the Gentiles; Prepare war, wake up the mighty men, let all the men of war draw near; let them come up:
10 Beat your plowshares into swords, and your pruning hooks into spears: let the weak say, I *am* strong.
11 Assemble yourselves, and come, all you heathen, and gather yourselves together round about: there cause your mighty ones to come down, O Yahweh.
12 Let the heathen be wakened, and come up to the valley of Jehoshaphat: for there will I sit to judge all the heathen round about.
13 Put you in the sickle, for the harvest is ripe: come, get you down; for the press is full, the vats overflow; for their wickedness *is* great.
14 Multitudes, multitudes in the valley of decision: for the day of Yahweh *is* near in the valley of decision.
15 The sun and the moon shall be darkened, and the stars shall withdraw their shining.
16 Yahweh also shall roar out of Zion, and utter his voice from Jerusalem; and the heavens and the earth shall shake: but Yahweh *will be* the hope of his people, and the strength of the children of Israel.
17 So shall you know that I *am* Yahweh your God dwelling in Zion, my holy mountain: then shall Jerusalem be holy, and there shall no strangers pass through her any more.
18 ¶ And it shall come to pass in that day, *that* the mountains shall drop down new wine, and the hills shall flow with milk, and all the rivers of Judah shall flow with waters, and a fountain shall come forth from the house of Yahweh, and shall water the valley of Shittim.
19 Egypt shall be a desolation, and Edom shall be a desolate wilderness, for the violence *against* the children of Judah, because they have shed innocent blood in their land.
20 But Judah shall dwell forever, and Jerusalem from generation to generation.
21 For I will cleanse their blood *that* I have not cleansed: for Yahweh dwells in Zion.

Amos

Amos 1

1:1 ¶ The words of Amos, who was among the herdsmen of Tekoa, which he saw concerning Israel in the days of Uzziah king of Judah, and in the days of Jeroboam the son of Joash king of Israel, two years before the earthquake.
2 And he said, Yahweh will roar from Zion, and utter his voice from Jerusalem; and the habitations of the shepherds shall mourn, and the top of Carmel shall wither.
3 ¶ Thus says Yahweh; For three transgressions of Damascus, and for four, I will not turn away *the punishment* thereof; because they have threshed Gilead with threshing instruments of iron:
4 But I will send a fire into the house of Hazael, which shall devour the palaces of Benhadad.
5 I will break also the bar of Damascus, and cut off the inhabitant from the plain of Aven, and him that holds the scepter from the house of Eden: and the people of Syria shall go into captivity to Kir, says Yahweh.
6 Thus says Yahweh; For three transgressions of Gaza, and for four, I will not turn away *the punishment* thereof; because they carried away captive the whole captivity, to deliver *them* up to Edom:
7 But I will send a fire on the wall of Gaza, which shall devour the palaces thereof:
8 And I will cut off the inhabitant from Ashdod, and him that holds the scepter from Ashkelon, and I will turn my hand against Ekron: and the remnant of the Philistines shall perish, says the Lord Yahweh.
9 Thus says Yahweh; For three transgressions of Tyrus, and for four, I will not turn away *the punishment* thereof; because they delivered up the whole captivity to Edom, and remembered not the brotherly covenant:
10 But I will send a fire on the wall of Tyrus, which shall devour the palaces thereof.
11 Thus says Yahweh; For three transgressions of Edom, and for four, I will not turn away *the punishment* thereof; because he did pursue his brother with the sword, and did cast off all pity, and his anger did tear perpetually, and he kept his wrath forever:
12 But I will send a fire upon Teman, which shall devour the palaces of Bozrah.
13 Thus says Yahweh; For three transgressions of the children of Ammon, and for four, I will not turn away *the punishment* thereof; because they have ripped up the women with child of Gilead, that they might enlarge their border:
14 But I will kindle a fire in the wall of Rabbah, and it shall devour the palaces thereof, with shouting in the day of battle, with a tempest in the day of the whirlwind:
15 And their king shall go into captivity, he and his princes together, says Yahweh.

Amos 2

2:1 ¶ Thus says Yahweh; For three transgressions of Moab, and for four, I will not turn away *the punishment* thereof; because he burned the bones of the king of Edom into lime:
2 But I will send a fire upon Moab, and it shall devour the palaces of Kerioth: and Moab shall die with tumult, with shouting, *and* with the sound of the trumpet:
3 And I will cut off the judge from the midst thereof, and will slay all the princes thereof with him, says Yahweh.
4 Thus says Yahweh; For three transgressions of Judah, and for four, I will not turn away *the punishment* thereof; because they have despised the law of Yahweh, and have not kept his commandments, and their lies caused them to err, after the which their fathers have walked:
5 But I will send a fire upon Judah, and it shall devour the palaces of Jerusalem.
6 Thus says Yahweh; For three transgressions of Israel, and for four, I will not turn away *the punishment* thereof; because they sold the righteous for silver, and the poor for a pair of shoes;
7 That pant after the dust of the earth on the head of the poor, and turn aside the way of the meek: and a man and his father will go in to the *same* maid, to profane my holy name:
8 And they lay *themselves* down upon clothes laid to pledge by every altar, and they drink the wine of the condemned *in* the house of their god.
9 ¶ Yet destroyed I the Amorite before them, whose height *was* like the height of the cedars, and he *was* strong as the oaks; yet I destroyed his fruit from above, and his roots from beneath.
10 Also I brought you up from the land of Egypt, and led you *for* forty years through the wilderness, to possess the land of the Amorite.
11 And I raised up of your sons for prophets, and of your young men for Nazarites. *Is it* not even thus, O you children of Israel? says Yahweh.
12 But you gave the Nazarites wine to drink; and commanded the prophets, saying, Prophesy not.
13 Behold, I am pressed under you, as a cart is pressed *that is* full of sheaves.
14 Therefore the flight shall perish from the swift, and the strong shall not strengthen his force, neither shall the mighty deliver himself:
15 Neither shall he stand that handles the bow; and *he that is* swift of foot shall not deliver *himself*: neither shall he that rides the horse deliver himself.
16 And *he that is* courageous among the mighty shall flee away naked in that day, says Yahweh.

Amos 3

3:1 ¶ Hear this word that Yahweh has spoken against you, O children of Israel, against the whole family which I brought up from the land of Egypt, saying,
2 You only have I known of all the families of the earth: therefore I will punish you for all your iniquities.
3 Can two walk together, except they be agreed?
4 Will a lion roar in the forest, when he has no prey? will a young lion cry out of his den, if he has taken nothing?
5 Can a bird fall in a snare upon the earth, where no gin *is* for him? shall *one* take up a snare from the earth, and have taken nothing at all?
6 Shall a trumpet be blown in the city, and the people not be afraid? shall there be evil in a city, and Yahweh has not done *it*?
7 Surely the Lord Yahweh will do nothing, but he reveals his secret to his servants the prophets.
8 The lion has roared, who will not fear? the Lord Yahweh has spoken, who can but prophesy?
9 ¶ Publish in the palaces at Ashdod, and in the palaces in the land of Egypt, and say, Assemble yourselves upon the mountains of Samaria, and behold the great tumults in the midst thereof, and the oppressed in the midst thereof.
10 For they know not to do right, says Yahweh, who store up violence and robbery in their palaces.
11 Therefore thus says the Lord Yahweh; An adversary *there shall be* even round about the land; and he shall bring down your strength from you, and your palaces shall be spoiled.
12 Thus says Yahweh; As the shepherd takes out of the mouth of the lion two legs, or a piece of an ear; so shall the children of Israel be taken out that dwell in Samaria in the corner of a bed, and in Damascus *in* a couch.
13 Hear you, and testify in the house of Jacob, says the Lord Yahweh, the God of hosts,
14 That in the day that I shall visit the transgressions of Israel upon him I will also visit the altars of Bethel: and the horns of the altar shall be cut off, and fall to the ground.
15 And I will smite the winter house *along* with the summer house; and the houses of ivory shall perish, and the great houses shall have an end, says Yahweh.

Amos 4

4:1 ¶ Hear this word, you cows of Bashan, that *are* in the mountain of Samaria, which oppress the poor, which crush the needy, which say to their masters, Bring, and let us drink.
2 The Lord Yahweh has sworn by his holiness, that, lo, the days shall come upon you, that he will take you away with hooks, and your posterity with fishhooks.
3 And you shall go out at the breaches, every *cow at* that which *is* before her; and you shall cast *them* into the palace, says Yahweh.
4 Come to Bethel, and transgress; at Gilgal multiply transgression; and bring your sacrifices every morning, *and* your tithes after three years:
5 And offer a sacrifice of thanksgiving with leaven, and proclaim *and* publish the free offerings: for this you like, O you children of Israel, says the Lord Yahweh.

Amos 4

6 ¶ And I also have given you cleanness of teeth in all your cities, and want of bread in all your places: yet have you not returned unto me, says Yahweh.

7 And also I have withheld the rain from you, when *there were* yet three months to the harvest: and I caused it to rain upon one city, and caused it not to rain upon another city: one piece was rained upon, and the piece whereupon it rained not withered.

8 So two *or* three cities wandered to one city, to drink water; but they were not satisfied: yet have you not returned unto me, says Yahweh.

9 I have smitten you with blasting and mildew: when your gardens and your vineyards and your fig trees and your olive trees increased, the palmerworm devoured *them*: yet have you not returned unto me, says Yahweh.

10 I have sent among you the pestilence after the manner of Egypt: your young men have I slain with the sword, and have taken away your horses; and I have made the stink of your camps to come up to your nostrils: yet have you not returned to me, says Yahweh.

11 I have overthrown *some* of you, as God overthrew Sodom and Gomorrah, and you were as a firebrand plucked out of the burning: yet have you not returned unto me, says Yahweh.

12 Therefore thus will I do unto you, O Israel: *and* because I will do this to you, prepare to meet your God, O Israel.

13 For, lo, he that forms the mountains, and creates the wind, and declares to man what *is* his thought, that makes the morning darkness, and treads upon the high places of the earth, Yahweh, The God of hosts, *is* his name.

Amos 5

5:1 ¶ Hear you this word which I take up against you, *even* a lamentation, O house of Israel.

2 The virgin of Israel is fallen; she shall no more rise: she is forsaken upon her land; *there is* none to raise her up.

3 For thus says the Lord Yahweh; The city that went out *by* a thousand shall leave a hundred, and that which went forth *by* a hundred shall leave ten, to the house of Israel.

4 ¶ For thus says Yahweh to the house of Israel, Seek you me, and you shall live:

5 But seek not Bethel, nor enter into Gilgal, and pass not to Beersheba: for Gilgal shall surely go into captivity, and Bethel shall come to nothing.

6 Seek Yahweh, and you shall live; lest he breaks out like fire in the house of Joseph, and devours *it*, and *there is* none to quench *it* in Bethel.

7 You who turn judgment to wormwood, and leave off righteousness in the earth,

8 *Seek him* that made the seven stars and Orion, and turns the shadow of death into the morning, and makes the day dark with night: that calls for the waters of the sea, and pours them out upon the face of the earth: Yahweh *is* his name:

9 That strengthens the spoiled against the strong, so that the spoiled shall come against the fortress.

10 They hate him that rebukes in the gate, and they abhor him that speaks uprightly.

11 Forasmuch therefore as your treading *is* upon the poor, and you take from him burdens of wheat: you have built houses of hewn stone, but you shall not dwell in them; you have planted pleasant vineyards, but you shall not drink wine of them.

12 For I know your manifold transgressions and your mighty sins: they afflict the just, they take a bribe, and they turn aside the poor in the gate *from their right*.

13 Therefore the prudent shall keep silence in that time; for it *is* an evil time.

14 Seek good, and not evil, that you may live: and so Yahweh, the God of hosts, shall be with you, as you have spoken.

15 Hate the evil, and love the good, and establish judgment in the gate: it may be that Yahweh God of hosts will be gracious unto the remnant of Joseph.

16 ¶ Therefore Yahweh, the God of hosts, the Lord, says thus; Wailing *shall be* in all streets; and they shall say in all the highways, Alas! alas! and they shall call the husbandman to mourning, and such as are skillful in lamentation to wailing.

17 And in all vineyards *shall be* wailing: for I will pass through you, says Yahweh.

18 Woe unto you that desire the day of Yahweh! to what end *is* it for you? the day of Yahweh *is* darkness, and not light.

19 As if a man did flee from a lion, and a bear met him; or went into the house, and leaned his hand on the wall, and a serpent bit him.

20 *Shall* not the day of Yahweh *be* darkness, and not light? even very dark, and no brightness in it?

21 ¶ I hate, I despise your feast days, and I will not smell in your solemn assemblies.

22 Though you offer me burnt offerings and your meat offerings, I will not accept *them*: neither will I regard the peace offerings of your fat beasts.

23 Take you away from me the noise of your songs; for I will not hear the melody of your viols.

24 But let judgment run down as waters, and righteousness as a mighty stream.

25 Have you offered unto me sacrifices and offerings in the wilderness *for* forty years, O house of Israel?

26 But you have borne the tabernacle of your Moloch and Chiun your images, the star of your god, which you made to yourselves.

27 Therefore will I cause you to go into captivity beyond Damascus, says Yahweh, whose name *is* The God of hosts.

Amos 6

6:1 ¶ Woe unto them *that are* at ease in Zion, and trust in the mountain of Samaria, *which are* named chief of the nations, to whom the house of Israel came!

2 Pass you to Calneh, and see; and from there go you to Hamath the great: then go down to Gath of the Philistines: *are they* better than these kingdoms? or their border greater than your border?

3 You that put far away the evil day, and cause the seat of violence to come near;

4 That lie upon beds of ivory, and stretch themselves upon their couches, and eat the lambs out of the flock, and the calves out of the midst of the stall;

5 That chant to the sound of the viol, *and* invent to themselves instruments of music, like David;

6 That drink wine in bowls, and anoint themselves with the chief ointments: but they are not grieved for the affliction of Joseph.

7 Therefore now shall they go captive with the first that go captive, and the banquet of them that stretched themselves shall be removed.

8 ¶ The Lord Yahweh has sworn by himself, says Yahweh the God of hosts, I abhor the excellency of Jacob, and hate his palaces: therefore will I deliver up the city with all that is therein.

9 And it shall come to pass, if there remain ten men in one house, that they shall die.

10 And a man's uncle shall take him up, and he that burns him, to bring out the bones out of the house, and shall say to him that *is* by the sides of the house, *Is there* yet *any* with you? and he shall say, No. Then shall he say, Hold your tongue: for we may not make mention of the name of Yahweh.

11 For, behold, Yahweh commands, and he will smite the great house with breaches, and the little house with clefts.

12 Shall horses run upon the rock? will *one* plow *there* with oxen? for you have turned judgment into gall, and the fruit of righteousness into hemlock:

13 You which rejoice in a thing of nothing, which say, Have we not taken to us horns by our own strength?

14 But, behold, I will raise up against you a nation, O house of Israel, says Yahweh the God of hosts; and they shall afflict you from the entering in of Hemath unto the river of the wilderness.

Amos 7

7:1 ¶ Thus has the Lord Yahweh shown unto me; and, behold, he formed grasshoppers in the beginning of the shooting up of the latter growth; and, lo, *it was* the latter growth after the king's mowings.

2 And it came to pass, *that* when they had made an end of eating the grass of the land, then I said, O Lord Yahweh, forgive, I beseech you: by whom shall Jacob arise? for he *is* small.

3 Yahweh repented for this: It shall not be, says Yahweh.

4 Thus has the Lord Yahweh shown unto me: and, behold, the Lord Yahweh called to contend by fire, and it devoured the great deep, and did eat up a part.

5 Then said I, O Lord Yahweh, cease, I beseech you: by whom shall Jacob arise? for he *is* small.

6 Yahweh repented for this: This also shall not be, says the Lord Yahweh.

7 Thus he showed me: and, behold, the Lord stood upon a wall *made* by a plumbline, with a plumbline in his hand.

8 And Yahweh said to me, Amos, what see you? And I said, A plumbline. Then said the Lord, Behold, I will set a plumbline in the midst of my people Israel: I will not again pass by them any more:

9 And the high places of Isaac shall be desolate, and the sanctuaries of Israel shall be laid waste; and I will rise against the house of Jeroboam with the sword.

10 ¶ Then Amaziah the priest of Bethel sent to Jeroboam king of Israel, saying, Amos has conspired against you in the midst of the house of Israel: the land is not able to bear all his words.

11 For thus Amos said, Jeroboam shall die by the sword, and Israel shall surely be led away captive out of their own land.

12 Also Amaziah said to Amos, O you seer, go, flee you away into the land of Judah, and there eat bread, and prophesy there:

13 But prophesy not again any more at Bethel: for it *is* the king's chapel, and it *is* the king's court.

14 Then answered Amos, and said to Amaziah, I *was* no prophet, neither *was* I a prophet's son; but I *was* a herdsman, and a gatherer of sycamore fruit:

15 And Yahweh took me as I followed the flock, and Yahweh said to me, Go, prophesy to my people Israel.

16 Now therefore hear you the word of Yahweh: You say, Prophesy not against Israel, and drop not *your word* against the house of Isaac.

17 Therefore thus says Yahweh; Your wife shall be a harlot in the city, and your sons and your daughters shall fall by the sword, and your land shall be divided by line; and you shall die in a polluted land: and Israel shall surely go into captivity forth from his land.

Amos 8

8:1 ¶ Thus has the Lord Yahweh shown to me: and behold a basket of summer fruit.

2 And he said, Amos, what see you? And I said, A basket of summer fruit. Then said Yahweh to me, The end is come upon my people of Israel; I will not again pass by them any more.

3 And the songs of the temple shall be howlings in that day, says the Lord Yahweh: *there shall be* many dead bodies in every place; they shall cast *them* forth with silence.

4 ¶ Hear this, O you that swallow up the needy, even to make the poor of the land to fail,

5 Saying, When will the new moon be gone, that we may sell corn? and the sabbath, that we may set forth wheat, making the ephah small, and the shekel great, and falsifying the balances by deceit?

6 That we may buy the poor for silver, and the needy for a pair of shoes; *yes,* and sell the refuse of the wheat?

7 Yahweh has sworn by the excellency of Jacob, Surely I will never forget any of their works.

8 Shall not the land tremble for this, and every one mourn that dwells therein? and it shall rise up wholly as a flood; and it shall be cast out and drowned, as *by* the flood of Egypt.

Amos 8

9 And it shall come to pass in that day, says the Lord Yahweh, that I will cause the sun to go down at noon, and I will darken the earth in the clear day:

10 And I will turn your feasts into mourning, and all your songs into lamentation; and I will bring up sackcloth upon all loins, and baldness upon every head; and I will make it as the mourning for an only *son*, and the end thereof as a bitter day.

11 ¶ Behold, the days come, says the Lord Yahweh, that I will send a famine in the land, not a famine of bread, nor a thirst for water, but of hearing the words of Yahweh:

12 And they shall wander from sea to sea, and from the north even to the east, they shall run to and fro to seek the word of Yahweh, and shall not find *it*.

13 In that day shall the fair virgins and young men faint for thirst.

14 They that swear by the sin of Samaria, and say, Your god, O Dan, lives; and, The manner of Beersheba lives; even they shall fall, and never rise up again.

Amos 9

9:1 ¶ I saw the Lord standing upon the altar: and he said, Smite the lintel of the door, that the posts may shake: and cut them in the head, all of them; and I will slay the last of them with the sword: he that flees of them shall not flee away, and he that escapes of them shall not be delivered.

2 Though they dig into hell, there shall my hand take them; though they climb up to heaven, there will I bring them down:

3 And though they hide themselves in the top of Carmel, I will search and take them out therefrom; and though they are hidden from my sight in the bottom of the sea, there will I command the serpent, and he shall bite them:

4 And though they go into captivity before their enemies, there will I command the sword, and it shall slay them: and I will set my eyes upon them for evil, and not for good.

5 And the Lord Yahweh of hosts *is* he that touches the land, and it shall melt, and all that dwell therein shall mourn: and it shall rise up wholly like a flood; and shall be drowned, as *by* the flood of Egypt.

6 *It is* he that builds his stories in the heaven, and has founded his troop in the earth; he that calls for the waters of the sea, and pours them out upon the face of the earth: Yahweh *is* his name.

7 *Are* you not as children of the Ethiopians to me, O children of Israel? says Yahweh. Have not I brought up Israel out of the land of Egypt? and the Philistines from Caphtor, and the Syrians from Kir?

8 Behold, the eyes of the Lord Yahweh *are* upon the sinful kingdom, and I will destroy it from off the face of the earth; saving that I will not utterly destroy the house of Jacob, says Yahweh.

9 For, lo, I will command, and I will sift the house of Israel among all nations, like as *corn* is sifted in a sieve, yet shall not the least grain fall upon the earth.

10 All the sinners of my people shall die by the sword, which say, The evil shall not overtake nor prevent us.

11 ¶ In that day will I raise up the tabernacle of David that is fallen, and close up the breaches thereof; and I will raise up his ruins, and I will build it as in the days of old:

12 That they may possess the remnant of Edom, and of all the heathen, which are called by my name, says Yahweh that does this.

13 Behold, the days come, says Yahweh, that the plowman shall overtake the reaper, and the treader of grapes him that sows seed; and the mountains shall drop sweet wine, and all the hills shall melt.

14 And I will bring again the captivity of my people of Israel, and they shall build the waste cities, and inhabit *them*; and they shall plant vineyards, and drink the wine thereof; they shall also make gardens, and eat the fruit of them.

15 And I will plant them upon their land, and they shall no more be pulled up out of their land which I have given them, says Yahweh your God.

Obadiah

Obadiah 1

1:1 ¶ The vision of Obadiah. Thus says the Lord Yahweh concerning Edom; We have heard a rumor from Yahweh, and an ambassador is sent among the heathen, Arise you, and let us rise up against her in battle.

2 Behold, I have made you small among the heathen: you are greatly despised.

3 The pride of your heart has deceived you, you that dwell in the clefts of the rock, whose habitation *is* high; that says in his heart, Who shall bring me down to the ground?

4 Though you exalt *yourself* as the eagle, and though you set your nest among the stars, there will I bring you down, says Yahweh.

5 If thieves came to you, if robbers by night, (how are you cut off!) would they not have stolen till they had enough? if the grape gatherers came to you, would they not leave *some* grapes?

6 How are *the things* of Esau searched out! how are his hidden things sought up!

7 All the men of your confederacy have brought you *even* to the border: the men that were at peace with you have deceived you, *and* prevailed against you; *they that eat* your bread have laid a wound under you: *there is* no understanding in him.

8 Shall I not in that day, says Yahweh, even destroy the wise *men* out of Edom, and understanding out of the mount of Esau?

9 And your mighty *men*, O Teman, shall be dismayed, to the end that every one of the mount of Esau may be cut off by slaughter.

10 ¶ For *your* violence against your brother Jacob shame shall cover you, and you shall be cut off forever.

11 In the day that you stood on the other side, in the day that the strangers carried away captive his forces, and foreigners entered into his gates, and cast lots upon Jerusalem, even you *were* as one of them.

12 But you should not have looked on the day of your brother in the day that he became a stranger; neither should you have rejoiced over the children of Judah in the day of their destruction; neither should you have spoken proudly in the day of distress.

13 You should not have entered into the gate of my people in the day of their calamity; yes, you should not have looked on their affliction in the day of their calamity, nor have laid *hands* on their substance in the day of their calamity;

14 Neither should you have stood in the crossway, to cut off those of his that did escape; neither should you have delivered up those of his that did remain in the day of distress.

15 For the day of Yahweh *is* near upon all the heathen: as you have done, it shall be done to you: your reward shall return upon your own head.

16 For as you have drunk upon my holy mountain, *so* shall all the heathen drink continually, yes, they shall drink, and they shall swallow down, and they shall be as though they had not been.

17 ¶ But upon mount Zion shall be deliverance, and there shall be holiness; and the house of Jacob shall possess their possessions.

18 And the house of Jacob shall be a fire, and the house of Joseph a flame, and the house of Esau for stubble, and they shall kindle in them, and devour them; and there shall not be *any* remaining of the house of Esau; for Yahweh has spoken *it*.

19 And *they of* the south shall possess the mount of Esau; and *they of* the plain the Philistines: and they shall possess the fields of Ephraim, and the fields of Samaria: and Benjamin *shall possess* Gilead.

20 And the captivity of this host of the children of Israel *shall possess* that of the Canaanites, *even* to Zarephath; and the captivity of Jerusalem, which *is* in Sepharad, shall possess the cities of the south.

21 And saviors shall come up on mount Zion to judge the mount of Esau; and the kingdom shall be Yahweh's.

Jonah

Jonah 1

1:1 ¶ Now the word of Yahweh came to Jonah the son of Amittai, saying,

2 Arise, go to Nineveh, that great city, and cry against it; for their wickedness has come up before me.

3 But Jonah rose up to flee to Tarshish from the presence of Yahweh, and went down to Joppa; and he found a ship going to Tarshish: so he paid the fare thereof, and went down into it, to go with them to Tarshish from the presence of Yahweh.

4 ¶ But Yahweh sent out a great wind into the sea, and there was a mighty tempest in the sea, so that the ship was likely to be broken.

5 Then the mariners were afraid, and cried every man to his god, and cast forth the wares that *were* in the ship into the sea, to lighten *it* of them. But Jonah had gone down into the sides of the ship; and he lay, and was fast asleep.

6 So the shipmaster came to him, and said to him, What mean you, O sleeper? arise, call upon your God, if so be that God will think upon us, that we perish not.

7 And they said every one to his fellow, Come, and let us cast lots, that we may know for whose cause this evil *is* upon us. So they cast lots, and the lot fell upon Jonah.

8 Then said they to him, Tell us, we pray you, for whose cause this evil *is* upon us; What *is* your occupation? and *from* where come you? what *is* your country? and of what people *are* you?

9 And he said to them, I *am* a Hebrew; and I fear Yahweh, the God of heaven, which has made the sea and the dry *land*.

10 Then were the men exceedingly afraid, and said to him, Why have you done this? For the men knew that he fled from the presence of Yahweh, because he had told them.

11 ¶ Then said they to him, What shall we do to you, that the sea may be calm to us? for the sea worked, and was tempestuous.

12 And he said to them, Take me up, and cast me forth into the sea; so shall the sea be calm to you: for I know that for my sake this great tempest *is* upon you.

13 Nevertheless the men rowed hard to bring *it* to the land; but they could not: for the sea worked, and was tempestuous against them.

14 Therefore they cried unto Yahweh, and said, We beseech you, O Yahweh, we beseech you, let us not perish for this man's life, and lay not upon us innocent blood: for you, O Yahweh, have done as it pleased you.

15 So they took up Jonah, and cast him forth into the sea: and the sea ceased from her raging.

16 Then the men feared Yahweh exceedingly, and offered a sacrifice unto Yahweh, and made vows.

17 Now Yahweh had prepared a great fish to swallow up Jonah. And Jonah was in the belly of the fish three days and three nights.

Jonah 2

2:1 ¶ Then Jonah prayed unto Yahweh his God out of the fish's belly,

2 And said, I cried by reason of my affliction unto Yahweh, and he heard me; out of the belly of hell cried I, *and* you heard my voice.

3 For you had cast me into the deep, in the midst of the seas; and the floods compassed me about: all your billows and your waves passed over me.

Jonah 2

4 Then I said, I am cast out of your sight; yet I will look again toward your holy temple.
5 The waters encompassed me about, *even* to the soul: the depth enclosed me round about, the weeds were wrapped about my head.
6 I went down to the bottom of the mountains; the earth with her bars *was* about me forever: yet have you brought up my life from corruption, O Yahweh my God.
7 When my soul fainted within me I remembered Yahweh: and my prayer came in unto you, into your holy temple.
8 They that observe lying vanities forsake their own mercy.
9 But I will sacrifice to you with the voice of thanksgiving; I will pay *that* that I have vowed. Salvation *is* of Yahweh.
10 ¶ And Yahweh spoke to the fish, and it vomited out Jonah upon the dry *land*.

Jonah 3

3:1 ¶ And the word of Yahweh came to Jonah the second time, saying,
2 Arise, go to Nineveh, that great city, and preach to it the preaching that I bid you.
3 So Jonah arose, and went to Nineveh, according to the word of Yahweh. Now Nineveh was an exceedingly great city of three days' journey.
4 And Jonah began to enter into the city a day's journey, and he cried, and said, Yet forty days, and Nineveh shall be overthrown.
5 ¶ So the people of Nineveh believed God, and proclaimed a fast, and put on sackcloth, from the greatest of them even to the least of them.
6 For word came to the king of Nineveh, and he arose from his throne, and he laid his robe from him, and covered *himself* with sackcloth, and sat in ashes.
7 And he caused *it* to be proclaimed and published through Nineveh by the decree of the king and his nobles, saying, Let neither man nor beast, herd nor flock, taste anything: let them not feed, nor drink water:
8 But let man and beast be covered with sackcloth, and cry mightily to God: yes, let them turn every one from his evil way, and from the violence that *is* in their hands.
9 Who can tell *if* God will turn and repent, and turn away from his fierce anger, that we perish not?
10 And God saw their works, that they turned from their evil way; and God repented of the evil, that he had said that he would do to them; and he did *it* not.

Jonah 4

4:1 ¶ But it displeased Jonah exceedingly, and he was very angry.
2 And he prayed unto Yahweh, and said, I pray you, O Yahweh, *was* not this my saying, when I was yet in my country? Therefore I fled before to Tarshish: for I knew that you *are* a gracious God, and merciful, slow to anger, and of great kindness, and repent you of the evil.
3 Therefore now, O Yahweh, take, I beseech you, my life from me; for *it is* better for me to die than to live.
4 Then said Yahweh, Do you well to be angry?
5 ¶ So Jonah went out of the city, and sat on the east side of the city, and there made him a booth, and sat under it in the shadow, till he might see what would become of the city.
6 And Yahweh God prepared a gourd, and made *it* to come up over Jonah, that it might be a shadow over his head, to deliver him from his grief. So Jonah was exceedingly glad for the gourd.
7 But God prepared a worm when the morning rose the next day, and it smote the gourd that it withered.
8 And it came to pass, when the sun did arise, that God prepared a vehement east wind; and the sun beat upon the head of Jonah, that he fainted, and wished in himself to die, and said, *It is* better for me to die than to live.
9 And God said to Jonah, Do you well to be angry for the gourd? And he said, I do well to be angry, *even* unto death.
10 Then said Yahweh, You have had pity on the gourd, for the which you have not labored, neither made it grow; which came up in a night, and perished in a night:
11 And should not I spare Nineveh, that great city, wherein are more than six score thousand persons that cannot discern between their right hand and their left hand; and *also* much cattle?

Micah

Micah 1

1:1 ¶ The word of Yahweh that came to Micah the Morasthite in the days of Jotham, Ahaz, *and* Hezekiah, kings of Judah, which he saw concerning Samaria and Jerusalem.
2 Hear, all you people; listen, O earth, and all that therein is: and let the Lord Yahweh be witness against you, the Lord from his holy temple.
3 For, behold, Yahweh comes forth out of his place, and will come down, and tread upon the high places of the earth.
4 And the mountains shall be molten under him, and the valleys shall be cleft, as wax before the fire, *and* as the waters *that are* poured down a steep place.
5 For the transgression of Jacob *is* all this, and for the sins of the house of Israel. What *is* the transgression of Jacob? *is it* not Samaria? and what *are* the high places of Judah? *are they* not Jerusalem?
6 Therefore I will make Samaria as a heap of the field, *and* as plantings of a vineyard: and I will pour down the stones thereof into the valley, and I will uncover the foundations thereof.
7 And all the graven images thereof shall be beaten to pieces, and all the hires thereof shall be burned with the

fire, and all the idols thereof will I lay desolate: for she gathered *it* of the hire of a harlot, and they shall return to the hire of a harlot.

8 ¶ Therefore I will wail and howl, I will go stripped and naked: I will make a wailing like the dragons, and mourning as the owls.

9 For her wound *is* incurable; for it has come to Judah; he has come to the gate of my people, *even* to Jerusalem.

10 Declare you *it* not at Gath, weep you not at all: in the house of Aphrah roll yourself in the dust.

11 Pass you away, you inhabitant of Saphir, having your shame naked: the inhabitant of Zaanan came not forth in the mourning of Bethezel; he shall receive from you his standing.

12 For the inhabitant of Maroth waited carefully for good: but evil came down from Yahweh to the gate of Jerusalem.

13 O you inhabitant of Lachish, bind the chariot to the swift beast: she *is* the beginning of the sin to the daughter of Zion: for the transgressions of Israel were found in you.

14 Therefore shall you give presents to Moreshethgath: the houses of Achzib *shall be* a lie to the kings of Israel.

15 Yet will I bring an heir to you, O inhabitant of Mareshah: he shall come to Adullam the glory of Israel.

16 Make you bald, and poll you for your delicate children; enlarge your baldness as the eagle; for they have gone into captivity from you.

Micah 2

2:1 ¶ Woe to them that devise iniquity, and work evil upon their beds! when the morning is light, they practice it, because it is in the power of their hand.

2 And they covet fields, and take *them* by violence; and houses, and take *them* away: so they oppress a man and his house, even a man and his heritage.

3 Therefore thus says Yahweh; Behold, against this family do I devise an evil, from which you shall not remove your necks; neither shall you go haughtily: for this time *is* evil.

4 In that day shall *one* take up a parable against you, and lament with a doleful lamentation, *and* say, We are utterly spoiled: he has changed the portion of my people: how has he removed *it* from me! turning away he has divided our fields.

5 Therefore you shall have none that shall cast a cord by lot in the congregation of Yahweh.

6 ¶ Prophesy you not, *say they to them that* prophesy: they shall not prophesy to them, *that* they shall not take shame.

7 O *you that are* named the house of Jacob, is the spirit of Yahweh shortened? *are* these his doings? do not my words do good to him that walks uprightly?

8 Even of late my people have risen up as an enemy: you pull off the robe with the garment from them that pass by securely as men returned from war.

9 The women of my people have you cast out from their pleasant houses; from their children have you taken away my glory forever.

10 Arise you, and depart; for this *is* not *your* rest: because it is polluted, it shall destroy *you*, even with a grievous destruction.

11 If a man walking in the spirit and falsehood does lie, *saying*, I will prophesy to you of wine and of strong drink; he shall even be the prophet of this people.

12 ¶ I will surely assemble, O Jacob, all of you; I will surely gather the remnant of Israel; I will put them together as the sheep of Bozrah, as the flock in the midst of their fold: they shall make great noise by reason of *the multitude of* men.

13 The breaker has come up before them: they have broken up, and have passed through the gate, and have gone out by it: and their king shall pass before them, and Yahweh on the head of them.

Micah 3

3:1 ¶ And I said, Hear, I pray you, O heads of Jacob, and you princes of the house of Israel; *Is it* not for you to know judgment?

2 Who hate the good, and love the evil; who pluck off their skin from off them, and their flesh from off their bones;

3 Who also eat the flesh of my people, and strip their skin from off them; and they break their bones, and chop them in pieces, as for the pot, and as flesh within the caldron.

4 Then shall they cry unto Yahweh, but he will not hear them: he will even hide his face from them at that time, as they have behaved themselves ill in their doings.

5 Thus says Yahweh concerning the prophets that make my people err, that bite with their teeth, and cry, Peace; and he that puts not into their mouths, they even prepare war against him.

6 Therefore night *shall be* unto you, that you shall not have a vision; and it shall be dark unto you, that you shall not divine; and the sun shall go down over the prophets, and the day shall be dark over them.

7 Then shall the seers be ashamed, and the diviners confounded: yes, they shall all cover their lips; for *there is* no answer from God.

8 ¶ But truly I am full of power by the spirit of Yahweh, and of judgment, and of might, to declare to Jacob his transgression, and to Israel his sin.

9 Hear this I pray you, you heads of the house of Jacob, and princes of the house of Israel, that abhor judgment, and pervert all equity.

10 They build up Zion with blood, and Jerusalem with iniquity.

11 The heads thereof judge for reward, and the priests thereof teach for hire, and the prophets thereof divine for money: yet will they lean upon Yahweh, and say, *Is* not Yahweh among us? no evil can come upon us.

Micah 3

12 Therefore shall Zion for your sake be plowed *as* a field, and Jerusalem shall become heaps, and the mountain of the house as the high places of the forest.

Micah 4

4:1 ¶ But in the last days it shall come to pass, *that* the mountain of the house of Yahweh shall be established in the top of the mountains, and it shall be exalted above the hills; and people shall flow unto it.
2 And many nations shall come, and say, Come, and let us go up to the mountain of Yahweh, and to the house of the God of Jacob; and he will teach us of his ways, and we will walk in his paths: for the law shall go forth from Zion, and the word of Yahweh from Jerusalem.
3 And he shall judge among many people, and rebuke strong nations afar off; and they shall beat their swords into plowshares, and their spears into pruning hooks: nation shall not lift up a sword against nation, neither shall they learn war any more.
4 But they shall sit every man under his vine and under his fig tree; and none shall make *them* afraid: for the mouth of Yahweh of hosts has spoken *it*.
5 For all people will walk every one in the name of his god, and we will walk in the name of Yahweh our God forever and ever.
6 In that day, says Yahweh, will I assemble her that limps, and I will gather her that was driven out, and her that I have afflicted;
7 And I will make her that limps a remnant, and her that was cast far off a strong nation: and Yahweh shall reign over them in mount Zion from now on, even forever.
8 ¶ And you, O tower of the flock, the strong hold of the daughter of Zion, unto you shall it come, even the first dominion; the kingdom shall come to the daughter of Jerusalem.
9 Now why do you cry out aloud? *is there* no king in you? has your counselor perished? for pangs have taken you as a woman in labor.
10 Be in pain, and labor to bring forth, O daughter of Zion, like a woman in labor: for now shall you go forth out of the city, and you shall dwell in the field, and you shall go *even* to Babylon; there shall you be delivered; there Yahweh shall redeem you from the hand of your enemies.
11 Now also many nations have gathered against you, that say, Let her be defiled, and let our eye look upon Zion.
12 But they know not the thoughts of Yahweh, neither understand they his counsel: for he shall gather them as the sheaves into the floor.
13 Arise and thresh, O daughter of Zion: for I will make your horn iron, and I will make your hoofs brass: and you shall beat in pieces many people: and I will consecrate their gain unto Yahweh, and their substance unto the Lord of the whole earth.

Micah 5

5:1 ¶ Now gather yourself in troops, O daughter of troops: he has laid siege against us: they shall smite the judge of Israel with a rod upon the cheek.
2 But you, Bethlehem Ephratah, *though* you are little among the thousands of Judah, *yet* out of you shall he come forth unto me *that is* to be ruler in Israel; whose goings forth *have been* from of old, from everlasting.
3 Therefore will he give them up, until the time *that* she which labors has brought forth: then the remnant of his brethren shall return to the children of Israel.
4 And he shall stand and feed in the strength of Yahweh, in the majesty of the name of Yahweh his God; and they shall stand: for now shall he be great unto the ends of the earth.
5 And this *man* shall be the peace, when the Assyrian shall come into our land: and when he shall tread in our palaces, then shall we raise against him seven shepherds, and eight principal men.
6 And they shall waste the land of Assyria with the sword, and the land of Nimrod in the entrances thereof: thus shall he deliver *us* from the Assyrian, when he comes into our land, and when he treads within our borders.
7 ¶ And the remnant of Jacob shall be in the midst of many people as a dew from Yahweh, as the showers upon the grass, that tarries not for man, nor waits for the sons of men.
8 And the remnant of Jacob shall be among the Gentiles in the midst of many people as a lion among the beasts of the forest, as a young lion among the flocks of sheep: who, if he goes through, both treads down, and tears in pieces, and none can deliver.
9 Your hand shall be lifted up upon your adversaries, and all your enemies shall be cut off.
10 And it shall come to pass in that day, says Yahweh, that I will cut off your horses out of the midst of you, and I will destroy your chariots:
11 And I will cut off the cities of your land, and throw down all your strong holds:
12 And I will cut off witchcrafts out of your hand; and you shall have no *more* soothsayers:
13 Your graven images also will I cut off, and your standing images out of the midst of you; and you shall no more worship the work of your hands.
14 And I will pluck up your groves out of the midst of you: so will I destroy your cities.
15 And I will execute vengeance in anger and fury upon the heathen, such as they have not heard.

Micah 6

6:1 ¶ Hear you now what Yahweh says; Arise, plead you before the mountains, and let the hills hear your voice.
2 Hear you, O mountains, Yahweh's controversy, and you strong foundations of the earth: for Yahweh has a controversy with his people, and he will plead with Israel.

3 O my people, what have I done to you? and wherein have I wearied you? testify against me.

4 For I brought you up out of the land of Egypt, and redeemed you out of the house of servants; and I sent before you Moses, Aaron, and Miriam.

5 O my people, remember now what Balak king of Moab consulted, and what Balaam the son of Beor answered him from Shittim to Gilgal; that you may know the righteousness of Yahweh.

6 ¶ With what shall I come before Yahweh, *and* bow myself before the high God? shall I come before him with burnt offerings, with calves of a year old?

7 Will Yahweh be pleased with thousands of rams, *or* with ten thousands of rivers of oil? shall I give my firstborn *for* my transgression, the fruit of my body *for* the sin of my soul?

8 He has shown you, O man, what *is* good; and what does Yahweh require of you, but to do justly, and to love mercy, and to walk humbly with your God?

9 ¶ Yahweh's voice cries to the city, and *the man of* wisdom shall see your name: hear you the rod, and who has appointed it.

10 Are there yet the treasures of wickedness in the house of the wicked, and the scant measure *that is* abominable?

11 Shall I count *them* pure with the wicked balances, and with the bag of deceitful weights?

12 For the rich men thereof are full of violence, and the inhabitants thereof have spoken lies, and their tongue *is* deceitful in their mouth.

13 Therefore also will I make *you* sick in smiting you, in making *you* desolate because of your sins.

14 You shall eat, but not be satisfied; and your casting down *shall be* in the midst of you; and you shall take hold, but will not deliver; and *that* which you deliver will I give up to the sword.

15 You shall sow, but you shall not reap; you shall tread the olives, but you shall not anoint you with oil; and sweet wine, but will not drink wine.

16 For the statutes of Omri are kept, and all the works of the house of Ahab, and you walk in their counsels; that I should make you a desolation, and the inhabitants thereof a hissing: therefore you shall bear the reproach of my people.

Micah 7

7:1 ¶ Woe is me! for I am as when they have gathered the summer fruits, as the grape gleanings of the vintage: *there is* no cluster to eat: my soul desired the first ripe fruit.

2 The good *man* has perished out of the earth: and *there is* none upright among men: they all lie in wait for blood; they hunt every man his brother with a net.

3 That they may do evil with both hands earnestly, the prince asks, and the judge *asks* for a reward; and the great *man*, he utters his mischievous desire: so they wrap it up.

4 The best of them *is* as a brier: the most upright *is sharper* than a thorn hedge: the day of your watchmen *and* your visitation comes; now shall be their perplexity.

5 Trust you not in a friend, put you not confidence in a guide: keep the doors of your mouth from her that lies in your bosom.

6 For the son dishonors the father, the daughter rises up against her mother, the daughter-in-law against her mother-in-law; a man's enemies *are* the men of his own house.

7 ¶ Therefore I will look unto Yahweh; I will wait for the God of my salvation: my God will hear me.

8 Rejoice not against me, O my enemy: when I fall, I shall arise; when I sit in darkness, Yahweh *shall be* a light unto me.

9 I will bear the indignation of Yahweh, because I have sinned against him, until he pleads my cause, and executes judgment for me: he will bring me forth to the light, *and* I shall behold his righteousness.

10 Then *she that is* my enemy shall see *it*, and shame shall cover her which said to me, Where is Yahweh your God? my eyes shall behold her: now shall she be trodden down as the mire of the streets.

11 *In* the day that your walls are to be built, *in* that day shall the decree be far removed.

12 *In* that day *also* he shall come even to you from Assyria, and *from* the fortified cities, and from the fortress even to the river, and from sea to sea, and *from* mountain to mountain.

13 Notwithstanding the land shall be desolate because of them that dwell therein, for the fruit of their doings.

14 ¶ Feed your people with your rod, the flock of your heritage, which dwell solitarily *in* the woods, in the midst of Carmel: let them feed *in* Bashan and Gilead, as in the days of old.

15 According to the days of your coming out of the land of Egypt will I show to him marvelous *things*.

16 The nations shall see and be confounded at all their might: they shall lay *their* hand upon *their* mouth, their ears shall be deaf.

17 They shall lick the dust like a serpent, they shall move out of their holes like worms of the earth: they shall be afraid of Yahweh our God, and shall fear because of you.

18 Who *is* a God like unto you, that pardons iniquity, and passes by the transgression of the remnant of his heritage? he retains not his anger forever, because he delights *in* mercy.

19 He will turn again, he will have compassion upon us; he will subdue our iniquities; and you will cast all their sins into the depths of the sea.

20 You will perform the truth to Jacob, *and* the mercy to Abraham, which you have sworn to our fathers from the days of old.

Nahum

Nahum 1

1:1 ¶ The burden of Nineveh. The book of the vision of Nahum the Elkoshite.

2 ¶ God *is* jealous, and Yahweh revenges; Yahweh revenges, and *is* furious; Yahweh will take vengeance on his adversaries, and he reserves *wrath* for his enemies.

3 Yahweh *is* slow to anger, and great in power, and will not at all acquit *the wicked*: Yahweh has his way in the whirlwind and in the storm, and the clouds *are* the dust of his feet.

4 He rebukes the sea, and makes it dry, and dries up all the rivers: Bashan languishes, and Carmel, and the flower of Lebanon languishes.

5 The mountains quake at him, and the hills melt, and the earth is burned at his presence, yes, the world, and all that dwell therein.

6 Who can stand before his indignation? and who can dwell in the fierceness of his anger? his fury is poured out like fire, and the rocks are thrown down by him.

7 Yahweh *is* good, a strong hold in the day of trouble; and he knows them that trust in him.

8 But with an overrunning flood he will make an utter end of the place thereof, and darkness shall pursue his enemies.

9 ¶ What do you imagine against Yahweh? he will make an utter end: affliction shall not rise up the second time.

10 For while *they are* folded together *as* thorns, and while they are drunken *as* drunkards, they shall be devoured as stubble fully dry.

11 There is *one* come out of you, that imagines evil against Yahweh, a wicked counselor.

12 Thus says Yahweh; Though *they are* quiet, and likewise many, yet thus shall they be cut down, when he shall pass through. Though I have afflicted you, I will afflict you no more.

13 For now will I break his yoke from off you, and will burst your bonds apart.

14 And Yahweh has given a commandment concerning you, *that* no more of your name be sown: out of the house of your gods will I cut off the graven image and the molten image: I will make your grave; for you are vile.

15 Behold upon the mountains the feet of him that brings good tidings, that publishes peace! O Judah, keep your solemn feasts, perform your vows: for the wicked shall no more pass through you; he is utterly cut off.

Nahum 2

2:1 ¶ He that dashes in pieces has come up before your face: keep the fortification, watch the way, make *your* loins strong, fortify *your* power mightily.

2 For Yahweh has turned away the excellency of Jacob, as the excellency of Israel: for the emptiers have emptied them out, and marred their vine branches.

3 The shield of his mighty men is made red, the valiant men *are* in scarlet: the chariots *shall be* with flaming torches in the day of his preparation, and the fir trees shall be terribly shaken.

4 The chariots shall rage in the streets, they shall jostle one against another in the broad ways: they shall seem like torches, they shall run like the lightnings.

5 He shall remember his nobles: they shall stumble in their walk; they shall make haste to the wall thereof, and the defense shall be prepared.

6 The gates of the rivers shall be opened, and the palace shall be dissolved.

7 And Huzzab shall be led away captive, she shall be brought up, and her maids shall lead *her* as with the voice of doves, beating upon their breasts.

8 But Nineveh *is* of old like a pool of water: yet they shall flee away. Stand, stand, *shall they cry*; but none shall look back.

9 Take you the spoil of silver, take the spoil of gold: for *there is* no end of the store *and* glory out of all the pleasant furniture.

10 She is empty, and void, and waste: and the heart melts, and the knees knock together, and much pain *is* in all loins, and the faces of them all gather blackness.

11 ¶ Where *is* the dwelling of the lions, and the feeding place of the young lions, where the lion, *even* the old lion, walked, *and* the lion's cub, and none made *them* afraid?

12 The lion did tear in pieces enough for his cubs, and strangled for his lionesses, and filled his holes with prey, and his dens with torn *flesh*.

13 Behold, I *am* against you, says Yahweh of hosts, and I will burn her chariots in the smoke, and the sword shall devour your young lions: and I will cut off your prey from the earth, and the voice of your messengers shall no more be heard.

Nahum 3

3:1 ¶ Woe to the bloody city! it *is* all full of lies *and* robbery; the prey departs not;

2 The noise of a whip, and the noise of the rattling of the wheels, and of the prancing horses, and of the jumping chariots.

3 The horseman lifts up both the bright sword and the glittering spear: and *there is* a multitude of slain, and a great number of carcasses; and *there is* no end of *their* corpses; they stumble upon their corpses:

4 Because of the multitude of the whoredoms of the well favored harlot, the mistress of witchcrafts, that sells nations through her whoredoms, and families through her witchcrafts.

5 Behold, I *am* against you, says Yahweh of hosts; and I will uncover your skirts upon your face, and I will show the nations your nakedness, and the kingdoms your shame.

6 And I will cast abominable filth upon you, and make you vile, and will set you as a spectacle.

7 And it shall come to pass, *that* all they that look upon you shall flee from you, and say, Nineveh is laid waste: who will bemoan her? *from* where shall I seek comforters for you?

8 ¶ Are you better than populous No, that was situated among the rivers, *that had* the waters round about it, whose rampart *was* the sea, *and* her wall *was* from the sea?

9 Ethiopia and Egypt *were* her strength, and *it was* infinite; Put and Lubim were your helpers.

10 Yet *was* she carried away, she went into captivity: her young children also were dashed in pieces at the top of all the streets: and they cast lots for her honorable men, and all her great men were bound in chains.

11 You also shall be drunken: you shall be hidden, you also shall seek strength because of the enemy.

12 All your strong holds *shall be like* fig trees with the first ripe figs: if they are shaken, they shall even fall into the mouth of the eater.

13 Behold, your people in the midst of you *are* women: the gates of your land shall be set wide open unto your enemies: the fire shall devour your bars.

14 Draw you waters for the siege, fortify your strong holds: go into clay, and tread the mortar, make strong the brick kiln.

15 There shall the fire devour you; the sword shall cut you off, it shall eat you up like the cankerworm: make yourself many as the cankerworm, make yourself many as the locusts.

16 You have multiplied your merchants above the stars of heaven: the cankerworm spoils, and flies away

17 Your crowned *are* as the locusts, and your captains as the great grasshoppers, which camp in the hedges in the cold day, *but* when the sun rises they flee away, and their place is not known where they *are*.

18 Your shepherds slumber, O king of Assyria: your nobles shall dwell *in the dust*: your people are scattered upon the mountains, and no man gathers *them*.

19 *There is* no healing of your bruise; your wound is grievous: all that hear the report of you shall clap the hands over you: for upon whom has not your wickedness passed continually?

Habakkuk

Habakkuk 1

1:1 ¶ The burden which Habakkuk the prophet did see.

2 O Yahweh, how long shall I cry, and you will not hear! *even* cry out to you *of* violence, and you will not save!

3 Why do you show me iniquity, and cause *me* to behold grievance? for spoiling and violence *are* before me: and there are *those that* raise up strife and contention.

4 Therefore the law is slacked, and judgment does never go forth: for the wicked does encompass about the righteous; therefore wrong judgment proceeds.

5 ¶ Behold you among the heathen, and regard, and wonder marvelously: for *I* will work a work in your days, *which* you will not believe, though it be told *you*.

6 For, lo, I raise up the Chaldeans, *that* bitter and hasty nation, which shall march through the breadth of the land, to possess the dwelling places *that are* not theirs.

7 They *are* terrible and dreadful: their judgment and their dignity shall proceed from themselves.

8 Their horses also are swifter than the leopards, and are more fierce than the evening wolves: and their horsemen shall spread themselves, and their horsemen shall come from afar; they shall fly as the eagle *that* hastens to eat.

9 They shall come all for violence: their faces shall sup up *as* the east wind, and they shall gather the captivity as the sand.

10 And they shall scoff at the kings, and the princes shall be a scorn to them: they shall deride every strong hold; for they shall heap dust, and take it.

11 Then shall *his* mind change, and he shall pass over, and offend. *imputing* this his power unto his god.

12 ¶ *Are* you not from everlasting, O Yahweh my God, my Holy One? we shall not die. O Yahweh, you have ordained them for judgment; and, O mighty God, you have established them for correction.

13 *You are* of purer eyes than to behold evil, and can not look on iniquity: why look you upon them that deal treacherously, *and* hold your tongue when the wicked devours *the* man that is more righteous than he?

14 And make men as the fishes of the sea, as the creeping things, *that have* no ruler over them?

15 They take up all of them with the angle, they catch them in their net, and gather them in their drag: therefore they rejoice and are glad.

16 Therefore they sacrifice unto their net, and burn incense unto their drag; because by them their portion *is* fat, and their meat plenteous.

17 Shall they therefore empty their net, and not spare continually to slay the nations?

Habakkuk 2

2:1 ¶ I will stand upon my watch, and set me upon the tower, and will watch to see what he will say to me, and what I shall answer when I am reproved.

2 And Yahweh answered me, and said, Write the vision, and make *it* plain upon tables, that he may run that reads it.

3 For the vision *is* yet for an appointed time, but at the end it shall speak, and not lie: though it tarries, wait for it; because it will surely come, it will not tarry.

4 Behold, his soul *which* is lifted up is not upright in him: but the just shall live by his faith.

5 ¶ Yes also, because he transgresses by wine, *he is* a proud man, neither keeps at home, who enlarges his

desire as hell, and *is* as death, and cannot be satisfied, but gathers unto him all nations, and heaps unto him all people:

6 Shall not all these take up a parable against him, and a taunting proverb against him, and say, Woe to him that increases *that which is* not his! how long? and to him that covers himself with thick clay!

7 Shall they not rise up suddenly that shall bite you, and awake that shall vex you, and you shall be for *a* booty unto them?

8 Because you have spoiled many nations, all the remnant of the people shall spoil you; because of men's blood, and *for* the violence of the land, of the city, and of all that dwell therein.

9 Woe to him that covets an evil covetousness to his house, that he may set his nest on high, that he may be delivered from the power of evil!

10 You have counseled shame to your house by cutting off many people, and have sinned *against* your soul.

11 For the stone shall cry out of the wall, and the beam out of the timber shall answer it.

12 Woe to him that builds a town with blood, and establishes a city by iniquity!

13 Behold, *is it* not of Yahweh of hosts that the people shall labor in the very fire, and the people shall weary themselves for very vanity?

14 For the earth shall be filled with the knowledge of the glory of Yahweh, as the waters cover the sea.

15 ¶ Woe to him that gives his neighbor drink, that puts your bottle to *him*, and makes *him* drunken also, that you may look on their nakedness!

16 You are filled with shame for glory: drink you also, and let your foreskin be uncovered: the cup of Yahweh's right hand shall be turned unto you, and shameful spewing *shall be* on your glory.

17 For the violence of Lebanon shall cover you, and the spoil of beasts, *which* made them afraid, because of men's blood, and for the violence of the land, of the city, and of all that dwell therein.

18 What profits the graven image that the maker thereof has graven it; the molten image, and a teacher of lies, that the maker of his work trusts therein, to make dumb idols?

19 Woe to him that said to the wood, Awake; to the dumb stone, Arise, it shall teach! Behold, it *is* laid over with gold and silver, and *there is* no breath at all in the midst of it.

20 But Yahweh *is* in his holy temple: let all the earth keep silence before him.

Habakkuk 3

3:1 ¶ A prayer of Habakkuk the prophet upon Shigionoth.

2 O Yahweh, I have heard your speech, *and* was afraid: O Yahweh, revive your work in the midst of the years, in the midst of the years make known; in wrath remember mercy.

3 ¶ God came from Teman, and the Holy One from mount Paran. Selah. His glory covered the heavens, and the earth was full of his praise.

4 And *his* brightness was as the light; he had horns *coming* out of his hand: and there *was* the hiding of his power.

5 Before him went the pestilence, and burning coals went forth at his feet.

6 He stood, and measured the earth: he beheld, and drove apart the nations; and the everlasting mountains were scattered, the perpetual hills did bow: his ways *are* everlasting.

7 I saw the tents of Cushan in affliction: *and* the curtains of the land of Midian did tremble.

8 Was Yahweh displeased against the rivers? *was* your anger against the rivers? *was* your wrath against the sea, that you did ride upon your horses *and* your chariots of salvation?

9 Your bow was made quite naked, *according* to the oaths of the tribes, *even your* word. Selah. You did divide the earth with rivers.

10 The mountains saw you, *and* they trembled: the overflowing of the water passed by: the deep uttered his voice, *and* lifted up his hands on high.

11 The sun *and* moon stood still in their habitation: at the light of your arrows they went, *and* at the shining of your glittering spear.

12 You did march through the land in indignation, you did thresh the heathen in anger.

13 You went forth for the salvation of your people, *even* for salvation with your anointed; you wounded the head out of the house of the wicked, by uncovering the foundation to the neck. Selah.

14 You did strike through with his staves the head of his villages: they came out as a whirlwind to scatter me: their rejoicing *was* as to devour the poor secretly.

15 You did walk through the sea with your horses, *through* the heap of great waters.

16 ¶ When I heard, my belly trembled; my lips quivered at the voice: rottenness entered into my bones, and I trembled in myself, that I might rest in the day of trouble: when he comes up to the people, he will invade them with his troops.

17 Although the fig tree shall not blossom, neither *shall* fruit *be* in the vines; the labor of the olive shall fail, and the fields shall yield no food; the flock shall be cut off from the fold, and *there shall be* no herd in the stalls:

18 Yet I will rejoice in Yahweh, I will joy in the God of my salvation.

19 Yahweh God *is* my strength, and he will make my feet like deer's *feet*, and he will make me to walk upon my high places. To the chief singer upon my stringed instruments.

Zephaniah

Zephaniah 1

1:1 ¶ The word of Yahweh which came to Zephaniah the son of Cushi, the son of Gedaliah, the son of Amariah, the son of Hezekiah, in the days of Josiah the son of Amon, king of Judah.
2 I will utterly consume all *things* from off the land, says Yahweh.
3 I will consume man and beast; I will consume the fowls of the heaven, and the fishes of the sea, and the stumbling blocks with the wicked; and I will cut off man from off the land, says Yahweh.
4 I will also stretch out my hand upon Judah, and upon all the inhabitants of Jerusalem; and I will cut off the remnant of Baal from this place, *and* the name of the Chemarims with the priests;
5 And them that worship the host of heaven upon the housetops; and them that worship *and* that swear by Yahweh, and that swear by Malcham;
6 And them that are turned back from Yahweh; and *those* that have not sought Yahweh, nor inquired for him.
7 ¶ Hold your peace at the presence of the Lord Yahweh: for the day of Yahweh *is* at hand: for Yahweh has prepared a sacrifice, he has bid his guests.
8 And it shall come to pass in the day of Yahweh's sacrifice, that I will punish the princes, and the king's children, and all such as are clothed with strange apparel.
9 In the same day also will I punish all those that leap on the threshold, which fill their masters' houses with violence and deceit.
10 And it shall come to pass in that day, says Yahweh, *that there shall be* the noise of a cry from the fish gate, and a howling from the second, and a great crashing from the hills.
11 Howl, you inhabitants of Maktesh, for all the merchant people are cut down; all they that bear silver are cut off.
12 And it shall come to pass at that time, *that* I will search Jerusalem with candles, and punish the men that are settled on their lees: that say in their heart, Yahweh will not do good, neither will he do evil.
13 Therefore their goods shall become a booty, and their houses a desolation: they shall also build houses, but not inhabit *them*; and they shall plant vineyards, but not drink the wine thereof.
14 ¶ The great day of Yahweh *is* near, *it is* near, and hastens greatly, *even* the voice of the day of Yahweh: the mighty man shall cry there bitterly.
15 That day *is* a day of wrath, a day of trouble and distress, a day of devastation and desolation, a day of darkness and gloominess, a day of clouds and thick darkness,
16 A day of the trumpet and alarm against the fenced cities, and against the high towers.
17 And I will bring distress upon men, that they shall walk like blind men, because they have sinned against Yahweh: and their blood shall be poured out as dust, and their flesh as the dung.
18 Neither their silver nor their gold shall be able to deliver them in the day of Yahweh's wrath; but the whole land shall be devoured by the fire of his jealousy: for he shall make even a speedy riddance of all them that dwell in the land.

Zephaniah 2

2:1 ¶ Gather yourselves together, yes, gather together, O nation not desired;
2 Before the decree brings forth, *before* the day passes as the chaff, before the fierce anger of Yahweh comes upon you, before the day of Yahweh's anger comes upon you.
3 Seek you Yahweh, all you meek of the earth, which have worked his judgment; seek righteousness, seek meekness: it may be you shall be hidden in the day of Yahweh's anger.
4 ¶ For Gaza shall be forsaken, and Ashkelon a desolation: they shall drive out Ashdod at the noon day, and Ekron shall be rooted up.
5 Woe unto the inhabitants of the sea coast, the nation of the Cherethites! the word of Yahweh *is* against you; O Canaan, the land of the Philistines, I will even destroy you, that there shall be no inhabitant.
6 And the sea coast shall be dwellings *and* cottages for shepherds, and folds for flocks.
7 And the coast shall be for the remnant of the house of Judah; they shall feed thereupon: in the houses of Ashkelon shall they lie down in the evening: for Yahweh their God shall visit them, and turn away their captivity.
8 ¶ I have heard the reproach of Moab, and the revilings of the children of Ammon, whereby they have reproached my people, and magnified *themselves* against their border.
9 Therefore *as* I live, says Yahweh of hosts, the God of Israel, Surely Moab shall be as Sodom, and the children of Ammon as Gomorrah, *even* the breeding of nettles, and salt pits, and a perpetual desolation: the residue of my people shall spoil them, and the remnant of my people shall possess them.
10 This shall they have for their pride, because they have reproached and magnified *themselves* against the people of Yahweh of hosts.
11 Yahweh *will be* terrible to them: for he will famish all the gods of the earth; and *men* shall worship him, every one from his place, *even* all the isles of the heathen.
12 ¶ You Ethiopians also, you *shall be* slain by my sword.
13 And he will stretch out his hand against the north, and destroy Assyria; and will make Nineveh a desolation, *and* dry like a wilderness.
14 And flocks shall lie down in the midst of her, all the beasts of the nations: both the cormorant and the bittern

Zephaniah 2

shall lodge in the upper lintels of it; *their* voice shall sing in the windows; desolation *shall be* in the thresholds: for he shall uncover the cedar work.

15 This *is* the rejoicing city that dwelt carelessly, that said in her heart, I *am*, and *there is* none besides me: how has she become a desolation, a place for beasts to lie down in! every one that passes by her shall hiss, *and* wag his hand.

Zephaniah 3

3:1 ¶ Woe to her that is filthy and polluted, to the oppressing city!

2 She obeyed not the voice; she received not correction; she trusted not in Yahweh; she drew not near to her God.

3 Her princes within her *are* roaring lions; her judges *are* evening wolves; they gnaw not the bones till the next day.

4 Her prophets *are* light *and* treacherous persons: her priests have polluted the sanctuary, they have done violence to the law.

5 The just Yahweh *is* in the midst thereof; he will not do iniquity: every morning does he bring his judgment to light, he fails not; but the unjust knows no shame.

6 I have cut off the nations: their towers are desolate; I made their streets waste, that none passes by: their cities are destroyed, so that there is no man, that there is no inhabitant.

7 I said, Surely you will fear me, you will receive instruction; so their dwelling should not be cut off, however I punished them: but they rose early, *and* corrupted all their doings.

8 ¶ Therefore wait you upon me, says Yahweh, until the day that I rise up to the prey: for my determination *is* to gather the nations, that I may assemble the kingdoms, to pour upon them my indignation, *even* all my fierce anger: for all the earth shall be devoured with the fire of my jealousy.

9 For then will I turn to the people a pure language, that they may all call upon the name of Yahweh, to serve him with one consent.

10 From beyond the rivers of Ethiopia my worshippers, *even* the daughter of my dispersed, shall bring my offering.

11 In that day shall you not be ashamed for all your doings, wherein you have transgressed against me: for then I will take away out of the midst of you them that rejoice in your pride, and you shall no more be haughty because of my holy mountain.

12 I will also leave in the midst of you an afflicted and poor people, and they shall trust in the name of Yahweh.

13 The remnant of Israel shall not do iniquity, nor speak lies; neither shall a deceitful tongue be found in their mouth: for they shall feed and lie down, and none shall make *them* afraid.

14 ¶ Sing, O daughter of Zion; shout, O Israel; be glad and rejoice with all the heart, O daughter of Jerusalem.

15 Yahweh has taken away your judgments, he has cast out your enemy: the king of Israel, *even* Yahweh, *is* in the midst of you: you shall not see evil any more.

16 In that day it shall be said to Jerusalem, Fear you not: *and to* Zion, Let not your hands be slack.

17 Yahweh your God in the midst of you *is* mighty; he will save, he will rejoice over you with joy; he will rest in his love, he will joy over you with singing.

18 I will gather *them that are* sorrowful for the solemn assembly, *who* are of you, *to whom* the reproach of it *was* a burden.

19 Behold, at that time I will undo all that afflict you: and I will save her that limps, and gather her that was driven out; and I will get them praise and fame in every land where they have been put to shame.

20 At that time will I bring you *again*, even in the time that I gather you: for I will make you a name and a praise among all people of the earth, when I turn back your captivity before your eyes, says Yahweh.

Haggai

Haggai 1

1:1 ¶ In the second year of Darius the king, in the sixth month, in the first day of the month, came the word of Yahweh by Haggai the prophet to Zerubbabel the son of Shealtiel, governor of Judah, and to Joshua the son of Josedech, the high priest, saying,

2 Thus speaks Yahweh of hosts, saying, This people say, The time has not come, the time that Yahweh's house should be built.

3 Then came the word of Yahweh by Haggai the prophet, saying,

4 *Is it* time for you, O you, to dwell in your paneled houses, and this house *lies* waste?

5 Now therefore thus says Yahweh of hosts; Consider your ways.

6 You have sown much, and bring in little; you eat, but you have not enough; you drink, but you are not filled with drink; you clothe you, but there is none warm; and he that earns wages earns wages *to put it* into a bag with holes.

7 Thus says Yahweh of hosts; Consider your ways.

8 Go up to the mountain, and bring wood, and build the house; and I will take pleasure in it, and I will be glorified, says Yahweh.

9 You looked for much, and, lo, *it came* to little; and when you brought *it* home, I did blow upon it. Why? says Yahweh of hosts. Because of my house that *is* waste, and you run every man to his own house.

10 Therefore the heaven over you is stayed from dew, and the earth is stayed *from* her fruit.

11 And I called for a drought upon the land, and upon the mountains, and upon the corn, and upon the new wine, and upon the oil, and upon *that* which the ground brings forth, and upon men, and upon cattle, and upon all the labor of the hands.
12 ¶ Then Zerubbabel the son of Shealtiel, and Joshua the son of Josedech, the high priest, with all the remnant of the people, obeyed the voice of Yahweh their God, and the words of Haggai the prophet, as Yahweh their God had sent him, and the people did fear before Yahweh.
13 Then spoke Haggai Yahweh's messenger in Yahweh's message to the people, saying, I *am* with you, says Yahweh.
14 And Yahweh stirred up the spirit of Zerubbabel the son of Shealtiel, governor of Judah, and the spirit of Joshua the son of Josedech, the high priest, and the spirit of all the remnant of the people; and they came and did work in the house of Yahweh of hosts, their God,
15 In the four and twentieth day of the sixth month, in the second year of Darius the king.

Haggai 2

2:1 ¶ In the seventh *month*, in the one and twentieth *day* of the month, came the word of Yahweh by the prophet Haggai, saying,
2 Speak now to Zerubbabel the son of Shealtiel, governor of Judah, and to Joshua the son of Josedech, the high priest, and to the residue of the people, saying,
3 Who *is* left among you that saw this house in her first glory? and how do you see it now? *is this* not in your eyes in comparison of it as nothing?
4 Yet now be strong, O Zerubbabel, says Yahweh; and be strong, O Joshua, son of Josedech, the high priest; and be strong, all you people of the land, says Yahweh, and work: for I *am* with you, says Yahweh of hosts:
5 *According to* the word that I covenanted with you when you came out of Egypt, so my spirit remains among you: fear you not.
6 For thus says Yahweh of hosts; Yet once, it *is* a little while, and I will shake the heavens, and the earth, and the sea, and the dry *land*;
7 And I will shake all nations, and the desire of all nations shall come: and I will fill this house with glory, says Yahweh of hosts.
8 The silver *is* mine, and the gold *is* mine, says Yahweh of hosts.
9 The glory of this latter house shall be greater than of the former, says Yahweh of hosts: and in this place will I give peace, says Yahweh of hosts.
10 ¶ In the four and twentieth *day* of the ninth *month*, in the second year of Darius, came the word of Yahweh by Haggai the prophet, saying,
11 Thus says Yahweh of hosts; Ask now the priests *concerning* the law, saying,
12 If one bears holy flesh in the skirt of his garment, and with his skirt does touch bread, or pottage, or wine, or oil, or any meat, shall it be holy? And the priests answered and said, No.
13 Then said Haggai, If *one that is* unclean by a dead body touches any of these, shall it be unclean? And the priests answered and said, It shall be unclean.
14 Then answered Haggai, and said, So *is* this people, and so *is* this nation before me, says Yahweh; and so *is* every work of their hands; and that which they offer there *is* unclean.
15 And now, I pray you, consider from this day and upward, from before a stone was laid upon a stone in the temple of Yahweh:
16 Since those *days* were, when *one* came to a heap of twenty *measures*, there were *but* ten: when *one* came to the press fat for to draw out fifty *vessels* out of the press, there were *but* twenty.
17 I smote you with blight and with mildew and with hail in all the labors of your hands; yet you *turned* not to me, says Yahweh.
18 Consider now from this day and upward, from the four and twentieth day of the ninth *month, even* from the day that the foundation of Yahweh's temple was laid, consider *it*.
19 Is the seed yet in the barn? yes, as yet the vine, and the fig tree, and the pomegranate, and the olive tree, has not brought forth: from this day will I bless *you*.
20 ¶ And again the word of Yahweh came to Haggai in the four and twentieth *day* of the month, saying,
21 Speak to Zerubbabel, governor of Judah, saying, I will shake the heavens and the earth;
22 And I will overthrow the throne of kingdoms, and I will destroy the strength of the kingdoms of the heathen; and I will overthrow the chariots, and those that ride in them; and the horses and their riders shall come down, every one by the sword of his brother.
23 In that day, says Yahweh of hosts, will I take you, O Zerubbabel, my servant, the son of Shealtiel, says Yahweh, and will make you as a signet: for I have chosen you, says Yahweh of hosts.

Zechariah

Zechariah 1

1:1 ¶ In the eighth month, in the second year of Darius, came the word of Yahweh to Zechariah, the son of Berechiah, the son of Iddo the prophet, saying,
2 Yahweh has been angrily displeased with your fathers.
3 Therefore say you to them, Thus says Yahweh of hosts; Turn you unto me, says Yahweh of hosts, and I will turn unto you, says Yahweh of hosts.
4 Be you not as your fathers, to whom the former prophets have cried, saying, Thus says Yahweh of hosts; Turn you now from your evil ways, and *from* your evil doings: but they did not hear, nor listen to me, says Yahweh.

Zechariah 1

5 Your fathers, where *are* they? and the prophets, do they live forever?

6 But my words and my statutes, which I commanded my servants the prophets, did they not take hold of your fathers? and they returned and said, Like as Yahweh of hosts thought to do unto us, according to our ways, and according to our doings, so has he dealt with us.

7 ¶ Upon the four and twentieth day of the eleventh month, which *is* the month *of* Sebat, in the second year of Darius, came the word of Yahweh to Zechariah, the son of Berechiah, the son of Iddo the prophet, saying,

8 I saw by night, and behold a man riding upon a red horse, and he stood among the myrtle trees that *were* in the bottom; and behind him *were there* red horses, speckled, and white.

9 Then said I, O my lord, what *are* these? And the angel that talked with me said to me, I will show you what these *are*.

10 And the man that stood among the myrtle trees answered and said, These *are they* whom Yahweh has sent to walk to and fro through the earth.

11 And they answered the angel of Yahweh that stood among the myrtle trees, and said, We have walked to and fro through the earth, and, behold, all the earth sits still, and is at rest.

12 Then the angel of Yahweh answered and said, O Yahweh of hosts, how long will you not have mercy on Jerusalem and on the cities of Judah, against which you have had indignation these threescore and ten years?

13 And Yahweh answered the angel that talked with me *with* good words *and* comfortable words.

14 So the angel that communed with me said to me, Cry you, saying, Thus says Yahweh of hosts; I am jealous for Jerusalem and for Zion with a great jealousy.

15 And I am very angrily displeased with the heathen *that are* at ease: for I was but a little displeased, and they helped forward the affliction.

16 Therefore thus says Yahweh; I have returned to Jerusalem with mercies: my house shall be built in it, says Yahweh of hosts, and a line shall be stretched forth upon Jerusalem.

17 Cry yet, saying, Thus says Yahweh of hosts; My cities through prosperity shall yet be spread abroad; and Yahweh shall yet comfort Zion, and shall yet choose Jerusalem.

18 ¶ Then lifted I up my eyes, and saw, and behold four horns.

19 And I said to the angel that talked with me, What *are* these? And he answered me, These *are* the horns which have scattered Judah, Israel, and Jerusalem.

20 And Yahweh showed me four carpenters.

21 Then said I, What come these to do? And he spoke, saying, These *are* the horns which have scattered Judah, so that no man did lift up his head: but these have come to terrify them, to cast out the horns of the Gentiles, which lifted up *their* horn over the land of Judah to scatter it.

Zechariah 2

2:1 ¶ I lifted up my eyes again, and looked, and behold a man with a measuring line in his hand.

2 Then said I, Where go you? And he said to me, To measure Jerusalem, to see what *is* the breadth thereof, and what *is* the length thereof.

3 And, behold, the angel that talked with me went forth, and another angel went out to meet him,

4 And said to him, Run, speak to this young man, saying, Jerusalem shall be inhabited *as* towns without walls for the multitude of men and cattle therein:

5 For I, says Yahweh, will be unto her a wall of fire round about, and will be the glory in the midst of her.

6 ¶ Ho, ho, *come forth*, and flee from the land of the north, says Yahweh: for I have spread you abroad as the four winds of the heaven, says Yahweh.

7 Deliver yourself, O Zion, that dwell *with* the daughter of Babylon.

8 For thus says Yahweh of hosts; After the glory has he sent me to the nations which spoiled you: for he that touches you touches the apple of his eye.

9 For, behold, I will shake my hand upon them, and they shall be a spoil to their servants: and you shall know that Yahweh of hosts has sent me.

10 ¶ Sing and rejoice, O daughter of Zion: for, lo, I come, and I will dwell in the midst of you, says Yahweh.

11 And many nations shall be joined to Yahweh in that day, and shall be my people: and I will dwell in the midst of you, and you shall know that Yahweh of hosts has sent me to you.

12 And Yahweh shall inherit Judah his portion in the holy land, and shall choose Jerusalem again.

13 Be silent, O all flesh, before Yahweh: for he is raised up out of his holy habitation.

Zechariah 3

3:1 ¶ And he showed me Joshua the high priest standing before the angel of Yahweh, and Satan standing at his right hand to resist him.

2 And Yahweh said to Satan, Yahweh rebuke you, O Satan; even Yahweh that has chosen Jerusalem rebuke you: *is* not this a brand plucked out of the fire?

3 Now Joshua was clothed with filthy garments, and stood before the angel.

4 And he answered and spoke to those that stood before him, saying, Take away the filthy garments from him. And to him he said, Behold, I have caused your iniquity to pass from you, and I will clothe you with *a* change of apparel.

5 And I said, Let them set a clean turban upon his head. So they set a clean turban upon his head, and clothed him with garments. And the angel of Yahweh stood by.

6 And the angel of Yahweh protested to Joshua, saying,

7 Thus says Yahweh of hosts; If you will walk in my ways, and if you will keep my charge, then you shall also judge my house, and shall also keep my courts, and I will give you places to walk among these that stand by.

8 ¶ Hear now, O Joshua the high priest, you, and your fellows that sit before you: for they *are* men wondered at: for, behold, I will bring forth my servant the BRANCH.

9 For behold the stone that I have laid before Joshua; upon one stone *shall be* seven eyes: behold, I will engrave the engraving thereof, says Yahweh of hosts, and I will remove the iniquity of that land in one day.

10 In that day, says Yahweh of hosts, shall you call every man his neighbor under the vine and under the fig tree.

Zechariah 4

4:1 ¶ And the angel that talked with me came again, and awakened me, as a man that is awakened out of his sleep

2 And said to me, What see you? And I said, I have looked, and behold a candlestick all *of* gold, with a bowl upon the top of it, and his seven lamps thereon, and seven pipes to the seven lamps, which *are* upon the top thereof:

3 And two olive trees by it, one upon the right *side* of the bowl, and the other upon the left *side* thereof.

4 So I answered and spoke to the angel that talked with me, saying, What *are* these, my lord?

5 Then the angel that talked with me answered and said to me, Know you not what these are? And I said, No, my lord.

6 Then he answered and spoke to me, saying, This *is* the word of Yahweh to Zerubbabel, saying, Not by might, nor by power, but by my spirit, says Yahweh of hosts.

7 Who *are* you, O great mountain? before Zerubbabel *you shall become* a plain: and he shall bring forth the headstone *thereof with* shouting, *crying*, Grace, grace unto it.

8 Moreover the word of Yahweh came to me, saying,

9 The hands of Zerubbabel have laid the foundation of this house; his hands shall also finish it; and you shall know that Yahweh of hosts has sent me to you.

10 For who has despised the day of small things? for they shall rejoice, and shall see the plummet in the hand of Zerubbabel *with* those seven; they *are* the eyes of Yahweh, which run to and fro through the whole earth.

11 ¶ Then answered I, and said to him, What *are* these two olive trees upon the right *side* of the candlestick and upon the left *side* thereof?

12 And I answered again, and said to him, What *are* these two olive branches which through the two golden pipes empty the golden *oil* out of themselves?

13 And he answered me and said, Know you not what these *are*? And I said, No, my lord.

14 Then said he, These *are* the two anointed ones, that stand by the Lord of the whole earth.

Zechariah 5

5:1 ¶ Then I turned, and lifted up my eyes, and looked, and behold a flying roll.

2 And he said to me, What see you? And I answered, I see a flying roll; the length thereof *is* twenty cubits, and the breadth thereof ten cubits.

3 Then said he to me, This *is* the curse that goes forth over the face of the whole earth: for every one that steals shall be cut off *as* on this side according to it; and every one that swears shall be cut off *as* on that side according to it.

4 I will bring it forth, says Yahweh of hosts, and it shall enter into the house of the thief, and into the house of him that swears falsely by my name: and it shall remain in the midst of his house, and shall consume it with the timber thereof and the stones thereof.

5 ¶ Then the angel that talked with me went forth, and said to me, Lift up now your eyes, and see what *is* this that goes forth.

6 And I said, What *is* it? And he said, This *is* an ephah that goes forth. He said moreover, This *is* their resemblance through all the earth.

7 And, behold, there was lifted up a talent of lead: and this *is* a woman that sits in the midst of the ephah.

8 And he said, This *is* wickedness. And he cast it into the midst of the ephah; and he cast the weight of lead upon the mouth thereof.

9 Then lifted I up my eyes, and looked, and, behold, there came out two women, and the wind *was* in their wings; for they had wings like the wings of a stork: and they lifted up the ephah between the earth and the heaven.

10 Then said I to the angel that talked with me, Where do these bear the ephah?

11 And he said to me, To build it a house in the land of Shinar: and it shall be established, and set there upon her own base.

Zechariah 6

6:1 ¶ And I turned, and lifted up my eyes, and looked, and, behold, there came four chariots out from between two mountains; and the mountains *were* mountains of brass.

2 In the first chariot *were* red horses; and in the second chariot black horses;

3 And in the third chariot white horses; and in the fourth chariot spotted and bay horses.

4 Then I answered and said to the angel that talked with me, What *are* these, my lord?

5 And the angel answered and said to me, These *are* the four spirits of the heavens, which go forth from standing before the Lord of all the earth.

6 The black horses which *are* therein go forth into the north country; and the white go forth after them; and the spotted go forth toward the south country.

7 And the bay went forth, and sought to go that they might walk to and fro through the earth: and he said, Get you away, walk to and fro through the earth. So they walked to and fro through the earth.

Zechariah 6

8 Then cried he upon me, and spoke to me, saying, Behold, these that go toward the north country have quieted my spirit in the north country.

9 ¶ And the word of Yahweh came to me, saying,

10 Take of *them of* the captivity, *even* of Heldai, of Tobijah, and of Jedaiah, which have come from Babylon, and come you the same day, and go into the house of Josiah the son of Zephaniah;

11 Then take silver and gold, and make crowns, and set *them* upon the head of Joshua the son of Josedech, the high priest;

12 And speak to him, saying, Thus speaks Yahweh of hosts, saying, Behold the man whose name *is* The BRANCH; and he shall grow up out of his place, and he shall build the temple of Yahweh:

13 Even he shall build the temple of Yahweh; and he shall bear the glory, and shall sit and rule on his throne; and he shall be a priest upon his throne: and the counsel of peace shall be between them both.

14 And the crowns shall be to Helem, and to Tobijah, and to Jedaiah, and to Hen the son of Zephaniah, for a memorial in the temple of Yahweh.

15 And they *that are* far off shall come and build in the temple of Yahweh, and you shall know that Yahweh of hosts has sent me to you. And *this* shall come to pass, if you will diligently obey the voice of Yahweh your God.

Zechariah 7

7:1 ¶ And it came to pass in the fourth year of king Darius, *that* the word of Yahweh came to Zechariah in the fourth *day* of the ninth month, *even* in Chisleu;

2 When they had sent to the house of God Sherezer and Regemmelech, and their men, to pray before Yahweh,

3 *And* to speak to the priests which *were* in the house of Yahweh of hosts, and to the prophets, saying, Should I weep in the fifth month, separating myself, as I have done these so many years?

4 Then came the word of Yahweh of hosts to me, saying,

5 Speak to all the people of the land, and to the priests, saying, When you fasted and mourned in the fifth and seventh *month*, even those seventy years, did you at all fast unto me, *even* to me?

6 And when you did eat, and when you did drink, did not you eat *for yourselves*, and drink *for yourselves*?

7 *Should you* not *hear* the words which Yahweh has cried by the former prophets, when Jerusalem was inhabited and in prosperity, and the cities thereof round about her, when *men* inhabited the south and the plain?

8 ¶ And the word of Yahweh came to Zechariah, saying,

9 Thus speaks Yahweh of hosts, saying, Execute true judgment, and show mercy and compassion every man to his brother:

10 And oppress not the widow, nor the fatherless, the stranger, nor the poor; and let none of you imagine evil against his brother in your heart.

11 But they refused to listen, and pulled away the shoulder, and stopped their ears, that they should not hear.

12 Yes, they made their hearts *as* an adamant stone, lest they should hear the law, and the words which Yahweh of hosts has sent in his spirit by the former prophets: therefore came a great wrath from Yahweh of hosts.

13 Therefore it has come to pass, *that* as he cried, and they would not hear; so they cried, and I would not hear, says Yahweh of hosts:

14 But I scattered them with a whirlwind among all the nations whom they knew not. Thus the land was desolate after them, that no man passed through nor returned: for they laid the pleasant land desolate.

Zechariah 8

8:1 ¶ Again the word of Yahweh of hosts came *to me*, saying,

2 Thus says Yahweh of hosts; I was jealous for Zion with great jealousy, and I was jealous for her with great fury.

3 Thus says Yahweh; I am returned to Zion, and will dwell in the midst of Jerusalem: and Jerusalem shall be called a city of truth; and the mountain of Yahweh of hosts the holy mountain.

4 Thus says Yahweh of hosts; There shall yet old men and old women dwell in the streets of Jerusalem, and every man with his staff in his hand because of great age.

5 And the streets of the city shall be full of boys and girls playing in the streets thereof.

6 Thus says Yahweh of hosts; If it is marvelous in the eyes of the remnant of this people in these days, should it also be marvelous in my eyes? says Yahweh of hosts.

7 Thus says Yahweh of hosts; Behold, I will save my people from the east country, and from the west country;

8 And I will bring them, and they shall dwell in the midst of Jerusalem: and they shall be my people, and I will be their God, in truth and in righteousness.

9 ¶ Thus says Yahweh of hosts; Let your hands be strong, you that hear in these days these words by the mouth of the prophets, which *were* in the day *that* the foundation of the house of Yahweh of hosts was laid, that the temple might be built.

10 For before these days there was no hire for man, nor any hire for beast; neither *was there any* peace to him that went out or came in because of the affliction: for I set all men every one against his neighbor.

11 But now I *will* not *be* to the residue of this people as in the former days, says Yahweh of hosts.

12 For the seed *shall be* prosperous; the vine shall give her fruit, and the ground shall give her increase, and the heavens shall give their dew; and I will cause the remnant of this people to possess all these *things*.

13 And it shall come to pass, *that* as you were a curse among the heathen, O house of Judah, and house of Israel; so will I save you, and you shall be a blessing: fear not, *but* let your hands be strong.

14 For thus says Yahweh of hosts; As I thought to punish you, when your fathers provoked me to wrath, says Yahweh of hosts, and I repented not:
15 So again have I thought in these days to do well unto Jerusalem and to the house of Judah: fear you not.
16 These *are* the things that you shall do; Speak you every man the truth to his neighbor; execute the judgment of truth and peace in your gates:
17 And let none of you imagine evil in your hearts against his neighbor; and love no false oath: for all these *are things* that I hate, says Yahweh.
18 ¶ And the word of Yahweh of hosts came to me, saying,
19 Thus says Yahweh of hosts; The fast of the fourth *month*, and the fast of the fifth, and the fast of the seventh, and the fast of the tenth, shall be to the house of Judah joy and gladness, and cheerful feasts; therefore love the truth and peace.
20 Thus says Yahweh of hosts; *It shall yet come to pass*, that there shall come people, and the inhabitants of many cities:
21 And the inhabitants of one *city* shall go to another, saying, Let us go speedily to pray before Yahweh, and to seek Yahweh of hosts: I will go also.
22 Yes, many people and strong nations shall come to seek Yahweh of hosts in Jerusalem, and to pray before Yahweh.
23 Thus says Yahweh of hosts; In those days *it shall come to pass*, that ten men shall take hold out of all languages of the nations, even shall take hold of the skirt of him that is a Jew, saying, We will go with you: for we have heard *that* God *is* with you.

Zechariah 9

9:1 ¶ The burden of the word of Yahweh in the land of Hadrach, and Damascus *shall be* the rest thereof: when the eyes of man, as of all the tribes of Israel, *shall be* toward Yahweh.
2 And Hamath also shall border thereby; Tyrus, and Zidon, though they are very wise.
3 And Tyrus did build herself a strong hold, and heaped up silver as the dust, and fine gold as the mire of the streets.
4 Behold, the Lord will cast her out, and he will smite her power in the sea; and she shall be devoured with fire.
5 Ashkelon shall see *it*, and fear; Gaza also *shall see it*, and be very sorrowful, and Ekron; for her expectation shall be ashamed; and the king shall perish from Gaza, and Ashkelon shall not be inhabited.
6 And a bastard shall dwell in Ashdod, and I will cut off the pride of the Philistines.
7 And I will take away his blood out of his mouth, and his abominations from between his teeth: but he that remains, even he, *shall be* for our God, and he shall be as a governor in Judah, and Ekron as a Jebusite.

8 And I will encamp about my house because of the army, because of him that passes by, and because of him that returns: and no oppressor shall pass through them any more: for now have I seen with my eyes.
9 ¶ Rejoice greatly, O daughter of Zion; shout, O daughter of Jerusalem: behold, your King comes to you: he *is* just, and having salvation; lowly, and riding upon a donkey, and upon a colt the foal of a donkey.
10 And I will cut off the chariot from Ephraim, and the horse from Jerusalem, and the battle bow shall be cut off: and he shall speak peace to the heathen: and his dominion *shall be* from sea *even* to sea, and from the river *even* to the ends of the earth.
11 As for you also, by the blood of your covenant I have sent forth your prisoners out of the pit wherein *is* no water.
12 ¶ Turn you to the strong hold, you prisoners of hope: even today do I declare *that* I will render double to you;
13 When I have bent Judah for me, filled the bow with Ephraim, and raised up your sons, O Zion, against your sons, O Greece, and made you as the sword of a mighty man.
14 And Yahweh shall be seen over them, and his arrow shall go forth as the lightning: and the Lord Yahweh shall blow the trumpet, and shall go with whirlwinds of the south.
15 Yahweh of hosts shall defend them; and they shall devour, and subdue with sling stones; and they shall drink, *and* make a noise as through wine; and they shall be filled like bowls, *and* as the corners of the altar.
16 And Yahweh their God shall save them in that day as the flock of his people: for they *shall be as* the stones of a crown, lifted up as an ensign upon his land.
17 For how great *is* his goodness, and how great *is* his beauty! corn shall make the young men cheerful, and new wine the maids.

Zechariah 10

10:1 ¶ Ask you of Yahweh rain in the time of the latter rain; *so* Yahweh shall make bright clouds, and give them showers of rain, to every one grass in the field.
2 For the idols have spoken vanity, and the diviners have seen a lie, and have told false dreams; they comfort in vain: therefore they went their way as a flock, they were troubled, because *there was* no shepherd.
3 My anger was kindled against the shepherds, and I punished the goats: for Yahweh of hosts has visited his flock the house of Judah, and has made them as his goodly horse in the battle.
4 Out of him came forth the corner, out of him the nail, out of him the battle bow, out of him every oppressor together.
5 ¶ And they shall be as mighty *men*, which tread down *their enemies* in the mire of the streets in the battle: and they shall fight, because Yahweh *is* with them, and the riders on horses shall be confounded.

Zechariah 10

6 And I will strengthen the house of Judah, and I will save the house of Joseph, and I will bring them again to place them; for I have mercy upon them: and they shall be as though I had not cast them off: for I *am* Yahweh their God, and will hear them.

7 And *they of* Ephraim shall be like a mighty *man*, and their heart shall rejoice as through wine: yes, their children shall see *it*, and be glad; their heart shall rejoice in Yahweh.

8 I will whistle for them, and gather them; for I have redeemed them: and they shall increase as they have increased.

9 And I will sow them among the people: and they shall remember me in far countries; and they shall live with their children, and turn again.

10 I will bring them again also out of the land of Egypt, and gather them out of Assyria; and I will bring them into the land of Gilead and Lebanon; and *place* shall not be found for them.

11 And he shall pass through the sea with affliction, and shall smite the waves in the sea, and all the deeps of the river shall dry up: and the pride of Assyria shall be brought down, and the scepter of Egypt shall depart away.

12 And I will strengthen them in Yahweh; and they shall walk up and down in his name, says Yahweh.

Zechariah 11

11:1 ¶ Open your doors, O Lebanon, that the fire may devour your cedars.

2 Howl, fir tree; for the cedar has fallen; because the mighty are spoiled: howl, O you oaks of Bashan; for the forest of the vintage has come down.

3 *There is* a voice of the howling of the shepherds; for their glory is spoiled: a voice of the roaring of young lions; for the pride of *the* Jordan is spoiled.

4 ¶ Thus says Yahweh my God; Feed the flock of the slaughter;

5 Whose possessors slay them, and hold themselves not guilty: and they that sell them say, Blessed *be* Yahweh; for I am rich: and their own shepherds pity them not.

6 For I will no more pity the inhabitants of the land, says Yahweh: but, lo, I will deliver the men every one into his neighbor's hand, and into the hand of his king: and they shall smite the land, and out of their hand I will not deliver *them*.

7 And I will feed the flock of slaughter, *even* you, O poor of the flock. And I took unto me two staves; the one I called Beauty, and the other I called Bands; and I fed the flock.

8 Three shepherds also I cut off in one month; and my soul loathed them, and their soul also abhorred me.

9 Then said I, I will not feed you: that that dies, let it die; and that that is to be cut off, let it be cut off; and let the rest eat every one the flesh of another.

10 And I took my staff, *even* Beauty, and cut it apart, that I might break my covenant which I had made with all the people.

11 And it was broken in that day: and so the poor of the flock that waited upon me knew that it *was* the word of Yahweh.

12 And I said to them, If you think good, give *me* my price; and if not, forbear. So they weighed for my price thirty *pieces* of silver.

13 And Yahweh said to me, Cast it to the potter: a goodly price that I was valued at by them. And I took the thirty *pieces* of silver, and cast them to the potter in the house of Yahweh.

14 Then I cut in two my other staff, *even* Bands, that I might break the brotherhood between Judah and Israel.

15 ¶ And Yahweh said to me, Take to you yet the instruments of a foolish shepherd.

16 For, lo, I will raise up a shepherd in the land, *which* shall not visit those that are cut off, neither shall seek the young one, nor heal that that is broken, nor feed that that stands still: but he shall eat the flesh of the fat, and tear their claws in pieces.

17 Woe to the idol shepherd that leaves the flock! the sword *shall be* upon his arm, and upon his right eye: his arm shall be completely withered, and his right eye shall be utterly darkened.

Zechariah 12

12:1 ¶ The burden of the word of Yahweh for Israel, says Yahweh, which stretches forth the heavens, and lays the foundation of the earth, and forms the spirit of man within him.

2 Behold, I will make Jerusalem a cup of trembling to all the people round about, when they shall be in the siege both against Judah *and* against Jerusalem.

3 And in that day will I make Jerusalem a burdensome stone for all people: all that burden themselves with it shall be cut in pieces, though all the people of the earth are gathered together against it.

4 In that day, says Yahweh, I will smite every horse with astonishment, and his rider with madness: and I will open my eyes upon the house of Judah, and will smite every horse of the people with blindness.

5 And the governors of Judah shall say in their heart, The inhabitants of Jerusalem *shall be* my strength in Yahweh of hosts their God.

6 In that day will I make the governors of Judah like a hearth of fire among the wood, and like a torch of fire in a sheaf; and they shall devour all the people round about, on the right hand and on the left: and Jerusalem shall be inhabited again in her own place, *even* in Jerusalem.

7 Yahweh also shall save the tents of Judah first, that the glory of the house of David and the glory of the inhabitants of Jerusalem do not magnify *themselves* against Judah.

8 In that day shall Yahweh defend the inhabitants of Jerusalem; and he that is feeble among them at that day shall be as David; and the house of David *shall be* as God, as the angel of Yahweh before them.

9 ¶ And it shall come to pass in that day, *that* I will seek to destroy all the nations that come against Jerusalem.
10 And I will pour upon the house of David, and upon the inhabitants of Jerusalem, the spirit of grace and of supplications: and they shall look upon me whom they have pierced, and they shall mourn for him, as one mourns for *his* only *son*, and shall be in bitterness for him, as one that is in bitterness for *his* firstborn.
11 In that day shall there be a great mourning in Jerusalem, as the mourning of Hadadrimmon in the valley of Megiddon.
12 And the land shall mourn, every family apart; the family of the house of David apart, and their wives apart; the family of the house of Nathan apart, and their wives apart;
13 The family of the house of Levi apart, and their wives apart; the family of Shimei apart, and their wives apart;
14 All the families that remain, every family apart, and their wives apart.

Zechariah 13

13:1 ¶ In that day there shall be a fountain opened to the house of David and to the inhabitants of Jerusalem for sin and for uncleanness.
2 And it shall come to pass in that day, says Yahweh of hosts, *that* I will cut off the names of the idols out of the land, and they shall no more be remembered: and also I will cause the prophets and the unclean spirit to pass out of the land.
3 And it shall come to pass, *that* when any shall yet prophesy, then his father and his mother that begot him shall say to him, You shall not live; for you speak lies in the name of Yahweh: and his father and his mother that begot him shall thrust him through when he prophesies.
4 And it shall come to pass in that day, *that* the prophets shall be ashamed every one of his vision, when he has prophesied; neither shall they wear a rough garment to deceive:
5 But he shall say, I *am* no prophet, I *am* a husbandman; for man taught me to keep cattle from my youth.
6 And *one* shall say to him, What *are* these wounds in your hands? Then he shall answer, *Those* with which I was wounded *in* the house of my friends.
7 ¶ Awake, O sword, against my shepherd, and against the man *that is* my fellow, says Yahweh of hosts: smite the shepherd, and the sheep shall be scattered: and I will turn my hand upon the little ones.
8 And it shall come to pass, *that* in all the land, says Yahweh, two parts therein shall be cut off *and* die; but the third shall be left therein.
9 And I will bring the third part through the fire, and will refine them as silver is refined, and will try them as gold is tried: they shall call on my name, and I will hear them: I will say, It *is* my people: and they shall say, Yahweh *is* my God.

Zechariah 14

14:1 ¶ Behold, the day of Yahweh comes, and your spoil shall be divided in the midst of you.
2 For I will gather all nations against Jerusalem to battle; and the city shall be taken, and the houses rifled, and the women ravished; and half of the city shall go forth into captivity, and the residue of the people shall not be cut off from the city.
3 Then shall Yahweh go forth, and fight against those nations, as when he fought in the day of battle.
4 And his feet shall stand in that day upon the mount of Olives, which *is* before Jerusalem on the east, and the mount of Olives shall cleave in the midst thereof toward the east and toward the west, *and there shall be* a very great valley; and half of the mountain shall remove toward the north, and half of it toward the south.
5 And you shall flee *to* the valley of the mountains; for the valley of the mountains shall reach to Azal: yes, you shall flee, like as you fled from before the earthquake in the days of Uzziah king of Judah: and Yahweh my God shall come, *and* all the saints with you.
6 And it shall come to pass in that day, *that* the light shall not be clear, *nor* dark:
7 But it shall be one day which shall be known to Yahweh, not day, nor night: but it shall come to pass, *that* at evening time it shall be light.
8 ¶ And it shall be in that day, *that* living waters shall go out from Jerusalem; half of them toward the former sea, and half of them toward the hinder sea: in summer and in winter shall it be.
9 And Yahweh shall be king over all the earth: in that day shall there be one Yahweh, and his name one.
10 All the land shall be turned as a plain from Geba to Rimmon south of Jerusalem: and it shall be lifted up, and inhabited in her place, from Benjamin's gate to the place of the first gate, to the corner gate, and *from* the tower of Hananeel to the king's winepresses.
11 And *men* shall dwell in it, and there shall be no more utter destruction; but Jerusalem shall be safely inhabited.
12 And this shall be the plague with which Yahweh will smite all the people that have fought against Jerusalem; Their flesh shall rot away while they stand upon their feet, and their eyes shall rot away in their holes, and their tongue shall rot away in their mouth.
13 And it shall come to pass in that day, *that* a great tumult from Yahweh shall be among them; and they shall lay hold every one on the hand of his neighbor, and his hand shall rise up against the hand of his neighbor.
14 And Judah also shall fight at Jerusalem; and the wealth of all the heathen round about shall be gathered together, gold, and silver, and apparel, in great abundance.
15 And so shall be the plague of the horse, of the mule, of the camel, and of the donkey, and of all the beasts that shall be in these tents, as this plague.

Zechariah 14

16 ¶ And it shall come to pass, that every one that is left of all the nations which came against Jerusalem shall even go up from year to year to worship the King, Yahweh of hosts, and to keep the feast of tabernacles.

17 And it shall be, that whoever will not come up of all the families of the earth to Jerusalem to worship the King, Yahweh of hosts, even upon them shall be no rain.

18 And if the family of Egypt goes not up, and comes not, that have no rain; there shall be the plague, with which Yahweh will smite the heathen that come not up to keep the feast of tabernacles.

19 This shall be the punishment of Egypt, and the punishment of all nations that come not up to keep the feast of tabernacles.

20 In that day shall there be upon the bells of the horses, HOLINESS UNTO YAHWEH; and the pots in Yahweh's house shall be like the bowls before the altar.

21 Yes, every pot in Jerusalem and in Judah shall be holiness unto Yahweh of hosts: and all they that sacrifice shall come and take of them, and boil therein: and in that day there shall be no more the Canaanite in the house of Yahweh of hosts.

Malachi

Malachi 1

1:1 ¶ The burden of the word of Yahweh to Israel by Malachi.

2 I have loved you, says Yahweh. Yet you say, Wherein have you loved us? Was not Esau Jacob's brother? says Yahweh: yet I loved Jacob,

3 And I hated Esau, and laid his mountains and his heritage waste for the dragons of the wilderness.

4 Whereas Edom said, We are impoverished, but we will return and build the desolate places; thus says Yahweh of hosts, They shall build, but I will throw down; and they shall call them, The border of wickedness, and, The people against whom Yahweh has indignation forever.

5 And your eyes shall see, and you shall say, Yahweh will be magnified from the border of Israel.

6 ¶ A son honors his father, and a servant his master: if then I am a father, where is my honor? and if I am a master, where is my fear? says Yahweh of hosts to you, O priests, that despise my name. And you say, Wherein have we despised your name?

7 You offer polluted bread upon my altar; and you say, Wherein have we polluted you? In that you say, The table of Yahweh is contemptible.

8 And if you offer the blind for sacrifice, is it not evil? and if you offer the lame and sick, is it not evil? offer it now to your governor; will he be pleased with you, or accept your person? says Yahweh of hosts.

9 And now, I pray you, beseech God that he will be gracious to us: this has been by your means: will he regard your persons? says Yahweh of hosts.

10 Who is there even among you that would shut the doors for nothing? neither do you kindle fire on my altar for nothing. I have no pleasure in you, says Yahweh of hosts, neither will I accept an offering at your hand.

11 For from the rising of the sun even to the going down of the same my name shall be great among the Gentiles; and in every place incense shall be offered unto my name, and a pure offering: for my name shall be great among the heathen, says Yahweh of hosts.

12 But you have profaned it, in that you say, The table of Yahweh is polluted; and the fruit thereof, even his meat, is contemptible.

13 You said also, Behold, what a weariness is it! and you have snuffed at it, says Yahweh of hosts; and you brought that which was torn, and the lame, and the sick; thus you brought an offering: should I accept this from your hand? says Yahweh.

14 But cursed be the deceiver, which has in his flock a male, and vows, and sacrifices unto the Lord a corrupt thing: for I am a great King, says Yahweh of hosts, and my name is dreadful among the heathen.

Malachi 2

2:1 ¶ And now, O you priests, this commandment is for you.

2 If you will not hear, and if you will not lay it to heart, to give glory unto my name, says Yahweh of hosts, I will even send a curse upon you, and I will curse your blessings: yes, I have cursed them already, because you do not lay it to heart.

3 Behold, I will corrupt your seed, and spread dung upon your faces, even the dung of your solemn feasts; and one shall take you away with it.

4 And you shall know that I have sent this commandment to you, that my covenant might be with Levi, says Yahweh of hosts.

5 My covenant was with him of life and peace; and I gave them to him for the fear with which he feared me, and was afraid before my name.

6 The law of truth was in his mouth, and iniquity was not found in his lips: he walked with me in peace and equity, and did turn many away from iniquity.

7 For the priest's lips should keep knowledge, and they should seek the law at his mouth: for he is the messenger of Yahweh of hosts.

8 But you have departed out of the way; you have caused many to stumble at the law; you have corrupted the covenant of Levi, says Yahweh of hosts.

9 Therefore have I also made you contemptible and base before all the people, according as you have not kept my ways, but have been partial in the law.

10 ¶ Have we not all one father? has not one God created us? why do we deal treacherously every man against his brother, by profaning the covenant of our fathers?

11 Judah has dealt treacherously, and an abomination is committed in Israel and in Jerusalem; for Judah has profaned the holiness of Yahweh which he loved, and has married the daughter of a strange god.

12 Yahweh will cut off the man that does this, the master and the scholar, out of the tabernacles of Jacob, and him that offers an offering unto Yahweh of hosts.

13 And this have you done again, covering the altar of Yahweh with tears, with weeping, and with crying out, insomuch that he regards not the offering any more, or receives *it* with good will at your hand.

14 Yet you say, Why? Because Yahweh has been witness between you and the wife of your youth, against whom you have dealt treacherously: yet *is* she your companion, and the wife of your covenant.

15 And did not he make one? Yet had he the residue of the spirit. And why one? That he might seek a godly seed. Therefore take heed to your spirit, and let none deal treacherously against the wife of his youth.

16 For Yahweh, the God of Israel, says that he hates putting away: for *one* covers violence with his garment, says Yahweh of hosts: therefore take heed to your spirit, that you deal not treacherously.

17 You have wearied Yahweh with your words. Yet you say, Wherein have we wearied *him*? When you say, Every one that does evil *is* good in the sight of Yahweh, and he delights in them; or, Where *is* the God of judgment?

Malachi 3

3:1 ¶ Behold, I will send my messenger, and he shall prepare the way before me: and the Lord, whom you seek, shall suddenly come to his temple, even the messenger of the covenant, whom you delight in: behold, he shall come, says Yahweh of hosts.

2 But who may endure the day of his coming? and who shall stand when he appears? for he *is* like a refiner's fire, and like fullers' soap:

3 And he shall sit *as* a refiner and purifier of silver: and he shall purify the sons of Levi, and purge them as gold and silver, that they may offer unto Yahweh an offering in righteousness.

4 Then shall the offering of Judah and Jerusalem be pleasant unto Yahweh, as in the days of old, and as in former years.

5 And I will come near to you for judgment; and I will be a swift witness against the sorcerers, and against the adulterers, and against false swearers, and against those that oppress the hireling in *his* wages, the widow, and the fatherless, and that turn aside the stranger *from his right*, and fear not me, says Yahweh of hosts.

6 For I *am* Yahweh, I change not; therefore you sons of Jacob are not consumed.

7 ¶ Even from the days of your fathers you have gone away from my ordinances, and have not kept *them*. Return unto me, and I will return to you, says Yahweh of hosts. But you said, Wherein shall we return?

8 Will a man rob God? Yet you have robbed me. But you say, Wherein have we robbed you? In tithes and offerings.

9 You *are* cursed with a curse: for you have robbed me, *even* this whole nation.

10 Bring you all the tithes into the storehouse, that there may be meat in my house, and prove me now herewith, says Yahweh of hosts, if I will not open you the windows of heaven, and pour you out a blessing, that *there shall* not *be room* enough *to receive it*.

11 And I will rebuke the devourer for your sakes, and he shall not destroy the fruits of your ground; neither shall your vine cast her fruit before the time in the field, says Yahweh of hosts.

12 And all nations shall call you blessed: for you shall be a delightsome land, says Yahweh of hosts.

13 ¶ Your words have been stout against me, says Yahweh. Yet you say, What have we spoken *so much* against you?

14 You have said, It *is* vain to serve God: and what profit *is it* that we have kept his ordinance, and that we have walked mournfully before Yahweh of hosts?

15 And now we call the proud happy; yes, they that work wickedness are set up; yes, *they that* tempt God are even delivered.

16 Then they that feared Yahweh spoke often one to another: and Yahweh listened, and heard *it*, and a book of remembrance was written before him for them that feared Yahweh, and that thought upon his name.

17 And they shall be mine, says Yahweh of hosts, in that day when I make up my jewels; and I will spare them, as a man spares his own son that serves him.

18 Then shall you return, and discern between the righteous and the wicked, between him that serves God and him that serves him not.

Malachi 4

4:1 ¶ For, behold, the day comes, that shall burn as an oven; and all the proud, yes, and all that do wickedly, shall be stubble: and the day that comes shall burn them up, says Yahweh of hosts, that it shall leave them neither root nor branch.

2 But unto you that fear my name shall the Sun of righteousness arise with healing in his wings; and you shall go forth, and grow up as calves of the stall.

3 And you shall tread down the wicked; for they shall be ashes under the soles of your feet in the day that I shall do *this*, says Yahweh of hosts.

4 ¶ Remember you the law of Moses my servant, which I commanded to him in Horeb for all Israel, *with* the statutes and judgments.

5 Behold, I will send you Elijah the prophet before the coming of the great and dreadful day of Yahweh:

6 And he shall turn the heart of the fathers to the children, and the heart of the children to their fathers, lest I come and smite the earth with a curse.

Section 5
The Gospels and Acts

Matthew

Matthew 1

1:1 ¶ The book of the generation of Yahshua the Messiah, the son of David, the son of Abraham.
2 Abraham begot Isaac; and Isaac begot Jacob; and Jacob begot Judah and his brothers;
3 And Judah begot Pharez and Zarah by Tamar; and Pharez begot Hezron; and Hezron begot Ram;
4 And Ram begot Amminadab; and Amminadab begot Nahshon; and Nahshon begot Salmon;
5 And Salmon begot Boaz of Rachab; and Boaz begot Obed of Ruth; and Obed begot Jesse;
6 And Jesse begot David the king; and David the king begot Solomon of her *that had been the wife* of Uriah;
7 And Solomon begot Rehoboam; and Rehoboam begot Abijah; and Abijah begot Asa;
8 And Asa begot Jehoshaphat; and Jehoshaphat begot Joram; and Joram begot Uzziah;
9 And Uzziah begot Jotham; and Jotham begot Ahaz; and Ahaz begot Hezekiah;
10 And Hezekiah begot Manasseh; and Manasseh begot Amon; and Amon begot Josiah;
11 And Josiah begot Jechoniah and his brothers, about the time they were carried away to Babylon:
12 And after they were brought to Babylon, Jechoniah begot Shealtiel; and Shealtiel begot Zerubbabel;
13 And Zerubbabel begot Abiud; and Abiud begot Eliakim; and Eliakim begot Azur;
14 And Azur begot Sadoc; and Sadoc begot Achim; and Achim begot Eliud;
15 And Eliud begot Eleazar; and Eleazar begot Matthan; and Matthan begot Jacob;
16 And Jacob begot Joseph the husband of Mary, of whom was born Yahshua, who is called the Messiah.
17 So all the generations from Abraham to David *are* fourteen generations; and from David until the carrying away into Babylon *are* fourteen generations; and from the carrying away into Babylon to the Messiah *are* fourteen generations.
18 ¶ Now the birth of Yahshua the Messiah was in this manner: When as his mother Mary was espoused to Joseph, before they came together, she was found with child of the Holy Ghost.
19 Then Joseph her husband, being a just *man*, and not willing to make her a public example, was minded to put her away privately.
20 But while he thought on these things, behold, the angel of the Lord appeared unto him in a dream, saying, Joseph, you son of David, fear not to take unto you Mary your wife: for that which is conceived in her is of the Holy Ghost.
21 And she shall bring forth a son, and you shall call his name YAHSHUA: for he shall save his people from their sins.
22 Now all this was done, that it might be fulfilled which was spoken of the Lord *Yahweh* by the prophet, saying,
23 Behold, a virgin shall be with child, and shall bring forth a son, and they shall call his name Immanuel, which being interpreted is, God with us.
24 Then Joseph being raised from sleep did as the angel of the Lord had invited him, and took unto him his wife:
25 And knew her not till she had brought forth her firstborn son: and he called his name YAHSHUA.

Matthew 2

2:1 ¶ Now when Yahshua was born in Bethlehem of Judaea in the days of Herod the king, behold, there came wise men from the east to Jerusalem,
2 Saying, Where is he that is born King of the Jews? for we have seen his star in the east, and have come to worship him.
3 When Herod the king had heard *these things*, he was troubled, and all Jerusalem with him.
4 And when he had gathered all the chief priests and scribes of the people together, he demanded of them where the Messiah should be born.
5 And they said unto him, In Bethlehem of Judaea: for thus it is written by the prophet,
6 And you Bethlehem, *in* the land of Judah, are not the least among the princes of Judah: for out of you shall come a Governor, that shall rule my people Israel.
7 Then Herod, when he had privately called the wise men, inquired of them diligently what time the star appeared.
8 And he sent them to Bethlehem, and said, Go and search diligently for the young child; and when you have found *him*, bring me word again, that I may come and worship him also.
9 ¶ When they had heard the king, they departed; and, behold, the star, which they saw in the east, went before them, till it came and stood over where the young child was.
10 When they saw the star, they rejoiced with exceedingly great joy.
11 And when they had come into the house, they saw the young child with Mary his mother, and fell down, and worshipped him: and when they had opened their treasures, they presented to him gifts; gold, and frankincense, and myrrh.

Matthew 2

12 And being warned of God in a dream that they should not return to Herod, they departed into their own country another way.

13 ¶ And when they had departed, behold, the angel of the Lord appeared to Joseph in a dream, saying, Arise, and take the young child and his mother, and flee into Egypt, and be you there until I bring you word: for Herod will seek the young child to destroy him.

14 When he arose, he took the young child and his mother by night, and departed into Egypt:

15 And was there until the death of Herod: that it might be fulfilled which was spoken of the Lord by the prophet, saying, Out of Egypt have I called my son.

16 ¶ Then Herod, when he saw that he was mocked by the wise men, was exceedingly angry, and sent forth, and slew all the children that were in Bethlehem, and in all the coasts thereof, from two years old and under, according to the time which he had diligently inquired of the wise men.

17 Then was fulfilled that which was spoken by Jeremiah the prophet, saying,

18 In Ramah was there a voice heard, lamentation, and weeping, and great mourning, Rachel weeping *for* her children, and would not be comforted, because they were not.

19 ¶ But when Herod was dead, behold, an angel of the Lord appeared in a dream to Joseph in Egypt,

20 Saying, Arise, and take the young child and his mother, and go into the land of Israel: for they are dead which sought the young child's life.

21 And he arose, and took the young child and his mother, and came into the land of Israel.

22 But when he heard that Archelaus did reign in Judaea in the room of his father Herod, he was afraid to go there: notwithstanding, being warned of God in a dream, he turned aside into the parts of Galilee:

23 And he came and dwelt in a city called Nazareth: that it might be fulfilled which was spoken by the prophets, He shall be called a Nazarene.

Matthew 3

3:1 ¶ In those days came John the Baptist, preaching in the wilderness of Judaea,

2 And saying, Repent you: for the kingdom of heaven is at hand.

3 For this is he that was spoken of by the prophet Isaiah, saying, The voice of one crying in the wilderness, Prepare you the way of the Lord *Yahweh*, make his paths straight.

4 And the same John had his garment of camel's hair, and a leather girdle about his loins; and his food was locusts and wild honey.

5 Then went out to him Jerusalem, and all Judaea, and all the region round about *the* Jordan,

6 And were baptized of him in *the* Jordan, confessing their sins.

7 ¶ But when he saw many of the Pharisees and Sadducees come to his baptism, he said unto them, O generation of vipers, who has warned you to flee from the wrath to come?

8 Bring forth therefore fruits befitting repentance:

9 And think not to say within yourselves, We have Abraham as *our* father: for I say to you, that God is able of these stones to raise up children to Abraham.

10 And now also the ax is laid to the root of the trees: therefore every tree which brings not forth good fruit is hewn down, and cast into the fire.

11 I indeed baptize you with water unto repentance: but he that comes after me is mightier than I, whose shoes I am not worthy to bear: he shall baptize you with the Holy Ghost, and *with* fire:

12 Whose fan *is* in his hand, and he will thoroughly purge his floor, and gather his wheat into the barn; but he will burn up the chaff with unquenchable fire.

13 ¶ Then came Yahshua from Galilee to *the* Jordan unto John, to be baptized by him.

14 But John forbade him, saying, I have need to be baptized by you, and come you to me?

15 And Yahshua answering said unto him, Allow *it to be so* now: for thus it becomes us to fulfill all righteousness. Then he allowed him.

16 And Yahshua, when he was baptized, went up straightway out of the water: and, behold, the heavens were opened unto him, and he saw the Spirit of God descending like a dove, and lighting upon him:

17 And behold a voice from heaven, saying, This is my beloved Son, in whom I am well pleased.

Matthew 4

4:1 ¶ Then was Yahshua led up by the Spirit into the wilderness to be tempted by the devil.

2 And when he had fasted *for* forty days and forty nights, he was afterward hungry.

3 And when the tempter came to him, he said, If you are the Son of God, command that these stones be made bread.

4 But he answered and said, It is written, Man shall not live by bread alone, but by every word that proceeds out of the mouth of God *Yahweh*.

5 Then the devil took him up into the holy city, and set him on a pinnacle of the temple,

6 And said unto him, If you are the Son of God, cast yourself down: for it is written, He shall give his angels charge concerning you: and in *their* hands they shall bear you up, lest at any time you dash your foot against a stone.

7 Yahshua said unto him, It is written again, You shall not tempt the Lord *Yahweh* your God.

8 Again, the devil took him up into an exceedingly high mountain, and showed him all the kingdoms of the world, and the glory of them;

9 And said unto him, All these things will I give you, if you will fall down and worship me.

10 Then said Yahshua unto him, Get you away, Satan: for it is written, You shall worship the Lord *Yahweh* your God, and him only shall you serve.

11 Then the devil left him, and, behold, angels came and ministered unto him.

12 ¶ Now when Yahshua had heard that John was cast into prison, he departed into Galilee;

13 And leaving Nazareth, he came and dwelt in Capernaum, which is upon the sea coast, in the borders of Zebulun and Naphtali:

14 That it might be fulfilled which was spoken by Isaiah the prophet, saying,

15 The land of Zebulun, and the land of Naphtali, *by* the way of the sea, beyond *the* Jordan, Galilee of the Gentiles;

16 The people which sat in darkness saw great light; and to them which sat in the region and shadow of death light has sprung up.

17 From that time Yahshua began to preach, and to say, Repent: for the kingdom of heaven is at hand.

18 ¶ And Yahshua, walking by the sea of Galilee, saw two brothers, Simon called Peter, and Andrew his brother, casting a net into the sea: for they were fishermen.

19 And he said unto them, Follow me, and I will make you fishers of men.

20 And they immediately left *their* nets, and followed him.

21 And going on from there, he saw other two brothers, James *the son* of Zebedee, and John his brother, in a ship with Zebedee their father, mending their nets; and he called them.

22 And they immediately left the ship and their father, and followed him.

23 ¶ And Yahshua went about all Galilee, teaching in their synagogues, and preaching the gospel of the kingdom, and healing all manner of sickness and all manner of disease among the people.

24 And his fame went throughout all Syria: and they brought unto him all sick people that were taken with various diseases and torments, and those which were possessed with devils, and those which were lunatic, and those that had the palsy; and he healed them.

25 And there followed him great multitudes of people from Galilee, and *from* Decapolis, and *from* Jerusalem, and *from* Judaea, and *from* beyond *the* Jordan.

Matthew 5

5:1 ¶ And seeing the multitudes, he went up into a mountain: and when he was seated, his disciples came unto him:

2 And he opened his mouth, and taught them, saying,

3 ¶ Blessed *are* the poor in spirit: for theirs is the kingdom of heaven.

4 Blessed *are* they that mourn: for they shall be comforted.

5 Blessed *are* the meek: for they shall inherit the earth.

6 Blessed *are* they which do hunger and thirst after righteousness: for they shall be filled.

7 Blessed *are* the merciful: for they shall obtain mercy.

8 Blessed *are* the pure in heart: for they shall see God.

9 Blessed *are* the peacemakers: for they shall be called the children of God.

10 Blessed *are* they which are persecuted for righteousness' sake: for theirs is the kingdom of heaven.

11 Blessed are you, when *men* shall revile you, and persecute *you*, and shall say all manner of evil against you falsely, for my sake.

12 Rejoice, and be exceedingly glad: for great *is* your reward in heaven: for so persecuted they the prophets which were before you.

13 ¶ You are the salt of the earth: but if the salt has lost its savor, with what shall it be salted? it is thereafter good for nothing, but to be cast out, and to be trodden under foot of men.

14 You are the light of the world. A city that is set on a hill cannot be hidden.

15 Neither do men light a candle, and put it under a bushel, but on a candlestick; and it gives light to all that are in the house.

16 Let your light so shine before men, that they may see your good works, and glorify your Father which is in heaven.

17 ¶ Think not that I have come to destroy the law, or the prophets: I have not come to destroy, but to fulfill.

18 For truly I say to you, Till heaven and earth pass, one jot or one tittle shall in no way pass from the law, till all is fulfilled.

19 Whoever therefore shall break one of these least commandments, and shall teach men so, he shall be called the least in the kingdom of heaven: but whoever shall do and teach *them*, the same shall be called great in the kingdom of heaven.

20 For I say unto you, That unless your righteousness shall exceed *the righteousness* of the scribes and Pharisees, you shall in no case enter into the kingdom of heaven.

21 ¶ You have heard that it was said by them of old time, You shall not kill; and whoever shall kill shall be in danger of the judgment:

22 But I say unto you, That whoever is angry with his brother without a cause shall be in danger of the judgment: and whoever shall say to his brother, Raca, shall be in danger of the council: but whoever shall say, You fool, shall be in danger of hell fire.

23 Therefore if you bring your gift to the altar, and there remember that your brother has anything against you;

24 Leave there your gift before the altar, and go your way; first be reconciled to your brother, and then come and offer your gift.

25 Agree with your adversary quickly, while you are in the way with him; lest at any time the adversary deliver you to the judge, and the judge deliver you to the officer, and you be cast into prison.

26 Truly I say unto you, You shall by no means come out therefrom, till you have paid the utmost farthing.

27 ¶ You have heard that it was said by them of old time, You shall not commit adultery:

28 But I say to you, That whoever looks on a woman to lust after her has committed adultery with her already in his heart.

29 And if your right eye offends you, pluck it out, and cast *it* from you: for it is profitable for you that one of your members should perish, and not *that* your whole body should be cast into hell.

30 And if your right hand offends you, cut it off, and cast *it* from you: for it is profitable for you that one of your members should perish, and not *that* your whole body should be cast into hell.

31 It has been said, Whoever shall put away his wife, let him give her a writing of divorce:

32 But I say unto you, That whoever shall put away his wife, saving for the cause of fornication, causes her to commit adultery: and whoever shall marry her that is divorced commits adultery.

33 ¶ Again, you have heard that it has been said by them of old time, You shall not forswear yourself, but will perform unto the Lord *Yahweh* your oaths:

34 But I say unto you, Swear not at all; neither by heaven; for it is God's throne:

35 Nor by the earth; for it is his footstool: neither by Jerusalem; for it is the city of the great King.

36 Neither shall you swear by your head, because you can not make one hair white or black.

37 But let your communication be, Yes, yes; No, no: for whatever is more than these comes of evil.

38 ¶ You have heard that it has been said, An eye for an eye, and a tooth for a tooth:

39 But I say unto you, That you resist not evil: but whoever shall smite you on your right cheek, turn to him the other also.

40 And if any man will sue you at the law, and take away your coat, let him have *your* cloak also.

41 And whoever shall compel you to go a mile, go with him two.

42 Give to him that asks you, and from him that would borrow of you turn not you away.

43 ¶ You have heard that it has been said, You shall love your neighbor, and hate your enemy.

44 But I say to you, Love your enemies, bless them that curse you, do good to them that hate you, and pray for them which despitefully use you, and persecute you;

45 That you may be the children of your Father which is in heaven: for he makes his sun to rise on the evil and on the good, and sends rain on the just and on the unjust.

46 For if you love them which love you, what reward have you? do not even the publicans the same?

47 And if you salute your brethren only, what do you more *than others*? do not even the publicans so?

48 Be you therefore perfect, even as your Father which is in heaven is perfect.

Matthew 6

6:1 ¶ Take heed that you do not your alms before men, to be seen by them: otherwise you have no reward of your Father which is in heaven.

2 Therefore when you do *your* alms, do not sound a trumpet before you, as the hypocrites do in the synagogues and in the streets, that they may have glory of men. Truly I say to you, They have their reward.

3 But when you do alms, let not your left hand know what your right hand does:

4 That your alms may be in secret: and your Father which sees in secret himself shall reward you openly.

5 ¶ And when you pray, you shall not be as the hypocrites *are*: for they love to pray standing in the synagogues and in the corners of the streets, that they may be seen by men. Truly I say unto you, They have their reward.

6 But you, when you pray, enter into your closet, and when you have shut your door, pray to your Father which is in secret; and your Father which sees in secret shall reward you openly.

7 But when you pray, use not vain repetitions, as the heathen *do*: for they think that they shall be heard for their much speaking.

8 Be not you therefore like unto them: for your Father knows what things you have need of, before you ask him.

9 ¶ After this manner therefore pray you: Our Father which are in heaven, Hallowed be your name.

10 Your kingdom come. Your will be done in earth, as *it is* in heaven.

11 Give us this day our daily bread.

12 And forgive us our debts, as we forgive our debtors.

13 And lead us not into temptation, but deliver us from evil: For yours is the kingdom, and the power, and the glory, forever. Amen.

14 For if you forgive men their trespasses, your heavenly Father will also forgive you:

15 But if you forgive not men their trespasses, neither will your Father forgive your trespasses.

16 ¶ Moreover when you fast, be not, as the hypocrites, of a sad countenance: for they disfigure their faces, that they may appear unto men to fast. Truly I say unto you, They have their reward.

17 But you, when you fast, anoint your head, and wash your face;

18 That you appear not unto men to fast, but to your Father which is in secret: and your Father, which sees in secret, shall reward you openly.

19 ¶ Lay not up for yourselves treasures upon earth, where moth and rust does corrupt, and where thieves break through and steal:

20 But lay up for yourselves treasures in heaven, where neither moth nor rust does corrupt, and where thieves do not break through nor steal:

21 For where your treasure is, there will your heart be also.

22 The light of the body is the eye: if therefore your eye be single, your whole body shall be full of light.

23 But if your eye is evil, your whole body shall be full of darkness. If therefore the light that is in you is darkness, how great *is* that darkness!
24 No man can serve two masters: for either he will hate the one, and love the other; or else he will hold to the one, and despise the other. You cannot serve God and mammon.
25 ¶ Therefore I say unto you, Take no thought for your life, what you shall eat, or what you shall drink; nor yet for your body, what you shall put on. Is not the life more than food, and the body than clothing?
26 Behold the fowls of the air: for they sow not, neither do they reap, nor gather into barns; yet your heavenly Father feeds them. Are you not much better than they?
27 Which of you by taking thought can add one cubit to his stature?
28 And why take you thought for clothing? Consider the lilies of the field, how they grow; they toil not, neither do they spin:
29 And yet I say unto you, That even Solomon in all his glory was not arrayed like one of these.
30 Moreover, if God so clothes the grass of the field, which today is, and tomorrow is cast into the oven, *shall he* not much more *clothe* you, O you of little faith?
31 Therefore take no thought, saying, What shall we eat? or, What shall we drink? or, With what shall we be clothed?
32 (For after all these things do the Gentiles seek:) for your heavenly Father knows that you have need of all these things.
33 But seek you first the kingdom of God, and his righteousness; and all these things shall be added unto you.
34 Take therefore no thought for tomorrow: for tomorrow shall take thought for the things of itself. Sufficient unto the day *is* the evil thereof.

Matthew 7

7:1 ¶ Judge not, that you be not judged.
2 For with what judgment you judge, you shall be judged: and with what measure you measure, it shall be measured to you again.
3 And why behold you the twig that is in your brother's eye, but consider not the beam that is in your own eye?
4 Or how will you say to your brother, Let me pull out the twig out of your eye; and, behold, a beam *is* in your own eye?
5 You hypocrite, first cast out the beam out of your own eye; and then shall you see clearly to cast out the twig out of your brother's eye.
6 Give not that which is holy unto the dogs, neither cast you your pearls before swine, lest they trample them under their feet, and turn again and tear you.
7 ¶ Ask, and it shall be given you; seek, and you shall find; knock, and it shall be opened unto you:
8 For every one that asks receives; and he that seeks finds; and to him that knocks it shall be opened.
9 Or what man is there of you, whom if his son asks bread, will he give him a stone?
10 Or if he asks a fish, will he give him a serpent?
11 If you then, being evil, know how to give good gifts to your children, how much more shall your Father which is in heaven give good things to them that ask him?
12 ¶ Therefore all things whatever you desire that men should do to you, do you even so to them: for this is the law and the prophets.
13 Enter you in at the narrow gate: for wide *is* the gate, and broad *is* the way, that leads to destruction, and many there are which go in through it:
14 Because narrow *is* the gate, and troubled *is* the way, which leads unto life, and few there be that find it.
15 ¶ Beware of false prophets, which come to you in sheep's clothing, but inwardly they are ravening wolves.
16 You shall know them by their fruits. Do men gather grapes of thorns, or figs of thistles?
17 Even so every good tree brings forth good fruit; but a corrupt tree brings forth evil fruit.
18 A good tree cannot bring forth evil fruit, neither *can* a corrupt tree bring forth good fruit.
19 Every tree that brings not forth good fruit is hewn down, and cast into the fire.
20 Therefore by their fruits you shall know them.
21 ¶ Not every one that says unto me, Lord, Lord, shall enter into the kingdom of heaven; but he that does the will of my Father which is in heaven.
22 Many will say to me in that day, Lord, Lord, have we not prophesied in your name? and in your name have cast out devils? and in your name done many wonderful works?
23 And then will I profess to them, I never knew you: depart from me, you that work iniquity.
24 Therefore whoever hears these sayings of mine, and does them, I will liken him unto a wise man, which built his house upon a rock:
25 And the rain descended, and the floods came, and the winds blew, and beat upon that house; and it fell not: for it was founded upon a rock.
26 And every one that hears these sayings of mine, and does them not, shall be likened unto a foolish man, which built his house upon the sand:
27 And the rain descended, and the floods came, and the winds blew, and beat upon that house; and it fell: and great was the fall of it.
28 And it came to pass, when Yahshua had ended these sayings, the people were astonished at his doctrine:
29 For he taught them as *one* having authority, and not as the scribes.

Matthew 8

8:1 ¶ When he had come down from the mountain, great multitudes followed him.
2 And, behold, there came a leper and worshipped him, saying, Lord, if you will, you can make me clean.
3 And Yahshua put forth *his* hand, and touched him, saying, I will; be you clean. And immediately his leprosy was cleansed.

Matthew 8

4 And Yahshua said to him, See you tell no man; but go your way, show yourself to the priest, and offer the gift that Moses commanded, for a testimony to them.

5 ¶ And when Yahshua was entered into Capernaum, there came to him a centurion, beseeching him,

6 And saying, Lord, my servant lies at home sick of the palsy, grievously tormented.

7 And Yahshua said to him, I will come and heal him.

8 The centurion answered and said, Lord, I am not worthy that you should come under my roof: but speak the word only, and my servant shall be healed.

9 For I am a man under authority, having soldiers under me: and I say to this *man*, Go, and he goes; and to another, Come, and he comes; and to my servant, Do this, and he does *it*.

10 When Yahshua heard *it*, he marveled, and said to them that followed, Truly I say to you, I have not found so great faith, no, not in Israel.

11 And I say to you, That many shall come from the east and west, and shall sit down with Abraham, and Isaac, and Jacob, in the kingdom of heaven.

12 But the children of the kingdom shall be cast out into outer darkness: there shall be weeping and gnashing of teeth.

13 And Yahshua said to the centurion, Go your way; and as you have believed, *so* be it done unto you. And his servant was healed in the very same hour.

14 ¶ And when Yahshua had come into Peter's house, he saw his wife's mother lying, and sick of a fever.

15 And he touched her hand, and the fever left her: and she arose, and ministered to them.

16 When the evening had come, they brought to him many that were possessed with devils: and he cast out the spirits with *his* word, and healed all that were sick:

17 That it might be fulfilled which was spoken by Isaiah the prophet, saying, Himself took our infirmities, and bore *our* sicknesses.

18 ¶ Now when Yahshua saw great multitudes about him, he gave commandment to depart to the other side.

19 And a certain scribe came, and said to him, Master, I will follow you wherever you go.

20 And Yahshua said to him, The foxes have holes, and the birds of the air *have* nests; but the Son of man has nowhere to lay *his* head.

21 And another of his disciples said to him, Lord, allow me first to go and bury my father.

22 But Yahshua said to him, Follow me; and let the dead bury their dead.

23 ¶ And when he had entered into a ship, his disciples followed him.

24 And, behold, there arose a great tempest in the sea, insomuch that the ship was covered with the waves: but he was asleep.

25 And his disciples came to *him*, and awoke him, saying, Lord, save us: we perish.

26 And he said to them, Why are you fearful, O you of little faith? Then he arose, and rebuked the winds and the sea; and there was a great calm.

27 But the men marveled, saying, What manner of man is this, that even the winds and the sea obey him!

28 ¶ And when he had come to the other side into the country of the Gergesenes, there met him two possessed with devils, coming out of the tombs, exceedingly fierce, so that no man might pass by that way.

29 And, behold, they cried out, saying, What have we to do with you, Yahshua, you Son of God? have you come here to torment us before the time?

30 And there was a good way off from them a herd of many swine feeding.

31 So the devils sought him, saying, If you cast us out, allow us to go away into the herd of swine.

32 And he said to them, Go. And when they had come out, they went into the herd of swine: and, behold, the whole herd of swine ran violently down a steep place into the sea, and perished in the waters.

33 And they that kept them fled, and went their ways into the city, and told everything, and what had happened to the possessed of the devils.

34 And, behold, the whole city came out to meet Yahshua: and when they saw him, they begged *him* that he would depart out of their coasts.

Matthew 9

9:1 ¶ And he entered into a ship, and passed over, and came into his own city.

2 And, behold, they brought to him a man sick of the palsy, lying on a bed: and Yahshua seeing their faith said to the sick of the palsy; Son, be of good cheer; your sins are forgiven you.

3 And, behold, certain of the scribes said within themselves, This *man* blasphemes.

4 And Yahshua knowing their thoughts said, Why think you evil in your hearts?

5 For which is easier, to say, *Your* sins are forgiven you; or to say, Arise, and walk?

6 But that you may know that the Son of man has power on earth to forgive sins, (then said he to the sick of the palsy,) Arise, take up your bed, and go to your house.

7 And he arose, and departed to his house.

8 But when the multitudes saw *it*, they marveled, and glorified God, which had given such power to men.

9 ¶ And as Yahshua passed forth from there, he saw a man, named Matthew, sitting at the receipt of custom: and he said to him, Follow me. And he arose, and followed him.

10 And it came to pass, as Yahshua sat to dine in the house, behold, many publicans and sinners came and sat down with him and his disciples.

11 And when the Pharisees saw *it*, they said to his disciples, Why eats your Master with publicans and sinners?

12 But when Yahshua heard *that*, he said to them, They that are whole need not a physician, but they that are sick.

13 But go you and learn what *that* means, I will have mercy, and not sacrifice: for I have not come to call the righteous, but sinners to repentance.

14 ¶ Then came to him the disciples of John, saying, Why do we and the Pharisees fast often, but your disciples fast not?

15 And Yahshua said to them, Can the children of the bride chamber mourn, as long as the bridegroom is with them? but the days will come, when the bridegroom shall be taken from them, and then shall they fast.

16 No man puts a piece of new cloth unto an old garment, for that which is put in to fill it up takes from the garment, and the tear is made worse.

17 Neither do men put new wine into old bottles: *or* else the bottles break, and the wine runs out, and the bottles perish: but they put new wine into new bottles, and both are preserved.

18 ¶ While he spoke these things to them, behold, there came a certain ruler, and worshipped him, saying, My daughter is even now dead: but come and lay your hand upon her, and she shall live.

19 And Yahshua arose, and followed him, and *so did* his disciples.

20 And, behold, a woman, which was diseased with an issue of blood *for* twelve years, came behind *him*, and touched the hem of his garment:

21 For she said within herself, If I may but touch his garment, I shall be whole.

22 But Yahshua turned himself about, and when he saw her, he said, Daughter, be of good comfort; your faith has made you whole. And the woman was made whole from that hour.

23 And when Yahshua came into the ruler's house, and saw the minstrels and the people making a noise,

24 He said to them, Give place: for the maid is not dead, but sleeps. And they laughed him to scorn.

25 But when the people were put forth, he went in, and took her by the hand, and the maid arose.

26 And the fame hereof went abroad into all that land.

27 ¶ And when Yahshua departed therefrom, two blind men followed him, crying, and saying, *You* Son of David, have mercy on us.

28 And when he had come into the house, the blind men came to him: and Yahshua said to them, Believe you that I am able to do this? They said to him, Yes, Lord.

29 Then touched he their eyes, saying, According to your faith be it unto you.

30 And their eyes were opened; and Yahshua sternly charged them, saying, See *that* no man knows *it*.

31 But they, when they were departed, spread abroad his fame in all that country.

32 As they went out, behold, they brought to him a dumb man possessed with a devil.

33 And when the devil was cast out, the dumb spoke: and the multitudes marveled, saying, It was never so seen in Israel.

34 But the Pharisees said, He casts out devils through the prince of the devils.

35 ¶ And Yahshua went about all the cities and villages, teaching in their synagogues, and preaching the gospel of the kingdom, and healing every sickness and every disease among the people.

36 But when he saw the multitudes, he was moved with compassion on them, because they fainted, and were scattered abroad, as sheep having no shepherd.

37 Then said he to his disciples, The harvest truly *is* plenteous, but the laborers *are* few;

38 Pray you therefore the Lord of the harvest, that he will send forth laborers into his harvest.

Matthew 10

10:1 ¶ And when he had called unto *him* his twelve disciples, he gave them power *against* unclean spirits, to cast them out, and to heal all manner of sickness and all manner of disease.

2 Now the names of the twelve apostles are these; The first, Simon, who is called Peter, and Andrew his brother; James *the son* of Zebedee, and John his brother;

3 Philip, and Bartholomew; Thomas, and Matthew the publican; James *the son* of Alphaeus, and Lebbaeus, whose surname was Thaddaeus;

4 Simon the Canaanite, and Judas Iscariot, who also betrayed him.

5 ¶ These twelve Yahshua sent forth, and commanded them, saying, Go not into the way of the Gentiles, and into *any* city of the Samaritans enter you not:

6 But go rather to the lost sheep of the house of Israel.

7 And as you go, preach, saying, The kingdom of heaven is at hand.

8 Heal the sick, cleanse the lepers, raise the dead, cast out devils: freely you have received, freely give.

9 Provide neither gold, nor silver, nor brass in your purses,

10 Nor sack for *your* journey, neither two coats, neither shoes, nor yet staffs: for the workman is worthy of his food.

11 And into whatever city or town you shall enter, inquire who in it is worthy; and there dwell till you go forth.

12 And when you come into a house, salute it.

13 And if the house is worthy, let your peace come upon it: but if it is not worthy, let your peace return to you.

14 And whoever shall not receive you, nor hear your words, when you depart out of that house or city, shake off the dust from your feet.

15 Truly I say to you, It shall be more tolerable for the land of Sodom and Gomorrah in the day of judgment, than for that city.

16 ¶ Behold, I send you forth as sheep in the midst of wolves: be you therefore wise as serpents, and harmless as doves.

17 But beware of men: for they will deliver you up to the councils, and they will scourge you in their synagogues;

18 And you shall be brought before governors and kings for my sake, for a testimony against them and the Gentiles.

19 But when they deliver you up, take no thought *of* how or what you shall speak: for it shall be given you in that same hour what you shall speak.

20 For it is not you that speak, but the Spirit of your Father which speaks in you.
21 And the brother shall deliver up the brother to death, and the father the child: and the children shall rise up against *their* parents, and cause them to be put to death.
22 And you shall be hated by all *men* for my name's sake: but he that endures to the end shall be saved.
23 But when they persecute you in this city, flee you into another: for truly I say to you, You shall not have gone over the cities of Israel, till the Son of man has come.
24 The disciple is not above *his* master, nor the servant above his lord.
25 It is enough for the disciple that he be as his master, and the servant as his lord. If they have called the master of the house Beelzebub, how much more *shall they call* them of his household?
26 Fear them not therefore: for there is nothing covered, that shall not be revealed; and hidden, that shall not be known.
27 What I tell you in darkness, *that* speak you in light: and what you hear in the ear, *that* preach you upon the housetops.
28 And fear not them which kill the body, but are not able to kill the soul: but rather fear him which is able to destroy both soul and body in hell.
29 Are not two sparrows sold for a farthing? and one of them shall not fall on the ground without your Father.
30 But the very hairs of your head are all numbered.
31 Fear you not therefore, you are of more value than many sparrows.
32 Whoever therefore shall confess me before men, him will I confess also before my Father which is in heaven.
33 But whoever shall deny me before men, him will I also deny before my Father which is in heaven.
34 Think not that I have come to send peace on earth: I came not to send peace, but a sword.
35 For I have come to set a man at variance against his father, and the daughter against her mother, and the daughter-in-law against her mother-in-law.
36 And a man's foes *shall be* they of his own household.
37 He that loves father or mother more than me is not worthy of me: and he that loves son or daughter more than me is not worthy of me.
38 And he that takes not his cross, and follows after me, is not worthy of me.
39 He that finds his life shall lose it: and he that loses his life for my sake shall find it.
40 He that receives you receives me, and he that receives me receives him that sent me.
41 He that receives a prophet in the name of a prophet shall receive a prophet's reward; and he that receives a righteous man in the name of a righteous man shall receive a righteous man's reward.
42 And whoever shall give to drink unto one of these little ones a cup of cold *water* only in the name of a disciple, truly I say to you, he shall by no means lose his reward.

Matthew 11

11:1 ¶ And it came to pass, when Yahshua had made an end of commanding his twelve disciples, he departed therefrom to teach and to preach in their cities.
2 Now when John had heard in the prison the works of the Messiah, he sent two of his disciples,
3 And said to him, Are you he that should come, or do we look for another?
4 Yahshua answered and said to them, Go and show John again those things which you do hear and see:
5 The blind receive their sight, and the lame walk, the lepers are cleansed, and the deaf hear, the dead are raised up, and the poor have the gospel preached to them.
6 And blessed is *he*, whoever shall not be offended in me.
7 ¶ And as they departed, Yahshua began to say to the multitudes concerning John, What went you out into the wilderness to see? A reed shaken with the wind?
8 But what went you out for to see? A man clothed in soft clothes? behold, they that wear soft *clothing* are in kings' houses.
9 But what went you out for to see? A prophet? yes, I say to you, and more than a prophet.
10 For this is *he*, of whom it is written, Behold, I send my messenger before your face, which shall prepare your way before you.
11 Truly I say unto you, Among them that are born of women there has not risen a greater than John the Baptist: notwithstanding he that is least in the kingdom of heaven is greater than he.
12 And from the days of John the Baptist until now the kingdom of heaven suffers violence, and the violent takes it by force.
13 For all the prophets and the law prophesied until John.
14 And if you will receive *it*, this is Elijah, which was for to come.
15 He that has ears to hear, let him hear.
16 ¶ But whereunto shall I liken this generation? It is like unto children sitting in the markets, and calling to their fellows,
17 And saying, We have piped unto you, and you have not danced; we have mourned unto you, and you have not lamented.
18 For John came neither eating nor drinking, and they say, He has a devil.
19 The Son of man came eating and drinking, and they say, Behold a man gluttonous, and a winebibber, a friend of publicans and sinners. But wisdom is justified of her children.
20 Then began he to upbraid the cities wherein most of his mighty works were done, because they repented not:
21 Woe unto you, Chorazin! woe unto you, Bethsaida! for if the mighty works, which were done in you, had been done in Tyre and Sidon, they would have repented long ago in sackcloth and ashes.
22 But I say to you, It shall be more tolerable for Tyre and Sidon at the day of judgment, than for you.

23 And you, Capernaum, which are exalted unto heaven, will be brought down to hell: for if the mighty works, which have been done in you, had been done in Sodom, it would have remained until this day.

24 But I say to you, That it shall be more tolerable for the land of Sodom in the day of judgment, than for you.

25 ¶ At that time Yahshua answered and said, I thank you, O Father, Lord of heaven and earth, because you have hidden these things from the wise and prudent, and have revealed them to babes.

26 Even so, Father: for so it seemed good in your sight.

27 All things are delivered unto me of my Father: and no man knows the Son, but the Father; neither knows any man the Father, save the Son, and *he* to whomever the Son will reveal *him*.

28 Come unto me, all *you* that labor and are heavy laden, and I will give you rest.

29 Take my yoke upon you, and learn of me; for I am meek and lowly in heart: and you shall find rest unto your souls.

30 For my yoke *is* easy, and my burden is light.

Matthew 12

12:1 ¶ At that time Yahshua went on the sabbath day through the corn; and his disciples were hungry, and began to pluck the ears of corn, and to eat.

2 But when the Pharisees saw *it*, they said to him, Behold, your disciples do that which is not lawful to do upon the sabbath day.

3 But he said to them, Have you not read what David did, when he was hungry, and they that were with him;

4 How he entered into the house of God, and did eat the showbread, which was not lawful for him to eat, neither for them which were with him, but only for the priests?

5 Or have you not read in the law, how that on the sabbath days the priests in the temple profane the sabbath, and are blameless?

6 But I say to you, That in this place is *one* greater than the temple.

7 But if you had known what *this* means, I will have mercy, and not sacrifice, you would not have condemned the guiltless.

8 For the Son of man is Lord even of the sabbath day.

9 And when he had departed therefrom, he went into their synagogue:

10 And, behold, there was a man which had *his* hand withered. And they asked him, saying, Is it lawful to heal on the sabbath days? that they might accuse him.

11 And he said to them, What man shall there be among you, that shall have one sheep, and if it fall into a pit on the sabbath day, will he not lay hold on it, and lift *it* out?

12 How much then is a man better than a sheep? Therefore it is lawful to do well on the sabbath days.

13 Then said he to the man, Stretch forth your hand. And he stretched *it* forth; and it was restored whole, like as the other.

14 ¶ Then the Pharisees went out, and held a council against him, how they might destroy him.

15 But when Yahshua knew *it*, he withdrew himself from there: and great multitudes followed him, and he healed them all;

16 And charged them that they should not make him known:

17 That it might be fulfilled which was spoken by Isaiah the prophet, saying,

18 Behold my servant, whom I have chosen; my beloved, in whom my soul is well pleased: I will put my spirit upon him, and he shall show judgment to the Gentiles.

19 He shall not strive, nor cry; neither shall any man hear his voice in the streets.

20 A bruised reed shall he not break, and smoking flax shall he not quench, till he sends forth judgment unto victory.

21 And in his name shall the Gentiles trust.

22 ¶ Then was brought to him one possessed with a devil, blind, and dumb: and he healed him, insomuch that the blind and dumb both spoke and saw.

23 And all the people were amazed, and said, Is not this the son of David?

24 But when the Pharisees heard *it*, they said, This *fellow* does not cast out devils, but by Beelzebub the prince of the devils.

25 And Yahshua knew their thoughts, and said to them, Every kingdom divided against itself is brought to desolation; and every city or house divided against itself shall not stand:

26 And if Satan casts out Satan, he is divided against himself; how shall then his kingdom stand?

27 And if I by Beelzebub casts out devils, by whom do your children cast *them* out? therefore they shall be your judges.

28 But if I cast out devils by the Spirit of God, then the kingdom of God has come unto you.

29 Or else how can one enter into a strong man's house, and spoil his goods, unless he first binds the strong man? and then he will spoil his house.

30 He that is not with me is against me; and he that gathers not with me scatters abroad.

31 Therefore I say to you, All manner of sin and blasphemy shall be forgiven unto men: but the blasphemy *against* the *Holy* Ghost shall not be forgiven unto men.

32 And whoever speaks a word against the Son of man, it shall be forgiven him: but whoever speaks against the Holy Ghost, it shall not be forgiven him, neither in this world, neither in the *world* to come.

33 Either make the tree good, and his fruit good; or else make the tree corrupt, and his fruit corrupt: for the tree is known by *his* fruit.

34 O generation of vipers, how can you, being evil, speak good things? for out of the abundance of the heart the mouth speaks.

35 A good man out of the good treasure of the heart brings forth good things: and an evil man out of the evil treasure brings forth evil things.

36 But I say to you, That every idle word that men shall speak, they shall give account thereof in the day of judgment.

Matthew 12

37 For by your words you shall be justified, and by your words you shall be condemned.

38 ¶ Then certain of the scribes and of the Pharisees answered, saying, Master, we would see a sign from you.

39 But he answered and said to them, An evil and adulterous generation seeks after a sign; and there shall no sign be given to it, but the sign of the prophet Jonah:

40 For as Jonah was three days and three nights in the whale's belly; so shall the Son of man be three days and three nights in the heart of the earth.

41 The men of Nineveh shall rise in judgment with this generation, and shall condemn it: because they repented at the preaching of Jonah; and, behold, a greater than Jonah *is* here.

42 The queen of the south shall rise up in the judgment with this generation, and shall condemn it: for she came from the utmost parts of the earth to hear the wisdom of Solomon; and, behold, a greater than Solomon *is* here.

43 When the unclean spirit has gone out of a man, he walks through dry places, seeking rest, and finds none.

44 Then he says, I will return into my house from where I came out; and when he has come, he finds *it* empty, swept, and garnished.

45 Then goes he, and takes with himself seven other spirits more wicked than himself, and they enter in and dwell there: and the last *state* of that man is worse than the first. Even so shall it be also to this wicked generation.

46 ¶ While he yet talked to the people, behold, *his* mother and his brothers stood outside, desiring to speak with him.

47 Then one said to him, Behold, your mother and your brothers stand outside, desiring to speak with you.

48 But he answered and said to him that told him, Who is my mother? and who are my brothers?

49 And he stretched forth his hand toward his disciples, and said, Behold my mother and my brothers!

50 For whoever shall do the will of my Father which is in heaven, the same is my brother, and sister, and mother.

Matthew 13

13:1 ¶ The same day went Yahshua out of the house, and sat by the sea side.

2 And great multitudes were gathered together unto him, so that he went into a ship, and sat; and the whole multitude stood on the shore.

3 And he spoke many things to them in parables, saying, Behold, a sower went forth to sow;

4 And when he sowed, some *seeds* fell by the way side, and the fowls came and devoured them up:

5 Some fell upon stony places, where they had not much earth: and immediately they sprung up, because they had no deepness of earth:

6 And when the sun was up, they were scorched; and because they had no root, they withered away.

7 And some fell among thorns; and the thorns sprung up, and choked them:

8 But others fell into good ground, and brought forth fruit, some a hundredfold, some sixtyfold, some thirtyfold.

9 Who has ears to hear, let him hear.

10 And the disciples came, and said to him, Why speak you to them in parables?

11 He answered and said to them, Because it is given to you to know the mysteries of the kingdom of heaven, but to them it is not given.

12 For whoever has, to him shall be given, and he shall have more abundance: but whoever has not, from him shall be taken away even that he has.

13 Therefore speak I to them in parables: because they seeing see not; and hearing they hear not, neither do they understand.

14 And in them is fulfilled the prophecy of Isaiah, which says, By hearing you shall hear, and shall not understand; and seeing you shall see, and shall not perceive:

15 For this people's heart has grown thick, and *their* ears are dull of hearing, and their eyes they have closed; lest at any time they should see with *their* eyes, and hear with *their* ears, and should understand with *their* heart, and should be converted, and I should heal them.

16 But blessed *are* your eyes, for they see: and your ears, for they hear.

17 For truly I say to you, That many prophets and righteous *men* have desired to see *those things* which you see, and have not seen *them*; and to hear *those things* which you hear, and have not heard *them*.

18 Hear you therefore the parable of the sower.

19 When any one hears the word of the kingdom, and understands *it* not, then comes the wicked *one*, and catches away that which was sown in his heart. This is he which received seed by the way side.

20 But he that received the seed into stony places, the same is he that hears the word, and immediately with joy receives it;

21 Yet has he not root in himself, but endures for a while: for when tribulation or persecution arises because of the word, by and by he is offended.

22 He also that received seed among the thorns is he that hears the word; and the cares of this world, and the deceitfulness of riches, chokes the word, and he becomes unfruitful.

23 But he that received seed into the good ground is he that hears the word, and understands *it*; which also bears fruit, and brings forth, some a hundredfold, some sixty, some thirty.

24 ¶ Another parable put he forth to them, saying, The kingdom of heaven is likened to a man which sowed good seed in his field:

25 But while men slept, his enemy came and sowed tares among the wheat, and went his way.

26 But when the blade was sprung up, and brought forth fruit, then appeared the tares also.

27 So the servants of the householder came and said to him, Sir, did not you sow good seed in your field? from where then has it tares?

28 He said to them, An enemy has done this. The servants said to him, Will you then that we go and gather them up?

29 But he said, No; lest while you gather up the tares, you root up also the wheat with them.

30 Let both grow together until the harvest: and in the time of harvest I will say to the reapers, Gather you together first the tares, and bind them in bundles to burn them: but gather the wheat into my barn.

31 Another parable put he forth to them, saying, The kingdom of heaven is like to a grain of mustard seed, which a man took, and sowed in his field:

32 Which indeed is the least of all seeds: but when it is grown, it is the greatest among herbs, and becomes a tree, so that the birds of the air come and lodge in the branches thereof.

33 Another parable spoke he to them; The kingdom of heaven is like unto leaven, which a woman took, and hid in three measures of meal, till the whole was leavened.

34 All these things spoke Yahshua to the multitude in parables; and without a parable spoke he not to them:

35 That it might be fulfilled which was spoken by the prophet, saying, I will open my mouth in parables; I will utter things which have been kept secret from the foundation of the world.

36 Then Yahshua sent the multitude away, and went into the house: and his disciples came to him, saying, Declare to us the parable of the tares of the field.

37 He answered and said to them, He that sows the good seed is the Son of man;

38 The field is the world; the good seed are the children of the kingdom; but the tares are the children of the wicked *one*;

39 The enemy that sowed them is the devil; the harvest is the end of the world; and the reapers are the angels.

40 As therefore the tares are gathered and burned in the fire; so shall it be in the end of this world.

41 The Son of man shall send forth his angels, and they shall gather out of his kingdom all things that offend, and them which do iniquity;

42 And shall cast them into a furnace of fire: there shall be wailing and gnashing of teeth.

43 Then shall the righteous shine forth as the sun in the kingdom of their Father. Who has ears to hear, let him hear.

44 ¶ Again, the kingdom of heaven is like unto treasure hidden in a field; the which when a man has found, he hides, and for joy thereof goes and sells all that he has, and buys that field.

45 Again, the kingdom of heaven is like unto a merchant man, seeking beautiful pearls:

46 Who, when he had found one pearl of great price, went and sold all that he had, and bought it.

47 Again, the kingdom of heaven is like unto a net, that was cast into the sea, and gathered of every kind:

48 Which, when it was full, they drew to shore, and sat down, and gathered the good into vessels, but cast the bad away.

49 So shall it be at the end of the world: the angels shall come forth, and sever the wicked from among the just,

50 And shall cast them into the furnace of fire: there shall be wailing and gnashing of teeth.

51 Yahshua said to them, Have you understood all these things? They said to him, Yes, Lord.

52 Then said he to them, Therefore every scribe *which is* instructed unto the kingdom of heaven is like unto a man *that is* a householder, which brings forth out of his treasure *things* new and old.

53 ¶ And it came to pass, *that* when Yahshua had finished these parables, he departed therefrom.

54 And when he had come into his own country, he taught them in their synagogue, insomuch that they were astonished, and said, *From* where has this *man* this wisdom, and *these* mighty works?

55 Is not this the carpenter's son? is not his mother called Mary? and his brothers, James, and Joses, and Simon, and Judas?

56 And his sisters, are they not all with us? *From* where then has this *man* all these things?

57 And they were offended in him. But Yahshua said to them, A prophet is not without honor, except in his own country, and in his own house.

58 And he did not many mighty works there because of their unbelief.

Matthew 14

14:1 ¶ At that time Herod the tetrarch heard of the fame of Yahshua,

2 And said unto his servants, This is John the Baptist; he is risen from the dead; and therefore mighty works do show forth themselves in him.

3 For Herod had laid hold upon John, and bound him, and put *him* in prison for Herodias' sake, his brother Philip's wife.

4 For John said to him, It is not lawful for you to have her.

5 And when he would have put him to death, he feared the multitude, because they counted him as a prophet.

6 But when Herod's birthday was kept, the daughter of Herodias danced before them, and pleased Herod.

7 Whereupon he promised with an oath to give her whatever she would ask.

8 And she, being before instructed of her mother, said, Give me here John *the* Baptist's head in a platter.

9 And the king was sorry: nevertheless for the oath's sake, and them which sat with him at meat, he commanded *it* to be given *her*.

10 And he sent, and beheaded John in the prison.

11 And his head was brought in a platter, and given to the damsel: and she brought *it* to her mother.

12 And his disciples came, and took up the body, and buried it, and went and told Yahshua.

13 ¶ When Yahshua heard *of it*, he departed therefrom by ship into a desert place apart: and when the people had heard *thereof*, they followed him on foot out of the cities.

14 And Yahshua went forth, and saw a great multitude, and was moved with compassion toward them, and he healed their sick.

Matthew 14

15 And when it was evening, his disciples came to him, saying, This is a desert place, and the time is now past; send the multitude away, that they may go into the villages, and buy themselves victuals.
16 But Yahshua said to them, They need not depart; give you them to eat.
17 And they said to him, We have here but five loaves, and two fishes.
18 He said, Bring them here to me.
19 And he commanded the multitude to sit down on the grass, and took the five loaves, and the two fishes, and looking up to heaven, he blessed, and broke, and gave the loaves to *his* disciples, and the disciples to the multitude.
20 And they did all eat, and were filled: and they took up of the fragments that remained twelve baskets full.
21 And they that had eaten were about five thousand men, besides women and children.
22 ¶ And immediately Yahshua constrained his disciples to get into a ship, and to go before him to the other side, while he sent the multitudes away.
23 And when he had sent the multitudes away, he went up into a mountain apart to pray: and when the evening had come, he was there alone.
24 But the ship was now in the midst of the sea, tossed with waves: for the wind was contrary.
25 And in the fourth watch of the night Yahshua went to them, walking on the sea.
26 And when the disciples saw him walking on the sea, they were troubled, saying, It is a spirit; and they cried out for fear.
27 But immediately Yahshua spoke to them, saying, Be of good cheer; it is I; be not afraid.
28 And Peter answered him and said, Lord, if it is you, bid me come to you on the water.
29 And he said, Come. And when Peter had come down out of the ship, he walked on the water, to go to Yahshua.
30 But when he saw the wind boisterous, he was afraid; and beginning to sink, he cried, saying, Lord, save me.
31 And immediately Yahshua stretched forth *his* hand, and caught him, and said to him, O you of little faith, why did you doubt?
32 And when they had come into the ship, the wind ceased.
33 Then they that were in the ship came and worshipped him, saying, Of a truth you are the Son of God.
34 ¶ And when they had gone over, they came into the land of Gennesaret.
35 And when the men of that place had knowledge of him, they sent out into all that country round about, and brought to him all that were diseased;
36 And begged him that they might only touch the hem of his garment: and as many as touched were made perfectly whole.

Matthew 15

15:1 ¶ Then came to Yahshua scribes and Pharisees, which were of Jerusalem, saying,
2 Why do your disciples transgress the tradition of the elders? for they wash not their hands when they eat bread.
3 But he answered and said to them, Why do you also transgress the commandment of God by your tradition?
4 For God commanded, saying, Honor your father and mother: and, He that curses father or mother, let him die the death.
5 But you say, Whoever shall say to *his* father or *his* mother, *It is* a gift, by whatever you might be profited by me;
6 And honor not his father or his mother, *he shall be free*. Thus have you made the commandment of God of no effect by your tradition.
7 *You* hypocrites, well did Isaiah prophesy of you, saying,
8 This people draw near to me with their mouth, and honors me with *their* lips; but their heart is far from me.
9 But in vain they do worship me, teaching *for* doctrines the commandments of men.
10 ¶ And he called the multitude, and said to them, Hear, and understand:
11 Not that which goes into the mouth defiles a man; but that which comes out of the mouth, this defiles a man.
12 Then came his disciples, and said to him, Know you that the Pharisees were offended, after they heard this saying?
13 But he answered and said, Every plant, which my heavenly Father has not planted, shall be rooted up.
14 Let them alone: they are blind leaders of the blind. And if the blind lead the blind, both shall fall into the ditch.
15 Then answered Peter and said to him, Declare to us this parable.
16 And Yahshua said, Are you also yet without understanding?
17 Do not you yet understand, that whatever enters in at the mouth goes into the belly, and is cast out into the toilet?
18 But those things which proceed out of the mouth come forth from the heart; and they defile the man.
19 For out of the heart proceed evil thoughts, murders, adulteries, fornications, thefts, false witness, blasphemies:
20 These are *the things* which defile a man: but to eat with unwashed hands defiles not a man.
21 ¶ Then Yahshua went therefrom, and departed into the coasts of Tyre and Sidon.
22 And, behold, a woman of Canaan came out of the same coasts, and cried unto him, saying, Have mercy on me, O Lord, *you* Son of David; my daughter is grievously possessed with a devil.
23 But he answered her not a word. And his disciples came and begged him, saying, Send her away; for she cries after us.

24 But he answered and said, I am not sent but to the lost sheep of the house of Israel.
25 Then came she and worshipped him, saying, Lord, help me.
26 But he answered and said, It is not good to take the children's bread, and to cast *it* to dogs.
27 And she said, Truth, Lord: yet the dogs eat of the crumbs which fall from their masters' table.
28 Then Yahshua answered and said to her, O woman, great *is* your faith: be it unto you even as you will. And her daughter was made whole from that very hour.
29 ¶ And Yahshua departed from there, and came near to the sea of Galilee; and went up into a mountain, and sat down there.
30 And great multitudes came to him, having with them *those that were* lame, blind, dumb, maimed, and many others, and cast them down at Yahshua's feet; and he healed them:
31 Insomuch that the multitude wondered, when they saw the dumb to speak, the maimed to be whole, the lame to walk, and the blind to see: and they glorified the God of Israel.
32 Then Yahshua called his disciples *unto him*, and said, I have compassion on the multitude, because they continue with me now three days, and have nothing to eat: and I will not send them away fasting, lest they faint on the way.
33 And his disciples said unto him, *From* where should we get so much bread in the wilderness, as to fill so great a multitude?
34 And Yahshua said to them, How many loaves have you? And they said, Seven, and a few little fishes.
35 And he commanded the multitude to sit down on the ground.
36 And he took the seven loaves and the fishes, and gave thanks, and broke *them*, and gave to his disciples, and the disciples to the multitude.
37 And they did all eat, and were filled: and they took up of the broken *food* that was left seven baskets full.
38 And they that did eat were four thousand men, besides women and children.
39 And he sent away the multitude, and took ship, and came into the coasts of Magdala.

Matthew 16

16:1 ¶ The Pharisees also with the Sadducees came, and tempting desired him that he would show them a sign from heaven.
2 He answered and said to them, When it is evening, you say, *It will be* fair weather: for the sky is red.
3 And in the morning, *It will be* foul weather today: for the sky is red and sorrowful. O *you* hypocrites, you can discern the face of the sky; but can you not *discern* the signs of the times?
4 A wicked and adulterous generation seeks after a sign; and there shall no sign be given to it, but the sign of the prophet Jonah. And he left them, and departed.

5 ¶ And when his disciples had come to the other side, they had forgotten to take bread.
6 Then Yahshua said to them, Take heed and beware of the leaven of the Pharisees and of the Sadducees.
7 And they reasoned among themselves, saying, *It is* because we have taken no bread.
8 *Which* when Yahshua perceived, he said to them, O you of little faith, why reason you among yourselves, because you have brought no bread?
9 Do you not yet understand, neither remember the five loaves of the five thousand, and how many baskets you took up?
10 Neither the seven loaves of the four thousand, and how many baskets you took up?
11 How is it that you do not understand that I spoke *it* not to you concerning bread, that you should beware of the leaven of the Pharisees and of the Sadducees?
12 Then understood they how that he told *them* not beware of the leaven of bread, but of the doctrine of the Pharisees and of the Sadducees.
13 ¶ When Yahshua came into the coasts of Caesarea Philippi, he asked his disciples, saying, Whom do men say that I the Son of man am?
14 And they said, Some *say that you are* John the Baptist: some, Elijah; and others, Jeremiah, or one of the prophets.
15 He said to them, But whom say you that I am?
16 And Simon Peter answered and said, You are the Messiah, the Son of the living God.
17 And Yahshua answered and said to him, Blessed are you, Simon Barjona: for flesh and blood has not revealed *it* to you, but my Father which is in heaven.
18 And I say also to you, That you are Peter, and upon this rock I will build my congregation; and the gates of hell shall not prevail against it.
19 And I will give to you the keys of the kingdom of heaven: and whatever you shall bind on earth shall be bound in heaven: and whatever you shall loose on earth shall be loosed in heaven.
20 Then charged he his disciples that they should tell no man that he was Yahshua the Messiah.
21 ¶ From that time forward began Yahshua to show to his disciples, how that he must go to Jerusalem, and suffer many things of the elders and chief priests and scribes, and be killed, and be raised again the third day.
22 Then Peter took him, and began to rebuke him, saying, Be it far from you, Lord: this shall not be unto you.
23 But he turned, and said to Peter, Get you behind me, Satan: you are an offense to me: for you savor not the things that are of God, but those that are of men.
24 ¶ Then said Yahshua to his disciples, If any *man* will come after me, let him deny himself, and take up his cross, and follow me.
25 For whoever will save his life shall lose it: and whoever will lose his life for my sake shall find it.
26 For what has a man profited, if he shall gain the whole world, and lose his own soul? or what shall a man give in exchange for his soul?

Matthew 16

27 For the Son of man shall come in the glory of his Father with his angels; and then he shall reward every man according to his works.
28 Truly I say unto you, There are some standing here, which shall not taste of death, till they see the Son of man coming in his kingdom.

Matthew 17

17:1 ¶ And after six days Yahshua took Peter, James, and John his brother, and brought them up into a high mountain apart,
2 And was transfigured before them: and his face did shine as the sun, and his clothes were white as the light.
3 And, behold, there appeared to them Moses and Elijah talking with him.
4 Then answered Peter, and said to Yahshua, Lord, it is good for us to be here: if you will, let us make here three tabernacles; one for you, and one for Moses, and one for Elijah.
5 While he yet spoke, behold, a bright cloud overshadowed them: and behold a voice out of the cloud, which said, This is my beloved Son, in whom I am well pleased; hear you him.
6 And when the disciples heard *it*, they fell on their face, and were greatly afraid.
7 And Yahshua came and touched them, and said, Arise, and be not afraid.
8 And when they had lifted up their eyes, they saw no man, save Yahshua only.
9 And as they came down from the mountain, Yahshua charged them, saying, Tell the vision to no man, until the Son of man is risen again from the dead.
10 And his disciples asked him, saying, Why then say the scribes that Elijah must first come?
11 And Yahshua answered and said to them, Elijah truly shall first come, and restore all things.
12 But I say to you, That Elijah has come already, and they knew him not, but have done unto him whatever they desired. Likewise shall also the Son of man suffer of them.
13 Then the disciples understood that he spoke to them of John the Baptist.
14 ¶ And when they had come to the multitude, there came to him a *certain* man, kneeling down to him, and saying,
15 Lord, have mercy on my son: for he is lunatic, and miserably suffering: for oftentimes he falls into the fire, and often into the water.
16 And I brought him to your disciples, and they could not cure him.
17 Then Yahshua answered and said, O faithless and perverse generation, how long shall I be with you? how long shall I forbear you? bring him here to me.
18 And Yahshua rebuked the devil; and he departed out of him: and the child was cured from that very hour.
19 Then came the disciples to Yahshua apart, and said, Why could not we cast him out?
20 And Yahshua said to them, Because of your unbelief: for truly I say to you, If you have faith as a grain of mustard seed, you shall say to this mountain, Remove away to yonder place; and it shall remove; and nothing shall be impossible unto you.
21 However this kind goes not out but by prayer and fasting.
22 ¶ And while they stayed in Galilee, Yahshua said to them, The Son of man shall be betrayed into the hands of men:
23 And they shall kill him, and the third day he shall be raised again. And they were exceedingly sorry.
24 ¶ And when they had come to Capernaum, they that received tribute *money* came to Peter, and said, Does not your master pay tribute?
25 He said, Yes. And when he had come into the house, Yahshua anticipated him, saying, What think you, Simon? of whom do the kings of the earth take custom or tribute? of their own children, or of strangers?
26 Peter said to him, Of strangers. Yahshua said to him, Then are the children free.
27 Notwithstanding, lest we should offend them, go you to the sea, and cast a hook, and take up the fish that first comes up; and when you have opened his mouth, you shall find a piece of money: that take, and give to them for me and you.

Matthew 18

18:1 ¶ At the same time came the disciples to Yahshua, saying, Who is the greatest in the kingdom of heaven?
2 And Yahshua called a little child unto him, and set him in the midst of them,
3 And said, Truly I say to you, Unless you are converted, and become as little children, you shall not enter into the kingdom of heaven.
4 Whoever therefore shall humble himself as this little child, the same is greatest in the kingdom of heaven.
5 And whoever shall receive one such little child in my name receives me.
6 But whoever shall offend one of these little ones which believes in me, it would be better for him that a millstone were hung about his neck, and *that* he were drowned in the depth of the sea.
7 ¶ Woe unto the world because of offenses! for it must need be that offenses come; but woe to that man by whom the offense comes!
8 Therefore if your hand or your foot offends you, cut them off, and cast *them* from you: it is better for you to enter into life lame or maimed, rather than having two hands or two feet to be cast into everlasting fire.
9 And if your eye offends you, pluck it out, and cast *it* from you: it is better for you to enter into life with one eye, rather than having two eyes to be cast into hell fire.
10 Take heed that you despise not one of these little ones; for I say to you, That in heaven their angels do always behold the face of my Father which is in heaven.

11 For the Son of man has come to save that which was lost.
12 How think you? if a man has a hundred sheep, and one of them has gone astray, does he not leave the ninety and nine, and go into the mountains, and seek that which has gone astray?
13 And if so be that he finds it, truly I say to you, he rejoices more over that *sheep*, than of the ninety and nine which went not astray.
14 Even so it is not the will of your Father which is in heaven, that one of these little ones should perish.
15 ¶ Moreover if your brother shall trespass against you, go and tell him his fault between you and him alone: if he shall hear you, you have gained your brother.
16 But if he will not hear *you, then* take with you one or two more, that in the mouth of two or three witnesses every word may be established.
17 And if he shall neglect to hear them, tell *it* to the congregation: but if he neglects to hear the congregation, let him be to you as a heathen man and a publican.
18 Truly I say unto you, Whatever you shall bind on earth shall be bound in heaven: and whatever you shall loose on earth shall be loosed in heaven.
19 Again I say unto you, That if two of you shall agree on earth as touching anything that they shall ask, it shall be done for them by my Father which is in heaven.
20 For where two or three are gathered together in my name, there am I in the midst of them.
21 ¶ Then came Peter to him, and said, Lord, how often shall my brother sin against me, and I forgive him? till seven times?
22 Yahshua said to him, I say not to you, Until seven times: but, Until seventy times seven.
23 Therefore is the kingdom of heaven likened to a certain king, which would take account of his servants.
24 And when he had begun to reckon, one was brought to him, which owed him ten thousand talents.
25 But forasmuch as he had nothing to pay, his lord commanded him to be sold, and his wife, and children, and all that he had, and payment to be made.
26 The servant therefore fell down, and worshipped him, saying, Lord, have patience with me, and I will pay you all.
27 Then the lord of that servant was moved with compassion, and dismissed him, and forgave him the debt.
28 But the same servant went out, and found one of his fellow servants, which owed him a hundred pence: and he laid hands on him, and took *him* by the throat, saying, Pay me what you owe.
29 And his fellow servant fell down at his feet, and begged him, saying, Have patience with me, and I will pay you all.
30 And he would not: but went and cast him into prison, till he should pay the debt.
31 So when his fellow servants saw what was done, they were very sorry, and came and told unto their lord all that was done.
32 Then his lord, after that he had called him, said to him, O you wicked servant, I forgave you all that debt, because you begged me:
33 Should not you also have had compassion on your fellow servant, even as I had pity on you?
34 And his lord was angry, and delivered him to the tormentors, till he should pay all that was due to him.
35 So likewise shall my heavenly Father do also unto you, if you from your hearts forgive not every one his brother their trespasses.

Matthew 19

19:1 ¶ And it came to pass, *that* when Yahshua had finished these sayings, he departed from Galilee, and came into the coasts of Judaea beyond *the* Jordan;
2 And great multitudes followed him; and he healed them there.
3 ¶ The Pharisees also came to him, tempting him, and saying to him, Is it lawful for a man to put away his wife for every cause?
4 And he answered and said to them, Have you not read, that he which made *them* at the beginning made them male and female,
5 And said, For this cause shall a man leave father and mother, and shall be joined to his wife: and they two shall be one flesh?
6 Therefore they are no more two, but one flesh. What therefore God has joined together, let not man put apart.
7 They said to him, Why did Moses then command to give a writing of divorce, and to put her away?
8 He said to them, Moses because of the hardness of your hearts permitted you to put away your wives: but from the beginning it was not so.
9 And I say unto you, Whoever shall put away his wife, unless *it is* for fornication, and shall marry another, commits adultery: and whoever marries her which is put away does commit adultery.
10 His disciples said unto him, If the case of the man is so with *his* wife, it is not good to marry.
11 But he said unto them, All *men* cannot receive this saying, except *they* to whom it is given.
12 For there are some eunuchs, which were so born from *their* mother's womb: and there are some eunuchs, which were made eunuchs of men: and there are eunuchs, which have made themselves eunuchs for the kingdom of heaven's sake. He that is able to receive *it*, let him receive *it*.
13 ¶ Then were there brought to him little children, that he should put *his* hands on them, and pray: and the disciples rebuked them.
14 But Yahshua said, Allow little children, and forbid them not, to come unto me: for of such is the kingdom of heaven.
15 And he laid *his* hands on them, and departed therefrom.
16 ¶ And, behold, one came and said to him, Good Master, what good thing shall I do, that I may have eternal life?

Matthew 19

17 And he said to him, Why call you me good? *there is* none good but one, *that is*, God: but if you will enter into life, keep the commandments.

18 He said to him, Which? Yahshua said, You shall do no murder, You shall not commit adultery, You shall not steal, You shall not bear false witness,

19 Honor your father and *your* mother: and, You shall love your neighbor as yourself.

20 The young man said to him, All these things have I kept from my youth up: what lack I yet?

21 Yahshua said to him, If you will be perfect, go *and* sell that you have, and give to the poor, and you shall have treasure in heaven: and come *and* follow me.

22 But when the young man heard that saying, he went away sorrowful: for he had great possessions.

23 ¶ Then said Yahshua to his disciples, Truly I say to you, That a rich man shall hardly enter into the kingdom of heaven.

24 And again I say to you, It is easier for a camel to go through the eye of a needle, than for a rich man to enter into the kingdom of God.

25 When his disciples heard *it*, they were exceedingly amazed, saying, Who then can be saved?

26 But Yahshua saw *them*, and said to them, With men this is impossible; but with God all things are possible.

27 Then answered Peter and said to him, Behold, we have forsaken all, and followed you; what shall we have therefore?

28 And Yahshua said to them, Truly I say to you, That you which have followed me, in the regeneration when the Son of man shall sit in the throne of his glory, you also shall sit upon twelve thrones, judging the twelve tribes of Israel.

29 And every one that has forsaken houses, or brothers, or sisters, or father, or mother, or wife, or children, or lands, for my name's sake, shall receive a hundred times, and shall inherit everlasting life.

30 But many *that are* first shall be last; and the last *shall be* first.

Matthew 20

20:1 ¶ For the kingdom of heaven is like unto a man *that is* a householder, which went out early in the morning to hire laborers into his vineyard.

2 And when he had agreed with the laborers for a penny a day, he sent them into his vineyard.

3 And he went out about the third hour, and saw others standing idle in the marketplace,

4 And said to them; Go you also into the vineyard, and whatever is right I will give you. And they went their way.

5 Again he went out about the sixth and ninth hour, and did likewise.

6 And about the eleventh hour he went out, and found others standing idle, and said to them, Why stand you here all the day idle?

7 They said to him, Because no man has hired us. He said to them, Go you also into the vineyard; and whatever is right, *that* shall you receive.

8 So when evening had come, the lord of the vineyard said to his steward, Call the laborers, and give them *their* hire, beginning from the last to the first.

9 And when they came that *were hired* about the eleventh hour, they received every man a penny.

10 But when the first came, they supposed that they should have received more; and they likewise received every man a penny.

11 And when they had received *it*, they murmured against the master of the house,

12 Saying, These last have worked *but* one hour, and you have made them equal to us, which have borne the burden and heat of the day.

13 But he answered one of them, and said, Friend, I do you no wrong: did not you agree with me for a penny?

14 Take *that* yours *is*, and go your way: I will give unto this last, even as unto you.

15 Is it not lawful for me to do what I will with my own? Is your eye evil, because I am good?

16 So the last shall be first, and the first last: for many are called, but few chosen.

17 ¶ And Yahshua going up to Jerusalem took the twelve disciples apart in the way, and said to them,

18 Behold, we go up to Jerusalem; and the Son of man shall be betrayed unto the chief priests and to the scribes, and they shall condemn him to death,

19 And shall deliver him to the Gentiles to mock, and to scourge, and to crucify *him*: and the third day he shall rise again.

20 ¶ Then came to him the mother of Zebedee's children with her sons, worshipping *him*, and desiring a certain thing of him.

21 And he said unto her, What will you? She said to him, Grant that these my two sons may sit, the one on your right hand, and the other on the left, in your kingdom.

22 But Yahshua answered and said, You know not what you ask. Are you able to drink of the cup that I shall drink of, and to be baptized with the baptism that I am baptized with? They said to him, We are able.

23 And he said unto them, You shall drink indeed of my cup, and be baptized with the baptism that I am baptized with: but to sit on my right hand, and on my left, is not mine to give, but *it shall be given to them* for whom it is prepared by my Father.

24 And when the ten heard *it*, they were moved with indignation against the two brothers.

25 But Yahshua called them *to him*, and said, You know that the princes of the Gentiles exercise dominion over them, and they that are great exercise authority upon them.

26 But it shall not be so among you: but whoever will be great among you, let him be your minister;

27 And whoever will be chief among you, let him be your servant:

28 Even as the Son of man came not to be ministered unto, but to minister, and to give his life a ransom for many.

29 ¶ And as they departed from Jericho, a great multitude followed him.

30 And, behold, two blind men sitting by the way side, when they heard that Yahshua passed by, cried out, saying, Have mercy on us, O Lord, *you* Son of David.

31 And the multitude rebuked them, because they should hold their peace: but they cried the more, saying, Have mercy on us, O Lord, *you* Son of David.

32 And Yahshua stood still, and called them, and said, What will you that I shall do to you?

33 They said to him, Lord, that our eyes may be opened.

34 So Yahshua had compassion *on them*, and touched their eyes: and immediately their eyes received sight, and they followed him.

Matthew 21

21:1 ¶ And when they drew near to Jerusalem, and had come to Bethphage, to the mount of Olives, then sent Yahshua two disciples,

2 Saying to them, Go into the village over against you, and straightway you shall find a donkey tied, and a colt with her: loose *them*, and bring *them* to me.

3 And if any man says anything to you, you shall say, The Lord has need of them; and straightway he will send them.

4 All this was done, that it might be fulfilled which was spoken by the prophet, saying,

5 Tell you the daughter of Zion, Behold, your King comes to you, meek, and sitting upon a donkey, and a colt the foal of a donkey.

6 And the disciples went, and did as Yahshua commanded them,

7 And brought the donkey, and the colt, and put on them their clothes, and they set *him* thereon.

8 And a very great multitude spread their garments in the way; others cut down branches from the trees, and strewed *them* in the way.

9 And the multitudes that went before, and that followed, cried, saying, Hosanna to the Son of David: Blessed *is* he that comes in the name of the Lord *Yahweh*; Hosanna in the highest.

10 And when he had come into Jerusalem, all the city was moved, saying, Who is this?

11 And the multitude said, This is Yahshua the prophet of Nazareth of Galilee.

12 ¶ And Yahshua went into the temple of God, and cast out all them that sold and bought in the temple, and overthrew the tables of the moneychangers, and the seats of them that sold doves,

13 And said to them, It is written, My house shall be called the house of prayer; but you have made it a den of thieves.

14 And the blind and the lame came to him in the temple; and he healed them.

15 And when the chief priests and scribes saw the wonderful things that he did, and the children crying in the temple, and saying, Hosanna to the Son of David; they were very displeased,

16 And said to him, Hear you what these say? And Yahshua said to them, Yes; have you never read, Out of the mouth of babes and sucklings you have perfected praise?

17 And he left them, and went out of the city into Bethany; and he lodged there.

18 ¶ Now in the morning as he returned into the city, he hungered.

19 And when he saw a fig tree in the way, he came to it, and found nothing thereon, but leaves only, and said to it, Let no fruit grow on you henceforward forever. And presently the fig tree withered away.

20 And when the disciples saw *it*, they marveled, saying, How soon is the fig tree withered away!

21 Yahshua answered and said to them, Truly I say to you, If you have faith, and doubt not, you shall not only do this *which is done* to the fig tree, but also if you shall say to this mountain, Be you removed, and be you cast into the sea; it shall be done.

22 And all things, whatever you shall ask in prayer, believing, you shall receive.

23 ¶ And when he had come into the temple, the chief priests and the elders of the people came to him as he was teaching, and said, By what authority do you these things? and who gave you this authority?

24 And Yahshua answered and said to them, I also will ask you one thing, which if you tell me, I in like wise will tell you by what authority I do these things.

25 The baptism of John, *from* where was it? from heaven, or of men? And they reasoned with themselves, saying, If we shall say, From heaven; he will say to us, Why did you not then believe him?

26 But if we shall say, Of men; we fear the people; for all hold John as a prophet.

27 And they answered Yahshua, and said, We cannot tell. And he said to them, Neither tell I you by what authority I do these things.

28 ¶ But what think you? A *certain* man had two sons; and he came to the first, and said, Son, go work today in my vineyard.

29 He answered and said, I will not: but afterward he repented, and went.

30 And he came to the second, and said likewise. And he answered and said, I *go*, sir: and went not.

31 Which of the two did the will of *his* father? They said unto him, The first. Yahshua said unto them, Truly I say unto you, That the publicans and the harlots go into the kingdom of God before you.

32 For John came to you in the way of righteousness, and you believed him not: but the publicans and the harlots believed him: and you, when you had seen *it*, repented not afterward, that you might believe him.

33 ¶ Hear another parable: There was a certain householder, which planted a vineyard, and hedged it round about, and dug a winepress in it, and built a tower, and let it out to husbandmen, and went into a far country:

34 And when the time of the fruit drew near, he sent his servants to the husbandmen, that they might receive the fruits of it.

Matthew 21

35 And the husbandmen took his servants, and beat one, and killed another, and stoned another.
36 Again, he sent other servants more than the first: and they did to them likewise.
37 But last of all he sent to them his son, saying, They will reverence my son.
38 But when the husbandmen saw the son, they said among themselves, This is the heir; come, let us kill him, and let us seize on his inheritance.
39 And they caught him, and cast *him* out of the vineyard, and slew *him*.
40 When the lord therefore of the vineyard comes, what will he do to those husbandmen?
41 They said to him, He will miserably destroy those wicked men, and will let out *his* vineyard to other husbandmen, which shall render him the fruits in their seasons.
42 Yahshua said to them, Did you never read in the scriptures, The stone which the builders rejected, the same has become the head of the corner: this is the Lord's [*Yahweh's*] doing, and it is marvelous in our eyes?
43 Therefore say I unto you, The kingdom of God shall be taken from you, and given to a nation bringing forth the fruits thereof.
44 And whoever shall fall on this stone shall be broken: but on whomever it shall fall, it will grind him to powder.
45 And when the chief priests and Pharisees had heard his parables, they perceived that he spoke of them.
46 But when they sought to lay hands on him, they feared the multitude, because they took him for a prophet.

Matthew 22

22:1 ¶ And Yahshua answered and spoke to them again by parables, and said,
2 The kingdom of heaven is like unto a certain king, which made a marriage for his son,
3 And sent forth his servants to call them that were invited to the wedding: and they would not come.
4 Again, he sent forth other servants, saying, Tell them which are invited, Behold, I have prepared my dinner: my oxen and *my* fatted calves *are* killed, and all things *are* ready: come to the marriage.
5 But they made light of *it*, and went their ways, one to his farm, another to his merchandise:
6 And the remnant took his servants, and entreated *them* spitefully, and slew *them*.
7 But when the king heard *thereof*, he was angry: and he sent forth his armies, and destroyed those murderers, and burned up their city.
8 Then said he to his servants, The wedding is ready, but they which were invited were not worthy.
9 Go you therefore into the highways, and as many as you shall find, invite to the marriage.
10 So those servants went out into the highways, and gathered together all as many as they found, both bad and good: and the wedding was filled with guests.
11 And when the king came in to see the guests, he saw there a man which had not on a wedding garment:
12 And he said to him, Friend, how came you in here not having a wedding garment? And he was speechless.
13 Then said the king to the servants, Bind him hand and foot, and take him away, and cast *him* into outer darkness; there shall be weeping and gnashing of teeth.
14 For many are called, but few *are* chosen.
15 ¶ Then went the Pharisees, and took counsel how they might entangle him in *his* talk.
16 And they sent out unto him their disciples with the Herodians, saying, Master, we know that you are true, and teach the way of God in truth, neither care you for any *man*: for you regard not the person of men.
17 Tell us therefore, What think you? Is it lawful to give tribute to Caesar, or not?
18 But Yahshua perceived their wickedness, and said, Why tempt you me, *you* hypocrites?
19 Show me the tribute money. And they brought to him a penny.
20 And he said to them, Whose *is* this image and superscription?
21 They said to him, Caesar's. Then said he to them, Render therefore to Caesar the things which are Caesar's; and to God the things that are God's.
22 When they had heard *these words*, they marveled, and left him, and went their way.
23 ¶ The same day came to him the Sadducees, which say that there is no resurrection, and asked him,
24 Saying, Master, Moses said, If a man dies, having no children, his brother shall marry his wife, and raise up seed unto his brother.
25 Now there were with us seven brothers: and the first, when he had married a wife, deceased, and, having no issue, left his wife to his brother:
26 Likewise the second also, and the third, to the seventh.
27 And last of all the woman died also.
28 Therefore in the resurrection whose wife shall she be of the seven? for they all had her.
29 Yahshua answered and said to them, You do err, not knowing the scriptures, nor the power of God.
30 For in the resurrection they neither marry, nor are given in marriage, but are as the angels of God in heaven.
31 But as touching the resurrection of the dead, have you not read that which was spoken unto you by God, saying,
32 I am the God of Abraham, and the God of Isaac, and the God of Jacob? God is not the God of the dead, but of the living.
33 And when the multitude heard *this*, they were astonished at his doctrine.
34 ¶ But when the Pharisees had heard that he had put the Sadducees to silence, they were gathered together.
35 Then one of them, *which was* a lawyer, asked *him a question*, tempting him, and saying,
36 Master, which *is* the great commandment in the law?

37 Yahshua said to him, You shall love the Lord *Yahweh* your God with all your heart, and with all your soul, and with all your mind.
38 This is the first and great commandment.
39 And the second *is* like unto it, You shall love your neighbor as yourself.
40 On these two commandments hang all the law and the prophets.
41 ¶ While the Pharisees were gathered together, Yahshua asked them,
42 Saying, What think you of the Messiah? whose son is he? They said to him, *The Son* of David.
43 He said to them, How then does David in spirit call him Lord, saying,
44 The LORD *Yahweh* said to my Lord, Sit you on my right hand, till I make your enemies your footstool?
45 If David then calls him Lord, how is he his son?
46 And no man was able to answer him a word, neither dared any *man* from that day forth ask him any more *questions*.

Matthew 23

23:1 ¶ Then spoke Yahshua to the multitude, and to his disciples,
2 Saying, The scribes and the Pharisees sit in Moses' seat:
3 All therefore whatever they bid you observe, *that* observe and do; but do not you after their works: for they say, and do not.
4 For they bind heavy burdens and grievous to be borne, and lay *them* on men's shoulders; but they *themselves* will not move them with one of their fingers.
5 But all their works they do for to be seen of men: they make broad their phylacteries, and enlarge the borders of their garments,
6 And love the uppermost rooms at feasts, and the chief seats in the synagogues,
7 And greetings in the markets, and to be called of men, Rabbi, Rabbi.
8 But be not you called Rabbi: for one is your Master, *even* the Messiah; and all you are brethren.
9 And call no *man* your father upon the earth: for one is your Father, which is in heaven.
10 Neither be you called masters: for one is your Master, *even* the Messiah.
11 But he that is greatest among you shall be your servant.
12 And whoever shall exalt himself shall be abased; and he that shall humble himself shall be exalted.
13 ¶ But woe unto you, scribes and Pharisees, hypocrites! for you shut up the kingdom of heaven against men: for you neither go in *yourselves*, neither allow you them that are entering to go in.
14 Woe unto you, scribes and Pharisees, hypocrites! for you devour widows' houses, and for a pretense make long prayer: therefore you shall receive the greater damnation.
15 Woe unto you, scribes and Pharisees, hypocrites! for you compass sea and land to make one proselyte, and when he is made, you make him twofold more the child of hell than yourselves.
16 Woe unto you, *you* blind guides, which say, Whoever shall swear by the temple, it is nothing; but whoever shall swear by the gold of the temple, he is a debtor!
17 *You* fools and blind: for which is greater, the gold, or the temple that sanctifies the gold?
18 And, Whoever shall swear by the altar, it is nothing; but whoever swears by the gift that is upon it, he is guilty.
19 *You* fools and blind: for which *is* greater, the gift, or the altar that sanctifies the gift?
20 Whoever therefore shall swear by the altar, swears by it, and by all things thereon.
21 And whoever shall swear by the temple, swears by it, and by him that dwells therein.
22 And he that shall swear by heaven, swears by the throne of God, and by him that sits thereon.
23 Woe unto you, scribes and Pharisees, hypocrites! for you pay tithe of mint and anise and cummin, and have omitted the weightier *matters* of the law, judgment, mercy, and faith: these ought you to have done, and not to leave the other undone.
24 *You* blind guides, which strain at a gnat, and swallow a camel.
25 Woe unto you, scribes and Pharisees, hypocrites! for you make clean the outside of the cup and of the platter, but within they are full of extortion and excess.
26 *You* blind Pharisee, cleanse first that *which is* within the cup and platter, that the outside of them may be clean also.
27 Woe unto you, scribes and Pharisees, hypocrites! for you are like unto whitewashed sepulchers, which indeed appear beautiful outward, but are within full of dead *men's* bones, and of all uncleanness.
28 Even so you also outwardly appear righteous to men, but within you are full of hypocrisy and iniquity.
29 Woe unto you, scribes and Pharisees, hypocrites! because you build the tombs of the prophets, and garnish the sepulchers of the righteous,
30 And say, If we had been in the days of our fathers, we would not have been partakers with them in the blood of the prophets.
31 Therefore you are witnesses unto yourselves, that you are the children of them which killed the prophets.
32 Fill you up then the measure of your fathers.
33 *You* serpents, *you* generation of vipers, how can you escape the damnation of hell?
34 ¶ Therefore, behold, I send to you prophets, and wise men, and scribes: and *some* of them you shall kill and crucify; and *some* of them shall you scourge in your synagogues, and persecute *them* from city to city:
35 That upon you may come all the righteous blood shed upon the earth, from the blood of righteous Abel to the blood of Zachariah son of Barachiah, whom you slew between the temple and the altar.
36 Truly I say to you, All these things shall come upon this generation.

Matthew 23

37 O Jerusalem, Jerusalem, *you* that kill the prophets, and stone them which are sent to you, how often would I have gathered your children together, even as a hen gathers her chickens under *her* wings, and you would not!

38 Behold, your house is left unto you desolate.

39 For I say to you, You shall not see me henceforth, until you shall say, Blessed *is* he that comes in the name of the Lord *Yahweh*.

Matthew 24

24:1 ¶ And Yahshua went out, and departed from the temple: and his disciples came to *him* for to show him the buildings of the temple.

2 And Yahshua said to them, See you not all these things? truly I say to you, There shall not be left here one stone upon another, that shall not be thrown down.

3 And as he sat upon the mount of Olives, the disciples came to him privately, saying, Tell us, when shall these things be? and what *shall be* the sign of your coming, and of the end of the world?

4 ¶ And Yahshua answered and said to them, Take heed that no man deceives you.

5 For many shall come in my name, saying, I am the Messiah; and shall deceive many.

6 And you shall hear of wars and rumors of wars: see that you are not troubled: for all *these things* must come to pass, but the end is not yet.

7 For nation shall rise against nation, and kingdom against kingdom: and there shall be famines, and pestilences, and earthquakes, in diverse places.

8 All these *are* the beginning of sorrows.

9 Then shall they deliver you up to be afflicted, and shall kill you: and you shall be hated of all nations for my name's sake.

10 And then shall many be offended, and shall betray one another, and shall hate one another.

11 And many false prophets shall rise, and shall deceive many.

12 And because iniquity shall abound, the love of many shall grow cold.

13 But he that shall endure to the end, the same shall be saved.

14 And this gospel of the kingdom shall be preached in all the world for a witness to all nations; and then shall the end come.

15 When you therefore shall see the abomination of desolation, spoken of by Daniel the prophet, stand in the holy place, (whoever reads, let him understand:)

16 Then let them which are in Judaea flee into the mountains:

17 Let him which is on the housetop not come down to take anything out of his house:

18 Neither let him which is in the field return back to take his clothes.

19 And woe unto them that are with child, and to them that give suck in those days!

20 But pray you that your flight be not in the winter, neither on the sabbath day:

21 For then shall be great tribulation, such as was not since the beginning of the world to this time, no, nor ever shall be.

22 And unless those days should be shortened, there should no flesh be saved: but for the elect's sake those days shall be shortened.

23 Then if any man shall say to you, Lo, here *is* the Messiah, or there; believe *it* not.

24 For there shall arise false Messiahs, and false prophets, and shall show great signs and wonders; insomuch that, if *it were* possible, they shall deceive the very elect.

25 Behold, I have told you before.

26 Therefore if they shall say to you, Behold, he is in the desert; go not forth: behold, *he is* in the secret chambers; believe *it* not.

27 For as the lightning comes out of the east, and shines even to the west; so shall also the coming of the Son of man be.

28 For wherever the carcass is, there will the eagles be gathered together.

29 Immediately after the tribulation of those days shall the sun be darkened, and the moon shall not give her light, and the stars shall fall from heaven, and the powers of the heavens shall be shaken:

30 And then shall appear the sign of the Son of man in heaven: and then shall all the tribes of the earth mourn, and they shall see the Son of man coming in the clouds of heaven with power and great glory.

31 And he shall send his angels with a great sound of a trumpet, and they shall gather together his elect from the four winds, from one end of heaven to the other.

32 ¶ Now learn a parable of the fig tree; When his branch is yet tender, and puts forth leaves, you know that summer *is* nigh:

33 So likewise you, when you shall see all these things, know that it is near, *even* at the doors.

34 Truly I say to you, This generation shall not pass, till all these things are fulfilled.

35 Heaven and earth shall pass away, but my words shall not pass away.

36 But of that day and hour knows no *man*, no, not the angels of heaven, but my Father only.

37 But as the days of Noah *were*, so shall also the coming of the Son of man be.

38 For as in the days that were before the flood they were eating and drinking, marrying and giving in marriage, until the day that Noah entered into the ark,

39 And knew not until the flood came, and took them all away; so shall also the coming of the Son of man be.

40 Then shall two be in the field; the one shall be taken, and the other left.

41 Two *women shall be* grinding at the mill; the one shall be taken, and the other left.

42 Watch therefore: for you know not what hour your Lord does come.

43 But know this, that if the master of the house had known in what watch the thief would come, he would

have watched, and would not have allowed his house to be broken up.

44 Therefore be you also ready: for in such an hour as you think not the Son of man comes.

45 Who then is a faithful and wise servant, whom his lord has made ruler over his household, to give them food in due season?

46 Blessed *is* that servant, whom his lord when he comes shall find so doing.

47 Truly I say to you, That he shall make him ruler over all his goods.

48 But and if that evil servant shall say in his heart, My lord delays his coming;

49 And shall begin to smite *his* fellow servants, and to eat and drink with the drunken;

50 The lord of that servant shall come in a day when he looks not for *him*, and in an hour that he is not aware of.

51 And shall cut him apart, and appoint *him* his portion with the hypocrites: there shall be weeping and gnashing of teeth.

Matthew 25

25:1 ¶ Then shall the kingdom of heaven be likened unto ten virgins, which took their lamps, and went forth to meet the bridegroom.

2 And five of them were wise, and five *were* foolish.

3 They that *were* foolish took their lamps, and took no oil with them:

4 But the wise took oil in their vessels with their lamps

5 While the bridegroom delayed, they all slumbered and slept.

6 And at midnight there was a cry made, Behold, the bridegroom comes; go you out to meet him.

7 Then all those virgins arose, and trimmed their lamps.

8 And the foolish said to the wise, Give us of your oil; for our lamps have gone out.

9 But the wise answered, saying, *Not so*; lest there be not enough for us and you: but go you rather to them that sell, and buy for yourselves.

10 And while they went to buy, the bridegroom came; and they that were ready went in with him to the marriage: and the door was shut.

11 Afterward came also the other virgins, saying, Lord, Lord, open to us.

12 But he answered and said, Truly I say to you, I know you not.

13 Watch therefore, for you know neither the day nor the hour wherein the Son of man comes.

14 ¶ For *the kingdom of heaven is* as a man traveling into a far country, *who* called his own servants, and delivered to them his goods.

15 And to one he gave five talents, to another two, and to another one; to every man according to his own ability; and immediately took his journey.

16 Then he that had received the five talents went and traded with the same, and made *them* another five talents.

17 And likewise he that *had received* two, he also gained another two.

18 But he that had received one went and dug in the earth, and hid his lord's money.

19 After a long time the lord of those servants came, and reckoned with them.

20 And so he that had received five talents came and brought another five talents, saying, Lord, you delivered to me five talents: behold, I have gained besides them five talents more.

21 His lord said to him, Well done, *you* good and faithful servant: you have been faithful over a few things, I will make you ruler over many things: enter you into the joy of your lord.

22 He also that had received two talents came and said, Lord, you delivered to me two talents: behold, I have gained two other talents besides them.

23 His lord said to him, Well done, good and faithful servant; you have been faithful over a few things, I will make you ruler over many things: enter you into the joy of your lord.

24 Then he which had received the one talent came and said, Lord, I knew you that you are a hard man, reaping where you have not sown, and gathering where you have not scattered:

25 And I was afraid, and went and hid your talent in the earth: lo, *there* you have *that is* yours.

26 His lord answered and said to him, *You* wicked and slothful servant, you knew that I reap where I sowed not, and gather where I have not scattered:

27 You ought therefore to have put my money to the exchangers, and *then* at my coming I should have received my own with usury.

28 Take therefore the talent from him, and give *it* to him which has ten talents.

29 For to every one that has shall be given, and he shall have abundance: but from him that has not shall be taken away even that which he has.

30 And cast you the unprofitable servant into outer darkness: there shall be weeping and gnashing of teeth.

31 ¶ When the Son of man shall come in his glory, and all the holy angels with him, then shall he sit upon the throne of his glory:

32 And before him shall be gathered all nations: and he shall separate them one from another, as a shepherd divides *his* sheep from the goats:

33 And he shall set the sheep on his right hand, but the goats on the left.

34 Then shall the King say to them on his right hand, Come, you blessed of my Father, inherit the kingdom prepared for you from the foundation of the world:

35 For I was hungry, and you gave me food: I was thirsty, and you gave me drink: I was a stranger, and you took me in:

36 Naked, and you clothed me: I was sick, and you visited me: I was in prison, and you came to me.

37 Then shall the righteous answer him, saying, Lord, when saw we you hungry, and fed *you*? or thirsty, and gave *you* drink?

38 When saw we you a stranger, and took *you* in? or naked, and clothed *you*?
39 Or when saw we you sick, or in prison, and came to you?
40 And the King shall answer and say to them, Truly I say to you, Inasmuch as you have done *it* to one of the least of these my brethren, you have done *it* unto me.
41 Then shall he say also to them on the left hand, Depart from me, you cursed, into everlasting fire, prepared for the devil and his angels:
42 For I was hungry, and you gave me no food: I was thirsty, and you gave me no drink:
43 I was a stranger, and you took me not in: naked, and you clothed me not: sick, and in prison, and you visited me not.
44 Then shall they also answer him, saying, Lord, when saw we you hungry, or thirsty, or a stranger, or naked, or sick, or in prison, and did not minister to you?
45 Then shall he answer them, saying, Truly I say to you, Inasmuch as you did *it* not to one of the least of these, you did *it* not to me.
46 And these shall go away into everlasting punishment: but the righteous into life eternal.

Matthew 26

26:1 ¶ And it came to pass, when Yahshua had finished all these sayings, he said to his disciples,
2 You know that after two days is *the feast of* the passover, and the Son of man is betrayed to be crucified.
3 Then assembled together the chief priests, and the scribes, and the elders of the people, to the palace of the high priest, who was called Caiaphas,
4 And consulted that they might take Yahshua by subtlety, and kill *him*.
5 But they said, Not on the feast *day*, lest there be an uproar among the people.
6 ¶ Now when Yahshua was in Bethany, in the house of Simon the leper,
7 There came to him a woman having an alabaster box of very precious ointment, and poured it on his head, as he sat *at dinner*.
8 But when his disciples saw *it*, they had indignation, saying, To what purpose *is* this waste?
9 For this ointment might have been sold for much, and given to the poor.
10 When Yahshua understood *it*, he said to them, Why trouble you the woman? for she has worked a good work upon me.
11 For you have the poor always with you; but me you have not always.
12 For in that she has poured this ointment on my body, she did *it* for my burial.
13 Truly I say to you, Wherever this gospel shall be preached in the whole world, *there* shall also this, that this woman has done, be told for a memorial of her.
14 ¶ Then one of the twelve, called Judas Iscariot, went to the chief priests,
15 And said *to them*, What will you give me, and I will deliver him to you? And they covenanted with him for thirty pieces of silver.
16 And from that time he sought opportunity to betray him.
17 ¶ Now the first *day* of the *feast of* unleavened bread the disciples came to Yahshua, saying to him, Where will you that we prepare for you to eat the passover?
18 And he said, Go into the city to such a man, and say to him, The Master said, My time is at hand; I will keep the passover at your house with my disciples.
19 And the disciples did as Yahshua had appointed them; and they made ready the passover.
20 Now when the evening had come, he sat down with the twelve.
21 And as they did eat, he said, Truly I say to you, that one of you shall betray me.
22 And they were exceedingly sorrowful, and began every one of them to say to him, Lord, is it I?
23 And he answered and said, He that dips *his* hand with me in the dish, the same shall betray me.
24 The Son of man goes as it is written of him: but woe unto that man by whom the Son of man is betrayed! it had been good for that man if he had not been born.
25 Then Judas, which betrayed him, answered and said, Master, is it I? He said to him, You have said.
26 ¶ And as they were eating, Yahshua took bread, and blessed *it*, and broke *it*, and gave *it* to the disciples, and said, Take, eat; this is my body.
27 And he took the cup, and gave thanks, and gave *it* to them, saying, Drink you all of it;
28 For this is my blood of the new testament, which is shed for many for the remission of sins.
29 But I say to you, I will not drink henceforth of this fruit of the vine, until that day when I drink it new with you in my Father's kingdom.
30 And when they had sung a hymn, they went out into the mount of Olives.
31 ¶ Then said Yahshua to them, All you shall be offended because of me this night: for it is written, I will smite the shepherd, and the sheep of the flock shall be scattered abroad.
32 But after I am risen again, I will go before you into Galilee.
33 Peter answered and said to him, Though all *men* shall be offended because of you, *yet* will I never be offended.
34 Yahshua said to him, Truly I say to you, That this night, before the cock crows, you shall deny me three times.
35 Peter said to him, Though I should die with you, yet will I not deny you. Likewise also said all the disciples.
36 ¶ Then came Yahshua with them to a place called Gethsemane, and said to the disciples, Sit you here, while I go and pray yonder.
37 And he took with him Peter and the two sons of Zebedee, and began to be sorrowful and very heavy.
38 Then said he to them, My soul is exceedingly sorrowful, even unto death: stay you here, and watch with me.

39 And he went a little further, and fell on his face, and prayed, saying, O my Father, if it is possible, let this cup pass from me: nevertheless not as I will, but as you *will*.

40 And he came to the disciples, and found them asleep, and said to Peter, What, could you not watch with me one hour?

41 Watch and pray, that you enter not into temptation: the spirit indeed *is* willing, but the flesh *is* weak.

42 He went away again the second time, and prayed, saying, O my Father, if this cup may not pass away from me, except I drink it, your will be done.

43 And he came and found them asleep again: for their eyes were heavy.

44 And he left them, and went away again, and prayed the third time, saying the same words.

45 Then came he to his disciples, and said to them, Sleep on now, and take *your* rest: behold, the hour is at hand, and the Son of man is betrayed into the hands of sinners.

46 Rise, let us be going: behold, he is at hand that does betray me.

47 ¶ And while he yet spoke, lo, Judas, one of the twelve, came, and with him a great multitude with swords and staves, from the chief priests and elders of the people.

48 Now he that betrayed him gave them a sign, saying, Whomever I shall kiss, that same is he: hold him fast.

49 And immediately he came to Yahshua, and said, Hail, master; and kissed him.

50 And Yahshua said unto him, Friend, why have you come? Then came they, and laid hands on Yahshua, and took him.

51 And, behold, one of them which was with Yahshua stretched out *his* hand, and drew his sword, and struck a servant of the high priest's, and cut off his ear.

52 Then said Yahshua to him, Put up again your sword into its place: for all they that take the sword shall perish with the sword.

53 Think you that I cannot now pray to my Father, and he shall presently give me more than twelve legions of angels?

54 But how then shall the scriptures be fulfilled, that thus it must be?

55 In that same hour said Yahshua to the multitudes, Have you come out as against a thief with swords and staves for to take me? I sat daily with you teaching in the temple, and you laid no hold on me.

56 But all this was done, that the scriptures of the prophets might be fulfilled. Then all the disciples forsook him, and fled.

57 ¶ And they that had laid hold on Yahshua led *him* away to Caiaphas the high priest, where the scribes and the elders were assembled.

58 But Peter followed him afar off to the high priest's palace, and went in, and sat with the servants, to see the end.

59 Now the chief priests, and elders, and all the council, sought false witness against Yahshua, to put him to death;

60 But found none: yes, though many false witnesses came, *yet* found they none. At the last came two false witnesses,

61 And said, This *fellow* said, I am able to destroy the temple of God, and to build it in three days.

62 And the high priest arose, and said to him, Answer you nothing? what *is it which* these witness against you?

63 But Yahshua held his peace. And the high priest answered and said to him, I adjure you by the living God, that you tell us whether you are the Messiah, the Son of God.

64 Yahshua said to him, You have said: nevertheless I say to you, Hereafter shall you see the Son of man sitting on the right hand of power, and coming in the clouds of heaven.

65 Then the high priest tore his clothes, saying, He has spoken blasphemy; what further need have we of witnesses? behold, now you have heard his blasphemy.

66 What think you? They answered and said, He is guilty of death.

67 Then did they spit in his face, and buffeted him; and others smote *him* with the palms of their hands,

68 Saying, Prophesy to us, you Messiah, Who is he that smote you?

69 ¶ Now Peter sat outside in the palace: and a damsel came to him, saying, You also were with Yahshua of Galilee.

70 But he denied before *them* all, saying, I know not what you say.

71 And when he had gone out into the porch, another *maid* saw him, and said to them that were there, This *fellow* was also with Yahshua of Nazareth

72 And again he denied with an oath, I do not know the man.

73 And after a while came to *him* they that stood by, and said to Peter, Surely you also are *one* of them; for your speech betrays you.

74 Then began he to curse and to swear, *saying*, I know not the man. And immediately the cock crowed.

75 And Peter remembered the word of Yahshua, which said to him, Before the cock crows, you shall deny me three times. And he went out, and wept bitterly.

Matthew 27

27:1 ¶ When the morning had come, all the chief priests and elders of the people took counsel against Yahshua to put him to death:

2 And when they had bound him, they led *him* away, and delivered him to Pontius Pilate the governor.

3 Then Judas, which had betrayed him, when he saw that he was condemned, repented himself, and brought again the thirty pieces of silver to the chief priests and elders,

4 Saying, I have sinned in that I have betrayed the innocent blood. And they said, What *is that* to us? see you *to that*.

5 And he cast down the pieces of silver in the temple, and departed, and went and hanged himself.

6 And the chief priests took the silver pieces, and said, It is not lawful for to put them into the treasury, because it is the price of blood.

Matthew 27

7 And they took counsel, and bought with them the potter's field, to bury strangers in.

8 Therefore that field was called, The field of blood, unto this day.

9 Then was fulfilled that which was spoken by Jeremiah the prophet, saying, And they took the thirty pieces of silver, the price of him that was valued, whom they of the children of Israel did value;

10 And gave them for the potter's field, as the Lord *Yahweh* appointed me.

11 ¶ And Yahshua stood before the governor: and the governor asked him, saying, Are you the King of the Jews? And Yahshua said to him, You say.

12 And when he was accused of the chief priests and elders, he answered nothing.

13 Then said Pilate to him, Hear you not how many things they witness against you?

14 And he answered him with nary a word; insomuch that the governor marveled greatly.

15 Now at *that* feast the governor was inclined to release to the people a prisoner, whom they would.

16 And they had then a notable prisoner, called Barabbas.

17 Therefore when they had gathered together, Pilate said to them, Whom will you that I release to you? Barabbas, or Yahshua which is called the Messiah?

18 For he knew that for envy they had delivered him.

19 When he had sat down on the judgment seat, his wife sent to him, saying, Have you nothing to do with that just man: for I have suffered many things this day in a dream because of him.

20 But the chief priests and elders persuaded the multitude that they should ask Barabbas, and destroy Yahshua.

21 The governor answered and said to them, Which of the two will you that I release to you? They said, Barabbas.

22 Pilate said to them, What shall I do then with Yahshua which is called the Messiah? *They* all said to him, Let him be crucified.

23 And the governor said, Why, what evil has he done? But they cried out the more, saying, Let him be crucified.

24 When Pilate saw that he could prevail nothing, but *that* rather a tumult was made, he took water, and washed *his* hands before the multitude, saying, I am innocent of the blood of this just person: see you *to it*.

25 Then answered all the people, and said, His blood *be* on us, and on our children.

26 ¶ Then released he Barabbas to them: and when he had scourged Yahshua, he delivered *him* to be crucified.

27 Then the soldiers of the governor took Yahshua into the common hall, and gathered unto him the whole band *of soldiers*.

28 And they stripped him, and put on him a scarlet robe.

29 And when they had platted a crown of thorns, they put *it* upon his head, and a reed in his right hand: and they bowed the knee before him, and mocked him, saying, Hail, King of the Jews!

30 And they spit upon him, and took the reed, and smote him on the head.

31 And after that they had mocked him, they took the robe off from him, and put his own clothes on him, and led him away to crucify *him*.

32 And as they came out, they found a man of Cyrene, Simon by name: him they compelled to bear his cross.

33 ¶ And when they had come to a place called Golgotha, that is to say, a place of a skull,

34 They gave him vinegar to drink mingled with gall: and when he had tasted *thereof*, he would not drink.

35 And they crucified him, and parted his garments, casting lots: that it might be fulfilled which was spoken by the prophet, They parted my garments among them, and upon my coat did they cast lots.

36 And sitting down they watched him there;

37 And set up over his head his accusation written, THIS IS YAHSHUA THE KING OF THE JEWS.

38 Then were there two thieves crucified with him, one on the right hand, and another on the left.

39 And they that passed by reviled him, wagging their heads,

40 And saying, You that destroy the temple, and build *it* in three days, save yourself. If you are the Son of God, come down from the cross.

41 Likewise also the chief priests mocking *him*, with the scribes and elders, said,

42 He saved others; himself he cannot save. If he is the King of Israel, let him now come down from the cross, and we will believe him.

43 He trusted in God; let him deliver him now, if he will have him: for he said, I am the Son of God.

44 The thieves also, which were crucified with him, cast the same in his teeth.

45 Now from the sixth hour there was darkness over all the land to the ninth hour.

46 And about the ninth hour Yahshua cried with a loud voice, saying, Eli, Eli, lama sabachthani? that is to say, My God, my God, why have you forsaken me?

47 Some of them that stood there, when they heard *that*, said, This *man* calls for Elijah.

48 And immediately one of them ran, and took a sponge, and filled *it* with vinegar, and put *it* on a reed, and gave him to drink.

49 The rest said, Let be, let us see whether Elijah will come to save him.

50 ¶ Yahshua, when he had cried again with a loud voice, yielded up the ghost.

51 And, behold, the veil of the temple was divided in two from the top to the bottom; and the earth did quake, and the rocks divided;

52 And the graves were opened; and many bodies of the saints which slept arose,

53 And came out of the graves after his resurrection, and went into the holy city, and appeared to many.

54 Now when the centurion, and they that were with him, watching Yahshua, saw the earthquake, and those

things that were done, they feared greatly, saying, Truly this was the Son of God.

55 And many women were there beholding afar off, which followed Yahshua from Galilee, ministering unto him:

56 Among which was Mary Magdalene, and Mary the mother of James and Joses, and the mother of Zebedee's children.

57 ¶ When the evening had come, there came a rich man of Arimathaea, named Joseph, who also himself was Yahshua's disciple:

58 He went to Pilate, and begged the body of Yahshua. Then Pilate commanded the body to be delivered.

59 And when Joseph had taken the body, he wrapped it in a clean linen cloth,

60 And laid it in his own new tomb, which he had hewn out in the rock: and he rolled a great stone to the door of the sepulcher, and departed.

61 And there was Mary Magdalene, and the other Mary, sitting over against the sepulcher.

62 Now the next day, that followed the day of the preparation, the chief priests and Pharisees came together unto Pilate,

63 Saying, Sir, we remember that that deceiver said, while he was yet alive, After three days I will rise again.

64 Command therefore that the sepulcher be made sure until the third day, lest his disciples come by night, and steal him away, and say to the people, He is risen from the dead: so the last error shall be worse than the first.

65 Pilate said to them, You have a watch: go your way, make *it* as sure as you can.

66 So they went, and made the sepulcher sure, sealing the stone, and setting a watch.

Matthew 28

28:1 ¶ In the end of the sabbath, as it began to dawn toward the first *day* of the week, came Mary Magdalene and the other Mary to see the sepulcher.

2 And, behold, there was a great earthquake: for the angel of the Lord descended from heaven, and came and rolled back the stone from the door, and sat upon it.

3 His countenance was like lightning, and his clothes white as snow:

4 And for fear of him the keepers did shake, and became as dead *men*.

5 And the angel answered and said to the women, Fear not you: for I know that you seek Yahshua, which was crucified.

6 He is not here: for he is risen, as he said. Come, see the place where the Lord lay.

7 And go quickly, and tell his disciples that he is risen from the dead; and, behold, he goes before you into Galilee; there shall you see him: lo, I have told you.

8 And they departed quickly from the sepulcher with fear and great joy; and did run to bring his disciples word.

9 And as they went to tell his disciples, behold, Yahshua met them, saying, All hail. And they came and held him by the feet, and worshipped him.

10 Then said Yahshua to them, Be not afraid: go tell my brethren that they go into Galilee, and there shall they see me.

11 ¶ Now when they were going, behold, some of the watch came into the city, and showed to the chief priests all the things that were done.

12 And when they had assembled with the elders, and had taken counsel, they gave much money to the soldiers,

13 Saying, Say you, His disciples came by night, and stole him *away* while we slept.

14 And if this comes to the governor's ears, we will persuade him, and secure you.

15 So they took the money, and did as they were taught: and this saying is commonly reported among the Jews until this day.

16 ¶ Then the eleven disciples went away into Galilee, into a mountain where Yahshua had appointed them.

17 And when they saw him, they worshipped him: but some doubted.

18 And Yahshua came and spoke to them, saying, All power is given unto me in heaven and in earth.

19 Go you therefore, and teach all nations, baptizing them in the name of the Father, and of the Son, and of the Holy Ghost:

20 Teaching them to observe all things whatever I have commanded you: and, lo, I am with you always, *even* to the end of the world. Amen.

Mark

Mark 1

1:1 ¶ The beginning of the gospel of Yahshua the Messiah, the Son of God;

2 As it is written in the prophets, Behold, I send my messenger before your face, which shall prepare your way before you.

3 The voice of one crying in the wilderness, Prepare you the way of the Lord *Yahweh*, make his paths straight.

4 John did baptize in the wilderness, and preach the baptism of repentance for the remission of sins.

5 And there went out to him all the land of Judaea, and they of Jerusalem, and were all baptized of him in the river of Jordan, confessing their sins.

6 And John was clothed with camel's hair, and with a girdle of a skin about his loins; and he did eat locusts and wild honey;

7 And preached, saying, There comes one mightier than I after me, the lace of whose shoes I am not worthy to stoop down and unloose.

8 I indeed have baptized you with water: but he shall baptize you with the Holy Ghost.

9 ¶ And it came to pass in those days, that Yahshua came from Nazareth of Galilee, and was baptized by John in *the* Jordan.

Mark 1

10 And straightway coming up out of the water, he saw the heavens opened, and the Spirit like a dove descending upon him:

11 And there came a voice from heaven, *saying*, You are my beloved Son, in whom I am well pleased.

12 And immediately the Spirit drove him into the wilderness.

13 And he was there in the wilderness *for* forty days, tempted by Satan; and was with the wild beasts; and the angels ministered to him.

14 ¶ Now after that John was put in prison, Yahshua came into Galilee, preaching the gospel of the kingdom of God,

15 And saying, The time is fulfilled, and the kingdom of God is at hand: repent you, and believe the gospel.

16 Now as he walked by the sea of Galilee, he saw Simon and Andrew his brother casting a net into the sea: for they were fishermen.

17 And Yahshua said to them, Come you after me, and I will make you to become fishers of men.

18 And immediately they forsook their nets, and followed him.

19 And when he had gone a little further there, he saw James the *son* of Zebedee, and John his brother, who also were in the ship mending their nets.

20 And immediately he called them: and they left their father Zebedee in the ship with the hired servants, and went after him.

21 And they went into Capernaum; and immediately on the sabbath day he entered into the synagogue, and taught.

22 And they were astonished at his doctrine: for he taught them as one that had authority, and not as the scribes.

23 ¶ And there was in their synagogue a man with an unclean spirit; and he cried out,

24 Saying, Let *us* alone; what have we to do with you, you Yahshua of Nazareth? have you come to destroy us? I know you who you are, the Holy One of God.

25 And Yahshua rebuked him, saying, Hold your peace, and come out of him.

26 And when the unclean spirit had torn him, and cried with a loud voice, he came out of him.

27 And they were all amazed, insomuch that they questioned among themselves, saying, What thing is this? what new doctrine *is* this? for with authority commands he even the unclean spirits, and they do obey him.

28 And immediately his fame spread abroad throughout all the region round about Galilee.

29 ¶ And immediately, when they had come out of the synagogue, they entered into the house of Simon and Andrew, with James and John.

30 But Simon's wife's mother lay sick of a fever, and immediately they told him of her.

31 And he came and took her by the hand, and lifted her up; and immediately the fever left her, and she ministered unto them.

32 And at evening, when the sun did set, they brought to him all that were diseased, and them that were possessed with devils.

33 And all the city was gathered together at the door.

34 And he healed many that were sick of various diseases, and cast out many devils; and permitted not the devils to speak, because they knew him.

35 And in the morning, rising up a great while before day, he went out, and departed into a solitary place, and there prayed.

36 And Simon and they that were with him followed after him.

37 And when they had found him, they said to him, All *men* seek for you.

38 And he said unto them, Let us go into the next towns, that I may preach there also: for therefore came I forth.

39 And he preached in their synagogues throughout all Galilee, and cast out devils.

40 ¶ And there came a leper to him, begging him, and kneeling down unto him, and saying to him, If you will, you can make me clean.

41 And Yahshua, moved with compassion, put forth *his* hand, and touched him, and said to him, I will; be you clean.

42 And as soon as he had spoken, immediately the leprosy departed from him, and he was cleansed.

43 And he sternly charged him, and immediately sent him away;

44 And said to him, See you say nothing to any man: but go your way, show yourself to the priest, and offer for your cleansing those things which Moses commanded, for a testimony to them.

45 But he went out, and began to publish *it* much, and to spread abroad the matter, insomuch that Yahshua could no more openly enter into the city, but was outside in desert places: and they came to him from every quarter.

Mark 2

2:1 ¶ And again he entered into Capernaum after *some* days; and it was heard that he was in the house.

2 And immediately many were gathered together, insomuch that there was no room to receive *them*, no, not so much as about the door: and he preached the word to them.

3 And they came unto him, bringing one sick of the palsy, which was carried by four.

4 And when they could not come near to him for the crowd, they uncovered the roof where he was: and when they had broken *it* up, they let down the bed wherein the sick of the palsy lay.

5 When Yahshua saw their faith, he said to the sick of the palsy, Son, your sins are forgiven you.

6 But there were certain of the scribes sitting there, and reasoning in their hearts,

7 Why does this *man* thus speak blasphemies? who can forgive sins but God only?

8 And immediately when Yahshua perceived in his spirit that they so reasoned within themselves, he said to them, Why reason you these things in your hearts?

9 Which is easier to say to the sick of the palsy, *Your* sins are forgiven you; or to say, Arise, and take up your bed, and walk?

10 But that you may know that the Son of man has power on earth to forgive sins, (he said to the sick of the palsy,)
11 I say unto you, Arise, and take up your bed, and go your way into your house.
12 And immediately he arose, took up the bed, and went forth before them all; insomuch that they were all amazed, and glorified God, saying, We never saw it on this fashion.
13 ¶ And he went forth again by the sea side; and all the multitude resorted unto him, and he taught them.
14 And as he passed by, he saw Levi the *son* of Alphaeus sitting at the receipt of custom, and said to him, Follow me. And he arose and followed him.
15 And it came to pass, that, as Yahshua sat at *a* meal in his house, many publicans and sinners sat also together with Yahshua and his disciples: for there were many, and they followed him.
16 And when the scribes and Pharisees saw him eat with publicans and sinners, they said to his disciples, How is it that he eats and drinks with publicans and sinners?
17 When Yahshua heard *it*, he said to them, They that are whole have no need of the physician, but they that are sick: I came not to call the righteous, but sinners to repentance.
18 ¶ And the disciples of John and of the Pharisees had been fasting: and they came and said to him, Why do the disciples of John and of the Pharisees fast, but your disciples fast not?
19 And Yahshua said to them, Can the children of the bride chamber fast, while the bridegroom is with them? as long as they have the bridegroom with them, they cannot fast.
20 But the days will come, when the bridegroom shall be taken away from them, and then shall they fast in those days.
21 No man also sews a piece of new cloth on an old garment: *or* else the new piece that filled it up takes away from the old, and the tear is made worse.
22 And no man puts new wine into old bottles: *or* else the new wine does burst the bottles, and the wine is spilled, and the bottles will be marred: but new wine must be put into new bottles.
23 And it came to pass, that he went through the corn fields on the sabbath day; and his disciples began, as they went, to pluck the ears of corn.
24 And the Pharisees said to him, Behold, why do they on the sabbath day that which is not lawful?
25 And he said to them, Have you never read what David did, when he had need, and was hungry, he, and they that were with him?
26 How he went into the house of God in the days of Abiathar the high priest, and did eat the showbread, which is not lawful to eat but for the priests, and gave also to them which were with him?
27 And he said to them, The sabbath was made for man, and not man for the sabbath:
28 Therefore the Son of man is Lord also of the sabbath.

Mark 3

3:1 ¶ And he entered again into the synagogue; and there was a man there which had a withered hand.
2 And they watched him, whether he would heal him on the sabbath day; that they might accuse him.
3 And he said to the man which had the withered hand, Stand forth.
4 And he said to them, Is it lawful to do good on the sabbath days, or to do evil? to save life, or to kill? But they held their peace.
5 And when he had looked round about on them with anger, being grieved for the hardness of their hearts, he said to the man, Stretch forth your hand. And he stretched *it* out: and his hand was restored whole as the other.
6 And the Pharisees went forth, and immediately took counsel with the Herodians against him, how they might destroy him.
7 But Yahshua withdrew himself with his disciples to the sea: and a great multitude from Galilee followed him, and from Judaea,
8 And from Jerusalem, and from Idumaea, and *from* beyond *the* Jordan; and they about Tyre and Sidon, a great multitude, when they had heard what great things he did, came unto him.
9 And he spoke to his disciples, that a small ship should wait on him because of the multitude, lest they should crush him.
10 For he had healed many; insomuch that they pressed upon him for to touch him, as many as had plagues.
11 And unclean spirits, when they saw him, fell down before him, and cried, saying, You are the Son of God.
12 And he sternly charged them that they should not make him known.
13 ¶ And he went up into a mountain, and called *unto him* whom he would: and they came to him.
14 And he ordained twelve, that they should be with him, and that he might send them forth to preach,
15 And to have power to heal sicknesses, and to cast out devils:
16 And Simon he surnamed Peter;
17 And James the *son* of Zebedee, and John the brother of James; and he surnamed them Boanerges, which is, The sons of thunder:
18 And Andrew, and Philip, and Bartholomew, and Matthew, and Thomas, and James the *son* of Alphaeus, and Thaddaeus, and Simon the Canaanite,
19 And Judas Iscariot, which also betrayed him: and they went into a house.
20 And the multitude came together again, so that they could not so much as eat bread.
21 And when his friends heard *of it*, they went out to lay hold on him: for they said, He is beside himself.
22 ¶ And the scribes which came down from Jerusalem said, He has Beelzebub, and by the prince of the devils casts he out devils.

Mark 3

23 And he called them *unto him*, and said to them in parables, How can Satan cast out Satan?
24 And if a kingdom is divided against itself, that kingdom cannot stand.
25 And if a house is divided against itself, that house cannot stand.
26 And if Satan rises up against himself, and is divided, he cannot stand, but has an end.
27 No man can enter into a strong man's house, and spoil his goods, unless he will first bind the strong man; and then he will spoil his house.
28 Truly I say unto you, All sins shall be forgiven to the sons of men, and blasphemies with which ever they shall blaspheme:
29 But he that shall blaspheme against the Holy Ghost has never forgiveness, but is in danger of eternal damnation:
30 Because they said, He has an unclean spirit.
31 ¶ There came then his brothers and his mother, and, standing outside, sent to him, calling him.
32 And the multitude sat about him, and they said to him, Behold, your mother and your brothers outside seek for you.
33 And he answered them, saying, Who is my mother, or my brothers?
34 And he looked round about on them which sat about him, and said, Behold my mother and my brothers!
35 For whoever shall do the will of God, the same is my brother, and my sister, and mother.

Mark 4

4:1 ¶ And he began again to teach by the sea side: and there was gathered unto him a great multitude, so that he entered into a ship, and sat in the sea; and the whole multitude was by the sea on the land.
2 And he taught them many things by parables, and said to them in his doctrine,
3 Listen; Behold, there went out a sower to sow:
4 And it came to pass, as he sowed, some fell by the way side, and the fowls of the air came and devoured it up.
5 And some fell on stony ground, where it had not much earth; and immediately it sprang up, because it had no depth of earth:
6 But when the sun was up, it was scorched; and because it had no root, it withered away.
7 And some fell among thorns, and the thorns grew up, and choked it, and it yielded no fruit.
8 And other fell on good ground, and did yield fruit that sprang up and increased; and brought forth, some thirty, and some sixty, and some a hundred.
9 And he said unto them, He that has ears to hear, let him hear.
10 And when he was alone, they that were about him with the twelve asked of him the parable.
11 And he said unto them, Unto you it is given to know the mystery of the kingdom of God: but unto them that are outside, all *these* things are done in parables:
12 That seeing they may see, and not perceive; and hearing they may hear, and not understand; lest at any time they should be converted, and *their* sins should be forgiven them.
13 And he said unto them, Know you not this parable? and how then will you know all parables?
14 The sower sows the word.
15 And these are they by the way side, where the word is sown; but when they have heard, Satan comes immediately, and takes away the word that was sown in their hearts.
16 And these are they likewise which are sown on stony ground; who, when they have heard the word, immediately receive it with gladness;
17 And have no root in themselves, and so endure but for a time: afterward, when affliction or persecution rises for the word's sake, immediately they are offended.
18 And these are they which are sown among thorns; such as hear the word,
19 And the cares of this world, and the deceitfulness of riches, and the lusts of other things entering in, choke the word, and it becomes unfruitful.
20 And these are they which are sown on good ground; such as hear the word, and receive *it*, and bring forth fruit, some thirty times, some sixty, and some a hundred.
21 ¶ And he said to them, Is a candle brought to be put under a bushel, or under a bed? and not to be set on a candlestick?
22 For there is nothing hidden, which shall not be manifested; neither was any thing kept secret, but that it should come abroad.
23 If any man has ears to hear, let him hear.
24 And he said to them, Take heed what you hear: with what measure you measure, it shall be measured to you: and to you that hear shall more be given.
25 For he that has, to him shall be given: and he that has not, from him shall be taken even that which he has.
26 And he said, So is the kingdom of God, as if a man should cast seed into the ground;
27 And should sleep, and rise night and day, and the seed should spring and grow up, he knows not how.
28 For the earth brings forth fruit of herself; first the blade, then the ear, after that the full corn in the ear.
29 But when the fruit is brought forth, immediately he puts in the sickle, because the harvest has come.
30 And he said, Whereunto shall we liken the kingdom of God? or with what comparison shall we compare it?
31 *It is* like a grain of mustard seed, which, when it is sown in the earth, is less than all the seeds that are in the earth:
32 But when it is sown, it grows up, and becomes greater than all herbs, and shoots out great branches; so that the fowls of the air may lodge under the shadow of it.
33 And with many such parables spoke he the word unto them, as they were able to hear *it*.
34 But without a parable spoke he not to them: and when they were alone, he expounded all things to his disciples.
35 ¶ And the same day, when the evening had come, he said to them, Let us pass over to the other side.

36 And when they had sent away the multitude, they took him even as he was in the ship. And there were also with him other little ships.
37 And there arose a great storm of wind, and the waves beat into the ship, so that it was now full.
38 And he was in the stern of the ship, asleep on a pillow: and they awoke him, and said to him, Master, care you not that we perish?
39 And he arose, and rebuked the wind, and said to the sea, Peace, be still. And the wind ceased, and there was a great calm.
40 And he said unto them, Why are you so fearful? how is it that you have no faith?
41 And they feared exceedingly, and said one to another, What manner of man is this, that even the wind and the sea obey him?

Mark 5

5:1 ¶ And they came over to the other side of the sea, into the country of the Gadarenes.
2 And when he had come out of the ship, immediately there met him out of the tombs a man with an unclean spirit,
3 Who had *his* dwelling among the tombs; and no man could bind him, no, not with chains:
4 Because that he had been often bound with fetters and chains, and the chains had been pulled apart by him, and the fetters broken in pieces: neither could any *man* tame him.
5 And always, night and day, he was in the mountains, and in the tombs, crying, and cutting himself with stones.
6 But when he saw Yahshua afar off, he ran and worshipped him,
7 And cried with a loud voice, and said, What have I to do with you, Yahshua, *you* Son of the most high God? I adjure you by God, that you torment me not.
8 For he said to him, Come out of the man, *you* unclean spirit.
9 And he asked him, What *is* your name? And he answered, saying, My name *is* Legion: for we are many.
10 And he begged him much that he would not send them away out of the country.
11 Now there was there near to the mountains a great herd of swine feeding.
12 And all the devils begged him, saying, Send us into the swine, that we may enter into them.
13 And immediately Yahshua gave them leave. And the unclean spirits went out, and entered into the swine: and the herd ran violently down a steep place into the sea, (they were about two thousand;) and were drowned in the sea.
14 And they that fed the swine fled, and told *it* in the city, and in the country. And they went out to see what it was that was done.
15 And they came to Yahshua, and saw him that was possessed with the devil, and had the legion, sitting, and clothed, and in his right mind: and they were afraid.
16 And they that saw *it* told them how it happened to him that was possessed with the devil, and *also* concerning the swine.
17 And they began to encourage him to depart out of their coasts.
18 And when he entered into the ship, he that had been possessed with the devil begged him that he might be with him.
19 However Yahshua permitted him not, but said unto him, Go home to your friends, and tell them how great things the Lord has done for you, and has had compassion on you.
20 And he departed, and began to publish in Decapolis how great things Yahshua had done for him: and all *men* did marvel.
21 ¶ And when Yahshua had passed over again by ship to the other side, many people gathered to him: and he was near to the sea.
22 And, behold, there came one of the rulers of the synagogue, Jairus by name; and when he saw him, he fell at his feet,
23 And begged him greatly, saying, My little daughter lies at the point of death: *I pray you*, come and lay your hands on her, that she may be healed; and she shall live.
24 And Yahshua went with him; and many people followed him, and thronged him.
25 And a certain woman, which had an issue of blood *for* twelve years,
26 And had suffered many things of many physicians, and had spent all that she had, and was not better, but rather grew worse,
27 When she had heard of Yahshua, came in the crowd behind, and touched his garment.
28 For she said, If I may touch but his clothes, I shall be whole.
29 And immediately the fountain of her blood was dried up; and she felt in *her* body that she was healed of that plague.
30 And Yahshua, immediately knowing in himself that power had gone out of him, turned him about in the crowd, and said, Who touched my clothes?
31 And his disciples said to him, You see the multitude thronging you, and say you, Who touched me?
32 And he looked round about to see her that had done this thing.
33 But the woman fearing and trembling, knowing what was done in her, came and fell down before him, and told him all the truth.
34 And he said unto her, Daughter, your faith has made you whole; go in peace, and be healed of your plague.
35 ¶ While he yet spoke, there came from the ruler of the synagogue's *house certain* which said, Your daughter is dead: why trouble you the Master any further?
36 As soon as Yahshua heard the word that was spoken, he said to the ruler of the synagogue, Be not afraid, only believe.
37 And he allowed no man to follow him, except Peter, and James, and John the brother of James.

Mark 5

38 And he came to the house of the ruler of the synagogue, and saw the tumult, and them that wept and wailed greatly.

39 And when he had come in, he said unto them, Why make you this commotion, and weep? the girl is not dead, but sleeps.

40 And they laughed him to scorn. But when he had put them all out, he took the father and the mother of the girl, and them that were with him, and entered in where the girl was lying.

41 And he took the girl by the hand, and said unto her, Talitha cumi; which is, being interpreted, Damsel, I say unto you, arise.

42 And immediately the girl arose, and walked; for she was *of the age* of twelve years. And they were astonished with a great astonishment.

43 And he charged them sternly that no man should know it; and commanded that something should be given her to eat.

Mark 6

6:1 ¶ And he went out from there, and came into his own country; and his disciples followed him.

2 And when the sabbath day had come, he began to teach in the synagogue: and many hearing *him* were astonished, saying, From where has this *man* these things? and what wisdom *is* this which is given to him, that even such mighty works are worked by his hands?

3 Is not this the carpenter, the son of Mary, the brother of James, and Joses, and of Judah, and Simon? and are not his sisters here with us? And they were offended at him.

4 But Yahshua said to them, A prophet is not without honor, but in his own country, and among his own kin, and in his own house.

5 And he could there do no mighty work, except that he laid his hands upon a few sick folk, and healed *them*.

6 And he marveled because of their unbelief. And he went round about the villages, teaching.

7 ¶ And he called *unto him* the twelve, and began to send them forth by two and two; and gave them power over unclean spirits;

8 And commanded them that they should take nothing for *their* journey, save a staff only; no sack, no bread, no money in *their* purse:

9 But *be* shod with sandals; and not put on two coats.

10 And he said to them, In whatever place you enter into a house, there remain till you depart from that place.

11 And whoever shall not receive you, nor hear you, when you depart there, shake off the dust under your feet for a testimony against them. Truly I say to you, It shall be more tolerable for Sodom and Gomorrah in the day of judgment, than for that city.

12 And they went out, and preached that men should repent.

13 And they cast out many devils, and anointed with oil many that were sick, and healed *them*.

14 ¶ And king Herod heard *of him*; (for his name was spread abroad:) and he said, That John the Baptist was risen from the dead, and therefore mighty works do show forth themselves in him.

15 Others said, That it is Elijah. And others said, That it is a prophet, or as one of the prophets.

16 But when Herod heard *thereof*, he said, It is John, whom I beheaded: he is risen from the dead.

17 For Herod himself had sent forth and laid hold upon John, and bound him in prison for Herodias' sake, his brother Philip's wife: for he had married her.

18 For John had said to Herod, It is not lawful for you to have your brother's wife.

19 Therefore Herodias had a quarrel against him, and would have killed him; but she could not:

20 For Herod feared John, knowing that he was a just man and holy, and observed him; and when he heard him, he did many things, and heard him gladly.

21 And when a convenient day had come, that Herod on his birthday made a supper to his lords, high captains, and chief *estates* of Galilee;

22 And when the daughter of the said Herodias came in, and danced, and pleased Herod and them that sat with him, the king said to the damsel, Ask of me whatever you will, and I will give *it* you.

23 And he swore to her, Whatever you shall ask of me, I will give *it* you, to the half of my kingdom.

24 And she went forth, and said to her mother, What shall I ask? And she said, The head of John the Baptist.

25 And she came in immediately with haste unto the king, and asked, saying, I will that you give me by and by in a platter the head of John the Baptist.

26 And the king was exceedingly sorry; *yet* for his oath's sake, and for their sakes which sat with him, he would not reject her.

27 And immediately the king sent an executioner, and commanded his head to be brought: and he went and beheaded him in the prison,

28 And brought his head on a platter, and gave it to the damsel: and the damsel gave it to her mother.

29 And when his disciples heard *of it*, they came and took up his corpse, and laid it in a tomb.

30 ¶ And the apostles gathered themselves together unto Yahshua, and told him all things, both what they had done, and what they had taught.

31 And he said unto them, Come you yourselves apart into a desert place, and rest a while: for there were many coming and going, and they had no leisure so much as to eat.

32 And they departed into a desert place by ship privately.

33 And the people saw them departing, and many knew him, and ran afoot there out of all cities, and preceded them, and came together unto him.

34 And Yahshua, when he came out, saw many people, and was moved with compassion toward them, because they were as sheep not having a shepherd: and he began to teach them many things.

35 And when the day was now far spent, his disciples came unto him, and said, This is a desert place, and now the time *is* far passed:
36 Send them away, that they may go into the country round about, and into the villages, and buy themselves bread: for they have nothing to eat.
37 He answered and said unto them, Give you them to eat. And they said unto him, Shall we go and buy two hundred pennyworth of bread, and give them to eat?
38 He said to them, How many loaves have you? go and see. And when they knew, they said, Five, and two fishes.
39 And he commanded them to make all sit down by companies upon the green grass.
40 And they sat down in ranks, by hundreds, and by fifties.
41 And when he had taken the five loaves and the two fishes, he looked up to heaven, and blessed, and broke the loaves, and gave *them* to his disciples to set before them; and the two fishes divided he among them all.
42 And they did all eat, and were filled.
43 And they took up twelve baskets full of the fragments, and of the fishes.
44 And they that did eat of the loaves were about five thousand men.
45 ¶ And immediately he constrained his disciples to get into the ship, and to go to the other side before to Bethsaida, while he sent away the people.
46 And when he had sent them away, he departed into a mountain to pray.
47 And when evening had come, the ship was in the midst of the sea, and he alone on the land.
48 And he saw them toiling in rowing; for the wind was contrary to them: and about the fourth watch of the night he came to them, walking upon the sea, and would have passed by them.
49 But when they saw him walking upon the sea, they supposed it had been a spirit, and cried out:
50 For they all saw him, and were troubled. And immediately he talked with them, and said to them, Be of good cheer: it is I; be not afraid.
51 And he went up to them into the ship; and the wind ceased: and they were very amazed in themselves beyond measure, and wondered.
52 For they considered not *the miracle* of the loaves: for their heart was hardened.
53 And when they had passed over, they came into the land of Gennesaret, and drew to the shore.
54 And when they had come out of the ship, immediately they knew him,
55 And ran through that whole region round about, and began to carry about in beds those that were sick, where they heard he was.
56 And wherever he entered, into villages, or cities, or country, they laid the sick in the streets, and begged him that they might touch if it were but the border of his garment: and as many as touched him were made whole.

Mark 7

7:1 ¶ Then came together unto him the Pharisees, and certain of the scribes, which came from Jerusalem.
2 And when they saw some of his disciples eat bread with defiled, that is to say, with unwashed, hands, they found fault.
3 For the Pharisees, and all the Jews, unless they wash *their* hands often, eat not, holding the tradition of the elders.
4 And *when they come* from the market, unless they wash, they eat not. And many other things there be, which they have received to hold, *as the* washing of cups, and pots, brazen vessels, and of tables.
5 Then the Pharisees and scribes asked him, Why walk not your disciples according to the tradition of the elders, but eat bread with unwashed hands?
6 He answered and said unto them, Well has Isaiah prophesied of you hypocrites, as it is written, This people honors me with *their* lips, but their heart is far from me.
7 However in vain do they worship me, teaching *for* doctrines the commandments of men.
8 For laying aside the commandment of God, you hold the tradition of men, *as* the washing of pots and cups: and many other such like things you do.
9 And he said unto them, Full well you reject the commandment of God, that you may keep your own tradition.
10 For Moses said, Honor your father and your mother; and, Whoever curses father or mother, let him die the death:
11 But you say, If a man shall says to his father or mother, *It is* Corban, that is to say, a gift, by whatever you might be profited by me; *he shall be free.*
12 And you allow him no more to do anything for his father or his mother;
13 Making the word of God of no effect through your tradition, which you have delivered: and many such like things do you.
14 And when he had called all the people *unto him*, he said to them, Listen to me every one *of you*, and understand:
15 There is nothing from outside a man, that entering into him can defile him: but the things which come out of him, those are they that defile the man.
16 If any man has ears to hear, let him hear.
17 And when he had entered into the house from the people, his disciples asked him concerning the parable.
18 And he said unto them, Are you so without understanding also? Do you not perceive, that whatever thing from outside enters into the man, *it* cannot defile him;
19 Because it enters not into his heart, but into the belly, and goes out into the toilet, purging all food?
20 And he said, That which comes out of the man, that defiles the man.
21 For from within, out of the heart of men, proceed evil thoughts, adulteries, fornications, murders,

Mark 7

22 Thefts, covetousness, wickedness, deceit, lasciviousness, an evil eye, blasphemy, pride, foolishness:
23 All these evil things come from within, and defile the man.
24 ¶ And from there he arose, and went into the borders of Tyre and Sidon, and entered into a house, and would have no man know *it*: but he could not be hidden.
25 For a *certain* woman, whose young daughter had an unclean spirit, heard of him, and came and fell at his feet:
26 The woman was a Greek, a Syrophoenician by nation; and she begged him that he would cast forth the devil out of her daughter.
27 But Yahshua said to her, Let the children first be filled: for it is not good to take the children's bread, and to cast *it* to the dogs.
28 And she answered and said to him, Yes, Lord: yet the dogs under the table eat of the children's crumbs.
29 And he said to her, For this saying go your way; the devil is gone out of your daughter.
30 And when she had come to her house, she found the devil gone out, and her daughter laid upon the bed.
31 ¶ And again, departing from the coasts of Tyre and Sidon, he came to the sea of Galilee, through the midst of the coasts of Decapolis.
32 And they brought to him one that was deaf, and had an impediment in his speech; and they begged him to put his hand upon him.
33 And he took him aside from the multitude, and put his fingers into his ears, and he spat, and touched his tongue;
34 And looking up to heaven, he sighed, and said to him, Ephphatha, that is, Be opened.
35 And straightway his ears were opened, and the string of his tongue was loosed, and he spoke plainly.
36 And he charged them that they should tell no man: but the more he charged them, so much the more a great deal they published *it*;
37 And were beyond measure astonished, saying, He has done all things well: he makes both the deaf to hear, and the dumb to speak.

Mark 8

8:1 ¶ In those days the multitude being very great, and having nothing to eat, Yahshua called his disciples *to him*, and said to them,
2 I have compassion on the multitude, because they have now been with me three days, and have nothing to eat:
3 And if I send them away fasting to their own houses, they will faint by the way: for some of them came from far.
4 And his disciples answered him, From where can a man satisfy these *men* with bread here in the wilderness?
5 And he asked them, How many loaves have you? And they said, Seven.
6 And he commanded the people to sit down on the ground: and he took the seven loaves, and gave thanks, and broke, and gave to his disciples to set before *them*; and they did set *them* before the people.
7 And they had a few small fishes: and he blessed, and commanded to set them also before *them*.
8 So they did eat, and were filled: and they took up of the broken *food* that was left seven baskets.
9 And they that had eaten were about four thousand: and he sent them away.
10 ¶ And immediately he entered into a ship with his disciples, and came into the parts of Dalmanutha.
11 And the Pharisees came forth, and began to question with him, seeking of him a sign from heaven, tempting him.
12 And he sighed deeply in his spirit, and said, Why does this generation seek after a sign? truly I say to you, There shall no sign be given to this generation.
13 And he left them, and entering into the ship again departed to the other side.
14 Now *the disciples* had forgotten to take bread, neither had they in the ship with them more than one loaf.
15 And he charged them, saying, Take heed, beware of the leaven of the Pharisees, and *of* the leaven of Herod.
16 And they reasoned among themselves, saying, *It is* because we have no bread.
17 And when Yahshua knew *it*, he said to them, Why reason you, because you have no bread? perceive you not yet, neither understand? have you your heart yet hardened?
18 Having eyes, see you not? and having ears, hear you not? and do you not remember?
19 When I broke the five loaves among five thousand, how many baskets full of fragments took you up? They said to him, Twelve.
20 And when the seven among four thousand, how many baskets full of fragments took you up? And they said, Seven.
21 And he said to them, How is it that you do not understand?
22 ¶ And he came to Bethsaida; and they brought a blind man to him, and begged him to touch him.
23 And he took the blind man by the hand, and led him out of the town; and when he had spit on his eyes, and put his hands upon him, he asked him if he saw anything.
24 And he looked up, and said, I see men as trees, walking.
25 After that he put *his* hands again upon his eyes, and made him look up: and he was restored, and saw every man clearly.
26 And he sent him away to his house, saying, Neither go into the town, nor tell *it* to any in the town.
27 ¶ And Yahshua went out, and his disciples, into the towns of Caesarea Philippi: and by the way he asked his disciples, saying to them, Whom do men say that I am?
28 And they answered, John the Baptist: but some *say*, Elijah; and others, One of the prophets.
29 And he said to them, But whom say you that I am? And Peter answered and said to him, You are the Messiah.
30 And he charged them that they should tell no man of him.
31 And he began to teach them, that the Son of man must suffer many things, and be rejected by the elders, and *of* the chief priests, and scribes, and be killed, and after three days rise again.

32 And he spoke that saying openly. And Peter took him, and began to rebuke him.

33 But when he had turned about and looked on his disciples, he rebuked Peter, saying, Get you behind me, Satan: for you mind not the things that are of God, but the things that are of men.

34 And when he had called the people *to him* with his disciples also, he said to them, Whoever will come after me, let him deny himself, and take up his cross, and follow me.

35 For whoever will save his life shall lose it; but whoever shall lose his life for my sake and the gospel's, the same shall save it.

36 For what shall it profit a man, if he shall gain the whole world, and lose his own soul?

37 Or what shall a man give in exchange for his soul?

38 Whoever therefore shall be ashamed of me and of my words in this adulterous and sinful generation; of him also shall the Son of man be ashamed, when he comes in the glory of his Father with the holy angels.

Mark 9

9:1 ¶ And he said to them, Truly I say to you, That there are some of them that stand here, which shall not taste of death, till they have seen the kingdom of God come with power.

2 And after six days Yahshua took *with him* Peter, and James, and John, and led them up into a high mountain apart by themselves: and he was transfigured before them.

3 And his clothes became shining, exceedingly white as snow; such as no fuller on earth can whiten them.

4 And there appeared to them Elijah with Moses: and they were talking with Yahshua.

5 And Peter answered and said to Yahshua, Master, it is good for us to be here: and let us make three tabernacles; one for you, and one for Moses, and one for Elijah.

6 For he knew not what to say; for they were very afraid.

7 And there was a cloud that overshadowed them: and a voice came out of the cloud, saying, This is my beloved Son: hear him.

8 And suddenly, when they had looked round about, they saw no man any more, except Yahshua only with themselves.

9 And as they came down from the mountain, he charged them that they should tell no man what things they had seen, till the Son of man was risen from the dead.

10 And they kept that saying with themselves, questioning one with another what the rising from the dead should mean.

11 And they asked him, saying, Why say the scribes that Elijah must first come?

12 And he answered and told them, Elijah truly comes first, and restores all things; and how it is written of the Son of man, that he must suffer many things, and be treated as nothing.

13 But I say to you, That Elijah has indeed come, and they have done to him whatever they desired, as it is written of him.

14 ¶ And when he came to *his* disciples, he saw a great multitude about them, and the scribes questioning with them.

15 And immediately all the people, when they saw him, were greatly amazed, and running to *him* saluted him.

16 And he asked the scribes, What question you with them?

17 And one of the multitude answered and said, Master, I have brought to you my son, which has a dumb spirit;

18 And wherever he takes him, he tears him: and he foams, and gnashes with his teeth, and pines away: and I spoke to your disciples that they should cast him out; and they could not.

19 He answered him, and said, O faithless generation, how long shall I be with you? how long shall I bear with you? bring him to me.

20 And they brought him to him: and when he saw him, immediately the spirit convulsed him; and he fell on the ground, and wallowed foaming.   21 And he asked his father, How long is it ago since this came to him? And he said, From a child.

22 And oftentimes it has cast him into the fire, and into the waters, to destroy him: but if you can do any thing, have compassion on us, and help us.

23 Yahshua said to him, If you can believe, all things *are* possible to him that believes.

24 And immediately the father of the child cried out, and said with tears, Lord, I believe; help you my unbelief.

25 When Yahshua saw that the people came running together, he rebuked the foul spirit, saying to him, *You* dumb and deaf spirit, I charge you, come out of him, and enter no more into him.

26 And *the spirit* cried, and tore him greatly, and came out of him: and he was as one dead; insomuch that many said, He is dead.

27 But Yahshua took him by the hand, and lifted him up; and he arose.

28 And when he had come into the house, his disciples asked him privately, Why could not we cast him out?

29 And he said to them, This kind can come forth by nothing, but by prayer and fasting.

30 ¶ And they departed therefrom, and passed through Galilee; and he would not that any man should know *it*.

31 For he taught his disciples, and said to them, The Son of man is delivered into the hands of men, and they shall kill him; and after that he is killed, he shall rise the third day.

32 But they understood not that saying, and were afraid to ask him.

33 And he came to Capernaum: and being in the house he asked them, What was it that you disputed among yourselves by the way?

34 But they held their peace: for by the way they had disputed among themselves, who *should be* the greatest.

35 And he sat down, and called the twelve, and said to them, If any man desires to be first, *the same* shall be last of all, and servant of all.

Mark 9

36 And he took a child, and set him in the midst of them: and when he had taken him in his arms, he said to them,
37 Whoever shall receive one of such children in my name, receives me: and whoever shall receive me, receives not me, but him that sent me.
38 And John answered him, saying, Master, we saw one casting out devils in your name, and he follows not us: and we forbade him, because he follows not us.
39 But Yahshua said, Forbid him not: for there is no man which shall do a miracle in my name, that can lightly speak evil of me.
40 For he that is not against us is on our part.
41 ¶ For whoever shall give you a cup of water to drink in my name, because you belong to the Messiah, truly I say to you, he shall not lose his reward.
42 And whoever shall offend one of *these* little ones that believes in me, it is better for him that a millstone was hung about his neck, and he was cast into the sea.
43 And if your hand offends you, cut it off: it is better for you to enter into life maimed, than having two hands to go into hell, into the fire that never shall be quenched:
44 Where their worm dies not, and the fire is not quenched.
45 And if your foot offends you, cut it off: it is better for you to enter lame into life, than having two feet to be cast into hell, into the fire that never shall be quenched:
46 Where their worm dies not, and the fire is not quenched.
47 And if your eye offends you, pluck it out: it is better for you to enter into the kingdom of God with one eye, than having two eyes to be cast into hell fire:
48 Where their worm dies not, and the fire is not quenched.
49 For every one shall be salted with fire, and every sacrifice shall be salted with salt.
50 Salt *is* good: but if the salt has lost its saltiness, with what will you season it? Have salt in yourselves, and have peace one with another.

Mark 10

10:1 ¶ And he arose from there, and came into the coasts of Judaea by the farther side of *the* Jordan: and the people assembled to him again; and, as he was inclined, he taught them again.
2 And the Pharisees came to him, and asked him, Is it lawful for a man to put away *his* wife? tempting him.
3 And he answered and said to them, What did Moses command you?
4 And they said, Moses allowed *a man* to write a bill of divorce, and to put *her* away.
5 And Yahshua answered and said to them, For the hardness of your heart he wrote you this precept.
6 But from the beginning of the creation God made them male and female.
7 For this cause shall a man leave his father and mother, and be joined to his wife;
8 And they two shall be one flesh: so then they are no more two, but one flesh.
9 What therefore God has joined together, let not man put apart.
10 And in the house his disciples asked him again of the same *matter*.
11 And he said to them, Whoever shall put away his wife, and marry another, commits adultery against her.
12 And if a woman shall put away her husband, and be married to another, she commits adultery.
13 ¶ And they brought young children to him, that he should touch them: and *his* disciples rebuked those that brought *them*.
14 But when Yahshua saw *it*, he was very displeased, and said to them, Allow the little children to come to me, and forbid them not: for of such is the kingdom of God.
15 Truly I say to you, Whoever shall not receive the kingdom of God as a little child, he shall not enter therein.
16 And he took them up in his arms, put *his* hands upon them, and blessed them.
17 ¶ And when he had gone forth into the way, there came one running, and kneeled to him, and asked him, Good Master, what shall I do that I may inherit eternal life?
18 And Yahshua said to him, Why call you me good? *there is* none good but one, *that is*, God.
19 You know the commandments, Do not commit adultery, Do not kill, Do not steal, Do not bear false witness, Defraud not, Honor your father and mother.
20 And he answered and said to him, Master, all these have I observed from my youth.
21 Then Yahshua beholding him loved him, and said to him, One thing you lack: go your way, sell whatever you have, and give to the poor, and you shall have treasure in heaven: and come, take up the cross, and follow me.
22 And he was sad at that saying, and went away grieved: for he had great possessions.
23 And Yahshua looked round about, and said to his disciples, How hardly shall they that have riches enter into the kingdom of God!
24 And the disciples were astonished at his words. But Yahshua answered again, and said to them, Children, how hard is it for them that trust in riches to enter into the kingdom of God!
25 It is easier for a camel to go through the eye of a needle, than for a rich man to enter into the kingdom of God.
26 And they were astonished out of measure, saying among themselves, Who then can be saved?
27 And Yahshua looking upon them said, With men *it is* impossible, but not with God: for with God all things are possible.
28 Then Peter began to say to him, Lo, we have left all, and have followed you.
29 And Yahshua answered and said, Truly I say to you, There is no man that has left house, or brothers, or sisters, or father, or mother, or wife, or children, or lands, for my sake, and the gospel's,
30 But he shall receive a hundred times now in this time, houses, and brothers, and sisters, and mothers, and children, and lands, with persecutions; and in the world to come eternal life.
31 But many *that are* first shall be last; and the last first.

32 ¶ And they were in the way going up to Jerusalem; and Yahshua went before them: and they were amazed; and as they followed, they were afraid. And he took again the twelve, and began to tell them what things should happen to him,

33 *Saying*, Behold, we go up to Jerusalem; and the Son of man shall be delivered to the chief priests, and to the scribes; and they shall condemn him to death, and shall deliver him to the Gentiles:

34 And they shall mock him, and shall scourge him, and shall spit upon him, and shall kill him: and the third day he shall rise again.

35 And James and John, the sons of Zebedee, came to him, saying, Master, we would that you should do for us whatever we shall desire.

36 And he said to them, What would you that I should do for you?

37 They said to him, Grant to us that we may sit, one on your right hand, and the other on your left hand, in your glory.

38 But Yahshua said to them, You know not what you ask: can you drink of the cup that I drink of? and be baptized with the baptism that I am baptized with?

39 And they said to him, We can. And Yahshua said to them, You shall indeed drink of the cup that I drink of; and with the baptism that I am baptized therewith shall you be baptized:

40 But to sit on my right hand and on my left hand is not mine to give; but *it shall be given to them* for whom it is prepared.

41 And when the ten heard *it*, they began to be very displeased with James and John.

42 But Yahshua called them *to him*, and said to them, You know that they which are accounted to rule over the Gentiles exercise lordship over them; and their great ones exercise authority upon them.

43 But so shall it not be among you: but whoever will be great among you, shall be your minister:

44 And whoever of you will be the most chief, shall be servant of all.

45 For even the Son of man came not to be ministered to, but to minister, and to give his life a ransom for many.

46 ¶ And they came to Jericho: and as he went out of Jericho with his disciples and a great number of people, blind Bartimaeus, the son of Timaeus, sat by the highway side begging.

47 And when he heard that it was Yahshua of Nazareth, he began to cry out, and say, Yahshua, *you* Son of David, have mercy on me.

48 And many charged him that he should hold his peace: but he cried the more a great deal, *You* Son of David, have mercy on me.

49 And Yahshua stood still, and commanded him to be called. And they called the blind man, saying to him, Be of good comfort, rise; he calls you.

50 And he, casting away his garment, rose, and came to Yahshua.

51 And Yahshua answered and said to him, What will you that I should do to you? The blind man said to him, Lord, that I might receive my sight.

52 And Yahshua said to him, Go your way; your faith has made you whole. And immediately he received his sight, and followed Yahshua in the way.

Mark 11

11:1 ¶ And when they came near to Jerusalem, to Bethphage and Bethany, at the mount of Olives, he sent forth two of his disciples,

2 And said to them, Go your way into the village over against you: and as soon as you have entered into it, you shall find a colt tied, whereon no man sat; loose him, and bring *him*.

3 And if any man says to you, Why do you this? say you that the Lord has need of him; and immediately he will send him here.

4 And they went their way, and found the colt tied by the door outside in a place where two ways met; and they loosed him.

5 And certain of them that stood there said to them, What do you, loosing the colt?

6 And they said to them even as Yahshua had commanded: and they let them go.

7 And they brought the colt to Yahshua, and cast their garments on him; and he sat upon him.

8 And many spread their garments in the way: and others cut down branches off the trees, and strewed *them* in the way.

9 And they that went before, and they that followed, cried, saying, Hosanna; Blessed *is* he that comes in the name of the Lord *Yahweh*:

10 Blessed *be* the kingdom of our father David, that comes in the name of the Lord *Yahweh*: Hosanna in the highest.

11 And Yahshua entered into Jerusalem, and into the temple: and when he had looked round about upon all things, and now the evening had come, he went out to Bethany with the twelve.

12 ¶ And on the next day, when they had come from Bethany, he was hungry:

13 And seeing a fig tree afar off having leaves, he came, if then he might find any thing thereon: and when he came to it, he found nothing but leaves; for the time of figs was not *yet*.

14 And Yahshua answered and said to it, No man eats fruit of you hereafter forever. And his disciples heard *it*.

15 And they come to Jerusalem: and Yahshua went into the temple, and began to cast out them that sold and bought in the temple, and overthrew the tables of the moneychangers, and the seats of them that sold doves;

16 And would not permit that any man should carry *any* vessel through the temple.

17 And he taught, saying to them, Is it not written, My house shall be called of all nations the house of prayer? but you have made it a den of thieves.

Mark 11

18 And the scribes and chief priests heard *it*, and sought how they might destroy him: for they feared him, because all the people were astonished at his doctrine.

19 And when evening had come, he went out of the city.

20 And in the morning, as they passed by, they saw the fig tree dried up from the roots.

21 And Peter calling to remembrance said to him, Master, behold, the fig tree which you cursed is withered away.

22 And Yahshua answering said to them, Have faith in God.

23 For truly I say to you, That whoever shall say to this mountain, Be you removed, and be you cast into the sea; and shall not doubt in his heart, but shall believe that those things which he said shall come to pass; he shall have whatever he says.

24 Therefore I say to you, Whatever things you desire, when you pray, believe that you receive *them*, and you shall have *them*.

25 And when you stand praying, forgive, if you have anything against anyone: that your Father also which is in heaven may forgive you your trespasses.

26 But if you do not forgive, neither will your Father which is in heaven forgive your trespasses.

27 ¶ And they came again to Jerusalem: and as he was walking in the temple, there came to him the chief priests, and the scribes, and the elders,

28 And said to him, By what authority do you these things? and who gave you this authority to do these things?

29 And Yahshua answered and said to them, I will also ask of you one question, and answer me, and I will tell you by what authority I do these things.

30 The baptism of John, was *it* from heaven, or of men? answer me.

31 And they reasoned with themselves, saying, If we shall say, From heaven; he will say, Why then did you not believe him?

32 But if we shall say, Of men; they feared the people: for all *men* counted John, that he was a prophet indeed.

33 And they answered and said to Yahshua, We cannot tell. And Yahshua answering said to them, Neither do I tell you by what authority I do these things.

Mark 12

12:1 ¶ And he began to speak to them by parables. A *certain* man planted a vineyard, and set a hedge about *it*, and dug *a place for* the wine vat, and built a tower, and let it out to husbandmen, and went into a far country.

2 And at the season he sent to the husbandmen a servant, that he might receive from the managers of the fruit of the vineyard.

3 And they caught *him*, and beat him, and sent *him* away empty.

4 And again he sent to them another servant; and at him they cast stones, and wounded *him* in the head, and sent *him* away shamefully handled.

5 And again he sent another; and him they killed, and many others; beating some, and killing some.

6 Having yet therefore one son, his wellbeloved, he sent him also last to them, saying, They will reverence my son.

7 But those husbandmen said among themselves, This is the heir; come, let us kill him, and the inheritance shall be ours.

8 And they took him, and killed *him*, and cast *him* out of the vineyard.

9 What shall therefore the lord of the vineyard do? he will come and destroy the husbandmen, and will give the vineyard to others.

10 And have you not read this scripture; The stone which the builders rejected has become the head of the corner:

11 This was the Lord's [*Yahweh's*] doing, and it is marvelous in our eyes?

12 And they sought to lay hold on him, but feared the people: for they knew that he had spoken the parable against them: and they left him, and went their way.

13 ¶ And they sent to him certain of the Pharisees and of the Herodians, to catch him in *his* words.

14 And when they had come, they said to him, Master, we know that you are true, and care for no man: for you regard not the person of men, but teach the way of God in truth: Is it lawful to give tribute to Caesar, or not?

15 Shall we give, or shall we not give? But he, knowing their hypocrisy, said to them, Why tempt you me? bring me a penny, that I may see *it*.

16 And they brought *it*. And he said to them, Whose *is* this image and superscription? And they said to him, Caesar's.

17 And Yahshua answering said to them, Render to Caesar the things that are Caesar's, and to God the things that are God's. And they marveled at him.

18 ¶ Then came to him the Sadducees, which say there is no resurrection; and they asked him, saying,

19 Master, Moses wrote to us, If a man's brother dies, and leaves *his* wife *behind him*, and leaves no children, that his brother should take his wife, and raise up seed to his brother.

20 Now there were seven brothers: and the first took a wife, and dying left no seed.

21 And the second took her, and died, neither left he any seed: and the third likewise.

22 And the seven had her, and left no seed: last of all the woman died also.

23 In the resurrection therefore, when they shall rise, whose wife shall she be of them? for the seven had her to wife.

24 And Yahshua answering said to them, Do you not therefore err, because you know not the scriptures, neither the power of God?

25 For when they shall rise from the dead, they neither marry, nor are given in marriage; but are as the angels which are in heaven.

26 And as touching the dead, that they rise: have you not read in the book of Moses, how in the bush God spoke to him, saying, I *am* the God of Abraham, and the God of Isaac, and the God of Jacob?

27 He is not the God of the dead, but the God of the living: you therefore do greatly err.

28 ¶ And one of the scribes came, and having heard them reasoning together, and perceiving that he had answered them well, asked him, Which is the first commandment of all?

29 And Yahshua answered him, The first of all the commandments *is*, Hear, O Israel; The Lord *Yahweh* our God is one Lord *Yahweh*:

30 And you shall love the Lord *Yahweh* your God with all your heart, and with all your soul, and with all your mind, and with all your strength: this *is* the first commandment.

31 And the second *is* like, *namely* this, You shall love your neighbor as yourself. There is no other commandment greater than these.

32 And the scribe said to him, Well, Master, you have said the truth: for there is one God; and there is none other but he:

33 And to love him with all the heart, and with all the understanding, and with all the soul, and with all the strength, and to love *his* neighbor as himself, is more than all whole burnt offerings and sacrifices.

34 And when Yahshua saw that he answered discreetly, he said to him, You are not far from the kingdom of God. And no man after that dared ask him *any question*.

35 ¶ And Yahshua answered and said, while he taught in the temple, How say the scribes that the Messiah is the Son of David?

36 For David himself said by the Holy Ghost, The LORD *Yahweh* said to my Lord, Sit you on my right hand, till I make your enemies your footstool.

37 David therefore himself calls him Lord; and *from* where is he *then* his son? And the common people heard him gladly.

38 And he said to them in his doctrine, Beware of the scribes, which love to go in long clothing, and *love* salutations in the marketplaces,

39 And the chief seats in the synagogues, and the uppermost rooms at feasts:

40 Which devour widows' houses, and for a pretense make long prayers: these shall receive greater damnation.

41 ¶ And Yahshua sat over against the treasury, and saw how the people cast money into the treasury: and many that were rich cast in much.

42 And there came a certain poor widow, and she threw in two mites, which make a farthing.

43 And he called *to him* his disciples, and said to them, Truly I say to you, That this poor widow has cast more in, than all they which have cast into the treasury:

44 For all *they* did cast in of their abundance; but she of her want did cast in all that she had, *even* all her living.

Mark 13

13:1 ¶ And as he went out of the temple, one of his disciples said to him, Master, see what manner of stones and what buildings *are here*!

2 And Yahshua answering said to him, See you these great buildings? there shall not be left one stone upon another, that shall not be thrown down.

3 And as he sat upon the mount of Olives over against the temple, Peter and James and John and Andrew asked him privately,

4 Tell us, when shall these things be? and what *shall be* the sign when all these things shall be fulfilled?

5 ¶ And Yahshua answering them began to say, Take heed lest any *man* deceive you:

6 For many shall come in my name, saying, I am *the Messiah*; and shall deceive many.

7 And when you shall hear of wars and rumors of wars, be you not troubled: for *such things* must need be; but the end *shall* not *be* yet.

8 For nation shall rise against nation, and kingdom against kingdom: and there shall be earthquakes in various places, and there shall be famines and troubles: these *are* the beginnings of sorrows.

9 But take heed to yourselves: for they shall deliver you up to councils; and in the synagogues you shall be beaten: and you shall be brought before rulers and kings for my sake, for a testimony against them.

10 And the gospel must first be published among all nations.

11 But when they shall lead *you*, and deliver you up, take no thought beforehand what you shall speak, neither do you premeditate: but whatever shall be given you in that hour, that speak you: for it is not you that speak, but the Holy Ghost.

12 Now the brother shall betray the brother to death, and the father the son; and children shall rise up against *their* parents, and shall cause them to be put to death.

13 And you shall be hated by all *men* for my name's sake: but he that shall endure to the end, the same shall be saved.

14 ¶ But when you shall see the abomination of desolation, spoken of by Daniel the prophet, standing where it ought not, (let him that reads understand,) then let them that are in Judaea flee to the mountains:

15 And let him that is on the housetop not go down into the house, neither enter *therein*, to take any thing out of his house:

16 And let him that is in the field not turn back again for to take up his garment.

17 But woe to them that are with child, and to them that give suck in those days!

18 And pray you that your flight is not in the winter.

19 For *in* those days shall be affliction, such as was not from the beginning of the creation which God created to this time, neither shall be.

20 And except that the Lord had shortened those days, no flesh should be saved: but for the elect's sake, whom he has chosen, he has shortened the days.

21 And then if any man shall say to you, See, here *is* the Messiah; or, see, *he is* there; believe *him* not:

22 For false Messiahs and false prophets shall rise, and shall show signs and wonders, to seduce, if *it were* possible, even the elect.

Mark 13

23 But take you heed: behold, I have foretold you all things.
24 ¶ But in those days, after that tribulation, the sun shall be darkened, and the moon shall not give her light,
25 And the stars of heaven shall fall, and the powers that are in heaven shall be shaken.
26 And then shall they see the Son of man coming in the clouds with great power and glory.
27 And then shall he send his angels, and shall gather together his elect from the four winds, from the utmost part of the earth to the utmost part of heaven.
28 ¶ Now learn a parable of the fig tree; When her branch is yet tender, and puts forth leaves, you know that summer is near:
29 So you in like manner, when you shall see these things come to pass, know that it is near, *even* at the doors.
30 Truly I say to you, that this generation shall not pass, till all these things are done.
31 Heaven and earth shall pass away: but my words shall not pass away.
32 But of that day and *that* hour knows no man, no, not the angels which are in heaven, neither the Son, but the Father.
33 Take you heed, watch and pray: for you know not when the time is.
34 *For the Son of man is* as a man taking a far journey, who left his house, and gave authority to his servants, and to every man his work, and commanded the porter to watch.
35 Watch you therefore: for you know not when the master of the house comes, at evening, or at midnight, or at the cock-crowing, or in the morning:
36 Lest coming suddenly he finds you sleeping.
37 And what I say to you I say to all, Watch.

Mark 14

14:1 ¶ After two days was *the feast of* the passover, and of unleavened bread: and the chief priests and the scribes sought how they might take him by craft, and put *him* to death.
2 But they said, Not on the feast *day*, lest there be an uproar of the people.
3 And being in Bethany in the house of Simon the leper, as he sat at *a* meal, there came a woman having an alabaster box of ointment of spikenard very precious; and she broke the box, and poured *it* on his head.
4 And there were some that had indignation within themselves, and said, Why was this waste of the ointment made?
5 For it might have been sold for more than three hundred pence, and have been given to the poor. And they murmured against her.
6 And Yahshua said, Let her alone; why trouble you her? she has worked a good work on me.
7 For you have the poor with you always, and whenever you will you may do them good: but me you have not always.
8 She has done what she could: she has come beforehand to anoint my body for the burying.
9 Truly I say to you, Wherever this gospel shall be preached throughout the whole world, *this* also that she has done shall be spoken of for a memorial of her.
10 And Judas Iscariot, one of the twelve, went to the chief priests, to betray him to them.
11 And when they heard *it*, they were glad, and promised to give him money. And he sought how he might conveniently betray him.
12 ¶ And the first day of unleavened bread, when they killed the passover, his disciples said to him, Where will you that we go and prepare that you may eat the passover?
13 And he sent forth two of his disciples, and said to them, Go you into the city, and there shall meet you a man bearing a pitcher of water: follow him.
14 And wherever he shall go in, say you to the master of the house, The Master says, Where is the guest room, where I shall eat the passover with my disciples?
15 And he will show you a large upper room furnished *and* prepared: there make ready for us.
16 And his disciples went forth, and came into the city, and found as he had said to them: and they made ready the passover.
17 And in the evening he came with the twelve.
18 And as they sat and did eat, Yahshua said, Truly I say to you, One of you which eats with me shall betray me.
19 And they began to be sorrowful, and to say to him one by one, *Is* it I? and another *said, Is* it I?
20 And he answered and said to them, *It is* one of the twelve, that dips with me in the dish.
21 The Son of man indeed goes, as it is written of him: but woe to that man by whom the Son of man is betrayed! good were it for that man if he had never been born.
22 And as they did eat, Yahshua took bread, and blessed, and broke *it*, and gave to them, and said, Take, eat: this is my body.
23 And he took the cup, and when he had given thanks, he gave *it* to them: and they all drank of it.
24 And he said to them, This is my blood of the new testament, which is shed for many.
25 Truly I say to you, I will drink no more of the fruit of the vine, until that day that I drink it new in the kingdom of God.
26 And when they had sung a hymn, they went out into the mount of Olives.
27 And Yahshua said to them, All you shall be offended because of me this night: for it is written, I will smite the shepherd, and the sheep shall be scattered.
28 But after I am risen, I will go before you into Galilee.
29 But Peter said to him, Although all shall be offended, yet *will* not I.
30 And Yahshua said to him, Truly I say to you, That this day, *even* in this night, before the cock crows twice, you shall deny me three times.
31 But he spoke the more vehemently, If I should die with you, I will not deny you in any way. Likewise also said they all.

32 ¶ And they came to a place which was named Gethsemane: and he said to his disciples, Sit you here, while I shall pray.
33 And he took with him Peter and James and John, and began to be very amazed, and to be very heavy;
34 And said to them, My soul is exceedingly sorrowful unto death: tarry you here, and watch.
35 And he went forward a little, and fell on the ground, and prayed that, if it were possible, the hour might pass from him.
36 And he said, Abba, Father, all things *are* possible to you; take away this cup from me: nevertheless not what I will, but what you will.
37 And he came, and found them sleeping, and said to Peter, Simon, sleep you? could not you watch one hour?
38 Watch you and pray, lest you enter into temptation. The spirit truly *is* ready, but the flesh *is* weak.
39 And again he went away, and prayed, and spoke the same words.
40 And when he returned, he found them asleep again, (for their eyes were heavy,) neither knew they what to answer him.
41 And he came the third time, and said to them, Sleep on now, and take *your* rest: it is enough, the hour has come; behold, the Son of man is betrayed into the hands of sinners.
42 Rise up, let us go; see, he that betrays me is at hand.
43 ¶ And immediately, while he yet spoke, came Judas, one of the twelve, and with him a great multitude with swords and staves, from the chief priests and the scribes and the elders.
44 And he that betrayed him had given them a token, saying, Whomever I shall kiss, that same is he; take him, and lead *him* away safely.
45 And as soon as he had come, he went immediately to him, and said, Master, master; and kissed him.
46 And they laid their hands on him, and took him.
47 And one of them that stood by drew a sword, and smote a servant of the high priest, and cut off his ear.
48 And Yahshua answered and said to them, Have you come out, as against a thief, with swords and *with* staves to take me?
49 I was daily with you in the temple teaching, and you took me not: but the scriptures must be fulfilled.
50 And they all forsook him, and fled.
51 And there followed him a certain young man, having a linen cloth cast about *his* naked *body*; and the young men laid hold on him:
52 And he left the linen cloth, and fled from them naked.
53 ¶ And they led Yahshua away to the high priest: and with him were assembled all the chief priests and the elders and the scribes.
54 And Peter followed him afar off, even into the palace of the high priest: and he sat with the servants, and warmed himself at the fire.
55 And the chief priests and all the council sought for witness against Yahshua to put him to death; and found none.
56 For many bore false witness against him, but their witness agreed not together.

57 And there arose certain *men*, and *they* bore false witness against him, saying,
58 We heard him say, I will destroy this temple that is made with hands, and within three days I will build another made without hands.
59 But neither so did their witness agree together.
60 And the high priest stood up in the midst, and asked Yahshua, saying, Answer you nothing? what *is it which* these witness against you?
61 But he held his peace, and answered nothing. Again the high priest asked him, and said to him, Are you the Messiah, the Son of the Blessed?
62 And Yahshua said, I am: and you shall see the Son of man sitting on the right hand of power, and coming in the clouds of heaven.
63 Then the high priest tore his clothes, and said, What need we any further witnesses?
64 You have heard the blasphemy: what think you? And they all condemned him to be guilty of death.
65 And some began to spit on him, and to cover his face, and to buffet him, and to say to him, Prophesy: and the servants did strike him with the palms of their hands.
66 ¶ And as Peter was beneath in the palace, there came one of the maids of the high priest:
67 And when she saw Peter warming himself, she looked upon him, and said, And you also were with Yahshua of Nazareth.
68 But he denied, saying, I know not, neither understand I what you say. And he went out into the porch; and the cock crowed.
69 And a maid saw him again, and began to say to them that stood by, This is *one* of them.
70 And he denied it again. And a little after, they that stood by said again to Peter, Surely you are *one* of them: for you are a Galilaean, and your speech agrees *thereto*.
71 But he began to curse and to swear, *saying*, I know not this man of whom you speak.
72 And the second time the cock crowed. And Peter called to mind the words that Yahshua said to him, Before the cock crows twice, you shall deny me three times. And when he thought thereon, he wept.

Mark 15

15:1 ¶ And immediately in the morning the chief priests held a consultation with the elders and scribes and the whole council, and bound Yahshua, and carried *him* away, and delivered *him* to Pilate.
2 And Pilate asked him, Are you the King of the Jews? And he answering said to him, You say *it*.
3 And the chief priests accused him of many things: but he answered nothing.
4 And Pilate asked him again, saying, Answer you nothing? behold how many things they witness against you.
5 But Yahshua yet answered nothing; so that Pilate marveled.
6 Now at *that* feast he released to them one prisoner, whomever they desired.

Mark 15

7 And there was *one* named Barabbas, *which lay* bound with them that had made insurrection with him, who had committed murder in the insurrection.
8 And the multitude crying aloud began to desire *him to do* as he had always done unto them.
9 But Pilate answered them, saying, Will you that I release to you the King of the Jews?
10 For he knew that the chief priests had delivered him for envy.
11 But the chief priests moved the people, that he should rather release Barabbas to them.
12 And Pilate answered and said again to them, What will you then that I shall do *to him* whom you call the King of the Jews?
13 And they cried out again, Crucify him.
14 Then Pilate said to them, Why, what evil has he done? And they cried out the more exceedingly, Crucify him.
15 ¶ And *so* Pilate, willing to content the people, released Barabbas to them, and delivered Yahshua, when he had scourged *him*, to be crucified.
16 And the soldiers led him away into the hall, called Praetorium; and they called together the whole band.
17 And they clothed him with purple, and platted a crown of thorns, and put it upon his *head*,
18 And began to salute him, Hail, King of the Jews!
19 And they smote him on the head with a reed, and did spit upon him, and bowing *their* knees worshipped him.
20 And when they had mocked him, they took off the purple from him, and put his own clothes on him, and led him out to crucify him.
21 And they compelled one Simon a Cyrenian, who passed by, coming out of the country, the father of Alexander and Rufus, to bear his cross.
22 ¶ And they brought him to the place Golgotha, which is, being interpreted, The place of a skull.
23 And they gave him to drink wine mingled with myrrh: but he received *it* not.
24 And when they had crucified him, they parted his garments, casting lots upon them, what every man should take.
25 And it was the third hour, and they crucified him.
26 And the superscription of his accusation was written over, THE KING OF THE JEWS.
27 And with him they crucified two thieves; the one on his right hand, and the other on his left.
28 And the scripture was fulfilled, which says, And he was numbered with the transgressors.
29 And they that passed by railed on him, wagging their heads, and saying, Ah, you that destroy the temple, and build *it* in three days,
30 Save yourself, and come down from the cross.
31 Likewise also the chief priests mocking said among themselves with the scribes, He saved others; himself he cannot save.
32 Let the Messiah the King of Israel descend now from the cross, that we may see and believe. And they that were crucified with him reviled him.
33 ¶ And when the sixth hour had come, there was darkness over the whole land until the ninth hour.
34 And at the ninth hour Yahshua cried with a loud voice, saying, Eloi, Eloi, lama sabachthani? which is, being interpreted, My God, my God, why have you forsaken me?
35 And some of them that stood by, when they heard *it*, said, Behold, he calls Elijah.
36 And one ran and filled a sponge full of vinegar, and put *it* on a reed, and gave him to drink, saying, Let alone; let us see whether Elijah will come to take him down.
37 And Yahshua cried with a loud voice, and gave up the ghost.
38 And the veil of the temple was divided in two from the top to the bottom.
39 And when the centurion, which stood over against him, saw that he so cried out, and gave up the ghost, he said, Truly this man was the Son of God.
40 There were also women looking on afar off: among whom was Mary Magdalene, and Mary the mother of James the less and of Joses, and Salome;
41 (Who also, when he was in Galilee, followed him, and ministered to him;) and many other women which came up with him to Jerusalem.
42 ¶ And now when the evening had come, because it was the preparation, that is, the day before the sabbath,
43 Joseph of Arimathaea, an honorable counselor, which also waited for the kingdom of God, came, and went in boldly to Pilate, and craved the body of Yahshua.
44 And Pilate wondered if he were already dead: and calling *to him* the centurion, he asked him whether he had been any while dead.
45 And when he knew *it* of the centurion, he gave the body to Joseph.
46 And he bought fine linen, and took him down, and wrapped him in the linen, and laid him in a sepulcher which was hewn out of a rock, and rolled a stone to the door of the sepulcher.
47 And Mary Magdalene and Mary *the mother* of Joses saw where he was laid.

Mark 16

16:1 ¶ And when the sabbath was past, Mary Magdalene, and Mary the *mother* of James, and Salome, had bought sweet spices, that they might come and anoint him.
2 And very early in the morning the first *day* of the week, they came to the sepulcher at the rising of the sun.
3 And they said among themselves, Who shall roll us away the stone from the door of the sepulcher?
4 And when they looked, they saw that the stone was rolled away: for it was very great.
5 And entering into the sepulcher, they saw a young man sitting on the right side, clothed in a long white garment; and they were afraid.
6 And he said to them, Be not afraid: You seek Yahshua of Nazareth, which was crucified: he is risen; he is not here: behold the place where they laid him.

7 But go your way, tell his disciples and Peter that he goes before you into Galilee: there shall you see him, as he said to you.

8 And they went out quickly, and fled from the sepulcher; for they trembled and were amazed: neither said they any thing to any *man*; for they were afraid.

9 ¶ Now when Yahshua was risen early the first *day* of the week, he appeared first to Mary Magdalene, out of whom he had cast seven devils.

10 *And* she went and told them that had been with him, as they mourned and wept.

11 And they, when they had heard that he was alive, and had been seen of her, believed not.

12 After that he appeared in another form to two of them, as they walked, and went into the country.

13 And they went and told *it* to the residue: neither believed they them.

14 ¶ Afterward he appeared to the eleven as they sat at the table, and upbraided them with their unbelief and hardness of heart, because they believed not them which had seen him after he was risen.

15 And he said to them, Go you into all the world, and preach the gospel to every creature.

16 He that believes and is baptized shall be saved; but he that believes not shall be damned.

17 And these signs shall follow them that believe; In my name shall they cast out devils; they shall speak with new tongues;

18 They shall take up serpents; and if they drink any deadly thing, it shall not hurt them; they shall lay hands on the sick, and they shall recover.

19 ¶ So then after the Lord had spoken to them, he was received up into heaven, and sat on the right hand of God.

20 And they went forth, and preached every where, the Lord working with *them*, and confirming the word with signs following. Amen.

Luke

Luke 1

1:1 ¶ Forasmuch as many have taken in hand to set forth in order a declaration of those things which are most surely believed among us,

2 Even as they delivered them to us, which from the beginning were eyewitnesses, and ministers of the word;

3 It seemed good to me also, having had perfect understanding of all things from the very first, to write to you in order, most excellent Theophilus,

4 That you might know the certainty of those things, wherein you have been instructed.

5 ¶ There was in the days of Herod, the king of Judaea, a certain priest named Zechariah, of the course of Abija: and his wife *was* of the daughters of Aaron, and her name *was* Elisabeth.

6 And they were both righteous before God, walking in all the commandments and ordinances of the Lord blameless.

7 And they had no child, because that Elisabeth was barren, and they both were *now* well stricken in years.

8 And it came to pass, that while he executed the priest's office before God in the order of his course,

9 According to the custom of the priest's office, his lot was to burn incense when he went into the temple of the Lord.

10 And the whole multitude of the people were praying outside at the time of incense.

11 And there appeared to him an angel of the Lord standing on the right side of the altar of incense.

12 And when Zechariah saw *him*, he was troubled, and fear fell upon him.

13 But the angel said to him, Fear not, Zechariah: for your prayer is heard; and your wife Elisabeth shall bear you a son, and you shall call his name John.

14 And you shall have joy and gladness; and many shall rejoice at his birth.

15 For he shall be great in the sight of the Lord, and shall drink neither wine nor strong drink; and he shall be filled with the Holy Ghost, even from his mother's womb.

16 And many of the children of Israel shall he turn to the Lord their God.

17 And he shall go before him in the spirit and power of Elijah, to turn the hearts of the fathers to the children, and the disobedient to the wisdom of the just; to make ready a people prepared for the Lord.

18 And Zechariah said to the angel, Whereby shall I know this? for I am an old man, and my wife well stricken in years.

19 And the angel answering said to him, I am Gabriel, that stands in the presence of God; and am sent to speak to you, and to show you these glad tidings.

20 And, behold, you shall be dumb, and not able to speak, until the day that these things shall be performed, because you believe not my words, which shall be fulfilled in their season.

21 And the people waited for Zechariah, and marveled that he tarried so long in the temple.

22 And when he came out, he could not speak to them: and they perceived that he had seen a vision in the temple: for he beckoned to them, and remained speechless.

23 And it came to pass, that, as soon as the days of his ministry were accomplished, he departed to his own house.

24 And after those days his wife Elisabeth conceived, and hid herself five months, saying,

25 Thus has the Lord dealt with me in the days wherein he looked on *me*, to take away my reproach among men.

26 ¶ And in the sixth month the angel Gabriel was sent from God to a city of Galilee, named Nazareth,

27 To a virgin espoused to a man whose name was Joseph, of the house of David; and the virgin's name *was* Mary.

28 And the angel came in unto her, and said, Hail, *you that are* highly favored, the Lord *is* with you: blessed *are* you among women.

Luke 1

29 And when she saw *him*, she was troubled at his saying, and cast in her mind what manner of salutation this should be.

30 And the angel said to her, Fear not, Mary: for you have found favor with God.

31 And, behold, you shall conceive in your womb, and bring forth a son, and shall call his name YAHSHUA.

32 He shall be great, and shall be called the Son of the Highest: and the Lord God shall give to him the throne of his father David:

33 And he shall reign over the house of Jacob forever; and of his kingdom there shall be no end.

34 Then said Mary to the angel, How shall this be, seeing I know not a man?

35 And the angel answered and said to her, The Holy Ghost shall come upon you, and the power of the Highest shall overshadow you: therefore also that holy thing which shall be born of you shall be called the Son of God.

36 And, behold, your cousin Elisabeth, she has also conceived a son in her old age: and this is the sixth month with her, who was called barren.

37 For with God nothing shall be impossible.

38 And Mary said, Behold the handmaid of the Lord; be it unto me according to your word. And the angel departed from her.

39 ¶ And Mary arose in those days, and went into the hill country with haste, into a city of Judah;

40 And entered into the house of Zechariah, and saluted Elisabeth.

41 And it came to pass, that, when Elisabeth heard the salutation of Mary, the babe leaped in her womb; and Elisabeth was filled with the Holy Ghost:

42 And she spoke out with a loud voice, and said, Blessed *are* you among women, and blessed *is* the fruit of your womb.

43 And *from* where *is* this to me, that the mother of my Lord should come to me?

44 For, lo, as soon as the voice of your salutation sounded in my ears, the babe leaped in my womb for joy.

45 And blessed *is* she that believed: for there shall be a performance of those things which were told her from the Lord.

46 And Mary said, My soul does magnify the Lord,

47 And my spirit has rejoiced in God my Savior.

48 For he has regarded the low estate of his handmaiden: for, behold, from now on all generations shall call me blessed.

49 For he that is mighty has done to me great things; and holy *is* his name.

50 And his mercy *is* on them that fear him from generation to generation.

51 He has shown strength with his arm; he has scattered the proud in the imagination of their hearts.

52 He has put down the mighty from *their* seats, and exalted them of low degree.

53 He has filled the hungry with good things; and the rich he has sent away empty.

54 He has helped his servant Israel, in remembrance of *his* mercy;

55 As he spoke to our fathers, to Abraham, and to his seed forever.

56 And Mary stayed with her about three months, and returned to her own house.

57 ¶ Now Elisabeth's full time came that she should be delivered; and she brought forth a son.

58 And her neighbors and her cousins heard how the Lord had shown great mercy upon her; and they rejoiced with her.

59 And it came to pass, that on the eighth day they came to circumcise the child; and they called him Zechariah, after the name of his father.

60 And his mother answered and said, Not *so*; but he shall be called John.

61 And they said to her, There is none of your kindred that is called by this name.

62 And they made signs to his father, how he would have him called.

63 And he asked for a writing tablet, and wrote, saying, His name is John. And they marveled all.

64 And his mouth was opened immediately, and his tongue *loosed*, and he spoke, and praised God.

65 And fear came on all that dwelt round about them: and all these sayings were noised abroad throughout all the hill country of Judaea.

66 And all they that heard *them* laid *them* up in their hearts, saying, What manner of child shall this be! And the hand of the Lord was with him.

67 ¶ And his father Zechariah was filled with the Holy Ghost, and prophesied, saying,

68 Blessed *be* the Lord God of Israel; for he has visited and redeemed his people,

69 And has raised up a horn of salvation for us in the house of his servant David;

70 As he spoke by the mouth of his holy prophets, which have been since the world began:

71 That we should be saved from our enemies, and from the hand of all that hate us;

72 To perform the mercy *promised* to our fathers, and to remember his holy covenant;

73 The oath which he swore to our father Abraham,

74 That he would grant to us, that we being delivered out of the hand of our enemies might serve him without fear,

75 In holiness and righteousness before him, all the days of our life.

76 And you, child, will be called the prophet of the Highest: for you shall go before the face of the Lord to prepare his ways;

77 To give knowledge of salvation to his people by the remission of their sins,

78 Through the tender mercy of our God; whereby the dayspring from on high has visited us,

79 To give light to them that sit in darkness and *in the* shadow of death, to guide our feet into the way of peace.

80 And the child grew, and became strong in spirit, and was in the deserts till the day of his showing to Israel.

Luke 2

2:1 ¶ And it came to pass in those days, that there went out a decree from Caesar Augustus, that all the world should be taxed.

2 (*And* this taxing was first made when Cyrenius was governor of Syria.)

3 And all went to be taxed, every one into his own city.

4 And Joseph also went up from Galilee, out of the city of Nazareth, into Judaea, to the city of David, which is called Bethlehem; (because he was of the house and lineage of David:)

5 To be taxed with Mary his espoused wife, being great with child.

6 And so it was, that, while they were there, the days were accomplished that she should be delivered.

7 And she brought forth her firstborn son, and wrapped him in swaddling clothes, and laid him in a manger; because there was no room for them in the inn.

8 ¶ And there were in the same country shepherds living in the field, keeping watch over their flock by night.

9 And, lo, the angel of the Lord came upon them, and the glory of the Lord shone round about them: and they were greatly afraid.

10 And the angel said to them, Fear not: for, behold, I bring you good tidings of great joy, which shall be to all people.

11 For unto you is born this day in the city of David a Savior, which is the Messiah the Lord.

12 And this *shall be* a sign unto you; You shall find the babe wrapped in swaddling clothes, lying in a manger.

13 And suddenly there was with the angel a multitude of the heavenly host praising God, and saying,

14 Glory to God in the highest, and on earth peace, good will toward men.

15 And it came to pass, as the angels had gone away from them into heaven, the shepherds said one to another, Let us now go even to Bethlehem, and see this thing which has come to pass, which the Lord has made known to us.

16 And they came with haste, and found Mary, and Joseph, and the babe lying in a manger.

17 And when they had seen *it*, they made known abroad the saying which was told them concerning this child.

18 And all they that heard *it* wondered at those things which were told them by the shepherds.

19 But Mary kept all these things, and pondered *them* in her heart.

20 And the shepherds returned, glorifying and praising God for all the things that they had heard and seen, as it was told to them.

21 ¶ And when eight days were accomplished for the circumcising of the child, his name was called YAHSHUA, which was so named of the angel before he was conceived in the womb.

22 And when the days of her purification according to the law of Moses were accomplished, they brought him to Jerusalem, to present *him* to the Lord;

23 (As it is written in the law of the Lord *Yahweh*, Every male that opens the womb shall be called holy to the Lord *Yahweh*;)

24 And to offer a sacrifice according to that which is said in the law of the Lord *Yahweh*, A pair of turtledoves, or two young pigeons.

25 ¶ And, behold, there was a man in Jerusalem, whose name *was* Simeon; and the same man *was* just and devout, waiting for the consolation of Israel: and the Holy Ghost was upon him.

26 And it was revealed to him by the Holy Ghost, that he should not see death, before he had seen the Lord's Messiah.

27 And he came by the Spirit into the temple: and when the parents brought in the child Yahshua, to do for him after the custom of the law,

28 Then took he him up in his arms, and blessed God, and said,

29 Lord, now let you your servant depart in peace, according to your word:

30 For my eyes have seen your salvation,

31 Which you have prepared before the face of all people;

32 A light to lighten the Gentiles, and the glory of your people Israel.

33 And Joseph and his mother marveled at those things which were spoken of him.

34 And Simeon blessed them, and said to Mary his mother, Behold, this *child* is set for the fall and rising again of many in Israel; and for a sign which shall be spoken against;

35 (Yes, a sword shall pierce through your own soul also,) that the thoughts of many hearts may be revealed.

36 And there was one Anna, a prophetess, the daughter of Phanuel, of the tribe of Asher: she was of a great age, and had lived with a husband seven years from her virginity;

37 And she *was* a widow of about fourscore and four years, which departed not from the temple, but served *God* with fastings and prayers night and day.

38 And she coming in that instant gave thanks likewise unto the Lord, and spoke of him to all them that looked for redemption in Jerusalem.

39 And when they had performed all things according to the law of the Lord, they returned into Galilee, to their own city Nazareth.

40 And the child grew, and became strong in spirit, filled with wisdom: and the grace of God was upon him.

41 ¶ Now his parents went to Jerusalem every year at the feast of the passover.

42 And when he was twelve years old, they went up to Jerusalem after the custom of the feast.

43 And when they had fulfilled the days, as they returned, the child Yahshua tarried behind in Jerusalem; and Joseph and his mother knew not *of it*.

44 But they, supposing him to have been in the company, went a day's journey; and they sought him among *their* kinsfolk and acquaintances.

Luke 2

45 And when they found him not, they turned back again to Jerusalem, seeking him.

46 And it came to pass, that after three days they found him in the temple, sitting in the midst of the doctors, both hearing them, and asking them questions.

47 And all that heard him were astonished at his understanding and answers.

48 And when they saw him, they were amazed: and his mother said to him, Son, why have you thus dealt with us? behold, your father and I have sought you sorrowing.

49 And he said to them, How is it that you sought me? knew you not that I must be about my Father's business?

50 And they understood not the saying which he spoke to them.

51 And he went down with them, and came to Nazareth, and was subject to them: but his mother kept all these sayings in her heart.

52 And Yahshua increased in wisdom and stature, and in favor with God and man.

Luke 3

3:1 ¶ Now in the fifteenth year of the reign of Tiberius Caesar, Pontius Pilate being governor of Judaea, and Herod being tetrarch of Galilee, and his brother Philip tetrarch of Ituraea and of the region of Trachonitis, and Lysanias the tetrarch of Abilene,

2 Annas and Caiaphas being the high priests, the word of God came to John the son of Zechariah in the wilderness.

3 And he came into all the country about *the* Jordan, preaching the baptism of repentance for the remission of sins;

4 As it is written in the book of the words of Isaiah the prophet, saying, The voice of one crying in the wilderness, Prepare you the way of the Lord *Yahweh*, make his paths straight.

5 Every valley shall be filled, and every mountain and hill shall be brought low; and the crooked shall be made straight, and the rough ways *shall be* made smooth;

6 And all flesh shall see the salvation of God.

7 Then said he to the multitude that came forth to be baptized by him, O generation of vipers, who has warned you to flee from the wrath to come?

8 Bring forth therefore fruits worthy of repentance, and begin not to say within yourselves, We have Abraham to *our* father: for I say to you, That God is able of these stones to raise up children unto Abraham.

9 And now also the ax is laid to the root of the trees: every tree therefore which brings not forth good fruit is hewn down, and cast into the fire.

10 And the people asked him, saying, What shall we do then?

11 He answered and said to them, He that has two coats, let him impart to him that has none; and he that has food, let him do likewise.

12 Then came also publicans to be baptized, and said to him, Master, what shall we do?

13 And he said to them, Exact no more than that which is appointed you.

14 And the soldiers likewise demanded of him, saying, And what shall we do? And he said to them, Do violence to no man, neither accuse *any* falsely; and be content with your wages.

15 ¶ And as the people were in expectation, and all men mused in their hearts about John, whether he was the Messiah, or not;

16 John answered, saying to *them* all, I indeed baptize you with water; but one mightier than I comes, the lace of whose shoes I am not worthy to unloose: he shall baptize you with the Holy Ghost and with fire:

17 Whose fan *is* in his hand, and he will thoroughly purge his floor, and will gather the wheat into his barn; but the chaff he will burn with fire unquenchable.

18 And many other things in his exhortation preached he to the people.

19 But Herod the tetrarch, being reproved by him for Herodias his brother Philip's wife, and for all the evils which Herod had done,

20 Added yet this above all, that he shut up John in prison.

21 ¶ Now when all the people were baptized, it came to pass, that Yahshua also being baptized, and praying, the heaven was opened,

22 And the Holy Ghost descended in a bodily shape like a dove upon him, and a voice came from heaven, which said, You are my beloved Son; in you I am well pleased.

23 And Yahshua himself began to be about thirty years of age, being (as was supposed) the son of Joseph, which was *the son* of Heli,

24 Which was *the son* of Matthat, which was *the son* of Levi, which was *the son* of Melchi, which was *the son* of Janna, which was *the son* of Joseph,

25 Which was *the son* of Mattathiah, which was *the son* of Amos, which was *the son* of Nahum, which was *the son* of Esli, which was *the son* of Nogah,

26 Which was *the son* of Maath, which was *the son* of Mattathiah, which was *the son* of Shimei, which was *the son* of Joseph, which was *the son* of Judah,

27 Which was *the son* of Joanna, which was *the son* of Rhesa, which was *the son* of Zerubbabel, which was *the son* of Shealtiel, which was *the son* of Neriah,

28 Which was *the son* of Melchi, which was *the son* of Addi, which was *the son* of Cosam, which was *the son* of Elmodam, which was *the son* of Er,

29 Which was *the son* of Jose, which was *the son* of Eliezer, which was *the son* of Jorim, which was *the son* of Matthat, which was *the son* of Levi,

30 Which was *the son* of Simeon, which was *the son* of Judah, which was *the son* of Joseph, which was *the son* of Jonan, which was *the son* of Eliakim,

31 Which was *the son* of Melea, which was *the son* of Menan, which was *the son* of Mattatha, which was *the son* of Nathan, which was *the son* of David,

32 Which was *the son* of Jesse, which was *the son* of Obed, which was *the son* of Boaz, which was *the son* of Salmon, which was *the son* of Nahshon,
33 Which was *the son* of Amminadab, which was *the son* of Ram, which was *the son* of Hezron, which was *the son* of Pharez, which was *the son* of Judah,
34 Which was *the son* of Jacob, which was *the son* of Isaac, which was *the son* of Abraham, which was *the son* of Terah, which was *the son* of Nahor,
35 Which was *the son* of Serug, which was *the son* of Reu, which was *the son* of Peleg, which was *the son* of Eber, which was *the son* of Salah,
36 Which was *the son* of Cainan, which was *the son* of Arphaxad, which was *the son* of Shem, which was *the son* of Noah, which was *the son* of Lamech,
37 Which was *the son* of Methuselah, which was *the son* of Enoch, which was *the son* of Jared, which was *the son* of Mahalaleel, which was *the son* of Cainan,
38 Which was *the son* of Enos, which was *the son* of Seth, which was *the son* of Adam, which was *the son* of God

Luke 4

4:1 ¶ And Yahshua being full of the Holy Ghost returned from *the* Jordan, and was led by the Spirit into the wilderness,
2 Being forty days tempted of the devil. And in those days he did eat nothing: and when they had ended, he afterward hungered.
3 And the devil said to him, If you are the Son of God, command this stone that it be made bread.
4 And Yahshua answered him, saying, It is written, That man shall not live by bread alone, but by every word of God *Yahweh*.
5 And the devil, taking him up into a high mountain, showed to him all the kingdoms of the world in a moment of time.
6 And the devil said to him, All this power will I give you, and the glory of them: for that is delivered to me; and to whomever I will I give it.
7 If you therefore will worship me, all shall be yours.
8 And Yahshua answered and said to him, Get you behind me, Satan: for it is written, You shall worship the Lord *Yahweh* your God, and him only shall you serve.
9 And he brought him to Jerusalem, and set him on a pinnacle of the temple, and said to him, If you are the Son of God, cast yourself down from here:
10 For it is written, He shall give his angels charge over you, to keep you:
11 And in *their* hands they shall bear you up, lest at any time you dash your foot against a stone.
12 And Yahshua answering said to him, It is said, You shall not tempt the Lord *Yahweh* your God.
13 And when the devil had ended all the temptation, he departed from him for a season.
14 ¶ And Yahshua returned in the power of the Spirit into Galilee: and there went out a fame of him through all the region round about.

15 And he taught in their synagogues, being glorified of all.
16 And he came to Nazareth, where he had been brought up: and, as his custom was, he went into the synagogue on the sabbath day, and stood up for to read.
17 And there was delivered to him the book of the prophet Isaiah. And when he had opened the book, he found the place where it was written,
18 The Spirit of the Lord *Yahweh is* upon me, because he has anointed me to preach the gospel to the poor; he has sent me to heal the brokenhearted, to preach deliverance to the captives, and recovering of sight to the blind, to set at liberty them that are bruised,
19 To preach the acceptable year of the Lord *Yahweh*.
20 And he closed the book, and he gave *it* again to the minister, and sat down. And the eyes of all them that were in the synagogue were fastened on him.
21 And he began to say to them, This day is this scripture fulfilled in your ears.
22 And all bore him witness, and wondered at the gracious words which proceeded out of his mouth. And they said, Is not this Joseph's son?
23 And he said to them, You will surely say unto me this proverb, Physician, heal yourself: whatever we have heard done in Capernaum, do also here in your country.
24 And he said, Truly I say unto you, No prophet is accepted in his own country.
25 But I tell you of a truth, many widows were in Israel in the days of Elijah, when the heaven was shut up *for* three years and six months, when great famine was throughout all the land;
26 But unto none of them was Elijah sent, save to Zarephath, *a city* of Sidon, to a woman *that was* a widow.
27 And many lepers were in Israel in the time of Elisha the prophet; and none of them was cleansed, except Naaman the Syrian.
28 And all they in the synagogue, when they heard these things, were filled with wrath,
29 And rose up, and thrust him out of the city, and led him to the brow of the hill whereon their city was built, that they might cast him down headlong.
30 But he passing through the midst of them went his way,
31 ¶ And came down to Capernaum, a city of Galilee, and taught them on the sabbath days.
32 And they were astonished at his doctrine: for his word was with power.
33 And in the synagogue there was a man, which had a spirit of an unclean devil, and cried out with a loud voice,
34 Saying, Let *us* alone; what have we to do with you, *you* Yahshua of Nazareth? have you come to destroy us? I know who you are; the Holy One of God.
35 And Yahshua rebuked him, saying, Hold your peace, and come out of him. And when the devil had thrown him in the midst, he came out of him, and hurt him not.
36 And they were all amazed, and spoke among themselves, saying, What a word *is* this! for with authority and power he commands the unclean spirits, and they come out.

Luke 4

37 And the fame of him went out into every place of the country round about.

38 And he arose out of the synagogue, and entered into Simon's house. And Simon's wife's mother was taken with a great fever; and they sought him for her.

39 And he stood over her, and rebuked the fever; and it left her: and immediately she arose and ministered unto them.

40 Now when the sun was setting, all they that had any sick with various diseases brought them to him; and he laid his hands on every one of them, and healed them.

41 And devils also came out of many, crying out, and saying, You are the Messiah the Son of God. And he rebuking *them* allowed them not to speak: for they knew that he was the Messiah.

42 And when it was day, he departed and went into a desert place: and the people sought him, and came to him, and restrained him, that he should not depart from them.

43 And he said to them, I must preach the kingdom of God to other cities also: for therefore am I sent.

44 And he preached in the synagogues of Galilee.

Luke 5

5:1 ¶ And it came to pass, that, as the people pressed upon him to hear the word of God, he stood by the lake of Gennesaret,

2 And saw two ships standing by the lake: but the fishermen were gone out of them, and were washing *their* nets.

3 And he entered into one of the ships, which was Simon's, and prayed him that he would thrust out a little from the land. And he sat down, and taught the people out of the ship.

4 Now when he had left speaking, he said to Simon, Launch out into the deep, and let down your nets for a catch.

5 And Simon answering said to him, Master, we have toiled all the night, and have taken nothing: nevertheless at your word I will let down the net.

6 And when they had this done, they enclosed a great multitude of fishes: and their net broke.

7 And they beckoned to *their* partners, which were in the other ship, that they should come and help them. And they came, and filled both the ships, so that they began to sink.

8 When Simon Peter saw *it*, he fell down at Yahshua's knees, saying, Depart from me; for I am a sinful man, O Lord.

9 For he was astonished, and all that were with him, at the catch of the fishes which they had taken:

10 And so *was* also James, and John, the sons of Zebedee, which were partners with Simon. And Yahshua said to Simon, Fear not; from now on you shall catch men.

11 And when they had brought their ships to land, they forsook all, and followed him.

12 ¶ And it came to pass, when he was in a certain city, behold a man full of leprosy: who seeing Yahshua fell on *his* face, and begged him, saying, Lord, if you will, you can make me clean.

13 And he put forth *his* hand, and touched him, saying, I will: be you clean. And immediately the leprosy departed from him.

14 And he charged him to tell no man: but go, and show yourself to the priest, and offer for your cleansing, according as Moses commanded, for a testimony to them.

15 But so much the more went there a fame abroad of him: and great multitudes came together to hear, and to be healed by him of their infirmities.

16 And he withdrew himself into the wilderness, and prayed.

17 ¶ And it came to pass on a certain day, as he was teaching, that there were Pharisees and doctors of the law sitting by, which had come out of every town of Galilee, and Judaea, and Jerusalem: and the power of the Lord was *present* to heal them.

18 And, behold, men brought in a bed a man which was taken with a palsy: and they sought *means* to bring him in, and to lay *him* before him.

19 And when they could not find by what *way* they might bring him in because of the multitude, they went upon the housetop, and let him down through the tiling with *his* couch into the midst before Yahshua.

20 And when he saw their faith, he said to him, Man, your sins are forgiven you.

21 And the scribes and the Pharisees began to reason, saying, Who is this which speaks blasphemies? Who can forgive sins, but God alone?

22 But when Yahshua perceived their thoughts, he answering said to them, What reason you in your hearts?

23 Which is easier, to say, Your sins are forgiven you; or to say, Rise up and walk?

24 But that you may know that the Son of man has power upon earth to forgive sins, (he said to the sick of the palsy,) I say to you, Arise, and take up your couch, and go into your house.

25 And immediately he rose up before them, and took up that whereon he lay, and departed to his own house, glorifying God.

26 And they were all amazed, and they glorified God, and were filled with fear, saying, We have seen strange things today.

27 ¶ And after these things he went forth, and saw a publican, named Levi, sitting at the receipt of custom: and he said to him, Follow me.

28 And he left all, rose up, and followed him.

29 And Levi made him a great feast in his own house: and there was a great company of publicans and of others that sat down with them.

30 But their scribes and Pharisees murmured against his disciples, saying, Why do you eat and drink with publicans and sinners?

31 And Yahshua answering said to them, They that are whole need not a physician; but they that are sick.

32 I came not to call the righteous, but sinners to repentance.

33 And they said to him, Why do the disciples of John fast often, and make prayers, and likewise *the disciples* of the Pharisees; but yours eat and drink?

34 And he said to them, Can you make the children of the bride chamber fast, while the bridegroom is with them?

35 But the days will come, when the bridegroom shall be taken away from them, and then shall they fast in those days.

36 And he spoke also a parable to them; No man puts a piece of a new garment upon an old; if otherwise, then both the new makes a tear, and the piece that was *taken* out of the new agrees not with the old.

37 And no man puts new wine into old bottles; else the new wine will burst the bottles, and be spilled, and the bottles shall perish.

38 But new wine must be put into new bottles; and both are preserved.

39 No man also having drunk old *wine* immediately desires new: for he said, The old is better.

Luke 6

6:1 ¶ And it came to pass on the second sabbath after the first, that he went through the corn fields; and his disciples plucked the ears of corn, and did eat, rubbing *them* in *their* hands.

2 And certain of the Pharisees said to them, Why do you that which is not lawful to do on the sabbath days?

3 And Yahshua answering them said, Have you not read so much as this, what David did, when himself was hungry, and they which were with him;

4 How he went into the house of God, and did take and eat the showbread, and gave also to them that were with him; which it is not lawful to eat but for the priests alone?

5 And he said to them, That the Son of man is Lord also of the sabbath.

6 And it came to pass also on another sabbath, that he entered into the synagogue and taught: and there was a man whose right hand was withered.

7 And the scribes and Pharisees watched him, whether he would heal on the sabbath day; that they might find an accusation against him.

8 But he knew their thoughts, and said to the man which had the withered hand, Rise up, and stand forth in the midst. And he arose and stood forth.

9 Then said Yahshua to them, I will ask you one thing; Is it lawful on the sabbath days to do good, or to do evil? to save life, or to destroy *it*?

10 And looking round about upon them all, he said to the man, Stretch forth your hand. And he did so: and his hand was restored whole as the other.

11 And they were filled with madness; and communed one with another what they might do to Yahshua.

12 ¶ And it came to pass in those days, that he went out into a mountain to pray, and continued all night in prayer to God.

13 And when it was day, he called *unto him* his disciples: and of them he chose twelve, whom also he named apostles;

14 Simon, (whom he also named Peter,) and Andrew his brother, James and John, Philip and Bartholomew,

15 Matthew and Thomas, James the *son* of Alphaeus, and Simon called Zelotes,

16 And Judas *the brother* of James, and Judas Iscariot, which also was the traitor.

17 And he came down with them, and stood in the plain, and the company of his disciples, and a great multitude of people out of all Judaea and Jerusalem, and from the sea coast of Tyre and Sidon, which came to hear him, and to be healed of their diseases;

18 And they that were troubled with unclean spirits: and they were healed.

19 And the whole multitude sought to touch him: for there went virtue out of him, and healed *them* all.

20 ¶ And he lifted up his eyes on his disciples, and said, Blessed *be you* poor: for yours is the kingdom of God.

21 Blessed *are you* that hunger now: for you shall be filled. Blessed *are you* that weep now: for you shall laugh.

22 Blessed are you, when men shall hate you, and when they shall separate you *from their company*, and shall reproach *you*, and cast out your name as evil, for the Son of man's sake.

23 Rejoice you in that day, and leap for joy: for, behold, your reward *is* great in heaven: for in the like manner did their fathers unto the prophets.

24 But woe unto you that are rich! for you have received your consolation.

25 Woe unto you that are full! for you shall hunger. Woe unto you that laugh now! for you shall mourn and weep.

26 Woe unto you, when all men shall speak well of you! for so did their fathers to the false prophets.

27 ¶ But I say to you which hear, Love your enemies, do good to them which hate you,

28 Bless them that curse you, and pray for them which spitefully use you.

29 And to him that smites you on the *one* cheek offer also the other; and him that takes away your cloak forbid not *to take your* coat also.

30 Give to every man that asks of you; and of him that takes away your goods ask *them* not again.

31 And as you would that men should do to you, do you also to them likewise.

32 For if you love them which love you, what thanks have you? for sinners also love those that love them.

33 And if you do good to them which do good to you, what thanks have you? for sinners also do even the same.

34 And if you lend *to them* of whom you hope to receive, what thanks have you? for sinners also lend to sinners, to receive as much again.

35 But love you your enemies, and do good, and lend, hoping for nothing again; and your reward shall be great, and you shall be the children of the Highest: for he is kind to the unthankful and *to* the evil.

36 Be you therefore merciful, as your Father also is merciful.

37 ¶ Judge not, and you shall not be judged: condemn not, and you shall not be condemned: forgive, and you shall be forgiven:

Luke 6

38 Give, and it shall be given to you; good measure, pressed down, and shaken together, and running over, shall men give into your bosom. For with the same measure that you measure therewith it shall be measured to you again.
39 And he spoke a parable to them, Can the blind lead the blind? shall they not both fall into the ditch?
40 The disciple is not above his master: but every one that is perfect shall be as his master.
41 And why behold you the twig that is in your brother's eye, but perceive not the beam that is in your own eye?
42 Either how can you say to your brother, Brother, let me pull out the twig that is in your eye, when you yourself behold not the beam that is in your own eye? You hypocrite, cast out first the beam out of your own eye, and then shall you see clearly to pull out the twig that is in your brother's eye.
43 For a good tree brings not forth corrupt fruit; neither does a corrupt tree bring forth good fruit.
44 For every tree is known by his own fruit. For of thorns men do not gather figs, nor of a bramble bush gather they grapes.
45 A good man out of the good treasure of his heart brings forth that which is good; and an evil man out of the evil treasure of his heart brings forth that which is evil: for of the abundance of the heart his mouth speaks.
46 And why call you me, Lord, Lord, and do not the things which I say?
47 Whoever comes to me, and hears my sayings, and does them, I will show you to whom he is like:
48 He is like a man which built a house, and dug deep, and laid the foundation on a rock: and when the flood arose, the stream beat vehemently upon that house, and could not shake it: for it was founded upon a rock.
49 But he that hears, and does not, is like a man that without a foundation built a house upon the earth; against which the stream did beat vehemently, and immediately it fell; and the ruin of that house was great.

Luke 7

7:1 ¶ Now when he had ended all his sayings in the audience of the people, he entered into Capernaum.
2 And a certain centurion's servant, who was dear to him, was sick, and ready to die.
3 And when he heard of Yahshua, he sent to him the elders of the Jews, asking him that he would come and heal his servant.
4 And when they came to Yahshua, they sought him instantly, saying, That he was worthy for whom he should do this:
5 For he loves our nation, and he has built us a synagogue.
6 Then Yahshua went with them. And when he was now not far from the house, the centurion sent friends to him, saying to him, Lord, trouble not yourself: for I am not worthy that you should enter under my roof:
7 Therefore neither thought I myself worthy to come to you: but say a word, and my servant shall be healed.
8 For I also am a man set under authority, having under me soldiers, and I say to one, Go, and he goes; and to another, Come, and he comes; and to my servant, Do this, and he does *it*.
9 When Yahshua heard these things, he marveled at him, and turned him about, and said to the people that followed him, I say to you, I have not found such great faith, no, not in Israel.
10 And they that were sent, returning to the house, found the servant whole that had been sick.
11 ¶ And it came to pass the day after, that he went into a city called Nain; and many of his disciples went with him, and many people.
12 Now when he came near to the gate of the city, behold, there was a dead man carried out, the only son of his mother, and she was a widow: and many people of the city were with her.
13 And when the Lord saw her, he had compassion on her, and said to her, Weep not.
14 And he came and touched the bier: and they that bore *him* stood still. And he said, Young man, I say to you, Arise.
15 And he that was dead sat up, and began to speak. And he delivered him to his mother.
16 And there came a fear on all: and they glorified God, saying, That a great prophet has risen up among us; and, That God has visited his people.
17 And this rumor of him went forth throughout all Judaea, and throughout all the region round about.
18 And the disciples of John showed him of all these things.
19 ¶ And John calling *to him* two of his disciples sent *them* to Yahshua, saying, Are you he that should come? or look we for another?
20 When the men had come to him, they said, John *the* Baptist has sent us to you, saying, Are you he that should come? or look we for another?
21 And in that same hour he cured many of *their* infirmities and plagues, and of evil spirits; and to many *that were* blind he gave sight.
22 Then Yahshua answering said to them, Go your way, and tell John what things you have seen and heard; how that the blind see, the lame walk, the lepers are cleansed, the deaf hear, the dead are raised, to the poor the gospel is preached.
23 And blessed is *he*, whoever shall not be offended in me.
24 And when the messengers of John had departed, he began to speak to the people concerning John, What went you out into the wilderness for to see? A reed shaken with the wind?
25 But what went you out for to see? A man clothed in soft garments? Behold, they which are gorgeously appareled, and live delicately, are in kings' courts.
26 But what went you out for to see? A prophet? Yes, I say to you, and much more than a prophet.
27 This is *he*, of whom it is written, Behold, I send my messenger before your face, which shall prepare your way before you.

28 For I say unto you, Among those that are born of women there is not a greater prophet than John the Baptist: but he that is least in the kingdom of God is greater than he.
29 And all the people that heard *him*, and the publicans, justified God, being baptized with the baptism of John.
30 But the Pharisees and lawyers rejected the counsel of God against themselves, being not baptized of him.
31 And the Lord said, Whereunto then shall I liken the men of this generation? and to what are they like?
32 They are like unto children sitting in the marketplace, and calling one to another, and saying, We have piped to you, and you have not danced; we have mourned to you, and you have not wept.
33 For John the Baptist came neither eating bread nor drinking wine; and you say, He has a devil.
34 The Son of man has come eating and drinking; and you say, Behold a gluttonous man, and a winebibber, a friend of publicans and sinners!
35 But wisdom is justified of all her children.
36 ¶ And one of the Pharisees desired him that he would eat with him. And he went into the Pharisee's house, and sat down to meat.
37 And, behold, a woman in the city, which was a sinner, when she knew that *Yahshua* sat at meat in the Pharisee's house, brought an alabaster box of ointment,
38 And stood at his feet behind *him* weeping, and began to wash his feet with tears, and did wipe *them* with the hairs of her head, and kissed his feet, and anointed *them* with the ointment.
39 Now when the Pharisee which had invited him saw *it*, he spoke within himself, saying, This man, if he were a prophet, would have known who and what manner of woman *this is* that touches him: for she is a sinner.
40 And Yahshua answering said to him, Simon, I have somewhat to say to you. And he said, Master, say on.
41 There was a certain creditor which had two debtors: the one owed five hundred pence, and the other fifty.
42 And when they had nothing to pay, he frankly forgave them both. Tell me therefore, which of them will love him most?
43 Simon answered and said, I suppose that *he*, to whom he forgave most. And he said to him, You have rightly judged.
44 And he turned to the woman, and said to Simon, See you this woman? I entered into your house, you gave me no water for my feet: but she has washed my feet with tears, and wiped *them* with the hairs of her head.
45 You gave me no kiss: but this woman since the time I came in has not ceased to kiss my feet.
46 My head with oil you did not anoint: but this woman has anointed my feet with ointment.
47 Therefore I say unto you, Her sins, which are many, are forgiven; for she loved much: but to whom little is forgiven, *the same* loves little.
48 And he said to her, Your sins are forgiven.
49 And they that sat at meat with him began to say within themselves, Who is this that forgives sins also?
50 And he said to the woman, Your faith has saved you; go in peace.

Luke 8

8:1 ¶ And it came to pass afterward, that he went throughout every city and village, preaching and showing the glad tidings of the kingdom of God: and the twelve *were* with him,
2 And certain women, which had been healed of evil spirits and infirmities, Mary called Magdalene, out of whom went seven devils,
3 And Joanna the wife of Chuza Herod's steward, and Susanna, and many others, which ministered to him of their substance.
4 ¶ And when many people were gathered together, and had come to him out of every city, he spoke by a parable:
5 A sower went out to sow his seed: and as he sowed, some fell by the way side; and it was trodden down, and the fowls of the air devoured it.
6 And some fell upon a rock; and as soon as it was sprung up, it withered away, because it lacked moisture.
7 And some fell among thorns; and the thorns sprang up with it, and choked it.
8 And other fell on good ground, and sprang up, and bore fruit a hundredfold. And when he had said these things, he cried, He that has ears to hear, let him hear.
9 And his disciples asked him, saying, What might this parable be?
10 And he said, Unto you it is given to know the mysteries of the kingdom of God: but to others in parables; that seeing they might not see, and hearing they might not understand.
11 Now the parable is this: The seed is the word of God.
12 Those by the way side are they that hear; then comes the devil, and takes away the word out of their hearts, lest they should believe and be saved.
13 They on the rock *are they*, which, when they hear, receive the word with joy; and these have no root, which for a while believe, and in time of temptation fall away.
14 And that which fell among thorns are they, which, when they have heard, go forth, and are choked with cares and riches and pleasures of *this* life, and bring no fruit to perfection.
15 But that on the good ground are they, which in an honest and good heart, having heard the word, keep *it*, and bring forth fruit with patience.
16 No man, when he has lit a candle, covers it with a vessel, or puts *it* under a bed; but sets *it* on a candlestick, that they which enter in may see the light.
17 For nothing is secret, that shall not be made manifest; neither *any thing* hidden, that shall not be known and come abroad.
18 Take heed therefore how you hear: for whoever has, to him shall be given; and whoever has not, from him shall be taken even that which he seems to have.
19 Then came to him *his* mother and his brothers, and could not come at him for the crowd.

Luke 8

20 And it was told *to* him *by some* which said, Your mother and your brothers stand outside, desiring to see you.

21 And he answered and said to them, My mother and my brothers are these which hear the word of God, and do it.

22 ¶ Now it came to pass on a certain day, that he went into a ship with his disciples: and he said to them, Let us go over to the other side of the lake. And they launched forth.

23 But as they sailed he fell asleep: and there came down a storm of wind on the lake; and they were filled *with water*, and were in jeopardy.

24 And they came to him, and woke him, saying, Master, master, we perish. Then he arose, and rebuked the wind and the raging of the water: and they ceased, and there was a calm.

25 And he said to them, Where is your faith? And they being afraid wondered, saying one to another, What manner of man is this! for he commands even the winds and water, and they obey him.

26 And they arrived at the country of the Gadarenes, which is over against Galilee.

27 And when he went forth to land, there met him out of the city a certain man, which had devils *a* long time, and wore no clothes, neither stayed in *any* house, but in the tombs.

28 When he saw Yahshua, he cried out, and fell down before him, and with a loud voice said, What have I to do with you, Yahshua, *you* Son of God most high? I beg you, torment me not.

29 (For he had commanded the unclean spirit to come out of the man. For oftentimes it had caught him: and he was kept bound with chains and in fetters; and he broke the bands, and was driven by the devil into the wilderness.)

30 And Yahshua asked him, saying, What is your name? And he said, Legion: because many devils had entered into him.

31 And they sought him that he would not command them to go out into the deep.

32 And there was there a herd of many swine feeding on the mountain: and they begged him that he would permit them to enter into them. And he permitted them.

33 Then went the devils out of the man, and entered into the swine: and the herd ran violently down a steep place into the lake, and were drowned.

34 When they that fed *them* saw what was done, they fled, and went and told *it* in the city and in the country.

35 Then they went out to see what was done; and came to Yahshua, and found the man, out of whom the devils had departed, sitting at the feet of Yahshua, clothed, and in his right mind: and they were afraid.

36 They also which saw *it* told them by what means he that was possessed of the devils was healed.

37 Then the whole multitude of the country of the Gadarenes round about asked him to depart from them; for they were taken with great fear: and he went up into the ship, and returned back again.

38 Now the man out of whom the devils had departed sought him that he might be with him: but Yahshua sent him away, saying,

39 Return to your own house, and show how great things God has done to you. And he went his way, and published throughout the whole city how great things Yahshua had done to him.

40 ¶ And it came to pass, that, when Yahshua had returned, the people *gladly* received him: for they were all waiting for him.

41 And, behold, there came a man named Jairus, and he was a ruler of the synagogue: and he fell down at Yahshua's feet, and begged him that he would come into his house:

42 For he had only one daughter, about twelve years of age, and she lay a dying. But as he went the people thronged him.

43 And a woman having an issue of blood *for* twelve years, which had spent all her living upon physicians, neither could be healed by any,

44 Came behind *him*, and touched the border of his garment: and immediately her issue of blood stopped.

45 And Yahshua said, Who touched me? When all denied, Peter and they that were with him said, Master, the multitude throng you and press *you*, and say you, Who touched me?

46 And Yahshua said, Somebody has touched me: for I perceive that virtue is gone out of me.

47 And when the woman saw that she was not hidden, she came trembling, and falling down before him, she declared to him before all the people for what cause she had touched him, and how she was healed immediately.

48 And he said to her, Daughter, be of good comfort: your faith has made you whole; go in peace.

49 While he yet spoke, there came one from the ruler of the synagogue's *house*, saying to him, Your daughter is dead; trouble not the Master.

50 But when Yahshua heard *it*, he answered him, saying, Fear not: believe only, and she shall be made whole.

51 And when he came into the house, he allowed no man to go in, except Peter, and James, and John, and the father and the mother of the maiden.

52 And all wept, and bewailed her: but he said, Weep not; she is not dead, but sleeps.

53 And they laughed him to scorn, knowing that she was dead.

54 And he put them all out, and took her by the hand, and called, saying, Maid, arise.

55 And her spirit came again, and she arose immediately: and he commanded *them* to give her food.

56 And her parents were astonished: but he charged them that they should tell no man what was done.

Luke 9

9:1 ¶ Then he called his twelve disciples together, and gave them power and authority over all devils, and to cure diseases.

2 And he sent them to preach the kingdom of God, and to heal the sick.

3 And he said to them, Take nothing for *your* journey, neither staves, nor sack, neither bread, neither money; neither have two coats apiece.

4 And whatever house you enter into, there stay, and therefrom depart.

5 And whoever will not receive you, when you go out of that city, shake off the very dust from your feet for a testimony against them.

6 And they departed, and went through the towns, preaching the gospel, and healing every where.

7 Now Herod the tetrarch heard of all that was done by him: and he was perplexed, because that it was said of some, that John was risen from the dead;

8 And of some, that Elijah had appeared; and of others, that one of the old prophets was risen again.

9 And Herod said, John have I beheaded: but who is this, of whom I hear such things? And he desired to see him.

10 ¶ And the apostles, when they had returned, told him all that they had done. And he took them, and went aside privately into a desert place belonging to the city called Bethsaida.

11 And the people, when they knew *it*, followed him: and he received them, and spoke to them of the kingdom of God, and healed them that had need of healing.

12 And when the day began to wear away, then came the twelve, and said to him, Send the multitude away, that they may go into the towns and country round about, and lodge, and get provisions: for we are here in a desert place.

13 But he said to them, Give you them to eat. And they said, We have no more but five loaves and two fishes; unless we should go and buy meat for all this people.

14 For they were about five thousand men. And he said to his disciples, Make them sit down by fifties in a company.

15 And they did so, and made them all sit down.

16 Then he took the five loaves and the two fishes, and looking up to heaven, he blessed them, and broke, and gave to the disciples to set before the multitude.

17 And they did eat, and were all filled: and there was taken up of fragments that remained to them twelve baskets.

18 ¶ And it came to pass, as he was alone praying, his disciples were with him: and he asked them, saying, Whom say the people that I am?

19 They answering said, John the Baptist; but some *say*, Elijah; and others *say*, that one of the old prophets is risen again.

20 He said to them, But whom say you that I am? Peter answering said, The Messiah of God.

21 And he sharply charged them, and commanded *them* to tell no man that thing;

22 Saying, The Son of man must suffer many things, and be rejected by the elders and chief priests and scribes, and be slain, and be raised the third day.

23 And he said to *them* all, If any *man* will come after me, let him deny himself, and take up his cross daily, and follow me.

24 For whoever will save his life shall lose it: but whoever will lose his life for my sake, the same shall save it.

25 For what is a man advantaged, if he gains the whole world, and lose himself, or be cast away?

26 For whoever shall be ashamed of me and of my words, of him shall the Son of man be ashamed, when he shall come in his own glory, and *in his* Father's, and of the holy angels.

27 But I tell you of a truth, there are some standing here, which shall not taste of death, till they see the kingdom of God.

28 ¶ And it came to pass about eight days after these sayings, he took Peter and John and James, and went up into a mountain to pray.

29 And as he prayed, the fashion of his countenance was altered, and his clothing *was* white *and* glistening.

30 And, behold, there talked with him two men, which were Moses and Elijah:

31 Who appeared in glory, and spoke of his decease which he should accomplish at Jerusalem.

32 But Peter and they that were with him were heavy with sleep and when they were awake, they saw his glory, and the two men that stood with him.

33 And it came to pass, as they departed from him, Peter said to Yahshua, Master, it is good for us to be here: and let us make three tabernacles; one for you, and one for Moses, and one for Elijah: not knowing what he said.

34 While he thus spoke, there came a cloud, and overshadowed them: and they feared as they entered into the cloud.

35 And there came a voice out of the cloud, saying, This is my beloved Son: hear him.

36 And when the voice was past, Yahshua was found alone. And they kept *it* close, and told no man in those days any of those things which they had seen.

37 ¶ And it came to pass, that on the next day, when they had come down from the hill, many people met him.

38 And, behold, a man of the company cried out, saying, Master, I beseech you, look upon my son: for he is my only child.

39 And, lo, a spirit takes him, and he suddenly cries out; and it tears him that he foams again, and bruising him hardly departs from him.

40 And I asked your disciples to cast him out; and they could not.

41 And Yahshua answering said, O faithless and perverse generation, how long shall I be with you, and endure you? Bring your son here.

42 And as he was yet coming, the devil threw him down, and tore *him*. And Yahshua rebuked the unclean spirit, and healed the child, and delivered him again to his father.

43 ¶ And they were all amazed at the mighty power of God. But while they wondered every one at all things which Yahshua did, he said to his disciples,

44 Let these sayings sink down into your ears: for the Son of man shall be delivered into the hands of men.
45 But they understood not this saying, and it was hidden from them, that they perceived it not: and they feared to ask him of that saying.
46 Then there arose a reasoning among them, which of them should be greatest.
47 And Yahshua, perceiving the thought of their hearts, took a child, and set him by him,
48 And said to them, Whoever shall receive this child in my name receives me: and whoever shall receive me receives him that sent me: for he that is least among you all, the same shall be great.
49 And John answered and said, Master, we saw one casting out devils in your name; and we forbade him, because he follows not with us.
50 And Yahshua said to him, Forbid *him* not: for he that is not against us is for us.
51 ¶ And it came to pass, when the time had come that he should be received up, he steadfastly set his face to go to Jerusalem,
52 And sent messengers before his face: and they went, and entered into a village of the Samaritans, to make ready for him.
53 And they did not receive him, because his face was as though he would go to Jerusalem.
54 And when his disciples James and John saw *this*, they said, Lord, will you that we command fire to come down from heaven, and consume them, even as Elijah did?
55 But he turned, and rebuked them, and said, You know not what manner of spirit you are of.
56 For the Son of man has not come to destroy men's lives, but to save *them*. And they went to another village.
57 ¶ And it came to pass, that, as they went in the way, a certain *man* said to him, Lord, I will follow you wherever you go.
58 And Yahshua said to him, Foxes have holes, and birds of the air *have* nests; but the Son of man has no where to lay *his* head.
59 And he said to another, Follow me. But he said, Lord, permit me first to go and bury my father.
60 Yahshua said to him, Let the dead bury their dead: but go you and preach the kingdom of God.
61 And another also said, Lord, I will follow you; but let me first go bid them farewell, which are at home at my house.
62 And Yahshua said to him, No man, having put his hand to the plough, and looking back, is fit for the kingdom of God.

Luke 10

10:1 ¶ After these things the Lord appointed another seventy also, and sent them two by two before his face into every city and place, where he himself would come.
2 Therefore said he to them, The harvest truly *is* great, but the laborers *are* few: pray you therefore the Lord of the harvest, that he would send forth laborers into his harvest.
3 Go your ways: behold, I send you forth as lambs among wolves.
4 Carry neither purse, nor sack, nor shoes: and salute no man by the way.
5 And into whatever house you enter, first say, Peace *be* to this house.
6 And if the son of peace is there, your peace shall rest upon it: if not, it shall return to you again.
7 And in the same house remain, eating and drinking such things as they give: for the laborer is worthy of his hire. Go not from house to house.
8 And into whatever city you enter, and they receive you, eat such things as are set before you:
9 And heal the sick that are therein, and say to them, The kingdom of God has come near unto you.
10 But into whatever city you enter, and they receive you not, go your ways out into the streets of the same, and say,
11 Even the very dust of your city, which clings on us, we do wipe off against you: notwithstanding be you sure of this, that the kingdom of God has come near to you.
12 But I say to you, that it shall be more tolerable in that day for Sodom, than for that city.
13 Woe unto you, Chorazin! woe unto you, Bethsaida! for if the mighty works had been done in Tyre and Sidon, which have been done in you, they had a great while ago repented, sitting in sackcloth and ashes.
14 But it shall be more tolerable for Tyre and Sidon at the judgment, than for you.
15 And you, Capernaum, which are exalted to heaven, will be thrust down to hell.
16 He that hears you hears me; and he that despises you despises me; and he that despises me despises him that sent me.
17 ¶ And the seventy returned again with joy, saying, Lord, even the devils are subject to us through your name.
18 And he said to them, I beheld Satan as lightning fall from heaven.
19 Behold, I give to you power to tread on serpents and scorpions, and over all the power of the enemy: and nothing shall by any means hurt you.
20 Notwithstanding in this rejoice not, that the spirits are subject to you; but rather rejoice, because your names are written in heaven.
21 In that hour Yahshua rejoiced in spirit, and said, I thank you, O Father, Lord of heaven and earth, that you have hidden these things from the wise and prudent, and have revealed them to babes: even so, Father; for so it seemed good in your sight.
22 All things are delivered to me by my Father: and no man knows who the Son is, but the Father; and who the Father is, but the Son, and *he* to whom the Son will reveal *him*.

23 And he turned him to *his* disciples, and said privately, Blessed *are* the eyes which see the things that you see:
24 For I tell you, that many prophets and kings have desired to see those things which you see, and have not seen *them*; and to hear those things which you hear, and have not heard *them*.
25 ¶ And, behold, a certain lawyer stood up, and tempted him, saying, Master, what shall I do to inherit eternal life?
26 He said to him, What is written in the law? how read you?
27 And he answering said, You shall love the Lord *Yahweh* your God with all your heart, and with all your soul, and with all your strength, and with all your mind; and your neighbor as yourself.
28 And he said to him, You have answered right: this do, and you shall live.
29 But he, willing to justify himself, said to Yahshua, And who is my neighbor?
30 And Yahshua answering said, A certain *man* went down from Jerusalem to Jericho, and fell among thieves, which stripped him of his clothing, and wounded *him*, and departed, leaving *him* half dead.
31 And by chance there came down a certain priest that way: and when he saw him, he passed by on the other side.
32 And likewise a Levite, when he was at the place, came and looked *on him*, and passed by on the other side.
33 But a certain Samaritan, as he journeyed, came where he was: and when he saw him, he had compassion *on him*,
34 And went to *him*, and bound up his wounds, pouring in oil and wine, and set him on his own beast, and brought him to an inn, and took care of him.
35 And on the next day when he departed, he took out two pence, and gave *them* to the host, and said to him, Take care of him; and whatever you spend more, when I come again, I will repay you.
36 Which now of these three, think you, was neighbor to him that fell among the thieves?
37 And he said, He that showed mercy on him. Then said Yahshua to him, Go, and do you likewise.
38 ¶ Now it came to pass, as they went, that he entered into a certain village: and a certain woman named Martha received him into her house.
39 And she had a sister called Mary, which also sat at Yahshua's feet, and heard his word.
40 But Martha was encumbered about much serving, and came to him, and said, Lord, do you not care that my sister has left me to serve alone? bid her therefore that she help me.
41 And Yahshua answered and said to her, Martha, Martha, you are careful and troubled about many things:
42 But one thing is needful: and Mary has chosen that good part, which shall not be taken away from her.

Luke 11

11:1 ¶ And it came to pass, that, as he was praying in a certain place, when he ceased, one of his disciples said to him, Lord, teach us to pray, as John also taught his disciples.
2 And he said to them, When you pray, say, Our Father which are in heaven, Hallowed be your name. Your kingdom come. Your will be done, as in heaven, so in earth.
3 Give us day by day our daily bread.
4 And forgive us our sins; for we also forgive every one that is indebted to us. And lead us not into temptation; but deliver us from evil.
5 And he said to them, Which of you shall have a friend, and shall go to him at midnight, and say to him, Friend, lend me three loaves;
6 For a friend of mine in his journey has come to me, and I have nothing to set before him?
7 And he from within shall answer and say, Trouble me not: the door is now shut, and my children are with me in bed; I cannot rise and give you.
8 I say to you, Though he will not rise and give him, because he is his friend, yet because of his persistence he will rise and give him as many as he needs
9 And I say to you, Ask, and it shall be given you; seek, and you shall find; knock, and it shall be opened to you.
10 For every one that asks receives; and he that seeks finds; and to him that knocks it shall be opened.
11 If a son shall ask bread of any of you that is a father, will he give him a stone? or if *he asks for* a fish, will he for a fish give him a serpent?
12 Or if he shall ask an egg, will he offer him a scorpion?
13 If you then, being evil, know how to give good gifts to your children: how much more shall *your* heavenly Father give the Holy Spirit to them that ask him?
14 ¶ And he was casting out a devil, and it was dumb. And it came to pass, when the devil had gone out, the dumb spoke; and the people wondered.
15 But some of them said, He casts out devils through Beelzebub the chief of the devils.
16 And others, tempting *him*, sought of him a sign from heaven.
17 But he, knowing their thoughts, said to them, Every kingdom divided against itself is brought to desolation; and a house *divided* against a house falls.
18 If Satan also is divided against himself, how shall his kingdom stand? because you say that I cast out devils through Beelzebub.
19 And if I by Beelzebub casts out devils, by whom do your sons cast *them* out? therefore shall they be your judges.
20 But if I with the finger of God cast out devils, no doubt the kingdom of God has come upon you.
21 When a strong man armed keeps his palace, his goods are in peace:
22 But when a stronger than he shall come upon him, and overcome him, he takes from him all his armor wherein he trusted, and divides his spoils.

Luke 11

23 He that is not with me is against me: and he that gathers not with me scatters.
24 When the unclean spirit has gone out of a man, he walks through dry places, seeking rest; and finding none, he says, I will return to my house wherefrom I came out.
25 And when he comes, he finds *it* swept and garnished.
26 Then goes he, and takes *to him* seven other spirits more wicked than himself; and they enter in, and dwell there: and the last *state* of that man is worse than the first.
27 ¶ And it came to pass, as he spoke these things, a certain woman of the company lifted up her voice, and said to him, Blessed *is* the womb that bore you, and the breasts which you have sucked.
28 But he said, yes rather, blessed *are* they that hear the word of God, and keep it.
29 ¶ And when the people were gathered thick together, he began to say, This is an evil generation: they seek a sign; and there shall no sign be given it, but the sign of Jonah the prophet.
30 For as Jonah was a sign to the Ninevites, so shall also the Son of man be to this generation.
31 The queen of the south shall rise up in the judgment with the men of this generation, and condemn them: for she came from the utmost parts of the earth to hear the wisdom of Solomon; and, behold, a greater than Solomon *is* here.
32 The men of Nineveh shall rise up in the judgment with this generation, and shall condemn it: for they repented at the preaching of Jonah; and, behold, a greater than Jonah *is* here.
33 No man, when he has lighted a candle, puts *it* in a secret place, neither under a bushel, but on a candlestick, that they which come in may see the light.
34 The light of the body is the eye: therefore when your eye is sound, your whole body also is full of light; but when *your eye* is evil, your body also *is* full of darkness.
35 Take heed therefore that the light which is in you is not darkness.
36 If your whole body therefore *is* full of light, having no part dark, the whole shall be full of light, as when the bright shining of a candle does give you light.
37 ¶ And as he spoke, a certain Pharisee asked him to dine with him: and he went in, and sat down to meat.
38 And when the Pharisee saw *it*, he marveled that he had not first washed before dinner.
39 And the Lord said to him, Now do you Pharisees make clean the outside of the cup and the platter; but your inward part is full of ravening and wickedness.
40 *You* fools, did not he that made that which is outside make that which is within also?
41 But rather give alms of such things as you have; and, behold, all things are clean to you.
42 But woe unto you, Pharisees! for you tithe mint and rue and all manner of herbs, and pass over judgment and the love of God: these ought you to have done, and not to leave the other undone.
43 Woe unto you, Pharisees! for you love the uppermost seats in the synagogues, and greetings in the markets.
44 Woe unto you, scribes and Pharisees, hypocrites! for you are as graves which appear not, and the men that walk over *them* are not aware *of them*.
45 Then answered one of the lawyers, and said to him, Master, thus saying you reproach us also.
46 And he said, Woe unto you also, *you* lawyers! for you load men with burdens grievous to be borne, and you yourselves touch not the burdens with one of your fingers.
47 Woe unto you! for you build the sepulchers of the prophets, and your fathers killed them.
48 Truly you bear witness that you allow the deeds of your fathers: for they indeed killed them, and you build their sepulchers.
49 Therefore also said the wisdom of God, I will send them prophets and apostles, and *some* of them they shall slay and persecute:
50 That the blood of all the prophets, which was shed from the foundation of the world, may be required of this generation;
51 From the blood of Abel to the blood of Zechariah, which perished between the altar and the temple: truly I say to you, It shall be required of this generation.
52 Woe unto you, lawyers! for you have taken away the key of knowledge: you entered not in yourselves, and them that were entering in you hindered.
53 And as he said these things to them, the scribes and the Pharisees began to urge *him* vehemently, and to provoke him to speak of many things:
54 Lying in wait for him, and seeking to catch something out of his mouth, that they might accuse him.

Luke 12

12:1 ¶ In the mean time, when there were gathered together an innumerable multitude of people, insomuch that they trod one upon another, he began to say to his disciples first of all, Beware you of the leaven of the Pharisees, which is hypocrisy.
2 For there is nothing covered, that shall not be revealed; neither hidden, that shall not be known.
3 Therefore whatever you have spoken in darkness shall be heard in the light; and that which you have spoken in the ear in closets shall be proclaimed upon the housetops.
4 And I say to you my friends, Be not afraid of them that kill the body, and after that have no more that they can do.
5 But I will forewarn you whom you shall fear: Fear him, which after he has killed has power to cast into hell; yes, I say to you, Fear him.
6 Are not five sparrows sold for two farthings, and not one of them is forgotten before God?
7 But even the very hairs of your head are all numbered. Fear not therefore: you are of more value than many sparrows.
8 Also I say to you, Whoever shall confess me before men, him shall the Son of man also confess before the angels of God:

9 But he that denies me before men shall be denied before the angels of God.

10 And whoever shall speak a word against the Son of man, it shall be forgiven him: but to him that blasphemes against the Holy Ghost it shall not be forgiven.

11 And when they bring you to the synagogues, and *to* magistrates, and powers, take you no thought how or what thing you shall answer, or what you shall say:

12 For the Holy Ghost shall teach you in the same hour what you ought to say.

13 ¶ And one of the company said to him, Master, speak to my brother, that he divides the inheritance with me.

14 And he said to him, Man, who made me a judge or a divider over you?

15 And he said to them, Take heed, and beware of covetousness: for a man's life consists not in the abundance of the things which he possesses.

16 And he spoke a parable to them, saying, The ground of a certain rich man brought forth plentifully:

17 And he thought within himself, saying, What shall I do, because I have no room where to gather my fruits?

18 And he said, This will I do: I will pull down my barns, and build greater; and there will I gather all my fruits and my goods.

19 And I will say to my soul, Soul, you have many goods laid up for many years; take your ease, eat, drink, *and* be merry.

20 But God said to him, *You* fool, this night your soul shall be required of you: then whose shall those things be, which you have provided?

21 So *is* he that lays up treasure for himself, and is not rich toward God.

22 ¶ And he said to his disciples, Therefore I say to you, Take no thought for your life, what you shall eat; neither for the body, what you shall put on.

23 The life is more than food, and the body *is more* than clothing.

24 Consider the ravens: for they neither sow nor reap; which neither have storehouse nor barn; and God feeds them: how much more are you better than the fowls?

25 And which of you by taking thought can add to his stature one cubit?

26 If you then are not able to do that thing which is least, why take you thought for the rest?

27 Consider the lilies how they grow: they toil not, they spin not; and yet I say to you, that Solomon in all his glory was not arrayed like one of these.

28 If then God so clothes the grass, which is today in the field, and tomorrow is cast into the oven; how much more *will he clothe* you, O you of little faith?

29 And seek not you what you shall eat, or what you shall drink, neither be you of doubtful mind.

30 For all these things do the nations of the world seek after: and your Father knows that you have need of these things.

31 But rather seek you the kingdom of God; and all these things shall be added unto you.

32 Fear not, little flock; for it is your Father's good pleasure to give you the kingdom.

33 Sell what you have, and give alms; provide yourselves bags which grow not old, a treasure in the heavens that fails not, where no thief approaches, neither moth corrupts.

34 For where your treasure is, there will your heart be also.

35 Let your loins be girded about, and *your* lights burning;

36 And you yourselves like unto men that wait for their lord, when he will return from the wedding; that when he comes and knocks, they may open unto him immediately.

37 Blessed *are* those servants, whom the lord when he comes shall find watching: truly I say to you, that he shall gird himself, and make them to sit down to meat, and will come forth and serve them.

38 And if he shall come in the second watch, or come in the third watch, and find *them* so, blessed are those servants.

39 And this know, that if the master of the house had known what hour the thief would come, he would have watched, and not have allowed his house to be broken through.

40 Be you therefore ready also: for the Son of man comes at an hour when you think not.

41 ¶ Then Peter said to him, Lord, speak you this parable to us, or even to all?

42 And the Lord said, Who then is that faithful and wise steward, whom *his* lord shall make ruler over his household, to give *them their* portion of food in due season?

43 Blessed *is* that servant, whom his lord when he comes shall find so doing.

44 Of a truth I say to you, that he will make him ruler over all that he has.

45 But and if that servant says in his heart, My lord delays his coming; and shall begin to beat the menservants and maidens, and to eat and drink, and to be drunken;

46 The lord of that servant will come in a day when he looks not for *him*, and at an hour when he is not aware, and will cut him in two, and will appoint him his portion with the unbelievers.

47 And that servant, which knew his lord's will, and prepared not *himself*, neither did according to his will, shall be beaten with many *stripes*.

48 But he that knew not, and did commit things worthy of stripes, shall be beaten with few *stripes*. For to whomever much is given, of him shall be much required: and to whom men have committed much, of him they will ask the more.

49 I have come to send fire on the earth; and what will I, if it is already kindled?

50 But I have a baptism to be baptized with; and how am I constrained till it is accomplished!

51 Suppose you that I have come to give peace on earth? I tell you, No; but rather division:

52 For from now on there shall be five in one house divided, three against two, and two against three.

53 The father shall be divided against the son, and the son against the father; the mother against the daughter, and the daughter against the mother; the mother-in-law against her daughter-in-law, and the daughter-in-law against her mother-in-law.

Luke 12

54 ¶ And he said also to the people, When you see a cloud rise out of the west, immediately you say, There comes a shower; and so it is.
55 And when *you see* the south wind blow, you say, There will be heat; and it comes to pass.
56 *You* hypocrites, you can discern the face of the sky and of the earth; but how is it that you do not discern this time?
57 Yes, and why even of yourselves judge you not what is right?
58 When you go with your adversary to the magistrate, *as you are* in the way, give diligence that you may be delivered from him; lest he drag you to the judge, and the judge deliver you to the officer, and the officer cast you into prison.
59 I tell you, you shall not depart there, till you have paid the very last mite.

Luke 13

13:1 ¶ There were present at that season some that told him of the Galileans, whose blood Pilate had mingled with their sacrifices.
2 And Yahshua answering said to them, Suppose you that these Galileans were sinners above all the Galileans, because they suffered such things?
3 I tell you, No: but, unless you repent, you shall all likewise perish.
4 Or those eighteen, upon whom the tower in Siloam fell, and slew them, think you that they were sinners above all men that dwelt in Jerusalem?
5 I tell you, No: but, unless you repent, you shall all likewise perish.
6 ¶ He spoke also this parable; A certain *man* had a fig tree planted in his vineyard; and he came and sought fruit thereon, and found none.
7 Then said he to the dresser of his vineyard, Behold, these three years I come seeking fruit on this fig tree, and find none: cut it down; why uses it *up* the ground?
8 And he answering said to him, Lord, let it alone this year also, till I shall dig about it, and fertilize *it*:
9 And if it bears fruit, *well*: and if not, *then* after that you shall cut it down.
10 ¶ And he was teaching in one of the synagogues on the sabbath.
11 And, behold, there was a woman which had a spirit of infirmity *for* eighteen years, and was bent over, and could in no way lift up *herself*.
12 And when Yahshua saw her, he called *her to him*, and said to her, Woman, you are loosed from your infirmity.
13 And he laid *his* hands on her: and immediately she was made straight, and glorified God.
14 And the ruler of the synagogue answered with indignation, because that Yahshua had healed on the sabbath day, and said to the people, There are six days in which men ought to work: in them therefore come and be healed, and not on the sabbath day.

15 The Lord then answered him, and said, *You* hypocrite, does not each one of you on the sabbath loose his ox or *his* donkey from the stall, and lead *him* away to watering?
16 And ought not this woman, being a daughter of Abraham, whom Satan has bound, lo, these eighteen years, be loosed from this bond on the sabbath day?
17 And when he had said these things, all his adversaries were ashamed: and all the people rejoiced for all the glorious things that were done by him.
18 ¶ Then said he, Unto what is the kingdom of God like? and unto what shall I compare it?
19 It is like a grain of mustard seed, which a man took, and cast into his garden; and it grew, and became a great tree; and the fowls of the air lodged in the branches of it.
20 And again he said, Whereunto shall I liken the kingdom of God?
21 It is like leaven, which a woman took and hid in three measures of meal, till the whole was leavened.
22 And he went through the cities and villages, teaching, and journeying toward Jerusalem.
23 ¶ Then said one to him, Lord, are there few that be saved? And he said to them,
24 Strive to enter in at the narrow gate: for many, I say to you, will seek to enter in, and shall not be able.
25 When once the master of the house is risen up, and has shut the door, and you begin to stand outside, and to knock at the door, saying, Lord, Lord, open to us; and he shall answer and say to you, I know you not from where you are:
26 Then shall you begin to say, We have eaten and drank in your presence, and you have taught in our streets.
27 But he shall say, I tell you, I know you not from where you are; depart from me, all *you* workers of iniquity.
28 There shall be weeping and gnashing of teeth, when you shall see Abraham, and Isaac, and Jacob, and all the prophets, in the kingdom of God, and you *yourselves* thrust out.
29 And they shall come from the east, and *from* the west, and from the north, and *from* the south, and shall sit down in the kingdom of God.
30 And, behold, there are last which shall be first, and there are first which shall be last.
31 ¶ The same day there came certain of the Pharisees, saying to him, Get you out, and depart away: for Herod will kill you.
32 And he said to them, Go you, and tell that fox, Behold, I cast out devils, and I do cures today and tomorrow, and the third *day* I shall be perfected.
33 Nevertheless I must walk today, and tomorrow, and the *day* following: for it cannot be that a prophet perishes outside of Jerusalem.
34 O Jerusalem, Jerusalem, which kills the prophets, and stones them that are sent to you; how often would I have gathered your children together, as a hen *does gather* her brood under *her* wings, and you would not!
35 Behold, your house is left unto you desolate: and truly I say to you, You shall not see me, until *the time* comes when you shall say, Blessed *is* he that comes in the name of the Lord *Yahweh*.

Luke 14

14:1 ¶ And it came to pass, as he went into the house of one of the chief Pharisees to eat bread on the sabbath day, that they watched him.

2 And, behold, there was a certain man before him which had the dropsy.

3 And Yahshua answering spoke to the lawyers and Pharisees, saying, Is it lawful to heal on the sabbath day?

4 And they held their peace. And he took *him*, and healed him, and let him go;

5 And answered them, saying, Which of you shall have a donkey or an ox fallen into a pit, and will not immediately pull him out on the sabbath day?

6 And they could not answer him again to these things.

7 ¶ And he put forth a parable to those which were invited, when he marked how they chose out the chief rooms; saying to them,

8 When you are invited of any *man* to a wedding, sit not down in the highest place; lest a more honorable man than you be invited by him;

9 And he that invited you and him come and say to you, Give this man *this* place; and you begin with shame to take the lowest place.

10 But when you are invited, go and sit down in the lowest place; that when he that invited you comes, he may say to you, Friend, go up higher: then shall you have glory in the presence of them that sit at meat with you.

11 For whoever exalts himself shall be abased; and he that humbles himself shall be exalted.

12 Then said he also to him that invited him, When you make a dinner or a supper, call not your friends, nor your brethren, neither your kinsmen, nor *your* rich neighbors; lest they also invite you again, and a recompense be made you.

13 But when you make a feast, call the poor, the maimed, the lame, the blind:

14 And you shall be blessed; for they cannot recompense you: for you shall be recompensed at the resurrection of the just.

15 ¶ And when one of them that sat at meat with him heard these things, he said to him, Blessed *is* he that shall eat bread in the kingdom of God.

16 Then said he to him, A certain man made a great supper, and invited many:

17 And sent his servant at supper time to say to them that were invited, Come; for all things are now ready.

18 And they all with one *consent* began to make excuses. The first said to him, I have bought a piece of ground, and I must needs go and see it: I pray you have me excused.

19 And another said, I have bought five yoke of oxen, and I go to prove them: I pray you have me excused.

20 And another said, I have married a wife, and therefore I cannot come.

21 So that servant came, and showed his lord these things. Then the master of the house being angry said to his servant, Go out quickly into the streets and lanes of the city, and bring in here the poor, and the maimed, and the lame, and the blind.

22 And the servant said, Lord, it is done as you have commanded, and yet there is room.

23 And the lord said to the servant, Go out into the highways and hedges, and compel *them* to come in, that my house may be filled.

24 For I say to you, That none of those men which were invited shall taste of my supper.

25 ¶ And there went great multitudes with him: and he turned, and said to them,

26 If any *man* comes to me, and hates not his father, and mother, and wife, and children, and brothers, and sisters, yes, and his own life also, he cannot be my disciple.

27 And whoever does not bear his cross, and come after me, cannot be my disciple.

28 For which of you, intending to build a tower, sits not down first, and counts the cost, whether he has *sufficient* to finish *it*?

29 Lest perhaps, after he has laid the foundation, and is not able to finish *it*, all that behold *it* begin to mock him,

30 Saying, This man began to build, and was not able to finish.

31 Or what king, going to make war against another king, sits not down first, and consults whether he is able with ten thousand to meet him that comes against him with twenty thousand?

32 Or else, while the other is yet a great way off, he sends an ambassador, and desires conditions of peace.

33 So likewise, whoever he is of you that forsakes not all that he has, he cannot be my disciple.

34 Salt *is* good: but if the salt has lost its savor, with which shall it be seasoned?

35 It is neither fit for the land, nor yet for the dunghill; *but* men cast it out. He that has ears to hear, let him hear.

Luke 15

15:1 ¶ Then drew near to him all the publicans and sinners for to hear him.

2 And the Pharisees and scribes murmured, saying, This man receives sinners, and eats with them.

3 And he spoke this parable to them, saying,

4 What man of you, having a hundred sheep, if he loses one of them, does not leave the ninety and nine in the wilderness, and go after that which is lost, until he finds it?

5 And when he has found *it*, he lays *it* on his shoulders, rejoicing.

6 And when he comes home, he calls together *his* friends and neighbors, saying to them, Rejoice with me; for I have found my sheep which was lost.

7 I say to you, that likewise joy shall be in heaven over one sinner that repents, more than over ninety and nine just persons, which need no repentance.

8 Either what woman having ten pieces of silver, if she loses one piece, does not light a candle, and sweep the house, and seek diligently till she finds *it*?

Luke 15

9 And when she has found *it*, she calls *her* friends and *her* neighbors together, saying, Rejoice with me; for I have found the piece which I had lost.

10 Likewise, I say to you, there is joy in the presence of the angels of God over one sinner that repents.

11 ¶ And he said, A certain man had two sons:

12 And the younger of them said to *his* father, Father, give me the portion of goods that falls *to me*. And he divided to them *his* living.

13 And not many days after the younger son gathered all together, and took his journey into a far country, and there wasted his substance with riotous living.

14 And when he had spent all, there arose a mighty famine in that land; and he began to be in want.

15 And he went and joined himself to a citizen of that country; and he sent him into his fields to feed swine.

16 And he would desire to have filled his belly with the husks that the swine did eat: and no man gave to him.

17 And when he came to himself, he said, How many hired servants of my father's have bread enough and to spare, and I perish with hunger!

18 I will arise and go to my father, and will say to him, Father, I have sinned against heaven, and before you,

19 And am no more worthy to be called your son: make me as one of your hired servants.

20 And he arose, and came to his father. But when he was yet a great way off, his father saw him, and had compassion, and ran, and fell on his neck, and kissed him.

21 And the son said to him, Father, I have sinned against heaven, and in your sight, and am no more worthy to be called your son.

22 But the father said to his servants, Bring forth the best robe, and put *it* on him; and put a ring on his hand, and shoes on *his* feet:

23 And bring here the fatted calf, and kill *it*; and let us eat, and be merry:

24 For this my son was dead, and is alive again; he was lost, and is found. And they began to be merry.

25 Now his elder son was in the field: and as he came and drew near to the house, he heard music and dancing.

26 And he called one of the servants, and asked what these things meant.

27 And he said to him, Your brother has come; and your father has killed the fatted calf, because he has received him safe and sound.

28 And he was angry, and would not go in: therefore came his father out, and called for him.

29 And he answering said to *his* father, Lo, these many years did I serve you, neither transgressed I at any time your commandment: and yet you never gave me a kid, that I might make merry with my friends:

30 But as soon as this your son has come, which has devoured your living with harlots, you have killed for him the fatted calf.

31 And he said to him, Son, you are ever with me, and all that I have is yours.

32 It was proper that we should make merry, and be glad: for this your brother was dead, and is alive again; and was lost, and is found.

Luke 16

16:1 ¶ And he said also to his disciples, There was a certain rich man, which had a steward; and the same was accused unto him that he had wasted his goods.

2 And he called him, and said to him, How is it that I hear this of you? give an account of your stewardship; for you may be no longer steward.

3 Then the steward said within himself, What shall I do? for my lord takes away from me the stewardship: I cannot dig; to beg I am ashamed.

4 I am resolved what to do, that, when I am put out of the stewardship, they may receive me into their houses.

5 So he called every one of his lord's debtors *to him*, and said to the first, How much owe you to my lord?

6 And he said, A hundred measures of oil. And he said to him, Take your bill, and sit down quickly, and write fifty.

7 Then said he to another, And how much owe you? And he said, A hundred measures of wheat. And he said to him, Take your bill, and write fourscore.

8 And the lord commended the unjust steward, because he had done wisely: for the children of this world are in their generation wiser than the children of light.

9 And I say to you, Make to yourselves friends of the mammon of unrighteousness; that, when you fail, they may receive you into everlasting habitations.

10 He that is faithful in that which is least is faithful also in much: and he that is unjust in the least is unjust also in much.

11 If therefore you have not been faithful in the unrighteous mammon, who will commit to your trust the true *riches*?

12 And if you have not been faithful in that which is another man's, who shall give you that which is your own?

13 No servant can serve two masters: for either he will hate the one, and love the other; or else he will hold to the one, and despise the other. You cannot serve God and mammon.

14 And the Pharisees also, who were covetous, heard all these things: and they derided him.

15 And he said to them, You are they which justify yourselves before men; but God knows your hearts: for that which is highly esteemed among men is abomination in the sight of God.

16 The law and the prophets *were* until John: since that time the kingdom of God is preached, and every man presses into it.

17 And it is easier for heaven and earth to pass, than one tittle of the law to fail.

18 Whoever puts away his wife, and marries another, commits adultery: and whoever marries her that is put away from *her* husband commits adultery.

19 ¶ There was a certain rich man, which was clothed in purple and fine linen, and fared sumptuously every day:

20 And there was a certain beggar named Lazarus, which was laid at his gate, full of sores,
21 And desiring to be fed with the crumbs which fell from the rich man's table: moreover the dogs came and licked his sores.
22 And it came to pass, that the beggar died, and was carried by the angels into Abraham's bosom: the rich man also died, and was buried;
23 And in hell he lifted up his eyes, being in torment, and saw Abraham afar off, and Lazarus in his bosom.
24 And he cried and said, Father Abraham, have mercy on me, and send Lazarus, that he may dip the tip of his finger in water, and cool my tongue; for I am tormented in this flame.
25 But Abraham said, Son, remember that you in your lifetime received your good things, and likewise Lazarus evil things: but now he is comforted, and you are tormented.
26 And besides all this, between us and you there is a great gulf fixed: so that they which would pass from here to you cannot; neither can they pass to us, that *would come* from there.
27 Then he said, I pray you therefore, father, that you would send him to my father's house:
28 For I have five brothers; that he may testify to them, lest they also come into this place of torment.
29 Abraham said to him, They have Moses and the prophets; let them hear them.
30 And he said, No, father Abraham: but if one went to them from the dead, they will repent.
31 And he said to him, If they hear not Moses and the prophets, neither will they be persuaded, though one rose from the dead.

Luke 17

17:1 ¶ Then said he to the disciples, It is impossible but that offenses will come: but woe *unto him*, through whom they come!
2 It were better for him that a millstone were hung about his neck, and he cast into the sea, than that he should offend one of these little ones.
3 Take heed to yourselves: If your brother trespasses against you, rebuke him; and if he repents, forgive him.
4 And if he trespasses against you seven times in a day, and seven times in a day turns again to you, saying, I repent; you shall forgive him.
5 And the apostles said unto the Lord, Increase our faith.
6 And the Lord said, If you had faith as a grain of mustard seed, you might say to this sycamine tree, Be you plucked up by the root, and be you planted in the sea; and it should obey you.
7 But which of you, having a servant plowing or feeding cattle, will say to him by and by, when he has come from the field, Go and sit down to meat?
8 And will not rather say to him, Make ready that which I may sup, and gird yourself, and serve me, till I have eaten and drunk; and afterward you shall eat and drink?
9 Does he thank that servant because he did the things that were commanded him? I think not.
10 So likewise you, when you shall have done all those things which are commanded you, say, We are unprofitable servants: we have done that which was our duty to do.
11 ¶ And it came to pass, as he went to Jerusalem, that he passed through the midst of Samaria and Galilee.
12 And as he entered into a certain village, there met him ten men that were lepers, which stood afar off:
13 And they lifted up *their* voices, and said, Yahshua, Master, have mercy on us.
14 And when he saw *them*, he said to them, Go show yourselves to the priests. And it came to pass, that, as they went, they were cleansed.
15 And one of them, when he saw that he was healed, turned back, and with a loud voice glorified God,
16 And fell down on *his* face at his feet, giving him thanks: and he was a Samaritan.
17 And Yahshua answering said, Were there not ten cleansed? but where *are* the nine?
18 There were none found that returned to give glory to God, except this stranger.
19 And he said to him, Arise, go your way: your faith has made you whole.
20 ¶ And when he was demanded of the Pharisees, when the kingdom of God should come, he answered them and said, The kingdom of God comes not with observation:
21 Neither shall they say, Lo here! or, lo there! for, behold, the kingdom of God is within you.
22 And he said to the disciples, The days will come, when you shall desire to see one of the days of the Son of man, and you shall not see *it*.
23 And they shall say to you, See here; or, see there: go not after *them*, nor follow *them*.
24 For as the lightning, that lightens out of the one *part* under heaven, shines to the other *part* under heaven; so shall also the Son of man be in his day.
25 But first must he suffer many things, and be rejected by this generation.
26 And as it was in the days of Noah, so shall it be also in the days of the Son of man.
27 They did eat, they drank, they married wives, they were given in marriage, until the day that Noah entered into the ark, and the flood came, and destroyed them all.
28 Likewise also as it was in the days of Lot; they did eat, they drank, they bought, they sold, they planted, they built;
29 But the same day that Lot went out of Sodom it rained fire and brimstone from heaven, and destroyed *them* all.
30 Even thus shall it be in the day when the Son of man is revealed.
31 In that day, he which shall be upon the housetop, and his goods in the house, let him not come down to take it away: and he that is in the field, let him likewise not return back.
32 Remember Lot's wife.
33 Whoever shall seek to save his life shall lose it; and whoever shall lose his life shall preserve it.

Luke 17

34 I tell you, in that night there shall be two *men* in one bed; the one shall be taken, and the other shall be left.
35 Two *women* shall be grinding together; the one shall be taken, and the other left.
36 Two *men* shall be in the field; the one shall be taken, and the other left.
37 And they answered and said to him, Where, Lord? And he said to them, Wherever the body *is*, there will the eagles be gathered together.

Luke 18

18:1 ¶ And he spoke a parable to them *to this end*, that men ought always to pray, and not to faint;
2 Saying, There was in a city a judge, which feared not God, neither regarded man:
3 And there was a widow in that city; and she came to him, saying, Avenge me of my adversary.
4 And he would not for a while: but afterward he said within himself, Though I fear not God, nor regard man;
5 Yet because this widow troubles me, I will avenge her, lest by her continual coming she weary me.
6 And the Lord said, Hear what the unjust judge said.
7 And shall not God avenge his own elect, which cry day and night to him, though he bears long with them?
8 I tell you that he will avenge them speedily. Nevertheless when the Son of man comes, shall he find faith on the earth?
9 ¶ And he spoke this parable unto some which trusted in themselves that they were righteous, and despised others:
10 Two men went up into the temple to pray; the one a Pharisee, and the other a publican.
11 The Pharisee stood and prayed thus with himself, God, I thank you, that I am not as other men *are*, extortioners, unjust, adulterers, or even as this publican.
12 I fast twice in the week, I give tithes of all that I possess.
13 And the publican, standing afar off, would not lift up so much as *his* eyes to heaven, but smote upon his breast, saying, God be merciful to me a sinner.
14 I tell you, this man went down to his house justified *rather* than the other: for every one that exalts himself shall be abased; and he that humbles himself shall be exalted.
15 ¶ And they brought to him also infants, that he would touch them: but when *his* disciples saw *it*, they rebuked them.
16 But Yahshua called them *to him*, and said, Allow little children to come to me, and forbid them not: for of such is the kingdom of God.
17 Truly I say to you, Whoever shall not receive the kingdom of God as a little child shall in no way enter therein.
18 ¶ And a certain ruler asked him, saying, Good Master, what shall I do to inherit eternal life?
19 And Yahshua said to him, Why call you me good? none *is* good, save one, *that is*, God.
20 You know the commandments, Do not commit adultery, Do not kill, Do not steal, Do not bear false witness, Honor your father and your mother.
21 And he said, All these have I kept from my youth up.
22 Now when Yahshua heard these things, he said to him, Yet lack you one thing: sell all that you have, and distribute to the poor, and you shall have treasure in heaven: and come, follow me.
23 And when he heard this, he was very sorrowful: for he was very rich.
24 And when Yahshua saw that he was very sorrowful, he said, How hardly shall they that have riches enter into the kingdom of God!
25 For it is easier for a camel to go through a needle's eye, than for a rich man to enter into the kingdom of God.
26 And they that heard *it* said, Who then can be saved?
27 And he said, The things which are impossible with men are possible with God.
28 Then Peter said, Lo, we have left all, and followed you.
29 And he said to them, Truly I say to you, There is no man that has left house, or parents, or brothers, or wife, or children, for the kingdom of God's sake,
30 Who shall not receive manifold more in this present time, and in the world to come life everlasting.
31 ¶ Then he took *to him* the twelve, and said to them, Behold, we go up to Jerusalem, and all things that are written by the prophets concerning the Son of man shall be accomplished.
32 For he shall be delivered unto the Gentiles, and shall be mocked, and spitefully treated, and spit on:
33 And they shall scourge *him*, and put him to death: and the third day he shall rise again.
34 And they understood none of these things: and this saying was hidden from them, neither knew they the things which were spoken.
35 ¶ And it came to pass, that as he had come near to Jericho, a certain blind man sat by the way side begging:
36 And hearing the multitude pass by, he asked what it meant.
37 And they told him, that Yahshua of Nazareth passes by.
38 And he cried, saying, Yahshua, *you* Son of David, have mercy on me.
39 And they which went before rebuked him, that he should hold his peace: but he cried so much the more, *You* Son of David, have mercy on me.
40 And Yahshua stood, and commanded him to be brought to him: and when he had come near, he asked him,
41 Saying, What will you that I shall do to you? And he said, Lord, that I may receive my sight.
42 And Yahshua said to him, Receive your sight: your faith has saved you.
43 And immediately he received his sight, and followed him, glorifying God: and all the people, when they saw *it*, gave praise to God.

Luke 19

19:1 ¶ And *Yahshua* entered and passed through Jericho.

2 And, behold, *there was* a man named Zacchaeus, which was the chief among the publicans, and he was rich.

3 And he sought to see Yahshua who he was; and could not for the crowd, because he was little of stature.

4 And he ran before, and climbed up into a sycamore tree to see him: for he was to pass that *way*.

5 And when Yahshua came to the place, he looked up, and saw him, and said to him, Zacchaeus, make haste, and come down; for today I must stay at your house.

6 And he made haste, and came down, and received him joyfully.

7 And when they saw *it*, they all murmured, saying, That he had gone to be guest with a man that is a sinner.

8 And Zacchaeus stood, and said unto the Lord; Behold, Lord, the half of my goods I give to the poor; and if I have taken any thing from any man by false accusation, I restore *him* fourfold.

9 And Yahshua said unto him, This day has salvation come to this house, because he also is a son of Abraham.

10 For the Son of man has come to seek and to save that which was lost.

11 ¶ And as they heard these things, he added and spoke a parable, because he was near to Jerusalem, and because they thought that the kingdom of God should immediately appear.

12 He said therefore, A certain nobleman went into a far country to receive for himself a kingdom, and to return.

13 And he called his ten servants, and delivered them ten pounds, and said to them, Occupy till I come.

14 But his citizens hated him, and sent a message after him, saying, We will not have this *man* to reign over us.

15 And it came to pass, that when he had returned, having received the kingdom, then he commanded these servants to be called to him, to whom he had given the money, that he might know how much every man had gained by trading.

16 Then came the first, saying, Lord, your pound has gained ten pounds.

17 And he said to him, Well, you good servant: because you have been faithful in a very little, have you authority over ten cities.

18 And the second came, saying, Lord, your pound has gained five pounds.

19 And he said likewise to him, Be you also over five cities.

20 And another came, saying, Lord, behold, *here is* your pound, which I have kept laid up in a napkin:

21 For I feared you, because you are an austere man: you take up that you laid not down, and reap that you did not sow.

22 And he said to him, Out of your own mouth will I judge you, *you* wicked servant. You knew that I was an austere man, taking up that I laid not down, and reaping that I did not sow:

23 Why then gave not you my money into the bank, that at my coming I might have required my own with usury?

24 And he said to them that stood by, Take from him the pound, and give *it* to him that has ten pounds.

25 (And they said to him, Lord, he has ten pounds.)

26 For I say to you, That to every one which has shall be given; and from him that has not, even what he has shall be taken away from him.

27 But those my enemies, which would not that I should reign over them, bring here, and slay *them* before me.

28 ¶ And when he had thus spoken, he went before, ascending up to Jerusalem.

29 And it came to pass, when he had come near to Bethphage and Bethany, at the mount called *the mount* of Olives, he sent two of his disciples,

30 Saying, Go you into the village over opposite *you*; in which at your entering you shall find a colt tied, whereon yet no man sat: loose him, and bring *him* here.

31 And if any man asks you, Why do you loose *him*? thus shall you say to him, Because the Lord has need of him.

32 And they that were sent went their way, and found even as he had said to them.

33 And as they were loosing the colt, the owners thereof said to them, Why loose you the colt?

34 And they said, The Lord has need of him.

35 And they brought him to Yahshua: and they cast their garments upon the colt, and they set Yahshua thereon.

36 And as he went, they spread their clothes in the way.

37 And when he had come near, even now at the descent of the mount of Olives, the whole multitude of the disciples began to rejoice and praise God with a loud voice for all the mighty works that they had seen;

38 Saying, Blessed *be* the King that comes in the name of the Lord *Yahweh*: peace in heaven, and glory in the highest.

39 And some of the Pharisees from among the multitude said to him, Master, rebuke your disciples.

40 And he answered and said to them, I tell you that, if these should hold their peace, the stones would immediately cry out.

41 ¶ And when he had come near, he beheld the city, and wept over it,

42 Saying, If you had known, even you, at least in this your day, the things *which belong* unto your peace! but now they are hidden from your eyes.

43 For the days shall come upon you, that your enemies shall cast a trench about you, and compass you round, and keep you in on every side,

44 And shall lay you even with the ground, and your children within you; and they shall not leave in you one stone upon another; because you knew not the time of your visitation.

45 And he went into the temple, and began to cast out them that sold therein, and them that bought;

46 Saying to them, It is written, My house is the house of prayer: but you have made it a den of thieves.

47 And he taught daily in the temple. But the chief priests and the scribes and the chief of the people sought to destroy him,
48 And could not find what they might do: for all the people were very attentive to hear him.

Luke 20

20:1 ¶ And it came to pass, *that* on one of those days, as he taught the people in the temple, and preached the gospel, the chief priests and the scribes came upon *him* with the elders,
2 And spoke to him, saying, Tell us, by what authority do you these things? or who is he that gave you this authority?
3 And he answered and said to them, I will also ask you one thing; and answer me:
4 The baptism of John, was it from heaven, or of men?
5 And they reasoned with themselves, saying, If we shall say, From heaven; he will say, Why then believed you him not?
6 But and if we say, Of men; all the people will stone us: for they are persuaded that John was a prophet.
7 And they answered, that they could not tell from where *it was*.
8 And Yahshua said to them, Neither tell I you by what authority I do these things.
9 ¶ Then began he to speak to the people this parable; A certain man planted a vineyard, and let it forth to husbandmen, and went into a far country for a long time.
10 And at the season he sent a servant to the husbandmen, that they should give him of the fruit of the vineyard: but the husbandmen beat him, and sent *him* away empty.
11 And again he sent another servant: and they beat him also, and treated *him* shamefully, and sent *him* away empty.
12 And again he sent a third: and they wounded him also, and cast *him* out.
13 Then said the lord of the vineyard, What shall I do? I will send my beloved son: it may be they will reverence *him* when they see him.
14 But when the husbandmen saw him, they reasoned among themselves, saying, This is the heir: come, let us kill him, that the inheritance may be ours.
15 So they cast him out of the vineyard, and killed *him*. What therefore shall the lord of the vineyard do to them?
16 He shall come and destroy these husbandmen, and shall give the vineyard to others. And when they heard *it*, they said, God forbid.
17 And he beheld them, and said, What is this then that is written, The stone which the builders rejected, the same has become the head of the corner?
18 Whoever shall fall upon that stone shall be broken; but on whomever it shall fall, it will grind him to powder.
19 And the chief priests and the scribes the same hour sought to lay hands on him; and they feared the people: for they perceived that he had spoken this parable against them.
20 ¶ And they watched *him*, and sent forth spies, which should feign themselves just men, that they might take hold of his words, that so they might deliver him to the power and authority of the governor.
21 And they asked him, saying, Master, we know that you say and teach rightly, neither accept you the person *of any*, but teach the way of God truly:
22 Is it lawful for us to give tribute to Caesar, or not?
23 But he perceived their craftiness, and said to them, Why tempt you me?
24 Show me a penny. Whose image and superscription has it? They answered and said, Caesar's.
25 And he said to them, Render therefore to Caesar the things which are Caesar's, and to God the things which are God's.
26 And they could not take hold of his words before the people: and they marveled at his answer, and held their peace.
27 ¶ Then came to *him* certain of the Sadducees, which deny that there is any resurrection; and they asked him,
28 Saying, Master, Moses wrote to us, If any man's brother dies, having a wife, and he dies without children, that his brother should take his wife, and raise up seed unto his brother.
29 There were therefore seven brothers: and the first took a wife, and died without children.
30 And the second took her to wife, and he died childless.
31 And the third took her; and in like manner the seven also: and they left no children, and died.
32 Last of all the woman died also.
33 Therefore in the resurrection whose wife of them is she? for seven had her to wife.
34 And Yahshua answering said to them, The children of this world marry, and are given in marriage:
35 But they which shall be accounted worthy to obtain that world, and the resurrection from the dead, neither marry, nor are given in marriage:
36 Neither can they die any more: for they are equal to the angels; and are the children of God, being the children of the resurrection.
37 Now that the dead are raised, even Moses showed at the bush, when he calls the Lord *Yahweh* the God of Abraham, and the God of Isaac, and the God of Jacob.
38 For he is not a God of the dead, but of the living: for all live unto him.
39 ¶ Then certain of the scribes answering said, Master, you have well said.
40 And after that they dared not ask him any *questions at all*.
41 And he said to them, How say they that the Messiah is David's son?
42 And David himself said in the book of Psalms, The LORD *Yahweh* said to my Lord, Sit you on my right hand,
43 Till I make your enemies your footstool.
44 David therefore calls him Lord, how is he then his son?
45 Then in the audience of all the people he said to his disciples,

46 Beware of the scribes, which desire to walk in long robes, and love greetings in the markets, and the highest seats in the synagogues, and the chief rooms at feasts;
47 Which devour widows' houses, and for a show make long prayers: the same shall receive greater damnation.

Luke 21

21:1 ¶ And he looked up, and saw the rich men casting their gifts into the treasury.
2 And he saw also a certain poor widow casting in there two mites.
3 And he said, Of a truth I say to you, that this poor widow has cast in more than they all:
4 For all these have of their abundance cast in to the offerings of God: but she of her poverty has cast in all the living that she had.
5 ¶ And as some spoke of the temple, how it was adorned with beautiful stones and gifts, he said,
6 *As for* these things which you behold, the days will come, in which there shall not be left one stone upon another, that shall not be thrown down.
7 And they asked him, saying, Master, but when shall these things be? and what sign *will there be* when these things shall come to pass?
8 And he said, Take heed that you be not deceived: for many shall come in my name, saying, I am *the Messiah*; and the time draws near: go you not therefore after them.
9 But when you shall hear of wars and commotions, be not terrified: for these things must first come to pass; but the end *is* not by and by.
10 Then said he to them, Nation shall rise against nation, and kingdom against kingdom:
11 And great earthquakes shall be in various places, and famines, and pestilences; and fearful sights and great signs shall there be from heaven.
12 But before all these, they shall lay their hands on you, and persecute *you*, delivering *you* up to the synagogues, and into prisons, being brought before kings and rulers for my name's sake.
13 And it shall turn to you for a testimony.
14 Settle *it* therefore in your hearts, not to meditate before what you shall answer:
15 For I will give you a mouth and wisdom, which all your adversaries shall not be able to deny nor resist.
16 And you shall be betrayed both by parents, and brothers, and relatives, and friends; and *some* of you shall they cause to be put to death.
17 And you shall be hated by all *men* for my name's sake.
18 But there shall not a hair of your head perish.
19 In your patience possess you your souls.
20 ¶ And when you shall see Jerusalem encompassed with armies, then know that the desolation thereof is near.
21 Then let them which are in Judaea flee to the mountains; and let them which are in the midst of it depart out; and let not them that are in the country enter there into.
22 For these are the days of vengeance, that all things which are written may be fulfilled.
23 But woe unto them that are with child, and to them that give suck, in those days! for there shall be great distress in the land, and wrath upon this people.
24 And they shall fall by the edge of the sword, and shall be led away captive into all nations: and Jerusalem shall be trodden down by the Gentiles, until the times of the Gentiles are fulfilled.
25 And there shall be signs in the sun, and in the moon, and in the stars; and upon the earth distress of nations, with perplexity; the sea and the waves roaring;
26 Men's hearts failing them for fear, and for looking after those things which are coming on the earth: for the powers of heaven shall be shaken.
27 And then shall they see the Son of man coming in a cloud with power and great glory.
28 And when these things begin to come to pass, then look up, and lift up your heads; for your redemption draws near.
29 ¶ And he spoke to them a parable; Behold the fig tree, and all the trees;
30 When they now shoot forth, you see and know of your own selves that summer is now near at hand.
31 So likewise you, when you see these things come to pass, know you that the kingdom of God is near at hand.
32 Truly I say to you, This generation shall not pass away, till all is fulfilled.
33 Heaven and earth shall pass away: but my words shall not pass away.
34 And take heed to yourselves, lest at any time your hearts be overcharged with binging, and drunkenness, and cares of this life, and *so* that day comes upon you unexpectedly.
35 For as a snare shall it come on all them that dwell on the face of the whole earth.
36 Watch you therefore, and pray always, that you may be accounted worthy to escape all these things that shall come to pass, and to stand before the Son of man.
37 And in the day time he was teaching in the temple; and at night he went out, and stayed in the mount that is called *the mount* of Olives.
38 And all the people came early in the morning to him in the temple, for to hear him.

Luke 22

22:1 ¶ Now the feast of unleavened bread drew near, which is called the Passover.
2 And the chief priests and scribes sought how they might kill him; for they feared the people.
3 Then entered Satan into Judas surnamed Iscariot, being of the number of the twelve.
4 And he went his way, and communed with the chief priests and captains, how he might betray him to them.
5 And they were glad, and agreed to give him money.

Luke 22

6 And he promised, and sought opportunity to betray him to them in the absence of the multitude.

7 ¶ Then came the day of unleavened bread, when the passover must be killed.

8 And he sent Peter and John, saying, Go and prepare us the passover, that we may eat.

9 And they said to him, Where will you that we prepare?

10 And he said to them, Behold, when you have entered into the city, there shall a man meet you, bearing a pitcher of water; follow him into the house where he enters in.

11 And you shall say to the master of the house, The Master said to you, Where is the guest room, where I shall eat the passover with my disciples?

12 And he shall show you a large upper room furnished: there make ready.

13 And they went, and found as he had said to them: and they made ready the passover.

14 And when the hour had come, he sat down, and the twelve apostles with him.

15 And he said to them, With desire I have desired to eat this passover with you before I suffer:

16 For I say to you, I will not any more eat thereof, until it is fulfilled in the kingdom of God.

17 And he took the cup, and gave thanks, and said, Take this, and divide *it* among yourselves:

18 For I say to you, I will not drink of the fruit of the vine, until the kingdom of God shall come.

19 And he took bread, and gave thanks, and broke *it*, and gave to them, saying, This is my body which is given for you: this do in remembrance of me.

20 Likewise also the cup after supper, saying, This cup *is* the new testament in my blood, which is shed for you.

21 ¶ But, behold, the hand of him that betrays me *is* with me on the table.

22 And truly the Son of man goes, as it was determined: but woe to that man by whom he is betrayed!

23 And they began to inquire among themselves, which of them it was that should do this thing.

24 And there was also a strife among them, which of them should be accounted the greatest.

25 And he said to them, The kings of the Gentiles exercise lordship over them; and they that exercise authority upon them are called benefactors.

26 But you *shall* not *be* so: but he that is greatest among you, let him be as the younger; and he that is chief, as he that does serve.

27 For which *is* greater, he that sits at meat, or he that serves? *is* not he that sits at meat? but I am among you as he that serves.

28 You are they which have continued with me in my temptations.

29 And I appoint to you a kingdom, as my Father has appointed to me;

30 That you may eat and drink at my table in my kingdom, and sit on thrones judging the twelve tribes of Israel.

31 And the Lord said, Simon, Simon, behold, Satan has desired *to have* you, that he may sift *you* as wheat:

32 But I have prayed for you, that your faith fail not: and when you are converted, strengthen your brethren.

33 And he said to him, Lord, I am ready to go with you, both into prison, and to death.

34 And he said, I tell you, Peter, the cock shall not crow this day, before that you shall three times deny that you know me.

35 And he said to them, When I sent you without purse, and sack, and shoes, lacked you anything? And they said, Nothing.

36 Then said he to them, But now, he that has a purse, let him take *it*, and likewise *his* sack: and he that has no sword, let him sell his garment, and buy one.

37 For I say to you, that this that is written must yet be accomplished in me, And he was reckoned among the transgressors: for the things concerning me have an end.

38 And they said, Lord, behold, here *are* two swords. And he said to them, It is enough.

39 ¶ And he came out, and went, as he was inclined, to the mount of Olives; and his disciples also followed him.

40 And when he was at the place, he said to them, Pray that you enter not into temptation.

41 And he was withdrawn from them about a stone's cast, and knelt down, and prayed,

42 Saying, Father, if you are willing, remove this cup from me: nevertheless not my will, but yours, be done.

43 And there appeared an angel to him from heaven, strengthening him.

44 And being in agony he prayed more earnestly: and his sweat was as it were great drops of blood falling down to the ground.

45 And when he rose up from prayer, and had come to his disciples, he found them sleeping for sorrow,

46 And said to them, Why sleep you? rise and pray, lest you enter into temptation.

47 ¶ And while he yet spoke, behold a multitude, and he that was called Judas, one of the twelve, went before them, and drew near to Yahshua to kiss him.

48 But Yahshua said to him, Judas, betray you the Son of man with a kiss?

49 When they which were about him saw what would follow, they said to him, Lord, shall we smite with the sword?

50 And one of them smote the servant of the high priest, and cut off his right ear.

51 And Yahshua answered and said, Allow you thus far. And he touched his ear, and healed him.

52 Then Yahshua said to the chief priests, and captains of the temple, and the elders, which had come to him, Have you come out, as against a thief, with swords and staves?

53 When I was daily with you in the temple, you stretched forth no hands against me: but this is your hour, and the power of darkness.

54 ¶ Then took they him, and led *him*, and brought him into the high priest's house. And Peter followed afar off.

55 And when they had kindled a fire in the midst of the hall, and had set down together, Peter sat down among them.

56 But a certain maid saw him as he sat by the fire, and earnestly looked upon him, and said, This man was also with him.

57 And he denied him, saying, Woman, I know him not.
58 And after a little while another saw him, and said, You are also of them. And Peter said, Man, I am not.
59 And about the space of one hour after another confidently affirmed, saying, Of a truth this *fellow* also was with him: for he is a Galilaean.
60 And Peter said, Man, I know not what you say. And immediately, while he yet spoke, the cock crowed.
61 And the Lord turned, and looked upon Peter. And Peter remembered the word of the Lord, how he had said to him, Before the cock crows, you shall deny me three times.
62 And Peter went out, and wept bitterly.
63 ¶ And the men that held Yahshua mocked him, and smote *him*.
64 And when they had blindfolded him, they struck him on the face, and asked him, saying, Prophesy, who is it that smote you?
65 And many other things blasphemously spoke they against him.
66 And as soon as it was day, the elders of the people and the chief priests and the scribes came together, and led him into their council, saying,
67 Are you the Messiah? tell us. And he said to them, If I tell you, you will not believe:
68 And if I also ask *you*, you will not answer me, nor let *me* go.
69 Hereafter shall the Son of man sit on the right hand of the power of God.
70 Then said they all, Are you then the Son of God? And he said to them, You say that I am.
71 And they said, What need we any further witness? for we ourselves have heard of his own mouth.

Luke 23

23:1 ¶ And the whole multitude of them arose, and led him to Pilate.
2 And they began to accuse him, saying, We found this *fellow* perverting the nation, and forbidding to give tribute to Caesar, saying that he himself is the Messiah a King.
3 And Pilate asked him, saying, Are you the King of the Jews? And he answered him and said, You say *it*.
4 Then said Pilate to the chief priests and *to* the people, I find no fault in this man.
5 And they were the more fierce, saying, He stirs up the people, teaching throughout all Judea, beginning from Galilee to this place.
6 When Pilate heard of Galilee, he asked whether the man was a Galilaean.
7 And as soon as he knew that he belonged to Herod's jurisdiction, he sent him to Herod, who himself also was at Jerusalem at that time.
8 And when Herod saw Yahshua, he was exceedingly glad: for he was desirous to see him for a long *time*, because he had heard many things about him; and he hoped to have seen some miracle done by him.

9 Then he questioned with him in many words; but he answered him nothing.
10 And the chief priests and scribes stood and vehemently accused him.
11 And Herod with his men of war despised him as nothing, and mocked *him*, and arrayed him in a gorgeous robe, and sent him again to Pilate.
12 And the same day Pilate and Herod were made friends together: for before they were at enmity between themselves.
13 ¶ And Pilate, when he had called together the chief priests and the rulers and the people,
14 Said to them, You have brought this man to me, as one that perverts the people: and, behold, I, having examined *him* before you, have found no fault in this man touching those things whereof you accuse him:
15 No, nor yet Herod: for I sent you to him; and, lo, nothing worthy of death is done to him.
16 I will therefore chastise him, and release *him*.
17 (For of necessity he must release one to them at the feast.)
18 And they cried out all at once, saying, Away with this *man*, and release to us Barabbas:
19 (Who for a certain sedition made in the city, and for murder, was cast into prison.)
20 Pilate therefore, willing to release Yahshua, spoke again to them.
21 But they cried, saying, Crucify *him*, crucify him.
22 And he said to them the third time, Why, what evil has he done? I have found no cause of death in him: I will therefore chastise him, and let *him* go.
23 And they were instant with loud voices, requiring that he might be crucified. And the voices of them and of the chief priests prevailed.
24 And Pilate gave sentence that it should be as they required.
25 And he released to them him that for sedition and murder was cast into prison, whom they had desired; but he delivered Yahshua to their will.
26 ¶ And as they led him away, they laid hold upon one Simon, a Cyrenian, coming out of the country, and on him they laid the cross, that he might bear *it* after Yahshua.
27 And there followed him a great company of people, and of women, which also bewailed and lamented him.
28 But Yahshua turning to them said, Daughters of Jerusalem, weep not for me, but weep for yourselves, and for your children.
29 For, behold, the days are coming, in which they shall say, Blessed *are* the barren, and the wombs that never bore, and the breasts which never gave suck.
30 Then shall they begin to say to the mountains, Fall on us; and to the hills, Cover us.
31 For if they do these things in a green tree, what shall be done in the dry?
32 ¶ And there were also two other, malefactors, led with him to be put to death.
33 And when they had come to the place, which is called Calvary, there they crucified him, and the malefactors, one on the right hand, and the other on the left.

Luke 23

34 Then said Yahshua, Father, forgive them; for they know not what they do. And they parted his garments, and cast lots.

35 And the people stood beholding. And the rulers also with them derided *him*, saying, He saved others; let him save himself, if he is the Messiah, the chosen of God.

36 And the soldiers also mocked him, coming to him, and offering him vinegar,

37 And saying, If you are the king of the Jews, save yourself.

38 And a superscription also was written over him in letters of Greek, and Latin, and Hebrew, THIS IS THE KING OF THE JEWS.

39 And one of the malefactors which was hanged railed on him, saying, If you are the Messiah, save yourself and us.

40 But the other answering rebuked him, saying, Do not you fear God, seeing you are in the same condemnation?

41 And we indeed justly; for we receive the due reward of our deeds: but this man has done nothing amiss.

42 And he said to Yahshua, Lord, remember me when you come into your kingdom.

43 And Yahshua said to him, Truly I say to you, Today shall you be with me in paradise.

44 ¶ And it was about the sixth hour, and there was a darkness over all the earth until the ninth hour.

45 And the sun was darkened, and the veil of the temple was divided in the middle.

46 And when Yahshua had cried with a loud voice, he said, Father, into your hands I commend my spirit: and having said thus, he gave up the ghost.

47 Now when the centurion saw what was done, he glorified God, saying, Certainly this was a righteous man.

48 And all the people that came together to that sight, beholding the things which were done, smote their breasts, and returned.

49 And all his acquaintances, and the women that followed him from Galilee, stood afar off, beholding these things.

50 ¶ And, behold, *there was* a man named Joseph, a counselor; *and he was* a good man, and just:

51 (The same had not consented to the counsel and deed of them;) *he was* of Arimathaea, a city of the Jews: who also himself waited for the kingdom of God.

52 This *man* went to Pilate, and begged *for* the body of Yahshua.

53 And he took it down, and wrapped it in linen, and laid it in a sepulcher that was hewn in stone, wherein never man before was laid.

54 And that day was the preparation, and the sabbath drew on.

55 And the women also, which came with him from Galilee, followed after, and saw the sepulcher, and how his body was laid.

56 And they returned, and prepared spices and ointments; and rested the sabbath day according to the commandment.

Luke 24

24:1 ¶ Now upon the first *day* of the week, very early in the morning, they came to the sepulcher, bringing the spices which they had prepared, and certain *others* with them.

2 And they found the stone rolled away from the sepulcher.

3 And they entered in, and found not the body of the Lord Yahshua.

4 And it came to pass, as they were much perplexed thereabout, behold, two men stood by them in shining garments:

5 And as they were afraid, and bowed down *their* faces to the earth, they said to them, Why seek you the living among the dead?

6 He is not here, but is risen: remember how he spoke to you when he was yet in Galilee,

7 Saying, The Son of man must be delivered into the hands of sinful men, and be crucified, and the third day rise again.

8 And they remembered his words,

9 And returned from the sepulcher, and told all these things to the eleven, and to all the rest.

10 It was Mary Magdalene, and Joanna, and Mary *the mother* of James, and other *women that were* with them, which told these things to the apostles.

11 And their words seemed to them as idle tales, and they believed them not.

12 Then arose Peter, and ran to the sepulcher; and stooping down, he beheld the linen clothes laid by themselves, and departed, wondering in himself at that which had come to pass.

13 ¶ And, behold, two of them went that same day to a village called Emmaus, which was from Jerusalem *about* threescore furlongs.

14 And they talked together of all these things which had happened.

15 And it came to pass, that, while they communed *together* and reasoned, Yahshua himself drew near, and went with them.

16 But their eyes were held that they should not know him.

17 And he said to them, What manner of communications *are* these that you have one to another, as you walk, and are sad?

18 And the one of them, whose name was Cleopas, answering said to him, Are you only a stranger in Jerusalem, and have not known the things which have come to pass there in these days?

19 And he said to them, What things? And they said to him, Concerning Yahshua of Nazareth, which was a prophet mighty in deed and word before God and all the people:

20 And how the chief priests and our rulers delivered him to be condemned to death, and have crucified him.

21 But we trusted that it had been he which should have redeemed Israel: and besides all this, today is the third day since these things were done.

22 Yes, and certain women also of our company made us astonished, which were early at the sepulcher;
23 And when they found not his body, they came, saying, that they had also seen a vision of angels, which said that he was alive.
24 And certain of them which were with us went to the sepulcher, and found *it* even so as the women had said: but him they saw not.
25 Then he said to them, O fools, and slow of heart to believe all that the prophets have spoken:
26 Ought not the Messiah to have suffered these things, and to enter into his glory?
27 And beginning at Moses and all the prophets, he expounded to them in all the scriptures the things concerning himself.
28 And they drew near to the village, where they went: and he made as though he would have gone further.
29 But they constrained him, saying, Stay with us: for it is toward evening, and the day is far spent. And he went in to tarry with them.
30 And it came to pass, as he sat at meat with them, he took bread, and blessed *it*, and broke, and gave to them.
31 And their eyes were opened, and they knew him; and he vanished out of their sight.
32 And they said one to another, Did not our hearts burn within us, while he talked with us by the way, and while he opened to us the scriptures?
33 And they rose up the same hour, and returned to Jerusalem, and found the eleven gathered together, and them that were with them,
34 Saying, The Lord is risen indeed, and has appeared to Simon.
35 And they told what things *were done* in the way, and how he was known of them in breaking of bread.
36 ¶ And as they thus spoke, Yahshua himself stood in the midst of them, and said to them, Peace *be* unto you.
37 But they were terrified and frightened, and supposed that they had seen a spirit.
38 And he said to them, Why are you troubled? and why do thoughts arise in your hearts?
39 Behold my hands and my feet, that it is I myself: handle me, and see; for a spirit has not flesh and bones, as you see me have.
40 And when he had thus spoken, he showed them *his* hands and *his* feet.
41 And while they yet believed not for joy, and wondered, he said to them, Have you here any food?
42 And they gave him a piece of a broiled fish, and of a honeycomb.
43 And he took *it*, and did eat before them.
44 And he said to them, These *are* the words which I spoke to you, while I was yet with you, that all things must be fulfilled, which were written in the law of Moses, and *in* the prophets, and *in* the psalms, concerning me.
45 Then opened he their understanding, that they might understand the scriptures,
46 And said to them, Thus it is written, and thus it behooved the Messiah to suffer, and to rise from the dead the third day:

47 And that repentance and remission of sins should be preached in his name among all nations, beginning at Jerusalem.
48 And you are witnesses of these things.
49 And, behold, I send the promise of my Father upon you: but tarry you in the city of Jerusalem, until you are endued with power from on high.
50 ¶ And he led them out as far as to Bethany, and he lifted up his hands, and blessed them.
51 And it came to pass, while he blessed them, he was parted from them, and carried up into heaven.
52 And they worshipped him, and returned to Jerusalem with great joy:
53 And were continually in the temple, praising and blessing God. Amen.

John

John 1

1:1 ¶ In the beginning was the Word, and the Word was with God, and the Word was God.
2 The same was in the beginning with God.
3 All things were made by him; and without him was not anything made that was made.
4 In him was life; and the life was the light of men.
5 ¶ And the light shines in darkness; and the darkness comprehended it not.
6 There was a man sent from God, whose name *was* John.
7 The same came for a witness, to bear witness of the Light, that all *men* through him might believe.
8 He was not that Light, but *was sent* to bear witness of that Light.
9 *That* was the true Light, which lights every man that comes into the world.
10 He was in the world, and the world was made by him, and the world knew him not.
11 He came to his own, and his own received him not.
12 But as many as received him, to them gave he power to become the sons of God, *even* to them that believe on his name:
13 Which were born, not of blood, nor of the will of the flesh, nor of the will of man, but of God.
14 And the Word was made flesh, and dwelt among us, (and we beheld his glory, the glory as of the only begotten of the Father,) full of grace and truth.
15 ¶ John bore witness of him, and cried, saying, This was he of whom I spoke, He that comes after me is preferred before me: for he was before me.
16 And of his fullness have all we received, and grace for grace.
17 For the law was given by Moses, *but* grace and truth came by Yahshua the Messiah.
18 No man has seen God at any time; the only begotten Son, which is in the bosom of the Father, he has declared *him*.

John 1

19 ¶ And this is the record of John, when the Jews sent priests and Levites from Jerusalem to ask him, Who are you?
20 And he confessed, and denied not; but confessed, I am not the Messiah.
21 And they asked him, What then? Are you Elijah? And he said, I am not. Are you that prophet? And he answered, No.
22 Then said they to him, Who are you? that we may give an answer to them that sent us. What say you of yourself?
23 He said, I *am* the voice of one crying in the wilderness, Make straight the way of the Lord *Yahweh*, as said the prophet Isaiah.
24 And they which were sent were of the Pharisees.
25 And they asked him, and said to him, Why baptize you then, if you are not that Messiah, nor Elijah, neither that prophet?
26 John answered them, saying, I baptize with water: but there stands one among you, whom you know not;
27 He it is, who coming after me is preferred before me, whose shoe's lace I am not worthy to unloose.
28 These things were done in Bethabara beyond *the* Jordan, where John was baptizing.
29 ¶ The next day John saw Yahshua coming to him, and said, Behold the Lamb of God, which takes away the sin of the world.
30 This is he of whom I said, After me comes a man which is preferred before me: for he was before me.
31 And I knew him not: but that he should be made manifest to Israel, therefore have I come baptizing with water.
32 And John bore record, saying, I saw the Spirit descending from heaven like a dove, and it stayed upon him.
33 And I knew him not: but he that sent me to baptize with water, the same said to me, Upon whom you shall see the Spirit descending, and remaining on him, the same is he which baptizes with the Holy Ghost.
34 And I saw, and bore record that this is the Son of God.
35 Again the next day after John stood, and two of his disciples;
36 And looking upon Yahshua as he walked, he said, Behold the Lamb of God!
37 ¶ And the two disciples heard him speak, and they followed Yahshua.
38 Then Yahshua turned, and saw them following, and said to them, What seek you? They said to him, Rabbi, (which is to say, being interpreted, Master,) where dwell you?
39 He said to them, Come and see. They came and saw where he dwelt, and stayed with him that day: for it was about the tenth hour.
40 One of the two which heard John *speak*, and followed him, was Andrew, Simon Peter's brother.
41 He first found his own brother Simon, and said to him, We have found the Messiah, which is, being interpreted, the Christ.
42 And he brought him to Yahshua. And when Yahshua saw him, he said, You are Simon the son of Jonah: you shall be called Cephas, which is by interpretation, A stone.
43 ¶ The day following Yahshua would go forth into Galilee, and found Philip, and said to him, Follow me.
44 Now Philip was of Bethsaida, the city of Andrew and Peter.
45 Philip found Nathanael, and said to him, We have found him, of whom Moses in the law, and the prophets, did write, Yahshua of Nazareth, the son of Joseph.
46 And Nathanael said to him, Can there any good thing come out of Nazareth? Philip said to him, Come and see.
47 Yahshua saw Nathanael coming to him, and said of him, Behold an Israelite indeed, in whom is no guile!
48 Nathanael said to him, *From* where know you me? Yahshua answered and said to him, Before that Philip called you, when you were under the fig tree, I saw you.
49 Nathanael answered and said to him, Rabbi, you are the Son of God; you are the King of Israel.
50 Yahshua answered and said to him, Because I said to you, I saw you under the fig tree, believe you? you shall see greater things than these.
51 And he said to him, Truly, truly, I say to you, Hereafter you shall see heaven open, and the angels of God ascending and descending upon the Son of man.

John 2

2:1 ¶ And the third day there was a marriage in Cana of Galilee; and the mother of Yahshua was there:
2 And both Yahshua was called, and his disciples, to the marriage.
3 And when they wanted wine, the mother of Yahshua said to him, They have no wine.
4 Yahshua said to her, Woman, what have I to do with you? my hour is not yet come.
5 His mother said to the servants, Whatever he says to you, do *it*.
6 And there were set there six water pots of stone, after the manner of the purifying of the Jews, containing two or three firkins apiece.
7 Yahshua said to them, Fill the water pots with water. And they filled them up to the brim.
8 And he said to them, Draw out now, and bring to the governor of the feast. And they brought *it*.
9 When the ruler of the feast had tasted the water that was made wine, and knew not from where it was: (but the servants which drew the water knew;) the governor of the feast called the bridegroom,
10 And said to him, Every man at the beginning does set forth good wine; and when men have well drunk, then that which is worse: *but* you have kept the good wine until now.
11 This beginning of miracles did Yahshua in Cana of Galilee, and manifested forth his glory; and his disciples believed on him.
12 ¶ After this he went down to Capernaum, he, and his mother, and his brothers, and his disciples: and they continued there not many days.

13 And the Jews' passover was at hand, and Yahshua went up to Jerusalem,
14 And found in the temple those that sold oxen and sheep and doves, and the changers of money sitting:
15 And when he had made a whip of small cords, he drove them all out of the temple, and the sheep, and the oxen; and poured out the changers' money, and overthrew the tables;
16 And said to them that sold doves, Take these things away; make not my Father's house a house of merchandise.
17 And his disciples remembered that it was written, The zeal of your house has eaten me up.
18 Then answered the Jews and said to him, What sign show you to us, seeing that you do these things?
19 Yahshua answered and said to them, Destroy this temple, and in three days I will raise it up.
20 Then said the Jews, Forty and six years was this temple in building, and will you raise it up in three days?
21 But he spoke of the temple of his body.
22 When therefore he was risen from the dead, his disciples remembered that he had said this to them; and they believed the scripture, and the word which Yahshua had said.
23 ¶ Now when he was in Jerusalem at the passover, in the feast *day*, many believed in his name, when they saw the miracles which he did.
24 But Yahshua did not commit himself to them, because he knew all *men*,
25 And needed not that any should testify of man: for he knew what was in man.

John 3

3:1 ¶ There was a man of the Pharisees, named Nicodemus, a ruler of the Jews:
2 The same came to Yahshua by night, and said unto him, Rabbi, we know that you are a teacher come from God: for no man can do these miracles that you do, unless God is with him.
3 Yahshua answered and said to him, Truly, truly, I say to you, Unless a man is born again, he cannot see the kingdom of God.
4 Nicodemus said to him, How can a man be born when he is old? can he enter the second time into his mother's womb, and be born?
5 Yahshua answered, Truly, truly, I say to you, Unless a man is born of water and *of* the Spirit, he cannot enter into the kingdom of God.
6 That which is born of the flesh is flesh; and that which is born of the Spirit is spirit.
7 Marvel not that I said to you, You must be born again.
8 The wind blows where it wants, and you hear the sound thereof, but cannot tell from where it comes, and where it goes: so is every one that is born of the Spirit.
9 Nicodemus answered and said to him, How can these things be?
10 Yahshua answered and said to him, Are you a master of Israel, and know not these things?
11 Truly, truly, I say to you, We speak that we do know, and testify that we have seen; and you receive not our witness.
12 If I have told you earthly things, and you believe not, how shall you believe, if I tell you *of* heavenly things?
13 And no man has ascended up to heaven, but he that came down from heaven, *even* the Son of man which is in heaven.
14 And as Moses lifted up the serpent in the wilderness, even so must the Son of man be lifted up:
15 That whoever believes in him should not perish, but have eternal life.
16 For God so loved the world, that he gave his only begotten Son, that whoever believes in him should not perish, but have everlasting life.
17 For God sent not his Son into the world to condemn the world; but that the world through him might be saved.
18 He that believes on him is not condemned: but he that believes not is condemned already, because he has not believed in the name of the only begotten Son of God.
19 And this is the condemnation, that light has come into the world, and men loved darkness rather than light, because their deeds were evil.
20 For every one that does evil hates the light, neither comes to the light, lest his deeds should be reproved.
21 But he that does truth comes to the light, that his deeds may be made manifest, that they are done in God.
22 ¶ After these things came Yahshua and his disciples into the land of Judaea; and there he continued with them, and baptized.
23 And John also was baptizing in Aenon near to Salim, because there was much water there: and they came, and were baptized.
24 For John was not yet cast into prison.
25 Then there arose a question between *some* of John's disciples and the Jews about purifying.
26 And they came to John, and said to him, Rabbi, he that was with you beyond *the* Jordan, to whom you bear witness, behold, the same baptizes, and all *men* come to him.
27 John answered and said, A man can receive nothing, unless it is given him from heaven.
28 You yourselves bear me witness, that I said, I am not the Messiah, but that I am sent before him.
29 He that has the bride is the bridegroom: but the friend of the bridegroom, which stands and hears him, rejoices greatly because of the bridegroom's voice: this my joy therefore is fulfilled.
30 He must increase, but I *must* decrease.
31 He that comes from above is above all: he that is of the earth is earthly, and speaks of the earth: he that comes from heaven is above all.
32 And what he has seen and heard, that he testifies; and no man receives his testimony.
33 He that has received his testimony has set to his seal that God is true.

34 For he whom God has sent speaks the words of God: for God gives not the Spirit by measure *to him*.
35 The Father loves the Son, and has given all things into his hand.
36 He that believes on the Son has everlasting life: and he that believes not the Son shall not see life; but the wrath of God remains on him.

John 4

4:1 ¶ When therefore the Lord knew how the Pharisees had heard that Yahshua made and baptized more disciples than John,
2 (Though Yahshua himself baptized not, but his disciples,)
3 He left Judaea, and departed again into Galilee.
4 ¶ And he must need go through Samaria.
5 Then came he to a city of Samaria, which is called Sychar, near to the parcel of ground that Jacob gave to his son Joseph.
6 Now Jacob's well was there. Yahshua therefore, being wearied with *his* journey, sat thus on the well: *and* it was about the sixth hour.
7 There came a woman of Samaria to draw water: Yahshua said to her, Give me to drink.
8 (For his disciples were gone away to the city to buy food.)
9 Then said the woman of Samaria to him, How is it that you, being a Jew, ask drink of me, which am a woman of Samaria? for the Jews have no dealings with the Samaritans.
10 Yahshua answered and said to her, If you knew the gift of God, and who it is that says to you, Give me to drink; you would have asked of him, and he would have given you living water.
11 The woman said to him, Sir, you have nothing to draw with, and the well is deep: from where then have you that living water?
12 Are you greater than our father Jacob, which gave us the well, and drank thereof himself, and his children, and his cattle?
13 Yahshua answered and said to her, Whoever drinks of this water shall thirst again:
14 But whoever drinks of the water that I shall give him shall never thirst; but the water that I shall give him shall be in him a well of water springing up into everlasting life.
15 The woman said to him, Sir, give me this water, that I thirst not, neither come here to draw.
16 Yahshua said to her, Go, call your husband, and come here.
17 The woman answered and said, I have no husband. Yahshua said to her, You have well said, I have no husband:
18 For you have had five husbands; and he whom you now have is not your husband: in that said you truly.
19 The woman said to him, Sir, I perceive that you are a prophet.
20 Our fathers worshipped in this mountain; and you say, that in Jerusalem is the place where men ought to worship.
21 Yahshua said to her, Woman, believe me, the hour comes, when you shall neither in this mountain, nor yet at Jerusalem, worship the Father.
22 You worship you know not what: we know what we worship: for salvation is of the Jews.
23 But the hour comes, and now is, when the true worshippers shall worship the Father in spirit and in truth: for the Father seeks such to worship him.
24 God *is* a Spirit: and they that worship him must worship *him* in spirit and in truth.
25 The woman said to him, I know that Messiah comes, which is called Christ: when he has come, he will tell us all things.
26 Yahshua said to her, I that speak to you am *he*.
27 ¶ And upon this came his disciples, and marveled that he talked with the woman: yet no man said, What seek you? or, Why talk you with her?
28 The woman then left her water pot, and went her way into the city, and said to the men,
29 Come, see a man, which told me all things that ever I did: is not this the Messiah?
30 Then they went out of the city, and came to him.
31 In the mean while his disciples begged him, saying, Master, eat.
32 But he said to them, I have food to eat that you know not of.
33 Therefore said the disciples one to another, Has any man brought him *something* to eat?
34 Yahshua said to them, My meat is to do the will of him that sent me, and to finish his work.
35 Say not you, There are yet four months, and *then* comes harvest? behold, I say to you, Lift up your eyes, and look on the fields; for they are white already to harvest.
36 And he that reaps receives wages, and gathers fruit unto life eternal: that both he that sows and he that reaps may rejoice together.
37 And herein is that saying true, One sows, and another reaps.
38 I sent you to reap that which you bestowed no labor: other men labored, and you are entered into their labors.
39 And many of the Samaritans of that city believed on him for the saying of the woman, which testified, He told me all that ever I did.
40 So when the Samaritans had come unto him, they sought him that he would remain with them: and he stayed there two days.
41 And many more believed because of his own word;
42 And said to the woman, Now we believe, not because of your saying: for we have heard *him* ourselves, and know that this is indeed the Messiah, the Savior of the world.
43 ¶ Now after two days he departed therefrom, and went into Galilee.
44 For Yahshua himself testified, that a prophet has no honor in his own country.
45 Then when he had come into Galilee, the Galileans received him, having seen all the things that he did at Jerusalem at the feast: for they also went to the feast.

46 So Yahshua came again into Cana of Galilee, where he made the water wine. And there was a certain nobleman, whose son was sick at Capernaum.

47 When he heard that Yahshua had come out of Judaea into Galilee, he went to him, and begged him *so* that he would come down, and heal his son: for he was at the point of death.

48 Then said Yahshua to him, Unless you see signs and wonders, you will not believe.

49 The nobleman said to him, Sir, come down before my child dies.

50 Yahshua said to him, Go your way; your son lives. And the man believed the word that Yahshua had spoken to him, and he went his way.

51 And as he was now going down, his servants met him, and told *him*, saying, Your son lives.

52 Then inquired he of them the hour when he began to improve. And they said to him, Yesterday at the seventh hour the fever left him.

53 So the father knew that *it was* at the same hour, in which Yahshua said to him, Your son lives: and himself believed, and his whole house.

54 This *is* again the second miracle *that* Yahshua did, when he had come out of Judaea into Galilee.

John 5

5:1 ¶ After this there was a feast of the Jews; and Yahshua went up to Jerusalem.

2 Now there is at Jerusalem by the sheep *market* a pool, which is called in the Hebrew tongue Bethesda, having five porches.

3 In these lay a great multitude of weak folk, of blind, lame, withered, waiting for the moving of the water.

4 For an angel went down at a certain season into the pool, and troubled the water: whoever then first after the troubling of the water stepped in was made whole of whatever disease he had.

5 And a certain man was there, which had an infirmity *for* thirty and eight years.

6 When Yahshua saw him lie, and knew that he had been now a long time *in that case*, he said to him, Will you be made whole?

7 The weak man answered him, Sir, I have no man, when the water is troubled, to put me into the pool: but while I am coming, another steps down before me.

8 Yahshua said to him, Rise, take up your bed, and walk.

9 And immediately the man was made whole, and took up his bed, and walked: and on the same day was the sabbath.

10 The Jews therefore said to him that was cured, It is the sabbath day: it is not lawful for you to carry *your* bed.

11 He answered them, He that made me whole, the same said to me, Take up your bed, and walk.

12 Then asked they him, What man is that which said to you, Take up your bed, and walk?

13 And he that was healed knew not who it was: for Yahshua had conveyed himself away, a multitude being in *that* place.

14 Afterward Yahshua found him in the temple, and said to him, Behold, you are made whole: sin no more, lest a worse thing comes unto you.

15 The man departed, and told the Jews that it was Yahshua, which had made him whole.

16 And therefore did the Jews persecute Yahshua, and sought to slay him, because he had done these things on the sabbath day.

17 ¶ But Yahshua answered them, My Father works till now, and I work.

18 Therefore the Jews sought the more to kill him, because he not only had broken the sabbath, but said also that God was his Father, making himself equal with God.

19 Then answered Yahshua and said to them, Truly, truly, I say to you, The Son can do nothing of himself, but what he sees the Father do: for whatever things he does, these also does the Son likewise.

20 For the Father loves the Son, and shows him all things that himself does: and he will show him greater works than these, that you may marvel.

21 For as the Father raises up the dead, and revives *them*; even so the Son revives whom he will.

22 For the Father judges no man, but has committed all judgment to the Son:

23 That all *men* should honor the Son, even as they honor the Father. He that honors not the Son honors not the Father which has sent him.

24 Truly, truly, I say to you, He that hears my word, and believes on him that sent me, has everlasting life, and shall not come into condemnation; but is passed from death unto life.

25 Truly, truly, I say to you, The hour is coming, and now is, when the dead shall hear the voice of the Son of God: and they that hear shall live.

26 For as the Father has life in himself; so has he given to the Son to have life in himself;

27 And has given him authority to execute judgment also, because he is the Son of man.

28 Marvel not at this: for the hour is coming, in which all that are in the graves shall hear his voice,

29 And shall come forth; they that have done good, to the resurrection of life; and they that have done evil, to the resurrection of damnation.

30 I can of my own self do nothing: as I hear, I judge: and my judgment is just; because I seek not my own will, but the will of the Father which has sent me.

31 ¶ If I bear witness of myself, my witness is not true.

32 There is another that bears witness of me; and I know that the witness which he witnesses of me is true.

33 You sent to John, and he bore witness to the truth.

34 But I receive not testimony from man: but these things I say, that you might be saved.

35 He was a burning and a shining light: and you were willing for a season to rejoice in his light.

36 But I have greater witness than *that* of John: for the works which the Father has given me to finish, the same works that I do, bear witness of me, that the Father has sent me.

John 5

37 And the Father himself, which has sent me, has borne witness of me. You have neither heard his voice at any time, nor seen his shape.

38 And you have not his word abiding in you: for whom he has sent, him you believe not.

39 Search the scriptures; for in them you think you have eternal life: and they are they which testify of me.

40 And you will not come to me, that you might have life.

41 I receive not honor from men.

42 But I know you, that you have not the love of God in you.

43 I have come in my Father's name, and you receive me not: if another shall come in his own name, him you will receive.

44 How can you believe, which receive honor one of another, and seek not the honor that *comes* from God only?

45 Do not think that I will accuse you to the Father: there is *one* that accuses you, *even* Moses, in whom you trust.

46 For had you believed Moses, you would have believed me: for he wrote of me.

47 But if you believe not his writings, how shall you believe my words?

John 6

6:1 ¶ After these things Yahshua went over the sea of Galilee, which is *the sea* of Tiberias.

2 And a great multitude followed him, because they saw his miracles which he did on them that were diseased.

3 And Yahshua went up into a mountain, and there he sat with his disciples.

4 And the passover, a feast of the Jews, was near.

5 When Yahshua then lifted up *his* eyes, and saw a great company come to him, he said to Philip, From where shall we buy bread, that these may eat?

6 And this he said to prove him: for he himself knew what he would do.

7 Philip answered him, Two hundred pennyworth of bread is not sufficient for them, that every one of them may take a little.

8 One of his disciples, Andrew, Simon Peter's brother, said to him,

9 There is a lad here, which has five barley loaves, and two small fishes: but what are they among so many?

10 And Yahshua said, Make the men sit down. Now there was much grass in the place. So the men sat down, in number about five thousand.

11 And Yahshua took the loaves; and when he had given thanks, he distributed to the disciples, and the disciples to them that were set down; and likewise of the fishes as much as they desired.

12 When they were filled, he said to his disciples, Gather up the fragments that remain, *so* that nothing is lost.

13 Therefore they gathered *them* together, and filled twelve baskets with the fragments of the five barley loaves, which remained over and above to them that had eaten.

14 Then those men, when they had seen the miracle that Yahshua did, said, This is of a truth that prophet that should come into the world.

15 ¶ When Yahshua therefore perceived that they would come and take him by force, to make him a king, he departed again into a mountain himself alone.

16 And when evening had *now* come, his disciples went down to the sea,

17 And entered into a ship, and went over the sea toward Capernaum. And it was now dark, and Yahshua had not come to them.

18 And the sea arose by reason of a great wind that blew.

19 So when they had rowed about five and twenty or thirty furlongs, they saw Yahshua walking on the sea, and drawing near to the ship: and they were afraid.

20 But he said to them, It is I; be not afraid.

21 Then they willingly received him into the ship: and immediately the ship was at the land where they went.

22 ¶ The day following, when the people which stood on the other side of the sea saw that there was no other boat there, except that one where into his disciples were entered, and that Yahshua went not with his disciples into the boat, but *that* his disciples had gone away alone;

23 (However there came other boats from Tiberias near to the place where they did eat bread, after that the Lord had given thanks:)

24 When the people therefore saw that Yahshua was not there, neither his disciples, they also took shipping, and came to Capernaum, seeking for Yahshua.

25 And when they had found him on the other side of the sea, they said to him, Rabbi, when came you here?

26 Yahshua answered them and said, Truly, truly, I say to you, You seek me, not because you saw the miracles, but because you did eat of the loaves, and were filled.

27 Labor not for the food which perishes, but for that meat which endures to everlasting life, which the Son of man shall give to you: for him has God the Father sealed.

28 ¶ Then said they to him, What shall we do, that we might work the works of God?

29 Yahshua answered and said to them, This is the work of God, that you believe on him whom he has sent.

30 They said therefore to him, What sign show you then, that we may see, and believe you? what do you work?

31 Our fathers did eat manna in the desert; as it is written, He gave them bread from heaven to eat.

32 Then Yahshua said to them, Truly, truly, I say to you, Moses gave you not that bread from heaven; but my Father gives you the true bread from heaven.

33 For the bread of God is he which comes down from heaven, and gives life to the world.

34 Then said they to him, Lord, evermore give us this bread.

35 And Yahshua said to them, I am the bread of life: he that comes to me shall never hunger; and he that believes on me shall never thirst.

36 But I said to you, That you also have seen me, and believe not.

37 All that the Father gives me shall come to me; and him that comes to me I will by no means cast out.
38 For I came down from heaven, not to do my own will, but the will of him that sent me.
39 And this is the Father's will which has sent me, that of all which he has given me I should lose nothing, but should raise it up again at the last day.
40 And this is the will of him that sent me, that every one which sees the Son, and believes on him, may have everlasting life: and I will raise him up at the last day.
41 The Jews then murmured at him, because he said, I am the bread which came down from heaven.
42 And they said, Is not this Yahshua, the son of Joseph, whose father and mother we know? how is it then that he said, I came down from heaven?
43 Yahshua therefore answered and said to them, Murmur not among yourselves.
44 No man can come to me, unless the Father which has sent me draws him: and I will raise him up at the last day.
45 It is written in the prophets, And they shall be all taught of God *Yahweh*. Every man therefore that has heard, and has learned of the Father, comes to me.
46 Not that any man has seen the Father, save he which is of God, he has seen the Father.
47 Truly, truly, I say to you, He that believes on me has everlasting life.
48 I am that bread of life.
49 Your fathers did eat manna in the wilderness, and are dead.
50 This is the bread which came down from heaven, that a man may eat thereof, and not die.
51 I am the living bread which came down from heaven: if any man eats of this bread, he shall live forever: and the bread that I will give is my flesh, which I will give for the life of the world.
52 The Jews therefore strove among themselves, saying, How can this man give us *his* flesh to eat?
53 Then Yahshua said to them, Truly, truly, I say to you, Unless you eat the flesh of the Son of man, and drink his blood, you have no life in you.
54 Whoever eats my flesh, and drinks my blood, has eternal life; and I will raise him up at the last day.
55 For my flesh is food indeed, and my blood is drink indeed.
56 He that eats my flesh, and drinks my blood, dwells in me, and I in him.
57 As the living Father has sent me, and I live by the Father: so he that eats me, even he shall live by me.
58 This is that bread which came down from heaven: not as your fathers did eat manna, and are dead: he that eats of this bread shall live forever.
59 These things said he in the synagogue, as he taught in Capernaum.
60 ¶ Many therefore of his disciples, when they had heard *this*, said, This is a hard saying; who can hear it?
61 When Yahshua knew in himself that his disciples murmured at it, he said to them, Does this offend you?
62 *What* and if you shall see the Son of man ascend up where he was before?
63 It is the spirit that quickens; the flesh profits nothing: the words that I speak to you, *they* are spirit, and *they* are life.
64 But there are some of you that believe not. For Yahshua knew from the beginning who they were that believed not, and who should betray him.
65 And he said, Therefore said I to you, that no man can come to me, except it were given to him by my Father.
66 From that *time* many of his disciples went back, and walked no more with him.
67 Then said Yahshua to the twelve, Will you also go away?
68 Then Simon Peter answered him, Lord, to whom shall we go? you have the words of eternal life.
69 And we believe and are sure that you are that Messiah, the Son of the living God.
70 Yahshua answered them, Have not I chosen you twelve, and one of you is a devil?
71 He spoke of Judas Iscariot *the son* of Simon: for he it was that should betray him, being one of the twelve.

John 7

7:1 ¶ After these things Yahshua walked in Galilee: for he would not walk in Judaea, because the Jews sought to kill him.
2 Now the Jews' feast of tabernacles was at hand.
3 His brothers therefore said to him, Depart away, and go into Judaea, that your disciples also may see the works that you do.
4 For *there is* no man *that* does anything in secret, and he himself seeks to be known openly. If you do these things, show yourself to the world.
5 For neither did his brothers believe in him.
6 Then Yahshua said to them, My time has not yet come: but your time is always ready.
7 The world cannot hate you; but me it hates, because I testify of it, that the works thereof are evil.
8 Go you up to this feast: I go not up yet to this feast; for my time is not yet fully come.
9 When he had said these words to them, he stayed *still* in Galilee.
10 But when his brothers had gone up, then went he also up to the feast, not openly, but as it were in secret.
11 Then the Jews sought him at the feast, and said, Where is he?
12 And there was much murmuring among the people concerning him: for some said, He is a good man: others said, No; but he deceives the people.
13 However no man spoke openly of him for fear of the Jews.
14 ¶ Now about the middle of the feast Yahshua went up into the temple, and taught.
15 And the Jews marveled, saying, How knows this man letters, having never learned?

16 Yahshua answered them, and said, My doctrine is not mine, but his that sent me.
17 If any man will do his will, he shall know of the doctrine, whether it is of God, or *whether* I speak of myself.
18 He that speaks of himself seeks his own glory: but he that seeks his glory that sent him, the same is true, and no unrighteousness is in him.
19 Did not Moses give you the law, and *yet* none of you keeps the law? Why go you about to kill me?
20 The people answered and said, You have a devil: who goes about to kill you?
21 Yahshua answered and said to them, I have done one work, and you all marvel.
22 Moses therefore gave to you circumcision; (not because it is of Moses, but of the fathers;) and you on the sabbath day circumcise a man.
23 If a man on the sabbath day receives circumcision, that the law of Moses should not be broken; are you angry at me, because I have made a man completely whole on the sabbath day?
24 Judge not according to the appearance, but judge righteous judgment.
25 Then said some of them of Jerusalem, Is not this he, whom they seek to kill?
26 But, see, he speaks boldly, and they say nothing to him. Do the rulers know indeed that this is the very Messiah?
27 However we know this man from where he is: but when the Messiah comes, no man knows from where he is.
28 Then cried Yahshua in the temple as he taught, saying, You both know me, and you know from where I am: and I have not come of myself, but he that sent me is true, whom you know not.
29 But I know him: for I am from him, and he has sent me.
30 Then they sought to take him: but no man laid hands on him, because his hour had not yet come.
31 And many of the people believed on him, and said, When the Messiah comes, will he do more miracles than these which this *man* has done?
32 The Pharisees heard that the people murmured such things concerning him; and the Pharisees and the chief priests sent officers to take him.
33 Then said Yahshua to them, Yet a little while am I with you, and *then* I go to him that sent me.
34 You shall seek me, and shall not find *me*: and where I am, *there* you cannot come.
35 Then said the Jews among themselves, Where will he go, that we shall not find him? will he go to the dispersed among the Gentiles, and teach the Gentiles?
36 What *manner of* saying is this that he said, You shall seek me, and shall not find *me*: and where I am, *there* you cannot come?
37 ¶ In the last day, that great *day* of the feast, Yahshua stood and cried, saying, If any man thirsts, let him come to me, and drink.
38 He that believes on me, as the scripture has said, out of his belly shall flow rivers of living water.
39 (But this spoke he of the Spirit, which they that believe on him should receive: for the Holy Ghost was not yet *given*; because that Yahshua was not yet glorified.)
40 Many of the people therefore, when they heard this saying, said, Of a truth this is the Prophet.
41 Others said, This is the Messiah. But some said, Shall the Messiah come out of Galilee?
42 Has not the scripture said, That the Messiah comes of the seed of David, and out of the town of Bethlehem, where David was?
43 So there was a division among the people because of him.
44 And some of them would have taken him; but no man laid hands on him.
45 ¶ Then came the officers to the chief priests and Pharisees; and they said to them, Why have you not brought him?
46 The officers answered, Never *has a* man spoke like this man.
47 Then answered them the Pharisees, Are you also deceived?
48 Have any of the rulers or of the Pharisees believed on him?
49 But this people who knows not the law are cursed.
50 Nicodemus said to them, (he that came to Yahshua by night, being one of them,)
51 Does our law judge *any* man, before it hears him, and know what he does?
52 They answered and said to him, Are you also of Galilee? Search, and look: for out of Galilee arises no prophet.
53 And every man went to his own house.

John 8

8:1 ¶ Yahshua went to the mount of Olives.
2 And early in the morning he came again into the temple, and all the people came to him; and he sat down, and taught them.
3 And the scribes and Pharisees brought to him a woman taken in adultery; and when they had set her in the midst,
4 They said to him, Master, this woman was taken in adultery, in the very act.
5 Now Moses in the law commanded us, that such should be stoned: but what say you?
6 This they said, tempting him, that they might have to accuse him. But Yahshua stooped down, and with *his* finger wrote on the ground, *as though he heard them not.*
7 So when they continued asking him, he lifted up himself, and said to them, He that is without sin among you, let him first cast a stone at her.
8 And again he stooped down, and wrote on the ground.
9 And they which heard *it*, being convicted by *their own* conscience, went out one by one, beginning at the oldest, *even* to the last: and Yahshua was left alone, and the woman standing in the midst.
10 When Yahshua had lifted up himself, and saw none but the woman, he said to her, Woman, where are those your accusers? has no man condemned you?
11 She said, No man, Lord. And Yahshua said to her, Neither do I condemn you: go, and sin no more.

12 ¶ Then spoke Yahshua again to them, saying, I am the light of the world: he that follows me shall not walk in darkness, but shall have the light of life.

13 The Pharisees therefore said to him, You bear record of yourself; your record is not true.

14 Yahshua answered and said to them, Though I bear record of myself, *yet* my record is true: for I know from where I came, and where I go; but you cannot tell from where I come, and where I go.

15 You judge after the flesh; I judge no man.

16 And yet if I judge, my judgment is true: for I am not alone, but I and the Father that sent me.

17 It is also written in your law, that the testimony of two men is true.

18 I am one that bears witness of myself, and the Father that sent me bears witness of me.

19 Then said they to him, Where is your Father? Yahshua answered, You neither know me, nor my Father: if you had known me, you should have known my Father also.

20 These words spoke Yahshua in the treasury, as he taught in the temple: and no man laid hands on him; for his hour had not yet come.

21 ¶ Then said Yahshua again to them, I go my way, and you shall seek me, and shall die in your sins: where I go, you cannot come.

22 Then said the Jews, Will he kill himself? because he said, Where I go, you cannot come.

23 And he said to them, You are from beneath; I am from above: you are of this world; I am not of this world.

24 I said therefore to you, that you shall die in your sins: for if you believe not that I am *he*, you shall die in your sins.

25 Then said they to him, Who are you? And Yahshua said to them, Even *the same* that I said to you from the beginning.

26 I have many things to say and to judge of you: but he that sent me is true; and I speak to the world those things which I have heard from him.

27 They understood not that he spoke to them of the Father.

28 Then said Yahshua to them, When you have lifted up the Son of man, then shall you know that I am *he*, and *that* I do nothing of myself; but as my Father has taught me, I speak these things.

29 And he that sent me is with me: the Father has not left me alone; for I do always those things that please him.

30 As he spoke these words, many believed on him.

31 ¶ Then said Yahshua to those Jews which believed on him, If you continue in my word, *then* are you my disciples indeed;

32 And you shall know the truth, and the truth shall make you free.

33 They answered him, We are Abraham's seed, and were never in bondage to any man: how say you, You shall be made free?

34 Yahshua answered them, Truly, truly, I say to you, Whoever commits sin is the servant of sin.

35 And the servant stays not in the house forever: *but* the Son stays forever.

36 If the Son therefore shall make you free, you shall be free indeed.

37 I know that you are Abraham's seed; but you seek to kill me, because my word has no place in you.

38 ¶ I speak that which I have seen with my Father: and you do that which you have seen with your father.

39 They answered and said to him, Abraham is our father. Yahshua said to them, If you were Abraham's children, you would do the works of Abraham.

40 But now you seek to kill me, a man that has told you the truth, which I have heard from God: this did not Abraham.

41 You do the deeds of your father. Then said they to him, We are not born of fornication; we have one Father, *even* God.

42 Yahshua said to them, If God were your Father, you would love me: for I proceeded forth and came from God; neither came I of myself, but he sent me.

43 Why do you not understand my speech? *even* because you cannot hear my word.

44 You are of *your* father the devil, and the lusts of your father you will do. He was a murderer from the beginning, and stayed not in the truth, because there is no truth in him. When he speaks a lie, he speaks of his own: for he is a liar, and the father of it.

45 And because I tell *you* the truth, you believe me not.

46 ¶ Which of you convinces me of sin? And if I say the truth, why do you not believe me?

47 He that is of God hears God's words: you therefore hear *them* not, because you are not of God.

48 Then answered the Jews, and said to him, Say we not well that you are a Samaritan, and have a devil?

49 Yahshua answered, I have not a devil; but I honor my Father, and you do dishonor me.

50 And I seek not my own glory: there is one that seeks and judges.

51 ¶ Truly, truly, I say to you, If a man keeps my saying, he shall never see death.

52 Then said the Jews to him, Now we know that you have a devil. Abraham is dead, and the prophets; and you say, If a man keeps my saying, he shall never taste of death.

53 Are you greater than our father Abraham, which is dead? and the prophets are dead: whom make you yourself?

54 Yahshua answered, If I honor myself, my honor is nothing: it is my Father that honors me; of whom you say, that he is your God:

55 Yet you have not known him; but I know him: and if I should say, I know him not, I shall be a liar like unto you: but I know him, and keep his saying.

56 Your father Abraham rejoiced to see my day: and he saw *it*, and was glad.

57 Then said the Jews to him, You are not yet fifty years old, and have you seen Abraham?

58 Yahshua said to them, Truly, truly, I say to you, Before Abraham was, I am.

59 Then took they up stones to cast at him: but Yahshua hid himself, and went out of the temple, going through the midst of them, and so passed by.

John 9

9:1 ¶ And as *Yahshua* passed by, he saw a man which was blind from *his* birth.
2 And his disciples asked him, saying, Master, who did sin, this man, or his parents, that he was born blind?
3 Yahshua answered, Neither has this man sinned, nor his parents: but that the works of God should be made manifest in him.
4 I must work the works of him that sent me, while it is day: the night comes, when no man can work.
5 As long as I am in the world, I am the light of the world.
6 When he had thus spoken, he spat on the ground, and made clay of the spittle, and he anointed the eyes of the blind man with the clay,
7 And said to him, Go, wash in the pool of Siloam, (which is by interpretation, Sent.) He went his way therefore, and washed, and came seeing.
8 ¶ The neighbors therefore, and they which before had seen him that he was blind, said, Is not this he that sat and begged?
9 Some said, This is he: others *said*, He is like him: *but* he said, I am *he*.
10 Therefore said they to him, How were your eyes opened?
11 He answered and said, A man that is called Yahshua made clay, and anointed my eyes, and said to me, Go to the pool of Siloam, and wash: and I went and washed, and I received sight.
12 Then said they to him, Where is he? He said, I know not.
13 ¶ They brought to the Pharisees him that formerly was blind.
14 And it was the sabbath day when Yahshua made the clay, and opened his eyes.
15 Then again the Pharisees also asked him how he had received his sight. He said to them, He put clay upon my eyes, and I washed, and do see.
16 Therefore said some of the Pharisees, This man is not of God, because he keeps not the sabbath day. Others said, How can a man that is a sinner do such miracles? And there was a division among them.
17 They said to the blind man again, What say you of him, that he has opened your eyes? He said, He is a prophet.
18 But the Jews did not believe concerning him, that he had been blind, and received his sight, until they called the parents of him that had received his sight.
19 And they asked them, saying, Is this your son, who you say was born blind? how then does he now see?
20 His parents answered them and said, We know that this is our son, and that he was born blind:
21 But by what means he now sees, we know not; or who has opened his eyes, we know not: he is of age; ask him: he shall speak for himself.
22 These *words* spoke his parents, because they feared the Jews: for the Jews had agreed already, that if any man did confess that he was the Messiah, he should be put out of the synagogue.
23 Therefore said his parents, He is of age; ask him.
24 Then again called they the man that was blind, and said to him, Give God the praise: we know that this man is a sinner.
25 He answered and said, Whether he is a sinner *or not*, I know not: one thing I know, that, whereas I was blind, now I see.
26 Then said they to him again, What did he to you? how opened he your eyes?
27 He answered them, I have told you already, and you did not hear: why would you hear *it* again? will you also be his disciples?
28 Then they reviled him, and said, You are his disciple; but we are Moses' disciples.
29 We know that God spoke to Moses: *as for* this *fellow*, we know not from where he is.
30 The man answered and said to them, Why herein is a marvelous thing, that you know not from where he is, and *yet* he has opened my eyes.
31 Now we know that God hears not sinners: but if any man is a worshipper of God, and does his will, him he hears.
32 Since the world began was it not heard that any man opened the eyes of one that was born blind.
33 If this man were not of God, he could do nothing.
34 They answered and said to him, You were altogether born in sins, and do you teach us? And they cast him out.
35 ¶ Yahshua heard that they had cast him out; and when he had found him, he said to him, Do you believe on the Son of God?
36 He answered and said, Who is he, Lord, that I might believe on him?
37 And Yahshua said to him, You have both seen him, and it is he that talks with you.
38 And he said, Lord, I believe. And he worshipped him.
39 ¶ And Yahshua said, For judgment I have come into this world, that they which see not might see; and that they which see might be made blind.
40 And *some* of the Pharisees which were with him heard these words, and said to him, Are we blind also?
41 Yahshua said to them, If you were blind, you should have no sin: but now you say, We see; therefore your sin remains.

John 10

10:1 ¶ Truly, truly, I say to you, He that enters not by the door into the sheepfold, but climbs up some other way, the same is a thief and a robber.
2 But he that enters in by the door is the shepherd of the sheep.
3 To him the porter opens; and the sheep hear his voice: and he calls his own sheep by name, and leads them out.
4 And when he puts forth his own sheep, he goes before them, and the sheep follow him: for they know his voice.

5 And a stranger will they not follow, but will flee from him: for they know not the voice of strangers.
6 This parable spoke Yahshua to them: but they understood not what things they were which he spoke to them.
7 Then said Yahshua to them again, Truly, truly, I say to you, I am the door of the sheep.
8 All that ever came before me are thieves and robbers: but the sheep did not hear them.
9 I am the door: by me if any man enters in, he shall be saved, and shall go in and out, and find pasture.
10 The thief comes not, but for to steal, and to kill, and to destroy: I have come that they might have life, and that they might have *it* more abundantly.
11 I am the good shepherd: the good shepherd gives his life for the sheep.
12 But he that is a hireling, and not the shepherd, whose own the sheep are not, sees the wolf coming, and leaves the sheep, and flees: and the wolf catches them, and scatters the sheep.
13 The hireling flees, because he is a hireling, and cares not for the sheep.
14 I am the good shepherd, and know my *sheep*, and am known of mine.
15 As the Father knows me, even so know I the Father: and I lay down my life for the sheep.
16 And other sheep I have, which are not of this fold: them also I must bring, and they shall hear my voice; and there shall be one fold, *and* one shepherd.
17 Therefore does my Father love me, because I lay down my life, that I might take it again.
18 No man takes it from me, but I lay it down of myself. I have power to lay it down, and I have power to take it again. This commandment have I received from my Father.
19 ¶ There was a division therefore again among the Jews for these sayings.
20 And many of them said, He has a devil, and is mad; why hear you him?
21 Others said, These are not the words of him that has a devil. Can a devil open the eyes of the blind?
22 ¶ And it was at Jerusalem the feast of the dedication, and it was winter.
23 And Yahshua walked in the temple in Solomon's porch.
24 Then came the Jews round about him, and said to him, How long do you make us to doubt? If you are the Messiah, tell us plainly.
25 Yahshua answered them, I told you, and you believed not: the works that I do in my Father's name, they bear witness of me.
26 But you believe not, because you are not of my sheep, as I said to you.
27 My sheep hear my voice, and I know them, and they follow me:
28 And I give to them eternal life; and they shall never perish, neither shall any *man* pluck them out of my hand.
29 My Father, which gave *them* to me, is greater than all; and no *man* is able to pluck *them* out of my Father's hand.
30 I and *my* Father are one.
31 Then the Jews took up stones again to stone him.
32 Yahshua answered them, Many good works have I shown you from my Father; for which of those works do you stone me?
33 The Jews answered him, saying, For a good work we stone you not; but for blasphemy; and because that you, being a man, make yourself God.
34 Yahshua answered them, Is it not written in your law, I said, You are gods?
35 If he called them gods, to whom the word of God came, and the scripture cannot be broken;
36 Say you of him, whom the Father has sanctified, and sent into the world, You blaspheme; because I said, I am the Son of God?
37 If I do not the works of my Father, believe me not.
38 But if I do, though you believe not me, believe the works: that you may know, and believe, that the Father *is* in me, and I in him.
39 ¶ Therefore they sought again to take him: but he escaped out of their hand,
40 And went away again beyond *the* Jordan into the place where John at first baptized; and there he stayed.
41 And many resorted to him, and said, John did no miracle: but all things that John spoke of this man were true.
42 And many believed on him there.

John 11

11:1 ¶ Now a certain *man* was sick, *named* Lazarus, of Bethany, the town of Mary and her sister Martha.
2 (It was *that* Mary which anointed the Lord with ointment, and wiped his feet with her hair, whose brother Lazarus was sick.)
3 Therefore his sisters sent to him, saying, Lord, behold, he whom you love is sick.
4 When Yahshua heard *that*, he said, This sickness is not unto death, but for the glory of God, that the Son of God might be glorified thereby.
5 Now Yahshua loved Martha, and her sister, and Lazarus.
6 When he had heard therefore that he was sick, he stayed two days still in the same place where he was.
7 Then after that said he to *his* disciples, Let us go into Judaea again.
8 *His* disciples said to him, Master, the Jews of late sought to stone you; and go you there again?
9 Yahshua answered, Are there not twelve hours in the day? If any man walks in the day, he stumbles not, because he sees the light of this world.
10 But if a man walks in the night, he stumbles, because there is no light in him.
11 These things said he: and after that he said to them, Our friend Lazarus sleeps; but I go, that I may awake him out of sleep.
12 Then said his disciples, Lord, if he sleeps, he shall do well.
13 However Yahshua spoke of his death: but they thought that he had spoken of taking of rest in sleep.

John 11

14 Then said Yahshua to them plainly, Lazarus is dead.
15 And I am glad for your sakes that I was not there, to the intent you may believe; nevertheless let us go to him.
16 Then said Thomas, which is called Didymus, to his fellow disciples, Let us also go, that we may die with him.
17 ¶ Then when Yahshua came, he found that he had *lain* in the grave four days already.
18 Now Bethany was near to Jerusalem, about fifteen furlongs off:
19 And many of the Jews came to Martha and Mary, to comfort them concerning their brother.
20 Then Martha, as soon as she heard that Yahshua was coming, went and met him: but Mary sat *still* in the house.
21 Then said Martha to Yahshua, Lord, if you had been here, my brother had not died.
22 But I know, that even now, whatever you will ask of God, God will give *it* you.
23 Yahshua said to her, Your brother shall rise again.
24 Martha said to him, I know that he shall rise again in the resurrection at the last day.
25 Yahshua said to her, I am the resurrection, and the life: he that believes in me, though he were dead, yet shall he live:
26 And whoever lives and believes in me shall never die. Believe you this?
27 She said to him, Yes, Lord: I believe that you are the Messiah, the Son of God, which should come into the world.
28 And when she had so said, she went her way, and called Mary her sister secretly, saying, The Master has come, and calls for you.
29 As soon as she heard *that*, she arose quickly, and came to him.
30 Now Yahshua had not yet come into the town, but was in that place where Martha met him.
31 The Jews then which were with her in the house, and comforted her, when they saw Mary, that she rose up hastily and went out, followed her, saying, She goes to the grave to weep there.
32 Then when Mary had come where Yahshua was, and saw him, she fell down at his feet, saying to him, Lord, if you had been here, my brother had not died.
33 ¶ When Yahshua therefore saw her weeping, and the Jews also weeping which came with her, he groaned in the spirit, and was troubled,
34 And said, Where have you laid him? They said to him, Lord, come and see.
35 Yahshua wept.
36 Then said the Jews, Behold how he loved him!
37 And some of them said, Could not this man, which opened the eyes of the blind, have caused that even this man should not have died?
38 Yahshua therefore again groaning in himself came to the grave. It was a cave, and a stone lay upon it.
39 Yahshua said, Take you away the stone. Martha, the sister of him that was dead, said to him, Lord, by this time he stinks: for he has been *dead* four days.
40 Yahshua said to her, Said I not to you, that, if you would believe, you should see the glory of God?
41 Then they took away the stone *from the place* where the dead was laid. And Yahshua lifted up *his* eyes, and said, Father, I thank you that you have heard me.
42 And I knew that you hear me always: but because of the people which stand by I said *it*, that they may believe that you have sent me.
43 And when he thus had spoken, he cried with a loud voice, Lazarus, come forth.
44 And he that was dead came forth, bound hand and foot with grave clothes: and his face was bound about with a napkin. Yahshua said to them, Loose him, and let him go.
45 ¶ Then many of the Jews which came to Mary, and had seen the things which Yahshua did, believed on him.
46 But some of them went their ways to the Pharisees, and told them what things Yahshua had done.
47 Then gathered the chief priests and the Pharisees a council, and said, What do we? for this man does many miracles.
48 If we let him thus alone, all *men* will believe on him: and the Romans shall come and take away both our place and nation.
49 And one of them, *named* Caiaphas, being the high priest that same year, said to them, You know nothing at all,
50 Nor consider that it is expedient for us, that one man should die for the people, and that the whole nation perish not.
51 And this spoke he not of himself: but being high priest that year, he prophesied that Yahshua should die for that nation;
52 And not for that nation only, but that also he should gather together in one the children of God that were scattered abroad.
53 Then from that day forth they took counsel together for to put him to death.
54 Yahshua therefore walked no more openly among the Jews; but went therefrom to a country near to the wilderness, into a city called Ephraim, and there continued with his disciples.
55 And the Jews' passover was near at hand: and many went out of the country up to Jerusalem before the passover, to purify themselves.
56 Then sought they for Yahshua, and spoke among themselves, as they stood in the temple, What think you, that he will not come to the feast?
57 Now both the chief priests and the Pharisees had given a commandment, that, if any man knew where he was, he should show *it*, that they might take him.

John 12

12:1 ¶ Then Yahshua six days before the passover came to Bethany, where Lazarus was which had been dead, whom he raised from the dead.
2 There they made him a supper; and Martha served: but Lazarus was one of them that sat at the table with him.
3 Then took Mary a pound of ointment of spikenard, very costly, and anointed the feet of Yahshua, and wiped his feet with her hair: and the house was filled with the odor of the ointment.

4 Then said one of his disciples, Judas Iscariot, Simon's *son*, which should betray him,
5 Why was not this ointment sold for three hundred pence, and given to the poor?
6 This he said, not that he cared for the poor; but because he was a thief, and had the bag, and bore what was put therein.
7 Then said Yahshua, Let her alone: against the day of my burying has she kept this.
8 For the poor always you have with you; but me you have not always.
9 Many people of the Jews therefore knew that he was there: and they came not for Yahshua's sake only, but that they might see Lazarus also, whom he had raised from the dead.
10 But the chief priests consulted that they might put Lazarus also to death;
11 Because that by reason of him many of the Jews went away, and believed on Yahshua.
12 ¶ On the next day many people that had come to the feast, when they heard that Yahshua was coming to Jerusalem,
13 Took branches of palm trees, and went forth to meet him, and cried, Hosanna: Blessed *is* the King of Israel that comes in the name of the Lord *Yahweh*.
14 And Yahshua, when he had found a young donkey, sat thereon; as it is written,
15 Fear not, daughter of Zion: behold, your King comes, sitting on a donkey's colt.
16 These things understood not his disciples at the first: but when Yahshua was glorified, then remembered they that these things were written of him, and *that* they had done these things to him.
17 The people therefore that were with him when he called Lazarus out of his grave, and raised him from the dead, bore record.
18 For this cause the people also met him, for that they heard that he had done this miracle.
19 The Pharisees therefore said among themselves, Perceive you how you prevail nothing? behold, the world has gone after him.
20 ¶ And there were certain Greeks among them that came up to worship at the feast:
21 The same came therefore to Philip, which was of Bethsaida of Galilee, and desired him, saying, Sir, we would see Yahshua.
22 Philip came and told Andrew: and again Andrew and Philip told Yahshua.
23 And Yahshua answered them, saying, The hour has come, that the Son of man should be glorified.
24 Truly, truly, I say to you, Unless a corn of wheat falls into the ground and dies, it stays alone: but if it dies, it brings forth much fruit.
25 He that loves his life shall lose it; and he that hates his life in this world shall keep it unto life eternal.
26 If any man serves me, let him follow me; and where I am, there shall also my servant be: if any man serves me, him will *my* Father honor.

27 ¶ Now is my soul troubled; and what shall I say? Father, save me from this hour: but for this cause came I to this hour.
28 Father, glorify your name. Then came there a voice from heaven, *saying*, I have both glorified *it*, and will glorify *it* again.
29 The people therefore, that stood by, and heard *it*, said that it thundered: others said, An angel spoke to him.
30 Yahshua answered and said, This voice came not because of me, but for your sakes.
31 Now is the judgment of this world: now shall the prince of this world be cast out.
32 And I, if I am lifted up from the earth, will draw all *men* unto me.
33 This he said, signifying what death he should die.
34 The people answered him, We have heard out of the law that the Messiah stays forever: and how say you, The Son of man must be lifted up? who is this Son of man?
35 Then Yahshua said to them, Yet a little while is the light with you. Walk while you have the light, lest darkness comes upon you: for he that walks in darkness knows not where he goes.
36 While you have light, believe in the light, that you may be the children of light. These things spoke Yahshua, and departed, and did hide himself from them.
37 ¶ But though he had done so many miracles before them, yet they believed not on him:
38 That the saying of Isaiah the prophet might be fulfilled, which he spoke, Lord *Yahweh*, who has believed our report? and to whom has the arm of the Lord *Yahweh* been revealed?
39 Therefore they could not believe, because that Isaiah said again,
40 He has blinded their eyes, and hardened their heart; that they should not see with *their* eyes, nor understand with *their* heart, and be converted, and I should heal them.
41 These things said Isaiah, when he saw his glory, and spoke of him.
42 ¶ Nevertheless among the chief rulers also many believed on him; but because of the Pharisees they did not confess *him*, lest they should be put out of the synagogue:
43 For they loved the praise of men more than the praise of God.
44 ¶ Yahshua cried and said, He that believes on me, believes not on me, but on him that sent me.
45 And he that sees me sees him that sent me
46 I have come a light into the world, that whoever believes on me should not abide in darkness.
47 And if any man hear my words, and believe not, I judge him not: for I came not to judge the world, but to save the world.
48 He that rejects me, and receives not my words, has one that judges him: the word that I have spoken, the same shall judge him in the last day.
49 For I have not spoken of myself; but the Father which sent me, he gave me a commandment, what I should say, and what I should speak.

John 12

50 And I know that his commandment is life everlasting: whatever I speak therefore, even as the Father said to me, so I speak.

John 13

13:1 ¶ Now before the feast of the passover, when Yahshua knew that his hour had come that he should depart out of this world to the Father, having loved his own which were in the world, he loved them to the end.

2 And supper being ended, the devil having now put into the heart of Judas Iscariot, Simon's *son*, to betray him;

3 Yahshua knowing that the Father had given all things into his hands, and that he had come from God, and went to God;

4 He rose from supper, and laid aside his garments; and took a towel, and girded himself.

5 After that he poured water into a basin, and began to wash the disciples' feet, and to wipe *them* with the towel with which he was girded.

6 Then came he to Simon Peter: and Peter said to him, Lord, do you wash my feet?

7 Yahshua answered and said to him, What I do you know not now; but you shall know hereafter.

8 Peter said to him, You shall never wash my feet. Yahshua answered him, If I wash you not, you have no part with me.

9 Simon Peter said to him, Lord, not my feet only, but also *my* hands and *my* head.

10 Yahshua said to him, He that is washed needs not save to wash *his* feet, but is clean completely: and you are clean, but not all.

11 For he knew who should betray him; therefore said he, You are not all clean.

12 So after he had washed their feet, and had taken his garments, and had sat down again, he said to them, Know you what I have done to you?

13 You call me Master and Lord: and you say well; for *so* I am.

14 If I then, *your* Lord and Master, have washed your feet; you also ought to wash one another's feet.

15 For I have given you an example, that you should do as I have done to you.

16 Truly, truly, I say to you, The servant is not greater than his lord; neither he that is sent greater than he that sent him.

17 If you know these things, happy are you if you do them.

18 ¶ I speak not of you all: I know whom I have chosen: but that the scripture may be fulfilled, He that eats bread with me has lifted up his heel against me.

19 Now I tell you before it comes, that, when it has come to pass, you may believe that I am *he*.

20 Truly, truly, I say to you, He that receives whomever I send receives me; and he that receives me receives him that sent me.

21 When Yahshua had thus said, he was troubled in spirit, and testified, and said, Truly, truly, I say to you, that one of you shall betray me.

22 Then the disciples looked one on another, doubting of whom he spoke.

23 Now there was leaning on Yahshua's bosom one of his disciples, whom Yahshua loved.

24 Simon Peter therefore beckoned to him, that he should ask who it should be of whom he spoke.

25 He then lying on Yahshua's breast said to him, Lord, who is it?

26 Yahshua answered, He it is, to whom I shall give a sop, when I have dipped *it*. And when he had dipped the sop, he gave *it* to Judas Iscariot, *the son* of Simon.

27 And after the sop Satan entered into him. Then said Yahshua to him, That you do, do quickly.

28 Now no man at the table knew for what intent he spoke this to him.

29 For some *of them* thought, because Judas had the bag, that Yahshua had said to him, Buy *those things* that we have need of against the feast; or, that he should give something to the poor.

30 He then having received the sop went immediately out: and it was night.

31 ¶ Therefore, when he had gone out, Yahshua said, Now is the Son of man glorified, and God is glorified in him.

32 If God is glorified in him, God shall also glorify him in himself, and shall immediately glorify him.

33 Little children, yet a little while I am with you. You shall seek me: and as I said to the Jews, Where I go, you cannot come; so now I say to you.

34 A new commandment I give to you, That you love one another; as I have loved you, that you also love one another.

35 By this shall all *men* know that you are my disciples, if you have love one to another.

36 ¶ Simon Peter said to him, Lord, where go you? Yahshua answered him, Where I go, you can not follow me now; but you shall follow me afterward.

37 Peter said to him, Lord, why cannot I follow you now? I will lay down my life for your sake.

38 Yahshua answered him, Will you lay down your life for my sake? Truly, truly, I say to you, The cock shall not crow, till you have denied me three times.

John 14

14:1 ¶ Let not your heart be troubled: you believe in God, believe also in me.

2 In my Father's house are many mansions: if *it were* not *so*, I would have told you. I go to prepare a place for you.

3 And if I go and prepare a place for you, I will come again, and receive you to myself; that where I am, *there* you may be also.

4 ¶ And where I go you know, and the way you know.

5 Thomas said to him, Lord, we know not where you go; and how can we know the way?

6 Yahshua said to him, I am the way, the truth, and the life: no man comes to the Father, but by me.

7 If you had known me, you should have known my Father also: and from now on you know him, and have seen him.

8 Philip said to him, Lord, show us the Father, and it suffices us.
9 Yahshua said to him, Have I been so long *a* time with you, and yet have you not known me, Philip? he that has seen me has seen the Father; and how say you *then*, Show us the Father?
10 Believe you not that I am in the Father, and the Father in me? the words that I speak to you I speak not of myself: but the Father that dwells in me, he does the works.
11 Believe me that I *am* in the Father, and the Father in me: or else believe me for the very works' sake.
12 ¶ Truly, truly, I say to you, He that believes on me, the works that I do shall he do also; and greater *works* than these shall he do; because I go to my Father.
13 And whatever you shall ask in my name, that will I do, that the Father may be glorified in the Son.
14 If you shall ask anything in my name, I will do *it*.
15 ¶ If you love me, keep my commandments.
16 And I will pray the Father, and he shall give you another Comforter, that he may abide with you forever;
17 *Even* the Spirit of truth; whom the world cannot receive, because it sees him not, neither knows him: but you know him; for he dwells with you, and shall be in you.
18 ¶ I will not leave you comfortless: I will come to you
19 Yet a little while, and the world sees me no more; but you see me: because I live, you shall live also.
20 At that day you shall know that I *am* in my Father, and you in me, and I in you.
21 He that has my commandments, and keeps them, he it is that loves me: and he that loves me shall be loved by my Father, and I will love him, and will manifest myself to him.
22 Judas said to him, not Iscariot, Lord, how is it that you will manifest yourself to us, and not to the world?
23 Yahshua answered and said to him, If a man loves me, he will keep my words: and my Father will love him, and we will come to him, and make our abode with him.
24 He that loves me not keeps not my sayings: and the word which you hear is not mine, but the Father's which sent me.
25 ¶ These things have I spoken to you, being *yet* present with you.
26 But the Comforter, *which is* the Holy Ghost, whom the Father will send in my name, he shall teach you all things, and bring all things to your remembrance, whatever I have said to you.
27 Peace I leave with you, my peace I give to you: not as the world gives, give I unto you. Let not your heart be troubled, neither let it be afraid.
28 ¶ You have heard how I said to you, I go away, and come *again* to you. If you loved me, you would rejoice, because I said, I go to the Father: for my Father is greater than I.
29 And now I have told you before it comes to pass, that, when it has come to pass, you might believe.
30 Hereafter I will not talk much with you: for the prince of this world comes, and has nothing in me.
31 But that the world may know that I love the Father; and as the Father gave me commandment, even so I do. Arise, let us go away.

John 15

15:1 ¶ I am the true vine, and my Father is the husbandman.
2 Every branch in me that bears not fruit he takes away: and every *branch* that bears fruit, he prunes it, that it may bring forth more fruit.
3 Now you are clean through the word which I have spoken to you.
4 Abide in me, and I in you. As the branch cannot bear fruit of itself, unless it abides in the vine; no more can you, unless you abide in me.
5 I am the vine, you *are* the branches: He that abides in me, and I in him, the same brings forth much fruit: for without me you can do nothing.
6 If a man abides not in me, he is cast forth as a branch, and is withered; and men gather them, and cast *them* into the fire, and they are burned.
7 If you abide in me, and my words abide in you, you shall ask what you will, and it shall be done unto you.
8 Herein is my Father glorified, that you bear much fruit; so shall you be my disciples.
9 ¶ As the Father has loved me, so have I loved you: continue you in my love.
10 If you keep my commandments, you shall abide in my love; even as I have kept my Father's commandments, and abide in his love.
11 These things have I spoken to you, that my joy might remain in you, and *that* your joy might be full.
12 This is my commandment, That you love one another, as I have loved you.
13 Greater love has no man than this, that a man lays down his life for his friends.
14 You are my friends, if you do whatever I command you.
15 From now on I call you not servants; for the servant knows not what his lord does: but I have called you friends; for all things that I have heard of my Father I have made known to you.
16 You have not chosen me, but I have chosen you, and ordained you, that you should go and bring forth fruit, and *that* your fruit should remain: that whatever you shall ask of the Father in my name, he may give it you.
17 These things I command you, that you love one another.
18 ¶ If the world hates you, you know that it hated me before *it hated* you.
19 If you were of the world, the world would love his own: but because you are not of the world, but I have chosen you out of the world, therefore the world hates you.
20 Remember the word that I said to you, The servant is not greater than his lord. If they have persecuted me, they will also persecute you; if they have kept my saying, they will keep yours also.

21 But all these things will they do to you for my name's sake, because they know not him that sent me.
22 If I had not come and spoken to them, they had not had sin: but now they have no cloak for their sin.
23 He that hates me hates my Father also.
24 If I had not done among them the works which no other man did, they had not had sin: but now have they both seen and hated both me and my Father.
25 But *this came to pass*, that the word might be fulfilled that is written in their law, They hated me without a cause.
26 ¶ But when the Comforter has come, whom I will send to you from the Father, *even* the Spirit of truth, which proceeds from the Father, he shall testify of me:
27 And you also shall bear witness, because you have been with me from the beginning.

John 16

16:1 ¶ These things have I spoken to you, that you should not be offended.
2 They shall put you out of the synagogues: yes, the time comes, that whoever kills you will think that he does God service.
3 And these things will they do to you, because they have not known the Father, nor me.
4 But these things have I told you, that when the time shall come, you may remember that I told you of them. And these things I said not to you at the beginning, because I was with you.
5 But now I go my way to him that sent me; and none of you asks me, Where go you?
6 But because I have said these things to you, sorrow has filled your heart.
7 ¶ Nevertheless I tell you the truth; It is expedient for you that I go away: for if I go not away, the Comforter will not come to you; but if I depart, I will send him to you.
8 And when he has come, he will reprove the world of sin, and of righteousness, and of judgment:
9 Of sin, because they believe not on me;
10 Of righteousness, because I go to my Father, and you see me no more;
11 Of judgment, because the prince of this world is judged.
12 I have yet many things to say to you, but you cannot bear them now.
13 However, when he, the Spirit of truth, has come, he will guide you into all truth: for he shall not speak of himself; but whatever he shall hear, *that* shall he speak: and he will show you things to come.
14 He shall glorify me: for he shall receive of mine, and shall show *it* to you.
15 All things that the Father has are mine: therefore said I, that he shall take of mine, and shall show *it* to you.
16 ¶ A little while, and you shall not see me: and again, a little while, and you shall see me, because I go to the Father.
17 Then said *some* of his disciples among themselves, What is this that he said to us, A little while, and you shall not see me: and again, a little while, and you shall see me: and, Because I go to the Father?
18 They said therefore, What is this that he said, A little while? we cannot tell what he said.
19 Now Yahshua knew that they were desirous to ask him, and said to them, Do you inquire among yourselves of that I said, A little while, and you shall not see me: and again, a little while, and you shall see me?
20 Truly, truly, I say to you, That you shall weep and lament, but the world shall rejoice: and you shall be sorrowful, but your sorrow shall be turned into joy.
21 A woman when she is in labor has sorrow, because her hour has come: but as soon as she is delivered of the child, she remembers no more the anguish, for joy that a man is born into the world.
22 And you now therefore have sorrow: but I will see you again, and your heart shall rejoice, and your joy no man takes from you.
23 ¶ And in that day you shall ask me nothing. Truly, truly, I say to you, Whatever you shall ask the Father in my name, he will give *it* you.
24 Till now have you asked nothing in my name: ask, and you shall receive, that your joy may be full.
25 These things have I spoken to you in proverbs: but the time comes, when I shall no more speak to you in proverbs, but I shall show you plainly of the Father.
26 At that day you shall ask in my name: and I say not to you, that I will pray the Father for you:
27 For the Father himself loves you, because you have loved me, and have believed that I came out from God.
28 ¶ I came forth from the Father, and have come into the world: again, I leave the world, and go to the Father.
29 His disciples said to him, See, now speak you plainly, and speak no proverb.
30 Now are we sure that you know all things, and need not that any man should ask you: by this we believe that you came forth from God.
31 Yahshua answered them, Do you now believe?
32 Behold, the hour comes, yes, has now come, that you shall be scattered, every man to his own, and shall leave me alone: and yet I am not alone, because the Father is with me.
33 These things I have spoken to you, that in me you might have peace. In the world you shall have tribulation: but be of good cheer; I have overcome the world.

John 17

17:1 ¶ These words spoke Yahshua, and lifted up his eyes to heaven, and said, Father, the hour has come; glorify your Son, that your Son also may glorify you:
2 As you have given him power over all flesh, that he should give eternal life to as many as you have given him.
3 And this is life eternal, that they might know you the only true God, and Yahshua the Messiah, whom you have sent.
4 I have glorified you on the earth: I have finished the work which you gave me to do.
5 And now, O Father, glorify you me with your own self with the glory which I had with you before the world was.

6 ¶ I have manifested your name to the men which you gave me out of the world: yours they were, and you gave them me; and they have kept your word.

7 Now they have known that all things whatever you have given me are of you.

8 For I have given to them the words which you gave me; and they have received *them*, and have known surely that I came out from you, and they have believed that you did send me.

9 I pray for them: I pray not for the world, but for them which you have given me; for they are yours.

10 And all mine are yours, and yours are mine; and I am glorified in them.

11 ¶ And now I am no more in the world, but these are in the world, and I come to you. Holy Father, keep through your own name those whom you have given me, that they may be one, as we *are*.

12 While I was with them in the world, I kept them in your name: those that you gave me I have kept, and none of them is lost, but the son of perdition; that the scripture might be fulfilled.

13 And now come I to you; and these things I speak in the world, that they might have my joy fulfilled in themselves.

14 I have given them your word; and the world has hated them, because they are not of the world, even as I am not of the world.

15 I pray not that you should take them out of the world, but that you should keep them from the evil.

16 They are not of the world, even as I am not of the world.

17 ¶ Sanctify them through your truth: your word is truth.

18 As you have sent me into the world, even so have I also sent them into the world.

19 And for their sakes I sanctify myself, that they also might be sanctified through the truth.

20 ¶ Neither pray I for these alone, but for them also which shall believe on me through their word;

21 That they all may be one; as you, Father, *are* in me, and I in you, that they also may be one in us: that the world may believe that you have sent me.

22 And the glory which you gave me I have given them; that they may be one, even as we are one:

23 I in them, and you in me, that they may be made perfect in one; and that the world may know that you have sent me, and have loved them, as you have loved me.

24 ¶ Father, I will that they also, whom you have given me, be with me where I am; that they may behold my glory, which you have given me: for you loved me before the foundation of the world.

25 O righteous Father, the world has not known you: but I have known you, and these have known that you have sent me.

26 And I have declared to them your name, and will declare *it*: that the love with which you have loved me may be in them, and I in them.

John 18

18:1 ¶ When Yahshua had spoken these words, he went forth with his disciples over the brook Kidron, where was a garden, into the which he entered, and his disciples.

2 And Judas also, which betrayed him, knew the place: for Yahshua often resorted there with his disciples.

3 Judas then, having received a band *of men* and officers from the chief priests and Pharisees, came there with lanterns and torches and weapons.

4 Yahshua therefore, knowing all things that should come upon him, went forth, and said to them, Whom seek you?

5 They answered him, Yahshua of Nazareth. Yahshua said to them, I am *he*. And Judas also, which betrayed him, stood with them.

6 As soon then as he had said to them, I am *he*, they went backward, and fell to the ground.

7 Then asked he them again, Whom seek you? And they said, Yahshua of Nazareth.

8 Yahshua answered, I have told you that I am *he*: if therefore you seek me, let these go their way:

9 That the saying might be fulfilled, which he spoke, Of them which you gave me have I lost none.

10 Then Simon Peter having a sword drew it, and smote the high priest's servant, and cut off his right ear. The servant's name was Malchus.

11 Then said Yahshua to Peter, Put up your sword into the sheath: the cup which my Father has given me, shall I not drink it?

12 Then the band and the captain and officers of the Jews took Yahshua, and bound him,

13 ¶ And led him away to Annas first; for he was father-in-law to Caiaphas, which was the high priest that same year.

14 Now Caiaphas was he, which gave counsel to the Jews, that it was expedient that one man should die for the people.

15 And Simon Peter followed Yahshua, and *so did* another disciple: that disciple was known to the high priest, and went in with Yahshua into the palace of the high priest.

16 But Peter stood at the door outside. Then went out that other disciple, which was known to the high priest, and spoke to her that kept the door, and brought in Peter.

17 Then said the damsel that kept the door to Peter, Are not you also *one* of this man's disciples? He said, I am not.

18 And the servants and officers stood there, who had made a fire of coals; for it was cold: and they warmed themselves: and Peter stood with them, and warmed himself.

19 The high priest then asked Yahshua of his disciples, and of his doctrine.

20 Yahshua answered him, I spoke openly to the world; I always taught in the synagogue, and in the temple, where the Jews always resort; and in secret have I said nothing.

21 Why ask you me? ask them which heard me, what I have said to them: behold, they know what I said.

22 And when he had thus spoken, one of the officers which stood by struck Yahshua with the palm of his hand, saying, Answer you the high priest so?

23 Yahshua answered him, If I have spoken evil, bear witness of the evil: but if well, why smite you me?
24 Now Annas had sent him bound to Caiaphas the high priest.
25 And Simon Peter stood and warmed himself. They said therefore to him, Are not you also *one* of his disciples? He denied *it*, and said, I am not.
26 One of the servants of the high priest, being *his* kinsman whose ear Peter cut off, said, Did not I see you in the garden with him?
27 Peter then denied again: and immediately the cock crowed.
28 ¶ Then led they Yahshua from Caiaphas to the hall of judgment: and it was early; and they themselves went not into the judgment hall, lest they should be defiled; but that they might eat the passover.
29 Pilate then went out to them, and said, What accusation bring you against this man?
30 They answered and said to him, If he were not a malefactor, we would not have delivered him up to you.
31 Then said Pilate to them, Take you him, and judge him according to your law. The Jews therefore said to him, It is not lawful for us to put any man to death:
32 That the saying of Yahshua might be fulfilled, which he spoke, signifying what death he should die.
33 Then Pilate entered into the judgment hall again, and called Yahshua, and said to him, Are you the King of the Jews?
34 Yahshua answered him, Say you this thing of yourself, or did others tell it *to* you of me?
35 Pilate answered, Am I a Jew? Your own nation and the chief priests have delivered you unto me: what have you done?
36 Yahshua answered, My kingdom is not of this world: if my kingdom were of this world, then would my servants fight, that I should not be delivered to the Jews: but now is my kingdom not from here.
37 Pilate therefore said unto him, Are you a king then? Yahshua answered, You say that I am a king. To this end was I born, and for this cause came I into the world, that I should bear witness to the truth. Every one that is of the truth hears my voice.
38 Pilate said to him, What is truth? And when he had said this, he went out again to the Jews, and said to them, I find in him no fault *at all*.
39 But you have a custom, that I should release to you one at the passover: will you therefore that I release to you the King of the Jews?
40 Then cried they all again, saying, Not this man, but Barabbas. Now Barabbas was a robber.

John 19

19:1 ¶ Then Pilate therefore took Yahshua, and scourged *him*.
2 And the soldiers platted a crown of thorns, and put *it* on his head, and they put on him a purple robe,
3 And said, Hail, King of the Jews! and they smote him with their hands.
4 Pilate therefore went forth again, and said to them, Behold, I bring him forth to you, that you may know that I find no fault in him.
5 Then came Yahshua forth, wearing the crown of thorns, and the purple robe. And *Pilate* said to them, Behold the man!
6 When the chief priests therefore and officers saw him, they cried out, saying, Crucify *him*, crucify *him*. Pilate said to them, Take you him, and crucify *him*: for I find no fault in him.
7 The Jews answered him, We have a law, and by our law he ought to die, because he made himself the Son of God.
8 When Pilate therefore heard that saying, he was the more afraid;
9 And went again into the judgment hall, and said to Yahshua, From where are you? But Yahshua gave him no answer.
10 Then said Pilate to him, Speak you not to me? know you not that I have power to crucify you, and have power to release you?
11 Yahshua answered, You could have no power *at all* against me, unless it were given you from above: therefore he that delivered me to you has the greater sin.
12 And from thereafter Pilate sought to release him: but the Jews cried out, saying, If you let this man go, you are not Caesar's friend: whoever makes himself a king speaks against Caesar.
13 When Pilate therefore heard that saying, he brought Yahshua forth, and sat down in the judgment seat in a place that is called the Pavement, but in the Hebrew, Gabbatha.
14 And it was the preparation of the passover, and about the sixth hour: and he said to the Jews, Behold your King!
15 But they cried out, Away with *him*, away with *him*, crucify him. Pilate said to them, Shall I crucify your King? The chief priests answered, We have no king but Caesar.
16 ¶ Then delivered he him therefore to them to be crucified. And they took Yahshua, and led *him* away.
17 And he bearing his cross went forth into a place called *the place* of a skull, which is called in the Hebrew Golgotha:
18 Where they crucified him, and two others with him, on either side one, and Yahshua in the middle.
19 ¶ And Pilate wrote a title, and put *it* on the cross. And the writing was, YAHSHUA OF NAZARETH THE KING OF THE JEWS.
20 This title then read many of the Jews: for the place where Yahshua was crucified was near to the city: and it was written in Hebrew, *and* Greek, *and* Latin.
21 Then said the chief priests of the Jews to Pilate, Write not, The King of the Jews; but that he said, I am King of the Jews.
22 Pilate answered, What I have written I have written.
23 Then the soldiers, when they had crucified Yahshua, took his garments, and made four parts, to every soldier

a part; and also *his* coat: now the coat was without seam, woven from the top throughout.

24 They said therefore among themselves, Let us not tear it, but cast lots for it, whose it shall be: that the scripture might be fulfilled, which says, They parted my garments among them, and for my coat they did cast lots. These things therefore the soldiers did.

25 Now there stood by the cross of Yahshua his mother, and his mother's sister, Mary the *wife* of Cleophas, and Mary Magdalene.

26 When Yahshua therefore saw his mother, and the disciple standing by, whom he loved, he said to his mother, Woman, behold your son!

27 Then said he to the disciple, Behold your mother! And from that hour that disciple took her to his own *home*.

28 After this, Yahshua knowing that all things were now accomplished, that the scripture might be fulfilled, said, I thirst.

29 Now there was set a vessel full of vinegar: and they filled a sponge with vinegar, and put *it* upon hyssop, and put *it* to his mouth.

30 When Yahshua therefore had received the vinegar, he said, It is finished: and he bowed his head, and gave up the ghost.

31 ¶ The Jews therefore, because it was the preparation, that the bodies should not remain upon the cross on the sabbath day, (for that sabbath day was a high day,) asked Pilate that their legs might be broken, and *that* they might be taken away.

32 Then came the soldiers, and broke the legs of the first, and of the other which was crucified with him.

33 But when they came to Yahshua, and saw that he was dead already, they broke not his legs:

34 But one of the soldiers with a spear pierced his side, and immediately came there out blood and water.

35 And he that saw *it* bore record, and his record is true: and he knows that he said truth, that you might believe.

36 For these things were done, that the scripture should be fulfilled, A bone of him shall not be broken.

37 And again another scripture says, They shall look on him whom they pierced.

38 ¶ And after this Joseph of Arimathaea, being a disciple of Yahshua, but secretly for fear of the Jews, asked Pilate that he might take away the body of Yahshua: and Pilate gave *him* permission. He came therefore, and took the body of Yahshua.

39 And there came also Nicodemus, which at the first came to Yahshua by night, and brought a mixture of myrrh and aloes, about a hundred pound *weight*.

40 Then took they the body of Yahshua, and wound it in linen clothes with the spices, as the manner of the Jews is to bury.

41 Now in the place where he was crucified there was a garden; and in the garden a new sepulcher, wherein was never man yet laid.

42 There laid they Yahshua therefore because of the Jews' preparation *day*; for the sepulcher was near at hand.

John 20

20:1 ¶ The first *day* of the week came Mary Magdalene early, when it was yet dark, to the sepulcher, and saw the stone taken away from the sepulcher.

2 Then she ran, and came to Simon Peter, and to the other disciple, whom Yahshua loved, and said to them, They have taken away the Lord out of the sepulcher, and we know not where they have laid him.

3 Peter therefore went forth, and that other disciple, and came to the sepulcher.

4 So they ran both together: and the other disciple did outrun Peter, and came first to the sepulcher.

5 And he stooping down, *and looking in*, saw the linen clothes lying; yet went he not in.

6 Then came Simon Peter following him, and went into the sepulcher, and saw the linen clothes lie,

7 And the napkin, that was about his head, not lying with the linen clothes, but wrapped together in a place by itself.

8 Then went in also that other disciple, which came first to the sepulcher, and he saw, and believed.

9 For as yet they knew not the scripture, that he must rise again from the dead.

10 Then the disciples went away again to their own homes.

11 ¶ But Mary stood outside at the sepulcher weeping: and as she wept, she stooped down, *and looked* into the sepulcher,

12 And saw two angels in white sitting, the one at the head, and the other at the feet, where the body of Yahshua had lain.

13 And they said unto her, Woman, why weep you? She said to them, Because they have taken away my Lord, and I know not where they have laid him.

14 And when she had thus said, she turned herself back, and saw Yahshua standing, and knew not that it was Yahshua.

15 Yahshua said to her, Woman, why weep you? whom seek you? She, supposing him to be the gardener, said to him, Sir, if you have taken him away, tell me where you have laid him, and I will take him away.

16 Yahshua said to her, Mary. She turned herself, and said to him, Rabboni; which is to say, Master.

17 Yahshua said to her, Touch me not; for I have not yet ascended to my Father: but go to my brethren, and say to them, I ascend to my Father, and your Father; and *to* my God, and your God.

18 Mary Magdalene came and told the disciples that she had seen the Lord, and *that* he had spoken these things to her.

19 ¶ Then the same day at evening, being the first *day* of the week, when the doors were shut where the disciples were assembled for fear of the Jews, came Yahshua and stood in the midst, and said to them, Peace *be* to you.

20 And when he had so said, he showed to them *his* hands and his side. Then were the disciples glad, when they saw the Lord.

John 20

21 Then said Yahshua to them again, Peace *be* to you: as *my* Father has sent me, even so send I you.
22 And when he had said this, he breathed on *them*, and said to them, Receive you the Holy Ghost:
23 Whose soever sins you remit, they are remitted to them; *and* whose soever *sins* you retain, they are retained.
24 But Thomas, one of the twelve, called Didymus, was not with them when Yahshua came.
25 The other disciples therefore said to him, We have seen the Lord. But he said to them, Unless I shall see in his hands the print of the nails, and put my finger into the print of the nails, and thrust my hand into his side, I will not believe.
26 ¶ And after eight days again his disciples were within, and Thomas with them: *then* came Yahshua, the doors being shut, and stood in the midst, and said, Peace *be* to you.
27 Then said he to Thomas, Reach here your finger, and behold my hands; and reach here your hand, and thrust *it* into my side: and be not faithless, but believing.
28 And Thomas answered and said to him, My Lord and my God.
29 Yahshua said to him, Thomas, because you have seen me, you have believed: blessed *are* they that have not seen, and *yet* have believed.
30 And many other signs truly did Yahshua in the presence of his disciples, which are not written in this book:
31 But these are written, that you might believe that Yahshua is the Messiah, the Son of God; and that believing you might have life through his name.

John 21

21:1 ¶ After these things Yahshua showed himself again to the disciples at the sea of Tiberias; and in this manner showed he *himself*.
2 There were together Simon Peter, and Thomas called Didymus, and Nathanael of Cana in Galilee, and the *sons* of Zebedee, and two others of his disciples.
3 Simon Peter said to them, I go a fishing. They say to him, We also go with you. They went forth, and entered into a ship immediately; and that night they caught nothing.
4 But when the morning had now come, Yahshua stood on the shore: but the disciples knew not that it was Yahshua.
5 Then Yahshua said to them, Children, have you any food? They answered him, No.
6 And he said to them, Cast the net on the right side of the ship, and you shall find. They cast therefore, and now they were not able to draw it for the multitude of fishes.
7 Therefore that disciple whom Yahshua loved said to Peter, It is the Lord. Now when Simon Peter heard that it was the Lord, he girt *his* fisher's coat *unto him*, (for he was naked,) and did cast himself into the sea.
8 And the other disciples came in a little ship; (for they were not far from land, but as it were two hundred cubits,) dragging the net with fishes.
9 As soon then as they had come to land, they saw a fire of coals there, and fish laid thereon, and bread.
10 Yahshua said to them, Bring of the fish which you have now caught.
11 Simon Peter went up, and drew the net to land full of great fishes, a hundred and fifty and three: and for all there were so many, yet was not the net broken.
12 Yahshua said to them, Come *and* dine. And none of the disciples dared ask him, Who are you? knowing that it was the Lord.
13 Yahshua then came, and took bread, and gave them, and fish likewise.
14 This is now the third time that Yahshua showed himself to his disciples, after that he was risen from the dead.
15 ¶ So when they had dined, Yahshua said to Simon Peter, Simon, *son* of Jonas, love you me more than these? He said to him, Yes, Lord; you know that I love you. He said to him, Feed my lambs.
16 He said to him again the second time, Simon, *son* of Jonas, love you me? He said to him, Yes, Lord; you know that I love you. He said to him, Feed my sheep.
17 He said to him the third time, Simon, *son* of Jonas, love you me? Peter was grieved because he said to him the third time, Love you me? And he said to him, Lord, you know all things; you know that I love you. Yahshua said to him, Feed my sheep.
18 Truly, truly, I say to you, When you were young, you girded yourself, and walked where you would: but when you shall be old, you shall stretch forth your hands, and another shall gird you, and carry *you* where you would not.
19 This spoke he, signifying by what death he should glorify God. And when he had spoken this, he said to him, Follow me.
20 ¶ Then Peter, turning about, saw the disciple whom Yahshua loved following; which also leaned on his breast at supper, and said, Lord, which is he that betrays you?
21 Peter seeing him said to Yahshua, Lord, and what *shall* this man *do*?
22 Yahshua said to him, If I will that he tarry till I come, what *is that* to you? follow you me.
23 Then went this saying abroad among the brethren, that that disciple should not die: yet Yahshua said not to him, He shall not die; but, If I will that he tarry till I come, what *is that* to you?
24 This is the disciple which testifies of these things, and wrote these things: and we know that his testimony is true.
25 And there are also many other things which Yahshua did, the which, if they should be written every one, I suppose that even the world itself could not contain the books that should be written. Amen.

Acts

Acts 1

1:1 ¶ The former treatise have I made, O Theophilus, of all that Yahshua began both to do and teach,

2 Until the day in which he was taken up, after that he through the Holy Ghost had given commandments to the apostles whom he had chosen:

3 To whom also he showed himself alive after his suffering by many infallible proofs, being seen of them *for* forty days, and speaking of the things pertaining to the kingdom of God:

4 And, being assembled together with *them*, commanded them that they should not depart from Jerusalem, but wait for the promise of the Father, which, *said he*, you have heard of me.

5 For John truly baptized with water; but you shall be baptized with the Holy Ghost not many days hence.

6 ¶ When they therefore had come together, they asked of him, saying, Lord, will you at this time restore again the kingdom to Israel?

7 And he said to them, It is not for you to know the times or the seasons, which the Father has put in his own power.

8 But you shall receive power, after that the Holy Ghost has come upon you: and you shall be witnesses to me both in Jerusalem, and in all Judaea, and in Samaria, and to the utmost part of the earth.

9 And when he had spoken these things, while they beheld, he was taken up; and a cloud received him out of their sight.

10 And while they looked steadfastly toward heaven as he went up, behold, two men stood by them in white apparel;

11 Which also said, You men of Galilee, why stand you gazing up into heaven? this same Yahshua, which is taken up from you into heaven, shall so come in like manner as you have seen him go into heaven.

12 ¶ Then returned they to Jerusalem from the mount called Olives, which is from Jerusalem a sabbath day's journey.

13 And when they had come in, they went up into an upper room, where stayed both Peter, and James, and John, and Andrew, Philip, and Thomas, Bartholomew, and Matthew, James *the son* of Alphaeus, and Simon Zelotes, and Judas *the brother* of James.

14 These all continued with one accord in prayer and supplication, with the women, and Mary the mother of Yahshua, and with his brothers.

15 ¶ And in those days Peter stood up in the midst of the disciples, and said, (the number of names together were about a hundred and twenty,)

16 Men *and* brethren, this scripture must needed *to* have been fulfilled, which the Holy Ghost by the mouth of David spoke before concerning Judas, which was guide to them that took Yahshua.

17 For he was numbered with us, and had obtained part of this ministry.

18 Now this man purchased a field with the reward of iniquity; and falling headlong, he burst open in the middle, and all his bowels gushed out.

19 And it was known to all the dwellers at Jerusalem; insomuch as that field is called in their proper tongue, Aceldama, that is to say, The field of blood.

20 For it is written in the book of Psalms, Let his habitation be desolate, and let no man dwell therein: and his office let another take.

21 Therefore of these men which have accompanied with us all the time that the Lord Yahshua went in and out among us,

22 Beginning from the baptism of John, to that same day that he was taken up from us, must one be made to be a witness with us of his resurrection.

23 And they appointed two, Joseph called Barsabas, who was surnamed Justus, and Matthias.

24 And they prayed, and said, You, Lord, which know the hearts of all *men*, show which of these two you have chosen,

25 That he may take part of this ministry and apostleship, from which Judas by transgression fell, that he might go to his own place.

26 And they gave forth their lots; and the lot fell upon Matthias; and he was numbered with the eleven apostles.

Acts 2

2:1 ¶ And when the day of Pentecost had fully come, they were all with one accord in one place.

2 And suddenly there came a sound from heaven as of a rushing mighty wind, and it filled all the house where they were sitting.

3 And there appeared unto them cloven tongues like as of fire, and it sat upon each of them.

4 And they were all filled with the Holy Ghost, and began to speak with other tongues, as the Spirit gave them utterance.

5 ¶ And there were dwelling at Jerusalem Jews, devout men, out of every nation under heaven.

6 Now when this was noised abroad, the multitude came together, and were confounded, because that every man heard them speak in his own language.

7 And they were all amazed and marveled, saying one to another, Behold, are not all these which speak Galileans?

8 And how hear we every man in our own tongue, wherein we were born?

9 Parthians, and Medes, and Elamites, and the dwellers in Mesopotamia, and in Judaea, and Cappadocia, in Pontus, and Asia,

10 Phrygia, and Pamphylia, in Egypt, and in the parts of Libya about Cyrene, and strangers of Rome, Jews and proselytes,

11 Cretes and Arabians, we do hear them speak in our tongues the wonderful works of God.

12 And they were all amazed, and were in doubt, saying one to another, What means this?

Acts 2

13 Others mocking said, These men are full of new wine.

14 ¶ But Peter, standing up with the eleven, lifted up his voice, and said to them, You men of Judaea, and all *you* that dwell at Jerusalem, be this known unto you, and listen to my words:

15 For these are not drunken, as you suppose, seeing it is *but* the third hour of the day.

16 But this is that which was spoken by the prophet Joel;

17 And it shall come to pass in the last days, says God *Yahweh*, I will pour out of my Spirit upon all flesh: and your sons and your daughters shall prophesy, and your young men shall see visions, and your old men shall dream dreams:

18 And on my servants and on my handmaidens I will pour out in those days of my Spirit; and they shall prophesy:

19 And I will show wonders in heaven above, and signs in the earth beneath; blood, and fire, and vapor of smoke:

20 The sun shall be turned into darkness, and the moon into blood, before that great and notable day of the Lord *Yahweh* comes:

21 And it shall come to pass, *that* whoever shall call on the name of the Lord *Yahweh* shall be saved.

22 You men of Israel, hear these words; Yahshua of Nazareth, a man approved of God among you by miracles and wonders and signs, which God did by him in the midst of you, as you yourselves also know:

23 Him, being delivered by the determinate counsel and foreknowledge of God, you have taken, and by wicked hands have crucified and slain:

24 Whom God has raised up, having loosed the pains of death: because it was not possible that he should be held of it.

25 For David speaks concerning him, I foresaw the Lord *Yahweh* always before my face, for he is on my right hand, that I should not be moved:

26 Therefore did my heart rejoice, and my tongue was glad; moreover also my flesh shall rest in hope:

27 Because you will not leave my soul in hell, neither will you allow your Holy One to see corruption.

28 You have made known to me the ways of life; you shall make me full of joy with your countenance.

29 Men *and* brethren, let me freely speak to you of the patriarch David, that he is both dead and buried, and his sepulcher is with us unto this day.

30 Therefore being a prophet, and knowing that God had sworn with an oath to him, that of the fruit of his loins, according to the flesh, he would raise up the Messiah to sit on his throne;

31 He seeing this before spoke of the resurrection of the Messiah, that his soul was not left in hell, neither his flesh did see corruption.

32 This Yahshua has God raised up, whereof we all are witnesses.

33 Therefore being by the right hand of God exalted, and having received of the Father the promise of the Holy Ghost, he has shed forth this, which you now see and hear.

34 For David has not ascended into the heavens: but he said himself, The LORD *Yahweh* said to my Lord, Sit you on my right hand,

35 Until I make your foes your footstool.

36 Therefore let all the house of Israel know assuredly, that God has made that same Yahshua, whom you have crucified, both Lord and the Messiah.

37 ¶ Now when they heard *this*, they were pricked in their heart, and said to Peter and to the rest of the apostles, Men *and* brethren, what shall we do?

38 Then Peter said to them, Repent, and be baptized every one of you in the name of Yahshua the Messiah for the remission of sins, and you shall receive the gift of the Holy Ghost.

39 For the promise is to you, and to your children, and to all that are afar off, *even* as many as the Lord our God shall call.

40 And with many other words did he testify and exhort, saying, Save yourselves from this perverse generation.

41 Then they that gladly received his word were baptized: and the same day there were added *to them* about three thousand souls.

42 ¶ And they continued steadfastly in the apostles' doctrine and fellowship, and in breaking of bread, and in prayers.

43 And fear came upon every soul: and many wonders and signs were done by the apostles.

44 And all that believed were together, and had all things common;

45 And sold their possessions and goods, and parted them to all *men*, as every man had need.

46 And they, continuing daily with one accord in the temple, and breaking bread from house to house, did eat their food with gladness and singleness of heart,

47 Praising God, and having favor with all the people. And the Lord added to the congregation daily such as should be saved.

Acts 3

3:1 ¶ Now Peter and John went up together into the temple at the hour of prayer, *being* the ninth *hour*.

2 And a certain man lame from his mother's womb was carried, whom they laid daily at the gate of the temple which is called Beautiful, to ask alms of them that entered into the temple;

3 Who seeing Peter and John about to go into the temple asked for alms.

4 And Peter, fastening his eyes upon him with John, said, Look on us.

5 And he gave attention to them, expecting to receive something of them.

6 Then Peter said, Silver and gold have I none; but such as I have give I you: In the name of Yahshua the Messiah of Nazareth rise up and walk.

7 And he took him by the right hand, and lifted *him* up: and immediately his feet and ankle bones received strength.

8 And he leaping up stood, and walked, and entered with them into the temple, walking, and leaping, and praising God.

9 And all the people saw him walking and praising God:

10 And they knew that it was he which sat for alms at the Beautiful gate of the temple: and they were filled with wonder and amazement at that which had happened to him.
11 And as the lame man which was healed held Peter and John, all the people ran together to them in the porch that is called Solomon's, greatly wondering.
12 ¶ And when Peter saw *it*, he answered unto the people, You men of Israel, why marvel you at this? or why look you so earnestly on us, as though by our own power or holiness we had made this man to walk?
13 The God of Abraham, and of Isaac, and of Jacob, the God of our fathers, has glorified his Son Yahshua; whom you delivered up, and denied him in the presence of Pilate, when he was determined to let *him* go.
14 But you denied the Holy One and the Just, and desired a murderer to be granted unto you;
15 And killed the Prince of life, whom God has raised from the dead; whereof we are witnesses.
16 And his name through faith in his name has made this man strong, whom you see and know: yes, the faith which is by him has given him this perfect soundness in the presence of you all.
17 And now, brethren, I know that through ignorance you did *it*, as *did* also your rulers.
18 But those things, which God before had shown by the mouth of all his prophets, that the Messiah should suffer, he has so fulfilled.
19 Repent you therefore, and be converted, that your sins may be blotted out, when the times of refreshing shall come from the presence of the Lord;
20 And he shall send Yahshua the Messiah, which before was preached unto you:
21 Whom the heaven must receive until the times of restoration of all things, which God has spoken by the mouth of all his holy prophets since the world began.
22 For Moses truly said to the fathers, A prophet shall the Lord *Yahweh* your God raise up unto you of your brethren, like unto me; him shall you hear in all things whatever he shall say unto you.
23 And it shall come to pass, *that* every soul, which will not hear that prophet, shall be destroyed from among the people.
24 Yes, and all the prophets from Samuel and those that follow after, as many as have spoken, have likewise foretold of these days.
25 You are the children of the prophets, and of the covenant which God *Yahweh* made with our fathers, saying to Abraham, And in your seed shall all the families of the earth be blessed.
26 Unto you first God, having raised up his Son Yahshua, sent him to bless you, in turning away every one of you from his iniquities.

Acts 4

4:1 ¶ And as they spoke to the people, the priests, and the captain of the temple, and the Sadducees, came upon them,
2 Being grieved that they taught the people, and preached through Yahshua the resurrection from the dead.
3 And they laid hands on them, and put *them* in hold unto the next day: for it was now evening.
4 However many of them which heard the word believed; and the number of the men was about five thousand.
5 ¶ And it came to pass on the next day, that their rulers, and elders, and scribes,
6 And Annas the high priest, and Caiaphas, and John, and Alexander, and as many as were of the family of the high priest, were gathered together at Jerusalem.
7 And when they had set them in the midst, they asked, By what power, or by what name, have you done this?
8 Then Peter, filled with the Holy Ghost, said to them, You rulers of the people, and elders of Israel,
9 If we this day are questioned of the good deed done to the weak man, by what means he is made whole;
10 Be it known to you all, and to all the people of Israel, that by the name of Yahshua the Messiah of Nazareth, whom you crucified, whom God raised from the dead, *even* by him does this man stand here before you whole.
11 This is the stone which was set at nothing by you builders, which has become the head of the corner.
12 Neither is there salvation in any other: for there is no other name under heaven given among men, whereby we must be saved.
13 Now when they saw the boldness of Peter and John, and perceived that they were unlearned and ignorant men, they marveled; and they took knowledge of them, that they had been with Yahshua.
14 And seeing the man which was healed standing with them, they could say nothing against it.
15 ¶ But when they had commanded them to go aside out of the council, they conferred among themselves,
16 Saying, What shall we do to these men? for that indeed a notable miracle has been done by them *is* manifest to all them that dwell in Jerusalem; and we cannot deny *it*.
17 But that it spreads no further among the people, let us straightly threaten them, that they speak henceforth to no man in this name.
18 And they called them, and commanded them not to speak at all nor teach in the name of Yahshua.
19 But Peter and John answered and said to them, Whether it is right in the sight of God to listen to you more than to God, judge you.
20 For we cannot but speak the things which we have seen and heard.
21 So when they had further threatened them, they let them go, finding nothing that they might punish them *for*, because of the people: for all *men* glorified God for that which was done.
22 For the man was above forty years old, on whom this miracle of healing was shown.

Acts 4

23 ¶ And being let go, they went to their own company, and reported all that the chief priests and elders had said to them.

24 And when they heard that, they lifted up their voice to God with one accord, and said, Lord, you *are* God, which has made heaven, and earth, and the sea, and all that in them is:

25 Who by the mouth of your servant David has said, Why did the heathen rage, and the people imagine vain things?

26 The kings of the earth stood up, and the rulers were gathered together against the Lord *Yahweh*, and against his Messiah.

27 For of a truth against your holy child Yahshua, whom you have anointed, both Herod, and Pontius Pilate, with the Gentiles, and the people of Israel, were gathered together,

28 For to do whatever your hand and your counsel determined before to be done.

29 And now, Lord, behold their threatenings: and grant to your servants, that with all boldness they may speak your word,

30 By stretching forth your hand to heal; and that signs and wonders may be done by the name of your holy child Yahshua.

31 And when they had prayed, the place was shaken where they were assembled together; and they were all filled with the Holy Ghost, and they spoke the word of God with boldness.

32 ¶ And the multitude of them that believed were of one heart and of one soul: neither said any *of them* that any of the things which he possessed was his own; but they had all things common.

33 And with great power gave the apostles witness of the resurrection of the Lord Yahshua: and great grace was upon them all.

34 Neither was there any among them that lacked: for as many as were possessors of lands or houses sold them, and brought the prices of the things that were sold,

35 And laid *them* down at the apostles' feet: and distribution was made to every man according as he had need.

36 And Joses, who by the apostles was surnamed Barnabas, (which is, being interpreted, The son of consolation,) a Levite, *and* of the country of Cyprus,

37 Having land, sold *it*, and brought the money, and laid *it* at the apostles' feet.

Acts 5

5:1 ¶ But a certain man named Ananias, with Sapphira his wife, sold a possession,

2 And kept back *part* of the price, his wife also being privy *to it*, and brought a certain part, and laid *it* at the apostles' feet.

3 But Peter said, Ananias, why has Satan filled your heart to lie to the Holy Ghost, and to keep back *part* of the price of the land?

4 While it remained, was it not your own? and after it was sold, was it not in your own power? why have you conceived this thing in your heart? you have not lied to men, but to God.

5 And Ananias hearing these words fell down, and gave up the ghost: and great fear came on all them that heard these things.

6 And the young men arose, wrapped him up, and carried *him* out, and buried *him*.

7 And it was about the space of three hours after, when his wife, not knowing what was done, came in.

8 And Peter answered unto her, Tell me whether you sold the land for so much? And she said, Yes, for so much.

9 Then Peter said to her, How is it that you have agreed together to tempt the Spirit of the Lord? behold, the feet of them which have buried your husband *are* at the door, and shall carry you out.

10 Then fell she down immediately at his feet, and yielded up the ghost: and the young men came in, and found her dead, and, carrying *her* forth, buried *her* by her husband.

11 And great fear came upon all the congregation, and upon as many as heard these things.

12 ¶ And by the hands of the apostles were many signs and wonders worked among the people; (and they were all with one accord in Solomon's porch.

13 And of the rest dared no man join himself to them: but the people magnified them.

14 And believers were the more added to the Lord, multitudes both of men and women.)

15 Insomuch that they brought forth the sick into the streets, and laid *them* on beds and couches, that at the least the shadow of Peter passing by might overshadow some of them.

16 There came also a multitude *out* of the cities round about to Jerusalem, bringing sick folks, and them which were troubled with unclean spirits: and they were healed every one.

17 ¶ Then the high priest rose up, and all they that were with him, (which is the sect of the Sadducees,) and were filled with indignation,

18 And laid their hands on the apostles, and put them in the common prison.

19 But the angel of the Lord by night opened the prison doors, and brought them forth, and said,

20 Go, stand and speak in the temple to the people all the words of this life.

21 And when they heard *that*, they entered into the temple early in the morning, and taught. But the high priest came, and they that were with him, and called the council together, and all the senate of the children of Israel, and sent to the prison to have them brought.

22 But when the officers came, and found them not in the prison, they returned, and told,

23 Saying, The prison truly found we shut with all safety, and the keepers standing outside before the doors: but when we had opened, we found no man within.

24 Now when the high priest and the captain of the temple and the chief priests heard these things, they doubted of themselves unto what this would become.

25 Then came one and told them, saying, Behold, the men whom you put in prison are standing in the temple, and teaching the people.

26 ¶ Then went the captain with the officers, and brought them without violence: for they feared the people, lest they should have been stoned.
27 And when they had brought them, they set *them* before the council: and the high priest asked them,
28 Saying, Did not we straightly command you that you should not teach in this name? and, behold, you have filled Jerusalem with your doctrine, and intend to bring this man's blood upon us.
29 Then Peter and the *other* apostles answered and said, We ought to obey God rather than men.
30 The God of our fathers raised up Yahshua, whom you slew and hanged on a tree.
31 Him has God exalted with his right hand *to be* a Prince and a Savior, for to give repentance to Israel, and forgiveness of sins.
32 And we are his witnesses of these things; and *so is* also the Holy Ghost, whom God has given to them that obey him.
33 When they heard *that*, they were cut *to the heart*, and took counsel to slay them.
34 Then stood there up one in the council, a Pharisee, named Gamaliel, a doctor of the law, held in honor among all the people, and commanded to put the apostles forth a little space;
35 And said to them, You men of Israel, take heed to yourselves what you intend to do as touching these men.
36 For before these days rose up Theudas, boasting himself to be somebody; to whom a number of men, about four hundred, joined themselves: who was slain; and all, as many as obeyed him, were scattered, and brought to nothing.
37 After this man rose up Judas of Galilee in the days of the taxing, and drew away many people after him: he also perished; and all, *even* as many as obeyed him, were dispersed.
38 And now I say unto you, Refrain from these men, and let them alone: for if this counsel or this work is of men, it will come to nothing:
39 But if it is of God, you cannot overthrow it; lest perhaps you be found even to fight against God.
40 And to him they agreed: and when they had called the apostles, and beaten *them*, they commanded that they should not speak in the name of Yahshua, and let them go.
41 And they departed from the presence of the council, rejoicing that they were counted worthy to suffer shame for his name.
42 And daily in the temple, and in every house, they ceased not to teach and preach Yahshua the Messiah.

Acts 6

6:1 ¶ And in those days, when the number of the disciples was multiplied, there arose a murmuring of the Grecians against the Hebrews, because their widows were neglected in the daily ministration.
2 Then the twelve called the multitude of the disciples *to them*, and said, It is not pleasing that we should leave the word of God, and serve tables.
3 Therefore, brethren, look you out among you seven men of honest report, full of the Holy Ghost and wisdom, whom we may appoint over this business.
4 But we will give ourselves continually to prayer, and to the ministry of the word.
5 And the saying pleased the whole multitude: and they chose Stephen, a man full of faith and of the Holy Ghost, and Philip, and Prochorus, and Nicanor, and Timon, and Parmenas, and Nicolas a proselyte of Antioch:
6 Whom they set before the apostles: and when they had prayed, they laid *their* hands on them.
7 And the word of God increased; and the number of the disciples multiplied in Jerusalem greatly; and a great company of the priests were obedient to the faith.
8 ¶ And Stephen, full of faith and power, did great wonders and miracles among the people.
9 Then there arose certain of the synagogue, which is called *the synagogue* of the Libertines, and Cyrenians, and Alexandrians, and of them of Cilicia and of Asia, disputing with Stephen.
10 And they were not able to resist the wisdom and the spirit by which he spoke.
11 Then they instigated men, which said, We have heard him speak blasphemous words against Moses, and *against* God.
12 And they stirred up the people, and the elders, and the scribes, and came upon *him*, and caught him, and brought *him* to the council,
13 And set up false witnesses, which said, This man ceases not to speak blasphemous words against this holy place, and the law:
14 For we have heard him say, that this Yahshua of Nazareth shall destroy this place, and shall change the customs which Moses delivered *to* us.
15 And all that sat in the council, looking steadfastly on him, saw his face as it had been the face of an angel.

Acts 7

7:1 ¶ Then said the high priest, Are these things so?
2 And he said, Men, brethren, and fathers, listen; The God of glory *Yahweh* appeared unto our father Abraham, when he was in Mesopotamia, before he dwelt in Haran,
3 And said to him, Get you out of your country, and from your relatives, and come into the land which I shall show you.
4 Then came he out of the land of the Chaldeans, and dwelt in Haran: and from there, when his father was dead, he removed him into this land, wherein you now dwell.
5 And he gave him no inheritance in it, no, not *so much as* to set his foot on: yet he promised that he would give it to him for a possession, and to his seed after him, when *as yet* he had no child.
6 And God *Yahweh* spoke in this way, That his seed should dwell in a strange land; and that they should bring them into bondage, and treat *them* evilly *for* four hundred years.

Acts 7

7 And the nation to whom they shall be in bondage will I judge, said God *Yahweh*: and after that shall they come forth, and serve me in this place.

8 And he gave him the covenant of circumcision: and so *Abraham* begot Isaac, and circumcised him the eighth day; and Isaac *begot* Jacob; and Jacob *begot* the twelve patriarchs.

9 And the patriarchs, moved with envy, sold Joseph into Egypt: but God was with him,

10 And delivered him out of all his afflictions, and gave him favor and wisdom in the sight of Pharaoh king of Egypt; and he made him governor over Egypt and all his house.

11 Now there came a famine over all the land of Egypt and Canaan, and great affliction: and our fathers found no sustenance.

12 But when Jacob heard that there was corn in Egypt, he sent out our fathers first.

13 And at the second *time* Joseph was made known to his brothers; and Joseph's family was made known to Pharaoh.

14 Then sent Joseph, and called his father Jacob to *him*, and all his relatives, threescore and fifteen souls.

15 So Jacob went down into Egypt, and died, he, and our fathers,

16 And were carried over into Shechem, and laid in the sepulcher that Abraham bought for a sum of money of the sons of Hamor *the father* of Shechem.

17 ¶ But when the time of the promise drew nigh, which God had sworn to Abraham, the people grew and multiplied in Egypt,

18 Till another king arose, which knew not Joseph.

19 The same dealt subtly with our kindred, and evilly treated our fathers, so that they cast out their young children, to the end *that* they might not live.

20 In which time Moses was born, and was exceedingly fair, and nourished up in his father's house three months:

21 And when he was cast out, Pharaoh's daughter took him up, and nourished him for her own son.

22 And Moses was learned in all the wisdom of the Egyptians, and was mighty in words and in deeds.

23 And when he was *a* full forty years old, it came into his heart to visit the brethren the children of Israel.

24 And seeing one *of them* suffer wrong, he defended *him*, and avenged him that was oppressed, and smote the Egyptian:

25 For he supposed the brethren would have understood how that God by his hand would deliver them: but they understood not.

26 And the next day he showed himself to them as they fought, and would have set them at one again, saying, Sirs, you are brethren; why do you wrong one to another?

27 But he that did his neighbor wrong thrust him away, saying, Who made you a ruler and a judge over us?

28 Will you kill me, as you did the Egyptian yesterday?

29 Then fled Moses at this saying, and was a stranger in the land of Midian, where he begot two sons.

30 ¶ And when forty years were expired, there appeared to him in the wilderness of mount Sinai an angel of the Lord *Yahweh* in a flame of fire in a bush.

31 When Moses saw *it*, he wondered at the sight: and as he drew near to behold *it*, the voice of the Lord *Yahweh* came to him,

32 *Saying*, I *am* the God of your fathers, the God of Abraham, and the God of Isaac, and the God of Jacob. Then Moses trembled, and dared not behold.

33 Then said the Lord *Yahweh* to him, Put off your shoes from your feet: for the place where you stand is holy ground.

34 I have seen, I have seen the affliction of my people which are in Egypt, and I have heard their groaning, and have come down to deliver them. And now come, I will send you into Egypt.

35 This Moses whom they refused, saying, Who made you a ruler and a judge? the same did God send *to be* a ruler and a deliverer by the hand of the angel which appeared to him in the bush.

36 He brought them out, after that he had shown wonders and signs in the land of Egypt, and in the Red Sea, and in the wilderness *for* forty years.

37 This is that Moses, which said to the children of Israel, A prophet shall the Lord *Yahweh* your God raise up unto you of your brethren, like unto me; him shall you hear.

38 This is he, that was in the congregation in the wilderness with the angel which spoke to him in the mount Sinai, and *with* our fathers: who received the lively oracles to give to us:

39 To whom our fathers would not obey, but thrust *him* from them, and in their hearts turned back again into Egypt,

40 Saying to Aaron, Make us gods to go before us: for *as for* this Moses, which brought us out of the land of Egypt, we know not what has become of him.

41 And they made a calf in those days, and offered sacrifice to the idol, and rejoiced in the works of their own hands.

42 ¶ Then God turned, and gave them up to worship the host of heaven; as it is written in the book of the prophets, O you house of Israel, have you offered to me slain beasts and sacrifices *by the space of* forty years in the wilderness?

43 Yes, you took up the tabernacle of Moloch, and the star of your god Remphan, figures which you made to worship them: and I will carry you away beyond Babylon.

44 Our fathers had the tabernacle of witness in the wilderness, as he had appointed, speaking to Moses, that he should make it according to the fashion that he had seen.

45 Which also our fathers that came after brought in with Joshua into the possession of the Gentiles, whom God drove out before the face of our fathers, unto the days of David;

46 Who found favor before God, and desired to find a tabernacle for the God of Jacob.

47 But Solomon built him a house.
48 However the most High dwells not in temples made with hands; as said the prophet,
49 Heaven *is* my throne, and earth *is* my footstool: what house will you build me? says the Lord *Yahweh*: or what *is* the place of my rest?
50 Has not my hand made all these things?
51 ¶ You stiffnecked and uncircumcised in heart and ears, you do always resist the Holy Ghost: as your fathers *did*, so *do* you.
52 Which of the prophets have not your fathers persecuted? and they have slain them which showed before of the coming of the Just One; of whom you have been now the betrayers and murderers:
53 Who have received the law by the disposition of angels, and have not kept *it*.
54 ¶ When they heard these things, they were cut to the heart, and they gnashed on him with *their* teeth.
55 But he, being full of the Holy Ghost, looked up steadfastly into heaven, and saw the glory of God, and Yahshua standing on the right hand of God,
56 And said, Behold, I see the heavens opened, and the Son of man standing on the right hand of God.
57 Then they cried out with a loud voice, and stopped their ears, and ran upon him with one accord,
58 And cast *him* out of the city, and stoned *him*: and the witnesses laid down their clothes at a young man's feet, whose name was Saul.
59 And they stoned Stephen, calling upon *God*, and saying, Lord Yahshua, receive my spirit.
60 And he knelt down, and cried with a loud voice, Lord, lay not this sin to their charge. And when he had said this, he fell asleep.

Acts 8

8:1 ¶ And Saul was consenting to his death. And at that time there was a great persecution against the congregation which was at Jerusalem; and they were all scattered abroad throughout the regions of Judaea and Samaria, except the apostles.
2 And devout men carried Stephen *to his burial*, and made great lamentation over him.
3 As for Saul, he made havoc of the congregation, entering into every house, and dragging off men and women committing *them* to prison.
4 ¶ Therefore they that were scattered abroad went everywhere preaching the word.
5 Then Philip went down to the city of Samaria, and preached the Messiah to them.
6 And the people with one accord gave heed to those things which Philip spoke, hearing and seeing the miracles which he did.
7 For unclean spirits, crying with *a* loud voice, came out of many that were possessed *with them*: and many taken with palsies, and that were lame, were healed.
8 And there was great joy in that city.
9 But there was a certain man, called Simon, which before in the same city used sorcery, and bewitched the people of Samaria, giving out that himself was some great one:
10 To whom they all gave heed, from the least to the greatest, saying, This man is the great power of God.
11 And to him they had regard, because that for a long time he had bewitched them with sorceries.
12 But when they believed Philip preaching the things concerning the kingdom of God, and the name of Yahshua the Messiah, they were baptized, both men and women.
13 Then Simon himself believed also: and when he was baptized, he continued with Philip, and wondered, beholding the miracles and signs which were done.
14 ¶ Now when the apostles which were at Jerusalem heard that Samaria had received the word of God, they sent to them Peter and John:
15 Who, when they had come down, prayed for them, that they might receive the Holy Ghost:
16 (For as yet he had fallen upon none of them: only they were baptized in the name of the Lord Yahshua.)
17 Then laid they *their* hands on them, and they received the Holy Ghost.
18 And when Simon saw that through laying on of the apostles' hands the Holy Ghost was given, he offered them money,
19 Saying, Give me also this power, that on whomever I lay hands, he may receive the Holy Ghost.
20 But Peter said to him, Your money perish with you, because you have thought that the gift of God may be purchased with money.
21 You have neither part nor lot in this matter: for your heart is not right in the sight of God.
22 Repent therefore of this your wickedness, and pray God, if perhaps the thought of your heart may be forgiven you.
23 For I perceive that you are in the gall of bitterness, and *in* the bond of iniquity.
24 Then answered Simon, and said, Pray you to the Lord for me, that none of these things which you have spoken come upon me.
25 And they, when they had testified and preached the word of the Lord, returned to Jerusalem, and preached the gospel in many villages of the Samaritans.
26 ¶ And the angel of the Lord spoke to Philip, saying, Arise, and go toward the south to the way that goes down from Jerusalem to Gaza, which is desert.
27 And he arose and went: and, behold, a man of Ethiopia, a eunuch of great authority under Candace queen of the Ethiopians, who had the charge of all her treasure, and had come to Jerusalem for to worship,
28 Was returning, and sitting in his chariot reading Isaiah the prophet.
29 Then the Spirit said to Philip, Go near, and join yourself to this chariot.
30 And Philip ran there to *him*, and heard him read the prophet Isaiah, and said, Understand you what you read?
31 And he said, How can I, unless some man should guide me? And he desired Philip that he would come up and sit with him.

Acts 8

32 The place of the scripture which he read was this, He was led as a sheep to the slaughter; and like a lamb dumb before his shearer, so opened he not his mouth:
33 In his humiliation his judgment was taken away: and who shall declare his generation? for his life is taken from the earth.
34 And the eunuch answered Philip, and said, I pray you, of whom speaks the prophet this? of himself, or of some other man?
35 Then Philip opened his mouth, and began at the same scripture, and preached to him Yahshua.
36 And as they went on *their* way, they came to a certain water: and the eunuch said, See, *here is* water; what does hinder me to be baptized?
37 And Philip said, If you believe with all your heart, you may. And he answered and said, I believe that Yahshua the Messiah is the Son of God.
38 And he commanded the chariot to stand still: and they went down both into the water, both Philip and the eunuch; and he baptized him.
39 And when they had come up out of the water, the Spirit of the Lord caught away Philip, that the eunuch saw him no more: and he went on his way rejoicing.
40 But Philip was found at Azotus: and passing through he preached in all the cities, till he came to Caesarea.

Acts 9

9:1 ¶ And Saul, yet breathing out threatenings and slaughter against the disciples of the Lord, went to the high priest,
2 And desired of him letters to Damascus to the synagogues, that if he found any of this way, whether they were men or women, he might bring them bound to Jerusalem.
3 And as he journeyed, he came near Damascus: and suddenly there shined round about him a light from heaven:
4 And he fell to the earth, and heard a voice saying to him, Saul, Saul, why persecute you me?
5 And he said, Who are you, Lord? And the Lord said, I am Yahshua whom you persecute: *it is* hard for you to kick against the pricks.
6 And he trembling and astonished said, Lord, what will you have me to do? And the Lord *said* to him, Arise, and go into the city, and it shall be told you what you must do.
7 And the men which journeyed with him stood speechless, hearing a voice, but seeing no man.
8 And Saul arose from the earth; and when his eyes were opened, he saw no man: but they led him by the hand, and brought *him* into Damascus.
9 And he was three days without sight, and neither did eat nor drink.
10 ¶ And there was a certain disciple at Damascus, named Ananias; and to him said the Lord in a vision, Ananias. And he said, Behold, I *am here*, Lord.
11 And the Lord *said* to him, Arise, and go into the street which is called Straight, and inquire in the house of Judas for *one* called Saul, of Tarsus: for, behold, he prays,
12 And has seen in a vision a man named Ananias coming in, and putting *his* hand on him, that he might receive his sight.
13 Then Ananias answered, Lord, I have heard by many of this man, how much evil he has done to your saints at Jerusalem:
14 And here he has authority from the chief priests to bind all that call on your name.
15 But the Lord said to him, Go your way: for he is a chosen vessel to me, to bear my name before the Gentiles, and kings, and the children of Israel:
16 For I will show him how great things he must suffer for my name's sake.
17 And Ananias went his way, and entered into the house; and putting his hands on him said, Brother Saul, the Lord, *even* Yahshua, that appeared to you in the way as you came, has sent me, that you might receive your sight, and be filled with the Holy Ghost.
18 And immediately there fell from his eyes as it had been scales: and he received sight immediately, and arose, and was baptized.
19 And when he had received food, he was strengthened. Then was Saul certain days with the disciples which were at Damascus.
20 And immediately he preached the Messiah in the synagogues, that he is the Son of God.
21 But all that heard *him* were amazed, and said; Is not this he that destroyed them which called on this name in Jerusalem, and came here for that intent, that he might bring them bound to the chief priests?
22 But Saul increased the more in strength, and confounded the Jews which dwelt at Damascus, proving that this is truly the Messiah.
23 ¶ And after that many days were fulfilled, the Jews took counsel to kill him:
24 But their lying in wait was known of Saul. And they watched the gates day and night to kill him.
25 Then the disciples took him by night, and let *him* down by the wall in a basket.
26 And when Saul had come to Jerusalem, he attempted to join himself to the disciples: but they were all afraid of him, and believed not that he was a disciple.
27 But Barnabas took him, and brought *him* to the apostles, and declared to them how he had seen the Lord in the way, and that he had spoken to him, and how he had preached boldly at Damascus in the name of Yahshua.
28 And he was with them coming in and going out at Jerusalem.
29 And he spoke boldly in the name of the Lord Yahshua, and disputed against the Grecians: but they went about to slay him.
30 *Which* when the brethren knew, they brought him down to Caesarea, and sent him forth to Tarsus.
31 Then had the assemblies rest throughout all Judaea and Galilee and Samaria, and were edified; and walking in the fear of the Lord, and in the comfort of the Holy Ghost, were multiplied.
32 ¶ And it came to pass, as Peter passed throughout all *quarters*, he came down also to the saints which dwelt at Lydda.

33 And there he found a certain man named Aeneas, which had kept his bed *for* eight years, and was sick of the palsy.
34 And Peter said to him, Aeneas, Yahshua the Messiah makes you whole: arise, and make your bed. And he arose immediately.
35 And all that dwelt at Lydda and Sharon saw him, and turned to the Lord.
36 ¶ Now there was at Joppa a certain disciple named Tabitha, which by interpretation is called Dorcas: this woman was full of good works and giving of alms which she did.
37 And it came to pass in those days, that she was sick, and died: whom when they had washed, they laid *her* in an upper chamber.
38 And forasmuch as Lydda was near to Joppa, and the disciples had heard that Peter was there, they sent to him two men, desiring *him* that he would not delay to come to them.
39 Then Peter arose and went with them. When he had come, they brought him into the upper chamber: and all the widows stood by him weeping, and showing the coats and garments which Dorcas made, while she was with them.
40 But Peter put them all forth, and kneeled down, and prayed; and turning *him* to the body said, Tabitha, arise. And she opened her eyes: and when she saw Peter, she sat up.
41 And he gave her *his* hand, and lifted her up, and when he had called the saints and widows, presented her alive.
42 And it was known throughout all Joppa; and many believed in the Lord.
43 And it came to pass, that he tarried many days in Joppa with one Simon a tanner.

Acts 10

10:1 ¶ There was a certain man in Caesarea called Cornelius, a centurion of the band called the Italian *band*,
2 *A* devout *man*, and one that feared God with all his house, which gave much alms to the people, and prayed to God always.
3 He saw in a vision evidently about the ninth hour of the day an angel of God coming in to him, and saying to him, Cornelius.
4 And when he looked on him, he was afraid, and said, What is it, Lord? And he said to him, Your prayers and your alms have come up for a memorial before God.
5 And now send men to Joppa, and call for *one* Simon, whose surname is Peter:
6 He lodges with one Simon a tanner, whose house is by the sea side: he shall tell you what you ought to do.
7 And when the angel which spoke to Cornelius had departed, he called two of his household servants, and a devout soldier of them that waited on him continually;
8 And when he had declared all *these* things to them, he sent them to Joppa.
9 ¶ On the next day, as they went on their journey, and drew near to the city, Peter went up on the housetop to pray about the sixth hour:
10 And he became very hungry, and would have eaten: but while they made ready, he fell into a trance,
11 And saw heaven opened, and a certain vessel descending unto him, as it had been a great sheet knit at the four corners, and let down to the earth:
12 Wherein were all manner of four footed beasts of the earth, and wild beasts, and creeping things, and fowls of the air.
13 And there came a voice to him, Rise, Peter; kill, and eat.
14 But Peter said, Not so, Lord; for I have never eaten anything that is common or unclean.
15 And the voice *spoke* to him again the second time, What God has cleansed, *that* call not you common.
16 This was done three times: and the vessel was received up again into heaven.
17 Now while Peter doubted in himself what this vision which he had seen should mean, behold, the men which were sent from Cornelius had made inquiry for Simon's house, and stood before the gate,
18 And called, and asked whether Simon, which was surnamed Peter, was lodged there.
19 ¶ While Peter thought on the vision, the Spirit said to him, Behold, three men seek you.
20 Arise therefore, and get you down, and go with them, doubting nothing: for I have sent them.
21 Then Peter went down to the men which were sent to him from Cornelius; and said, Behold, I am he whom you seek: what *is* the cause why you have come?
22 And they said, Cornelius the centurion, a just man, and one that fears God, and of good report among all the nation of the Jews, was warned from God by a holy angel to send for you into his house, and to hear words from you.
23 Then called he them in, and lodged *them*. And on the next day Peter went away with them, and certain brethren from Joppa accompanied him.
24 And the next day after they entered into Caesarea. And Cornelius waited for them, and had called together his relatives and near friends.
25 And as Peter was coming in, Cornelius met him, and fell down at his feet, and worshipped *him*.
26 But Peter took him up, saying, Stand up; I myself also am a man.
27 And as he talked with him, he went in, and found many that had come together.
28 And he said to them, You know how that it is an unlawful thing for a man that is a Jew to keep company, or come to one of another nation; but God has shown me that I should not call any man common or unclean.
29 Therefore came I *to you* without gainsaying, as soon as I was sent for: I ask therefore for what intent you have sent for me?

Acts 10

30 And Cornelius said, Four days ago I was fasting until this hour; and at the ninth hour I prayed in my house, and, behold, a man stood before me in bright clothing,
31 And said, Cornelius, your prayer is heard, and your alms are had in remembrance in the sight of God.
32 Send therefore to Joppa, and call here Simon, whose surname is Peter; he is lodged in the house of *one* Simon a tanner by the sea side: who, when he comes, shall speak to you.
33 Immediately therefore I sent to you; and you have well done that you have come. Now therefore are we all here present before God, to hear all things that are commanded you of God.
34 ¶ Then Peter opened *his* mouth, and said, Of a truth I perceive that God is no respecter of persons:
35 But in every nation he that fears him, and works righteousness, is accepted with him.
36 The word which *God* sent to the children of Israel, preaching peace by Yahshua the Messiah: (he is Lord of all:)
37 That word, *I say*, you know, which was published throughout all Judaea, and began from Galilee, after the baptism which John preached;
38 How God anointed Yahshua of Nazareth with the Holy Ghost and with power: who went about doing good, and healing all that were oppressed of the devil; for God was with him.
39 And we are witnesses of all things which he did both in the land of the Jews, and in Jerusalem; whom they slew and hanged on a tree:
40 Him God raised up the third day, and showed him openly;
41 Not to all the people, but to witnesses chosen before of God, *even* to us, who did eat and drink with him after he rose from the dead.
42 And he commanded us to preach to the people, and to testify that it is he which was ordained of God *to be* the Judge of quick and dead.
43 To him give all the prophets witness, that through his name whoever believes in him shall receive remission of sins.
44 ¶ While Peter yet spoke these words, the Holy Ghost fell on all them which heard the word.
45 And they of the circumcision which believed were astonished, as many as came with Peter, because that on the Gentiles also was poured out the gift of the Holy Ghost.
46 For they heard them speak with tongues, and magnify God. Then answered Peter,
47 Can any man forbid water, that these should not be baptized, which have received the Holy Ghost as well as we *have*?
48 And he commanded them to be baptized in the name of the Lord. Then prayed they him to tarry certain days.

Acts 11

11:1 ¶ And the apostles and brethren that were in Judaea heard that the Gentiles had also received the word of God.
2 And when Peter had come up to Jerusalem, they that were of the circumcision contended with him,
3 Saying, You went in to men uncircumcised, and did eat with them.
4 But Peter rehearsed *the matter* from the beginning, and expounded *it* by order to them, saying,
5 I was in the city of Joppa praying: and in a trance I saw a vision, A certain vessel descend, as it had been a great sheet, let down from heaven by four corners; and it came even to me:
6 Upon which when I had fastened my eyes, I considered, and saw four footed beasts of the earth, and wild beasts, and creeping things, and fowls of the air.
7 And I heard a voice saying to me, Arise, Peter; slay and eat.
8 But I said, Not so, Lord: for nothing common or unclean has at any time entered into my mouth.
9 But the voice answered me again from heaven, What God has cleansed, *that* call not you common.
10 And this was done three times: and all were drawn up again into heaven.
11 And, behold, immediately there were three men already come to the house where I was, sent from Caesarea to me.
12 And the Spirit told me to go with them, nothing doubting. Moreover these six brethren accompanied me, and we entered into the man's house:
13 And he showed us how he had seen an angel in his house, which stood and said to him, Send men to Joppa, and call for Simon, whose surname is Peter;
14 Who shall tell you words, whereby you and all your house shall be saved.
15 And as I began to speak, the Holy Ghost fell on them, as on us at the beginning.
16 Then remembered I the word of the Lord, how that he said, John indeed baptized with water; but you shall be baptized with the Holy Ghost.
17 Forasmuch then as God gave them the like gift as *he did* to us, who believed on the Lord Yahshua the Messiah; what was I, that I could withstand God?
18 When they heard these things, they held their peace, and glorified God, saying, Then has God also to the Gentiles granted repentance unto life.
19 ¶ Now they which were scattered abroad upon the persecution that arose about Stephen traveled as far as Phenice, and Cyprus, and Antioch, preaching the word to none but to the Jews only.
20 And some of them were men of Cyprus and Cyrene, which, when they had come to Antioch, spoke to the Grecians, preaching the Lord Yahshua.
21 And the hand of the Lord was with them: and a great number believed, and turned unto the Lord.
22 Then tidings of these things came to the ears of the congregation which was in Jerusalem: and they sent forth Barnabas, that he should go as far as Antioch.

23 Who, when he came, and had seen the grace of God, was glad, and exhorted them all, that with purpose of heart they would cling unto the Lord.
24 For he was a good man, and full of the Holy Ghost and of faith: and many people were added unto the Lord.
25 Then departed Barnabas to Tarsus, for to seek Saul:
26 And when he had found him, he brought him to Antioch. And it came to pass, that a whole year they assembled themselves with the congregation, and taught many people. And the disciples were called Christians first in Antioch.
27 ¶ And in these days came prophets from Jerusalem to Antioch.
28 And there stood up one of them named Agabus, and signified by the Spirit that there should be great famine throughout all the world: which came to pass in the days of Claudius Caesar.
29 Then the disciples, every man according to his ability, determined to send relief to the brethren which dwelt in Judaea:
30 Which also they did, and sent it to the elders by the hands of Barnabas and Saul.

Acts 12

12:1 ¶ Now about that time Herod the king stretched forth *his* hands to afflict certain of the congregation.
2 And he killed James the brother of John with the sword.
3 And because he saw it pleased the Jews, he proceeded further to take Peter also. (Then were the days of unleavened bread.)
4 And when he had apprehended him, he put *him* in prison, and delivered *him* to four quaternions of soldiers to keep him; intending after passover to bring him forth to the people.
5 ¶ Peter therefore was kept in prison: but prayer was made without ceasing of the congregation to God for him.
6 And when Herod would have brought him forth, the same night Peter was sleeping between two soldiers, bound with two chains: and the keepers before the door kept the prison.
7 And, behold, the angel of the Lord came upon *him*, and a light shined in the prison: and he smote Peter on the side, and raised him up, saying, Arise up quickly. And his chains fell off from *his* hands.
8 And the angel said to him, Gird yourself, and bind on your sandals. And so he did. And he said to him, Cast your garment about you, and follow me.
9 And he went out, and followed him; and knew not that it was true which was done by the angel; but thought he saw a vision.
10 When they were past the first and the second ward, they came to the iron gate that leads to the city; which opened to them of its own accord: and they went out, and passed on through one street; and immediately the angel departed from him.
11 And when Peter had come to himself, he said, Now I know for sure, that the Lord has sent his angel, and has delivered me out of the hand of Herod, and *from* all the expectation of the people of the Jews.
12 And when he had considered *the thing*, he came to the house of Mary the mother of John, whose surname was Mark; where many were gathered together praying.
13 And as Peter knocked at the door of the gate, a damsel came to listen, named Rhoda.
14 And when she knew Peter's voice, she opened not the gate for gladness, but ran in, and told how Peter stood before the gate.
15 And they said to her, You are mad. But she constantly affirmed that it was even so. Then said they, It is his angel.
16 But Peter continued knocking: and when they had opened *the door*, and saw him, they were astonished.
17 But he, beckoning to them with the hand to hold their peace, declared to them how the Lord had brought him out of the prison. And he said, Go show these things to James, and to the brethren. And he departed, and went into another place.
18 Now as soon as it was day, there was no small stir among the soldiers, *about* what had become of Peter.
19 And when Herod had sought for him, and found him not, he examined the keepers, and commanded that *they* should be put to death. And he went down from Judaea to Caesarea, and *there* stayed.
20 ¶ And Herod was highly displeased with them of Tyre and Sidon: but they came with one accord to him, and, having made Blastus the king's chamberlain their friend, desired peace; because their country was nourished by the king's *country*.
21 And upon a set day Herod, arrayed in royal apparel, sat upon his throne, and made an oration to them.
22 And the people gave a shout, *saying, It is* the voice of a god, and not of a man.
23 And immediately the angel of the Lord smote him, because he gave not God the glory: and he was eaten of worms, and gave up the ghost.
24 But the word of God grew and multiplied.
25 And Barnabas and Saul returned from Jerusalem, when they had fulfilled *their* ministry, and took with them John, whose surname was Mark.

Acts 13

13:1 ¶ Now there were in the congregation that was at Antioch certain prophets and teachers; as Barnabas, and Simeon that was called Niger, and Lucius of Cyrene, and Manaen, which had been brought up with Herod the tetrarch, and Saul.
2 As they ministered to the Lord, and fasted, the Holy Ghost said, Separate me Barnabas and Saul for the work whereunto I have called them.
3 And when they had fasted and prayed, and laid *their* hands on them, they sent *them* away.

Acts 13

4 ¶ So they, being sent forth by the Holy Ghost, departed to Seleucia; and from there they sailed to Cyprus.

5 And when they were at Salamis, they preached the word of God in the synagogues of the Jews: and they had also John as *their* minister.

6 And when they had gone through the isle to Paphos, they found a certain sorcerer, a false prophet, a Jew, whose name *was* Barjesus:

7 Which was with the deputy of the country, Sergius Paulus, a prudent man; who called for Barnabas and Saul, and desired to hear the word of God.

8 But Elymas the sorcerer (for so is his name by interpretation) withstood them, seeking to turn away the deputy from the faith.

9 Then Saul, (who also *is called* Paul,) filled with the Holy Ghost, set his eyes on him,

10 And said, O full of all subtlety and all mischief, *you* child of the devil, *you* enemy of all righteousness, will you not cease to pervert the right ways of the Lord?

11 And now, behold, the hand of the Lord *is upon* you, and you shall be blind, not seeing the sun for a season. And immediately there fell on him a mist and a darkness; and he went about seeking some to lead him by the hand.

12 Then the deputy, when he saw what was done, believed, being astonished at the doctrine of the Lord.

13 Now when Paul and his company loosed from Paphos, they came to Perga in Pamphylia: and John departing from them returned to Jerusalem.

14 ¶ But when they departed from Perga, they came to Antioch in Pisidia, and went into the synagogue on the sabbath day, and sat down.

15 And after the reading of the law and the prophets the rulers of the synagogue sent to them, saying, *You* men *and* brethren, if you have any word of exhortation for the people, say on.

16 Then Paul stood up, and beckoning with *his* hand said, Men of Israel, and you that fear God, give audience.

17 The God of this people of Israel chose our fathers, and exalted the people when they dwelt as strangers in the land of Egypt, and with a high arm brought he them out of it.

18 And about the time of forty years endured he their manners in the wilderness.

19 And when he had destroyed seven nations in the land of Canaan, he divided their land to them by lot.

20 And after that he gave *to them* judges about the space of four hundred and fifty years, until Samuel the prophet.

21 And afterward they desired a king: and God gave to them Saul the son of Kish, a man of the tribe of Benjamin, by the space of forty years.

22 And when he had removed him, he raised up unto them David to be their king; to whom also he gave testimony, and said, I have found David the *son* of Jesse, a man after my own heart, which shall fulfill all my will.

23 Of this man's seed has God according to *his* promise raised unto Israel a Savior, Yahshua:

24 When John had first preached before his coming the baptism of repentance to all the people of Israel.

25 And as John fulfilled his course, he said, Whom think you that I am? I am not *he*. But, behold, there comes one after me, whose shoes of *his* feet I am not worthy to loose.

26 Men *and* brethren, children of the stock of Abraham, and whoever among you fears God, to you is the word of this salvation sent.

27 For they that dwell at Jerusalem, and their rulers, because they knew him not, nor yet the voices of the prophets which are read every sabbath day, they have fulfilled *them* in condemning *him*.

28 And though they found no cause for death *in him*, yet desired they Pilate that he should be slain.

29 And when they had fulfilled all that was written of him, they took *him* down from the tree, and laid *him* in a sepulcher.

30 But God raised him from the dead:

31 And he was seen many days of them which came up with him from Galilee to Jerusalem, who are his witnesses to the people.

32 And we declare to you glad tidings, how that the promise which was made to the fathers,

33 God *Yahweh* has fulfilled the same to us their children, in that he has raised up Yahshua again; as it is also written in the second psalm, You are my Son, this day have I begotten you.

34 And as concerning that he raised him up from the dead, *now* no more to return to corruption, he said in this manner, I will give you the sure mercies of David.

35 Therefore he said also in another *psalm*, You shall not allow your Holy One to see corruption.

36 For David, after he had served his own generation by the will of God, fell asleep, and was laid to his fathers, and saw corruption:

37 But he, whom God raised again, saw no corruption.

38 Be it known unto you therefore, men *and* brethren, that through this man is preached to you the forgiveness of sins:

39 And by him all that believe are justified from all things, from which you could not be justified by the law of Moses.

40 Beware therefore, lest that comes upon you, which is spoken of in the prophets;

41 Behold, you despisers, and wonder, and perish: for I work a work in your days, a work which you shall in no way believe, though a man declares it unto you.

42 ¶ And when the Jews were gone out of the synagogue, the Gentiles sought that these words might be preached to them the next sabbath.

43 Now when the congregation was broken up, many of the Jews and religious proselytes followed Paul and Barnabas: who, speaking to them, persuaded them to continue in the grace of God.

44 And the next sabbath day came almost the whole city together to hear the word of God.

45 But when the Jews saw the multitudes, they were filled with envy, and spoke against those things which were spoken by Paul, contradicting and blaspheming.

46 Then Paul and Barnabas became bold, and said, It was necessary that the word of God should first have been spoken to you: but seeing you put it from you, and judge yourselves unworthy of everlasting life, behold, we turn to the Gentiles.
47 For so has the Lord *Yahweh* commanded us, *saying*, I have set you to be a light of the Gentiles, that you should be for salvation to the ends of the earth.
48 And when the Gentiles heard this, they were glad, and glorified the word of the Lord: and as many as were ordained to eternal life believed.
49 And the word of the Lord was published throughout all the region.
50 But the Jews stirred up the devout and honorable women, and the chief men of the city, and raised persecution against Paul and Barnabas, and expelled them out of their coasts.
51 But they shook off the dust of their feet against them, and came to Iconium.
52 And the disciples were filled with joy, and with the Holy Ghost.

Acts 14

14:1 ¶ And it came to pass in Iconium, that they went both together into the synagogue of the Jews, and so spoke, that a great multitude both of the Jews and also of the Greeks believed.
2 But the unbelieving Jews stirred up the Gentiles, and made their minds evilly affected against the brethren.
3 Long time therefore stayed they speaking boldly in the Lord, which gave testimony to the word of his grace, and granted signs and wonders to be done by their hands.
4 But the multitude of the city was divided: and part held with the Jews, and part with the apostles.
5 And when there was an assault made both by the Gentiles, and also by the Jews with their rulers, to use *them* spitefully, and to stone them,
6 They were aware of *it*, and fled to Lystra and Derbe, cities of Lycaonia, and to the region that lies round about:
7 And there they preached the gospel.
8 ¶ And there sat a certain man at Lystra, weak in his feet, being a cripple from his mother's womb, who never had walked:
9 The same heard Paul speak: who steadfastly beholding him, and perceiving that he had faith to be healed,
10 Said with a loud voice, Stand upright on your feet. And he leaped and walked.
11 And when the people saw what Paul had done, they lifted up their voices, saying in the speech of Lycaonia, The gods have come down to us in the likeness of men.
12 And they called Barnabas, Jupiter [Zeus]; and Paul, Mercurius [Hermes], because he was the chief speaker.
13 Then the priest of Jupiter [Zeus], which was before their city, brought oxen and garlands to the gates, and would have done sacrifice with the people.
14 *Which* when the apostles, Barnabas and Paul, heard *of*, they tore their clothes, and ran in among the people, crying out,
15 And saying, Sirs, why do you these things? We also are men of like passions with you, and preach to you that you should turn from these vanities unto the living God, which made heaven, and earth, and the sea, and all things that are therein:
16 Who in times past allowed all nations to walk in their own ways.
17 Nevertheless he left not himself without witness, in that he did good, and gave us rain from heaven, and fruitful seasons, filling our hearts with food and gladness.
18 And with these sayings scarcely restrained they the people, that they had not done sacrifice to them.
19 ¶ And there came there *certain* Jews from Antioch and Iconium, who persuaded the people. and, having stoned Paul, drew *him* out of the city, supposing he had been dead.
20 However, as the disciples stood round about him, he rose up and came into the city: and the next day he departed with Barnabas to Derbe.
21 And when they had preached the gospel to that city, and had taught many, they returned again to Lystra, and *to* Iconium, and Antioch,
22 Confirming the souls of the disciples, *and* exhorting them to continue in the faith, and that we must through much tribulation enter into the kingdom of God.
23 And when they had ordained them elders in every congregation, and had prayed with fasting, they commended them to the Lord, on whom they believed.
24 And after they had passed throughout Pisidia, they came to Pamphylia.
25 And when they had preached the word in Perga, they went down into Attalia:
26 And there sailed to Antioch, from where they had been recommended to the grace of God for the work which they fulfilled.
27 And when they had come, and had gathered the congregation together, they told all that God had done with them, and how he had opened the door of faith to the Gentiles.
28 And there they stayed *a* long time with the disciples.

Acts 15

15:1 ¶ And certain men which came down from Judaea taught the brethren, *and said*, Unless you are circumcised after the manner of Moses, you cannot be saved.
2 When therefore Paul and Barnabas had no small dissension and disputation with them, they determined that Paul and Barnabas, and certain other of them, should go up to Jerusalem to the apostles and elders about this question.
3 And being brought on their way by the congregation, they passed through Phenice and Samaria, declaring the conversion of the Gentiles: and they caused great joy to all the brethren.

Acts 15

4 And when they had come to Jerusalem, they were received of the congregation, and *of* the apostles and elders, and they declared all things that God had done with them.

5 But there rose up certain of the sect of the Pharisees which believed, saying, That it was needful to circumcise them, and to command *them* to keep the law of Moses.

6 ¶ And the apostles and elders came together for to consider of this matter.

7 And when there had been much disputing, Peter rose up, and said to them, Men *and* brethren, you know how that a good while ago God made choice among us, that the Gentiles by my mouth should hear the word of the gospel, and believe.

8 And God, which knows the hearts, bears them witness, giving them the Holy Ghost, even as *he did* unto us;

9 And put no difference between us and them, purifying their hearts by faith.

10 Now therefore why tempt you God, to put a yoke upon the neck of the disciples, which neither our fathers nor we were able to bear?

11 But we believe that through the grace of the Lord Yahshua the Messiah we shall be saved, even as they.

12 Then all the multitude kept silent, and gave audience to Barnabas and Paul, declaring what miracles and wonders God had worked among the Gentiles by them.

13 And after they had held their peace, James answered, saying, Men *and* brethren, listen to me:

14 Simeon has declared how God at the first did visit the Gentiles, to take out of them a people for his name.

15 And to this agree the words of the prophets; as it is written,

16 After this I will return, and will build again the tabernacle of David, which has fallen down; and I will build again the ruins thereof, and I will set it up:

17 That the residue of men might seek after the Lord *Yahweh*, and all the Gentiles, upon whom my name is called, says the Lord *Yahweh*, who does all these things.

18 Known to God are all his works from the beginning of the world.

19 Therefore my sentence is, that we trouble not them, which from among the Gentiles are turned to God:

20 But that we write to them, that they abstain from pollutions of idols, and *from* fornication, and *from* things strangled, and *from* blood.

21 For Moses of old time has in every city them that preach him, being read in the synagogues every sabbath day.

22 ¶ Then pleased it the apostles and elders, with the whole congregation, to send chosen men of their own company to Antioch with Paul and Barnabas; *namely*, Judas surnamed Barsabas, and Silas, chief men among the brethren:

23 And they wrote *letters* by them after this manner; The apostles and elders and brethren *send* greetings to the brethren which are of the Gentiles in Antioch and Syria and Cilicia:

24 Forasmuch as we have heard, that some which went out from us have troubled you with words, subverting your souls, saying, *You must* be circumcised, and keep the law: to whom we gave no *such* commandment:

25 It seemed good to us, being assembled with one accord, to send chosen men to you with our beloved Barnabas and Paul,

26 Men that have hazarded their lives for the name of our Lord Yahshua the Messiah.

27 We have sent therefore Judas and Silas, who shall also tell *you* the same things by mouth.

28 For it seemed good to the Holy Ghost, and to us, to lay upon you no greater burden than these necessary things;

29 That you abstain from foods offered to idols, and from blood, and from things strangled, and from fornication: from which if you keep yourselves, you shall do well. Fare you well.

30 So when they were dismissed, they came to Antioch: and when they had gathered the multitude together, they delivered the epistle:

31 *Which* when they had read, they rejoiced for the consolation.

32 And Judas and Silas, being prophets also themselves, exhorted the brethren with many words, and confirmed *them*.

33 And after they had worked *there* a while, they were let go in peace from the brethren to the apostles.

34 Notwithstanding it pleased Silas to remain there still.

35 Paul also and Barnabas continued in Antioch, teaching and preaching the word of the Lord, with many others also.

36 ¶ And some days after Paul said to Barnabas, Let us go again and visit our brethren in every city where we have preached the word of the Lord, *and see* how they *are* doing.

37 And Barnabas determined to take with them John, whose surname was Mark.

38 But Paul thought not good to take him with them, who departed from them from Pamphylia, and went not with them to the work.

39 And the contention was so sharp between them, that they departed apart one from the other: and so Barnabas took Mark, and sailed to Cyprus;

40 And Paul chose Silas, and departed, being recommended by the brethren to the grace of God.

41 And he went through Syria and Cilicia, confirming the congregations.

Acts 16

16:1 ¶ Then came he to Derbe and Lystra: and, behold, a certain disciple was there, named Timotheus, the son of a certain woman, which was a Jewess, and believed; but his father *was* a Greek:

2 Which was well reported of by the brethren that were at Lystra and Iconium.

3 Him would Paul have to go forth with him; and took and circumcised him because of the Jews which were in those quarters: for they knew all that his father was a Greek.

4 And as they went through the cities, they delivered them the decrees for to keep, that were ordained of the apostles and elders which were at Jerusalem.

5 And so were the congregations established in the faith, and increased in number daily.

6 ¶ Now when they had gone throughout Phrygia and the region of Galatia, and were forbidden by the Holy Ghost to preach the word in Asia,

7 After they had come to Mysia, they tried to go into Bithynia: but the Spirit allowed them not.

8 And they passing by Mysia came down to Troas.

9 And a vision appeared to Paul in the night; There stood a man of Macedonia, and called for him, saying, Come over into Macedonia, and help us.

10 And after he had seen the vision, immediately we endeavored to go into Macedonia, assuredly gathering that the Lord had called us for to preach the gospel to them.

11 Therefore sailing from Troas, we came with a straight course to Samothracia, and the next *day* to Neapolis;

12 And from there to Philippi, which is the chief city of that part of Macedonia, *and* a colony: and we were in that city abiding certain days.

13 And on the sabbath we went out of the city by a river side, where prayer was inclined to be made; and we sat down, and spoke to the women which resorted *there*.

14 And a certain woman named Lydia, a seller of purple, of the city of Thyatira, which worshipped God, heard *us*: whose heart the Lord opened, that she attended unto the things which were spoken by Paul.

15 And when she was baptized, and her household, she sought *us*, saying, If you have judged me to be faithful to the Lord, come into my house, and stay *there*. And she constrained us.

16 ¶ And it came to pass, as we went to prayer, a certain damsel possessed with a spirit of divination met us, which brought her masters much gain by soothsaying:

17 The same followed Paul and us, and cried, saying, These men are the servants of the most high God, which show unto us the way of salvation.

18 And this did she many days. But Paul, being grieved, turned and said to the spirit, I command you in the name of Yahshua the Messiah to come out of her. And he came out the same hour.

19 And when her masters saw that the hope of their gains was gone, they caught Paul and Silas, and drew *them* into the marketplace unto the rulers,

20 And brought them to the magistrates, saying, These men, being Jews, do exceedingly trouble our city,

21 And teach customs, which are not lawful for us to receive, neither to observe, being Romans.

22 And the multitude rose up together against them: and the magistrates tore off their clothes, and commanded to beat *them*.

23 And when they had laid many stripes upon them, they cast *them* into prison, charging the jailer to keep them safely:

24 Who, having received such a charge, thrust them into the inner prison, and made their feet fast in the stocks

25 ¶ And at midnight Paul and Silas prayed, and sang praises to God: and the prisoners heard them.

26 And suddenly there was a great earthquake, so that the foundations of the prison were shaken: and immediately all the doors were opened, and every one's bands were loosed.

27 And the keeper of the prison awaking out of his sleep, and seeing the prison doors open, he drew out his sword, and would have killed himself, supposing that the prisoners had been fled.

28 But Paul cried with a loud voice, saying, Do yourself no harm: for we are all here.

29 Then he called for a light, and sprang in, and came trembling, and fell down before Paul and Silas,

30 And brought them out, and said, Sirs, what must I do to be saved?

31 And they said, Believe on the Lord Yahshua the Messiah, and you shall be saved, and your house.

32 And they spoke unto him the word of the Lord, and to all that were in his house.

33 And he took them the same hour of the night, and washed *their* stripes; and was baptized, he and all his, immediately.

34 And when he had brought them into his house, he set food before them, and rejoiced, believing in God with all his house.

35 ¶ And when it was day, the magistrates sent the sergeants, saying, Let those men go.

36 And the keeper of the prison told this saying to Paul, The magistrates have sent to let you go: now therefore depart, and go in peace.

37 But Paul said to them, They have beaten us openly uncondemned, being Romans, and have cast *us* into prison; and now do they thrust us out privately? no truly; but let them come themselves and fetch us out.

38 And the sergeants told these words to the magistrates: and they feared, when they heard that they were Romans.

39 And they came and summoned them, and brought *them* out, and asked *them* to depart out of the city.

40 And they went out of the prison, and entered into *the house of* Lydia: and when they had seen the brethren, they comforted them, and departed.

Acts 17

17:1 ¶ Now when they had passed through Amphipolis and Apollonia, they came to Thessalonica, where was a synagogue of the Jews:

2 And Paul, as his manner was, went in to them, and three sabbath days reasoned with them out of the scriptures,

3 Opening and alleging, that the Messiah must need *to* have suffered, and risen again from the dead; and that this Yahshua, whom I preach unto you, is the Messiah.

4 And some of them believed, and consorted with Paul and Silas; and of the devout Greeks a great multitude, and of the chief women not a few.

Acts 17

5 But the Jews which believed not, moved with envy, took to them certain lewd fellows of the baser sort, and gathered a company, and set all the city on an uproar, and assaulted the house of Jason, and sought to bring them out to the people.

6 And when they found them not, they drew Jason and certain brethren to the rulers of the city, crying, These that have turned the world upside down have come here also;

7 Whom Jason has received: and these all do contrary to the decrees of Caesar, saying that there is another king, *one* Yahshua.

8 And they troubled the people and the rulers of the city, when they heard these things.

9 And when they had taken security of Jason, and of the other, they let them go.

10 ¶ And the brethren immediately sent away Paul and Silas by night to Berea: who coming *there* went into the synagogue of the Jews.

11 These were more noble than those in Thessalonica, in that they received the word with all readiness of mind, and searched the scriptures daily, whether those things were so.

12 Therefore many of them believed; also of honorable women which were Greeks, and of men, not a few.

13 But when the Jews of Thessalonica had knowledge that the word of God was preached by Paul at Berea, they came there also, and stirred up the people.

14 And then immediately the brethren sent away Paul to go as it were to the sea: but Silas and Timotheus stayed there still.

15 And they that conducted Paul brought him to Athens: and receiving a commandment unto Silas and Timotheus for to come to him with all speed, they departed.

16 ¶ Now while Paul waited for them at Athens, his spirit was stirred in him, when he saw the city wholly given to idolatry.

17 Therefore disputed he in the synagogue with the Jews, and with the devout persons, and in the market daily with them that met with him.

18 Then certain philosophers of the Epicureans, and of the Stoicks, encountered him. And some said, What will this babbler say? and others *said*, He seems to be a setter forth of strange gods: because he preached to them Yahshua, and the resurrection.

19 And they took him, and brought him to Areopagus, saying, May we know what this new doctrine, whereof you speak, *is*?

20 For you bring certain strange things to our ears: we would *like to* know therefore what these things mean.

21 (For all the Athenians and strangers which were there spent their time in nothing else, but either to tell, or to hear some new thing.)

22 ¶ Then Paul stood in the midst of Mars' hill, and said, *You* men of Athens, I perceive that in all things you are too superstitious.

23 For as I passed by, and saw your devotions, I found an altar with this inscription, TO THE UNKNOWN GOD. Whom therefore you ignorantly worship, him declare I to you.

24 God that made the world and all things therein, seeing that he is Lord of heaven and earth, dwells not in temples made with hands;

25 Neither is worshipped with men's hands, as though he needed anything, seeing he gives to all life, and breath, and all things;

26 And has made of one blood all nations of men for to dwell on all the face of the earth, and has determined the times before appointed, and the bounds of their habitation;

27 That they should seek the Lord, if then they might feel after him, and find him, though he is not far from every one of us:

28 For in him we live, and move, and have our being; as certain also of your own poets have said, For we are also his offspring.

29 Forasmuch then as we are the offspring of God, we ought not to think that the Godhead is like unto gold, or silver, or stone, graven by art and man's device.

30 And the times of this ignorance God winked at; but now commands all men every where to repent:

31 Because he has appointed a day, in which he will judge the world in righteousness by *that* man whom he has ordained; *whereof* he has given assurance to all *men*, in that he has raised him from the dead.

32 ¶ And when they heard of the resurrection of the dead, some mocked: and others said, We will hear you again of this *matter*.

33 So Paul departed from among them.

34 However certain men clung to him, and believed: among the which *was* Dionysius the Areopagite, and a woman named Damaris, and others with them.

Acts 18

18:1 ¶ After these things Paul departed from Athens, and came to Corinth;

2 And found a certain Jew named Aquila, born in Pontus, lately come from Italy, with his wife Priscilla; (because that Claudius had commanded all Jews to depart from Rome:) and came to them.

3 And because he was of the same craft, he stayed with them, and worked: for by their occupation they were tentmakers.

4 And he reasoned in the synagogue every sabbath, and persuaded the Jews and the Greeks.

5 And when Silas and Timotheus had come from Macedonia, Paul was pressed in the spirit, and testified to the Jews *that* Yahshua *was* the Messiah.

6 And when they opposed themselves, and blasphemed, he shook *his* garments, and said to them, Your blood *be* upon your own heads; I *am* clean: from now on I will go to the Gentiles.

7 ¶ And he departed from there, and entered into a certain *man's* house, named Justus, *one* that worshipped God, whose house joined hard to the synagogue.

8 And Crispus, the chief ruler of the synagogue, believed on the Lord with all his house; and many of the Corinthians hearing believed, and were baptized.

9 Then spoke the Lord to Paul in the night by a vision, Be not afraid, but speak, and hold not your peace:
10 For I am with you, and no man shall set on you to hurt you: for I have many people in this city.
11 And he continued *there* a year and six months, teaching the word of God among them.
12 ¶ And when Gallio was the deputy of Achaia, the Jews made insurrection with one accord against Paul, and brought him to the judgment seat,
13 Saying, This *fellow* persuades men to worship God contrary to the law.
14 And when Paul was now about to open *his* mouth, Gallio said to the Jews, If it were a matter of wrong or wicked lewdness, O *you* Jews, reason would that I should bear with you:
15 But if it is a question of words and names, and *of* your law, look you *to it*; for I will be no judge of such *matters*.
16 And he drove them from the judgment seat.
17 Then all the Greeks took Sosthenes, the chief ruler of the synagogue, and beat *him* before the judgment seat. And Gallio cared for none of those things.
18 ¶ And Paul *after this* continued *there* yet a good while, and then took his leave of the brethren, and sailed away into Syria, and with him Priscilla and Aquila; having shorn *his* head in Cenchrea: for he had a vow.
19 And he came to Ephesus, and left them there: but he himself entered into the synagogue, and reasoned with the Jews.
20 When they desired *him* to remain *a* longer time with them, he consented not;
21 But told them farewell, saying, I must by all means keep this feast that comes in Jerusalem: but I will return again to you, if God wills. And he sailed from Ephesus.
22 And when he had landed at Caesarea, and gone up, and saluted the congregation, he went down to Antioch.
23 And after he had spent some time *there*, he departed, and went over *all* the country of Galatia and Phrygia in order, strengthening all the disciples.
24 ¶ And a certain Jew named Apollos, born at Alexandria, an eloquent man, *and* mighty in the scriptures, came to Ephesus.
25 This man was instructed in the way of the Lord; and being fervent in the spirit, he spoke and taught diligently the things of the Lord, knowing only the baptism of John.
26 And he began to speak boldly in the synagogue: whom when Aquila and Priscilla had heard, they took him unto *them*, and expounded to him the way of God more perfectly.
27 And when he was intending to pass into Achaia, the brethren wrote, exhorting the disciples to receive him: who, when he had come, helped them much which had believed through grace:
28 For he mightily convinced the Jews, *and that* publicly, showing by the scriptures that Yahshua was the Messiah.

Acts 19

19:1 ¶ And it came to pass, that, while Apollos was at Corinth, Paul having passed through the upper coasts came to Ephesus: and finding certain disciples,
2 He said to them, Have you received the Holy Ghost since you believed? And they said to him, We have not so much as heard whether there is any Holy Ghost.
3 And he said to them, Unto what then were you baptized? And they said, Unto John's baptism.
4 Then said Paul, John truly baptized with the baptism of repentance, saying to the people, that they should believe on him which should come after him, that is, on the Messiah Yahshua.
5 When they heard *this*, they were baptized in the name of the Lord Yahshua.
6 And when Paul had laid *his* hands upon them, the Holy Ghost came on them; and they spoke with tongues, and prophesied.
7 And all the men were about twelve.
8 ¶ And he went into the synagogue, and spoke boldly for the space of three months, disputing and persuading the things concerning the kingdom of God.
9 But when some were hardened, and believed not, but spoke evil of that way before the multitude, he departed from them, and separated the disciples, disputing daily in the school of one Tyrannus.
10 And this continued over the space of two years; so that all they which dwelt in Asia heard the word of the Lord Yahshua, both Jews and Greeks.
11 And God worked special miracles by the hands of Paul:
12 So that from his body were brought to the sick handkerchiefs or aprons, and the diseases departed from them, and the evil spirits went out of them.
13 ¶ Then certain of the vagabond Jews, exorcists, took upon them to call over them which had evil spirits the name of the Lord Yahshua, saying, We adjure you by Yahshua whom Paul preaches.
14 And there were seven sons of *one* Sceva, a Jew, *and* chief of the priests, which did so.
15 And the evil spirit answered and said, Yahshua I know, and Paul I know; but who are you?
16 And the man in whom the evil spirit was leaped on them, and overcame them, and prevailed against them, so that they fled out of that house naked and wounded.
17 And this was known to all the Jews and Greeks also dwelling at Ephesus; and fear fell on them all, and the name of the Lord Yahshua was magnified.
18 And many that believed came, and confessed, and showed their deeds.
19 Many of them also which used curious arts brought their books together, and burned them before all *men*: and they counted the price of them, and found *it* fifty thousand *pieces* of silver.
20 So mightily grew the word of God and prevailed.
21 ¶ After these things were ended, Paul purposed in the spirit, when he had passed through Macedonia and Achaia, to go to Jerusalem, saying, After I have been there, I must also see Rome.

Acts 19

22 So he sent into Macedonia two of them that ministered to him, Timotheus and Erastus; but he himself stayed in Asia for a season.

23 And the same time there arose no small stir about that way.

24 For a certain *man* named Demetrius, a silversmith, which made silver shrines for Diana [Artemis], brought no small gain to the craftsmen;

25 Whom he called together with the workmen of like occupation, and said, Sirs, you know that by this craft we have our wealth.

26 Moreover you see and hear, that not alone at Ephesus, but almost throughout all Asia, this Paul has persuaded and turned away many people, saying that they are no gods, which are made with hands:

27 So that not only this our craft is in danger to be set at nothing; but also that the temple of the great goddess Diana [Artemis] should be despised, and her magnificence should be destroyed, whom all Asia and the world worships.

28 And when they heard *these sayings*, they were full of wrath, and cried out, saying, Great *is* Diana [Artemis] of the Ephesians.

29 And the whole city was filled with confusion: and having caught Gaius and Aristarchus, men of Macedonia, Paul's companions in travel, they rushed with one accord into the theatre.

30 And when Paul would have entered in to the people, the disciples allowed him not.

31 And certain of the chief of Asia, which were his friends, sent to him, desiring *him* that he would not adventure himself into the theater.

32 Some therefore cried one thing, and some another: for the assembly was confused; and the more part knew not why they had come together.

33 And they drew Alexander out of the multitude, the Jews putting him forward. And Alexander beckoned with the hand, and would have made his defense unto the people.

34 But when they knew that he was a Jew, all with one voice about the space of two hours cried out, Great *is* Diana [Artemis] of the Ephesians.

35 And when the town clerk had appeased the people, he said, *You* men of Ephesus, what man is there that knows not how that the city of the Ephesians is a worshipper of the great goddess Diana [Artemis], and of the *image* which fell down from Jupiter [Zeus]?

36 Seeing then that these things cannot be spoken against, you ought to be quiet, and to do nothing rashly.

37 For you have brought here these men, which are neither robbers of temples, nor yet blasphemers of your goddess.

38 Therefore if Demetrius, and the craftsmen which are with him, have a matter against any man, the law is open, and there are deputies: let them accuse one another.

39 But if you inquire anything concerning other matters, it shall be determined in a lawful assembly.

40 For we are in danger to be called in question for this day's uproar, there being no cause whereby we may give an account of this concourse.

41 And when he had thus spoken, he dismissed the assembly.

Acts 20

20:1 ¶ And after the uproar had ceased, Paul called unto *him* the disciples, and embraced *them*, and departed for to go into Macedonia.

2 And when he had gone over those parts, and had given them much exhortation, he came into Greece,

3 And *there* stayed three months. And when the Jews laid wait for him, as he was about to sail into Syria, he purposed to return through Macedonia.

4 And there accompanied him into Asia Sopater of Berea; and of the Thessalonians, Aristarchus and Secundus; and Gaius of Derbe, and Timotheus; and of Asia, Tychicus and Trophimus.

5 These going before waited for us at Troas.

6 And we sailed away from Philippi after the days of unleavened bread, and came unto them to Troas in five days; where we stayed seven days.

7 ¶ And upon the first *day* of the week, when the disciples came together to break bread, Paul preached to them, ready to depart on the next day; and continued his speech until midnight.

8 And there were many lights in the upper chamber, where they were gathered together.

9 And there sat in a window a certain young man named Eutychus, was falling into a deep sleep: and as Paul was long preaching, he sunk down with sleep, and fell down from the third loft, and was taken up dead.

10 And Paul went down, and fell on him, and embracing *him* said, Trouble not yourselves; for his life is in him.

11 When he therefore had come up again, and had broken bread, and eaten, and talked a long while, even till *the* break of day, so he departed.

12 And they brought the young man alive, and were not a little comforted.

13 ¶ And we went before to *the* ship, and sailed to Assos, there intending to take in Paul: for so had he arranged, intending himself to go afoot.

14 And when he met with us at Assos, we took him in, and came to Mitylene.

15 And we sailed there, and came the next *day* over against Chios; and the next *day* we arrived at Samos, and stayed at Trogyllium; and the next *day* we came to Miletus.

16 For Paul had determined to sail by Ephesus, so that he would not spend the time in Asia: for he hurried, if it were possible for him, to be at Jerusalem the day of Pentecost.

17 ¶ And from Miletus he sent to Ephesus, and called the elders of the congregation.

18 And when they had come to him, he said to them, You know, from the first day that I came into Asia, after what manner I have been with you at all seasons,

19 Serving the Lord with all humility of mind, and with many tears, and temptations, which befell me by the lying in wait of the Jews:
20 *And* how I kept back nothing that was profitable *to you*, but have shown you, and have taught you publicly, and from house to house,
21 Testifying both to the Jews, and also to the Greeks, repentance toward God, and faith toward our Lord Yahshua the Messiah.
22 And now, behold, I go bound in the spirit to Jerusalem, not knowing the things that shall befall me there:
23 Save that the Holy Ghost witnesses in every city, saying that bonds and afflictions await me.
24 But none of these things move me, neither count I my life dear to myself, so that I might finish my course with joy, and the ministry, which I have received of the Lord Yahshua, to testify the gospel of the grace of God.
25 And now, behold, I know that you all, among whom I have gone preaching the kingdom of God, shall see my face no more.
26 Therefore I take you to record this day, that I *am* pure from the blood of all *men*.
27 For I have not shunned to declare to you all the counsel of God.
28 Take heed therefore unto yourselves, and to all the flock, over the which the Holy Ghost has made you overseers, to feed the congregation of God, which he has purchased with his own blood.
29 For I know this, that after my departing shall grievous wolves enter in among you, not sparing the flock.
30 Also of your own selves shall men arise, speaking perverse things, to draw away disciples after them.
31 Therefore watch, and remember, that by the space of three years I ceased not to warn every one night and day with tears.
32 And now, brethren, I commend you to God, and to the word of his grace, which is able to build you up, and to give you an inheritance among all them which are sanctified.
33 I have coveted no man's silver, or gold, or apparel.
34 Yes, you yourselves know, that these hands have ministered to my necessities, and to them that were with me.
35 I have shown you all things, how that so laboring you ought to support the weak, and to remember the words of the Lord Yahshua, how he said, It is more blessed to give than to receive.
36 ¶ And when he had thus spoken, he kneeled down, and prayed with them all.
37 And they all wept much, and fell on Paul's neck, and kissed him,
38 Sorrowing most of all for the words which he spoke, that they should see his face no more. And they accompanied him to the ship.

Acts 21

21:1 ¶ And it came to pass, that after we withdrew from them, and had launched, we came with a straight course to Coos, and the *day* following to Rhodes, and from there to Patara:
2 And finding a ship sailing over to Phenicia, we went aboard, and set forth.
3 Now when we had discovered Cyprus, we left it on the left hand, and sailed into Syria, and landed at Tyre: for there the ship was to unload her burden.
4 And finding disciples, we stayed there seven days: who said to Paul through the Spirit, that he should not go up to Jerusalem.
5 And when we had accomplished those days, we departed and went our way; and they all brought us on our way, with wives and children, till *we were* out of the city: and we knelt down on the shore, and prayed.
6 And when we had taken our leave one of another, we took ship; and they returned home again.
7 And when we had finished *our* course from Tyre, we came to Ptolemais, and saluted the brethren, and stayed with them one day.
8 ¶ And the next *day* we that were of Paul's company departed, and came to Caesarea: and we entered into the house of Philip the evangelist, which was *one* of the seven; and stayed with him.
9 And the same man had four daughters, virgins, which did prophesy.
10 And as we stayed *there* many days, there came down from Judaea a certain prophet, named Agabus.
11 And when he had come to us, he took Paul's girdle, and bound his own hands and feet, and said, Thus says the Holy Ghost, So shall the Jews at Jerusalem bind the man that owns this girdle, and shall deliver *him* into the hands of the Gentiles.
12 And when we heard these things, both we, and they of that place, begged him not to go up to Jerusalem.
13 Then Paul answered, What mean you to weep and to break my heart? for I am ready not to be bound only, but also to die at Jerusalem for the name of the Lord Yahshua.
14 And when he would not be persuaded, we ceased, saying, The will of the Lord be done.
15 ¶ And after those days we took up our carriages, and went up to Jerusalem.
16 There went with us also *certain* of the disciples of Caesarea, and brought with them one Mnason of Cyprus, an old disciple, with whom we should lodge.
17 And when we had come to Jerusalem, the brethren received us gladly.
18 And the *day* following Paul went in with us to James; and all the elders were present.
19 And when he had saluted them, he declared particularly what things God had worked among the Gentiles by his ministry.
20 And when they heard *it*, they glorified the Lord, and said to him, You see, brother, how many thousands of Jews there are which believe; and they are all zealous of the law:

21 And they are informed of you, that you teach all the Jews which are among the Gentiles to forsake Moses, saying that they ought not to circumcise *their* children, neither to walk after the customs.

22 What is it therefore? the multitude must surely come together: for they will hear that you have come.

23 Do therefore this that we say to you: We have four men which have a vow on them;

24 Them take, and purify yourself with them, and be at charges with them, that they may shave *their* heads: and all may know that those things, whereof they were informed concerning you, are nothing; but *that* you yourself also walk orderly, and keep the law.

25 As touching the Gentiles which believe, we have written *and* concluded that they observe no such thing, save only that they keep themselves from *things* offered to idols, and from blood, and from strangled, and from fornication.

26 Then Paul took the men, and the next day purifying himself with them entered into the temple, to signify the accomplishment of the days of purification, until that an offering should be offered for every one of them.

27 ¶ And when the seven days were almost ended, the Jews which were of Asia, when they saw him in the temple, stirred up all the people, and laid hands on him,

28 Crying out, Men of Israel, help: This is the man, that teaches all *men* every where against the people, and the law, and this place: and further brought Greeks also into the temple, and has polluted this holy place.

29 (For they had seen before with him in the city Trophimus an Ephesian, whom they supposed that Paul had brought into the temple.)

30 And all the city was moved, and the people ran together: and they took Paul, and drew him out of the temple: and immediately the doors were shut.

31 And as they went about to kill him, tidings came to the chief captain of the band, that all Jerusalem was in an uproar.

32 Who immediately took soldiers and centurions, and ran down to them: and when they saw the chief captain and the soldiers, they left beating of Paul.

33 Then the chief captain came near, and took him, and commanded *him* to be bound with two chains; and demanded who he was, and what he had done.

34 And some cried one thing, some another, among the multitude: and when he could not know the certainty for the uproar, he commanded him to be carried into the castle.

35 And when he came upon the stairs, so it was, that he was borne of the soldiers for the violence of the people.

36 For the multitude of the people followed after, crying, Away with him.

37 And as Paul was to be led into the castle, he said to the chief captain, May I speak to you? Who said, Can you speak Greek?

38 Are not you that Egyptian, which before these days made an uproar, and led out into the wilderness four thousand men that were murderers?

39 But Paul said, I am a man *which am* a Jew of Tarsus, *a city* in Cilicia, a citizen of no mean city: and, I ask of you, allow me to speak to the people.

40 And when he had given him license, Paul stood on the stairs, and beckoned with the hand to the people. And when there was made a great silence, he spoke to *them* in the Hebrew tongue, saying,

Acts 22

22:1 ¶ Men, brethren, and fathers, hear you my defense *which I make* now to you.

2 (And when they heard that he spoke in the Hebrew tongue to them, they kept the more silent: and he said,)

3 ¶ I am truly a man *which am* a Jew, born in Tarsus, *a city* in Cilicia, yet brought up in this city at the feet of Gamaliel, *and* taught according to the perfect manner of the law of the fathers, and was zealous toward God, as you all are this day.

4 And I persecuted this way unto the death, binding and delivering into prisons both men and women.

5 As also the high priest does bear me witness, and all the estate of the elders: from whom also I received letters unto the brethren, and went to Damascus, to bring them which were there bound to Jerusalem, for to be punished.

6 And it came to pass, that, as I made my journey, and had come near to Damascus about noon, suddenly there shone from heaven a great light round about me.

7 And I fell to the ground, and heard a voice saying to me, Saul, Saul, why persecute you me?

8 And I answered, Who are you, Lord? And he said to me, I am Yahshua of Nazareth, whom you persecute.

9 And they that were with me saw indeed the light, and were afraid; but they heard not the voice of him that spoke to me.

10 And I said, What shall I do, Lord? And the Lord said to me, Arise, and go into Damascus; and there it shall be told you of all things which are appointed for you to do.

11 And when I could not see for the glory of that light, being led by the hand of them that were with me, I came into Damascus.

12 And one Ananias, a devout man according to the law, having a good report of all the Jews which dwelt *there*,

13 Came to me, and stood, and said to me, Brother Saul, receive your sight. And the same hour I looked up upon him.

14 And he said, The God of our fathers has chosen you, that you should know his will, and see that Just One, and should hear the voice of his mouth.

15 For you shall be his witness to all men of what you have seen and heard.

16 And now why wait you? arise, and be baptized, and wash away your sins, calling on the name of the Lord.

17 And it came to pass, that, when I had come again to Jerusalem, even while I prayed in the temple, I was in a trance;

18 And saw him saying to me, Make haste, and get you quickly out of Jerusalem: for they will not receive your testimony concerning me.
19 And I said, Lord, they know that I imprisoned and beat in every synagogue them that believed on you:
20 And when the blood of your martyr Stephen was shed, I also was standing by, and consenting to his death, and kept the garments of them that slew him.
21 And he said to me, Depart: for I will send you far away to the Gentiles.
22 ¶ And they gave him audience unto this word, and then lifted up their voices, and said, Away with such a *fellow* from the earth: for it is not fit that he should live.
23 And as they cried out, and cast off *their* clothes, and threw dust into the air,
24 The chief captain commanded him to be brought into the castle, and said that he should be examined by scourging; that he might know why they cried so against him.
25 And as they bound him with straps, Paul said to the centurion that stood by, Is it lawful for you to whip a man that is a Roman, and uncondemned?
26 When the centurion heard *that*, he went and told the chief captain, saying, Take heed what you do: for this man is a Roman.
27 Then the chief captain came, and said to him, Tell me, are you a Roman? He said, Yes.
28 And the chief captain answered, With a great sum obtained I this freedom. And Paul said, But I was *free* born.
29 Then straightway they departed from him which should have examined him: and the chief captain also was afraid, after he knew that he was a Roman, and because he had bound him.
30 On the next day, because he desired *to* have known the certainty *of* why he was accused by the Jews, he loosed him from *his* bands, and commanded the chief priests and all their council to appear, and brought Paul down, and set him before them.

Acts 23

23:1 ¶ And Paul, earnestly beholding the council, said, Men *and* brethren, I have lived in all good conscience before God until this day.
2 And the high priest Ananias commanded them that stood by him to smite him on the mouth.
3 Then said Paul to him, God shall smite you, *you* whitened wall: for sit you to judge me after the law, and command me to be smitten contrary to the law?
4 And they that stood by said, Revile you God's high priest?
5 Then said Paul, I knew not, brethren, that he was the high priest: for it is written, You shall not speak evil of the ruler of your people.
6 ¶ But when Paul perceived that the one part were Sadducees, and the other Pharisees, he cried out in the council, Men *and* brethren, I am a Pharisee, the son of a Pharisee: of the hope and resurrection of the dead I am called in question.
7 And when he had so said, there arose a dissension between the Pharisees and the Sadducees: and the multitude was divided.
8 For the Sadducees say that there is no resurrection, neither angel, nor spirit: but the Pharisees confess both.
9 And there arose a great cry: and the scribes *that were* of the Pharisees' part arose, and strove, saying, We find no evil in this man: but if a spirit or an angel has spoken to him, let us not fight against God.
10 And when there arose a great dissension, the chief captain, fearing lest Paul should have been pulled in pieces by them, commanded the soldiers to go down, and to take him by force from among them, and to bring *him* into the castle.
11 And the night following the Lord stood by him, and said, Be of good cheer, Paul: for as you have testified of me in Jerusalem, so must you bear witness also at Rome.
12 ¶ And when it was day, certain of the Jews banded together, and bound themselves under a curse, saying that they would neither eat nor drink till they had killed Paul.
13 And they were more than forty which had made this conspiracy.
14 And they came to the chief priests and elders, and said, We have bound ourselves under a great curse, that we will eat nothing until we have slain Paul.
15 Now therefore you with the council signify to the chief captain that he bring him down to you tomorrow, as though you would inquire something more perfectly concerning him: and we, before he comes near, are ready to kill him.
16 And when Paul's sister's son heard of their lying in wait, he went and entered into the castle, and told Paul.
17 Then Paul called one of the centurions unto *him*, and said, Bring this young man to the chief captain: for he has a certain thing to tell him.
18 So he took him, and brought *him* to the chief captain, and said, Paul the prisoner called me to *him*, and asked me to bring this young man to you, who has something to say to you.
19 Then the chief captain took him by the hand, and went *with him* aside privately, and asked *him*, What is that you have to tell me?
20 And he said, The Jews have agreed to ask you that you would bring down Paul tomorrow into the council, as though they would inquire somewhat of him more perfectly.
21 But do not you yield to them: for there lie in wait for him of them more than forty men, which have bound themselves with an oath, that they will neither eat nor drink till they have killed him: and now are they ready, looking for a promise from you.
22 So the chief captain *then* let the young man depart, and charged *him, See you* tell no man that you have shown these things to me.
23 And he called unto *him* two centurions, saying, Make ready two hundred soldiers to go to Caesarea, and horsemen threescore and ten, and spear men two hundred, at the third hour of the night;

Acts 23

24 And provide *them* beasts, that they may set Paul on, and bring *him* safely to Felix the governor.
25 And he wrote a letter after this manner:
26 Claudius Lysias to the most excellent governor Felix *sends* greetings.
27 This man was taken of the Jews, and should have been killed of them: then came I with an army, and rescued him, having understood that he was a Roman.
28 And when I would have known the cause *of* why they accused him, I brought him forth into their council:
29 Whom I perceived to be accused of questions of their law, but to have nothing laid to his charge worthy of death or of bonds.
30 And when it was told *to* me how that the Jews laid wait for the man, I sent immediately to you, and gave commandment to his accusers also to say before you what *they had* against him. Farewell.
31 Then the soldiers, as it was commanded them, took Paul, and brought *him* by night to Antipatris.
32 On the next day they left the horsemen to go with him, and returned to the castle:
33 Who, when they came to Caesarea, and delivered the epistle to the governor, presented Paul also before him.
34 And when the governor had read *the letter*, he asked of what province he was. And when he understood that *he was* of Cilicia;
35 I will hear you, said he, when your accusers have also come. And he commanded him to be kept in Herod's judgment hall.

Acts 24

24:1 ¶ And after five days Ananias the high priest descended with the elders, and *with* a certain orator *named* Tertullus, who informed the governor against Paul.
2 And when he was called forth, Tertullus began to accuse *him*, saying, Seeing that by you we enjoy great quietness, and that very worthy deeds are done unto this nation by your providence,
3 We accept *it* always, and in all places, most noble Felix, with all thankfulness.
4 Notwithstanding, that I be not further tedious to you, I beg you that you would hear us by your clemency a few words.
5 For we have found this man *a* pestilent *fellow*, and a mover of sedition among all the Jews throughout the world, and a ringleader of the sect of the Nazarenes:
6 Who also has gone about to profane the temple: whom we took, and would have judged according to our law.
7 But the chief captain Lysias came *upon us*, and with great violence took *him* away out of our hands,
8 Commanding his accusers to come to you: by examining of whom yourself may take knowledge of all these things, whereof we accuse him.
9 And the Jews also assented, saying that these things were so.
10 ¶ Then Paul, after that the governor had beckoned to him to speak, answered, Forasmuch as I know that you have been of many years a judge to this nation, I do the more cheerfully answer for myself:
11 Because that you may understand, that there are yet but twelve days since I went up to Jerusalem for to worship.
12 And they neither found me in the temple disputing with any man, neither raising up the people, neither in the synagogues, nor in the city:
13 Neither can they prove the things whereof they now accuse me.
14 But this I confess to you, that after the way which they call heresy, so worship I the God of my fathers, believing all things which are written in the law and in the prophets:
15 And have hope toward God, which they themselves also allow, that there shall be a resurrection of the dead, both of the just and unjust.
16 And herein do I exercise myself, to have always a conscience void of offense toward God, and *toward* men.
17 Now after many years I came to bring alms to my nation, and offerings.
18 Whereupon certain Jews from Asia found me purified in the temple, neither with multitude, nor with tumult.
19 Who ought to have been here before you, and object, if they had anything against me.
20 Or else let these same *here* say, if they have found any evil doing in me, while I stood before the council,
21 Except it be for this one voice, that I cried standing among them, Touching the resurrection of the dead I am called in question by you this day.
22 ¶ And when Felix heard these things, having more perfect knowledge of *that* way, he deferred them, and said, When Lysias the chief captain shall come down, I will know accurately of your matter.
23 And he commanded a centurion to keep Paul, and to let *him* have liberty, and that he should forbid none of his acquaintances to minister or come to him.
24 And after certain days, when Felix came with his wife Drusilla, which was a Jewess, he sent for Paul, and heard him concerning the faith in the Messiah.
25 And as he reasoned of righteousness, temperance, and judgment to come, Felix trembled, and answered, Go your way for this time; when I have a convenient season, I will call for you.
26 He hoped also that money should have been given him by Paul, that he might loose him: therefore he sent for him more often, and communed with him.
27 But after two years Porcius Festus came into Felix' room: and Felix, willing to show the Jews a pleasure, left Paul bound.

Acts 25

25:1 ¶ Now when Festus had come into the province, after three days he ascended from Caesarea to Jerusalem.
2 Then the high priest and the chief of the Jews informed him against Paul, and sought him,
3 And desired favor against him, that he would send for him to Jerusalem, laying wait in the way to kill him.

4 But Festus answered, that Paul should be kept at Caesarea, and that he himself would depart shortly *there*.

5 Let them therefore, said he, which among you are able, go down with *me*, and accuse this man, if there is any wickedness in him.

6 And when he had tarried among them more than ten days, he went down to Caesarea; and the next day sitting on the judgment seat commanded Paul to be brought.

7 And when he had come, the Jews which came down from Jerusalem stood round about, and laid many and grievous complaints against Paul, which they could not prove.

8 While he answered for himself, Neither against the law of the Jews, neither against the temple, nor yet against Caesar, have I offended anything at all.

9 But Festus, willing to do the Jews a pleasure, answered Paul, and said, Will you go up to Jerusalem, and there be judged of these things before me?

10 Then said Paul, I stand at Caesar's judgment seat, where I ought to be judged: to the Jews have I done no wrong, as you very well know.

11 For if I am an offender, or have committed anything worthy of death, I refuse not to die: but if there are none of these things whereof these accuse me, no man may deliver me to them. I appeal to Caesar.

12 Then Festus, when he had conferred with the council, answered, Have you appealed unto Caesar? unto Caesar shall you go.

13 ¶ And after certain days king Agrippa and Bernice came to Caesarea to salute Festus.

14 And when they had been there many days, Festus declared Paul's cause to the king, saying, There is a certain man left in bonds by Felix:

15 About whom, when I was at Jerusalem, the chief priests and the elders of the Jews informed *me*, desiring *to have* judgment against him.

16 To whom I answered, It is not the manner of the Romans to deliver any man to die, before that he which is accused has the accusers face to face, and has license to answer for himself concerning the crime laid against him.

17 Therefore, when they had come here, without any delay on the next day I sat on the judgment seat, and commanded the man to be brought forth.

18 Against whom when the accusers stood up, they brought no accusation of such things as I supposed:

19 But had certain questions against him of their own superstition, and of one Yahshua, which was dead, whom Paul affirmed to be alive.

20 And because I doubted of such manner of questions, I asked *him* whether he would go to Jerusalem, and there be judged of these matters.

21 But when Paul had appealed to be reserved for the hearing of Augustus, I commanded him to be kept till I might send him to Caesar.

22 Then Agrippa said to Festus, I would also hear the man myself. Tomorrow, said he, you shall hear him.

23 And on the next day, when Agrippa had come, and Bernice, with great pomp, and had entered into the place of hearing, with the chief captains, and principal men of the city, at Festus' commandment Paul was brought forth.

24 And Festus said, King Agrippa, and all men which are here present with us, you see this man, about whom all the multitude of the Jews have dealt with me, both at Jerusalem, and *also* here, crying that he ought not to live any longer.

25 But when I found that he had committed nothing worthy of death, and that he himself has appealed to Augustus, I have determined to send him.

26 Of whom I have no certain thing to write to my lord. Therefore I have brought him forth before you, and especially before you, O king Agrippa, that, after examination is made, I might have something to write.

27 For it seems to me unreasonable to send a prisoner, and not therewith to signify the crimes *laid* against him.

Acts 26

26:1 ¶ Then Agrippa said to Paul, You are permitted to speak for yourself. Then Paul stretched forth his hand, and answered for himself:

2 I think myself happy, king Agrippa, because I shall answer for myself this day before you touching all the things whereof I am accused by the Jews:

3 Especially *because I know* you to be expert in all customs and questions which are among the Jews: therefore I beseech you to hear me patiently.

4 My manner of life from my youth, which was at the first among my own nation at Jerusalem, know all the Jews;

5 Which knew me from the beginning, if they would testify, that after the most strict sect of our religion I lived a Pharisee.

6 And now I stand and am judged for the hope of the promise made by God to our fathers:

7 Unto which *promise* our twelve tribes, instantly serving God day and night, hoped to come. For which hope's sake, king Agrippa, I am accused of the Jews.

8 Why should it be thought a thing incredible with you, that God should raise the dead?

9 I truly thought with myself, that I ought to do many things contrary to the name of Yahshua of Nazareth.

10 Which things I also did in Jerusalem: and many of the saints did I shut up in prison, having received authority from the chief priests; and when they were put to death, I gave my voice against *them*.

11 And I punished them often in every synagogue, and compelled *them* to blaspheme; and being exceedingly mad against them, I persecuted *them* even unto strange cities.

12 ¶ Whereupon as I went to Damascus with authority and commission from the chief priests,

13 At midday, O king, I saw in the way a light from heaven, above the brightness of the sun, shining round about me and them which journeyed with me.

14 And when we had all fallen to the earth, I heard a voice speaking to me, and saying in the Hebrew tongue, Saul, Saul, why persecute you me? *it is* hard for you to kick against the pricks.

Acts 26

15 And I said, Who are you, Lord? And he said, I am Yahshua whom you persecute.

16 But rise, and stand upon your feet: for I have appeared unto you for this purpose, to make you a minister and a witness both of these things which you have seen, and of those things in which I will appear to you;

17 Delivering you from the people, and *from* the Gentiles, to whom now I send you,

18 To open their eyes, *and* to turn *them* from darkness to light, and *from* the power of Satan unto God, that they may receive forgiveness of sins, and inheritance among them which are sanctified by faith that is in me.

19 Whereupon, O king Agrippa, I was not disobedient to the heavenly vision:

20 But showed first to them of Damascus, and at Jerusalem, and throughout all the coasts of Judaea, and *then* to the Gentiles, that they should repent and turn to God, and do works befitting repentance.

21 For these causes the Jews caught me in the temple, and went about to kill *me*.

22 Having therefore obtained help from God, I continue unto this day, witnessing both to small and great, saying no other things than those which the prophets and Moses did say should come:

23 That the Messiah should suffer, *and* that he should be the first that should rise from the dead, and should show light unto the people, and to the Gentiles.

24 ¶ And as he thus spoke for himself, Festus said with a loud voice, Paul, you are beside yourself; much learning does make you mad.

25 But he said, I am not mad, most noble Festus; but speak forth the words of truth and soberness.

26 For the king knows of these things, before whom also I speak freely: for I am persuaded that none of these things are hidden from him; for this thing was not done in a corner.

27 King Agrippa, believe you the prophets? I know that you believe.

28 Then Agrippa said to Paul, Almost you persuade me to be a Christian.

29 And Paul said, I would to God, that not only you, but also all that hear me this day, were both almost, and altogether such as I am, except these bonds.

30 And when he had thus spoken, the king rose up, and the governor, and Bernice, and they that sat with them:

31 And when they had gone aside, they talked among themselves, saying, This man does nothing worthy of death or of bonds.

32 Then said Agrippa unto Festus, This man might have been set at liberty, if he had not appealed unto Caesar.

Acts 27

27:1 ¶ And when it was determined that we should sail into Italy, they delivered Paul and certain other prisoners unto *one* named Julius, a centurion of Augustus' band.

2 And entering into a ship of Adramyttium, we launched, meaning to sail by the coasts of Asia; *one* Aristarchus, a Macedonian of Thessalonica, being with us.

3 And the next *day* we landed at Sidon. And Julius courteously treated Paul, and gave *him* liberty to go to his friends to refresh himself.

4 And when we had launched from there, we sailed under Cyprus, because the winds were contrary.

5 And when we had sailed over the sea of Cilicia and Pamphylia, we came to Myra, *a city* of Lycia.

6 And there the centurion found a ship of Alexandria sailing into Italy; and he put us therein.

7 And when we had sailed slowly many days, and scarcely had come over against Cnidus, the wind not permitting us, we sailed under Crete, over against Salmone;

8 And, hardly passing it, came unto a place which is called the Fair Havens; near whereunto was the city *of* Lasea.

9 Now when much time was spent, and when sailing was now dangerous, because the fast was now already past, Paul admonished *them*,

10 And said to them, Sirs, I perceive that this voyage will be with hurt and much damage, not only of the lading and ship, but also of our lives.

11 Nevertheless the centurion believed the master and the owner of the ship, more than those things which were spoken by Paul.

12 ¶ And because the harbor was not fit to winter in, the more part advised to depart therefrom also, if by any means they might attain to Phenice, *and there* to winter; *which is* a harbor of Crete, and lies toward the south west and north west.

13 And when the south wind blew softly, supposing that they had obtained *their* purpose, loosing *therefrom*, they sailed close by Crete.

14 But not long after there arose against it a tempestuous wind, called Euroclydon.

15 And when the ship was caught, and could not bear up into the wind, we let *her* drive.

16 And running under a certain island which is called Clauda, we had much work to secure the boat:

17 Which when they had taken up, they used helps, under girding the ship; and, fearing lest they should fall into the quicksands, lowered sail, and so were driven.

18 And we being exceedingly tossed with a tempest, the next *day* they lightened the ship;

19 And the third *day* we cast out with our own hands the tackling of the ship.

20 And when neither sun nor stars in many days appeared, and no small tempest lay on *us*, all hope that we should be saved was then taken away.

21 ¶ But after long abstinence Paul stood forth in the midst of them, and said, Sirs, you should have listened to me, and not have loosed from Crete, and to have gained this harm and loss.

22 And now I exhort you to be of good cheer: for there shall be no loss of *any man's* life among you, but of the ship.

23 For there stood by me this night the angel of God, whose I am, and whom I serve,

24 Saying, Fear not, Paul; you must be brought before Caesar: and, behold, God has given you all them that sail with you.

25 Therefore, sirs, be of good cheer: for I believe God, that it shall be even as it was told *to* me.
26 However we must be cast upon a certain island.
27 But when the fourteenth night had come, as we were driven up and down in Adria, about midnight the shipmen deemed that they drew near to some country;
28 And sounded, and found *it* twenty fathoms: and when they had gone a little further, they sounded again, and found *it* fifteen fathoms.
29 Then fearing lest we should have fallen upon rocks, they cast four anchors out of the stern, and wished for the day.
30 And as the shipmen were about to flee out of the ship, when they had let down the boat into the sea, under color as though they would have cast anchors out of the bow,
31 Paul said to the centurion and to the soldiers, Unless these stay in the ship, you cannot be saved.
32 Then the soldiers cut off the ropes of the boat, and let her fall off.
33 And while the day was coming on, Paul encouraged *them* all to take food, saying, This day is the fourteenth day that you have waited and continued fasting, having taken nothing.
34 Therefore I encourage you to take *some* food: for this is for your health: for there shall not a hair fall from the head of any of you.
35 And when he had thus spoken, he took bread, and gave thanks to God in *the* presence of them all: and when he had broken *it*, he began to eat.
36 Then were they all of good cheer, and they also took *some* food.
37 And we were in all in the ship two hundred threescore and sixteen souls.
38 And when they had eaten enough, they lightened the ship, and cast out the wheat into the sea.
39 And when it was day, they knew not the land: but they discovered a certain creek with a shore, into the which they were determined, if it were possible, to thrust in the ship.
40 And when they had taken up the anchors, they committed *themselves* to the sea, and loosed the rudder bands, and hoisted up the mainsail to the wind, and made toward shore.
41 And falling into a place where two seas met, they ran the ship aground; and the bow stuck fast, and remained unmovable, but the stern was broken with the violence of the waves.
42 And the soldiers' counsel was to kill the prisoners, lest any of them should swim out, and escape.
43 But the centurion, willing to save Paul, kept them from *their* purpose; and commanded that they which could swim should cast *themselves* first *into the sea*, and get to land:
44 And the rest, some on boards, and some on *broken pieces* of the ship. And so it came to pass, that they escaped all safely to land.

Acts 28

28:1 ¶ And when they had escaped, then they knew that the island was called Melita [Malta].
2 And the barbarous people showed us no little kindness: for they kindled a fire, and received us every one, because of the present rain, and because of the cold.
3 And when Paul had gathered a bundle of sticks, and laid *them* on the fire, there came a viper out of the heat, and fastened on his hand.
4 And when the barbarians saw the *venomous* beast hang on his hand, they said among themselves, No doubt this man is a murderer, whom, though he has escaped the sea, yet vengeance allows not to live.
5 And he shook off the beast into the fire, and felt no harm.
6 However they looked when he should have swollen, or fallen down dead suddenly: but after they had looked a great while, and saw no harm come to him, they changed their minds, and said that he was a god.
7 In the same quarters were possessions of the chief man of the island, whose name was Publius; who received us, and lodged us three days courteously.
8 And it came to pass, that the father of Publius lay sick of a fever and of a bloody flux: to whom Paul entered in, and prayed, and laid his hands on him, and healed him.
9 So when this was done, others also, which had diseases in the island, came, and were healed:
10 Who also honored us with many honors: and when we departed, they loaded *us* with such things as were necessary.
11 ¶ And after three months we departed in a ship of Alexandria, which had wintered in the isle, whose sign was Castor and Pollux.
12 And landing at Syracuse, we tarried *there* three days.
13 And from there we wandered about, and came to Rhegium: and after one day the south wind blew, and we came the next day to Puteoli:
14 Where we found brethren, and were desired to stay with them seven days: and so we went toward Rome.
15 And from there, when the brethren heard of us, they came to meet us as far as Appii Forum, and the Three Taverns: whom when Paul saw, he thanked God, and took courage.
16 And when we came to Rome, the centurion delivered the prisoners to the captain of the guard: but Paul was allowed to dwell by himself with a soldier that kept him.
17 ¶ And it came to pass, that after three days Paul called the chief of the Jews together: and when they had come together, he said to them, Men *and* brethren, though I have committed nothing against the people, or customs of our fathers, yet was I delivered prisoner from Jerusalem into the hands of the Romans.
18 Who, when they had examined me, would have let *me* go, because there was no cause of death in me.
19 But when the Jews spoke against *it*, I was compelled to appeal to Caesar; not that I had anything to accuse my nation of.

Acts 28

20 For this cause therefore have I called for you, to see *you*, and to speak with *you*: because that for the hope of Israel I am bound with this chain.

21 And they said to him, We neither received letters out of Judaea concerning you, neither any of the brethren that came showed or spoke any harm of you.

22 But we desire to hear of you what you think: for as concerning this sect, we know that every where it is spoken against.

23 ¶ And when they had appointed him a day, there came many to him into *his* lodging; to whom he expounded and testified the kingdom of God, persuading them concerning Yahshua, both out of the law of Moses, and *out of* the prophets, from morning till evening.

24 And some believed the things which were spoken, and some believed not.

25 And when they agreed not among themselves, they departed, after that Paul had spoken one word, Well spoke the Holy Ghost by Isaiah the prophet to our fathers,

26 Saying, Go unto this people, and say, Hearing you shall hear, and shall not understand; and seeing you shall see, and not perceive:

27 For the heart of this people has grown thick, and their ears are dull of hearing, and their eyes have they closed; lest they should see with *their* eyes, and hear with *their* ears, and understand with *their* heart, and should be converted, and I should heal them.

28 Be it known therefore unto you, that the salvation of God is sent to the Gentiles, and *that* they will hear it.

29 And when he had said these words, the Jews departed, and had great reasoning among themselves.

30 ¶ And Paul dwelt two whole years in his own rented house, and received all that came in to him,

31 Preaching the kingdom of God, and teaching those things which concern the Lord Yahshua the Messiah, with all confidence, no man forbidding him.

Section 6
The Epistles

Romans

Romans 1

1:1 ¶ Paul, a servant of Yahshua the Messiah, called *to be* an apostle, separated unto the gospel of God,

2 (Which he had promised before by his prophets in the holy scriptures,)

3 Concerning his Son Yahshua the Messiah our Lord, which was made of the seed of David according to the flesh;

4 And declared *to be* the Son of God with power, according to the spirit of holiness, by the resurrection from the dead:

5 By whom we have received grace and apostleship, for obedience to the faith among all nations, for his name:

6 Among whom are you also the called of Yahshua the Messiah:

7 To all that are in Rome, beloved of God, called *to be* saints: Grace to you and peace from God our Father, and the Lord Yahshua the Messiah.

8 ¶ First, I thank my God through Yahshua the Messiah for you all, that your faith is spoken of throughout the whole world.

9 For God is my witness, whom I serve with my spirit in the gospel of his Son, that without ceasing I make mention of you always in my prayers;

10 Making request, if by any means now at length I might have a prosperous journey by the will of God to come to you.

11 For I long to see you, that I may impart to you some spiritual gift, to the end you may be established;

12 That is, that I may be comforted together with you by the mutual faith both of you and me.

13 Now I would not have you ignorant, brethren, that oftentimes I purposed to come to you, (but was hindered till now,) that I might have some fruit among you also, even as among other Gentiles.

14 I am debtor both to the Greeks, and to the Barbarians; both to the wise, and to the unwise.

15 So, as much as in me is, I am ready to preach the gospel to you that are at Rome also.

16 ¶ For I am not ashamed of the gospel of the Messiah: for it is the power of God unto salvation to every one that believes; to the Jew first, and also to the Greek.

17 For therein is the righteousness of God revealed from faith to faith: as it is written, The just shall live by faith.

18 For the wrath of God is revealed from heaven against all ungodliness and unrighteousness of men, who hold the truth in unrighteousness;

19 ¶ Because that which may be known of God is manifest in them; for God has shown *it* to them.

20 For the invisible things of him from the creation of the world are clearly seen, being understood by the things that are made, *even* his eternal power and Godhead; so that they are without excuse:

21 Because that, when they knew God, they glorified *him* not as God, neither were thankful; but became vain in their imaginations, and their foolish heart was darkened.

22 Professing themselves to be wise, they became fools,

23 And changed the glory of the uncorruptible God into an image made like to corruptible man, and to birds, and four footed beasts, and creeping things.

24 Therefore God also gave them up to uncleanness through the lusts of their own hearts, to dishonor their own bodies between themselves:

25 Who changed the truth of God into a lie, and worshipped and served the creature more than the Creator, who is blessed forever. Amen.

26 For this cause God gave them up to vile affections: for even their women did change the natural use into that which is against nature:

27 And likewise also the men, leaving the natural use of the woman, burned in their lust one toward another; men with men performing that which is shameful, and receiving in themselves that repayment for their error which was necessary.

28 And even as they did not like to retain God in *their* knowledge, God gave them over to a reprobate mind, to do those things which are not convenient;

29 Being filled with all unrighteousness, fornication, wickedness, covetousness, maliciousness; full of envy, murder, debate, deceit, malignity; whisperers,

30 Backbiters, haters of God, despiteful, proud, boasters, inventors of evil things, disobedient to parents,

31 Without understanding, covenant breakers, without natural affection, implacable, unmerciful:

32 Who knowing the judgment of God, that they which commit such things are worthy of death, not only do the same, but have pleasure in them that do them.

Romans 2

2:1 ¶ Therefore you are inexcusable, O man, whoever you are that judge: for wherein you judge another, you condemn yourself; for you that judge do the same things.

2 But we are sure that the judgment of God is according to truth against them which commit such things.

3 And think you this, O man, that judge them which do such things, and do the same, that you shall escape the judgment of God?

Romans 2

4 Or despise you the riches of his goodness and forbearance and longsuffering; not knowing that the goodness of God leads you to repentance?
5 But after your hardness and impenitent heart treasure up unto yourself wrath against the day of wrath and revelation of the righteous judgment of God;
6 Who will render to every man according to his deeds:
7 To them who by patient continuance in well doing seek for glory and honor and immortality, eternal life:
8 But to them that are contentious, and do not obey the truth, but obey unrighteousness, indignation and wrath,
9 Tribulation and anguish, upon every soul of man that does evil, of the Jew first, and also of the Gentile;
10 But glory, honor, and peace, to every man that works good, to the Jew first, and also to the Gentile:
11 For there is no respect of persons with God.
12 For as many as have sinned without law shall also perish without law: and as many as have sinned in the law shall be judged by the law;
13 (For not the hearers of the law *are* just before God, but the doers of the law shall be justified.
14 For when the Gentiles, which have not the law, do by nature the things contained in the law, these, having not the law, are a law to themselves:
15 Which show the work of the law written in their hearts, their conscience also bearing witness, and *their* thoughts the mean while accusing or else excusing one another;)
16 In the day when God shall judge the secrets of men by Yahshua the Messiah according to my gospel.
17 ¶ Behold, you are called a Jew, and rest in the law, and make your boast of God,
18 And know *his* will, and approve the things that are more excellent, being instructed out of the law;
19 And are confident that you yourself are a guide of the blind, a light of them which are in darkness,
20 An instructor of the foolish, a teacher of babes, which have the form of knowledge and of the truth in the law.
21 You therefore which teach another, teach you not yourself? you that preach a man should not steal, do you steal?
22 You that say a man should not commit adultery, do you commit adultery? you that abhor idols, do you commit sacrilege?
23 You that make your boast of the law, through breaking the law dishonor you God?
24 For the name of God *Yahweh* is blasphemed among the Gentiles through you, as it is written.
25 For circumcision truly profits, if you keep the law: but if you are a breaker of the law, your circumcision is made uncircumcision.
26 Therefore if the uncircumcised keeps the righteousness of the law, shall not his uncircumcision be counted for circumcision?
27 And shall not uncircumcision which is by nature, if it fulfills the law, judge you, who by the letter and circumcision do transgress the law?
28 For he is not a Jew, which is one outwardly; neither *is that* circumcision, which is outward in the flesh:
29 But he *is* a Jew, which is one inwardly; and circumcision *is that* of the heart, in the spirit, *and* not in the letter; whose praise *is* not of men, but of God.

Romans 3

3:1 ¶ What advantage then has the Jew? or what profit *is there* of circumcision?
2 Much every way: chiefly, because that to them were committed the oracles of God.
3 For what if some did not believe? shall their unbelief make the faith of God without effect?
4 God forbid: yes, let God be true, but every man a liar; as it is written, That you might be justified in your sayings, and might overcome when you are judged.
5 But if our unrighteousness commends the righteousness of God, what shall we say? *Is* God unrighteous who takes vengeance? (I speak as a man)
6 God forbid: for then how shall God judge the world?
7 For if the truth of God has more abounded through my lie to his glory; why yet am I also judged as a sinner?
8 And not *rather*, (as we be slanderously reported, and as some affirm that we say,) Let us do evil, that good may come? whose damnation is just.
9 What then? are we better *than they*? No, in no way: for we have before proved both Jews and Gentiles, that they are all under sin;
10 As it is written, There is none righteous, no, not one:
11 There is none that understands, there is none that seeks after God.
12 They are all gone out of the way, they have together become unprofitable; there is none that does good, no, not one.
13 Their throat *is* an open sepulcher; with their tongues they have used deceit; the poison of asps *is* under their lips:
14 Whose mouth *is* full of cursing and bitterness:
15 Their feet *are* swift to shed blood:
16 Destruction and misery *are* in their ways:
17 And the way of peace have they not known:
18 There is no fear of God before their eyes.
19 ¶ Now we know that whatever things the law says, it says to them who are under the law: that every mouth may be stopped, and all the world may become guilty before God.
20 Therefore by the deeds of the law there shall no flesh be justified in his sight: for by the law *is* the knowledge of sin.
21 But now the righteousness of God without the law is manifested, being witnessed by the law and the prophets;
22 Even the righteousness of God *which is* by faith of Yahshua the Messiah to all and upon all them that believe: for there is no difference:
23 For all have sinned, and come short of the glory of God;
24 Being justified freely by his grace through the redemption that is in the Messiah Yahshua:
25 Whom God has set forth *to be* a propitiation through faith in his blood, to declare his righteousness for the remission of sins that are past, through the forbearance of God;

26 To declare, *I say*, at this time his righteousness: that he might be just, and the justifier of him which believes in Yahshua.
27 Where *is* boasting then? It is excluded. By what law? of works? No: but by the law of faith.
28 Therefore we conclude that a man is justified by faith without the deeds of the law.
29 *Is he* the God of the Jews only? *is he* not also of the Gentiles? Yes, of the Gentiles also:
30 Seeing *it is* one God, which shall justify the circumcised by faith, and uncircumcised through faith.
31 Do we then make void the law through faith? God forbid: rather, we establish the law.

Romans 4

4:1 ¶ What shall we say then that Abraham our father, as pertaining to the flesh, has found?
2 For if Abraham were justified by works, he has *whereof* to glory; but not before God.
3 For what says the scripture? Abraham believed God *Yahweh*, and it was counted to him for righteousness.
4 Now to him that works is the reward not reckoned of grace, but of debt.
5 But to him that works not, but believes on him that justifies the ungodly, his faith is counted for righteousness.
6 Even as David also describes the blessedness of the man, to whom God imputes righteousness without works,
7 *Saying*, Blessed *are* they whose iniquities are forgiven, and whose sins are covered.
8 Blessed *is* the man to whom the Lord *Yahweh* will not impute sin.
9 ¶ *Comes* this blessedness then upon the circumcised *only*, or upon the uncircumcised also? for we say that faith was reckoned to Abraham for righteousness.
10 How was it then reckoned? when he was in circumcision, or in uncircumcision? Not in circumcision, but in uncircumcision.
11 And he received the sign of circumcision, a seal of the righteousness of the faith which *he had yet* being uncircumcised: that he might be the father of all them that believe, though they are not circumcised; that righteousness might be imputed unto them also:
12 And the father of circumcision to them who are not of the circumcision only, but who also walk in the steps of that faith of our father Abraham, which *he had* being *yet* uncircumcised.
13 For the promise, that he should be the heir of the world, *was* not to Abraham, or to his seed, through the law, but through the righteousness of faith.
14 For if they which are of the law *are* heirs, faith is made void, and the promise made of no effect:
15 Because the law works wrath: for where no law *is*, *there is* no transgression.
16 Therefore *it is* of faith, that *it might be* by grace; to the end *that* the promise might be sure to all the seed; not to that only which is of the law, but to that also which is of the faith of Abraham; who is the father of us all,
17 ¶ (As it is written, I have made you a father of many nations,) before him whom he believed, *even* God, who revives the dead, and calls those things which are not as though they were.
18 Who against hope believed in hope, that he might become the father of many nations, according to that which was spoken, So shall your seed be.
19 And being not weak in faith, he considered not his own body now dead, when he was about a hundred years old, neither yet the deadness of Sarah's womb:
20 He staggered not at the promise of God through unbelief; but was strong in faith, giving glory to God;
21 And being fully persuaded that, what he had promised, he was able also to perform.
22 And therefore it was imputed to him for righteousness.
23 ¶ Now it was not written for his sake alone, that it was imputed to him;
24 But for us also, to whom it shall be imputed, if we believe on him that raised up Yahshua our Lord from the dead;
25 Who was delivered up for our offenses, and was raised again for our justification.

Romans 5

5:1 ¶ Therefore, being justified by faith, we have peace with God through our Lord Yahshua the Messiah:
2 By whom also we have access by faith into this grace wherein we stand, and rejoice in hope of the glory of God.
3 And not only *so*, but we glory in tribulations also: knowing that tribulation works patience;
4 And patience, experience; and experience, hope:
5 And hope makes not ashamed; because the love of God is shed abroad in our hearts by the Holy Ghost which is given to us.
6 ¶ For when we were yet without strength, in due time the Messiah died for the ungodly.
7 For scarcely for a righteous man will one die: yet perhaps for a good man some would even dare to die.
8 But God commends his love toward us, in that, while we were yet sinners, the Messiah died for us.
9 Much more then, being now justified by his blood, we shall be saved from wrath through him.
10 For if, when we were enemies, we were reconciled to God by the death of his Son, much more, being reconciled, we shall be saved by his life.
11 And not only *so*, but we also joy in God through our Lord Yahshua the Messiah, by whom we have now received the atonement.
12 Therefore, as by one man sin entered into the world, and death by sin; and so death passed upon all men, for that all have sinned:
13 (For until the law sin was in the world: but sin is not imputed when there is no law.
14 Nevertheless death reigned from Adam to Moses, even over them that had not sinned after the likeness of Adam's transgression, who is the figure of him that was to come.
15 But not as the offense, so also *is* the free gift. For if through the offense of one many are dead, much more the grace of God, and the gift by grace, *which is* by one man, Yahshua the Messiah, has abounded unto many.

16 And not as *it was* by one that sinned, *so is* the gift: for the judgment *was* by one to condemnation, but the free gift *is* of many offenses unto justification.

17 For if by one man's offense death reigned by one; much more they which receive abundance of grace and of the gift of righteousness shall reign in life by one, Yahshua the Messiah.)

18 Therefore, as by the offense of one *judgment came* upon all men to condemnation; even so by the righteousness of one *the free gift came* upon all men unto justification of life.

19 For as by one man's disobedience many were made sinners, so by the obedience of one shall many be made righteous.

20 Moreover the law entered, that the offense might abound. But where sin abounded, grace did much more abound:

21 That as sin has reigned unto death, even so might grace reign through righteousness unto eternal life by Yahshua the Messiah our Lord.

Romans 6

6:1 ¶ What shall we say then? Shall we continue in sin, that grace may abound?

2 God forbid. How shall we, that are dead to sin, live any longer therein?

3 Know you not, that as many of us as were baptized into Yahshua the Messiah were baptized into his death?

4 Therefore we are buried with him by baptism into death: that like as the Messiah was raised up from the dead by the glory of the Father, even so we also should walk in newness of life.

5 For if we have been planted together in the likeness of his death, we shall be also *in the likeness* of *his* resurrection:

6 Knowing this, that our old man is crucified with *him*, that the body of sin might be destroyed, that henceforth we should not serve sin.

7 For he that is dead is freed from sin.

8 Now if we are dead with the Messiah, we believe that we shall also live with him:

9 Knowing that the Messiah being raised from the dead dies no more; death has no more dominion over him.

10 For in that he died, he died to sin once: but in that he lives, he lives unto God.

11 Likewise reckon you also yourselves to be dead indeed to sin, but alive unto God through Yahshua the Messiah our Lord.

12 Let not sin therefore reign in your mortal body, that you should obey it in the lusts thereof.

13 Neither yield you your members *as* instruments of unrighteousness unto sin: but yield yourselves unto God, as those that are alive from the dead, and your members *as* instruments of righteousness unto God.

14 For sin shall not have dominion over you: for you are not under the law, but under grace.

15 What then? shall we sin, because we are not under the law, but under grace? God forbid.

16 Know you not, that to whom you yield yourselves servants to obey, his servants you are to whom you obey; whether of sin unto death, or of obedience unto righteousness?

17 But God be thanked, that you were the servants of sin, but you have obeyed from the heart that form of doctrine which was delivered *unto* you.

18 Being then made free from sin, you became the servants of righteousness.

19 I speak after the manner of men because of the infirmity of your flesh: for as you have yielded your members servants to uncleanness and to iniquity unto iniquity; even so now yield your members *as* servants to righteousness unto holiness.

20 For when you were the servants of sin, you were free from righteousness.

21 What fruit had you then in those things whereof you are now ashamed? for the end of those things *is* death.

22 But now being made free from sin, and *having* become servants to God, you have your fruit unto holiness, and the end *unto* everlasting life.

23 For the wages of sin *is* death; but the gift of God *is* eternal life through Yahshua the Messiah our Lord.

Romans 7

7:1 ¶ Know you not, brethren, (for I speak to them that know the law,) how that the law has dominion over a man as long as he lives?

2 For the woman which has a husband is bound by the law to *her* husband so long as he lives; but if the husband is dead, she is loosed from the law of *her* husband.

3 So then if, while *her* husband lives, she is married to another man, she shall be called an adulteress: but if her husband is dead, she is free from that law; so that she is no adulteress, though she is married to another man.

4 Therefore, my brethren, you also have become dead to the law by the body of the Messiah; that you should be married to another, *even* to him who is raised from the dead, that we should bring forth fruit unto God.

5 For when we were in the flesh, the afflictions of sins, which were by the law, did work in our members to bring forth fruit unto death.

6 But now we are delivered from the law, that being dead wherein we were held; that we should serve in newness of spirit, and not *in* the oldness of the letter.

7 ¶ What shall we say then? *Is* the law sin? God forbid. No, I had not known sin, but by the law: for I had not known lust, except the law had said, You shall not covet.

8 But sin, taking occasion by the commandment, worked in me all manner of lusts. For without the law sin *was* dead.

9 For I was alive without the law once: but when the commandment came, sin revived, and I died.

10 And the commandment, which *was ordained* to life, I found *to be* unto death.

11 For sin, taking occasion by the commandment, deceived me, and by it slew *me*.

12 Therefore the law *is* holy, and the commandment holy, and just, and good.

13 Was then that which is good made death unto me? God forbid. But sin, that it might appear sin, working death in me by that which is good; that sin by the commandment might become exceedingly sinful.

14 ¶ For we know that the law is spiritual: but I am carnal, sold under sin.

15 For that which I do I understand not: for what I would *do*, that do I not; but what I hate, that do I.

16 If then I do that which I would not, I consent to the law that *it is* good.

17 Now then it is no more I that do it, but sin that dwells in me.

18 For I know that in me (that is, in my flesh,) dwells no good thing: for to will is present with me; but *how* to perform that which is good I find not.

19 For the good that I would I do not: but the evil which I would not, that I do.

20 Now if I do that *which* I would not, it is no more I that do it, but sin that dwells in me.

21 I find then a law, that, when I would do good, evil is present with me.

22 For I delight in the law of God after the inward man:

23 But I see another law in my members, warring against the law of my mind, and bringing me into captivity to the law of sin which is in my members.

24 O wretched man that I am! who shall deliver me from the body of this death?

25 I thank God through Yahshua the Messiah our Lord. So then with the mind I myself serve the law of God; but with the flesh the law of sin.

Romans 8

8:1 ¶ *There is* therefore now no condemnation to them which are in the Messiah Yahshua, who walk not after the flesh, but after the Spirit.

2 For the law of the Spirit of life in the Messiah Yahshua has made me free from the law of sin and death.

3 For what the law could not do, in that it was weak through the flesh, God sending his own Son in the likeness of sinful flesh, and for sin, condemned sin in the flesh:

4 That the righteousness of the law might be fulfilled in us, who walk not after the flesh, but after the Spirit.

5 For they that are after the flesh do mind the things of the flesh; but they that are after the Spirit the things of the Spirit.

6 For to be carnally minded *is* death; but to be spiritually minded *is* life and peace.

7 Because the carnal mind *is* enmity against God: for it is not subject to the law of God, neither indeed can be.

8 So then they that are in the flesh cannot please God.

9 But you are not in the flesh, but in the Spirit, if so be that the Spirit of God dwells in you. Now if any man has not the Spirit of the Messiah, he is none of his.

10 ¶ And if the Messiah *is* in you, the body *is* dead because of sin; but the Spirit *is* life because of righteousness.

11 But if the Spirit of him that raised up Yahshua from the dead dwells in you, he that raised up the Messiah from the dead shall also quicken your mortal bodies by his Spirit that dwells in you.

12 Therefore, brethren, we are debtors, not to the flesh, to live after the flesh.

13 For if you live after the flesh, you shall die: but if you through the Spirit do mortify the deeds of the body, you shall live.

14 For as many as are led by the Spirit of God, they are the sons of God.

15 For you have not received the spirit of bondage again to fear; but you have received the Spirit of adoption, whereby we cry, Abba, Father.

16 The Spirit itself bears witness with our spirit, that we are the children of God:

17 ¶ And if children, then heirs; heirs of God, and joint-heirs with the Messiah; if so be that we suffer with *him*, that we may be also glorified together.

18 For I reckon that the sufferings of this present time *are* not worthy *to be compared* with the glory which shall be revealed in us.

19 For the earnest expectation of the creature waits for the manifestation of the sons of God.

20 For the creature was made subject to vanity, not willingly, but by reason of him who has subjected *the same* in hope,

21 Because the creature itself also shall be delivered from the bondage of corruption into the glorious liberty of the children of God.

22 For we know that the whole creation groans and travails in pain together until now.

23 And not only *they*, but ourselves also, which have the firstfruits of the Spirit, even we ourselves groan within ourselves, waiting for the adoption, *that is*, the redemption of our body.

24 For we are saved by hope: but hope that is seen is not hope: for what a man sees, why does he yet hope for?

25 But if we hope for that we see not, *then* do we with patience wait for *it*.

26 ¶ Likewise the Spirit also helps our infirmities: for we know not what we should pray for as we ought: but the Spirit itself makes intercession for us with groanings which cannot be uttered.

27 And he that searches the hearts knows what *is* the mind of the Spirit, because he makes intercession for the saints according to *the will of* God.

28 And we know that all things work together for good to them that love God, to them who are the called according to *his* purpose.

29 ¶ For whom he did foreknow, he also did predestinate *to be* conformed to the image of his Son, that he might be the firstborn among many brethren.

30 Moreover whom he did predestinate, them he also called: and whom he called, them he also justified: and whom he justified, them he also glorified.

31 ¶ What shall we then say to these things? If God *is* for us, who can be against us?

32 He that spared not his own Son, but delivered him up for us all, how shall he not with him also freely give us all things?

Romans 8

33 Who shall lay anything to the charge of God's elect? *It is* God that justifies.
34 Who *is* he that condemns? *It is* the Messiah that died, yes rather, that is risen again, who is even at the right hand of God, who also makes intercession for us.
35 Who shall separate us from the love of the Messiah? *shall* tribulation, or distress, or persecution, or famine, or nakedness, or peril, or sword?
36 As it is written, For your sake we are killed all the day long; we are accounted as sheep for the slaughter.
37 No, in all these things we are more than conquerors through him that loved us.
38 For I am persuaded, that neither death, nor life, nor angels, nor principalities, nor powers, nor things present, nor things to come,
39 Nor height, nor depth, nor any other creature, shall be able to separate us from the love of God, which is in the Messiah Yahshua our Lord.

Romans 9

9:1 ¶ I say the truth in the Messiah, I lie not, my conscience also bearing me witness in the Holy Ghost,
2 That I have great heaviness and continual sorrow in my heart.
3 For I could wish that myself were accursed from the Messiah for my brethren, my kinsmen according to the flesh:
4 Who are Israelites; to whom *pertains* the adoption, and the glory, and the covenants, and the giving of the law, and the service *of God*, and the promises;
5 Whose *are* the fathers, and of whom as concerning the flesh the Messiah *came*, who is over all, God blessed forever. Amen.
6 ¶ Not as though the word of God has taken no effect. For they *are* not all Israel, which are of Israel:
7 Neither, because they are the seed of Abraham, *are they* all children: but, In Isaac shall your seed be called.
8 That is, They which are the children of the flesh, these *are* not the children of God: but the children of the promise are counted as the seed.
9 For this *is* the word of promise, At this time will I come, and Sarah shall have a son.
10 And not only *this*; but when Rebecca also had conceived by one, *even* by our father Isaac;
11 (For *the children* being not yet born, neither having done any good or evil, that the purpose of God according to election might stand, not of works, but of him that calls;)
12 It was said to her, The elder shall serve the younger.
13 As it is written, Jacob have I loved, but Esau have I hated.
14 ¶ What shall we say then? *Is there* unrighteousness with God? God forbid.
15 For he said to Moses, I will have mercy on whom I will have mercy, and I will have compassion on whom I will have compassion.
16 So then *it is* not of him that wills, nor of him that runs, but of God that shows mercy.
17 For the scripture says unto Pharaoh, Even for this same purpose have I raised you up, that I might show my power in you, and that my name might be declared throughout all the earth.
18 Therefore has he mercy on whom he will *have mercy*, and whom he will he hardens.
19 You will say then to me, Why does he yet find fault? For who has resisted his will?
20 No but, O man, who are you that replies against God? Shall the thing formed say to him that formed *it*, Why have you made me thus?
21 Has not the potter power over the clay, of the same lump to make one vessel to honor, and another to dishonor?
22 *What* if God, willing to show *his* wrath, and to make his power known, endured with much longsuffering the vessels of wrath fitted to destruction:
23 And that he might make known the riches of his glory on the vessels of mercy, which he had before prepared to glory,
24 Even us, whom he has called, not of the Jews only, but also of the Gentiles?
25 ¶ As he said also in Hosea, I will call them my people, which were not my people; and her beloved, which was not beloved.
26 And it shall come to pass, *that* in the place where it was said to them, You *are* not my people; there shall they be called the children of the living God.
27 Isaiah also cries concerning Israel, Though the number of the children of Israel be as the sand of the sea, a remnant shall be saved:
28 For he will finish the work, and cut *it* short in righteousness: because a short work will the Lord *Yahweh* make upon the earth.
29 And as Isaiah said before, Except the Lord of Sabaoth had left us a seed, we had been as Sodom, and been made like unto Gomorrah.
30 ¶ What shall we say then? That the Gentiles, which followed not after righteousness, have attained to righteousness, even the righteousness which is of faith.
31 But Israel, which followed after the law of righteousness, has not attained to the law of righteousness.
32 Why? Because *they sought it* not by faith, but as it were by the works of the law. For they stumbled at that stumbling stone;
33 As it is written, Behold, I lay in Zion a stumbling stone and rock of offense: and whoever believes on him shall not be ashamed.

Romans 10

10:1 ¶ Brethren, my heart's desire and prayer to God for Israel is, that they might be saved.
2 For I bear them record that they have a zeal of God, but not according to knowledge.
3 For they being ignorant of God's righteousness, and going about to establish their own righteousness, have not submitted themselves to the righteousness of God.

4 For the Messiah *is* the end of the law for righteousness to every one that believes.

5 For Moses describes the righteousness which is of the law, That the man which does those things shall live by them.

6 But the righteousness which is of faith speaks in this manner, Say not in your heart, Who shall ascend into heaven? (that is, to bring the Messiah down *from above*:)

7 Or, Who shall descend into the deep? (that is, to bring up the Messiah again from the dead.)

8 But what says it? The word is near you, *even* in your mouth, and in your heart: that is, the word of faith, which we preach;

9 That if you shall confess with your mouth the Lord Yahshua, and shall believe in your heart that God has raised him from the dead, you shall be saved.

10 For with the heart man believes unto righteousness; and with the mouth confession is made unto salvation.

11 For the scripture says, Whoever believes on him shall not be ashamed.

12 ¶ For there is no difference between the Jew and the Greek: for the same Lord over all is rich unto all that call upon him.

13 For whoever shall call upon the name of the Lord *Yahweh* shall be saved.

14 How then shall they call on him in whom they have not believed? and how shall they believe in him of whom they have not heard? and how shall they hear without a preacher?

15 And how shall they preach, unless they are sent? as it is written, How beautiful are the feet of them that preach the gospel of peace, and bring glad tidings of good things!

16 But they have not all obeyed the gospel. For Isaiah says, Lord *Yahweh*, who has believed our report?

17 So then faith *comes* by hearing, and hearing by the word of God.

18 But I say, Have they not heard? Yes truly, their sound went into all the earth, and their words to the ends of the world.

19 But I say, Did not Israel know? First Moses says, I will provoke you to jealousy by *them that are* no people, *and* by a foolish nation I will anger you.

20 But Isaiah is very bold, and says, I was found of them that sought me not; I was made manifest to them that asked not after me.

21 But to Israel he said, All day long I have stretched forth my hands to a disobedient and gainsaying people.

Romans 11

11:1 ¶ I say then, Has God cast away his people? God forbid. For I also am an Israelite, of the seed of Abraham, *of* the tribe of Benjamin.

2 God has not cast away his people which he foreknew. Know you not what the scripture says of Elijah? how he makes intercession to God against Israel, saying,

3 Lord *Yahweh*, they have killed your prophets, and dug down your altars; and I am left alone, and they seek my life.

4 But what says the answer of God *Yahweh* to him? I have reserved to myself seven thousand men, who have not bowed the knee to *the image of* Baal.

5 Even so then at this present time also there is a remnant according to the election of grace.

6 And if by grace, then *is it* no more of works: otherwise grace is no more grace. But if *it is* of works, then is it no more grace: otherwise work is no more work.

7 What then? Israel has not obtained that which he seeks for; but the election has obtained it, and the rest were blinded

8 (According as it is written, God *Yahweh* has given them the spirit of slumber, eyes that they should not see, and ears that they should not hear;) unto this day.

9 And David says, Let their table be made a snare, and a trap, and a stumbling block, and a recompense to them:

10 Let their eyes be darkened, that they may not see, and bow down their back always.

11 I say then, Have they stumbled that they should fall? God forbid: but *rather* through their fall salvation *has come* unto the Gentiles, for to provoke them to jealousy.

12 Now if the fall of them *is* the riches of the world, and the diminishing of them the riches of the Gentiles; how much more their fullness?

13 For I speak to you Gentiles, inasmuch as I am the apostle of the Gentiles, I magnify my office:

14 If by any means I may provoke to emulation *them which are* my flesh, and might save some of them.

15 For if the casting away of them *is* the reconciling of the world, what *shall* the receiving *of them be*, but life from the dead?

16 For if the first fruit *is* holy, the lump *is also holy*: and if the root *is* holy, so *are* the branches.

17 And if some of the branches are broken off, and you, being a wild olive tree, were grafted in among them, and with them partake of the root and fatness of the olive tree;

18 Boast not against the branches. But if you boast, you bear not the root, but the root you.

19 You will say then, The branches were broken off, that I might be grafted in.

20 Well; because of unbelief they were broken off, and you stand by faith. Be not high minded, but fear:

21 For if God spared not the natural branches, *take heed* lest he also spare not you.

22 Behold therefore the goodness and severity of God: on them which fell, severity; but toward you, goodness, if you continue in *his* goodness: otherwise you also will be cut off.

23 And they also, if they continue not still in unbelief, shall be grafted in: for God is able to graft them in again.

24 For if you were cut out of the olive tree which is wild by nature, and were grafted contrary to nature into a good olive tree: how much more shall these, which are the natural *branches*, be grafted into their own olive tree?

25 For I would not, brethren, that you should be ignorant of this mystery, lest you should be wise in your own conceits; that blindness in part has happened to Israel, until the fullness of the Gentiles has come in.

26 And so all Israel shall be saved: as it is written, There shall come out of Zion the Deliverer, and shall turn away ungodliness from Jacob:
27 For this *is* my covenant unto them, when I shall take away their sins.
28 As concerning the gospel, *they are* enemies for your sakes: but as touching the election, *they are* beloved for the fathers' sakes.
29 For the gifts and calling of God *are* without repentance.
30 For as you in times past have not believed God, yet have now obtained mercy through their unbelief:
31 Even so have these also now not believed, that through your mercy they also may obtain mercy.
32 For God has concluded them all in unbelief, that he might have mercy upon all.
33 ¶ O the depth of the riches both of the wisdom and knowledge of God! how unsearchable *are* his judgments, and his ways past finding out!
34 For who has known the mind of the Lord *Yahweh*? or who has been his counselor?
35 Or who has first given to him, and it shall be recompensed to him again?
36 For of him, and through him, and to him, *are* all things: to whom *be* glory forever. Amen.

Romans 12

12:1 ¶ I beseech you therefore, brethren, by the mercies of God, that you present your bodies a living sacrifice, holy, acceptable unto God, *which is* your reasonable service.
2 And be not conformed to this world: but be you transformed by the renewing of your mind, that you may prove what *is* that good, and acceptable, and perfect, will of God.
3 For I say, through the grace given to me, to every man that is among you, not to think *of himself* more highly than he ought to think; but to think soberly, according as God has dealt to every man the measure of faith.
4 For as we have many members in one body, and all members have not the same function:
5 So we, *being* many, are one body in the Messiah, and every one members one of another.
6 Having then gifts differing according to the grace that is given to us, whether prophecy, *let us prophesy* according to the proportion of faith;
7 Or ministry, *let us wait* on *our* ministering: or he that teaches, on teaching;
8 Or he that exhorts, on exhortation: he that gives, *let him do it* with simplicity; he that presides over, with diligence; he that shows mercy, with cheerfulness.
9 *Let* love be without hypocrisy. Abhor that which is evil; cling to that which is good.
10 *Be* kindly affectioned one to another with brotherly love; in honor preferring one another;
11 Not slothful in business; fervent in spirit; serving the Lord;
12 Rejoicing in hope; patient in tribulation; continuing instant in prayer;
13 Distributing to the necessity of saints; given to hospitality.
14 Bless them which persecute you: bless, and curse not.
15 Rejoice with them that do rejoice, and weep with them that weep.
16 *Be* of the same mind one toward another. Mind not high things, but condescend to men of low estate. Be not wise in your own conceits.
17 Recompense to no man evil for evil. Provide things honest in the sight of all men.
18 If it is possible, as much as lies in you, live peaceably with all men.
19 Dearly beloved, avenge not yourselves, but *rather* give place unto wrath: for it is written, Vengeance *is* mine; I will repay, says the Lord *Yahweh*.
20 Therefore if your enemy hungers, feed him; if he thirsts, give him drink: for in so doing you shall heap coals of fire on his head.
21 Be not overcome of evil, but overcome evil with good.

Romans 13

13:1 ¶ Let every soul be subject to the higher powers. For there is no power but of God: the powers that be are ordained of God.
2 Whoever therefore resists the power, resists the ordinance of God: and they that resist shall receive to themselves damnation.
3 For rulers are not a terror to good works, but to the evil. Will you then not be afraid of the power? do that which is good, and you shall have praise of the same:
4 For he is the minister of God to you for good. But if you do that which is evil, be afraid; for he bears not the sword in vain: for he is the minister of God, an avenger to *execute* wrath upon him that does evil.
5 Therefore *you* must need be subject, not only for wrath, but also for conscience sake.
6 For for this cause pay you tribute also: for they are God's ministers, attending continually upon this very thing.
7 ¶ Render therefore to all their dues: tribute to whom tribute *is due*; custom to whom custom; fear to whom fear; honor to whom honor.
8 Owe no man anything, but to love one another: for he that loves another has fulfilled the law.
9 For this, You shall not commit adultery, You shall not kill, You shall not steal, You shall not bear false witness, You shall not covet; and if *there is* any other commandment, it is briefly comprehended in this saying, namely, You shall love your neighbor as yourself.
10 Love works no ill to his neighbor: therefore love *is* the fulfilling of the law.
11 ¶ And that, knowing the time, that now *it is* high time to awake out of sleep: for now *is* our salvation nearer than when we believed.
12 The night is far spent, the day is at hand: let us therefore cast off the works of darkness, and let us put on the armor of light.

13 Let us walk honestly, as in the day; not in revelling and drunkenness, not in cohabitation and promiscuousness, not in strife and envying.

14 But put you on the Lord Yahshua the Messiah, and make not provision for the flesh, to *fulfill* the lusts *thereof*.

Romans 14

14:1 ¶ Him that is weak in the faith receive you, *but* not to doubtful disputations.

2 For one believes that he may eat all things: another, who is weak, eats herbs.

3 Let not him that eats despise him that eats not; and let not him which eats not judge him that eats: for God has received him.

4 Who are you that judges another man's servant? to his own master he stands or falls. Yes, he shall be held up: for God is able to make him stand.

5 One man esteems one day above another: another esteems every day *alike*. Let every man be fully persuaded in his own mind.

6 He that regards the day, regards *it* unto the Lord; and he that regards not the day, to the Lord he does not regard *it*. He that eats, eats to the Lord, for he gives God thanks; and he that eats not, to the Lord he eats not, and gives God thanks.

7 For none of us lives to himself, and no man dies to himself.

8 For if we live, we live unto the Lord; and if we die, we die unto the Lord: whether we live therefore, or die, we are the Lord's.

9 For to this end the Messiah both died, and rose, and revived, that he might be Lord both of the dead and living.

10 But why do you judge your brother? or why do you set at nothing your brother? for we shall all stand before the judgment seat of the Messiah.

11 For it is written, *As* I live, says the Lord *Yahweh*, every knee shall bow to me, and every tongue shall confess to God.

12 So then every one of us shall give account of himself to God.

13 Let us not therefore judge one another any more: but judge this rather, that no man put a stumbling block or an occasion to fall in *his* brother's way.

14 I know, and am persuaded by the Lord Yahshua, that *there is* nothing unclean of itself: but to him that esteems anything to be unclean, to him *it is* unclean.

15 But if your brother is grieved with *your* meat, now walk you not charitably. Destroy not him with your meat, for whom the Messiah died.

16 Let not then your good be evilly spoken of:

17 For the kingdom of God is not meat and drink; but righteousness, and peace, and joy in the Holy Ghost.

18 For he that in these things serves the Messiah *is* acceptable to God, and approved of men.

19 Let us therefore follow after the things which make for peace, and things with which one may edify another.

20 For meat destroys not the work of God. All things indeed *are* pure; but *it is* evil for that man who eats with offense.

21 *It is* good neither to eat flesh, nor to drink wine, nor *anything* whereby your brother stumbles, or is offended, or is made weak.

22 Have you faith? have *it* to yourself before God. Happy *is* he that condemns not himself in that thing which he allows.

23 And he that doubts is damned if he eats, because *he eats* not of faith: for whatever *is* not of faith is sin.

Romans 15

15:1 ¶ We then that are strong ought to bear the infirmities of the weak, and not to please ourselves.

2 Let every one of us please *his* neighbor for *his* good to edification.

3 For even the Messiah pleased not himself; but, as it is written, The reproaches of them that reproached you fell on me

4 For whatever things were written aforetime were written for our learning, that we through patience and comfort of the scriptures might have hope.

5 ¶ Now the God of patience and consolation grant you to be likeminded one toward another according to the Messiah Yahshua:

6 That you may with one mind *and* one mouth glorify God, even the Father of our Lord Yahshua the Messiah.

7 ¶ Therefore receive you one another, as the Messiah also received us to the glory of God.

8 Now I say that Yahshua the Messiah was a minister of the circumcision for the truth of God, to confirm the promises *made* to the fathers:

9 And that the Gentiles might glorify God *Yahweh* for *his* mercy; as it is written, For this cause I will confess to you among the Gentiles, and sing unto your name.

10 And again he said, Rejoice, you Gentiles, with his people.

11 And again, Praise the Lord *Yahweh*, all you Gentiles; and laud him, all you people.

12 And again, Isaiah says, There shall be a root of Jesse, and he that shall rise to reign over the Gentiles; in him shall the Gentiles trust.

13 ¶ Now *may* the God of hope fill you with all joy and peace in believing, that you may abound in hope, through the power of the Holy Ghost.

14 ¶ And I myself also am persuaded of you, my brethren, that you also are full of goodness, filled with all knowledge, able also to admonish one another.

15 Nevertheless, brethren, I have written the more boldly to you in some sort, as putting you in mind, because of the grace that is given to me by God,

16 That I should be the minister of Yahshua the Messiah to the Gentiles, ministering the gospel of God, that the offering up of the Gentiles might be acceptable, being sanctified by the Holy Ghost.

17 ¶ I have therefore whereof I may glory through Yahshua the Messiah in those things which pertain to God.

18 For I will not dare to speak of any of those things which the Messiah has not worked by me, to make the Gentiles obedient, by word and deed,

Romans 15

19 Through mighty signs and wonders, by the power of the Spirit of God; so that from Jerusalem, and round about to Illyricum, I have fully preached the gospel of the Messiah.
20 Yes, so have I strived to preach the gospel, not where the Messiah was named, lest I should build upon another man's foundation:
21 But as it is written, To whom he was not spoken of, they shall see: and they that have not heard shall understand.
22 ¶ For which cause also I have been much hindered from coming to you.
23 But now having no more place in these parts, and having a great desire these many years to come to you;
24 Whenever I take my journey into Spain, I will come to you: for I trust to see you in my journey, and to be brought on my way there by you, if first I am somewhat filled with your *company*.
25 But now I go to Jerusalem to minister to the saints.
26 For it has pleased them of Macedonia and Achaia to make a certain contribution for the poor saints which are at Jerusalem.
27 It has pleased them truly; and their debtors they are. For if the Gentiles have been made partakers of their spiritual things, their duty is also to minister unto them in carnal things.
28 When therefore I have performed this, and have sealed to them this fruit, I will come by you into Spain.
29 And I am sure that, when I come to you, I shall come in the fullness of the blessing of the gospel of the Messiah.
30 ¶ Now I beseech you, brethren, for the Lord Yahshua the Messiah's sake, and for the love of the Spirit, that you strive together with me in *your* prayers to God for me;
31 That I may be delivered from them that do not believe in Judaea; and that my service which *I have* for Jerusalem may be accepted of the saints;
32 That I may come to you with joy by the will of God, and may with you be refreshed.
33 Now the God of peace *be* with you all. Amen.

Romans 16

16:1 ¶ I commend to you Phebe our sister, which is a servant of the congregation which is at Cenchrea:
2 That you receive her in the Lord, as becomes saints, and that you assist her in whatever business she has need of you: for she has been a succorer of many, and of myself also.
3 Greet Priscilla and Aquila my helpers in the Messiah Yahshua:
4 Who have for my life laid down their own necks: to whom not only I give thanks, but also all the congregations of the Gentiles.
5 Likewise *greet* the congregation that is in their house. Salute my wellbeloved Epaenetus, who is the firstfruits of Achaia unto the Messiah.
6 Greet Mary, who bestowed much labor on us.
7 Salute Andronicus and Junia, my kinsmen, and my fellow prisoners, who are of note among the apostles, who also were in the Messiah before me.
8 Greet Amplias my beloved in the Lord.
9 Salute Urbane, our helper in the Messiah, and Stachys my beloved.
10 Salute Apelles approved in the Messiah. Salute them which are of Aristobulus' *household*.
11 Salute Herodion my kinsman. Greet them that are of the *household* of Narcissus, which are in the Lord.
12 Salute Tryphena and Tryphosa, who labor in the Lord. Salute the beloved Persis, which labored much in the Lord.
13 Salute Rufus chosen in the Lord, and his mother and mine.
14 Salute Asyncritus, Phlegon, Hermas, Patrobas, Hermes, and the brethren which are with them.
15 Salute Philologus, and Julia, Nereus, and his sister, and Olympas, and all the saints which are with them.
16 Salute one another with a holy kiss. The congregations of the Messiah salute you.
17 ¶ Now I beseech you, brethren, mark them which cause divisions and offenses contrary to the doctrine which you have learned; and avoid them.
18 For they that are such serve not our Lord Yahshua the Messiah, but their own belly; and by good words and fair speeches deceive the hearts of the simple.
19 For your obedience has come abroad unto all *men*. I am glad therefore on your behalf: but yet I would have you wise to that which is good, and simple concerning evil.
20 And the God of peace shall bruise Satan under your feet shortly. The grace of our Lord Yahshua the Messiah *be* with you. Amen.
21 ¶ Timotheus my work fellow, and Lucius, and Jason, and Sosipater, my kinsmen, salute you.
22 I Tertius, who wrote *this* epistle, salute you in the Lord.
23 Gaius my host, and of the whole congregation, salutes you. Erastus the chamberlain of the city salutes you, and Quartus a brother.
24 The grace of our Lord Yahshua the Messiah *be* with you all. Amen.
25 ¶ Now to him that is of power to establish you according to my gospel, and the preaching of Yahshua the Messiah, according to the revelation of the mystery, which was kept secret since the world began,
26 But now is made manifest, and by the scriptures of the prophets, according to the commandment of the everlasting God, made known to all nations for the obedience of faith:
27 To God only wise, *be* glory through Yahshua the Messiah forever. Amen. <<*Written to the Romans from Corinth, and sent by Phebe servant of the congregation at Cenchrea.*>>

1 Corinthians

1 Corinthians 1

1:1 ¶ Paul, called *to be* an apostle of Yahshua the Messiah through the will of God, and Sosthenes *our* brother,

2 Unto the congregation of God which is at Corinth, to them that are sanctified in the Messiah Yahshua, called *to be* saints, with all that in every place call upon the name of Yahshua the Messiah our Lord, both theirs and ours:

3 Grace *be* to you, and peace, from God our Father, and *from* the Lord Yahshua the Messiah.

4 I thank my God always on your behalf, for the grace of God which is given *to* you by Yahshua the Messiah;

5 That in every thing you are enriched by him, in all utterance, and *in* all knowledge;

6 Even as the testimony of the Messiah was confirmed in you:

7 So that you come behind in no gift; waiting for the coming of our Lord Yahshua the Messiah:

8 Who shall also confirm you to the end, *that you may be* blameless in the day of our Lord Yahshua the Messiah.

9 God *is* faithful, by whom you were called unto the fellowship of his Son Yahshua the Messiah our Lord.

10 ¶ Now I beg *of* you, brethren, by the name of our Lord Yahshua the Messiah, that you all speak the same thing, and *that* there be no divisions among you; but *that* you are perfectly joined together in the same mind and in the same judgment.

11 For it has been declared unto me of you, my brethren, by them *which are of the house* of Chloe, that there are contentions among you.

12 Now this I say, that every one of you said, I am of Paul; and I of Apollos; and I of Cephas; and I of the Messiah.

13 Is the Messiah divided? was Paul crucified for you? or were you baptized in the name of Paul?

14 ¶ I thank God that I baptized none of you, but Crispus and Gaius;

15 Lest any should say that I had baptized in my own name.

16 And I baptized also the household of Stephanas: besides, I know not whether I baptized any other.

17 ¶ For the Messiah sent me not to baptize, but to preach the gospel: not with wisdom of words, lest the cross of the Messiah should be made of no effect.

18 For the preaching of the cross is to them that perish foolishness; but to us which are saved it is the power of God.

19 For it is written, I will destroy the wisdom of the wise, and will bring to nothing the understanding of the prudent.

20 Where *is* the wise? where *is* the scribe? where *is* the disputer of this world? has not God made foolish the wisdom of this world?

21 For after that in the wisdom of God the world by wisdom knew not God, it pleased God by the foolishness of preaching to save them that believe.

22 For the Jews require a sign, and the Greeks seek after wisdom:

23 But we preach the Messiah crucified, unto the Jews a stumbling block, and to the Greeks foolishness;

24 But to them which are called, both Jews and Greeks, the Messiah the power of God, and the wisdom of God.

25 Because the foolishness of God is wiser than men; and the weakness of God is stronger than men.

26 For you see your calling, brethren, how that not many wise men after the flesh, not many mighty, not many noble, *are called*:

27 But God has chosen the foolish things of the world to confound the wise; and God has chosen the weak things of the world to confound the things which are mighty;

28 And base things of the world, and things which are despised, has God chosen, *yes,* and things which are not, to bring to nothing things that are:

29 That no flesh should glory in his presence.

30 But of him are you in the Messiah Yahshua, who of God is made to us wisdom, and righteousness, and sanctification, and redemption:

31 That, according as it is written, He that glories, let him glory in the Lord *Yahweh*.

1 Corinthians 2

2:1 ¶ And I, brethren, when I came to you, came not with excellency of speech or of wisdom, declaring to you the testimony of God.

2 For I determined not to know anything among you, save Yahshua the Messiah, and him crucified.

3 And I was with you in weakness, and in fear, and in much trembling.

4 And my speech and my preaching *was* not with enticing words of man's wisdom, but in demonstration of the Spirit and of power:

5 That your faith should not stand in the wisdom of men, but in the power of God.

6 ¶ However we speak wisdom among them that are perfect: yet not the wisdom of this world, nor of the princes of this world, that come to nothing:

7 But we speak the wisdom of God in a mystery, *even* the hidden *wisdom,* which God ordained before the world unto our glory:

8 Which none of the princes of this world knew: for had they known *it,* they would not have crucified the Lord of glory.

9 But as it is written, Eye has not seen, nor ear heard, neither have entered into the heart of man, the things which God has prepared for them that love him.

10 But God has revealed *them* to us by his Spirit: for the Spirit searches all things, yes, the deep things of God.

11 For what man knows the things of a man, save the spirit of man which is in him? even so the things of God knows no man, but the Spirit of God.

12 Now we have received, not the spirit of the world, but the spirit which is of God; that we might know the things that are freely given to us by God.

13 Which things also we speak, not in the words which man's wisdom teaches, but which the Holy Ghost teaches; comparing spiritual things with spiritual.

1 Corinthians 2

14 But the natural man receives not the things of the Spirit of God: for they are foolishness unto him: neither can he know *them*, because they are spiritually discerned.
15 But he that is spiritual judges all things, yet he himself is judged by no man.
16 For who has known the mind of the Lord *Yahweh*, that he may instruct him? But we have the mind of the Messiah.

1 Corinthians 3

3:1 ¶ And I, brethren, could not speak to you as unto spiritual, but as unto carnal, *even* as to babes in the Messiah.
2 I have fed you with milk, and not with meat: for till now you were not able *to bear it*, neither yet now are you able.
3 For you are yet carnal: for whereas *there is* among you envying, and strife, and divisions, are you not carnal, and walk as men?
4 For while one says, I am of Paul; and another, I *am* of Apollos; are you not carnal?
5 ¶ Who then is Paul, and who *is* Apollos, but ministers by whom you believed, even as the Lord gave to every man?
6 I have planted, Apollos watered; but God gave the increase.
7 So then neither is he that plants anything, neither he that waters; but God that gives the increase.
8 Now he that plants and he that waters are one: and every man shall receive his own reward according to his own labor.
9 For we are laborers together with God: you are God's field, *you are* God's building.
10 According to the grace of God which is given to me, as a wise master builder, I have laid the foundation, and another builds thereon. But let every man take heed how he builds thereupon.
11 ¶ For another foundation can no man lay than that is laid, which is Yahshua the Messiah.
12 Now if any man build upon this foundation gold, silver, precious stones, wood, hay, stubble;
13 Every man's work shall be made manifest: for the day shall declare it, because it shall be revealed by fire; and the fire shall try every man's work of what sort it is.
14 If any man's work endures which he has built thereupon, he shall receive a reward.
15 If any man's work shall be burned, he shall suffer loss: but he himself shall be saved; yet so as by fire.
16 ¶ Know you not that you are the temple of God, and *that* the Spirit of God dwells in you?
17 If any man defiles the temple of God, him shall God destroy; for the temple of God is holy, which *temple* you are.
18 ¶ Let no man deceive himself. If any man among you seems to be wise in this world, let him become a fool, that he may be wise.
19 For the wisdom of this world is foolishness with God. For it is written, He takes the wise in their own craftiness.
20 And again, The Lord *Yahweh* knows the thoughts of the wise, that they are vain.
21 ¶ Therefore let no man glory in men. For all things are yours;
22 Whether Paul, or Apollos, or Cephas, or the world, or life, or death, or things present, or things to come; all are yours;
23 And you are the Messiah's; and the Messiah *is* God's.

1 Corinthians 4

4:1 ¶ Let a man so account of us, as of the ministers of the Messiah, and stewards of the mysteries of God.
2 Moreover it is required in stewards, that a man be found faithful.
3 But with me it is a very small thing that I should be judged by you, or by man's judgment: yes, I judge not my own self.
4 For I know nothing by myself; yet am I not hereby justified: but he that judges me is the Lord.
5 Therefore judge nothing before the time, until the Lord comes, who both will bring to light the hidden things of darkness, and will make manifest the counsels of the hearts: and then shall every man have praise of God.
6 And these things, brethren, I have in a figure transferred to myself and *to* Apollos for your sakes; that you might learn in us not to think *of men* above that which is written, that no one of you be puffed up for one against another.
7 ¶ For who makes you to differ *from another*? and what have you that you did not receive? now if you did receive *it*, why do you glory, as if you had not received *it*?
8 Now you are full, now you are rich, you have reigned as kings without us: and I would to God you did reign, that we also might reign with you.
9 For I think that God has set forth us the apostles last, as it were appointed to death: for we are made a spectacle to the world, and to angels, and to men.
10 We *are* fools for the Messiah's sake, but you *are* wise in the Messiah; we *are* weak, but you *are* strong; you *are* honorable, but we *are* despised.
11 Even unto this present hour we both hunger, and thirst, and are naked, and are buffeted, and have no certain dwelling place;
12 And labor, working with our own hands: being reviled, we bless; being persecuted, we suffer it:
13 Being defamed, we entreat: we are made as the filth of the world, *and are* the offscouring of all things unto this day.
14 ¶ I write not these things to shame you, but as my beloved sons I warn *you*.
15 For though you have ten thousand instructors in the Messiah, yet *have you* not many fathers: for in the Messiah Yahshua I have begotten you through the gospel.
16 Therefore I encourage you, be you followers of me.
17 ¶ For this cause have I sent to you Timotheus, who is my beloved son, and faithful in the Lord, who shall bring you into remembrance of my ways which are in the Messiah, as I teach every where in every congregation.

18 Now some are puffed up, as though I would not come to you.
19 But I will come to you shortly, if the Lord wills, and will know, not the speech of them which are puffed up, but the power.
20 For the kingdom of God *is* not in word, but in power.
21 What will you? shall I come to you with a rod, or in love, and *in* the spirit of meekness?

1 Corinthians 5

5:1 ¶ It is reported commonly *that there is* fornication among you, and such fornication as is not so much as named among the Gentiles, that one should have his father's wife.
2 And you are puffed up, and have not rather mourned, that he that has done this deed might be taken away from among you.
3 For I truly, as absent in body, but present in spirit, have judged already, as though I were present, *concerning* him that has so done this deed,
4 In the name of our Lord Yahshua the Messiah, when you are gathered together, and my spirit, with the power of our Lord Yahshua the Messiah,
5 To deliver such a one unto Satan for the destruction of the flesh, that the spirit may be saved in the day of the Lord Yahshua.
6 Your glorying *is* not good. Know you not that a little leaven leavens the whole lump?
7 ¶ Purge out therefore the old leaven, that you may be a new lump, as you are unleavened. For even the Messiah our passover is sacrificed for us:
8 Therefore let us keep the feast, not with old leaven, neither with the leaven of malice and wickedness; but with the unleavened *bread* of sincerity and truth.
9 ¶ I wrote to you in an epistle not to company with fornicators:
10 Yet not altogether with the fornicators of this world, or with the covetous, or extortioners, or with idolaters; for then must you need *to* go out of the world.
11 But now I have written to you not to keep company, if any man that is called a brother is a fornicator, or covetous, or an idolater, or a reviler, or a drunkard, or an extortioner; with such a one not so much as to eat.
12 For what have I to do to judge them also that are outside? do not you judge them that are within?
13 But them that are outside God judges. Therefore put away from among yourselves that wicked person.

1 Corinthians 6

6:1 ¶ Dare any of you, having a matter against another, go to law before the unjust, and not before the saints?
2 Do you not know that the saints shall judge the world? and if the world shall be judged by you, are you unworthy to judge the smallest matters?
3 Know you not that we shall judge angels? how much more things that pertain to this life?
4 If then you have judgments of things pertaining to this life, set them to judge who are least esteemed in the congregation.
5 I speak to your shame. Is it so, that there is not a wise man among you? no, not one that shall be able to judge between his brethren?
6 But brother goes to law with brother, and that before the unbelievers.
7 Now therefore there is utterly a fault among you, because you go to law one with another. Why do you not rather take wrong? why do you not rather *allow yourselves to* be defrauded?
8 No, you do wrong, and defraud, and that *your* brethren.
9 ¶ Know you not that the unrighteous shall not inherit the kingdom of God? Be not deceived: neither fornicators, nor idolaters, nor adulterers, nor effeminate, nor those who lie with males as with females,
10 Nor thieves, nor covetous, nor drunkards, nor revilers, nor extortioners, shall inherit the kingdom of God.
11 And such were some of you: but you are washed, but you are sanctified, but you are justified in the name of the Lord Yahshua, and by the Spirit of our God.
12 ¶ All things are lawful unto me, but all things are not expedient: all things are lawful for me, but I will not be brought under the power of any.
13 Foods for the belly, and the belly for food: but God shall destroy both it and them. Now the body *is* not for fornication, but for the Lord; and the Lord for the body.
14 And God has both raised up the Lord, and will also raise up us by his own power.
15 Know you not that your bodies are the members of the Messiah? shall I then take the members of the Messiah, and make *them* the members of a harlot? God forbid.
16 What? know you not that he which is joined to a harlot is one body? for two, said he, shall be one flesh.
17 But he that is joined unto the Lord is one spirit.
18 Flee fornication. Every sin that a man does is outside the body; but he that commits fornication sins against his own body.
19 What? know you not that your body is the temple of the Holy Ghost *which is* in you, which you have of God, and you are not your own?
20 For you are bought with a price: therefore glorify God in your body, and in your spirit, which are God's.

1 Corinthians 7

7:1 ¶ Now concerning the things whereof you wrote to me: *It is* good for a man not to touch a woman.
2 Nevertheless, *to avoid* fornication, let every man have his own wife, and let every woman have her own husband.
3 Let the husband render to the wife due benevolence: and likewise also the wife to the husband.
4 The wife has not power of her own body, but the husband: and likewise also the husband has not power of his own body, but the wife.
5 Defraud you not one the other, unless *it be* with consent for a time, that you may give yourselves to fasting and prayer; and come together again, that Satan tempts you not for your lack of self-control.

1 Corinthians 7

6 But I speak this by permission, *and* not of commandment.
7 For I would that all men were even as I myself. But every man has his proper gift of God, one after this manner, and another after that.
8 I say therefore to the unmarried and widows, It is good for them if they remain even as I.
9 But if they cannot abstain, let them marry: for it is better to marry than to burn.
10 ¶ And to the married I command, *yet* not I, but the Lord, Let not the wife depart from *her* husband:
11 But and if she departs, let her remain unmarried, or be reconciled to *her* husband: and let not the husband put away *his* wife.
12 But to the rest speak I, not the Lord: If any brother has a wife that believes not, and she is pleased to dwell with him, let him not put her away.
13 And the woman which has a husband that believes not, and if he is pleased to dwell with her, let her not leave him.
14 For the unbelieving husband is sanctified by the wife, and the unbelieving wife is sanctified by the husband: or else were your children unclean; but now are they holy.
15 But if the unbelieving depart, let him depart. A brother or a sister is not under bondage in such *cases*: but God has called us to peace.
16 For what know you, O wife, whether you shall save *your* husband? or how know you, O man, whether you shall save *your* wife?
17 ¶ But as God has distributed to every man, as the Lord has called every one, so let him walk. And so ordain I in all congregations.
18 Is any man called being circumcised? let him not become uncircumcised. Is any called in uncircumcision? let him not be circumcised.
19 Circumcision is nothing, and uncircumcision is nothing, but the keeping of the commandments of God.
20 Let every man remain in the same calling wherein he was called.
21 Are you called *being* a servant? care not for it: but if you may be made free, use *it* rather.
22 For he that is called in the Lord, *being* a servant, is the Lord's freeman: likewise also he that is called, *being* free, is the Messiah's servant.
23 You are bought with a price; be not you the servants of men.
24 Brethren, let every man, wherein he is called, therein remain with God.
25 ¶ Now concerning virgins I have no commandment of the Lord: yet I give my judgment, as one that has obtained mercy of the Lord to be faithful.
26 I suppose therefore that this is good for the present distress, *I say*, that *it is* good for a man so to be.
27 Are you bound to a wife? seek not to be loosed. Are you loosed from a wife? seek not a wife.
28 But and if you marry, you have not sinned; and if a virgin marries, she has not sinned. Nevertheless such shall have trouble in the flesh: but I spare you.
29 But this I say, brethren, the time *is* short: it remains, that both they that have wives be as though they had none;
30 And they that weep, as though they wept not; and they that rejoice, as though they rejoiced not; and they that buy, as though they possessed not;
31 And they that use this world, as not abusing *it*: for the fashion of this world passes away.
32 But I would have you without carefulness. He that is unmarried cares for the things that belong to the Lord, how he may please the Lord:
33 But he that is married cares for the things that are of the world, how he may please *his* wife.
34 There is *a* difference *also* between a wife and a virgin. The unmarried woman cares for the things of the Lord, that she may be holy both in body and in spirit: but she that is married cares for the things of the world, how she may please *her* husband.
35 And this I speak for your own profit; not that I may cast a snare upon you, but for that which is honorable, and that you may attend upon the Lord without distraction.
36 ¶ But if any man thinks that he behaves himself unbecomingly toward his virgin, if she passes the flower of *her* age, and need so requires, let him do what he intends, he sins not: let them marry.
37 Nevertheless he that stands steadfast in his heart, having no necessity, but has power over his own will, and has so decreed in his heart that he will keep his virgin, does well.
38 So then he that gives *her* in marriage does well; but he that gives *her* not in marriage does better.
39 ¶ The wife is bound by the law as long as her husband lives; but if her husband is dead, she is at liberty to be married to whom she will; only in the Lord.
40 But she is happier if she so remains, after my judgment: and I think also that I have the Spirit of God.

1 Corinthians 8

8:1 ¶ Now as touching things offered to idols, we know that we all have knowledge. Knowledge puffs up, but charity edifies.
2 And if any man thinks that he knows anything, he knows nothing yet as he ought to know.
3 But if any man loves God, the same is known by him.
4 ¶ As concerning therefore the eating of those things that are offered in sacrifice to idols, we know that an idol *is* nothing in the world, and that *there is* no other God but one.
5 For though there are *those* that are called gods, whether in heaven or in earth, (as there are gods many, and lords many,)
6 But to us *there is but* one God, the Father, of whom *are* all things, and we in him; and one Lord Yahshua the Messiah, by whom *are* all things, and we by him.
7 ¶ However *there is* not in every man that knowledge: for some with conscience of the idol to this hour eat *it* as a thing offered to an idol; and their conscience being weak is defiled.
8 But meat commends us not to God: for neither, if we eat, are we the better; neither, if we eat not, are we the worse.

9 But take heed lest by any means this liberty of yours becomes a stumbling block to them that are weak.
10 For if any man sees you which has knowledge sit at meat in the idol's temple, shall not the conscience of him which is weak be emboldened to eat those things which are offered to idols;
11 And through your knowledge shall the weak brother perish, for whom the Messiah died?
12 But when you sin so against the brethren, and wound their weak conscience, you sin against the Messiah.
13 Therefore, if meat makes my brother to offend, I will eat no flesh while the world stands, lest I make my brother to offend.

1 Corinthians 9

9:1 ¶ Am I not an apostle? am I not free? have I not seen Yahshua the Messiah our Lord? are not you my work in the Lord?
2 If I am not an apostle to others, yet doubtless I am to you: for the seal of my apostleship are you in the Lord.
3 ¶ My answer to them that do examine me is this,
4 Have we not power to eat and to drink?
5 Have we not power to lead about a sister, a wife, as well as other apostles, and *as* the brethren of the Lord, and Cephas?
6 Or I only and Barnabas, have not we power to forbear working?
7 Who goes to war any time at his own expense? who plants a vineyard, and eats not of the fruit thereof? or who feeds a flock, and eats not of the milk of the flock?
8 Say I these things as a man? or says not the law the same also?
9 For it is written in the law of Moses, You shall not muzzle the mouth of the ox that treads out the corn. Does God take care of oxen?
10 Or says he *it* altogether for our sakes? For our sakes, no doubt, *this* is written: that he that plows should plow in hope; and that he that threshes in hope should be partaker of his hope.
11 If we have sown to you spiritual things, *is it* a great thing if we shall reap your carnal things?
12 If others are partakers of *this* power over you, *are* not we rather? Nevertheless we have not used this power; but bear all things, lest we should hinder the gospel of the Messiah.
13 Do you not know that they which minister about holy things live *of the things* of the temple? and they which wait at the altar are partakers with the altar?
14 Even so has the Lord ordained that they which preach the gospel should live from the gospel.
15 ¶ But I have used none of these things: neither have I written these things, that it should be so done to me: for *it were* better for me to die, than that any man should make my glorying void.
16 For though I preach the gospel, I have nothing to glory of: for necessity is laid upon me; yes, woe is unto me, if I preach not the gospel!

17 For if I do this thing willingly, I have a reward: but if against my will, a stewardship *of the gospel* is committed unto me.
18 What is my reward then? *Truly* that, when I preach the gospel, I may make the gospel of the Messiah without charge, that I abuse not my power in the gospel.
19 ¶ For though I am free from all *men*, yet have I made myself servant to all, that I might gain the more.
20 And to the Jews I became as a Jew, that I might gain the Jews; to them that are under the law, as under the law, that I might gain them that are under the law:
21 To them that are without law, as without law, (being not without law to God, but under the law to the Messiah,) that I might gain them that are without law.
22 To the weak became I as weak, that I might gain the weak: I am made all things to all *men*, that I might by all means save some.
23 And this I do for the gospel's sake, that I might be partaker thereof with *you*.
24 ¶ Know you not that they which run in a race run all, but one receives the prize? So run, that you may obtain.
25 And every man that strives for the mastery is temperate in all things. Now they *do it* to obtain a corruptible crown; but we an incorruptible.
26 I therefore so run, not as uncertainly; so fight I, not as one that beats the air:
27 But I keep under my body, and bring *it* into subjection: lest that by any means, when I have preached to others, I myself should be a castaway.

1 Corinthians 10

10:1 ¶ Moreover, brethren, I would not that you should be ignorant, how that all our fathers were under the cloud, and all passed through the sea;
2 And were all baptized unto Moses in the cloud and in the sea;
3 And did all eat the same spiritual food;
4 And did all drink the same spiritual drink: for they drank of that spiritual Rock that followed them: and that Rock was the Messiah.
5 But with many of them God was not well pleased: for they were overthrown in the wilderness.
6 ¶ Now these things were our examples, to the intent we should not lust after evil things, as they also lusted.
7 Neither be you idolaters, as *were* some of them; as it is written, The people sat down to eat and drink, and rose up to play.
8 Neither let us commit fornication, as some of them committed, and fell in one day three and twenty thousand.
9 Neither let us tempt the Messiah, as some of them also tempted, and were destroyed by serpents.
10 Neither murmur you, as some of them also murmured, and were destroyed by the destroyer.
11 Now all these things happened to them for examples: and they are written for our admonition, upon whom the ends of the world have come.
12 Therefore let him that thinks he stands take heed lest he fall.

1 Corinthians 10

13 There has no temptation taken you but such as is common to man: but God *is* faithful, who will not allow you to be tempted above that you are able; but will with the temptation also make a way to escape, that you may be able to bear *it*.
14 Therefore, my dearly beloved, flee from idolatry.
15 ¶ I speak as to wise men; judge you what I say.
16 The cup of blessing which we bless, is it not the communion of the blood of the Messiah? The bread which we break, is it not the communion of the body of the Messiah?
17 For we *being* many are one bread, *and* one body: for we are all partakers of that one bread.
18 Behold Israel after the flesh: are not they which eat of the sacrifices partakers of the altar?
19 What say I then? that the idol is anything, or that which is offered in sacrifice to idols is anything?
20 But I *say*, that the things which the Gentiles sacrifice, they sacrifice to devils, and not to God: and I would not that you should have fellowship with devils.
21 You cannot drink the cup of the Lord, and the cup of devils: you cannot be partakers of the Lord's table, and of the table of devils.
22 Do we provoke the Lord to jealousy? are we stronger than he?
23 ¶ All things are lawful for me, but all things are not expedient: all things are lawful for me, but all things edify not.
24 Let no man seek his own, but every man another's *wealth*.
25 Whatever is sold in the shambles, *that* eat, asking no question for conscience sake:
26 For the earth *is* the Lord's [*Yahweh's*], and the fullness thereof.
27 If any of them that believe not bid you *to a feast*, and you be disposed to go; whatever is set before you, eat, asking no question for conscience sake.
28 But if any man says to you, This is offered in sacrifice to idols, eat not for his sake that showed it, and for conscience sake: for the earth *is* the Lord's [*Yahweh's*], and the fullness thereof:
29 Conscience, I say, not your own, but of the other: for why is my liberty judged by another *man's* conscience?
30 For if I by grace be a partaker, why am I evilly spoken of for that for which I give thanks?
31 Whether therefore you eat, or drink, or whatever you do, do all to the glory of God.
32 Give no offense, neither to the Jews, nor to the Gentiles, nor to the congregation of God:
33 Even as I please all *men* in all *things*, not seeking my own profit, but the *profit* of many, that they may be saved.

1 Corinthians 11

11:1 ¶ Be you followers of me, even as I also *am* of the Messiah.
2 Now I praise you, brethren, that you remember me in all things, and keep the ordinances, as I delivered *them* to you.
3 But I would have you know, that the head of every man is the Messiah; and the head of the woman *is* the man; and the head of the Messiah *is* God.
4 Every man praying or prophesying, having *his* head covered, dishonors his head.
5 But every woman that prays or prophesies with *her* head uncovered dishonors her head: for that is even all one as if she were shaven.
6 For if the woman is not covered, let her also be shorn: but if it is a shame for a woman to be shorn or shaven, let her be covered.
7 For a man indeed ought not to cover *his* head, forasmuch as he is the image and glory of God: but the woman is the glory of the man.
8 For the man is not of the woman; but the woman of the man.
9 Neither was the man created for the woman; but the woman for the man.
10 For this cause ought the woman to have power on *her* head because of the angels.
11 Nevertheless neither is the man without the woman, neither the woman without the man, in the Lord.
12 For as the woman *is* of the man, even so *is* the man also by the woman; but all things of God.
13 Judge in yourselves: is it becoming that a woman pray unto God uncovered?
14 Does not even nature itself teach you, that, if a man has long hair, it is a shame to him?
15 But if a woman has long hair, it is a glory to her: for *her* hair is given her for a covering.
16 But if any man seems to be contentious, we have no such custom, neither the congregations of God.
17 ¶ Now in this that I declare *to you* I praise *you* not, that you come together not for the better, but for the worse.
18 For first of all, when you come together in the congregation, I hear that there are divisions among you; and I partly believe it.
19 For there must be also heresies among you, that they which are approved may be made manifest among you.
20 When you come together therefore into one place, *this* is not to eat the Lord's supper.
21 For in eating every one takes before *others* his own supper: and one is hungry, and another is drunken.
22 What? have you not houses to eat and to drink in? or despise you the congregation of God, and shame them that have not? What shall I say to you? shall I praise you in this? I praise *you* not.
23 ¶ For I have received of the Lord that which also I delivered to you, That the Lord Yahshua the *same* night in which he was betrayed took bread:
24 And when he had given thanks, he broke *it*, and said, Take, eat: this is my body, which is broken for you: this do in remembrance of me.
25 After the same manner also *he took* the cup, when he had supped, saying, This cup is the new testament in my blood: this do you, as often as you drink *it*, in remembrance of me.
26 For as often as you eat this bread, and drink this cup, you do show the Lord's death till he comes.

27 Therefore whoever shall eat this bread, and drink *this* cup of the Lord, unworthily, shall be guilty of the body and blood of the Lord.
28 But let a man examine himself, and so let him eat of *that* bread, and drink of *that* cup.
29 For he that eats and drinks unworthily, eats and drinks damnation to himself, not discerning the Lord's body.
30 For this cause many *are* weak and sickly among you, and many sleep.
31 For if we would judge ourselves, we should not be judged.
32 But when we are judged, we are chastened by the Lord, that we should not be condemned with the world.
33 Therefore, my brethren, when you come together to eat, wait one for another.
34 And if any man hungers, let him eat at home; that you come not together to condemnation. And the rest will I set in order when I come.

1 Corinthians 12

12:1 ¶ Now concerning spiritual *gifts*, brethren, I would not have you ignorant.
2 You know that you were Gentiles, carried away unto these dumb idols, even as you were led.
3 Therefore I give you to understand, that no man speaking by the Spirit of God calls Yahshua accursed: and *that* no man can say that Yahshua is the Lord, but by the Holy Ghost.
4 Now there are diversities of gifts, but the same Spirit.
5 And there are differences of administrations, but the same Lord.
6 And there are diversities of operations, but it is the same God which works all in all.
7 But the manifestation of the Spirit is given to every man to profit therewith.
8 For to one is given by the Spirit the word of wisdom; to another the word of knowledge by the same Spirit;
9 To another faith by the same Spirit; to another the gifts of healing by the same Spirit;
10 To another the working of miracles; to another prophecy; to another discerning of spirits; to another *diverse* kinds of tongues; to another the interpretation of tongues:
11 But all these works that one and the very same Spirit, dividing to every man individually as he will.
12 ¶ For as the body is one, and has many members, and all the members of that one body, being many, are one body: so also *is* the Messiah.
13 For by one Spirit are we all baptized into one body, whether *we are* Jews or Gentiles, whether *we are* bond or free; and have been all made to drink into one Spirit.
14 For the body is not one member, but many.
15 If the foot shall say, Because I am not the hand, I am not of the body; is it therefore not of the body?
16 And if the ear shall say, Because I am not the eye, I am not of the body; is it therefore not of the body?
17 If the whole body *were* an eye, where *is* the hearing? If the whole *were* hearing, where *is* the smelling?
18 But now has God set the members every one of them in the body, as it has pleased him.
19 And if they were all one member, where *is* the body?
20 But now *are they* many members, yet but one body.
21 And the eye cannot say to the hand, I have no need of you: nor again the head to the feet, I have no need of you.
22 No, much more those members of the body, which seem to be more feeble, are necessary:
23 And those *members* of the body, which we think to be less honorable, upon these we bestow more abundant honor; and our unseemly *parts* have more abundant modesty.
24 For our honorable *parts* have no need: but God has tempered the body together, having given more abundant honor to that *part* which lacked:
25 That there should be no schism in the body; but *that* the members should have the same care one for another.
26 And whether one member suffers, all the members suffer with it; or one member is honored, all the members rejoice with it.
27 ¶ Now you are the body of the Messiah, and members in particular.
28 And God has set some in the congregation, first apostles, secondarily prophets, thirdly teachers, after that miracles, then gifts of healings, helps, governments, diversities of tongues.
29 *Are* all apostles? *are* all prophets? *are* all teachers? *are* all workers of miracles?
30 Have all the gifts of healing? do all speak with tongues? do all interpret?
31 But covet earnestly the best gifts: and yet show I to you a more excellent way.

1 Corinthians 13

13:1 ¶ Though I speak with the tongues of men and of angels, and have not charity, I have become *as* sounding brass, or a tinkling cymbal.
2 And though I have *the gift of* prophecy, and understand all mysteries, and all knowledge; and though I have all faith, so that I could remove mountains, and have not charity, I am nothing.
3 And though I bestow all my goods to feed *the poor*, and though I give my body to be burned, and have not charity, it profits me nothing.
4 ¶ Charity suffers long, *and* is kind; charity envies not; charity boasts not itself, is not puffed up,
5 Does not behave itself unseemly, seeks not her own, is not easily provoked, thinks no evil;
6 Rejoices not in iniquity, but rejoices in the truth;
7 Bears all things, believes all things, hopes all things, endures all things.
8 ¶ Charity never fails: but whether *there are* prophecies, they shall fail; whether *there are* tongues, they shall cease; whether *there is* knowledge, it shall vanish away
9 For we know in part, and we prophesy in part.
10 But when that which is perfect has come, then that which is in part shall be done away.

1 Corinthians 13

11 When I was a child, I spoke as a child, I understood as a child, I thought as a child: but when I became a man, I put away childish things.
12 For now we see through a glass, darkly; but then face to face: now I know in part; but then shall I know even as also I am known.
13 And now remains faith, hope, charity, these three; but the greatest of these *is* charity.

1 Corinthians 14

14:1 ¶ Follow after charity, and desire spiritual *gifts*, but rather that you may prophesy.
2 For he that speaks in an *unknown* tongue speaks not to men, but to God: for no man understands *him*; however in the spirit he speaks mysteries.
3 But he that prophesies speaks to men *to* edification, and exhortation, and comfort.
4 He that speaks in an *unknown* tongue edifies himself; but he that prophesies edifies the congregation.
5 I would that you all spoke with tongues, but rather that you prophesied: for greater *is* he that prophesies than he that speaks with tongues, unless he interprets, that the congregation may receive edification.
6 ¶ Now, brethren, if I come to you speaking with tongues, what shall I profit you, except I shall speak to you either by revelation, or by knowledge, or by prophesying, or by doctrine?
7 And even things without life giving sound, whether pipe or harp, unless they give a distinction in the sounds, how shall it be known what is piped or harped?
8 For if the trumpet gives an uncertain sound, who shall prepare himself to the battle?
9 So likewise you, unless you utter by the tongue words easy to be understood, how shall it be known what is spoken? for you shall speak into the air.
10 There are, it may be, so many kinds of voices in the world, and none of them *is* without speech.
11 Therefore if I know not the meaning of the voice, I shall be to him that speaks a barbarian, and he that speaks *shall be* a barbarian unto me.
12 Even so you, forasmuch as you are zealous of spiritual *gifts*, seek that you may excel to the edifying of the congregation.
13 Therefore let him that speaks in an *unknown* tongue pray that he may interpret.
14 For if I pray in an *unknown* tongue, my spirit prays, but my understanding is unfruitful.
15 ¶ What is it then? I will pray with the spirit, and I will pray with the understanding also: I will sing with the spirit, and I will sing with the understanding also.
16 Else when you shall bless with the spirit, how shall he that occupies the room of the unlearned say Amen at your giving of thanks, seeing he understands not what you say?
17 For you truly give thanks well, but the other is not edified.
18 I thank my God, I speak with tongues more than you all:
19 Yet in the congregation I had rather speak five words with my understanding, that *by my voice* I might teach others also, than ten thousand words in an *unknown* tongue.
20 Brethren, be not children in understanding: however in malice be you children, but in understanding be men.
21 ¶ In the law it is written, With *men of* other tongues and other lips will I speak to this people; and yet for all that will they not hear me, says the Lord *Yahweh*.
22 Therefore tongues are for a sign, not to them that believe, but to them that believe not: but prophesying *serves* not for them that believe not, but for them which believe.
23 If therefore the whole congregation has come together into one place, and all speak with tongues, and there comes in *those that are* unlearned, or unbelievers, will they not say that you are mad?
24 But if all prophesy, and there comes in one that believes not, or *one* unlearned, he is convinced by all, he is judged by all:
25 And thus are the secrets of his heart made manifest; and so falling down on *his* face he will worship God, and report that God is in you of a truth.
26 ¶ How is it then, brethren? when you come together, every one of you has a psalm, has a doctrine, has a tongue, has a revelation, has an interpretation. Let all things be done unto edifying.
27 If any man speaks in an *unknown* tongue, *let it be* by two, or at the most *by* three, and *that* by course; and let one interpret.
28 But if there is no interpreter, let him hold his peace in the congregation; and let him speak to himself, and to God.
29 Let the prophets speak two or three, and let the others judge.
30 If *anything* is revealed to another that sits by, let the first hold his peace.
31 For you may all prophesy one by one, that all may learn, and all may be comforted.
32 And the spirits of the prophets are subject to the prophets.
33 For God is not *the author* of confusion, but of peace, as in all congregations of the saints.
34 ¶ Let your women keep silence in the congregations: for it is not permitted unto them to speak; but *they are commanded* to be under obedience, as also says the law.
35 And if they will learn anything, let them ask their husbands at home: for it is a shame for women to speak in the congregation.
36 ¶ What? came the word of God out from you? or came it to you only?
37 If any man thinks himself to be a prophet, or spiritual, let him acknowledge that the things that I write to you are the commandments of the Lord.
38 But if any man is ignorant, let him be ignorant.
39 Therefore, brethren, covet to prophesy, and forbid not to speak with tongues.
40 Let all things be done decently and in order.

1 Corinthians 15

15:1 ¶ Moreover, brethren, I declare to you the gospel which I preached to you, which also you have received, and wherein you stand;

2 By which also you are saved, if you keep in memory what I preached to you, unless you have believed in vain.

3 For I delivered to you first of all that which I also received, how that the Messiah died for our sins according to the scriptures;

4 And that he was buried, and that he rose again the third day according to the scriptures:

5 And that he was seen by Cephas, then by the twelve:

6 After that, he was seen by above five hundred brethren at once; of whom the greater part remain to this present, but some have fallen asleep.

7 After that, he was seen by James; then by all the apostles.

8 And last of all he was seen by me also, as of one born out of due time.

9 For I am the least of the apostles, that am not worthy to be called an apostle, because I persecuted the congregation of God.

10 But by the grace of God I am what I am: and his grace which *was bestowed* upon me was not in vain; but I labored more abundantly than they all: yet not I, but the grace of God which was with me.

11 Therefore whether *it were* I or they, so we preach, and so you believed.

12 ¶ Now if the Messiah is preached that he rose from the dead, how say some among you that there is no resurrection of the dead?

13 But if there is no resurrection of the dead, then is the Messiah not risen:

14 And if the Messiah is not risen, then *is* our preaching vain, and your faith *is* also vain.

15 Yes, and we are found false witnesses of God; because we have testified of God that he raised up the Messiah: whom he raised not up, if so be that the dead rise not.

16 For if the dead rise not, then is not the Messiah raised:

17 And if the Messiah is not raised, your faith *is* vain; you are yet in your sins.

18 Then they also which are fallen asleep in the Messiah are perished.

19 If in this life only we have hope in the Messiah, we are of all men most miserable.

20 ¶ But now is the Messiah risen from the dead, *and* become the firstfruits of them that slept.

21 For since by man *came* death, by man *came* also the resurrection of the dead.

22 For as in Adam all die, even so in the Messiah shall all be made alive.

23 But every man in his own order: the Messiah the firstfruits; afterward they that are the Messiah's at his coming.

24 Then *comes* the end, when he shall have delivered up the kingdom to God, even the Father; when he shall have put down all rule and all authority and power.

25 For he must reign, till he has put all enemies under his feet.

26 The last enemy *that* shall be destroyed *is* death.

27 For he has put all things under his feet. But when he said all things are put under *him, it is* manifest that he is excepted, which did put all things under him.

28 And when all things shall be subdued unto him, then shall the Son also himself be subject to him that put all things under him, that God may be all in all.

29 Else what shall they do which are baptized for the dead, if the dead rise not at all? why are they then baptized for the dead?

30 And why stand we in jeopardy every hour?

31 I protest by your rejoicing which I have in the Messiah Yahshua our Lord, I die daily.

32 If after the manner of men I have fought with beasts at Ephesus, what advantages it *to* me, if the dead rise not? let us eat and drink; for tomorrow we die.

33 Be not deceived: evil communications corrupt good manners.

34 Awake to righteousness, and sin not; for some have not the knowledge of God: I speak *this* to your shame.

35 ¶ But some *man* will say, How are the dead raised up? and with what body do they come?

36 *You* fool, that which you sow is not quickened, unless it dies:

37 And that which you sow, you sow not that body that shall be, but bare grain, it may *by* chance *be* of wheat, or of some other *grain*:

38 But God gives it a body as it has pleased him, and to every seed his own body.

39 All flesh *is* not the same flesh: but *there is* one *kind of* flesh of men, another flesh of beasts, another of fishes, *and* another of birds.

40 *There are* also celestial bodies, and bodies terrestrial: but the glory of the celestial *is* one, and the *glory* of the terrestrial *is* another.

41 *There is* one glory of the sun, and another glory of the moon, and another glory of the stars: for *one* star differs from *another* star in glory.

42 So also *is* the resurrection of the dead. It is sown in corruption; it is raised in incorruption:

43 It is sown in dishonor; it is raised in glory: it is sown in weakness; it is raised in power:

44 It is sown a natural body; it is raised a spiritual body. There is a natural body, and there is a spiritual body.

45 And so it is written, The first man Adam was made a living soul; the last Adam *was made* a quickening spirit.

46 However that *was* not first which is spiritual, but that which is natural; and afterward that which is spiritual.

47 The first man *is* of the earth, earthly: the second man *is* the Lord from heaven.

48 As *is* the earthly, such *are* they also that are earthly: and as *is* the heavenly, such *are* they also that are heavenly.

49 And as we have borne the image of the earthly, we shall also bear the image of the heavenly.

1 Corinthians 15

50 Now this I say, brethren, that flesh and blood cannot inherit the kingdom of God; neither does corruption inherit incorruption.
51 ¶ Behold, I show you a mystery; We shall not all sleep, but we shall all be changed,
52 In a moment, in the twinkling of an eye, at the last trump: for the trumpet shall sound, and the dead shall be raised incorruptible, and we shall be changed.
53 For this corruptible must put on incorruption, and this mortal *must* put on immortality.
54 So when this corruptible shall have put on incorruption, and this mortal shall have put on immortality, then shall be brought to pass the saying that is written, Death is swallowed up in victory.
55 O death, where *is* your sting? O grave, where *is* your victory?
56 The sting of death *is* sin; and the strength of sin *is* the law.
57 But thanks *be* to God, which gives us the victory through our Lord Yahshua the Messiah.
58 ¶ Therefore, my beloved brethren, be you steadfast, unmovable, always abounding in the work of the Lord, forasmuch as you know that your labor is not in vain in the Lord.

1 Corinthians 16

16:1 ¶ Now concerning the collection for the saints, as I have given order to the congregations of Galatia, even so do you.
2 Upon the first *day* of the week let every one of you lay by him in store, as *God* has prospered him, that there be no gatherings when I come.
3 And when I come, whomever you shall approve by *your* letters, them will I send to bring your liberality to Jerusalem.
4 And if it is fitting that I go also, they shall go with me.
5 ¶ Now I will come to you, when I shall pass through Macedonia: for I do pass through Macedonia.
6 And it may be that I will remain, yes, and winter with you, that you may bring me on my journey wherever I go.
7 For I will not see you now by the way; but I trust to tarry a while with you, if the Lord permits.
8 But I will tarry at Ephesus until Pentecost.
9 For a great and powerful door has opened to me, and *there are* many adversaries.
10 ¶ Now if Timotheus comes, see that he may be with you without fear: for he works the work of the Lord, as I also *do*.
11 Let no man therefore despise him: but conduct him forth in peace, that he may come to me: for I look for him with the brethren.
12 As touching *our* brother Apollos, I greatly desired him to come to you with the brethren: but his will was not at all to come at this time; but he will come when he shall have convenient time.
13 ¶ Watch you, stand fast in the faith, be you like men, be strong.
14 Let all your things be done with charity.
15 I beseech you, brethren, (you know the house of Stephanas, that it is the firstfruits of Achaia, and *that* they have appointed themselves to the ministry of the saints,)
16 That you submit yourselves to such, and to every one that helps with *us*, and labors.
17 I am glad of the coming of Stephanas and Fortunatus and Achaicus: for that which was lacking on your part they have supplied.
18 For they have refreshed my spirit and yours: therefore acknowledge you them that are such.
19 ¶ The congregations of Asia salute you. Aquila and Priscilla salute you much in the Lord, with the congregation that is in their house.
20 All the brethren greet you. Greet you one another with a holy kiss.
21 The salutation of *me* Paul with my own hand.
22 If any man loves not the Lord Yahshua the Messiah, let him be Anathema Maranatha.
23 The grace of our Lord Yahshua the Messiah *be* with you.
24 My love *be* with you all in the Messiah Yahshua. Amen. <<*The first epistle to the Corinthians was written from Philippi by Stephanas and Fortunatus and Achaicus and Timotheus.*>>

2 Corinthians

2 Corinthians 1

1:1 ¶ Paul, an apostle of Yahshua the Messiah by the will of God, and Timothy *our* brother, to the congregation of God which is at Corinth, with all the saints which are in all Achaia:
2 Grace *be* to you and peace from God our Father, and *from* the Lord Yahshua the Messiah.
3 ¶ Blessed *be* God, even the Father of our Lord Yahshua the Messiah, the Father of mercies, and the God of all comfort;
4 Who comforts us in all our tribulation, that we may be able to comfort them which are in any trouble, by the comfort with which we ourselves are comforted of God.
5 For as the sufferings of the Messiah abound in us, so our consolation also abounds by the Messiah.
6 And whether we are afflicted, *it is* for your consolation and salvation, which is effectual in the enduring of the same sufferings which we also suffer: or whether we are comforted, *it is* for your consolation and salvation.
7 ¶ And our hope for you *is* steadfast, knowing, that as you are partakers of the sufferings, so *shall you be* also of the consolation.
8 For we would not, brethren, have you ignorant of our trouble which came to us in Asia, that we were pressed out of measure, above strength, insomuch that we despaired even of life:
9 But we had the sentence of death in ourselves, that we should not trust in ourselves, but in God which raises the dead:

10 Who delivered us from so great a death, and does deliver: in whom we trust that he will yet deliver *us*;

11 You also helping together by prayer for us, that for the gift *bestowed* upon us by the means of many persons thanks may be given by many on our behalf.

12 ¶ For our rejoicing is this, the testimony of our conscience, that in simplicity and godly sincerity, not with fleshly wisdom, but by the grace of God, we have had our conversation in the world, and more abundantly toward you.

13 For we write no other things to you, than what you read or acknowledge; and I trust you shall acknowledge even to the end;

14 As also you have acknowledged us in part, that we are your rejoicing, even as you also *are* ours in the day of the Lord Yahshua.

15 ¶ And in this confidence I was minded to come to you before, that you might have a second benefit;

16 And to pass by you into Macedonia, and to come again out of Macedonia to you, and of you to be brought on my way toward Judaea.

17 When I therefore was thus minded, did I use lightness? or the things that I purpose, do I purpose according to the flesh, that with me there should be yes yes, and no no?

18 But *as* God *is* true, our word toward you was not yes and no.

19 For the Son of God, Yahshua the Messiah, who was preached among you by us, *even* by me and Silvanus and Timotheus, was not yes and no, but in him was yes.

20 For all the promises of God in him *are* yes, and in him Amen, unto the glory of God by us.

21 Now he which establishes us with you in the Messiah, and has anointed us, *is* God;

22 Who has also sealed us, and given the earnest of the Spirit in our hearts.

23 Moreover I call God for a record upon my soul, that to spare you I came not as yet to Corinth.

24 Not because we have dominion over your faith, but are helpers of your joy: for by faith you stand.

2 Corinthians 2

2:1 ¶ But I determined this with myself, that I would not come again to you in heaviness.

2 For if I make you sorry, who is he then that makes me glad, but the same which is made sorry by me?

3 And I wrote this same to you, lest, when I came, I should have sorrow from them of whom I ought to rejoice; having confidence in you all, that my joy is *the joy* of you all.

4 For out of much affliction and anguish of heart I wrote to you with many tears; not that you should be grieved, but that you might know the love which I have more abundantly unto you.

5 ¶ But if any has caused grief, he has not grieved me, but in part: that I may not overcharge you all.

6 Sufficient to such a man *is* this punishment, which *was* inflicted by many.

7 So that contrarily you *ought* rather to forgive *him*, and comfort *him*, lest perhaps such a one should be swallowed up with much more sorrow.

8 Therefore I beseech you that you would confirm *your* love toward him.

9 For to this end also did I write, that I might know the proof of you, whether you are obedient in all things.

10 To whom you forgive anything, I *forgive* also: for if I forgave anything, to whom I forgave *it*, for your sakes *forgave I it* in the person of the Messiah;

11 Lest Satan should get an advantage of us: for we are not ignorant of his devices.

12 ¶ Furthermore, when I came to Troas to *preach* the Messiah's gospel, and a door was opened to me by the Lord,

13 I had no rest in my spirit, because I found not Titus my brother: but taking my leave of them, I went from there into Macedonia.

14 Now thanks *be* to God, which always causes us to triumph in the Messiah, and makes manifest the savor of his knowledge by us in every place.

15 For we are to God a sweet savor of the Messiah, in them that are saved, and in them that perish:

16 To the one *we are* the savor of death unto death; and to the other the savor of life unto life. And who *is* sufficient for these things?

17 For we are not as many, which corrupt the word of God: but as of sincerity, but as of God, in the sight of God speak we in the Messiah.

2 Corinthians 3

3:1 ¶ Do we begin again to commend ourselves? or need we, as some *others*, epistles of commendation to you, or *letters* of commendation from you?

2 You are our epistle written in our hearts, known and read of all men:

3 *Forasmuch as you are* manifestly declared to be the epistle of the Messiah ministered by us, written not with ink, but with the Spirit of the living God; not in tables of stone, but in fleshy tables of the heart.

4 And such trust have we through the Messiah toward God:

5 Not that we are sufficient of ourselves to think anything as of ourselves; but our sufficiency *is* of God;

6 ¶ Who also has made us able ministers of the new testament; not of the letter, but of the spirit: for the letter kills, but the spirit gives life.

7 But if the ministration of death, written *and* engraved in stones, was glorious, so that the children of Israel could not steadfastly behold the face of Moses for the glory of his countenance; which *glory* was to be done away:

8 How shall not the ministration of the spirit be rather glorious?

2 Corinthians 3

9 For if the ministration of condemnation *is* glory, much more does the ministration of righteousness exceed in glory.
10 For even that which was made glorious had no glory in this respect, by reason of the glory that excels.
11 For if that which is done away *was* glorious, much more that which remains *is* glorious.
12 ¶ Seeing then that we have such hope, we use great plainness of speech:
13 And not as Moses, *which* put a veil over his face, that the children of Israel could not steadfastly look to the end of that which is abolished:
14 But their minds were blinded: for until this day remains the same veil not taken away in the reading of the old testament; which *veil* is done away in the Messiah.
15 But even unto this day, when Moses is read, the veil is upon their heart.
16 Nevertheless when it shall turn to the Lord, the veil shall be taken away.
17 Now the Lord is that Spirit: and where the Spirit of the Lord *is*, there *is* liberty.
18 But we all, with open face beholding as in a glass the glory of the Lord, are changed into the same image from glory to glory, *even* as by the Spirit of the Lord.

2 Corinthians 4

4:1 ¶ Therefore seeing we have this ministry, as we have received mercy, we faint not;
2 But have renounced the hidden things of dishonesty, not walking in craftiness, nor handling the word of God deceitfully; but by manifestation of the truth commending ourselves to every man's conscience in the sight of God.
3 But if our gospel is hidden, it is hidden to them that are lost:
4 In whom the god of this world has blinded the minds of them which believe not, lest the light of the glorious gospel of the Messiah, who is the image of God, should shine unto them.
5 For we preach not ourselves, but the Messiah Yahshua the Lord; and ourselves your servants for Yahshua's sake.
6 For God, who commanded the light to shine out of darkness, has shined in our hearts, to *give* the light of the knowledge of the glory of God in the face of Yahshua the Messiah.
7 But we have this treasure in earthen vessels, that the excellency of the power may be of God, and not of us.
8 ¶ *We are* troubled on every side, yet not distressed; *we are* perplexed, but not in despair;
9 Persecuted, but not forsaken; cast down, but not destroyed;
10 Always bearing about in the body the dying of the Lord Yahshua, that the life also of Yahshua might be made manifest in our body.
11 For we which live are always delivered unto death for Yahshua's sake, that the life also of Yahshua might be made manifest in our mortal flesh.
12 So then death works in us, but life in you.
13 We having the same spirit of faith, according as it is written, I believed, and therefore have I spoken; we also believe, and therefore speak;
14 Knowing that he which raised up the Lord Yahshua shall raise up us also by Yahshua, and shall present *us* with you.
15 For all things *are* for your sakes, that the abundant grace might through the thanksgiving of many abound to the glory of God.
16 For which cause we faint not; but though our outward man perishes, yet the inward *man* is renewed day by day.
17 For our light affliction, which is but for a moment, works for us a far more exceeding *and* eternal weight of glory;
18 While we look not at the things which are seen, but at the things which are not seen: for the things which are seen *are* temporal; but the things which are not seen *are* eternal.

2 Corinthians 5

5:1 ¶ For we know that if our earthly house of *this* tabernacle were dissolved, we have a building of God, a house not made with hands, eternal in the heavens.
2 For in this we groan, earnestly desiring to be clothed upon with our house which is from heaven:
3 If so be that being clothed we shall not be found naked.
4 For we that are in *this* tabernacle do groan, being burdened: not for that we would be unclothed, but clothed upon, that mortality might be swallowed up by life.
5 Now he that has worked us for the very same thing *is* God, who also has given to us the earnest of the Spirit.
6 Therefore *we are* always confident, knowing that, while we are at home in the body, we are absent from the Lord:
7 (For we walk by faith, not by sight:)
8 We are confident, *I say*, and willing rather to be absent from the body, and to be present with the Lord.
9 Therefore we labor, that, whether present or absent, we may be accepted by him.
10 For we must all appear before the judgment seat of the Messiah; that every one may receive the things *done* in *his* body, according to that he has done, whether *it is* good or bad.
11 Knowing therefore the terror of the Lord, we persuade men; but we are made manifest to God; and I trust also are made manifest in your consciences.
12 ¶ For we commend not ourselves again to you, but give you occasion to glory on our behalf, that you may have somewhat to *answer* them which glory in appearance, and not in heart.
13 For whether we are beside ourselves, *it is* for God: or whether we are sober, *it is* for your cause.
14 For the love of the Messiah constrains us; because we thus judge, that if one died for all, then were all dead:

15 And *that* he died for all, that they which live should not henceforth live unto themselves, but to him which died for them, and rose again.

16 ¶ Therefore henceforth know we no man after the flesh: yes, though we have known the Messiah after the flesh, yet henceforth now on know we *him* no more.

17 Therefore if any man *is* in the Messiah, *he is* a new creature: old things are passed away; behold, all things have become new.

18 And all things *are* of God, who has reconciled us to himself by Yahshua the Messiah, and has given to us the ministry of reconciliation;

19 That is, that God was in the Messiah, reconciling the world to himself, not imputing their trespasses to them; and has committed to us the word of reconciliation.

20 Now then we are ambassadors for the Messiah, as though God did call *you* through us: we pray *you* in the Messiah's stead, be you reconciled to God.

21 For he has made him *to be* sin for us, who knew no sin; that we might be made the righteousness of God in him.

2 Corinthians 6

6:1 ¶ We then, *as* workers together *with him*, beseech you also that you receive not the grace of God in vain.

2 (For he said, I have heard you in a time accepted, and in the day of salvation have I helped you: behold, now *is* the accepted time; behold, now *is* the day of salvation.)

3 Giving no offense in anything, that the ministry be not blamed:

4 But in all *things* approving ourselves as the ministers of God, in much patience, in afflictions, in necessities, in distresses,

5 In stripes, in imprisonments, in tumults, in labors, in watchings, in fastings;

6 By pureness, by knowledge, by longsuffering, by kindness, by the Holy Ghost, by love unfeigned,

7 By the word of truth, by the power of God, by the armor of righteousness on the right hand and on the left,

8 By honor and dishonor, by evil report and good report: as deceivers, and *yet* true;

9 As unknown, and *yet* well known; as dying, and, behold, we live; as chastened, and not killed;

10 As sorrowful, yet always rejoicing; as poor, yet making many rich; as having nothing, and *yet* possessing all things.

11 ¶ O *you* Corinthians, our mouth is open to you, our heart is enlarged.

12 You are not distressed in us, but you are distressed in your own bowels.

13 Now for a recompense in the same, (I speak as to my children,) be you also enlarged.

14 Be you not unequally yoked together with unbelievers: for what fellowship has righteousness with unrighteousness? and what communion has light with darkness?

15 And what concord has the Messiah with Belial? or what part has he that believes with an infidel?

16 And what agreement has the temple of God with idols? for you are the temple of the living God; as God *Yahweh* has said, I will dwell in them, and walk in *them*; and I will be their God, and they shall be my people.

17 Therefore come out from among them, and be you separate, says the Lord *Yahweh*, and touch not the unclean *thing*; and I will receive you,

18 And will be a Father to you, and you shall be my sons and daughters, says the Lord *Yahweh* Almighty.

2 Corinthians 7

7:1 ¶ Having therefore these promises, dearly beloved, let us cleanse ourselves from all filthiness of the flesh and spirit, perfecting holiness in the fear of God.

2 Receive us; we have wronged no man, we have corrupted no man, we have defrauded no man.

3 I speak not *this* to condemn *you*: for I have said before, that you are in our hearts to die and live with *you*.

4 Great *is* my boldness of speech toward you, great *is* my glorying of you: I am filled with comfort, I am exceedingly joyful in all our tribulation.

5 ¶ For, when we had come into Macedonia, our flesh had no rest, but we were troubled on every side; outside *were* fightings, within *were* fears.

6 Nevertheless God, that comforts those that are cast down, comforted us by the coming of Titus;

7 And not by his coming only, but by the consolation with which he was comforted in you, when he told us your earnest desire, your mourning, your fervent mind toward me; so that I rejoiced the more.

8 For though I made you sorry with a letter, I do not repent, though I did repent: for I perceive that the same epistle has made you sorry, though *it were* but for a season.

9 Now I rejoice, not that you were made sorry, but that you sorrowed to repentance: for you were made sorry after a godly manner, that you might receive damage by us in nothing.

10 For godly sorrow works repentance to salvation not to be repented of: but the sorrow of the world works death.

11 For behold this very same thing, that you sorrowed after a godly sort, what carefulness it worked in you, yes, *what* clearing of yourselves, yes, *what* indignation, yes, *what* fear, yes, *what* vehement desire, yes, *what* zeal, yes, *what* revenge! In all *things* you have approved yourselves to be clear in this matter.

12 ¶ Therefore, though I wrote to you, *I did it* not for his cause that had done the wrong, nor for his cause that suffered wrong, but that our care for you in the sight of God might appear to you.

13 Therefore we were comforted in your comfort: yes, and exceedingly the more rejoiced we for the joy of Titus, because his spirit was refreshed by you all.

14 For if I have boasted anything to him of you, I am not ashamed; but as we spoke all things to you in truth, even so our boasting which *I made* before Titus, is found a truth.

15 And his inward affection is more abundant toward you, while he remembers the obedience of you all, how with fear and trembling you received him.
16 I rejoice therefore that I have confidence in you in all *things*.

2 Corinthians 8

8:1 ¶ Moreover, brethren, we make known *to* you of the grace of God bestowed on the congregations of Macedonia;
2 How that in a great trial of affliction the abundance of their joy and their deep poverty abounded to the riches of their liberality.
3 For to *their* power, I bear record, yes, and beyond *their* power *they were* willing of themselves;
4 Praying us with much urging that we would receive the gift, and *take upon us* the fellowship of the ministering to the saints.
5 And *this they did*, not as we hoped, but first gave their own selves to the Lord, and to us by the will of God.
6 Insomuch that we desired Titus, that as he had begun, so he would also finish in you the same grace also.
7 ¶ Therefore, as you abound in every *thing, in* faith, and utterance, and knowledge, and *in* all diligence, and *in* your love to us, *see* that you abound in this grace also.
8 I speak not by commandment, but by occasion of the forwardness of others, and to prove the sincerity of your love.
9 For you know the grace of our Lord Yahshua the Messiah, that, though he was rich, yet for your sakes he became poor, that you through his poverty might be rich.
10 And herein I give *my* advice: for this is expedient for you, who have begun before, not only to do, but also to be forward a year ago.
11 Now therefore perform the doing *of it*; that as *there was* a readiness to will, so *there may be* a performance also out of that which you have.
12 For if there is first a willing mind, *it is* accepted according to that a man has, *and* not according to that he has not.
13 For *I mean* not that other men be eased, and you burdened:
14 But by an equality, *that* now at this time your abundance *may be a supply* for their want, that their abundance also may be *a supply* for your want: that there may be equality:
15 As it is written, He that *had gathered* much had nothing over; and he that *had gathered* little had no lack.
16 ¶ But thanks *be* to God, which put the same earnest care into the heart of Titus for you.
17 For indeed he accepted the exhortation; but being more forward, of his own accord he went to you.
18 And we have sent with him the brother, whose praise *is* in the gospel throughout all the congregations;
19 And not *that* only, but who was also chosen of the congregations to travel with us with this grace, which is administered by us to the glory of the same Lord, and *declaration of* your ready mind:
20 Avoiding this, that no man should blame us in this abundance which is administered by us:
21 Providing for honest things, not only in the sight of the Lord, but also in the sight of men.
22 And we have sent with them our brother, whom we have oftentimes proved diligent in many things, but now much more diligent, upon the great confidence which *I have* in you.
23 Whether *any do inquire* of Titus, *he is* my partner and fellow helper concerning you: or our brethren *are inquired of, they are* the messengers of the congregations, *and* the glory of the Messiah.
24 Therefore show you to them, and before the congregations, the proof of your love, and of our boasting on your behalf.

2 Corinthians 9

9:1 ¶ For as touching the ministering to the saints, it is superfluous for me to write to you:
2 For I know the forwardness of your mind, for which I boast of you to them of Macedonia, that Achaia was ready a year ago; and your zeal has provoked very many.
3 Yet have I sent the brethren, lest our boasting of you should be in vain in this behalf; that, as I said, you may be ready:
4 Lest perhaps if they of Macedonia come with me, and find you unprepared, we (that we say not, you) should be ashamed in this same confident boasting.
5 Therefore I thought it necessary to exhort the brethren, that they would go before to you, and make up beforehand your bounty, whereof you had notice before, that the same might be ready, as *a matter of* bounty, and not as *of* covetousness.
6 ¶ But this *I say*, He which sows sparingly shall reap also sparingly; and he which sows bountifully shall reap also bountifully.
7 Every man according as he purposes in his heart, *so let him give*; not grudgingly, or of necessity: for God loves a cheerful giver.
8 And God *is* able to make all grace abound toward you; that you, always having all sufficiency in all *things*, may abound to every good work:
9 (As it is written, He has dispersed abroad; he has given to the poor: his righteousness remains forever.
10 Now he that ministers seed to the sower both minister bread for *your* food, and multiply your seed sown, and increase the fruits of your righteousness;)
11 Being enriched in every thing to all bountifulness, which causes through us thanksgiving to God.
12 For the administration of this service not only supplies the want of the saints, but is abundant also by many thanksgivings to God;
13 While by the experiment of this ministration they glorify God for your professed subjection to the gospel of the Messiah, and for *your* liberal distribution to them, and to all *men*;

14 And by their prayer for you, which long after you for the exceeding grace of God in you.
15 Thanks *be* to God for his unspeakable gift.

2 Corinthians 10

10:1 ¶ Now I Paul myself beseech you by the meekness and gentleness of the Messiah, who in presence *am* base among you, but being absent am bold toward you:
2 But I beseech *you*, that I may not be bold when I am present with that confidence, with which I think to be bold against some, which think of us as if we walked according to the flesh.
3 For though we walk in the flesh, we do not war after the flesh:
4 (For the weapons of our warfare *are* not carnal, but mighty through God to the pulling down of strong holds;)
5 Casting down imaginations, and every high thing that exalts itself against the knowledge of God, and bringing into captivity every thought to the obedience of the Messiah;
6 And having in a readiness to revenge all disobedience, when your obedience is fulfilled.
7 ¶ Do you look on things after the outward appearance? If any man trusts to himself that he is the Messiah's, let him of himself think this again, that, as he *is* the Messiah's, even so *are* we the Messiah's.
8 For though I should boast somewhat more of our authority, which the Lord has given us for edification, and not for your destruction, I should not be ashamed.
9 That I may not seem as if I would terrify you by letters.
10 For *his* letters, say they, *are* weighty and powerful; but *his* bodily presence *is* weak, and *his* speech contemptible.
11 Let such a one think this, that, such as we are in word by letters when we are absent, such *will we be* also in deed when we are present.
12 ¶ For we dare not make ourselves of the number, or compare ourselves with some that commend themselves: but they measuring themselves by themselves, and comparing themselves among themselves, are not wise.
13 But we will not boast of things without *our* measure, but according to the measure of the rule which God has distributed to us, a measure to reach even to you.
14 For we stretch not ourselves beyond *our measure*, as though we reached not unto you: for we have come as far as to you also in *preaching* the gospel of the Messiah:
15 Not boasting of things without *our* measure, *that is*, of other men's labors; but having hope, when your faith is increased, that we shall be enlarged by you according to our rule abundantly,
16 To preach the gospel in the *regions* beyond you, *and* not to boast in another man's line of things made ready to our hand.
17 But he that glories, let him glory in the Lord *Yahweh*.
18 For not he that commends himself is approved, but whom the Lord commends.

2 Corinthians 11

11:1 ¶ Would to God you could bear with me a little in *my* folly: and indeed bear with me.
2 For I am jealous over you with godly jealousy: for I have espoused you to one husband, that I may present *you as* a chaste virgin to the Messiah.
3 But I fear, lest by any means, as the serpent deceived Eve through his subtlety, so your minds should be corrupted from the simplicity that is in the Messiah.
4 For if he that comes preaches another Yahshua, whom we have not preached, or *if* you receive another spirit, which you have not received, or another gospel, which you have not accepted, you might well bear with *him*.
5 ¶ For I suppose I was not at all behind the very most chief apostles.
6 But though *I am* rude in speech, yet not in knowledge; but we have been thoroughly made manifest among you in all things.
7 Have I committed an offense in abasing myself that you might be exalted, because I have preached to you the gospel of God freely?
8 I robbed other congregations, taking wages *from them*, to do you service.
9 And when I was present with you, and wanted, I was chargeable to no man: for that which was lacking to me the brethren which came from Macedonia supplied: and in all *things* I have kept myself from being burdensome to you, and *so* will I keep *myself*.
10 As the truth of the Messiah is in me, no man shall stop me of this boasting in the regions of Achaia.
11 Why? because I love you not? God knows.
12 But what I do, that I will do, that I may cut off occasion from them which desire occasion; that wherein they glory, they may be found even as we.
13 For such *are* false apostles, deceitful workers, transforming themselves into the apostles of the Messiah.
14 And no marvel; for Satan himself is transformed into an angel of light.
15 Therefore *it is* no great thing if his ministers also are transformed as the ministers of righteousness; whose end shall be according to their works.
16 ¶ I say again, Let no man think me a fool; if otherwise, yet as a fool receive me, that I may boast myself a little.
17 That which I speak, I speak *it* not after the Lord, but as it were foolishly, in this confidence of boasting.
18 Seeing that many glory after the flesh, I will glory also.
19 For you endure fools gladly, seeing you *yourselves* are wise.
20 For you endure, if a man brings you into bondage, if a man devours *you*, if a man takes *of you*, if a man exalts himself, if a man smites you on the face.
21 I speak as concerning reproach, as though we had been weak. But in whatever any is bold, (I speak foolishly,) I am bold also.

2 Corinthians 11

22 ¶ Are they Hebrews? so *am* I. Are they Israelites? so *am* I. Are they the seed of Abraham? so *am* I.
23 Are they ministers of the Messiah? (I speak as a fool) I *am* more; in labors more abundant, in stripes above measure, in prisons more frequently, in deaths often.
24 Of the Jews five times received I forty *stripes* save one.
25 Three times was I beaten with rods, once was I stoned, three times I suffered shipwreck, a night and a day I have been in the deep;
26 *In* journeys often, *in* perils of waters, *in* perils of robbers, *in* perils by *my own* countrymen, *in* perils by the heathen, *in* perils in the city, *in* perils in the wilderness, *in* perils in the sea, *in* perils among false brethren;
27 In weariness and painfulness, in watchings often, in hunger and thirst, in fastings often, in cold and nakedness.
28 Besides those things that are without, that which came upon me daily, the care of all the congregations.
29 Who is weak, and I am not weak? who is offended, and I burn not?
30 If I must need glory, I will glory of the things which concern my infirmities.
31 The God and Father of our Lord Yahshua the Messiah, which is blessed forevermore, knows that I lie not.
32 In Damascus the governor under Aretas the king kept the city of the Damascenes with a garrison, desirous to apprehend me:
33 And through a window in a basket was I let down by the wall, and escaped his hands.

2 Corinthians 12

12:1 ¶ It is not expedient for me doubtless to glory. I will come to visions and revelations of the Lord.
2 I knew a man in the Messiah before fourteen years ago, (whether in the body, I cannot tell; or whether out of the body, I cannot tell: God knows;) such a one caught up to the third heaven.
3 And I knew such a man, (whether in the body, or out of the body, I cannot tell: God knows;)
4 How that he was caught up into paradise, and heard unspeakable words, which it is not lawful for a man to utter.
5 Of such a one will I glory: yet of myself I will not glory, but in my infirmities.
6 For though I would desire to glory, I shall not be a fool; for I will say the truth: but *now* I forbear, lest any man should think of me above that which he sees me *to be*, or *that* he hears from me.
7 And lest I should be exalted above measure through the abundance of the revelations, there was given to me a thorn in the flesh, the messenger of Satan to buffet me, lest I should be exalted above measure.
8 For this thing I sought the Lord three times, that it might depart from me.
9 And he said to me, My grace is sufficient for you: for my strength is made perfect in weakness. Most gladly therefore will I rather glory in my infirmities, that the power of the Messiah may rest upon me.
10 Therefore I take pleasure in infirmities, in reproaches, in necessities, in persecutions, in distresses for the Messiah's sake: for when I am weak, then am I strong.
11 ¶ I have become a fool in glorying; you have compelled me: for I ought to have been commended by you: for in nothing am I behind the very most chief apostles, though I am nothing.
12 Truly the signs of an apostle were worked among you in all patience, in signs, and wonders, and mighty deeds.
13 For what is it wherein you were inferior to other congregations, except *it was* that I myself was not burdensome to you? forgive me this wrong.
14 Behold, the third time I am ready to come to you; and I will not be burdensome to you: for I seek not yours, but you: for the children ought not to lay up for the parents, but the parents for the children.
15 And I will very gladly spend and be spent for you; though the more abundantly I love you, the less I am loved.
16 But be it so, I did not burden you: nevertheless, being crafty, I caught you with guile.
17 Did I make a gain of you by any of them whom I sent to you?
18 I desired Titus, and with *him* I sent a brother. Did Titus make a gain of you? walked we not in the same spirit? *walked we* not in the same steps?
19 Again, think you that we excuse ourselves to you? we speak before God in the Messiah: but *we do* all things, dearly beloved, for your edifying.
20 For I fear, lest, when I come, I shall not find you such as I would, and *that* I shall be found to you such as you would not: lest *there be* debates, envyings, wraths, strifes, backbitings, whisperings, swellings, tumults:
21 *And* lest, when I come again, my God will humble me among you, and *that* I shall bewail many which have sinned already, and have not repented of the uncleanness and fornication and lasciviousness which they have committed.

2 Corinthians 13

13:1 ¶ This *is* the third *time* I am coming to you. In the mouth of two or three witnesses shall every word be established.
2 I told you before, and foretell you, as if I were present, the second time; and being absent now I write to them which already have sinned, and to all others, that, if I come again, I will not spare:
3 Since you seek a proof of the Messiah speaking in me, which toward you is not weak, but is mighty in you.
4 For though he was crucified through weakness, yet he lives by the power of God. For we also are weak in him, but we shall live with him by the power of God toward you.
5 Examine yourselves, whether you are in the faith; prove your own selves. Know you not your own selves, how that Yahshua the Messiah is in you, unless you are reprobates?
6 But I trust that you shall know that we are not reprobates.

7 ¶ Now I pray to God that you do no evil; not that we should appear approved, but that you should do that which is honest, though we are as reprobates.
8 For we can do nothing against the truth, but for the truth.
9 For we are glad, when we are weak, and you are strong: and this also we wish, *even* your perfection.
10 Therefore I write these things being absent, lest being present I should use sharpness, according to the power which the Lord has given me to edification, and not to destruction.
11 ¶ Finally, brethren, farewell. Be perfect, be of good comfort, be of one mind, live in peace; and the God of love and peace shall be with you.
12 Greet one another with a holy kiss.
13 All the saints salute you.
14 The grace of the Lord Yahshua the Messiah, and the love of God, and the communion of the Holy Ghost, *be* with you all. Amen. <<*The second epistle to the Corinthians was written from Philippi, a city of Macedonia, by Titus and Lucas.*>>

Galatians

Galatians 1

1:1 ¶ Paul, an apostle, (not of men, neither by man, but by Yahshua the Messiah, and God the Father, who raised him from the dead;)
2 And all the brethren which are with me, to the congregations of Galatia:
3 Grace *be* to you and peace from God the Father, and *from* our Lord Yahshua the Messiah,
4 Who gave himself for our sins, that he might deliver us from this present evil world, according to the will of God and our Father:
5 To whom *be* glory forever and ever. Amen.
6 ¶ I marvel that you are so soon removed from him that called you into the grace of the Messiah unto another gospel:
7 Which is not another; but there are some that trouble you, and would pervert the gospel of the Messiah.
8 But though we, or an angel from heaven, preach any other gospel to you than that which we have preached to you, let him be accursed.
9 As we said before, so say I now again, If any *man* preaches any other gospel to you than that you have received, let him be accursed.
10 ¶ For do I now persuade men, or God? or do I seek to please men? for if I yet pleased men, I should not be the servant of the Messiah.
11 But I certify you, brethren, that the gospel which was preached of me is not after man.
12 For I neither received it of man, neither was I taught *it*, but by the revelation of Yahshua the Messiah.
13 For you have heard of my conversation in time past in the Jews' religion, how that beyond measure I persecuted the congregation of God, and wasted it:
14 And profited in the Jews' religion above many my equals in my own nation, being more exceedingly zealous of the traditions of my fathers.
15 But when it pleased God, who separated me from my mother's womb, and called *me* by his grace,
16 To reveal his Son in me, that I might preach him among the heathen; immediately I conferred not with flesh and blood:
17 Neither went I up to Jerusalem to them which were apostles before me; but I went into Arabia, and returned again to Damascus.
18 Then after three years I went up to Jerusalem to see Peter, and stayed with him fifteen days.
19 But others of the apostles saw I none, except James the Lord's brother.
20 Now the things which I write to you, behold, before God, I lie not.
21 Afterward I came into the regions of Syria and Cilicia;
22 And was unknown by face to the congregations of Judaea which were in the Messiah:
23 But they had heard only, That he which persecuted us in times past now preaches the faith which once he destroyed.
24 And they glorified God in me.

Galatians 2

2:1 ¶ Then fourteen years after I went up again to Jerusalem with Barnabas, and took Titus with *me* also.
2 And I went up by revelation, and communicated to them that gospel which I preach among the Gentiles, but privately to them which were of reputation, lest by any means I should run, or had run, in vain.
3 But not even Titus, who was with me, being a Greek, was compelled to be circumcised:
4 And that because of false brethren secretly brought in, who came in privately to spy out our liberty which we have in the Messiah Yahshua, that they might bring us into bondage:
5 To whom we gave place by subjection, no, not for an hour; that the truth of the gospel might continue with you.
6 But of these who seemed to be something, (whatever they were, it makes no matter to me: God accepts no man's person:) for they who seemed *to be something* in conference added nothing to me:
7 But *on the* contrary, when they saw that the gospel of the uncircumcision was committed unto me, as *the gospel* of the circumcision *was* unto Peter;
8 (For he that worked effectually in Peter to the apostleship of the circumcision, the same was mighty in me toward the Gentiles:)
9 And when James, Cephas, and John, who seemed to be pillars, perceived the grace that was given to me, they gave to me and Barnabas the right hands of fellowship; that we *should go* to the heathen, and they to the circumcision.

Galatians 2

10 Only *they would* that we should remember the poor; the same which I also was forward to do.
11 ¶ But when Peter had come to Antioch, I withstood him to the face, because he was to be blamed.
12 For before that certain came from James, he did eat with the Gentiles: but when they had come, he withdrew and separated himself, fearing them which were of the circumcision.
13 And the other Jews acted hypocritically likewise with him; insomuch that Barnabas also was carried away with their hypocrisy.
14 But when I saw that they walked not uprightly according to the truth of the gospel, I said to Peter before *them* all, If you, being a Jew, live after the manner of Gentiles, and not as do the Jews, why compel you the Gentiles to live as do the Jews?
15 We *who are* Jews by nature, and not sinners of the Gentiles,
16 Knowing that a man is not justified by the works of the law, but by the faith of Yahshua the Messiah, even we have believed in Yahshua the Messiah, that we might be justified by the faith of the Messiah, and not by the works of the law: for by the works of the law shall no flesh be justified.
17 But if, while we seek to be justified by the Messiah, we ourselves also are found sinners, *is* therefore the Messiah the minister of sin? God forbid.
18 For if I build again the things which I destroyed, I make myself a transgressor.
19 For I through the law am dead to the law, that I might live unto God.
20 I am crucified with the Messiah: nevertheless I live; yet not I, but the Messiah lives in me: and the life which I now live in the flesh I live by the faith of the Son of God, who loved me, and gave himself for me.
21 I do not frustrate the grace of God: for if righteousness *comes* by the law, then the Messiah is dead in vain.

Galatians 3

3:1 ¶ O foolish Galatians, who has bewitched you, that you should not obey the truth, before whose eyes Yahshua the Messiah has been evidently set forth, crucified among you?
2 This only would I learn of you, Received you the Spirit by the works of the law, or by the hearing of faith?
3 Are you so foolish? having begun in the Spirit, are you now made perfect by the flesh?
4 Have you suffered so many things in vain? if *it is* yet in vain?
5 He therefore that ministers to you the Spirit, and works miracles among you, *does he it* by the works of the law, or by the hearing of faith?
6 ¶ Even as Abraham believed God *Yahweh*, and it was accounted to him for righteousness.
7 Know you therefore that they which are of faith, the same are the children of Abraham.
8 And the scripture, foreseeing that God would justify the heathen through faith, preached before the gospel to Abraham, *saying*, In you shall all nations be blessed.
9 So then they which are of faith are blessed with faithful Abraham.
10 For as many as are of the works of the law are under the curse: for it is written, Cursed *is* every one that continues not in all things which are written in the book of the law to do them.
11 But that no man is justified by the law in the sight of God, *it is* evident: for, The just shall live by faith.
12 And the law is not of faith: but, The man that does them shall live in them.
13 The Messiah has redeemed us from the curse of the law, being made a curse for us: for it is written, Cursed *is* every one that hangs on a tree:
14 That the blessing of Abraham might come on the Gentiles through Yahshua the Messiah; that we might receive the promise of the Spirit through faith.
15 Brethren, I speak after the manner of men; Though *it is* but a man's covenant, yet *if it is* confirmed, no man annuls, or adds thereto.
16 Now to Abraham and his seed were the promises made. He said not, And to seeds, as of many; but as of one, And to your seed, which is the Messiah.
17 And this I say, *that* the covenant, that was confirmed before of God in the Messiah, the law, which was four hundred and thirty years after, cannot annul, that it should make the promise of no effect.
18 For if the inheritance *is* of the law, *it is* no more of promise: but God gave *it* to Abraham by promise.
19 ¶ What then *serves* the law? It was added because of transgressions, till the seed should come to whom the promise was made; *and it was* ordained by angels in the hand of a mediator.
20 Now a mediator is not *a mediator* of one, but God is one.
21 *Is* the law then against the promises of God? God forbid: for if there had been a law given which could have given life, truly righteousness should have been by the law.
22 But the scripture has concluded all under sin, that the promise by faith of Yahshua the Messiah might be given to them that believe.
23 But before faith came, we were kept under the law, shut up to the faith which should afterward be revealed.
24 Therefore the law was our schoolmaster *to bring us* to the Messiah, that we might be justified by faith.
25 But after that faith has come, we are no longer under a schoolmaster.
26 For you are all the children of God by faith in the Messiah Yahshua.
27 For as many of you as have been baptized into the Messiah have put on the Messiah.
28 There is neither Jew nor Greek, there is neither bond nor free, there is neither male nor female: for you are all one in the Messiah Yahshua.
29 And if you *are* the Messiah's, then are you Abraham's seed, and heirs according to the promise.

Galatians 4

4:1 ¶ Now I say, *That* the heir, as long as he is a child, differs nothing from a servant, though he is lord of all;
2 But is under tutors and governors until the time appointed by the father.
3 Even so we, when we were children, were in bondage under the elements of the world:
4 But when the fullness of the time had come, God sent forth his Son, made of a woman, made under the law,
5 To redeem them that were under the law, that we might receive the adoption of sons.
6 And because you are sons, God has sent forth the Spirit of his Son into your hearts, crying, Abba, Father.
7 Therefore you are no more a servant, but a son; and if a son, then an heir of God through the Messiah.
8 ¶ However then, when you knew not God, you did service to them which by nature are no gods.
9 But now, after that you have known God, or rather are known of God, how turn you again to the weak and beggarly elements, whereunto you desire again to be in bondage?
10 You observe days, and months, and times, and years.
11 I am afraid for you, lest I have bestowed upon you labor in vain.
12 ¶ Brethren, I beseech you, be as I *am*; for I *am* as you *are*: you have not injured me at all.
13 You know how through infirmity of the flesh I preached the gospel to you at the first.
14 And my temptation which was in my flesh you despised not, nor rejected; but received me as an angel of God, *even* as the Messiah Yahshua.
15 Where is then the blessedness you spoke of? for I bear you record, that, if *it had been* possible, you would have plucked out your own eyes, and have given them to me.
16 Have I therefore become your enemy, because I tell you the truth?
17 ¶ They zealously affect you, *but* not well; yes, they would exclude you, that you might affect them.
18 But *it is* good to be zealously affected always in *a* good *thing*, and not only when I am present with you.
19 ¶ My little children, of whom I labor in birth again until the Messiah is formed in you,
20 I desire to be present with you now, and to change my voice; for I stand in doubt of you.
21 ¶ Tell me, you that desire to be under the law, do you not hear the law?
22 For it is written, that Abraham had two sons, the one by a bondmaid, the other by a free woman.
23 But he *who was* of the bondwoman was born after the flesh; but he of the free woman *was* by promise.
24 Which things are an allegory: for these are the two covenants; the one from the mount Sinai, which genders to bondage, which is Hagar.
25 For this Hagar is mount Sinai in Arabia, and answers to Jerusalem which now is, and is in bondage with her children.
26 But Jerusalem which is above is free, which is the mother of us all.
27 For it is written, Rejoice, *you* barren that bear not; break forth and cry, you that labor not: for the desolate has many more children than she which has a husband.
28 Now we, brethren, as Isaac was, are the children of promise.
29 But as then he that was born after the flesh persecuted him *that was born* after the Spirit, even so *it is* now.
30 Nevertheless what says the scripture? Cast out the bondwoman and her son: for the son of the bondwoman shall not be heir with the son of the free woman.
31 So then, brethren, we are not children of the bondwoman, but of the free.

Galatians 5

5:1 ¶ Stand fast therefore in the liberty with which the Messiah has made us free, and be not entangled again with the yoke of bondage.
2 Behold, I Paul say to you, that if you are circumcised, the Messiah shall profit you nothing.
3 For I testify again to every man that is circumcised, that he is a debtor to do the whole law.
4 The Messiah has become of no effect to you, whoever of you are justified by the law; you are fallen from grace.
5 For we through the Spirit wait for the hope of righteousness by faith.
6 For in Yahshua the Messiah neither circumcision avails anything, nor uncircumcision; but faith which works by love.
7 You did run well; who did hinder you that you should not obey the truth?
8 This persuasion *comes* not from him that calls you.
9 A little leaven leavens the whole lump.
10 I have confidence in you through the Lord, that you will be none otherwise minded: but he that troubles you shall bear his judgment, whoever he is.
11 And I, brethren, if I yet preach circumcision, why do I yet suffer persecution? then is the offense of the cross ceased.
12 I would they were even cut off which trouble you.
13 ¶ For, brethren, you have been called to liberty; only *use* not liberty for an occasion to the flesh, but by love serve one another.
14 For all the law is fulfilled in one word, *even* in this; You shall love your neighbor as yourself.
15 But if you bite and devour one another, take heed that you are not consumed one of another.
16 *This* I say then, Walk in the Spirit, and you shall not fulfill the lust of the flesh.
17 For the flesh lusts against the Spirit, and the Spirit against the flesh: and these are contrary the one to the other: so that you cannot do the things that you would.

Galatians 5

18 But if you are led of the Spirit, you are not under the law.
19 Now the works of the flesh are manifest, which are *these*; Adultery, fornication, uncleanness, lasciviousness,
20 Idolatry, witchcraft, hatred, variance, jealousies, wrath, strife, seditions, heresies,
21 Envyings, murders, drunkenness, revelings, and such like: of the which I tell you before, as I have also told *you* in time past, that they which do such things shall not inherit the kingdom of God.
22 But the fruit of the Spirit is love, joy, peace, longsuffering, gentleness, goodness, faith,
23 Meekness, temperance: against such there is no law.
24 And they that are the Messiah's have crucified the flesh with the affections and lusts.
25 If we live in the Spirit, let us also walk in the Spirit.
26 Let us not be desirous of vain glory, provoking one another, envying one another.

Galatians 6

6:1 ¶ Brethren, if a man is overtaken in a fault, you which are spiritual, restore such a one in the spirit of meekness; considering yourself, lest you also be tempted.
2 Bear you one another's burdens, and so fulfill the law of the Messiah.
3 For if a man thinks himself to be something, when he is nothing, he deceives himself.
4 But let every man prove his own work, and then shall he have rejoicing in himself alone, and not in another.
5 For every man shall bear his own burden.
6 Let him that is taught in the word communicate to him that teaches in all good things.
7 Be not deceived; God is not mocked: for whatever a man sows, that shall he also reap.
8 For he that sows to his flesh shall of the flesh reap corruption; but he that sows to the Spirit shall of the Spirit reap life everlasting.
9 And let us not be weary in well doing: for in due season we shall reap, if we faint not.
10 As we have therefore opportunity, let us do good to all *men*, especially to them who are of the household of faith.
11 ¶ You see how large a letter I have written to you with my own hand.
12 As many as desire to make a fair show in the flesh, they constrain you to be circumcised; only lest they should suffer persecution for the cross of the Messiah.
13 For neither they themselves who are circumcised keep the law; but desire to have you circumcised, that they may glory in your flesh.
14 But God forbid that I should glory, save in the cross of our Lord Yahshua the Messiah, by whom the world is crucified unto me, and I unto the world.
15 For in the Messiah Yahshua neither circumcision avails anything, nor uncircumcision, but a new creature.
16 And as many as walk according to this rule, peace *be* on them, and mercy, and upon the Israel of God.
17 From now on let no man trouble me: for I bear in my body the marks of the Lord Yahshua.
18 Brethren, the grace of our Lord Yahshua the Messiah *be* with your spirit. Amen. <<*To the* Galatians written from Rome.>>

Ephesians

Ephesians 1

1:1 ¶ Paul, an apostle of Yahshua the Messiah by the will of God, to the saints which are at Ephesus, and to the faithful in the Messiah Yahshua:
2 Grace *be* to you, and peace, from God our Father, and *from* the Lord Yahshua the Messiah.
3 ¶ Blessed *be* the God and Father of our Lord Yahshua the Messiah, who has blessed us with all spiritual blessings in heavenly *places* in the Messiah:
4 According as he has chosen us in him before the foundation of the world, that we should be holy and without blame before him in love:
5 Having predestinated us to the adoption of children by Yahshua the Messiah to himself, according to the good pleasure of his will,
6 To the praise of the glory of his grace, wherein he has made us accepted in the beloved.
7 In whom we have redemption through his blood, the forgiveness of sins, according to the riches of his grace;
8 Wherein he has abounded toward us in all wisdom and prudence;
9 Having made known to us the mystery of his will, according to his good pleasure which he has purposed in himself:
10 That in the dispensation of the fullness of times he might gather together in one all things in the Messiah, both which are in heaven, and which are on earth; *even* in him:
11 In whom also we have obtained an inheritance, being predestinated according to the purpose of him who works all things after the counsel of his own will:
12 That we should be to the praise of his glory, who first trusted in the Messiah.
13 In whom you also *trusted*, after that you heard the word of truth, the gospel of your salvation: in whom also after that you believed, you were sealed with that holy Spirit of promise,
14 Which is the earnest of our inheritance until the redemption of the purchased possession, to the praise of his glory.
15 ¶ Therefore I also, after I heard of your faith in the Lord Yahshua, and love unto all the saints,
16 Cease not to give thanks for you, making mention of you in my prayers;
17 That the God of our Lord Yahshua the Messiah, the Father of glory, may give to you the spirit of wisdom and revelation in the knowledge of him:

18 The eyes of your understanding being enlightened; that you may know what is the hope of his calling, and what *are* the riches of the glory of his inheritance in the saints,
19 And what *is* the exceeding greatness of his power toward us who believe, according to the working of his mighty power,
20 Which he worked in the Messiah, when he raised him from the dead, and set *him* at his own right hand in the heavenly *places*,
21 Far above all principality, and power, and might, and dominion, and every name that is named, not only in this world, but also in that which is to come:
22 And has put all *things* under his feet, and gave him *to be* the head over all *things* to the congregation,
23 Which is his body, the fullness of him that fills all in all.

Ephesians 2

2:1 ¶ And you *has he quickened*, who were dead in trespasses and sins;
2 Wherein in time past you walked according to the course of this world, according to the prince of the power of the air, the spirit that now works in the children of disobedience:
3 Among whom also we all had our conversation in times past in the lusts of our flesh, fulfilling the desires of the flesh and of the mind; and were by nature the children of wrath, even as others.
4 ¶ But God, who is rich in mercy, for his great love with which he loved us,
5 Even when we were dead in sins, has quickened us together with the Messiah, (by grace you are saved;)
6 And has raised *us* up together, and made *us* sit together in heavenly *places* in the Messiah Yahshua:
7 That in the ages to come he might show the exceeding riches of his grace in *his* kindness toward us through the Messiah Yahshua.
8 For by grace are you saved through faith; and that not of yourselves: *it is* the gift of God:
9 Not of works, lest any man should boast.
10 For we are his workmanship, created in the Messiah Yahshua unto good works, which God has before ordained that we should walk in them.
11 ¶ Therefore remember, that you *being* in time past Gentiles in the flesh, who are called Uncircumcision by that which is called the Circumcision in the flesh made by hands;
12 That at that time you were without the Messiah, being aliens from the commonwealth of Israel, and strangers from the covenants of promise, having no hope, and without God in the world:
13 But now in the Messiah Yahshua you who sometimes were far off are made near by the blood of the Messiah.
14 ¶ For he is our peace, who has made both one, and has broken down the middle wall of partition *between us*;
15 Having abolished in his flesh the enmity, *even* the law of commandments *contained* in ordinances; for to make in himself of two one new man, *so* making peace;
16 And that he might reconcile both to God in one body by the cross, having slain the enmity thereby:
17 And came and preached peace to you which were afar off, and to them that were near.
18 For through him we both have access by one Spirit to the Father.
19 Now therefore you are no more strangers and foreigners, but fellow citizens with the saints, and of the household of God;
20 And are built upon the foundation of the apostles and prophets, Yahshua the Messiah himself being the chief corner *stone*;
21 In whom all the building fitly framed together grows unto a holy temple in the Lord:
22 In whom you also are built together for a habitation of God through the Spirit.

Ephesians 3

3:1 ¶ For this cause I Paul, the prisoner of Yahshua the Messiah for you Gentiles,
2 If you have heard of the dispensation of the grace of God which is given me toward you:
3 How that by revelation he made known to me the mystery; (as I wrote before in few words,
4 Whereby, when you read, you may understand my knowledge in the mystery of the Messiah)
5 Which in other ages was not made known to the sons of men, as it is now revealed to his holy apostles and prophets by the Spirit;
6 That the Gentiles should be fellow heirs, and of the same body, and partakers of his promise in the Messiah by the gospel:
7 Whereof I was made a minister, according to the gift of the grace of God given to me by the effectual working of his power.
8 Unto me, who am less than the least of all saints, is this grace given, that I should preach among the Gentiles the unsearchable riches of the Messiah;
9 And to make all *men* see what *is* the fellowship of the mystery, which from the beginning of the world has been hidden in God, who created all things by Yahshua the Messiah:
10 To the intent that now unto the principalities and powers in heavenly *places* might be known by the congregation the manifold wisdom of God,
11 According to the eternal purpose which he purposed in the Messiah Yahshua our Lord:
12 In whom we have boldness and access with confidence by the faith of him.
13 Therefore I desire that you faint not at my tribulations for you, which is your glory.
14 ¶ For this cause I bow my knees to the Father of our Lord Yahshua the Messiah,

Ephesians 3

15 Of whom the whole family in heaven and earth is named,
16 That he would grant you, according to the riches of his glory, to be strengthened with might by his Spirit in the inner man;
17 That the Messiah may dwell in your hearts by faith; that you, being rooted and grounded in love,
18 May be able to comprehend with all saints what *is* the breadth, and length, and depth, and height;
19 And to know the love of the Messiah, which passes knowledge, that you might be filled with all the fullness of God.
20 Now to him that is able to do exceedingly abundantly above all that we ask or think, according to the power that works in us,
21 Unto him *be* glory in the congregation by the Messiah Yahshua throughout all ages, world without end. Amen.

Ephesians 4

4:1 ¶ I therefore, the prisoner of the Lord, beseech you that you walk worthy of the vocation with which you are called,
2 ¶ With all lowliness and meekness, with longsuffering, forbearing one another in love;
3 Endeavoring to keep the unity of the Spirit in the bond of peace.
4 *There is* one body, and one Spirit, even as you are called in one hope of your calling;
5 One Lord, one faith, one baptism,
6 One God and Father of all, who *is* above all, and through all, and in you all.
7 But to every one of us is given grace according to the measure of the gift of the Messiah.
8 Therefore he said, When he ascended up on high, he led captivity captive, and gave gifts to men.
9 (Now that he ascended, what is it but that he also descended first into the lower parts of the earth?
10 He that descended is the same also that ascended up far above all heavens, that he might fulfill all things.)
11 And he gave some, apostles; and some, prophets; and some, evangelists; and some, pastors and teachers;
12 For the perfecting of the saints, for the work of the ministry, for the edifying of the body of the Messiah:
13 Till we all come in the unity of the faith, and of the knowledge of the Son of God, to a perfect man, to the measure of the stature of the fullness of the Messiah:
14 That we *henceforth* be no more children, tossed to and fro, and carried about with every wind of doctrine, by the sleight of men, *and* cunning craftiness, whereby they lie in wait to deceive;
15 But speaking the truth in love, may grow up into him in all things, which is the head, *even* the Messiah:
16 From whom the whole body fitly joined together and compacted by that which every joint supplies, according to the effectual working in the measure of every part, makes increase of the body to the edifying of itself in love.

17 ¶ This I say therefore, and testify in the Lord, that you henceforth walk not as other Gentiles walk, in the vanity of their mind,
18 Having the understanding darkened, being alienated from the life of God through the ignorance that is in them, because of the blindness of their heart:
19 Who being past feeling have given themselves over to lasciviousness, to work all uncleanness with greediness.
20 But you have not so learned the Messiah;
21 If so be that you have heard him, and have been taught by him, as the truth is in Yahshua:
22 That you put off concerning the former conversation the old man, which is corrupt according to the deceitful lusts;
23 And be renewed in the spirit of your mind;
24 And that you put on the new man, which after God is created in righteousness and true holiness.
25 Therefore putting away lying, speak every man truth with his neighbor: for we are members one of another.
26 Be you angry, and sin not: let not the sun go down upon your wrath:
27 Neither give place to the devil.
28 Let him that stole steal no more: but rather let him labor, working with *his* hands the thing which is good, that he may have to give to him that needs.
29 Let no corrupt communication proceed out of your mouth, but that which is good to the use of edifying, that it may minister grace to the hearers.
30 And grieve not the holy Spirit of God, whereby you are sealed unto the day of redemption.
31 Let all bitterness, and wrath, and anger, and clamor, and evil speaking, be put away from you, with all malice:
32 And be you kind one to another, tenderhearted, forgiving one another, even as God for the Messiah's sake has forgiven you.

Ephesians 5

5:1 ¶ Be you therefore followers of God, as dear children;
2 And walk in love, as the Messiah also has loved us, and has given himself for us an offering and a sacrifice to God for a sweet smelling savor.
3 ¶ But fornication, and all uncleanness, or covetousness, let it not be once named among you, as becomes saints;
4 Neither filthiness, nor foolish talking, nor jesting, which are not convenient: but rather giving of thanks.
5 For this you know, that no whoremonger, nor unclean person, nor covetous man, who is an idolater, has any inheritance in the kingdom of the Messiah and of God.
6 Let no man deceive you with vain words: for because of these things comes the wrath of God upon the children of disobedience.
7 Be not you therefore partakers with them.
8 For you were sometimes darkness, but now *are you* light in the Lord: walk as children of light:
9 (For the fruit of the Spirit *is* in all goodness and righteousness and truth;)
10 Proving what is acceptable unto the Lord.

11 And have no fellowship with the unfruitful works of darkness, but rather reprove *them*.
12 For it is a shame even to speak of those things which are done by them in secret.
13 But all things that are reproved are made manifest by the light: for whatever does make manifest is light.
14 Therefore he said, Awake you that sleep, and arise from the dead, and the Messiah shall give you light.
15 See then that you walk circumspectly, not as fools, but as wise,
16 Redeeming the time, because the days are evil.
17 Therefore be you not unwise, but understanding what the will of the Lord *is*.
18 And be not drunk with wine, wherein is excess; but be filled with the Spirit;
19 Speaking to yourselves in psalms and hymns and spiritual songs, singing and making melody in your heart to the Lord;
20 Giving thanks always for all things to God and the Father in the name of our Lord Yahshua the Messiah;
21 ¶ Submitting yourselves one to another in the fear of God.
22 Wives, submit yourselves to your own husbands, as unto the Lord.
23 For the husband is the head of the wife, even as the Messiah is the head of the congregation: and he is the savior of the body.
24 Therefore as the congregation is subject to the Messiah, so *let* the wives *be* to their own husbands in every thing.
25 Husbands, love your wives, even as the Messiah also loved the congregation, and gave himself for it;
26 That he might sanctify and cleanse it with the washing of water by the word,
27 That he might present it to himself a glorious congregation, not having spot, or wrinkle, or any such thing; but that it should be holy and without blemish.
28 So ought men to love their wives as their own bodies. He that loves his wife loves himself.
29 For no man ever yet hated his own flesh; but nourishes and cherishes it, even as the Lord the congregation:
30 For we are members of his body, of his flesh, and of his bones.
31 For this cause shall a man leave his father and mother, and shall be joined to his wife, and they two shall be one flesh.
32 This is a great mystery: but I speak concerning the Messiah and the congregation.
33 Nevertheless let every one of you in particular so love his wife even as himself; and the wife *see* that she reverence *her* husband.

Ephesians 6

6:1 ¶ Children, obey your parents in the Lord: for this is right.
2 Honor your father and mother; (which is the first commandment with promise;)
3 That it may be well with you, and you may live long on the earth.
4 And, you fathers, provoke not your children to wrath: but bring them up in the nurture and admonition of the Lord.
5 Servants, be obedient to them that are *your* masters according to the flesh, with fear and trembling, in singleness of your heart, as to the Messiah;
6 Not with eyeservice, as men pleasers; but as the servants of the Messiah, doing the will of God from the heart;
7 With good will doing service, as to the Lord, and not to men:
8 Knowing that whatever good thing any man does, the same shall he receive of the Lord, whether *he is* bond or free.
9 And, you masters, do the same things to them, forbearing threatening: knowing that your Master also is in heaven; neither is there respect of persons with him.
10 ¶ Finally, my brethren, be strong in the Lord, and in the power of his might.
11 Put on the whole armor of God, that you may be able to stand against the wiles of the devil.
12 For we wrestle not against flesh and blood, but against principalities, against powers, against the rulers of the darkness of this world, against spiritual wickedness in high *places*.
13 Therefore take to you the whole armor of God, that you may be able to withstand in the evil day, and having done all, to stand.
14 Stand therefore, having your loins girt about with truth, and having on the breastplate of righteousness;
15 And your feet shod with the preparation of the gospel of peace;
16 Above all, taking the shield of faith, with which you shall be able to quench all the fiery darts of the wicked.
17 And take the helmet of salvation, and the sword of the Spirit, which is the word of God:
18 Praying always with all prayer and supplication in the Spirit, and watching thereunto with all perseverance and supplication for all saints;
19 ¶ And for me, that utterance may be given to me, that I may open my mouth boldly, to make known the mystery of the gospel,
20 For which I am an ambassador in bonds: that therein I may speak boldly, as I ought to speak.
21 But that you also may know my affairs, *and* how I do, Tychicus, a beloved brother and faithful minister in the Lord, shall make known to you all things:
22 Whom I have sent to you for the same purpose, that you might know our affairs, and *that* he might comfort your hearts.
23 Peace *be* to the brethren, and love with faith, from God the Father and the Lord Yahshua the Messiah.
24 Grace *be* with all them that love our Lord Yahshua the Messiah in sincerity. Amen. <<*To the* Ephesians written from Rome, by Tychicus.>>

Philippians

Philippians 1

1:1 ¶ Paul and Timotheus, the servants of Yahshua the Messiah, to all the saints in the Messiah Yahshua which are at Philippi, with the overseers and deacons:
2 Grace *be* to you, and peace, from God our Father, and *from* the Lord Yahshua the Messiah.
3 ¶ I thank my God upon every remembrance of you,
4 Always in every prayer of mine for you all making request with joy,
5 For your fellowship in the gospel from the first day until now;
6 Being confident of this very thing, that he which has begun a good work in you will perform *it* until the day of Yahshua the Messiah:
7 ¶ Even as it is right for me to think this of you all, because I have you in my heart; inasmuch as both in my bonds, and in the defense and confirmation of the gospel, you all are partakers of my grace.
8 For God is my record, how greatly I long after you all in the inward affection of Yahshua the Messiah.
9 ¶ And this I pray, that your love may abound yet more and more in knowledge and *in* all judgment;
10 That you may approve things that are excellent; that you may be sincere and without offense till the day of the Messiah;
11 Being filled with the fruits of righteousness, which are by Yahshua the Messiah, to the glory and praise of God.
12 ¶ But I would you should understand, brethren, that the things *which happened* to me have fallen out rather to the furtherance of the gospel;
13 So that my bonds in the Messiah are manifest in all the palace, and in all other *places*;
14 And many of the brethren in the Lord, becoming confident by my bonds, are much more bold to speak the word without fear.
15 Some indeed preach the Messiah even of envy and strife; and some also of good will:
16 The one preaches the Messiah of contention, not sincerely, supposing to add affliction to my bonds:
17 But the other of love, knowing that I am set for the defense of the gospel.
18 What then? notwithstanding, every way, whether in pretense, or in truth, the Messiah is preached; and I therein do rejoice, yes, and will rejoice.
19 For I know that this shall turn to my salvation through your prayer, and the supply of the Spirit of Yahshua the Messiah,
20 According to my earnest expectation and *my* hope, that in nothing I shall be ashamed, but *that* with all boldness, as always, *so* now also the Messiah shall be magnified in my body, whether *it be* by life, or by death.
21 ¶ For to me to live *is* the Messiah, and to die *is* gain.
22 But if I live in the flesh, this *is* the fruit of my labor: yet what I shall choose I know not.
23 For I am in a bind between two, having a desire to depart, and to be with the Messiah; which is far better:
24 Nevertheless to continue in the flesh *is* more needful for you.
25 And having this confidence, I know that I shall remain and continue with you all for your furtherance and joy of faith;
26 That your rejoicing may be more abundant in Yahshua the Messiah for me by my coming to you again.
27 ¶ Only let your conversation be as it becomes the gospel of the Messiah: that whether I come and see you, or else be absent, I may hear of your affairs, that you stand fast in one spirit, with one mind striving together for the faith of the gospel;
28 And in nothing terrified by your adversaries: which is to them an evident token of perdition, but to you of salvation, and that of God.
29 For to you it is given in the behalf of the Messiah, not only to believe on him, but also to suffer for his sake;
30 Having the same conflict which you saw in me, and now hear *to be* in me.

Philippians 2

2:1 ¶ If *there is* therefore any consolation in the Messiah, if any comfort of love, if any fellowship of the Spirit, if any inward affections and mercies,
2 Fulfill you my joy, that you be likeminded, having the same love, *being* of one accord, of one mind.
3 *Let* nothing *be done* through strife or vainglory; but in lowliness of mind let each esteem others better than themselves.
4 Look not every man on his own things, but every man also on the things of others.
5 Let this mind be in you, which was also in the Messiah Yahshua:
6 Who, being in the form of God, thought it not robbery to be equal with God:
7 But made himself of no reputation, and took upon him the form of a servant, and was made in the likeness of men:
8 And being found in fashion as a man, he humbled himself, and became obedient unto death, even the death of the cross.
9 Therefore God also has highly exalted him, and given him a name which is above every name:
10 That at the name of Yahshua every knee should bow, of *things* in heaven, and *things* in earth, and *things* under the earth;
11 And *that* every tongue should confess that Yahshua the Messiah *is* Lord, to the glory of God the Father.
12 ¶ Therefore, my beloved, as you have always obeyed, not as in my presence only, but now much more in my absence, work out your own salvation with fear and trembling.
13 For it is God which works in you both to will and to do of *his* good pleasure.

14 ¶ Do all things without murmurings and disputings:
15 That you may be blameless and harmless, the sons of God, without rebuke, in the midst of a crooked and perverse nation, among whom you shine as lights in the world;
16 Holding forth the word of life; that I may rejoice in the day of the Messiah, that I have not run in vain, neither labored in vain.
17 Yes, and if I am offered upon the sacrifice and service of your faith, I joy, and rejoice with you all.
18 For the same cause also do you joy, and rejoice with me.
19 But I trust in the Lord Yahshua to send Timotheus shortly to you, that I also may be of good comfort, when I know your state.
20 For I have no man likeminded, who will naturally care for your state.
21 For all seek their own, not the things which are Yahshua the Messiah's.
22 But you know the proof of him, that, as a son with the father, he has served with me in the gospel.
23 Him therefore I hope to send presently, so soon as I shall see how it will go with me.
24 But I trust in the Lord that I also myself shall come shortly.
25 Yet I supposed it necessary to send to you Epaphroditus, my brother, and companion in labor, and fellow soldier, but your messenger, and he that ministered to my wants.
26 For he longed after you all, and was full of heaviness, because that you had heard that he had been sick.
27 For indeed he was sick near unto death: but God had mercy on him; and not on him only, but on me also, lest I should have sorrow upon sorrow.
28 I sent him therefore the more carefully, that, when you see him again, you may rejoice, and that I may be the less sorrowful.
29 Receive him therefore in the Lord with all gladness; and hold such in reputation:
30 Because for the work of the Messiah he was near unto death, not regarding his life, to supply your lack of service toward me.

Philippians 3

3:1 ¶ Finally, my brethren, rejoice in the Lord. To write the same things to you, to me indeed *is* not grievous, but for you *it is* safe.
2 Beware of dogs, beware of evil workers, beware of the mutilation.
3 For we are the circumcision, which worship God in the spirit, and rejoice in the Messiah Yahshua, and have no confidence in the flesh.
4 ¶ Though I might also have confidence in the flesh. If any other man thinks that he has whereof he might trust in the flesh, I more:
5 Circumcised the eighth day, of the stock of Israel, *of* the tribe of Benjamin, a Hebrew of the Hebrews; as touching the law, a Pharisee;
6 Concerning zeal, persecuting the congregation; touching the righteousness which is in the law, blameless.
7 But what things were gain to me, those I counted loss for the Messiah.
8 Yes doubtless, and I count all things *but* loss for the excellency of the knowledge of the Messiah Yahshua my Lord: for whom I have suffered the loss of all things, and do count them *but* dung, that I may win the Messiah,
9 ¶ And be found in him, not having my own righteousness, which is of the law, but that which is through the faith of the Messiah, the righteousness which is of God by faith:
10 That I may know him, and the power of his resurrection, and the fellowship of his sufferings, being made conformable to his death;
11 If by any means I might attain unto the resurrection of the dead.
12 Not as though I had already attained, either were already perfect: but I follow after, if that I may apprehend that for which also I am apprehended of the Messiah Yahshua.
13 Brethren, I count not myself to have apprehended: but *this* one thing *I do*, forgetting those things which are behind, and reaching forth to those things which are before,
14 I press toward the mark for the prize of the high calling of God in the Messiah Yahshua.
15 ¶ Let us therefore, as many as be perfect, be thus minded: and if in anything you be otherwise minded, God shall reveal even this to you.
16 Nevertheless, whereto we have already attained, let us walk by the same rule, let us mind the same thing.
17 ¶ Brethren, be followers together of me, and mark them which walk so as you have us for an example.
18 (For many walk, of whom I have told you often, and now tell you even weeping, *that they are* the enemies of the cross of the Messiah:
19 Whose end *is* destruction, whose God *is their* belly, and *whose* glory *is* in their shame, who mind earthly things.)
20 For our commonwealth is in heaven; from where also we look for the Savior, the Lord Yahshua the Messiah:
21 Who shall change our vile body, that it may be fashioned like unto his glorious body, according to the working whereby he is able even to subdue all things to himself.

Philippians 4

4:1 ¶ Therefore, my brethren dearly beloved and longed for, my joy and crown, so stand fast in the Lord, *my* dearly beloved.
2 I beseech Euodias, and beseech Syntyche, that they be of the same mind in the Lord.
3 And I entreat you also, true yoke fellow, help those women which labored with me in the gospel, with Clement also, and *with* other my fellow laborers, whose names *are* in the book of life.
4 Rejoice in the Lord always: *and* again I say. Rejoice.
5 Let your moderation be known to all men. The Lord *is* at hand.

Philippians 4

6 Be anxious for nothing; but in every thing by prayer and supplication with thanksgiving let your requests be made known to God.

7 And the peace of God, which passes all understanding, shall keep your hearts and minds through the Messiah Yahshua.

8 Finally, brethren, whatever things are true, whatever things *are* honest, whatever things *are* just, whatever things *are* pure, whatever things *are* lovely, whatever things *are* of good report; if *there is* any virtue, and if *there is* any praise, think on these things.

9 Those things, which you have both learned, and received, and heard, and seen in me, do: and the God of peace shall be with you.

10 ¶ But I rejoiced in the Lord greatly, that now at the last your care of me has flourished again; wherein you were also careful, but you lacked opportunity.

11 Not that I speak in respect of want: for I have learned, in whatever state I am, *therewith* to be content.

12 I know both how to be abased, and I know how to abound: every where and in all things I am instructed both to be full and to be hungry, both to abound and to suffer need.

13 I can do all things through the Messiah which strengthens me.

14 Notwithstanding you have well done, that you did communicate with my affliction.

15 Now you Philippians know also, that in the beginning of the gospel, when I departed from Macedonia, no congregation communicated with me as concerning giving and receiving, but you only.

16 For even in Thessalonica you sent once and again to my necessity.

17 Not because I desire a gift: but I desire fruit that may abound to your account.

18 But I have all, and abound: I am full, having received of Epaphroditus the things *which were sent* from you, an odor of a sweet smell, a sacrifice acceptable, well pleasing to God.

19 But my God shall supply all your need according to his riches in glory by the Messiah Yahshua.

20 ¶ Now to God and our Father *be* glory forever and ever. Amen.

21 Salute every saint in the Messiah Yahshua. The brethren which are with me greet you.

22 All the saints salute you, chiefly they that are of Caesar's household.

23 The grace of our Lord Yahshua the Messiah *be* with you all. Amen. <<*To the* Philippians written from Rome, by Epaphroditus.>>

Colossians

Colossians 1

1:1 ¶ Paul, an apostle of Yahshua the Messiah by the will of God, and Timotheus *our* brother,

2 To the saints and faithful brethren in the Messiah which are at Colosse: Grace *be* to you, and peace, from God our Father and the Lord Yahshua the Messiah.

3 ¶ We give thanks to God and the Father of our Lord Yahshua the Messiah, praying always for you,

4 Since we heard of your faith in the Messiah Yahshua, and of the love *which you have* for all the saints,

5 For the hope which is laid up for you in heaven, whereof you heard before in the word of the truth of the gospel;

6 Which has come to you, as *it is* in all the world; and brings forth fruit, as *it does* also in you, since the day you heard *of it*, and knew the grace of God in truth:

7 As you also learned of Epaphras our dear fellow servant, who is for you a faithful minister of the Messiah;

8 Who also declared to us your love in the Spirit.

9 ¶ For this cause we also, since the day we heard *it*, do not cease to pray for you, and to desire that you might be filled with the knowledge of his will in all wisdom and spiritual understanding;

10 That you might walk worthy of the Lord unto all pleasing *of Him*, being fruitful in every good work, and increasing in the knowledge of God;

11 Strengthened with all might, according to his glorious power, unto all patience and longsuffering with joyfulness;

12 ¶ Giving thanks to the Father, which has made us able to be partakers of the inheritance of the saints in light:

13 Who has delivered us from the power of darkness, and has translated *us* into the kingdom of his dear Son:

14 In whom we have redemption through his blood, *even* the forgiveness of sins:

15 Who is the image of the invisible God, the firstborn of every creature:

16 For by him were all things created, that are in heaven, and that are in earth, visible and invisible, whether *they are* thrones, or dominions, or principalities, or powers: all things were created by him, and for him:

17 And he is before all things, and by him all things consist.

18 And he is the head of the body, the congregation: who is the beginning, the firstborn from the dead; that in all *things* he might have the preeminence.

19 For it pleased *the Father* that in him should all fullness dwell;

20 And, having made peace through the blood of his cross, by him to reconcile all things to himself; by him, *I say*, whether *they are* things in earth, or things in heaven.

21 And you, that were sometimes alienated and enemies in *your* mind by wicked works, yet now has he reconciled

22 In the body of his flesh through death, to present you holy and blameless and above reproach in his sight:

23 If you continue in the faith grounded and settled, and *are* not moved away from the hope of the gospel, which you have heard, *and* which was preached to every creature which is under heaven; whereof I Paul am made a minister;
24 Who now rejoice in my sufferings for you, and fill up that which is behind of the afflictions of the Messiah in my flesh for his body's sake, which is the congregation:
25 Whereof I am made a minister, according to the stewardship of God which is given to me for you, to fulfill the word of God;
26 *Even* the mystery which has been hidden from ages and from generations, but now is made manifest to his saints:
27 To whom God would make known what *are* the riches of the glory of this mystery among the Gentiles; which is the Messiah in you, the hope of glory:
28 Whom we preach, warning every man, and teaching every man in all wisdom; that we may present every man perfect in the Messiah Yahshua:
29 Whereunto I also labor, striving according to his working, which works in me mightily.

Colossians 2

2:1 ¶ For I would that you knew what great conflict I have for you, and *for* them at Laodicea, and *for* as many as have not seen my face in the flesh;
2 That their hearts might be comforted, being knit together in love, and unto all riches of the full assurance of understanding, to the acknowledgement of the mystery of God, and of the Father, and of the Messiah;
3 In whom are hidden all the treasures of wisdom and knowledge.
4 ¶ And this I say, lest any man should beguile you with enticing words.
5 For though I am absent in the flesh, yet am I with you in the spirit, rejoicing and beholding your order, and the steadfastness of your faith in the Messiah.
6 As you have therefore received the Messiah Yahshua the Lord, *so* walk you in him:
7 Rooted and built up in him, and established in the faith, as you have been taught, abounding therein with thanksgiving.
8 Beware lest any man spoils you through philosophy and vain deceit, after the tradition of men, after the rudiments of the world, and not after the Messiah.
9 For in him dwells all the fullness of the Godhead bodily.
10 And you are complete in him, which is the head of all principality and power:
11 In whom also you are circumcised with the circumcision made without hands, in putting off the body of the sins of the flesh by the circumcision of the Messiah:
12 Buried with him in baptism, wherein also you are risen with *him* through the faith of the operation of God, who has raised him from the dead.
13 ¶ And you, being dead in your sins and the uncircumcision of your flesh, has he quickened together with him, having forgiven you all trespasses;
14 Blotting out the handwriting of ordinances that was against us, which was contrary to us, and took it out of the way, nailing it to his cross;
15 *And* having spoiled principalities and powers, he made a show of them openly, triumphing over them in it.
16 ¶ Let no man therefore judge you in food, or in drink, or in respect of a holy day, or of the new moon, or of the sabbath *days*:
17 Which are a shadow of things to come; but the body *is* of the Messiah.
18 Let no man beguile you of your reward in a voluntary humility and worshipping of angels, intruding into those things which he has not seen, vainly puffed up by his fleshly mind,
19 And not holding the Head, from which all the body by joints and bands having nourishment ministered, and knit together, grows with the increase of God.
20 Therefore if you are dead with the Messiah from the rudiments of the world, why, as though living in the world, are you subject to ordinances,
21 (Touch not; taste not; handle not;
22 Which all are to perish with the using;) after the commandments and doctrines of men?
23 Which things have indeed a show of wisdom in arbitrary worship, and humility, and neglecting of the body; not in any honor to the satisfying of the flesh.

Colossians 3

3:1 ¶ If you then are risen with the Messiah, seek those things which are above, where the Messiah sits on the right hand of God.
2 Set your affection on things above, not on things on the earth.
3 For you are dead, and your life is hidden with the Messiah in God.
4 When the Messiah, *who is* our life, shall appear, then shall you also appear with him in glory.
5 ¶ Mortify therefore your members which are upon the earth; fornication, uncleanness, inordinate affection, evil lusts, and covetousness, which is idolatry:
6 For which things' sake the wrath of God comes on the children of disobedience:
7 In which you also walked some time, when you lived in them.
8 ¶ But now you also put off all these; anger, wrath, malice, blasphemy, filthy communication out of your mouth.
9 Lie not one to another, seeing that you have put off the old man with his deeds;
10 And have put on the new *man*, which is renewed in knowledge after the image of him that created him:
11 Where there is neither Greek nor Jew, circumcision nor uncircumcision, Barbarian, Scythian, bond *nor* free: but the Messiah *is* all, and in all.
12 ¶ Put on therefore, as the elect of God, holy and beloved, tender mercies, kindness, humbleness of mind, meekness, longsuffering;

Colossians 3

13 Forbearing one another, and forgiving one another, if any man has a quarrel against any: even as the Messiah forgave you, so also *do* you.
14 And above all these things *put on* charity, which is the bond of perfection.
15 And let the peace of God rule in your hearts, to which also you are called in one body; and be you thankful.
16 Let the word of the Messiah dwell in you richly in all wisdom; teaching and admonishing one another in psalms and hymns and spiritual songs, singing with grace in your hearts to the Lord.
17 And whatever you do in word or deed, *do* all in the name of the Lord Yahshua, giving thanks to God and the Father by him.
18 ¶ Wives, submit yourselves to your own husbands, as it is fit in the Lord.
19 Husbands, love *your* wives, and be not bitter against them.
20 Children, obey *your* parents in all things: for this is well pleasing unto the Lord.
21 Fathers, provoke not your children *to anger*, lest they be discouraged.
22 Servants, obey in all things *your* masters according to the flesh; not with eyeservice, as men pleasers; but in singleness of heart, fearing God:
23 And whatever you do, do *it* heartily, as to the Lord, and not unto men;
24 Knowing that of the Lord you shall receive the reward of the inheritance: for you serve the Lord the Messiah.
25 But he that does wrong shall receive for the wrong which he has done: and there is no respect of persons.

Colossians 4

4:1 ¶ Masters, give to *your* servants that which is just and equal; knowing that you also have a Master in heaven.
2 ¶ Continue in prayer, and watch in the same with thanksgiving;
3 Therewith praying also for us, that God would open unto us a door of utterance, to speak the mystery of the Messiah, for which I am also in bonds:
4 That I may make it manifest, as I ought to speak.
5 ¶ Walk in wisdom toward them that are without, redeeming the time.
6 Let your speech *be* always with grace, seasoned with salt, that you may know how you ought to answer every man.
7 ¶ All my state shall Tychicus declare to you, *who is* a beloved brother, and a faithful minister and fellow servant in the Lord:
8 Whom I have sent to you for the same purpose, that he might know your estate, and comfort your hearts;
9 With Onesimus, a faithful and beloved brother, who is *one* of you. They shall make known to you all things which *are done* here.
10 Aristarchus my fellow prisoner salutes you, and Marcus, sister's son to Barnabas, (touching whom you received commandments: if he comes to you, receive him;)
11 And Jesus, which is called Justus, who are of the circumcision. These only *are my* fellow workers unto the kingdom of God, which have been a comfort to me.
12 Epaphras, who is *one* of you, a servant of the Messiah, salutes you, always laboring fervently for you in prayers, that you may stand perfect and complete in all the will of God.
13 For I bear him record, that he has a great zeal for you, and them *that are* in Laodicea, and them in Hierapolis.
14 Luke, the beloved physician, and Demas, greet you.
15 Salute the brethren which are in Laodicea, and Nymphas, and the congregation which is in his house.
16 And when this epistle is read among you, cause that it be read also in the congregation of the Laodiceans; and that you likewise read the *epistle* from Laodicea.
17 And say to Archippus, Take heed to the ministry which you have received in the Lord, that you fulfill it.
18 The salutation by the hand of me Paul. Remember my bonds. Grace *be* with you. Amen. <<*Written from Rome to Colossians by Tychicus and Onesimus.*>>

1 Thessalonians

1 Thessalonians 1

1:1 ¶ Paul, and Silvanus, and Timotheus, to the congregation of the Thessalonians *which is* in God the Father and *in* the Lord Yahshua the Messiah: Grace *be* to you, and peace, from God our Father, and the Lord Yahshua the Messiah.
2 ¶ We give thanks to God always for you all, making mention of you in our prayers;
3 Remembering without ceasing your work of faith, and labor of love, and patience of hope in our Lord Yahshua the Messiah, in the sight of God and our Father;
4 Knowing, brethren beloved, your election by God.
5 For our gospel came not to you in word only, but also in power, and in the Holy Ghost, and in much assurance; as you know what manner of men we were among you for your sake.
6 ¶ And you became followers of us, and of the Lord, having received the word in much affliction, with joy of the Holy Ghost:
7 So that you were examples to all that believe in Macedonia and Achaia.
8 For from you sounded out the word of the Lord not only in Macedonia and Achaia, but also in every place your faith unto God is spread abroad; so that we need not to speak anything.
9 For they themselves show of us what manner of entering in we had to you, and how you turned to God from idols to serve the living and true God;
10 And to wait for his Son from heaven, whom he raised from the dead, *even* Yahshua, which delivered us from the wrath to come.

1 Thessalonians 2

2:1 ¶ For yourselves, brethren, know our entering in unto you, that it was not in vain:

2 But even after that we had suffered before, and were shamefully treated, as you know, at Philippi, we were bold in our God to speak to you the gospel of God with much contention.

3 For our exhortation *was* not of deceit, nor of uncleanness, nor in guile:

4 But as we were allowed by God to be put in trust with the gospel, even so we speak; not as pleasing men, but God, which tries our hearts.

5 For neither at any time used we flattering words, as you know, nor a cloak of covetousness; God *is* witness:

6 Nor of men sought we glory, neither of you, nor *yet* of others, when we might have been burdensome, as the apostles of the Messiah.

7 ¶ But we were gentle among you, even as a nurse cherishes her children:

8 So being affectionately desirous of you, we were willing to have imparted to you, not the gospel of God only, but also our own souls, because you were dear to us.

9 For you remember, brethren, our labor and hardship: for laboring night and day, because we would not be chargeable to any of you, we preached to you the gospel of God.

10 You *are* witnesses, and God *also*, how holy and justly and blamelessly we behaved ourselves among you that believe:

11 As you know how we exhorted and comforted and charged every one of you, as a father *does* his children,

12 That you would walk worthy of God, who has called you unto his kingdom and glory.

13 ¶ For this cause also thank we God without ceasing, because, when you received the word of God which you heard from us, you received *it* not *as* the word of men, but as it is in truth, the word of God, which effectually works also in you that believe.

14 For you, brethren, became followers of the congregations of God which in Judaea are in the Messiah Yahshua: for you also have suffered like things from your own countrymen, even as they *have* of the Jews:

15 Who both killed the Lord Yahshua, and their own prophets, and have persecuted us; and they please not God, and are contrary to all men:

16 Forbidding us to speak to the Gentiles that they might be saved, to fill up their sins always: for the wrath has come upon them to the utmost.

17 ¶ But we, brethren, being taken from you for a short time in presence, not in heart, endeavored more abundantly to see your face with great desire.

18 Therefore we would have come to you, even I Paul, once and again; but Satan hindered us.

19 For what *is* our hope, or joy, or crown of rejoicing? *Are* not even you in the presence of our Lord Yahshua the Messiah at his coming?

20 For you are our glory and joy.

1 Thessalonians 3

3:1 ¶ Therefore when we could no longer forbear, we thought it good to be left at Athens alone;

2 And sent Timotheus, our brother, and minister of God, and our fellow laborer in the gospel of the Messiah, to establish you, and to comfort you concerning your faith:

3 That no man should be moved by these afflictions: for yourselves know that we are appointed thereunto.

4 For truly, when we were with you, we told you before that we should suffer tribulation; even as it came to pass, and you know.

5 For this cause, when I could no longer forbear, I sent to know your faith, lest by some means the tempter had tempted you, and our labor was in vain.

6 ¶ But now when Timotheus came from you to us, and brought us good tidings of your faith and charity, and that you have good remembrance of us always, desiring greatly to see us, as we also *to see* you:

7 Therefore, brethren, we were comforted over you in all our affliction and distress by your faith:

8 For now we live, if you stand fast in the Lord.

9 For what thanks can we render to God again for you, for all the joy with which we joy for your sakes before our God;

10 Night and day praying exceedingly that we might see your face, and might perfect that which is lacking in your faith?

11 ¶ Now God himself and our Father, and our Lord Yahshua the Messiah, direct our way to you.

12 And the Lord make you to increase and abound in love one toward another, and toward all *men*, even as we *do* toward you:

13 To the end he may establish your hearts blameless in holiness before God, even our Father, at the coming of our Lord Yahshua the Messiah with all his saints.

1 Thessalonians 4

4:1 ¶ Furthermore then we beseech you, brethren, and exhort *you* by the Lord Yahshua, that as you have received from us how you ought to walk and to please God, *so* you would abound more and more.

2 For you know what commandments we gave you by the Lord Yahshua.

3 For this is the will of God, *even* your sanctification, that you should abstain from fornication:

4 That every one of you should know how to possess his vessel in sanctification and honor;

5 Not in the lust of desire, even as the Gentiles which know not God:

6 That no *man* go beyond and defraud his brother in *any* matter: because that the Lord *is* the avenger of all such, as we also have forewarned you and testified.

7 For God has not called us to uncleanness, but to holiness.

1 Thessalonians 4

8 He therefore that despises, despises not man, but God, who has also given to us his holy Spirit.

9 ¶ But as touching brotherly love you need not that I write to you: for you yourselves are taught of God to love one another.

10 And indeed you do it toward all the brethren which are in all Macedonia: but we beseech you, brethren, that you increase more and more;

11 And that you study to be quiet, and to do your own business, and to work with your own hands, as we commanded you;

12 That you may walk honestly toward them that are outside, and *that* you may have lack of nothing.

13 ¶ But I would not have you to be ignorant, brethren, concerning them which are asleep, that you sorrow not, even as others which have no hope.

14 For if we believe that Yahshua died and rose again, even so them also which sleep in Yahshua will God bring with him.

15 For this we say to you by the word of the Lord, that we which are alive *and* remain unto the coming of the Lord shall not prevent them which are asleep.

16 For the Lord himself shall descend from heaven with a shout, with the voice of the archangel, and with the trump of God: and the dead in the Messiah shall rise first:

17 Then we which are alive *and* remain shall be caught up together with them in the clouds, to meet the Lord in the air: and so shall we ever be with the Lord.

18 Therefore comfort one another with these words.

1 Thessalonians 5

5:1 ¶ But of the times and the seasons, brethren, you have no need that I write to you.

2 For yourselves know perfectly that the day of the Lord so comes as a thief in the night.

3 For when they shall say, Peace and safety; then sudden destruction comes upon them, as labor upon a woman with child; and they shall not escape.

4 But you, brethren, are not in darkness, that that day should overtake you as a thief.

5 You are all the children of light, and the children of the day: we are not of the night, nor of darkness.

6 ¶ Therefore let us not sleep, as *do* others; but let us watch and be sober.

7 For they that sleep sleep in the night; and they that are drunken are drunken in the night.

8 But let us, who are of the day, be sober, putting on the breastplate of faith and love; and for a helmet, the hope of salvation.

9 For God has not appointed us to wrath, but to obtain salvation by our Lord Yahshua the Messiah,

10 Who died for us, that, whether we wake or sleep, we should live together with him.

11 ¶ Therefore comfort yourselves together, and edify one another, even as also you do.

12 And we beseech you, brethren, to know them which labor among you, and are over you in the Lord, and admonish you;

13 And to esteem them very highly in love for their work's sake. *And* be at peace among yourselves.

14 Now we exhort you, brethren, warn them that are unruly, comfort the feebleminded, support the weak, be patient toward all *men*.

15 See that none render evil for evil unto any *man*; but ever follow that which is good, both among yourselves, and to all *men*.

16 ¶ Rejoice evermore.

17 Pray without ceasing.

18 In every thing give thanks: for this is the will of God in the Messiah Yahshua concerning you.

19 Quench not the Spirit.

20 Despise not prophesyings.

21 Prove all things; hold fast that which is good.

22 Abstain from all appearance of evil.

23 ¶ And the very God of peace sanctify you wholly; and *I pray God* your whole spirit and soul and body be preserved blameless unto the coming of our Lord Yahshua the Messiah.

24 Faithful *is* he that calls you, who also will do *it*.

25 Brethren, pray for us.

26 Greet all the brethren with a holy kiss.

27 I charge you by the Lord that this epistle be read to all the holy brethren.

28 The grace of our Lord Yahshua the Messiah *be* with you. Amen. <<*The first epistle to the Thessalonians was written from Athens.*>>

2 Thessalonians

2 Thessalonians 1

1:1 ¶ Paul, and Silvanus, and Timotheus, to the congregation of the Thessalonians in God our Father and the Lord Yahshua the Messiah:

2 Grace to you, and peace, from God our Father and the Lord Yahshua the Messiah.

3 We are bound to thank God always for you, brethren, as it is fitting, because that your faith grows exceedingly, and the charity of every one of you all toward each other abounds;

4 So that we ourselves glory in you in the congregations of God for your patience and faith in all your persecutions and tribulations that you endure:

5 ¶ *Which is* a manifest token of the righteous judgment of God, that you may be counted worthy of the kingdom of God, for which you also suffer:

6 Seeing *it is* a righteous thing with God to recompense tribulation to them that trouble you;

7 And to you who are troubled rest with us, when the Lord Yahshua shall be revealed from heaven with his mighty angels,

8 In flaming fire taking vengeance on them that know not God, and that obey not the gospel of our Lord Yahshua the Messiah:
9 Who shall be punished with everlasting destruction from the presence of the Lord, and from the glory of his power;
10 When he shall come to be glorified in his saints, and to be admired in all them that believe (because our testimony among you was believed) in that day.
11 ¶ Therefore also we pray always for you, that our God would count you worthy of *this* calling, and fulfill all the good pleasure of *his* goodness, and the work of faith with power:
12 That the name of our Lord Yahshua the Messiah may be glorified in you, and you in him, according to the grace of our God and the Lord Yahshua the Messiah.

2 Thessalonians 2

2:1 ¶ Now we beseech you, brethren, by the coming of our Lord Yahshua the Messiah, and *by* our gathering together to him,
2 That you be not soon shaken in mind, or be troubled, neither by spirit, nor by word, nor by letter as from us, as that the day of the Messiah is at hand.
3 ¶ Let no man deceive you by any means: for *that day shall not come*, unless there comes a falling away first, and that man of sin is revealed, the son of perdition;
4 Who opposes and exalts himself above all that is called God, or that is worshipped; so that he as God sits in the temple of God, showing himself that he is God.
5 Remember you not, that, when I was yet with you, I told you these things?
6 And now you know what restrains that he might be revealed in his time.
7 For the mystery of iniquity does already work: only he who now restrains *will restrain*, until he is taken out of the way.
8 And then shall that Wicked be revealed, whom the Lord shall consume with the spirit of his mouth, and shall destroy with the brightness of his coming:
9 *Even him*, whose coming is after the working of Satan with all power and signs and lying wonders,
10 And with all deceivableness of unrighteousness in them that perish; because they received not the love of the truth, that they might be saved.
11 And for this cause God shall send them strong delusion, that they should believe a lie:
12 That they all might be damned who believed not the truth, but had pleasure in unrighteousness.
13 ¶ But we are bound to give thanks always to God for you, brethren beloved of the Lord, because God has from the beginning chosen you to salvation through sanctification of the Spirit and belief of the truth:
14 Whereunto he called you by our gospel, to the obtaining of the glory of our Lord Yahshua the Messiah.

15 Therefore, brethren, stand fast, and hold the traditions which you have been taught, whether by word, or our epistle.
16 ¶ Now our Lord Yahshua the Messiah himself, and God, even our Father, which has loved us, and has given *us* everlasting consolation and good hope through grace,
17 Comfort your hearts, and establish you in every good word and work.

2 Thessalonians 3

3:1 ¶ Finally, brethren, pray for us, that the word of the Lord may have *free* course, and be glorified, even as *it is* with you:
2 And that we may be delivered from unreasonable and wicked men: for all *men* have not faith.
3 But the Lord is faithful, who shall establish you, and keep *you* from evil.
4 And we have confidence in the Lord touching you, that you both do and will do the things which we command you.
5 And the Lord direct your hearts into the love of God, and into the patient waiting for the Messiah.
6 ¶ Now we command you, brethren, in the name of our Lord Yahshua the Messiah, that you withdraw yourselves from every brother that walks disorderly, and not after the tradition which he received from us.
7 For yourselves know how you ought to follow us: for we behaved not ourselves disorderly among you;
8 Neither did we eat any man's bread for nothing; but worked with labor and hardship night and day, that we might not be chargeable to any of you:
9 Not because we have not power, but to make ourselves an example to you to follow us.
10 For even when we were with you, this we commanded you, that if any would not work, neither should he eat.
11 For we hear that there are some which walk among you disorderly, working not at all, but are busybodies.
12 Now them that are such we command and exhort by our Lord Yahshua the Messiah, that with quietness they work, and eat their own bread.
13 But you, brethren, be not weary in well doing.
14 And if any man obeys not our word by this epistle, note that man, and have no company with him, that he may be ashamed.
15 Yet count *him* not as an enemy, but admonish *him* as a brother.
16 ¶ Now the Lord of peace himself give you peace always by all means. The Lord *be* with you all.
17 The salutation of Paul with my own hand, which is the token in every epistle: so I write.
18 The grace of our Lord Yahshua the Messiah *be* with you all. Amen. <<*The second epistle to the Thessalonians was written from Athens.*>>

1 Timothy

1 Timothy 1

1:1 ¶ Paul, an apostle of Yahshua the Messiah by the commandment of God our Savior, and Lord Yahshua the Messiah, *which is* our hope;
2 To Timothy, *my* own son in the faith: Grace, mercy, *and* peace, from God our Father and Yahshua the Messiah our Lord.
3 As I sought you to remain still at Ephesus, when I went into Macedonia, that you might charge some that they teach no other doctrine,
4 Neither give heed to fables and endless genealogies, which minister questions, rather than godly edifying which is in faith: *so do.*
5 ¶ Now the end of the commandment is charity out of a pure heart, and *of* a good conscience, and *of* faith unfeigned:
6 From which some having swerved have turned aside to vain talking;
7 Desiring to be teachers of the law; understanding neither what they say, nor whereof they affirm.
8 But we know that the law *is* good, if a man uses it lawfully;
9 Knowing this, that the law is not made for a righteous man, but for the lawless and disobedient, for the ungodly and for sinners, for unholy and profane, for murderers of fathers and murderers of mothers, for manslayers,
10 For whoremongers, for those who lie with males as with females, for kidnappers, for liars, for perjured persons, and if there is any other thing that is contrary to sound doctrine;
11 According to the glorious gospel of the blessed God, which was committed to my trust.
12 ¶ And I thank the Messiah Yahshua our Lord, who has enabled me, for that he counted me faithful, putting me into the ministry;
13 Who was before a blasphemer, and a persecutor, and injurious: but I obtained mercy, because I did *it* ignorantly in unbelief.
14 And the grace of our Lord was exceedingly abundant with faith and love which is in the Messiah Yahshua.
15 This *is* a faithful saying, and worthy of all acceptance, that the Messiah Yahshua came into the world to save sinners; of whom I am chief.
16 However for this cause I obtained mercy, that in me first Yahshua the Messiah might show forth all longsuffering, for a pattern to them which should hereafter believe on him to life everlasting.
17 Now unto the King eternal, immortal, invisible, the only wise God, *be* honor and glory forever and ever. Amen.
18 ¶ This charge I commit unto you, son Timothy, according to the prophecies which went before upon you, that you by them might war a good warfare;
19 Holding faith, and a good conscience; which some having put away concerning faith have made shipwreck:
20 Of whom is Hymenaeus and Alexander; whom I have delivered to Satan, that they may learn not to blaspheme.

1 Timothy 2

2:1 ¶ I exhort therefore, that, first of all, supplications, prayers, intercessions, *and* giving of thanks, be made for all men;
2 For kings, and *for* all that are in authority; that we may lead a quiet and peaceable life in all godliness and honesty.
3 For this *is* good and acceptable in the sight of God our Savior;
4 Who will have all men to be saved, and to come to the knowledge of the truth.
5 For *there is* one God, and one mediator between God and men, the man the Messiah Yahshua;
6 Who gave himself a ransom for all, to be testified in due time.
7 Whereunto I am ordained a preacher, and an apostle, (I speak the truth in the Messiah, *and* lie not;) a teacher of the Gentiles in faith and truth.
8 I will therefore that men pray every where, lifting up holy hands, without wrath and doubting.
9 ¶ In like manner also, that women adorn themselves in modest apparel, with reverence and self-control; not with braided hair, or gold, or pearls, or costly array;
10 But (which becomes women professing godliness) with good works.
11 Let the woman learn in silence with all subjection.
12 But I permit not a woman to teach, nor to usurp authority over the man, but to be in silence.
13 For Adam was first formed, then Eve.
14 And Adam was not deceived, but the woman being deceived was in the transgression.
15 Notwithstanding she shall be saved in childbearing, if they continue in faith and charity and holiness with self-control.

1 Timothy 3

3:1 ¶ This *is* a true saying, If a man desires the office of an overseer, he desires a good work.
2 An overseer then must be blameless, the husband of one wife, vigilant, sober, of good behavior, given to hospitality, apt to teach;
3 Not given to wine, no striker, not greedy of filthy profit; but patient, not a brawler, not covetous;
4 One that rules well his own house, having his children in subjection with all gravity;
5 (For if a man knows not how to rule his own house, how shall he take care of the congregation of God?)
6 Not a novice, lest being lifted up with pride he falls into the condemnation of the devil.
7 Moreover he must have a good report of them which are outside; lest he falls into reproach and the snare of the devil.

8 ¶ Likewise *must* the deacons *be* devout, not double tongued, not given to much wine, not greedy of filthy profit;

9 Holding the mystery of the faith in a pure conscience.

10 And let these also first be proven; then let them use the office of a deacon, being *found* blameless.

11 Even so *must their* wives *be* devout, not slanderers, sober, faithful in all things.

12 Let the deacons be the husbands of one wife, ruling their children and their own houses well.

13 For they that have used the office of a deacon well purchase to themselves a good degree, and great boldness in the faith which is in the Messiah Yahshua.

14 ¶ These things write I to you, hoping to come to you shortly:

15 But if I tarry long, that you may know how you ought to behave yourself in the house of God, which is the congregation of the living God, the pillar and ground of the truth.

16 And without controversy great is the mystery of godliness: God was manifest in the flesh, justified in the Spirit, seen of angels, preached to the Gentiles, believed on in the world, received up into glory.

1 Timothy 4

4:1 ¶ Now the Spirit speaks expressly, that in the latter times some shall depart from the faith, giving heed to seducing spirits, and doctrines of devils;

2 Speaking lies in hypocrisy; having their conscience seared with a hot iron;

3 Forbidding to marry, *and commanding* to abstain from foods, which God has created to be received with thanksgiving of them which believe and know the truth.

4 For every creature of God *is* good, and nothing to be refused, if it is received with thanksgiving:

5 For it is sanctified by the word of God and prayer.

6 ¶ If you put the brethren in remembrance of these things, you shall be a good minister of Yahshua the Messiah, nourished up in the words of faith and of good doctrine, whereunto you have attained.

7 But refuse profane and old wives' fables, and exercise yourself *rather* unto godliness.

8 For bodily exercise profits little: but godliness is profitable to all things, having promise of the life that now is, and of that which is to come.

9 This *is* a faithful saying and worthy of all acceptance.

10 For therefore we both labor and suffer reproach, because we trust in the living God, who is the Savior of all men, especially of those that believe.

11 These things command and teach.

12 Let no man despise your youth; but be you an example to the believers, in word, in conversation, in charity, in spirit, in faith, in purity.

13 Till I come, give attendance to reading, to exhortation, to doctrine.

14 Neglect not the gift that is in you, which was given you by prophecy, with the laying on of the hands of the presbytery.

15 Meditate upon these things; give yourself wholly to them; that your profiting may appear to all.

16 Take heed to yourself, and to the doctrine; continue in them: for in doing this you shall both save yourself, and them that hear you.

1 Timothy 5

5:1 ¶ Rebuke not an elder, but treat *him* as a father; *and* the younger men as brethren;

2 The elder women as mothers; the younger as sisters, with all purity.

3 ¶ Honor widows that are widows indeed.

4 But if any widow have children or nephews, let them learn first to show piety at home, and to repay their parents: for that is good and acceptable before God.

5 Now she that is a widow indeed, and desolate, trusts in God, and continues in supplications and prayers night and day.

6 But she that lives in pleasure is dead while she lives.

7 And these things give in charge, that they may be blameless.

8 But if any provides not for his own, and especially for those of his own house, he has denied the faith, and is worse than an infidel.

9 Let not a widow be taken into the number under threescore years old, having been the wife of one man,

10 Well reported of for good works; if she has brought up children, if she has lodged strangers, if she has washed the saints' feet, if she has relieved the afflicted, if she has diligently followed every good work.

11 But the younger widows refuse: for when they have begun to grow wanton against the Messiah, they will marry;

12 Having damnation, because they have cast off their first faith.

13 And therewith they learn *to be* idle, wandering about from house to house; and not only idle, but tattlers also and busybodies, speaking things which they ought not.

14 I will therefore that the younger women marry, bear children, guide the house, give no occasion to the adversary to speak reproachfully.

15 For some are already turned aside after Satan.

16 If any man or woman that believes have widows, let them relieve them, and let not the congregation be charged; that it may relieve them that are widows indeed.

17 ¶ Let the elders that rule well be counted worthy of double honor, especially they who labor in the word and doctrine.

18 For the scripture says, You shall not muzzle the ox that treads out the corn. And, The laborer *is* worthy of his reward.

19 Against an elder receive not an accusation, but before two or three witnesses.

20 Them that sin rebuke before all, that others also may fear.
21 I charge *you* before God, and the Lord Yahshua the Messiah, and the elect angels, that you observe these things without preferring one before another, doing nothing by partiality.
22 Lay hands suddenly on no man, neither be partaker of other men's sins: keep yourself pure.
23 Drink no longer water, but use a little wine for your stomach's sake and your often infirmities.
24 Some men's sins are open beforehand, going before to judgment; and some *men* they follow after.
25 Likewise also the good works *of some* are manifest beforehand; and they that are otherwise cannot be hidden.

1 Timothy 6

6:1 ¶ Let as many servants as are under the yoke count their own masters worthy of all honor, that the name of God and *his* doctrine be not blasphemed.
2 And they that have believing masters, let them not despise *them*, because they are brethren; but rather do *them* service, because they are faithful and beloved, partakers of the benefit. These things teach and exhort.
3 If any man teaches otherwise, and consents not to wholesome words, *even* the words of our Lord Yahshua the Messiah, and to the doctrine which is according to godliness;
4 He is proud, knowing nothing, but doting about questions and strifes of words, whereof comes envy, strife, railings, evil suspicions,
5 Perverse disputings of men of corrupt minds, and destitute of the truth, supposing that gain is godliness: from such withdraw yourself.
6 ¶ But godliness with contentment is great gain.
7 For we brought nothing into *this* world, *and it is* certain we can carry nothing out.
8 And having food and clothing let us be therewith content.
9 But they that will be rich fall into temptation and a snare, and *into* many foolish and hurtful lusts, which drown men in destruction and perdition.
10 For the love of money is the root of all evil: which while some coveted after, they have erred from the faith, and pierced themselves through with many sorrows.
11 But you, O man of God, flee these things; and follow after righteousness, godliness, faith, love, patience, meekness.
12 Fight the good fight of faith, lay hold on eternal life, whereunto you are also called, and have professed a good profession before many witnesses.
13 ¶ I give you charge in the sight of God, who revives all things, and *before* the Messiah Yahshua, who before Pontius Pilate witnessed a good confession;
14 That you keep *this* commandment without spot, blameless, until the appearing of our Lord Yahshua the Messiah:
15 Which in his times he shall show, *who is* the blessed and only Potentate, the King of kings, and Lord of lords;
16 Who only has immortality, dwelling in the light which no man can approach unto; whom no man has seen, nor can see: to whom *be* honor and power everlasting. Amen.
17 Charge them that are rich in this world, that they be not high-minded, nor trust in uncertain riches, but in the living God, who gives us richly all things to enjoy;
18 That they do good, that they be rich in good works, ready to distribute, willing to communicate;
19 Laying up in store for themselves a good foundation against the time to come, that they may lay hold on eternal life.
20 O Timothy, keep that which is committed to your trust, avoiding profane *and* vain babblings, and oppositions of science falsely so called:
21 Which some professing have erred concerning the faith. Grace *be* with you. Amen. <<*The first to Timothy was written from Laodicea, which is the most chief city of Phrygia Pacatiana.*>>

2 Timothy

2 Timothy 1

1:1 ¶ Paul, an apostle of Yahshua the Messiah by the will of God, according to the promise of life which is in the Messiah Yahshua,
2 To Timothy, *my* dearly beloved son: Grace, mercy, *and* peace, from God the Father and the Messiah Yahshua our Lord.
3 I thank God, whom I serve from *my* forefathers with pure conscience, that without ceasing I have remembrance of you in my prayers night and day;
4 Greatly desiring to see you, being mindful of your tears, that I may be filled with joy;
5 When I call to remembrance the unfeigned faith that is in you, which dwelt first in your grandmother Lois, and your mother Eunice; and I am persuaded that *is* in you also.
6 ¶ Therefore I put you in remembrance that you stir up the gift of God, which is in you by the putting on of my hands.
7 For God has not given us the spirit of fear; but of power, and of love, and of a sound mind.
8 Be not you therefore ashamed of the testimony of our Lord, nor of me his prisoner: but be you partaker of the afflictions of the gospel according to the power of God;
9 Who has saved us, and called *us* with a holy calling, not according to our works, but according to his own purpose and grace, which was given us in the Messiah Yahshua before the world began,
10 But is now made manifest by the appearing of our Savior Yahshua the Messiah, who has abolished death, and has brought life and immortality to light through the gospel:
11 Whereunto I am appointed a preacher, and an apostle, and a teacher of the Gentiles.

12 For which cause I also suffer these things: nevertheless I am not ashamed: for I know whom I have believed, and am persuaded that he is able to keep that which I have committed to him against that day.
13 Hold fast the form of sound words, which you have heard from me, in faith and love which is in the Messiah Yahshua.
14 That good thing which was committed to you keep by the Holy Ghost which dwells in us.
15 ¶ This you know, that all they which are in Asia have turned away from me; of whom are Phygellus and Hermogenes.
16 The Lord give mercy to the house of Onesiphorus; for he often refreshed me, and was not ashamed of my chains:
17 But, when he was in Rome, he sought me out very diligently, and found *me*.
18 The Lord grant to him that he may find mercy of the Lord in that day: and in how many things he ministered to me at Ephesus, you know very well.

2 Timothy 2

2:1 ¶ You therefore, my son, be strong in the grace that is in the Messiah Yahshua.
2 And the things that you have heard of me among many witnesses, the same commit you to faithful men, who shall be able to teach others also.
3 You therefore endure hardness, as a good soldier of Yahshua the Messiah.
4 No man that wars entangles himself with the affairs of *this* life; that he may please him who has chosen him to be a soldier.
5 And if a man also strives for masteries, *yet* is he not crowned, unless he strives lawfully.
6 The husbandman that labors must be first partaker of the fruits.
7 Consider what I say; and the Lord give you understanding in all things.
8 ¶ Remember that Yahshua the Messiah of the seed of David was raised from the dead according to my gospel:
9 Wherein I suffer trouble, as an evil doer, *even* unto bonds; but the word of God is not bound.
10 Therefore I endure all things for the elect's sake, that they may also obtain the salvation which is in the Messiah Yahshua with eternal glory.
11 *It is* a faithful saying: For if we are dead with *him*, we shall also live with *him*:
12 If we suffer, we shall also reign with *him*: if we deny *him*, he also will deny us:
13 If we believe not, *yet* he remains faithful: he cannot deny himself.
14 ¶ Of these things put *them* in remembrance, charging *them* before the Lord that they strive not about words to no profit, *but* to the subverting of the hearers.
15 Study to show yourself approved unto God, a workman that needs not to be ashamed, rightly dividing the word of truth.
16 But shun profane *and* vain babblings: for they will increase unto more ungodliness.
17 And their word will eat as does a canker: of whom is Hymenaeus and Philetus;
18 Who concerning the truth have erred, saying that the resurrection is past already; and overthrow the faith of some.
19 ¶ Nevertheless the foundation of God stands sure, having this seal, The Lord knows them that are his. And, Let every one that names the name of the Messiah depart from iniquity.
20 But in a great house there are not only vessels of gold and of silver, but also of wood and of earth; and some to honor, and some to dishonor.
21 If a man therefore purges himself from these, he shall be a vessel unto honor, sanctified, and useful for the master's use, *and* prepared unto every good work.
22 ¶ Flee also youthful lusts: but follow righteousness, faith, charity, peace, with them that call on the Lord out of a pure heart.
23 But foolish and unlearned questions avoid, knowing that they do engender strifes.
24 And the servant of the Lord must not strive; but be gentle unto all *men*, apt to teach, patient,
25 In meekness instructing those that oppose themselves; if God perhaps will give them repentance to the acknowledging of the truth;
26 And *that* they may recover themselves out of the snare of the devil, who are taken captive by him at his will.

2 Timothy 3

3:1 ¶ This know also, that in the last days perilous times shall come
2 For men shall be lovers of their own selves, covetous, boasters, proud, blasphemers, disobedient to parents, unthankful, unholy,
3 Without natural affection, trucebreakers, false accusers, incontinent, fierce, despisers of those that are good,
4 Traitors, heady, high-minded, lovers of pleasures more than lovers of God;
5 Having a form of godliness, but denying the power thereof: from such turn away.
6 For of this sort are they which creep into houses, and lead captive silly women loaded with sins, led away with diverse lusts,
7 Ever learning, and never able to come to the knowledge of the truth.
8 Now as Jannes and Jambres withstood Moses, so do these also resist the truth: men of corrupt minds, reprobate concerning the faith.
9 But they shall proceed no further: for their folly shall be manifest unto all *men*, as theirs also was.
10 ¶ But you have fully known my doctrine, manner of life, purpose, faith, longsuffering, charity, patience,
11 Persecutions, afflictions, which came to me at Antioch, at Iconium, at Lystra; what persecutions I endured: but out of *them* all the Lord delivered me.

2 Timothy 3

12 Yes, and all that will live godly in the Messiah Yahshua shall suffer persecution.
13 But evil men and seducers shall grow worse and worse, deceiving, and being deceived.
14 But continue you in the things which you have learned and have been assured of, knowing of whom you have learned *them*;
15 And that from a child you have known the holy scriptures, which are able to make you wise unto salvation through faith which is in the Messiah Yahshua.
16 All scripture *is* given by inspiration of God, and *is* profitable for doctrine, for reproof, for correction, for instruction in righteousness:
17 That the man of God may be perfect, thoroughly furnished to all good works.

2 Timothy 4

4:1 ¶ I charge *you* therefore before God, and the Lord Yahshua the Messiah, who shall judge the quick and the dead at his appearing and his kingdom;
2 Preach the word; be instant in season, out of season; reprove, rebuke, exhort with all longsuffering and doctrine.
3 For the time will come when they will not endure sound doctrine; but after their own lusts shall they heap to themselves teachers, having itching ears;
4 And they shall turn away *their* ears from the truth, and shall be turned unto fables.
5 But watch you in all things, endure afflictions, do the work of an evangelist, make full proof of your ministry.
6 For I am now ready to be offered, and the time of my departure is at hand.
7 I have fought a good fight, I have finished *my* course, I have kept the faith:
8 Henceforth there is laid up for me a crown of righteousness, which the Lord, the righteous judge, shall give me at that day: and not to me only, but to all them also that love his appearing.
9 ¶ Do your diligence to come shortly to me:
10 For Demas has forsaken me, having loved this present world, and has departed to Thessalonica; Crescens to Galatia, Titus to Dalmatia.
11 Only Luke is with me. Take Mark, and bring him with you: for he is profitable to me for the ministry.
12 And Tychicus have I sent to Ephesus.
13 The cloak that I left at Troas with Carpus, when you come, bring *with you*, and the books, *but* especially the parchments.
14 Alexander the coppersmith did me much evil: the Lord reward him according to his works:
15 Of whom you beware also; for he has greatly resisted our words.
16 ¶ At my first answer no man stood with me, but all *men* forsook me: *I pray God* that it may not be laid to their charge.
17 Notwithstanding the Lord stood with me, and strengthened me; that by me the preaching might be fully known, and *that* all the Gentiles might hear: and I was delivered out of the mouth of the lion.
18 And the Lord shall deliver me from every evil work, and will preserve *me* unto his heavenly kingdom: to whom *be* glory forever and ever. Amen.
19 Salute Prisca and Aquila, and the household of Onesiphorus.
20 Erastus stayed at Corinth: but Trophimus have I left at Miletum sick.
21 Do your diligence to come before winter. Eubulus greets you, and Pudens, and Linus, and Claudia, and all the brethren.
22 The Lord Yahshua the Messiah *be* with your spirit. Grace *be* with you. Amen. <<*The second epistle to Timotheus, ordained the first overseer of the congregation of the Ephesians, was written from Rome, when Paul was brought before Nero the second time.*>>

Titus

Titus 1

1:1 ¶ Paul, a servant of God, and an apostle of Yahshua the Messiah, according to the faith of God's elect, and the acknowledging of the truth which is after godliness;
2 In hope of eternal life, which God, that cannot lie, promised before the world began;
3 But has in due times manifested his word through preaching, which is committed to me according to the commandment of God our Savior;
4 To Titus, *my* own son after the common faith: Grace, mercy, *and* peace, from God the Father and the Lord Yahshua the Messiah our Savior.
5 ¶ For this cause left I you in Crete, that you should set in order the things that are wanting, and ordain elders in every city, as I had appointed you:
6 ¶ If any is blameless, the husband of one wife, having faithful children not accused of riot or unruly.
7 For an overseer must be blameless, as the steward of God; not self-willed, not soon angry, not given to wine, no striker, not given to filthy profit;
8 But a lover of hospitality, a lover of good men, sober, just, holy, temperate;
9 Holding fast the faithful word as he has been taught, that he may be able by sound doctrine both to exhort and to convince the contradictors.
10 For there are many unruly and vain talkers and deceivers, especially they of the circumcision:
11 Whose mouths must be stopped, who subvert whole houses, teaching things which they ought not, for filthy profit's sake.
12 One of them, *even* a prophet of their own, said, The Cretians *are* always liars, evil beasts, slow bellies.

13 This witness is true. Therefore rebuke them sharply, that they may be sound in the faith;
14 Not giving heed to Jewish fables, and commandments of men, that turn from the truth.
15 Unto the pure all things *are* pure: but to them that are defiled and unbelieving *is* nothing pure; but even their mind and conscience is defiled.
16 They profess that they know God; but in works they deny *him*, being abominable, and disobedient, and to every good work reprobate.

Titus 2

2:1 ¶ But speak *to* you the things which *are* fitting *for* sound doctrine:
2 That the aged men be sober, devout, temperate, sound in faith, in charity, in patience.
3 The aged women likewise, that *they be* in behavior as becomes holiness, not false accusers, not given to much wine, teachers of good things;
4 That they may teach the young women to be sober, to love their husbands, to love their children,
5 *To be* discreet, chaste, keepers at home, good, obedient to their own husbands, that the word of God be not blasphemed.
6 Young men likewise exhort to be sober minded.
7 In all things showing yourself a pattern of good works: in doctrine *showing* soundness, gravity, sincerity,
8 Sound speech, that cannot be condemned; that he that is of the contrary part may be ashamed, having no evil thing to say of you.
9 *Exhort* servants to be obedient to their own masters, *and* to please *them* well in all *things*; not answering again;
10 Not embezzling, but showing all good fidelity; that they may adorn the doctrine of God our Savior in all things.
11 ¶ For the grace of God that brings salvation has appeared to all men,
12 Teaching us that, denying ungodliness and worldly lusts, we should live soberly, righteously, and godly, in this present world;
13 Looking for that blessed hope, and the glorious appearing of the great God and our Savior Yahshua the Messiah;
14 Who gave himself for us, that he might redeem us from all iniquity, and purify unto himself a peculiar people, zealous of good works.
15 ¶ These things speak, and exhort, and rebuke with all authority. Let no man despise you.

Titus 3

3:1 ¶ Put them in mind to be subject to principalities and powers, to obey magistrates, to be ready to every good work,
2 To speak evil of no man, to be no brawlers, *but* gentle, showing all meekness to all men.
3 For we ourselves also were sometimes foolish, disobedient, deceived, serving diverse lusts and pleasures, living in malice and envy, hateful, *and* hating one another.
4 But after that the kindness and love of God our Savior toward man appeared,
5 Not by works of righteousness which we have done, but according to his mercy he saved us, by the washing of regeneration, and renewing of the Holy Ghost;
6 Which he shed on us abundantly through Yahshua the Messiah our Savior;
7 That being justified by his grace, we should be made heirs according to the hope of eternal life.
8 *This is* a faithful saying, and these things I will that you affirm constantly, that they which have believed in God might be careful to maintain good works. These things are good and profitable to men.
9 ¶ But avoid foolish questions, and genealogies, and contentions, and strivings about the law; for they are unprofitable and vain.
10 A man that is a heretic after the first and second admonition reject;
11 Knowing that he that is such is subverted, and sins, being condemned of himself.
12 When I shall send Artemas to you, or Tychicus, be diligent to come unto me to Nicopolis: for I have determined there to winter.
13 Bring Zenas the lawyer and Apollos on their journey diligently, that nothing be wanting unto them.
14 And let ours also learn to maintain good works for necessary uses, that they be not unfruitful.
15 All that are with me salute you. Greet them that love us in the faith. Grace *be* with you all. Amen.
<<*It was written to Titus, ordained the first overseer of the congregation of the Cretians, from Nicopolis of Macedonia*>>

Philemon

Philemon 1

1:1 ¶ Paul, a prisoner of Yahshua the Messiah, and Timothy *our* brother, to Philemon our dearly beloved, and fellow laborer,
2 And to *our* beloved Apphia, and Archippus our fellow soldier, and to the congregation in your house:
3 Grace to you, and peace, from God our Father and the Lord Yahshua the Messiah.
4 I thank my God, making mention of you always in my prayers,
5 Hearing of your love and faith, which you have toward the Lord Yahshua, and toward all saints;
6 That the communication of your faith may become effectual by the acknowledging of every good thing which is in you in the Messiah Yahshua.

Philemon 1

7 For we have great joy and consolation in your love, because the bowels of the saints are refreshed by you, brother.
8 ¶ Therefore, though I might be greatly bold in the Messiah to command you that which is convenient,
9 Yet for love's sake I rather beseech *you*, being such a one as Paul the aged, and now also a prisoner of Yahshua the Messiah.
10 I beseech you for my son Onesimus, whom I have begotten in my bonds:
11 Which in time past was to you unprofitable, but now profitable to you and to me:
12 Whom I have sent again: you therefore receive him, that is, my own inward affection:
13 Whom I would have retained with me, that in your stead he might have ministered to me in the bonds of the gospel:
14 But without your mind would I do nothing; that your benefit should not be as it were of necessity, but willingly.
15 For perhaps he therefore departed for a season, that you should receive him forever;
16 Not now as a servant, but above a servant, a brother beloved, especially to me, but how much more to you, both in the flesh, and in the Lord?
17 If you count me therefore a partner, receive him as myself.
18 If he has wronged you, or owes *you* anything, put that on my account;
19 I Paul have written *it* with my own hand, I will repay *it*: albeit I do not say to you how you owe to me even your own self besides.
20 Yes, brother, let me have joy of you in the Lord: refresh my inward affection in the Lord.
21 Having confidence in your obedience I wrote to you, knowing that you will also do more than I say.
22 But therewith prepare me also a lodging: for I trust that through your prayers I shall be given to you.
23 There salute you Epaphras, my fellow prisoner in the Messiah Yahshua;
24 Marcus, Aristarchus, Demas, Lucas, my fellow laborers.
25 The grace of our Lord Yahshua the Messiah *be* with your spirit. Amen. <<*Written from Rome to Philemon, by Onesimus a servant.*>>

Hebrews

Hebrews 1

1:1 ¶ God, who at many times and in diverse manners spoke in time past to the fathers by the prophets,
2 Has in these last days spoken to us by *his* Son, whom he has appointed heir of all things, by whom also he made the worlds;
3 Who being the brightness of *his* glory, and the express image of his person, and upholding all things by the word of his power, when he had by himself purged our sins, sat down on the right hand of the Majesty on high;
4 ¶ Being made so much better than the angels, as he has by inheritance obtained a more excellent name than they.
5 For unto which of the angels said he at any time, You are my Son, this day have I begotten you? And again, I will be to him a Father, and he shall be to me a Son?
6 And again, when he brings in the first begotten into the world, he says, And let all the angels of God worship him.
7 And of the angels he says, Who makes his angels spirits, and his ministers a flame of fire.
8 But to the Son *he says*, Your throne, O God, *is* forever and ever: a scepter of righteousness *is* the scepter of your kingdom.
9 You have loved righteousness, and hated iniquity; therefore God, *even* your God, has anointed you with the oil of gladness above your fellows.
10 And, You, Lord *Yahweh*, in the beginning have laid the foundation of the earth; and the heavens are the works of your hands:
11 They shall perish; but you remain; and they all shall grow old as does a garment;
12 And as a cloak shall you fold them up, and they shall be changed: but you are the same, and your years shall not fail.
13 But to which of the angels said he at any time, Sit on my right hand, until I make your enemies your footstool?
14 Are they not all ministering spirits, sent forth to minister for them who shall be heirs of salvation?

Hebrews 2

2:1 ¶ Therefore we ought to give the more earnest heed to the things which we have heard, lest at any time we should let *them* slip.
2 For if the word spoken by angels was steadfast, and every transgression and disobedience received a just recompense of reward;
3 How shall we escape, if we neglect so great *a* salvation; which at the first began to be spoken by the Lord, and was confirmed to us by them that heard *him*;
4 God also bearing *them* witness, both with signs and wonders, and with diverse miracles, and gifts of the Holy Ghost, according to his own will?
5 ¶ For unto the angels has he not put in subjection the world to come, whereof we speak.
6 But one in a certain place testified, saying, What is man, that you are mindful of him? or the son of man, that you visit him?
7 You made him a little lower than the angels; you crowned him with glory and honor, and did set him over the works of your hands:
8 You have put all things in subjection under his feet. For in that he put all in subjection under him, he left nothing *that is* not put under him. But now we see not yet all things put under him.
9 But we see Yahshua, who was made a little lower than the angels for the suffering of death, crowned with glory and honor; that he by the grace of God should taste death for every man.

10 ¶ For it became him, for whom *are* all things, and by whom *are* all things, in bringing many sons unto glory, to make the captain of their salvation perfect through sufferings.

11 For both he that sanctifies and they who are sanctified *are* all of one: for which cause he is not ashamed to call them brethren,

12 Saying, I will declare your name to my brethren, in the midst of the congregation will I sing praise to you.

13 And again, I will put my trust in him. And again, Behold I and the children which God *Yahweh* has given me.

14 ¶ Forasmuch then as the children are partakers of flesh and blood, he also himself likewise took part of the same; that through death he might destroy him that had the power of death, that is, the devil;

15 And deliver them who through fear of death were all their lifetime subject to bondage.

16 For truly he took not on *him the nature of* angels; but he took on *him* the seed of Abraham.

17 Therefore in all things it behooved him to be made like unto *his* brethren, that he might be a merciful and faithful high priest in things *pertaining* to God, to make reconciliation for the sins of the people.

18 For in that he himself has suffered being tempted, he is able to help them that are tempted.

Hebrews 3

3:1 ¶ Therefore, holy brethren, partakers of the heavenly calling, consider the Apostle and High Priest of our profession, the Messiah Yahshua;

2 Who was faithful to him that appointed him, as also Moses *was faithful* in all his house.

3 For this *man* was counted worthy of more glory than Moses, inasmuch as he who has built the house has more honor than the house.

4 For every house is built by some *man*; but he that built all things *is* God.

5 And Moses truly *was* faithful in all his house, as a servant, for a testimony of those things which were to be spoken after;

6 But the Messiah as a son over his own house; whose house are we, if we hold fast the confidence and the rejoicing of the hope firm unto the end.

7 ¶ Therefore (as the Holy Ghost said, Today if you will hear his voice,

8 Harden not your hearts, as in the provocation, in the day of temptation in the wilderness:

9 When your fathers tempted me, proved me, and saw my works *for* forty years.

10 Therefore I was grieved with that generation, and said, They do always err in *their* heart; and they have not known my ways.

11 So I swore in my wrath, They shall not enter into my rest.)

12 Take heed, brethren, lest there be in any of you an evil heart of unbelief, in departing from the living God.

13 But exhort one another daily, while it is called Today; lest any of you be hardened through the deceitfulness of sin.

14 For we are made partakers of the Messiah, if we hold the beginning of our confidence steadfast unto the end;

15 While it is said, Today if you will hear his voice, harden not your hearts, as in the provocation.

16 For some, when they had heard, did provoke: however not all that came out of Egypt by Moses.

17 But with whom was he grieved *for* forty years? *was it* not with them that had sinned, whose carcasses fell in the wilderness?

18 And to whom swore he that they should not enter into his rest, but to them that believed not?

19 So we see that they could not enter in because of unbelief.

Hebrews 4

4:1 ¶ Let us therefore fear, lest, a promise being left *us* of entering into his rest, any of you should seem to come short of it.

2 For unto us was the gospel preached, as well as unto them: but the word preached did not profit them, not being mixed with faith in them that heard *it.*

3 For we which have believed do enter into rest, as he said, As I have sworn in my wrath, if they shall enter into my rest: although the works were finished from the foundation of the world.

4 For he spoke in a certain place of the seventh *day* in this manner, And God did rest the seventh day from all his works.

5 And in this *place* again, If they shall enter into my rest.

6 Seeing therefore it remains that some must enter therein, and they to whom it was first preached entered not in because of unbelief:

7 Again, he limits a certain day, saying in David, Today, after so long a time; as it is said, Today if you will hear his voice, harden not your hearts.

8 For if Joshua had given them rest, then would he not afterward have spoken of another day.

9 There remains therefore a rest to the people of God.

10 For he that is entered into his rest, he also has ceased from his own works, as God *did* from his.

11 ¶ Let us labor therefore to enter into that rest, lest any man falls after the same example of unbelief.

12 For the word of God *is* quick, and powerful, and sharper than any two-edged sword, piercing even to the dividing apart of soul and spirit, and of the joints and marrow, and *is* a discerner of the thoughts and intents of the heart.

13 Neither is there any creature that is not manifest in his sight: but all things *are* naked and opened to the eyes of him with whom we have to do.

14 Seeing then that we have a great high priest, that is passed into the heavens, Yahshua the Son of God, let us hold fast *our* profession.

Hebrews 4

15 For we have not a high priest which cannot be touched with the feeling of our infirmities; but was in all points tempted like as *we are, yet* without sin.

16 Let us therefore come boldly unto the throne of grace, that we may obtain mercy, and find grace to help in time of need.

Hebrews 5

5:1 ¶ For every high priest taken from among men is ordained for men in things *pertaining* to God, that he may offer both gifts and sacrifices for sins:

2 Who can have compassion on the ignorant, and on them that are out of the way; for that he himself also is compassed with infirmity.

3 And by reason hereof he ought, as for the people, so also for himself, to offer for sins.

4 And no man takes this honor unto himself, but he that is called of God, as *was* Aaron.

5 So also the Messiah glorified not himself to be made a high priest; but he that said to him, You are my Son, today have I begotten you.

6 As he said also in another *place*, You *are* a priest forever after the order of Melchizedek.

7 Who in the days of his flesh, when he had offered up prayers and supplications with strong crying and tears to him that was able to save him from death, and was heard in that he feared;

8 Though he were a Son, yet learned he obedience by the things which he suffered;

9 And being made perfect, he became the author of eternal salvation unto all them that obey him;

10 ¶ Called of God a high priest after the order of Melchizedek.

11 Of whom we have many things to say, and hard to be uttered, seeing you are dull of hearing.

12 For when for the time you ought to be teachers, you have need that one teach you again which *are* the first principles of the oracles of God; and have become such as have need of milk, and not of strong meat.

13 For every one that uses milk *is* unskillful in the word of righteousness: for he is a babe.

14 But strong meat belongs to them that are of full age, *even* those who by reason of use have their senses exercised to discern both good and evil.

Hebrews 6

6:1 ¶ Therefore leaving the principles of the doctrine of the Messiah, let us go on to perfection; not laying again the foundation of repentance from dead works, and of faith toward God,

2 Of the doctrine of baptisms, and of laying on of hands, and of resurrection of the dead, and of eternal judgment.

3 And this will we do, if God permits.

4 For *it is* impossible for those who were once enlightened, and have tasted of the heavenly gift, and were made partakers of the Holy Ghost,

5 And have tasted the good word of God, and the powers of the world to come,

6 If they shall fall away, to renew them again unto repentance; seeing they crucify to themselves the Son of God afresh, and put *him* to an open shame.

7 For the earth which drinks in the rain that comes often upon it, and brings forth herbs useful for them by whom it is dressed, receives blessings from God:

8 But that which bears thorns and briers *is* rejected, and *is* near to cursing; whose end *is* to be burned.

9 ¶ But, beloved, we are persuaded *of* better things of you, and things that accompany salvation, though we thus speak.

10 For God *is* not unrighteous to forget your work and labor of love, which you have shown toward his name, in that you have ministered to the saints, and do minister.

11 And we desire that every one of you do show the same diligence to the full assurance of hope to the end:

12 That you be not slothful, but followers of them who through faith and patience inherit the promises.

13 For when God made *a* promise to Abraham, because he could swear by no greater, he swore by himself,

14 Saying, Surely blessing I will bless you, and multiplying I will multiply you.

15 And so, after he had patiently endured, he obtained the promise.

16 For men truly swear by the greater: and an oath for confirmation *is* to them an end of all strife.

17 Wherein God, willing more abundantly to show to the heirs of promise the immutability of his counsel, confirmed *it* by an oath:

18 That by two immutable things, in which *it was* impossible for God to lie, we might have a strong consolation, who have fled for refuge to lay hold upon the hope set before us:

19 Which *hope* we have as an anchor of the soul, both sure and steadfast, and which enters into that within the veil;

20 Where the forerunner is for us entered, *even* Yahshua, made a high priest forever after the order of Melchizedek.

Hebrews 7

7:1 ¶ For this Melchizedek, king of Salem, priest of the most high God, who met Abraham returning from the slaughter of the kings, and blessed him;

2 To whom also Abraham gave a tenth part of all; first being by interpretation King of righteousness, and after that also King of Salem, which is, King of peace;

3 Without father, without mother, without genealogy, having neither beginning of days, nor end of life; but made like unto the Son of God; remains a priest continually.

4 Now consider how great this man *was*, unto whom even the patriarch Abraham gave the tenth of the spoils.

5 And truly they that are of the sons of Levi, who receive the office of the priesthood, have a commandment to take

tithes of the people according to the law, that is, of their brethren, though they come out of the loins of Abraham:
6 But he whose genealogy is not counted from them received tithes of Abraham, and blessed him that had the promises.
7 And without all contradiction the less is blessed of the better.
8 And here men that die receive tithes; but there he *receives them*, of whom it is witnessed that he lives.
9 And as I may so say, Levi also, who received tithes, paid tithes in Abraham.
10 For he was yet in the loins of his father, when Melchizedek met him.
11 ¶ If therefore perfection was by the Levitical priesthood, (for under it the people received the law,) what further need *was there* that another priest should arise after the order of Melchizedek, and not be called after the order of Aaron?
12 For the priesthood being changed, there is made of necessity a change also of the law.
13 For he of whom these things are spoken pertains to another tribe, of which no man gave attendance at the altar.
14 For *it is* evident that our Lord sprang out of Judah; of which tribe Moses spoke nothing concerning priesthood.
15 And it is yet far more evident: for that after the likeness of Melchizedek there arises another priest,
16 Who is made, not after the law of a carnal commandment, but after the power of an endless life.
17 For he testifies, You *are* a priest forever after the order of Melchizedek.
18 For there is truly an annulling of the commandment going before for the weakness and unprofitableness thereof.
19 For the law made nothing perfect, but the bringing in of a better hope *did*; by which we draw near unto God.
20 And inasmuch as not without an oath *he was made priest*:
21 (For those priests were made without an oath; but this with an oath by him that said to him, The Lord *Yahweh* swore and will not repent, You *are* a priest forever after the order of Melchizedek:)
22 By so much was Yahshua made a surety of a better testament.
23 And they truly were many priests, because they were not allowed to continue by reason of death:
24 But this *man*, because he continues on, has an unchangeable priesthood.
25 Therefore he is able also to save them to the utmost that come to God by him, seeing he ever lives to make intercession for them.
26 For such a high priest *was* becoming unto us, *who is* holy, harmless, undefiled, separate from sinners, and made higher than the heavens;
27 Who needs not daily, as those high priests, to offer up sacrifice, first for his own sins, and then for the people's: for this he did once, when he offered up himself.
28 For the law makes men high priests which have infirmity; but the word of the oath, which was since the law, *makes* the Son, who is consecrated forevermore.

Hebrews 8

8:1 ¶ Now of the things which we have spoken *this is* the sum: We have such a high priest, who is set on the right hand of the throne of the Majesty in the heavens;
2 A minister of the sanctuary, and of the true tabernacle, which the Lord pitched, and not man.
3 For every high priest is ordained to offer gifts and sacrifices: therefore *it is* of necessity that this man has something also to offer.
4 For if he were on earth, he should not be a priest, seeing that there are priests that offer gifts according to the law:
5 Who serve unto the example and shadow of heavenly things, as Moses was admonished of God when he was about to make the tabernacle: for, See, said he, *that* you make all things according to the pattern shown to you in the mount.
6 ¶ But now has he obtained a more excellent ministry, by how much also he is the mediator of a better covenant, which was established upon better promises.
7 For if that first *covenant* had been faultless, then should no place have been sought for the second.
8 For finding fault with them, he said, Behold, the days come, says the Lord *Yahweh*, when I will make a new covenant with the house of Israel and with the house of Judah:
9 Not according to the covenant that I made with their fathers in the day when I took them by the hand to lead them out of the land of Egypt; because they continued not in my covenant, and I regarded them not, says the Lord *Yahweh*.
10 For this *is* the covenant that I will make with the house of Israel after those days, says the Lord *Yahweh*; I will put my laws into their mind, and write them in their hearts: and I will be to them a God, and they shall be to me a people:
11 And they shall not teach every man his neighbor, and every man his brother, saying, Know the Lord *Yahweh*: for all shall know me, from the least to the greatest.
12 For I will be merciful to their unrighteousness, and their sins and their iniquities will I remember no more.
13 In that he says, A new *covenant*, he has made the first old. Now that which decays and becomes old *is* ready to vanish away.

Hebrews 9

9:1 ¶ Then truly the first *covenant* had also ordinances of divine service, and a worldly sanctuary.
2 For there was a tabernacle made; the first, wherein *was* the candlestick, and the table, and the showbread; which is called the sanctuary.
3 And after the second veil, the tabernacle which is called the Holiest of all;

Hebrews 9

4 Which had the golden censer, and the ark of the covenant overlaid round about with gold, wherein *was* the golden pot that had manna, and Aaron's rod that budded, and the tables of the covenant;
5 And over it the cherubims of glory shadowing the mercy seat; of which we cannot now speak particularly.
6 Now when these things were thus ordained, the priests went always into the first tabernacle, accomplishing the service *of God*.
7 But into the second *went* the high priest alone once every year, not without blood, which he offered for himself, and *for* the errors of the people:
8 ¶ The Holy Ghost this signifying, that the way into the holiest of all was not yet made manifest, while as the first tabernacle was yet standing:
9 Which *was* a figure for the time then present, in which were offered both gifts and sacrifices, that could not make him that did the service perfect, as pertaining to the conscience;
10 *Which stood* only in foods and drinks, and diverse washings, and carnal ordinances, imposed *on them* until the time of reformation.
11 But the Messiah coming *as* a high priest of good things to come, by a greater and more perfect tabernacle, not made with hands, that is to say, not of this building;
12 Neither by the blood of goats and calves, but by his own blood he entered in once into the holy place, having obtained eternal redemption *for us*.
13 For if the blood of bulls and of goats, and the ashes of a heifer sprinkling the unclean, sanctifies to the purifying of the flesh:
14 How much more shall the blood of the Messiah, who through the eternal Spirit offered himself without spot to God, purge your conscience from dead works to serve the living God?
15 ¶ And for this cause he is the mediator of the new testament, that by means of death, for the redemption of the transgressions *that were* under the first testament, they which are called might receive the promise of eternal inheritance.
16 For where a testament *is*, there must also of necessity be the death of the testator.
17 For a testament *is* in force after men are dead: otherwise it is of no strength at all while the testator lives.
18 Whereupon not even the first *testament* was dedicated without blood.
19 For when Moses had spoken every precept to all the people according to the law, he took the blood of calves and of goats, with water, and scarlet wool, and hyssop, and sprinkled both the book, and all the people,
20 Saying, This *is* the blood of the testament which God has commanded unto you.
21 Moreover he sprinkled with blood both the tabernacle, and all the vessels of the ministry.
22 And almost all things are by the law purged with blood; and without shedding of blood is no remission.
23 ¶ *It was* therefore necessary that the patterns of things in the heavens should be purified with these; but the heavenly things themselves with better sacrifices than these.
24 For the Messiah has not entered into the holy places made with hands, *which are* the figures of the true; but into heaven itself, now to appear in the presence of God for us:
25 Nor yet that he should offer himself often, as the high priest enters into the holy place every year with blood of others;
26 For then must he often have suffered since the foundation of the world: but now once in the end of the world has he appeared to put away sin by the sacrifice of himself.
27 And as it is appointed unto men once to die, but after this the judgment:
28 So the Messiah was once offered to bear the sins of many; and to them that look for him shall he appear the second time without sin unto salvation.

Hebrews 10

10:1 ¶ For the law having a shadow of good things to come, *and* not the very image of the things, can never with those sacrifices which they offered year by year continually make the comers thereunto perfect.
2 For then would they not have ceased to be offered? because that the worshippers once purged should have had no more conscience of sins.
3 But in those *sacrifices there is* a remembrance again *made* of sins every year.
4 For *it is* not possible that the blood of bulls and of goats should take away sins.
5 Therefore when he came into the world, he said, Sacrifice and offering you would not, but a body have you prepared me:
6 In burnt offerings and *sacrifices* for sin you have had no pleasure.
7 ¶ Then said I, Lo, I come (in the volume of the book it is written of me,) to do your will, O God.
8 Above when he said, Sacrifice and offering and burnt offerings and *offering* for sin you would not, neither had pleasure *therein*; which are offered by the law;
9 Then said he, Lo, I come to do your will, O God. He takes away the first, that he may establish the second.
10 By that will we are sanctified through the offering of the body of Yahshua the Messiah once *for all*.
11 And every priest stands daily ministering and offering oftentimes the same sacrifices, which can never take away sins:
12 But this man, after he had offered one sacrifice for sins forever, sat down on the right hand of God;
13 From now on expecting till his enemies are made his footstool.
14 For by one offering he has perfected forever them that are sanctified.
15 *Whereof* the Holy Ghost also is a witness to us: for after that he had said before,

16 This *is* the covenant that I will make with them after those days, says the Lord *Yahweh*, I will put my laws into their hearts, and in their minds will I write them;
17 And their sins and iniquities will I remember no more.
18 Now where remission of these *is, there is* no more offering for sin.
19 ¶ Having therefore, brethren, boldness to enter into the holiest by the blood of Yahshua,
20 By a new and living way, which he has consecrated for us, through the veil, that is to say, his flesh;
21 And *having* a high priest over the house of God;
22 Let us draw near with a true heart in full assurance of faith, having our hearts sprinkled from an evil conscience, and our bodies washed with pure water.
23 Let us hold fast the profession of *our* faith without wavering; (for he *is* faithful that promised;)
24 And let us consider one another to provoke unto love and to good works:
25 Not forsaking the assembling of ourselves together, as the manner of some *is*; but exhorting *one another*: and so much the more, as you see the day approaching.
26 For if we sin willfully after that we have received the knowledge of the truth, there remains no more sacrifice for sins,
27 But a certain fearful looking for of judgment and fiery indignation, which shall devour the adversaries.
28 He that despised Moses' law died without mercy under two or three witnesses:
29 Of how much worse punishment, suppose you, shall he be thought worthy, who has trodden under foot the Son of God, and has counted the blood of the covenant, with which he was sanctified, an unholy thing, and has done insult unto the Spirit of grace?
30 For we know him that has said, Vengeance *belongs* to me, I will recompense, says the Lord *Yahweh*. And again, The Lord *Yahweh* shall judge his people.
31 *It is* a fearful thing to fall into the hands of the living God.
32 But call to remembrance the former days, in which, after you were illuminated, you endured a great fight of afflictions;
33 Partly, while you were made a spectacle both by reproaches and afflictions; and partly, while you became companions of them that were so used.
34 For you had compassion on me in my bonds, and took joyfully the spoiling of your goods, knowing in yourselves that you have in heaven a better and an enduring substance.
35 Cast not away therefore your confidence, which has great recompense of reward.
36 For you have need of patience, that, after you have done the will of God, you might receive the promise.
37 For yet a little while, and he that shall come will come, and will not tarry.
38 Now the just shall live by faith: but if *any man* draws back, my soul shall have no pleasure in him.
39 But we are not of them who draw back unto perdition; but of them that believe to the saving of the soul.

Hebrews 11

11:1 ¶ Now faith is the substance of things hoped for, the evidence of things not seen.
2 For by it the elders obtained a good report.
3 Through faith we understand that the worlds were framed by the word of God, so that things which are seen were not made of things which do appear.
4 ¶ By faith Abel offered unto God a more excellent sacrifice than Cain, by which he obtained witness that he was righteous, God testifying of his gifts: and by it he being dead yet speaks.
5 By faith Enoch was translated that he should not see death; and was not found, because God had translated him: for before his translation he had this testimony, that he pleased God.
6 But without faith *it is* impossible to please *him*: for he that comes to God must believe that he is, and *that* he is a rewarder of them that diligently seek him.
7 By faith Noah, being warned of God of things not seen as yet, moved with fear, prepared an ark to the saving of his house; by the which he condemned the world, and became heir of the righteousness which is by faith.
8 By faith Abraham, when he was called to go out into a place which he should after receive for an inheritance, obeyed; and he went out, not knowing where he went.
9 By faith he sojourned in the land of promise, as *in* a strange country, dwelling in tabernacles with Isaac and Jacob, the heirs with him of the same promise:
10 For he looked for a city which has foundations, whose builder and maker *is* God.
11 Through faith also Sarah herself received strength to conceive seed, and was delivered of a child when she was past age, because she judged him faithful who had promised.
12 Therefore sprang there even of one, and him as good as dead, *so many* as the stars of the sky in multitude, and as the sand which is by the sea shore innumerable.
13 These all died in faith, not having received the promises, but having seen them afar off, and were persuaded of *them*, and embraced *them*, and confessed that they were strangers and pilgrims on the earth.
14 For they that say such things declare plainly that they seek a country.
15 And truly, if they had been mindful of that *country* from where they came out, they might have had opportunity to have returned.
16 But now they desire a better *country*, that is, a heavenly: therefore God is not ashamed to be called their God: for he has prepared for them a city.
17 By faith Abraham, when he was tried, offered up Isaac: and he that had received the promises offered up his only begotten *son*,
18 Of whom it was said, That in Isaac shall your seed be called:
19 Accounting that God *was* able to raise *him* up, even from the dead; from where also he received him in a figure.

Hebrews 11

20 By faith Isaac blessed Jacob and Esau concerning things to come.
21 By faith Jacob, when he was dying, blessed both the sons of Joseph; and worshipped, *leaning* upon the top of his staff.
22 By faith Joseph, when he died, made mention of the departing of the children of Israel; and gave commandment concerning his bones.
23 By faith Moses, when he was born, was hidden three months by his parents, because they saw *he was* a proper child; and they were not afraid of the king's commandment.
24 By faith Moses, when he had come of age, refused to be called the son of Pharaoh's daughter;
25 Choosing rather to suffer affliction with the people of God, than to enjoy the pleasures of sin for a season;
26 Esteeming the reproach of the Messiah greater riches than the treasures in Egypt: for he had respect unto the recompense of the reward.
27 By faith he forsook Egypt, not fearing the wrath of the king: for he endured, as seeing him who is invisible.
28 Through faith he kept the passover, and the sprinkling of blood, lest he that destroyed the firstborn should touch them.
29 By faith they passed through the Red Sea as by dry *land*: which the Egyptians attempting to do were drowned.
30 By faith the walls of Jericho fell down, after they were compassed about seven days.
31 By faith the harlot Rahab perished not with them that believed not, when she had received the spies with peace.
32 ¶ And what shall I more say? for the time would fail me to tell of Gideon, and *of* Barak, and *of* Samson, and *of* Jephthah; *of* David also, and Samuel, and *of* the prophets:
33 Who through faith subdued kingdoms, worked righteousness, obtained promises, stopped the mouths of lions,
34 Quenched the violence of fire, escaped the edge of the sword, out of weakness were made strong, became valiant in fight, turned to flight the armies of the aliens.
35 Women received their dead raised to life again: and others were tortured, not accepting deliverance; that they might obtain a better resurrection:
36 And others had trial of *cruel* mockings and scourgings, yes, moreover of bonds and imprisonment:
37 They were stoned, they were sawn in two, were tempted, were slain with the sword: they wandered about in sheepskins and goatskins; being destitute, afflicted, tormented;
38 (Of whom the world was not worthy:) they wandered in deserts, and *in* mountains, and *in* dens and caves of the earth.
39 And these all, having obtained a good report through faith, received not the promise:
40 God having provided some better thing for us, that they without us should not be made perfect.

Hebrews 12

12:1 ¶ Therefore seeing we also are compassed about with so great a cloud of witnesses, let us lay aside every weight, and the sin which does so easily beset *us*, and let us run with patience the race that is set before us,
2 Looking unto Yahshua the author and finisher of *our* faith; who for the joy that was set before him endured the cross, despising the shame, and has set down at the right hand of the throne of God.
3 For consider him that endured such contradiction of sinners against himself, lest you be wearied and faint in your minds.
4 ¶ You have not yet resisted unto blood, striving against sin.
5 And you have forgotten the exhortation which speaks unto you as to children, My son, despise not you the chastening of the Lord *Yahweh*, nor faint when you are rebuked of him:
6 For whom the Lord *Yahweh* loves he chastens, and scourges every son whom he receives.
7 If you endure chastening, God deals with you as with sons; for what son is he whom the father chastens not?
8 But if you are without chastisement, whereof all are partakers, then are you bastards, and not sons.
9 Furthermore we have had fathers of our flesh which corrected *us*, and we gave *them* reverence: shall we not much rather be in subjection to the Father of spirits, and live?
10 For they truly for a few days chastened *us* after their own pleasure; but he for *our* profit, that *we* might be partakers of his holiness.
11 Now no chastening for the present seems to be joyous, but grievous: nevertheless afterward it yields the peaceable fruit of righteousness unto them which are exercised thereby.
12 Therefore lift up the hands which hang down, and the feeble knees;
13 And make straight paths for your feet, lest that which is lame be turned out of the way; but let it rather be healed.
14 Follow peace with all *men*, and holiness, without which no man shall see the Lord:
15 Looking diligently lest any man fail of the grace of God; lest any root of bitterness springing up troubles *you*, and thereby many be defiled;
16 Lest there *be* any fornicator, or profane person, as Esau, who for one morsel of food sold his birthright.
17 For you know how that afterward, when he would have inherited the blessing, he was rejected: for he found no place for repentance, though he sought it carefully with tears.
18 ¶ For you have not come to the mount that might be touched, and that burned with fire, nor to blackness, and darkness, and tempest,
19 And the sound of a trumpet, and the voice of words; which *voice* they that heard entreated that the word should not be spoken to them any more:

20 (For they could not endure that which was commanded, And if so much as a beast touches the mountain, it shall be stoned, or thrust through with a dart:
21 And so terrible was the sight, *that* Moses said, I exceedingly fear and quake:)
22 But you have come unto mount Zion, and unto the city of the living God, the heavenly Jerusalem, and to an innumerable company of angels,
23 To the general assembly and congregation of the firstborn, which are written in heaven, and to God the Judge of all, and to the spirits of just men made perfect,
24 And to Yahshua the mediator of the new covenant, and to the blood of sprinkling, that speaks better things than *that of* Abel.
25 See that you refuse not him that speaks. For if they escaped not who refused him that spoke on earth, much more *shall not* we *escape*, if we turn away from him that *speaks* from heaven:
26 Whose voice then shook the earth: but now he has promised, saying, Yet once more I shake not the earth only, but also heaven.
27 And this *word*, Yet once more, signifies the removing of those things that are shaken, as of things that are made, that those things which cannot be shaken may remain.
28 Therefore we *are* receiving a kingdom which cannot be moved, let us have grace, whereby we may serve God acceptably with reverence and godly fear:
29 For our God *Yahweh is* a consuming fire.

Hebrews 13

13:1 ¶ Let brotherly love continue.
2 Be not forgetful to entertain strangers: for thereby some have entertained angels unaware.
3 Remember them that are in bonds, as bound with them; *and* them which suffer adversity, as being yourselves also in the body.
4 Marriage *is* honorable in all, and the bed undefiled: but whoremongers and adulterers God will judge.
5 *Let your* conversation *be* without covetousness; *and be* content with such things as you have: for he has said, I will never leave you, nor forsake you.
6 So that we may boldly say, The Lord *Yahweh is* my helper, and I will not fear what man shall do to me.
7 Remember them which have the rule over you, who have spoken to you the word of God: whose faith follow, considering the end of *their* conversation.
8 Yahshua the Messiah the same yesterday, and today, and forever.
9 Be not carried about with diverse and strange doctrines. For *it is* a good thing that the heart be established with grace; not with foods, which have not profited them that have been occupied therein.
10 We have an altar, whereof they have no right to eat which serve the tabernacle.
11 For the bodies of those beasts, whose blood is brought into the sanctuary by the high priest for sin, are burned outside the camp.
12 Therefore Yahshua also, that he might sanctify the people with his own blood, suffered outside the gate.
13 Let us go forth therefore to him outside the camp, bearing his reproach.
14 For here have we no continuing city, but we seek one to come.
15 By him therefore let us offer the sacrifice of praise to God continually, that is, the fruit of *our* lips giving thanks to his name.
16 But to do good and to communicate forget not: for with such sacrifices God is well pleased.
17 Obey them that have the rule over you, and submit yourselves: for they watch for your souls, as they that must give account, that they may do it with joy, and not with grief: for that *is* unprofitable for you.
18 ¶ Pray for us: for we trust we have a good conscience, in all things willing to live honestly.
19 But I beseech *you* more earnestly to do this, that I may be restored to you the sooner.
20 Now the God of peace, that brought again from the dead our Lord Yahshua, that great shepherd of the sheep, through the blood of the everlasting covenant,
21 Make you perfect in every good work to do his will, working in you that which is well pleasing in his sight, through Yahshua the Messiah; to whom *be* glory forever and ever. Amen.
22 And I beseech you, brethren, endure the word of exhortation: for I have written a letter to you in few words.
23 Know you that *our* brother Timothy is set at liberty; with whom, if he comes shortly, I will see you.
24 Salute all them that have the rule over you, and all the saints. They of Italy salute you.
25 Grace *be* with you all. Amen.

James

James 1

1:1 ¶ James, a servant of God and of the Lord Yahshua the Messiah, to the twelve tribes which are scattered abroad, greetings.
2 ¶ My brethren, count it all joy when you fall into diverse temptations;
3 Knowing *this*, that the trying of your faith works patience.
4 But let patience have *her* perfect work, that you may be perfect and entire, wanting nothing.
5 If any of you lacks wisdom, let him ask of God, that gives to all *men* liberally, and reproaches not; and it shall be given him.
6 But let him ask in faith, nothing wavering. For he that wavers is like a wave of the sea driven with the wind and tossed.

James 1

7 For let not that man think that he shall receive anything of the Lord.
8 A double minded man *is* unstable in all his ways.
9 Let the brother of low degree rejoice in that he is exalted:
10 But the rich, in that he is made low: because as the flower of the grass he shall pass away.
11 For the sun has no sooner risen with a burning heat, but it withers the grass, and the flower thereof falls, and the grace of the fashion of it perishes: so also shall the rich man fade away in his ways.
12 Blessed *is* the man that endures temptation: for when he is tried, he shall receive the crown of life, which the Lord has promised to them that love him.
13 ¶ Let no man say when he is tempted, I am tempted by God: for God cannot be tempted with evil, neither tempts he any man:
14 But every man is tempted, when he is drawn away of his own lust, and enticed.
15 Then when lust has conceived, it brings forth sin: and sin, when it is finished, brings forth death.
16 Do not err, my beloved brethren.
17 Every good gift and every perfect gift is from above, and comes down from the Father of lights, with whom is no variation, neither shadow of turning.
18 Of his own will begot he us with the word of truth, that we should be a kind of firstfruits of his creatures.
19 ¶ Therefore, my beloved brethren, let every man be swift to hear, slow to speak, slow to wrath:
20 For the wrath of man works not the righteousness of God.
21 Therefore lay apart all filthiness and superfluity of naughtiness, and receive with meekness the engrafted word, which is able to save your souls.
22 But be you doers of the word, and not hearers only, deceiving your own selves.
23 For if any is a hearer of the word, and not a doer, he is like unto a man beholding his natural face in a glass:
24 For he beholds himself, and goes his way, and immediately forgets what manner of man he was.
25 But whoever looks into the perfect law of liberty, and continues *therein*, he being not a forgetful hearer, but a doer of the work, this man shall be blessed in his deed.
26 If any man among you seems to be religious, and bridles not his tongue, but deceives his own heart, this man's religion *is* vain.
27 Pure religion and undefiled before God and the Father is this, To visit the fatherless and widows in their affliction, *and* to keep himself unspotted from the world.

James 2

2:1 ¶ My brethren, have not the faith of our Lord Yahshua the Messiah, *the Lord* of glory, with respect of persons.
2 For if there comes unto your congregation a man with a gold ring, in goodly apparel, and there comes in also a poor man in filthy clothing;
3 And you have respect to him that wears the splendid clothing, and say unto him, Sit you here in a good place; and say to the poor, Stand you there, or sit here under my footstool:
4 Are you not then partial in yourselves, and have become judges of evil thoughts?
5 Listen, my beloved brethren, Has not God chosen the poor of this world rich in faith, and heirs of the kingdom which he has promised to them that love him?
6 But you have despised the poor. Do not rich men oppress you, and draw you before the judgment seats?
7 Do not they blaspheme that worthy name by which you are called?
8 ¶ If you fulfill the royal law according to the scripture, You shall love your neighbor as yourself, you do well:
9 But if you have respect of persons, you commit sin, and are convicted of the law as transgressors.
10 For whoever shall keep the whole law, and yet offends in one *point*, he is guilty of all.
11 For he that said, Do not commit adultery, said also, Do not kill. Now if you commit no adultery, yet if you kill, you have become a transgressor of the law.
12 So speak you, and so do, as they that shall be judged by the law of liberty.
13 For he shall have judgment without mercy, that has shown no mercy; and mercy rejoices against judgment.
14 ¶ What *does it* profit, my brethren, though a man says he has faith, and has not works? can faith save him?
15 If a brother or sister is naked, and destitute of daily food,
16 And one of you says unto them, Depart in peace, be *you* warmed and filled; notwithstanding you give them not those things which are needful to the body; what *does it* profit?
17 Even so faith, if it has not works, is dead, being alone.
18 Yes, a man may say, You have faith, and I have works: show me your faith without your works, and I will show you my faith by my works.
19 You believe that there is one God; you do well: the devils also believe, and tremble.
20 But will you know, O vain man, that faith without works is dead?
21 Was not Abraham our father justified by works, when he had offered Isaac his son upon the altar?
22 See you how faith worked with his works, and by works was faith made perfect?
23 And the scripture was fulfilled which says, Abraham believed God *Yahweh*, and it was imputed unto him for righteousness: and he was called the Friend of God.
24 You see then how that by works a man is justified, and not by faith only.
25 Likewise also was not Rahab the harlot justified by works, when she had received the messengers, and had sent *them* out another way?
26 For as the body without the spirit is dead, so faith without works is dead also.

James 3

3:1 ¶ My brethren, be not many masters, knowing that we shall receive the greater condemnation.
2 For in many things we offend all. If any man offends not in word, the same *is* a perfect man, *and* able also to bridle the whole body.
3 Behold, we put bits in the horses' mouths, that they may obey us; and we turn about their whole body.
4 Behold also the ships, which though *they are* so great, and *are* driven by fierce winds, yet are they turned about with a very small helm, wherever the governor wants.
5 Even so the tongue is a little member, and boasts great things. Behold, how great a woods a little fire kindles!
6 And the tongue *is* a fire, a world of iniquity: so is the tongue among our members, that it defiles the whole body, and sets on fire the course of nature; and it is set on fire by hell.
7 For every kind of beasts, and of birds, and of serpents, and of things in the sea, is tamed, and has been tamed of mankind:
8 But the tongue can no man tame; *it is* an unruly evil, full of deadly poison.
9 Therewith bless we God, even the Father; and therewith curse we men, which are made after the likeness of God.
10 Out of the same mouth proceeds blessing and cursing. My brethren, these things ought not so to be.
11 Does a fountain send forth at the same place sweet *water* and bitter?
12 Can the fig tree, my brethren, bear olive berries? either a vine, figs? so *can* no fountain both yield salt water and fresh.
13 ¶ Who *is* a wise man and endued with knowledge among you? let him show out of a good conversation his works with meekness of wisdom.
14 But if you have bitter envying and strife in your hearts, glory not, and lie not against the truth.
15 This wisdom descends not from above, but *is* earthly, sensual, devilish.
16 For where envying and strife *is*, there *is* confusion and every evil work.
17 But the wisdom that is from above is first pure, then peaceable, gentle, *and* easy to be entreated, full of mercy and good fruits, without partiality, and without hypocrisy.
18 And the fruit of righteousness is sown in peace by those that make peace.

James 4

4:1 ¶ From where *come* wars and fightings among you? *come they* not *from* here, *even* from your lusts that war in your members?
2 You lust, and have not: you kill, and desire to have, and cannot obtain: you fight and war, yet you have not, because you ask not.
3 You ask, and receive not, because you ask amiss, that you may consume *it* upon your lusts.
4 You adulterers and adulteresses, know you not that the friendship of the world is enmity with God? whoever therefore will be a friend of the world is the enemy of God.
5 Do you think that the scripture says in vain, The spirit that dwells in us desires to envy?
6 But he gives more grace. Therefore he says, God *Yahweh* resists the proud, but gives grace to the humble.
7 Submit yourselves therefore to God. Resist the devil, and he will flee from you.
8 Draw near to God, and he will draw near to you. Cleanse *your* hands, *you* sinners; and purify *your* hearts, *you* double minded.
9 Be afflicted, and mourn, and weep: let your laughter be turned to mourning, and *your* joy to heaviness.
10 Humble yourselves in the sight of the Lord, and he shall lift you up.
11 ¶ Speak not evil one of another, brethren. He that speaks evil of *his* brother, and judges his brother, speaks evil of the law, and judges the law: but if you judge the law, you are not a doer of the law, but a judge.
12 There is one lawgiver, who is able to save and to destroy: who are you that judge another?
13 Go to now, you that say, Today or tomorrow we will go into such a city, and continue there a year, and buy and sell, and get gain:
14 Whereas you know not what *shall be* on the next day. For what *is* your life? It is even a vapor, that appears for a little time, and then vanishes away.
15 For that you *ought* to say, If the Lord wills, we shall live, and do this, or that.
16 But now you rejoice in your boastings: all such rejoicing is evil.
17 Therefore to him that knows to do good, and does *it* not, to him it is sin.

James 5

5:1 ¶ Go to now, *you* rich men, weep and howl for your miseries that shall come upon *you*.
2 Your riches are corrupted, and your garments are moth eaten.
3 Your gold and silver is corroded; and the rust of them shall be a witness against you, and shall eat your flesh as it were fire. You have heaped treasure together for the last days.
4 Behold, the hire of the laborers who have reaped down your fields, which is by you kept back by fraud, cries: and the cries of them which have reaped have entered into the ears of the Lord of Sabaoth.
5 You have lived in pleasure on the earth, and been *in* luxury; you have nourished your hearts, as in a day of slaughter.
6 You have condemned *and* killed the just; *and* he does not resist you.

7 Be patient therefore, brethren, unto the coming of the Lord. Behold, the husbandman waits for the precious fruit of the earth, and has long patience for it, until he receives the early and latter rain.

8 Be you also patient; establish your hearts: for the coming of the Lord draws near.

9 Grudge not one against another, brethren, lest you be condemned: behold, the judge stands before the door.

10 Take, my brethren, the prophets, who have spoken in the name of the Lord *Yahweh*, for an example of suffering affliction, and of patience.

11 Behold, we count them happy which endure. You have heard of the patience of Job, and have seen the end of the Lord; that the Lord is very full of pity, and of tender mercy.

12 ¶ But above all things, my brethren, swear not, neither by heaven, neither by the earth, neither by any other oath: but let your yes be yes; and *your* no, no; lest you fall into condemnation.

13 Is any among you afflicted? let him pray. Is any merry? let him sing psalms.

14 Is any sick among you? let him call for the elders of the congregation; and let them pray over him, anointing him with oil in the name of the Lord:

15 And the prayer of faith shall save the sick, and the Lord shall raise him up; and if he has committed sins, they shall be forgiven him.

16 Confess *your* faults one to another, and pray one for another, that you may be healed. The effectual fervent prayer of a righteous man avails much.

17 Elijah was a man subject to like passions as we are, and he prayed earnestly that it might not rain: and it rained not on the earth by the space of three years and six months.

18 And he prayed again, and the heaven gave rain, and the earth brought forth her fruit.

19 Brethren, if any of you do err from the truth, and one converts him;

20 Let him know, that he which converts the sinner from the error of his way shall save a soul from death, and shall hide a multitude of sins.

1 Peter

1 Peter 1

1:1 ¶ Peter, an apostle of Yahshua the Messiah, to the strangers scattered throughout Pontus, Galatia, Cappadocia, Asia, and Bithynia,

2 Elect according to the foreknowledge of God the Father, through sanctification of the Spirit, unto obedience and sprinkling of the blood of Yahshua the Messiah: Grace unto you, and peace, be multiplied.

3 ¶ Blessed *be* the God and Father of our Lord Yahshua the Messiah, which according to his abundant mercy has begotten us again to a lively hope by the resurrection of Yahshua the Messiah from the dead,

4 To an inheritance incorruptible, and undefiled, and that fades not away, reserved in heaven for you,

5 Who are kept by the power of God through faith unto salvation ready to be revealed in the last time.

6 ¶ Wherein you greatly rejoice, though now for a season, if need be, you are in heaviness through manifold temptations:

7 That the trial of your faith, being much more precious than of gold that perishes, though it is tried with fire, might be found to praise and honor and glory at the appearing of Yahshua the Messiah:

8 Whom having not seen, you love; in whom, though now you see *him* not, yet believing, you rejoice with joy unspeakable and full of glory:

9 Receiving the end of your faith, *even* the salvation of *your* souls.

10 ¶ Of which salvation the prophets have inquired and searched diligently, who prophesied of the grace *that should come* unto you:

11 Searching what, or what manner of time the Spirit of the Messiah which was in them did signify, when it testified beforehand the sufferings of the Messiah, and the glory that should follow.

12 Unto whom it was revealed, that not unto themselves, but to us they did minister the things, which are now reported to you by them that have preached the gospel to you with the Holy Ghost sent down from heaven; which things the angels desire to look into.

13 ¶ Therefore gird up the loins of your mind, be sober, and hope to the end for the grace that is to be brought to you at the revelation of Yahshua the Messiah;

14 As obedient children, not fashioning yourselves according to the former lusts in your ignorance:

15 But as he which has called you is holy, so be you holy in all manner of conversation;

16 Because it is written, Be you holy; for I am holy.

17 And if you call on the Father, who without respect of persons judges according to every man's work, pass the time of your sojourning *here* in fear:

18 Forasmuch as you know that you were not redeemed with corruptible things, *as* silver and gold, from your vain conversation *received* by tradition from your fathers;

19 But with the precious blood of the Messiah, as of a lamb without blemish and without spot:

20 Who truly was foreordained before the foundation of the world, but was manifest in these last times for you,

21 Who by him do believe in God, that raised him up from the dead, and gave him glory; that your faith and hope might be in God.

22 Seeing you have purified your souls in obeying the truth through the Spirit unto unfeigned love of the brethren, *see that you* love one another with a pure heart fervently:

23 Being born again, not of corruptible seed, but of incorruptible, by the word of God, which lives and remains forever.

24 ¶ For all flesh *is* as grass, and all the glory of man as the flower of grass. The grass withers, and the flower thereof falls away:

25 But the word of the Lord endures forever. And this is the word which by the gospel is preached to you.

1 Peter 2

2:1 ¶ Therefore laying aside all malice, and all guile, and hypocrisies, and envies, and all evil speakings,
2 As newborn babes, desire the sincere milk of the word, that you may grow thereby:
3 If so be you have tasted that the Lord *is* gracious.
4 ¶ To whom coming, *as to* a living stone, disallowed indeed of men, but chosen of God, *and* precious,
5 You also, as lively stones, are built up a spiritual house, a holy priesthood, to offer up spiritual sacrifices, acceptable to God by Yahshua the Messiah.
6 Therefore also it is contained in the scripture, Behold, I lay in Zion a chief corner stone, elect, precious: and he that believes on him shall not be confounded.
7 Unto you therefore which believe *he is* precious: but to those which are disobedient, the stone which the builders disallowed, the same is made the head of the corner,
8 And a stone of stumbling, and a rock of offense, *even to them* which stumble at the word, being disobedient: whereunto also they were appointed.
9 But you *are* a chosen generation, a royal priesthood, a holy nation, a peculiar people; that you should show forth the praises of him who has called you out of darkness into his marvelous light:
10 Which in time past *were* not a people, but *are* now the people of God: which had not obtained mercy, but now have obtained mercy.
11 Dearly beloved, I beseech *you* as strangers and pilgrims, abstain from fleshly lusts, which war against the soul;
12 Having your conversation honest among the Gentiles: that, whereas they speak against you as evildoers, they may by *your* good works, which they shall behold, glorify God in the day of visitation.
13 ¶ Submit yourselves to every ordinance of man for the Lord's sake: whether it is to the king, as supreme;
14 Or to governors, as to them that are sent by him for the punishment of evildoers, and for the praise of them that do well.
15 For so is the will of God, that with well doing you may put to silence the ignorance of foolish men:
16 As free, and not using *your* liberty for a cloak of maliciousness, but as the servants of God.
17 Honor all *men*. Love the brotherhood. Fear God. Honor the king.
18 Servants, *be* subject to *your* masters with all fear; not only to the good and gentle, but also to the crooked.
19 For this *is* thank worthy, if a man for conscience toward God endures grief, suffering wrongfully.
20 For what glory *is it*, if, when you are buffeted for your faults, you shall take it patiently? but if, when you do well, and suffer *for it*, you take it patiently, this *is* acceptable with God.
21 For even hereunto were you called: because the Messiah also suffered for us, leaving us an example, that you should follow his steps:
22 Who did no sin, neither was guile found in his mouth:
23 Who, when he was reviled, reviled not again; when he suffered, he threatened not; but committed *himself* to him that judges righteously:
24 Who his own self bore our sins in his own body on the tree, that we, being dead to sins, should live unto righteousness: by whose stripes you were healed.
25 For you were as sheep going astray; but are now returned to the Shepherd and Overseer of your souls.

1 Peter 3

3:1 ¶ Likewise, you wives, *be* in subjection to your own husbands; that, if any obey not the word, they also may without the word be won by the conversation of the wives;
2 While they behold your chaste conversation *coupled* with fear.
3 Whose adorning let it not be that outward *adorning* of braiding the hair, and of wearing of gold, or of putting on of apparel;
4 But *let it be* the hidden man of the heart, in that which is not corruptible, *even the ornament* of a meek and quiet spirit, which is in the sight of God of great price.
5 For after this manner in the old time the holy women also, who trusted in God, adorned themselves, being in subjection to their own husbands:
6 Even as Sarah obeyed Abraham, calling him lord: whose daughters you are, as long as you do well, and are not afraid with any amazement.
7 Likewise, you husbands, dwell with *them* according to knowledge, giving honor to the wife, as to the weaker vessel, and as being heirs together of the grace of life; that your prayers be not hindered.
8 ¶ Finally, *be you* all of one mind, having compassion one of another, love as brothers, *be* pitiful, *be* courteous:
9 Not rendering evil for evil, or railing for railing: but on the contrary blessing; knowing that you are thereunto called, that you should inherit a blessing.
10 For he that will love life, and see good days, let him refrain his tongue from evil, and his lips that they speak no guile:
11 Let him avoid evil, and do good; let him seek peace, and ensue it.
12 For the eyes of the Lord *Yahweh are* over the righteous, and his ears *are* open to their prayers: but the face of the Lord *Yahweh is* against them that do evil.
13 And who *is* he that will harm you, if you are followers of that which is good?
14 But and if you suffer for righteousness' sake, happy *are you*: and be not afraid of their terror, neither be troubled;
15 But sanctify the Lord God in your hearts: and *be* ready always to *give* an answer to every man that asks you a reason of the hope that is in you with meekness and fear:

1 Peter 3

16 ¶ Having a good conscience; that, whereas they speak evil of you, as of evildoers, they may be ashamed that falsely accuse your good conversation in the Messiah.
17 For *it is* better, if the will of God be so, that you suffer for well doing, than for evil doing.
18 ¶ For the Messiah also has once suffered for sins, the just for the unjust, that he might bring us to God, being put to death in the flesh, but quickened by the Spirit:
19 By which also he went and preached to the spirits in prison;
20 Which sometimes were disobedient, when once the longsuffering of God waited in the days of Noah, while the ark was *in* preparation, wherein few, that is, eight souls were saved by water.
21 ¶ The like figure whereunto *even* baptism does also now save us (not the putting away of the filth of the flesh, but the answer of a good conscience toward God,) by the resurrection of Yahshua the Messiah:
22 Who has gone into heaven, and is on the right hand of God; angels and authorities and powers being made subject to him.

1 Peter 4

4:1 ¶ Forasmuch then as the Messiah has suffered for us in the flesh, arm yourselves likewise with the same mind: for he that has suffered in the flesh has ceased from sin;
2 That he no longer should live the rest of *his* time in the flesh to the lusts of men, but to the will of God.
3 For the time past of *our* life may suffice us to have worked the will of the Gentiles, when we walked in lasciviousness, lusts, excess of wine, revelings, drinking parties, and abominable idolatries:
4 ¶ Wherein they think it strange that you run not with *them* to the same excess of riot, speaking evil of *you*:
5 Who shall give account to him that is ready to judge the living and the dead.
6 For for this cause was the gospel preached also to them that are dead, that they might be judged according to men in the flesh, but live according to God in the spirit.
7 ¶ But the end of all things is at hand: be you therefore sober, and watch unto prayer.
8 And above all things have fervent charity among yourselves: for charity shall cover the multitude of sins.
9 Use hospitality one to another without grudging.
10 As every man has received the gift, *even so* minister the same one to another, as good stewards of the manifold grace of God.
11 If any man speaks, *let him speak* as the oracles of God; if any man ministers, *let him do it* as of the ability which God gives: that God in all things may be glorified through Yahshua the Messiah, to whom be praise and dominion forever and ever. Amen.
12 ¶ Beloved, think it not strange concerning the fiery trial which is to try you, as though some strange thing happened to you:

13 But rejoice, inasmuch as you are partakers of the Messiah's sufferings; that, when his glory shall be revealed, you may be glad also with exceeding joy.
14 If you are reproached for the name of the Messiah, happy *are you*; for the spirit of glory and of God rests upon you: on their part he is evil spoken of, but on your part he is glorified.
15 But let none of you suffer as a murderer, or *as* a thief, or *as* an evildoer, or as a busybody in other men's matters.
16 Yet if *any man suffers* as a Christian, let him not be ashamed; but let him glorify God on this behalf.
17 For the time *has come* that judgment must begin at the house of God: and if *it* first *begins* at us, what shall the end *be* of them that obey not the gospel of God?
18 And if the righteous scarcely be saved, where shall the ungodly and the sinner appear?
19 Therefore let them that suffer according to the will of God commit the keeping of their souls *to him* in well doing, as unto a faithful Creator.

1 Peter 5

5:1 ¶ The elders which are among you I exhort, who am also an elder, and a witness of the sufferings of the Messiah, and also a partaker of the glory that shall be revealed:
2 Feed the flock of God which is among you, taking the oversight *thereof*, not by constraint, but willingly; not for filthy profit, but of a ready mind;
3 Neither as being lords over *God's* heritage, but being examples to the flock.
4 And when the chief Shepherd shall appear, you shall receive a crown of glory that fades not away.
5 ¶ Likewise, you younger, submit yourselves unto the elder. Yes, all *of you* be subject one to another, and be clothed with humility: for God *Yahweh* resists the proud, and gives grace to the humble.
6 Humble yourselves therefore under the mighty hand of God, that he may exalt you in due time:
7 Casting all your cares upon him; for he cares for you.
8 ¶ Be sober, be vigilant; because your adversary the devil, as a roaring lion, walks about, seeking whom he may devour:
9 Whom resist steadfast in the faith, knowing that the same afflictions are accomplished in your brethren that are in the world.
10 ¶ But the God of all grace, who has called us unto his eternal glory by the Messiah Yahshua, after that you have suffered a while, make you perfect, establish, strengthen, settle *you*.
11 To him *be* glory and dominion forever and ever. Amen.
12 By Silvanus, a faithful brother to you, as I suppose, I have written briefly, exhorting, and testifying that this is the true grace of God wherein you stand.
13 The *congregation that is* at Babylon, elected together with *you*, salutes you; and *so does* Marcus my son.

14 Greet you one another with a kiss of charity. Peace *be* with you all that are in the Messiah Yahshua. Amen.

2 Peter

2 Peter 1

1:1 ¶ Simon Peter, a servant and an apostle of Yahshua the Messiah, to them that have obtained like precious faith with us through the righteousness of God and our Savior Yahshua the Messiah:

2 Grace and peace be multiplied unto you through the knowledge of God, and of Yahshua our Lord,

3 According as his divine power has given to us all things that *pertain* unto life and godliness, through the knowledge of him that has called us to glory and virtue:

4 Whereby are given to us exceedingly great and precious promises: that by these you might be partakers of the divine nature, having escaped the corruption that is in the world through lust.

5 ¶ And besides this, giving all diligence, add to your faith virtue; and to virtue knowledge;

6 And to knowledge temperance; and to temperance patience; and to patience godliness;

7 And to godliness brotherly kindness; and to brotherly kindness charity.

8 For if these things are in you, and abound, they make *you that you shall* neither *be* barren nor unfruitful in the knowledge of our Lord Yahshua the Messiah.

9 But he that lacks these things is blind, and cannot see afar off, and has forgotten that he was purged from his old sins.

10 Therefore the rather, brethren, give diligence to make your calling and election sure: for if you do these things, you shall never fall:

11 For so an entrance shall be ministered to you abundantly into the everlasting kingdom of our Lord and Savior Yahshua the Messiah.

12 ¶ Therefore I will not be negligent to put you always in remembrance of these things, though you know *them*, and are established in the present truth.

13 Yes, I think it right, as long as I am in this tabernacle, to stir you up by putting *you* in remembrance;

14 Knowing that shortly I must put off *this* my tabernacle, even as our Lord Yahshua the Messiah has shown me.

15 Moreover I will endeavor that you may be able after my decease to have these things always in remembrance.

16 ¶ For we have not followed cunningly devised fables, when we made known to you the power and coming of our Lord Yahshua the Messiah, but were eyewitnesses of his majesty.

17 For he received from God the Father honor and glory, when there came such a voice to him from the excellent glory, This is my beloved Son, in whom I am well pleased.

18 And this voice which came from heaven we heard, when we were with him in the holy mount.

19 ¶ We have also a more sure word of prophecy; whereunto you do well that you take heed, as unto a light that shines in a dark place, until the day dawns, and the day star arises in your hearts:

20 Knowing this first, that no prophecy of the scripture is of any private interpretation.

21 For the prophecy came not in old time by the will of man: but holy men of God spoke *as they were* moved by the Holy Ghost.

2 Peter 2

2:1 ¶ But there were false prophets also among the people, even as there shall be false teachers among you, who secretly shall bring in damnable heresies, even denying the Lord that bought them, and bring upon themselves swift destruction.

2 And many shall follow their pernicious ways; by reason of whom the way of truth shall be evilly spoken of.

3 ¶ And through covetousness shall they with feigned words make merchandise of you: whose judgment now of a long time lingers not, and their damnation slumbers not.

4 For if God spared not the angels that sinned, but cast *them* down to hell, and delivered *them* into chains of darkness, to be reserved unto judgment;

5 And spared not the old world, but saved Noah the eighth *person*, a preacher of righteousness, bringing in the flood upon the world of the ungodly;

6 And turning the cities of Sodom and Gomorrah into ashes condemned *them* with an overthrow, making *them* an example to those that after should live ungodly;

7 ¶ And delivered just Lot, oppressed with the filthy conversation of the wicked:

8 (For that righteous man dwelling among them, in seeing and hearing, tormented *his* righteous soul from day to day with *their* unlawful deeds;)

9 The Lord knows how to deliver the godly out of temptations, and to reserve the unjust unto the day of judgment to be punished:

10 ¶ But chiefly them that walk after the flesh in the lust of uncleanness, and despise government. Presumptuous *are they*, self-willed, they are not afraid to speak evil of dignities.

11 Whereas angels, which are greater in power and might, bring not railing accusation against them before the Lord.

12 But these, as natural brute beasts, made to be taken and destroyed, speak evilly of the things that they understand not; and shall utterly perish in their own corruption;

13 And shall receive the reward of unrighteousness, *as* they that count it pleasure to riot in the day time. Spots *they are* and blemishes, sporting themselves with their own deceitfulness while they feast with you;

14 Having eyes full of adultery, and that cannot cease from sin; beguiling unstable souls: a heart they have exercised with covetous practices; cursed children:

2 Peter 2

15 Which have forsaken the right way, and are gone astray, following the way of Balaam *the son* of Beor, who loved the wages of unrighteousness;
16 But was rebuked for his iniquity: the dumb donkey speaking with man's voice forbade the madness of the prophet.
17 These are wells without water, clouds that are carried with a tempest; to whom the mist of darkness is reserved forever.
18 For when they speak great swelling *words* of vanity, they allure through the lusts of the flesh, *through much* promiscuity, those that were clean escaped from them who live in error.
19 While they promise them liberty, they themselves are the servants of corruption: for of whom a man is overcome, of the same is he brought in bondage.
20 For if after they have escaped the pollutions of the world through the knowledge of the Lord and Savior Yahshua the Messiah, they are again entangled therein, and overcome, the latter end is worse with them than the beginning.
21 For it had been better for them not to have known the way of righteousness, than, after they had known *it*, to turn from the holy commandment delivered to them.
22 But it has happened to them according to the true proverb, The dog *has* turned to his own vomit again; and the sow that was washed to her wallowing in the mire.

2 Peter 3

3:1 ¶ This second epistle, beloved, I now write to you; in *both* which I stir up your pure minds by way of remembrance:
2 That you may be mindful of the words which were spoken before by the holy prophets, and of the commandment of us the apostles of the Lord and Savior:
3 ¶ Knowing this first, that there shall come in the last days scoffers, walking after their own lusts,
4 And saying, Where is the promise of his coming? for since the fathers fell asleep, all things continue as *they were* from the beginning of the creation.
5 For this they willingly are ignorant of, that by the word of God the heavens were of old, and the earth standing out of the water and in the water:
6 Whereby the world that then was, being overflowed with water, perished:
7 But the heavens and the earth, which are now, by the same word are kept in store, reserved unto fire against the day of judgment and perdition of ungodly men.
8 ¶ But, beloved, be not ignorant of this one thing, that one day *is* with the Lord as a thousand years, and a thousand years as one day.
9 ¶ The Lord is not slack concerning his promise, as some men count slackness; but is longsuffering toward us, not willing that any should perish, but that all should come to repentance.
10 But the day of the Lord will come as a thief in the night; in which the heavens shall pass away with a great noise, and the elements shall melt with fervent heat, the earth also and the works that are therein shall be burned up.
11 ¶ *Seeing* then *that* all these things shall be dissolved, what manner *of persons* ought you to be in *all* holy conversation and godliness,
12 Looking for and hastening unto the coming of the day of God, wherein the heavens being on fire shall be dissolved, and the elements shall melt with fervent heat?
13 Nevertheless we, according to his promise, look for new heavens and a new earth, wherein dwells righteousness.
14 Therefore, beloved, seeing that you look for such things, be diligent that you may be found of him in peace, without spot, and blameless.
15 And account *that* the longsuffering of our Lord *is* salvation; even as our beloved brother Paul also according to the wisdom given to him has written to you;
16 As also in all *his* epistles, speaking in them of these things; in which are some things hard to be understood, which they that are unlearned and unstable twist, as *they do* also the other scriptures, unto their own destruction.
17 You therefore, beloved, seeing you know *these things* before, beware lest you also, being led away with the error of the wicked, fall from your own steadfastness.
18 But grow in grace, and *in* the knowledge of our Lord and Savior Yahshua the Messiah. To him *be* glory both now and forever. Amen.

1 John

1 John 1

1:1 ¶ That which was from the beginning, which we have heard, which we have seen with our eyes, which we have looked upon, and our hands have handled, of the Word of life;
2 (For the life was manifested, and we have seen *it*, and bear witness, and show to you that eternal life, which was with the Father, and was manifested to us;)
3 That which we have seen and heard declare we unto you, that you also may have fellowship with us: and truly our fellowship *is* with the Father, and with his Son Yahshua the Messiah.
4 And these things write we unto you, that your joy may be full.
5 ¶ This then is the message which we have heard of him, and declare to you, that God is light, and in him is no darkness at all.
6 If we say that we have fellowship with him, and walk in darkness, we lie, and do not the truth:

7 But if we walk in the light, as he is in the light, we have fellowship one with another, and the blood of Yahshua the Messiah his Son cleanses us from all sin.

8 ¶ If we say that we have no sin, we deceive ourselves, and the truth is not in us.

9 If we confess our sins, he is faithful and just to forgive us *our* sins, and to cleanse us from all unrighteousness.

10 If we say that we have not sinned, we make him a liar, and his word is not in us.

1 John 2

2:1 ¶ My little children, these things write I unto you, that you sin not. And if any man sins, we have an advocate with the Father, Yahshua the Messiah the righteous:

2 And he is the propitiation for our sins: and not for ours only, but also for *the sins of* the whole world.

3 ¶ And hereby we do know that we know him, if we keep his commandments.

4 He that says, I know him, and keeps not his commandments, is a liar, and the truth is not in him.

5 But whoever keeps his word, in him truly is the love of God perfected: hereby know we that we are in him.

6 He that says he dwells in him ought himself also so to walk, even as he walked.

7 ¶ Brethren, I write no new commandment unto you, but an old commandment which you had from the beginning. The old commandment is the word which you have heard from the beginning.

8 Again, a new commandment I write unto you, which thing is true in him and in you: because the darkness is past, and the true light now shines.

9 He that says he is in the light, and hates his brother, is in darkness even until now.

10 He that loves his brother remains in the light, and there is no occasion of stumbling in him.

11 But he that hates his brother is in darkness, and walks in darkness, and knows not where he goes, because that darkness has blinded his eyes.

12 ¶ I write unto you, little children, because your sins are forgiven you for his name's sake.

13 I write unto you, fathers, because you have known him *that is* from the beginning. I write to you, young men, because you have overcome the wicked one. I write unto you, little children, because you have known the Father.

14 I have written unto you, fathers, because you have known him *that is* from the beginning. I have written unto you, young men, because you are strong, and the word of God remains in you, and you have overcome the wicked one.

15 Love not the world, neither the things *that are* in the world. If any man loves the world, the love of the Father is not in him.

16 For all that *is* in the world, the lust of the flesh, and the lust of the eyes, and the pride of life, is not of the Father, but is of the world.

17 And the world passes away, and the lust thereof: but he that does the will of God remains forever.

18 ¶ Little children, it is the last time: and as you have heard that antichrist shall come, even now are there many antichrists; whereby we know that it is the last time.

19 They went out from us, but they were not of us; for if they had been of us, they would *no doubt* have continued with us: but *they went out*, that they might be made manifest that they were not all of us.

20 ¶ But you have an anointing from the Holy One, and you know all things.

21 I have not written unto you because you know not the truth, but because you know it, and that no lie is of the truth.

22 Who is a liar but he that denies that Yahshua is the Messiah? He is antichrist, that denies the Father and the Son.

23 Whoever denies the Son, the same has not the Father: *(but) he that acknowledges the Son has the Father also*.

24 Let that therefore dwell in you, which you have heard from the beginning. If that which you have heard from the beginning shall remain in you, you also shall continue in the Son, and in the Father.

25 And this is the promise that he has promised us, *even* eternal life.

26 These *things* have I written to you concerning them that seduce you.

27 But the anointing which you have received of him continues in you, and you need not that any man teach you: but as the same anointing teaches you of all things, and is truth, and is no lie, and even as it has taught you, you shall remain in him.

28 ¶ And now, little children, remain in him; that, when he shall appear, we may have confidence, and not be ashamed before him at his coming.

29 If you know that he is righteous, you know that every one that does righteousness is born of him.

1 John 3

3:1 ¶ Behold, what manner of love the Father has bestowed upon us, that we should be called the sons of God: therefore the world knows us not, because it knew him not.

2 Beloved, now are we the sons of God, and it does not yet appear what we shall be: but we know that, when he shall appear, we shall be like him; for we shall see him as he is.

3 And every man that has this hope in him purifies himself, even as he is pure.

4 ¶ Whoever commits sin transgresses also the law: for sin is the transgression of the law.

5 And you know that he was manifested to take away our sins; and in him is no sin.

6 Whoever remains in him sins not: whoever sins has not seen him, neither known him.

7 Little children, let no man deceive you: he that does righteousness is righteous, even as he is righteous.

8 He that commits sin is of the devil; for the devil sinned from the beginning. For this purpose the Son of God was manifested, that he might destroy the works of the devil.

9 Whoever is born of God does not commit sin; for his seed remains in him: and he cannot sin, because he is born of God.

10 In this the children of God are manifest, and the children of the devil: whoever does not righteousness is not of God, neither he that loves not his brother.

11 ¶ For this is the message that you heard from the beginning, that we should love one another.

12 Not as Cain, *who* was of that wicked one, and slew his brother. And why slew he him? Because his own works were evil, and his brother's righteous.

13 Marvel not, my brethren, if the world hates you.

14 ¶ We know that we have passed from death unto life, because we love the brethren. He that loves not *his* brother remains in death.

15 Whoever hates his brother is a murderer: and you know that no murderer has eternal life abiding in him.

16 Hereby perceive we the love *of God*, because he laid down his life for us: and we ought to lay down *our* lives for the brethren.

17 But whoever has this world's goods, and sees his brother has need, and shuts up his bowels *of compassion* from him, how dwells the love of God in him?

18 My little children, let us not love in word, neither in tongue; but in deed and in truth.

19 And hereby we know that we are of the truth, and shall assure our hearts before him.

20 ¶ For if our heart condemns us, God is greater than our heart, and knows all things.

21 Beloved, if our heart condemns us not, *then* have we confidence toward God.

22 And whatever we ask, we receive of him, because we keep his commandments, and do those things that are pleasing in his sight.

23 ¶ And this is his commandment, That we should believe on the name of his Son Yahshua the Messiah, and love one another, as he gave us commandment.

24 And he that keeps his commandments dwells in him, and he in him. And hereby we know that he remains in us, by the Spirit which he has given us.

1 John 4

4:1 ¶ Beloved, believe not every spirit, but try the spirits whether they are of God: because many false prophets have gone out into the world.

2 Hereby know you the Spirit of God: Every spirit that confesses that Yahshua the Messiah has come in the flesh is of God:

3 And every spirit that confesses not that Yahshua the Messiah has come in the flesh is not of God: and this is that *spirit* of antichrist, whereof you have heard that it should come; and even now already is it in the world.

4 ¶ You are of God, little children, and have overcome them: because greater is he that is in you, than he that is in the world.

5 They are of the world: therefore speak they of the world, and the world hears them.

6 We are of God: he that knows God hears us; he that is not of God hears not us. Hereby know we the spirit of truth, and the spirit of error.

7 ¶ Beloved, let us love one another: for love is of God; and every one that loves is born of God, and knows God.

8 He that loves not knows not God; for God is love.

9 In this was manifested the love of God toward us, because that God sent his only begotten Son into the world, that we might live through him.

10 Herein is love, not that we loved God, but that he loved us, and sent his Son *to be* the propitiation for our sins.

11 Beloved, if God so loved us, we ought also to love one another.

12 No man has seen God at any time. If we love one another, God dwells in us, and his love is perfected in us.

13 Hereby know we that we dwell in him, and he in us, because he has given us of his Spirit.

14 ¶ And we have seen and do testify that the Father sent the Son *to be* the Savior of the world.

15 Whoever shall confess that Yahshua is the Son of God, God dwells in him, and he in God.

16 And we have known and believed the love that God has to us. God is love; and he that dwells in love dwells in God, and God in him.

17 ¶ Herein is our love made perfect, that we may have boldness in the day of judgment: because as he is, so are we in this world.

18 There is no fear in love; but perfect love casts out fear: because fear has torment. He that fears is not made perfect in love.

19 We love him, because he first loved us.

20 If a man says, I love God, and hates his brother, he is a liar: for he that loves not his brother whom he has seen, how can he love God whom he has not seen?

21 And this commandment have we from him, That he who loves God love his brother also.

1 John 5

5:1 ¶ Whoever believes that Yahshua is the Messiah is born of God: and every one that loves him that begot loves him also that is begotten of him.

2 By this we know that we love the children of God, when we love God, and keep his commandments.

3 For this is the love of God, that we keep his commandments: and his commandments are not grievous.

4 For whatever is born of God overcomes the world: and this is the victory that overcomes the world, *even* our faith.

5 Who is he that overcomes the world, but he that believes that Yahshua is the Son of God?

6 ¶ This is he that came by water and blood, *even* Yahshua the Messiah; not by water only, but by water and blood. And it is the Spirit that bears witness, because the Spirit is truth.

7 For there are three that bear record in heaven, the Father, the Word, and the Holy Ghost: and these three are one.

8 And there are three that bear witness in earth, the Spirit, and the water, and the blood: and these three agree in one.

9 If we receive the witness of men, the witness of God is greater: for this is the witness of God which he has testified of his Son.

10 ¶ He that believes on the Son of God has the witness in himself: he that believes not God has made him a liar; because he believes not the record that God gave of his Son.

11 And this is the record, that God has given to us eternal life, and this life is in his Son.

12 He that has the Son has life; *and* he that has not the Son of God has not life.

13 These things have I written unto you that believe on the name of the Son of God; that you may know that you have eternal life, and that you may believe on the name of the Son of God.

14 ¶ And this is the confidence that we have in him, that, if we ask anything according to his will, he hears us:

15 And if we know that he hears us, whatever we ask, we know that we have the petitions that we desired of him.

16 If any man sees his brother sin a sin *which is* not unto death, he shall ask, and he shall give him life for them that sin not unto death. There is a sin unto death: I do not say that he shall pray for it.

17 All unrighteousness is sin: and there is a sin not unto death.

18 ¶ We know that whoever is born of God sins not; but he that is begotten of God keeps himself, and that wicked one touches him not.

19 *And* we know that we are of God, and the whole world lies in wickedness.

20 And we know that the Son of God has come, and has given us an understanding, that we may know him that is true, and we are in him that is true, *even* in his Son Yahshua the Messiah. This is the true God, and eternal life.

21 Little children, keep yourselves from idols. Amen.

2 John

2 John 1

1:1 ¶ The elder to the elect lady and her children, whom I love in the truth; and not I only, but also all they that have known the truth;

2 For the truth's sake, which dwells in us, and shall be with us forever.

3 Grace be with you, mercy, *and* peace, from God the Father, and from the Lord Yahshua the Messiah, the Son of the Father, in truth and love.

4 I rejoiced greatly that I found of your children walking in truth, as we have received a commandment from the Father.

5 ¶ And now I beseech you, lady, not as though I wrote a new commandment to you, but that which we had from the beginning, that we love one another.

6 And this is love, that we walk after his commandments. This is the commandment, That, as you have heard from the beginning, you should walk in it.

7 ¶ For many deceivers have entered into the world, who confess not that Yahshua the Messiah has come in the flesh. This is a deceiver and an antichrist.

8 Look to yourselves, that we lose not those things which we have worked, but that we receive a full reward.

9 Whoever transgresses, and abides not in the doctrine of the Messiah, has not God. He that abides in the doctrine of the Messiah, he has both the Father and the Son.

10 ¶ If there comes any to you, and brings not this doctrine, receive him not into *your* house, neither bid him God speed:

11 For he that bids him God speed is partaker of his evil deeds.

12 ¶ Having many things to write unto you, I would not *write* with paper and ink: but I trust to come unto you, and speak face to face, that our joy may be full.

13 The children of your elect sister greet you. Amen.

3 John

3 John 1

1:1 ¶ The elder to the wellbeloved Gaius, whom I love in the truth.

2 Beloved, I wish above all things that you may prosper and be in health, even as your soul prospers.

3 ¶ For I rejoiced greatly, when the brethren came and testified of the truth that is in you, even as you walk in the truth.

4 I have no greater joy than to hear that my children walk in truth.

5 Beloved, you do faithfully whatever you do to the brethren, and to strangers;

6 Which have borne witness of your charity before the congregation: whom if you bring forward on their journey after a godly sort, you shall do well:

7 Because that for his name's sake they went forth, taking nothing of the Gentiles.

8 We therefore ought to receive such, that we might be fellow helpers to the truth.

9 ¶ I wrote to the congregation: but Diotrephes, who loves to have the preeminence among them, receives us not.

3 John 1

10 Therefore, if I come, I will remember his deeds which he does, talking idly against us with malicious words: and not content therewith, neither does he himself receive the brethren, and forbids them that would, and casts *them* out of the congregation.

11 Beloved, follow not that which is evil, but that which is good. He that does good is of God: but he that does evil has not seen God.

12 ¶ Demetrius has good report of all *men*, and of the truth itself: yes, and we *also* bear record; and you know that our record is true.

13 I had many things to write, but I will not with ink and pen write unto you:

14 But I trust I shall shortly see you, and we shall speak face to face. Peace *be* to you. *Our* friends salute you. Greet the friends by name.

Jude

Jude 1

1:1 ¶ Jude, the servant of Yahshua the Messiah, and brother of James, to them that are sanctified by God the Father, and preserved in Yahshua the Messiah, *and* called:

2 Mercy unto you, and peace, and love, be multiplied.

3 ¶ Beloved, when I gave all diligence to write unto you of the common salvation, it was needful for me to write unto you, and exhort *you* that you should earnestly contend for the faith which was once delivered to the saints.

4 For there are certain men crept in unnoticed, who were before of old ordained to this condemnation, ungodly men, turning the grace of our God into lasciviousness, and denying the only Lord God, and our Lord Yahshua the Messiah.

5 I will therefore put you in remembrance, though you once knew this, how that the Lord *Yahweh*, having saved the people out of the land of Egypt, afterward destroyed them that believed not.

6 And the angels which kept not their first estate, but left their own habitation, he has reserved in everlasting chains under darkness unto the judgment of the great day.

7 Even as Sodom and Gomorrah, and the cities about them in like manner, giving themselves over to fornication, and going after strange flesh, are set forth for an example, suffering the vengeance of eternal fire.

8 ¶ Likewise also these *filthy* dreamers defile the flesh, despise dominion, and speak evil of dignities.

9 Yet Michael the archangel, when contending with the devil he disputed about the body of Moses, dared not bring against him a railing accusation, but said, The Lord *Yahweh* rebuke you.

10 But these speak evil of those things which they know not: but what they know naturally, as brute beasts, in those things they corrupt themselves.

11 Woe unto them! for they have gone in the way of Cain, and ran greedily after the error of Balaam for reward, and perished in the gainsaying of Korah.

12 These are spots in your feasts of charity, when they feast with you, feeding themselves without fear: clouds *they are* without water, carried about of winds; trees whose fruit withers, without fruit, twice dead, plucked up by the roots;

13 Raging waves of the sea, foaming out their own shame; wandering stars, to whom is reserved the blackness of darkness forever.

14 And Enoch also, the seventh from Adam, prophesied of these, saying, Behold, the Lord comes with ten thousands of his saints,

15 ¶ To execute judgment upon all, and to convince all that are ungodly among them of all their ungodly deeds which they have ungodly committed, and of all their hard *speeches* which ungodly sinners have spoken against him.

16 These are murmurers, complainers, walking after their own lusts; and their mouth speaks great swelling *words*, having men's persons in admiration because of advantage.

17 But, beloved, remember you the words which were spoken before of the apostles of our Lord Yahshua the Messiah;

18 How that they told you there should be mockers in the last time, who should walk after their own ungodly lusts.

19 These are they who separate themselves, sensual, having not the Spirit.

20 But you, beloved, building up yourselves on your most holy faith, praying in the Holy Ghost,

21 Keep yourselves in the love of God, looking for the mercy of our Lord Yahshua the Messiah to eternal life.

22 And of some have compassion, making a difference:

23 And others save with fear, pulling *them* out of the fire; hating even the garment spotted by the flesh.

24 Now unto him that is able to keep you from falling, and to present *you* faultless before the presence of his glory with exceeding joy,

25 To the only wise God our Savior, *be* glory and majesty, dominion and power, both now and ever. Amen.

Section 7
Prophecy

Revelation

Revelation 1

1:1 ¶ The Revelation of Yahshua the Messiah, which God gave to him, to show to his servants things which must shortly come to pass; and he sent and signified *it* by his angel to his servant John:

2 Who bore record of the word of God, and of the testimony of Yahshua the Messiah, and of all things that he saw.

3 ¶ Blessed *is* he that reads, and they that hear the words of this prophecy, and keeps those things which are written therein: for the time *is* at hand.

4 John to the seven congregations which are in Asia: Grace *be* to you, and peace, from him which is, and which was, and which is to come; and from the seven Spirits which are before his throne;

5 And from Yahshua the Messiah, *who is* the faithful witness, *and* the first begotten of the dead, and the ruler of the kings of the earth. To him that loved us, and washed us from our sins in his own blood,

6 And has made us kings and priests unto God and his Father; to him *be* glory and power forever and ever. Amen.

7 Behold, he comes with clouds; and every eye shall see him, and they *also* which pierced him: and all families of the earth shall wail because of him. Even so, Amen.

8 I am Alpha and Omega, the beginning and the ending, says the Lord, which is, and which was, and which is to come, the Almighty.

9 ¶ I John, who also am your brother, and companion in tribulation, and in the kingdom and patience of Yahshua the Messiah, was in the isle that is called Patmos, for the word of God, and for the testimony of Yahshua the Messiah.

10 I was in the Spirit on the Lord's day, and heard behind me a great voice, as of a trumpet,

11 Saying, I am Alpha and Omega, the first and the last: and, What you see, write in a book, and send *it* to the seven congregations which are in Asia; to Ephesus, and to Smyrna, and to Pergamos, and to Thyatira, and to Sardis, and to Philadelphia, and to Laodicea.

12 And I turned to see the voice that spoke with me. And being turned, I saw seven golden candlesticks;

13 And in the midst of the seven candlesticks *one* like unto the Son of man, clothed with a garment down to the foot, and girt about the breasts with a golden girdle.

14 His head and *his* hair *were* white like wool, as white as snow; and his eyes *were* as a flame of fire;

15 And his feet like unto fine brass, as if they burned in a furnace; and his voice as the sound of many waters.

16 And he had in his right hand seven stars: and out of his mouth went a sharp two-edged sword: and his face *was* as the sun shines in its strength.

17 And when I saw him, I fell at his feet as dead. And he laid his right hand upon me, saying to me, Fear not; I am the first and the last:

18 I *am* he that lives, and was dead; and, behold, I am alive forevermore, Amen; and have the keys of hell and of death.

19 Write the things which you have seen, and the things which are, and the things which shall be hereafter;

20 The mystery of the seven stars which you saw in my right hand, and the seven golden candlesticks. The seven stars are the angels of the seven congregations: and the seven candlesticks which you saw are the seven congregations.

Revelation 2

2:1 ¶ Unto the angel of the congregation of Ephesus write; These things says he that holds the seven stars in his right hand, who walks in the midst of the seven golden candlesticks;

2 I know your works, and your labor, and your patience, and how you can not bear them which are evil: and you have tried them which say they are apostles, and are not, and have found them liars:

3 And have borne, and have patience, and for my name's sake have labored, and have not fainted.

4 Nevertheless I have *something* against you, because you have left your first love.

5 Remember therefore from where you have fallen, and repent, and do the first works; or else I will come to you quickly, and will remove your candlestick out of his place, unless you repent.

6 But this you have, that you hate the deeds of the Nicolaitans, which I also hate.

7 He that has an ear, let him hear what the Spirit says to the congregations; To him that overcomes will I give to eat of the tree of life, which is in the midst of the paradise of God.

8 ¶ And to the angel of the congregation in Smyrna write; These things says the first and the last, which was dead, and is alive;

9 I know your works, and tribulation, and poverty, (but you are rich) and *I know* the blasphemy of them which say they are Jews, and are not, but *are* the synagogue of Satan.

10 Fear none of those things which you shall suffer: behold, the devil shall cast *some* of you into prison, that you may be tried; and you shall have tribulation ten days: be you faithful unto death, and I will give you a crown of life.

11 He that has an ear, let him hear what the Spirit says to the congregations; He that overcomes shall not be hurt by the second death.

Revelation 2

12 ¶ And to the angel of the congregation in Pergamos write; These things says he which has the sharp sword with two edges;

13 I know your works, and where you dwell, *even* where Satan's seat *is*: and you hold fast my name, and have not denied my faith, even in those days wherein Antipas *was* my faithful martyr, who was slain among you, where Satan dwells.

14 But I have a few things against you, because you have there them that hold the doctrine of Balaam, who taught Balak to cast a stumbling block before the children of Israel, to eat things sacrificed to idols, and to commit fornication.

15 So have you also them that hold the doctrine of the Nicolaitans, which thing I hate.

16 Repent; or else I will come to you quickly, and will fight against them with the sword of my mouth.

17 He that has an ear, let him hear what the Spirit says to the congregations; To him that overcomes will I give to eat of the hidden manna, and will give him a white stone, and in the stone a new name written, which no man knows saving he that receives *it*.

18 ¶ And to the angel of the congregation in Thyatira write; These things says the Son of God, who has his eyes like unto a flame of fire, and his feet *are* like fine brass;

19 I know your works, and charity, and service, and faith, and your patience, and your works; and the last *to be* more than the first.

20 Notwithstanding I have a few things against you, because you allow that woman Jezebel, which calls herself a prophetess, to teach and to seduce my servants to commit fornication, and to eat things sacrificed to idols.

21 And I gave her space to repent of her fornication; and she repented not.

22 Behold, I will cast her into a bed, and them that commit adultery with her into great tribulation, unless they repent of their deeds.

23 And I will kill her children with death; and all the congregations shall know that I am he which searches the reins and hearts: and I will give to every one of you according to your works.

24 But to you I say, and to the rest in Thyatira, as many as have not this doctrine, and which have not known the depths of Satan, as they speak; I will put upon you no other burden.

25 But that which you have *already* hold fast till I come.

26 And he that overcomes, and keeps my works unto the end, to him will I give power over the nations:

27 And he shall rule them with a rod of iron; as the vessels of a potter shall they be broken to pieces: even as I received of my Father.

28 And I will give him the morning star.

29 He that has an ear, let him hear what the Spirit says to the congregations.

Revelation 3

3:1 ¶ And to the angel of the congregation in Sardis write; These things says he that has the seven Spirits of God, and the seven stars; I know your works, that you have a name that you live, and are dead.

2 Be watchful, and strengthen the things which remain, that are ready to die: for I have not found your works perfect before God.

3 Remember therefore how you have received and heard, and hold fast, and repent. If therefore you shall not watch, I will come upon you as a thief, and you shall not know what hour I will come upon you.

4 You have a few names even in Sardis which have not defiled their garments; and they shall walk with me in white: for they are worthy.

5 He that overcomes, the same shall be clothed in white garments; and I will not blot out his name out of the book of life, but I will confess his name before my Father, and before his angels.

6 He that has an ear, let him hear what the Spirit says to the congregations.

7 ¶ And to the angel of the congregation in Philadelphia write; These things says he that is holy, he that is true, he that has the key of David, he that opens, and no man shuts; and shuts, and no man opens;

8 I know your works: behold, I have set before you an open door, and no man can shut it: for you have a little strength, and have kept my word, and have not denied my name.

9 Behold, I will make them of the synagogue of Satan, which say they are Jews, and are not, but do lie; behold, I will make them to come and worship before your feet, and to know that I have loved you.

10 Because you have kept the word of my patience, I also will keep you from the hour of temptation, which shall come upon all the world, to try them that dwell upon the earth.

11 Behold, I come quickly: hold that fast which you have, that no man take your crown.

12 Him that overcomes will I make a pillar in the temple of my God, and he shall go no more out: and I will write upon him the name of my God, and the name of the city of my God, *which is* new Jerusalem, which comes down out of heaven from my God: and *I will write upon him* my new name.

13 He that has an ear, let him hear what the Spirit says to the congregations.

14 ¶ And to the angel of the congregation of the Laodiceans write; These things says the Amen, the faithful and true witness, the beginning of the creation of God;

15 I know your works, that you are neither cold nor hot: I would you were cold or hot.

16 So then because you are lukewarm, and neither cold nor hot, I will spew you out of my mouth.

17 Because you say, I am rich, and increased with goods, and have need of nothing; and know not that you are wretched, and miserable, and poor, and blind, and naked:

18 I counsel you to buy of me gold tried in the fire, that you may be rich; and white garments, that you may be clothed, and *that* the shame of your nakedness does not appear; and anoint your eyes with eye salve, that you may see.

19 As many as I love, I rebuke and chasten: be zealous therefore, and repent.

20 Behold, I stand at the door, and knock: if any man hears my voice, and opens the door, I will come in to him, and will sup with him, and he with me.

21 To him that overcomes will I grant to sit with me in my throne, even as I also overcame, and am set down with my Father in his throne.

22 He that has an ear, let him hear what the Spirit says to the congregations.

Revelation 4

4:1 ¶ After this I looked, and, behold, a door *was* opened in heaven: and the first voice which I heard *was* as it were of a trumpet talking with me; which said, Come up here, and I will show you things which must be hereafter.

2 And immediately I was in the spirit: and, behold, a throne was set in heaven, and *one* sat on the throne.

3 And he that sat was to look upon like a jasper and a sardius stone: and *there was* a rainbow round about the throne, in sight like unto an emerald.

4 And round about the throne *were* four and twenty seats: and upon the seats I saw four and twenty elders sitting, clothed in white garments; and they had on their heads crowns of gold.

5 And out of the throne proceeded lightnings and thunderings and voices: and *there were* seven lamps of fire burning before the throne, which are the seven Spirits of God.

6 And before the throne *there was* a sea of glass like unto crystal: and in the midst of the throne, and round about the throne, *were* four beasts full of eyes before and behind.

7 And the first beast *was* like a lion, and the second beast like a calf, and the third beast had a face as a man, and the fourth beast *was* like a flying eagle.

8 ¶ And the four beasts had each of them six wings about *him*; and *they were* full of eyes within: and they rest not day and night, saying, Holy, holy, holy, Lord God Almighty, which was, and is, and is to come.

9 And when those beasts give glory and honor and thanks to him that sits on the throne, who lives forever and ever,

10 The four and twenty elders fall down before him that sits on the throne, and worship him that lives forever and ever, and cast their crowns before the throne, saying,

11 You are worthy, O Lord, to receive glory and honor and power: for you have created all things, and for your pleasure they are and were created.

Revelation 5

5:1 ¶ And I saw in the right hand of him that sat on the throne a book written within and on the backside, sealed with seven seals.

2 And I saw a strong angel proclaiming with a loud voice, Who is worthy to open the book, and to loose the seals thereof?

3 And no man in heaven, nor in earth, neither under the earth, was able to open the book, neither to look thereon.

4 And I wept much, because no man was found worthy to open and to read the book, neither to look thereon.

5 And one of the elders said to me, Weep not: behold, the Lion of the tribe of Judah, the Root of David, has prevailed to open the book, and to loose the seven seals thereof.

6 ¶ And I beheld, and, lo, in the midst of the throne and of the four beasts, and in the midst of the elders, stood a Lamb as it had been slain, having seven horns and seven eyes, which are the seven Spirits of God sent forth into all the earth.

7 And he came and took the book out of the right hand of him that sat upon the throne.

8 And when he had taken the book, the four beasts and four *and* twenty elders fell down before the Lamb, having every one of them harps, and golden vials full of incense, which are the prayers of saints.

9 And they sung a new song, saying, You are worthy to take the book, and to open the seals thereof: for you were slain, and have redeemed us to God by your blood out of every kindred, and tongue, and people, and nation;

10 And have made us unto our God kings and priests: and we shall reign on the earth.

11 And I beheld, and I heard the voice of many angels round about the throne and the beasts and the elders: and the number of them was ten thousand times ten thousand, and thousands of thousands;

12 Saying with a loud voice, Worthy is the Lamb that was slain to receive power, and riches, and wisdom, and strength, and honor, and glory, and blessing.

13 And every creature which is in heaven, and on the earth, and under the earth, and such as are in the sea, and all that are in them, heard I saying, Blessing, and honor, and glory, and power, *be* to him that sits upon the throne, and to the Lamb forever and ever.

14 And the four beasts said, Amen. And the four *and* twenty elders fell down and worshipped him that lives forever and ever.

Revelation 6

6:1 ¶ And I saw when the Lamb opened one of the seals, and I heard, as it were the noise of thunder, one of the four beasts saying, Come and see.

2 And I saw, and behold a white horse: and he that sat on him had a bow; and a crown was given to him: and he went forth conquering, and to conquer.

3 ¶ And when he had opened the second seal, I heard the second beast say, Come and see.

4 And there went out another horse *that was* red: and *power* was given to him that sat thereon to take peace from the earth, and that they should kill one another: and there was given to him a great sword.

Revelation 6

5 And when he had opened the third seal, I heard the third beast say, Come and see. And I saw, and behold a black horse; and he that sat on him had a pair of balances in his hand.

6 And I heard a voice in the midst of the four beasts say, A measure of wheat for a penny, and three measures of barley for a penny; and *see* you hurt not the oil and the wine.

7 And when he had opened the fourth seal, I heard the voice of the fourth beast say, Come and see.

8 And I looked, and behold a pale horse: and his name that sat on him was Death, and Hell followed with him. And power was given to them over the fourth part of the earth, to kill with sword, and with hunger, and with death, and with the beasts of the earth.

9 ¶ And when he had opened the fifth seal, I saw under the altar the souls of them that were slain for the word of God, and for the testimony which they held:

10 And they cried with a loud voice, saying, How long, O Lord, holy and true, do you not judge and avenge our blood on them that dwell on the earth?

11 And white robes were given to every one of them; and it was said to them, that they should rest yet for a little season, until their fellow servants also and their brethren, that should be killed as they *were*, should be fulfilled.

12 And I saw when he had opened the sixth seal, and, behold, there was a great earthquake; and the sun became black as sackcloth of hair, and the moon became as blood;

13 And the stars of heaven fell to the earth, even as a fig tree casts her untimely figs, when she is shaken of a mighty wind.

14 And the heaven departed as a scroll when it is rolled together; and every mountain and island were moved out of their places.

15 And the kings of the earth, and the great men, and the rich men, and the chief captains, and the mighty men, and every bondman, and every free man, hid themselves in the dens and in the rocks of the mountains;

16 And said to the mountains and rocks, Fall on us, and hide us from the face of him that sits on the throne, and from the wrath of the Lamb:

17 For the great day of his wrath has come; and who shall be able to stand?

Revelation 7

7:1 ¶ And after these things I saw four angels standing on the four corners of the earth, holding the four winds of the earth, that the wind should not blow on the earth, nor on the sea, nor on any tree.

2 And I saw another angel ascending from the east, having the seal of the living God: and he cried with a loud voice to the four angels, to whom it was given to hurt the earth and the sea,

3 Saying, Hurt not the earth, neither the sea, nor the trees, till we have sealed the servants of our God in their foreheads.

4 And I heard the number of them which were sealed: *and there were* sealed a hundred *and* forty *and* four thousand of all the tribes of the children of Israel.

5 Of the tribe of Judah *were* sealed twelve thousand. Of the tribe of Reuben *were* sealed twelve thousand. Of the tribe of Gad *were* sealed twelve thousand.

6 Of the tribe of Asher *were* sealed twelve thousand. Of the tribe of Naphtali *were* sealed twelve thousand. Of the tribe of Manasseh *were* sealed twelve thousand.

7 Of the tribe of Simeon *were* sealed twelve thousand. Of the tribe of Levi *were* sealed twelve thousand. Of the tribe of Issachar *were* sealed twelve thousand.

8 Of the tribe of Zebulun *were* sealed twelve thousand. Of the tribe of Joseph *were* sealed twelve thousand. Of the tribe of Benjamin *were* sealed twelve thousand.

9 After this I beheld, and, behold, a great multitude, which no man could number, of all nations, and families, and people, and tongues, stood before the throne, and before the Lamb, clothed with white robes, and palms in their hands;

10 And cried with a loud voice, saying, Salvation to our God which sits upon the throne, and unto the Lamb.

11 And all the angels stood round about the throne, and *about* the elders and the four beasts, and fell before the throne on their faces, and worshipped God,

12 Saying, Amen: Blessing, and glory, and wisdom, and thanksgiving, and honor, and power, and might, *be* unto our God forever and ever. Amen.

13 ¶ And one of the elders answered, saying to me, What are these which are arrayed in white robes? and from where came they?

14 And I said to him, Sir, you know. And he said to me, These are they which came out of great tribulation, and have washed their robes, and made them white in the blood of the Lamb.

15 Therefore are they before the throne of God, and serve him day and night in his temple: and he that sits on the throne shall dwell among them.

16 They shall hunger no more, neither thirst any more; neither shall the sun light on them, nor any heat.

17 For the Lamb which is in the midst of the throne shall feed them, and shall lead them to living fountains of waters: and God shall wipe away all tears from their eyes.

Revelation 8

8:1 ¶ And when he had opened the seventh seal, there was silence in heaven about the space of half an hour.

2 And I saw the seven angels which stood before God; and to them were given seven trumpets.

3 And another angel came and stood at the altar, having a golden censer; and there was given to him much incense, that he should offer *it* with the prayers of all saints upon the golden altar which was before the throne.

4 And the smoke of the incense, *which came* with the prayers of the saints, ascended up before God out of the angel's hand.

5 And the angel took the censer, and filled it with fire of the altar, and cast *it* into the earth: and there were voices, and thunderings, and lightnings, and an earthquake.

6 And the seven angels which had the seven trumpets prepared themselves to sound.

7 ¶ The first angel sounded, and there followed hail and fire mingled with blood, and they were cast upon the earth: and the third part of trees was burnt up, and all green grass was burnt up.

8 And the second angel sounded, and as it were a great mountain burning with fire was cast into the sea: and the third part of the sea became blood;

9 And the third part of the creatures which were in the sea, and had life, died; and the third part of the ships were destroyed.

10 And the third angel sounded, and there fell a great star from heaven, burning as it were a lamp, and it fell upon the third part of the rivers, and upon the fountains of waters;

11 And the name of the star is called Wormwood: and the third part of the waters became wormwood; and many men died of the waters, because they were made bitter.

12 And the fourth angel sounded, and the third part of the sun was struck, and the third part of the moon, and the third part of the stars; so as the third part of them was darkened, and the day shone not for a third part of it, and the night likewise.

13 And I beheld, and heard an angel flying through the midst of heaven, saying with a loud voice, Woe, woe, woe, to the inhabitants of the earth by reason of the other voices of the trumpet of the three angels, which are yet to sound!

Revelation 9

9:1 ¶ And the fifth angel sounded, and I saw a star fall from heaven to the earth: and to him was given the key of the bottomless pit.

2 And he opened the bottomless pit; and there arose a smoke out of the pit, as the smoke of a great furnace; and the sun and the air were darkened by reason of the smoke of the pit.

3 And there came out of the smoke locusts upon the earth: and to them was given power, as the scorpions of the earth have power.

4 And it was commanded them that they should not hurt the grass of the earth, neither any green thing, neither any tree; but only those men which have not the seal of God in their foreheads.

5 And to them it was given that they should not kill them, but that they should be tormented five months: and their torment *was* as the torment of a scorpion, when it stings a man.

6 And in those days shall men seek death, and shall not find it; and shall desire to die, and death shall flee from them.

7 And the shapes of the locusts *were* like unto horses prepared to battle; and on their heads *were* as it were crowns like gold, and their faces *were* as the faces of men.

8 And they had hair as the hair of women, and their teeth were as *the teeth* of lions.

9 And they had breastplates, as it were breastplates of iron; and the sound of their wings *was* as the sound of chariots of many horses running to battle.

10 And they had tails like unto scorpions, and there were stings in their tails: and their power *was* to hurt men five months.

11 And they had a king over them, *which is* the angel of the bottomless pit, whose name in the Hebrew tongue *is* Abaddon, but in the Greek tongue has *his* name Apollyon.

12 One woe is past; *and*, behold, there come two woes more hereafter.

13 ¶ And the sixth angel sounded, and I heard a voice from the four horns of the golden altar which is before God,

14 Saying to the sixth angel which had the trumpet, Loose the four angels which are bound in the great river Euphrates

15 And the four angels were loosed, which were prepared for an hour, and a day, and a month, and a year, for to slay the third part of men.

16 And the number of the army of the horsemen *was* two hundred thousand thousand: and I heard the number of them.

17 And thus I saw the horses in the vision, and them that sat on them, having breastplates of fire, and of jacinth, and brimstone: and the heads of the horses *were* as the heads of lions; and out of their mouths issued fire and smoke and brimstone.

18 By these three was the third part of men killed, by the fire, and by the smoke, and by the brimstone, which issued out of their mouths.

19 For their power is in their mouth, and in their tails: for their tails *were* like unto serpents, and had heads, and with them they do hurt.

20 And the rest of the men which were not killed by these plagues yet repented not of the works of their hands, that they should not worship devils, and idols of gold, and silver, and brass, and stone, and of wood: which neither can see, nor hear, nor walk:

21 Neither repented they of their murders, nor of their sorceries, nor of their fornication, nor of their thefts.

Revelation 10

10:1 ¶ And I saw another mighty angel come down from heaven, clothed with a cloud: and a rainbow *was* upon his head, and his face *was* as it were the sun, and his feet as pillars of fire:

2 And he had in his hand a little book open: and he set his right foot upon the sea, and *his* left *foot* on the earth,

3 And cried with a loud voice, as *when* a lion roars: and when he had cried, seven thunders uttered their voices.

Revelation 10

4 And when the seven thunders had uttered their voices, I was about to write: and I heard a voice from heaven saying to me, Seal up those things which the seven thunders uttered, and write them not.

5 And the angel which I saw stand upon the sea and upon the earth lifted up his hand to heaven,

6 And swore by him that lives forever and ever, who created heaven, and the things that therein are, and the earth, and the things that therein are, and the sea, and the things which are therein, that there should be time no longer:

7 But in the days of the voice of the seventh angel, when he shall begin to sound, the mystery of God should be finished, as he has declared to his servants the prophets.

8 ¶ And the voice which I heard from heaven spoke to me again, and said, Go *and* take the little book which is open in the hand of the angel which stands upon the sea and upon the earth.

9 And I went to the angel, and said to him, Give me the little book. And he said to me, Take *it*, and eat it up; and it shall make your belly bitter, but it shall be in your mouth sweet as honey.

10 And I took the little book out of the angel's hand, and ate it up; and it was in my mouth sweet as honey: and as soon as I had eaten it, my belly was bitter.

11 And he said to me, You must prophesy again before many peoples, and nations, and tongues, and kings.

Revelation 11

11:1 ¶ And there was given me a reed like unto a rod: and the angel stood, saying, Rise, and measure the temple of God, and the altar, and them that worship therein.

2 But the court which is outside the temple leave out, and measure it not; for it is given to the Gentiles: and the holy city shall they tread under foot *for* forty *and* two months.

3 ¶ And I will give *power* to my two witnesses, and they shall prophesy a thousand two hundred *and* threescore days, clothed in sackcloth.

4 These are the two olive trees, and the two candlesticks standing before the God of the earth.

5 And if any man will hurt them, fire proceeds out of their mouth, and devours their enemies: and if any man will hurt them, he must in this manner be killed.

6 These have power to shut heaven, that it rain not in the days of their prophecy: and have power over waters to turn them to blood, and to smite the earth with all plagues, as often as they will.

7 And when they shall have finished their testimony, the beast that ascends out of the bottomless pit shall make war against them, and shall overcome them, and kill them.

8 And their dead bodies *shall lie* in the street of the great city, which spiritually is called Sodom and Egypt, where also our Lord was crucified.

9 And they of the people and families and tongues and nations shall see their dead bodies three days and a half, and shall not allow their dead bodies to be put in graves.

10 And they that dwell upon the earth shall rejoice over them, and make merry, and shall send gifts one to another; because these two prophets tormented them that dwelt on the earth.

11 And after three days and a half the Spirit of life from God entered into them, and they stood upon their feet; and great fear fell upon them which saw them.

12 And they heard a great voice from heaven saying to them, Come up here. And they ascended up to heaven in a cloud; and their enemies saw them.

13 And the same hour was there a great earthquake, and the tenth part of the city fell, and in the earthquake were slain of men seven thousand: and the remnant was afraid, and gave glory to the God of heaven.

14 ¶ The second woe is past; *and*, behold, the third woe comes quickly.

15 And the seventh angel sounded; and there were great voices in heaven, saying, The kingdoms of this world have become *the kingdoms* of our Lord, and of his Messiah; and he shall reign forever and ever.

16 And the four and twenty elders, which sat before God on their seats, fell upon their faces, and worshipped God,

17 Saying, We give you thanks, O Lord God Almighty, which is, and was, and is to come; because you have taken to you your great power, and have reigned.

18 And the nations were angry, and your wrath has come, and the time of the dead, that they should be judged, and that you should give reward to your servants the prophets, and to the saints, and them that fear your name, small and great; and should destroy them which destroy the earth.

19 And the temple of God was opened in heaven, and there was seen in his temple the ark of his testament: and there were lightnings, and voices, and thunderings, and an earthquake, and great hail.

Revelation 12

12:1 ¶ And there appeared a great wonder in heaven; a woman clothed with the sun, and the moon under her feet, and upon her head a crown of twelve stars:

2 And she being with child cried, laboring in birth, and pained to be delivered.

3 And there appeared another wonder in heaven; and behold a great red dragon, having seven heads and ten horns, and seven crowns upon his heads.

4 And his tail drew the third part of the stars of heaven, and did cast them to the earth: and the dragon stood before the woman which was ready to be delivered, for to devour her child as soon as it was born.

5 And she brought forth a man child, who was to rule all nations with a rod of iron: and her child was caught up to God, and *to* his throne.

6 And the woman fled into the wilderness, where she has a place prepared of God, that they should feed her there a thousand two hundred *and* threescore days.

7 And there was war in heaven: Michael and his angels fought against the dragon; and the dragon fought and his angels,
8 And prevailed not; neither was their place found any more in heaven.
9 And the great dragon was cast out, that old serpent, called the Devil, and Satan, which deceives the whole world: he was cast out into the earth, and his angels were cast out with him.
10 And I heard a loud voice saying in heaven, Now has come salvation, and strength, and the kingdom of our God, and the power of his Messiah: for the accuser of our brethren is cast down, which accused them before our God day and night.
11 And they overcame him by the blood of the Lamb, and by the word of their testimony; and they loved not their lives unto the death.
12 ¶ Therefore rejoice, *you* heavens, and you that dwell in them. Woe to the inhabitants of the earth and of the sea! for the devil has come down unto you, having great wrath, because he knows that he has but a short time.
13 And when the dragon saw that he was cast to the earth, he persecuted the woman which brought forth the man *child*.
14 And to the woman were given two wings of a great eagle, that she might fly into the wilderness, into her place, where she is nourished for a time, and times, and half a time, from the face of the serpent.
15 And the serpent cast out of his mouth water as a flood after the woman, that he might cause her to be carried away of the flood.
16 And the earth helped the woman, and the earth opened her mouth, and swallowed up the flood which the dragon cast out of his mouth.
17 And the dragon was angry with the woman, and went to make war with the remnant of her seed, which keep the commandments of God, and have the testimony of Yahshua the Messiah.

Revelation 13

13:1 ¶ And I stood upon the sand of the sea, and saw a beast rise up out of the sea, having seven heads and ten horns, and upon his horns ten crowns, and upon his heads the name of blasphemy.
2 And the beast which I saw was like unto a leopard, and his feet were as *the feet* of a bear, and his mouth as the mouth of a lion: and the dragon gave him his power, and his seat, and great authority.
3 And I saw one of his heads as it were wounded to death; and his deadly wound was healed: and all the world wondered after the beast.
4 And they worshipped the dragon which gave power to the beast: and they worshipped the beast, saying, Who *is* like unto the beast? who is able to make war with him?
5 And there was given to him a mouth speaking great things and blasphemies; and power was given to him to continue *for* forty *and* two months.

6 And he opened his mouth in blasphemy against God, to blaspheme his name, and his tabernacle, and them that dwell in heaven.
7 And it was given to him to make war with the saints, and to overcome them: and power was given him over all families, and tongues, and nations.
8 And all that dwell upon the earth shall worship him, whose names are not written in the book of life of the Lamb slain from the foundation of the world.
9 If any man has an ear, let him hear.
10 He that leads into captivity shall go into captivity: he that kills with the sword must be killed with the sword. Here is the patience and the faith of the saints.
11 ¶ And I saw another beast coming up out of the earth; and he had two horns like a lamb, and he spoke as a dragon.
12 And he exercises all the power of the first beast before him, and causes the earth and them which dwell therein to worship the first beast, whose deadly wound was healed.
13 And he does great wonders, so that he makes fire come down from heaven on the earth in the sight of men,
14 And deceives them that dwell on the earth by *the means of* those miracles which he had power to do in the sight of the beast; saying to them that dwell on the earth, that they should make an image to the beast, which had the wound by a sword, and did live.
15 And he had power to give life to the image of the beast, that the image of the beast should both speak, and cause that as many as would not worship the image of the beast should be killed.
16 And he causes all, both small and great, rich and poor, free and bond, to receive a mark in their right hand, or in their foreheads:
17 And that no man might buy or sell, save he that had the mark, or the name of the beast, or the number of his name.
18 Here is wisdom. Let him that has understanding count the number of the beast: for it is the number of a man; and his number *is* Six hundred threescore *and* six.

Revelation 14

14:1 ¶ And I looked, and, behold, a Lamb stood on the mount Zion, and with him a hundred forty *and* four thousand, having his Father's name written in their foreheads.
2 And I heard a voice from heaven, as the voice of many waters, and as the voice of a great thunder: and I heard the voice of harpers harping with their harps:
3 And they sung as it were a new song before the throne, and before the four beasts, and the elders: and no man could learn that song but the hundred *and* forty *and* four thousand, which were redeemed from the earth.
4 These are they which were not defiled with women; for they are virgins. These are they which follow the Lamb wherever he goes. These were redeemed from among men, *being* the firstfruits to God and to the Lamb
5 And in their mouth was found no guile: for they are without fault before the throne of God.

Revelation 14

6 ¶ And I saw another angel fly in the midst of heaven, having the everlasting gospel to preach to them that dwell on the earth, and to every nation, and kindred, and tongue, and people,

7 Saying with a loud voice, Fear God, and give glory to him; for the hour of his judgment has come: and worship him that made heaven, and earth, and the sea, and the fountains of waters.

8 And there followed another angel, saying, Babylon is fallen, is fallen, that great city, because she made all nations drink of the wine of the wrath of her fornication.

9 And the third angel followed them, saying with a loud voice, If any man worships the beast and his image, and receives *his* mark in his forehead, or in his hand,

10 The same shall drink of the wine of the wrath of God, which is poured out without mixture into the cup of his indignation; and he shall be tormented with fire and brimstone in the presence of the holy angels, and in the presence of the Lamb:

11 And the smoke of their torment ascends up forever and ever: and they have no rest day nor night, who worship the beast and his image, and whoever receives the mark of his name.

12 Here is the patience of the saints: here *are* they that keep the commandments of God, and the faith of Yahshua.

13 ¶ And I heard a voice from heaven saying to me, Write, Blessed *are* the dead which die in the Lord from now on: Yes, said the Spirit, that they may rest from their labors; and their works do follow them.

14 And I looked, and behold a white cloud, and upon the cloud *one* sat like unto the Son of man, having on his head a golden crown, and in his hand a sharp sickle.

15 And another angel came out of the temple, crying with a loud voice to him that sat on the cloud, Thrust in your sickle, and reap: for the time has come for you to reap; for the harvest of the earth is ripe.

16 And he that sat on the cloud thrust in his sickle on the earth; and the earth was reaped.

17 And another angel came out of the temple which is in heaven, he also having a sharp sickle.

18 And another angel came out from the altar, which had power over fire; and cried with a loud cry to him that had the sharp sickle, saying, Thrust in your sharp sickle, and gather the clusters of the vine of the earth; for her grapes are fully ripe.

19 And the angel thrust in his sickle into the earth, and gathered the vine of the earth, and cast *it* into the great winepress of the wrath of God.

20 And the winepress was trodden outside the city, and blood came out of the winepress, even to the horse bridles, by the space of a thousand *and* six hundred furlongs.

Revelation 15

15:1 ¶ And I saw another sign in heaven, great and marvelous, seven angels having the seven last plagues; for in them is filled up the wrath of God.

2 And I saw as it were a sea of glass mingled with fire: and them that had gotten the victory over the beast, and over his image, and over his mark, *and* over the number of his name, stand on the sea of glass, having the harps of God.

3 And they sing the song of Moses the servant of God, and the song of the Lamb, saying, Great and marvelous *are* your works, Lord God Almighty; just and true *are* your ways, you King of saints.

4 Who shall not fear you, O Lord, and glorify your name? for *you* only *are* holy: for all nations shall come and worship before you; for your judgments are made known.

5 ¶ And after that I looked, and, behold, the temple of the tabernacle of the testimony in heaven was opened:

6 And the seven angels came out of the temple, having the seven plagues, clothed in pure and white linen, and having their breasts girded with golden girdles.

7 And one of the four beasts gave to the seven angels seven golden vials full of the wrath of God, who lives forever and ever.

8 And the temple was filled with smoke from the glory of God, and from his power; and no man was able to enter into the temple, till the seven plagues of the seven angels were fulfilled.

Revelation 16

16:1 ¶ And I heard a great voice out of the temple saying to the seven angels, Go your ways, and pour out the vials of the wrath of God upon the earth.

2 And the first went, and poured out his vial upon the earth; and there fell a noisome and grievous sore upon the men which had the mark of the beast, and *upon* them which worshipped his image.

3 And the second angel poured out his vial upon the sea; and it became as the blood of a dead *man*: and every living soul died in the sea.

4 And the third angel poured out his vial upon the rivers and fountains of waters; and they became blood.

5 And I heard the angel of the waters say, You are righteous, O Lord, which are, and were, and shall be, because you have judged thus.

6 For they have shed the blood of saints and prophets, and you have given them blood to drink; for they are worthy.

7 And I heard another out of the altar say, Even so, Lord God Almighty, true and righteous *are* your judgments.

8 ¶ And the fourth angel poured out his vial upon the sun; and power was given to him to scorch men with fire.

9 And men were scorched with great heat, and blasphemed the name of God, which has power over these plagues: and they repented not to give him glory.

10 And the fifth angel poured out his vial upon the seat of the beast; and his kingdom was full of darkness; and they gnawed their tongues for pain,

11 And blasphemed the God of heaven because of their pains and their sores, and repented not of their deeds.

12 ¶ And the sixth angel poured out his vial upon the great river Euphrates; and the water thereof was dried up, that the way of the kings of the east might be prepared.

13 And I saw three unclean spirits like frogs *come* out of the mouth of the dragon, and out of the mouth of the beast, and out of the mouth of the false prophet.
14 For they are the spirits of devils, working miracles, *which* go forth to the kings of the earth and of the whole world, to gather them to the battle of that great day of God Almighty.
15 Behold, I come as a thief. Blessed *is* he that watches, and keeps his garments, lest he walk naked, and they see his shame.
16 And he gathered them together into a place called in the Hebrew tongue Armageddon.
17 ¶ And the seventh angel poured out his vial into the air; and there came a great voice out of the temple of heaven, from the throne, saying, It is done.
18 And there were voices, and thunders, and lightnings; and there was a great earthquake, such as was not since men were upon the earth, so mighty an earthquake, *and* so great.
19 And the great city was divided into three parts, and the cities of the nations fell: and great Babylon came in remembrance before God, to give to her the cup of the wine of the fierceness of his wrath.
20 And every island fled away, and the mountains were not found.
21 And there fell upon men a great hail out of heaven, *every stone* about the weight of a talent: and men blasphemed God because of the plague of the hail; for the plague thereof was exceedingly great.

Revelation 17

17:1 ¶ And there came one of the seven angels which had the seven vials, and talked with me, saying to me, Come here; I will show to you the judgment of the great whore that sits upon many waters:
2 With whom the kings of the earth have committed fornication, and the inhabitants of the earth have been made drunk with the wine of her fornication.
3 So he carried me away in the spirit into the wilderness: and I saw a woman sit upon a scarlet colored beast, full of names of blasphemy, having seven heads and ten horns.
4 And the woman was arrayed in purple and scarlet color, and decked with gold and precious stones and pearls, having a golden cup in her hand full of abominations and filthiness of her fornication:
5 And upon her forehead *was* a name written, MYSTERY, BABYLON THE GREAT, THE MOTHER OF HARLOTS AND ABOMINATIONS OF THE EARTH.
6 And I saw the woman drunken with the blood of the saints, and with the blood of the martyrs of Yahshua: and when I saw her, I wondered with great admiration.
7 ¶ And the angel said to me, Why did you marvel? I will tell you the mystery of the woman, and of the beast that carries her, which has the seven heads and ten horns.
8 The beast that you saw was, and is not; and shall ascend out of the bottomless pit, and go into perdition: and they that dwell on the earth shall wonder, whose names were not written in the book of life from the foundation of the world, when they behold the beast that was, and is not, and yet is.

9 And here *is* the mind which has wisdom. The seven heads are seven mountains, on which the woman sits.
10 And there are seven kings: five are fallen, and one is, *and* the other has not yet come; and when he comes, he must continue a short space.
11 And the beast that was, and is not, even he is the eighth, and is of the seven, and goes into perdition.
12 And the ten horns which you saw are ten kings, which have received no kingdom as yet; but receive power as kings one hour with the beast.
13 These have one mind, and shall give their power and strength to the beast.
14 ¶ These shall make war with the Lamb, and the Lamb shall overcome them: for he is Lord of lords, and King of kings: and they that are with him *are* called, and chosen, and faithful.
15 And he said to me, The waters which you saw, where the whore sits, are peoples, and multitudes, and nations, and tongues.
16 And the ten horns which you saw upon the beast, these shall hate the whore, and shall make her desolate and naked, and shall eat her flesh, and burn her with fire.
17 For God has put in their hearts to fulfill his will, and to agree, and give their kingdom to the beast, until the words of God shall be fulfilled.
18 And the woman which you saw is that great city, which reigns over the kings of the earth.

Revelation 18

18:1 ¶ And after these things I saw another angel come down from heaven, having great power; and the earth was lightened with his glory.
2 And he cried mightily with a strong voice, saying, Babylon the great is fallen, is fallen, and has become the habitation of devils, and the hold of every foul spirit, and a cage of every unclean and hateful bird.
3 For all nations have drunk of the wine of the wrath of her fornication, and the kings of the earth have committed fornication with her, and the merchants of the earth have become rich through the abundance of her delicacies.
4 And I heard another voice from heaven, saying, Come out of her, my people, that you be not partakers of her sins, and that you receive not of her plagues.
5 For her sins have reached to heaven, and God has remembered her iniquities.
6 Reward her even as she rewarded you, and double to her double according to her works: in the cup which she has filled fill to her double.
7 How much she has glorified herself, and lived deliciously, so much torment and sorrow give her: for she says in her heart, I sit a queen, and am no widow, and shall see no sorrow.
8 Therefore shall her plagues come in one day, death, and mourning, and famine; and she shall be utterly burned with fire: for strong *is* the Lord God who judges her.

Revelation 18

9 ¶ And the kings of the earth, who have committed fornication and lived deliciously with her, shall bewail her, and lament for her, when they shall see the smoke of her burning,

10 Standing afar off for the fear of her torment, saying, Alas, alas, that great city Babylon, that mighty city! for in one hour has your judgment come.

11 And the merchants of the earth shall weep and mourn over her; for no man buys their merchandise any more:

12 The merchandise of gold, and silver, and precious stones, and of pearls, and fine linen, and purple, and silk, and scarlet, and all thyine wood, and all manner vessels of ivory, and all manner vessels of most precious wood, and of brass, and iron, and marble,

13 And cinnamon, and odors, and ointments, and frankincense, and wine, and oil, and fine flour, and wheat, and beasts, and sheep, and horses, and chariots, and bodies, and souls of men.

14 And the fruits that your soul lusted after are departed from you, and all things which were dainty and goodly are departed from you, and you shall find them no more at all.

15 The merchants of these things, which were made rich by her, shall stand afar off for the fear of her torment, weeping and wailing,

16 And saying, Alas, alas, that great city, that was clothed in fine linen, and purple, and scarlet, and decked with gold, and precious stones, and pearls!

17 For in one hour so great riches has come to nothing. And every shipmaster, and all the company in ships, and sailors, and as many as trade by sea, stood afar off,

18 And cried when they saw the smoke of her burning, saying, What *city is* like unto this great city!

19 And they cast dust on their heads, and cried, weeping and wailing, saying, Alas, alas, that great city, wherein were made rich all that had ships in the sea by reason of her costliness! for in one hour is she made desolate.

20 Rejoice over her, *you* heaven, and *you* holy apostles and prophets; for God has avenged you on her.

21 And a mighty angel took up a stone like a great millstone, and cast *it* into the sea, saying, Thus with violence shall that great city Babylon be thrown down, and shall be found no more at all.

22 And the voice of harpers, and musicians, and of pipers, and trumpeters, shall be heard no more at all in you; and no craftsman, of whatever craft *he is*, shall be found any more in you; and the sound of a millstone shall be heard no more at all in you;

23 And the light of a candle shall shine no more at all in you; and the voice of the bridegroom and of the bride shall be heard no more at all in you: for your merchants were the great men of the earth; for by your sorceries were all nations deceived.

24 And in her was found the blood of prophets, and of saints, and of all that were slain upon the earth.

Revelation 19

19:1 ¶ And after these things I heard a great voice of many people in heaven, saying, Halleluyah. Salvation, and glory, and honor, and power, *belong* unto the Lord our God:

2 For true and righteous *are* his judgments: for he has judged the great whore, which did corrupt the earth with her fornication, and has avenged the blood of his servants at her hand.

3 And again they said, Halleluyah. And her smoke rose up forever and ever.

4 And the four and twenty elders and the four beasts fell down and worshipped God that sat on the throne, saying, Amen; Halleluyah.

5 ¶ And a voice came out of the throne, saying, Praise our God, all you his servants, and you that fear him, both small and great.

6 And I heard as it were the voice of a great multitude, and as the voice of many waters, and as the voice of mighty thunderings, saying, Halleluyah: for the Lord God omnipotent reigns.

7 Let us be glad and rejoice, and give honor to him: for the marriage of the Lamb has come, and his wife has made herself ready.

8 And to her was granted that she should be arrayed in fine linen, clean and white: for the fine linen is the righteousness of saints.

9 And he said to me, Write, Blessed *are* they which are called to the marriage supper of the Lamb. And he said to me, These are the true sayings of God.

10 And I fell at his feet to worship him. And he said to me, See *you do it* not: I am your fellow servant, and of your brethren that have the testimony of Yahshua: worship God: for the testimony of Yahshua is the spirit of prophecy.

11 ¶ And I saw heaven opened, and behold a white horse; and he that sat upon him *was* called Faithful and True, and in righteousness he does judge and make war.

12 His eyes *were* as a flame of fire, and on his head *were* many crowns; and he had a name written, that no man knew, but he himself.

13 And he *was* clothed with a coat dipped in blood: and his name is called The Word of God.

14 And the armies *which were* in heaven followed him upon white horses, clothed in fine linen, white and clean.

15 And out of his mouth goes a sharp sword, that with it he should smite the nations: and he shall rule them with a rod of iron: and he treads the winepress of the fierceness and wrath of Almighty God.

16 And he has on *his* coat and on his thigh a name written, KING OF KINGS, AND LORD OF LORDS.

17 And I saw an angel standing in the sun; and he cried with a loud voice, saying to all the fowls that fly in the midst of heaven, Come and gather yourselves together to the supper of the great God;

18 That you may eat the flesh of kings, and the flesh of captains, and the flesh of mighty men, and the flesh of horses, and of them that sit on them, and the flesh of all *men, both* free and bond, both small and great.

19 And I saw the beast, and the kings of the earth, and their armies, gathered together to make war against him that sat on the horse, and against his army.
20 And the beast was taken, and with him the false prophet that worked miracles before him, with which he deceived them that had received the mark of the beast, and them that worshipped his image. These both were cast alive into a lake of fire burning with brimstone.
21 And the remnant was slain with the sword of him that sat upon the horse, which *sword* proceeded out of his mouth: and all the fowls were filled with their flesh.

Revelation 20

20:1 ¶ And I saw an angel come down from heaven, having the key of the bottomless pit and a great chain in his hand.
2 And he laid hold on the dragon, that old serpent, which is the Devil, and Satan, and bound him *for* a thousand years,
3 And cast him into the bottomless pit, and shut him up, and set a seal upon him, that he should deceive the nations no more, till the thousand years should be fulfilled: and after that he must be loosed a little season.
4 And I saw thrones, and they sat upon them, and judgment was given to them: and *I saw* the souls of them that were beheaded for the witness of Yahshua, and for the word of God, and which had not worshipped the beast, neither his image, neither had received *his* mark upon their foreheads, or in their hands; and they lived and reigned with the Messiah *for* a thousand years.
5 But the rest of the dead lived not again until the thousand years were finished. This *is* the first resurrection.
6 Blessed and holy *is* he that has part in the first resurrection: on such the second death has no power, but they shall be priests of God and of the Messiah, and shall reign with him *for* a thousand years.
7 And when the thousand years are expired, Satan shall be loosed out of his prison,
8 And shall go out to deceive the nations which are in the four quarters of the earth, Gog and Magog, to gather them together to battle: the number of whom *is* as the sand of the sea.
9 And they went up on the breadth of the earth, and encircled the camp of the saints about, and the beloved city: and fire came down from God out of heaven, and devoured them.
10 And the devil that deceived them was cast into the lake of fire and brimstone, where the beast and the false prophet *are*, and shall be tormented day and night forever and ever.
11 ¶ And I saw a great white throne, and him that sat on it, from whose face the earth and the heaven fled away; and there was found no place for them.
12 And I saw the dead, small and great, stand before God: and the books were opened: and another book was opened, which is *the book* of life: and the dead were judged out of those things which were written in the books, according to their works.
13 And the sea gave up the dead which were in it; and death and hell delivered up the dead which were in them: and they were judged every man according to their works.
14 And death and hell were cast into the lake of fire. This is the second death.
15 And whoever was not found written in the book of life was cast into the lake of fire.

Revelation 21

21:1 ¶ And I saw a new heaven and a new earth: for the first heaven and the first earth were passed away; and there was no more sea.
2 And I John saw the holy city, new Jerusalem, coming down from God out of heaven, prepared as a bride adorned for her husband.
3 And I heard a great voice out of heaven saying, Behold, the tabernacle of God *is* with men, and he will dwell with them, and they shall be his people, and God himself shall be with them, *and be* their God.
4 And God shall wipe away all tears from their eyes; and there shall be no more death, neither sorrow, nor crying, neither shall there be any more pain: for the former things are passed away.
5 And he that sat upon the throne said, Behold, I make all things new. And he said to me, Write: for these words are true and faithful.
6 And he said to me, It is done. I am Alpha and Omega, the beginning and the end. I will give to him that is thirsty of the fountain of the water of life freely.
7 He that overcomes shall inherit all things; and I will be his God, and he shall be my son.
8 But the fearful, and unbelieving, and the abominable, and murderers, and whoremongers, and sorcerers, and idolaters, and all liars, shall have their part in the lake which burns with fire and brimstone: which is the second death.
9 ¶ And there came to me one of the seven angels which had the seven vials full of the seven last plagues, and talked with me, saying, Come here, I will show you the bride, the Lamb's wife.
10 And he carried me away in the spirit to a great and high mountain, and showed me that great city, the holy Jerusalem, descending out of heaven from God,
11 Having the glory of God: and her light *was* like unto a stone most precious, even like a jasper stone, clear as crystal;
12 And had a wall great and high, *and* had twelve gates, and at the gates twelve angels, and names written thereon, which are *the names* of the twelve tribes of the children of Israel:
13 On the east three gates; on the north three gates; on the south three gates; and on the west three gates.
14 And the wall of the city had twelve foundations, and in them the names of the twelve apostles of the Lamb.
15 And he that talked with me had a golden reed to measure the city, and the gates thereof, and the wall thereof.

Revelation 21

16 And the city lies foursquare, and the length is as large as the breadth: and he measured the city with the reed, twelve thousand furlongs. The length and the breadth and the height of it are equal.

17 And he measured the wall thereof, a hundred *and* forty *and* four cubits, *according to* the measure of a man, that is, of the angel.

18 And the building of the wall of it was *of* jasper: and the city *was* pure gold, like unto clear glass.

19 And the foundations of the wall of the city *were* garnished with all manner of precious stones. The first foundation *was* jasper; the second, sapphire; the third, a chalcedony; the fourth, an emerald;

20 The fifth, sardonyx; the sixth, sardius; the seventh, chrysolite; the eighth, beryl; the ninth, a topaz; the tenth, a chrysoprasus; the eleventh, a jacinth; the twelfth, an amethyst.

21 And the twelve gates *were* twelve pearls; every single gate was of one pearl: and the street of the city *was* pure gold, as it were transparent glass.

22 And I saw no temple therein: for the Lord God Almighty and the Lamb are the temple of it.

23 And the city had no need of the sun, neither of the moon, to shine in it: for the glory of God *Yahweh* did lighten it, and the Lamb *is* the light thereof.

24 And the nations of them which are saved shall walk in the light of it: and the kings of the earth do bring their glory and honor into it.

25 And the gates of it shall not be shut at all by day: for there shall be no night there.

26 And they shall bring the glory and honor of the nations into it.

27 And there shall by no means enter into it anything that defiles, neither *whatever* works abomination, or *makes* a lie: but they which are written in the Lamb's book of life.

Revelation 22

22:1 ¶ And he showed me a pure river of water of life, clear as crystal, proceeding out of the throne of God and of the Lamb.

2 In the midst of the street of it, and on either side of the river, *was there* the tree of life, which bore twelve *manner of* fruits, *and* yielded her fruit every month: and the leaves of the tree *were* for the healing of the nations.

3 And there shall be no more curse: but the throne of God and of the Lamb shall be in it; and his servants shall serve him:

4 And they shall see his face; and his name *shall be* in their foreheads.

5 And there shall be no night there; and they need no candle, neither light of the sun; for the Lord God gives them light: and they shall reign forever and ever.

6 ¶ And he said to me, These sayings *are* faithful and true: and the Lord God of the holy prophets sent his angel to show to his servants the things which must shortly be done.

7 Behold, I come quickly: blessed *is* he that keeps the sayings of the prophecy of this book.

8 And I John saw these things, and heard *them*. And when I had heard and seen, I fell down to worship before the feet of the angel which showed me these things.

9 Then said he to me, See *you do it* not: for I am your fellow servant, and of your brethren the prophets, and of them which keep the sayings of this book: worship God.

10 And he said to me, Seal not the sayings of the prophecy of this book: for the time is at hand.

11 He that is unjust, let him be unjust still: and he which is filthy, let him be filthy still: and he that is righteous, let him be righteous still: and he that is holy, let him be holy still.

12 And, behold, I come quickly; and my reward *is* with me, to give every man according as his work shall be.

13 I am Alpha and Omega, the beginning and the end, the first and the last.

14 Blessed *are* they that do his commandments, that they may have right to the tree of life, and may enter in through the gates into the city.

15 For without *are* dogs, and sorcerers, and whoremongers, and murderers, and idolaters, and whoever loves and makes a lie.

16 I Yahshua have sent my angel to testify to you these things in the congregations. I am the root and the offspring of David, *and* the bright and morning star.

17 And the Spirit and the bride say, Come. And let him that hears say, Come. And let him that is thirsty come. And whoever will, let him take the water of life freely.

18 For I testify to every man that hears the words of the prophecy of this book, If any man shall add to these things, God shall add to him the plagues that are written in this book:

19 And if any man shall take away from the words of the book of this prophecy, God shall take away his part out of the book of life, and out of the holy city, and *from* the things which are written in this book.

20 ¶ He which testifies these things says, Surely I come quickly. Amen. Even so, come, Lord Yahshua.

21 The grace of our Lord Yahshua the Messiah *be* with you all. Amen.

Section 8
Concordance

Aaron
Ex 4:14 Aaron the Levite
Ex 7:12 Aaron's rod
Ex 28:2 garments for Aaron
Ex 32:35 calf, which Aaron
Nu 33:38 Aaron the priest
De 9:20 angry with Aaron
Mic 6:4 Moses, Aaron
Ac 7:40 Aaron, Make us gods
Heb 9:4 order of Aaron

Abaddon
Re 9:11 Hebrew tongue *is* Abaddon

Abase
Job 40:11 proud, and abase
Isa 31:4 nor abase himself
Eze 21:26 abase *him that is*
Da 4:37 he is able to abase

Abased
Mt 23:12 shall be abased
Lu 14:11 shall be abased
Lu 18:14 shall be abased
Php 4:12 how to be abased

Abated
Ge 8:3 waters were abated
De 34:7 natural force abated
Jud 8:3 anger was abated

Abba
Mr 14:36 said, Abba, Father
Ro 8:15 we cry, Abba, Father
Ga 4:6 crying, Abba, Father

Abednego
Da 1:7 Azariah, of Abednego
Da 2:49 Meshach, and Abednego
Da 3:16 Meshach, and Abednego

Abel
Ge 4:2 his brother Abel
Ge 4:25 Abel, whom Cain
Mt 23:35 righteous Abel
Lu 11:51 blood of Abel
Heb 11:4 By faith Abel
Heb 12:24 than *that of* Abel

Abiathar
1Sa 23:6 Abiathar the son
1Sa 30:7 Abiathar brought
2Sa 15:27 son of Abiathar
2Sa 19:11 Abiathar the priests
1Ki 1:7 Abiathar the priest
1Ki 2:27 thrust out Abiathar
Mr 2:26 Abiathar the high priest

Abib
Ex 13:4 month *of* Abib
Ex 23:15 month *of* Abib
Ex 34:18 month *of* Abib
De 16:1 Abib, and keep

Abide
Ge 22:5 Abide you here
Nu 31:19 abide outside
1Sa 22:5 Abide not in
Eo 11:6 sword shall abide
Joh 12:46 abide in darkness.
Joh 14:16 that he may abide
Joh 15:4 Abide in me

Abigail
1Sa 25:14 Abigail, Nabal's
1Sa 30:5 Abigail the wife

Abihu
Le 10:1 Nadab and Abihu
Nu 3:4 Abihu died before
1Ch 24:2 Abihu died

Abijah
1Ki 14:1 Abijah the son
2Ch 11:22 Abijah the son
2Ch 12:16 Abijah his son
2Ch 13:1 Abijah to reign over
2Ch 29:1 Abijah, the daughter
Mt 1:7 Rehoboam begot Abijah
Lu 1:5 course of Abijah

Abimelech
Ge 20:3 God came to Abimelech
Ge 21:32 Abimelech rose up
Ge 26:1 Abimelech king of
Jud 9:1 Abimelech the son
1Ch 18:16 Abimelech the son

Abinadab
1Sa 7:1 house of Abinadab
1Sa 16:8 Jesse called Abinadab
2Sa 6:3 house of Abinadab
1Ch 13:7 house of Abinadab

Abiram
Nu 26:9 Dathan and Abiram
Ps 106:17 company of Abiram

Abishai
1Sa 26:7 David and Abishai
2Sa 3:30 Joab and Abishai
2Sa 10:10 hand of Abishai
2Sa 23:18 Abishai, the brother
1Ch 18:12 Abishai the son

Abner
1Sa 14:50 host *was* Abner
1Sa 17:57 Abner took him
1Sa 26:5 Abner the son of Ner
2Sa 4:1 Abner was dead
1Ki 2:32 Abner the son
1Ch 26:28 Kish, and Abner

Abomination(s)
Ge 43:32 abomination to the Egyptians
Ex 8:26 the abomination of the Egyptians
Le 11:11 an abomination to you
De 7:26 an abomination into your house
De 20:18 after all their abominations
1Sa 13:4 an abomination to the Philistines
1Ki 11:5 the abomination of the Ammonites
2Ch 34:33 took away all the abominations
Isa 1:13 incense is an abomination unto me
Isa 66:3 delights in their abominations
Eze 8:13 see greater abominations that they do
Da 11:31 the abomination that makes desolate
Da 12: the abomination that makes desolate
Mt 24:15 see the abomination of desolation
Mr 13:14 see the abomination of desolation
Re 17:5 ABOMINATIONS OF THE EARTH

Abraham (Abram)
Ge 11:27 Terah begot Abram
Ge 12:1 Abram, Get you out
Ge 15:1 Fear not, Abram
Ge 17:5 shall be Abraham
Ge 21:2 bore Abraham a son
Ge 22:8 Abraham said, My son
De 1:8 Abraham, Isaac
Mt 1:1 son of Abraham
Lu 1:73 our father Abraham
Joh 8:58 Before Abraham was
Ro 4:3 Abraham believed God
Ro 9:7 the seed of Abraham
Ga 3:7 the children of Abraham
Ga 3:18 to Abraham by promise
Ga 3:29 Abraham's seed
Heb 11:17 By faith Abraham
1Pe 3:6 Sarah obeyed Abraham

Absalom
2Sa 13:1 Absalom the son
2Sa 14:24 Absalom returned
2Sa 15:10 Absalom sent spies
2Sa 18:10 Absalom hanged
2Sa 19:4 O my son Absalom

Abstain
Ac 15:20 abstain from pollutions
1Co 7:9 abstain, let them marry
1Th 5:22 Abstain from all
1Ti 4:3 abstain from fornication
1Pe 2:11 abstain from fleshly

Achan
Jos 7:1 Achan, the son of Carmi
Jos 7:20 Achan answered

Accord
Le 25:5 its own accord
Jos 9:2 with one accord
Ac 1:14 one accord in prayer
Ac 4:24 God with one accord
Ac 8:6 people with one accord
Ac 12:10 its own accord
Ac 15:25 with one accord

Accord

Ac 18:12 one accord against
Ac 19:29 with one accord
Php 2:2 accord, of one mind

Accursed
Jos 6:17 shall be accursed
Jos 7:13 accursed thing
1Co 12:3 Yahshua accursed
Ga 1:9 let him be accursed

Adam
Ge 2:20 Adam gave names
Ge 3:20 Adam called his wife's
Ge 5:2 their name Adam
Ro 5:14 reigned from Adam
1Co 15:22 as in Adam all die

Adar
Jos 15:3 went up to Adar
Ezr 6:15 the month of Adar
Es 3:7 the month of Adar
Es 9:21 fourteenth day of the month of Adar

Adder
Ge 49:17 adder in the path
Ps 91:13 lion and adder
Pr 23:32 stings like an adder

Adoption
Ro 8:15 Spirit of adoption
Ro 9:4 *pertains* the adoption
Ga 4:5 receive the adoption
Eph 1:5 us to the adoption

Adulteress
Le 20:10 the adulteress
Pr 6:26 adulteress will hunt
Ho 3:1 yet an adulteress
Ro 7:3 called an adulteress

Adulterer(s)
Job 24:15 adulterer waits for
Isa 57:3 adulterer and the whore
Jer 9:2 they *are* all adulterers
Jer 23:10 full of adulterers
Ho 7:4 They *are* all adulterers
Mal 3:5 against the adulterers
Lu 18:11 unjust, adulterers
1Co 6:9 nor adulterers, nor
Heb 13:4 adulterers God will
Jas 4:4 adulterers and adulteresses

Adultery
Ex 20:14 not commit adultery
Le 20:10 commits adultery
Pr 6:32 adultery with a woman
Jer 3:8 Israel committed adultery
Eze 16:32 that commits adultery
Ho 4:13 shall commit adultery
Mt 5:28 adultery with her
Mt 19:9 does commit adultery
Joh 8:3 woman taken in adultery
Ga 5:19 Adultery, fornication
Re 2:22 adultery with her

Agag
Nu 24:7 higher than Agag
1Sa 15:8 Agag the king
1Sa 15:9 people spared Agag
1Sa 15:33 hewed Agag

Agagite
Es 3:10 Agagite, the Jews'
Es 8:3 Haman the Agagite
Es 9:24 Hammedatha, the Agagite

Agrippa
Ac 25:13 king Agrippa
Ac 26:1 Agrippa said to Paul
Ac 26:32 Agrippa unto Festus

Ahab
1Ki 16:29 Ahab the son
1Ki 18:2 himself to Ahab
1Ki 19:1 Ahab told Jezebel
1Ki 21:2 Ahab spoke
1Ki 22:40 Ahab slept
2Ki 3:5 Ahab was dead
2Ki 9:8 house of Ahab
2Ki 10:18 Ahab served Baal
2Ch 21:13 house of Ahab

Ahasuerus
Es 1:2 king Ahasuerus
Es 2:16 to king Ahasuerus
Es 3:1 Ahasuerus promote
Es 10:1 Ahasuerus laid

Ahaz
2Ki 16:1 Ahaz the son
1Ch 3:13 Ahaz his son
2Ch 28:19 Ahaz king of
Isa 7:12 Ahaz said, I will
Isa 38:8 sun dial of Ahaz
Mt 1:9 Ahaz begot Hezekiah

Ahaziah
1Ki 22:51 Ahaziah the son
2Ki 8:25 Ahaziah the son
2Ki 11:1 mother of Ahaziah
2Ch 20:35 Ahaziah king
2Ch 22:1 Ahaziah the son

Ahijah
1Ki 11:30 Ahijah caught
1Ki 14:2 Ahijah the prophet
1Ki 15:29 his servant Ahijah
1Ki 15:33 Ahijah to reign
1Ch 26:20 Ahijah *was* over

Ahimelech
1Sa 21:1 Ahimelech the priest
1Sa 22:14 Ahimelech answered
1Sa 23:6 Ahimelech fled
1Sa 30:7 priest, Ahimelech's
1Ch 24:31 and Ahimelech

Aholah
Eze 23:5 Aholah played
Eze 23:44 Aholah and unto

Aholibah
Eze 23:11 her sister Aholibah
Eze 23:36 Aholah and Aholibah
Eze 23:44 Aholibah, the lewd

Ai
Jos 7:2 Jericho to Ai
Jos 8:17 man left in Ai
Jos 10:1 had taken Ai
Ezr 2:28 Bethel and Ai
Ne 7:32 Bethel and Ai
Jer 49:3 Ai is spoiled

Alabaster
Mt 26:7 alabaster box
Mr 14:3 alabaster box
Lu 7:37 alabaster box

Alexander
Mr 15:21 Alexander and Rufus
Ac 4:6 John, and Alexander
Ac 19:33 Alexander out
1Ti 1:20 and Alexander
2Ti 4:14 Alexander the

Alexandria
Ac 18:24 born at Alexandria
Ac 27:6 ship of Alexandria
Ac 28:11 ship of Alexandria

Aliens
La 5:2 houses to aliens.
Eph 2:12 being aliens from
Heb 11:34 armies of the aliens

Alms
Mt 6:1 alms before men
Lu 11:41 give alms of such
Ac 3:2 ask alms of them
Ac 10:4 your alms

Alpha
Re 1:8 I am Alpha
Re 21:6 Alpha and Omega
Re 22:13 I am Alpha

Altar
Ge 8:20 built an altar
Ge 22:9 built an altar
Ex 17:15 built an altar
Ex 20:25 altar of stone
Ex 29:37 altar shall be holy
2Ch 29:24 blood upon the altar
2Ch 32:12 before one altar
Isa 6:6 from off the altar
Am 9:1 upon the altar
Mt 5:23 gift to the altar
Heb 13:10 We have an altar
Re 8:3 golden altar which

Amalek
Ge 36:12 Eliphaz Amalek
Ex 17:8 Amalek, and fought
Nu 24:20 Amalek *was* the first
De 25:17 what Amalek
Jud 3:13 Ammon and Amalek
Jud 5:14 against Amalek
1Sa 15:3 smite Amalek
1Sa 28:18 wrath upon Amalek

Amalekites
Ge 14:7 the Amalekites
Nu 13:29 Amalekites dwell
Nu 14:43 Amalekites and the
1Sa 14:48 smote the Amalekites
1Sa 15:7 smote the Amalekites

Anoint

1Sa 30:1 Amalekites had invaded
2Sa 1:1 of the Amalekites
1Ch 4:43 rest of the Amalekites

Amariah
1Ch 6:7 Meraioth begot Amariah
1Ch 6:11 Azariah begot Amariah
2Ch 19:11 Amariah the chief priest
Ezr 7:3 Amariah, the son of Azariah
Ne 11:4 Amariah, the son of Shephatiah
Zep 1:1 Amariah, the son of Hezekiah

Amasai
1Ch 6:25 sons of Elkanah; Amasai
Ch 12:18 spirit came upon Amasai
1Ch 15:24 Amasai, and Zechariah

Amaziah
2Ki 12:21 Amaziah his son
2Ki 14:1 Amaziah the son
2Ki 15:1 Amaziah king
2Ch 25:1 Amaziah was twenty
2Ch 26:1 his father Amaziah
Am 7:10 Amaziah the priest

Ambassador(s)
Jos 9:4 had been ambassadors
2Ch 32:31 ambassadors of the
Isa 18:2 ambassadors by the sea
Isa 33:7 ambassadors of peace
Jer 49:14 ambassador is sent
Eze 17:15 ambassadors into Egypt
Ob 1:1 ambassador is sent
Lu 14:32 sends an ambassador
2Co 5:20 ambassadors for the
Eph 6:20 ambassador in bonds

Ambush
Jos 8:2 lay you an ambush
Jos 8:9 lie in ambush
2Ch 13:13 caused an ambush

Amen
De 27:15 say, Amen
1Ch 16:36 Amen, and praised
Ne 8:6 Amen, Amen
Ps 106:48 Amen. Praise
Mt 6:13 forever. Amen
Mt 28:20 the world. Amen
Ro 1:25 forever. Amen
2Co 1:20 in him Amen
Re 22:20 quickly. Amen

Ammonites
1Sa 11:11 slew the Ammonites
1Ki 11:5 of the Ammonites
2Ch 26:8 Ammonites gave gifts
2Ch 27:5 king of the Ammonites
Ezr 9:1 Jebusites, the Ammonites
Ne 4:7 Ammonites, and the
Jer 49:1 Concerning the Ammonites
Eze 21:28 concerning the Ammonites

Amorites
Ge 14:7 Amorites, that dwelt
Nu 13:29 Amorites, dwell
Nu 21:21 king of the Amorites
De 1:4 king of the Amorites
Jos 2:10 kings of the Amorites
Jos 10:5 kings of the Amorites
Jos 24:15 gods of the Amorites
Jud 1:34 Amorites forced
1Sa 7:14 Israel and the Amorites
2Sa 21:2 remnant of the Amorites

Amos
Am 1:1 words of Amos
Am 7:8 Amos, what see you
Am 8:2 Amos, what see you
Lu 3:25 Amos, which was

Amram
Ex 6:18 Kohath; Amram
Nu 26:58 Kohath begot Amram
1Ch 1:41 Dishon; Amram
1Ch 6:3 Amram; Aaron,
1Ch 23:13 Amram; Aaron

Anak
Nu 13:33 sons of Anak
De 9:2 children of Anak
Jos 15:13 father of Anak
Jud 1:20 three sons of Anak

Anakims
De 1:28 sons of the Anakims
De 2:11 giants, as the Anakims
De 9:2 children of the Anakims
Jos 11:21 cut off the Anakims
Jos 14:12 day how the Anakims

Anammelech
2Ki 17:31 and Anammelech

Ananias
Ac 5:3 Ananias, why has Satan
Ac 9:10 Damascus, named Ananias
Ac 22:12 Ananias, a devout man
Ac 23:2 high priest Ananias

Anathema
1Co 16:22 Anathema Maranatha.

Anathoth
Jos 21:18 Anathoth with her
1Ki 2:26 Get you to Anathoth
1Ch 6:60 Anathoth with her
Ezr 2:23 men of Anathoth
Jer 1:1 Anathoth in the land
Jer 29:27 Jeremiah of Anathoth
Jer 32:7 that is in Anathoth

Anchor
Heb 6:19 anchor of the soul

Ancient of Days
Da 7:9 Ancient of days did

Andrew
Mt 4:18 Peter, and Andrew
Mr 13:3 Andrew asked him
Lu 6:14 Andrew his brother,
Joh 1:40 Andrew, Simon Peter's
Joh 6:8 disciples, Andrew
Joh 12:22 came and told Andrew
Ac 1:13 John, and Andrew

Angel(s)
Ge 19:1 came two angels to Sodom
Ge 22:11 angel of Yahweh
Ge 28:12 behold the angels of God
Nu 22:35 angel of Yahweh said
Jud 6:12 angel of Yahweh appeared
2Sa 24:17 angel that smote
1Ki 13:18 angel spoke to me
1Ki 19:5 angel touched him
2Ki 1:3 angel of Yahweh said
2Ki 19:35 angel of Yahweh went
Ps 8:5 a little lower than the angels
Ps 91:11 give his angels charge
Ps 104:4 makes his angels spirits
Da 6:22 angel, and has shut
Zec 1:9 angel that talked
Mt 2:13 angel of the Lord
Mt 4:6 give his angels charge
Mt 13:39 reapers are the angels
Mt 24:31 he shall send his angels
Mt 25:41 for the devil and his angels
Mt 28:2 angel of the Lord
Mr 1:13 the angels ministered to him.
Lu 1:26 angel Gabriel
Lu 4:10 give his angels charge
Lu 12:9 denied before the angels
Ac 7:30 Sinai an angel
Ac 8:26 angel of the Lord
Ac 27:23 angel of God
2Co 11:14 angel of light
Heb 1:4 so much better than the angels
Heb 1:7 makes his angels spirits
Heb 12:22 innumerable company of angels
2Pe 2:4 if God spared not the angels
Jude 1:6 angels which kept not
Re 1:20 seven stars are the angels
Re 7:1 I saw four angels
Re 7:2 angel ascending
Re 8:2 I saw the seven angels
Re 9:15 the four angels were loosed
Re 12:9 his angels were cast out
Re 15:8 plagues of the seven angels
Re 21:9 one of the seven angels

Anger
Ge 49:7 be their anger
Ex 4:14 anger of Yahweh
Ex 32:19 anger grew hot
De 29:20 anger of Yahweh
Jud 2:12 Yahweh to anger
Ps 145:8 slow to anger
Isa 1:4 Israel to anger
Joe 2:13 slow to anger
Mic 7:18 his anger forever
Na 1:3 is slow to anger
Eph 4:31 wrath, and anger
Col 3:8 off all these; anger

Anna
Lu 2:36 Anna, a prophetess

Anoint
Ex 28:41 anoint them
Ex 29:36 anoint it, to sanctify
Ex 30:26 anoint the tabernacle
Ex 40:10 anoint the altar
Le 16:32 whom he shall anoint
Jud 9:8 anoint a king over
1Sa 15:1 sent me to anoint

Anoint

1Ki 19:16 anoint to be prophet
Isa 21:5 anoint the shield.
Da 9:24 anoint the most Holy
Mr 14:8 anoint my body
Mr 16:1 come and anoint him.
Re 3:18 anoint your eyes

Anointed

Ge 31:13 anointed the pillar
Ex 29:2 anointed with oil
Le 7:12 anointed with oil
Le 8:10 oil, and anointed
Nu 7:1 anointed it
1Sa 16:13 anointed him
1Ki 1:39 anointed Solomon
1Ch 11:3 anointed David king
Ps 89:20 oil have I anointed
Isa 61:1 Yahweh has anointed
Eze 28:14 anointed cherub
Lu 4:18 anointed me to preach
Lu 7:38 feet, and anointed
Ac 10:38 God anointed Yahshua
Heb 1:9 anointed you with the oil

Anointing

Ex 25:6 spices for anointing
Ex 30:25 holy anointing oil
Ex 40:9 take the anointing
Le 7:35 anointing of Aaron
Le 21:10 the anointing oil
Nu 4:16 the anointing oil
Nu 18:8 anointing, and to
Jas 5:14 over him, anointing
1Jo 2:20 anointing from the

Antichrist

1Jo 2:18 antichrist shall
1Jo 2:22 He is antichrist
1Jo 4:3 spirit of antichrist
2Jo 1:7 and an antichrist

Antioch

Ac 6:5 proselyte of Antioch
Ac 11:19 Antioch, preaching
Ac 13:14 Antioch in Pisidia
Ac 14:19 Jews from Antioch
Ac 15:35 continued in Antioch
Ga 2:11 had come to Antioch
2Ti 3:11 came to me at Antioch

Apollos

Ac 18:24 Jew named Apollos
Ac 19:1 Apollos was at
1Co 1:12 Apollos; and I
1Co 3:4 I am of Apollos
1Co 4:6 myself and to Apollos
1Co 16:12 our brother Apollos
Tit 3:13 lawyer and Apollos

Apostles

Mt 10:2 twelve apostles
Lu 6:13 named apostles
Ac 1:2 to the apostles
Ac 2:43 by the apostles
Ac 4:33 apostles witness
Ac 5:2 the apostles' feet
1Co 4:9 the apostles last
1Co 12:28 apostles, secondarily
1Co 15:9 least of the apostles
2Co 11:13 false apostles
Eph 2:20 apostles and prophets
2Pe 3:2 apostles of the Lord
Re 2:2 apostles, and are not
Re 21:14 apostles of the Lamb

Apothecary

Ex 30:25 art of the apothecary
Ex 37:29 work of the apothecary
Ec 10:1 ointment of the apothecary

Appeal

Ac 25:11 appeal to Caesar
Ac 28:19 appeal to Caesar

Aquila

Ac 18:2 Jew named Aquila
Ac 18:18 Priscilla and Aquila
Ac 18:26 Aquila and Priscilla had
Ro 16:3 Priscilla and Aquila my
1Co 16:19 Aquila and Priscilla salute
2Ti 4:19 Salute Prisca and Aquila

Arabia

1Ki 10:15 kings of Arabia
2Ch 9:14 Arabia and governors
Isa 21:13 burden upon Arabia
Jer 25:24 kings of Arabia
Eze 27:21 Arabia, and all
Ga 1:17 I went into Arabia
Ga 4:25 mount Sinai in Arabia

Arabians

2Ch 17:11 Arabians brought him
2Ch 21:16 Arabians, that were
2Ch 26:7 Arabians that dwelt
Ne 4:7 Arabians, and the
Ac 2:11 Cretes and Arabians

Aram

Ge 10:22 Arphaxad, and Lud, and Aram
Ge 22:21 Kemuel the father of Aram
Nu 23:7 has brought me from Aram
1Ch 1:17 Arphaxad, and Lud, and Aram, and Uz, and Hul, and Gether, and Meshech.
1Ch 2:23 he took Geshur, and Aram

Ararat

Ge 8:4 mountains of Ararat
Jer 51:27 kingdoms of Ararat

Araunah

2Sa 24:16 Araunah the Jebusite

Archangel

1Th 4:16 voice of the archangel
Jude 1:9 Michael the archangel

Ariel

Ezr 8:16 Eliezer, for Ariel
Isa 29:1 Woe to Ariel
Isa 29:7 fight against Ariel

Arimathaea

Mt 27:57 rich man of Arimathaea
Mr 15:43 Joseph of Arimathaea
Lu 23:51 Arimathaea, a city of
Joh 19:38 Joseph of Arimathaea

Ark

Ge 6:14 ark of gopher wood
Ge 8:4 ark rested in
Ex 2:3 ark of bulrushes
Ex 25:10 ark of shittim
Ex 26:33 ark of the
Nu 7:89 was upon the ark
De 31:25 bore the ark
Jos 4:5 over before the ark
Jos 6:4 ark seven trumpets
1Sa 3:3 ark of God was
1Sa 5:1 Philistines took the ark
2Sa 6:17 ark of Yahweh
1Ch 28:2 rest for the ark
Mt 24:38 into the ark
Heb 11:7 ark to the saving
Re 11:19 temple the ark

Arm of Yahweh

Isa 51:9 arm of Yahweh
Isa 53:1 arm of Yahweh

Armageddon (see also Meggido)

Re 16:16 tongue Armageddon

Armor

1Sa 14:1 bore his armor
1Sa 17:6 leg armor of brass
1Sa 31:9 stripped off his armor
2Sa 2:21 take you his armor
2Sa 18:15 Joab's armor turned
1Ki 22:38 washed his armor
2Ch 26:14 armor, and bows
Ne 4:16 body armor
Isa 39:2 house of his armor
Eze 38:4 all sorts of armor
Lu 11:22 armor wherein he
Ro 13:12 armor of light
2Co 6:7 armor of righteousness
Eph 6:11 whole armor of God

Armory

Ne 3:19 armory at the turning
So 4:4 built for an armory
Jer 50:25 opened his armory

Army

Ge 26:26 captain of his army
Ex 14:9 army, and overtook
1Sa 4:2 slew of the army
1Sa 17:21 army against army
2Ki 25:5 army of the Chaldees
Isa 43:17 horse, the army
Jer 32:2 Babylon's army
Eze 17:17 mighty army
Da 11:7 come with an army
Joe 2:11 army: for his camp
Re 9:16 number of the army

Arpad (Arphad)

Ki 18:34 Hamath, and of Arpad
2Ki 19:13 king of Arpad
Isa 10:9 Hamath as Arpad
Isa 36:19 Hamath and Arphad
Jer 49:23 confounded, and Arpad

Artaxerxes
Ezr 4:7 Artaxerxes king
Ne 13:6 Artaxerxes king

Artemis
Ac 19:24 shrines for Diana *Artemis*
Ac 19:35 goddess Diana *Artemis*

Asa
1Ki 15:11 Asa did *that which*
1Ki 22:41 Asa began to reign
2Ch 14:2 Asa did *that*
2Ch 15:17 heart of Asa
Jer 41:9 Asa the king
Mt 1:7 Abijah begot Asa

Asaph
2Ki 18:37 Asaph the recorder
1Ch 16:5 Asaph the chief
1Ch 25:1 sons of Asaph
2Ch 29:30 Asaph the seer
Ezr 2:41 children of Asaph
Ne 2:8 Asaph the keeper
Ne 11:22 Asaph, the singers
Isa 36:22 Asaph, the recorder

Asher
Ge 35:26 Asher: these *are*
Nu 34:27 children of Asher
Jos 19:31 children of Asher
Jud 1:31 Asher drive out
2Ch 30:11 some of Asher
Lu 2:36 tribe of Asher
Re 7:6 Asher *were* sealed

Ashes
Ge 18:27 dust and ashes
Ex 9:10 ashes of the furnace
Le 6:11 ashes outside the
Nu 19:9 ashes of the heifer
2Sa 13:19 ashes on her head
1Ki 20:38 ashes upon his face
2Ki 23:4 carried the ashes
Job 42:6 repent in dust and ashes
Isa 61:3 beauty for ashes
Jer 6:26 wallow yourself in ashes
Da 9:3 sackcloth, and ashes
Jon 3:6 sat in ashes
Lu 10:13 sackcloth and ashes
Heb 9:13 ashes of a heifer
2Pe 2:6 Gomorrah into ashes

Ashima
2Ki 17:30 Hamath made Ashima

Ashtaroth (Ashtoreth)
Jos 9:10 *was* at Ashtaroth
Jud 2:13 Baal and Ashtaroth
Jud 10:6 Baalim, and Ashtaroth
1Sa 7:3 gods and Ashtaroth
1Sa 12:10 Baalim and Ashtaroth
1Sa 31:10 house of Ashtaroth
1Ki 11:5 Ashtoreth the goddess
2Ki 23:13 Ashtoreth the abomination

Asia
Ac 6:9 Cilicia and of Asia
Ac 16:6 the word in Asia
Ac 19:10 dwelt in Asia
Ac 20:16 time in Asia
Ac 24:18 Jews from Asia
Ac 27:2 coasts of Asia
1Co 16:19 congregations of Asia
2Ti 1:15 Asia have turned
Re 1:4 which are in Asia

Asshur
Ge 10:11 Asshur, and built
Nu 24:24 shall afflict Asshur
1Ch 1:17 Shem; Elam, and Asshur
Eze 27:23 Asshur, and Chilmad
Ho 14:3 Asshur shall not save

Assyria
2Ki 15:20 king of Assyria
2Ki 17:23 land to Assyria
2Ki 18:11 Israel to Assyria
Ki 19:20 king of Assyria
1Ch 5:6 king of Assyria
Isa 11:16 left, from Assyria
Isa 27:13 land of Assyria
Ho 8:9 gone up to Assyria
Mic 5:6 the land of Assyria
Zep 2:13 destroy Assyria
Zec 10:10 out of Assyria

Astrologers
Isa 47:13 the astrologers, the stargazers
Da 1:20 all the magicians *and* astrologers
Da 2:2 the magicians, and the astrologers
Da 4:7 the magicians, the astrologers
Da 5:7 bring in the astrologers
Da 5:11 master of the magicians, astrologers

Athens
Ac 17:16 for them at Athens
Ac 18:1 departed from Athens
1Th 3:1 left at Athens alone

Atonement
Ex 29:33 atonement was made
Ex 30:15 atonement for your
Ex 32:30 atonement for your sin
Le 1:4 make atonement for him
Le 19:22 make an atonement
Nu 8:21 made an atonement
Nu 15:25 atonement for all
1Ch 6:49 atonement for Israel
Ne 10:33 atonement for Israel
Ro 5:11 received the atonement

Atonement, Day of
Le 23:27 be a day of atonement

Augustus
Lu 2:1 from Caesar Augustus
Ac 25:21 hearing of Augustus
Ac 25:25 appealed to Augustus
Ac 27:1 centurion of Augustus

Avenger of Blood
De 19:12 the avenger of blood
Jos 20:5 avenger of blood pursues
Jos 20:9 the avenger of blood

Ax
De 19:5 ax to cut down
De 20:19 forcing an ax
Jud 9:48 ax in his hand
1Ki 6:7 ax *nor* any tool
Jer 10:3 with the ax
Jer 51:20 ax *and* weapons
Mt 3:10 ax is laid to

Azariah (also see Uzziah)
1Ki 4:2 Azariah the son of Zadok
1Ki 4:5 Azariah the son of Nathan
2Ki 15:1 Azariah son of Amaziah
1Ch 2:8 son of Ethan; Azariah
1Ch 2:38 Jehu begot Azariah
1Ch 6:9 Ahimaaz begot Azariah
1Ch 9:11 Azariah the son of Hilkiah
2Ch 15:1 Azariah the son of Oded
2Ch 22:6 Azariah the son of Jehoram
2Ch 26:17 Azariah the priest
2Ch 29:12 Azariah the son of Jehalelel
2Ch 31:10 Azariah the chief priest
Ne 3:23 Azariah the son of Maaseiah
Jer 43:2 Azariah the son of Hoshaiah
Da 1:6 Mishael, and Azariah

Baal
Nu 22:41 places of Baal
Jud 2:13 served Baal
Jud 6:25 altar of Baal
1Ki 16:32 altar for Baal
2Ki 10:18 Ahab served Baal
Jer 2:8 prophesied by Baal
Ho 2:8 prepared for Baal
Zep 1:4 remnant of Baal
Ro 11:4 *image of* Baal

Baalberith (Berith)
Jud 8:33 Baalberith their god
Jud 9:4 house of Baalberith
Jud 9:46 the god Berith

Baalim
Jud 3:7 Baalim and the groves
Jud 10:6 Baalim, and Ashtaroth
1Sa 7:4 put away Baalim
2Ch 17:3 not unto Baalim
2Ch 28:2 images for Baalim
Jer 2:23 not gone after Baalim
Ho 2:17 names of Baalim
Ho 11:2 sacrificed to Baalim

Baali
Ho 2:16 no more Baali

Baalis
Jer 40:14 Baalis the king

Baalpeor
Nu 25:3 himself to Baalpeor
De 4:3 followed Baalpeor
Ps 106:28 Baalpeor, and ate
Ho 9:10 went to Baalpeor

Baalzebub
2Ki 1:2 Baalzebub the god

Baasha
1Ki 15:16 Baasha king
1Ki 16:3 posterity of Baasha
2Ki 9:9 Baasha the son
2Ch 16:1 Baasha king
Jer 41:9 fear of Baasha

Babel

Babel
Ge 10:10 kingdom was Babel
Ge 11:9 called Babel

Babes
Ps 8:2 mouth of babes
Isa 3:4 babes shall rule
Lu 10:21 revealed them to babes
Ro 2:20 teacher of babes
1Co 3:1 babes in the Messiah
1Pe 2:2 newborn babes

Babylon
2Ki 17:24 *men* from Babylon
2Ki 24:1 king of Babylon
1Ch 9:1 Babylon for their
Ezr 1:11 Babylon to Jerusalem
Ne 13:6 king of Babylon
Isa 13:1 burden of Babylon
Jer 20:4 captive into Babylon
Eze 12:13 Babylon *to* the land
Da 2:48 province of Babylon
Ac 7:43 away beyond Babylon
1Pe 5:13 *that is* at Babylon
Re 17:5 MYSTERY, BABYLON

Backsliding
Pr 14:14 backslider in heart
Isa 57:17 backsliding in the
Jer 5:6 perpetual backsliding
Jer 49:4 backsliding daughter
Ho 11:7 bent to backsliding
Ho 14:4 heal their backsliding

Balaam
Nu 22:5 Balaam the son
Nu 31:8 Balaam also the
De 23:4 against you Balaam
Jos 24:10 listen to Balaam
Ne 13:2 hired Balaam
2Pe 2:15 way of Balaam
Jude 1:11 error of Balaam
Re 2:14 doctrine of Balaam

Balak
Nu 22:4 Balak the son
Nu 23:2 Balak did as Balaam
Nu 24:10 Balak's anger
Jos 24:9 Balak the son
Mic 6:5 Balak king of Moab
Re 2:14 who taught Balak

Balance(s)
Le 19:36 Just balances
Job 31:6 an even balance
Pr 11:1 false balance
Isa 46:6 in the balance
Jer 32:10 in the balances
Eze 5:1 balances to weigh
Da 5:27 in the balances
Re 6:5 pair of balances

Bamah
Eze 20:29 called Bamah

Baptism
Mt 3:7 come to his baptism
Mt 21:25 baptism of John
Mr 1:4 baptism of repentance
Lu 3:3 preaching the baptism
Ac 1:22 from the baptism
Ro 6:4 baptism into death
Eph 4:5 faith, one baptism
Col 2:12 him in baptism
1Pe 3:21 baptism does also

Baptize
Mt 3:6 baptized of him
Mt 28:19 baptizing them
Mr 1:8 baptize you with
Lu 3:21 being baptized
Joh 1:25 Why baptize you
Ac 1:5 be baptized with
Ac 2:38 and be baptized
Ac 10:48 baptized in the name
Ro 6:3 baptized into Yahshua
1Co 12:13 baptized into one

Barabbas
Mt 27:16 called Barabbas
Mr 15:15 released Barabbas
Lu 23:18 release to us Barabbas
Joh 18:40 Barabbas was a robber

Barley
Ex 9:31 flax and the barley
Le 27:16 barley seed
Ru 1:22 barley harvest
2Ki 4:42 loaves of barley
Jer 41:8 wheat, and of barley
Eze 4:12 barley cakes
Joe 1:11 for the barley
Joh 6:9 five barley loaves
Re 6:6 measures of barley

Barn
2Ki 6:27 the barn floor
Job 39:12 *into* your barn
Hag 2:19 seed yet in the barn
Mt 3:12 wheat into the barn
Lu 3:17 wheat into his barn
Lu 12:24 storehouse nor barn

Barnabas
Ac 4:36 surnamed Barnabas
Ac 9:27 Barnabas took him
Ac 11:30 Barnabas and Saul
Ac 13:2 Separate me Barnabas
Ac 15:12 Barnabas and Paul
Ga 2:1 Jerusalem with Barnabas
Col 4:10 son to Barnabas

Barren
Ge 11:30 barren; she *had* no
Ge 29:31 Rachel *was* barren
Ex 23:26 nor be barren
Jud 13:3 barren, and bear
1Sa 2:5 barren has born
2Ki 2:19 ground barren
Pr 30:16 barren womb
Joe 2:20 barren and desolate
Lu 1:7 Elisabeth was barren
Lu 23:29 barren, and the
2Pe 1:8 barren nor unfruitful

Baruch
Ne 3:20 Baruch the son
Jer 32:12 Baruch the son
Jer 36:4 Baruch wrote
Jer 43:3 Baruch the son
Jer 45:1 spoke to Baruch

Bashan
Nu 21:33 king of Bashan
De 1:4 king of Bashan
De 32:14 breed of Bashan
Jos 20:8 Golan in Bashan
1Ch 5:16 Gilead in Bashan
Ps 68:22 from Bashan
Isa 2:13 oaks of Bashan
Jer 50:19 Carmel and Bashan
Zec 11:2 oaks of Bashan

Basket
Ex 29:3 into one basket
Le 8:2 basket of unleavened
De 28:5 basket and your
Jud 6:19 put in a basket
2Ki 10:7 heads in baskets
Jer 6:9 into the baskets
Am 8:1 basket of summer
Mt 14:20 twelve baskets
Mt 15:37 seven baskets

Bathsheba
2Sa 11:3 Bathsheba, the daughter
2Sa 12:24 Bathsheba his wife
1Ki 1:11 Bathsheba the mother
1Ki 2:13 came to Bathsheba

Beard
Le 13:29 or the beard
Le 14:9 beard and his
Le 19:27 of your beard
1Sa 17:35 by his beard
2Sa 19:24 his beard
2Sa 20:9 by the beard
Ezr 9:3 of my beard
Jer 48:37 beard clipped
Eze 5:1 your beard

Beast (of the Sea)
Re 13:1 beast rise up out of the sea
Re 15:2 victory over the beast

Beast (of the Earth)
Ge 1:24 beast of the earth
Ge 9:2 every beast of the earth
Re 13:11 beast coming up out of

Beast (Image of the)
Re 13:14 image to the beast
Re 14:9 beast and his image
Re 15:2 beast, and over his image
Re 20:4 beast, neither his image

Beast (Mark of the)
Re 13:17 mark, or the name of the beast
Re 16:2 mark of the beast
Re 19:20 mark of the beast

Beast, Venomous
Ac 28:4 venomous beast hang

Beasts
Ge 36:6 all his beasts
Ge 45:17 load your beasts
Le 20:25 clean beasts
1Sa 17:46 wild beasts

2Ch 32:28 beasts, and stalls
Ps 8:7 beasts of the field
Da 7:3 four great beasts
Zec 14:15 beasts that shall
Ac 7:42 to me slain beasts
Ro 1:23 four footed beasts
1Co 15:39 flesh of beasts
Jas 3:7 kind of beasts
Re 4:6 beasts full of eyes

Beauty
Ex 28:2 and for beauty
1Ch 16:29 beauty of holiness
Es 1:11 princes her beauty
Ps 27:4 beauty of Yahweh
Ps 45:11 desire your beauty
Ps 96:6 strength and beauty
Pr 20:29 beauty of old men
Isa 33:17 king in his beauty
Isa 53:2 no beauty that we
Eze 28:17 of your beauty
Zec 11:7 I called Beauty

Bee(s)
De 1:44 chased you, as bees
Jud 14:8 swarm of bees
Ps 118:12 about like bees
Isa 7:18 bee that *is* in

Beelzebub
Mt 10:25 house Beelzebub
Mt 12:24 Beelzebub the prince
Mr 3:22 Beelzebub, and by
Lu 11:15 Beelzebub the chief

Beersheba
Ge 21:14 of Beersheba
Ge 26:33 city *is* Beersheba
Ge 28:10 out from Beersheba
Jos 19:2 inheritance Beersheba
1Sa 3:20 even to Beersheba
1Ki 19:3 Beersheba, which
2Ch 30:5 from Beersheba
Am 8:14 Beersheba lives

Behemoth
Job 40:15 Behold now behemoth

Bel
Isa 46:1 Bel bows down
Jer 50:2 Bel is confounded
Jer 51:44 punish Bel

Belial
De 13:13 children of Belial
Jud 19:22 sons of Belial
1Sa 2:12 *were* sons of Belial
1Sa 25:25 man of Belial,
2Sa 16:7 you man of Belial
2Sa 20:1 man of Belial
2Ch 13:7 children of Belial
2Co 6:15 Messiah with Belial

Believe(d)(s)
Ge 15:6 he believed in Yahweh
Ex 4:31 And the people believed
Nu 14:11 before they believe me
De 1:32 you did not believe Yahweh
2Ki 17:14 that did not believe in Yahweh
Ps 78:22 they believed not in God
Ps 106:12 believed they his words
Ps 116:10 I believed, therefore
Pr 14:15 The simple believes every word
Isa 53:1 Who has believed our report?
Da 6:23 he believed in his God
Jon 3:5 Nineveh believed God
Hab 1:5 you will not believe, though
Mt 21:32 and the harlots believed
Mt 24:23 believe *it* not
Mr 1:15 repent you, and believe
Mr 5:36 Be not afraid, only believe
Mr 15:32 that we may see and believe
Mr 16:16 He that believes and is baptized
Lu 1:45 blessed *is* she that believed
Lu 8:50 Fear not: believe only
Joh 1:12 them that believe on his name
Joh 3:16 that whoever believes in him
Joh 6:47 that believes on me has
Joh 20:31 believe that Yahshua is
Ac 8:37 If you believe with all
Ro 10:9 and shall believe in your heart
1Co 7:13 has a husband that believes not
2Th 2:11 that they should believe a lie
1Ti 3:16 believed on in the world,
Heb 4:3 must believe that he is,
Jas 2:19 the devils also believe
1Jo 4:1 believe not every spirit
1Jo 5:13 that believe on the name of
Jude 1:5 destroyed them that believed not

Bell(s)
Ex 28:34 bell and a pomegranate
Ex 39:25 bells *of* pure gold
Zec 14:20 bells of the horses

Belshazzar
Da 5:1 Belshazzar the king
Da 5:30 Belshazzar the king
Da 7:1 Belshazzar king
Da 8:1 king Belshazzar

Belteshazzar
Da 1:7 *name* of Belteshazzar
Da 2:26 name *was* Belteshazzar
Da 4:9 Belteshazzar, master
Da 5:12 named Belteshazzar
Da 10:1 called Belteshazzar

Benjamin
Ge 35:24 Joseph, and Benjamin
Ge 44:12 Benjamin's sack
Nu 26:38 sons of Benjamin
Jos 18:20 children of Benjamin
Jud 20:10 Gibeah of Benjamin
1Sa 9:1 Benjamin, whose name
1Ch 9:3 children of Benjamin
1Ch 12:29 Benjamin, the kindred
Ne 11:7 sons of Benjamin
Jer 32:44 land of Benjamin
Php 3:5 tribe of Benjamin
Re 7:8 Benjamin *were* sealed

Berea
Ac 17:10 by night to Berea
Ac 17:13 by Paul at Berea

Bethany
Mt 21:17 city into Bethany
Mt 26:6 Yahshua was in Bethany
Mr 11:1 Bethany, at the mount
Mr 14:3 Bethany in the house
Lu 19:29 Bethany, at the mount
Lu 24:50 far as to Bethany
Joh 11:1 Bethany, the town
Joh 12:1 came to Bethany

Bethel
Ge 28:19 that place Bethel
Ge 31:13 God of Bethel
Jos 8:9 Bethel and Ai
Jud 4:5 Bethel in mount
1Ki 12:29 one in Bethel
1Ki 13:1 Bethel: and Jeroboam
2Ki 10:29 *were* in Bethel
Am 3:14 altars of Bethel

Bethlehem (Bethlehemjudah)
Ge 35:19 which *is* Bethlehem
Jud 19:1 out of Bethlehemjudah
Ru 2:4 came from Bethlehem
1Sa 20:6 Bethlehem his city
1Ch 11:17 well of Bethlehem
Ezr 2:21 children of Bethlehem
Mic 5:2 Bethlehem Ephratah
Mt 2:1 Bethlehem of Judaea
Lu 2:4 called Bethlehem
Joh 7:42 town of Bethlehem

Bethpeor
De 3:29 against Bethpeor
De 4:46 against Bethpeor
De 34:6 against Bethpeor
Jos 13:20 Bethpeor

Bethphage
Mt 21:1 Bethphage, to the mount
Mr 11:1 Bethphage and Bethany
Lu 19:29 near to Bethphage

Bethsaida
Mt 11:21 you, Bethsaida
Mr 6:45 before to Bethsaida
Mr 8:22 came to Bethsaida
Lu 9:10 city called Bethsaida
Lu 10:13 unto you, Bethsaida
Joh 1:44 was of Bethsaida
Joh 12:21 Bethsaida of Galilee

Bethshemesh
Jos 15:10 to Bethshemesh
Jos 19:22 Bethshemesh
Jud 1:33 of Bethshemesh
1Sa 6:19 men of Bethshemesh
2Ki 14:11 face at Bethshemesh
2Ch 25:21 Bethshemesh, which
2Ch 28:18 taken Bethshemesh
Jer 43:13 of Bethshemesh

Bird(s)
Ge 7:14 bird of every sort
Ge 40:17 birds did eat
Le 14:4 two birds alive
De 14:11 clean birds
Ps 124:7 bird out of
Pr 27:8 bird that wanders
Ec 10:20 bird of the air
Isa 31:5 birds flying

Bird(s)

Jer 5:27 is full of birds
Lu 9:58 birds of the air
Re 18:2 hateful bird

Birth
Ex 28:10 to their birth
Ru 2:11 land of your birth
Ps 58:8 untimely birth
Isa 37:3 come to the birth
Isa 66:9 bring to the birth
Eze 16:3 birth and your
Lu 1:14 rejoice at his birth
Joh 9:1 blind from *his* birth
Ga 4:19 I labor in birth
Re 12:2 laboring in birth

Birthright
Ge 25:31 your birthright
Ge 27:36 my birthright
Ge 43:33 to his birthright
1Ch 5:1 bed, his birthright
Heb 12:16 sold his birthright

Bitter Herbs
Ex 12:8 bitter *herbs* they
Nu 9:11 and bitter *herbs*

Bitter Water
Nu 5:18 bitter water that causes
Nu 5:24 drink the bitter water
Jas 3:11 sweet *water* and bitter

Blaspheme(s)
Le 24:16 blasphemes the name
Ps 44:16 and blasphemes
Mt 9:3 *man* blasphemes
Mr 3:29 he that shall blaspheme
Lu 12:10 blasphemes against
Joh 10:36 blaspheme; because
Ac 26:11 *them* to blaspheme
Jas 2:7 blaspheme that worthy
Re 13:6 blaspheme his name

Blasphemy
Isa 37:3 and of blasphemy
Mt 12:31 blasphemy *against*
Mt 26:65 heard his blasphemy
Mr 14:64 heard the blasphemy
Re 2:9 *know* the blasphemy
Re 13:1 name of blasphemy
Re 17:3 names of blasphemy

Blasting
De 28:22 blasting, and with
1Ki 8:37 pestilence, blasting
2Ch 6:28 blasting, or mildew
Am 4:9 blasting and mildew

Blessing
Ge 12:2 be a blessing
Ex 32:29 upon you a blessing
De 11:26 blessing and a curse
De 23:5 curse into a blessing
Ps 129:8 blessing of Yahweh
Ps 133:3 blessing, *even* life
Eze 34:26 showers of blessing
Mal 3:10 you out a blessing
Lu 24:53 blessing God
1Co 10:16 cup of blessing

Ga 3:14 blessing of Abraham

Blind
Ex 4:11 seeing, or the blind
Le 21:18 a blind man
De 15:21 blind, *or has* any
De 28:29 blind gropes
2Sa 5:6 blind and the lame
Isa 29:18 eyes of the blind
Mt 11:5 blind receive
Mt 15:14 blind leaders
Lu 4:18 sight to the blind
Joh 9:25 blind, now I see
2Co 4:4 world has blinded
Re 3:17 blind, and naked

Blindness
Ge 19:11 house with blindness
De 28:28 madness, and blindness
2Ki 6:18 them with blindness
Zec 12:4 people with blindness
Ro 11:25 blindness in part
Eph 4:18 blindness of their

Blood
Ge 4:10 brother's blood
Ex 4:9 become blood
Ex 12:13 blood shall be
Le 7:26 manner of blood
Le 15:19 flesh is blood
Nu 35:19 revenger of blood
Zec 9:11 blood of your
Mt 26:28 blood of the new
Mt 27:4 innocent blood
Mr 5:29 fountain of her blood
Joh 1:13 born, not of blood
Joh 6:56 drinks my blood
Ac 15:29 and from blood
Ro 3:25 faith in his blood
Eph 1:7 through his blood
Eph 6:12 flesh and blood
Heb 9:14 blood of the Messiah
Re 1:5 his own blood
Re 6:12 became as blood
Re 19:13 dipped in blood

Body
2Ki 8:5 dead body to life
1Ch 10:12 body of Saul
Ps 132:11 fruit of your body
Pr 5:11 flesh and your body
Da 10:6 body also *was* like
Mt 6:22 light of the body
Mr 14:8 body for the burying
Lu 12:23 body *is* more
Joh 2:21 temple of his body
Ro 12:5 body in the Messiah
1Co 6:19 body is the temple
1Co 7:4 her own body
1Co 12:13 into one body
1Co 15:44 natural body
Eph 5:30 body, of his flesh
Col 1:18 head of the body
Heb 10:10 body of Yahshua
Jas 2:26 body without

Boil(s)
Ex 9:11 of the boils
Le 13:20 out of the boil

De 28:27 boils of Egypt
Job 2:7 with grievous boils
Isa 38:21 upon the boil

Bondage
Ex 1:14 hard bondage
Ex 13:3 house of bondage
De 26:6 us hard bondage
Ezr 9:9 in our bondage
Isa 14:3 hard bondage
Joh 8:33 bondage to any
Ro 8:15 spirit of bondage
Ga 5:1 yoke of bondage
Heb 2:15 subject to bondage
2Pe 2:19 brought in bondage

Bone(s)
Ge 2:23 bone of my bones
Ex 13:19 bones of Joseph
Nu 9:12 break any bone
2Sa 21:12 bones of Saul
2Ki 13:21 bones of Elisha
Ps 34:20 keeps all his bones
Eze 37:4 you dry bones
Lu 24:39 flesh and bones
Heb 11:22 his bones

Booth
Ge 33:17 booths for his
Le 23:42 dwell in booths
Ne 8:14 booths in the feast
Jon 4:5 booth, and sat

Born Again
Joh 3:3 man is born again
Joh 3:7 must be born again
1Pe 1:23 Being born again

Borrow
Ex 3:22 borrow of her
Ex 12:35 borrowed of the
De 15:6 shall not borrow
Ne 5:4 borrowed money
Ps 37:21 wicked borrows
Pr 22:7 borrower *is* servant
Isa 24:2 with the borrower
Mt 5:42 that would borrow

Bottle(s)
Ge 21:14 bottle of water
Jos 9:4 wine bottles, old
Jud 4:19 opened a bottle
1Sa 10:3 bottle of wine
Isa 22:24 vessels of bottles
Jer 13:12 bottle shall be
Ho 7:5 bottles of wine
Lu 5:37 into old bottles

Bottomless Pit
Re 9:1 the bottomless pit
Re 11:7 of the bottomless pit
Re 17:8 bottomless pit, and go
Re 20:1 bottomless pit and

Bow(ed)
Ge 9:13 set my bow
Ge 24:26 bowed down
Ge 49:8 shall bow down
Ex 20:5 shall not bow

1Ki 1:16 bowed, and did
Ne 8:6 bowed their heads
Ps 95:6 worship and bow
Isa 45:23 knee shall bow
Mt 27:29 bowed the knee
Joh 19:30 bowed his head
Ro 14:11 knee shall bow
Php 2:10 knee should bow

Branch
Ge 40:12 branches *are* three
Le 23:40 branches of palm
Isa 4:2 branch of Yahweh
Isa 11:1 Branch shall grow
Jer 23:5 righteous Branch
Eze 19:10 full of branches
Zec 3:8 servant the BRANCH
Mt 24:32 branch is yet tender
Ro 11:16 *are* the branches

Brazen Serpent
Nu 21:9 Moses made a serpent of brass
2Ki 18:4 brazen serpent that Moses
Joh 3:14 Moses lifted up the serpent

Bread
Ge 19:3 unleavened bread
Ge 25:34 bread and pottage
Ge 47:19 land for bread
Ex 12:17 unleavened bread
Ex 16:4 bread from heaven
Nu 6:15 bread, cakes
De 8:3 live by bread only
Jos 9:5 bread of their
1Sa 2:36 piece of bread
2Sa 9:7 bread at my table
Ec 11:1 Cast your bread
Am 8:11 famine of bread
Mt 6:11 our daily bread
Mt 26:26 Yahshua took bread
Lu 4:4 not live by bread
Joh 6:35 I am the bread
1Co 11:26 eat this bread

Breast
Ge 49:25 breasts, and of
Ex 29:27 sanctify the breast
Job 3:12 breasts that I
Ps 22:9 mother's breasts
Pr 5:19 breasts satisfy you
So 1:13 between my breasts
So 4:5 Your two breasts
So 8:1 breasts of my mother
So 8:10 my breasts like towers
Isa 28:9 from the breasts
Eze 23:8 breasts of her
Ho 9:14 and dry breasts
Na 2:7 upon their breasts
Lu 11:27 breasts which you
Lu 18:13 upon his breast
Joh 21:20 leaned on his breast
Re 1:13 breasts with a golden

Breastplate(s)
Ex 28:4 breastplate, and
Ex 39:8 breastplate *of*
Le 8:8 breastplate the Urim
Eph 6:14 breastplate of
1Th 5:8 breastplate of faith
Re 9:9 breastplates of iron

Breath
Ge 2:7 breath of life
Ge 7:22 the breath of life
1Ki 17:17 breath left in him
Job 33:4 breath of the
Isa 11:4 breath of his lips
Jer 10:14 no breath in them
Eze 37:5 breath to enter
Ac 17:25 life, and breath

Brick
Ge 11:3 brick for stone
Ex 1:14 mortar, and in brick
2Sa 12:31 the brick kiln
Isa 9:10 bricks have fallen
Isa 65:3 upon altars of brick
Jer 43:9 clay in the brick kiln
Na 3:14 strong the brick kiln

Bride
Isa 61:10 bride adorns
Isa 62:5 over the bride
Jer 33:11 voice of the bride
Joe 2:16 bride out of her
Mt 9:15 bride chamber
Mr 2:19 bride chamber
Joh 3:29 bride is the
Re 21:2 bride adorned
Re 22:17 Spirit and the bride

Bridegroom
Ps 19:5 bridegroom coming
Isa 62:5 bridegroom rejoices
Jer 25:10 of the bridegroom
Joe 2:16 let the bridegroom
Mt 25:5 bridegroom delayed
Mr 2:19 bridegroom with
Joh 2:9 called the bridegroom
Joh 3:29 is the bridegroom
Re 18:23 bridegroom and of

Bridle(s)
2Ki 19:28 bridle in your
Ps 32:9 bit and bridle
Ps 39:1 mouth with a bridle
Isa 30:28 bridle in the jaws
Isa 37:29 bridle in your lips
Jas 1:26 bridles not his
Re 14:20 horse bridles

Brimstone
Ge 19:24 brimstone and fire
De 29:23 thereof *is* brimstone
Ps 11:6 fire and brimstone
Isa 34:9 into brimstone
Eze 38:22 and brimstone
Lu 17:29 brimstone from
Re 9:17 and brimstone
Re 14:10 fire and brimstone
Re 19:20 with brimstone
Re 20:10 fire and brimstone

Brother(s)
Ge 20:13 is my brother
Ge 37:4 his brothers saw
Ge 42:8 knew his brothers
Ex 7:1 Aaron your brother
De 25:5 If brothers dwell
Ho 12:3 brother by the heel
Mt 4:18 two brothers, Simon
Mt 10:21 brother shall deliver
Mt 13:55 and his brothers
Mt 22:24 brother shall marry
Mr 6:17 brother Philip's
Lu 15:27 brother has come
Joh 2:12 and his brothers
1Co 8:13 brother to offend
Ga 1:19 the Lord's brother
1Jo 3:15 hates his brother
Re 1:9 brother, and companion

Brethren
Ex 2:11 of his brethren
Jos 1:15 brethren rest
2Ch 29:15 their brethren
Ps 133:1 brethren to dwell
Mt 23:8 you are brethren
Ac 15:22 the brethren
1Co 14:20 Brethren, be not
2Co 11:26 false brethren
Ga 4:28 brethren, as Isaac
1Th 5:26 all the brethren
Re 12:10 of our brethren

Bulrush(es)
Ex 2:3 ark of bulrushes
Isa 18:2 vessels of bulrushes
Isa 58:5 head as a bulrush

Burial
2Ch 26:23 field of the burial
Ec 6:3 has no burial
Isa 14:20 with them in burial
Jer 22:19 burial of a donkey
Mt 26:12 for my burial
Ac 8:2 Stephen *to his burial*

Bury
Ge 23:4 bury my dead
Ge 49:29 bury me with
1Ki 13:31 bury me in
1Ki 14:13 and bury him
Jer 14:16 none to bury them
Eze 39:11 bury Gog and all
Mt 8:21 bury my father
Mt 27:7 to bury strangers
Lu 9:60 bury their dead
Joh 19:40 Jews is to bury

Busybody
1Pe 4 15 busybody in other

Butler
Ge 40:9 chief butler told
Ge 41:9 butler to Pharaoh

Butter
Ge 18:8 butter, and milk
De 32:14 Butter of cows
Jud 5:25 butter in a lordly
2Sa 17:29 honey, and butter
Job 20:17 honey and butter
Ps 55:21 smoother than butter
Pr 30 33 brings forth butter
Isa 7:15 Butter and honey

Caesar

Caesar
Mr 12:14 tribute to Caesar
Lu 2:1 Caesar Augustus
Lu 3:1 of Tiberius Caesar
Joh 19:15 king but Caesar
Ac 11:28 Claudius Caesar
Ac 25:10 Caesar's judgment
Ac 28:19 appeal to Caesar
Php 4:22 Caesar's household

Caesarea
Mt 16:13 coasts of Caesarea
Mr 8:27 Caesarea Philippi
Ac 8:40 he came to Caesarea
Ac 9:30 down to Caesarea
Ac 10:1 Caesarea called
Ac 12:19 Judaea to Caesarea
Ac 21:8 came to Caesarea
Ac 23:23 go to Caesarea
Ac 25:1 Caesarea to Jerusalem

Cage
Jer 5:27 cage is full
Re 18:2 cage of every

Caiaphas
Mt 26:3 called Caiaphas
Lu 3:2 Caiaphas being the
Joh 11:49 *named* Caiaphas
Joh 18:13 to Caiaphas
Ac 4:6 priest, and Caiaphas

Cain
Ge 4:1 and bore Cain
Ge 4:9 Cain, Where *is* Abel
Heb 11:4 sacrifice than Cain
1Jo 3:12 Not as Cain,
Jude 1:11 way of Cain

Caleb
Nu 13:6 Caleb the son
Nu 26:65 save Caleb
Jos 14:13 gave to Caleb
Jud 1:13 Caleb's younger
Jud 1:20 Hebron to Caleb
1Sa 25:3 house of Caleb
1Ch 2:18 Caleb the son

Calf
Ge 18:7 calf tender
Ex 32:4 molten calf
Le 9:2 calf for a sin
1Ki 12:28 calves *of* gold
2Ki 10:29 golden calves
2Ch 13:8 calves, which
Jer 34:18 cut the calf in two
Ho 13:2 kiss the calves
Lu 15:23 fatted calf
Ac 7:41 made a calf
Heb 9:12 goats and calves
Re 4:7 beast like a calf

Calvary
Lu 23:33 Calvary, there

Camel(s)
Ge 12:16 donkeys, and camels
Le 11:4 camel, because he
1Sa 30:17 rode upon camels
1Ki 10:2 camels that bear
Job 1:17 upon the camels
Isa 21:7 chariot of camels
Isa 30:6 humps of camels
Mt 3:4 garment of camel's
Lu 18:25 easier for a camel

Cana
Joh 2:1 marriage in Cana
Joh 2:11 Cana of Galilee
Joh 4:46 again into Cana
Joh 21:2 Nathanael of Cana

Canaan
Ge 9:18 father of Canaan
Ge 11:31 land of Canaan
Ge 17:8 Canaan, for an
Ge 42:5 land of Canaan
Ex 16:35 land of Canaan
Nu 13:2 land of Canaan
Nu 33:51 land of Canaan
Zep 2:5 you; O Canaan
Mt 15:22 woman of Canaan
Ac 7:11 Egypt and Canaan
Ac 13:19 land of Canaan

Canaanites
Ge 10:18 Canaanites spread
Ex 3:8 of the Canaanites
Nu 21:3 up the Canaanites
Jos 3:10 you the Canaanites
Jos 16:10 Canaanites dwell
Jud 1:1 against the Canaanites
1Ki 9:16 slain the Canaanites
Ne 9:8 land of the Canaanites

Candlestick
Ex 25:31 candlestick *of* pure
Ex 40:4 candlestick, and light
Le 24:4 pure candlestick
Nu 8:2 against the candlestick
1Ch 28:15 every candlestick
2Ch 13:11 candlestick of gold
Da 5:5 against the candlestick
Mt 5:15 candlestick; and it
Lu 8:16 on a candlestick
Heb 9:2 candlestick, and
Re 1:12 golden candlesticks
Re 2:5 your candlestick
Re 11:4 candlesticks standing

Capernaum
Mt 4:13 dwelt in Capernaum
Mt 8:5 into Capernaum
Mt 11:23 you, Capernaum
Mr 2:1 into Capernaum
Lu 4:31 Capernaum, a city
Lu 10:15 Capernaum, which
Joh 2:12 down to Capernaum
Joh 4:46 sick at Capernaum
Joh 6:59 taught in Capernaum

Captain
Ge 21:22 chief captain
Jos 5:15 captain of Yahweh's
1Sa 9:16 him *to be* captain
2Sa 2:8 captain of Saul's
2Sa 17:25 Amasa captain
2Ki 5:1 Naaman, captain
2Ki 20:5 Hezekiah the captain
2Ki 25:8 Nebuzaradan, captain
2Ch 13:12 for *our* captain
Joh 18:12 captain and officers
Ac 21:32 captain and the soldiers
Ac 28:16 captain of the guard
Heb 2:10 captain of their salvation

Captivity
De 28:41 go into captivity
2Ki 24:15 captivity from
2Ch 6:37 of their captivity
Ezr 3:8 out of the captivity
Ps 53:6 back the captivity
Jer 15:2 captivity, to the
Jer 33:7 captivity of Judah
La 1:3 gone into captivity
Da 5:13 of the captivity
Am 5:27 captivity beyond
Ro 7:23 captivity to the law
2Co 10:5 captivity every
Re 13:10 leads into captivity

Carmel
1Sa 15:12 came to Carmel
1Sa 25:2 sheep in Carmel
2Ki 4:25 to mount Carmel
Isa 35:2 Carmel and Sharon
Isa 37:24 forest of his Carmel
Jer 50:19 feed on Carmel
Am 9:3 top of Carmel
Mic 7:14 midst of Carmel

Carnal(ly)
Le 18:20 not lie carnally
Nu 5:13 with her carnally
Ro 7:14 carnal, sold under
Ro 8:6 carnally minded
1Co 3:3 are yet carnal
1Co 9:11 reap your carnal
2Co 10:4 *are* not carnal
Heb 7:16 carnal commandment
Heb 9:10 carnal ordinances

Carpenters
2Sa 5:11 carpenters, and masons
2Ki 12:11 carpenters and builders
1Ch 14:1 masons and carpenters
2Ch 24:12 carpenters to repair
Ezr 3:7 and to the carpenters
Isa 44:13 carpenter stretches
Jer 29:2 carpenters, and the
Zec 1:20 four carpenters
Mr 6:3 this the carpenter

Castle
1Ch 11:5 castle of Zion
Pr 18:19 bars of a castle
Ac 21:34 into the castle
Ac 22:24 into the castle
Ac 23:10 into the castle

Cattle
Ge 1:24 his kind, cattle
Ge 2:20 names to all cattle
Ge 8:1 and all the cattle
Ge 30:39 cattle striped
Ge 46:32 to feed cattle

Ex 34:19 among your cattle
Nu 32:16 for our cattle
1Ki 1:25 oxen and fat cattle
Ps 50:10 cattle upon a
Eze 34:17 between cattle
Joe 1:18 herds of cattle
Lu 17:7 feeding cattle
Joh 4:12 and his cattle

Cave
Ge 19:30 dwelt in a cave
Ge 23:19 wife in the cave
Ge 25:9 him in the cave
Jos 10:16 in a cave
1Sa 22:1 cave Adullam
1Sa 24:3 sides of the cave
1Ki 18:4 fifty in a cave
1Ki 19:9 cave, and lodged
1Ch 11:15 cave of Adullam
Joh 11:38 It was a cave

Chain(s)
Ge 41:42 chain about his
Ex 28:22 breastplate chains
1Ki 7:17 wreaths of chain
Ps 68:6 bound with chains
Ps 149:8 kings with chains
La 3:7 chain heavy
Na 3:10 bound in chains
Lu 8:29 chains and in fetters
Ac 12:6 with two chains
2Ti 1:16 of my chains
2Pe 2:4 chains of darkness
Jude 1:6 everlasting chains
Re 20:1 pit and a great chain

Chaldea
Jer 50:10 Chaldea shall be
Jer 51:24 inhabitants of Chaldea
Eze 11:24 God into Chaldea
Eze 16:29 Canaan to Chaldea
Eze 23:15 Babylonians of Chaldea

Chaldeans
Isa 23:13 land of the Chaldeans
Isa 48:20 from the Chaldeans
Jer 21:4 *against* the Chaldeans
Jer 37:5 Chaldeans that besieged
Jer 40:9 serve the Chaldeans
Jer 52:8 Chaldeans pursued
Eze 1:3 land of the Chaldeans
Eze 23:14 of the Chaldeans
Da 1:4 of the Chaldeans
Da 5:7 Chaldeans, and the
Ac 7:4 land of the Chaldeans

Chaldees
Ge 11:28 in Ur of the Chaldees.
Ge 11:31 from Ur of the Chaldees
Ge 15:7 out of Ur of the Chaldees
2Ki 25:5 army of the Chaldees pursued
2Ki 25:13 did the Chaldees break in pieces
2Ki 25:24 servants of the Chaldees
2Ki 25:26 afraid of the Chaldees
2Ch 36:17 king of the Chaldees
Ne 9:7 out of Ur of the Chaldees
Isa 13:19 beauty of the Chaldees'

Chamberlain
2Ki 23:11 the chamberlain
Es 2:3 king's chamberlain
Ac 12:20 chamberlain their
Ro 16:23 the chamberlain

Chariot(s)
Ge 41:43 second chariot
Jos 17:16 chariots of iron
2Sa 1:6 chariots and
1Ki 4:26 for his chariots
1Ki 7:33 a chariot wheel
2Ki 2:11 chariot of fire
Ps 68:17 chariots of God
Jer 22:4 riding in chariots
Ac 8:38 chariot to stand
Re 9:9 chariots of many

Charity
1Co 8:1 charity edifies
1Co 13:1 have not charity
Col 3:14 *put on* charity
1Ti 1:5 charity out of
1Ti 2:15 faith and charity
2Ti 2:22 faith, charity
1Pe 4:8 fervent charity
Jude 1:12 feasts of charity
Re 2:19 works, and charity

Charmers
De 18:11 charmer, or a
Ps 58:5 voice of charmers
Isa 19:3 to the charmers
Jer 8:17 not *be* charmed

Chaste
2Co 11:2 chaste virgin
Tit 2:5 chaste, keepers
1Pe 3:2 chaste conversation

Chemosh
Nu 21:29 people of Chemosh
Jud 11:24 Chemosh your god
1Ki 11:33 Chemosh the god
2Ki 23:13 Chemosh the
Jer 48:7 Chemosh shall go forth

Cherub
Ex 25:19 one cherub on
Ex 37:8 cherub on the end
2Sa 22:11 upon a cherub
1Ki 6:24 wing of the cherub
2Ch 3:12 cherub *was* five
Eze 10:14 face of a cherub
Eze 28:14 anointed cherub
Eze 41:18 cherub had two

Cherubims
Ge 3:24 of Eden Cherubims
Ex 26:1 cherubims of cunning
1Sa 4:4 *between* the cherubims
1Ki 8:7 cherubims covered
1Ch 28:18 of the cherubims
2Ch 5:8 cherubims spread
Eze 11:22 cherubims lift up
Heb 9:5 cherubims of glory

Children
Ge 3:16 bring forth children
Ge 30:1 Jacob no children
Ex 1:1 names of the children
Ex 3:14 children of Israel
Ex 13:15 of my children
1Ch 28:8 for your children
Jer 38:23 and your children
Mt 18:3 as little children
Mr 10:14 children to come
Ro 8:17 children, then heirs
1Jo 4:4 God, little children

Christ (see also Messiah)
Joh 1:41 being interpreted, the Christ
Joh 4:25 which is called Christ

Circumcise (Circumcision)
Ge 17:11 circumcise the flesh
De 30:6 circumcise your heart
Jer 4:4 Circumcise yourselves
Lu 1:59 circumcise the child
Ac 7:8 of circumcision
Ac 10:45 of the circumcision
Ac 15:5 needful to circumcise
Ro 2:29 circumcision *is that*
1Co 7:19 Circumcision is
Ga 5:6 circumcision avails

Cistern
2Ki 18:31 of his cistern
Pr 5:15 your own cistern
Ec 12:6 at the cistern
Isa 36:16 his own cistern

Clay
Da 2:41 with miry clay
Na 3:14 clay, and tread
Hab 2:6 with thick clay
Joh 9:6 clay of the spittle
Ro 9:21 power over the clay

Cloud(s)
Ge 9:13 bow in the cloud
Ex 13:22 pillar of the cloud
De 4:11 clouds, and thick
Jud 5:4 clouds also dropped
2Sa 22:12 clouds of the skies
Ps 18:12 clouds passed, hail
Ps 77:17 clouds poured
Ec 12:2 clouds return after
Mt 24:30 coming in the clouds
Lu 12:54 cloud rise out
1Th 4:17 in the clouds
Heb 12:1 cloud of witnesses
2Pe 2:17 clouds that are
Re 10:1 clothed with a cloud
Re 14:16 sat on the cloud

Colt
Ge 49:11 donkey's colt
Zec 9:9 colt the foal
Mt 21:5 colt the foal
Mr 11:7 colt to Yahshua
Lu 19:30 find a colt tied
Lu 19:33 upon the colt
Joh 12:15 donkey's colt

Comforter
Joh 14:16 another Comforter
Joh 14:26 Comforter, *which is*

Comforter

Joh 15:26 Comforter has come
Joh 16:7 Comforter will not

Commandment(s)
Ex 20:6 my commandments
Ex 24:12 commandments which
Ex 36:6 gave commandment
Le 26:3 my commandments
Nu 14:41 commandment of
De 6:1 *are* the commandments,
De 8:6 keep the commandments

Communion
1Co 10:16 communion of the
2Co 6:14 communion has light
2Co 13:14 communion of the

Concubine(s)
Ge 35:22 father's concubine
Ge 36:12 concubine to Eliphaz
Jud 8:31 concubine that *was*
Jud 19:2 concubine played
2Sa 3:7 Saul had a concubine
2Sa 5:13 concubines and wives
1Ki 11:3 hundred concubines
1Ch 1:32 Abraham's concubine
Da 5:2 and his concubines

Congregation
Ex 12:6 of the congregation
Ex 27:21 of the congregation
Ex 40:24 tent of the congregation
Le 4:13 congregation of Israel
Nu 1:18 all the congregation
Jos 9:15 of the congregation
1Ki 8:14 all the congregation
2Ch 1:5 and the congregation
2Ch 29:28 congregation worshipped
Ezr 10:1 congregation of men
Ps 82:1 stands in the congregation
Ps 89:5 congregation of the saints
Joe 2:16 sanctify the congregation
Mt 16:18 build my congregation
Ac 2:47 added to the congregation
Ac 8:1 against the congregation
Ac 11:22 congregation which was
Ac 20:28 congregation of God
1Co 4:17 every congregation
1Co 12:28 congregation, first
Eph 5:27 glorious congregation
Col 1:18 body, the congregation
2Ti 4:22 overseer of the congregation
Heb 12:23 assembly and congregation
Re 2:1 angel of the congregation

Coniah (see also Jeconiah)
Jer 22:24 Coniah the son
Jer 37:1 instead of Coniah

Conscience
Joh 8:9 *own* conscience
Ac 23:1 conscience before
Ac 24:16 conscience void
Ro 2:15 conscience also
2Co 1:12 of our conscience
1Ti 3:9 pure conscience
1Ti 4:2 conscience seared
2Ti 1:3 pure conscience
Heb 9:14 your conscience

1Pe 3:16 good conscience

Conspiracy
2Sa 15:12 conspiracy was strong
2Ki 12:20 made a conspiracy
2Ki 15:30 conspiracy against
2Ch 25:27 conspiracy against
Jer 11:9 A conspiracy is found
Eze 22:25 conspiracy of her
Ac 23:13 made this conspiracy

Constellations
Isa 13:10 the constellations

Content(ment)
Jos 7:7 content, and dwelt
Pr 6:35 he rest content
Mr 15:15 willing to content
Lu 3:14 content with your
Php 4:11 to be content
1Ti 6:6 with contentment
Heb 13:5 *be* content with

Converts
Isa 1:27 converts with
Jas 5:20 converts the sinner

Convicted
Joh 8:9 being convicted
Jas 2:9 convicted of the

Convocation
Ex 12:16 holy convocation
Le 23:3 holy convocation
Nu 28:18 holy convocation
Nu 29:1 holy convocation

Corban
Mr 7:11 Corban, that is

Corinth
Ac 18:1 came to Corinth
Ac 19:1 was at Corinth
1Co 1:2 is at Corinth
2Co 1:1 Corinth, with
2Co 1:23 yet to Corinth
2Ti 4:20 stayed at Corinth

Corn
Ge 27:28 corn and *new*
Ge 41:5 ears of corn
Le 2:14 corn dried
Ru 2:2 ears of corn
Ne 5:3 corn, because of
Isa 62:8 corn *to be* food
Mt 12:1 ears of corn
Mr 4:28 corn in the ear
Lu 6:1 ears of corn
Ac 7:12 corn in Egypt
1Co 9:9 out the corn

Cornelius
Ac 10:1 Cornelius, a centurion
Ac 10:31 Cornelius, your prayer

Corner
Ps 118:22 of the corner
Pr 21:9 corner of the
Isa 28:16 corner *stone*

Zec 14:10 the corner gate
Mt 21:42 head of the corner
Ac 4:11 head of the corner
Eph 2:20 chief corner *stone*
1Pe 2:6 a chief corner

Council
Mt 26:59 council, sought false
Mr 15:1 council, and bound
Ac 4:15 council, they
Ac 5:27 before the council
Ac 6:12 *him* to the council
Ac 23:1 beholding the council

Counsel
Jos 9:14 *counsel* at the mouth
1Sa 14:37 counsel of God
1Ki 12:8 forsook the counsel
1Ch 10:13 asking *counsel* of

Counselor
2Ch 22:3 counselor to do
Isa 9:6 Wonderful, Counselor
Isa 40:13 counselor has taught
Isa 41:28 *was* no counselor
Lu 23:50 Joseph, a counselor
Ro 11:34 been his counselor

Countenance
Ge 31:5 father's countenance
Jud 13:6 countenance of an
1Sa 1:18 countenance was
1Sa 16:12 beautiful countenance
Ne 2:2 countenance sad
Pr 15:13 cheerful countenance
Da 1:13 countenance of the
Mt 6:16 sad countenance
Mt 28:3 countenance was
Lu 9:29 countenance was

Country
Ge 12:1 of your country
Ge 24:4 go to my country
De 26:3 country which
Jos 2:2 out the country
2Ch 6:32 a far country
Isa 1:7 country *is* desolate
Jer 2:7 plentiful country
Jon 1:8 *is* your country
Mt 2:12 own country
Mt 13:57 country, and in
Lu 1:39 the hill country
Lu 15:13 a far country
Heb 11:14 seek a country

Covenant
Ge 6:18 establish my covenant
Ge 17:2 covenant between me
Ex 2:24 covenant with Abraham
Ex 24:8 blood of the covenant
Ex 34:28 covenant, the ten
Nu 10:33 ark of the covenant
2Ki 23:2 book of the covenant
Jer 31:31 new covenant with
Eze 37:26 covenant of peace
Ro 11:27 this *is* my covenant
Heb 8:6 better covenant
Heb 13:20 everlasting covenant

Covet(ousness)
Ex 20:17 shall not covet
Ps 119:36 not to covetousness
Jer 6:13 given to covetousness
Mr 7:22 Thefts, covetousness
Lu 12:15 of covetousness
Ro 7:7 You shall not covet
Ro 13:9 You shall not covet
1Co 12:31 covet earnestly
Heb 13:5 without covetousness

Craftiness
Job 5:13 own craftiness
Lu 20:23 their craftiness
1Co 3:19 their own craftiness
2Co 4:2 walking in craftiness
Eph 4:14 cunning craftiness

Creation
Mr 10:6 of the creation
Ro 1:20 creation of the
Ro 8:22 creation groans

Creator
Isa 40:28 Yahweh, the Creator
Isa 43:15 creator of Israel
Ro 1:25 than the Creator

Creature
Ge 1:21 living creature
Eze 1:20 the living creature
Eze 10:15 creature that I
Mr 16:15 to every creature
Ro 1:25 served the creature
Ro 8:19 of the creature
2Co 5:17 is a new creature
Col 1:15 of every creature
1Ti 4:4 creature of God
Heb 4:13 there any creature
Re 5:13 creature which is in

Creditor
Ex 22:25 as a creditor
De 15:2 creditor that lent
2Ki 4:1 creditor is coming
Lu 7:41 certain creditor

Creeping Things
Ge 7:23 creeping things
Le 11:23 creeping things
Ps 148:10 creeping things
Eze 8:10 creeping things
Eze 38:20 creeping things
Ac 10:12 creeping things
Ro 1:23 creeping things

Cross
Mt 16:24 take up his cross
Mr 10:21 cross, and follow
Mr 15:30 down from the cross
Lu 23:26 they laid the cross
Joh 19:17 bearing his cross
1Co 1:17 cross of the Messiah
Ga 5:11 offense of the cross
Eph 2:16 body by the cross
Php 2:8 death of the cross
Col 1:20 blood of his cross
Col 2:14 nailing it to his cross
Heb 12:2 endured the cross

Crown(ed)
Es 2:17 royal crown
Ps 8:5 crowned him
Ps 21:3 crown of pure
Mr 15:17 crown of thorns
1Co 9:25 corruptible crown
2Ti 4:8 crown of
Heb 2:7 crowned him
Jas 1:12 receive the crown
Re 2:10 crown of life
Re 12:1 crown of twelve
Re 14:14 golden crown

Crucified
Mt 26:2 to be crucified
Mt 28:5 was crucified
Mr 15:24 had crucified him
Joh 19:18 crucified him
Ac 2:23 crucified and slain
Ro 6:6 man is crucified
1Co 1:23 Messiah crucified
Ga 2:20 crucified with
Re 11:8 Lord was crucified

Crucify
Mt 20:19 and to crucify
Mt 23:34 kill and crucify
Mr 15:14 Crucify him
Lu 23:21 saying, Crucify
Joh 19:6 and crucify him
Heb 6:6 seeing they crucify

Cruelty
Ps 27:12 breathe out cruelty
Ps 74:20 habitations of cruelty
Eze 34:4 and with cruelty

Cubit(s)
Ge 6:16 and in a cubit
Ex 25:10 cubits and a half
Nu 35:4 thousand cubits
1Sa 17:4 was six cubits
1Ki 6:2 threescore cubits
2Ch 3:3 length by cubits
Ezr 6:3 threescore cubits
Eze 40:5 cubit and a hand
Da 3:1 threescore cubits
Zec 5:2 twenty cubits
Mt 6:27 add one cubit
Re 21:17 cubits, *according*

Cup
Ge 44:2 silver cup
Ne 1:11 king's cup bearer
Ps 23:5 my cup runs over
Ps 116:13 cup of salvation
Jer 25:15 cup of this fury
Jer 51:7 golden cup in
Zec 12:2 cup of trembling
Mt 20:22 drink of the cup
Mt 26:27 cup, and gave
Mr 14:36 away this cup
Lu 11:39 outside of the cup
Lu 22:20 cup *is* the new
1Co 10:21 cup of the Lord
1Co 11:26 drink this cup
Re 14:10 cup of his
Re 17:4 cup in her hand

Curse(d)
Ge 3:17 cursed *is* the
Ge 8:21 curse the ground
Ge 27:29 cursed *be* every
De 11:26 and a curse
De 27:15 Cursed *is* the man
Job 2:9 curse God, and die
Jer 11:3 Cursed *be* the man
Zec 5:3 curse that goes
Mt 5:44 them that curse
Mr 14:71 curse and to swear
Ro 12:14 and curse not
Ga 3:13 curse of the law
Re 22:3 no more curse

Cursing
De 30:19 blessing and cursing
2Sa 16:12 cursing this day
Ps 10:7 cursing and deceit
Ps 109:17 he loved cursing
Pr 29:24 hears cursing
Ro 3:14 cursing and bitterness
Jas 3:10 blessing and cursing

Cush
Ge 10:6 Ham; Cush
1Ch 1:10 Cush begot
Isa 11:11 and from Cush

Cut
Ge 17:14 cut off from
Ex 29:17 cut the ram
Ex 34:13 cut down their
Jos 4:7 cut off before
Jud 20:6 cut her in pieces
1Sa 24:4 cut off the skirt
Da 2:34 stone was cut
Mt 5:30 cut it off
Mt 26:51 cut off his ear

Cyprus
Ac 15:39 sailed to Cyprus
Ac 27:4 sailed under Cyprus

Cyrene
Mt 27:32 man of Cyrene

Cyrus
2Ch 36:22 Cyrus king
Ezr 1:2 says Cyrus king
Isa 44:28 Cyrus, *He is* my
Isa 45:1 anointed, to Cyrus
Da 1:21 year of king Cyrus

Dagon
Jud 16:23 Dagon their god
1Sa 5:3 Dagon *had* fallen
1Ch 10:10 temple of Dagon

Damascus
So 7:4 toward Damascus
Isa 17:1 Damascus is taken
Jer 49:23 Concerning Damascus
Eze 47:16 border of Damascus
Am 1:3 of Damascus
Ac 9:3 came near Damascus
Ac 22:5 went to Damascus
Ac 26:12 I went to Damascus
Ga 1:17 again to Damascus

Damnation (Damned)

Damnation (Damned)
Mt 23:14 greater damnation
Mr 3:29 eternal damnation
Mr 16:16 shall be damned
Joh 5:29 of damnation
Ro 13:2 themselves damnation
Ro 14:23 doubts is damned
1Co 11:29 drinks damnation
2Th 2:12 might be damned
1Ti 5:12 Having damnation

Dan
Ge 30:6 his name Dan
Ge 49:17 Dan shall be
Jos 19:47 Dan, after
Jud 1:34 Dan into the
Jud 18:30 children of Dan
1Ki 12:29 put he in Dan
Am 8:14 Your god, O Dan

Dance (Dancing)
Ex 32:19 the dancing
Jud 21:21 dance in dances
1Sa 18:6 singing and dancing
1Sa 30:16 drinking, and dancing
2Sa 6:16 dancing before Yahweh
Ps 30:11 mourning into dancing
Ec 3:4 time to dance
Jer 31:13 rejoice in the dance
La 5:15 our dance has turned
Lu 15:25 music and dancing

Daniel
Eze 14:14 Noah, Daniel
Eze 28:3 wiser than Daniel
Da 1:6 Judah, Daniel
Mt 24:15 Daniel the prophet
Mr 13:14 by Daniel the prophet

Darius
Ezr 4:24 Darius king
Ne 12:22 reign of Darius
Da 5:31 Darius the Median
Hag 1:1 Darius the king
Zec 1:1 year of Darius

Darkness
Ge 1:2 darkness *was* upon
Ex 10:21 darkness over
1Ki 8:12 thick darkness
Isa 9:2 walked in darkness
Isa 60:2 darkness shall cover
Mt 4:16 sat in darkness
Mt 22:13 into outer darkness
Mt 27:45 darkness over all
Joh 1:5 shines in darkness
Joh 3:19 men loved darkness
Ro 13:12 works of darkness
Eph 6:12 of the darkness
Re 16:10 full of darkness

Daughter
Ex 1:22 daughter you shall
Ex 2:5 daughter of Pharaoh
Jud 11:34 daughter came
1Sa 18:20 Saul's daughter
Es 2:7 his own daughter
Isa 1:8 daughter of Zion
Mal 2:11 daughter of a
Mt 9:18 daughter is even
Mt 14:6 daughter of Herodias
Mr 7:25 young daughter

David
Ru 4:22 Jesse begot David
1Sa 16:13 came upon David
1Sa 17:39 David girded
2Sa 5:4 David *was* thirty
1Ki 8:1 city of David
1Ch 11:9 David grew greater
Mt 12:23 the son of David
Lu 2:11 city of David
Re 22:16 offspring of David

Day
Ge 1:5 the light Day
Ex 13:21 day in a pillar
Ezr 9:7 unto this day
Ps 118:24 day which
Eze 7:19 day of the wrath
Mt 6:11 day our daily
Mt 27:64 the third day
Joh 9:4 while it is day
2Co 4:16 renewed day
2Pe 3:10 day of the Lord
Re 6:17 day of his wrath

Day of Yahweh
Isa 2:12 day of Yahweh
Eze 30:3 day of Yahweh
Joe 2:1 day of Yahweh
Am 5:18 day of Yahweh
Zep 1:7 day of Yahweh
Zep 1:14 great day of Yahweh
Mal 4:5 day of Yahweh

Day star
2Pe 1:19 day star arises

Deacon
1Ti 3:10 office of a deacon

Dead
Ge 23:4 bury my dead
Ex 4:19 men are dead
2Sa 12:23 now he is dead
2Ki 4:32 child was dead
2Ki 19:35 all dead corpses
Mt 8:22 bury their dead
Lu 7:15 was dead sat up
Lu 20:38 God of the dead
Joh 11:25 dead, yet shall
Ro 10:9 from the dead
1Th 4:16 dead in the
Heb 11:35 dead raised
Re 20:13 gave up the dead

Deaf
Le 19:14 curse the deaf
Ps 38:13 deaf *man*, heard
Isa 29:18 deaf hear
Isa 35:5 ears of the deaf
Isa 42:18 Hear, you deaf
Mic 7:16 shall be deaf
Mt 11:5 deaf hear
Mr 7:32 that was deaf
Mr 9:25 dumb and deaf

Death
Le 24:16 put to death
De 30:15 death and evil
Ps 23:4 shadow of death
Ec 7:1 day of death
Mt 4:16 shadow of death
Lu 18:33 put him to death
Ac 22:20 consenting to his death
Ro 5:10 death of his Son
Ro 6:23 wages of sin *is* death
1Co 11:26 Lord's death
Php 2:8 obedient unto death
1Jo 5:17 sin not unto death
Re 20:13 death and hell

Deborah
Ge 35:8 Deborah Rebekah's
Jud 4:4 Deborah, a prophetess
Jud 5:1 Deborah and Barak

Debt
1Sa 22:2 that *was* in debt
2Ki 4:7 pay your debt
Ne 10:31 of every debt
Mt 18:27 him the debt
Ro 4:4 grace, but of debt

Debtor
Eze 18:7 debtor his pledge
Mt 23:16 he is a debtor
Ro 1:14 I am debtor
Ga 5:3 debtor to do the

Deceit
Ge 27:35 came with deceit
Nu 25:18 with their deceit
Job 27:4 tongue utter deceit
Job 31:5 hurried to deceit
Ps 10:7 deceit and fraud
Ps 55:11 deceit and guile
Ps 119:118 deceit *is* falsehood
Pr 12:20 Deceit *is* in
Jer 9:8 speaks deceit
Jer 14:14 deceit of their heart
Am 8:5 balances by deceit
Mr 7:22 wickedness, deceit
Ro 1:29 deceit, malignity

Deceived
Ge 31:7 father has deceived
De 11:16 is not deceived
Pr 20:1 deceived thereby
Jer 20:7 you have deceived
Eze 14:9 prophet is deceived
Lu 21:8 you be not deceived
2Co 11:3 serpent deceived
Ga 6:7 Be not deceived
1Ti 2:14 as not deceived
Re 18:23 all nations deceived
Re 20:10 devil that deceived

Decision, Valley of
Joe 3:14 valley of decision

Decrees
Isa 10:1 unrighteous decrees
Ac 16:4 decrees for to keep
Ac 17:7 decrees of Caesar

Dedication
Nu 7:84 dedication of the
2Ch 7:9 kept the dedication

Ezr 6:16 dedication of this
Ne 12:27 dedication of the
Ps 30:1 dedication of
Da 3:2 dedication of the
Joh 10:22 of the dedication

Defile
Le 11:44 shall you defile
Le 15:31 defile my
Le 18:20 defile yourself
Eze 9:7 Defile the house
Eze 33:26 defile every
Eze 44:25 person to defile
Mt 15:18 defile the man
Mr 7:15 into him can defile
Jude 1:8 defile the flesh

Delaiah
1Ch 24:18 Delaiah, the four
Ezr 2:60 children of Delaiah
Ne 6:10 Delaiah the son
Ne 7:62 children of Delaiah
Jer 36:12 Delaiah the son
Jer 36:25 Elnathan and Delaiah

Delilah
Jud 16:4 name *was* Delilah
Jud 16:13 Delilah said to

Deliver
Ge 37:22 deliver him to
Ge 40:13 deliver Pharaoh's
Nu 35:25 deliver the slayer
De 7:2 God shall deliver
Jos 2:13 deliver our lives
Jud 13:5 to deliver Israel
Mt 5:25 judge deliver you
Mt 6:13 deliver us from evil
Ac 7:25 hand would deliver
Ro 7:24 shall deliver me
1Co 5:5 deliver such a one
Ga 1:4 deliver us from this
2Pe 2:9 deliver the godly

Deliverer
Jud 3:9 raised up a deliverer
Jud 3:15 deliverer, Ehud
2Sa 22:2 and my deliverer
Ps 18:2 deliverer; my God
Ps 40:17 and my deliverer
Ps 70:5 deliverer; O Yahweh
Ps 144:2 and my deliverer
Ac 7:35 ruler and a deliverer
Ro 11:26 Zion the Deliverer

Demetrius
Ac 19:24 Demetrius, a silversmith
3Jo 1:12 Demetrius has good

Demons (see Devils)

Devil
Mt 4:1 by the devil
Mt 17:18 the devil
Mt 25:41 for the devil
Mr 5:15 with the devil
Lu 9:42 devil threw him
Joh 8:44 father the devil
Eph 6:11 wiles of the devil
Heb 2:14 that is, the devil
Jas 4:7 Resist the devil
1Pe 5:8 adversary the devil
1Jo 3:8 sins of the devil
Re 12:9 called the Devil

Devils
Le 17:7 offer their sacrifices to devils
De 32:17 they sacrificed unto devils
2Ch 11:15 for the high places, and for the devils
Ps 106:37 sons and their daughters unto devils
Mt 4:24 were possessed with devils
Mt 8:16 that were possessed with devils
Mt 10:8 raise the dead, cast out devils
Mt 12:24 prince of the devils
Mr 1:39 cast out devils
Mr 16:9 he had cast seven devils
Mr 16:17 in my name shall they cast out devils
Lu 4:41 devils also came out of many
Lu 8:2 out of whom went seven devils
Lu 9:1 authority over all devils
Lu 10:17 even the devils are subject to us
Lu 11:15 the chief of the devils
1Co 10:20 they sacrifice to devils
1Ti 4:1 doctrines of devils
Jas 2:19 the devils also believe
Re 9:20 they should not worship devils
Re 16:14 For they are the spirits of devils
Re 18:2 the habitation of devils

Dew
Ge 27:28 dew of heaven
Ex 16:13 dew lay round
De 33:28 drop down dew
Jud 6:37 dew is on the
2Sa 1:21 dew, neither *let*
1Ki 17:1 dew nor rain
Pr 3:20 down the dew
Pr 19:12 dew upon the
Da 4:23 dew of heaven
Zec 8:12 give their dew

Diadem
Job 29:14 and a diadem
Isa 28:5 diadem of beauty
Isa 62:3 royal diadem
Eze 21:26 the diadem

Diana
Ac 19:24 Diana *Artemis*
Ac 19:35 Goddess Diana

Diligence
Pr 4:23 with all diligence
Lu 12:58 give diligence that
Ro 12:8 over, with diligence
2Co 8:7 diligence, and *in*
2Ti 4:9 diligence to come
Heb 6:11 same diligence
2Pe 1:5 giving all diligence
Jude 1:3 diligence to write

Dinah
Ge 30:21 her name Dinah
Ge 34:1 Dinah the daughter
Ge 46:15 daughter Dinah

Disciple
Mt 10:24 disciple is not above
Mt 27:57 Yahshua's disciple
Lu 14:26 be my disciple
Joh 18:15 disciple was known
Joh 19:26 disciple standing by
Joh 20:2 disciple, whom
Ac 9:10 disciple at Damascus
Ac 21:16 an old disciple

Dispersion (see Scatter)

Divination
Nu 22:7 rewards of divination
De 18:10 divination, *or* an
2Ki 17:17 divination and
Jer 14:14 vision and divination
Eze 13:6 lying divination
Eze 21:21 use divination
Ac 16:16 spirit of divination

Divorce
De 24:1 bill of divorce
Isa 50:1 mother's divorce
Jer 3:8 bill of divorce
Mt 5:31 writing of divorce
Mt 19:7 divorce, and to put
Mr 10:4 bill of divorce

Doctrines
Mt 15:9 doctrines the
Mr 7:7 *for* doctrines
Col 2:22 doctrines of men
1Ti 4:1 doctrines of devils
Heb 13:9 strange doctrines

Door
Ge 4:7 lies at the door
Ge 6:16 door of the ark
Ge 18:1 tent door in the
Ge 19:10 shut to the door
Ex 33:9 door of the
Jud 19:26 door of the
1Ki 14:17 of the door
Eze 8:16 door of the temple
Am 9:1 lintel of the door
Mt 6:6 shut your door
Mt 27:60 door of the
Joh 10:9 I am the door
Ac 12:13 at the door
Col 4:3 door of utterance
Re 3:20 stand at the door

Dorcas
Ac 9:36 Dorcas: this woman
Ac 9:39 which Dorcas

Dove
Ge 8:8 sent forth a dove
Ps 68:13 wings of a dove
So 5:2 my love, my dove
Isa 38:14 mourn as a dove
Jer 48:28 dove *that* makes
Ho 11:11 dove out of
Mt 3:16 like a dove
Mr 1:10 Spirit like a dove
Lu 3:22 shape like a dove
Joh 1:32 heaven like a dove

Drink Offering
Ge 35:14 a drink offering

Drink Offering

Drink Offering
Ex 29:40 a drink offering
Nu 6:17 his drink offering
Nu 29:28 his drink offering
Isa 65:11 drink offering unto
Joe 1:9 drink offering is cut
Joe 2:14 drink offering unto

Drink, Strong
Le 10:9 wine nor strong drink
De 29:6 wine or strong drink
Jud 13:4 strong drink, and eat
Pr 20:1 mocker, strong drink
Pr 31:6 Give strong drink
Isa 5:22 mingle strong drink
Isa 24:9 strong drink shall be
Isa 28:7 through strong drink
Mic 2:11 of strong drink
Lu 1:15 wine nor strong drink

Dross
Ps 119:119 earth *like* dross
Pr 25:4 Take away the dross
Pr 26:23 with silver dross
Isa 1:22 has become dross
Eze 22:18 become dross

Drought
Ge 31:40 drought consumed
De 8:15 drought, where
Job 24:19 Drought and heat
Ps 32:4 drought of summer
Jer 2:6 land of drought
Jer 17:8 year of drought
Jer 50:38 drought *is* upon
Ho 13:5 of great drought
Hag 1:11 drought upon

Drunkard
De 21:20 and a drunkard
Pr 23:21 drunkard and the
Pr 26:9 of a drunkard
Isa 24:20 like a drunkard
1Co 5:11 or a drunkard

Drunkenness
De 29:19 drunkenness to
Ec 10:17 for drunkenness
Jer 13:13 with drunkenness
Eze 23:33 drunkenness and
Lu 21:34 and drunkenness
Ro 13:13 and drunkenness
Ga 5:21 murders, drunkenness

Duke(s)
Ge 36:15 dukes of the sons of Esau
Jos 13:21 dukes of Sihon
1Ch 1:51 the dukes of Edom

Dust
Ge 2:7 dust of the ground
Ge 3:14 dust shall you eat
Ge 13:16 dust of the earth
Ex 8:16 smite the dust
Nu 5:17 dust that is in
Jos 7:6 dust upon their
Isa 65:25 dust *shall* be
Eze 24:7 cover it with dust
Na 1:3 clouds *are* the dust
Mt 10:14 shake off the dust
Lu 9:5 dust from your feet
Ac 13:51 shook off the dust
Ac 22:23 dust into the air
Re 18:19 cast dust on

Eagle
De 14:12 eat: the eagle
De 28:49 the eagle flies
Pr 30:19 eagle in the air
Jer 48:40 fly as an eagle
Eze 10:14 face of an eagle
Eze 17:3 eagle with great
Da 7:4 had eagle's wings
Mic 1:16 as the eagle
Re 4:7 like a flying eagle
Re 12:14 of a great eagle

Ear
Ex 9:31 *was* in the ear
Ex 21:6 bore his ear
Le 8:23 Aaron's right ear
2Ki 19:16 ear and hear
Job 13:1 ear has heard
Pr 20:12 hearing ear
Isa 48:8 my ear to hear
Mt 10:27 hear in the ear
Mr 4:28 corn in the ear
Lu 22:51 touched his ear
Joh 18:26 ear Peter cut off
1Co 2:9 nor ear heard
Re 2:7 He that has an ear

Earnest
Ro 8:19 earnest expectation
2Co 1:22 earnest of the Spirit
2Co 5:5 to us the earnest
2Co 7:7 earnest desire
Eph 1:14 earnest of our
Php 1:20 earnest expectation
Heb 2:1 more earnest heed

Earring
Ge 24:22 golden earring
Ge 24:30 earring and bracelets
Ge 24:47 earring upon her face
Job 42:11 every one an earring
Pr 25:12 earring of gold

Earth
Ge 1:1 heaven and the earth
Ge 2:5 rain upon the earth
Ge 9:1 replenish the earth
Jos 5:14 earth trembled
Ps 67:6 earth yield her
Isa 26:15 ends of the earth
Eze 1:15 upon the earth
Hab 3:6 measured the earth
Mt 5:13 salt of the earth
Mt 6:19 treasures upon earth
Mr 4:28 earth brings forth
Ac 17:26 face of the earth
Heb 1:10 of the earth
Heb 6:7 earth which drinks
Jas 5:7 fruit of the earth
2Pe 3:5 earth standing out
Re 9:4 grass of the earth

Earthquakes
1Ki 19:11 an earthquake
Isa 29:6 earthquake, and
Zec 14:5 earthquake in the
Mt 27:54 saw the earthquake
Ac 16:26 great earthquake
Re 8:5 and an earthquake.
Re 11:13 earthquake, and
Re 11:19 earthquake, and

Eating
Ru 3:3 eating and drinking
1Sa 14:34 Yahweh in eating
2Ki 4:40 eating of the pottage
Isa 22:13 eating flesh
Isa 66:17 eating swine's
Am 7:2 eating the grass
Mt 11:18 eating nor drinking
Mt 24:38 eating and drinking
Mt 26:26 eating, Yahshua
Lu 7:33 neither eating
1Co 8:4 eating of those things

Ebenezer
1Sa 4:1 beside Ebenezer
1Sa 5:1 it from Ebenezer
1Sa 7:12 of it Ebenezer

Eber
Ge 10:21 children of Eber
Ge 11:16 Eber lived four
Nu 24:24 shall afflict Eber
1Ch 1:18 Shelah begot Eber
1Ch 8:12 of Elpaal; Eber
Lu 3:35 *son* of Eber

Eden
Ge 2:8 eastward in Eden
Ge 3:24 garden of Eden
2Ki 19:12 children of Eden
2Ch 29:12 Eden the son
Eze 28:13 Eden the garden
Eze 31:9 trees of Eden
Joe 2:3 garden of Eden
Am 1:5 house of Eden

Edom
Ge 36:8 Esau *is* Edom.
Nu 20:14 king of Edom
Jos 15:1 border of Edom
Jud 5:4 Edom, the earth
2Sa 8:14 garrisons in Edom
2Ch 25:20 the gods of Edom
Jer 49:7 Concerning Edom
Eze 25:12 Edom has dealt
Joe 3:19 Edom shall be
Am 1:6 *them* up to Edom
Ob 1:1 concerning Edom

Edomites
Ge 36:9 of the Edomites
1Ki 11:17 Edomites of his
2Ki 8:21 smote the Edomites
1Ch 18:13 Edomites became
2Ch 21:10 Edomites revolted
25:19 smitten the Edomites

Egypt
Ge 12:10 down into Egypt
Ge 37:28 Joseph into Egypt
Ge 50:22 dwelt in Egypt

Ex 3:7 which *are* in Egypt
Ex 6:11 king of Egypt
Le 25:38 the land of Egypt
Nu 11:18 with us in Egypt
Nu 34:5 the river of Egypt
De 28:60 diseases of Egypt
Mt 2:13 flee into Egypt
Ac 7:9 Joseph into Egypt
Heb 11:27 he forsook Egypt
Re 11:8 Sodom and Egypt

Egyptians
Ge 41:56 to the Egyptians
Ex 3:9 Egyptians oppress
Ex 12:27 smote the Egyptians
Ex 14:9 Egyptians pursued
Isa 31:3 Egyptians *are* men
Jer 43:13 of the Egyptians
Eze 16:26 with the Egyptians
Eze 30:26 scatter the Egyptians
Ac 7:22 of the Egyptians.
Heb 11:29 Egyptians attempting

Ekron
Jos 13:3 borders of Ekron
Jud 1:18 Ekron with the
1Sa 5:10 God came to Ekron.
1Sa 7:14 Israel, from Ekron
2Ki 1:2 god of Ekron
Am 1:8 hand against Ekron
Zep 2:4 Ekron shall be rooted
Zec 9:7 Ekron as a Jebusite

Elah
1Sa 17:2 valley of Elah
1Ki 16:6 Elah his son
2Ki 15:30 Elah made
2Ki 17:1 son of Elah
1Ch 1:52 duke Elah, duke
1Ch 9:8 Elah the son

Elam
Ge 10:22 Shem; Elam
Ge 14:1 king of Elam
1Ch 26:3 Elam the fifth
Ezr 10:2 sons of Elam
Isa 11:11 Elam, and from
Isa 22:6 Elam bore
Jer 49:38 set my throne in Elam
Da 8:2 Elam; and I saw

Elamites
Ezr 4:9 *and* the Elamites
Ac 2:9 Medes, and Elamites

Elbethel
Ge 35:7 called the place Elbethel

Eldaah
Ge 25:4 Abida, and Eldaah
1Ch 1:33 Eldaah. All these

Elder
Ge 25:23 elder shall serve
Ge 27:42 Esau her elder
Ge 29:16 elder *was* Leah
1Ki 2:22 my elder brother
Eze 16:46 elder sister *is*
Eze 23:4 Aholah the elder
Lu 15:25 elder son was
1Ti 5:1 Rebuke not an elder
1Pe 5:1 also an elder
3Jo 1:1 elder to the well

Eleazar
Ex 6:25 Eleazar Aaron's
Le 10:16 with Eleazar
Nu 3:4 Eleazar and Ithamar
Nu 16:39 Eleazar the priest
Nu 20:28 Eleazar came
De 10:6 Eleazar his son
Jos 21:1 Eleazar the priest
1Sa 7:1 sanctified Eleazar
1Ch 6:4 Eleazar begot
Mt 1:15 Eliud begot Eleazar

Eli
1Sa 1:9 Eli the priest
1Sa 2:12 sons of Eli
1Sa 2:20 Eli blessed
1Sa 3:6 Eli, and said
1Sa 3:16 Eli called Samuel
1Sa 4:15 Eli was ninety
1Ki 2:27 Eli in Shiloh
Mt 27:46 Eli, Eli, lama

Elihu
1Sa 1:1 son of Elihu
1Ch 26:7 men, Elihu
1Ch 27:18 Judah, Elihu
Job 32:2 wrath of Elihu
Job 32:4 Elihu had waited

Elijah
1Ki 17:1 Elijah the Tishbite
1Ki 19:1 all that Elijah
2Ki 1:3 said to Elijah
2Ki 2:1 Elijah into heaven
Mal 4:5 Elijah the prophet
Mt 16:14 some, Elijah
Mt 27:49 Elijah will come
Mr 9:13 Elijah has indeed
Lu 1:17 power of Elijah
Lu 9:33 one for Elijah
Joh 1:21 Are you Elijah
Jas 5:17 Elijah was a man

Elim
Ex 15:27 they came to Elim
Ex 16:1 journey from Elim
Nu 33:9 Elim *were* twelve
Nu 33:10 removed from Elim

Elimelech
Ru 1:3 Elimelech Naomi's
Ru 2:1 family of Elimelech
Ru 4:9 that *was* Elimelech's

Elizabeth
Lu 1:7 Elisabeth was barren
Lu 1:24 Elisabeth conceived
Lu 1:40 saluted Elisabeth
Lu 1:57 Elisabeth's full time

Elisha
1Ki 19:16 Elisha the son
2Ki 2:1 went with Elisha
2Ki 4:1 prophets unto Elisha
2Ki 5:9 house of Elisha
2Ki 6:17 round about Elisha
2Ki 8:1 spoke Elisha to
2Ki 8:5 Elisha restored to
2Ki 13:14 Elisha had fallen

Elishua
2Sa 5:15 Elishua, and Nepheg
1Ch 14:5 Elishua, and Elpalet

Eloi
Mr 15:34 Eloi, Eloi, lama

Enchantment
Nu 23:23 enchantment against
Ec 10:11 without enchantment

Endor
Jos 17:11 inhabitants of Endor
1Sa 28:7 spirit at Endor
Ps 83:10 perished at Endor

Enemy
Nu 10:9 enemy that
De 28:57 enemy shall
1Sa 18:29 David's enemy
1Ki 8:44 against their enemy
Es 7:6 adversary and enemy
Ps 143:3 enemy has
Zep 3:15 out your enemy
Mt 5:43 hate your enemy
Mt 13:25 enemy came
Lu 10:19 of the enemy
Ac 13:10 devil, *you* enemy
Ro 12:20 enemy hungers
Jas 4:4 enemy of God

Engraving
Ex 32:4 engraving tool
2Ch 2:14 manner of engraving
Zec 3:9 engrave the engraving

Enoch
Ge 4:18 Enoch was born
Ge 5:24 Enoch walked
Lu 3:37 Enoch, which
Heb 11:5 Enoch was
Jude 1:14 Enoch also

Enos
Ge 4:26 his name Enos
Ge 5:6 begot Enos:
Ge 5:11 days of Enos
Lu 3:38 Enos, which

Ephah
Ge 25:4 Midian; Ephah
Ex 16:36 of an ephah
Le 19:36 a just ephah
Jud 6:19 ephah of flour
Ch 2:46 Ephah, Caleb's
Eze 45:10 just ephah
Am 8:5 ephah small
Zec 5:7 of the ephah

Ephesians
Ac 19:28 of the Ephesians.
Ac 19:35 of the Ephesians
2Ti 4:22 Ephesians

Ephesus

Ephesus
Ac 18:19 came to Ephesus
Ac 19:17 dwelling at Ephesus
Ac 20:16 sail by Ephesus
1Co 15:32 beasts at Ephesus
1Co 16:8 Ephesus until
Eph 1:1 which are at Ephesus
1Ti 1:3 still at Ephesus
Re 1:11 Asia; to Ephesus
Re 2:1 of Ephesus

Ephod
Ex 25:7 ephod, and in
Ex 28:6 ephod *of* gold
Ex 39:5 of his ephod
Nu 34:23 son of Ephod
Jud 8:27 made an ephod
Jud 17:5 ephod, and teraphim
1Sa 2:18 linen ephod
1Sa 14:3 wearing an ephod
2Sa 6:14 linen ephod
Ho 3:4 without an ephod

Ephraim
Ge 41:52 called he Ephraim
Ge 48:20 set Ephraim before
Nu 1:10 Joseph: of Ephraim
Nu 13:8 tribe of Ephraim
Jos 24:30 mount Ephraim
Jud 1:29 Ephraim drive out
2Ch 17:2 cities of Ephraim
Jer 31:9 Ephraim *is* my
Ho 5:9 Ephraim shall be
Ob 1:19 fields of Ephraim
Zec 9:10 chariot from Ephraim
Joh 11:54 city called Ephraim

Ephratah
Ru 4:11 worthily in Ephratah
1Ch 2:50 firstborn of Ephratah
Ps 132:6 of it at Ephratah
Mic 5:2 Bethlehem Ephratah

Ephrath
Ge 35:16 come to Ephrath
Ge 48:7 Ephrath: and I
1Ch 2:19 to him Ephrath

Ephron
Ge 23:8 Ephron the son
Ge 23:10 Ephron dwelt
Ge 25:9 field of Ephron
Ge 49:29 Ephron the Hittite
Ge 50:13 place of Ephron

Epistles
2Co 3:1 epistles of
2Pe 3:16 all *his* epistles

Erech
Ge 10:10 Babel, and Erech

Errors
Ps 19:12 understand *his* errors
Jer 10:15 work of errors
Jer 51:18 errors: in the time
Heb 9:7 errors of the people

Esau
Ge 25:26 on Esau's heel
Ge 26:34 Esau was forty
Ge 27:1 Esau his oldest
Ge 35:29 Esau and Jacob
Ge 36:1 Esau, who *is* Edom
De 2:4 Esau, which dwell
Jos 24:4 Jacob and Esau
Jer 49:8 calamity of Esau
Ob 1:6 Esau searched out
Mal 1:3 I hated Esau
Ro 9:13 Esau have I hated
Heb 11:20 Jacob and Esau

Esther
Es 2:7 that *is*, Esther
Es 5:1 Esther put on
Es 7:1 Esther the queen
Es 9:12 Esther the queen

Eternal Life
Mt 19:16 have eternal life
Joh 3:15 have eternal life
Joh 6:54 has eternal life
Joh 10:28 them eternal life
Ac 13:48 eternal life believed
Ro 6:23 God *is* eternal life
Tit 1:2 hope of eternal life
1Jo 2:25 *even* eternal life
1Jo 5:20 God, and eternal life
Jude 1:21 Messiah to eternal life

Eternal Fire (see Everlasting)
Jude 1:7 vengeance of eternal fire

Eternity
Isa 57:15 inhabits eternity

Ethiopia
Ge 2:13 land of Ethiopia.
2Ki 19:9 king of Ethiopia
Es 8:9 India to Ethiopia
Ps 68:31 Egypt; Ethiopia
Isa 18:1 rivers of Ethiopia
Isa 45:14 of Ethiopia
Eze 38:5 Persia, Ethiopia
Na 3:9 Ethiopia and Egypt
Zep 3:10 Ethiopia my
Ac 8:27 man of Ethiopia

Eunuch
Isa 56:3 let the eunuch
Ac 8:27 eunuch of great
Ac 8:38 and the eunuch

Euphrates
Ge 2:14 river *is* Euphrates
De 1:7 the river Euphrates
Jos 1:4 river Euphrates
2Ch 35:20 by *the* Euphrates
Jer 13:4 go to *the* Euphrates
Jer 51:63 of *the* Euphrates
Re 9:14 great river Euphrates

Euroclydon
Ac 27:14 called Euroclydon

Eve
Ge 3:20 wife's name Eve
Ge 4:1 Adam knew Eve
2Co 11:3 serpent deceived Eve
1Ti 2:13 formed, then Eve

Everlasting
Ge 9:16 everlasting covenant
Ex 40:15 everlasting priesthood
De 33:27 everlasting arms
Ps 100:5 mercy *is* everlasting
Pr 10:25 everlasting foundation
Isa 9:6 everlasting Father
Isa 45:17 everlasting salvation
Jer 10:10 everlasting king
Da 7:14 everlasting dominion
Mt 18:8 everlasting fire
Mt 25:46 into everlasting punishment
2Th 1:9 everlasting destruction
Heb 13:20 everlasting covenant
Re 14:6 everlasting gospel

Everlasting Fire
Mt 18:8 everlasting fire
Mt 25:41 everlasting fire

Everlasting Life
Da 12:2 to everlasting life
Mt 19:29 inherit everlasting life
Joh 3:16 have everlasting life
Joh 5:24 has everlasting life,
Joh 6:47 has everlasting life
Ac 13:46 of everlasting life
Ro 6:22 *unto* everlasting life

Everlasting Punishment
Mt 25:46 everlasting punishment

Evil
Ge 2:9 good and evil
Ge 48:16 from all evil
Jud 3:7 Israel did evil
1Sa 12:19 sins *this* evil
Ne 13:27 great evil, to
Ps 10:15 the evil *man*
Isa 1:16 away the evil
Isa 5:20 call evil good
Jer 26:3 evil of their
Jon 3:10 heir evil way
Mt 6:13 us from evil
Mr 7:21 proceed evil
Joh 3:20 evil hates
Ac 19:12 evil spirits
Ro 7:19 evil which I
Ga 1:4 evil world
Eph 5:16 days are evil
1Ti 6:10 root of all evil
Re 2:2 which are evil

Evilmerodach
2Ki 25:27 Evilmerodach king of Babylon
Jer 52:31 Evilmerodach king of Babylon

Eye
Ex 21:24 Eye for eye
De 34:7 eye was not dim
Ezr 5:5 eye of their God
Ps 33:18 eye of Yahweh
Pr 20:12 the seeing eye
Jer 13:17 eye shall weep
Mic 4:11 let our eye look

Zec 2:8 apple of his eye
Mt 5:29 right eye offends
Mt 19:24 eye of a needle
Lu 11:34 body is the eye
1Co 2:9 Eye has not seen
Re 1:7 eye shall see him

Ezekiel
Eze 1:3 Ezekiel the priest
Eze 24:24 Ezekiel is unto

Ezra
1Ch 4:17 sons of Ezra
Ezr 7:11 Ezra the priest
Ne 8:1 Ezra the scribe
Ne 12:26 Ezra the priest
Ne 12:33 Azariah, Ezra

Fables
1Ti 1:4 heed to fables and
1Ti 4:7 old wives' fables
2Ti 4:4 turned unto fables
Tit 1:14 heed to Jewish fables
2Pe 1:16 cunningly devised fables

Face
Ge 1:2 face of the waters
Ge 1:29 face of all the earth
Ge 16:8 face of my
Ge 17:17 upon his face
Ge 19:13 face of Yahweh
Ge 32:30 God face to face
Le 13:41 toward his face
De 1:17 face of man
Eze 1:10 face of a man
Da 10:6 face as the
Mt 6:17 wash your face
Joh 11:44 face was bound
1Co 13:12 then face to face
Jas 1:23 face in a glass
Re 4:7 beast had a face

Faith
Hab 2:4 live by his faith
Mt 9:29 faith be it unto
Mt 17:20 faith as a grain
Mt 21:21 faith, and doubt
Mr 11:22 faith in God
Lu 7:50 faith has saved
Ac 3:16 faith in his name
Ro 3:25 faith in his blood
1Co 13:13 remains faith
2Co 5:7 faith, not by sight
Ga 3:11 shall live by faith
Eph 2:8 saved through faith
1Ti 4:1 depart from the faith
2Ti 4:7 have kept the faith
Heb 11:1 faith is the
Jas 5:15 prayer of faith

Faithful
De 7:9 faithful God
1Sa 2:35 faithful priest
Ne 9:8 heart faithful
Isa 8:2 faithful witnesses
Isa 49:7 that is faithful
Jer 42:5 true and faithful
Da 6:4 faithful, neither was
Mt 25:21 faithful servant
1Co 10:13 God is faithful
Heb 2:17 faithful high priest
1Jo 1:9 faithful and just
Re 3:14 faithful and true

Faithfulness
1Sa 26:23 his faithfulness
Ps 36:5 faithfulness reaches
Ps 40:10 your faithfulness
Ps 89:33 faithfulness to fail
Ps 92:2 faithfulness every
Ps 119:90 faithfulness is
Isa 25:1 faithfulness and
La 3:23 your faithfulness

False Prophets
Ac 13:6 a false prophet
Re 16:13 the false prophet
Re 19:20 false prophet that
Re 20:10 the false prophet

False Teachers
2Pe 2:1 false teachers among

Familiar Spirit
Le 20:27 a familiar spirit
1Sa 28:7 familiar spirit at
1Ch 10:13 familiar spirit
2Ch 33:6 a familiar spirit
Isa 29:4 familiar spirit, out

Family
Le 20:5 against his family
Nu 26:57 Gershon, the family
Nu 36:12 tribe of the family
Jud 18:19 family in Israel
Es 9:28 every family
Zec 12:12 family of the
Ac 4:6 family of the high
Ac 7:13 Joseph's family
Eph 3:15 family in heaven

Famine
Ge 41:27 years of famine
Ge 42:33 food for the famine
2Ch 20:9 pestilence, or famine
Ne 5:3 because of the famine
Jer 14:16 of the famine
Eze 5:16 increase the famine
Eze 6:12 die by the famine
Eze 14:13 will send famine
Am 8:11 famine of bread
Lu 15:14 mighty famine
Ac 7:11 famine over all
Ro 8:35 famine, or nakedness
Re 18:8 mourning, and famine

Fasting
Ne 9:1 fasting, and with
Es 4:3 fasting, and weeping
Ps 109:24 through fasting
Da 6:18 night fasting
Da 9:3 with fasting
Mt 15:32 fasting, lest
Mr 8:3 them away fasting
Ac 10:30 I was fasting
Ac 27:33 fasting, having
1Co 7:5 yourselves to fasting

Fat
Ge 41:2 cows and fat
Ge 45:18 eat the fat
Ex 29:13 fat that covers
Le 4:35 fat of the lamb
Nu 13:20 fat or lean
De 32:38 fat of their
Jud 3:17 very fat man
1Sa 2:29 yourselves fat
Ne 8:10 eat the fat
Ne 9:35 large and fat land
Job 15:27 fat on his flanks
Isa 10:16 fat ones leanness
Eze 39:19 shall eat fat
Hab 1:16 fat, and their meat
Zec 11:16 flesh of the fat

Father
Ge 2:24 father and his
Ge 17:4 father of many
Ge 20:12 of my father
Ex 3:6 God of your father
Le 20:9 curses his father
Isa 9:6 everlasting Father
Zec 13:3 father and his
Mal 2:10 all one father
Mt 6:9 Our Father which
Mr 10:29 father, or mother
Joh 1:14 of the Father
Joh 8:44 father the devil
Joh 10:30 I and my Father
Ro 8:15 cry, Abba, Father
Heb 7:10 loins of his father
1Pe 1:3 Father of our Lord
1Jo 4:14 Father sent the Son
Re 14:1 Father's name written

Fatherless
Ex 22:22 fatherless child
De 16:14 the fatherless
Ps 109:9 children be fatherless
Isa 9:17 fatherless and widows
Jer 49:11 fatherless children
La 5:3 orphans and fatherless
Zec 7:10 nor the fatherless
Mal 3:5 and the fatherless
Jas 1:27 fatherless and widows

Fatted Calf
Isa 11:6 the fatted calf
Lu 15:23 fatted calf, and kill
Lu 15:27 killed the fatted calf
Lu 15:30 him the fatted calf

Favor
Ge 39:21 gave him favor
Ex 3:21 people favor
1Sa 29:6 lords favor you
Es 2:17 grace and favor
Job 10:12 life and favor
Ps 30:7 by your favor
Pr 22:1 loving favor
Pr 31:30 Favor is deceitful
Isa 60:10 my favor have
Lu 1:30 found favor with God
Ac 7:10 favor and wisdom

Fear
Ge 9:2 fear of you

Fear

Ge 15:1 Fear not, Abram
Ex 15:16 Fear and dread
Le 25:36 fear your God
Jud 6:10 fear not the gods
Ps 23:4 I will fear no evil
Ec 12:13 Fear God, and keep
Isa 8:12 fear, nor be afraid
Da 6:26 tremble and fear
Mal 4:2 fear my name
Mt 10:28 fear not them
Mt 14:26 cried out for fear
Lu 8:50 Fear not: believe
Lu 12:5 you shall fear
Joh 20:19 fear of the Jews
Ac 5:11 fear came upon
Ro 8:15 bondage again to fear
1Co 2:3 fear, and in much
2Ti 1:7 spirit of fear
Heb 2:15 fear of death
Heb 12:28 godly fear
1Jo 4:18 no fear in love
Re 1:17 Fear not; I am
Re 14:7 Fear God, and give

Fear of God

Ge 20:11 fear of God is not
2Sa 23:3 in the fear of God
Ne 5:15 of the fear of God
Ro 3:18 no fear of God
2Co 7:1 in the fear of God
Eph 5:21 in the fear of God

Feast of Tabernacles

Le 23:34 the feast of tabernacles
De 16:16 the feast of tabernacles
De 31:10 the feast of tabernacles
2Ch 8:13 the feast of tabernacles
Ezr 3:4 the feast of tabernacles
Zec 14:16 the feast of tabernacles
Joh 7:2 Jews' feast of tabernacles

Feast of Unleavened Bread

Ex 12:17 the *feast of* unleavened bread
Ex 23:15 the feast of unleavened bread
Ex 34:18 The feast of unleavened bread
Le 23:6 the feast of unleavened bread
De 16:16 the feast of unleavened bread
2Ch 8:13 the feast of unleavened bread
2Ch 30:13 the feast of unleavened bread
2Ch 35:17 the feast of unleavened bread
Ezr 6:22 the feast of unleavened bread
Mt 26:17 the *feast of* unleavened bread
Lu 22:1 the feast of unleavened bread

Feast of Weeks (see Pentecost)

Ex 34:22 the feast of weeks
De 16:16 the feast of weeks
2Ch 8:13 the feast of weeks

Feasts

Le 23:4 feasts of Yahweh
Nu 15:3 solemn feasts
Ne 10:33 set feasts
Isa 1:14 appointed feasts
La 1:4 solemn feasts
Eze 46:11 feasts and in
Am 8:10 feasts into mourning
Mr 12:39 rooms at feasts
Lu 20:46 rooms at feasts
Jude 1:12 feasts of charity

Feet

Ge 19:2 wash your feet
Ex 3:5 off your feet
Ex 12:11 shoes on your feet
Ex 30:19 hands and their feet
Le 8:24 toes of their right feet
Le 11:21 legs above their feet
De 11:24 soles of your feet
Jud 4:15 fled away on his feet
2Sa 9:13 lame on both his feet
Ps 22:16 hands and my feet
Zec 14:4 feet shall stand
Mt 10:14 dust from your feet
Mt 18:8 hands or two feet
Lu 7:38 feet with tears
Lu 24:39 hands and my feet
Joh 13:5 disciples' feet
Ac 3:7 feet and ankle bones
Ro 10:15 feet of them
Eph 6: feet shod
Re 1:15 feet like unto

Felix

Ac 23:24 Felix the governor
Ac 24:25 Felix trembled
Ac 25:14 bonds by Felix

Fellowship

Ac 2:42 doctrine and fellowship
1Co 1:9 fellowship of his Son
1Co 10:20 fellowship with devils
2Co 6:14 fellowship has
Ga 2:9 hands of fellowship
Eph 3:9 fellowship of the
Eph 5:11 fellowship with the
Php 2:1 fellowship of the Spirit
Php 3:10 fellowship of his
1Jo 1:7 fellowship one

Fig tree

Ge 3:7 fig leaves
De 8:8 fig trees
So 2:13 fig tree puts
Joe 2:22 fruit, the fig
Am 4:9 your fig trees
Hab 3:17 fig tree shall
Mt 24:32 of the fig tree
Mr 11:13 seeing a fig tree
Lu 13:6 fig tree planted
Joh 1:50 under the fig tree
Re 6:13 fig tree casts

Figure

De 4:16 figure, the likeness
Isa 44:13 figure of a man
Ro 5:14 figure of him
1Co 4:6 figure transferred
Heb 9:9 figure for the time
Heb 11:19 him in a figure
1Pe 3:21 like figure

Fire

Ge 19:24 fire from Yahweh
Ex 3:2 flame of fire
Ex 13:21 pillar of fire
Ex 24:17 devouring fire
Le 4:12 wood with fire
Nu 26:61 offered strange fire
Jud 18:27 city with fire
Ne 2:17 burned with fire
Isa 43:2 fire, you shall not
Eze 1:4 fire enfolding itself
Da 3:24 midst of the fire
Mal 3:2 like a refiner's fire
Mt 3:11 Ghost, and *with* fire
Mt 5:22 danger of hell fire
Mt 18:8 everlasting fire
Ac 2:3 tongues like as of fire
Ac 28:3 laid *them* on the fire
Jas 3:6 tongue *is* a fire
2Pe 3:12 heavens being on fire
Re 1:14 as a flame of fire

First and the Last

Re 1:11 the first and the last
Re 2:8 the first and the last
Re 22:13 the first and the last

First Fruit

De 18:4 first fruit *also*
Ro 11:16 first fruit *is* holy

Fish

Ge 1:26 fish of the sea
Ex 7:18 fish that *are* in
Nu 11:5 fish, which we
Eze 29:4 fish of your
Eze 47:10 nets; their fish
Jon 1:17 fish to swallow
Mt 17:27 fish that first
Lu 11:11 *asks for* a fish
Joh 21:9 fish laid thereon

Fishermen

Mt 4:18 they were fishermen
Mr 1:16 they were fishermen
Lu 5:2 fishermen were gone

Fish Gate

2Ch 33:14 at the fish gate
Ne 3:3 But the fish gate
Ne 12:39 above the fish gate
Zep 1:10 from the fish gate

Fishhooks

Am 4:2 with fishhooks

Fetch

Ge 18:5 fetch a morsel
Ge 42:16 fetch your brother
Nu 20:10 fetch you water
Jud 20:10 fetch provisions
1Sa 4:3 fetch the ark
1Sa 20:31 fetch him
Jer 36:21 fetch the roll
Ac 16:37 and fetch us

Flax

Ex 9:31 flax and the barley
Jos 2:6 stalks of flax
Jud 15:14 flax that was
Jud 16:9 as a thread of flax
Pr 31:13 wool, and flax
Isa 42:3 smoking flax
Eze 40:3 line of flax
Ho 2:9 flax *given* to cover
Mt 12:20 smoking flax

Flesh
Ge 2:23 flesh of my flesh
Ge 6:12 flesh had corrupted
Ge 29:14 bone and my flesh
Ex 12:8 eat the flesh
Nu 11:18 flesh to eat
Jer 32:27 God of all flesh
Eze 36:26 heart of flesh
Joe 2:28 spirit upon all flesh
Mt 16:17 flesh and blood
Mr 10:8 two shall be one flesh
Joh 1:14 was made flesh
Joh 3:6 flesh is flesh
Joh 6:51 give is my flesh
1Co 15:50 flesh and blood
2Co 10:3 walk in the flesh
2Co 12:7 thorn in the flesh
Ga 2:20 live in the flesh
Eph 2:3 lusts of our flesh
Eph 6:12 flesh and blood
Heb 10:20 to say, his flesh

Flood
Ge 6:17 flood of waters
Ge 9:11 waters of a flood
Job 22:16 with a flood
Isa 28:2 flood of mighty
Isa 59:19 in like a flood
Jer 47:2 overflowing flood
Am 8:8 the flood of Egypt
Lu 6:48 flood arose
Lu 17:27 flood came
2Pe 2:5 flood upon the
Re 12:16 flood which

Food
Ge 1:30 herb for food
Ge 3:6 good for food
Ge 9:3 shall be food
Ge 41:48 up all the food
1Ki 5:11 wheat *for* food
1Ki 19:8 food *for* forty
Eze 16:19 My food also
Mt 3:4 food was locusts
Mt 25:35 gave me food
Joh 6:55 my flesh is food
1Co 6:13 belly for food
1Co 10:3 spiritual food

Fool
Ps 14:1 fool has said
Pr 11:29 fool *shall be*
Pr 18:2 fool has no delight
Ec 5:3 fool's voice *is*
Lu 12:20 fool, this night
2Co 12:6 not be a fool

Foot
Ex 21:24 foot for foot
Le 8:23 his right foot
De 25:9 off his foot
Jos 1:3 foot shall tread
Ps 26:12 My foot stands
Ps 66:6 flood on foot
Isa 20:2 from your foot
Mt 4:6 foot against a stone
Mr 9:45 foot offends you
1Co 12:15 foot shall say
Re 10:2 right foot upon

Forgive
Ex 32:32 forgive their sin
Nu 30:8 shall forgive
2Ch 6:30 forgive, and
Ps 86:5 forgive; and
Jer 31:34 forgive their
Mt 6:12 forgive us our
Mt 18:21 forgive him
Mr 2:10 to forgive sins
Lu 6:37 forgive, and you
Lu 23:34 forgive them
1Jo 1:9 just to forgive

Forgiveness
Ps 130:4 forgiveness with
Da 9:9 and forgiveness
Mr 3:29 never forgiveness
Ac 5:31 forgiveness of sins
Ac 13:38 forgiveness of sins
Ac 26:18 forgiveness of sins
Eph 1:7 blood, the forgiveness
Col 1:14 forgiveness of sins

Fornication
2Ch 21:11 commit fornication
Isa 23:17 fornication with
Eze 16:29 your fornication
Mt 5:32 cause of fornication
Joh 8:41 born of fornication
Ac 21:25 from fornication
1Co 5:1 fornication among
1Co 7:2 avoid fornication
Ga 5:19 Adultery, fornication
Jude 1:7 fornication, and going
Re 2:14 commit fornication
Re 17:2 wine of her fornication.

Forty
Ge 7:4 forty days
Ex 16:35 manna forty
Nu 1:21 forty and six
De 2:7 these forty years
De 25:3 Forty stripes
Eze 41:2 forty cubits
Lu 4:2 forty days tempted
Ac 7:23 forty years old
2Co 11:24 forty *stripes*
Re 7:4 hundred *and* forty
Re 11:2 forty *and* two

Fountain
Ge 16:7 fountain of water
De 33:28 fountain of Jacob
Ne 3:15 gate of the fountain
Ps 36:9 fountain of life
So 4:15 fountain of gardens
Jer 2:13 fountain of living
Ho 13:15 fountain shall be
Mr 5:29 fountain of her blood
Jas 3:12 fountain both yield
Re 21:6 fountain of the water

Friends
2Sa 19:6 hate your friends
1Ki 16:11 of his friends
Job 2:11 Job's three friends
Pr 14:20 many friends
La 1:2 friends have dealt
Mr 5:19 to your friends
Lu 14:12 not your friends
Lu 15:29 with my friends
Lu 16:9 friends of the
Joh 15:13 life for his friends
Ac 10:24 near friends

Friendship
Pr 22:24 friendship with
Jas 4:4 friendship of the

Frogs
Ex 8:2 borders with frogs
Ps 78:45 frogs, which
Ps 105:30 brought forth frogs
Re 16:13 spirits like frogs

Frontlets
Ex 13:16 frontlets between
De 6:8 shall be as frontlets
De 11:18 frontlets between

Furnace
Ge 15:17 smoking furnace
Ex 9:8 ashes of the furnace
De 4:20 iron furnace, *even*
Ps 12:6 tried in a furnace
Eze 22:20 furnace, to blow
Da 3:6 burning fiery furnace
Mt 13:42 furnace of fire
Re 9:2 of a great furnace

Gabriel
Da 8:16 Gabriel, make
Da 9:21 Gabriel, whom
Lu 1:19 I am Gabriel
Lu 1:26 angel Gabriel

Gad
Ge 30:11 his name Gad
Ge 35:26 handmaid; Gad
Nu 1:25 tribe of Gad
Nu 32:2 children of Gad
De 33:20 enlarges Gad
2Ch 29:25 Gad the king's
Jer 2:36 Why gad you
Re 7:5 Gad *were* sealed

Galatia
Ac 16:6 region of Galatia
Ac 18:23 country of Galatia
1Co 16:1 congregations of Galatia
Ga 1:2 congregations of Galatia
2Ti 4:10 Crescens to Galatia
1Pe 1:1 Pontus, Galatia

Galilee
Jos 20:7 Galilee in mount
1Ki 9:11 land of Galilee
Mt 4:15 Galilee of the Gentiles
Mt 15:29 sea of Galilee
Mr 1:14 Galilee, preaching
Lu 1:26 city of Galilee
Lu 4:14 Spirit into Galilee
Joh 2:1 Cana of Galilee
Joh 12:21 Bethsaida of Galilee

Gall
De 29:18 gall and wormwood

Gall

De 32:32 grapes of gall
Job 16:13 pours out my gall
Ps 69:21 gall for my food
Jer 8:14 gall to drink
Mt 27:34 mingled with gall
Ac 8:23 gall of bitterness

Garment
Le 6:10 linen garment
De 22:11 wear a garment
Es 8:15 garment of fine linen
Ps 102:26 garment; as a coat
Eze 18:7 with a garment
Da 7:9 garment *was* white
Mt 3:4 garment of camel's
Mr 16:5 long white garment
Lu 5:36 new garment upon
Re 1:13 garment down to

Gates
De 3:5 gates, and bars
Jos 6:26 up the gates
1Sa 23:7 has gates and bars
1Ch 9:19 keepers of the gates
1Ch 22:3 doors of the gates
Ne 2:8 beams for the gates
Ps 100:4 into his gates with
Isa 38:10 gates of the grave
Eze 44:17 gates of the inner
Mt 16:18 gates of hell
Re 21:12 twelve gates

Gedaliah
2Ki 25:22 Gedaliah the son
1Ch 25:3 Jeduthun; Gedaliah
Jer 38:1 Gedaliah the son of Pashur
Jer 39:14 Gedaliah the son of Ahikam
Jer 40:8 came to Gedaliah
Zep 1:1 Gedaliah, the son of Amariah

Genealogy
1Ch 4:33 and their genealogy
1Ch 5:7 genealogy of their
1Ch 7:40 genealogy of them
1Ch 9:22 genealogy in their
2Ch 31:16 genealogy of males
Ezr 2:62 reckoned by genealogy
Ezr 8:1 *this is* the genealogy
Ne 7:5 reckoned by genealogy
Heb 7:3 without genealogy

Gentiles
Isa 11:10 Gentiles seek
Isa 42:6 light of the Gentiles
Isa 62:2 Gentiles shall see
Jer 46:1 against the Gentiles
Mt 4:15 Galilee of the Gentiles
Mt 20:19 him to the Gentiles
Lu 2:32 lighten the Gentiles
Ac 9:15 before the Gentiles
Ac 28:28 sent to the Gentiles
Ro 2:14 Gentiles, which have
1Co 12:13 Jews or Gentiles
Col 1:27 among the Gentiles
Re 11:2 given to the Gentiles

Gethsemane
Mt 26:36 called Gethsemane
Mr 14:32 named Gethsemane

Gezer
Jos 10:33 king of Gezer
Jos 16:10 dwelt in Gezer
Jos 21:21 slayer; and Gezer
Jud 1:29 dwelt in Gezer
1Ki 9:15 Megiddo, and Gezer
1Ch 20:4 war at Gezer

Giants
Ge 6:4 giants in the earth
Nu 13:33 giants, the sons
De 2:11 giants, as the Anakims
De 3:11 remnant of giants
Jos 12:4 giants, that dwelt
Jos 15:8 valley of the giants
Jos 17:15 and of the giants

Gibeah
Jos 15:57 Cain, Gibeah
Jud 19:12 pass over to Gibeah
Jud 20:4 Gibeah that *belongs*
1Sa 10:26 went home to Gibeah
1Sa 13:15 Gibeah of Benjamin
1Sa 22:6 stayed in Gibeah
2Sa 6:3 that *was* in Gibeah
2Sa 21:6 Yahweh in Gibeah
Ho 5:8 cornet in Gibeah
Ho 9:9 days of Gibeah

Gideon
Jos 9:3 of Gibeon heard
Jos 10:2 Gibeon *was* a
2Sa 2:24 wilderness of Gibeon
1Ki 3:4 king went to Gibeon
1Ki 9:2 to him at Gibeon.
1Ch 16:39 that *was* at Gibeon
Jer 41:12 that *are* in Gibeon

Gilead
Ge 31:21 the mount Gilead
Nu 26:29 Machir begot Gilead
Nu 32:40 Moses gave Gilead
De 3:10 Gilead, and all Bashan
De 4:43 Ramoth in Gilead
Jos 12:5 Gilead, the border
Jud 5:17 Gilead stayed beyond
1Sa 13:7 Gad and Gilead
Ps 60:7 Gilead *is* mine
Jer 8:22 balm in Gilead
Ho 6:8 Gilead *is* a city
Zec 10:10 Gilead and Lebanon

Gilgal
De 11:30 over against Gilgal
Jos 4:19 encamped in Gilgal
Jos 5:9 place is called Gilgal
Jos 10:7 ascended from Gilgal
Jud 3:19 that *were* by Gilgal
1Sa 13:4 after Saul to Gilgal
2Sa 19:15 Judah came to Gilgal
2Ki 2:1 Elisha from Gilgal
Ne 12:29 house of Gilgal
Ho 9:15 wickedness *is* in Gilgal
Am 4:4 Gilgal multiply
Mic 6:5 Shittim to Gilgal

Girdle
Ex 28:8 girdle of the
Le 16:4 linen girdle
1Sa 18:4 and to his girdle
2Sa 20:8 girdle *with* a
1Ki 2:5 girdle that *was*
2Ki 1:8 girdle of leather
Isa 11:5 be the girdle
Jer 13:1 a linen girdle
Mt 3:4 leather girdle
Mr 1:6 girdle of a skin
Ac 21:11 Paul's girdle
Re 1:13 golden girdle

Giving
De 10:18 giving him food
Ru 1:6 giving them bread
Ezr 3:11 giving thanks
Ac 9:36 giving of alms
Ac 15:8 giving them
Ro 9:4 giving of the law
2Co 6:3 Giving no offense
Eph 5:20 Giving thanks
1Ti 4:1 giving heed
1Pe 3:7 giving honor

Glory
Ex 33:22 glory passes by
Ex 40:34 glory of Yahweh
De 5:24 glory and his
1Sa 2:8 throne of glory
1Sa 4:21 glory is departed
Ps 24:10 King of glory
Isa 2:19 glory of his majesty
Jer 2:11 changed their glory
Hab 3:3 glory covered
Mt 6:29 all his glory
Mr 8:38 comes in the glory
Lu 2:14 Glory to God
Joh 1:14 beheld his glory
1Co 2:8 Lord of glory
2Co 4:17 weight of glory
1Ti 3:16 received up into glory
Heb 1:3 brightness of *his* glory
Re 1:6 glory and power

Glory of God
Ps 19:1 declare the glory of God
Joh 11:4 for the glory of God
Ac 7:55 saw the glory of God
Ro 3:23 short of the glory of God
1Co 10:31 to the glory of God
2Co 1:20 unto the glory of God
2Co 4:6 of the glory of God
Php 2:11 glory of God the Father
Re 15:8 from the glory of God

Glory of Yahweh
Ex 16:10 the glory of Yahweh
Ex 24:16 glory of Yahweh
Ps 138:5 the glory of Yahweh
Isa 35:2 the glory of Yahweh
Eze 1:28 of the glory of Yahweh
Eze 43:5 glory of Yahweh filled
Hab 2:14 of the glory of Yahweh

Glutton
De 21:20 glutton, and a
Pr 23:21 and the glutton

God
Ge 1:1 In the beginning God
Ge 2:4 Yahweh God made
Ge 24:7 Yahweh God of heaven
Ex 3:15 Yahweh God of your fathers
Ge 6:9 Noah walked with God
Ge 9:8 And God spoke to Noah
Ge 17:1 the Almighty God
Ge 26:24 the God of Abraham
Ex 3:14 And God said to Moses
Ex 4:5 Yahweh God of their fathers
Ex 13:17 God led them
Ex 15:26 Yahweh your God
Ex 34:14 a jealous God
Le 21:6 to their God
De 1:6 Yahweh our God spoke
De 4:25 Yahweh your God
De 16:1 passover unto Yahweh your God
De 16:22 which Yahweh your God hates
Jos 1:17 God be with you
1Sa 2:2 any rock like our God
Isa 43:12 says Yahweh, that I *am* God
Isa 46:9 God, and *there is* none else
Da 3:25 like the Son of God
Mt 14:33 you are the Son of God
Mr 12:32 there is one God
Joh 1:34 this is the Son of God
Joh 3:18 only begotten Son of God
Joh 9:35 believe on the Son of God
Joh 11:27 Messiah, the Son of God
Ro 8:14 led by the Spirit of God
1Co 3:16 Spirit of God dwells in you
1Co 8:4 no other God but one
1Jo 4:12 God dwells in us
Re 2:18 says the Son of God
Re 22:9 worship God

GOD (see Yahweh)

Gods
Ge 3:5 gods, knowing
Ge 31:30 stolen my gods
Ex 20:3 no other gods
Ex 34:15 after their gods
De 4:28 gods, the work
Jos 24:14 away the gods
Jud 2:3 gods shall be a snare
1Sa 7:3 strange gods
1Ki 11:4 after other gods
Isa 21:9 images of her gods
Jer 44:3 serve other gods
Da 2:47 God of gods
Ac 19:26 gods, which are

Gog
1Ch 5:4 Gog his son
Eze 38:2 face against Gog
Eze 39:1 against Gog
Re 20:8 Gog and Magog

Gold
Ge 2:11 *there is* gold
Ge 24:35 silver, and gold
Ge 41:42 put a gold chain
Ex 25:3 gold, and silver
Ex 39:30 *of* pure gold
De 7:25 silver or gold
1Ki 9:14 talents of gold
2Ch 3:9 shekels of gold
Ezr 1:9 chargers of gold
Ne 7:71 drams of gold
Jer 4:30 ornaments of gold
Da 2:32 *was* of fine gold
Mt 2:11 gifts; gold
1Ti 2:9 gold, or pearls
Jas 2:2 gold ring
Re 3:18 gold tried in
Re 21:18 *was* pure gold

Golgotha
Mt 27:33 called Golgotha
Mr 15:22 place Golgotha.
Joh 19:17 Hebrew Golgotha

Goliath
1Sa 17:4 named Goliath,
1Sa 21:9 sword of Goliath
1Sa 22:10 sword of Goliath
2Sa 21:19 Goliath the Gittite
1Ch 20:5 brother of Goliath

Gomer
Ge 10:2 Japheth; Gomer
1Ch 1:5 Gomer, and Magog
Eze 38:6 Gomer, and all his
Ho 1:3 Gomer the daughter

Gomorrah
Ge 10:19 Sodom, and Gomorrah
Ge 13:10 Gomorrah, *even* as the
Ge 14:8 king of Gomorrah
Ge 19:24 Gomorrah brimstone
Isa 1:9 been like unto Gomorrah
Zep 2:9 Ammon as Gomorrah
Mt 10:15 Gomorrah in the day
Mr 6:11 Sodom and Gomorrah
Ro 9:29 made like unto Gomorrah
2Pe 2:6 Sodom and Gomorrah
Jude 1:7 Gomorrah, and the cities

Gospel
Mt 4:23 preaching the gospel
Mt 9:35 gospel of the kingdom
Mt 24:14 gospel of the kingdom
Mr 1:1 gospel of Yahshua
Lu 4:18 gospel to the poor
Ac 15:7 word of the gospel
Ac 20:24 gospel of the grace
Ro 1:1 the gospel of God
Ro 10:15 gospel of peace
1Co 9:12 gospel of the Messiah
Ga 1:9 any other gospel
Eph 1:13 gospel of your salvation
Eph 6:19 mystery of the gospel
Re 14:6 everlasting gospel

Government
Isa 9:6 government shall be
Isa 9:7 government and peace
Isa 22:21 government into his
2Pe 2:10 despise government

Grace
Ge 6:8 Noah found grace
Ex 33:12 grace in my sight
Ru 2:2 shall find grace
1Sa 1:18 find grace
Ezr 9:8 grace has been
Ps 84:11 will give grace
Zec 12:10 spirit of grace
Lu 2:40 grace of God was
Joh 1:14 full of grace
Ac 15:11 grace of the Lord
Ro 3:24 freely by his grace
Ro 5:15 gift by grace
Ro 11:6 And if by grace
2Co 12:9 grace is sufficient
Ga 5:4 fallen from grace
Eph 2:5 grace you are saved
Heb 4:16 throne of grace
1Pe 5:5 grace to the humble

Grape
Le 19:10 grape of your
De 32:14 blood of the grape
Job 15:33 unripe grape
So 7:12 tender grape appears
Isa 18:5 grape is ripening
Jer 6:9 grape gatherer
Jer 31:29 eaten a sour grape
Jer 49:9 If grape gatherers
Ob 1:5 grape gatherers
Mic 7:1 grape gleanings

Greece
Da 8:21 king of Greece
Da 10:20 prince of Greece
Da 11:2 realm of Greece
Zec 9:13 O Greece
Ac 20:2 came into Greece

Groves
Ex 34:13 down their groves
De 12:3 burn their groves
Jos 24:13 and olive groves
Jud 3:7 Baalim and the groves
1Sa 8:14 olive groves
1Ki 14:23 images, and groves
2Ch 17:6 places and groves
2Ch 19:3 away the groves
Ne 5:11 olive groves
Ne 9:25 groves, and fruit
Isa 17:8 groves, or the images
Isa 27:9 groves and images
Jer 17:2 groves by the green
Mic 5:14 pluck up your groves

Habakkuk
Hab 1:1 Habakkuk the prophet
Hab 3:1 prayer of Habakkuk

Hagar
Ge 16:15 Hagar bore Abram
Ge 21:17 God called to Hagar
Ge 25:12 Hagar the Egyptian
Ga 4:25 Hagar is mount Sinai

Haggai
Ezr 5:1 Haggai the prophet
Hag 1:1 word of Yahweh by Haggai
Hag 2:13 Then said Haggai

Hail
Ex 9:18 grievous hail
Job 38:22 treasuries of the hail
Ps 78:47 vines with hail,
Ps 105:32 them hail for rain
Ps 148:8 Fire, and hail; snow
Isa 28:2 tempest of hail
Mt 26:49 Hail, master

Hail

Joh 19:3 Hail, King of
Re 8:7 hail and fire
Re 16:21 plague of the hail

Hair
Ex 25:4 goats' *hair*
Le 13:3 hair in the plague
Le 14:9 hair he shall shave
Jud 16:22 hair of his head
2Sa 14:26 *hair* was heavy
Isa 3:24 hair baldness
Eze 5:1 divide the *hair*
Da 7:9 hair of his head
Mt 3:4 camel's hair
Joh 12:3 feet with her hair.
1Co 11:14 man has long hair
1Pe 3:3 braiding the hair
Re 1:14 hair *were* white

Halleluyah
Re 19:1 Halleluyah. Salvation
Re 19:3 said, Halleluyah
Re 19:6 Halleluyah: for the Lord

Hallowed
Ex 20:11 day, and hallowed
Le 22:32 I will be hallowed
Nu 18:8 hallowed things
1Sa 21:6 hallowed *bread*
1Ki 9:3 hallowed this house
2Ki 12:18 hallowed things
2Ch 7:7 Solomon hallowed
Mt 6:9 Hallowed be your

Ham
Ge 5:32 Ham, and Japheth
Ge 9:18 Ham *is* the father
Ge 14:5 Zuzims in Ham
1Ch 1:8 sons of Ham
1Ch 4:40 Ham had dwelt
Ps 78:51 tabernacles of Ham
Ps 105:23 land of Ham

Haman
Es 3:1 promote Haman
Es 3:6 Haman sought
Es 6:5 Haman stands
Es 9:24 Haman the son

Hannah
1Sa 1:19 Hannah his wife
1Sa 1:20 Hannah had conceived

Haran
Ge 11:28 Haran died
Ge 12:4 departed out of Haran
2Ki 19:12 Gozan, and Haran
1Ch 2:46 bore Haran
1Ch 23:9 Haziel, and Haran
Eze 27:23 Haran, and Canneh
Ac 7:4 dwelt in Haran

Harlot
Ge 38:24 played the harlot
Jos 6:17 Rahab the harlot
Jud 16:1 saw there a harlot
Pr 7:10 attire of a harlot
Jer 3:1 played the harlot
Eze 23:5 played the harlot
Ho 4:15 play the harlot
Am 7:17 shall be a harlot
Mic 1:7 hire of a harlot
Na 3:4 well favored harlot
1Co 6:16 joined to a harlot
Heb 11:31 harlot Rahab

Harp
Ge 31:27 and with harp
1Sa 16:23 harp, and played
1Ch 25:3 with a harp
Ps 150:3 psaltery and harp
Da 3:5 cornet, flute, harp
1Co 14:7 pipe or harp

Hart
De 12:15 as of the hart
De 14:5 hart, and the
Ps 42:1 the hart pants
So 2:17 young hart upon
Isa 35:6 leap as a hart

Harvest
Ge 8:22 seedtime and harvest
Le 19:9 reap the harvest
De 24:19 harvest in your
Ru 2:23 barley harvest
Isa 18:5 before the harvest
Jer 8:20 harvest is past
Joe 3:13 harvest is ripe
Mt 9:37 harvest truly *is*
Mt 9:38 Lord of the harvest
Re 14:15 harvest of the earth

Harvest, Feast of
Ex 23:16 feast of harvest

Hatred
2Sa 13:15 hatred with which
Ps 139:22 perfect hatred
Pr 10:12 Hatred stirs up strife
Ec 9:6 love, and their hatred
Ho 9:7 the great hatred
Ga 5:20 hatred, variance

Heart
Ge 45:26 Jacob's heart
Ex 36:2 heart stirred him
De 6:5 with all your heart
De 8:2 *was* in your heart
De 30:6 circumcise your heart
1Sa 10:9 him another heart
1Ki 3:9 understanding heart
1Ch 22:19 set your heart
2Ch 7:16 eyes and my heart
Ps 44:21 secrets of the heart
Ps 51:10 me a clean heart
Ps 57:7 My heart is fixed
Pr 3:5 with all your heart
Jer 17:9 heart *is* deceitful
Eze 36:26 new heart also
Mt 5:8 pure in heart
Mr 7:6 heart is far from
Ro 10:9 in your heart

Heathen
Le 26:45 of the heathen
2Sa 22:44 heathen: a
2Ch 20:6 of the heathen
Ezr 6:21 of the heathen
Ne 5:8 sold to the heathen
La 4:20 among the heathen
Eze 23:30 after the heathen
Mt 18:17 heathen man and
Ga 1:16 among the heathen

Heaven
Ge 1:8 firmament Heaven
Ge 28:12 reached to heaven
Ex 20:11 heaven and earth
De 1:10 the stars of heaven
Jos 8:20 ascended up to heaven
1Ki 8:30 heaven your dwelling
2Ch 7:13 shut up heaven
Job 26:11 pillars of heaven
Ps 103:11 heaven is high
Isa 13:10 stars of heaven
Isa 14:12 heaven, O Lucifer
Da 11:4 four winds of heaven
Mt 6:9 which are in heaven
Mt 26:64 clouds of heaven
Ac 7:49 Heaven *is* my throne
1Th 4:16 descend from heaven
Re 21:1 saw a new heaven

Heaven, Kingdom of
Mt 3:2 kingdom of heaven
Mt 5:3 kingdom of heaven
Mt 7:21 kingdom of heaven
Mt 13:11 kingdom of heaven
Mt 13:24 kingdom of heaven
Mt 16:19 kingdom of heaven
Mt 18:1 kingdom of heaven

Hebrew
Ge 14:13 Abram the Hebrew
Ge 39:14 Hebrew to us to mock
Ex 1:16 midwife to the Hebrew
De 15:12 brother, a Hebrew
Jer 34:9 Hebrew or a Hebrewess
Jon 1:9 I *am* a Hebrew
Lu 23:38 Hebrew, THIS IS
Joh 19:20 written in Hebrew
Php 3:5 Hebrew of the Hebrews
Re 9:11 Hebrew tongue *is*

Hebron
Ge 13:18 which *is* in Hebron
Ge 23:2 Hebron in the land
Nu 3:19 Izehar, Hebron
Jos 14:13 Jephunneh Hebron
Jud 1:10 dwelt in Hebron
2Sa 5:5 Hebron he reigned
2Ch 11:10 Hebron, which

Hedge
Job 1:10 hedge about him
Isa 5:5 away the hedge
Eze 13:5 hedge for the house
Eze 22:30 hedge, and stand
Mr 12:1 set a hedge

Heifer
Nu 19:2 heifer without spot
De 21:3 heifer, which has
1Sa 16:2 Take a heifer
Jer 50:11 fat as the heifer
Ho 10:11 heifer *that is* taught

Heb 9:13 ashes of a heifer

Heir
Ge 15:4 heir; but he that
2Sa 14:7 destroy the heir
Jer 49:1 has he no heir
Mt 21:38 This is the heir
Ro 4:13 heir of the world
Ga 4:1 heir, as long
Ga 4:7 heir of God
Heb 1:2 appointed heir
Heb 11:7 heir of the

Hell
De 32:22 lowest hell
Ps 9:17 turned into hell
Ps 55:15 quick into hell
Pr 15:11 Hell and destruction
Isa 5:14 hell has enlarged
Eze 31:17 down into hell
Mt 5:22 danger of hell
Mt 10:28 body in hell
Mt 16:18 gates of hell
Lu 12:5 cast into hell
2Pe 2:4 down to hell
Re 1:18 keys of hell
Re 6:8 Death, and Hell
Re 20:13 death and hell

Helmet
1Sa 17:38 helmet of brass
Isa 59:17 helmet of salvation
Eze 23:24 shield and helmet
Eph 6:17 helmet of salvation
1Th 5:8 for a helmet, the hope

Heresy
Ac 24:14 they call heresy

Herod
Mt 14:1 Herod the tetrarch
Mr 6:20 Herod feared John
Lu 1:5 Herod, the king
Lu 3:1 Herod being tetrarch
Lu 23:7 Herod's jurisdiction
Ac 4:27 Herod, and Pontius
Ac 12:6 Herod would have

Herodians
Mt 22:16 the Herodians
Mr 3:6 Herodians against
Mr 12:13 Herodians, to

Herodias
Mt 14:6 Herodias danced
Mr 6:17 prison for Herodias'
Mr 6:19 Herodias had a quarrel
Lu 3:19 Herodias his brother

Hezekiah
2Ki 18:1 Hezekiah the son
1Ch 4:41 Hezekiah king
2Ch 29:1 Hezekiah began
Isa 36:1 king Hezekiah
Jer 15:4 son of Hezekiah
Mt 1:9 Ahaz begot Hezekiah

High Places
Le 26:30 your high places
Nu 22:41 high places of Baal
1Ki 3:2 sacrificed in high places
2Ki 12:3 high places were not
2Ch 33:17 in the high places
Ps 18:33 upon my high places
Isa 41:18 rivers in high places
Am 4:13 high places of the
Eph 6:12 in high *place*

High Priest
Nu 35:25 of the high priest
2Ki 22:4 Hilkiah the high priest
Hag 2:2 high priest, and to the
Zec 3:8 Joshua the high priest
Mr 14:63 high priest tore his
Joh 18:24 the high priest
Heb 2:17 faithful high priest
Heb 3:1 Apostle and High Priest
Heb 5:1 every high priest
Heb 6:20 made a high priest
Heb 9:25 high priest enters

Highway
Jud 21:19 highway that goes
2Sa 20:12 highway into the field
2Ki 18:17 highway of the fuller's
Pr 16:17 highway of the upright
Isa 11:16 highway for the remnant
Isa 19:23 highway out of Egypt
Isa 35:8 highway shall be there
Isa 40:3 highway for our God
Mr 10:46 highway side begging

Hiram
2Sa 5:11 Hiram king of Tyre
1Ki 5:1 Hiram was ever a lover
1Ki 7:40 Hiram made the lavers
1Ki 10:11 navy also of Hiram
1Ch 14:1 Hiram king of Tyre

Hire
Ge 31:8 shall be your hire
1Ki 5:6 give hire
1Ch 19:6 hire them chariots
Isa 46:6 hire a goldsmith
Mic 3:11 teach for hire
Mt 20:1 hire laborers
Lu 10:7 worthy of his hire
Jas 5:4 hire of the laborers

Hittites
Ex 3:8 and the Hittites
Nu 13:29 Hittites, and the
Jos 1:4 land of the Hittites
1Ki 10:29 kings of the Hittites
2Ch 8:7 left of the Hittites

Hivites
Ex 3:8 Hivites, and the
Jos 9:7 said to the Hivites
Jos 11:19 Hivites the inhabitants
Jud 3:3 Hivites that dwelt
2Sa 24:7 cities of the Hivites
2Ch 8:7 Hivites, and the Jebusites

Holiness
Ex 28:36 signet, HOLINESS
2Ch 31:18 in holiness
Ps 29:2 beauty of holiness
Isa 35:8 he way of holiness
Jer 2:3 Israel *was* holiness
Lu 1:75 holiness and
Ro 1:4 spirit of holiness
Ro 6:22 fruit unto holiness
2Co 7:1 perfecting holiness
1Th 4:7 but to holiness
Heb 12:14 holiness, without

Holy Ghost
Mt 1:18 of the Holy Ghost
Mt 12:31 a*gainst* the *Holy* Ghost
Mr 1:8 with the Holy Ghost
Lu 1:15 with the Holy Ghost
Lu 3:22 Holy Ghost descended
Joh 14:26 *is* the Holy Ghost
Ac 2:38 gift of the Holy Ghost
Ro 15:16 by the Holy Ghost
1Co 6:19 of the Holy Ghost
Heb 9:8 Holy Ghost this
2Pe 1:21 by the Holy Ghost
1Jo 5:7 and the Holy Ghost
Jude 1:20 in the Holy Ghost

Holy Spirit
Ps 51:11 holy spirit from me
Isa 63:10 grieved his holy Spirit
Lu 11:13 give the Holy Spirit
Eph 1:13 with that holy Spirit
Eph 4:30 not the holy Spirit
1Th 4:8 us his holy Spirit

Honey
Ex 3:8 milk and honey
Ex 16:31 *made* with honey
Jud 14:8 bees and honey
1Sa 14:29 of this honey
1Ki 14:3 cruse of honey
Ps 19:10 honey and the
Pr 24:13 eat you honey
Mt 3:4 and wild honey
Re 10:9 sweet as honey

Horn
Jos 6:5 ram's horn
1Sa 2:1 horn is exalted
2Sa 22:3 horn of my
1Ki 1:39 horn of oil
Da 7:8 another little horn
Da 8:5 *had* a notable horn
Lu 1:69 horn of salvation

Horse
Ex 15:1 horse and his rider
1Ki 20:20 escaped on a horse
Es 6:8 horse that the king
Job 39:19 horse strength
Ps 76:6 chariot and horse
Pr 26:3 whip for the horse
Zec 1:8 upon a red horse
Re 6:2 behold a white horse
Re 19:11 white horse

Hosanna
Mt 21:9 Hosanna in the
Mr 11:9 Hosanna; Blessed
Joh 12:13 Hosanna: Blessed

Hosea

Hosea
Ho 1:1 Hosea, the son
Ro 9:25 also in Hosea

Hoshea
De 32:44 Hoshea the son
2Ki 15:30 Hoshea the son
2Ki 17:4 conspiracy in Hoshea
1Ch 27:20 Hoshea the son
Ne 10:23 Hoshea, Hananiah

House
1Sa 1:21 and all his house
2Ki 20:1 your house in order
Ps 31:2 house of defense
Ps 69:9 zeal of your house
Jer 21:12 O house of David
Eze 18:15 house of Israel
Hag 1:8 build the house
Mt 7:24 built his house upon
Mt 21:13 house of prayer
Mr 3:25 house is divided

House of God
Jud 18:31 house of God was
Jud 20:18 the house of God
1Ch 6:48 the house of God
2Ch 3:3 the house of God
Ezr 1:4 house of God that
Da 5:3 the house of God
Mt 12:4 the house of God
Heb 10:21 the house of God
1Pe 4:17 the house of God

Huldah
2Ki 22:14 Huldah the prophetess
2Ch 34:22 Huldah the prophetess

Humility
Pr 15:33 honor *is* humility
Pr 22:4 humility *and* the fear
Ac 20:19 Lord with all humility
Col 2:18 humility and worshipping
1Pe 5:5 clothed with humility

Hunger
De 8:3 hunger, and fed
De 28:48 hunger, and in
Jer 38:9 die from hunger
La 4:9 slain with hunger
Mt 5:6 hunger and thirst
Lu 15:17 perish with hunger
Joh 6:35 shall never hunger
Re 7:16 hunger no more

Huram
1Ch 8:5 Shephuphan, and Huram
2Ch 2:3 Huram the king of Tyre
2Ch 8:2 Huram had restored
2Ch 9:21 servants of Huram

Husband
Le 19:20 betrothed to a husband
Nu 5:20 besides your husband
De 21:13 husband, and she shall
De 22:22 married to a husband
Jud 20:4 husband of the woman
Ru 1:5 sons and her husband
Isa 54:5 Maker *is* your husband
Mt 1:16 husband of Mary
Lu 16:18 husband commits adultery
Ro 7:2 which has a husband
1Co 7:4 body, but the husband
Eph 5:23 husband is the head
1Ti 3:2 husband of one wife
Re 21:2 adorned for her husband

Hypocrisy
Mt 23:28 hypocrisy and
Mr 12:15 their hypocrisy
Lu 12:1 which is hypocrisy
Ro 12:9 without hypocrisy
Ga 2:13 with their hypocrisy
1Ti 4:2 lies in hypocrisy
Jas 3:17 without hypocrisy

Hyssop
Ex 12:22 bunch of hyssop
Le 14:4 scarlet, and hyssop
Nu 19:6 hyssop, and scarlet
1Ki 4:33 hyssop that springs
Ps 51:7 me with hyssop
Joh 19:29 *it* upon hyssop
Heb 9:19 hyssop, and sprinkled

I Am That I Am
Ex 3:14 I AM THAT I AM

Idol
1Ki 15:13 destroyed her idol
2Ch 33:7 image, the idol
Isa 66:3 he blessed an idol
Ac 7:41 sacrifice to the idol
1Co 8:4 idol *is* nothing
1Co 10:19 idol is anything

Idolatry
1Sa 15:23 iniquity and idolatry
Ac 17:16 wholly given to idolatry
1Co 10:14 flee from idolatry
Ga 5:20 Idolatry, witchcraft
Col 3:5 which is idolatry

Ignorance
Le 4:2 sin through ignorance
Le 5:15 sins through ignorance
Nu 15:24 committed by ignorance
Ac 3:17 that through ignorance
1Pe 1:14 lusts in your ignorance

Illyricum
Ro 15:19 about to Illyricum

Image
Ge 1:26 man in our image
Ge 9:6 the image of God
Ex 20:4 any graven image
Jud 18:18 carved image
2Ki 10:27 image of Baal
2Ch 33:7 image, the idol
Ps 106:19 molten image
Da 2:32 image's head
Ro 8:29 image of his Son
Col 1:15 image of the invisible
Re 13:15 image of the beast

Immanuel
Isa 7:14 name Immanuel
Isa 8:8 land, O Immanuel
Mt 1:23 name Immanuel

Inheritance
Ge 31:14 portion or inheritance
Le 25:46 inheritance for your
Nu 16:14 inheritance of fields
De 29:8 for an inheritance
Jos 13:7 land for an inheritance
Jud 2:6 inheritance to possess
Ru 4:10 inheritance, that the
1Ch 28:8 inheritance for your
Ps 78:71 Israel his inheritance
Eze 44:28 their inheritance
Mr 12:7 inheritance shall be
Ac 26:18 sins, and inheritance
Eph 1:11 obtained an inheritance
Eph 5:5 inheritance in the kingdom
Heb 9:15 eternal inheritance
1Pe 1:4 inheritance incorruptible

Iniquity
Ex 20:5 iniquity of the fathers
Ex 34:9 pardon our iniquity
Le 26:40 confess their iniquity
Nu 14:18 iniquity and transgression
De 19:15 iniquity, or for any sin
1Sa 15:23 iniquity and idolatry
Ne 4:5 cover not their iniquity
Ps 32:5 iniquity have I not hidden
Ps 51:2 iniquity, and cleanse me
Isa 6:7 iniquity is taken away
Jer 31:34 forgive their iniquity
Da 9:5 committed iniquity
Mic 2:1 iniquity, and work evil
Zep 3:13 iniquity, nor speak lies
Mt 13:41 which do iniquity
Ro 6:19 uncleanness and to iniquity
Jas 3:6 world of iniquity

Interpretation
Ge 40:5 interpretation of his
Jud 7:15 and the interpretation
Pr 1:6 and the interpretation
Da 2:4 show the interpretation
Joh 1:42 interpretation, A stone
1Co 12:10 interpretation of tongues
1Co 14:26 has an interpretation
Heb 7:2 by interpretation King
2Pe 1:20 private interpretation

Iron
Ge 4:22 brass and iron
Nu 31:22 iron, the tin
De 28:48 yoke of iron
Jos 6:19 brass and iron
Jos 17:16 chariots of iron
2Sa 12:31 tools of iron
1Ch 22:3 iron in abundance
Jer 11:4 iron furnace
Eze 27:12 iron, tin
Da 2:33 legs of iron
Am 1:3 instruments of iron
Re 2:27 rod of iron
Re 9:9 breastplates of iron

Isaac
Ge 17:19 name Isaac
Ge 21:3 bore to him, Isaac
Ge 25:28 Isaac loved Esau

Le 26:42 covenant with Isaac
De 1:8 Abraham, Isaac
1Ki 18:36 God of Abraham, Isaac
Mt 1:2 Abraham begot Isaac
Ac 7:8 Isaac, and circumcised
Ro 9:7 In Isaac shall your seed
Ga 4:28 Isaac was, are
Heb 11:17 offered up Isaac
Jas 2:21 offered Isaac his

Isaiah
2Ki 19:2 Isaiah the prophet
2Ch 32:20 Isaiah the son
Isa 1:1 vision of Isaiah
Isa 7:3 Yahweh unto Isaiah
Isa 20:3 servant Isaiah has
Lu 4:17 prophet Isaiah
Joh 1:23 the prophet Isaiah
Ac 8:28 Isaiah the prophet
Ac 28:25 Holy Ghost by Isaiah
Ro 10:20 Isaiah is very bold

Ishbosheth
2Sa 2:10 Ishbosheth Saul's
2Sa 3:8 words of Ishbosheth
2Sa 3:14 to Ishbosheth
2Sa 4:8 head of Ishbosheth

Ishi
1Ch 2:31 of Appaim; Ishi
1Ch 4:20 sons of Ishi
1Ch 5:24 Ishi, and Eliel
Ho 2:16 call me Ishi

Ishmael
Ge 16:11 name Ishmael
Ge 17:23 Ishmael his son
Ge 25:9 Ishmael buried him
1Ch 1:28 Isaac, and Ishmael
1Ch 9:44 Ishmael, and Sheariah
2Ch 23:1 Ishmael the son
Ezr 10:22 Maaseiah, Ishmael
Jer 40:14 Ishmael the son

Ishmaelites
Jud 8:24 they *were* Ishmaelites
Ps 83:6 Ishmaelites; of Moab

Israel
Ge 32:28 no more Jacob, but Israel
Ge 37:3 Now Israel loved Joseph
Ge 49:28 twelve tribes of Israel
Ex 1:1 names of the children of Israel
Ex 12:27 children of Israel in Egypt
Ex 15:22 So Moses brought Israel
Ex 16:2 children of Israel murmured
Ex 34:23 the God of Israel
De 6:4 Hear, O Israel
Jos 4:7 children of Israel forever
Jos 23:1 given rest to Israel
1Sa 7:4 Israel did put away Baalim and Jer
9:26 Israel *are* uncircumcised in the heart
Jer 23:6 Israel shall dwell safely
Jer 31:7 the remnant of Israel
Eze 48:31 the tribes of Israel
Da 9:20 sin of my people Israel
Ho 1:11 Israel be gathered together
Joe 2:27 I *am* in the midst of Israel
Am 7:15 prophesy to my people Israel
Mic 1:5 sins of the house of Israel

Zec 12:1 word of Yahweh for Israel
Mt 2:6 rule my people Israel
Ac 2:36 let all the house of Israel know
Ro 9:6 not all Israel, which are of Israel
Eph 2:12 from the commonwealth of Israel
Re 7:4 all the tribes of the children of Israel
Re 21:12 tribes of the children of Israel

Issachar
Ge 30:18 name Issachar
Nu 1:28 children of Issachar
Jos 19:17 came out to Issachar
Jud 5:15 princes of Issachar
1Ki 15:27 house of Issachar
2Ch 30:18 Issachar, and Zebulun
Re 7:7 Issachar *were* sealed

Ivory
1Ki 10:18 throne of ivory
1Ki 22:39 ivory house which
2Ch 9:21 silver, ivory
Eze 27:15 ivory and ebony
Am 6:4 lie upon beds of ivory
Re 18:12 vessels of ivory

Jacob
Ge 25:26 Jacob: and Isaac
Ge 29:18 Jacob loved Rachel
Ge 32:28 Jacob, but Israel
Ex 1:5 loins of Jacob
Le 26:42 covenant with Jacob
Ps 135:4 Yah has chosen Jacob
Isa 29:23 Holy One of Jacob
Jer 31:11 redeemed Jacob
Eze 37:25 Jacob my servant
Mic 5:7 remnant of Jacob
Mt 1:2 Jacob begot Judah
Mt 1:16 Jacob begot Joseph
Joh 4:6 Jacob's well was there
Ac 7:8 Jacob *begot* the twelve
Ro 9:13 Jacob have I loved

Jahaziel
1Ch 16:6 Jahaziel the priests
1Ch 23:19 Jahaziel the third
2Ch 20:14 Jahaziel the son
Ezr 8:5 son of Jahaziel

James
Mt 10:2 James *the son*
Mt 27:56 mother of James
Mr 6:3 brother of James
Ac 12:2 killed James
1Co 15:7 seen by James
Ga 1:19 James the Lord's
Jas 1:1 James, a servant
Jude 1:1 brother of James

Japheth
Ge 5:32 Ham, and Japheth
Ge 7:13 Japheth, the sons
Ge 9:23 Japheth took a
Ge 10:2 sons of Japheth
1Ch 1:4 Ham, and Japheth
1Ch 1:5 Japheth; Gomer

Jealousy
Nu 5:14 spirit of jealousy
De 29:20 his jealousy

1Ki 14:22 jealousy with their
Ps 78:58 jealousy with their
Pr 6:34 jealousy *is* the rage
Eze 8:3 image of jealousy
Zep 1:18 fire of his jealousy
Zec 8:2 with great jealousy
Ro 10:19 you to jealousy
2Co 11:2 with godly jealousy

Jebus
Jud 19:10 Jebus, which *is*
1Ch 11:4 Jebus; where

Jebusites
Ex 3:8 and the Jebusites
Ex 13:5 Jebusites, which
Ex 23:23 Jebusites: and
Jos 15:63 Jebusites which
Jud 1:21 out the Jebusites
2Sa 5:6 to the Jebusites
1Ki 9:20 Jebusites, which
1Ch 11:4 where the Jebusites

Jeconiah (see also Coniah)
1Ch 3:16 Jeconiah his son
Es 2:6 Jeconiah king
Jer 24:1 Jeconiah the son
Jer 27:20 captive Jeconiah
Jer 28:4 this place Jeconiah
Jer 29:2 Jeconiah the king

Jehoahaz
2Ki 10:35 Jehoahaz his son
2Ki 13:1 Jehoahaz the son
2Ki 14:1 Jehoahaz king
2Ki 23:30 Jehoahaz the son
2Ch 21:17 Jehoahaz, the
2Ch 25:17 Jehoahaz, the son

Jehoiachin (see also Jeconiah)
2Ki 24:12 Jehoiachin the king
2Ki 25:27 captivity of Jehoiachin
2Ch 36:8 Jehoiachin his son
Jer 52:31 Jehoiachin king
Eze 1:2 Jehoiachin's captivity

Jehoiada
2Sa 8:18 son of Jehoiada
2Ki 11:9 Jehoiada the priest
2Ki 12:2 Jehoiada the priest
1Ch 12:27 Jehoiada *was* the leader
1Ch 27:34 Ahithophel *was* Jehoiada
2Ch 24:12 king and Jehoiada
2Ch 24:25 sons of Jehoiada
Ne 3:6 repaired Jehoiada
Jer 29:26 Jehoiada the priest

Jehoiakim
2Ki 23:34 name to Jehoiakim
2Ki 24:1 Jehoiakim became
1Ch 3:15 second Jehoiakim
2Ch 36:4 name to Jehoiakim
Jer 1:3 Jehoiakim the son
Da 1:1 Jehoiakim king

Jehoram
1Ki 22:50 Jehoram his son
2Ki 1:17 Jehoram the son
2Ki 3:1 Jehoram the son
2Ki 9:24 smote Jehoram

Jehoram

2Ch 17:8 Jehoram, priests
2Ch 21:3 gave he to Jehoram

Jehoshaphat
2Sa 8:16 Jehoshaphat the son
1Ki 4:17 Jehoshaphat the son
1Ki 22:2 Jehoshaphat the king
2Ki 3:1 Jehoshaphat king
2Ki 9:2 Jehoshaphat the son
2Ch 17:3 was with Jehoshaphat
Joe 3:2 valley of Jehoshaphat
Mt 1:8 Asa begot Jehoshaphat

Jehoshua
Nu 13:16 son of Nun Jehoshua
1Ch 7:27 Jehoshua his son

Jehu
1Ki 16:1 Jehu the son of Hanani
1Ki 19:16 Jehu the son of Nimshi
2Ki 9:2 Jehu the son of Jehoshaphat
2Ki 10:1 Jehu wrote letters
1Ch 2:38 Obed begot Jehu
1Ch 4:35 Jehu the son of Josibiah
1Ch 12:3 Jehu the Antothite
2Ch 25:17 Jehu, king of Israel
Ho 1:4 upon the house of Jehu

Jeremiah
2Ki 23:31 Jeremiah of Libnah
2Ch 35:25 Jeremiah lamented
2Ch 36:12 Jeremiah the prophet
Jer 1:1 words of Jeremiah
Jer 20:2 Jeremiah the prophet
Jer 29:30 Yahweh to Jeremiah
Jer 38:7 Jeremiah in the dungeon
Da 9:2 Yahweh came to Jeremiah
Mt 2:17 Jeremiah the prophet
Mt 16:14 Jeremiah, or one
Mt 27:9 spoken by Jeremiah

Jericho
Nu 22:1 Jordan *by* Jericho
Nu 36:13 Jordan *near* Jericho
De 32:49 Jericho; and behold
Jos 6:1 Jericho was closely
1Ki 16:34 build Jericho
2Ch 28:15 Jericho, the city
Jer 52:8 plains of Jericho
Mr 10:46 came to Jericho
Lu 10:30 Jerusalem to Jericho
Lu 19:1 passed through Jericho
Heb 11:30 walls of Jericho fell

Jeroboam
1Ki 11:26 Jeroboam the son
1Ki 12:25 Jeroboam built
1Ki 13:4 king Jeroboam heard
1Ki 15:6 Rehoboam and Jeroboam
2Ki 14:28 acts of Jeroboam
1Ch 5:17 Jeroboam king
Ho 1:1 Jeroboam the son
Am 1:1 Jeroboam the son

Jerusalem
Jos 15:8 same *is* Jerusalem
Jos 18:28 which *is* Jerusalem
Jud 19:10 which *is* Jerusalem
2Sa 11:1 tarried still at Jerusalem

2Sa 24:16 Jerusalem to destroy
2Ki 18:22 altar in Jerusalem
2Ki 19:31 out of Jerusalem shall
Ne 2:11 came to Jerusalem
Ne 11:4 Jerusalem dwelt *certain*
Ps 68:29 temple at Jerusalem
Ps 122:6 peace of Jerusalem
Ps 135:21 dwells at Jerusalem
Ps 147:2 build up Jerusalem
Jer 1:3 Jerusalem captive
Jer 25:18 Jerusalem, and the
La 1:8 Jerusalem has grievously
Eze 5:5 Jerusalem: I have set it
Da 5:2 *was* in Jerusalem
Joe 3:17 Jerusalem be holy
Zec 1:16 Jerusalem with mercies
Mt 2:1 east to Jerusalem
Mt 23:37 Jerusalem, Jerusalem
Mr 11:11 entered into Jerusalem
Lu 4:9 Jerusalem, and set him on
Ac 1:12 Jerusalem from the mount
Ga 1:17 went I up to Jerusalem
Heb 12:22 the heavenly Jerusalem
Re 3:12 *which is* new Jerusalem
Re 21:2 holy city, new Jerusalem

Jeshua
Ezr 2:2 Jeshua, Nehemiah
Ezr 3:8 Jeshua the son
Ne 3:19 Jeshua, the ruler
Ne 8:17 Jeshua the son of Nun
Ne 10:9 Jeshua the son of Azaniah
Ne 12:10 Jeshua begot Joiakim

Jesus (see Yahshua)

Jesse
Ru 4:17 Jesse, the father
1Sa 16:1 Jesse the Bethlehemite
1Sa 17:12 Jesse; and he had
2Sa 23:1 son of Jesse
1Ch 2:12 Obed begot Jesse
Isa 11:1 stem of Jesse
Mt 1:6 Jesse begot David
Ac 13:22 of Jesse, a man
Ro 15:12 root of Jesse

Jews
2Ki 18:26 Jews' language
Ezr 4:23 Jerusalem to the Jews
Ne 1:2 Jews that had escaped
Jer 40:11 Jews that *were* in
Da 3:12 certain Jews whom
Lu 23:38 KING OF THE JEWS
Joh 2:6 purifying of the Jews
Ac 12:3 pleased the Jews
Ac 18:5 testified to the Jews
1Co 1:22 Jews require a sign
Ga 1:14 Jews' religion
Re 2:9 say they are Jews

Jezebel
1Ki 16:31 Jezebel the daughter
1Ki 19:1 Ahab told Jezebel
2Ki 9:10 shall eat Jezebel
Re 2:20 Jezebel, which calls

Jezreel
Jos 17:16 valley of Jezreel
1Sa 29:11 went up to Jezreel
1Ki 18:45 went to Jezreel

1Ki 21:1 Jezreel, next to
2Ki 9:10 portion of Jezreel
2Ch 22:6 healed in Jezreel
Ho 1:4 name Jezreel

Joab
2Sa 2:13 Joab the son
2Sa 3:22 David and Joab
2Sa 11:1 David sent Joab
2Sa 19:5 Joab came into
1Ki 1:19 Joab the captain
1Ki 11:15 Joab the captain
1Ch 27:34 army *was* Joab
Ezr 8:9 sons of Joab
Ne 7:11 Jeshua and Joab
Ps 60:1 when Joab returned

Joash
Jud 6:11 Joash the Abiezrite
Jud 7:14 Joash, a man of Israel
1Ki 22:26 Joash the king's son
2Ki 11:2 Joash the son of Ahaziah
2Ki 13:10 Joash king of Judah
2Ki 13:14 Joash the king of Israel
1Ch 3:11 Joash his son
2Ch 24:1 Joash *was* seven years
Ho 1:1 Joash, king of Israel
Am 1:1 Joash king of Israel

Job
Job 1:1 name *was* Job
Job 2:3 my servant Job
Job 42:7 Job, Yahweh said
Job 42:12 latter end of Job
Ec 1:13 job has God given
Eze 14:14 Daniel, and Job
Jas 5:11 patience of Job

Joel
1Sa 8:2 firstborn was Joel
1Ch 5:12 Joel the chief
1Ch 11:38 Joel the brother
1Ch 27:20 Joel the son of Pedaiah
2Ch 29:12 Joel the son of Azariah
Ne 11:9 Joel the son of Zichri
Joe 1:1 Joel the son of Pethuel
Ac 2:16 prophet Joel

John, The Apostle
Mt 4:21 Zebedee, and John
Mr 3:17 John the brother
Mr 9:2 John, and led them
Mr 10:35 John, the sons
Lu 6:14 James and John
Lu 9:28 Peter and John
Ac 3:1 John went up
Ac 12:12 mother of John
Ga 2:9 John, who seemed
Re 1:1 servant John
Re 21:2 I John saw

John, The Baptist
Mt 3:1 John the Baptist
Mt 11:11 John the Baptist
Mt 14:2 John the Baptist
Mt 16:14 John the Baptist
Mr 6:14 John the Baptist
Lu 7:20 John *the* Baptist
Lu 9:19 John the Baptist

Jonah
2Ki 14:25 Jonah, the son
Jon 1:1 Jonah the son
Jon 2:1 Jonah prayed
Mt 12:39 prophet Jonah
Mt 16:4 prophet Jonah
Lu 11:30 Jonah was a sign
Joh 1:42 son of Jonah

Jonathan
Jud 18:30 Jonathan, the son
1Sa 14:1 Jonathan the son
1Sa 18:1 soul of Jonathan
2Sa 1:4 Saul and Jonathan
2Sa 21:12 bones of Jonathan
1Ch 8:33 Saul begot Jonathan
1Ch 20:7 Jonathan the son
1Ch 27:32 Jonathan, David's
Ezr 10:15 Jonathan the son
Ne 12:11 Joiada begot Jonathan
Jer 37:15 Jonathan the scribe

Joram
2Ki 8:16 Joram the son
2Ki 9:14 against Joram.
2Ki 11:2 king Joram, sister
1Ch 3:11 Joram his son
2Ch 22:5 smote Joram
Mt 1:8 Joram begot Uzziah

Jordan
Nu 22:1 Jordan by Jericho
Nu 26:3 Moab by the Jordan
Jos 1:2 go over this Jordan
Jud 3:28 fords of the Jordan
2Sa 19:15 king over the Jordan
1Ki 7:46 plain of Jordan
Jer 12:5 swelling of the Jordan
Eze 47:18 Israel by the Jordan
Mt 3:6 in the Jordan
Lu 4:1 Jordan, and was led
Joh 1:28 Jordan, where John

Joseph
Ge 30:25 birthed Joseph
Ge 37:3 Israel loved Joseph
Ge 50:26 Joseph died
Ex 13:19 bones of Joseph
Jos 14:4 Joseph were two
Ps 105:17 Joseph, who was
Am 5:15 remnant of Joseph
Mt 1:16 Jacob begot Joseph
Mr 15:43 Joseph of Arimathaea
Lu 2:16 Mary, and Joseph
Ac 1:23 Joseph called Barsabas
Heb 11:22 By faith Joseph
Re 7:8 Joseph were sealed

Joshua
Ex 17:9 said to Joshua
De 1:38 Joshua the son
Jos 1:1 spoke to Joshua
Jud 1:1 death of Joshua
1Sa 6:14 Joshua, a Bethshemite
2Ki 23:8 Joshua the governor
Hag 1:1 Joshua the son
Zec 3:1 Joshua the high
Ac 7:45 Joshua into the
Heb 4:8 Joshua had given

Josiah
2Ki 22:1 Josiah was eight
2Ch 33:25 Josiah his son
Jer 1:2 days of Josiah
Jer 22:11 Josiah king
Zec 6:10 Josiah the son
Mt 1:10 Amon begot Josiah

Joy
Ezr 3:12 aloud for joy
Ne 8:10 joy of Yahweh
Ps 30:5 joy comes in the
Isa 22:13 joy and gladness
Jer 31:13 mourning into joy
Mt 25:23 joy of your lord
Lu 1:14 joy and gladness
Joh 16:20 turned into joy
Ro 14:17 joy in the Holy
Ga 5:22 Spirit is love, joy
Heb 12:2 joy that was set
Jas 1:2 count it all joy
1Pe 1:8 joy unspeakable

Jubilee
Le 25:9 of the jubilee
Le 25:10 shall be a jubilee
Le 27:17 year of jubilee
Nu 36:4 jubilee of the

Judah
Ge 35:23 Levi, and Judah
Jos 15:1 children of Judah
Ru 1:7 land of Judah
1Ki 4:20 Judah and Israel
2Ch 11:17 kingdom of Judah
Ezr 1:2 which is in Judah
Jer 31:31 house of Judah
Da 1:1 Judah came
Zep 2:7 house of Judah
Mt 1:2 Jacob begot Judah
Mt 2:6 land of Judah
Heb 7:14 out of Judah
Re 5:5 tribe of Judah

Judas
Mt 13:55 Simon, and Judas
Mt 26:25 Judas, which betrayed
Lu 6:16 Judas the brother
Ac 1:16 Judas, which was
Ac 5:37 Judas of Galilee
Ac 9:11 house of Judas
Ac 15:22 Judas surnamed

Jude
Jude 1:1 Jude, the servant

Judea
Ezr 5:8 province of Judea
Lu 23:5 throughout all Judea

Judge
Ge 16:5 Yahweh judge
Ge 18:25 Judge of all
Ex 2:14 prince and a judge
Ex 18:13 judge the people
De 1:16 judge righteously
1Sa 2:25 judge shall judge
Ezr 7:25 which may judge
Mt 5:25 judge, and the judge
Mt 7:1 Judge not, that
Joh 5:30 I judge
Ac 10:42 God to be the Judge
1Co 6:3 shall judge angels
Heb 10:30 Yahweh shall judge
Re 19:11 he does judge

Judging
2Ki 15:5 judging the people
2Ch 26:21 judging the people
Ps 9:4 throne judging right
Isa 16:5 David, judging
Mt 19:28 judging the twelve
Lu 22:30 thrones judging

Judgment
Ex 12:12 execute judgment
Nu 27:21 judgment of Urim
Jud 4:5 her for judgment
Isa 9:7 judgment and with justice
Eze 18:8 judgment between man
Da 7:22 came, and judgment
Mt 5:21 danger of the judgment
Mt 10:15 day of judgment
Joh 5:22 judgment to the Son
Joh 12:31 judgment of this world
Joh 18:28 hall of judgment
Heb 6:2 eternal judgment
Heb 9:27 after this the judgment
1Pe 4:17 judgment must begin
Re 14:7 hour of his judgment

Judgment Seat
Mt 27:19 the judgment seat
Joh 19:13 judgment seat in
Ac 18:12 the judgment seat
Ac 25:6 judgment seat
Ro 14:10 judgment seat of
2Co 5:10 the judgment seat

Jupiter
Ac 14:12 Barnabas, Jupiter
Ac 14:13 priest of Jupiter
Ac 19:35 from Jupiter Zeus

Justification
Ro 4:25 for our justification
Ro 5:16 unto justification
Ro 5:18 justification of life

Kenites
Ge 15:19 Kenites, and the
Nu 24:21 looked on the Kenites
Jud 4:11 Kenites, and pitched
1Sa 15:6 said to the Kenites
1Sa 27:10 south of the Kenites
1Ch 2:55 are the Kenites

King
Jer 10:10 everlasting king
1Sa 10:24 God save the king
Ps 5:2 my King, and my God
Ps 10:16 Yahweh is King forever
Mt 1:6 David the king
Mt 27:37 KING OF THE JEWS
Joh 18:37 Are you a king
Ti 1:17 King eternal, immortal

Kingdom of God

Kingdom of God
Mt 6:33 kingdom of God
Mt 21:43 kingdom of God
Mr 1:14 kingdom of God
Mr 10:15 kingdom of God
Lu 4:43 kingdom of God
Joh 3:3 kingdom of God
Ac 14:22 kingdom of God
Ro 14:17 kingdom of God
1Co 6:9 kingdom of God
Ga 5:21 kingdom of God

Kingdom of Heaven
Mt 3:2 kingdom of heaven
Mt 5:3 kingdom of heaven
Mt 7:21 kingdom of heaven
Mt 13:11 kingdom of heaven
Mt 16:19 kingdom of heaven
Mt 19:23 kingdom of heaven
Mt 22:2 kingdom of heaven
Mt 25:1 kingdom of heaven

Kiss
Ge 31:28 kiss my sons
Ps 2:12 Kiss the Son
Pr 24:26 kiss *his* lips
So 1:2 kiss me with
Mt 26:48 I shall kiss
Lu 22:47 Yahshua to kiss
Ro 16:16 holy kiss
1Pe 5:14 kiss of charity

Knowledge
Ge 2:9 tree of knowledge
1Sa 2:3 God of knowledge
2Ch 1:10 wisdom and knowledge
Pr 1:7 beginning of knowledge
Isa 11:2 spirit of knowledge
Ho 4:6 lack of knowledge
Lu 1:77 knowledge of salvation
Ro 11:33 knowledge of God
1Co 8:1 Knowledge puffs up
Php 3:8 knowledge of the Messiah
Heb 10:26 knowledge of the truth
2Pe 1:5 to virtue knowledge

Kore
1Ch 9:19 son of Kore
1Ch 26:1 Kore, of the sons
1Ch 26:19 sons of Kore
2Ch 31:14 Kore the son

Laban
Ge 25:20 Laban the Syrian
Ge 28:2 daughters of Laban
Ge 29:5 Laban the son
Ge 31:12 seen all that Laban
Ge 46:18 Laban gave to Leah
De 1:1 Tophel, and Laban,

Lamb
Ge 22:7 lamb for a burnt
Ex 12:3 lamb for a house
Ex 12:5 lamb shall be without
Ex 29:39 lamb you shall offer
Le 14:21 lamb *for* a trespass
Isa 53:7 lamb to the slaughter
Ac 8:32 lamb dumb before
1Pe 1:19 Messiah, as of a lamb
Re 5:6 Lamb as it had been
Re 21:9 Lamb's wife

Lamb of God
Joh 1:29 Lamb of God
Joh 1:36 Lamb of God

Lamp
Ge 15:17 burning lamp
Ex 27:20 lamp to burn
1Sa 3:3 lamp of God
1Ki 15:4 lamp in Jerusalem
Ps 119:105 word *is* a lamp
Pr 6:23 lamp; and the law
Pr 20:20 thereof as a lamp
Re 8:10 as it were a lamp

Language
Ge 11:1 language, and of one
Ge 11:9 confound the language
Es 3:12 after their language
Isa 19:18 speak the language
Isa 36:13 Jews' language
Jer 5:15 language you know
Eze 3:5 hard language
Da 3:29 nation, and language
Zep 3:9 pure language
Ac 2:6 own language

Lasciviousness
Mr 7:22 deceit, lasciviousness
2Co 12:21 and lasciviousness
Ga 5:19 lasciviousness
Eph 4:19 over to lasciviousness
1Pe 4:3 lasciviousness, lusts
Jude 1:4 into lasciviousness

Law
Ge 47:26 made it a law
Ex 13:9 Yahweh's law may
De 31:11 read this law
Jos 1:8 law shall not depart
2Ki 10:31 law of Yahweh
Jer 31:33 law in their inward
Mt 22:40 law and the prophets
Joh 19:7 law he ought to die
Ro 7:4 dead to the law
Ga 2:16 works of the law
Heb 7:19 law made nothing
Heb 9:22 law purged with blood
Heb 10:1 law having a shadow

Lazarus
Lu 16:20 beggar named Lazarus
Joh 11:1 Lazarus, of Bethany
Joh 11:43 Lazarus, come forth
Joh 12:17 called Lazarus out

Leah
Ge 29:30 more than Leah
Ge 33:1 children unto Leah
Ge 34:1 daughter of Leah
Ge 46:15 sons of Leah
Ge 49:31 buried Leah
Ru 4:11 Leah, which two

Leaven
Ex 12:15 put away leaven
Ex 34:25 sacrifice with leaven
Le 2:11 burn no leaven
Le 10:12 eat it without leaven
Mt 13:33 like unto leaven
Mt 16:6 leaven of the Pharisees
Lu 12:1 of the leaven
1Co 5:6 little leaven leavens
Ga 5:9 leaven leavens

Lebanon
De 1:7 Lebanon, to
Jos 11:17 valley of Lebanon
Jud 9:15 cedars of Lebanon
1Ki 7:2 forest of Lebanon.
Ps 29:5 cedars of Lebanon
Isa 33:9 Lebanon is ashamed
Jer 22:20 up to Lebanon
Ho 14:5 roots as Lebanon
Zec 10:10 Gilead and Lebanon

Legion
Mr 5:9 My name is Legion
Mr 5:15 and had the legion
Lu 8:30 And he said, Legion

Lend
Ex 22:25 lend money
Le 25:37 nor lend him
De 15:6 lend to many
De 23:19 lend upon usury
De 28:44 lend to you
Ne 5:10 lend them money
Lu 6:34 lend to sinners

Leprosy
Le 13:2 plague of leprosy
Le 14:3 leprosy is healed
Le 14:57 law of leprosy
De 24:8 plague of leprosy
2Ki 5:3 him of his leprosy
Mt 8:3 leprosy was cleansed
Mr 1:42 leprosy departed
Lu 5:12 man full of leprosy

Levi
Ge 29:34 name called Levi
Ge 34:25 Levi, Dinah's
Ex 1:2 Simeon, Levi
Ex 2:1 house of Levi
Nu 17:3 rod of Levi
De 10:8 Levi, to bear the ark
Mal 2:4 might be with Levi
Mr 2:14 Levi the *son*
Lu 5:27 publican, named Levi
Heb 7:5 sons of Lev
Re 7:7 Levi *were* sealed

Leviathan
Job 41:1 leviathan with a hook
Ps 74:14 heads of leviathan
Ps 104:26 *is* that leviathan
Isa 27:1 leviathan the piercing

Levites
Ex 6:25 of the Levites
Le 25:32 Levites redeem
Nu 1:50 Levites over
De 18:1 priests the Levites
Jos 3:3 Levites bearing
1Ch 6:48 Levites *were*
2Ch 5:4 Levites took up
Ezr 1:5 Levites, with all
Joh 1:19 priests and Levites

Liars
De 33:29 found liars
Ps 116:11 men *are* liars
Isa 44:25 of the liars
Jer 50:36 upon the liars
1Ti 1:10 liars, for perjured
Tit 1:12 *are* always liars
Re 21:8 and all liars

Liberty
Le 25:10 proclaim liberty
Ps 119:45 walk at liberty
Isa 61:1 proclaim liberty
Jer 34:16 set at liberty
Eze 46:17 year of liberty
Lu 4:18 set at liberty
Ac 24:23 *him* have liberty
Ro 8:21 glorious liberty
2Co 3:17 there *is* liberty
Ga 5:1 in the liberty
Jas 1:25 law of liberty
2Pe 2:19 promise them liberty

Life
Ge 2:7 breath of life
Ge 3:24 tree of life
Ex 21:23 give life for life
De 12:23 blood *is* the life
2Sa 15:21 death or life
Lu 10:25 inherit eternal life
Joh 3:16 everlasting life
Joh 5:24 death unto life
Joh 6:48 bread of life.
Ac 3:15 Prince of life
Ro 6:4 newness of life
Heb 11:35 raised to life
Jas 1:12 crown of life
1Jo 1:1 Word of life
1Jo 2:16 pride of life
1Jo 5:12 Son has life
Re 2:7 tree of life

Light
Ge 1:3 Let there be light
Ex 25:37 light the lamps
1Sa 14:36 morning light
Ps 43:3 light and your truth
Ec 12:2 sun, or the light
Isa 2:5 light of Yahweh
Isa 5:20 darkness for light
Eze 8:17 Is it a light thing
Da 5:11 light and understanding
Mt 5:14 light of the world
Mt 6:22 light of the body
Mt 11:30 burden is light
Joh 1:7 witness of the Light
Joh 8:12 I am the light
2Co 11:14 angel of light
1Jo 1:5 God is light
Re 21:23 Lamb *is* the light

Lightning
Job 38:25 lightning of thunder
Ps 144:6 Cast forth lightning
Jer 10:13 lightning with rain
Eze 1:14 flash of lightning
Da 10:6 lightning, and his
Zec 9:14 as the lightning
Mt 24:27 lightning comes out
Lu 10:18 Satan as lightning
Lu 17:24 lightning, that lightens

Linen
Ge 41:42 garments of fine linen
Ex 26:1 fine twined linen
De 22:11 woolen and linen
1Sa 2:18 linen ephod
1Ki 10:28 linen yarn
Pr 7:16 linen of Egypt
Da 12:6 clothed in linen
Mt 27:59 a clean linen
Joh 20:5 linen clothes
Re 15:6 and white linen

Lion
Jud 14:8 carcass of the lion
1Sa 17:34 lion, and a bear
Job 4:10 roaring of the lion
Ps 10:9 lion in his den
Isa 65:25 lion shall eat
Eze 1:10 face of a lion
Eze 19:3 young lion
Da 7:4 *was* like a lion
1Pe 5:8 as a roaring lion
Re 4:7 *was* like a lion
Re 5:5 Lion of the tribe

Locust
Ex 10:19 locust in all
Le 11:22 locust after his kind
De 28:38 locust shall consume
1Ki 8:37 locust, *or* if there
Ps 78:46 labor to the locust
Joe 2:25 locust has eaten

Lord, the
Ge 18:27 to speak to the Lord,
Ge 42:33 the lord of the country
Ex 23:17 appear before the Lord Yahweh
Ex 34:23 appear before the Lord Yahweh
Jos 3:13 Yahweh, the Lord of all the earth
2Ki 7:17 king appointed the lord on
Ps 71:16 strength of the Lord YahwehIsa
7:14 the Lord himself shall give you a sign
Isa 40:10 the Lord Yahweh will come
Isa 61:1 Spirit of the Lord Yahweh *is* upon
Jer 50:31 says the Lord Yahweh of hosts
Eze 8:1 the hand of the Lord Yahweh fell
Zep 1:7 the presence of the Lord Yahweh
Mal 3:1 the Lord, whom you seek
Mt 1:20 the angel of the Lord appeared
Lu 1:9 into the temple of the Lord
Lu 24:3 the body of the Lord Yahshua
Joh 12:13 comes in the name of the Lord
Ac 13:48 the word of the Lord
2Th 2:8 the Lord shall consume with
2Pe 3:8 one day *is* with the Lord as
Re 1:8 and the ending, says the Lord
Re 22:5 the Lord God gives them light

LORD, the (see Yahweh; see Yah)

Lot
Ge 11:31 Lot the son
Ge 13:11 Lot chose him
Le 16:8 lot for the scapegoat
Nu 26:55 divided by lot
Es 3:7 that *is*, the lot
Pr 16:33 lot is cast
Jer 13:25 lot, the portion
Lu 1:9 office, his lot
Lu 17:32 Remember Lot's
Ac 1:26 lot fell upon
2Pe 2:7 delivered just Lot

Love
Ge 22:2 whom you love
Le 19:18 love your neighbor
De 6:5 love Yahweh your
Pr 10:12 love covers all sins
Ec 3:8 time to love
Jer 31:3 everlasting love
Zec 8:19 love the truth
Mt 5:44 Love your enemies
Lu 10:27 love the Lord
Joh 13:34 love one another
Joh 21:15 Jonas, love you me
Ro 8:39 the love of God
Ga 5:22 Spirit is love, joy
Eph 5:25 love your wives
1Ti 6:10 love of money
1Jo 2:15 Love not the world
1Jo 4:8 for God is love
Re 2:4 left your first love

Lucifer
Isa 14:12 Lucifer, Son of

Luke
Col 4:14 Luke, the beloved
2Ti 4:11 Only Luke is

Lust
Ps 78:18 food for their lust
Ps 81:12 own hearts' lust
Pr 6:25 Lust not after
Mt 5:28 woman to lust
Ro 1:27 burned in their lust
Ro 7:7 not known lust
Ga 5:16 lust of the flesh
Jas 4:2 lust, and have not
2Pe 1:4 world through lust
1Jo 2:16 lust of the flesh

Macedonia
Ac 16:9 man of Macedonia
Ac 18:5 from Macedonia
Ro 15:26 Macedonia to make
2Co 9:4 Macedonia come
2Co 11:9 from Macedonia
1Th 1:7 believe in Macedonia

Magician
Da 2:10 magician, or astrologer

Malachi
Mal 1:1 Israel by Malachi

Man
Ge 1:26 man in our image
Ge 2:7 man *of* the dust
Ex 30:12 man a ransom
Nu 1:4 man of every tribe
2Sa 12:7 You *are* the man
Mt 6:24 No man can serve
Mt 19:5 man leave father
Joh 3:3 man is born
Ro 3:28 man is justified
Ro 7:24 wretched man
1Co 11:3 head of every man

Man

Heb 10:12 man, after he
Re 22:19 man shall take

Manna
Ex 16:31 Manna: and it
Nu 11:9 manna fell
De 8:3 manna know that
Jos 5:12 manna ceased
Ne 9:20 not your manna
Ps 78:24 rained down manna
Joh 6:58 did eat manna
Heb 9:4 pot that had manna
Re 2:17 hidden manna

Mantle
Jud 4:18 with a mantle
1Sa 15:27 skirt of his mantle
1Sa 28:14 with a mantle
1Ki 19:19 cast his mantle
2Ki 2:14 mantle of Elijah
Ezr 9:3 my mantle
Job 2:12 one his mantle

Mark
Ge 4:15 mark upon Cain
Ru 3:4 mark the place
1Sa 20:20 shot at a mark
Job 7:20 set me as a mark
Ps 56:6 mark my steps
Ps 130:3 mark iniquities
Eze 44:5 Son of man, mark
Ro 16:17 mark them which
Php 3:14 mark for the prize

Mark the Apostle
Ac 12:12 surname was Mark
Ac 15:39 Barnabas took Mark
2Ti 4:11 Take Mark, and bring

Mark of the Beast
Re 13:16 mark in their right hand
Re 14:9 mark in his forehead
Re 15:2 his mark, and over
Re 16:2 mark of the beast
Re 19:20 mark of the beast
Re 20:4 mark upon their foreheads

Marriage
Ex 21:10 duty of marriage
Ps 78:63 given to marriage
Mt 22:30 given in marriage
Mt 25:10 to the marriage
Joh 2:1 marriage in Cana
1Co 7:38 her in marriage
Heb 13:4 Marriage is
Re 19:9 marriage supper

Martha
Lu 10:38 named Martha
Joh 11:5 Yahshua loved Martha
Joh 12:2 Martha served

Mary, mother of Yahshua
Mt 1:16 Mary, of whom
Mt 2:11 Mary his mother
Mt 13:55 mother called Mary
Mr 6:3 son of Mary
Lu 1:27 name was Mary
Lu 2:16 Mary, and Joseph
Ac 1:14 Mary the mother

Mary Magdalene
Mt 27:56 Mary Magdalene
Mt 28:1 came Mary Magdalene
Mr 15:40 was Mary Magdalene
Lu 8:2 Mary called Magdalene
Joh 20:16 said to her, Mary

Mary, sister of Lazarus
Lu 10:39 Mary, which also
Lu 10:42 Mary has chosen
Joh 11:19 Martha and Mary
Joh 12:3 Mary a pound

Master
Ge 24:12 God of my master
Ge 39:20 Joseph's master
Ex 21:4 master has given
2Ki 5:20 master has spared
Mt 8:19 Master, I will follow
Mt 23:8 Master, even the
Mt 26:49 master; and kissed
Mr 9:5 Master, it is good
Lu 6:40 above his master
Lu 8:24 Master, master

Matthew
Mt 9:9 Matthew, sitting
Mt 10:3 Matthew the publican
Lu 6:15 Matthew and Thomas
Ac 1:13 and Matthew

Medes
2Ki 17:6 the cities of the Medes
Ezr 6:2 the province of the Medes
Es 1:19 laws of the Persians and the Medes
Isa 13:17 stir up the Medes against them
Jer 25:25 all the kings of the Medes
Jer 51:11 spirit of the kings of the Medes
Da 5:28 given to the Medes and Persians
Da 6:8 law of the Medes and Persians
Da 9:1 seed of the Medes
Ac 2:9 Parthians, and Medes, and Elamites

Media
Es 1:3 power of Persia and Media
Isa 21:2 besiege, O Media
Da 8:20 the kings of Media and Persia

Megiddo (see also Armageddon)
Jos 12:21 king of Megiddo
Jos 17:11 inhabitants of Megiddo
Jud 1:27 Megiddo and her towns
Jud 5:19 waters of Megiddo
2Ki 9:27 fled to Megiddo
2Ki 23:29 slew him at Megiddo
2Ch 35:22 valley of Megiddo

Melchizedek
Ge 14:18 Melchizedek king
Ps 110:4 order of Melchizedek
Heb 5:10 order of Melchizedek
Heb 7:1 Melchizedek, king

Melech
1Ch 8:35 Pithon, and Melech

Memorial
Ex 3:15 memorial unto
Ex 17:14 for a memorial
Ex 28:12 stones of memorial
Le 2:2 burn the memorial
Le 23:24 sabbath, a memorial
Jos 4:7 be for a memorial
Es 9:28 memorial of them
Ho 12:5 is his memorial
Zec 6:14 memorial in the
Mr 14:9 for a memorial
Ac 10:4 memorial before God

Mephibosheth (also see Meribaal)
2Sa 4:4 was Mephibosheth
2Sa 9:6 Mephibosheth, the son of Jonathan
2Sa 16:1 servant of Mephibosheth
2Sa 19:24 Mephibosheth the son
2Sa 21:7 spared Mephibosheth

Meribbaal (also see Mephibosheth)
1Ch 9:40 son of Jonathan was Meribbaal

Merodach
Jer 50:2 Merodach is broken

Mesopotamia
Ge 24:10 Mesopotamia, to the
De 23:4 Pethor of Mesopotamia
Jud 3:8 king of Mesopotamia
1Ch 19:6 out of Mesopotamia
Ac 2:9 dwellers in Mesopotamia
Ac 7:2 was in Mesopotamia

Messenger
Ge 50:16 messenger to Joseph
2Sa 11:19 charged the messenger
1Ki 19:2 messenger to Elijah
2Ki 5:10 Elisha sent a messenger
Job 33:23 messenger with him
Eze 23:40 messenger was sent
Hag 1:13 Yahweh's messenger
Mal 2:7 messenger of Yahweh
Mt 11:10 I send my messenger
2Co 12:7 messenger of Satan

Messiah
Da 9:25 to the Messiah the Prince
Mt 1:1 generation of Yahshua the Messiah
Mt 1:16 Yahshua, who is called the Messiah
Mt 24:5 saying, I am the Messiah
Mr 1:1 Yahshua the Messiah, the Son of God
Joh 1:41 Messiah, which is, being interpreted
Joh 4:25 Messiah comes, which is called Christ
Joh 11:27 you are the Messiah, the Son of God
Ac 16:18 in the name of Yahshua the Messiah
Ro 3:22 by faith of Yahshua the Messiah
1Co 10:4 that Rock was the Messiah
1Co 15:3 the Messiah died for our
2Co 4:6 God in the face of Yahshua the Messiah
2Co 5:19 God was in the Messiah
2Co 13:5 Yahshua the Messiah is in you
Php 4:13 Messiah which strengthens me
Heb 13:8 Yahshua the Messiah the same
1Jo 4:2 confesses that Yahshua the Messiah
Re 1:1 The Revelation of Yahshua the Messiah
Re 22:21 Yahshua the Messiah be with you all

Micah
Jud 17:5 Micah had a house
Jud 18:18 Micah's house

1Ch 9:15 son of Micah
Jer 26:18 Micah the Morasthite
Mic 1:1 Micah the Morasthite

Micaiah
1Ki 22:8 one man, Micaiah
2Ch 18:8 Micaiah the son

Michael
Nu 13:13 son of Michael
1Ch 5:13 fathers *were*, Michael
1Ch 6:40 son of Michael
1Ch 27:18 son of Michael
Ezr 8:8 son of Michael
Da 10:13 Michael, one of
Da 12:1 Michael stand up
Jude 1:9 Michael the archangel
Re 12:7 Michael and his angels

Michaiah
2Ki 22:12 son of Michaiah
2Ch 13:2 also *was* Michaiah
2Ch 17:7 Michaiah, to teach
Ne 12:35 son of Michaiah
Jer 36:13 Michaiah declared

Midian
Ge 25:4 sons of Midian
Ex 3:1 priest of Midian
Ex 4:19 Moses in Midian
Nu 22:7 elders of Midian
Nu 31:3 Yahweh of Midian
Jud 6:1 hand of Midian
1Ki 11:18 out of Midian
Isa 10:26 slaughter of Midian
Hab 3:7 Midian did tremble
Ac 7:29 land of Midian

Midianites
Ge 37:36 Midianites sold him
Nu 25:17 Attack the Midianites
Jud 6:2 of the Midianites
Jud 7:2 give the Midianites
Ps 83:9 as *to* the Midianites

Mildew
De 28:22 with mildew
1Ki 8:37 blasting, mildew
2Ch 6:28 mildew, locust
Am 4:9 blasting and mildew
Hag 2:17 with mildew

Milk
Ex 3:8 milk and honey
Ex 23:19 mother's milk
Jud 4:19 bottle of milk
1Sa 6:7 two milk cows
Job 21:24 full of milk
Isa 28:9 from the milk
1Co 3:2 fed you with milk
Heb 5:12 milk, and not
1Pe 2:2 milk of the word

Ministers
1Ki 10:5 of his ministers
Ezr 8:17 ministers for the
Ps 104:4 ministers a flaming
Isa 61:6 Ministers of our God
Eze 44:11 ministers in my
Lu 1:2 ministers of the word
Ro 13:6 God's ministers
1Co 3:5 ministers by whom
2Co 9:10 ministers seed
Ga 3:5 ministers to you
1Pe 4:11 man ministers

Miracles
Nu 14:22 my miracles
Joh 2:11 beginning of miracles
Joh 3:2 do these miracles
Ac 2:22 miracles and wonders
Ac 19:11 special miracles
1Co 12:10 working of miracles
Heb 2:4 diverse miracles
Re 13:14 miracles which
Re 16:14 working miracles
Re 19:20 worked miracles

Miriam
Ex 15:20 Miriam the prophetess
Nu 12:15 Miriam was shut
Nu 20:1 Miriam died
Nu 26:59 Moses, and Miriam
De 24:9 God did unto Miriam
1Ch 4:17 she bore Miriam
Mic 6:4 Aaron, and Miriam

Moab
Ge 19:37 name Moab
Ge 36:35 field of Moab
Nu 22:8 plains of Moab
Ru 1:1 country of Moab
1Sa 12:9 king of Moab
Ps 60:8 Moab *is* my wash
Isa 15:1 burden of Moab

Moabites
De 2:29 Moabites which dwell
Jud 3:28 enemies the Moabites
1Ki 11:33 god of the Moabites
2Ki 13:20 of the Moabites
2Ki 23:13 of the Moabites
1Ch 18:2 Moabites became

Molech
Le 18:21 *fire* to Molech
Le 20:2 seed to Molech
1Ki 11:7 Molech, the
Jer 32:35 *fire* unto Molech

Money
Ge 17:12 bought with money
Ge 23:9 money as it is worth
Ge 33:19 pieces of money
Ex 30:16 atonement money
De 2:28 food for money
1Ki 21:6 vineyard for money
2Ki 12:10 money in the chest
Isa 55:1 has no money
Mt 17:24 tribute *money*
Mr 12:41 money into the
1Ti 6:10 love of money

Month
Ge 7:11 second month
Nu 3:15 a month old
Nu 9:22 month, or a year
Nu 11:20 whole month
1Ch 27:1 month by month
Zec 8:19 fourth *month*
Lu 1:26 month the angel
Re 9:15 day, and a month
Re 22:2 fruit every month

Moon
Ge 37:9 sun and the moon
1Sa 20:18 *is* the new moon
Ps 104:19 moon for seasons
Ps 136:9 moon and stars
Isa 13:10 moon shall not
Jer 31:35 of the moon
Joe 2:31 moon into blood
Mt 24:29 moon shall not
Re 6:12 moon became as
Re 21:23 neither of the moon

Mordecai
Es 2:5 name *was* Mordecai
Es 3:2 Mordecai bowed not
Es 6:13 Mordecai *is* of
Es 10:3 Mordecai the Jew

Moriah
Ge 22:2 land of Moriah
2Ch 3:1 mount Moriah

Moses
Ex 2:10 name Moses
Ex 24:2 Moses alone shall
Jos 1:1 Moses the servant
1Ch 23:14 Moses the man
Mr 12:26 book of Moses
Lu 24:27 beginning at Moses
Joh 1:17 given by Moses
Joh 3:14 Moses lifted up
Joh 6:32 Moses gave you
Ac 6:14 Moses delivered
2Co 3:13 Moses, *which* put
Heb 11:23 By faith Moses
Jude 1:9 body of Moses
Re 15:3 song of Moses

Mother
Ge 3:20 mother of all living
Ex 20:12 and your mother
De 13:6 son of your mother
Jud 16:17 mother's womb
Jer 22:26 mother that bore
Zec 13:3 mother that begot
Mr 3:33 Who is my mother
Lu 1:15 mother's womb
Joh 2:1 mother of Yahshua
Joh 3:4 mother's womb
Re 17:5 MOTHER OF HARLOTS

Mother-In-Law
De 27:23 mother-in-law
Ru 1:14 mother-in-law
Ru 3:1 mother-in-law
Mic 7:6 mother-in-law
Mt 10:35 mother-in-law
Lu 12:53 mother-in-law

Naaman
Ge 46:21 and Ashbel, Gera, and Naaman
2Ki 5:1 Now Naaman, captain of the host
2Ki 5:20 spared Naaman this Syrian

Naaman

2Ki 5:27 The leprosy therefore of Naaman
Lu 4:27 except Naaman the Syrian

Name
Ge 2:19 that *was* the name
Ge 3:20 wife's name Eve
Ge 5:2 their name Adam
Ge 11:4 make us a name
De 14:24 set his name
De 18:5 minister in the name
Jud 13:18 name, seeing it
Isa 7:14 name Immanuel
Isa 9:6 name shall be
Mr 11:10 name of the Lord
Joh 14:13 ask in my name
Joh 20:31 life through his name
Ro 10:13 call upon the name
Re 13:17 name of the beast
Re 19:16 name written
Re 22:4 name *shall be*

Name of Yahweh
Ge 4:26 name of Yahweh
Ex 20:7 name of Yahweh
Le 24:11 name *of Yahweh*
De 18:22 name of Yahweh
1Ki 5:3 name of Yahweh
Job 1:21 name of Yahweh
Ps 102:15 name of Yahweh
Isa 56:6 name of Yahweh
Am 6:10 name of Yahweh
Mic 5:4 name of Yahweh
Zep 3:12 name of Yahweh

Name of Yahshua
Ac 2:38 name of Yahshua
Ac 4:18 name of Yahshua
Ac 5:40 name of Yahshua
Ac 8:12 name of Yahshua
Ac 9:27 name of Yahshua
Ac 16:18 name of Yahshua
Ac 26:9 name of Yahshua
1Co 1:2 name of Yahshua
Php 2:10 name of Yahshua

Naomi
Ru 1:3 Naomi's husband died
Ru 2:1 Naomi had a kinsman
Ru 3:1 Naomi her mother-in-law
Ru 4:17 son born to Naomi

Naphtali
Ge 30:8 name Naphtali
Nu 26:50 families of Naphtali
Jos 19:39 children of Naphtali
Jud 1:33 Neither did Naphtali
1Ch 6:62 tribe of Naphtali
Ps 68:27 princes of Naphtali
Eze 48:34 gate of Naphtali
Mt 4:13 Zebulun and Naphtali
Re 7:6 Naphtali *were* sealed

Nathan
2Sa 12:1 Yahweh sent Nathan
1Ki 1:8 Nathan the prophet
1Ch 3:5 Nathan, and Solomon
1Ch 29:29 Nathan the prophet
2Ch 9:29 book of Nathan
Ezr 8:16 and for Nathan
Ps 51:1 Nathan the prophet
Zec 12:12 house of Nathan
Lu 3:31 Nathan, which was

Navy
1Ki 9:26 made a navy
1Ki 10:11 navy also of Hiram
1Ki 10:22 navy of Tharshish

Nazareth
Mt 2:23 city called Nazareth
Mt 21:11 prophet of Nazareth
Mr 1:9 Nazareth of Galilee
Mr 14:67 Yahshua of Nazareth
Lu 1:26 named Nazareth
Lu 2:4 Nazareth, into Judaea
Joh 1:46 out of Nazareth
Joh 19:19 OF NAZARETH
Ac 3:6 Messiah of Nazareth
Ac 22:8 Yahshua of Nazareth

Nazarite
Nu 6:13 law of the Nazarite
Jud 13:5 Nazarite unto God
Jud 16:17 Nazarite unto God

Nebo
Nu 32:3 Nebo, and Beon
Nu 33:47 before Nebo.
De 32:49 mount Nebo
De 34:1 Nebo, to the top
1Ch 5:8 Nebo and Baalmeon
Ezr 2:29 children of Nebo
Ezr 10:43 sons of Nebo
Isa 46:1 Nebo stoops
Jer 48:1 Woe unto Nebo

Nebuchadnezzar
2Ki 24:1 Nebuchadnezzar
1Ch 6:15 Nebuchadnezzar
2Ch 36:7 Nebuchadnezzar
Ezr 5:12 Nebuchadnezzar
Es 2:6 Nebuchadnezzar
Jer 27:6 Nebuchadnezzar
Da 2:1 Nebuchadnezzar
Da 3:1 Nebuchadnezzar
Da 4:33 Nebuchadnezzar:

Necromancer
De 18:11 or a necromancer

Nehemiah
Ezr 2:2 Jeshua, Nehemiah
Ne 1:1 words of Nehemiah
Ne 3:16 Nehemiah the son
Ne 8:9 Nehemiah, which
Ne 10:1 sealed *were*, Nehemiah
Ne 12:26 Nehemiah the governor

Neighbor
Ex 12:4 and his neighbor
Ex 20:16 against your neighbor
Le 19:13 defraud your neighbor
Jos 20:5 smote his neighbor
Ru 4:7 *it* to his neighbor
1Sa 28:17 neighbor, *even* to
Isa 19:2 against his neighbor
Jer 49:18 and the neighbor
Hab 2:15 gives his neighbor
Zec 8:10 against his neighbor

Nethinims
1Ch 9:2 and the Nethinims
Ezr 2:58 Nethinims, and
Ezr 2:70 Nethinims, dwelt
Ezr 8:20 Nethinims, whom
Ne 3:26 Nethinims dwelt
Ne 7:46 Nethinims: the
Ne 10:28 Nethinims, and all

Nicodemus
Joh 3:1 Nicodemus, a ruler
Joh 7:50 Nicodemus said
Joh 19:39 also Nicodemus

Nicolaitans
Re 2:6 deeds of the Nicolaitans
Re 2:15 doctrine of the Nicolaitans

Night
Ge 1:5 he called Night
Ge 8:22 day and night
Ge 28:11 night, because
Ex 13:21 night in a pillar
2Ch 7:12 Solomon by night
Jer 33:20 night in their season
Da 7:13 saw in the night
Mt 28:13 by night, and stole
Joh 3:2 Yahshua by night
Ro 13:12 night is far spent
Re 22:5 no night there

Nimrod
Ge 10:8 Cush begot Nimrod
1Ch 1:10 Nimrod: he began
Mic 5:6 land of Nimrod

Nineveh
Ge 10:11 built Nineveh
Isa 37:37 dwelt at Nineveh
Jon 1:2 Nineveh, that great
Jon 3:3 Nineveh was
Na 1:1 burden of Nineveh
Zep 2:13 Nineveh a desolation
Mt 12:41 men of Nineveh

Nisan
Ne 2:1 month *of* Nisan
Es 3:7 month *of* Nisan

Noah
Ge 6:8 Noah found grace
Ge 7:9 Noah into the ark
Ge 8:1 remembered Noah
1Ch 1:4 Noah, Shem, Ham
Isa 54:9 waters of Noah
Eze 14:14 Noah, Daniel
Mt 24:37 days of Noah
Heb 11:7 By faith Noah
1Pe 3:20 Noah, while the ark
2Pe 2:5 saved Noah

North
Jer 25:9 families of the north
Jer 25:26 kings of the north
Eze 26:7 from the north
Da 11:6 king of the north
Da 11:40 king of the north

Oath
Ge 26:3 oath which I swore
Ge 50:25 took an oath

Ex 22:11 <u>oath</u> of Yahweh
De 29:14 and this <u>oath</u>
2Sa 21:7 Yahweh's <u>oath</u>
1Ch 16:16 his <u>oath</u> to Isaac
Ne 10:29 <u>oath</u>, to walk
Eze 16:59 despised the <u>oath</u>
Da 9:11 <u>oath</u> that *is* written
Zec 8:17 no false <u>oath</u>
Jas 5:12 any other <u>oath</u>

Obadiah
1Ki 18:3 <u>Obadiah</u>, which
1Ch 3:21 sons of <u>Obadiah</u>
2Ch 34:12 Jahath and <u>Obadiah</u>
Ezr 8:9 <u>Obadiah</u> the son
Ne 10:5 Meremoth, <u>Obadiah</u>
Ob 1:1 vision of <u>Obadiah</u>

Oil
Ex 25:6 <u>Oil</u> for the light
Ex 27:20 pure olive <u>oil</u>
Ex 30:25 anointing <u>oil</u>
Le 2:4 mingled with <u>oil</u>
Le 14:16 finger in the <u>oil</u>
2Ki 18:32 land of olive <u>oil</u>
Ps 23:5 head with <u>oil</u>
Mt 25:3 took no <u>oil</u>
Mr 6:13 anointed with <u>oil</u>
Re 18:13 wine, and <u>oil</u>

Ointment
Ex 30:25 holy <u>ointment</u>
2Ki 20:13 precious <u>ointment</u>
1Ch 9:30 <u>ointment</u> of the
Pr 27:9 <u>Ointment</u> and perfume
Ec 10:1 <u>ointment</u> of the
Mt 26:7 precious <u>ointment</u>
Mr 14:3 <u>ointment</u> of spikenard
Joh 11:2 <u>ointment</u>, and wiped

Olive
Ge 8:11 <u>olive</u> leaf
Ex 23:11 <u>olive</u> grove
1Ki 6:23 <u>olive</u> tree
2Ki 18:32 land of <u>olive</u>
Ne 8:15 <u>olive</u> branches
Isa 17:6 <u>olive</u> tree
Zec 4:3 two <u>olive</u> trees
Ro 11:17 wild <u>olive</u> tree
Re 11:4 two <u>olive</u> trees

Olives, Mount of
2Sa 15:30 *mount of* <u>Olives</u>
Zec 14:4 mount of <u>Olives</u>
Mt 21:1 mount of <u>Olives</u>
Mt 24:3 mount of <u>Olives</u>
Mr 14:26 mount of <u>Olives</u>
Lu 19:37 mount of <u>Olives</u>
Lu 22:39 mount of <u>Olives</u>
Joh 8:1 mount of <u>Olives</u>

Omega
Re 1:8 Alpha and <u>Omega</u>
Re 1:11 Alpha and <u>Omega</u>
Re 21:6 <u>Omega</u>, the
Re 22:13 Alpha and <u>Omega</u>

Omri
1Ki 16:16 <u>Omri</u>, the captain
1Ki 16:23 <u>Omri</u> to reign
1Ki 16:25 <u>Omri</u> worked evil
1Ki 16:30 son of <u>Omri</u>
2Ki 8:26 <u>Omri</u> king of Israel
1Ch 7:8 <u>Omri</u>, and Jerimoth
1Ch 9:4 <u>Omri</u>, the son
1Ch 27:18 <u>Omri</u> the son
Mic 6:16 statutes of <u>Omri</u>

Onesimus
Col 4:9 <u>Onesimus</u>, a faithful
Phm 1:10 my son <u>Onesimus</u>

Oracle
2Sa 16:23 at the <u>oracle</u>
1Ki 6:5 of the <u>oracle</u>
1Ki 6:16 for the <u>oracle</u>
1Ki 6:23 <u>oracle</u> he made
1Ki 8:8 before the <u>oracle</u>
2Ch 3:16 *as* in the <u>oracle</u>
2Ch 5:9 before the <u>oracle</u>
Ps 28:2 holy <u>oracle</u>

Orion
Ob 9:9 <u>Orion</u>, and Pleiades
Job 38:31 bands of <u>Orion</u>
Am 5:8 stars and <u>Orion</u>

Ornan
1Ch 21:21 came to <u>Ornan</u>
2Ch 3:1 <u>Ornan</u> the Jebusite

Ospray
Le 11:13 and the <u>ospray</u>
De 14:12 and the <u>ospray</u>

Ossifrage
Le 11:13 <u>ossifrage</u>, and
De 14:12 <u>ossifrage</u>, and

Othniel
Jos 15:17 <u>Othniel</u> the son
Jud 1:13 <u>Othniel</u> the son
1Ch 4:13 <u>Othniel</u>, and Seraiah
1Ch 27:15 <u>Othniel</u>: and in

Oven
Le 26:26 in one <u>oven</u>
Ps 21:9 fiery <u>oven</u>
La 5:10 like an <u>oven</u>
Ho 7:4 <u>oven</u> heated
Mal 4:1 as an <u>oven</u>
Mt 6:30 into the <u>oven</u>

Overseer
Ge 39:4 <u>overseer</u> over his
Ne 11:9 *was* their <u>overseer</u>
Ne 11:22 <u>overseer</u> also
Pr 6:7 <u>overseer</u>, or ruler
1Ti 3:1 of an <u>overseer</u>
2Ti 4:22 <u>overseer</u> of the
Tit 1:7 <u>overseer</u> must be
1Pe 2:25 <u>Overseer</u> of your

Owl
Le 11:17 <u>owl</u>, and the
De 14:16 little <u>owl</u>
Ps 102:6 <u>owl</u> of the desert
Isa 34:15 <u>owl</u> make her nest

Ox
Ex 21:28 <u>ox</u> gores a man
Ex 22:1 oxen for an <u>ox</u>
Jud 3:31 an <u>ox</u> goad
Job 40:15 grass as an <u>ox</u>
Isa 1:3 <u>ox</u> knows his
Jer 11:19 lamb *or* an <u>ox</u>
Eze 1:10 face of an <u>ox</u>
1Co 9:9 mouth of the <u>ox</u>

Ozem
1Ch 2:15 <u>Ozem</u> the sixth
1Ch 2:25 Oren, and <u>Ozem</u>

Passover
Ex 12:21 kill the <u>passover</u>
Nu 9:5 <u>passover</u> on the
2Ki 23:21 Keep the <u>passover</u>
Eze 45:21 <u>passover</u>, a feast
Mt 26:18 <u>passover</u> at your
Lu 22:1 called the <u>Passover</u>
Joh 6:4 <u>passover</u>, a feast
Joh 18:39 one at the <u>Passover</u>
Ac 12:4 <u>passover</u> to bring
1Co 5:7 Messiah our <u>passover</u>
Heb 11:28 kept the <u>passover</u>

Paul
Ac 13:9 *is called* <u>Paul</u>
Ac 15:2 <u>Paul</u> and Barnabas
Ac 21:39 <u>Paul</u> said, I am
Ro 1:1 <u>Paul</u>, a servant
Ga 1:1 <u>Paul</u>, an apostle
Eph 3:1 <u>Paul</u>, the prisoner
Col 1:23 <u>Paul</u> am made
2Ti 4:22 <u>Paul</u> was brought
Tit 1:1 <u>Paul</u>, a servant
Phm 1:9 <u>Paul</u> the aged
2Pe 3:15 brother <u>Paul</u>

Peace Offerings
Ex 24:5 peace <u>offerings</u>
Le 7:11 peace <u>offerings</u>
Jud 20:26 peace <u>offerings</u>
2Sa 6:17 peace <u>offerings</u>
1Ki 8:63 peace <u>offerings</u>
2Ki 16:13 peace <u>offerings</u>
2Ch 7:7 peace <u>offerings</u>
2Ch 30:22 peace <u>offerings</u>
Eze 45:17 peace <u>offerings</u>
Eze 46:12 peace <u>offerings</u>

Peacocks
1Ki 10:22 apes, and <u>peacocks</u>
2Ch 9:21 apes, and <u>peacocks</u>
Job 39:13 to the <u>peacocks</u>

Pentecost (see Feast of Weeks)
Ac 2:1 <u>Pentecost</u> had fully
Ac 20:16 day of <u>Pentecost</u>
1Co 16:8 until <u>Pentecost</u>

Penuel
Ge 32:31 passed over <u>Penuel</u>
Jud 8:8 up there to <u>Penuel</u>
1Ki 12:25 built <u>Penuel</u>
1Ch 4:4 <u>Penuel</u> the father
1Ch 8:25 <u>Penuel</u>, the sons

Peor
Nu 23:28 the top of Peor
Nu 25:18 matter of Peor
Nu 31:16 matter of Peor
Jos 22:17 iniquity of Peor

Persia
2Ch 36:22 king of Persia
Ezr 4:5 king of Persia
Ezr 9:9 kings of Persia
Es 1:3 power of Persia
Eze 27:10 They of Persia
Da 8:20 Media and Persia
Da 10:13 kingdom of Persia

Persians
Es 1:19 laws of the Persians and the Medes
Da 5:28 given to the Medes and Persians
Da 6:8 law of the Medes and Persians

Peter
Mt 10:2 called Peter
Mt 16:18 Peter, and upon
Mr 3:16 surnamed Peter
Lu 9:20 Peter answering
Lu 22:34 Peter, the cock
Joh 13:6 Peter said to him
Joh 21:15 Peter, Simon
Ac 1:15 Peter stood up
Ac 2:38 Peter said to them
Ac 4:8 Peter, filled with
Ac 5:29 Peter and the

Pharaoh
Ge 40:2 Pharaoh was angry
Ge 41:25 dream of Pharaoh
Ex 10:1 Pharaoh: for I have
Ex 12:29 firstborn of Pharaoh
1Sa 6:6 Pharaoh hardened
1Ki 3:1 Pharaoh king
Isa 36:6 Pharaoh king
Eze 30:22 against Pharaoh
Ac 7:10 Pharaoh king
Ro 9:17 says unto Pharaoh

Pharez
Ge 38:29 called Pharez
Ge 46:12 sons of Pharez
Nu 26:20 Pharez, the family
1Ch 2:4 bore him Pharez
1Ch 9:4 Pharez the son
Mt 1:3 Judah begot Pharez
Lu 3:33 Pharez, which was

Pharisees
Mt 5:20 scribes and Pharisees
Mt 12:14 Pharisees went out
Mt 16:12 doctrine of the Pharisees
Mt 23:2 Pharisees sit in Moses'
Lu 5:17 Pharisees and doctors
Lu 11:42 unto you, Pharisees
Joh 3:1 Pharisees, named
Joh 7:45 priests and Pharisees
Joh 11:57 Pharisees had given
Ac 15:5 Pharisees which believed
Ac 23:7 between the Pharisees

Philemon
Phm 1:1 Philemon our dearly

Philip
Mt 10:3 Philip, and
Lu 3:1 Philip tetrarch
Joh 1:44 Philip was of
Joh 6:5 said to Philip
Joh 14:8 Philip said to
Ac 8:5 Philip went down
Ac 21:8 Philip the evangelist

Philistine(s)
Ge 26:1 king of the Philistines
Ex 13:17 land of the Philistines
Jud 3:3 lords of the Philistines
Jud 15:11 Philistines are rulers
1Sa 5:1 Philistines took the ark
1Sa 17:4 Philistines, named
1Sa 17:45 said David to the Philistine
1Sa 27:7 country of the Philistines
Jer 25:20 land of the Philistines
Am 6:2 Gath of the Philistines
Ob 1:19 plain the Philistines
Zep 2:5 land of the Philistines

Pilate, Pontius
Mt 27:2 Pontius Pilate
Lu 3:1 Pontius Pilate
Ac 4:27 Pontius Pilate
1Ti 6:13 Pontius Pilate

Pillar
Ge 19:26 pillar of salt
Ge 28:22 set for a pillar
Ex 13:21 pillar of a cloud
Ex 33:9 pillar descended
Nu 12:5 pillar of the cloud
Jud 20:40 pillar of smoke
2Sa 18:18 himself a pillar
2Ki 23:3 stood by a pillar
Jer 52:21 of one pillar
1Ti 3:15 pillar and ground
Re 3:12 I make a pillar

Pillow
1Sa 19:13 pillow of goats'
1Sa 26:7 at his pillow
Mr 4:38 on a pillow

Plague
Ex 9:3 grievous plague
Ex 11:1 plague more upon
Nu 16:46 plague is begun
Nu 25:9 died in the plague
De 24:8 plague of leprosy
1Sa 6:4 plague was on you
2Sa 24:21 plague may be
1Ki 8:38 plague of his own
Zec 14:12 plague with which
Mr 5:29 of that plague
Re 16:21 plague of the hail

Plowshares
Isa 2:4 into plowshares
Joe 3:10 plowshares into
Mic 4:3 into plowshares

Poor
Ge 41:19 poor and very ill
Ex 22:25 that are poor
De 15:11 poor shall never
1Sa 2:7 poor, and makes rich
2Sa 12:3 poor man had nothing
Job 24:4 poor of the earth
Pr 10:15 poor is their poverty
Isa 66:2 poor and of a contrite
Mt 5:3 poor in spirit
Mt 26:11 poor always with
Mr 12:43 poor widow has
Lu 4:18 gospel to the poor
2Co 8:9 he became poor
Jas 2:2 poor man in filthy
Re 3:17 miserable, and poor
Re 13:16 rich and poor

Praise
Ge 29:35 I praise Yahweh
De 10:21 He is your praise
Ne 12:46 songs of praise
Ps 50:23 praise glorifies me
Isa 61:3 garment of praise
Jer 17:26 sacrifices of praise
Da 4:37 Nebuchadnezzar praise
Joh 12:43 praise of men
2Co 8:18 praise is in the gospel
Eph 1:6 praise of the glory
Php 4:8 if there is any praise

Prayer
2Sa 7:27 pray this prayer
1Ki 8:45 prayer and their
Pr 15:8 prayer of the upright
Isa 26:16 poured out a prayer
Isa 56:7 house of prayer
Da 9:3 seek by prayer
Mt 17:21 prayer and fasting
Mt 21:13 house of prayer
Lu 6:12 all night in prayer
Ac 1:14 one accord in prayer
Ac 3:1 hour of prayer
Php 4:6 every thing by prayer
Col 4:2 Continue in prayer
Jas 5:15 prayer of faith shall

Preacher
Ec 1:1 words of the Preacher
Ec 7:27 preacher, counting
Ec 12:9 preacher was wise
Ro 10:14 without a preacher
1Ti 2:7 preacher, and an
2Ti 1:11 appointed a preacher
2Pe 2:5 person, a preacher

Preaching
Jon 3:2 to it the preaching
Mt 3:1 Baptist, preaching
Mr 1:14 preaching the gospel
Lu 3:3 preaching the baptism
Lu 11:32 preaching of Jonah
Ac 8:4 preaching the word
Ac 11:19 preaching the word
Ro 16:25 preaching of Yahshua
1Co 1:18 preaching of the cross
2Ti 4:17 preaching might be
Tit 1:3 through preaching

Priscilla
Ac 18:2 with his wife Priscilla
Ac 18:18 Priscilla and Aquila

Ac 18:26 Aquila and Priscilla had
Ro 16:3 Priscilla and Aquila my
1Co 16:19 Aquila and Priscilla salute
2Ti 4:19 Salute Prisca and Aquila

Preparation Day
Joh 19:42 Jews' preparation *day*

Pride
Le 26:19 pride of your power
2Ch 32:26 pride of his heart
Pr 8:13 pride, and arrogance
Pr 16:18 Pride *goes* before
Isa 9:9 pride and stoutness
Da 5:20 hardened in pride
Ob 1:3 pride of your heart
Zep 3:11 pride, and you shall
Mr 7:22 blasphemy, pride
1Ti 3:6 lifted up with pride
1Jo 2:16 pride of life

Priest
Ge 14:18 priest of the most
Ex 28:1 priest's office
Le 1:7 Aaron the priest
Le 4:6 priest shall dip
De 18:3 priest's due
1Sa 2:35 faithful priest
Jer 14:18 prophet and the priest
Zec 3:8 Joshua the high priest
Ac 4:6 the high priest
Heb 2:17 faithful high priest
Heb 3:1 Apostle and High Priest
Heb 5:6 priest forever after
Heb 9:7 high priest alone once

Prison
Ge 39:20 prison, a place
Jud 16:21 grind in the prison
1Ki 22:27 prison, and feed
Ps 142:7 soul out of prison
Isa 24:22 shut up in the prison
Isa 61:1 opening of the prison
Jer 29:26 prison, and in the
Mt 25:36 prison, and you
Lu 3:20 John in prison
Ac 16:26 of the prison
1Pe 3:19 spirits in prison
Re 2:10 you into prison
Re 20:7 out of his prison

Prize
1Co 9:24 receives the prize
Php 3:14 mark for the prize

Promise
1Ki 8:56 his good promise
2Ch 1:9 promise to David
Ps 105:42 his holy promise
Lu 24:49 promise of my Father
Ac 2:33 promise of the Holy
Ac 13:23 promise raised
Ro 4:13 promise, that he
Ro 9:8 of the promise
Ga 3:14 promise of the Spirit
Eph 1:13 Spirit of promise
2Ti 1:1 promise of life
Heb 6:13 God made *a* promise
Heb 9:15 promise of eternal

2Pe 3:13 promise, look for

Prophecy
2Ch 9:29 in the prophecy
Da 9:24 vision and prophecy
Mt 13:14 fulfilled the prophecy
Ro 12:6 prophecy, *let us*
1Co 12:10 prophecy; to
1Co 13:2 *gift of* prophecy
1Ti 4:14 prophecy, with the
2Pe 1:19 word of prophecy
Re 1:3 of this prophecy
Re 19:10 spirit of prophecy
Re 22:7 of the prophecy

Prophet
De 13:1 prophet, or a dreamer
De 18:22 prophet speaks
1Sa 9:9 Prophet was before
1Ki 18:22 prophet of Yahweh
2Ki 5:8 prophet in Israel
Jer 1:5 you a prophet
Jer 28:9 word of the prophet
Eze 7:26 vision of the prophet
Eze 14:7 prophet to inquire
Ho 12:13 prophet Yahweh
Mt 8:17 Isaiah the prophet
Mt 21:11 prophet of Nazareth
Lu 1:76 prophet of the Highest
Re 16:13 false prophet
Re 19:20 false prophet

Prophetess
Ex 15:20 Miriam the prophetess
Jud 4:4 Deborah, a prophetess
2Ki 22:14 Huldah the prophetess
Ne 6:14 prophetess Noadiah
Isa 8:3 prophetess; and she
Lu 2:36 Anna, a prophetess
Re 2:20 herself a prophetess

Propitiation
Ro 3:25 propitiation through
1Jo 2:2 propitiation for our
1Jo 4:10 *be* the propitiation

Prosperity
1Sa 25:6 lives *in prosperity*
1Ki 10:7 prosperity exceeds
Job 36:11 days in prosperity
Ps 35:27 prosperity of his
Ps 73:3 prosperity of the
Ec 7:14 day of prosperity
Jer 22:21 in your prosperity
Jer 33:9 prosperity that I
Zec 1:17 prosperity shall yet
Zec 7:7 and in prosperity

Punish
Le 26:18 punish you seven
Isa 13:11 punish the world
Isa 26:21 punish the inhabitants
Jer 21:14 punish you according
Ho 12:2 will punish Jacob
Am 3:2 punish you for all
Zep 1:8 punish the princes

Punishment
Le 4:13 punishment *is*

Le 26:41 punishment of
Pr 19:19 punishment
La 4:6 punishment of
Eze 14:10 the punishment
Am 1:3 *the punishment*
Mt 25:46 punishment
Heb 10:29 punishment
1Pe 2:14 punishment of

Purification
Nu 19:9 purification for sin
2Ch 30:19 purification of
Ne 12:45 purification, according
Es 2:3 things for purification
Lu 2:22 purification according
Ac 21:26 days of purification

Queen
1Ki 10:1 queen of Sheba
1Ki 15:13 *being* queen
2Ki 10:13 of the queen
Ne 2:6 queen also sitting
Es 2:4 queen instead of
Da 5:10 queen, by reason
Lu 11:31 queen of the south
Ac 8:27 Candace queen of
Re 18:7 I sit a queen

Queen of Heaven
Jer 7:18 queen of heaven
Jer 44:17 queen of heaven

Rabbi
Mt 23:7 of men, Rabbi
Joh 1:49 Rabbi, you are
Joh 3:2 Rabbi, we know
Joh 3:26 Rabbi, he that
Joh 6:25 Rabbi, when came

Rachel
Ge 29:6 Rachel his daughter
Ge 35:19 Rachel died
Ge 46:19 Rachel Jacob's
Ru 4:11 Rachel and like
Jer 31:15 Rachel weeping
Mt 2:18 Rachel weeping

Rahab
Jos 2:1 named Rahab
Ps 87:4 mention of Rahab
Ps 89:10 Rahab in pieces
Isa 51:9 Rahab, *and* wounded
Heb 11:31 Rahab perished not
Jas 2:25 Rahab the harlot

Rain
Ge 2:5 caused it to rain
Ge 7:4 rain upon the earth
Ex 16:4 rain bread
De 32:2 drop as the rain
1Ki 17:1 dew nor rain
Ps 147:8 rain for the earth
Ec 11:3 clouds are full of rain
Isa 55:10 rain comes down
Jer 5:24 rain, both the former
Eze 38:22 rain, and great
Mt 7:25 rain descended
Ac 14:17 rain from heaven
Re 11:6 heaven, that it rain

Rainbow
Re 4:3 rainbow round
Re 10:1 rainbow *was* upon

Raisins
1Sa 25:18 clusters of raisins
1Sa 30:12 clusters of raisins
2Sa 16:1 bunches of raisins
1Ch 12:40 bunches of raisins

Ram
Ge 22:13 ram caught in
Ex 29:15 one ram; and Aaron
Le 5:15 ram without blemish
Le 9:2 ram for a burnt
Nu 5:8 ram of the
Jos 6:5 ram's horn
Ru 4:19 Hezron begot Ram
Da 8:3 ram which had

Raven
Ge 8:7 sent forth a raven
Le 11:15 raven after his
Job 38:41 for the raven
So 5:11 black as a raven.
Isa 34:11 raven shall dwell

Read
De 31:11 read this law
2Ki 23:2 read in their ears
Ne 8:8 read in the book
Jer 36:6 read in the roll
Da 5:7 read this writing
Mt 12:3 read what David
Lu 4:16 stood up for to read
Ac 8:30 read the prophet
2Co 3:2 known and read
2Co 3:15 Moses is read
Re 5:4 open and to read

Reading
Ne 8:8 understand the reading
Jer 36:8 reading in the book
Ac 8:28 chariot reading Isaiah
Ac 13:15 reading of the law
2Co 3:14 reading of the old
1Ti 4:13 attendance to reading

Reaping
1Sa 6:13 reaping their wheat
Mt 25:24 reaping where you
Lu 19:22 reaping that I did

Rebekah
Ge 24:15 Rebekah came
Ge 25:20 Rebekah to wife
Ge 26:7 kill me for Rebekah
Ge 27:6 Rebekah spoke
Ge 49:31 Isaac and Rebekah

Rechabites
Jer 35:2 the Rechabites
Jer 35:18 Rechabites

Reconciliation
Le 8:15 reconciliation
2Ch 29:24 reconciliation
Eze 45:15 reconciliation
Da 9:24 reconciliation
2Co 5:18 reconciliation
Heb 2:17 reconciliation

Red Heifer
Nu 19:2 red heifer without

Red Sea
Ex 10:19 into the Red Sea
Ex 13:18 of the Red Sea
Ex 15:4 in the Red Sea
Nu 21:4 way of the Red Sea
Jos 2:10 of the Red Sea
Ne 9:9 by the Red Sea
Ps 136:13 divided the Red Sea
Ac 7:36 Red Sea, and in
Heb 11:29 Red Sea as by

Redeem(ed)
Ge 48:16 The Angel which redeemed me
Ex 6:6 I will redeem you with
Ex 13:13 your children shall you redeem
Ex 21:8 shall he let her be redeemed
Ex 34:20 of your sons you shall redeem
Le 19:20 not at all redeemed, nor freedom
Le 27:20 if he will not redeem the field
Nu 3:51 money of them that were redeemed
De 7:8 redeemed you out of the house of
De 24:18 Yahweh your God redeemed you
Ru 4:4 If you will redeem *it,* redeem *it*
1Ki 1:29 that has redeemed my soul out
Ne 5:8 redeemed our brethren the Jews
Ps 25:22 Redeem Israel, O God
Ps 72:14 He shall redeem their soul from
Isa 1:27 shall be redeemed with judgment
Isa 29:22 Yahweh, who redeemed Abraham
Isa 51:11 the redeemed of Yahweh shall
Isa 52:3 redeemed without money
Jer 31:11 For Yahweh has redeemed Jacob
Ho 13:14 redeem them from death
Mic 4:10 Yahweh shall redeem you
Zec 10:8 I have redeemed them
Lu 1:68 redeemed his people
Lu 24:21 should have redeemed Israel
Ga 3:13 The Messiah has redeemed us from
Tit 2:14 that he might redeem us from all
1Pe 1:18 not redeemed with corruptible
Re 5:9 redeemed us to God by your blood
Re 14:3 were redeemed from the earth

Redeemer
Job 19:25 I know *that* my redeemer lives
Isa 43:14 Thus says Yahweh, your redeemer
Isa 49:7 the Redeemer of Israel
Isa 60:16 your Savior and your Redeemer
Isa 63:16 our father, our redeemer
Jer 50:34 Their Redeemer *is* strong

Redeeming
Eph 5:16 Redeeming the time
Col 4:5 redeeming the time

Redemption
Jer 32:7 the right of redemption
Lu 2:38 redemption in Jerusalem
Ro 3:24 redemption that is in the Messiah
1Co 1:30 sanctification, and redemption
Eph 1:7 redemption through his blood
Eph 4:30 sealed unto the day of redemption
Col 1:14 redemption through his blood
Heb 9:12 obtained eternal redemption

Refiner('s)
Pr 25:4 a vessel for the refiner
Mal 3:2 he *is* like a refiner's fire,

Refining
Pr 27:21 refining pot

Refuge, Cities of
Nu 35:11 be cities of refuge
Nu 35:14 be cities of refuge
Jos 20:2 you cities of refuge
1Ch 6:67 cities of refuge

Regeneration
Mt 19:28 regeneration when
Tit 3:5 washing of regeneration

Rehoboam
1Ki 12:6 king Rehoboam
1Ki 14:21 Rehoboam the son
1Ch 3:10 son *was* Rehoboam
2Ch 10:13 Rehoboam forsook
2Ch 11:3 Rehoboam the son
2Ch 13:7 Rehoboam was young
Mt 1:7 begot Rehoboam

Repentance
Mt 3:8 befitting repentance
Mt 9:13 sinners to repentance
Mr 1:4 baptism of repentance
Lu 15:7 need no repentance
Ac 5:31 repentance to Israel
Ac 11:18 repentance unto life
Ro 2:4 you to repentance
Ro 11:29 without repentance
2Co 7:10 repentance to salvation
Heb 6:1 repentance from dead
2Pe 3:9 come to repentance

Respect of Persons
2Ch 19:7 respect of persons
Pr 28:21 respect of persons
Ro 2:11 no respect of persons
Eph 6:9 respect of persons
Col 3:25 no respect of persons
Jas 2:1 respect of persons
1Pe 1:17 respect of persons

Rest
Ge 8:9 the dove found no rest
Ex 16:23 the rest of the holy Sabbath
Ex 23:11 let it rest and lie still
Ex 31:15 the sabbath of rest
Le 23:3 the sabbath of rest
Le 25:5 rest unto the land
Jos 1:13 God has given you rest
Jos 21:44 Yahweh gave them rest
Jud 3:11 the land had rest
Ne 9:28 after they had rest
Es 9:16 rest from their enemies
Job 3:26 neither had I rest
Ps 37:7 Rest in Yahweh
Ps 95:11 not enter into my rest
Isa 14:3 Yahweh shall give you rest
Jer 46:27 be in rest and at ease
Zec 1:11 earth sits still, and is at rest

Salvation

Mt 11:28 I will give you rest
Lu 11:24 dry places, seeking rest
Heb 4:9 a rest to the people of God
Re 6:11 rest yet for a little season
Re 14:11 no rest day nor night

Resurrection
Mt 27:53 his resurrection
Lu 20:27 any resurrection
Joh 5:29 resurrection of life
Joh 11:25 am the resurrection
Ac 2:31 resurrection of the
1Co 15:12 no resurrection
Php 3:10 his resurrection
Heb 11:35 better resurrection
1Pe 1:3 resurrection of
Re 20:5 first resurrection

Revelation
Ro 16:25 revelation of
1Co 14:6 revelation, or
Ga 1:12 revelation of
Eph 1:17 and revelation
Eph 3:3 revelation he made
1Pe 1:13 at the revelation
Re 1:1 Revelation of

Revenge
Jer 15:15 revenge me of
Jer 20:10 take our revenge
Eze 25:15 dealt by revenge
2Co 7:11 what revenge
2Co 10:6 readiness to revenge

Rich, The
Ex 30:15 The rich shall
2Sa 12:2 The rich *man*
Pr 14:20 the rich *has*
Pr 22:2 The rich and
Ec 5:12 of the rich
Isa 53:9 with the rich
Jer 9:23 let not the rich
Lu 16:21 the rich man
Re 6:15 the rich men

Riches
1Sa 17:25 great riches
2Ch 1:11 riches, wealth
Ps 104:24 full of your riches
Pr 11:4 Riches profit not
Eze 27:12 all *kind of* riches
Mt 13:22 deceitfulness of riches
Mr 10:23 riches enter into
Lu 16:11 the true *riches*
Ro 11:33 depth of the riches
Eph 3:8 unsearchable riches
Php 4:19 riches in glory
Col 1:27 riches of the glory
Heb 11:26 greater riches
Re 5:12 power, and riches

Riddle
Jud 14:12 forth a riddle
Eze 17:2 forth a riddle

Righteous
Ge 7:1 seen righteous
Ge 18:23 destroy the righteous
Ex 9:27 Yahweh *is* righteous
1Ki 8:32 justifying the righteous
Job 34:5 I am righteous
Ps 7:9 righteous God tries
Ps 34:15 upon the righteous
Ps 37:25 righteous forsaken
Pr 11:30 righteous *is* a tree
Pr 13:5 righteous *man* hates

Righteousness
Ge 15:6 for righteousness
De 6:25 our righteousness
De 9:5 your righteousness
1Ki 3:6 in righteousness
Job 27:6 righteousness
Ps 15:2 works righteousness
Pr 12:17 forth righteousness
Pr 16:8 a little with righteousness
Isa 1:26 city of righteousness
Isa 5:16 in righteousness

Rising Early
Job 24:5 rising early for
Pr 27:14 rising early in
Jer 11:7 rising early and
Jer 25:3 rising early and
Jer 35:14 you, rising early
Jer 44:4 rising early and

Robbers
Jer 7:11 den of robbers
Eze 7:22 robbers shall enter
Da 11:14 robbers of your
Ob 1:5 robbers by night
Joh 10:8 thieves and robbers
2Co 11:26 perils of robbers

Robbery
Pr 21:7 robbery of the
Isa 61:8 I hate robbery
Eze 22:29 exercised robbery
Am 3:10 violence and robbery
Na 3:1 lies and robbery
Php 2:6 not robbery to be

Rock
Ex 17:6 you shall smite the rock
Ex 33:22 in a cleft of the rock
Nu 20:8 speak you to the rock
De 32:4 He is the Rock
De 32:15 Rock of his salvation
Jud 6:21 fire out of the rock
2Sa 22:3 The God of my rock
2Sa 22:32 who is a rock
Ps 18:2 Yahweh is my rock
Ps 42:9 God my rock
Ps 62:7 rock of my strength
Ps 105:41 He opened the rock
Isa 48:21 flow out of the rock
Mt 16:18 upon this rock I will build
Lu 6:48 foundation on a rock
Ro 9:33 rock of offense
1Co 10:4 that Rock was the Messiah
1Pe 2:8 a rock of offense

Roe
2Sa 2:18 as a wild roe
Pr 5:19 pleasant roe
Pr 6:5 yourself as a roe
So 2:9 roe or a young
Isa 13:14 chased roe

Rome
Ac 2:10 strangers of Rome
Ac 18:2 depart from Rome
Ac 19:21 also see Rome
Ac 23:11 also at Rome
2Ti 1:17 was in Rome

Ruth
Ru 1:14 Ruth clung to her
Ru 3:9 Ruth your handmaid
Ru 4:5 Ruth the Moabitess
Mt 1:5 begot Obed of Ruth

Sabbath
Ex 16:23 holy sabbath
Le 23:3 *is* the sabbath
Le 25:2 keep a sabbath
Nu 28:9 sabbath day
Nu 28:10 every sabbath
Ne 13:17 profane the sabbath
Jer 17:21 on the sabbath
Mt 12:2 upon the sabbath
Lu 23:54 sabbath drew

Sackcloth
Ge 37:34 sackcloth upon
2Sa 3:31 you with sackcloth
Ne 9:1 and with sackcloth
Es 4:1 sackcloth with ashes
Da 9:3 fasting, and sackcloth
Mt 11:21 ago in sackcloth
Lu 10:13 sitting in sackcloth
Re 6:12 black as sackcloth
Re 11:3 clothed in sackcloth

Sadducees
Mt 3:7 Sadducees come
Mt 16:6 of the Sadducees
Ac 5:17 of the Sadducees
Ac 23:6 part were Sadducees

Salt
Ge 14:3 the salt sea
Ge 19:26 pillar of salt
Le 2:13 season with salt
Nu 18:19 covenant of salt
De 29:23 brimstone, and salt
Jos 15:62 city of Salt
Jud 9:45 sowed it with salt
Job 6:6 eaten without salt
Eze 43:24 shall cast salt
Zep 2:9 salt pits
Mt 5:13 salt of the earth
Mr 9:49 salted with salt

Salutations
Mr 12:38 *love* salutations

Salvation
Ex 14:13 salvation of Yahweh
Ex 15:2 my salvation
De 32:15 Rock of his salvation
Lu 3:6 salvation of God
Ac 4:12 is there salvation
Ro 1:16 salvation to every
Ro 10:10 made unto salvation
2Co 7:10 repentance to salvation
Eph 1:13 gospel of your salvation

Salvation

Eph 6:17 helmet of salvation
Php 2:12 your own salvation
2Th 2:13 salvation through
Heb 1:14 heirs of salvation
Heb 5:9 eternal salvation
1Pe 1:5 faith unto salvation
Re 19:1 Salvation, and glory

Samson

Jud 13:24 name Samson
Jud 15:16 Samson said
Jud 16:6 said to Samson
Heb 11:32 and *of* Samson

Samuel

1Sa 1:20 name Samuel
1Sa 7:15 Samuel judged Israel
1Sa 16:1 said to Samuel
1Sa 25:1 Samuel died
1Sa 28:11 me up Samuel
1Ch 9:22 Samuel the seer
1Ch 29:29 book of Samuel
2Ch 35:18 Samuel the prophet
Jer 15:1 Samuel stood before
Ac 13:20 Samuel the prophet

Sanctify

Ex 28:41 sanctify them
Ex 29:44 sanctify the tabernacle
Ex 31:13 that does sanctify
Nu 20:12 to sanctify me
1Ch 23:13 sanctify the most
Ne 13:22 sanctify the sabbath
Isa 8:13 Sanctify Yahweh
Isa 29:23 sanctify my name
Eze 37:28 do sanctify Israel
Joh 17:17 Sanctify them through
Eph 5:26 sanctify and cleanse
1Th 5:23 sanctify you wholly
Heb 13:12 sanctify the people

Sarah

Ge 17:15 Sarah *shall* her
Ge 20:2 Sarah his wife
Ge 21:2 Sarah conceived
Ge 49:31 Abraham and Sarah
Nu 26:46 Asher *was* Sarah
Ro 4:19 Sarah's womb
Ro 9:9 Sarah shall have
Heb 11:11 faith also Sarah
1Pe 3:6 Sarah obeyed Abraham

Satan

1Ch 21:1 Satan stood up
Job 1:6 Yahweh, and Satan
Zec 3:1 Satan standing at
Mr 1:13 tempted by Satan
Lu 4:8 behind me, Satan
Lu 22:3 Satan into Judas
2Co 11:14 Satan himself
2Co 12:7 messenger of Satan
Re 2:9 synagogue of Satan
Re 20:2 Devil, and Satan

Savior

2Sa 22:3 refuge, my savior
2Ki 13:5 Israel a savior
Ps 106:21 God their savior
Isa 43:3 Israel, your Savior
Isa 60:16 Savior and your
Ho 13:4 no savior besides
Lu 2:11 of David a Savior
Joh 4:42 Messiah, the Savior
Ac 13:23 Savior, Yahshua
1Jo 4:14 Savior of the world

Scarlet

Ge 38:28 scarlet thread
Ex 25:4 purple, and scarlet
Le 14:4 scarlet, and hyssop
Jos 2:18 scarlet thread
Isa 1:18 sins are as scarlet
Mt 27:28 scarlet robe
Heb 9:19 scarlet wool
Re 17:3 scarlet colored
Re 18:16 scarlet, and decked

Scatter (Scattered)

Ge 11:4 lest we be scattered
Le 26:33 I will scatter you
Nu 10:35 enemies be scattered
De 4:27 Yahweh shall scatter
De 28:64 Yahweh shall scatter
De 30:3 God has scattered you
1Ki 14:15 shall scatter them
2Ch 18:16 see all Israel scattered
Es 3:8 people scattered abroad
Ps 44:11 scattered us among
Jer 9:16 I will scatter them
Jer 10:21 flocks shall be scattered
Eze 5:10 will I scatter
Eze 34:5 they were scattered
Da 12:7 scatter the power
Zec 1:19 which have scattered
Mt 26:31 scattered abroad
Joh 10:12 scatters the sheep
Ac 11:19 scattered abroad
Jas 1:1 scattered abroad
1Pe 1:1 strangers scattered

Scepter

Ge 49:10 scepter shall not
Es 4:11 golden scepter
Isa 14:5 scepter of the
Eze 19:14 scepter to rule
Eze 21:13 even the scepter
Am 1:5 holds the scepter
Zec 10:11 scepter of Egypt
Heb 1:8 scepter of

Science

Da 1:4 understanding science
1Ti 6:20 science falsely

Scorpion

Lu 11:12 him a scorpion
Re 9:5 of a scorpion

Scourging

Ac 22:24 by scourging

Scribe

2Ki 12:10 king's scribe
2Ki 22:9 Shaphan the scribe
2Ki 25:19 principal scribe
Ezr 4:8 scribe wrote
Ezr 7:6 scribe in the law
Ne 8:1 scribe to bring
Ne 8:4 Ezra the scribe
Ne 12:26 priest, the scribe
Jer 36:20 Elishama the scribe
Mt 13:52 scribe *which*

Scribes

1Ch 2:55 scribes which dwelt
2Ch 34:13 scribes, and officers
Jer 8:8 pen of the scribes
Mt 7:29 not as the scribes
Mt 23:13 scribes and Pharisees
Mr 9:14 scribes questioning
Mr 12:38 Beware of the scribes
Mr 15:1 elders and scribes
Lu 22:2 priests and scribes

Scriptures

Mt 21:42 read in the scriptures
Mt 26:54 scriptures be fulfilled
Lu 24:27 all the scriptures
Joh 5:39 Search the scriptures
Ac 17:2 out of the scriptures
Ac 17:11 searched the scriptures
Ac 18:28 by the scriptures
Ro 16:26 scriptures of
1Co 15:4 to the scriptures
2Ti 3:15 holy scriptures

Scurvy

Le 21:20 scurvy, or scabbed
Le 22:22 ulcer, or scurvy

Sea

Ge 1:26 fish of the sea
Ex 14:16 sea, and divide
2Sa 22:16 sea appeared
1Ch 18:8 brazen sea
Ps 89:9 raging of the sea
Da 7:3 up from the sea
Mic 7:19 depths of the sea
Mt 4:18 sea: for they
Joh 6:19 walking on the sea
Re 4:6 sea of glass

Seal

Es 8:8 seal *it* with the
Da 12:4 seal the book
Joh 3:33 set to his seal
Ro 4:11 seal of the
2Ti 2:19 having this seal
Re 6:3 second seal
Re 9:4 seal of God
Re 22:10 Seal not the

Seasons

Ge 1:14 seasons, and
Ex 18:22 at all seasons
Le 23:4 in their seasons
Ps 104:19 moon for seasons
Da 2:21 and the seasons
Mt 21:41 in their seasons
Ac 1:7 times or the seasons
Ac 14:17 fruitful seasons

Second Death

Re 2:11 the second death
Re 20:6 second death has
Re 21:8 is the second death

Secret
Nu 5:13 kept secret
De 29:29 secret *things*
1Sa 19:2 secret place
Job 20:26 secret places
Ps 25:14 secret of Yahweh *is*
Ps 64:2 from the secret
Ps 90:8 secret *sins*
Isa 48:16 spoken in secret
Jer 49:10 secret places
Eze 28:3 secret that
Da 2:19 secret revealed
Am 3:7 reveals his secret
Mt 6:4 be in secret
Joh 7:10 were in secret
Ro 16:25 kept secret

Seed
Ge 1:11 seed *is* in itself
Ge 3:15 seed and her seed
Ge 47:19 seed, that we
Ex 16:31 coriander seed
Le 18:21 seed pass through
1Sa 8:15 tenth of your seed
2Ch 22:10 all the seed royal
Es 6:13 seed of the Jews
Ps 126:6 bearing precious seed
Eze 17:5 seed of the land
Hag 2:19 seed yet in the barn
Mt 13:19 received seed
Mt 13:37 good seed is the Son
Lu 8:11 seed is the word
1Pe 1:23 corruptible seed
Re 12:17 remnant of her seed

Sepulcher
De 34:6 of his sepulcher
Jud 8:32 in the sepulcher
1Sa 10:2 Rachel's sepulcher
1Ki 13:31 in the sepulcher
Mt 27:60 of the sepulcher
Mr 16:2 sepulcher at the
Joh 19:41 a new sepulcher
Ac 7:16 in the sepulcher

Seraiah
2Sa 8:17 Seraiah *was*
2Ki 25:23 Seraiah the son
1Ch 4:14 Seraiah begot Joab
1Ch 6:14 Azariah begot Seraiah
Ezr 7:1 son of Seraiah
Ne 11:11 Seraiah the son of Hilkiah
Jer 51:59 Seraiah the son of Neriah

Seraphims
Isa 6:2 stood the seraphims
Isa 6:6 one of the seraphims

Serpent
Ge 3:1 serpent was more
Ex 7:9 become a serpent
Nu 21:8 You a fiery serpent
2Ki 18:4 brazen serpent
Ps 140:3 serpent; adders'
Isa 14:29 poisonous serpent
Mic 7:17 dust like a serpent
Mt 7:10 give him a serpent
Joh 3:14 lifted up the serpent
Re 12:9 serpent, called the Devil
Re 20:2 that old serpent

Servant
Ge 39:17 Hebrew servant
Ge 49:15 servant unto tribute
Ex 12:44 servant that is bought
Le 25:40 hired servant
Jos 12:6 servant of Yahweh
2Sa 13:17 servant that ministered
Job 1:8 my servant Job
Isa 49:5 *to be* his servant
Zec 3:8 servant the BRANCH
Mt 12:18 servant, whom I have
Mr 10:44 chief, shall be servant
Lu 16:13 servant can serve two
Lu 17:7 servant plowing
Re 19:10 your fellow servant

Seven
Ge 7:4 yet seven days
Ge 29:20 served seven years
Ge 41:2 seven well favored
Ex 12:15 Seven days shall
De 15:1 seven years you
Jos 6:4 seven priests shall
1Ki 11:3 seven hundred wives
Pr 6:16 seven *are* an
Eze 43:26 Seven days shall
Da 9:25 *shall be* seven weeks
Mt 15:36 seven loaves
Mr 16:9 cast seven devils
Lu 17:4 against you seven
Re 1:4 seven congregations

Seventy
Ex 24:1 seventy of the elders
Nu 7:13 seventy shekels
1Ch 21:14 seventy thousand
Jer 25:11 Babylon seventy
Da 9:24 Seventy weeks
Mt 18:22 seventy times
Lu 10:1 another seventy

Shaalbim
Jud 1:35 Shaalbim: yet
1Ki 4:9 Shaalbim, and

Shaaph
1Ch 2:47 Ephah, and Shaaph
1Ch 2:49 Shaaph the father

Shadrach
Da 2:49 Shadrach, Meshach
Da 3:13 bring Shadrach
Da 3:26 Shadrach, Meshach
Da 3:30 promoted Shadrach

Shallum
2Ki 15:10 Shallum the son
2Ki 22:14 wife of Shallum
1Ch 2:40 begot Shallum
1Ch 6:12 Zadok begot Shallum
1Ch 9:17 porters *were*, Shallum
Ne 3:12 repaired Shallum
Ne 7:45 children of Shallum
Jer 22:11 Shallum the son

Shame
Jud 18:7 put *them* to shame
2Ch 32:21 returned with shame
Ps 35:26 clothed with shame
Pr 11:2 then comes shame
Isa 30:3 be your shame
Eze 16:52 shame for your sins
Da 12:2 shame *and* everlasting
Php 3:19 glory *is* in their shame
Heb 12:2 despising the shame
Re 3:18 shame of your

Shaphan
Ki 22:3 Shaphan the son
2Ch 34:16 Shaphan carried
Jer 26:24 Shaphan was with
Jer 29:3 son of Shaphan
Jer 36:10 Shaphan the scribe
Eze 8:11 son of Shaphan

Shave
Le 14:8 shave off all his hair
Le 21:5 shave off the corner
Nu 8:7 shave all their flesh
De 21:12 shave her head
Jud 16:19 shave off
Isa 7:20 shave with a razor

Shechem
Ge 33:18 city of Shechem
Ge 34:2 Shechem the son
Ge 37:12 flock in Shechem
Nu 26:31 Shechem, the family
Jos 21:21 Shechem with her
Jud 9:25 Shechem set liers
Jud 21:19 Bethel to Shechem
1Ki 12:25 Shechem in mount

Sheshach
Jer 25:26 king of Sheshach shall drink
Jer 51:41 How is Sheshach taken

Sheep
Ge 4:2 keeper of sheep
Ge 38:12 sheep shearers
Le 1:10 sheep, or of the goats
Nu 27:17 sheep which have
1Sa 8:17 tenth of your sheep
1Sa 17:34 his father's sheep
Job 31:20 fleece of my sheep
Isa 53:6 sheep have gone
Jer 50:6 been lost sheep
Mt 9:36 sheep having no
Mt 10:6 lost sheep of the
Lu 15:4 hundred sheep
Joh 10:2 shepherd of the sheep
Joh 21:16 Feed my sheep
Ro 8:36 sheep for the slaughter

Sheep Gate
Ne 3:1 built the sheep gate
Ne 3:32 unto the sheep gate
Ne 12:39 to the sheep gate

Sheet
Ac 10:11 great sheet knit
Ac 11:5 sheet, let down

Shemaiah
1Ki 12:22 Shemaiah the man
1Ch 3:22 Shechaniah; Shemaiah
1Ch 9:14 Levites; Shemaiah
1Ch 15:8 Shemaiah the chief
1Ch 24:6 Shemaiah the son

Shemaiah

1Ch 26:4 Shemaiah the firstborn
2Ch 12:5 Shemaiah the prophet
Ne 10:8 Shemaiah: these *were*
Jer 29:24 Shemaiah the Nehelamite

Shepherd
Ge 46:34 shepherd *is* an
1Ki 22:17 not a shepherd
Ps 23:1 *is* my shepherd
Isa 40:11 flock like a shepherd
Eze 34:12 shepherd seeks out
Mt 25:32 shepherd divides *his*
Joh 10:11 am the good shepherd
Heb 13:20 shepherd of the sheep
1Pe 2:25 Shepherd and Overseer
1Pe 5:4 Shepherd shall appear

Shield
Ge 15:1 I *am* your shield
Jud 5:8 shield or spear
2Sa 22:3 shield, and the horn
1Ch 5:18 shield and sword
Job 39:23 spear and the shield
Ps 3:3 Yahweh, *are* a shield
Eze 23:24 shield and helmet
Eph 6:16 shield of faith

Shiloh
Jos 18:1 Shiloh, and set
Jos 19:51 Shiloh before
Jud 18:31 God was in Shiloh
1Sa 1:3 hosts in Shiloh
1Sa 3:21 again in Shiloh
1Ki 2:27 Eli in Shiloh
Ps 78:60 tabernacle of Shiloh

Shinar
Ge 10:10 land of Shinar
Ge 11:2 the land of Shinar
Ge 14:1 king of Shinar
Isa 11:11 from Shinar
Da 1:2 land of Shinar
Zec 5:11 land of Shinar

Shittim
Ex 25:10 ark *of* shittim wood
Ex 26:15 tabernacle *of* shittim
Ex 30:1 shittim wood
Ex 38:1 offering *of* shittim
Nu 25:1 stayed in Shittim
Jos 2:1 sent out of Shittim
Joe 3:18 valley of Shittim

Shoe
De 25:9 shoe from off
De 29:5 shoe has not
Jos 5:15 Loose your shoe
Ru 4:7 plucked off his shoe
Isa 20:2 shoe from your
Joh 1:27 shoe's lace I am

Sickle
De 16:9 sickle to the corn
De 23:25 move a sickle
Jer 50:16 handles the sickle
Joe 3:13 sickle, for the harvest
Re 14:15 sickle, and reap

Sickness
Ex 23:25 take sickness away
Le 20:18 having her sickness
De 7:15 all sickness
De 28:61 sickness, and every
2Ch 21:19 reason of his sickness
Mt 9:35 healing every sickness
Joh 11:4 sickness is not unto

Sidon
Ge 10:15 Canaan begot Sidon
Mt 15:21 Tyre and Sidon
Mr 7:24 of Tyre and Sidon
Lu 4:26 *a city* of Sidon
Lu 6:17 of Tyre and Sidon
Ac 12:20 of Tyre and Sidon
Ac 27:3 landed at Sidon

Sihon
Nu 21:21 Sihon king
De 2:24 Sihon the Amorite
De 31:4 Sihon and to Og
Jos 12:5 Sihon king
Jos 13:21 kingdom of Sihon
Ne 9:22 land of Sihon

Silas
Ac 15:32 Silas, being
Ac 16:25 Silas prayed
Ac 17:4 Paul and Silas
Ac 18:5 Silas and Timotheus

Silence
Job 4:16 there was silence, and I heard
Job 29:21 waited, and kept silence
Ps 31:18 lying lips be put to silence;
Ps 35:22 Yahweh: keep not silence
Ps 115:17 go down into silence
Ec 3:7 a time to keep silence
Isa 15:1 and brought to silence
Isa 41:1 Keep silence before me
Isa 62:6 of Yahweh, keep not silence
Jer 8:14 God has put us to silence
La 2:10 the ground, and keep silence
Am 5:13 prudent shall keep silence
Am 8:3 cast them forth with silence
Hab 2:20 keep silence before him
Mt 22:34 put the Sadducees to silence
Ac 21:40 there was made a great silence
1Co 14:34 Let your women keep silence
1Ti 2:11 Let the woman learn in silence
1Pe 2:15 put to silence the ignorance
Re 8:1 there was silence in heaven

Silent
Jud 3:19 king: who said, Keep silent
1Sa 2:9 the wicked shall be silent
Ps 28:1 O Yahweh my rock; be not silent
Ps 31:17 let them be silent in the grave
Ps 50:3 and shall not keep silent
Isa 47:5 Sit you silent, and get you
Isa 65:6 I will not keep silent,
La 3:28 He sits alone and keeps silent
Zec 2:13 Be silent, O all flesh
Ac 15:12 all the multitude kept silent
Ac 22:2 they kept the more silent

Silk
Pr 31:22 clothing *is* silk
Eze 16:10 you with silk
Eze 16:13 linen, and silk
Re 18:12 silk, and scarlet

Siloam
Lu 13:4 tower in Siloam
Joh 9:7 pool of Siloam
Joh 9:11 pool of Siloam

Silvanus
2Co 1:19 Silvanus and Timotheus
1Th 1:1 Paul, and Silvanus
2Th 1:1 Paul, and Silvanus
1Pe 5:12 Silvanus, a faithful

Silver
Ge 13:2 silver, and in gold
Ge 23:16 silver, current *money*
Ge 37:28 *pieces* of silver
Ex 20:23 gods of silver
Ex 26:19 sockets of silver
2Ch 32:27 treasuries for silver
Isa 1:22 silver has become
Da 2:32 arms of silver
Mal 3:3 purifier of silver
Mt 27:9 thirty pieces of silver
Re 9:20 gold, and silver

Silversmith
Ac 19:24 Demetrius, a silversmith

Simeon
Ge 29:33 his name Simeon
Nu 1:22 children of Simeon
Jos 19:1 forth to Simeon
1Ch 2:1 Reuben, Simeon
Eze 48:24 west side, Simeon
Lu 2:25 name *was* Simeon
Ac 13:1 Simeon that was
Ac 15:14 Simeon has declared
Re 7:7 tribe of Simeon

Similitude
De 4:16 similitude of any

Sin
Ge 4:7 sin lies at the door
Ge 39:9 sin against God
Ex 34:7 transgression and sin
De 21:22 sin worthy of death
2Ch 25:4 die for his own sin
Ps 51:3 sin *is* ever before me
Isa 6:7 sin purged
Isa 53:12 bore the sin
Mt 12:31 sin and blasphemy
Mt 18:21 brother sin against
Joh 1:29 sin of the world
Ro 5:12 one man sin
Ro 6:23 wages of sin

Sin, Wilderness of
Ex 16:1 wilderness of Sin
Ex 17:1 wilderness of Sin
Nu 33:11 wilderness of Sin

Sinai
Ex 19:1 wilderness of Sinai
Ex 34:2 mount Sinai
Nu 1:1 Sinai, in the
Nu 10:12 Sinai; and the
Nu 33:16 desert of Sinai
Ps 68:8 Sinai itself
Ac 7:30 Sinai an angel
Ga 4:24 mount Sinai

Sinner
Pr 11:31 and the sinner
Pr 13:22 of the sinner
Ec 8:12 sinner does evil
Ec 9:18 sinner destroys
Lu 7:37 which was a sinner
Lu 15:7 sinner that repents
Jas 5:20 converts the sinner
1Pe 4:18 and the sinner

Skin
Ex 22:27 for his skin
Ex 34:29 skin of his face
Le 1:6 skin the burnt
Le 4:11 skin of the bullock
Le 13:2 skin of his flesh
Job 19:20 skin and to
Eze 37:6 you with skin
Mr 1:6 girdle of a skin

Sleep
Ge 2:21 deep sleep to fall
De 31:16 sleep with your fathers
Jud 16:14 out of his sleep
1Sa 3:3 lain down *to sleep*
1Sa 26:12 a deep sleep
Ps 132:4 sleep to my eyes
Isa 29:10 spirit of deep sleep
Mt 26:45 Sleep on now
Lu 9:32 heavy with sleep
Joh 11:11 awake him out of sleep
Ac 20:9 into a deep sleep
Ro 13:11 awake out of sleep
1Co 15:51 shall not all sleep
Eph 5:14 Awake you that sleep
1Th 4:14 sleep in Yahshua

Slime
Ge 11:3 slime had they
Ge 14:10 *full of slime* pits
Ex 2:3 daubed it with slime

Sling
Jud 20:16 could sling stones
1Sa 17:50 sling and with
1Sa 25:29 middle of a sling
Jer 10:18 will sling out
Zec 9:15 with sling stones

Slothfulness
Pr 19:15 Slothfulness casts
Ec 10:18 slothfulness the

Smith
1Sa 13:19 no smith found
Isa 44:12 smith with the tongs
Isa 54:16 smith that blows

Smoke
Ex 19:18 in a smoke
Jos 8:20 smoke of the city
Jud 20:38 flame with smoke
Job 41:20 nostrils goes smoke
Pr 10:26 smoke to the eyes
Isa 4:5 cloud and smoke
Isa 51:6 away like smoke
Ho 13:3 smoke out of the
Re 9:2 smoke out of the pit
Re 14:11 smoke of their
Re 15:8 smoke from the glory

Snare
Ex 23:33 surely be a snare
Jud 2:3 shall be a snare
Jud 8:27 snare to Gideon
Job 18:8 walks upon a snare
Ps 124:7 snare of the fowlers
Ec 9:12 caught in the snare
Isa 24:17 pit, and the snare
1Ti 3:7 snare of the devil

Snow
Ex 4:6 leprous as snow
2Sa 23:20 time of snow
Job 24:19 consume the snow
Ps 51:7 whiter than snow
Ps 148:8 hail; snow
Isa 1:18 white as snow
Isa 55:10 snow from heaven
Da 7:9 white as snow
Mr 9:3 white as snow
Re 1:14 white as snow

Sodom
Ge 13:12 tent toward Sodom
Ge 18:26 Sodom fifty righteous
Ge 19:24 rained upon Sodom
Eze 16:49 Sodom, pride
Am 4:11 God overthrew Sodom
Re 11:8 is called Sodom

Sodomites
1Ki 14:24 sodomites in the land
1Ki 15:12 away the sodomites
1Ki 22:46 of the sodomites
2Ki 23:7 of the sodomites

Soldiers
1Ch 7:4 soldiers for war
2Ch 25:13 soldiers of the
Mt 27:27 soldiers of the
Joh 19:2 soldiers platted
Joh 19:23 soldiers, when
Ac 12:4 quaternions of soldiers
Ac 27:42 soldiers' counsel

Solomon
2Sa 12:24 Solomon: and Yahweh
1Ki 1:43 made Solomon king
1Ki 2:12 Solomon upon the
1Ki 3:5 appeared to Solomon
1Ki 6:2 Solomon built for
1Ki 10:23 Solomon exceeded
1Ki 11:6 Solomon did evil
Pr 1:1 proverbs of Solomon
So 1:1 which *is* Solomon's
Mt 1:6 king begot Solomon
Mt 12:42 wisdom of Solomon
Ac 7:47 Solomon built him

Son
Ge 4:25 she bore a son
Ge 17:19 bear you a son
Ex 4:22 Israel is my son
De 13:6 son of your mother
Jer 27:7 son, and his son's
Da 3:25 the Son of God
Ho 1:3 bore him a son
Mt 1:1 the son of David
Mt 1:25 firstborn son
Mt 4:3 Son of God,
Mr 1:1 Son of God
Mr 2:28 Son of man
Lu 1:13 bear you a son
Lu 1:32 Son of the Highest
Joh 3:16 only begotten Son
Joh 6:69 Son of the living God
Joh 17:12 son of perdition
Ro 5:10 death of his Son
Heb 5:5 You are my Son
1Jo 1:7 Son cleanses us
1Jo 5:11 life is in his Son
Re 14:14 like unto the Son

Song
Ex 15:1 Israel this song
Nu 21:17 sang this song
De 31:19 you this song
1Ch 15:27 song with the
Ps 30:1 Psalm *and* Song
Ps 120:1 Song of degrees
Eze 33:32 lovely song
Re 5:9 sung a new song
Re 15:3 song of the Lamb

Soothsayer
Jos 13:22 the soothsayer

Sorcery
Ac 8:9 used sorcery

Sorrow
Ge 3:16 multiply your sorrow
Ge 44:29 sorrow to the grave
Le 26:16 sorrow of heart
De 28:65 sorrow of mind
Pr 15:13 sorrow of the heart
Joh 16:20 sorrow shall be
2Co 7:10 godly sorrow works
1Th 4:13 you sorrow not
Re 21:4 sorrow, nor crying

Soul
Ge 2:7 a living soul
Ge 35:18 soul was departing
Le 5:1 if a soul sins
De 4:9 keep your soul
De 6:5 soul, and with all
Job 33:22 soul draws near
Eze 18:20 soul that sins
Mt 10:28 soul and body
Mt 26:38 soul is exceedingly
Ac 2:27 my soul in hell
Ro 13:1 soul be subject
1Co 15:45 a living soul
Heb 4:12 soul and spirit
Re 16:3 soul died in the sea

South
Da 11:5 king of the south
Da 11:14 king of the south
Da 11:25 king of the south
Da 11:40 king of the south
Zec 14:10 Rimmon south of Jerusalem
Mt 12:42 queen of the south
Lu 11:31 queen of the south

Sower
Isa 55:10 seed to the sower

Sower

Jer 50:16 sower from Babylon
Mr 4:14 sower sows the word
Lu 8:5 sower went out to sow
2Co 9:10 seed to the sower

Speaking
Ge 24:45 speaking in my heart
Ex 31:18 speaking with him
Nu 7:89 voice of one speaking
Nu 16:31 speaking all these
De 4:33 God speaking
2Ch 36:12 prophet *speaking*
Jer 38:4 speaking such words
Da 7:8 mouth speaking great
Ac 1:3 speaking of the things
Ac 26:14 voice speaking
1Co 12:3 speaking by the Spirit
1Co 14:6 speaking with tongues
Eph 5:19 Speaking to yourselves
Re 13:5 mouth speaking

Spices
Ge 43:11 honey, spices
Ex 25:6 spices for anointing
Ex 30:23 spices, of pure
1Ch 9:30 of the spices
2Ch 16:14 *spices* prepared
So 4:14 the chief spices
Joh 19:40 with the spices

Spies
Ge 42:9 You *are* spies
Nu 21:1 way of the spies
Jos 6:23 that were spies
1Sa 26:4 sent out spies
2Sa 15:10 Absalom sent spies
Lu 20:20 sent forth spies
Heb 11:31 received the spies

Spirit
Ge 1:2 Spirit of God moved
Ge 6:3 My spirit shall not
De 2:30 hardened his spirit
1Sa 28:7 familiar spirit
Eze 2:2 spirit entered into me
Da 5:11 spirit of the holy gods
Joe 2:29 pour out my spirit
Zec 4:6 by my spirit, says
Mt 4:1 Spirit into the wilderness
Mr 7:25 an unclean spirit
Lu 11:13 give the Holy Spirit
Lu 13:11 spirit of infirmity
Joh 1:32 Spirit descending
Joh 3:5 water and *of* the Spirit
Joh 14:17 Spirit of truth
Ro 8:2 the Spirit of life
1Th 5:19 Quench not the Spirit
2Th 2:13 sanctification of the Spirit
Heb 9:14 eternal Spirit offered
1Jo 4:1 believe not every spirit
1Jo 4:6 spirit of truth
1Jo 5:8 Spirit, and the water
Re 2:7 hear what the Spirit

Spiritual Blessings
Eph 1:3 spiritual blessings

Spoils
Jos 7:21 spoils a goodly
1Ch 26:27 spoils won in
Ps 35:10 that spoils him
Ho 7:1 robbers spoils
Na 3:16 cankerworm spoils
Lu 11:22 divides his spoils
Col 2:8 spoils you through
Heb 7:4 tenth of the spoils

Spring
De 8:7 spring out of valleys
1Sa 9:26 spring of the day
2Ki 2:21 spring of the waters
Job 38:27 herb to spring
Isa 58:11 spring of water
Eze 17:9 leaves of her spring
Mr 4:27 spring and grow up

Sprinkling
Heb 9:13 sprinkling the unclean
Heb 11:28 sprinkling of blood
Heb 12:24 blood of sprinkling
1Pe 1:2 sprinkling of the blood

Stammering
Isa 28:11 stammering lips
Isa 33:19 stammering tongue

Standard
Nu 1:52 his own standard
Nu 2:2 his own standard
Nu 10:14 standard of the
Isa 49:22 set up my standard
Isa 59:19 lift up a standard
Jer 51:12 standard upon the

Stars
Ge 1:16 *he made* the stars
Ex 32:13 stars of heaven
De 4:19 moon, and the stars
Jud 5:20 stars in their courses
Isa 13:10 stars of heaven
Jer 31:35 stars for a light
Am 5:8 stars and Orion
Mr 13:25 stars of heaven
1Co 15:41 glory of the stars
Re 1:16 hand seven stars
Re 6:13 stars of heaven fell
Re 12:4 third part of the stars

Stephen
Ac 6:5 Stephen, a man
Ac 7:59 stoned Stephen
Ac 8:2 Stephen *to his burial*
Ac 11:19 arose about Stephen
Ac 22:20 martyr Stephen

Steward
Ge 15:2 steward of my house
Ge 43:19 steward of Joseph's
Mt 20:8 steward, Call the
Lu 12:42 wise steward
Lu 16:1 steward; and the
Tit 1:7 steward of God

Stocks
Job 33:11 feet in the stocks
Pr 7:22 correction of the stocks
Jer 20:2 him in the stocks
Jer 29:26 and in the stocks
Ac 16:24 fast in the stocks

Stones
Ge 28:11 stones of that place
Ex 28:9 onyx stones
Ex 39:7 stones for a memorial
Le 20:2 stone him with stones
De 23:1 wounded in the stones
De 27:5 altar of stones
Jos 4:8 twelve stones out
Jos 10:11 stones from heaven
1Ki 5:17 stones, costly stones
Isa 9:10 with hewn stones
Zec 9:15 with sling stones
Mt 4:3 stones be made bread
1Pe 2:5 stones, are built up
Re 18:12 precious stones

Stool
2Ki 4:10 table, and a stool

Stork
Le 11:19 stork, the heron
Ps 104:17 *as for* the stork
Jer 8:7 stork in the heaven
Zec 5:9 wings of a stork

Straight
1Sa 6:12 straight way
Ps 5:8 your way straight
Pr 4:25 be made straight
Ec 7:13 make *that* straight
Isa 40:3 straight in the desert
Eze 1:9 straight forward
Lu 3:5 be made straight
Ac 9:11 called Straight
Ac 21:1 straight course

Strangers
Ex 6:4 they were strangers
Ex 23:9 strangers in the land
Jos 8:35 strangers that were
Ne 9:2 from all strangers
Pr 5:17 strangers' with you
Jer 5:19 serve strangers
La 5:2 strangers, our houses
Eze 16:32 strangers instead
Eph 2:12 strangers from the
Heb 13:2 entertain strangers

Strangled
Na 2:12 strangled for his
Ac 15:20 strangled, and *from*
Ac 21:25 strangled, and from

Strength
Ge 4:12 you her strength
Ex 13:3 strength of hand
Ex 15:2 Yah *is* my strength
Jud 16:5 great strength *lies*
1Sa 15:29 Strength of Israel
1Ki 19:8 strength of that food
Job 9:19 strength, lo, *he*
Isa 44:12 strength of his arms
Da 10:8 remained no strength
Mr 12:30 all your strength
2Co 12:9 strength is made
Re 3:8 strength, and have

Strife
Ge 13:7 strife between
Ps 55:9 violence and strife

Ps 106:32 waters of strife
Pr 10:12 stirs up strife
Pr 26:17 meddles with strife
Pr 29:22 man stirs up strife
Jer 15:10 man of strife
1Co 3:3 envying, and strife
Ga 5:20 strife, seditions
Php 2:3 strife or vainglory
Jas 3:14 envying and strife

Suffering
Mt 17:15 suffering: for
Ac 1:3 suffering by many
Heb 2:9 suffering of death
Jas 5:10 example of suffering
1Pe 2:19 suffering wrongfully
Jude 1:7 suffering the vengeance

Summer
Ge 8:22 summer and winter
Jud 3:20 summer parlor
2Sa 16:1 summer fruits
Ps 32:4 drought of summer
Jer 8:20 summer is ended
Mt 24:32 summer is nigh

Sun
Ge 15:12 sun was going
Ge 19:23 sun had risen
Ex 16:21 sun became hot
De 4:19 sun, and the moon
Jos 10:13 sun stood still
2Sa 23:4 the sun rises
Ps 136:8 sun to rule by day
Ec 1:5 sun also rises
Isa 38:8 the sun dial
Eze 8:16 sun toward the east
Mal 4:2 Sun of righteousness
Lu 21:25 signs in the sun
Jas 1:11 sun has no sooner
Re 6:12 sun became black
Re 21:23 no need of the sun

Surety
Ge 43:9 surety for him
Ge 44:32 surety for the lad
Pr 6:1 surety for your friend
Pr 11:15 surety for a stranger
Pr 20:16 that is surety
Heb 7:22 surety of a better

Swaddling
Job 38:9 swaddling band
Lu 2:7 him in swaddling
Lu 2:12 in swaddling clothes

Swine
Le 11:7 swine, though he
Isa 65:4 eat swine's flesh
Mt 8:30 swine feeding
Lu 8:32 a herd of many swine
Lu 15:16 swine did eat

Sword
Ge 3:24 flaming sword
Ge 27:40 sword shall you live
Ex 32:27 sword by his side
Jos 10:11 slew with the sword
Jud 7:18 sword of Yahweh

1Sa 13:22 sword nor spear
1Sa 17:39 sword upon his
Ps 57:4 tongue a sharp sword
Eze 21:9 sword is sharpened
Mt 10:34 peace, but a sword
Eph 6:17 sword of the Spirit
Heb 4:12 two-edged sword
Re 1:16 two-edged sword
Re 19:21 with the sword

Tabernacle
Ex 26:1 make the tabernacle
Ex 40:34 filled the tabernacle
Ex 40:38 upon the tabernacle
Nu 1:1 Sinai, in the tabernacle
De 31:15 in the tabernacle
2Sa 6:17 midst of the tabernacle
1Ch 23:26 carry the tabernacle
Ps 27:5 secret of his tabernacle
Ac 7:44 tabernacle of witness
2Co 5:1 house of this tabernacle
Heb 8:2 true tabernacle
Heb 9:11 tabernacle, not made
2Pe 1:13 I am in this tabernacle
Re 15:5 tabernacle of the
Re 21:3 tabernacle of God

Tabernacles, Feast of
Le 23:34 feast of tabernacles
De 16:13 feast of tabernacles
De 31:10 feast of tabernacles
Ezr 3:4 feast of tabernacles
Zec 14:16 feast of tabernacles
Joh 7:2 feast of tabernacles

Tabitha
Ac 9:36 disciple named Tabitha
Ac 9:40 Tabitha, arise

Table
Ex 25:23 table of shittim
Ex 31:8 table and his furniture
Nu 3:31 ark, and the table
Nu 4:7 table of showbread
Jud 1:7 under my table
2Sa 9:7 bread at my table
1Ki 7:48 table of gold
1Ki 10:5 food of his table
Jer 17:1 table of their heart
Lu 16:21 rich man's table
Lu 22:30 table in my kingdom
1Co 10:21 Lord's table

Tahpanhes
Jer 43:7 even to Tahpanhes.
Jer 44:1 and at Tahpanhes
Jer 46:14 and in Tahpanhes

Talebearer
Le 19:16 talebearer among
Pr 11:13 talebearer reveals
Pr 18:8 talebearer are as
Pr 20:19 talebearer reveals
Pr 26:20 no talebearer, the strife

Tamar
Ge 38:6 name was Tamar
Ru 4:12 Tamar bore unto
2Sa 13:1 name was Tamar
2Sa 14:27 name was Tamar

Eze 47:19 Tamar even to
Mt 1:3 Zarah by Tamar

Tammuz
Eze 8:14 weeping for Tammuz

Tares
Mt 13:25 tares among the wheat
Mt 13:29 gather up the tares
Mt 13:36 parable of the tares
Mt 13:38 tares are the children

Tarshish
Ge 10:4 Elishah, and Tarshish
2Ch 9:21 went to Tarshish
Ps 72:10 Tarshish and of the
Isa 23:1 ships of Tarshish
Isa 66:19 Tarshish, Pul
Eze 27:12 Tarshish was your
Jon 1:3 flee to Tarshish

Tarsus
Ac 9:11 Saul, of Tarsus
Ac 9:30 forth to Tarsus
Ac 11:25 Tarsus, for to seek
Ac 21:39 Tarsus, a city

Taxes
Da 11:20 raiser of taxes

Teachers
Ac 13:1 prophets and teachers
1Co 12:28 thirdly teachers
Eph 4:11 pastors and teachers
1Ti 1:7 teachers of the law
2Ti 4:3 teachers, having itching
Heb 5:12 thought to be teachers
2Pe 2:1 false teachers

Tears
De 33:20 tears the arm
2Ki 20:5 seen your tears
Es 8:3 him with tears
Job 16:9 tears me in his
Ps 6:6 couch with my tears
Ps 116:8 eyes from tears
Ps 126:5 tears shall reap
Isa 25:8 wipe away tears
Jer 9:1 fountain of tears
La 1:2 tears are on her
Mal 2:13 tears, with weeping
Lu 7:38 feet with tears
Heb 5:7 crying and tears
Re 21:4 wipe away all tears

Temperance
Ac 24:25 temperance
Ga 5:23 Meekness, temperance
2Pe 1:6 knowledge temperance

Temple
1Sa 3:3 temple of Yahweh
2Ki 11:11 corner of the temple
Ezr 3:6 foundation of the temple
Ne 6:10 within the temple
Isa 6:1 train filled the temple
Eze 41:1 temple, and measured
Zec 6:12 build the temple
Mt 4:5 pinnacle of the temple
Mt 24:1 buildings of the temple

Temple

Mt 26:61 veil of the temple
Mr 11:15 temple, and began
Lu 18:10 temple to pray
Joh 2:21 temple of his body
1Co 3:16 temple of God
1Co 6:19 temple of the Holy
Re 7:15 measure the temple

Temptation
Ps 95:8 day of temptation
Mt 6:13 not into temptation
Lu 4:13 all the temptation
1Co 10:13 no temptation taken
Ga 4:14 temptation which was
Re 3:10 hour of temptation

Ten Commandments
Ex 34:28 ten commandments
De 4:13 ten commandments
De 10:4 ten commandments

Tent
Ge 12:8 pitched his tent
Ex 26:12 curtains of the tent
Ex 35:11 tabernacle, his tent
Ex 40:2 tent of the congregation
2Ch 1:4 pitched a tent
Isa 40:22 tent to dwell in

Terah
Ge 11:25 he begot Terah
Ge 11:27 Terah begot Abram
Ge 11:31 Terah took Abram
Lu 3:34 *son* of Terah

Teraphim
Jud 17:5 ephod, and teraphim
Jud 18:14 teraphim, and a graven
Ho 3:4 *without* teraphim

Theft
Ex 22:3 sold for his theft
Ex 22:4 theft is certainly

Thief
Ex 22:2 thief is found
Pr 6:30 thief, if he steals
Mt 24:43 watch the thief
Lu 12:33 thief approaches
Joh 10:10 thief comes not
Joh 12:6 he was a thief
2Pe 3:10 thief in the night
Re 16:15 come as a thief

Thieves
Isa 1:23 companions of thieves
Ob 1:5 thieves came to you
Mt 6:19 thieves break through
Mt 21:13 den of thieves
Mt 27:38 thieves crucified
Lu 10:30 fell among thieves
Joh 10:8 thieves and robbers

Thirst
De 28:48 thirst, and in
2Ch 32:11 famine and by thirst
Ne 9:15 rock for their thirst
Ps 69:21 thirst they gave me
Isa 41:17 tongue fails for thirst
Am 8:11 thirst for water
Mt 5:6 thirst after
Joh 4:13 water shall thirst

Thomas
Mt 10:3 Bartholomew; Thomas
Joh 11:16 Thomas, which
Joh 14:5 Thomas said to him
Joh 20:24 Thomas, one of
Joh 20:28 Thomas answered

Thorn
Isa 55:13 thorn shall come
Eze 28:24 grieving thorn
Ho 10:8 thorn and the thistle
Mic 7:4 *sharper* than a thorn
2Co 12:7 thorn in the flesh

Threshing
1Sa 23:1 threshing floors
2Sa 24:22 threshing instruments
1Ch 21:20 threshing wheat
Isa 21:10 threshing, and the corn
Isa 28:27 threshing instrument
Isa 41:15 threshing instrument
Da 2:35 summer threshing floors

Thummim
Ex 28:30 the Thummim
Le 8:8 and the Thummim
De 33:8 Thummim and
Ezr 2:63 with Thummim

Thunder
Ex 9:23 thunder and hail
1Sa 2:10 shall he thunder
1Sa 12:17 thunder and rain
Job 28:26 lightning of the thunder
Ps 77:18 voice of your thunder
Mr 3:17 sons of thunder
Re 6:1 noise of thunder
Re 14:2 great thunder

Timothy
2Co 1:1 Timothy *our* brother
1Ti 1:2 Timothy, *my* own son
1Ti 6:20 Timothy, keep that
2Ti 1:2 Timothy, *my* dearly
Phm 1:1 Timothy *our* brother
Heb 13:23 Timothy is set

Tin
Nu 31:22 iron, the tin
Isa 1:25 all your tin
Eze 22:18 brass, and tin
Eze 22:20 lead, and tin
Eze 27:12 iron, tin

Tithes
Ge 14:20 gave him tithes
Nu 18:24 tithes of the
De 12:6 tithes, and heave
De 26:12 tithes of your
Ne 10:38 Levites take tithes
Ne 12:44 and for the tithes
Ne 13:5 tithes of the corn
Mal 3:10 tithes into the
Heb 7:5 tithes of the people

Titus
2Co 2:13 Titus my brother
2Co 7:6 coming of Titus
2Co 8:6 we desired Titus
2Co 12:18 Titus, and with
Ga 2:3 Titus, who was
Tit 1:4 Titus, *my* own son

Tobiah
Ezr 2:60 children of Tobiah
Ne 2:10 Tobiah the servant
Ne 6:12 Tobiah and Sanballat
Ne 6:19 Tobiah sent letters
Ne 13:4 allied unto Tobiah
Ne 13:7 Tobiah, in preparing

Tophet
Isa 30:33 Tophet *is* ordained
Jer 7:31 high places of Tophet
Jer 19:6 called Tophet
Jer 19:13 place of Tophet

Torment
Mt 8:29 here to torment us
Lu 16:23 being in torment
Lu 16:28 place of torment
1Jo 4:18 fear has torment
Re 9:5 torment of a scorpion
Re 14:11 of their torment
Re 18:7 torment and sorrow

Torments
Mt 4:24 diseases and torments

Tower
Ge 11:4 city and a tower
Jud 9:46 tower of Shechem
2Sa 22:3 high tower
2Ki 9:17 on the tower
Ps 144:2 my high tower
Jer 6:27 tower *and* a fortress
Hab 2:1 upon the tower
Mt 21:33 built a tower
Lu 13:4 tower in Siloam

Tradition
Mt 15:2 tradition of the elders
Mr 7:9 your own tradition
Mr 7:13 your tradition
Col 2:8 tradition of men
2Th 3:6 after the tradition
1Pe 1:18 tradition from your

Traitor
Lu 6:16 was the traitor

Trance
Nu 24:4 *into a trance*
Ac 10:10 into a trance
Ac 11:5 trance I saw
Ac 22:17 was in a trance

Transfigured
Mt 17:2 transfigured before
Mr 9:2 he was transfigured

Translation
Heb 11:5 his translation

Treasure
Ge 43:23 treasure in your
Ex 1:11 treasure cities
Ex 19:5 peculiar treasure
De 28:12 his good treasure
Ezr 5:17 king's treasure
Mt 6:21 treasure is, there
Mt 19:21 treasure in heaven
Lu 12:21 lays up treasure
2Co 4:7 treasure in earthen
Jas 5:3 heaped treasure

Tree
Ge 1:11 tree yielding fruit
Ge 2:17 tree of the knowledge
Ge 3:17 eaten of the tree
1Ki 4:33 from the cedar tree
1Ki 6:23 *of* olive tree
Isa 41:19 shittah tree
Mt 7:17 good tree brings
Lu 6:44 tree is known by
Ac 5:30 hanged on a tree
Ga 3:13 hangs on a tree
Re 2:7 eat of the tree of life
Re 22:2 the tree of life

Trespasses
1Ki 8:31 trespasses against
Eze 39:26 all their trespasses
Mt 6:14 men their trespasses
Mt 18:35 their trespasses
Mr 11:25 your trespasses
Lu 17:4 trespasses against
2Co 5:19 their trespasses
Eph 2:1 trespasses and sins
Col 2:13 you all trespasses

Trial
Job 9:23 trial of the
Eze 21:13 it is a trial
2Co 8:2 trial of affliction
Heb 11:36 trial of cruel
1Pe 4:12 fiery trial which

Tribulation
De 4:30 tribulation, and all
1Sa 26:24 of all tribulation
Mt 13:21 tribulation or
Mt 24:21 great tribulation
Joh 16:33 have tribulation
Ac 14:22 tribulation enter
Ro 2:9 Tribulation and anguish
Ro 8:35 tribulation, or distress
1Th 3:4 suffer tribulation
Re 2:9 works, and tribulation
Re 7:14 of great tribulation

Tribute
Nu 31:28 levy a tribute
De 16:10 tribute of a freewill
Jud 1:28 Canaanites to tribute
1Ki 9:21 tribute of slavery
2Ch 8:8 pay tribute until
Ezr 4:20 toll, tribute
Mr 12:14 give tribute
Ro 13:7 tribute to whom

Trumpet
Ex 19:16 voice of the trumpet
Nu 10:4 with one *trumpet*
Jos 6:5 sound of the trumpet
Jud 7:16 trumpet in every
Ps 150:3 sound of the trumpet
Eze 33:3 trumpet, and warns
Ho 8:1 trumpet to your mouth
Joe 2:1 Blow you the trumpet
Mt 24:31 sound of a trumpet
1Co 15:52 trumpet shall sound
Re 1:10 voice, as of a trumpet
Re 9:14 had the trumpet

Truth
Ge 42:16 truth in you
Ex 18:21 men of truth
De 32:4 God of truth
1Ki 17:24 mouth *is* truth
Job 9:2 *is* so of a truth
Ps 15:2 truth in his heart
Ps 51:6 truth in the inward
Zec 8:16 truth to his neighbor
Mal 2:6 truth was in
Mt 14:33 truth you are
Mr 5:33 him all the truth
Joh 1:17 truth came by
Joh 4:23 spirit and in truth
Joh 5:33 witness to the truth
Joh 8:32 truth shall make
Joh 14:6 the way, the truth
Joh 15:26 Spirit of truth
Joh 17:17 your word is truth
Joh 18:38 What is truth
Ro 1:25 truth of God into

Tumors
De 28:27 tumors, and with
1Sa 5:6 them with tumors
1Sa 6:4 Five golden tumors

Twins
Ge 25:24 twins in her womb
Ge 38:27 twins *were* in her
So 4:2 one bears twins
So 7:3 roes *that are* twins

Tyre
2Sa 24:7 hold of Tyre
1Ki 5:1 king of Tyre
1Ki 7:14 man of Tyre
Ne 13:16 men of Tyre
Isa 23:8 against Tyre
Joe 3:4 Tyre, and Zidon
Mt 15:21 Tyre and Sidon
Ac 21:3 landed at Tyre

Tyrus
Jer 25:22 kings of Tyrus
Eze 26:4 walls of Tyrus
Eze 28:2 prince of Tyrus
Ho 9:13 Tyrus, is planted
Am 1:9 of Tyrus
Zec 9:3 Tyrus did build

Uncircumcised
Ge 17:14 uncircumcised man
Ex 6:30 uncircumcised lips
Le 26:41 uncircumcised hearts
Isa 52:1 uncircumcised and
Jer 6:10 ear *is* uncircumcised
Eze 44:7 uncircumcised in heart
Ac 7:51 uncircumcised in heart
Ac 11:3 uncircumcised, and did
Ro 2:26 uncircumcised keeps
Ro 4:12 *yet* uncircumcised

Unclean
Le 15:25 *shall be* unclean
Nu 6:7 himself unclean
Nu 19:7 shall be unclean
Isa 6:5 man of unclean lips
Isa 64:6 an unclean *thing*
Mt 10:1 unclean spirits
Lu 4:33 unclean devil
Ac 10:28 common or unclean
2Co 6:17 the unclean *thing*
Heb 9:13 sprinkling the unclean
Re 16:13 unclean spirits

Uncleanness
Le 5:3 the uncleanness
Le 15:3 his uncleanness
Nu 19:13 uncleanness is
De 24:1 some uncleanness
Eze 39:24 their uncleanness
Ro 1:24 uncleanness through
Ro 6:19 to uncleanness
2Co 12:21 uncleanness and
Eph 4:19 work all uncleanness
1Th 4:7 us to uncleanness

Understand(ing)
Ge 41:15 you can understand a dream
Nu 16:30 then you shall understand
1Ch 28:19 Yahweh made me understand
Ne 8:8 to understand the reading
Ps 119 169 understanding according to
Pr 1:2 perceive the words of understanding
Pr 13:15 Good understanding gives favor
Isa 29:24 shall come to understanding
Da 12:10 the wise shall understand
Ho 4:14 *that* do not understand shall fall
Lu 24:45 opened he their understanding

Unfaithful
Pr 25:19 unfaithful man

Unfruitful
Mt 13:22 becomes unfruitful
1Co 14:14 is unfruitful
Eph 5:11 unfruitful works
Tit 3:14 be not unfruitful
2Pe 1:8 barren nor unfruitful

Unicorn
Nu 23:22 of an unicorn
Nu 24:8 strength of a unicorn
Job 39:9 Will the unicorn
Ps 29:6 young unicorn
Ps 92:10 horn *of* a unicorn

Unity
Ps 133:1 together in unity
Eph 4:3 unity of the Spirit
Eph 4:13 unity of the faith

Unleavened Bread
Ex 12:15 unleavened bread
Ex 29:2 unleavened bread

Unleavened Bread

Le 6:16 unleavened bread
Mr 14:12 unleavened bread
1Co 5:8 unleavened *bread*

Unleavened Bread, Feast of
Ex 12:17 *feast of* unleavened bread
Ex 23:15 feast of unleavened bread
Le 23:6 feast of unleavened bread
De 16:16 feast of unleavened bread
2Ch 30:13 feast of unleavened bread
Mt 26:17 *feast of* unleavened bread
Lu 22:1 feast of unleavened bread

Ur
Ge 11:28 Ur of the Chaldees
Ge 15:7 you out of Ur
1Ch 11:35 son of Ur
Ne 9:7 Ur of the Chaldees

Uriah
2Sa 11:21 Uriah the Hittite
2Sa 12:15 Uriah's wife
2Sa 23:39 Uriah the Hittite.
1Ki 15:5 Uriah the Hittite
Ezr 8:33 Uriah the priest
Mt 1:6 *wife* of Uriah

Urijah
2Ki 16:11 Urijah the priest
Ne 3:4 son of Urijah
Jer 26:20 Urijah the son
Jer 26:21 Urijah heard it

Urim
Ex 28:30 Urim and the
Nu 27:21 judgment of Urim
De 33:8 Urim *be* with your
1Sa 28:6 Urim, nor by
Ezr 2:63 priest with Urim

Usury
Le 25:37 money upon usury
De 23:19 lend upon usury
Ne 5:7 exact usury
Pr 28:8 usury and unjust
Isa 24:2 taker of usury
Eze 18:8 forth upon usury
Mt 25:27 own with usury
Lu 19:23 own with usury

Uzziah (also see Azariah)
2Ki 15:13 Uzziah king
1Ch 6:24 Uzziah his son
2Ch 26:3 Uzziah when he
2Ch 26:21 Uzziah the king
Ezr 10:21 Jehiel, and Uzziah
Isa 1:1 days of Uzziah
Isa 6:1 king Uzziah died
Zec 14:5 Uzziah king of
Mt 1:8 Joram begot Uzziah

Vanity
2Ki 17:15 vanity, and
Ps 12:2 speak vanity every
Ec 1:2 Vanity of vanities
Ec 7:15 days of my vanity
Ec 11:10 youth *are* vanity
Isa 5:18 cords of vanity
Isa 30:28 sieve of vanity
Isa 44:9 of them vanity
Jer 16:19 vanity, and *things*
Zec 10:2 spoken vanity
2Pe 2:18 *words* of vanity

Veil
Ge 24:65 veil, and covered
Ex 26:31 veil *of* blue
Ex 30:6 veil that *is* by
Ex 34:35 put the veil
Ex 40:3 ark with the veil
Le 16:2 veil before the
Mt 27:51 veil of the temple
2Co 3:15 veil is upon their
Heb 10:20 veil, that is

Vine
Le 25:5 grapes of your vine
De 32:32 vine *is* of the vine
1Ki 4:25 vine and under
Job 15:33 grape as the vine
Eze 17:6 spreading vine
Ho 10:1 an empty vine
Zec 8:12 vine shall give
Mal 3:11 vine cast her fruit
Mr 14:25 fruit of the vine
Joh 15:1 I am the true vine
Re 14:18 clusters of the vine

Vinegar
Nu 6:3 drink no vinegar
Ru 2:14 morsel in the vinegar
Ps 69:21 me vinegar to drink
Mt 27:34 vinegar to drink
Joh 19:30 vinegar, he said

Vineyard
Ge 9:20 planted a vineyard
Le 25:3 prune your vineyard
De 22:9 sow your vineyard
De 24:21 of your vineyard
1Ki 21:2 me your vineyard
Isa 5:4 more to my vineyard
Mt 20:1 into his vineyard
Mr 12:1 planted a vineyard

Viol
Isa 5:12 harp, and the viol
Am 6:5 sound of the viol

Virgin
Ge 24:16 virgin, neither
1Ki 1:2 young virgin
2Ki 19:21 virgin the daughter
Isa 7:14 virgin shall conceive
Isa 62:5 marries a virgin
Mt 1:23 virgin shall be
Lu 1:27 virgin espoused
1Co 7:36 virgin, if she
2Co 11:2 chaste virgin

Virtue
Lu 6:19 virtue out of him
Lu 8:46 virtue is gone out
Php 4:8 *is* any virtue
2Pe 1:5 your faith virtue

Voice
Ge 3:8 voice of Yahweh
Ge 16:2 voice of Sarai
Ge 26:5 obeyed my voice
Ex 5:2 obey his voice
Ex 18:19 now to my voice
Nu 7:89 voice of one
De 1:34 voice of your words
1Sa 1:13 but her voice
Mt 3:3 voice of one crying
Lu 9:35 voice out of
Joh 10:3 hear his voice
Heb 3:15 hear his voice
Re 1:12 voice that spoke
Re 18:23 voice of the

Wages
Ge 31:7 changed my wages
Le 19:13 wages of him
Jer 22:13 wages, and gives
Mal 3:5 hireling in *his* wages
Lu 3:14 with your wages
Joh 4:36 receives wages
Ro 6:23 wages of sin
2Pe 2:15 wages of

War
Ex 1:10 any war, they join
Ex 15:3 a man of war
Ex 32:17 noise of war
Nu 1:3 war in Israel
De 1:41 weapons of war
1Sa 8:12 instruments of war
Eze 27:10 men of war
Mic 4:3 they learn war
2Co 10:3 war after the flesh
Jas 4:1 war against the soul
Re 11:7 war against them
Re 12:7 war in heaven
Re 17:14 war with the Lamb

Warfare
1Sa 28:1 for warfare
Isa 40:2 warfare is
2Co 10:4 of our warfare
1Ti 1:18 good warfare

Washing
Le 13:56 after the washing
2Sa 11:2 washing herself
Ne 4:23 off for washing
Mr 7:4 washing of cups
Lu 5:2 washing *their* nets
Eph 5:26 washing of water
Tit 3:5 washing of

Watch
Ge 31:49 Yahweh watch
Ex 14:24 morning watch
Jud 7:19 middle watch
2Ki 11:7 keep the watch
2Ch 20:24 the watch tower
Job 14:16 watch over my sin
Hab 2:1 upon my watch
Mt 24:42 Watch therefore
2Ti 4:5 watch you in all
1Pe 4:7 sober, and watch

Watchful
Re 3:2 watchful, and strengthen

Watchman
2Sa 18:24 watchman went
2Ki 9:17 watchman on the
Isa 21:6 set a watchman
Eze 3:17 watchman unto
Eze 33:6 watchman sees
Ho 9:8 watchman of Ephraim

Water
Ge 2:10 water the garden
Ge 24:17 water from your
Ex 15:27 wells of water
Nu 5:17 holy water
De 8:7 brooks of water
Ps 77:17 poured out water
Eze 16:9 you with water
Da 1:12 water to drink
Am 8:11 thirst for water
Mt 3:11 baptize you with water
Mt 14:29 walked on the water
Mr 9:41 water to drink
Joh 3:5 born of water
Joh 4:11 that living water
Eph 5:26 washing of water
1Jo 5:8 water, and the blood
Re 21:6 water of life freely

Wedding
Mt 22:3 invited to the wedding
Mt 22:12 wedding garment
Lu 12:36 from the wedding
Lu 14:8 *man* to a wedding

Weeping
De 34:8 weeping *and* mourning
Ezr 3:13 noise of the weeping
Es 4:3 weeping, and wailing
Jer 31:16 weeping, and your
Mt 2:18 Rachel weeping
Mt 25:30 weeping and gnashing
Lu 7:38 weeping, and began
Re 18:19 weeping and wailing

Wells
Ge 26:18 again the wells
Ex 15:27 wells of water
Nu 20:17 water of the wells
2Ki 3:19 wells of water
Isa 12:3 wells of salvation
2Pe 2:17 wells without water

Wheat
Ex 9:32 wheat and the rye
Jud 6:11 wheat by the
1Sa 6:13 reaping their wheat
1Ki 5:11 wheat *for* food
1Ch 21:23 wheat for the meat
Ps 81:16 finest of the wheat
Mt 3:12 wheat into the barn
Mt 13:25 among the wheat
Joh 12:24 corn of wheat falls
1Co 15:37 wheat, or of some

Wheel
1Ki 7:33 chariot wheel
Ec 12:6 wheel broken
Isa 28:28 wheel of his cart
Eze 1:16 wheel in the middle
Eze 10:9 wheel by one cherub

White
Le 13:4 spot *is* white
Isa 1:18 white as snow
Da 12:10 and made white
Mt 17:2 clothes were white
Mr 9:3 white as snow
Re 1:14 hair were white
Re 4:4 clothed in white
Re 6:11 white robes
Re 7:14 white in the blood
Re 20:11 great white throne

Whirlwind
2Ki 2:1 by a whirlwind
Job 38:1 of the whirlwind
Pr 1:27 as a whirlwind
Isa 66:15 like a whirlwind
Eze 1:4 whirlwind came
Da 11:40 whirlwind, with
Na 1:3 whirlwind and
Zec 7:14 with a whirlwind

Whisper
Ps 41:7 whisper together
Isa 29:4 whisper out of

Whisperer
Pr 16:28 whisperer separates

Whore
Le 19:29 to be a whore
Le 21:7 wife *that is* a whore
De 23:18 hire of a whore
Jud 19:2 played the whore
Isa 57:3 and the whore
Re 17:1 whore that sits
Re 19:2 the great whore

Whoredom
Ge 38:24 child by whoredom
Le 20:5 whoredom with Molech
Jer 13:27 of your whoredom
Eze 16:17 commit whoredom
Ho 1:2 whoredom, *departing*
Ho 4:13 whoredom, and your

Whoremonger
Eph 5:5 whoremonger, nor

Wicked
Ge 13:13 Sodom *were* wicked
2Sa 4:11 wicked men have slain
Ps 101:3 no wicked thing
Pr 2:14 perversity of the wicked
Pr 17:23 wicked *man* takes a gift
Ec 3:17 righteous and the wicked
Jer 17:9 desperately wicked
Eze 18:24 that the wicked
Eze 33:19 wicked turns from
Mt 25:26 wicked and slothful
Eph 6:16 darts of the wicked
2Th 2:8 Wicked be revealed
1Jo 2:14 overcome the wicked

Widow
Ge 38:14 widow's garments
Ex 22:22 widow, or fatherless
Le 21:14 widow, or a divorced
2Sa 14:5 widow woman
Lu 2:37 widow of about
Lu 4:26 *that was* a widow
Lu 21:2 widow casting in
1Ti 5:4 widow have children

Wife
Ge 3:20 wife's name Eve
Ge 17:19 wife shall bear
Ex 4:20 took his wife
Le 20:10 man's wife
Nu 5:29 wife goes aside
De 20:7 betrothed a wife
Ru 4:13 was his wife
Job 2:9 said his wife
Ho 1:2 wife of whoredoms
Mt 5:32 away his wife
Mr 6:18 brother's wife
Mr 12:23 had her to wife
Lu 17:32 Lot's wife
1Co 7:14 by the wife
Eph 5:23 head of the wife
1Ti 3:2 husband of one wife
Re 21:9 the Lamb's wife

Wilderness
Ge 16:7 in the wilderness
Ex 3:18 into the wilderness
Le 16:10 into the wilderness
Nu 14:33 in the wilderness
Jud 8:16 of the wilderness
Isa 41:18 wilderness a pool
Isa 43:19 in the wilderness
Eze 19:13 wilderness, in a dry
Ho 13:5 wilderness, in the land
Zep 2:13 like a wilderness
Mt 3:1 in the wilderness
Lu 4:1 into the wilderness
Joh 3:14 in the wilderness
Joh 6:49 in the wilderness
Ac 7:44 in the wilderness
Re 12:6 into the wilderness

Will
Mt 6:10 will be done
Mt 7:21 will of my Father
Joh 4:34 will of him
Joh 6:39 Father's will
Ac 21:14 will of the Lord
Ro 8:27 the *will of* God.
Eph 1:9 mystery of his will
Php 2:13 to will and to do
Re 22:17 whoever will

Wind
Ge 8:1 wind to pass over
Ex 10:13 east wind brought
Ex 10:19 strong west wind
1Ki 19:11 wind tore the
Job 30:22 up to the wind
Ps 107:25 stormy wind
Ec 1:6 wind goes toward
Jon 4:8 vehement east wind
Mt 14:24 wind was contrary
Mr 4:41 wind and the sea
Joh 6:18 a great wind
Ac 2:2 mighty wind

Wine
Ge 9:21 wine, and was

Wine

Ge 14:18 bread and <u>wine</u>
Ge 49:12 red with <u>wine</u>
Nu 6:3 <u>wine</u> and strong
Nu 28:7 <u>wine</u> to be poured
De 28:39 drink *of* the <u>wine</u>
2Sa 13:28 merry with <u>wine</u>
1Ch 27:27 for the <u>wine</u>
Ne 2:1 took up the <u>wine</u>
Job 1:13 drinking <u>wine</u>
Mr 15:23 <u>wine</u> mingled
Joh 4:46 water <u>wine</u>
1Ti 5:23 <u>wine</u> for your

Wine, New

Ge 27:37 *new* <u>wine</u> have
Nu 18:12 of the *new* <u>wine</u>
2Ch 31:5 *new* <u>wine</u>, and oil
Isa 65:8 *new* <u>wine</u> is found
Joe 3:18 own *new* <u>wine</u>
Mt 9:17 *new* <u>wine</u> into
Ac 2:13 full of *new* <u>wine</u>

Wine Press

Nu 18:27 of the <u>winepress</u>
De 15:14 your <u>winepress</u>
Jud 6:11 by the <u>winepress</u>
2Ki 6:27 out of the <u>winepress</u>
Isa 5:2 made a <u>winepress</u>
Isa 63:3 the <u>winepress</u>
La 1:15 *as* in a <u>winepress</u>
Ho 9:2 and the <u>winepress</u>
Mt 21:33 dug a <u>winepress</u>
Re 14:19 <u>winepress</u> of the

Winter

Ge 8:22 summer and <u>winter</u>
So 2:11 <u>winter</u> is past
Isa 18:6 earth shall <u>winter</u>
Mt 24:20 not in the <u>winter</u>
Joh 10:22 it was <u>winter</u>
Ac 27:12 not fit to <u>winter</u>

Wisdom

Ex 31:3 <u>wisdom</u>, and in
Ex 36:1 <u>wisdom</u> and
2Sa 14:20 <u>wisdom</u> of an angel
1Ki 4:30 Solomon's <u>wisdom</u>
Job 38:36 <u>wisdom</u> in the
Ps 111:10 beginning of <u>wisdom</u>
Pr 1:2 <u>wisdom</u> and instruction
Pr 2:6 Yahweh gives <u>wisdom</u>
Pr 4:7 <u>Wisdom</u> *is* the principal
Pr 16:16 <u>wisdom</u> than gold
Eze 28:17 your <u>wisdom</u>
Lu 2:52 increased in <u>wisdom</u>
1Co 1:30 made to us <u>wisdom</u>

Wise Men

Ge 41:8 all the <u>wise</u> <u>men</u>
Ex 7:11 <u>wise</u> <u>men</u> and the
De 1:13 you <u>wise</u> <u>men</u>
Pr 10:14 <u>Wise</u> *men* lay up
Da 2:12 all the <u>wise</u> *men*
Da 5:15 <u>wise</u> *men*, the
Mt 2:1 <u>wise</u> <u>men</u> from
Mt 23:34 and <u>wise</u> <u>men</u>

Witchcraft

1Sa 15:23 sin of <u>witchcraft</u>
2Ch 33:6 used <u>witchcraft</u>
Ga 5:20 Idolatry, <u>witchcraft</u>

Witness

Ge 31:50 God *is* <u>witness</u>
Ex 20:16 false <u>witness</u>
Nu 17:7 tabernacle of <u>witness</u>
Nu 35:30 <u>witness</u> shall not
Pr 14:5 faithful <u>witness</u>
Mt 24:14 for a <u>witness</u>
Mr 14:55 sought for <u>witness</u>
Joh 1:7 <u>witness</u> of the Light
Joh 5:33 <u>witness</u> to the truth
Ac 1:22 <u>witness</u> with us
Ac 4:33 apostles <u>witness</u>
Ac 14:17 without <u>witness</u>
Ro 8:16 itself bears <u>witness</u>

Women

Ge 18:11 manner of <u>women</u>
Ex 1:19 Hebrew <u>women</u>
Ex 35:22 men and <u>women</u>
De 3:6 the men, <u>women</u>
Ru 1:4 <u>women</u> of Moab
1Sa 15:33 <u>women</u> childless
Am 1:13 ripped up the <u>women</u>
Mt 11:11 born of <u>women</u>
Ac 1:14 <u>women</u>, and Mary
Ro 1:26 <u>women</u> did change
1Ti 2:9 <u>women</u> adorn
1Ti 5:14 <u>women</u> marry
Re 14:4 defiled with <u>women</u>

Wonderful

2Sa 1:26 was <u>wonderful</u>
Job 42:3 things too <u>wonderful</u>
Ps 78:4 <u>wonderful</u> works
Ps 107:8 <u>wonderful</u> works
Ps 139:6 *is* too <u>wonderful</u>
Isa 9:6 <u>Wonderful</u>, Counselor
Mt 7:22 <u>wonderful</u> works
Ac 2:11 tongues the <u>wonderful</u>

Wool

Jud 6:37 fleece of <u>wool</u>
2Ki 3:4 rams, with the <u>wool</u>
Pr 31:13 seeks <u>wool</u>, and flax
Isa 1:18 they shall be as <u>wool</u>
Eze 34:3 with the <u>wool</u>
Eze 44:17 no <u>wool</u> shall
Da 7:9 the pure <u>wool</u>
Ho 2:9 <u>wool</u> and my flax
Heb 9:19 scarlet <u>wool</u>
Re 1:14 white like <u>wool</u>

Word

Ge 41:40 to your <u>word</u>
Nu 11:23 <u>word</u> shall come
Nu 23:5 <u>word</u> in Balaam's
De 4:2 not add to the <u>word</u>
De 8:3 *word* that proceeds
1Ki 2:42 <u>word</u> *that* I have
Isa 30:21 hear a <u>word</u>
Da 4:31 <u>word</u> *was* in
Mt 12:36 idle <u>word</u>
Mr 4:14 sows the <u>word</u>
Joh 1:1 <u>Word</u> was with God
Joh 17:17 <u>word</u> is truth
Ac 15:7 <u>word</u> of the gospel
1Co 12:8 <u>word</u> of wisdom
Eph 5:26 water by the <u>word</u>
Jas 1:22 doers of the <u>word</u>
1Jo 1:1 <u>Word</u> of life
Re 12:11 Lamb, and by the <u>word</u>

Word of God

1Sa 9:27 the <u>word</u> of God
Pr 30:5 <u>word</u> of God *is* pure
Mr 7:13 <u>word</u> of God of no effect
Lu 8:11 seed is the <u>word</u> of God
Lu 11:28 hear the <u>word</u> of God
Ac 4:31 spoke the <u>word</u> of God
Ro 10:17 by the <u>word</u> of God
Eph 6:17 is the <u>word</u> of God
1Ti 4:5 by the <u>word</u> of God
Heb 4:12 <u>word</u> of God *is* quick
1Pe 1:23 <u>word</u> of God, which
Re 1:2 <u>word</u> of God, and of
Re 19:13 called The <u>Word</u> of God

Word of Yahweh

Ge 15:1 <u>word</u> of Yahweh came
Nu 15:31 the <u>word</u> of Yahweh
Nu 22:18 the <u>word</u> of Yahweh
1Sa 3:1 <u>word</u> of Yahweh was
2Sa 22:31 <u>word</u> of Yahweh *is*
1Ki 22:19 <u>word</u> of Yahweh: I
2Ch 36:21 the <u>word</u> of Yahweh
Ps 33:6 <u>word</u> of Yahweh were
Isa 28:13 <u>word</u> of Yahweh was
Zep 2:5 <u>word</u> of Yahweh *is*
Mal 1:1 of the <u>word</u> of Yahweh

Words

Mt 10:14 hear your <u>words</u>
Mt 12:37 <u>words</u> you shall
Mt 22:22 heard *these words*
Mt 24:35 <u>words</u> shall not
Mt 26:44 the same <u>words</u>

Work

Ge 2:3 from all his <u>work</u>
Ge 5:29 <u>work</u> and toil
Ex 31:5 <u>work</u> in all manner
Ex 32:16 <u>work</u> of God
Le 23:7 laborious <u>work</u>
Ne 4:21 labored in the <u>work</u>
Ps 8:3 <u>work</u> of your fingers
Isa 32:6 heart will <u>work</u>
Mt 21:28 <u>work</u> today in
Joh 4:34 finish his <u>work</u>
Joh 6:29 <u>work</u> of God
Ro 2:15 <u>work</u> of the law
Ro 8:28 all things <u>work</u>
1Co 16:10 works the <u>work</u>
Php 1:6 good <u>work</u> in you
Php 2:12 <u>work</u> out your own
Jas 1:4 *her* perfect <u>work</u>
Jas 1:25 doer of the <u>work</u>

Works

De 2:7 <u>works</u> of your hand
Jos 24:31 <u>works</u> of Yahweh
Ps 66:5 <u>works</u> of God
Da 6:27 <u>works</u> signs
Mt 5:16 good <u>works</u>
Joh 10:25 not: the <u>works</u>
Ac 26:20 <u>works</u> befitting
Ro 4:6 without <u>works</u>

2Co 7:10 works repentance
Ga 2:16 works of the law
Eph 2:9 Not of works
Heb 6:1 from dead works
Jas 2:17 not works, is dead
1Jo 3:8 works of the devil
Re 2:2 works, and your labor

Worm
Ex 16:24 there any worm
Job 24:20 worm shall feed
Job 25:6 *which is* a worm
Ps 22:6 I *am* a worm
Isa 51:8 worm shall eat
Isa 66:24 worm shall not
Jon 4:7 prepared a worm
Mr 9:44 worm dies not

Wormwood
De 29:18 gall and wormwood
Pr 5:4 bitter as wormwood
Jer 9:15 wormwood, and give
La 3:19 wormwood and the gall
Am 5:7 judgment to wormwood
Re 8:11 is called Wormwood

Worship
Ge 22:5 yonder and worship
Ex 34:14 worship no other
Ps 29:2 worship Yahweh
Ps 95:6 worship and bow
Jer 44:19 cakes to worship
Da 3:5 worship the golden
Mic 5:13 worship the work
Zep 1:5 worship the host
Mt 2:2 to worship him
Lu 4:8 worship the Lord
Joh 4:24 worship *him*
Re 4:10 worship him
Re 14:11 worship the beast

Wrath
Ge 49:7 wrath for it
Ex 22:24 wrath shall grow
2Ch 30:8 of his wrath
Job 20:23 fury of his wrath
Job 21:30 day of wrath
Job 42:7 wrath is kindled
Pr 15:1 turns away wrath
Mt 3:7 flee from the wrath
Ro 2:5 wrath and revelation
Ro 12:19 place unto wrath
Eph 4:31 bitterness, and wrath
Re 6:16 wrath of the Lamb
Re 15:7 full of the wrath

Wrestle
Eph 6:12 wrestle not against

Writing
Ex 32:16 writing of God
Ex 39:30 writing, *like to*
De 31:24 writing the words
Ezr 4:7 writing of the letter
Es 4:8 writing of the decree
Da 5:7 read this writing
Mt 5:31 writing of divorce
Lu 1:63 writing tablet
Joh 19:19 writing was

Yah
Ex 15:2 Yah *is* my strength
Ps 68:4 the heavens by his name YAH
Ps 68:18 Yah God might dwell
Ps 111:1 Praise you Yah
Ps 118:14 Yah *is* my strength and song
Ps 150:6 has breath praise Yah
Isa 12:2 Yah Yahweh *is* my strength
Isa 26:4 Yah, even Yah

Yahshua
Mt 1:1 book of the generation of Yahshua
Mt 1:21 you shall call his name YAHSHUA
Mt 2:1 Yahshua was born in Bethlehem
Mt 4:1 Yahshua led up by the Spirit
Mt 12:25 And Yahshua knew their thoughts
Mt 17:18 And Yahshua rebuked the devil
Mt 27:37 YAHSHUA THE KING OF THE
Mr 1:1 the Messiah, the Son of God;
Joh 1:17 grace and truth came by Yahshua
Joh 8:1 Yahshua went to the mount of Olives
Joh 21:17 Yahshua said to him, Feed my sheep
Ac 5:42 teach and preach Yahshua the Messiah
Ac 7:59 Lord Yahshua, receive my spirit
Ac 10:38 anointed Yahshua of Nazareth
Ac 22:8 I am Yahshua of Nazareth
Ro 3:24 the Messiah Yahshua
Ro 8:1 the Messiah Yahshua
1Co 1:2 the Messiah Yahshua
1Co 8:6 one Lord Yahshua the Messiah
2Co 1:19 Son of God, Yahshua the Messiah
2Co 4:5 the Messiah Yahshua
Ga 2:4 the Messiah Yahshua
Ga 3:28 all one in the Messiah Yahshua
Eph 1:5 adoption of children by Yahshua
Php 2:11 tongue should confess that Yahshua
Col 1:4 your faith in the Messiah Yahshua
1Th 5:9 Yahshua the Messiah
1Ti 1:15 Yahshua came
1Ti 6:3 Yahshua the Messiah
Heb 3:1 profession, the Messiah Yahshua
Heb 13:8 Yahshua the Messiah
1Pe 3:21 Yahshua the Messiah
1Jo 1:7 Yahshua the Messiah
1Jo 3:23 on the name of his Son Yahshua
1Jo 4:15 confess that Yahshua
2Jo 1:7 Yahshua the Messiah
Re 1:1 of Yahshua the Messiah
Re 12:17 have the testimony of Yahshua
Re 14:12 the faith of Yahshua
Re 17:6 blood of the martyrs of Yahshua
Re 20:4 beheaded for the witness of Yahshua
Re 22:21 The grace of our Lord Yahshua

Yahweh
Ge 2:4 Yahweh God made
Ge 4:26 call upon the name of Yahweh
Ge 8:20 Noah built an altar unto Yahweh
Ge 12:1 Yahweh had said to Abram
Ge 12:8 called upon the name of Yahweh
Ge 13:4 Abram called on the name of Yahweh
Ge 16:13 And she called the name of Yahweh
Ex 3:15 Yahweh God of your fathers
Ex 6:2 I *am* Yahweh
Ex 12:11 it *is* Yahweh's passover
Ex 12:14 keep it a feast to Yahweh
Ex 20:7 name of Yahweh your God in vain
Ex 33:19 I will proclaim the name of Yahweh
Ex 34:14 Yahweh, whose name *is* Jealous
De 21:5 bless in the name of Yahweh
De 28:10 you are called by the name of Yahweh
1Ki 8:17 build a house for the name of Yahweh
1Ki 18:32 an altar in the name of Yahweh
2Ch 28:9 But a prophet of Yahweh
Ps 7:17 sing praise to the name of Yahweh
Ps 96:8 Yahweh the glory *due unto* his name
Ps 104:35 Bless you Yahweh, O my soul
Pr 18:10 The name of Yahweh *is* a strong tower
Isa 12:2 Yah Yahweh *is* my strength
Isa 12:4 Praise Yahweh, call upon his name
Isa 26:4 Yah Yahweh *is* everlasting strength
Isa 42:8 I *am* Yahweh: that *is* my name
Isa 47:4 redeemer, Yahweh of hosts
Isa 56:6 love the name of Yahweh
Jer 15:16 I am called by your name, O Yahweh
Jer 23:6 YAHWEH OUR RIGHTEOUSNESS
Joe 2:32 shall call on the name of Yahweh
Mic 4:5 we will walk in the name of Yahweh
Zep 3:9 all call upon the name of Yahweh
Zec 13:9 they shall say, Yahweh *is* my God
Mt 23:39 in the name of the Lord *Yahweh*
Ac 2:21 of the Lord *Yahweh* shall be saved

Yahweh-Yireh
Ge 22:14 Yahweh-yireh

Yahweh-Nissi
Ex 17:15 Yahweh-nissi

Yahweh-Shalom
Jud 6:24 Yahweh-shalom

Year
Ge 47:18 year had ended
Ex 23:14 me in the year
Ex 30:10 once in a year
Le 25:4 seventh year
Ezr 1:1 year of Cyrus
Isa 6:1 year that king
Eze 4:6 day for a year
Lu 4:19 year of the Lord
Heb 10:1 year by year
Re 9:15 month, and a year

Yoke
Ge 27:40 yoke from off
De 28:48 yoke of iron
1Ki 12:4 yoke grievous
Jer 27:8 yoke of the king
Mt 11:29 yoke upon you
Ga 5:1 yoke of bondage

Young Men
Jos 6:23 young men that
Ru 3:10 not young men
1Sa 25:5 ten young men
1Ki 12:14 of the young men
Pr 20:29 glory of young men
Jer 31:13 both young men
Joe 2:28 young men shall
Am 2:11 young men for

Young Women
Tit 2:4 young women to be sober

Zacchaeus
Lu 19:2 Zacchaeus, which was
Lu 19:5 Zacchaeus, make haste

Zachariah
2Ki 14:29 Zachariah his son
2Ki 15:8 Zachariah the son
2Ki 18:2 daughter of Zachariah
Mt 23:35 blood of Zachariah

Zadok
2Sa 8:17 Zadok the son
2Sa 15:27 Zadok the priest
1Ki 1:32 Zadok the priest
1Ch 6:8 Ahitub begot Zadok
1Ch 29:22 Zadok *to be* priest
Ne 3:4 Zadok the son
Ne 13:13 Zadok the scribe
Eze 43:19 seed of Zadok

Zeal
2Sa 21:2 them in his zeal
2Ki 10:16 zeal for Yahweh
Ps 119:139 zeal has consumed
Isa 9:7 zeal of Yahweh
Joh 2:17 zeal of your house
Co 9:2 zeal has provoked
Php 3:6 Concerning zeal

Zebulun
Ge 30:20 name Zebulun
Ge 49:13 Zebulun shall dwell
Ex 1:3 Zebulun, and Benjamin
Jos 19:27 reaches to Zebulun
Jud 5:18 Zebulun and Naphtali
Jud 12:12 country of Zebulun
Eze 48:33 one gate of Zebulun
Mt 4:13 borders of Zebulun
Re 7:8 Zebulun *were* sealed

Zechariah
1Ch 9:21 Zechariah the son
1Ch 16:5 next to him Zechariah
2Ch 24:20 Zechariah the son
2Ch 26:5 Zechariah, who
Ezr 5:1 Zechariah the son
Zec 1:1 Yahweh to Zechariah
Lu 1:12 Zechariah saw *him*
Lu 11:51 blood of Zechariah

Zedekiah
1Ki 22:11 Zedekiah the son
2Ki 24:18 Zedekiah *was* twenty
2Ch 36:10 Zedekiah his brother
Jer 1:3 Zedekiah the son
Jer 21:7 deliver Zedekiah king
Jer 39:7 put out Zedekiah's eyes

Zephaniah
2Ki 25:18 Zephaniah the
Jer 21:1 Zephaniah the son
Zep 1:1 Zephaniah the son
Zec 6:14 son of Zephaniah

Zerubbabel
1Ch 3:19 Zerubbabel, and
Ezr 3:2 Zerubbabel the son
Ne 7:7 came with Zerubbabel
Ne 12:47 days of Zerubbabel
Hag 1:1 prophet to Zerubbabel
Hag 2:21 Zerubbabel, governor
Zec 4:6 Yahweh to Zerubbabel
Lu 3:27 *son* of Zerubbabel

Zidon
Jud 10:6 gods of Zidon
1Ki 17:9 *belongs* to Zidon
1Ch 1:13 Canaan begot Zidon
Ezr 3:7 Zidon, and to them
Isa 23:4 ashamed, O Zidon
Jer 25:22 kings of Zidon
Eze 27:8 inhabitants of Zidon
Eze 28:21 face against Zidon

Zimri
Nu 25:14 Zimri, the son
1Ki 16:10 Zimri went
1Ch 2:6 of Zerah; Zimri
1Ch 8:36 Zimri begot Moza
Jer 25:25 kings of Zimri

Zion
2Sa 5:7 hold of Zion
Ps 2:6 holy hill of Zion
Ps 69:35 will save Zion
Ps 74:2 this mount Zion
Isa 62:11 daughter of Zion
Mic 4:2 go forth from Zion
Ro 9:33 lay in Zion
Ro 11:26 Zion the Deliverer
Heb 12:22 mount Zion
1Pe 2:6 lay in Zion
Re 14:1 mount Zion

Zipporah
Ex 2:21 gave Moses Zipporah
Ex 4:25 Zipporah took a sharp
Ex 18:2 Zipporah, Moses' wife

www.ingramcontent.com/pod-product-compliance
Lightning Source LLC
Chambersburg PA
CBHW080526300426
44111CB00017B/2627